# Music Lovers' Cyclopedia

*Author of*
*"Contemporary American Composers," "The*
*Love Affairs of Musicians," "Gyges'*
*Ring," "The Whirlwind,"*
*Etc.*

# Music Lovers' Cyclopedia

Containing a pronouncing and defining Dictionary of Terms, Instruments, &c., including a Key to the Pronunciation of sixteen Languages; many Charts; an Explanation of the Construction of Music for the Uninitiated; a pronouncing Biographical Dictionary; the Stories of the Operas; and numerous biographical and critical Essays by distinguished Authorities

EDITED BY

## RUPERT HUGHES, M.A.

GARDEN CITY      NEW YORK
DOUBLEDAY, DORAN & COMPANY, INC.
1931

*Copyright*, 1912, *by*
DOUBLEDAY, PAGE & COMPANY

ALL RIGHTS RESERVED

COPYRIGHT, 1903, BY MCCLURE, PHILLIPS & CO.

PRINTED IN THE UNITED STATES
AT
THE COUNTRY LIFE PRESS, GARDEN CITY, N. Y.

# Music Lovers' Cyclopedia

## PUBLISHER'S PREFACE TO THE REVISED EDITION

WHEN the "Music Lovers' Cyclopedia" was first compiled, it was the editor's effort to make it the most nearly complete reference work of its kind in existence. That this effort did not fail is proved by a comparison of the original edition with other works since issued. A careful checking, item by item, proves that where other musical dictionaries and cyclopædias, however voluminous, contain at most a few hundreds of biographies and definitions omitted from this work, the best of them omit many thousands of biographies and definitions contained in the "Music Lovers' Cyclopedia."

On account of the completeness of its contents and their extremely convenient arrangement, the book at once took its place on the reference shelves of libraries, public and private, large and small; and everywhere the worn condition of its bindings, and the testimony of its readers have proved how invaluable it has been found.

Originally published in two volumes at six dollars, we are now able to issue it at a great reduction, and the editor has seized the opportunity to bring it down to date by the addition of several thousand biographies. Great changes have taken place in music in the nine years since the "Music Lovers' Cyclopedia" was published in 1903. Two widely contrasted instances will prove this: Caruso, and "Parsifal."

Caruso swam into the ken of London and New York just

after the "Music Lovers' Cyclopedia" went to press. "Parsifal" was, of course well known, but its libretto was omitted from the "Stories of the Operas" for the reason that it was then supposed to be the exclusive property of Bayreuth. Only a few months later it was produced in New York City, after a sensational controversy. The story of "Parsifal," therefore, appears in this new edition of the "Music Lovers' Cyclopedia," along with the stories of many other operas that have since entered the repertoire of the leading opera houses. This means that the "Music Lovers' Cyclopedia" now contains the detailed plots of sixty operas.

Attention may be called again to the fact that the stories as told here give the places and dates of original production, and, where discoverable, the names of the creators of the rôles, the pronunciation of the names of the characters, and a full outline of the plot as it is unfolded on the stage by exits and entrances, with the titles of the principal musical numbers as they appear.

We beg to acknowledge here our indebtedness to G. Schirmer for permission to give the plots of the following operas whose American copyright he controls: "Louise," "Pelléas et Mélisande," "Ariane et Barbe-Bleu," "Hänsel und Gretel," "I Pagliacci," "Le Cid," "Le Jongleur," "Thaïs," "Manon," "I Giojelli della Madonna" and "Le Donne Curiose."

The phonetic pronunciation of every proper name and term is a further distinguishing feature.

Emphasis should also be laid on the number of special contributions by the most eminent musical authorities in

America and England, men of the calibre of Sir Hubert H. Parry, Ernest Newman, James Huneker, W. J. Henderson, Richard Aldrich, and many others of distinction.

The fault to be found with dictionaries in general is that they are inclined to be provincial; those published in England have been parsimonious of German, French, Italian, and American names; and those published in these other countries have returned the discourtesy. It has been the ambition of the editor of the "Music Lovers' Cyclopedia" to avoid this disproportion by collecting the greatest possible number of important names from every country.

The compactness of the "Music Lovers' Cyclopedia" compels a decided brevity of presentation, but this in itself is rather a virtue than a fault, and it has been a great source of gratification to be constantly informed by musicians, both lay and professional, that the "Music Lovers' Cyclopedia" is the book to which they refer first, and the one in which they are least often disappointed.

The need for a book of this kind has become increasingly evident during the past few years. People everywhere have been awakened to a new and finer appreciation of music. Many who were once content merely to listen to music, now find expression for themselves in some favorite instrument.

One of the elements responsible for the great present day interest in musical instruction is the method of teaching perfected by the U. S. School of Music. This method has reached out into every hamlet and village throughout the country, planting the seed of musical appreciation. This famous school has already provided more than half a mil-

lion men and women with a musical training, and has
achieved an inestimable good in placing within reach of all
the chance to acquire a sound, thorough musical education.

With this greater interest in music, the need for a more
complete and authentic musical reference work has been
felt. Students of music find this one of the most essential
phases of their education. And the "Music Lovers' Cyclopedia" fills just this need—clearly, simply and authentically
it gives the complete background of music.

It is a book compiled for the convenience of the lover of
music who seeks information on the simplest subjects, as
well as for the trained musician who has more abstruse
needs.

Now that it is possible to issue the work in one greatly
enlarged tome, the "Music Lovers' Cyclopedia" can be
confidently announced as a musical reference book of un-
approached completeness, a concise musical library in itself,
an invaluable addition to any musical collection, however
large.

THE PUBLISHERS.

# The Preface

**M**USIC is, indeed, the universal language. It passes current everywhere like gold. But none the less every nation puts a different stamp on its coinage, and each new sovereign of the realm makes some change in the design and the legend. In consequence a musical dictionary becomes largely a polyglot affair.

The object of this book is to present in a condensed and convenient form all the essential facts that may be required to guide the student of music, or needed as a reference for the professional musician.

To fit this work for the non-professional mind has been no easy task, but it has been the chief effort, and an introduction into the mysteries has been written especially for the uninitiated, who wish to be told some necessary truths without submitting to hard study or teaching.

The marriage of completeness with conciseness is a hard knot to tie. The present work cannot hope to compete with the great musical encyclopædias in certain respects. Yet, in other respects, it outdoes even the greatest of them. It has more biographies and more definitions than any of them. Each of the large encyclopædias shows a distinct bias toward one nation, period, or idea. *The Music Lovers' Cyclopedia* has practically every |name and definition in each of them; by its catholicity it covers many fields quite unnoticed by any one book, and it has many names and definitions to be found in none of them.

*The pronunciation of practically every name and term in musical use,* forms a unique feature of the *Music Lovers' Cyclopedia.* This alone makes it a desirable and important supplement to any musical library, however large. Not only have general rules of pronunciation for sixteen languages been tabulated in a novel and convenient manner, but the pronunciation of names, terms, and frequently of phrases has been represented as closely as possible. Even the "given names" have been pronounced, for it is of little comfort, for instance, to be saved from calling "Bāt'-hôf-ĕn," "Bee-tho'-ven," and to be left to miscall his first name "Lŭd-wĭg" for "Loot'-vĭkh."

The *Definitions* are given as plainly as is compatible with succinctness. Space has been greatly saved, not by sacrificing fulness of explanation, but rather by grouping together words of similar meaning in different languages, so far as this could be done without undue violence to alphabetical arrangement. So far as possible the *Music Lovers' Cyclopedia* avoids that exasperating abuse of cross-reference, by which some of the Dictionaries bandy the reader from one term to another in a wearisome zigzag, finally, at times, to send him to a word that has been omitted.

In the *Biographies* the scheme has been to crowd the multitude of minor personages into very narrow space in order that a hundred or more of the greatest should find liberal room. The major dead musicians and those still living, minor as well as major, have been chiefly favoured. The work is particularly rich in living musicians, and the great masters are given biographies which, although condensed, are quite complete. As to the rest, the mere list of dates, with an abbreviated indication of special activities, must suffice, compensation being found, it is hoped, in the great number of these names.

The *Contributed Essays* are in many respects the most valuable part of the work, written as they are by notable authorities who have reviewed certain subjects peculiarly their own, in a brief yet luminous manner especially for the layman. Nothing is a more valuable mental property than a somewhat definite and decisive summing-up of the actual meaning and the true proportions of the great personages, schools, and phases of a subject; such a summing-up is rare, largely because it is so difficult. As one contributor wrote: "It is very hard to compress these oxen into cups of beef-tea." That these prominent scholars have expressed themselves so definitely and with such rounded completeness on the subjects explained here, is a matter of greatest value in a work of this kind, and of greatest interest to every one that cares for music.

The *Stories of the Operas* are told here in the only way in which, surely, they should be told; and that is by telling the story as it is unfolded on the stage, not by acts and by scenes only, but by the entrances and exits and by the principal songs. The pronunciations of the names of the operas in different languages, and of the characters, have also been given, as well as the dates and casts of the first productions.

A few *Charts* of actual value have been preferred to the mere ornaments of portraits. These latter would have to be very numerous to be at all comprehensive, and their introduction would defeat the prime purpose of the book, which is to be informing within limited compass.

In fact, the one idea of the work has been to present as much information as possible, as conveniently as possible — *andante quasi allegretto*.

That mistakes occur is inevitable. Every dictionary the Editor has examined has abounded in them, ranging from what scientists call the personal equation to what they call downright blunders. It is only to be hoped that most of the errors of this book will be rather amusing than exasperating or misleading. In any case, corrections and suggestions of any kind for future editions will be most gratefully welcomed.

The code of pronunciation as used in the book is explained on the top line of the Table of Pronunciations. It cannot hope to give more than approximate shades of sound.

The Editor is indebted to Miss Annie C. Muirhead for many valuable suggestions and a large contribution to the accuracy of the work. The stories of the three operas, "Louise," "La Bohême," and "The Cid," are from her pen. For everything else not specially signed or credited, the Editor must be held responsible. He wishes here to make grateful acknowledgment to his publishers, who first suggested the idea of preparing such a work, and to the distinguished gentlemen who have lent to the *Music Lovers' Cyclopedia* the prestige and value of their contributions.

# Table of Contents

## PART II

# TABLE OF CONTENTS

# Stories of the Operas:

PA

# List of Charts

# CONTRIBUTORS *and* SUBJECTS *of* SPECIAL ESSAYS

*All Essays will be found in their Alphabetical Sequence*

...s in father ; $\bar{a}$ as in fate ; $\breve{a}$ as in
at ; $\ddot{a}\dot{n}$ and $\breve{a}\dot{n}$ as in French *élan* and
*in ;* see note 1, vol. I, page 396.

...s in bob.

...sed only in *ch*, as in church. The
Scotch and German guttural as in *loch*
and *ich* is indicated by *kh ;* see note
.., vol. I.

...s in deed ; *dh* as *th* in these ; *dj* as
in adjoin.

...s in bean ; $\breve{e}$ as in pet—at the end of
words it is almost like $\breve{u}$.

...s in fife.

...s in gig.

...s in hate.

...s in fight ; $\bar{\imath}$ as in pin.

...s in jug.

...s in kiek ; *kh* is used here to indicate
the German or Scotch *ch* or *g ;* see
note 3, vol. I.

...s in lull.

*m* as in mum.

*n* as in nun ; $\dot{n}$ indicates the French
nasal *n* or *m ;* see note 1, vol. I.

$\eth$ as in note ; *oi* as in noise ; *oo* as in
moon or foot ; $\delta$ as in wrong ; *ow* as
in cow ; $\delta\dot{n}$ as in French *bon ;* see
note 1, vol. I.

*p* as in pop.

*r* as in roar.

*s* as in sense.

*t* as in tot ; *th* as in think ; the sound of
*th* in these is indicated by *dh*.

$\bar{u}$ always with the sound of you ; the
French *u* and the German long $\bar{u}$ are
both indicated by $\ddot{u} ;$ **see note 2,**
vol. I.

*v* as in revive.

*w* as in will.

*x* as in fix.

*y* as in yoke.

*z* as in zone.

# *An* Introduction *to* Music

## FOR THE UNINITIATED

### Free Translation of its Technicalities into Untechnical Language (especially for those who do not Read Music and do not Care to Study it).

THERE is almost as much humbug about the mysteries of music as there was about the oracles of Delphi. And the vast majority of music-lovers have as meek and uninquiring a ~~h~~ead of the inner art and science of composition as the ol~~d~~ pagans had of priestcraft.

There is no deeper mystery about the tools and the trade o~~f~~ music than about those of any other carpentry and joi~~n~~ery. It is far easier for some people to write a melody th~~an~~ to drive a nail straight. But anybody who will earn-~~es~~tly try, can learn to do the one as easily as the other. ~~A~~nd there are thousands of professional composers who ~~o~~ught to be earning honest livings driving nails home instead o~~f~~ starving to death dishonestly driving audiences home.

The one mystery of music is the one mystery of all art ~~an~~d all other human intercourse—personality. Everybody ~~ca~~n write a novel or a play. Almost everybody does. So ~~ev~~eryone can write a sonata or a string-quartet. But the ~~nu~~mber of those who possess the spark (divine, prenatal, ~~ac~~cidental or howsoever secured)—the spark of magnetism, ~~fel~~icity, and eloquence, that number is small and is no more

superabundant than on the day when little Hermes fou
the old tortoise-shell and made the first harp out of it.

The reason the Editor is desirous of taking the veil fr
certain of the arcana of music is not that he wishes to
crease the number of composers—Heaven forbid! T
one object is to increase the number of those who will l
ten to music intelligently and know just what they
hearing, and pretty well why they like this and dislike th
For like and dislike by pure instinct are relics of m
animalism.

The open highway to the enjoyment of so-called clas
music is the hearing of it in large quantities. There i
short cut for those who lack the time or the inclination
this long training—and it is by way of learning the e
ments of musical form. For it is the crystallisation
human passion into some graceful and powerful form t
gives music long life. Many wretched pedants think t
the number of forms is limited; but this is a fallacy tha
disproved every day.

Some form, however, is as necessary in music as in scu
ture. And though the number and variety of forms av
able are as infinite and illimitable in music as in sculpt
still some definite shape must be in the artist's mind a
must be discoverable by an unprejudiced, attentive, a
educated audience

If you do not already know the skeleton that under
the shapely contours and full, fair flesh of melody and l
mony, you can find some enlightenment in the anatom
lecture that follows, provided you will use your own s
pel, and carry out the suggestions made. It is not eas
avoid asking the reader to master the language and s
bols of music, but much that is important can be lear
from the following, without this long special study, if
occasional general truth will be allowed to stand witl

tating its exceptions, and if permission be granted to arrive
t certain facts in a homely and button-hole manner.

## I

FIRST, turn to a piano or organ—either of these is
more convenient for illustration than a bow or
wind-instrument. The highly-organized instrument before you is the result of centuries of blind groping
n the dark, of unnumbered great failures for every little
iumph. This is true not only of the mechanism of strings,
ammers, keys, shape, size and materials of wood and
etal, but of the very music the instrument is intended to
nd out upon the air.

If you will simply glide your finger-nail along the white
eys you will produce a scale which in itself is the result
ot only of ages of experiment but of the bitterest conflict
etween scholarly musicians,—a conflict still raging. But
is cannot be discussed here. Let us for the present take
e instrument as we find it.

Opposite the next page will be found a picture of the
iddle portion of the key-board, with the letter-names that
ve been, for convenience' sake, given to the tones marked
n it. They are easily recognisable by the alternation of
e black keys in groups of twos and threes. For con-
enience it might be well to transfer the letter-names to the
hite keys with ink, which will be easily washed off with a
et cloth.

The first thing noteworthy about the diagram is that this
ries of letter-names is made of only seven letters and be-
ns over again at every eighth tone. This is because the
ghth tone (or octave) is produced by a string or a col-
nn of air making just twice as many vibrations as the
iginal tone ; the 15th tone by 4 times as many, etc., and
cause each group of seven steps plus the octave or 8th

step, is built on a uniform model of ratios. The seri
from one letter-name to its reappearance, as from c to c′,
subdivided into 12 half-steps or semitones.

This extended series of tones thus divided into octav
is the material from which all European and America
music is made. Save for a few changes and choices mad
for convenience, this scale is based on human nature an
physical law, and is not likely to be materially altered
our generation. Other fundamental facts will be disco
ered on studying this array of *whole-steps* (white keys—e
cept e to f and b to c) and *half-steps* (from a black key
the next white—also from b to c and e to f).

You will observe that the black keys carry the sam
names as the white keys they interpose between, exce
that the letter-name carries the symbol ♯ (" sharp ") for t
key next below or the symbol ♭ (" flat ") for the key ne
above. The same black key represents two white key
If you are advancing from f to g, for instance, the blac
key between is a half-step above f ; it is said to " sharpen
the note, by a half-step (or a " chromatic " degree) ;
however, you are moving down the scale from g to f t
black key is said to " flatten " the note g by a half-step (
a " chromatic " degree). The same black key serves co
veniently then both as f♯ (f" sharp ") and g♭ (g" flat ")
our system of music. Tones not thus " chromatically a
tered " by a sharp or flat are said to be " natural."
you have struck g♭ or f♯ and wish to reassert the whi
key, the tone is now called g♮ (g " natural ") or
natural.

The signs, ♯'s, ♭'s and ♮'s are called " sharps, flats an
naturals," or in general " chromatics."

Put your finger at random on any of the white keys an
move downwards on the white keys in strict successio
You will find (if you have a normal ear) that, whatever t

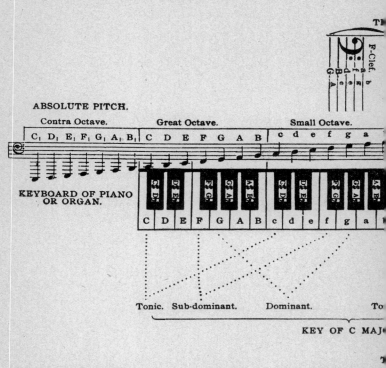

ABSOLUTE PITCH.

| Contra Octave. | Great Octave. | Small Octave. |
|---|---|---|
| C₁ D₁ E₁ F₁ G₁ A₁ B₁ | C D E F G A B | c d e f g a |

KEYBOARD OF PIANO
OR ORGAN.

Tonic.   Sub-dominant.        Dominant.            To

KEY OF C MAJ

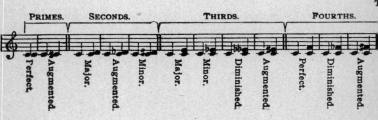

| PRIMES. | SECONDS. | THIRDS. | FOURTHS. |
|---|---|---|---|
| Perfect. Augmented. | Major. Augmented. Minor. | Major. Minor. Diminished. Augmented. | Perfect. Diminished. Augmented. |

G-Clef.

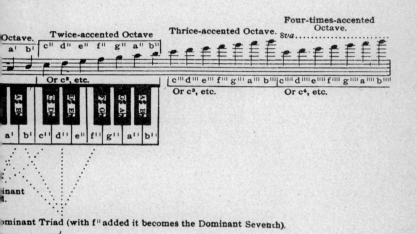

Four-times-accented Octave.

Thrice-accented Octave. *8va* ....................

Octave.     Twice-accented Octave

a' b'    c'' d'' e'' f'' g'' a'' b''

Or c³, etc.

c'''d'''e'''f'''g'''a'''b'''   c''''d''''e''''f''''g''''a''''b''''

Or c³, etc.       Or c⁴, etc.

a' b' c'' d'' e'' f'' g'' a'' b''

inant

ominant Triad (with f'' added it becomes the Dominant Seventh).

ALS.

SIXTHS.      SEVENTHS.     OCTAVES.     NINTHS.

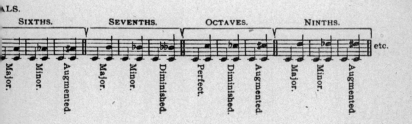

etc.

Major. Minor. Augmented. Major. Minor. Diminished. Perfect. Diminished. Augmented. Major. Minor. Augmented.

ne you sounded first, you do not feel a willingness to
op till you reach a certain tone or one of its octaves.
hat tone will invariably be one of the notes lettered C.

If now you begin at random on any note and move up-
rd keeping to the white keys except in the case of f, for
ich you substitute f♯, you will find that the letter c no
nger gives a sense of repose, but that you unconsciously
sire and demand one of the letters marked g.

If you run a scale on all the white keys except b, and
bstitute for this note the b♭, you will find no resting-place
cept upon one of the letters marked f.

It is a physical fact, then, that a scale with neither sharps
r flats finds its end on the note c; a scale with one sharp
hich is always f) is based on the note g; a scale with
e flat (b flat) is based on the note f. Hence one speaks
the scale of C, or of G, or of F.

If you try the substitution of some other single sharp
flat for the f sharp or b flat, you will get no satisfactory
int of repose at all. But by keeping b flat and adding
lat you will find b flat a comfortable pausing-place; by
ding a flat to the b♭ and e♭, you will find a pleasant scale
ding on e♭. By adding flats in the following order (and
ly in the following order), b, e, a, d, g, c, you will con-
uct symmetrical scales reposing always on the next to
e last flat added.

By substituting sharps for the natural tones of the origi-
l scale of C, you build scales satisfactorily only by heap-
g up sharps in the following order, f, c, g, d, a, e, which
les are based respectively on the notes g, d, a, e, b, f,
e point of repose being in each case a half-tone above the
t sharp added.

The scales take their names from the note of repose. A
le together with all the chords that can be built upon its
tes is called a *key*. The word "key" is often loosely

used (and has been used in this essay thus far) to indi
a finger-lever which causes a string to sound; this is b
called a "digital." From now on the word "key" wil
used only to designate a group of harmonies and a s
belonging to some series of progressions ending on a
tain note, as the "key of C," the "key of G" (which (
tains f sharp), the "key of D" (which contains f sharp
c sharp), the "key of E flat" (which contains b flat, e
and a flat), and the others.

Since practically every musical composition has some principal key to v
it harks back as its home, however far or often it may wander away, so
will find at the beginning of every new line of a composition a list o
sharps or flats in that key which predominates, and these sharps or flats a
every tone not otherwise marked throughout the composition. This gro
called the *key-signature*.

A convenient trick of deciding the key from the number of sharps or
is as follows : where there are flats the key is next to the last flat ; v
there are sharps the key is always the next letter-name above the last sl
This is true of every key except three which are easily remembered, F
one flat, G with one sharp, C with neither flats nor sharps.

Before studying chords, it will be necessary to have
other look at the diagram of the key-board. We h
spoken of half-steps and whole steps. But it is poss
also (and often desirable) to desert the monotonous p
gression of whole and half-steps and skip several st
as one does in singing a tune. The space covered b
skip is called an *interval*. As geography has its imagin
equator, and as geometry has its imaginary lines with
breadth and its planes without depth, so music has
imaginary interval which is no interval at all, but ident
The distance from a note to the very same note is calle
*prime*. (This is sometimes useful when speaking, for
stance, of a♭ and a♯, which are a prime apart, and are ca
*primes* of each other.) The interval from one white di
to the next white digital is called a *second*, the skip to

: but one is called a *third* (the original note being always
nbered one), the skip to the third white digital is called
*urth*, and so on; the interval of an eighth being called
*ctave*. Also the tones separated by an interval may be
:d by the names of the interval as c and g, or d and a
called *fifths*; f and d, or g and e are called *sixths*, etc.
t will greatly clear the belt of fog we are now going
ugh if you will pick out the examples on the key-board.
'he skip from a white to a black digital results in an in-
al which is either greater or less than the nearest inter-
on the white digitals alone. The normal or greater of
similarly named intervals as c to e is called a *major*
d, while c to e♭ is called a lesser or *minor* third. C to e♯
reater even than the major and is called an *augmented*
d, while c to e♭♭ ("double flat") is a *diminished* third.
)wing to the elasticity of the letter-names of the notes,
interval may be expressed or *spelled* in different ways,
s c to e♭ is called a *minor* third, but the very same tones
 be called c to d♯, an *augmented* second, c–f♭♭ a *dimin-
d* fourth, b♯–d♯ a *major* third, etc. The name of the in-
al depends upon the key we happen to have most in
d at the time.
t is a curious fact that all scales are made up of exactly
same intervals in exactly the same order. Try over any
he scales you wish, and you will find that you move up-
d by the following degrees, in the following order: (1)
hole step, (2) a whole step, (3) a half-step, (4) a whole
, (5) a whole step, (6) a whole step, (7) a half-step; this
 bringing you to the octave of the note you started
n.
As earnestly as the soul demands that in the last act of a
 we shall see the villain sent to prison and the hero and
oine locked in each other's arms, so our nature demands
 arrangement of tones, and when it says half-step or

whole step we must move so, or leave the key we starte
and take up another.

This explains why there is no black digital between
notes, b – c, and e – f: the scale of C, which has no sh
or flats, must still have its two half-steps at these poi
there is accordingly no sharp or flat to be put there.

## II

WE have now had a bird's-eye view of the nat
arrangement of tones, one at a time. But
grow tired of one note at a time. Four
singing along a midnight street or a picnic group ri
home in a moonstruck mood fall to singing favourite m
dies and naturally avoid singing in unison. They s{
taneously sing in chords. These chords are formed
dividually and succeed one another according to ce
fundamental demands of the ear just as noticeably as
tones of the scale followed a rigid pattern.

First, let us combine various tones. Take the mi
c′ and strike this tone with the right thumb while ano
finger strikes another tone above. c′ and c′♯ do not so
well together, nor yet c′ and d′; c′ and d′♯ (or e′♭) is
unpleasant, but rather sombre (it is indeed a minor
mony, the interval c′–e′♭ being a minor third); c′ an
make a pure, sweet concord, however. Let us keep c′
e′ and see if we can add another tone, c′ + e′ + f′, is
bad; c′ + e′ + f′♯ is also rough; c′ + e′ + g′ is very c
fortable. We have now a three-tone chord, which we
call a *triad*; it happens to be based on the 1st, 3d and
degrees of the scale.

Let us see if we can build triads on other tones of
C scale. We find by trying all the combinations on
note d′, that while the triad d′–f′–a′ is pleasant but son

t is minor), the only clear harmony is d′–f♯–a′; but as f♯ oes not belong to the scale of C, we cannot include it. On the note e′ we find e′–g′–b′, minor, and e′–g′♯–b′ pleasnt; this again is outlawed by the g♯. On f′, however, we an form a triad f′–a′–c′, which has no foreign chromatics nd is yet satisfying. On g′ we find another triad, g′–b′–d″, hich is native to the C scale and which impels us strongly o substitute the e″ above for the d″, and c″ for the b′; hen we have done this we find we have the chord c′–e′–g′ ain, only now arranged differently, as g′–c″–e″.

If we rearrange the chord on g′ differently, as b′–d″–g″, e shall be impelled to move on to c″–e″–g″, which is ain our old friend the original triad on c′ in its original rm.

This hankering after the original triad on the key-note henever we form a triad on the fifth tone of the scale, is ne of the most noteworthy and inescapable factors of the ord-world.

But let us proceed with our triads; on a′ we find a′–c″–e″ be minor; the major chord b′–d♯″–f♯″ is doubly ruled at; while b′–d″–f″ is doubly minor, the fifth (b′–f″) beg imperfect and the third (b′–d″) being minor.

It may be well to state here a handy way of telling the majority or minorof intervals; imagine the lower note to be the key-note; if the upper note uld occur in a major scale on that key-note its interval is major or diatonic. us on b : the key of B has 5 sharps, f, c, g, d, and a; both d and f are rp, therefore b–d♮–f♮ has neither interval major.

Looking back over the chords of the scale of C, we find e only major triads to be those on c′, f′ and g′. Since at on g′ is so urgent in demanding the main triad on C, is called the *dominant* triad, and the tone g is called the *minant* of the scale of C. f′ being beneath it is called *subminant*, and its chord the *subdominant chord*; the note c

being the foundation note of the whole scale and key
called the *tonic* (*tonus* being an old name for scale).

The principal chord-material of any scale is, then, m
up of the triads on the tonic (or 1st), the dominant
5th) and the subdominant (or 4th).

Try another Key, F for instance, which has b♭.    A
testing all the combinations on the key-note or toni
we find only f′–a″–c″ ; on g′ the triad, to be in the k
must be g′–b′♭–d″ (since b♭ is a characteristic of the ?
of F), and this is a minor chord ; a′–c″–e″ is also min
but b′♭–d″–f″ is a major triad ; it is indeed a chord on
*subdominant*.    We should expect also to find a major t.
on the dominant (which, in the key of F, is the tone
and so we find c″–e″–g″, which we recognise as the t
chord of the scale of C.    But strange to say it offers
repose in its new environment with the other chords of
key of F ; on the contrary, we have an irresistible desir
move on from it to c″–f″–a″ (the same as the key-chor
tonic chord, f′–a′–c″, where we feel at home).    The two
maining tones of the scale of F offer no satisfactory cho

Let us try a key with one sharp in it, that is to say,
key of G.    Beginning on g′ we find after groping ak
that the only chord endurable is g′–b′–d″.    Building tr
on all the other tones, a, b, c, d, e and f♯, we find all of tl
outlawed as unpleasant or at least minor, except two, w.
again, are on the *subdominant* and the *dominant* tones of
key of G, and are c″–e″–g″, and d″–f″♯–a″.

Taking the sum-total of the chords of these three k
c, f, and g, we have the following chords : (C) c–e–g, f–
g–b–d ; (F) f–a–c, b♭–d–f, c–e–g ; (G) g–b–d, c–e–g, d–f
You will see that each of the two subordinate keys has
of the chords of the key of C.    This will be found
case with any group of three keys similarly differing
by one sharp or flat, that is to say, having their tonics a

ove or below. On this account the keys based on the
ominant and subdominant tones of the scale of any given
ey are said to be closely *related* in the first degree of re-
tionship.

Add another flat and another sharp, that is, take the key
Bb and the key of D, and we find the following princi-
l chords: (Bb) bb –d–f, eb –g–bb and f–a–c; (D) d–f#–a,
-b–d, a–c#–e. Each of these keys has only one of the
ords belonging to the key of C. These keys are then
*lated*, but only in the *second* degree

If we add three flats or three sharps and study the keys
Eb and A we find the chords (Eb) eb–g–bb, ab c–eb,
–d–f; (A) a–c#–e, d–f#–a, e–g# bb. None of these
ords occur in C, and these keys are said to be *remote* from

On the other hand comparing Eb with the key which had
ly 2 flats (Bb), we find that Eb has two chords belonging
Bb. We also find that A has two of the chords belong-
g to the key with one sharp less, viz., D. We may
neralise, then, by saying that the most closely related keys
e those that differ by one flat or one sharp; the next near-
t relations are those differing by two flats or sharps.

## III

WHILE we are on the subject of heredity take
another point of view of this family-tree:
The tone f′, which is four steps above c′, is
lled its subdominant; on looking below the note c, we find
other f, but where it was four tones above, it is five tones
low. The Key of F has added one flat to the key of C.
ounting five more whole steps down (always counting the
te you began on as first) we find the note Bb. The
ale on that tone has yet another flat, two more than C.
he tone a full fifth below (Eb) has three flats. So we

find that moving downward by fifths we add one flat eve
step.   Ab has 4, Db has 5, and Gb has 6 flats.

Now counting upwards from our starting point on c',
find that the key based on the fifth (g') adds one shar
a fifth above G is D, a key with two sharps; a fifth abo
is A with three sharps, a fifth further is E with four shar
and, as we continue, B with five sharps and F♯ with
sharps.

But the key of F♯ on our piano or organ passes o
the very same digitals as the key of Gb, is identical with
in fact.   We have therefore been personally conduct
through the grand tour of keys by way of the *circle of fift*
twelve in all.

We see therefore that all keys are related, and by care
procedure in chords a player can move through them all
succession with the greatest smoothness.   The more m
ern the composition the more widely does it rove from k
to key until in some works, Wagner's for instance, it
sometimes hard to say just what key we are driving
Instead of keeping to the iron rails of one key as ear
music aimed to do, and only leaving the main line at c
tain definite set switches, the art has recently left the h
and fast railroad and taken to the pathless waters where,
use Wagner's words, it " swims in a sea of tone."

Some very formal minds grow speedily sea-sick and p
fer the rigid grooves of the older school.   Each one to
tastes.   But the broadest mind will find pleasure both
land-travel and sea-change, insisting only that the compo
shall have a plan and know what he is about, and not s
his locomotives slashing and sinking in the buxom wa
nor drag his yacht gratingly along the hard ground.   L
and let live is the best art motto.

One more point is worth noting in this increasingly
portant subject of key-relationships.   Reverting for a

nent to the key of C with its first cousins f and g, we find
f we take the tonic triads of the three keys and arrange
hem as follows :

$$\underset{\text{subdominant}\qquad\text{dominant}}{\underset{\text{tonic,}}{f–a–c–e–g–b–d.}}$$

These tones include the complete scale of C.   So it will be
ound of every key-scale that it contains within itself the
onic triads of itself, of its subdominant and its dominant
:eys.

This scale and key principle is further justified by a
tudy of the mathematics and physics of music.   And the
Relationship of Keys is given a still greater importance in
he more recent writers on the theory of music, especially in
Riemann's beautiful theory of clang-keys (see this word in
he Dictionary of Definitions).

## IV

NOW that we have laboriously picked out our triads,
they will be found more elastic than they look.
Take the triad c′–e′–g′, the tonic triad of the key
f C, which is now said to be in the root or first position,
′ being the root or generator of the triad.   We can place
he C′ uppermost and have e′–g′–c″, which is in effect the
ame chord, though a chord is said to be *inverted* when
ny note except its root is in the bass.   The second *inver-
ion* places the fifth in the bass, as g′–c″–e″ or g–c′–e′–g′ or
–e′–g′–c″.   These 3 *positions* are all we have for a 3-tone
hord or triad.   They can be sounded anywhere on the
:ey-board, however.

Still another possibility is to repeat some of these letter-
1ames, as to sound the triad c′–e′–g′ with the right hand

and touch the tone c an octave below with the left hand
or the tones c–g with the left hand and e'–g'–c" with the
right. This process called *doubling* may be carried on in
definitely. In a piano-duet, sometimes twenty notes or
more are struck, all of them repetitions of the inner kernel
or triad of three notes.

Strike the left hand note c first, then the right hand
triad c'–e–'g' twice; then strike the note f with the left
hand and the subdominant triad c'–f'–a' twice, now c and
the tonic triad again; then strike g with the left hand and
the dominant triad b–d'–g' twice; and return finally to c
and the tonic triad. This little plot in three instalments
constitutes the whole harmonic accompaniment of many
a modern popular song and many an old work of classic
reputation.

You can usually tell the key of a song by humming it
and picking out on the piano or organ its very last note;
nine times in ten this will be the *tonic* or homenote of
the composition. Suppose this to be B♭. How shall
one find chords to accompany it? Build a major triad on
b'♭; it will be b'♭–d'–f'; build a triad on the dominant or
fifth (f), f–a'–c"; build another on the subdominant or
fourth (e♭), e'♭ –g'–b'♭. Play these three notes (B♭, f,
e♭) with the left hand, and use triads with the right, re
arranging the three notes in any of the inversions as they
run most smoothly into one another. Your ear will help
you find the right order of the chords. This will serve as
a recipe for easy accompaniments.

More elaborate songs rove through so many keys with
so little warning that only trained ears and hands can pick
out their accompaniment; but it will clear up a deal of the
construction of music if you will take some simple tune and
study out its accompaniment on these lines, however pain
ful the operation may be to yourself and your neighbor.

amiliar songs requiring only these three chords are " The
ar Spangled Banner," " God Save the Queen," " Home
reet Home," " Suwanee River," " Dixie," etc., and most
the hymn-tunes.)

## V

BUT the simple triads grow monotonous, and it is
desirable, if possible, to enrich them. Take the
all important dominant triad of the key of C
amely, g′–b′–d″) and see if we can lay another third on
p of it like a musical brick. The next major third above
is f″♯. But f♯ does not belong to the key of C. The
nor third f″♮ does beautifully, however, and we have a
rm rich chord which more than ever goads us on to the
nic triad; the g′ holding over, the b′ and the d″ both
erging into c″, and the f″ subsiding blissfully into e″.

A chord of 4 tones is called a *chord of the seventh* or
venth chord, because the interval between the first and last
nes is a *seventh* (g′–f″). This chord, g′–b′–d″–f″, is a
minant 7th, then. If we wish, we can add another third,
, and make a chord g–b–d–f–a, called a *ninth chord*. The
ominant 7th, however, is far the more useful. In fact it
the most energetic chord in all music, and whatever key
u may be in, if you stray into the dominant seventh of a
reign key, it drags you along eagerly and hales you into
at foreign key to which it belongs and for which it is a
ost eager usher.

This seventh chord, pleasant as it is, is only a go-
tween, it offers no point of repose, but requires an almost
amediate dissolution into another chord. The musical
rm for one of these restless chords is *dissonance*; the mu-
cal term for the necessity and process of merging it into
aother is called *resolution*. The word *dissonant* does not

necessarily mean " ugly " or " harsh " in music, but mere
implies lack of stability.

This dominant 7th chord has magical powers for trans
tion.   Take the tonic triad of the key of C major in th
second inversion, that is, touch g with the left hand an
e′–g′–c″ with the right.   Now lift the finger off the upp
g′ and place it on b′♭.   Instantly you find it undesirab
to go back to the c′–e′–g′ triad and you are impelled
lower that b′♭ to a′, bring the e′ up to f′, keep the c″ whe
it is and lower the g in the left hand to f.   Now you fe
at rest; if you will pause and look, you will find that th
b′♭, which is characteristic of the key of F, has led you in
the triad f′–a′–c″, which is the tonic triad of the key of
If you revert to the state of affairs existing when that fo
eigner b′♭ entered the peaceful key of C, you will find th
the chord formed by its entrance could be arranged to re
c′–e′–g′–b′♭.   This is a 7th chord on the tone c.   B
while the tone c′ is tonic of the key of C, it is the fifth
dominant of the key of F.   Yet, though this 7th chord w
built on the tonic of C, as it happened to be the domina
of F, it forced the key over into the tonality of F.   Th
is the case with every dominant 7th chord.

It is possible by a slight diversion to throw the resol
tion of the chord into other keys, but this always comes
a surprise to the hearer.   It may be justified and it may l
pleasurable, but it is a surprise, and in a sense abnormal.

Going back to the first formation of the 7th chord,
will be found that the 7th chord, on other tones than th
dominant, are rather murky or even distressing.   The
are called *secondary* 7ths and must be handled in ginger
manner.

## VI

NOW if we take our dominant 7th of the key of C, that is, g'–b'–d''–f'', and raise the g' a half-step so that the chord reads g♯ b'–d''–f'', it will most naturally *resolve* itself into this chord, a'–c''–e'', a sombre chord which is minor because its third from a–c is minor (the major third being a–c♯, as c♯ would be characteristic of the key of A). This chord, a'–c''–e'', has the look of a chord in the key of C, but it seems to offer a sense of dejected repose and makes no demand for progress to the tonic chord, c'–e'–g'. We arrived at this chord by way of a curious chord with f♮ but g♯. The chord g'–b'–d''–f'' had been a minor 7th (the interval from g' to f'' being less than the major interval, which would be g' to f''♯), but this chord, g'♯–b'–d''–f'', is even narrower than minor. It is hence called a *diminished 7th chord.*

We have been led to believe that the first sharp of a major key was f, and that c followed, then g. This is true of a major key, but here we are under a different flag. You can construct a scale out of these two chords, the diminished 7th and its resolution, and g♯–b–d–f; a–c–e gives us a–b–c–d–e–f–g♯–a as an octave scale. This scale, which is closely related to the C major scale, is founded on a', which is a minor third below c''. So it will be found that every major key has one of these disappointed relative keys a minor third below and differing from it, for harmonic purposes, only in the fact that the 7th tone of this minor scale is raised a half-step above the tone of the same name in the major scale (in the scale of A minor, the 7th tone, g♯, is the only tone foreign to the scale of C major, and it is a half-tone higher than the tone g; the key of

C minor corresponds exactly with the major key a minor third above, that is E♭, except that where b is flattened in the key of E♭ major, it is made natural in the scale of C minor). This is the case with every major and minor key; the related minor key is a minor third below and raises the 7th tone of its major scale a half-step (as g to g♯; e♭ to e♮). Thus far we have concerned ourselves only with major scales, keys and intervals. But life would be very monotonous if it were all sunshine, blue sky and laughter. Music could not represent or stimulate human emotion, as it does, without a large armoury of sombre colours, bitter dissonances and, in place of a sense of cheerful repose, a feeling of resigned despair. These purposes are subserved by the minor key.

In looking at scales and intervals we find that certain of the intervals were to be distinguished as "greater" and "lesser." The Latin words meaning greater and lesser are *major* and *minor*. (And as the mediæval Latinity of the Catholic Church was the fountain-head of modern music, many of its terms persist.) On the major scale there were indeed four minor triads to only three major. There is abundance of minor material then in music. Its arrangement into scales and keys cannot be so easily explained as that of the major mode; indeed upon this subject scientists are mutually discordant and commonly as " troubled " (*betrübt*) as the great musical scientist Helmholtz found the minor scale itself.

Where doctors disagree, the layman would do best to pass by on the other side. Let us take the minor keys as we find them and thank Heaven for their existence as mirrors to the chillier, grayer moods of the mind. Music has indeed laid up something for a rainy day.

To go any further into the construction of chords would be to write a text-book on Harmony.

Those who wish to pursue the subject of chord construction and progression will find further information in such articles as Chord, Harmony, Thorough-bass, Parallel, Covered, Anticipation, Suspension, Interval, Altered, etc., in the Dictionary of Definitions.

## VII

GIVEN the scales for melody and the chords for harmony, with an unlimited variety of progressions, the subject of rhythm enters. There was a time when the music of the scholars was all in notes of equal length; such music was well called plain-song (*planus* meaning literally " smooth "). But popular instinct and popular music still had drum-rhythms and dances and finally forced the music of the scholars to return to humanity; and so-called mensurable (i. e., measurable) music began.

The definition of rhythm is so native and instinctive in everyone that it would be impertinence to foist it on the reader. It is to be noted, however, that in music it depends on the relative accent and duration of notes following a pattern more or less closely. The rhythm of a composition can be expressed by thumping it on a table with your fingers, for rhythm is independent of height or lowness of the tone and the volume of sound. Strum out in this way such tunes as " Comin' Thro' the Rye," " Yankee Doodle," " We Won't Go Home Until Morning," or the like, or airs of more dignity. If you mark the accents forcefully, the regularity of the rhythmical pattern becomes evident, and almost as monotonous as certain styles of wall-paper. If you tap with the left hand a regular beat like a clock's, only faster, the rhythm of the air will assume new vividness.

Take " Comin' Thro' the Rye " for example, the rhythm

could be expressed by underlining with the right hand a
series of numbers to be ticked off by the left hand :

If  a bod-y  meet a bod - y  com - in' thro' the  rye————
1-2, 3, 4-5, 6, 7-8, 9, 10-11, 12, 13-14, 15, 16-17, 18, 19, 20, 21, 22, 23, 24

If  a bod-y  kiss a bod-y  need a bod-y  cry————
25-26, 27, 28-29, 30, 31-32, 33, 34-35, 36, 37-38, 39, 40-41, 42, 43, 44, 45, 46, 47, 4

This covers two lines of the song, the rest of which fol
lows the same model.  We find 48 beats in the two line
of verse, 24 to each line.  The rhythm is almost exactl
stencilled all the way through ; it begins over again, afte
every sixth count, each 7th count having a marked accen
the 4th of each group of 6 having a lighter accent.  I
since the rhythm is the same, we simply repeat the first
numerals and cut off with a line every group of 6, we sha
have the song pictured in as simple a pattern as that of th
maid's own print gown.

If  a body  meet a body  com-in' thro' the  rye————
/ 1-2, 3, 4, 5, 6 / 1-2, 3, 4-5, 6 / 1-2, 3, 4-5, 6 / 1, 2, 3, 4, 5, 6 /

Call each of these groups a *measure*, the slanted line
*bar*, take a certain time or *note*-value as the unit in place c
these numbers and you will have the musical terminology
As the notes are short the quick eighth note (one-eighth c
a whole note) may be taken as the unit ; there are 6 c
these in each measure, and the *time* of the song is said t
be *six-eighths* or 6-8 time.  This is a combination of tripl
and duple rhythm, for, while each measure contains
counts, these counts are divided into two groups of thre
each and there are two accents to each measure, conse
quently 6-8 time is sometimes used for marches.

But the typical march time for marches (as well as fo
many other moods, as " Auld lang syne," etc.) is, as yo
will find, divisible into measures of 4 counts each, with tw

cents to each measure. As the whole note is taken as the whole extent of each measure, the presence of four beats to the measure gives each beat a fourth or quarter-note value. is therefore called *4–4 time*, or simply *common-time*. Very quick marches are sometimes written in 2–4 time with one beat to the measure. Waltzes are written with 3 beats and only one accent to the measure. This time is called 3–4 time. Other rhythms are 3–2, a slow time (with 3 half-notes and 3 accents to the measure); 3–8 time (a light quick time with 3 eighth notes and one accent to the measure); 6–4 time (a slower form of 6–8 measure, differing from 3–2 only in having two accents to the measure); 9–8 (with eighth notes and 3 accents), &c. (v. article on Time).

## VIII

NO way of submitting music to the all-devouring decimal system has yet been brought into play. The measure-notes are all multiples of 2 and 4: whole notes, half, quarter, 8th, 16th, 32d, and 64th notes. The larger divisions of music also fail to follow the decimal system. In the analysis of "Comin' Thro' the Rye" the measures themselves can be collected into groups of 2, 4 and 8. There is a slight pause after every other measure, a perceptible pause at the end of the 4th measure, a longer pause at the end of the 8th. The next group of 8 measures is likewise divisible into groups of 2 and 4.

This quality of divisibility into 4 and 8 measures is a fundamental law of musical structure. · Because it is such a law many composers strive to hide its nakedness or re-shape it to special purposes, but these are exceptions which by their very sense of novelty and oddity prove and emphasise the general rule.

A group of eight measures is called a *period*; this peri
contains two *phrases* of four measures each; each *phra*
contains two *sections*, of 2 measures; and each section
generally divisible into its melodic or rhythmic *motive
subject*. The song "Comin' Thro' the Rye" is especial
clean-cut in its divisions. They correspond in spirit to t
comma, semicolon, colon and period of ordinary pros
but occur with far more regularity. Frequently the perio
themselves can be collected into larger groups or *compou
periods* corresponding to paragraphs. The first accent of
measure has a stronger accent than the second or third. S
the first accent of the first measure of a period should r
ceive a greater stress than the first accent of the first mea
ure of a phrase, and so on. In the proper distribution
accents lies the larger part of musical punctuation, or, as
is called, *phrasing*.

## IX

IN the first group of 8 measures of "Comin' Thro' t
Rye" there is a general upward tendency to t
melody. The second *period* begins on a high no
(at the words "Ilka body") and has a downward te
dency. This desire for a contrast is at the root of a
musical form. This song is condensed even beyond t
usual popular form, partly because of the stanza-form o
its poetry. "The Last Rose of Summer" fulfils the typic
*song-form* which contains a *theme* of one or more period
followed by a contrasting or *subsidiary theme* of one or mor
periods, the song concluding with a repetition of the firs
or principal theme. Practically the same idea governs th
typical dance-form though the themes are likely to be mor
elaborate and the second theme is still stupidly called a *tr*
(from the fact that it was actually in old times given to

rio of instruments in order to contrast its simple song-like manner with the more ornate and broken progress of the principal theme).

It would naturally occur to composers seeking variety, to put this subsidiary theme into a different key, to emphasise the contrast. The key naturally chosen would be a closely related key. This is usually the case, and the contrast of keys is a most important part of classic forms.

The elaboration or variation of the themes in a way to show off the composer's scholarship and cleverness, was also as inevitable as human pride in skill.

The word *variations* has, in the general mind, a thought of " The Old Oaken Bucket " and " Nearer my God to Thee " " with variations." " *Variations* " is an incorrect word here : the proper term for these cheap and gaudy works being *embellishments*, for the air is simply made a trellis for all manner of running vines and frippery.

The true variation of a theme is its genuine manipulation. Take the first 2 measures of " Comin' Thro' the Rye " as a theme; i.e., the notes to the words " Gin a body meet a body," sit down again before the piano and play this theme, picking out the notes as indicated from their letter-names as shown in the Chart.

Suppose the notes to be placed—

$$/c', c', c', e'/, d', c', d', e'/g g a g/c'.$$

If with the right hand you play the theme as indicated, and shortly after follow in with the left hand (as you would follow the leading voice in singing such a round as " Three Blind Mice "), you will use the frequent device called for evident reasons *imitation*, as here :

Right hand/c' c' c' e'/d' c' d' e'/g g a g/c' - - -/&c.
Left hand /- - - - -/-----------/c c c e/d c d e/&c.

This is imitation *at the octave* and at two measures' *dis tance*; imitation may be at a different interval and distance *at the fifth*, for instance :

Right hand / c' c' c' e / d' c' d' e' / &c.
Left  hand / ———— / f f f a / &c.

Imitation need not be so *strict* as this; it may be *free* the intervals being slightly changed to enrich the harmony for it is not every air that can be treated smoothly and strict ly at the same time.   Here, for instance, the a in the lef hand might be reduced to a g.   Imitation in the orchestr has vast scope.   The trombones may proclaim a splendid phrase which the oboes will cackle over ludicrously, the flutes whistle gaily, the clarinets echo gurgingly, the 'cello bemoan nasally, and the violins murmur deliciously.

But in piano or organ composition, imitation is more restricted.   Sometimes a composer in mathematical mood will set an elaborate air jogging, and when it has gone a few spaces along, will start after it its very double.   The two will race like twin snakes.

When the imitation is exact, whole step by whole step skip by skip, whole note by whole note, and half-note by half-note, the composition is said to be a *canon*.   The canon may set more than two snakes wriggling swiftly along always the same distance from head to head.   Fugue i only a special form of composition in which the canon play a large part, the word "*fuga*" meaning "flight."

## X

THE devices for varying a theme are infinite. It
can be played in longer notes while another theme
chosen from another part of the song ripples
about it; or the duration of the notes can be shortened.
The new treatment of a theme by lengthening its notes
is called *augmentation*; the shortening of the notes is *diminution*.

The upper of two themes can be made the lower at different intervals than the octave; this is called *inversion*.
Another form of inversion is the turning of a theme upside
down, so that whenever it went up before, it goes down
now, and *vice versa*; this is *imitation by contrary motion*.

A theme can be picked to pieces and different fragments of it tossed to and fro with the skill of a juggler (and
about as much importance). The first 4 notes of " Comin'
Thro' the Rye" could be taken as a figure and repeated.
Thus :

$$c'\ c'\ c'\ e',\ e'\ e'\ e'\ g'\sharp,\ g'\sharp\ g'\sharp\ g'\sharp\ b',\ \text{etc.}$$

This would be called a *sequence*. The themes could be
played in octaves, or in varied and key-changing chords as :

If       a       bod    -y

$$e\flat\text{-}g\text{-}c^{1},\ f\text{-}a\flat\text{-}c^{1},\ g\text{-}b\flat\text{-}c^{1},\ g\text{-}b\flat\text{-}e^{1}$$

It could be ornamented as :

If       a       bod    -y

$$c',\ c',\ d',\ c',\ b',\ c',\ d',\ c',\ e',\ e',\ e',\ e'.$$

In fact, there is no hinting here the dissection and recon struction of which a theme is capable. As opposed to melodious or lyric treatment, this method is called *themati* Common names for this sort of treatment are " develop ment, elaboration, variation, working-out, free fantasy, &c., &c., the Germans calling it Durchführung, "goin through."

## XI

THE highest and noblest form of strictly academ and formal composition is the *sonata*, for th symphony is only a sonata for orchestra. W have now arrived hastily at a point where a rough explana tion of this form is possible.

This is the way you should set about writing a sonata or rather, one of the ways, for the sonata is elastic an has some room for individual tastes.

First you select a melody, one with an elocutionary an sententious manner, and containing many good texts t develop. You write it out plainly and emphatically in th key that suits it best. As a sidelight and a foil you se lect some more lyrical and song-like air, and for contras you put it in another key, naturally one of the related key most naturally the nearest related key, or the dominan Or you might put the second melody in the relative minor Having stated your two subjects, you may choose to repea them word for word, or note for note, so that there shall b no mistaking them ; you may then add a concluding reflec tion more or less elaborate. This is the first section of th sonata.

Having stated the two texts, the *principal* and the *subsi iary*, you now propose to show their true profoundnes and your own true skill as an orator. You employ the de

ices of elaboration mentioned above, and you play battle-
ore and shuttlecock with the two themes in all the keys
ou wish till they fly to pieces; then you juggle the pieces;
ou modulate from grave to gay; from cold to tropical,
om whisper to shriek, from insinuation to fervid appeal,
om metaphor to homely paraphrase; in fact, you invoke
very art and artifice you can borrow from the schools
r can find in the promptings of your own emotions.
When you have exhausted all the devices propriety or your
nowledge permits, you have finished the second section of
he sonata, the so-called Working-out, or Development, or
ree Fantasy, or Elaboration.

The third section consists of a re-statement of the first
heme in the original or tonic key, followed by the second
heme, not in its related key, but now *in the same key as the
irst theme,* in order that a definite key may be left in the
nind to give an effect of unity. A short peroration or
oda ends the sermon like a welcome benediction.

This is what is strictly called the sonata form. It is
easonable and based on a natural and artistic arrangement
f ideas and their development.

The sonata is not complete in this one composition, or
movement as it is called. Three or usually four contrasted
movements are strung together. They usually have some
aint suggestion of similarity of theme, but variety of mood
nd key is the chief endeavor. A slow movement (called
rom its slowness by one of the Italian words meaning
" slow "—Andante, lento, largo), marked by deep pathos
r tragedy, usually follows the passionate outburst. Then
:omes a lighter mood in one or two movements in the form
►f (a) an optimistic and prettily braided Rondo with one
hief theme and two attendant themes; (b) a gallant Minuet; or (c) a witty and jocose scherzo.

The sonata ends with a Finale of stormy and brilliant

character generally built on the same scheme as the firs
movement and written in the same key.

The whole group of three or four movements makes u
a sonata.   The first movement of the sonata is often als
called the " sonata-form."

An *overture* (excepting one that is a medley of airs
is merely the first movement of a sonata, written out fc
an orchestra.   A *symphony* is merely a whole sonata writte
to take advantage of the enlarged opportunities of a grea
orchestra of from 50 to 120 instruments.   The sonata
formula is also the basis of the *string-quartet*, -quintet, etc
and of *concertos* for solo instruments with orchestra.

A *symphonic poem* is a symphony only in the breadth c
its orchestration and its high demands.   Like many smalle
forms it forsakes the somewhat rigid arrangement of th
sonata and other classical forms and lets the moods or th
story it tells furnish the programme of musical events.  *A
composition which has some programme other than th
classic arrangement of keys and sections ;—a programme fc
instance representing musically a storm or the tragedy c
" Romeo and Juliet "—such a composition is said to b
*programme music.*   In its worst form, when programm
music descends to cheap and unconvincing imitations c
natural sounds instead of contenting itself with an artist
suggestion of them to the hearers' imagination, such musi
if music it can be called, becomes quite as hopeless trash a
that school of music which stoops to cheap and unconvinc
ing imitations of classical masters and parrots devices whic
only the original spontaneity of the old master himself ca
keep alive.   But generalisations are vain.   What is poiso
as one man serves it up, is meat from another's hand
One failure or one triumph no more makes a rule than on
bluebird brings the spring.

This hasty and incomplete sketch will have failed in its purpose if it leads its reader to the delusion that he need investigate no further the real mysteries of the art of music ; if it lead to the delusion that because the art is founded on certain physical laws of inner and outer nature, the artistic imagination is to be hobbled to them ; or if it lead to the delusion that any one form, symmetrical or natural soever, can suffice for all generations or all moods, or that any school of masters can hope to embody all that is good and solid in the art.

The classic masters were once living, breathing, passionate young artists, impatient of precedent and breaking rules for sheer pleasure as wanton boys smash windows. He who approaches them with intelligence and sympathy will find them still made of bone and blood, sinew and spirit. But once he has had the inestimable delight of their acquaintance, he must, above all things, avoid the belief that art and glory died with them. He should approach every new work, howsoever startling, with a readiness to be convinced that the new trumpeter, standing on the outer hilltop which we thought was the rim of the art, may, after all, be looking into a further world and be proclaiming to us new fields and streams, and a new horizon. And though his music may seem strange, blatant and incoherent to us at first, perhaps the fault is not with him, nor with us, but only with the great new wonder-land he sees beyond.

Music, like any other living speech, is always growing and must always be newly studied. If we would not have it a dead language we must be prepared for change, and be willing to learn.

# The National Schools

*Five Essays*

*by*

IRENÆUS PRIME-STEVENSON

## With an Appendix on the American School by the Editor

## Italial Music

WHATEVER currents of emotion, or of the me chanics of music, have varied and developed th art in Italy, two traits have been fundamental t distinctively Italianistic compositions—in each instance ap parently spontaneous vital pulsations and principles. Th first is the notion that without melody—especially sensuou warm, obvious melody—music has no eloquence for th heart, no matter how admirable the harmonic structure ma be. The second trait is lyricalism—the tendency to kee music ever in touch with the art of actual song, with the ex pressiveness that the human voice alone can afford.

It is true that in view of many widening phases of Italia musical genius we cannot claim that on these two command ments have hung all the law and the prophets which se Italy to creating for the rest of the world the most recentl perfected of the arts; that gave Italy her long-time sov ereignty in music; even now distinguish her in it. Stil they are the quintessence of Italianism in all "schools and phases really reproductive. Let us note, along wit these two general Italian concepts of music, the tendenc to unite melodic beauty with melodic strength, a feminine not a masculine, emotionality and melodiousness, and a failure, first and last, to reach in abstract music that interest and dignity which Germany, Austria, France, Scandinavia, and Russia have achieved. Thus we have two other salient Italian traits before us. The Italian "schools" of music, not excluding even the lofty ecclesiastical composers, if compared with the workers in the North, stand for Music as a thing of mere human heart and nerves and artless passion as contrasted with a vaguer, more mystic psychologic message. Only Italy could produce a Rossini or a Verdi ; we cannot think of an Italian Bach, Beethoven, or Brahms ; and *vice versa* the feeling holds good.

It is logical, therefore, that we find Italy to be really shining in only two forms of music. Both are her own special discoveries, or re-creation. The first is polyphonic church-music. The second is opera. Neither of these forms is of the more abstract and independent utterances of the art. But in each instance Italy has never been surpassed in dealing with them, either in principles or practice, and it is not likely that she ever will be, till music as a science and as an emotion is revolutionised. Let us add, in passing, that a third form—also lyric—is also Italy's direct invention, the sacred oratorio. But her accents in oratorio, as in her early developments of almost all other kinds of music, have been so outdone by French and German musicians that the Italian oratorio is to-day a fact for the student, not the auditor.

It would be as impossible to essay even a general historical sketch of Italy in music in a few pages, as to condense the story of Italian painting into equally few paragraphs. In Italy, the modern ideas of music, sacred or secular, all found creation or resurrection. All the rest of the world owes the art, as it is to-day, to one or another phase of Italy's early intense sensibility to it. Perhaps, indeed, music is *the* Italian art, in chief, rather than any other. Out of the mists of the early Christian Era, out of the thunders of mediæval wars and sieges, come to us the harsh but noble chants of Saint Ambrose of Milan (A.D. 333–397) and of Pope Gregory the Great (540–604) ; and as we reach the fifteenth and sixteenth centuries, we hear, clear and full, some of the most magnificent and pure church-song ever written, in the masses, motets, anthems, psalms and other great polyphonic works by the Roman masters of vocal scoring, Palestrina (1524 ?–1594), and Allegri (1560–1652) and their contemporaries. At the same time, sacred oratorios began under Cavalieri (1550–15—) a course to which in a course of 200 years Handel, Haydn, and Mendelssohn were to give such dignity. But the great burst of Italian church-music occurs after the beginning of the seventeenth century, when Carissimi (1604–1674), the Venetian Marcello (1686–1739), the Neapolitans Durante (1684–1755) and Leo (1694–1746), Pergolesi (1710–1736), Jommelli of Naples (1714–1744) and Scarlatti, the Sicilian (1659–1725), shone out as suns in Italian church-music, by styles and principles not yet weakened. Thereafter, however, Italian church-music declined in excellence ; and save for a few special and relatively recent works by Zingarelli, Rossini, and Verdi (quite of other voice and structure), its message has finished. In early instrumental composition Domenico Scarlatti of Naples (1683–1757) is of mark.

Opera, as has been observed, presents the phase of Italian genius in music at its most prolific, most powerful and—apparently—most natural eloquence. As is well known, it was in trying to revive old Greek drama, with its musical element, that, in 1681, a group of wealthy Italian *dilettanti* originated modern lyric drama. Under Caccini and Peri, by the broader ideas of Monteverde, Lotti, and others, the structure of opera became firm. In Alessandro Scarlatti, Pergolesi, Sacchini, and Piccini—mostly southern Italians—

n enormous Italian operatic growth occurred; soon trans-
ormed or grafted to France, Germany and Austria. The
onsummation of the classical Italian opera appears in the
Austrian Mozart, whose operatic voice is—fundamentally
—Italian. From this point we pass, in Italian opera, to the
greater modernists and romanticists, always Italian in their
concept of opera, whatever their actual birth or locality—
Paesiello, Cimarosa, Salieri, Zingarelli, Spontini, Rossini,
Donizetti, Bellini, Mercadante, mostly Neapolitan or of
meridional Italy. Their works have given place, in large
measure, to the Contemporary School of Italian Opera,
strikingly eclectic and much influenced for better or worse by
Northern phases. The supremest and noblest figure here
met is the gigantic Verdi (1813–1901), beyond doubt, one
of the most astonishing and consummate emotional composers in all the story of music. Verdi is elsewhere in this
book so fully treated, as are Rossini, Donizetti and Bellini,
as to need no long essay here on his merits and career. Of
his contemporaries, especially of what we may call the Neo-
talian "School" of operatic writing, the most important
are Ponchielli, Boito, Cagnoni, Gomez, Puccini, Franchetti,
Cilta and Giordano; with less distinct merits attaching to two
other much advertised names, Mascagni and Leoncavallo.

At present, Italy is, beyond doubt, in the same plight
of musical decadence (creatively estimated and measured
by her past importance) as is almost every other land and
ace in the art. Only in opera has the Italian composer
to-day a really attractive, spontaneous musical communication. For we can scarcely think that the few superior
Italian symphonists and pianoforte writers are of general
and real significance. Whether Italy can give any further
impetus, indeed, to a form of art that appears to be thought-
out and written-out is a question: but if the Italian fail to-
day in his æsthetics it is easy to forgive the failure, considering his splendidly Hellenic utterances in the past.

# German Music

NO other art is so indebted to distinctively Teutonic influences, no other art has been so civilised and dignified by the German minds and by the German temperaments as music. A special office of the Teutonic soul seems to be the bringing of intellect to bear on all those things for which it possesses emotional receptiveness and creative power. It is true that this very tendency sometimes ties down the wings of Pegasus, and dulls the lyre of this or that muse. Sensuous beauty can be the less in its being Germanized. But we can forgive the turgidness and clumsiness that come often as if in an intellectual extreme when we think of Peter Fischer, of Albrecht Dürer, of the architects who have built the Cologne Cathedral or St. Stephen's, and of that sparkling galaxy of musicians whose names are peculiarly linked to Austria—Haydn, Mozart, Gluck, Beethoven, Schubert and Brahms; and of the more strictly German group that shows us as central figures Bach, Handel, Mendelssohn, Weber, Schumann, and Wagner.

Whenever we ask ourselves what constitutes distinctively the high and true German school of musical creativeness, we are face to face with the same concept and result: the making of music an intellectual matter; a psychological thing to a degree not originative in any other country. The passion and fire of Italy's idea of music, as well as her lighter sensuousness in it, these are seized by the German heart and made into something deeper and more eloquent. The dance-forms of the South are transformed to a Ciaconna by Bach, a Minuet in Mozart's G minor symphony, or to the mystery of a Scherzo in Beethoven's terrific utterance. The symphony in German and Austrian concert-halls reached the supreme disclosure of music yet known to us. The love-ditties that merrily sighed or prattled or languished, *alla mandolinata*, in less serious lands, grew under the hand of Schubert and Schumann to be outcries from the world's heart. A romantic ballad could reach the height of tragedy, when Löwe gave it German voice. As for opera, Mozart so infused Italian principles with the force of his dramatic instinct as to give the world three consummate advances on all Italian models preceding, advances beyond which music in operatic conditions never has gone and never can go. Beethoven speaks with the soul forever in the three acts of " Fidelio." Weber and Marschner have built up the structure of a truly German-romantic opera to perfect effect. Wagner has brought into an absolutely stupendous demonstration a group of theories as to the lyric-dramatic opera—theories which, with all their error of expression even from so great a workman, are of psychological power overwhelming to the mass of opera-hearers to-day (not necessarily even musical) and which have indeed put a period for the time to any new phase of opera as drama.

In church-music and in religious music (to use a false term) the Germans and the German-Austrians have said what no other schools seem to have conceived in any ecclesiastic or devotional or spiritually reflective connection. The suave beauty of Italian polyphony as we find it in the church-music of Palestrina and Leo and of Marcello and Pergolesi grows colourless when our ears contrast it with the Mass in B minor of Bach and the D minor Mass of Beethoven. True, a lovely and devout Italianism created oratorio ; but it was left for Handel to write " Israel in Egypt " and the " Messiah," and for Mendelssohn to consummate such a form of musical and of religious receptiveness as " Elijah."

In fact it is through a subtle appeal to the very core and essence of human nature just as it is, just as we meet it daily

about us, as we know it to be struggling or repressed in ou
very selves, in our heart of hearts, that the German schoo
has so influenced music. Its voice is the voice of mysti
humanity in us ; and something more. Haydn, Mozart
Gluck, Beethoven, Schumann, Schubert, and Brahms hav
not degraded music in relation to our merely artistic idea
of it. They have not laid violent hands on it as art, and
wrested it away from its earlier mysteriousness. They hav
brought it near to us by a wonderful natural gift and in
sight. But they have made music psychologically as near
ly an articulate and organic thing as it is possible to mak
it. From Bach to the second Johann Strauss this is ou
of question. There is no clear outlook at present for any
further mastery over it—mystic and ever-elusive art tha
it is—none for any more articulate soul messages. The
German has entered within the holy of holies of musica
art. To him has been granted the freest foot in its vagu
realm yet granted to any mortal.

Whether after such a glorious and dominant past th
German is likely to go further for us than he has already
done, we may well believe is not in the bounds of even th
most thoughtful and the most psychologic of prophets ir
æsthetics to decide for us. All the future of music is a
present a strange problem. We are certainly swinging back
to the highest ideals and the truest expressions of them, ir
such large measure the express embodiments of Germar
composers. We do so daily not only because the " Ger
man " symphony, concert overture, concerto, string quartet
pianoforte sonata, song, oratorio and opera are what they
are, but because with the departure from the world of the
last set of greater " German " composers a twilight seem
to be settling down over all mortal musical creativeness.

The youngest, the most suddenly and prodigally flores
cent of all æsthetics, seems to demand a time of silence, o

epose, or inaction. It seems to say, " I have done enough
or awhile, I have given you enough for awhile. Let me
leep for a century or more." And such being music's
ood pleasure, we cannot deny that the German mind and
emperament have given the most beautiful and solemn
last word " the art has published.

## French Music

THE history and scholastic aspects of France in
music are like the relationship of France to the development of the sister arts—of painting, of archi-
ecture, of sculpture, and even of literature. We do not find
he gift of high origination—of invention—of striking out a
ew ground of principles—fresh forms and phrase. Instead,
ve find that the mission of the French composers from the
irst fruits of their musical creativeness (often so lavish and
ich) to our own day has been to clarify, to refine, to suggest,
often to imitate with a most subtle and elegant technical
mprovement, what Germany and Italy may have invented
n one or another form, but have not carried out in the
ame degree of a lucid and logical eloquence. More than
hat, in several of the most dignified forms of music, in
hat music which approaches the abstract, as the symphony
nd the deepest expressiveness of chamber-music approach
t, we find France has ever been singularly lacking in her
contributions; and has not only made no advance on the
ame foundation, no successful rivalry, but has distinctly
ailed to take a firm place and to win universal recognition.
Between the symphonies of Mozart or Beethoven and
hose of Saint-Saëns or Franck; between the songs of
Schubert and Brahms and the lyrics of Godard and Massenet, from the string quartets of Haydn or Smetana to

the best works of the Gallic hand, there is a long musica
distance; and in sonata-writing for the pianoforte th
French temperament has not in any wise distinguishe
itself.

The French troubadour (corresponding to the minne
singer of Germany's early musical day), a development un
der Italian influences in the South of France, is now
romantic and venerable figure before us as we study th
mediæval growth of secular music in French social life
If we include the Franco-Flemish masters of religiou
church-music in the seventh, eighth, ninth and later cen
turies until the close of the sixteenth, France offers a serie
of composers for the Church of great learning and ofte
lastingly instructive work.   Such are de Meurs (1300?-
1370?), Dufay (1350), Ockeghem (1430?-1495?) and Gou
dimel (1505?-1572).   With this group, we are near to th
great Italian church-composers represented by Palestrin
(1514?-1594), who was taught by Goudimel.

The element of concrete, human emotion is strong i
French temperament and art.   We are therefore not sur
prised to find the opera a vigourous phrase in France'
music-story; but with the establishment of Italian opera i
France under Mazarin a foreign form for dramatic mu
sic was seized on by French composers and soon mad
into something their own, and unlike that which they im
itated; and such it has continued even to our day.   Cam
bert (1628?-1677), pioneer, and the great founder o
French opera, Lulli (1633-1687), and the equally gifte
Rameau (1683-1764), defined opera for France with grac
and force.

The noble, sincere art of Gluck (who though a Germa
by birth belongs to France in his purest glory) is elo
quent to us to-day, though his "Orphée" and "Iphi
génie" and "Armide" date from the last year before th

rench Revolution. Every dramatic and musical princi-
le re-proclaimed by Wagner is contained in Gluck's best
cores. From Gluck we advance to the truly modern
poch. The works of Lesueur (1764–1837) are not vital
ow.; but Cherubini, "the French Beethoven," holds a
igh place for his best operas and his austere Requiem, a
masterpiece of church-music. The galaxy of French opera-
riters is met herewith—Méhul (1763–1817), Boieldieu
1775–1834), Grétry (1741–1813), Auber (1782–1871),
Hérold (1791–1833), Meyerbeer (1791–1864), the most
istinctively French composer as a stylist in opera of the
eriod, Halévy (1799–1862), and Berlioz (1803–1869).
With Berlioz (who is truly a Titanesque figure in modern
French music, either for opera or concert, but ever gran-
iose rather than grand) we are in quite our own epoch.
Gounod, Bizet, and Lalo are its strongest and most widely
ecognized creators of serious lyric drama. "Faust" and
Carmen" are of universal acceptance. To these masters
as succeeded a prolific Germano-Gallic school of music,
oth secular and religious, under Wagnerian or Neo-Ital-
an or other influence. The most salient, if not always
igorous expressions of this group, we soon find in the
cores of Massenet, Salvayre, Chabrier, Reyer, Saint-Saëns,
nd Franck, de Lara, Leroux and Charpentier. We must
ot forget that Offenbach, the creator of satiric opera-
bouffe, not only was a figure of brilliant originality under
he second Empire, but, like Johann Strauss in Austria,
eems destined to a longer vitality than was expected a
decade ago and has created a school of imitators of wide
rogue.

It is not likely that in any form of music France will
originate more in the future than her brilliant and most
epresentative composers have done in the past. But it is
omething—a great thing—in modern music to hold our

interest and admiration by the art with which a work, from
a song to a symphony, is written for us, the skill of men
means even to an imitated purpose. In this gift it is not
likely that the French composers soon will fail us. We
can hear them with pleasure where their message is neither
new nor valuable in itself—a racial trait and grace.

## English Music

IT is under restricted meaning that we can speak at all of
an "English" school of musical art. However flexi-
bly the word "school" be employed in defining mu-
sical utterances, after all it should stand for a distinctive individual product; and in case of a country and race, for an
accent in symphony, oratorio, opera, chamber-music and
song, that is national and individualised. It should not be
reckoned as merely a product of influences from outside.
In England nearly every form of music has been an importation; and almost every expression of the art that is effec-
tively represented in the present or the past history of musical
composition in England is derived or reflects Italy, France
or Germany. Musical composition and musical taste in
England itself in the old-time of the art lagged behind
the popular developments in Wales, Scotland, and Ireland
(where the bardic expressions of music early were enjoyed
by all classes), and creative productiveness was proportion-
ately slow. The Italian musical influences in due course
obtained, as did Italian literary influences, and later the
German and French; and English composition to-day is a
more or less disguised and eloquent product of Continental developments of the art, and English popular taste
for music in abeyance and instructed by the Continental
product.

There are, however, three exceptions to this general mmary. The English Ballad—the true ballad—with its ecise, definite rhythms and clear periods has an individlity at once strong in song, and admirable in sincerity d beauty. The Scotch and Irish lyric, or instrumental pression, is also distinct; and both interesting and beauul. The second exception is represented by the finest velopments of music for the organ and for its churchly age; and the choral English anthem, and what apperns to English liturgical offices in music. Here we can view a noble musical structure. It was gradually perted from the time of Elizabeth (in particular) as a prodt of English, Italian and German musical art fused tother. Bright lights in it have been Dunstable, Tallis, rd, and the gifted Purcell; the majestic Gibbons and Blow; e great organist Bull; the English fraction of Handel's ork in oratorio and for the Protestant church service; and e busy group of contemporary English composers for the fices of the National church, who are not much under reign influences of one sort or another. Although Hanl is always to be reckoned as of England, and as developg the English "oratorio" to its climax, we cannot speak "the great Saxon" as uttering an "English style," so uch as a modification of German and Italian musical rms and accents, whether in an oratorio or an opera, a ntata, a suite or an organ-piece. Purcell, after all, was eratically Italian. Costa said little to be reckoned English." Nevertheless in one field of opera to-day ngland has an assured and a brilliant individuality. It has t come in the serious opera, whatever successes have been n by such skilled workers as Benedict, Balfe, Stanford, d MacKenzie, Goring Thomas and others; but in the nius of Sir Arthur Sullivan for light opera. By Sullivan d in a lesser degree by Cellier, an English operatic mes-

sage firmly and graciously has been given forth, allowing f
all suggestions of influences from abroad.   Sullivan's "Pi
afore," "Mikado," "Ruddygore," and "The Yeoman
the Guard," are masterpieces of invention and of music
diction—not to be confused with Italian, French, or Germa
products.

In modern secular music for the orchestra some sup
rior symphonic work has come from Bennet, Cowen, ar
others; and particularly contemporaneous high lights i
composition in large form for the orchestra or choral cho
are Edward Elgar and Coleridge-Taylor.   Both these vi
orous writers are, however, of the modern German scho
rather than of any English style !

Altogether we must accept the fact that in England mus
is not an original art-expression, compared with the produc
in other and more genial lands.   The English temperame
is not yet to the manner born, musical.   Musical produ
tivity is a process of kindly foreign sunshine and of enricl
ment of a more or less England-born and England-workii
musical talent.   If a genius of world-wide importance is
be expected from England and as " an English composer
he has been long on the way, and will now have hard wor
to win any " towering pride of place."   Dignified nation
productivity is not national originality ; nor a national voi
and school in æsthetics.

# Russian  Music

THE youngest school (as a strictly national develo
ment of composition) of which the average stude
of music must seriously take account at present,
that of Russia.   It has, however, reached a clear and, in lar
measure, a singularly impressive unfolding for the extr
Slavic world's notice within the century, in which distinc

ely Russian musicianship has made its place good in the
ncert-rooms, in the drawing-room, and in the operatic es-
blishments of almost every corner of æsthetic Europe and
merica.

Like the Italian, and the Hungarian, and the Pole, so
the Russian, by nature, intensely musical. Often he is
orbidly so. The peasant and the prince alike are born
quick musical *Empfindlichkeit.* The folk-songs and
lk-melodies for the dance or more serious mood are im-
emorial, beautiful, and countless. All truly Russian mel-
dies have a peculiar voice and character of their own—scale
d rhythms are rich in melancholy, in passionate gaiety, in
amatic accent and in varied hints of the psychologic. A
rain of Orientalism is not absent. The Russian sings or
akes instrumental music by impulse and feels music by
ipulse (the *balaika,* a three-stringed guitar, is the original
usical instrument of Russia).

Such being the popular aspect noted, we turn to the
rmal development of the art in Russia. This, as has
en mentioned, is little more than a century old in culti-
ated activity. Its chief classic is—curiously—an operatic
riter, Michel Glinka, of Smolensk (1804–1869), a gifted
an in many other traits than music, a pupil of Dehn along
th the two Rubinsteins. His two finest operas, " A Life
r the Czar " and " Ruslan and Ludmilla," are, to Russian
ric drama, what Mozart, Gluck, and Weber are to Italian,
rench and German opera. Dargomizsky (1813–1869) is
link between Glinka and Anton Rubinstein. Anton Ru-
nstein, however, although popularly accounted as a Rus-
n master-worker and although so great an influence for
usic in Russia (I am not speaking here only of his career
a pianist), was less a Russian than a German composer
matter and manner. His best music is superb ; his birth
d works honour Russia, but in symphony, pianoforte

music and opera, Anton Rubinstein was Germanised earl
and stayed thus to the end, *nolens volens.*

Far more national in " school " is Borodin, a writer o
the first order, whose opera, " Prince Igor," is a classi
though its composer has been dead only some fourtee
years. Yet a further height of national Russian utteranc
in music comes with Balakireff, a native of Nijni-Novgoro
whose heart ever turns toward the folk-tunes of all Russ
for thematic material. The most national Russian com
poser, however, and a veritable giant in the technical use o
Slav themes is Tschaikowski, whose masterpieces are not t
be questioned as to their being Russian music and stron
developments of composition scientifically, measured by an
school.

The contemporary Russian movement is represente
especially in Rimsky-Korsakow, a giant for modern orche
tration and a magician in orchestral effectiveness ; in Cés
Cui, a brilliant operatic writer ; and in Alexander Glazounov
a pupil of Rimsky-Korsakow, and a symphonist of stron
Slavic diction, as well as a technicist of orchestration equalle
only by the most eminent writers of the day.

The actual profession of composition in music is yet
recent—one might almost say experimental—profession
Russia. We find one distinguished composer is a soldie
another a lawyer, another a marine officer, another a milita
official by his legal standing. Which gives us rather a cu
ous perspective of amateurism, if of magnificent amateurisr
However, this older aspect is each year passing away, th
Russian conservatory system is widening and taking root
the greater cities ; and while the most gifted contemporari
are not always concentrated on their own home-material f
subjects, they have fairly impressed the world as a distin
school. Often they have astonished and fascinated it.

## American Music

THE youth and lack of uniformity of the United
States citizenry furnish excuses for the absence of
a strictly national art hitherto. But, after all,
ere are not many countries that have preserved one form
government so long as the Constitution has been presid-
g over the assimilation of the world-pilgrims. Youth is
disease for which time is an almost certain cure, and too
uch uniformity of thought and character is favourable
ther to stagnation than life.

At last, however, American music has arrived. It is
ıly a healthy and somewhat bewildered child as yet, but
has the beginnings of an accent quite its own. The
merican composer has had a combination of advantage
ıd disadvantage in the thoroughly foreign nature of most
f his tuition. But so Germany and France took their start
ı Italy. As they gradually learned the importance of mak-
ıg their alien dexterity a medium for the expression of nave and national emotions and personalities, so has Amer-
a finally reached the stage of true introspection expressed
ith outward polish of manner.

The high favour of the foreign executant as pianist, violin-
t, 'cellist, opera and concert singer, and also as orchestral
:ader and yeoman, has been an obstacle to the wide and
ısy promulgation of the native composer's experiments
ıd achievements.

Through the fog of a thousand discouragements and dis-
·actions, however, the cause has groped until a few sturdy
gures have emerged already into prominence and even
ıto importance. The forms in which the earliest successes
ave been found have naturally been the smaller. In
rand opera there has been absolutely nothing achieved in
public sense, though doubtless there are enough manu-

script grand operas to bankrupt a dozen impresarios. I
the symphony there have been only a few works of larg
worth, though John Knowles Paine's " Spring Sympho
ny," Edgar S. Kelley's humourous symphony " Gulliver,
and Henry K. Hadley's " Youth " are full of personality
art, and genuine vitality. A number of overtures, syn
phonic poems and prologues have shown a right to exis
notably George W. Chadwick's " Melpomene," Arthu
Foote's " In the Mountains," Frank van der Stuck
en's " Ratcliffe," and various works by Johann H. Beck
Harry Rowe Shelley, C. C. Converse, and Mrs. H. H. A
Beach, while Edward MacDowell's " Indian Suite," Henr
Schoenefeld's " Sunny South Overture " and Kelley
" Aladdin " have exploited fields of local colour in whic
the American finds much novelty ready to hand. Variou
symphonic poems and orchestral suites deserve the men
tion space forbids them here. Of concertos there ar
many, Henry Holden Huss having written an especiall
excellent work for piano.

In the field of the sonata MacDowell has written tw
masterworks, the sonatas " Eroica " and " Tragica," and
piano " Fantasy " by Arthur Whiting is a notable innova
tion in the free manipulation of the sonata form. Th
religious choral works of Dudley Buck and Horatio W
Parker deserve serious acceptance. The marches for bras
band written by John Philip Sousa have gained world-wid
note for their military fire and novelty. In the realm o
smaller piano pieces, cantatas, and songs, there is an em
barrassment of riches. The piano-works of MacDowel
who gains eminence in all fields, and of Harvey Worthing
ton Loomis are genuine creations.

In the short-song form these two men collaborate witl
such sterling individualities as Kelley, Ethelbert Nevin
Foote, Wilson G. Smith, James H. Rogers, Fred Fiel

ullard, Margaret Ruthven Lang, Ad. M. Foerster, Ho-
er A. Norris, Howard Brockway and others, to give
merica a song literature whose importance is not sur-
assed in contemporary composition. There is also a large
ody of naturalised foreigners who, while hardly justifying
ne epithet American, are yet aiding to make American
usical life one of great activity, a life which has accom-
lished more than might have been fairly expected, and
ves promise most glowing.

# Two Essays

*by*

## LOUIS C. ELSON

*on*

## I. The Great Instrumentalists.
## II. The Great Singers.

I

# Great Instrumentalists

IF the time of Beethoven, Schubert, and Haydn was golden epoch in the field of musical creation, the presen has become, in even a greater degree, the era of musica execution, for we have attained a standard of musical excel lence far beyond anything ever dreamed of by the classica composers. Feats which Beethoven's critics derided a being too difficult for the violin (the high C in the " Eg mont" overture for example) are now readily within th scope of all good orchestral players, and our concert pian ists have now definitely shelved the cadenzas which the ol masters wrote for their concertos as being too simple t display the modern points of technique.

Piano technique, beginning with Bach's " Well-tempere Clavichord," advancing with Clementi and Cramer, foun its transition period in the time of Moscheles, and the culminated in two diverse ways—the poetry of Chopin an the brilliancy of Liszt. All of the pianists cited in thes pages will be most easily measured by four standards, viz. —Bach, for intellectuality; Chopin, for emotion; Beet hoven, for a combination of both in equipoise; and Liszt

such works as the " Don Juan " Fantasie, for technique
are and simple, or rather pure and difficult.

D'Albert achieves his chief triumphs in the Beethoven
hool; Von Bülow was pre-eminent in the last five Beet-
oven sonatas; De Pachmann leads the Chopin band;
aderewski is famous in Chopin as well as in the entire
odern school; Rosenthal scintillates with all the pyro-
chnics of the latest specialists. Occasionally one finds a
iszt who is almost equally great in all the schools, or a
ubinstein in whom intellectuality and emotion are well
mbined.

Less diverse are the schools of violin-playing, for here
e evolution has taken two rather distinct roads: pyro-
chnics on the one hand, and soulful expression on the
her. While these two styles are sometimes combined,
for example, in the Mendelssohn concerto, they are
fficiently distinct to enable one to classify every soloist
belonging chiefly to the one or the other school.

Paganini, the greatest violinist that ever lived (as Liszt
ight be called the greatest pianist), was distinctly de-
ted to technical display, in which he so entirely dis-
nced all competitors that some of his cadenzas cannot
played exactly as originally written by even the greatest
chnicists of our time. He was able to produce the
velfth harmonic with absolute clearness (his strings were
ade especially thin for this effect), the most intricate
uble harmonics had no terrors for him; special ways
tuning were studied out by him for special effects; but
learn from contemporary authorities, that his tone was
ither broad nor especially sympathetic. Joachim, in our
vn day, has held the violin sceptre, and combined tech-
que and expression in a marvellous degree. A host of
oman-violinists has arisen, with Lady Hallé at their head,
d as will be seen in other parts of this volume, the

modern school has brought forth numerous young violinis'
of both sexes, among whom it might be hard to select a
absolute monarch of violin-playing—such as Paganini ur
doubtedly was—from the technical side.

On other instruments, too, one can find definite leader
as for example, Servais, on the violoncello ; Dragonetti, o
the contrabass ; Thomas Harper, in trumpet-playing, etc.
all illustrating in a large degree the triumph of technic:
skill and the modern tendency toward specialisation o
effort in the music of the last hundred years.

# II

# Great Singers

IF, as may be seen in the article on " Great Instrumenta
ists " (pages 48–50), their technique has been advancin
in modern times, almost the opposite may be said i
regard to the art of singing.    The studies required of th
vocalist in the seventeenth and eighteenth centuries woul
be appalling to the singers of to-day, and every operat
manager finds more difficulty in finding an adequate qua
tette for the " Barber of Seville " than in selecting force
for " La Bohême," or even such great works as " Aïda
or " Otello " ; even Wagnerian singers are becoming mor
plentiful than thorough *coloratura* singers.

The study of vocal art is the most ancient branch o
technical musical work.    Gaditanian singers were traine
for performance in imperial Rome eighteen centuries ag
the Phonarci, vocal teachers of Athens, preceded eve
these ; the early Christians made vocal conservatories o
their orphan asylums in the third century ; Julian, a litt
later, endeavoured (in opposition) to found a Pagan sing
ing-school in Alexandria ; the Copts in earliest times ga

ong cadenzas upon almost every syllable of their religious
ongs; Notker, in the tenth century, trained many digni-
aries of the Church in singing; Guido, of Arezzo, in the
leventh century, taught sight-singing and the vocal sylla-
les; the list might be carried on in an almost unbroken
ne down to our own times.

But the period of greatest vocal development is found in
taly in the seventeenth century. A whole race of vocal teach-
rs culminated in Nicolò Porpora, whose pupils, Farinelli,
enesino, Caffarelli and many more, won the highest fame.

It may be mentioned *en passant* that Italy has always
een prolific in natural tenors, and Spain even more so.
Russia is the land of phenomenal basses; England is
he natural home of the alto; America of the soprano.
Vhether such vocal characteristics are racial, alimentary or
limatic has not yet been decided.

Yet the greatest sopranos of the world, Catalani, Mali-
ran, Patti, do not belong to America. The highest soprano
hat history tells us of was Agujari, sometimes called " La
Bastardella," who really sang, not squeaked, a full octave
igher than the highest of our famous sopranos of to-day,
nd we have Mozart's authority for the good quality of her
igh notes.

It is not our purpose in such a very brief synopsis to
peak of many of the famous singers, the list of whom
lone would form a long article; we desire only to speak
f those who are especially representative of some epoch
r are recognised as absolute leaders in their field.

Such a leader was Luigi Lablache, the most wonderful of
ll bass singers. His ponderous voice could easily overtop
he heaviest orchestra, yet was modulated with the skill
nd flexibility of a flute; the most showy cadenzas could
e sung by him as easily as if he were a *soprano leggiero*,
et he could also sing the Priest's part in "The Magic

Flute," or any rôle requiring ponderous majesty. Amor
great altos one thinks first of Alboni.

The list of leading tenors would be a difficult one
compile, yet Rubini, Mario, and the modern Jean de Reszl
are representative.

A special list of Wagnerian singers might be adde
but it may be observed that the title will soon lose i
especial meaning, for many of the Italian and French a
tists are entering this field and proving that the same a
plication of vocal technique is necessary in the singing
Wagner's rôles that is required in Mozart or Rossini. O
may learn in Italy the vocal method to be applied to th
operas of Germany

# *A*

# List

## of

# Abbreviations, Titles, Dignities, Institutions, Etc.

:ad., Academy.
:app. (*I.*, *a cappella*), unaccompanied.
c., according(ly).
comp., accompaniment.
g., allgem. (*G.*, *allgemein*), universal, general.
p., appointed.
t., appointment.
rab., Arabian.
rchbp., Archbishop.
r., arranged, arrangement.
st., assistant.

, born.
ndm., bandmaster.
r., barytone.
D., used of the Biographical Dictionary in this volume.
og., biography, biographical.

, composed.
, circa (*L.*), about.
th., cathedral.
av. (*I.*, *Cavaliere*), Chevalier.
nt., century, as *18th cent.*
, (*L.*, *confer*), compare.
., church, chorus, choir.
apelle (*F.*), chapel, choir.
hev., Chevalier.
oirm., choirmaster.
ar., clarinet.
ll., collected, collection, collector, college.
ollab., collaborated, collaboration.
mp(s)., composition(s).
nd., conducted, conductor (this abbreviation is here used for the equivalents

in various languages, *Kapellmeister*, *maestro di cappella*, *maître de chapelle*, etc.).
**Cons.**, Conservatory (Conservatoire, Conservatorio, Conservatorium).
cpt., counterpoint.
cptist., contrapuntist (used of an early composer of highly contrapuntal works).
ct., court ; **ct.-cond.**, court-conductor ; **ct.-Th.**, court-theatre ; **ct.-opera,** court-opera.

d., died.
**D. D.**, used of the Dictionary of Definitions in this volume.
dict., dictionary.
dir., director.
do., ditto.
dram., dramatic.
**Dr. jur.** (*L.*, *doctor juris*), Doctor of Law(s).
**Dr. phil.** (*L.*, *doctor philosophiæ*), Doctor of Philosophy. *h. c.* (*L.*, *honoris causa*, i. e., honorarily.)

eccl., ecclesiastical.
ed., edited, editor, edition.
e. g. (*L.*, *exempli gratia*), for example.
eng., engaged.
**Engl.**, England, English.
est., establ., established.
et seq. (*L.*, *et sequentes*, *sequentia*) and the following.

**F., Fr.**, French.
**Fest.**, Festival.

53

fl., flute.
fragm., fragmentary ; fragment(s).
F. (R.) C. O., Fellow of the (Royal) College of Organists, London.
Frl. (*G.*, *Fräulein*), Miss.

G., Ger., German.
gen., general.
Govt., Government.
Gr., Greek.
gr., grand.
grossherzöglich (grôs-hăr-tsākh-lĭkh, *G.*), Grandducal.
Gym., Gymnasium.

harm., harmony.
harps., harpsichord.
h. c. (*L.*, *honoris causa*), used of honorary titles.
Heb., Hebrew.
herzöglich (*G.*), Ducal.
H. M.'s Th., Her Majesty's Theatre, London.
Hochschule (hôkh' - shoo - lĕ, *G.*), "High School," college, university.
Hof (hôf, *G.*), court ; a frequent prefix, as in *Hof-kapelle*, court-chapel, or court-orchestra ; *Hof Kapellmeister*, court-conductor ; *Hofmusikintendant*, superintendent of the court-music, etc.
hon., honorary.
Hun., Hungarian.

I., It., Ital., Italian.
ib., ibid. (*L.*, *ibidem*), in the same place.
id. (*L.*, *idem*), the same.
i. e. (*L.*, *id est*), that is.
Imp., Imperial.
incid. music, incidental music (to a drama).
incl., including.
inst., institute, institution.
instr(s)., instrument(s), instrumental.
introd., introduction, introduced.
inv., invented, inventor.

Jap., Japanese.

L., Latin.
libr., librarian.
lit., literally.
lyr., lyric.

m., married.
M(aestro) (*I.*), teacher, conducto[r]
    *m. al cembalo*, the conductor, w[ho]
    formerly sat at the harpsichord ;
    *dei putti*, Master of the choir-boys.
m. de chap. (*F.*, *maître de chappel[le]*) conductor.
m. di capp. (*I.*, *maestro di cappell[a]*) conductor.
M. E., Methodist Episcopal.
melodr., melodrama.
Met. Op., Metropolitan Opera Hou[se] New York.
mfr., manufacturer.
mgr., manager.
mid., middle.
min., minor.
mod., moderately.
m.-sopr., mezzo-soprano.
M. T. (N.) A., Music Teachers' (N[a]tional) Association.
mus., music, musical, musician.
Mus. Antiq. Soc., Musical Antiqu[a]rian Society, London.
Mus. Bac. (Doc.), Bachelor (Docto[r] of Music. Vide D. D.

n., near.
Nat. Cons., National Conservator[y] New York.
N. E. Cons., New England Conserv[a]tory, Boston.
n. s., new style (referring to the use [of] our calendar in place of the Russia[n] or old style).
N. Y., New York, U. S. A.

O., Ohio, U. S. A.
obbl., obbligato.
obs., obsolete.
op., opus, opera.
Op. com., opéra-comique ; or t[he] Opéra Comique at Paris.
Oper (*G.*), opera.
Opéra, used of the Grand Opéra at Pari[s]
orch., orchl., orchestra, orchestral.
org., organ, organist.
o. s., old style, see n. s. above.
Oxon. (*L.*, *Oxonia*), of Oxfor[d]

p., part.
pcs., pieces.

E., Protestant Episcopal.
erf., performed.
., pianoforte.
hilh., **Philharm.**, Philharmonic.
ol., Polish.
*p., popular.
ort., Portuguese.
es., president.
resb., Presbyterian.
od., produced.
rof., Professor (a special title of great distinction in Germany).
seud., pseudonym.
t., pianist.
ub., published, publisher.

., Royal.
. A. M., Royal Academy of Music, London.
. C., Roman Catholic.
. C. M., Royal College of Music, London.
egius musicus, Royal musician.
et., retired, retiring, returned.
ev., revised.
ev., Reverend.
us., Russian.

ch., school.
ec., secretary.
oc., society.
opr., soprano.
p., Spanish.

**st.**, studied, studying, student.
**succ.**, successfully, success.
**supt.**, superintendent.
**symph.**, symphonic, symphony.

**t.**, teacher, taught.
**th.**, theatre.
**th.**, theorist (writer of treatises).
**th.-cond.**, conductor of theatre-orchestra.
**transcr.**, transcribed, transcription.
**transl.**, translated, translation, translator.
**Tur.**, Turkish.

**Unit.**, Unitarian.
**U. S.**, United States.
**U., Univ.**, university.

**v.**, 1. (*L.*, *vide*) see ; as *v.* B. D., see the Biographical part of this volume. *v.* D. D., see the Defining Dictionary. 2. very, as *v. succ.*, very successful(ly).
**var(s)**, variation(s).
**vla.**, viola.
**vln.**, violin.
**vt.**, violinist.

**w.**, with.
**Wis.**, Wisconsin, U. S. A.

**Ztg.** (*G.*, *Zeitung*). Gazette.

# A

## PRONOUNCING & DEFINING
## 𝕯𝖎𝖈𝖙𝖎𝖔𝖓𝖆𝖗𝖞
*of*
## Musical Terms, Instruments
*&c.*

### A

**A** (*G.* ä; *F. I.* & *Sp.* lä.) 1. A musical pitch (435 vibrations per second, according to the standard adopted in France 1879 and at Vienna 1887, and called diapason normal). 2. Any octave of this pitch. 3. This tone designated in Absolute Pitch (q.v.) as *a′* is invariable on the oboe, and is accordingly used as the tone to which the whole orchestra is attuned. It is hence called the normal tone. 4. The major key with three sharps. 5. The minor key relative to C major.

**a** or **ab**, *L., I., F.* By, from, for, to, at, in, etc.[1]

**â** (äp), *G.* "Off." Used of stops.

**'acus harmon′icus**, *L.* 1. A table of notes. 2. The arrangement of the keys and pedals of an instrument.

**anera** (ă-bä-nä′-rä), *Sp.* Vide HA-BANERA.

**andon** (ă-bäṅ-dôṅ), *F.* Lack of all restraint in emotion.

**badare** (äb-bä-dä′-rĕ), *I.* To take care.

**bandonar′si, abbandonatamen′te, abbando′ne, abbando′no,** *I.* With abandon.

**bassamen′to,** *I.* Lowering. **A. di mano,** (a) down-beat; (b) the carrying of one hand below the other in piano playing. **A. di voce** (vō-chĕ), *I.* Lowering of the voice. Diminution.

**abbatimen′to,** *I.* Down-beat.

**abbellare** (äb-bel-lä′-rĕ), *I.* To orna. ment. **abbelitura(e)** (too′-rä), **a. bellimen′to**(i). Embellishment(s).

**abbetont** (äp′-bä-tōnt), *G.* With final emphasis.

**a-b-c-d-i(e)ren** (ä-bā-tsä-dē′rĕn), *G.* To sing the notes by their letter names.

**Abend** (ä′-bĕnt), *G.* Evening. **-glocke.** Curfew. **-lied** (lēt). Even song. **-musik** (moo-zēk′). Evening music.

**abenteuerlich** (ä′-bĕn-toi-ĕr-lĭkh), *G.* Venturesome.

**abfal′len,** *G.* To deteriorate. **-gebrochen** (äp′-gĕ-brôkh-ĕn). Interrupted. Vide CADENCE. **Abgesang** (äp′-gĕ-zängk). Refrain. It followed the two *Stollen* in the songs of the Meistersänger. **-gestossen** (äp′-gĕ-shtôs-sĕn). Staccato. **-gleiten** (äp′-glī-tĕn). To slide the finger from a black key to the next white key. **Abkürzung** (äp′-kür-tsoongk). Abbreviation. **-leiten** (äp′-lī-tĕn). To derive from. **-lösen** (äp′-lā-zĕn). To change fingers on a sustained tone. **-nehmend** (äp′-nā-mĕnt). Diminuendo.

**abrégés** (äb-rā-zhā), *F.* Trackers.

**abreichen** (äp′-rī-khĕn), *G.* On the violin, to extend the little, or draw back the first, finger.

**Abreissung** (äp′-rīs-soongk), *G.* Sudden pause.

---

[1] Phrases beginning with these and other prepositions will be found under their principal words.

**abrup'tio,** *L.* An abrupt halt.

**Absatz** (äp'-zäts), *G.* 1. Cadence. 2. A phrase.

**Abschnitt** (äp'-shnĭt), *G.* Section.

**abschwellen** (äp'-schvĕl-len), *G.* Diminuendo.

**absetzen** (äp'-zĕt-zĕn), *G.* To strike two keys successively with the same finger.

**absolute.** Used of music that is self-derived and complete in its own form, meaning, and beauty, as opposed to operatic or programme music.

**abstammen** (äp'-shtäm-men), *G.* To be derived from.

**Abstand** (äp'-shtänt), *G.* Interval.

**ab'stossen,** *G.* To play staccato. **Ab'stosszeichen** (tsī-khĕn). Staccato mark(s).

**Abstrak'ten,** *G.* Trackers.

**Abstufung** (äp'-shtoo-foongk), *G.* Shading.

**abtönen** (äp'-tā-nĕn), *G.* To err from the key.

**ab(h)ub** (ä'-boob). A Hebrew horn.

**abun'dans,** *L.* Augmented.

**abwechselnd** (äp'-vĕkhs-ĕlnt), *G.* Alternating.

**Abweichung** (äp'-vīkh-oongk), *G.* A variant.

**Abyssinian flute.** A beak flute.

**Abzug** (äp'-tsookh). 1. Lifting of a finger or a bow. 2. The sliding of the finger from one key to the next.

**académie spirituelle** (ăk-ăd-ā-mē spĭr-ēt-wĕl), *F.* A sacred concert.

**acathis'tus,** *Gr.* Ancient Greek Church hymn in honor of the Virgin.

**accademia** (ak-käd-ā-mē'-ä), *I.* 1. An Academy. 2. A concert.

**accarezzevole** (äk-kä-rĕd-zā'vō-lĕ), *I.* Caressing. **accarezzevolmen'te.** Pleadingly.

**accell., acceldo.** Abbr. of accelerando.

**accelerando** (ät-chä-lĕ-rän'-dō), *I.* Accelerating (the velocity). **acceleratemen'te.** Swiftly. **accelerato,** (rä'-tō). Swift.

**accent** (in *F.*, ăk-säṅ). **accento** (ät-chĕn'-to), *I.* 1. Emphasis, force, on a tone, a chord, a beat. 2. An cent mark (q.v.). The first beat every measure receives a *primary* cent. In 4-4 time, the third beat ceives a lighter or *secondary* or *s accent.* 3. In 6-8 or 6-4 time fourth beat takes a *secondary* acc In 9-8 time the fourth beat ha *secondary a.,* and the seventh a *te ary a.* still lighter. The regular s etonic accent of the standard meas is called the *grammatical, metri natural* or *regular a.;* this is m fied by the *rhythmical* and the *thetic, emotional, pathetic, poetica rhetorical* accent.

**accent-mark.** One of the numer signs of stress; as > *sfzorzando* ∧ (strictly tenuto); 'or,, used (a) indicate *pitch* (q. v.) as *c'* and C,, = and C₂; (b) as an abbreviation *foot* (q. v.) as 8' = 8-foot.

**accent'or.** Leader of a chorus.

**accentuare** (too-ä'-rĕ), *I.* **accentui ren** (ak-tsĕn-too-ē'-rĕn), *G.* To cent. To accentuate. **accentua'** With marked accent

**accentuation.** The aċċ oṙ äṙṫ oṙ pr erly distributing emphasis.

**accen'tus,** *L.* Portion(s) of the ri song of the Church, chanted by priest at the altar; in contradisti tion to the Concentus, sung by assistants or choir. **A. ecclesi tici,** *L.* Melodic formulæ used the Church in reciting, the colle etc. They correspond with the c ma, semicolon, interrogation, etc., ordinary writing, and are of se kinds, called *immutab'ilis,* monoto *me'dius,* a minor third; *grav'is,* fifth; *acu'tus,* sol mi mi sol; *moder tus,* rising a second and returnir *interrogati'vus,* falling a second a returning; *final'is,* sol la sol fa re—thus closing in the Dorian key

**Accessis'ten,** *G.* Unpaid choriste

**accessory notes.** The subordin notes of an ornament. **accesso tones.** Overtones.

**acciaccato** (ät-chĭ-äk-kä'-tō), *I.* olent.

**ciaccatur** (ät-tsĭ-äk-kä-toor'), *G.* The doubling of the 6-4 chord on the dominant, the right hand alone resolving it.

**ciaccatura** (ät-chäk-kä-too'-rä), *I.* A short appoggiatura, usually a grace-note, struck at the same time with its principal, but instantly released.

**cidentals,** *E.* **accidenti** (ät-tshĭ-dĕn'-tē), *I.* **accidents** (äk-sĭ-dän), *F.* Sharps, flats, and naturals, foreign to the key-signature.

**colade** (äk-kô-läd), *F.* Brace.

**compagnamento** (äk-kom-pän-ya-nĕn'-to), *I.* Accompaniment; figured bass. **accompagnare** (yä'-rĕ). To accompany. **accompagnato** (yä'-ō). Accompanied.

**commodare** (dä'-rĕ), *I.* To tune. **compagner** (äk-kôm-pīn-yā), *F.* To accompany. **accompagné** (äk-kôm-pīn-yā). Accompanied. **accompagnement** (äk-kôm-pīn-yŭ-mäñ). Accompaniment.

**companiment.** A part or parts added to other principal parts. **a. ad libitum.** Optional accompaniment. **a. obbligato.** Accompaniment essential. **accompanist.** One who plays accompaniments.

**coppiato** (äk-kôp-pī-ä'-tō), *I.* Tied. **cord,** *E* (in *F.*, äk-kŏr), 1. Consonance. 2. A chord; **à l'ouvert,** on the open strings; **natural,** a fundamental chord; **parfait,** a triad; **renversé,** inverted; **de sixte ajoutée,** chord of the added sixth. Vide ALTERED.

**accordant** (äk-kôr-däñ), *F.* In concord. **accorder** (äk-kôr-dā). To tune. **accordeur** (dŭr). 1. A tuner; 2. a set of 12 tuning forks giving the tempered scale. 3. Monochord. **accordoir** (äk-kôr-dwär). A tuning-key, hammer, or cone.

**cordamen'to, accordanza** (dän'-sä), *I.* Consonance.

**cor'dance, accor'dature,** *E.* **accordatura** (too'-rä), *I.* The system of tuning the strings of an instrument; thus, the **a.** of a violin is g-d-a-e.

**accordare** (dä-rĕ), *I.* To tune. **accordan'do.** Tuning; in tune.

**accor'deon.** A free-reed instr. inv. by Damian of Vienna, 1829. The tone is produced by a double set of bellows acting upon metallic tongues. The right hand presses buttons or keys giving an incomplete chromatic scale; the left hand has a few bass tones.

**accor'do,** *I.* 1. A chord. 2. An old Italian instrument of twelve or more strings.

**accoupler** (äk-koo-plā), *F.* To couple. **accouplez** (äk-koo-plā). "Draw the coupler."

**accrescendo** (ak-krĕs-shĕn'-do). *I.* Crescen'do. **accrescimento** (ac-crä-shē-mĕn-tō). Augmentation as of a fugal theme. **punto d'a.,** the dot placed after a note to prolong it. **accresciuto** (shoo'-tō), *I.* Augmented.

**acetab'ulum,** *L.* An ancient instr. of percussion. Earthen vessels beaten as drums or clashed as cymbals.

**achromat'ic.** Lacking accidentals and modulations.

**acht** (äkht), *G.* Eight. **Achtfusston** (äkht'-foos-tōn) or **8-füssig** (füs-sĭkh). Eight-foot tone. **8-stimmig** (shtĭm-mĭkh). For eight voices or instruments.

**Achtel** (äkhtl), **Achtelnote,** *G.* Eighth note; quaver. **Achtelpause,** *G.* Eighth-rest.

**A Chula** (ä choo'-lä), *Port.* A dance like the fandango.

**ac'ocotl.** A Mexican plant from whose stalk an aboriginal wind-instr. of the same name was made.

**acolyth'ia,** *Gr.* The order of service in the Greek Church.

**acous'tics** (ä-kow'-stix, or ä-koo'stix), *E.,* **acoustique** (ä-koos-tēk), *F.* The science of sounds.

## Acoustics.

### By J. S. Shedlock.

THE term Acoustics is derived from a Greek verb signifying to hea
and the science of acoustics tells us about the production and pro
agation, also the comparison, of sounds. When a pianoforte stri
is struck by a hammer or a violin string by a bow, it trembles, sways to ar
fro and thus sets the surrounding air a-trembling ; the air-particles sway
and fro producing a wave as a light breeze sets a corn-field waving; so v
speak of waving air, or waves of air. These waves strike the ear and the
motion is passed on to the brain and becomes what is called sound; but l
what wonderful process one changes into the other does not concern us her
¶When the swaying to and fro of the particles of an elastic body is stea
and sufficiently rapid, a musical sound results, otherwise, only noise. Tl
word *sound* indeed is generally understood to mean a musical one, her
sound is contrasted with noise. We speak of the noise of thunder or of battl
but of the sound of an instrument or of the human voice. Nature frequent
offers a mixture of sound and noise, as in a waterfall, in which sometimes t
one sometimes the other predominates. ¶*Vibration* is the name given to t
swaying to and fro of the particles of an elastic body, and of this motion t
clock pendulum gives a clear and simple idea. The particles only sway b
the motion is passed on. When a glass ball is pushed against one end of
row of glass balls touching one another, the ball at the other end flies o
The motion of the first ball has been passed on from ball to ball until it h
reached the extreme one. Vibrations when steady and sufficiently rap
produce sounds which may be higher or lower, and the higher the sound t
greater the number of swayings to and fro, or vibrations, within a given tim
There are two special instruments by means of which air-vibrations can
easily counted : one is Savart's toothed wheel, the other the Siren. Wh
one sound is higher than another, it is said to be of higher pitch ; wh
lower, of lower pitch. The shorter a string, the higher its pitch. If a vi
linist, setting one of the strings of his instrument in motion by means of t
bow, slides his finger along that string toward the bridge, the sound will b
come continually of higher pitch : for the string is gradually shortened, t
ever-increasing portion behind the finger being cut off from the vibrato
movement caused by the bow. There is, therefore, a topsy-turvy conne
tion between the number of vibrations produced by a string, and the leng
of that string. ¶Vibration can be felt if a glass jar over which a bow h
been drawn is touched lightly with the finger. Vibration can be seen wh
the string of a piano or violin is struck by a hammer or bow. Vibration c
be shown by attaching a strip of sheet copper tapering to a point to one of t

ongs of a tuning-fork. If the latter be set in motion, and the copper point placed on a piece of smoked glass, it will give the exact record of the exact raying to and fro of the fork. ¶ Strings such as are used in the pianoforte d violin when set in motion would of themselves create very faint sound-aves. The sound has to be strengthened. In the pianoforte the motion not communicated directly to the air, but first to a massive sound-board. a violin the little sound-post plays an important part in passing on the orations from the string to the back of the instrument. The strengthening tone by such means is apt to be overlooked. ¶ Particles of air when set motion by a vibrating body first move from their point of rest to a certain stance and then back through the point of rest to a similar distance in an oposite direction ; the distance between these extreme points is the extent, as it is named, the *amplitude* of the vibration. As the vibrating body turns to a state of rest, that distance gradually diminishes and finally vanishes, st as it does when, the chain giving out, the clock pendulum slows down d finally stops. The degree of loudness or softness of a sound depends on e extent or amplitude of the vibration, the wider the one the louder the her. Sound travels at freezing temperature at the rate of 1090 feet per cond ; with increase of temperature there is increase of velocity, for the air us becomes more elastic. Sound travels faster in water than in air because the rmer is more elastic. The degree of closeness of the particles of the medium, r, water, gases of different kinds, through which sound travels has also an fluence on velocity. ¶ Sound diminishes in intensity according to the dis-nce. Throw a stone into a pond and see how the expanding waves be-ome feebler and feebler in proportion as they are distant from the spot which enerated them. So it is with sound-waves. Intensity varies inversely as e square of the distance, *i.e.*, if a sound is heard twenty feet away from the nstrument producing it, at forty feet, twice the distance, it will only be a uarter as loud : the square of $2 = 4$, and the relationship of the two sounds s as one to four, or $\frac{1}{4}$. This is of course theory; in practice sound is mostly ntensified in various ways, so that it does not lose its strength at this exact rate. A string set in motion, that is into a state of vibration, produces a note igher or lower according to its length. That note, however, is not a simple ound, but one made up of many sounds. For in addition to the whole tring vibrating, it divides into two, three, four, and indeed into many por-ions, all of which vibrate in themselves at the same time that the whole string s vibrating. And these portions being shorter give out higher sounds than hat of the whole string, and they bear themselves the self-evident name of Overtones. They are also called *upper partials* because they are higher ounds produced by parts of the string. The swaying to and fro of these parts is not so great as that of the whole string, therefore the sounds they pro-

duce are fainter. The halves give a louder sound than the thirds, the thirds th
the quarters and so on. All these sounds mix so thoroug̱ḫ
together as to give the impression of one simple sound, and it
*etc.* upon their order and number, which differ in different instr
ments, that quality of tone depends. Here are the first elev
notes of such a compound sound—they can be heard and an
lyzed by pressing the "loud" pedal of a pianoforte, striking t
low c indicated and listening intently and long. Out of the overtones whi
are repeated we secure easily the simplest of all chords in ha
mony. ¶If the key of the lowest note is pressed down on
pianoforte without producing any sound, and so held, then if the above cho.
is struck sharply, the fingers after the blow being instantly removed from tl
keys, then that chord will continue to sound, although the strings which pr
duced it have ceased to vibrate. Portions of the string of the lowest note hav
been set swaying to and fro, for the key pressed down removing the damp
from its string left it free to vibrate. These portions vibrate by what is calle
*sympathetic attraction.* Repeat the experiment, but immediately after tl
chord has been struck, raise the key of the lowest note, and the chord is n
longer heard. ¶It has already been stated that by means of certain instr
ments the numbers of vibrations of sounds can be counted, and they ca
therefore also be compared. Of any two notes an octave apart the upp
one has twice as many vibrations as the lower. Of any two notes a perfe
fifth apart the relationship between upper and lower is as 3 to 2. Of an
two notes a major third apart as 5 to 4, and a minor third as 6 to 5. W
see then that the perfect consonances, the 8th, 5th, and 4th, have the sin
plest relationship, 2 to 1, 3 to 2, 4 to 3. Next in order come the imperfe
consonances, the major and minor thirds, 5 to 4, and 6 to 5 ; in no case is
higher figure than 6 required. From these relationships the major diatoni
scale can easily be constructed, and then if the relationships between each not
of the scale and the succeeding one be taken, it will be found that the inter
vals between c and d, f and g, a and b are equal, that d to e and g to ar
slightly smaller and that e to f and b to c are alike. The former are calle
tones, either major or minor, and the last two semitones.

---

**acte de cadence** (ăkt-dŭ-kă-däns), *F.*
A progression to or toward a cadence.

**action.** The mechanism of an instrument.

**actin′ophone.** A device for producin₉
sound by means of actinic rays.

**act music.** Cantatas composed by th
Professor of Music at Oxford for spe
cial occasions.

-tune. Music between the acts of play.

ité (äk-wē-té), *F.* Acuteness.

stica (ä-koos'-tǐ-kä), *I.*, **Acustik** .-koos-tĕk'), *G.* Acoustics. acus- sch (tǐsh), *G.* Acoustical.

ta (ä-koo'-tä), *I.* I. Acute, shrill. . A shrill 2-ft. mixture-stop.

'tæ clav'es, *L.* The name given y Guido to the tones from a to g.

te. High in pitch, shrill.

tus, *L.* Vide ACCENTUS.

*L.* To, for, at.

gio (ä-dä'-jo), *I.* I. Slow, slower ian andante, not so slow as lento. . A slow movement or division of a ymphony or sonata. **adagietto** (ä- ä-jĕt'-tō). A little faster than ada- io. **adagissimo** (jĭs-sĭ-mo). Ex- remely slow.

ptation, *E.*, **adattazione** (ä-dät- ä-tsǐ-ō'-nĕ), *I.* An arrangement or ranscription.

sio (ä-dä'-sǐ-ō), *I.* Adagio.

led lines. Ledger lines. **added** ixth. Vide SIXTH.

litato (äd-dǐ-tä'-tō), *I.* Fingered.

litional keys. Those above f''' n the piano. **additional accom- ⸱animents.** Accompaniments or ⸱arts added to a work by another and than that of the composer.

lolorato (äd-dō-lō-rä'-tō), *I.* Mel- ncholy.

el (ä'-dĕl), *G.* Majesty.

i'aphone. Vide GABELKLAVIER.

i'aphonon, *G.* A piano of perma- ⸱ent tune, inv. in 1820 by Schuster. The tone was produced by metal ⸱ars.

irato (ä-dǐ-rä'-tō), *I.* Angry. **adi- ⸱atamen'te.** Angrily.

junct notes. Unaccented auxiliary ⸱otes.

ljuvant (ät'-yoo-fänt), *G.* Assistant :o a chorister.

ller (ät'-lĕr), *G.* A rarely used organ- stop.

o'nia. An ancient musical feast.

⸱ornamen'to (pl. -i), *I.* An embel- ⸱ishment.

adoucir (ä-doo-sēr), *F.* To soften, to flatten.

adquis'ta or **adsuma'ta vox,** *L.* The extreme low tone.

adufe (ä-dhoo'-fĕ), *Sp.* Tambourine. **adufero** (fä'-rō). Player of it.

A-dur (ä-door), *G.* The key of A major.

æ'rophone. A kind of harmonium.

ængstlich (ĕnkst-lǐkh), *G.* Anxious- ly.

æol'harmon'ica. A kind of seraphine.

Æo'lian. I. Vide MODES. 2. The fifth of the authentic Gregorian modes. 3. An automatic reed instrument in which the performer controls the time, the stops, and the expression.

Æo'lian Harp or **Lyre.** An instr. inv. by Kircher in the 17th century. It is usually a box set in a window and fit- ted with 6 or more strings of silk or gut, tuned in unison, passing over bridges about ¾-inch high. The strings are so arranged that the air causes vibration among them. The varying humours of the wind produce a strangely sweet and various har- mony, the different overtones being audible in a shifting concord of eerie beauty.

Æolian mute. A combination of the pitch-pipe and mute.

Æolian pianoforte. A piano inv. by T. Gilbert about 1850, and provided with free reeds and a bellows for giv- ing the piano a sustaining power.

æoli'na. I. A small free-reed mouth instr., inv. by Wheatstone, 1829. 2. An organ-stop.

æolo'dicon or **æolo'dion,** *Gr.* A keyed instr. in which the tone is produced by steel springs, put in vibration by bellows.

æolomelo'dicon. The same instru- ment with brass tubes to reinforce the springs.

æolopan'talon. An æolodicon com- bined with a piano.

Æolsharfe (ä'-ôls-här'-fĕ), *G.* Æol- ian harp.

Æolsklavier (ä'-ôls-klä-fēr), *G.* A keyboard wind instr., inv. 1825, by

Schortmann, with reeds of wood instead of metal.

**Æota′na,** *Gr.* A small mouth instr. of short metallic reeds.

**Æqual** (ā-kwäl), *G.*, from Lat., signifying " 8-ft." Vide STOP.

**æquiso′nus,** *L.* Unison. **æquiso′nans.** Concordant.

**æquiva′gans,** *L.* Simultaneously syncopated or varied in all the parts.

**Æquivoken** (ā′-kwĭ-fō-kĕn), *G.* Meistersinger airs of the same name.

**ære recurvo.,** *L.* Bucena.

**æ′rophone.** A French melodeon.

**aevia** (ē′-vĭ-ä), *L.* Abbr. (the vowels only) of Alleluia.

**affabile** (äf-fä′-bĭ-lĕ), *I.* Affable. **affabilità** (bē-lĭ-tä′). Cordiality. **affabilmen′te.** Affably.

**affanna′to, affano′so,** *I.* Tormented, distressed.

**affectirt** (äf-fĕk-tērt′), *G.* With affectation.

**affectueux** (äf-fĕk-tü-ŭ′), *F.* Affectionate.

**affettazione** (tä-tsĭ-ō′-nĕ), *I.* Affectation. **affettatamen′te.** Affectedly.

**affet′to,** *I.* Affection. **affettuoso.** Affectionate. **affettuosamente.** Affectionately. **affettivo** (tē′-vo). Affecting.

**affilar′,** *I.* Vide FILAR.

**affinity.** Close relation (as of keys).

**afflizione** (äf-flē-tsĭ-ō′-nĕ). Sorrow. **afflit′to.** Sorrowful.

**affrettan′do, affrettate** (tä′-tĕ). Hurrying. **affretto′so.** Hurried.

**afofa′.** Portuguese fandango.

**after-beat.** Two notes used as ending a trill. **after note.** A small unaccented note taking its time from the preceding.

**agevole** (ä-ja′-vō-lĕ), *I.* Agile. **agevolmen′te.** Nimbly. **agevolezza** (ä-jä-vō-lĕd′-zä). Agility.

**aggiustato** (äd-joos-tä′-tō), *I.* Adjusted, arranged, adapted. **aggiustatamen′te.** In strict time.

**aggraver la fugue** (ăg-grä-vä lä füg), *F.* To augment the (subject of a) fugue.

**agiatamente** (ä-jät-*ä̇*-m*ĕ̇n*′-tĕ̇). Easily.

**agilità** (ä-jēl-ĭ-tä′), *I.* Agility. **ag men′te.** Nimbly.

**agitato** (ä-jĭ-tä′-tō), *I.* Agitated, h ried. **agitamen′to, agitazione** jē-tä′-tsĭ-ō′-nĕ). Agitation.

**agité** (ä-zhē-tä′), *F.* Agitated.

**agli** (äl′-yē), *I.* Vide AL.

**Ag′nus De′i.** *L.* "Lamb of Go Vide MASS.

**ago′ge,** *Gr.* 1. The order of int vals of melodic progression. Rhythmical order of accents a duration. 3. Expression. **Ago′g** *G.* The art of expression by ruba acceleration, &c. **ago′gic acce** Expression mark.

**agraffe** (ä-gräff), *F.* A small pin check the vibration of a piano strir

**agréments** (ä-grä-män), *F.* 1. E bellishments. 2. Incidental music a dancing.

**ai** (ä′-ē), *I.* To the. Vide AL.

**aigre** (ĕgr), *F.* Harsh, sharp. **aig** ment (ĕgr-män). Sharply.

**aigu** (ĕ-gü), *F.* Acute, shrill.

**air,** *E.* and *F.* A melody, or tur an aria. **a. à boire** (bwär). A dri ing song. **a. à reprises** (rŭ-prē Catch. **a. chantant** (shän-tän). lyric. **a. détaché** (dä-tä-shä). A s gle air detached from a larger wo **a. rapide** (rä-pēd). A flourish. **varié** (vă-rĭ-ä). Theme with var tions.

**Ais** (ä-ĭs), *G.* The note or key "*A* sharp.

**aisé** (ĕ-zä), *F.* Easy. **aisément** (ĕ- män). Easily, freely.

**aiuton** (ĭ′-ū-tän), *Gr.* An organ ma of tuning-forks, inv. by Charles Cla get and guaranteed never to requ retuning.

**ajakli-keman** (a-yäk′-le-kä-män). Turkish violin.

**Akkord** (äk-kôrt′), *G.* A chord. *A* **passage.** An arpeggio. **A.-zith** 1. The auto-harp. 2. A set of inst ments.

**Akromat** (ä-krō-mät′), *G.* A musica **akromatisch** (ä-krŏ-mä′-tĭsh), *G.* A romatic.

**Akustik** (ä-koos′-tēk), *G.* Acoustic

**, au, aux, al, all', alla, alle,
lo, agli, ai,** *F.* and *I.* Varying
mbinations of the different genders
the article "the" with the prepo-
ion "to," meaning "in the manner
," as *à la grecque,* and *alla cappella.*

**moth,** *Heb.* Obscure and disputed
usical term in Psalm LXVIII, 25.

**'um,** *L.* **all' armi,** *I.* A call to
ms.

**da** (äl-bä'-dhä), *Sp.* A morning
renade.

**erti Bass.** A bass consisting of
onotonous simple broken chords.
called after its alleged inventor.
de B.D.

**gue** (äl-bō-gā'), *Sp.* An instr. of
e flute species.

**umblatt** (äl'-boom-blät). Album-
af. Plural, **A.-blätter** (blĕt-ter).

**na** (al-koo'-na), *I.* Some ; as **con
licenza,** with some licence.

**u'ya,** *Sp.* Hallelujah.

**nana** (äl-ĕ-mä'-nä), *Sp.* Old Span-
h dance.

**xandre organ.** Vide AMERICAN
RGAN.

**uot.** Used of the parts into which
vibrating string is subdivided in
oducing overtones. **Aliquotflü-
l,** *G.* A piano inv. by Blüthner
th a sympathetic octave string for
ch note. **Aliquottheorie** (äl'-ı-
vôt-tā-ō-rē) *G.* The theory of over-
nes.

**.** Vide AL.

**rgan'do,** *I.* Gradually slower
d broader.

**ova.** Vide OTTAVA.

(äl'lĕ), *G.* All : **alle Instrumente.**
ll the instruments ; *tutti.*

**grativo** (al-lā-grä-te'-vō) ; **alle-
ramen'te, allegran'te,** *I. ;* **allé-
rement** (äl-lā-grŭ-mäṅ), *F.* Gayly
d quickly.

**grettino** (äl-lā-grĕt-tē'-nō), *I.* A
tle slower than allegretto.

**gret'to,** *I.* Slower than allegro,
t blithe and cheery.

**grezza** (äl-lā-grĕd'-za) ; **allegria**
rē'-ä), *I.* Joy, cheer.

**gro** (äl-lā'-grō), *I.* Very fast.

though slower than Presto ; it usually
indicates a high rate of speed. This
may be modified by additional phrases
as *allegro ma non troppo.* **allegri
di bravura** (äl-lā-grē dē brä-voora),
*I.* Compositions to display virtuosity. **allegrissimamen'te, allegris'-
simo,** *I.* Extremely fast. **allegro
con moto,** *I.* **a. di molto.** Very
fast. **a. moderato, a. non molto,
a. non troppo,** *I.* Moderately fast.
**a. giusto** (joos'-to), *I.* Fast ; but
exactly in time.

**allein** (äl-līn'), *G.* Alone, single. **A.-
sang.** Solo. **A.-sänger,** or **-spieler.**
Solo-singer (or player).

**alleluia, allelujah** (äl-lā-loo'-yä),
*Heb.* " Praise the Lord ; " Hallelujah.

**Allemande** (äl-mänd), *F.* **1.** A German national or peasant dance in 3-4
or 3-8 time ; in some places 2-4 time
**2.** A French imitation of this dance
**3.** A movement in the classic Suite of
Bach, etc. ; in 4-4 time, *andantino,*
with a short note on the up-take.

**allentato** (tä'-tō), **allentamen'to, al-
lentan'do,** *I.* Retarding.

**allgemeiner Bass** (äl-khĕ-mī'-nĕr bäs),
*G.* Thorough bass.

**allied.** Accessory.

**allmählich, allmählig** (äl'-mä-lĭkh), *G.*
Gradually.

**allonger l'archet** (äl-lôṅ-zhä lär-shà),
*F.* To prolong the bow stroke.

**allo'ra,** *I.* Then.

**Almain, Alman, Almand.** Allemande.

**Alma Redemp'toris,** *L.* Hymn to
the Virgin.

**al'penhorn, alp'horn.** A horn used
by the Alpine herdsmen ; it is made
of strips of firwood from 3 to 8 feet
long. It has a limited range.

**alphabet.** The 7 letters used in music,
'A-G.

**alt** (ält), *I.* High. **In alt** is applied
to tones in the first octave above the
treble staff, as b'' ; **in altissimo** refers to tones in the second octave
above the treble staff, as d'''.

**al'ta,** *I.,* **alt,** *G.* High, or alto ; as
**Althorn. octava alta.** An octave
above.

al'ta, *Sp.* An old Spanish dance.

alterata (ä'-tä), *I.* Scales with notes foreign to the Church modes.

altera'tio, *L.* The doubling of the time value.

alterato (äl-tĕ-rä'-tō), *I.*, altéré tä-rä), *F.*, altered, *E.* Char chromatically, especially applie certain inverted chords.

## Altered Chords.

### BY CHARLES W. PEARCE, MUS. DOC.

A CHORD originally formed by a combination of notes belon to the Diatonic Scale of any key can be chromatically altered the addition of an accidental ♯, ♭, or ♮, to one or more of its tervals. A chord ceases to be chromatic when it induces modulati being then a diatonic chord in the new key. In modern harmc the combinational tendency of the Diatonic Scale is to arrange itsel a perpendicular series of thirds above the 5th degree or dominant of the scale, according to this formula :
¶Reckoned from the lower note (or root) the intervals are : 1. Major 3d ; 2. Perfect 5th ; 3. Minor 7th ; 4. Major (or minor) 9th ; 5. Eleventh (compound 4th) ; 6. Major (or minor) 13th (compound 6th). ¶Thus the first sign of chromatic alteration is the interchange-ability of the major and minor 3d and 6th of the scale. The harmonic formula shown in Fig. 1 can be built up on the dominant notes of the two adjacent keys,

Fig. 1. — The s black notes ind those intervals a the Dominant w are most suscep of chromatic al tion.

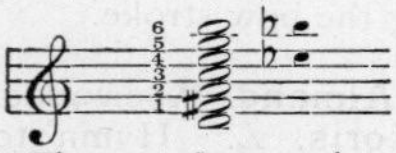

(viz.: those keys having one sharp or one flat more or less than the si ture of the tonic key). And as these additional formulæ can be use

Fig. 2.—Supertonic Formula.

the tonic key without modulation to either of its adja keys, their roots are conveniently called supertonic tonic to show their relationship to the scale of the to ¶The supertonic root is dominant of the next s key. ¶The tonic root is dominant of the next flat ¶In the supertonic formula the necessary major 3d of the root (1 of the series) is an invariable chromatic alteration. The interchangeability of the major and minor 3d of the scale (4 of the series) is a confirma-tion of No. 6 of the Dominant formula (Fig. 1). The interchangeability of the major and minor 7th of the

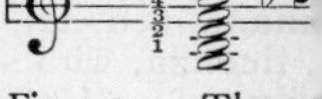

Fig. 3.—Tonic F mula.

scale (6 of the series) is the characteristic chromatic alteration of the su tonic formula. ¶In the tonic formula the necessary minor 7th of the (3 of the series) is an invariable chromatic alteration. The intercha ability of the major and minor 6th of the scale (6 of the series) is a

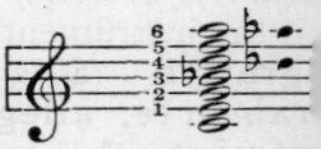

nation of No. 4 of the Dominant formula (Fig. 1). The interchange-
ity of the major and minor 2d of the scale (4 of the series) is the
racteristic chromatic alteration of the tonic formula. ¶ From the harmonic
nulæ shown in Figs. 1, 2, 3, the chromatic scale is derived. This
omatic scale is the same for both major and minor keys having the same
ic; but the difference of key signature induces changes in the number of
identals used. Compare Figs. 4 and 5. ¶ With the introduction of the

Fig. 4.—Signature of C Major.

Fig. 5.—Signature of C Minor.

omatic element into harmony, the absolute distinction of major and minor
ppears, and the key tonality becomes one. ¶ To facilitate the notational
venience of the chromatic element in harmony, the enharmonic equiva-
s of several degrees of the chromatic scale are freely admitted. ¶ Chro-
ic alteration is chiefly observable in triads and in chords of the seventh
n their inversions. ¶ Fig. 6 shows the triads on the seven degrees of
diatonic scale. Fig. 7 shows how these triads may be chromatically
red in the same key without necessitating modulation to any other key.

I II III IV V VI VII

Fig. 6.

Fig. 7.

f these Nos. 1, 4, 18, 19, and 28, show an enharmonic substitution of
harp for D flat; Nos. 4, 5, 11, 22, and 25 have G sharp instead of A
; Nos. 10, 21, 25, and 34 have D sharp for E flat; Nos. 3 and 15,
e G flat for F sharp; and No. 30 has C flat for B. It may also be re-
ked that Nos. 30 and 15 are the only triads of the series which have all

three of their notes altered from the notation of the diatonic scale of C ;
it will be observed that in No. 30 two of these altered notes (A flat and
flat) are the notes shown in Fig. 1 to be those first susceptible of chrom
alteration in the key of E ; and in No. 15 two of the altered notes belong to
supertonic formula shown in Fig. 2. A glance at Fig. 7 is sufficient to sl
that " enharmonic substitution " is only made use of in modern music in or
to throw the altered chords into an easily recognizable harmonic shape suc
triads or sevenths (or their inversions). ¶Distinguishing names of a pu
fanciful character have been given to the first inversions of several of
chords in Fig. 7 (see Fig. 8). ¶One other triad containing three alte

*Neapolitan Sixth.*      *Italian Sixths.*

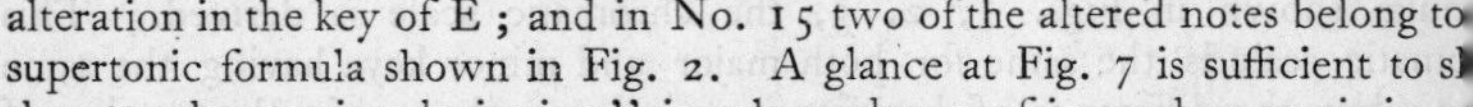

1st inversion of    1st inversion of    1st inversion of    1st inversio
No. 8, Fig. 7.      No. 10, Fig. 7.    No. 20, Fig. 7.    No. 36, Fig

Fig. 8.

notes remains to be shown—this can be written either as the major tria
the flattened dominant or its enharmonic equivalent, the sharpened subdc
nant of the key, as in Fig. 9. ¶Figure 9 exemplifies also the ordir

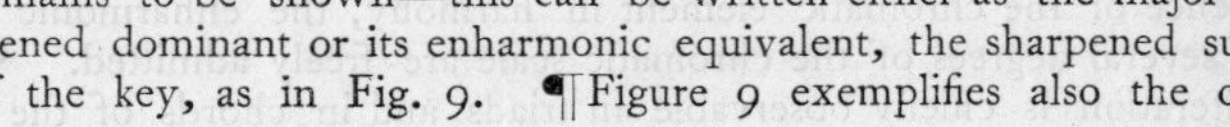

Fig. 9.

treatment of chromatically altered triads, viz. : they are usually followed
some form of dominant harmony. ¶The chords of the seventh built on
seven degrees of the diatonic scale (see Fig. 10) may (like the triads in
6) undergo chromatic alteration. ¶A chromatic alteration of Fig. 10

I    II    III    IV    V    VI    VII

Fig. 10.

III, V, VII, has already been shown in Fig. 3 by the flattening of the le
ing note of the scale ; and similar alterations of Fig. 10, II, and IV, h
been observed in Fig. 2 by the sharpening of the subdominant of the s
(see Fig. 11). ¶Fig. 11 shows that a chord of the seventh may consis

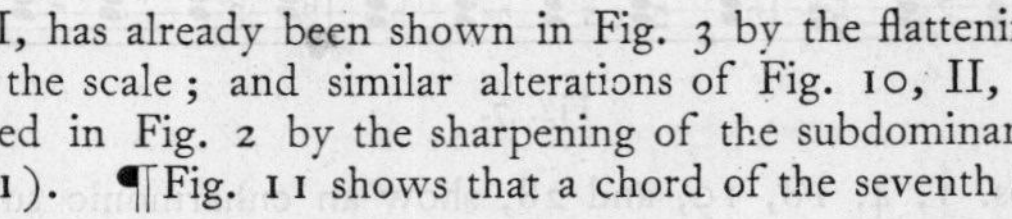

I    III    V    VII      II    IV

Fig. 11.

following different series of intervals from the bass : ¶I, and II, Major
: Perfect 5th : Minor 7th ; III, and IV, Minor 3d : Dim. 5th :
ʌor 7th ; V, Minor 3d : Perfect 5th : Minor 7th ; VII, Major 3d :
fect 5th : Major 7th. ¶A further reference to Figs. 1, 2, and 3, shows
the harmonic superposition of three minor 3ds one above the other—that
iliar combination of notes known as the chord of the Diminished 7th—is
sible over every note of the unaltered Diatonic Scale by chromatic or
armonic alteration without necessitating modulation. ¶Accordingly each

*Enharmonic Equivalents.*

I   II   III   IV   V   VI   VII      I   II   IV   V   VI

Fig. 12.

of the Diatonic Scale may bear the chromatic alteration of its own chord
he 7th as shown in Fig. 13. ¶And with the chromatic alteration (Fig. 14)

Fig. 13.

he root itself the permutations are almost endless. ¶It only remains to
the distinguishing names which have been fancifully applied to one or
of the chromatically altered chords of the 7th in an inverted shape.

*French Sixth.*          *German Sixth.*

(1)   (2)   (3)      (4)   (5)   (6)

Fig. 14.

)f these (1) is the second inversion of VII in Fig. 10, with the sixth of
bass chromatically raised. (2) is the second inversion of II in Fig. 11
ι its bass chromatically lowered. (3) is the second inversion of V in
, 10, with its bass chromatically lowered. (4) is the first inversion of
ι Fig. 10 with its root chromatically raised. (5) and (6) are respect-
y chromatic alterations of the first inversions of IV in Fig. 11, and VII
Fig. 12. ¶It will be observed that the distinguishing feature of the
rds in Fig. 14 is the interval of the *Augmented 6th*. In the usual reso-
on of such chords, care should be taken to let the two notes forming the
gmented 6th proceed outwardly, each by step of a semitone.

**alterezza** (äl-tĕ-rĕd′-zä), *I.* Haughtiness.

**alternamen′te, alternan′do,** *I.* Alternating.

**alternations.** Tunes for bells.

**alternativo** (tē′-vō), *I.* 1. Alternative ; a choice of methods. 2. A short trio.

**Altgeige** (ält′-gī-khe), *G.* The viola.

**Althorn.** Vide SAXHORN.

**altieramente** (tĭ-ä′-rä), *I.* Haughtily.

**alti naturali.** Male altos, or countertenors, as opposed to castrati.

**altisonan′te, altiso′no.** Sonorous.

**altis′onous.** High-sounding, used of the highest male voice.

**altis′simo,** *L.* Vide ALT.

**altist, altista** (äl-tēs′-tä), *I.*, **altiste** (äl-tēst), *F.* An alto singer.

**Alt′klausel** (ält′-klow-zĕl), *G.* The progression of the alto part in a cadence.

**alto** (äl′-tō), *I.* 1. High ; originally applied to the high range of the artificial or falsetto tenors (*castrati, alti naturali, tenori acuti, falsetti*, counter-tenors). Thence the term has been applied to the lower range of women's or boys' voices, ordinarily extending from g below the treble staff to c′′ (an octave above middle C). 2. Viola, also alto viola. **a. primo,** *I.* The higher alto. **a. secondo,** *T.* The lower alto. **a. tenore,** *I.* The higher tenor.

**al′to-basso,** *I.* An obs. dulcimer with a few gut strings, struck with a stick in the left hand, while the performer held a flageolet in the right hand.

**alt′ottava,** *I.* Vide ALTA.

**Altposaune** (ält′-pō-zow-nĕ), *G.* Alto trombone.

**al′tra, al′tro,** *I.* Another. **altra volta.** Encore. **altro modo.** Alternate manner.

**Altsänger** (ält′-zĕng-er), *G.* Alto, or counter-tenor.

**Altschlüssel** (ält-shlüs′-sĕl), *G.* The alto clef.

**Altviole,** *G.* The viola.

**al′tus,** *L.* Alto or counter-tenor.

**alzamento** (äl-tsä-mĕn′-to), *I.* elevating, as of the voice. **a. di ma** Up-beat.

**alzando** (äl-tsan′do), *I.* Raising.

**amabile** (ä-mä′-bĭ-lĕ), *I.* **amabilmen′te.** Amiably. **am lità** (bē-lĭ-tä′). Tenderness.

**amarezza** (ä-mä-rĕd′-zä), *I.* Bit ness. **amaro** (ä-mä′-rō). Bit **amarissimamen′te, amarissi** Very bitter(ly).

**amateur** (ăm-ä-tŭr′), *F.* A "lov of an art, who does not make it profession ; makes it rather an av tion than a vocation.

**Amati.** A violin made by the brot Amati. Vide B. D.

**am′bira.** An African wooden d with vibrating tongues of wood iron.

**am′bitus,** *L.* Compass or range.

**am′bo** or **ambon.** The platf where canons were sung in the diæval Eastern Church.

**Ambro′sian, Ambrosia′nus.** In duced by Ambrose. Vide B. D. **Hymn.** The "Te Deum" do fully credited to him.

**ambuba′ja** (äm-boo-bä′-yä), *L.* strolling flute-player from Syria. ANBUBA.

**ambulant** (äñ-bü-läñ), *F.* Vagab musician.

**âme** (äm), *F.* Soundpost.

**amen** (ä-mĕn′), *Heb.* "So be it."

**American fingering.** That sys of fingering in which x indicates thumb ; in foreign fingering, thumb is called the first finger marked 1.

**American organ.** Originally ca "Melodeon" or "Melodie." A f reed instrument differing from older harmonium (q. v.) in that air is drawn through the reeds suction, instead of forced outw through them ; this gives a supe control and shading ; inv. by J miah Carhart. Its superiority, re nised in Europe more than at ho is also due to the better voicing the reeds and the resonant air-ch

rs developed by Mason & Hamlin.
ae stops are many, and imitate va-
us instruments.

**re** (ä-mō'-rĕ), *I.* Love; affection.

**norevole** (rä'-vō-lĕ), **amorevol-
en'te, amoro'so, amorosamen-
, Loving(ly).

**hichord.** Lira barberina (q. v.).

**orschall** (ä'-môr-shäll), **Amors-
ang,** *G.* An imperfectly valved
ench horn, inv. by Kölbel, 1760.

**ho'ter,** *Gr.* A series of tones com-
n to two registers.

**ollo'so, ampollosamen'te,** *I.* **am-
ulé** (än-poo-lä'), *F.* Pompous(ly).

**sement** (ä-müz-män), *F.* A light
nposition.

än), *G.* On (of an organ-stop);
draw."

**'asis,** *Gr.* A series of ascending
es.

**ath'mi,** *Gr.* Certain antiphons
the Greek Church.

**ru'sis, anakrusis,** *Gr.* 1. The
-beat. 2. The up-take, or ac-
ated part of a measure beginning a
me or air.

**il** (ä-nä-fēl'), *Sp.* A Moorish pipe.
**afilero** (fē-lä-rō) A player of it.

**aza** (ä-nä-gä'-thä), *Sp.* A bird-
l.

**camp'sis, anakamp'tos,** *Gr.* A
ies of descending tones.

**ca'ra,** *Gr.* Ancient kettle-drum.
**akaris'ta,** *Gr.* Kettle-drummer.

**isi** (ä-na-lē'-zē), *I.,* **analyse** (än-ä-
), *F.* Analysis.

**'ba (ya).** Syrian flute.

e (änsh), *F.* A reed. **libre.** Free-
d. **jeu d'a.,** or **a. d'orgue.** A
d-stop.

a (än-chē'ä), *I.* A reed.

**'ra,** *I.* Once more; yet; still, as
**cor più mosso.** Still more quick-

**acht** (än'-däkht), *G.* Devotion.
**dächtig** (än-dĕkh'-tĭkh). Devo-
nal.

**men'to,** *I.* 1. Rate of speed.
An episode as in a fugue. 3. A
al theme.

**nte** (än-dän'-tĕ), *I.* Literally—

"going"; moderately slow, repose-
ful. Often much qualified by other
words, as *con moto, largo, mæstoso, più
tosto allegretto*=(nearly *allegretto*).

**andantino,** *I.* Literally, slower than
Andante; but usually considered to
mean slightly faster.

**andare** (än-dä'-rä), *I.* To move; as **a
diritto,** go straight on; **a. a tempo,**
keep strict time.

**anem'ochord** or **anim'ocorde.** An
instr. inv. by Schnell, 1789, aiming to
imitate the Æolian harp by means
of keys pressing bellows and forcing
air against strings.

**anemom'eter.** Wind-gauge.

**ane'sis,** *Gr.* 1. Descent from a higher
to a lower tone. 2. The lowering of
the pitch of strings. Reverse of **ep-
itasis.**

**Anfang** (än'-fängk), *G.* Beginning.
**vom A.,** = *Da capo.* **Anfänger**
(än'-fĕng-ĕr). A beginner. **Anfangs-
grunde.** Rudiments. **Anfangsri-
tornell.** Prelude.

**Anführer** (än'-fü-rĕr), *G.* Conductor,
leader.

**angeben** (än'gä-bĕn), *G.* To give.
**den Ton a.** to give the pitch.

**Angelica** (än-jä'-lĭ-kä), *G.* **angélique**
(än-zhä-lēk), **angélot** (än-zhŭ-lō), *F.*
1. An organ-stop. Vide vox. 2. A
17th century keyboard instr. with 17
strings.

**angel'ophone.** Early form of harmonium.

**angemes'sen,** *G.* Appropriate.

**angenehm** (än'-khĕ-näm), *G.* Pleasing.

**angkloung** (änk'-loong). A Javanese
xylophone.

**anglaise** (än-glĕz), *F.,* **anglico** (än-
glē'-kō), *I.* 1. In the "English"
style. 2. An English country dance,
ballad or hornpipe. 3. A sprightly
French dance in 3-4 time.

**ango're** (än-gō'-rĕ), **angoscia** (än-
gō'-shä), *I.* Anguish.

**angoscevole** (än-go-shä'-vō-lĕ), **an-
gosciamen'te, angosciosamen'te,
angoscio'so,** *I.* With anguish or
anxiety.

**ängstlich** (ĕngsht' lĭkh), *G.* Anxious-(ly).

**anhaltend** (än'-häl-tĕnt), *G.* Continuous. **a. Cadenz.** A pedal point or prolonged cadence.

**Anhang** (än'-hängk), *G.* Coda.

**am'ma,** *I.* Soul spirit.

**animan'do, animato** (ä'-to), *I.,* **anime'** (än-ĭ-mā), *F.* Animated. **animazione** (ä-nĭ-mä-tsĭ-ō'-nĕ), *I.* Animation.

**animo** (än'-ĭ-mō), *I.* Spirit. **animo'so, animosamen'te,** *I.* Boldly.

**animocorde.** Vide ANEMOCHORD.

**An'klang,** *G.* Harmony.

**Anlage** (än'-lä-khĕ), *G.* Outline.

**anlaufen** (än'-low-fen), *G.* To increase ; to swell.

**Anleitung** (än'-lĭ-toongk), *G.* Introduction ; instruction.

**Anmuth** (än'moot), *G.* Sweetness, grace. **anmuthig** (an'-moo-tĭkh). Sweetly. **anmuthvoll** (fôl). Full of grace.

**anom'aly.** Deviation from exactitude due to temperament (q. v.). **anomalous.** As a chord ; characterized by a much tempered interval.

**anonner** (ă-nŭn-nā), *F.* To hesitate, blunder.

**anpfeifen** (än'-pfī-fen), *G.* To whistle at ; to hiss.

**An'sa.** In Hindu music the note corresponding to our tonic.

**Ansatz** (än'-zäts), *G.* 1. Embouchure. 2. Attack.

**Anschlag** (än'-shläkh), *G.* 1. Touch. 2. A short double appoggiatura.

**anschwellen** (än-'shvĕl-lĕn), *G.* To increase ; swell.

**an'singen,** *G.* To greet with song.

**ansio'so, ansiosamen'te,** *I.* Anxiously.

**anspielen** (än'-shpē-lĕn), *G.* To play first.

**Ansprache** (än'-spräkh-ĕ), *G.* " Speaking " or intonation.

**an'sprechen, anstimmen,** *G.* To speak ; sound.

**Anstimmung** (än'-shtĭm-moongk), *G.* Intonation.

**answer.** Vide FUGUE.

**antelu'dium,** *L.* A prelude.

**antece'dent.** 1. A subject 2. FUGUE.

**anthem.** In the Anglican Church vice, a sacred vocal work wit without accompaniment. " Ther five species of anthems. 1. V and chorus a., consisting of v and chorus, but beginning in ch 2. **Verse a.,** containing verse solo) and chorus, but beginnin verse. 3. **Full a.,** consisting wl of chorus. 4. **Solo a.,** consi of solos and choruses, but wit verse, and 5. **Instrumental** [*Busby*].

**anthe'ma.** Greek dance with song

**Anthologie** (än-tō-lō-zhē'), **Anthe gium,** *F.* and *G.* The collectio hymns, prayers, and lections of Greek Church.

**an'thropoglossa,** *Gr.* The vox mana ; a stop.

**anticipation, anticipamento** (är chē-pä-men'-to), or **anticipazi** (än-tē-chē-pä'-tsĭ-ō'-nĕ), *I.* The so ing of one or more parts of a mony before the natural and pected tone.

**antico** (än-tē'-kō), *I.* Ancient. **a.** In the ancient style.

**antienne** (äns-yĕn), *F.,* **antifona** tē'fō-nä), *I.* Anthem , antip atifona'rio, *I.,* atifonero (än-t nä'-rō), *Sp.* A precentor ; ant singer.

**antifonal',** *Sp.* A book of anthem

**an'tiphon, an'tiphone, antipho' antiph'ony.** 1. In Greek m accompaniments in the octave. Responsive singing by parts of a vided choir, or congregation. short scriptural sentence sung be and after the Psalms or Canti The chant or alternate singin churches and cathedrals.

**antiphona,** *Gr.* An anthem.

**antiphonal, antiphonaire** (änt när), *F.,* **antiphona'rium,** *L.* an **phonary.** A collection of Cat antiphons.

**antiphonel.** Vide PLANCHETTE.

phonic. Not in unison ; made up 2 or more parts.

stro'fa. An ancient Spanish dance.

th'esis. 1. Contrast. 2. Counsubject. 3. In fugues applied to answer.

'de, *Gr.* Responsive singing.

wort (änt'-vôrt), *G.* Answer.

achsend (än'väkh-zěnt), *G.* Cresndo.

los, *Gr.* Singer.

'to, *I.* 1. Open, broad. 2. In no music, "use the damper pedal."

'tus, *L.* Open ; as diapason, ca-n, pipes.

lregal (äp'fěl-räkh-äl), *G.* "Ap--register," an obsolete reed-stop.

ony, aphonie (ă-fô-nē), *F.* Dumb-ss. aph'onous. Without voice.

giatura. Vide APPOGGIATURA.

li'no, *Gr.* An invention combin-; the qualities of several instru-nts.

lo, apol'lon. A 20-stringed lute . in 1678, by Prompt, of Paris.

lo lyra. An improvement made Schmidt in 1832, on the Psalmmelo-on (q. v.).

lo'nicon. A gigantic orchestrion ibited in 1817, by Flight & Robson, l containing 5 manuals, 45 stops, oo pipes, and kettle-drums. It ld be played automatically or by performers at once.

lo'nion. An instr. inv. by Voller in oo ; a piano with double key-board, an-pipes and automatic performer.

'trophe. In singing, used to mark reathing-place.

'ome, *Gr.* A major semitone, in eek music.

ssionato (äp-päs'-sǐ-ō-nä'-tō), ap-ssionatamente, *I.* Passionate-.

au (ăp-pō), *F.* Bird-like tone.

el (äp-pěl'), *F. & G.* Drum call ; embly.

nato (ap-pā-nä'-tō), *I.* Dis-ssed.

cation (ăp-plǐ-kăs-yôṅ), *F.,* ap-catura (äp-plǐ-kä-too'-ra), *I.,* Ap-katur (toor'), *G.* Fingering.

**appoggiando** (äp-pôd-jän'-dō), **appoggiato** (jä'-tō), *I.* Leaning upon, as a tone that slides into the next *legato.*

**appoggiatura** (äp-pôd-jä-too'-rä), pl. e, *I.* "Leaning note." 1. The short or lesser **a.**, or grace note, is written small with a line through its hook, it receives the accent, but has the minimum of duration ; the double, or compound **a.**, contains more than one note and follows the same rule, the first note taking the stress ; the unaccented **a.** (*Nachschlag*) follows its principal, is connected with it by a slur, and like other grace notes borrows its time from the principal, but unlike them has no accent. 2. The long **a.** was written small in old music but played at its full value. It is now written large as an unprepared suspension. Almost any dissonantial note can be introduced unprepared as an **a.** 3. A superior **a.** is one placed above its principal ; an inferior **a.** one below. Vide GRACE.

**apprestare** (äp-prä-stä'-rě), *I.,* **appreti(e)ren** (äp-prě-tē'-rěn), *G.* To prepare, as an instrument.

**Appretur** (äp-prě-toor'), *G.* The proper set-up of an instrument.

**âpre** (äpr), *F.* Harsh. **âprement** (äpr-män). Harshly. **âpreté** (äp-rǔ-tä). Harshness.

**Ar** (är), *Port.* All.

**Arabeske** (är-ä-běs'-kě), *G.,* **arabesque** (är-ä-běsk), *F.* 1. An embellishment. 2. A light and graceful form of music, resembling the rondo.

**arbit'rio.** Pleasure. *A suo a.=ad lib.* **arbit'rii** (trǐ-ē). Embellishments improvised at pleasure while singing.

**arc,** *I.* The bow ; an abbr. of arco **arcata** (är-kä'-tä). Use of the bow **arca'to.** Played with the bow.

**Arche** (är-khě), *G.* Sounding-board.

**arch-,** *E. & F.,* **archi-,** *L.,* **arci-** *I.* A prefix, meaning "chief, principal" ; of instruments "the greatest."

**archeggiare** (är-kěd-jä'-rě), *I.* To use the bow, to fiddle.

**archet** (är-shā), *F.*, **archetto** (är-ket'-to), *I.* Violin bow.

**archlute, archiluth** (är-shĭ-lüt), *F.*, **arciliuto** (är-chēl-yoo'-tō), *I.* A theorbo in which the bass strings were doubled with an octave and the small strings with a unison.

**arcicembalo** (är-chĭ-chäm'-bä-lō), *I.* A harpsichord inv. by Vincentino in the 16th century with 6 key-boards and a diatonic, chromatic, and enharmonic scale. He also inv. the so-called arci-organ.

**arco** (är'-kō), *I.* The bow. **a pun'ta** or **colla punta d'arco.** With the point of the bow. **coll' arco,** or simply **arco** after **pizzicato.** "Resume the bow." **a. in giù** (joo). Down-bow. **a. in su** (soo). Up-bow. **contr' arco.** Bowing against the rule.

**arden'te, ardentemen'te, ardentis'-simo,** *I.* Ardent(ly).

**arditezza** (ar-di-tĕd'-za), *I.* Boldness.

**ardito, arditamen'te.** Bold(ly).

**Aretin'ian.** Concerning Guido D'Arezzo or Aretinus, as the **A. syllables.** Vide ꜱᴏʟᴍɪꜱᴀᴛɪᴏɴ (and ɢᴜɪᴅᴏ in the B. D.).

**argentin** (är-zhäṅ-tăṅ), *F.* Silvery.

**arghool'.** An Egyptian cane pipe with reed mouthpiece.

**aria** (ä'-rĭ-ä) (pl. **e**), *I.* A song; a melodic composition for a solo voice with instrumental accompaniment. It is usually elaborate. The **a. da capo** with two parts (the first repeated after the second) was the first important form, though the rondo and even the sonata idea have been used. Various sorts of aria are **a. buffa** (boof'-fä), humorous; **cantabile,** lyrical; **concertante** (côn-chĕr-tän'-tĕ) or **da concerto,** for concert use, elaborately accompanied; **d'abilità** (dä-bē-lē-tä'), for a display of virtuosity; **d'entrata** (dĕn-trä'-tä), or **sortita** (sôr-tē'-tä), for the first appearance or entrance of an operatic character; **di bravura,** highly florid; **da chiesa,** for church with accompaniments of full orchestra; **fuga'ta parlan'te,** declamatory; **tedes'ca,** with closely related

accompaniment. **A. d'ostinaz** (dôs-tĭ-nä'-tsĭ-ō'-nĕ), *I.* An aria a *basso ostinato*. **aggiunte.** introduced into an opera. **ariet** (tē'-na), **ariet'ta,** *I.* A short a melody.

**ariette** (är-ĭ-ĕt), *F.* Literally "a s aria," actually a grand aria.

**arigot** (ä-rĭ-gō), *F.* A fife.

**ario'sa** (or-o), *I.* Melodious(ly), tabile. **ariose cantate** (ä-rĭ-ō'sĕ tä'tĕ), *I.* Airs in a style betw a song and recitative, introdu frequent changes in time and mar **ario'so.** In the style of an air; tween an aria and a recitation rather melodious declamation.

**arm.** Iron end-piece in an or roller.

**Armandine** (är-mäṅ-dēn), *F.* A g piano with gut-strings and no board, invented by Pascal Ta and named after the singer ᴹ Armand.

**arma'rius,** *L.* Precentor.

**armer la clef** (är-mā lä klā), *F.* mark the signature on the clef.

**Armgeige** (ärm'-gī-khĕ), *G.* Viol braccia.

**armoneggiare** (är-mō-nĕd-jä'-rĕ To harmonize.

**armonia** (är-mō-nē'-ä), *I.* Harm union. **a. militare.** Military b **armonia'co** (ä'-kō), **armonia'le monia'to, armo'nico, armoni armoniosamen'te,** *I.* Harmoni harmonious(ly).

**armo'nica,** *I.* 1. Early form of accordeon. 2. Musical glasses. ʜᴀʀᴍᴏɴɪᴄᴀ. **armonica guida** ( dä). Text-book in harmony.

**armure** (är-mür), *F.* 1. The key nature. 2. Action, mechanism.

**ar'pa** (pl. **e**), *I.* Harp. **a. d'eolo.** lian harp. **a. doppia.** 1. Forme harp with double strings for each 2. Now a double-action. **arpa ta, arpinel'la.** A small harp or Vide ꜱᴘɪᴛᴢʜᴀʀꜰᴇ.

**arpège** (är-pĕzh), **arpègement** pĕzh-mäṅ), *F.* Arpeggio. **arp** (är-pĕ-zhä). To arpeggiate.

ggi (är-pĕd'-jē), *I.* Pl. of Arpeg-
o.

ggiare (är-pĕd-jä'rĕ), *I.* 1. To
y the harp. 2. To play chords in
rp-manner, i. e., waved, broken.
peggiamento (är-pĕd-jä-mĕn'-tō),
peggian'do (pĕd-jän'-dō), **arpeg-
ato** (jä'-to). Played arpeggio, in
itation of the harp.

ggiatura (too'-rä), *I.* A series
arpeggi.

ggio (är-pĕd'-jō), *I.* 1. The play-
g of the notes of a chord quickly,
e after another, in the harp style,
plingly. 2. Such a chord written
c.

ggione (jō'-nĕ). A small 6-
inged 'cello tuned like a guitar,
. by Stauffer in 1823.

cor'do, *I.* Harpsichord.

'ne, *I.* A harp with horizontal
ings, inv. in the 18th century by
rbieri.

ngement. The translation of a
nposition to an instr. or instrs. for
ich it was not originally written.

nger (ăr-rän-zhā), *F.* **arrangiren**
-rän-zhēr'en), *G.* To arrange.

s, *Gr.* A raising as opposed to
esis. In accent it means the stress ;
metre it means the up-beat, and
erefore the unaccented part. It is
isically most common in the latter
ise.

nusica, *L.* The art of music.

(ärt), *G.* Species, quality, as **Ton-
t**, key.

olare (är-tē-kō-lä'-rĕ), *I.* **articu-
** (är-tē-kŭ-lä), *F.*, **artikuliren**
-tē-koo-lē'-rĕn), *G.* To articulate.

ticolato (lä'tō), *I.* Articulated.

ticolazione (lä'-tsĭ-ō'-nĕ), *I.* Ex-
and distinct pronunciation ; articu-
ion.

ic'ial. Vide HARMONIC.

'lich (är'tĭkh-lĭkh), *G.* Neat(ly).

äs), *G.* The note A flat. **Asas,
Ases**. The note A double flat.

ulos or askau'los, *Gr.* A bag-
e.

ur (äs-door), *G.* The key of A
t major.

**Ashantee trumpet.** One made of
the tusk of an elephant.

**asheor** (ä-'shĕ-ôr). Hebrew instr. of
10 strings.

**As-moll** (äs-môll), *G.* The key of A
flat minor.

**Asper'ges me,** *L.* "Cleanse me."
The opening of the Catholic Mass.

**aspirare** (äs-pĭ-rä'-rĕ), *I.* To breathe
audibly.

**aspira'tion.** 1. The dot indicating
*Spiccato.* 2. An obsolete grace note
having the effect of a beat in a sustained tone.

**asprezza** (äs-prĕd'-zä), *I.* Harshness.

**assai** (äs-sä'-ē), *I.* Very ; as **allegro
a.**, very fast.

**assemblage** (äs-säṅ-bläzh), *F.* Double
tonguing ; rapid execution.

**assembly.** A rallying call for troops.

**assez** (ăs-sä), *F.* Enough ; rather.

**assoluto** (loo'-to), *I.* Absolute ; alone ;
of a chief singer.

**as'sonant,** *E.*, **assonan'te,** *I.* Having
resemblance in sounds, concordant.
**Assonanz** (äs-sō-nänts'), *G.*, **asso-
nanza** (äs-sō-nän'-tsa), *I.* Consonance.

**assourdir** (ăs-soor-dēr), *F.* To muffle ; to deafen. **assourdissant** (dĭs-
säṅ). Deafening.

**at'abal.** A large Moorish drum.

**Athem** (ä'tām), *G.* Breath. **a.-ios.**
Breathless. **A.-zug** (tsookh). Res-
piration.

**athmen** (ät'-män), *G.* To blow softly.

**attacca** (ät-täk'-kä), *I.*, **attaquer** (ät-
tä-kä'), *F.* To attack. **attacca subito,** *I.* Attack or begin what follows immediately. **attacca-Ansatz,**
*G.* The attack-touch, a quick stroke
from near the keys.

**attacco,** *I.*, **attaque** (ät-täk), *F.* 1.
A brief fugue theme. 2. A subject
for imitation in fugue.

**attack.** The manner or act of beginning a tone, a phrase or a movement.

**atten'dant.** Related.

**atto** (ät'-tō), *I.* An act. **a. di cadenza.** Point where a cadence may
occur.

**au** (ō), *F.* "To the; in the style of the." Vide AL, etc.

**aubade** (ō-bǎd), *F.* Morning music; a day-break serenade.

**audace** (ä-oo-dät'-che), *I.* Audacious.

**auf** (owf), *G.* On, upon, in, at, etc. **-blassen.** To blow upon. **-fassung.** Conception; interpretation. **-führung** (fü-roongk). Performance. **-geregt** (-ge-räkht). Agitated. **-geweckt** (-gě-věkt). Lively. **-gewecktheil** (tīl). Cheer.

**aufhalten,** *G.* To retard, to suspend. **Aufhaltung** (owf'-häl-toongk), *G.* A suspension. Vorhalt.

**Auflage** (owf'-lä-khě), *G.* Edition.

**auflösen** (owf-lā'-zěn). To resolve. **Auflösung** (owf'-lā-zoongk). 1. Resolution. 2. The solution of a riddle canon. 3. A natural (♮) sign.

**Aufsatz** (owf'-zäts), *G.* Tube (of a reed-pipe).

**Aufschlag** (owf'-shläkh), *G.* Up-beat.

**Aufschnitt** (owf'-shnĭtt), *G.* Mouth (of a pipe).

**aufsteigende** (owf-shtī'-khěn-dě), *G.* Ascending.

**Aufstrich** (owf'-shtrĭkh), *G.* An up-bow.

**Auf'takt,** *G.* Anacrusis; up-take.

**Auf'tritt,** *G.* A scene.

**Aufzug** (owf-'tzookh), *G.* An act.

**augmentant, en** (ä-nōg-mäṅ-täṅ), *F.* Crescendo.

**augmenta'tio,** *L.*, **augmenta'tion** (in *F.* ōg-mäṅ-tăs'-yôṅ). Increase. 1. Of interval (q. v.) a semitone larger than major, as an **augmented** fifth. 2. Of note-values, as in counterpoint, where a theme may appear with quarter notes changed to half, etc.

**augmented,** *E.*, **augmenté** (ōg-mäṅ-tā'), *F.* Used of 1. Intervals a semitone greater than major. 2. Chords containing such intervals. Vide ALTERED CHORDS.

**aul'os,** *Gr.* Most important Greek instrument, probably a flute, possibly like the oboe. **aul'etes.** Flute-player.

**aulozo'num,** *Gr.* The tuning-wire of reeds.

**aus** (ows), *G.* From, out of. **-arbei** (-är-bī-toongk). Elaboration. **nung** (-dä-noongk). Developm **-druck** (-drook). Expres **-drucksvoll.** Full of expres **-führung** (fü-roongk). Performa exposition. **-füllung.** The m parts. **-gabe** (-gä-bě). Ed **-gang.** Exit; conclusion. **-g** **ten.** Sostenuto. **-geigen** (gī-k To finish. **-gelassen.** Wild ; governable. **Aus'gelassenheit** Extravagance; wantonness. **ten.** To sustain. **Aus'halt** Sustaining. **Aushaltungszei** (tsī-khěn). The fermate. **-lö** (-lä-zoongk). The device that rel the hammer of a piano.

**äusserste Stimmen** (īs'-sěr-stě s mĕn), *G.* Extreme parts.

**ausweichen** (ows-vikh'n), *G.* To ulate. **Ausweichung** (vī-khoo *G.* Modulation; transition.

**authentic,** *E.*, **autentico** (ä-oo-tě kō), *I.*, **authentisch** (ow-ten'-tĭs That part of a scale between the and the dominant above; the pa tween the tonic and the dominar low being called *Plagal.* Vide M **a. cadence.** Vide CADENCE **melody.** One whose range cove octave above its tonic or final.

**au'toharp.** A zither whose string stopped by a series of dampers ranged that pressing one down, l free certain strings. When the swept with the plectrum a chor sults.

**au'tophon.** A barrel-organ, music is cut in heavy pasteboard

**autos sacrementale** (ä'-oo-tos rä-měn-tä'-lě), *Sp.* Oratorio, or sion music.

**auxiliary.** Said of tones one d above or below the true harmonic particularly in a grace; of scal longing to auxiliary or related k

**avanera.** Vide HABANERA.

**ave** (ä'-vā), *L.* "Hail." **Ave** **ria.** "Hail Mary," the salutat the angel at the Annunciation, v with the words of Elizabeth (L

) and a concluding hymn, has ⁻med a favorite text for music since ℮ 7th century. **Ave maris stella,** *L.* Hail, star of the sea." A Catholic ₥n.

⁚ (ă-vĕk), *F.* With.

₥a, *L.* A reed ; a pipe.

₥in'ium. A bird-like organ-stop.

₥ded. Prepared and then omitted, a cadence (q. v.).

⁚r du retentissement (ă-vwär-rŭ-täṅ-tēs-mäṅ), *F.* To be re-₥ated and echoed.

₥ne sacra (ä'-tsĭ-ō-nĕ sä'-krä). ⁻atorio ; passion music.

# B

₥ I. A musical pitch, one whole step higher than A, and its octaves. In France and Italy called " si." In Germany B ₥tural is called H (hä), and the term ₥(bä) confined to B flat. 2. The major ₥y having five sharps ; the minor key ₥lative to D major. In old works ₥nd modern German) **square B** (or **B** ₥adratum or **quadrum** or **durum,** *F.* **Bé carré**) stands both for B nat-₥a⁴ and for the natural sign (♮) itself.

₥ rotundum (or **molle,** in *F,* **bé-**₥ol) stands for B flat, and for the flat ₥gn itself (♭), the tone B having been ₥e first to be chromatically lowered.

₥ cancellatum stands for the sharp ₥gn (♯) first formed by crossing the flat ₥) and originally equivalent merely to ₥llifying or naturalizing the flat.

In old solmization B flat was *B fa ;* ₥ natural, *B mi.*

As abbr. B—*basso ;* c. b.—*col* ₥sso ;* C. B.—*Contrabasso.* Mus. B. ⁻*Bachelor of music.*

₥s (bäs) or **base dance.** A dance ₥sembling the minuet.

₥zas (bä-zä), *F.* A kind of guitar.

₥ara (bä-bä'-rä), *Sp.* A Spanish ₥untry dance.

₥orack'a, bab'orak. Bohemian ₥ances of eccentric rhythm.

₥calaureus musicæ, *L.,* **bachel-**₥r (băsh-ŭl-yä), *F.* Bachelor of Mu-sic. A degree granted to those who have proved a certain standard of proficiency. Inferior to Doctor of Music.

**bacchanale** (năl), *F.* A Bacchic revel.

**bacchanalian songs.** Drinking songs.

**bacchia.** A Kamschatkan dance in 2-4 time.

**bacciocolo** (bät-tchĭ-ō-kō'-lō), *I.* A Tuscan guitar.

**bachelor.** Vide BACCALAUREUS.

**back-block.** Wrest-block.

**badinage** (bă-dĭ-näzh), *F.* Banter.

**baga'na.** 10-stringed Abyssinian lyre.

**back.** The under side of a violin.

**back-fall.** I. An obsolete sign and the grace note it indicated. Vide GRACES. 2. A lever in the organ.

**back-turn.** Vide TURN.

**bagatelle** (băg-ă-tĕl), *F.* A trifle.

**bagpipe(s).** An instr. of great antiquity and wide favour, consisting of a series of pipes furnished with wind from a bag in the player's mouth or a bellows under his arm, or both. It has usually one *chanter* or melody pipe with a reed, and 6 or 8 holes, played with the fingers ; 3 *drone pipes* sounding continuously an octave and a fifth.

**baguette** (bă-gĕt), *F.* I. A drumstick. 2. Bow.

**baile** (bä-ē'-lĕ), *Sp.* National Spanish dances.

**baisser** (bĕs-sä), *F.* To lower, as the pitch.

**bal'afo.** A Senegambian xylophone.

**balalaika** (bä-lä-lĭ'-kä). A rude Russian or Gipsy guitar with 2 to 4 strings.

**balancement** (băl-äṅs-mäṅ), *F.* A tremolo (as of a violinist's finger).

**balance-rail.** The wooden strip on which piano keys are balanced.

**Bal(c)ken** (bäl'-ken), *G.* I. Bass-bar. 2. The heavy lines connecting the stems of a series of small notes.

**Balg** (bälkh), *G.* Bellows. **B.-zug.** Bellows-stop.

**ballabile** (bäl-lä'-bĭ-lĕ), *I.* In a dance manner.

bal'lad, Ballade (băl-lăd'), F. (bäl-lä'-dĕ), G. ballata (bäl-lä'-tä), I. Originally a dance tune (from *ballare*, to dance); it now means a simple song of popular tone. In instrumental work, it may be as elaborate as " Chopin's Ballades," but it still has an idea of directness and melodiousness, if not narrative. balladenmässig (mĕs-sĭkh), G. Ballad style. ballad of ballads. Solomon's song. ballad opera. Light tuneful opera. alla ballata. In ballad style. ballatella, ballatetta. A short ballata.

ballet (băl-lä), F., Ballett (bäl-lĕt'), G., ballet'to, I. 1. An elaborate dance by professionals, often spectacular and narrative. 2. A light glee of the 16th cent. Vide FA-LA. 3. balletto was used by Bach for an allegretto in common time.

bal'lo (pl-ī), I. A dance, or dance tune, as b. della stira, Styrian dance like the waltz ; b. ungaresi, a syncopated 2-4 Hungarian dance ; da ballo, in dance style.

ballonchio (bäl-lôn'kĭ-ō), I. A country dance.

band. A group of instrumentalists, usually a military band, sometimes an orchestra ; oftener a part of the orchestra, as the string-band. bandmaster. The leader of a band.

Band (bänt), G. A volume.

ban'da, I. 1. The brass and the drums of a theatre-orchestra. 2. An orchestra on the stage.

Bande (bän'-dĕ, G., bäṅd, F.). 1. The 24 court-violins. 2. A strolling band.

bando'la, bandolon. bandalo're, bandelo're. bando'ra, bandura (ban-doo'ra), I. Instrs. of the lute kind, played with a plectrum.

bando'nion. A concertina named after the Heinrich Band, invented by Uhlig, 1830.

bandurria (bän-door'-rĭ-a), Sp. A wire-strung guitar.

ban'ia, ban'ja. African instrs. from which the banjo may have been derived.

banjo. A long-necked stringed instru-

ment with a broad, round body, ered with a tight skin, which give five to nine strings a quaint soun

Bänkelsänger (bĕnk'el-zĕng-er), " Bench-singer(s)," vagabond cian(s).

bar. 1. A vertical line drawn a the stave just before the major a of each measure ; since the bar arates the measures, the word i correctly used to denote the mea itself. In psalmody used to mar end of lines and phrases. 2. A eral division of the song of the M tersänger ; it included 2 Stollen an Abgesang. 3. Vide BARRER.

bar'baro, I. Barbarous(ly).

barbarism. Crudeness of progres or combination.

barbet', bar'biton, bar'bitos. 1. cient Greek lyre. 2. In 16th ce violin.

barcaro'la, barcaruola (bär-kä-ro lä), barca'ta, I., barcarolle (bä rôl), F. 1. An air sung by gondol or boatmen. 2. Hence, a lyrica strumental composition usually i time (Chopin's are in 12-8).

bard. A Celtic minstrel.

bardd alan (bärd-ä'-lăn). A W prof. of music.

Bardiet, Bardit (bär-dēt'), G. Anc German war-song.

bardo'ne, I. Vide BARYTONE.

bare. Open ; parallel, as bare fif

Barem (bä'-räm), G. Obs. soft or; stop.

Bärentanz (bär'-ĕn-tänts), G. B dance.

bargaret, bargeret, barginet. V BERGERET.

baribas'so. A deep barytone.

bariolage (băr-ĭ-ō-läzh), F. 1. A m ley. 2. A rapid passage showin distinct design, or " waist-coat tern."

bar'itenor. The deeper tenor voic

bariton(e). Vide BARYTON.

baroc'co, I., barock', G., baroque rôk), F. Eccentric ; uncouth.

Bärpfeife (bär'-pfī-fĕ), G. Bear-p an old growling organ-stop.

quade (băr-kăd), *F.* Old form of
arcarolle.

'ra, *I.* Bar.

rage (băr-räzh), *F.* Vide BARRER.

re (băr), *F.* 1. A bar ; also **b. de
iesure ; b. de répétition,** repeti-
on mark. 2. A bridge.

ré (băr-rā), *F.* Vide BARRER.

red C. The mark for common time.
with a bar through it ; a mark of
*lla breve.*

rel. The body of a bell.

rel chime. Portion of a mechanism
nging a chime of bells.

rel organ. 1. An instrument, com-
only portable, in which the bellows
re worked, the pipes blown and the
une automatically played by a crank
irning a cylinder set with pegs, so
-rranged as to open valves in melodic
nd harmonic order. 2. The same
rinciple is used in street-pianos, the
egs releasing hammers which strike
ires.

rer (băr-rā), *F.* To bar. Pressing
ie strings of a guitar or lute with the
orefinger of the left hand to raise
ieir pitch ; **great,** *or* **grand b.,** press-
ng all the strings ; **small b.,** pressing
or 3 strings ; hence **barré** and **bar-
age.**

t, *G.* Ear, as of an organ-pipe.

yton(e), *E.*, **baryton** (băr-ĭ-tôn),
aryton (bä-rĭ-tōn'), *G.*, **barito'no,**
, 1. The male voice, between bass
nd tenor, with a compass between low
and g (vide PITCH). If low in qual-
y it is **bass-baryton,** if high, **tenor-
aryton.** 2. A brass valved instr.
ride SAX-HORN). 3. The **viola di
ordone** (*or* **bardone).** An obsolete
8th cent. instr. resembling the viola
a gamba ; its 6 gut-strings being re-
nforced by the sympathetic vibration
f from 8 to 27 wires. 4. An epithet
or any instr. between bass and tenor,
s b. clarinet. 5. **b. clef.** The obsote F clef on the 3d line.

z (bärz), *Welsh.* A Welsh bard.

(bä), *F.* Low. **bas-dessus** (děs-
i). Mezzo-soprano.

e, **bass,** *E.*, **Bass** (bäs), *G.*, **basse**

(băs), *F.*, **basso** (bäs'-sō), *I.* 1. The
base or lowest part of a chord, progression, chorus, etc. 2. An epithet
denoting the deepest instr. of a class,
as bass clarinet. The double-bass,
q. v. 3. Formerly an instr. of 5 or 6
strings between 'cello and double-
bass. 4. Affixed to the name of an
organ-pipe or stop, it restricts it to the
pedal. 5. The lowest male voice,
ranging usually from low F to mid. C ;
**basse chantante** (shäṅ-täṅt), **basso
cantan'te,** a flexible " lyric " bass
voice ; **basse-contre** (kôṅtr), **basso
profundo** (pro-foon'-do), a very low
voice ; **basse taille** (tī-yŭ), a high
bass ; **basso buffo,** bass comedian.
6. **Thorough bass, continued bass,
figured bass, Generalbass** (gä-ně-
räl'-bäs), **bezifferte Bass, basse
chiffrée** (shĭf-frā), **basse continue**
(kôṅ-täṅ-ü), **basse figurée** (fē-gü-
rä), **basso contin'uo, basso figura'-
to, basso numera'to**—a species of
musical shorthand in which only the
bass-part is written with Arabic and
Roman numerals indicating the chords
(vide CHORD). 7. **Fundamentalbass,
basse fondamentale, basso fon-
damentalo,** vide FUNDAMENTAL. 8.
**Ground-bass, drone-bass, basse
contrainte** (kôṅ-träṅt), **basso con-
strutto, basso ostinato, basso tenuto,** a bass phrase or figure obsti-
nately repeated. 9. **basse-contre,**
a very deep voice ; also the double-
bass ; **b. de cremo(r)ne,** or, **de cromorne** or **d'hautbois** or **de flûte
traversière,** old names for the bassoon ; **b. de cornet,** the serpent ;
**b. d'harmonie,** the ophicleide ; **b.
guerrière,** a bass clarinet ; **bass
orgue,** an instr. inv. in 1812 by
Sautermuiter. 10. **Bassflöte,** an
obsolete bassoon ; an 8-foot organ-
stop on the pedal. **Bassgeige,**
'cello ; **grosse Bassgeige,** double-bass. **Bass-schlüssel,** or **-zei-
chen**—F clef. 11. **basso concertante,** the principal bass in recitatives
etc. ; also florid music for the lower
strings ; **basso obbligato,** a neces-

sary bass-part; **b. ottava,** an octave lower; **b. ripieno,** vide RIPIENO; **b. rivoltato,** inverted bass. 12. **bass clef,** the F clef. **Alberti bass,** vide ALBERTI. **given bass,** a bass on which harmony is to be built. **supposed bass,** a bass tone not the root of the chord. **murky bass,** vide MURKY. **bassanello,** an obsolete instr. **bass-bar, bass-bram,** in violins, etc., a strip of wood glued inside the belly near the bass string.

**basset horn.** An obsolete clarinet.

**Bassett', bassett'l, Bass'l,** *G.* 1. Old name for 'cello. 2. As a prefix= tenor. 3. A 4-ft. flute-stop on the pedal.

**basset'to,** *I.* 1. The little bass. 2. An obsolete instr. with 4 strings. 3. An 8 or 16 ft. reed-stop. 4. The lowest voice when the bass is silent.

**Bassklausel** (bäs'-klow-zēl). The progression of the bass in a cadence.

**Basslade** (bäs'-lä-dĕ), *G.* Soundboard.

**basson** (bäs-sôn), *F.* Bassoon. **b. quart** (kär). One whose tones are a fourth lower. **b. quinte** (kănt). One whose tones are a fifth higher.

**bassoon.** The bass voice of the wood-wind. A 9-foot conical tube doubled on itself, with a long double-reed mouth-piece. Its original was the long bombardon, from which it was derived in 1539. It is the bass of the oboes; its natural scale is G major; its music is written in the F clef, save for higher notes which use the tenor clef. All keys are available by means of cross fingering, and it is capable of considerable brilliance. It has three registers, the lowest being very reedy, the highest resembling partly a 'cello and partly a tenor voice, the medium is rather colourless. The compass B♭-c'' (sometimes to f'').

**basta, bastante,** *I.* " Enough ! stop !"

**bastardilla** (bäs-tär-dēl'-yä), *Sp.* A kind of flute.

**bath'yphon,** *Gr.* An obsolete clarinet inv. 1829.

**batil'lus,** *L.* An Armenian instr. in the place of bells; a board st with a hammer.

**battant(e)** (băt-tăn(t) ), *F.* Beat

**bâton de mesure** (bă-tôṅ dŭ mŭ- *F.* 1. Stick used in beating 2. A conductor's manner. 3. A of 2 or more measures. 4. bâ The thick line of a measure-rest. **de reprise.** Repeat.

**battement** (băt'-mäṅ), *F.* battin to, *I.* Beat.

**battere** (băt'-tĕ-rĕ), *I.* The down st

**batterie** (băt-rē), *F.* 1. The ro the drum. 2. Smiting the g strings. 3. Broken chords on s instrs. 4. The group of percu instruments.

**battery.** A harpsichord effect amo ing to a quick sharp repetition chord.

**battre** (bătr), *F.* To beat.

**battuta** (băt-too'-tä), *I.* 1. A b so a b., with the beat, strictly *a po.* 2. A measure. 3. A progres from the 10th on an up-beat to octave on the down, forbidden ir counterpoint.

**Bau** (bow), *G.* Construction.

**bäuerisch** (bī'-ĕr-ĭsh), *G.* Ru coarse.

**Bauernflöte** (bow'-ĕrn-flä-tĕ), **Bau pfeife, Bäuerlein,** *G.* 1. R flute. 2. A stopped register in organs.

**Bauernlied** (bow'-ĕrn-lēt), *G.* A r ballad.

**baxoncillo** (bäx-ōn-thēl'-yō), *Sp.* Small bassoon. 2. Open diapa stop.

**bayla, bayle** (bä'-ē-lä), *Sp.* A da

**b b** (bā-bä), *G.* Double flat.

**B-cancellatum.** Vide B.

**B-dur** (bā-door), *G.* B. **durum,** The key of B flat major.

**bearbeitet** (bĕ-är'-bī-tĕt), *G.* ranged. **Bearbeitung** (bī'-toon Adaptation.

**beards.** Small projections on the of, or beneath, the mouth of a p to improve the speech; hence, **cr and side-beards.**

rings. The tones and intervals
rst established by a tuner as a
asis.

t, beating. 1. The hand-motions
f a conductor. 2. That part of a
measure marked by one beat. 3.
One pulsation of a trill. 4. An old
rnament consisting of a short prelim-
mary trill with the next note below.
Vide GRACES. 5. The throb produced
y the interference of two tones of
ightly different pitch. Vide ACOUS-
ICS.

isation. Vide SOLMISATION.

bung (bā'-boongk), *G*. 1. A tremolo ;
n the clavichord, a tremolo made by
ibrating the finger upon the key. 2.
Also, German organ-stop.

(běk), *F.*, bec'co, *I*. The mouth-
iece, as of a clarinet. becco polac-
o. A large bagpipe.

arre (bā-kǎr), *F*. The natural
gn (♮).

cher (běkh'ěr), *G*. 1. The cup or
ell of a wind-instr. 2. The tube of a
eed-pipe.

cken (běk-n), *G*. Cymbals.

eckt', *G*. Covered ; stopped.

on (bŭ-dôǹ), *F*. Old name for
rum. b. de Biscaye. A tam-
ourine.

(bā), *G*. B flat. Be-be. B dou-
le flat.

roi (bŭf-frwä), *F*. 1. Belfry. 2.
ocsin.

lzen (bě-fēl'-tsěn), *G*. To put felt
n. Befilzung. Felt.

geisterung (bě-gīs'-těr-oongk), *G.*
nthusiasm.

leiten (bě-glī'-těn), *G*. To accom-
any. Begleitung. Accompani-
ent. Begleitstimmen. The ac-
ompanying parts. beglei'tete
u'ge. A fugue with free parts.

de (bī'-dě), *G*. Both, usually die
eiden.

spiel (bī'-shpēl), *G*. Example.

sser (bīs'sěr), *G*. A mordent.

töne (bī'-tä-ně), *G*. Accessory
ones ; harmonics.

zeichen (bī'-tsī-khěn), *G*. Accidentals.

bekielen (bě-kē'-lěn), *G*. To fit with
quills.

beklemmt', *G*. Oppressed.

bel (běl), *I*. Beautiful, perfect, as il
bel canto. The perfect (art of) song.

belebend (bě-lā'-běnt), *G*. Accelerat
ing. belebt (bě-lāpt). Lively. Be-
lebtheit (hīt). Belebung. Vivac
ity.

beledern (bě-lā'-děrn), *G*. To cover
with leather or felt. Belederung
Felt.

belegt (bě-lākht'), *G*. Hoarse ; veiled.

belieben (bě-lē'-běn), *G*. Pleasure ; at
pleasure.

beliebig (bě-lē'-bǐkh), *G*. At pleasure.

bell. 1. A hollow metallic instrument
set in vibration by a clapper, or ball,
within, or by hammers from outside.
2. The wide opening of horns, etc.
3. B. diapason. A diapason stop
with flaring pipes. b.-gamba. A stop
whose pipes are topped with a bell.
b.-harp. An old form of harp which
was swung when played. b.-metro-
nome. A met. with a bell-indicator.
b.-scale. A diapason for testing bells.
b.-piano. Vide GLOCKENSPIEL.

bellezza (běl-lěd'zä). *I*. Beauty.

bellico'so, bellicosamen'te, *I*. Belli-
cose(ly).

bello'nion. An automatic instr. inv. in
1812, consisting of 24 trumpets and 2
drums.

bel'lows. A pneumatic device for sup-
plying air to various instruments.

bel'ly. A soundboard of an instr.,
violin or piano, over which strings are
stretched.

bemerk'bar, *G*. Marked.

bémol (bā-mǔl), *F.*, bemolle (bā-môl-
lě), *I*. The mark called a flat (♭). bé-
moliser (bā-mô-lǐ-zā), *F.*, bemol-
lizzare (bā-môl-lǐd-zä'rě), *I*. To
mark with a flat. bémolisée(zā).
Flattened.

ben (bān), ben' (bā'-ně), *I*. Well,
good ; as ben tenuto, well-sustained ;
a bene placito, at the good pleasure.

Benedic'ite, Omnia Opera. "All ye
works (of the Lord) praise Him," *I.*
A canticle for morning prayer.

**"Benedictus, Domine,"** Blessed be Thou, O Lord. A canticle. **Benedic'tus Qui Venit,** *L.* "Blessed is He that cometh," vide MASS.

**bequadro** (bā-kwä'drō), *I.* The natural sign (♮).

**berceuse** (bĕr-sŭz), *F.* A cradle-song; hence, an instrumental piece in that spirit.

**bergamask,** *E.,* **bergamas'ca,** *I.,* **bergamasque** (mäsk), *F.* A rustic dance, imitating the clumsy peasants of Bergamask in Italy.

**bergeret** (bĕr-zhĕ-rā), *F.* A rustic song or dance.

**Bergkreiyen, Bergreigen** (bärkh-rī'-khen), *G.* Mountain melodies.

**berlingozza** (bĕr-lĭn-gôd'zä), *I.* A rustic dance.

**Bes** (bās), *G.* The note B double flat.

**besaiten** (bĕ-zī'-tĕn), *G.* To string.

**beschleunigend** (bĕ-shloi'-nĭ-gĕnt), *G.* Accelerating.

**befiedern** (bĕ-fē'-dĕrn), *G.* To quill.

**bestimmt** (bĕ-shtĭmt), *G.* Distinct. **B.-heit** (hīt), *G.* Precision.

**betonend, betont** (bĕ-tōnt), *G.* Accented. **Betonung.** Accentuation.

**betrübt** (bĕ-trüpt'), *G.* Troubled.

**Bet'tlerleier** (lī-ĕr), *G.* Hurdy-gurdy; **Bettleroper.** "Beggar's opera."

**bewegen** (bĕ-vä'-khĕn), *G.* To agitate. **bewegt** (väkht). Agitated. **Bewegung.** Motion, emotion. **Bewegungsart.** Tempo, a movement.

**beziffert** (bĕ-tsĭf'-fĕrt), *G.* Figured. Vide BASS.

**Bezug** (bĕ-tsookh'), *G.* The set of strings for an instrument.

**bhat.** A Hindu bard.

**bianca** (bĭ-än'-kä), *I.* A "white" or half note.

**bibi** (bē-bē), *F.* A pianette.

**Bible-regal.** A regal that folded up into the size of a tome.

**bichord,** *L.* An instr. (a) having two strings. (b) Having two strings to each note.

**bicin'ium.** A 2-part composition.

**bien** (b'yăn), *F.* Well.

**bifara** (bē'-fä-rä), **bif'fara, bif'ra,** *I.* A

stop with paired pipes slightly out of tune, so as to produce a tremolo.

**biju'ga.** The two-necked cither.

**bina.** Vide VINA.

**bimmolle** (bĭm-môl'-lĕ), *I.* B flat, the flat mark.

**bin'ary.** Two-fold; two-part. **form.** A movement with 2 ch themes or sections. **b. measu** Common time with its two accents

**bind.** A line, usually curved, bindi two notes into a sustained tone; or brace binding staves.

**Bindebogen** (bĭn'-dĕ-bō-khĕn), *G.* slur.

**bin'den,** *G.* To bind; to perform gato. **Bindung.** A slur; hence suspension or syncopation; the leg manner. **Bindungszeichen.** 1 slur.

**biquadro** (bē-kwä'-dro), *I.* The n ural sign.

**bird-organ.** A small organ for tea ing tunes to birds.

**Birn(e)** (bĕr'nĕ), *G.* The socket o mouthpiece.

**bis** (bēs), *L.* 1. Twice, **bis unca,** 1 note. 2. Used by the French stead of our pseudo-French " core!" meaning "please repeat."

**biscan'to,** *I* A duet.

**bischero** (bēs'-kā-rō), *I.* A peg pin.

**biscroma** (bēs-kro'-ma), *I.,* **biscro** (bēs-krôm), *F.* A 16th note.

**bisdiapa'son,** *L.* A double octave fifteenth.

**biseau** (bē-sō), *F.* Stopper of a pi

**bisin'ium,** *L.* A duet.

**bisogna** (bē-sōn'-yä), *I.* "It is ne sary."

**bisqua'dro** (kwä'-drō), *I.* A natu sign.

**bissare** (bĭs-sä'-rĕ), *I.,* **bisser** (bēs-s *F.* To encore.

**bis'sex,** *L.* A 12-stringed guitar.

**bit.** A small tube to supplemen crook.

**Bit'terkeit** (kīt), *G.* Bitterness.

**bizzarria** (bĭd-zär-rē'-ä), *I.* Eccent ity. **biz'zar'ro.** Curious. **bizz ramen'te.** Oddly.

ache (bläñsh), *F.* A "white" or
alf note.

sebalg (blä'-zě-bälkh), *G.* Bel-
ows.

sen (blä'-zěn), *G.* To blow. **Bla'-**
er. A blower; an instrument for
lowing. **Blasemusik.** Music for
ind instrs. **Blas'instrument.** A
ind-instrument.

tt (blät), *G.* A leaf; a reed.

chinstrumente (blěkh'-ĭn-stroo-
ěn-tě), *G.* The brass instruments.

d (blĭnt), *G.* "Blind," simulated,
s a dummy pipe.

ckflöte (blŏk'-flä-tě), *G.* 1. A stop,
f large-scale pipes. 2. A 16th cen-
ury flute.

ol (bē-môl), *F.* The flat mark ♭.
ide BEMOL.

noll (bā-môl), *G.* The key of B
at minor.

cks. Supporting strips in violins,
tc.

t-songs. Water-music, vocal or
nstrumental.

. The changes to which a set of
ells can be rung; 6 bells give **bob**
ninor; 8, **b. major**; 10, **b. royal**;
2, **b. maximus.**

bisation, bocedisation. Vide SOL-
ISATION.

al (bô-kăl), *F.*, **boc'ca**, *I.* Mouth-
iece; mouth. **bocca ridente.**
" Smiling mouth," believed to aid the
roduction of pure tone. **con bocca**
hiusa (kĭ-oo'-zä). With mouth
losed, humming. **bocchino** (kě'no),
. Mouthpiece.

cina (bō-thē'-nä), *Sp.* A large trum-
et.

ckpfeife (bôk'-pfī-fě), *G.* A bag-
ipe.

ckstriller (bôks'-trĭl-lěr), *G.* A goat-
sh bleat.

den (bō'-děn), *G.* The back (of vio-
ins, etc.).

ehm Flöte (bām flä'-tě). An im-
roved flute inv. 1834 by Boehm, in
vhich a series of keys simplify the
ingering and intonation; the system
s also fitted to oboes and clarinets.
Vide the B. D.

**Bogen** (bō'-khěn), *G.* 1. A bow. 2. A
slur, as *Haltebogen.* **Bogenführung.**
Bowing. **Bogenstrich.** A stroke of the
bow. **Bogeninstrumente.** Stringed
instruments. **Bogenflügel, -ham-
merklavier,** or **-klavier.** Piano-
violin.

**bois** (bwä), *F.* Wood. **les** (lä) **bois.**
The wood-wind.

**boîte** (bwät). Box; swell box. **ouvrez
(fermez) la b.** Open (close) the swell.

**bolero** (bō-la'-rō), *Sp.* A lively Spanish dance, in 3-4 time, with castanets.
See chart of dance-rhythms.

**bom'bard,** *E.,* **bombarde** (bôñ-bărd),
*F.,* **bombar'do,** *I.* 1. A very long
obsolete shawm, the original of the
bassoon (q. v.). 2. A powerful reed-
stop of 16-ft. tone.

**bombar'don,** *E.* (in *F.* bôñ-băr-dôñ;
in *G.* bôm-bär-dōñ'). 1. A large,
valved bass trumpet. 2. The bass
saxhorn. 3. A 16-ft. reed-stop.

**bom'bix,** *Gr.* Ancient Greek reed
instrument.

**Bom'bart, bom'mert,** *G.* Bombard.

**bom'bo,** *I.* A figure in repeated tones.

**bon** (bôñ), *F.* Good. **bon temps de
la mesure,** *F.* The accented part of
a measure.

**bonang.** A Javanese series of gongs.

**bones.** Castanets made of bone.

**Bonn's bridge.** A violin bridge inv. by
Bonn of London with a foot under
each string, aiming at more resonance for the interior strings.

**boot.** The foot of a reed-pipe.

**bo'ra.** A tin trumpet used by the Turkish.

**bordone** (bôr-do'-ně), *I.,* **Bordun** (bôr'-
doon), *G.* 1. A covered 16-ft. or 32-
ft. stop; the French have 4 and 8
foot bourdons. 2. The lowest string
of 'cello and double bass; the free
string of a hurdy-gurdy. 3. A great-
bell. 4. A drone bass. **B. Flöte,**
*G.* A stop. **bourdon de cornemuse**
(-kôrn-müz), or **bourdon de musette,**
*F.* The drone of a bagpipe.

**bouché** (boo-shā), *F.* 1. Stopped (of
horn, etc., tones). 2. Covered (of
pipes).

**bouche fermée** (boosh fĕr-mā), *F.* With closed mouth ; humming.

**bouffe** (boof), *F.* A buffoon. **opera b.** Comic opera.

**boulon.** A Senegambian harp.

**bour'don**, *E.* (in *F.*, boor-dôṅ). Vide BORDONE.

**bourrée** (boor-rā), *F.* A lively old Spanish or French dance in 4-4 or 2-4 time. The second and fourth quarters of the measure divided. Used as an alla breve movt. in old suites. See chart of dance-rhythms.

**boutade** (boo-tăd), *F.* 1. An instrumental spectacular fantasia. 2. An old French dance. 3. A short ballet, impromptu.

**bow.** An elastic wooden rod with horsehairs (in recent cases, gut-thread) stretched from the bent head or *point* to a movable *nut ;* the hair being drawn over strings sets them in vibration. **bowhair.** Hair used in making the bows. **bowhand.** The right hand. **bowing.** 1. The art of using the bow. 2. The sign for bowing. The direction in which the bow is drawn is indicated by *down-bow* (marked ⊓) from nut to point ; or *up-bow* (marked ∨ or ∧) from point to nut. The back of the bow is sometimes used, and indicated by *sul* or *col legno*, "with the wood." The bow may be allowed to bounce on the strings (the *bounding* or *springing* bow), the *spiccato* (marked by dots over the notes) being played with a loose wrist near the middle of the bow ; the *saltato* being with higher leaps. **bow instruments.** String instruments played with a bow. **bow guitar.** A violin shaped like a guitar ; vide also PIANO-VIOLIN, and BOW-ZITHER.

**boyau** (bwä-yō), *F.* Gut-strings. **boyaudier** (bwä-yōd-yā). A maker of them.

**bozzetto** (bōd-zĕt'-tō), *I.* Sketch.

**B-quadratum, B-quadrum,** *L.* 1. Vide B. 2. B-natural.

**brabançonne** (brä-bäṅ-sŭn). The Belgian or Brabantine national hymn.

**braccio** (brät'-shō), *I.* "Arm." A term applied to instruments held to the neck, as **viola da b.**, an [a] cello. Vide VIOLA.

**brace.** 1. A character used to conn[ect] staves. 2. Leather slides on dr[um] cords.

**branches.** Parts of a trumpet that c[on]duct the air.

**bran de inglaterra** (brän dĕ ēn-[glä]tĕr'-ra), *Sp.* An old Spanish dan[ce] the English Brawl.

**bran(s)le** (bräṅ'-lŭ), *F.* A lively [ ] dance, 4-4 time, led in turn [by] couples.

**brass.** General term for the ins[truments] made of brass (or **brass-wi[re]**). **brass-band.** A military band of [ ] brass instruments.

**Bratsche** (brät'-shĕ) (pl. -en), *G.* [vi]ola.

**Brautlied** (browt'lēt), *G.* A wedd[ing] song. **Brautmesse.** Music be[fore] the wedding.

**Bravour** (brä-foor'). *G.* Bravura. **B[ra]vour-arie** or **-stück**, *G.* A fl[orid] song or piece.

**bravura** (brä-voo'rä), *I.*, **bravo[ure]** (brä-voor), *F.* Dexterity, dash. [ ] **di b.** A show-piece. **con b.** V[ith] brilliancy. **b. mezza.** Medium d[iffi]culty.

**brawl(e).** An old dance in a circle[ ]

**break.** 1. The point at which one [reg]ister ends and another begins. [2.] Slips of various kinds in tone proc[duc]tion. 3. In a stop, the abrupt ret[urn] to an octave lower, due to insuffic[ient] pipes. 4. In compound-stops, a p[oint] where the relative pitch changes.

**breakdown.** An hilarious negro d[ance].

**breit** (brīt), *G.* Broad, slow.

**Brettgeige** (brĕt'-gī-gĕ), *G.* A p[ock]et fiddle.

**breve** (*E.*, brēv—in *I.*, brä've). br[eve] (brĕv), *F.* 1. Formerly the shor[t] note, now the longest, equal to [two] whole notes. 2. In old music [a] half the longa. **alla breve.** To [the] breve, i. e., a half note to each b[eat] formerly four minims to the meas[ure] and in quick time ; it is indicate[d by] a common-time signature, with a [ ]

cal bar through it ; also called **alla**
appella, or **tempo maggiore.**

viary. A book of matins, lauds,
nd vespers.

vis, *L.* and *G.* A breve.

ge. 1. A piece of wood on which
rings rest ; itself rests on the reso-
ance box or board, to which it trans-
its vibrations.

f. 1. A bass-viol bridge. 2. Breve.

lant(e) (brē-yän(t) in *F.*, in *I.* brĭl-
n'tĕ). Brilliant.

lenbässe (brĭl'-lĕn-bĕs-sĕ), *G.*
Spectacle basses," on account of
s resemblance to a pair of spectacles ;
name for the abbreviated form of a
ass tremolo, two half notes with thick
nnecting bar.

disi (brĭn'-dē-zē), *I.* A drinking-
ng.

(brē'ō), *I.* Vigour ; fire. **con brio,**
brio'so. With spirit ; vivacity.

é (brē-zā), *F.* Broken, as chords.
adence b. A trilling grace.

ach. An old instr. played with a
ank.

deries (brôd-rē), *F.* Ornaments.

ken. Vide (interrupted) CADENCE ;
chords whose notes are not taken
multaneously, but in arpeggio ; so
roken octaves.

k'king. Quavering.

otundum, *L.* 1. Flat sign, ♭. 2.
he note B flat.

mmeisen (broom'mī-zĕn), *G.* Jew's
arp.

mmen (broom'mĕn), *G.* To hum, to
um. **Brummer.** Drone. **Brumm-**
n. Drone. **Brummstimmen.**
umming voices.

scamen'te, *I.*, **brusquement**
rüsk-män), *F.* Brusquely.

st (broost), *G.* The breast or chest,
ence **B.-ton** or **-stimme.** Chest
ice. **Brust'werk.** The middle
pes of an organ.

a (boo'-ka), *I.* Sound-hole.

e'na, *L.*, **buccina** (boot-chē'-na), *I.*
n ancient curved trumpet.

hse (bükh'-sĕ), *G.* Boot (q. v.).

h'stabentonschrift, *G.* Alpha-
etical notation.

**bucol'ic,** *E.*, **buccol'ica,** *I.*, **bucolique**
(bü-kô-lēk), *F.* Pastoral.

**buffa** (boof'fä), or (**-o**), *I.* Comic ; a
comic singer. **buffo carica'to.** Comic
character. **aria buffa.** Comic aria.
**opera buffa.** Comic opera. **buf-**
**fo'ne.** Comic singer. **buffonesco,**
**-amente.** Burlesque(ly).

**buffet.** Organ case. **buffet organ.**
A small organ.

**bugle.** 1. A hunting and military horn
in 3 or more keys (B♭, C, E♭) having
7 harmonic tones. 2. The key-bugle
with 6 keys (inv. in 1815 by Halliday,
and named by him after the Duke of
Kent) has a chromatic compass b-c'''.
3. Valve-bugle. Vide SAXHORN.

**bugle horn.** A hunting-horn.

**Bühnenweihfestspiel** (bü'-nĕn-vi-
fĕsht-shpēl), *G.* "Stage-consecrat-
ing-festival-piece." Wagner's name
for his opera "Parsifal."

**Bund** (boont), *G.* Fret. **bundfrei.**
Fret free. Vide CLAVICHORD.

**Bunge** (boong'-ĕ), *G.* A kettle-drum.

**bungen** (boong'-ĕn), *G.* To drum.

**buonaccordo** (boo-ōn-äk-kôr'-dō), *I.*
A child's spinet.

**buono(-a)** (boo-ō-nō(ä)), *I.* Good. **b.**
**nota.** An accented note. **b. mano.**
A skilful hand.

**buras'ca,** *I.* A comp. descriptive of
a storm.

**bur'den.** 1. A regular refrain. 2.
The bass. 3. The drone.

**burla** (boor'-la), *I.* A quip. **burlan'-**
**do, burles'co, burlescamen'te.** Fa-
cetious(ly). **burles'ca,** *I.*, **burlesque**
(bür-lĕsk), *F.* A travesty. **burlet'-**
**ta,** *I.* A light farcical work.

**burre** (bür), *F.* A dance melody.

**bur'then.** Burden.

**busain** (bü-săn), *F.*, **Busaun** (boo-
zown'), *G.* A 16-ft. reed-stop on the
pedal.

**busna** (boos'na), *I.* A species of trumpet.

**bussone** (boos-sō'-nĕ), *I.* Obs. instr.
of bassoon type.

**button.** 1. The knob on a violin-base,
etc. 2. An accordeon-key. 3. A
leather-disk on the wire of a tracker.

**bux'ea tibia, bux'us,** *L.* Ancient 3-holed flute.

**bys'synge songes.** Early English lullabies.

## C

(For German words not found here look under **K**.)

C (*G.*, **C** (tsā), *F.*, ut ; *I.*, do.) 1. A musical pitch (mid-C or c' has 256 vibrations, "philosophical pitch" ; c'', 522, international pitch). c' called **middle-c** from its position on the piano key-board, is the tonic or key-note of the normal major scale. 2. All the octaves of this pitch. 3. The major key having neither flats nor sharps; the minor key relative to E flat major. **C reversed,** an old sign indicating a decrease of one half of the note-values. 4. Vide TIME and NOTATION.

**cabalet'ta,** *I.* "A little horse." Hence a song (usually a rondo with variations) with an accompaniment in triplets suggesting hoof-beats.

**cabinet d'orgue** (kăb-i-nā dôrg), *F.* Organ-case.

**cabinet organ.** A small reed-organ.

**cabinet pianoforte.** An upright piano.

**cabis'cola,** *L.* Precentor.

**caccia** (kät'chä), *I.* A hunt. **alla c.** In hunting style.

**cachée** (kǎ-shā), *F.* Hidden (as fifths).

**cachucha** (kǎ-choo'-chä), *Sp.* A dance like the bolero.

**cacofonia** (kä-kō-fō-nē'-ä), *I.*, **cacophonie** (kǎk-ô-fō-nē), *F.*, **cacoph'ony,** *E.* Discord. **cacofon'ico,** *I.* Discordant.

**ca'dence,** *E.* (in *F.* kǎ-däns), **ca'dens,** *L.*, **cadenza** (kä-děn-tsä), *I.*, **Kadenz** (kä-děnts'), *G.* 1. Literally "a fall," hence, the subsidence of a melody or harmony to a point of rest ; thence any concluding strain, rising or falling. Harmonic cadences are of the following sorts : (a) When the chord of the dominant is followed

by the chord of the tonic, with roots of both chords in the bass the root of the second chord dou in the highest voice, it is called a **fect authentic cadence** ; when first chord has other than the roo the bass, or when the highest v does not take the tonic in the chord (takes the third for instan this cadence is called an **imper authentic cadence.** Other na for the **authentic cadence whole, perfect, full** or **comp cadence** ; **cadence parfaite** (fĕt), *F.* **voll'kommene,** or **eige liche** (ī-'khěnt-lĭkh-ě)**Kadenz,** *G* When the cadence is formed by a dominant chord followed with a to the cadence is called **plagal** (popul **church** or **amen** cadence) ; **cade plagale** (plǎ-gǎl), *F.* ; **Plagal denz,** *G.* (c) When a subdomi chord is followed by a dominant a tonic, it is called a **mixed** cadence When the mediant is prominent th is called a **medial** cadence. (e) W the tonic or some other chord is lowed by the dominant the caden called a **half-cadence, semi dence, imperfect cadence, h close** ; c. **imparfaite** (ăn-păr-fĕt) **sur la dominante** or c. **irréguli** (ĕr-rǎg-ül-yăr), *F.* ; **unvollkomm** or **Mittel Kadenz,** *G.* (f) Wher chord of the dominant apparently paring a close, is followed by o than the tonic harmony the progres is called a **deceptive, avoided, ken, interrupted, irregular** or **prise cadence** ; **cadence évi** (ä-vĭ-tä) or **interrompue** (ăn rôn-pü), or **rompue,** *F.* ; **cade d'ingann'o,** c. **sfuggita** (sfood tä) or **fin'ta,** *I.* ; **Trug'kadena -schluss,** or **ab'gebrochene K.** (g) When various modulations are troduced between the dominant its tonic, the cadence is said to **suspended** ; or **sospesa** (sôs-pā'- *I.* (h) When any dissonant harmo followed by a consonance the Fre call this a **cadence pleine** (pl

(i) A cadence of any kind in which the chords have their roots in the bass is called a **radical** cadence.

2. When the cadence is highly ornate it is called **fioritu'ra** or **fiorita** (fē-ō-rē'-tä). So the word **cadenza** has in English and Italian, and the word **Kadenz** in German, a wide use for designating the florid passage preceding the actual cadence. This may be vocal or instrumental, may go up as well as down, and may be written out by the composer or some other musician or left to the skill of the performer. This cadenza usually follows a sustained chord in the second inversion (a 6-4 chord) with a fermate or hold-mark over it (in *F. pointe d'orgue*). The Germans accordingly call this an **auf'gehaltene Kadenz**, the *F.* call it a **pointe d'orgue**.

3. The French use **cadence** of a brief trilling ornament as **c. brillan-te**, or **c. perlée**; **c. pleine** is a trill.

4. Cadence is used of rhythm and velocity also as the "cadence" of double-time in a military sense, is 180 steps to the minute.

**'dent.** An old ornament like a short anticipation.

**a)esu'ra**, *E., I.*, and *L.* **caesure** (sē-zür), *F.* 1. A minor rhythmic pause dividing a line or period; hence, 2. The last accented note preceding a **caesura. c. tedesca.** A 10-stringed zither.

**isse** (kĕs), *F.* A drum. **c. plate** (plät). A shallow side-drum. **grosse** (grôs) **c.** The bass-drum. **c. roulan-te** (-roo-länt). The side-drum, of wood. **caisses claires** (kĕs-klăr). The drums.

**'amus, c. pastoralis**, or **tibialis**, *L.* A reed used by shepherds.

**an'do**, *I.* Diminishing and retarding.

**andro'ne**, *I.* A small clarinet.

**ascione** (kä-lä-shi-ō'-nĕ), *I.* A 2-stringed guitar of lower Italy.

**ata** (kä-lä'-tä), *I.* A lively dance in -4 time.

**calcando** (kal-kän'-do), *I.* Hurrying.

**Calcant** (käl'-känt), *G.* Bellows-treader.

**Calli'ope.** 1. The Greek muse of heroic verse. 2. An instr. played by an engine that fills its metal pipes with steam instead of air.

**callithump'ian.** Vide SHIVAREE.

**calma** (käl-mä), *I.* Calm. **calma'to.** With calm.

**calore** (kä-lō'-rĕ), *I.* Warmth. **Caloro'so.** Animated.

**cambiare** (käm-bĭ-ä'rĕ), *I.* To change. **nota cambia'ta.** Changing note.

**cam'era**, *I.* Chamber, used in distinction from a large auditorium, as *musica di c., sonata di c., alla c.*

**camminan'do**, *I.* Andante.

**campana** (käm-pä'-nä), *I.* A bell. **campanel'la** (or **o**), *I.* A little bell. **campanile** (nē'-lĕ), *I.* A belfrey. **campanol'ogy.** The art of ringing or making bells. **campano'ne**, *I.* A great bell. **campana'rum concer'tus**, or **modula'tio**, *L.* Chimes. **campanarum pulsa'tor**, *L.* A ringer of bells.

**canarder** (kă-năr-dā), *F.* To imitate a duck; to *couac.*

**canarie** (kă-nă-rē), *F.*, **cana'ry, cana'ries**, *E.*, **canario** (kä-nä'-rĭ-ō), *I.* A lively dance in 3-8, 6-8 or 12-8 time. Named from the Canary Islands.

**cancan** (käṅ-käṅ). A boisterous French dance.

**cancel.** The natural sign, ♮. **cancellatum**, *L.* Vide B.

**Cancellen** (kän'-tsel-lĕn), *G.* Grooves in an organ.

**can'crizans, cancrica'nus**, *L.*, **cancrizzante** (kän'-krĭd-zän'-tĕ), *I.* Retrograde. Vide CANON.

**canere** (ka'nĕ-rĕ), *L.* To sing; to play.

**cangiare** (kän-jä'-rĕ), *I.* To change; to alter.

**can'na**, *I.* A reed, or pipe. **c. d'anima.** Flue-pipe. **c. a lingua.** Reed-pipe.

**cannon-drum.** East Indian tomtom.

**can'on** (in *F.*, kă-nôṅ), **canone** (kä-nō'-nĕ), *I., G.* **Canon** or **Kanon** (kä'-

nōn). The most rigid form of imitation, a subject (antecedent) being followed accurately by an answer (consequent); once the playground of musical ingenuity, all forms of complication being indulged in. A canon written out completely was **full** or **aper'to.** Often only the antecedent (or canon) was written out, the consequent (now called fuga or consequenza) being left to the performer's skill; this was called **close** or **chiuso** (kĭ-oo′-zo). If the entrances of the other parts were indicated by cabalistic signs, it was a **riddle-canon (Räthsel-Kan**on), or **enigmatical** or **enigmatico.** Canons were named by the interval between answer and antecedent and by the general treatment as in **Imitation** (q. v.).

**canonic hours.** Vide HORÆ.

**cano′nici,** *L.* The Pythagoreans, who developed musical science from the abstract mathematics of intervals; opposed to Aristoxenos and the **harmonici,** who developed it from the actual practice of music.

**cantabile** (kän-tä′-bĭ-lĕ), *I.* Lyrical.

**cantajuolo** (kän-tä-yoo-ō′-lō), **cantamban′ca,** *I.* A street singer.

**cantamen′to,** *I.* Air; cantilena.

**cantan′do** (kän-tän′-dō), *I.* In a melodious, singing style.

**can′tans,** *L.* Singing.

**cantan′te,** *I.* A singer; also a vocal part. **c. ariose.** A form of melody transitional between air and recitative.

**cantare** (tä′-rĕ), *I.* To sing. **c. di maniera** (män-yä′-rä) or **maniera′-ta.** To sing with mannerism. **c. a orecchio** (o-rĕk′-kĭ-ō). To sing by ear. **c. a aria.** To sing with improvised cadenzas.

**cantarina** (rē′-nä), *Sp.* A woman-singer.

**cantata** (kän-tä′-tä), *I.,* **cantate** (kän-tät), *F.,* **Cantate** (kän-tä′-tĕ), *G.* 1. Originally, something sung, in distinction to something played (*sonata*). 2. Now a work for chorus and solo, often with orchestral accompaniment;

a short oratorio of a narrative sty
a short opera not meant for the t
atre. **c. amoro′sa,** *I.* A cantata h
ing love for its subject. **c. mora**
or **spiritua′le.** A *sacred* cantata
signed for the church. **cantatil**
**cantatille** (tē′-yŭ), **cantati′na.**
short cantata; an air preceded b
recitative.

**canta′tor,** *L.* A singer; a chanter.
**cantato′re,** *I.* A male singer. **c**
**tatrice** (trē-chĕ). A female sin
**c. buffa.** A woman who sings
comic opera.

**cantato′rium,** *L.* The Roman Ca
olic book containing the music of
Antiphonary and Gradual.

**Canterei** (kän′-tĕ-rī), *G.* 1. The dw
ing-house of the cantor. 2. A c
of choristers.

**canterellare** (kän-tĕ-rĕl-lä′-rĕ), *I.*
sing softly. **canterellan′do.** Si
ing softly.

**canti carnascialeschi** (cär-nä-shä-
kĕ), **canti carnevali** (kär-nĕ-vä′-lĕ
Songs of the carnival week.

**can′ticles,** *E.,* **can′tico,** *I.,* **c**
**tique** (kän-tēk), *F.,* **can′ticum,** *L.*
Biblical lyrics, the Song of So
**(canticum canticorum).** 2. A
cred chant with scriptural text.
The **cantica majora** include
Magnificat, Benedictus and N
dimittis. The **cantica minora**
seven texts from the Old Testame

**can′tillate,** *E.* To recite with o
sional musical tones; hence, **can**
**lation.**

**cantilena** (kän-tĭ-lä′-nä), *I.* The r
ody; air.

**cantilla′tio,** *L.* A singing style
declamation.

**cantino** (tē′-nō), *I.* The sma
string.

**can′to,** *I.* 1. A song; a melody;
voice. **col canto.** "With" (i.
adopting the time and expression
the voice or melody. 2. The ar
singing, as **il bel canto,** the old
of allegedly perfect production.
The highest part in concert music
The soprano voice. 5. The hi

st string of an instrument. **c. a cappella.** Vocal music without accompaniment. **c. ambrosiano.** Ambrosian chant (Vide CANTUS). **c. armonico.** A part song. **c. clef.** The C clef on the first line. **c. concertante** (kôn-chĕr-tän′-tĕ). The treble of the principal concerting parts. **c. cromat′ico.** Chromatic melody. **c. fermo.** 1. A chant or melody. 2. Choral unison. 3. Cantus firmus. **c. figurato.** A figured melody instead of figured bass (q. v.). **c. fiorit′to.** A much ornamented air. **c. fune′bre.** Funeral song. **c. grego′riano.** The Gregorian chant. **c. plano.** Plain chant. **c. necessa′rio.** A principal part. **c. primo.** The first treble or soprano. **c. recitativo.** Recitative. **c. ripie′no.** Vide RIPIENO. **c. rivolta′to.** The treble inverted. **c. secondo.** The second treble. **c. simplice.** A simple song. **ntolla′no,** *Sp.* Precentor. **ntor,** *L.* Singer. **c. choralis.** Precentor. **cantori** are the singers that sit near the cantor, on the left side; opposite to **decani,** those on the dean's side.

**n′tus,** *L.* 1. A song; a melody. 2. The treble or soprano part. **c. Ambrosia′nus.** The four chants introduced by St. Ambrose, in the fourth century, supposed to be derived from Greek melodies. **c. figura′lis** (or **figuratus).** Mensurable music; melody with figurate embellishment. **c. fir′mus.** (a) The melody originally given to the tenors, later to the sopranos; (b) plain song; (c) a theme or air chosen for counterpoint; this air remains the same, i. e., "firm," as the different voices take it, while the accompanying voices always change; in distinction to the **c. f.** they are called the *counterpoint* (q. v.). **coronatus,** A *c. fractus* when accompanied by a fa-burden. **c. durus.** A song modulating into a key with one or more sharps, almost the same as "major key." **c. eccle-**siasticus. Church-music, particularly plain song; also the singing of the liturgy. **c. fractus.** Broken melody. **c. Gregorianus.** A melody introduced by St. Gregory. **c. planus.** Plain song. **c. mensurabilis.** Regular, or measured, melody. Vide MENSURABLE MUSIC. **c. mollis.** Song in the minor.

**ca′nun,** *Tur.* A Turkish zither.

**canzona, canzone** (kän-tsō′-nĕ), *I.* 1. A folk-song. 2. A part-song. 3. An instrumental work, in two or three parts, with passages in imitation, somewhat like the madrigal. **canzonaccia** (nät′-chä). A low song. **canzoncina** (chĕ′-nä). A short canzone, or song. **c. sacra.** A sacred song. **canzonet, canzonnet′ta, canzonina.** A short canzone. **canzoniere** (tsōn-ya′-rĕ). A song-book.

**caoine, caoineadh** (kŭ-ēn′-ē-ŭ), *Irish.* A funeral song.

**capis′col.** A precentor.

**capis′trum.** A face bandage worn by ancient trumpeters.

**capo** (kä′-pō), *I.* The head or beginning. **da capo** (return and play again), from the beginning. **capo d'opera, capo-lavoro.** Master-piece, chief work. **c. violino.** The first violin. **capo-dastro, c. di tasto.** Vide CAPOTASTO. **c. d'instrumenti.** Leader. **c. d'orchestra.** The conductor.

**capodastre** (kăp-ô-dästr), *F.* Capotasto.

**capo′na.** A Spanish dance.

**capotasto** (kä-pō-täs′-to), *I.* 1. The nut of a fingerboard. 2. A strip fastened across a fretted fingerboard and serving as a movable nut to raise the pitch of all the strings at once.

**cappel′la,** *I.* 1. A chapel, or church. 2. A band of musicians. **A c.** or **alla c.** (a) Without instrumental accompaniment. (b) Alla breve. **da c.** In solemn church style.

**cappello chinese** (kē-nä′-zĕ), *I.* Vide CHAPEAU.

**caprice,** *E.* and *F.,* **capriccio** (kä-prĕt′-chō), *I.* A whimsical work of irregular form. **capriccietto** (chĕt'-tō), *I.* A short caprice. **capricciosamen- te, capriccio'so**, *I.*, **capricieuse- ment** (kǎ-prĕs-yŭz'-män), **capricieux** (kǎ-prĕs-yŭ), *F.* Capricious(ly).

**captan'dum, ad**, *L.* Takingly, brilliantly.

**caput scho'lae**, *L.* Precentor.

**caractères de musique** (kǎr-ǎk-tǎr dǔ mü-zēk), *F.* Musical symbols.

**caramillo** (kä-rä-mēl'yō), *Sp.* A flageolet.

**carattere** (kä-rät'-tä-rĕ), *I.* Character, dignity.

**caressant** (kä-rĕs-sän'), *F.*, **carez- zando** (kä-rĕd-zän'-dō), **carezze- vole** (zä'-vō-lĕ), *I.* Caressing; tender.

**carica'to** (kä'-tō), *I.* Exaggerated.

**carillon** (kä-rē-yôn), *F.* 1. A set of fixed bells on which tunes may be played by hand or mechanism. 2. A composition suggesting or using bells. 3. The simultaneous clashing of many large bells. 4. A bell-like stop. **c. à clavier**, *F.* A set of keys and pedals, acting on bells. **carillonner** (kä-rē-yô-nä'), *F.* To ring bells. **carillonneur** (nŭr), *F.* A bell- ringer.

**carità** (kä-rē-tä'), *I.* Tenderness.

**Carmagnole** (kǎr-mǐn-yôl), *F.* A famous French revolutionary song. It derived its name from the town Carmagnola.

**carmen**, *L.* A song. **c. natalitium.** A carol of the Nativity.

**carol.** 1. A song of joy and devotion. 2. Ballads for Christmas and Easter. 3. An old circling dance.

**caro'la**, *I.* A circling dance, resembling the Carmagnole. **carolet'ta.** A little dance.

**carrée** (kǎr-rā), *F.* A breve.

**carrure des phrases** (kǎr-rür-dä frǎz), *F.* The balance of the phrases.

**cart'el**, *E.*, **cartelle** (kǎr-tĕl), *F.* 1. The first draft of a score. 2. A sheet of hide or varnished cloth on which music could be sketched and erased.

**cartellone** (lō'-nĕ), *I.* A catalogue of operas to be performed.

**cas'sa**, *I.* The drum. **c. grande militare.** The great drum. **c. monica.** The body (as of a 'cell

**cassa'tio**, *L.*, **cassazione** (käs- tsǐ-ō'-nĕ), *I.* 1. The final num 2. A serenade consisting of ins mental pieces.

**castagnetta** (käs-tän-yĕt'tä), *I.*, c **tagnettes** (käs-tīn-yĕt), *F.*, **cast nole** (käs-tän-yō'-lĕ), **castañ as** (käs-tän-yä'täs), **castanue** (käs-tän-yoo-ā'-läs), *Sp.*, **castan ta** (käs-tänyä'-tä), *Port.*, **castane** *E.* Small, concave shells of ivory hard wood, carried in the hand rhythmically snapped by dancers Spain and other countries.

**castrato** (käs-trä'-tō), *I.* An artifi male soprano or alto; a eunuch.

**catch.** A round in which the sing catch up their lines at the cue; u ally with humourous and ambigu effect.

**catena di trilli** (kä-tä'-nä), *I.* A ch of trills.

**catgut.** A small string for violi made of the intestines of sheep a lambs, rarely of cats.

**catling.** A lute-string of smallest si

**cattivo** (kät-te'-vō), *I.* "Bad." **tempo.** The weak beat.

**catzoze'rath.** Hebrew trumpet.

**cauda**, *L.* The tail of a note.

**cavallet'to**, *I.* 1. A cabaletta. 2. small bridge. 3. The break in registers.

**cavata** (kä-vä'-tä), *I.* 1. Tone-p duction. 2. A recitative; a ca tina.

**cavatina** (kä-vä-tē'nä), *I.*, **cavati** (kǎv-ǎ-tēn), *F.* A melody of o strain only.

**c-barré** (üt-bǎr-rä), *F.* Vide BARREL

**c-clef.** The tenor clef; wherever stands it indicates middle C.

**C-dur** (tsä-door), *G.* The key of major.

**cebell'.** A theme in common time w variations and alternation of high a low notes. A sort of English gavot

**cecilium** (sǔ-sē'-lǐ-ŭn), *F.* A key-boa reed instr. the size and shape of

cello, the left hand playing keys, the
right working bellows.

**dez** (sā-dā), *F.* Decrease !

**amustel** (sā-lä-mü-stĕl), *F.* A harmonium with unusual imitative stops.

**ere** (chä'-lä-rĕ), *I.* Rapid. **celerità**
(-ri-tä'). Rapidity.

**este** (sā-lĕst), *F.* Celestial, applied
to stops of soft, sweet tone, and to a
piano pedal of the same effect.

**estina** (chä-lĕs-tē'nä), *I.* 1. A 4-ft.
stop. 2. A tremolo stop in reed organs.

**l.** Vide ELLIS (B. D.).

**llo** (chĕl'lō). Abbr. and common
name of *violoncello.* **cello'ne.** A
cello inv. by Stelzner gaining increased sonority by its method of
stringing.

**mbalo** (chäm'bä-lō), **cembolo** (chäm'-
bō-lō), *I.*, **cembal** (säṅ-băl), *F.* 1. A
harpsichord. 2. A cymbal. **cembalis-
a,** *I.* A player on either. **cembal d'-
amour,** *F.* A very large harpsichord.
**c. tutto il c.,** *I.* Loud pedal. **c. onni-
cordo,** *I.* Proteus. **cembalist,** *E.*
A player on the harpsichord.

**nbanel'la, cennamel'la,** *I.* A
flute.

**nt,** *E.* The hundredth part of an
equal semitone. Vide ELLIS (B. D.).

**nto** (chän'-tō), **cento'ne,** *I.*, **centon**
(säṅ-tôn), *F.* 1. The Gregorian antiphonary. 2. A patchwork or medley.

**rcare** (chär-kä'-rĕ), *I.* To search. **c.
a nota.** A common effect in singing where a note taken by skip is
lightly anticipated with a short grace.

**r' valet, cervelat.** An obsolete clarinet.

**es** (tsĕs), *G.* The note C flat. **Ces-
es.** C double flat.

**sura, cesure.** Vide CÆSURA.

**tera** (chä'-tĕ-rä), *I.* A cittern.

**f.** Abbr. of *Cantus firmus.*

**a chi** (chä-chē), *Chinese.* A chromatic kin.

**acona** (chä-kō'-nä), *Sp.*, **chaconne**
(shă-kŭn), *F.*, **ciaccona** (chäk-kō'-
nä), *I.* A slow dance probably Spanish in origin; in 3-4 time with a

groundbass ; almost always in major,
in contrast with the *passacaglia ;* and
generally in form of variations.

**chair organ.** Vide CHOIR ORGAN.

**chalmeau,** *E.*, **chalumeau** (shăl-ŭ-
mō), *F.*, **Chalämau, Chalämaus**
(shäl'-ä-mows), *G.* 1. An ancient
pipe blown through a calamus, or
reed. 2. The low register of the
clarinet ; as a direction it means "an
octave lower," being cancelled by
*clar.* or *clarinet.* 3. The chanter of
a bag-pipe.

**chalil** (kä-lel), *Heb.* Hebrew pipe or
flute.

**chalotte** (shă-lôt'). A tube to receive
a reed.

**chamber music.** Music composed for
a small auditorium, as a string quartet
or a pianoforte trio.

**chamber-organ.** A cabinet organ.

**chang.** A Persian harp.

**change.** 1. A tune rung on a chime.
2. Vide MODULATION. 3. Mutation.
4. (a) **changing-note.** A note foreign to the immediate harmony and
entering (unlike the passing-note) on
a strong beat ; when two or more appear simultaneously they make a
**changing-chord.** (b) In old counterpoint, a passing discord entering unaccented and then skipping.

**changeable.** Used of chants that may
be sung either in the major or minor
mode.

**changer de jeu** (shäṅ-zhä dŭ zhŭ), *F.*
To change the stops.

**chanson** (shäṅ-sôṅ), *F.* A song ; a
ballad. **c. bachique** (bă-shēk). A
drinking-song. **c. des rues** (dä-rü).
A street-song ; a vaudeville. **chan-
sonnette** (nĕt). A little or short
song. **chansonnier** (sŭn-yä). A
song-writer ; a book of songs.

**chant.** 1. Originally a song, and still
so meant in the French word (vide below), since the Gregorian time used of
vocal music marked by the recitation
of many syllables on one tone, and
employed for prose texts such as the
Canticles and Psalms. There are two
sorts of chant, the Gregorian and the

Anglican. (a) The Gregorian is a short tune to be repeated in successive sections of prose ; it has 8 tones and is in four parts ; the *intonation* (or *inchoatio*) or opening notes ; the *first reciting note* (or *dominant*) ; the *mediation ;* the *second reciting note* (or *dominant*) ; the *termination* (ending or cadence). (b) The Anglican omits the *intonation* and differs in the rhythm and mode but has the same monotone recitation with modulations in the middle (mediation) and end (termination). The Anglican has two parts of 3 and 4 measures, 7 in all ; this is the *single* chant, there are also *double, triple,* and *quadruple* forms of proportionate length. In chanting, the fitting of the unequal phrases to the music is called *pointing,* and consists of reciting them strictly within the duration of the notes except those of the 1st and 4th measures which are enlarged to fit the words. Words to be sung to the cadence are cut off from those to be sung to the reciting-note, by a vertical line called the *cadence-mark.* 2. Any recitation of chant-like character. 3. A tone. 4. A *cantus firmus.* 5. Vide PLAIN-CHANT. 6. Vide CHANGEABLE. 7. **Free-chant.** A form in which the hemistichs consist of only 2 measures. 8. Roman Chant-Gregorian. 9. **Phrygian chant.** One intended to provoke wrath.

**chant** (shäṅ), *F.* Song ; tune ; vocal part. **c. amoureux.** Love song. **c. d'église,** or **grégorien.** Gregorian chant. **c. égal, c. en ison.** Chant on one tone, or with one interval of two tones. **c. figuré.** Figured counterpoint. **c. funèbre.** Funeral song. **c. royal.** A sacred song ; or a prayer for the monarch ; the mode in which such prayer was sung. **c. sur le livre,** i. e., "on the book," vocal counterpoint extemporized on a printed *cantus firmus.*

**chanter,** *E.* 1. One who chants. **arch-c.** The leader of the chants. **2.** The tenor or melodic pipe of a bag-pipe.

**chanter** (shäṅ-tä), *F.* To sing. **c. livre ouvert** (ä lēv-roovĕr). To si at sight. **chantant(e).** Lyric. **bas c.** Vide BASS. **café c.** (kă-fä-chä täṅ). A music hall. **chant é(e)** (shä tā). Sung. **chanteur (euse).** male (female) singer. **chantonne** Canterellare.

**chanterelle** (shänt-ŭ-rĕl), *F.* T highest and smallest string of instrument.

**chanterie** (shäṅ-trē), *F.* **chantry,** A chapel endowed for daily mass.

**chanterres** (shäṅ-tĕr), *F.* 10th ce tury ballad-singers.

**chan'tor,** *E.* A singer in a cathedral choir.

**chantre** (shäṅtr), *F.* Choir - lead **grand c.** Precentor. **second c.** chorister.

**chapeau** (shă-pō), *F.* A "hat ;" a t **c. chinois** (shĕn-wä). A set of sm bells arranged on a frame like a Cl nese hat. Cf. CRESCENT.

**chapel.** Musicians in the retinue of great personage.

**chapelle** (shă-pĕl), *F.* Cappella.

**characteristic.** Strongly individu in character, or mood, used of a co position (as **Charakterstück,** *G.*). **note** or **tone.** The leading-tone any tone peculiar to a key. **c. chor** The principal chord. **Charakte stimme,** *G.* A solo-sto.

**charivari** (shă-rĭ-vä'-rĭ), *F.* Vi SHIVAREE.

**chasse** (shăs), *F.* The hunt. **à la** In hunting style.

**chatsoteroth.** A Hebrew trumpet.

**che** (kā), *I.* Than, that, which.

**che chi** (kā-kē). One of the eig species of Chinese music.

**chef** (shĕf), *F.* Leader, chief. **che d'attaque** (dăt-tăk). 1. The leade or first violin. 2. Leader of a choru **chef-d'œuvre** (shä-dŭvr). Maste piece. **chef-d'orchestre** (shĕf-dô kĕstr). The leader. **ch. du chan** Leader of an opera chorus.

**cheipour.** A Persian trumpet.

**chel'idonizing.** Singing a spring "swallow song."

el'ys. 1. Vide LYRE. 2. Old name or viol.

eng (chĕng). A Chinese mouth-organ, a gourd with many free reeds ; it suggested the invention of the harmonium.

eng chi (chĕng-chē). One of the eight species of Chinese music.

erub'ical hymn. The Prisagion.

est of viols. A group or set of viols, two basses, two tenors, and two trebles.

est tone, chest voice. The lowest register of the voice.

evalet (shĕv-ä-lä), F. Bridge.

eville (shĕ-vē'-yĕ), F. Peg.

evroter (shĕv-rô-tā), F. To bleat like a goat, hence, **chevrotement** (shĕ-vrôt-môṅ). A tremor or shake in singing.

iarenta'na, I. An Italian country dance.

iarina (kē-ä-rē'nä), I. A clarion.

iaro (kē-ä'-rō), I. Clear, pure. **chiaramen'te.** Brightly, purely. **chiarezza** (rĕd'-zä). Clearness. **di c.** Clearly.

iave (kē-ä'-vĕ), I. 1. A clef. 2. Key. 3. Tuning-key. 4. A failure. 5. **c. maestro.** The fundamental key or note.

iavette (vĕt'-tĕ), I. pl. Transposing clefs of the 16th century ; of which the **high c.** indicated that its line was to be read a third higher, the **low c.,** a third lower. Thus the C clef might indicate e or eɂ ; or a, or aɂ.

ickera (kē'-kĕ-rä) or **chikarah.** A Hindu bow instrument.

iesa (kē-ā'-zä), I. A church. **da c.** For the church, or in sacred style, as *sonata* or *concerto da chiesa.*

iffre (shĭfr), F. A figure in thorough bass. **basse chiffrée** (shĭf-frā). Figured bass.

ifonie (shē-fō-nē'), F. Old name for hurdy-gurdy.

ime. A set of bells tuned to a scale.

chime-barrel. Portion of the mechanism for ringing a chime.

imney. A tube in the cap of a stopped pipe

Chinese flute. Bamboo flute.

Chinese hat. Vide CHAPEAU.

Chinese scale. Five notes without semitones ; the music is written on five perpendicular lines, the pitches indicated by distinctive names.

chinnor, chinor. Vide KINNOR.

chirimia (chē-rē-mē'-ä), Sp. The oboe ; clarion.

chirogym'nast. A mechanical contrivance for exercising the fingers.

chi'roplast (kī'rō). A device of gloves and bars, inv. 1814 by Logier, to keep the hands and fingers of piano players in the right position.

chitarra (kē-tär'-rä), I. 1. A guitar, a cithara. **c. coll' arco.** A violin with guitar-shaped body. **chitarris'ta.** One who plays on the guitar. **chittarrina** (rē'-nä). Small Neapolitan guitar. **chitarro'ne.** A double guitar.

chiterna (kē-tĕr'-nä), I. Quinterna.

chiuso (kē-oo'-zō), I. Closed. Vide CANON and BOCCA. **chiuden'do.** Closing.

Chladni's figures. Vide NODAL FIGURES.

choeur (kŭr), F. Choir, chorus. **à grand c.** For full chorus.

choice note. An alternative note.

choir. 1. A body of singers usually in a church. 2. Their place in the church. 3. A subdivision of a chorus or orchestra. **c. organ.** Vide ORGAN. **grand c.** The combination of all the reed-stops.

Chor (kôr), G. Same as Choir 1, 2, 3 ; also on the piano, or organ, a unison, i. e., all the strings or pipes belonging to one digital or pipe ; hence a piano with 3 strings to each tone is **dreichörig.**

chora'gus, chore'gus (kō). The donor of a choral or dramatic work. At Oxford the director of Church music.

cho'ral. Pertaining to a choir or chorus. **choral service.** A service in which the entire liturgy is intoned or chanted.

cho'rale, Choral (kō-räl'), G. 1. Choral psalm or hymn. 2. Early German Protestant hymn.

**chora′leon.** Vide ÆOLOMELODICON.

**choraliter** (kō-räl′-ĭ-tĕr), **choralmäs-sig** (mĕs-sikh), *G.* In choral style.

**Choramt** (kôr′-ämt), *G.* Choral service.

**choraul′es.** A Greek flutist.

**chord.** 1. A string. 2. Vide VOCAL C. 3. A combination of three or more tones, whether pleasant or discordant.

The chords which are the building-material of all our music are made up of thirds laid brick-wise one upon another. A single third is not counted a chord, two thirds (for instance the two intervals, g-b-d) make up a **triad ;** another third (d to f) makes a chord, called a **seventh** (g-b-d-f) because the interval (q. v.) from g to f is a seventh ; adding another third gives a **chord of the ninth** or a **ninth chord** (g-b-d-f-a), two other additions give the **chords of the eleventh** and **thirteenth** (g-b-d-f-a-c-e) (these last are usually cacophonous, and their existence as special chords is denied by some theorists). To add another third brings us back, on the tempered scale, to g, from which the chord grew and which is known as the **fundamental** or **root** of the chord.

Chords are distinguished in mode major or minor, from the majorit minority of their intervals, a mi triad differing from a **major** in ing a minor third, the fifth being p fect in both cases. When the ch has been constructed as above ( d-f) it is said to be in the **first** **root** or **fundamental** or **perfect sition ;** it may re-appear with of its notes as the lowest (thoug always remains the **root**). When 3d (b) is in the bass, it is said t in the 2d position; when the fifth (d is in its 3d position. With any o notes other than the root in the the chord is said to be **inverted.** names of these **inversions** have b cumbrously taken from the inter between the lowest note and the oth no interval being stated in term over an octave, the greatest inte being named first, and some of the tervals being unmentioned, especi those of doubled notes : thus the tervals in that inversion of a seve chord in which the seventh is in bass might be, counting upward (-4), 16 (-2), 20 (-6), but it would called, for short, a 4-2 chord, or ch of the second and fourth.

In the following table the names of all the inversions are given. In thorou bass these inversions are indicated by Arabic numerals above the bass notes.

A triad in the root or fundamental position is marked —3 or $\frac{5}{3}$ or $\frac{8}{5}$.

A triad in the 1st inversion is called a **chord of the 6th** and marked 6.

A triad in the 2d inversion is called **a chord of the 4th and 6th** or a **six-f** chord and marked $\frac{6}{4}$.

A 7th chord in the root or fundamental position is marked 7 or $\frac{7}{5}$.

A 7th chord in the 1st inversion is called **a chord of the 5th and 6th** or a **six-** chord, and marked $\frac{6}{5}$ or $\frac{6}{5}$. 3

A 7th chord in the 2d inversion is called **a chord of the 3d, 4th and 6th,** four-three chord and marked $\frac{6}{4}$ or $\frac{6}{4}$. 3

h chord in the 3d inversion is called **a chord of the 2d and 4th** or a four-
vo chord and marked $\frac{4}{2}$ or $\frac{6}{4}$.

h chord in the root or fundamental position is marked 9 or $7\frac{9}{3}\frac{9}{3}$ according as the
h or 7th is omitted.

line or dash through any Arabic nu-
eral as ⚡ means that the note it
presents is sharpened ; it may be
so preceded by a natural or flat.
sharp or flat standing over a bass
ote means that the *third* of the
ord is to be sharpened or flattened ;
dash or horizontal line following a
imeral continues its tone in the next
ord.

he character (but not the inversion)
' chords may be indicated by Roman
imerals indicating the degree of the
ale on which they are founded, the
ale being noted by a large letter for
ajor (as C), and a small for minor
s c). Thus IV means a triad on
e fourth degree with a major third
id perfect fifth ; iv. a triad on the
urth degree with minor 3d and per-
ct fifth. An accent after the numeral
dicates an augmented fifth, as IV';
small cipher indicates a diminished
fth, as VII° ; a small 7 indicates a
ord of the seventh. These devices
e an heirloom from an age of little
odulation and formal counterpoint ;
ey were shorthand then, but to our
usic they are handcuffs. They have
nly a dry text-book career, and alert
eorists are rapidly denying them
e right even to this existence.

ther kinds of chords are **character-
stic**, the leading chord ; **chromatic**,
ontaining a chromatic tone ; **com-
ion**, a triad ; **accidental**, produced
y anticipation or suspension ; **al-
ered**, having some tone chromatical-
changed with modulatory effect (one
f the bugaboos of the theorists), vide
LTERED ; **anomalous**, vide ANOM-
LY ; **augmented**, having an aug-
ented fifth ; **broken**, vide BROKEN ;
erivative**, formed by inversion ; **di-**

**atonic**, a triad ; **diminished**, having
an imperfect 5th and diminished 7th ;
**dominant**, the triad or 7th chord on
the dominant ; **doubtful, equivocal**,
resolvable in many ways, as the diminished 7th ; **imperfect**, having an
imperfect fifth, or having some tone
omitted ; **leading**, the dominant
chord ; **related** or **relative**, containing a tone in common ; **solid**,
opposed to broken ; **threefold**, a
triad ; **transient**, modulatory.

**chord'a**, *L.* A string ; a note. **c.
characteristica.** The leading note.
**c. dominant septima.** The dominant chord of the seventh ; **no'na,** the
ninth. **chordæ essentia'les.** The
tonic, third and fifth. **chordæ voca'-
les.** Vocal chords.

**chordaulo'dian, chordomelo'dion.** A
large automatic barrel organ, inv. by
Kaufmann, 1812.

**Chordienst** (kôr'-dēnst), *G.* Choral
service. **Chordirektor.** A director
who trains a chorus at the opera
house.

**chordom'eter.** A gauge for measuring
strings.

**Chöre** (kär'ĕ), *G. plural.* Choirs, choruses.

**Chorist'**, *G.*, **choriste** (kô-rēst), *F.*,
**chorister**, *E.* 1. A leader of a choir.
2. A choral singer. **Chorsänger,
C.-schüler, C.-knabe** (kôr'-knä-bĕ),
*G.* Choir-boy.

**Chorstimme** (kôr-shtĭm-mĕ), *G.* Chorus part.

**Chorton** (kôr-tōn), *G.* "Choir-pitch."
1. The pitch at which choruses formerly sang in Germany. 2. Choral
tune.

**chorus.** 1. A company of singers ; especially in opera, etc., the supporting body of vocalists who do not

sing solos. 2. A composition for a chorus, usually in 4 parts—a "double chorus" requires 8 parts. 3. A refrain. 4. The compound stops. 5. The bagpipe, or drone-pipe. 7. Marine trumpet. 8. The free-staves of the crwth. **chorusmaster.** The chief singer in a chorus.

**choutarah.** Vide TAMBOURA.

**Chris'te eleison** (ā-lā'-ē-sōn), *Gr.* "Christ have mercy ;" part of the Kyrie.

**Christmesse, Christmette** (krēst'-mĕt-tĕ), *G.* Christmas matins.

**chro'ma,** *Gr.* 1. A chromatic modification of the Greek tetrachord. 2. A sharp or a flat. **c. duplex.** A double sharp. 3. **c. diesis.** A semitone. 4. (Or **c. simplex.**) An eighth note. **c. duplex.** A 16th note.

**chromam'eter.** A tuning-fork.

**chromat'ic, chromatique** (tēk), *F.,* **chromatisch** (mä'-tĭsh), *G.,* **cromat'ico,** *I.* 1. Literally, "coloured" and implying a foreign or added tinge, specifically that given to the sober diatonic notes natural to a key, by an unrelated sharp, flat or natural that is not of modulatory effect. A whole scale may be **chromatic** (i. e., progress by semitones) ; a chord, an interval or a progression altered by a flat or sharp is called **chromatic,** and the process of so modifying it is called **c. alteration ;** an instr. playing semitones is called **c.,** and the signs themselves that sharpen or flatten a tone are called **c. signs,** or **chromatics.** 2. Vide MODES.

**chronom'eter.** Metronome, particularly Godfrey Weber's.

**chronomètre** (krôn-ô-mĕtr), *F.* A form of monochord inv. 1827, by Raller, to teach piano-tuning.

**chrotta** (krot'ta). Vide CROWD.

**church cadence.** The plagal cadence.

**church modes.** Vide MODES.

**chute** (shüt), *F.* An obsolete sliding embellishment.

**ciaconne.** Vide CHACONNE.

**ciaramella** (chä-rä-mĕl'-lä), *I.* A bagpipe.

**cicogna** (chē-cōn-yä), *I.* Mouthpie[

**cicu'ta,** *L.* A Pan's pipe.

**cicutrenna** (chē-koo-trĕn'-na), *I.* pipe.

**cifrato** (chē-frä'-to), *I.* Figured.

**cimbalo** (chēm'-bä-lō), *I.* 1. Cymb 2. Tambourine. 3. Harpsichord dulcimer.

**cimbalon.** Vide CZIMBALON.

**Cimbel** (tsĭm'-bĕl), *G.* A high mi ure stop. **Cimbelstern.** A gro of star-shaped cymbals attached old organs.

**cinelli** (chē-nĕl'-lē), *I.,* **Cinellen** (t nĕl'-lĕn), *G.* Cymbals.

**Cink** (tsĭnk), *G.* 1. A small reed-sto 2. Vide ZINK.

**cinq** (sănk), *F.,* **cinque** (chēn'kwĕ), Five ; the fifth voice or part in quintet. **a c.**—in 5 parts. **cinqu pace** (sănk-păs). Old French dar in quintuple time.

**cin'yra.** Old name for harp.

**ciphering.** The sounding of org pipes, when the keys are not touche due to leakage. **cipher system.** old notation using numerals instead letters.

**circle of fifths.** A method of mod lation by dominants. Vide TEMP AMENT and preliminary essay, INTl DUCTION TO MUSIC.

**circular canon.** A canon goi through the major keys.

**circular scale.** The curved row of t ing-pins.

**Cis** (tsēs), *G.* The note C sharp. **C is.** C double sharp. **Cis-dur.** major. **Cis-moll.** C ♯ minor.

**cistel'la,** *L.* A dulcimer.

**cistre** (sēstr), *F.* Cither.

**cistrum,** *L.* Vide SISTRUM.

**citara** (chē-tä'-rä), *I.* Cither.

**citaredo** (thē-tä-rä'-dhō), *Sp.,* **citari** (chē-tä-rēs'-tä), *I.* A minstrel, a pla upon the harp or cittern.

**citerna** (chē-tĕr'-nä), *I.* Quinterna.

**cith'ara,** *L.* The large lyre from whi the guitar and zither are derived. **biju'ga.** A 2-necked **c. c. hispanic** The Spanish guitar. **keyed c.** T **clavicitherium. cith'aris.** The t

orbo. **citharoe′dus.** A singing lutenist.

**th′er, cithera, cithern, cittern,
cythorn.** An old guitar-like instr.,
strung with wire and played with a
plectrum ; sometimes with a bow, or
by means of keys.

**to′le.** A dulcimer.

**:′tam.** Ancient English guitar.

**vetteria** (chĕ-vĕt-tĕ-rē′-ä), *I.* Coquetry.

**air** (klăr), *F.* Clear, shrill, loud.

**aircylindre** (klăr-si-lăṅdr), *F.* Vide
CLAVICYLINDER.

**airon** (klăr-ôṅ), *F.* 1. Trumpet. **2.**
Reed-stop. 3. Vide CLARINET. **4.**
A bugler.

**ang.** 1. A bell-tone. 2. In acoustics a fundamental tone with its group
of over and under-tones, their completeness giving the **clang-colour** or
**clang-tint,** Tyndall's word.

**ang-key,** *E.,* **Klangschlüssel,** *G.*
Riemann's word for his system of
chord designation intended to supplant
thorough-bass as a better method of
describing a combination by its qualities. Intervals are reckoned, not from
the bass, but from the principal tone
of each chord. He uses Arabian figures for major, Roman for minor
chords, the former indicating an interval upwards from a tone, the latter an interval below, as follows:
**1** (I). Principal tone. 2 (II). Major
2d. 3 (III). Major 3d. 4 (IV).
Perfect 4th. 5 (V). Perfect 5th.
6 (VI). Major 6th. 7 (VII). Minor 7th. 8 (VIII). Octave. 9 (IX).
Major 9th. 10 (X). Major 10th.
< indicates raising a tone by a semi-
tone. > Lowering it a semitone ;
' tones doubly raised or lowered being inconceivable musically." The
major chord (or upper-clang) is abbreviated + (for 5-3-1), the minor
chord (or under-clang) is abbr. o (for
I-III-V)—thus a+ or ao. Feeling that,
for instance, the tone C in the major
triad ab-c-eb has a different meaning
from the tone c in the minor triad
a-c-e, he has coined for this " sub-

stitution of clangs " the word
**Klangvertretung** (kläng′-fĕr-trä′-
toongk). **clang-succession** is a
chord-progression with regard to its
**clang-meaning,** that is, a tonality
which does not consider every chord
in its proper absolute key but in its
relation to some other chord to which
it plays the part of **principal** or related **clang.** Fuller particulars of
this interesting philosophy must be
sought in Riemann's Dictionary of
Music, and other of his writings.

**claquebois** (klăk-bwä), *F.* A xylophone.

**clar.** Abbr. of *Clarinet.*

**clarabel′la,** *L.* A soft-voiced wood
organ-stop.

**claribel flute.** 1. A flute. 2. A 4-ft.
clarabella.

**clar′ichord, clarico′lo, clar′igold.** An
old harp, or a clavichord.

**Clarin** (klä-rēn′, *G.* In *F.* klăr-ăṅ). 1.
A ' clarion. 2. A 4-ft reed-stop.
**Clarinblasen.** Soft notes of the
trumpet.

**clar′inet, clarinette** (nĕt), *F.,* **clarinetto,** *I.* An important wood-wind
instr. with a single beating reed, cylindrical tube and bell. It is in effect a
stopped pipe (q. v.) and sounds an
octave lower than other wood-wind
of its length ; it has only the odd-
numbered partials in the overtone-
scale, and requires a different fingering from the oboe, etc. It has
18 holes, including 13 with keys, by
means of which it has a range of
3 octaves and a sixth, which range
is sharply divided into four distinct
qualities of tone: 1. The **highest,**
or **superacute,** being (in the normal
soprano clarinet in C) d‴ -c⁗. 2. The
**high** or **clarinette** or **clarion** register (whence the instr. took its name)
b′-c‴. 3. The **medium,** f′ -b′b. 4. The
**chalumeau** (shăl′-ŭ-mō) or **Schalmei**
(shäl-mī) g-e′ ; the qualities being respectively. 1. Shrill. 2. Liquid and
clear. 3. Veiled and feeble. 4. Rich
and sonorous like a contralto voice.
The clarinet is a transposing instr.

written in the C clef; it is made in many sizes to adapt it to different keys; the **large soprano** in C, B♭ (often called simply "clarinet in B") and A; the **small soprano** in D, E, F, A♭; the **alto** or **barytone** in F and E♭, the **bass** (an octave lower than the sopranos) in C, B♭ and A. The soprano in B♭ is the most brilliant; the soprano in A is very tender in tone. The **small sopranos** are too shrill for use except in military bands in which the clarinet group serves the substantial purpose served by the strings in the orchestra.

The clarinet is an improvement (made by Denner of Nürnberg, 1700) upon the old **chalumeau** or **Schalmei**, whose name still persists in the low register of the clarinet. The **ch.** had a single, beating reed, a cylindrical tube and nine holes, each of which produced a tone giving a compass of these natural tones, f -a'. By placing a hole and a key at a nodal point dividing the tube into 3 equal parts, overblowing became possible in the twelfth, i. e., the 3d partials (vide ACOUSTICS). This new register was called *clarinetto* or *clarion* for its clarity of tone, and from this word came the present name of the instr., all of whose gaps have been filled by means of the Böhm key-mechanism, etc., though the fingering is still difficult and a slip gives a squawk called the "goose" or *couac*. 2. A soft 8-ft. reed-stop. **clarinet flute.** A flue-stop with holes in the cover.

**clarino** (klä-rē'-nō), *I.*, **clarion**, *E.* (in *F.* klär-yôṅ). 1. A small trumpet. 2. A 4-foot organ reed-stop, an octave above the trumpet. 3. The trumpet parts in score. **c. harmonique.** A reed-stop.

**clarionet.** Obsolescent spelling of clarinet.

**clarionet-flute.** A stop.

**clarone** (klä-rō'-nĕ), *I.* A clarinet.

**clàrseach** (klär'-säkh), **clarseth** (klär'-sĕ). The old Irish harp.

**claus'ula**, *L.* A dance.

**clavecin** (klăv-săṅ), *F.* 1. The har chord. 2. The keys a bell-rin plays on. **c. acoustique.** An in of the 18th cent. imitating var instruments.

**Claviatur** (klä-fĭ-ä-toor'), *G.* key-board.

**clav'ichord.** Prototype of the pia the strings being set in vibration by hammers, but by small br wedges (called tangents) on the e of the keys; these set only one s tion of the string in vibration.

**clavicyl'inder.** An instr. inv. Chladni, about 1800, consisting cylinders of glass attuned.

**clavicymbalum**, *L.*, **clavicem'balo** The harpsichord.

**clavicythe'rium**, *L.* An upright ha sichord of the 13th Century.

**Clavier** (clăv-yā, *F.*, in *G.* klä-fē 1. The key-board. 2. An old name the clavichord. 3. **c. de récit.** 1 swell manual. 4. In French use, gamut included in the stave. 5. V KLAVIER.

**clav'is**, *L.* and *G.* 1. A key. A clef. 3. A note. 4. Handle c bellows.

**clé** (klā), **clef** (klā), *F.* (In Eng pron. "klĕf.") A florid form o letter, used as a symbol with a fi note-meaning, from which it takes name, as the so-called "c" clef noting that whichever line it grip middle C (c'). The most comm clefs are the "G" (or **treble c. clef sol**, or **clef descant**, or v **lin c.**) which is always seen now the 2d line; the F. (or **bass** or **de fay**). (These two are those u in piano music.) The C (or **clef d'** is used movably and is called **soprano** (or **German soprano** **discant c.**; or the **alto**; or the te (or **mean** or **counter-tenor**) clef, cording as it is placed on the fi the 3d or the 4th line, in each which cases it marks middle C. 1 C clef is found in various forms a is still used in music for the 'cello a

ther instruments and in contrapuntal
writing.

The obsolete clefs are the F on the
,d line (the **barytone clef**), the C on
he 2d line (the **mezzo soprano**), the
G on the 1st line (the **French violin,**
or **French treble clef**).

ar flute. Organ-stop.

f d'accordeur (dăk-kôr-dŭr), *F.*
Cuning-hammer.

c'ca, *L.*, cloche (klôsh), *F.* A bell.

clochette. A hand-bell.

ck. To swing the clapper of a sta-
ionary bell.

g, *Irish.* A shuffling dance.

ro'ne, *I.* Alto clarinet.

se (klōz). A cadence.

se harmony or position. That in
which the chords spread over little
pace ; when a chord extends beyond
n octave it is said to be in **open** po-
ition.

se play. Lute-playing in which the
ngers remain on the strings.

se score. That with more than one
oice on a stave.

noll (tsä-môl), *G.* The key of C
ninor.

). Abbr. of *choir-organ.*

.lotino (kō-ä-lôt-tē'nō), *I.* Concer-
ino.

china (kôk-kē'-na), *I.* An Italian
ountry-dance.

da, *I.* "Tail." 1. An additional
ermination to the body of a compo-
ition, ranging from a few chords to
long passage. 2. The stem of a
ote.

let'ta. 1. A short coda. 2. A
hort passage in fugue, between the
nd of the subject and the entry of
he answer.

don, *Gr.* 1. A little bell. 2. The
ell of a trumpet.

lesti'no (or-a). A name formerly
pplied to various keyed instruments.

fre (kôfr), *F.* The frame of an
nstrument.

gli (kōl'-yē), coi (kō'-e), col, coll',
olla, collo, *I.* Forms of the prepo-
ition "con," and the definite article
neaning "with the."

colachon (kō-lă-shôn), *F.* An instr. like
a lute with longer neck.

colascione. Vide CALASCIONE.

collet (kôl-lā), *F.* The neck, as of a violin.

collinet (kôl-lĭ-nā). A flageolet, named
from a famous virtuoso on it.

colofo'nia, *I.*, colophane (kôl-ō-făn),
*F.*, Colophonium (kô-lô-fō'-nĭ-oom),
*G.*, col'ophony, *E.* Resin.

colorato (kō-lō-rä'-to), *I.* Florid.

coloratura (kō-lō-rä-too'rà) (pl e), *I.*,
Coloraturen (kô-lô-rä-too'-rĕn), *G.*
Ornaments and ornamental passages,
in vocal or instrumental music ; brilliant vocalization.

coloris (kô-lō-rē'), *F.*, Colorit (rēt'),
*G.* The "colour"-scheme of a work.

colour. 1. Vide NOTATION. 2. Timbre.
3. Literally colour ; to some minds
each tone, or each key, has a distinctive actual colour, as C is red to some,
C♯ scarlet, C♮ blood red, C♭ darker,
etc. The Editor has even met a
painter who claimed the ability to play
any picture or paint any composition.

colpo, di, *I.* "At a blow," abruptly.

combinational tones. Vide RESULT-
ANT TONES.

combination mode. The ambiguous
mode resulting from resolving a dominant chord in a minor key to the
tonic major.

combination pedals. Vide COMPO-
SITION PEDALS.

come (kō'mĕ), *I.* As, like, the same as.
c. prima. As before or at first. c.
sopra. As above. c. sta. Exactly
as it stands.

co'mes, *L.* 1. In fugue, the companion
or answer, to the dux (leader), or subject. 2. In canon, the consequent.

comiquement (kō-mĕk-măn), *F.* Comically.

com'ma. 1. A breathing-mark. 2. A
theoretical term indicating the minute
difference between two tones nearly
identical. (a) The comma syntonum, or c. of Didymus, is that between a major and a minor tone 80: 81.
(b) The comma ditonicum, or c. of
Pythagoras, is that by which six

whole notes with the ratio 9 : 8 exceed the octave, or 531 + : 524 +.

**com(m)odamen'te, com'(m)odo,** *I.* With ease.

**common.** Vide CHORD and TURN. **c. measure** or **time.** 4-4 time.

**compass.** Range of a voice or instr.

**compiacevole** (kôm-pïä-chä'-võ-lĕ), **compiacevolmen'te,** *I.* Pleasant-(ly).

**complainte** (kôn-plănt), *F.* A religious ballad.

**com'plement.** That quantity or interval which fills up an octave, as a fourth is **c.** to a fifth.

**complementary part.** In fugue, the part added to the subject and counter-subject.

**complete.** Vide CADENCE.

**completo'rium,** *L.*, **com'pletory,** *E.* 1. An Ambrosian anthem supplementary to the antiphon. 2. A compline.

**complin(e),** *L.* Vide HORAE CANON-ICAE.

**componis'ta,** *I.* A composer.

**compo'num.** A machine inv. by Winkel to present a given theme in endless variety of forms.

**composition,** *I.* The act, art or science of writing original music.

**composition pedals.** Pedals inv. by J. C. Bishop, connected with a mechanism for bringing into use several stops simultaneously.

**composizione di tavolino** (kôm-põ-zē-tsï-ō'-nĕ dē tä-võ-lē'-nõ), *I.* Table-music.

**compos'to,** *I.* Composed, quiet.

**compound.** Of intervals, those exceeding the octave. **c. stop.** One having more than one rank of pipes. **c. measures** or **times.** Those which contain more than one principal accent, as 6-4, 9-8, etc.

**compressed score.** Close score.

**comprimaria** (kôm-prē-mä'-rï-ä), *I.* The next in rank to a *prima donna*.

**con** (kõn), *I.* "With ; " it is often combined with the article "the," vide COGLI, etc. *con. 8va*, vide OTTAVA.

**concave pedals.** Radiating pedals.

**concealed.** Vide HIDDEN.

**concento** (kôn-chĕn'-to), *I.* 1. Concor 2. Non-arpeggiation.

**concen'tus,** *L.* 1. Concord, vide CENTUS.

**concert** (in *F.* kôn-sär'). 1. A pub performance. 2. **c. spirituel.** cred concert. **Dutch c.** An imp vised chorus of little regularity a much hilarity. 3. A concerto. 4. set of instrs. of different size, v CHEST OF VIOLS.

**concertante** (kôn-chĕr-tän'-tĕ), *I.* A piece in which each part is alt nately principal, as a *duo conc tante*. 2. A concerto for two more instrs., with orchestral accom **c. style.** In brilliant concert sty **c. parts.** Parts for solo instrs. in orchestral work.

**concertato** (tä'-tõ), *I.*, **concerted,** Used of music for several voices instruments.

**concert-grand.** The largest size the piano.

**concertina** (kŏn-sĕr-tē'nä). Ch Wheatstone's improved accorde (q. v.) inv. 1829. It is double-acti producing tone on being drawn or compressed. Its 2 key-boards hexagonal, and the *English treble* (much superior to the German) ha range of four octaves from g bel middle C with all the chromatic ton The **c** is to be had also in *alto, ten bass* and *double-bass* ranges.

**concertino** (kôn-chĕr-tē'-nõ), *I.* 1. small concerto. 2. Principal as posed to *ripieno*, e. g., violino principal violin. 3. The first-vio part.

**concertis'ta,** *I.* Virtuoso.

**Concertmeister** (kôn-tsĕrt-mïshtĕ *G.* 1. The leader. 2. The first the first-violins.

**concerto** (kôn-chĕr'-tõ), *I.* 1. A c cert. 2. A composition for on two (*double*) three (*triple*)—or m solo instruments with orchestral companiment. It is usually in son form with modifications to all of virtuosity, notably the caden played by the performer of the s part just before the concluding tutti of the first and last movement. Formerly the word was applied to **concertante.** Torelli is credited with the modern form. The **c.** without orchestral accompaniment (**c. a. solo**) is very rare. **c. da camera.** Chamber concerto, opposed to *grosso*. **c. da chiesa** (kĭ-ā′-zä) or **c. ecclesiastico.** (a) In Viadana's work, merely motets with accomp. for organ. (b) A concerto for church use. **c. doppio. a c.** for two or more instruments. **c. gros′so.** A composition for full orchestra. **c. spirituale.** Sacred concert.

**ncert pitch.** Vide A, of which the French standard is now generally adopted. By this all the tones are regulated. In England **c. p.** refers to a pitch almost half a tone higher than the international pitch.

**ncertspieler** (kôn-tsĕrt′-shpē-lĕr), *G.* A solo or concerto player. **Concert′stück** (shtük). 1. A concert-piece. 2. A concerto.

**ncitato** (kôn-chĭ-tä′-tō), *I.* Agitated.

**nclusione** (kloo-zĭ-ō′-nĕ), *I.* Conclusion.

**ncord.** An harmonious combination. **concordant.** 1. Harmonious. 2. In French use (pron. kôn-kôr-däŋ), a barytone.

**n-dissonant.** Used of a triad which is consonant with each of two mutually dissonant triads.

**nducten** (dook′-tĕn), *G.* Wind-tubes.

**nductor.** The time-beater and director of a chorus or orchestra.

**nduct′us,** *L.* That form of discant in the 12th century in which not only the improvised counterpoint of the singers was original, but the central melody (or *cantus firmus*) also.

**nduit** (kôn-dwē), *F.* 1. A wind-trunk. 2. Conductus.

**ne-gamba.** The bell-gamba.

**nfinal.** Vide FINAL.

**njoint,** or **conjunct,** *E.,* **congiunto** (joon′-to), *I.* 1. Used of notes lying immediately next to each other; of

*motion* or *succession* proceeding regularly by single degrees. 2. Applied by the Greeks to tetrachords, in which the highest note of the lower, was also the lowest note of the upper, tetrachord.

**connecting note.** One common to successive chords.

**consecutive.** Following in immediate succession. Chiefly applied to progressions of intervals such as perfect fifths and octaves, strictly forbidden in most cases.

**conseguente** (gwĕn′-tĕ), *I.,* **con′sequent,** *E.* In fugue or canon, the imitation or answer of the subject.

**conservatoire** (kôŋ-sĕr-vä-twär), *F.,* **conservato′rio,** *I.,* **Conservatorium** (oom), *G.,* **conservatory,** *E.* A school of music.

**consolan′te,** *I.* Consoling. **consolatamen′te.** Cheeringly.

**con′sonance,** *E.,* **consonanza** (nän′-tsä), *I.* An accord of sounds, not only agreeable but restful, cf. DISSONANCE. **imperfect c.** A major or minor third or sixth. **perfect c.** An octave, fifth or fourth. **consonant.** Harmonious. **c. chord.** One without a dissonant interval.

**consort.** 1. To be in accord. 2. A set, as of viols, cf. CHEST.

**constit′uents.** Partial tones.

**cont.** Abbr. of *contano*.

**contadines′co,** *I.* Rustic.

**contano,** *I.* "They count," of instrs. which "rest."

**continua′to** (tĭn-oo-ä′-tō), *I.* Sustained.

**continued bass.** Vide BASS (6).

**continuo,** *I.* Vide BASS (6).

**con′tra.** Against or under. As a prefix to names of instruments, or of organ-stops, it indicates a pitch an octave lower than the standard, as **Contraposaune, contra - octave.** (Vide PITCH). **contra-arco.** Bowing against the rule. **contra-tempo.** Syncopation. **contrabass** (kôn-trä-bäs). The double-bass. **contrabombarde.** A 32-ft. stop in the pedal.

**contraddanza** (kôn-träd-dän′tsä), *I.* A country-dance.

**contralto** (kôn-träl'-tô), *I.* The deepest female voice. The term means lower than the *alto* (high), the former name of male soprano.

**contrappunto** (poon'-tō), *I.* Counterpoint. **contrappuntista.** One skilled in cpt. **c. alla decima.** Double counterpoint in the tenth. **c. alla mente.** Improvised cpt. **alla zoppa,** or **syncopata.** Syncopated cpt. **c. doppio.** Double cpt. **c. doppio alla duo decima.** Double cpt. in the twelfth. **c. sciolto** (shôl'-tō). Free cpt. **c. sopra (sotto) il soggetto** (sôd-jĕt'-to). Cpt. above (below) the subject.

**contrapunct'us,** *L.* Counterpoint. **c. flo'ridum,** *L.* Florid cpt. **c. in decima gradi.** Double cpt. in which the parts move in tenths or thirds below the subject. **c. simplex.** Simple cpt.

**con'trapuntal.** Relating to counterpoint. **contrapunt'ist.** One skilled in counterpoint.

**contrario** (trä'-rĭ-ō), *I.* Contrary. Vide MOTION. **contrary bow.** A reversed stroke.

**contrasogetto** (sôd-jĕt'-to), *I.* Counter-subject.

**contratenor.** Vide COUNTER-TENOR.

**Contratöne** (kôn'trä-tä-nĕ). *G.* The deeper bass tones.

**contraviolo'ne,** *I.* Double-bass.

**contre** (kôntr), *F.* Contra, or counter, as **contrebasse.** Double-bass. **c. éclisse.** Lining. **c. partie.** A part contrasted with another, as bass and soprano. **contrepoint** (kôntr-pwăn). Counterpoint. **contresujet.** Counter-subject. **contre-temps.** Syncopation.

**contredanse** (kôn-trŭ-däns), *F.* A country-dance, in which the dancers stand in opposite ranks.

**conver'sio,** *L.* Inversion.

**coper'to,** *I.* 1. Covered (as fifths). 2. Muffled (as drums).

**cop'ula,** *I.* 1. A coupler. 2. A stop requiring a coupler.

**cor.** Abbr. of *cornet*.

**cor** (kôr), *F.* Horn. **cor-alt.** Alto

horn. **cor-basse.** Bass-horn. **c-a glais.** " English horn," in real an alto oboe (q. v.). **c. de bass** Basset-horn. **c. de chasse** (shä Hunting-horn ; the French horn. **de postillon.** Postilion's horn. **de signal.** A bugle. **c. de nu** The Cremona stop. **c. de vache** Cow-horn. **c. omnitonique.** A Sa horn.

**corale** (kō-rä'lĕ), *I.* Chora.

**coranto** (kō-rän'-to), *I.* Vide co RANTE.

**corda** (kôr'-dä), *I.* A string ; *una cora* one string, i. e., the soft pedal ; *a* (two) or *tre* (three) or *tutte* (all) *corde* (the strings), " release the s pedal !" In violin-playing, *due-cor* means " play the same note on 2 strin simultaneously ; " *1ma. 2da, 3za,* *4ta corda,* means that the passage all to be played on the string in cated.

**cordatura** (too'-ra), *I.* Vide / CORD (3).

**corde** (kôrd), *F.* A. A string. **c. boyau.** Catgut. **c. à jour** (zhoo **c. à vide** (vēd). Open string. **de luth.** A lute-string. **c. faus** (fōs). A false string. **c. sourc** (soord). A mute-string.

**cordier** (kôrd-yä), *F.* **cordiera** (k dĭ-ä-rä'), *I.* Tail-piece.

**cordomètre** (kôr-dō-mĕtr), *F.* Strin gauge.

**corifeo** (kō-rĭ-fä'-ō), *I.* Leader of ballet. **corimagistro** (mä-jēs'-tr Leader of a chorus.

**corista** (kō-rēs'-tä), *I.* 1. Chorister. Tuning-fork or pitch-pipe.

**cormorne.** 1. A soft-toned horn. A reed-stop.

**corn** (kôrn). *Welsh.* Horn.

**cornamusa** (kôr-nä-moo'-zä), *I.,* c nemuse (kôrn-müz), *F.* Bagpipe.

**cor'net** (not cornet'), *E.* (in *F.* kôr-n Cornett', *G.* 1. Loosely used of t *cornet à pistons* (q. v.) 2. An ob lete wind instr. of the 15th cent. ma *straight* (*diritto* or *muto*) and *b* (*curvo* or *torto*) ; the latter was a called **cornon** or **cornetto bas**

nd was the original of the serpent.
Various reed-stops as **echo c.**,
ounted **c.**, **grand c.**, **c. de récit**,
. **dreifach** (or 3-ranked).

neta (kôr-nä´-tä), **cornet´to**, *I.* A
-ft. reed-stop.

net à **bouquin** (boo-kăṅ), *F.* Bugle-
orn.

net à **pistons** (kôr-nä tä pēs-tôṅ),
. A 3-valved chromatic brass in-
rument of the trumpet family. It
as a plebeian voice of great agility.
: is a transposing instr. written in
ne G clef. It is usually in B♭, and
as crooks (A, A♭, G). It has a
aromatic compass, f♯ -c´´´

'no, *I.* Horn. **c. alto.** A horn
f high pitch. **c. basso.** A bass-
orn. **c. di basset´to.** 1. The bas-
et-horn. 2. A soft-reed stop. **c. di
accia** (kät´-chä). The hunting or
rench horn. **c. dolce** (dōl´chĕ).
n organ-stop. **c. in B basso.** A
ow B horn. **c. inglese** (ēn-glä´zĕ).
he English horn (vide OBOE). **c.
entile** (vĕn-tē´-lĕ). Chromatic horn.
. **sor´do.** A horn with dampers.

nope´an. 1. Cornet à pistons. 2.
n 8-ft. reed-stop.

ro, *I.* and *Sp.* Chorus. **c. della
hiesa,** *I.* Church-choir. **c. primo.**
The first chorus.

o´na, *I.* A pause or fermate (⌢).

onach (kôr´-ō-näkh). A Gaelic
irge.

rps (kôr), *F.* Body (as of an instru-
nent). **c. de ballet** (băl-lā). All
he dancers in a ballet. **c. d'har-
nonie** (dăr-mō-nē). A fundament-
l chord. **c. de musique.** A band.
:. **de réchange.** The crook of a
orn. **c. de voix.** Body or range
f a voice.

rren´te, *I.* Vide COURANTE.

ryphæus, *G.* 1. The conductor of
he chorus. 2. At Oxford, a special
nstructor in music.

ryphée (kō-rĭ-fā), *F.* 1. The leader
f dancers. 2. A ballet-dancer.

saque (kō-săk), *F.* The Cossack
lance.

tillon (kō-tē-yôṅ), *F.* " Petticoat."

---

An elaborate ceremonial dance of
many couples, not unlike the German.

**couac** (kwăk), *F.* Vide GOOSE.

**couched harp.** Spinet.

**coulé** (koo-lā), *F.* 1. Slurred. 2. A
grace note consisting of two or three
sliding notes, indicated by a dash between the notes.

**coulisse** (koo-lēs), *F.* 1. Slide (vide
TROMBONE). 2. Side-scene, wing (of
a theatre).

**count.** A beat. To *count time*, to
measure the beats audibly or men-
tally.

**counter-.** A prefix indicating contrast,
as *counter-tenor* (once a name for the
alto voice), is higher than the usual
tenor ; often falsetto or artificial tenor ;
*counter-bass* is lower than the usual
bass ; *counter-tenor clef*, vide CLEF ;
*counter-subject*, vide FUGUE.

**counterpoint.** Originally notes were
called " points ; " the literal meaning
of counterpoint is therefore "note
against (or in accompaniment with)
note ; " it is loosely used of the combination of independent voices as in a
quartet. It is more strictly used (a) of
the art of writing simultaneous melodies or (b) of the melodic part added to
a given part called the *cantus firmus*
(q. v.). The contrapuntal style differs from the harmonic in that while
the latter consists of melody accompanied by chords, the former is a combination of melodic parts. The supreme contrapuntal forms are Canon
and Fugue. Of counterpoint there
are five *species :* 1. Note against note
—a semibreve against a semibreve.
2. Two notes against one ; 3. Four
notes against one. 4. Syncopation.
5. Florid counterpoint—a mixture of
the preceding species. Counterpoint
is also *Simple* and *Double*. In the
latter, the parts are invertible, i. e.,
may be transposed an octave, or
ninth, tenth, twelfth, etc., above or
below one another. Counterpoint is
*triple* (or *quadruple*) when 3 or 4
parts are mutually invertible.

## Counterpoint.

### By Homer A. Norris.

THE art of combining melodies is called counterpoint. When a pian "plays ' Old Hundred ' in one hand, and ' Yankee Doodle ' in t other " he illustrates the contrapuntal idea. Weingartner's arrang ment of Weber's " Invitation to the Dance " represents most ingenic counterpoint. In *strict* (plain, simple) counterpoint, no combination notes representing more than three sounds is allowed ; no dissonances exce passing notes ; no chromatics. ¶Counterpoint is *double* when it may correctly used either as an upper, or a lower part ; i. e., when it admits double employment. Double counterpoint may be so written as to invert the 8th, 9th, 12th, or any other interval. The following is an example

*Inversion of above example.*

double counterpoint. ¶Within the confines of strict counterpoint ecclesiasti music reached its loftiest expression through Palestrina, in about 1600. ¶ modern harmony chords may be built up of three, four, five, and even mc different sounds. When the contrapuntal idea is applied to modern harmon

ssult is called *free* counterpoint. Free counterpoint is simply a contra-
l manipulation of modern harmony, as opposed to strict counterpoint
1 is limited to chords of three sounds. Bach re-established the counter
of Palestrina on the modern harmonic bass. In his fugues the contra-
l, or polyphonic, idea is found in its most perfect form. ¶The very
ce of Wagner's music is counterpoint. When the melodies of "Die
tersinger" are brought together in the overture it is modern counter-
; not an end in itself, but as a means to direct, emotional expression.
from out this old counterpoint has come a new, which to-day permeates
isic. Neither Brahms nor Richard Strauss could exist but for the industry
ose early *savants*, who, piling notes upon notes, laid a foundation for
athedral of music which has risen majestically under Bach, Handel,
irt, Beethoven, Brahms, and Wagner. It is modern counterpoint,
erpoint with a soul in it, which distinguishes all great work to-day and
os it for posterity.

---

erynge ye songe (kown'-tĕr-
the sóng) (old *E.*). Descant.

ry-dance. Whatever the ety-
ogy, a country-dance is a contra-
ce (in duple or triple time) in
ch partners are ranged opposite
1 other.

(koo), *F.* Blow. c. d'archet
-shä). A stroke of the bow. c.
glotte (glôt). A snappy vocal at-
c. double c. de langue. Double-
guing. c. de baguette (bă-gĕt).
t of the drum. c. de cloche
sh). Stroke of a bell.
er le sujet (koo-pä lŭ soo-zhä), *F.*
cut or contract the subject.
ier. An organ mechanism con-
cing 2 manuals, or manuals with
als.
et. Two notes occupying the time
triplet.
nte (koo-ränt), *F.* "Running,"
old dance in 3-2 and 6-4 time.
ice an instrumental piece in the
e style. Vide SUITE. The sec-
part of the suite, usually in pas-
e work.
nne (koo-rŭn), *F.* A hold.
e. A group of strings sounding
nison.
al (koor-tăl), courtaud (koor-tō),

courtaut (koor-tō), *F.* An old short
bassoon.

couvre-feu (koovr-fŭ), *F.* Curfew.

covered. 1. Hidden, used of progressions (q. v.). 2. Used of pipes and
stops (q. v.). 3. Used of strings
wrapped with fine wire.

c. p. Abbr. of *colla parte*, or *counterpoint.*

cr., cres., cresc. Abbr. of *crescendo.*

crackle. In lute-playing, to play chords
brokenly.

cracoviak, *Pol.*, cracovienne (krä-
kō'vĭ-ĕn), *F.* A Polish dance in
syncopated 2-4 time.

creanluidh (krän'-loo-ē). Vide PI-
BROCH.

Cre'do, *L.* "I believe." Vide MASS.

crem'balum, *L.* Jew's harp.

Cremona (krä-mō'-nä), *I.* 1. A town in
Italy, hence an instr. made there by
the Stradivari, the Amati, or Guarnerius. 2. A corrupt form of crom-
horn.

cremorn. Vide CROM-HORN.

crepitac'ulum or crepun'dia, *L.*
Ancient frictional castanets.

crescendo (krĕ-shĕn'-dō), *I.* "Increasing," i. e., in loudness. c. il tempo.
Increasing in speed. C-zug, *G.* The
swell-box, or crescendo pedal.

**cres'cent.** A Turkish instr. of crescent-shaped metal plates hung on a pavilion ; or small bells on an inverted crescent.

**criard(e)** (krē-ăr(d)), *F.* Bawling.

**crib'rum,** *L.* Sound-board.

**croche** (krôsh), *F.* An eighth note. **c. double.** Sixteenth note. **c. quadruple.** A sixty-fourth note. **c. triple.** 32d note.

**crochet** (krŏ-shā), *F.* The hook of a note. **croche'ta,** *L.* A quarter note.

**croisement** (kwäz-mäṅ), *F.* Crossing (as of parts).

**croma** (krŏ'-mä) (pl. e), *I.* An eighth note. "**crome,**" written under notes of larger value indicates that they are to be played as eighth notes.

**cromat'ica,** *I.* Chromatic.

**crom'-horn.** 1. A melancholy double-reed wood-wind instr. of the 16th cent. 2. A 4, 8 or 16-ft. reed-stop.

**crom'mo,** *I.* A choral dirge.

**cromor'na,** *I.,* **cromorne** (krŏ-môrn), *F.* Crom-horn.

**cronach.** Same as **coronach.**

**crook.** 1. A curved tube inserted in horns, etc., altering the length of the tube, therefore the key. 2. The mouth-piece of a bassoon. 3. A device in old harps for raising a string a half tone.

**crooked flute.** An Egyptian instrument.

**crooked horn** or **trumpet.** Buccina.

**crope'zia,** *Gr.* Wooden clogs worn by the Greeks in beating time.

**croque-note** (krôk-nŏt), *F.* An unintelligent virtuoso.

**cross.** 1. The head of a lute. 2. Vide FINGERING.

**cross-beards.** Vide BEARDS.

**cross-fingering.** A method of playing old flutes.

**cross flute.** A transverse flute.

**cross-relation.** Vide FALSE.

**crotale** (krŏ-tăl), *F.,* **crota'lo,** *I.,* **cro'talum,** *L.* An ancient small cymbal or castanet.

**crot'chet.** A quarter note. **crot'-het rest.** A quarter rest.

**crowd.** The crwth (q. v.).

**crowie.** Old English instr. o bassoon type.

**Crucifix'us,** *L.* "Crucified," pa the Credo. Vide MASS.

**cruit** (krŭ'ĭt), *Irish.* Old Irish C

**crush-note.** Acciaccatura.

**crutch'etam.** Name originally to the crotchet.

**crwth** (krooth), *Welsh.* An old of Welsh or Irish origin ; it somewhat lyre-shaped, had strings, and was the first Eur instr. played with a bow.

**c. s.** Abbr. of *Con sordino.*

**csárdás** (tsär-däsh), *Magyar.* A garian (Magyar) dance in 2-4 time. Triple time is very ⟨ tional, and not true to the na character. The Csardas (from da, "inn on the heath") is ofte ceded by a moderate movement **lassu** (from *lassan,* slow). The movement is called **fris** or **f** (cf. the German *frisch,* fresh, lively).

**C–Schlüssel** (tsä'-shlüs-sĕl}, *G* clef (vide CLEF).

**cto.** Abbr. of *Concerto.*

**cue.** Notes from another part in as a guide.

**cuivre** (kwēvr), *F.* **les cuivres.** brasses. *faire cuivrer* (făr kw To half-stop a French horn with gourous effect.

**Cum sancto spiritu,** *L.* "Wi Holy Ghost." Part of the ⟨ Vide MASS.

**cupo** (koo'-po), *I.* Dark, reserve

**Currenda'ner, Curren'de,** *G.* carol-singers.

**cushion dance.** An old English dance in triple time, each ⟨ placing before another of his choice a cushion on which both and kiss.

**custo** (koos'-tō), *I.,* **custos,** direct.

**cuvette** (kü-vĕt), *F.* Pedestal harp.

**cycle.** A complete set (as of s **cyclical forms** (*G.* cyclische

n). Those made up of a set or
.e of movements, as the sonata,
.e or symphony.

.der, *G.* Ventil piston.

.als, *E.*, **cymbales** (săn-băl), *F.*
Circular metal plates, clashed to-
.ler. 2. A steel triangle with a
.ber of rings. 3. A high-pitched
ture-stop.

.alum, *L.* 1. Cymbal. 2. A medi-
.l series of eight drums to a scale.

.an (tshäk'-än). A Bohemian bam-
.flute.

.as (tshär'-dăsh). Vide CSÁRDÁS.

.en (tschĭm'-kĕn). A Polish
.ntry-dance.

.balom (tshĭm'-bä-lôm). The
.garian dulcimer.

## D

In *G.* pron. dä, *F.* **ré** (rā),
*I.* re (rā). 1. A musical pitch,
the next full step above C in
all its octaves. 2. The ma-
.key having two sharps ; the minor
.relative to F major. 3. Abbr. **d** =
*antus,* or *dessus ,* in *da capo, dal*
*.o, main droit, mano dritto,* **d'**
r. of *de* before a vowel.

.), *L.* By, from, for, through, in
style of, etc.

.da (däb-boo'-da), *I.* A psaltery.

.apo (dä kä'-pō), *I.* "From the
.inning." A sign of repetition.

(däkh), *G.* "Roof." The belly
.violin, etc.

.schweller (däkh'-shvĕl-ler), *G.*
.ll-box.

.l'ion, *Gr.* An apparatus of 10
's hung from steel springs above
.key-board, used to strengthen the
ers ; inv. by Herz, 1835.

A term in drum music—the left
d.

.y-mammy. A colloquial term
a roll on the side-drum.

(däl-yē), **dai** (dä-ē), **dal, dall'**,
le, **dal'lo,** *I.* Combinations of
prep. **da** with the article "the."

, (dä-ē'-nä), **dainos.** A tender
.uanian folk-song.

**daire** (dä-ē'-rä), *I.* The tambourine.

**dal,** *I.* Vide DAGLI.

**dalzimr.** An Egyptian reed instrument.

**damenisa'tion.** Vide SOLMISATION.

**damper.** 1. In pianos a cushion which
when raised by the touch of the key
or the use of the *damper pedal* (often
called the " loud pedal ") permits the
vibration of strings ; when released
it silences the vibration. 2. A mute
for brass instruments.

**dämpfen** (dĕmp'-fen), *G.* To muffle.
**Dämp'fer.** A mute or damper.
**Dämp'fung.** Damping mechanism.

**Danklied** (dänk'-lēt), *G.* A thanksgiving song.

**danse** (däns), *F.* A dance, or dance-
tune. **contre d.** (kôṅtr). A country-
dance, **a** quadrille. **d. de matelot**
(măt-lō). A horn-pipe. **danseries**
(däns-rē). D**a**nce-tunes.

**danza** (dän'-tsä), *I.* A dance or dance-
tune. **danzet'ta.** A little dance.

**daraboo'ka** or **darabuk'keh.** A small
Arabian drum.

**dar la voce** (där lä vō'-chĕ), *I.* Give
the key-note.

**Darmsaite** (därm'zī-tĕ) (pl. **en**), *G.*
Gut-string.

**Darsteller** (där'-shtĕl-ler), *G.* A performer. **Darstellung.** Performance.

**dash.** 1. A staccato mark. 2. Vide
CHORD. 3. Vide COULÉ.

**Da'sian-notierung,** *G.* Hucbald's notation, using forms of the letter F for
14 tones.

**Dauer** (dow-ĕr), *G.* Duration.

**Daumen** (dow'-mĕn), *G.* The thumb.
**D.-aufsatz.** Thumb-position. **D.-
klapper.** Castanet.

**D. C.** Abbr. of *da capo.*

**D-dur** (dä-door), *G.* D major.

**de** (dŭ), *F.* Of, in, from, by. *De plus*
*en plus vite.* More and more quickly.

**dead march.** Funeral march.

**debile, debole** (dā'-bō-lā), *I.* Feeble.

**dec'achord, decachor'don, deca-
cor'do,** *L.* An ancient harp or guitar with ten strings.

**dec'ad.** Vide ELLIS (B. D.).

**dé'cani,** *L. pl.* Vide CANTORI.

## Chart of Dance-Rhythms.

m (dā-tsĕm), _G._ Vide DECIMA (2).

otive. Vide CADENCE.

ant (dā-shän), _F._ Discant.

lé (dā-sē-dā), **décidément** (dā-sē-
män), _F._ Decisive(ly).

ma, _L._ 1. A tenth. 2. An organ-
p sounding the tenth. **d. plena
tonis.** A major tenth. **d. non
na de tonis.** A minor tenth. **d.
tia, quarta, quinta.** Intervals
:he 13th, 14th, 15th.

ime (dā sēm), _F._ (dā-tsēm'), _G._ A
th.

mole. A group of ten equal
es.

sif (dā-sē-sēf), **décisivement**
v-män), _F._ Decisive(ly).

sione (dā-chē'-zĭ-ō'nĕ), _I._ Decis-
. **decisivo** (dā-chĭ-sē'vō). **de-
o** (dā-chē'-zō). In a bold manner,
:isively.

ke (dĕk'ĕ), _G._ 1. Sound-board. 2.
lly. 3. Cover or top for organ-
ps.

aman'do (dā-clā-män'-dō), _I._ With
:lamatory expression.

amation, declamazione (dā-klä-
-tsĭ-ō'-nĕ), _I._ Singing in declam-
ory style.

aver' (dā-klă-vā), _F._ To change
: key.

mposé (dā-kôṅ-pō-zā), _F._ Dis-
nnected.

mpter (dā-kôṅ-tā), _F._ To use
: portamento.

ration (dā-kō-răs-yôṅ), _F._ The
nature.

rative notes. Notes of embel-
nment.

uplez (dā-koo-plā), _F._ Uncouple.

usu(e) (dā-koo-sü), _F._ Disjointed.

., decres. Abbr. of _decrescen-

escendo (dā-krĕsh-ĕn'-dō), _I._ Di-
nishing in loudness.

uplet. A group of ten equal
tes.

cato (dā-dĭ-kä'tō), _I._, **dédié** (dād-
), _F._ Dedicated.

ict'io, _L._ 1. Resolution. 2. In
ido d'Arezzo's hexachords, the as-
nding series.

**deficiendo** (da-fē-chĕn'-dō), _I._ Dying
away.

**degli** (dāl'-yē), **dei** (dā-ē), **del, dell',
del'la, del'le, del'lo,** _I._ Of the ;
than the.

**degré** (dŭ-grā), _F._, **degree,** _E._ 1.
Line or space on the staff. 2. One
of the diatonic tones of a scale.

**dehnen** (dā'-nĕn), _G._ To extend.
**gedehnt** (gĕ-dānt). Prolonged, slow.
**Dehnung.** Prolongation. **Deh-
nungsstrich.** 1. The line or dot in
vocal music holding one syllable over
several notes. 2. A long bow-stroke.

**délassement** (dā-lăs-män), _F._ A light
piece.

**deliberato** (dā-lē-bĕ-rä'-to), **deliber-
atamen'te,** _I._ Deliberate(ly).

**délicatesse** (dā-lĭ-kä-tĕs), _F._, **deli-
catezza** (dā-lĭ-kä-tĕd'-zä), _I._ Delicacy.

**delicato** (dā-lĭ-kä'-tō), **delicatamen'-
te,** _I._ Delicate(ly). **delicatissima-
men'te, delicatis'simo.** Most del-
icate(ly).

**délié** (dāl-yā), _F._ Light, easy.

**delir'io,** _I._ Frenzy, excitement.

**delizio'so** or **-amente,** _I._ Delicious-
(ly).

**dem** (dām), _G._ "To the." Dative of
"the."

**démancher** (dā-mäṅ-shā), _F._ To
change or cross hands ; to shift on
the 'cello or violin ; hence **déman-
ché, démanchement** (dā-mäṅsh-
män).

**demande** (dŭ-mänd), _F._ The "question," subject of a fugue.

**demi** (dŭ-mē), _F._ Half. **d.-baton.**
(bă-tôṅ). A semibreve ; or 2-meas-
ure rest. **d.-cadence** (kā-däṅs). A
half cadence. **d.-croche.** A 16th
note **d.-jeu.** With half power, _mf._
**d.-mesure.** Half measure. **d.-stac-
cato.** Lightly staccato. **d.-pause.**
A half rest. **d.-quart de soupir.**
A 32d rest. **d.-soupir.** An 8th rest.
**d.-temps.** A half beat. **d.-ton.** A
half tone.

**demi-dit'onus,** _L._ A minor 3d.

**demi-quaver.** A 16th note, or semiquaver.

**dem'isemiquaver.** A 32d note.

**dem'itone.** A semitone.

**demoiselle** (dĕm-wä-zĕl), *F.* Tracker.

**Denis d'or** (dŭn-ĕ-dôr). A piano with pedals and many qualities of sound, inv. 1762 by Procopius Divis.

**depen'dent.** Used of a chord requiring resolution.

**depres'sio,** *I.* Lowering, as of the hand in time-beating ; or of a tone chromatically.

**De profun'dis,** *L.* "From the depths." One of the penitential ps**a**lms.

**der** (dĕr), *G.* 1. The. 2. Of the.

**deriv'ative.** 1. The root of a chord. 2. An inversion.

**dérivé** (dā-rē-vā), *F.* 1. Derivative. 2. An inversion. 3. Inverted.

**dernière** (dĕrn-yǎr), *F.* Last. **d. fois.** The last time.

**Des** (dĕs), *G.* 1. The note' D♭. 2. From the ; of the.

**désaccorder** (dā-zǎk-kôr-dā), *F.* To untune. **désaccordé.** Untuned.

**des'cant.** Vide DISCANT.

**descend.** To pass from higher to lower pitch. **descent.** Such a passing.

**descendere** (dā-shĕn'-dĕ-rĕ), *I.*, **descendre** (dŭ-sändr), *F.* To descend. **d. d'un ton.** To descend a step. **descendant** (dŭ-säṅ-däṅ). Descending.

**deschant** (dŭ-shäṅ) *F.* Discant.

**Desdes** (dāsdās) or **Deses** (dāsās), *G.* D double flat.

**Des-dur** (dās'door), *G.* D♭ major.

**desiderio** (dā-sē-dā'-rǐ-ō), *I.* Desire, passion.

**desinvolturato** (vōl-too-rä'-to), *I.*, **avec désinvolture** (ǎ-vĕk dā-sǎṅ-vôl-tür), *F.* Free, easy.

**Des-moll** (dās-môl), *G.* D♭ minor.

**desperazione.** Vide DISPERAZIONE.

**Dessauer Marsch** (dĕs' sow-er märsh), *G.* One of the national march-songs of Germany.

**dessin** (dus-sǎṅ), *F.* Sign.

**dessus** (dŭs-sü), *F.* 1. Treble or upper part. 2. Old name for violin.

**desto** (dās'-tō), *I.* Brisk, sprightly.

**desterità** (tā-rĕ-tä'), *I.* Dexterity.

**destra** (dās'-trä), *I.* Right. **d. m** Right hand. **colla d.** With the hand.

**détaché** (dā-tă-shā), *F.* Detac with separate bow movements, not staccato. **grand d.** Wi whole bow-stroke to each note.

**determinazione** (dā-tĕr-mǐ-nä-t nĕ), *I.* Determination. **determ to** (nä'-tō). Determined, resolut

**detoni(e)ren** (dā-tō-nē'-rĕn), *G.*, **tonner** (dā-tǔn-nā), *F.* To sin play off the key ; hence **déto tion** (dā-tun-nǎs'-yôṅ).

**detto** (dĕt'-tō), *I.* The same ; dit

**deut'erus.** Vide MODES.

**deutlich** (doit'-lĭkh), *G.* Distinctl

**Deutsch** (doitsh), *G.* "Germ **deutsche Flöte.** The Germa transverse flute. **deutscher B** An obsolete 5 or 6 stringed do bass. **deutsche Tabulatur.** TABLATURE. **deutsche Tänze.** slow waltzes.

**deux** (dŭ), *F.* Two. **à deuxhuit** wēt). In 2-8 time. **à d. ma** For 2 hands. **d.-quatre.** 2-4 **d.-temps.** The two-step, or a waltz with two measures to the also called *Valse à d. t.* **deux** twice.

**deuxième** (dŭz-yĕm), *F.* Second. **position** (pō-zēs-yôṅ). 1. The ond fret. 2. The second positio half-shift.

**development.** Working out ; free tasy. Vide FORM.

**devo'to,** *I.* Devout. **devozione** vō-tsĭ-ō'-nĕ). Devotion.

**dex'tra,** *L.*, **dextre** (dĕxtr), *F.* Right ; the right hand. 2. Vide T.

**Dezem** (dā-tsäm'), *G.* Vide DECI

**Dezime** (dā'-tsē-mĕ), *G.* A tenth.

**di** (dē), *I.* Of, with, for, from, by, **di molto.** Extremely, as *allegr molto.*

**di'a,** *Gr.* Through.

**diacon'icon,** *Gr.* Collects in the G Church.

**di'adrom,** *Gr.* Vibration.

**diagonal bellows.** The old form slanting flap.

am'ma, *Gr.* Diagram. 1. The
ek scale. 2. The staff. 3. A
.e.

go (dē-ä-lō'-gō), *I.*, **dialogue** (dē-
g), *F.* Dialogue : a duet.

**ond-shaped notes.** Vide HAR-
NICS.

(dē-ä'-nä), *I.*, **Diane** (dǐ-ăn), *F.*
e reveille.

Abbr. of *diapason.*

son, *Gr.* pron., in *E.* (dī-ä-pā'-
; in *F.*, dē-ăp-ä-sôn). 1. An oc-
e. **d.** (cum) **diapente.** An octave
h the fifth—a twelfth. **d. con di-
sseron.** An octave with the fourth
n eleventh. 2. Range. 3. Abso-
e pitch, as **d. normal,** internation-
pitch, vide A (1). 4. In the organ,
sonorous chief foundation-stops,
of 8 and one of 16-foot pitch on
manual, on the pedal, 16-foot ;
*open d.* has metal pipes open at
top, the *stopped d.* has wooden
es closed at the top. In other
ntries they are called *principal.*

en'te, *Gr.* A perfect fifth ; vide
APASON (4). **d. col dito'no.** A ma-
7th. **d. col semidito'no.** A mi-
7th. **d. cum semito'nio.** A
or 6th. **d. cum tono.** A major

entisa're, *Mediæval L.* 1. To
cant at the interval of a 5th. 2.
proceed by 5ths. 3. To tune by
s. 4. In French usage, discant at
intervals of the 2d, 3d, 6th, and

honics. The science of refracted
nds.

h'ony. 1. In Greek music, dis-
nance. 2. In the middle ages, the
liest form of 2-voiced counter-
nt.

la'sion. Vide VIS-A-VIS.

chis'ma or **diaskhisma,** *Gr.*
de SCHISMA and ELLIS (B. D.).

tema, *Gr.* An interval.

tolic(s), *Gr.*, **Diastolik** (lēk'), *G.*
t of phrasing.

es'seron, *Gr.* Interval of a fourth.

on'ic, *E.*, **diato'nico,** *I.*, **diaton-
ue** (dē-ä-tôn-ēk), *F.*, **diatonisch**

(dē-ä-tōn'-ǐsh), *G.* 1. Going through,
or confined to, the tones of any one key.
with no flats, sharps, or naturals belonging to another key—opposed to
*chromatic;* hence a *d. scale* is the regular scale of any predominant key ; a *d.
interval, chord,* or *progression* is an
unaltered interval, chord, or progression containing no tones foreign to the
key ; a *d. melody* or *harmony* clings to
one scale ; a *d. instrument* sounds only
the tones of the one key from which it
takes its name ; a *d. modulation* goes
to the nearest related key. 2. One of
the three genera in Greek music.
Vide MODES.

**diaul'os,** *Gr.* A double flute with 2
tubes, 1 mouthpiece.

**diazeux'is,** *Gr.* The separation of two
tetrachords by a tone ; the tone sep-
arating them ; hence the adjective
**diazeuc'tic.** Vide MODES.

**di'chord.** An instrument (a) with 2
strings ; (b) with 2 strings to each
note.

**dicta'tion, dictée musicale** (dĕk-tä
mü-zǐ-kăl), *F.* The performance of
musical phrases to be written on
paper by the listener(s).

**die** (dē), *G.* The.

**die,** *E.* A steel punch for engraving
music.

**diecetto** (dē-ä-chĕt'-tō), *I.* A composition for 10 instruments.

**diesare** (dē-ä-sä'-rĕ), *I.*, **diéser** (dē-ä-
zā), *F.* To sharpen a tone or note.

**dièse** or **dièze** (dē-ĕz), *F.* Sharp (#).

**Di'es i'ræ,** *L.* "Day of wrath," second movement of the Requiem.

**diesis** (dē-ä'sǐs), *Gr.* and *I.*, **diésis** (dǐ-
ā'sē), *F.* 1. The sharp (#). 2. The
*enharmonic d.* is the difference between a diatonic and a chromatic semitone (ratio 128 : 125), or between 3
major thirds and one octave. 3. A
quarter tone, the unit of tone-division
in Aristotle's system. 4. The Pythagorean semitone or limma.

**diezeug'menon,** *Gr.* Disjunct. Vide
MODES.

**dif'ference tones.** Vide RESULTANT
TONES.

**differen'tiale** or **distinct'io tonorum,**
*L.* **Differenzen** (ĕn'-tsĕn), *G.* The
different cadences available for the
**saeculorum amen** of each psalm-
tone.

**difficile** (dĭf-fē'chē-lā), *I.* (dĭf-fĭ-sēl), *F.*
Difficult.

**dig'ital.** A key to be pressed by a
finger (as opposed to *pedal* = foot-
key).

**digito'rium.** A dumb instr. with five
keys for exercising the fingers.

**dignità** (dēn-yĭ-tä'), **dignita'de, dig-
nitate** (tä'-tĕ), *I.* Dignity.

**digressio'ne,** *I.* Deviation.

**dilettant(e)** (dē-lĕt-tän(t)), *I.* An amateur.

**dilet:osamen'te,** *I.* Pleasantly.

**dilicato** (de-lĭ-kä'-tō), **dilicatamen'te,**
*I.* Delicate(ly). **dilicatezza** (tĕd'-
zä). Delicateness. **dilicatis'simo.**
Most delicate.

**diligenza** (dē-lĭ-jĕn'-tsä), *I.* Diligence,
care.

**dilu'dium,** *L.* An interlude.

**diluendo** (dē-loo-en'dō), *I.* Fading
away.

**dim, dimin.** Abbr. of *diminuendo.*

**diminished. 1.** Used of intervals
which are a semitone smaller than
the minor intervals; used also of
chords containing such intervals.
Fourths, fifths and octaves, however,
being called "perfect" instead of
"major," are, when contracted a
semitone, said to be, not "minor,"
but *diminished.* When inverted, *d.
intervals* become *augmented* and vice
versa. A *d. triad* contains a minor
3d and an imperfect (or diminished)
fifth. The *chord of the d. seventh*
is the 7th chord built on the leading
tone of a minor key. *d. imitation,
subject* or *theme,* is used when the answer reappears in notes of lessened
time-value.

**diminuendo** (dē-mē-noo-ĕn'-dō), *I.* Diminishing gradually in loudness. **d.
molto.** With extreme diminution of
power.

**diminuer** (dĭ-mē-nü-ā), *F.* To diminish. **diminué** (dĭ-mēn-ü-ā). Di-

minished. **en diminuant beauc**
Diminuendo molto.

**diminu'tion,** *E.* (in *F.* dē-mē
yôn), **diminuzione** (dē-mĭ-no‹
ō'-nĕ), *I.* In cpt., the repetiti‹
imitation of a theme, in notes of sha
duration; opposed to *augmenta‹*

**diox'ia,** *Gr.* Diapente.

**dip.** The extent to which a k‹
pedal may be depressed.

**dipho'nium.** A vocal duet.

**direct'.** 1. A mark placed at the
of a staff (a) to indicate the positi‹
the note next following (∿); (
&c. 2. Vide TURN. 3. To con‹
**d. motion.** Similar or parallel
tion.

**directeur** (dĭ-rĕk-tŭr), *F.,* **dirett**
*I.* Director; conductor.

**diriger** (dē-rē-zhā), *F.,* **dirig**
(dē-rē-jē'-rĕn), *G.* To conduct.

**dirit'to(a),** *I.* Direct. **alla d.** Str‹
on.

**Dis** (dēs), *G.* The note D sharp.

**disaccentato** (ät-chĕn-tä'-tō), *I.*
accented.

**disarmo'nico,** *I.* Discordant.
**armonia** (nĕ'-ä). Discord.

**dis'cant,** *E.,* **discant'us,** *L.* "Di‹
song." 1. The early form of cpt.
addition, usually by improvisatio‹
one or more parts to a given me‹
Contrary motion was much used
elaborate rules made. *Double, tr‹
quadruple d.* refer to the numbe‹
parts. 2. The highest part, voi‹
register; the highest of a family c
strs. **d. clef.** The soprano clef.

**discendere** (dē-shän'-dĕ-rĕ), *I.* T‹
scend.

**disciolto** (dĕ-shôl'tō), *I.* Skilful,
terous.

**discord,** *E.,* **discorde** (dēs-kôrd),
**discor'dia,** *L.,* **discordanza** (‹
tsä), *I.* 1. Ug'iness of sound ‹
inharmonious combination of to‹
2. Loosely used for DISSONANCE (q
**discordan'te, discordantemer**
*I.* Discordant(ly).

**discreto** (dĭs-krä'-tō), *I.* Disc‹
**discrezione** (dĭs-krä-tsĭ-ō'nĕ).
cretion.

apa'son. In mediæval music, a
ble octave, a 15th.
lis (dēs-dēs), *G.* D double sharp.
lur (dēs-door), *G.* D ♯ major.
armonie (dēs-här-mō-nē'), *G.* Dis-
d. disharmo'nisch (nĭsh). Dis-
dant.
vol'to, disinvolturato (vōl-too-
tō), *I.* Easy. **disinvoltura**
'-rä). Ease.
. (dēs-ēs), *G.* D double sharp.
nct'. Disjoined. A term applied
the Greeks to tetrachords where
lowest sound of the upper was
degree higher than the highest
nd of the lower. Vide MODES.
nct succession. A succession of
os.
ant (dēs-känt'), *G.* Discant 1.
. 2. D.-schlüssel. The soprano
. D.-geige. The soprano
strings, i. e., the violin. Diskan'-
t, D.-sänger. Treble singer. D.-
ister, D.-stimme. Half-stops.
-saite. The highest string.
noll (dēs-môl), *G.* D♯ minor.
ir'te, *I.* Aside.
era'to (ä'-tō), *I.* Desperate. dis-
-azione (dĭs-pĕ-rä-tsĭ-ō'-nĕ), *I.*
spair.
ersed. Used of chords or har-
nies whose elements are at wide
ervals.
osition. 1. Arrangement of parts
a score, chorus, or orchestra. 2.
:imate as to make-up and cost of
organ.
nance, *E.* (*F.* dĭs-sō-näns), Dis-
anz (dēs-sō-nänts'), *G.*, disso-
nza (dĭs-sō-nän'-tsä), *I.* 1. Loose-
used for discord. 2. In acoustics
d of combinations producing
.ts. 3. In composition used of
es or combinations (irrespective
their pleasantness or unpleasant-
s of effect) that do not give a
se of rest, but demand motion and
olution in some other tone or
ord.
onant, *E.* (*F.* dĭs-sō-nän), disso-
n'te, *I.* Dissonant.
onare (dĭs-sō-nä'-rĕ), *I.*, dissoner

(dēs-sō-nä), *F.*, dissoniren (dĭs-sō-
nē'-rĕn), *G.* To form dissonance.
**distance.** Interval.
**distanza** (dēs-tän'-tsä), *I.* Interval.
distance. **in d.** In the distance.
**distinct'io.** 1. Vide DIFFERENTIALE. 2.
A pause in Gregorian vocal music.
**distin'to, distintamen'te,** *I.* Dis
tinct(ly).
**distonare** (tō-nä'-rĕ), *I.*, **distoniren**
(dēs-tō-nē'-rĕn), *G.* To be out of
tune.
**distro'pha.** In plain-song, a double
square note of lesser stress than the
tristropha.
**di'tal.** A key raising the string of a
lute or guitar a semitone. **d. harp.**
A chromatic lute with a dital to each
of its 12 to 18 strings; inv. by Light,
1778.
**diteggiatura** (dē-tĕd-jä-too'-rä), *I.*
Fingering.
**dith'yramb,** *E.*, **dithyrambe** (dē-tĭ-
rämb), *F.*, **Dithyrambe** (dē-tĭ-räm'-
bĕ), *G.*, **ditirambo** (dē-tē-räm'-bō),
*I.* A rhapsody in honour of Bacchus;
a wine-rapture.
**dito** (dē'tō), *I.* Finger. **d. grosso.**
The thumb.
**di'tone,** *E.*, **diton** (dē-tôṅ), *F.*, **dito-
no** (dē-tō'-nō), *I.*, **dito'nus,** *L.* A
Pythagorean major third greater by a
comma than our major third.
**ditty.** A naïve little song.
**div.** Abbr. of *divisi*.
**diver'bia,** *L.*, **diver'bio,** *I.* A musical dialogue.
**divertimen'to,** *I.*, **divertissement**
(dĭ-vĕr'-tēs-mäṅ), *F.* 1. A musical diversion; a potpourri, a series of
songs or dances inserted in operas
and plays; a short ballet, in one or
several movements. 2. In fugue, an
episode.
**divide.** Vide DIVISION.
**divisi** (dē-vē'-zē), *I.* Divided. When
2 parts are written on one stave, to
ensure their not being played as doub-
le-stops by one instr. they are
marked "*divisi.*" When a single
note is to be played by two instrs. the
sign is *a due*, separated.

**divisio modi,** *L.* A point formerly serving the purpose of the present bar.

**division.** 1. A variation. 2. A long note divided into short notes. 3. A series of notes sung to one syllable. To "divide" or "run a division" is to execute such a series. **d.-viol.** The viola da gamba. **division-mark.** A figure and a slur binding a number of notes of foreign rhythm, as a triplet or quintole.

**division** (dĕ-vēz'-yôṅ), *F.* A double bar.

**divo'to,** **divotamen'te,** *I.* Devout(ly). **divozione** (dē-vō-tsǐ-ō'-nĕ). Devotion.

**dixième** (dēz-yĕm), *F.* A tenth.

**d. m.** Abbr. of *destra mano*.

**D-moll** (dā-môl), *G.* D minor.

**do** (dō), *I.* 1. A syllable applied to the first note of a scale in solmisation. In the "*fixed do*" system, the name **do** is always applied to C. In the "*movable do*" system, **do** is always the tonic or key-note; it has displaced the original syllable *ut.* Vide SOLMISATION. 2. In France and Italy, the name for C.

**Dock'e** (dôk'-ĕ), *G.* A wooden jack.

**Doctor of Music.** The highest musical degree, generally honorary, frequently meaningless. In England secured by examination.

**dodechachor'don,** *Gr.* 1. The bissex. 2. Vide GLAREANUS in the B. D.

**dodec'upla di cro'me,** *I.* 12-8 time. **d. di semicrome.** 12-16 time.

**dodec'uplet.** A group of 12 equal notes.

**doglia** (dōl'-yä), *I.* Grief.

**doh** (dō). Vide TONIC-SOL-FA.

**doigt** (dwä), *F.* Finger. **doigté** (dwä-tā). Fingered, or fingering. **doigter** (dwä-tā). To finger; the art of fingering any instrument. **doigtés fourchus** (dwä-tā foor-shü). Cross-fingerings.

**dol.** Abbr. of *dolce*.

**dolce** (dōl'-chĕ), *I.* Sweet, soft. **dolcezza** (dōl-chĕd'-zä). Sweetness. **dolcemen'te.** Softly. **dolcis'simo.**

1. With extreme sweetness. very soft flute-stop.

**Dolcian** (dôl-tsǐ-än'), *G.*, **dolc** (o) (dōl-chĕ-ä'-nä), **dolcino** (chē-no), *I.* 1. An obsolete smal soon. 2. A reed-stop.

**dolciato** (dol-chä'-tō), *I.* Soften

**dolciss.** Abbr. of *dolcissimo*.

**dolemment** (dô-lĕm-mäṅ), *F.* fully.

**dolen'do, dolente,** *I.* Sad. dol men'te. Sadly.

**dolent** (dō-läṅ), *F.* Sorrowful, m ful.

**dolore** (dō-lō'rĕ), *I.* Grief, so **doloro'so, dolorosamen'te.** rowful(ly).

**Dolzflöte** (dôlts'-flä-tĕ), *G.* 1 obsolete flute. 2. A flute-stop.

**Dom** (dôm) or **Domkirche** (kĕr' *G.* A cathedral. **Domchor** The cathedral choir.

**dom'inant,** *E.*, **dominante** (d nänt), *F.*, **Dominante** (dō-mǐ-nä *G.* & *I.* 1. The fifth tone of a sca called because it is the principal after the tonic and its chord o mony indicates the key and der resolution in the tonic; hen **chord,** the triad or the 7th built on the dominant. 2. Th whose tonic is the dominant c principal key; hence the expre "to modulate to the dominant." the key of G is the dominant t key of C. In the sonata formu dominant key is the one usually c for the contrasting second su after which the tonic key is re-lished; hence the *dominant se* 3. Vide CHANT (1) **a.**

**Domine, salvum fac,** *L.* " make him hale," first words of a olic prayer for the health of the ereign.

**Domin'icali Psalmi,** *L.* Psalms Vespers.

**Do'na no'bis pa'cem,** *L.* "Gr Thy peace." Vide MASS.

**donna,** *I.* Lady. **prima d** Leading lady in opera.

**do'po,** *I.* After.

el (dôp'l), *G.* Double. **doppel-**
or **doppel-Be** (dôp''l-bā). The
ble flat (♭♭). **D.-blatt.** Double
l. **D.-chor.** Double chorus. **D.-**
ott. Double bassoon. **D.-flöte.**
Double flute. 2. A stop-pipe with
mouths. **D.-fuge.** Double
ue. **D.-flügel.** 1. Vide VIS-A-VIS.
Vide PIANO A CLAVIERS REN-
RSES. **d.-gedeckt.** Double-stopped
pason. **D.-geige.** An organ-stop.
**-griff.** Double stop on the violin,
; paired notes on other instru-
nts. **D.-kanon.** Canon with two
jects. **D.-kreuz** (kroits). The
ble sharp. **D.-okta've.** Double
ave. **D.-punkt.** Double dot after
ote. **D.-quintpommer.** A large
nbard. **D.-schlag.** A double
t, a turn. **D.-schritt.** A quick
rch. **D.-zunge.** Double tongu-

elt (dôp'-plt), *G.* Doubled. **d.**
llerlauf. Double cadence. **dop-**
**tgestrichene Note.** A 16th
e. **doppelte Noten.** Double
es.

io (or a), *I.* Double; sometimes
d to mean "play also the octave";
n names of instrs. it means larger
deeper. **d. movimento** or **d.**
npo. Twice as fast. **d. pedale.**
ying the pedals in octaves. **d.**
a. A double lyre.

-mi. Vide SOLMISATION.

an, Doric, *E.*, dorien (dō-rĭ-äñ),
Vide MODES.

ologia (dôs-sō-lō'-jä), *I.* Doxol-
.

1. A point placed after a note to
rease its duration one half. **double**
. Two dots placed after a note to
rease its duration three fourths. 2.
oint placed above or below a note
ndicate that it is to be played stac-
o ; if slurred, mezzo-staccato. 3. A
ies of dots above a note indicate
t it is to be divided into that num-
of small notes. 4. Vide REPEAT.
le. *As a noun.* 1. A repetition.
A variation. 3. Any 16-foot stop.
A change rung on 5 bells. *As a*

*verb.* 1. To add the superior or inferior octave to the written tones of
any part. 2. To give the same tones
to different instrs.
*As an adjective.* 1. Doubled, paired,
as the 2-mouthed d. flageolet. 2.
Repeated in the octave or in other
instrs. 3. Vide PITCH, concerning
**double C, double octave. d. chant,**
vide CHANT 1 b. **d. drum.** One beaten
at both ends. **d. reed.** The combination of 2 reeds in the mouthpiece of one
instr. **d. flute.** (a) A flute capable of
producing two tones at once. (b) An
organ-stop. **d. grand pianoforte.**
An instr. inv. by James Pierson, of
New York, with a set of keys at either
end. **d. action harp.** Vide HARP.
**d. lyre.** A double lyre. **d. demi-**
**semiquaver.** A 64th note. **double**
**flat.** A symbol of two flats (♭♭) lowering its note two semitones. **dou-**
**ble sharp.** A symbol ( × ) raising a
note two semitones. **d. note.** A
breve. **d. time.** (a) 2-4 time. (b) In
the army a running step or cadence of
180 to the minute. **d. concerto** or
**sonata.** A concerto or sonata for two
solo instrs., as violin and piano. **d.**
**octave.** An interval of a 15th or 2
octaves. **d. quartet.** Eight singers.
**d. chorus.** Two choirs. **d. after-**
**note.** 2 after-notes. **d. beat.** A beat
repeated. **d. shake** or **trill.** Two
notes (3ds or 6ths) shaken together. **d.**
**backfall.** An old grace. **d. relish,**
vide RELISH. **d. suspension.** The
suspension of two notes of a chord.
**d. triplet.** A sextole. **d. pedal.**
Pedal-point on 2 notes. **double bar.**
Two thin or thick lines vertically cleav-
ing the stave to show the end of a
major part, or of the whole composition.
"**doubled**" is used of notes repeated
in the octave or in other instruments,
as "the 'cellos are *d.* by the bassoons."
Concerning the **double letters** (AA,
BB, etc., or D.A, D.B, etc.), vide
PITCH. In England d. is applied to
the tones from G to F inclusive.

4. Deeper by an octave. **d. bassoon.**
An instr. an octave lower than the
bassoon. Its compass extends from
B‿♭ to F. **d. bourdon.** A 32-ft. stop.
**d. diapason.** A stop an octave below
diapason, 16-ft. on the manuals, 32-ft.
on the pedals. **d. dulciana.** A 16-ft.
dulciana. **d. hautboy.** A 16-ft. stop.
5. **double counterpoint** and **d. descant** refer to parts so written that
they may be inverted. Vide COUN-
TERPOINT. **d. fugue.** A fugue with
2 subjects.
6. **double stopping.** The playing of
two or more notes at once on a stringed
instr. **d.-stopped diapason.** A double diapason with covered pipes. **double tonguing** or **d. tonguing.** In flute
and trumpet playing, the production
of rapid staccato tones by striking
the upper teeth and the hard palate
alternately with the tongue. **double
trouble.** A quick shuffle of the feet in
The breakdown. **double trava′le.**
The trill of a tambourine made by
drawing the wet thumb across it.
**d. twelfth.** A stop sounding the fifth
above the foundation-stops. The **double-bass** got its name from an obsolete higher instr., the *bass* of the
stringed instrs., and of the orchestra.
Its compass is from E‿ or G‿ to *a*, its
3 strings being tuned by the Italian
and French system, G‿-D-A, by the
English, A‿-D-G. With 4 strings it
is tuned E‿-A‿-D‿-G. Its music is
written an octave higher than it
sounds.
**double** (doo-bl), *F.* 1. Repetition with
variations, pl. **doubles.** Obsolete. 2.
In the minuet, a short trio with the
main harmonies of the first subject
retained. *As an adjective.* Double,
**d.-barre.** Double bar. **D.-bémol.**
Double flat. **d.-corde.** (a) Double
stopping. (b) Playing the same note
on 2 strings simultaneously. **d. coup
de langue** (koo-dŭ läng). Double
tonguing. **d. croche.** A 16th note.
**d. dièse.** Double sharp. **d. main.**
An octave-coupler. **d. octave.**
Double octave. **d. touche** (toosh).

In harmoniums, etc., a key-fa‖
justable at two heights to regula‖
volume of tone. **d. triple.** 3-2
**doublé** (doo-blä), *F.* 1. A turr‖
Doubled.
**doublette′** (ĕt), *F.* 1. A 2-ft. stop.
stop with 2 ranks of pipes. Vid‖
TEENTH.
**doublophone.** A combination‖
euphonium and trombone in‖
Besson, Paris, 1891.
**doubtful.** Vide EQUIVOCAL.
**douleur** (doo-lŭr), *F.* Grief. **do‖
reux** (doo-loo-rŭ′). Sad. **do‖
reusement** (doo-loor-ŭz-män).
ly.
**doux** (doo), **douce** (doos), *F.*
sweet. **doucement** (doos-män).
ly.
**douzième** (dooz-yĕm), *F.* A twel‖
**downbeat.** 1. The fall of the ha‖
time-beating, marking the majo‖
cent of the measure. 2. The a‖
itself, or thesis.
**downbow.** Vide BOW.
**doxolo′gia,** *L.,* **doxologie** (dô‖
zhē), *F.,* **doxol′ogy,** *E.* A s‖
hymn of praise ; strictly, the *G‖*
(or *major* or *magna*) **D.** is the‖
**ria in excelsis.** The *Lesser* (c‖
*nor* or *parva*) **D.** is the **gloria F‖**
**drag.** 1. A retardation. 2. In‖
music, a portamento downward.
**Drahtsaite** (drät′-zī-tĕ), *G.*‖
string.
**dramma lir′ico** or **per musica** (‖
zĭ-kä), *I.* An opera or m‖
drama.
**drammat′ico,** *I.* Dramatic. **d‖
maticamen′te.** Dramatically.
**drängend** (drĕng′-ĕnt), *G.* Hur‖
**drawknob** or **drawstop.** In‖
organ a knob which when pulle‖
mits the wind to a stop, or cc‖
certain stops. **d. s. action.**‖
mechanism of stops.
**Dreher** (drā′ĕr), *G.* An obsolete‖
trian waltz like the Ländler.
**Drehorgel** (drā′-ôrg-ĕl), *G.* Barr‖
gan.
**Drehsessel** (drā′-zĕs-sĕl), **Dreh‖**
(drā-shtool), *G.* A music-stool.‖

(drī), *G.* Three. **Dreiachtel-**
**:t** (drī-äkht'-ĕl-täkt). 3-8 time.
**ndig** (hĕn-dĭkh). For three hands.
**gel** (drī'-äng-ēl). Triangle.
**örig**(kär-ĭkh). Three-choired. Ap-
:d to (a) pianos having three strings
each note. (b) Compositions for
ee choirs. **-gesang** (drī'ge-zäng).
**o. -gestrichen.** 3-lined ; vide
**CH. -klang.** A triad. **-mal** (drī'-
l). Thrice. **-spiel** (drī'shpēl). A
**. -stimmig.** Three-voiced. **Drei-**
**erteltakt** (drī-fēr'tĕl-täkt). 3-4
**ie. Dreizweiteltakt** (drī-tsvī'-tel-
:t). 3-2 time.
**st** (drīsht), *G.* Brave, confident.
**eistigkeit** (drīs'tĭkh-kīt). Bold-
ss.
**'la,** *Pol.* A Jew's harp.
**gend** (drĭng'ĕnt), *G.* Hastening.
**te** (drĭt'-tĕ), *G.* Third.
**to,** *I.* Right. **mano d.** Right
nd.
**ing note.** A syncopated note.
**t** (dwä), **droite** (dwät), *F.* Right.
**ain droite.** Right hand.
**mmete** (drôm-mā'tĕ), *G.* A trum-
t.
**e** or **drone-pipe.** Vide BAGPIPE.
**e-bass.** A form of monotonous
dal-point suggesting a bagpipe.
de MUSETTE.
**en** (drā'nĕn), *G.* To drone.
**cker** (drook'er), *G.* 1. A tour-de-
rce in performance. 2. Sticker.
**ckwerk** (vĕrk), *G.* In an organ,
action exerted through stickers.
**ruckbalg** (drook-bälkh). A con-
ssion bellows.
**m.** An instr. of percussion, of great
ntiquity and variety ; it consists of
ne or two membranes stretched taut
ver the ends of a hollowed chamber
wood or metal. The tightness of
is membrane regulates the pitch of
e one tone of which it is capable.
Many drums do not produce a musi-
al tone, but are merely of rhythmic
alue ; besides the savage forms, there
re (a) the small, shrill **side drum**
or **tenor-drum**) with two heads, the
pper only being beaten with two

wooden sticks ; this is capable of a
sharp rattling roll, which may be
emphasized by drawing strings (or
snares) of gut across the lower head;
the drum is then called a **snare-**
**drum ;** (b) the **tambourine ;** (c) the
big deep-booming **bass-drum** beaten
on both sides or on one, with padded
sticks. The musical drum is the
**kettle-drum** (q. v.). **drum-major.**
The officer conducting a band on the
march.

**dru'ma,** *Irish.* A drum.

**drum-bass.** The monotonous giving
out of the tonic and dominant in
double-bass music.

**D. S.** Abbr. of *Dal Segno.*

**duc'tus,** *L.* Melodic progression. 1.
**d. rectus.** Ascending. 2. **d. rever-**
**sus** or **revertens.** Descending ; or
3. **d. circumcurrens.** Ascending
and descending.

**Dudeler** (doo'dĕl-er), *G.* A wretched
singer or player.

**Du'delkasten,** *G.* Barrel-organ.

**Dudelsack** (doo'd'l-zäk), **Dudelkas-**
**tensack,** *G.* A bagpipe.

**due** (doo'-ĕ), *I.* Two ; in two parts.
Vide DIVISI. **d. corde.** Vide CORDA.
**d. cori.** Two choirs or choruses.
**d. pedali,** *I.* Both pedals to be used.
**due volti.** Twice. *A due,* vide
DIVISI.

**duet, Duett** (doo-et'), *G.,* **duet'to,** *I.*
A composition for two singers, or instrumentalists ; a 2-hand piece for
two manuals of an organ. **duettino**
(tē'no), *I.* A short duet.

**dulçáina** (dool-sä-ē'na), *Port.* A beak
flute. Also doçaina.

**dulcet.** A stop.

**dulcian.** 1. Vide DOLCIAN. 2. An
organ-stop.

**dulciana stop, dolcan, dolcin, dul-**
**can,** or **dulzain.** 1. An 8-ft. stop of
soft sweet quality. **d. principal.** A
4-ft. stop. 2. A dolcian.

**dulcimer.** A very ancient instr. with
a wooden frame, a sound-board with
sound-holes, two bridges, and wire
strings. It is played upon with two
padded hammers ; compass g to d."

The czimbalom is a very familiar form.

**dulzaina** (dool-thä-ē'-nä), *Sp.* A small trumpet.

**dumb piano, dumb spinet.** A keyboard without strings or hammers meant for silent practice.

**dummy pipes.** Ornamental organ pipes that make no sound.

**dump.** An obsolete slow dance in 4-4 time.

**dumpf** (doompf), **dumpfig** (doomp'-fĭkh), *G.* Dull, muffled. **Dumpfigkeit** (kĭt). Dulness.

**duo** (doo' ō), *I.* Two; in two parts; a duet, especially of 2 voices or instrs. of the same kind. **d. concertante.** A duo in which each part is alternately principal.

**duodecima** (doo-ō-dā'chĭ-mä), *I.* The twelfth; a stop, a twelfth above the diapasons. **d. acuta**, *L.* A twelfth above. **d. gravi**, *L.* A twelfth below.

**duodecimole**, *I.* A group of twelve equal notes.

**duode'nal, duodena'rium, duodena'-tion.** See A. J. ELLIS in the B. D.

**duodram'ma**, *I.* A dramatic piece for 2 actors or singers.

**duoi** (doo-ō'e), *I.* Two.

**duole**, *G.* Vide COUPLET.

**duolo** (doo-ō'lō), *I.* Sorrow, grief.

**duomo** (doc-ō'mō), *I.* A cathedral.

**dupla** (doo'-plä), *L.* Double. Vide NOTATION.

**duple time.** Double time; 2 beats to the measure. Vide TIME.

**duplex longa.** Vide NOTATION.

**duplication.** Doubling.

**duplo** (doo-plō), *I.* Double.

**dur** (door), *G.* Major, as A-dur.

**dur** (dür), *F.* 1. Hard, harsh of tone. 2. Major.

**durament'te** (doo-rä-měn'-tě), *I.* Sternly.

**durchaus** (doorkh-ows), *G.* Throughout.

**durchdringend** (doorkh'-drĭng ĕnt), *G.* Penetrating, shrill.

**Durch'führung** (für-oongk), *G.* Development; working out. Vide FORM.

**Durchgang** (gäng), *G.* Pas: **Durch'gangston.** Passing not changing note, called *regelmä* when on a weak beat; *unregelmä* on a strong beat (or *schwerer Du gang*).

**durchgehend** (doorkh'gā-ěnt), *G.* Passing, transitional. 2. Comp d. **Stimmen.** Complete organ-s

**durch'komponirt** (nĕrt), *G.* "( posed through," used of a song w every stanza has individual t ment. Through-composed.

**durchschlagende** (shläkh-ĕnt-ě), *G.* Free (of a reed).

**durchstechen** (stĕkh-ĕn), *G.* RUN (2). **D.-stecher.** Notes r by running.

**durée** (dü-rā), *F.* Length, duratic

**durezza** (doo-rĕd'-zä), *I.* Hard, harshness.

**dur-moll Tonart** (door'-môl-tōn'-*G.* Major-minor-mode. Vide ( BINATION MODE.

**duro(a)** (dooro), *I.* Rude, harsh.

**durus**, *L.* 1. Major, as *cantus d.* Natural, as *b. durum.*

**Dutch concert.** Vide CONCERT.

**Dütchen** (düt'-khěn), *G.* A small net.

**duten** (doo'-ten), *G.* To toot.

**dux**, *L.* "Leader, guide;" the ject of a fugue (q. v.)

**dy'ad.** A concord of two tones.

**dynam'ics.** The theory of the di ent degrees of power applied to n

**Dystonie** (des-to-nē'), *G.* and *Gr.* intonation.

## E

**E** Pron. ā in *G.*; in *F.* and called *mi* (mě). 1. A mus pitch, two full steps abov 2. All its octaves. 3. major scale having four sharps; minor scale relative to G major.

**e** (ā), *I.* And; written *ed* before v els.

**ear.** 1. A projecting metal plate either side of the mouth of org pipes. 2. A musical sense of pi

erval, etc.; the capability of dis-
guishing between tone-qualities.

**izione** (ā-bôl-lēt-tsĭ-ō´-nĕ), *I.*
ullition, overflow of emotion.
**ollimen´to.** Ebullient(ly).

t (ā-kăr), *F.* A long stretch on the
ano.

**ole,** *Gr.* The sharpening of a
ne.

**dente** (ĕt-chĕ-dĕn´-tĕ), *I.* Aug-
ented.

**esia** (ĕk-klā´zĭ-ä), *L.* and *I.*
urch. ecclesiastical **modes.**
de MODES. **ecclesiastico,** *I.* Ec-
esiastic.

(ĕk´-ko). 1. Behold. 2. Echo.
**appement** (ā-shăp-män), *F.* Rease. **double é.** Repeating-mech-
ism.

**eggiare** (ā-kĕd-jä´-rĕ), *I.* To echo.
**ei´on** (pl. **a**), *Gr.* 1. A drum or
ong. 2. A sound-screen. 3. Res-
ance-box of a lyre.

**elette** (ash-lĕt), *F.* Xylophone.
**elle** (ā-shĕl), *F.* The scale or
amut.

**elon** (ash-lôn), *F.* A degree.
o (in *F.* ā-ko). 1. An imitation of an
ho. 2. An echo-stop. 3. A harpsi-
ord-stop. **e. cornet, e. dulciana.**
rgan-stops. **e. organ.** A set of
pes inside a box or at a distance
ving an echo effect.

**´ometer.** A device for measuring
e power of an echo.

**sses** (ā-klēs), *F.* Ribs (of a violin,
c.).

**ogue.** A pastoral.

**ysis,** *Gr.* The flattening of a tone.
(ā-ko), *I.* Echo.

**le** (ā-kŭl), *F.* School, method.

**ssais** (ā-kôs-sā), **écossaise** (ā-kôs-
ēz), *F.,* **Ecossäse** (ā-kôs-sä´zĕ), *G.*
Scotch.'' 1. A grave old dance, in
-2 or 3-4 time. 2. A lively country-
ance in 2-4 time.

(ā-kü), *F.* A shield on the face of
andolins, etc.

**(ĕd),** *I.* And.

**l** (ā´dl), *G.* Noble.

**dur** (ā-door), *G.* E major.

**´ekt´,** *G.,* **effet** (ĕf-fä), *F.,* **effet´-**

to, *I.* Effect. **Effekt-piano**, *G.*
The effect marked '' fp '' (forte piano).

**effort** (ĕf-fôr), *F.* A guttural vocal
attack.

**également** (ā-găl-män), *F.* Equally,
evenly. **égalité** (ā-găl-ĭ-tā), *F.*
Equality, evenness.

**egloga** (āl´yō-ga), *I.,* **églogue** (āg-
lôg), *F.* A pastoral.

**eguale** (ā-goo-ä´lĕ), *I.* 1. Equal, even.
2. Applied to a composition for
voices or instrs. of one kind, as female
voices only. **egualezza** (lĕd´zä),
**egualanza** (än´-tsä). Evenness.
**egualmen´te.** Evenly, alike.

**ei´domusikon.** A melograph.

**eifrig** (if̣-rĭkh), *G.* Ardent.

**eigentlich** (īkh´-ĕnt-lĭkh), *G.* Right,
strict, in perfect time. **e. Fuge.** A
strict fugue. **e. Kadenz.** Perfect
cadence.

**Eigenton** (ĭ´-khĕn-tōn), *G.* The tone
natural to a wind or other instr., its
'' own tone.''

**eight** or **8.** The octave. **con 8va.**
With the octave below or above.
Vide OTTAVA.

**eighteenth.** A double octave plus a
fourth.

**eight-foot. 8-ft.** Vide FOOT.

**eighth.** 1. An octave. 2. An eighth
note. **eighth note.** A quaver, of half
the value of a quarter note. **eighth
rest.** A rest of an eighth-note duration.

**eilen** (ĭ´lĕn), *G.* To hurry. **eilend**
(lĕnt). Accelerating. **eilig** (ĭ´-lĭkh).
Swift.

**ein** (īn), **eine** (ĭ´nĕ), **eins** (īns), *G.*
One, once. **einchörig** (kā´-rĭkh).
Used, 1. Of an instr. which has but
one string to each note. 2. Of a
comp. for one choir. **eingestrichen**
(īn-ghĕ-strĭkh´-ĕn). Once-accented.
Vide PITCH.

**einfach** (īn-fäkh), *G.* Simple, plain.
**einfache Kontrapunkt.** Simple
counterpoint. **Einfalt.** Simplicity.

**Eingang** (īn´-gäng), *G.* Introduction.
**Eingang der Messe.** The Introit.
**Eingang´schlüssel.** Introductory
key.

**eingreifen** (īn'-grī-fĕn), *G.* (a) To strike (of strings). (b) To interlace (of the fingers in piano-playing).
**Einheit** (īn'-hīt), *G.* Unity. **einhelfen.** To prompt. **Einhelfer.** Prompter. **einige(n)** (ī'nĭkh-ĕn). Some, any. **Einigkeit** (kīt). Unity, harmony. **Einklang** (īn'kläng). Unison. **Einlage** (īn-läkh-ĕ). A short interpolation. **Einleitung** (īn'lī-toongk). Introduction. **Einleitungssatz** (zäts) or **spiel.** Overture, prelude. **einmal** (īn-mäl). Once. **Einmüthigkeit** (īn-müt'-ĭkh-kīt). Unanimity. **Einsaiter** (zī'-ter). The monochord. **Einsang.** A solo. **Einsatz.** (a) Attack. (b) Entrance. **Einsatzstück.** Crook. **Einsatzzeichen** (īn'zätz-tsīkh'n). 1. The sign the leader gives the performers to commence. 2. In a canon the mark indicating the entrance of the imitating voice. **einschlagen.** To strike in. **einschlafend.** Dying away. **einschmeichelnd** (shmīkh-ĕlnt). Insinuating. **Einschnitt** (shnĭt). A phrase. **einsetzen.** To enter, attack. **einsetzender Hornist.** A horn-player, whose thick lips must surround, instead of press the mouthpiece. **einsingen.** (a) To learn singing by practice. (b) To lull to sleep. **einspielen.** (a) To get an instr. in good working order. (b) To attain command of a piece. **einstimmen.** To tune. **einstimmig.** For one part. **Einstimmigkeit.** Literally, one-voiced-ness. **eintönig.** Monotonous. **Eintracht.** Accord. **einträchtig** (trĕkh-tĭkh). Concordant. **eintretend** (trā-tĕnt). Entering. **Eintritt.** Entrance, entry, beginning. **Einverständniss** (fershtĕnt-nĭs). Agreement.
**Eïs** (ā'-ēs), *G.* E sharp. **Eïsis.** E double sharp.
**Eisenvicline** (ī-'zĕn), *G.* A nail-fiddle.
**Eisteddfod** (ēs'-tĕd-fôd), *Welsh.* An assemblage of Welsh bards and musicians; first held in 1078.
**Eklog(u)e** (āk'-lôkh-ĕ), *G.* Eclogue.

**éla.** Name of the highest tone i Aretinian scale ; e''.
**electric organ.** One having tric connections in place of track
**electric piano.** A piano inv. and unsuccessfully attempted since, till Dr. Eisenmann of Ber 1891 succeeded in obtaining an capable of swelling on a sust. tone, and securing many beautif fects.
**élégamment** (āl-ā-găm-mäń), *F.*, **gantemen'te,** *I.* Elegantly, g fully. **elegante** (āl-ĕ-gän'tĕ), *I.* gant. **eleganza** (āl-ĕ-gän'tsä) Elegance, grace.
**elegia** (ā-lä-jē'-ä), *I.*, **élégie** zhē), *F.*, **Elegie** (ĕl-ä-jē'), *G.*, **el** *E.* A mournful composition or d **elegiaco** (jäk'-ō), *I.*, **élégi** (ä-lä-zhäk), *F.* elegiac.
**élément** (ā-lā-mäń), *F.* The seri tones in a scale. **é. métrique** measure-note.
**elevamen'to, elevatezza** (āl-ā-vä zä), *I.*, **elevazione** (vä-tsǐ-ō'nĕ). vation. **elevato** (vä'to). Elev. exalted, sublime.
**eleva'tio,** *L.*, **elevation.** 1. upbeat. 2. The rising of a me beyond the compass of a mode. motet or other comp. performed ing the elevation of the Host.
**eleventh.** An octave plus a fourth **Elfte** (ĕlf'tĕ), *G.* Eleventh.
**Ellenlänge** (ĕllĕn-lĕng-ĕ), *G.* A (in pipe-measuring).
**Ellis's system.** See A. J. ELLI the B. D.
**embellir** (äń-bĕl-lēr), *F.* To embel **embellissement** (lēs-mäń), *F.* bellishment.
**embellishment.** Ornament, dec tion. Vide GRACE.
**embouchure** (äń-boo-shür), *F.* 1. mouthpiece of a wind instr. 2. position the mouth assumes in ing the instrument.
**E-moll** (ā-môl), *G.* E minor.
**emmelei'a,** *Gr.* 1. Consonance. A tragic dance.
**emozione** (ā-mō-tsǐ-ō'-nĕ), *I.* Emot

npâter les sons (än-pä-tā lä sön), *F.* To produce a legato. **exécution** or **voix empâtée.** A blurred style.

mpfindung (ĕmp-fĭnt′-oongk), *G.* Feeling, emotion. **e. svoll.** Full of feeling.

mphase (*G.* ĕm-fä′-zĕ, *F.* än-fåz). Emphasis. **emphasis.** Stress or accent.

nphatique (än-fä-tēk), *F.* **emphatisch** (ĕm-fä′-tĭsh), *G.* Emphatic. **emphatiquement** (tēk-män), *F.* Emphatically.

npito (ĕm′-pē-tō), *I.* Impetuosity. **empituosamen′te.** Impetuously.

nporté (än-pôr-tā), *F.* Passionate, hurried. **emportement** (pôrt-män). Passion, transport.

npressé (än-prĕs-sā), *F.* Hurried. **empressement** (prĕs-män), *F.* Zeal.

**n** (än), *F.* In; often used with the participle, as *en déscendant,* descending; *en badinant,* scherzando.

**narmo′nico,** *I.* Enharmonic.

**nclavure du manche** (än-klä-vür dü mänsh). Space for the insertion of the neck (of a violin) into the belly.

**ncore** (än-kôr), *F.* Again; a recall. Used by the English to demand a repetition; the French use " *bis.*"

**nde** (ĕnt′ĕ), *G.* End, conclusion.

**nd-man.** One of the chief negro minstrels who sits at either end of their semicircle.

**nergia** (ĕn-ĕr-jē′ä), *I.*, **energie** (ĕn-ĕr-zhē), *F.* Energy. **energico** (ĕn-är′jĭ-kō), **energicamen′te,** *I.* Energetic(ally). **energique** (ĕn-ĕr-zhēk), *F.*, **energisch** (ĕn-är′zhĭsh), *G.* Energetic. **energiquement** (zhēk-män), *F.* Energetically.

**nfasi** (ĕn-fä′zē), *I.* Emphasis. **nfat′ico, enfaticamen′te,** *I.* Emphatic(ally).

**nfiatamente** (ĕn-fē-ä′-tä-mĕn′-tĕ), *I.* Proudly.

**nfler** (än-flā), *F.* To swell, increase.

**ng** (ĕngk), *G.* Close, compressed; applied, (a) to the stretto in fugue, (b) to narrow straight organ-pipes. **enge Harmonie (or Lage).** Close harmony.

**Engelstimme** (ĕng′ĕl-shtĭm-mĕ), *G.* "Angel voice." Angelica; a stop.

**Engführung** (ĕng′-für-oongk), *G.* Stretto.

**englisch** (ĕng′lĭsh), *G.* English. **e. Horn.** English horn. **e. Mechanik,** in pianos, the English action. **e. Tanz.** Vide ANGLAISE. **e. Viollet** (vē-ō-lĕt′). (a) An old way of tuning the violin—e-a-e′-a′. (b) An obsolete *viola a'amore* with 14 sympathetic strings beneath the others.

**English fingering.** Same as American fingering.

**English horn.** A species of oboe (q. v.)

**enguichure** (än-gē-shür), *F.* Embouchure.

**enharmonic, enharmon′icus,** *L.*, **enharmonique** (ĕn-är-môn-ēk), *F.*, **enharmonisch** (ĕn-här-mō′-nīsh), *G.* **1.** Differing in name or notation, but not in sound, as c sharp and d flat. Mathematically and actually c ♯ and d ♭ differ by an appreciable interval, but for convenience' sake and in the name of *temperament* (q. v.) they are the same tone on the keyboard instruments and, by contagion, have become so in singing and the playing of stringed and wind instruments. Tones that are identical in our present artificial scale, but not in actuality or acoustics, are called enharmonic; hence *chords and intervals* written differently and sounding alike are called **enharmonic,** and the change of the key by such chords is called **enharmonic modulation;** the writing of the same chord in 2 notations is **e. change.** Instruments have been frequently invented making a distinction between such tones as c sharp and d flat, and giving them separate digitals. These instrs. are called **enharmonic.** The **e. scale** is, strictly, a scale with more than the twelve semitones of our usual scale; the term is loosely applied *to* scales as c sharp and d flat, having the same sound. **2.** Vide MODES. **3.** Vide DIESIS.

**enigmatical.** Vide CANON.

**énoncer** (ā-nôn-sā), *F.* To enunciate. **énonciation** (ā-nôn-săs-yôn). Enunciation.

**eno'plia,** *Gr.* Spartan war-music.

**ensemble** (än-sän'bl), *F.* 1. Together; the whole; all the factors considered as a unit. 2. The quality of their co-operation. **morceau d'e.** A number requiring more than one performer.

**entgegen** (ĕnt-gā'khĕn),e. **-gesetzt,** *G.* Contrary. opposite.

**entr'acte** (än-träkt), *F.* Music played between the acts, or of such character.

**entran'te, entrata** (ĕn-trä'-tä), *I.*, **entrada** (ĕn-trä'-dhä), *Sp.*, **entrée** (än-trā), *F.* 1. Entrance; introduction, or music of such character, as in a ballet. 2. An old polonaise-like dance in 4-4 time.

**entre-chats** (änt-rŭ-shä), *F.* The entering bounds of a dancer.

**entremese** (ĕn-trĕ-mā'-sä), *Sp.* A burlesque interlude.

**entremets** (änt-rŭ-mā), *F.* Slight interlude.

**entry** (obs). An act.

**Entscheidung** (ĕnt'-shī-doongk), *G.* Decision. **entschieden** (ĕnt-shē'-dĕn), *G.* Decided.

**entschlafen** (ĕnt-shlä'fĕn), *G.* To die away (lit. to fall asleep).

**Entschliessung** (ĕnt'-shlēs-soongk), *G.* Resolution.

**entschlossen** (ĕnt-shlôs'sĕn), *G.* Resolute. **Entschluss** (ĕnt'-shloos), *G.* Resolution.

**Entwurf** (ĕnt'-voorf), *G.* Sketch, outline.

**enunciato** (ā-noon-chī-ä'-tō), *I.* Enunciated. **enunciazione** (ä'-tsī-ō'-nĕ), *I.* Enunciation.

**en'voy.** Postscript, or ending, of a ballad.

**Eolia** (ē-ō'lī-ä), **Eolian** (ē-ō'lī-än), *I.* Vide ÆOLIAN.

**epicède** (ĕp-i-sĕd), *F.*, **epicedio** (ĕp-ī-chä'dī-ō), *I.*, **epice'dium,** *L.* An elegy, dirge, funeral-song, or ode.

**epigo'nion,** *Gr.*, **epigo'nium.** *L.* An ancient Greek lyre, with 40 string named from Epigon.

**epile'nia,** *Gr.* Vineyard songs.

**epinic'ion,** *Gr.* 1. A triumphal son 2. The Triumphal Sanctus in t Greek Church.

**epio'dion,** *Gr.* A dirge.

**episode, épisode** (ā-pē-sôd), *F.*, **ep so'dio,** *I.* All incidental portions composition. Vide FUGUE. **epis disch** (ĕp-ī-zō-dĭsh), *G.* Episodic.

**epistle side.** The left or south si of the altar; the right or north the **gospel side.**

**epis'trophe,** *Gr.* A refrain.

**epitalamio** (ĕp-ī-tä-lä'mī-ō), *I.*, **e th'alme** (ĕp-ī-tălm), *F.*, **epith lami'on,** *Gr.*, **epithalamium, e thal'amy,** *L.* and *E.* Wedding-oc

**epit'asis,** *Gr.* Vide ANESIS.

**epito'nion,** *Gr.* 1. A pitch-pipe. A tuning-wrench.

**ep'ode,** *Gr.* After-song. 1. A refra 2. The conclusion of an ode. 3. retraction.

**ep'tacorde** (ĕp-tä-kôrd), *F.*, **eptaco do,** *I.* 1. A heptachord. 2. seventh. 3. A scale of seven note

**equabile** (ā-kwä'bī-lā), *I.* Equal, alik **equabilmen'te.** Smoothly.

**equal.** 1. Of counterpoint, consisti of notes of equal duration. 2. Vi TEMPERAMENT. 3. Of voices, al (all male, for instance); not mixed

**e'quisonance, equisonnance** (ā-l sŭn-näns), *F.* Unison, as of octav **e'quisonant.** Of like sound; in u son. In guitar music used of diff ent ways of stopping the same no **equiso'no** (ā-kwē'sō-nō), *I.* In t unison or octave.

**equiv'ocal.** Used of chords wh may by slight change in notation I long to more than one key.

**Erard action.** Vide HARP.

**erbeb,** *Arab.* Rebec.

**erfreulich** (ĕr-froi'-lĭkh), *G.* Joyous

**ergrif'fen,** *G.* Stirred, affected. **É-h** (hīt). Agitation.

**erhaben** (ĕr-hä'bĕn), *G.* Exalted, su lime. **Erhabenheit** (hīt). Subli ity.

neben (ĕr-hä′bĕn), *G.* To raise, to elevate ; as the hand, in beating time. höhen (ĕr-hä′ĕn), *G.* To raise. Er-nöhung (ĕr-hä′oongk), *G.* Raising, sharpening. **E.-szeichen.** Sharps, double sharps, or naturals following flats.

nattet (ĕr-mät′-tĕt), *G.* Exhausted. niedrigung (ĕr-nē′-drĭkh-oongk), *G.* Depression by means of a flat or natural. **E.-szeichen.** A sign for lowering a note.

nst (ĕrnsht), **ernsthaft** (ĕrnst′häft), *G.* Earnest. **Ernsthaftigkeit** (ĕrnst′häf-tĭkh-kīt), **Ernstlichkeit** (lĭkh-kīt). Earnestness.

ntelied (ĕrn′tĕ-lēt), *G.* Harvest-song.

öffnung (ĕr-ĕf′noongk), *G.* Opening, beginning. **E.-sstück.** Over-ture.

oico (ā-ro′ĭ-kō or -a), *I.* Heroic. " *Sinfonia eroica,*" Beethoven's 3d symphony.

ot′ico, *I.*, **érotique** (ā-rô-tēk), *F.*, erot′ic. 1. Amorous. 2. An amorous composition.

st (ĕrsht), *G.* First. **erste Mal.** First time.

sterben, *G.* To die away.

tönen (ĕr-tä′-nĕn), *G.* To sound.

weckung (ĕr-vĕk′oongk), *G.* Animation.

weitern (ĕr-vī′-tĕrn), *G.* To develop, expand. **erweitert.** Expanded, as **erweiterte Harmonie.** Open harmony. **erweiterter Satz.** A movement fully developed thematically. **Erweiterung.** The widening of an interval in a fugal theme.

rzähler (ĕr-tsä′lĕr), *G.* The narrator in Passion music.

rzlaŭte (ĕrts′-low-tĕ), *G.* The arch-lute.

s (ĕs), *G.* The note E flat.

acordo (ā-sä-kôr′do), *I.* 1. Hexachord. 2. A sixth.

at′to, *I.* Exact, strict.

s-dur (ĕs-door), *G.* E flat major.

ecuzione (ās-ĕ-koot-sĭ-ō′nĕ), *I.* Execution. **esecuto′re.** Performer. eguire (ā-sä-goo-ē′-rĕ). To execute.

esem′pio, *I.* Example.

esercizio (ā-sĕr-chē′tsĭ-ō) (pl. **i**), *I.* An exercise.

Es-es (ĕs-ĕs), *G.* E double flat.

esitamento (ā-sē-ta-mĕn′tō), **esita-zione** (ā-sē-tä-tsĭ-ō′nĕ), *I.* Hesitation.

Es-moll (ĕs-môl), *G.* E flat minor.

espace (ŭs-pǎs), *F.* A space in the staff.

espagnol (ĕs-pīn-yôl), *F.*, **espagnuolo** (ĕs-pän-yoo-ō′lō), *I.* " Spanish ;" in Spanish style.

esper′to, *I.* Expert.

espiran′do, *I.* Dying.

espr., **espress.** Abbr. of *Espressivo.*

espressione (sĭ-ō′nĕ), *I.* Expression, feeling. **espressivo** (sē′vo), *I.* Expressive.

espringale (ĕs-prĭn-gä′-lĕ), *I.* Spring-dance.

essem′pio, *I.* Example.

essen′tial. (a) Of *harmonies*, the three chief harmonies in any key, *viz.*, the tonic, dominant, and subdominant. (b) Of *notes*, those that make up a chord, in distinction from ornamental, and other foreign notes. **e. seventh.** (a) The leading note. (b) The 7th chord in the dominant.

estemporale (rä′lĕ), **estemporaneo** (rä′-nĕ-ō), *I.* Extemporaneous.

estinguendo (ĕs-tĭn-goo-ĕn′dō), *I.* Dying away.

estinto (ĕs-tēn′-tō) (or **a**), *I.* Extinguished, almost inaudible.

estravaganza (ĕs-trä-vä-gän′tsä), *I.* Extravaganza.

estremamente (ĕs-trä-mä-men′-tĕ), *I.* Extremely.

estribilho (ĕs-trĭ-bēl′-yō). A familiar Portuguese air.

estrinciendo (ĕs-trēn-chän′dō), *I.* Playing incisively.

estriniendo (ĕs-trēn-yän′dō), *I.* Very legato.

es′tro, *I.* Poetic fire.

et, *L.* And.

et (ā), *F.* And.

étalon (ā-tä-lôṅ), *F.* Vide SCALE 3.

éteinte (ā-tăṅt), *F.* Almost inaudible.

**étendre** (ā-täṅdr), *F.* To extend, spread. **étendue** (ā-täṅ-dü). Compass.

**Et Incarna'tus,** *L.* "And He was born," etc. Part of the Credo.

**étoffé** (ā-tôf-fā), *F.* Having " body," as a voice.

**étouffer** (ā-toof-fā), *F.* To deaden the tone. **étouffé** (ā-toof-fā). Stifled, muffled ; in harp-playing a deadening of the tones by touching the strings. **étouffoir** (ā-toof-wär). Damper.

**être en répétition** (ĕt'räṅ rā-pā-tēs-yôṅ), *F.* To be in rehearsal.

**Et Res'urrexit,** *L.* "And rose again." A part of the Credo.

**-et'to** (or **a**), *I.* Little ; an Italian suffix, as *trombetta.* A little trumpet.

**et'tacordo,** *I.* Instr. with 7 strings.

**étude** (ā-tüd), *F.* A study. A comp. outwardly intended for practice and facility in some special difficulty of technic ; often marked with much art, and in the **é. de concert** (dŭ-kôṅ-săr), concert-study, intended for public display. **étudier** (ā-tüd-yā). To study, to practise. Vide STUDY.

**Et Vi'tam,** *L.* "And life everlasting." Part of the Credo.

**etwas** (ĕt'väs), *G.* Some, somewhat. **e. langsamer.** A little slower.

**eufonia** (ā-oo-fō-nē'ä), *I.* Euphony. **eufo'nico.** Harmonious.

**euharmon'ic** (ū). Producing harmony or concordant sounds. Well-harmonied, not tempered. **e. organ.** An instr. of American origin, inv. by H. W. Poole, 1848, and containing the untempered intervals. Vide ENHARMONIC.

**euouae.** The vowels in the words "Seculorum, Amen," at the end of the "Gloria Patri ; " (a) the trope of the Gregorian Lesser Doxology ; (b) any trope (q. v.)

**Euphon** (yoo-fōn). A glass harmonica (compass from c to f''') inv. by Chladni, about 1790 ; the tone produced by rubbing with wet fingers strips of glass, connected with metal rods ; also called **eupho'nium.**

**eupho'niad.** An instr. of Ameri origin, containing thirty keys, a tones of the organ, horn, basso clarinet, and violin.

**euphonic-horn, eupho'nion.** Som rophone.

**eupho'nious.** Harmonious.

**eupho'nium.** A bass brass instr. u in military bands. It has two tub played from a single mouthpiece.

**Euter'pe,** *G.* The seventh mu patroness of flute-music and song.

**evacua'tio,** *L.* In old notation, reduction by one-half of a solid not value by writing only its outline.

**Evakuant** (ā-väk-oo-änt'), *G.* exhaust-pallet ; also **evacuant,** *E*

**éveillé** (ā-vā-yā), *F.* Gay, sprightly

**evening,** or **even, song.** Even service in the Anglican Church.

**ever'sio,** *L.* In cpt., inversion.

**evirato** (ā-vē-rä'-tō), *I.* A eun with a soprano or alto voice.

**evolu'tio,** *L.* In cpt., inversion.

**evovae.** Vide EUOUAE.

**exécutant** (ĕx-ā-kü-täṅ), *F.* A p former.

**exe'quiae,** *L.,* **Exequien** (ĕx-ā'k ĕn), *G.* Obsequies ; requiems.

**exercice** (ĕx-ĕr-sēs), *F.,* **Exercit'i** (ĕx-ĕr-tsē'tsĭ-oom), *G.,* **exercise.** practice piece ; a problem in com sition, or technic.

**exhaust pallet** or **valve.** A st opening a valve which exhausts t bellows of an organ.

**exposi'tion.** Development , the wo ing out of a theme. Vide FORM a FUGUE.

**expressif** (ĕx-prŭs-ēf), *F.* Expressi

**expres'sion** (in *F.* ĕx-prŭs-yôṅ). T psychological and spiritual eleme of music, its message and eloquen The delivery of a composition w fidelity to its meaning. Hence **expression-mark** is any sign th will aid in the interpretation of composition. In French the word is also used specifically of the vibr effect. **expression-stop.** An h monium-stop giving the pedals l control of the expression.

pressive-organ, **Expressivorgel** (sĕf-ôr-khĕl), *G.*, **orgue expressif**, *F.* The harmonium.

tempora'neous. Without premed-tation. **extem'pore**, *L.* Improvised; off-hand. **extemporize.** To improvise. **extemporizing machine.** A melograph for recording extemporization.

tended. 1. Dispersed, as a chord. 2. Enlarged, as a development. **e. phrase.** One with three measures instead of the usual two, etc. **e. section.** One containing from 5 to 8 measures.

:tension (ĕz-täns-yôn), *F.* Stretch, or compass on the violin; the extension of the forefinger or little finger of the left hand. **extension pedal.** Loud pedal.

:tra'neous. Foreign to the key. **e. modulation.** Transition to an unrelated key.

:travaganza (ĕx-trä-vä-gän'tsä), *I.* 1. An ornament in bad taste. 2. A musical burlesque, usually spectacular.

:treme, **extrême** (ĕx-trĕm), *F.* 1. The highest and lowest parts. 2. Augmented. **chord of the e. sixth.** An altered chord. (Vide ALTERED.)

## F

**F** E. and *G.*; in *F.* and *I.* called **fà** (fä). 1. A musical pitch, a perfect fourth above C in all its octaves. 2. The major key having one flat; the minor key relative to A flat minor. **F clef**, *F* **Schlüssel**, *G.* The bass clef gripping the line F. **f. holes** (in *G.* **F. Löcher** (ĕf-lĕkh-ĕr); in *F.* **les F.** (lä-zĕf). The f-shaped sound-holes in the belly of violins, etc. **f, ff, fff, etc.** Abbr. of *forte* and *fortissimo*.

(fä), *I.* 1. The fourth of the syllables of solmisation (q. v.). 2. Name of F. in France and Italy, **fa-feint** (fän), *F.*, **fa fint'o**, *I.*, **fa fict'um**, *L.* Obsolete term for any flatted note. **fa mi.** Formerly the descent of half

a tone from F to E; now any such descent. **fa bémol**, F flat. **fa dièse.** F sharp. **faburden.** 1. A counterpoint of thirds and sixths added by ear to a *cantus firmus*. 2. Later any improvised accompaniment. 3. A burden. 4. A drone-bass. 5. Intonation of the Psalms.

**fabliau** (fäb-lĭ-ō), *F.* An old narrative poem. **fablier** (lĭ-ā). A trouvère.

**faces d'un accord** (fäs d'ŭn äk-kôr), *F.* The positions of a chord; a triad has 3, a seventh 4, etc.

**fach** (fäkh), *G.* (lit. -fold). Ranked; as **dreifach.** Three-ranked (of pipes).

**fächerförmiges Pedal** (fĕkh'-ĕr-fĕr-mĭkh-ĕs pä-däl), *G.* A fan-shaped pedal-board.

**facile** (fă-sēl), *F.*, **facile** (fä'-chē-lĕ). Light, easy. **'facilità** (fä-chē-lĭ-tä'), *I.*, **facilité** (fä-sēl-ĭ-tä), *F.* 1. Facility. 2. An easier arrangement of a piece or passage. **facilement** (fä-sēl-män), *F.*, **facilmente** (fä-chēl-mĕn'-tä), *I.* Easily.

**Fackeltanz** (fäk'ĕl-tänts), *G.* Dance with flambeaux in a minuet form, 4-4 time.

**facture** (fäk-tür), *F.*, **Faktur** (fäk-toor'), *G.* 1. Scheme or construction, workmanship. 2. The scale of pipes.

**-fädig** (fä-dĭkh), *G.* Threaded (of violin-strings), as **vierfädig.** 4-threaded.

**fading** (fäd'-ĭng), *Irish.* A dance; a refrain.

**fag.** Abbr. of *fagotti*.

**fag'ot**, *E.*, **Fagott** (fä-gôt'), *G.*, **fagot'-to**, *I.* 1. A bassoon. 2. A reed-stop (also **Fagottzug**). **fagottino** (tē'no), *I.* A small bassoon. **Fagottist** (fä-gôt-test'), *G.* **fagottista** (tēs'-tä), *I.* A performer on the bassoon. **fagotto contro**, *I.* A bassoon, an octave, a fifth, or a fourth lower. **fagotto'ne.** A large obs. bassoon, an octave lower.

**fah.** Fa in Tonic sol-fa.

**Fähnenmarsch** (fä'-nĕn-märsh), *G.* The march played when the colours are lodged.

**faible** (fĕb'l) *F.* Weak. **temps f.** Weak-beat.

**faire** (făr), *F.* To do, make. **f. des fredons.** A trill. **faites bien sentir la mélodie** (fĕt-bĭ-ăṅ-săṅ-tēr lä mä-lō-dē), *F.* Keep the melody very distinct.

**fa-la.** 1. An old refrain. 2. A song with such refrain, or a dance. **falal-el'la**, *I.* A nonsense song.

**fall.** 1. A cadence. 2. Vide FLY.

**falo'tico**, *I.* Fantastic.

**falsa** (fäl'-sä) (or o), *I.,* **false**, *E.,* **falsch** (fälsh), *G.* False, wrong, out of tune. **false accent.** Accent removed from the first to the second or fourth beat. **f. bordone.** (a) Faburden. (b) The reciting-notes. **f. cadence.** An imperfect or interrupted cadence. **f. fifth.** An imperfect fifth. **f. relation.** (a) The appearance simultaneously or consecutively in different voices of the same notes chromatically altered, as C sharp and C flat, implying a disagreement or incompatibility. (b) The appearance of the tritone (q. v.) in different voices. Though strictly forbidden in the text-books, late composers ignore the rule altogether. **f. string.** An ill-made string giving a bad tone. **f. triad.** The diminished triad having a false fifth.

**Falsett** (fäl-zĕt'), *G.,* **falset'to**, *I.* 1. The top or artificial register of the voice, having an unnatural or effeminate sound. 2. One who uses this register.

**fan'cy.** 1. A slight tune. 2. A fantasy.

**fandan'go**, *Sp.* A popular Spanish dance in triple time, accompanied with castanets (or tambourine) and guitar, the dance being interpolated between vocal couplets.

**fanfare**, *E.* (pron. in *F.* făṅ-fär), **fanfara** (fän-fä'-rä), *I.* 1. A trumpet-flourish. 2. A brass-band.

**fantaisie** (fäṅ-tĕ-zē), *F.,* **fantasia** (fän-tä-zē'ä), *I.,* **Fantasie** (fän-tä-zē'), *G.* 1. Fantasy, caprice, a composition free in spirit and form. 2. An ar-

peggiated prelude. 3. A potpou 4. An improvisation. 5. Forme a work, vocal or instrumental, full **free imitation free fantasia fantasy**, same as Developme Vide FORM. **fantasio'so**, *I.* F tastic. **fantasiren** (zē'rĕn), *G.* improvise.

**fantas'tico**, **fantasticamen'te**, **fantastique** (fän-täs-tēk), *F.,* **fanta tisch** (fän-täs'-tĭsh), *G.* Capricio

**faran'dola**, *I.,* **farandole** (fär-äṅ-dō **farandoule** (fär-äṅ-dool), *F.* A c cle dance in 6-8 time.

**farneticamen'te**, *I.* Deliriously.

**farsa in musica** (moo'zi-ka), *I.* burletta.

**farsia** (fär'sĭ-ä), *I.* A canticle Italian and Latin sung at Catho festivals.

**fascia** (fä'-shä), *I.* 1. A tie. 2. rib.

**fasto'so**, **fastosamen'te**, *I.* Po pous(ly).

**fattura** (fät-too'-rä), *I.* Vide FACTUR

**faucette** (fō-sĕt), **fausset** (fō-sä), *l* Falsetto.

**faux** (fō) or **fausse** (fōs), *F.* Fals out of tune. **f. accord** (fō zăk-kō A dissonance. **f. bourdon** (fō-boo dôṅ). Vide FABURDEN. **f. quint** Imperfect fifth.

**F clef.** The bass-clef. Vide CLEF.

**F-dur** (ĕf-door), *G.* F major.

**feathering.** The bowing of swi staccato.

**Federklavier** (fā-dĕr-klä-fēr'), Spinet.

**feeders.** Small bellows to supp large.

**Feier** (fī'ĕr), *G.* Festival, celebratio **F.-gesang.** Anthem. **feierlic** Festive, solemn. **F.-keit.** Soler nity.

**feigned voice.** Falsetto voice.

**feilen** (fī-lĕn), *G.* To polish.

**fein** (fīn), *G.* Fine, refined.

**feint.** In drum music, a figure.

**feinte** (fĕnt), *F.* Old name for sem tone ; accidental.

**Feld** (fĕlt), *G.* Field. **F. flöte.** peasant flute. **F. Kunstpfeife**

(koonst'pfī-fĕr). A military musician.
**Feldmusik** (fĕlt-moo-zĕk'). Military music. **Feldrohr** (rōr). *G.* A rural pipe. **F.-stück.** A cavalry call. **F. -ton.** The key-note of a military wind instr. **F. -trompete.** Military trumpet.

**'rial.** Non-festal, secular.

**r'ma,** *I.* Firm. **fermamen'te,** *I.* Firmly.

**rmare il tuono.** Vide MESSA DI VOCE.

**r'mate,** *E.* (in *G.* fĕr-mä'-tĕ), **fermata** (fĕr-mä'-tä), *I.* 1. A symbol ⌒ or ⌄ above or below a note, rest or bar indicating a long pause upon it, *f. ad libitum*, often occurring before a cadenza. 2. A stop, on the violin.

**rmato** (mä'-tō). *I.* Firmly, **fermezza** (fĕr-mĕd'-zä). Firmness. **fermo** (fĕr'mo). Firm. Vide CANTUS FIRMUS

**rmement** (fĕrm-mäń). *F.* Firmly.

**erne** (fĕr'nĕ), *G.* Distance. **wie aus der F.** (vē-ows-dĕr). As if from the distance. **Fern-flöte.** A covered 8-ft. stop. **Fern-werk.** Echo-organ.

**roce** (fä-rō'-chĕ), **ferocemen'te,** *I.* Fierce(ly). **ferocità** (fä-rō-chĭ-tä'). Fierceness.

**rtig** (fĕr-tĭkh), *G.* Ready, nimble. **F.-keit** (kīt). Dexterity.

**rvemment** (fär-vĕ-mäń), *F* Fervently.

**rven'te, fer'vido,** *I.* Fervent. **ferventemen'te, fervidamen'te.** Vehemently.

**es** (fĕs), *G.* The note F♭. **Feses** (fĕs'ĕs). F double flat.

**est** (fĕsht), *G.* 1. Feast, festival. 2. Firm, steady. **Festigkeit** (fĕs-tĭkh-kīt). Firmness, steadiness. **festlich** (fĕst-lĭkh). Festive, solemn. **Festlichkeit.** Solemnity. **Festlied.** A festive-song. **Festouvertüre.** A brilliant overture. **Festzeit** (tsīt). Festival-time.

**estivo** (fĕs-tē'vō), **festivamen'te,** *I.* Gay(ly). **festività** (fĕs-tē-vĭ-tä'). Festivity, gayety.

**esto'so,** *I.* Merry cheerful, gay.

**Feuer** (foi'ĕr), *G* Fire, ardour, passion. **feurig** (rĭkh). Ardent, passionate.

**fff.** Abb. of *Fortissimo.*

**F holes.** Vide F.

**fiacco** (fĭ-äk'kō), *I.* Feeble, languishing.

**fiasco** (fĭ-äs'-kō), *I.* A failure; not so used in Italy.

**fiato** (fĭ-ä'-tō), *I.* Breath; voice.

**fictus(a)-(um),** *L.* "Feigned." 1. Vide FA. 2. **musica ficta.** Former name for music transposed.

**fiddle.** Violin. **iron f.** An arrangement of nails or rods played with a bow, inv. by Jn. Wilde, 18th cent. **fiddler.** Violinist, commonly a poor player. **fiddlestick.** Violin-bow.

**Fidel** (fē'-dĕl), *G.* Violin.

**fi'des,** *L* 1. A string. 2. A stringed instr. **fid'icen.** One who plays a stringed instr. **fidicina.** A woman-player.

**fidic'ula,** *L.* A small lute.

**fiducia** (fĭ-doo̅'-chä), *I.* Confidence.

**Fiedel** (fē'dl). *G.* A violin. **Strohfiedel.** Xylophone. **F.-bogen** (bōkh'-ĕn). A violin-bow. **F.-brett** (brĕt). A squeaky violin. **Fiedler** (fēt'-lĕr). A fiddler.

**fiel.** An old name for violin.

**field-music.** Martial music.

**fier** (fē-ăr), **fière** (fĭ-är). *F.* Proud, lofty, fierce. **fièrement** (fĭ-är-mäń). Fiercely. **fièrté** (f'yär-tä'). Fierceness.

**fiero** (fe-ä'-rō), **fieramen'te,** *I.* Fierce(ly). **fierezza** (rĕd'-zä). Fierceness.

**fife.** 1. A 6-holed octave cross-flute, usually in the key of F or B♭, chiefly used in military music, differing from the piccolo in lacking keys, compass d'-d'''. 2. A 2-foot stop.

**fif'faro,** *I.* Fife.

**f.fre** (fēfr), *F.* 1. A fife. 2. A fifer. 3. An harmonium-stop.

**fifteenth.** 1. An interval of two octaves. 2. A 2-ft. stop, two octaves above the diapasons.

**fifth.** 1. The fifth tone of a scale, the dominant. 2. An interval containing five tones, the extremes included.

# THE MUSICAL GUIDE

128

as C-G (the ratio being 2 : 3). The
tonic and the dominant of a key con-
stitute a *perfect* (or less strictly, *major*) *fifth*. To widen the interval by
lowering the lower (or raising the upper) tone a half-step results in an *augmented* (or *superfluous, extreme,
sharp* or *pluperfect*) *fifth*, as c-g♯, or
c♭-g ; to narrow the interval a semitone by raising the lower or lowering
the upper tone a half-step results
in a *diminished* (or *imperfect, false,
flat, minor* or *defective*) *fifth*. Two
parts or voices according to the rules
may not progress by perfect fifths
either in *consecutive* or *parallel* manner, whether the fifths are *open* or
(*covered, concealed*), *hidden*, (q. v.).
Though this rule is the very ABC
of harmonic law, it is not justified by
science, by history, or by latest practice. **Circle of fifths.** Vide TEM-
PERAMENT. **fifthy.** With the second
partial (a fifth) noticeably marked.
**Figur** (fē-goor'), *G.* A figure, or numeral.
**figura** (fē-goo'-rä), *L.* and *I.* Vide
FIGURE. **f. liga'ta.** A ligature. **f.
muta** (moo-ta). A rest. **f. obli'qua.**
In old music, an oblique symbol indicating that two superimposed notes
(as g-b) were to be sung obliquely
(thus g-b-b-g).
**figural,** *E.* (in *G.* fē-goo-räl'). Figurate. **F.-gesang.** Cantus figuratus, counterpoint.
**figuration.** 1. The use of figures or
ornamented passages in the variation
of a theme. 2. The writing or the
filling out of figured bass. 3. In
cpt. the interpolation of figures,
changing notes, etc.
**figurato** (fē-goo-rä'-tō), *I.*, **figuré** (fē-
gü-rä), *F.* **figurate,** or **figured.** 1.
Ornamented with figures, hence
florid, free. 2. Provided with numerals, as **figured bass.** Vide BASS 6,
and CHORD.
**figure,** *E.* (in *F.* pron. fī-gür). 1. A
pattern or design in grouped notes
which may be repeated variously. 2.
**A numeral. f. of diminution. A**

number diminishing the duration of
note.
**fil** (fēl), *F.* Thread (of a string).
**filar il tuono** or **la voce** (fē-lär
too-ō'-nō or lä vō' chě), *I.*, **filer
son** or **la voix** (fē-lā rŭṅ sôṅ or
vwä), *F.* To draw the tone out to
thread of sound.
**filarmo'nico,** *I.* Music-loving.
**filet de voix** (fē-lā dŭ vwä), *F.*
mere thread of tone.
**filling-up.** 1. Of parts, those of ha
monic but not melodic use. 2.
stops, mutation.
**filo** (fē'-lō), *I.* Thread. **f. di voc**
Softest possible tone.
**filpen** (fēl'-pěn), *G.* Vide FISTULIRE
**fi'lum,** *L.* Stem, of a note.
**fin** (fǎṅ), *F.* The end ; fine. **f. à q**
(fǎ nä kē). End here.
**fi'nal.** The note of rest in churc
modes corresponding to our Toni
in authentic modes the *F.* is on t
first degree ; in plagal, on the 4
These are called *regular fina*
Others occur frequently and are *irr*
*ular* or *confinals*. Vide MODES.
**close.** A finishing cadence.
**finale** (fē-nä'-lě, *I. ;* in *F.* fī-näl).
The conclusio.ι, usually elaborate,
the closing chorus of an act in oper
in sonatas, symphonies, an indepen
ent movement. 2. A final.
**final'is,** *L.* Vide ACCENTUS ECCLE
ASTICI.
**fine** (fē'-ně), *I.* The end ; it may a
pear sometimes before a *da ca*
sign, in which case the movement
to be played to the repeat-bar a
then repeated to the Fine, where
ends.
**Finger** (In *E.* fĭng'-gěr ; in *G.* fĭng
ěr). Finger. **F.-bildner, finger-d**
**veloper.** A device for keeping t
last joint of the fingers up ; in
by Seeber. **F.-brett.** Finger-boa
**F.-fertigkeit.** Agility. **F.-leit**
(lĭt'-ěr). The chiroplast. **F.-sat**
**F.-setzung.** Fingering. **Enger**
**gedehnter, Fingersatz.** Close (
stretched) fingering. **F.-wechs**
(věkhs'l). Change of fingers. **finge**

oard. In a stringed instr. the neck
n which the strings are stopped.

nger-cymbals. Tiny cymbals
xed on the fingers. finger-holes.
he holes on wind-instrs. by which
he pitch is regulated.

gering. 1. The manner of using
ne fingers on instrs. 2. The symbols
ndicating a fingering. In the *Ger-
nan F.* the thumb is marked 1, the
ngers 2, 3, 4, 5 ; in an older German
nethod the thumb was marked by a
rcle O ; in the *English*, or *Ameri-
an F.* the thumb is marked with a
ross, the fingers, 1, 2, 3, 4.

re il tuono, *I.* Vide MESSA DI
OCE.

ite. Of a canon, not repeated, end-
ng with the finish of the theme ; not
infinite."

to(a) (fĭ-nĕ′-tō), *I.* Finished.

(fē′-nō), *I.* To, as far as, till.

o(a) (fĕn′-tō), *I.* Feigned. cadenza
Vide CADENCE (f). fa finto. Vide
A.

o(a) (fĭ-ô′-kō), *I.* Hoarse, faint.
ochetto. Rather hoarse. fiocchez-
a (fē-ō-kĕd′-zä). Hoarseness.

e (fĭ-ō′-rĕ), *I.* Flower. a f. di
abbre. Lightly on the lip.

eggiare (fē-ō-rĕd-jä′-rĕ), *I.* To
dd figures to.

et′to, *I.* A little ornament.

iscente (fē-ō-rĭ-shĕn′-tĕ), *I.*, fiorito
ē-ō-rē′-tō). Florid. fioritezza (fē-ō-
-tĕd′-zä). Embellishment.

itura (fē-ō-rĭ-too′rä) (pl. e), *I.*
lorid ornament.

t. 1. The highest voice-part or
tring ; the lowest line or space. 2.
unison or prime.

(fēs), *G.* The note F♯. Fis-dur
ēs-door). F♯ major. Fis-fis. The
ote F double sharp. Fis-moll. F♯
ninor.

tel (fĭsh-tel), *G.* Falsetto (also F.-
timme).

tola (fēs′-tō-lä), *I.*, fis′tula, *L.*
reed, a pipe. f. dulcis. The *flûte
bec.* f. germanica. German flute.
panis or f. pastoralis. The Pan-
ean pipes. f. pastorica. An oaten

pipe used in Roman theatres to express disapprobation. fistulator, *L.*,
fistulato′re, *I.* A piper. fistuli-
ren (fĭs-too-lē′rĕn), *G.* 1. To sing falsetto. 2. Of organ-pipes, to over-blow.

fith′ele. Old English name for fiddle.

fixed-Do. That system of solmisation
in which the syllables are fixed, i. e.,
do is given always to C (sharp, flat,
or natural), re to D, etc.

fixed tone or intonation. Used of
the piano and instrs. in which the
player cannot change the pitch of a
tone, as on the violin, etc.

Flachflöte (fläkh′flä-tĕ), *G.* 1. Flageolet. 2. An organ-stop.

flag. 1. Abbr. for *flageolet*, or *fla-
olet tones*. 2. A hook.

flageolet′, *E.* (*F.* flăzh-ō-lā), Flage-
olett (flä-jĕ-ō-lĕt′), *G.*, flagioletta
(flä-jō-lĕt′ta), *I.* 1. A small flute played
at the end, compass g′-b‴ flat.
double f. An instr. with 2 different-
sized flageolets meeting in one mouthpiece, inv. by Bainbridge, 1800. 2.
flageolet or flageolet-tones or
Töne. Vide HARMONICS. 3. A 1-
or 2-ft. stop.

flam. In drum music a grace note,
*close f.*, as short as possible ; *open f.*,
with a brief interval.

Fla′minenorgel, *G.* Pyrophone.

Flaschinett (fläsh′ĭ-nĕt′), *G.* The
flageolet.

flat. 1. A symbol (♭) lowering the note
before which it is placed one semitone ; placed in the signature it affects every note occurring on its line
or space. The double flat (♭♭),
formerly a *great flat*, lowers the note
two semitones. flat fifth. Vide
FIFTH. flat tuning. Of a lute tuned
to the former lower French pitch. 2.
*As a verb*, to lower a note a semitone ; preferably to flatten.

flatter la corde (flăt-tā lá′ kôrd), *F.*
To flatter or caress the string.

flautando (flä-oo-tän′dō), flautato
(tä′to), *I.* 1. Drawing the bow gently across the strings near the bridge,
producing a "fluty" tone. 2. Producing harmonics.

**flauto** (fla'oo-tō), *I.* Flute. **flautis'-ta.** Performer on the flute. **flau-tino** (tē'-no). 1. A small octave-flute. 2. A piccolo. 3. Same as *flautando.* **f. piccolo.** The shrill octave-flute. **f. a bec'co.** Beak-flute. **f. alto.** A tenor-flute used in bands. **f. amabile.** An organ-stop. **f. amoroso.** A 4-foot organ-stop. **f. dolce.** 1. A beak-flute. 2. An organ-stop. **flauto'ne.** A large bass-flute. **f. tedesco, transverso, tra-verso.** 1. The German or transverse flute. 2. An organ-stop.

**flebile** (flā'-bĭ-lĕ), **flebilmen'te,** *I.* Sad-(ly), doleful(ly).

**flessibile** (flĕs-sē'-bĭ-lā), *I.* Flexible. **flessibilità** (lĭ-tä'), *I.* Flexibility.

**Flick'opera,** *G.* An opera with new words to old tunes.

**fling.** A Scotch Highland dance in 4-4 time.

**F-Löcher,** *G.* F holes. Vide F.

**flon-flon** (flôṅ-flôṅ), *F.* A refrain to old vaudevilles ; hence, trash.

**flor'id.** Ornamental, embellished.

**Flöte** (flā'tĕ), *G.* Flute. **flötchen** (flĕt'-khĕn). A little flute. **F.-bass.** A bass-flute. **flöten.** To play the flute. **F.-spieler.** A flute-player. **F.-stimme, F.-zug.** A flute-stop. **Flötenwerk.** A small organ with only flue-pipes. **F. traverso.** 1. The transverse flute. 2. An organ-stop. **Flötist** (flā'-tēst). A flute-player.

**flour'ish.** 1. A trumpet-fanfare. 2. An embellishment.

**flüchtig** (flükh'tĭkh), *G.* Light(ly). **Flüchtigkeit** (kīt). Fleetness.

**flue-pipe-stop-work.** Vide PIPE.

**Flügel** (flü'-gĕl), *G.* "Wing," hence, 1. A wing-shaped instr. ; or the modern grand piano. 2. The ear of a pipe. **F.-harfe.** A small table-harp with upright sound-board. **F.-horn.** 1. A bugle. 2. A keyed bugle or other keyed brass instrument.

**flute,** *E.,* **flu'ta,** *L.,* **flûte** (flüt), *F.* 1. Now generally used of the *transverse* (or *cross,* or *German*) *flute.* The *beak-* (or *direct*) *flute* (in various sizes) obsolete. This latter was blown one end. The *cross-flute* is blo through a hole in the side near larger end. It is a long tube (f merly slightly conical) with the lar end closed. Usually made of wo it is sometimes of silver or other m als. The principle is that of the fl pipe (vide PIPE), and the tone clear, pure, and especially rich in lower range, which is too little us A very ancient instrument (appe ing often with two tubes and mouthpiece as the *double-flute,* tube furnishing probably a m drone-bass); its modern form o much to the improvements of Boe and controls with its keys fourt orifices, with an extreme range b-c'''♯. It is made in six sizes cluding the *piccolo,* or *octave*-fl and sounds as written, is non-tra posing. The normal flute is the there are two others in D flat an flat. The *piccolo* is in the same k but the lower octave is not used is written an octave lower than sounds. A *fourth* (or *quart*) fl sounds a fourth higher than the mal flute. 2. An organ-stop. **flu work.** Vide STOP. **harmonic f. f. armonique.** An organ-stop. **tave-f.** The piccolo. **pastora shepherd's f.** A short beak-fl **f. à bec** (ä bĕk), *F.,* **Schnab flöte** (shnä-bĕl), *G.* Beak-flute. **allemande** (ăl-mänd), *F.* The cr **flute. f. conique** (kôn-ēk), *F.* Conical flute. 2. An organ-st **f. d'amour** (dä-moor). 1. An solete flute in A or in B flat. A 4- or 8-ft. stop. **f. d'Ang terre** (däṅ-glŭ-tăr). The flaged **f. du Poitou**( dŭ pwä-too). The b pipe. **f. douce** (doos). The be flute. **f. minor** (mē-nôr). A 2 4-foot stop. **f. octaviante** (ôk vĭ-änt). Octave-flute ; an org stop. **f. ouverte** (oo-vărt). An o stop. **f. traversière** (trä-vĕr-sĭ The cross-flute.

.e, *F.* *As a direction*—"use har-
1onics." flûtée (tā). Fluty.
The lid covering a key-board.
noll (ĕf-môl), *G.* F minor.
:o, *I.* Fire, passion. focosamen'-
e. Ardently. focosis'simo. Very
rdent. focoso. Passionate.
·lietto (fōl-yĕt'-to), *I.* A part which
ontains all the obbligato passages,
sed often by conductors instead of a
core.
re des enfants (fwär-dā-zäṅ-fäṅ), *F.*
" Children's fair." Toy symphony.
s (fwä), *F.* Time. première f.

(prŭm-yĕr). The first time. deuxième f. (dŭz-yĕm). The second time.
deux f. (dŭ-fwä). Twice. dernière f. The last time.
folia (fō-lē'-ä), *Sp.*, follia(e) di spagna
(spän-yä), *I.*, folies d'espagne
(fō-lē-dĕs-spīn), *F.* 1. A slow Spanish solo-dance in 3-4 time. 2. A
species of air with variations.
folia'ted. Ornamented.
folk-music. The body of folk-songs
dances, etc.
folk-song. A strongly racial popula:
song that has become a tradition.

## Folk-Song.

### By H. E. KREHBIEL.

THE bea:ing which Folk-music (*i.e.*, Folk-song and Folk-dance) has
on national schools of composition gives propriety to an attempt at
accurate definition of the subject to which this article is devoted.
k-song is not popular song in the sense in which the word is most fre-
:ntly used, but the song of the folk ; not only the song admired of the
•ple but, in a strict sense, the song created by the people. It is a body or
:try and music which has come into existence without the influence of
iscious art, as a spontaneous utterance, filled with characteristic expression
he feelings of a people. Such songs are marked by certain peculiarities of
·thm, form, and melody which are traceable, more or less clearly, to racial
national) temperament, modes of life, climatic and political conditions,
graphical environment and language. Some of these elements, the spirit-
, are elusive, but others can be determined and classified. Peoples living
northern climates, for instance, are predisposed to the minor mode, which
meiancholy for its most marked characteristic. Here the influence is
erally climatic and geographical. But peoples living in cheerful and salu-
ous climes may also be dominated by gloom if they have long suffered under
oressive political and social conditions. ¶Both propositions are illustrated
the case of Russian Folk-song, which is overwhelmingly minor in spite of
fact that the Czar's empire extends over nearly thirty degrees of latitude
l has a mean temperature varying from thirty-two degrees Fahrenheit at
changel, to fifty-eight degrees in the Caucasus. It would seem to be a
adox, moreover, that heavy-hearted song should be paired almost univer-
y with singularly boisterous and energetic dances ; but the reason of this
omes plain when it is remembered that a measured and decorous mode of

popular amusement is the general expression of equable popular life, wh
wild and desperate gayety is frequently the sign of reaction from sufferi
There is a gayety of despair as well as of contentment and happine
¶ Intervallic peculiarities are more difficult to explain than rhythmic, a
may be said to be survivals of primitive artistic conditions.  The mode
scale was an evolution, not an inspiration, and the study of savage music d
closes many rudimentary forms of it.  The most idiomatic music of the Fir
is confined to the first five tones of the minor scale, which was the comp
of the ancient Finnish harp—the *kantele*.  Old Irish and Scotch songs sha
the pentatonic scale (*i.e.*, the modern diatonic scale omitting the fourth a
seventh steps) with the popular music of China, Japan, and Siam.  In
songs of the negro slaves of America, I have found the same scale, a ma
scale with a flat seventh and a minor scale with a raised sixth, to be predo
nant.  César Cui mentions the prevalence in Russia of two major scales, c
without the fourth, the other without the third and seventh.  Hungar
melodies make frequent use of the interval called the augmented secor
which compasses three semitones and is common to Oriental music.  Th
is a hint in this of the origin of the Magyars, who are not Slavs, as is so co
monly supposed, but Scythians ; they belong to the Finno-Ungrian sto
and are more nearly related to the Turks than to their neighbours, the Po
and Russians.  The profusion of ornament which characterises Hungar
music is an importation from the Orient by the Gypsies who, while
national musicians of Hungary, are nevertheless a Hindu people.  ¶ Th
facts, gathered at random from the vast but as yet unexplored storehouse
Folk-music indicate the possibility of using the study as an aid in the det
mination of many things in ethnology and ethnography ; for Folk-sc
elements have a marvellous tenacity of life.  In the study of Folk-mus
however, the purpose of the student should be primarily to discover and
possible, account for the elements which differentiate the creations of c
race, people, or tribe from those of another.  This done it will be possible
explain and describe the distinguishing characteristics of the national scho
of composition based upon Folk-song idioms, such as the Scandinavi
Russian, Polish, Bohemian, and Hungarian.

**folk-tone.**  The folk-song manner or
spirit (**cf. Volkston**).

**fondamental(e),** (fôn-dă-män-tăl) *F.*,
**fondamentale** (tä'lĕ), *I.*  Fundamental. **son f.** Root.  **basse,** or **basso, f.**  Vide BASS 6.

**fondamen'to,** *I.*  Fundamental bass.

**fonds d'orgue** (fôn dôrg), *F.*  The
foundation-stops.

**foot.**  1. The unit of metre, a disti
rhythmic unit of two or more sy
bles.  2. Of a pipe, the part below
mouth.  3. Old term for a refrain, c
drone-bass.  4. A unit for the des
nation of the pitch of pipes and ins
arrived at as follows.  Sound trav
1056 feet per second, the tone $C_{,,}$
33 vibrations a second : 1056 ÷ 3.

32 feet, the length of one sound-wave ; a 32-foot pipe will therefore sound $C_{,,}$. The pipe giving C (two octaves below middle C) is about 8 feet long. This is taken as the normal length, and while the pipes that make up a so-called 8-foot stop (q. v.) decrease in length as they ascend the scale, they are considered as belonging to the 8-foot tone and they sound as written or played, i. e., when an 8-foot stop is on and the key of mid. C is depressed, mid. C sounds, etc. If this key is depressed when a 4-foot stop is on, the tone an octave higher sounds ; when a 32-foot is on, a tone two octaves lower sounds ; the 2-foot and 1-foot stops produce tones respectively two and three octaves higher than the key depressed. A stop then is named from the length of its longest pipe and lowest tone. From this use arises the designation of instruments by *foot-measure*, or *foot-tone ;* an instr. sounding *as written* (e. g., the flute) is called an 8-foot instr., one sounding an octave higher (e. g., the piccolo-flute) is called a 4-foot instr. Furthermore, this designation is used of octaves ; the letters in the great octave (vide PITCH) are known as 8-foot (as 8-ft. C, D, etc.), those in the small octave, as 4-ft. *c, d,* etc. ; those in the once-accented as 2-foot, and those in the twice-accented as 1-foot. The word *foot* is sometimes abbreviated by an ( ´ ) as 8´, 16´.

The metrical system has been applied with much inaccuracy ; 8-feet $= \frac{5}{2}$ metre ; 4-feet $= \frac{5}{4}$ m. ; 2-feet $= \frac{5}{8}$ m. ; 16-ft. $=$ 5 m. ; 32-ft. $=$ 10 m. ;

Quinte (10 $\frac{2}{3}$, 5 $\frac{1}{3}$, 2 $\frac{2}{3}$, 1 $\frac{1}{3}$, and $\frac{2}{3}$ feet) $= \frac{10}{3}, \frac{5}{3}, \frac{5}{6}, \frac{5}{12}$ and $\frac{5}{24}$ metres respectively.

Tierce (6 $\frac{2}{5}$, 3 $\frac{1}{5}$, 1 $\frac{3}{5}$, and $\frac{4}{5}$ feet) $= \frac{10}{5}$ (or 2), $\frac{5}{5}$ (or 1), $\frac{5}{10}$ ($\frac{1}{2}$), and $\frac{5}{20}$ ($\frac{1}{4}$) metres respectively.

**foot-key.** Pedal-key.

**forbidden.** Contrary to musical grammar. Vide HARMONY.

**foreign.** Alien to the given key, or tonality.

**forlana** (för-lä´-nä), *I.*, **forlane** (fôr-län), *F.* A lively Venetian dance in 6-8 or 6-4 time.

## Form.

### By John F. Runciman.

A DEFINITION of Form would have this disadvantage : that it would convey absolutely nothing save to those who understood perfectly what the meaning is ; and, further, it would occupy much [m]ore space than is here available. So instead of trying to reach a perfect [de]finition, let us try what is a much better plan from the lay point of view—[let] us trace the growth of the mass of principles and their methods of appli[ca]tion which are included in this one comprehensive term Form. ¶ In the [be]ginning, we may assume, music was without Form, though not always [qu]ite void. The savage tootled his melody, caring nothing about repeating [ph]rases, nothing about middle sections, nothing about development. But in [th]e earliest traditional melodies that come down to us we find the germ of all [th]at is now known as Form. ¶ In any collection of popular songs the reader

will find examples built on the following plan :—first a strain is delivered
then another strain, in another key, is delivered ; and finally the first strain
repeated, bringing the whole thing to a satisfactory close. Let us consid
for a moment the inwardness of this arrangement. No one wants to sing on
one strain and be done with it. To sing a second strain in the same ke
would prove tiresome, so a feeling of relief, of variety is produced when th
thing is lengthened by the addition of a second strain in a new key. But
end in the new key would be quite unsatisfactory : it would be like breakin
off in the middle of a sentence. So the first key is re-introduced and th
whole song rounded off and made to end with a sense of perfect complet
ness by a repetition of the first strain in the first key. ¶From this simp
example, then, we may infer the whole object of Form : it is to secur
whether in songs or in instrumental movements or in choruses, a piece
music sufficiently long and combining variety with unity. ¶Length, variet
and unity—to attain these is, so far as instrumental music, music witho
words, is concerned, the whole aim and object of Form. When once mus
is used in association with words, other than the simplest lyrics, other co
siderations enter. These we will touch upon later ; let us for the prese
try to get as far as the first instrumental music written in anything approac
ing regular Form. Naturally this grew out of the polyphonic vocal musi
which came before it. If we examine the old music, in a great deal of
we find nothing corresponding to Form as we understand the word to-da
A phrase is delivered by one voice. Let us call that phrase A ; it may l
two, four, or six bars, or indeed any length. After the first voice has su
it a second voice takes it up, while the first voice proceeds to a second then
or strain which we will call B—a third voice enters with A, the second tak
up B, while the first proceeds to yet another new strain, C. Roughly, th
is the way in which whole movements are spun out. The modulations a
more or less haphazard and dictated entirely by the composer's desire
achieve expression : there is nothing done in obedience to any rule. Th
first instrumental pieces are built after this plan. ¶These pieces may l
compared to the harmless amœba, the tiny speck of protoplasm which swir
about, sans eyes, ears, mouth or limbs : simply a shapeless bit of life capab
of existing, so long as it remains small. But even the older composers we
not content to let their musical creations remain small. They wanted l
display their skill in weaving a longer web of music ; some of them ha
something to say, something which demanded length ; most of them had th
architectonical instinct which forces man to build out of any material he ca
lay his hands on. Now a long movement, a too long movement, spun o
the old plan necessarily becomes tedious, monotonous and difficult to follow—
it is at best like a very long sentence or paragraph with never a comma or

iod. Moreover, if the music is all the same, if it is homogeneous, it is
rious that one of the principal methods of getting expression, contrast, is
ed out. Last, no musical architecture is possible with a mere series of
sical phrases that can only be compared with a lot of strips of wood more
less carelessly nailed together. So gradually the principle of the popular
g already referred to was adopted, probably, nay, certainly, quite uncon-
ously, and there was evolved a very simple and useful Form, one which
been vastly used by all composers and will doubtless be used constantly
the future, however music may develop. ¶In place of the one strain of
simple song one section consisting of many strains was introduced. Fol-
ing that, in a new key, for the sake of variety, came a second section,
o consisting of many strains. Finally the first section was repeated in the
ginal key, bringing the whole movement to a satisfying conclusion. Of
s form there are hundreds of examples in the shorter movements of Haydn,
ozart and Beethoven. When a more modern composer uses it, however,
by no means sticks to a couple of keys. Our sense of tonality has grown,
perceive relations between keys, which our forefathers were totally unable
perceive ; and the first and second sections may both pass through many
s. But the general principle remains the same. Now this very excel-
t Form is also very primitive. In Haydn's time, and before it, the in-
ct to build, to crystallise, music was still at work ; more than ever com-
ers wanted to express something ; and more than ever it was necessary to
ure contrast. ¶So what is commonly called *sonata form* came to be
ented. In the simplest examples of this a first theme—corresponding to
first strain of a popular song, as aforesaid—is announced. Then comes
second theme in a fresh key. But after that, instead of a repetition of
first section, there is what is called a *development* or *working-out section*,
which both first and second themes are treated with all the skill and fancy
composer possesses and shown in a dozen or more unsuspected lights.
ly after that does the first theme return, and then the second theme.
is is called the *Reprise*. But the second theme, if repeated in the key in
ich it first appeared, would of course end the work inconclusively : where-
e it is placed, on its last appearance, in the key of the first theme. ¶The
enious reader will observe that if variety is obtained only by change of
then there would be no more variety from the beginning of what is called
reprise. Nor, for that matter, is the mere change from the original key
hat of the dominant enough to produce any great variety. The second
ne therefore is made as unlike the first in every respect as possible : if the
, is bold and rugged, the second may be gentle and soothing ; if the first
ves rapidly, the second may be long drawn out ; if rhythm is strongly
ked in the first, the second is in a more subtle and elusive rhythm—in
contrast is secured by any of the thousand ways open to the composer.

and quite easily understood when heard, though anything but easy to
scribe. ¶Now if we take a symphonic movement of Mozart we find a fi
theme of marked character ; after its delivery (and perhaps brief expansio
all the orchestra goes to work at a cadence in a hammer-and-tongs fash
and lets you know unmistakably that you have reached the end of a sectio
Then the second theme is announced, clearly. Then we have "develo
ment" in which the old tunes are turned into new ones as unlike the old
possible, yet obviously growing out of them. Finally we have the repri
and then the *coda*, a few bars in the case of Haydn and Mozart stuck on
make an effective conclusion. ¶This is simple sonata form. There was
enormous lot of waste in it : those thumping conventional series of chords
the end of each section, for example, never mean and never did mean an
thing. At the time they were written the tendency to formulate music,
get conscious control of the material of music, was at its strongest ; one
the most powerful desires of Mozart and Haydn was to make their form
clear and distinct as possible ; and to that everything else was, in an em
gency, sacrificed. In fact, composers of that time seem to have felt as kee
pleasure in the mere regularity and balance of the various parts of moveme
as in the poetic and sheer musical quality of the parts, even when the bala
was secured by the introduction of conventional padding altogether at v
with beauty and expression, quite destructive of both. ¶With Beethov
came a change. His music must at first have been very difficult to und
stand, for instead of the trumpet and drum passages marking the close of
different sections, one section leads straight into another by means of passa
of as high musical and poetic quality as any other portions of his moveme
Further, he went in for third themes following the second (the second a
third being so proportioned as to balance the first), and he mightily exten
the coda. Instead of a few noisy bars to end up each movement he star
out and developed his theme in new ways, thus adding a fourth main sect
to the three existing before his time—the first, in which the themes are
nounced ; the second, in which they are developed ; the third, in wh
they are repeated. This was an inevitable corollary of the enormous incre
he made in the size of the forms he used. After such huge themes, s
lengthy developments, a few chords were not sufficient to wind up ; be
was needed by the symphonic movement before it could be felt to be sa
factory, just as much as a tail is needed by a kite before it will asce
¶Let us pause for a moment to sum up. In the early days music had fo
as a flower or a blade of grass has form ; each piece grew more or less
haphazard into some shape, starting from its one theme. The utmost t
could be done in that way was done by Bach in his fugues. But the fu
itself was the result of the tendency to formulate music, to press it into
bonds of strict rule, to get a conscious mastery of the material. That t

y, together with the desire to express more complex emotions and the
al instinct of man to build, resulted in certain clearly defined forms, with
outlines, so to speak. Beethoven came and softened the outlines, hiding
ones of music, as it were, under a beautiful expressive veil of tone.
form is there just the same, and can easily be grasped by anyone who
the trouble to listen carefully. The fact that for the sake of expression,
odiously varied his themes on their repetition, does not alter the fact
hey are repeated in a satisfying way. The reader who can follow the
of say the first movement of the Eroica symphony (a symphony being
an orchestral sonata) understands not only the abstract principles of
but the manner of applying those principles to the concrete. ¶The
s of these applications are various forms—the Rondo, the Minuet and
: all are based on one of the two plans ; in short pieces one theme is
set forth and finished with ; in longer pieces variety and unity are se-
. by two or three (or even more) themes of different character placed
ferent keys. The mere setting of themes one after another can always
e variety of a kind ; but whether there is at the same time unity depends
ly upon whether the composer is or is not an artist. There is no rule
at : only genius can solve the problem. So much then for pure music.
e application of the principles may be widened in a thousand ways ;
emes may be used instead of two or three or four, the order and rela-
of the keys used may be altered and added to ; but the principles remain
ame. ¶But when music ceases to be pure music, when words are
t to it, or it is intended to tell a story, then these principles can no
r be applied—or rather, there is no longer any need to apply them.
id of following the architectonical faculty, the composer must follow the
es of the dramatic or lyrical faculty. The number, character, mode of
opment, etc., of the themes is derived from the thing to be conveyed to
stener ; and then we get what is called Programme music. But just as
ine novel the writer reveals architectonical sense, so in a really fine piece
ogramme it is revealed. There is very little difference in form, for
ple—at any rate no essential difference—between a Bach fugue and the
ries' Ride of Wagner ; the themes are stated and developed in a certain
, and all one's faculties are satisfied—the emotions, the sense of pure
y in melody and harmony, the architectonical sense, the intellectual
ciation of right handling of the material. ¶Whether music is pure
or Programme music, it must satisfy all these. And though, in the
, we may use quarters and eighths of tones, and though we may arrive
nplexities unknown to-day and be able to express subtleties of feelings
: never felt, the principles by which our feelings are expressed in noble
eautiful Form cannot but remain the same.

**formare il tuono.** Vide MESSA DI VOCE.

**formula.** A word respectfully submitted by the editor to obviate the loose use of " sonata-form," which is employed both of a movement and a group of movements—both for the part and the whole ; by speaking of the dual-theme movement as written in the *sonata formula* and the group of formulæ, largo, rondo, etc., as in the sonata-*form* much ambiguity will be avoided.

**fort,** *G.* Off (of an organ-stop).

**fort** (fôr), **forte** (fôrt), *F.* 1. Loud. 2. **Temps f.** Strong beat.

**fortbien** (fôrb-yăṅ), *F.* A modification of the old fortepiano, by Friederici, 1758.

**forte** (fôr'-tĕ), *I.* 1. Loud. (Abbr. f.) **f. possibile.** As loud as possible. **più f.** Louder. **poco f.** Rather loud. **f. piano.** (Abbr. fp.) Loud, then immediately soft. **fortamen'te.** Loudly.

**fortement** (fôrt-mäṅ), *F.* Loudly.

**forte-piano.** 1. Vide PIANOFORTE. 2. Loud ! then soft !

**fortezza** (fôr'-tĕd'-zä). Force.

**fortiss.** Abbr. of *fortissimo.*

**fortissimo** (fôr-tēs'-sĭ-mo), *I.* Very loud. **fortissis'simo.** Double superlative of *forte.* **f. quanto possibile** (kwän'-to pös-sē'-bĭ-lĕ). As loud as possible.

**Fortrücken** (fôrt'-rükĕn), *G.* The advance of the hand (as in ascending figuration) with the same fingering.

**Fortschreitung** (fôrt'shrī-toongk), *G.* Progression. **F. einer Dissonanz.** Resolution. **fortschreiten.** To progress.

**Fortsetzung** (fôrt'zĕt-zoongk), *G.* Continuation, development.

**forza** (fôr'-tsä), *I.* Force, power. **forzan'do,** **forzato** (fôr-tsä'-tō). Forced, sharply emphasized (marked ∨ ∧ >). **forzare** (fôr-tsä'-rĕ). To strengthen. **f. la voce** (lä vō'chĕ). To force the voice.

**foundation-stop.** Vide STOP.

**fourchette tonique** (foor-shĕt tô[...] *F.* Tuning-fork.

**fourniture** (foor-nĭ-tür), *F.* A mi[...] stop.

**four-part.** Written for four part[...]

**fourth.** 1. The fourth tone of a [...] the subdominant. 2. An in[...] containing four tones, the ext[...] included, as d-g, the ratio being [...] Fourths are *perfect* and *imp*[...] rather than *major* or *minor.* *augmented* (*superfluous, ex*[...] *sharp* or *pluperfect*) *fourth* [...] whose upper tone has been rai[...] half-step, or its lower lowere[...] *diminished* (*imperfect, false,*[...] or *defective*) *fourth* one whose [...] tone has been lowered half a ste[...] lower raised (cf. FIFTH). **Ch**[...] **the second and fourth, cho**[...] **the 3d, 4th, and 6th, cho**[...] **the 4th and 6th.** Vide c[...] **four-three, four-two.** Vide c[...] **f. flute, f. shift.** Vide FLUT[...] SHIFT.

**fp.** Abbr. Vide FORTE (2).

**français** (fräṅ-sĕ'), **française** (sĕz), *F.* 1. French. 2. A co[...] dance in 3-4 time.

**francamen'te,** *I.* Frankly, bold[...]

**franchezza** (fräṅ-kĕd'-zä), *I.*, **chise** (fräṅ-shēz), *F.* Bol[...] frankness.

**franzese** (fräṅ-tsä'zĕ), *I.*, **franzö**[...] (fräṅ-tsä-zĭsh), *G.* " French [...] French style. **Franzton** (fräṅ[...] *G.* French pitch.

**frappe** (fräp), *F.* A manner of [...] ing time with force. **frappé** [...] pä). The down-beat.

**frapper** (fräp-pä), *F.* To stri[...] beat time.

**frase** (frä'-zĕ) (pl. i), *I.* A phras[...] **larga.** With broad phrasing. [...] **seggiare** (frä-zĕd-jär'rĕ). To p[...]

**Frauenstimme** (frow'-ĕn-shtĭ[...] *G.* Female voice.

**freddo** (frĕd'-dō), **freddamen'**[...] Cold(ly). **freddezza** (frĕd-d[...] Coldness.

**fredon** (frŭ-dôṅ), *F.* A trill, or [...] ornament. **fredonneme**[...] (fr[...]

i). Humming, trilling. **fre-**
**ner** (frü-dŭn-nä). To trill, also
um.

Unrestrained, not according to
t rule, as *f. composition,* or
e. **f. fugue.** Vide FUGUE. **f.**
d. Vide REED. **f. part.** An in-
endent part added to fill up the
mony of canon or fugue. **f. chant.**
orm of reciting the Psalms or Can-
es using a group of two chords for
h hemistich. Vide FRET-FREE.
en's songs. Little compositions
three or four voices, in use about
o.
are (frä-jä're), *I.* To adorn.
giatura (too' rä). An ornament.
(frī), *G.* Free. **Freiheit** (frī-
. License. **f. Schreibart** (shrīp'-
. Free composition.
ch horn. Vide HORN. **French**
th. Vide ALTERED.
ch treble clef. The G on the
est line of the staff.
o (frĕs'-ko), *I.,* **frescamen'te**
sh(ly).
One of the thin projecting ridges
oss the neck of stringed instrs.
divide the strings into differ-
lengths, thus producing different
hes, on pressure. **fretted** and
t-free. In the early precursors of
piano, there were fewer strings
n keys, each string serving for
eral notes, through the action of
gents acting as frets. These were
ed *tied* or *fretted* or *gebunden.*
ter instruments were given a string
each note, and these were called
dfrei, or *ungebunden* or *free* or
t-free.
au, fretian, frestel, fretel (frü-
, fretèle, fretetel. A Pan's pipe.
a, *I.* Haste.
de (froi'-dĕ), *G.* Joy, rejoicing.
eudengesang. Song of joy.
udig (froi'dĭkh). Joyfully. **Freu-**
keit (kīt). Joyfulness.
ssée (frē-kăs-sä), *F.* A dance with
ntomime in the 18th cent. In the
h cent. a part-song, each part hav-
different words.

**Fries** (frēs), *G.* Purfling.
**frisch** (frĭsh), *G.* Fresh, lively.
**fris'ka** (frĭsh'-kä). The quick movement in the Czardas, and the Hungarian Rhapsody.
**frivolo** (frē'vō-lo), *I.* Trifling, trashy.
**fröhlich** (frä-lĭkh), *G.* Joyous, gay.
**F.-keit** (kīt). Gayety. **Frohgesang**
(frō-khĕ-zäng). Song of joy.
**Frohnamt** (frōn'ämt), *G.* High Mass.
**Frontpfeife** (frônt'-pfī-fĕ), *G.* Front
pipes of an organ.
**Frosch** (frôsh), *G.* Nut (of a bow).
**frottola** (frôt'-tō-lä), *I.* A 16th century ballad.
**Frühlingslied** (frü'lings-lēt), *G.* Spring-
song.
**Frühmesse** (frü'mĕs-sĕ), **Frühstück**
(frü'shtŭk), *G.* Matins.
**F-Schlüssel** (ĕf-shlüs'ĕl), *G.* The F-
clef.
**fuga** (foo'-gä), *L.* and *I.* "A flight."
Vide FUGUE. **f. ad quintam (octav-**
**am).** Fugue (also canon) at the 5th (octave). **f. aequalis motus (or recta).**
In similar motion, the answer conform-
ing to the ascent and descent of the
subject. **f. al contrario (or riverso**
**or roves'cio)** or **fuga contraria (or**
**per motum contrarium).** One whose
answer is the subject inverted. **f.**
**authentica.** A fugue with an ascending subject. **f. canonica (or**
**inconseguenza or perpetua or**
**totalis).** A canon. **f. compo-**
**sita (or inaequalis).** One whose
subject moves by degrees, not by
leaps, as does **f. incomposita f. del**
**tuono,** *I.* A tonal fugue, opposed
to **f. reale,** a real fugue. **f. dop-**
**pia,** *I.* A double fugue. **f. homopho'-**
**na.** One whose answer is at the
unison. **f. impro'pria (or irregu-**
**laris or sciolta o. soluta).** An irregular free fugue. **f. in contrario**
**tempo (or per ar'sin et the'sin).**
One in which the accented notes of
the subject are the unaccented of the
answer, and vice versa. **f. in nomine.**
A fugue "in name only," i. e., a free
fugue. **f. inversa.** One in double
counterpoint and contrary motion.

**f. libera.** One with free episodes, opposed to **f. ligata** (or **obbligata**), whose episodes are entirely derived. **f. mixta.** One whose answer is varied by augmentation, etc. **f. partialis** (or **periodica**). One without full and perpetual canonic imitation, the usual fugue. **f. per augmentationem** (or **diminutionem**). One whose answer is by augmentation (diminution). **f. per imitationem interruptam.** One whose answer is broken by rests, etc. **f. plagalis.** One with subjects descending below the key-note. **f. propria** (or **regularis**). One in regular form. **f. reddita** or **redita.** One in which canonic progression occurs at the middle or end. **f. retrograda.** One whose answer is in *retrograde* progression. **f. retrograda per motum contrarium.** One whose answer is in contrary motion as well as retrograde progression. **f. ricercata** (rēt-chĕr-kä′-tä). A fugue of the highest development.

**fugara** (foo-gä′-rä), *I.* A 4- or 8-ft. organ-stop.

**fugato** (foo-gä′-to), *I.* 1. Fre[e] the manner of fugue. 2. A pa[ssage] in such manner.

**Fuge** (foo′-khĕ), *G.* Fugue. F[ugé] **ante** (gä-län′tĕ), *G.* A free fu[gue] chamber-music style.

**fuggire la cadenza** (food-jē-rĕ), [I.] write a deceptive cadence.

**fughetta** (foo′gĕt′-tä), *I.* A [little] fugue.

**fugirt** (foo-gērt′), *G.* In fugue [form]; also used of the ranks of a mi[xture] stop.

**fugue** (*E.* fūg, in *F.* füg). See b[elow.] **counter f.** One whose subjects [move] in contrary directions. **double [f.]** fugue on two subjects. **f. renv[ersée]** (rän-vĕr-sā), *F.* An inverted f[ugue.] **strict f.** One in which the [strict] form and its laws are strictly obse[rved]. **perpetual f.** A canon. **f. simp[le.]** A fugue containing but a single [sub]ject. **fugued** (fūgd) or **fuguin[g]** [In] fugue form, or loosely in [such] manner. **fuguist.** A compos[er or] performer of fugues. Also FUGA.

## Fugue.

### By Homer A. Norris.

A FUGUE is a composition in which a theme, called the *subje[ct]* announced by one voice and imitated by other voices. The [word] comes from the Latin *fuga* (a flight), suggesting the thoug[ht of] one part starting alone after which the others enter in pursuit. A fugue [may] be written for any number of voices, but we shall here discuss a four-v[oiced] fugue. ¶The subject is usually short and of such marked character as t[o fix] itself readily on the mind, and is usually so constructed as to admit of o[ver]lapping ; *i.e.*, so that a second voice may enter without musical fri[ction] before the first voice has completed the phrase. This overlapping proce[ss is] called *stretto*. ¶The subject may be announced by any voice. A[t its] completion there comes a very short passage called *codetta*, after whi[ch the] second voice sings the subject-matter in another key. This is called [the] *answer.* ¶In the majority of fugues the answer is a transposition of the [sub]ject into the key a perfect fifth above the subject, so that subject and an[swer] correspond to the keys of tonic and dominant. Certain subjects instea[d] reproduced literally are changed. Subjects which are changed are n as *tonal* subjects ; subjects which remain unchanged are known as *real* cts. ¶While the second voice is singing the answer, the first voice npanies it, and usually in one of the forms of double counterpoint. It :n intended for subsequent use. Such an accompanying part is called *er-subject*. ¶The answer is followed by another codetta, leading back e original key, where a third voice sings the subject, but in a different e than that in which the first voice announced it. The other voices nue with contrapuntal accompaniment. Another codetta follows, leading fourth voice which sings the answer in the dominant. The part of th : that we have discussed is called the *exposition*. The exposition closes rst of the three big divisions of the fugue. ¶The exposition is followed ie first *episode*. In the episode the composer has more freedom than in other portion of the fugue. New material may be presented ; brief ilations to related keys introduced, together with free imitation. ¶After first episode comes the *middle section*. ¶Here the four voices again :nt the subject-matter in somewhat the same order as in the first section n other keys. The principal keys are altogether avoided or only inci- ally touched. In this group often occur variations of the subject ; it be shortened or lengthened ; the answer may be presented in contrary on, etc. ¶In the third, and (usually) *final* section a return is made e original keys. Here the subject and answer are generally combined retto. ¶A *strict fugue* is one in which there are either no episodes, which the episodic material is drawn entirely from the subject or counter- :ct. Nearly all the fugues in Bach's "Das Wohltemperirte Clavier" are : fugues. ¶In a *free fugue* the episodes are constructed of new material. a *fugato* passage one voice announces a theme, after which other voices · in free imitation. ¶A *fughetta* is to a fugue what a sonatina is to a ta : *i.e.*, it is a little fugue. ¶An academic fugue is the most elaborate, cial, and purely intellectual expression of musical art.

rer (fü-rĕr), *G.* 1. Conductor. 2. bject of a fugue.
- (ffl), *G.* Filling. **F.-flöte.** "Fill- flute," a 4-ft. stop. **F.-pfeife** (f̄'fĕ). A dummy pipe. **F.-quinte.** shrill quint-stop useful only in com- nation. **F.-stelle.** Padding. **F.- imme.** 1. A part used to fill out rmony. 2. A mutation-stop a 3d 5th above normal pitch. 3. A rt doubling another in the octave unison.

**full.** For the voices or instrs. complete. **f. anthem.** Vide ANTHEM. **f. band.** A complete band or orchestra. **f. cadence** or **close.** Vide CADENCE. **f. chord.** A complete chord ; in part-music, one in which all the parts join. **f. score.** Vide SCORE. **f. stop** (on the lute). A chord using all the fingers ; full chord followed by a pause. **full choir** (or **great** or **swell**). "Draw all the stops of the choir (or great or swell) organ." **full organ.**

"Draw all the stops and couplers."
**f. service.** 1. One for the whole choir. 2. An office using music as far as permissible. **f. orchestra.** One in which all the instrs. are employed.
**fundamental.** 1. The root of a chord. 2. The generator of a series of partials. **f. position.** Vide POSITION. **f. tone.** 1. A generator of partials. 2. One of the three principal tones, tonic, dominant or subdominant. **f. bass.** Vide BASE.
**Fundamentalbass** (foon-dä-měn-täl'-bäs), *G.* Vide BASE. **F.-ton.** Fundamental tone.
**funèbre** (fü-něbr), *F.*, **funebre** (foo-nä-brě), *I.*, **funerale** (foo-ně-rä'-lě), *I.*, **funereo** (foo-nä'-rě-ō), *I.* Funereal; mournful. *marcia f.* Funeral march.
**fünf** (fínf), *G.* Five. **f.-fach.** Fivefold, in five ranks, of pipes. **f.-stimmig.** For five voices. **f.-stufige.** Pentatonic. **Fünfte** (fínf'-tě). Fifth. **Fünfzehnte** (fínf'tsän-tě). Fifteenth.
**funzioni** (foon-tsǐ-ō'ně), *I.* (pl.) Masses, and other sacred music in the R. C. Church.
**fuoco** (fo-ô'kō), *I.* Fire, energy, passion. **fuoco'so.** Fiery.
**für** (für), *G.*, *preposition.* For.
**fureur** (fü-rŭr), *F.*, **furia** (foo'-rǐ-ä), *I.* Fury, passion. **Furiant** (foo'rǐ-änt), *G.*, **furie** (foo-rē), *F.* A quick Bohemian dance with irregular rhythm and accent. **furibon'do, furioso,** *I.* Furious, mad. **furieusement** (für-yŭz-mäṅ), *F.*, **furiosamen'te,** *I.* Furiously, madly.
**furlando** (foor-iän'-dō), **furlano** (foor-lä'-ṉō), *I.* Forlana.
**furniture stop.** Vide STOP.
**furore** (foo-rō'-rě), *I.* Rage; a great success.
**fu'sa,** *L.*, **fuse** (füz), *F.*, **Fusel** (foo-zěl'), *G.* An eighth note.
**fusée** (fü-zä), *F.* A roulade or rapid passage, a skip or slide.
**fusel'la,** *L.* A 32d note. **fusel'lala.** A 64th note.
**Fuss** (foos), pl. **Füsse** (fís-se), *G.* Foot (q. v.). **Fussklavier.** The

pedals of an organ. **füssig** (füs-*G.* Foot, as *8-füssig,* 8-foot. **ton** (foos-tōn). Foot-tone, as *fusston,* 8-foot tone.
**fut** (füt), *F.* Barrel (of a drum).
**Fütterung** (füt'-těr-oongk), *G.* ings.
**Future, music of the.** Vide KUNFTSMUSIK.
**fz.** Abbr. of *Forzando.*

# G

**G** Pron. in *G.* gä ; in *F.* a sol (sŭl in *F.*, sôl in *I.*). musical pitch, a perfec above C ; all its oc 2. The major key having one s the minor key relative to B flat n
**G clef.** The treble clef.
**g.** Abbr. for *main gauche,* left ! or *grand orgue,* full, or great-or
**Gabel** (gä'běl), *G.* A fork. **G.** The fork-tone, *a'* used for tu **G.-grif'fe.** Cross-fingering. **St** **g.** Tuning-fork. **G.-klavier** b'l-klä-fer). A key-board instr. a scale of tuning-forks, and a sy thetic fork an octave higher for tone ; inv. by Fischer & Frit Leipzig, 1882.
**gagliarda** (gäl-yär'dä), *I.*, **Gagli** (gäl-yär'-dě), *G.* A galliard.
**gagliardo** (gäl-yär'-do), **gaglia men'te,** *I.* Gayly.
**gaillarde** (gī-yärd), *F.* 1. Merry A galliard. **gaillardement** (gī-) mäṅ). Merrily.
**gaio** (gä'ǐ-ō), *I.* Gay.
**gaita** (gä-ē-tä'), *Sp.* 1. Bagpipe A flageolet. **gaitero** (gä-ē-tä A player on the street-organ.
**gajo** (gä'-yō), *I.* Gay. **gajame** Gayly.
**gala** (gä'la), *I.* Gala. *di g.* Ga
**galamment** (gäl-ä-mäṅ), *F.*, **ga** **temente** (tě-men-tě), *I.* Graci
**galant(e)** (gä-läṅ(t)), *F.*, **galante** läṅ'-tě), *I.* Graceful, gallant. **antemen'te,** *I.* Gallantly. **ga** **tria** (gä-län-trě'-ä), *I.* Gallantr **galant** (gä-läṅt'), *G.* Free. **G. St**

reibart). The free (as opp. to the *undener* or strictly contrapuntal) e of harpsichord composition in the century. **Galanterien** (gä-län-'-ĕn). Ornaments in old harpsi-rd music. **Galanteriestück** (gä-tĕ-rē'stük). A piece in the orna-tal style.

rd (găl-yärd), *E.* An old dance ilar to the Pavan.

p, *E.* (in *F.* găl-ō), **galopade** -ō-păd), *F.*, **Galopp** (gä-lôp'), *G.*, op po, *I.* A hopping round-ace in 2-4 time.

bé (gä-loo-bä), **galoubet** (gä-bä'), *F.* A small fife with three es and range of 17 notes, found in vence.

a (gäm'-bä), *I.*, **gambe** (gämb), **Gambe** (gäm'-bĕ), *G.* 1. Leg; ce, viol di g. Vide VIOLA. 2. An an-stop; the whole family of stops ned after stringed instrs. **Gamben-mme.** A gamba-stop. **Gamben-rk.** A piano-violin. **Gambabass.** 16-ft. stop on the pedals. **G.** jor. A 16-ft. stop. **Gambette** m-bĕt'-tĕ), *G.* An octave gamba-p. **Gambist'.** A player on the **Gambviole** (gämp-fē-ō'lĕ), *G.* l di gamba.

beta (gäm-bä'-tä), *Sp.* An ancient ace, a caper.

ma, *Gr.*, **gamme** (găm), *F.* The eek G. (Γ). 1. The lowest note ) of the Aretinian scale. 2. The me of that scale. 3. Scale gener-y. 4. Compass. 5. A clef for scale of G. **g. chromatique** escendante, montante). Chro-tic (descending, ascending) scale. mmes (găm). Scale-exercises. ma ut or Γ ut. G, in the old solmi-ion.

ut. (From gamma ut.) 1. The le of any key. 2. The staff. 3. old English church-music, the key G. **gamut G.** The G on the st line of the bass staff. **Guido's** The scale of two octaves and a xth introduced by Guido of Arezzo : e tones called by name, ut, re, mi,

fa, sol, la, and written in the first octave Γ (gamma) (the lowest tone) A, B to G, in the second g-g ; and in the upper sixth gg-dd.

**ganascione** (gä-nä-shō'nĕ), *I.* A lute.

**Gang** (gäng), *G.* 1. Rate of movement. 2. A passage.

**ganz** (gänts), *G.* Whole, all, very. **Ganzinstrumente.** Those brass instrs. of such width that they speak the lowest sound natural to the tube, i. e., they reach the depth of an open organ-pipe of equal length. Narrower instrs. speak only the octave above this natural tone and are called **Halbinstrumente. ganz langsam.** Very slowly. **ganze Note** (gän'tsĕ nō'tĕ). A whole note. **ganzer Ton** (gän'-tser-tōn). **Ganzton.** A whole tone. Vide SECOND. **ganzes Werk.** The full organ. **Ganz-schluss.** Final cadence. **ganzver-hallend** (fĕr-häl'lent). Dying away entirely.

**garbo** (gär'-bo), *I.* Grace, elegance. **garbato** (bä'-tō), **garbatamen'te.** Graceful(ly).

**garibo** (gä-rē'-bō), *I.* Dance, ball.

**gariglione** (gä-rēl-yō'nĕ), *I.* Chime.

**garnir** (gär-nēr), *F.* To string a violin.

**garrire** (gär-rē'rĕ), *I.* To chirp, warble.

**Gassenhauer** (gäs'-sĕn-hower), *G.* Street-song, trash. **Gassenhauer-lin** (lĕn). Popular songs of the 16th century.

**Gastrollen** (gäst'rōl-lĕn), *G.* To go "guesting," i. e., "starring."

**gathering note.** A pause on a final note of recitation to give time for the chorus to gather.

**gauche** (gōsh), *F.* Left. **main g.** (mäṅ). The left hand.

**gaudente** (gä-oo-dĕn'-tĕ), **gaudio'so, gaudentemen'te,** *I.* Joyful(ly).

**Gaumenton** (gow'-mĕn-tōn), *G.* Guttural tone.

**gavot'**, *E.*, **gavot'ta**, *I.*, **gavotte** (gä-vôt), *F.* An old French dance (named probably from the people of Gap, called Gavots). It is in 4-4 time, strongly marked ; begins on the weak half of a measure and ends on the accented ; no notes smaller than eighth notes occur.

**gazel'.** A piece with a brief constant refrain.

**gazzarra** (gäd-zär'-rä), *I.* A fête with music and cannon.

**G clef.** The treble clef.

**G-dur** (gä-door), *G.* G major.

**Gebläse** (gĕ-blä'-zĕ), *G.* Bellows.

**gebrochen** (gĕ-brô'-khĕn), *G.* Broken.

**gebunden** (gĕ-boon'dĕn), *G.* 1. Tied. **g. Dissonanz.** A prepared (and tied) dissonance. **g. Spiel.** Legato-playing. **g. Stil.** Strict, connected style. 2. Vide FRETTED.

**Geburtslied** (gĕ-boorts'lēt), *G.* Birthday-song.

**gedackt** (gĕ-däkt'), **gedeckt** (ge-dĕkt'), *G.* Stopped, of pipes. **Gedacktstimmen.** Stops with covered pipes. **G.-flöte.** Stopped flute, in an organ.

**gedämpft** (gĕ-dĕmpft), *G.* Muffled, muted.

**gedehnt** (ge-dänt'), *G.* Lengthened, slow.

**Gefährte** (gĕ-fär'-tē), *G.* Answer (in fugue).

**Gefallen** (gĕ-fäl'lĕn). Pleasure. **nach G.** Ad libitum.

**gefällig** (gĕ-fäl'lĭkh), *G.* Pleasing(ly), agreeably.

**Gefiedel** (gĕ-fē'dĕl), *G.* Fiddling.

**Gefühl** (gĕ-fül'), *G.* Feeling, expression. **mit G.** or **gefühlvoll.** With feeling.

**gegen** (gä'-khĕn), *G.* Against, contrary, contrasted with. **G.-bewegung** (be-vākh'-oongk). Contrary motion. **G.-fuge.** A fugue whose answer is an inversion of the subject. **G.-gesang.** Antiphony. **G.-hall, G.-schall.** Resonance, echo. **G.-harmonie.** Counter-subject in fugue. **Gegenpunkt** (poonkt). Counterpoint. **G.-satz.** 1. Contrast. 2. A movement. **G.-stimme.** 1. Counter-tenor or alto. 2. Counter-subject. 3. Any contrapuntal part. **g.-stimmig.** Dissonant. **G.-subjekt.** Counter-subject, in a fugue.

**gegit'tertes B.** B. cancellatum, v

**gehend** (gā'-ĕnt), *G.* Andante.

**Gehörlehre** (gĕ-här'-lā-rĕ), *G.* A tics. **gehörspielen.** To play b

**Geige** (gī'-khĕ) (pl. **en**), *G.* V **geigen** (gī'-khen). To pla the violin. **G.-blatt.** Finger-l of a violin. **G.-bogen** (bō' Bow. **G.-clavicymbel** or **G.** vier. Bow-piano. **G.-futter** ( ter). Case for a violin. **G.-** The neck of a violin. **G.-** (härts). Resin. **G.-holz** (hōlts Wood used in making violins. **macher** (mäkh'-ĕr). A violin-m **G.-principal.** A diapason stop **saite.** Violin-string. **G.-satte steg** (stäkh). Bridge of a violin **schule.** A violin method. **G.-s** (strĭkh). A stroke of the bow. **stück.** A comp. for the violin. **werk.** 1. Piano-violin. 2. A organ-stop. **G.-wirbel** (vēr'-be violin-peg. **G.-zettel** (tsĕt' The violin-maker's label. **G.-** A violin-stop. **Geiger** (gī'khĕr) lin-player.

**Geist** (gīst), *Gr.* Spirit, soul, mind nius. **g.-reich** (rīkh), **g.-voll** Spiritual. **Geisterharfe.** Æ harp. **geistlich.** Ecclesias sacred. **G.-gesänge.** Psalms, hy

**Geklingel** (gĕ-klĭng'-ĕl), *G.* Tink

**gekneipt** (gĕ-knīpt'), *G.* Pizzica

**gelassen** (gĕ-läs'-sen), *G.* Calm, q ly. **G.-heit** (hīt). Tranquillity.

**geläufig** (gĕ-lī'fĭkh), *G.* Easy, r **G.-keit** (kīt). Fluency, ease.

**Geläut** (gĕ-līt), *G.* A peal.

**gelinde** (gĕ-lĭn'-de), *G.* Soft, ge **Gelindigkeit.** Sweetness.

**gellen** (gĕl'lĕn), *G.* To sound lo **G.-flöte**, *G.* Clarinet.

**Geltung** (gĕl'-toongk), *G.* Value, portion (of a note).

**gemächlich** (gĕ-mĕkh'-lĭkh), **gem sam** (gĕ-mäkh'zäm), *G.* Quie calm, slow.

**gemählig** (gĕ-mä'lĭkh), *G.* Gradua

**gemässigt** (gĕ-mĕs-sĭkht), *G.* N erato. **gemes'sen.** Measured, r erato.

isch (gĕ-mïsh'), *G.* Mixture (of ps).

shorn (gĕms'-hôrn), *G.* 1. A pipe de of a chamois horn. 2. A stop h tapering pipes, 2, 4, 8-ft. on : manuals, 16-ft. on the pedals, -quinte. A quint-stop of this ss.

üt(h) (gĕ-müt), *G.* Mind, soul. mütlich (lïkh). Expressive.

:ra, plural of **genus** (q. v.).

ral (gā-nĕ-räl'), *G.* General. **G.-ss** (gā-nĕ-räl'-bäs). Thorough-ss. **G.-b.-schrift.** Thorough-bass tation. **G.-pause** (pow-ze). A t or pause for all the instrs. **G.-**obe. A general rehearsal.

erator, *E.*, **générateur** (zhā-nā-rǎ-), *F.* Root, fundamental.

:re (jā'-nĕ-rĕ), *I.* 1. A mode or key. A genus.

:ro'so (jā-nĕ-rō'sō), *I.* Noble, dig-ied.

al'ia, *L.* Cymbals.

e (zhā-nē), *F.*, **Genie** (gā'-nē), *G.*, nio (jā'-nï-ō), *I.* Genius, talent. .rit.

•uillère (zhŭn-wï-yăr), *F.* Knee-rer.

:e (zhäṅr), *F.* 1. Style. **g. ex-essif.** The expressive style. 2. :nus, as **g. chromatique, g. dia-nique, g. enharmonique.**

:il(le) (zhäṅ-tē(l)), *F.*, **gentile** (jĕn--lĕ), *I.* Graceful, elegant. **genti-zza** (lĕd'-zä), *I.* Refinement of -le. **gentilmen'te.** Gracefully.

us, pl. **genera,** *L.* 1. Greek clas--ication of tetrachords. Vide MODES. A scale or mode. 3. Class. **g. in-.tile.** Wind instrs. **g. percussi-**le. Instrs. of percussion. **g. ten-**le. Stringed instruments.

.de (gĕ-rä'-dĕ), *G.* Straight, reg-.r. **G.-bewegung** (be-va'khoong). milar motion. **G.-taktart** or ge-der **Takt.** Common time.

.man. Vide FINGERING, FLUTE. **G.** .dals. Pedal key-board. **G. scale.** , H, C, D, E, F, G. (Vide H.) . sixth. Vide ALTERED CHORDS. . soprano clef. Vide CLEF.

**Ges** (gĕs), *G.* The note G flat. **Ge-ses** (gĕs'-ĕs). G double flat.

**Gesang** (gĕ-zäng'), pl. **Gesänge** (zĕng'ĕ), *G.* Song, melody, air. **G.-buch** (bookh). Song-book. **G.-kunst.** Art of song. **G.-(s)mässig** (mĕs-sïkh). Adapted for or congenial to the voice. **G.-sgruppe** (groop-pe). Sc¬ng-group; the second subject of a sonata formula, which should be lyri-cal in nature. **g.-sweise** (vï-ze). In the style of song. **G.-verein** (fĕr-ïn). A choral society.

**Geschlecht** (gĕ-shlĕkht'), *G.* Genus.

**geschleift** (gĕ-shlïft'), *G.* Slurred, le-gato.

**Geschmack** (gĕ-shmäks), *G.* Taste. **g.-voll.** Tasteful.

**geschwänzte Noten** (gĕ-shvĕnts'tĕ no'tĕn), *G.* Notes with tails.

**geschwind** (gĕ-shvïnt'), *G.* Quick, rapid. **G.-igkeit** (kït). Rapidity. **Geschwindmarsch.** A quick-step.

**Ges-dur** (gĕs-door), *G.* Major. **Geses** (gŏs-ĕs), *G.* G double flat.

**Gesicht** (ge-zïkht'), *G.* Face, front (of an organ). **G.-spfeifen.** Front pipes.

**Gesinge** (gĕ-zïng'ĕ), *G.* Bad sing-ing, sing-song.

**gesponnen** (gĕ-shpôn'-nĕn), *G.* Spun. **gesponnene saite.** Covered string. **gesponnener Ton.** A tone drawn out to a mere thread.

**gesteigert** (gĕ-shtï'-khĕrt), *G.* Cres-cendo.

**gestossen** (gĕ-shtôs'sĕn), *G.* Sepa-rated, detached.

**gestrichen** (gĕ-strïkh'ĕn), *G.* 1. Hav-ing hooks (as notes). 2. Having lines or accents, as *eing. Oktave,* one-lined octave. Vide PITCH. 3. Crossed, as a numeral, raising the in-terval a half-tone. Vide CHORD. 4. Cut, as a movement or scene.

**get'ern, get'ron.** The cittern.

**get(h)eilt** (gĕ-tïlt'), *G.* Divided. Vide DIVISI. **g. Stimmen.** Partial stops.

**Getön** (gĕ-ṫän), *G.* Clamour.

**getragen** (gĕ-trä'khĕn), *G.* Sustained.

**getrost** (gĕ-trôst'), *G.* Confident.

**gewichtig** (ge-vïkh'-tïkh), *G.* Heavy.

**gewidmet** (gĕ-vēt'-mĕt), *G.* Dedicated.

**Gewirbel** (gĕ-vēr'bĕl), *G.* Roll of drums.

**gewiss** (gĕ-vĭs'), *G.* Firm, sure. **G.-heit** (hīt). Firmness.

**geworfener Strich** (gĕ-vôrf'-ĕn-ĕr strĭkh), *G.* A springing bow-stroke. Vide BOW.

**geziert** (gĕ-tsērt'), *G.* Affected, prim.

**geyta'rah.** Eastern guitar.

**ghazel'**, *Arab.* A piece with simple recurrent theme.

**ghiribizzi** (gē-rĭ-bĕd'-zĭ), *I.* Unexpected intervals, fantastic passages. **ghiribizzo'so.** Fantastic.

**ghironda** (gē-rôn'-dä), *I.* Hurdygurdy.

**ghit'tern.** Old name for cittern.

**gicheroso** (jē-kĕ-rō'-sō), *I.* Merry.

**giga** (jē'-gä), *I.*, **gigue** (zhēg), *F.*, **Gigue** (jē'gĕ), *G.* 1. Jig. 2. Old form of viol. **gighardo** (jē-gär'-dō), *I.* A jig.

**gigelira** (jē-gĕ-lĭ'rä), *I.* Xylophone.

**ging'larus, ging'ras**, or **gingri'na.** A small Phœnician flute.

**gioco** (jô'-kō), *I.* A joke, merriment. **giocoso, giocosamen'te.** Jocose(ly). **giochevole** (jō-kā'vō-lĕ). Merry. **giocolarmen'te.** Merrily.

**giocondo** (jō-kôn'-dō), **giocondamen'-te,** *I.* Cheerful(ly).

**gioja** (jō'-yä), *I.* Joy. **giojan'te, giojo'so, giojosamen'te.** Joyful(ly).

**gioviale** (jō-vĭ-ä'lĕ), *I.* Jovial. **giovialità** (ĭ-tä). Gayety.

**giraffe** (jĭ-räf'). An upright spinet.

**giro** (jē'-rō), *I.* A turn.

**Gis** (gēs), *G.* G sharp. **Gisis** (gēs-ēs). G double sharp. **Gis-moll,** G. sharp minor.

**gitana** (he-tä'-nä), *Sp.* A gipsy.

**gittana** (jĭt-tä'-na), *I.* A Spanish dance.

**git'tern, git'teron, git'tron.** Cittern.

**gitteth** (jĭt'tĕth), *Heb.* An instr. of the harp kind.

**giubilazione** (joo-bĭ-lä-tsĭ-ō'nĕ), **giubilio** (joo-bĭ-lē'-ō), **giubilo** (joo'bĭ-lō), *I.* Jubilation. **giubbilo'so.** Jubilant.

**giucante** (joo-kän'-tĕ), **giuchevole** (joo-kä'-vō-lĕ), *I.* Merry, joyful.

**giulivo** (joo-lē'vō), **giulivamen't** Joyful(ly).

**giuoco** (joo-ô'kō), *I.* 1. A joke, s 2. A stop. **giuoco'so, giuoca** Playful.

**giusto** (joos'-to), *I.* Exact, pr proper. **tempo g.** Strict **allegro g.** Rather fast. **gi** men'te. Strictly.

**given bass.** A figured bass.

**glais** (glĕ), *F.* The passing-bell **funèbre.** A knell.

**glänzend** (glĕn'-tsĕnt), *G.* Brillia

**glapissant** (glä-pĭs-sän), *F.* Shr

**Glas'harmonika,** *G.* Vide HARMO

**glasses, musical.** Goblets tune partial filling with water and p by rubbing their edges evenly w wet finger.

**glatt** (glät), *G.* Smooth, even. **G.** (glĕt'tĕ). Smoothness.

**glee.** An unaccompanied secular c for three or more voices ; its mood be grave or gay, its counterpoi not usually elaborate.

**gleich** (glīkh), *G.* Equal, consonant. **gleicher Klang.** sonance, unison. **gleicher Ko punkt.** Equal cpt. **gleichsch** **ende Temperatur** (shvä'-bĕr Equal temperament. **gleiche S men.** Voices of the same sor *male.* **gleichstimmig** (shtĭm-m Harmonious.

**gleiten** (glī'tĕn), *G.* To glide th gers.

**gli** (lē), *I.* Pl. The.

**glicibarifona** (glē-chē-bä-rĭ-fō'-na A wind-instr. inv. by Catterini, 1 a small expressive organ.

**glide.** Portamento ; glissando.

**Glied** (glēt), *G.* Link.

**glissade** (glĭs-säd), *F.*, **glissa** **glissato** (glĭs-sä'tō), **glissica** **glissicato** (kä'tĕh), *I.*, **glisser** (glēs-män), *F.* Gliding, i. e., by ing the finger quickly along the or the strings ; in piano-playi is done with the finger-nail usu **glisser** (glĭs-sä), *F.*, **glitschen** shĕn), *G.* 1. To glide. 2. An bellishment executed by glissa

issez la pouce (glĭs-sä lä-poos), *F.* de the thumb.

:ke (glôk'ĕ), *G.* A bell. **Glock-** ,geläute (glô'kĕn-gĕ-lī-tĕ). The .ging or chiming of bells. **Glock'-** .ist. Bell-ringer. **G.-klang.** The .nd of bells. **G.-spiel.** 1. Chimes. A stop imitating bells, or causing em to tinkle. 3. An orchestral str. of bells or tuned steel rods ·uck with a hammer. **Glöckchen** lĕk'khĕn). A little bell. **glöck-** n (glĕk'-ĕln). To ring little bells. lockner (glôk'ner). Bell-ringer. lockleinton (glôk'-līn-tōn). An gan-stop of very small scale and de measure.

ria or **Gloria in excel'sis Deo,** *L.* Glory to God in the highest," Vide .ss and DOXOLOGY.

ria **Pa'tri,** *L.* " Glory to the .ather." Vide DOXOLOGY.

:te (glôt), *F.* The glottis. **coup de** , (koo dŭ). A short snappy attack ·ught by some vocal teachers, but .nerally believed to be pernicious.

:tis (glät'tis). 1. The upper part the wind-pipe, an aperture in the ·rynx controlling vocal production. A reed used by ancient flutists.

.end (glü'ĕnt), *G.* Ardent, glowing. .oll (gä-môl). G minor.

.ccare (näk-kä'-rä), *I.* Castanets. .cchera (näk-kä'rä), *I.* A tambou- .ne, kettle-drum.

·mo (nō'-mō). In neumatic nota- .on, a long bar used to indicate a .stained note.

**goathorn.** Vide GEMSHORN.

**gola** (gō'lä), *I.* 1. Throat. 2. A gut- tural voice.

**goll trompo.** Trumpet used by Danes, Normans, etc.

**Gondellied** (gôn'dĕl-lēt), *G.,* **gondo- liera** (gôn-dōl-yä'rä), *I.,* gondolier- song. Song composed and sung by the Venetian gondoliers ; barcarolle. 2. Music in the same style.

gon'dolin. An instr. of the zither- class with four octaves of strings and .one octave of piano-keys above them. The pressure of one key submits one tone in all its octaves to the sweep of the plectrum. Chords can thus be played in different posi- tions.

**gong.** A Chinese instr., a circular plate of metal struck with a padded stick. Also called tam-tam.

**goose.** A squawk accidentally occur- ring in the tone of an oboe or other reed instrument.

**gorgheggiare** (gôr-gĕd-jä'rĕ), *I.* To trili, shake. **gorgheggiamen'to.** Trilling ; the art of florid song. **gor- gheggio** (gĕd'jō). A trill, a shake. **gorgheggi.** Rapid vocalises.

**gos'ba.** An Arabian flute.

**gospel side.** Vide EPISTLE SIDE.

**go'to.** Japanese dulcimer.

**Gottesdienst** (gôt'tĕs-dēnst), *G.* Di- vine service.

**goût** (goo), *F.* Taste, judgment.

**governing key.** Principal key.

**Grabgesang** (gräp'-gĕ-zäng), *G.* **lied** (lēt), *G.* Dirge.

## Grace.

### BY THE EDITOR.

)NE of the innumerable decorative details of melodic progression. Grace notes are musical parasites borrowing their entire sustenance and duration from the note to which they are tied by a slur. They consequently vitally affected by the rapidity of the tempo. They are ost invariably written small, and are frequently abbreviated, or indicated some form of musical shorthand. It is to be noted in playing old music : the appoggiatura was written small merely as a bit of academic hypocrisy

## Modern Graces.

**Acciacatura, or Short Appog-
giatura,** I. and E.  Kurzer Vorschlag or Zusammenschlag G.
Pincé étouffé, F.  (Sometimes
struck simultaneously and instantly released.)

**Long Appoggiatura.**  Langer Vorschlag or Vo
(Written small but taking its full value.)

Written.

Played.

**Double Appoggiatnra, or Slide,** E.  Anschlag, or
Schleifer, or Schneller. G.

**Unaccented Appoggiatur
After-beat.** Nacnschlag or
schleifer.  (Also double N

Written.

Played.

**Shake, or Trill,** E. Trillo, I.  Trille, F.  Triller, G.  [Old abbreviations, *t*, +, (*w*
*w*, etc.]  (The length of the trill varies with the length of the note and the tempo.)

Written.

Begun on the
principal.

Begun on the
auxiliary.

With After-
beat.

With a chromatic sign.

Played.

**Chain of Trills,** E.  Catena di trilli, I.  Trillerkette, G..  (May be with or without
afterbeat, at discretion.)

Written.

*a*

or

Played.

*b*

Passing Shake, or Inverted Mor-, Praller, Pralltriller, or Schneil-, Pincé renversé, or mordant, F.

The Mordent, E.
Mordent or Beis-ser, G. Pincé, F. [Old signs, ◆|◆, or '.]

The Double Mordent (dop-pelte M; pincé double). Given here with a chromatic.

Turn, E. Doppelschlag, G. Groupe, F. Gruppetto, I. [Sign, ∾ or ∿, formerly ∾ or ⅔ now used for *back-turn.*

(a) With sign *over* the note. (b) With sign following a note.

With chromatic sign. Back turn. Double turn.

## Old Graces.

*(Those used in Bach's works from his own explanation.)*

Trillo. Mordant. Trillo and Mordant. Cadence. Double or Doppelt Cadence.

Doppelt Cadence. Doppelt Cadence and Mordant. Doppelt Cadence and Mordant. Doppelt Cadence and Mordant.

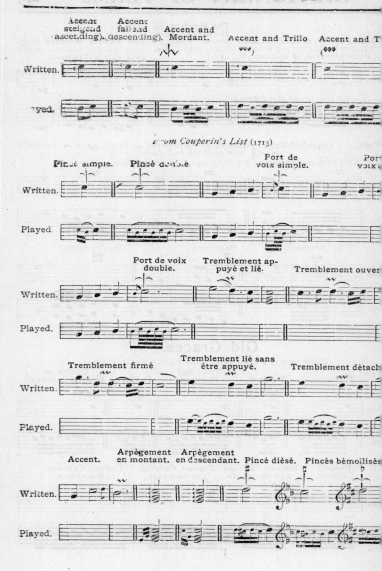

From *Couperin's List* (1713).

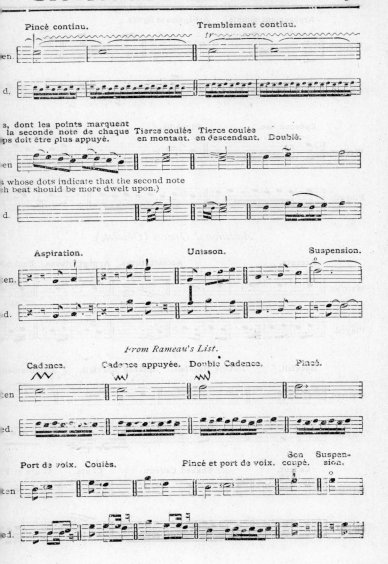

Pincé continu.    Tremblement continu.

s, dont les points marquent la seconde note de chaque ps doit être plus appuyé.    Tierce coulée en montant.    Tierce coulée en descendant.    Doublé.

s whose dots indicate that the second note h beat should be more dwelt upon.)

Aspiration.    Unisson.    Suspension.

*From Rameau's List.*

Cadence.    Cadence appuyée.    Double Cadence.    Pincé.

Port de voix.    Coulés.    Pincé et port de voix.    Son coupé.    Suspension.

Arpègement simple.   Arpègement figuré.

Cadence liée.   Pincé lié.   Liaison.

## Additional Graces (*Obsolete*).

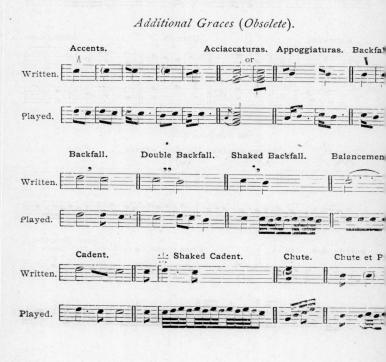

Accents.   Acciaccaturas.   Appoggiaturas.   Backfall

Backfall.   Double Backfall.   Shaked Backfall.   Balancemen

Cadent.   Shaked Cadent.   Chute.   Chute et P

to smuggle in thus an unprepared suspension. Though written small it ·
given one-half (sometimes only a third) the value of the note it was bo
to, and two-thirds of the value if the note were dotted. ¶The C
gives first the modern graces, as written and executed, then a series of
graces made up from Bach's own list, and from those of Couperin :
Rameau. ¶Composers who desire to escape the wide diversity of interp
tation put on all grace-abbreviations are coming, more and more, to w
their ornaments out in full, a procedure for which there is every reason
the one of laziness.

**Grad** (grät), *G.* Step, degree.

**gradare** (dä're), *I.* To descend by degrees.

**grada'tion.** A series of diatonic chords ascending or descending.

**gradation** (grä-däs-yôn), *F.*, **gradazi-one** (grä-dä-tsï-ō'nĕ), *I.* A gradual increase cr diminution of speed or volume.

**gradevole** (grä-dā'-vō-lĕ), **gradevole-men'te,** *I.* Graceful(ly). **gradita-men'te, graditis'simo.** Very sweetly.

**gradire** (grä-dē'-rĕ), *I.* To ascend by degrees.

**Gradleiter** (grät'-lī-tĕr), *G.* A scale.

**grado** (grä'-do), *I.* A degree; single step. **g. ascendente** (or **descen-dente**). Ascending (or descending) degree. **di grado.** Moving by step, opposed to **di salto,** moving by skip.

**grad'ual,** *E.,* **gradua'le,** *L.* 1. Part of the R. C. service sung between the Epistle and Gospel, anciently sung on the altar-steps. 2. A book containing the gradual and other antiphons. The Roman G or Graduale Romanum. A celebrated ancient volume of ritual music of the 16th century. 3. **gradual modulation.** That in which the principal modulating chord is reached by others.

**gradualmen'te, graduatamen'te,** *I.,* **graduellement** (grad-ü-ĕl-män), *F.* By degrees.

**graduare** (grä-doo-ä'rĕ), *I.* To divide into degrees. **graduazione,** *I.* Vide GRADAZIONE. **gradweise** (grät-vī-ze), *G.* Gradually, by degrees.

**gra'dus ad Parnas'sum,** *L.* "·road to Parnassus." Name app by Fux to his text-book in coun point; by Clementi to his book études; hence, any text-book.

**graha** (grä'-hä), *Hindu.* The op ing tone of a song.

**grail** (grāl). *Early E.* The Ron gradual.

**graillement** (grĕ-yŭ-män), *F.* hoarse sound.

**grammar.** Rules of composition.

**grammatical accent.** Vide ACCEN

**gran** (grän), *I.* Great, grand. **g. ca** or **tamburo.** The great, or ba drum. **g. prova.** Final rehearsa

**grand.** Abbr. of *Grand piano.* V PIANO. **g. action.** The action c grand piano. **grand opera.** S ous opera in which there is no spo dialogue. **g. stave.** Vide STAFF. **choir.** Union of all the reed-sto **g. cornet.** 16-ft. reed-stop. **g. nata.** An extended sonata.

**grand(e)** (grän(d)), *F.,* **grande** (grä dĕ), *I.* Grand, great. **g.barré,** *F.* V BARRÉ. **g. bourdon.** A 32-ft. st on the pedal. **g. chantre** (shän Precentor. **g. chœur** (kŭr). F organ, all the stops. **g. orgue** (gr dorg). 1. Great organ. 2. Full gan. **g. jeu.** 1. Full organ. 2. stop bringing all the stops of an h monium into play. **g. messe.** Hi Mass. **g. mesure à deux temp** Duple time. **g. orchestre** (gra dôr-kĕstr). Full orchestra.

**grandeur** (grän-dŭr), *F.* 1. Grandeu 2. Width (of intervals).

ndezza (grän-děd'-zä), *I.* Grand-
ur.

ndio'so, *I.* Noble. **grandison-**
**n'te.** Sonorous.

ndsire. Changes on 5 bells. Vide
OUBLE (4).

nulato (grä-noo-lä'-tō), *I.* Slightly
:accato.

ppa (gräp'pa), *I.* Brace.

sseyer (gräs-sŭ-yä), *F.* To pro-
ounce the *r* or *l* thickly; hence,
rasseyement (grăs-yŭ-mäṅ), such
ronunciation.

a'tias ag'imus, *L.* "We give
nanks to Thee." Vide MASS.

tioso (grä'-tsi-ō'so), *I.* Gracious.

ve (grä'vě in *I.*; in *F.* grăv).
. Grave, deep, slow. 2. A slow
novement. **grave harmonics.**
Combinational tones. **gravement**
grăv-mäṅ), *F.* **gravemente** (grä-vě-
něn'tě), *I.* Gravely. **gravezza** (gra-
ěd'-zä), *I.* Gravity.

avicembalo (grä-vē-chäm'-bä-lō), *I.*,
:ravicem'bolo, *I.*, **gravecem'bal-**
im, *L.* Harpsichord.

a'vis, *L.* Heavy. Vide ACCENTUS
:CCLESIASTICI.

avisonan'te, *I.* Loud-sounding.

avità (grä-vǐ-tä'), *I.*, **Gravität** (grä-
ē-tāt'), *G.*, **gravité** (grä-vǐ-tä), *F.*
:. Solemnity. 2. Relative depth of a
one.

ayle (grāl). *Early E.* The "Ro-
nan gradual."

azia (gräts'-yä), *I.*, **grazie** (gräts-
ʸä), *G.* Grace, elegance. **graziös**
'grä-tsǐ-äs), *G.*, **grazio'so**, *I.* Grace-
ul. **graziosamen'te.** Gracefully.

eater. Major (of a scale, sixth, or
third).

**eat octave.** Vide PITCH. **great**
**organ.** Vide ORGAN. **great sixth.**
A 6-5 chord with perfect 5th and major 6th.

ec (grěk), *F.* Greek. *Chorus à la*
*G.* A chorus at the end of an act, as
in Greek tragedy.

**reek Modes and Music.** Vide
MODES.

**rego'rian, gregorianisch** (grě-gō-rǐ-
äṅ'-ǐsh), *G.*, **grégori'ano** (grä-gō-rǐ-

ä'no), *I.*, **grégorien** (grä-gō-rǐ-äṅ), *F.*
Introduced or regulated by Pope
Gregory I. in the sixth century (vide
his name in the B. D.). Chiefly
used as a synonym for plain-chant.
Gevaert in his "Les origines du chant
lyrique," 1890, has shown how little
reason there is for continuing the traditional view of St. Gregory as a
great innovator; he may have been a
codifier of music. Much credit belonging to St. Ambrose has been
given to him; he did not originate
the notation by letters (a-g), sometimes called the *Gregorian letters*.
The so-called *Gregorian chant* or
*song* is diatonic, without definite
rhythm (the words dictating the metre) and keeping to the Church modes.
Of *Gregorian chant, modes, tones,
etc.* Vide PLAIN-CHANT, and MODES.

greifen (grī'-fěn), *G.* To take, to
finger, to play; to stop (of violin-
playing); to stretch.

grel (grěl), *G.* Shrill. **G.-heit** (hīt).
Sharpness.

grelot (grŭ-lō), *F.* A small bell.

Griff (grǐf), *G.* Touch, manipulation,
fingering, stretch. **G.-brett.** Finger-
board. **G.-loch** (lôkh). Hole (as of
a flute). **G.-saite** (zī-te). A stopped,
or melody, string as opposed to a
sympathetic string.

grillig (grǐl'-lǐkh), *G.* Capricious.

gringotter (grăṅ-gô-tā), *F.* To hum.

grisoller (grē-sô-lā), *F.* To warble.

grob (grôp), *G.* Coarse, deep, broad.
As a prefix (of organ-pipes); "of
broad scale." **G.-gedackt.** A
stopped diapason of full, rough tone.

grop po, groppet'to. Vide GRUPPO,
GRUPPETTO.

gros (grō), *F.* Great. **g. tambour.**
Great drum.

gros-fa (grō-fä). The old square notation.

gross (grôs), *G.*, **grosse** (grôs), *F.*
Great, major. **grosse caisse** (grôs
kěs), *F.* The great drum. **Grosse-**
**nazard**, *G.* A stop a fifth above the
diapasons. **grosse Oktave.** The
great octave. Vide PITCH. **grosse**

**Quinte, grosses Quintenbass.** A stop in the pedals, a fifth or twelfth to the great bass. **grosse Sonate.** Grand sonata. **grosses Principal.** A 32-ft. stop. **grosses Terz.** Major third. **grosse Tierce.** Stop producing the third or tenth above the foundation-stops. **grosse Trommel.** The great drum. **grossgedackt** (gĕ-däkt). Double-stopped 16-ft. diapason.

**grosso** (grôs´-sō), *I.* Full, great, grand.

**Grossvatertanz** (grôs´fä-tĕr-tänts), *G.* "Grandfather's dance"; an old-fashioned dance.

**grottes´co,** *I.* Grotesque.

**ground bass.** Vide BASE (8).

**group.** 1. A series of short notes tied, or sung to one syllable. 2. A division or run. 3. A set of instruments, as *the brass.* 4. The arrangement of parts in score.

**Grund** (groont), *G.* Ground, foundation. **G.-akkord.** An uninverted chord. **G.-bass.** Fundamental bass. **G.-lage.** Fundamental position. **G.-ton.** Root; tonic. Fundamental of a compound tone. **G.-tonart.** The prevailing key. **G.-stimme.** The bass part.

**gruppo** (groop´pō), *I.* A group, formerly a trill, shake, or turn. **gruppet´to.** 1. A small group. 2. A turn.

**G-Schlüssel** (gä´-shlüs-sĕl), *G.* The G clef. Vide CLEF.

**guaracha** (gwa-rä´chä), *Sp.* A Spanish dance, with one part in triple and one in 2-4 time, the dancer often accompanying himself on the guitar.

**guaranita** (gwä-rä-nē´-tä), *Sp.* A small guitar.

**Guarnerius.** Vide the B. D.

**guddok** (goo-dôk), *Rus.* A 3-stringed violin.

**gue.** An obsolete Shetland violin with 2 horsehair strings played 'cello-fashion.

**guerriero** (goo-ĕr-rĭ-ā´-rō), *I.* Martial.

**guet** (gĕ), *F.* A trumpet flourish.

**guia** (gē-ä), *Sp.* Fugue; conductor; leader.

**guida** (goo-ē´-dä), *I.* (a) Guide 1, (b) Vide PRESA. (c) Also, a through which the voice glide singing an interval legato.

**guide.** 1. Subject, of fugue. 2. tecedent of imitation. 3. A dire

**guide** (gēd), *F.* Guide 1, 2. gu main (măṅ). A chiroplast, inv Kalkbrenner.

**guidon** (gē-dôṅ), *F.* A direct.

**Guido´nian.** Relating to Guido d'A zo. (Vide B. D.) **G. hand.** A diag on an outstretched left hand of *Aretenian syllables.* Vide SOLM TION.

**guil´tern** (gĭl´-tern). Cither.

**guimbard, guimbarde** (găṅ-bär(d) A jew's harp.

**guion** (gē´-ōn), *Sp.* A repeat sign.

**guitar,** *E.*, **guitare** (gĭ-tär), *F.*, **gui ra** (gē-tär´rä), *Sp.*, **Guitarre** (gĭ-rĕ), *G.* A modern form of the l long-necked with frets; six-string compass E-a″ (plus an octave harmonics). The accordature is A-d-g-b-e´ (or E-B-e-g-b-e´). music is written an octave higher t it sounds. **g. d'amour.** Vide ARI GIONE. **g. lyre.** A French stringed instr. of lyre-shape.

**guiterne** (gē-tĕrn), *F.* Ancient gui

**gu´nibry.** A 2-stringed guitar.

**Gunst** (goonst), *G.* Grace, ten ness.

**guracho** (goo-rä´-chō), *Sp.* Vide GU ACHA.

**gusla** (goosh´-la). Servian 1-strin instr. with skin sound-board.

**gusli, gussel.** A Russian zither.

**gusto** (goos-to), *I.* Taste, express **gran g.** The grand manner. g **toso** (goos-to´so), **gustosamer** Tasteful(ly).

**G-ut.** Vide GAMMA UT.

**gut.** Strings made of entrails of she

**gut** (goot), *G.* Good. **gutdün** (dünk´ĕn). At pleasure. gu **Takteil.** Strong beat.

**gutturale** (goot-too-rä´lĕ), **guttu men´te,** *I.* Gutteral(ly).

**gyta´rah.** Nubian guitar. **g. b barych.** The Berber guitar.

## H

**H** (In *G.* pron. hä). German name for *B-natural;* B being reserved for *B flat.* **h.** Abbr. for *horn, heel,* and.

**banera** (ä-bä-nä´-rä), *Sp.* A dance popular in Havana; it is in 2-4 time with the first eighth note dotted; ncopation and caprice play a large art. Vide DANCE-RHYTHMS.

**berrohr** (hä´-bĕr-rōr), *G.* Shepherd's ute.

**ckbrett** (häk´-brĕt), *G.* Dulcimer. **b** (hälp), *G.* Half, lesser. **halbe Apikatur.** Half-shift. **Halb-bass, ello,** or **violine.** A small doubleass, 'cello or violin. **H.-violon.** A nall double-bass. **halbgedackt** (ĕ-däkt). Half covered (of stops). **.-instrumente.** Vide GANZINSTRUENTE. **H.-kadenz** or **-schluss.** alf-cadence. **H.-mond.** Crescent. **.-note.** Half-note, or **H.-taktnote.** and-note; in horn-playing, a opped note. **H.-orgel,** or **-werk.** n organ with no stops lower than ft. pitch. **H.-prinzipal.** An obsote 4-ft. stop. **H.-rüdenhorn.** Vide EFHORN. **h.-stark.** Mezzoforte. **.-stimme.** A half or partial stop. **.-ton,** or **halber Ton.** Semitone. **alf-cadence** or **half-close.** Vide DENCE. **half-note.** A minim. **alf-note rest.** A pause equal to a alf-note. **half-shift.** Vide SHIFT. **alf-step.** The smallest interval sed. **half-stop.** Vide STOP.

**il.** Vide KHALIL.

**l** (häl), *G.* Sound, clang. **hallen** äl´lĕn). To sound, to clang. **Hallrommete** (drôm-mä-te) or **-tromete.** A powerful trumpet.

**elujah** (häl-lĕ-loo´yä), *Heb.* Alluia.

**ling.** Norwegian country-dance.

**mpfeife** (pfī´fĕ), *G.* Shepherd's pe.

**s** (häls), *G.* 1. Neck (of a violin, c.). 2. Throat. 3. Stem.

**t** (hält), *G.* A pause, a hold.

**Hammer** (pron. in *G.* häm´mĕr). 1. That part of the mechanism of a piano which strikes the strings and produces the tone. 2. Mallet for playing the dulcimer. 3. The striker of a bell. **tuning h.** An instr. for tightening the pegs of a piano or harp. **Hammerklavier** (klä-fēr´), *G.* The modern piano.

**hanacca** (hä-näk´-kä), *I.,* **hanaise** (ä-nĕz), *F.,* **Hanakisch** (hä-nä´-kĭsh), *G.* A rapid polonaise-like Moravian dance in 3-4 time.

**Hand, harmonic.** Vide GUIDONIAN. **hand-guide.** Chiroplast. **h.-harmonic.** Accordeon. **h.-horn.** One without valves or pistons. **h.-organ.** A portable barrel organ (q. v.). **h.-note.** In horn-playing, a stopped note.

**Hand** (hänt), pl. **Hände** (hĕnt´-ĕ), *G.* Hand. **H.-bassl.** An obsolete instr. between viola and 'cello. **H.-bildner** (or **-leiter**). A chiroplast. **H.-lage.** Position of the hand. **H.-stücke.** Finger-exercises. **H.-trommel.** Tambourine.

**handle-piano.** Vide BARREL ORGAN 2

**Harfe** (här´-fĕ), *G.* A harp. **Harfen bass** (här´fĕn-bàss). A bass of broken chords. **Harfensaite.** Harpstring. **Harfenspieler.** Harpist. **Harfenett.** Vide SPITZHARFE. **Harfeninstrumente.** Instrs. whose strings are plucked. **H.-laute.** Vide DITAL.

**Harke** (här´-ke), *G.* Fork for ruling staves.

**Harmo'nia,** *L.* Daughter of Mars and Venus; music in general.

**Harmonic.** *As an adjective.* Musical, concordant; relating to harmony (i. e., to chords, etc. as opposed to melody) and to the theory of music. **h. chord.** A generator and its harmonics. (Vide below.) **h. curve.** The figure described by a string in vibration. **h. figuration.** Broken chords, often with passing notes. **h. hand.** Vide GUIDONIAN. **h. mark.** A small circle over a note to be played as an harmonic. **h. note, tone,** vide the noun HARMONIC. **h. scale.**

The series of partials (vide ACOUSTICS). **h. stop.** A flute or reed stop having its pipes pierced midway, so that the harmonics predominate over the fundamental tone, hence **h. flute** and **h. reed. h. triad.** Major triad. **h. trumpet.** The sackbut.

*As a noun* (frequently used in the plural). 1. One of the many partial tones that go to make up the compound vibration we call tone, this compound being called by the name of its generator. (Vide ACOUSTICS.) 2. A vibrating string when lightly touched at a nodal point (as that of a half, 3d, 4th, or 5th, etc., of the string's length) will vibrate in divisions (2, 3, 4, or 5, etc.), each division sounding the same tone respectively an octave, a 12th, 15th or 17th, etc., higher than the string. These produce a choir-like unison of exquisite sweetness whose flutiness has given them the name **flageolet-tones.** These harmonics if produced from an open string are called **natural ;** from a stopped string, **artificial.** Harmonics are called for by the word *flageolet* or its abbr. *fl. ;* or the words *flautando, flautato,* or *flûte,* or by a small circle (o) called the **harmonic-mark** over the note to be touched, or by writing a black note indicating the open string, a diamond-headed note above it showing where the string is to be touched, and a small note above to indicate the actual sound. **Grave Harmonics.** Combinational tones. "Properly speaking, the harmonics of any compound tone are other compound tones of which the primes are partials of the original compound tone of which they are said to be harmonics." —A. J. ELLIS.

**Harmon'ica.** 1. An arrangement by Benj. Franklin of musical glasses in a scale, on a spindle turned by a treadle. The glasses were moistened in a trough, and as they revolved melodies and chords could be played. F. called his device **armonica.** 2.

The **mouth-harmonica** or ▮ **monicon** is a reed mouth-instr. ducing different tones when breath is inhaled and exhaled. delicate stop. **Harmonica-ä risch** (ä'-tĕr-ĭsh), *G.* A delicate n ure-stop. **harmonichord.** PIANO-VIOLIN.

**harmonicello** (chĕl'-lō). A 'cello instr. with 15 strings (5 of them ▮ inv. by J. K. Bischoff, Nürnb 18th century.

**harmonici.** Vide CANONICI.

**harmon'icon.** 1. Vide HARMONICA A keyed harmonica with flue-stop, by W. C. Müller. 3. An orchestr

**harmoni-cor,** *F.* A wind-instr. ▮ harmonium-like reeds in a clarinet-tube, inv. by Jaulin, Paris.

**harmo'nicum.** An improved ba nion ; virtually an accordeon wor with treadles, inv. by Brendl Klosser, Saxony, 1893.

**Harmonie** (här-mō-nē'), *G.* 1. I mony. 2. A chord. 3. (a) The w instruments collectively, or (b) m for them. **h.-eigen,** Chordal ; ap priate or native to the harmony ; posed to **h.-fremd,** foreign. **H.-le** (lā-rĕ). Theory of music. **H.-mu** Vide HARMONIE 3. **H.-trompete** trumpet employing stopped tones ▮ success. **H.-verständiger** (fĕr-sht dĭkh'-r). A harmonist. **harm ren** (här-mō-nē'-rĕn). To harmon **harmo'nisch.** Harmonious.

**harmonist.** One versed in the ▮ of music.

**harmonie** (ăr-mō-nē), *F.* 1. Harm 2. Harmonics. **harmonieux** mōn-yŭ'). Harmonious. **harm eusement** (yŭz-män). Harmoni ly.

**Harmo'nika,** *G.* 1. Accordeon. Concertina. **H.-töne.** Vide HARM ICS.

**Harmo'niker,** *G.* Harmonici.

**harmon'iphon.** An instr. with ▮ board, inv. 1837, by Panis, of Pari supply the place of oboes in orc tras. The sounds are produced f reeds acted upon by currents of

rmonique (ăr-mō-nēk), *F.* Harmonic, applied to pipes of double length.

rmoniquement (ăr-mō-nēk-män), *F.* Harmonically.

rmo'nium. Vide REED-ORGAN.

r'monise. To combine two or more parts in accordance with the laws of music ; to add accompanying chords to a melody.

rmonom'eter. A monochord.

rmony, chromatic (or diatonic). That characterised by chromatic (or diatonic) progression. close h. That in which the 3 highest parts do not cover more than an octave ; opposed to open, dispersed, or extended h. compound h. That in which some of the tones are doubled ; op-posed to simple h. essential h. (a) The fundamental chords of a key. (b) The harmonic outline stripped of embellishment. figured h. That in which the chord progressions are embellished variously ; opposed to plain or natural h., the common triad. forbidden h. A chord whose construction or approach is contrary to the rules of Harmony. suspended h. That in which one or more notes is suspended. pure h. (as of a stringquintet). Opposed to tempered h., as of a piano. Vide TEMPERAMENT. strict h. That which is rigidly obedient to the rules ; opposed to free h. Two-part (etc.) h. That in which two (or more) parts appear.

## Modern Harmony in Practice.

### By A. J. Goodrich.

[NOTE.—Many of the terms touched upon here will be found treated in more detail under their names.—*Ed.*]

N its broader sense Harmony embraces the origin and classification of chords, their rearrangement, inversion, and progression ; modulation, resolution, transition, false relation, sequence, suspension, chromatic rmonisation and other topics too numerous to mention here. Yet the idamental principles of harmony may be easily explained and readily under-od. ¶We begin with concords because they are most euphonious and t subject to the somewhat complex theories of resolution. A concord or nsonant triad consists of a normal ("perfect") 5th and a major or minor from the root. When the intervals stand in this order the lowest note the root, or the name-note of the chord. It would thus appear to the eye *upon lines or all upon spaces :* thus *G b d* form the chord of **G** ajor. *G, b flat, and d,* would form the chord of *G* minor. ¶Every ajor key bears six concords, the imperfect triad on the leading note not be-; a concord. ¶The reader may now sound upon a piano or organ these concords, each in its first or root position. After sounding the first chord d before proceeding to the next, ascertain the gender,—that is, whether it masculine (major), or feminine (minor). These distinctions should be termined by the auricular sense, and also by the visual sense. Practice d theory should be thus combined. ¶From the theory of scales and keys,

and intervals [vide these terms] the reader is supposed to know whethe
given chord represents a major or a minor key. The 1st, 3d, and 5th,
every major scale form a major concord : the same numbers in a minor
yield a minor concord. But it is still more important that the ear shall
trained to distinguish between these genders, because music appeals m
directly to the auricular faculties.

### Concords Classified.

When all the concords have been sounded and their characteristics rec
nised, they should be classified. How many major? How many mine
Which degrees of the scale bear major and which minor concords? ¶Te-
nical terms may be then applied : chord of the tonic, 1 ; chord of the s-
dominant, 4 ; chord of the dominant, 5 ; chord of the super-dominant (relat
minor of the tonic), 6 ; chord of the super-tonic, 2 ; chord of the mediant,
In other words we have as elemental material, the chords of the tonic, s-
dominant, and dominant (always major in a major key) and the relat
minors [vide RELATIVE] of these. This process should be repeated in
the major keys.

### Concords Rearranged.

A chord has as many close positions as it has letters. In the first positi
the root is lowest. In the second position the root is highest, while the th
is below. In the third position the root is in the middle, the 5th
below and the 3d above. ¶At first the different positions are to be effec
by rearranging the letters thus : *C*, *e*, *g*, root position of the *C* cho:
Place the *C* last (an octave higher), and the second position will result *e, g,*
Now place the *e* last (an octave higher), and the third position will appe
—*g*, *C*, *e*. Since no new element has been introduced it is evident that
chord still remains and that *C* is the root. The capital letter serves to in
cate to the eye whether the theoretical root is below, in the middle, or
the top. (A distinction is to be made between these simple rearrangeme
of concords and the actual *inversion* of chords. Inversion comes much late:
Every concord in the key is to be rearranged by means of letters, as in
cated, and the different positions are to be numbered in regular order 1, 2,
¶The six concords are now to be rearranged on the key-board, using
letter schemes as a preliminary guide. After the six chords have thus be
played in their three close positions the process should be continued in ot
keys without the aid of letters or written notes. ¶Care must be exerci:
not to add any new element to the tones of a given chord while its rearran;
ments are being played. For instance, in the second position of the *F* ch
pupils sometimes produce the *A* minor triad by playing *a*, *C*, *e*, instead

*c*, *F*. Sound all the concords in their three close positions in every major
. (See Ex. 1.) ¶ Also it is desirable to play the rearrangements in this

EXAMPLE I.

inner descending, as well as ascending. (Interesting examples in this style
y be invented.)

### PRELIMINARY HARMONISATION.

The six rearranged chords in any given key are now selected as a guide.
ese must appear in notation. Every tone in the major scale of *C* is to be
monised with as many concords as contain the note to be illustrated.
is is to be accomplished at the instrument. 1. Select *c″* (an octave
ve middle *c*). This is a stationary tone representing, for instance, a soprano
t. 2. How many of the six concords in this key contain *c*? (Examine
chart of rearranged chords in *C*, always beginning with the first chord,
ascertain how many contain *c*,—whether above or below is immaterial.)
What is the first chord that contains a *c*? What position has *c* at the
? 4. Play this. 5. What is the next chord containing *c*? 6. What
ition has *c* uppermost? 7. Play this, keeping the same finger (5) upon
space *c″*. 8. What is the third chord containing *c*? In what position
uppermost? 9. Play this, the *c* being still in the soprano part, highest.
this much has been correctly executed the following results will appear:
e *C* chord will be in its second position, the *F* chord in its first position,
the *A* minor chord in its third position, *e*, *A*, *c*. Each chord is to be
nded simultaneously, the letters which represent notes are read from below,
vard, therefore *e*, *g*, *C*, indicate that the chord of *C* is to be struck, *C*
ng uppermost. Repeat the process at the piano : *C* chord, 2. *F* chord, 1.

minor chord, 3. The fingering should be 2 3 3 (See Ex. 2.) ¶ The
5 5 5 (above)
1 1 1 (below)

EXAMPLE II.

ond chord of the scale is now selected, and this is to be harmonically illus-
ed in the same manner. 1. How many concords in the key of *C* con-
*d*? (Do not use the imperfect triad in any of these elementary exercises.)
What is the first chord containing *d*? 3. What position has *d* at the

top? 4. Play this. 5. What is the other chord having a *d*? (Mention
letter-name of the chord and say whether it be masculine or feminine.)
What position of the *G* chord has *d* at the top? 7. Play it, then rep
In this manner every tone in the key of *C* should be harmonically illustrat
Only the six concords in this key are to be used, though each one may
played in any of its three close positions, according to circumstances. Tra
pose to other major keys.

### SIMPLE THEORY OF STRICT CHORD PROGRESSION.

Any tone which occurs in any two different chords is called a *connect
tone*. Every connecting tone is played by the same finger in both chords
sung by the same voice. When there are two notes in common between t
chords in progression, the connecting tones are retained, or remain station
—tied or played by the same finger. (The previous elementary progr
sions agree with this theory.) ¶Now arrange a score of four staves,
bass staff below and three treble staves above. On the first treble staff w
the progression *C, F, A* minor, keeping the connecting notes stationa
On the second treble staff write the *C* chord in its next position above, *g, C*
Then write the *F* chord (with *c* in the middle) and the *A* minor chord w
*a* and *c* tied from the preceding. On the third or highest treble staff w
the *C* chord in its first position and proceed to make the same progressi
*i. e., C* to *F*, and *F* to *A*. It is to be understood that the progressions on
two upper staves are similar to those on the lowest treble staff, 2 and 3 be
rearrangements of 1. In each instance the same principles are to be appli

EXAMPLE III.

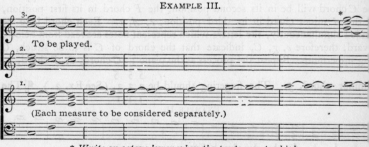

To be played.

(Each measure to be considered separately.)

*Write an octave lower when the parts run too high.*

For instance in progressing from the *C* to the *F* the connecting note (*c*) v
appear alternately in the soprano, mezzo-soprano, and contralto parts. W
the first measure is completed in the three treble parts, vertically, add
roots in the bass staff immediately beneath the treble chords. The bass p

es fundamentally, from root to root, while the treble parts progress
odically, that is without skipping. Do not skip the bass part up or down
e than a 5th. ¶Proceed to harmonise d with the two concords which
ompany it : then write two rearrangements above. Observe strictly the
necting-note principle. When the second measure is completed in the
le parts add the roots in the bass as before. Every tone in the scale is
be treated similarly—2, 4 and 7 having but two chords each as accom-
ying harmonies. (See Ex. 3.) ¶After this scheme has been worked
on paper, choose another key and proceed to make a similar example at
key-board, without the aid of notes except perhaps the rearranged chords,
ch may be used as a chart. Continue this process in several other major
s, until the progressions can be played readily and correctly.

## MELODIC SKIPS OF A 3D.

When the melody skips up or down a 3d the accompanying harmony
ains the same. In other words the melody skip may be accompanied by
chord in the key which contains both notes of the melodic interval. This
been partially illustrated in the rearrangement of concords. Therefore
nd e may be accompanied by the C chord or the A minor chord, but *not
both chords.* When the melody skips, the bass remains stationary as a con-
ting note. Consequently there is always a connecting note either above
below in the present examples. A skipping theme is given and this should
harmonised at the piano and on paper. (See Ex. 4.)

### EXAMPLE IV.

(Continuous.)

### SKIPS OF A 4TH.

These are harmonised by the same principle, though a skip of a fourth
mits but one chord as accompaniment : that chord which contains both
es of the skip furnishes the solution. During the skip the bass remains,
acts as a connecting note. Example 5 is to be harmonised practically
theoretically, as explained.

### EXAMPLE V.

(8-measure theme.)

## Harmonic Warnings for Composers.

### By A. J. Goodrich.

1. Don't use any intervals in parallel movement *except* these :

(*a*) Unisons, and octaves when the latter are above or below, with harmony between the octaves.

(*b*) Major or minor thirds, ascending or descending diatonically.

(*c*) Minor thirds ascending or descending chromatically.

(*d*) Major thirds ascending or descending chromatically. (These w formerly forbidden, but modern composers use them freely for certain p poses. They are, however, rather harsh and incisive.)

(*e*) Major or minor sixths ascending or descending diatonically—like thirds.

(*f*) Major sixths up or down chromatically.

(*g*) Minor sixths up or down chromatically. (These are inversions the major thirds, and therefore the same remarks apply.)

(*h*) Augmented fourths may ascend or descend chromatically where th form parts of diminished chords in succession. (The exigencies of notat will require that the imperfect fifth—which is an harmonic equivalent of augmented fourth—shall appear occasionally in place of the latter. Thus and *f* sharp may be followed by *b* and *f* natural. Practically the two in vals are identical and interchangeable.)

(*i*) Descending augmented fourths may occur in a series of domin seventh chords proceeding according to the dominant relation—up a fourth down a fifth.

2. Don't use *any* of these intervals in parallel movement :

(*a*) Major or minor seconds, ascending or descending.

(*b*) Normal or "perfect" fifths, especially between bass and soprano, contralto and soprano. The imperfect may follow the perfect fifth. But reverse of this is rather rough and generally ineffective.

(*c*) [Normal fourths, when they are accompanied by diatonic thir above or below, have been frequently employed. A succession of triads their second or third close positions necessarily involves parallel fourths, as the Finale to Beethoven's op. 2, *II*.] Parallel fourths ought to be exclud from strict two-part counterpoint, as they are too much inclined to vacuousne

(*d*) Major or minor sevenths are not to be used in parallel successie Diminished sevenths sound like major sixths. Therefore these two interv may succeed each other alternately.

(*e*) Parallel octaves have always been forbidden, and usually their effec awkward or confusing. Yet hundreds of instances might be quoted from

ters. A simple illustration is the little Romance from Schumann usually
pled with his "Träumerei"—the theme above is doubled by a solo
s part below.

f ) Cross relation or false relation is another pitfall into which the young
poser is likely to stumble. The effect is sometimes very unpleasant and
ther times perfectly satisfactory. ¶The student should avoid at all times
nterdicted or suspicious progressions, even though the "evil" be more
:ied than real. If he becomes a creative artist he must eventually act on
own responsibility, free and independent of all prescription and formula.

p, *E.*, **harpe** (ärp), *F.* A stringed
iangular instr. of great antiquity
nd variety. The gut-strings which
re plucked with both hands are nec-
sarily diatonic. In the old single-
ction harp (key of E flat, compass
-d'''') the notes could be raised a half-
ne by the use of pedals. Thanks
to the ingenuity of Sebastian Erard,
ho in 1820 perfected the "double-
ction harp," all keys are obtainable
n the modern harp in fairly quick suc-
ssion, by the manipulation of seven
edals each raising a string and all its
ctaves a half or a whole tone. Thus
y sharpening or flattening the proper
nes, any key may be obtained. The
atural scale is C♭, and the more
arps in the key the less the sonor-
y; double flats and sharps are im-
ssible, and remote modulation diffi-
lt. There are 46 (or 47) strings,
mpass C' flat–f'''' (or g'''' flat).
uble **h.** One with 2 rows of dif-
rently tuned strings. **triple h.**
ich as the Welsh). One with 3 rows.
olian **h., h. éolienne.** Vide
OLIAN. **couched h.** The spinet.
inted **h.** Vide SPITZHARFE. **chro-**
atic **h.** Inv. by Pfranger; it has,
wever, too many strings. **jew's**
arp. A small instr. with metal
ngue, played upon by placing it
tween the teeth, and striking with
e tongue and the finger; the breath
termines the tone; known in the
ade as "Irish harp." **h. instru-**
ents. Those whose strings are not
wed.

**harpechorde** (ärp-kôrd), *F.*, **harpi-**
**cordo** (är-pǐ-kôr'-dō), *I.* The harpsichord.

**harpeggiren** (här-pĕd-jē'rĕn), *G.* Vide
ARPEGGIATE.

**harpe-lute.** Vide DITAL. **harp-pedal.**
The soft pedal of a piano.

**harpo-lyre.** A 3-necked, 21-stringed
guitar, inv. by Salomon, 1829.

**harp'secol.** Vide HARPSICHORD.

**harp'sichord.** A precursor of the modern piano, whose strings were set in
vibration by jacks carrying quills or
bits of hard leather (instead of tangents, as in the clavichord). Sometimes
it had more than one key-board as in
the **vis-à-vis** (vē-zä-vē), which had
a key-board at each end. The **double**
**h.** had 2 unison strings and an octave
for each tone; and stops for varying the use of these. The **harmon-**
**ica h.** is an harmonica with key-
board.

**harp-style.** Arpeggio style.

**harp-way tuning.** Early English ac-
cordatures of the viol da gamba fa-
cilitating arpeggios.

**harsur** or **hasur** (hä'-zoor), *Heb.* A
Hebrew instr. of 10 strings.

**hart,** *G.* Major; hard; unprepared. **h.**
**verminderter Dreiklang.** A triad
with major 3d and diminished 5th.

**hartklingend.** Harsh-sounding.

**hâte** (ät), *F.* Haste, speed.

**haubois** (ō-bwä), *F.* An oboe.

**Haupt** (howpt), *G.* Head, principal.
**H.-accent.** Principal accent. **H.-**
**akkord.** Fundamental triad. **H.-ge-**
**sang, H.-melodie.** Principal mel-

ody. **H.-kadenz.** Full cadence. **H.-kirche.** Cathedral. **H.-manual.** The great manual ; the great organ. **H.-note.** 1. The principal note in a shake, turn or trill. 2. The chord-note. 3. Accented note. 4. Melody-note. **H.-periode.** Principal period. **H.-probe.** The final rehearsal. **H.-satz.** Principal theme, subject or idea. **H.-schluss.** Final cadence. **H.-septime.** Dominant 7th. **H.-stimme.** Principal part. **H.-thema.** Principal theme. **H.-ton.** 1. Funda-mental or principal tone. 2. The tonic. 3. The 5th in a minor triad. **H.-tonart.** The principal key. **H.-werk.** Great organ.

**hausse** (ōs), *F.* Nut of a bow.

**hausser** (ōs-sā), *F.* To raise the pitch.

**haut** (ō), **haute** (ōte), *F.* Acute, shrill, high. **haute-contre** (ōt-kôntr). High tenor. **haute-dessus** (ōt-děs-sü). High treble, soprano. **hautement** (ōt-män). Haughtily. **haute-taille** (ōt-tä-ē). High tenor.

**hautb.** Abbr. of *Hautboy.*

**hautbois** (ō-bwä), *F.,* **hautboy** (ho'-boy), *E.* 1. The oboe. 2. An 8-ft. reed-stop. **h.-d'amour.** An organ-stop. Vide OBOE. **hautboy-clarion.** Vide OCTAVE HAUTBOY.

**H.-bes** (hä-běs), *G.* B double flat. **H.-dur** (hä-door). B major.

**head.** 1. The part of the note which marks its position on the staff. 2. Point of a bow. 3. Membrane of a drum. 4. The part above the neck of violins, etc., containing the pegs. **head voice.** The upper or highest register of the voice.

**heel.** The wooden brace fastening the neck of violins, etc., to the body.

**Heerhorn** (hār'-hôrn), *G.* A military trumpet. **Heerpauke** (hār'pow-ke), *G.* Old kettle-drum, tymbal. **Heer-pauker.** Kettle-drummer.

**heftig** (hěf'-tǐkh), *G.* Boisterous, pas-sionate. **Heftigkeit** (kīt). Vehe-mence.

**heimlich** (hīm'-lǐkh), *G.* Secret, stealthy, mysterious.

**heiss** (hīs), *G.* Hot, ardent.

**heiter** (hī'těr), *G.* Serene, glad.

**Heldenlied** (hěl'děn-lēt), *G.* He[ song. **heldenmüthig** (mü-tǐkh). [ roic. **Heldentenor.** Dramatic ten

**hel'icon,** *E.,* **Hel'ikon,** *G.* 1. A [ itary bass brass wind-instr., car[ over the shoulder ; scales, F, E [ C and B flat (the lowest tone of bass of which is B,,). 2. Ancien[ stringed device showing the theor[ intervals.

**hell** (hěl), *G.* Clear, bright.

**helper.** An octave-pipe set beside [ of 8-ft. pitch to add to its brilliance[

**hem'i,** *G.* Half. **hemidemise[ quaver (-rest).** A 64th note (or re[ **hemidiapen'te.** Diminished fi[ **hemidit'onos,** *Gr.* Minor third[

**hemio'la, hemio'lia,** *Gr.* 1. The r[ 3 : 2. 2. Quintuple time. 3. In[ val of a 5th. 4. A triplet. 5. [ NOTATION (COLOUR).

**hemiope,** *Gr.* An ancient three-h[ flute.

**hemiphrase.** One bar of a phrase[

**hemito'nium,** *Gr.* A semitone in G[ music (ratio 256 : 243).

**heptachord.** 1. Interval of a seve[ 2. A 7-stringed instr. 3.` A G[ series of 7 tones with half-tone [ between the 3d and 4th.

**heptade** (hěp'-täd), **hep'tadechord[** Vide ELLIS.

**heptam'eris,** *Gr.* A seventh part [ meris.

**Herabstrich** (hār'-äp'strǐkh), *G.* Do[ bow. **Heraufstrich** (hār'-owf-strǐ[ Up-bow.

**heraufgehen** (hār-owf'gāěn), *G.* [ ascend.

**hero'ic,** *E.,* **heroisch** (hār'-ō-ǐsh), **héroïque** (ā-rō-ēk), *F.* Bold, bra[ Vide EROICA.

**Herstrich** (hār-strǐkh), *G.* Down-[ (on 'cello and double-bass). **Her[ terstrich,** *G.* Down-bow (on the [ lin, etc.).

**hervorgehoben** (hār-fôr'ghě-hō'b[ **hervorhebend** (hä'běnt), **herv[ tretend** (trä-těnt), *G.* With emp[ sis.

**z** (hĕrts), *G.* "Heart." Vide TAS-
CAU.

**zig** (hĕrts-ikh), **herzlich** (lĭkh), *G.*
ender.

**s** (hĕs), *G.* B flat when directly
erived from B natural (or H).
**eses,** B double flat.

**len** (hoi'-lĕn), *G.* To cipher.

**achord,** *Gr.*, **hexachorde** (ĕx-ä-
ŏrd), *F.* 1. A scale, or system, of
x sounds. 2. A sixth. 3. A six-
ringed lyre.

**am'eron,** *Gr.* Group of six pieces.

**aphonic.** Composed of six voices.

**de guise** (ĕ-dŭ-gēze), *F.* A
ountry-dance.

**tus.** A gap.

**den.** 1. Obscured, covered, yet im-
lied; thus in the skip, say, from
to *g*, the tone *f* is implied though
ot struck or dwelt on; it could be
alled **hidden.** But the term is used
ather of intervals similarly implied,
ius in the progression, say from e–c
o g–d, the tone *f* is passed over,
nd as *f* makes with *c* the same in-
erval as *g* with *d*, that is, a perfect
fth, the progression becomes a **hid-
en** or **implied fifth,** and is put
nder the same ban by stricter theo-
sts, though sanctioned by free prac-
ce. Similarly a progression, as of
–b' to c–c' contains **hidden octaves.**
. **h. canon.** Close canon.

**f** (hēf), **Hiefstoss** (shtôss), *G.*
ound of the hunting-horn. **Hief-
orn, Hifthorn** (hĭft), **Hüfthorn**
ĭft). A wooden hunt-horn with 2
r 3 notes, and in 3 pitches: **H.-
inke** (tsĭnk-kĕ). High. **Rüden-
orn** (rüd'-n). Low. **Halb-rüden-
orn.** Medium.

**rophon** (hēr'-ō-fōn), *Gr.* Singer of
ymns.

**gai'on se'lah,** *Heb.* A term, per-
aps calling for stringed instr. and
rumpets.

**h.** 1. Acute in pitch. 2. Upper,
r first, as **h.** *soprano.* **high bass.**
. baritone. **higher rhythm.** A
iythm composed of smaller ones.
**igh mass.** Vide MASS. **h. tenor.**

Counter-tenor. **h. treble clef.** The
G clef on the first line.

**hilfs-.** Same as **hülfs-.**

**Hinaufstrich** (hĭn-owf'strĭkh), *G.* Up-
bow on the violin, etc. **Hinstrich**
(hĭn'-strĭkh), *G.* Up-bow on 'cello
and double-bass.

**Hintersatz,** *G.* An old mixture-stop,
re-enforcing the open diapason.

**Hirtenflöte** (hĭrt'-ĕn-flā'-tĕ), *G.* Shep-
herd's flute. **Hirtengedicht** (gĕ-
dĭkht). Pastoral poem. **H.-lied** (lēt).
Pastoral song. **H.-pfeife** (pfī-fe).
Pastoral pipe. **hirtlich** (hĭrt'-lĭkh).
Pastoral, rural.

**His** (hĭs), *G.* B♯. **hisis** (hĭs'ĭs), *G.* B
double sharp.

**H.-moll** (hä'môl), *G.* B minor.

**Hoboe** (hō-bō'-ĕ), **Hoboy** (hō-bōē), *G.*
Oboe. **Hobo'ist,** *G.* Oboist.

**hoch** (hôkh), *G.* High, sharp, very.
**Hochamt** (hôkh ämt). High Mass.
**h. feierlich** (fī'-ĕr-likh). Very solemn. **H.-gesang, H.-lied** (lēt).
Ode, hymn. **H.-horn.** Oboe. **H.-
muth** (moot). Elevation, pride.
**Hochzeitsgedicht** (tsīts), **Hochzeitslied.** Wedding-song. **Hoch-
zeitsmarsch.** Wedding - march.
**höchsten** (hĕkh'-shtĕn), *G.* Highest.

**hock'et, hocqu'etus.** 1. An abrupt
rest. 2. Old English part-music full
of rests and abruptness.

**Hof** (hôf), *G.* Court; hence, **H.-kapelle
(Konzert).** Court orchestra (concert).
**H.-musikant** (moo-zi-kant). Court
musician. **H.-organist.** Court organist.

**höflich** (hĕf'lĭkh), *G.* Graceful. **Hof-
lichkeit** (kīt). Grace.

**Höhe** (hā'ĕ), *G.* Height, acuteness;
upper register of; as *Oboen-höhe.*

**hoheit** (hō'hīt), *G.* Dignity, lofti-
ness.

**Hohlflöte** (hōl'flā-tĕ), *G.* "Hollow-
toned flute." Open flue-stop of various pitches; in the smaller called
**Hohlpfeifen.** The mutation-stop in
the fifth is called **Hohlquinte.**

**hok'et, hock'et.** A quint-stop.

**hold** (hōlt), *G.* Pleasing, sweet.

**hold.** The fermate. **holding-note.**

A note sustained while others are in motion.

**hold'ing.** *Old F.* Burden.

**Holzbläser** (hôlts'blā-zĕr), *G.* Player(s) on **Holz'blasinstrumente,** or wood-wind instruments.

**hölzernes Gelächter** (hĕlts'-ĕr-nĕs gĕ-lĕkh'-tĕr), *G.* Xylophone.

**Holzflöte** (hôlts'flā-tĕ), *G.* "Wood-flute "; a stop.

**Holz'harmonika,** *G.* Xylophone.

**hom'ophone.** A letter or character denoting the same sound as another ; thus a♯ and b♭ are homophones. **homophon'ic, homoph'onous.** 1. Noncontrapuntal, lyric, marked by one melody in predominance. Vide POLYPHONIC. 2. In unison. Vide ANTIPHONIC. **homoph'ony,** *E.,* **homophonie** (ôm-ôf-ôn-ē), *F.* Music that is homophonic 1 or 2.

**hook.** The stroke added to the stem of notes smaller than ¼ notes.

**hop'per.** In piano action, the escapement-lever.

**Hop'ser, Hops-tanz** (tänts), *G.* Country-dance. **Hopswalzer** (hôps' väl-tsĕr), *G.* Quick waltzes.

**hoq'uetus.** Hocket.

**hora** (pl. **horae**), *L.* Hour(s). **horae canonicae.** Canonic hours, those at which services are held : **lauds.** Sunrise. **prime.** First hour (6 a.m.). **tierce** (or **terce**). 3d (9 a.m.). **Sext.** 6th (noon). **nones.** 9th (3 p.m.). **vespers.** Evening. **compline.** Final. Services during the night are called **nocturns ;** the word **matins** includes both nocturns and lauds. **horae regulares.** Chant sung at regular hours.

**horn** (*G.* pl. **Hörner**) (hĕrn'ĕr), *E.* & *G.* General name for all metal wind-instruments. Specifically, the **French horn,** a brass conical tube variously curved, with a flaring bell at one end, and a cupped mouthpiece at the other ; the shape of this mouthpiece, and the ratio of the width to the length of the tube determining the quality of the instr. The old *natural horn* was diatonic, producing only the tones of its natural scale, some intermediate tones being obtained by putting the hand in the bell, or "stopping " the tone. The key of the horn was changed by taking out one section of its tube (a *crook*), and inserting a section longer or shorter, thus lowering or raising the key. The series was thus incomplete, and its *stopped tones* were inaccurate. The natural tones depend on the amount of wind-pressure (or in F, embouchure, lipping) which must vary with each note according to the natural scale (see ACOUSTICS).

The horn of this century has gradually displaced the natural horn. It is provided with valves (or auxiliary tubes), which practically lengthen or shorten the tube instantaneously. The tone is produced by embouchure combined with valve-manipulation until a complete chromatic scale is obtainable. *Stopped tones* are not necessary, though available for special effects ; they are called for by the sign +, by the word "stopped," or by "son bouché " (sôn boo-shā), and are weirdly tragic or romantic. The range of the horn depends upon its key, the scale of each consisting of a fundamental tone, and the natural series of partials (vide ACOUSTICS), the intermediate tones between the 3d and the 16th partial being obtained by valves or stopping. A horn in C thus sounds *C, c, g,* from *g* to *c''* being nearly complete chromatically, the upper notes being risky. The other horns are lower, the interval between their key and C ; they are B flat, A, A flat, G, F, E flat, D, C *basso,* B flat *basso.* The keys F♯ (G flat), C♯ (D flat), B and A *basso* are obtained not by changing crooks, but by drawing out a special slide which lowers the key a semitone. In valve-horns the F horn is by far most common. Music for horn is now always written in the G clef, the F clef being used for the lower notes, which are always written

tave lower than they sound. For
nvenience of embouchure, the notes
e written as if the horn were always
C, and the player so plays it ; but
e crook used governs the tone, and
C on the staff sounds as the F below
an **F horn**, as A flat on the A flat
rn, etc. **Alpine h.** A wooden horn
t. long. **basset h.** Vide BASSET.
nting-h. The primitive *natural*
*French horn.* **horn-band.** A
nd of trumpeters. A *Russian H-*
is one in which each hunting-horn
ays but one note. **horning.** Vide
VAREE. **Hornmusik',** *G.* Music for
brass. **Hornquinten,** *G.* The hid-
a fifths prevalent in music for two
rns. **Hornsordin',** *G.* A conical or
ar-shaped mute inserted in the bell.
pipe. A old E. shawm with a
l of horn ; hence, an old E. dance
great vivacity, in 3-4 or 4-4 time.
an'na, Hosian'na, *Heb.* "Save,
pray," an interjection in prayer,
ace part of the Sanctus. Vide MASS.
(hŏ'-zĕ), *G.* Boot of a pipe.
(howl). A Persian military drum.
s. Vide HORÆ.
(wrā'ôl). A Danish peasant-dance.
Abbr. for *Hauptsatz.*
uetl, huehuitl (wā-wāt'-'l). An
ec drum 3 feet high with a mem-
ne that could be tightened at will,
nging the pitch and furnishing an
monic bass.
horn (hĭft-hôrn), *G.* Bugle-horn.
gab, *Heb.* 1. An organ. 2. Pan's
es.
ied (wēt-pĭ-ā), *F.* Eight feet (of
ps). **huitpieds.** An organ with
stops larger than 8 ft.
igungsmarsch (hool-dĭ-goongks-
sh), *G.* A solemn march for re-
ws.

**Hülfs-** (hĭlfs), *G.* Auxiliary. **Hülfslinien**
(lē'-nĭ-ĕn). Ledger-lines. **H.-note,**
**H.-ton.** Auxiliary, accessory note.
**H.-stimme** (shtĭm'mĕ). A mutation-
stop.

**Hummel** (hoom'mel), **Hümmelchen**
(hĭm'mĕl-khĕn), *G.* 1. A bagpipe.
2. In organs the thorough-bass drone.
3. The Balalaika, because it had a
sympathetic or drone-string. 4. The
drones in a hurdy-gurdy.

**hummen** (hoom'mĕn), *G.* To hum.

**Humor** (hoo'-mor), *G.* Humour, whim.
**Humoreske** (hoo'mo-rĕs'ke), *G.,* **hu-
moresque** (ü-môr-ĕsk), *F.* A humorous or whimsical composition.

**hunting-horn.** A bugle or French
horn. **hunting-song.** Song in
praise of the chase. **hunt's-up.** A
boisterous morning-song.

**hurdy-gurdy.** An old instr. with
four strings, acted on by a wheel
rubbed in resin. Two of the strings
are stopped by certain keys, the
others act as a drone-bass ; compass
$g$-$g''$.

**hurry.** Premonitory roll of drum or
tremolo of strings in stage-music.

**hurtig** (hoor'tĭkh), *G.* Quick, allegro.
**H.-keit** (kīt). Agility.

**hydraul'icon, hydraulic organ.** An
instr. older than the wind-organ, inv.
180 B.C., by Ktesibios of Alexandria,
the wind-pressure being regulated by
water.

**hymn,** *F.,* **hymne** (ēmn), *F.,* **Hymne**
(hēm'nĕ), *G.* A sacred or patriotic
song. **h. vesper.** A hymn sung in
the R. C. Vesper service. **hymnal,**
**hymn-book.** A collection of hymns.
**hymnology, hymnologie** (ēm-n'ŏl-
ō-zhē). Vide next page.

**hymnus,** *L.* A hymn. **h. Ambro-
sianus.** The Ambrosian chant.

## Hymnology.

### By H. E. Krehbiel.

HYMNS, in the sense in which we apply the term, as an adjunc
Christian worship, appear to have been used from the earliest c
of the Church.    The early Christians naturally borrowed t
music from their forefathers in Judea, Greece, and Rome, and the Church
was quite lacking in any uniformity in this element of worship.    Not till
various branches of the Church in the Roman Empire were united und
Christian Emperor, Constantine, is there evidence of attempts to form a syst
The first result of this was the Ambrosian chant, and later, the Gregorian, at
congregational, later confined exclusively to the priest.    Famous Latin hyn
like the " Te Deum," " Magnificat," " Benedictus," etc., were in
from very early days of the Church, being sung to plain-chant melodies.
the period of the great Church composers—Josquin des Prés, Palestr
Orlando di Lasso, and others, these hymn-tunes were often used as c
fermi for masses and motets ; and Palestrina also used them as the basis
a set of " Hymns for the Entire Year," one of the most important of
works.    ¶In the meantime a more popular development of hymnal m
had been going on in the Mysteries and Miracle-plays, outside the immec
supervision of the Church, that were so conspicuous a feature of popular life
worship in the Middle Ages.    In the Church itself the music had been
tirely in the hands of the priests and the regular choirs.    At the time of
Reformation, however, Luther introduced a great change in this respect,
which the ground was already prepared by the popular development of hy
singing just mentioned.    The chief note of the Reformation was individu
in worship, the transfer of its chief features from the priest to the congr
tion ; and in line with this principle Luther laid great stress on the rein
duction of congregational singing, which had been abandoned since the e
days of the Church.    Luther produced a great number of hymns, the w
of which he fitted to popular melodies of the day.    The first Lutheran hy
book was published in 1524 ; it was in the vernacular and its popularit
Germany soon became enormous, leading to the speedy issue of innumer
other works of the same kind.    Luther not only used the melodies of s
songs for these hymns, but caused new tunes to be written, and som
them—notably the most famous, " Ein' feste Burg ist unser Gott,"—h
said to have composed himself.    It ought to be said, however, that his
thorship of the music of this " Battle Hymn of the Reformation " has k
disputed.    They were all broad choral tunes simply harmonised, such as
main to-day in constant use in Germany, and formed the model for the hy

e whole Protestant Church. In France the metrical psalms of Marot
Beza were as enthusiastically received by the Protestants as Luther's
as in Germany; they were originally sung to popular tunes of the day
ntained in a psalter published in 1542, by Calvin, in Geneva. There-
numerous other collections were published, notably one by Claude Gou-
l, in 1565. ¶In England the general cultivation of part-singing in the
rigals made the acceptance of popular hymnody as a part of the new
ous movement facile and speedy. Here, as in France, the first hymns
metrical versions of the Psalms in English, and numerous collections of
were published in the last half of the sixteenth century, at first for one
only. "The Whole Psaimes in foure parts," harmonised in the sim-
manner possible, published in 1563, was the first harmonised collection
nglish hymn-tunes. Numerous collections of such tunes were issued
after, the most notable being Ravenscroft's, in 1621, and Playford's,
71. ¶With the composition of hymns by Wesley and his followers in
ighteenth century came a new poetic material of which musicians were
low to avail themselves, and which resulted in new hymn-tunes of greater
th of feeling, differing entirely from the older school of hymns in both
dy and harmony. These have had a great, if not always beneficial, ince on the modern development of hymnal music. ¶Hymnology has
a notable place in the history of American music. The stern piety of
Puritan immigrants in New England developed a great activity in this
ch of musical art, after it had been freed from the shackles that at first
ned it, and the number of early American hymn-tune composers was
. Among these were William Billings (who in 1770 published "The
rican Psalm Singer : or American Chorister," containing hymns of his
composition), Samuel Holyoke, Andrew Law, Jacob Kimball, Oliver
en, and others. In the earlier years of the nineteenth century Thomas
ngs, Lowell Mason—whose influence in a secular way on the develop-
of music and musical taste in America was marked—and Nathaniel
d were the most prominent.

te, *Gr*. The uppermost lyre-string
the lowest in tone. **hypaton.**
west tetrachord. Vide MODES.
**tho'ides.** The lower tones in the
ek scale.
**r** (hī'-per), *Gr*. Over, above, of in-
vals, "super," or "upper" (as **hy-
diapa'son,** the octave above ; **h.-
pen'te,** the 5th above ; **h.-dito'-
,** the 3d above, etc.) ; of the Greek
nsposition scales and ecclesiastical
ave species, "a fourth higher"; the

Greek octave species "a fifth higher,"
or "a fourth lower." Vide MODES for
such words as **hyper-æolian,** etc.
**hypo,** *Gr*. Below, under; of intervals,
"sub," or "lower." **hypodiapa'son.**
The lower octave. **h-diapen'te.** The
fifth below. **h-dito'nos.** The third
below. For the names of the Greek
transposition scales and ecclesiastical
modes, as **hypoæo'lian,** etc., vide
MODES.
**Hzbl.** Abbr. of **Holzbläser (q. v.).**

# I

**I** (ē) *I.*, pl. " The." Also the letter is used by Kirnberger, to indicate a major seventh, as b♮ in place of b♭ in the 7th chord on c. Tartini used *u.*

**Ias'tian**, *Gr.* The Ionian mode.

**ic'tus**, *Gr.* Stress, accent, emphasis.

**idea.** A theme, subject, figure, or motive.

**idée fixe** (ē-dā fēx), *F.* Berlioz's name for a recurring theme or motive.

**idyl, idillio** (ē-dēl'lĭ-ō), *I.*, **idylle** (ē-dē-yŭ in *F.*, in *G.* ē-dĭl'lĕ). A pastoral.

**il** (ēl), *I.* The. **il più** (ēl pē-oo'). The most, e. g., *il più forte possibile.* As loud as possible.

**ilarità** (ē-lä-rĭ-tä'), *I.* Hilarity.

**imboccatura** (ĭm-bŏk-kä-too'rä), *I.* 1. Mouthpiece. 2. Embouchure.

**imbroglio** (ĭm-brōl'yō), *I.* "Confusion," a passage of complicated rhythms.

**imitando** (ĭm-ĭ-tän'dō), *I.* Imitating. **i. la voce** (vō'-chĕ). Imitating the voice.

**imitation** (pron. in *F.* ĭm-ĭ-tăs-yôṅ), **imitatio** (ēm-ĭ-tä'tsĭ-ō), *I.* The repetition by a second voice (the consequent or answer) of a figure, subject or theme first announced by another (the antecedent or subject). If this repetition be exact, interval for interval, note-value for note-value, the **imitation** is *strict* or *canonic*, vide CANON ; otherwise *free.* **i. at the 5th, octave, etc.** That in which the answer follows the subject at the interval of a 5th, octave, etc. **i. augmented** or **i. by augmentation.** That in which the answer is in notes of greater value than those of the subject. **diminished i.** or **i. by diminution.** A style of imitation in which the answer is given in notes of less value than those of the subject. **freely inverted i.** That in which the order of successive notes is not strictly retained. **i. in contrary motion.** That in which the rising

intervals of the subject descen the answer and vice versa. **i. in ferent divisions.** That in w the subject is answered in a diffe division of a measure ; for insta beginning on the accented is swered on the unaccented. **i. in ilar motion.** That in which answer retains the order of not the subject. **retrograde i.** ( **per recte e retro), cancrizan cancrizante.** That in which subject is taken backwards in answer. **reversed retrograd** That in which the subject is t backwards and also in contrary tion in the answer. **strictly inv ed i.** That in which note-value precisely answered in contrary tion. **tonal i.** That which doe alter the key.

**imitation pipes and draw-knob** dummies of more beauty than us

**imitative music.** That aimin mimic the operations of natur water-falls, thunder, etc.

**imitato** (ĭm-ĭ-tä'tō), *I.* Imitated. **itazione** (tä-tsĭ-ō'nĕ). Imitatio

**immer** (ĭm'mĕr), *G.* Always, constantly.

**immutab'ilis,** *L.* Vide ACCE ECCLESIASTICI.

**imparfait** (ăṅ-păr-fĕ'), *F.* Imper

**impaziente** (ĭm-pät-sĭ-ĕn'-tĕ), *I.* patient. **impazientemen'te.** riedly.

**imperfect.** Not perfect or com Vide CADENCE and INTERVAL. **i. cords, consonances.** Thirds sixths, so called because they ch from major to minor, still rema consonant. **i. measure.** Old for two-fold measure. **i. time.** term for common time. **i. t** The chord of the third, fifth eighth, on the seventh degre consists of two minor thirds.

**imperfection.** 1. Vide LIGATUR Vide NOTATION.

**imperfet'to,** *I.* Imperfect.

**imperioso** (ĭm-pā-rĭ-ō'-so), *I.* pous. **imperiosamen'te.** Imperi

erturbabile (ĭm-pĕr-toor-bä′bĭ-lĕ),
  Quiet.
eto (im′-pĕ-tō). impetuosità (im-
  -too-ō-zĭ-tä′), I. Impetuosity, ve-
  mence. impetuo′so, impetuosa-
  en′te. Impetuous(ly).
onente (nĕn′tĕ), I. Imposingly.
lied discord. A concord con-
  ined in a dissonant chord as a major
  ird in an augmented 5th (as f-a-c♯).
lied interval. One not specifically
  dicated by its numeral but implied by
  other numeral. Vide HIDDEN.
resario (ĭm-prĕ-sä′-rĭ-ō), I. Man-
  er of opera, concerts, etc.
romp′tu (in F. ăṅ-prôṅ-tü). An
  temporaneous comp., or one having
  spirit of informality and caprice.
rope′ria, L. "Reproaches." In
  . C. ritual, a series of antiphons
  d responses for Good Friday morn-
  g. In Rome sung to old Faux
  urdons arranged by Palestrina ;
  sewhere to plain-song from the
  raduale Romanum.
ropri′etas. Vide LIGATURE.
rovise, impro(v)visare (zä′rĕ), I.,
  iproviser (äṅ-prô-vē-zä), F. To
  ig or play without premeditation.
rovisateur (äṅ-prô-vē-ză-tŭr′),
  iprovisatrice (trēs), F., Impro-
  sator (ĭm-prō-fĭ-zä′-tôr), G., Im-
  ovvisato′re, I. An improviser.
  rovisation. Extemporaneous per-
  rmance. Improvisier maschine
  n-prō-fĭ-zēr′ mä-shē′-nĕ), G. A
  elograph. improvvisata (zä′tä), I.
  n extempore composition. im-
  ovviso (ĭm-prôv-vē′-zō), improv-
  samen′te, I. Extemporaneous(ly).
  n), I., G. and L. In, into, in the.
  utire (in-ä-koo-tē′-rĕ), I. To
  arpen.
etont, G. With medial emphasis.
runst (ĭn′broonst), G. Fervour.
  brünstig (ĭn-brĭn′-shtĭkh). Ar-
  nt.
lzando (ĭn-käl-tsän′dō), I. Has-
  ning.
arna′tus, L. "Was born" (of the
  irgin Mary). Part of the Credo.
ide MASS.

inch (of wind). In an organ, wind-
  pressure is gauged by a graduated U
  tube in which water rises, the mean
  pressure being 3 inches.
inchoa′tio, L. Vide CHANT.
incisore (ĭn-chĭ-sō′-rĕ), I. Engraver
  of music.
inconsola′to (lä′-tō), I. Mournful.
incordare (dä′-rĕ), I. To string.
incrociamen′to (krō-chä), I. Crossing.
indeciso (ĭn-dĕ-chē′-zō), I. Undecided
  (implying slight changes of time, a
  somewhat capricious tempo).
indegnato (ĭn-dān-yä′-tō), indegna-
  tamen′te, I. Wrathful(ly).
independent. Used of non-dissonant
  harmony requiring no resolution.
index. 1. A direct. 2. Forefinger.
indifferen′te (rĕn′-tĕ), indifferente-
  men′te, I. Indifferent(ly). indiffer-
  enza (rĕn′-tsä), I. Indifference.
infantile (ĭn-fän-tē′lĕ), I. Child-like
  (of the quality of upper notes of some
  voices).
infe′rior, L. Lower.
infernale (ĭn-fĕr-nä′lē), I. Infernal.
infervorato (rä′-tō), I. Fervent.
infiammatamen′te, I. Ardently.
in′finite, E., infinito (ĭn-fĭ-nē′-tō), I.
  Used of canon which can be continued indefinitely unless given a special
  cadence.
inflatil′ia, L. Instrs. of inflation ; wind-
  instruments.
inflection. 1. Modification in the
  pitch of the voice. 2. In chanting a
  change from the monotone.
in′fra, L. Beneath. Infrabass, G.
  Sub-bass.
infuriante (ĭn-foo-rĭ-än′tĕ), infuriato
  (ä′-tō), I. Furious.
inganno (ĭn-gän′-nō), I. "Deception" ; applied to a deceptive cadence ; also to unexpected resolutions
  or modulations. d′inganno. Unexpected.
in′gemination. Old term for repetition of words.
ingressa. Vide INTROIT.
Inhalt (ĭn′hält), G. Contents ; idea.
inharmonic relation. Vide FALSE
  RELATION.

**inner.** 1. Used of the alto or tenor part as distinguished from the bass and soprano. 2. Used of a pedal-point on an inner part.

**innig, inniglich** (ĭn'-nĭkh-lĭkh), *G.* Sincere, tender, heartfelt. **Innigkeit** (kīt). Deep feeling.

**inno** (ĭn'-nō), *I.* A hymn, canticle, ode.

**innocente** (ĭn-no-chĕn'tĕ), **innocent-emen'te,** *I.* Innocent(ly), artless-(ly). **innocenza** (ĭn-nō-chĕn'-tsä). Innocence.

**inquieto** (ĭn-kwĭ-ā'-tō), *I.* Restless.

**insensible** (ĭn-sĕn-sē'bĭ-lĕ), **insensi-bilmen'te,** *I.* Imperceptibly, by small degrees.

**insisten'do,** *I.* Urgent. **insistenza** (tĕn'-tsä). Insistence.

**inständig** (ĭn-shtĕn'dĭkh), *G.* Urgent, pressing.

**instante** (ĭn-stän'tĕ), **instantemen'te,** *I.* Vehement(ly), urgent(ly).

**in'strument** (in *F.* ăn-strü-män̈). A sonorous body constructed for the production of musical sounds. **i. à cordes** (ä-kôrd). A stringed instr. **i. à l'archet** (ä-lär-shä). Instr. played with a bow. **i. à percussion** (ä păr-küs-yôn̈). Instr. of percussion. **i. à vent** (ä vän̈). Wind-instrument.

**instrumental,** *E.,* **instrumentale** (ĭn-stroo-mĕn-tä'lĕ), *I.* Of music for instrs. as opposed to vocal music.

**instrumentare** (tä'rĕ), *I.* To compose instrumental music.

**in'strumenta'tion** (in *F.* ăn-strü-män̈-tăs'yôn̈), **instrumentazione** (tä-tsĭ-ō'nĕ), *I.,* **Instrumenti(e)rung** (ĭn-stroo-mĕn-tē'-roongk), *G.* The art or act of writing or arranging a composition for instrs., particularly the orchestra (vide article on THE ORCHESTRA AND ORCHESTRATION); sometimes used of piano-playing that produces the effect of other instrs. **Instrumentenmacher** (mäkh'ĕr), *G.* An instr.-maker.

**instrumen'to,** *I.,* An instrument. **i. d'arco** (or **a corda**) (där'-kō). A stringed instrument. **i. da campanel'la.** Glockenspiel. **i. da fiato**

(fĭ-ä'-tō). Wind-instr. **i. da qu** A spinet.

**intavolare** (ĭn-tä-vō-lä'-rĕ), *I.* write out or copy music. **intav tura** (lä-too'-rä). 1. Notation. Figured bass. 3. Tablature.

**integer valor (notarum),** *L.* " integral value" (of notes), i. e., average duration at a mode movement. Michael Pretorius the **i. v.** of the brevis at about a minute (i. e., 80 to 7¼ minutes)

**intendant** (än̈-tän̈-dän̈), *F.,* **in den'te.** *I.* Director, conductor.

**intenzionato** (ĭn-tĕn-tsĭ-ō-nä'-tō). phatic.

**in'terlude.** 1. A piece, usually s played between acts, moveme stanzas, or portions of service. A short operetta.

**interlu'dium,** *L.,* **intermède** (än̈ mĕd), *F.,* **intermedio** (ĭn-tĕr-mä'd **intermezzo** (ĭn-tĕr-mĕd'-zō), *I.* interlude.

**interme'diate.** 1. Accidental. Transitional.

**intermedietto** (ĭn-tĕr-mä'dĭ-ĕt-tō). A short interlude.

**interrogati'vus.** Vide ACCENTUS E

**interrotto** (rôt'-tō), *I.* Interrupte

**interrupted.** Vide CADENCE.

**interruzione** (root-sĭ-ō'nĕ), *I.* In ruption.

**interval, Intervall** (ĭn-tĕr-fäl'), *G.,* **tervale** (än̈-tĕr-văl), *F.,* **interv** (väl'lō), *I.,* **interval'lum,** *L.* distance, or difference in pitch, tween tones, reckoned upwards (un specially stated). The intervals the *first* or *prime* (which is identity for instance being its own prime) ; *second* (as c–d) ; the *third* or *tierce* c–e) ; the *fourth* or *quart* (as c–f) ; *fifth* or *quint* (as c–g) ; the *sixt* *sext* (as c–a) ; the *seventh* or *sept* c–b) ; the *eighth* or *octave* (as c– the *ninth* (as c–d'), etc. Those w in the octave are called *simple ;* t over the octave, *compound,* sinc *tenth* is an octave plus a third, et Intervals are qualified also by t mode ; those in the major key of t

wer tone (as a–c♯) being called *major*,
ose a semitone greater than major
e *augmented* or *extreme*, *superflu-*
*es*, *redundant* or *sharp ;* those a
mitone less than major are *minor*
s a–c) ; those a semitone less than
inor are *diminished* or *flat* (as a–c♭).
he first, fourth, fifth and octave are
lled *perfect* instead of major, be-
use they do not change their quality
do the others on inversion (q. v.).
ther names for intervals are *chro-*
*atic*, containing a note foreign to
e key, opposed to *diatonic*, *dis-*
*nant*, needing resolution ; opposed
*consonant*, *enharmonic* (q. v.) ;
*armonic* when struck simultaneous-
instead of separately, hence op-
sed to *melodic*. *Forbidden*. Con-
ary to the rules of Harmony (q. v.).
*nsecutive* (q. v.). A *natural* inter-
l is that between two tones of a
ajor scale.

he ratios of the vibrations of diaton-
intervals are prime, 1 : 1 ; second,
: 9 ; third, 4 : 5 ; fourth, 3 : 4 ; fifth,
: 3 ; sixth, 3 : 5 ; seventh, 8 : 15 ;
tave, 1 : 2.

*rvening*. Intermediate (of a fugue
bject).

**mo** (ĭn'-tĭ-mō), *I.* Intimate, ex-
ressive. **intimis'simo.** Most ex-
ressive.

**nare** (ĭn-tō-nä'rě), *I.* To in-
ne.

**na'tion.** 1. The production of
und by voice or instr., as regards
uality and pitch. **false i.** That
hich is untrue to the key or pitch.
The initial phrase of the antiphon.
. Method of singing plain-chant. 4.
ide CHANT. **fixed i.** Vide FIXED
ONE.

**nato** (ĭn-tō-nä'-tō), *I.* Tuned, set
music.

**onator.** Monochord.

**natura** (ĭn-tō-nä-too'rä), **intona-**
**ione** (ĭn-tō-nä-tsĭ-ō'ně), *I.* Intona-
on.

**ni(e)ren** (ĭn-tō-nē'rěn), *G.* 1. To
tone. 2. To voice, as pipes. 3.
he voicing.

**Intonireisen** (nēr'-ī-zěn), *G.* A knife
used in trimming and tuning pipes.

**Intrade** (ĭn-trä'-dě), *G.* A prelude or
entrance-music.

**intreccio** (ĭn-trĕt'-chō), *I.* " Intrigue."
A short dramatic work.

**intrepidezza** (ĭn-trä-pĭ-dĕd'-zä), *I.* In-
trepidity. **intrepido** (ĭn-trä'-pĕ-dō),
**intrepidamen'te.** Bold(ly).

**introduc'tion**, *E.*, **introducimen'to**
(doo-chĭ), **introduzione** (doo-tsĭ-ō'-
ně), *I.* The preliminary measures,
or movement preparatory for the
main subject.

**intro'it** (in *F.* ăṅ-trwä), **introito** (ĭn-
trō-ē'-tō), *I.*, **intro'itus**, *L.* " Entrance " ; a hymn or antiphon sung
in R. C. service while the priest goes
to the altar ; in the Anglican Church
Communion, when the minister goes
to the table. In the Ambrosian ritual called *Ingressa*.

**intuonare** (in-too-ō-nä'-rě), *I.* To intone.

**inven'tion** (in *F.* ăṅ-väṅs-yôṅ), **in-**
**venzione** (ĭn-věn-tsĭ-ō'-ně), *I.* A
short informal contrapuntal study
with one theme.

**Inventions** (horn) (ĭn-věn'tsĭ-ōns), *F.*
A Waldhorn fitted with crooks by
Werner, 1760.

**inver'sio**, *L.*, **inver'sion**, *E.* The
transposition of the elements of (a),
chords, (b) intervals, (c) themes, (d)
parts. (a) The triad is " inverted "
from its fundamental position with
the root in the bass, to the *first in-*
*version* with the 3d in the bass, and
the *second i.* when the fifth is in the
bass (a 6–4 chord), etc., vide CHORD.
(b) The inversion of intervals is the
lowering of the upper tone an octave,
thus bringing the lower note above,
and the upper below ; for example,
to invert a major 6th, *e'♭–c'*, we lower
*c'* an octave, securing *c–e'♭*, a minor
3d. The new product of an inversion is always the difference between
the first interval and the number 9,
e. g., a 6th inverted becomes a 3d,
a 5th inverted becomes a 4th, etc.
The result of inversion is to change

major intervals to minor, and vice versa; and augmented to diminish, and vice versa; but perfect remain perfect. (c) A theme is inverted by being repeated backwards, hence, **retrograde inversion**, or **inversio cancrizans**, "crab-like." (d) Two parts are inverted when the lower is raised by an octave (**inversio in octavam acutam**), or by a fifth, tenth, twelfth, etc., or when the higher is lowered by an octave (**inversio in octavam gravem**, or **inferiorem**), a fifth, tenth, twelfth, etc. (vide COUNTER-POINT).

**invert, inverted.** Vide INVERSION. A *pedal-point* in any part other than the lowest is called *inverted*. A *turn* commencing with the lowest note is *inverted*.

**invi'tatory,** *E.*, **invitato'rio,** *Sp.*, **invitato'rium,** *L.* 1. An antiphon in the R. C. Matins. 2. In the Anglican Church, the versicle "Praise ye the Lord," and the response sung at matins. 3. In the Greek Church the "O come let us worship" sung thrice before the psalms at the canonical hours.

**invocazione** (kä-tsĭ-ō'-nĕ), *I.* Invocation.

**Io'nian, Ion'ic.** Vide MODES.

**ira** (ē'-rä), *I.* Anger, wrath. **irato** (ē-rä'-tō), **iratamen'te.** Passionate(ly).

**Irish harp.** 1. An ancient instr. having more strings than the lyre. 2. Trade name for "Jew's harp."

**irlandais** (ēr-läṅ-dĕ'), *F.*, **irländisch** (ēr'-lĕnt-ĭsh), *G.* An air or dance in the Irish style.

**iron harp.** A semicircular arrangement of tuned iron rods which vibrate sympathetically when a violin is played.

**ironico** (ē-rō'-nĭ-kō), *I.*, **ironicamen'te.** Ironical(ly).

**irregular,** *E.*, **irregolare** (ēr-rā-gō-lä'rĕ), *I.* Not according to strict rule or practice. Vide CADENCE.

**irresoluto** (ēr-rā-zō-loo'-tō), *I.* Irresolute.

**isdegno** (ēs-dān'-yō), *I.* Indigna

**i'sochronal,** *Gr.*, **isoch'ronous.** form in time.

**i'son.** In Greek Church chant movable tonic.

**isoton'ic.** Used of a system of vals in which all concords are pered alike, and contain twelve semitones.

**istes'so,** *I.* The same. **i. tempo.** same time (as before).

**istrepito** (ēs-trä-pē'-tō), *I.* Noise, ter.

**istrionica** (ēs-trĭ-ō'nĭ-kä), *I.* H onic.

**istrumentale** (ēs-troo-měn-tä'lĕ) Instrumental. **istrumentazion** tsĭ-ō'në). Instrumentation. i **men'to.** An instrument.

**Italian mordent.** Shake or trill tone with the next above. **Ita sixth.** Vide ALTERED CHO **Italian strings.** Catgut st largely made in Rome.

**italiano** (ē-tä-lĭ-ä'-nō), *I.*, **italier** (ē-tä-lĭ-ä'-nĭsh), *G.*, **italien(ne)** ( yäṅ [or-yĕn]), *F.* Italian.

**i'te, mis'sa est** (ecclesia), *L.* ' part, the congregation is dismis Vide MASS; from the word *miss* word mass is derived.

## J

**JACK,** *I.* 1. An upright slip of on the back end of a key-k carrying a crow-quill or pie hard leather which projecte right angles (in the harpsichord a metal tangent (in the clavich and which struck and set in m a string. The quill or the le served as a plectrum. 2. The " per."

**Jagd** (yäkht), *G.* Hunt, hunting. **J horn, Jagdzink** (tsĭnk). Hun horn, bugle-horn. **Jagdruf** (r Sound of the horn. J-lied Hunting-song. **J-sinfonie** (sĭ nĕ'). A symphony of the hunt. **stück.** A hunting-piece.

erchor (jä'-khĕr-kôr), *G.* Chorus
hunters. **Jägerhorn.** Hunting-
orn.

:age (yäl'-täj). The sole musical
str. of Tartary, a slender box of fir,
out 4 ft. long, over which six wire
rings are stretched. It is played
ith both hands.

o (hä-lä'-ō), *Sp.* A Spanish dance
3-8 time, moderato, for one per-
n.

usieschweller (yäl-oo-zē'-shvĕl-
r), *G.* "Venetian-blind" swell.

itscharenmusik (yä-nĭt-shä'rĕn-
oo-zēk'), *G.*, **jan'izary music.** Mil-
ary music for cymbals, triangles,
c.

kó. Vide KEY-BOARD.

(zhŭ) pl. **jeux** (zhŭ), *F.* 1. Play;
yle of playing on an instr. 2. A
op on the organ, harmonium, etc.
The organ-power, as **grand j.**
-rän), or **plain j.** (plăn). Full organ.
emi-j. Half-power. **j. à bouche** (ä
posh). Flue-stop. **j. céleste** (sä-
st). Vide CELESTE. **j. d'anche**
(länsh). Reed-stop. **j. d'anges**
(änzh). Vox angelica. **j. d'échos**
(lä'-kō). Echo-stop. **j. de flûtes**
(lüt). Flute-stop. **j. de mutation**
(nü-tăs-yôn). Mutation, or a mixt-
re-stop. **j. de timbres** (tănbr).
lockenspiel. **j. de violes** (vē-ôl).
onsort of viols. **j. de voix hu-**
**maine** (vwä ü-mĕn). Vox humana.
**d'orgues** (dôrg). Register, or
w of pipes. **jeux forts** (fôr). Loud
ops.

r's harp or jewstrump. Vide
ARP.

A light, brisk dance in 6-8 or 12-8
me. Vide SUITE.

:les. The disks of metal on a tam-
ourine

el (yō'-bĕl), *Heb.* Trumpets or
orns.

ulator. A jongleur.

ler (yōt'-lĕr), *G.* A style of sing-
g affected by the Tyrolese, falsetto
lternating rapidly with chest-regis-
r. **jodeln** (yō'dĕln). To sing in
ich style.

**jongleur** (zhôn-glŭr), *F.* A hired or
strolling musician. Vide TROUBA-
DOUR.

**jota** (hō'-tä), *Sp.* A Spanish dance in
rapid 3-8 time.

**jouer de** (zhoo-ä-dŭ), *F.* To play
upon (as an instr.).

**jour** (zhoor), *F.* "Day." **corde à j.**
Open string.

**ju'ba.** Part of the breakdown dance of
the American negro.

**Jubal** (yoo'-bäl), *G.* A 2 or 4 ft.
stop.

**Jubelflöte** (yoo-bĕl-flä'-tĕ), *G.* A stop.
**Jubelgesang, Jubellied** (lēt). Song
of jubilee. **Jubelhorn.** Key-bugle.

**jubelnd** (yoo'-bĕlnt), *G.* Rejoicing.

**Jubila'te,** *L.* "Be joyful." The name
for the 10th Psalm in the Anglican
Church.

**jubila'tio,** *L.* The cadence on the last
syllable of "Alleluia" in R. C. music.

**jubiloso** (yoo-bĭ-lō'-sō). *I.* Jubilant.

**ju'bilus,** *L.* 1. An elaborate passage
sung to one vowel. 2. Jubilatio.

**Judenharfe** (yoo'-dĕn), *G.* Jew's harp.

**Jula** (yoo'-la), *G.* An old 5 ½-ft. stop.

**jump.** 1. A progression by a skip. 2.
Vide DUMP.

**Jungfernregal** (yoonk-fărn-rä'-gäl) or
**J-stimme,** *G.* Vox angelica.

**Jupiter symphony.** Mozart's 49th,
in C major.

**just.** Used of consonant intervals,
voices, strings, pipes, etc., that speak
or sound with exactness.

**juste** (zhüst), *F.* Accurate, perfect (of
intervals). **justesse** (zhüs-tĕs'). Exactness of intonation.

# K

[*NOTE.—Many German words are
spelt either with "C" or "K," preferably the latter.*]

**KABARO** (kä-bä'-rō). A small
Egyptian drum.
**Kadenz** (kă-dents'), *G.* 1.
Cadence (q. v.). 2. Cadenza.
**kalamaika** (kăl-ä-mä'-kä). A lively
Hungarian dance in 2-4 time.

**Kalkant** (käl-känt'), *G.* Bellows-treader. **K.-glocker.** Signal-bell to the blower.

**Kammer** (käm'-mĕr), *G.* Chamber (q. v.). **K.-kantate** (kän-tä'-tĕ). Chamber-cantata. **K. komponist.** Court-composer. **K. konzert.** Chamber-concert, or concerto. **K. duet.** C. duet. **K. musik, K. spiel** (shpēl). Chamber-music. **K. musikus** (moo'-zĭ-koos). Member of a prince's private band. **K. sänger** (zĕng-ĕr). Court-singer. **K. stil** (shtēl). Style of chamber-music. **K. suiten.** Chamber-suites. Vide SUITE. **K. ton.** International pitch. **K. virtuose.** Court-virtuoso.

**kampoul** (käm-pool'). A Malay gong.

**kandele** (kän-dä'-lĕ). 1. Ancient Finnish harp. 2. A dulcimer.

**Kanon** (kä'-nōn), *G.* "A rule." 1. A canon. 2. A monochord with movable bridge; sometimes it had a second string in unison. **kanonik** (kä-nŏ'-nĕk). Canonic.

**kanoon', kanun'.** Turkish instr. of the dulcimer variety; the canun.

**Kantate** (kän-tä'-tĕ), *G.* Cantata.

**Kan'tor,** *G.* Cantor.

**Kanzelle** (kän-tsĕl'-lĕ), *G.* Groove in a wind-chest.

**Kanzellied** (lēt), *G.* Hymn before the sermon.

**Kanzone** (kän-tsō'-nĕ). *G.* Canzone.

**Kapelle** (kä-pĕl'-lĕ), *G.* A chapel. 1 A musical establishment, a choir o a band connected with a church or court. 2. Any orchestra. **Kapellknabe(n)** (knä'-bĕ(n). Choir-boy(s). **Kapellmeister** (kä-pĕl'-mīsh-ter), *G.* 1. Conductor. 2. Chapel-master. **Kapellmeister-musik.** Music full of such strains as must sound reminiscent to the conductor. **K. stil** (kä-pĕi'-shtēl) *G.* Same as *A cappella*, i. e., unaccompanied.

**Kapodas'ter,** *G.* Capotasto.

**Karfreitag** (kär-frī'täkh), *G.* Good Friday.

**Kassation** (käs-sä'-tsĭ-ōn), *G.* Cassation.

**Kastagnetten** (käs-tän-yĕt'-tĕn), Castanets.

**Kat'zenmusik** (moo-zēk'), *G.* " music." Charivari.

**Kavatine** (käv-ä-tē'-nĕ), *G.* Cava

**kazoo .** A tube with a vibrating st which gives the voice an amu quality when spoken or sung thro

**keck** (kĕk), *G.* Fresh, bold. **Ke heit** (kĕk'-hīt). Boldness, vigor.

**keen'ers.** Irish paid mourners.

**Kehle** (kā'-lĕ), *G.* The voice, throat. **K.-fertigkeit** (fĕr-tĭkh- Vocal agility. **K.-kopf.** Lar **K.-schlag** (shläkh). Coup de gl **K.-laut** (lowt). A guttural soun

**Kehrab** (kär'-äp), **Kehraus** (ows) Colloquial term, for the final danc a ball.

**kemangeh** (kĕ-män-gäh'). A T ish stringed instrument.

**kenet** (kĕn'-ĕt). Abyssinian trump

**Ken'ner,** *G.* A connoisseur, " who knows."

**Kent bugle** (*G.*, **Kenthorn**). BUGLE. So named in honor of Duke of Kent.

**kerana** (kë-rä'-nä). A Persian sounded at sunset and midnight.

**ker'anim.** Vide KEREN.

**ke'ras,** *Gr.* A horn.

**Keraulophon** (kĕ-row'-lô-fōn), *G.* 8-ft. stop, a small round hole b in the pipe near the top promc the overtones; inv. by Gray Davidson.

**keren** (kĕr'-ĕn), pl. **keranim,** *Heb.* horn. **keren-Jcbel** (ya-bel). bilee horn.

**Kern** (kärn), *G.* The languid (q. **K. stimmen.** The fundame stops.

**kerrena** (kĕr-rä'-nä). The kerana.

**Kes'sel,** *G.* Cup (of a mouthpie **Kesselpauke** (pow-kĕ). Ke drum.

**ketch.** Old name for catch.

**Ket'tentriller,** *G.* Chain of trills.

**ket'tledrum.** A brass or copper tle over the top of which is stret a head of vellum, tightened by a and tuned by screws, or by cor-is

races. **Kettledrums** are usually
layed in pairs with sticks having
exible handles and soft knobs.
ach has a compass of a fifth ; the
wer may be tuned to any note from
to c, and the higher B flat to f.
. 1. A family of chords and a
ain of tones (i. e., a scale) finding
eir centre and point of rest in a cer-
in tone (the tonic) from which the
ey takes its name. All keys con-
rm to the standard for major keys,
to that for minor keys. The
gnature in which the number of
arps or flats of a major key is
ritten serves as the signature for
related minor key, the tonic
which is a minor third below.
he key of C has neither sharps nor
ats, the key a fifth above (G) has
e sharp, the key a fifth below (F)
s one flat, and so the progression con-
ues, forming (in a tempered instru-
ent. Vide TEMPERAMENT) what is
lled the circle of fifths, as F♯ and G♭
e enharmonic keys traversing the
me tones. The following ingenious
art from Riemann's Dictionary
bulates the keys and their signatures
ncisely, the flats and sharps ap-
aring in the same order on the
gnatures as here :

Major Keys.

Flats.       Sharps.

7 6 5 4 3 2 1 0 1 2 3 4 5 6 7
Cb Gb Db Ab Eb Bb F C G D A E B F♯ C♯ G♯ D♯ A♯
7 6 5 4 3 2 1 0 1 2 3 4 5 6 7

Flats.       Sharps.

Minor Keys.

tendant, or related k. Vide RE-
TED. **chromatic k.** One with
arps or flats, opposed to **natural
extreme k.** A remote, unrelated
**parallel k.** a. Related. b. Used
a major and a minor key with the
me tonic but different signatures.
Old name for clef. 3. A me-
anical lever for controlling tone,
ether digital or foot-key. 4. One
such keys as those on the outside
a flute covering certain holes. 5.

A tuning-hammer. 6. A lever controlling organ-pallets.
**key-action.** The entire mechanism
of a keyed instr.
**key-board.** The series of digitals or
pedals of a piano, organ or such instr.
The idea of having a key-board so
arranged that each digital can be
struck in 3 different places seems to
have occurred first to Paul von Jankó,
who in 1882 inv. the **Jankó key-
board**, which has the look of six
contiguous key-boards on a rising
plane. The advantages are that all
scales are fingered alike and that the
reach of the hand is greatly increased,
so that a good hand can cover 14 digitals. The consequent simplification
and enrichment of piano-resources
are inestimably valuable. It may
be applied to any key-board and is
sometimes called a **chromatic key-
board.**
**key-bugle.** Vide BUGLE.
**key-chord.** The triad on the tonic.
**keyed.** Furnished with keys, as a
flute, or piano. **keyed violin.** Piano-violin.
**key-stop violin.** One having a finger-
board fitted with thirty-three keys
acting as stops perpendicularly upon
the strings.

**key-harp.** An adjustment of tuning-
forks over cavities of sonorous metal,
with piano-key action, inv. by Dietz
and Second, 1819.
**key-note, key-tone.** The tonic. **key-
ship.** Tonality.
**key-trumpet.** One with keys or
valves.
**khal'il.** Hebrew flute or oboe.
**khasan** (khä´zän), Heb. Chief singer
in a synagogue.
**Kicks,** G. Vide GOOSE

**Kielflügel** (kēl'-flü-khĕl), *G.* Wing-shaped harpsichord.

**kin chi** (kĭn chē). A Chinese dulcimer with 5 to 25 silk strings.

**Kinderscenen** (kĭnt'-ĕr-zā-nĕn), *G.* Childhood scenes. **Kinderstück** (shtük). An easy piece.

**king chi** (kĭng chē). A Chinese instr. with sixteen pendent stones graduated and struck with a hammer.

**kinnor** (kĭn'-nôr), *Heb.* A small harp, or lyre.

**kin'tal.** Small Indian cymbals.

**Kirche** (kēr'-khĕ), *G.* (in compounds **Kirchen**). Church. **K. kantate** (kän-tä'-tĕ). A cantata for church service. **K. komponist'.** Composer of church music. **K. dienst** (dēnst). Church service. **K. fest** (fĕsht). Church festival. **K. gesang** (gĕ-zäng), **K. lied** (lēt). Canticle, psalm, or hymn. **K. musik** (moo-zēk'). Church music. **K. schluss** (shloos). Plagal cadence. **K. stil** (shtēl). "Church style"; in an ecclesiastical mode. **K. töne** (tān'-ĕ). The church modes.

**kis'sar.** 5-stringed Nubian lyre.

**kit.** A small pocket violin, with 3 strings, *c'-g'-d"*.

**kitra** (kĭ-trä'). A guitar-like instr. of the Arabs.

**kitha'ra,** *Gr.* Greek lyre.

**Klage** (klä'-khĕ), *G.* Lamentation. **K.-gedicht** (gĕ-dĭkht), **K.-lied** (lēt). Elegy. **K.-ton** (tōn). Plaintive tune, or melody. **klagend** (klä'-khĕnt). Plaintive.

**Klang** (kläng), pl. **Klänge** (klĕng'-ĕ), *G.* 1. Sound, ringing. 2. Vide CLANG. **K.-boden.** Sound-board. **K.-far'-be.** Sound-color, clang-tint. **K.-geschlecht** (gĕ-shlĕkht). A genus, or mode. **K.-lehre** (lā-rĕ). Acoustics. **K.-folge** (fôl-khĕ). A chord-progression in point of tonality. **K.-figuren** (fĭ-goo'-rĕn). Nodal figures. **K.-leiter** (lī-tĕr). A scale. **K.-saal** (zäl). Concert-room. **K.-schlüssel, K.-vertretung.** Vide KLANG-KEY. **klanglos** (kläng'lōs), *G.* Soundless.

**Klappe** (kläp'pĕ), *G.* Valve (of a [    ] inst.). **Klappenflügelhorn** (flü [    ] *G.* Keyed bugle. **Klappen[    ]** Keyed horn. **Klapptrompete[    ]** keyed trumpet.

**klar** (klär), *G.* Clear, bright. [    ] **heit** (klär'-hīt). Clearness, plain [    ] **klärlich** (klĕr-lĭkh), *G.* Clearly [    ] tinctly.

**Klarinette** (klä-rĭ-nĕt'-tĕ), *G.* [    ] inet.

**klassisch** (kläs'sĭsh), *G.* C [    ] cal.

**Klausel** (klow'-zĕl), *G.* A cad [    ] **Bassklausel.** The progression [    ] bass in a final cadence from dom [    ] to tonic.

**Klaviatur** (klä-fĭ-ä-toor'), *G.* [    ] board. **K. harfe** (or **Klavier-ha[    ]** A harp inv. by Lutz, Vienna, [    ] in which the strings are plucke [    ] plectra manipulated by a key-b [    ] The same man in the same yea[    ] the **K.-zither,** a small piano [    ] single strings, plucked by means [    ] key-board.

**Klavier** (klä-fēr'). 1. Key-board [    ] Key-board instr., especially the [    ] ichord (formerly the piano). **K.[    ] erauszug** (ows-tzookh). Arr [    ] ment for piano. **K.-harfe.** KLAVIATUR-HARFE. **K.-harmon[    ]** An harmonium shaped like a [    ] piano, inv. by Woroniecki, [    ] **K.-hoboe.** The harmoniphon. [    ] **mässig** (mĕs-sĭkh). Suitable f[    ] the style of the piano. **K.-[    ]** Piano-music, or manner. **K.-so[    ]** (klä-fēr'-sō-nä-tĕ). Piano-sonata [    ] **spieler** (shpē'-lĕr), *G.* Piano-p[    ] **K.-violoncello.** A 'cello in a [    ] with a key-board arrangement f[    ] left hand, of special advantages [    ] by de Vlaminck, Brussels, 1893.[    ] **viola.** A viola with key-boar[    ] tachment.

**klein** (klīn), *G.* Small, minor. [    ] **bass** (klīn-bäs), **K.-bassgeige** [    ] khĕ), *G.* Violoncello. **Klein[    ] dacht.** A flute-stop. **klein[    ]** (lowt), *G.* Small or low in to[    ] voice.

gbar (klĭng'-bär), *G.* Resonant.
ingel (klĭng'-ēl). A bell. **klingeln**
Ing'-ĕln). To jingle. **klingend**
Ing-ĕnt). Ringing. **klingende**
imme. Speaking (as opposed to
mmy) pipes. **Klingklang** (klĭng-
ing). Tinkling, bad music.
tter (kloot'-tĕr), *G.* A bird-call.
.benstimme (knä'-bĕn-shtĭm-mĕ),
" Boy's voice," counter-tenor.
e-stop. A lever worked by the
ee, and (a) controlling the wind,
) opening the swell-box, (c) drawing
the stops.
ll. The tolling of a bell.
e (knē, not nē). Knee. **K.-gui-
rre.** Guitarre d'amour. **K.-zug**
ookh). Knee-stop. **K.-geige** (knē-
-khĕ), *G.* Viol da gamba. **K.-
**hre** (rō-rĕ), *G.* A mitred pipe.
**pfregal** (knôpf-rä'-gäl), *G.* An
s. reed-stop.
te (knō'-tĕ), *G.* Node. **K.-punkt.**
odal point.
sa (kôb'-shä), *Rus.* A crude lute-
ke instrument.
lectivzug (kôl-lĕk-tēf'-tsookh), or
**ombinationspedale** (kôm-bĭ-nä-
-ōns-pĕ-dä'-lĕ), *G.* Combination
dal.
o (kôl'-lō), *Jap.* A Japanese harp.
lern, *G.* To sing in a thin reedy
ice.
ophon'. Resin.
nbinationstöne (kôm-bĭ-nä-tsĭ-
s'-tä-nĕ). Resultant tones. Vide
so KOLLEKTIVZUG.
miker (kō'-mĭ-kĕr), *G.* A writer of
arlettas ; comic performer.
nisch (kō'-mĭsh), *G.* Comical.
mma (kôm'-mä), *G.* Comma.
nponi(e)ren (kôm-pō-nē'-rĕn), *G.*
o compose. **komponi(e)rt.** Com-
osed. **Komponist'.** A composer.
mposition (kôm-pō-zē'-tsĭ-ōn), *G.*
composition. **Kompositionslehre**
ä-rĕ). The art of composition.
nservatorium (tō'-rĭ-oom), *G.* A
onservatory.
'tra, *G.* Contra. **Kontrabass.**
Double-bass. **K.-fagott.** Double-
assoon. **K.-oktave.** Contra-octave.

**K.-punkt.** Counterpoint. **K.-
subjekt.** Counter-subject. **K.-töne**
(tä-nĕ). The deepest tones of a bass
voice.
**Konzert** (kôn-tsärt'). Concert ; concerto. **K.-meister** (mī-shtĕr). First
violin ; leader. **K.-oper.** Concert
opera. **K.-stück** (shtük). A free
concerto in one movement, or any
short concert-solo.
**koous.** A Persian brass drum.
**Kopfstimme** (kôpf'-shtĭm-mĕ), *G.* Falsetto.
**Koppel** (kôp'-pel), *G.* Coupler, coup-
ling-stop. **K. ab** (or **an**). " Coupler
off (or on)."
**Kornett** (kôr-nĕt'), *G.* Cornet.
**koryphæ'us,** *Gr.* Chief, or leader of
the dances.
**kos** (kōz), *Hun.* A Hungarian dance.
**Kosake** (kō-sä'-kĕ). A national dance
of the Cossacks in 2-4 time.
**ko'to.** Japanese zither with 13 silk
strings, compass 2 octaves.
**Kraft** (kräft), *G.* Power, energy. **kräf-
tig** (krĕf'-tĭkh). Powerful, vigorous.
**Kragen** (krä'-khĕn), *G.* Lute peg-box.
**Kräusel** (krī'-zĕl), *G.* Mordent.
**Krakoviak** (krä-kō'-vĭ-äk), **Krako-
vienne** (krä-kō-vĭ-ĕn), *F.* The cracovienne.
**krebsgängig** (kräps'-gĕng-ĭkh), *G.*
"Crab-going" ; retrograde imitation.
**Krebskanon.** Canon cancrizans.
**kreischend** (krī'-shĕnt), *G.* Shrieking.
**Kreisfuge** (krīs'-foo-khĕ), *G.* A canon.
**Kreisleriana** (krīs'-lä-rĭ-ä'-nä), *G.* A
series of piano pieces by Schumann,
named after an eccentric conductor
called Kreisler, in one of Hoffman's
novels.
**Kreistanz** (krīs'-tänts), *G.* Dance in a
circle.
**kreol** (krā'-ôl). A Danish reel.
**Kreuz** (kroits), *G.* A sharp. **doppelt K.** A double sharp. **K.-
saitig** (zī-tĭkh). Overstrung. **K.-
tonart.** Sharp key.
**Kriegsgesang** (krĕkhs'-gĕ-zäng),
**Kriegslied** (lēt), *G.* A war-song.
**K.-spieler** (shpē'-ler). A military
musician.

**kriegerisch** (krē'-khĕr-ĭsh). Martial.

**Krome** (krō'-mĕ), *G.* Vide CHROMA.

**kro'talon,** *Gr.* Crotalum.

**krumm** (kroom), *G.* Crooked, curved, bent. **K.-bogen** (bō'-khĕn). A crook. **K.-horn.** Crooked horn. 1. An obs. wind-instr. resembling a small cornet; it had a range of nine notes, and was made in several sizes; its plaintive tone has led to its imitation in (2) an organ-stop of 4 and 8 ft. pitch (and in the **Krummhorn-bass,** of 16 ft.). Same as **cromhorn.**

**krustische Instrumente** (kroos'-tĭsh-ĕ), *G.* Instr. of percussion.

**kuhn** (koon), *G.* Bold, decided.

**Kuhhorn** (koo-hôrn), *G.* Swiss "cowhorn."

**Kuh-kuk** (koo'-kook), *G.* The cuckoo used in toy symphonies.

**Kuhreigen** (koo'-rī-khĕn), *G.* "Cowround-up." Vide KANZ DES VACHES.

**kuit'-ra.** Kitra.

**Kunst** (koonst), *G.* Art, skill. **K.-fuge** (foo-khe), *fuga ricercata.* Vide FUGUE. **Künstler** (kĭnst'-lr). Artist. **K.-lied** (lēt). An art (as opp. to a folk) song. **K.-pfeifer** (pfī'-fĕr). Street musician. **Kunstwerk der Zukunft** (koonst'-vărk dĕr tsoo'-koonft). "Art work of the future." A term given by Richard Wagner to his theory of music.

**ku'rum.** Curved trumpet of the Western Nile.

**kurz** (koorts), *G.* Short, detached, staccato. **kürzen.** To abridge. **kurzer Mordent.** Short mordent. **kurze Oktave.** Short-octave. **kurzer Singesatz.** Cavatina. **Kürzung** (kür'-tsoongk). Abbreviation. **Kürzungszeichen** (tsī'-khen). Sign of abbreviation.

**kussir** (küs-sĕr), *F.* Turkish instrument.

**Kyrie eleison** (kē'-rĭ-ā ā-lā'-ĕ-sōn), *Gr.* "Lord, have mercy (upon us)." Vide MASS.

**kyrielle** (kē-rĕ-ĕl), *F.* Litany.

**kyr'riole.** Old E. for Carol.

## L

Abbr. for *Left* (*G.,* Links). *left hand.* l', abbr. for *la,* "the."

**la.** 1. Vide SOLMISATION. The note A (*F.* and *I.*). **la bemolle, ab**; **la dièse** (lä dĭ *F.,* a♯.

**la** (lä). *I.* and *F.* The.

**labecedisa'tion.** Vide SOLMISAT]

**la'bial.** Lipped (of flue-pipes). **bialstimme** (lä-bĭ-äl'-shtĭm-mĕ) **pfeife** (pfī'-fĕ), *G.* Flue-stops.

**labisa'tion.** Vide SOLMISATION.

**Labien** (lä'-bĭ-ĕn), pl., *G.* Pipes.

**Labium** (la'-bĭ-oom), *L.* and *G.* lip of a pipe.

**lacrimando** (lä-krĭ-män'-do), **la mo'so,** *I.* Mournful.

**Lacrimosa** (lä-krĭ-mō'-sä), *L.* "W ing." An occasional part of the quiem.

**Lade** (lä'-dĕ), *G.* Wind-chest of organ.

**Lage** (lä'-khĕ), *G.* Position. 1. a chord. 2. Of the hand in vi shifts. **eng'e L.** Close harm opposed to **weite** (vī'-tĕ), open.

**Lagenwechsel** (vĕkhs-ĕl), *G.* S] ing.

**lagnoso** (län-yō'-sō), *I.* Plaintive, d ful.

**lagrimando** (lä-grĭ-män'-dō), **la mo'so,** *I.* Weeping.

**lah.** Vide TONIC SOL-FA.

**lai** (lĕ), *F.* Lay, ditty.

**lament'.** Old name for harp musi songs of pathos.

**lamentabile** (lä-mĕn-tä'-bĭ-lĕ), **lam tabilmen'te,** *I.* Mournful(ly). **mentan'do, lamentevole** (lä-m tä'-vō-lĕ), **lamento'so.** Plaintive

**Lamenta'tions.** Words from J miah sung at Vespers in Pass week.

**lampon** (län-pôn), *F.* Drinking-so

**lan'cers,** *E.,* **lanciers** (läns-yä), *F.* set of quadrilles.

**Länderer** (lĕn'-dĕ-rĕr), **Ländler** (lĕ lĕr), *G.* Slow German or Austr waltz in 3-4 or 3-8 time, the last n

each measure a dotted 8th and a
5th note.

**derisch** (lĕn'-dĕr-ĭsh), *G.* In the
ändler style.

**dlich** (lĕnt'-lĭkh), *G.* Rural.

**ndlied** (länt'-lēt), *G.* Rustic-song.

**du** (län'-doo), *Port.* A Portuguese
ance in duple time.

**dums** (län'-dooms), *Port.* Portu-
nese music of sentimental tone.

**g** (läng), *G.* Long.

**gsam** (läng'-zäm). *G.* Slow(ly),
**rgo.** **langsamer** (läng'-zäm-ĕr).
ower.

**guage, languid.** In a flue-pipe a
orizontal strip of metal or wood just
side the mouth.

**guendo** (län-gwĕn'-dō). **languen'-**
**e, languido** (län-gwē'-dō), *I.* Lan-
uishing. **languemen'te.** Lan-
uishingly.

**guette** (län-gĕt), *F.* 1. The tongue
f reed-pipes. 2. Pallet. 3. Key on
wind-instr. 4. Tongue carrying the
uill of a jack.

**guid.** Vide LANGUAGE.

**tum.** A large hurdygurdy with
otary bellows and reeds played by
uttons.

**id'eon.** A scale of flint-stones
layed with hammers; inv. by Bau-
ry.

**gamente** (lär-gä-mĕn'-tĕ). Broadly,
obly. Vide LARGO.

**gando** (lär-gän'-dō), *I.* Broadening,
ecoming largo (q. v.).

**ge.** The longest note in ancient
nusic equal to four brevos (eight of
ur whole notes). Vide N ATION.

**ge** (lärzh) *F.* Broad. **large-**
**ment** (lärzh-mäṅ). Broadly.

**ghetto** (lär-gĕt'-tō), *I.* Not quite
o slow as largo.

**ghezza** (lär-gĕd'-zä), *I.* Breadth,
lowness. **larghissimo** (lär-gĭs'-sĭ-
nō). Very slow.

**go** (lär'-gō), *I.* Slow, noble, broad,
sually taken as slower than **lento.**
**, assai** (äs-sä'-ē), **l. di molto** (dē-
nōl'-to). Very slow. **l. ma non**
**roppo.** Slow, but not too slow. **l.**
**n poco** (oon pō'-kō). Rather slow.

**larigot** (lär-ĭ-gō), *F.* 1. Shepherd's
pipe. 2. A very shrill 1⅓-ft. stop.

**laringe** (lä-rēn'-jĕ), *I.* Larynx.

**larmoyant** (lärm-wä-yäṅ), *F.* Weeping.

**lar'ynx.** Upper part of the trachea or
wind-pipe; a human reed-pipe varying at will the tones of the voice.

**laud** (lä-oodh), *Sp.* Lute.

**laud, lauda** (lä'-oo-dä), *I.* and *L.*, *I.* pl.
*laude,* *L.* pl. *laudes.* 1. Hymn(s) of
praise. 2. Vide HORA.

**Lau'da Si'on, Salvato'rem.** "Zion,
praise the Saviour"; a sequence sung
at the High Mass of Corpus Christi.

**laudis'ti,** *L.* Psalm-singers.

**Lauda'mus Te,** *L.* "We praise Thee."
Part of the Gloria. Vide MASS.

**Lauf** (lowf), *G.* 1. Peg-box. 2. A
run, a trill. **Lauftanz** (lowf'-tänts).
A running dance, corante. **Läufe**
(lī'-fĕ). Rapid divisions. **Läufer** (lī'-
fĕr). A run, trill, or shake.

**Launenstück** (low'-nĕn-shtük), *G.* A
voluntary.

**launig** (low'-nĭkh). Humorous.

**lauréate** (lō-rā-ăt), *F.* A winner of
the Grand Prix de Rome (q. v.).

**laut** (lowt), *G.* 1. Loud. 2. A sound.
**lautlos** (lowt-lōs). Soundless, mute.

**Laute** (lowt'-ĕ), *G.* The lute. **Laut-**
**enist', Lautenschläger** (shlä'-khĕr),
or **spieler** (shpē-lĕr), *G.* Lutenist.

**Lautenfutter** (foot-ter), **lautenkas-**
**ten.** Lute-case. **Lauteninstru-**
**mente.** Instrs. whose strings are
plucked. **L.-geige.** Viol. **L.-zug.**
Lute compass. **L.-macher** (mä'-khĕr).
Lutemaker.

**läuten** (lī'-tĕn). To toll, to sound.

**lavol'ta.** Old Italian waltz.

**lay.** Song.

**le** (lŭ), *F.*, **le** (lā), *I.*, pl. The.

**lead** (lēd). 1. The announcement by
one part of a theme to reappear in
others. 2. A sign giving the cue for
the entry of the various parts of a
canon, etc.

**leader.** 1. Conductor, director. In
older times the first violinist was the
actual conductor and is still called
"leader" though he has lost his

function as conductor. 2. The first cornet (in bands). 3. The first soprano (in chorus).

**leading.** 1. *As a noun.* A melodic progression or tendency. 2. *As an adjective.* Guiding, compelling, characteristic, predominant. **l.-chord.** The dominant. **l.-tone,** or **note.** The 7th degree of a scale (because it leads in and demands the toni **l.-melody.** The chief melody.

**leading-motive.** A musical phrase figure (as those in Wagner's opera used as a sort of autograph or tra mark of a certain character, mood sentiment, and recurring whenev that character or mood is to appe or is remembered.

## Leading-Motives.

### By Gustave Kobbé.

OTHER composers before Wagner have used typical phrases express some personal characteristic or idea, and have repeated th in a manner which suggests what is now termed a leading-moti Such is the "*Idée fixe*" in Berlioz's "Fantastique" symphony ; or phrase in Weber's "Euryanthe" which occasionally even is spoken of the "Tomb Motive." I, however, have always considered that Beethov in the use he made of the opening theme of his Fifth Symphony more nea approached the leading-motive than any of Wagner's predecessors. T theme recurs with great variety of effect throughout the symphony, second movement excepted. It is found as a mysterious threatening fig accompanying the second theme of the first movement, while in the Alleg the scherzo of the symphony, it partakes of a joyous character, to reapp as a disturbing element in the finale. It has the plasticity of a leadi

motive, but it may be questioned whether Beethoven intended to use it for other than a purely musical effect. In fact any suggestions Wagner n

received from other composers were so slight that the leading-motive
the modern sense may unhesitatingly be said to be his invention. ¶It
sier to say what a leading-motive is not, than to give it a fixed defi-
n. The first idea to disabuse one's self of is that a leading-motive
anything like a label. The "Walhalla" motive in the "Ring of the
elung" is not a guide-post which reads "Walhalla to the right—3
s"—nor does it even represent Walhalla as a pile of masonry. It
esses, in its simple yet lofty measures, the rulership of *Wotan*, the
monia of the gods. A leading-motive is a musical searchlight or X-ray
ch illuminates and enables us to look deep into every character, thought,
d, purpose, idea, and impulse in the drama. Even conscience itself
not escape Wagner. Witness how he lays it bare with his scalpel of
ing-motives in the first meeting of *Siegfried* and *Hagen* in "Goetterdaem-
ing" with the Curse Motive, which hints at *Hagen's* fell purpose,
ening the noble Siegfried Motive. The use of the Curse in this episode
rly foreshadows the death of the Volsung hero at *Hagen's* hand and lays
gloom of impending tragedy heavily upon the hearer's soul. ¶How
tic a leading-motive may be, how closely welded to the ever-changing
es of the drama and how clearly it expresses them, the wonderful

ants of the motive of Siegfried the Fearless—the call *Siegfried* sounds on
silver horn—will show. Joyous and buoyant in its simplest form, it
omes when he takes leave of *Brünhilde* to sally forth in quest of adven-
, heroically grand, and in the Death Music, that strain of triumphant
urning which thrills every hearer and stamps the episode as the greatest
ax ever achieved in a musical work for the stage. Indeed, the whole
e is a triumph for the leading-motive idea, since here, as *Siegfried's* life-

less body is borne up on the mountain crest, the orchestra gives a mu
epitome of his career by voicing successively the motives most intim
relating to him which have been heard in the cycle of music-dramas.
Wagner's use of leading-motives singly and in complex combinations
cording to the trend of the drama however interesting analytically w
wholly have failed were not the motives themselves musically valuable.
are enunciated chiefly by the orchestra (which thus forms a constant c
mentary upon the proceedings of the stage) and they are considered by t
who are in the van of musical opinion to have resulted in the most eloq
and sublime—if at times the most tedious—scores ever penned. To
preciate what a genius Wagner really was, it is only necessary to listen t
works of some of his imitators.

Liszt in his Symphonic Poems has adapted the leading-motive to in
mental music, in which respect Richard Strauss may be regarded as foll
ing him.

---

**lean'ing note.** Appoggiatura.

**leap.** 1. Skip. 2. In piano-playing a long jump for the hand. 3. A distance composed of several intermediate intervals.

**Leben** (lā´-běn), *G.* Life, vivacity. **lebendig** (lā´-běn-dĭkh), **lebhaft** (lāp´-häft). Lively. **Lebhaftigkeit** (kīt). Vivacity.

**leçon** (lŭ-sôn), *F.* Lesson, exercise.

**ledger line, leger line.** A short additional line above or below the staff, for notes too high or too low to be written on the staff. **l. l.** are counted away from the staff, the nearest being the first. **ledger space.** The space between two **l. l.**

**leere Saiten** (lā-rě zī´-ten), *G.* Open strings.

**legabile** (lë-gä´-bǐ-lě), **legan'do,** *I.* Legato.

**legare** (le-ga-re). To bind, or tie.

**legato** (lě-gä´-tō), *I.* "Bound." In a smooth, connected manner, opposed to staccato, and indicated by a slur, or **legato-mark** (*G.*, **legato-bogen**) thus, ⌢. **L. touch.** A touch prolonging the tone, till it exactly connects with the next. **legatis'simo.** Exceedingly legato.

**legatura** (lā-gä-too´-rä), *I.* 1. A 2. Syncopation. **l. di voce.** LIGATURE (2).

**legend, légende** (lā-zhänd), *F.,* **gende** (lā-gěn´-dě), *G.* A com tion in romantic or narrative s im **Le'gendenton,** *G.* In the mance manner.

**leger.** Vide LEDGER.

**leger** (lā-zhā), **legère** (lā-zhăr), Light, nimble. **legèrement** (n Lightly. **legèreté** (lā-zhăr-tā). ity.

**leggenda** (lěd-jěn´-dä), *I.* A leg **leggeramente** (lěd-jěr-ä-měn´-te), germen'te, *I.* Lightly. **legge za** (lěd-jěr-än´-tsä). **leggere** (lěd-jěr-ěd´-zä). Lightness.

**leggiadro** (lěd-jä´-drō), **leggia** men'te, *I.* Graceful(ly).

**leggiere** (lěd-jä´-rě), **leggiero,** gieramen'te, leggiermen'te Light(ly). **leggierezza** (lěd-jě-zä). Delicacy.

**leggieruco'lo.** Rather light.

**legno** (lān´-yō), *I.* Wood. **col** To be played with the back or v of the bow.

**Lehrer** (lā´-rěr), feminine **Lehr** *G.* Teacher, master.

**h** (līkh), *G.* A lay.

**chenmusik** (lī'-khĕn-moo-zēk'), *G.* uneral-music. **Leichenton** (tōn). lugubrious sound.

**ht** (līkht), *G.* Light, easy, facile. **. bewegt** (bĕ-vākht), (a) delicately vift. (b) agitatedly. **Leichtheit** īt), **Leichtigkeit** (līkh'-tīkh-kīt). ightness, facility. **leichtfertig** ĕr-tīkh). Light(ly), careless(ly).

**denschaft** (lī'-dĕn-shäft), *G.* Passon. **leidenschaftlich** (līkh). Passonate.

**er** (lī'-er), *G.* A lyre. **L.-kasten** äst'en). A hurdygurdy. **Leierädchen** (māt'-khĕn). A girl who ays on a hurdygurdy. **Leiermann** nän). A male player of a hurdyurdy. **Leierorgel** (lī'-ĕr-ôrkh-ĕl). and-organ. **Leierspieler** (shpē-r). One who plays on a lyre.

**ne** (lī'-nĕ), *G.* A line on the staff. **e** (lī'-zĕ), *G.* Low, soft, gentle. **l. ie für sich** 've für zīkh). Softly, as to one's self.

**takkord** (līt'-äk-kôrd', *G.* A harony progressing naturally to anher, as the dominant. **Leitmotiv** t'-mō-tēf). Leading-motive (q. v.). **eitton** (līt'-tōn). The leading note. **ter** (lī'-tĕr), *G.* 1. Leader. 2. Ladder," the scale of any key. **ereigen** (lī-'ĕr-īkh'-n). Proper and cuҺiar to a key, opposed to foreign otes which are **l.-fremd** (frĕmt). **.** Old term for a note sustained, hile other parts move.

**o** (lä'-no), *I.* Weak, feeble, faint. **nezza** (lä-nĕd'-zä). Gentleness. **(län)**, *F.* Slow. **lentemente** (länt-än), *F.* Slowly. **lenteur** (län-r'). Slowness, delay.

**ando** (lĕn-tän'-dō), *I.* Retarding. **o** (lĕn'-tō), *I.* Slow; usually condered between andante and largo. **assai, l. di molto** (dē mōl'-tō), **l. nto.** Very slow. **lentis'simo.** xtremely slow. **lentamen'te, len-men'te.** Slowly. **lentezza** (lĕn-d'-zä). Slowness.

**er.** Minor, as the **l. third. l. ppoggiatura.** Vide APPOGG.

**l. barbiton.** The kit. **l. comma.** The diaschisma.

**lesson.** A piece of two or three movements for the harpsichord or pianoforte, often combined into a suite.

**lesto** (lĕs'-tō), *I.* Lively. **lestissimo.** Very quick. **lestezza** (lĕs-tĕd'-zä), *I.* Agility.

**letterale** (lĕt-tĕ-rä'-lĕ), **letteralmen'te,** *I.* Literal(ly). Exactly as written.

**letter-name.** A letter designating a tone, key, etc., as a, b, c. Letter-notation is old as the Greeks.

**leuto** (lä-oo'-tō), *I.* Lute.

**leva** (lä'-vä), *I.* Lift, release, *si leva il sordino,* "lift the mute"; *si levano i sordini,* "release the dampers."

**levé** (lŭ-vā'), *F.* Up-beat.

**levet.** A blast of a trumpet; reveille.

**levezza** (lĕ-vĕd'-zä), *I.* Lightness.

**levier pneumatique** (lĕv-ĭ-ā'-nŭ-mă-tēk'), *F.* The pneumatic lever.

**leziosamen'te** (lä-tsĭ-ō), *I.* Affectedly.

**lezzioni** (lĕd-zĭ-ō'-nē), *I.*, pl. Lessons.

**Leyer** (lī'-ĕr), *G.* Lyre.

**L. H.** Abbr. for "left hand."

**liaison** (lē-ĕz'-ôn), *F.* 1. A bind or tie. 2. Vide LIGATURE, 2. 3. **l. d'harmonie** (där-mō-nē). Syncopation. **l. de chant** (dŭ-shän). Sostenuto singing.

**libero** (lē'-bĕ-rò), **liberamen'te,** *I.* Free(ly), unrestrained(ly).

**libitum,** *L.* Pleasure, will. **ad libitum.** At the pleasure of the performer, who may decide tempo, expression, etc., or even omit the section so marked.

**librement** (lēbr-män), *F.* Freely.

**libret'to.** The text of an opera, oratorio, etc. **libret'tist.** A writer of such texts.

**li'cence** (in *F.* lē-säns), **licenza** (lē-chĕn'-tsä), *I.* A deviation from the rules. **con' alcuna** (äl-koo'-nä) **licenza.** With some freedom.

**liceo** (lē-chä'-ō), *I.* Lyceum; academy.

**-lich-** (līkh), *G.* Suffix, equivalent to "-like," or "-ly."

**lich'anos,** *Gr.* Vide LYRE.

**lié** (lē-ā'), *F.* Smooth(ly), legato. **lié coulant** (koo-laṅ). Slurred but flowing.

**Liebeslied** (lē'-bĕs-lēt). Love-song. **Liebesflöte.** A flute-stop. **Liebhaber** (lēp'-hä-bĕr). Amateur. **lieblich** (lēp'-lĭkh). Lovely, charming. **Lieb'lichgedacht** (gĕ-däkht). A stopped-diapason organ register.

**Lied** (lēt), pl. **Lieder** (lē'-dĕr), *G.* Loosely, any song; technically, a song (as opposed to the ballad or **Strophenlied**), in which the text predominates over merely melodic rights, and the music interprets, rather than disregards, the words. Such a song in which each stanza has special music is often called **durchkompon-i(e)rtes** (doorkh-kôm-pō-nēr'-tĕs), or one "composed all through." LIED (or LIEDER) **ohne Worte** (ō'-nĕ vôr'-tĕ), *G.* Song (or songs) without words. **Lied form** (fôrm). The form, or theme of a song. **Liedchen** (lēt'-khĕn). A short song. **Liederbuch** (bookh). A song or hymn-book. **L.-bund** (boont). A society of singers. **L.-cyclus** (tsē'-kloos). A cycle of songs. **L.-dichter** (dĭkh'-tĕr). A song-writer. **L.-kranz** (kränts). Glee-club. **L.-kreis** (krīs). A "wreath" of songs. **L.-sammlung** (zäm'-loongk). Collection of songs. **L.-sänger** (zĕng'-ĕr). A ballad-singer. **L.-spiel** (shpēl). An operetta. **L.-sprache** (sprä'-khĕ). Words adapted to songs. **L.-tafel** (tä'-fĕl). "Song-table"; a glee-club of male voices. **L.-täfler** (tĕf'-lĕr). Glee-singers. **L.-tanz** (tänts). A dance with songs.

**lier** (lēr), *Dutch.* A lyre.

**ligare** (lĭ-gä'-rĕ), **ligato** (lē-gä'-tō). Vide LEGARE, LEGATO.

**Ligatur** (lē-gä-toor'), *G.*, **ligatura** (lē-gä-too'-rä), *I.*, **lig'ature**, *E.* (pron. in *F.* lē-gä-tür'). 1. A succession of notes sung to one syllable or in one breath, or played with one stroke of the bow. 2. A tie. 3. A syncopation. 4. In old music a succession of

notes sung to one syllable. Vide NOTATION.

**ligne** (lēn'-yu), *F.* A line. **l. additnelle** (äd-dēs-yŭ-nĕl), or **aj** (ä-zhoo-tä'), or **postiche** (pôs-tĕ or **supplémentaire** (süp-plā-r tăr'). A ledger line.

**lig'neum psalte'rium,** *L.* Xyloph

**limite** (lē'-mĭ-tĕ), *I.* Limit.

**lim'ma,** *Gr.* An interval in G music, less by a comma than a m semitone.

**linea** (lē'-nĕ-ä), *I.* A line of the st

**line.** One of the five lines making the staff (q. v.). **added,** or led **line.** Vide LEDGER.

**lingua** (lĭn'-gwä), *I.* 1. The tongu a reed. 2. The reed itself.

**Lingualpfeife** (lēn-goo-äl'-pfī-fĕ), A reed-pipe.

**lin'gula,** *L.* Glottis.

**Linie** (lē'-nē), pl. **Linien,** *G.* Lin **Liniensystem** (lē'-nĭ-ĕn-zēs-t The staff.

**lining-out.** The old practice of r ing out one or two lines of a h before singing them.

**li'nings.** The supporting strips g to the ribs of violins, etc.

**link** (lĭnk), **links** (lĭnks), *G.* l **linke Hand** (hänt). The left ha

**li'nos,** *Gr.* 1. A rustic air. 2 dirge.

**lip,** *E.*, **Lippe** (lĭp'-pĕ), *G.* 1. flat surface above or below the m of a flue-pipe. 2. Vide EMBOUCH' **Lippenpfeife.** A flue-pipe.

**lira** (lē'-rä), *I.* 1. The Greek lyre. In 16th–18th cent. a viol, hence **barberi'na.** A small viol inv. Doni in 17th century. **l. da bra** (dä brät'-shō). Obsolete instr. the tenor viol, with seven stri **l. da gam'ba.** An instr. held tween the knees and having 12 t strings. **l. dop'pia.** Double **l. grande** (grän'-dĕ). A viol wit strings, formerly used in Germ **l. pagana** (pä-gä'-nä), **l. rus** (roos'-tĭ-kä), **l. tedesca** (tä-dĕs' A hurdygurdy.

**lire** (lēr), *F.* To read.

ssa (lē-rĕs'-sä).  A bad lyre

o (lē'-rĭ-kō), *I.*  Lyric.

ne (lē-rō'-nĕ), *I.*  The large bass
ol with 24 strings.

io (lē'-shō), *I.*  Smooth.

elnd (lĭs'-pĕlnt), *G.*  Lisping.

esso (lēs-tĕs'-sō), *I.*  The same.

neia, *Gr.,* litania (lē-tä-nē'-ä),
, and *I.,* litanie (lĭ-tä-nē'), *F.,*
itanei (lē-tä-nī'), *G.,* lit'any, *E.*  A
lemn form of supplication, the min-
ter offering prayers, to which the
ongregation add "Lord have mer-
." *kyrie eleison* is the lesser l.

erae significa'tivae, *L.*  Letters
doubtful meaning, used in neu-
atic notation.

us, *L.*  A kind of trumpet.

o (lē-oo'-tō), *I.*  A lute.

e (lēvr), *F.*  A book; à l' ouvert
o-vār).  At first sight.

et (lē'-vrä), *F.*  A libretto.

lō), *I.*  The.

ogesang (lōp'-gĕ-zäng), Loblied
op'-lēt), *G.*  A hymn of praise.

ch (lôkh) in der Stimme, *G.*
Hole in the voice," used of that
art of a register where certain tones
re weak or wanting.

o (lō'-kō), *I.*  "Place."  1. A word
ullifying *8va* or *all ottava,* and
eaning that the notes are to be
layed as written, not an octave
igher or lower as before.  2. A sign
or a violinist to return to his original
osition, form or shift.

crian (lo'-krĭ-än), lokrisch (lō'-
rĭsch), *G.*  Vide MODES.

geum, *L.*  1. A stage.  2. A motet.

gier'ian system.  The system of in-
truction of John Bernard Logier,
icluding class-work, harmony, etc.,
nd use of the chiroplast.

ibar'do.  A dance of Lombardy.

g, longa, *L.*  An obsolete note half
he length of the *large,* or equal to
our of our whole notes.  long double.
n old character equal to four breves.
*As adjective,* long appoggiatura.
n accented app. of a single note
orming part of the theme, and borrow-
ng half the length of the next note.  l.

drum.  The bass-drum of military
bands.  l. mordent.  A mordent
of four notes.  l. roll.  A drumbeat
to arms.  l. spiel.  An ancient long
and narrow Icelandic bow instrument.

longue pause (lông'-pōz), *F.*  A long
pause.

lontano (lôn-tä'-nō), *I.*  Distant, re
mote.  da l.  At a distance.  lon-
tananza (lôn-tä-nän'-tsä).  Distance.

loop.  1. The vibrating part between 2
nodes.  2. The chord binding the tail-
pieces of violins, etc., to the button.

Lösung, fortschreitende (fôrt-shrī-
tĕn-dĕ-lä'-zoongk), *G.*  Resolution.

loud pedal.  Vide DAMPER.

lourde (loord), *F.*  Heavy.  lourdement
(män).  Heavily.

loure (loor), *F.*  1. An old F. bagpipe,
thence;  2. A slow dance in 6-4 time,
strongly accented.

louré (loo-rā'), *F.*  Smooth(ly), legato.

louvre (loovr), *F.*  Applied to an air,
called "L' Amiable Vainqueur," a
favourite of Louis XIV. ; thence a
dance.

lu'dus, *L.*  Play.  ludi moderator.
Organist.  ludi spirituali.  Miracle-
plays.

lugubre (loo-goo'-brĕ), *I.*  Lugubrious,
sad.

luinig.  A plaintive song of the Hebrides sung by the women at work.

lul'laby.  A cradle-song.

lu-lu.  The Chinese official laws of
music.

lundu (loon'-doo), *Port.*  A Portuguese
dance in duple time.

lunga (loon'-gä), pl. lunghe (loon-ge).
*I.*  Long, prolonged.

luogo (loo-ô-gō), *I.*  Same as LOCO.

lur (loor), *Dan.*  1. A birch-bark instr.
similar to the alp-horn.  2. A pre-
historic curved and conical bronze
instr.  5 to 7 feet long, with cupped
mouthpiece, and, instead of a bell, a
circular flat plate, ornamented with
bosses and bronze tassels.

lusing.  An abbr. of lusingato.

lusingando (loo-sēn-gän'-dō), lusin-
gan'te, lusingato (gä'-to), lusin-

**ghevole** (gä'-vō-lĕ), *I.*, **lusinghiere** or **o** (gĭ-ä'-rĕ). Coaxing **lusinghevol-men'te.** Insinuatingly, persuasively.

**lustig** (loos'-tĭkh), *G.* Merry, cheerful.

**Lustlied** (loost'-lēt), *G.* A gay song.

**lute** (lūt, not loot), *E.*, **lut** or **luth** (lüt), *F.* A very ancient string instr. now obsolete except in the small form of the mandolin and the modified form of the guitar. It was pearshaped, and had a neck with fretted finger-board. The stringing was various; the largest having paired strings tuned in unisons, and, besides, a series of strings that did not cross the finger-board but were played upon as a bass. This form required a double neck and was called a **theorbo, arch-lute,** or **chitarrone.** The strings, sometimes as many as 13 pairs, were played as in the guitar. Lute-music was written in tablature. Lute-players were called **lutists, luters, lutanists, lutenists,** or **lutinists.** A lute-maker was a **luthier** (lüt-yä), a name also given then, and now, to violin-makers. The trade and its product are called **lutherie** (lüt-rē'). **lutina.** A small lute, or mandolin.

**luttuoso** (loot-too-ō'-sō), **luttuosamen'te,** *I.* Mournful(ly).

**Lyd'ian,** *E.*, **lydisch** (lēt'-ĭsh), *G.* Vide MODES. **Lydian chant.** A chant of a sorrowful, melancholy style.

**Lyon catlins.** Thick bass-strings.

**lyre** (līr in *E.* ; in *F.* lēr), **lyra** (lē'-rä), *L.*, *I.*, and *G.* 1. A most ancient instr. consisting of a sound-box or board with 2 long curved arms carrying a cross-bar from which descended, across a bridge, the 3 to 10 strings, struck with a plectrum. On the 8-stringed lyre, the strings thus named, beginning nearest the body: **hy'pate** (hī'-pä-tĕ) (the lowest in tone), **parhy'pate, lich'anos, me'se, par'amese, trite** (trē'-tĕ), **paranete, nete** (nä'-tĕ). The largest lyre was the **cithara,** the treble was

the **chelys.** A large 20-str[ing] instr. on which octaves were p[layed], was the **magadis.** 2. The m[odern] **lyra** is a rebec, and various instrs. have been called lyres, or **viols,** since the 14th cent. ; [some] have a double neck or bijuga[te,] the theorbo (Vide LUTE), inclu[ding] the **lyra di braccio** (brä' ch[io]), arm-viol and **archeviola di l.,** **doppia.** The l. **di gamba** is a [bass] viol. l. **barbarina.** An old i[nstr.] resembling the guitar, but pl[ayed] with the bow. l. **hex'achordis,** A six-stringed lyre. l. **mendico'[?]** *L.* " Beggar's lyre," a hurdy[-gur]dy. **Lyra-sänger** (zĕng'-ĕr), [-**säng**] **-spieler** (shpē'-lĕr), *G.* Performe[r on] the lyre. 3. The modern Stahls[piel?]

**lyr'ic, lyr'ical, lyrisch** (līr'-ĭsh), " Fitted to be sung to the l[yre,] hence used of subjective moods, [usu]ally brief and enthusiastic as opp[osed] to narrative, dramatic, or epic. l[yric] **drama** is opera. **lyric tragedy,** [a] tragic opera. l. **comedy.** Co[mic] opera. l. **opera.** A ballad ope[ra.]

## M

**M** Abbr. of *Mezzo, Metrono[me,]* *Mano, Main ;* m. f., *Mezzo-forte ;* m. p., *Me[zzo]* *piano ;* m. v., *Mezzo-vo[ce].*

**M. M.** Abbr. for Maelzel's Me[tro]nome (q. v.).

**ma** (mä), *I.* But ; as *allegro ma [non] troppo,* quick, but not too much so.

**machalath** (mä'-kä-läth), *Heb.* A te[rm] employed in the Psalms, supposed [by] some to mean a flute, but by oth[ers] to indicate familiar tunes.

**machête** (mä-shĕ'-tĕ). *Port.* A sm[all] guitar with 4 strings, tuned *d'[-g'-]* *b'-e''.*

**mach-icotage** (mäsh-ĭ-kô-täzh), **macicota'ticum,** *L.* Embellishm[ent] added to the *cantus firmus* of pla[in]chant, customary in France in t[he] 18th cent. The clergy alone sa[ng] the embellished or **machicot[ed]** (mäsh-ĭ-kō-tä) plain-song, and we[re] ₑd **machicots** (măsh-ĭ-kō) or **ma-ico'nici**. The choir sang the *tus firmus* without embellishment ₙe macicota'tico).

**ₗine-head**. A rack and pinion ₗliance to be used in place of ordi-y tuning-pegs.

**ₗol** (mä'-kōl), *Heb*. Instr. sup-ₑd to be either string or pulsatile.

**re, alla** (äl'-lä mäd'-rĕ). "To the ₜher." Used of hymns to the Vir-

**iale** (mä-drĭ-ä'-lĕ), *I*. Madrigal. **drialet'to**. A short madrigal. **ₗigal** (in *F*. mäd-rĭ-gäl; in *G*. mä--häl'), **madrigale** (mäd-rĭ-gäl'-ĕ), ₁. Loosely, a short amorous or pas-ₐl lyric. 2. Strictly an unaccom-ₙied chorus in from 2 to 8 parts, ₛed on a *cantus firmus*, and written ₕ elaborate counterpoint. Begin-ₙg in Italy in the 15th cent. it ₑad all over Europe. **madrigal-co**, *I*. Pertaining to the madri-ₗ.

**ₛta** (mä-äs'-tä), **maëstade** (mä-tä'-dĕ), **maëstate** (tä'-tĕ), *I*. ₐjesty, grandeur. **maëstevole** '-vō-lĕ), **maëstevolmen'te, ma-to'so, maëstosamen'te**. Majes-ₗ(ally), noble (nobly).

**stria** (mä-äs-trē'-ä), *I*. Mastery, ₗl.

**stro** (mä-äs'-trō), fem., **maestra** ä-äs'-trä), *I*. Master. **m. al mbale**. A conductor, since he ₋merly sat at the harpsichord. **al piano**. Pianist of an orches-₋. **m. del coro**. Master of the ₒir. **m. di camera**. Conduc-ᵣ of chamber-music. **m. di ₙto**. A singing-master. **m. di ₚpella** (dē käp-pĕl'-lä). 1. Chap-master. 2. Conductor.

**ₛadis**, *Gr*. 1. Vide LYRE. 2. ₜh cent. name for monochord. **ₛadizing**. A vocal performance in ₜaves. **ₛas**, *Gr*. 1. Bridge. 2. Fret. 3. ₗde MAGADIS, 2. **ₛazinbalg** (mäkh-ä-tsēn'-bälkh), *G*. ₑservoir-bellows

**maggiolata** (mäd-jō-lä'-tä), *I*. A song in praise of May.

**maggiore** (mäd-jō'-re), *I*. "Greater," major.

**maggot**. An impromptu fantasy.

**magistrale** (mä-jĭs-trä'-lĕ), *I*. Vide MAESTRALE.

**Magnificat**, *L*. A part of the Vespers from "Magnificat anima mea Dominum," My soul magnifies the Lord.

**main** (män), *F*. The hand. **m. droite** (drwät). Right hand. **m. gauche** (gōsh). Left hand. **m. harmonique** (mä-när-mŭn-ēk). Harmonic hand.

**maître** (mĕtr), *F*. A master, a director. **m. de chappelle** (shä-pĕl). Chapel-master; conductor; director of a choir. **m. de musique** (dŭ mü-zēk'). Musical director, or teacher.

**maîtrise** (mĕt-rēz), *F*. A music school connected with a cathedral.

**majestà** (mä-yäs-tä'), *I*., **majesté** (mä-zhĕs-tä), *F*. Majesty. **majestueux** (mä-zhĕst-yŭ'). Majestic. **majestätisch** (mä-yĕs-tä'-tĭsh), *G*. Majestic.

**ma'jor**, *E*., **majeur** (mä-zhŭr), *F*. "Greater," as opp. to minor ("less"), and used of intervals greater than a semitone than the minor (though less by a semitone than the augmented); hence, those major chords and major scales and keys in which major intervals predominate. **m. triad**. One with a major 3d and perfect 5th. **m. cadence**. One ending on a major triad.

**Mal** (mäl), *G*. Time, as **zum ersten M.**, for the first time.

**malagueña** (mä-lä-gwän'-yä), *Sp*. A fandango.

**malanconia** (mä-län-kō-nē'-ä), **malinconi'a**, *I*. Melancholy. **malenco'-nico, malincol'ico, malinco'nico, malinconio'so, malincono'so, malinconicamen'te**, *I*. In a melancholy style.

**mama** (mä'-mä), *I*. In drum-music the right hand.

**manca** (män'-kä), *I*. The left.

**mancando** (män-kän'-dō), *I*. Decreasing and retarding.

**manche** (mänsh), *F*. Neck (of a violin, etc.).

**mandolin(e)** (măn′-dō-lĭn), *E.*, **mandolino** (män-dō-lē′-nō), *I.* A small lute with fretted neck, and paired strings played with a plectrum. The compass g-g.‴ The **Neapolitan** (*mandolino napolita′no*) has 4 pairs tuned g–d′–a′–e″ ; the **Milanese** (*m. lombardo*) has five or six pairs tuned g–c′–a′–d″–e″, or g–b–e′–a′–d″–e″.

**mandolinata** (ä′-tä). To be played with mandolin-like effect. **mando′la, mando′ra, mando′re.** A large mandolin.

**mangeot** (män-zhō), *F.* A piano *à claviers renversé.*

**manico** (mä′nĭ-kō), *I.* Neck (of violin, etc.).

**man′ichord**, *E.*, **manichord′ium**, *L.*, **manichord′on**, *Gr.* An old term for various string instrs. **Manichordiendraht** (drät), *G.* Wire for the manichord.

**maniera** (mä-nĭ-ä′-rä), *I.*, **manière** (män yăr), *F.* Manner, style. m. **affettata** (äf-fĕt-tä′-tä), *I.* Affected delivery. m. **languida** (län′gwĭ-dä), *I.* A languid style.

**Manier** (mä-nēr′), pl. **Manieren** (mä-nē′-rĕn), *G.* Grace(s), embellishment(s).

**man′ifold fugue.** One with two or more subjects.

**Männerchor** (mĕn-nĕr-kōr), *G.* Male chorus. **Männergesangverein** (gĕ-zäng′-fĕr-īn). A male choral society. **Män′nerstimmen.** Male voices.

**mano** (mä′-nō), *I.* The hand. m. **destra** (däs′-trä), m. **diritta** (dĭ-rĭt′-tä), or **dritta** (drĭt′-tä). The right hand. m. **sinistra** (sĭ-nēs′-trä). The left hand.

**man′ual**, *E.*, **Manual** (mä-noo-äl′), *G.*, **manuale** (mä-noo-ä′-lĕ), *I.* and *L.* 1. Key-board of an organ. 2. A digital, especially **man′ual-key. manual′iter.** Without pedals, " on the manuals alone." **M.-koppel**, *G.* A coupler connecting one manual with another. m.-**mente** (mä-noo-äl-mĕn′-tĕ), *I.* Manually. **M.-untersatz** (oon-tĕr-zäts), *G.* A 32-ft. stop.

**manubrio** (mä-noo′-brĭ-ō), *I.*, **Man-**

ubrien (mä-noo′-brĭ-ĕn), pl., *G.* handle(s) by which a stop is dr... **M. koppel.** A draw-stop colla...

**marcan′do, marcato** (mär-kä′-tō) Marked, accented. **marcatis′si** Very strongly marked.

**march.** A composition to accom... marching. There are two kinds *quick m.* or *quickstep*, and the sol processional, *funeral* or *dead* Usually in 4-4 time, the m. may 2-4, 3-4 or 6-8 time. The m usually includes a second part, or and a repetition of the first sub The second part is often lyrical r... than rhythmic. The cadence fo... quick step in the American arm 120 to the minute.

**marche** (märsh), *F.* 1. A march. A progression, as m. **harmon** (är-mŭn-ēk).

**marcia** (mär′-chä), *I.* A march. **funèbre** (foo-nä′-brĕ). Fun... march. **marcia′le**, or **marz** (mär-tsĭ-ä′-lĕ), or **alla m.** In m... style. **marciata** (mär-chä′-tä). march.

**marked.** Accented.

**mark.** A sign. **cadenc***ɔ***-m.** CHANT. **harmonic-m.** Vide MONIC. **metronomic-m.** Vide RONOME. **expression-m.** Vid PRESSION. **tempo-m.** Vide TE

**markiren** (mär-kē′-ren), *G.*, **mar** (mär-kä), *F.* To mark, empha **markirt** (mär-kērt′), *G.*, **ma** (märkä′), *F.* Well marked. **mar** un p...u la mélodie (mär-kä′ ŭ lä mä′-lô-dē′), *F.* " Emphasize melody slightly."

**Marsch** (märsh), pl. **märsche** (... shĕ), *G.* March(es). **märscha** (märsh′-är-tĭkh). In the style march.

**Marseillaise, la** (lä mă1-sĕ-y˟z) The French national anthem, w1 and composed by Capt. Roug Lisle, April 24, 1792, and calle him " Chant de guerre de l'arm Rhin," but first popularized by always named after, the soldiers Marseilles.

eau (măr-tō), *F.* 1. Hammer, in
no-action. 2. Tuning-key.
elé (măr-tŭ-lā'), *F.*, **martellato**
ir-tĕl-lä'-tō), **martellan'do**, *I.*
ongly marking the notes, as if
mering.
ellement (măr-tĕl-män), *F.* 1.
yed with the acciacatura. 2. In
music a mordent.
iale (măr-tsĭ-ä'-lĕ), *I.* Vide MAR-
herata (mä-skĕ-rä'-tä). Masque-
e.
chera (mä'-skä-rä), *I.* A mask.
chinen (mä-shē'-nĕn), *G.* Pistons.
le VALVE. **M.-pauken.** Kettle-
ms with a mechanical adjuster of
ch.
k, *E.*, **masque** (măsk), *F.*, **Mas-
nspiel** (mäs'-kĕn-shpēl), *G.* A spec-
ular entertainment usually allegor-
l and dramatic, with music. Very
borately done in Elizabethan
es.
s. In the R. C. service, that por-
n accompanying the consecration
the Host. Before this service,
se not permitted to take part are
missed with the words, "Ite
ssa est" (vide ITE)—hence, by cor-
otion, the name "mass." The
vice up to the dismissal was called
Mass of the catechumens," that
er it, "Mass of the faithful"
*issa fidelium*). A mass without
sic is **low m.**; with music **high**
The musical service is as follows :
The **kyrie**, (a) Kyrie Eleison, (b)
riste Eleison, (c) Kyrie Eleison.
The **gloria**, or **doxology**, (a)
atias agimus, (b) Qui tollis, (c)
oniam, (d) Cum sancto spiritu. 3.
e **credo**, (a) Et incarnatus, (b)
ucifixus, (c) Et resurrexit. 4. The
**nctus.** Benedictus and Hosanna.
The **agnus dei**, and Dona Nobis.
ese divisions are named from the
st words of their text (which will be
ind translated under the separate
ads).
e **short m.** is that of tne Protes-
nt Church, which uses only the **kyrie**
the **gloria.**

Masses have been written in all elaborations from simple unison to fullest
counterpoint and to chora'. works in
from 8 to 32 parts with orchestral accompaniment. (Vide PALESTRINA in
the B. D.)
**Mass** (mäs), *G.* Measure, time.
**mässig** (mĕs'-sĭkh), *G.* 1. Moderato,
moderate(ly). 2. As a suffix, "appropriate to," as *klaviermässig*, etc.
**massima** (mäs'-sĭ-mä), *I.* The "greatest." 1. A whole note. 2. Augmented
intervals. 3. A maxim. Vide NOTA-
TION.
**master chord.** The dominant. **m.
fugue.** An elaborate *fuga ricercata*.
**m. note.** The leading-tone. **m.-
singer.** Vide MEISTERSINGER.
**Masure** (mä-zoo'-rĕ), *G.*, **Masure(c)k**
(mä-zoo'-rĕk), *Pol.*, **Masurka** (mä-
zoor'-kä), *G.* Vide MAZURKA.
**matachin** (mă-tä-chēn'), *Sp.* A grotesque Merry Andrew dance.
**mat'alan.** A small Indian flute.
**matassins** (mä-tăs-săn), *F.* 1. Matachin. 2. The dancers of it.
**matelotte** (măt-lôt), *F.* Sailor's horn-
pipe.
**matinare** (mä-tĭ-nä'-rĕ), *I.* To sing
matins.
**matinata** (mä-tĭ-nä'-tä), *I.* Morning
serenade.
**mat'ins.** The first morning service in
the R. C. Church. Vide HORÆ.
**Maultrommel** (mowl'-trôm-mĕl), *G.*
A Jew's harp. **M.-t.-klavier.** Melodicon.
**maxim(a)**, *L.* Vide NOTATION.
**Mazourk** (mä-tsoork'). **Maz(o)urka**
(mä-tsoor'-kä), **mazur** (ma-tsoor'),
**Mazur'ca, Mazurek** (mä-tsoo'-rĕk),
**Mazurka** (mä-tsoor'-kä ; pl. **Mazur-
ke**, mä-tsoor'-kĕ), *G.* **mazurka,** *E.*
(mä-zoor'-kä). A Polish national
dance of whimsical mood ; in triple
time with the 3d beat variously
treated.
**m. d.** Abbr. of Main Droite, right hand.
**me.** Vide TONIC-SOL-FA.
**mean.** Inner, as tenor, or alto (of
voices) ; as the *d* or *a* strings (of a violin). **mean clef.** Tenor clef. **mean-
tone system.** Vide TEMPERAMENT

**measurable.** Vide MENSURABLE.

**meas'ure.** 1. The unit of rhythm, corresponding to the metrical foot and including the notes between two bars; each measure has one and only one major accent. Vide TIME. 2. Loosely for tempo. 3. A stately dance as the **passy m.**, a cinque-pace. **measure-note,** the typical standard note of a measure as the 8th note in 3-8 time. **measure-rest.** Vide REST.

**mécanisme** (mā-kăn-ēzm), *F.* Technic.

**Mechanik** (mĕ-kä'-nēk), *G.* 1. Action. 2. Machine-head. 3. The mechanism of fingering and wrist-action. 4. Technic.

**mech'anism.** 1. Action. 2. Finger and wrist action.

**medesimo** (mĕ-dā'-sĭ-mō), **medes'mo,** *I.* The same. **m. tempo.** The same time, as before.

**me'dial.** 1. Concerning the Mediant. 2. Intermediate or secondary (of accent). Vide CADENCE.

**me'diant, médiante** (mā'-dĭ-ănt), *F.,* **mediante** (mā-dĭ-än'-tĕ), *G.* and *I.* 1. The third note of the scale. 2. One of the 3 pivotal tones of a mode, midway between final and dominant.

**mediation.** Vide CHANT.

**medius.** Vide ACCENTUS ECCL.

**medley.** A conglomerate of unrelated and usually familiar tunes.

**M e e r t r o m p e te** (mār-trôm-pā'-tĕ), **Meerhorn,** *G.* Sea-trumpet.

**mehr** (mār), *G.* More. **m. chörig** (kä-rïkh). For several choruses. **mehrfach** (mār-fäkh). Manifold, of an interval, a canon, or a compound stop. **mehrstimmig** (shtĭm'-mĭkh). For several voices. **Mehrstimmigkeit durch Brechung** (kĭt-doorkh-brĕkh-oongk). Polyphony that consists only of broken chords.

**Meister** (mī'-stĕr), *G.* Master. **M. fuge** (foo'-ge). A ricercata fugue. **M.-gesang** (gĕ-zäng'). Minstrelsong. **M.-sänger** (zĕng-ĕr), or **singer** (zĭng-ĕr). A member of the singing guild founded at Mainz in the 14th cent. and lasting till 1839 at

Ulm. Wagner's opera de their strict and elaborate ru Tabulatur. (Vide Stories o Operas, " Die Meistersinger.") **terstück** (shtük). Masterpiece

**melancolia** (mā-län-kō-lē'-ä), *I.* **lancolie** (mā-lăn-kô-lē'), *F.* choly.

**mélange** (mā-länzh), *F.* A med

**melis'ma,** *Gr.* 1. A vocal emb ment or run. 2. **melismat'ic** That in which one syllable is to many notes, opposed to sy song.

**melode** (mā-lō'-dĕ), or **melodia** lō-dē'-ä), *I.* 1. Melody. 2. much like the clarabella.

**melo'deon.** Vide AMERICAN ORG

**melod'ic interval,** or **step.** O which the tones are taken in s sion, as opposed to harmon which they are simultaneously

**melo'dica.** A tiny pipe-organ compass of 3½ octaves, inv. 17 Stein, of Augsburg.

**melodico** (mā-lō'-dĭ-kō). Cantar

**melod'icon.** A key-board instr. by Riffel, in Copenhagen, the produced from tuning-forks.

**melod'ics.** Theory of melody.

**mélodie** (mā-lō-dē), *F.* Melod **m. bien sentie** (bĭ-ăn sän-tē'). melody well accented.

**mélodieuse** (mā-lōd-yŭz). Melo **mélodieusement** (män). M ously.

**Melodik** (mĕ-lō'-dēk), *G.* Vide N DICS.

**melo'diograph.** Melograph.

**melo'dion.** A key-board instr. range of 6 octaves inv. by Di Emmerich, the tone produce tuned steel bars pressed by a ro cylinder.

**melodio'so** (mĕ-lō-dĭ-ō'-so), *I.,* **disch** (mĕ-lō'-dĭsh), *G.* Melod

**melodista** (mā-lō-dēs'-tä), *I.,* **diste** (mā-lō-dēst), *F.* Melodi

**Melodistik** (mĕ-lō-dĕs'-tēk), *G.* dics.

**melo'dium.** 1. American orga Alexandre organ.

◦drama, *E.*, **Melodram** (mā´-lō-
m), *G.*, **mélodrame** (mā-lō-drăm),
**melodramma** (mā-lō-dräm´-mä),
1. Originally opera. 2. Spoken
ma accompanied with instr. music,
ce the music accompanying action.
A play of sensational nature.

◦dy. 1. A tune. 2. A succession
tones, rhythmically and symmetri-
y arranged, as opposed to har-
ny, a combination of simultaneous
es 3. The leading part. **lead-
◦m.** A principal melody.

◦graph. A piano inv. 1827, which
orded what was improvised. Many
mpts of this sort have been made,
most successful an electric **m.**, *the
◦naut´ograph*, by Fenby, of Eng-
d, recording after the manner of
graphy. This record cut into
dboard is run through a key-board
achment, the *melotrope*, to repro-
e the music.

◦logue. Recitative and music

◦man, *Gr.*, **mélomane** (mā´-lō-
n), *F.*, **Melómániàc**, *E.* A pas-
nate lover of music. **me´lomanie**
◦-lō-mă-nē), *F.*, **mel´omany.** Mu-
mania.

◦pea (mā-lō-pā´-ä), *I.*, **mélopée**
◦-lō-pā), *F.* The art of melody.

◦phare. A lantern with oiled
sic paper sides for use in sere-
les.

◦piano. A device inv. 1870 by
dera, of Turin, for giving the
no power to increase the volume
a sustained tone. A treadle works
ll hammers acting rapidly on the
ngs.

◦plaste (měl´-ō-plăst). Pierre Gal-
s simplified method of teaching the
iments by singing popular airs and
nting the place of the notes on the
ff, and by using two metronomes
beats and measures.

◦poea (mě-lō-pē´-ä), *Gr.* Art of
nposition.

◦s (mā´-lōs). Melody. Used by
gner for the melody, also the en-
implied harmony, the musical
a. *V*ide RECITATIVE.

**mel´otrope.** Vide MELOGRAPH.

**même** (měm), *F.* The same. **à la m.
tempo.** In the original tempo.

**men** (mān), *I.* Abbr. of **meno** before
a vowel. **men allegro.** Less quick.

**menéstrel** (mŭ-nās-trĕl´), *F.* Minstrel.
Vide TROUBADOUR.

**mené´trier** (mŭ´nä-trĭ-ā), *F.* A minstrel or rustic musician. Vide TROU-
BADOUR.

**meno** (mā´-nō), *I.* Less; not so fast.
**m. mosso.** Less speed.

**Mensur** (měn-zoor´), *G.* Measure, of
time, intervals, scale of pipes, and
sizes of instr. strings, etc.

**men´sura,** *L.* Measure, time.

**men´surable,** *E.*, **mensural** (měn-
zoo-räl´), *G.* The original plain-
chant was in notes of equal duration ;
in the 12th cent. the old square
notes were modified and given a
" measurable " value. The first **mensurable notes** were the *maxima,
longa, brevis* and *semibrevis ;* in
1300, the *minima* and *semiminima*
were added. In the 15th cent. white
notes displaced the black, which were
chiefly used for smaller values. The
music so written, or **mensurable
music,** was governed by many complicated laws. Vide NOTATION.

**mente** (měn´-tě). Mind. **alla m.** Improvised.

**menuet** (mŭ-noo-ā´), *F.*, **Menuett**
(měn-oo-ĕt´), *G.*, **menuetto** (mā-
noo-ĕt´-tō), *I.* Minuet.

**mer´ula,** *L.* A set of pipes in water
producing a warbling tone.

**me´ris,** *Gr.* The 6th part of an octave.

**mesau´lion,** *Gr.* Symphony, ritornello.

**mès´cal.** A Turkish instr. of twenty-
three cane pipes; each giving three
different sounds.

**mescolanza** (měs-kō-län´-tsä), *I.* A
medley.

**me´se, me´son,** *Gr.* Vide CHART OF
GREEK MODES and LYRE.

**me´sotonic.** 1. Mean-tone. Vide TEM-
PERAMENT. 2. Vide LYRE.

**mes´sa.** *I.* A mass.

**messa di voce** (mĕs'-sa dĭ vō'-chĕ), *I.*
The gradual swelling and diminishing
of a tone ; to attack and swell is **formare il tuono** (fŏr-mä'-rĕ ēl too-ō'-
nō) ; to sustain loudly is **fermare il
t.** (fĕr-mä'-rĕ) ; to diminish is **finire**
(fē-nē'-rĕ) **il t.**

**messanza** (mĕs-sän'-tsä), *I.* Quodlibet (q. v.).

**messe** (mĕs), *F.*, **Messe** (mĕs'-sĕ), *G.*
A mass.

**mes'sel**, *Arab.* " Measure." The Arabian method of reckoning intervals,
the lower notes receiving greater
values than the higher because the
vibrating portion of the string which
produces them is longer.

**mesto** (mās'-to), *I.* Melancholy. **mesto'so.** Sad.

**mesure** (mŭ-zür'), *F.* Measure. **à la
m.** In time. **m. à deux temps** (dŭ
täṅ). Common time. **m. à trois
temps** (trwä täṅ). Triple time. **m.
demi** (d'mē). Half measure.

**met.** Abbr. of Metronome.

**metal** (mā-tăl'), *Sp.* Strength, compass
of the voice.

**metallico** (mĕ-täl'-lĭ-kō), *I.* (Of a voice)
" metallic " in a good sense, clear,
ringing, hence **metal'lo**, " metal."

**metamor'phoses.** Variations.

**meter,** or **metre,** *E.*, **mètre** (mĕtr), *F.*
In music as in verse, the arrange-
ment of rhythmic units, or measures.
The **m.** of hymns is classified by the
number of syllables to a line, the metrical foot and the number of lines to a
stanza. In Iambic **m.** are **common
m.** (C. M.), 4 lines alternately 8 and
6 syllables long ; **common particular,** or **hallelujah m.** (C. P. M.),
886886 ; **long m.** (L. M.), 4 lines of 8
syllables ; **long particular m.** (L.
P. M.), or **long· m. six lines,** 6
lines of 8 ; **short m.** (S. M.), 6686 ;
**short particular m.** (S. P. M.,),
668668 ; stanzas of 8 lines are called
**double** (C. M. D. ; L. M. D. ; S. M.
D.). Other line-lengths are **sevens**
and **sixes** (7676), **tens** (four 10's),
**hallelujah** (666688, or 66664444).
In trochaic **m.** are **sixes** (four 6's),
**sixes** and **fives** (6562) **sevens**

(four 7's), **eights** and **sevens** (8
In Dactylic **m.** are **eights, eig
sevens** and **fours,** etc. ; **ele
(four 11's), and **elevens** and
(11, 10, 11, 10), etc. Classic
French metres depend on *qua
or length of syllables, instead o
their stress or accentuation as
us. Vide FOOT.

**method,** *E.*, **méthode** (mā-tôd),
**metodo** (mā'-tō-dō), *I.* A cour
instruction ; classification ; syste

**Metrik** (māt'-rēk), *G.* Metrical
**metrisch** (mĕt'-rĭsh). Metrical

**metro** (mā'-tro), *I.* and *Sp.* Metr
**Metrometer** (mĕ-trō-mā'-tĕr), *G.*,
**tromètre** (mā-trō-mĕtr), *F.*, **m
metro** (mā-trō-mā'-trō), *I.* M
nome.

**met'ronome,** *E.*, **Metronom**
trō-nôm'), *G.*, **métronome** (m
nŭm), *F.*, **metronomo** (mā-trō
mō), *I.* A pendulum worke
clock-work, and weighted below ;
vided with a movable slide, ar
graduated that its rate of vibr
per minute can be fixed by the sl
with the slider at 60 it beats 60
a minute, etc. It moves with a
dible click ; the **bell-metronom
also a bell which rings every thi
fourth, etc., beat. Perfected by
kel it was put on the marke
Maelzel (vide B. D.), and is c
**Maelzel's metronome** (abbr. M
It is useful as a composer's in
tion of the standard time of a co
sition ; hence the **metronome-m
thus M. M. ♩–90, means a rat
quarter notes equal to 90 per mi
as indicated by the slider set a
It is used also to beat time for
dents. It is made also in w
form as a **pocket m.**

**met'rum,** *L.* Metre.

**Mette** (mĕt'-tĕ), *G.* Matins.

**metter la voce,** *I.* Same as mes
voce.

**mettere in musica** (mĕt'-tĕ-rĕ ĭn
zĭ-kä), *I.* To set to music.

**mettez** (mĕt-tā), *F.* " Draw (a st

**mettre d'accord** (mĕtr dăk-kôr
To tune. **m. en musique** (äṅ

). To set to music. **m. en ré-
:ition** (rä-pä-tēs'-yôṅ). To put in
:earsal.

:**illoth, metzilltheim,** *Heb.* Cym-
..s.

.. Abbr. of Mezzo.

:o (mĕd'-zō), *I.* Medium, half.
.**aria.** Vide ARIA PARLANTE. **m.
.vura.** Moderate difficulty. **m.
.za** (fôr'-tsä). Moderately loud.
.**manica** (mä'-nĭ-kä). The half-
..t. **mezzana** (mĕd-zä'-nä). Middle
.ng of a lute. **m. orchestra.** Half
. string-band. **m. voce** (vō'-chĕ),
.Half the voice, with moderate
.e. **m. forte** (fôr'-tĕ). Moderately
.d. **m. piano** (pĭ-ä'-nō), *I.* Rather
.t. **m. soprano.** A voice lower
.n soprano, higher than contralto.
.**ezzo soprano clef.** The C clef on
.e second line, in old church-music
.madrigals. The treble, or soprano,
.f now supplies its place. **m. stac-
.to.** A little detached. **m. teno're.**
.ow tenor voice, nearly barytone. **m.
.ono** (too-ō'-nō), *I.* A semi-tone.

.. Abbr. of mezzo forte.

.g. Abbr. of main gauche (left
.nd).

.mē), *I.* and *F.* 1. The note E.
. **bémol** (bā'-môl). E flat. **mi
.èse** (dĭ-ĕz'). The note E sharp.
.Vide SOLMISATION. 3. The 3d
.the scale. *mi contra fa est diabo-
.s in musica,* "mi against fa is the
.vil in music," was the mediæval ob-
.-gation against the tritone (q. v.),
.being B natural in the hard hexa-
.ord, fa being F in the natural
.xachord. **mi-re-ut.** Vide OCTAVE.

.**rophone.** An instr. for the mag-
.'ying of sounds.

.-**c.,** or **middle c.** *c'* (vide PITCH),
.cause it is in the centre of the piano
.d between the treble and bass
.aves.

.**dle voices.** Tenor and alto.

.**non** (mēn-yôṅ), *F.* 1. Favourite,
.t. 2. Delicate.

.**taire** (mĭl-ĭ-tăr), *F.,* **militare** (mē-
.tä'-rĕ), *I.,* **militairement** (mĭl-ĭ-
.r'-mäṙ,), *F.,* **militarmen'te,** *I.*
.artial(ly).

**Militärmusik** (mē-lĭ-tär'-moo-zēk').
Military band or music.

**military band.** An orchestra for out-
of-doors, substituting for stringed
instrs. additional and more powerful
clarinets, and using saxophones, cornets, etc., freely.

**milote** (mē-lō'-tĕ), *Sp.* An Indian
dance.

**mi'modrama,** *E.,* **mimodrame** (mē-
mô-dräm'), *F.* Pantomime.

**minacciando** (mē-nät-chän'-dō), **min-
accievole** (chä'-vō-lĕ), **minaccio'so,
minaccie'volmente, minaccio'samente.** Threatening(ly).

**minagnghinim** (mĭ-nängd'-gĭ-nĭm),
*Heb.* A table over which was stretched
an iron chain and a hempen cord
through balls of wood or brass; striking against the table they made a
ringing sound.

**minder** (mĭnt'-ĕr), *G.* Minor, less.

**mineur** (mē-nŭr'), *F.* Minor.

**min'im, minima** (mē'-nĭ-mä), *I.,* **min-
ime** (mĭn-ēm'), *F.* A half-note. Vide
NOTATION.

**Minnedichter** (mĭn'-nĕ-dĭkh'-tĕr), **M.-
sänger** (zĕng-ĕr), **M.-singer** (zĭng-
ĕr), *G.* From the 12th to the 14th
century a German troubadour of
noble birth celebrating pure love in
song (**Minne-gesang**). The singers wrote both words and music, singing and playing on the arpanetta or
the viol. Their festivals of contest
are reproduced in Wagner's "Tannhäuser." They were less formulaic
than their successor the "Meistersinger." In the opera of the latter
name, Wagner (vide "Stories of the
Operas" in this book) shows Walter
the **Minnesinger** in conflict with the
dogmas of the Meistersinger.

**mi'nor,** *E.,* **minore** (mē-nō'-rĕ), *I.*
"Smaller," of intervals, etc., as op-
posed to **major.** Vide INTERVAL, MA-
JOR, MODE, SCALE. **m. tone.** The
lesser whole tone, 10:9. **m. triad.**
One with minor 3d and perfect 5th.

**min'strels.** Singers, usually of a servile
or vagabond class, sometimes acting
as attendants on the trouvères and
troubadours (q. v.), and generally play-

ing the rebec. **negro m.** One who gives an imitation (usually remote) of the songs, dances, etc., of the American negro.

**minue** (mē-noo-ā'), *Sp.* A minuet.

**minuet** (mĭn-ū-ĕt'), *E.*, **minuetto** (mē-noo-ĕt'-tō), *I.* A stately and deliberate dance (originating probably in Poitou in the 17th century) in triple time, with gallant and amorous spirit. As one of the most important music-forms, it contains usually a principal subject and a trio each in contrasted sections. Appearing first as a movement in the suite and partita it became a part of the sonata and symphony, Beethoven substituting for it the Scherzo, and Tchaïkovsky, in one case, a Viennese waltz. **minuettina** (tē'nä), *I.* A little minuet.

**miracle, miracle-play.** Vide MYSTERY.

**mi-re-ut.** Vide OCTAVE.

**miscel'la,** *L.* Mixture-stop.

**mise de voix** (mēz-dŭ-vwä). Vide MESSA DI VOCE.

**miserere** (mē-zĕ-rā'-rĕ), *L.* First word of Psalm LI.beginning **miserere mei, domine,** "Pity me, Lord." Hence a setting of this Psalm sung in the R. C. service for the dead, and during Holy Week.

**misericordia** (mē'-zā-rĭ-kôr'-dĭ-ä), *L.* A miserere.

**misk'in.** A little bagpipe.

**mis'sa,** *L.* and *I.* A mass (q. v.). **m. brevis.** Short mass. **m. can'onica.** A canonical mass. **m. canta'ta.** Chanted mass. **m. pro defunc'tis.** "Mass for the dead." Requiem. **m. solen'nis.** High mass.

**mis'sal,** *E.*, **missa'le,** *L.*, **Missel** (mĭs'-sĕl), *G.* The mass-book containing the forms of the year.

**misshällig,** or **misshellig** (mĭs-hĕl'-lĭkh), *G.* Discordant. **Misshalligkeit** (kīt). Dissonance. **Missklang** (kläng). Discord. **missklingen** (mĭs -klĭng-ĕn), **misslauten** (lowtĕn). To be discordant. **Misslaut** (lowt). Discordant sound. **Misslautend** (low-tĕnt). Dissonant, dis-

cordant. **misstimmen** (shtĭm'- To put out of tune.

**misterio** (mĭs-tā'-rĭ-o), **mistero** tā'-rō), *I.* Mystery. **mister misteriosamen'te.** Mysteriou

**mistichanza** (mēs-tĭ-kän'-tsä), Quodlibet (q. v.).

**mis'to,** *Gr.* Mixed. Vide MODES

**misura** (mē-soo'-rä), *I.* Measure. **urato** (mē-soo-rä'-tō), *I.* In time.

**mit** (mĭt), *G.* With, by.

**Mitklang** (mĭt'-kläng), *G.* Reson **mitklingende Töne** (mĭt'-l ĕnt-ĕ tā'-nĕ). Overtones.

**Mitlaut** (mĭt'-lowt), *G.,* **Mitla** (mĭt'-low-ter). Concord, conson **mitlauten.** To sound with.

**mitleidsvoll** (mĭt'-lĭts-fôl), *G.* Cor sionate.

**Mittel** (mĭt'-tĕl), *G.* Middle, **mittel c.** (tsä). Middle C. **Mi kadenz** (kä-dĕnts'). A half-cad Vide CADENCE. **Mittel-laut** (l Middle sound. **mittelmässig.** different. **M.-stimme** (shtĭm' Inner part.

**mixed.** Vide CADENCE. **m. ca** Vide CANON. **m. chorus,** etc. with both male and female voices in organ, the mixture-stops.

**mix'olydian.** Vide MODES.

**mixt'ure,** *E.,* **mixtu'ra,** *L.,* **Mi** (mĕx-toor'), *G.* A compound stop consisting of 2 to 6 rank pipes, giving 2 to 6 harmonics o tone. The **m.** is auxiliary usually sounding only the octave the fifth, and aiming to brighte foundation-stops. Ancient **m.'s** from 8 to 24 ranks, the result d less being atrocious discord.

**mobile** (mō'-bĭ-lĕ), *I.* Facile, ir sive, fickle.

**moderato** (mō-dĕ-rä'-tō), *I.* Mode in time. **moderatis'simo,** or **assai** (äs-sä'-ē). In very mode time. **moderamen'te.** Modera **moderanza** (rän'-tsä), **moderaz** (rä-tsĭ-ō'-nĕ). Moderation.

**moderna, alla** (äl'-lä mō-dĕr'-nä) In the modern style.

## Modes.

### By the Editor.

ᗞERHAPS the most graphic definition of modes to the modern mind
would be :—overlapping portions of the C major scale : or successive octave-stretches along the white keys of the pianoforte. *Eccle-
ical modes* were the Middle Age perversion of the *Greek Modes*. While
thrown by Nineteenth Century scales and tonality, traces of their
ence persevere, and many of the old chants still in use in the Roman
ᶥolic and Anglican services are more or less exact specimens of the
bilities of the modes. The Twenty-first Century will probably qualify
develop our own system of keys out of shape and recognition. The
ᵖlete overthrow of the ideas of tonality and modulation of the earlier part
ᵗhe Twentieth Century is indeed even now beginning. We are already
the doorsill of the nullitonic or omnitonic harmonies, and the multitude
ᴄcidental sharps and flats and naturals required to notate the highly
ᵐatic music of our day renders inevitable some radical change in the
ᵗm of keys ; meanwhile, the obsolete modal systems have at least a keen
ᵗrical interest and importance. There is place here for only an allusion
few of the salient points. Full statement of the details and the contro-
es on them would fill a large library. ¶Though the Greeks properly
music a very high place in their educational system, they were too
ᵗh engrossed in theories, rules, and restrictions to build up large material.
ᶤr musical resources were of the slenderest. While their noble tragedies
· exactly Wagner's idea of opera, the music to which they were set
ᵏs to have been of the most limited range and variety ; and furthermore,
ᶥutely lacking in harmony even in the Middle Age sense. ¶The Greek
ᵗm differs from ours in being all of a minor tendency, in having the
ᵏs named downwards, and in paying attention only to melody and not at
ᵗo chords. The white piano keys from e′ (just above middle C) to the
ᵃ octave below, represent their oldest and central mode, the Dorian. By
ᵉmbering that all these steps are whole tones except the two semitones
ᵃ c′ to b and F to E, and by representing a whole step by a ( + ) and a
step by a ( — ), it will be seen that this Dorian mode descends by the
wing steps, + + — + + —. These make two similar groups of three
ᵏs or four notes, which were called *tetrachords*. The word chord with
ᵃ meant " string " not " harmony," for their whole music took its rise
ᵃ their lyre, a stiff and limited, unfretted instrument of many poetical
ᴄᵢations but stinted in practical possibilities. The pattern of tetrachord
+ — ) into which this Dorian mode divided was called the Dorian tetra-

## Chart of the Greek Modes.

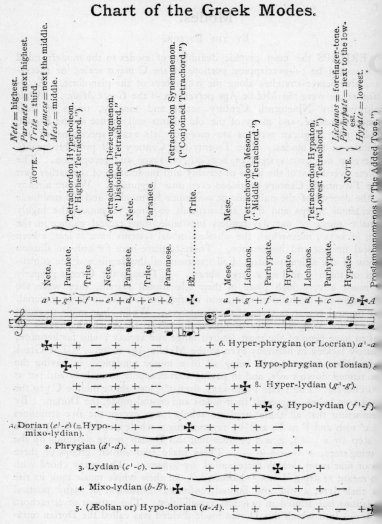

The whole steps are indicated by + ; the half-steps by — ; the Diazeuxis is indicated by ✠.

They superimposed on the top note e′ a similar tetrachord of the tones f′, e, and added below another e, d, c, B. To these they added the as a supplementary (in Greek *proslambanomenos*). The outer couples achords overlap. Between the middle two is an imaginary line of sep- (*diazeuxis*). Each of these was therefore a "disjunct" (*diazeng-* ) tetrachord. The "complete system" (*systema teleion*) of two octaves wn to A) was divided thus into four tetrachords, each of them given me which (with its English translation) is shown in the chart here-

For purposes of modulation they laid across the middle of this system rlapping or "conjunct" (*synemmenon*) tetrachord in which the b was ed, d′, c′, b♭, a ( + + — ). ¶The octave from e′ down to E was, ady stated, called the *Dorian mode*. Other portions of the systema given other names, d to D being called the *Phrygian*, c′ to C the , and b to B the *Mixo-Lydian*. ¶They conceived a way of extend- ese octaves by duplicating one of the tetrachords below (in Greek ''). Thus, if the upper tetrachord (e′ to a) of the Dorian mode nsferred an octave below, and fastened to the lower tetrachord, we o longer have e′, d′, c′, b, a, g, f, e, ( + + — + + — ) but a, g, , c, B, A, which also is + + — + + —, with the added step + mbanomenos). This is called the *Hypo-Dorian mode*. ¶The Phryg- dian, and Mixo-Lydian modes do not descend by the same whole lf steps as the Dorian, but as follows : Phrygian ( + — + + + — + ), ( — + + — + + — ), Mixo-Lydian ( + + + — + + — ). It will d, however, that these modes are capable of the same *hypo*-treatment, aking two more modes, *Hypo-Phrygian* and *Hypo-Lydian*,—for the Lydian (b to B) being too low to add a tetrachord beneath, it is above, giving e′ to e, which is identical with the Dorian. The al note (*tonic*) of the regular modes was the top note. Each hypo- kept for its chief note the chief note of the original (or its octave). ames and ranges of these seven modes with two others added later are in the chart, which shows also the names (and their translations) given ote and each tetrachord. ¶With this system as a foundation and he use of the conjunct tetrachord and its b flat as an entering wedge, eeks gradually added several notes above and below their systema, and half steps between the full steps until they acquired a complete tic scale on which they transposed their scales with much melodic n. Harmony, of course, they did not have. These transposed scales ot named like the original modes from their chief notes, but were he name of the scale whose steps they resembled. By making use of and — , or other signs for indicating half or whole steps, it is easy to t the steps of any scale and find its prototype and its name in the

original modes. ¶The Greek notation was by letters and symbols.
too complicated to explain here. ¶A method of manipulating their
melodically may be mentioned. The tetrachords as described were c
diatonic, but in the Dorian e, d, c, b, if the d were omitted, the tetrac
became e — c, b, and was called the *older enharmonic.* A later plan w
keep the d, but lower it by half a tone (that is, to tune the d string
sharp), making the four strings e, c♯, c, b. This was the *chromatic g*
A still later plan, called the *newer enharmonic,* was to tune the d to a
third with the e, making the tetrachord e, c, c, b ; the two c strings d
ing slightly in tone (see the word COMMA). ¶This group of three tone
c, b, or c♯, c, b, was the *pyknon* (plural *pykna*). Other variations i
treatment were called *chroai* (colourings). Definite melodies were
definite names, a melody being a *nomos* (i. e., arrangement, order, or
ting). ¶Upon this false, but elaborate, system, enormous ingenuity
spent, and appalling complexity and scholarship of a kind were made pos
to the delight of the typical theorist. In respect of melody the Greek n
offered far more freedom than the church modes, which, however, poss
the modern invention of harmony.

### ECCLESIASTICAL MODES.

Music, along with all the other early Christian arts, borrowed la
from the Greeks, but rejected their warmth and ornate sophistication
stark rigidity. ¶Early church musicians took the Greek modes as best
could understand them, making as many mistakes as was usual in th
generate classicism of those times. The Byzantine school perverted (
music and passed it along, as it had done with painting and archite
The range and the chromatic graces of later Greek melody were desert
a heavy march through one octave of one key. Furthermore, the scal
considered now as ascending, instead of descending. ¶St. Ambrose i
ditionally credited with establishing four modes for church music.
these St. Gregory was believed to have derived four new modes.
original four are called *Authentic,* i. e., " governing," or " chief."
latter four are called *Plagal,* i. e., " oblique " or " inferior." To
were added other modes, some of them being denied a right to exist.
with all the old Greek modes, all the church modes are to be found o
white keys of the piano ; no chromatic was allowed except, finally, I
which was admitted to avoid the forbidden tritone and the diminished
A melody that did not stray out of its octave mode was called *perfect*
that did not use all of its range was *imperfect ;* one that overstepp
octave was *superfluous ;* one that used up both a mode and its plagal wa
*mixed mode.* ¶Greek names were used for the church modes, but

AUTHENTIC MODES,
OR
MODI AUTHENTICI.

Each authentic mode is connected with its plagal by a line through the key-note or finalis of both.

PLAGAL MODES,
OR
MODI PLAGALES.

## Chart of the Church Modes.

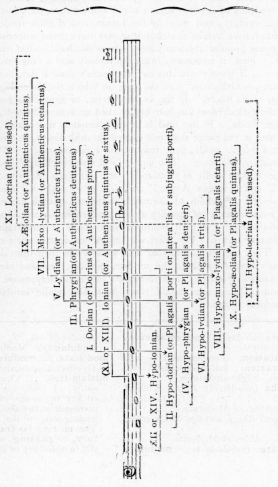

XI. Locrian (little used).

IX. Æolian (or Authenticus quintus).

VII. Mixo-lydian (or Authenticus tetartus).

V. Lydian (or Authenticus tritus).

III. Phrygian (or Authenticus deuterus).

I. Dorian (or Dorius or Authenticus protus).

(XI or XIII) Ionian (or Authenticus quintus or sixtus).

(XII or XIV. Hypo-ionian.

XII. Hypo-dorian (or Plagalis porti or lateralis or subjugalis porti).

IV. Hypo-phrygian (or Plagalis deuteri).

VI. Hypo-lydian (or Plagalis triti).

VIII. Hypo-mixo-lydian (or Plagalis tetarti).

X. Hypo-æolian (or Plagalis quintus).

XII. Hypo-locrian (little used).

many differences from the old nomenclature. ¶An authentic mode i: on its *Final* or lowest note ; the next most important note, usually a a third above, is its *dominant*. A plagal mode is found a fourth be. authentic, and the *final* of the authentic serves also for the plagal. dominant of a plagal is a third below that of its authentic (save where on b, in which case c is used). ¶Curiously enough, the two moder which we think of as white keys, c major and a minor, were not added u sixteenth century, and then as the Ionian and Æolian modes. ¶I many impressive hymns the church modes have been unconsciously a to fit many popular modern tunes. It is not hard to test the mode- any air. First, if necessary, bring the melody into a range requiring n signature. If it now contains any accidentals save b flat, it is not in the modes. Otherwise note the tone on which the air ends. This the *final* of its mode. If this is the lowest, or almost the lowest note and if the melody does not soar higher than an octave above it, the air authentic mode. If the final is in approximately the centre of the r range, and if the range does not exceed the fifth above, or the fourth it is in a *plagal* mode, or it may be in a *mixed mode. The name final indicates the mode.* The airs " God save the King" (or " Ame and the " Blue Bells of Scotland " are *authentic* melodies. The 100th " and " Eileen Aroon " are *plagal.* " Jock o' Hazeldean " *mixed mode.* ¶Much of the music in the old church modes is as sh to the modern sense of tonality as our modern music would seem ana to an old master. Superb treasures were given to immortality in th and arbitrary forms. Yet, after all, the modes deserve their eternal ob ness. They were unsatisfactory and arbitrary in their own day. Th hopelessly inappropriate to the modern musical ideas and ideals. Th jestic beauties of some of their results are but as the impressive fossils of evolution. Their fate should warn us against stolid satisfaction wi own musical system.

**modesto** (mō-dās'-tō), **modestamente.** Modest(ly).
**mod'ification.** Temperament (q. v.).
**modificazioni** (mō-dē-fī-kä-tsī-ō'-ne), *I.*, pl. Slight alterations.
**modinha** (mō-dēn'-ä), *Port.* A short song.
**mod.** Abbr. of Moderato.
**modo** (mō'-dō), *I.* and *Sp.* Mode, scale, style.
**modto.** Abbr. of Moderato.
**modolare** (mō-dō-lä'-rĕ), **modulare**

(mō-doo-lä'-rĕ), *I.* To mo
**modulan'te.** Modulating.
**mod'ulate,** *E.,* **moduler** (mŏd-ü To effect a modulation.
**modula'tion.** 1. Change of k nality, or mode (usually to a ed key by means of chords dominant of the new major, or leading-tone of the new min The **m.** may be **transient,** tory, or **passing,** when it le still a third key or back to th

ıy be **final** when it establishes a
tonality. **enharmonic m.** is that
means of enharmonic (q. v.)
ges of notation. 2. *Obsolete.*
ɔdic, or rhythmic measurement,
ction.

a'tor. Vide TONIC-SOL-FA.

atore (mō-doo-lä-tō'-rĕ), *I.* 1.
er. 2. Tuner.

azione (mō-doo-lä-tsĭ-ō'-nĕ), *I.*
ulation.

iren (mô-doo-lē'-rĕn), *G.* To
ulate.

s, *L.* Key, mode, scale.

ch (mäkh'-lĭkh), *G.* Possible.
asch wie m. (zō-räsh-vē). As
as possible.

da (mō-ēn'-dä). A short Portu-
e love-song.

entanz (mō-rĕn-tänts), *G.* Mo-
.

(mwăṅ), *F.* Less.

môl), *G.* Minor. **Mollakkord,**
**Molldreiklang.** Minor chord or
l, etc.

(môl'-lä), *I.* A key (of the flute),

, *L.* Soft. 1. Vide "B." 2.
d of the hexachord f–d in which
at was substituted for the older
tural. 3. Minor.

(môl), *F.* Soft, delicate.

mente (môl-lĕ-mĕn'-tĕ), *I.* Softly,
ly.

s, *L.* Vide MOLLE.

onart (môl'-tōn-ärt), *G.* Minor
**Molltonleiter** (lī-tĕr). Minor
e.

sonante (mōl-tē-sō-nän'-tĕ), *I.*
ounding, very sonorous.

(mōl'-tō), *I.* Much, very. **di m.**
remely. **m. adagio.** Very slow.
allegro. Very quick, etc.

n'tulum, *L.* A 16th rest.

n'tum, *L.* An 8th rest.

u'los, *Gr.* An ancient beak-

cordo (mō'-nō-kôr'-dō), *I.*, **mon'-
ord,** *F.*, **monochorde** (môn-ō-
l), *F.* 1. An instr. of one string
ı a movable bridge, for determin-
intervals and pitch. 2. Marine

trumpet. 3. A clavichord. 4. A
German 1-stringed zither with fretted
finger-board and resonance-box. 5.
**a monocordo =** "on one string,"
i. e., with the soft (or **monochord)**
pedal down.

**monferina** (môn-fĕ-rē'-nä), *I.* Livelv
dance in 6-8 time.

**monodia** (mô-nō-dē'-ä), *I.*, **Monodie**
(môn-ō-dē'), *F.* and *G.* Monody.

**monod'ic.** For one voice ; or with one
voice predominant.

**monodra'ma, monodrame** (dräm). A
musical drama with only one actor.

**mon'ody.** Homophony.

**monophon'ic.** Homophonic.

**monoph'onous.** Producing but one
tone, as the drum.

**mon'otone.** 1. Uniformity of sound.
2. Recitation on one tone.

**Monotonie** (mō-nô-tō-nē'), *G.* Monot-
ony.

**monot'onous.** Monophonous ; lacking variety.

**montant** (môṅ-tän), *F.* Ascending.

**monter** (môṅ-tā), *F.* 1. To string. 2.
To tune. 3. To put an instr. together. 4. To ascend.

**montre** (môṅtr), *F.* The pipes (usually the diapason) erected and
"shown" at the front of the organ.

**Moor'ish drum.** A tambourine.

**Moralitäten** (mōräl-ĭ-tä'-tĕn), *G.*, **mo-
ralités** (mô-räl-ĭ-tā'), *F.*, **moralities,**
*E.* Allegorical moral plays of the
middle ages, a later form of the mysteries.

**morbidezza** (mŏr-bĭ-dĕd'-zä), *I.* Lux-
urious delicacy.

**morceau** (môr-sō), *F.* A "piece."
1. A short composition. 2. A phrase.
**m. d'ensemble** (dän-säṅbl). A piece
harmonised for voices. **m. de genre**
(dŭ zhäṅr). Characteristic piece.

**mordant** (môr-dän), *F.* A trilled
grace (q. v.).

**mor'dent,** *E.*, **Mordent',** *G.*, **mordente**
(môr-dĕn'-tĕ), *I.* A grace (q. v.), *long,*
*short,* or *inverted.*

**moren'do, moriente** (mō-rĭ-ĕn'-tĕ), *I.*
Dying away ; diminishing in volume
and speed.

**moresca** (mō-rĕs'-kӭ), *I.*, **moresque** (mô-rĕsk), *F.* Moorish dance with jingling anklets and clashing swords.

**Morgengesang** (môr'gen-gĕ-zäng), **M.-lied** (lēt), *G.* Morning song. **M. -ständchen** (sthtĕnt'-khĕn). Morning serenade.

**morisco** (mō-rēs'-kō), *I.* Moorish. Vide MORESCA.

**mo'risk.** Morris-dance.

**mormoramen'to,** *I.* A murmur. **mormorando** (rän'-dō), **mormorevole** (rā'-vō-lĕ), **mormoro'so.** Gently murmuring.

**morrice-dance, morris-dance, morriske-dance.** An English country-dance of supposedly Moorish origin in 4-4 time, the dancers wearing ankle-bells and grotesque costumes.

**mort** (in *F.* môr). A tune at "the death" of the game.

**mosso** (môs'-sō), *I.* "Moved," rapid. **molto m.** Very fast. **meno m.** Less fast, etc.

**mostra** (mōs'-trä), *I.* A direct.

**mot** (mō, *F.* A note or strain on the bugle.

**motet(t),** *E.*, **Motette** (mō-tĕt'-tĕ), *G.*, **motet** (mō-tā), *F.*, **motet'to,** *I.* 1. An almost always unaccompanied vocal composition contrapuntally developed, and using biblical text; a sacred madrigal. 2. Loosely, an anthem.

**mote'tus,** *L.* 1. A motet. 2. An obscure mediæval term.

**motif** (mō-tēf'), *F.* Motive, subject.

**motion.** Progression. 1. Of a single part by degrees (**conjunct m.**), or by skip (**disjunct m.**). 2. Of two parts relatively considered; **contrary** or **opposite** if one ascends as the other descends; **oblique,** if one is stationary while the other progresses; **parallel** or **consecutive,** if both move in the same direction by the same interval; **similar,** if both move in the same direction by unequal intervals (the latter terms are loosely used as synonymous); **mixed,** if, in the case of several parts, two of the above motions occur simultaneously between different parts. 3. **perpet-**

ual m. Vide PERPETUAL. 4. p motion. That in which the pr ing tone-length is that of the star note of the measure, as ½ notes dominating in 3-2 time; **half-p** that in which the prevailing mot in notes of half the pulse-value, notes in 3-2 time, etc. 5. **eighth-motion.** That in which the prev: entrances of tones fall uniform eighth notes.

**motive,** *E.*, **Motiv** (mō-tēf'), *G.,* tivo (mō-tē'-vō), *I.* 1. Theme, ject, a brief phrase or figure. 2. LEADING-MOTIVE. 3. In Forr measure. **measure-m.** One w accent is that of the measure.

**moto** (mō'-tō), *I.* 1. Motion (q 2. Speed. **con moto.** With mo rather fast. **m. contrario** (kôn rĭ-ō). Contrary motion. **m. mi** Mixed motion. **m. obliquo** lē'-kwō). Oblique motion. **m. to.** Parallel motion. **m. perpe** Vide PERPETUAL. **m. precid** (prā-chĭ-dĕn'-tĕ). The same tim the preceding movement. **m. p** (prē'-mō). The same time as the

**motteggiando** (mōt-tĕd-jän'-dō) Mocking(ly), jocose(ly).

**mottetto** (mōt-tĕt'-tō), *I.* Motet.

**mo'tus,** *L.* 1. Motion (q. v.). 2. M ment. **m. contrarius.** Con motion. **m. obliquus.** Oblique tion.

**mouth.** The opening in the front pipe. **m.-harmonica,** or **m. or** 1. Vide HARMONICA. 2. Pan's p

**mouth'piece.** The part of a w instr. applied to the lips.

**mouvement** (moov-mäṅ), *F.*, **m** men'to, *I.* 1. Motion. 2. M ment. **m. de l'archet** (dŭ-lär-s *F.* Bowing. **bien mouveme** (b'yäṅ moov-mäṅ-tā). Rhythmi< elegant; well regulated.

**movement.** 1. Rate of speed. Style of rhythm, as *waltz*-m. major division of a composition, ing a certain integrity in itself, a: slow or the 2d **m.** of a symph etc.

, Abbr. of Mezzo-piano.

, Abbr. of Mano Sinistra (left
nd).

nce (mü-äṅs), *F.* A change or
iation of note. Vide MUTATION

(mü), *F.* See MUTATION.

t (mü-ā), *F.* Mute.

d (moont), *G.* Mouth. **M. har-
·'nika.** Mouth-harmonica. Vide
RMONICA. **M.-loch** (lôkh). Mouth
a pipe. **M. stück** (shtük). Mouth-
·ce.

eira (moon-yä-ē'-rä), *Sp.* A mod-
ately fast Galician dance, in 2-4
1e, beginning on the unaccented
at, with the strong beat in casta-
·-rhythm.

ter (moon'-tĕr), *G.* Lively, spright-
**Munterkeit** (kīt). Vivacity.

·'y. Used of a harpsichord comp.
ving a bass in broken octaves
lled **murky-bass**).

neln (moor'-mĕln), *G.* To mur-
r. **murmelnd** (moor'melṅt). Mur-
·uring.

. **Bac.** Abbr. of Bachelor (q. v.)
Music.

. **Doc.** Abbr. of Doctor (q. v.) of
isic.

e (mūz). 1. One of the nine god-
sses of art. 2. The muzzle or tube
a bagpipe.

etta (moo-zĕt'-tä), *I.,* **musette** (in
mü-zet', in *F.* mü-zĕt). 1. A
all, imperfect oboe. 2. A bag-
e with bellows. 3. Hence, a short
storal dance-tune (often part of the
votte) in duple or triple time with
rone-bass. 4. A reed-stop.

ca (moo'-zĭ-kä), *L.* and *I.* Music.
**da camera** (dä kä'-mĕ-rä). Cham-
·-music. **m. da teatro** (tä-ä'-trō).
amatic music. **m. di gat'ti.**
Cat-music." Vide CHARIVARI. **m.
ına.** Plain-chant.

cale (moo-zĭ-kä'-lĕ), **musical-
·n'te,** *I.* Musical(ly).

cale (mū'-zĭ-kăl). An "at home"
icert.

·c-box. A box containing an au-
natic musical instr. The *Swiss*

m. b. has a steel comb of graduated
teeth set in vibration by small pegs in
a revolving cylinder.

**music-drama.** An opera (particularly
of the Wagnerian school) in which
the text and the action determine
the music, and are not interrupted by
set arias, dvets, etc.

**musicien** (mü-zēs'-yäṅ), *F.* Musician.

**musicista** (moo-zĭ-chē'-stä), *I.* Musician.

**musico** (moo'-zĭ-kō), *I.* 1. Musician.
2. A male soprano, particularly a
eunuch.

**musicone** (moo-zĭ-kō'-nĕ), *I.* A great
musician.

**music-pen.** 1. A 5-pointed pen for
ruling the staff. 2. A broad-pointed
pen for writing music.

**music-recorder.** A melograph.

**music-timekeeper.** An English instr.
enabling a performer to keep time.

**Musik** (moo-zēk'), *G.* Music. **Musiker** (moo'-zĭ-kĕr). **Musikus** (koos').
A musician. **Musikalien** (käl'-ĭ-ĕn).
Trade name for compositions. **Musikant** (moo-zĭ-känt'). A vagabond
musician. **M.-fest.** A musical festival.
**Musik'bande,** or **Musikanten-
bande** (bän-de). A band of strolling
musicians. **Musik'diktät** (dēk-tät).
Vide DICTATION. **M.-direktor.** Conductor. **M.-lehrer** (lā'-rĕr). Music-
teacher. **M.-meister** (mī-shtĕr).
Bandmaster. **M.-probe** (prō'-bĕ).
Rehearsal. **M.-verein** (fĕ-rīn). A
musical society. **M.-zeitung** (tsī-
toongk). A musical periodical.

**musique** (mü-zēk'), *F.,* Music. **m.
d'église** (dā-glēz). Church-music.

**musiquette** (mü-zĭ-kĕt). 1. A short
composition. 2. Light music.

**muta** (moo'-ta). "Change!" A direction in scores to change the crooks
or tuning of an instr. in preparation
for a change of key.

**muta'tion,** *E.* (in *F.* mü-tăs'-yôṅ),
**mutazione** (moo-tä-tsĭ-ō'-nĕ), *I.* 1.
The transformation of the male voice
at puberty (in *F.* **mue** (mü)). 2. Vide
SOLMISATION. 3. Shifting. 4. *As
prefix*, used of all tierce. quint, etc.,

**stops** not producing the unison or octave of the foundation-stop.

**mute.** A device for muffling tone ; in string-instrs. a clamp of brass, wood or ivory placed on the bridge and deadening the resonance ; in wind-instrs. a pear-shaped leather pad, a cylinder of perforated wood or a pasteboard cone introduced into the bell.

**mut(h)ig** (moo'-tĭkh), *G.* Courageous, spirited.

**muthwillig** (moot'-vĭl-likh), *G.* Mischievous.

**Muterung** (moo'-tĕ-roongk), *G.* Mutation, 1.

**mystères** (mĭs-tăr), *F.*, **Mysterien** (mē-stā'-rĭ-ĕn), *G.*, **mysteries**, *E.* Mediæval sacred dramas dealing with the Last Judgment and other mysteries, as the **moralities** dealt with allegorical virtues and vices, and **miracleplays** with the miracles of Christ. The idea persists in the Passion Play dealing with Christ's sufferings. In these dramas, often accompanied with music, oratorio had its beginning

## N

**N** ABLA (nä'-blä), *Heb.* The nebel.
**nacaire** (nä-kăr), *F.*, **nacara** (nä-kä'-rä), *I.* An obs. kettledrum.

**naccara** (näk-kä'-ra), **nacchera** (näk-kä'-rä), *I.* Kettledrum.

**nach** (näkh), *G.* After ; according to. **Nach'ahmung** (ä-moongk). Imitation. **nach Belieben** (bĕ-lēb'n). Ad libitum. **Nachdruck** (drook). Emphasis, accent. **nachdrücklich** (drük-lĭkh), **nachdrucksvoll** (drooks'fôl). Emphatic. **nachgi(e)biger** (gē'-bĭkh-ĕr). More slow and sustained. **Nachhall** (häl), **Nachklang** (kläng). Resonance, echo. **nachklingen** (klĭng-ĕn), **nachlassend** (läs'-sĕnt). Slackening in time. **nachlässig** (lĕs-sĭkh). Carelessly. **Nachruf** (roof). A farewell. **Nachsatz** (zäts).

The second part of a period, ing the **Vordersatz. Nac** (shläkh). (a) An after-note, poggiatura following its princip. (the opposite of *Vorschlag*) An auxiliary note at the en shake, also **Nachschliefe** (s **Nachspiel** (shpēl). Postlude. **und nach** (oont). By degrees. **tanz** (tänts), *F.* Second mo of a dance.

**nächtsverwandte Töne** (nĕk vänt'-tĕ-tä'-nĕ), *G.* The neare ative keys.

**Nacht** (näkht). Night. **N.-hor schall.** An 8-ft. flue-stop. **N. bass.** The same stop on the **N.-musikständchen**, *G.*, **N.-** (shtük). Nocturne, serenade.

**Nachtschläger** (nakht'-shlä **Nachtigall** (näkht'-ĭ-gäl), Nightingale ; an imitative instr

**nae'nia**, *Gr.* A dirge.

**nafie** (nä'-fē). A Persian trumpe

**nafiri** (nä-fē'-rē). An Indian tr

**nagârah** (nä-gä'-rä), **nagaret gareet'.** Oriental kettledrums

**nag'uar.** An Indian drum.

**Nagelgeige** (nägh'-ĕl-gī-khĕ), **fiddle.** Vide FIDDLE (I:ron).

**naïf** (nä-ēf), *F.*, fem. **naïve** (nä-ē **naïy** (nä-ēf'), *G.* Artless, na **naïvement** (nä-ēv-män). Nat **naïveté** (nä-ēv-tä). Artlessness plicity.

**naked.** Of intervals, as fourt fifths lacking the third or oth companiment.

**na'ker, nakeres.** *Old E.* metal drum(s).

**nakokus** (nä-kō'-kŭs), *Egypt.* brass plates suspended and stru

**nan'ga.** Negro harp.

**Nänien** (nä-nĭ-ĕn), *G.* Dirges.

**narrante** (när-rän'-tĕ), *I.* In nai style.

**narra'tor.** The chief performer oratorio or Passion Play.

**Narrentanz** (när'-rĕn-tänts), *G* dance.

**nasard** (nä-zăr), *F.*, **Nas(s)at'** (näs *G.*, **nazard'.** An old name for

ned a twelfth above the diapasons.
...asar'do, *I.* and *Sp.*, **nasarde** (nä-
rd), *F.*, **nassart** (näs'-särt), **na'-sil-
rd**. A 2⅔-foot stop. The **Grosnas-
d** (grō-nä-zăr), *F.*, or **Grossnasat**
...ōs-nä-zät'), *G.*, i.. a quint stop on
anual or pedal. **petit-nasard** (p'tē),
**larigot**, is a 1⅓-ft. stop.
...on. A 4-ft. flute-stop.
...ionallied (nä-tsɪ-ō-näl'-lēt), *G.* Na-
...nal song.
...ur (nä-toor'), *G.* Nature. **N. horn.**
valveless Waldhorn. **N.-scala.**
...atural scale. **N.-töne.** Vide NAT-
...AL TONE. **N. trompete.** Valve-
...ss trumpet. **natürliche** (nä-tür'-
...h-ĕ). Natural. **Naturalist'.** A
...f-taught singer. **naturalistisch**
...t'-ɪsh). Untrained.
...ural. 1. The sign ♮ nullifying a
...arp or flat. 2. A white digital.
...harmonics. Those on an open
...ing. **n. hexachord.** That based
...C. **n. modes.** The authentic
...urch modes. **n. modulation.**
...aat to a nearly related key. **n. key,**
...scale. That of C major. **n. pitch.**
...nat of a pipe not overblown. **n.**
...nes. Those producible on a wind-
...str., as the horn, without altering
...e length of the tube with valves,
...ys, etc., hence **natural horn**, etc.,
...e producing tones without valves
...keys.
...rale (nä-too-rä'-lĕ), *I.* Natural.
...turali suoni (soo-ō'-nē). Sounds in
...e compass of the voice. **natural-
...en'te.** Naturally.
...ral'is, *L.* Natural; *Cantus* **n.,**
...sic in the *hexachordum* **N.** (the
...xachord based on C).
...rel(le) (nät-ü-rĕl), *F.* Natural.
...lum (nô'-bloom), *Heb.* Vide
...BEL.
...(nä). A Turkish flute.
...politan sixth. Vide ALTERED
...ORDS.
...el (nä-bĕl), **nebel nassor** (nä-bĕl-
...s'-sôr), *Heb.* Ten-stringed harp.
...en (nä'-bĕn), *G.* Accessory. **N.-
...minant.** The dominant of the
...minant. **N.-dreiklang.** Second-

ary triad. **N.-gedanke.** Subsidiary
theme, or idea. **N.-klang.** Accessory tone. **N.-note.** Auxiliary note.
**N.-register, N.-züge** (tsü-khĕ).
Acessory stops. **N.-septimenak-
korde.** Secondary sevenths. **N.-
stimme.** Subordinate voice or part.
**N.-werk.** Choir-organ.

**necessario** (nā-chĕs-sä'-rĭ-ō), *I.* Necessary.

**nechiloth** (nĕk'-ɪ-lôt), **neg(h)inoth**
(nĕ'-gĭ-nôt), *Heb.* A wind-instrument.

**neck.** That part of an instr. which
carries the finger-board.

**ne'fer.** Egyptian guitar.

**negligente** (näl-yē-jĕn'-tĕ), **negligent-
emen'te,** *I.* Negligent(ly). **negli-
genza** (jĕn'-tsä). Carelessness.

**negli** (näl'-yē), **nei** (nä'-ē), *I.*, pl. In
the.

**nei** (nä'-ē), *Tur.* A flute made of-cane.

**nekeb** (nä'-kĕb), *Heb.* A wind-instr.
formed of a single tube.

**nel, nella, nelle, nello, nell',** *I.* In
the, at the.

**nenia.** Vide NAENIA.

**neo-German.** Used of the programmatic school.

**nero** (nä'-rō), *I.* "Black." A quarter
note.

**nete** (nä'-tĕ), *Gr.* Vide LYRE and
MODE.

**net** (nĕt), **nette** (nĕt), *F.*, **nett** (nĕt),
*G.*, **net'to,** *I.* Neat, clear. **nettetè**
(nĕt-tä), *F.*, **Nettheit** (nĕt-hīt),
**Nettigkeit** (nĕt'-tɪkh-kīt), *G.* Neat-
ness, distinctness. **nettamen'te,** *I.*
Crisply.

**neu** (noi), *G.* New. **n.-deutsche
Schule** (doit-shĕ shool'-ĕ). Vide NEO-
GERMAN SCHOOL.

**neu'ma, neume** (nūm). 1. One of the
characters in the early notation by
points, commas, hooks, etc. Lines
were introduced later, but they were
always rather an aid to memory than
a notation. 2. Melisma. 3. A slur.
The neumes somewhat resembled
modern shorthand and served somewhat the same function. The earlier
forms before lines are quite indeciph-

erable. A single note was called *Virga, virgula, punctus,* or *punctum ;* a rising inflection sign, *pes,* or *podatus ;* a falling inflection, *clinis* or *flexa ;* various nuances of performance and special note values were the *ancus, bivirga, cephalicus, distropha epiphonus, gnomo, oriscus, plica* (turn), *quilisma* (shake), *semivocalis, sinuosa, strophicus, tramea, tremula, trivirga,* etc.

**neun** (noin), *G.* Nine. **Neunachteltakt** (äkh'-tel-täkt), *G.* Nine-eighth time. **Neunte** (noin'-tĕ). A ninth. **Neunzehnte** (tsän-tĕ). Nineteenth.

**neuvième** (nŭv-yĕm'), *F.* A ninth.

**nex'us,** *L.* A binding together.

**nicht** (nĭkht), *G.* Not.

**nicolo** (nē'-kō-lō). A 17th cent. bombardon.

**nieder** (nē'-dĕr), *G.* Down. **N.-schlag.** Down-beat, or accented part. **N.-strich.** The down bow.

**niedrig** (nē'-drĭkh), *G.* Deep, in voice.

**nina** (nē'-nä), *I.* Lullaby (or, **ninnananna**). **ninnare** (nĭn-nä'-rĕ). To sing a lullaby.

**nine-eighth.** Vide TIME.

**nineteenth.** 1. An interval of two octaves and a fifth. 2. A stop tuned a nineteenth above the diapasons. Vide LARIGOT.

**ninth.** 1. An interval of an octave and a second. 2. Vide CHORD.

**nobile** (nō'-bĭ-lĕ), **nobilmente,** *I.,* **noble** (nôbl), **noblement** (nô-blŭ-mäñ), *F.* Noble (nobly). **nobilità** (nō-bē-lĭ-tä'), *I.* Nobility.

**noch** (nôkh), *G.* Still, yet ; as **noch schneller** (shnĕl'-ler). Still quicker.

**nocturn(e),** *E.,* **nocturne** (nôk-türn) *F.,* **notturno** (nôt-toor'-nō), *I.* 1. Term first used by John Field for a composition of dreamy, night-like mood. 2. Vide HORÆ CANONICÆ.

**node, nodalpoint, no'do,** *I.* One of the axis-like points or lines in a vibrating body, where there is no vibration (cf. LOOP). **nodal figures.** The chart of vibration produced by sand strewn upon a flat vibrating plate ; discovered by Chladni.

**no'dus,** *L.* "A knot," an enigmati[c] canon.

**noël** (nō-ĕl'), *F.* A Christmas ca[rol] Vide NOWELL.

**noeud** (nŭ), *F.* 1. A turn. 2. A no[de]

**no fer.** Vide NEFER.

**noire** (nwär), *F.* "Black," a quar[ter] note.

**noise.** Early *E.* 1. Music. 2. [A] band.

**no'lae,** *L.* Tintinnabulæ.

**nomes** (nōmz), *Gr.* 1. Airs ancien[tly] sung to Cybele, Pan, and other div[in]ities. 2. Compositions regulated [by] inviolable rules, as canon. 3. A ca[n]on. Vide NOMOS.

**nomine, in** (in nō'-mĭ-nä), *L.* 1. "[In] the name" (of the Lord). A mot[et]. Vide FUGA.

**no'mos,** pl. **nomoi,** *Gr.* Law(s). Gr[eek] songs fulfilling all the rules.

**non** (nōn), *I.* Not, no.

**nona** (nō'-nä), *I.,* **None** (nō'-nĕ), *G* ninth (interval). **Nonachord'-o, No'nenakkord,** *G.* A ninth. V[ide] CHORD.

**no'nes.** Vide HORÆ CANONICÆ.

**nonet(t)',** *E.,* **Nonett',** *G.,* **nonet'** *I.* Music for 9 parts.

**Non'nengeige** (gī-khĕ). "Nun's-[fid]dle." Vide MARINE TRUMPET.

**Nonole** (nō-nō'-lĕ), *G.* Nonuplet.

**nonny hey nonny.** An old *E.* refra[in]

**non'uplet.** A group of nine eq[ual] notes.

**nor'mal** (in *G.* nôr-mäl')[.] Norm[al] standard. **Normalton** (tōn), *G.* [The] tone A. **Normaltonleiter** (lī-t[er]) *G.* The natural scale (of C).

**nota** (nō'-tä), *I.* and *L.* Note. **bianca.** "White" or half-note, [e]tc. **n. buo.na** (boo-ō'-nä). Accented n[ote] **n. cambiata** (käm-bĭ-ä'-tä), or **ca**[mbiata] **bita,** *I.* 1. A changing note. 2. Resolution by skip. **n. caratteri**[s]**tica.** Leading-note. **n. catti**[va] (kät-tē'-vä). Unaccented note. **n[.]** **contra notam.** "Note agai[nst] note." Vide COUNTERPOINT. **corona'ta.** A note marked wit[h a] hold. **n. d'abbellimen'to.** A n[ote] of embellishment. **n. di passagg[io.]**

päs-säd'-jō). A passing note. **di piacere** (dē-pī-ä-chā'-rě). An ...ional embellishment. **n. falsa.** A ...nging note. **n. principale** (prěn- ...-pä'-lě). Principal note. **n. quad- ...ta.** A plain-song note. **n. ro- ...na.** A neume. **n. scolta** (shōl'- ta). Staccato. **n. sensible** (sěn-sē'-bǐ-lě), *I.*, **sensi'bilis**, *L.* The leading-note. **n. digna'ta**, *L.* A note marked with a sign. **n. sostenuta** (sōs-tě-noo'-tä). A sustained note. **nota'tion** (in *F.* nō-tăs -yôn), **notazi-one** (nō-tä'-tsi-ō -ně), *I.* Notation.

## Notation.

### By the Editor.

HE musical parallel of writing and printing as the means of expressing in universal and permanent symbols the ideas, emotions and memories of the mind. ¶The Greeks, having only unharmonised ...dies to record, made use of the letters of the alphabet in positions and ...binations of a most complex yet definitive variety. These letters had ...ence to tetrachords and transpositions of the most subtle sort (see ...es). The business-like Romans swept away a mass of detail by giving ...letter a definite position on the whole scale without reference to tetra-...d relations. These letters were written on a straight line over the text ...e sung. In the Eighth Century this *alphabetical notation* had given way ...re a system of symbols looking much like the hooks and curves of modern ...thand. These were called *neumæ* (q. v.) and were of numberless sorts ...names. Thus a short single note was a *punctum*; two or three of these in ...oup were *bipunctum* or *tripunctum*; the standard long note was the *virga* ...ch could be grouped as *bivirga* or *trivirga*. Other terms were *podatus* ...ow note joined to a higher), and its reverse called *clivis*, *clinis*, or *flexa*; ...*scandicus* (three ascending notes) and its reverse, *climacus*; the *quilisma* ...repeated note), the *gnomo*, *ancus*, *distropha* and many others. These ...mæ were written over the text and were set higher or lower in a rough ...n of melodic contour. They were only an aid to the memory and fre-...ntly defy decipherment. In time, a few letters were added as abbreviations ...peed or force. ¶But about the year 900 a genius (who in his way was ...ost as great as the inventor of the wheel) hit upon the inspiration of ruling ...ve the text a thin red line and calling it "F." Every neuma on this ...stood positively for the tone F, and those above or below the lines were ...higher or lower pitch. The genius was soon followed by a man of ...nt who ruled a yellow line a little higher and called it "C." The ...amental letters set at the head of these lines soon took the forms known ...lay as the *clefs*. Not long after, the monk Hucbald erected a series of ...s and used the spaces between them to indicate definite pitches, writing at ...beginning *T* for a whole step and *S* for a semitone. The hymn to be

sung was written in these spaces, each syllable being placed on its pi
space. (This gave the verse a stepladder effect resembling the refrains of
tain modern humorous poems.) Spaces were added above or below a
melody needed them and each voice had its own set of shelves. ¶
awkward plan suggested the use of the lines instead of the spaces, for i
instead of syllables. Each line was given a definite pitch marked by a le
¶ Recurrence was now made to the two-line system and somebody ( G
of Arezzo was usually credited with the scheme) added two black lines
made a 4-line staff in which both lines and spaces had fixed pitch values
only needed the later addition of one more line to give the five-lined staff
still use to-day. ¶ The neumæ gradually exchanged their scraggly out
for the square black heads of the *choral note* (the *nota quadrata* or *qu*
*quarta*). ¶ It now being possible to express the relative pitch of note:
effort was made to express their relative duration, for the old Plain Song
its notes all of the same length could not satisfy many human musical n
The modern division into measures of equal length by means of bars w
long time coming. There were two centuries of clumsy *mensurable* (*i*
measurable) *music*. Notes to be sung to the same syllable were gro
together by *ligatures;* they were either set so close together as to to
or were if ascending, placed one above the other like a chord; if
scending, they were merged in a thick black slanting line (*figura obliq*
When white or open notes came into use the thick line became an
rectangle sloping in the desired direction. When the first note of the
ture was a breve, it was said to be "*cum proprietate*"; if the first note i
a long, it was *sine proprietate;* if a semibreve, it was *cum opposita pro*
*tate;* if the last note were a breve it was *imperfecta;* it was a *ligatura*
*fecta* when the last note was a long. ¶ The method of expressing rhy
was, as said, very cumbersome. Rhythm was classified under three rat
mode (*modus*), time-value (*tempus*), prolation. ¶ The *Modus n*
or "Great Mode" concerned the division of the large into longs, t
*perfect*(*us*) if there were three longs to a large, and *imperfect*(*us*
there were two. *Modus minor* or the "Lesser Mode" concerned
division of the long into breves, with the same classes *perfect* or *imper*
¶ The division of the breves into semibreves was the *tempus* and was s
larly called *perfect*(*um*) or *imperfect*(*um*), a circle indicating perfect time
a semicircle, imperfect. ¶ The relation of semibreve to minims was c
*prolatio*(*n*), being major or minor (greater or lesser) prolation as the semib
equalled 3 or 2 minims. The former was indicated by a dot in the
signature. ¶ The *position* of the notes also indicated their proportion; a
or a breve followed by a note of its own value was *perfect by position*
note accompanied by another of less value was imperfect. ¶ *Colour* pl

t; the red (*notula rubra*) or white (*alba*) or black (*nigra*) note
g others of a different colour marked a change from perfection to imper-
n. There was later the *proportio hemiol(i)a*, or 2 : 3, indicated by
ed black notes among white. ¶Speed was open to slackening (*aug-
atio*) or acceleration (*diminutio*), the latter being marked by a bar through
me-signature, or by the use of numerals or fractions, called signs of pro-
on, a term referring to the rhythm of simultaneous voices. ¶The value
note was open to *alteratio(n)* by position or by use of the *dot (punctum
entationis, alterationis, (im)perfectionis* or *divisionis*). ¶Expression
s appeared, along with many other symbols, in the Seventeenth Cen-
; the bar was brought over from lute-tablature, and *mensurable music*
peared before the convenient complexities of our own era.

---

A character representing a musi-
tone; by its shape indicating the
ation, by its position on the staff,
pitch, of the tone. **connecting
:e.** A note common to two
rds.

(nôt), *F.* Note. **n. d'agrément**
-grä-mäṅ). Ornamental note. **n.
passage** (dŭ päs-säzh). Passing
e. **n. dièsée** (dĭ-ĕ-zā), *F.* Note
rked with a sharp. **notes coulées**
o-lā). Slurred notes. **n. de goût**
-goo). Note of embellishment.
**sensible** (säṅ-sēbl'). Leading
e. **n. surabondantes** (sür-ă-bôṅ-
it). Such incommensurate groups
triplets, quintoles, etc. **n. liée**
ā). Tied note. **n. syncopées**
i-kô-pā). Syncopated notes.
en (nō'-tĕn), *G.*, pl. Notes. **No-
iblatt** (blät). A sheet of music.
**-buch** (bookh). Music-book. **N.-
sser.** "Note-gobbler," one who
s facility but no taste. **N.-schrift**
rĭft). Musical manuscript. **N.-
stem** (zēs-tām). The staff.
**r** (nō-tā), *F.* To write out a tune.
**graph.** Melograph.
irno (nôt-toor'-nō), *I.* A noc-
ne.
**la,** *L.* Note used in ligature.
rir le son (noor-rēr lŭ sôṅ), *F.*
attack a note forcibly, and sus-
n it. **un son nourri** (noor-rē). A
stained tone.

**nourrisson** (noor-rēs-sôṅ), *F.* Bard.
**nour'singh.** A straight Indian trumpet.
**no'va,** *I.* A small flute.
**Novelette** (nôf-ĕ-lĕt'), *G.* From *F.*, a
short musical romance. Name first
given by Schumann to pieces containing considerable freedom of form,
treatment, and idea.
**novemole** (nō-vĕ-mō'-lĕ), *I.* A group
of nine equal notes.
**no'well.** Old *E.* "Good news." 1.
A refrain of Christmas carols, hence
2. Carol. Cf. NOEL.
**nuances** (nü-äṅs), *F.*, pl. 1. Lights
and shades of expression; variety.
2. A notation.
**null.** 1. A cipher. Vide O. 2. Vide
TASTO SOLO.
**number.** 1. An integral portion of an
opera, symphony, or programme, etc.
2. A favourite method of designating
compositions, as Chopin's "5th"
waltz.
**numer'ical notation.** A scheme introduced by Rousseau, to substitute
numerals as names of tones. A similar notation in Massachusetts was
called Day's & Beal's "One-line system."
**nu'merus,** *L.* 1. Number. 2. Rhythm.
**Nunc dimit'tis,** *L.* "Now dismiss
(us)." The text, Luke II. 10–12,
often used as a final number.
**nun's-fiddle.** Marine trumpet.

**nuovo** (noo-ō'-vō), *I*. New. **di nuovo.** Again.

**nut.** 1. The small bridge at the upper end of the finger-board of violins, etc. 2. The movable fastening of the hair of a bow. 3. The "lowest nut," the ridge between tail-piece and tail-pin.

# O

O A small circle, or cipher, means : 1. An open string. 2. Harmonic. 3. Diminished fifth (or a chord containing one). 4. Tasto solo. 5. To be played with the thumb. 6. Tempus perfectum. Vide NOTATION. 7. Harmonium-stops are marked with a numeral in a circle. 8. In neume-notation, the fourth church mode.

**O** (ō), **od** (ōd), *I*. Or, as, either.

**O** (ō) *L*. Exclamation. *les* **O** *de Noël* (lā-zō dŭ nō-ĕl), *F*. The Christmas antiphons to the Magnificat, all beginning with "O!"

**oaten-pipe.** A simple straw cut to form a reed-pipe.

**ob.** Abbr. for oboe(s).

**obbligato** (ôb-blĭ-gä'-tō), *I*., **obligé** (ôb-lĭ-zhā), *F*., **Obligat** (ôp-lĭ-gät'), *G*. "Indispensable," of a part which cannot be omitted without injury to completeness ; though latterly the term has come almost to mean "optional," as in songs "with violin obb." in which the violin part is frequently omitted.

**ob(b)liquo** (ôb-blē'-kwō), *I*. Oblique. Vide MOTION.

**ober** (ō'-bĕr), *G*. Upper, higher. **O.-dominante.** Dominant. **O.-labium.** Upper lip (of a pipe). **O.-manual.** The upper manual. **O.-stimme.** Upper part. **O.-taste** (täs'-tĕ). Black key. **O.-theil** (tīl). The upper part. **O.-ton.** Harmonic. **phonischer O.-ton** The 15th partial. **O.-werk.** In an organ with 2 manuals, the choir-organ ; with 3, the sweli ; with 4, the solo.

**oblique, obli'quus**, *L*. Vide MOTION.

**oblique pf.** An upright pf. with agonal strings.

**oboe** (ō'-bō ; in *G*. ō-bō'-ĕ), **oboe** bō-ā'), *I*. *Plurals :* **oboes, Oboen**, *G*., **oboi** (ō-bō'-ē), *I*. double-reed instr. with conical woo tube, and 9 to 14 keys ; extreme c pass *bb–f'''*. It is non-transpo (except in the case of the B♭ an oboes for military bands), a fingered somewhat like a flute. tone is reedy and quaint, al homely ; it gives a pastoral at phere, or is capable of great me choly, but rarely of much floridity The alto of the oboe is the so-ca **cor anglais** (kôr än-glĕ'), *F*., **cc inglese** (kôr-nō-ēn-glā'-zĕ), *I*., **glisches Horn** (ĕng'-lĭsh-ĕs not glĭsh-ĕs), *G*., or **English horn.** oboe with a double long tube, a pitch a fifth lower, extreme com *g♭–b."* This is now written as instr. transposing a fifth. It is more sombre than the treble obo indeed it is the most mournful inconsolable of instruments. I a development from the old **oboe caccia** (dä kät'-shä), in F. or written in the alto clef. The **o. more** (dä-mō'-rĕ), **o. basso**, an **lungo** (loon'-gō) were lower b minor third than the modern tr oboe, which was formerly calle **piccolo.** 2. A reed-stop of 4 a ft. pitch, also called **orchestral ol**

**obois'ta**, *I*. Oboist.

**Obw.** Abbr. for **Oberwerk**.

**ocarina** (ō-kä-rē'-nä). A terra-c bird-shaped instr. of fluty tone.

**occhiali** (ôk-kĭ-ä'-lē). 1. White no 2. Brillenbasse.

**occhetto** (ôk-kĕt'-tō), *I*., **oche'tu** Hocket.

**oct'achord.** 1. An 8-stringed instr. A series of 8 tones.

**oct'aphonic.** Eight-voiced.

**oc'tave** (in *F*. ôk-tăv, in *G*. ôk-fĕ). 1. A consecutive series of e diatonic tones as from *c'–c''*. 2. interval of an eighth. 3. A tone 8th above (or below) another.

.rge octave, once-marked or lined
, etc. Vide PITCH. 5. The diapa-
on of the Greek system. 6. The
ght days following a Church festival.
   A stop sounding an octave higher
ian the digital pressed, as octave-
ute (also used for the *piccolo* (q v.).
onsecutive covered, broken, etc.,
ctaves, vide the adjectives. rule
f the o. A 17th century system of
armonising the scale giving a bass
cale with the normal chords and
versions to accompany it. short
. The lowest octave in an organ,
here the scale is incomplete or com-
ressed, also called *mi–re–ut*. o.-
cale. Vide MODES. o.-coupler.
ide COUPLER. o.-staff. A notation
troduced by Adams, of New Jersey,
aree groups of lines combined in
aree octaves, dispensing with the
ats and sharps, and giving each tone
s own place. octave stop. 1. A
ft. stop. 2. The position of fingers
opping an octave on the finger-
oard. 3. A mechanical stop in
ed-organs, coupling the octave
pove.
aviana (ôk-tä-vĭ-ä'-nä), octavina
k-tä-vē'-nä), *I.*, octavin (ôk-tä-
iä), *F.* 1. An octave-spinet. 2.
he piccolo. 3. A harpsichord oc-
ve-stop. 4. A 2-ft. organ-stop.
avin (ôk-tä-fēn'), *G.* A single reed,
onical wood-wind instr. fingered like
ae oboe ; compass *c'–c''''*, keys Bb and
. Inv. by O. Adler.
a'vo attachment. Vide PEDAL
octave).
et(t)', octet'to, *I.* A composition
or eight parts.
pho'nium, *L.* Octet.
obass, *E.*, octobasse (bäs), *F.* A
ouble-bass of huge size, about 12-ft.
gh. Inv. by Vuillaume. The 3
rings are stopped by means of keys
nd pedals.
ochord, *L.* 8-stringed lute.
ole (ôk-tō'-lĕ), *G.* Octuplet.
uplet. A group of eight equal
otes.
uor (ôk-twôr), *F.* Octet.

od (ōd), *I.* Or.
ode (ōd). An elaborate lyric, almost
   a cantata. odische (ō'-dĭsh-ĕ) Musik, *G.* Music for an ode.
Odem (ō'-däm), *G.* Breath.
Odeon (ō-dā'-ōn), *Gr.*, ode'um, *L* A
   public building for music.
oder (ō'-dĕr), *G.* Or, or else.
ode-symphonie (ôd-săn-fō-nē), *F.* A
   symphony with chorus.
œuvre (ŭvr), *F.* Work, composition.
off. 1. A direction to push in an organ-
   stop or coupler. 2. False.
offen (ôf'-fĕn), *G.*, of'fenbar. 1. Open.
   2. Parallel. Offenflöte (flä'-te). An
   open flute-stop.
offertoire (ôf'-fĕr-twär), *F.*, offerto'rio,
   *I.* and *Sp.*, offerto'rium, *L.*, of fer-
   tory. The part of the Mass or service, the motet or instrumental piece,
   performed during the taking of the
   collection.
offic'ium, *L.* A service. o. defunc-
   to'rum. Funeral service. o. diur'-
   num. Daily s. o. matuti'num
   (nocturn'um) morning (evening) s.
   o. vesperti'num. Vespers.
oficleida (ō-fĭ-klä'-ĭ-dä), pl. e., *I.* Ophicleide.
ohne (ō'-nĕ), *G.* Without.
oioueae. The vowels of " World
   without end, Amen." Cf. EVOVAE.
Oktave (ôk-tä'-fĕ), *G.* Octave (q. v.).
   oktavi(e)ren (fē'-rĕn). To produce
   the octave by overblowing. Oktäv-
   chen (ôk-tāf'-khĕn), Oktavflöte (flä'-
   tĕ), or -flötlein (līn). Piccolo. Ok-
   tavengattungen (gät-toong-ĕn).
   Octave-scales. Oktav-folgen (fôl-
   khĕn), or -parallelen, or Oktaven-
   verdoppelungen (fĕr-dôp-pĕl-oong-
   ĕn). Parallel, or consecutive octaves.
Oktavwaldhorn. A Waldhorn inv. by
   Eichborn & Heidrich.
Oktavin, *G.* Vide OCTAVIN.
ole, el (ĕl ō'-lĕ), *Sp.* Slow 3-4 dance
   with castanets.
ol'iphant. A horn made of a tusk.
o'lio. A miscellany.
olivettes (ô-lĭ-vĕt), *F.* Provençal
   dance after the olives are gathered.

**olla podrida** (ôl'-lä pō-drē'-dhä). Medley.

**om'bi.** An African harp.

**om'bra,** *L.* Shade ; nuance.

**om'nes, omnia,** *L.* All. Vide TUTTI.

**om'nitonic, omnitonique** (ôm-nĭ-tônĕk), *F.* Having all the tones of the chromatic scale, as a horn.

**once-accented,** or **once-marked octave.** Vide PITCH.

**ondeggiamen'to** (ôn-dĕd-jä-mĕn'-tō). Undulation. **ondeggian'te,** *I.* **ondulé** (ôn-dü-lä), *F.* Waving, undulating, trembling. **onduliren** (ôn-doo-lē-rĕn), *G.* To make a tremulous tone.

**one-lined.** Vide PITCH.

**ongarese** (ôn-gä-rä'-zĕ), **ongherese** (ôn-gĕ-rä'-zĕ), *I.* Hungarian.

**onzième** (ôṅz-yĕm), *F.* Eleventh.

**op.** Abbr. of Opus.

**open.** 1. Of pipes, open at the top. 2. Of chords, not in *close* position. 3. Of strings, not stopped. 4. Of tone, (a) produced by an open string

or by a wind-instr. not stoppe not prod. by valve or key. scores, in which a stave is giv each part or instrument.

**Oper** (ō'-pĕr), *G.,* **op'era,** *E.* ō'-pĕ-rä), *I.,* **opéra** (ō-pä-rä) Drama set to music. **o.-bouffe** ( or **buffon** (büf-fôn), *F.,* **o.-** (boof'-fä), *I.* Farcical, or low-cc opera, what we call comic c **opéra comique** (kō-mēk), *F.* Li ly " comic opera," but generally only to indicate that the dialog spoken, not sung. The plot m as serious as **grand opera, c seria** (sä'-rĭ-ä), *I.,* **opéra sér** (sä-rĭ-ŭ), *F.,* in which all dialog in recitative and the ensemble more elaborate. **o. di camera** mĕ-rä). Opera for a small a rium. **o. lyrique** (lē-rēk), **ba opera.** One in which lyricisn the preference over dramatic a **o.-drammat'ica,** *I.* Romantic c **O.-haus** (hows). Opera-house. **sänger.** Operatic singer.

## The Opera.

### By Ernest Newman.

COMBINATIONS of poetry and music, in a more or less dra form, must have been usual from very ancient times ; and, matter of fact, we can trace this form of art back to 1350. the opera proper, in the modern sense of the word, sprang up in Italy a the end of the sixteenth century. It was the invention of certain Flore amateurs, lovers of the antique, who wished to give to music somethir the importance it was thought to have had in the Greek drama ; anc *Dafne* (1594), and *Euridice* (1600), of Peri and Caccini, mark the be nings of opera. These works were mostly in a kind of recitative, with s orchestral accompaniment. The object was to imitate in music the inflec of the speaking voice, the Florentine scholars imagining that the music i Greek drama had been simply an intensification of the tones of ordi speech. *Musica parlante,* " speaking music," was the ideal they aime As the opera progressed, it inevitably became less speaking and more mus The orchestra became larger and more capable of colour ; recitative d oped into the aria, the duet, and the concerted piece. As the opera sp

Italy, however, it tended to degenerate. It relied too much on imita-
of the antique; it had no healthy poetical drama with which to compare
, and so became ever more inane in sentiment; it was corrupted first by
fashionable courts and then by the ignorant, pleasure-loving Italian public;
ue prominence was given to the mere scenery and spectacle; and the star
ers tried to subordinate everything to their own vanity. All this while
e existed, among the people, an ancient form of rural comedy—the *Com-
ia dell' Arte*—full of healthy life and sincere sentiment, and free from the
ctation of the pseudo-antique. From this there grew up, at a later date, the
rming and sparkling *opera buffa*. ¶France had long had a form of enter-
ment—the ballet—with many points of similarity with the opera. The
real French opera seems to have been *La pastorale*, by Perrin and Cam-
t (1659); but no great progress was made till Lully—an Italian by birth,
French in sympathies—became the head of the opera in Paris (1671).
France, the verbal element always resisted the encroachment of the mu-
l, this being partly due to the highly developed, rather than to that of the
ving, aria. In the course of time, Italian influences tended to cultivate
merely musical element at the expense of the dramatic; but the balance
s restored by Rameau, who, with a greater musical gift than Lully's, made
vocal portion of the opera free and interesting in itself, without losing
ht of the dramatic expression. When the Italian *opera buffa* was intro-
ed into Paris (1752), it strengthened the already existent French comic
era, and even taught the serious writers some lessons in naturalness and
ectness. ¶In Germany, opera first found favour at the Courts. Singers,
mposers, librettists, conductors—all were Italian; and, if, in an isolated
e, the recitatives were sung in German, the airs, which were held to be
essential parts of the opera, were generally given in Italian. It was at
mburg that the German element had its stronghold. Keiser (1673–
39) relied on the German *Lied* rather than the Italian *aria*, and preferred
German libretto to an Italian one. But on the whole the German passion
s for thoroughly Italian opera. ¶Neither in Italy, Germany, nor France
1 the opera seem, in the middle of the eighteenth century, to have any real
or any chance of development. From this miserable condition it was de-
ered by Gluck, who added to a musical gift greater than that of the major-
of his predecessors, a strong sense of the value of a dramatic basis for the
sic. ¶The history of the opera in England in the seventeenth and eigh-
nth centuries is somewhat curious. Purcell's influences were mainly French,
rived through his master, Pelham Humphreys, who had studied under
lly. Purcell's striking individuality, however, transformed this influence
to something quite English. Later on, the English stage was ruled almost
tirely for a time by Handel, who made no alterations in the general form

of the opera, but fi'led each separate part with a wealth of musical inven
ness previously unknown. ¶In the early work of Mozart, Italian influe
struggled with German. His experiences in Paris, where he heard the
operas of all kinds, in 1778, deepened both his technical powers and his
matic sense. "The Marriage of Figaro," and "Don Giovanni," show
most wonderful art of character-drawing, interpenetrated with a musical s
of unfailing and surpassing loveliness. They seem to combine Handel's
odic beauty and power with Gluck's intensity of dramatic expression. G
and Mozart were the two men whose influence was most felt by later ope
writers. ¶The next great development came with Weber and the Ger
Romantic movement. Between the true classical and Romantic epoch, h
ever, came a body of work, half ancient, half modern, both in France
Germany. It is typified by such men as Hérold, Méhul, Cherubini, B
dieu, and Spontini, and by Beethoven's solitary opera "Fidelio," and re
sents the crossing of the old culture with the new, the forms of the eighte
century with the post-Revolution spirit. Under Weber and the Roma
the German opera entered on a new career. Its essence was a heartfelt
cerity—almost simplicity—of musical feeling, subtilised and enriched by
warm, expansive culture of that day. Most of the sensations of the eightee
century opera are found in the work of Weber and his fellows, together v
some quite novel ones ; and in every case a deeper or subtler tinge is gi
them by the superior orchestral resources. In the painting of scenes of
vous horror, for example, the Romantics added considerably to the ~alett
their predecessors. ¶While this movement was going on in Germany, R
sini was galvanising the almost extinct art of Italy. His sparkling melody,
verve, his audacity, his superficiality, produced a new type of Italian ope
appealing to fashionable and uncultured audiences, who asked for nothing fr
the opera but amusement, and that in a form not too subtle for them. T
really dramatic passages in his operas, as in those of Donizetti and Bellini,
comparatively few. Their general style of work was carried on by a stron
musician, Meyerbeer, who was weak enough to sacrifice, for the applause
Paris, the genuine musical gifts he had brought with him from Germa
¶Concurrently with this vogue of Italian opera there ran the career of W
ner, who reflected more upon his art than any opera composer except Glu
Dissatisfied with both the independent musical and poetical elements out
which previous operas had been built, he modified each to suit the dema
of the other. He aimed at a form of expression in which poetry and mu
should combine in one indissoluble speech. This was to be the "mean
of the opera ; its "end" was the drama itself. Wagner's reforms were
entirely the outcome of his own peculiar individuality, and depended so mu
on his own stupendous gifts, that no one has been able to take up his wo

him. He has influenced almost all his countrymen; but their work, as
ole, is plainly imitative and reminiscent. ¶Similarly Berlioz, who also
ed on his own lines, occasionally casting his eyes back to Gluck and
er, left no successor. The line on which composers like Halévy and
r must be strung derives from Meyerbeer and the Italians. But the
modern French opera-writers strike a more original, more national note.
od and Bizet, Reyer, Saint-Saëns, and Massenet are really French, each
is own way; while in the very modern work of Bruneau we get the
of French realistic fiction, and in that of Vincent d'Indy we have a
us expression of the subtlety and mysticism of the Celtic revival.
rise of serious French opera has been accompanied by a consolidation of
lighter form—the *opéra bouffe*. ¶In Italy, the most remarkable phe-
enon has been the change of Verdi's style. Beginning as a common-
, though sometimes dramatic, writer of Italian operas, he has developed
a composer who, while never losing his southern grace and litheness, has
ilated some of the best elements of northern art. In the work of the
ger men of his school there seems to be, at present, a contest between
ild ideals and the new. In many cases, unfortunately, their musical gifts
not on a par with their dramatic intentions. ¶The first great name in
ian music is that of Glinka, who, about the middle of the century, worked
a national form of opera. Though Wagner's influence has necessarily
felt here and there, the Russian opera as a whole has developed freely
ts own account; and the two representatives of it best known to the
t—Rubinstein and Tschaïkowsky—are in no way Wagnerian.

---

et′ta, *I.*, **Operette** (ôp-ĕ-rĕt′-tĕ),
A small light opera, cf. SING-
iELE. **Op′erist.** An operatic singer.
rndichter (ō′pärn-dĭkh-tĕr), *G.* Li-
etto writer.
icleide (ôf′-ĭ-klīd). 1. An obsoles-
nt brass instr. the bass of the key-
igle family. The **bass. o.** in C, B♭
id A♭ (compass A♭–a′♮) the **alto**
in F and E♭ (compass 2½ oc-
ves); the **contrabass o.** same com-
iss as the **alt. o.** but an octave
wer. The bass tuba (q. v.) has a
cher tone and has displaced it. 2.
powerful 4 or 8 ft. reed-stop.
, Abbr. of **oppure.**
osite. Contrary (of motion, q. v.).
ure (ôp-poo′-rĕ), *I.* Or, or else.

**opus** (ō′-poos), *L.* Work, composition;
as, Op. 10, the 10th composition, or,
more commonly, the 10th publication
of a composer. **opus′culum.** A little work. **opus post′humum.** A
work published after the death of
the composer.
**orage** (ō-räzh), *F.* "Storm." 1. An
imitative composition. 2. A stop.
**O′ra pro no′bis,** *L.* "Pray for us!" A
response to a litany in R. C. service.
**oratoire** (ôr-ä-twär), *F.*, **orato′rio,** *I.*
and *E.*, **orato′rium,** *L.* (in *G.* ō′-
rä-tō′-rĭ-oom). A sacred work constructed like an opera, but performed
now without action, costume, or
scenery. See next page.

## The Oratorio.

### By H. E. Krehbiel.

AN oratorio is a musical composition for chorus and solo voices, w orchestral accompaniment, to a poem on a religious or sacred s ject, generally in narrative form, though often with dramatic sodes, but without scenery, action, or costume. The origin of the oratori to be found in the so-called mysteries and miracle-plays of the thirteenth fourteenth centuries, which enacted an important part in the life of the c mon people. These were sung and acted, and though, on account of ab that crept into them they were frowned upon by the Church, their popula was never destroyed. The oratorio was brought into existence upon model of these religious plays by St. Philip of Neri (1515–95), who ognised in them a means of opposing the influence of the Reformation u the common people. In his chapel or oratory (whence the name orator in Rome he had spiritual songs sung after sermons and other devotions "allure young people to pious offices." St. Philip induced capable Ita poets to write the words, and the best composers to furnish the music. degrees the spiritual songs gave place to musical settings of sacred sto sometimes in dialogue form. The invention of dramatic recitative at the of the sixteenth century had a marked influence on oratorio. The first use it was Emilio Cavaliere, whose allegory, "The Soul and the Body performed in a Roman Church, was the first oratorio corresponding to modern form. It was, however, intended to be acted in costume, and o gradually did this feature fall into disuse. The later Italian composers, Ca simi, Stradella, Cesti and Alessandro Scarlatti, first developed the new fo on the lines in which it has come down to us. Carissimi greatly impro the recitative, giving it more character and musical expressiveness than predecessors had done, and ventured more boldly into the field of bro choral writing. Cesti and Stradella cultivated still further the natural sources of the chorus at a time when the general tendency in Italy was to ard the more obvious and pleasing forms of solo song. Alessandro Scarla who was one of the chief forces in this direction, also contributed to the dev opment of the oratorio by the increased stress he put upon the solo arias in But on the whole, as Dr. Parry has remarked, the oratorio had to w for representatives of more strenuous nations for its ultimate developme ¶That development was destined to come in Germany. While oratorio h thus been taking shape in Italy, there was an important movement going in Germany by which the Passion was brought into existence. This ca about, after a long line of tentative and experimental efforts, through works of Heinrich Schütz, who had received his training in Italy and carr ce to his native land some of the new ideals of music. His first Passion produced in 1645. The various attempts that followed this culminated 1e settings by J. S. Bach. These works were intended for performance 1urch in Passion Week, as a religious service partly narrative, partly dra-c and partly reflective in character. The narrative was put into the th of the Evangelist, usually the principal tenor, who related the Passion Christ ; the personages in the story spoke for themselves. The chorus often treated dramatically, representing the emotions of the onlookers, e the solo airs were of a piously reflective character. There was a plen-interspersion of chorales in which the congregation joined. In the mid-there was an intermission for the sermon. The Passion music was also utgrowth of the mediæval miracle-plays, but it soon fell into disuse and layed no vitality after the great creations of Bach, the " Passions accord-to St. Matthew " and " St. John," respectively, composed in the first ter of the eighteenth century. German art was thenceforward turned the channels of the oratorio as it was developed in Italy ; and the form brought to its highest perfection by George Frederick Handel. As thus ected it was not, like the Passions, a part of religious exercises, nor a ct expression of devotional feeling, but epic or narrative, with certain i-dramatic traits and sometimes with the use of vivid local colour ; but ays with the most impressive use of the chorus as the most important ium of expression. Handel's first oratorio " Esther " was written in o and performed first in England in 1732, oratorio being then quite nown in that country. The long line of masterpieces he produced there-r gave the final and definite character to the oratorio form which has ained to this day. The greatest of them are " The Messiah," " Judas ccabæus," " Israel in Egypt," and " Samson." Handel's strength lay fly in broad choral writing, and it was natural that the oratorio should elop mainly on this line, as affording a vehicle for more descriptive and racteristic music, thus making up for a lack of pantomime, costume, and 1ery. ¶ For a considerable period after Handel's death, little of impor-e in the field of oratorio was produced. Haydn's " Creation " and The Seasons," written in 1795 and 1801 respectively, still retain some heir vitality and freshness. Beethoven's " Mount of Olives " does not. torios by Spohr and Schneider attained a great but transient popularity, the next really important works in this form were Mendelssohn's " St. l," performed first in 1836, and " Elijah," in 1846. In both of these dramatic element is foremost, and the musical characterisation of the ous persons presented is perhaps more vivid than any previous attempts in line. Works like Liszt's " St. Elizabeth " and Rubinstein's " Moses " conceived as operas in which descriptive directions take the place of 1ery, costume, and incident.

**orchésographie** (ôr-kā'-zō-grǎ-fē), *F.*
The science and explanation of dancing. **orchestique** (tēk), *F.* Relating to dancing. **Orchestik** (ôr-kĕs-
tēk'), *G.* Art of dancing.
**or'chestra**, *E.* (in *I.* or-kās-tra), **Orchester** (ôr-kĕs'-ter), *G.*, **orchestre**
(ôr-kĕstr), *F.* Literally "dancing-
place," that used in front of the stage
in Greek tragedy for the chorus; the
name was given by the first opera-
writers (vide PERI, B. D.) to the place
occupied by the musicians, thence to
the musicians themselves. The word
now means the place and its occu-

pants, and the instrs. in general
modern **o.** may be (a) **large,
grand. symphony**; (b) **small.**
of the orchestra may be desigr
as *string orchestra*, etc. **Orche
verein** (fĕr-īn). An orchestra
ciety. **O-stimmen.** Orchestral
**orchestral flute** or **oboe.** A
**or'chestra'tion.** The art or a
arranging music for orchestra.
**chestrate**, *E.*, **orchestrare** (ôr
trä-rĕ), *I.*, **orchestri(e)ren** (trē
*G.*, **orchestrer** (ôr-kĕs-trā), *F.*
write for orchestra.

## The Orchestra and Orchestration.

### By W. J. Henderson.

THE modern orchestra dates from the early part of the sevente
century. Previous to that no attempts at a systematic comb
tion of instruments can be found. The original use of the orch
was in the accompaniments of operas, and even here the earliest combina
were fortuitous and without special purpose. The earliest writer who see
to have distinct ideas as to instrumental effects was Claudio Montev
(1568–1643). His orchestra was the first in which a considerable b
of strings, including two violins, figured. He invented some special in
mental effects, and led the way toward the establishment of the string qu
as the foundation of the orchestra. Alessandro Scarlatti (born 1659) w
for a string quartet similar to that employed in the present orchestra, and
oboes and flutes as his principal wind-instruments. ¶ Handel (1658–17
used all the ordinary instruments of the present orchestra except the clar
but not in the same combinations as those of to-day. The orchestra of
time contained a much larger number of oboes and bassoons than ours,
cause these instruments then were much less powerful. In the early pa
the eighteenth century, when the seeds of symphonic music were just be
ning to sprout, the orchestra consisted of the same body of strings as
used, but the violoncello was not yet appreciated at its true value, trum
and tympani being added when brilliancy was needed. Clarinets had
entered the orchestra, but flutes were common. The trombone was
ployed only in the opera, where alone also the harp was heard. ¶ Jo
Haydn (1732–1809) wrote his first symphony in 1759 for first and
ond violins, violas and basses, two oboes and two horns. Mozart (17
91) introduced clarinets and Haydn learned their use from him, so that n
major symphony, written in 1795, is scored for 2 flutes, 2 oboes, 2 clari

rns, 2 kettle-drums, violins, violas, 'cellos and basses, adding in the
movement 2 bassoons and 2 trumpets. In the "Eroica" he introduced
d horn, and in the fifth symphony a piccolo, a contra-bassoon and three
ones. Four horns were used in the Ninth symphony, and this work
ins the entire modern orchestra, except such instruments as have since
introduced for special effects. The operatic writers in their search after
atic colouring led the way in such introductions, and the romantic com-
s of symphonic music, building up their great colour schemes, were not
to accept every suggestion. ¶ Nevertheless the orchestra as now con-
ed is practically that of Beethoven. As ordinarily distributed it is com-
l of a piccolo, 2 flutes, 2 oboes, 2 clarinets, 2 bassoons, 4 horns, 2
pets, 3 trombones, 2 kettle-drums, first and second violins, violas, 'cellos,
basses. The wood-wind instruments are now frequently used in triplets
ad of pairs, and the whole wind choir is extended at will by the use of
English horn, the bass clarinet, the tuba, the saxophone or other less
mon instruments. The harp is also employed at times. ¶ORCHESTRATION,
rt of writing for orchestra, has developed rapidly in recent years, yet the
amental principles are those which guided Mozart and Beethoven. The
ern efforts have been in the direction of increased sonority and richness
lour. These ends are obtained by writing for a larger number of instru-
s and by dividing the old ones into a greater number of parts. The
estra naturally separates itself into three groups of melodic instruments
one of merely rhythmic ones. The first three groups are the wood-wind,
rass, and the strings, and the other is the "battery," as the group of
assive instruments is called. In this last group only the kettle-drums
musical pitch, except when bells are employed. ¶The wood-wind is
ded into flutes, which have no reed mouthpieces ; oboes and bassoons,
h have mouthpieces with two vibrating reeds ; and clarinets, which have
thpieces with one reed. Flutes used in triplets are capable of indepen-
harmony, but all of a high pitch. Bassoons are the basses of the oboe
ly, and hence with two oboes and two bassoons, composers can write in
four-part harmony for this class of reed instruments, and let them play by
selves when their peculiar thin, reedy quality is desired. The English
, the alto of the oboe, can be used as another part. Clarinets have a
pass extending through the alto and soprano ranges of the human voice,
e the bass clarinet covers the tenor and the bass. Here again the com-
r can get a full harmony in one family of wood. Thus the wood alone
s three distinct orchestral tints. But the instruments of the different
lies combine to make new tints. Flutes go well with clarinets or oboes,
clarinets combine admirably with bassoons. Furthermore, the whole
d-band can be used at once with fine effect. The older composers
conventional methods of writing for these instruments, almost always

allotting the same parts of the harmony to the same instruments.
moderns have learned to vary this practice with excellent results.   All
wood-wind instruments can be used profitably as solo voices.   ¶The b
offers three groups, horns, trumpets and trombones, each of which is cap
of independent harmony, while each may be combined with the other
with any part of another to make variety of effects.   All are useful for
effects, the horn being especially good for this purpose.   The brass can
be used in many combinations with the wood-wind.   Horns, clarinets,
bassoons, for example, are frequently combined.   The foundation of the
chestra, however, is the string quartet, as it is called, though it is rea
quintet.   Violins supply the soprano and alto parts of the harmony, vi
part of the alto and all of the tenor ;  'cellos run from bass up to low sopra
and basses give the deepest notes.   The older composers made but poor
of the viola and the 'cello, but the moderns take every advantage of t
compass and their individuality of timbre.   Furthermore, the moderns su
vide the strings very often, writing at times for first and second violins i
many as six parts, for violas in two parts, and 'cellos in the same way.
this way the harmony becomes many-voiced and extremely rich.   ¶
essential requirements of good orchestration are solidity, balance of tone, c
trast and variety.   Solidity is obtained by a proper distribution, among
instruments, of the notes of each chord, so that the proper sounds are m
the more prominent.   The foundation of solidity is good writing for
strings, the mainstay of the orchestra.   Balance of tone also depends
proper dispersal of the harmony, so that the instruments which are provic
the harmonic support will not drown out the voices of those which are s
ing the melody.   A perfect understanding of the relative powers of the v
ous instruments is necessary to success in these two matters.   Especially n
the middle voices be skilfully treated to obtain solidity.   If they are too lc
the effect is "muddy"; if they are too weak, the orchestra is "all top
bottom," as the musicians say.   ¶Contrast is obtained by transferring
melodic ideas frequently from one of the three divisions of the orchestra
another, while variety is the result of mixing the tints.   A theme is n
confined to the strings, but is often handed over to the brass, or the wo
wind.   But even this would not be sufficient.   Consequently the var
effects of mingling the voices of the different instruments, flutes and ho
or clarinets and 'cellos, or oboes and violas, are employed.   The comp
must, of course, know his orchestral colours thoroughly before endeavouring
mix them.   Students of orchestral music will find the simplest and most s
colour schemes in the scores of the classic symphonists, while in the mod
operas and symphonic works of the romanticists he will hear all the result
the most complex treatment of orchestral tinting.

:hestrina (trē'-nä). **di ca'mera**, *I.* A
mall free-reed key-board instr., imi-
ating some orchestral instr. Inv. by
V. E. Evans, 1860.

:hestrino (trē'-nō), *I.* A piano vio-
in, inv. by Pouleau, 1808.

:hes'trion. 1. A large automatic
arrel-organ with many imitative
tops. 2. A chamber-organ devised
nd used on his tours by Abbé Vogler.

**ordinario** (ôr-dĭ-nä'-rĭ-ō), *I.* Ordinary
usual, common. **tempo o.** 1. The
usual time. 2. 4-4 time.

**ordre** (ôrdr), *F.* A suite.

**orecchio** (ō-rĕk'-kĭ-ō), *I.* Ear. **orec-
chiante** (ō-rĕk-kĭ-än'-tĕ). Singing
by ear.

**oreille** (ō-rā'-yŭ), *F.* Ear.

**organ,** *E.*, **organo** (ôr-gä'-nō), *I.*, **or-
gane** (ôr-gän), *F.* See below.

## Organ.

### BY THE EDITOR.

THOUGH many instruments are loosely called *organs* (such as the
mouth-organ, hand-organ, etc.), the word is generally given to
the *pipe-organ*, a microcosmic wind-instrument which contains in
forest of resources almost all the powers and qualities of almost all other
ruments. In the course of time while its powers have grown ever
ater, their control has become always easier and more centralised.
The HISTORY of the organ is, in any completeness, beyond the space of
work. Its prototypes are the primeval Pan's pipes and the bagpipe.
e 2d century B.C. finds it with a key-board, and pipes supplied by
ows with air compressed by water. Ctesibius (170 B.C.) invented
*water-organ* (Organon hydraulicon) which his pupil Heron described
Greek. There are many accounts and representations of organs from that
nt on. The mediæval monks used organs abundantly, the pipes being
o 15 in number and of no greater than 4-ft. length, the range being
ally one octave from middle *c'* downward, the key-board consisting of
ered plates to be pressed. In the 10th century there was at Winchester,
gland, an organ with 2 manuals for 2 performers, 20 digitals each, and
pipes to each digital, 400 in all. In the 12th century the pipes began to
divided into registers or stops (q. v.). For two centuries the action
ame so clumsy that keys were struck with fists or elbows. Pedals were
ented about 1325. Till the 15th century, reed pipes were unknown.
e that time the resources have been vastly increased, the variety of tone
dered almost illimitable, and the introduction of water, steam or electric
to work the bellows has displaced the need of a man to serve as organ-
per or bellows-treader. Electricity has also been called into play for
ging remote parts of the organ into convenient control, till the performer
h his draw-knobs has almost as easy command as the conductor with his
on. ¶The CONSTRUCTION of the organ is too complicated for detail, but
y of the terms following will be found more fully explained under their

separate heads. When looking at an organ, in a church for example
eye is first caught by the great array of pipes. These ornamental or *di*
*pipes* (some of which may be only for show, *dummy-pipes*) conceal
plain pipes of wood or metal, which are of various shapes and sizes
cording to the quality and pitch of the tone of the *pipe* (q. v.). These
are grouped together into *registers* or *stops* (q. v.), each being of un
quality of tone and furnishing a complete or partially complete scale (or
of pipes of graduated lengths). Though these pipes are merely colossal f
oboes, trumpets, etc. (each pipe, however, sounding only one tone),
are too large to be blown by human lungs, and an elaborate mechanis
used. This is concealed from the eye, which sees only the series of
boards for the hands and feet, and the multitude of little *draw-knobs* gro
within easy reach. ¶Of these key-boards the numbers vary, those fo
hands, the *manuals*, being from 1 to 5 in number and appearing in the fo
ing order counting from below, and giving both English and foreign na

| ENGLISH. | GERMAN. | FRENCH. | ITAL |
|---|---|---|---|
| Great (Gt.) organ lmanua | Hauptwerk (Manual I.) | Grand-orgue (1er clavier) | Principa |
| Choir " | Unterwerk ( " II.) | Positierif (2e " ) | Organo |
| Swell (Sw.) " | Schwellwerk ( " III.) | Clav, de récit (3e " ) | " d'e |
| Solo " | Soloklavier ( " IV.) | " des bombardes (4e " ) | " d'a |
| Echo " | Echoklavier ( " V.) | " d'écho (5e " ) | " d'e |

Each of these key-boards may be said to control a separate instrumen
*partial organ;* and one often speaks of the *choir-organ, swell organ,*
¶The *pedal-key-board, Pedalklaviatur* (pā-däl'-klä-fi-ä-toor'), *G.,* or *cl*
*des pédales* (klāv-yā-dā-pā-dāl') *Fr.,* or *pedallera* (pā-däl-lā'-rā), *I.,* is wc
by the feet and is also a separate instrument with stops of its own (vide PED
¶By means of *couplers,* any two of these key-boards (manuals or pe
may be connected; or they may all be combined into the *full-organ.*
*coupling-action* is worked by draw-knobs. ¶The organ as a whole,
is divided into three chief parts: (1) The *action* (key-boards and stops).
The *pipe-work.* (3) The *wind-supply.* The *action* we have exami
The pipes (vide PIPE and STOP) are set upright above the wind-chest,
cover of which is called the *sound-board;* the lower part of the pipe, pa
through an *upper-board,* which grips its *nose,* sets its *foot* in the *pipe-r*
below this is a *slider* (worked by a draw-knob), a thin strip of wood w
hole for each pipe of its particular stop. ¶(4) The *wind* is collected
the outer air by *bellows* and led by *feeders* into a *storage-bellows,* where
compressed by heavy weights; it is next led by a wooden channel or *w*
*trunk* into a wooden reservoir, or *wind-chest,* the top of which (the *so*
*board*) is pierced by *grooves* closed by valves or *pallets,* and separate
*bars.* ¶To play the organ, we first pull out a *draw-knob,* which
along a *slider* until its holes are beneath the feet of the pipes of its

stop is now said to be *on* (before being brought into play it was *off*). ...ng also pulled out a draw-knob setting the wind-supply to work (or ...g signalled the person working the bellows), we next press down one of ...igitals on the key-board whose stop we have drawn. In pressing down ... digital lever we raise its opposite end, which lifts an upright rod (a ...*er*), this in turn raising the front end of a horizontal lever (or *back-fall*) ...se rear end is thus depressed and pulls down a thin upright strip of wood ...*acker*) which in turn pulls a wire (a *pull-down* or *pallet-wire*) fastened ... valve (or *pallet*) which opens and lets the air (which was waiting in ...groove from the wind-chest) rush up through the slider into the pipe to ... it sound or speak. (*Squares* and *roller-boards* sometimes intervene ...een the stickers and trackers, while *pneumatic* or *electric* actions give ...more direct connection between digital and pallet.) This is the mech-...n by which each tone is secured. By means of a multitude of stops ...couplers, what would be a simple tone or chord on another instrument ... become a vast group of tones of various pitches and colours. ¶ By ...s of the *swell* (q. v.) the volume of sound may be gradually increased ...minished while it is sustained.

---

...n-bellows. A machine for sup-ing wind. **o.-blower.** One who ...rks the bellows. **o.-loft.** The part ... the church where the organ is ...ced. **o. metal.** A tin and lead ...xture used in pipes. **o. tabla-**...e. Vide TABLATURE. **o. point.** ...le PEDAL POINT. **o. tone.** A ...e sustained with uniform power. ...ffet o. Very small organ. **enhar-**...nic, enharmonic organ. An ...erican instr. giving three or four ...es the usual sounds within an oc-...e, furnishing the precise intervals ... every key, the scale of each key ...ng produced by pressing a pedal. ...l organ. All the power of the ...an. **hand-organ** or **barrel-o.** A ...nder turned by hand and acting ...keys to produce set tunes. **harmo-**...m o. A reed instr. voiced to im-...e organ-stops. **organet'to,** *I.* A ...all organ. **organier** (ôr-găn-yā), ... Organ-builder. **organique** (ôr-...-ēk), *F.* Relating to the organ. ...anista (ôr-gä-nēs'-tä), *I.* and *Sp.* ...An organ-player. 2. Formerly a ...nposer.

**organic.** Old term for instrumental. **orga'nicen,** *L.* Organ-player. **organis'trum,** *L.* A hurdygurdy of about 1100 A.D. **organo** (ör-gä'-nō), *I.* Organ (q. v.). **o. di campan'a.** Organ with bells. **o. di legno** (lān-yō). Xylophone. **o. pieno** (pĭ-ā'-nō), or **pleno** (plā'-no). Full organ. **o. portatile** (pôr-tä-tē'-lĕ). Portable organ. **organi voca-li** (ôr-gä'-nē-vō-kä'-lĕ), *I.,* pl. The vocal organs. **organo, in,** *L.* Vide ORGANUM. **orga'nochor'dium.** A combination of pf. and pipe-organ inv. by Abbé Vogler. **organophon'ic.** Name adopted by a band of Polish performers imitating various instrs. vocally. **organographie** (grä-fē), *F.* The description of an organ. **organologie** (zhē). The science of building and playing the organ. **or'ganum,** *L.,* **or'ganon,** *Gr.* 1. Any instrument, thence the organ. 2. The earliest polyphonic music, a con-tinual progression of two parts in fourths or fifths (also called *diapho-*

*ny*); later it developed into 3 parts (*tripho'nia*), the third part called *triplum*, hence our term **treble**; then into 4 parts (*tetrapho'nia*). 3. The part added to another in 2 part organum. **in organo**. *Old term for* in more than two parts. **o. hydraul'-icum**. Hydraulic o. **o. pneumaticum**. The ordinary wind o. **o. simplex**, *L.* A mediæval term probably meaning the unisonal accompaniment of a single voice.

**Orgell** (ôr'-gĕl), *G.* An organ. **O.-bälge** (bĕlkh-ĕ). Organ-bellows. **O.-bank** (bänk). Organist's seat. **O.-bauer** (bow-ĕr). Organ-builder. **O.-bühne** (bü-nĕ), or **-chor** (kōr), or **-platz** (pläts). Organ-loft. **O.-gehäuse** (gĕ-hī'-zĕ). Organ-case. **O.-kasten** (käs'tĕn). 1. Cabinet organ. 2. Organ-case. **O.-klang**. Tone of an organ. **O.-kunst** (koonst). The art of playing, or constructing an organ. **O.-metall** (mā-täl'). Organ-metal. **O.-pfeife** (pfī'-fĕ). Organ-pipe. **O.-punkt** (poonkt). Pedal-point. **O.-register** (rĕ-gĕs'-tĕr). Organ-stop. **O.-schule** (shoo'lĕ). Organ-school or method. **O.-spiel** (shpēl). Playing the organ; or the piece played. **O.-spieler** (shpē-lĕr). Organ-player. **O.-stein** (shtīn). Pan's pipes. **O.-stimmen** (shtĭm'-mĕn). Row of organ-pipes. **O.-stücke** (shtü'-kĕ). Organ-pieces. **O.-treter** (trā'-tĕr). Organ-treader, bellows-blower. **O.-virtuose** (fēr-too-ō'-zĕ). Organ-virtuose. **O.-wolf** (vôlf). Ciphering. **O.-zug** (tsookh). Organ-stop or row of pipes.

**orgeln** (ôr'-gĕln). To play on the organ.

**orgue** (ôrg), *F.* Organ. **o. de salon** (dŭ să-lôṅ), **orgue expressif**. (a) The harmonium. (b) The swell organ. **o. hydraulique** (ē-drō-lēk). Hydraulic organ. **o. à percussion** (pĕr-küs'-yôṅ). A reed **o.** made by De Provins & Alexandre, Paris. **o. plein** (plăṅ). Full organ. **o. portatif** (pôr-tä-tēf). A portable organ. **o. de barbarie** (dŭ băr-bä-rē). A

barrel-organ, hurdygurdy. **o. p____ tif** (pô-zĭ-tēf). 1. The choir-org____ 2. A small fixed organ.

**orguinette** (ôr-gĭ-nĕt), *F.* A s____ reed-organ played with a crank, music being perforated to admit to the reeds.

**orificcio** (ôr-ĭ-fĭt'-chō), *I.* Orifice (____ pipe).

**oris'cus**. Vide NEUME.

**or'nament**, *E.*, **ornamen'to**, *I.*, **nement** (ôrn-mäṅ), *F.* An embell____ ment, as the turn, grace (q. v.), **ornamental note**. An access____ note.

**ornato** (ôr-nä'-tō), **ornatamen'te**, Ornate(ly).

**orpha'rion, orphéor(e)on** (ôr-fä-ō-r____ *F.* A kind of cither.

**Orphéon** (ôr-fä-ôṅ). 1. A piano-vi____ 2. A popular male singing society enormous proportions in France 1881 it had 60,000 members). **orp____ oniste** (nēst). A member of s____ society.

**Orpheus** (ôrf'-yūs, or ôr'-fĕ-ŭs). ____ bled Greek lyre-player and singe____ supernatural power. **O.-harmo'ni____** *G.* Pan harmonikon.

**orthog'raphy**. Spelling and gramm____ are as necessary in music as in any o____ written language. Bad spelling occ____ in music where, for instance, a ch____ is written in sharps when the k____ relationship shows it to belong in ____ enharmonic flat notes. Sometim____ however, a note is mis-written inte____ tionally for the sake of easier re____ ing.

**os'cillation**, *E.*, **Oszillation** (ôs-____ lä-tsĭ-ōn'), *G.* Beating, vibration.

**osia** (ō'-sē-ä), **ossia** (ôs'-sĭ-ä), *I.* otherwise, or else. **o. più fa____** (pĭ-oo' fä'-chĭ-lĕ). Or else this m____ easy way.

**osservanza** (vän'-tsä), *I.* Observati____ strictness. **osservato** (vä'-tō). Str____ exact.

**ostinato** (ôs-tĭ-nä'-tō), *I.* 1. Obstin____ continuous. 2. A ground-bass, so____ times **basso o.**

**otez** (ō-tā), *F.* "Off!" (of a stop)

ava (ôt-tä´-vä), *I.* Octave, eighth.
. alta (äl´-tä). The octave above ;
n octave higher (abbreviated 8va.) ;
. bassa (bäs´-sä). The octave be-
w (abbreviated 8va. bassa). *e.*
upra (soo´-prä). The octave above.
oil´ o. To be played with the octave
dded.

avina (öt-tä-vē´-nä), *I.* Vide OCTA-
IANA.

avino (ôt-tä-vē´-nō), *I.* The pic-
olo.

emole (ôt-tĕ-mō´-lĕ). A group of
ight equal notes.

et´to, *I.* Octet.

(oo), *F.* Or, or else.

ṛab (oo´-gäb), *Heb.* Ancient reed-
nstrument.

e (oo-ē), *F.* Soundhole.

er voices. The highest and lowest
oices.

vert (oo-vǎr´), *F.* Open. Vide
.IVRE.

verture (oo-vǎr-tür), *F.*, Ouvertüre
oo´-fĕr-tü-rĕ), *G.*, overtura (ō-vĕr-
´-rä), *I.*, overture (ō´-vĕr-tūr, not
oor). An elaborate prelude to an
pera, oratorio or play, often based
in the concert o.) on the sonata
ormula ; often (in the opera o.) a
nere medley of airs ; sometimes an
ndependent composition. o. di bal-
o (dē bäl´-lō), *I.* An overture intro-
lucing dance melodies.

erblow. 1. To blow with enough
orce to produce harmonics on a wind-
nstr. Vide ACOUSTICS and HORN.
This feat is constantly necessary in
laying many wind-instrs. 2. Of de-
ective pipes, to sound a partial instead of the fundamental.

erchord. Vide PHONE.

erspun. Used of covered strings.

erstrung. Of a piano in which the
strings of two or more of the lowest
octaves are stretched diagonally under
other strings, the object being to
economise space.

vero (ôv-vä´-rō), *I.* Or.

W. Abbr. for Oberwerk.

typyc´ni. Church modes with a
pyknon high in the tetrachord.

# P

**P** Abbr. of *pedale ; piano ; più,*
as *più forte* (pf.); *poco*, as p. a.
p., *poco a poco ; parte* (as colla
p.) ; *pointe*, *F.* (toe) ; and *positif* (choir-organ).

**pad.** Vide PIANOFORTE.

**padiglione** (pä-dēl-yō´-nĕ), *I.* The
bell (of a wind-instr.).

**Padova´o** (pä-do-vä´-nō), **Padava´ne,**
or, **Paduane** (pä - doo - ä´ - nĕ), *I.*
"From Padua." An Italian dance
in ternary rhythm. Perhaps the same
as Pavan.

**paean** (pē´-än), *Gr.* Hymn of invocation, usually to Apollo.

**pair of organs.** An organ with a
complete set of pipes.

**paired notes.** Thirds, sixths, etc., in
pf.-playing.

**paisana** (pä-ĭ-zä´-nä), *Sp.* A country
dance.

**palalaika.** Vide BALALAIKA.

**palco** (päl´-kō), *I.* Stage of a theatre ;
box.

**Palestrinastil** (shtēl), *G.* The style of
Palestrina (vide B. D.), i. e., a cappella.

**palettes** (pǎl-ĕt´), *F.* The white keys.

**pal´let.** A spring valve in the wind-
chest of an organ.

**palmadilla** (pǎl-mä-dēl´-yä), *Sp.* A
dance.

**pam´be.** Small Indian drum.

**panathe´næa,** *Gr.* An Athenian festival
at which musical contests were held.

**Pan´dean pipes, Pan's pipes.** A
primitive group of reeds or tubes of
different lengths, fastened together
and tuned, named for the god Pan.

**pando´ran,** *Gr.*, **Pandore** (pän-dō´-rĕ),
*G.*, **pando´ra, pandoura, pandura**
(pän-doo´-rä), *I.*, **pandure** (pän̄dür),
*F.* Vide BANDORA.

**Panflöte** (pän´-flä´-tĕ), *G.* Pandean
pipes.

**panharmo´nicon.** A kind of orchestrion inv. by Maelzel.

**panmelo´deon.** A key-board instr. of
wheels impinging on metal rods, inv.
1810, by Leppich.

**panorgue** (ôrg), *F.* A little reed-organ to be attached to a pf. inv. by J. Jaulin.

**pan'sympho'nikon.** An orchestrion inv. by Peter Singer, 1839.

**pantaleone** (păn-tä-lĕ-ō-'nĕ), **pantalon.** An instr. inv. by Pantaleon Hebenstreit, in the 18th century. It was 9 ft. long, 4 ft. wide, and had 186 gut strings, played on with two small sticks. **P.-zug,** *G.* A harpsichord-stop.

**pantalon** (păṅ-tä-lôṅ), *F.* First movement of the quadrille.

**Papagenoflöte** (pä'-pä-gā-nō-flā'-tĕ), *G.* Pan's pipes, from Mozart's *Papageno* (vide " Magic Flute " in " Stories of the Operas ").

**papillons** (păp-ē-yôṅ), *F.* " Butterflies." A frail and flitting composition.

**parallel.** Of intervals, consecutive ; of keys, related. Of motion, the progression of two voices in the same direction at a fixed interval. It requires care in handling. **Parallelen** (pä-räl-lā'-lĕn), *G.* 1. Sliders. 2. Consecutives. **Parallelbewegung** (bĕ - väkh' - oongk), *G.* Similar or parallel motion. **Parallel-tonarten** (tōn-är-tĕn), *G.* Related keys.

**parame'se, parane'te.** Vide LYRE.

**par'aphrase.** Free or florid transcription.

**parfait** (păr-fĕ'), *F.* Perfect (of intervals), etc.

**parlan'do, parlante** (păr-län'-tĕ), *I.* "Speaking," in a recitative manner.

**parhy'pate.** Vide LYRE.

**Parnas'sus.** A mountain in Greece, sacred to Apollo, the Muses, and inspiration generally. *Gradus ad Parnas'sum.* Vide METHOD.

**parole(s)** (pă-rôl'), *F.* Word(s).

**part,** *E.* and *G.* 1. The music of an individual voice or instr. 2. A division.

**part-book.** 1. The music of any one voice or instr. 2. In the 15th–16th cent. a book with separate parts on facing pages.

**part-song.** A song for three or more voices.

**part-writing.** Counterpoint.

**parte** (pär'-tĕ), pl. **i,** *I.* Part(s). **co p.** With the part, i. e., adopting tempo of the singer or soloist. **cantan'te.** The vocal part, the le ing voice. **parti di ripieno** (rē-ä'-nō). Supplementary parts. **equale.** With more than one vo of leading importance.

**partial.** 1. An harmonic. Vide ACO TICS. 2. Vide STOP. 3. Vide TU

**partic'ipating.** Accessory. **parti pa'tum syste'ma,** *L.* Equal te perament.

**Partie** (pär-tē'), *G.* 1. Variations. Vide SUITE.

**partie(s)** (pär-tē), *F.* Parts. **p. de re plissage** (dŭ räṅ-plĭ-säzh), *F.* cessory parts.

**partimen'to,** *I.* 1. An exercise. Figured bass.

**partita** (pär-tē'-tä), *I.* 1. Variatio 2. Vide SUITE.

**partitino** (tē'-no). A small supp mentary score.

**partition,** *E.* (in *F.* pär-tēs-yôṅ), **P titur** (pär-tĭ-toor'), *G.*, **partit** (pär-tĭ-too'-rä), partizione (pär tsĭ-ō'-nĕ), *I.* A full score for vo or instrs. **p. cancella'ta.** A se staves with vertical lines for the b

**Partiturspiel** (toor'-shpēl), *G.* P ing from the score.

**partito** (par-tē'-tō), *I.* Scored, vided.

**pas** (pä), *F.* 1. Step, dance. **p. o naire** (pä-zôr-dĭ-năr). March ti **p. de charge** (dŭ shärzh). Dou time. **p. seul** (sŭl). A dance one performer ; **p. de deux** (dŭ For two, etc. **p. redoublé** (pä doo-blā'). A quick-step. 2. Not **pas trop vite** (pä trō vēt). Not fast.

**paspié** (päs'-pĭ-ā), *Sp.* A kind dance.

**pas'py.** Vide PASSEPIED.

**passacaglio** (päs-sä-käl'-yō), *I.*, **p sacaille** (päs-sä-kĭ'-yŭ), *F.*, **pas col'le,** *Sp.*, **passagall'o,** *I.* chaconne with a ground-bass in time, always in minor.

age (in *F.* păs-säzh). 1. A phrase section. 2. A figure. 3. A run. ...tes de p. Grace notes. **passage-ards.** Boards on which an organ-...er may walk.

...aggio (päs-säd'-jō), *I.* 1. A pas-...ge. 2. Modulation.

...amezzo (päs-sä-měd'-zō). A slow ...lian dance, in 2-4 time, resembling ...Pavan.

...ant (păs-säṅ), *F.* Slide (of a ...v).

...epied (păs-pĭ-ā), *F.* A lively old ...ench dance in 3-4, 3-8, or 6-8 time; ...quick minuet with three or more re-...ses, the first of eight bars.

...e-rue (păs-rü). Passacaglio.

...ing. Unessential, as a **passing** ...dulation. A transient modulation.

...ssing tone, or note, a brief dis-...nance on the weak beat, leading ...m one consonant tone to another; ...does not need to be prepared.

...sion, Passion-music. Oratorio, or ...y. A dramatic or musical setting ...the "Passion" (suffering) of Christ. ...differs from the oratorio (q. v.) in ...tory and form only in the facts of ...being always concerned with the ...e subject, and in the introduction ...ually of spiritual reflections.

...ionata or -o (päs-sĭ-ō-nä'-tä), **pas-**...onatamen'te, *I.* Passionate(ly).

...ione (päs-sĭ-ō'-ně). 1. Passion, ...ling. 2. Vide PASSION.

...sionsmusik (päs-sĭ-ōns-moo-zēk'), ...Vide PASSION.

...so, *I.* Step.

...sy-measure. Old *E.* Passamezzo.

...tete (päs-tā'-tě), *G.* Pasticcio.

...iccio (päs-tē'-chō), *I.*, **pastiche** ...äs-tēsh), *F.* 1. An opera, or other ...ork in which old airs are used to ...w words. 2. A medley.

...toral, **pastorale** (päs-tō-rä'-lě in ...; in *F.* păs-tō-räl'). An opera, can-...ta, song or instrumental composi-...on of rustic nature or subject. p. ...ite. Shepherd's pipe. p. organ-...int. Vide PEDAL-POINT. **pasto-**...l'la, *I.*, **pastorelle** (rěl), *F.* A ...tle pastoral.

**pastorita** (ē'-tä). 1. A shepherd's pipe. 2. A stop, the Nachthorn.

**pastourelle** (păs-too-rěl), *F.* 1. A 6-8 movement of a quadrille. 2. A troubadour lyric.

**patetica** or -o (pä-tā'-tĭ-kä), *I.*, **pathétique** (pä-tä-tēk), *F.*, **pathetisch** (pä-tā'-tĭsh), *G.* Pathetic; a piano sonata in C minor by Beethoven is so-called; and a symphony by Tchaikovski. **pateticamen'te,** *I.* Pathetically.

**patimen'to,** *I.* Grief, suffering.

**patouille** (pät-oo-ē'-yŭ), *F.* Xylophone.

**patte** (păt), *F.* 1. A special clarinet key. 2. A music-pen.

**Pauke(n)** (pow'-kě(n)), *G.* Kettledrum(s).

**pause,** *E.*, **pausa** (pä'-oo-zä), *I.*, **pause** (pōz), *F.* 1. A rest of variable length; if very protracted called **lunga** (or long) **pausa.** 2. A fermate. 3. *F.* and *G.* A whole rest. **demi-pause** (dě-mě'-pōz), *F.* A half-rest.

**pavan',** *F.*, **pavana** (pä-vä'-nä), *I.*, **pavane** (pä-văn'), *F.* A grave stately dance in 3-4 time, generally in three strains, each repeated; once supposed to be derived from *pavo,* peacock, now from *Paduna* (q. v.).

**paventato** (pä-věn-tä'-tō), **pavento'so,** *I.* Fearful, timid.

**pavillon** (pä-vē'-yôṅ), *F.* The bell of a wind-instr. **p. en l'air** (äṅ lăr). "The bell upwards" (direction to horn-players). **flûte à p.** A stop with flaring pipes. **p. chinois** (shěn-wä). Chinese hat, crescent.

**peal.** 1. A chime. 2. A change, of bells.

**pean.** A pæan.

**pearly** (of runs, etc.). Bright, distinct.

**ped.** Abbr. of Pedal.

**ped'al,** *E.* (in *G.* pä-däl'), **pédale** (pä-dăl), *F.*, **pedale** (pä-dä'-lě), *I.* 1. Abbr. of Pedal-point (q. v.). 2. A foot lever of various musical uses. The piano has usually two pedals: (a) The **damper (open, loud,** or **extension) pedal,** which raises all the dampers from the strings, allowing the tones struck to be sustained and broadened by sympathetic (q. v.) vibration. The use of the damper-pedal is indicated by Ped., and its cessation by the mark ✳ or ⊕. Wm. H. Sherwood (vide B. D.) has introduced a more accurate system of continuous lines ⌐⌐ to indicate just when this pedal is to be pressed, how long held and when released. (b) The **soft pedal** (pétite (pā-tĕt), **pédale**) in some cases merely lets a cloth fall over the strings, but usually shifts the action so that the hammers strike only one of the two, or three strings allotted each tone. Hence its use is indicated by **una corda** (oo'-na kôr'-dä, one string), or **Verschiebung** (tĕr-shē'-boongk), and its discontinuance by "**tre corde**" (trā kôr'-dā, " 3 strings "). In the upright pf. this pedal simply moves the hammers nearer the strings. Some pianos are fitted with a (c) **sustaining**, or **prolongation pedal**. A damper-pedal holding the dampers from only those strings struck at the moment, until the pedal is released, thus permitting the sustention of a chord or tone while the hands are busy elsewhere. (d) A. B. Chase has inv. an **octave-pedal**, or **octavo-attachment**, sounding also the higher octave. Both pedals (a and b) may be pressed together ; this is indicated by **pedale doppio**, or **doppelte**.

The harp (q. v.) has 8 pedals, one opening or closing a panel in the sounding-case with loud or soft effect. Reed-organs, etc., have double pedals or treadles for working the bellows. In the pipe-organ (and in the **pedalier**, q. v.) the pedals are of great variety. There is a pedal key-board, **Pedalklaviatur** (pä - däl' - klä - fï - ä-toor'), or **Pedalklavier**, *G.*, **clavier des pédales** (dä pä-däl'), *F.*, **pedaliera**, *I.*, with a compass of C–f, or, counting stops, from C͵͵ up. This is played by the feet (⋁ over a note indicating the right toe ; under it, the left : ◯ similarly marking the heel). To this

part of the organ, called the **ped** **organ,** many stops are often allott‹ hence **pedal - pipe, stop - sou** **board,** etc. ; it is locked from sou ing by a **pedal-check** (worked b stop-knob), a bar running beneath The pedal-stops may be made to so‹ with any of the manuals by mean‹ mechanism, called **pedal-couple** **coupler - pedals,** or **reversib** **pedal.**

The word pedal is also given to ‹ organ, to such foot-levers as the **c‹** **bination,** or **composition ped** (**pédales de combinaison),** whic single-acting draw out certain n‹ or push in certain old, stops ; **double-acting** produce certain c‹ binations regardless of the previ‹ registration. The **forte-pedal** dr‹ out all the stops of its key-board ; **mezzo - p.** the chief 4-8 ft. stop the **piano-pedal** leaving only ‹ softest on ; the **crescendo-p.** dr‹ out the full power gradually, the **minuendo** withdraws it ; the **sf** **zando** produces a sudden fuln‹ Vide also CELESTE.

The **swell-pedal** works the shutt‹ of the swell-box ; if it remains at ‹ where left, it is called a **bala** **swell-pedal.**

**Pedalflügel** (flü'-ghĕl), *G.* Pedalier **Pedalharfe** (pĕ-däl'-härfĕ), *G.*, **ped** **harp.** A double-action harp.

**pedalier** (pĕd-ä-lēr'), *E.*, **pédalier** (‹ däl-yä'), *F.*, **pedal'ion.** A ped‹ key-board attachable to a piano a‹ playing the bass-strings.

**pedal-note,** or **tone.** A tone s‹ tained by the pedal or some voi‹ usually the bass, while the other pa‹ move independently. As the w‹ " point " originally meant " not‹ **pedal-point** (abbr. to **pedal**) is s‹ onymous with pedal-note, but is m‹ used rather of the phrase in wh‹ the pedal-note occurs. It is displ‹ ing the word **organ-point**, deri‹ not from organ, but from *organ‹* (q. v.) and referring to the long no‹ of the *cantus firmus* against wh‹

other voices moved, these notes ng called *organici puncti*, or *or-ium notes*. Pedal-point is then a rase in which one tone is sus-ned through independent harmo-s. The tonic or the dominant is ually the tone sustained. If both used at once it is called **pastoral.** the pedal-pt. occurs in other voices n the bass it is **inverted.** It is netimes **exterior,** or **interior.** It y be figurated, trilled, or florid.

A tuning-pin; in the violin, etc., s set in the head, in a space called **peg-box.**

(pāl-yē), *I.* For the (from *per*

:is, *Gr*. A Greek lute.

**pel'lo,** *I.* For the (from *per il, lo*).

'lion. A Welsh improvisation of ses.

ant. Hook.

ata (pĕn-nä'-tä), *I.* Quilled (of spinet, etc.).

rçon (pŭ-nôr'-sôṅ), *F.,* from **pe-** r'kon, *Gr.* An ancient guitar.

ieroso (pĕn-sē-ä-rō'-sō), **pen-so,** *I.* Pensive, thoughtful.

achium, *Gr.* A composition in 5 ts.

achord. I. A series of 5 diatonic es. 2. An instr. with 5 strings.

atone, *E.,* pen'taton, *Gr.* I. interval of 5 whole tones, an aug-nted sixth. **pentaton'ic.** Having whole tones. **pentatonic scale.** five-toned scale, the same as the al major scale, with the fourth and enth tones skipped; called also Scotch scale. The black keys of piano represent a pentatonic le.

*L.* and *I.* For, by, through, in, m.

as'sion, *E.,* percussione (pĕr-s-sĕ-ō'-nĕ), *I.* I. The actual nding of a tone or chord (as op-ed to its preparation or resolution). nstrs. of percussion are those in ch the tone is secured by striking, ticularly the drums, cymbals, and

triangle, also the piano, and so forth. **percussion-stop.** One in which the reed is struck just as it is blown, to emphasise its tone. **percussive.** An instr. of percussion.

**perden'do, perden'dosi,** *I.* Dying away in both speed and power.

**perdu'na.** Bourdon.

**perfect,** *E.,* pɛrfet'to, *I.* I. Vide IN-TERVAL, CADENCE, CHORD. 2. An obsolete name for triple time. **per-fection.** Vide NOTATION and LIGA-TURE.

**Périgourdine** (pā-rĭ-goor-dēn), *F.* Cheerful old French dance, in triple time, so called from the province of Perigord.

**period, période** (pā-rĭ-ôd), *F.,* **periodo** (pā-rĭ-ō'-dō), *I.* A passage contain-ing two or more sections and some form of cadence. Vide FORM. **Perio-denbau** (pā'-rĭ-ōd-ĕn-bow), *G.* The building of periods, or composition.

**perpetual, perpetuo** (pĕr-pā'-too-ō), *I.* I. Vide CANON. 2. **Perpetual mo-tion,** or pɛrpet'uum mo'bile, *L.* A piece of great rapidity and no pause till the end.

**pes,** *L.* Foot. A ground-bass to a round.

**pesante** (pā-sän'-tĕ), **pesantemen'te,** *I.* Heavy(ly), impressive(ly), forcibly.

**peso, di** (dē pā'-sō), *I.* At once.

**petit** (pŭ-tē'), **petite** (pŭ-tēt), *F.* Small. **choeur p.** A three-part chorus. **p. flute.** Piccolo. **p. mesure à deux temps.** 2-4 time. **petits notes** (pŭ-tē' nŏt). Grace notes. **p. pedale.** Soft pedal.

**pet'to,** *I.* The chest. **voce de p.** Chest voice. **di p.** From the chest.

**peu** (pŭ), *F.* Little. **un p.** A little. **p. à p.** Little by little.

**pezzo** (pĕd'-zō), pl. **i,** *I.* A piece or number. **pezzi concertanti.** Con-certed numbers.

**pf.** Abbr. of, I. Pianoforte. 2. Poco forte.

**Pfeife** (pfī'-fĕ), *G.* I. A fife. 2. A pipe, as of an organ. **Pfeifendeckel.** The covering of a pipe. **P.-werk.** The pipe-work. **Pfei'fer.** A fifer.

**Phantasie** (fän-tä-zē'), *G.* Fantasy, or fantasia. **P.-bilder, P.-stücke.** Fanciful pieces of no strict form. **phantasieren** (zē'-rĕn). To improvise. **Phantasier'-maschine.** A melograph. **phantasi(e)rte** (zĕr'-tĕ). Improvised.

**phil'harmon'ic.** Music-loving.

**philomèle** (fē-lō-mĕl). Vide ZITHER.

**phonas'cus,** *L.,* from *Gr.* Singing-teacher.

**phisharmon'ica.** An octagonal accordeon.

**phonaut'ograph.** 1. A name given first to a melograph, inv. by Abbé Moigno, a pencil fitted to a vibrating membrane. 2. An electric melograph for key-board instrs. inv. by Fenby.

**phone,** *Gr.* 1. Voice or tone. 2. Sound, a term appropriated by Dr. Th. Baker, to represent Riemann's term "clang" (q. v.), hence **homophone, under phone, contro-phone,** and **phonic.**

**phonet'ics, pho'nics.** The science of sounds.

**pho'nikon.** A metal wind-instr. with globular bell inv. by Czerveny, 1848.

**phonom'eter,** *E.,* **phonomètre** (fôn-ō-mĕtr), *F.* A device for measuring vibration.

**phor'minx,** *Gr.* An ancient lyre-like instrument.

**pho'tinx,** *Gr.* An ancient crooked flute.

**phrase,** *E.* (in *F.* fräz, in *G.* frä'-zĕ). 1. A musical clause. Vide FORM. 2. A short passage or figure. **phrase-mark.** A long curve covering a phrase ; or any musical punctuation-mark. **phrasi(** )ren (zē'-rĕn), *G.* To phrase. **phrasé** (frä-zā), *F.,* **phrasing,** *E.,* **Phrasierung**(zē'-roongk),*G.* (a) The act or art of delivering music with due regard ⌣ its melodic and rhythmic punctuation, relation and contrast. (b) Signs for such phrasing.

**Phrygian** (frĭ'-jän), *E.,* from *Gr.* **phrygische** (frē'-jĭsh-ĕ). Vide MODES.

**physharmo'nica.** 1. A small reed and bellows attachment to a piano key-board for sustaining and colouring tones ; inv. by Häckel, Vienna,

1818 ; the forerunner of the ha nium. 2. A free-reed-stop.

**piacere, a** (ä pĭ-ä-chā'-re), **a pi men to,** *I.* At pleasure. **piace** (pĭ-ä-chā'-vō-lĕ), **piacevolme** Pleasant(ly). **piacevolezza** (lĕd' Suavity.

**piagendo** (pĭ-ä-jĕn'-dō), *I.* Plaint

**piagnevole** (pĭ-än-yā'-vō-lĕ), *I.* mournful.

**pianar'tist,** *G.* A mechanical att ment for playing the piano.

**pianente** (pĭ-ä-nĕn'-tĕ), *I.* Ge softly. **pianet'to.** Very soft.

**pianette** (nĕt'). A small piano.

**piangevole** (pĭ-än-jä'-vō-lĕ), **pia volmen'te,** *I.* Doleful(ly).

**pianino** (nē'-nō), *I.* An upright pi **pianis'simo,** *I.* Very soft. **pia sis'simo.** Extremely soft.

**pianist** (pĭ-än'-ĭst, not pē'-än-ĭst) A piano-player.

**pianista** (nē'-stä), *I.* 1. A pianis A mechanical piano.

**pianiste** (pĭ-än-ēst'), *F.* Pianis either sex.

**piano** (pĭ-ä'nō), *I.* 1. Soft, so abbr. (*p*). hence **piano-pedal.** The common form of the word pi forte (q. v.) ; this shorter form is gether used in France, and comm elsewhere. Many terms are use indicate sizes and forms of the pi as the **concert grand** and **par grand** or **piano à queue** (ä-the **semi-grand** or **boudoir** or **queue écourtée** (ä-koor-tä), **baby-grand.** Smaller form. **square** or **carré** (cär-rä) ; **p. à volins** ; the upright or **cabine p. à sécretaire** (sä-krŭ-tär), or **(drwä), oblique,** or **à pilastre vertical,** and still smaller sizes as the **cottage,** or the **pic** inv. by Wornum, of London, For practice there are the **dumb** **p. muet** (mü), and the **Virgil** **tice-clavier,** etc. **electric p.** employing electro-magnets in of hammers. **p-quatuor,** or **archet** (ä är-shä). Vide PIANO LIN. **p. éolien.** Vide AM

ORD. The **p. harmon'icorde.** A
mbination with an harmonium, inv.
Debain. **the p. à claviers ren-**
rsés (ä-klǎv-yä rän-vĕr-sä). One
h 2 key-boards, one above the
er, the scale of the upper ascend-
from right to left. **p. méchanique**

(mä-kä-nēk). A mechanical or automatic piano. **p. organisé** (ôr-gǎ-
nĭ-zā). One with phys-harmonica attached.
**pianoforte** (pĭ-ä′-nō-fôr-tĕ, or commonly pĭ-ä′-nō-fōrt), *E.* and *I.* **piano‧**
**forté** (fôr-tā), *F.*

## Pianoforte.

### By the Editor.

IANOFORTE (in *G.* usually restricted to the square piano). The
most used and most abused of instruments—a combination of the
strings of the harp with a key-board system derived from the organ
he 14th cent. there is mention of a " stringed instrument of the organ
y : the *Exaquir, Sp., Eschiquier d' Angleterre* " i.e., " English chess-
," *F.* or *Esquakiel, G.*). ¶Its History is obscure and owes much
ly to the monochord and elaborations from it. In the monochord,
urdygurdy, or organistrum, etc., a single string produced various
by means of a movable bridge. So the early forms of the piano
a few strings serving for many digitals. The word *monochord* was
even after the strings were increased in number, but was finally
ed to *clavichord* (*clavis*=key) or *clavier;* the movable bridge was
ced by *tangents* which served both to divide the strings as with
and to sound them. ¶Simultaneously with the fretted clavichord, in
n each string served for several tones (as a guitar-string does) prospered
elopment from the dulcimer, a key-board dulcimer, or *clavicymbal* (from
al meaning dulcimer), called in France, *clavecin;* in I*al*y, *clavi-cembalo*
picordo ;* in England, *harpsichord;* in Germany, *Flügel, Kielflügel,*
tstück or *Schweinskopf.* Small forms of this were the *Virginal*(*s*), the
ed harp* or *spinet* (from *spina*=quill), etc. In this variety there was a
for each tone, and the string was sharply plucked with a quill carried
end of a wooden *jack.* In time the clavichord was also given a string
ch tone and was now said to be " fret-free " (*bundfrei*) instead of
ted " (*gebunden*). The tone was capable of a beautiful trembling
(*Bebung*) and considerable virtuosity, but there was little possibility of
ng from loud to soft. The appearance of the elaborate dulcimer, the
aleon seems to have set the clavichordists to thinking, and Cristofori,
11, invented the hammer-mechanism, which he called, from its power
ind loudly or softly, *piano forte,* literally " loud-and-soft " (this name
been used as early as 1598). In Germany, Silbermann, the organ-
r, won Bach's approval for a *Hammer-klavier* of the same general

idea. This idea, with many improvements in detail, but little fundam
change, persists to-day in the magnificent instrument on which great g
nasts combine brute force with legerdemain. ¶The CONSTRUCTION of
piano of our time shows the triumph of ingenuity over a total string-ter
of twelve to twenty tons. A powerful cast-iron *frame*, usually cast in one p
and braced with *trusses* and *cross-bars*, braces the wooden *sound-board* be
on which is a raised *bridge* of hard wood, over which are stretched
*strings*. The strings are of steel wire, the bass strings being covered wi
finely-wound copper wire. The lowest octave of the bass has one strir
each tone, the next octave or more has two strings to each tone, the res
the instrument has three strings tuned exactly alike as *unisons* for each
Some of the strings are generally carried back across the others to save sp
this is called *overstringing*. The hammer of each tone strikes all
strings at once, except when the soft pedal by shifting lets it strike only
string (hence " tre corde " and " una corda "). ¶The ACTION of the p
consists of a key-board of finger-levers or digitals (loosely called keys)
*white* digitals forming the scale of C major, the *black* digitals furnishing
necessary semitones to give the piano (by means of temperament, q.
command of all the major and minor keys—the fingering differing for
key except with the Jankó (q. v.) key-board. The pressure of a digital
not, as in the old clavichord or harpsichord, immediately affect the st
but reaches it by a complicated series of levers which bring the hammer
position for a new stroke instantly, so that a tone can, in a proper actio
repeated as rapidly as the fingers can strike the digital. (This is called
*repetition* or *double escapement*—the *double échappement* of Erard being
origin of the many forms of escapement.) The digital carries at the
end a vertical *pilot* which supports a nearly horizontal *carrier*, at abo
right angle to which is the rod called the *hopper*, which fits against the
*mer* by a notch or projection. As soon as the hopper has forced the han
against the string, it slips loose from the hammer and is brought inst
back (by devices hard to describe briefly) into position so that the har
on rebounding from the strings finds the hopper ready for an immediate
stroke. The *hammer* is hinged at the *butt ;* at the other end of its *sha*
the hammer-shaped *head* with a *pad* of *felt* (or leather). The action v
throws the hammer against the strings, and makes it rebound instantly,
away from the strings the little *damper*, which muffles the strings when r
use ; this damper remains off the strings as long as the digital is held d
¶By means of the *damper-pedal* (commonly called the " loud pedal ") a
dampers may be lifted from all the strings, thus permitting sustained
and sympathetic vibrations while the hands play other chords. Some p
have also a *sustaining* as well as a *piano,* or soft pedal (vide PER

ie piano has a complete chromatic scale with a compass of about
n octaves $A_{,,}-a''''$. It is capable of a rapidity and clarity of utterance
hich the organ is incapable ; and no other instrument but the organ ap-
ches its resources in chords, range, and brilliance. Except the organ,
the only self-supporting instrument ; it can furnish absorbing employ-
t for the four hands of two performers. The chief lack is the inability
well a sustained tone, and some method of adding this final touch or
an interest will doubtless be devised in time by some of the many minds
ged upon the problem.

## Piano Studies.

### By James Huneker.

CENTURY of experience in piano pedagogy has not been fruit-
less ; skilled masters of the instrument no longer burden their
pupils with futile finger exercises, and the precious morning hours
ad of being devoted to mere digital tortures are now utilised for the
orising of a *répertoire* and the study of especial difficulties in a composi-
. Since Karl Tausig, the vast and useless étude literature has been sent
imbo ; for in the music itself may be studied the precise technical difficulty
overcome. ¶After the independence of the fingers, the scales in single
double notes, arpeggios and octaves have been thoroughly mastered, the
wing studies are generally employed for style, for endurance and the musi-
development of the scholar : Cramer—edited by Von Bülow ; Clementi
dited by Tausig ; Kessler—a judicious selection ; Kullak's octave school ;
the Chopin Etudes, opus 10 and opus 25. After these latter the studies
iszt and Rubinstein, and Schumann's Symphonic Etudes may be essayed.
special studies, the Toccata of Czerny, the Schumann Toccata, the Ru-
tein Staccato study in C, and Thalberg's study in A minor, opus 45,
ated notes, are recommended. For beginners, Heller's studies in phrasing
later Czerny's finishing studies may be tried. But the Czerny school—
the exception of his excellent special studies for the left hand—is obso-
. ¶All the latter day writers of piano studies, Scharwenka, Moszkowski,
abine, Godowsky, and Joseffy, build on the Chopin-Liszt technics. For
quick grasp of the Brahms technique, study his fifty-one exercises. Isi-
Philipp, taking his cue from Tausig, has given us the marrow of Chopin's
nique in a volume of Daily Exercises. For pure polyphony, nothing is
er than Bach. For daily gymnastics, use Tausig's studies, but in frugal
ner. ¶For the rest, read all piano music from Alkan to Zaremski.

**piano score.** An arrangement of vocal or orchestral music for piano.

**pian'ograph.** A melograph, inv. by Guérin.

**pianoharp.** Vide KLAVIER HARFE.

**piano'la.** A detachable pneumatic attachment by which a piano may be played mechanically, the performer controlling the speed, the force, and, in a remarkable degree, also the expression ; inv. by E. S. Votey of New York, in 1897. It has 65 felt-covered fingers brought into play by air-power forced through perforated music by treadle action.

**piano-organ.** Vide BARREL - ORGAN (2).

**piano'tist.** A mechanical attachment for playing the piano.

**piano quatuor** (kât-ü-ôr), *F.* Piano-violin.

**piano-violin.** A numerous group of instrs. endeavouring to combine the fulness and range of the piano with the violin's expression and power of increasing the volume of a sustained tone. In 1610 Hans Heydn of Nürnberg inv. the **Gambenwerk,** in which catgut strings were pressed by resined parchment rollers actuated by a wheel (other authorities say that Heydn's instr. was called **Geigenwerk,** and had wire strings ; and that the **Gambenwerk,** or **Klaviergamba,** was inv. by Reich or Gleichmann of Ilmenau, about 1750, and had gut strings). In 1754 Hohlfeld inv. the **Bogenflügel** or **Bogenklavier,** with a horse-hair bow ; von Meyer in 1794 provided each string with a bow. In 1800 Hübner devised the **clavecin harmonique,** which Pouleau developed into the **orchestrin.** Other instrs. of the same general idea were the **gambe-clavier,** inv. by Le Voirs, Paris, 1741 ; the **Bogenklavier** of Garbrecht, Königsberg, 1710 ; the **Xänorphika** of Röllig, Vienna, 1797 ; the **Bogenhammer-klavier,** of Karl Greiner, 1779 ; the **harmonichord** of Kaufman, 1785 ; the **piano-violino,** 1837.

The most successful is the **pi** **quatuor** or **piano-violin,** inv. 18 H. C. Baudin, of Paris, consistin thick single strings to each of w is attached at a nodal point a jecting piece of stiff catgut, whic the pressure of the key, is bro in contact with a linen roller tu by pedals, the communicated v tion causing the string to sound general principle of these instrs sembles that of the hurdygurdy.

**pian piano** (pĭ-än' pĭ-ä'-nō), *I.* softly.

**piatti** (pĭ-ät'-tē), *I.,* pl. Cymbals.

**pib** (pēb), **pibcorn.** A Welsh pip

**pibroch** (pē'-brôkh), *Scotch.* A like composition for the bagp consisting of three or four varia on a theme called the **urlar ;** the of increasing speed and close w quick movement called the **cr** **luidh.**

**piccanteria** (pĭk-kän-tĕr-ē'-ä), *I.* quancy.

**picchetta'to,** or **picchiettato** (pĭ ĕt-tä'-tō). *I.* Staccato, in violin ing made with a bounding bow, indicated by slur over dots.

**picciolo** (pĭt-chō'-lō), *I.* Small.

**piccolo** (pĭk'-kŏ-lō), *I.* 1. Small. PIANO. 2. The octave flute (q. 3. A 2-ft. stop. **piccolino** (lē Very small.

**pic'co, picco pipe.** A small wh with 3 holes ; it was named aft blind Sardinian peasant who pl it in London (1856) with great b iancy, securing a compass of 3 taves.

**pick.** 1. A plectrum. 2. To p (of strings).

**Pic'kelflöte,** *G.* The octave flute.

**piece.** 1. A composition. 2. An strument (generally used in pl.).

**pièce** (pĭ-ĕs'), *F.* 1. A piece ; a con sition. 2. An opera, or dram work. **suite de pièces** (swēt dŭ ĕs). A set of pieces.

**pieno** (pĭ-ā'-nō), *I.* Full. **p. cord** **p. organo.** Full chorus, or full gan. **pienamen'te.** Fully.

(pī-ā'), *F.* Foot. **avec les eds** (lā pĭ-ā). With the feet (on an gan).

**à** (pĭ-ā-tä'), *I.* Pity. **pieto'so, etosamen te.** Tender(ly).

**ced gamba.** Keraulophon.

**ra** (pĭ-fä'-rä), *I.* A fife.

**rare** (rä-rĕ), *I.* To play the fife.

**f fero.** 1. A fife. 2. A primitive **oe.** 3. A stop, the bifara. **pif-ra'ro.** A player on the fife.

**eren** (pĭ-kĕ'-rĕn), *G.* Vide PIQUER.

**a'ta,** *L.* "Capped" (of a covered ɔe).

**é** (păn-sā), or **pincement** (păns-in), *F.* "Pinched." 1. Plucked (as rings). 2. Pizzicato. 3. A mordent. **étouffé.** Acciaccatura. **p. ren-rsé.** Inverted mordent. **instru-ents à cordes pincées.** Instrs. to plucked, as guitar, etc., hence **pin-r** (păn-sā). To play such an in-rument. **pincé bemolisé** (or **diè-**). Trill with a flattened (or sharp-ed) note.

**.** A tone-producing tube of reed, ɔod or metal. 1. One of the ear-st musical-instrs., a simple straw. 2. ne tone-producing tubes of an or-n. (a) **flue-pipe,** or **lip-pipe.** One which the column of air produces ne by being forced through a small ɔening with a sharp edge. The **ɔ-pipe** may be compared to a great te standing on end (the flute is in ct a lip-pipe). The **foot** rests on e **pipe-rack;** the lower part of the **ɔdy** is the **throat;** just above it is , opening called the **mouth,** with upper and lower **lip;** the **upper ɔ** is bevelled to an edge called the **af.** An **ear** projects on each side the **mouth;** inside the mouth is a ɔjection called the **block** (if it is ry thin it is called the **language).** ne passage between lower lip and ɔck is the **windway;** through this e air is driven againt the **leaf,** which, ɔrating, produces a tone from the r column that fills the upper part or **ɔdy** of the pipe. **flue-pipes** may be **ɔen** at the top, or **covered (stopped** or **plugged),** the **stopped-p.** sounding an octave lower than the same pipe open. **flue-pipes** are tuned, or voiced, if metal, by flaps at the top called **tuners;** if wood, by small adjustable boards. (b) **reed-pipe.** One depending upon a reed for its tone, the body governing the quality of the tone only. The lowest part of the **reed-p.** is the **boot;** it contains a sheet of metal called the **block,** which contains two apertures, one holding an adjustable **tuning-wire,** the other a **reed,** or **conical tube** (called a **shallot)** with an opening giving play to a vibrating **tongue.** 3. **bent-pipe.** A rectangular bent tube connecting the bellows with the wind-trunk; also a secondary channel from the wind-chest to the wind-trunk. *Speaking pipes* may be *bent* without altering their tone, to fit them into smaller space. **pipe-metal.** That of which organ-pipes are made, usually an alloy of lead and tin

**pipe-organ.** Vide ORGAN.

**pique** (pĕk), *F.* Peg of a 'cello.

**piqué** (pē-kā'), *F.* Same as **picchie-tato. piquer** (pē-kā), *F.,* **piquiren** (pē-kĕ'-rĕn), *G.* To play in such a manner.

**pirolino** (pē-rō-lē'-nō), *I.* Button.

**piston(s).** Vide VALVE and CORNET-À-PISTONS. **piston-solo,** *G.* Solo for cornet-à-pistons.

**pitch.** The height or depth of a tone *relatively* to others, or its *absolute* position on the complete scale adopted as the standard and divided into octaves definitely named (see the CHART OF PITCH). The vibration-number of a tone also gives it an **absolute pitch** according to the particular pitch accepted as the standard. The opinion of the civilised races, with the chief exception of England, has settled on the **International (low** or **French)** pitch adopted in France in 1859, and at the Vienna Congress in 1887. This gives the tone *a'* 435 vibrations a second and c" 522 vibrations An older pitch was the classical or mean pitch, in which *a'* lay between 415 and 429 vibrations (apparently about the same as the most ancient standards). The desire to secure a more and more brilliant tone led instrument-makers to raise the pitch to outrageous heights. A congress of physicists adopted in 1834 the **Stuttgart Pitch** with *a'* at 440. The **high** or **concert** or **English** pitch gives *a'* about 450, which is a severe and needless strain and distortion. For convenience of calculation a theoretical middle *c'* has been given 256 vibrations, the number being a high power of 2; this so-called **philosophical pitch** gives *a'* about 427 vibrations.

The subject of **Pitch-relationships** is too abstruse for explanation here—though important in the tuning and temperament of instruments. The old Pythagorean theorists did not consider the third (as *c* to *e*) to be a legitimate interval; they reached it by four steps of a fifth (ignoring octaves) thus, *c–g, g–d, d–a, a–e*. This gives it the ratio of 64 : 81. But we now accept both the third and the fifth as intervals, and the ratio of a third is 4 : 5, or in larger terms 64 : 80. The note *e* may then be considered a *quinttone* if reached by steps of a fifth; or a *tierce-tone* if reached by a step of a third. But 64 : 80 differs from 64 : 81 by the ratio of 80 : 81, which is called the *comma syntonum*. Starting from *c'* any tone may be reached by quint or tierce steps up or down. Every tierce step up is $\frac{80}{81}$ less than a quint step and the letter name of a tone reached by a tierce step may be marked with a line under it for every tierce step upward, or a line over it for every tierce step downward, required to reach it. These lines therefore indicate the number of *commas* by which it is lower or higher than the same tone reached by quint steps.

Relative pitches may also be expressed in (a) fractions showing the relative string lengths required produce them; (b) in decimals sh ing relative vibrations; and (c logarithms showing comparat the interval-ratios.

**pitch-fork.** A tuning-fork.

**pitch-pipe.** Small reed-pipe of pitch.

**più** (pē-oo'), *I.* More; as **p. mo** More speed; **più tosto.** Rathe **p. t. allegro.** Rather faster.

**piva** (pē'-vä), *I.* 1. A bag-pipe. composition in bag-pipe manner.

**pizzican do, pizzicato** (pĭd-zĭ-kä *I.* "Pinched," indicating that strings are not to be bowed, plucked with the fingers.

**placido** (plä'-chē-dō), **placidame** *I.* Placid(ly).

**placito** (plä'-chē-tō), *I.* Pleasure. **bene p.** At pleasure, same as *a bitum.*

**pla gal,** *E.,* **pla galis,** *L.,* **plagal** (plä-gä'-lĭsh), *G.* Used of t modes accessory to the authentic ( MODES), and formed from them taking the fourth below as the tonic. Vide also CADENCE.

**plagiau los,** *Gr.* Cross-flute.

**plain-chant** (in French pron. shäṅ), **plain-song.** The old gorian Church-music, so-called its smooth progress in notes of e length. It employs 8 modes (q. and is written on four-line staves, ploying 3 notes, the long, the b and semibreve, and two clefs. still employed in the R. C. ca lation of priests at the altar, ar the basis of the Episcopal Ch service.

**plainte** (plăṅt), *F.* A lament. **pl** **tif** (plăṅ-tēf). Plaintive.

**plaisant** (plĕz-äṅ), *F.* Pleasant.

**plaisanterie** (plĕz-äṅ-tŭ-rē), *F.*, **ple** **anterie.** A cheerful harpsich piece.

**plana** (plä'-nä), *L.* and *I.* Plain. *mu p.* plain=chant.

**planchette** (plăṅ-shĕt), *F.* 1. A mec ical piano. 2. A part of its mec ism, a board fitted with pegs.

**ita'tion.** The manner in which e pipes of a stop are arranged on e sound-board.

**ix'ty.** Literally, "lament," though metimes applied to lively melodies ed by Welsh harpers.

**qué** (plă-kā), *F.* Played simultaously (as a chord); opposed to broken."

**'toral, plec'tron, plec'trum.** A all bit of ivory, metal or shell for ucking the strings of mandolins, c.

**'traphone.** A piano attachment iitating the mandolin.

**-house tune.** Old name for tr'act music.

**n-jeu** (plăn-zhŭ), *F.* 1. Full-organ. A mixture-stop.

**no orga'no,** *L.* Full-organ.

**'tro,** *I.* 1. Bow. 2. Plectrum.

**a,** *L.* "Fold." A neume, used a concluding ornament, indicated a stroke up or down on the last te of a ligature.

**res ex u'na,** *L.* "Many from e." Old name for canon.

**s** (plü), *F.* More.

**uma** (nū'-mä), *Gr.* "Breath." 1. eume. 2. The exhausting vocalition of the closing syllable of the rly Christian Alleluia. 3. A jubition.

**umat'ic.** 1. Used of all windstrs. 2. **p. action,** or **lever.** A lows attachment for lightening the uch of an organ, inv. 1832, by Barr. 3. **p. organ.** The modern windgan, so called originally in distincn to the hydraulic.

**etta** (pō-chet'-tä), *I.,* **poche** (pôsh), **ochette** (pŏ-shĕt), *F.* Pocketddle.

**hessimo** (pō-kĕs'-sĭ-mō), *I.* As tle as possible. **pochettino** (pōt-tē'-nō), **pochet'to, pochino** (pō'-nō), *I.* Just a little.

**o** (pō'-kō), *I.* A little; rather: mewhat. **poco a poco.** Little little.

**giato** (pôd-jä'-tō). *I.* "Leant" ı, dwelt upon.

**poi** (pō'-ē). *I.* Then, afterwards, as **piano poi forte.** Soft then loud. **poi segue,** then follows ; **poi a poi.** By degrees.

**point.** 1. Old name for note. Vide NOTATION. 2. A dot. 3. Staccatomark. 4. Head of a bow. 5. The entrance of an important theme. 6. To divide words for chanting, hence **pointing.** 7. **organ-point.** Vide PEDAL-POINT. 8. Vide SIGNS. (In French pronounced pwăn.) A dot. **p. détaché** (dā-tă-shā). Staccatomark. **sur tête**(sür-tĕt). Dot above or below a note. **p. d'arrêt** (dăr-rĕ'), or **p. de repos** (dŭ rŭ-pō). A hold, **p. d'augmentation** (dōg-măn-tăsyôn). A dot of augmentation. **p. final** (fĭ-năl'). Final pause. **p. d'orgue** (dôrg). 1. A hold, hence also a cadenza or flourish. 2. Pedalpoint.

**pointe** (pwănt), *F.* 1. Toe, in organplaying. Abbr. **p.** or **tp.** Talon pointe.

**pointé** (pwän-tā), *F.* Dotted, from **pointer** (pwän-tā). To dot, or play staccato.

**poitrine** (pwä-trēn), *F.* Chest.

**polacca** (pō-läk'-kä), *I.* Polonaise. **alla p.** In the style of a polonaise.

**polichinelle** (pōl - ĭ - shĭ - nĕl'), *F.* "Punch." A clown-dance.

**pol'ka.** A round dance in lively 2-4 time, originated in Bohemia about 1830. **p.mazurka.** A slower dance in triple time with accent on the last beat. **p. redowa.** Is faster than the **p. m.,** with accent on first beat.

**pollice** (pôl'-lĭ-chě), *I.* Thumb.

**polonaise** (pôl-ō-něz'), *F.,* **Polonäse** (pôl-ō-nä'-zě), *G.* A Polish dance in moderate 3-4 time ; strictly a marchpast. Its rhythm resembles that of the bolero ; it begins with a sharply accented 8th note followed by two 16th notes, and four 8th notes ; its closing measure is an 8th and two 16th notes ; a sharply accented quarter note, an 8th note, and an 8th rest. Also spelt **polonoise** (pôl-ôn-wäz). Vide CHART OF DANCE RHYTHMS.

**polska** (pôls'-ka), *Swedish*. A dance in 3-4 time, usually in the minor.

**poly-**. A Greek prefix, meaning "many."

**polychord**. An instr. inv. by Fr. Hillmer, of Berlin, resembling a double-bass with 10 gut-strings and movable finger-board. **polymorphous**. Used of counterpoint, with a widely varied theme. **polyphon'ic**, or **polyph'onous**. 1. Used of compositions in which more than one theme at a time is given individuality; loosely used of compositions of many parts, but to be sharply distinguished from a mere melody with an accompanying harmony. 2. Used of instrs. that can produce more than one tone at a time (compare homophonic, and homophonous), hence **polyphony** (pŏl-ĭ-fō'-nĭ or pō-lĭf'-ō-nĭ). The treatment of simultaneous parts each independently, i. e., counterpoint.

**Pommer** (pôm'-mĕr), *G*. Vide BOMBARD.

**pompös** (pôm'-pās), *G.*, **pompo'so**, **pomposamen'te**, *I.* Pompous(ly). Majestic(ally).

**ponctuation**(pônkt-ü-ăs-yôn), *F*. Phrasing, from **ponctuer** (pônk-tü-ā). To phrase.

**pondero'so**, *I.* Ponderous, heavily marked.

**ponticello** (pôn-tĭ-chĕl'-lō), *I.* 1. Bridge. **sul. p.** A direction for bow instrs., "play near the bridge." (Abbr. **s. pont.**) 2. The break in the voice.

**pont-neuf** (pôn-nŭf), *F*. A bridge in Paris, hence a street ballad.

**poo'gye**. Hindoo nose-flute.

**popolare** (pō-pō-lä'-rĕ), *I.* Popular.

**porrec'tus**. Gnomo. Vide NEUME.

**port** (pôr), *F*. 1. Portamento. 2. Vide CHUTE.

**portamen'to**. The passage across an interval by means of gliding with imperceptible gradations through all the intermediate tones in one continuous sound (such an effect as is gained by sliding the finger along a string while the bow presses it). Hence a legato style; so a singer is said to have a *true* **portamento**.

**portan'do**, *I.* Carrying across, i producing the *portamento* effect; **portare** (pôr-tä'-rĕ). To carry.

**portar** (pôr-tär'), *I.* Carry ! **p. la tuta**. Follow the beat. **p. la v** Sustain the tone. Pl. **portate**.

**portata** (pôr-tä-tä), *I.* Staff.

**portatif**, *F.*, **portativ**, *G.* (pôr-tä-**por'tative**. A portable organ.

**portato** (pôr-tä'-tō), *I.* Sustained.

**portée** (pôr-tā'), *F.* Staff.

**porter** (pôr-tā), *F*. To carry. **p voix**. Produce the portamento.

**por'tunal flute**. A flue-stop wide-top pipes.

**Portunen** (pôr-too'-nĕn), *G.* Bour

**Pos.** Abbr. for **Posaune**.

**posato** (pō-zä'-tō), *I.* Sedate.

**Posaune** (pō-zow'-nĕ), pl. **-en**, *G.* Trombone. 2. A trumpet. He **Posauner**. A trombonist. 3. A r stop. **Posaunzug** (tsookh). S but.

**Poschette** (pō-shĕt'-tĕ), *G.* Po violin.

**posé'ment** (pō-zā-män), *F.* Seda

**poser** (pō-zā), *F.* To poise. **p voix**. To attack a tone exactly

**positif**, *F.*, **positiv**, *G.* (pō-zē-**pos'itive**. Stationary organ; French choir-organ.

**posi'tion**, *E.* (pron. in *F.* pō-zēs'-y **posizione** (pō-zē-tsĭ-ō'-nĕ), *I.* Vide CHORD. 2. Vide CLOSE. 3. place of the first finger of the hand on the finger-board of vio etc. The **first position** is th which the fore-finger presses the semi-tone or tone of the open str the **half position** that in which second finger presses the first s tone of the open string. By ma a **shift**, the hand reaches the **sec position**, that in which the finger presses at the place occu by the second finger in the first tion; in the **third position** in finger occupies the place held by third finger in the first position; so on.

**possibile** (pôs-sē'-bĭ-lĕ), *I.* Poss as *presto p.*, as fast as possible.

horn. 1. A straight valveless
gle. 2. A piece or passage imi-
ing a postman's call.
a, di (dē pōs'-tä), *I.* At once.
hume (pôs-tüm), *F.* Posthumous,
b. after the composer's death.
lu'deum, *L.* A concluding phrase,
mposition, or church voluntary.
nza (pō-těn'-tsä), *I.* 1. Old name
· musical note or sign. 2. The
und any instr. produces.
pourri (pō-poor'-rē), *F.* Medley.
·e (poos), *F.* Thumb. In guitar
usic a direction to sweep the strings
ith the thumb.
e, la (lä pool), *F.* "The hen." A
adrille figure; the third.
· (poor), *F.* For, in order to, as *p.*
·ir, in order to close.
·ssé (poos-sā'), *F.* "Pushed."
ie up-bow.
    Abbr. of **pianissimo**.
htig (prěkh'-tǐkh), *G.* Pompous.
rachtvoll (präkht'-fōl), *G.* Full of
andeur.
is (prä-tsēs'), *G.* Precise.
cen'tor, *L.* Choir-leader.
am'bulum, *L.* Prelude.
fa'tio, *L.* The prayers said or sung
the Mass before the Transubstan-
tion.
fec'tus cho'ri, *L.* Chorus-leader.
l'triller, *G.* Inverted mordent.
de GRACE.
udiren (prä-loo-dē'-rěn), *G.* To
eludise.
stant (prä'-shtänt), *G.* Principal
t. stop.
ent'or. Choir-director in the An-
can Church.
hantre (prä-shäntr), *F.* Choir-di-
ctor.
ipitare (prä-chē-pǐ-tä'-rě), *I.* To
rry precipitately, hence **precipi-
to** (tä'-tō). **precipitan'do**, **preci-
to'so**. Hurried. **precipitamen'-**
  Hurriedly. **precipitazione**
·-tsǐ-ō'-ně). Haste.
cisione (prä-chē-zǐ-ō'-ně), *I.* Pre-
sion. **preciso** (prä-chē'-sō). Exact.
ghiera (prä-gǐ-ā'-rä), *I.* Prayer.
ude (prē'-lüd or prěl'-ūd), *E.*, **pré-**

lude (prä-lüd), *F.*, **preludio** (prä-
loo'-dǐ-ō), *I.* 1. An introductory
phrase, section, or composition.
Hence, a composition of an improvised manner, and brief length. 2.
*As a verb*, to improvise such an
introductory piece.

**premier** (prŭm-yā), **première** (prŭm-
yǎr), *F.* First, as **premier dessus**
(děs-sü). First treble or soprano.
**première fois** (fwä). First time.
**à première vue** (vü). At first sight.
As a noun, **première** is used of a first
production.

**prepara'tion, préparation** (prä-pǎ-
răs-yôṅ), *F.*, **preparazione** (prä-pä-
rä-tsǐ-ō'-ně), *I.* A musical device for
softening a discord by preparing the
mind for it through the introduction
of the dissonant note in a previous
chord in which it is consonant. Vide
HARMONY. Custom has greatly
changed from the early period in
which no unprepared dissonance was
permitted, for now in free writing
almost any dissonance can appear
without warning.

**prepar'ative note.** Appoggiatura.

**prepared.** 1. Used of a note which
had preparation (q. v.). 2. Used of
a shake or trill which had two or
more introductory notes.

**près de** (prě dŭ), *F.* Near.

**presa** (prā'-sä), *I.* Vide LEAD (2).

**pressant** (prěs-säṅ), *F.*, **pressante**
(prěs-sänt), *F.*, **pressan'do**, *I.*, **pres-
sirend** (prěs-sē'-rěnt), *G.* "Pressing,"
accelerating.

**pressez** (prěs-sā), *F.* Accelerate.

**pressure note or tone.** One marked
thus $\widehat{\phantom{=}}$, and to be attacked softly and
suddenly increased in volume.

**prestamen'te,** *I.* Very rapidly.

**prestant** (prŭ-stäṅ), *F.* Principal, 4-
foot open stop.

**prestezza** (prěs-těd'-zä), *I.* Rapidity.

**presto** (präs'-tō), *I.* 1. Fast, faster than
allegro, the fastest rate in music except its own superlatives as **prestis'-
simo** and **prestis'samente.** 2. A
movement in very rapid time.

**prick.** 1. *As a noun,* the head of a note, hence 2. *as a verb,* to write music. **prick-song.** The first written music, in contrast with improvised music. 3. The counterpoint written to a cantus firmus.

**prière** (prĭ-ăr'), *F.* Prayer.

**prima** (prē'-mä), *I.* First, principal. **da p.** From the beginning. **p. buffa.** Leading woman in comic opera. **prima donna.** "Leading lady" in opera, chief soprano. **p. vista.** First sight. **p. volta.** The first time (abbr. 1ma. **Volta**), and used to mark measures to be played before a repetition, and to be skipped after that repetition for the measures marked **seconda volta** (2da. **volta**).

**pri'mary.** 1. Used of an accent beginning a measure. 2. Of a triad or chord which constitutes one of the three fundamental triads of a key, viz., those on the tonic, dominant, and the subdominant.

**prime** (prīm), *E.* (in *G.* and *F.* prēm). 1. The first tone of a scale, the tonic. 2. Used of that interval which is indicated by two notes on the same line or space, but separated by a chromatic distinction. Used also of two notes in unison. Vide INTERVAL. 3. Vide HORA.

**Primgeiger** (prēm'-gī-gěr), *G.* First violin, leader.

**primo** (prē'-mō), *I.* First, principal. **tempo p.** At the original tempo. **p. buffo.** Leading man in a comic opera. **p. uomo** (oo-ō'-mō). Old term for first male soprano or tenor. **primo** as a noun, is used of the leading part of a duet.

**Primtöne** (prēm'-tä-ně), *G.* Fundamental tones. **Primzither.** Treble zither.

**primice'rio** (prē'-mĭ-chā'-rĭ-ō), *I.,* **primicerius,** *L.* Cantor.

**prin'cipal,** *E.* (pron. in *G.* prēn-tsĭ-päl', in *F.* prăn-sĭ-päl'). 1. In France and Germany used of the open diapason ; in England used of an open flue-stop of 4-ft. pitch, on the manual (8 ft. on the pedal) an octave higher

than the open diapason. 2. Old n[...] for fugue subject. 3. Old name [...] trumpet.
*As an adjective.* 1. Vide PRIMARY[...] **principal key.** The predomi[...] key of the composition. 3. Th[...] voices are the soprano and bass. **p. close** or **cadence.** One in[...] principal key. 5. **p. subject** **theme,** one to which others are [...] ordinate. **principal-bass.** An [...] diapason stop on the pedals. **pri[...]pal-work.** The flue-pipes of di[...] son quality. Vide STOP.

**principale** (prēn-chĭ-pä'-lě), *I.* 1. [...] pason-stop. 2. Principal or lead[...] as an adjective. 3. Old name fo[...] trumpet. **principalino.** 8-ft. s[...]

**principio** (prĭn-chē'-pĭ-ō), *I.* Be[...]ning.

**prise,** or **p. du sujet** (prēz dŭ sü-[...] *F.* Entry of the subject.

**Probe** (prō'-bě), *G.* Rehearsal. [...] **eralprobe.** Final rehearsal.

**procéder** (prō-sā-dā), *F.* To prog[...]

**procella** (prō-chěl'-lä), *I.* Storm.

**pro'em.** Ancient heroic song with [...] ara accompaniment.

**programme,** *F.,* **program** (prō'-g[...] not prō'-grŭm), *E.,* **program'ma** **Programm** (prō-gräm'), *G.* A li[...] compositions to be performed.

**gram - music, Programm - m[...]** (prō-gräm' moo-zēk'), *G.* Music [...] a programme, i. e., with a more o[...] definite description of events [...] moods. It usually aims to prese[...] suggestion (rarely in decent musi[...] imitation) of some music of natu[...] a brook, bird-improvisations, fo[...] sounds, or of some narrative, the[...] its main effort is to deploy the e[...] tions arising from such scenes [...] thoughts. Beethoven's ideal is [...] pressed in his famous characterisa[...] of his Pastoral Symphony as *m[...] Ausdruck als Malerei,* "more an [...] pression than a painting." So lor[...] the "descriptive" element is a m[...] suggestion, music is capable of m[...] felicitous hints, and programme-[...] sic has most ancient and vener[...]

uthority, traceable farther back even
.an Bach (who wrote a musical sug-
.stion of a postilion), to Jannequin,
.d others. When programme-music
.oops to imitation direct it either
.ows ludicrously incompetent or
.ases to be music and becomes noise.
.rogrammist. A devotee of pro-
.ramme-music.

grès (prō-grĕ), F. Progression.

gres'sion, E. progressione (sĭ-
-nĕ), I. 1. melodic progression.
.he advance of the melody from one
.ne to another. 2. harmonic p.
.he advance of the harmony from one
.nord to another. These two pro-
.esses, particularly the latter, are
.edged round with continual difficul-
.es and restrictions, some of them
.ased on human nature and acous-
.cs, others deriving no sustenance
.rom either, but depending for their
.xistence in the text-books entirely on
.radition, history, conservatism, fash-
.on, or a sense of hearing rendered
.rtificial by long pedantry. The sci-
.nce of progressions constitutes the
.reater part of the Theory of Music,
.nd of harmony and counterpoint
.q. v.).

.gres'sio harmo'nica, I. A mixture-
.top.

.ogressions-schweller (prŏ-grĕs-sĭ-
.ns'-shvĕl-lĕr), G. A device inv. by
.bbé Vogler, for gradually calling in
.lay, then gradually closing off, the
.tops of an organ, to produce a cres-
.endo, then a diminuendo.

.ogressive. 1. Of a stop in which the
.umber of ranks increases with the
.itch. 2. Through-composed.

.ola'tion, E., prola'tio, L., prolazi-
.ne (prŏ-lä-tsĭ-ō'-nĕ), I. 1. The clas-
.ification of the relative value of
.he notes in mensurable (q. v.) mu-
.sic, almost corresponding in its four
.lasses to our musical metre. 2. The
.neasurement of the semibreve, pro-
.latio major, indicating that it is to
.e divided into three minims; p.
.minor, indicating two minims. Vide
.NOTATION.

prolongement (prō-lônzh-män) F. 1. A
pedal, inv. by Debain, for holding
down harmonium keys. 2. That part
of the piano action which holds the
hammer from its place of rest ; a sustaining pedal.

promptement (prônt-män), F., prom-
tamen te, I. Promptly, quickly.
pron'to, I. Prompt, quick.

pronunziato (prō-noon-tsĭ-ä'-tō), I.
Enunciated, marked.

proper-chant. Old name for the key
of C major.

propor'tio, L., propor'tion, E. 1.
The determination of time in mensur-
able music by means of fractions.
Vide NOTATION. 2. The second part
of 16th cent. dance-tunes. Vide SAL-
TARELLA.

propos'ta, I. Subject of a fugue.

prosa'rium, L. A book of prosae, the
prosa being the Sequence (q. v.),
sung between the gradual and the
Gospel in the R. C. Service.

propri'etas, L. A ligature whose first
note is a breve. opposita p. One in
which the first two notes are semibreves. sine proprietate. Impro-
prietas. Vide NOTATION.

proslambanom'enos. Vide MODES.

Prospekt', G. Organ front, hence P.-
pfeife(n). Display pipe(s).

pro'teus. A key-board stringed inst.
inv. 1650 by Nigetti.

pro'tus. Middle-age term for the first
church mode.

pro'va, I. Proof, rehearsal. p. gen-
erale (jän-ā-rä'-lĕ), or p. grande.
Final rehearsal.

Provençales (proo-vän-säl'). Troubadours from Provence.

prycke. In Merbecke's notation of
1550 a minim. Vide PRICK.

psallette (säl-lĕt), F. A maîtrise.

psalm (in E. säm, in G. psäl-'m),
psaume (psôm), F. From a Greek
word meaning to pluck a string, hence
a harp-song, taken from Jewish religion by the Christian and highly developed, in various manners. Psalm-
buch, G. A Psalter. Psalm-
gesang, G. Psalmody. P.-lied (lĕt)

Psalm. **P.-sänger**, *G.* Psalm-singer. **psalm'ody**, *E.*, **psalmo-die** (psăl-mō-dē), *F.* The art or practice of psalm-singing. **psalm'ista.** An order of clergy.

**psalm-melo'dicon.** An instr. inv. by Weinrich, in 1828, with eight finger-holes and 25 keys, giving it a compass of 4 octaves, and the power of producing chords of 6 tones.

**psalter** (săl'tĕr, in *G.* psăl'-tĕr), **psautier** (psŏt-yā), *F.* A book of psalms. **Psalter** (psăl'-tĕr), *G.*, **psaltérion** (psăl-tā'-rĭ-ôṅ), *F.*, **psalte'rium**, *L.*, **psaltery** (săl'-tĕ-rĭ), *E.* An ancient stringed instr. with a sound-board, the strings being plucked with the fingers or a plectrum.

**psalte'riæ**, *L.* Women who played and sang during a feast.

**psaume.** Vide PSALM.

**pulcha** (pool'-chä), *Rus.*, **pul'ka**, *Bohemian.* Polka.

**pulpit'ium.** 1. A stage. 2. Motet.

**pul'satile.** Used of instrs. of percussion.

**pulsa'tor organo'rum**, *L.* Organ-player.

**punct'us**, *L.* 1. A note, hence **punctus contra punctum.** "Note against note," i. e., counterpoint. 2. A dot. **Punkt** (poonkt), *G.*, **punto** (poon'-tō), *I.* Dot. **punktiert** (tĕrt'), *G.*, **puntato** (tä'-tō), *I.* Dotted, stacca-to.

**punta** (poon'-tä) *I.* Point (of a bow). **p. d'organo** (dôr-gä'-nŏ). Pedal-point. **p. per p.** Note for note. **p. coronato.** Fermate.

**pupitre** (pü-pētr) *F* Music-desk. **p.-improvisateur** (pü-pēt'-răṅ-prō-vĕ'-zä-tŭr'). A melograph inv. by F. A. E. Keller, 1835.

**purf'ling.** The ornamental border of violins, etc.

**put'ti** (poot'-tē), *I.* Choir-boys.

**pyk'na**, *Gr.* 1. Half and quarter tone progressions, in Greek music. 2. Close notes (q. v.). 3. A semi-tone.

**pyram'idon.** A 16 or 32 ft. stop, with top 4 times as wide as the mouth.

**py'rophon**, *Gr.* "Organ of flam An instr. inv. by Fr. Kastner, 1 A key-board with electric attachm producing gas flames in tubes tune the compass C–c″.

**Pyr'rhic, Pyrrich'ius.** A G dance.

**Pyth'ian.** Games in honour of Ap including musical contests.

**Pythagore'an.** 1. Used of the m ematical investigations in music b by Pythagoras. 2. Used of a ł said to have been inv. by him.

## Q

**Q** This letter inverted in 'c music indicates that the th is to be laid across the str as a nut.

**Quadrat** (kvä-drät'), *G.*, **quad'r** *E.*, **quadra'tum**, *L.* " A squa 1. A natural sign (♮), in *L.* B. **qu ratum.** 2. In mensurable musi breve, hence **Quadramusik** (n zēk'), *G.* Old music in square no

**quad'rible.** Quatrible.

**quadricin'ium**, *L.* A 4-voiced com sition.

**quadriglio** (kwä-drēl'-yō), *I.*, **quadr** (in *E.* kwä-drĭl', in *F.* kăd-rē'-yü). square dance in 6-8 and 2-4 time five different figures : le pantal " Pantaloon." l'été (lā-tā). " S mer." la poule. "The hen." la p tourelle, or la trenise ; and finale.

**quadripar'tite.** A four-voices com sition.

**quad'ro**, *I.*, **quad'rum**, *L.* 1. A natu sign (♮). 2. Tableau.

**quad'ruple.** Four-fold. 1. V COUNTERPOINT. 2. Used of a qua with four tails, a 64th note. 3. rhythm, that with four beats to measure.

**quad'ruplet.** A group of four eq notes.

**quad'riplum**, *L.* Vide TRIPLUM.

**quan'tity.** The duration of a note syllable.

**rt** (in *E.* kwärt, in *F.* kär), **quar'-**, *L.* and *I.* 1. The interval of fourth. 2. A fourth. **quart de esure.** A quarter rest. **quart de oupir** (soo-pēr'). A sixteenth rest. **uart de son**, or **ton**. A quarter ne. **quarta modi**, or **toni**. The ubdominant.

**rt-** (kvärt), *G.* A prefix indicat- g that an inst. is a fourth higher s **Quart-flöte**, **-geige**, etc.), or fourth lower (as **Q.-fagott**, or **posaune**, etc.), than the normal str.

**artsext'akkord**, *G.* A 6-4 chord. ide CHORD.

**arte** (in *F.* kärt, in *G.* kvär'- ). The interval of a fourth. **q. de azard** (dŭ nä-zär'), *F.* A 15th. also 2-ft. organ-stop. **q. de ton.** *F.* he subdominant. **Quartenfolgen**, **r parallelen**, *G.* Consecutive urths.

**rter**, or **quarter note.** A crotchet, alf of a half-note. **quarter rest.** rest of a quarter note's duration.

**arter tone.** An interval less than a emi-tone, the difference for example etween D sharp and E flat on the iolin.

**artet'**, **Quartett'**, *G.*, **quartet'to**, *I.* A composition for 4 voices or strs. 2. A 4-part composition in onata form, as a string-quartet. **ar'to**, *I.* Fourth. **q. d'aspet'to.** 16th rest. **q. di tuono** (too-ō'-nō). Quarter tone.

**asi** (kwä'-sē), *L.* and *I.* As if; al- most; somewhat like. **andante q.** **ento** = andante, nearly lento. **q. sonata.** Almost (but not strictly) n sonata form.

**atre** (kätr), *F.* Four.

**atorzième** (kä-tôrz'-yĕm), *F.* A ourteenth.

**at'rible.** In old music a progression n parallel fourths, a quinible, being n parallel fifths.

**atricin'ium.** Four-part composi- ion.

**attricro ma**, *I.* 64th note.

**at'tro**, *I.* Four.

**quatuor** (kăt-ü-ôr), *F.* Quartet.

**qua'ver.** An 8th note.

**quer-** (kvär), *G.* Prefix meaning cross, or transverse, as **Q.-flöte**. The trans- verse flute. **Q.-pfeife.** Swiss fife, with 6 holes and with a compass of two octaves. **Q.-stand** (shtänt). Cross or false relation. **Q.-strich.** 1. Ledger line. 2. The single thick tail for a group of notes.

**questo** or **-a** (kwās'-to), *I.* This; or that.

**queue** (kŭ), *F.* Tail. 1. Of notes. 2. Tail-piece of vlns., and so forth. **piano à q.** Grand piano.

**quick-step.** A rapid march.

**quieto** (kwē-ā'-tō), **quietamen'te**, *I.* Calm(ly), serene(ly).

**quilis'ma.** Vide NEUME.

**quindecima** (kwēn-dā'-chē-mä), *I.* A 15th. 1. Interval. 2. Organ-stop. **a la q.**, or **15ma.** = 2 octaves higher or lower.

**Quindezime** (kvēn-dā'-tsē-mě), *G.* A 15th.

**quin'ible.** Vide QUATRIBLE.

**quin'quegrade.** Pentatonic.

**quint** (in *E.* kwĭnt; in *G.* kvēnt). 1. A 5th. 2. A 5⅓-ft. stop, sounding a fifth higher than the normal. 3. The *e* string of the violin. **q. stride.** Progression of a fifth. **Q.-absatz**, or **abschluss**, *G.* Imperfect cadence. **Q.-fagott**, *G.* A bassoon pitched a fifth higher than the normal. **Q.- gedackt** or **Q.-stimme**, *G.* Same as 2. **Q.-bass**, *G.* A stop on the pedal sounding a fifth above the double diapason. **Q.-fuge** (foo'-gě). A fugue with the answer a fifth above the subject. **Q.-saite.** A treble string. **Q.-töne.** Quint tone. Vide PITCH. **Q.-viola.** 1. Quin- ton. 2. A stop a fifth above the gamba.

**quin'ta**, *L.* and *I.* A fifth; vide also QUINTUS. **q. decima.** Quindecima. **q. ed una** or **quintadena.** Vide QUIN- TATON. **q. falsa.** The diminished fifth formerly prohibited. **q. modi** or **toni.** The dominant. **alla q.** At the fifth.

**Quintaton** (kvĕn'-tä-tōn), *G.* A covered 8-, 16-, or 32-ft. flue-stop sounding the 12th as well as the fundamental.

**quinte** (in *F.* kănt, in *G.* kvĕn'-tĕ). Vide QUINT 1, 2, 3. **q. octaviante** (ôk-tăv-ĭ-ănt), *F.* The 12th. **Quinten-folgen**, or **-parallelen**, *G.* Parallel fifths. **Quinten-zirkel** (tsĕr'-kĕl), *G.* Circle of fifths. Vide TEMPERAMENT. **quinten-rein** (rīn), *G.* " Pure in fifths," used of bow instrs.

**quinter** (kăn-tä), *F.* To sing in quinible.

**quinter'na**, *I.*, **quin'terne**, *E.* Old Italian lute with 3 or 5 pairs of gut-strings, sometimes also 2 single strings covered with wire.

**quinti(e)ren** (kvĕn-tĕ'-rĕn), *G.* To overblow and sound the twelfth.

**quintoier**, or **quintoyer** (kwĕn-twä-yā), *F.* 1. To sing in quinible. 2. To overblow and sound the 12th.

**quintet'**, *E.*, **Quintett'**, *G.*, **quintette** (kwĕn-tĕt), *F.*, **quinta'to**, *I.* A five-part composition.

**Quintole** (in *E.* quĭn'-tōl ; in *G.* kvĕn-tō'-lĕ). Quintuplet.

**quinton** (kwĕn-tôn), *F.* 1. The 5-stringed treble viol. 2. The tenor viol.

**quintuor** (kwĕn-tü-ôr), *F.* Quintet.

**quintu'plum**, *L.* Vide TRIPLUM.

**quin'tuple.** Five-fold.

**quin'tuplet.** A group of five equal notes.

**quin'tus**, *L.*, or **quin'ta.** A fifth part in compositions ; as it occasionally wandered from one voice to another it was called **q. vagans.**

**quinzième** (kănz-yĕm), *F.* Fifteenth.

**quire.** Choir. **qui'rister.** Chorister.

**quodlibet**, or **quotlibet**, *L.* "What (or " as many as ") you please." 1. A comic medley, without connecting links. 2. A charivari.

**Qui tollis**, *L.* " Who takest away (the sins of the world)." Vide GLORIA.

**quitter** (kĭt-tä), *F.* To leave.

**Quo'niam tu so'lus**, *L.* " For Thou only (art Holy)." Part of the Gloria.

# R

**R** Abbr. for 1. *Right*, as *r.* right hand. 2. *Responsor* (*r. g.=r. Graduale*) in Ca lic music. 3. *Ripieno. Clavier de récit* (swell-manual). organ music.

**raban', raban'na.** Hindu tambour

**rabbia** (räb-bē'-ä). Mad rage, fury

**rabé** (rä-bā'), **rabel'**, *Sp.* Rebec.

**raccontan'do**, *I.* As if relating or scribing.

**Rackett', Rankett'**, *G.* 1. An obso bombard with many curves in tube, and a weak voice. Made in sizes, it was simplified as the **R. gott** by Denner. 2. A reed-st obsolete.

**raccourcir** (răk-koor-sēr'), *F.* abridge.

**racler** (ră-klā'), *F.* To saw, scratch, hence **racleur** (ră-klŭr). bad fiddler.

**raddolcen'do, raddolcente** (räd-chĕn'-tĕ). Growing softer and sw er. **raddolcito** (chĕ'-tō). Pacifi

**raddoppiamen'to**, *I.* 1. Doubling the notes of a chord. 2. Multiply copies. **raddoppiato** (pĭ-ä'- Doubled.

**Radel** (rä'-dĕl), *G.* A solo with chor

**radia'ting.** Used of a fan-shap pedal key-board.

**rad'ical.** Fundamental. Vide DENCE.

**Radleier** (rät'-lī-ĕr), *G.* Hurdygur

**Radlmaschine** (rätl-mä-shē'-nĕ). Va mechanism.

**rag.** The clog dance of the Americ negro, perhaps related to the Span verb *raer*, to scrape. The mu has some resemblance to the Al nera in spirit and syncopation, but in 4-4 time and of an hilarious ch acter, hence the verb to **rag**, a **rag-time** music in this style.

**raggione** (räd-jō'-nĕ), *I.* Proportio

**rago'ke.** Small Russian horn.

**rake.** A 5-pointed device for ruli off staves.

**rall.** Abbr. of **rallentando.**

ntare (tä'-rĕ). To become slower,
ice **rallentan'do** (abbr. *rall*). With
dually reduced speed. **rallenta-
n'to.** Retardation. **rallentato**
-tō). Retarded. **rallenta'te.** Re-
d!

(rän), *F.* Rank.

e. Compass, as of a voice.

. A row of pipes belonging to one
p.

An old country-dance; a reel.

**des vaches** (rän-dä-väsh), *F.*
Calling of the cows." A Swiss tune
ag or played on long horns by
dsmen.

lo (rä'-pē-dō), **rapidamen'te,** *I.*
pid(ly). **rapidità** (rä-pē-dĭ-tä').
pidity.

odie (răp-sō-dĕ), *F.* Rhapsody.

el', *F.* A military call.

a (räsh), *G.* Fast. **rascher.** Faster.

ad (rä-zĕnt), *G.* Raging, hence
segesang, and **Raselied** (rä'-zĕ-
. Dithyramb.

ado (răs-gä-dhō), *Sp.* "Scrap-
," hence in guitar playing, sweep-
the strings with the thumb to
duce an arpeggio.

ral, ras'trum. Vide RAKE.

selkanon (rät'-zĕl-kä-nōn), *G.*
e CANON.

. Used of the relative value of
ration-numbers.

nen'do, **rattenuto** (noo'-tō), *I.*
straining, or restrained, i. e., re-
ded.

zza (rät-tĕd'-zä), *I.* Speed.

(rä'-oo-kō), *I.*, **rauh** (rŏw), *G.*,
que (rōk), *F.* Harsh, hoarse,
gh. **raucedine** (rä-oo-chĕ-dĕ'-nᵉ),
Harshness.

scher (row'-shĕr), *G.* The rapid
etition of a note.

ch- (rowsh). *G.* Prefix denoting a
p of **2** ranks soun ling the twelfth
i fifteenth, or fifteenth and oc-
e twelfth; hence **Rauschflöte,
eife, -quinte, -werk;** and also
szpipe (roos'-pē-pē).

nas'tron. A primitive violin with
e or two strings, claimed by the
ylonese as the invention of a king

who reigned about 5000 B.C. It is still
used by the Buddhists.

**rav(v)ivare** (vä'-rĕ), *I.* To accelerate,
hence, **ravivan'do.** Accelerating.
**ravivato** (vä'-tō). Accelerated.

**ray.** Name for **re,** in the Tonic-Sol-fa.

**re** (rä), *I.*, **ré** (rä), *F.* 1. Vide SOLMI-
SATION. 2. In France and Italy, the
note D.

**rebab,** *Arab.* Rebec.

**re'bec(k), rebec'ca, re'bet, rebed, re-
bibe, re'bible.** Old *E.* An early violin with 3 gut-strings. Its origin has
been credited to the Moors, who are
said to have brought it into Spain;
it has been claimed that the Spanish
gave it to the Moors; it has been
also derived from the British Chrotta,
or crwth.

**re'al.** Vide FUGUE.

**récension** (rä-säṅs-yôṅ), *F.* An analytical editing.

**rechange** (rŭ-shäṅzh). "Change."
Hence, **corps** (kôr) or **tons** (tôṅ) **de
r.** Crooks.

**recheat'.** A hunting recall.

**recht(e)** (rĕkht(ĕ)), *G.* Right, as *r.
Hand.*

**récit** (rä-sē), *F.* 1. Recitative. 2. A
solo part. 3. The chief of several
parts. **clavier de r.** (klăv-yā dŭ).
Swell manual on the organ.

**recitado** (rä-thē-tä'-dhō), *Sp.* Recitative.

**reci'tal.** A musical performance given
entirely by one performer, or from
one composer's works. Said to have
been initiated by Liszt in 1840.

**recitan'do, recitan'te, recitato** (rä-
chē-tä'-tō). In recitative style.

**récitant** (rä-sē-täṅ), **Recitante** (rä'-
tsē-tänt), *F.* A man (or woman) soloist.

**recitative** (rĕs-ĭ-tä-tēv'), *E.*, **recitatif**
(rä-sē-tä-tēf'), *F.*, **Recitativ** (rä-tsē-
tä-tēf'), *G.*, **recitativo** (rä-chē-tä-
tē'-vō), *I.* Musical declamation or
recitation, as opposed to strict melody. It usually aims to be a sort of
musical colloquialism. In modern
form it began in the first operatic
works of Peri (vide B.D.), and the
others; it was more or less a sing-

song declamation with an accompaniment consisting of occasional chords to keep the singer on the key; it was well-called "dry," or **recitativo secco**, or **parlante**, and the accompaniment was indicated merely by figured bass. This accompaniment was gradually elaborated into the **recitativo stromentato**. "Instrumented," or **accompagnato**, or con **accompagnamento** or **obbligato** (in *F*. **accompagné**, or **obligé**). In later opera, particularly Wagner's, the whole musical structure is inclined to be in recitative with a descriptive and complicated orchestral background. Recitative is usually delivered at the singer's pleasure except when specially marked *a tempo*.

**réciter** (rā-sē-tā), *F*. To perform a récit, or solo.

**reci'ting note.** That tone of a church-mode on which most of the chanting is done, usually the dominant.

**rec'ord.** Old *É*. To play the **rec-ord'er.** An obsolete flageolet with 9 holes, one of them covered with gold beater's skin, compass 2 octaves f'–f'''.

**recreation**, **récréation** (rā-krā-ăs-yôn), *F*. A light composition.

**rec'te et re'tro**, *L*. Forward and backward. Vide CANON.

**rec'tus**, *L*. Similar (of motion).

**reddi'ta, redita** (rā-dē'-tä), *I.*, **redite** (rŭ-dēt), *F*. A repeat.

**redondilla** (rā-dôn-dēl'-yä), *Sp*. Roundelay.

**redoub'led.** Compound (of an interval).

**redoublement** (rŭ-doob-lŭ-män), *F*. Doubling.

**red'owa, redowak', redowazka** (rā-dō-väts'-kä), *Bohemian*. A dance in lively 3-4 time; in the Bohemian form 2-4 time is also employed.

**redublicato** (rā'-doob-lĭ-kä'-tŏ), *I*. Redoubled.

**reduciren, reduziren** (rā-doo-tsē'-rĕn), *G.*, **réduire** (rā-dwēr), *F*. To arrange or transcribe a composition in a smaller form. Hence, such con-

densation is called **reduction**, **réduction** (rā-dūks-yôn), *F.*, **duktion** (rĕ-dook'-tsĭ-ōn), *G.*, **zione** (re-doo-tsĭ-ō'-nĕ), *I.*

**reduc'tio,** *L*. Reduction (of a to its original key).

**red-note.** Vide NOTATION.

**reed.** Originally a thin and elastic of cane, now made of other fibre of metal. It is fixed in an ope by one end; its free end is s motion by the breath or by a cu of air, and transmits this vibra with musical effect to the colum air in the main tube, to which it s as a sort of quivering valve. human larynx has a membra reed, and the lips of horn-pla serve the same purpose, the being determined by the tensio the lips and the length of the in ment. Vide EMBOUCHURE. **reeds** vibrate without striking edges of their sockets. Those w strike the edges are called **bea (impinging, percussion,** or **st ing) reeds.** They are used in organ for brass effects. Some in as the oboe and bassoon, have 2 which strike each other, and are c **double.** Reeds are usually tune a sliding *wire* by which the vibra portion is shortened or lengthene

**reed-instruments.** A general n for those employing the reed mec ism, particularly the oboe and cla groups of the orchestra.

**reed-pipe, r. stop, r. work.** Re the pipes and stops of an organ w employ reeds.

**reed-organ.** Originally, a small p able organ called the **regal**, or a of **regals** (if it had 2 pipes for digital). This small instr. w could sometimes be folded up li book or Bible [hence **Bibel-re** (bē'-bĕl-rā'-gäl)], employed bea reeds, in the pipes. In 1810 G inv. what he called the **orgue pressif**, because he could swell diminish the tone. In 1843, De developed the *Harmonium*, w

ssessed several stops. The air
essure is usually applied by pedals
rked by treadles; with levers,
rked by the knees, to produce a
ell. The *American Organ* (q. v.)
ployed a suction mechanism. The
*calion* returns to the harmonium
le with elaborate improvements.
ere are many other instrs. which
fer chiefly in name from the typical
d-organ.

A lively dance usually in 4-4
metimes 6-8) time, perhaps of
andinavian origin, but chiefly pop-
r in Scotland. It is danced by 2
ples. The **Virginia reel** of
nerica is danced by 2 long facing
es, the men on one side, and the
men on the other.

in'. A burden, or stanza, repeated
the end of each new stanza of a
ng.

al (in *G*. rä'-gäl), **régale** (rä-gäl),
1. Vide REED-ORGAN. 2. An
l suffix indicating a reed-stop. 3.
obsolete xylophone.

el (rä'-gĕl), *G*. Rule.

enschori, *L*. Choirmaster.

i'na cœ'li, *L*. "Queen of Heav-
." A hymn to the Virgin.

ister (rĕj'-ĭs-tĕr in *E*.; in *G*. rä-
'-tĕr). 1. The handle or draw-
ob which bears the name of a stop.
ence, 2. A complete stop, or the
: of pipes controlled by a single
aw-knob. Accordingly **register-
g** and **registration** are the act or
: of bringing into play and com-
nation the different stops of an
gan. **Regis'ter-knopf** (knôpf), *G*.
aw-knob. **R.-stange** (shtäng-ĕ).
op-lever. **R.-zug** (tsookh). The
echanism of the draw-stop. Speak-
g stops (**R.-stimmen**, or **tönende**
) are distinguished from mechanical
ps. **stumme** (shtoom'-mĕ) **R.** 3.
frame through which trackers run.
A distinct section of the tone-qual-
· of a voice or instr. Vide VOICE.

stre (rŭ-zhĕst'r), *F*., **registro** (rä-
s'-trō), *I*. 1. A stop-knob. 2. Vide
GISTER (4).

**registri(e)ren** (rä-jēs-trē'-rĕn), *G*.
To register. **Registri(e)ung** (trē'-
roongk). Registration.

**règle** (rĕgl), *F*., **regola** (rä'-gō-lä), *I*.
Rule.

**reg'ula**, *L*. 1. Register. 2. Rule.

**reg'ular**. 1. Strict (of fugue). 2. Similar (of motion).

**regula'tion**. Adjustment of touch.

**Reigen** (rī'-gĕn), or **Reihen** (rī'-ĕn),
*G*. A circular dance.

**rein** (rīn), *G*. Pure, perfect (of intervals), exact, hence **reingreifen** (grī-
fĕn). To play accurately.

**Reiselied** (rī'-zĕ-lēt), *G*. Traveller's
or pilgrim's song.

**Reitertrompete** (rī'-tĕr-trôm-pā'-tĕ),
*G*. A clarion, obsolete straight trumpet 30 inches long.

**rela'ted**. Vide RELATION.

**rela'tion** (in *F*. rŭ-lăs-yôn),
*L*., **relazione** (rä-läts-ĭ-ō'-nĕ), *I*. The
affinity of keys based upon the similarity or identity of certain chords.
Upon key-relationship the whole subject of harmony and modern counterpoint is largely based, and upon this
split hair more great theorists jostle
than there were angels dancing upon
the needle-point of the old monkish
dogmatists. In a liberal sense all
keys are closely related. For purposes of distinction those keys are
said to be *related* (*attendant, accessory,*
or *auxiliary*) which have one or more
chords in common. The most nearly
related (or least *remote*) keys to any
key are those founded on its dominant and subdominant (as the keys of
G and F are most nearly related to
the key of C), also the absolute and
relative major and minor (as *c* minor
is the absolute minor of C major
while the relative minor to C major is
*a* minor, which has the same signature). **false-relation**, or **rela'tio non
harmon'ica**. Vide FALSE.

**rel'ative key**, *E*., **mode-relatif** (môd-
rŭl-ä-tēf'), *F*., **tono relativo** (tĕ'-vō),
*I*. 1. The relative key to a major is
the minor key whose tonic is a minor
third below. The relative major of a

minor key has its tonic a minor third above. Vide RELATION.

**religio'so** (rä-lē-jĭ-ō'-sō), *I.*, **religiosamen'te**. Solemn(ly), devout(ly).

**rel'ish.** An old grace (q. v.).

**remote'.** Unrelated. Vide RELATION.

**remo'tus,-a,** *L.* Remote; open (as harmony).

**remplissage** (rän-plĭs-säzh), *F.* 1. "Filling," as the inner parts of a harmony. 2. Padding. 3. Cadenzas, and bravura passages.

**rentrée** (rän-trä), *F.* Re-entrance (of a part).

**renverser** (rän-vĕr-sä), *F.* To invert, hence **renversé** (rän-vĕr-sä). Inverted. **renversement** (vĕrs-män). Inversion.

**renvoi** (rän-vwä), *F.* A repeat; a sign of repetition.

**repeat.** A sign indicating the repetition of certain measures—marked by two or more dots in the spaces between the lines, before (or. after) the double bar, which indicates the end (or beginning) of the portion to be repeated.

**repeating.** 1. Of action in which the hammer rebounds quickly enough to permit a rapid reiteration of the tone. 2. Of mixed stops whose overtones do not keep always the same height above the pitch, but sound an octave lower, as the pitch rises.

**repercus'sa** (*vox*), *L.* A "repeated tone." 1. In neumes the notes called *bi-*, *di-*, or *tri*. 2. In Gregorian music, the principal note of a mode.

**repercus'sion, repercus'sio,** *L.* 1. Repetition, of a chord or note. 2. The reappearance of the subject of the fugue after the exposition. 3. The dominant of a church-mode.

**repeti(e)ren** (rā-pā-tē'-rĕn), *G.* 1. Vide to BREAK (3). Hence **repeti(e)ren-de Stimme.** A mixture-stop with a break. 2. To repeat.

**Repeti'tion** (in *G.* rā-pā-tē'-tsĭ-ōn). 1. The rapid repeating of a note or chord. 2. (In *G.* **Repetions'mecha'nik**). Vide REPEATING (1). 3. Vide BREAK (3).

**répétition** (rā-pā-tēs-yôn), *F.* 1 hearsal. 2. Repetition.

**répétiteur** (rä'-pā -tē-tŭr'), *F.*, re itore (rä-pā-tē-tō'-rĕ), *I.* Train an opera chorus; the rehearser.

**repetizione** (rā-pā-tē-tsĭ-ō'-nĕ), **petimen'to,** *I.* Repetition.

**replica** (rä'-plē-kä), *I.* A repeat; etition, hence **replicato** (kä'-tō). peated; doubled.

**rep'licate.** The octave of a tone.

**Replik** (rā-plēk'). Complementar terval.

**réplique** (rā-plēk), *F.* 1. The o of a tone. 2. The answer fugue. 3. Complementary inte 4. Cue.

**reply.** Answer (of a fugue).

**répons** (rā-pôn), *F.* Response (1)

**réponse** (rā-pôns), *F.* Answer.

**report.** Answer.

**repos** (rŭ-pō), *F.* Point of repose lowing a cadence.

**reprise** (rē-prīz'), *E.* The reapp ance of the first theme of a sona symphony after the development

**reprise** (rŭ-prēz), *F.* 1. Repetition Vide REPRISE. 3. Reappearanc a theme. 4. Vide BREAK (3) Revival of a work.

**reprendre** (rŭ-prändr), *F.* To sume.

**Requiem** (rā'-kwĭ-ĕm), *L.* The word and title of the Mass for Dead (*missa pro defunctis*). Be ning "*Requiem æternam dona domine*" "rest eternal, grant t Lord." The requiem is divided the introit, kyrie, gradual (with t us, "*Absolve*," and sequence " *iræ*"). Offertory, "*Domine Christe*"; Sanctus, and Benedic Agnus Dei; and Communion " *æterna*."

**research'.** An improvisation as a prelude to a composition made up of its chief theme.

**res'ervoir.** The portion of a bel in which wind is stored.

**resin** (rĕz'-ĭn). A refined gum ap to the hair of the bow to improv grip on the strings.

u'tion, **résolution** (rā-zō-lüs-yôṅ), **resolu'tio**, *L.*, **resoluzione** (rā-oo-tsĭ-ō'-nĕ), *I.* 1. Firmness, determination. 2. The dissolving of sonance into concord ; the satisfaction of the mental demand for that tial repose found only in consonance. Dissonant tones are generally solved by progressing half a tone or whole tone down or up.

nance, *E.*, **Resonanz** (rā-zō-äts'), *G.* The sympathetic response a vibrating body to its own particular tone or tones, under the impulse of vibrations received from other vibrating body sounding the one tone or tones. Thus if one unds the note a' on a violin, a tuning-fork of the same pitch will give th the same tone spontaneously, as o will a piano with the damper lal down ; a pane of glass or a se plate of metal of the proper natural will also reply ; furthermore each rtial tone will be affected similarly. is acoustic fact is used for the reorcing of tones ; as cavities of air d sheets of wood have this same property of resonance to all the tones d partials which they themselves ntain. The violin, etc., employ hollow space called the **resonance x**, or **Resonanzkasten**, *G.* Certain old instrs. used a *sympathetic ing* or **Resonanzsaite**, *G.* The ano, etc., use a **resonance board**, *sound-board*, **Resonanz'boden**, *G.* iro (rā-spē'-rô), *I.* "A breath"; sixteenth rest.

ond'. A psalm (or part of one) ng between lessons at canonical urs.

onse', *E.*, **respon'sum**, *L.*, **respon-o'ne**, **respon'so**, *I.* 1. The reply of oir or congregation to a phrase read chanted by a priest or officiant, in , C. and Episcopal churches. 2. esponsory. 3. The answer in fugue. on'sory, *E.*, **responso'rium**, *L.* 1. he psalm or portion of one sung between Missal lessons. 2. The gradue. 3. A respond.

**responsivo** (rā-spôn-sē'-vō), *I.* Responsive(ly).

**resserrement** (rŭs-sĕr-mäṅ), *F.* Stret

**ressort** (rŭs-sôr'), *F.* Bass-bar.

**rest.** 1. A period of rhythmic silence, the tempo continuing to be counted passively. 2. A symbol indicating such rest. The rests are usually named according to the portion of a measure they occupy, as 16*th rest ;* sometimes being called after the note which has the same duration, as *quarter-note rest, breve rest.* They may be augmented by dots and may extend beyond the limits of one measure, as the *four-measure rest.* Vide SIGNS AND SYMBOLS. **large-rest, long-rest.** Vide NOTATION.

**restric'tio**, *L.* Stretto.

**result'ant.** Used of secondary tones formed by the combined vibration of two independent tones. Vide ACOUSTICS. When sounded together they produce a *difference tone* or *differential tone* whose vibration equals the difference between theirs ; also a *summational tone* whose vibration is the sum of theirs.

**Resurrex'it**, *L.* "And rose again." Part of the Credo. Vide MASS.

**retard'.** 1. To diminish the velocity. 2. To suspend and then resolve upwards, hence **retarded progression,** or **retarda'tion, retarda'tio**, *L.* 1. A suspension resolving upwards. 2. A decrease in velocity.

**retraite** (rŭ-trĕt'), *F.* Retreat, tattoo.

**ret'ro**, *L.* Backwards. Vide CANON.

**ret'rograde, retrogra'dus**, *L.*, **retrogrado** (rā-trō-grä'-dō), *I.* Vide IMITATION.

**ret'to**, *I.* Direct, similar. Vide MOTION.

**réveil** (rā-vĕ'), *F.*, **reveille** (rŭ-vā'-yŭ, in *E.* rĕ-vĕl'-yĕ. In the American army rĕv-ĕ-lē', in *G.* rā-fil'-lĕ). "Awakening," the first morning military signal. In old *E.* **reveill'**, or **revel'ly.**

**rev'erie.** A contemplative composition.

**reversed.** Contrary (of motion). **re-ver'sion.** Retrograde imitation.

**revoice.** To tune an organ-pipe.

**rf., rfz.** Abbr. for **Rinforzando.**

**r. h.** Abbr. for right hand.

**rhapsodie** (răp-sō-dē'), *F.* and *G.*, **rhap'sody,** *E.* " A song of patches." In ancient music a fragment of an epic poem, sung by a minstrel or rhapsode, or rhapsodist. In modern music a brilliant composition which combines the idea of a medley with the acquired idea of great joy or ecstasy.

**rhythm,** *E.*, **rhyth'mus,** *L.* (in *G.* rēt'-moos), **rhythme** (rēdhm), *F.* The " flow " and undulation of progression, marked by the rise and fall of stress and duration. The arrangement of accented and unaccented, and of long and short sounds. Rhythm usually follows some pattern which is repeated with more or less variation through an entire movement or composition. Rhythm might be called the melody of monotone. It is distinct from melodic or harmonic progression, and can be vividly shown on such an instr. as the drum, and it can be written on a single line without reference to pitch. The rhythm sometimes is so complicated that it is not completed in less than a musical period, vide FORM ; but it is usually based upon a fundamental series of pulsations that can be expressed within the limits of three or four or nine beats. These are accordingly taken as a unit and grouped within the limits of a *measure*, and cut off by two bars ; the first bar being placed before the strongest accent of the group, the second after the weakest. Time may be expressed by the regular swing of a bâton ; rhythm embellishes this bâton pulsation, and usually coincides with it in accentuation, except in a syncopated rhythm.

**rhythmique** (rēdh-mēk), *F.*, **rhythmisch** (rēt'-mĭsh), *G.* Rhythmical.

**ribattuta** (rē-băt-too'-tä), *I.* " Restriking." The slow beginning of a trill.

**ribe'ba, ribeca** (rē-bä'-kä), *I.* Ret **ribbechino** (kē'-nō). Small Ret

**ribs.** The sides connecting back belly of violins, etc.

**ricerca're, ricercata** (rē-chĕr-kä' *I.*, **ricercar** (rē-tsĕr-kär'), " Searched out," cf. *récherché.* of compositions or passages, us of fugal form, and employing al resources and learning of the poser. Vide FUGUE.

**richiamare** (rē-kĭ-ä-mä'-rĕ), *I.* imitate the **Richia'mo** or bird-ca

**ricordanza** (rē-kôr-dän'-tsä), *I.* ollection.

**riddo'ne,** *I.* A roundelay.

**ridevolmente** (rē-dä'-vōl-mĕn'-tĕ) Laughingly.

**ridicolosamen'te,** *I.* Ridiculous

**rid'dle-canon.** Vide CANON.

**ridot'to,** *I.* 1. Reduced (cf. **reducir** 2. A reduction.

**riduzione** (rē-doo-tsĭ-ō'-nĕ), *I.* rangement, reduction.

**Riesenharfe** (rē'-zĕn-här-fĕ), *G.* lian harp.

**rifiormento** (rē-fĭ-ôr-mĕn'-tō), *I.* nament.

**riga** (rē'-gä), *I.* Staff.

**rigabel'lo,** *I.*, **rigabel'lum,** *L.* Re

**rigadoon',** *E.*, **rigaudon, rigodon** gō-dôń), *F.* A lively and humo dance of Provençal origin, and sisting of three or four reprises, third in a lower position. The is usually 4-4, with an uptake o quarter note.

**rigals, rigol(e)s.** Regals.

**rigore** (rē-gō'-rĕ), *I.* Rigour, ex ness of tempo. **rigoro'so.** Exa

**rilasciando** (rē-lä-shän'-dō), *I.* laxing the speed. **rilasciar** With reduced speed.

**rikk.** Egyptian tambourine.

**rilch** (rĭlsh), **ril'ka.** Russian lute.

**rimett.** Abbr. for **rimettendo,** *I.* tarding.

**rinforzare** (rĭn-fôr-tsä'-rĕ), *I.* To inforce, emphasise. **rinforzamen rinforzo** (fôr'-tsō). Reinforcem **rinforzan'do, -a'to.** Suddenly phasised and accented.

**elpauke** (rĭng'-ĕl-pow-kĕ), *G.* A
le with rings on bars.

**eltanz** (rĭng'-ĕl-tänts), *G.* Circu-
dance.

**cussio'ne,** *I.* Repercussion.

**izione** (rē-pā-tē-tsĭ-ō'-nē), **ripet-
ra** (too'-rä), *I.* 1. Repetition. 2.
frain.

**no,** pl. **-i** (rē-pē-ā'-nō[ē]), *I.*
"illing." 1. Used of a part or an
tr. which merely strengthens and
unds out the harmony, as opposed
*solo* or *concertante.* 2. Used in
res to indicate the entrance of the
l band. One who plays a ripieno
*G.* **Ripienstimme,** rē-pĭ-ān-
ĭm-mě) is called **Ripienist,** or **ri-
enis'ta.** 3. A mixture-stop called
**ieno** *di due, tre, quattro* or *cinque,*
:ording as it has 2, 3, 4, or 5 ranks.
**nino** (nē'-nō). 4-ft. stop.

**liare** (rē-pēl-yä'-rě), **ripren'dere**
ěn'-dě-rě), *I.* To resume, hence,
**iglan'do, riprenden'do.** Resum-
. **ripiglio** (rē-pēl'-yō). Reprise.

**so,** *I.* Repose, hence **riposa'to**
'-tō), **reposatamen'te.** Repose-
ily.)

**esa** (rē-prā'-zä), *I.* 1. Reprise.
Repeat. 3. The repeat mark.

**utito** (rē-sěn-tē'-tō), *I.* With en-
etic expression.

**uzione** (rē-zō-loo-tsĭ-ō'-ně), *I.*
solution, 1 and 2. **risoluto** (loo'-
, **risolutamen'te.** Decided(ly),
ergetic(ally).

**anza, risuonanza** (rē-soo-o-nän'-
), *I.* Resonance.

**osta** (rēs-spō'-stä), *I.* 1. Conse-
ent. 2. Answer in fugue.

**,** *G.* "Gap," between registers.

**et'to,** *I.* Stretto.

**egliato** (rēs-vāl-yä'-tō), *I.* Ani-
ated.

**ritard.** Abbr. for **ritardando** (rē-
-dän'-dō). Retarding gradually.
**ardato** (dä'-to). Retarded. **ri-
r'do, -azio'ne.** Retardation.

**a.** Abbr. for **ritenuto** (rē-tā-noo'-
), *I.* Immediately slower, to be
stinguished from *ritardando* and
:lentando as well as from **ritenen-**

**do,** and **ritenen'te,** which refer to
gradual retardation.

**ritmo** (rēt'-mō), *I.* Rhythm. **r. di
due (tre) battute** (dē doo-ā-bät-too'-
tä). Rhythm in 2 (or 3) *measures* to
the beat, not in duple or triple time,
which means 2 (or 3) beats to the
measure. **ritmico.** Rhythmic.

**ritornare** (rē-tôr-nä'-rě), *I.* To return.
**ritornan'do.** Returning. **ritorna-
to** (ä'-tō). Reverted.

**ritornel', ritornel'lo,** *I.,* **ritour-
nelle** (rē-toor-nĕl'), **ritornelle,** *F.*
1. A burden or repeated portion, such
as the instrumental prelude, inter- and
post-lude of a song, sometimes called
the symphony. 2. The tutti parts in
a concerto. 3. A repeat. 4. A
burden, or refrain.

**river'so, riverscio** (rē-věr'-shō), *I*
1 Reversed. 2. Retrograde.

**rivoglimento** (rē-vōl-yĭ-měn'-tō), *I.*
Inversion or transposition, in counterpoint. **rivoltato** (rē-vôl-tä'-tō),
**rivolto** (rē-vôl'-tō). Inversion.

**robusto** (rō-boos'-tō), *I.* Robust. Vide
TENOR. **robustamen'te.** Firmly.

**roccoco, rococo** (rō-kō'-kō), *I.* Old-
fashioned, eccentric.

**rock-harmon'icon.** A graduated series
of rock crystals played with hammers.

**Roger de Coverley.** Vide SIR R. DE
C.

**Rohr** (1ōr), pl. **Röhre** (rā'-rě), *G.* 1
Tube. 2. Reed, usually **R.-blatt.**
reed of oboe, bassoon and clarinet.
**R.-flöte.** "Reed-flute" a half-cov-
ered 4, 8 or 16 ft. flue-stop. **R.-
schelle** (shĕl-lě). The same stop in
1 or 2 ft. pitch. **Doppelröhrflöte.**
One with double mouth. **R.-quint.**
One sounding a fifth above. **Rohr-
werk.** The reed-stops.

**roll** (rōl), *E.,* **rollo** (rôl'-lō), *I.* 1. The
trill on drum or tambourine, produced
on the kettle-drum by rapid taps with
the two sticks ; on the side-drum with
two taps with the left stick, then two
with the right ; on the tambourine
with the knuckles. 2. **long r.** (a)
Battle or rally signal for troops. (b)

Swift arpeggio on the organ. **rollan'-do.** Rolling.

**Rolle** (rôl'-lĕ), *G.* Rapid up-and-down passages of one figure.

**roller.** 1. A 2-armed wooden bar on gudgeons connecting two trackers, one to a draw-stop, one to a valve, usually **roller-board.** 2. Cylinder of music-box or carillon.

**Roman.** 1. Used of the school of Rome from Goudimel and Palestrina to the 19th century. 2. Of strings made in Italy.

**romance** (in *F.* rō-mäns), **romanza** (rō-män'-tsä), *I.,* **Romanze** (rō-män'-tsĕ), *G.,* **romaunt,** Old *E.* 1. A composition of romantic character, as *r. sans paroles,* a story without words. 2. In *F.* a love-song.

**romanesca** (rō-mä-näs'-kä), *I.,* **roman-esque** (rō-mǎn-ĕsk'). The galliard.

**romantic, romantique** (rō-mǎn-tĕk), **romanzesco** (tsäs'-kō). A term much fought for and much evaded. In general, it means the striving after individuality, novelty, and personality of musical expression as opposed to the repetition of classic forms—the reaction of the molten against the mold. As every generation tries to modify, assimilate and re-spin the art of the preceding, and always meets an opposition from the schoolmen and conservatives, the word really means little more than " modern."

**Rome, prix de** (prē dŭ rôm), *F.* 1. A stipend granting four years' study in Rome, annually awarded by the French government to competing pupils of the Paris Conservatoire. This is the **grand prix** (grän prē), the **second** (sŭ-kôn) being a gold medal. 2. Stipend awarded every other year by the Brussels Cons.

**romera** (rō-mä'-rä). A Turkish dance.

**Romanusbuchstaben** (rō-mä'-noos-bookh'-shtä-bĕn), *G.* " Letters of Romanus." Vide LITTERÆ SIGNIFI-CATÆ.

**ro'mischer Gesang',** *G.* " Roman " Catholic plain-song.

**ron'da,** *I.* Round.

**ronde** (rônd), *F.* A whole note.

**rondel'lus.** An early form of imitation.

**rondeau** (rôn-dō), *F* , **ron'do** (rôn *I.* and *E.* 1. A form originally on a dance with alternating (couplets), and chorus (rondeaux form is characterised by a ch humour. 2. In classic music a cipal subject preceding and inte ing two episodes, with much var of key and many bridge-passage The more modern form consis three themes with the first recu thus A–B–A–C–A–B and coda. second theme appears in the dom at first, finally in the tonic, g the Rondo a close relation wi sonata formula. Vide FORM. A or easy rondo is called various **mignon** (mēn-yôn), *F.,* **rond ta, rondinet'to, rondino** (rô nō), **rondolet'to.**

**rondeña** (rôn-dän'-yä), *Sp.* Fand

**root.** Fundamental tone of a cho

**rosalia** (rō-zä'-lĭ-ä), **Rosalie** (rō-z *G.* 1. A sequence (q. v.) adva a whole tone each time. 2. consisting of cheap and trite sequ and harmonies.

**rose** (in *G.* rō'-zĕ), **rosa** (rō'-zä **rosette** (rō-zĕt'), *F.* The ornam border of the sound-hole of guitar

**rosin** (räz'-ĭn). Resin.

**Rostral** (rôs'-träl), *G.* A music-p

**rote,** *E.,* **ro'ta, rot'ta,** *I.,* **Rot't** " Wheel." 1. Canon, round. Rondeau 3. Hurdygurdy.

**rotondo** (rō-tôn'-dō), *I.* Round, **rot'to,** *I.* Broken, interrupted.

**ro'tula.** A small round or carol.

**roulade** (roo-läd), *F.* A florid pas division, a grace.

**roulement** (rool-män), *F.* A roll.

**round.** 1. Popular form of canon i unison or octave, without coda, with a frequent harmonic suppo *pes.* 2. A circle-dance. **round** A rondo.

**round'el, roun'delay.** A ballad o fourteenth century with a re u refrain. Also a ring-dance.

sciamento (rō-vā-shä-měn'-tō) *I.*, Reversion. 2. Inversion.

scio (rō-vā'-shō), *I.* 1. Retro-de. 2. Inverted. Hence, **al r.** inversion.

..a. Hindu violin.

to (roo-bä'-tō), *I.* " Robbed," rowed, used of a tempo whose ct values are to be disregarded at rice, the long notes stealing time m the short, etc. It should not de-t so far from the tempo as to de-oy the sense of rhythm.

fall (rük'-fäl), *G.* Back-fall.

ck - positiv'. Vide POSITIVE.

ck'gang. Return of the leading me.

kung (rük'-oongk), *G.* 1. Synco-tion. 2. Change.

enhorn (rü'-děn-hôrn). Vide HIEF-RN.

rung (rü'-roongk), *G.* Emotion.

epunkt (roo'-ě-poonkt), *G.* Rest. stelle, -zeichen. A pause t.

g (roo'-ĭkh), *G.* Calm, gentle.

rtrommel (rür'-). An old-fash-ed drum.

1. Old name for line. 2. In sic as in science, not an edict by authority, but a recorded observa-n by more or less qualified judges what has happened with some reg-rity before. It need not neces-ily happen always again. Vide TAVE.

n'do, rullante (rool-län'-tě), *I.* lling. tamburo r. Side-drum.

1. A rapid flight of notes usually scales, used in singing on one syl-le. 2. Of air in an organ, to leak m the wind-chest into a groove, ere it causes certain pipes to give aint sound called **running**.

dgedicht (roont'-gě-dĭkht), *G.* 1. ndo. 2. Solo with chorus. Also -gesang.

e (rüs), *F.* Russian. **à la r.** In ssian style.

spfeife, **Ruszpfeife** (roos'-pfī-fě), **ruispipe** (rois'-pē-pě), *Dutch.* de RAUSCHQUINTE.

**Rus'sian bassoon.** A deep-toned military instrument.

**Russian horn band.** One in which each horn plays but one tone.

**rustico** (roos'-tĭ-kō), *I.* Rural, rustic.

**Rutscher** (root'-shěr), *G.* A galop.

**ruvido** (roo'-vĭ-dō), **ruvidamen'te**, *I.* Rough(ly).

**ry'mour.** Old *E.* Minstrel

**rythme, rythmé,** *F.* Same as *rhythm(é)*.

## S

**S** Abbr. (*dal*) *segno; senza* (*pe-dale*); *sinistra; solo; sordino,* (*volti*) *subito.*

**sab(b)eca.** Hebrew harp.

**sabot** (să'-bō), *F.* 1. A disk turned by one of the pedals of a double-action harp and carrying two studs which engage and shorten the vibrating portion of a string. 2. A cheap fiddle.

**saccade** (săk-kăd), *F.* A firm pressure of the bow against two or more strings.

**sack'but, sag'but.** 1. An old instr. resembling the trombone. 2. Translation of sabeca.

**Sackpfeife** (säk'-pfī-fě), *G.* A bag-pipe.

**sacque-boute** (săk-boot), *F.* Sackbut.

**sa'cring-bell.** Small bell marking the divisions of the Mass.

**sac'rist.** Music librarian, and copyist of a church.

**sa'cred music.** Religious music.

**Saite** (zī'-tě), pl. **Saiten,** *G.* String (s). **Sai'teninstrument.** A stringed instrument. **S.-chor.** A group of strings tuned in unison. **S.-fessel,** or **-halter.** Tailpiece. **S.-harmo'-nika.** A key-board instr. with diminuendo device, inv. by Stein, 1788. **S.-orgel.** A trichord piano with a fourth string for each note. This string is fanned by a reed of the same pitch, with leather head, thus obtaining a sustained tone, capable of swell and decrease. Treadles and bellows control this part of the instr., which may

serve as piano, or organ, or both, or
part of either. This instr. was inv.
by a Prussian, Karl Gümbel, 1890.
**S.-klang**, or **-ton**. The sound of a
string. **S.-spieler**. Player on a
stringed instr. **saitig** (zī'-tĭkh).
Stringed.

**saint's bell.** Vide SACRING-BELL.

**sal'amie.** Oriental flute.

**salcional** (săl-sĭ-ō-năl). **salicet** (sä-lĭ-sä). **sali'cionell, salicional** (să-lē'-sĭ-ō-năl), _F._ A reed-stop of stringy
tone.

**Salm** (sälm), _G._, **salmo** (säl'-mō), pl. **i**,
_I._ A psalm.

**salmi** (säl'-mē), _F._ Quodlibet.

**Salon'flügel**, _G._ Parlour grand piano.
**Salonmusik** or **-stück**. Music for
the drawing-room.

**sal'pinx.** Ancient Greek trumpet.

**saltando** (säl-tän'-dō), _I._ 1. Proceeding by skips. 2. With bounding
bow.

**saltarella** or (**o**) (säl-tä-rĕl'-lō), _I._ 1. A
very quick dance, in 2-4, 6-8, or 6-4
measure with wide skips. 2. The
triple-timed, second part of a 16th
century dance in duple time (also
called _Hop'peltanz_ (tänts). _Nachtanz_,
_G._, _proportio_, _L._, _tourdion_, _F._ 3. A
jack. 4. A _cantus firmus_ with accompaniment of sextuplets.

**saltato** (säl-tä'-tō), _I._ Springing. Vide
SALTANDO.

**salteret'to**, _I._ 1. A rhythmic figure in
6-8 time, the first and fourth quavers
dotted.

**salter(i)'o** (säl-tä-rĭ-ō), _I._, **Salteire**
(zäl-tī'-rĕ), **Saltirsanch** (zäl-tērs'-änkh), _G._ 1. Psaltery. **s. tedesco.**
Dulcimer.

**salto** (säl'-tō), _I._ 1. Leap, skip. 2.
Dance. **di s.** By skip.

**Sal've Regi'na**, _L._ "Hail Queen";
R. C hymn to the Virgin Mary.

**salvar'(e)** (säl-vä'-rĕ), _I._ To resolve.

**salvation** (săl-văs-yôṅ), _F._ Resolution.

**sambuca** (säm-boo'-kä), _I._, **Sambat'**,
**Sambiut** (zäm'-bĭ-oot), _G._ Word used
variously and ambiguously for various mediæval instrs., bagpipe, hurdy-

gurdy, etc. **sambucis'tria.**
who plays such an instrument.

**Sammlung** (zäm'-loongk), _G._ C
tion.

**sampogna** (säm-pōn'-yä), **sampo
sampu'nia**, _I._ 1. A flageolet
Sambuca.

**san'cho.** A negro guitar.

**Sanct'us**, _L._ "Holy." 1. F
movement of the Mass. 2.
SACRING.

**sanft** (zänft), _G._ Soft, mild. **S.
dackt.** A soft-toned stopped
**S.-heit.** Softness, smoothness, ge
ness. **sänftig** (zĕnf'-tĭkh), **sa
müthig.** Soft, gentle. **S.-m
S.-müthigkeit** (mü-tĭkh-kīt).
ness.

**Sang** (zäng), _G._ Song.

**Sänger** (zĕng'-ĕr), _G._ Singer(s).
**bund** (boont). A society or cor
tion of singers. **S.-verein** (fĕ
Singers' union.

**sanglot** (säṅ-glō), _F._ "Sob."
old grace in singing, an interjec

**sans** (säṅ), _F._ Without.

**san'toral**, _Sp._ Choir-book.

**santur'.** A Turkish inst., the psal

**saquebute** (săk-büt), _F._ Sackbut

**saraband** (săr'-ä-bănd), _E._, **sarab**
(sär-ä-bän'-dä), _I._, **sarabande** (s
bänd in _F._ ; in _G._ zä-rä-bän'-dĕ)
stately Spanish dance, perhaps der
from the Saracens, and danced
castanets ; it is in slow 3-4 or
time, with the second note us
prolonged through the second
third beats of the measure.

**sarrus'ophone.** A double-reed in
inv. by Sarrus, Paris, 1863. I
made in 6 sizes besides a sopra
and a contra-bass in E♭, and
sembles a bassoon in appearan
trombone in tone.

**sartarella** (or **-o**), _I._ A tarant
like dance in 6-8 time.

**Sattel** (zät'-t'l), _G._ Nut. **S.-mac**
To use the thumb as a nut for
ducing harmonics on the 'cello.
lage. Half-position.

**Satz** (zäts), _G._ 1. Theme or sub
2. Phrase, half a period, the fo

f being the **Vordersatz,** the sec-
, the **Nachsatz.** 3. Section of
novement. 4. Movement. 5. A
position. 6. Style, school, as
ner S. Pure, strict style.

, Burmese harp.

(sō), *F.* Skip. **sauter** (sō-tā).
overblow. **sautereau** (sō-tĕ-rō).
k. sau'terie, Old *E.* Psaltery.
llé (sō-tē'-yā), *F.* Springing bow.
er (sō-vä). To resolve. **sauve-**
**nt** (sōv-mäň). Resolution.
try. Psaltery.

(zäx). A prefix for the numerous in-
tions or improvements of Adolphe
, the Christopher Columbus of
tallic instruments, whose impor-
ce lies largely in the application of
valve-mechanism to old *natural*
ed instruments. **saxhorn.** An
provement in various sizes on the
-bugle and ophicleide, used chiefly
military bands except the tuba
v.). Saxhorns are made in the
owing seven principal sizes (va-
usly named), and are also made a
itone lower than each of the fol-
ing, the compass of each being
en in brackets :

*gles à Pistons :* 1. Sopranino sax-
n (petit saxhorn, petit bugle à pis-
s, piccolo in *Es.* or e♭, [range
' flat]). 2. Soprano saxhorn (con-
to saxhorn, bugle-tenor, Flügel-
n in *B* or B flat) [g–b'' flat]. 3.
o saxhorn (Althorn in *Es.*) E flat
-e'']. 4. Tenor saxhorn (baryton
si♭, Tenorhorn in *B*, Bassflügel-
n), in B flat [E–b' flat]. *Tubas or*
*rbardons :* 1. Bass saxhorn (tuba-
se en *si♭*, Basstuba, Euphonium,
yton, Tenorbass in *B*) in B flat
–b' flat], also made in C. 2. Low
ss saxhorn (bombardon in *mi♭*) in
flat [G, flat–e' flat], also made in
3. Contrabass saxhorn (bombar-
en *si♭* grave, Kontrabasstuba)
B flat [E flat–b flat], also in C.
**x'ophone.** A keyed brass instr.
gle-reeded and mouthed like a clar-
t and combining in its tone that
the 'cello, cor anglais and clarinet.

It is a transposing instr. written in
the G clef, made in six sizes with two
keys to each, the compass being nearly three octaves : 1. Sopranino or
piccolo or aigu in *F* and *E♭.* 2. Soprano in *C* and *B♭.* 3. Contralto in
*F* and *E♭.* 4. Tenor in *C* and *B♭.*
5. Barytone in *F* and *E♭.* 6. Bass
in *C* and *B♭.* Also **saxofo'nia,** *I.*
**sax'otromba.** An instr. in seven
sizes standing in tone between the
key-bugles, or saxhorns, and the
horns. **sax-tuba.** Vide SAXHORNS
(*Tubas*).

**saynete** (sä-ē-nā'-tĕ), *Sp.,* **saynete**
(sĕ-nĕt), *F.* Comedietta for two singers.

**sbalzo** (sbäl'-tsō), *I.* Skip. **sbalzato**
(tsä'-tō). Dashing.

**sbar ra,** *I.* Bar. **s. doppia.** Double-bar.

**scagnello** (skän-yĕl'-lō), *I.* Bridge.

**scala** (skä'-lä), *I.* Scale, gamut.

**scald.** Scandinavian poet-musician.

**scale.** From the Latin *scala* "a ladder," applied to the Aretinian syllables, ut, re, mi, fa, sol, la. In
modern usage : 1. The tones of any
key (q. v.) taken in succession up or
down according to pitch ; according
to Riemann a chord of the tonic
with passing notes, as *c,* d, *e,* f,
*g,* a, b, and *c,* those passing notes being chosen which lead most inevitably
to the next chord-note. **chromatic,**
**diatonic, enharmonic, major,**
**minor, pentatonic,** etc., **scales,** vide
the adjectives. Vide also MODES. The
so-called **German s.** is a–h–c–d–e–f–
g ; "b," being reserved for b♭. Vide H.
**natural** or **normals.** That of the key
of C, which has no chromatics. 2. A
series of semitones in successive order. 3. The series of tones belonging to any instr. as a natural horn,
**harmonic** or **natural s.** The series
of over-tones (vide ACOUSTICS). 4.
A compass or range. 5 Dimensions
and proportions, as the **s.** of organ-
pipes, determined by the ratio of
diameter to height, a **broad s.** giving a broad, smooth tone, a **narrow**
**s.** giving a thin, sharp tone.

**scannet'to, scanel'la** (skä-něl'-lä), *I.* Bridge.

**scemando** (shě-män'-dō), *I.* Diminishing.

**scena** (shā'-nä), *I.*, **scène** (sěn), *F.*, **scene** (sēn), *E.* The portion between the entrances of different actors, hence a dramatic recitative usually followed by an aria, often **s. d'entrata** or **d'entrée** (dän-trä). Entry-song. **scenic music.** Dramatic music.

**Schablonen** (shäp-lō'-něn), *G.* Stencil-patterns, hence **S.-musik.** Trite and formal music. **S.-haft** (häft). Academic.

**Schäfer** (shā'-fěr), *G.* Shepherd. **S.-lied** (lēt). Pastoral song. **S.-pfeife.** Shepherd's pipe. **S.-tanz.** Rustic dance.

**schalkhaft** (shälk'-häft), *G.* Sportive, roguish.

**Schall** (shäl), *G.* Sound, ringing, resonance. **S.-becher, S.-horn, S.-stück,** or **S.-trichter.** Bell (of an instr.). **S.-becken,** *G.* Cymbals. **S.-loch.** Sound-hole. f.-hole. **S.-stab** (shtäp). Triangle.

**Schalmay, Schalmei** (shäl'-mī), *G.* 1. Shawm. 2. Chalumeau. 3. A reed-stop.

**Schanzune** (shän-tsoo'-ně), *G.* Chanson.

**scharf** (shärf), *G.* 1. Sharp. 2. Acute, of a stop.

**schaurig** (show'-rĭkh), *G.* Weird, ghastly.

**Schauspiel** (show'-shpēl). *G.* Dramatic piece. **Schauspieler.** Actor.

**Scheitholt** (shīt-hōlt), *G.* Marine trumpet.

**Schellen** (shěl'-lěn), *G.* Bells, jingles. **S.-baum** (bowm). "Jingle-tree"; Crescent.

**Scherz** (shěrts), pl. **en,** *G.,* **scherzo** (skěr'-tsō). pl. **i,** *I.* "Jest." 1. A style of instrumental composition in which humour prevails (though those of Chopin are merely moody and whimsical). Those of Beethoven, the greatest master of this style, are often hilariously funny and provoke audible laughter. 2. A form devel-

oped from the Minuet and by [t]hoven and his successors gen[erally] substituted as the 3d (or 2d) [move]ment of the sonata (q. v.) or [sym]phony. The structure varies gr[eatly] but the time is usually triple. **s[cher]zan'do, scherzan'te, scherz[oso]** (tsä-vō-lě), **scherzo'so,** *I.,* **sc[herz-]haft** (shěrts'häft), *G.* Sportive, [mirth]ful. **scherzosamen'te,** *I.* Ga[y.]

**schietto** (skī-ět'-tō), **schiettame[nte]** *I.* Simp(ly). **schietezza** (tě[d]) neatness.

**schisma** (skīz'-ma'), *Gr.* A minu[te dif]ference between intervals. In a[ny] music, equal to the half of a co[mma] or the 18th of a tone; in m[odern] acoustics, the 11th of a syntonic [com]ma (the difference between t[he] tierce of the 8th quint and the o[ctave] of a given tone). Vide TE[MPER]AMENT, QUINT, and TIERCE.

**Schlachtgesang** (shläkht'-gě-z[ang]) *G.* War-song.

**Schlag** (shläkh), *G.* 1. Stroke, 2. Beat, impulse. **schlagen.** To [strike] **Schlagfeder** (fā'-děr). Plectrum [of an] **instrument.** Inst. of percu[ssion.] **S.-mani(e)'ren.** The stroke [of the] down-beating. **S.-zither.** [The] common zither as opposed t[o the] bow-zither.

**Schlägel** (shlā'-khěl), *G.* Drum[-stick;] hammer.

**schlecht** (shlěkht), *G.* Faulty, [weak.] **Schlechtertaktt(h)eil** (shlěk[hter-]täkt-tīl), *G.* The unaccented [part] of a measure.

**schleifen** (shlī'-f'n), *G.* To [bind,] slur. **Schleifbogen** (bō-gěn). [Slur.] **Schleifer** (shlī'-fěr). 1. Slurred [note.] 2. Slow waltz. **Schleifzeichen.** [Slur.]

**schleppen** (shlěp'-pěn), *G.* To [drag.] **schleppend.** Dragging.

**Schlummer-lied** (shloom'-měr-lē[t]) Slumber-song.

**Schluss** (shloos), *G.* 1. The en[d.] Cadence, also **S.-fall, S.-kade[nz]** note). Fina[l] cadence or note.

**Schlüssel** (shlüs'-sěl), *G.* A clef. [S.-]**fiedel.** Nail-fiddle. **S. G.** The [clef] *g'* occupied by the G clef. **S.-**

closing passage or movement.
**striche.** Double bar. **S.-zeich-**
1. A firmate. 2. Double bar.
**reim** (rīm). Refrain.
**achtend** (shmäkh´-tĕnt), *G.* Lan-
shing.
**eichelnd** (shmī´-khĕlnt), *G.* Coax-
, caressing.
**elzend** (shmĕl´-tsĕnt), *G.* Melt-
.
**erz** (shmĕrts), *G.* Grief, sorrow.
**shaft, s.-lich.** Sorrowful.
**abel** (shnä´-bĕl), *G.* "Beak,"
uthpiece. **S.-flöte.** Vide FLUTE.
**arr** (shnär), *G.* Rattle. **S.-pfeifen,**
**-werk.** 1. Reed-pipes, reed-work.
Regal. **S.-töne.** A series of
gh under-tones exactly paralleling
l drowning the overtones as in
uning-fork vibrating loosely on a
.
**ecke** (shnĕk´-ĕ), *G.* "Snail,"
oll.
**ell** (shnĕl), *G.* Quick, rapidly.
**hnel´le, Schnelligkeit** (shnĕl´-
-kīt). Rapidity. **schnel´ler,** *G.*
Quicker. 2. Inverted mordent.
**hnell´walzer.** Quick waltz.
**llrohr** (shôl´-rōr), *G.* Brass wind-
trument.
**ttisch** (shôt´-tĭsh), *G.*, **schot-**
**che** (*E.* and *F.*, shŏt´-tĭsh). "Scot-
," rather slow 2-4 time round
nce.
**ag** (shräkh), *G.* Oblique.
**eibart** (shrīp´-ärt), *G.* Style.
**hreiber.** Music copyist.
**eiend** (shrī´-ĕnt), *G.* Screaming,
te. **Schreiwerk.** Acute (mixt-
-stop).
**ei´erpfeife.** A sharp 3-rank mixt-
-stop in octaves.
**yari** (shrē´-ä-rē), *G.* 1. An obso-
e wind-instr. 2. Schreierpfeife.
**ttmäs´sig** (shrĭt´-mĕs-sĭkh), *G.*
dante.
**b** (shoop), *G.* Slide (of a bow).
**h** (shooh), *G.* "Shoe"; bridge of
marine trumpet. **S.-plattltanz.**
. Austrian clog-dance.
**iftrommpet** (shwĭf´-trôm-pĕt).
*tch.* Sackbut.

**Schule** (shoo´-lĕ), *G.* A school or
method. **schulgerecht** (ghĕ-rĕkht).
Academic.
**Schultergeige** (shool-tĕr-gī´-khe), *G.*
Shoulder-violin.
**Schusterfleck** (shoos´-tĕr-flĕk), *G.* Rosalia.
**schwach** (shväkh), *G.* Weak,
**schwacher Taktteil.** Weak beat.
**schwächer** (shvĕ´-khĕr). Softer.
**Schwärmer** (shwĕr´-mĕr), *G.* Rauscher.
**Schwebung** (shvä´-boongk), *G.* Waving. 1. Tremulant. 2. Beat (of vibration).
**Schweige** (shvī´-khĕ), *G.* A rest. **S.-**
**zeichen.** Rest-mark.
**Schwegel** (shvä´-khĕl). 1. A wind-instr.
2. A flue-pipe. **S.-pfeife.** A 4 or
8 ft. stop with tapering pipes.
**Schweinskopf** (shvīns´-kôpf), *G.* "Pig's
head." Used of the profile of a grand
piano.
**Schweizerflöte** (shvī´-tsĕr-flä-tĕ).
"Swiss flute." 1. Fife. 2. 8-ft metal
flue-stop. **S.-bass.** The 16-ft. stop
on the pedal. **Schweizerpfeife.** 1.
4-ft. stop. 2. Old name of cross flute.
**schwellen** (shvĕl´lĕn), *G.* To swell,
increase. **Schweller.** The swell.
**Schwellwerk.** Swell-organ.
**Schwellton.** Messa di voce.
**schwer** (shvär), *G.* 1. Heavy, ponderous. 2. Difficult. **S.-mut(h)ig.**
Melancholy.
**Swiegel** (shvĕ´-gĕl), *G.* Schwegel.
**Schwindend** (shvĭn´-dĕnt). Dying
away.
**Schwingung** (shvĭng´-oongk), *G.* Vibration.
**scialumo** (shäl-oo-mō´), *I.* Chalumeau.
**scintillant(e)** (săn-tē-yän(t) in *F.*;
shĕn-tĭl-län´-tĕ in *I.*). Brilliant.
**scioltezza** (shôl-tĕd´-zä), *I.* Ease
**sciolto** (shôl´-tō). 1. Light. 2. Free
(of fugue). **scioltamen´te.** Easily.
**scivolando** (shē´-vō-län-dō), *I.* Glissando.
**scolia** (skō´-lĭ-ä), *Gr.* Festive lyrics.
**scordato** (skôr-dä´-tō), *I.* 1. Out of
tune. 2. Tuned in an unmusical accordature.

**scordatura** (too'-rä), *I.*, **scord'ature,**
*E.* The unusual tuning of an instr.
for special effects, as a violin b-d'-a'-
e'' (Paganini).

**score.** 1. An arrangement of the parts
of a composition with bars drawn (or
" scored ") across all the parts to
connect the simultaneous measures.
**full** or **orchestral s.** One with a
stave to each part, voice or instr.
**close, compressed,** or **short s.** (*a.*)
One with more than one part on a
single stave. (*b.*) An abridged score
or sketch. **piano s.** A compression
of score to two staves for the instruments with two additional staves for
the voice, also **vocal s.** The **organ s.**
has a 3d stave for the pedal. **supplementary s.** Staves pasted on
when the parts are too numerous for
the page. 2. *As a verb,* to arrange
for instrs., hence **scoring** is instrumentation ; **score-reading** or **playing,** the mental transposition of the
different keys and clefs of a full score
into one key.

**scorren'do, scorrevole** (rä'-vō-lĕ), *I.*
Gliding, flowing.

**Scotch scale.** Vide PENTATONIC.

**Scotch catch,** or **snap.** A rhythmic
peculiarity in tunes ; as the placing
of an accented 16th note before a
dotted eighth note with a snapping
electric effect. It is a characteristic
of Scotch music and also of American
negro tunes.

**scozzese** (skôd-zā'-sĕ), *I.* Scotch.
**alla s.** In Scotch style.

**scriva** (skrē'-vä). Written. **si s.** As
written.

**scroll.** The curved head of violins, etc.

**sdegno** (sdān'-yō), *I.* Disdain, wrath.
**sdegnan'te.** Angry. **sdegno'so.**
Disdainful.

**sdrucciolare** (sdroot-chō-lä'-rĕ), *I.* To
slide the fingers along the strings or
the keys of an instr., hence the noun
**sdrucciolamen'to,** and the adjective,
**sdrucciolato** (ä'-tō).

**se** (sĕ), *I.* If, as, etc. **se bisogna**
(bē-sōn'-yä). If necessary. **se piace**
(pĭ-ä'-chĕ). If it please (you).

**sea-trumpet.** Marine trumpet.

**sec** (sĕk), *F.*, **secco** (sĕk'-kō), *I.*
unornamented, cold, sharp.
RECITATIVO. **à tabl**2 **sec** (ä
sĕk). Without accompaniment.

**seccarara** (sĕk-kä-rä'-rä), *I.* Nea
tan dance.

**sechs** (zĕkhs). Six. **S.-achtelt**
6-8 time. **S.-vierteltakt.** 6-4

**Sechs'er, sechstaktiger** (täk-tĭkh
**Satz,** *G.* A passage or period
measures. **sechstheilig** (tī'-l
Six-fold, e. g., in 6 parts.

**sechzehn** (zĕkhs'-tsän), *G.* Six
**S.-tel.** 16th note. **S.-telpa**
(pow-zĕ). 16th rest. **S.-fü**
(füs-sĭkh). 16-ft. pipe.

**second(e)** (in *F.* sŭ-kôṅ(d)), **sec**
or **o** (sā-kôn'-dä), *I.*, **Secunde**
koon'-dĕ), *G.* 1. *As a noun,* (a)
interval (q. v.) between a tone
the next above or below. (b)
voice or part. (c) **secondo.**
part or player in a duet. (d) c
**of the second** (Secund'akk
6-4-2 chord. 2. *As an adjec*
(a) Lower in pitch, as 2d st
(b) Of lower rank or importanc
2d violin. **seconde dessus.**
soprano, **secon'da don'na,** etc
Higher, as the 2d space of a s
(d) Second in order, as **seconde**
subject, etc. **secondan'do.** Follow

**secondaire, temps** (täṅ-sŭ-kôn-ĕ
*F.* Weak beat.

**sec'ondary.** Subordinate (of cl
or themes), related (of keys).

**sec'tio can'onis,** *L.* " The secti
the canon." The mathematica
vision of a string, upon a monoc

**sec'tion.** Portion of a composi
variously used as (a) Half a ph
(b) what is often called a phrase
a group of periods with a dis
completeness. Vide FORM.

**sec'ular music.** Music that is
sacred.

**Secun'de,** *G.* Vide SECOND.

**secun'dum ar'tem,** *L.* Accordir
art or rule.

**sedecima** (sā-dā'-chē-mä), *I.* an
Sixteenth. 1. Interval. 2. Sto

(zā´-lĕ), *G.* 1. Soul, feeling. 2.
nd-post. **Seelenamt** (sā´-lĕn-
۰ or **-mes´se.** Requiem.
Bard or rhapsodist.
(sān´-yō), *I.* A sign :S:. **al s.**
rn), "to the sign." **dal s.** (re-
) "from the sign," to the *Fine.*
(sā´-gwĕ), *I.* 1. Follows, now
ws, as *s. la finale.*—The finale
follows. 2. In a similar manto that which precedes. 3. Go
*s. senza rit,* go on without retard-

ndo (sĕ-gwĕn´-dō), **seguen´te,** *I.*
owing next. **seguenza** (sā-
n´-tsä). A sequence.
dilla (sā-gwē-dēl´-yä), *Sp.* Span-
dance in 3-4 time, usually slow
in minor, with vocal and castanet
uitar accompaniment.
te (sĕ-gwē´-tā), *I.* Plural of
.e.
to (sĕ-gwē´-tō), *I.* Followed,
ated.
ch (zān´-lĭkh), *G.* Longing(ly).
sucht (zān´-zookht), *G.* Desire,
ing. **s.-svoll.** Full of longing.
nsüchtig (zān´-zükh-tĭkh), Long-
y.
zär), *G.* Very much.
ĕ), *I.* Six.
nbewegung (zeit´-ĕn-bĕ-vā´-
ĝk), *G.* "Side-wise," i. e.,
que motion (q. v.). **Seitensatz**
s). A "side-piece"; episode, or
nd subject.
me (sĕz-yĕm), *F.* Sixteenth.
ide (zĕ-koon´-dĕ), *G.* Second.
undi(e)ren (dē´-rĕn) To play a
nd part.
(sā´-lä), *Heb.* A term used per-
s to mark a pause or a place for
priests to blow the trumpets.
)iog´raphy. Notation by signs
otes.
omelodicon (zā-mĭ´-ō-mĕ-lōd´-ĭ-
-. A device inv. by Fruh, 1820,
iding beginners; it consists of a
es of note-heads which the finger
ses, producing the corresponding
.
sĕm´-ĭ), *L.* and *I.* Half. **s. bis-**

croma. 32d note. **semibreve rest.**
Whole rest. **s. chorus.** A chorus
to be sung by half of the voices.
**s. cro´ma.** A 16th note. **semi-
demisemiquaver (rest).** 64th note
(or rest). **s. diapa´son, diapen´te,
diates´seron, di´tonus (or di´tone).**
Diminished or minor octave, fifth,
fourth, third. **semidi´tas.** The
diminution due to a stroke through
the time-signature. **semidi´tone,
semi-fusa,** or **semiquaver.** 16th
note. **semigrand.** Small grand
piano. **s. min´im(a).** Quarter note.
**semipausa** (pä´-oo-zä) Whole rest.
**semiserio** (sā´-rĭ-ō). Serio-comic.
**s. sus´pirium.** Quarter rest. **s.
trillo.** Inverted mordent.
sem´itone, *E.*, **semito´nium,** *L.*, **se-
mituono** (sĕ-mĭ-too-ō´-nō), *I.* A
half-tone, smallest interval written.
semito´nium mo´di. The leading
note. **s. fic´tum (naturale).** A
chromatic (diatonic) half-tone.
semi-tonique (tô-nēk´), *F.* Chromatic.
semplice (sĕm´-plĭ-chĕ), *I.* Simple.
**semplicità** (sĕm-plē-chĭ-tä´). Sim
plicity. **semplicemen´te.** Plainly,
without ornament. **semplicis´simo.**
With utmost simplicity.
sempre (sĕm´-prĕ), *I.* Always, continually, throughout.
sen´net. Old *E.* Repeating a note
seven times.
sensibile (sĕn-sē´-bĭ-lĕ), *I.* Sensitive,
expressive. **nota s.** Leading note.
**sensibilità** (bē-lĭ-tä´). Feeling. **sen-
sibilmen´te.** Expressively.
sensible (in *F.* sän-sēbl). Leading
note, usually **note s.**
sen´tence. 1. An interlude strain in
the Anglican Church service. 2. Short
anthem. 3. Passage, or phrase.
sentimen´to, *I.* Feeling, sentiment.
senza (sĕn´-tsä), *I.* (Without, sometimes followed by the infinitive with
or without **di,** as *s. (di) rallentare,*
without retarding.
separa´tion. 1. A device for keeping
the great organ-stops from speaking.
2. A passing note in a tierce.

**sept-chord.** Chord of the 7th.

**Septdezime** (zĕpt-dä´-tsē-mĕ), *G.* A 17th.

**septet** (sĕp-tĕt´), *E.*, **septet´to,** *I.*, **Septett** (zĕp-tĕt´), *G.* Composition for seven voices or instruments.

**septième** (sĕt-yĕm), *F.*, **Septime** (zĕp´-tē-mĕ), *G.* Interval of a seventh. **Sep´timenakkord.** Chord of the seventh.

**septimole** (mō´-lĕ), **septio´le, septo´le, sep´tuplet,** *L.* and *I.* A group of seven equal notes.

**septuor** (sĕp-tü-ôr) *F.* Septet.

**sequence** (in *F.* sā-käns), **Sequenz** (zā-kvĕnts´), *G.*, **sequenza** (sĕ-kwĕn´-tsä). *I.* 1. The repetition at least three times in succession of a musical pattern, a *melodic* or *harmonic* design, it may proceed chromatically or by whole tones. Vide ROSALIA. 2. A R. C. Church poem (Pro´sa) of the 9th century adopted to the long coda (or sequentia) of vocalising on the vowels of the Hallelujah. In 1568 Pope Pius V. abolished all but these five: Victimae paschali laudes; Veni Sancte Spiritus; Lauda sion Salvatorem; Stabat Mater; Dies irae. These are still in use (vide also the separate titles).

**ser´aphine** (or **-a**). An early harmonium.

**serenade,** *E.*, **sérénade** (sā-rā-nǎd), *F.*, **serenata** (sā-rĕ-nä´-tä), *I.* "Evening music." 1. An open-air concert under the window of the person addressed. 2. An instrumental piece of like character. 3. A dramatic cantata of the 18th cent. 4. A composition in chamber-style of several movements.

**sereno** (sĕ-rä´-nō), *I.* Serene.

**sérieusement** (sā-rɤ-ŭz´-män), *F.* Seriously.

**serinette** (sŭr-ɤ-nĕt´), *F.* A bird-organ used for training birds to sing tunes.

**sering´ɥi** (sĕ-rēn´-gē), *Hin.* Hindu violin.

**serio** (**-a**) (sä´-ri-ō), **serio´so,** *I.* Serious, grave.

**ser´pent, serpente** (sĕr-pĕn´-tĕ), **pento´no,** *I.* 1. Long curved ɥ instr. of coarse tone and comp 2 octaves. It is practically obs having yielded to the tuba. **serpentcleide** is wooden but like the ophicleide. The **co serpent,** descended to E♭. reed-stop.

**ser´vice.** The music for a complet of the solo and chorus numbers in the Anglican Church ritua morning and evening prayer communion: Venite exultemus Deum, Benedicite, Benedictus inus, Jubilate, Kyrie, Credo, San Agnus Dei, Benedictus fui Gloria magnificat, Cantate Do Nunc dimittis, Deus misereatur the separate titles).

**sesqui** (sĕs´-kwɤ), *L.* Latin pref whole, and a half " joined with **ra, ter´za, quar´ta,** etc., it exp a kind of ratio. **sesquialtera** kwɤ-äl´-tĕ-rä) 1. The ratio of fect fifth which ncludes one a half to one (3:2). 2. A 2 to 5 mixture-stop producing the 3d and 5th partials. **sesquino´na,** ser, whole tone (ratio 9:10). **ta´va.** Greater whole tone **s.-ter´tia.** Perfect 4th (3:4) **quar´ta.** Major 3d (4:5). **s.-** **ta,** or **s.-tone.** Minor 3d (3:4

**sesto** (sĕs´-tō), *I.* Interval of a si

**sestet** (sĕs-tĕt´), *E.*, **sestet´to,** *I* tet.

**sestina** (sĕs-tē´-nä), **sesto´la,** sextole.

**sette** (sĕt´-tĕ), *I.* Seven.

**settimo** (sĕt´-tɤ-mō), *I.* Interval seventh. **settimo´la.** A sept

**Setzart** (zĕts´-ärt), *G.* Style of c sition. **Setzkunst** (koonst) composition. **Setzstück.** Cɪ

**seul(e)** (sŭl), *F.* "Alone," solo.

**seventeenth´.** 1. Two octaves tierce. 2. A tierce-stop.

**sev´enth.** Vide INTERVAL, CHOF

**severamente** (sĕ-vär-ä-mĕn´-tĕ Strictly. **severità** (sĕ-vä-rɤ-tä´) actness, strictness.

. 1. Interval of a 6th. 2. Vide
▸RAE 3. A compound stop with 2
ıks a 6th apart.

ta, *L.* Sixth ; interval of a 6th.

te (zĕx'-tĕ), *G.* 1. Sixth. 2. A
▸p with two ranks.

quial'tera. Vide SESQUI.

et', *E.*, Sextett', *G.*, sextuor
x-tü-ôr), *F.* A composition for
voice-parts, or instrs. Usually a
nposition in sonata form for six
truments.

ole, sex'tolet, sex'tuplet, *L.* A
▸up of six equal notes. The false
is a double triplet.

:uple measure. Compound double
asure.

:us, *L.* Sixth.

Abbr. of Sforzando.

ato (sfō-gä'-tō), *I.* "Exhaled.'
ightly executed note. soprano s.
nigh voice.

a (sfôr'-tsä), *I.* Force. sforzan'-
, sforzato (ä'-tō). "Forced," of
·articular chord or note to be struck
h immediate emphasis. If followed
a softer tone, it is sfp., or fzp. sfor-
·e la voce. To overstrain the
ce. sforzatamen'te. Energet-
·lly.

gito (sfood-jē'-tō), *I.* Avoided.
le CADENCE.

ato (sfoo-mä'-tō), *I.* Exhausted
breath).

inacciare (sgäl-lï-nä-chä'-rĕ), *I.*
sing like a rooster (galinaccio).

e. 1. To place anything near
ugh to the tip of a pipe to affect
vibration. 2. To observe grada-
·s of force in executing music.

e. 1. Trill. double s. Simul-
·eous shakes as on sixths or thirds.
·sing s. A short trill. prepared
A shake preceded by introduc-
▸ notes shaked graces. The
·t, backfall, cadent, elevation, and
ble Relish. Vide GRACE.

1. Shawm.

▸. 1. A character (♯) raising the
▸wing note a half-tone ; if in the
·ature, raising every note on the
or space it occupies. The double

s. (×) marks an elevation of two
half-steps. 2. *As an adj.* (a) Too
high in pitch. (b) Augmented or
major (of intervals). (c) With sharps
in the key-signature. (d) Shrill (of
stops). (e) A black piano-digital ;
also white digital regarded as a
semitone above another. to sharpen,
or sharp. To raise the pitch a semitone.

shawm. 1. Ancient Hebrew wind-
instr., supposed to be of the reed
class. 2. An early form of the oboe
with double reeds in a mouthpiece ;
it still persists in the chanter of the
bagpipe. 3. Vide CHALUMEAU.

shem'inith, *Heb.* 1. A stringed instr.
2. Species of music. 3. Section.

shepherd's flute. A short flute, blown
through a lip-piece at the end.

shift. 1. A change of the left hand's
position on the violin, etc. (vide PO-
SITION), half-shift being the 2d
position, whole s. the 3d, the
double s. the 4th. 2. Any position
except the first, hence "on the shift"
and shifting.

shiv'aree. Corruption, probably of
charivari ; a grotesque discordant
serenade with an orchestra of tin
pans, cat-calls, etc., to bridal couples
or to other objects of general ridicule. Philip Hale quotes from Gabriel Peignot's "Histoire morale,
civile, politique, et littéraire sur Charivari, depuis son origine vers le iv*
siècle," the exact make-up of such an
orchestra for a town of 15,000 or 20,-
000 inhabitants ; "12 copper kettles,
10 saucepans, 4 big boilers, 3 drip-
ing-pans, 12 shovels, and 12 tongs, 12
dish covers for cymbals, 6 frying-
pans and pipkins, 4 warming-pans, 8
basins, 6 watering-pots, 10 hand-
bells and mule bells, 4 strings of
bells, 2 tambourines, 1 gong, 1 or 2
empty casks, 3 cornets-à-bouquins, 3
big hunting horns, 3 little trumpets,
4 clarinets (badly keyed), 2 oboes,
ditto, 2 whistles (these will be enough),
1 musette, 4 wretched violins to
scrape, 2 hurdygurdies, 1 marine·

trumpet (if you can find one), 4 rattles, 10 screeching voices, 8 howling voices, 3 sucking pigs, 4 dogs to be well whipped. This is all that is necessary. I can assure you that when all this is vigorously set a-going at the same time, the ear will experience all desirable joy."

**sho'far.** A Heb. trumpet.

**short.** Vide METER, MORDENT, APPOGGIATURA, SCORE, SHAKE, OCTAVE.

**shut'ter.** One of the blinds of a swell-box. Vide ORGAN.

**si** (sē), *F.* and *I.* 1. The note or key of B. 2. Vide SOLMISATION. 3. One (cf. French **on**), almost equal to "**you**," as **si leva.** One lifts, you lift. **si piace.** One pleases, if you please, etc.

**sib'ilus,** *L.* A little flute.

**Siciliana** (sē-chē-lı̄-ä'-nä), or **-o,** *I.,* **Sicilienne** (sē-sēl-yěn), *F.* A Sicilian peasant dance of slow pastoral nature in 6-8 or 12-8 time. **alla s.** In Siciliana style.

**side-drum.** Vide DRUM.

**side-beards.** Vide BEARD.

**Sieb** (zēp), *G.* Sound-board.

**sieben** (zē'-běn), *G.* Seven. **S.-pfeife.** Pan's pipes. **S.-klang.** Heptachord. **Siebente** (zē'-běn'-tě). Seventh. **Siebenzehnte** (zē'-běntsän-tě), *G.* Seventeenth.

**Siegesgesang** (zēkh'-ěs-gě-zäng), or **Siegeslied** (lēt), *G.* Triumphal song. **Sieges marsch.** A triumphal march.

**si(e)fflöte** (zēf'-flä-tě), *G.* A 1 or 2 ft. stop of the Hohlflute species.

**siffler** (sı̄f-flä), *F.* To whistle. **sifflet** (sı̄f-flä). 1. A whistle. **s. de pan.** (pän) Pan's pipes. **s. diapa son.** 1. Pitchpipe. 2. A cat-call.

**Signalhorn** (zēkh-näl'-hôrn), *G.* A bugle. **Signalist** (lēst) *G.* Trumpeter.

**sign, musical.** One of the numerous devices for expressing music visually. Vide chart, SIGNS AND SYMBOLS.

**signatur** (zēkh'-nä-toor), pl. **-en,** *G.,* **sig'nature,** *E.* 1. The tabulation at the beginning of a composition section or stave, showing (a) the key of the piece (*key-signature*), with such

tones as are to be sharpened or tened unless otherwise marked. The governing time or rhythm ( *signature*). 2. In Germany a f̄ bass sign.

**signe** (sēn'-yŭ). *F.* Sign, as **s. dental.** An accidental. **s. de si** (dŭ sē-läṅs). 1. A rest. 2. Vide si

**sig'net.** Sennet.

**sig'num,** *L.* Sign.

**siguidilla** (sē-gwē-dēl'-yä), *Sp.* S dilla.

**Silbendehnung** (zēl'-běn-dā-noo *G.* Singing a syllable to more one note.

**silence** (sē-läṅs). *F.,* **silenzio** (sē tsı̄-ō), *I.* A rest.

**sillet** (sē-yä). *F.* Nut. **petit s.** nut at the neck of violins, etc. g **s.** That at the tailpiece.

**silver trumpet.** Chatsoteroth. instrs. and strings are made of s

**sim'icon,** *Gr.* 35-stringed harp.

**sim ilar.** Vide MOTION.

**simile** (sēm'-ı̄-lě), *I.,* **simil'iter,** *L* ilarly. An indication that a c manner of pedalling or playing be continued till otherwise indi

**simp la, low,** *L.* Quarter note.

**simple,** *E.* (in *F.* sän-pl). 1. Not pound (of intervals). Vide cou: POINT, IMITATION, RHYTHM, ete Plain, easy. 3. Without valves. **plement** (sän-plü-mäṅ). Simp

**sin** (sı̄n), *I.* As far as. Vide SINO. **al.** As far as the.

**sincopa** (sı̄n'-kō-pä), or **-e,** *I.* Sir tion.

**sinfonia** (sı̄n-fō-nē'-ä), *I.,* **Sinfon** *G.* zēn-fō-nē'; in *F.* säṅ-fō-nē Symphony. 2. In early operas, ture. **s. pittor'ica.** Descr symphony. **s. concertan'te,** **certa'ta, concertate** (tä'-tě). certo for many instrs., a co symphony. **s. da cam'era.** Ch quartet.

**singen** (zı̆ng'-ěn), *G.* To sing, to **Singakademie** (ä-kä-dě-mē'), stalt or **-verein.** Vocal socie

**Singart** (zı̆ng'-ärt). Vocal ar **chor.** Choir.

## SIGNS AND SYMBOLS

*(See also* GRACES *and* NOTATION,)

### NUMERALS AND ACCENTS.

3, etc.  See CHORD, METRONOME,
GERING, TEMPO and REST.

a.  See OTTAVA.

8′, 16′.  See FOOT.

②), etc.  See HARMONIUM.

6/8, etc.  See TEMPO.

5
or ⌐,  } See TRIPLET, QUARTOLE,
...·. ,  }  etc.

, b″, B″, etc.  )
or            }
, a³, C₁, C₂, etc.  } See PITCH.
etc.  )

4-tette, 5-tette, etc.  Quartette, Quintette, etc.

1-ma, 2-da, etc.  Prima (Seconda, etc.)
volta.

Man. 1.  The Great Organ.

Man. 2.  The Choir Organ.

⌀, ♯, etc.        )
I, II, II₇, VII⁰, etc.  } See CHORD.

O.  1. Open string.  2. See HARMONIC.
3. Tasto solo.  4. The heel, in organ-
playing.  See below.

## DOTS, COMMAS, CURVES, LINES, ETC.

DOT and NOTATION.

ccato.

Slightly staccato.

- Slightly staccato and marcato.

Very staccato.  Martellato.

— Forte tenuto.

- Placed under notes sung to one
syllable; in Tonic Sol-fa, placed
under the letters.

ermate.

/ Abbreviation indicating a repetition of the figure preceding.
f the previous measure(s) or part
measure.

:S:  Presa.

⊕ ⸕  Segno.

▦▦▦  Repeat.

+ Thumb (pfte.-music).

Sharp, Flat, Natural.

× Double-sharp.

’ or // // or v v  Breathing-place.

— Tenuto.  Pesante.

⏜ Mezzo legato.

⌒ Bind.  Slur.  Tie.

≋ Sign of a measure where no bar
is required.

> ∧ ∨ <  1. Forte-piano (*fp*).  2. Rin-
forzando.  3. Sforzato (*sf*).

∧ ∨ or o ∧ or ‿ ∨  Heel and toe; in
organ-playing placed above the notes
for the right foot; below, for the left.

∧ ‿ ∧  Slide the toe to the next note.

∨ — ∧  Change toes on the same note.

∨ ∨  1. Up-bow.  2. Breathing place.

∧ Down-bow in 'cello music.

⨆ ⨅  Down-bow on the violin.

⨅ ⨆  1. In organ music, alternately heel and toe f the same foot.
2. Bind.

# DICTIONARY OF TERMS

⌐ Notes thus connected are to be played with the same finger or hand; or to be sung *divisi*.

▭ Pesante.

{ Brace.

⌐ or ⌐ Notes so connected are to be played with the same hand, or continue a melody or a resolution from one staff to another.

〜〜 Sign of the continuation of a TRILL (q.v.) or of ALL' OTTAVA (q.v.).

{ Arpeggio. A chord preceded by this mark is to be played broken.

〜 ⁓ or √ Direct.

⁓ Inverted Mordent.

⋏ Mordent.

*tr* ⁓ etc. Trill.

∾ Turn.

✳ ⊕ + Release damper-pedal.

└─┐ or └─┘ A recent improve( marking exactly the points whe pedal is to be pressed and relea

♪ Thumb-position on the 'ce'lo

◁ Crescendo.

▷ Diminuendo.

## NOTES, RESTS, AND SIGNATURES.

KEY SIGNATURES.—Capital letters indicate Major keys; small letters, the re Minor keys which use the same signatures. White notes indicate the tonics of keys; black notes, the tonics of Minor keys.

bar (zǐng'-bär). Singable. **sing-**
**d** (zǐng'-ĕnt). Cantabile. **Sing (e)-**
**uz** (tänts). Dance-song. **Sing-**
**re.** Vocal fugue. **Singmärchen**
är'-khĕn). A ballad. **Singma-**
**e)ren** (mä-nē'-rĕn). Vocal embel-
ıment. **Singschauspiel** (show-
ɔēl). Drama with songs. **Sing-**
**hule** (shoo-lĕ). Vocal school or
·thod. **Singspiel** (shpēl). I. The
·ginal form of German opera in
ɛ 18th cent. Simple tunes were
·en to peasants, etc., florid songs
· the aristocracy. (Vide J. A. HILLER
·the B. D.) **Singstimme.** Voice,
ːal part. **Singstück, Singweise.**
·r, melody.

**hiozzando** (sǐn-gǐ-ôd-zän'-dō), _I._
bbing.

·le-action. Vide HARP.

·le-chant. A simple melody to
ɛ verse of a psalm.

·estra (sē-nǐ-äs'-trä), _Sp._, **sinistra**
n'-ǐs-trä), _L._ (in _I._ sē-nēs'-trä). Left
and). **colla sinistra (mano).**
·ith the left hand. **sinis'trae,** _L._
de TIBIA.

·apace. A five-step dance. Cin-
·epace.

· (sē'nō), _I._ To, as far as; usually
n'al.

·n, _E._, **Sirene** (zē-rā'-nĕ), _G._, **sirène**
ɛ-rĕn'), _F._ I. A mythological be-
·g whose vocal powers captivated
ɛ human beings on whom she
·eyed; hence, a prima donna. 2.
· instr. for counting vibrations.

**Roger de Coverley.** An imaginary
·ntleman of the old school described
· Addison; hence an English coun-
·y-dance in 9-4 time.

·entes (sēr-vänt̪), _F._ Troubadour
·ngs of homage.

·ema (sēs-tä'-mä), _I._ Staff.

·er (zēs-tĕr), _G._ Old 7-stringed
·itar.

·rum, _L._ An ancient inst., con-
·sting of an iron frame with a num-
·r of movable rings; when shaken
· struck it sounded.

·ır. Hindu guitar.

·le. Citole.

---

**Sitz** (zǐts), _G._ Position, place.

**six** (in _F._ sēs). Six. Vide METER;
6-8 time, that in which there are six-
eighth notes, the accent resting on
the first and fourth. **six pour quatre**
(poor kătr). Sextuplet.

**sixte** (sēkst), **sixième** (sēz-yĕm), _F._
A sixth.

**sixteenth note.** A semiquaver; one-
fourth of a quarter note. **sixteentr**
**rest.** A pause of equal duration.

**sixth.** I. An interval (q. v.). 2. A
chord. **chord of the s.** or **s. chord.**
The first inversion of a chord (q. v.),
chord of the **added s. (de la s.**
**ajoutée).** Subdominant triad, with
sixth added as f-a-c-d. Vide ALTERED.
**little sharp s.** The 2d inversion
of the seventh on the second degree.
**extreme s.** Vide EXTREME and
ALTERED. **six-four, six-five,** etc.
Vide CHORD.

**sixtine** (sĕx-tēn'), _F._ Sextuplet.

**sixty-fourth (note).** A hemidemi-
semiquaver. **s. rest.** A pause of
equal duration.

**Skalde** (skäl'-dĕ), _G._ Vide SCALD.

**skim'mington.** A shivaree described
in Hardy's novel "The Mayor of Cas-
terbridge."

**skip.** A progression exceeding a whole
step.

**Skizze** (skǐts'-zĕ), _G._ Sketch, a short
piece.

**slancio** (slän'-chō), _I._ Vehemence.

**slargando** (slär-gän'-dō), **slargan-**
**do si,** _I._ Enlarging, gradually slower.

**slentan'to,** _I._ Becoming slower.

**slide.** I. A movable tube in the shape
of a U, used in the **slide-trumpet,**
**slide-horn,** and the **trombone** (q. v.).
2. A grace of two or more notes
moving diatonically. 3. A portamento. 4. A sliding lath strip which
cuts off a rank of pipes from th wind,
also **slider.** 5. **tuning-s.** ſ ⹀liding
pitch - pipe sounding thirteen semitones. **sliding-relish.** 6. An old
grace, a slide (2).

**slo'gan.** Highland war-cry or rallying
word.

**slur.** 1. A curved line above or beneath two or more notes, which are, (a) to be played legato, (b) to be sung to one syllable, hence **slurred** as opposed to *syllabic* melody.

**small octave.** Vide PITCH.

**smaniante** (smä-nĭ-än'-tĕ), **smaniato** (ä'-tō), **smanio'so,** *I.* Frantic.

**sminuendo** (smē-noo-ĕn'-dō). Diminishing. **siminuito** (smē-noo-ē'-tō). Softer.

**smoran'do,** *I.* Dying away.

**smorfioso** (smôr-fĭ-ō'-zō), *I.* Affected.

**smorz.** Abbr. of **smorzando** (smôrtsän'-dō), *I.* Dying away. Extinguished.

**snap.** Vide SCOTCH.

**snare-drum.** Side-drum. Vide DRUM.

**snuff-box.** 1. A musical box combined with a snuff-box. 2. A famous waltz written for it.

**soave** (sō-ä'-vĕ), **soavemen'te,** *I.* Suave(ly), sweet(ly).

**sobb.** Damping (on the lute).

**sock'et.** The round joint which holds the mouthpiece of a clarinet.

**soggetto** (sôd-jĕt'-tō), *I.* Subject, theme, motive. **s. invariato** (ä'-tō). The invariable subject. **s. variato** (vä-rĭ-ä'-tō), *I.* Variable subject of a counterpoint.

**sognando** (sōn-yän'-dō), *I.* Dreamy.

**soh.** Tonic Sol-fa, for Sol.

**sol** (sōl). 1. Vide SOLMISATION. 2. The note G in France and Italy.

**sola** (sō'-lä), *I.* Alone, solo.

**solem'nis,** *L.* Solemn.

**solenne** (sō-lĕn'-nĕ), **solennemen'te,** *I.* Solemn(ly). **solennità** (ĭ-tä'). Solemnity.

**solfà** (sōl-fä'), *I.* 1. Gamut; scale. 2. A bâton. 3. Time, a *bat'tere la* **s.,** to beat time.

**solfa,** *E.* 1. Solmisation (q. v.). 2. Solfeggio. 3. To sing in solmisation or solfeggio. 4. Vide TONIC SOL-FA.

**solfège** (sŭl-fĕzh), *F.,* **solfeggio** (sôl-fĕd'-jō), *I.* Exercise for the voice in solmisation or on one syllable. **solfeggiare** (sôl-fĕd-jä'-rĕ), *I.,* **solfeggi(e)ren** (zôl-fĕd-jē'-rĕn), *G.,* **sol-**

**fier** (sŭl-fĭ-ā), *F.* To sing a s... gio.

**soli** (sō-lē), *I.* 1. Plural of solo. ... passage played by one perform... each part.

**sol'id.** Of a chord not *broken* (q. ...

**so'list.** Soloist, solo-player.

**solito** (sō-lē'-tō), *I.* Usual. **al s...** usual.

**sollecito** (sôl-lā'-chē'-tō), *I.* Ca... exact.

**solmisation.** "The singing of th... lables *do, re,* **sol, mi,** etc." A v... able method of teaching and sin... scales and intervals ascribed to G... D'Arezzo (or Aretinus). It is a ... venient crutch for those who ar... going far; but must soon be ... carded.

Greek music (Vide MODES) divide... complete scale into groups of ... consecutive degrees or *tetrach...* Guido or a disciple divided it ... groups of six degrees, or *hexach...* It happened that the initial syll... of the six phrases of a certai... miliar hymn to St. John forme... ascending scale of one of these ... chords (the one called *naturale*). ... device was hit upon (as an aid ... weak memories) of using these s... bles as names of the notes; h... the notes of this hexachord beg... be called ut, re, mi, fa, sol, la. ... hymn ran as follows: "*Ut* qu... laxis, *R*esonare fibris *Mi*ra gest... *Fa*muli tuorum *Sol*ve polluti ... reatum, Sancte Johannes.") It ... later found convenient to use t... syllables for other hexachords, th... being movable. A crude form ... modulation was developed called ... *tation.* When the modern s... came into play early in the 17th ... it brought into use the heptac... or scale of seven degrees. A ... syllable *si* was therefore dev... and the so-called *Aretinian sylla...* used for singing in all the keys ... being always the tonic, *sol,* the ... inant, etc. The syllables have ... sisted for primary use and for v...

rcises ever since. In many coun-
es they have been since used as the
inite names of the notes of the
le of C, except that the syllable
(being more easily sung) has dis-
ced *ut* except in France, since its
t use (perhaps by Bononcini), in
73. This is the only change that
s been accepted among the many
t have been advocated, such as
*bocedisation*, or *bodisation* (bo, ce,
ga, lo, ma, ni) of Waelraut, 1550
dro d'Urenna in 1620 proposing
for si), and the *bebisation*, or *labe-
ation* (la, be, ce, de, me, fe, ge)—
irically called *labisation*—of Hitz-
in 1628. The *damenisation* (da,
, ni, po, tu, la, be) of Graun, 1750,
s not for solmisation but for use in
ce of words in vocalising.

(sō'-lō). *I.* 1. As adjective,
alone." 2. A passage or compo-
on for a single voice or instr.
olino **solo** may mean either "vio-
only"; or the solo (i. e., leading)
. **solo-organ.** A manual of the
gan (q. v.). **solo pitch.** A scor-
ture (q. v.) used by a soloist. **solo
artet.** A group of four soloists;
composition for such a group; a
o with 3-part accompaniment. **solo-
p.** Vide STOP. The word is used
compounds of various languages,
**Solo-sänger,** *G.* Solo-singer, etc.
nanie (sō-lō-mä-nē'). A Turkish
te, without reed.
rer (sôn-brä), *F.* To give a som-
, veiled tone.
na (sôm'-mä), *I.* Greatest, high-
, extreme.
mer'ophone. A bombardon-like
tr. inv. by Sommer of Weimar, 1843
so called *euphonion, euphonic horn*).
(sôn), *F.,* son (sōn), *Sp.* Sound.
harmonique (sō-năr-mō-nēk).
armonic.
bile (sō-nä'-bǐ-lě), sonante (nän'-
, *I.* Sounding, sonorous.
re (sō-nä'-rě), *I.* To sound; to
g; to play. **s. alla mente.** To
provise.
ta (sō-nä'-tä), *I.,* Sonate (in *F.* sō

năt, in *G.* zō-nä'-tě). Music "sounded or played" as opposed to music
sung (*cantata*). Originally any instrumental piece, as **s. da chies..**,
For church. **s. da camera.** For
the salon. Later the term was applied
to a group of three to five dance-tunes
of varied rhythms. The treatment
came to be less and less lyrical and
more and more thematic (q. v.). Such
were Bach's organ and violin sonatas.
The very human Haydn added a
lyric interest as contrast in the form
both of counter-themes to the principal theme and of separate movements
of melodious character. Mozart made
no formal change but added more
human interest and warmth. The
sonata now consisted of 3 or 4 movements; first an allegro written on
what is confusedly called the sonata-
form (the editor suggests "sonata-
formula" (q. v.) as a substitute term
for describing the structure of this one
movement, retaining the word "sonata-form" for the entire group of
movements); second, a slow movement; third a minuet; fourth, a rondo,
or finale on the same formula as the
first movement. Beethoven substituted for the minuet a light and witty
scherzo (q. v.); other composers have
made other substitutions. This general group of varied movements and
moods is applied to many forms, notably the symphony, the classic overture, the concerto, the string quartet,
and chamber-music generally, which
are hence said to be "in sonata-
form." The **sonata-formula, son
ata-piece,** or **Sonatasatz** (zäts),
the structure of the first movement,
marks the highest period of classic
formalism. It is described under
Form (q. v.). The word is qualified
in many ways as *grand,* a highly
elaborate form, *double,* for two solo
instrs. A short easy composition with
few movements and little development is called **sonatina** (sōn-ä-tē'-
nä). **sonatil'la,** *I.,* **Sonatine** (zō-
nä-tě'-ně), *G.*

**sonatore** (to'-rĕ), feminine **sona-trice** (trē'-chĕ), *I.* A man (or woman) instrumentalist.

**sonevole** (sō-nā'-vo-lĕ), *I.* Resounding.

**sonetto** (sō-nĕt'-tō), *I.* A composition based on a poetic sonnet.

**song.** 1. A melody for voice. 2. Lyric piece for any instr.

**song-form.** A structure of 3 chief sections, (a) a first theme, (b) a contrasting second theme, (c) a return of the first theme. In poems of many stanzas, the same air is commonly used for all the stanzas regardless of changed language and emphasis. This *strophic* treatment is discarded by more conscientious composers for a treatment in which each stanza is individually set to music with intelligent deference to its meaning. This is the *through-composed* or *durchkomponi(e)rt* (doorkh-kôm-pō-nērt') style.

**song without words.** A lyric instrumental piece.

**sonnante** (sôn-nänt), *F.* A scale of hanging steel bars struck with a hammer.

**sonner** (sŭn-nā), *F.* To sound. **s. le tambour** (lŭ tän-boor). To sound the drum, used of a jarring G string in the 'cello.

**sonnerie** (sŭn-rē), *F.* 1. Chime. 2. Military call.

**sono** (sō'-nō), *I.* Sound, tone.

**sonomètre** (sō-nō-mĕtr), *F.*, **sono-me'ter.** 1. A monochord inv. by Loulis to aid piano-tuners. 2. A sounding-board with two strings for acoustic experiments.

**sonore** (sō-nôr), *F.*, **sonoro** (sō-nō'-rō), *I.*, **sonoramen'te.** Sonorous-(ly). **sonoridad** (sō-nō-rĭ-dädh'), *Sp.*, **sonorità** (sō-nō-rĭ-tä'), *I.*, **son-orité** (sō-nō-rĭ-tā), *F.* Sonority.

**sonor'ophone.** A form of bombardon.

**sonorous** (sō-nō'-rous). Capable of musical sound; sounding.

**so'nus,** *L.* Sound, tone.

**so'pra,** *I.* Over, above, upon, before.

**come s.** As above. **di s.** A[...] **s. u'na cor'da.** On one st[...] **par'te di s.** Higher part. **s.[...] minante.** The dominant. **s.** c[...] **ta.** Upper dominant. **s. to'[...]** Supertonic.

**soprano** (sō-prä'-nō), *I.* (pl.[...] **Sopran** (zō-prän'), *G.* 1. The [...] est kind of human voice, diff[...] from the alto in lying chiefly i[...] " head-register "; this voice is [...] cally a woman's voice, but is [...] found in boys. It occurs natura[...] some men (called *falsetti, a.ti[...] urali,* or *tenorini*), but was obta[...] artificially in others (called *evi[...] castrati*), particularly in the last [...] tury when the eunuch "artifi[...] sopranos achieved marvellous p[...] and agility. The soprano voice[...] an average range from c'–a''(...) PITCH), the tones from f' up [...] head-tones. The voice occasio[...] reaches lower, and often higher [...] this normal range, c''', being no[...] usual. A voice that reaches f''' o[...] is phenomenal (Agujari sang [...] three octaves above mid-C). (...) also **mezzo-soprano.**) Sop[...] voices are divided into the [...] powerful or *dramatic* (*drammat[...]* and the flexible, and light or [...] *legg'iero* (lĕd-jä'-rō) or *lég'er* (lä-[...] 2. The part sung by the highest [...] or the highest instrument. 3.[...] instr. which is the *highest* of its [...] (sometimes an extra high inst[...] called **sopranino**). 4. The posse[...] of a soprano voice. **soprana che[...]** (kôr-dä). The E string of a vi[...] **sopran'ist.** A male soprano.[...] **prano clef.** The C clef on the [...] line of the staff; sometimes use[...] the G clef.

**sordo** (sôr'-dō), *I.* Muffled, v[...] tone. **sordamen'te.** Soft(ly).

**sordellina** (lē'-nä), *I.* A small 4-p[...] bagpipe.

**sor'dine,** *E.*, **Sordino** (sôr-dē'-nō[...] -i,** German pl. -en), *I.* 1. A s[...] tone-softening device, damper or [...] to set against piano-strings, in [...]

nouth of a trumpet, or, on the ridge of a violin. 2. A kit. **con**. In piano-playing "use the soft edal"; in playing violin, horn, etc., use the mute." **senza** (sĕn'-tsä), **s. r s. levato** (lĕ-vä'-tō). "Remove ne mute or damper."

**do'no**, *I.*, **sordone** (sôr-dŭn), *F.*, **sordun** (zôr-doon'), *G.* 1. Obs. bombard of 5 sizes, and 12 ventages. 2. An old stop. 3. In *G.* a trumpetnute.

**gfältig** (zôrkh'-fĕl-tĭkh), *G.* Careul(ly).

**tita** (sôr-tē'-tä), *I.* 1. Entrance aria. . Voluntary for close of service.

**pensione** (sĭ-ō'-nĕ), *I.* Suspension. **ospensivamen'te.** Doubtfully.

**piran'do, sospirante** (rän'-tĕ), **sos-irevole** (rä'-vō-lĕ), **sospiro'so**, *I.* . Sighing, doleful. 2. A sobbing atch in the breath.

**stenen'do, sostenen'te**, *I.* Sustaining the tone.

**stenuto** (sōs-tĕ-noo'-tō), *I.* 1. Sustained, prolonged, retarded. 2. Gradually retarded. 3. Andante.

**stinen'te**, *I.* Used of instrs. with pecial device for sustaining tones. **'to** (sôt'-tō), *I.* Under, below. **s. roce** (vō'-chĕ). In an undertone. **s. lominan'te.** Sub-dominant.

**ubass** (soo-băs), *F.* Sub-bass.

**uf farah.** Oriental reedless windnstrs. in general.

**um.** Burmese harp.

**ufflerie** (soof-flĕ-rē), *F.* The bellows .ction. **soufflet** (soof-flä). Bellows. **souffler** (soof-flä). To blow. **souf-leur** (flŭr), fem. **souffleuse** (flŭz). .. Organ-blower. 2. Prompter.

**und.** Vide ACOUSTICS.

**und-board, sounding-board.** 1. A hin resonant board which by sympathetic vibrations enlarges, enriches and prolongs the tone of the strings stretched across it (as in pianos, the pelly of violins, etc.). 2. The cover of the wind-chest, **sound-body** or box, a resonance box; **s. bow**, the rim of a bell; **s. hole**, a hole in the resonance box to give communication

from the resonance chamber to the air. **s. post.** Vide VIOLIN. **s. register.** A sound-recorder inv. in Paris, 1858. **s. waves.** The alternate condensation and rarefaction of air in vibration (q. v.).

**soupape** (soo-păp), *F.* Valve.

**soupir** (soo-pēr), *F.* A quarter rest. **demi-s.** 8th rest. **quart de s.** 16th rest **huitième** (or **demi quart**) **de s.** 32d rest. **seizième.** 64th rest.

**sourdeline** (soor-dĕ-lēn), *F.* Sordellina.

**sourdement** (soord-mäṅ), *F.* In a subdued manner.

**sourdine** (soor-dēn), *F.* 1. Sordino. 2. A soft harmonium-stop. 3. Céleste pedal. 4. An old spinet.

**sous** (soo), *F.* Under, below. **s.-chantre** (shäntr). Subcantor. **s.-dominante.** Sub-dominant. **s.-médiante.** Sub-mediante. **s.-tonique.** Leading note.

**soutenir** (soo-tĕ-nēr), *F.* To sustain.

**souvenir** (soo-vĕ-nēr), *F.* Reminiscence.

**Sp.** Abbr. of **Spitz.**

**space.** The interval between 2 lines of the staff, or between 2 ledger lines.

**spagnuola** (spän-yoo-ō'-lä), *I.* The guitar.

**spalla** (späl'-lä), *I.* Vide VIOL.

**spanisch** (spän-ĭsh), *G.*, **spagnolesco** (spän-yō-lĕs'-kō), *I.* Spanish. **span-ischer Reiter** (rī'-ter), *G.* Tones made by *running*. **spanisches Kreuz** (kroits), *G.* Double sharp.

**spar'ta, spartita** (spär-tē'-tä), or **-o**, *I.*, **Sparte** (spär'-tĕ), *G.* Partitura.

**spartire** (tē'-rĕ), *I.* To score; particularly to rescore an old work.

**spassapensiero** (pĕn-sĭ-ā'-rŏ), *I.* Jew's harp.

**spasshaft** (späss'-häft), *G.* Sportive(ly). **S.-tigkeit** (tĭkh-kīt). Sportiveness, playfulness.

**spa'tium**, *L.*, **spazio** (spä'-tsĭ-ō), *I.* A space.

**spe'cies.** Kind. Vide COUNTERPOINT.

**Sperrventil**, *G.* Vide VENTIL 2.

**spezzato** (spĕd-zä'-tō), *I.* Divided.

**spianato** (spī-ä-nä´-tō). 1. Legato. 2. Calm.

**spiccato** (spĭk-kä´-tō), *I.* Separated. pointed. Vide BOW.

**Spiel** (shpēl), *G.* Playing : style of playing. **S.-art.** 1. Style of performance. 2. Touch. **s.-bar.** Playable. **S.-leute** (loi-tě). 1. The drummer and fifers of a band. 2. Strolling players. **S.-manieren** (mä-nē´-rĕn). Ornaments, graces. **S.-oper.** Light opera. **S.-tenor**, etc. Light opera tenor, etc.

**Spillflöte**, *G.* Spitzflöte.

**spina** (spē´-nä), *L.* " Thorn," jack, quill of a spinet (q. v.).

**Spin´delflöte**, *G.* Spitzflöte.

**spinet** (spĭn´-ĕt or spĭ-nĕt´), *E.*, **Spinett** (spĭ-nĕt´), *G.*, **spinet´ta**, *I.* Obsolete and small square form of harpsichord, originally called the couched harp, later called **spinet**, from its quills, or **spinae**.

**spirito** (spē´-rĭ-tō), *I.* Spirit, energy. **spirituo´so, spirito´so, spiritosamen´te.** Spirited(ly).

**spirituale** (spē-rĭ-too-ä´-lě), *I.*, **spirituel** (spĭr-ĭ-too-ĕl´), *F.* Spiritual.

**spis´si gravis´simi**, *L.* Hypatoides— the deep sounds of the Greek system.

**spis´sus**, *L.* " Thick ; " full (of intervals).

**Spitz** (shpĭts), *G.* Point (of bow), toe (of foot) **S.-flöte** (flä-tě). A soft stop with pointed pipes. **S.-quint.** Its quint. **S.-harfe** (här´-fě). Pointed harp. A small harp with strings on each side of its sounding-board.

**spondau´lium.** Greek hymn with flute.

**spread.** Open.

**springing bow.** Vide BOW.

**spressione** (ĭ-ō´-ně), *I.* Expression.

**Sprung** (sproongk), *G.* A skip. **s. weise** (vī-zě). By skip.

**square.** Vide ORGAN. **square B.** Vide B. **square piano.** Vide PIANO.

**squil´la**, *I.* A little bell. **squillan´te.** Tinkling.

**srou´tis.** The 22 degrees of the Hindu scale.

**sta** (stä), *I.* " Let it stand ; " i. e., to be played just as it stands.

**Stab´at Ma´ter Do´loro´sa**, *L.* " grieving Mother stood," a hymn the Crucifixion, written by Jacopo 14th cent. Vide SEQUENCE.

**stabile** (stä´-bĭ-lě), *I.* Firm.

**stac.** Abbr. of Staccato.

**staccare** (stäk-kä´-rě), *I.* To staccato.

**staccato** (stäk-kä´-tō), *I.* " Detache used of short, non-legato notes o touch which leaves the key or str immediately. This crispness is mar over the notes by round dots ca **staccato marks** ; it may be m fied by a slur over the dots, or phasised by small wedge-like d **staccatis simo.** As staccato as p sible.

**Stadt** (shtät), *G.* Town, city ; u of a salaried municipal musician **S.-musikus, -pfeifer**, etc.

**staff, stave.** The five horizontal p allel lines on, between, above and low which the notes are placed, pitch of the note being determined the key-signature and the clef, fr which the **s.** takes its name. T usual arrangement is a **bass s.** (w F clef) under a **treble s.** (with clef) ; they form a continuous no tion except for the middle C, whic sometimes given a line, making **11-line** or great **s. s. notation** opp. to alphabetical notation. Gregorian **s.** had 4 lines.

**Stahlharmo´nika** (shtäl), *G.* St bars played (a) with a bow, inv. Nobe, 1796, (b) with a hammer ; m commonly **Stahlspiel** (shtäl-shpēl

**Stamentienpfeife** (shtä-mēn´-tĭ-pfī´-fě), *G.* Vide SCHWEGEL.

**Stamm** (shtäm), *G.* Stem, trunk. **akkord.** A chord in root positi unaltered and uninverted. **S.-t** Natural tone. **S.-tonleiter.** Key C major.

**stampita** (stäm-pē´-tä), *I.* A song.

**Ständchen** (shtěnt´-khěn), *G.* S nade.

**Standhaftigkeit** (shtänt´-häf-tĭkh-k *G.* Firmness.

**stanghetta** (stän-gĕt´-tä), *I.* A ba

**ple.** The tube which holds the
oe's reed.

**k** (shtärk), *G.* Strong, loud. **stär-
er** (shtĕr'-kĕr). Louder.

**ve.** Staff.

**am-organ.** Calliope.

**c'ca,** *I.* A choked and strained
one-production.

**cher** (stĕkh'-ĕr), *G.* Sticker. Vide
RGAN.

**g** (stäk), *G.* Bridge.

**llung** (shtĕl'-loongk), *G.* Position.

**n.** The thin stroke attached to the
ead of a note.

**ntan'do,** *I.* Retarding. **stentato**
ä'-tō). Slow and forced.

**p.** A progression to the adjoining
ote or tone, hence **whole-step,** and
alf-step or **chromatic-step**; a
iatonic-step is a progression to
he next note of the key.

**rbend** (shtĕr'-bĕnt), *G.* Dying
way. **Sterbelied** (shtĕr'-bĕ-lēt).
Death-song.

**so** (stä'-sō), *I.* Extended, prolonged,
low.

**s'so,** *I.* The same. **s. tempo.**
ame time.

**énocire** (stä-nō-sēr), *F.* A finger-
trengthener.

**bbacchiato** (stĭb-bäk-kĭ-ä'-tō), *I.*
Retarded.

**cca'do, sticcato** (stĭk-kä'-tō). *I.*
Xylophone.

**ck'er.** Vide ORGAN.

**iefel** (shtē'-fĕl), *G.* Boot (of a pipe).
**iel** (shtēl), *G.* 1. Stem. 2. Neck.
**ift** (shtĭft), *G.* Jack (of violin).
**il** (shtēl), *G.,* **stile** (stē'-lĕ), **stilo**
stē'-lō), *I.,* **sti'lus,** *L.* Style. **s.
igoro'so,** or **osservato** (vä'-tō).
Strict style. **s. rappresentativo**
tē'-vō). Vide OPERA.

**ll** (shtĭl), *G.* Calm, quietly. **S.-
gedakt.** A stopped diapason.

**imme** (shtĭm'-mĕ), pl.**-en,** *G.* 1. The
voice. **2. Part. mit der S.** Colla
parte. 3. Organ-stop. 4. Sound-
post. **Stim'menssatz.** Vocal
attack. **Stimm'bänder** (bĕnt-ĕr).
Vocal cords. **S.-bildung.** Voice-
building. **S.-bruch** (brookh). Change

of voice. Vide MUTATION. **S.-buch.**
Part-book. **Stimmer.** Tuner ; drone.
**stimmen.** To tune, or voice.
**Stimmflöte,** or **-pfeife.** Pitch-pipe.
**S.-führer.** Chorus-leader. **S.-mit-
tel.** Vocal capacity. **S.-ritze** (rĭt-
zĕ). Glottis. **S.-holz** (hōlts), or
**-hölzchen** (hĕlts'-khĕn), or **-stock.**
Sound-post ; wrestplank. **S.-werk-
zeuge** (vĕrk'-tsoi-khĕ). Vocal organs. **S.-führung** (fü-roongk).
Part-progression. **S.-gabel** (gä-bĕl)
Tuning-fork. **S.-hammer** (häm-mĕr).
Tuning-hammer. **S.-horn.** Tuning-
cone. **S.-keil.** Tuning-wedge. **S.-
krucke.** Tuning-wire. **S.-zange.**
Tuning-tongs. **S.-umfang, S.-weite**
(vī-tĕ). Compass.

**Stimmung** (shtĭm'-moongk), *G.* 1.
Tune. 2. Accordature. 3. Pitch.
4. Mood. **S. halten.** To keep the
key. **S.-bild.** Tone-picture.

**stinguendo** (stĭn-gwĕn'-dō), *I.* Dying
away.

**stiracchiato** (stē-räk-kĭ-ä'-tō), **stirato**
(stē-rä'-tō), *I.* Retarded.

**sti'va,** *L.* Neuma.

**Stock** (shtôk), *G.* Bundle of 30 strings.
**S.-fagott.** Rackett. **S.-flöte.** 1.
Bamboo flute. 2. A flute in a walk-
ing-stick. **Stöckchen** (shtĕk'-khĕn).
Heel (of violin, etc.).

**Stollen** (shtôl'-lĕn), *G.,* pl. Vide
STROPHE.

**stolz** (shtôlts), *G.* Proud.

**stonante** (nän'-tĕ), *I.* Dissonant.

**stone-harmon'ica.** Lapideon.

**stop.** 1. Loosely used for (a) draw-
knob and stop-knob and draw-stop,
which only carry the label and, by
admitting wind, bring into play the
stop proper. (b) A mechanical stop,
which does not sound or speak, but
acts as a coupler, a bell-signal, a
tremulant, etc. Strictly, the **sounding,** or **speaking stop** is a complete
graduated series of organ-pipes of
uniform quality. It is this quality
which gives the stop its individual
name (as *dulciana, cremona,* etc.).
Stops are divided into two chief classes, (a) those with flue-pipes, **flue-**

**work,** or **flue-stops,** and (b) those with reed-pipes (q. v.), **reed-work,** or **reed-stops. flue-work** is again divided, according to the character of the pipes, into (a) the cylindrical open pipes that give the **diapason,** or typical organ-quality, also called **principal-stops,** or **-work ;** (b) covered, plugged, or stopped pipes (without chimneys), **gedackt-work ;** (c) pipes too broad or too narrow of scale to give diapason tone, 3 or 4 sided wooden pipes, and stopped pipes with chimneys.

**stops** are further grouped according to the length of their pipes as 2-ft., 4-ft., 8-ft., etc., the standard being the 8-ft.. or foundation-stops, which are the basis of the organ, and to which the other stops are tuned (vide FOOT).

**stops** which do not produce the unison or the octave of the key-board, but sound the third (tierce), fifth (quint) and such of their octaves as the tenth (double tierce), fifteenth, etc., are called **mutation-stops.**

**furniture, mixture,** or **compound stops** are composed of 2 or more ranks of pipes and produce the octave of the key depressed and also one or more of its other overtones.

A stop may have its pipes *divided* between two draw-knobs. If it has a pipe for every key of the key-board, it is *complete ;* otherwise it is an im-*perfect, incomplete, partial* or *half-stop.*

Some stops are given only to the *pedal ;* or to only one of the manuals ; these are said to be *on* the pedal, *on* the swell, etc. A **solo-stop** is one complete enough in itself to sound a melody. **stopped.** Vide PIPE.

**stop.** 2. A fret, or similar position on an unfretted instr. 3. The pressure of the finger at a nodal point of a string. **double stop.** The stopping, hence sounding, of two or more notes at once on the violin, etc. 4. On a wind-instr. the closing with key or finger of a ventage. 5. On

horns, etc., the inserting of the [hand] in the bell to produce a raised to muffled quality. Such a tone is to be **stopped,** as opposed to op[en] natural.

**stop'fen,** *G.* To stop (of trumpet, [etc.]) **stopftöne** (shtôpf'-tä-ně). Sto[pped] tones.

**stop-knob.** Vide STOP.

**stor'ta,** *I.* A serpent. **stortina** nä). A small serpent.

**Stosszeichen** (shtôs'-tsī-khěn) Staccato mark.

**str.** Abbr. for String(s).

**straccicalando** (strät-chī-kä-län'-[dō], *I.* Prattling.

**straccinato** (strä-chī-nä'-tō), *I.* tarded.

**Strad., Stradivari, Stradivarius,** A violin made by Stradivari (vid[e] D.), A.D. 1650.

**strain.** Section, motive, theme, ai[r]

**strascicando** (strä-shī-kän'-dō), **st**[ra]**cinan'do,** *I.* Dragging, pla[y] slowly. **s. l'arco.** Keeping the [bow] of the violin close to the strings to [slur] the notes. **strascinato** (ä'-tō). S[ee] **strascino** (strä-shē'-nō). A dra[g], slurring race, in slow vocal music.

**strath'spey.** A lively Scotch da[nce] in common time, employing the Sco[tch] snap freely.

**stravagante** (gän'-tě), *I.* Extravaga[nt], odd. **stravaganza** (gän'-tsä). E[c]centricity.

**straw-fiddle.** Xylophone, because [the] bars are often laid on straw cords.

**straziante** (strä-tsī-än'-tě), *I.* Mo[urn]ing.

**street-organ.** Hand-organ.

**Streich** (strīkh), *G.* Stroke (as [of] a bow), hence **S.-instrumen**[t]. Stringed instrs. **S.-quartett.** Str[ing] quartet. **S.-orchester.** The stri[ng] of the orch. **S.-zither.** Bow-zith[er] **streichen** 1. To draw the bow. To cut (as a scene). **streicher** "Stringy" (of the violin quality [of] certain stops). **Strei'cher,** Bo[w] instr. player(s).

**strene.** A breve

**streng** (shtrěng), *G.* Firm(ly), strict(l[y])

epito (strä′-pĭ·tō), *I.* Noise. **stre-
ito′so, strepitosamen′te.** Bois-
erous(ly).

etch. The interval covered by the
ngers of one hand.

etta (strĕt′-tä), *I.* A concluding
assage, or finale, in an opera, taken
1 quicker time to enhance the effect.
et′to, sometimes **stretta,** *I.,* **strette**
strĕt), *F.* 1. "Compressed." In
ugue a closing treatment in which
ubject and answer are so compressed
s to overlap. **s. maëstrale,** or **maestrale.** A strictly canonic **stretto.
.lla s.** In stretto-style. **andante s.
, slow agitato. 2. "Hastened." A
losing movement at increased speed.
·ich** (strĭkh), *G.* Stroke. 1. A dash.
. A cut. **Strichart.** Manner of
»owing.

ict. Used of a composition follow-
ng the most rigid and severe rules.
/ide CANON, FUGUE, etc.

ident** (strē-däṅ), *F.,* **striden′te,
tridevole** (dä′-vō-lĕ), *I.* Sharp,
hrill.

iking reed.** Vide REED.

ing. A sonorous cord made of va-
ious materials, the strings of violins,
»tc., being of **gut,** or **cat-gut** (so-
alled, although made of the entrails
»f sheep). Guitar, etc., strings are
»f brass, copper, or a core of steel
vire or silk, sometimes *covered* (wound
ound with silver or other wire) ; piano strings are of drawn cast steel.
Strings are measured in thickness by
. **string-gauge.** "The strings" is
. general term for the stringed instru-
nents of an orchestra (also **string-
oand,** etc., or **string orchestra).
s. pendulum.** A Weber chronome-
:er. **s. quartet.** 1. A group of four
nstrs. of the violin species, 1st and
2d violin, a viola, and 'cello. 2. All
:he instrs. of these kinds in the orchestra. 3. A composition for these
4 instrs. **s. quintet, sextet,** etc., (a)
:he string-quartet with addition of
some other stringed instr. (as double-
bass), or more of the same kind (as
an extra violin).

The strings of an instr. are numbered
beginning with the highest (or soprano
or chanterelle). **stringy** is used of
tone (such as that of an organ-stop),
which resembles a bow and string
instr.). **open strings** are those
which are not pressed with the finger,
or stopped. **string-organ.** Vide
SAITENORGEL.

**stringendo** (jĕn′-dō), *I.* Accelerating.

**Stroh-** (shtrō), *G.* Straw. **S.-bass.**
The husky lower tones of a bass voice.
**S.-fiedel** (fē-dĕl). Xylophone.

**stroke.** 1. Vide SIGNS. 2. The rise
and fall of a pedal.

**strombazzata** (strôm-bäd-zä′-tä),
**strombettata** (bĕt-tä′-tä), *I.* Sound
of a trumpet. **strombettare** (tä′-rĕ).
To play on the trumpet. **strombet-
tiere** (tĭ-ā′-rĕ). Trumpeter.

**stromentato** (tä′-tō), *I.* Instrumented.
Vide RECITATIVE.

**stromen′to, strumen′to** (pl. **-i**), *I.* In-
strument(s). **s. da fiato** (dä fĭ-ä′-tō),
or **s. di ven′to.** Wind-instr. **s.
d'arco** (där′-kō). Bow-instr. **s. da
cor′da.** String-instr. **s. da tacto.**
Key-board instr. **s. di legno** (di
**metallo).** Wooden (metal) instr.
**s. di rinforzo** (fôr′-tsō). An instr.
used to support or strengthen an effect.

**Stuben-orgel** (shtoo′-bĕn-ôr-gĕl), *G.*
Chamber-organ.

**Stück** (shtük), pl. **Stücke** (shtük-ĕ),
*G.* Piece. **S.-chen** (khĕn). Little
tune.

**Studie** (stoo′-dē), pl. **-ien** (ĭ-ĕn), *G.,*
**studio** (stoo′-dĭ-ō), *I.,* **stu′dium,** *L.,*
**stud′y,** *E.* Vide ÉTUDE and PIANO
STUDIES.

**Stufe** (stoo′-fĕ), pl. **en,** *G.* Step, degree. **stufenweise** (vī-zĕ). By degrees.

**stumm** (shtoom), *G.* Dumb. **S.-reg-
is′ter.** Mechanical stop.

**stürmisch** (shtür′-mĭsh), *G.* Stormy.

**Stürze** (shtür′-tsĕ), *G.* Bell (of horns,
etc.). **S. in der Höhe** (hā′-ĕ).
"The bell turned upwards."

**Stutt′gart pitch.** Vide PITCH.

**Stuzflügel** (shtoots'-flü-gĕl), *G.* " Baby " grand piano.

**Styl** (shtēl), *G.* Style.

**su** (soo), *I.* Above, upon. **arco in su.** Up-bow.

**suabe-flute.** A soft stop.

**suave** (soo-ä'-vĕ), *I.*, **suave** (swäv), *F.* Suave. **suavità** (soo-ä-vĭ-tä'), *I.* Suavity.

**sub,** *L.* Under, below, beneath.

**Subbass** (soop'-bäs) *G.*, **subbour'don.** A double-stopped 16 or 32 ft. stop.

**subcan'tor.** Assistant cantor.

**subdiapen'te.** The 5th below.

**subdom'inant.** The fourth tone of a scale or key.

**Subflöte,** *G.* Sifflöte.

**subito** (soo'-bĭ-tō), *I.*, **subitamen'te.** Sudden(ly), immediate(ly). **volti s.** Turn quickly. **p. subito.** A soft touch immediately after a loud.

**sub'ject,** *E.*, **Subjekt** (soop'-yĕkht), *G.* A motive or theme for development usually followed by an answer, or second (*secondary* or *subsidiary*) subject, or counter-subject. Vide FORM.

**subme'diant.** The sixth tone of a scale or key.

**suboct'ave.** 1. The octave below. 2. Coupler producing the octave below.

**subor'dinate.** Not principal or fundamental, used of chords on the 2d, 3d, 6th, and 7th degrees of a scale, and of all 7th chords except that on the 5th degree.

**subprin'cipal.** Below the pedal diapason, a double open bass 32-ft. stop.

**subsemifu'sa,** *L.* A 32d note.

**subsemi'tone, subsemito'nium mo'-di,** *L.* Leading note.

**substitu'tion.** The resolution of a dissonance in some other part an octave removed.

**substitution** (süb-stĭ-tüs-yôn), *F.* Change of fingers.

**subton'ic.** Leading note.

**succen'tor,** *L.* 1. Subcantor. 2. Bass-singer.

**succes'sion.** 1. Sequence. 2. Progression.

**Sufflöte** (soof-flä-tĕ), *G.* Sifflöte.

**sudden modulation.** Modulation remote key without intermediate mony.

**suffocato** (soof-fō-kä'-tō), *I.* " S cated," muffled.

**sugli** (sool-yē), **sui** (soo-ē), *I.* Vide

**suite** (swēt), *F.*, or **suite de piè** (dŭ pĭ-ĕs'). A set or series of piè Originally a group of dances, th has followed the line deserted by sonata. Strictly it is a cycle seri classic dance-forms in one key. number varies from three to five, o with a prelude. The dance-fo are chosen from the following : mande, courante, sarabande, bou gigue, gavotte, minuet, passep loure, anglaise, polonaise, pava The allemande is usually first, gigue last ; the first dances na were the regular constituents, others being called *intermezzi.* modern suite aims chiefly at light even when extended to the orches and great liberty is now taken keys and forms.

**suivez** (swē-vā), *F.* " Follow " soloist) ; continue similarly.

**sujet** (sü-zhä), *F.* Subject.

**sul** (sool), **sull', sulla** (sool'-lä), *I.* the, near the, as **sul a.** On th string. **sulla tastiera.** Near finger-board (of bowing). **sul po cel'lo.** Near the bridge.

**suma'ra.** A two-piped Turkish flu

**summa'tional tones.** Vide RESU ANT.

**sumpun'jah,** *Heb.* Sambuca.

**sumsen** (zoom'-zĕn), *G.* To hum.

**suonare** (soo-o-nä'-rĕ), *I.* To p sound, ring. **suonata** (soo-o-nä'- Sonata. **suonatina** (tē'-nä). natina.

**suono** (soo-ō'-nō), *I.* Sound. **su armonichi** (är-mō'-nĭ-kē). Har nics.

**su'per,** *L.* Over, above.

**superano** (soo-pĕr-ä'-nō), *Sp.* Sopra

**superdom'inant.** The 6th tone in scale.

**super'fluous,** *E.*, **superflu** (sü-flü), *F.* Augmented.

e′rius, *L.* Higher, i. e., the high-
t part.

eroc′tave. 1. The octave above.
A stop two octaves above the dia-
sons. 3. Coupler producing the
tave above.

erton′ic, *E.*, **supertonique** (sü-
r-tôn-ēk′), *F.* The second tone o′ a
ale.

plican′do, **supplichevole** (soop-
ĭ-kä′-vō-lĕ), **supplichevolmen′te,**
Pleading(ly), appealing(ly).

port′. Accompaniment, reinforce-
ent.

posed bass. The lowest note of
inverted chord (q. v.).

(soor). *I.*, **sur** (sür), *F.* On, upon,
ver. **sur une corde.** On one string.
abondant(es) (sür-ă-bôṅ-däṅ(t)), *F.*
sed of triplets, quintoles, etc.
aïgu (sür-ĕ-gü), *F.* Over-acute.
delina (soor-dā-lē′-nä), *I.* Small
gpipe.

prise. 1. Vide CADENCE. 2. Name
Haydn's 6th symphony with an un-
pected crash breaking in on a long,
ft movement.

dominante (sü-), *F.* Superdomi-
ant.

pended cadence. 1. Vide CA-
ENCE. 2. Vide SUSPENSION.

pen′sion. 1. The holding back of
ne note of a chord with the result
at it causes, with the following
ord, a clash that earnestly demands
s progress to the destined note in
hich it will find resolution (q. v.).
. The note so suspended. A **s.** may
e *unprepared,* that is, it may be the
nly note of a group that is not
roper to a sudden chord. **s.** may
e *double* or *triple,* by occurring in
ore than one note of a group at
nce.

spir′ium, *L.* 1. A quarter rest. 2.
More anciently, a half-rest.

ss (züs), *G.* Sweet(ly). **Sussflöte.**
A soft flute-stop.

(s) **s u r a n d o** (soo(s)-soo-rän′-dō),
su(s)surante (rän′-tĕ), *I.* Whisper-
ng, murmur. **sussura′tion,** *E.* A
oft murmur.

**sustain.** To hold a note during its
full time-value ; to perform in legato
manner, vide also PEDAL-POINT. Vide
PEDAL.

**svegliato** (svāl-yä′-tō), *I.* Lively.

**svelto** (svĕl′-tō), *I.* Light, easy.

**sw.** Abbr. of Swell-organ.

**swell.** 1. Gradual increase (and decrease) of sound. 2. The device for
increasing and diminishing a sustained tone on an organ, hence
**swell-organ,** and **swell key-board.**
Part of an organ (the **swell-organ**),
is surrounded by a **swell-box,** the
front of which is filled with **Venetian
swell-blinds (Jalousie,** *G.*), opened
or closed by a lever worked by a
**swell-pedal.** In old organs, there
was but one shutter (**nag's-head
swell**) ; in harpsichords the cover
moved.

**Sylbe** (zēl′-bĕ), *G.* Syllable.

**syllab′ic,** *E.*, **syllabisch** (zēl-läp′-
ĭsh), *G.*, **syllabique** (sēl-läb-ēk), *F.*
Of an air in which each syllable has
its own note.

**syllable-names.** Do, re, mi, etc., as
opposed to *letter-names,* C, d, e, etc.
Vide SOLMISATION.

**sym′bal.** Cymbal.

**sympathet′ic.** Of strings, etc., which
are made to sound by sympathetic
vibration (q. v.), and strengthen some
other tone by unison or by sounding
some overtone.

**symphone′ta,** *L.* Polyphony.

**sympho′nia,** *Gr.* 1. Agreement. 2.
Hurdygurdy. 3. A symphony.

**symphon′ic,** *E.*, **symphonique** (säṅ-
fō-nēk), *F.*, **symphonisch** (zēm-fō′-
nĭsh), *G.* Pertaining to or relating to
the symphony. **symphonic poem,
poème s.** (pō-ĕm′ säṅ-fō-nēk), *F.*,
**sympho′nische Dichtung** (dĭkh-
toongk), *G.* A composition of symphonic demands on orchestra and intelligence, but not built on the sonata
form and rather descriptive than
thematic. The name was first given
by Liszt to some of his best works.

**Symphonie** (säṅ-fō-nē in *F.,* in *G.*
zēm-fō-nē′). 1. Symphony. 2. Con-

**cord.** 3. Instrumental accompaniment. 4. String-band. 5. Orchestra. **Symphonie-Ode** (ō'-dĕ), *G.* Choral symphony.

**sympho'nion.** 1. A combination of flute-stop with piano, inv. by Kaufmann. 2. A music-box with interchangeable disk in place of a cylinder.

**sym'phonist, symphoniste** (săn'-fō-nĕst'), *F.*, **Sympho'niker, symphonienr²:·ar** (zĕm-fō'-nĭ-ĕn-zä'-zĕr), *G.* A composer of symphonies ; in *F.* also a church-composer, or member of an orchestra.

**sympho'nious.** Harmonious.

**sym'phony, Symphonie** (in *F.* săn-fō-nē', in *G.* zĕm-fō-nē'). 1. A sonata for orchestra with all the elaboration and extension permitted by the larger resources. Beethoven (and followers of him) even added a chorus, hence *choral symphony*. Historically founded on the overture, Haydn, the father of the sonata (q. v.), established the form, which has survived with minor substitutions (as in the sonata) till now. 2. In E. and elsewhere the instrumental pre-, inter-, and postludes, of vocal composition. 3. Old name for hurdygurdy, etc.

**sympo'sia.** Convivial compositions.

**syn'copate.** To perform syncopation.

**syncopato** (sĭn-kō-pä'-tō), *I.*, Syncopated.

**syn'copation,** *E.*, **syncopa'tio,** *L.*, **syncope** (săn-kŏp in *F.*, in *G.* zĕn'-kō-pĕ). A pleasantly confusing rhythmic "intersection" caused by suppressing a natural accent or strong-beat, or moving it from its natural place to a weak beat, usually by means of tie-ing over a note on a weak beat across the time belonging to a strong beat. The note so prolonged is said to be **syncopated.** In piano-music, only one hand usually has the syncopation.

**Synkope** (zĕn'-kō-pĕ), *G.* Syncopation. **synkopi(e)ren** (pē'-rĕn). To syncopate.

**synnem'enon.** Vide MODES.

**synonyme** (sē-nō-nĕm), *F.* Ho phone.

**synton'ic.** Vide COMMA.

**syntonolyd'ian.** Hypolydian.

**sy'ren.** Siren.

**syr'inx,** *Gr.*, **syringe** (sē-rănzh), 1. Pandean pipes. 2. A portion hymn to Apollo sung by candida for Pythian prizes.

**sys'tem** (in *G.* zĕs'-tām). 1. A grou staves. 2. In *G.* a staff.

**syste'ma,** *Gr.* 1. A tetrachord, other interval. 2. In *L.* Staff. Hexachord series. Vide MODES.

**système** (sĕs-tĕm), *F.* 1. All mus tones. 2. Compass.

**syzygi'a,** *Gr.* and *L.* A chord. **perfecta,** or **simplex.** Triad. **composita.** Triad with a tone do led. **s. propin'qua** (*remo'ta*). C (open) chord.

**szopelka** (shō-pĕl'-kä). Russian o with brass mouthpiece.


# T

**T** Abbr. of *Talon, Tasto, Tem Tenor, Toe, Tre, Tutti* **tabal'lo,** *I.* A kettle-drun **tabar** (tä-bär'), *I.*, **tab'ar tab'arte,** Old *E.* A tabor.

**tabl.** Egyptian drum.

**tablatura** (täb-lä-too'-rä), *I.*, **tab ture** (tă-blä-tür'), *F.*, **tablature** (t lä-tür), *E.*, **Tabulatur** (tä-boo toor'), *G.* 1. The Tonic Sol notation. 2. The rules of poetic a musical composition established the Meistersinger. Vide "STORIES THE OPERAS." 3. An early form of tation from which our present syst got its vertical character, the bar a the tails of its notes. Old tablat had many forms. In **lute-tablatu** the French and English used lette the Italians, numerals, designating frets to be touched on the lu These were written on a staff with many lines as the instr. written had strings ; beneath were stems w tails, indicating the time-value of

es ; these tails represent our mod-
values except that our whole note
(eir semibreve) had a stem like that
our half-note ; our half-note (their
hima) had the tail of an eighth
e ; our ¼ note (semiminima) a
able-hooked-stem, our ⅛ note (fusa)
ee hooks, our 1/16 note (semifusa)
tail of a 64th note. The hooks
consecutive notes were often run
ether in thick lines as in our music.
gan (or **German**) t. was used
key-board instrs., and employed
letter-names of the notes, the
lody being marked on a staff with
ord-accompaniment in vertical rows
letters beneath.

e d'harmonie (tăbl dăr-mō-nē), *F.*
A table of chords, intervals, etc.
Sound-board.

e d'instrument (tăbl dăṅ-strü-
kṅ), *F.* Belly.

e-music. 1. Part-songs. 2. Music
inted so that singers at opposite
les of a table could read it.

or, taboret', *E.*, tabourin (tă-boo-
ḣ), *F.*, tab'ret. A small drum ; a
mbourine without jingles.

et, pl. ta'cent, *L.*, tace (tä'-chĕ),
. taci (tä'-chē), taciasi (tä-chī-ä'-
, *I.* "Be silent!" as *oboe tacet*, let
e oboe be silent.

tus, *L.* The stroke of the hand or
ton in conducting.

el (tä'-fĕl), *G.* Table. **T.-förmiges**
r-mĭkh-ĕs) **klavier**, or **T.-kla-**
er. Square piano. **T.-musik** (moo-
k'). 1. Music sung at a banquet.
Vide TABLE-MUSIC.

Stem. **tail-piece.** The wooden
ace which holds the strings of vio-
is, etc., below the bridge.

e (tī'-yŭ), *F.* 1. Tenor. 2. Viola,
so t. de violin, t. de basson. Oboe
caccia.

igo'to. 1. Japanese dulcimer.

ct (täkt), *G.* 1. Time. 2. Measure.
Beat. im T. In time. ein T.
ie vorher zwei. Double the for-
er time. **T.-accent.** Primary ac-
nt. **T.-art.** Species of time, as
aple or triple. **T.-erstickung** (ĕr-

shtĭk-oongk). Syncopation. **T.-fach**
(fäkh). Space. **T.-fest.** Steady in
keeping time. **T.-glied** (glēt). Measure-note. **T.-führer** (fü -rĕr). Conductor ; leader. **T -halten.** To
keep time. **takti(e)ren** (täk-tēr'-ĕn}
or **t.-schlagen.** To beat time. **T.-**
**linie** (lĭn'ē), **T.-strich** (strĭkh).
Bar-line. **t.-mässig** (mĕs-sĭkh). In
time. **T.-messer.** Metronome. **T.-**
**note.** Whole note. **T.-pause.** Whole
rest. **T.-stock.** Bàton. **guter T.-**
**teil.** Strong beat. **schlechter T.-**
**teil.** Weak beat. **T.-vorzeichnung,**
or **Taktzeichen** (tsī-khĕn). Signature.

talabalac'co, *I.* Moorish drum.

ta'lan. Hindu cymbals.

talon (tă-lôṅ), *F.* Heel. 1. Of a bow.
2. Of the foot.

tambour (täṅ-boor), *F.* 1. Drum. 2.
Drummer. **t. de basque** (dŭ băsk).
Tambourine. **t. chromatique.** Tim-
balarion. **t. roulante** (roo-länt).
Long drum. **t. major** (mă-zhôr).
Drum-major.

tamb(o)u'ra. An ancient instr., used
in the East, like a guitar, struck with
a plectrum.

tambouret (täṅ-boo-rā), *F.*, tambourine (tăm'boo-rĕn), *E.*, **Tambourin**
(täm-boo-rēn'), *G.* 1. A small drum,
with little bells (called *jingles*) pivoted
in the rim. Notes with waved stems
indicate a *roll;* notes with vertical
lines above, call for the *jingles.*
tambourineur (nŭr'), *F.* Tambou-
rine-player.

tambourin (täṅ-boo-răṅ), *F.* 1. A tambourine without jingles. 2. A lively
dance in 2-4 time with **t.** accompaniment.

tamburaccio (täm-boo-rät'-chō), *I.* A
large drum. **tamburel'lo, tambu-**
ret'to, *I.* 1. Tabor. 2. Drummer.

tamburino (täm-boo-rē'-nō), *I.* 1.
Drummer. 2. Tambourine.

tamburo (täm-boo'-rō), *I.* Side-drum.

tamburone (täm-boo-rō'-nē), *I.* The
great drum.

tamis (tă-mē'), *F.* Pipe-rack.

tam'tam'. 1. Indian drum. 2. Gong

**Tanbur** (tän-boor′), *G.* Tamburo.

**tändelnd** (tĕn′-dĕlnt), *G.* Playful, trifling.

**tan′gent**, *E.*, **Tangente** (tän-jĕn′-tĕ), *G.* Vide CLAVICHORD. **Tangentenflügel.** A " wing-shaped " clavichord.

**tantino** (tän-tē′-nō), *I.* A little.

**tanto** (tän′-tō), *I.* So much ; as much ; but **allegro non t.** Not too quick. **allegro t. possibile.** As fast as possible.

**Tan′tum er′go**, *L.* " So much therefore." A hymn sung at the Benediction in the R. C. service.

**Tanz** (tänts), *G.*, pl. **Tänze** (tĕn′-tsĕ). A dance. **Tänzer** (tĕn′-tsĕr). A dancer. **Tänzerin** (tĕn′-tsĕ-rĭn). A female dancer. **T.-lied** (lēt). Dancesong. **T.-musik**, or **T.-stück** (shtük). Dance-tune.

**tap.** A single note on the drum. **taps.** The last military signal at night. It is also used at the funeral of a soldier.

**tapada** (tä-pädh′-ä), *Sp.* Stop. **tapadillo** (dhĕl-yō). Baxoncillo.

**ta′rabouk.** Instr. used by Turks, a parchment over the bottom of a large earthen vessel.

**tarantella** (tä-rän-tĕl′-lä), **tarentelle** (tär-äṅ-tĕl′), *F.* Perhaps of Tarentine origin, but claimed to be derived from the tarantula, two explanations being given, one that the bite of the spider incites a mania for dancing ; a more probable one that the fatal effects of the poison find an antidote in violent exercise. The dance is a wild presto in 3-8 or 6-8 time, with increasing frenzy and alternatingly major and minor.

**tarau, theyau thro.** Burmese violin with 3 silk strings.

**tar′do, tardato** (tär-dä′-tō), **tardan′do, tardamen′te**, *I.* Slow(iy).

**Tartini′s tones.** Resultant tones, first observed by Tartini. (Vide B. D.).

**Taschengeige** (täsh′-ĕn-gī-khĕ), *G.* Kit.

**tasseau** (täs-sō), *F.* The mould on which violins are built.

**tastame** (täs-tä′-mĕ), *I.*, **Tastatur** tä-toor ), *G.*, **tastatura** (täs-tä-rä), *I.*, **tastiera** (täs-tĭ-ā′-rä), *I.* board ; finger-board. **sulla tast** Near the finger-board (of a vln.)

**Taste** (täs′-tĕ), *G.* The touch, h a key. **Tas′tenbreit.** Key-be **Tastenstäbchen** (stĕp-khĕn). **Tasteuschwanz** (shvänts). tremity of key-board. **Tastenw** A keyed instrument.

**tasto** (täs′-tō), *I.* 1. Touch. 2. 3. Fret. 4. Finger-board. su " Near the finger-board." **t. s** " One key alone," a note to be pl without other harmony than the taves.

**tatto** (tät′-tō), *I.* Touch.

**tattoo′.** The drum-beat at night calling soldiers to quarters for s It precedes taps (q. v.).

**tche** (chē). A Chinese stringed in ment.

**te.** Tonic Sol-fa name for the 7th *si.*

**té** (tā), *F.* C sharp.

**technic(s)** (tĕk′-nĭk(s)), *E.*, **Tech** (tĕkh-nĕk′), *G* , **technique** (tĕk-n *F.* The mechanical side of mu performance, including dexterity locity, distinctness, shading as posed to the poetical or interpr tive side. The means, not the ● of a properly balanced musical a tion.

**tech′nicon.** A device for training fingers, inv. by J. Brotherhood, 1

**tech′niphone.** First name of the gil Practice-Clavier.

**technisch** (tĕkh′-nĭsh), *G.* Techni used to indicate proficiency.

**tedesco (-a)** (tĕ-dĕs′-kō), *I.* Germ **alla t.** In the German style, in wa rhythm. **lira t.** Hurdygurdy.

**Te De′um Lauda′mus**, *L.* " T Lord, we praise," a hymn attribu to St. Ambrosius. Vide MASS.

**Teil** (tīl), *G.* Vide THEIL.

**tel′ephone-harp.** An instr. for tra mitting music by telephone.

**tell′tale.** An indicator of wind-pr ure.

. (tä'-mä), *I.* Theme; subject; lody.

perament, *E.*, **tempérament** n̈-pä-rä-mäṅ), *F.*, **temperamen´**- *I.* A method of tuning, repre- ating the triumph of practice over ory; of art over science. It is a tem of compromise, whereby, for actical musical purposes, the octave livided into twelve intervals, none which is quite true. In the pres- : piano, and similar instrs. the nes *c♯* and *d♭*, for example, are ntical, and are given the same ing and digital. As a matter of ustical fact there is a difference ween them. If they were given ferent digitals and tuned exactly, : present freedom of modulation m one key to another would be possible without some elaborate vice, and the piano, organ, etc., uld need a greatly increased fin- r-board, with 53 digitals to the oc- e instead of 12 as now. The sent tuning was not reached with- : a war of the bitterest sort; but ce the 18th century began, only degrees have been given to the ave. The earliest method was **equal temperament,** the key of major being tuned true, and the ner tones forced to conform. In e **twelve-semitone system,** the ave was divided into twelve equal rts, no interval being quite true. e **mean-tone** system had the ma- thirds tuned true, the intermediate ace being divided into two equal ervals; this system produced much scord called the *wolf.* **equal tem- rament** is now generally em- yed; it is the practice of tuning by ths. A series of twelve fifths be- nning with c lacks only 74/73 of form- a perfect seven octaves; by dividing s slight discrepancy equally among e 12 fifths, the *circle of fifths* is npered and made perfect; thus in ajor C-G-D-A-E-B-F♯- (or G♭)- -A♭-E♭-D♮ F- C (B♯); in minor e-b-f♯-c♯-g♯-d♯ (or e♭)-b♭-f-c-g-

d-a; and one can modulate by means of dominant harmony (chords on the fifths) through the whole suc- cession of keys with almost imper- ceptible acoustic falsehood. It is this great convenience and simplicity of Equal Temperament that has pre- vented thus far the acceptance of any of the many instruments invented with the rival method of **just intona- tion.** Nevertheless the music we know and enjoy has no perfect inter- vals except the octave; the fifths are a 12th of a *comma* flat; the fourths a 12th of a *comma* sharp; the major thirds ¼th of a *comma* sharp, etc.

**Temperatur** (tăm-pĕ-rä-toor´), *G.* Temperament.

**tempesto´so, tempestosamen´te.** Tempestuous(ly), furious(ly).

**tempête** (täṅ-pĕt), *F.* "Tempest." A boisterous quadrille in 2-4 time.

**tem´po,** *I.* "Time." 1. Rate of speed, ranging from the slowest to the fastest, thus Grave, largo, lento, adagio, andante, moderato, allegro, presto, prestissimo. 2. Rhythm, measure. 3. Beat. **a tempo.** In exact time (usually appearing after retarda- tion). **t. primo** (or 1mo), or **pri- miero.** Original speed. **t. alla breve** (brä'-vĕ). Vide BREVE. **t. a. piacere,** or **senza t.** The time at pleasure. **t. bina´rio (terna´rio).** Duple (triple) time. **t. como´do.** Convenient, moderate time. **t. de- bole** (dā'-bŏ-lĕ). Weak beat. **t. di bal´lo.** Dance-time. **t. di bole´ro, gavot´ta, mar´cia,** etc. In the time of a bolero, gavotte, march, etc. **t. di cappel´la.** In the Church-time. Vide BREVE. **t. di pri´ma par´te.** In the same time as the first part. **t. for´te.** Strong beat. **t. giusto** (joos'-tō). In strict time. **l'istesso** (or **lo stesso**), **t.** Continue at "the same speed." **t. maggiore** (mäd-jō'-rĕ). Vide BREVE. **t. mi- no´re,** or **t. ordina´rio.** 1. Common time, 4 beats to the measure. 2. The original time of the piece. **t. perdu´to.** "Lost." unsteady time. **t.**

**reggiato** (rĕd-jä´-tō), same as colla parte. **t. rubato.** Vide RUBATO. **T. wie vorher** (vē fôr-hār), *G.* Same time as before.

**tempo-mark, Tempo-Bezeichnung** (bĕ-tsīkh´-noongk), *G.* A word or phrase indicating the standard or unit of time for a composition, as *andante;* or indicating some deviation from this unit, as *meno mosso.*

**temporiser** (tän-pôr-ĭ-zā), *F.* In an accompaniment, to follow the soloist's time.

**temps** (tän), *F.* 1. Time. 2. Beat. **t. faible** (fĕbl), or **levé** (lŭ-vā). Weak beat. **t. fort** (fôr), **frappé** (frăp-pā´). Strong beat.

**tem´pus,** *L.* Time, i. e., of the breve. **t. perfec´tum** (marked O). That in which the breve equalled 3 semibreves. **t. im´perfectum** (marked ( ). That in which it equalled 2 semibreves. **t. bina´rium** (or **terna´-rium**). Duple or triple time. Vide NOTATION.

**tenete** (tĕ-nā´-tĕ), *I.* Hold.

**Ten´ebræ,** *L.* "Shadows, Darkness"; R. C. Evening Service, during Holy Week, in commemoration of the Crucifixion, the candles being extinguished one by one.

**tenen´do,** *I.* Sustaining (as the melody).

**tenero** (tā´-nĕ-rō), **tenero´so, teneramen´te,** *I.* Tender(ly). **tenerez-za** (tā-nĕ-rĕd´-zä). Tenderness.

**teneur** (tŭ-nŭr), *F. Cantus firmus* of a hymn.

**tenor** (in *G.* tā-nôr´), **ténor** (tā-nôr). *F.* **tenore** (tā-nō´-rĕ), *I.* 1. The highest male voice produced "in the cr´ st." Vide SOPRANO. (a) The more powerful tenor is almost a barytone and is called **dramatic (Heldentenor´),** **teno´re robus´to,** or **di mezzo carrattere** (dē mĕd´-zō kä-răt-tā´-rĕ), or **di forza** (dē fôr´-tsä). Compass c–b´ (♮). The more light and flexile tenor is called **lyric, lyrischer** (lēr-ĭsh-ĕr). **T. tenore leg-giero** (lĕd-jä-rō), **légier** (lā-zhä), or **di grazia** (dē gräts´-yä). Compass d–c´´, sometimes higher. 2. The part cor-

responding to the tenor voice in pass. 3. The highest of a chi▨ bells. 4. The viola, as tenor ▨ 5. As a prefix for instrs. of range ; e. g., tenor trombone (*T posaune*), etc. 6. **tenor C** is a tave below mid-c. 7. **tenor Tenor-schlüssel** or **-zeichen** C clef on the fourth line. 8. Th▨ est string of the viola. 9. In G▨ rian music, the principal melody by a medium male voice, above ▨ sang the. **counter-** or **contra-t**▨ or the *altus* or *alto.* 10. In m▨ val music, (a) fermate, (b) am (c) tone of a mode of the *e▨*

**tenorino** (tā-nō-rē´-nō), *I.* Fa▨ or **castrato** tenor. **Tenorist** ō-rēst´), *G.,* **tenorista** (tān-c̄ tä), *I.,* **ténoriste** (tā-nō-rēst´), tenor-singer.

**tenoroon´.** 1. Old tenor oboe, co▨ downward to tenor C. 2. A that does not go below E.

**ten´sile.** Applied to stringed i▨ ments.

**tenth.** 1. An interval of an o▨ and a third. 2. A stop a tenth ▨ the diapasons. 3. Decima.

**tenu(e)** (tŭ nü), *F.,* **tenuto** (tā-no▨ *I.* "Held." 1. Sustained. sustained note or pedal-point. L´egato. 4. Constantly, as for Pl. **tenute (note).**

**téorbe** (tā-ôrb), *F.* Theorbo.

**teoretico** (tā-ō-rā´-tĭ-kō), *I.* Th▨ ical.

**teoria** (tā-ō-rē´-ä), *I.* Theory.

**tepidità** (tā-pē-dĭ-tä´), *I.* Indiffer▨ lukewarmth. **tepidamen´te.** Ca▨

**teponaz´tli.** An Aztec drum still in Central America ; a log ab▨ yard long, hollowed from below, cut through till two tongues of are left. These sound an int▨ when struck with padded sticks.

**ter** (tĕr), *L.* Thrice, three times passage to be repeated twice). **un´ca.** "Three-hooked"; 16th **ter sanctus.** "Thrice holy," ring to the "Holy, holy, hol▨ the Te Deum.

1. Tierce. 2. Vide HORÆ
ONICÆ.

t (tĕr-sä), *F.* Triplet.

ire (tĕr-năr). *F.*, ternario (tĕr-
rĭ-ō), *I.*, ter´nary, *E.* Triple,
ee-fold. ternary form. Rondo-
n. ternary measure. Triple
e.

´dion. 1. An instr. inv. 1816 by
chmann, resembling the harmo-
n, the tone being produced from
ks of wood. 2. An 8-ft. stop.

sichore (tĕrp-sĭk´-ō-rĕ). The muse
lance and song.

a, *L.*, Terzia (tĕr´-tsĭ-ä), *G.* 1.
rd, tierce. tertia modi. The
degree. 2. A stop sounding a
d or tenth above.

n Zweifach (tĕr-tsĭ-än tsvĭ´-
n), *G.* A stop combining tierce
larigot.

(tĕrts) (pl. en), *G.*, terzo(-a) (tĕr´-
, *I.* 1. Third, (a) the interval,
in number. 2. Tierce, terzo
no. Octave-coupler. terzadec-
a, Terzde´zime. A 13th. Terz-
rt´akkord, or Terzquartsext´-
kord, 6–4–3 chord. (Vide CHORD.)
rzquintsext´akkord, 6 – 5 – 3
rd. (Vide CHORD.) Terztöne.
rce-tones. Terzflöte. 1. Small
e, a minor third above. 2. A
.

decimole (dä-tsĭ-mō´-lĕ). A group
hirteen equal notes.

ett (tĕr-tsĕt´), *G.*, terzetto (tĕr-
´-tō), *I.* A trio.

na (tĕr-tsē´-nä), *I.* A triplet.

:ura (tĕs-sĭ-too´-rä), *I.*, tessiture
´-sĭ-tūr), *E.* "The web." The
eral "lie" of a song or phrase—
average pitch, whether high or

a, *I.* Head. di t. In the head
he voice.

(tĕs´-tō), *I.* "Text." 1. Subject,
heme. 2. The words of a song.

´do, *L.* "Tortoise." The lyre.
(tĕt not tāt), *F.* Head, of a note ;
a vln., etc.

achord, *E.*, tetrachorde (tĕt-rä-
d), *F.*, tetracor´do, *I.* 1. A 4-

stringed instr. 2. The interval of a
fourth. 3. The 4 diatonic tones of
a perfect fourth. (Vide MODES.) tetra-
chordal system. Original form of
Tonic Sol-fa.

tetrachor´don. A small piano-like
instr. with a rubber cylinder, impinging on strings.

tetrato´non, *Gr.*, tet´ratone. An interval of four whole tones.

tet´rad. Chord of the seventh.

tet´radiapa´son. Interval of 4 octaves.

tet´raphone. Tetratone.

tetrapho´nia. Organum in 4 parts.

T(h)eil (tīl), *G.* Part. T.-ton. Partial
tone.

the´ma, *Gr.*, Thema (tä´-mä), *G.*,
thème (tĕm), *F.*, theme, *E.* Loosely,
the general idea of a composition.
Strictly, the structural molecule, of
which motive or subject and answer
are the component atoms. The
theme of a "theme with variations,"
tema con variazioni, is an extended
air. Such a work as a sonata has
contrasting themes which are developed. themat´ic treatment refers
to the contrapuntal handling of a
musical design as opposed to a lyric
treatment, though the theme itself
may be lyric in nature.

Theorbe (tĕ-ôr´-bĕ), *G.*, théorbe (tä-
ôrb), *F.*, theorbo (thē-ôr´-bō), *E.*
A large bass lute with two necks,
the longer carrying a set of bass
strings.

Theoretiker (tĕ - ō - rā´ - tĭ - kĕr), *G.*,
théoricien (tä-ō-rĕs-yäṅ), *F.* A
theorist.

theoria, *Gr.* and *L.*, théorie (tä-ō-rē),
*F.*, theory (thē´-ō-rĭ), *E.* The
science of music, particularly of its
composition.

the´sis, *Gr.* The accented downbeat.
Vide ARSIS.

Theur´gic hymns. Songs performed
in Greek mysteries.

theyau. Vide TARAU.

thin. Used of chords and harmonies
that lack support and fulness.

thior´bo. Theorbo.

**third.** 1. Vide INTERVAL. 2. The mediant. **third-flute.** Vide TERZFLÖTE.
**third-tones.** Vide QUINT-TONES.

**thirteenth.** An octave and a sixth.

**thirty-second note.** A demisemiquaver. **32d rest.** A rest of equal
duration.

**thorough-bass.** Vide BASS.

**thorough-composed.** Vide SONG.

**three-eighth time.** That in which
each measure contains three eighth
notes.

**threefold.** Used of triads.

**three-lined.** Vide PITCH.

**three-time.** Triple time.

**threno′dia,** *L.* and *Gr.* A song.
**thren′ody.** Lamentation.

**thrice-marked,** or **lined.** Vide
PITCH.

**thro.** Vide TARA.

**through-composed.** Vide SONG.

**thumb-position.** On the 'cello, a high
position where the thumb quits the
neck.

**thumb-string.** Banjo melody-string.

**Thürmer** (tür′-měr), *G.* Town-musician.

**tib′ia** (pl. **tib′iae**), *L.* "Shin-bone." 1.
Ancient name of all wind-instrs. with
holes, such as the flute, pipe and fife,
originally made from the human leg-
bone. **tibiae pa′res,** *L.,* pl. Two
flutes of the same length. **t. impares.**
Unequal flutes, one for the right hand
and the other for the left, which were
played on by the same performer;
those for the right hand, **t. dextrae,**
being perhaps of higher pitch than
those for the left (**sinistrae**). **t. ob-
li′qua,** or **vas′ca.** Cross-flute. 2.
Name of various flute-stops, as **t.
major,** a 16-ft. covered stop. 3. **t.
utric′ularis.** The bagpipe.

**tib′icen** (pl. **tibic′ines**, feminine **tibi-
ci′na**), *L.* Flute-player. **tibicin′ium.**
Piping.

**tie.** A slur; a curved line placed over
notes on the same degree which are
to be sustained as one tone. Vide
SIGNS. **tied-notes.** 1. Those thus
tied. 2. A series of notes (16th notes,
etc.) with a single tail.

**tief** (tēf), *G.* Deep, low. **tiefe**
fěr). Lower. **8va tiefer.**
below. **tieftönend** (tēf-tā′-
Deep-toned.

**tier** (tēr). Rank (of pipes).

**tierce** (tērs), *E.* 1. A third,
**tierce-tones,** those reached by
of major thirds. Vide PITCH.
4th in a series of harmonics.
mutation stop 2⅓ octaves abo
apason. 4. Vide HORÆ CANO

**tierce** (tĭ-ĕrs′), *F.* 1. A third. 2
HORÆ CANONICÆ. **t. de Pic**
(dŭ pē-kăr-dē), *F.* Tierce of Pi
a major third introduced in tl
chord of a composition in n
supposed to have originated in
dy. **t. coulée** (koo-lā). A s
grace in thirds. Vide GRACE.

**timbala′rion.** A series of 8
chromatically tuned and fitted
pedals.

**timbale** (tăn-băl), *F.,* **timbal′lo,**
kettle-drum. **timbalier** (tăn-ba
A kettle-drummer.

**timbre** (tăn-br), *F.,* **tim′bro,**
Quality and color of tone. 2.
struck with a hammer. **jeu**
**timbres** (zhŭ-dŭ-tănbr). A
matic series of small bells or
bars. 3. The snare of a drum.

**tim′brel.** Hebrew tambourine.

**time.** A word used loosely and
changeably with its Italian e
lent *tempo*, to indicate: 1. R
movement, or speed. 2. Rhytl
Speed is indicated in various wa
descriptive words, such as slov
*dante, langsam*, etc., or by th
tronome mark.
Rhythm is generally indicated
fraction, as 2-4 or 3-8 set at th
ginning of the composition or
ment. The denominator indicat
unit of note-value; the num
fixes the number of those unit
in each measure. Thus 2-4 r
that the quarter-note is the sta
of value, and that each measure
tains two quarter notes or their
alents.
With the exception of such

## Duple. or Common Time. (mesures à deux ou quatre temps. F. gerader Takt, G. tempi pari, I.)

### A. Simple. (binaire, F. einfacher, G. semplice, I.)

| No. of beats to meas. | English. | French. | German. | Italian. |
|---|---|---|---|---|
| 2 | Two-two (alla breve). | Deux-deux. | Zweizweiteltakt. | A cappella (alla breve). |
| 2 | Two-four. | Deux-quatre. | Zweivier " | Due-quarti (quarttro-due). |
| 2 | Two-eight. | Deux-huit. | Zweiach " | Due-ottavi (otto-due). |
| 4 | Four-two. | Quatre-deux. | Vierzwei " | Quattro-mezzi (due-quattro). |
| 4 | Four-four. (common). | Quatre quatre. | Viervier " | Quattro-quarti (quattro-quattro, binario, ordinario). |
| 4 | Four-eight. | Quatre-huit. | Viverach " | Quattro-ottavi (otto-quattro). |
| 4 | Four-sixteen. | Quatre-seize. | Viersechzehn " | Quattro-sedicesimi (sedici-quattro). |
| 8 | Eight-eight. | Huit-huit. | Achtach " | Otto-ottavi (otto-otto). |

### B. Compound. (ternaire, F. zusammengesetzer. G. compost., I.)

| No. of beats to meas. | English. | French. | German. | Italian. |
|---|---|---|---|---|
| 2 | Six-two. | Six-deux. | Sechszweiteltakt. | Sei-mezzi (due-sei). |
| 2 | Six-four. | Six-quatre. | Sechsvier " | Sei-quarti (quattro-sei). |
| 2 | Six-eight. | Six-huit. | Sechsach " | Sei-ottavi (otto-sei). |
| 2 | Six-sixteen. | Six-seize. | Sechssechzehn " | Sei-sedicesimi (sedici-sei). |
| 4 | Twelve-four. | Douze-quatre. | Zwölfvier " | Dodici-quarti (quattro-dodici). |
| 4 | Twelve-eight. | Douze-huit. | Zwölfach " | Dodici-ottavi (otto-dodici). |
| 4 | Twelve-sixteen. | Douze-seize. | Zwölfsechzehr ' | Dodici-sedicesimi (sedici-dodici). |
| 8 | Twenty-four-sixteen. | Vingt quatre-seize. | Vierundzwanzigsechzehn " | Ventiquattro-sedici. |

## Triple time. (mesures à trois temps, F. ungerader, or Tripel Takt, G. tempi dispari, I.)

### A. Simple.

| No. of beats to meas. | English. | French. | German. | Italian. |
|---|---|---|---|---|
| 3 | Three-one. | Mesure à trois un. | Dreieintelta t. | Uno-tre. |
| 3 | Three-two. | à trois deux. | Dreizwei " | Tre-mezzi (due-tre). |
| 3 | Three-four. | à trois-quatre. | Dreivier " | Tre-quarti (quattro-tre). |
| 3 | Three-eight. | à trois-huit. | Dreiach " | Tre ottavi (otto-tre) |

### B. Compound.

| No. of beats to meas. | English. | French. | German. | Italian. |
|---|---|---|---|---|
| 3 | Nine-four | à neuf-quatre. | Neunvierteltakt. | Nove-quarti (quattro-nove). |
| 3 | Nine-eight. | à neuf-huit. | Neunach " | Nove-ottavi (otto-nove). |
| 3 | Nine-sixteen. | à neuf-seize. | Neunsechzehn " | Nove-sedicesimi (sedici-nove). |
| 5 | Five-four. | à cinq-quatre. | Fünfvier " | Cinque-quarti (quattro-cinque). |
| 5 | Five-eight. | a cinq-huit. | Fünfach " | Cinque-ottavi (otto-cinque) |

some English writers classify times also as *quadruple* and *octuple*, and indicate compound times atures of the correspondir g simple times with a dot added after the denominator.

rhythms as the 5-8 time, all musical time-patterns are divisible by 2 or 3, and are called *duple* or *triple.* Thus in 2-4 time there are two beats to the measure, in 3-4 time there are three. In more elaborate times the beats may themselves be divided by twos or threes. These are called *compound duple* or *compound triple* times.

The chart gives the various times in various languages. (See also Accent and Tempo.)

**timido** (tē′-mĭ-dō), *I.* Timid. **timidezza** (tē-mĭ-dĕd′-zä). Timidity.

**timoro so, timorosamen′te,** *I.* Timid(ly). **timore** (tĭ-mō′-rĕ). Fear.

**timpano** (tĭm′-pä-nō) (Pl. **-i**), *I.* Kettle-drum. **t. coper′to.** Muffled drum. **timpanis′to.** Drummer

**tin′termell.** An old dance.

**tintinnab′ulum,** *L.,* **tintinnabolo** *I.* (tĭn-tĭn-nä′-bō-lō), **tintinna′bulo** (boo-lō). 1. A little bell. 2. A small rattle of bells.

**tintinnamen′to,** **tintinnio** (nē′-ō) **tintin′no,** *I.* Tinkling.

**tin′to,** *I.* Shading.

**tiorba** (tē-ôr′-bä), *I.* Theorbo.

**tipping.** Vide DOUBLE-TONGUING.

**tirade** (tē-răd). *F.* A slide across an interval.

**tiran′na,** *Sp.* A national air with guitar.

**tirant** (tē-räṅ), *F.* Stop-knob. **t. à coupler** (ä-koo-plā). 1. Coupler 2. Button. 3. Drum-cord.

**tirarsi, da** (dä tē-rär′-sē), *I.* "With a slide," as **tromba da t.**

**tirasse** (tĭ-răs), *F.* 1. A pedal-coupler. 2. A pedal key-board acting only on the manual pipes.

**tirata** (tē-rä′-tä), *I.* A group of equal notes, moving in joint degrees.

**tirato** (tē-rä′-tō), *I.* 1. Down-bow. 2. Pedal-coupler.

**tira tutto** (tē-rä toot′-tō), *I.* A pedal mechanism controlling the full power of an organ.

**tiré** (tē-rā), *F.* Drawn, pulled; a down-bow. **tirez** (tē-rā). "Use the down-bow."

**Tischharfe** (tĭsh′-här-fĕ), *G.* harp," an autoharp.

**tlap′anhuehue′tl.** Huehuetl.

**tit′ty.** Hindu bagpipe.

**tirolienne.** Tyrolienne.

**toccata** (tōk-kä′-tä), *I.* From **care,** to touch, to play. In it century form, a prelude made runs and arpeggios. The m toccata develops with great the hilarity and contrapuntal infor a brilliant, swift and showy im sation. **toccatina** (tē′-nä), **t tel la.** Short toccata.

**toccato** (tōk-kä′-tō), *I.* A fourth pet part in place of kettle-drum

**toc′sin.** An alarm-bell.

**To(d)tesgesang** (tōt′ ĕs-gĕ **To(d)teslied** (lēt), *G.* A **To(d)tenglöckchen** (glĕk′-l Funeral bell **To(d)tenm** (märsh). Funeral ("dead") m

**tombeau** (tôṅ-bō). *F.* "Tomb matic elegy.

**tomb estere.** Old *E.* A dance tambourine.

**tom′tom.** Hindu drums.

**Ton** (tōn), pl. **Töne** (tä-nĕ), Tone. **T.-bestimmung,** or sung. Calculation of tones. **gattung** (gät′-toongk). The di of the octave. The selection of Hence, mode. **T.-rein.** T pitch. **T.-bildung.** Tone-p tion, voice-training. **T.-b** Orchestra. **T.-dichter.** Tone composer (also **T.-setzer**). **dichtung** (dĭkh-toongk) or Composition. **T.-farbe** (fä Tone-colour, timbre. **T.-folge.** of tones. **T.-führung.** M progression, modulation. **T.- T.-fall** (or **-schluss**). Cad **T.-setzung,** or **-verhalt.** Rh measure. **T.-gang.** Melody. **gebung.** Intonation. **T.-k** Science of music. **T.-kunst** (ko Music; the art of music. **Tonk schule.** School of music. **lehre** (tōn′-lā-rĕ). Acoustics. **leiter** (lī-tĕr). Scale. **T.-** Ventage. **T.-malerei.** "

nting," programme music. **T.-
sser.** Monochord, siren, sono-
ter. **Tonschlüssel** (shlüs'-sĕl).
y-note. **T.-runge.** Fugue. **T.-
zkuast.** Art of composition. **T.-
rache.** Music. **T.-stück** or
erk. Piece of music. **T -schrift.**
isical notes. **T.-verwandschaft.**
lation of tones. **T.-verziehung.**
mpo rubato. **T.-veränderung.**
odulation. **T.-werkzeug.** In-
iment (including the voice). **T.-
stem,** or **wissenschaft.** Theory
music. **T.-zeichen.** Note or
er musical sign.
Pitch. **den T. angaben** (hal-
i). To give (keep) the pitch. **T.-
he.** Pitch. **T.-lage.** Register.
Key, octave-scale, mode, usually
nart (tōn -ärt). **T.-anverwand-
haft** (fĕr-vänt -shäft). Key-rela-
nship. **T.-geschlecht** (gĕ-
ĕkht') Mode (i. e major or minor).
nabstand (äp-shtänt). Interval.
-achtel. Eighth note. **T.-stufe.**
gree **T.-umfang.** Compass.
(tōn), *F.* 1. Tone. **t. bouché**
o-shä). Stopped tone of a horn.
entier (än-tĭ-ä). Whole tone. **t.
nt** (tän). Old term for flatted tone.
**ouvert** (oo-vär). Open tone, of
wind-instr. **t. générateur** (zhā-
rä-tŭr). Fundamental. 2. Pitch.
ner le t. Give the pitch. 3. Key.
le, mode. **t. majeur (mineur).**
ajor (minor) key. **t. relatif.** Reed key. **t. de l'église** (dŭ lā-
z). Church-mode. 4. Crook of a
n. **t. de réchange,** or **du cor.**
ning-fork.
dica (tō-nä-dē'-kä), **tonadilla**
l'-yä), *Sp.* Cheerful song with
tar.
e **fic'ti,** *L.* Transposed church-
des.
l. Relating to a tone, a key,
de, etc. Vide FUGUE, and IMITA-
ON.
alität (tōn-äl-ĭ-tät'), *G.,* **tonali-
**(tôn-äl-ĭ-tä), *F.,* **tonal'ity,** *E.*
e unity in key-relationship of a
rase or composition. It may pass

out of the predominant key, but so
long as it does not stray beyond
the limits of easy return and constant
relationship with this key, the composition has not overstepped its general
**tonality.**
**ton do,** *I.* Round, full (of tone).
**tone.** 1. A sound of musical quality
and regular vibration as opposed to
noise. 2. A sound, (a) of definite
pitch, (b) of a definite quality. 3. A
full interval of two semitones. 4. A
mode. 5. Of *aliquot, combinational,
differential, partial, resultant, summational,* etc., tones or *difference-
tones, overtones,* etc. Vide those words,
also ACOUSTICS. Of *fifth-tones. quint-
tones, third-tones.* Vide QUINT-TONES.
**bridge-tone.** Vide TONIC SOL-FA.
**tone-colour.** The distinctive quality or timbre of a tone. **tone-paint-
ing.** Description by music. **tone-
poem.** A musical expression of
sentiment. **determination** of t.
The investigation of vibrations, or
tone-values, tone-relationship, etc.
**tone-relationship.** Tones which
concur in a major or minor chord are
said to be of the first degree of relationship c is so related to g. f. e, a♭
a, and e♭, etc.
**tönen** (tä -nĕn). *G.* To sound. **tö nend**
Sounding
**tongue.** 1. Reed , or the vibrating
metal slip of a reed , hence, **tongue-
pipes.** 2. *As a verb,* to use the
tongue in playing wind-instr., called
**tonguing.** Vide DOUBLE-TONGUING.
*Triple-tonguing* is the rapid iteration
by tongue-thrust with the consonants.
t-k-t, t-k-t, etc.
**ton ic,** *E.,* **tonica** (tō'-nē-kä), *I.,* **To'-
nika,** *G.,* **tonique** (tō-nēk), *F.* 1
The key-note of a key, that on which
the scale begins and ends, the tone
from which a key takes its name,
as C. 2. The **tonic-chord,** the
diatonic chord built on the key-note.
**t.-pedal.** Pedal-point on the key-
note. **t. section.** One which closes
with a cadence to the tonic of the
chief key of the movement.

**Tonic Sol-fa.** A system of teaching singing, inv. by Sarah Ann Glover, of Norwich, and improved by Rev. John Curwen, and his son John Spencer Curwen. It consists, first, in analysis with constant reference to key-relations, or "tones in key", the second element is a notation modified from solmisation (q. v.), and consisting of doh for do, ray for re, me for mi, fah for fa, soh for sol, lah for la, te for si. These take the place of notes and are written on one line by their initials, d, r, m, etc. an accent being affixed below or above the letter to indicate an octave lower or higher as d' r. Sharps are sung dē, rē etc. flats dä, rä, etc. In modulation. *bridge-tones* are indicated by the new key-value of the tone large with its old key value small as ᵈd. In notation, rhythm is expressed by time-spaces, the number varying according to the beats or pulses in the bar, a thick bar before a letter marks a strong accent, a colon a weak accent, a dot and a comma mark half and quarter beats, a dash indicates prolongation of tone, a rest is marked by a vacant space.

**to no,** *I.* 1. Tone. 2. Key.

**to nos,** *Gr.,* **to nus,** *L.* 1. A whole tone. **t. grav'is, tris'tis, mys'ticus, harmon'icus, laet'us, devo'tus, angel'icus, perfect'us,** respectively the 1st, 2d, 3d, 4th, 5th, 6th, 7th, and 8th tones in church-music. **t. cur rens.** Reciting note. **t. peregri'nus.** Foreign tone. 2. Mode.

**toquet** (tō-kā) **touquet,** *F.* Toccato.

**toomour'ah.** Hindu tambourine.

**too'rooree'.** Brahmin trumpet.

**toph** (tôf), *Heb.* Hebrew tambourine.

**torcelli** (tôr-chĕl'-lē). *I.* Organs.

**tosto** (tôs'-tō). Quick, rapid. **più tosto.** Rather; sooner.

**touch.** 1. Act or style of pressing the keys of a key-board instr. 2. The response or resistance of the action.

**touche** (toosh). *F.* 1. Touch. 2. A digital. 3. A fret. 4. A finger-board.

**toucher** (too-shā). *F.* 1. *As a* touch. 2. *As a verb,* to touch,

**touchette** (too-shĕt'). *F.* Fret.

**toujours** (too-zhoor). *F.* Always. SEMPRE.

**touquet** (too-kā). *F.* Toccato.

**tourdion** (toor-dĭ-ôṅ). *F.* Saltare

**tourmenté** (toor-mäṅ-tā), *F.* elaborated.

**tourne-boute** (toorn-boot), *F.* instr. like a flute.

**tour de force** (toor dŭ fôrs). *F* vura passage, etc.

**tourniquet** (toor-nĭ-kā). *F* Plug

**touta'ri.** Hindu bagpipe.

**tout** (too), pl. **touts** (too), or to (toot), *F.* All. **t. ensemble** täṅ · säṅ' - bl). All the whol gether , the general effect.

**toy.** A trivial air or dance. **toy phony.** A comic work, partic one by Haydn employing toy cu trumpet, etc.

**tp.** Abbr. of Timpani.

**tr.** Abbr. for trumpet or trill.

**track'ers,** *E.* Tractur (träk-toor Vide ORGAN.

**tract,** *E.* **trac'tus,** *L.* Solemn dies sung from the Psalms d Lent in the Requiem Mass. words are taken from the Psalm

**tradolce** (trä-dōl'-chĕ). *I.* Very s

**tradotto** (trä-dôt'-tō) *I* Transl arranged.

**Tra'gen der Stim'me,** *G.* Portam

**trainé** (trĕ-nā). *F* 1. Slurred. slow waltz.

**trait** (trĕ), *F.* 1. Passage as t chant. Vocal run. 2. A ph progression **t. d'harmonie.** quence. 3. Rule. **t. d'oct** Rate of the octave.

**traité** (trĕ-tā). *F* A treatise.

**Traktur** (träk-toor'). *G.* Trac Vide ORGAN.

**tranquillezza** (trän-kwĭl-lĕd'-zä), t **quillità** (trän-kwĭl-lĭ-tä'). *I.* T quillity. **tranquil'lo, tranqu men'te.** Calm(ly).

**transcription** (in *F.* träṅ-skrĕps- A rearrangement of a compos for a different instr. or instrs

iforme. The notation, common
French bands, of writing all the
nsposing instrs. in the G clef.

sient. Used of notes, chords and
dulations that are merely passing
l secondary, the means, not the
l.

sito, *L.*, transit'ion (in *F.* trän-
-yŏń). I. A modulation of tran-
nt value, so also in Tonic Sol-

situs, *L.* A passing note (usu-
y t. re'gularis). t. irre'gularis.
anging note.

sponi(e)ren (pō-nē'-rĕn), *G.* To
nspose. transponi'rende In'-
rumente. Transposing instrs.

spose, *E.*, transposer (trän-spô-
, *F.* To change the pitch of a
nposition to a key higher or lower.
uus the tonic is replaced by the
ıic of the new key, the old domi-
nt by the new, etc.

sposing. I. Used of instruments,
ıch are not written as they sound,
t always in the key of C major.
ais is done so that the player's ease
d accuracy may be insured, by
eping the fingering, etc., the same
all keys, the key of the instr. be-
ç changed by changing the instr.
tirely or merely changing a crook.
ıe extent of this transposition is the
erval between the key of the instr.
d the key of C major. So an instr.
B, sounds a half-tone lower than
itten; an instr. in E♭ sounds a ma-
ç 6th below or a minor 3d above
e actual note. 2. t. piano, etc.,
e in which, by a mechanism, the
tion is shifted to higher or lower
tch. t.-scale. Vide MODES.

spositeur (träns-pō-zĭ-tŭr'), *F.* I.
ıe who transposes. 2. A single-
lve inv. by Gautrot as a substitute
ç the series usually used. 3. A
y-board instr., piano t., inv. by A.
olff. 1873.

asposition (in *G.* träns-pō-zē-tsĭ-
ı). The changing of the key of a
mposition. T.-skalen. Trans-
»sing Scales. Vide MODES.

transverse flute. Vide FLUTE.

traquenard (träk-när), *F.* A brisk
dance.

trascinando (trä-shǐ-nän'-dō), *I.* Dragging, retarding.

trascrit'to, *I.* Copied, transcribed.

trasportato (trä-spôr-tä'-tō), *I.* Transposed. chiavi trasportati. Vide
CHIAVETTE.

tratt. Abbr. of trattenuto.

trattato (trät-tä'-tō), *I.* Treatise.

trattenuto (noo'-tō), *I.* Retarded.

Trauergesang (trow'-ĕr-gĕ-zäng), *G.*
Dirge. Trauermarsch (märsh).
Funeral-march. trauervoll. Sad.
traurig (trow'-rĭkh). Heavy, sad.

travailler (trä-vī-yā), *F.* To work;
to lead, play solo part. travaillé
(vī-yā). Worked up elaborately.

Travers'flöte. I. A cross-flute. 2.
A 4-ft. stop.

traversière (trä-vĕrs-yär), *F.*, traverso (trä-vĕr'-sō). Vide FLUTE.

tre (trä), *I.* Three. a tre. For three
voices or instrs. tre cor'de. Loud-
pedal. Vide PIANO. tre volte. Three
times.

treble. I. The highest voice, sopranⱺ
(from *triplum*, q. v.). 2. Highest
part of a comp. 3. Highest register. 4. The highest of a group of
instrs. t. clef. The G clef. t.
forte stop. A stop for cabinet organs, increasing the treble at will,
while the bass remains soft. t. staff.
The staff on which the treble clef is
placed.

Tredezime (trä-dä'-tsē-mĕ), *G.* Thirteenth.

treibend (trī'-bĕnt), *G.* Hurrying, accelerating.

treizième (trĕz-yĕm), *F.* Thirteenth.

tremblant (trän-blän), *F.*, tremen'do,
*I.* Shaking. trembler (blä), *F.*
To trill. Vide TREMULANT. tremblement (trän-bl-män), *F.* A trill,
shake.

tremolando (träm-ō-län-dō), tremo-
late (lä'-tĕ), tremolo (trä'-mō-lō),
tremulo (trä'-moo-lō), *I.* Trembling,
trilling, quivering, reiterated with
great rapidity

**trem'olant, trem'ulant.** A stop which gives to the tone a waving or trembling effect.

**tremore** (trā-mō'-rě), **tremoro'so,** *I.* Tremor(ous).

**tremuli(e)ren** (trā-moo-lē'-rěn). To trill.

**trench'more.** An old dance in triple or compound duple time.

**trénise** (trā-nēz), *F.* Vide QUA-DRILLE.

**trenodia** (trā-nō'-dǐ-ä), *I.* A funeral-dirge.

**très** (trě), *F.* Very.

**tres'ca, trescone** (trěs-kō'-ně), *I.* A country-dance.

**Treter** (trā'-těr), *G.* Bellows treader.

**tri'ad,** *E.,* **triade** (in *F.* trě-ăd ; in *I.* trě-ä'-dě). A chord of three tones. Vide CHORD. **harmonic t.** Major triad.

**tri'angle,** *E.* (in *F.* trě-äṅgl), **Triangel** (trě'-äṅg-ěl), *G.,* **triangolo** (trě-än'-gō-lō), *I.,* **triangulo** (trě-än'-goo-lō). *Sp.,* **triang'ulus,** *L.* A small steel rod bent into a triangle and tapped with a straight rod, for emphasising rhythm. **Triangular harp.** Vide HARP.

**tri'as,** *L.* Triad. **t. defic'iens.** Imperfect chord. **t. harmo'nica.** Perfect chord.

**tri'chord.** The three-stringed lyre. **t. piano.** One with three strings tuned in unison for each note. **trichord'-on.** 3-stringed colachon.

**Trichter** (trǐkh'-těr), *G.* 1. Tube of a reed-pipe. 2. Bell of horn, etc.

**tricin'ium,** *L.* An unaccompanied trio.

**tricorde** (trǐ-kôr'-dě), *I.* 3-stringed.

**tridiapa'son,** *Gr.* A triple octave.

**tri'gon, trigo'num.** A 3-stringed lyre-like instrument.

**trihemito'nium,** *Gr.* Minor third.

**trill, trille** (trě'-yǔ), *F.,* **Triller** (trǐl'-lěr), *G.* **rillo** (trǐl'-lō), *I.* The rapid alternation of a principal note with an auxiliary, usually the major or minor second above (a small chromatic sign being set above the note when its auxiliary is not to be diatonic). The trill begins on the auxiliary note only

when the auxiliary is written grace note before the princip this case the trill ends on the cipal ; normally it ends on the iliary. A trill is *long* or (**trillette** (trě-yět), *F.,* **trillet'ta let'to,** *I.*) according to the durat the principal, the short trill some amounting only to a morder series of trills on different note **chain of trills** (Trillerket'te mere rough rattle on one note i of two notes crisply trilled is **goat-trill, Bockstriller, ch.èv ment,** or **trillo caprino. trille** (tě'nō). *I.* A soft trill. **imperf** One without a turn at the close Caccini's Method, 1601, the tril the reiteration of a single not trill being called **grup'po. tril** (trěl-län'-dō), *I.* 1. Trilling. success on, or chain, of shakes o ferent notes. **trillern** (trǐl'-lěr To trill. Vide GRACES and SIG

**trine** (trēn). A triad, with 2 thirds.

**Trinkgesang** (trǐnk'-gě-zäng), T (lět), *G.* Drinking-song.

**trino'na.** Open 8-ft. stop.

**trio** (trě'-ō), *I.* 1. A compositio three instrs. or voices, often in s form. **pianoforte trio.** pf., vln cello. **string trio** (vln., viola ( vln.), and cello). (The name formerly used for 3 instrs., acc nied by a fourth playing basso tinuo.) **organ trio.** A strongl trasted work for 2 manuals and or for 3 manuals. 2. In the d form, the contrastingly quiet or l second division. Gaining its from being once written in 3 the word should now be laid as meaningless and confusing, an phrase second part, or second su used instead.

**Triole** (trǐ-ō'-lě), *G.,* **triolet** (in *F* ō-lä). A triplet.

**triomphale** (trě-ôṅ-fäl), *F.,* **trio** (trě-ōṅ-fä'-lě), *I.* Triumphal. **t** **phant** (trě-ôṅ-fäṅ), *F.,* **trion** (trě-ôṅ-fän'tě), *I.* Triumphant.

ar'tite. In three parts.
el (trē'-pĕl), G. Triple, as T.
ge, triple fugue. T.-konzert. iple concerto. T.-takt. Triple
ie. T.-zunge. Triple-tonguing.
'ony. Three sounds heard at ce. tripho'nia. Organum in 3 rts. triphonisch (trē-fō'-nĭsh), G. iphonic, 3-voiced.
a (trē'-plä), I. Triple time. t. de n'ima. 1. 3-2 time. 2. Triplet.
e (in F. trēp'-l). Threefold. Vide UNTERPOINT, TIME, etc. t.-croche ŏsh). 32d note.
let. A group of three equal notes.
ublet. A sextole.
lum, L. The third part in organ-
i, hence the highest ; in 4-part next the highest, the 4th being called adruplum ; if there is a 5th it is led quintuplum, etc.
ola (trē'-pö-lä). I. Tripla.
a'gion, Gr., Trisa'gium, L. Thrice Holy," the Sanctus.
emito'nium, L. Minor third.
ezza (trĭs-tĕd'-zä), I. Sadness.
ro'pha, Gr. Triple square note of e greater stress.
n (trē-tôn), F., tritone (trī'-tōn), , tritono (trē-tō'-nō), I., tri'to-s, L. (in G. trē-tō-noos'). An aug-ented forbidden ; long a forbidden erval in strict writing, since it was gmented and was said to be hard sing. mi chord of the t. Third version of the dominant seventh, iich contains the tritone. Vide MI.
on a'vis, L. "3-toned bird," a est-Indian bird, capable of singing note, and its twelfth and seven-enth, all at the same time.
t (trĭt), G. Treadle, pedal. Tritt'-huh (shoo). Place for the foot on llows. Tritt'harfe. Pedal-harp.
ritt'bret or T.-holz. The board which the bellows-treader steps.
us, L. Lydian Church-mode.
iphirend (trē-oom-fē'-rĕnt), G. iumphant. Triumphlied (lēt).
ng of triumph.
(trwä), F. Three. mesure à is-deux (trwä-dŭ). 3-2 time. A

*trois-huit* (trwä zwēt). 3-8 time.
*trois-quatre* (trwä kätr). 3-4 time.
troll. 1. Round or catch. 2. *As a verb*, to sing a catch.
tromba (trōm'-bä), I. 1. A trumpet 2. 8-ft. reed-stop. t. croma'tica, I. Valve trumpet. t.-bas'sa, or di bas'so, or spezzata (spĕd-zä-tä). The bass trumpet. t. da tirar si. Old slide trumpet, perhaps a soprano trombone. t.-marina (ma-rē'-nä), I. Marine trumpet. spezzata (spĕd-zä'-tä), I. An obsolete name for the bass trombone. t. sor'da. Muted trumpet. trombadore (dō'-rĕ), trom-bacelloclyde. A B♭ ophicleide.
trombet'ta, trombettino (tē'-no), trombettatto're- or iere (ĭ-ā'-rĕ). 1. Trumpet. 2. A small trumpet.
trombone (in E. träm'-bōn, in I. trôm-bō'-nĕ, in F. trôṅ-bŭn), I., pl. -i. 1. A trumpet-like instr. with valves : or more anciently, with a tube that may be lengthened or shortened by means of a U-shaped portion to be pushed in or drawn out. This *slide* moving by semitones has seven positions, each of which virtually makes a separate instr. of it with a distinct key, the partial tones of this being obtained by variations of press-ure (vide EMBOUCHURE). The tone of the instr., though suffering from misuse in bad hands, is of the utmost richness, dignity and humanity. Ber-lioz calls it "epic." It is a non-trans-posing instr. in four sizes, the tenor being most used , the tenor and alto are written on the C clef , the bass and contrabass on the F clef ; com-passes , *tenor*, chromatic E–b'♭ (with *pedal-tones* G,–B, ♭, and difficult tones b'–d''), *alto*, A–e''♭; bass B,–t'. 2. A powerful 8, 16 or 32 ft. stop.
Trommel (trôm'-mĕl), G. Drum. gros'se T. Bass drum. Militär-t., or Wirbel-t. Side drum. Roll-t Tenor drum. T.-bass. A bass note thumped drum-wise. T.-boden (bō'-den). Bottom of a drum. T.-kas-ten. The body of a drum. T.-klöpfel (klĕp-fĕl), or T.-schlägel

(shlä-gĕl). Drumsticks. **T.-schlä-ger.** Drummer. **trom′meln.** To drum; drumming.

**Trommelstück** ( trôm′-mĕl-shtük), *G.* Tambourine, tabor.

**trompe** (trônp), *F.* 1. Hunt-horn. 2. Reed-stop. **t. de Béarn** (dŭ bā-ărn), or **à laquais** (ä lăk-ĕ′). Jew's harp.

**Trompete** (trôm-pā′-tĕ), *G.* 1. Trumpet. 2. A reed-stop. **Trompeten-geige.** Marine trumpet. **Trompe-tenzug** (tsookh). Trumpet-stop. **Trompeter** (trôm-pā′-tĕr), **trompé-teur** (trôn-pā-tŭr), *F.* Trumpeter.

**trompette** (trôn-pĕt), *F.* 1. A trumpet. 2. Trumpeter. 3. A reed-stop. **t. à coulisse** (ä koo-lēs). Slide-trumpet. **t. à clefs** (ä klā). The trumpet with keys. **t. à pistons** (ä pēs-tôn). Valve trumpet. **t. d'har-monie** (dăr-mŭ-nē). Orchestral t. **t. harmonieuse** (ăr-môn-yŭz). Trom-bone. **t. marine.** Marine trum-pet. **t. harmonique** (ăr-mŭn-ēk). A reed-stop.

**troop.** 1. A quick march for trooping the colors. 2. The 2d drum-beat as a march-signal.

**trope, tro′pus.** 1. A Gregorian for-mula for the close of the lesser doxol-ogy. 2. Mode.

**troppo** (trôp′-pō), *I.* Too, too much. *lento ma non* **t.** Slow, but not too slow.

**troubadour** (troo-bä-door), *F.,* **trova-dor** (trō-vä-dhôr), *Sp.,* **trovatore** (trō-vä-tō′-rĕ), *I.* A poet musician, usually of noble rank, skilled in sing-ing, chiefly of love. The cult arising in Southern France, flourished widely from the 11th Century. The **t.** sometimes had hired minstrels (mé-nestrels, ménétriers, or jongleurs) in attendance on him. **trouvères** (troo-văr), *F.* A cult of poet-musicians contemporary with and often con-fused with the troubadours, but more characteristic of the north of France, and singing songs rather of war and epic struggle than of love.

**trüb(e)** (trüp or trü′-bĕ), *G.* Sad.

**Trug** (trookh), *G.* Deception. **T.-**

fortschreitung. Progression dissonance, not to its resolution to another dissonance. **T.-kad** or **-schluss.** Vide CADENCE.

**Trumbscheit** (troomp′-shīt), *G.* rine trumpet.

**trump.** 1. Trumpet. 2. Jew's h

**trump′et.** 1. A metal wind-instr. a tube half as long as that of the h but bent in longer folds, and wi smaller bell. The tube is narrow cylindrical till near the bell; mouthpiece is hemispherical cupped. It is a transposing i written in the G clef (almost alwa and in the key of C. Its pitch i octave higher than that of the h and it is used in fewer keys. It i most commanding of all brass ins but its stopped tones are unpleas It should be written for in a dist ly vocal manner. It is fitted crooks to give it any key, the being produced by embouchure (o except in the **valve;** or chroma **trumpet;** which is displacing the o form. Its extreme compass is d– In England the **slide trumpet** is u working like a trombone but shorter slide. Trumpets of the s key but sounding an octave apart called *alto* (high), and *basso* (l 2. An 8-ft. reed-stop.

**marine trumpet.** An old in once used for signalling in the I lish navy, hence its name; also in convents, whence it was ca "*nun's fiddle.*" It was played cl ly in harmonics, and had one t gut string, sometimes an oc string, and one or more drone-stri The box was long and thin with s neck and flat belly; one foot of bridge rested loosely producing powerful resonance. **harmonic** A sackbut. **reed-t.** A trumpet 36 brass-reeded pipes inclosed, ranged in a circle, so that each was brought in turn between mouthpiece and the bell.

**Trumscheit** (troom′-shīt), *G.* Ma trumpet.

Abbr. of Tasto Solo.

ng (chĕng). Cheng.

ng (choong). Chinese gong.

(too'-bä), *I.* 1. The lowest of the horns (q. v.), an enormous brass n with four pistons, a trombone- mouthpiece, and a compass of 4 aves. It is a non-transposing instr. cept in the case of a tenor-tuba in , and a bass-tuba in F so written Wagner), and is written in the G . It is usually made of 3 sizes, **bass** or the **euphonium**, in B flat mpass available B♭–f'), or in E♭, **bombardon**, a fifth lower, and the ntrabass tuba (or **bombardon**) b an octave lower than the Eupho- m. 2. The straight Roman trum- , or t. **communis** ; the t. **duc- s**, being curved. 3. t. **curva.** A ited natural French trumpet of the h Century. 4. A powerful 8-ft. d-stop. t. **major**, t. **mirabilis**, t. rion. A 4-ft. stop.

cen, *L.* A trumpeter.

et. A flourish of trumpets.

u (twē-ō), *F.* Tuyau.

ltuoso (too-mool-too-ō-sō), *I.* gitated.

Ancient Yucatan drum.

. An air or melody, usually short d simple.

er. 1. One who tunes instruments. The flap or cut in the top of a pe by which it is tuned. 3. Tun- g-cone.

ing. 1. The correction of the tone- oduction of an instr. 2. Accorda- e. t.-**cone** or **horn.** A cone of rn or metal which can be inserted the top of an organ-pipe, by coning out" or increasing its flare d raising its pitch, by "coning ' or pressing it point upwards. er the top of a pipe, it decreases e flare and lowers the pitch. t.- ook. Vide CROOK. t.-**fork.** A nall steel instr. with two prongs hich upon being struck sounds a rtain fixed tone. t.-**hammer** or ey. A hand-wrench. t. **slide.** An English instr. for producing

thirteen semitones. 2. An adjustable U-shaped portion of the tube of cer- tain brass instrs. t. **wire.** Vide REED and PIPE.

**tuono** (too-ō'-nō), *I.* 1. Mode, as t. **ecclesias'tico.** Church-mode. 2. Tone.

**tuorbe** (twôrb), *F.* Theorbo.

**tur'ba**, pl. -æ, *L.* "Crowd, multi- tude." The heathen or Jewish chorus in Passion music.

**turbinoso** (toor-bĭ-nō'-so), *I.* Tempes- tuous.

**turbo** (toor'-bō), *Gr.* A seashell trum- pet.

**turco** (toor'-kō), *I.* Turkish. **alla turca.** In the style of Turkish music.

**turdion** (toor'-dĭ-ōn), *Sp.*, **turchesco** (toor-kā'-skō), *I.* An old dance.

**türkish** (tür'-kĭsh), *G.* Turkish. **Turk- isch-muzik.** Janizary music.

**turn.** An embellishment consisting of a principal tone (struck twice) and one higher and one lower auxiliary a diatonic second removed, unless a chromatic sign accompanies the sym- bol ; if a sharp or flat is placed above the turn-mark, it alters the higher auxiliary ; if below, the lower. The **common, direct,** or **regular** turn usually begins on the upper auxiliary ; the **back** or **inverted t.** begins with the lower ; the **rebounding** or **trilled** t. begins with a passing shake ; the **double t.** affects two notes at once. Vide GRACES.

turr. 3-stringed Burmese violin.

**Tusch** (toosh), *G.* A triple flourish of trumpets and drums.

**Tute** (too'-tĕ). *G.* Cornet.

**tutta** (toot'-tä), **tutto**, pl. **tutte** (toot'- tĕ). or **tutti** (toot'-tē), *I.* All ; the entire band or chorus ; in a solo or con- certo it means that the full orchestra is to come in. **tutte corde** (kôr'-dĕ). "All the strings" ; i. e., release the soft pedal. **tutti.** Full band or chorus—the entire force. **tutto ar'- co.** With the whole bow.

**tuyau** (twē'-yō), *F.* 1. Tube, as of a horn. 2. Pipe. t. **à anche.** Reed- pipe. t. **à bouche.** Flue-pipe.

**twelfth.** 1. An interval of an octave pius a fifth. 2. A stop twelve tones above the diapasons.

**twenty-second.** A triple octave.

**twice-marked,** or **-accented.** Vide PITCH.

**two-lined.** Vide PITCH. **two-time.** Duple time. **two-step.** A dance in 6-8 time, somewhat resembling the waltz, but in duple accent.

**tymb'estere.** Vi.le TOMBESTERE.

**tym'pan.** 1. Timbrel. 2. Drum. 3. Irish instr., perhaps the crowd. **tympani** (tĭm'-pä-nē), *I.*, pl. Kettle-drums. **tympanis'ta.** Kettle-drummer.

**tympanischi'za.** Marine trumpet.

**tympan'on** (tĕm-pä-nôn), *F.* 1. Dulcimer. 2. Kettle-drum.

**tym'panum,** *L.* 1. Ancient drum resembling the kettle-drum. 2. Kettle-drum. 3. The water-wheel in old hydraulic organs.

**ty'pophone.** A piano-like instr., with steel wands instead of strings, compass c'–c''''.

**tyrolienne** (tē-rōl-yĕn), *F.* 1. Song, or dance peculiar to the Tyrolese ; and characterised by the jodel. 2. Round dance in 3-4 time.

**tzeltze'lim,** *Heb.* Cymbals.

**tzet'ze.** Abyssinian guitar.

**tzi'ti.** Hindu bagpipe.

# U

**U**BELKLANG (ü'-bĕl-kläng) or **-laut** (lowt), *G.* Discord. **üben** (ü'-bĕn), *G.* To practise.

**über** (ü'-bĕr), *G.* Over, above. **Ü.-einstimmung** (īn-shtĭm-moongk). Harmony **ü.-geführt** (gĕ-fürt). Divided (of stops). **ü.-greifen** (grī-fĕn). (a) To cross the hands ; (b) to lift the thumb from the neck of a 'cello. **ü.-greifendes System** (zēs'-tăm). Hauptmann's plan of forming ъ new key-system by adding to the group of triads of one key, a triad in its dominant or sub-dominant key.

**Ü.-blasen** (blä-zĕn). Overblowing,

to overblow. **Ü.-gang** (g Transition, modulation. **Ü.-le** (lī-toongk). Transition passage **mässig** (mĕs-sĭkh). Augmented **schlagen** (shlä'-gĕn). (a) To over (the hands). (b) To over (c) To break. **ü.-setzen** (zĕt' To pass a finger over the thum one foot over the other. **ü.-ste** (shtī'-ghĕn). For a part to soar porarily higher than the part nor above it.

**Übung** (ü-boongk), *G.* (pl. **-en**). ercise ; a study. **Ubungsabend.** piis' concert.

**ugab** (oo'-gäb), *Heb.* An organ.

**uguale** (oo-gwä'-lĕ), *I.* Equal. **ugualità** (lĭ-tä'). Equality. **ug men'te.** Equality, alike.

**umana** (oo-mä'-nä), *I.* Human. **ce u.** (vō'-chĕ). 1. The human v 2. A stop.

**Umfang** (oom'-fäng), *G.* Compa

**umgekehrt** (oom-gĕ-kārt'), *G.* versed, inverted.

**Umkehrung** (oom-kā'-roongk), *G.* version.

**umore** (oo-mō'-rĕ), *I.* Humour.

**um** (oom), *G. Prefix* about, arc

**umschlagen** (slä'-gĕn). 1. To b to make a pronounced change of ister. 2. To overblow. 3. To the goose. **Um'stimmung** (sł moongk). (a) Change. (b) C ture, pitch or key.

**un.** Abbr. of Unison.

**un** (ŭn), *F.,* **un** (oon), **una** (oo' **uno** (oo'-nō), *I.* A, an, one.

**unaccented.** Vide PITCH.

**unaccompanied.** Without instru tal accompaniment.

**unacknowledged.** Used of pas or unessential notes.

**un'ca,** *L.* " Hooked " ; quarter **bis unca.** 16th note.

**uncoupled.** With coupler release **und** (oont). *G.* And.

**un'da ma'ris,** *L.* " Wave of the A stop tuned sharp or flat and ducing an undulating effect by m of beats ; sometimes a pipe with mouths, one higher than the oth

ima (oon-dä-chĕ'-mä), *L.* and *I.*
eleventh.

imole (oon-dä-chĭ-mō'-lĕ), *I.* A
p of eleven equal notes.

chord. The minor triad.

part. That beneath, or subor-
te to others.

song. A burden.

tone. A lower partial sometimes
uced by the simultaneous sound-
of two higher tones. (Vide
USTICS.)

zime (oon-dä'-tsē-mĕ), *G.* An
enth. Unde'zimo'le. Undeci-
.

a'tion, *E.*, undulazione (oon-
lä-tsĭ-ō'-nĕ), *I.* Vibrato effect on
instruments.

n), *F.* A, an, one.

entliche (oon-ī'-gĕnt-lĭkh-ĕ). Ir-
lar (of fugue).

lich(er) (oon-ĕnt'-lĭkh-(ĕr) ), *G.*
less (of canon).

al. 1. Vide TEMPERAMENT. 2.
oices = mixed.

en'tial. Used of passing and
e notes, etc.

'ted. Vide FRETTED.

(oon'-gär), ungarisch (oon-gä'-
, *G.* Hungarian.

unden (oon-gĕ-boont'-ĕn), *G.*
de FRETTED. 2. Unconstrained.

uldig (oon-gĕ-dool'-dĭkh), *G.*
atient.

ade Takt (oon-gĕ-rä'-dĕ täkt),
Triple time.

trichen (oon-gĕ-strĭkh'-ĕn). Un-
nted. Vide PITCH.

tüm (oon'-gĕ-shtüm), *G.* Impet-
.

wungen (oon-gĕ-tsvoong'-ĕn),
Easy.

ch (oon'-glĭkh). Unequal. Vide
NTERPOINT. ungleichschwe-
de (shvä-bĕn-dĕ). Unequal, of
erament (q. v.).

mo'nischer Querstand (kwär'-
nt) or umstand (oom'-shtänt).
e relation.

ord, *E.*, unichor'dum, *L.* 1.
ochord. 2. Marine trumpet.

(ün-yôn), *F.* Union. u. des

régistres (dä rä-zhĕstr). Blending
of registers.

unione (oo-nĭ-ō'-nĕ), *I.* Coupler.

u'nison (in *G.*, oo-nĭ-zōn'), uniso'nus,
*L.*, unisono (oo-nē-sō'-nō), *I.*; unisson (ü-nĭs-sôṅ), *F.* 1. Identity of
pitch. 2. Any octave of a pitch. 3.
A tone of the same or octave pitch.
4. A prime, hence augmented unison. 5. A group of 2 or 3 strings
tuned in the piano to one note. all'
unisono, à l'unisson, in unison, or
progressing · in the unison or the octave.

unis'onant, unis'onous. In unison
or octave.

unito (oo-nē'-tō), unitamen'te, *I.*
United(ly). uniti cancels divisi
(q. v.).

unmeasured. Without definite measure.

uno (oo'-nō), una (oo'-nä), *I.* One;
a, an. uno a uno. One by one; one
after another.

unrein (oon'-rīn'), *G.* Impure; out of
tune.

unruhig (oon-roo'-ĭkh), *G.* Restless;
uneasy.

unschuldig (oon-shool'-dĭkh), *G.* Innocent.

unsingbar (oon-zĭng'-bär), *G.* Not
singable.

unstrung. Of strings (a) relaxed in
tension, (b) removed entirely.

unter (oon'-tĕr), *G.* Under, below,
sub. U.-bass (bäs). Double bass.
U.-brechung (brĕkh'-oongk). Inter-
ruption. u.-brochen (brôkh-ĕn). Interrupted. U.-dominante (dō-mĭ-
nän'-tĕ). Subdominant. U.-halbton
(hälp-tōn). Half-step below. U.-
haltungsstück (häl-toongs-shtük).
Divertissement. U.-leitton (līt-tōn).
Dominant seventh. U.-mediante
(mä-dĭ-änt'-ĕ). Submediant. U.-
satz (zäts). Supporter; a 32-ft. stop
on the pedal. u.-setzen (zĕt'-zĕn).
To pass the thumb under a finger; or
one foot under another. U.-stimme.
Lowest voice, or part. U.-tasten
(täs-tĕn). The white keys of the
piano or organ. U.-töne (tā-nĕ)

**Untertönreihe** (rī-ĕ).    Vide UNDER-
TONES.

**unverziert** (oon-fĕr-tsērt'), *G.*   Unornamented.

**unvolkommen** (oon'-fôl-kôm-mĕn), *G.*
Incomplete.

**uomo** (oo-ō'-mō), *I.*   A man.   Vide
PRIMO.

**up-beat.**   1. The raising of the hand
or bâton, hence  2. An unaccented
part of a measure.

**up-bow.**   Vide BOW.

**upright.**   Vide PIANO.

**ura'nion.**   An instrument like the harpsichord or piano.

**uhr-heen.**   Chinese violin.

**upper-clang.**   Vide CLANG.

**uscir di tuono** (oo'-shēr dē too-ō-'nō), *I.*
To get out of tune.

**u'sus**, *L.*   1. The rules of music.   2.
Old synonym for neumes and the
neume system.

**ut** (üt in *F.;* in *I.* and *L.* oot).   1. In
France the key and note C, so used
also in indicating pitch, as *ut 2.*   2.
Vide SOLMISATION.   3. In Latin, as,
like that. **ut supra.**  As above, as
before.

**Ut que'ant lax'is**, *L.*  Vide SOLMISA-
TION.

## V

**V** Abbr. for *vide* = see ;  *vio-
lin(s) ; volti ; voce.*
**va** (vä), *I.*   Go on.  **va crescendo** (krĕ-shĕn'-dō), *I.*   Go
on increasing the volume.

**vaccilando** (vät-chǐ-län'-dō), **vacci-
lante** (län'-tĕ), *I.*   Wavering, irregular.

**va'gans**, *L.*   Vague.   Vide QUINTUS.

**vago** (vä'-gō), *I.*   Vague, rambling.

**valce** (väl'-chĕ), *I.*   Waltz.

**valeur** (vä-lŭr), *F.*, **val'or**, *L.*, **valore**
(vä-lō'-rĕ), *I.*   Duration (of a note).

**valse** (väls), *F.*   Waltz ; used in *E.*
rather of a concert-piece (**v. de salon**), than of a strict dance-tune.
**v. chantée** (shän-tā), vocal waltz.
**v. à deux temps** (dŭ tän).   A quick
waltz, with two steps in each measure.

**value.**   Duration of a note or rest

**valve, valvola** (väl'-vō-lä), *I.*   1.
device inv. by Claggett, 1790,
Blühmel, 1813, by which na
brass instrs. are made chromatic
natural horn produces the fu
mental tone naturally made by ɑ
umn of air of its exact length ;  ɨ
be made to produce a series of
tials of this tone by the meth
blowing.   Vide EMBOUCHURE
ACOUSTICS.   The key of the hor
be changed by substituting fo
section of its tube a longer or sh
section called a crook, which ɑ
the length of the horn, and the
umn of air, and alters therefo
fundamental key and gives it ɑ
series of partials.   Until the ʋ
mechanism was invented a horn
therefore play only in one key
time.   Valve instrs. have aux
tubes fitted to the main tube ;
are, in fact, merely stationary cr
The pressure of a certain valve
as an instantaneous change of
by shutting off the air in one ɔ
and turning it into another of ɛ
ent length.   This device permi
sounding of a complete chro
scale along the instrument's ʋ
range.   The valves are usually
in number, the first lowering
pitch a semitone, the second a
the third three semitones, thus g
a command of all keys (cf. ʜ
(a) **the piston,** or **piston-val**
a *plunger* in an air-tight cylinde
means of two holes the plung
rest carries the air through the
tube ; when pressed it shuts oɨ
main tube and opens a side-tube
changing the key ; a spiral spri
stores it after pressure to the nɑ
position.   (b) **the rotary valv**
stop-cock with four holes whicʜ
duce the same effect.   2. oɨ
**valves** are (a) **suction-valve**
**suckers,** which admit the wiʜ
the bellows and retain it there
**joint-valves** which regulate th
density in the wind channels

-valves or **pallets,** which are
⸱ed by a draw-stop ; and (d) the
⸱te-pallet relieving the bellows
⸱rplus air.

⸱ (väl-tsär), *I.* Waltz. **v. a due
⸱si.** Two-step.
  1. To improvise an accompa-
⸱nt or prelude. 2. Such an ac-
⸱paniment or prelude.

⸱nento (vä-rĭ-ä-mĕn'-tō), *I.* Va-
⸱on, difference. **variamen'te.**
⸱ed, freely.

⸱tion, *E.* (in *G.* fä-rĭ-ä-tsĭ-ōn', pl.
⸱ in *F.* vär-ĭ-äs-yôṅ), **variazione**
⸱ĭ-ä-tsĭ-ō'-nĕ, pl. -i), *I.* The ma-
⸱lation of a given theme or air.
⸱the old sense (called **doubles**),
⸱ in cheap modern usage such as
⸱ome, sweet Home with varia-
⸱s," the air is simply smothered in
⸱ments, arpeggios, etc.; in the
⸱er sense (**character variations**)
⸱ theme is subjected to as much re-
⸱elling, inversion, change of note-
⸱e, etc., as is possible without losing
⸱re sight of its original meaning ;
⸱etimes merely the chord-relations
⸱preserved. **variato** (vä-rĭ-ä'-tō),
⸱**varié** (vä-rĭ-ä), *F.* Treated with
⸱ation.

⸱viana (ä'-nä), *I.*, **varsovienne**
⸱n), *F.* "Warsaw dance." Slow
⸱sh dance in 3-4 time with an up-
⸱of a quarter note, and an ac-
⸱ed down-beat in every other meas-

⸱ville (vōd-vĕl), *F.* I₄ A coun-
⸱pallad or roundelay, usually satir-
⸱ 2. Operatic or musical comedy.
⸱cello. Abbr. for violoncello.
⸱ente (vä-ä-mĕn'-tĕ), *I.* Vehe-
⸱t. **veemenza** (mĕn'-tsä). Force.
⸱**, velato** (vä-lä'-tō), *I.* Marked
⸱ desirable softening of the metal-
⸱uality of a tone ; usually acquired
⸱ slight escape of breath.
⸱ato (vĕl-loo-tä'-tō), *I.* Velvety,
⸱oth.
⸱ (vĕ-lō'-chĕ), **velocemen'te,** *I.*
⸱t(ly). **velocis'simo.** With ex-
⸱ᴇe rapidity. **velocità** (chĕ-tä').
⸱idity.

**veneziana** (vĕ-nä-tsĭ-ä'-nä), *I.* Venetian.
**vent'age.** A hole in flutes, etc., to be
stopped with finger or key.
**Ventil** (in *G.* fĕn'-tĭl), **ventile** (vĕn-
tē'-lĕ), *I.* 1. Valve, hence **Ventil-
horn** or **-kornett.** 2. Organ-valve.
**vêpres** (vĕpr), *F.* Vespers.
**venusto** (vä-noos'-tō), *I.* Beautiful,
charming.
**Veränderungen** (fĕr-ĕn'-dĕr-oong-ĕn),
*G.*, pl. Variations.
**Verbindung** (fĕr-bĭn'-doongk) *G.*
Binding, combination. **V.-szeichen**
(tsĭ-khĕn), *G.* Tie.
**verdeckt** (fĕr-dĕkt'), *G.* Hidden.
**verdoppelt** (fĕr-dôp'-pĕlt), *G.* Doubled.
**Verdop'pelung** (oongk). Doubling.
**Verengung** (fĕr-ĕng'-oongk), *G.* Diminution of value or interval.
**vergellen** (fĕr-gĕl'-lĕn), *G.* To diminish.
**vergliedern** (fĕr-glē'-dĕrn), *G.* To
articulate.
**vergnügt** (fĕr-gnükht), *G.* Cheerful.
**Vergrösserung** (fĕr-grĕs'-sĕr-oongk),
*G.* Augmentation.
**Verhältniss** (fĕr-hĕlt'-nĭs), *G.* Ratio
or proportion.
**verhallend** (fĕr-häl'-lĕnt), *G.* Dying
away.
**ver'ilay.** Vaudeville.
**Verkehrung** (fĕr-kā'-roongk), *G.* Imitation in contrary motion,
**Verkleinerung** (fĕr-klī'-nĕr-oongk), *G.*
Diminution.
**Verkürzung** (fĕr-kür'-tsoongk), *G.*
Diminution of value.
**Verlängerungszeichen** (fĕr-lĕng'-ĕr-
oongs-tsī'-khĕn), *G.* Dot of prolongation.
**verlöschend** (fĕr-lĕsh'-ĕnt), *G.* Dying
away.
**vermindert** (fĕr-mĭn'-dĕrt), *G.* Diminished.
**Vermittelungssatz** (fer-mĭt'-tĕl-
oongks-zäts), *G.* Episode.
**verrillon** (vĕr-ē-yôṅ), *F.* Mouth-harmonica.
**Verschiebung** (fĕr-shē'-boongk), *G.*
"Shift," soft pedal. **ohne V.** Without
soft pedal. **mit V.** With soft pedal.

**verschwindend** (fĕr-shvĭn'-dĕnt), *G.* Dying away.

**verse.** 1. Portion of an anthem or service to be sung by a soloist to each part, and not by the full chorus; hence **Verse-anthem**, and **Verse-service** for solo voices. 2. Line. 3. Stanza.

**verset'** (in *F.* vĕr-sā), **versetto** (vĕr-sĕt'-tō), *I.*, **Versette** (fĕr-sĕt'-tĕ), *G.* 1. Short piece for the organ. 2. Versicle. **versetzen** (fĕr-zĕt'-sĕn), *G.* To transpose. **Verset'zung** (zoongk). Transposition. **Verset'-zungszeichen** (tsī'-khĕn). The sharp, flat, and natural.

**ver'sicle,** *E.*, **Versikel** (fĕr'-sĭk-ĕl), *G.* A short phrase or line, combining with the response to form one sentence.

**versila're,** *L.* To sing antiphonally.

**verso** (vĕr'-sō), *I.* 1. Verse. 2. Air.

**Verspätung** (fĕr-shpā'-toongk), *G.* Retardation.

**verstärkt** (fĕr-shtĕrkt'), *G.* Sforzando.

**verstimmt** (fĕr-shtĭmt'), *G.* 1. Out of tune. 2. Depressed.

**ver'tatur, ver'te,** *L.* Turn over. **v. subito.** Turn quickly.

**ver'tical.** Of piano-strings, in one plane; opposed to overstrung.

**vertönen** (fĕr-tā'-nĕn), *G.* To die away.

**verve** (vĕrv), *F.* Spirit, energy.

**verwandt** (fĕr-vänt'), *G.* Related, relative. **V.-schaft** (shäft). Relationship.

**Verwechselung** (fĕr-vĕkh'-sĕl-oongk), *G.* Change, mutation, of key, etc.

**verweilend** (fĕr-vī'-lĕnt), *G.* Retarding.

**Verwerfung** (fĕr-vĕrf'-oongk), *G.* Transposing.

**verzi(e)rt** (fĕr-tsĕrt'), *G.* Embellished. **Verzi(e)rung** (tsē'-roongk). Ornament. **Verzögerung** (fĕr-tsäkh'-ĕ-roongk), *G.* Retardation.

**verzweiflungsvoll** (fĕr-tsvī'-floongs-fôl), *G.* Full of despair.

**Vesper** (fĕs'-pĕr), *G.*, **vespero** (vĕs'-pĕ-rō), **vespro** (vĕs'-prō), *I.*, **ves'peræ,** *L.* Vespers. Vide HORÆ.

**vesperti'ni psal'mi,** *I.*, pl. Ev psalms.

**vezzoso** (vĕd-zō'-sō), *I.*, **vezzosar te,** *I.* Graceful(ly), tender(ly).

**vi.** Abbr. for violini.

**vibrante** (vē-brän'-tĕ), *I.* Vibra quivering.

**vibrato** (vē-brä'-tō), *I.* 1. Vibra resonant. 2. A strongly trem tone of distinct vibrations.

**vibra'tion** (in *F.* vĕ-brăs-yôn). regular oscillation of an elastic as a string, sounding ‧ board, contributing rapid periodic chan the density of the air, which co the motion in sound-waves to th (without the air the vibrations a conveyed to the air as sound ; vacuum, a bell, for example, ̇ audible). The strength of th varies according to the *amplit* breadth of vibrations (travellin tance of the elastic body bac forth); the pitch of the tone directly with the *rapidity* of t brations. The vibration-numbe sounds vary in inverse ratio wi length of their sound-wave. A vibration is from the point of 
one extreme of motion, but is calculated from one extreme opposite. A double vibration is ured from one extreme to the site and back again. **sympat v.** is that which is set up in an (as a string, tuning-fork or e plate) when the tone to which brates naturally is sounded by other instrument. Thus pres loud pedal of a piano, to remo dampers, and sing or play on a any note. This note will be he once sounding on the piano-s Furthermore, its partials will b larly heard.

**vic'ar-choral.** Lay vicar of a dral choir.

**vicenda** (vē-chĕn'-dä), *I.* Ch **vicendevole** (dä'vō-lĕ). Vacil

**Vic'timæ pas'chali lau'aes** "Praise the paschal offering." SEQUENCE.

, vi′di, *L.* See. vi- is often put
the beginning of a passage to be
:, and -de at the end.
(vēd), *F.* "Empty"; open, of
ings, as corde à v. opp. to corde
ouer, a string to be stopped.
:l (fē′-děl), *G.* Fiddle.
(fèl), *G.* Much, many. v.-chörig
ä-rĭkh). For several choruses. v.-
:her (fäkh-ěr). Polymorphous.
·stimmig (shtĭm-mĭkh). Poly-
onic.
l)e (vĭ-ěl), *F.*, viella (vĭ-ěl′-lä), *I.*
Hurdygurdy. 2. Old viol. viel-
ır (vĭ-ěl-lŭr), *F.* Player of the viol.
(fēr), *G.* Four. V.-achteltakt.
³ time. v.-doppelt. Quadruple.
·fach (fěr′-fäkh). With four ranks
pipes, etc. v.-füssig (fēr′-füs-
h). Four-foot (of pipes). V.-
sang. 4-part song. v.-gestri-
ene Note. 32d note. v.-ges-
chene Oktave. Four-marked.
de PITCH. v.-händig (hěn-dĭkh).
·r four hands. V.-klang (fēr′-
ĭng). Chord of four tones; a
·enth chord. v.-mässig (fěr-měs-
h). Containing four measures.
·saitig. Four-stringed. v.-stim-
g. In four-parts. V.-stück.
ɪartet. vierte (fēr′-tě). Fourth.
ertel or viertelnote. Quarter
te. Viertelpause. Quarter rest.
ertelton. Quarter note. Vierund-
chzigstel (fēr-oont-zěkhs′-ĭkh-
·ěl). 64th note. Vierviertel-
kt (fēr-fēr′-těl-täkt). 4-4 time.
erzehn (fēr′-tsān). Fourteen. vier-
hnte. Fourteenth. Vierzweitel-
ct (fēr-zvĭ′-těl-täkt). 4-2 time.
ato (vē-ä-tä′-tō), *I.* Forbidden.
·ēf), *F.* Brisk, quick.
·roso (vē-gŏ-rō′-sō), vigorosa-
·en′te, *I.* Bold(ly).
·ela (vē-goo-ā′-lä), vihuela (vē-
·ɔ-ä′-lä), *Sp.* A primitive guitar.
·geois (vē-lă-zhwä), villageoise
·ıwäz), *F.* Rustic.
·ncico (věl-yän′-thē-kō), villancio
·l-yän′-thĭ-ō), *Sp.* 1. A church
·tivaľ anthem. 2. A beginning
·d ending with chorus.

villanella (věl-lä-něl′-lä), *I.*, villanelle
(vē-yä-něl), *F.* "Village song," 15th
cent. Italian folk-song of rustic tone
and artless grace.
villanesco (něs′-kö), villareccio (věl-
lä-rět′-chō), *I.* Rustic.
villot′to, *I.* Secular song; cf. VILLA-
NELLA.
vi′na. Ancient fretted 7-stringed Hindu instr. with body of bamboo, and
two gourds for resonance.
vinata (vē-nä′-tä), *I.* A vintage-song.
vinet′ta. Little vinata.
vi′ol, viola (vē-ō′-lä), *I.*, viole (in *F.*
vē′-ôl; in *G.* fē-ō′-lě). 1. The viola
in modern usage is the tenor or alto
violin, a little larger in size than the
normal violin, and tuned a fifth lower
c-g-d′-a′. It is written on the C
clef (except high notes, which are
written in the G clef). Its tone is
more sombre (very richly melancholy
and elegiac indeed), and its harmonics are more limited. 2. The prototype of the viclin. A fretted bow-
instr. with 6 strings (sometimes 5 to
8); flat and tapering back; belly usually flat; sound-holes circular; bridge
low to facilitate chords; tuned in
fourths with one midway third. In 4
sizes *treble* (*alta*), *alto* (*alt* or *tenore*),
*bass* (*bassa*), *contrabass* (*violone*).
The bass-viol still persists in England. v. di bardone (bär-dō′-ně), *I.* A
barytone viol, of the size cf the 'cello,
with 6 or 7 gut strings, and a number of wire resonance strings lying
along the belly and tuned diatonically. v. bastarda (bäs-tär′-dä), *I.*
"Bastard viol." Large viol da gamba. v. da braccio (dä brät′-chō).
"Arm-viol" as opposed to v. da
gamba, "Leg-viol." v. da spalla.
"Shoulder-viol," a larger arm-viol.
viola d'amore (dä-mō′-rě), *I.*, viole
d'amour (dä-moōr′), *F.* 1. Richiy
beautiful, but obsolete instr., larger
than the viola, furnished with frets
and more strings, some above, and
some below the finger-board. 2. A
stop. v. pic′cola or marina (mä-
rē′-nä). An instr. resembling the v.

d'amore. v. pomposa (pôm-pō'-sä). A large viol of the compass of the 'cello, but with a fifth string. Inv. by J. S. Bach. **viol da gamba** (dä gäm'-bä), **viol di** (dē) **gamba.** "Leg-viol." A small obsolete violoncello, with frets, and five or six strings. **viola alta.** An enlarged viola inv. by Hermann Ritter of Wismar, Germany, 1877.

**violento** (vē-ō-lĕn'-tō), **violentemen-te** (lĕn-tĕ-mĕn'-tĕ), *I.* Violently. **vio-lenza** (lĕn'-tsä). Fury.

**vi'olin'**, *E.*, **Violine** (fē-ō-lē'-nĕ), *G.*, **violino** (vē-ō-lē'-nō), *I.*, **violon** (vē-ō-lôn), *F.* 1. "Small viol." A universally popular 4-stringed bow-instr. Developed possibly from the Viol, it has also been traced to the *lira da braccio ;* it passed through many changes from about 1480–1530, when it assumed a shape little varied since. Though the name usually applies to one size, it may also be stretched to include the whole string quartet (which is the harmonic basis of the modern orchestra) : the violin (or treble), the tenor violin or viola, the violoncello and the double bass. The violin proper has four gut strings with the accordature, g–d'–a'–e". Its tone is capable of great variety, sentiment and brilliance, its range extending from g to the highest note in the orchestra, e''''. It is rich in harmonics, but its resources in chords are limited and must be handled with great care for the fingering.

Instrs. of the violin family consist of a curved *body*, or *resonance-box*, whose upper surface or *belly* is joined to a vaulted *back* by *ribs ;* the body is curved in at the *waist*, the incurving being accented by *bouts*, whose *cor-ners* are braced with *triangular blocks;* the belly (on which the *bridge* rests between slits called *sound-holes*, or from their shape *f-holes*) is braced with a thin strip (under the G string) called the *bass-bar.* A round prop or *soundpost* beneath the treble foot of the bridge connects the back and

the belly. The *finger-board* is *neck*, which terminates in a *head* mented with a *scroll* and contai *peg-box*, in which are four mc *pegs* from each of which a passes across a ridge called th along the finger-board and ov bridge to the flat *tail-piece* wh fastened by a *loop* of gut to a ( in the lower end of the body. 2, 4, and 8 ft. stop. **Violinb** (fē-ō-lēn'-bō-khĕn), *G.* A vln. **Violin-clef, Violinschlüsse** **-zeichen,** *G.* The G clef. **nier** (lĭn-ĭ-ā), **violiniste** (nēst **violinista** (nēs'-tä), *I.*, **Violin ler,** *G.* A violin-player. **vi alto,** *I.* A small tenor viol. **lino picciolo** (pĭt'-chō-lō), **pic' pochetto** (kĕt'-tō), *I.* A small tuned a fifth higher. **v. pomp** *I.* A viola with an additional h string. **violin-principal.** A 4 ft. stop. **Violinsaite.** Violin-s **Violinsteg** (stäkh). Violin-b **Violinstimme.** Violin-part. **lin-tenor.** A vln. of low tone. **lon de fer** (dŭ fĕr). Iron fiddle. **linata.** A piece for violin, violin style. **violinzo'li.** 8-ft. on the swell.

**Violon** (fē-ō-lôn'), *G.* The double-**violier** (vē-ôl-yā), **violiste** (lēst' Viola-player.

**violonar** (vē-ō-ō-när'), *F.* Double-**violonaro** (när'-ō). Octo-bass.

**Violoncell** (fē-ō-lōn-tsĕl'), *G.*, **vi celle** (vē-ō-lôn-sĕl), *F.*, **violon** (vē-ō-lōn-chĕl'-lō), *I.* "Little lone." Commonly abbr. 'cello. I 4-stringed instr. of vln.-family VIOLIN) held between the knees resting on a *standard* or *peg.* tuned an octave below the viol G, d, a. Its music is written c in the C clef, save high notes in clef, and low in the F clef (for it was all written in the G clef, a tave higher than it sounded). Cl and harmonics are little used, e in solos. The 'cello is one of most important of orchestral in

one of the most expressive, espe-
y of the graver or more yearning
tions, its gayety being rather sar-
.c.

ꭩe (vē-ō-lō′-nĕ), **violono** (lō′-no),
" Large viol." 1. Double-bass.
ꞋꞋedal-stop.

Ꞌta. A large viola devised by
zner, Dresden, 1895, and tuned G,
, eꞋ.

ay. Vaudeville (also from the
n of Vaux de Vire).

l, *L.* A neume.

l **practice-clavier.** A mechan-
piano inv. by A. K. Virgil, 1883,
practice-purposes, the heaviness
ouch being adjustable in 6 grada-
ꞇs ; a click answering the depression
ꞇ key, and another click its release.

nal(s). A small spinet-like instr.
ꞇular in the time of Queen Eliza-
h, and placed upon a table.

ꞇos (fĕr-too-ōz′), *G.,* **virtuoso**
ꞇ-too-ō′-sō), *I.,* **virtuose** (vĭr-tü-
, *F.* A performer of marked skill.
ꞇtuosität (ō-zĭ-tät′), *G.* Virtuos-
Remarkable execution.

-vis (vē-zä-vē′), *F.* " Face to
ꞇe." A large double piano with 2
ꞇosite key-boards.

, (vēs′-tä), *I.* Sight. **a prima v.**
(first) sight.

ꞇ (vēs′-tō), **vito** (vē′-tō), **vi(s)ta-**
ꞇn′te, *I.* Swift(ly).

(vēt), **vitement** (vēt-mäṅ), *F.*
ick(ly).

ꞇse (vē-tĕs), *F.* Swiftness.

ꞇe (vē-vä′-chĕ), *I.* Lively, faster
ꞇn *Allegro.* **vivacemen′te.** Brisk-
quickly. **vivacet′to** (chĕt′-tō).
ther lively. **vivacezza** (chĕd′-
, **vivacità** (vē-vä-chĭ-tä′). Vivac-
. **vivacis′simo.** Very fast. **vi-**
ꞇmen′te. Briskly.

(vēv), *F.* Brisk, quick.
ꞇꞌdum, ad. *L.* " To live " i. e., for
ꞇmanence. Written, as opposed to
ꞇprovised, counterpoint.

ꞇnte (vē-vĕn′-tĕ), **vivido** (vē′-vĭ-dō),
ꞇꞇo (vē′-vō), *I.* Animated. **vivezza**
ꞇ-vĕd′-zä). Liveliness.

Abbr. for viola.

**vo′cal, vocale** (vō-kä′-lĕ in *I. ;* in *F.* vō-
kăl′), **voca′lis**, *L.* Relating or appropriate to the human voice. **vocal
chords.** The two membranes in the
larynx whose tensity is regulated at
will to produce desired pitches. Vide
GLOTTIS. **rima vocalis.** The opening between the vocal chords.

**vocalezzo** (vō-kä-lĕd′-zō), *I.* A vocal
exercise.

**voca′lion.** Vide REED-ORGAN.

**vocali′ses** (in *F.* vō-kä-lēz′). Solfeggio exercises for the voice.

**vocaliser** (vō-kăl-ĭ-zā), *F.,* **vocaliz-
zare** (vō-kä-lĭd-zä′-rĕ), *I.,* **vo′calize,**
*E.* To practise exercises for the
voice without words.

**vocalisa′tion** (in *F.* vō-kä-lĕ-zäs-yôṅ).
1. The practice of exercises for the
voice. 2. Display of vocal agility.

**vocalizzo** (lĭd′-zō, pl. -i), *I.* Vocal exercise.

**voce** (vō′-chĕ), *I.* Voice. **colla v.**
" With the voice," i. e., adopting the
tempo of the solo part. **v. angelica** (ăn-jā′-lĭ-kä). " Angel voice."
Delicate reed-stop. **v. di bianca**
(dē bĭ-än′-kä), *I.* " White voice."
Applied to pale and colourless tones,
such as the voices of young women,
children and poorly trained adults.
**v. di ca′mera.** A small voice for
the chamber. **v. di go′la.** A guttural,
throaty voice. **v. di pet′to.** The
chest voice. **v. di tes′ta.** Head
voice, the falsetto, upper register. **v.
granità** (grä-nē-tä′). A " granite "
or massive voice. **mezza voce**
(mĕd′-zä). Half the power of the
voice ; a moderate tone. **v. pasto′sa.**
A soft, flexible voice. **v. principale**
(prēn-chĭ-pä′-lĕ). Principal voice. **v.
rauca** (ra′-oo-kä). A hoarse, rough
voice. **v. so′la.** The voice alone. **v.
spianata** (spē-ä-nä′-tä). Drawn out ;
smooth, sustained voice. **v. spiccata**
(spĭk-kä′-tä). A clear, distinct voice ;
well articulated. **v. umana** (oo-mä′-
nä). The human voice. Vide VOX
HUMANA. **vociaccia** (vō-chĭ-ät′-chä).
A bad, disagreeable voice. **vocina**
(vō-chē′-nä). Thin little voice.

**voces,** *L.,* pl. of **vox. v. aequa'les.** Voices of the same kind.

**Vogar** (fō'-gär), *G.* Fugara.

**Vogel** (fō'-gĕl), *G.* Bird. **V.-flöte** or **pfeife.** A bird-whistle. **V.-gesang.** " Singing of birds " ; stop in old German organs, of small pipes standing in water, through which the wind passes ; a merula.

**voglia** (vōl'-yä), *I.* Ardour.

**voice.** 1. The sound produced by the larynx of human beings or animals. 2. Part (for any instr.), often **voicepart.** 3. The tuning and tone of organ-pipes.
Of the human voice, these are the following divisions : *basso, tenor, counter-tenor, contralto* or *alto, mezzo-soprano, soprano* (Vide each of these words). Each voice is also divided into registers (or groups of tones of a uniform quality) the transition from one to another register being sometimes distinct enough to be called a *break ;* there are usually two breaks in a male, and three in the female voice. The registers are chest, head and falsetto (q. v.).

**voicing.** The adjustment of the pitch and quality of a pipe.

**voilée** (vwä-lā), *F.* Veiled.

**voix** (vwä), *F.* 1. Voice(s). 2. Part(s). **v. angélique** (vwä-zäṅ-jā-lĕk). Vox angelica. **v. céleste** (sā-lĕst), *F.* " Celestial voice," a stop formed of two dulcianas, one slightly sharp, thus giving a vibrato. **v. de poitrine** (dŭ pwä-trēn), *F.* Chest voice. **v. de tête** (dŭ tĕt). Head voice, falsetto voice. **v. glapissante** (glä-pē-sänt). A shrill voice. **v. gréle** (vwä grĕl). A sharp, thin voice. **v. humaine** (ü-mĕn). Vox humana.

**vokal** (fō-käl'), *G.* Vocal. **V.-stil** (shtēl). Vocal style.

**volante** (vō-län'-tĕ), *I.* " Flying," light, swift.

**volata** (vō-lä'-tä), *I.,* **Volate** (vō-lä'-tĕ), *G.,* **volatine** (vō-lä-tēn), *F.* " Flight," run, rapid series of notes. **volatina** (vō-lä-tē'-nä), *I.* A little volata.

**volée** (vō-lā), *F.* A volata.

**Volk** (fôlk), *G.* Folk ; of the com people. **V. gesang** (fôlk'-gĕ-z V. s-lied** (slēt), **V. stückchen** ( kh'n), **V. s-weise.** Folk-son folk-music. **im Volkston'** or **V weise.** In folk-tone or style. **v t(h)ümliches** (tüm-lĭkh-ĕs). Popular folk-song.

**voll** (fôl), *G.* 1. Full ; *mit vollem V Chore, Orchester,* with the full o chorus or orchestra. **völler** lĕr). Fuller, louder. **volles V** (fôl'-lĕs vărk). Full organ. **Vo sang.** Chorus. **vollgriffig**(grif-l " Full-handed," with full ch **vollkom'men.** Perfect, com **vollstimmig.** Full-toned, full-vc **Vollstimmigkeit.** Fullness of **volltönend,** *G.* Sonorous. 2. suffix = full, as **gedanken** Thoughtful.

**volonté** (vō-lŏṅ-tä), *F.* Will, plea **à v.** At will.

**volta** (vōl'-tä), *I.* 1. Time. 2. A of galliard. **prima v.** (prē' First time. **una v.** One. **due v** Twice.

**voltare** (vōl-tä'-rĕ), *I.* To turi turn over.

**volte** (vōl'-tĕ, *I.;* in *F.* vōlt). 1. A solete bounding dance in 3-4 resembling the galliard. 2. I VOLTA.

**volteggiando** (vōl-tĕd-jän'-dō), Crossing the hands. **voltegg** To cross hands.

**volti** (vōl'-tĕ), *I.* Turn over. **v. bitc.** Turn quickly.

**volubilità** (vō-loo-bē-lĭ-tä'), *I.* ubility. **volubilmen'te.** Fluer

**vol'ume.** Quality of tone.

**vol'untary.** 1. An introductory or piece often extemporaneous. 2 introductory anthem. 3. A sp of toccata in two or three movem

**volver a la misma cancion** (vō ä lä mēs'-mä kän'-thĭ-ōn), *Sp.* return to the same (original) air.

**vom** (fōm), *G.* = *von dem.* I the. **vom Anfang.** From the b ning. **vom Blatte** (blät'-tĕ). " I the page," i. e., at first sight.

ōn), *G.* By, of, from, on.

ōr), *G.* Before, pre-.

usnahme (fōr-ows'-nä-mĕ), **Vor-**
ifung (fōr-grī'-foongk), **Vorgriff**
'-grĭf), *G.* Anticipation. **Vor-**
eitung (fōr'-bĕ-rī-toongk). Prep-
ion. **Vorberei'tungsunterricht**
ı'-tĕr-rīkht). Preparatory instruc-

ersatz (zäts). *G.* First sub-
wesentliche Dissonanz.

eiger (gī-khĕr), *G.* First violin,
er.

alt (fōr'-hält), *G.* 1. Suspension.
haltslösung (lä-zoongk). Its
lution. 2. Syncopation.

r (fōr-hār), *G.* Before. **tempo**
vorher, *G.* The time as be-

(fō'-rĭkh), *G.* Former, preceding.
iges Zeitmass. In the original
po.

ang (fōr'-zäng), *G.* Act of begin-
a song. **Vorsänger** (fōr'-zĕng-
Precentor.

hlag (fōr'-shläkh). Accentuated,
oggiatura.

etzzei'chen, *G.* Chromatic sign.
piel (fōr'-shpēl), *G.* Prelude; over-
. **Vor'spieler** (shpē-lĕr). Lead-
principal performer. **Vortän-**
Chief dancer. **Vorsteller.**
former.

ag (fōr'-träkh), *G.* Execution,
rpretation. **Vortragsbezeich-**
ıg (bĕ-tsīkh-noongk). Expression
k. **vortragsstück.** Concert-
e.

ärts (fōr'-värts), *G.* "Forward,"
, faster.

eichnung (tsīkh'-noongk). 1. Sig-
ure. 2. Outline of a composi-
.

vōx), *L.* Voice. **v. acu'ta.** 1.
hrill voice. 2. In ancient music.
highest note in the bisdiapason.
ange'lica, *L.* "Angelic voice," a
oot stop of sweet tone, also **v.**
gin'ea. "Girlish voice." **v. ante-**
dens. The antecedent. **v. con'-**
quens. The consequent. **v. grav'-**
Low voice. **v. huma'na.** "Human

voice," 8-foot reed-stop usually with
tremulous effect. **v. retu'sa.** 8-foot
stop. Plural **vo'ces. v. aequales.**
Voices of the same kind, as male
voices. **v. areti'niæ.** Aretinian syllables. **v. bel'gicæ.** The syllables
of bocedisation.

**v. s.** Abbr. of Volti subito.

**vue** (vü), *F.* Sight. **à premier v.**
(ä prŭm-yā vü). At first sight.

**vulgans (tibia),** *L.* A flute-stop.

**vuide** (vwĕd), *F.* Open (of a string).

**vuoto** (voo-ō'-tō), *I.* 1. Open (of a
string). 2. Empty (of a stage).

**v. v.** Abbr. for violini.

## W

**W** 1. In *F.* = **v. v.,** i. e., **Vi-**
olins. 2. Vide the let-
ter i.
**Wachtel** (väkht'-ĕl), *G.*
"Quail." A toy pipe.

**wahnsinnig** (vän'-zĭn-nĭkh), *G.* Frantic.

**waits,** *E.* 1. Hautboys. 2. Players
on the hautboys. 3. Night-watch-
men. 4. Christmas carollers.

**Wald** (vält), *G.* Forest. **Wald-**
**flöte,** *G.,* or **-pfeife.** Forest-flute.
**W.-quinte.** A stop. **W.-flöten-**
**quinte.** A stop a fifth higher.
**Waldhorn** (vält'-hôrn), *G.* "Forest-
horn"; a winding-horn. (Vide
HORN.)

**walnika** (väl-nē'-kä). Russian bagpipe.

**wals** (wäls), *Dutch.* A waltz.

**waltz,** *E.,* **Walzer** (väl'-tsĕr), *G.* 1.
A popular modern round dance in 3-4
time, perhaps of Bohemian origin.
The speed and rhythm vary, the
**Ländler,** or **German,** being slow;
the **Vienna,** or **Schleif-walzer** being quicker; the **Zweitritt, deux-**
**temps,** or **two-step,** having but
two steps to the measure. 2. A concert-piece in triple time, usually brilliant.

**walynka** (vā-lēn'-kä). Russian bagpipe.

**Walze** (väl'-tsĕ), *G.* "Roller." An undulating figuration.

**wankend** (vän'-kĕnt), *G.* Wavering, hesitating.

**war'ble.** A bagpipe grace.

**Wärme** (vĕr'-mĕ), *G.* Warmth.

**Washington Post.** In England a dance (so called from J. P. Sousa's march of that name) in which the man dances behind the woman.

**was'sail.** A convivial song.

**Wasserorgel** (väs'-sĕr-ôr-khĕl), *G.* Hydraulic organ.

**waste-pallet.** Vide VALVE.

**water music.** Handel's name for certain airs, performed on the water, for the King.

**water-organ.** Hydraulic organ.

**wayghtes.** Old *E.* Waits.

**Web'er chronom'eter.** Metronome, inv. by Weber. A cord divided into five inch-spaces, with a weight at the lower end. Abbr. **Web. Chron.**

**Wechsel** (vĕkh'-sĕl), *G.* Change. **W.-chor** (kōr). Alternate choir. **W.-gesang.** Antiphonal song. **W.-note** (nō'-tĕ). Changing note.

**Wehmuth** (vā'-moot), *G.* Sadness. **wehmüthig** (vā'-mü-tĭkh). Sad, sorrowful.

**Weiberstimme** (vī'-bĕr-shtĭm'-mĕ), *G.* A female voice.

**weich** (vīkh), *G.* 1. Soft. 2. Minor.

**weight of wind.** Vide INCH.

**Weihnachtslied** (vī'-näkhts-lēt), *G.* Christmas hymn.

**weinend** (vī'-nĕnt), *G.* Weeping.

**Weise** (vī'-zĕ), *G.* 1. Melody. 2. Manner; as a suffix= -wise.

**weisse Note** (vīs'-sĕ nō'-tĕ), *G.* "White" note; half or whole note.

**weit** (vīt), *G.* Dispersed, open (of harmony).

**Welle** (vĕl'-lĕ), *G.* Roller of an organ. **Wellatur** (toor'). Roller-system. **Wel'lenbrett.** Roller-board.

**well-tempered.** In equal temperament, as in Bach's "Well-tempered Clavichord," a series of clavichord pieces ranging through all the keys. Vide TEMPERAMENT.

**Welsh-harp.** Vide HARP.

**weltlich** (vĕlt'-lĭkh), *G.* Secula~

**wenig** (vā'-nĭkh), *G.* Little. **ei~ nig.** A little, rather.

**Werk** (vĕrk), *G.* 1. Work. 2. ~ ment. 3. Action. Vide H WERK and OBERWERK. 4. A 5. The set of stops belonging t key-board.

**Wert(h)** (vĕrt), *G.* Value, durat

**wesentlich** (vā'-zĕnt-lĭkh), *G.* I tial. **wesentliche Dissonan** dissonant chord-tone, oppose passing-note. **wesentliche time.** Dominant seventh.

**Wetter-harfe** (vĕt'-tĕr-här-fĕ) "Weather-harp." Æolian har

**Wettgesang** (vĕt'-gĕ-zäng), *G* singing-match.

**wheel.** Refrain, burden.

**whiffler.** A fifer.

**whipping bow.** A swift and ~ violin attack.

**whistle.** A small, shrill wind blown at the end, like an old E flute.

**whole note, rest, shift, step,** etc. Vide the NOUNS.

**wie** (vē), *G.* As. **wie aus der ne.** As from a distance. **wie ** Again as above. **wie vorher** här). As before.

**wieder** (vē'-dĕr), *G.* Again. **gabe** (gä'-bĕ). Performance. **herstellungszeichen** (tsī'-~ The natural sign (♮). **w.-anfa~** To begin again. **W.-holung** loongk). Repetition. **W.~ ungszeichen.** Sign of repe~ **W.-klang** (kläng), **W.-s~** (shäl). Echo.

**Wiegenlied** (vē'-gĕn-lēt), *G.* C~ song.

**wild** (vēlt), *G.* Wild.

**wind** (wīnd). To blow, as a hor

**Wind** (in *G.* vĭnt). Air. **w~ban~** A band of wind-instrs. 2. The ~ or the music for them. **windc** Vide ORGAN. **w. instrument** general name for all instrs. ~ tone is produced by the breath bellows. **windtrunk.** A p~ conveying air from the bello~

e wind-chest. **Windmesser** (mĕs-
r), *G.*, **windgauge.** Vide INCH.
J.-harfe, *G.* Æolian harp. **Wind-
de** (lä-dĕ), *G.* Wind-chest. Vide
ʀGAN. **Windstock** (shtôk), *G.*
ver of organ-pipes. **Windzunge**
soong-ĕ), *G.* Tongue of a pipe.
J.-harmo′nika, *G.* Æolodion.
selig (vĭn′-zĕ-lĭkh), *G.* Plaintive.
Jinselstimme. Plaintive voice.
·bel (vēr′-bĕl), *G.* 1. Peg (of a
olin). **Wirbelkasten.** Peg-box.
Stopper of a pipe. 3. Drumstick.
Roll (on a drum). **Wirbeltanz**
ints). A whirling dance.
·end (vō′-gĕnt), *G.* Waving.
.l (vōl), *G.* Well. **Wohlklang**
ōl′-kläng), **Wohllaut** (lowt). Harony. **wohlklingend.** Harmonious.
ohltemperi(e)rt (vōl-tĕm-pĕ-rērt′),
" Well-tempered " (q. v.).
If (in *G.* vôlf). 1. The disagree-
le snarling of two pipes not quite in
rfect tune. 2. Vide TEMPERAMENT.
In bow-instr. the roughness of cer-
n tones due to faulty workmanship.
Vide ORGELWOLF. 5. The 12th
d most troublesome of the circle of
chs. Vide TEMPERAMENT.
d-wind. 1. The whole group of
oden instrs. in the orchestra. 2.
gan-stops of wood.
king-out. Development. Vide
ʀM.
rtklang (vôrt′-kläng), *G.* Accent,
ne.
st. A tuning-hammer. **wrest-
ıs.** In a piano movable pins round
ich one end of the string is wound ;
turning this the instr. is tuned.
·estplank. A plank of several
ers of wood in which the wrestpins
e driven.
tguide. Vide CHIROPLAST.
htig (vookh′-tĭkh). Weighty, em-
atic.
de (vür′-dĕ), *G.* Dignity. **wür-
voll, würdig** (vür′-dĭkh). Digni-
l.
(h) (voot), *G.* Madness. **wüthend**
·-tĕnt), **wüthig** (tĭkh). Furi-
s.

## X

**XÆNORPHIKA** (ksän′-ôr-fī-
kä), *G.* A piano-violin with
a bow to each string, inv. by
Röllig, 1797 ; he also inv.
the somewhat similar *orphika*.

**xylharmo′nica** or **-con,** *Gr.* Utro's
improvement in 1810 upon his **xylo-
siston,** inv. 1807 ; a euphonion with
wooden, instead of glass, rods.

**Xylorganon** (ksĕl-ôr′-gä-nōn), *Gr.*
Xylophone.

**xylophone** (zĭl′-ō-fōn). A graduated
series of bars of wood upon bands of
straw or cord, played with wooden
mallets, compass 2 octaves.

## Y

**YABAL** (yä′-bäl), *Heb.* Trumpet blast.

**yang kin.** A Chinese dulcimer
with brass strings.

**yo.** Indian flute.

**yo′del, yod′ler.** Vide JODEL, JODLER.

**yue kin.** Chinese guitar.

## Z

**ZA** (zä). Formerly applied by the
French to *B♭* to distinguish
it from *B♮* or *Si*.

**zahlen** (tsä′-lĕn), *G.* To count.
**zahle.** " Count ! " **Zahlzeit** (tsīt).
A count.

**zaleo** (thä-lä′-ō), *Sp.* Vide JALEO.

**zampogna** (tsäm-pōn′-yä), **zampugna**
(poon′-ya), *I.* 1. Ancient bagpipe.
2. A shawm. Vide CORNAMUSA and
CHALUMEAU. **zampognare** (pōn-
yä′-rĕ). To play the pipes. **zampo-
gnato′re.** A piper. **zampognet′-
ta** or **-ina** (pōn-yĕ′-nä). A small
bagpipe.

**za′ner.** Egyptian bassoon.

**zanze.** Vide AMBIRA.

**zapateado** (thä-pä-tä′-ä-dhō), *Sp.* A
dance whose rhythm is emphasised by
stamping the heel.

**Zapfenstreich** (tsä′-pfĕn-strīkh), *G.* The tattoo.

**zarabanda** (thä-rä-bän′-dhä), *Sp.* Saraband.

**zaramel′la** (tsä-rä-), *I.* Rustic double-reed pipe with bell-mouth.

**Zargen** (tsär′-khĕn), *G.*, pl. Sides of violin, etc.

**zart** (tsärt), *G.*, **zärtlich** (tsärt-likh). Tender, delicate. *mit zarten Stimmen*, with delicate stops. **Zartflöte.** A very soft 4-foot flute-stop.

**zarzuela** (thär-thoo-ā′-lä), *Sp.* A 2-act drama with music, something like the vaudeville; originating in the 17th century at the royal castle Zarzuela.

**Zauber** (tsow′-bĕr), *G.* Magic. **Z.-lied** (lēt). Magic song.

**zeffiro′so** (tsĕf), *I.* Zephyr-like.

**zehn** (tsān), *G.* Ten. **Zehnte** (tsān′-tĕ). Tenth.

**Zeichen** (tsī′-khĕn), *G.* Sign(s).

**Zeit** (tsīt), *G.* Time. **Z.-mass** (tsīt′-mäs), *G.* Tempo. **Zeitmes′ser.** Metronome. **Z.-werth.** Time value.

**zèle** (zĕl), *F.*, **zelo** (tsā′-lō), *I.* Zeal, ardour. **zelo′so**, **zelosamen′te.** Zealous(ly).

**zeng** (tsĕng). Persian cymbals.

**Zergliederung** (tsĕr-glēt′-ĕr-oongk),*G.* Dissection, or analysis of a subject.

**zerstreut** (tsĕr-stroit′), *G.* Dispersed.

**ze′ze.** An African guitar.

**Ziehharmo′nica** (tsē), *G.* The accordion.

**ziemlich** (tsēm′-lĭkh), *G.* Rather; moderately.

**Zierathen** (tsē-rä′-tĕn), *G.*, pl. Ornaments.

**zierlich** (tsēr-lĭkh), *G.* Neat, graceful.

**Ziffer** (tsĭf′-fĕr), *G.* Figure, Arabic numeral.

**ziganka** (chĭ-gän′-kä), *Russian.* Country-dance.

**Zigeunerartig** (tsē-goin′-ĕr-är-tĭkh), *G.* In gypsy style. **Z.-musik** (moo-zēk′). Gipsy music.

**zikrs.** Dances of Egyptian dervishes.

**zillo** (tsĭl′-lō), *I.* Chirp, chirping.

**zimbalon.** Vide CZIMBALON.

**Zimbel** (tsēm′-bĕl), *G.* Cymbal. **Z.-stern.** A star hung with small bells

in front of an organ and sounded current of air.

**zingana** (chēn-gä′-nä). Bohemian s

**zingarese** (tsēn-gä-rä′-zĕ), *I.* Gi **zingaresca** (rĕs′-kä). In the sty gipsies. **zingaro** (tsēn′-gä-rō). Gi

**Zinke** (tsĭnk′-ĕ), pl. **-en**, *G.* Corn ancient or modern. **Zinkbl** (tsĭnk′-blä-zĕr), *G.* Cornet-playe

**zith′er** (in *G.* tsĭt′-ĕr). 1. The moder **Schlagzither**) is a flat, shallow onance-box without a neck, about thirty-six strings of various terial—wire and gut—some overs Under some of the strings at one lies a fretted finger-board; on this the melody is stopped out wit left hand. These strings, tuned a′, d′, g, c, are plucked with a trum attached to the right thu the rest of the strings are tune fourths, and plucked with the fingers of the right hand. It is usually in 3 sizes, the Treble or (prēm) **-z**; the **concert**; and el (ĕl-ĕ-jē′) (or **Alt** or **Lieder**) **-z**, is tuned a fourth lower. 2. **zither** or **Strich-zither** (str *G.* Was originally heart-shaped the **philomèle** now resembles a pointed viola with shallow bouts **viola-zither** having a still clos semblance). The **bow-z.** has in the head, which is rested u table, the body being held in the It has four metal strings, g, d, 3. A cither. 4. An old German with a sound-box, a neck, a fr finger-board, and eight or more s tuned in unison two and two plucked with a quill. **Z.-harfe** form of keyed auto-harp. **Zi spieler** (shpē′-lĕr), **Zitherschl** (shlä-khĕr), *G.* Guitar-player. **tera** (tsĭt′-tĕ-rä), *I.* Zither.

**zitternd** (tsĭt′-tĕrnt), *G.* Trembl

**zittino** (tsĭt-tē′-nō), *I.* Silence.

**zögernd** (tsā′-gĕrnt), *G.* Retardi

**zolfà** (tsôl-fä′), *I.* Vide SOLFA.

**zoppa** (tsôp′-pä), or **-o**, *I.* Lame, ing. **alla z.** Syncopated; use of a jerky Magyar rhythm.

ig (tsôr'-nĭkh), *G.* Angry.

ou (zoo-loo), *F.* "Zulu." A pia-
te.

na. Oriental oboe.

soo), *G.* To, at, by, in, unto.

llig (tsoo'-fĕl-lĭkh), *G.* Accidental
arp, flat, or natural).

o (tsoo'-fō-lō), *I.* Flageolet, small
d-flute. **zúfolone** (lō¯-nĕ). A
ge whistle.

(tsookh), pl. **Züge** (tsü'-khĕ). 1.
aw-stop or register. 2. Slide.
gtrompete (trôm-pā'-tĕ), *G.*
le-trumpet ; the trombone. **Zug-**
**erke** (vĕr'-kĕ). Tracker-mechanism.
eglöckchen (glĕk-khĕn), *G.* The
ssing bell ; a knell.
ang (tsoo'-kläng), *G.* Concord.
nftsmusik (tsoo-koonfts'-moo-
), *G.* "Music of the future." A
m applied satirically to Wagner's
rk by L. F. C. Bischoff, 1850 ; but
er adopted as a watchword by the
agnerians.

(tsoom), *G.* = *zu dem*. To the.
na'rah. An Egyptian reed instr.
e a bassoon.
hmend (tsoo-nā'-mĕnt), *G.* In-
asing.
ge (tsoong'-ĕ), *G.* 1. Tongue.
p'pelzunge. Vide TONGUING.
**Z.-pfeife.** Reed-pipe. **Z.-blatt.**
arinet reed. **Z.-stimme.** Reed-
p. **Z.-werk.** The reed-stops
lectively. **auf-** (or **durch-**) **schlag-**
de Z. Beating (or free) reed.
aa. Turkish oboe.
ck (tsoo-rük'), *G.* Back. **z.-ge-**
nd (gā'-ĕnt), *G.* Returning to the
ginal tempo. **z.-halten.** To re-
rd. **z.-haltend.** Retarding. **Z.-**
ltung (häl-toongk). Retardation.
-tönen (tā-nen) or **z.-treiben** (trī-
n). To reverberate. **z.-schlag.**
de RIBATTUTA.
mmen (tsoo-zäm'-mĕn), *G.* Tother. **z.-gesetzt.** Combined,
mpound (of time). **Z.-klang, Z.-**
ut (lowt). Harmony. **Z.-schlag.**
de ACCIACCATURA. **z.-streichen.**
slur. **Z.-streichung** (strī-
oongk). Slurring.

---

**zutraulich** (tsoo-trow'-lĭkh), *G.* Con-
fident(ly).
**Zuversicht** (tsoo'-fĕr-zĭkht), *G.* Confidence.
**zwanzig** (tsvän'-tsĭkh), *G.* Twenty.
**Zwanzigste** (tsvän'-tsĭkh-stĕ).
Twentieth.
**zwei** (tsvī), *G.* Two. **z.-chörig** (khā-
rĭkh). Two-choired. **z.-fach** (fäkh),
**z.-fältig** (fĕl-tĭkh). 1. In two ranks
(organ-pipes). 2. Compound (of intervals). 3. Double (of counterpoint).
**z.-füssig.** Two-foot. Vide PIPE and
PITCH. **Z.-gesang.** A duet. **z.-**
**gestrichen.** Twice-marked. Vide
PITCH. **Z.-glied** (glēt). Sequence
of two chords. **Z.-halbertakt.** 2-2
time. **z.-händige** (hĕnt'-ĭkh-ĕ). For
two hands. **Z.-klang.** A chord of
two tones. **z.-mal** (tsvī-mäl). Twice.
**z.-stimmig.** For two parts. **Z.-**
**spiel** (shpēl). A duet. **Zweite** (tsvī'-
tĕ). Second. **Zweitel (-note).**
Half-note. **Z.-tritt.** Vide WALTZ.
**Z.-unddreissigstel** (oont-drī-zĭkh-
shtĕl). 32d note. **Z.-viertelnote**
(fĕr'-tĕl-nō-tĕ). Half-note. **Z.-**
**viertelpause** (pow-zĕ). A half rest.
**Z.-vierteltakt.** 2-4 time. **Z.-**
**zählighertakt** (tsā-lĭkh-ĕr-takt).
Duple time. **Z.-zweiteltakt** (tsvī-
tsvī-tĕl-takt). 2-2 time.
**zwerchflöte** (tsvĕrkh-) or **pfeife,** *G.*
Transverse flute.
**zwischen** (tsvĭsh'-ĕn), *G.* Between.
**Z.-akt.** Intermezzo. **Z.-gesang,**
**Z.-handlung, Z.-harmonie, Z.-**
**satz.** The episode (in fugue). **Z.-**
**raum** (-rowm). Space between the
lines. **Z.-spiel.** Interlude. **Z.-**
**stille** (shtĭl'-lĕ). Pause. **Z.-stim-**
**me** (shtĭm-mĕ). Middle voice. **Z.-**
**ton.** Intermediate tone.
**Zwitscherharfe** (tsvĭtsh-ĕr), *G.* Vide
SPITZHARFE.
**zwölf** (tsvĕlf), *G.* Twelve. **Z.-ach-**
**teltakt** (äkh-tĕl-täkt). 12-8 time.
**Z.-saiter** (zī-tĕr). "12-stringed"
bissex.
**zymbel** (tsēm'-bĕl), *G.* Vide CYMBAL.
**zzxjoanw** (shaw). *Maori.* 1. Drum.
2. Fife. 3. Conclusion.

# Music Lovers' Cyclopedia
## Part 11

...ate (äb'-bä-tě), *I.* abbé (ăbbā), *F.* ...bbot (often honorary).

...né (lěn-ā), *F.* The elder. cadet (...ä-dā), *F.* The younger. Usually of ...rothers.

...ıerlingo (kä-měr-lēn'-gō), *I.* Chamberlain.

...tab(rigiensis). Of Cambridge University.

...aliere (kä-väl-yā'-rě), *I.* Knight. ...r.

...valier (shŭ-väl-yä), *F.* Knight.

, *F.* Company ; et cie (ā sē). & Co.

...nte (kônt), *F.*

...te (kōn'-tě), *I.* Count.

...to or -a (dět'-tō). "Called."

: (dük), *F.* duca (doo'-kä), *I.* ...Ɔuke.

...ler von (āt'-ler fōn). Nobleman of.

(fēs), *F.* Son.

...au (frow), *G.* Mrs. Fräulein (frī'-...n). Miss.

...eiherr (frī'-hăr), *G.* Baron.

...heimrath (gě-hīm'-rät), *G.* Privy ...ounsellor.

...sellschaft (gě-zěl'-shäft), *G.* Association, society.

...af (gräf), *G.* Count. Gräfin (grā-...n). Countess.

...rr (hăr), *G.* Mr.

...uptkirche (howpt-kēr'-khě), *G.* Chief church.

...fkapellmeister (mī-shtěr). Court-conductor. Hofmusik'intendant (...moo-zek'), *G.* Supt. of court-music.

...jeune (lŭ zhŭn), *F.* The younger.

...stizrath (yoos'-tēts-rät), *G.* Counsellor of justice ; often honorary.

...mmersänger (zěngk-ěr), *G.* Chamber-singer (to the court).

...estro (mä-ās'-tro), *I.* Master.

...maggiore (ěl mäd-jō'-rě), *I.* The greater.

maistre (old French), or maître (mětr), *F.* Master.

marchesa (mär-kā'-zä), *I.* Marchioness.

il minore (ēl-mē-nō'-rě), *I.* The lesser.

mus. bach(elor) and mus. doc(tor). Vide the D. D.

oxon(ensis). Of Oxford University.

père (pär), *F.* Father.

Reichsfreiherr (rīkhs'-frī-hăr), *G.* Baron of the empire.

Ritter (rĭt'-těr), *G.* Knight, chevalier.

sieur (s'yŭr), *F.* Sir, Mr.

und Sohn (oont zōn), *G.* & Son. und Söhne (oont zā'-ně), *G.* & Sons.

van (vän), *Dutch.* von (fōn), *G.* de (dŭ), *F.* di (dē), *I.* and *Sp.* From, of.

vicomtesse (vē-kôn-těs). Viscountess.

le vieux (lŭ v'yŭ), *F.* The elder.

y (ē), *Sp.* "And," used in joining two proper names somewhat as we use a hyphen ; the Spaniard keeping his mother's, as well as his father's, name.

zu (tsoo), *G.* To.

(Others will be found in the D. D.)

NOTE.—In the Biographical Dictionary, given names are regularly abbreviated as in the following list, the same abbreviation serving for one name in its different forms in different languages.

Abramo (ä'-brä-mō), *I.*
Adam (ä'-däm), *G.*
Adalbert (ä'-däl-běrt), *G.*
Adelaide (ä-dä-lä-ē'-dě), *I.* and *G.*
(Ad.) Adolf (ä'-dôlf), *G.*
(Ad.) Adolph, *G.*
(Ad.) Adolphe (ăd-ôlf), *F.*
(Adr.) Adriano (ä-drĭ-ä'-nō), *I.*
Adrien (ăd'-rĭ-äṅ), *F.*
Agathon (ä'-gä-tōn), *G.*

(Ag.) **Agostino** (ä-gôs-tē′-nō), *I.*
**Aimable** (ĕm-äb′′l), *F.*
(Alb.) **Albrecht** (äl′-brĕkht), *G.*
(Ales.) **Alessandro** (ä-lĕs-sän′-drō), *I.*
(Alex.) **Alexan′der.**
(Alex.) **Alexandre** (äl-ĕx-äṅdr′), *F.*
**Alexis** (ăl-ĕx-ēs), *F.*
**Aloys** (ä -lois).
**Aloysia** (ä-loi′-zĭ-ä), *G.*
**Amadeo** (äm-ä-dā′-ō), *I.* -deus (dā′-oos), *G.*
**Amalie** (ä′-mäl-ē), *G.*
**Ambroise** (äṅ-bwäz), *F.*
**Amédée** (ăm′-ā-dā), *F.*
**Amélie** (äm′-ā-lē), *F.*
**Anatole** (ăn-ä-tôl), *F.*
**André** (äṅ-drä), *F.*
(And.) **Andrea** (än′-drā-ä), *I.*
(Ands) **Andreas** (än′-drā-äs), *G.*
**Ange** (äṅzh), *F.*
**Angelica** (än-jä′-lē-kä), *I.*
(Ang.) **Angelo** (än′-jä-lō), *I.*
(A. or Ant.) **Antoine** (äṅ′-twăn), *F.*
(Ant.) **Anton** (än′-tōn), *G.*
(A. or Ant.) **Anto′nio,** *I.*
(Ap.) **Apollon** (ăp-ôl-lôṅ), *F.*
**Aristide** (är-ĭs-tēd), *F.*
**Armin** (är′-mēn), *G.*
**Arnaud** (är-nō), *F.*
**Arrigo** (är′-rē-gō), *I.*
**Arsène** (är-sĕn), *F.*
**Arthur** (ăr-tür), *F.*
**Attilio** (ät-tē′-lĭ-ō), *I.*
(Aug.) **August** (ow′-goost), *G.*
**Auguste** (ō-güst), *F.*
**Augustin** (ow′-goos-ten, *G.*) (ō-güs-täṅ, *F.*).
(Aug.) **Augusto** (ä-oo-goost′-ō), *I.*

**Baldassare** (bäl-däs-sä′-rě), *I.*
(Bal.) **Balthasar** (bäl-tä-zär′), *F.*
(Bap.) **Baptiste** (bă-tēst), *F.*
(Bart.) **Bartolommeo** (bär-tō-lôm-mä′-ō), *I.*
(Bat.) **Battista** (bät-tē′-stä), *I.*
**Benedikt** (bā′-ně-dēkt), *G.*
**Beniamino** (bän-yĕ-mē′-nō), *I.*
(Bv.) **Benvenuto** (bän-vě-noo′-tō), *I.*
(Bdo.) **Bernardo** (bĕr-när′-dō), *I.*
(Bd.) **Bernhard** (bärn′-härt), *G.*
**Bertrand** (bär-träṅ), *F.*
**Bianca** (bē-än′-kä), *I.*

**Blasius** (blä′-zĭ-oos), *G.*
**Bonaventure** (bôn-ăv-äṅ-tür′), *F.*
**Bonifacio** (bō-nē-fä′-chō), *I.*
**Bonafazio** (bōn-ē-fä′-tsĭ-ō), *I.*
**Brigida** (brē′-jē-dä), *I.*

**Camille** (kăm-ē′-yŭ), *F.*
**Carlo** (kär′-lō), *I.*
**Casimir** (käs-ĭ-mēr), *F.*
**Catherino** (kät-tĕr-rē′-nō), *I.*
**Caytan** (kä′ ē-tän), *Sp.*
**César** (sā-zär), *F.*
**Cesare** (chā-zä′-rě), *I.*
(Chas.) **Charles** (shärl), *F.*
**Chrisostomus** (krē-sôs′-tō-moos),
(Chr.) **Christian** (krēst′-ĭ-än), *G.*
(Chp.) **Christoph** (krēs′-tôph) *G.*
**Cinthie** (săṅ-tē), *F.*
**Claude** (klōd), *F.*
**Clément** (klä-mäṅ), *F.*
**Clotilde** (klō-tēl′-dě), *G.*
**Colin** (kô-lăṅ), *F.*
**Constance** (kôn-stäṅ′-tsě), *F.*
**Cornelius** (kôr-nā′-lĭ-oos), *G.*
**Costanzo** (kō-stän′-tsō), *I.*

**Damaso** (dä-mä′-sō), *Sp.*
(D.) **David** (dä-vēd), *F.*
(D.) **David** (dä′-fēt), *G.*
**Delphin** (dĕl-fäṅ), *F.*
**Dietrich** (dēt′-rĭkh), *G.*
**Dieudonné** (d′yŭ-dŭn-nä), *F.*
**Diogenio** (dē-ō-jä-nē′-ō), *I.*
**Dioma** (dē-ō′-mä), *I.*
(Dion.) **Dionisio** (dē-ō-nē′-sĭ-ō), *Sp.*
**Dionys** (dē′-o-nēs), *G.*
(Dom.) **Domenico** (dō-mā′-nĭ-kō),
(Dom.) **Dominique** (dôm-ĭ-nēk), *F.*
**Dufrèsne** (dü-frĕn), *F.*

(Edm.) **Edmond** (ĕd-môṅ), *F.*
(Edm.) **Edmund** (ät′-moont), *G.*
(Edw.) **Edward** (äd-văr), *F.*
**Egidio** (ä-jē′-dĭ-ō), *I.*
**Eleonore** (ā-lā-ō-nō′-rě), *G.*
**Eléonore** (ā-lā-ō-nôr), *F.* Also a masculine name.
**Elias** (ā-lē′-äs), *G.*
**Eligio** (ā-lē′-jō), *I.*
**Eliodoro** (ā-lĭ-ō-dō′-rō), *I.*
**Eliseo** (ā-lē′-zä-ō), *I.*

za (ā-lē′-zä), *I.*
ı.) Emanuel (ā-män-wĕl), *F.*
il (ā-mēl), *G.*
ilie (ā′-mĭ-lē), *F.*
ı.) Emilio (ā-mēl′-yō), *I.*
ım.) Emmanuele (ĕm-män-oo-ā′-), *I.*
g.) Engelbert (ĕng′-ĕl-bĕrt), *G.*
rico (ĕn-rē′-kō), *I.*
ısmc (ā-räs′-mō), *I.*
ole (ār′-kō-lä′), *I.*
h.) Erhard (ăr′-härt), *G.*
ıst (ărnst), *G.*
ico (ĕr′-rĭ-kō), *I.*
.) Étienne (āt′-yĕn), *F.*
ıg.) Eugen (oi′-gān), *G.*
ıg.) Eugène (ŭ-zhĕn′), *F.*
ıg.) Eugenio (ā-oo-jā′-nē-ō), *I.*
stache (ŭs-täsh), *F.*
arista (ā-vä-rē′-stä), *I.*

bio (fäb′-yō), *I.*
) Felice (fä-lē′-chĕ).
licien (fä-lĕs-yäń), *F.*
) Félix (fā′-lēx), *F.*
) Felix (fā-lēx), *G.*
l.) Ferdinand (făr′-dĭ-nänt, *G.*)
ār-dĭ-näń, *F.*).
lo.) Ferdinando (fĕr-dē-nän′-dō), *I.*
rencz (fĕr′-ĕns), *Hung.*
réol (fā-rā-ôl), *F.*
rnandez (fĕr-nän′-dĕth), *Sp.*
rnando (fĕr-nän′-dō), *I.*
rruccio (fĕr-root′-chō), *I.*
min (fĕr-mäń), *F.*
rence (flôr-äńs), *F.* Commonly a
ıasculine name.
rian (flôr-yäń, *F.*) (flôr′-ĭ-än, *G.*).
.) Fortunato (fôr-too-nä′-tō), *I.*
an.) Francesco (frän-chās′-kō), *I.*
ancesco (frän-thās′-kō), *Sp.*
ancisco (frän-thēs′-kō), *Sp.*
an.) François (fräń-swä), *F.*
antisek (frän′-tĭ-shĕk), *Bohemian.*
z.) Franz (fränts), *G.*
.) Frédéric (frā-dā-rēk), *F.*
dolin (frē′-dō-lēn), *G.*
.) Friedrich (frēt′-rĭkh), *G.*

briele (gä-brĭ-ā′-lĕ), *I.*
aet.) Gaetano (gä-ā-tä′-nō), *I.*
asp.) Gasparo (gäs-pä′-rō), *I.*

Gellio (jĕl′-lĭ-ō), *I.*
Geminiano (jĕm-ēn-ĭ-ä′-nō), *I.*
Gennaro (gĕn-nä′-rō), *I.*
(G.) Georg (gā-ôrkh′), *G.*
(G.) George, *E.*
(G.) Georges (zhôrzh), *F.*
(Ger.) Gerolamo (jĕ-rō′-lä-mō), *I.*
(Geron.) Geronimo (jĕ-rō′-nĭ-mō), *I.*
Gervais (zhĕr-vĕ′), *F.*
Gesu (hä′-zoo), *Sp.*
Ghislein (gés-läń), *F.*
Giacinto (jä-chēn′-tō), *I.*
Giacomo (jäk′-ō-mō), *I.*
Gialdino (jäl-dē′-nō), *I.*
Gioacchino (jō-ä-kē′-nō), *I.*
Giordano (jôr-dä-nō), *I.*
Gioseffo (jō-sĕf′-fō), *I.*
(Giov.) Giovanne (jō-vän′-nĕ), *I.*
Giuditta (joo-dĭt′-tä), *I.*
Giulia (jool′-yä), *I.*
Giulio (jool′-yō), *I.*
(Gius.) Giuseppe (joo-sĕp′-pĕ), *I.*
Gjula (gū′-lä), *Hung.*
Gotifredo (gō-tĕ-frä′-dō), *I.*
(Gf.) Gottfried (gôt′-frēt), *G.*
Gotthard (gôt′-härt), *G.*
(Gh.) Gotthilf (gôt′-hĭlf), *G.*
(Gl.) Gottlieb (gôt′-lēp), *G.*
Gottlob (gôt′-lōp), *G.*
Gregorio (grā-gō′-rĭ-ō), *I.*
Guido (goo-ē′-dō), *I.*
(Guil.) Guillaume (gē-yōm), *F.*
(Gv.) Gustav (goos′-täf), *G.*
(Gve.) Gustave (güs-tăv), *F.*

Hamish (hä′-mēsh), *Gaelic.*
Hans (häns), *G.*
(H.) Heinrich (hīn′-rĭkh).
(H.) Henri (äń-rē), *F.*
(H.) Hen′ry.
(Hn.) Hermann (här′-män), *G.*
Hieronymus (hē-ĕr-ōn′-ē-moos), *G.*
(Hip.) Hippolyte (ēp-ō-lēt), *F.*
Hugo (hoo′-gō, *G.*) (ü-gō, *F.*).

(Ign.) Ignace (ēn-yăs), *F.*
(Ign.) Ignazio (ēn-yät′-sĭ-ō), *I.*
(I.) Igraz (ēkh′-räts), *G.*
Ilitch (ē′-lĭtsh). *Rus.*
Ilja (ēl′-jä), *Rus.*
Ingeborg (ĭng′-ĕ-bôrkh), *G.*
(Ipp.) Ippolito (ēp-pō-lē′-tō). *I.*

Isidore (ē-zē-dôr), *F.*
Ítalo (ēt'-ä-lō), *I.*

Jacob (yäk'-ōp), *G.*
Jacopo (yäk'-ō-pō), *I.*
(Jac.) Jacques (zhăk), *F.*
Jan (yän), *Dutch.*
Jan (yän), *Polish.*
Javier (häv-yěr), *Sp.*
(J.) Jean (zhän), *F.*
Jefte (yěf'-tě), *I.*
Jérome (zhā-rôm), *F.*
(Joa.) Joachim (yō'-ä-khēm), *G.*
Joaquin (wä'-kēn), *Sp.*
(Jn.) Johann (yō'-hän), *G.*
(Jns.) Johannes (yō-hän'-něs), *G.*
(J.) John.
José (hō-zā'), *Sp.*
(Jos.) Josef, or Joseph (yō'-zěf, *G.*) (zhō-zěf, *F.*).
Josquin (zhôs-kǎn), *F.*
Juan (hoo-än'), *Sp.*
Jules (zhül), *F.*
Julie (zhü-lē), *F.*
Julien (zhül-yǎn), *F.*
Juliette (zhül-yět), *F.*
Julius (yoo'-lĭ-oos), *G.*
Juste (zhüst), *F.*
Justin (zhüs-tǎn), *F.*

Karl (kärl), *G.*
Karoline (kä-rō-lē'-ně), *G.*
Kasper (käs'-pěr), *G.*
(Kd.) Konrad (kôn'-rät), *G.*
(Konst.) Konstantin (kōn-stän-tēn), *G.*

Ladislaw (lăd'-ĭs-läf), *Pol.*
Laure (lōr), *F.*
Laurent (lō-räṅ), *F.*
Leberecht (lā'-bě-rěkht), *G.*
Léon (lā'-ôṅ), *F.*
Léonard (lā-ō-nǎr), *F.*
Léonce (lā-ôṅs), *F.*
Leone (lā-ō'-ně), *I.*
(Ld.) Léopold (lā-ŭ-pôld), *F.*
(Ld.) Leopold (lā-ō-pōlt), *G.*
Lopez (lō'-pěth), *Sp.*
(Lor.) Lorenz (lō'-rěnts), *G.*
(L.) Louis (loo-ē), *F.*
Louise (loo-ēz), *F.*

Luca (loo'-kä), *I.*
Lucien (lüs-yǎn), *F.*
Lucrezia (loo-krā'-tsē-ä), *I.*
(Lud.) Ludovico (loo-dō-vē'-kō), *I.*
(L.) Ludwig (loot'-vĭkh), *G.*
(L.) Luigi (loo-ē'-jē), *I.*
Luigia (loo-ē'-jä), *I.*
Luise (loo-ē'-zě), *G.*

Manfredo (män-frā'-dō), *I.*
Manuel (män'-oo-ěl), *G.*
Marcello (mär-chěl'-lō), *I.*
Marco (mär'-kō), *I.*
Marguerite (mär-gŭ-rēt'), *F.*
(M.) Maria (mä-rē'-ä), *G., I.* and *I.*
   Commonly a masculine name.
Marie (mă-rē), *F.* Commonly a masculine name.
Mathias (mä-tē'-ăs), *F.* and *G.*
Mathieu (măt-yŭ), *F.*
(Mat.) Matteo (mät-tā'-ō), *I.*
Matthäus (mät-tā'-oos), *G.*
Mattia (mät-tē'-ä), *I.*
Maturin (măt-ŭ-răṅ), *F.*
Maurice (mō-rēs), *F.*
Max (măx), *G.*
Maximilian (mäx-ĭ-mēl'-ĭ-än), *G.*
Melchior (měl-shĭ-ôr), *F.*
Melchiore (měl-kĭ-ō'-rě), *I.*
Michael (mē'-kä-ěl), *I.*
Michel (mē-shěl), *F.*
Michele (mē-kā'-lě), *I.*
Miroslaw (mē'-rō-släf), *Russian.*
Modeste (mō-děst), *F.*
Moritz (mō'-rēts), *G.*
Muzio (moo'-tsĭ-ō), *I.*

Napoléon (nă-pō'-lā-ôṅ), *F.*
Natale (nä-tā'-lě), *I.*
Nepomuk (nā'-pō-mook), *G.*
Niccola (nēk'-kō-lä), *I.*
(N.) Nich'olas, *E.*
(N.) Nicolas (nē-kō-läs), *F.*
(N.) Nicolò (nē-kō-lō'), *I.*
Nikolai (nē'-kō-lā'), *G.*
(N.) Nikolaus (ne'-kō-lows), *G.*

Octave (ôk-tăv), *F.*
Orazio (ō-rä'-tsĭ-ō), *I.*
Otto (ôt'-tō), *G.*
Ottokar (ôt'-tō-kär), *Pol.*

taléon (pän-tä-lā-ôn), *F.*
lo (pä'-ō-lō), *I.*
cal (păs-kăl), *F.*
quale (päs-kwä'-lĕ), *I.*
l (pōl), *F.*
ro (pä'-dhrō), *Sp.*
egrino (pā-rā-grē'-nō), *I.*
Peter.
Peter (pā'-tĕr), *G.*
ibert (fē-lǐ-băr), *F.*
) Philipp (fē'-lǐp), *G.*
) Philippe (fē-lēp), *F.*
luigi (pē-är-loo-ē'-jē), *I.*
Pierre (pǐ-ăr'), *F.*
Pietro (pǐ-ā'-trō), *I.*
bio (pō-lē'-bē-ō), *I.*
peo (pôm-pā'-ō), *I.*
no (prē'-mō), *I.*
sper (prôs'-pār), *F.*
dent (prü-dän), *F.*

ael (rä'-fä-ĕl), *I.* and *Sp.*
gnault (rĕn-yō), *F.*
chardt (rīkh'-ärt), *G.*
nhold (rīn'-hōlt), *G.*
né (rā-nā), *F.*
) Rob'ert, *E.* (in *F.* rō'-băr, in *G.*
'-bärt).
erte (rō-bărt), *F.*
) Rober'to, *I.*
mano, *I.*
mualdo (rōm-oo-äl'-dō), *I.*
se (rôz), *F.*
d.) Rudolf (roo'-dôlf), *G.*
ggiero (rood-jä'-rō), *I.*
precht (roo'-prĕkht), *G.*

bine (zä-bē'-nĕ), *G.*
) Salvatore (säl-vä-tō'-rĕ), *I.*
nl.) Samuel (zäm'-oo-ĕl), *G.*
pione (shē-pǐ-ō'-nĕ), *I.*
bald (zä'-bält), *G.*
b.) Sébastian (sā-băst-yän), *F*

(Seb.) Sebastiano (sā-bäs-tǐ'-ä'-nō), *I.*
and *Sp.*
Siegfried (zēkh'-frēt), *G.*
Siegmund (zēkh'-moont), *G.*
Simon (zē'-mōn), *G.*
(Sim.) Simone (sē'-mō-nĕ), *I.*
Spiro (spē'-rō).
Steffano (stĕf-fä'-nō), *I.*
Sylvain (sēl-văn), *F.*

Teodulo (tā-ō-doo'-lo), *I.*
Teresa (tā-rā'-sä), *I.*
Theobald (tä'-ō-bält), *G.*
Theodor (tä'-ō-dôr), *G.*
(The.) Théodore (tä-ŭ-dôr), *F.*
(T.) Thomas.
Thueskon (too-ĕs'-kōn), *G.*
(Tim.) Timothée (tē-mô-tä'), *F.*
(T.) Tommasso (tôm-mäs'-sō), *I.*
Traugott (trow'-gôt), *G.*
Turlogh (toor'-lôkh), *G.*

(Val.) Valentin (văl-än-tăn), *F.*
Venanzio (vā-nän'-tsǐ-ō), *I.*
(V.) Vincent (văn-sän), *F.*
(V.) Vincent (fēn'-tsĕnt), *G.*
(V.) Vincenzo (vēn-chän'-tsō), *I.*
Vincesleo (vēn-chĕs-lā'-ō), *I.*
Violante (vē-ō-län'-tĕ), *I.*

Wendela (vĕn'-dĕ-lä), *G.*
Wenzel (vĕn'-tsĕl), *G.*
Werner (văr'-nĕr), *G.*
(Wm.) Wilhelm (vēl'-hĕlm), *G.*
Wilhelmine (vēl-hĕl-mē'-nĕ), *G.*
Wilibald (vē'-lǐ-bält), *G.*
Willem (wǐl'-lĕm), *Dutch.*
(Wm.) William, *E.*
Woldemar (vōl'-dĕ-mär), *G.*
(Wg.) Wolfgang (vôlf-gäng), *G.*
Wulf (voolf), *G.*

(X.) Xavier (ksăv-yā), *F.*
(X.) Xavier (zä-fēr'), *G.*

.B.  The German modified vowels
, ü, are often spelled ae, oe, ue.
convenience they will here be ar-
ged alphabetically as if a, o, u.
or the system on which given names
abbreviated, and for their pronun-
ion, see the pages devoted to them.
he word " Gerbert," or " Cousse-
er " in a parenthesis means that
e of the composer's works are in
great collections of Gerbert or Cous-
aker (q. v.).  Where not otherwise
ed the man is a composer.

*A*

ron (ä'-rōn), (1) d. Cologne, 1052 ;
bbot and theorist. (2) (or **Aron**),
'ietro, Florence, 1480 or '90—bet.
545–62 ; theorist.
aco (děl ä'-bä-kō), **E. Fel. dell'**,
'erona, 1662—Munich, 1726, court-
onductor and composer.
bà-Cornaglia (äb-ba' kôr-näl'-yä),
lessandria, Piedmont, 1851—1894;
omposed operas and church-music.
badia (äb-bä-dē'-ä), (1) **Natale**,
enoa, 1792—Milan, ca. 1875; dram.
nd ch. composer. (2) **Luigia**, daugh-
er of above, b. Genoa, 1821 ; mezzo-
oprano.
batini (äb-bä-tē'-nē), **A. M.**, Castel-
, 1595 ?—1677 : composer.
bé (äb-bä), (1) **Philippe P. de St.
Sevin**, lived 18th cent.; 'cellist. (2)
'ierre de St. Sevin, bro. of above ;
cellist.
bey, **J.**, Northamptonshire, 1785—
'ersailles, 1859 ; organ-builder.
'bott, (1) **Emma**, Chicago, 1850—
New York, 1888 ; operatic soprano ;
oured America with great popular
uccess. (2) **Bessie (Pickens)**, b.
America ; soprano ; pupil of Mrs.
ashford, N. Y., and of Koenig,

Paris ; début 1902 at the Opéra there,
after singing in ballad concerts in
England.
**Abd el Kadir (Abdolkadir)** (kä'-dēr),
**Ben Isa**, lived 14th cent. ; Arabian
theorist and collector.
**Abd El Mumin (or Abdolmumin).**
Vide SSAFFIDDIN.
**Abeille** (ä-bī'-lě), **Jn. Chr. L.**, Bayreuth, 1761—Stuttgart, 1838, composer and court-conductor.
**Abel** (ä'-běl), (1) **Clamor H.**, b.
Westphalia 17th cent.; court-mus.
(2) **Chr. Fd.**, gambist at Köthen,
1720–37. (3) **Ld. Aug.**, b. Köthen,
1720, son of above ; court-violinist.
(4) **K. Fr.**, Köthen, 1725—London,
1787 ; bro. of above and the last virtuoso on the gamba. (5) **L.**, Eckarts-
berga, Thuringia, Jan. 14, 1835—Neu-
Pasing, Aug. 13, 1895 ; violinist.
**Abela** (ä-bä'-lä), (1) **Don Placido**
(dōn plä-thē'-dō), Syracuse, 1814—
Monte Cassino, 1876 ; prior. (2) **K.
Gl.**, Borne, Saxony, 1803—Halle,
1841 ; cantor and composer.
**Abel'la**,—singing-teacher; lived in New
York, 1867.
**Abell'**, **J.**, London, ca. 1660—Cambridge (?) ca. 1724; alto (musico)
and lutenist ; collector and composer.
**Abenheim** (ä'-běn-hīm), **Jos.**, Worms,
1804—Stuttgart, 1891 ; conductor and
violinist.
**Abert** (ä'-běrt), **Jn. Jos.**, b. Kocho-
witz, Bohemia, Sept. 21, 1832 ;
double-bass virtuoso and important
composer for the instr. ; also composed operas, etc.
**Abes'ser**, **Edm.**, Matgolitz, Saxony,
1837—Vienna, 1889 ; dram. composer.
**Abos** (ä'-bōs) (or **Avos, Avos'sa**),
**Gir.**, Malta, ca. 1700 — Naples,
1786 (?) ; composer of operas, etc.

**A'braham,** (1) **Jonn.** Vide BRAHAM. (2) (Dr.) **Max.** Vide PETERS, C. F.

**A'brams,** three English sisters, 1775–84. (1) **Harriet,** soprano and composer. (2) **Theodosia,** contralto. (3) **Eliza.**

**Abrányi** (ä-brän'-yē), **Kornel,** b. Szent Gyorgz Ábrányi, 1822; Hungarian nobleman; editor and composer.

**Abt** (äpt), (1) **Franz,** Eilenburg, Dec. 22, 1819—Wiesbaden, March 31, 1885; court-conductor at Bernburg, Zurich and Brunswick; visited America, 1872; immensely popular as a writer in the folk-song spirit, of such simple and pure songs as " *When the Swallows Homeward Fly,*" etc.; c. 500 works comprising over 3,000 numbers (the largest are 7 secular cantatas) and numerous choruses and other cantatas. (2) **Alfred,** Brunswick, 1855— (of consumption) Geneva, April 29, 1888; son of above; conductor.

**Ab'yngdon, Henry,** d. Wells, England, 1497; composer.

**Achard** (ä-shär), **Léon,** b. Lyons, Feb. 16, 1831; tenor.

**Achenbach.** Vide ALVARY.

**Ack'ermann, A. J.,** b. Rotterdam, April 2, 1836; composer.

**Ac'ton, J. B.,** b. Manchester (?), 1863; singing-teacher and composer.

**Adam** (äd-äṅ), (1) **Louis,** Muttersholtz, Alsatia, 1758—Paris, 1848; teacher and composer. (2) **Adolphe Charles,** Paris, July 24, 1802—May 3, 1856; son of above; c. many successful operas; *Pierre et Catherine* (1829), *Le Châlet* (1834), *Postillon de Longjumeau* (1836), *Le Fidèle Berger, Le Brasseur de Preston* (1838), *Le Roi d' Yvetot* (1842), *La Poupée de Nuremberg, Cagliostro,* and *Richard en Palestine* (1844), the ballets *Giselle, Le Corsaire, Faust,* etc.; in 1847 he founded the Théâtre National, but was made bankrupt by the revolution of 1848, and entered the Conservatoire as prof. of composition to succeed his father.

**Adam** (ät'-äm), **K. F.,** Zadel, 180 Leisnig, 1868; cantor and compo

**Adam de la Hale** (or **Halle**) (äd dŭ lä äl), Arras, ca. 1240—Nap 1287; called "Le bossu d'Arr (Hunchback of Arras); a pictures trouvère of great historical imp tance; c. chansons, jeux (operettas) motets; his works were pub. 1872

**Adam Von Fulda** (ät'-äm fōn fo dä), ca. 1450—ca. 1537. (Gerbert

**Adamberger** (ät'-äm-bĕrkh-ĕr), **Val** tin (not **Joseph**), Munich, 1743— enna, 1804; dram. tenor; assur name "Adamonti"; Mozart wr the rôle of Belmonte, etc., for him

**Adami da Bolsena** (or **da Volter** (ä'-dä-mē dä bōl-sā'-nä), **And.,** logna, 1664—Rome, 1742; theori

**Adamon'ti.** Vide ADAMBERGER.

**Adamowski** (äd-ä-môf'-shkĭ), **Timothée,** b. Warsaw, March 1858; violinist and composer; p of Kontchi, Warsaw Cons. and M sart, Paris Cons.; 1879 travelled America as soloist with Clara Lo Kellogg, and later with a compa of his own 1885–86; teacher, N Engl. Cons., Boston; organised Adamowski String-quartet (1888). **Joseph,** bro. of above.; 'celli member of the same quartet; mar Szumowska.

**Ad'ams,** (1) **Th.,** London, 1785—18 organist. (2) **Charles R.,** Charlest Mass., ca. 1834—July 3, 1900; ter (3) **Stephen.** Vide MAYBRICK, M

**Ad'cock, Jas.,** Eton, England, 177 Cambridge, 1860; choir-master a composer.

**Ad'dison, J.,** London, 1765—18 double-bass player, dram. compos

**Adelboldus** (ä'-dĕl-bōl-doos), d. 10 Bishop of Utrecht; theorist. (G bert.)

**Adelburg** (fōn ä'-dĕl-boorkh), **A** **Ritter von,** Constantinople, 183 (insane) Vienna, 1873; violinist.

**Adler** (ät'-lĕr), (1) **G.,** b. Ofen, 18 violinist, pianist, teacher and c poser. (2) **Guido,** b. Eibenscht Moravia, Nov. 1, 1855; pupil

ademic Gym. in Vienna, and Vien-
Cons.; ('78) Dr. jur., and ('80)
. D.; 1885 prof. of mus. science
ague Univ.; ('95) prof. of mus.
tory, Univ. of Vienna (vice Hans-
κ). (3) **V.,** Raab, Hungary, April
1826—Geneva, Jan. 4, 1871; son
above; teacher and composer.

asser (ät'-'l-gäs-sĕr), **Anton Ca-**
an, Innzell, Bavaria, 1728—1777;
ganist.

ung (ät'-loongk), or **A'delung, Ja-**
b, Bindersleben, near Erfurt,
99—1762; organist, teacher and
iter.

fati (ä-dōl-fä'-tē), **And.,** Venice,
11—Genoa (?) 1760; composer.

as'tos, lived Philippopolis ca. 330
.; pupil of Aristotle, and theorist.
ano di Bologna. Vide BAN-
IERI.

iansen (or **Hadrianus**), **Eman-**
l; lived Antwerp 16th cent.;
enist and collector.

en (ăd-rĭ-äṅ) or **Andrien.** (1)
artin Joseph (called **la Neu-**
le, or **l'Ainé**), Liège, 1767—
ris, 1832; bass and composer; he
d two brothers. (2) Name un-
own, b. Liège, 1765. (3) **Ferdi-**
nd, chorus-master Paris Opera
99-1801), composer.

d'ius **Zamoren'sis, Joannes,**
anciscan monk, Zamora, Spain,
70; theorist.

d'ius **de Muri'no,** 15th cent.;
orist. (Coussemaker.)

ters (ĕl-stĕrs), **Georges Jacques,**
ent, 1770—1849.

s (ĕrts), (1) **Egide,** Boom, Ant-
rp, 1822—Brussels, 1853. (2)
lix, St. Trond, Belgium, 1827—
velles, 1888 ('89?); violinist and
iter.

ard (lăf'-fē-lăr'), **Michel l',** 1683—
8; singer to Louis XIV.

nio (ä-frä'-nĭ-ō), b. Pavia, end of
th cent.; canon at Ferrara; inv.
bassoon.

lius (äf-tsä'-lĭ-oos), **Arvid A.,**
köping, Sweden, 1785—1871; col-
tor.

**Agazza'ri** (ä-gäd-zä'-rē), **Ag.,** Siena,
1578—1640; church-conductor.

**Agela'os of Tegea,** lived 559 B.C.;
considered the first solo virtuoso on
the cithera.

**Agnelli** (än-yĕl'-lē), **Salv.,** b. Palermo, 1817; pupil of Naples Cons.;
lived Marseilles and c. operas, cantata *Apothéose de Napoléon I.,*
etc.

**Agnesi** (dän-yā'-sē), (1) **M. Theresia**
d', Milan, 1724—1780 (?); pianist and
dram. composer. (2) **Luigi** (rightly **F. L. Agniez**), Erpent, Namur,
1833—London, 1875; bass.

**Agniez** (än-yĕz). Vide AGNESI (2).

**Agobar'dus,** d. Saintonge, 840; arch
bishop of Lyons; theorist.

**Agostini** (äg-ôs-tē'-nē), (1) **Lud.**
Ferrara, 1534—1590; court-conductor. (2) **Paolo,** Vallerano, 1593—
Rome, 1629; wonderful contrapuntist, some of his works being in 48
parts. (3) **P. Simone,** b. Rome,
ca. 1650. c. an opera, etc.

**Agramonte** (äg-rä-mŏn'-tä), **Emilio,**
b. Puerto Principe, Cuba, Nov. 28,
1844; eminent vocal teacher, lecturer, conductor, and friend of American music; studied comp. under
Malden in Spain, and David in
Paris; piano in Paris; singing under
Roger, Selva, and Delle Sedie; 1865
LL.D. at Univ. of Madrid; taught
singing in Barcelona, 1865, Cuba,
1866-68; lived since in New York;
c. (in MS.) a Stabat Mater, etc.

**Agrel** (ä'-grĕl), **J.,** Loth, Sweden, 1701
—Nürnberg, 1769; court-violinist and
conductor.

**Agric'ola,** (1) **Alex.,** Germany (?)
ca. 1470—Valladolid, Spain, 1530;
court-singer and church-composer.
(2) **Martin,** Sorau, Saxony, 1486—
Magdeburg, June 10, 1556; eminent writer and theorist. (3) **Jn.,** b.
Nürnberg ca. 1570; prof. and composer. (4) **Wolfgang Chp.,** German composer (1651); (5) **G. L.,
Grossfurra,** 1643—Gotha, 1676;
conductor. (6) **Jn. Fr.,** Dobitschen,
1720—Berlin, 1774; court-cond.

**Agthe** (äkh'-tĕ), **K. Ch.,** (1) Hettstadt, 1762—Ballenstedt, 1797; composer. (2) **W. Jos. Albrecht,** Ballenstedt, 1790—ca. 1848; son of above; teacher. (3) **Fr. W.,** Sangershausen, 1794—(insane) Sonnenstein, ca. 1828; cantor.

**Aguado** (ä-gwä'-dhō), **Dionisio,** Madrid, 1784—1849; performer and composer for guitar.

**Aguilar** (ä'-gwē-lär), **Emanuel,** b. 1824; composer.

**Aguiari, Lucrezia.** Vide AGUJARI.

**Aguilera de Heredia** (ä-gwĭ-lā'-rä dä ā-rä'-dhē-ä), **Seb.,** b. Sargossa, 17th cent.; monk and composer.

**Agujari** (ä-goo-hä'-rē), **Lucrezia** (called **La Bastardina,** or **Bastardella,** being the natural daughter of a nobleman), Ferrara, 1743—Parma, May 18, 1783; a phenomenal singer; Mozart remarked her "lovely voice, flexible throat, and incredibly high range," which reached from middle C three octaves up; she could shake on f''' (vide CHART OF PITCH); she m. Colla, 1780, and retired from the stage.

**Agus** (ä-zhüs), **H.,** France, 1749—1798; singing-teacher and composer.

**Ahle** (ä'-lĕ), (1) **Jn. Rud.,** Mühlhausen, 1625—1673; theorist and church-composer. (2) **Jn. G.,** Mülhausen, 1650—1706; son of above; organist, poet and theorist.

**Ahlström** (äl'-shträm), (1) **A. J. R.,** Stockholm, 1762—ca. 1827; organist. (2) **Johan Niklas,** Wisby, Sweden, June 5, 1805—Stockholm, May 14, 1857; probably son of above; dram. composer.

**Ahna.** Vide DE AHNA.

**Aibl** (ĭ'-bl), **Jos.,** founded publishing firm, Munich, 1824; later heads were Eduard Spitzweg (1836) and his sons, Eugen and Otto.

**Aiblinger** (ĭ'-blĭng-ĕr), **Jn. Kasper,** Wasserburg, Bavaria, 1779—Munich, 1867; court-conductor, collector and composer.

**Aichinger** (ĭ'-khĭng-ĕr), **Gregor,** Augsburg (?) ca. 1561—1628; canon and composer.

**Aïdé** (ä-ē-dā'), **Hamilton,** b. [ 1830, of Greek parents; poet, [poser of pop. songs.

**Aigner** (īkh'-nĕr), **Engelbert,** Vie[ 1798—ca. 1852; dram. compose[

**Aimo** (ä'-ē-mō). Vide HAYM, N. [

**Aimon** (ĕm-ôn), **Pamphile Ld. F[.** b. L'Isle, near Avignon, 1779; [ list, conductor, theorist.

**Aireton** (är'-tŭn), **Edw.,** Lor[ 1727—1807; violin-maker.

**Ajolla.** Vide LAYOLLE.

**Á Kem'pis, Florentino;** org. at [ sels, 1650.

**Akeroyde** (ăk'-ĕ-roid), **Samuel[** Yorkshire ca. 1650; song-writer[

**Ala** (ä'-lä), **Giov. Bat.,** Monza, 15[ 1612 (?); organist and composer[.

**Alabieff** (ä-lä-bĭ-ĕf), **Alex.,** Mos[ 1802—1852; composer.

**Alard** (äl-är), (1) **César,** b. G[ lies, Belgium, May 4, 1837; 'ce[ entered Brussels Cons. at 9, as [ linist; took up the 'cello and [ prizes; travelled as soloist. (2[ **Delphin,** Bayonne, March 8, 18[ Paris, Feb. 22, 1888; violinist, t[ er and composer.

**Alary** (äl-ä'-rē), **Giulio Eug[** **Abramo,** Mantua, 1814—Paris, [ flutist.

**Al'ayrac.** Vide DALAYRAC.

**Albanese** (äl-bä-nä'-zĕ), Albano, [ —Paris, 1800; musico and [ poser.

**Albanesi** (äl-bä-nä'-zē), **Carlo,** b. [ ples, 1856—London, 1893; p[ prof. R. A. M.

**Albani** (äl-bä'-nĭ) (stage name of [ **rie Louise Cecilia Emma [ Jeunesse),** b. Chambly, near M[ treal, Nov. 1, 1852; operatic sop[ sang in Cathedral, Albany, N.[ whence her name was mista[ supposed to have been taken; [ of Duprez, and of Lamperti; d[ at Messina in 1870.

**Albani, Mathias,** Bozen, 1621—1[ famous father of more famous s[ same name and trade, violin-mak[ the younger A.'s violins (17[ rival Amati's.

niz (ăl-bā'-nĕth), (1) **Pedro**, Lo-
ño, 1795—Madrid, 1855 ; court-or-
nist. (2) **Isaac**, b. Camprodon,
ain, May 20, 1861 ; grandnephew
above ; lives in London as pianist ;
nposed operas, etc. (3) **Pedro**, b.
scay, San Sebastian, 1821 ; monk,
arch-cond. and composer.

rgati (däl-bĕr-gä'-tē), (1) **Pirro**
pacelli, Conte d'. Lived in Bona, 17th cent. ; composer. (2) **Al-
brandini**, lived in Bologna, 17th
t.; dram. composer.

ert, Prinz von **Sachsen-Coburg
tha**, Schloss Rosenau, 1819—1861;
asort of Queen Victoria, patron of
sic and composer of an opera,
n le Fol (Bagnières de Bigorre,
55), an operetta, masses, etc.

rt (äl'-bĕrt), (1) **H.**, Lobenstein,
xony, 1604 — Königsberg, 1651 ;
et, organist and composer ; called
: father of the German *Lied*, and,
he alludes to a " Comödien-musik "
44), he must have been, with
ültz, one of the founders of Ger-
n opera. (2) **Max**, Munich, 1833
Berlin, 1882 ; zither-virtuoso and
entor. (3) **Charles L. N. d'**,
enstetten, near Hamburg, 1809—
ndon, 1866 ; dancing master and
nposer. (4) **Eugen d'**, rightly
gène (**Francis Charles**) (däl-
, or däl'-bĕrt), b. Glasgow, April
1864 ; son and pupil of above;
nist ; Newcastle scholar in the
ndon Nat. Training School, 1876 ;
pil of Pauer (pf.) and Stainer,
out and Sullivan (harm. and comp.);
31, Mendelssohn scholar and pu-
of Richter and Liszt, who called
n " the young Tausig "; 1881, he
yed the Schumann concerto at the
ystal Palace, London ; Oct. 24,
oncerto of his own, at a Richter
acert ; he performed 5 Beethoven
natas (op. 31, 53, 90, 109, 110) at a
wandhaus recital, 1893 ; he mar-
d the pianist Carreño in 1892 (di-
rced 1895) ; first conductor at Wei-
r, vice Lassen, but soon resigned ;
mposed a symphony, 2 overtures,

(*Hyperion* and *Esther*), 2 pf.-concer-
tos, libretto and music of the operas
*Der Rubin* (Carlsruhe, Oct. 12, 1893),
*Ghismonda* (Dresden, 1895), *Gernot*
(Mannheim, 1897), 1-act mus. comedy
*Die Abreise* (Frankfort, 1898), etc.

**Albertazzi** (äl-bĕr-täd'-zē), **Emma**
(née **Howson**), London, 1814—1847 ;
operatic contralto.

**Alberti** (äl-bĕr'-tē),(1)**Jn. Fr.**,Tonning,
1642 — Merseburg, 1710 ; organist.
(2) **Giuso Matteo**, Bologna, 1685—
1746 ; violinist and composer. (3)
**Domenico**, Venice, 1707—Formio,
1740 ; singer then pianist ; in his
piano music he made use of the since-
called " Alberti bass " (vide D. D.). (4)
**K. Edm. Robt.**, Danzig, 1801—Berlin, 1874 ; writer.

**Alberti'ni** (äl-bĕr-tē'-nē), (1) **Gioacchino**, b. 1751 — Warsaw, April,
1811 ; conductor and dram. composer. (2) **Michael** (called **Momolet'to**), soprano musico at Cassel,
18th cent., where his sister (3) **Giovanna** (called **Romanina**) was prima
donna.

**Albicas'tro**, **Henrico** (rightly, **Weissenburg**), b. Switzerland, 17th cent. ;
court-violinist.

**Albino'ni**, **Tommaso**, Venice, 1674—
1745 ; violinist.

**Albo'ni**, **Marietta**, Cesena, Romagna,
March 10, 1823—Ville d'Avray, near
Paris, June 23, 1894 ; eminent dram.
contralto, compass g-g" (vide PITCH,
D. D.); pupil of Rossini ; début La
Scala, Milan, 1843 ; m. Count Pe-
poli, 1854.

**Albrecht** (äl'-brĕkht), (1) **Jn. Lor.**,
Gormar (Thuringia), 1732—Mühl-
hausen, 1773 ; writer. (2) **Jn. Matt.**,
Osterbehringen, near Gotha, 1701—
Frankfort, 1769 ; organist. (3) **Karl**,
Breslau, 1817 (?) — Moscow, 1893 ;
court-conductor. (4) **Eugen Maria**,
St. Petersburg, 1842—1894 ; son of
(3) ; violinist and conductor.

**Albrechtsberger** (äl-brĕkhts-bĕrkh-ĕr),
**Jn. G.**, Klosternenburg, near Vienna, Feb. 3, 1736—Vienna, March
7, 1809 ; eminent composer, court-

organist, theorist and teacher (Beethoven was his unappreciated pupil).

**Albri'ci** (äl-brē'-chē), **V.**, Rome, 1631 —Prague, 1696 ; court-conductor.

**Alcarrot'ti, Giov. Fran.**, lived in Italy 16th cent. ; organist, 1740–91.

**Al'cock,** (1) **John,** London, 1715— Lichfield, 1806 , organist. (2) **J.**, son of above ; organist.

**Alday** (äl-dĕ'), French family. (1) The father (b. Perpignan, 1737), a mandolinist. His two sons (2) **A.** *le vieux* (b. 1763) ; violinist. (3) **A.** *le jeune* (b. 1764) ; violinist.

**Al'den, J. Carver,** b. Boston, Mass., Sept. 11, 1852 ; pupil of Carl Faelten, and of Paul, Plaidy, and Papperitz in Leipzig ; teacher at the N. E. Cons., later at Wollaston, Mass. ; c. pf.-concerto, etc.

**Aldovrandini** (äl-dō-vrän-dē'-nē), **Gius. A. V.**, b. Bologna, 1665 ; court-conductor and dram. composer.

**Al'drich,** (1) **H.**, Westminster, 1647— Oxford, 1710 , theorist and composer. (2) **Richard,** b. Providence, R. I., July 31, 1863 ; graduated Harvard, 1885, where he took several scholarships and honours ; studied music under J. K. Paine ; 1885 he went on the staff of the *Providence Journal,* soon reaching an editorial position, and being put in charge of the musical and other critical departments of the paper ; 1888 he spent in study abroad, chiefly of music ; 1889 to 1891, private secretary to U. S. Senator N. F. Dixon ; 1891 joined the staff of the *New York Tribune* as associate musical critic with H. E. Krehbiel, and as collaborator in their "*History of the Philharmonic Society ;*" author of various magazine articles, and editor of a series of musical biographies to be published in New York, the volume on Schumann being in preparation by him.

**Alembert** (dăl-äṅ-băr), **J. Le Rond d'**, Paris, 1717—1783 ; theorist.

**Alessan'dri,** (1) **Giulio,** c. an oratorio (ca. 1690). (2) **Felice,** Rome, 1742—Berlin (?), 1811.

**Alessan'dro Merlo** (or **Alless. mano**), called **Della Viola,** Rome (?) ca. 1530 ; monk, singe composer.

**Alexan'der, John** (or **Joseph**), 'c at Duisburg, 1801.

**Alfarâbi** (äl-fä-rä'-bē), or **Alpha bius,** properly **El Farâbi** (a **Farâbi**) Farâb (now Othrax,) 9 —Damascus, 950 ; Arabian the who vainly advocated Greek theo

**Alfieri** (äl-fē-ä'-rē), Abbate **Pi** Rome, 1801 — 1863 ; Camad monk ; teacher and theorist.

**Al'ford, J.**, lutenist at London, 15

**Algarot'ti,** Count **Fran.**, Venice, —Pisa, 1764 ; writer

**Aliani** (äl-ĭ-ä'-nē), **Francesco,** b. cenza ; 'cellist, 1820 ; son and pu a violinist.

**Alipran'di,** (1) **Bdo.,** b. Tusc Bavaria, ca. 1730 ; his son (2) **E** 'cellist at Munich, 1780.

**Alizard** (ăl-ĭ-zăr'), **Ad. Jos. L.,** F 1814— (of consumption) Marse 1850 ; bass, later barytone.

**Alkan** (äl-käṅ), (1) **Chas. H.** (*l'ainé*), Paris, Nov. 30, 1813—M 29, 1888; pianist, teacher, and bri composer for piano. (2) **Napol Morhange** (môr-änzh) (*le jeun* Paris, Feb. 2, 1826 ; brother of ab pianist.

**Allacci** (äl-lät'-chē), **Leone** (or **Allatius**), Chios, 1586—Rome, 1 writer.

**Al'lanson,** 1690—1705 ; English ganist, and church-composer.

**All'chin ;** conductor Oxford Music ciety, 1869–81.

**Allegran'ti, Maddalena ;** dram prano ; début, Venice, 1771.

**Allegri** (äl-lā'-grē), (1) **Greg** Rome, 1584—Feb. 18, 1662 ; of Nanini ; composed a celeb Miserere in 9 parts, sung d Holy Week at the Sistine Cha its publication was forbidden on of excommunication ; but M after twice hearing it, wrote it and it has since been frequently blished. (2) **Dom.;** lived 1610–

me ; one of the first to write in-
umental accompaniments not in
re unison with the voices.

n, (1) **H. R.**, Cork, 1809—Lon-
n, 1876; bass. (2) **G. B.**, Lon-
n, 1822—Brisbane, Queensland,
97 ; singer, organist, conductor,
nager, and composer. (3) **Na-
an H.**, b. Marion, Mass., 1848 ;
pil cf Haupt, Berlin ; organist and
cher in Hartford, Conn.; compos-
of cantatas, etc.

n (äl-lēn'), **H. Max.**, b. Halle-on-
ale, Aug. 31, 1841 ; writer on or-
n-building.

son, (1) **Richard**, teacher at
ndon, 1592. (2) **Robt.**, member
Chapel Royal till 1609.

tsen, **Frances**, English singer and
mposer ; début, London, 1882.

voode, ——, English church-
mposer, 16th cent.

a'gro, **A. Lopez**, b. Murcia,
ain, Sept. 17, 1839 ; pianist and
mposer.

eida (däl-mä'-ē-dhä), **Fernando**
, Lisbon, ca. 1618—1660 ; monk
d church-composer.

enräder (äl'-měn-rä-děr), **Karl**,
nsdorf, 1786—Nassau, 1843; virtu-
o and manufacturer of the bassoon.

sius, Baini's name for PALESTRINA
v.).

ara'bius. Vide ALFARABI.

en (däl-käń or däl'-kwän), (1) **P.
. d'**, Arnsberg, Westphalia, 1795
Mülheim-on-Rhine, 1863 ; com-
ser. (2) **Fz. d'**, Arnsberg, 1810
London, 1887, bro. of above ;
anist.

ager, **Thos. Massa**, Cheshire,
79—1846 ; English amateur and
tron.

ala'bi, **Mohammed**, 15th cent.;
abian theorist.

eben (äls'-lä-běn), **Julius**, Berlin,
32—1894 ; editor and writer.

ed(t) (äl'-shtät), **Jn. H.**, Herborn,
ssau, 1588—Weissenburg, 1638 ;
iter.

nburg (äl'-těn-boorkh), (1) **Mi-
ael**, Alach, near Erfurt, 1584—Er-

furt, 1640 ; pastor and composer. (2)
**Jn. Ernst**, Weissenfels, 1734—Bitter-
field, 1796 ; trumpet-virtuoso ; son of
(3) **Jn. Kasper**, do.

**Altès** (äl-těs), (1) **Jos. H.**, Rouen, 1826
—Paris, 1895 ; flutist. (2) **Ernest-
Eugène**, b. Paris, March 28, 1830,
bro. of above ; pupil Paris Cons.;
violinist and conductor ; 1871 deputy
conductor of the Opéra; 1879-87,
conductor.

**Altnikol** (ält'-nē-kôl), **Jn. Chp.**, d.
Naumberg. 1759 ; son-in-law and pupil of J. S. Bach ; organist and composer.

**Alvary** (äl-vä-rē), **Max** (rightly
**Achenbach**), Hamburg (?) 1858—
Datenberg, Thuringia, Nov. 8, 1898 ;
eminent Wagnerian tenor; début at
Weimar.

**Alvsleben, Melitta.** Vide OTTO-ALVS-
LEBEN.

**Alyp'ios**, lived ca. 360 B.C. Greek
theorist.

**Amadé** (ăm-ä-dā), (1) **Ladislaw**,
Baron von, Kaschau, Hungary, 1703
—Felbar, 1764 ; poet and composer.
(2) **Thaddäus**, Graf von Pressburg.
1783—Vienna, 1845 ; pianist.

**Amadei** (äm-ä-dä'-ē), **R.**, b. Loreto,
Italy, Nov. 29, 1840 ; succeeded his
father as organist and conductor.

**Amalia** (ä-mä-lī-ä). the name of three
princesses who composed. (1) **Anna
A.**, sister of Frederick the Great
1723—1782. (2) **Anna A.**, mother
of the Grand Duke Ernst August,
1739—1807. (3) **Marie A. Friederike**, sister of King John of Saxony,
Dresden, 1794—1870.

**Amati** (ä-mä'-tē), a family of famous
violin-makers at Cremona, Italy. (1)
**Andrea**, 1520 (?)—1577 (?), evolved
the violin from the viol ; his younger
bro..(2) **Niccolò**, made fine bass-viols.
1568-86. A.'s 2 sons, (3) **Antonio**,
1550—1635, and (4) **Geronimo**, d.
1638, produced violins of the same
style. The most famous was Geronimo's son, (5) **Niccolò**, Sept. 3,
1596—Aug. 12, 1684, who built the
" Grand Amatis," large violins of

powerful tone; his label is "Nicolaus Amati Cremonens. Hieronimi filius Antonii nepos. Fecit anno 16–"; he trained Andrea Guarneri and Antonio Stradivari. (6) His son **Geronimo**, the last of the family, was inferior. (7) **Giuseppe A.**, b. 17th cent., Bologna, a violin-maker, may have been of the same family. (8) **V.** (called **Amatus**), Cimmina, Sicily. 1629—Palermo, 1670; conductor and composer. (9) **Antonio** and (10) **Angelo**, brothers, and organ-builders at Pavia, ca. 1830

**Ambragetti** (äm-brä-jĕt'-tē). **G.**, 1817 —1838, basso-buffo.

**Ambros** (äm'-brôs), **Aug. W.**, Mauth, near Prague, Nov. 17, 1816—Vienna, June 28, 1876; eminent historian and critic.

**Ambrose (Ambro'sius)**, Trèves. A.D. 333—Milan, April 4, 397; Bishop of Milan; regulated (384) and developed Western church-music by introducing ritual as practised in the Eastern Church; the adoption of the four authentic church-modes was probably due to him; he has been called "The Father of Christian Hymnology," though his authorship of the so-called Ambrosian Hymn is discredited, further than the translation of the text into the "*Te Deum*"; it is improbable that he was acquainted with the use of letters for notation.

**Ames, John Carlowitz**, b. Bristol, England, 1860; composer of opera *The Last of the Incas* (1898).

**Ameyden** (ä'-mī-dĕn). **Christ**, 16th century church-composer.

**Am(m)erbach** (äm'-ĕr-bäkh), **Elias Nikolaus**, ca. 1540—Leipzig, 1597; organist, theorist, and composer.

**Amiot** (ăm-yō), **Father**, b. Toulon, 1718, Jesuit missionary and writer on Chinese music.

**Am(m)on** (äm'-mōn), (1) **Blasius**, b. in the Tyrol—d. Vienna, June, 1590; court-sopranist, later Franciscan friar; composer. (2) **Jn. Ands.**, Bamberg, 1763—Ottingen, 1825; virtuoso on the Waldhorn.

**Am'ner,** (1) **John**, b. late 16th c —d. 1641; organist. (2) His **Ralph**, bass at Windsor, 1623—1

**Amphi'on**, the earliest traditi Greek musician.

**Amorevoli** (ä-mō-rä'-vō-lē), **Ang** Venice, 1716—Dresden, 1798; sin

**Anacker** (ä'-näk-ĕr), **Aug. Fd.**, l berg, Saxony, 1790—1854; ca and composer.

**Ancot** (än-kō), a family of pia and composers at Bruges. (1) **J** (*père*), 1779—1848. His two s (2) **Jean** (*fils*), 1799—Boulogne, 1 (3) **Louis**, 1803—Bruges, 1836.

**Ander** (än'-dĕr), **Aloys**, Liebititz, hemia. 1824—Bad Wartenberg,18 tenor.

**An'ders, Gf. Eng.**, Bonn. 17( Paris. 1866, writer.

**An'dersen, Joachim**, b. Copenhag April 29, 1847 flute-virtuoso, so at 14 toured widely 1877, co musician Petersburg 1881, Be soloist court-opera, from 1895 l in Copenhagen as court-conduc composed notable flute-pieces, etc

**Anderson-Boker, Orleana**, b. N York, 1835, pianist and compose

**An'derson**, (1) **Lucy**, née Phil Bath, 1790—London, 1878; pia (2) **Geo. Fr.**, King's bandmaste England, 1848. (3) **Angela**, New York; great-granddaughte da Ponte; pianist, pupil of Stojo and Paderewski, début, Paris 1

**An'derton, Thos.**, b. Birmingh England, April 15, 1836; orga critic and composer.

**An'ding, Jn. Michael**, near Mein en. 1810—Hildburghausen. 18 teacher.

**Andrade** (dän-drä-dhĕ) **Fran. d** Lisbon, 1859 barytone stu with Miraglia and Ronconi, s leading rôles in many Europ cities.

**André** (än-drä), a musical family Offenbach. (1) **Jn.**, 1741—1799; l lisher and pianist, he originated 1783 the *durchkomponirte Bal* (vide D. D.). (2) **Jn. Ant.**, 177

42; third son of above; pianist, ublisher, theorist. (3) **Karl Aug.,** 06 — Frankfort, 1887; publisher d writer. (4) **Julius,** 1808— rankfort, 1880; organist. (5) **Jn. ug.,** 1817—1887; publisher; his 2 ns, (6) **Karl** (b. 1853) and (7) dolf (b. 1885), are the present pro- ietors. (8) **Jean Baptiste** (de St. lles), 1823—Frankfort, 1882; pian- : and composer.

reoli (än-drä-ō′-lē), (1) **Evanga- sta,** 1810—1875; organist at Mi- ndola; his two sons, (2) **Guglieno** odena, 1835—Nice, 1860) and (3) arlo (b. Mirandola, 1840), were anists, the latter also organist and mposer. (4) **Giuseppe,** Milan, 57—1832; double-bassist and harp-

reozzi (än-drä-ôd′-zē), **Gaetano,** aples, 1763—Paris, 1826, dram. mposer.

revi (än-drä′-vē), **Fran.,** Sana- ya, near Lerida, 1786—Barcelona, 53; critic and writer.

rien. Vide ADRIEN.

dries, **Jean,** Ghent, 1798—1872; acher and writer

riessen. Vide STAHMER.

rio (ä-nä′-rē-ō), (1) **Felice,** Rome, . 1560—ca. 1630, successor to Pa- strina. (2) **Giovanni Fran.,** ome, ca. 1569—1620 (?), bro. of ove; conductor and church-com- ser.

t, **Baptiste.** Vide BAPTISTE.

orge (än′-fôrkh-ĕ), **Kd.,** b. Buch- ld, near Liebau, Oct. 15, 1862; anist; pupil, Leipzig Cons. and of szt; toured Europe and America; es in Berlin; composer.

os′si, **Pasquale,** Taggia, near aples, 1727—Rome, 1797, pupil d rival of Piccinni: composed 54 eras. etc.

elet (än′-zhŭ-lä), **Chas. Fran.,** ent, 1797—Brussels, 1832.

elini (än-jä-lē′-nĭ), **Bontempi** le₀. **And.,** Perugia, ca. 1624— 05; court-singer and dram. com- ser.

**Angeloni** (än-jä-lō′-nĭ), **Luigi,** Frosi- none, Papal States, 1758—London, 1842; writer.

**Anglebert** (dän-glŭ-bӑr), **J. Bapt. H. d′,** 1628 (?)—Paris, 1691; court-cla- vicembalist to Louis XIV.

**Animuccia** (än-ē-moot′-chä), (1) **Giov.,** Florence, ca. 1500—Rome, March 1571; wrote the first *Laudi spirituali* for the lectures of Neri in the oratory of S. Philippo, has hence been called "Father of Oratorio"; he was Pa- lestrina's predecessor as conductor at the Vatican. (2) **Paolo,** d. Rome, 1563, bro. of above.

**Ankerts, D′.** Vide DANKERS, GHISE- LIN.

**Anna Amalia.** Vide AMALIA.

**Annibale** (än-nĭ-bä′-lĕ), (1) (called **Il Padova′no,** or **Patavi′nus,** from Padua, where he was born in the 15th cent.) organist and composer. (2) **Domenico,** Italian sopranist in London, 1756.

**Ansani** (än-sä′-nē) **Giovanni,** b. Rome, 18th cent., dram. tenor.

**Anschütz** (än′-shüts), (1) **Jn. And.,** Coblenz, 1772—1858, pianist. (2) **K.,** Coblenz, 1815—New York, 1870; son of above, cond. and composer.

**Anselm** of **Parma (Anselmus Par- mensis),** b. Parma, 1443, theorist.

**Antegnati** (än-tän-yä′-tĭ), **Costanzo,** Brescia, ca. 1550—ca. 1620; organ- builder, etc.

**An′tico, Andrea.** Vide ANTIQUUS, ANDREAS.

**Antiquis** (än′-tē-kwēs), **Johannes** (or **Giovanni) de,** l. 1574. Bari, Na- ples, composer.

**Antiquus** (än′-tē-kwoos), **Andreas** (or **A. de Antiquiis Venetus,** or **Andrea Antico),** b. Montana (Istria), 15th cent.; music-printer in Rome.

**Anton** (än′-tōr), **Konrad G.,** Lauban, Prussia, 1746—1819; writer.

**Anto′nio da Bologna** (bō-lōn′-yä) 1543; organist and composer.

**Antony** (än′-tō-nē), (1) **Joseph,** 1758 —1836; writer and composer. (2) **Fz. Jos.,** Münster, Westphalia,

1790—1836; son of above; organist, conductor, and composer.

**Apel** (ä'-pĕl), **Jn. Aug.**, Leipzig, 1771 —1816; writer.

**Apell** (ä-pĕl'), **Jn. D. von**, Cassel, 1754—1833; conductor and dram. composer.

**Apol'lo**, Greek sun-god, and god of music.

**Appel** (äp'-pĕl), **K.**, b. Dessau, 1812; violinist, court-leader composed opera *Die Rauberbraut* (Dessau, 1840), and humorous male quartets.

**Appun** (äp-poon'), **G. A. I.**, Hanau, 18.6—1885, versatile performer on nearly every instr., writer on and experimenter in acoustics, made an harmonium of 53 degrees to the octave.

**Aprile** (ä-prē'-lĕ), **Gius**, Bisceglia, 1738—Martins. 1814, celebrated contralto musico and vocal teacher; writer and composer.

**Ap'thorp**, **W. Foster**, b. Boston, Mass., Oct. 24, 1848. Harvard, '69, studied piano, harmony, cpt. with J. K. Paine, and B J Lang, teacher of theory, and for many years distinguished critic and writer on music; author of "*Hector Berlioz*, *Musicians and Music-Lovers and other Essays*"; "*By the Way. About Music and Musicians*" (1899), "*Opera and Opera Singers*" (1901), etc.

**Aptom'mas**, (1) **John**, (2) **Thomas**, brothers, b. Bridgend England, 1826, and 1829, harp-players and teachers.

**Araja** (ä-rä'-yä). **Fran.**, Naples, ca. 1700—Bologna, ca. 1770, dram. composer: composed the first opera written in Russian.

**Aranaz** (är-ä-näth'), **Pedro**, d Cuenca, Spain, 1825; priest and composer.

**Aranda d'** (dä-rän'-dhä), Pasha, b. Spain, contemporary court-conductor to the sultan with rank of Général de Division.

**Aranda** (ä-rän'-dä), **Matheo de**, Portuguese prof. of mus. (1544).

**Arando** (där-än'-dō), **del Sessa d'**, Italian composer. 16th cent.

**Arauxo** (ä-rä-ooks-ō) (or **Arauj(** rä-oo'-hō)), **Francisco Correa** ca. 1581—Segovia. 1663, bishop, orist.

**Arban** (är-bän), **Jos. J. Bap. I** rent, Lyons 1825—Paris, 1( cornet-virtuoso teacher at Paris ( servatoire.

**Arbeau**, **Thoinot** (twä-nō är- Vide TABOUROT.

**Ar'buckle**, **Matthew**, 1828—, York. 1883 cornetist and band( ter.

**Ar'cadelt**, **Jacob** (or **Jachet Ai delt, Archadet, Arcadet, Ha delt**), 1541—bet. 1570-75 di guished Flemish composer and te er 1540 singer in Paris, 1 *Regius musicus*, composed ma etc.

**Arcais** (där-kä-ēs) **Fran., March d'**, Cagliari Sardinia, 1830— Rome, 1890 writer and compos( **Archadet** (är-chä-dä'). Vide A DELT.

**Archambeau** (där-shän-bō), **J. chel d'**, b. Hervé, Belgium, M 3, 1823 organist and composer.

**Ar'cher**, **Fredk.**, Oxford, Engl June 16. 1838—Pittsburg, Pa., 22, 1901, pupil of his father; s ied in London and Leipzig, ganist and opera-director in Lon 1881. organist of Plymouth Chu Brooklyn. later in New York, 1 conductor of Boston Oratorio S 1895-98 Pittsburg (Pa.) Orches composed cantata organ-pieces,

**Archy'tas**, Tarentum. ca. 400— B.C., Greek mathematician.

**Arditi** (är-dē-tē). (1) **Michele**, ] chese, Naples 1745—1838, poser. (2) **Luigi**, b. Crescen Piedmont, J(y 16, 1822; pupi Milan Cons., violinist, then dir( of opera, 1843. Milan, Turin, Havana. He visited New York the Havana opera company; since travelled widely. Comp 3 operas, vocal waltzes, *Il B* etc.; wrote "*My Reminiscer* (London. 1896).

(ä'-rĕns), **Fz. Xavier,** b. near
Mosel, Germany, Oct. 28, 1856;
e to America early in youth; pu-
f his father, and of Rheinberger,
conductor, organist; composer
mphonic fantasia, etc.

ky (ä-rĕn'-shkĭ), **Anton Step-
vitch,** b. Novgorod, Russia,
30, 1862, composer and pianist;
l of Johanssen and Rimsky-Kor-
v Prof. Imp. Cons. Moscow,
conductor Imperial Court Choir,
posed a symphony, 4 suites for
1-act opera *Rafaello,* string
tets, concerto for piano, etc., in-
ng *Essais sur des rythmes ou-
*f. pf. 4 hands.

**o.** Vide GUIDO D'AREZZO.
e (däl är -jē-nĕ), **Constantino
',** Parma. 1842—Milan, 1877,
posed pop. operas and ballets.
i -rĭ-ä). **Cesare,** Bologna, 1820—
singing-teacher.

(ä-rē bō). **Scholas'ticus,** d. ca.
probably from the Nether-
s writer (Gerbert.)

zo (där-ĭ-ĕn'-tsō), **Nicolà d',** b.
les Dec. 24, 1843 (or '42)
posed 5 operas in Neapolitan dia-
*Monzu Gnazio* (Naples, 1860)
*l Due Mariti* (Naples, 1866)
most successful, realistic and orig-
also an oratorio, a *Pensiero
onico* overtures, etc.; wrote a
ise (1879) advocating pure in-
tion instead of temperament, and
rd mode (the Minor Second), be-
the usual major and minor.

, partly traditional Greek singer
lyrist (7th cent., B.C., 3ence, the
e of a vocal society.

ti, **Attilio,** Bologna, 1660—ca.
. composed 15 operas; 1716 a
of Buononcini, and of Händel,
ondon in 1720, the three com-
d the opera *Muzio Scaevola.*

'des Quintilia'nus, Greek teach-
nd writer on music, ca. 160.

otle, (1) Stagyra, 384 B.C.—
B.C.; Greek philosopher, whose
ks include valuable information
erning Greek music. **(2)** Pseu-

donym of a writer on mensurable
music, 12th—13th cent.

**Aristox'enos,** b. Tarentum, ca. 354
B.C.; one of the first Greek writers on
music.

**Armbrust** (ärm'-broost), **K. F.,** Hamburg, 1849—Hanover, 1896; teacher
and critic.

**Armbruster** (ärm'-broo-stĕr), **K.,** b
Andernach-on-Rhine, July 13, 1846,
pupil of Hompesch; pianist and lecturer; Hans Richter's assistant con
ductor at the Wagner concerts, 1882-
84; later conducted at various London theatres.

**Armes, Philip,** b. Norwich, England,
1836; Mus. Doc. Oxon, 1864; organ composer.

**Armingaud** (är-măṅ-gō), **Jules,** b. Bayonne, May 3. 1820; was refused admission to the Paris Cons. at 19 since
he was ' too far advanced"; leader
of a string quartet enlarged to the
*Société Classique ;* said to have introduced Beethoven's quartets into Paris.

**Arnaud** (är-nō). (1) Abbé **Fran.,** Au-
bignan, 1721—Paris, 1784; writer.
(2) **J. Et. Guil.,** Marseilles, 1807—
Jan., 1863 , composer.

**Arne** (ärn), (1) Dr. **Thomas Augustine,** London, March 12, 1710—March
5, 1778 , by secret nightly practice he
learned the spinet and violin, his father wishing him to study law ; 1736,
m. Cecilia Young, a favourite singer
of Händel's 1738, he was composer
to the Drury Lane Th. and set Dal-
ton's adaptation of Milton's *Comus ,*
in his masque *Alfred* (1740) is " Rule
Britannia " in Dublin (1742-44) he
produced two operas, *Britannia* and
*Eliza,* and a musical farce *Thomas
and Sally ,* 1745, composer to Vauxhall Gardens, London , set to music the songs in *As You Like It,
" Where the Bee Sucks,"* in *The
Tempest,* etc. , Mus. Doc. Oxon
1759, he was the first to use female
voices in oratorio-choruses ( *Judith,*
composed 2 oratorios, many masques
orch. overtures, vln.-sonatas, organ
music, harpsichord-sonatas, glees

catches, canons, etc.    (2) **Michael,**
London, 1741—Jan. 14, 1786 (not
1806) ; natural son of above ; con-
ductor and dram. composer.
**Arneiro** (där-nā'-ē-rō), **Jose Aug.
Ferreira Veiga,** Viscount d', b.
Macao, China, Nov. 22, 1838, of
Portuguese parents ; composed 2
operas.
**Arnold** (är'-nôlt), (1) **G.,** b. Welds-
berg, Tyrol, 17th cent.; organist.
(2) **Samuel,** London, 1740—1802 ;
organist Westminster Abbey. (3) **Jn.
Gottf.,** near Oehringen, 1773—
Frankfort, 1806 ; 'cellist, etc. (4)
**Ignaz Ernst Fd.,** Erfurt, 1774—
1812 ; writer. (5) **K.,** near Mergen-
theim, Würtemberg, 1794—Christiania, 1873 ; son of (3) **J. G.** ; pianist
and composer. (6) **K.,** b. St. Petersburg, 1820 ; son of (5) ; 'cellist in
Royal Orch. ; studied Stockholm.
(7) **Fr. W.,** near Heilbronn, 1810—
Elberfeld, 1864 ; collector and composer.    (8) **Yourij von,** St. Petersburg, 1811—Simferopol, Crimea,
1898 ; singing-teacher and dram.
composer.    (9) **Richard,** b. Eilenburg, Jan. 10, 1845 ; at 8 taken to U.
S.; pupil of Fd. David, 1869—76 ; 1st
violinist of Theo. Thomas' orch.,
1878 ; leader New York Philh. Club,
1891 ; 1897, organised a sextet. (10)
**Maurice** (real name Strothotte), b.
St. Louis, Jan. 19, 1865 ; pupil of
his mother ; then at the Cincinnati
Coll., 1883 ; Vierling and Urban, Berlin ; Cologne Cons. and Max Bruch,
Breslau ; lived St. Louis, then New
York as teacher in the Nat. Cons. and
pupil of D^vořák ; composed notable
" *Plantation Dances,*" a " *Dramatic
Overture,*" 2 comic operas, etc. Wrote
" *Some Points on Modern Orchestra-
tion.*" (11) **Hubert,** talented violin-
ist ; lives in N. Y.
**Ar'noldson,** (1) **Oscar,** 1843 (?)—
Stockholm, 1881 ; tenor. (2) **Sigrid,**
b. Stockholm, ca. 1865, daughter of
above ; operatic soprano ; pupil of
Maurice Strakosch ; début, Moscow,
1886 ; has sung in Europe and Amer-

ica with success, particularly in ┊
sia ; m. Alfred Fischof ; lives in P┊
singing at the Op. Com., 1901—2.┊
**Arnould** (är-noo), **Madeleine Sop**
Paris, 1744—1803 ; soprano, cre
Gluck's " *Iphigénie.*"
**Ar'nulf von St. Gillen,** 15th c┊
theorist.    (Gerbert.)
**Arquier** (är-kǐ-ā'), **Jos.,** Toulon,┊
—Bordeaux, 1816 ; 'cellist and d
composer.
**Arrhen** (är'-ĕn), **V. K.,** Swedish s┊
compo.er ; early part of 19th cen
**Arriaga y Balzola** (där-rǐ-ä'-gä e
thō-lä), **Juan C. J. A. d'.** Bi┊
1806—1825.
**Arrieta** (är-rǐ-ā'-tä), **J. Emilio,** Pu
la Reina, 1823—Madrid, 1894 ; d
composer.
**Arrigo** (är-rē'-gō), **Tedesco** (H
the German), pseud. of **Isaac**
Italy.
**Arrigoni** (är-rē-gō'-nĕ), **Carlo, I**
ence, ca. 1705—Tuscany (?) ca. 1
lutenist and composer, rival in ┊
don to Händel.
**Arrange** (lär-rônzh), **Adolf l',**
Hamburg, March 8, 1838 ; pupi
Genée, and at Leipzig Cons.; ┊
theatre-manager, Breslau ; comp
comic operas, " *Singspiele,*" etc.
**Artaria** (är-tä-rē'-ä), music publis
house in Vienna, founded by ┊
A., 1780.
**Artchibousheff**    (ärt-shē'-boo-s┊
**Nicholas Vassilievitch,** b. T
koje-Sielo, Russia, March 7, ┊
lawyer, pianist and composer ; ┊
of Soloviev and Rimsky-Korsak┊
**Arteaga** (är-tä-äg'-ä), **Stefano,**
drid (?), 1730 (?)—Paris, 1799 ; S
ish Jesuit ; theorist.
**Ar'thur, Alfred,** b. near Pittsb┊
Pa., Oct. 8, 1844 ; studied in Bo┊
1869—71, tenor ; since 1878 as c
master, Cleveland, O. ; cond┊
since 1873 Vocal Society ; dir┊
Cleveland School of Music ; ┊
posed three operas, etc.
**Artot** (är-tō), (1) **Maurice Mon**
**ney** (ancestor of a line of musi┊
named Montagney), Gray 'H

e), 1772—Brussels, 1829; band-
ter. (2) **J. Désiré M.**, Paris,1803
:. Josse ten Noode, 1887; son of
/e; horn-player and teacher. (3)
**x. Jos.**, son of Maurice, Brussels,
,—Ville-d'Avray, 1845; notable
nist and composer. (4) **Margue-
Josephine Désirée**, b. Paris,
21, 1835; daughter of (2) Jean-
ré; dram.-soprano, pupil of Viar-
Garcia (1855-57); début Brus-
1857; sang Grand Opera, Paris,
, etc., m. the Spanish baritone,
illa, in 1869.

**hibuschew.** Vide ARTSCHIBOUS-
F.

i (är-too'-zē), **Giov. M.**, Bologna
1550—1613; canon and theo-

:chevski (**Asantschewski,
antchevski**) (ä-sänt-shĕf'-shkĭ),
hael **Pavlovitch**, Moscow, 1838
881; composer.

enbren'ner (ä'-shĕn-) **Chr. H.**,
tettin, 1654—Jena, 1732; violin-
nd court-conductor.

er (äsh'-ĕr), **Jos.**, Groningen, Hol-
, 1829—London, 1869; pianist.

own, **Edwin**, London music-
isher, succeeded (1884) Ashdown
arry, who succeeded (1860) Wes-
Co.

**Andrew**, Lisburn, Ireland, ca.
—London after 1822; flutist and
luctor; 1799 married Miss Comer,
, as **Mrs. Ashe**, was a public
er; their two daughters were harp-
nd pianist.

ey, (1) **John**, b. 1805; bassoonist
manager; his three sons were (2)
eral, d. 1818, violinist. (3)
s. **Jane**, 1773—1843, 'cellist and
ager. (4) **J. Jas.**, 1771—1815,
nist and singing teacher. (5) **J.**,
shley of Bath," 1780—1830, bas-
iist. (6) **Richard**, 1775—1837,
don viola-player.

on, **Algernon Bennet Lang-**
, b. Durham, England, Dec. 9,
; pupil of Leipzig Conservatory,
teacher, R. C. M., London: comer.

**Ash'well, Thos.**, 16th cent., organist
and composer in England.

**Asioli** (äs-ē-ō'-lē), **Bonifacio**, Correggio, 1769—1832; at the age of 8
he had composed 3 masses, 20 other
sacred works, a harpsichord-concerto,
a vln. concerto, with orch., and 2
harp-sonatas for 4 hands; pupil of
Morigi; successful cembalist, improviser; his first opera buffa, *La Volu-
bile* (1785) was successful; his opera
*Cinna*, favourably received in 1793;
prof. of cpt. at Milan Cons.

**Asola** (or) **Asula** (ä'-sō-lä), **Giov.
Mat.**, Verona ca. 1560 — Venice,
1609; church-composer.

**Aspa** (äs'-pä), **Mario**, Messina, 1799
—1868; composed 42 operas.

**As'pull, G.**, 1814—(of consumption),
Leamington, England, 1833; pianist
ard composer.

**Assantsheffsky.** Vide ASANTCHEVSKI.

**Assmayer** (äs'-mī-ĕr), **Ignaz**, Salzburg, 1790—Vienna, 1862; conductor.

**Astarit'ta, Gennaro**, Naples, ca. 1749
—1803; composed 20 operas.

**As'ton, Hugh**, English organist and
composer in reign of Henry VIII.

**Astorga** (däs-tôr'gä), **Emmanuele**,
Baron d', Palermo, 1681—Prague,
1736; church-composer.

**Attaignant** (ät-tīn'-yäṅ), **Pierre** (also
**Attaingnant, Atteignant**), 16th
cent. music-printer.

**Attenhofer** (ät'-tĕn-hôf-ĕr), **K.**, b.
Wettingen, Switzerland, May 5,
1837; pupil of Leipzig Cons.; cond.,
organist, and teacher; notable composer of male choruses.

**At'terbury, Luffmann**, d. London,
1796; ct.-mus. and composer.

**At'tey, J.**, d. Ross, England, ca. 1640;
composer.

**Attrup** (ät'-troop), **K.**, b. Copenhagen,
March 4, 1848: pupil of Gade, whom
he succeeded as organ-teacher Copenhagen Cons.; composed studies for
organ and songs.

**Att'wood, Thos.**, London, Nov. 23,
1765—Chelsea, March 24, 1838; important English composer; chorister

2nd court-organist ; pupil of Mozart ; 
1796 organist St. Paul's Cathedral, 
composed 19 operas, anthems, sonatas 
for piano, etc.

**Auber** (ō-băr), **Daniel François Es-prit**, Caen, Normandy, Jan. 29, 1782 
—Paris, May 14, 1871 ; notable 
opera-composer ; his father an art-dealer in Paris, sent him to London 
to learn the trade ; but in 1804 he re-turned to Paris ; composed opera 
*Julie*, produced by amateurs in 1812 
with an orch. of six stringed instrs. ; 
Cherubini heard of it, recognised A.'s 
talent and taught him ; 1842 dir. the 
Cons. of Music, Paris, as Cherubi-ni's successor; 1857 imperial conduct-or to Napoleon III. A.'s first public 
productions were 2 unsuccessful 
operas ; *La Bergère Chatelaine* (1820) 
was a success ; before 1869, he com-posed over forty operas ; his one se-rious opera, *Masaniello ou la Muette 
de Portici* (1828), with Meyerbeer's 
*Robert le Diable* and Rossini's *Guil-laume Tell*, established French grand 
opera ; its vivid portrayal of popular 
fury caused riots in Brussels ; his 
comic operas (to Scribe's librettos) 
are the best of France ; his last opera 
*Rèves d'Amour*, was produced when 
he was 87 years old. Other operas 
are : *La Marquise de Brinvilliers* 
(1831 with eight other composers), 
*Le Domino Noir* (1837), *Zanetta* 
(1840), *Les Diamants de la Couronne* 
(1841), *La Sirène* (1844), *Haydée* 
(1847), *L'Enfant Prodigue* (1850), 
*Zerline, Manon Lescaut* (1856).

**Aubert** (ō-băr), (1) **Jac.** (" le vieux "), 
b. 1668—Belleville, 1753 ; violinist. 
(2) **Louis**, 1720—after 1771 ; son of 
above ; violinist, etc. (3) **T. Fran. 
Olivier**, b. Amiens, 1763 ; 'cellist 
and composer.

**Aubery du Boulley** (ō-bă-rē' dŭ bool-lĕ'), **Prudent-L.**, Verneuil, Eure, 
1796—1870 ; teacher and composer.

**Audran** (ō-dräṅ), (1) **Marius-P.**, Aix, 
Provence, 1816—Marseilles, 1887 ; 1st 
tenor at the Paris Opéra-Comique. 
(2) **Edmond**, Lyons, April 11, 

1842—Tierceville, n. Gisors, 
17, 1901 ; son of above ; p 
École Niedermeyer, Paris ; Ma 
1862, his first opera ; produ 
others, chiefly of a light cha 
Among his most pop. works a 
*vette*, *La Mascotte* (1880), giv 
1700 times ; *Miss Helyett*, *La 1* 
etc.

**Auer** (ow'-ĕr), (1) **Ld.**, b. Ves 
Hungary, May 28, 1845; vln.-vi 
pupil of Khonetol at Pesth, of 
Vienna, then of Joachim ; so 
the Czar, who conferred on h 
order of St. Vladimir, carrying 
itary nobility ; violin-Prof. at 
Petersburg Cons. (2) **Carl** 
FROTZLER.

**Au'gener & Co.**, London fi 
music pub., founded by **G. A.** 

**Auletta** (ä-oo-lĕt'-tä), (1) 
dram. composer, Naples, 176 
**Pietro**, ct.-cond., 1728–52 ; p 
operas.

**Aulin** (ow'-lēn), **Tor**, b. Stoc 
Sept. 10, 1866 ; violinist ; p 
Sauret and Ph. Scharwenka 
1889 Konzertmeister Stoc 
court-opera ; 1887 organise 
Aulin Quartet.

**Aulnaye, de l'**. Vide DE L'AUL 

**Aurelia'nus Reomen'sis**, 9th 
theorist. (Gerbert.)

**Aurenhammer** (ow-rĕn-häm 
**Josepha**, 1776—1814 ; pianist 

**Aus der Ohe** (ows'-dĕr ō'-ĕ), 
contemporary pianist ; pu 
Kullak and Liszt ; composed 2 
suites, concert étude, etc. Has 
widely with great success.

**Auspitz-Kolar** (ow'-shpĭts-k 
**Auguste**, Prague, ca. 1843—V 
1878 ; pianist and composer.

**Auteri-Manzocchi** (ä-oo-tā'-r 
tsôk'-kē), **Salv.**, b. Palermo, L 
1845 ; pupil of Platania at Pa 
and Mabellini at Florence ; 
posed successful operas, amon 
*Graziella* (Milan, 1894) ; li 
Trieste.

**Auvergne** (dō-vĕrn), **A. d'**, Cle 
Ferrand, Oct. 4, 1713—Lyons

1797; violinist and dram. com-
r.

i'nus, Jns. (rightly Thurnmay-
r Turmair), Abensberg (whence
ntinus), July 4, 1477—Jan. 9,
; writer.

y, J., d. England, 1808 ; organ-
der.

n, Chas., Newcastle-on-Tyne,
—May 9, 1770 ; organist, writer
composer ; vide Robert Brown-
" PARLEYINGS."

lio (ä-vōl'-yō), —— Italian so-
o in England, 1741.

ard (äl'-wärd), Th., ca. 1730—
; teacher and composer.

(ī'-rĕr), Jakob, lived in Ger-
y 1618 ; reformed the Singspiel.
le D.D.)

n (är'-tŭn), (1) Edm., Ripon,
ks, 1734 — Westminster, 1898 ;
poser. (2) W., London, 1777—
; son of above, writer and ed-

n (ā'-tŭn), Fanny, b. Maccles-
l, 1806 ; English dram. singer.

pardi (äd-zō-pär'-dē), Frances-
conductor and theorist at Malta,
6.

do (äth-vā'-dhō), Alexis Jacob,
deaux, 1813—Paris, 1875 ; writer.

# B

er (bä'-dĕr), K., viola-player,
d in Vienna and Liverpool, re-
d 1869.

n (bä'-bän), Gracian, cathe-
l conductor and composer, Valen-
, 1650-65.

ell, Wm., ca. 1690—Canonbury,
gland, 1723 ; organist, teacher and
nposer ; son of a bassoon-player.

i (bäb'-bē), Christoph (or Cris-
oro), Cesena, 1748 — Dresden,
4 ; violinist and composer.

ni (bä-bē'-nē), Mat., Bologna,
4—1816 ; tenor , début, 1780.

hi'us (Senior), ca. 150 A.D., Greek
orist.

usi (bäk-koo'-sē), Ippolito, monk ;

composer and cathedral cond., Verona, 1590.

Bac'fart (or Bacfarre), Valentin
(rightly Graew (gräv)), Transylvania,
1515—Padua, 1576 ; lutenist and
writer.

Bach (bäkh), the name of a Thurin-
gian family prominent for two centuries in music and furnishing so many
organists, Kapellmeisters and cantors
that town musicians were called " the
Bachs," after them. See the CHART.
(19) Bach, Jn. Sebastian, Eisenach,
March 21, 1685—Leipzig, July 28,
1750 ; youngest son of Jn. Ambrosius B. and Elizabeth (née Lam-
merhit), of Erfurt (vide CHART OF
BACHS) ; both parents died when he
was 10, his father having begun teaching him the violin. He went to the
home of his brother Jn. Christoph,
who taught him the clavichord, but
forbade him inspection of a MS. vol. of
works by Frohberger, Buxtehude, etc.,
obtaining it secretly B. copied it by
moonlight for 6 months, though near-
sighted, with results fatal to his eyes
in later life. This desire to study
other men's work characterised his
whole career. At 15 his fine soprano
voice secured him free tuition at St.
Michael's Ch. in Lüneberg (he having already attended the Ohrdruff
Lyceum). He went on foot on holi-
days to Hamburg to hear the great
Dutch organist Reinken, and at Celle
he heard the French instr. music used
in the Royal Chapel. He studied
also the work of Böhm, organist at
Lüneberg, and practised violin, clavichord and org. often all night ; 1703,
in the Weimar ct.-orch. , 1704, organist at Arnstadt ; 1705, walked 50
miles to Lübeck to hear Buxtehude,
and stayed till a peremptory recall from
the Church at Arnstadt ; 1707, organist at Mühlhausen. On Oct. 17, he
m. Maria Barbara Bach, his cousin,
who bore him 7 children, of whom
4 died, leaving a daughter, Wm
Friedemann, and K. P. E. (See
below.) 1708, he played before the

Duke at Weimar, and was made ct.-organist ; 1714 Konzertmeister. In his vacations he made clavichord and org. tours. 1714, he furnished the organ-music for a service conducted in the Thomaskirche, Leipzig, and produced a cantata. Dresden, 1717, he challenged Marchand, a French organist of high reputation, who was afraid to compete. 1717 Kapellmeister to Prince Leopold of Anhalt, at Köthen, and composed much orch.- and chamber-music. In 1719 he revisited Halle, to meet Händel, but he had just gone to England. 1720, his wife died. He applied for the organ of the Jacobskirche, Hamburg. **B.** was now famous, but a young rival offered to pay 4,000 marks for the place and got it. In 1721 he m. Anna Magdalene Wülken, daughter of the ct.-trumpeter at Weissenfels. She bore him 13 children, 9 of them sons, of whom only 2 survived him : Jn., Christoph, Fr., and Jn. Christian. His second wife had a fine voice and musical taste, and wrote out the parts of many of his cantatas ; for her he prepared 2 books of music. In May, 1723, cantor at the Thomasschule, Leipzig, vice Jn. Kühnau ; also organist and dir. of mus. at the Thomaskirche and the Nicolaikirche, continuing as " Kapellmeister vom Haus aus." to Prince Leopold. He was made, 1736, hon. cond. to the Duke of Weissenfels, and court-composer to the King of Poland, and Elector of Saxony. He kept his place at Leipzig for twenty-seven years, and there wrote most of his sacred music. He often visited Dresden, where he could hear the Italian opera, cond. by Hasse. Frederick the Great having asked to hear him, on May 7, 1747, with his son Wilhelm Friedemann, **B.** arrived at Potsdam. He improvised upon the various Silbermann pianos in the palace, followed from room to room by the king and his musicians. The next day he tried the principal organs in Potsdam, improvising a 6-

part fugue on a theme propose the king. He afterward wrote part fugue on this theme, a Rice in 6 parts, several canons insc " Thematis regii elaborationes ca icae," and a trio for flute, violin bass, dedicating the " *Musikali Opfer* " to the king. 1749, two ations to restore his sight, weak by copying his own and other works and engraving his " *A Fugue,*" left him totally blind ruined his previous vigour. His was suddenly restored, July 10, 1 but 10 days later he died of apop He dictated the choral " *Vor nen Thron tret' ich hiemit,* sh before his death.

Among his distinguished pupils Krebs, Homilius, Agricola, Kir ger, Goldberg, Marpurg; J. K Vogler ; Altnikol, his son-in-law, his sons, for whom he wrote " *Klavierbüchlein,*" and the " *K der Fuge.*" He engraved on cop invented the " viola pomposa " the " Lauten-Clavicembalum " ; advocated equal temperament D. D.), tuning his own pianos and ing "*Das Wohltemperirte Klavier* further the cause. This work (kn in English as " *The well-temp Clavichord,*" or " *The 48-Fugu* is a set of 48 preludes and fug two of each to each key, major minor. The works are very chron and use the keys enharmonic Some of his improvements in fin ing still survive. Bach was known as a composer during his and few of his works were publi then. He was not indeed establi on his present pinnacle till Men sohn took up his cause, in 18 Franz was also an important age preparing his scores for general In 1850, a hundred years after death, the BACH-GESELLSCHAFT gan to publish his complete wo Many other Bach societies now e **B's.** enormous list of works inclu VOCAL, 5 sets of church Cantatas ndays and feast-days, " *Gottes Zeit die beste Zeit*," etc., secular be-thal cantatas, 2 comic cantatas, the *Bauern Cantate* " and " *Coffee-Can-e*." a protest against the excessive e of the beverage, and *Trauerode*, the death of the Electress of Sax-y; 5 Passions, incl. the *St. Mat-ew*, the *St. John*, and the *St. Luke* [s]ubtful); a *Christmas Oratorio*, in parts; 4 small masses and the and Mass in B min. ; motets; 2 agnificats; 5 Sanctus. INSTRU-NTAL, numerous pieces for clav-ord: inventions in 2 and 3 parts;

6 " small " French suites; 6 " large " English suites; Preludes and Fugues, incl. "*Das Wohltemperirte Klavier*"; pf.-sonatas with instrs., incl. 6 famous sonatas for pf. and vln. ; solo son-atas for vln. and 'cello ; solos. trios, etc., for various combinations of instrs., concertos for 1 to 4 pfs., vln. and other instrs., concertos with orch. overtures and suites, and fantasias, toccatas, preludes, fugues, and chor-ale-arrangements for organ. The best biography of **B.** is by Spitta (Leipzig, 1873–80, 2 vols.; Eng. transl., London, 1884–85).

## The Art of Johann Sebastian Bach.

### By Sir Charles Hubert H. Parry.

FOR more than a century before J. S. Bach came upon the scene, a succession of exceptionally gifted and earnest composers had been hard at work developing the methods and style of organ-music. Andrea rieli and his nephew Giovanni Gabrieli and Claudio Merulo in Venice [J]an Pieterzoon Swelinck in Amsterdam had already done much to define [t]rue sphere and style before the era of pure choral-music was ended. The [early] years of the seventeenth century saw Frescobaldi in the zenith of his [fame], and his pupil Froberger following worthily in his footsteps ; and through-[out] the century rapid progress in the accumulation of artistic methods and the [deve]lopment of true instrumental forms was made by such famous organists as [Sche]idt, Scheidemann, Pachelbel, Muffat, Reinken, and Buxtehude. And [whe]n it is considered that this branch of art already enjoyed an advantage [over] the new secular form of art which began to be cultivated at the end of [the] sixteenth century, through having its foundation securely laid in the old [form]e of sacred choral-music, it seems natural that by the beginning of the [eigh]teenth century it should appear to be the most mature of all the branches of [art] then cultivated. ¶ These circumstances had profound and far-reaching [influ]ence upon J. S. Bach's musical character. In unravelling the secrets of [art h]e was naturally attracted by that branch which possessed methods most [fully] developed for the formulation of the artistic impulses which were urging [him] to utterance. But the attraction was enhanced by the fact that organ-[mus]ic had already become a kind of appanage of German composers, and [ap]proved the one special form of art in which the fervent religion of Teutonic [Prot]estants found the highest artistic expression. ¶ Hence it came about

that, great as his powers were as a composer of choral-music and of
and secular instrumental music, he was first and foremost a writer of o
music, and inasmuch as organ-music was the only branch of art which
even approximately mature in his youthful and most impressionable day
methods and diction of organ-music permeated and served as the found
of his style in all branches of art which he attempted.    In his earlier
he copied out and studied the works of great composers for the organ
watched with critical appreciation the performances of great organists su
Reinken and Buxtehude.    It is easy to trace in his own work the impre
made on him by the interlinked suspensions of Frescobaldi and Frob
and by the vivacity of their fugue subjects ; by the treatment of chorale
dies with elaborate figuration of accompanying counterpoint in which Pack
excelled, by the copious picturesqueness of detail and the richness and
tional force of the harmonisation of Buxtehude.    ¶ He brought all such sp
ities of earlier composers into the sphere of his own operations, and
them into consistency by the force of his personality, and this assimilatio
came the foundation of his life's work.    Most of his best organ-music,
as the sonatas, preludes, fugues, fantasias, canzonas and movements fou
on chorales, and the great passacaglio in C minor, belong to compara
early years, and his concentration on this branch of work was only re
by the production of a few church cantatas, which showed that he had b
to consider other forms of art, in which in later years he attained such
prehensive mastery.    After many years spent in several organistships,
the singular central episode of his life, when the appointment as Capellm
to the Prince of Anhalt-Cöthen caused him to apply his mind almost e
sively for some years to secular instrumental music, mainly of a domestic
¶ He sought for his models and types of procedure in the suites and o
of the French composers, such as Couperin and Dieupart ; and amon,
examples of the so-called French overture, which came into prominen
Lulli's operas, and had found such a brilliant imitator in Muffat.
studied also the instrumental compositions of the Italians, such as the
certos of Vivaldi, and the sonatas for stringed instruments of other I
composers such as Albinoni and Legrenzi and even German imitatio
such works like Reinken's " *Hortus Musicus* " ; and the outcome was a
fect outpouring of suites and partitas for the domestic keyed instruments,
sonatas for violin, flute, viole de gamba and concertos for strings and va
combinations of orchestral instruments ; and last and perhaps most notab
all, the collection of the twenty-four preludes and fugues in all keys, w
he called—as a sort of manifesto of his belief in the system of equal temp
ment, which made all keys equally available for the purposes of the
poser—" *Das Wohltemperirte Clavier.*"    Underlying a very large

on of the works of various kinds, even dance tunes or movements for a
instrument like the violin, fugue principles of procedure are predominant.
lightest dance tunes have a contrapuntal texture, and in the more serious
artistic examples it is so woven as to display beautiful combinations of
ment and melodic designs, ingenious sophistications of accent and subtleties
ythm such as are only possible in the style of instrumental counterpoint
h had sprung up in the development of the artistic requirements of organ
es. ¶ In the famous collection of preludes and fugues, which he ultimately
ased to forty-eight by the addition of a second collection, the style of in-
mental counterpoint which had been developed for organ-music found a
but most congenial sphere. As the works are written for the domestic
d instruments such as the tender expressive clavichord, or the pict-
ue harpsichord, they necessarily illustrated different artistic intentions
such as characterised genuine organ-music. Large scope of design and
erful effects of tune were obviously out of place, and more subtle treat-
and greater intrinsic interest of detail were inevitable. ¶Thus the
e became much more compact than the organ-fugues, and the treatment
elodic line and expressive harmony more intimately human. The com-
deals with more variety of style than in his organ-compositions, and
of the fugues may be taken as studies in human moods, such a play-
ss and gaiety, pathos and melancholy, contemplation and fervour,
iment, dignity, and confidence. The adaptation of known principles of
ic procedure to a purpose, at that time so novel, was characteristic of
's attitude toward art; and this is as true of the preludes as of the
es. The genealogy of the preludes may in some cases be traced back as
s the figurate preludes and little fantasias of such early types as were
uced by the Elizabethan composers of virginal music and their con-
oraries in other countries; though the form is enormously enhanced in
Bach's hands by the skilful use of more definite and attractive figures,
a higher balance of organisation in each work. However, the forms of
preludes are extremely various. Some seem to be almost without prec-
t. As, for instance, the rapturous instrumental song with solo part and
npaniment all combined for one instrument. ¶Among the preludes are
a few of the rare anticipations of complete sonatas of the harmonic kind,
ements with distinct contrast of key in the first half, "working out,"
modulation in the central part, and a recapitulation of the concrete
rial of the opening portion to conclude with. These occasional excur-
out of what seemed to be his most congenial ground, are often thoroughly
essful, but all the same his venture into the Italian manner and the
in type of form prove rather that he grasped their artistic meaning fully
that he believed in their efficiency as vehicles for the highest aspirations

of the composer.   In the latter part of his life J. S. Bach dealt more in
grand forms which bring into play the methods and resources of m
subordinate forms of art, both instrumental and vocal—such as the n
settings of the Passion, the masses—especially the great one in B minor—
work known as the "*Christmas Oratorio*" and the immense collectior
church cantatas written for Sundays and festivals in the churches in Leip
In all of these branches of art he had precursors, and the types of var
kinds had been explored.   The Italian aria-form had been more or
transformed for German purposes before he gave it his own exceptic
character and high artistic organisation.   ¶ The peculiar form of expres
recitative, so earnest and deeply emotional, which became a characteri
feature of German music and prefigured much in its latest dramatic m
festations, had found worthy exposition.   The treatment of chorales v
rich harmonisation and elaborate part-writing and the development of the
called motet choruses and choral fugues and even the peculiar contrapu
treatment of the accompanying instruments had all found characteristic G
man exponents.   Moreover, the form of Passion music had engaged the
tention of composers for nearly two hundred years and had arrived a
considerable degree of development recently in the hands of Kuhnau, Ke
and Händel himself.   But Bach's treatment of the scheme so immeasura
distanced all those who went before him that in later time his settings "
*cording to St. Matthew*" and "*St. John*" seem to stand almost alone
their pre-eminent glory.   The same is the case with his church canta
¶ The best work even of such composers as Buxtehude and John Christo
Bach seems singularly bald by the side of the copious variety and the inv
tive vigour of his work of this kind.   True it is that in all such cases,
even in such mighty phenomena as the choruses in the B minor mass,
built upon the foundation his predecessors supplied and with methods t
had helped to make available.   ¶ His peculiar quality was to divine how
resources of art which he found in being could be applied to purposes
grand and comprehensive that it is difficult to realise that the methods w
in truth the same as had been used by his forerunners.   His artistic pow
and insight were at such an immeasurably higher plane than those who p
ieded him that music seems at once to have stepped out of childishness i
maturity at his bidding.   ¶ In a sense his work is final and isolated.
work stands alone as the summing-up of a long period of preparation ;
the summing-up in his characteristically Teutonic direction seemed so co
plete that nothing remained to be said in the lines which he had illustrat
No composer followed in his footsteps.   Those who understood him s
that they could not approach him ; and the world in general wanted a m
easy-going and accommodating standard of art.   So the succeeding generat

nposers cultivated the more plausible Italian manner and the easily manip-
l Italian form.    ¶It was not for a century that his style and methods be-
o exert influence, and they came back to regenerate the world growing
with the overpersistency of harmonic forms of the sonata order.    ¶In-
it was the rise of what was called the romantic movement which
ght J. S. Bach back into the hearts of men, and made his ways of pro-
e suggestive of new developments.    The foremost prophets of the
antic movement, Schumann and Chopin, were his most ardent admirers.
the Classicists the style of J. S. Bach had seemed somewhat archaic.
s men began to long for human expression in art and the greater elasticity
m which helps to closer characterisation of mood and feeling, the richness
ssibilities and the greater pliancy of the forms Bach used became more
nore apparent.    At the same time the perfect adaptation of means to
which his perfect self-containment manifest may serve as a corrective
counterpoise in the turbulent times which follow the opening of the
gates of dramatic passion.    Those who cherish a constant love of the
n art of John Sebastian Bach have still a guiding light which will not
y them.

**Karl Philipp Emanuel** ("the
rlin" or "Hamburg Bach"), Wei-
r, March (8 ?) 14, 1714—Hamburg
pt. ?) Dec. 14, 1788. Son of above
le CHART OF BACHS). Studied phi-
ophy and law at Leipzig and
ankfort; cond. a singing society at
ankfort, for which he composed.
37 (38 ?) in Berlin.  Chamber-mus.
l clavecinist to Frederick the Great,
46–57. [or 1740–67 ?].  1757 Ham-
rg as Ch. mus.-dir. ; 1767 as Musik-
ector of the principal church there,
e Telemann, a position held till
ith.  He was one of the chief vir-
sos of the day.  He was the found-
of the modern school of piano-
ying, and a pioneer of greatest
portance in the sonata and sym-
ony-forms and orchestration, his
rks having a graceful modernity
possessed even by most of his
her's.  He wrote "*Versuch über
wahre Art das Clavier zu spie-*
" (2 parts, 1753–62), an impor-
at work containing detailed expla-
ions concerning ornaments.  His
y numerous comps. include **210**

solo pieces ; 52 concertos with orch. ;
quartets, trios, duets, sonatas, sonatinas, minuets, polonaises, solfeggi,
fugues, marches, etc., for clavier ; 18
symphonies ; 34 miscellaneous pieces
for wind-instrs., trios ; flute-, 'cello-,
and oboe-concertos ; soli for flute,
viola di gamba, oboe, cello, and harp,
etc., and 2 oratorios (" *Die Israeliten
in der Wüste*," and " *Die Auferstehung und Himmelfahrt Jesu*"), 22
Passions ; cantatas, etc.
(26) **Aug. Wm.**, Berlin, 1796—1869 ;
organist, teacher, and composer. (27)
(Rightly **Bak**), **Albert Ed.**, b.
Gyula, Hungary, March 22, 1844 ;
teacher, critic, writer and dram. bass ;
début, 1871. (28) (Dr.) **Otto**, Vienna,
1833—Unter-Waltersdorf, 1893 ; conductor and composer. (29) **Leonhard Emil**, b. Posen, March 11,
1849; pianist, pupil of Kullak, Wuerst
and Kiel ; 1874, court-pianist to
Prince George of Prussia ; ca. 1890,
London.  Composed opera *Irmen-
gard* (London, 1892) ; succ. 1-act
opera, *The Lady of Longford* (London, 1894) ; succ. 1-act comic opera,

*Des Kònigs Garde* (Cologne, 1895), etc.

**Bache** (bāch), (1) **Francis Edw.**, Birmingham, 1833—1858; violinist. (2) **Walter**, Birmingham, 1842—London, 1888, bro. of above; pianist and teacher. (3) **Constance**, b. Birmingham, sister and pupil of above; pupil of Klindworth and Hartvigson; since 1883 teacher, translator, and composer in London.

**Bachmann** (bäkh'-män), (1) **Anton**, 1716—1800; court-musician at Berlin, instr.-maker; inv. the machinehead. His son and successor, (2) **Karl L.**, 1743—1800, court-violinist, player, married the pianist and singer (3) **Charlotte Karoline Wilhelmine Stowe**, Berlin, 1757—1817. (4) Pater **Sixtus**, Ketterhausen, Bavaria, July 18, 1754—Marchthal, near Vienna, 1818; organist and pianist of unusual precocity, and memory; said to have played by heart over 200 pieces at 9; at 12 equalled Mozart, then 10 years old, in organ-competition, at Biberach; became a Premonstrant monk, composed masses, etc. (5) **G. Chr.**, Paderborn, 1804—Brussels, 1842; clarinet-maker, soloist and teacher. (6) **Georges**, ca. 1848—Paris, 1894. (7) **Gottlob**, Bornitz, Saxony, 1763—Zeitz, 1840, organist.

**Bachofen** (bäkh'-ôf-ĕn), **Jn. Kaspar**, Zurich, 1692—1755; organist.

**Bachrich** (bäkh'-rĭkh), **Sigismund**, b. Zsambokreth, Hungary, Jan. 23, 1841; violinist, pupil and now teacher at Vienna Cons.; composed 4 comic operas incl. *Der Fuchs-Major* (Prague, 1889), etc.

**Ba(c)ker-Gróndahl** (bäk'-ĕr grōn'-däl), **Agathe**, b. Holmestrand, Norway, Dec. 1, 1847; pianist and composer; pupil of Kjerulf, Bülow and Liszt; she married 1875, Gróndahl, singing-teacher in Christiania.

**Back'ers, Americus.** Vide BROADWOOD.

**Back'ofen, jn. G. H.**, Durlach, Baden, 1768 — Darmstadt, 1839; virtuoso

and manufacturer of wind-inst. Darmstadt; writer and compose

**Ba'con, Richard Mackenzie,** wich, Engl., 1776—1844; te and writer.

**Badarczevska** (bä-där-chĕf'-s **Thela,** Warsaw, 1838 — 1862 composed "*La prière d'une vi* etc.

**Bader** (bä'-dĕr), **K. Adam,** Bam 1789—Berlin, 1870; cathedral-o ist, Bamberg (1807); later first Berlin court opera (1820–45).

**Badia** (bä-dē'-ä), (1) **Carlo Ag.,** ice, 1672—Vienna, 1738; court poser at Vienna. (2) **Luigi,** Ti Naples, 1822—Milan, 1899; posed 4 operas.

**Bagge** (bäg'-gĕ), **Selmar,** Co 1823—Basel, 1896; editor and poser.

**Bagnolesi** (bän-yō-lā'-zē), Italian tralto in London, 1732.

**Bahn, Martin.** Vide TRAUTWEI

**Bähr** (or **Bär**, or **Beer**) (bār), **Jn** Georg (Austria), 1652—1770; conductor and writer of sat musical pamphlets signed "*U murmurat*," "*Ursus triump* etc.

**Bai** (or **Baj**) (bä'-ē), **Tommaso,** valcuore, near Bologna, ca. 1 Rome, Dec. 22, 1714; tenor a Vatican; conductor, 1713; com a *Miserere*, sung in the Papal el, during Holy Week, altern with those by Allegri and Baini.

**Baif** (bīf), **Jn. A. de,** Venice, 1 Paris, 1589; composer.

**Baildon** (bäl'-dŭn), d. London, Gentleman of the Chapel Roya composer.

**Bai'ley, Marie Louise,** b. Nash Tenn., Oct. 24, 1876; Leipzig, Pupil of C. Reinecke, winni scholarship, and with Lesche début, 1893, Gewandhaus, Lei Chamber-virtuoso to King Alb Saxony; now lives in Vienna.

**Baillot** (bī'-yō), (1) **P. M. Fra Sales,** Passy, Oct. 1, 1771 — Sept. 15, 1842; eminent violinist,

Polidori, Sainte, Marie, and Poll-
; later prof. of vln. at the Paris
ıs.; toured Europe ; 1821, leader at
Grand Opera ; 1825, solo violinist,
ʸal Orch.; wrote famous " *L'Art
Violon*" (1834) and "*Méthode du
ˑlon ;*" composed 10 vln. concer-
3 string-quartets, 24 preludes in
ɪeys, etc. (2) **Réné Paul**, Paris,
3—1889 ; son of above, Prof. at
is Cons.

ɪ (bä-ē'-nē), **Abbate, Gins.**,
ne, 1775 — 1844 ; composer and
ductor at St. Peter's ; wrote famous
of Palestrina.

ɒä'-ē). Vide BAI.

ɕti (bä-yĕt'-tē), **Giov.**, Brescia, ca.
5 — Milan, 1876 ; violinist, con-
tor and dram. composer.

ɛr., (1) **G.**, Exeter, England, 1773
ɾugeley, 1847 ; organist, violinist,
ɪ composer. (2) **Benj. Franklin**,
Wenham, Mass., July 10, 1811 ;
ɡer, teacher, and editor.

ɪkirew (bä-lä-kē'-rĕf), **Mily Al-
ɛjevitch**, b. Nijni-Novgorod,
ssia, 1836 ; studied at Kasan
iv., as a musician, self-taught ;
ɔut as pianist in St. Petersburg,
5 ; founded the " Free Music
ɪool," 1862 ; 1866, opera-conductor
ɪgue ; 1867-70, conductor Imp.
ɪsic Society, St. Petersburg, re-
ɛd 1872 ; composed a symph.
ɛm " *Tamara* " ; music to " *King
ɪr* " ; Russian, Czech and Spanish
ɛrtures ; an Oriental fantasia,
ʳslamei*," for pf., etc.; pub. 1866, a
ɪ. of Russian Folk-songs. 1901,
mphony in C.

ɪrt (bä-lärt'), **Gabriel**, Barcelona,
ɪ4—1893 ; studied in Paris ; con-
ɕtor, later director Barcelona Cons.;
nposed zarzuelas (Vide D. D.).

ɪt'ka, **Hans**, Hoffnungsthal, Mo-
ʲia, 1827—Chicago, 1899 ; studied
Vienna ; 1849, America ; **1851**,
ɪnded the Milwaukee Musikverein ;
ɔo, conductor of Chicago Philh.
c.; composed cantatas, etc.

ɪâtre or **Balbastre** (bäl-bätr),
ɪaude Louis, Dijon, 1729 — Paris,

1799 ; pupil and friend of Rameau ;
organist and composer.

**Balbi**, (bäl'-bē), (1) **Ludovico**, composer and conductor at S. Antonio,
Padua ; ca. 1606, Franciscan monastery, Venice. (2) (Cav.), **Melchiore**, Venice, 1796 — Padua, 1879ʹ
church-conductor, theorist and com
poser.

**Baldassari** (bäl-däs-sä'-rē), **Benedetto**, Italian tenor in London, 1721.

**Bal'denecker**, (1) **Nikolaus**, b.
Mayence, 1782 ; violinist. (2) **Konrad**, b. 1828 ; pianist.

**Baldewin** (bäl-dĕ-vēn). Vide BAUL-
DEWIJN.

**Balfe** (bälf), **Michael Wm.**, Dublin,
May 15, 1808—Rowney Abbey, Hert-
fordshire, Oct. 20, 1870 ; operatic
composer ; pupil of O'Rourke, Ireland, and C. F. Horn, London ;
1824, violinist Drury Lane ; also
sang in London ; went to Italy with
his patron Count Mazzara, and studied comp. with Frederici at Rome,
and singing with F. Galli at Milan ;
his ballet *La Pérouse*, prod. there
(1826) ; pupil of Bordogni, and first
barytone at the Ital. Opera, Paris
(1828), and elsewhere till 1835 ; composed several Italian operas ; m. the
Hungarian singer **Lina Rosen** (1808
—London, 1888) ; he ret. to England
1835, and prod. *The Siege of Rochelle* (Drury Lane) ; failed as manager ; went to Paris, returned 1843,
and prod. *The Bohemian Girl*, very
successful everywhere ; prod. Paris,
1856, in 5-act version as "*La Bohé-
mienne.*" In 1857. his daughter
**Victorie** made her début in Italian
opera ; 1864, he retired to his country-
seat, Rowney Abbey ; he composed
31 operas in all, including *The Rose
of Castile* (1857) ; *Satanella* (1858):
*Il Talismano* (1874) ; biog. by C. L.
Kenny (London, 1878), and W. A.
Barrett (do. 1882).

**Ballabene** (bäl-lä-bā'-nĕ), **Gregorio**,
lived 18th cent. (?) ; composed a remarkable Kyrie and Gloria in 48 **real**
parts, performed at Rome, **1770.**

**Ballazarini** (bäl-lä-tsä-rē'-nē) (or **Baltagerini**), Italian violinist; came from Piedmont to Paris, 1577, and was court-intendant to Catherine de Medicis, who gave him the name " **M. de Beaujoyeulx** "; founder of the ballet, and indirectly of French opera.

**Ballard** (bäl'-lär'), a family of French music-printers; founded 1552 by **Robert B.**, with a patent, from Henri II., as " Seul imprimeur de la musique de la chambre, chapelle et menus plaisirs du roy." The patent expired 1776 after being held by **R.**, and his brother-in-law, **Adrien la Roy**; by **Pierre B.**, 1633; **Robt. Ed. Christophe**, 1673; **J. Bapt. Christophe**, 1695; **Chp. J. Fran.**, 1750, **P. Robt. Chp.**, 1763.

**Baltagerini.** Vide BALLAZARINI.

**Balthasar** (called **Balthasar-Florence**) (bäl-tä-zär flô-räńs), **H. Mat.**, b. Arlon, Belgium, Oct. 21, 1844; pupil of Fétis, m. (1863) a daughter of the instr.-maker Florence; composed operas, etc.

**Baltzar** (bält'-tsär), **Thos.**, Lübeck, ca. 1630—London, 1663; eminent court-violinist in England from 1656.

**Balt'zell, Willard J.**, b. Philadelphia, U. S. A., d. 1900; teacher Ohio Wesleyan University, Ohio; composed songs.

**Banchieri** (bän-kĭ-ā'-rē), **Adr.**, Bologna, 1567 (?)—1634; theorist and organist.

**Banck** (bänk), **K.**, Magdeburg, 1809—Dresden, 1889; critic and vocal teacher.

**Banderali** (bän-dä-rä'-lē), **Davidde**, Lodi, 1780—Paris, 1849, buffo tenor, then teacher at Paris Cons.

**Bandini** (bän-dē'-nē), (1) **Primo**, b. Parma, Nov. 29, 1857; pupil R. School of Music there; composed successful operas *Eufemio di Messina* (Parma, 1878), *Fausta* (Milan, 1886), *Janko* (Turin, 1897). (2) **Uberto Rieti**, b. Umbria, March 28, 1860, pupil of Giustiniani, Bolloni, Rossi Tergiani, and Sgambati;

composed prize overture " *Eleono* symphony, etc

**Bandrowski** (bän-drôf'-shkĭ), **A** Ritter **von**, b. Lubackzon, Ga April 22, 1860, operatic tenor, s ied Cracc w University, then with giovanni, Milan, and Salvi, Vie début Berlin, for some years lea tenor Cologne opera. has sung in Russia, and oratorio in Engl sang Paderewski's *Manru* at Wa and in New York 1902.

**Banès** (bä-nĕs), **A. Anatole**, b. P June 8, 1856, pupil of E. Dur officer of pub. instruction; com of operettas, lives in Paris.

**Ban'ester, Gilbert**, 16th cent., I lish composer of Flemish influenc

**Ban'ister**, (1) **J.**, London, 16 1676(79?); court-violinist and com er. (2) **J. (Jr.)**, d. 1735, son of ab court-violinist. (3) **Chas. Wm.**, —1831; composer. (4) **Hy. Jos** London, 1803—1847. (5) **Hy. Ch** London, 1831—1897, son of pianist, teacher, and writer; I " *Lectures on Musical Analy*. etc.

**Banks**, (1) **Benj.**, vln.-maker, I don, 1750—1795, succeeded by son (2) **Benj. (Jr.)**. Two other s (3) **James**, and (4) **H.**, were also makers.

**Bannelier** (bä-nĕl-yā), **Chas.**, P 1840—1899; writer.

**Banti-Giorgi** (bän'-tē-jôr'-jē), I gida, Crema, Lombardy, 1759— logna, Feb. 18, 1806; dram. sopr first a *chanteuse* in a Paris café, I engaged at the Grand Opera; to Europe with great success, her v was remarkable in compass and e ness, but she was musically illiter m. the dancer Zaccaria Banti.

**Ban'tock, Granville**, b. London, A 7, 1868, studied R. A. M.. took Macfarren Prize for comp., his work, dram. cantata " *The Fire-W shippers*," successfully prod., 18 successful 1-act romantic opera *C mar* (London, 1892); conductor Gaiety Theatre Troupe, compo

her operas (text and mus.), also
mph. overture *Saul*" dram.
mphony in 24 parts, " *The Curse
Kehama*," etc.

'tie, **David**, b. Edinburgh, Nov.
, 1822, lives in Glasgow, com-
sed anthems, etc.; compiled hymn-
oks.

tiste (rightly **Baptiste Anet**)
(ăp-tĕst-ă-nā). violinist at Paris,
oo, where he introduced Corelli's
orks.

baco'la. Vide BARBIREAU.

bedette (bărb-dĕt). **H.**, b. 1825;
riter and composer.

baja (bär-bä'-yä), **Domenico**, Mi-
n, 1778—Posilippo, 1841; impre-
rio.

barieu. Vide BARBIREAU.

barini (bär-bä-rē'-nē), **Manfredo
upi**; lived 16th cent.; composed
otets under the name of " Lupi "
. v.).

bel'la, **Emanuele**, d. Naples,
773; violinist and composer.

bereau (bär-bŭ-rō), (1) **Maturin**-
ug. **Bal.**, Paris, 1799—1879, conuctor and theorist. (2) Vide BAR-
REAU.

bier (bărb-yā), (1) **Fr. Ét.**, Metz,
329—Paris, 1889; teacher and lead-
r; composed over 30 operas. (2)
ules Paul, Paris, 1825—Jan., 1901.
ollaborator with Carré, in the lib-
tti of many operas, including *Les
Voces de Jeannette* (Massé); *Le Par-
on de Ploërmel* (Meyerbeer); *Faust*
Gounod), *Philémon et Baucis* (Gou-
od); *Roméo et Juliette* (Gounod);
Hamlet (Ambr. Thomas). (3) **Paul**,
. Paris, 1854, son of above, libret-
st.

rbieri (bär-bĭ-ā'-rē), (1) **Carlo
Emm. di**, b. Genoa, 1822—Pesth,
867; conductor and dram. compos-
r. (2) **Francisco Asenjo**, Ma-
rid, 1823—1894; very pop. com-
oser of *Zarzuelas* (Vide D. D.).

rbireau (bär-bĭ-rō) (or **Barbiriau,
Barbarieu, Barbyria'nus, Barbe-
au, Barbingaut** (bär-băṅ-gō), or
**Barbaco'la**), d. Aug. 8, 1491; from

1448 choirmaster of Nôtre-Dame.
notable cptist., composed masses, etc.

**Barbot** (bär-bō), **Jos. Th. Désiré**,
Toulouse, 1824—Paris, 1897; tenor;
created " *Faust*," 1859; 1875. prof.
Paris Cons.

**Bardi** (bär'-dē), **Giov.**, conte del Ver-
nio, Florentine nobleman and patron
of the 16th cent., under whose influence the attempted revival of the
Greek lyric drama led to modern
opera. At his house "*Dafne*" was
performed. (Vide PERI.)

**Bargaglia** (bär-gäl'-yä), **Scipione**,
Neapolitan composer, said to have
first used the word " concerto " (1587).

**Barge** (bär'-gĕ), **Jn. H. Wm.**, b.
Wulfsahi, Hanover, Nov. 23, 1836;
self-taught flutist; 1867-95 first flute,
Leipzig Gewandhaus Orch., retired
on pension; teacher Leipzig Cons.;
wrote " Method for Flute ", composed 4 orchestral flute-studies, etc.

**Bargheer** (bär'-khār), (1) **K. Louis**, b.
Bückeburg, Dec. 31, 1833; violinist;
pupil of Spohr, David, and Joachim;
1863, court-conductor at Detmold,
made concert-tours; 1879-89, leader
Hamburg Phil. Soc., teacher in the
Cons.; later leader in Bülow orch.
(2) **A.**, b. Bückeburg, Oct. 21, 1840,
brother of above, pupil of Spohr;
court-violinist Detmold; since 1866,
Prof. Basel Sch. of Music.

**Bargiel** (bär'-gēl), **Woldemar**, Ber-
lin, Oct. 3, 1828—Feb. 23, 1897;
important composer; pupil, Leipzig
Cons.; later Prof. in Cologne Cons.;
1865, dir. and cond. of the Mus.
Sch., Amsterdam; 1874 Prof. R.
Hochschule, Berlin; 1882, Pres.
" Meisterschule für musikalische
Komposition "; composed 3 overtures
" *Zu einem Trauerspiel* (*Romeo and
Juliet*)" "*Prometheus*," " *Medea*"; a
symphony; 2 psalms for chorus and
orchestra; pf.-pcs., etc.

**Baril'li, A.**, 1826—Naples, 1876; half-
brother of Adelina Patti.

**Bar'ker, Chas. Spackmann**, b. Bath,
1806—Maidstone, 1879; organ-build
er; invented the pneumatic lever.

**Bärman** (bär'-män), (1) **H. Jos.**, Potsdam, 1784—Munich, 1847, clarinet-
virtuoso and composer. His brother
(2) **K.**, 1782—1842, was a bassoonist.
(3) **K.**, (Sr.), son of **H. J. B.**, was a
clarinettist ; his son (4) **K.**, (Jr.), b.
Munich, July 9, 1839 ; pupil of Liszt
and Lachner ; teacher at Munich
Cons., lives in Boston, Mass., as
pianist and teacher ; composed piano
pieces.

**Bar'nard**, (1) Rev. **Jn.**, canon St.
Paul's Cathedral, London ; pub. 1641
the first coll. of cathedral-music. (2)
Mrs. **Chas.** (née **Alington**), 1830—
Dover, 1869, composed popular
songs, etc. under name " **Claribel.** "

**Barn'by**, (1) **Rob.**, York, England,
1821 — London, 1875 ; alto-singer
Chapel Royal. (2) Sir **Jos.**, York,
Engl., Aug. 12, 1838—London, Jan.
28, 1896 ; choirboy at 7 ; at 10 taught
other boys, at 12 organist ; at 15
music-master ; 1854 entered the R. A.
M., London ; then organist various
churches and cond. ; 1875, precentor
and dir. at Eton ; 1892 Principal of
Guildhall Sch of Mus. ; knighted,
July, 1892 ; composed " *Rebekah* "
a sacred idyll (1870) ; Psalm 97 ; Service in E, etc.

**Barnes, Robt.**, violin-maker, London,
1760—1800.

**Barnett**, (1) **J.**, Bedford, England,
July 1, 1802—Cheltenham, April 17,
1890," The father of English opera " ;
pupil of C. E. Horn, Price, and
Ries ; brought out his first opera
" *Before Breakfast,*" 1825 ; " *The
Mountain Sylph* " (1834) ; the very
succ. " *Fair Rosamond* " (1837), and
" *Farinelli* " (London, 1838) ; 1841,
singing teacher at Cheltenham ; left
2 unfinished oratorios, a symphony,
etc. (2) **Jos. Alfred**, London, 1810
—(?), 1898 ; bro. of above ; composer. (3) **J. Francis**, b. London, Oct.
16, 1837, nephew of above ; studied
with Dr. Wylde (1849) ; and at R. A.
M., and Leipzig Cons. ; début as
pianist, 1853 ; 1883, prof. at R. Coll

of Mus. ; composed oratorio '
*Raising of Lazarus* " (1876), sym
ny in A min., " Ouverture sym
nique " (1868), overture to *Wi
Tale* (1871), cantatas, etc.

**Baron** (bä'-rōn), **Ernst Gl.**, Bre
1696—Berlin, 1760 ; court-lu
and theorbist ; writer and compe

**Barré** (or **Barra**) (bär-rā or bär
(1) **Léonard**, b. Limoges ; sing
Papal Chapel (1537) and special
sical envoy to the Council of
(1545) ; composed madrigals
motets. (2) **A.**, printer, etc., R
1555-70, later Milan.

**Barret** (bär-rā), **A. M. Rose**, 18
Paris, 1879 ; oboist.

**Bar'rett**, (1) **J.**, 1674—London,
(8 ?) ; organist. (2) **Thos.**, v
maker, London, 1710-30. (3) **
Alex.**, Hackney, Middlesex, 18
London (?), 1891 ; editor and w
co-editor with Sir John Stainer
" Dict. of Music. Terms."

**Barrien'tos, Maria**, b. Barcelona
1884 ; singing with wonderful
cess in Rome at 11 years ; took
medals for violin-playing.

**Bar'rington, Daines**, London,
—1800 ; lawyer and musical e
ist.

**Bar'ry, Chas. Ainslie**, b. Lon
June 10, 1830 ; pupil of Col
Cons. and Leipzig Cons. ; editor
organist ; composed a sympho
overtures, etc.

**Barsanti** (bär-sän'-tē), **Fran.**, L
ca. 1690—1760 ; flutist, oboist,
composer ; 1750, viola-player at
don.

**Barsot'ti, Tommaso G. F.**,
ence, 1786—Marseilles, 1868 ; te
er and composer.

**Bartay** (bär'-tä-ē), (1) **Andr
Széplak**, Hungary, 1798—Maye
1856 ; 1838 Dir. Nat. Th. Pe
composed Hungarian operas,
(2) **Ede**, Oct. 6, 1825—Sept.,
son of above ; pupil Nat. Mus. A
emy, Pesth ; founded pension-fun
musicians ; composed overture," 
*es.*" etc.

tei (bär-tä'-ē), **Girolamo**, general of ugustinian monks at Rome; publsher and composer (1607–18).

tel (bär'-tĕl), (1) **Aug.**, Sonderslausen, 1800—1876; son of (2) **H. .., trumpeter in the court-band; and rother to (3) Adolf**, 1809—1878, member of the same band. **Aug.** as an excellent teacher, and trained s 'cellists, his sons, (4) **Ernst**, 1824 -Remschied, 1868, and (5) **Gunher**, b. 1833; pupil also of Dehn; ves in Düsseldorf, as writer and omposer.

rt (bärt), (1) **Chr. Samuel**, Glauhen, Saxony, 1735—Copenhagen, 809; oboist. (2) **F. Phil. K. Ant.**, b. Cassel, ca. 1773; son of bove; composer. (3) **Jos. Jn. Aug.**, . Gresslippen, Bohemia, 1781; 810–30, tenor, Vienna. (4) **Gusav**, Vienna, 1800—Frankfort, 1897; on of (3); pianist and conductor. 5) **K. H.**, b. Pillau, Prussia, July 2, 1847; pianist, pupil of Von 3ülow, Bronsart, and Tausig; 1871, eacher at R. Hochschüle für Musik, onductor of the Philh. concerts at Hamburg (vice von Bülow). (6) **Richard**, left-handed violin-virtuoso; Jniv. Mus. Dir. Marburg, till 1894; ince then Dir. of Hamburg Philh. Concerts.

rthe, **Grat-Norbert** (grä-nôr-bĕrpärt), b. Bayonne, France, June 7, 828; pupil Paris Cons., 1854: won he Grand Prix de Rome; wrote canata "*Francesca da Rimini*"; composed operas "*Don Carlos*" and "*La Fiancée d'Abydos*" (1865); oraorio, "*Judith*," etc.

arthel (bär'-tĕl), **Jn. Chr.**, Plauen, Saxony, 1776—Altenburg, 1831; court-organist.

arthélemon (bär-tā-lŭ-môṅ) (in English **Bar'tleman**), **Fran. Hip.**, Bordeaux, 1741—London, 1808; violinist and composer.

artholdy (bär-tôl-dē), **Jakob Salomon** (of Jewish parents), Berlin, 1779—Rome, 1825; diplomatist and writer.

**Barthol'omew, Wm.**, London, 1793—1867; translator.

**Bart'lett,** (1) **J.**, 17th century, English composer. (2) **Homer Newton**, b. Olive, N. Y., Dec. 28, 1846; pupil of S. B. Mills, Max Braun, Jacobson, etc. From 14 organist New York churches; now at Madison Av. Bapt. Ch.; published a sextet, a cantata "*The Last Chieftain*," many songs, etc.; opera, "*La Vallière*," oratorio, "*Samuel*," etc., in MS.

**Bartoli** (bär-tō'-lē), Padre **Erasmo**, Gaeta, 1606—Naples, 1656; churchcomposer under the name "Padre Raimo."

**Bartolini** (lē'-nē), **V.**, Italian male soprano, in London, 1782.

**Bartolo** (bär-tō'-lō), Padre **Daniele**, Ferrara, 1608—Rome, 1685; Jesuit theorist.

**Baselt** (bä'-zĕlt), **Fritz (Fr. Gv. O.)**, b. Oels, Silesia, May 26, 1863; pupil of Köhler and Bussler; music-dealer, teacher and conductor Breslau, Essen and Nürnberg; since 1894, director of Philh. Verein, and "Sängervereinigung" (ca. 1,200 voices), Frankfort-on-Main; composed 9 operettas, nearly 100 male choruses, etc.

**Basevi** (bä-sā'-vē), **Abramo**, Leghorn, 1818—Florence, 1885; journalist and composer.

**Ba'sil** (Saint), **The Great**, Caesarea, 329—Cappadocia, 379; bishop; reputed introducer of congregational (antiphonal) singing into the Eastern Ch., preceding St. Ambrose in the Western.

**Basili** (bä-zē'-lē), (1) **Dom. Andrea**, 1720—Loreto, 1775; conductor and composer; his son (2) **Fran.**, Loreto, 1766—Rome, 1850; prod. 11 operas, and several dram. oratorios in Rome; 1837, conductor at St. Peter's, Rome; composed also symphonies, etc.

**Basiron** (bä'-sĭ-rôṅ), **Giovanni**, developed the motet, ca. 1430—1480.

**Bassani** (bäs-sä'-nē), (1) **Giov.**, ca. 1600; conductor at St. Mark's, Venice. (2) (or **Bassiani**), **Giov. Bat.**, Padua, ca. 1657—Ferrara, 1716; viô7 linist, conductor and composer. (3) **Geron.**, b. Padua, 17th cent.; singer, teacher and composer.

**Bassano** (bäs-sä'-nō) ,————; woman pianist ; début, London, Philh. Society, 1842.

**Basselin** (bäs-lăṅ), **Olivier,** lived at Vire, France, 15th cent.; a fuller whose songs were said to have been first given the name " Vau de Vire," whence, vaudeville.

**Bassevi** (bäs-sä'-vē), **Giacomo.** Vide CERVETTO.

**Bass'ford, Wm. Kipp,** b. New York, April 23, 1839 ; pupil of Samuel Jackson ; toured the U. S. as pianist ; now organist at East Orange, N. J.; also composer.

**Bassi** (bäs'-sē), **Luigi,** Pesaro, 1766—Dresden, 1825 ; barytone and director ; Mozart wrote the rôle of " Don Giovanni " for him.

**Bassiron** (bäs-sĭ-rôṅ), **Ph.,** 15th cent.; Netherland contrapuntist ; composed masses.

**Bastardella.** Vide AGUJARI.

**Bastiaans** (bäs'-tē-äns), (1) **J. G.,** Wilp, 1812—Haarlem, 1875 ; organist and teacher at Amsterdam and at St. Bavo's ; his son and successor (2) **Jn.,** 1854—1885; teacher and composer.

**Baston** (bäs-tôṅ), **Josquin,** lived, 1556, Netherlands ; contrapuntist.

**Batch'elder, J. C.,** b. Topsham, Vt., 1852 ; pianist and organist ; pupil of Haupt, Ehrlich, Loeschhorn, Berlin ; organ-teacher in Detroit (Mich.) Cons.

**Bates,** (1) **Joah,** Halifax, 1741—London, 1799 ; conductor ; promoter and conductor of the famous " Händel Commemoration " festivals in London (1784–91). (2) His wife was a singer. (3) **Wm.,** 1720—1790 (?) ; English opera composer.

**Ba'teson, T.,** England, ca. 1575—after 1611 ; organist and composer of madrigals.

**Bathe** (bāth), **Wm.,** Dublin, 1564—Madrid, 1614 ; writer.

**Batiste** (bă-tēst), **A. Éd.,** Paris, 1820—

1876; organist, teacher and poser.

**Batistin** (bă-tēs-tăṅ). Vide STR J. B.

**Bâton** (bä-tôṅ). (1) **H.,** 18th musette-player. His brother **Chas.** (le jeune) performed on vielle ; also composer and wr 1757.

**Batta** (bät'-tä), (1) **Pierre,** M tricht, Holland, 1795—Brussels, 1 'cellist and teacher. His sons (2) **Alex.,** b. Maastricht, July 1816 ; 'cellist and composer. (3 **Laurent,** Maastricht, 1817—Na 1880 ; pianist and teacher. (4) **J** b. Maastricht, April 24, 1824 ; 'ce pupil of Brussels Cons., took Grand Prix for comp. in 1845 ; s 1846 player at the Opéra-Comi Paris ; composed symphonies, etc

**Battaille** (bät-tī'-yŭ), **Chas.** Aima Nantes, 1822—Paris, 1872 ; dr bass.

**Batanchon** (băt-täṅ-shôṅ), **F.,** Pa 1814—1893 ; 'cellist ; inv. (1846 small 'cello, the " barytone."

**Bat'tan, Adrian,** ca. 1585—ca. 16 English organist.

**Bat'tishill, Jonathan,** London, 1 —Islington, 1801 ; conductor dram. composer.

**Battista** (bät-tēs'-tä), **V.,** Naples, 1 —1873 ; dram. composer.

**Battistini** (bät-tēs-tē'-nē), **Mattia** Rome (?) Nov. 27, 1857 ; dram. ba tone ; début, Rome, 1878 ; sang Buenos Ayres and principal thea in Europe.

**Battmann** (bät'-män), **Jacques** Maasmünster, Alsatia, 1818—Dij 1886 ; organist.

**Batton** (bät-tôṅ), **Désiré Alex.,** Pa 1797—Versailles, 1855 ; teacher ɛ dram. composer.

**Battu** (băt-tü), **Pantaléon,** Pa 1799—1870 ; violinist and compos€

**Baudet** (bō-dā), **Hubert Cyrille ;** vented " piano-violin," or " pia quatuor," 1865.

**Baudiot** (bōd-yō), **Chas. N.,** Nan 1773—Paris, 1849 ; 'cellist.

doin (or **Baudouyn**) (bō-dwǎṅ).
de BAULDEWIJN.

er (bow'-ĕr), (1) **Chrysostomus,**
th cent. organ-builder at Würtem-
rg. (2) **Harold,** b. London, 1873,
English mother and German father;
iyed violin in public at 9; studied
th Gorski, Paris; then the piano,
1892, under Paderewski; début
pianist, Paris, 1893; has toured
irope and, since 1900, America,
th great success.

ldewijn (bōd-wǎṅ) (or **Baulduin,**
aldewin, **Balduin, Baudoin,**
audouyn), **Noël (Natalis),** Ant-
rp, 1513 (or 1518 ?)—1529; conduc-
r at Nôtre Dame; and composer.

mbach (bowm'-bäkh), (1) **Fr.**
ug., 1753—Leipzig, 1813; con-
ctor and writer. (2) **Ad.,** Ger-
any, 1830 (?)—Chicago, 1880;
acher and composer.

mfelder (bowm'-fĕlt-ĕr), **Fr.,** b.
resden, May 28, 1836; pianist; pu-
l of J. Otto, and Leipzig Cons.

mgart (bowm'-gärt), **E. Fr.,** Gross-
ogau, 1817—Warmbrunn, 1871;
itor.

mgarten(bowm'-gärt-ĕn),(1)**Gott-**
lf von, Berlin, 1741—Gross-Stre-
z, Silesia, 1813; composed 3 operas.
) **K. Fr.,** Germany, 1754—Lon-
n, 1824; violinist and dram. com-
ser.

mgärtner (bowm'-gĕrt-nĕr), (1)
ug., Munich, 1814—1862; writer on
musical shorthand," etc. (2) **Wm.**
uillaume), 1820—Zurich, 1867;
mposer and mus. dir. at St. Gallen.

imker (bīm'-kĕr), **Wm.,** b. Elber-
ld, Oct. 25, 1842; chaplain and
hool-inspector, Niederkrüchten;
rote biogs. of Palestrina, Lassus,etc.

isch (bowsh), (1) **L. Chr. Aug.,**
aumburg, 1805—Leipzig, 1871;
aker of violins and bows. His 2
ns were vln.-makers: (2)
udwig (1829—Leipzig, 1871); lived
ew York, then in Leipzig; and (3)
tto, 1841—1874.

isznern (bows'-nĕrn), **Waldemar**
on, b. Berlin, Nov. 29, 1866; studied

at Kronstadt, Pesth, Vienna and with
Bargiel and Fr. Kiel at the Berlin
Hochschule; since 1894 lives in Dresden, as dir. Singakademie and Leid-
ertafel; composed a symphony, overtures, a Zigeuner suite, a music-drama
" *Dichter und Welt* " (Weimar, 1897),
etc.

**Bayer** (bī'-ĕr), **Josef,** b. Austria, ca.
1851 — 1871; 2d violinist, Court
Opera, Vienna, 1882, ballet-director,
composed operettas, etc.

**Bay'ly,** Rev. **Anselm,** 1719—1792;
English writer.

**Bazin** (bǎ-zǎṅ), **Fran. Ém. Jos.,** Marseilles, 1816 — Paris, 1878; dram.
composer.

**Bazzini** (bäd-zē'-nē), **A.,** Brescia,
March 11, 1818—Milan, Feb. 10,
1897; violinist; pupil of Camisani;
at 17 conductor Church of S. Filippo,
where he prod. masses and vespers,
and 6 oratorios with full orch., and
gave successful concert-tours through
Europe. 1873, prof. of comp., 1882,
dir. of Milan Cons. In his compositions his native melodiousness gained
unusual value from a German solidity
of harmony.

**Bazzino** (bäd-zē'-nō), (1) **Fr. M.,**
Lovere (Bergamo), 1593—Bergamo,
1660; theorbo virtuoso. (2) **Natale,**
d. 1639; composed masses.

**Bé, Le.** Vide LE BÉ.

**Beach,** Mrs. **H. H. A.** (née **Amy
Marcy Cheney),** b. Henniker, N.
H., Sept. 5, 1867; pianist and com-
poser; pupil of E. Perabo and K.
Baermann (pf.), and Junius W. Hill
(harmony); self-taught in cpt., comp.
and orchestration, having transl.
Berlioz and Gevaert for her own use;
Pres. Board of Councillors, N. E.
Cons., Boston; composed " *Gaelic* "
symphony, Mass with orch., songs,
etc.

**Beale,** (1) **Wm.,** Landrake, Cornwall,
1784—London, 1854; famous glee-
composer. (2) **J.,** London, ca. 1796;
pianist. (3) **Thos. Willert,** b. London, 1828; a lawyer and pupil of
Roeckel; one of the founders of the

New Philh. Soc. ; composed operettas ; used pen-name " Walter Maynard."

**Béanon** (bā-ä-nôn), **Lambert de**, conductor at Sistine Chapel, Rome, before Josquin des Prés.

**Beard, J.**, England, ca. 1717—Hampton, 1791 ; eminent tenor for whom Händel wrote the tenor rôles in his chief oratorios.

**Beauchamps** (bō-shän), **P. Fran. Godard de**, Paris, ca. 1689—1761 ; writer.

**Beaujoyeulx** (bō-zhwä-yŭ), **de.** Vide BALLAZARINI.

**Beaulieu** (rightly **Martin**) (bŏl-yŭ', or mär-tän), **M. Désiré**, Paris, 1791—Niort, 1863 ; patron, writer and composer.

**Beaumavielle** (bō-mäv-yĕl), d. Paris, 1688 ; barytone ; he sang in the first French opera, 1671.

**Beauquier** (bŏk-yā), **Chas.**, b. ca. 1830 ; writer of " Philosophie de musique " (1865), and librettist.

**Beaz'ley, Jas. Chas.**, b. Ryde, Isle of Wight, 1850 ; lives there as composer, pupil of R. A. M.

**Beccatel'li, Giov. Fran.**, d. Florence, 1734 ; cond. at Prato and writer.

**Becher** (bĕkh'-ĕr), (1) **Alfred Julius**, Manchester, 1803—Vienna, 1848 ; editor. (2) **Jos.**, b. Neukirchen, Bavaria, Aug. 1, 1821 ; composed over 60 masses, etc.

**Bechstein** (bĕkh'-shtīn), **Fr. Wm. K.**, b. Gotha, June 1, 1826 ; 1856, worked in German factories ; later established the well-known piano factory in Berlin.

**Beck**, (1) **David**, Germany, ca. 1590 ; organ-builder. (2) **Reichardt K.**, lived in Strassburg, ca. 1650 ; composer. (3) **Jn. Philip**, 1677 ; editor. (4) **Michael**, b. Ulm, 1653 ; writer. (5) **Gf. Jos.**, Podiebrad, Bohemia, 1723—Prague, 1787 ; Dominican (later Provincial) friar ; organist. (6) **Chr. Fr.**, b. Kirchheim, ca. 1755 ; composer. (7) **Fz.**, Mannheim, 1730 —Bordeaux, 1809 ; court-violinist. (8) **Fr. Ad.**, pub. at Berlin, "*Dr. M. Luther's Gedanken über die*

*Musik*," 1825. (9) **K.**, 1814—enna, 1879 ; tenor ; created " *Lo grin.*" (10) **Jn. Nepomuk**, Pe: 1828—Vienna (?) 1893 ; dram. b: tone. (11) **Jos.**, b. June 11, 18 son of above ; barytone, sang Austria, Berlin (1876), and Frank (1880). (12) **Johann Heinrich**, Cleveland, Ohio, Sept. 12, 18 violinist ; pupil Leipzig Cons. ; li Cleveland ; founded the " Schul Quartet " ; composed overtures Byron's " *Lara*," to " *Romeo Juliet* ;" cantata "*Deukalion*" (B ard Taylor), etc.

**Becké** (bĕk'-ā), **Jn. Baptist**, b. Nü berg, 1743 ; court-flutist, in Mün 1776.

**Beck'el, James Cox**, b. Philadelpl Dec. 20, 1811 ; pupil there of T jetta ; later music-publisher in Phil and editor of " *Musical Clipper* composed cantatas, etc.

**Beck'er**, (1) **Dietrich** (1668), cc poser at Hamburg, 1668. (2) **J** Helsa, near Cassel, 1726—18c court-organist. (3) **K. Fd.**, Leip: 1804—1877, organist and writ (4) **Konstantin Julius**, Freibe Saxony, 1811—Oberlössnitz, 18; editor. (5) **Val. Ed.**, Würzbu 1814—Vienna, 1890 ; dram. cc poser. (6) **Georg**, b. Frankenth Palatinate, June 24, 1824 ; piar and writer ; lives in Geneva ; p " *La Musique en Suisse*" (1874), e (7) **Albert Ernst Ant.**, Quedl burg, June 13, 1834—Berlin, Jan. : 1899 ; pupil of Bonicke and Deh 1881, teacher of comp. at Sch wenka's Cons. ; also conductor Ber cathedral choir ; composed a no worthy symphony. a Grand Mass B♭ min. (1878), and oratorio " *Se aus Gnade*," etc. (8) **Jean**, Mar heim, May 11, 1833—Oct. 10, 188 violinist, leader Mannheim orcl after concert-tours, lived in Floren and founded the famous " Florenti Quartet " ; toured with his childr (9) His daughter **Jeanne**, b. Mar heim, June 9, 1859 ; pianist, pupil

einecke and Bargiel. (10) **Hans.,**
. Strassburg, May 12, 1860; viola-
layer, pupil of Singer. (11) **Hugo,**
. Strassburg, Alsatia, Feb. 13, 1833;
oted 'cellist, son and pupil of (8), pu-
il of Kundiger, then of Grützmacher;
884, soloist at opera, Frankfort; since
894, Prof. at the Hoch Cons. there;
ured, U. S. 1900–1901. (12) **Rhein-
old,** b. Adorf, Saxony, 1842; vio-
nist; lives in Dresden; composed
ucc. operas *Frauenlob* (Dresden,
892), and *Ratbold* (Mayence, 1896),
-act; symph. poem *Der Prinz von
Homburg,* etc. (13) **K.,** b. Kirr-
veiler, near Trier, June 5, 1853;
eacher at Neuwied; pub. song-
ooks. (14) **Jakob,** founder (1841)
f large Russian pf.-factory; present
ead (since 1871), Paul Petersen.

ck'mann, Jn. Fr. Gl., 1737—Celle,
792; organist, harpsichord-virtuoso,
nd dram. composer.

ck'with, J. Christmas, Norwich,
England, 1750—1809; organist and
vriter.

cquié (bĕk-yā), (1) Jean Marie (?),
Toulouse, ca. 1800—Paris, 1825;
lutist. His brother (2) (" De Peyre
Ville"), Jean Marie, Toulouse,
797—Paris 1876; violinist.

čvařovsky (bĕch'-var-shôf'-shkǐ),
Ant. F., Jungbunzlau, Bohemia,
1754—Berlin, 1823; organist and
composer.

d'ford, Mrs. H. Vide LEHMANN,
LIZA.

dos de Celles (bŭ-dō' du sĕl), Caux,
near Bézières, 1706—St. Maur, 1779;
Benedictine monk and writer.

eechgard (or Beehgard) (bākh'-
gärt), Julius, b. Copenhagen, Dec.
19, 1843, pupil Leipzig Cons., and
of Gade, lives at Copenhagen; composed operas "*Frode,*" "*Frau
Inge*" (Prague, 1894), etc.

eecke (bā'-kĕ), Ignaz von, ca. 1730
—Wallerstein, 1803; captain of dra-
goons, then "Musikintendant" to
Prince of Otting-Wallerstein; harpsichordist; composer of 7 operas,
etc.

**Beellaerts** (bāl-lärts), **Jean.** Vide
BELLERE.

**Beer** (bār), (1) **Jacob Liebmann.**
Vide MEYERBEER. (2) **Josef,** Grünwald, Bohemia, 1744—Potsdam,
1811; player of the clarinet, for which
he invented the fifth key. (3) **Jules,**
b. ca. 1833; lives in Paris; composed 5 comic operas, etc. (4) **Max
Josef,** b. Vienna, Aug. 25, 1851;
pianist; pupil of Dessoff; lives in
Vienna; composed 4 operas, incl. the
succ. "*Der Striek der Schmied,*"
(Augsburg, 1897), etc. (5) **Anton,**
Kohlberg, June 29, 1864; studied
with Rheinberger; leader in Regens
burg orch.; later lived in Munich;
composed an opera "*Sühne,*" etc.

**Beeth** (bāt), **Lola,** b. Cracow, 1864;
soprano; pupil of Dustman, Viardot-
Garcia, and Désirée Artot; début,
1882, at Berlin Court Opera, then
Vienna, after various tours; sang in
New York; engaged at Vienna, 1897,
for 5 years.

**Beethoven** (bāt'-hō-fĕn, not bā-tō'-vĕn),
**Ludwig van,** b. Bonn-on-Rhine,
Dec. 16 (baptised, Dec. 17, 1770)
(Beethoven said Dec. 16, 1772), d.
Vienna, March 26, 1827; grandson of
**Ludwig van B.** (a native of Maestricht, bass singer, opera composer,
and conductor to the Elector Clemens
August, at Bonn), 2d child of **Jn.
van B.** (a tenor singer in the Electoral choir), who had m. a widow,
Magdalena Laym (née Keverich), a
daughter of the chief cook at Ehren-
breitstein. **B.** studied at the public
schools at Bonn till 14. From his
fourth year, his father taught him
music with great severity till 1779.
He played the vln. well at 8; at 11
he knew Bach's "*Wohltemperirte
Clavier.*" Became pupil of Pfeiffer,
a music-dir. and oboist; and Van der
Eeden, court-organist, who predicted
that he would be "a second Mozart"; 1785, studied vln. with Franz
Ries; 1787, took a few lessons of Mozart; 1792, Haydn, passing through
Bonn, praised a cantata of his (now

lost). The Elector sent **B.** to Vienna, where he studied cpt. with Haydn, who seemed to neglect him, so that he secretly studied with Schenck, later he went to Albrechtsberger, who said " he has learnt nothing, and will never do anything in decent style "; he studied the vln. with Schuppanzigh and consulted Salieri and Aloys Förster; 1781, he is believed to have written a Funeral Cantata in memory of the English *chargé d'affaires* at Bonn, who had advanced money to the family; 1781 (1782?). his first publication. 3 pf.-sonatas 1782 deputy organist 1783, cembalist for rehearsals of the opera-orch., without compensation 1784-92. asst. organist at an annual salary of 150 florins (about $63) from 1788 also 2d viola of the theatre orch. Visited Vienna. 1787. and made a sensation by extemporising Mozart exclaiming " He will make a noise in the world some day." In July his tenderhearted mother died of consumption; his father lost his voice and became a sot. **B.**'s only home was in the family of the widow von Breuning, to whose daughter and son he gave lessons. Here he acquired his passion for English literature. He now made acquaintance of young Count Waldstein, who became his life-long patron, and in 1792 sent him to Vienna, where he henceforward lived. The decade 1782-92 does not show much fertility in composition; half a dozen songs, a rondo, a minuet, and 3 preludes for pf., 3 pf.-quartets, a pf.trio; a string-trio, op. 3; 4 sets of pf. variations; a rondino for wind; the " *Ritter Ballet* " with orch. (pub. 1872); " *The Bagatelles*," op. 33; 2 vln.-rondos, op. 51; the " *Serenade Trio* " op. 8; the lost cantata, a lost trio for pf., flute, and bassoon, and an Allegro and Minuet for 2 flutes. 1792, he was sent to Vienna by the Elector, who paid him his salary for 2 years, he had growing royalties from his comps., also 600 florins annually

from Prince Lichnowsky, his war[m] admirer. March 29, 1795, he pl[ayed] his C major pf.-concerto in the B[urg] theater his first public appeara[nce] 1796, he played before King Fr. [William] II.; 1798, at Prague, he gave 2 [sen] sational concerts and met two pi[ano] virtuosi; Steibelt. who challe[nged] **B.** to extemporise and was s[oundly] worsted, and Wölffl, who became [a] friend. 1800 ends what is ca[lled] (after von Lenz's book " *B. et ses t[rois] styles* ") his " first period," of com[po] sition, the " second period," exte[nd] ing to 1815 the " third " to 1[822]. This first period includes op. 1[-20?] pf. and string-trios, string-quart[ets], 9 pf.-sonatas. 7 variations on " [God] *Save the Queen*," and 5 on " *[Rule] Britannia*," the aria " *Ah perf[ido]* " etc. Now a severe and early ve[ry] real trouble affected his liver, and [be] gan to ruin his hearing, which [by] 1822 was entirely gone. Though [he] had always been brusque (especi[ally] with the aristocracy, among whom [he] had an extraordinarily long list [of] friendships and love-affairs), his [for] mer generosity and geniality spee[dily] developed into atrocious suspicio[us] ness and violence toward his b[est] friends. The wild life of a nep[hew] whom he supported, brought h[im] great bitterness. Until the beg[in] ning of the " third period," howev[er] he had large stores of joy in l[ife], open-air Nature, and the details [of] his compositions. which were work[ed] up with utmost care from " sket[ch] books." always carried with him, a[nd] still extant as a unique exam[ple] of genius at work. In the arbitr[ary] but somewhat convenient von Le[nz] classification. the 2d period inclu[des] the symphonies III — VIII; [the] opera " *Fidelio* "; the music to " *[Eg] mont* "; the ballet " *Prometheus* "; the Mass in C, op. 86; the orato[rio] " *Christus am Oelberg* " (1803), [the] " *Coriolanus* " overture; 2 pf.-c[on] certos; 1 vln.-concerto; 3 quarte[ts]; 4 pf.-trios. and 14 pf.-sona[tas] nong them op. 27, op. 28, 31, No. 53, 57. and 81); the "*Lieder-eis*," etc. The "third period" :l. the five pf. sonatas, op. 101, I, the "*Missa solennis*," the nth Symphony, the overture *Ruins of Athens*"; the overtures . 115, 124; the grand fugue for ing-quartet, and the string-quar-s op. 127, 130, 131, 132, 135 (F). *Fidelio*," first named "*Leonore*," as prod. Nov. 20, 1805, just a week er the French army entered Vien-. It was withdrawn after three nsecutive performances; revised d prod. March 29, 1806, but with-awn by **B.** after two performances. ace more revised, it was revived in 14, very successfully; the present erture is the result of various ver-ons known as the *Leonore* overtures 2, and 3. The "*Eroica*" sym-iony (No. 3) was called "*Sinfonia ande Napoleon Bonaparte*" in hon-r of his advocacy of "liberty, quality, and fraternity." When apoleon proclaimed himself em-ror, **B.** tore up the title-page in rath and changed the name to *Sinfonia eroica composta per fes-ggiare il sovvenire d'un gran mo*" (Heroic symphony, com-sed to celebrate the memory of a eat man). In the Ninth Sym-iony, a choral Finale is used as e final addition to the orchestral imax of ecstasy (the words from chiller's "*Hymn to Joy*"). In 1809 erome Bonaparte invited **B.** to be-me conductor at Cassel with a lary of 600 ducats (about $1,500); it his Viennese patrons Archduke udolf, and the Princes Lobkowitz id Kinsky, settled on him an annu-y of 4,000 florins ($2,000). Dec., 826, a violent cold resulted in pneu-onia; dropsy followed, **B.** saying the doctors who tapped him three mes and drew out the water, "Bet-er from my belly than from my pen." fter an illness of 3 months he took ie Roman Catholic sacraments, a

two-days' agony of semi-consciousness followed and he died, just after shak-ing his clenched fist in the air, during a terrific thunderstorm, the evening of March 26, 1827. 20,000 persons attended his funeral.

His complete works comprise **138** opus-numbers, and about 70 unnum-bered comp. The following are those published. INSTRUMENTAL.— 9 Symphonies.—No. 1, op. 21, in C; 2, op. 36, in D; 3, op. 55, in E♭ (the "*Eroica*"); 4, op. 60, in B♭; 5, op. 67, in C min.; 6, op. 68, in F ("*Pas-toral*"); 7, op. 92, in A; 8, op. 93, in F; 9, op. 125, in D min. ("*Choral*"). "*The Battle of Vittoria*" (op. 91); music to the ballet "*Prometheus*" (op. 43), and to Goethe's "*Egmont*" (op. 84), both with overtures, besides, nine overtures—"*Coriolanus*"; "*Leo-nore*" (Nos. 1, 2, and 3); "*Fidelio*"; "*King Stephen*", "*Ruins of Ath-ens*"; "*Namensfeier*," op. 115; "*Weihe des Hauses*" (op. 124). Also for orch.: Allegretto in E♭; March from "*Tarpeia*," in C; *Military March*, in D; "*Ritter-Ballet*"; 12, Minuets; 12, "deutsche Tänze"; 12, Contretänze; violin - concerto, op. 61. Five pf.-concertos, the last op. 73, in E ("*Emperor*"); also a pf.-concerto arranged from the vio-lin-concerto. A triple-concerto, op. 56, for pf., vln., 'cello and orch.; a "*Choral Fantasia*" for pf., chorus and orch., a Rondo in B, for pf. and orch.; cadences to the pf.-concertos. Two Octets for wind, both in E♭. Septet for strings and wind. Sextet for strings and 2 horns. One sextet for wind, E♭. Two quintets for strings, fugue for string-quintet; also quintet arr. from pf.-trio in C min. Sixteen string-quartets: Op. 18, Nos. 1–6 in F. G, D. C min., A and B♭ (first period). op. 59, Nos. 1–3; op. 74, in E♭ (the "*Harfenquartett*"); op. 95 (second period); op. 127; op. 130; op. 131; op. 132, op. 135. A grand fugue for string-quartet, op. 133, in B♭ (third period). One pf.-quartet (arr. from the pf.-quintet) ; 3 juvenile pf.-quartets ; five string-trios ; eight pf.-trios, that in E♭ being juvenile ; an arr. of the "*Eroica*" symphony. Grand trios for pf., clar. and 'cello op. 11 ; in B♭ and in E♭ (arr. from septet, op. 20) ; trio for 2 oboes and *cor anglais*, in C op. 87.

Ten sonatas for pf. and violin, incl. op. 47 ("*Kreutzer*"), rondo for pf. and vln. ; 12 variations for do. Five sonatas and 31 variations for pf. and 'cello. Sonata for pf. and horn. Sonata for pf., 4 hands.

38 Sonatas for piano, incl. op. 27. Nos. 1 and 2 ("*Quasi Fantasia*"), op. 28 ("*Pastorale* ") in D ; op. 53 ("*Waldstein*") in C ; op. 57 ("*Appassionata*") in F min. ; op. 81 ("*Caractéristique*"—"*Les adieux, l'absence, le retour* ") in E♭. Also 6 easy sonatas, 3 of them composed at age of 10 ; 21 sets of variations for pf. , 3 sets of bagatelles ; 4 rondos ; fantasia in G min. ; 3 preludes ; polonaise ; andante in F ("*Favori* ") ; 7 minuets ; 13 Ländler. for 4 hands ; 3 marches ; 14 variations.

VOCAL.—Opera "*Fidelio*," in 2 acts, op. 72. 2 Masses, in C and D ("*Solennis*"). Oratorio "*Christus*

am Oelberg*," op. 85. Cantata " glorreiche Augenblick*," op. (1814) ; also arr. as *Preis der* kunst. Meeresstille und Glück Fahrt, op. 112 (poem by Goe Scena and aria for soprano, " Perfido," with orch., op. 65. for soprano, tenor and bass, " mate, Empi, Tremate," op. 116. " ferlied" for soprano solo, chorus orch. "Bundeslied" for 2 solo voi 3-part chorus and wind. " Elegi Gesang" for 4 voice-parts and stri 66 songs with pf.-accomp. , one d " Gesang der Mönche" ; 3 voice-p a capp. 18 vocal canons. 7 book English, Scotch, Irish, Welsh Italian songs, with pf., vln. and 'c The best biography is Alex. Thayer's " L. van Beethoven's ben." 3 vols. in German, transl. f the English MS. by H. Deiters ; vol. in preparation. Partial col tions of Beethoven's letters are and his sketch-books are discusse Ignaz von Seyfried's " Ludwig Beethoven's Studien im Generalb Kontrapunkt und in der Komp tionslehre." Biogs. also by Schind Nohl, Crowest. etc. Wagner wr an estimate.

# Beethoven : A Study of Influences.

## By H. E. KREHBIEL.

IN one respect Beethoven stands alone in the history of music. T influence of all his fellows, from Bach to Wagner and Brahms, can determined in matter as well as manner, and set down in plain ter his full significance is yet to be grounded. Beethoven was a gigantic res voir into which a hundred proud streams poured their waters ; he is a mig lake out of which a thousand streams have flowed through all the territor which the musical art has peopled, and from which torrents are still pour to irrigate lands that are still *terrae incognitae*. ¶In some respects his gen is an enigma. Whence came his profound knowledge of the musical art a existed before him ? He was not precocious as Mozart was. He wa diligent pupil, but not an orderly one. Except in childhood he was unru and impatient of discipline. The sternness and cruelty of a dissipated fat

de his earliest studies a suffering and an oppression. In later years he
formed his duties toward Albrechtsberger, but refused to yield himself to
t teacher's domination as he had already refused to bow to the authority of
ydn——an authority which he felt was too carelessly exercised. Yet the world
ws how conscious he was of the potency of the learned forms into which
rechtsberger strove to induct him, and the charm of romantic expression
mplified in Haydn. ¶He refused to acknowledge these men as his teachers,
le they returned the compliment by refusing to own him as their pupil.
ydn condemned his first trios ; Albrechtsberger advised his other pupils to
e nothing to do with him because, as he said, " he had never learned
thing, and would never do anything in decent style." Yet Beethoven
s proud of his ability in the department of study for which he had gone to
teacher of counterpoint. In his old age he considered Cherubini the
atest of his living contemporaries, and Händel the greatest of the great
d. Note the significance : both were masters in the severe forms.
king no account of the canons, fugues, and variations which occur incident-
in his symphonies, sonatas, and quartets, we find that Beethoven left an
raordinarily large number of compositions in these forms behind him——no
than thirty-five canons, five independent fugues and thirty-two sets of
iations for different instruments. Could there be a more convincing dem-
tration of his devotion to the scientific side of his art ? ¶But he was no
re and no less an iconoclast in these forms than in the romantic. Proof
another kind I found in an anecdote recorded in Mr. Thayer's note-book
elated to him by the nephew of the observer of the incident. ¶In 1809
lhelm Rust sat in a coffee-house in Vienna with Beethoven. A French
cer happening to pass, Beethoven doubled up his fist and exclaimed : " If I
e a general and knew as much about strategy as I know about coun-
oint, being a composer——I'd cut out some work for you fellows."
he great difference between him and his teachers was one of conception
ching the uses to which counterpoint and fugue should be put. To
rechtsberger the sciences existed for their own sake ; for Beethoven they
ted only as a medium of expression. There was nothing sacrosanct about
n. As he himself said, it was a good thing to learn the rules in order
rward to know what was contrary to them, and, he might have added,
to know how to violate them when musical expression could thereby be
moted. ¶Yet Beethoven's greatest significance as an influence is not as a
royer of forms and contemner of rules, as so many would have us believe
justify all manner of lawlessness to-day and quote Beethoven as an excuse ;
as a widener of forms and a creator of rules for the development of
ression, which is and must ever remain the aim of musical art. He was
prototype of Wagner's *Hans Sachs,* who wished due respect paid to the

laws of the poet's craft so that poetical creation might go on within the
of beauty, but who also wished spontaneous creative impulse to have its rig
Where he differed from the pedants who sought to stem the original flo
his utterance, was in realising better than they, that art-works are the so
of rules quite as much as their outcome. He felt, with *Faust*, that " In
beginning was the Deed," neither the " Word," nor the " Thought,"
the " Power," but the " Deed," ; from that can be deduced the o
potencies. ¶ " Beethoven was not only the embodiment of all that
before him, but also of that which was yet to come. In his works m
returned to its original purpose with its power raised a hundred-fold." 
have said this before and elsewhere, but as I cannot say it better and wa
said again, I say it again, and here. It is easy rhetoric to descant upon
tremendous strides which music has made in the last half century, the tr
formation of forms, the augmentation of expressive potencies (rhyth
melodic, harmonic, instrumental), the widening of the horizon of the th
proper to musical expression and much else ; but he has not yet learned
Beethoven who does not see all that has yet appeared to be essential in t
things distinctly foreshadowed in the music of the master who, in a lar
more comprehensive, more luminous sense than was dreamed of before
since, was priest, king, hero, and seer. A priest unceasing in his offering
the Temple Beautiful ! A king whose dominion is over the despotic ru
in man's emotional nature ! A hero who knew his mission and subordin
to it himself, his longings, his loves, his very life ! A seer, as Ruskin
of Imagination, " in the prophetic sense, calling the things that are no
though they were, and forever delighting to dwell on that which is
tangibly present." ¶Like *Faust* he ever heard the dread words ringing in
ears : " *Entbehren sollst du, sollst entbehren !* " His art asked his
he knew it and gave his all ; and then the *Gottheit* which he was wont
invoke, hushed the noises of the material world that he might the better
the whisperings of the spirit pervading it ; and raised a barrier between
and mankind to force him to be a witness and historian of the stru
between the human and the divine reflected in his own soul. All the m
anthropy which filled his later years could not shake his devotion to an ie
which had sprung from truest artistic appreciation and been nurtured
enforced introspection. This is the key to Beethoven's music. ¶ Bu
will not serve the purposes of this study merely to generalise. If the o
tention set forth is to be maintained, there must be some martialling
evidence. Confining ourselves to the cyclical form, the symphony, we r
that Beethoven introduced a wider range and a freer use of keys than w
employed by his models, Haydn and Mozart ; abolished much of w
sounds like mere *remplissage* in the connecting portions between them

tituting therefor phrases developed out of the themes themselves ; intro-
ed original episodic matter ; extended the free fantasia and coda ; devel-
ed the old minuet into the scherzo, which could better carry on the psycho-
cal story which he wished to tell in the four chapters of his instrumental
an ; infused unity into his works, not only by bringing the spiritual bonds
veen the movements more clearly before our percipience, but also by
ing the material bonds obvious and incontrovertible. This last achieve-
t has its simplest as well as most eloquent illustrations in the community
hythms between the first, third, and last movements of the *Fifth Sym-*
*y,* and all the movements of the *Seventh;* the recurrence of themes
lifferent movements of the *Fifth* and *Ninth;* the family likenesses,
siognomical resemblances, between the principal melodies of the *Ninth ;*
ly the programmatic conceit back of the *Sixth.* ¶ The acceptance and
inuation of the hints contained in these innovations is published in the
ition of pauses between the movements in the "Scotch" symphony of
adelssohn, the adoption of the same device by Schumann, together with
munity of theme in the symphony in D minor, the invention of "*l'idée*
" by Berlioz for his "*Symphonie Fantastique*" and the successive
pitulation of material already used in the second, third, and fourth move-
ts in the symphony, "*From the New World,*" by Dvôrák. ¶ It has
been necessary to go far afield for examples ; the proofs are surely coning and come down to our own day. Moreover we find an illustration
he same principle, coupled with an exposition of Beethoven's system of
natic, instead of melodic, development—another form of variation, in brief
a all the symphonic poems of Liszt and his imitators down to Richard
uss. ¶ Beethoven's license may have degenerated into lawlessness, but he
ted a way that has been followed in all the particulars enumerated, and
broke down the barriers between voices and instruments in the symphonic
as to the delight of many successors. His revolutionary proceeding in the
th symphony found imitation by Mendelssohn in his "*Hymn of Praise,*"
Berlioz in his "*Romeo and Juliet,*" by Liszt in his "*Faust*" and
*)ante*" symphonies, by Nicodé in "*Das Meer,*" and by Mahler in his
phony with contralto solo.

---

:ara (běf'-fä-rä), **Louis François,**
onancourt, Eure, 1751—Paris,
+38 ; 1792–1816, commissaire de
)lice, at Paris ; musical historian.

:roy de Reigny (běf-frwä dŭ rěn'-
:), **Louis Abel** (called "Cousin
icques"), Laon, Nov. 6, 1757—
aris, Dec. 18, 1811 ; composed very
icc. operettas.

**Begnis** (bān'-yēs), (1) **Gius** or **Wm.**
de, Lugo, Papal States, 1793—Bath(?)
England, 1849 ; buffo singer ; in 1816,
he m. (2) Signora **Ronzi,** Paris,
1800 (?)—Italy, 1853 ; comic soprano.

**Begrez** (bā'-grětz), **Pierre Ignace,**
Namur, 1783 — Brunswick, Ger.;
1863, dram. tenor.

**Behm** (bām), **Eduard,** b. Settin, April 8, 1862 ; studied with Paul, Weidenbach, Reinecke, Härtel, Raif and Kiel ; pianist and teacher in various cities, then at Berlin as dir. Schwantzer Cons.; composed an opera, " *Schelm von Bergen* " (Dresden, 1899), a symphony, pf.-concerto, etc.

**Behnke** (bān'-kē), **Emil,** Stettin, 1836 —Ostend, 1892 ; teacher and writer.

**Behr** (bār), (1) **Fz.,** b. Lubtheen, Mecklenburg, July 22, 1837 ; composed pf.-pieces, under pseud. of " William Cooper," " Charles Morley," or " Francesco d'Orso." (2) **Therese,** b. Stuttgart, Sept. 14, 1876 ; alto ; pupil of J. Stakhausen, of Schulz Demberg and of Etelka Gerster ; lives in Mainz.

**Behrens** (bā'-rĕns), **Konrad,** 1835— New York, 1898 ; operatic bass.

**Beier** (bī'-ĕr), Dr. **Fz.,** b. Berlin, April 18, 1857—Cassel, 1889, son of a military band-master ; pupil Stern and Kullak Cons. ; cond. at the Royal Theatre; composed succ. opera " *Der Posaunist von Scherkingen*" (Cassel, 1889), a parody on Nessler's wellknown " *Der Trompeter von Säkkingen;* " succ. comic operetta " *der Gaunerkönig* " (Cassel, 1890), etc.

**Belce.** Vide REUSS-BELCE.

**Belcke** (bĕl'-kĕ), (1) **Fr. Aug.,** Lucka, Altenburg, 1795—1874; the first trombone virtuoso. (2) **Chr. Gl.,** Lucka, 1796—1875 ; bro. of above ; flutist.

**Beldoman'dis** (or **Beldeman'dis, Beldeman'do), Prosdo'cimus de,** b. Padua, 14th cent. ; prof. of philosophy, ca. 1422 ; theorist.

**Beliczay** (bā'-lǐ-chä-ĕ), **Julius von,** Komorn, Hungary, 1835—Pesth, 1893 ; violinist.

**Belin** (or **Bellin**) (bŭ-lăṅ), (1) **Guil.,** ca. 1547; tenor Chapelle Royale, Paris. (2) **Julien,** b. Le Mans, ca. 1530 ; lutenist.

**Beliso'nius, Paul,** a canon said to have inv. quills for harpsichords, 16th century.

**Bella** (dĕl'-lä bĕl'-lä), **Dom. della,** 'cellist, Venice, 1704.

**Bel'la, Jn., Ld.,** b. St. Nicholan, per Hungary, 1843 ; canon at N sohl ; composed church-music, etc

**Bel'lamy,** (1) **Richard,** d. Londo 1813 ; church-composer. (2) His s **Thos. Ludford,** Westminster, 1 —London, 1843, bass.

**Bellasio** (bĕl-lä'-sǐ-ō), **Paolo,** 15 95 ; pub. madrigals, etc., at Veni

**Bel'lasis, Edw.,** b. Jan. 28, 18 English writer and composer.

**Bell'avere** (or **Bell'haver**) (bĕl-ä rĕ), **V.,** Venice, 1530 (?)—1588 organist and composer.

**Bellazzi** (bĕl-läd'-zē), **Fran. C.,** Venice, 1618–28.

**Bellère** (bĕl-lăr') (or **Belle'rus,** rig **Beellaerts**) (bāl-lärts'), (1) **Jean** Antwerp, ca. 1595 ; publisher. son and successor was (2) **Balthas**

**Bel'lermann,** (1) **Konstantin,** furt, 1696—Münden, 1763 ; re and composer. (2) **Jn. Fr.,** Erf 1795—Berlin, 1874 ; writer on Gi music. His son (3), **Jn. Gf. H.** Berlin, March 10, 1832 ; pupil Inst. for Ch.-music, 1866 ; prof mus. Berlin U. (vice Marx.) · thec and composer.

**Bellet'ti, Giov. Bat.,** b. Sarza 1815 ; barytone ; pupil of Pilotti Bologna ; début, 1838, Stockho sang with Jenny Lind on tour ; tired, 1862.

**Belleville-Oury** (bĕl-vē'-yŭ-oo'- **Emilie,** Munich, 1808—1880 ; p ist.

**Bell'haver, V.** Vide BELL'AVERE.

**Belli** (bĕl'-lē), (1) **Gir.,** pub., 15 94, madrigals, etc. (2) **Giulio,** Longiano, ca. 1560 ; ch.-comp and cond. (3) **Dom.,** 1616 ; co musician at Parma.

**Bellin, G.** Vide BELIN.

**Bellincioni** (bĕl-lǐn-chō'-nē), **Gem** notable Italian soprano ; toured U in opera, 1899 ; lives in Florence.

**Bellini** (bĕl-lē'-nē), (1) **Vincenzo, C** nia, Sicily, Nov.3,1802—Puteaux, r Paris, Sept. 23, 1835 ; opera com er ; son and pupil of an organist nobleman sent him (1819) to

ons. at Naples; studied under
urno, Tritto, and Zingarelli, until
827; privately studied with Haydn
nd Mozart, and chiefly Pergolesi;
s a student composed a symphony, 2
nasses, several psalms, a cantata, etc.;
is first opera, "*Adelson e Salvini*,"
as performed by Cons. pupils, 1825,
hereupon the manager of La Scala,
lilan, commissioned him to write an
pera; 1826, "*Bianca e Fernando*"
as prod. with succ., 1827, "*Il Pi-
ata;*" 1829, "*La Stranier.*" The
brettist of the latter 2 was Felice
Romani, who wrote the books of all
B.'s operas, except "*I Puritani.*"
"*Zaira*" (1829) was a failure; "*I
'apuleti e Montecchi*," written in forty
ays (1830), was a great succ.; "*La
connambula*," and "*Norma*" (1831),
ith Malibran in the title-rôle, estab-
shed his fame; "*Beatrice di Ten-
a*" (Venice, 1833) failed; "*I Puri-
ini*" (libretto by Count Pepoli),
ritten to order 1834, for the Théâtre
alien, Paris, was a great success,
nd his last finished work. **B.**'s work
s a compendium of all the virtues
nd vices of Italian opera, passionate
nd eminently vocal lyrics with empty
nd slovenly accompaniment. He
ied youngest of all prominent com-
osers—at the age of 33, from dysen-
ery due to overwork. Biog. by
cherillo (Milan, 1885), Pougin
Paris, 1868), etc. (2) **Carmelo**,
Catania, 1802—1884; brother of
bove; composed Church-music.

**Il'man**, (1) **Carl Mikael**, Stock-
olm, 1740—1795; Swedish poet who
et his own burlesques to music. (2)
**K. Gf.**, Schellenberg, Saxony, 1760
—Dresden, 1816; pf.- and bassoon-
naker. (3) **K. Gl.**, Muskau, 1772,
chleswig, 1862; organist.

**Iloc** (bĕl-lôk'), **Teresa** (**G. Trom-
et'ta-Belloc**), San Begnino, Can-
vese, 1784—S. Giorgio, 1855; mezzo-
oprano; repertoire of 80 operas.

**Iloli** (bĕl-lō'-lē), (1) **Luigi**, Castel-
ranco, Bologna, 1770—Milan, 1817;
orn-player and composer. (2) **Ag.,**

b. Bologna; first horn (1819–29) at
La Scala, Milan, and dram. composer.

**Bemberg** (bän-bĕrg), **Hermann**, b.
Paris, March 29, 1861; pupil of
Dubois, Franck and Massenet, Paris
Cons.; 1887 took Rossini prize;
composed 1-act opera "*Le Baiser de
Suzon*" (Paris, Op.-com., 1888), mod.
succ.; opera *Elaine* (London, 1892;
New York, 1894), and songs.

**Bemetzrieder** (bā'-mĕts-rē-dĕr), **T.**, b.
Alsatia, 1743; Benedictine monk;
then composer and writer.

**Ben'da**, (1) **Franz**, Alt-Benátek, Bohemia, Nov. 25, 1709—Potsdam,
March 7, 1786; court-violinist to
Frederick II., whom he accompanied
for 40 years in flute-concertos;
composed symphonies, etc. His 3
brothers (2) **Jn.**, Alt-Benátek, 1713
—Potsdam, 1752; violinist. (3) **G.**,
Jungbunzlau, Bohemia, 1722—Koes-
tritz, Nov. 6, 1795; court-cond., 1748
(Gotha); 1764–66, Italy; prod. at
Gotha 10 operas in which he originated the idea of spoken words with
orchestral accompaniment, literal
"melodrama." (4) **Jos.**, 1724—Berlin,
1804; violinist. His sister, (5) **Anna
Frangiska**, b. 1726—Gotha, 1780;
singer. (6) **Fr. Wm. H.**, Potsdam,
1745—1814; son and pupil of (1);
composed operas, etc. (7) **Fr. L.**,
Gotha, 1746—Königsberg, 1793; son
of (3); cond. and composer. (8) **K.
Hermann H.**, Potsdam, 1748—
1836; son of rich father; court.-
violinist and composer.

**Ben'dall**, **Wilfred Ellington**, b.
London, April 22, 1850; pupil of
Lucas, Silas and Leipzig Cons.; com-
poser.

**Ben'del**, **Fz.**, Schönlinde, northern
Bohemia, March 23, 1833—Berlin,
July 3, 1874; pianist; composed
symphonies, 4 masses, songs, etc., and
piano pieces of great lusciousness of
harmony and fervour of melody.

**Ben'deler**, **Jn. Ph.**, Riethnordhausen,
near Erfurt, 1660 — Quedlinburg
1708; clavecinist, organist and
writer.

**Ben'der,** (1) **Jakob,** Bechtheim, 1798
—Antwerp, 1844 ; dir. Antwerp wind-
band ; clarinettist and composer. (2)
**Jean Val.,** Bechtheim, near Worms,
1801—Brussels, 1873 ; bro. of above ;
clarinet-virtuoso and band-master.

**Ben'dix,** (1) **Ottɔ,** b. Copenhagen,
1850 ; pupil of Ree and Gade, Kullak and Liszt ; pf.-teacher in Copenh.
Cons. and oboist in theatre-orch. ;
lives in Boston, Mass., since 1880, as
teacher and composer. (2) **Victor
E.,** b. Copenhagen, 1851 ; pianist,
pupil and protégé of Gade ; lives in
Copenh. as pf.-teacher and cond. ;
composed 3 symphonies, incl. "*Zur
Höhe,*" in C (1891) (also named
"*Felsensteigung*") ; and "*Sommer-
klänge aus Südrussland*" in D.

**Ben'dl** (bĕnt'-'l), **K.,** Prague, April 16,
1838 — Sept. 20, 1897 ; important
Czech composer ; pupil of Blažok and
Pitsch, at Prague ; chorus-master,
Amsterdam (1864) ; 1866, cond.
Prague choral society, "Hlahol" ;
composed Czech operas incl. "*Dite
Tábora*" (Child of the Camp), 1892,
(3 acts) ; still given at Prague ; 3
masses, cantatas, an overture, a
"*Dithyramb,*" "*Slavonic Rhap-
sody,*" for orch., etc.

**Bendler** (bĕnt'-lĕr), **Salmon,** Quedlinburg, 1683—1724 ; singer.

**Ben'edict,** (1) Sir **Julius,** Stuttgart,
Nov. 27, 1804—London, June 5,
1885 ; son of a Jewish banker ; pupil of
Abeille, Hummel, and Weber, 1825 at
Naples, where his first opera was
prod. 1829, without success ; his next
(Stuttgart, 1830) was not a success ;
settled in London as pf.-teacher and
concert-giver ; 1836, cond. opera
buffa ; 1837 at Drury Lane, there his
first English opera, "*The Gypsy's
Warring,*" was prod. (1838) ; he accompanied Jenny Lind to America,
then cond. at Her Majesty's Th., and
Drury Lane; 1859 at Covent Garden ,
and "Monday Popular Concerts" ;
cond. also Norwich festivals, and
(1876–80) the Liverpool Philharmonic ; knighted in 1871 ; composed

11 operas ; 2 oratorios, "*St. Ceci*
(1866), and "*St. Peter*" (1870)
symphonies, 2 pf.-concertos, e
wrote a biog. of Weber. (2) **M
Ellsworth,** b. Cornwall, June
1866 ; pupil of C. Petersilea (pf.)
K. Paine (theory); 1883–84 in Eur
spending 3 mos. with Liszt ; live
Boston, as pf.-teacher and compo

**Benedic'tus Appenzelders** (äp'-
tsĕlt-ĕrs) (**B.** of **Appenzell**), b.
penzell, Switzerland ; choir-maste
Brussels (1539–55) and compos
often confused with Benedi
Ducis.

**Benel'li,** (1) **Alemanno.** Vide
TRIGARI. (2) **A. Peregrino,** F
Romagna, 1771—Bornichau, Saxo
1830 ; tenor.

**Benes** (bā'-nĕsh) (*Ger.* **Benes
Josɘf,** b. Batelov, Moravia, 17
conductor, violinist and composer

**Benevoli** (bā-nā'-vō-lē), **Orazio,** Ro
1602—1672 ; natural son of D
Albert of Lorraine, but lived in p
erty ; cond. at the Vatican (16.
remarkable contrapuntist ; in w
ing chorals with instrs. he was
pioneer ; his Salzburg mass be
written on 54 staves.

**Benfey** (bĕn-fī'), **Theodor,** Nör
near Göttingen, 1809—1881 ; writ

**Benini** (bā-nē'-nē), Signora, Ita
singer in London, 1787, comic ope
exquisite sweetness but little powe

**Beninco'ri, Ang. M.,** Brescia, 177
Paris, 1821 ; dram. composer.

**Ben'nat, Fz.,** b. Bregenz, Aug.
1844 ; 'cellist ; studied Munich Co
and with Servais ; since 1864
Munich court-orch.; since 1888 in
Walter Quartet, chamber-mus.

**Ben'net,** (1) **J.,** English compo
(1599). (2) **Saunders,** d. 18
English organist and composer.
**Theodore.** Vide TH. RITTER.

**Ben'nett,** (1) **Wm.,** b. Teignmou
ca. 1767 ; organist. (2) **Thos.,**
1774—1848 ; organist. (3) **Alfr**
1805—1830 ; English organist.
Sir **Wm. Sterndale,** Sheffield, A
13, 1816—London. Feb. 1, 18

of an organist (who died 1819);
8 entered the choir of King's Col-
e Chapel; at 10 pupil of R. A. M.;
17 played there an original pf.-
certo, later pub. by the Academy,
t 1837 by the Broadwoods to Leip-
for one year; friend of Schumann
. Mendelssohn; 1844 m. **Mary
ne Wood**, founded the Bach So-
y, 1849; cond. Philh. Society,
6–66; 1856. Mus. Doc. Cam-
lge and prof. of mus. there; 1866,
icipal there; 1871, knighted;
ied in Westminster Abbey; com-
ed 1 symphony, an oratorio " *The
man of Samaria*," music to So-
kles' "*Ajax*"; 5 overtures, "*Fa-
ina*," " *The Naiads*," " *The
od-nymph*," " *Paradise and the
i*," " *Merry Wives of Windsor*,"
atas, etc. (5) **Jos.**, b. Berkeley,
ucestershire, Nov. 29, 1831; orist of Westminster Chapel; then
sic critic for various London news-
ers; finally *The Telegraph*;
te various libretti; pub. "*Letters
m Bayreuth*" (1877); " *The
sical Year*" (1883), etc.

ewitz (běn'-ně-vēts), (1) **Wm.**,
lin, 1832—1871; dram. composer.
**Anton**, b. Privat, Bohemia,
rch 26, 1833; violinist; 1882, dir.
Prague Cons.

is (bŭn-wä), **Marie**, b. St. Peters-
g, Jan. 1, 1861; pianist; pupil of
schetizky (1876), won gold medal
Petersburg Cons.; toured with
cess; (1878) m. her cousin Wassi-
Benois.

ist (bŭn-wä), **François**, Nantes,
4—Paris, 1878; organ-prof. Paris
is.; composed operas, etc.

it (bŭn-wä), **Pierre Léonard**
.., Harlebecke, Belgium, Aug. 17,
4—Antwerp, Mar. 4, 1901; Flemish
poser and writer; pupil Brussels
is., 1851–55; at same time prod.
small opera and wrote music for
mish melodramas; 1856, cond.
rk Th.; 1857, won the Prix de
me, with the cantata " *Le Meurtre
bel*"; studied at Leipzig, Dres-

den, Munich, and Berlin, and wrote a
thesis for the Brussels Academy
" *L'école de musique flamande et son
avenir*." In 1861 his opera " *Le Roi
des Aulnes*," was accepted by Théâtre
Lyrique, Paris, but not given; cond.
at the Bouffes-Parisiennes; from
1867, dir. Antwerp Cons.; 1882,
member of the R. A., Berlin; composed *Messe solennelle* (1862); *Te
Deum* (1863); *Requiem* (1863); 2
oratorios "*Lucifer*," and "*De
Schelde*"; 2 operas "*Het Dorp int
Gebergte*" and "*Isa*"; "*Drama
Christi*," a sacred drama in Flemish;
a cantata "*De Oorlog War*"; "*Children's Oratorio*"; a choral symphony, "*De Maaiers*" (The Reap-
ers); music to "*Charlotte Corday*,"
and to "*Willem de Zwijger*" (1876);
the "Rubens cantata" "*Flanderens
kunstroem*"; "*Antwerpen*," for triple
male chorus (1877); vocal works
with orch. incl. "*Joncfrou Kathc-
lijne*," scena for alto (1879); "*Muse
der Geschiednis*" (1880); and "*Hucbald*," "*Triomfmarsch*" (1880);
grand cantata " *De Rhyn*" (1889); a
mass, etc. Wrote "*De vlaamsche
Musiek-school van Antwerpen*"
(1873), "*Verhandelung over de nationale Toonkunde*" (2 vols., 1877–
79), etc.

**Benson, Harry,** b. Birmingham, England, Dec. 14, 1848; pupil of Dea-
kin and Browning in England and
at N. E. Cons., Boston, where he
was for years instructor; since 1891
with Boston Training School of Music; cond. of various choral societies,
active devotee of Tonic Sol-fa.

**Benvenuti** (běn-vā-noo'-tē), **Tommaso,** b. Venice, 1832; dram. composer.

**Berardi** (bā-rär'-dē), **Ang.**, b. Bologna,
1681; conductor and theorist.

**Bérat** (bā-rä), **Fr.**, Rouen, 1800—
Paris, 1855; composer.

**Berbiguier** (běr-bǐg-yä), **Benoît
Tranquille,** Caderousse Vaucluse,
1782—near Blois, 1838; flute-vir
tuoso and composer.

**Berchem** (or **Berghem**) (bĕrkh'-ĕm), **Jachet de** (also **Jaquet, Jacquet,** and **Giachetto di Mantova**), Berchem (?) near Antwerp, ca. 1500—1580; contrapuntist and conductor.

**Berens** (bā'-rĕns), (1) **Hermann,** Hamburg, 1825 (?)—Stockholm, 1880; son and pupil of (2) **K. B.** (1801—1857); court-conductor and composer.

**Beret'ta, Giov. Batt,** Verona, 1819—Milan, 1876; theorist, editor, and composer.

**Berg** (bĕrkh), (1) **Adam,** 1540—1599; music-printer, Munich. (2) **Jn. von,** 1550; music-printer, Ghent, Nürnberg. (3) **G.,** German composer in England, 1763–71. (4) **Kon. Mat.,** Colmar, Alsatia, 1785—Strassburg, 1852; violinist, pianist, and writer.

**Berger** (bĕr'gĕr), (1) **L.,** Berlin, 1777—1839; from 1815 pf.-teacher and composer. (2) **Francesco,** b. London, June 10, 1834; pupil of Ricci and Lickl (pf.), Hauptmann and Plaidy; pf.-prof. R. A. M., and Guildhall Sch. of Mus.; for years dir., now sec., Philh.; composed an opera, a mass (prod. in Italy), etc.; wrote "*First Steps at the Pianoforte.*" (3) **Wm.,** b. Boston, Mass., U. S. A., Aug. 9, 1861; taken by parents to Bremen, pupil of Kiel, etc.; lives Berlin as teacher and composer; 1898 won a prize of 2,000 marks, with a setting of Goethe's "*Meine Göttin*" (op. 72); composed "*Gesang der Geister über den Wassern,*" mixed choir and orch. in overture form, a dram. fantasy, etc. (4) **Siegfried.** Vide CHELIUS. (5) **Otto,** Machau, Bohemia, 1873 (?)—1897; 'cellist.

**Berggreen** (bĕrkh'-grān),**Andreas P.,** Copenhagen, 1801—1880 ; teacher.

**Berghem.** Vide BERCHEM.

**Bergmann** (bĕrkh'-män), **K.,** Ebersbach, Saxony, 1821—New York, Aug. 16, 1876; in America, 1850, with "Germania" Orch., later its cond., till 1854 ; cond. "Händel and Haydn" Soc., Boston, 1852–54 ; in 1855 alter-

nate cond. Philh. Soc., New Yo[rk] 1862–76, sole cond; also co "Arion" Society ; active in intro[ducing] Wagner, Liszt, etc., to Amer[ica].

**Bergner** (bĕrkh'-nĕr), **Wm.,** b. R[iga] Nov. 4, 1837 ; organist ; founde[d] Bach Society and a cathedral cho[ir].

**Bergonzi** (bĕr-gôn'-tsē), (1) **Ca[rlo,]** 1716–1755 ; vln.-maker at Crem[ona] best pupil of Stradivari. His son[s] **Michelangelo,** and his 2 nephe[ws] (3) **Niccolò** and (4) **Carlo,** were important. (5) **Benedetto,** Crem[ona] 1790—1840 ; horn-player and inv[ent]or.

**Bergson** (bĕrkh'-zōn), **Michael,** Warsaw, May, 1820; pianist [and] composer; pupil of Schneider, [Co]genhagen, and Taubert, Paris (18[45]); Italy, 1846, where his opera "*Lo[redan?] di Montfort*" was succ. (Flore[nce,] 1847) ; Paris, 1859, prod. a 1-act [op]eretta ; 1863, 1st pf.-teacher [and] soon dir. Geneva Cons.; later in [Lon]don as teacher.

**Bergt** (bĕrkht), **Chr. Gl. Aug.,** Öderan, Saxony, 1772 — Baut[zen,] 1837 ; organist, violinist and [con]ductor.

**Beringer** (bā'-rĭng-ĕr), (1) **Robert,** Fürtwangen, June 14, 1841 ; [at?] pianist at the Crystal Palace ; co[nd.] of societies, and lecturer. (2) **Os[car,]** b. Fürtwangen, July 14, 1844 ; bro[ther of] above; pupil of Plaidy, Mosche[les,] Leipzig Cons., 1864–66; later [under] Tausig, Ehrlich, and Weitzma[nn,] Berlin ; teacher there, 1869 ; Lond[on,] 1871 ; since 1873 pf.-prof. in R. [A.] M. ; composed Technical Exerci[ses,] etc.

**Bériot** (dŭ bār-yō), (1) **Chas. Augu[ste] de,** Louvain, Feb. 20, 1802—B[rus]sels, April 8, 1870 ; vln.-virtuo[so,] pupil of Viotti and Baillot, but ch[iefly] of his guardian, Tiby ; at 9 he pla[yed] a concerto ; 1821, made a brill[iant] début, Paris ; chamber-violinist [to] the King of France, solo-violinis[t to] the King of the Netherlands (1826—) 1830–35 toured Europe with M[me.] Garcia-Malibran, whom he m[arried]

6 ; from 1843–52, prof. at Brussels
ns.; became blind and paralysed
eft arm ; pub. method and 7 con-
tos, etc., for vln. (2) **Chas. Vil-**
le de, b. Paris, Feb. 12, 1835 ; son
above ; pupil of Thalberg ; prof.
pf., Paris Cons. ; composed sym-
onies, etc.; wrote with his father
*Méthode d'accompagnement.*"

jn (or **Berlyn**) (băr'-lēn), **Anton
Aron Wolf**(?), Amsterdam, 1817
870 ; conductor.

n (băr'-lēn), **Jn. Daniel**, Memel,
o—Drontheim, Norway, 1737 ;
anist and writer.

oz (băr-lĭ-ōs not băr-lĭ-ō), **Hec-
(Louis)**, Côte-Saint-André, near
noble, France, Dec. 11, 1803—
is, March 9, 1869; " Father of
lern orchestration "; conductor,
ic, writer of verse and electric
se ; sent to Paris to study med-
e, he accepted disinheritance and
k up music, though he could never
y any instr. save the guitar and
eolet ; while pupil at the Cons., he
led a bare living ; joined the chorus
he Gymnase Dramatique ; left the
s. in disgust with Reicha's forma-
a, and plunged with characteristic
rgy—or rather fury—into the cause
omanticism ; 1825, an orchestral
ss given at St. Roch brought the
cule he usually had in France
re he was little thought of as a
poser though admired as a writer ;
8 saw the production of two over-
s " *Waverley* " and " *Les Francs-
es*," and a Symphonie fantastique,
*pisode de la vie d'un artiste* " ;
9, his " *Concerts des Sylphes*,"
licly produced at 26, show him
ardent believer in programme-
sic (vide D. D.) and a marvellous
uoso in instrumentation. He re-
red the Cons. under Lesueur, in
e of Cherubini, who fought his ad-
sion ; 1830, he took the Prix de
me with a cantata, " *Sardana-
* " ; after 18 months in Italy
returned to Paris and took up
ralism with marked success. His

symphony " *Harold en Italie* " (1834),
the " *Messe des Morts* " (1837), the
dram. symphony " *Roméo et Juliette*," with vocal soli and chorus
(1839), and the overture " *Carnéval
romain*," were well received, but the
2-act opera semi-seria " *Benvenuto
Cellini* " failed both in Paris and in
London, 1838. In 1839 he was made
Conservator of the Cons. ; librarian,
1852, but was never made professor
as he desired. Concert tours through
Germany and Russia, 1843–47, were
very successful and are described in
his book " *Voyage musical.*" London
(1852) he cond. the " New Philh.
Concerts "; prod. comic opera " *Béatrice et Bénédict* " (1862, Baden-Baden) ; 1865, member of the Académie,
and decorated with cross of Legion
of Honour. He m. Henrietta Smith-
son, an Irish actress who made a sensation in Paris in Shakespearian
rôles, but later was hissed off, and
became a peevish invalid. His opera,
" *Les Troyens à Carthage* " (1863)
was a failure. His son Louis died
1867. " *Les Troyens*," in two
parts ; *La Prise de Troie*, 3 acts,
and *Les Troyens à Carthage*, in 5
acts was given complete for the first
time, at Carlsruhe, 1897. His most
succ. work was his " oratorio," " *La
Damnation de Faust* " (1846). His
" *Traité d'instrumentation* " is a classic in orchestration, though its then
sensational modernity is lost. **B.**
strangely despised Wagner, who, however, confessed his large indebtedness
to **B.** Other books are " *Soirées
d'orchestre* " (1853), " *Grotesques de
la musique* " (1859), " *A travers
chants* " (1862), and an autobiography, " *Mémoires*," from 1803–65.
In original verse are the text to the
sacred trilogy " *L'Enfance du Christ* "
(*Part I., Le songe d'Hérode ; II., La
fuite en Égypte ; III., L'Arrivée à
Sais*) ; and his operas " *Les Troyens* " and " *Béatrice et Bénédict.*" He
composed also a " *Te Deum* " for 3
choirs, orch. and org. ; a " *Grand*

*symphonie funèbre et triomphale"* for full military band, with strings and chorus ad lib. ; overture to *"Le*

*Corsaire";* *"Le Cinq Mai,* chorus and orch. (on the annive of Napoleon's death), etc.

## Berlioz.

### BY ERNEST NEWMAN.

**B**ERLIOZ'S early influences were as much literary as musical. reading was mainly romantic ; his musical gods were Beeth Weber, and Gluck, whose orchestral works influenced him He knew little of Beethoven's piano writings, and did not like Bach. ¶ the intellectual world of the Beethoven symphony and the operas of ( and Weber he breathed the newer, more nervous life of the French Ro ticists. Colour and sensation became as important as form and the pure ¶ These influences and his literary instincts led him to graft the progr form on the older symphony. All his music aims at something conc Instead of the abstract world of the classical symphonists he gives us de emotions, or paints definite scenes. Colour, passion, and veracity wer prime needs ; form had to follow their guidance. Hence both his cesses and his failures. His virtue is truth and vivacity of expression defect the pursuit of these to the detriment of the musical interest. modern programmists have built upon him—Liszt, Richard Strauss, Tschaikowsky. Wagner felt his influence, though he belittled it. own words, " I have taken up music where Beethoven left it," indicat position. He is the real beginner of that interpenetration of music and poetic idea which has transformed modern art.

**Berlyn, Anton.** Vide BERLIJN.
**Bermudo** (bĕr-moo'-dhō), **Juan,** As-torga, ca. 1510 ; writer.
**Bernabei** (bĕr-nä-bā'-ē), (1) **Gius. Ercole,** Caprarola, ca. 1620—Munich, 1687 ; 1672 cond. at the Vatican ; 1674 cond. at Munich ; composed three operas (prod. in Munich), etc. (2) **Gius. A.,** Rome, 1659—Munich, 1732 ; son of above and his successor at Munich.
**Bernacchi** (bĕr-näk'-kē), **A.,** Bologna, ca. 1690—1756 ; soprano-musico, engaged by Händel for London, 1729, as the greatest living dram. singer ; 1736 founded a singing-school at Bologna.

**Bernard** (bĕr-năr, in *F.*), (1) **Émes** Orleans, France, 16th cent.; method of singing. (2) (bĕr'-nä *G.*), **Moritz,** Kurland, 1794 Petersburg, 1871; pianist and tea (3) **Paul,** Poitiers, 1827—Paris, composer and writer. (4) **Da** 1841—Paris, 1883 ; writer. **Émile,** b. Marseilles, Aug. 6, organist of Nôtre-Dame-des-Cha Paris ; important composer of concerto ; concert-stück for pf. orch.; overture *"Beatrice"; 2* tatas ; much chamber-music, etc
**Bernardel.** Vide LUPOT.
**Bernar'di,** (1) **Steffano,** ca. canon at Salzburg : theorist and

er. (2) **Francesco.** Vide SENE-
o. (3) **Enrico,** b. Milan, 1838—
o; conductor and dram. com-
ser.

.ardini (bĕr-när-dē'-nē), **Marcello
Marcello di Capua ''**), b. Capua,
1762; dram. composer.

.asco'ni, (1) **Andrea,** Marseilles,
2—Munich, 1784; court-conduc-
, (2) **P.,** d. Varese, May 27,
5; organ-builder.

.eli'nus, lived in Paris, 1000;
bably a Benedictine monk; theo-
and writer.

1er, **Fr. Wm.,** Breslau, 1780—
7; organist.

.hard (bĕr-när), (**St.**), Fontaines,
rgundy, 1091—1153; abbot and
orist.

.hard (bĕrn'-härt), (1) **der
utsche** (dĕr doit'-shĕ); organist,
nice, 1445–59; known as "Ber-
do di Steffanino Murer"; perhaps
., certainly introduced, into Italy,
organ-pedal. (2) **Chr.,** Danzig,
2—Dresden, 1692; court-con-
ctor and notable contrapuntist.

.icat (bĕr-nĭ-kä), **Firmin,** 1841—
ris, 1883; dram. composer.

.no, **Augien'sis,** d. Riechenau,
48; abbot and theorist.

.ouilli (băr-noo-ē'-yē), (1) **Jn.,**
sel, 1667—1747. His son (2)
.niel, Groningen, 1700—Basel,
32, also was prof. and writer on
oustics.

.s'dorf, **Eduard,** Dessau, March
1825—1901; Leipzig critic and
mposer.

.uth (băr'-noot), **Julius von,** b.
es, Rhine Province, Aug. 8, 1830;
died law and music at Berlin,
54; studied at Leipzig Cons. till
57; founded the "Aufschwung
ciety," and 1859 "Dilettante's Or-
stral Society"; also cond. 3 other
ieties; later cond. at Hamburg;
73, dir. of a cons. there; 1878,
Royal Prussian Professor."

(bĕr), **Fr.,** Mannheim, 1794—
ris, 1838; bandmaster; 1831, prof.
clar., Paris Cons.; 1836, dir. School
of Military Music; writer and composer.

**Berré** (bĕr-rā), **F.,** b. Ganshoren, near
Brussels, Feb. 5, 1843; composed
operas.

**Bersel'li, Matteo,** Italian tenor;
London, 1720–21.

**Bertali** (bĕr-tä'-lē), **Ant.,** Verona,
1605—Vienna, 1669; court-conductor
and dram. composer.

**Bertani** (bĕr-tä'-nē), **Telio,** 16th cent.;
court-conductor.

**Ber'telmann, Jan. G.,** Amsterdam,
1782—1854; prof. and composer.

**Ber'telsmann, K. Aug.,** Gütersioh,
Westphalia, 1811—Amsterdam, 1861;
director and composer.

**Berthaume** (bĕr-tōm), **Isidore,** Paris,
1752—St. Petersburg, 1802; violinist
and conductor.

**Berthelier** (bĕr-tĕl-yā), **H.,** solo-violinist, Paris Opéra, 1894.

**Berthold** (bĕr'-tôlt), **K. Fr. Theodor,**
Dresden, 1815—1882; court-organist.

**Berti** (bĕr-tē), **M. A.,** Vienna, 1721—
1740; barytone-player.

**Bertin** (bĕr'-tän), **Louise Angélique,**
Roches, near Paris, 1805—Paris,
1877; singer, pianist and dram. composer.

**Bertini** (bĕr-tē'-nē), (1) **Abbate Gius.,**
Palermo, 1756—1849 (?); court-cond.
and lexicographer. (2) **Benoît
Auguste,** b. Lyons, 1780; writer.
(3) **H. Jérome,** London, 1798—
Meylau, near Grenoble, 1876; bro.
and pupil of above; pianist and
composer; at 12, toured the Netherlands and Germany; retired, 1859;
wrote technical studies. (4) **Dom.,**
Lucca, 1829—Florence, 1890; teacher, critic, theorist and director.

**Bertinot'ti, Teresa,** Piedmont, 1776—
Bologna, 1854; operatic soprano; m.
**Felix Radicati,** a violinist and
composer.

**Bertolli** (tôl'-lĭ), **Fran.,** Italian singer
in Händel's operas, London, 1729-
37.

**Berton** (bĕr-tôn), (1) **P. Montan,**
Paris, 1727—1780; conductor grand
opera and dram. composer. (2) **H.**

**Montan,** Paris, 1767—1844 ; son of above ; composer. (3) **François,** Paris, 1784—1832 ; natural son of (2) ; pupil, later prof. of singing, at Cons. ; composed operas and songs.

**Berto′ni, Fdo. Giu.,** Venice, 1725—Desenzano, 1813 ; organist and dram. composer.

**Bertram** (bĕr′-träm), **Th.,** b. Stuttgart, Feb. 12, 1869 ; barytone ; studied with his father ; sang in various German cities lately with his wife, **Fanny Moran Olden.**

**Bertrand** (bĕr-trän), **J. Gᵥ.,** Vaugirard, near Paris, 1834—Paris, 1880 ; writer and critic.

**Berwald** (bĕr′-vält), (1) **Jn. Fr.,** Stockholm, 1788—1861 ; precocious violinist, etc.; pupil of Abbé Vogler ; composed a symphony at 9. (2) **Fz.,** Stockholm, 1796—1868 ; nephew of above ; dram. composer.

**Berwillibald** (bĕr′-vĭl-lĭ-bält), **G. G.,** German singer in London, 1716.

**Berwin** (bĕr′-vēn), **Adolf,** Schwersenz, near Posen, 1847—Rome, 1900 ; dir. Cecilia Academy, Rome ; writer.

**Besard** (bŭ-zăr′), **Jn. Bap.,** b. Besançon, ca. 1576 ; writer.

**Beschnitt** (bĕ-shnĭt′), **Jns.,** Bockau, Silesia, 1825—Stettin, 1880 ; conductor.

**Besekirsky** (bā-zĕ-kēr′-shkĭ), **Vasil Vasilevitch,** b. Moscow, 1836 ; concert violinist and composer.

**Besler** (bās′-lĕr), (1) **Samuel,** Brieg, Silesia, 1574—Breslau, 1625 ; rector and composer. (2) **Simon,** cantor at Breslau, and composer, 1615–28.

**Besozzi** (bā-sôd′-zē), the name of 4 brothers, all oboists except (3). (1) **Ales.,** Parma, 1700—Turin, 1775. (2) **Antonio,** Parma, 1707—Turin, 1781 ; (3) **Hieronimo,** Parma, 1713 —Turin (?), bassoonist. (4) **Gaetano,** b. Parma, 1727. (5) **Carlo,** b. Dresden, 1745 ; oboist, son of (2). (6) **Hieronimo,** d. 1785 ; son of (3) ; oboist. His son (7) **Henri** was a flutist, and father of (8) **Louis Désiré,** Versailles, 1814—Paris, 1879 ; teacher and composer.

**Bessems** (bĕs′-sāms), **A.,** Antᵥ 1809—1868 ; violinist and compo

**Besson** (bŭs-sôn), **Gv. Aug.,** 1820—1875 ; improver of valve wind-instruments.

**Best, Wm. T.,** Carlisle, Engl., 13, 1826—Liverpool, May 10, 1 org.-virtuoso ; pupil of Young ; ganist at various ch., and the P Society ; in 1880, declined kn hood, but accepted Civil-List sion of £100 per annum ; retired ; 1890 went to Sydney, tralia, to inaugurate the organ i new Town Hall ; composed overt sonatas, preludes, etc., for o also 2 overtures and march for o and pf.-pcs. ; wrote " *The Art o gan-playing.*" etc.

**Betts, J. & Edward,** London ; makers ; pupils and successors o Duke, 1760–80.

**Betz** (bĕts), **Fz.,** Mayence, Marcl 1835—Berlin, Aug. 12, 1900 ; l tone ; created " Wotan. " and "I Sachs."

**Beuer** (boi′-ĕr), **Elise,** b. Carls soprano, studied in 1892 at Vie City-Theatre, Leipzig ; 1899, I burg City Theatre.

**Beunter** (boin′-tĕr), **Benj., M** hausen, 1792—1837 ; organist composer.

**Bev′an, Fr. Chas.,** b. London, Jᵤ 1856 ; pupil of Willing and Hᵤ organist various churches ; then ied singing with Schira, Deacon Walker ; 1877 Gentleman of Chapel Royal ; composed pop. sᵤ

**Bevignani** (bā-vēn-yä′-nē), Cavₐ **Enrico,** b. Naples, Sept. 29, 1 pupil of Albanese, Lillo, etc., opera, " *Caterina Bloom,*" sᵥ Czar made him Knight of the C of St. Stanislas, which gives no and a life-pension ; chiefly note cond. in London, Moscow and York.

**Bev′in, Elway,** Wales, 1560(— —1640 (?) ; Gentleman of the Cl Royal ; organist, writer and poser.

'field, **Wm. Rd.**, Norwich, 1824
London, 1853 ; organist and com-
ser.

er (bī'-ĕr), (1) **Jn. Samuel,**
otha, 1669—Carlsbad, 1744 ; direc-
r. (2) **Rudolf,** Wilther, 1828—
resden, 1853 ; composer. (3) **Fd.,**
uerfurt, 1805 — Mayence, 1863 ;
mposer.

ggi (bē-äd'-jē), **Gir. Ales.**, Milan,
15—Florence, 1897 ; prof., dram.
mposer, writer under pseudonym
**Ippolito d'Albano.''**

(bē'-äl), (1) **Rudolf,** Habelschwerdt,
lesia, 1834—New York, 1881 ; vi-
inist, writer and cond. (2) **K.,**
abelschwerdt, 1833—Steglitz, near
erlin, 1892 ; bro. of above ; pianist.

nchi (bē-än'-kē), (1) **Fran.,** Cre-
ona, 1752—Bologna, 1811 ; organist;
mposed 47 operas. (2) **Valentine,**
ilna, 1839—Candau, Kurland,
84 ; dram. soprano ; début, 1855.
) **Bianca** (rightly **Schwarz**), b. in
village on the Neckar, June 27,
58 ; dram.-soprano ; pupil of Wil-
ek and Viardot-Garcia ; Pollini
id her tuition and then engaged
r for 10 years; début Carlsruhe,
73. (4) **Eliodoro,** composed
peras ; " *Gara d'Amore* " (Bari,
73) ; " *Sarah* " ; " *Almanzor*."

nchini (bē-än-kē'-nē), **P.,** b. Ven-
e, Oct., 18, 1828 ; violinist, cond.,
78–87, teacher at Trieste, then dir.
chool of the Padri Armeni, Venice ,
mposer.

er (bē'-bĕr), (1) **H. Jn. Fz. von,**
artenberg, Bohemia, 1644—Salz-
urg, May 3, 1704 ; violinist, and
ne of the founders of the German
chool of vln.-playing ; Leopold I.
nnobled him. (2) **Aloys,** Ellingen,
804—Munich, 1858 ; piano-maker.

l (bēb'-'l), (1) **Andreas,** Vienna,
797 ; organist and composer, as was
s son (2) **Rudolph,** b. 1832.

dermann (bē'-dĕr-män), (1) —,
bout 1786 tax-receiver at Beichlingen,
huringia ; a real virtuoso on, and
nprover of, the hurdygurdy. (2)
dw. **Julius,** b. Milwaukee, Wis.,

Nov. 8, 1849 (son and pupil of (3)
**A. Julius**) ; studied in Germany ;
since 1888 organist St. Mary's R. C.
Church, New York.

**Biehl** (bēl), **Albert,** b. Rudolstadt,
Germany, Aug. 16, 1833 ; writer of
valuable works on finger technic ; and
composer.

**Bierey** (bēr'-ī), **Gl. Benedikt,** Dresden, 1772—Breslau, 1840 ; conductor
and dram. composer.

**Biese** (bē'-zĕ), **Wm.**, b. Rathenow
1822 ; piano-maker, Berlin.

**Bigaglia** (bē-gäl'-yä), Padre **Diogenio,** 1725 ; Benedictine monk and
composer.

**Bignami** (bēn-yä'-mē), (1) **Carlo,** Cremona, Dec. 6, 1808—Voghera, Aug.
2, 1848 ; cond., violinist and dir.,
Cremona ; Paganini called him " the
first violinist of Italy." (2) **Enrico,**
1842 (?) — Genoa, 1894 ; violinist.
dram. composer.

**Bignio** (bēn'-yō), **Louis von,** b. Pesth,
1839 ; lyric barytone ; Vienna Court-
Opera ; pensioned, 1883.

**Bigot** (bē-gō), **M.** (née **Kiene**), Colmar, Upper Alsatia, 1786—Paris,
1820 ; pianist.

**Bilhon** (or **Billon**) (bē-yôṅ), **J. de,**
16th cent. ; composer and singer in
the Papal Chapel.

**Billema** (bēl-lä'-mä), (1) **Carlo** (b.
Naples, ca. 1822) and (2) **Raffaele**
(Naples, 1820—Saintes, Dec. 25,
1874), brothers ; pianists, and com
posers.

**Billert** (bēl'-lĕrt), **K. Fr. Aug.**, Alt-
stettin, 1821—Berlin, 1875 ; painter
and writer.

**Billet** (bēl-yā), **Alex. Ph.**, b. St.
Petersburg, March 14, 1817 ; pianist
and composer.

**Billeter** (bē-yŭ-tä), **Agathon,** Manne
dorf, Lake of Zurich, Nov. 21, 1834 ;
organist, conductor and composer of
pop. part-songs.

**Bil'lings,** **Wm.**, Boston, Mass.,
Oct. 7, 1749—Sept. 29, 1800 ; composed hymns ; introduced the pitch-
pipe and the 'cello into American
church-choirs, and is said to have

given the first concert in New England.

**Bil'lington,** (1) **Th.,** pianist, harpist and composer, latter part of 18th cent. (2) **Elizabeth** (née **Weichsel**), London, ca. 1768—near Venice, Aug. 23, 1818 ; pupil of her father, a clarinettist ; then of J. Chr. Bach ; handsome operatic soprano, had a compass of 3 octaves, *a-a″* (Vide PITCH, D. D.), 1784, Dublin ; 1786, Covent Garden ; retired, 1818.

**Billrot(h)** (bĕl'-rōt), (1) **Jn. Gv. Fr.,** Halle, near Lübeck, 1808—Halle, 1836 ; composer and writer. (2) **Theodor,** Bergen, Isle of Rügen, 1829—Abbazia, 1894 ; surgeon and writer.

**Bilse** (bēl'-sĕ), **Benj.,** b. Liegnitz, Aug. 17, 1816 ; "Stadtmusikus" at Liegnitz, and trained a remarkable orchestra ; retired 1894 as "Hofmusikus."

**Binchois (Gilles de Binche,** called **Binchois)** (bănsh-wä), Binche, in Belgian Hainault, ca. 1400—Lille, 1460 ; one of the early Netherland composers ; 3-part chanson, rondeaux, etc., of his are extant.

**Binder** (bĭnt'-ĕr), (1) **K. Wm. Fd.,** b. Dresden, 1764 ; harp-maker at Weimar, ca. 1797. (2) **K.,** Vienna, 1816—1860 ; conductor and dram. composer.

**Bini** (bē'-nē), **Pasqualino,** b. Pesaro, ca. 1720 ; violinist.

**Bioni** (bē-ō'-nē), **A.,** b. Venice, 1698 ; composed 26 operas.

**Biordi** (bē-ôr'-dē), **Giov.,** Commissioned by Pope Benedict XIII. to supplement Palestrina's service ; this was used till 1731.

**Birch,** (1) **C. Anne,** b. ca. 1815 ; pop. singer ; retired 1856. (2) **Eliza,** ca. 1830—1857 ; sister of above ; soprano.

**Birch'all, Robt.,** d. 1819 ; music-publisher, London.

**Birckenstock** (bĕr'-kĕn-shtôk), Alsfeld, 1687 — Eisenach, 1733 ; conductor.

**Bird,** (1) **Wm.** Vide BYRD. (2) **Arthur,**

b. Cambridge, Mass., July 23, 1 pupil of Haupt, Löschhorn, Rohde, Berlin, 1875-77 ; organist teacher at Halifax, N. S.; fou the first male chorus in N. S., 18 studied comp. and orchestration Urban, Berlin ; 1885-86 with Lis Weimar ; 1886, gave a succe concert, and has lived since, in Be Grünewald ; composed symphony 3 suites for orch.; various pieces piano ; comic opera "*Daphne*" ( York, 1897) ; and a ballet, "*K zahl.*"

**Birkler** (bĕr'-klĕr), **G. Wm.,** 18; 1877 ; composer and writer.

**Birnbach** (bērn'-bäkh), (1) **K. J** Kopernick, Silesia, 1751—Wars 1805 ; conductor. (2) **Jos. B H.,** Breslau, 1795—Berlin, 18 pianist and composer ; son and p of above.

**Bisaccia** (bē-sät'-chä), **Giov.,** 181 Naples, 1897 ; singer, conductor dram. composer.

**Biscaccianti** (bēs-kät-chän'-tē), za (née **Ostinelli**), Boston, Ma 1824 (7 ?)—1896 ; sang in Ame and Europe, in opera and conce teacher in Rome and elsewhere ; Marquis B.

**Bischoff** (bēsh'-ôf), (1) **G. Fr.,** Ellr Harz Mts., 1780—Hildesheim, 18 conductor ; founded the German n festivals. (2) **L. Fr. Ch.,** Dess 1794 — Cologne, 1867 ; translat son of (3) **K. B.,** court-mus., D den. (4) **Kasper Jakob,** Ansba 1823—Munich, 1893 ; teacher composer. (5) **Hans,** Berlin, 185 Niederschönhausen, near Berlin, 18 pf.-teacher, conductor and editor.

**Bish'op,** (1) Sir **H. Rowley,** Lond Nov. 18, 1786—April 30, 1855 ; nc Engl. composer ; pupil of Bianca ; first opera, "*The Circassian Bri* was prod. Drury Lane, when he v 20 ; 1810-11 comp. and cond. at vent Garden ; 1813 alternate co Philh. Soc.; 1825 cond. at Dr Lane ; 1830 musical dir. at Vauxh 1841-43, prof. music, Edinburg ighted, 1842 ; 1848 prof. of music Oxford ; 1853, Mus. Doc. (Oxon); od. over 80 operas, farces, ballets, oratorio, cantata, etc. (2) **J.**, Cheltenham, 1814 ; organist, editor d composer.

**ham** (bĭsp´-hăm), **David,** b. Philelphia, ca. 1860 ; dram. barytone ; ng in church and oratorio ; 1885–87 pil of Vannuccini and Wm. Shakesare ; from 1891 in opera at Covent arden, and America, with much ccess and versatility; and also in reals, in both of which fields his high amatic intelligence plays an unusual rt ; is brilliant in comic or tragic uations ; knows more than 40 rôles.

ter, **K. Hermann,** Schwedt-onder, 1813—Berlin, 1855 ; Prussian inister of Finance, and writer.

o´ni, **Bdo.,** Fabriano, 1755—1829 ; ganist.

et (bē-zā), **G. (Alex. César Léopld),** Paris, Oct. 25, 1838—Bougil, June 3, 1875 ; brilliant pianist d distinguished composer. At 9, pil at Paris Cons. of Marmontel f.), Benoist (org.), Zimmerman arm.), and Halévy (whose opera Noë" he finished, and whose ughter Geneviève he m.) ; 1857,

took Offenbach 1st prize for an opera buffa, " *Le Docteur Miracle,*" prod. at Bouffes Parisiens, 1863 ; also won the Grand Prix de Rome. In place of the Mass prescribed he sent from Rome a 2-act Ital. opera buffa " *Don Procopio*" ; 2 movements of a symphony, " *La Chasse D Ossian,*" an overture ; and " *La Guzla de l'Émir,*" a comic opera. 1836, his grand opera " *Les Pêcheurs de Perles,*" was prod. Paris (Th. Lyrique) ; it failed, as did " *La Jolie Fille de Perth* " (1867), and the 1-act " *Djamileh* " (1872). In all his music **B.** revealed a strong leaning toward Wagner, then so unpopular in France ; but 1872, his overture "*Patrie,*" the 2 symphonic movements, and incidental music to Daudet's *L'Arlésienne,* brought him success ; and " *Carmen* " (Opéra-Com., March 3, 1875) brought him a fame, which he hardly knew, as he died three months later of heart disease ; he composed also 2 operas, " *Numa*" (1871) and "*Ivan le Terrible*" ; 150 pf.-pcs., songs, etc.; collaborated with Délibes, Jonah and Legouix in opera " *Malbrough, s'en va-t-en-guerre.*" Biog. by Pigot, 1886.

---

## Bizet.

### BY EDWARD E. ZIEGLER.

AS Bizet's last work was his best, it is logical to argue that his untimely death has cheated us of compositions more valuable than "*Carmen ;*" but beyond mere conjecture such an estimate can e no value and his rank among opera-composers must be determined by *men*. That the stage was his real field, is proven clearly by the perency with which he composed for it, and a study of his different efforts ves he wisdom of his choice, for there are no masterpieces among his gs, or among his piano-compositions, and even his most successful orchesnumber is the "*First Suite*" compiled for his incidental music to det's "*L'Arlésienne.*" ¶His early letters confess his musical creed : zart and Beethoven, Rossini and Meyerbeer ; this is catholic, to say least, but later he acknowledged his preference for the Germans in gen-

eral and Beethoven as the master of all. But Bizet was a stranger to
larger forms in music—for two years he toiled intermittingly at a symph
and produced only the " Roman Suite " as a result—and his work sh
more tendency to follow Gounod's teaching than that of his high ide
He was bitterly accused of being a follower of Wagner ; Paris, knowin;
lamentably little of Wagner's music, then condemned that of Bizet's, wh
it did not like or could not understand, by labelling it " Wagnerian,"
thus put it hopelessly beyond the possibility of discussion. As a matte
fact there is no trace of Wagner to be found in Bizet's music, and the c
resemblance between the two is that both were innovators who presei
their theories about dramatic art in practical forms, proving them by t
operas. ¶ Bizet realised the sorry state of the French operatic stage,
contented himself with an effort at reforming the minor stage of the Op
Comique, and it is doubtless due in a great measure to the precedent
" Carmen " that to-day the Opéra-Comique is on a higher artistic pl
than the Opéra. ¶ A direct musical influence it would be difficult to tı
to Bizet. As an orchestral colourist he had been outdone and outdared
even his contemporaries ; nor did he bequeath to us a new art-form.
because he demanded a more sincere libretto than any of those with wl
that maker of marionette opera-books, Scribe, had conjured all Paris,
because in his music he did not fear contact with throbbing life, he cc
mands our respect. His work shows a musical sincerity foreign to Fre
composers generally, and he deserved a better fate than a sequence of failı
ending with an early death.

---

Blaes (blās), (1) Arnold Jos., Brussels, 1814—1892 ; clarinettist. (2)
M. Elisa, Antwerp, 1820, wife of
above ; teacher.

Bla'grove, (1) H. Gamble, Nottingham, 1811—London, 1872 ; violinist.
(2) Richard Manning, Nottingham, 1827—London, 1895 ; bro. of
above ; viola prof. R. A. M.

Blahag (blä'-häkh) (or Blahak), Josef, Raggendorf, Hungary, 1779—
Vienna, 1846 ; tenor, conductor, and
composer.

Blahet'ka (or Piahet'ka), Marie-
Léopoldine, Guntramsdorf, near
Vienna, 1811—Boulogne, 1887 ; pi-
anist and dram. composer.

Blainville (blän-vě'-yŭ), Chas. H.,
near Tours, 1711—Paris, 1769 ; 'cellist, writer and composer.

Blake, (1) Rev. Ed., b. Salisbury
1765. (2) Chas. Dupee, b. Walp
Mass., Sept. 13, 1847 ; pupil of J
D. Parker, J. K. Paine, etc.; orga
Union Ch., Boston, and composei

Blamont (blä-môṅ), Fran. Colin
Versailles, 1690—1760 ; supt. of
King's music and composer.

Blanc (bläṅ), Adolphe, b. Manoso
Basses-Alpes, June 24, 1828 ; pı
Paris Cons. and of Halévy ; cı
posed 3 operas.

Blanchard (blän-shär), H. L., I
deaux, 1778—Paris, 1858 ; violi
and critic.

Blanckenburgh (blänk'-ĕn-boork
Gerbrandt van, organist at Gou
17th century. Vide BLANKENBUR

Blancks, Edw., English compo
16th cent.

**d** (blänt), (1) **Maria Theresa** (e **Romanzini**), 1769—1838; pop. lian singer in England; married actor, Bland, and had two sons. **Chas.**, tenor. (3) **James**, 1798— 51, bass.

**gini** (blän-jĕ'-nē), **Giu. Marco,** **Felice,** Turin, 1781 — Paris, 41; organist.

**kenburg** (blänk-ĕn-boorkh), (1) **irin van,** Gouda, Holland, 1654 The Hague, 1749; probably son GERBRANDT VAN BLANCKEN-RGH (q. v.); organist and writer. (2) **r. Fr. von,** Kolberg, Pomerania, 14—Leipzig, 1796; Prussian offi-· and composer.

**amberg** (blä'-räm-bĕrkh), **Paul I.,** Orenburg, Russia, Sept. 26, 1841; pil of Balakirew; lawyer, then ed-r; composed succ. operas, "*Maria udor*" (St. Petersburg, 1882); "*The rst Russian Comedian*"; "*Tusch-sky*" (Moscow, 1895).

**.** Vide BLAES.

**ius** (bläz'-yüs), **Mathieu Fr.,** uterburg, Alsatia, 1758 — Ver-lles, 1829; cond. Op. Comique, ris; composer.

**smann** (bläs'-män), **Ad. Jos. M.,** esden, 1823—Bautzen, 1891; pi-ist, court-conductor and writer.

**t** (blät), **Fz. Thaddäus,** Prague, 93—(?); clarinettist and writer.

**wa.rt** (blow'-värt), **Emil,** St. cholas, Belgium, 1845—Brussels, 91; barytone.

**velt** (blou'-fĕlt), **Lillian,** b. Brook-a, N. Y., 1870(?); soprano; studied t. Cons., N. Y., and in Paris; af-· years of success at home, toured rope since 1900; decorated in Italy th the order of St. Cecilia; m. Royal ith (1898 divorced); m. again 1901. **ze** (bläz), (1) (Called **Castil-Blaze**) **an. H. Jos.,** Cavaillon Vaucluse, 84—Paris, 1857; "The father of dern French musical criticism"; n and pupil of Henri Sebastian B.; ote scathing "*L'Opéra en France*" 820); was made critic on "*Journal Débats,*" where his articles were

signed "*XXX*"; transl. libretti of German and Italian operas; com-posed 3 operas, several "pastiches," etc. (2) **H.,** Baron de Bury, Avig-non, 1813—Paris, 1888; son of above; writer.

**Bletzacher** (blät'-tsäkh-ĕr), **Jos.,** Schwoich, Tyrol, 1835 — Hanover, 1895; bass.

**Bleuer** (bloi'-ĕr), **L.,** Buda-Pesth, 1863 —Berlin, 1897; violinist; 1883-93, leader of Philh. orch., Berlin; 1894, of Philh. Club, Detroit (Michigan).

**Blewitt,** (1) **Jonathan,** London, 1782—1853; organist and director; son and pupil of (2) **Jonas,** organist and writer.

**Blied** (blēt), **Jacob,** Brühl-on-Rhine, 1844—1884; teacher and composer.

**Blitheman, Wm.,** d. 1591; organ.st, etc., at Oxford.

**Bloch** (blôkh), **G.,** b. Breslau, Nov. 1847; pupil of Hainsch, J. Schuber}, Taubert, and F. Geyer; teacher in Breslaur's Cons., Berlin; founded Opera Society, 1879; composer.

**Blockx** (blôx), **Jan.,** b. Antwerp, Jan. 25, 1851; pianist and composer; pu-pil, Flemish Mus. School; from 1886, teacher of harm. there; 1901 suc-ceeded Bénoît, at Antwerp cons.; composed succ. operas, incl. "*Maître Martin,*" etc.

**Blodek** (blôd-ĕk), (1) **P. Aug. L.,** Paris, 1784—1856; viola-player and dram. composer. (2) **Wm.,** Prague, 1834—1874; prof. and dram. composer.

**Bloom field-Zeisler** (tsīs'-lĕr), **Fanny,** b. Bielitz, Austrian Silesia, July 16, 1866; pianist; at 2 was brought to Chicago, where she still lives; played in public at 10; was pupil of Ziehn and Karl Wolfsohn, and 1876-81 of Leschetizky; from 1883 has toured America with distinction; from 1893, Germany, Austria, England and France with great success.

**Blow, John** (Mus. Doc. Oxon.), Col-lingham, Nottinghamshire, 1648— Westminster (London), Oct. 1. 1708; organist Westminster Abbey, 1680; was superseded by Purcell, whom he in turn succeeded ; he is buried in the Abbey ; 1674, organist and (1699) composer to the Chapel Royal ; beginning to compose as a boy, he achieved a vast amount of church-music.

**Blum** (bloom), **K. L.**, Berlin, 1786—July 2, 1844 ; actor, singer, poet, organist, 'cellist, cond., and composer ; chamber-musician to the Prussian Ct., 1822 ; stage mgr. ; prod. nearly 30 operas, ballets, songs, etc.; also vaudevilles, which he introduced to the German stage.

**Blumenfeld** (bloo'-měn-fĕlt), **F.**, b. Kovalevska, Russia, April 7, 1863 ; pianist, pupil of Th. Stein ; took gold medal at St. Petersburg Cons.; composed *"Allegro de Concert,"* with orchestra, etc.

**Blumenthal** (bloo'-měn-täl), (1) **Jos. von**, Brussels, 1782—Vienna, 1850, violinist and dram. composer. (2) **Jacob (Jacques)**, b. Hamburg, Oct. 4, 1826 ; pupil of Grund, Bocklet, and Sechter (Vienna), and 1846 of Herz and Halévy ; after 1848 in London ; pianist to the Queen, and composer. (3) **Paul**, b. Steinau-on-Oder, Silesia, Aug. 13, 1843 ; pupil of R. A., Berlin, 1870 ; organist. Frankfort-on-Oder ; from 1870, " R. mus. dir. "; composed masses, motets, etc.

**Blumner** (bloom'-nĕr), (Dr.) **Martin**, Fürstenberg, Mecklenburg, Nov. 21, 1827—Berlin, Nov. 6, 1901 ; pupil of S. W. Dehn ; 1876, cond. of Berlin Singakademie ; titles " R. Musik-dir." and " Prof."; composed 2 oratorios, *"Abraham"* (1860), and *" Der Falt Jerusalems"* (1881) ; cantata *Columbus* (1853); *Te Deum*, etc.

**Blüthner** (blüt'-nĕr), **Julius Fd.**, b. Falkenhain, near Merseburg, March 11, 1824 ; piano-maker, Leipzig, from 1853.

**Boccabadati** (bôk-kä-bä-dä'-tē), **Luigia**, Parma—Turin, 1850 ; soprano.

**Boccherini** (bôk-kĕ-rē'-nē), **Luigi**, Lucca, Italy, Feb. 19, 1743—Madrid, May 28. 1805; 'cellist; toured with suc-

cess ; 1797, made chamber-com to Friedrich Wilhelm II., of Pr in return for a dedication ; aft king's death **B.**'s fortune left him he died in dire poverty. His p and often fascinatingly graceful positions include 20 symphonic opera, an orchestral suite, a concerto, 2 octets, 16 sextets string-quintets, 12 pf.-quintets quintets for strings and flute (or o 91 string-quartets, 54 string-trio trios, sonatas and duets for vln., biog. by Picquot (Paris, 1851), Schletternd (Leipzig).

**Boch** (bôkh), **Fz. de**, b. Potens Bohemia, Feb. 14, 1808 ; 'cellist.

**Bochkoltz-Falco'ni** (bôkh'-kôlts) **na** (rightly **Bockholtz**), Frank 1820—Paris, 1870 ; singer and poser.

**Bochsa** (bôkh'-sä), (1) **K.**, Bohem Paris, 1821 ; oboist ; music-s (2) **Rob. Nic. Chas.**, Montm Meuse, Aug. 9, 1789—Sydney, tralia, Jan. 6, 1856 ; son and pu above ; composed a symphony an opera at 16 ; pupil of Fr. B harpist to Napoleon and to I XVIII.; he eloped with Sir H Bishop's wife, made tours in Eu and America, and finally to Austr composed 9 French operas, prod Lyons (1804), and in Paris (1813-4 ballets ; an oratorio, etc.; wro standard method for harp.

**Böckeler** (bĕk'-ĕ-lĕr), **H.**, b. Colo July 11, 1836—1862 ; cond. at le-Chapelle , editor and composer

**Böckh** (bĕkh), **Aug.**, Carlsruhe, —Berlin, 1867 ; writer.

**Bocklet** (bôk'-lĕt), **K. M. von**, Pra 1801—Vienna, 1881 ; violinist.

**Bockmühl** (bôk'-mül), **Robt. E** Frankfort, 1820—1881 ; 'cellist.

**Bockshorn** (bôks'-hôrn) (" **Capri nus** "), **Samuel**, Germany, 16 Stuttgart, 1669 (?) ; composer conductor.

**Bocquillon-Wilhem** (bôk'-ē-yôr äṅ), **G. L.** Vide WILHEM.

**Bode** (bō'-dĕ), **Jn. Jos. Chp.**, Bar

unswick, 1730—Weimar, 1793 ;
oist, publisher and composer.

enschatz (bō'-d'n-shäts), Erhard,
chtenberg, Saxony, 1570—Gross-
sterhausen, near Querfurt, 1638 ;
blisher.

decker (bā'-dĕk-ĕr), Louis, Ham-
rg, 1845—1899 ; teacher, critic,
d composer.

hm, Boehme. Vide BÖHM (E).

kelman (bā'-kĕl-män), Bernar-
s, b. Utrecht, Holland, 1838 ; pu-
l and son of A. J. B. ; director,
died with Moscheles, Richter and
auptmann, at Leipzig Cons. ; von
llow, Kiel, and Weitzmann, at
erlin ; from 1866, lives in New
ork ; founded and cond. (till 1888)
e N. Y. Trio Club ; 1883–97, mus.
r. Miss Porter's School, Farming-
n, Conn. ; later pianist and teacher
New York ; composed orch.-pcs.,
c. ; ed. an analytical edition of
ach's " Well-tempered Clavichord,"
colours, etc.

llmann (bwĕl'-män), Léon, Ensi-
eim, Alsatia, 1862—Paris, 1897 ;
mposer and teacher.

ly (bwĕl'-ē), Alex. P. Fran.,
ersailles, 1785—Paris, 1858 ; pian-
t and composer.

rs (boors), Jos. Karel, Nymwe-
en, Holland, 1812—Delft, 1896 ;
nd. and writer.

sset (bwôs-sā), (1) A., Sieur de
illedieu, ca. 1585—1673 ; intendant
f music to Louis XIII. (2) J. B., 1612
-1685 ; son and successor of above ;
d in turn succeeded by his son. (3)
. J. B., b. ca. 1636.

'tius (or Boethius), Ani'cius
Ian'lius Torqua'tus Severi'nus,
ome ca. 475—executed 524 (?) ; ement poet and writer on music.

lmann (bōl'-män), Th. H. Fr., b.
sterwieck am Harz, Germany, June
3, 1865 ; pianist ; pupil of Dr.
tade, Barth, Klindworth, Tiersch,
'Albert, and Moszkowski ; début
erlin, 1890 ; toured Germany ; since
890 pf. - prof. Cincinnati Cons.
J. S. A.

Boise (bois)

Bohm (bōm), K., b. Berlin, Sept. 11,
1844 ; pupil of Löschhorn, Reissmann and Geyer ; pianist and composer in Berlin.

Böhm (bām), (1) G., Goldbach,
Thuringia, 1661—Lüneburg, 1734 ;
organist and clavichordist ; composed
important organ preludes and suites.
(2) Elizabeth Riga, 1756—1797 ;
soprano, m. the actor B. (3) Theobald, Münich, April 9, 1794—Nov.
15, 1881 ; inv. the "Böhm flute"
(vide D. D.) ; flutist and composer for
flute ; "Hofmusikus," and player in
royal orch. (4) Jos., Pesth, 1795—
Vienna, 1876 ; son and pupil of above ;
violinist and prof. (5) Heinrich, b.
Blassia, Bohemia, 1836 ; composed
35 operas in Bohemian. (6) Jos.,
Kühnitz, Moravia, 1841 — Vienna,
1893 ; organist, comp. and director.

Böhme (bā'-mĕ), (1) Jn. Aug., 1794 ;
founder of pub. house at Hamburg.
His son, (2) Justus Eduard, succeeded him in 1839 ; and his grandson, (3) August Eduard, in 1885.
(4) Aug. Julius Fd., Ganderheim,
Brunswick, 1815—1883 ; conductor.
(5) Fz. Magnus, Wellerstedt, near
Weimar, 1827 — Dresden, 1898 ;
teacher, Dresden, later prof. ; composer, writer and collector.

Böhmer (bā'-mĕr), K. (Hermann
Ehrfried), The Hague, 1799—Berlin, 1884 ; dram. composer.

Bohn (bōn), Emil, b. Bielau, near
Neisse, Jan. 14, 1839 , organist, 1884,
founded the Bohn Choral Society,
giving historical concerts ; lecturer,
writer, critic and composer ; R. Prof.
of Music.

Böhner (bā'-nĕr), Jn. L., Tôttelstedt,
Gotha, 1787 — near Gotha, 1860 ;
composer ; led a roving life of drunk-
enness and talent ; said to be the
original of Hofmann's "Kreisler"
[vide SCHUMANN] ; composed opera,
etc.

Bohrer (bō'-rĕr), (1) Anton, Munich,
1783 — Hanover, 1852 ; violinist ;
composer for vln. : a co-member of
the Bavarian Court-orch. and concert-

giver with his brother, (2) **Max,** Münich, 1785—Stuttgart, 1867 ; 'cellist.

**Boie** (boi'-ĕ), (1) **John,** b. Altona, March 8, 1822 ; violinist. (2) **H.,** Altona, Sept. 16, 1825 ; bro. of above ; violinist and dram. composer.

**Boïeldieu** (bō-ĕld-yŭ'), (1) **Fran. Adrien,** Rouen, Dec. 16 (not 15), 1775—Jarcy, near Grosbois, Oct. 8, 1834 ; son of secretary of Archp. Larochefoucauld and a milliner ; apprenticed to the intemperate, brutal cathedral organist Broche, he ran away, at 12, and walked to Paris, but was brought back. He is not known to have had other teaching. At 18, he prod. succ. "*La fille coupable*" (Rouen, 1793) ; 1795, "*Rosalie et Myrza,*" text of both by his father. Discouraged in a planned Cons. at Rouen, he again walked to Paris, and subsisted as teacher and piano-tuner to Erard. The tenor Garat sang his still pop. songs, in public, and won him a publisher. 1796, "*La Dot de Suzette,*" in one act, was prod. with succ. (Opéra-Com.) ; 1797, "*La famille Suisse*" (ran 30 nights at the Th. Feydeau) ; 1798, he pub. sonatas, and a pf.-concerto, etc. ; 1800, prof. of piano, Paris Cons. "*Zoraime et Zulnare*" (1798), "*Beniowski,*" and "*Le Calife de Bagdad*" (1800) were succ. and ended his first period, one of light gracefulness. He now studied cpt. seriously, probably with Cherubini, who had criticised him. After 3 years' silence, he reappeared with enlarged powers, succ. in "*Ma Tante Aurore*" (Th. Feydeau, 1803). In 1802 he m. Clotilde Mafleuroy, a ballet-dancer ; 1803, he went to St. Petersburg, partially perhaps (but not surely) because of domestic unhappiness, and became cond. of the Imperial Opera, writing by contract 3 operas annually, and a number of marches. He returned to Paris, 1811 ; had immense succ., particularly with "*Jean de Paris,*" 1812 ; 1817

prof. of comp. at the Cons. member of Institut ; 1821, Chév of the Legion of Honour ; 1818, *Petit Chaperon rouge*" was succ. lowed, after 7 years' silence, by *Dame Blanche,*" his masterpiece. last opera, "*Les Deux N* (1829), failed. His wife d. 1825, 1827 he m. Mlle. Phillis, a er, who was a devoted wife. poverty of their last years was lieved by Thiers, minister of I Philippe, who made him an an of 6,000 francs. He died at country-home, of pulmonary tro **B.**'s work has great vivacity vitality combined with musical s ness, and rhythm without jingle. large gifts in the construction ensembles are seen in the septet chorus at the end of the 2d ac "*La Dame Blanche,*" which u 1875 had been performed 1340 t at the same theatre ; its libretto combination of 2 of Scott's no "The Monastery" and "Guy M nering." He collaborated with rubini in "*La Prisonnière*" (17 with Méhul, Kreutzer, and otl in "*Le Baiser et la Quittance*" (18 with Cherubini, Catel, and Nic Isouard, in "*Bayard à Mézière* with Kreutzer in "*Henri IV Voyage*" (1814) ; with Mme. in *Angela* (1814) ; with Hérol "*Charles de France*" ; with Ch bini, Berton, and others, in " *Cour des Fées*" (1821) and "*Ph mond*" ; with Auber, in "*Les 7 Genres*" ; with Berton, and otl in "*La Marquise de Brinvillie* Biog. by A. Pougin, 1875. (2) **A en L. V.,** b. Paris, 1816—near P. 1883 ; son and pupil of above ; d composer.

**Boisdeffre** (bwä-dĕfr), **Chas. H. R de,** b. Vesoul (Haute-Savoie), 18 Chev. of Legion of Honour ; c poser of religious and chamber m the latter taking Chartier prize, 18 lives in Paris.

**Boise** (bois), **Otis Bardwell,** b. Obe

ηio, Aug. 13, 1845; organist; 1861
pil of Hauptmann, Richter, Mos-
eles, etc., Leipzig; 1864, of Kullak,
Berlin; 1864–70 organist and
acher in Cleveland; 1870–76, in
ew York; 1876–78, spent in Eu-
pe; for some years prominent in
erlin as a teacher; 1901, settled in
altimore; composed symphonies,
ertures, pf.-concertos, etc., wrote
*Music and Its Masters*" (1902), etc.
sselot (bwäs-lō), (1) **J. Louis,**
ontpellier, 1785—Marseilles, 1847;
ano-maker at Marseilles; his eldest
n, (2) **Louis** (1809—1850), was
e manager. His grandson, (3)
**rançois,** is the present proprietor.
) **Xavier,** Montpellier, 1811—Mar-
illes, 1893; second son of above;
>mposer.

to (bō-ē'-tō), **Arrigo,** b. Padua,
eb. 24, 1842; poet, soldier, novel-
t, editor, essayist, librettist, and
>mposer; son of an Italian painter
nd a Polish woman. Pupil, 1853–
2, of Milan Cons., almost dismissed
»r mus. incompetence (cf. VERDI);
>mposed 2 cantatas, "*Il 4 di Giug-
.o*" (1860), and "*Le Sorelle d'Ita-
a*" (1862), in collab. with Faccio;
ιey met with such great succ. that
ιe Govt. gave F. and **B.** funds for 2
ears in Paris and Germany. **B.** had
lready taken up Goethe's "*Faust,*"
»ng before Gounod, at the suggestion
f his bro. Camillo, an eminent ar-
hitect. **B.** brought back from Ger-
ιany a passion for Beethoven, then
ttle heeded in Italy. 1867 at Paris,
s journalist; then Poland, where he
ketched out text and music of "*Mef-
stofeles,*" which was prod. at Milan,
868 (*La Scala*), after 52 rehearsals,
nd with great hopes; but it was
hen in a rather shapeless state, and
Gounod's "*Faust*" having mean-
vhile been prod. at Milan with succ.,
B.'s work was hissed by some, and
ιaving provoked riots and duels was
.vithdrawn by order of the police. It
.vas remodelled with more attention
to stage requirements and prod. with

great succ. at Bologna, Oct. 4, 1875.
An earlier opera, "*Ero e Leandro,*"
was never prod., **B.** lending his own
libretto to Bottesini, and later to
Mancinelli. Other libretti of his are,
Ponchielli's "*Gioconda,*" Verdi's
"*Otello*" and "*Falstaff,*" Faccio's
"*Amleto*" and Coronaro's "*Un Tra-
monto.*" Two operas diligently pre-
pared but still refused to the public
are "*Nerone*" and "*Orestiade.*" He
has translated 2 of Wagner's libretti
into Italian, and writes often under
the pseud. "**Tobios Gorria.**" The
King made him "Cavaliere," and
"Commendatore"; 1892, Inspector-
Gen. of Technical Instruction in the
Italian Cons. and Lyceums; 1895
Chevalier of the Legion of Honour.
He lives in Milan.

**Bolck** (bôlk), **Oskar,** Hohenstein,
1837—Bremen, 1888; dram. composer.

**Bol'la,** ——, Italian prima buffa soprano; last of 18th century.

**Bolsetti** (bōl-sĕt'-tē), 1789; buffo;
with his wife played principal rôles in
comic operas, London.

**Bolte** (bôl'-tē), **Jns.,** contemporary
German writer.

**Bomtempo** (bōm-tām'-pō), **João Do-
mingos,** Lisbon, 1775—1842; pianist, director and writer.

**Bona** (bō'-nä), **Giov.,** Mondovi, 1609—
Rome, 1674; cardinal and composer.

**Bonawitz** (bō'-nä-vĕts) (or **Bonewitz**),
**Jn. H.,** b. Durkheim-on-Rhine, Dec.
4, 1839; pupil Liège Cons. till 1852,
then brought to America; 1872–73
cond. "Popular Symphony Concerts,"
New York; 1873, toured U. S.; prod. 2
operas in Philadelphia; 1876, ret. to
Europe; lives in Vienna and London.

**Bond, Hugh,** d. England, 1792; organist.

**Bönicke** (bā'-nĭ-kĕ), **Hermann,** Endorf, 1821—Hermannstadt, Transylvania, 1879; conductor, composer
and writer.

**Boniventi** (bō-nĭ-vĕn'-tē) (or **Bone-
venti), Gius,** b. Venice, ca. 1660;
conductor and dram. composer.

**Bonnet** (bŭn-nā), (1) **Jacques**, Paris, 1644—1724 ; writer. (2) **J. Bap.**, b. Montauban, 1763 ; organist and composer.

**Bonuo** (bôn'-nō) (or **Bono**), **Jos.**, Vienna, 1710—1788 ; court-cond. and dram. composer.

**Bonomet'ti, Giov. Bat.**, Italian composer ; pub. motets, Venice, 1615. Vide BUONAMENTE.

**Bononcini** (bō-nôn-chē'-nē), (1) **Giov. M.**, Modena, 1640—Nov. 19, 1678 ; conductor, composer and writer of Bologna. (2) Who usually wrote it **Buononcini** (boo-ō-nôn-chē'-nē), **Giov. Bat.**, Modena, 1660—Venice (?), 1750 (?) ; son and pupil of above ; studied with Colonna and Buoni ('cello), at Bologna ; 1685-91, pub. 7 vols. masses and instr. mus. ; in 1690, court 'cellist of Vienna ; 1694, Rome, prod. 2 operas " *Tullo Ostilio*" and " *Serse* " ; 1699-1701 prod. 2 operas at Vienna ; 1703-5, at Berlin as court-composer ; prod. " *Polifemo*" (1703) ; ret. to Vienna, where 6 new operas were prod. In 1716, invited to London as cond. and composer for the new King's Theatre, and to rival Händel ; this provoked a famous and bitter war with some success for **B.**, who prod. 8 opêras, 1702-27 ; but in 1731 he was caught in a plagiarism from A. Lotti (a crime of which Händel was by no means guiltless himself) ; 1733 an alchemist swindled him from affluence to bankruptcy. Later he appeared in Paris and prod. a motet for the " Chapelle royale," playing the 'cello-accomp. before the King ; 1737 his opera " *Alessandro in Sidone*," and an oratorio, " *Ezechia*," were prod. in Vienna ; 1748, he was called to Vienna to write peace-festival music and later went to Venice as theatre-composer, a post retained at least till he was 90. (3) **Marco An.**, Modena, 1675 (?)— 1726 ; bro. of above ; court-cond. there ; prod. 11 operas highly rated by Padre Martini ; also composed an oratorio

**Bonporti** (bôn-pôr'-tē), **F. A.**, Tr ca. 1660 ; Imperial Counsellor composer.

**Bontempi** (bôn-tĕm'-pē) (surna Angelini), **Giov. Andrea**, Peru ca. 1624—Bruso, near Perugia, 17 dram. composer and writer.

**Bonvin** (bôn-văn), **L.**, b. Siders, Sw erland, Feb. 17, 1850 ; mainly s taught ; studied medicine, Vien entered Jesuit novitiate in Holla became organist and choirmas from 1887, mus. dir. Canisius Colle Buffalo, N. Y.; pub. 3 masses, et

**Boom** (bōm), (1) **Jan. E. G.** (Senior), b. Rotterdam, April 1783 ; flutist and composer for fl (2) **Jan. (Jns.) van**, Utrecht, 180 Stockholm, 1872 ; son of above ; p ist, professor and dram. composer. **Hermann M. van**, Utrecht, 180 1883 ; son and pupil of (1) ; flutist

**Boorn** (bōrn), **Eduard van den**, i —Liège, 1898 ; pianist and critic.

**Boo'sey, Thos.** (1825), founded London pub. house of Boosey & (

**Boott, Francis**, b. Boston, Ma June 21, 1813 ; pupil of L. Picc anti, in Florence ; lived in Ca bridge, Mass.; composed under pse " **Telford.**"

**Bord** (bôr), **Antoine**, Toulouse, 181 Paris, 1888 ; pf. maker and invent

**Bordese** (bôr-dā'-zě), **Luigi**, Nap 1815—Paris, 1886 ; singing teacl and dram. composer.

**Bordier** (bôrd-yā), (1) **L. Chas.**, Pa 1700—1764 ; abbé, conductor, co poser and writer. (2) **Jules**, 1846 —Paris, 1896 ; dram. composer.

**Bordogni** (bôr-dōn'-yē), **Giulio Ma co**, Gazzaniga, Bergamo, 1788 Paris, July 31, 1856 ; distinguish tenor and singing teacher ; pr Paris Cons. ; pub. standard " *Voc ises.*"

**Bordo'ni, Faustina.** Vide HASSE, FA STINA.

**Borghi** (bôr'-gē), **Luigi**, Italian violi ist, came to London, ca. 1780 ; pu symphonies, excellent music for vi etc.

ghi-Mamo (mä'-mō), (1) Adelaide, Bologna, 1829—1901; mezzo-soprano; début, 1846, at Urbino, where she was engaged ; then in Vienna and Paris ; later lived in Florence ; her daughter (2) Erminia, soprano ; début 1875, Bologna; sang in Italy and Paris.

rjon (bôr-zhôn), C. E., 1633—Paris, 691 ; musette-virtuoso and composr.

rodin (bō'-rō-dēn), Alex. Porphyrevitch, St. Petersburg, Nov. 12, 834—Feb. 27 (28 ?), 1887 ; composer f the neo-Russian school ; Prof. at he St. P. medico-surg. Institute ; Counsellor of State ; Knight ; pres. f Mus. Soc. of Amateurs ; at Balakiev's suggestion studied music ; composed opera, "Prince Igor" (finished after his death by Rimsky-Korsakov, and prod. succ. 1891) ; symphonies ; symphonic poem ; cherzo for orch., 2 string-quartets, f. pcs., etc.; biog. by A. Habets, n English, London, 1895.

roni (bō-rō'-nē) (or Buroni), A., Rome, 1738—1797 ; court-conductor.

rtnianski (bôrt-nyän'-shkî) (or Bartñansky), Dimitry Stefanovitch, Gluchov, Ukraine, 1752—St. Petersburg, Sept. 28 (Oct. 9), 1825 ; choir dir. and dram. composer, called "the Russian Palestrina ; " pupil of Galuppi, under patronage of Empress Catherine , 1779—96 dir. of her choir; then of her orchestra.

r'wick, Leonard, b. Walthamstow, Essex, Engl., 1868 ; London pianist ; pupil H. R. Bird, and Clara Schumann, B. Scholtz, and Ivan Knorr at Frankfort Cons.; début, at London Philh. Concert, 1890 ; toured Germany, 1895-96.

os (bōs), Coenraad V., b. Leiden, Dec. 7, 1875 ; studied Amsterdam Cons.; played in Berlin, a member of the " Dutch Trio " with J. M. van Veen and J. van Lier.

oschi (bôs'-kē), (1) Gius, celebrated basso, 18th cent.; his wife was (2) Franceska Vanini, contralto.

Bösendorfer (bā'-zĕn-dôrf-ĕr), firm of Vienna pf.-makers founded by (1) Ignaz B., Vienna, 1795—1859 , later managed by his son (2) Ludwig, b. Vienna, 1835.

Bosio (bō'-zī-ō), Angiolina, Turin, 1830—St. Petersburg, 1859 ; mezzo-soprano.

Bossi (bôs'-sē), (1) Pietro B., Morbegno, 1834—1896 ; organist. (2) Marco Enrico, b. Salo, Brescia, Italy, April 25, 1861 ; son and pupil of above , 1881-91, conductor and organist at Como Cath.; then till 1895, prof. of org. and harm. Naples ; since 1896, dir. and prof. Liceo Benedetto Marcello, Venice ; member of the permanent govt. commission for musical art , Chevalier of the Italian Crown and of the Spanish order of Isabella la Catolica , composed 2 1-act operas, "Paquita" and "Il Veggente"; 4-act melodrama "L'Angelo Della Notte" (Como) ; symph. poem "Il Cieco" (1897), with tenor solo, and chorus ; "Westminster Abbey," Inno di Gloria, for chorus and organ , Requiem Masses, etc.; wrote important "Metodo di Studio per l'Organo moderno," with G. Tebaldini (Milan, 1893).

Bote und Bock (bō'-tĕ oont bôk), firm of mus. pubs., Berlin, est. 1838 by Eduard Bote and Gustav Bock. (2) Hugo Bock, present head.

Bötel (bā'-tĕl), H., b. Hamburg, May, 1858 ; tenor , as cab-driver was "discovered " by Pollini ; now leading lyric tenor, Hamburg City Theatre.

Botgorschek (bôt-gôr'-shĕk), Fz., Vienna, 1812—The Hague, 1882 ; teacher, flutist, and composer.

Bott (bôt), Jean Jos., Cassel, March 9, 1826—New York, April 30, 1895 ; violinist ; son and pupil of a court-musician ; 1852, court-conductor ; 1878 pensioned ; 1885 came to New York ; composed 2 operas, etc.

Bottée, de Toulmon (dŭ toomôn bôt-tā'), Aug., Paris, 1797—1850 ; 'cellist and writer.

**Bottesini** (bôt-tĕ-sē'-nē), **Giov.**, Crema, Lombardy, 1823—Parma, 1889; double-bass virtuoso , conductor and dram. composer.

**Bot'tomley, Jos.**, b. Halifax, Yorkshire, 1786 ; organist, violinist and writer.

**Bottrigari** (bôt-trē-gä'-rē), **Ercole**, Bologna, Aug. 1531—S. Alberto, Sept. 30, 1612 ; wrote 3 learned theoretical treatises, each called by the name of a friend (a) Patrizio (b) Desiderio, and (c) Melone.

**Boucher** (boo-shā), **Alex J.**, Paris, April 11, 1778—Dec. 29, 1861 , vln.-virtuoso ; a charlatan but amazing in technic ; played before the court at 6; composed vln.-concertos ; his wife was a clever harpist, also eccentric, playing duets with one hand on harp and one on a piano.

**Bouichèrt** (bwē-shăr), **Émile**, 1860 (?)—Paris, Sept. 4, 1895 ; pupil of G. Lefèvre's Acad. , est. a vocal acad. 1892 ; composed valuable sacred and chamber music.

**Boulanger** (boc-län-zhā), (1) **Marie Julie** (née **Halliger**), 1786—1850 , dram. singer. (2) **Henri Alex. André Ernest**, b. Paris, Dec. 16, 1815. Son of above. Pupil of Lesueur and Halévy at the Cons., taking Grand Prix de Rome, 1835 ; prof. there 1871. Composed many operettas for Opéra Comique. Legion of Honour, 1868.

**Bourgault-Ducoudray** (boor-gō-dü-koo-drē), **Louis-Aibert**, b. Nantes, Feb. 2, 1840. Pupil of Thomas at Paris Cons., taking Grand Prix de Rome, 1862 , prof. of mus. hist. at the Cons. 1878 ; wounded as volunteer at siege of Paris ; later visited Greece and wrote on Oriental music.

**Bourgeois** (boor'-zhwä), (1) **Loys (Louis)**, Paris. ca. 1510— ? ; disciple of Calvin , 1545-57, Geneva ; one of the first to harmonise the French melodies ; wrote " Le droict chemin de musique," proposing the naming the tones after solmisation-syllables, a system since prevalent in France.

(2) **Louis Thomas**, Fontaine vēque, 1676—Paris, 1750 ; tenor composer ; d. in poverty.

**Bourges** (boorzh), (1) **Clémentine** d. 1561 ; notable woman-composer (2) **J. Maurice**, Bordeaux, 18 Paris, 1881 ; critic and dram. composer.

**Bousqué** (boos-kā), **G.**, Perpign 1818—St. Cloud, 1854 ; conductor the Paris Opéra (1847) ; critic dram. composer.

**Bovéry** (bō-vā-rē), **Jules** (right) **Bovy** (bō'vē), **A. Nic. Jos.**), Liège 808—Paris, 1868 ; self-taught vio ist conductor and dram. composer

**Bovicelli** (bō-vĭ-chĕl'-lē), **Giov. B.** b. Assisi ; writer at Milan, 1594.

**Bovy** (bō'-vē), (1) **Chas. Sml.** (known under pseud **Lysberg**), Lysberg near Geneva, 1821—Geneva, 18 composer. (2) Vide BOVÉRY.

**Bow'ley, R. K.**, London, 1813—18 conductor and composer.

**Bow'man, Ed. Morris**, b. Barnard Vt., July 18, 1848 ; pupil Wm. M son, and J. P. Morgan, at New Yo 1866 ; 1867-70, organist St. Lo Mo. , studied in Berlin and Pa 1873 , 1874, St. Louis , 1881 stud under Bridge, Macfarren, Turpin, Guilmant ; was the first American pass the examination of the Lond R. Coll. for Organists ; 1884, one the founders of Amer. Coll. of M sicians ; organist, Brooklyn, N. Y 1891-95, prof. of music Vassar Col 1895 founded the " Temple Choi Brooklyn (200 voices) , cond. also Newark Harmonic Soc. and the C cilian Choir.

**Boyce** (bois), **Wm.**, London, 1710 Kensington, 1779 ; organist and co poser.

**Boyer** (bwä-yā) (**L. Jos. Victo Georges**, b. Paris, July 21, 185 won Prix Rossini, with libretto " Hérode" (vide CHAUMET), wro libretti for " Le Portrait de Manor (Massenet), etc.

**Brad'bury, Wm. Batchelder**, Yor Me., 1816—Montclair, N. J., 186

eacher, conductor, piano-maker, and
ditor.

.de (brä′-dĕ), **Wm.**, b. England,
ved and died at Frankfort, 1647 ;
layer of the viol., etc.

.dsky (brät′-shkē), **Wenzel Th.**,
.akovnik, Bohemia, 1833 — 1881 ;
ram. composer.

.ga (brä′-gä), **Gaetano**, b. Giulia-
ova, Abruzzi, June 9, 1829 ; 'cellist,
upil of C. Gaetano (1841–52) ; lived
: Florence, Vienna, Paris, and Lon-
on and toured Europe ; dram. com-
oser ; also wrote " *Metodo di Vio-
ncello.*"

.ham (rightly **Abraham**), **J.**, b.
ondon, 1774—Feb. 17, 1856 ; noted
nor ; compass 3 octaves ; composed
op. ballads.

.hmig (brä′-mĭkh), **Julius Bd.**,
irschfeld (Merseburg), 1882—Det-
old, 1872 ; teacher and writer.

.hms (bräms), **Jns.**, Hamburg,
ay 7, 1833—Vienna, April 3, 1897,
on and pupil of a double-bass
ayer in the Hamburg City Theatre,
ter studied with Marxsen of Altona ,
:but Hamburg, at 14, playing his
wn variations on a folk-song ; 1853,
ured with Remenyi. Joachim heard
m and sent him to Schumann, at
üsseldorf. Schumann, with charac-
ristic openness of mind and enthusi-
om, pub. an article in the *Neue
:itschrift für Musik*, greeting **B.** as
e new Messiah of music, a welcome
at was a mixture of blessing and
ine, embarrassing the young **Brahms**
ith a mission that was a white ele-
nant on his hands ; for he forsook
e romanticism which Schumann,
nd later Liszt expected of him, and
ok up a determined classicism in the
atter of form, in which, however,
e made many modifications to suit
s enormous intellectuality and tech-
cal resource. This early welcome
so gave him over to be bandied be-
ween believers like Hanslick who
ere frantic to find an opponent to
.e progress of Wagner, and sceptics
ho would not have him praised for

any quality. Schumann's advocacy did
not save **B.**'s publication and concert
performance of his 3 pf.-sonatas and
3 books of songs from failure. After
serving for a time as cond. to the
Prince of Lippe-Detmold, he retired
for study to Hamburg, 1858–62. 1862
Vienna ; 1863–64 cond. of the *Singakademie* there ; 1864–69 Hamburg,
Zurich, Baden-Baden, etc., and
made tours with Stockhausen ; 1869,
Vienna, which was afterward his
head-quarters. In 1871–74, cond.
" Gesellschaft der Musikfreunde."
In 1877 Cambridge University offered
him the degree of Mus. Doc., which
offer he ignored, accepting, 1881, Dr.
phil. from Breslau and writing in
acknowledgment the " *Akademische
Festouvertüre ;*" 1886, a knight of the
Prussian Ordre pour le Mérite, with
voting privilege, and a member of
the Berlin Acad. of Arts. 1889 presented with the freedom of Hamburg.
His " *German Requiem*," op. 45 (the
first 3 choruses given in Vienna, 1867),
was given complete in the Bremen
cathedral, April, 1868, and established him on a peak where he has
since remained while the storms of
debate rage below him. He wrote in
almost every form but opera (he had
considered that at one time) but admitted he " knew nothing about the
theatre." He valued Wagner's
scores, and owned several Wagner
autographs ; Wagner, however, said
" Brahms is a composer whose importance lies in not wishing to create
any striking effect." His first symphony, on which he had spent 10
years, made a sensation when prod.
1876. His vln.-concerto when first
shown to Joachim was so impossible
to the vln. that J. laughed at it till
tears poured down his cheeks ; he is
said to have materially assisted in its
revision. **Brahms** was a brilliant pianist in his youth ; in his 20th year, at a
concert with Remenyi, the piano was
discovered to be a semitone below
concert-pitch , **B.**, playing without

notes, transposed the accompaniment to Beethoven's "*Kreutzer*" *sonata*, a semitone higher throughout. [Beethoven similarly transposed his own concerto in C to C♯ at a rehearsal.] Biog. by H. Deiters (Leipzig, 1880, Part II., 1898, in Engl., London, 1888); B. Vogel (Leipzig); Widmann (Berlin, 1898); A. Dietrich (Leipzig, 1898).

COMPOSITIONS (exclusive of Songs for one voice with pf.). For orch. Symphonies, Op. 68, in C minor, Op. 73, D, op. 90, F. op. 98. E minor; overtures, op. 80, *Akademische Festovertüre;* op. 81, *Pragische Ouvertüre;* op. 11—16, serenades; op. 56, variations on a theme of Haydn's. CHAMBER MUSIC. Op. 8, trio for pf., vln., 'cello; 18, 36, sextet for strings; 40, trios, pf., vln., horn; 114, pf., clar. and 'cello; 51, two string-quartets; 67, string-quartet; 88, 111, string-quintet; 115, quintet for clar. and strings.

For Piano, op. 1, 2 and 5, sonatas, 4, scherzo; 9, variations on a theme by Schumann; 10, four ballads; 15, 83, concertos; 21, 35, variations; 24, variations and fugue on theme by Händel; op. 76, 8 pcs.; 79, 2 Rhapsodies; 116, Fantasien; 117, 3 Intermezzi; 118, 6 Clavierstücke (3 Intermezzi, Ballades, Romanze); 119, 4 Clavierstücke (3 Intermezzi, Rhapso-

die;—unnumbered—Gluck's gavo and 2 studies). For piano, 4 hands, 23, variations on a theme by S mann; 34, sonata arr. from op. 39, 16 waltzes; op. 25, 26, 60, quartets; 34, pf.-quintet; 87, 101, trios. For piano and 'cello, op. and 99; sonatas; for vln., 77, certo; 78, 100—108, sonatas and vln; for vln. and 'cello, 102, concerto; for clarinet viola) and pf., op. 120, 2 sonatas; organ, Prelude and fugue, and fu (unnumbered). For voices, op. "*Rinaldo*" cantata (Goethe); Rhapsodie (from Goethe's "*H reise*"), for alto solo, male chor. orch., 54, "*Schicksalslied*" (Son, Destiny), for chor. and orch.; "*Triumphlied*" (Revelations, XIX.), for 8-part chor. and orch.; "*Nänie*" (Schiller), for chor. orch.; 89, "*Gesang der Parz* (Goethe), for 6-part chor. and orch op. 12, "*Ave Maria*," female c with orch. (or org.); 13, fun hymn, 109, Deutsche Fest-und denkspruche, for double chorus, numerous works for choruses of sorts accompanied or a capp Brahms' songs are generally mired even by those opposed to h they are very numerous and are p in sets, op. 121 being his last p lished work.

## Johannes Brahms.

### BY JAMES HUNEKER.

SCHUMANN, in his much-discussed article "New Paths," ca Brahms the true successor to Beethoven. His prediction was v fied. To-day Johannes Brahms stands for the ultra-classic in sy phonic music, though singularly enough he is really a hardy romantic who has widened and deepened the symphonic form. The career Brahms compared to Wagner's was a quiet, scholarly, uneventful one. severe student and self-critic, he made his way slowly, for the Wag furor was at hand, and the modest writer or chamber-music, of songs symphonies, was completely eclipsed by the glory of his so-called riva'

Von Bülow's audacious epigram, "The three B's,—Bach, Beethoven, Brahms," that drew down upon the head of the innocent composer the
of the Wagner camp. As a matter of record Brahms never posed as an
onent, much less as a rival of the Bayreuth hero ; indeed he was an ader, and knew his scores as only he could know a score—absolutely.
he was not in the least affected by Wagner—how could he be, working
e did in such a totally different *genre ?* This *genre,* however, was not the
worked vein it was so contemptuously christened by the new men.
-day Brahms is a modern among the moderns—indeed his has also been
ed the music of the future. ¶To old forms like the symphony, to the
ller forms, he has brought an abounding invention, a vitality in execu-
, and a musical intellect the most profound since Beethoven's. To
complex symphonic structure of Beethoven he had superadded a poly-
ny almost Bachian in its mastery of intricate voicing and the weaving of a
vellous contrapuntal web. The dignity of his themes, the depth and
etness of his *cantilena,* the massiveness of his musical architecture—he is
music the born builder—combined with a fecund fantasy, a grim but
tic humour, and no little susceptibility, mark Brahms as one of the elect,
aster among masters. His control of the orchestra is absolute in its elo-
nce, though he is no painter, no seeker after the unique word, the only
ur. ¶He has been reproached for a colour monotone by those critics
o are easily moved by brilliant and showy externals. But that reproach
to earth when the adaptability of the garb to the musical idea is dis-
ered. Brahms never erred in this matter ; his taste was impeccable.
e had a message and he delivered it in tones that befitted its weight, its
ortance. He is a symphonist primarily ; his themes as if carven from
ite are symphonic and not dramatic themes, and in his development of
n he is second only to Beethoven. A philosopher, he views his subject
every possible side, and the result is an edifice of tone comparable to a
hic Cathedral. In his songs he is the sweet-voiced, the tender German
st, deep in feeling, capricious, noble and moving as Schumann or Schu-
. He will rank with these song writers. In chamber-music, in the
able conjunction of piano and strings, trios, quartettes, quintettes, horn-trio
two clarinet-quintettes, Brahms is supreme. He has written a sterling
in-concerto dedicated to Joachim and played first by him. His two piano-
certos in D minor and B flat major, introduced here by Rafael Joseffy,
masterpieces ; though pianists complain of the dearth of display passages,
are sincere in feeling and perfect concertos in the balance of the solo
rument with the orchestra. ¶The Brahms solo piano-music is a new and
ependent literature. He wrote three sonatas ; of these the last is the most
ular ; its andante and scherzo are beautiful specimens of piano-writing.

The solo scherzo in E flat minor, opus 4, was a great favourite with Li
who saw in it trace of Chopin.   The little pieces written during the c
ing years of the composer's life are exquisite and poetic gems, concei
by a poet, executed with all the dainty cunning of a lapidary.   Tl
miniatures are Brahms in his most genial mood.   The forger of thunderb
was now resting and plotting lovely little gardens of fragrant flowers.   ¶
extraordinary technical invention is nowhere better evidenced than in
Paganini variations for the piano, the Ultima Thule of pianists.   Tl
variations are paralleled in his St. Anthony variations for orchestra, a n(
disapproval of the assertion that Brahms had no intimate feeling for
orchestra.   His *German Requiem* written in 1868 is tremendous in
scope and elemental power.   It is the apotheosis of a nation's grief.   ¶
was not uniformly successful—little wonder, for his published works num
130.   But if this Titian stumbled, was intermittent in his inspiration,
main body of his work stands out marmoreal, of overwhelming grand(
truly German, and withal, sounding the big note as no one has sounde(
in music since Beethoven.

**Brah-Müller** (brä-mül'-lĕr) (rightly
 **Müller**), **K. Fr. Gv.**, Kritschen,
 Silesia, 1839—Berlin, 1878; 1867,
 dramatic composer.
**Brambach** (bräm'-bäkh), (1). **Kaspar Jos.**, b. Bonn, July 14, 1833;
 pupil in Comp. of A. zur Nieden,
 then of Cologne Cons.; won Mozart
 scholarship, and studied under Fd.
 Hiller, Frankfort; 1858–61, teacher
 Cologne Cons.; 1861–69, dir. at Bonn,
 where he composed important secular
 cantatas; also an opera "*Ariadne*";
 concert - overture "*Tasso*"; pf.-
 concerto, etc. (2) **Wm.**, b. Bonn,
 Dec. 17, 1841; since 1872, librarian
 Carlsruhe; writer.
**Brambilla** (bräm-bēl'-lä), (1) **Paolo**,
 Milan, 1786—(?); dram. composer.
 (2) **Marietta**, Cassano D'Adda,
 1807—Milan, 1875; singer, teacher,
 and composer; contralto and eldest
 of five singers. (3) **Teresa**, Cassano
 d'Adda, 1813—Milan, 1895; sister of
 above, soprano; she created "Gilda" in "*Rigoletto*," 1851.
**Branca** (brän'-kä), **Guglielmo**, b. Bologna, April 13, 1849; pupil of A.
 Busi, Bologna Cons.; composed succ.

operas "*La Catalana*" (Flore
 1876); "*Hermosa*" (Florence, 18
 and "*La Figlia di Jorio*" (Crem(
 1897).
**Brancaccio** (brän-kät'-chō), **A.**,
 ples, 1813—1846; dram. compos(
**Brandeis** (brän'-dīs), **Fr.**, Viel
 1835—New York, 1899; toured
 U. S., then lived in N. Y., I
 Brooklyn, as organist and pr(
 composer.
**Brandenburg** (brän'-dĕn-boorkh), I
 b. Erfurt—d. Rudolstadt, 18
 violinist and dram. composer.
**Brandes** (brän'-dĕs), **Emma**, b. l
 Schwerin, Jan. 20, 1854; piar
 pupil of Aloys Schmitt and Gol
 mann; m. Prof. Engelmann, Utre(
**Brandl** (bränt'-'l), (1) **Jn.**, Klos
 Rohr, near Ratisbon, 1760—Ca
 ruhe, 1837; dir. and dram. compo(
 (2) **Jn.**, composer of operettas, liv
 in Vienna; has prod. 15 or 20 p
 works since 1869.
**Brandstetter.** Vide GARBRECHT.
**Brandt** (bränt), **Marianne** (rig
 **Marie Bischof**), b. Vienna, Sept.
 1842; dram. contralto; pupil I
 Marschner and of Viardot-Gar(

68–86 at Berlin Ct. Opera; created Kundry " in *Parsifal* at Bayreuth, 82; 1886 sang in New York.

dt-Buys (bränt-bois), (1) Corne-is Alex., b. Zalt-Bommel, April 3, 12; from 1840 lived in Deventer as ganist and cond. His sons are (2) arius Adrianus (b. 1840); (3) L. , (1847), organist and conductor at otterdam : (4) H. (1851), conduc-r at Amsterdam and dram. com-ser.

ndus, Dufour et Cie, Paris firm mus.-pubs. founded 1834, by M. chlesinger, and bought in 1840 by e brothers Louis (d. 1837) and emmy B. (d. 1873).

nt (bränt), Jobst (or Jodocus) m, Junior, 16th cent. captain d gov. of Liebenstein; optist.

ssin (bräs-săn), (1) Louis, Aix--Chapelle, 1840—St. Petersburg, 84; pianist. (2) Ld., Strassburg, 43—Constantinople, 1890; bro. d pupil of above; pianist. (3) erhard, b. Aix-la-Chapelle, June , 1844; leader; teacher at Stern ons., Berlin; 1875–80, cond. of *onkünstlerverein* in Breslau; since en, St. Petersburg.

tsch (brätsh), Jn. G., Zell, 1817— schaffenburg, 1887; director.

uer (brow'-ĕr), Max, b. Mannheim, ay 9, 1855; pupil of V. Lachner, iller, Jensen and De Lange; from 80–88, dir. Kaiserslautern; since 88, dir. court-church at Carlsruhe; od. " *Der Lotse*," succ. 1-act opera, arlsruhe, 1885.

bos, Gilles. Vide GILLES.

e (brä) (Jn. Bernardus), J. Ber-ard van, Amsterdam, 1801—1857; olinist; 1840, founded the " Ce-lia."

idenstein (brī'-dĕn-shtīn), H. K., Steinau, Hesse, 1796—Bonn, 876; dir., composer and writer.

eitkopf und Härtel (brīt'-kôpf ont hĕrt'-l), mus.-publishers, found-d (as a printing-office) 1719 by B. . Breitkopf; Klausthal, Harz, 695—1777. His son, J. G. Im-

n a nuel Breitkopf (1719—1794), suc-ceeded and revived Petrucci's inven-tion of movable types and took up music printing. 1795, Gottfr. Chr. Härtel (Schneeberg, 1763—1827), added a piano-factory, founded the "Allg. musikalische Zeitung " (1798); later heads were Florenz Härtel (1827–35), Dr. Hermann Härtel (d. 1882), and his bro. Reimund (d. 1888); two nephews, Wm. Volkmann (1837 — 1893 ?) and Dr. Oskar von Hase (b. 1846).

Breitner (brīt'-nĕr), Ludovic, b Triest, March 22, 1855; pianist and composer; studied Milan Cons., and with Rubinstein and Liszt; toured, Germany; Chev. of the Legion of Honour, officer of Public Instruction, etc., composed music to " *Wilhelm Meister*," song cycles, etc.

Brema (brā'-mä), Marie, b. of German parents, in England; notable dra-matic soprano in pop. concerts Lon-don; début in opera, Shaftesbury Theatre, 1891; sang in New York in frequent seasons; 1897 at Bay-reuth.

Brem'ner, Robt., Scotland, 1720— Kensington, 1789; teacher.

Brendel (brĕnt'-'l), K. Fz., Stolberg, 1811—Leipzig, 1868; critic, prof. and writer.

Brenet (brŭ-nā), Michel, b. France, 1882; wrote " *Histoire de la sym-phonie à orchestre depuis ses orig-ines*" (prize-essay), etc.

Brenner (brĕn'-nĕr), L., Ritter von, Leipzig, 1833—1902; pupil of the Cons.; toured the Continent; 15 years member of the Imp. orch.; 1872–76, cond. Berlin Symphony Orch.; 1897, cond. Meyder's Concert Orch., Bres-lau; composed 4 grand masses; sym-phonic poems.

Brent, Charlotte, d. 1802, Engl.; soprano; m. Pinto, a violinist, 1766.

Breslaur (bräs'-lowr), Emil, b. Kott-bus, May 20, 1836; pupil Stern Cons., Berlin; 1868–79, teacher Kul-lak's Acad.; since 1883 choirm., Re-formed Synagogue; founder and dir.

Piano - Teachers' Seminary ; ed. "*Klavierlehrer*" ; wrote technical works, etc.

**Brethol.** Vide PIERSON-BRETHOL.

**Breuer** (broi'-ĕr), **Hans,** b. Cologne, 1869 ; tenor ; studied at the Cons. at Stolzenberg. Sang "Mime" and "David" at Bayreuth.

**Breüning** (broi'-nĭng), **Fd.,** Brotterode, Thuringia, 1830 — Aix-la-Chapelle, 1883 ; pf. prof., Cologne Cons. ; 1865, director.

**Bréval** (brā-văl), (1) **J. Bap.,** Dept. of l'Aisne, France, 1765—Chamouille, 1825 ; 'cellist and teacher. (2) **Lucienne,** b. France, 1870 (?) ; notable dramatic soprano at Grand Opéra, Paris, for years ; début there in *L'Africaine,* 1892, created *Brünnhilde* in French, has sung at Covent Garden, and 1900 in New York.

**Brew'er,** (1) **Thos.,** 1609—1676 ; viol.-player, "father of the glee." (2) **J. Hyatt,** b. Brooklyn, N. Y., 1856 ; for 7 years boy-soprano ; studied with Dudley Buck and others ; since 1871 organist various churches, since 1881 at the Lafayette Av. Presby. Ch. ; cond. various vocal societies ; composed cantatas, etc.

**Briccialdi** (brēt-chäl'-dē), **Giulio,** Terni, Papal States, 1818—Florence, 1881 ; flutist.

**Bridge,** (1) Sir **J. Fr.,** b. Oldbury, Worcestershire, Engl., Dec. 5, 1844 ; son and pupil of **J. Bridge,** lay-clerk ; pupil later of J. Hopkins and Sir J. Goss ; organist 1869 Manchester cathedral ; 1882 of Westminster Abbey ; 1868 Mus. Bac. (Oxford), with the oratorio "*Mount Moriah*" ; now prof. of harm. and cpt. R. A. M.; cond. Western and the Madrigal Societies ; 1897, knighted ; composed cantatas, overtures, etc. (2) **Jos. Cox,** b. Rochester, Engl., 1853 ; pupil and bro. of above ; since 1877 organist of Chester cathedral ; Mus. Bac. Oxon., 1876 ; Mus. Doc., 1884 ; composed oratorios, etc.

**Bridge'tower, G. A. P.,** Poland, 1779 —ca. 1845 ; son of an African father and European mother ; brilliant linist.

**Briegel** (brē'-gĕl), **Wg. K.,** many, 1626—Darmstadt, 1712 ; ductor and composer.

**Brighenti** (or **Brighetti**) (brē-gĕt' **Mana** (née **Giorgi**), b. Bolo 1792 ; soprano ; created "Ros in "*Barbiere di Siviglia.*"

**Brind, Richard,** d. 1718 ; organist Paul's Cathedral from 1707.

**Brink, Jules Ten** (tän brĕnk), sterdam, 1838—Paris, 1889 ; dire and dram. composer.

**Brins'mead,** (1) **J.,** b. North Dev Oct. 13, 1814 ; 1835, founded pi factory, London ; inv. "Per Check Repeater Action", in his sons (2) **Thomas** and (3) **Ed** were taken in partnership.

**Brissler** (brĕs'-lĕr), **Fr. Fd.,** Ins burg, 1818—Berlin, 1893 ; pia and dram. composer.

**Brisson** (brĭs'-sòn), **Fr.,** b. Ang lême, Charente, 1821—Orléans, 1ç teacher and dram. composer.

**Bris'tow,** (1) **W. R.,** England, —N. Y., 1867 ; cond. in New Y (2) **G. Fr.,** Brooklyn, N. Y., 19, 1825—New York, Dec. 13, 18 son of above ; violinist N. Y. Ph Soc.; cond. of the Harmonic S later of the Mendelssohn Union ; ganist various churches ; compo operas, oratorios, etc.

**Brito** (brē'-tō), **Estéban de,** ca. 16 Portuguese director and composer.

**Brit'ton, Thos.,** 1651—1714 ; ca "Musical Small-coal Man," beca he earned his living by hawking co gave concerts in a room over his sh which were patronised by the arist racy ; Händel and Pepusch were p formers at these concerts.

**Brixi** (brĕx'-ē), **Fz. Xaver,** Prag 1732—1771 ; conductor and cc poser.

**Broad'wood & Sons,** firm of Lon pf.-makers ; est. 173ᶜ by the Sʋ harpsichord-maker **Burkhard Tscl** **di** (or **Shudi**), succeeded by his s in-law **J. Broadwood** (1732—18

ter by **James** and **Thos. Shudi**;
ney by **H. Fowler Broadwood** (d.
London, 1893).

ck'way, **Howard A.**, b. Brooklyn,
N. Y., Nov. 22, 1870; studied pf.
with Kortheuer; 1890–95, Berlin;
upil of Barth (pf.) and O. B. Boise
comp.); since 1895, l. N. Y. teaching and touring; his symphony in D
ucc., prod. Berlin; composed also
antata, Ballade and Scherzo for
rch., etc.

od (brō), **H.**, Paris, 1801—1839;
boist and conductor.

de (brō'-dĕ), **Max**, b. Berlin, Feb.
7, 1850; studied with Paul Mendels-
ohn and at Stern Cons., Leipzig
Cons. and Berlin Hochschule; dé-
ut Frankfort-on-Main; prof. and
eacher at Königsberg.

o'derip, (1) **Wm.**, England, 1683—
726; organist, etc., Wells Cathe-
ral. (2) **J.**, d. 1770; son of above
rganist; (3) **Robt.**, d. 1808; bro. of
bove; writer and composer.

odsky (brōd-shkĭ), **Adolf**, b. Ta-
anrog, Russia, March 21, 1851; vio-
inist; pupil of J. Hellmesberger and
Vienna Cons.; member Hellmes-
erger Quartet; 1868–70 Imp. Opera-
rch.; pupil of Laub, Moscow, later
rof. at the Cons.; 1879, cond. sym-
hony concerts at Kiev; toured, 1881;
883, vln.-prof. at Leipzig Cons.;
891–94, N. Y.; 1894 in Berlin;
895, prof. of vln., later dir. R. C.
M., Manchester, England.

oekhoven (brāk'-hō-fĕn), **J. A.**, b.
Holland, 1852; prof. of harm. and
omp. Cincinnati Coll. of Mus.; com-
osed grand overture "*Columbia*," etc.

ör (brār), **Ernst**, Silesia, 1809—
Tarnopol, 1886; 'cellist, organist, and
inging teacher.

onsart (brôn'-zärt), (1) **von Schel-**
**endorf, Hans** (**Hans von Bron-**
**sart**), b. Berlin, 1830; pupil, Dehn,
Kullak, Liszt; concerts in Paris;
1867, intendant R. Th. at Hanover;
1887 "Hofmusikintendant," Berlin;
composed opera, cantata, symphony
"*In den Alpen*," etc. (2) **Ingeborg,**

**von** (née **Starck**), b. St. Petersburg,
1840; wife (since 1862) of above;
pupil of Liszt; composed 3 operas,
etc.

**Brooks, Walter M.**, b. Birmingham,
March 19, 1861; pupil of King Edw.
School, later of Prout; lives in Lon-
don as writer and teacher; composed
Allegro for orch. (prize at Belfast,
1891), etc.

**Bros** (brōs), **Juan**, Tortosa, Spain,
1776—Oviedo, March 12, 1852; conductor; composed important masses.
etc.

**Brosig** (brō'-zĭkh), **Moritz**, Fuchs-
winkel, Upper Silesia, 1815—Breslau, 1887; organist and theorist.

**Brossard** (dŭ brôs-săr), (1) **Sébastien**
**de**, 1660—Meux, France, 1730; conductor, lexicographer, and composer.
(2) **Noël Matthieu**, Châlon-sur-
Saône, Dec. 25, 1789—after 1853;
magistrate and theorist.

**Brouck** (brook), **Jakob de** (or **de**
**Prugg**), collector, Antwerp, 1579.

**Broustet** (broo-stā), **Ed.**, b. Toulouse,
April 29, 1836; pupil of Stamaty,
Litolff and Ravina; pianist and com-
poser; toured Russia, etc., lives in
Toulouse.

**Brown**, (1) **Dr. J.**, Northumberland,
1715—1766; writer. (2) **Obadiah**
**Bruen**, b. Washington, D. C., July
2, 1829; pupil of Zerrahn, Parker,
Kreissmann, Hause and D. Paine,
and of Lobe and Plaidy, Leipzig,
1869; teacher and organist; pub.
school-songs, etc.

**Browne, Lennox**, Dr., b. London,
1841; prominent throat-specialist and
writer on the voice, lives in London.

**Brown'smith, J. Leman**, Westminster, 1809—1866; organist.

**Brozel', Philip**, b. in Russia; tenor;
studied at R. A. M., London; début
1896 at Covent Garden in *I Pagliac-*
*ci;* 1901 in New York.

**Bruch** (brookh), **Max**, b. Cologne,
Jan. 6, 1838; Jewish pianist and
composer; at first, pupil of his mother (née Almenrader), a singer; later
with Breidenstein, Bonn.; 1853 he

gained the four-year scholarship of
the Mozart Foundation at Frankfort,
and studied with Hiller, Reinecke,
and Breuning; at 14, prod. a symphony, Cologne; 1858, his first dram.
work, Goethe's *Singspiel*, "*Scherz
List und Rache*" (op. 1); 1864, prod.
opera "*Loreley*," etc.; male chorus
"*Frithjof*"; 1865–67, at Coblenz,
composed his first pop. vln.-concerto
(G minor); 1867–70, court-cond. at
Sondershausen; in 1878 cond. Stern
Choral Union, Berlin; in 1880,
cond. Liverpool Philh. Soc.; 1883,
dir. Breslau Orchestral Soc.; 1881,
m. Frl. Tuczek, of Berlin, a
singer; lived in Breslau till 1890;
1892, with K. Hochschule in Berlin,
prod. 1872, opera "*Hermione*," based
on "*Winter's Tale*"; 1873–78,
prod. the chorals "*Arminius*" and
"*Lied von der Glocke*," and the 2d
vln.-concerto; 1883, came to U. S.
and prod. his "*Arminius*," Boston.
The epic cantata is his special field;
among his works of this sort, are
"*Odysseus, Arminius, Lied von der
Glocke*, and *Achilleus*"; for male
chorus, "*Frithjof, Salamis, Nor-
mannenzug* and *Leonidas*" (op.
66). He arranged the old Hebrew
melody *Kol Nidre*, and composed
a cantata "*Das Feuerkreuz*" (op.
52, 1888); three symphonies; oratorio, "*Moses*" (1895); 3 vln.-
concertos.

**Bruck** (brook) (or **Brouck**), **Arnold
von** (a German Swiss (?)), d. 1545;
conductor and composer.

**Brückler** (brük'-lĕr), **Hugo,** Dresden,
1845—1871; composer.

**Bruckner** (brook'-nĕr), **Anton,** Aus-
felden, Upper Austria, Sept. 4, 1824
—Vienna, Oct. 11, 1896; mainly self-
taught as organist; 1867, court-organist at Vienna; prof. of org., harm.
and cpt. at Vienna Cons.; 1875,
"Lektor" of music at Vienna Univ.;
1891, Dr. hon. causa; one of the
chief contemporary organ-virtuosi, and
a disciple of Wagner; he composed
9 symphonies, the 4th called "*Ro-

*mantic.*" Biog. by Fz. Brur
(Linz-on-Danube, 1895).

**Brückner** (brük'-nĕr), **Oscar,** b.
furt, Jan. 2, 1857; 'cellist; pupi
Grützmacher and Draeseke; tou
Germany, Russia, etc.; Ducal chä
ber-virtuoso at Strelitz; since 1
teacher in the Wiesbaden Cons., a
composer.

**Bruhns** (broons), **Nikolaus,** Schw
stadt, Schleswig, 1665—Husi
1697; organist and violinist.

**Brüll** (brĭl), **Ignaz,** b. Moravia, Nov
1846; pianist; pupil of Epstein, I
finatscha and Dessoff; 1872–78, I
prof. Horak Institute, Vienna;
first opera "*Die Bettler von Sc
markand*" (1864) was not succ., l
"*Das Goldene Kreuz*" (Berli
1875) was very pop.; followed b
other operas and the succ. co
opera "*Der Husar*" (Vienna, Ma
2, 1898); composed also hunti
overture "*Im Walde*," etc.

**Brumel** (broo'-mĕl), **Anton,** ca. 1480
ca. 1520; Flemish cptist.

**Bruneau** (brü-nō) (**Louis Cha
Bonaventure), Alfred,** b. Par
March 3, 1857; pupil of Franchom
at the Cons.; took first 'cello pri
1876; studied with Savart and M.
senet; 1881, took first prize with ca
tata "*Sainte Geneviève*"; compos
operas "*Kerim*" (Opéra-Populai
1887), "*Le Rêve*" (Paris, 1892), a
the very succ. drame lyrique "*L'A
taque du Moulin*" (Opéra-Comiq
Paris, 1893); unsucc. drame lyriq
"*Messidor*" (Paris, Gr. Opera, Fe
19, 1897); the last three are on te
from Zola, some of the music bei
set to plain prose, as also in the son
set to Catulle Mendès' "*Lieds
prose*"; 1893–95, critic of "(
*Blas*," 1895 of "*Le Figaro*," Che
of Legion of Honour; composed al
Heroic overture; légende "*Pe
thésilée, Reine des Amazones*
etc.

**Brunelli** (broo-nĕl'-lē), **A.,** 17th cen
conductor to Duke of Florenc
writer and composer.

netti (broo-nĕt'-tē), **Gaetano**, Pisa,
53—Madrid, 1808 ; composer.

ai (broo'-nē), **A. Bart.**, Coni, Pied-
ont, 1759—1823 ; violinist, cond.
d dram. composer.

ner (broon'-nĕr), **Chr. Trau-
ott**, Brünlos, 1792—Chemnitz,
74 ; organist and conductor.

yck (broik), **K. Bebroid van**, b.
ünn, March 14, 1828 ; studied law,
enna, 1850 ; and theory with Rufi-
tscha ; writer on Bach, etc.

cison **Bros.**, London ; organ-
ilders.

en'nius, **Manuel**, lived ca. 1320 ;
st Greek theorist.

ne, **Albertus**, ca. 1621—after 1677;
ganist St. Paul's and Westminster
obey, London.

hholz (bookh'-hôlts), (1) **Jn. Si-
eon**, Schlosswippach, 1758—Berlin,
25 , founded firm of organ-builders ;
cceeded by his son (2) **K. Aug.**
796—1884), whose on (3) **K. Fr.**,
Feb. 17, 1885.

hner (bükh'-nĕr), **Emil**, b. Oster-
ld, near Naumburg, Dec. 25, 1826 ;
pil of Leipzig Cons., 1865, court-
nductor ; composed 2 operas, etc.

k, (1) **Zechariah**, Norwich, Eng-
nd, 1798—Newport, Essex, 1879 ;
ganist Norwich Cathedral ; teacher
d composer. (2) **Dudley**, b. Hart-
rd, Conn., March 10, 1839 ; pupil
. J. Babcock (pf.), then of Plaidy
d Moscheles (pf.) ; Hauptmann
omp.) and J. Reitz (instrumenta-
on), Leipzig Cons. ; later Dresden,
der Reitz and Johann Schneider
rgan); and 1861–62 in Paris ; 1862,
ganist of the Park Ch. , Hartford,
. S. A. ; St. James, Chicago, 1872,
. Paul's and of the Music Hall As-
ciation, Boston ; 1875, organist
ncinnati May Festival ; then, asst.
nd. to Th. Thomas, New York ,
ce organist of Holy Trinity Ch.,
ooklyn ; director Apollo Club ;
mposed comic opera "*Deseret*"
rod. 1880) , symphonic overture
*Marmion*" (1880), many cantatas ,
e 5th Psalm ; "*The Christian*

*Year*," a series of 5 cantatas ; wrote
2 books of Pedal-phrasing Studies,
and "*Illustrations on Choir-accompa-
niment, with Hints on Registration*";
pub. "*The Organist's Repertoire*"
(with A. P. Warren) ; "*The Influence of the Organ in History*" (1882) ,
and a "*Dictionary of Musical
Terms*."

**Bühler** (bü'-lĕr), **Fz. P. Gregorius**,
Schneidheim, 1760—Augsburg, 1824 ;
Benedictine monk, 1794 ; conducto
at Botzen ; dram. composer and theorist.

**Bull, John, Dr.**, Somersetshire, England, 1563—Antwerp, March 12,
1628 ; 1582, organist ; 1592, Mus
Doc. Oxon.; 1596, Prof. of music at
Gresham Coll. on Queen Elizabeth's
recommendation ; resigned on his
marriage, 1607 ; 1617, organist Nôtre
Dame, Antwerp ; an early English
composer whom Oscar Bie credits
with remarkable originality in the
midst of over-ornamentation.

**Bull** (bool), **Ole (Bornemann)**, Bergen, Norway, Feb. 5, 1810—Lysoen,
Aug. 17, 1880 ; enormously popular
and brilliant violin-virtuoso, a whit
charlatanic ; pupil of Paulsen ; then
self-taught, using a bridge almost
level and a flat fingerboard ; studied
theology, but failed in examinations ;
1828, dir. Philh. and Dram. Soc.,
Bergen ; 1829, studied with Spohr
briefly ; 1832, début, Paris, after living there a year observing Paganini's
methods ; toured Europe frequently,
and North America 5 times (1843–
79): he died at his country-seat. He
played his own comps. almost altogether ; wrote 2 concertos, and characteristic solos ; biog. by Sara C. Bull,
his second wife, Boston, 1883, and by
Vlik (Bergen, 1890).

**Bul'lard, Fred. F.**, b. Boston, Mass
Sept. 21, 1864  1888–92, studied
comp. under Rheinberger, Munich ;
teacher of comp., critic and composer,
Boston ; has pub. many successful bal
lads and four-part songs for male
voices, also sacred music.

**Bülow** (fōn bü'-lō), **Hans Guido von,**
Dresden, Jan. 8, 1830—Cairo, Egypt,
Feb. 12, 1894; versatile and influential musician; pianist and conductor
of remarkable accuracy and memory,
popularising the custom of conducting
without score; often called the best
interpreter of Beethoven, but rather
cold as a pianist; at 9, studied pf.
with Fr. Wieck; harmony with Ebe-
wein; 1848, entered Leipzig Univ.
as law-student, but studied cpt. with
Hauptmann; 1849, Wagner's "*Die
Kunst und die Revolution*" stirred
him deeply, and having heard
"*Lohengrin*" at Weimar under
Liszt's direction, he joined Wagner,
then exiled at Zurich, 1850–51; studied conducting with him, and acted as
cond. in theatres at Zurich and St.
Gallen, and later with Liszt; 1853
and 1855 toured Germany and Austria, with success; 1855–64, first pf.-
teacher Stern Cons., Berlin. 1857,
m. Cosima, Liszt's natural daughter,
whom he later surrendered to his
friend Wagner (q. v.); 1858, court-
pianist; 1863, Dr. Phil. *hon. causa*,
Univ. of Jena; 1864, court-pianist,
Munich; 1867–69, court-conductor
and dir. School of Music; 1869–72,
teacher and pianist in Florence;
1875–76, gave 139 concerts in America; 1878–80, court-conductor at
Hanover; then till 1885, Hofmusikintendant, Saxe-Meiningen; 1882,
m. Marie Schanzer; 1885–88, teacher Raff Cons., Frankfort, Klindworth
Cons., Berlin, and dir. Berlin Philh.
Concerts; in 1888, founded the succ.
"Subscription Concerts." Composed
music to "*Julius Cæsar*" (op. 10); a
Ballade for orch., "*Des Sängers
Fluch*" (op. 16); "*Nirwana*," a
symphonic Stimmungsbild (op. 20);
4 Charakterstücke for orch. (op. 23);
a few pf.-pcs. and songs; also many
piano arrangements. His critical ed.
of Beethoven's sonatas, and Cramer's
études, are standard; biog. by his
2d wife (Leipzig, 1895).

**Bulss** (bools), **Paul,** Birkholz Man-

or, Priegnitz, Dec. 19, 1847—Te
var, Hungary, March 20, 1902;
of G. Engel; barytone at Dre
(1876–89), later at Berlin court o

**Bulthaupt** (boolt'-howpt), **H.**
Bremen, Oct. 26, 1849; wrote a
able "*Dramaturgie der Oper*" (
zig, 1887).

**Bungert** (boong'-ĕrt), **August**
Mühlheim-on-Ruhr, March 14, 1
pupil of Kufferath (pf.), later at
logne Cons.; for 4 years at
Cons.; then (1869) with Matt
lived (1873–81) at Berlin, and
ied cpt. with Kiel; since lives
Genoa. His life-work has
"*Das Homerische Welt*," in 2
meric opera-cycles, occupyin
"evenings" (*Abende*), each wi
"Vorspiel;" The Iliad ("*Die Il
is unfinished: (a) *Achilles*; (b)
*temnestra*. The Odyssey ('
*Odyssee*") consists of "*Circe*;
*sikaa*; *Odysseus' Heimkehr* (Be
March 31, 1898; succ.), and *
seus' Tod* (Dresden, 1902). *
comp. are (comic opera) "*Die
denten von Salamanca*" (Lei
1884); symph. poem, "*Auf der V
burg*"; "*Hohes Lied der L
with orch.; overture, "*Tasso*,"
quartet, op. 18; Florentine qu
(prize, 1878); "*Italienishe F
bilder*," etc., for pf.; songs to
men Sylva's "*Lieder einer Köni*
etc.

**Bunnett, Edw.,** b. Norfolk, Engl
1834; articled to Dr. Buck, 1849
ganist various churches, Mus.
Oxon, 1869; 1871–92, cond.
wich Mus. Union; since 1872 o
ist of the Norwich Festivals;
posed cantata, etc.

**Bunning, Herbert,** b. London,
2, 1863; pupil of V. Ferroni
Italian scena, "*Ludovico il M
(prod. with succ., 1892), also 2
phonic poems, opera "*The
Days of Pompeii*" (MS.), etc.

**Bunting, Edw.,** Armagh, Feb.,
—Belfast, 1843; historian and
lector of Irish music.

amente (boo-ō-nä-měn´-tě), **Giov.
t.**, cond. Franciscan monastery at
.isi ; early and important composer
violin, also cornetti (1623-36) ;
.fused by Fétis with Bonometti.

.amici (boo-ō-nä-mē´-chē), **Giu.**,
.lorence, 1846 ; pianist ; pupil of
uncle Ceccherini, and of Bülow
.l Rheinberger at Munich ; 1873,
.d. Florentine Choral Society
.herubini" ; founded the Flor.
.rio Society" ; pub. études, etc.

.ONCINI. Vide BONONCINI.

.ure de Wesembeck (bür-bür dŭ
.zän-běk), **Léon Ph. M.**, Chevalier
. Termonde, 1812—Antwerp, 1889 ;
.mish nobleman ; writer and com-
.ser.

.e-Ney (bür´-dě-nī´), **Jenny**,
.az, 1826—Dresden, 1886 ; sono ; 1855, m. the actor E.
.rde.

.tte (bü-rět), **P. J.**, Paris, 1665—
.7 ; Prof. of Medicine, Paris Univ.;
.ter on Greek music.

.el (bür´-gěl), **Konstantin**, b.
.esia, June 24, 1837 ; pupil of Bro-
.and Kiel ; 1869-70 pf. teacher in
.llak's Acad., now private teacher ;
.mposer.

.er (bür´-gěr), **Sigmund**, b. Vien-
1856 ; pupil of Popper ; 'cel-
. since 1887 soloist at R. Opera,
.sth, and teacher in the Cons.

.rk (boorkh´), **Joachim Moller (or
üller)**, called **Joachim A. Burgk
Burg**, or **Burck**), Burg, near
.gdeburg ; ca. 1541—Mülhausen,
.uringia, May 24, 1610 ; organist
.l eminent composer of Protestant
.sic.

.rmein, **J.**, pen-name of " Giulio
.ordi."

.rmüller (boorkh´-mül-lěr), (1) **Jn.
. Fz.**, Ratisbon, 1806—Beaulieu,
.74 ; composer. (2) **Norbert**, Düs-
dorf, 1810—Aix-la-Chapelle, 1836 ;
.nist and composer.

.gstaller (boorkh´-shtäl-lěr), **Alois**,
Holzki:chen, Sept. 27, 1871 ;
.or ; studied with Bellurth and
.iese ; sang small rôles at Bayreuth

from 1894, " Siegfried " (1897) ;
" Siegmund " (1899).

**Burke, Jos.**, Ireland, 1818—New
York, Jan. 19, 1902 ; came to America at 12 as prodigy violinist ; pupil
of de Bériot ; retired about 1855.

**Burkhard** (boorkh´-härt), **Jn. Andreas
Chrn.**, Pastor, Leipheim, Swabia ;
theorist and editor.

**Burmeister** (boor´-mī-shtěr), (1) **Richard**, b. Hamburg, Dec. 7, 1860; pianist ; pupil of Liszt, accompanying him
as he travelled ; teacher Hamburg
Cons.; for 12 years head of pf. dept.,
Peabody Inst., Baltimore ; 1898, dir.
N. Y. Scharwenka Cons.; c. pf.-con-
certo (op. 1), " *The Chase after Fortune* " (" *Die Jagd nach dem Glück* "),
a symphonic fantasy in 3 movements ;
rescored Chopin's F minor concerto,
and wrote orch. accomp. for Liszt's
" *Pathetic* " concerto. (2) **Dory**
(née **Peterson**), b. Oldenburg, 1860 ;
pianist ; wife of above.

**Burmester** (boor´-mä-shtěr), **Willy**, b.
Hamburg, 1869 ; violin-virtuoso ;
studied with his father and Joachim ;
toured with his sister, a concert-pianist. Von Bülow aided him and brought
public attention to his abilities ; has
toured Europe, and 1899, America.

**Bur´ney, Chas.**, Shrewsbury, England, 1726—Chelsea, 1814 ; toured
Europe ; Mus. Doc. Oxon, 1769 ;
pub. very interesting and gossipy
" *The Present State of Music in
France and Italy*," etc. (1771) ;
" do. *in Germany, the Netherlands*,"
etc. (1773) ; " *General History of
Music* " (4 vols., 1776-89), etc.

**Burr, Willard**, b. Ohio, Jan. 17, 1852 ;
graduated Oberlin Cons. ; pupil of
Haupt, Berlin ; lives in Boston, Mass.;
composed grand sonata for pf. and
vln., etc.

**Bur´rowes, J. Freckleton**, London,
1787—1852 ; organist, pianist and
writer.

**Bur´ton**, (1) **Avery**, composer in reign
of Henry VIII. (2) **J. Yorkshire**,
1730—1785 ; harpsichord. (3) **Frederick R.**, graduated at Harvard ; ι

Yonkers, N. Y.; founded there, 1896, a choral society ; c. pop. cantata "Hiawatha," etc.

**Bur'tius** (or **Burci** (boor'-chē)) or **Burzio** (boor'-tsĭ-ō), **Nicolaus,** Parma, 1450—ca. 1520; wrote the earliest specimen of printed mensural music.

**Bus'by, Thos.,** Westminster, England, 1755—London, 1838 ; Mus. Doc. ; composer and writer.

**Busi** (boo'-zē), (1) **Giu.,** Bologna, 1808 —1871 ; Prof. (2) **Alessandro,** Bologna, 1833—1895 ; son of above ; 'cellist and conductor.

**Busnois** (bün-wä), **A.** (rightly **de Busne** (dŭ bün)), d. 1481 ; Netherland contrapuntist.

**Busoni** (boo-sō'-nē), **Ferruccio Benvenuto,** b. Empoli, near Florence, April 1, 1866 ; pianist ; pupil of his father (**Fdo.**), clarinettist, and his mother (*née* **Weiss**), a pianist ; at 8, début at Vienna ; then studied with W. A. Remy ; 1881, toured Italy ; at 15, elected a member of the Reale Accademia Filarmonica, Bologna ; 1886, Leipzig, where he c. a fantastic opera, a string-quartet (D min.), symphonic suite, etc. ; 1888–89, Prof. Helsingfors Cons.; 1890, won Rubinstein prizes for comp. and pf.-playing, with a *Concertstück* for pf. and orch., op. 31a ; sonata for pf. and vln.; pf. arr. of Bach's E♭ *Organ Prelude,* and *Fugue ;* and other pf. pcs. incl. 2 Cadenzas to Beethoven's *Concerto in G ;* 1890, Prof. in the Moscow Imp. Cons.; 1891–93 at New England Cons., Boston, U. S. A.; 1895, toured ; now lives in Berlin ; edited Bach's "*Well-tempered Clavichord*" with études ; other comps., "*Lustspiel Ouvertüre*"; 4 choruses with orch. ; 2 suites for orch. ; a "*Symphonisches Tongedicht*" for orch., etc.

**Büsser** (büs-sä), **H. Paul,** b. Toulouse, 1872 ; pupil of Guira..d and Gounod ; took first Grand Prix de Rome, with cantata "*Antigone*"; since 1892, organist at St. Cloud ; c. succ. 1-act pastorale "*Daphnis et*

*Chloe*" (Paris, Op. Com.), 1897 ; tata "*Amadis de Gaule*," 1892 ing 2d Grand Prix de Rome); or tral suite "*A la Villa Medicis* lyric drama "*Colomba*," and o "*Le Miracle des Perles.*"

**Busshop** (büs-shôp), **Aug. G** Paris, 1810—Bruges, 1896 ; taught ; c. prize-cantata, "*Le* peau Belge," 1834, etc.

**Bussler** (boos'-lĕr), **L.,** Berlin, 26, 1838—Jan. 18, 1900 ; theo son of the painter-author, Ro Bussler ; pupil of von Hertzb Dehn, Grell, and Wieprecht ; i teacher of theory, Ganz Schoo Music ; from 1879, at the Stern Co Berlin ; critic and writer of var treatises.

**Bussmeyer** (boos'-mī-ĕr), (1) **Hug** Brunswick, 1842 ; pianist ; pupi K. Richter, Litolff (pf.), and M fessel (comp.) ; 1860, toured in S America ; 1860, N. Y. ; comp and writer. (2) **Hans,** b. Brunsw 1853 ; bro. of above ; pianist ; p of Royal School of Music at Mur and teacher there since 1874 ; studied with Liszt ; toured S. A ica, 1872–74 ; 1879, founded Mu Choral Society.

**Bustini** (boos-tē'-nē), **Aless. ;** yo Italian composer, prod. succ. o "*Maria Dulcis*," Rome, 1902 ; bretto by Luigi Ilica.

**Buths** (boots), **Julius,** b. Wiesba May 7, 1851 ; pianist ; pupil of father (an oboist), also of Gernsh Hiller and Kiel ; 1871–72, cond. "Cecilia," at Wiesbaden ; 1873, Meyerbeer Scholarship, and live Milan and Paris ; 1875–79, cond Breslau ; in Elberfeld, 1879–90; s cond. Mus. Soc. at Elberfeld ; concerto, etc., for pf.

**Butt, Clara,** Eng. contralto ; wo scholarship at London R. C. M.; but, London, 1892 ; toured Amer 1899 ; m. Kennerly Rumford, b tone, 1900. Her great success been emphasised by her impos beauty (she is 6 ft. 2¼ inches tall).

tstedt (boot'-shtĕt), **Jn. H.**, Bin-
rsleben, 1666—Erfurt, 1727 ; writer
a famous defence of sol-mi-sa-tion ;
so organist and composer.

**s** (boos), **Jachet (Jacques) de,**
Bruges (?), 1510 ; Flemish cptist ;
541, asst. organist, San Marco.

ctehude (boox'-tĕ-hoo-dĕ), **Die-**
**rich,** Helsingör (Elsinore), Den-
ark, 1639—Lübeck, 1707; organist;
573, he established the "Abend-
usiken," which J. S. Bach walked
miles to hear ; great composer of
gues and suites.

zzola (bood-zō'-lä), **A.,** Adria, 1815
-Venice, 1871; conductor at San
arco and dram. composer.

d **(Byrde, Bird,** or **Byred), Wm. ;**
ccording to his will, discovered in
697, he was born London, 1542, or
543 (not 1538 or 1546, as stated); d.
ily 4, 1623 ; organist and notable
nglish composer, in whose work there
much modernity; 1554, organist ;
563, choirmaster and organist Lin-
oln Cathedral ; 1575, procured with
allis, his former teacher, an exclu-
ve patent for the privilege of print-
g music and selling music-paper.

## C

allero (kä-bäl-lä'-rō), **Manuel**
ernandez, b. Murcia, March 14,
835 ; pupil of Fuertes (harm.) and
slava (comp.), Madrid Cons. ; c.
op. *Zarzuelas* (v. D.D.) and churchusic.

el (kä-bĕl), rightly **Cabu,** (1) **Ed.,**
nger Op. Com.. Paris. (2) **Marie**
osephe (née **Dreulette**), Liège,
827—1885 ; sister-in-law, or perhaps
other, of above ; soprano.

o (kä'-bō), **Francisco Javier,** b.
aguera, near Valencia, 1832 ; or-
anist, conductor and composer.

cini (kät-chē'-nē), **Giulio** (called
omano), Rome, ca. 1546—Flor-
nce, ca. 1615 ; a Revolutionary com-
oser well called " The father of a new
yle of music " ; studied singing and
ute-playing with Scipione della Pal-

la. Wrote and sang *"Musica in Stile
Rappresentativo,"* and c. *"Il Rapti-
mento di Cefalo"* (Oct. 9, 1600), the
first opera ever publicly prod. ; he
had also set to music other works by
Bardi (q. v.), and collaborated with
Peri (q. v.) in *"Dafne,"* the first
opera ever composed. He c. also
a novel set of madrigals justly called
*"Le nuove musiche,"* and other
works of notable originality and importance to progress.

**Cadaux** (kä-dō), **Justin,** Albi, France,
1813—Paris, 1874 ; dram. composer.

**Cadiac** (käd-yäk), **P.,** choirmaster at
Auch, France, and composer (1543-
58).

**Cadore** (kä-dō'-rĕ), **Arturo,** young
Italian composer, prod. comic opera
*"I Vespri"* (Milan, 1898 ?) and succ.
1-act *"Il Natale"* (Milan, 1902).

**Cæsar, Julius,** M.D., b. Rochester,
England ; amateur composer, 17th
cent.

**Cafaro** (kä-fä'-rō), **Pasq.** (called **Caf-**
**fariel'lo**), San Pietro, Galatina, Italy,
1706—Naples, 1797 ; noted composer;
c. operas, oratorios, a notable *" Stabat
mater,"* etc.

**Caffarelli** (rightly **Gaetano Majora-**
**no**) (käf-fä-rĕl'-lī), Bari, April 16,
1703—Santo-Dorato, near Naples,
Nov. 30, 1783 ; famous male soprano ; discovered as a peasant boy,
by Caffaro, a musician, he took the
name Caffarelli out of gratitude ; he
studied 5 years with Porpora ; was a
skilful sight-reader and harpsichordist, a marvellous singer of florid music, and also gifted with pathos ; had
most successful début, Rome, 1724,
in a female rôle, and sang with enormous success everywhere except London ; made money enough to buy a
dukedom.

**Caffi** (käf'-fē), **Fran.,** Venice, 1786—
Padua, 1874 ; writer.

**Caffiaux** (käf-fī-ō), **Dom. Phillippe
Jos.,** Valenciennes, 1712—Paris,
1777 ; abbé and writer.

**Cagniar de la Tour** (kïn'-yăr dŭ lä
toor'), Baron, **Chas.,** Paris, 1777—

1859; improved the "Syren" (v. D. D.).

**Cagnoni** (kän-yō'-nǐ), **A.**, Godiasco, 1828—Bergamo, 1896; conductor and dram. composer.

**Cahen** (kä-äṅ), (1) **Ernest**, Paris, 1828—1893 ; pianist and dram. composer. (2) **Albert**, b. Paris (?), Jan. 8, 1846 ; pianist ; pupil of Mme. Szarvady and César Franck ; c. "*Jean le Précurseur*," biblical poem (1874) ; com. opera "*Le Bois*" (1880, Op. Com.) ; fairy opera "*La Belle au Bois Dormant*" (Geneva, 1886); 4-act opera "*Le Vénitien*" (Rouen, 1890) ; unsucc. opera "*La Femme de Claude*" (Paris, Op. Com., 1896) ; lives in Paris.

**Caillot** (kī-yō), **Jos.**, Paris, 1732—1816 ; tenor-barytone.

**Cain** (käṅ), **Henri**, b. Paris, 1859 ; painter ; and librettist to Massenet, etc.

**Caimo** (kä'-ē-mö), **Joseffo**, b. Milan, ca. 1540 ; composer.

**Cal'ah, J.,** 1758—1798, English organist.

**Caldara** (käl-dä'-rä), **A.**, Venice, 1678 —Vienna, Dec. 28, 1763 ; court-conductor and noted composer, Vienna ; c. operas, 70 sacred dramas, etc.

**Cal'dicott, Alfred Jas.,** Worcester, England, 1842—near Gloucester, Oct. 24, 1897 ; organist of St. Stephen's Church, Worcester, and Corporation organist ; 1883, prof. at R. C. M., London ; from 1885, cond. at the Albert Palace ; c. cantatas, 13 operettas, etc.

**Calegari** (käl-ā-gä'-rē), (1) (or **Callegari**) **Fran. A.**, d. Padua, 1742 ; a Franciscan monk, 1702-24 ; conductor and writer at Venice, then Padua. (2) **A.**, Padua, 1758—1828 ; dram. composer and writer.

**Cal'kin, J. Bapt.,** b. London, March 16, 1827 ; pianist, organist and composer ; prof. Guildhall School of Mus. ; pub. services, etc.

**Call, Leonard de,** 1779—Vienna, 1815 ; guitar virtuoso and composer.

**Callaerts** (käl'-lärts), **Jos.,** b. [A]werp, Aug. 22, 1838 ; pupil at B[rus]sels Cons. of Lemmens ; organis[t] Antwerp Cathedral, and teache[r at] the Music School from 1867 ; [c.] prize symphony and pf. trio, c[om.] opera ; "*Le Retour Imprévu*" (A[nt]werp, 1889), etc.

**Call'cott,** (1) **J. Wall,** Kensing[ton,] Nov. 20, 1766—May 15, 1821 ; m[ain]ly self-taught ; organist ; 1789 [he] won all the prizes offered by [the] "Catch Club ; " 1790, pupil of Hay[dn,] 1800, Mus. Doc. (Oxon) ; 1806, [fig]ured at the Royal Institute ; [his] work on an unfinished mus[ic] dictionary destroyed his reason ; [his] "*Grammar of Music*" (1806) [a] standard. (2) **Wm. Hutchins,** K[ens]ington, 1807—London, 1882 ; so[n of] above ; organist and pianist.

**Calliope** (käl-lī'-ō-pě or käl-lē'-ō-[pē),] the Greek muse of heroic verse.

**Calo'ri, Angiola,** Milan, 1732—1[?]; soprano.

**Calsabigi** (käl-sä-bē'-je), **Raniero** [b.] Livorno, 1715 — Naples, 1[?]; Gluck's librettist and aide in o[pera] reformation.

**Calvé** (käl-vä), **Emma (de Roqu[er),]** b. Madrid, 1864 ; eminent oper[atic] actress and soprano ; pupil of M[ar]chesi and Pugets ; 1882, débu[t in] Massenet's "*Hérodiade*," Th. d[e la] Monnaie, Brussels ; 1884, Paris [Th.] Italien ; 1885, Op. Com. ; has s[ung] constantly in New York, London, [etc.;] she is an Officier d'Académie, and [lives] in Paris.

**Calvis'ius, Sethus** (rightly S[eth] **Kallwitz** (käl'-vēts), Feb. 21, 15[9?] Leipzig, Nov. 24, 1615 ; son [of a] peasant ; singer for alms, then [as] teacher obtained funds to st[udy] (1581) mus. dir. ; writer of impor[tant] treatises and composer.

**Calvör** (käl'-fär), **Kaspar,** Hildesh[eim,] 1650—Clausthal, 1725 ; theorist.

**Cambert** (käṅ-bär), **Rob.,** Paris, [ca.] 1628—London, 1677 ; first comp[oser] of French operas ; organist at [St.] Honoré ; 1659, "*La Pastorale*"

cc. prod. at the Château d'Issy ;
d followed by others on the texts of
:rrin, who received letters patent for
:tablishing the "Académie royale de
usique" (now the Gr. Opéra) ; with
:rrin he also wrote the first genu-
e opera, "*Pomone*," prod. 1671,
fore Lully, who later took the pat-
t for himself ; he went to England
ere he died as Master of the Music
Charles II.

bini (käm-bē'-nē), **Giov. Giu.**,
ghorn, 1746—Bicêtre, 1825 (?);
nd. at Paris, and prolific but cheap
mposer of over 60 symphonies, 144
ing-quartets, several operas, etc. ;
died in the almshouse.

erana (käm-ā-rā'-nä), **Luigi**, b. in
edmont, 1846 ; theatre - cond. in
vona ; dram. composer.

'idge, (1) **J.**, ca. 1735 — York,
gl., 1803 ; organist York cath., 47
ars ; composer. (2) **Mat.**, York,
58—1844 ; son and successor of
ove. (3) **J.**, York, 1790—1859 ;
n and successor of (2).

pagnoli (käm-pän-yŏ'-lē), **Bart.**,
nto, 1751—Neustrelitz, 1827 ; vio-
ist and court-conductor.

pana (käm-pä'-nä), **Fabio**, Leg-
rn, 1819—London, 1882 ; singing-
acher and dram. composer.

panari (käm-pä-nä'-rē), (1) **Lean-
o**, b. Rovigo, Italy, Oct. 20, 1857 ;
pil at Milan Cons. ; toured Europe
years ; America, 1879 ; lived in
ston ; organised " C. String-quar-
" ; 1883 1st prof. of vln. in N.
Cons. ; 1890, 1st prof. of vln.
head of orch. dept. Cincinnati
ns. ; since 1897 conductor at
ilan ; writer and composer. (2)
useppe, eminent dram. barytone,
o. of above, sings at Met. Op., N.Y.

panini (käm-pä-nē'-nē), **Italo**,
rma, 1845—Vigatto, near Parma,
ov. 22, 1896 ; operatic tenor, a
acksmith when discovered ; début,
69, at Odessa, without much suc-
ss ; then studied with Lamperti,
d reappeared, Florence, 1871, as
Lohengrin," with great succ. ;

toured Europe and U. S. with Nilsson, Patti, etc.

**Camp'bell, Alex.**, organist, editor,
and publisher, 18th century.

**Campenhout** (käm'-pĕn-oot), **François van**, Brussels, 1779—1848 ; violinist, then tenor, then dram. composer.

**Campio'li A. Gualandi**, called **Cam-
piole**, b. Germany, of Sp. parents ;
male contralto ; début Berlin, 1708.

**Cam'pion**, (1) **Thos.**, d. London, Feb.
1619 ; English physician, poet, dramatist and noteworthy writer and
composer ; pub. two books of Ayres,
etc. (1610); 2 more (1612). (2) **Fran.**,
1703-19, theorbist, Paris Gr. Opéra.

**Campio'ni**, **Carlo A.**, Leghorn, ca.
1720—Florence, 1793 ; court-conductor.

**Camporese** (käm-pō-rā'-zĕ), **Violante**,
b. Rome, 1785 ; operatic sopr. of
Napoleon's private music ; début,
London, 1817 ; retired, 1829.

**Campos** (käm'-pōs), **João Ribeiro de
Almeida de**, b. Vizen, Portugal, ca.
1770 ; cond., and professor.

**Campra** (käṅ-prä), (1) **André**, Dec. 4,
1660—Versailles, July 29, 1744 ; cond.
at Nôtre Dame ; prod. 2 succ. operas
under his bro's name and gave up
church-mus. ; cond. Royal Orch. and
c. 18 operas. (2) **Jos.**, bro. of above ;
double-bass player.

**Camps y Soler** (kämps ē sō'-lär), **Oscar**, b. Alexandria, Egypt, Nov. 21,
1837; Spanish pianist ; pupil of Döhler
and Mercadante ; played in public at
13; lives in Madrid ; writer and theorist.

**Candeille** (käṅ-dĕ'-yŭ), (1) **P. Jos.**,
Estaires, 1744 — Chantilly, 1827 ;
dram. composer. (2) **(Simons-
Candeille) Amélie Julie**, Paris,
1767—1834 ; operatic sopr., actress,
and composer ; daughter of above ;
lived in Paris as teacher ; she wrote
libretto and music of the succ. operetta " *La Belle Fermière*" (1792) ;
she played the leading rôle and sang
to her own accomp. on piano and
harp.

**Cange** (dü känzh), **Chas.-Dufrèsne,** sieur **du,** Amiens, 1610—Paris, 1688 ; lawyer and lexicographer.

**Cannabich** (kän'-nä-bĭkh), (1) **Chr.,** Mannheim, ᵮ731—Frankfort, 1798 ; noteworthy violinist and conductor, a pioneer in orchestral diminuendo ; son of (2) **Mathias,** a flutist in the Electoral Orch. at Mannheim of which **Chr. C.** became leader in 1765, and cond. 1775. (3) **K.,** Mannheim, 1769—Munich, 1805 ; son of (1) ; court-conductor. (4) **Rose,** b. about 1762 according to Mozart, whose pupil she was ; daughter of (1) ; notable pianist.

**Canniciari** (kän-nē-chä'-rĕ), Don **Pompeo,** Rome, 1670—1744 ; conductor and composer.

**Canthal** (kän'-täl), Aug., b. Lübeck (?); flutist 1832 Hamburg Th.; 1847, succ. concerts, Copenhagen ; 1848, bandmaster, Leipzig ; composer.

**Cantor, Otto,** Engl. song-writer, lives in London.

**Campel'la Martianus Minucius (Mineus),** Felix, 5th cent., Latin scholar at Carthage ; writer.

**" Capel'li,"** pen-name of **Jn. D. von** Apell.

**Capocci** (kä-pôt'-chē), (1) **Gaetano,** Rome, Oct. 16, 1811—Jan. 11, 1898 ; notable teacher ; pub. much sacred music. (2) **Filippo,** b. Rome, May 11, 1840 ; son of above ; Italian organist, perhaps the best living ; since 1875 organist of San Giovanni in Laterano ; c. for organ.

**Caporale** (kä-pō-rä'-lĕ), **Andrea,** d. London, ca. 1756 ; 'cellist.

**Capoul** (kä-pool) (**Jos. Amédée**) (**Victor,** b. Toulouse, Feb. 27, 1839 ; tenor ; pupil of Révial and Mocker, Paris Cons. ; 1861–72 at the Op. Com. ; 1892 prof. of operatic singing in Nat. Cons., New York ; asst. dir. Gr. Opéra, Paris, 1899 ; 1902 (?) director Op. Com., Paris.

**Caraccio** (kä-rät'-chō) (or **Caravac- cio**), **Giov.,** Bergamo, ca. 1550— Rome, 1626 ; conductor.

**Caraccioli** (kä-rät-chō'-lē), **Luigi,**

Adria (Bari), 1849—London, 18 dram. composer.

**Carado'ri-Allan, Maria C. R.** **de Munck**), Milan, 1800—Lon 1865 ; soprano.

**Carafa de Colobrano** (kä-rä'-fä kō-lō-brä'-nō), **Michele Enr** Naples, Nov. 17, 1787—Paris, 26, 1872 ; son of Prince Colobra while very young c. an opera, 2 tatas, etc., with much success ; 1 member of the Academy ; 1840, ᵱ of comp. at Cons. ; c. also ba cantatas, and good church-music.

**Caramuel' de Lob'kowitz** (v **Juan,** Madrid, 1606—Vigevano,I 1682 ; bishop and writer.

**Cardon** (kär-dôn̄), (1) **Louis,** P: 1747—Russia, 1805 ; harpist. **P.,** b. Paris, 1751 ; 'cellist and sin

**Cardo'so, Manuel,** Fronteira, 1; Spanish priest and composer.

**Caresana** (kär-ä-sä'-nä), **Cristof** b. Tarentum, 1655 ; lives in Na as composer.

**Carestini** (kä-räs-tē'-nē), **Giov.** (s name **Cusanino**), Mente Filat (Ancona), ca. 1705—1760 ; male prano (musico).

**Ca'rey, Henry,** 1685 (?)—London, 4, 1743 ; a reputed natural sor Marquis of Halifax, and disp composer of " *God save the Kin* c. the song " *Sally in our Alle* ballad operas, etc.

**Cario** (kä'-rĭ-ō), **Jn. H.,** Eckernfo Holstein, 1736—after 1800 ; t1 peter.

**Carissimi** (kä-rĭs'-sē-mē), **Giaco** Marino, near Rome, ca. 1604—R0 Jan. 12, 1674 ; ca. 1624, chu conductor at Rome ; important composer and writer ; many of MSS. are lost ; 5 oratorios and o pieces remain.

**Carl, Wm. Crane,** b. Bloomfield J., March 2, 1865 ; pupil of S. Warren (org. and theory), M Schiller (pf.) and Guilmant, Pa since 1892, organist First Pre Ch., N. Y. ; cond. of N. Y. " Ga Club " ; tours as concert-organist

michael, **Mary Grant,** b. Birken-
ad, Engl.; pupil of O. Beringer,
Bache, and F. Hartivigson (pf.)
d E. Prout (comp.); accompanist;
operetta, "*The Snow Queen*";
f.-suite; and many pop. songs.

naby, **Wm.,** London, 1772—1839,
an composer.

icer (kär'-nē-thär), **Ramon,** Tar-
ge, Catalonia, Oct. 24, 1789—
drid, March 17, 1855; cond.
yal Opera, Madrid, 1830–54, prof.
comp. Madrid Cons.; one of
creators of the *Zarzuela* (v.
D.).

n (kä-rôñ), (1) **Firmin,** 15th cent.,
ist. of Netherlands? (2) **Rose,**
ed soprano Gr. Opéra, Paris.

ani (kär-pä'-nē), **Giu. A.,** b. Vil-
ese (Como), 1752—Vienna, 1825;
ter.

entras **(Il Carpentras'so).**
le ELEAZER GENET.

, **Frank Osmond,** b. Yorkshire,
1857; 1882 Mus. Bac. Oxon;
1, Mus. Doc.; c. farces, bur-
ques, and comic operas; "*Joan of
c*" (1891), "*Blue-Eyed Susan*"
ndon, 1892), "*In Town*" (1892),
*'is Excellency*" (1894, libretto by
Gilbert), etc.

é (kär-rā), (1) **Louis,** Clofontaine
e, 1663—Paris, 1711; writer. (2)
ert, b. Strasbourg, June 22, 1852;
8, dir. Op.-Com., Paris; lib-
ist.

eño (kär-rän'-yō), **Teresa,** b. Ca-
as, Venezuela, Dec. 22, 1853;
il of L. M. Gottschalk, and G.
thias; notable pianist; played in
lic at 12; at 22 toured the U. S.;
9–90 toured Germany with much
cess; for some years wife of E.
ret; then of Giov. Tagliapietra;
2–95, wife of Eugen d'Albert;
2, m. Arturo Tagliapietra, bro. of
v. T.; c. a string-quartet and pf.
n pieces. Her daughter **Teresita**
gliapietra is a pianist.

dus, **J. Tiplady,** Keighley
rkshire), 1836 — London, 1895;
inist.

**Car'ter,** (1) **Thos.,** Ireland, ca. 1735—
London, 1804; composer. (2) **H.,**
b. London, March 6, 1837; organist; pupil of Haupt (org.), Pauer (pf.),
Kiel and Hiller (comp.); at 9, church
organist; later at Quebec, Boston,
etc.; 1880, prof. in Coll. of Music,
Cincinnati; 1883 organist Brooklyn,
later N. Y.; composer.

**Cartier** (kärt-yä), **J. Bap.,** Avignon,
1765—Paris, 1841; violinist and dram.
composer,

**Carulli** (kä-rool'-lē), (1) **Fdo.,** Naples,
1770—Paris, 1841; self-taught guitar-virtuoso and teacher; c. 400
concertos. (2) **Gustavo,** Leghorn,
1880—Boulogne, 1877; son of above;
teacher and dram. composer.

**Caruso** (kä-roo'-zō), **Luigi,** Naples,
1754—Perugia, 1821; conductor, c.
69 operas.

**Carvalho** (kär-väl'-ō) (rightly **Car-
vaille),** (1) **Léon,** in a French colony,
1825—Paris, 1897; from 1875 dir.
Op. Com. (2) **Carvalho-Miolan**
(mē-ô-läñ), **Caroline M.-Félix,**
Marseilles, 1827—Puys, near Dieppe,
1895; soprano; wife of above; debut 1849.

**Ca'ry, Annie Louise,** b. Wayne (Ken-
nebec County, Me.), Oct. 22, 1842,
distinguished operatic and concert
contralto; studied in Boston and
Milan, and with Viardot-Garcia, etc.;
début 1868, at Hamburg; later
Stockholm, Copenhagen, Brussels,
London, New York (1870), St. Petersburg (1875); 1882, m. C. M. Raymond, Cincinnati.

**Casali** (kä-sä'-lē), **Giov. Bat.,** d. 1792;
conductor and dram. composer.

**Casamorata** (kä-sä-mō-rä'-tä), **Luigi
Fdo.,** Würzburg, 1807—Florence,
1881; editor, writer, and composer.

**Casarini** (or **-a**) (kä-sä-rē'-nē), Italian
soprano in Händel's operas, London,
1748.

**Casel'la,** **P.,** Pieve (Umbria), 1769—
Naples, 1843; dram. composer.

**Caser'ta, Philippe de,** Neapolitan
theorist, 15th century.

Casini (kä-sē'-nē), G. M., b. 1675 (?) ;
Florentine priest ; he tried to revive
Greek modes.

Cassell', Guillaume, Lyons, 1794—
Brussels, 1836 ; singer and teacher.

Cassiodo'rus Magnus Aurelius, b.
Syllaceum (Lucania), ca. 470 ; writer.

Castel (käs-tĕl), Louis Bertrand,
Montpellier, 1688—Paris, 1757 ; a
Jesuit writer who attempted without
success to construct a "Clavecin
oculaire," to prod. colour harmonies.

Castellan (käs-tel-län), Jeanne A., b.
Beaujeu, Oct. 26, 1819; retired,
1859 ; singer.

Castel'li, (1) Ignaz Fz., Vienna, 1781
—1862 ; editor. (2) ———, soprano in London, 1825–28.

Castelmary (käs-tĕl-mä-rē) (stage
name of Comte Armand de Castan), Toulouse, Aug. 16, 1834—
New York, Feb. 9, 1897 ; barytone ;
died on the stage of the Met. Op.,
N. Y., just after the first act of
"Martha."

Cas'tro, Jean de, played Lyons, 1570;
composer and lutist.

Castil-Blaze. Vide BLAZE, F. H. J.

Castrucci (käs-troot'-chē), P., Rome,
1689—London, 1769 ; violinist ; leader of Händel's opera-orch. ; inv. and
played the violetta marina. His
bro. (2) Prospero (d. London, 1769);
violinist and composer.

Catalani (kät-ä-lä'-nē), Angelica,
Sinigaglia, Oct., 1779—Paris, June
12, 1849 ; famous operatic soprano of
great beauty ; her voice was notably
flexible and reached to g''' (v. CHART
OF PITCH) ; in 1806, at London, she
earned over £16,000 ($80,000) in one
year ; 1814–17, she took up management of the Th. Italien, Paris, without
succ. After final appearance, York
festival, in 1828, she retired to her
country-seat, near Florence.

Catalini (kä-tä-lē'-nē), Alfredo, Lucca, July 19, 1854—Milan, Aug. 7,
1893 ; pupil of his father a musician
at Milan ; gained admission without
exam. to Paris Cons. ; 1886 prof. of
comp., Milan Cons. ; c. 6 operas, of

which the most succ. were, "
nire," "Loreley," and "La W

Catel (kä-tĕl), Chas. Simon, L':
Orne, 1773—Paris, 1830 ;
composer and writer.

Catelani (kät-ä-lä'-nē), Angelo,
talla, 1811—S. Martino di Mug
1866 ; dram. composer and writ

Catenhausen            (kä'-tĕn-how'
Ernst, b. Ratzeburg, 1841 ; co
tor and composer.

Cat'ley, Anne, London, 1745—
soprano, début, 1762 ; m. Gen.
celles.

Catrufo (kä-troo'-fō), Giu., N
1771—London, 1851 ; dram.
poser.

Caurroy (kōr-wä), Fran. Eust
du, sieur de St.-Fremin, Gerb
1549—Paris, 1609 ; singer and
ductor.

Caus'ton, Thos., d. Oct. 28, 156
the Chapel Royal ; English
poser.

Cavaccio (kä-vät'-chō), Giov
Bergamo, ca. 1556—Rome,
conductor.

Cavaillé-Coll. (kä-vī'-yä-kôl') (
Hyacinthe), Aristide, Montp
1811—Paris, 1899 ; son of fa
org.-builder ; 1771—1862, org.-
er and inv. of separate wind-
with different pressures, etc.

Cavalieri (dĕl kä-väl-yä'-rē), (1) E
del, Rome, ca. 1550—Floren
1599 (?) ; "Inspector-Gen. of A
Artists" to the Tuscan court
vocated non-polyphonic music ;
"Rappresentazione di Anima
Corpo" (Rome, 1600) is the firs
torio. (2) Katherina, Vienna,
—1801 ; singer, whom Mozart
for and praised. (3) Lina, b. R
Dec. 24, 1874, daughter of a
dress ; won notoriety as beaut
singer in cafés chantants ;
studied with Mme. Mariani-M
succ. début in "Pagliacci," Li
1900 ; sang Naples, Warsaw,
1902, engaged at Dal Verme
Milan.

Caval'li, Fran., Crema, ca. 16

ice, Jan. 14, 1676 (rightly Pier
ncesco, **Caletti-Bruni**, son of
mbatt. **Caletti**, called **Bruni,**
estro at Crema. A Venetian
leman, Federigo Cavalli, had him
ght and he took his name. He sang
S. Marco, 1665 ; first organist
e ; 1668, conductor ; he was a pu-
of Monteverde and developed M.'s
ciples, composing 41 operas, the
t succ. being " *Giasone* " (Venice,
9) ; " *Serse*" (1654) ; " *Ercole
ante* " (Paris, 1662) ; he c. also a
able requiem, and other church-
sic.

llini (lē'-nē), **Ernesto,** Milan, 1807
873 ; clarinettist and composer.

l'lo, **Peter,** Munich, 1819—Paris,
2 ; organist.

ndish, **Michael,** English comer, 1599.

s (kä-vōs), **Catterino,** Venice,
5—St. Petersburg, 1840 ; 1799,
rt-conductor; c. 13 Russian operas;
others.

us (kĕ'-lüs), **Anne Claude Phi-
pe de Tubières,** comte de, Paris,
2—1765 ; writer.

ati (käd-zä'-tē), **Maurizio,** Man-
, 1625—1677 ; composer and con-
tor.

'ia (Saint), d. Rome, A.D. 230, in
ristian martyrdom ; her feast-day
ov. 22d ; legendary inventor of the
an, and patron saint of Christian
sic.

stino (chä-lĕs-tē'-nō), **Eligio,**
ne, 1739—Ludwigslust, 1812 ;
inist and conductor.

r, **Ludovic.** Vide LECLERQ.

er (sĕl'-yĕr), **Alfred,** Hackney,
ndon, Dec. 1, 1844—Dec. 28,
1 ; conductor in London, etc. ; c.
operettas, incl. the very succ.
*Dorothy*" (1886) ; " *The Mounte-
ks* " (London, 1892), etc.

ohorsky (or **Czernohorsky**),
ĕr-nō-hôr'-shkĭ), **Bohuslav,** Nim-
g, Bohemia, 17th cent.—Italy,
0 ; a Minorite monk ; conductor ;
comps. are still sung in Bohemian
rches.

**Cerone** (chä-rō'-nè), **Dom. P.,** b. Bergamo, ca. 1566 ; theorist.

**Cerreto** (chĕr-rä'-tō), **Scipione,** Naples, 1551—ca. 1632 ; lutist and theorist.

**Certon** (sĕr-tôń), **P.,** 16th cent., contrapuntist ; choirm. Sainte Chapelle,
Paris.

**Cerù** (chä-roo'), **Dom. Ag.,** b. Lucca,
Aug. 28, 1817 ; engineer and writer.

**Červeny** (chär'-vä-nē), **V. F. (Wenzel Fz.),** Dubec, Bohemia, 1819—
Königgrätz, Jan. 19, 1896 ; maker
and improver of brass instrs. and inv.
of the important "roller" cylinder
mechanism, also of the contrabass
(1845), metal contrafagotto ('56), althorn obbligato ('59), primhorn ('73),
and the complete waldhorn quartet
(primhorn, E♭ alto, waldhorn in F,
tenor in B♭, basso, 11 in D♭), sub-
contrabass and subcontrafagotto ; improved the family of cornets, the euphonion, the screwdrum, and the
church-kettledrum, etc.

**Cervera** (thĕr-vä'-rä), **Fran.,** b. Valencia, 16th cent. ; theorist.

**Cervetti.** Vide GELINEK.

**Cervetto** (chĕr-vĕt'-tō), (1) **Giacomo**
(rightly **Bassevi**), Italy, ca. 1682—
London, Jan. 14, 1783 ; 'cellist. (2)
**Giacomo,** d. Feb. 5, 1837 ; son of
above ; 'cellist and composer.

**Cesbron** (sĕ'-brôń), **Suzanne Catherine,** b. Paris, May 29, 1879, soprano;
pupil of the Cons., taking prizes 1899,
1900, 1901 ; début, 1901, Opéra Comique as Griséldis in Massenet's opera.

**Cesi** (chä'-zē), **Beniamino,** b. Naples,
Nov. 6, 1845 ; pupil of Naples Cons.
under Mercadante and Pappalardo,
pf.-pupil of Thalberg ; since, 1866,
prof. Naples Cons. ; c. an opera,
" *Vittor Pisani* " (not prod.), etc.

**Cesti** (chäs'-tē), **Marc A.,** Arezzo,
1620 — Venice, 1669 ; Franciscan
monk ; conductor and tenor singer ;
first opera, " *Orontea*," succ. at Venice, 1649 ; wrote 10 other operas
mainly succ.; all lost now except "*La
Dori*" (Venice, 1663) ; his cantatas

are better preserved ; he wrote them for the stage.

**Cevallos** (thě-văl'-lōs), **Fran.**, 1535—1572 ; Spanish composer.

**Chabrier** (shăb-rǐ-ā), **Alexis Emm.**, Auvergne, Jan. 18, 1842—Paris, Sept. 13, 1894 ; studied law in Paris, then music ; 1881, choirm. under Lamoureux ; c. operettas, a rhapsodie " *Espaňi* " for orch., etc.

**Chad'wick, G. Whitfield**, b. Lowell, Mass., Nov. 13, 1854 ; studied organ, etc., under Eugene Thayer at Boston; 1876 head of mus. dept. of Olivet Coll., Mich.; 1877–78 studied Leipzig Cons. (Reinecke, Jadassohn), his graduation piece being an overture to " *Rip Van Winkle ;* " studied at Munich with Rheinberger ; 1880, organist Boston and teacher of harm., comp. and instrumentation at the N. E. Cons., of which he is dir. ; cond. the Worcester Mus. Festivals, resigned, 1902 ; c. 3 symphonies ; 4 overtures, " *Rip Van Winkle* " ('79), " *Thalia* " ('83), " *Melpomene* " ('87), " *The Miller's Daughter* " ('88) ; 3 symphonic sketches for orch. ; comic opera " *Tabasco* " (New York, '94) ; many choral works ; " *The Columbian Ode* " (Chicago, '93), etc.; wrote a text-book on " Harmony " (Boston, 1898).

**Challier** (shäl'-lǐ-ĕr), **Ernst**, b. Berlin, July 9, 1843; music-publisher, Berlin.

**Chamberlain, Houston Stewart**, b. Portsmouth, England, Sept. 9, 1855 ; son of a British Admiral, took doctor's degree in Germany, and lived at Vienna because of his health ; pub. famous book " Richard Wagner " (Leipzig, 1892), followed by others.

**Chambonnières** (shäṅ-bǔn-yȧr), **Jacques Champion** (called " **Champion de Chamb.** "), d. ca. 1670 ; first chamber cembalist to Louis XIV.

**Chaminade** (shăm'-ǐ-năd'), **Cécile (Louise Stéphanie)**, b. Paris, Aug. 8, 1861 ; pianist and composer of unusual spirit and originality ; pupil of Lecouppey, Savard, Marsick and Godard ; she lives in Paris ; c. the

succ. "ballet-symphonie" "*Cali*[
(Marseilles, 1888) ; the " symp
lyrique " " *Les Amazones* " (A
1888) ; 2 suites for orch. ; " Cc
stück " for pf. with orch. and
pop. songs and pf.-pieces ; op
MS., book by A. Silvester.

**Champein** (shäṅ-păṅ), **Stan**
Marseilles, 1753—Paris, 1830 ;
composer.

**Champion** (shäṅp-yôṅ), **Jac**
Vide CHAMBONNIÈRES.

**Champ'ington, J.**, English o
builder ; 1597.

**Channay** (shän-ně), **Jean de**,
cent. music-printer, Avignon.

**Chanot** (shä-nō), **Fran.**, Mire
1787—Brest, 1823 ; retired as a
engineer ; designed a violin
the Academy pronounced equ
Stradivari's ; his bro., a Paris
ier, manufactured it, but found
practicable.

**Chap'man, Wm. Rogers**, b. I
ver, Mass., Aug. 4, 1855 ; liv
New York as chorus-leader, co
tor and composer.

**Chap'pel & Co.**, music-publi
London ; founded 1812 by (1) S
uel C., the pianist, Cramer, an
T. Latour (1809—1888). (2)
C. became the head of the firr
1840 he founded the " Antiqu
Society," and pub. colls. of Old
music. His brothers, (3) Tho
founded, and (4) Arthur, condu
the Monday and Saturday Pop.
certs.

**Chap'ple, Samuel**, Crediton (De
1775—Ashburton, 1833 ; organis
pianist, blind from infancy ; cor
er.

**Chapuis** (shäp-wē), **Aug. Pau
Bap.**, b. Dampierre - sur - S
France, April 20, 1862 ; pup
Dubois, Massenet, and César Fr
Paris Cons., took first prize in h
1st prize for org., and the R
prize ; organist at Saint Roch.;
1894, prof. of harm. at the C
since 1895, inspector-gen. of 
instruction in Paris schools ; c

c. lyric drama, "*Enguerrande*"
p. Com., 1892); lyric drama
*Tancred*" (Op. Com., 1898?); an
atorio ; a pf.-suite " on the oriental
le," etc.; pub. a treatise on harm.

r (khär), **Fr. Ernst ("Fritz")**, b.
eve-on-Rhein, May 5, 1865 ; pupil
C. Kistler, Wüllner and Neitzel ;
nd. opera at Zwichau, Stettin, and
Gallen ; now at Ulm ; wrote book
d music of succ. opera "*Der
helm von Bergen*" (Zwickau, 1895);
cantata ' Spielmann," etc.

rd, **G. W.**, ca. 1765—May 23,
49 ; English organist and compos-

rpentier (shär-pänt-yā), (1) **Marc**
, Paris, 1634—March, 1702 ; con-
ctor to the Dauphin ; c. 16 operas
- the stage and many "tragédies
rituelles " for the Jesuits, masses,
. (2) **Gustave**, b. Dieuze, Lor-
ne, June 25, 1860 ; pupil of Mas-
rt, Pessard, and Massenet, Paris
ns. ; 1887, took grand prix de
me ; c. orch. suite "*Impressions
Italie*" ; scène lyrique "*Didon*";
mphonic drama (or concert opera)
*La Vie du Poète*" (Grand Opera,
92), and "*Italien*" (Hamburg,
02) ; symph. poem "*Napoli*"
891) ; book and music of succ. op-
a *Louise* (Op. Com., 1900) ; also c.
*Marie*," "*Orphée*," and "*Tête
uge*," unprod. ; and songs, "*Les
eurs du Mal*," "*Quinze poèmes*,"
me of them with chorus and orches-
a.

t'terton, **J. B.**, Norwich, 1810—
ondon, 1871; court-harpist and com-
ser.

ulieu (shōl-yŭ), **Chas.**, Paris,
88—London, 1849 ; pianist, teacher
d composer.

umet (shō-mā), **J. B. Wm.**, b.
ordeaux, April 26, 1842 ; won the
ix Cressent, with the comic opera
*Bathyle*" (prod. 1877), also the Prix
ossini ; c. comic operas ; lyric drama
*auprat* (MS.), etc.

uvet (shō-vā), **Chas. Alexis**,
arnes, June 7, 1837—Argentan,

Jan. 28, 1871; organist; c. noteworthy
org.-music.

**Chavanne** (shä-vän'-nĕ), **Irène von**,
b. Gratz, ca. 1867 ; contralto ; pupil,
Vienna Cons., 1882–85 ; since 1885 at
the Dresden court-Opera.

**Cheese, G. J.**, organist, London
1771 ; writer.

**Chelard** (shŭ-lär), **Hippolyte André
J. Bap.**, Paris, Feb. 1, 1789—Weimar, Feb. 12, 1861 ; 1815, prod. his
first opera, "*La Casa a Vendere*,"
Naples ; entered the Paris Operatic
orch. as violinist ; in 1827 his opera "*Macbeth*" (text by Rouget de
Lisle), was prod., but failed ; he
went to Munich, and 1828 prod. a
revised version of "*Macbeth*" with
such succ. that he was made court-
conductor ; he returned to Paris,
1829, and failed with 3 other operas ;
conducted the German Opera in London, which failed ; returned to Munich, and prod. his best work, "*Die
Hermannsschlacht*," 1835 ; 1836,
court-conductor at Weimar, where he
prod. 2 comic operas.

**Chelleri** (kĕl'-lĕ-rē), **Fortunato** (rightly **Keller**), Parma, 1686—Cassel,
1757 ; court-conductor and dram.
composer.

**Chéri** (shä-rē), **Victor** (rightly **Cizos**),
Auxerre, 1830—suicide, Paris, 1882 ;
cond. and dram. composer.

**Cherubini** (kā-roo-bē'-nē) **(M.) Luigi
(Carlo Zenobio Salvatore)**, Florence, Sept. 14, 1760—Paris, March
15, 1842 ; one of the greatest masters
of counterpoint ; pupil of his father,
(cembalist, at the Pergola Th.), then
of B. and A. Felici, Bizarri and Castrucci ; 1779 sent (under patronage of
the future Emperor Leopold III.) to
Milan, to study cpt. with Sarti ; at 13,
had c. a mass and an intermezzo for a
society theatre ; at 15, another intermezzo ; 1780, "*Quinto Fabio*" was
prod. without succ. though with better
results in a revised version (1783) ; he
had succ. with 6 other operas, and
was in 1784 invited to London, where
he prod. an opera buffa, with some

success, and another with none ; he was court composer for one year ; 1788 he prod. " *Ifigenia in Aulide* " at Turin ; and then lived in Paris, where his French opera " *Démophon* " (Grand Opéra, 1788) failed ; he then cond. at a small opera house, until 1792. His opera " *Lodoïska*," 1791, showed a new style of emotional strength, powerful ensemble, and novel orchestral colour that founded a school of imitators. 7 other operas and a ballet followed, incl. his masterpiece (1800), " *Les deux journées* " (in Germany called " *Der Wasserträger* " ; in England, " The Water-carrier "). 1795 he had been made one of the inspectors of the new Cons., Paris, but was not liked by Napoleon, whose musical opinion he had not flattered. On invitation he wrote for Vienna " *Faniska*," a great succ. (1806) ; an invitation to write a mass for the Prince of Chimay, resulted in the famous 3-part mass in F. He wrote 4 more operas, but found church-music more satisfactory. 1815, visited London ; wrote a symphony, an overture, and a *Hymn to Spring*, for the Philh. Soc. After many vicissitudes he became in 1816 prof. of comp. at the Cons., Paris, and 1821-41 dir. His enormous list of works includes 15 Italian and 14 French operas, 17 cantatas, 11 solemn masses, 2 requiems, 1 oratorio ; 1 symphony, 1 overture ; 6 string quartets ; 6 pf.-sonatas, and a mass of smaller works, mus. for pf., etc. The best biog. is by Bellasis (London, 1874).

**Chevé** (shŭ-vā), **Emile Jos. Maurice**, Douarnenez, Finistere, 1804—1864 ; a physician ; wrote pamphlets attacking the methods at the Paris Cons. His wife (née **Manine**, Paris) collaborated with him.

**Chevillard** (shŭ-vē-yăr), **Camille**, b. Paris, Oct., 1859 ; pupil of G. Mathias ; took 2d pf. prize at Cons.; till 1897, asst.-cond. of the Lamoureux Concerts ; then cond. ; c. a symph.

ballade, " *Le chêne et le roseau* symph. poem, a symph. fantasie

**Chiabran** (shä-brän) (or **Chabra Chiabrano**), **Fran.**, b. Pied[ ca. 1723 ; violinist and compose

**Chiaromonte** (kē-är-ō-môn´-tě) Castrogfovanni, Sicily, 1809— sels, 1886 ; tenor ; prof. of si and dram. composer.

**Chic** (shěk), **Léon**, b. April 28, 1 son and pupil of army musiciar rector of marine and military ba c. various pieces.

**Chick´ering & Sons**, American fi pf.-makers, est. 1823, by (1) **J Chickering** (New Ipswich, N. 1798—Boston, 1853) ; his sc.1 **Col. Thos. E. C.** (Boston, 18 1871), was named Chev. of the gion of Honour, and took firs: prize at the Paris Exposition, 1 he was in turn succeeded by his s the present firm.

**Chilcot** (chĭl´-kôt), **Thos.**, orga Bath, 1733, till end of century.

**Child, Wm.**, Bristol, 1606—Win 1697 ; organist.

**Chilesotti** (kē-lā-sôt´-tē), **Oscare** Bassano, Italy, July 12, 1848 ; graduate Padua Univ. ; flutist 'cellist ; self-taught in harm.; liv Milan ; wrote important histo works.

**Chimenti** (kē-měn´-tē), **Marga** (called **la Dragherina**), sang London, 1737.

**Chipp, Edm. Thos.** (Mus. D London, 1823—Nice, 1886 ; orga

**Chladni** (khlät´-nē), **Ernst Flor Fr.**, Wittenberg, Nov. 30, 17! Breslau, April 3, 1827 ; prof. of and investigator in physics and ac tics ; discovered the sound-fig which sand assumes on a vibra plate, and which bear his name ; the euphonium and clavicylinder D,D.).

**Chollet** (shôl-lā), **J. B. M.**, b. P. May, 1798 ; violinist and singe opera.

**Chopin** (shô-păň) (**François**) **Fré ric**, Zelazowa Wola (Jeliasovaya

, near Warsaw, March 1, 1809
atalie Janotha declares it to be
b. 22, 1810)—Paris, Oct. 17, 1849;
inent composer for the piano ; son
Nicholas C. (a native of Nancy,
ance, who was at first bookkeeper
a cigar factory, then teacher in the
arsaw Gymnasium), and a Polish
man (née Justine Kryzanowska).
studied at his father's private school,
ong young Polish noblemen ; Al-
rt Zwyny taught him pf. and Jo-
•h Elsner, harm., etc. At 9 he
yed in public a pf.-concerto and
provisations ; c. polonaises, ma-
·kas, and waltzes ; in 1825, pub.
op. 1 a rondo ; op. 2 a fantasie
ch orch. He played in German
ies and had at 19 an individual
le of comp., having written his 2
-concertos, mazurkas, nocturnes,
ndos, etc. He started for London,
d played in Vienna, 1829, with such
ccess that a critic called him " one
the most remarkable meteors blaz-
g on the musical horizon " : and at
ris he had such succ. in his first
ncert, 1831, that he settled there
· life as a teacher of the pf. and
casional giver of concerts. His
pils were of the most aristocratic,
d his friends included Liszt, Ber-
z, Meyerbeer, Bellini, Balzac, and
eine. Schumann with typical spon-
neity (cf. BRAHMS) was moved in
31 by Chopin's op. 2, to say, " Hats
, gentlemen :—a genius " ; and in
39, in reviewing certain of his prel-
es, mazurkas, and valses, to say
He is and remains the keenest and
aunchest poet-soul of the time."
,'s liaison with Mme. Dudevant
George Sand "), begun in 1836 and
ded in 1844, has caused endless
ntroversy. In 1838 an attack of

bronchitis drove him to Majorca,
where she seems to have been a devoted nurse, but the peevishness and
weakness due to his developing consumption caused bitter quarrels, and
she is believed to have caricatured
him as Prince Karol in her novel
" *Lucrezia Floriani.*" Concert tours
and social life in England and Scotland in 1841 – 49 destroyed his
strength. A collection of his letters
was pub. (Dresden, 1877). His many
biographers include Liszt, M. Kara-
sowski (Dresden, 1877), M. A. Audley, Fr. Niecks (Leipzig, 1889). The
latest, in many ways the best balanced,
estimate of **C.** and his works, is
James Huneker's " *Chopin* " (New
York, 1900). His comps. include
beside those mentioned (74, with opus-
number 12 lacking) : " *Don Giovanni,*" fantasia, op. 2 ; " *Krakoviak,*"
rondo, op. 14 ; *E♭ Polonaise*, op. 22 ;
and a fantasia on Polish airs for pf.
with orch ; duo concertant on themes
from " *Robert le Diable* "; an introd.
et Polonaise, op. 3, and a sonata, op.
65 for pf. and 'cello ; pf. trio, op. 8 ;
and a rondo for 2 pfs. op. 73. FOR
PF. SOLO : *Allegro de concert ;* 4
ballades ; barcarolle, op. 60 ; berceuse, op. 57 ; bolero, op. 19 ; 3 écos-
saises, op. 72 ; 12 grandes études, op.
10 ; 12 études, op. 25 ; 3 études ; 4
fantasies ; 3 impromptus ; marche
funèbre, op. 72 ; 52 mazurkas.
" *Morceau de concert sur la Marche
des Puritains de Bellini* " ; 19 nocturnes, 11 polonaises ; 24 préludes,
op. 28 ; prélude, op. 45 ; 3 rondos ;
4 scherzos ; 3 sonatas ; tarantelle,
op. 43 ; 13 vaises ; variations on " *Je
vends des scapulaires,*" op. 12 ;
" *Variation dans l'Hexaméron* " ; 16
Polish songs op. 74.

## Frédéric François Chopin.

### By James Huneker.

CHOPIN'S home education doubtless preserved in him a certain
nine delicacy which never deserted him.  ¶ At the age of
he played a Gyrowetz concerto in public and improvised,
seemed more solicitous about the impression his new collar made on
audience, than for the success of his music.  ¶ As a composer of ninetee
was remarkable and far in advance of his critics and audiences.  The
turbed political atmosphere of Poland coupled with an unsuccessful
affair—he vainly adored the singer Constantia Gladowska—decided him
residence in Vienna.  There his playing did not create any enthusiasm,
in the fall of the year he went to Stuttgart *en route* for Paris.  It was ir
German city that he heard of the downfall of Warsaw and of his patr
hopes ; for Chopin was a fierce patriot, but because of his slender physiq
non-combatant.  He journeyed at once to Paris and settled there.  ¶
intimacy with the famous novelist George Sand lasted ten years, and
influence, hurtful according to some, and valuable according to others,
most potent and enduring.  His sensitive nature was subject to many
shocks during his companionship with the coarser-fibred and more intelle
woman.  Yet it cannot be denied that from his most ardent pangs,
artist-like, contrived to wring some of his sweetest and most subtle m
The shock of the separation, a separation that was inevitable, shatt
Chopin's bruised spirit, and two years later he died, if not of a broken h
partially of disappointment, chagrin, and spleen.  His lungs, always w
became hopelessly diseased, and after a profitless tour in England and Scotl
where he was really too weak to play, he died of consumption and
buried in Père-Lachaise, near the graves of Cherubini and Bellini.
funeral, an imposing one, called out the representative artistic spirits of
city.  Seldom has genius been so accompanied to its last resting-pl
¶ During his lifetime Chopin was the centre of a circle of wit, talent,
fashion.  Balzac, Delacroix, Liszt, Meyerbeer, Heine, Bellini, Ber
Mendelssohn, were a few among his intimate associates.  His spiritual
original piano-playing admitted him into the inner circle of aristocracy,
he was sought for persistently until his life was sapped by sorrow and cons
social duties.  ¶ Chopin played but seldom in public, for he was unfitted
nature to cope with the audiences of the larger concert halls.  That task
gratefully resigned to Liszt.  But in the twilight of the salon among
favoured choice souls, his playing took on almost unearthly qualities.
touch, light in weight, was exquisite in *timbre ;* his ton ranged from *fort*
a feathery *pianissimo,* while his style was absolutely unique.  Tender, mar

ical, capricious, gay, and sad, this young Pole held in bondage the entire
otional gamut. Never had the piano sounded so before, sounded so
ial, so witty, so passionate ; and it may be doubted if it has sounded thus
e ; for, while Liszt, Rubinstein, Tausig, Joseffy, Heyman, DePachmann,
ipoff, Rosenthal, and Paderewski were, and are, remarkable interpreters,
those who heard Chopin the pianist despair in their efforts to describe his
itual performances. His light, finely articulated hand explains some of
characteristics of his technics ; the wide-spread harmonies, the changeful
y of inner voices ; the novel figuration ; and the lovely melodic life.
Chopin is the poet of his instrument, the musical poet of Poland. He
ght up and treasured the folk-songs of his country, and gave them to the
rld in an idealised form. His mazurkas are tiny poems full of caprice,
unded pride, ecstatic moments ; his four ballads are epical in scope, coning noble melodies, the form absolutely original ; the four scherzos are
dences of Chopin's creative powers, for here the form is again novel ; the
tent startling. Bitterness, frantic and cruel, followed by rapturous out-
sts of melody arouse in the listener the most vivid emotions. It is Chopin
the apex of his power. The polonaises are passionate and patriotic, or
fantastic and graceful, but always wonder-breeding. His waltzes are for
salon, and for the soul—like the mazurkas. Of the three sonatas, the
in B flat minor is the most satisfactory. Without organic unity it never-
less astonishes by its originality and depth. Its slow movement is the
eral march, now a banal concert number. In his four Impromptus Chopin
full of charm, while in the *Barcarolle* and in the *Fantaisie*, *Opus 49* he
ost achieves perfection. The nocturnes and *Cradle Song*, now for the
st part war-worn from repetition, contain much beautiful music. *The
dies, opus 10* and *25* with the *Preludes, opus 28* are Chopin in all his
zling invention, his never-failing fancy, poetry, daring harmonic innova-
ns and moving melodic richness. ¶He changed the modern map of
sic by his subtle and profound experimentings with the possibilities of
omatic harmonies, and for this ranks among the great composers. Within
range he is the most perfect lyrist that ever sang, and the ethereal sono-
es of his style, his discreet and original use of the *tempo rubato*, make him
orerunner of all that is free, individual and exotic in latter-day music.
Chopin was not happiest in writing for ochestra or for piano in conjunction
th violin or violoncello. His two concertos contain charming episodes, but
not cohere, do not make the eloquent appeal of the smallest of his
zurkas. He was not fashioned for the epic, this master of intimate moods.
wrote variations, fantasies, a 'cello-sonata, a piano-trio and bolero, a tar-
elle and songs. ¶We have forgotten them ; but never so long as the piano
nains the piano, will Chopin be forgotten. He is, as Rubinstein said, its
l.

**Chor'ley, H. Fothergill,** Blackley Hurst, Lancashire, 1808—London, 1872; critic and widely travelled writer.

**Choron** (shô-rôń), **Alex. Ét.,** Caen, Oct. 21, 1772—Paris, June 29, 1834; an ardent student of musical theory and practice, historian and benefactor who devoted his fortune to the advance of the art.

**Choudens** (shoo-däńs), **A.,** b. Paris, 1849; son of a music publisher; c. 2 operas, "*Graziella*" (Paris, 1877); and "*La Jeunesse de Don Juan,*" etc.

**Chouquet** (shoo-kā), **Ad. Gv.,** Havre, 1819—Paris, 1886; teacher and writer of historical works.

**Christiani** (krĕs-tĭ-ä'-nē), (1) **Ad. Fr.,** Cassel, 1836—Elizabeth, N. J., 1885; pianist and writer; lived in London, then America. (2) **Élise,** Paris, 1827—Tobolsk, 1853; remarkable 'cellist; début, Paris, 1845.

**Christ'mann,** (1) **Jn. Fr.,** Ludwigsburg, Würtemberg, 1752—Heutingsheim, 1817; composer and writer. (2) **Fz. X.,** Austrian organ-builder, d. Rottenmann, Styria, 1875.

**Chrysander** (krĕ'-zänt-ĕr), **Fr.,** Lübtheen, Mecklenburg, July 8, 1826—1902; editor and writer of the standard biography of Händel, etc.

**Chrysan'thos** of Madyton; writer 19th century; teacher of church singing, Constantinople, later Archbishop of Durazzo in Albania.

**Church, J.,** Windsor, 1675—Jan. 5, 1741, composer.

**Chwatal** (khwä'-täl), (1) **Fz. Xaver,** Rumburg, Bohemia, 1808—Elmen (Soolbad), 1879; teacher and composer (2) **Jos.,** b. Rumburg, Jan. 12, 1811, bro. of above; org.-builder in Merseburg; inv. minor improvements.

**Ciaja** (chä'-yä), **Azzolino Bdo. della,** b. Siena, 1671; organist, amateur org.-builder, and composer.

**Ciampi** (chäm'-pē). **Legrenzio V.,** b. Piacenza, 1719; dram. composer.

**Cianchettini** (chän-kĕt-tē'-nē), (1) **Ver-**

**onica** (née **Dussek,** Czaslau, B mia, 1779; composer and teac (2) **Pio,** London, 1799—1849; so above; composer and pianist; appearance at 5 years; at 10 formed an original concerto in pu

**Cibber** (sĭb'-bĕr), **Susanna M. Arne),** 1714—1766; great En actress and notable singer, siste Dr. Arne.

**Cieutat** (s'yŭ-tä), **H. Maurice,** Paris, July 15, 1861; pupil o Rousseau; c. vaudevilles and ops. from 1885.

**Cifra** (chē'-frä), **A.,** Rome, ca. 15 Loreto, ca. 1636; important c poser of the Roman School; p of Palestrina and B. Nanini; cc conductor.

**Cimador** (chē'-mä-dôr), **Giambat ta,** Venice, 1761—London, ca. 18 violinist, 'cellist, pianist and c poser.

**Cimarosa** (chē-mä-rō'-sä), **Domen** Aversa, near Naples, Dec. 17, 174 Venice, Jan. 11, 1801; the orpha a poor mason; studied at Min charity-school, his first teacher b Polcano, monastery organist; whe years old was given a scholarship the Cons. di S. Maria di Lor where he studied singing with Ma and Sacchini, cpt. with Fenaroli, comp. with Piccinni. 1770 his e torio "*Giuditta*" was prod. in Ro 1772, his first opera, "*Le Str ganze del Conte,*" at Naples, with succ., which was won, however, 1 year by "*La Finta Parigina.*" phenomenal facility, he c. 76 opera 29 years. He lived alternately Rome and Naples. 1781, he p two operas in Naples, one in Ro and two in Turin; invited 1789 to court-composer at St. Petersb (vice Paesiello), he spent 5 month triumphal progress thither, be lionised at various courts, he sta there 3 years, prod. 3 operas and wi 500 pieces of music for the cou but he could not tolerate the clim and was reluctantly released, be

gaged as cond. to Emperor Leo-
ld at Vienna, with a salary of 12,-
o florins. He prod. 3 operas incl.
s masterpiece "*Il Matrimonio Se-
eto*" (1787), which won an all-
acing success. 1793, he returned to
aples. 1799, he took part in the
eapolitan revolutionary demonstra-
n on the entrance of the French
my, and was condemned to death
King Ferdinand, but banished in-
ead; he died suddenly at Venice.
being everywhere claimed that he
d been poisoned by order of Queen
aroline of Naples, the Pope's phy-
cian made an examination, and
ore that he died of a gangrenous
dominal tumour. Particularly in
mic, but at times also in serious
era, C. almost challenges compari-
n with Mozart for fluency of melo-
 and orchestral richness. His best
eras are "*La Finta*" (Naples, 1773),
*L'Italiana in Londra*" (Rome, 1774),
*Il Fanatico per gli Antichi Romani*"
Naples. 1777), in which were intro-
ced dramatically vocal-trios and
artets, "*La Ballerina Amante*"
Naples, 1782), "*Le Trame Deluse*"
Naples, 1786), "*L'Impresario in An-
astie*" (Naples, 1786), "*Giannina e
ernadone*" (Naples, 1788), "*La Ver-
ne del Sole*" (St. Petersburg, 1791),
*Il Matrimonio Segreto*" (Vienna,
792), "*Le Astuzie Femminile*" (Na-
es, 1794). He also prod. 2 orato-
os, 7 symphonies, several cantatas;
asses, etc.

ollini (chē-pôl-lē'-nē), **Gaetano,** b.
ropea, Italy, Feb. 8, 1857; pupil of
rancesco Coppa; now lives at Mi-
an as dram. composer.

ollone (chē-pôl-lō'-ně), **Alfonso,** b.
ara S. Martino (Chieti), Nov. 25,
843; pupil of M. Rute; lives at
'erano as teacher and composer.

randi (chē-prän'-dē), **Ercole,** ca.
738—after 1790; tenor.

assen (kläs'-sěn), **Arthur,** b. Star-
ard, Prussia, Feb. 19, 1859; grad-
ated from Danzig Gym.; 1875,
tudied under Müller-Hartung, Gott-

schalk and Sulze, Weimar Music
School; 1880–84, cond. Göttingen
and Magdeburg; 1884, cond. "Ari-
on" and other societies of Brooklyn,
N. Y.; est. the "Claassen Mus.
Inst."; c. choruses, incl. "*Der Kam-
erad*" (prize); and symph. poem
"*Hohenfriedberg*," etc.

**Clag'get, Chas.,** London, 1755—
1820; violinist and inventor.

**Clapisson** (klă-pĭs-sôn), **Antoine L.,**
Naples, 1808—Paris, 1866; violinist,
professor and dram. composer.

**Clari** (klä'-rē), **Giov. M.,** Pisa, 1669—
Pistoia, ca. 1745; conductor and
composer.

**Clar'ibel.** Vide MRS. CHAS. BARNARD.

**Clark(e),** (1) **Jeremiah,** London, 1670
—(?), ca. 1707; organist and dram.
composer; a suicide for love. (2)
**Richard,** Datchet (Bucks), 1780—
London, 1856; composer and writer.
(3) Vide SCOTSON CLARK.

**Clarke,** (1) **Jas. Peyton,** Scotland,
1808—Toronto, Canada, 1877; organist and professor. (2) **Hugh
Archibald,** b. near Toronto, Canada, Aug. 15, 1839; son and pupil of
above; organist in Philadelphia
churches; 1875, prof. of music in the
Univ. of Pennsylv.; made Mus. Doc.
(1886) by the Univ. when his music
to Aristophanes' "*Acharnians*" was
prod.; also c. an oratorio, "*Jerusalem*" (Phila., 1891), etc. (3)
**J. (Whitfield-Clarke),** Gloucester,
England, 1770—Holmer, 1836; organist, professor and editor. (4)
**James Hamilton Smee,** b. Birmingham, England, Jan. 25, 1840; at
12 organist; 1866 at Queen's College,
Oxford; Mus. Bac., 1867; cond.
various theatres; 1893, cond. Carl
Rosa Opera Co.; c. operettas, 2 symphonies, etc. (5) **Wm. Horatio,** b.
Newton, Mass., March 8, 1840; 1878-
87, organist at Tremont Temple,
Boston, then retired to Reading,
Mass., where he has an estate and a
chapel of music, Clarigold Hall, containing a large 4-manual organ with
100 stops; wrote 15 instructive works

"*Outline of the Structure of the Pipe-Organ*" (1877), etc. (6) **Maria Victoria (Cowden-Clarke)**. Vide NOVELLO.

**Clarus** (klä'-roos), **Max.**, b. Mühlberg-on-Elbe, March 31, 1852; pupil of his father, the municipal mus. dir. there, and of Haupt, Schneider, and Löschorn, Berlin; cond. in various German, Austrian and Hungarian theatres; 1890, mus. dir. Brunswick court; from 1884 cond. the "Orpheus," and from 1890 the "Chorgesangverein"; c. "Patriotic spectacular" opera, "*Des Grossen Königs Rekrut*" (Brunswick, 1889); succ. romantic opera "*Ilse*" (Brunswick, 1895); ballets, etc.

**Clasing** (klä'-zĭng), **Jn. H.**, Hamburg, 1779—1829; teacher and dram. composer.

**Claudin** (klō-dăn), (1). Vide SERMISY. (2) **Le Jeune.** Vide LEJEUNE.

**Claudius** (klow'-dĭ-oos), **Otto**, Kamenz, Saxony, 1793—Naumburg, 1877; cantor and dram. composer.

**Claussen** (klows'-sĕn), **Wm.**, Schwerin, 1843—1869; composer.

**Clausz-Szarvady** (klows'-shär-vä'-dē), **Wilhelmine**, Prague, 1834—Paris, 1882; pianist.

**Clay, Fr.** (of English parents), Paris, 1840—Great Marlow, near London, 1889; dram. composer.

**Cleaver**, Mrs. **Eleanor** (née **Beebe**), b. Detroit, Mich.; alto; sang two years as soprano in New York; after short stage career, studied with Delle Sedie, and Bertin (acting), Paris; concert début, London, 1900; has sung there frequently with much success; 1902, sang in New York.

**Cleeman** (klä'-män), **Fr. Jos. Chp.**, Kriwitz, Mecklenburg, 1771—Parchim, 1827; writer.

**Clegg, J.**, Ireland (probably), 1714—Nisane, 1742; remarkable violinist and composer.

**Clem'ens**, Jacob (called "**Cl. Non Papa**") (i. e., "not the Pope" Clement VII.); d. ca. 1557 (?); played several instrs. and composed.

**Clement** (klä'-mĕnt), **Fz.**, Vie 1784—1842; violinist and dram. poser.

**Clément** (klä-män), (1) **Chas. F**ᵣ b. in Provence, ca. 1720; live Paris as pf.-teacher, writer and d composer. (2) **Félix**, Paris, 18 1885; organist.

**Clementi** (klä-mĕn'-tē), **Muzio**, R 1 7 5 2 — near Evesham, Engl March 10, 1832; son of a golds and musical amateur who had taught by A. Buroni, then by organist Condicelli. At 9 he chosen as an organist in compet with older players; until 14, stu under G. Carpani (comp.) and tartelli (voice); 1766, an English named Beckford secured permissio educate him in England, and till he lived and studied in Dorsets then made a sensation as pianis London. 1773, pub. pf.-sonatas icated to Haydn, and highly pra by Emmanuel Bach; 1777–80, balist at the Italian Opera; toured the continent, meeting Mo in "friendly" rivalry, without vic for either; lived in London, 17 1802; he amassed a fortune a teacher, pianist and composer in s of losses from the failure of L man and Broderip, instr.-makers; estab. a succ. piano-factory and house (now Collard's). 1802, made a brilliant tour with his p Field; he taught other famous pu incl. Moscheles, Kalkbrenner, Me beer. His comps. incl. sympho and overtures; 106 pf.-sonatas with vln., 'cello, or flute); fug preludes and exercises in canon fo toccatas, etc. His book of étu the "*Gradus ad Parnassum*," 18 is a standard; biog. by Giov. F (Milan, 1878); O. Chilesotti (Mil 1882) and Clement (Paris, 1878).

**Clement y Cavedo** (klä'-mĕnt ē vä'-dhō), b. Gandia, Spain, Jan. 1810; organist at Valencia; 18 52. at Gueret, France; lived in M rid as composer.

rice (klā-rēs), **Justin,** b. Buenos
yres, Oct. 16, 1863 ; 1882, pupil of
élibes and Pessard, Paris Cons. ;
ves in Paris ; prod. 4 comic operas,
c.

quot (klē-kō), **Fran. H.,** Paris,
728—1791 ; organ-builder.

'ford, Rev. **Jas.,** Oxford, 1622—
ondon, 1698 ; composer.

'ton, **J. Chas.,** London, 1781—
ammersmith, 1841 ; teacher, con-
actor and dram. composer ; inv. the
idomusicon (v. D. D.).

ve, **Catherine** (née **Raftor**) (called
Kitty Clive "), London, 1711—Dec.
, 1785 ; famous actress, also singer.

'er, **J.,** d. London, 1729, English
ublisher, reputed inventor of engrav-
g on tin plates.

ob, **Gerard Francis,** b. Nettle-
ead, Kent, Oct. 15, 1838 ; Fellow
'rinity Coll., Cambridge, 1863 ;
udied music, Dresden ; 1877–92,
airman Board of Music Studies,
ambridge ; c. Psalm 62, with orch.,
tc.

cchi (kôk'-kē), **Gioacchino,** Padua,
720—Venice, 1804; dram. composer.

ccia (kôt'-chä), **Carlo,** Naples,
782—Novara, 1873; cond. and dram.
omposer.

ccius (kôk'-tsï-oos), **Th.,** Knaut-
ain, near Leipzig, 1824—Leipzig,
897 ; pf.-teacher.

ccon (kôk-kōn), **Nicolò,** b. Venice,
ug. 10, 1826 ; pupil of E. Fabio ;
856 organist, 1873 conductor at San
Marco ; c. over 450 numbers, an
ratorio, " Saul," 8 requiem masses,
o " messe da gloria," 2 operas,
tc.

chläus (kôkh'-lĕ-oos), **Jns.** (rightly
ns. Dobnek, pseud. " **Wendel-
tein** "), 1479—Breslau, 1552 ; writer;
pponent of Luther.

cks, **Robt., & Co.,** firm of London
aus. publishers, founded, 1827, by
1) **Robt. C.,** succeeded by his sons,
2) **Arthur Lincoln C.,** and (3)
**Stroud Lincoln C.,** d. 1868 ; (4)
**Robt. Macfarlane C.** is now in
harge.

**Coclico** (kō'-klē-ko) (**Co'clicus**), **Adrian Petit,** b. in the Hennegau
(Hainaut), ca. 1500 ; singer and composer.

**Coenen** (koo'-něn), (1) **Jns. Meinardus,** b. The Hague, Jan. 28, 1824 ;
bassoonist, pupil of Lübeck Cons.
1864, cond. at Amsterdam ; latei
municipal mus. dir.; c. ballet-mus.,
2 symphonies, cantatas, etc. (2) **Fz.,**
b. Rotterdam, Dec 26, 1826 ; violinist; pupil of Vieuxtemps and Molique;
lived in Amsterdam, 1895, dir. of the
Cons. and prof. of vln. and comp. ;
solo violinist to the Queen ; leader of
a quartet ; and composer of a notable
symphony, cantatas, etc. (3) **Willem,** b. Rotterdam, Nov. 17, 1837 ;
bro. of above ; pianist, toured S.
America, and W. Indies ; since 1862,
concert-giver in London ; c. oratorio,
" *Lazarus* " (1878), etc. (4) **Cornelius,** b. The Hague, 1838 ; violinist ;
1859, cond. at Amsterdam ; 1860
bandm. Garde Nationale, Utrecht ; c.
overtures, etc.

**Coerne** (kĕr'-ně), **Louis Adolphe,** b.
Newark, N. J., 1870 ; 1876 – 80
studied at Stuttgart and Paris, then
entered Harvard College and studied
with Paine and Kneisel, Boston, U.
S. A.; 1890 studied with Rheinberger
and Hieber, Munich ; 1893 organist
at Boston, also at the Columbian
Exposition ; 1893–96 dir. Liedertafel,
Buffalo ; c. an opera " *The Maid of
Marblehead*," symph. poem " *Hiawatha*," etc.

**Co'gan, Phillip,** b. Cork, 1750 ; organist, teacher and composer.

**Cohen** (kow'-ěn or kō'-ěn), (1) **H.,**
Amsterdam, 1808—Brie-sur-Marne,
1880 ; writer. (2) **Léonce,** b. Paris,
Feb. 12, 1829 ; violinist and dram.
composer ; pupil Leborne Cons.;
1851 Grand prix de Rome. (3)
**Jules Émile David,** b. Marseilles,
Nov. 2, 1835 ; pupil of Zimmerman,
Marmontel, Benoist, and Halévy,
Paris Cons.; won first prize for pf.,
organ, cpt. and fugue ; 1870, teacher of
ensemble singing at the Cons. ; since

1877 *Chef de Chant*, and chorus-master Gr. Opéra ; prod. 4 operas ; c. 3 cantatas, several symphonies, masses, oratorios, etc. (4) **K. Hubert**, b. Laurenzkirg (near Aix), Oct. 18, 1851 ; a priest, studied at Aix and Raliston, 1879–87 cond. Bamberg ; now at Cologne Cath. ; c. masses, etc. (5) **Isidore**. Vide LARA, DE.

**Colasse** (kô-lăs), **Pascal**, Rheims (or Paris), 1639 (?) — Versailles, 1709 ; cond. and dram. composer.

**Col'bran**, (1) **Gianni**, court-musician to King of Spain, 18th century. (2) **Isabella A.**, Madrid, 1785—Boulogne, 1845, daughter of above ; singer and composer.

**Cole, Blanche**, d. London, 1888, concert-singer ; 1868, m. Sidney Naylor.

**Co'leridge-Taylor, Samuel**, b. London, Aug. 15, 1875 (of African descent ; his father a native of Sierra Leone, his mother, English) ; one of the leading living English composers ; pupil (vln.) of the R. A. M., 1890 ; won composition-scholarship in 1893 ; until 1896 pupil of V. Stanford ; 1892 pub. an anthem ; c. a nonet for pf., strings, and wind (1894) ; a symphony (1896) ; a quintet for clar. and strings (1897), a string-quartet, and a Morning and Evening Service ; pub. a ballade for viola and orch., operetta "*Dream Lovers*," 4 waltzes for orch. ; succ. cantata "*Hiawatha*," etc.

**Colin** (kô-lăn), **P. Gilbert** (**Colinus, Colinaus, Chamault**), singer and notable composer, Paris, 1532.

**Colins** (kô-lăns), **Jean Bapt.**, b. Brussels, Nov. 25, 1834 ; pupil of Wery ; from 1863 teacher at the Cons., from 1888 also at Antwerp school of music.

**Col'la,**—cond. at Parma, 1780, when he m. Agujari, who preferred his compositions to all others.

**Collard** (kôl-lăr'), a London family of pf.-makers. (1) **Fr. W. Collard** (1772—1860), in partnership with Clementi, bought out Longman & Broderip, 1798, then **C.** bought out

Clementi ; he inv. various dev the firm name now Collard & Col (2) **Chas. Lukey C.** being the b

**Col'lins**, (1) **Isaac**, 1797—Lon 1871 ; violinist, gave concerts his 5 children, (2) **Viotti** (vi ist) and (3) **G.** ('cellist, d. being the best known.

**Col'man**, (1) **Chas.**, d. in Fetter L London, in 1664 ; teacher and poser. (2) **Edward**, d. Aug. 1669, son of above ; teacher, poser and singer.

**Colombani** (kō-lôm-bä'-nē), **Ora** monk, conductor, and cptist. at V na, 1576–92.

**Colom'bi, Vincenzo**, Italian or builder, Rome, 1549.

**Colonna** (kō-lôn'-nä), **Giov. Pa** Bologna (or Brescia), ca. 1640— logna, 1695 ; organist, conduc and dram. composer.

**Colonne** (kô-lŭn'), **Édouard** (rig **Judas**), b. Bordeaux, July 23, 18 pupil of Girard and Sauzay (v Elwart, and A. Thomas (con Paris Cons. ; 1874, founded the mous "Concerts du Châtelet"; 1 cond. official Exposition conce 1892 cond. at the Gr. Opéra ; c often in London, and 1902, Vien

**Coltellini** (lē'-nē'), **Céleste**, b. L horn, 1764—retired, 1795 ; celebra mezzo-sopr. ; m. Mélicofre.

**Combs, Gilbert Raynolds**, b. Pl delphia, Jan. 5, 1863, son and p of a pianist, organist and compos organist and conductor in Phila phia ; 1885 founded the Broad Cons. of Mus.

**Comes** (kō'-mäs), **Juan Baptista,** lencia, ca. 1560 ; conductor and c poser.

**Comettant** (kôm-ĕt-tän), (**J. P.**) car, Bordeaux, Gironde, 1819 Montvilliers, 1898 ; writer and c poser.

**Commer** (kôm'-mĕr), **Fz.,** Colog 1813—Berlin, 1887 ; editor and c poser.

**Compenius** (kôm-pā'-nĭ-oos), (1) b. Nordhausen, 1540 ; organ-buil

c. His bro (?), (2) **Esajas**, organ-
ilder, inv. the "Duiflöte" pipe.

père (kôn-păr), **Louis** (diminutive,
**oyset**), Flanders, 15th cent.—St.
uentin, Aug. 16, 1518 ; famous con-
apuntist.

**acker & Co.**, organ-builders,
uddersfield, since 1854.

cone (kôn-kō'-nĕ), **Giu.**, Turin, ca.
10—June, 1861 ; organist, famous
nging-teacher in Paris, 1832–48,
ter court-organist Turin ; c. 2 operas
d famous vocal exercises.

'dell, **H.**, d. June, 1824 ; English
olinist and composer.

forti (kôn-fôr'-tē), **Giov.**, b. near
ileto, 1560 ; singer.

frèrie de St. Julien, a musical
ciety, Paris, 1330–1761.

ninck, (1) **Jacques Félix de**, Ant-
erp, 1791 — Schaerbeck-les-Brux-
les, 1866 ; conductor at Berlin, and
mposer. (2) **Fran. de**, b. Leb-
eke, Belgium, Feb. 20, 1810 ; pian-
t ; pupil of Pixis and Kalkbrenner,
aris ; teacher and composer, at
russels. (3) **Jos. Bernard de**, b.
stend, March 10, 1827 ; dram. com-
oser ; son of (1) ; pupil of de Leun,
ntwerp, and Leborne, Paris Cons. ;
ved in Paris.

radi (kōn-rä'-dē), (1) **Jn. G.**, 17th
ent. ; conductor ; one of the first
mposers of German opera, his
orks prod. at Hamburg. (2) **Joan G.**, Norway, ca. 1820—Christi-
nia, 1896 ; composer. (3) **Aug.**,
erlin, 1821—1873 ; organist and
ram. composer. (4) **Jules**, b. Liège,
an. 27, 1834 ; pupil of Decharneux
nd of Daussoigne-Méhul at Liège
`ons. (comp.) ; he won second grand
rix de Rome at Brussels ; 1864, prof.
f solfeggio at the Cons. ; c. 5 1-act
omic operas, etc.

nstantin (kôn-stän-tăn), **Titus
Chas.**, b. Marseilles, Jan. 7, 1835 ;
upil of Thomas, Paris Cons., 1860 ;
ond. of the "Fantasies Parisi-
nnes"; 1875, Op. Com. ; c. a
omic-opera, "*Dans la Forêt*"
1872), etc.

**Conti** (kôn'-tē), (1) **Fran. Bart.**, Florence, 1681—1732 ; court-theorbist
and dram. composer. (2) ("**Conti-
ni**") **Ignazio**, Florence, 1699—
Vienna, 1759 ; son and successor of
above ; composer. (3) **Gicacchino**
(named **Gizziello**, after his teacher
Dom. Gizzi), Arpino, Naples, 1714—
Rome, 1761 ; famous male soprano ;
1739, in London with Händel ; retired to Arpino in 1753. (4) **Carlo**,
Arpino, Naples, 1797—Naples, 1868 ;
prof. and dram. composer. (5) **Giacinto**, Brescia, 1815—1895 ; violinist and composer ; son and pupil of
(6) **Defendente**, theatre-dir. at
Brescia.

**Continuo** (kōn-tē'-noo-ō), **Giov.**, d.
Mantua, 1556 ; conductor and contrapuntist.

**Con'verse, Chas. Crozat** (pen-names,
**K. Redan, C. Nevers**, etc.), b.
Warren, Mass.. Oct. 7, 1832 ; pupil
of Richter, Plaidy, Leipzig Cons. ;
lawyer, Erie, Pa. ; pub. Amer. Concert-overture, "*Hail Columbia*," for
orch. (Paris, 1869) ; *Fest-Ouvertüre*
(1870) ; cantata (on the 126th Psalm)
for soli, chorus and orch. (1888),
"*Jesus, lover of my soul*" (very
pop.) ; in MS. 2 symphonies, 2 oratorios, etc.

**Cooke**, (1) **H.**, d. July 13, 1672 ; buried
Westminster Abbey ; court-composer
and teacher. (2) **Nathaniel**, b.
Bosham, 1773 ; organist. (3) **Benj.**,
London, 1734—1793 ; conductor and
composer. (4) **Thos. Simpson**,
Dublin, 1782—London, 1848 ; con-
ductor, later tenor, then prof. at the
R. A. M. ; prod. nearly 20 operas at
Drury Lane. (5) **H. Angelo Mi-
chael** (called **Grattan**), son of above;
oboist and bandmaster.

**Coombe, Wm. Francis**, b. Plymouth,
1786 ; son of a singing teacher ; composer.

**Coombs**, (1) **Jas. Morrison**, Salisbury, 1769—1820 ; organist and composer. (2) **Chas. Whitney**, b.
Bucksport, Maine, Dec. 25, 1859;
pupil of Speidel (pf.) and Max Sei

friz, Draeseke (comp.), Hermann
John, P. Janssen, and Lamperti;
1887–91, organist Amer. Ch, in
Dresden; returned as organist Church
of the Holy Communion, New York,
still there ; pub. "*The Vision of St.
John,*" cantata with orch. and org.,
songs, etc.

**Coo′per,** (1) **H. Christopher,** Bath,
Engl., 1819—Glasgow, 1881, conductor. (2) **G.,** Lambeth, London,
1820—London, 1876 ; organist and
composer.

**Coote, Chas.,** England, 1809—London, 1880 ; bandmaster, etc.

**Coperario** (kō-pĕr-ä′-rĭ-ō) (rightly **J.
Cooper),** famous English lutenist
and viola-da-gambist, 16th century.

**Cop′pola,** (1) **Giu.,** singer in London,
1777. (2) **P. A. (Pierantonio),**
Castrogiovanni, Sicily, 1793—Canta-
nia, 1877 ; dram. composer and conductor.

**Coquard** (kô-kăr), **Arthur,** b. Paris,
1846 ; pupil of César Franck ; mus.
prof. Nat. Inst. of the Young Blind ;
critic for "*Le Monde*" *;* c. operas
"*L'Epée du Roi*" (Angers, 1884) ;
"*Le Mari d'un Jour*" (Paris,
1886) ; lyric dramas, "*L'oiseau bleu*"
(Paris, 1891) ; "*La Jacquerie*" (Monte
Carlo and Paris, 1895), etc.

**Corbet** (kôr-bā), **Francisque,** Pavia,
ca. 1630—Paris, 1700 ; guitar virtuoso and composer.

**Cor′bett, Wm.,** 1669 (?)—London
(?), 1748 ; Engl. violinist and composer.

**Cordans** (kôr-däns), **Bart.,** Venice,
1700—Udine, 1757 ; Franciscan monk,
then conductor and dram. composer.

**Cordel′la, Giacomo,** Naples, 1786—
1846 ; dram. composer.

**Cor′der, Fr.,** b. Hackney, London,
Jan. 26, 1852 ; pupil of R. A. M. ;
1875, won the Mendelssohn Scholarship ; 1875–78, pupil of Ferd. Hiller ;
1880, cond. of Aquarium Concerts
at Brighton where he lives as a transl.
and critic, and composer of operas,
cantatas, etc.; wrote "*The Orchestra
and how to write for it,*" etc.

**Cordier** (kôrd-yā), **Jacques,** Lorra[i]
ca. 1580—Paris, ca. 1629 ; vi[o]
ist.

**Corel′li, Arcangelo,** Fusignano, [near]
Imola, Italy, Feb. 1, 1653—R[o]
Jan. 13, 1713 ; pupil of Bessani [and]
Simonelli ; toured Germany, [etc.;]
lived under patronage of Card[inal]
Ollobone ; one of the founders [of]
vln.-style, systematiser of bowing [and]
shifting, introducer of chord-playi[ng;]
a composer for the vln. whose w[orks]
still hold favour. On invitation f[rom]
the King of Naples he gave a s[eries]
court-concert, but at a second m[ade]
various blunders and returned [to]
Rome, in chagrin, increased [to]
fatal results on finding or imagin[ing]
himself supplanted there by a [young]
violinist named Valentini. His [mas-]
terpieces "*Concerti grossi,*" were [pub.]
just before his death. Many sp[uri-]
ous comps. were issued under [his]
name.

**Corfe,** (1) **Jos.,** Salisbury, 1740—1[820;]
organist and composer. (2) **Art[hur]
T.,** Salisbury, 1773—1863 ; so[n of]
above ; pianist, organist and wr[iter.]
(3) **Chas. W.,** son of above ; or[gan-]
ist Christ Church, Oxford.

**Cornelius** (kôr-nā′-lĭ-oos), **Peter,** [Ma-]
yence, Dec. 24, 1824—Oct. 26, 1[874;]
unsucc. actor ; then studied cpt. [with]
Dehn at Berlin, and joined the W[ag-]
nerian coterie at Weimar. His o[pera]
"*Der Barbier von Bagdad*" wa[s a]
failure through organised opposi[tion]
which led Liszt to leave the to[wn;]
but in 1886–87 it succeeded. [He]
wrote his own libretti and tra[ns.]
others. 1886–87, at Dresden, [and]
other cities ; 1859, with Wagner [to]
Vienna, and Munich, where he [be-]
came reader to King Ludwig, [and]
prof. ; prod. the opera "*Der C[id*"]
Weimar, 1865 ; he left "*Gunl[öd*"]
unfinished ; Lassen completed it, [and]
it was prod., Strassburg, 1892 ; [he]
pub. many songs. Biog. by Sa[ndt-]
berger (Leipzig, 1887).

**Cornell′, J. H.,** New York, 182[?—]
1894 ; organist, composer and wri[ter]

ayshe, ´1) **Wm.**, d. before 1526;
glish teacher and composer. (2)
m., son of above; composer.

et (kôr´-nāt), (1) **Julius**, S. Can-
lo, Tyrol, 1792—Berlin, 1860;
or and dir. His wife, (2) **Franz-
ka** (1806—1870) was also a singer.
naro (kō-rō-nä´-rō), (1) **Gaetano**,
Vincenza, Italy, Dec. 18, 1852; vio-
ist; till 1873, pupil, Milan Cons.,
en in Germany; prod. the succ.
era "*Un Tramonto*" (Milan Cons.
1., 1873); 3-act "*La Creola*"
ologna, 1878); "*Il Malacarne*"
rescia, 1894); for several years
of. of harm., and since 1894,
of. of comp., Milan Cons. (2)
ellio **Bv.**, b. Italy, ca. 1863; pian-
(protégé of Sonzogno); début at 8;
9, organist in Vincenza; at 13. th.
nd., Marosteca; at 15, chorusm.;
16, pupil Bologna Cons.; graduat-
g with first prizes; c. a symphony;
era, "*Jolanda*" (1889?); unsucc.
*Claudia*" (Milan, 1895).

ri (kôr´-rē), **Dom.**, Rome, 1744—
ondon, 1825; dram. composer and
riter.

si, **Jacopo**, b. ca. 1560; Florentine
obleman, in whose house and in
ardi´s, Peri, Caccini, Emilio del
avaliere, Galilei, Rinuccini, and
hers met and inaugurated modern
era (v. PERI); **C.** was a skilful gra-
cembalist.

teccia (kôr-tĕt´-chä), **Fran. Bdo.**
, Arezzo, 16th cent., Florence,
571; organist, conductor and com-
oser.

ss´mann, **B.**, b. Dessau, May 17,
822; ´cellist; pupil of Espenhahn,
rechsler, Theo. Müller and Kum-
er; 1840, member of Gr. Opéra
rch., Paris; 1847–48, solo ´cellist at
ewandhaus, Leipzig; then studied
omp. under Hauptmann; 1850, at
Weimar, with Liszt; 1866, prof. Mos-
ow Cons.; 1870–78 at Baden-Baden;
nce prof. of ´cello, Frankfort Cons.;
omposer.

s´ta, (1) Sir **Michael** (rightly
**Michele**), Naples, Feb. 4, 1810

(1807 ?)—Brighton, England, April
29. 1884, son and pupil of (2) **Pasquale C.** (composer ch.-mus.); pupil
also of Tritto, Zingarelli (comp.),
and Crescentini (singing) at the
Naples Cons.; prod. 4 succ. operas
at Naples, was sent to Birmingham
England, to cond. a psalm of Zin
garelli's, but through a misunder-
standing, had to sing the tenor part;
he thereafter lived in England as dir.
and cond. of King's Th., London,
where he prod. three ballets; 1846,
cond. of the Philh. and the new Ital.
Opera; 1848, Sacred Harmonic Society; from 1849, cond. Birmingham
festivals; from 1857, the Handel festivals; knighted in 1869; 1871 dir. of
the music and cond. at H. M.'s
Opera; c. 3 oratorios, 6 operas, 3
symphonies, etc. (3) **Andrea**, b.
Brescia, settled London, 1825; composer and teacher. (4) **Carlo, Naples**
1826—1888; teacher Naples Cons.
(5) **P. Mario**, *brother of above*, July 26,
1858, nephew of above; c. chamber-music and pop. songs in Neapolitan dialect; also 2 pantomimes, "*Le
Modèle Rêve*," and the succ. "*L'Histoire d'un Pierrot*" (Paris, 1894?).

**Costantini** (tē´-nē), **Fabio**, b. Rome,
ca. 1570; composer and teacher.

**Costanzi** (kō-stän´-tsǐ), **Juan** (or **Gio-
annino**), Rome, 1754—1778; con-
ductor.

**Coste** (kôst), **Gaspard**, composer at
Avignon, 1530.

**Cost´eley, Wm.**, Scotland, 1531—Er-
reux, 1606; organist and writer.

**Cotta** (kôt´-tä), **Jn.**, Ruhla, Thuringia,
1794—Wilterstet, near Weimar, 1868;
pastor and composer.

**Cot´to (Cotto´nius), Jns.**, 11th to
12th cent.; writer.

**Cottrau** (kôt-trō, or kôt-trä´-oo), (1)
**Guillaume (Guglielmo)**, Paris, 1797
—Naples, 1847; composer. His
sons (2) **Teodoro** (pen-name **Euta-
lindo Martelli**) (Naples, 1827—
1879) and (3) **Giulio (Jules)**, also
song-composers; the latter c. 2
operas.

**Cotumacci** (ko-too-mät'-chē), **Carlo**, Naples, 1698—1775 ; organist and composer.

**Coucy** (dŭ koo-sē), **Regnault**, Chatelain, **de**, d. Palestine, 1192 ; troubadour to Richard Cœur de Lion ; a poem of ca. 1228 tells that he begged that his heart be sent to his love, whose husband intercepted it, and had it roasted and served up to his wife, who died broken-hearted on being told of her menu ; his songs are in MSS. in the Paris Library, and have been re-published.

**Couperin** (koo-pŭ-răṅ), a family of French musicians, famous for two centuries. The first known were three brothers : (1) **Louis**, 1630—1665 ; organist of St. Gervais and composer. (2) **Fran.** (Sieur de Crouilly), 1631—1701 ; organist and composer. (3) **Chas.**, 1638—1669 ; organist ; his son, (4) **Fran.** (called **Le Grand**), Paris, 1668—1733 ; the first great composer to write exclusively for the harpsichord (or clavecin) ; pupil of Thomelin, and successor of his uncle François, at St. G., 1698 ; 1701, clavecinist and organist to the King ; c. brilliant and fascinating music pub. at Paris, and wrote "*L'Art de toucher du Clavecin*" (1711). (5) His son **Nicholas**, Paris, 1680—1748, was organist. (6) **Armand Louis**, Paris, 1721—1789, son of (5), a remarkable org.-virtuoso. His wife (7) **Élisabeth Antoinette** (née **Blanchet**), b. 1721, was an organist and clavecinist, and played in public at 81. They had 2 sons (8) **P. Louis** (d. 1789), his father's asst. organist, and (9) **Gervais Fran.**, his father's successor.

**Courtois** (koor-twä), **Jean**, 16th cent., French contrapuntist ; conductor and composer.

**Courtville** (koort'-vĭl), (1) **Raphael**, d. 1675 ; of the Chapel Royal. (2) d. ca. 1735 ; organ-composer, son of above. (3) **Raphael**, d. 1771, son of (2) ; organist and writer.

**Courvoisier** (koor-vwäs-yā, or koor'-

foi-sēr), **K.**, b. Basel, Nov. 12, ? violinist ; pupil of David, Röї and Joachim ; 1871, a member oї Thalia Th., orch., Frankfort ; till 1875, cond. of singing with tav Barth ; '76, cond. Düsse Th., orch., and choral socie since 1885 singing-teacher at L pool ; c. a symphony, 2 concert-ї tures, aₐvln.-concerto (MS.), є wrote "*Die Violintechnik*" (trї by H. E. Krehbiel ; N. Y., 18 an "*École de la velocité*" and a ' *thode*" (London, 1892).

**Coussemaker** (koos-mä-kăr'), **C Ed. H.**, Bailleul, Nord, April 1805—Bourbourg, Jan. 10, 187ї remarkable sight-reader, studied with V. Lefêbvre ; while serving judge he made musical researcі avocation, and pub. important w on Hucbald and mediæval in ments, theory and composeї s, incі "*Scriptores de musica medii nova series*" (1864-76, 4 vols. great collection intended as suї ment to Gerbert.

**Cousser.** Vide KUSSER.

**Coverley** (kŭv'-ĕr-lĭ), **Robert**, Oporto, Portugal, Sept. 6, 186ї Scotch father and aristocratic Po guese mother ; studied cpt., orch. vln. with Hill, Ludwig, and Jac not, in London ; lived in New Y many years, since 1898 in Lond pub. many graceful and succ. so orch. and pf.-pieces ; c. the imme ly succ. march " The Passing R ment" and a comic opera (MS.).

**Cow'ard**, (1) **Jas.**, London, 182 1880 ; organist, conductor and c poser. (2) **H.**, b. Liverpool, N 26, 1849 ; grad. Tonic-sol-fa С 1889 Mus. Bac.; 1894 Mus. I Oxon ; singing-teacher and conс Sheffield.

**Cow'en, Frederic Hymen**, b. Kі ton, Jamaica, Jan. 29, 1852 ; а brought to London to study, puї Benedict and Goss, then of Haї mann, Moscheles, Reinecke, Rich and Plaidy, Leipzig ; and Kiel, І

; 1882, dir. Edinburgh Acad. of
sic ; 1887, cond. London Philh. ;
8-9, mus.-dir. Melbourne Centen-
l Exhibition ; 1896, cond. Liver-
ol Phil., and the Manchester
ncerts ; prod. four operas ; two
torios, *The Deluge* (1878), and
*th* (1887) ; 7 cantatas ; 6 sympho-
s (No. 3 " *Scandinavian* " (1880),
" *Welsh*," 6 " *Idyllic* ") ; four or-
estral suites, " *The Language of
wers*," " *In the Olden Time*,"
*In Fairyland*," *Suite de Ballet* ,
fonietta in A for orch. ; 2 over-
es ; pf.-concerto ; pf.-trio ; pf.-
artet ; pf.-pcs. ; over 250 songs.

ner (krä'-mĕr or krä'-mĕr), (1)
'm., Mannheim, 1745 (1743 ?)—
ndon, 1799 (1800 ?) ; violinist and
nductor. (2) **K. Fr.**, Quedlinburg,
52—Paris, Dec. 1807 ; professor. (3)
. **Bap.**, Mannheim, Feb. 24, 1771
London, April 16, 1858 ; eldest son
d pupil of (1). Brought to London
en a year old ; pupil of Benser,
hroeter, then of Clementi ; in comp.,
efly self-taught ; toured as concert-
nist at 17 ; in 1828 est. a mus.-
b. firm (now Cramer & Co.) in
rtnership with Addison ; managed
till 1842 ; 1832–45, lived in Paris ,
b. "a Method for pf. (" *Grosse
aktische Pfte.-Schule* "), in 5
rts," the last containing the cele-
ated " *84 Studies* " (op. 50), still a
ndard ; c. 7 concertos, 105 sonatas,
artet, quintet, and many pf.-pcs.
**Fz.**, b. Munich, 1786 ; nephew of
, first flute in the Munich orch.,
d composer. (5) **Josef Hubert**,
Wageningen, Holland, Feb. 29,
44 ; violinist ; studied with Graven-
in and van Bree, Leonard and
avid ; at 12 played in public at
nsterdam where he now lives as
acher in the Cons., and com-
ser.

ne, **Helen**, American composer ;
pil of Fh. Scharwenka, Berlin, for
years ; c. symphonic poem " The
ast Tournament," suite and sere-
de for orch., etc.

**Crang & Hancock**, organ-builders in
London during 18th cent.

**Cranz** (kränts), **August**, Hamburg,
mus.-pub. firm, founded 1813 by **A.
H. Cranz** (1789–1870). His son **Alwin** (b. 1834), is now the head.

**Craywinckel** (krī'-vĭnk-ĕl), **Fd. Manuel Martin Louis Barthélemy
de**, b. Madrid, Aug. 24, 1820 ; pupil
of Bellon ; cond. St. Bruno, at Bordeaux, where he lived from 1825 ; c.
excellent masses and other church-
mus.

**Cre(c)quillon** (krĕk-wē-yôṅ), **Thos.**,
n. Ghent, (?)—Béthune, 1557 ; ca.
1544–47 conductor and composer.

**Crescentini** (krā-shĕn-tē'-nē), **Girolamo**, Urbania, near Urbino, Feb. 2,
1766—Naples, April 24, 1846 ; famous male soprano and composer.

**Crespel** (krĕs-pĕl'), **Guillaume**, Belgian composer 15th cent.

**Cressent** (krĕs-säṅ), **Anatole**, Argen-
teuil, 1824—Paris, 1870 ; lawyer and
founder of the triennial prize " prix
Cressent," endowed with 120,000
francs, to be equally divided between
the librettist, and the composer of the
best opera ; first awarded to Chaumet,
1875.

**Creyghton** (krā'-tŭn), Rev. **Robt.**, b.
ca. 1639 ; English composer.

**Cristofori**, **Bart.** (wrongly **Cristo-
fali** and **Cristofani**), Padua, May 4,
1653—Florence, March 17, 1731 ; inv.
the first practical hammer-action to
which he gave the name " pianoforte " (v. D. D.) ; in 1711 he substituted for the plucking quills " a row
of little hammers striking the strings
from below," the principle adopted by
Broadwood, and called the " English
action."

**Crivelli**, (1) **Arcangelo**, Bergamo, (?)
—1610 ; tenor and composer. (2) **Giov.
Bat.**, Scandiano, Modena (?)—Modena, 1682 ; organist and conductor.
(3) **Gaetano**, Bergamo, 1774—Brescia, 1836 ; famous tenor. (4) **Dom.**,
b. Brescia, 1794 son of above , dram.
composer.

**Croce** (krō'-chĕ), **Giov. dalla** (called " Il Chiozzotto "), Chioggia, ca. 1560 —Venice, 1609 ; conductor and composer.

**Croes** (kroos), **H. Jas. de,** Antwerp, 1705—Brussels, 1786 ; violinist and conductor.

**Croft(s), Wm.,** Nether-Eatington, Warwickshire, Engl., 1678—Bath, 1727 (buried Westm. Abbey) ; 1704, joint organist, 1707, sole organist Westm. Abbey ; pub. "*Musica sacra* " (the first English church-music engraved in score on plates).

**Crogaert** (krō'-gärt), **J. Ed.,** b. Antwerp ; pupil of Benoît ; 1882 cond. at Antwerp, since 1882 lives in Paris; writer of treatises.

**Croisez** (krwä-sā), **Alex.,** b. Paris (?), 1816 ; composer and writer.

**Cros'dill, J.,** London, 1751—Escrick, Yorkshire, 1825 ; 'cellist.

**Cross, Michael Hurley,** Philadelphia, 1833—1897 ; composer and director.

**Cross'ley, Ada,** Australian soprano ; début, Melbourne as a girl ; has sung with succ. in London for many years, also in Paris, etc.

**Crotch, Wm.,** Norwich, Engl., July 5, 1775—Taunton, Dec. 29, 1847 ; at the age of 2½ he played on a small organ, built by his father, a master-carpenter ; at 10 played in public at London ; at the age of 11 asst. organist of Trinity and King's Colleges Cambridge ; at 14 c. an oratorio, "*The Captivity of Judah*" (perf. 1789), became organist of Christ Ch., Oxford; 1797, prof. of mus. Oxford ; 1799, Mus. Doc. there; 1822 principal of the new R.A.M., c. 2 oratorios.

**Crouch,** (1) Mrs. **Anna M.** (née **Phil-lips**), 1763—Brighton, 1805 ; Engl. operatic singer. (2) **Fr. Nicholls,** London, July 31, 1808—Portland, Me., Aug. 18, 1896 ; basso, 'cellist and singing-teacher ; c. 2 operas, and songs, incl. "*Kathleen Mavourneen.*"

**Crow, Ed. J.,** b. Sittingbourne, Engl., Sept. 11, 1841; organist Leicester, 1861--73 ; since, at Ripon Cath. ; 1882, **Mus. Doc.** Cantab. ; c. oratorio,

" *Harvest-time* " ; Psalm CX for orch. and chorus, etc.

**Cro'west, Fr. F.,** b. London, organist Christ's Church, Kil writer and composer.

**Cro'ziar, Wm.,** b. Upper Norv Dec. 20, 1870 ; celebrated oboist.

**Crüger** (krü'-gĕr), **Jns.,** Gross-Bre near Guben, 1598—Berlin, organist.

**Crussel** (kroos'-sĕl), **Bernhard,** land, 1775—1838 ; composer.

**Cruvel'li** (rightly **Crüwell**) (krü' (1) **Friederike M.,** Bielefeld, phalia, 1824—1868 ; contralto in don, but lost her voice and died broken heart. (2) **Jne. Sophie C lotte,** b. Bielefeld, Mar. 12, sister of above ; also contralto, ill-trained, but had enormous su Paris Gr. Opéra, 1854, at a sala 100,000 francs ; in 1856 m. C Vigier, and left the stage.

**Cud'more, Richard,** Chichester, —Manchester, 1840 ; organist, linist and conductor.

**Cui** (kwē), **César Antonovitch** Vilna, Russia, Jan. 6, 1835 ; or the most important of Russian posers ; pupil of Moniuszko an lakirev ; a military engineer ; of fortification at the St. Peters Engineering Acad. ; from 18 critic of the St. P. "*Gazet* 1878-9, pub. articles in Paris "*La musique en Russie*" ; c. eras, "*William Ratcliffe*" (St 1869) ; "*The Prisoner in the casus* " (1873) ; "*Angelo*" (1 "*The Mandarin's Son*" (1878 ric comedy, "*Le Filibustier*" ( 1894) ; the very succ. "*Sarazin* P., 1899) ; symphonies, etc., 2 s zos and a tarantella for orch. ; for pf. and vln. ; pf.-pcs. ; 50 s "*Esquisse critique*" on Cui an works by the Comtesse de M Argenteau.

**Cum'mings, Wm. Hayman,** b. bury, Devon, Eng., Aug. 22, 1 organist Waltham Abbey ; pro

ging R. Coll. for the Blind, Nor-
od ; 1896, principal of Guildhall
1. of Mus. ; founded the Purcell
:iety, edits its pubs. ; wrote biog.
Purcell (London, 1882) ; has also
b. a music "*Primer*," 1877 ; and
" *Biog. Dictionary of Musicians*"
92) ; c. a cantata, "*The Fairy
ng*," etc.
:i (koor'-chē), **Giu.**, Barletta, 1808
877 ; singing teacher and dram.
mposer.

oni (koo-rĭ-ō'-nē), (1) (——), sono in London, 1754, perhaps the
ther of (2) **Alberico**, b. ca. 1790,
lian tenor.

schmann (koorsh'-män), **K. Fr.**,
rlin, 1805—Langfuhr, near Dan-
, 1841 ; singer, dram. composer
l pop. song-writer.

i (koor'-tē), **Fz.** (or **Francesco**),
ssel, 1854—Dresden, 1898 ; dram.
mposer.

is, Dr. **H. Holbrook**, b. New
rk, Dec. 15, 1856 ; grad. Yale,
77 ; 1880, M.D. ; vice-pres. Am.
cial Science Assn.,prominent throat
ecialist and writer on the voice,
b. "Voice Building and Tone
cing," 1898.

wen, (1) Rev. **J.**, Heckmondwike,
rkshire, Engl., 1816—near Man-
ester, 1880 ; 1862, resigned his pas-
ate, and founded a college, also a
b.-house, to exploit Tonic-sol-fa. (2)
**Spencer,** b. Plaistow, 1847 ; son
d pupil of above ; pupil also of G.
key and R.A.M.; writer, and since
80 pres. Tonic-sol-fa Coll.

ani no. Vide CARESTINI.

ns (kŭz'-ĭns), Sir **Wm. G.**, London,
33 — Remouchamps (Ardennes),
93 ; pf.-prof. R.A.M. ; knighted
92 ; conductor and composer.

ll', **Richard**, English writer of
th century.

ler, **Wm. H.**, b. London, 1792 ;
ganist and singer.

llon (kü-vē-yòn), **J. Bapt. Philé-
on de,** b. Dunkirk, 1809 ; pupil,
er prof. Paris, Cons.; notable vio-
ist and teacher.

**Cuzzoni** (kood-zō'-nē), **Fran.**, Parma,
1700—Bologna, 1770 ; début 1719 :
m. the pianist Sandoni ; very successful contralto till her latter days, when
it is said she earned a pittance by
covering silk buttons.

**Czartoryska** (chär-tō-rē'-shkä), **Marcelline** (née **Princess Radziwill**),
b. Vienna, 1826 ; pianist ; lives since
1848 in Paris ; pupil of Czerny.

**Czarwenka** (chär-věn'-kä), **Jos.**, Be-
madek, Bohemia, 1759 — Vienna,
1835 ; oboist and professor.

**Czerny** (**Černy**) (chär'-nē), **Karl**, Vienna, Feb. 21, 1791—July 15, 1857 ;
pupil of his father **Wenzel C.**, later
of Beethoven ; and had advice from
Clementi and Hummel ; made an
early reputation as pianist and was an
eminent teacher from his 16th year ;
Liszt, Döhler, and Thalberg were
among his pupils ; pub. over 1,000
works, his pf.-studies, still standard,
incl. many such works as "*Die Schule
der Geläufigkeit*" (School of Velocity)
(op. 299) ; c. also masses, symphonies, overtures, etc.

**Czersky** (chär'-shkĭ). Vide TSCHIRCH.

**Czibulka** (chē-bool'-kä), **Alphons,**
Szepes-Várallya, Hungary, May 14,
1842—Vienna, Oct. 27, 1894 ; pianist
and conductor ; c. 5 operettas, incl.
"*Der Bajazzo*" (Vienna, 1892),
waltzes, etc.

# D

**Daase** (dä'-zě), **Rudolf,** b. Berlin,
Feb. 21, 1822 ; pupil of A. W. Bach,
Marx and Wilsing ; lives in Berlin as
conductor and teacher ; c. orch. and
choral-pieces, etc.

**Dachs** (däkhs), **Jos.**, Ratisbon, 1825
—Vienna, 1896 ; teacher and pianist.

**Dachstein** (däkh'-shtĭn), **Wolfgang,**
ex-priest and composer at Strassburg, 1554.

**Dalayrac** (or **D'Alayrac**) (däl-ě-räk),
**Nicolas,** Muret, Haute-Garonne,
June 13, 1753—Paris, Nov. 27, 1809
prod. about 60 operas.

**Dalberg** (däl'-bărkh), **Jn. Fr. Hugo,** Reichsfreiherr **von,** Aschaffenburg, 1752—1812 ; writer and composer.

**D'Albert, Eugen.** Vide ALBERT, d'.

**Dall** (däl), **Roderick,** lived at Athol, 1740 ; the last of the Scotch "wandering harpists."

**Dal'lam,** Engl. family of organ-builders 17th cent. (also spelled **Dallans, Dallum, Dalham**).

**Dal'lery,** organ-builders 18th cent. at Amiens.

**Dall' Argine** (däl-är'-zhē-nä), **Const.,** Parma, 1842—Milan, 1877 ; dram. composer.

**Dalvimare** (däl-vē-mä'-rĕ) or **d'Alvimare** (däl-vĭ-mär), **Martin P.,** Dreux, Eure-et-Loire, 1772—Paris, 1839 ; composer.

**Damascene** (dä-mă-shä'-nĕ), **Alex.,** Italian, b. in France ; d. July 14, 1719 ; alto singer and song-writer in England.

**Damcke** (däm'-kĕ), **Berthold,** Hanover, 1812 — Paris, 1875 ; conductor.

**Damm** (däm). (1) **Fr.,** b. Dresden, March 7, 1831 ; pianist and composer ; pupil of Krägen, J. Otto, and Reichel ; lived in North Germany, then in the U. S., then in Dresden. (2) **G., v.** STEINGRÄBER.

**Damoreau** (dăm-ō-rō), **Laure-Cinthie** (née **Montalant,** first known as "Mlle. **Cinti**"), Paris, 1801—Chantilly, 1863 ; soprano, later prof. of singing, Paris Cons. ; wrote *Méthode de chant.*"

**Damrosch** (däm'-rôsh). (1) **Dr. Leopold,** Posen, Prussia, Oct. 22, 1832 —New York, Feb. 15, 1885 ; 1854, M. D. ; took up music as solo-violinist ; then as cond. at minor theatres ; 1855, solo violinist Grand Ducal Orch., at Weimar ; here he m. Helene von Heimburg, a singer ; 1859-60 cond. Breslau Phil. Soc., etc. ; 1871, invited to New York to conduct the Arion Society, made his first appearance as conductor and composer and violinist ; 1873, founded the Oratorio Society ; 1878 the

Symphony Society ; 1880 Mus. Columbia Coll. ; 1884, cond. Ge opera at Met. Op. ; c. 7 cant symphony; music to Schiller's " *of Arc,*" etc. (2) **Frank,** b. Bre June 22, 1859 ; son and pup above ; pupil of Pruckner, Jean and von Inten (pf.), Moszk (comp.) ; 1882–85, cond. D (Col.) Chorus Club ; 1884–85, s visor of music in public schools, organist in various churches ; 91, chorusm. Met. Op.; till cond. the Newark Harmonic Soc 1892 organized the People's Si Classes ; 1897, supervisor of m N. Y. City public schools ; now c the " Musurgia," Oratorio So and Mus. Art Soc. (N. Y.), Ora Soc., Bridgeport (Conn.) "Orph and " Eurydice " Phila., etc.; p few songs and choruses, and a i od of sight - singing. (3) **W.** **(Johannis),** b. Breslau, Silesia, 30, 1862 ; son and pupil of (1) pil of Rischbieter and Dra (harm.), von Inten, Boekelman, Max Pinner, (pf.), von Bülow ducting) ; 1885–99 cond. N. Y. torio and Symphony Societies ; founded the N. Y. Symphony O 1894, organized and cond. the rosch Opera Co. ; 1899, cond Philadelphia ; 1902, cond. N Philh. (vice Paur) ; prod. op " *The Scarlet Letter* " (Boston, 1 text by Geo. Parsons Lathrop MS. opera " Cyrano de Berger text by W. J. Henderson ; " *M Te Deum* " ; " *Danny Deever,*"

**Da'na,** (1) **Chas. Henshaw,** Newton, Mass., 1846 — Worce 1883 ; pianist, organist and con er. (2) **Wm. H.,** b. Warren, June 10, 1846 ; pupil of Haupt, Kullak's Cons., also R.A.M., don ; dir. Dana's Mus. Inst., Wa Ohio ; wrote text-books ; c. " *Profundis* " for ch. and orch.

**Danbé** (dän-bā), **Jules,** b. C France, Nov. 15, 1840 ; violi pupil of Paris Cons.; till 1892

of the Cons. Concerts ; 1895,
d. Op. Com., Paris ; composer.

by, J., 1757—London, May 16,
8 ; English organist and compos-

:e, Wm., 1755—1840, musician ;
of the founders of the Phil.
., London.

do, Jos. H. B., b. Somers Town,
ndon, 1806 ; violinist.

la (dän-klä), (1) J. Bap. Chas.,
Bagnères-de-Bigorre, Dec. 19,
8 ; 1828 pupil of Baillot, Halévy,
l Berton, Paris Cons.; 1834, 2nd
o vln. Op.-Com.; 1857, prof. of vln.
the Cons., giving famous quartet
rées ; c. four symphonies, over 130
rks for vln., etc.; wrote 5 techni-
books, " Les compositeurs chefs
rchestre," etc. (2) Arnaud, Bag-
es-de-Bigorre, 1820—1862, bro. of
ove ; 'cellist and writer. (3) Léo-
ld, Bagnères-de-Bigorre, 1823—
ris, 1895, bro. of above ; compos-

el (dä-nël), L. A. J., Lille, 1787
¤875 ; a printer who inv. a nota-
n.

hauser (dän-how'-zĕr or dän-ō-
), Ad. Ld., Paris, 1835—1896 ;
of. of solfeggio at Cons. and dram.
mposer.

ican. V. PHILIDOR.

iel, (1) Hn. Adalbert, b. Cöthen,
¤2 ; theologian and writer. (2)
lvador, for a few days dir. Paris
ns., under the Commune ; killed
battle, May 23, 1871 ; writer.

jou (dän'-zhoo), J. L. F., Paris,
¤2—Montpellier, 1866 ; 1840, or-
nist and erudite historian.

kers (or Danckerts), Ghiselin,
Tholen, Zealand ; chorister in Pa-
l chapel, 1538-65 ; composer and
iter.

ks, Hart Pease, b. New Haven,
nn., April 6, 1834 ; bass and mus.
. in various churches ; pupil G. E.
hiting ; c. over 1200 hymns and
ngs, and operetta "Pauline"
872).

neley (dän'-lǐ), John Feltham,

Oakingham, Berkshire, England, 1786
—London, 1836 ; organist and publisher.

Dannreuther (dän'-roi-tĕr), (1) Edward, b. Strassburg, Nov. 4, 1844 ;
at 5 taken to Cincinnati, where he
studied with F. L. Ritter ; later, pupil
of Richter, Moscheles, Hauptmann,
Leipzig Cons.; 1863, London, as
pianist ; 1872 founded and cond.
London Wagner Society ; wrote
"Richard Wagner, His Tendencies
and Theories" (London, 1873) ; also
composer. (2) Gustav, b. Cincinnati, July 21, 1853 ; pupil of de
Ahna and Joachim (vln.) and Heitel
(theory), Berlin ; lived in London till
1877 ; joined Mendelssohn Quintet
Club of Boston, where in 1880 he
settled as a member of the newly
formed Symphony Orch. ; 1882–84
dir. Philh. Soc. Buffalo, N. Y. ;
founded the "Beethoven String-
Quartet" of N. Y. (called "Dannr.
Q." from 1894) ; for 3 years leader
Symphony and Oratorio Societies,
N. Y.; wrote "Chord and S.
Studies for Young Players."

Danzi (dän'-tsē), (1) Fz., Mannheim,
May 15, 1763—Carlsruhe, April 13,
1826 ; dram. composer ; son and pu-
pil of (2) Innocenz D., 'cellist to the
Elector. (3) Franziska. Vide LE-
BRUN.

Da Ponte (dä pôn'-tĕ), Lorenzo, Cen-
eda, near Venice, March 10, 1749—
New York, Aug. 17, 1838 ; of Jewish race ; poet-laureate to Joseph II.
at Vienna, until 1792 ; wrote text of
Mozart's "Don Giovanni" and "Cosi
Fan Tutte"; London, 1803, teacher
of Italian and poet to the Italian
Opera ; made a failure of different
pursuits in the U. S. A., and was
finally teacher of Italian at Columbia
College, N. Y. ; pub. "Memorie"
(Memoirs). There is a sketch of his
life in Krehbiel's "Music and Manners" (N. Y., 1899).

Daquin (dä-kăn), L. Claude, Paris,
1694—1772 ; notable organist and
composer.

**Darcours** (där-koor), **Charles.** Vide RETY.

**Dargomyžsky** (där-gō-mēsh'-shkē), **Alex. Sergievitch,** Toula, Feb. 2, 1813—St. Petersburg, Jan. 29, 1869; pianist and composer; pupil of Schoberlechner; his opera "*Esmeralda*" (c. 1839) was prod. 1847 with succ.; his best opera "*Russalka*" followed in 1856; in 1867, at Moscow, an opera-ballet, "*The Triumph of Bacchus*" (written 1847), was instrumented; left an unfinished opera, "*Kammennoi Gost*" ("The Marble Guest") (finished by Rimsky-Korsakov). "*Rogdana*," a fantasy-opera, was only sketched; it follows the latest operatic creeds; c. also pop. orch. works.

**Da(s)ser** (dä'-sĕr), **(Dasserus) Ludwig,** until 1562 conductor and composer at Munich, predecessor of Lassus.

**Daube** (dow'-bĕ), **Fr.,** Cassel (Augsburg ?), 1730—Vienna, 1797; composer and writer.

**Daublaine et Callinet,** Paris firm of org.-builders, founded 1838.

**Daucresme** (dō-krĕm), **Lucien,** Elbeuf, Normandy, 1826—Paris, 1892; dram. composer.

**Dau'ney, Wm.,** Aberdeen, 1800—Demerara, 1843; writer.

**Dauprat** (dō-prä), **L. Fr.,** Paris, 1781 —July 16, 1868; notable horn-player and composer.

**Daussoigne-Méhul** (dōs'-swăn-mā'-ül), **L. Jos.,** Givet, Ardennes, 1790—Liège, 1875; dram. composer.

**Dauvergne** (dō-vĕrn), **Ant. C.,** Ferrand, 1713—Lyons, 1797; violinist and dram. composer.

**Davenport, Francis W.,** b. Wilderslowe, near Derby, England, 1847; pupil of Macfarren, whose daughter he m.; 1879, prof. R. A. M., and 1882 Guildhall Sch. of Music; c. two symphonies (the 1st winning 1st prize at Alexandra Palace, 1876), and other comps.; wrote text-books.

**David** (dä'-fĕt), **(1) Fd.,** Hamburg, Jan. 19, 1810—near Klosters, Switzerland,

July 18, 1873; pupil of Spohr Hauptmann; at 15 played in th wandhaus, Leipzig; 1827, in K stadt Th. orch., Berlin; at 1 vln. in the private quartet o wealthy Baron von Liphardt, at pat, whose daughter he m.; concerts till 1835 in Russia; leader of the Gewandhaus Orc Mendelssohn's invitation; his ous precision of drill is still a te ing tradition. In the compositi Mendelssohn's vln.-concerto he almost a collaborator (cf. Joachin Brahms). The Cons. was esta 1843, and **D.'s** unsurpassed gif a teacher had a large influenc making its reputation, among hi pils being Wilhelmj and Joachin a leader he had a wonderful fa of inspiring the players with his enthusiasm. His student editior classical works embrace nearl compositions of standard vln. li ture; edited many classics, inclu the "*Hohe Schule des Violinsp* His comp. include an opera, "*A Wacht*" (Leipzig, 1852); 2 sym nies; 5 vln.-concertos, etc.; wro standard meth. for vln. (2) **P Paul,** b. Leipzig, Aug. 1, 1840, of above; violinist; 1862–65, le Carlsruhe orch.; then teacher at pingham, England.

**David** (dä-vēd), **(3) Félicien Cé** Cadenet, Vaucluse, April 13, 18 St. Germain-en-Laye, Aug. 29, 1 at 7 a pupil and chorister in the trise of Saint-Sauveur at Aix hymns, motets, etc.; 1825–28 stu in the Jesuit college, but ran awa continue his music, and became a cond. in the theatre at Aix, an 19 cond. at Saint-Sauveur; Paris Cons., under Bénoist (o Reber and Millot, (harm.), Fétis and fugue). 1831, his rich uncle v drew his allowance of 50 fran month, and he took up Saint-Sir ism, composing hymns for this so istic sect, which coming under ba the law in 1833, he went with c

.mbers on a tour through Turkey,
:ypt, etc.; he returned in 1835 with
fund of Oriental musical impres-
.ns, resulting in an unsucc. volume
" *Mélodies Orientales*." He re-
:ed to the country home of a friend
d c. 2 symphonies, 24 string-quin-
s, etc. 1838 his first symphony
.s prod.; and 1844, his ode-sym-
.onie " *Le Désert*" had a "deliri-
s succ."; the oratorio, "*Moïse au
naï*," 1846 , a second symphonic-
:e " *Christophe Colombe*" and
*L'Eden*," a " mystery " in 2 parts
rand Opéra, 1848) had no succ.;
. opera " *La Perle du Brésil*" (Th.
rique, 1851), is still popular ; the
era " *La Fin du Monde*" was re-
ted by the Gr. Opéra, and put in
.earsal, but not produced, by the
.. Lyrique, and in 1859 produced
the Gr. Opéra as " *Herculaneum*,"
: great state prize of 20,000 francs
ng awarded it in 1867 ; " *Lalla
okh* " (1862) was a decided succ.,
t " *Le Saphir* " (1865) also at the
.. Com., failed, and he now aban-
.ned dram. comp., withdrawing " *La
ptive*," 1869, Academician and li-
.arian of the Cons. Biog. by Aze-
.do (Paris, 1863). (4) **Samuel**,
ris, 1838—1895 ; professor, direc-
: and dram. composer. (5) **Ad.
.aac**, Nantes, 1842–Paris, 1897 ;
.m. composer. (6) **Ernst**, Nancy,
.4—Paris, 1886 ; writer.

**.de** (dä-vě'-dě),(1) **Giacomo** (called
père) Presezzo, near Bergamo,
50—Bergamo, 1830 ; famous tenor.
(2) **Giovanni**, 1789, St. Petersburg,
1851 ; son of above ; tenor of
.narkable range B♭-b″.

**.doff** (dä'-vĭ-dôf), **Karl**, Goldingen,
.rland, 1838—Moscow, 1889 ; solo
.llist to the Czar ; 1876–87, dir. St.
.tersburg Cons.; c. symph. poem,
*The Gifts of Perek*." etc.

**.es** (dä'-vĭs), (1) **Ben**, b. Ponadawz,
.ar Swansea. Wales, Jan. 6, 1858 ;
.eratic and concert tenor ; 1880–3
.pil of Randegger at R. A. M. ;
.n bronze, **silver**, and gold medals,

and the Evill prize for declamatory
Engl. singing ; 3 years with Carl
Rosa Opera-troupe ; most prominent
in oratorio; since 1893 has often sung
in U. S. (2) **David Ffrangcon**, b.
Bethesda, Carnarvonshire, Dec. 11,
1860 ; barytone ; M. A. Oxford ; pupil of Shakespeare ; début Manchester, 1890 ; sang with Carl Rosa Opera Co., then oratorio ; toured U. S.
(3) **Fanny**, b. Guernsey, June 17
1861 ; pianist ; pupil of Reinecke
Paul and Jadassohn, Leipzig Cons. ;
later of Frau Schumann and Dr.
Scholz ; début Crystal Palace, London, 1885 ; has toured in England,
Germany and Italy. (4) **Henry Wal-
ford**, b. Oswestry, Engl., Sept. 6,
1869 ; pupil and asst. of Sir Walter
Parratt ; 1898 organist of the Temple
Church ; 1898, Mus. Doc., Cantab. ;
1895 prof. of cpt. R. C. M.; c. Symphony in D, cantata " *Hervé Riel*,"
etc.

**Da'vison**, (1) **Arabella**. Vide GOD-
DARD. (2) **J. W.**, London, 1815—
Margate, 1885 ; pianist, critic and
composer.

**Da'vy**, (1) **Richard**, Engl., comp. 16th
century. (2) **John**, Upton-Helion.
Exeter, 1765—London, 1824 ; violinist.

**Day**, Dr. **Alfred**, London, 1810—1849,
physician and theorist.

**Dayas** (dī'-äs), **W. Humphries**, b.
New York, Sept. 12, 1864 ; pupil of S.
Jackson, Warren, S. B. Mills and
Joseffy ; organist of various churches ;
then studied with Kullak, Haupt,
Erlich, Urban, and Liszt ; made
concert-tour 1888 ; 1890 pf.-teacher
Helsingfors Cons. ; in Düsseldorf
(1894), Wiesbaden Cons., and Cologne Cons. ; c. organ and piano
sonatas, etc.

**De Ahna** (dä-ä'-nä), (1) **H. K. Hermann**, Vienna, 1835—Berlin, 1892 ;
violinist, teacher and composer. His
sister (2) **Eleonore**, Vienna, 1838—
Berlin, 1865 ; mezzo-soprano.

**De Angelis** (dä än'-jä-lēs), **Girolamo**,
b. Civita Vecchia, Jan. 1, 1858 ; pupil

of Bazzini, Milan Cons. ; 1881, prof. there of vln. and vla. ; 1879-97, solo . violinist at La Scala ; 1897 teacher Royal Irish Acad. of Music, Dublin ; c. (text and music) " *L'Innocente* " (Novi Ligure, 1896).

**Deane, Thos.**, English organist, violinist and composer, 17th cent.

**Debain** (dŭ-băṅ), **Alex. Fran.**, Paris, 1809—Dec. 3, 1877 ; 1834 made pianos and organs in Paris ; inv. the harmonium 1840, also " antiphonel " and " harmonichorde " ; improved the accordion.

**Debillemont** (dŭ-bē'-yŭ-môṅ), **J. Jacques**, Dijon, 1824—Paris, 1879 ; dram. composer.

**Debois** (dŭ-bwä), **F.**, Brünn, 1834—1893 ; cond. and composer.

**Debussy** (dŭ-büs-sē), **Achille Claude**, b. Paris (?), 1862, French composer of much individuality; prod. " *Pelléas et Mélisande*," libretto based on Maeterlinck's play, Op. Comique, Paris, Apr. 30, 1902, with sensational effect ; he was a pupil of Guiraud, Paris Cons., took grand Prix de Rome, 1884, with cantata " *L'Enfant prodigue*"; began " *Pelléas et M.*" in 1893 ; c. also orch. prelude " *l'Après-midi d'un Faune ;*" pf. suite for 4 hands ; " *Chansons de Bilitis*," " *Proses lyriques*," etc.

**Dechert** (děkh'-ĕrt), **Hugo**, b. Potschappel near Dresden, Sept. 16, 1860 ; 'cellist ; studied with his father, then with H. Tiets, and at the Berlin Hochschule ; toured ; since 1894 soloist court-chapel, Berlin.

**Deck'er, Konst.**, Fürstenau, Brandenburg, 1810—Stolp, Pomerania, 1878 ; pianist and dram. composer.

**Dedekind** (dā'-dĕ-kĭnt), (1) **Henning**, abt. 1590 cantor, theorist and composer at Langensalza, Thuringia. (2) **Konst. Chr.**, Reinsdorf, Anhalt-Köthen, 1628—ca. 1697 comp.

**Dedler** (dāt'-lĕr), **Rochus**, Oberammergau, Jan. 15, 1779—Vienna, Oct. 15, 1822 ; c. music still used in the Passion-Play.

**De(e)r'ing, Richard**, b. Kent, d. Lon-

don (?), 1630 ; studied in Italy ; c organist ; pub. the oldest ex comp. with basso continuo, etc.

**Defesch** (dā-fĕsh'), **Wm.**, d. ca. 1 Flemish organist and violinist.

**Deffès** (dŭf-fĕs), **L. P.**, b. Toul July 25, 1819 ; pupil of Halévy Barbereau, Paris Cons., took G prix de Rome for cantata " *L'.et Tobie*"; his 1-act com.-op. " *neau d'argent*" was prod. P 1855 ; 14 others since, the last succ., " *Jessica*" (Toulouse, 18 now dir. of the Toulouse branc the Cons. ; c. also masses, etc.

**Degele** (dā'-gĕ-lĕ), **Eugen**, Mu 1834—Dresden, 1866 ; barytone composer.

**De Giosa** (dā jō'-sä), **Nicola**, 1820—1885 ; cond. and compose

**De Haan**, (1) **Willem**, b. Rotter Sept. 24, 1849 ; pupil of Nicola Lange, and Bargiel, also at Le Cons. ; 1873 dir. at Bingen ; c " Mozartverein " at Darms 1876 ; 1895 court-conductor h c. 2 operas " *Die Kaiserstochter*' the succ. " *Die Inkasöhne*" (D stadt, 1895) ; 3 cantatas. (2) **M farges, A. Pauline**, b. Rotter April 4, 1872 ; concert and ora alto, pupil of Julius Stockhausen

**Dehn** (dān), **Siegfried Wm.**, Alt Feb. 25, 1796—Berlin, April 12, 1 noteworthy theorist and teac among his pupils Rubinstein, lak, Glinka, Kiel, Hofmann, etc.

**Deiters** (dī'-tĕrs), **Hermann**, b. B June 27, 1833 ; 1858, Dr. jur., Dr. phil., at Bonn ; dir. of gymr at Bonn, 1858, and other cities ; of the " Provincial Schulrath ' Coblentz ; writer and translator.

**De Ko'ven (Henry Louis) Regin** b. Middletown, Conn., April 3, 1 educated in Europe, took degre Oxford, Engl., 1879 ; pupil of Speidel (pf.) at Stuttgart, Le (pf.), and Pruckner (harm.), Hauff (comp.), Vanuccini (sing Genée (operatic comp.) ; 1902 or ised and cond. Philharmonic Orc

ashington, D. C., where he has ed since 1900; c. many succ. mic operas, incl. "*Robin Hood*" hicago, 1890); "*The Fencing aster*" (Boston, 1892); "*The High- ayman*" (New Haven, 1897); *Maid Marian*" (1901); also many ngs; an orch. suite, and a pf.- nata in MS.

aborde (dŭ-lä-bôrd), (1) **J. Benj.**, aris, 1734—guillotined, 1794; dram. mposer and writer. (2) **Élie Mi- am**, b. Chaillot, France, Feb. 8, 39; pupil of Alkan, Liszt, and Mo- heles; pf.-prof. at Paris Cons. and am. composer.

acour (dŭ-lä-koor'), **Vincent Con- d Félix**, Paris, 1808—1840; harp- and composer.

âtre (dŭ-lăt'r), (1) **Olivier**, Belgian usic-pub. Antwerp, (1539-55). (2) **laude Petit Jan.**, conductor and mposer at Liège, 1555.

**Lattre** (dŭ-lătr), **Roland.** Vide ASSO, DI.

l'Aulnaye (dŭ-lōl-nä), **Fran. tanislas**, Madrid, July 7, 1739— haillot, 1830; writer and theor- t.

devez (dŭl-dŭ-věs), **Ed. Ernest**, aris, 1817—1897; 1859, asst.-cond. r. Opéra and Paris Cons.; dram. mposer and writer.

edicque (děl-děk), **Ld.**, b. La aye, Feb. 7, 1821; violinist and acher; pupil Paris Cons.; founder d cond. "Soc. des Symphonistes," 61-83; c. vln. pieces, etc.

**Leva** (dä-lä'-vä), **Enrico**, b. aples, Jan. 19, 1867; pupil of Pan- ani and Rossomandi (pf.); Puzzoni d d'Arienzo (harm.); his Canzo- tta Napoletana "É Spingole Fran- ese," was very succ., as are many of s songs; c. opera "*La Carmargo*" ot prod.).

ezenne (dŭ-lŭ-zěn), **Chas. Ed.** os., Lille, 1776—1866; writer.

hasse (děl-äs), **Félix**, b. Spaa, n. 8, 1809; lives in Brussels; rite.

ibes (dŭ-lēb'), **Clément Philibert**

**Léo**, St. Germain-du-Val, Sarthe, Feb. 21, 1836—Paris, Jan. 16, 1891; a composer of fascinating grace and polish; entered the Paris Cons. in 1848, Le Couppey, Bazin, Adam, and Bénoist being his chief teachers; 1853 organist at the Ch. of St.-Jean et St.- Francois; his first operetta "*Deux Sacs de Charbon*," was followed by 12 more; 1865, 2nd chorus-master Gr. Opera; his first ballet "*La Source*" was prod. here 1866, later in Vienna as "*Naila*"; the second, "*Coppe- lia*" (Gr. Opéra, 1870), is still popu- lar, as is "*Sylvia*" (1876); 1881, prof. of comp. at the Cons.; c also the succ. opera "*Lakmé*" (v. STORIES OF OPERAS), and others.

**Delicati** (dā-lǐ-kä'-tē), **Margherita**, Italian soprano in London with her husband, 1789.

**Delioux (De Savignac)** (dŭl-yoo dŭ săv-ēn-yăk), **Chas.**, b. Lorient, Mor- bihan, April, 1830; self-taught as pianist; studied harmony with Barbe- reau, and comp. with Halévy; 1846 took Grand Prix for cpt.; prod. 1-act comic opera "*Yvonne et Loie*" (Gym- nase, 1854); c. pf.-pcs and wrote tech- nical works.

**Della Maria** (děl'-lä mä-rē'-ä), **Do- minique**, Marseilles, 1768—Paris, March 9, 1800; son of an Italian mandolinist; played mandolin and 'cello; at 18 prod. a grand opera; studied comp. in Italy, and c. 7 operas, incl. the very succ. "*Le Prisonnier*" (1798).

**Delle Sedie** (děl-lě säd'-yě), **Enrico**, b. Leghorn, June 17, 1826; pupil of Galeffi, Persanola, and Domeniconi; 1848, imprisoned as a Revolutionist; then studied singing; début, Flor- ence, 1851; later prof. of singing Paris Cons.; has lived in Paris since as singing teacher.

**Dellinger** (děl'-lǐng-ěr), **Rudolf**, b. Graslitz, Bohemia, July 8, 1857; 1883, conductor at Hamburg; 1893 Dresden Ct. Opera; c. operettas, incl. succ. "*Capitän Fracasse*" (Hamburg, 1889), and "*Die Chansanette*" (Dresden, 1894); Prague, 1895, "*Die Säng-erin.*"

**Dell' Orefice** (dĕl ō-rä-fē'-chĕ), **Giu.**, Fara, Abruzzio, Chietino, 1848—Naples, 1889 ; cond. and dram. composer.

**Del Mela** (dĕl mä'-lä), Don **Domeni-co**, an Italian priest; 1730, inv. the "upright" piano.

**Delmotte** (dĕl-môt), **Henri Florent**, Mons, Belgium, 1799—1836 ; writer.

**Delprat** (dŭl-prä'), **Chas.**, 1803—Pau, Pyrenees, 1888 ; singing-teacher and writer there.

**Delsarte** (dŭl-särt), **Fran. Alex. Nicholas Chéri**, Solesme, Nord, 1811—Paris, 1871; tenor ; teacher of a well-known physical culture; 1855 inv. the Guide-Accord, or Sonotype, to facilitate piano-tuning.

**Del Valle de Paz** (dĕl väl'-lä dä pätz), **Edgardo**, b. Alexandria, Egypt, Oct. 18, 1861 ; pf.-pupil at Naples Cons., of Cesi (pf.), and Serrao (comp.) ; at 16 toured in Italy and Egypt, now prof. in Florence Cons. ; pub. pf.-method, etc.; c. orchestral suites, etc.

**Demantius** (dä-män'-tsĭ-oos), **Chr.**, Reichenberg, 1567—Freiburg, Saxony, 1643 ; prolific composer of church-music and songs; wrote a vocal method.

**Demelius** (dä-mä'-lĭ-oos), **Chr.**, Schlettau, Saxony, 1643 — Nordhausen, 1711 ; composer.

**Demeur** (dŭ-mŭr'), (1) **Anne Arsène** (née **Charton**), Sanjon, Charente, 1827—Paris (?), 1892 ; soprano ; m. (2) **J. A. Demeur**, flutist and composer.

**Demol** (dŭ-môl), (1) **Pierre**, Brussels, 1825—Alost, Belgium, 1899 ; dir. and composer. (2) **Fran. M.**, Brussels, 1844—Ostend, 1883 ; nephew of above ; cond., prof., and dram. composer.

**Demunck'**, (1) **François**, Brussels, 1815—1854 ; 'cellist and prof. (2) **Ernest**, b. Brussels, Dec. 21, 1840 ; son and pupil of above ; pupil of Servais ; lived in London, then Paris ;

1870, 'cellist Weimar Court o? 1879 m. Carlotta Patti ; 1893, ? R.A.M., London.

**Demuth** (dä-moot'), **Ld.**, b. Br Nov. 2, 1861 ; barytone ; stu Vienna Cons., with Gansbac? sang at Halle, etc., later Ham and Vienna.

**Denefve** (dŭ-nŭf), **Jules**, b. Chi? 1814 ; 'cellist and dram. compos?

**Dennée** (dĕn-nä), **Chas.**, b. Osw N. Y., Sept. 1, 1863 ; studied Emery, Boston ; lives there as tea and composer of comic operas, e?

**Dengremont** (däṅ-grŭ-môṅ), **Mau** b. of French parents, Rio de Jan? 1866—Buenos Ayres, 1893 ; violi at 11 played with succ. in Europ

**Den'ner**, **Jn. Chp.**, Leipzig, 16 Nürnberg, 1707 ; maker of v insts.; inv. 1690 or 1700 the clar perhaps also the Stockfagott and? Rackettenfagott.

**Denza** (dĕn'-tsä), **Luigi**, b. Castel? mare di Stabbia, Feb. 24, 1846 ; pil of Naples Cons.; c. opera " ? *lenstein* " (Naples, 1876), many songs (some in Neapolitan dia? incl. " Funiculi-Funicula."

**Deppe** (dĕp'-pĕ), **Ludwig**, Alverdi Lippe, 1828—Pyrmont, Sept. 1890 ; notable pf.-teacher and ductor.

**Desprès** (or **Després**) (dŭ-prĕ' o? prä), **Jossé** (known as **Josq** Condé (?) in Hainault, Burgundy 1450—Condé, Aug. 27, 1521. [Hi? taph reads " **Jossé Despres** "; spellings are Desprès, De(s) Depret, De(s)pret(s), Dupré, an? the Italians, Del Prato, Latinize a Prato, a Pratis, Pratensis, **Josquin** appears as Jossé, Jos Jusquin, Giosquin, Josquinus, J bo, Jodocus, Jodoculus, etc.] of the most eminent of musician? the chief contrapuntist of his pupil of Okeghem ; 1471–84 a s? in the Sistine Chapel, and a 1488 in Ferrara ; he was already accepted as " princeps musicor? and had international vogue. He?

ceived with honour by various
inces, and was court-musician to
Duis XII., many amusing anecdotes
his musical humour being told. He
ally returned to Condé as Provost
the Cathedral Chapter. Burney
lled him " the father of modern
rmony." The florid and restless
t. of his church-works and the sec-
ar *cantus firmus* (v. D.D.) that was
e basis of most of them, brought
s school into disfavour and disuse
en the revolutionary Palestrina ap-
ared. But he was at least the culmi-
tion of his style, and his erudition
s moulded into suave and emo-
nal effects, so that Ambros says
at he was the " first musician who
presses us as being a genius." His
riod coinciding with the use of
Dvable types for music, his works
e preserved in large quantities in
lumes and in the collections of Pe-
icci and Peutinger. His French
ansons were pub. by T. Susato,
45, P Attaignant, 1549, and Du
emin, 1553; excerpts in modern
tation are in the "*Bibliothek für
irchenmusik*," 1844; in Commer's
*Collectio*," Rochlitz' "*Sammlung
rzüglicher Gesangstücke*," 1838,
10ron's "*Collection*," and in the
stories of Ambros, Burney, Haw-
1s, etc.

rosse (dĕ-prôs'-sĕ), **Anton**, Much, 1838—Berlin, 1878; dram. com-
ser.

Reszké (dŭ rĕsh'-kā), (1) **Jean**, b.
arsaw, Jan. 14, 1852; perhaps the
ief tenor of his generation, great in
era of all schools; pupil of Ciaf-
, Cotogni, etc.; 1874, début as
rytone at Venice, as Alfonso in
*La Favorita*," under the name " De
eschi"; after singing in Italy and
ris and studying with Sbriglia, he
de his début as tenor in "*Robert
Diable*" (Madrid, 1879); 1884, Th.
s Nations; 1885 at the Gr. Opéra,
ris, creating Massenet's "*Le Cid*";
ice '87 has sung constantly in Lon-
n, and since '95 in New York. (2)

**Édouard**, b. Warsaw, Dec. 23, 1855,
bro. of above; pupil of his brother, of Ciaffei, Steller, and Coletti;
début, Paris, April 22, 1876, as the
King in "*Aïda*" (Th. des Italiens),
sang there two seasons, then at Turin and Milan; 1880–84 at the Italian
Opera, London; since then, Paris,
London, America; a magnificent
basso of enormous repertory and
astonishing versatility as an actor,
a master in tragic comic, or buffa
opera. His sister. (3) **Josephine**,
was a soprano of greatest promise,
but left the stage on her marriage.

**Dering**, v. DEERING.

**De Sanctis** (dā sänk'-tēs), **Cesare**, b.
Allbano, Rome, 1830; 1876, prof. of
harm. in the Liceo; c. overture,
Requiem Mass, " 100 fugues," a cappella in strict style; pub. treatises.

**Désaugiers** (dā-sō-zhā), **Marc Ant.**,
Fréjus, 1742—Paris, 1793; prod. numerous succ. short operas.

**Deshayes** (dŭz-ĕz), **Prosper Didier**,
prod., 1780, oratorio " *Les Macha-
bées*"; c. operettas and ballets, etc.

**Desmarets** (dā-mä-rā), **H.**, Paris, 1662
—Luneville, 1741; dram. composer.

**Desormes** (dā-zôrm), **L. C.**, Algiers,
1845—Paris, 1898; composer and
conductor.

**Dessau** (dĕs'-sow), **Bd.**, b. Hamburg,
March 1, 1861; violinist; pupil of
Schradieck, Joachim, and Wieniawski; leader at various theatres;
1898 Konzertmeister at the court-
opera, Berlin, and teacher Stern cons.

**Dessauer** (dĕs'-sow-ĕr), **Jos.**, Prague.
May 28, 1798—Mödling, near Vien-
na, July 8, 1876; c. 5 operas and
many pop. songs.

**Dessoff** (dĕs'-sôf), **Felix Otto**, Leipzig, 1835—Frankfort, 1892; court-
cond. at Carlsruhe.

**Destinn** (dā'-shtĭn), **Eminy**, b. Prague,
Feb. 26, 1878; soprano; studied
with Loewe-Destinn; 1898 court
opera, Berlin.

**Destouches** (dā-toosh), (1) **André
Cardinal**, Paris, 1672—1749; dram.
composer. (2) **Franz Seraph von**,

b. Munich, 1772—1844; dram. composer.

**Desvignes** (dā-vēn'-yŭ), **Frai.**, Trier, 1805—Metz, 1853; violinist; founded conservatory at Metz; dram. composer.

**Deswert** (dā-vär), (1) **Gaspard Isidore**, Louvain, 1830—Schaerbeck, near Brussels, 1896; 'cellist; prof. Brussels Cons. (2) **Jules**, Louvain, 1843—Ostend, 1891, brother of above; conductor and dram. composer.

**Deszczyński** (dĕsh-chēn´-shkĭ), **Jos.**, b. Wilno, 1781; Polish composer.

**Dett'mer, Wm.**, b. Breinum, near Hildesheim, 1808; operatic bass; son of a peasant; joined a troupe of players; sang minor rôles at Hanover; 1842 engaged for leading rôles Dresden; retired 1874.

**Deutz** (doits). Vide MAGNUS.

**Devienne** (dŭv-yĕn), **Fran.**, Joinville, Haute - Marne, Jan. 31, 1759 — (insane), Charenton, Sept. 5, 1803; flutist and bassoonist; important in improving wind instr.; prof., composer and writer.

**Dew'ey, Ferdinand**, Montpelier, Vt., U. S. A., 1851—Beverley, U. S. A., 1900; pianist, composer, and teacher.

**Dezède** (or **Dezaides**) (dŭ-zĕd), Lyons (?) 1740—Paris, 1792; prod. 15 pop. operas and operettas.

**Diabelli** (dē-ä-bĕl'-lē), **Antonio**, Mattsee, near Salzburg, Sept. 6, 1781—Vienna, April 8, 1858; pf.- and guitar-teacher; partner of Cappi, the music-publisher; c. opera and pop. sonatinas, etc.

**Diamandy.** Vide NUOVINA.

**Diaz (de la Peña)** (dē´-äth dŭ-lä-pān´-yä), **Eugène Émile**, Paris, Feb. 27, 1837—Oct., 1901; son of the painter; pupil of Paris Cons. (Halévy, Réber); prod. the com. opera "*Le Roi Candaule*" (1865, Th. Lyrique); 1867 won the prize for opera, "*La Coupe du Roi de Thule*" (Grand Opéra); 1890 prod. lyric drama "*Benvenuto*" (Op.-Com.); pub. many songs.

**Dib'din**, (1) **Chas.**, Dibdin, near Southampton, 1745—London, 1814;

composer, singer, accompanist, a[..] manager and writer. (2) **Henry ward**, Sadlers Wells, 1813—1[..] harpist, organist, violinist and [..] poser; youngest son of above.

**Dick, Chas. Geo.** Cotsford, London, Sept. 1, 1846; law-stu[..] at Worcester Coll., Oxford; musician; produced succ. opere[..] and 2 comic operas, a "child[..] opera," etc.

**Dic'kons, Mrs.** (née **Poole**), Lon[..] ca. 1770—May 4, 1833; soprano[..]

**Did'ymus**, b. Alexandria, Egypt[..] B.C.; wrote 4,000 works in all, [..] a treatise on harmony. Vide TE[..] CHORDS and COMMA (D. D.).

**Diehl** (dēl), **Louis**, b. Mannheim, 1[..] 1863, m. Alice Mangold; comp[..]

**Diem** (dēm), **Jos.**, Kellmunz, Memmingen, 1836—Constance, 1[..] 'cellist.

**Diémer** (d'yā-mā), **Louis**, b. P[..] Feb. 14, 1843; pianist; pupil at C[..] of Marmontel; took 1st pf.-priz[..] 13, later 1st harm., 2nd org. and cpt.-prizes; pupil Ambr. Tho[..] and Bazin; 1887 pf.-prof. at [..] Cons. (vice Marmontel); bes[..] brilliant concerts of modern m[..] he has organised most delightful [..] certs of ancient music played on [..] cient instrs.; c. pf.-concerto, ch[..] ber-music, etc., ed. collections.

**Dienel** (dē´-nĕl), **Otto**, b. Tiefenf[..] Silesia, Jan. 11, 1839; pupil Go[..] Gym., Bunzlau Seminary, R. [..] for church music, Berlin, and[..] Academy, organist Marienkir[..] Berlin; 1881 "Royal Musikd[..] tor."

**Diener** (dē´-nĕr), **Fz.**, Dessau, 18[..] 1879; tenor.

**Dierich** (dē´-rĭkh), **Carl**, b. Hein[..] au, March 31, 1852; tenor in [..] cert, opera and oratorio; studied Graben-Hoffman.

**Diës** (dē´-ĕs), **Albert K.**, Hano[..] 1755—Vienna, 1832; writer.

**Diet** (dē-ā), **Edmond M.**, b. P[..] Sept. 25, 1854; pupil of César Fra[..] and Guiraud; officier of the Acade[..]

od. 3 operas, incl. "*Stratonice*"
387), many ballets and pantomimes,
.

(t)er (dē'-tĕr), **Chr. L.,** Ludwigs-
rg, 1757—Stuttgart, 1822 ; dram
mposer.

rich (dē'-trĭkh) (or **Dieterich**), (1)
xtus, Augsburg (?) 1490 (95)—St.
llen, Switzerland, 1548 ; composer.
**Albert Hn.,** b. Golk, near Meis-
n, Aug. 28, 1829 ; important com-
ser ; pupil of J. Otto, Moscheles,
eitz and Schumann ; 1855–61, con-
rt-cond., 1859, principal mus.-
. at Bonn ; 1861, court-cond. at
denburg ; 1894 Leipzig ; c. succ.
era "*Robin Hood*" (Frankfort,
79) ; a notable symphony ; over-
re, "*Normannenfahrt*" ; cantatas
th orch., 'cello- and vln.-concertos,
. (3) **Marie,** b. Weinsberg ;
died Stuttgart and with Viardot-
rcia ; coloratura soprano at Stutt-
rt court-opera ; then at Berlin.

sch (dĕtsh), **Pierre L. Ph.,** Di-
n, 1808—1865 ; composer and con-
ctor.

z (dĕts), (1) **Jn. Chr.,** Darmstadt,
38—in Holland, 1845 ; instr.-mak-
; inv. melodeon (1805), etc. ; his
n and assistant (2) **Chr.,** a famous
-maker, inv. the Polypiectron.

apart (d'yŭ-părt), **Chas.,** 18th cent.,
linist and harpsichordist.

(dĕts), **Sophie** (née **Hartmann**),
nich, 1820—1887 ; soprano.

num, **Chas.,** Rotherhithe, 1765—
37 ; Engl. singer and composer.

iger, **Jn.,** Eisfeld, 1590—Coburg,
47, cantor and composer.

gelstedt (dĭng'-ĕl-shtĕt), **Jenny**
e **Lutzer**), Prague, 1816—Vienna,
77 ; a coloratura singer ; m. the poet
. D.

el (dĭp'-pĕl), **Andreas,** b. Cassel,
ov. 30, 1866 ; notable tenor ; stud-
with Hey, Leoni and Rau ; 1887—
Bremen opera, then in New York
several seasons, also in Breslau,
enna ; 1889 at Bayreuth, from 1897,
Covent Garden.

ta (dē-roo'-tä), (1) **Gir.,** b. Perugia,

---

ca. 1560 ; organist ; pub. technical
books on org., cpt., etc. (2) **Ag.,** b.
Perugia, 1622 ; Augustine monk ;
composer.

**Dis'tin,** (1) **John,** 1793—1863 ; Engl.
trumpeter, inv. key-bugle. (2) **Theodore,** Brighton, England, 1823—London, 1893 ; son of above ; barytone ;
later bass singer and composer.

**Dit'son,** (1) **Oliver,** 1811—1888 ;
founder of the music-pub. firm O.
Ditson Co., at Boston, Mass.; 1867,
his eldest son, (2) **Chas.,** took charge
of N. Y. branch (C. H. Ditson &
Co.). Since 1875 (3) **J. Edward
Ditson** has cond. Philadelphia branch
(J. E. D. & Co.). A branch for the
importation of instrs., etc., was est. at
Boston in 1860 as John C. Haynes &
Co.; and since 1864 a Chicago
branch, Lyon & Healy.

**Ditters** (dĭt'-tĕrs) (**von Dittersdorf**),
**Karl,** Vienna, Nov. 2, 1739—Neuhaus, Bohemia, Oct. 24, 1799; noteworthy as forerunner of Mozart, and
early writer of programme-music (v.
D. D.); pupil of König and Ziegler,
of Trani (vln.), and Bono (comp.); he
played in the orch. of his patron
Prince Joseph of Hildburghausen,
1759, and then in the ct.-Th. at Vienna
(1761) ; toured Italy with Gluck, and
made great succ. as violinist ; 1764–
69 conductor to the Bishop of Gross-
Wardein, Hungary. Prod. his first
opera, "*Amore in Musica*," 1767 ;
followed by various oratorios, and
much orchestral and chamber-music.
Later conductor to the Prince-Bishop
of Breslau ; built a small theatre and
prod. several pieces. 1770 the Pope
bestowed on him the Order of the
Golden Spur ; 1773 the Emperor ennobled him as "von Dittersdorf."
Prod. 28 operas ; "*Doctor und Apo
theker*" (Vienna, 1786), still pop. ,
several oratorios and cantatas, 12
symphonies on Ovid's "*Metamor-
phoses*" (Vienna, 1785) (noteworthy
as early attempts at programme-music) ; 41 other symphonies ; a "Concerto grosso" for 11 concerted instrs.

with orch.; 12 vln.-concertos, etc. Autobiography (Leipzig, 1801).

**Divitis** (dē'-vĭ-tēs), **Antonius** (rightly **Antoine Le Riche**), French contrapuntist and singer, 16th century.

**Dizi** (dē-zē), **Fran. J.**, Namur, France, Jan. 14, 1780—Paris, Nov., 1847; composer and harpist.

**Dlabacz** (dlä'-bäch), **Gottf. J.**, Böhmisch-Brod, Bohemia, 1758--Prague, 1820; pub. a biog. dict., etc.

**Djemil, Bey** (jĕm'-ĕl bä), b. Constantinople ca. 1858; court-'cellist to the Sultan.

**Dobrzynski** (dō-brŭ-tsēn'-shkĭ), **Ignacy Félix**, Romanoff, Volhynia, Feb. 25, 1807—Oct. 9, 1867; pupil of Elsner; pianist and dram. composer.

**Doebber** (dĕp'-bĕr), **Js.**, b. Berlin, March 28, 1866; pupil of Radecke, Bussler and Agghazy, Stern Cons.; taught the 1st pf.-class in Kullak's Cons.; then conductor at Kroll's Th.; at Darmstadt ct.-Th.; since 1895 cond. at the ct.-Th. in Coburg-Gotha, and tutor to Princess Beatrice; c. succ. operas, "*Die Strassensängerin*" (Gotha, 1890); "*Der Schmied von Gretna-Green*" (Berlin, 1893); burlesque-opera "*Dolcetta*" (Brandenburg, 1894); "*Die Rose von Genzanó*" (Gotha, 1895); "*Die Grille*" (Leipzig, 1897), etc.

**Döhler** (dä'-lĕr), **Th.**, Naples, 1814—Florence, 1856; pianist and dram. composer.

**Dohnanyi** (dō-nän'-yē), **Ernst von**, b. Pressburg, Hungary, July 27, 1877; notable pianist and promising composer; first lessons from his father, an amateur 'cellist; later studied with Foerstner, Kessler, Thoman, and Eugen D'Albert; début, Vienna; 1898, won prize there with his pf.-concerto. 1900 and 1901 toured in America with great succ.; began composing early and was favorably noticed by Brahms; c. also symphony, pf.-quintet, pf.-pcs., etc.

**Doles** (dō'-lĕs), **J. Fr.**, Steinbach, Saxe-Meiningen, 1715—Leipzig, 1797; director and composer.

**Dominiceti** (dō-mē-nē-chä'-tē), **sare,** Desenzano, Lago di G 1821—Sesto di Monza, 1888; of comp. at Milan Cons., and c composer.

**Dom'mer, Arrey von,** b. Danzig, 9, 1828; pupil of Richter and (comp.), and Schallenburg (c 1863 Hamburg as a lecturer, c and (1873–79) sec. to the Tow brary; 1892, Dr. phil. hon. (Marburg Univ.); writer and poser.

**Donati** (dō-nä'-tē), (1) **Ignazio, C** maggiore, near Cremona, 16th c composer and conductor. (2) **dassaro,** d. Venice, 1603; cond composer.

**Done** (dōn), **Wm.**, Worcester, 18 1895; Engl. organist and condu

**Doni** (dō'-nē), (1) **A. Fran.**, Flor 1519—Monselice, near Padua, 1 pub. a "*Dialogue on Music.*" **Giov. Bat.**, 1593—1647; Flore nobleman of great learning ar search in ancient music; i 1v. Lyra Barberina or Amphichord.

**Donizetti** (dō-nē-tsĕt'-tē), (1) **Ga no,** Bergamo, Nov. 25, 1797—Ap 1848; son of a weaver; pupil o lari (voice), Gonzales (pf. and comp.), and Mayr (harm.); F and Padre Mattei (cpt.); his f opposing his making mus. a pr sion, he entered the army, was pe at Venice, where he c. and prod. succ. "*Enrico di Borgogna*" (1: "*Il Falegname di Livonia*" (Ve 1820), first given as "*Pietr Grande,*" also succeeded; "*Le l in Villa*" (Mantua, 1820) fa "*Zoraide di Granata*" (1822) ceeded and he left the army; 18. m. Virginie Vasselli (d. 1837); 1 29 he c. 23 operas, none of the great originality or importance. "*Anna Bolena*" (Milan, 1830 began a better period, incl. great successes "*L'Elisir d'Am* (Milan, 1832), "*Lucrezia Bor* (La Scala, Milan, 1833), "*Lu( Lammermoor*" (Naples, 1835).

Paris he prod. " *Marino Faliero*."
37 dir. Naples Cons. The censor
bade his " *Poliuto* " (it was prod.
Naples after his death, 1848), and
wrath he left for Paris, where he
od. with much succ. " *La Fille du
'giment*" (Op.-Com., 1840), " *Les
artyrs* " (a new version of *Poliuto*)
péra, 1840) ? and " *La Favorita*"
péra, 1840). Returned to Italy,
d succ. prod. "*Adelasia*" (Rome,
41), and " *Maria Padilla* " (Milan,
41). At Vienna, 1842, c. and prod.
th great succ. " *Linda di Chamou-
x.*" The Emperor made him Court
mposer and Master of the Imperial
apel ; c. a Miserere and an Ave
aria in strict style. " *Don Pas-
ale*" was prod. in Paris, 1843.
olent headaches and mental depres-
n now assailed him, but he contin-
d to write and prod. " *Caterino
rnaro*" (Naples, 1844), his last
rk ; he was found stricken with
ralysis, never recovered, and died
1848 at Bergamo. Besides 67
eras, all of them produced, he c. 6
sses, a requiem ; cantatas ; 12
ing-quartets ; pf.-pcs. and songs.
og. by Cicconetti (Rome, 1864).

**Alfredo,** b. Smyrna, Sept. 2,
57 ; pupil of Ponchielli and Domi-
eti, Milan Cons., graduating with
noteworthy " Stabat Mater " with
h. ; lives at Milan as cond. and
cher of cpt. ; c. 1-act operas
*ana*" (Milan, 1889), and " *Dopo
ve Maria*" (Milan, 1897), very
cc., " *La Locandiera* " (comedy in
cts), a symphony, etc.

t (dônt), (1) Jos. **Val.**, Georgen-
l, Bohemia, 1776—Vienna, 1833 ;
llist. (2) **jakob,** Vienna, 1815—
38; son of above; violinist and com-
ser.

**gelli** (dôn-jĕl'-lē), **Dom.,** Berga-
, 1790—Bologna, 1873 ; tenor.

- (dōr), **Anton,** b. Vienna, June
1833 ; pupil of Czerny and Sech-
; court pianist at Stockholm ; 1859
cher at the Imp. Inst., Moscow ;
4 prof. at the Cons. ; 1869 1st

prof. Vienna Cons., resigned 1901 ;
has edited classical and instructive
works.

**Dopp'ler,** (1) **Albert Fr.,** Lemberg,
1821—Baden, near Vienna, 1883 ;
flutist, conductor, professor, and
dram. composer. (2) **Karl,** b. Lemberg, 1826 ; bro. of above ; flutist,
and conductor; c. operas, incl. " *Er-
zebeth*" in collab. with his bro. and
Erkel. (3) **Arpad,** b. Pesth, June
5, 1857 ; son and pupil of (2) ; pupil
of Stuttgart Cons., later pf.-teacher ;
1880–83 New York ; returned to
Stuttgart Cons., also since 1889
chorusm. at the ct.-Th. ; c. opera
" *Viel Lärm um Nichts*" (Leipzig,
1896) ; suite, *Festouvertüre*, etc.

**Dörffel** (dĕrf'-fĕl), **Alfred,** b. Walden-
burg, Saxony, Jan. 24, 1821 ; pupil
at Leipzig of Fink, Muller, Mendelssohn, etc. ; mus.-libr. Leipzig City
Library ; critic and editor ; 1885 Dr.
phil. h. c., Leipzig U.

**Do'ria, Clara,** (1) v. MRS. C. K.
ROGERS. (2) v. KLOUS, A.

**Döring** (dā'-ring), (1) **G.,** Pomeren-
dorf, near Elbing, 1801—1869 ; cantor ; pub. choral books and historical
essays. (2) **Karl,** b. Dresden, July
4, 1834 ; pupil Leipzig Cons. ; 1858,
Dresden Cons. ; 1875, prof. ; c. suites
for string-orch., Grand Mass, etc.

**Dorn,** (1) **H. (L. Edm.),** Königsberg,
Nov. 14, 1804—Berlin, Jan. 10, 1892;
pupil of Berger, Zelter, and Klein,
Berlin ; ct.-cond. at Königsberg ;
cond. Cologne ; founded the " Rheinische Musikschule," which, 1850, became the Cologne Cons.; cond. Royal
Opera, Berlin ; teacher and critic ;
notable composer of 12 operas, symphonies, etc. (2) **Julius Paul,** b.
Riga, June 8, 1833 ; son and pupil of
above ; pianist ; teacher in Poland,
Cairo, and Alexandria ; 1865-68
cond. the Crefeld " Liedertafel " ;
since pf.-teacher at the R. Hochschule, Berlin, with title " Royal
Prof." ; c. over 400 works, incl. **3**
masses with orch. (3) **Otto,** b. Cologne, Sept. 7, 1848 ; son and pupil

c. (1); studied at Stern Cons., took the Meyerbeer scholarship (1st prize), 1873; lives in Wiesbaden; c. succ. opera "*Afraja*" (Gotha, 1891); symphony, "*Prometheus*"; overtures, "*Hermannsschlacht*," and "*Sappho*," etc. (4) **Edward,** Pen-name of **J. L. Röckel.**

**Dörner** (děr'-něr), **Armin W.,** b. Marietta, Ohio, June 22, 1852; studied in Berlin, Stuttgart and Paris; pf.-prof. Cincinnati Coll. of Music; pub. "*Technical Exercises.*"

**Dornheckter** (dôrn'-hěk-těr), **Robert,** Franzburg, Pomerania, 1839—Stralsund, 1890; conductor. organist and composer.

**Dorus - Gras** (dō - rü - gräs), **Julie Aimée Josèphe** (rightly) **Van Steenkiste** (Dorus, stage-name); Valenciennes, 1805 — Paris, 1896; operatic soprano; created important rôles.

**Doss** (dôs), **Adolf von,** Pfarrkirchen, Lower Bavaria, 1825—Rome, 1886; Jesuit priest and dram. composer.

**Dötssch** (dětsh), **Aug.,** 1858—Wiesbaden, 1882; 'cellist.

**Dotzauer** (dôt'-tsow-ěr), (1) **Justus J. Fr.,** Hasselrieth, near Hildburghausen, 1783—Dresden, 1860; 'cellist, and dram. composer. (2) **Justus B. Fr.,** Leipzig, 1808—Hamburg, 1874; son of above; teacher. (3) **K. L.** ("**Louis**"), b. Dresden, Dec. 7, 1811; son and pupil of (1); 'cellist.

**Douay** (doo-ě'), **Georges,** Paris, Jan. 7, 1840; pupil of Duprato; amateur composer of operettas, etc.

**Dourlen** (door-lăn), **Victor Chas. Paul,** Dunkirk, 1780—Batignolles, near Paris, 1864; prof. and dram. composer.

**Dcw'land,** (1) **John,** Westminster, London, 1562—London, April, 1626; lutenist and composer to Christian IV. of Denmark. (2) **Robert,** 1641; son of above; lutenist and editor.

**Draeseke** (drā'-zě-kě), **Felix Aug. Bhd.,** b. Coburg, Oct. 7, 1835; important composer; pupil of Rietz,

Leipzig Cons., and of Liszt at mar; 1864–74 Lausanne Cons. cept 1868–69, in the R. M. S. at nich; 1875 Geneva, then Dresde teacher; 1884 prof. of comp. at Cons.; c. 4 operas; "*Sign Gudrun*" (Hanover, 1884), "*trand de Born*" (book and mu and the succ. "*Herrat*" (Dres 1892); 3 symphonies (op. 40 "*T ica*," in C); Grand Mass with or "*Akademische Festouvertüre*"; phonic preludes to Calderon's "*a Dream*," Kleist's "*Penthes* (both MS.), etc.; wrote treatises a "*Harmony*" in verse.

**Draghi** (drä'-gē), (1) **Antonio,** Fer 1635—Vienna, 1700; c. 87 op 87 festival plays, etc. (2) **Gio. F** 1667—1706, harpsichordist, org and composer, London.

**Dragonnet'ti, Dom.,** Venice, 7, 1763—London, April 16, 1 called "the Paganini of the co basso"; composed, played taught.

**Drath** (drät), **Th.,** b. Winzig, Sil June 13, 1828; pupil of Marx; tor at Bunzlau Seminary: R "Musikdirector"; composer and orist.

**Draud** (drowt) (**Drau'dius**), **Ge** Davernheim, Hesse, 1573—Butzb 1635; pub. "*Bibliotheca Class* and other musical works of grea formational value.

**Drechsler** (drěkhs'-lěr), (1) **Jos., V** isch-Birken (Vlachovo Brezi), B mia, 1782—Vienna, 1852; orga conductor and dram. composer. **Karl,** Kamenz, 1800 — Dres 1873; 'cellist teacher.

**Dregert** (drä'-gěrt), **Alfred,** Fr fort-on-Oder, 1836—Elberfeld, 1 conductor, dir. and composer.

**Dresel** (drä'-zěl), **Otto,** Andern 1826—Beverly, Mass., 1890; poser.

**Dress'ler,** (1) **Louis Raphael,** b. York, 1861; son and pupil o **Wm.** (a conductor at N. Y.): there as pianist and composer.

zer (drĕsh'-ĕr), **Anastasius W.,** Kalisch, Poland, April 28, 1845 ; a lliant pianist at 12 ; studied with ring, Krebs, and Früh, Dresden ns.; lived in Leipzig ; 1868, Halle ; .nded a music-school of which he is l dir. ; c. 2 symphonies, opera *Valmoda,"* etc.

`schock (drī'-shôk), (1) **Alex.,** ck, Bohemia, Oct. 15, 1818—Ven-, April 1, 1869 ; one of the most xtrous of pf.-virtuosi ; c. an opera, . (2) **Raimund,** Zack, 1824— ipzig, 1869, br. of above ; leader. s wife (3) **Elisabeth** (née Nose), logne, 1832. a contralto. (4) **Felix,** ipzig, Dec. 27, 1860; son of (1) ; nist ; student under Grabau, Ehr-, Taubert, and Kiel at the Ber- Royal Hochschule ; prof. Stern ns., Berlin ; c. a vln.-sonata (op. , etc.

berg (drĕ'-bĕrkh), **Fr. J. von,** arlottenburg, 1780—1856 ; writer Greek music ; dram. composer.

isch (drō'-bĭsh), (1) **Moritz W.,** Leipzig, Aug. 16, 1802; from 1842 of. of phil., Leipzig Univ. ; pub. portant treatises on the mathemat- l determination of relative pitches. **Karl L.,** Leipzig, 1803—Augs-g, 1854 ; bro. of above ; c. 3 ora-ios.

s (drĕps), **J. And.,** near Erfurt, 4—Leipzig, 1825 ; organist.

uet (droo-ā), **L. Franç. Ph.,** Am-rdam, 1792—Bern, Sept. 30, 1873 ; ist and composer.

ois (dü-bwä) (1) **(Clément Fran.)** ., b. Rosnay, Marne, Aug. 24, 37 ; studied at Rheims, then under rmontel, Bénoist, Bazin, and omas (fugue and cpt.) at Paris ns.; took Grand prix de Rome h the cantata "*Atala*"; also first zes in all departments ; sent from me a Solemn Mass (perf. at the adeleine in 1870), a dram. work, *La Prova d'un Opera Seria,"* and overtures ; returned to Paris as a cher ; cond. at Saint-Clotilde ; ce organist at the Madeleine ;

1871 prof. of harm. at the Cons. ; 1891 prof. of comp. ; 1894, elected to Acad. ; 1896, dir. of the Cons., and officier of the Legion of Honour ; c. 4 operas ; oratorios : "*Les Septs Paroles du Christ*" (1867), "*Le Paradis Perdu*" (1878) (city of Paris prize), and "*Nôtre Dame de la Mer*" (1897) ; cantatas ; masses, etc. ; 3 overtures, incl. "*Frithiof.*" (2) **Léon,** b. Brussels, Jan. 9, 1849 ; pupil of the Cons., took Grand prix de Rome. Since 1890 second cond., Th. de la Monnaie, Brussels ; c. 3 operas, ballet, symphonic poem, "*Atala,*" etc.

**Duburg',** Matthew, London, 1703—1767 ; violinist and conductor.

**Ducange.** Vide CANGE, DU.

**Ducis** (dü-sē), **Benoît (Benedictus Ducis),** b. Bruges, 1480 ; important composer ; not to be confused with Benedictus of Appenzell.

**Dufay** (dü-fē'), **Guill.,** ca. 1400—Cambrai, Nov. 27, 1474 ; a canon ; said to have inv. white (open) notes.

**Dugazon** (dü-gă-zôn), **Louise-Rosalie** (née **Lefèvre**), Berlin, 1753—Paris, 1821 ; untrained singer in light opera, so charming in both young and old rôles as to give rise to the descriptive terms "Jeunes Dugazon," and "Mères Dugazon."

**Dug'gan, Jos. Francis,** b. Dublin, July 10, 1817 ; opera-conductor and teacher in various cities in America, also Paris and London ; c. succ. operas, "*Pierre,*" and "*Léonie,*" and 3 not produced ; 2 symphonies, etc.

**Duiffopruggar** (rightly **Tieffenbrücker**) (dwĕf'-fō-proog'-gär or tēf'-fĕn-brük-ĕr), (1) **Gaspar,** Freising, Bavaria, 1514—Lyons, 1572 ; long considered the first vln.-maker ; went to Lyons in 1553, naturalised in 1559, and made violas da gamba and lutes. Other instr.-makers of the same surname were (2) **Wendelin,** (3) **Leonhard,** (4) **Leopold,** (5) **Ulrich,** and (6) **Magnus.** The latest made lutes at Venice, 1607.

**Dulcken** (dool'-kĕn), (1) **Louise** (née **David**), Hamburg, 1811—London, 1850, a sister of Fd. David ; pianist. (2) **Fd. Quentin**, London, June 1, 1837—Astoria, N. Y., 1902 ; son of above ; pupil of Mendelssohn, Moscheles, Gade, Hauptmann, Becker and F. Hiller ; prof. Warsaw Cons. ; toured in Europe ; lived for years in New York ; c. an opera, " *Wieslav* " ; a mass, etc.

**Dulon** (doo'-lōn), **Fr. L.**, Oranienburg, near Potsdam, 1769 — Würzburg, 1826 ; a blind flutist and composer.

**Dulong** (doo'-lôngk), (1) **Fz. Henri von**, b. Hamm, Westphalia, Feb. 26, 1861 ; tenor, studied with Vannucini in Florence ; toured as concert-singer. (2) **Magda von** (née **John**), b. Halle, Feb. 29, 1872 ; wife of above ; concert-alto ; studied with Hromada, Frau Joachim, and Gerster ; first sang as **Magda Lossen.**

**Dun, Finlay,** Aberdeen, 1795—1853 ; viola-player, singing-teacher, editor and composer.

**Dun'ham, H. Morton,** b. Brockton, Mass., July 27, 1853 ; pupil N. E. Cons., and Boston Univ. Coll. of Mus. ; has taught in both places since ; pub. " *Organ School* "; 2 organ-sonatas, etc.

**Duni** (doo'-nē), **Egidio Romualdo,** Matera, near Otranto, Feb. 9, 1709 —Paris, June 11, 1775 ; pupil of Durante ; his first opera, " *Nerone*," prod. Rome, 1735, with great succ., triumphing over Pergolesi's last opera " *Olimpiado*," which the generous Duni said was too good for the public, declaring himself " frenetico contre il pubblico Romano " ; he c. French operettas with such succ. that he settled in Paris, where he is considered the founder of French opera-bouffe ; c. 13 Italian operas and 20 French.

**Dunk'ley, Fd. (Louis),** b. London, England, July 16, 1869 ; pupil of G. A. Higgs, Bainbridge, J. Higgs (cpt.), and E. H. Turpin (comp.) ; and at R. A. M. (Scholarship), under Parry,

Bridge, Martin, Gladstone, S[ and Barnet ; 1893, dir. at St. A School, Albany, N. Y. ; also o ist since 1897 at Trinity M. E. pub. " *The Wreck of the Hespe* ballade for soli, chor., and ( etc. ; 1889 took prize of 50 gu with orch. suite.

**Dunoyer** (dün-wä-yā'). Vide ( QUIER.

**Dun'stable (Dunstaple), John,** stable, Bedfordshire, England, (?)—Walbrook, Dec. 24, 1453 ; c by Tinctor one of the " father counterpoint.

**Dupont** (dü-pôn), (1) **Pierre,** R taillée, near Lyons, April 23, 18 Saint-Étienne, July 25, 1870 ; c words and tunes of popular political songs which Reyer ( out ; provoked such riots that I leon banished him, 1851. (2 **seph** (ainé), Liège, 1821—1861 ; linist ; prof. and dram. comp (3) **J. Fran.,** Rotterdam, 1 Nürnberg, 1875 ; violinist and ( composer. (4) **Aug.,** Ensival, Liège, 1828—Brussels, 1890 ; poser. (5) **Alex.,** Liège, 1833— bro. of above ; pub. a " *Répe dramatique Belge.*" (6) **Jos** jeune), b. Ensival, near Liège, 3, 1838 ; bro. of (3), pupil at and Brussels Cons., took Grand de Rome at Brussels ; 1867 con Warsaw ; 1871, in Moscow ; prof. of harm., Brussels Cons. ; Th. de la Monnaie, the Socie Musicians, and the Popular Con (7) **Jos. D.,** d. The Hague, Jur 1867 ; bro. of above ; dir. Ge Op. at Amsterdam.

**Duport** (dü-pôr), (1) **J. P.,** Paris, —Berlin, 1818 ; 'cellist. (2) **J** Paris, 1749—1819 ; more fa bro. of above ; also 'cellist ; com and writer.

**Duprato** (dü-prä'-tō), **Jules Lau** Nîmes, 1827—Paris, 1892 ; pr harm. and dram. composer.

**Duprez** (dü-prä'), **L. Gilbert,** 1806—1896 ; tenor and compos(

uis (dü-pwē), (1) **José** (**Joseph
ambert**), Liège, 1833—Nogent-
-Marne, 1900; opera-bouffe singer.
**Sylvain**, Liège, Nov. 9, 1856 ;
pil Liège Cons., 1881 Prix de Rome;
w teacher of cpt. and cond. of a
ging-society ; c. 3 operas, incl.
e succ. com. opera " *L'idylle,*" 3
atatas, symphonic poem, "*Mac-
h,*" etc.

uy (dü-pwē). Vide PUTEANUS.

and (rightly **Duranowski**) (dü-
h or doo-rän-ôf'-shkï), (1) **Auguste
édéric**, b. Warsaw, 1770 ; violin-
and cond., son of a court-mus. (2)
mile, b. St.-Brieuc, Côtes du Nord,
b. 16, 1830 ; while still a pupil at
e Paris Cons. he was appointed
acher of an elementary singing-
ass ; 1871 prof. of harm ; dram.
mposer and writer. (3) **Marie
uguste**, Paris, July 18, 1830 ; pu-
of Benoist, 1849–74 organist at
rious churches ; 1870 est. mus.-pub.
siness of " Durand et Schöne-
erk," later " Durand et Fils " ; a
tic and composer.

ante (doo-rän'-tě), **Fran.**, Fratta
aggiore, Naples, March 15, 1684—
aples, Aug. 13, 1755 ; director and
nductor, with salary of less than
oo per annum ; he is an important
acher and composer of the " Nea-
litan School " ; c. 13 masses, etc.

astanti (doo-rä-stän'-tē), **Mar-
arita**, ca. 1695 Italian prima don-
, of wonderful popularity in Lon-
n.

r'fey, **Thos.**, Exeter, ca. 1649—
eb. 26, 1723 ; operatic composer
d editor.

rner (dǐr'-něr), **Ruprecht Jns.**
lius, Ansbach, Bavaria, 1810—Ed-
burgh, 1859 ; composer, writer, ed-
or.

utte (dü-rüt), **Fran. Camille
nt.**, Ypres, East Flanders, 1803—
aris, 1881 ; wrote a new but errone-
s system of harm.; c. operas, etc.

s)sek (**Dušek, Duschek**) (doos'-
k or better doo'-shěk), (1) **Fz.**, Chot-
orz, Bohemia, 1736—Prague, 1799 ;

composer, pianist and teacher. (2)
**Joséphine**, b. Prague, 1756 ; pianist,
composer, singer. (3) **J. Ladislaus**,
Caslav (Tschaslau), Bohemia, Feb.
9, 1761—Saint-Germain-en-Laye,
March 20, 1812 ; a boy-soprano at
Iglau, pupil of Father Spenar at the
Jesuit College ; organist Jesuit
Church, Kuttenburg, for 2 years ;
studied theology at Prague Univ.,
also music ; became organist of Saint-
Rimbaut's, Mechlin ; lived Bergen-
op-Zoom ; Amsterdam ; The Hague,
1783 ; studied with C. P. E. Bach,
Hamburg ; became famous pianist
and performer on Hessel's " Harmonica," Berlin and St. Petersburg ;
lived in Lithuania a year at Prince
Radziwill's Court ; lived Italy,
Paris, London ; 1792 m. (4) **Sofia
Corri** (b. Edinburgh, 1775 ; a singer,
harpist and composer). He entered
a mus.-business with his father-in-
law, 1800, failed and fled to Hamburg to escape creditors. He was in
the service of various Princes, and
(1808) of Prince Talleyrand in Paris.
A pioneer among Bohemian and Polish virtuosi and composers he disputed with Clementi the invention of
the " singing-touch." Prod. 2 English
operas in London with success, and
pub. a Mass (comp. at the age of 13),
oratorios and church-music ; pub.
nearly 100 works for pf., incl. 12 concertos, 80 sonatas with vln. ; 53 sonatas for pf.-solo, etc. ; pub. a
" *Method.*"

**Dustmann** (doost'-män), **Marie Luise**
(née **Meyer**), Aix-la-Chapelle, 1831
—1899 ; soprano.

**Dütch** (dütsh), b. Denmark—d. Frank-
furt-on-Main, 1863 ; prominent Russian composer.

**Duval** (dü-văl'), **Edmond**, b. Enghien,
Hainault, Aug. 22, 1809 ; pupil Paris
Cons., 1828–32, when he was dismissed for irregular attendance ; at
Mechlin became interested in Janssen's studies of Gregorian music ;
was commissioned by the Bishop to
revise the church-ritual, and visited

Rome ; he pub. "revised version," etc., of ecclesiastical song, which Fétis declares altogether wrong.

**Duvernoy** (or **Duvernois**) (dü-věrn-wä), (1) **Fr.**, Montbéliard, 1765—Paris, 1838 ; prof. at the Cons.; composer. (2) **Charles**, Montbéliard, 1766—Paris, 1845 ; bro. of above ; clarinettist ; prof. and composer. (3) **Chas. Fran.**, Paris, 1796—1872 ; singer. (4) **H. L. Chas.**, b. Paris, Nov. 16, 1820 ; son of (3) ; pupil of Halévy and Zimmermann, Paris Cons.; 1839, assist.-prof.; 1848, prof. there of solfeggio ; composer. (5) **Victor Alphonse**, Paris, Aug. 31, 1842 ; pupil of Bazin and Marmontel Paris Cons.; took first pf. prize ; now teacher of piano at the Cons.; a Chev. of the Legion of Honour, and officier of public instruction ; 1892 prod. the succ. opera " *Sardanapale* " (Lyons), also opera " *Helle* " (Gr. Opéra, 1896) ; his symph. poem, " *La Tempête*," won the City of Paris prize. (6) **J. Bapt.**, composer and pf.-teacher, Paris, 1825.

**Duysen** (doi´-sĕn), **Jes Lewe**, b. Flensburg, Aug. 1, 1820 ; 1860 founded a pf. factory at Berlin.

**Dvořák** (dvôr´-shäk), **Antonin**, b. Mühlhausen, Bohemia, Sept. 8, 1841 ; chief of Bohemian composers ; son of an inn-keeper, who wished him to be a butcher, but he learned the vln. from the schoolmaster, and at 16 entered the Prague Org.-Sch. under Pitzsch, earning a livelihood as violinist in a small orchestra ; graduated in 1862, became vla.-player at the Nat. Theatre. He was 33 before an important comp. was prod.,a hymn for male chorus and orch., which attracted such attention that 1875 he received a government stipend and devoted himself to composition. 1891 Mus. Doc. Cambridge Univ.; 1892–95 dir. Nat. Cons., New York ; since has lived at Prague ; 1901, director of the Prague Cons ; 1902, prod. opera " *Armida*," Pilsen Nat. Th. He is a strong believer in nationalism in mu-

sic, and provoked much controver advising American composers to f their school on the harmonic and odic elements of plantation-m In his 5th symphony, op. 95, " *the New World*," he made som of such a manner. His other c are : Bohemian operas " *The and the Charcoal-Burner* " (Pr 1874) ; " *Wanda* " (1876) ; " *S Sedlák* " (1878) ; " *Turde Pa* (1881) ; " *Dimitrije* " (1882) ; ' *Jacobins* " (1889) ; " *Rusalka, Water Nixie* " (Nat. Th. Pr 1901) ; oratorio " *St. Ludm* (Leeds Mus. Fest., 1886) ; *Req Mass*, op. 89, with orch. (Birr ham Fest., 1891) ; cantatas " *Spectre's Bride*," op. 69, with (Birmingham Fest., 1885), and " *American Flag* " (N. Y., 18 *Hymn of the Bohemian Peas* for mixed ch. ; hymn for mixed and orch. ; " *Stabat Mater* " orch. (London, 1883) ; Psalm with orch. ; 5 symphonies ; 3 chestral ballades, " *Der Wa mann*," " *Die Mittagshexe*," " *Das goldene Spinnrad*"; 2 se symphonic variations for orch. ; tures, " *Mein Heim*," " *Husits* " *In der Natur*," " *Othello*," " *neval*"; concertos for 'cello, pf., " *Slavische Tänze*," and " *Slav Rhapsodien*"; scherzo cappric for orch. ; string-sextet ; 2 st quintets ; pf.-quintet ; 6 string-c tets ; 2 pf.-quartets ; a string-tri pf.-trios ; mazurek for vln. orch. ; serenade for wind with " and double-bass ; notturno string-orch. ; pf. music, " *Legend* " *Dumka* " (Elegy), " *Furia* (Boh. natl. dances) ; " *Klänge Mahren*," and " *Silhouetten* " fo 4-hands ; violin-sonata, op. songs, etc.

**Dwight, J. Sullivan**, Boston, M. 1813—1893 ; editor and critic ; of the founders of the Harvard M cal Association ; was a membe the Brook Farm Community ; 1

, edited "*Dwight's Journal of
*usic.*"

:es (Rev.), **J. Bacchus**, Kingston-
₃on-Hull, Eng., 1823—St. Leon-
d's, 1876 ; conductor.

₃e, **John**, suicide, Oct. 30, 1788 ;
₃glish alto singer and composer.

# E

₃er, **John**, b. Norwich, 1782 ; violin-
: and teacher.

₃nes (āmz), **Emma**, b. (of American
₃rents) at Shanghai, Aug. 13, 1867 ;
₃ 5 went with her mother, her first
₃acher, to Bath, Maine ; pupil of
₃iss Munger at Boston ; 1886–88 at
₃aris, of Madame Marchesi (voice),
₃d Pluque (acting, etc.) ; 1888, en-
₃ged at the Op.-Com., but made dé-
₃it with succ. at the Gr. Opéra,
₃arch 13, 1889, as Juliette in Gou-
₃od's "*Roméo et Juliette*," a rôle pre-
₃ously sacred to Patti ; sang at the
₃pera for 2 years, creating "Co-
₃mbe" in St.-Saens' "*Ascania*" and
₃ "Zäire" in De La Nux's opera ;
₃91, Covent Garden in "*Faust;*" m.
₃e painter Julian Story the same year,
₃d in Oct. appeared in New York ;
₃nce then she has sung regularly in
₃. Y. and London, except 1892–93,
: Madrid, and 1895–96, during ill-
₃ealth ; her "Sieglinde" is perhaps
₃er best rôle.

₃st'cott, **Richard**, Exeter, 1740—
₃ivery Dale, Devonshire, 1828 ; writ-
₃r and composer.

₃den, **Thos.**, Durham, 1738—1811 :
₃rganist and composer.

₃eling (ā'-bĕ-lĭng), (1) **J. G.**, Lüne-
₃urg, ca. 1620—Stettin, 1676 ; prof.
₃nd composer. (2) **Chp. Daniel**,
₃armissen, near Hildesheim, 1741
₃–Hamburg, 1817 ; prof. and writer.

₃ell (ā'-bĕl), **H. K.**, Neuruppin,
₃775—Oppeln, 1824 ; conductor and
₃ram. composer.

₃erhard (1) **von Freisingen** (ā'-bĕr-
₃ärt fōn frī'-zĭng-ĕn), **Eberhar'dus
₃risengen'sis**, Benedictine monk,
₃ith cent. ; wrote on the scale of

pipes and bell-founding. (2) **J.
Aug.**, Halberstadt, 1739 — Halle,
1809 ; professor.

**Eberl** (ā'-bĕrl), **Anton**, Vienna, June
13, 1766—March 11, 1807 ; famous
pianist, conductor and dram. composer.

**Eberlin** (ā'-bĕr-lēn), (1) **Daniel**, Nürnberg, ca. 1630—Cassel, 1691 ; contrapuntist and violinist ; famous as a
composer in his day. (2) (or **Eberle**) **J. Ernst**, Jettenbacht, Swabia,
1702—Salzburg, 1762 ; conductor and
composer.

**Ebers** (ā'-bĕrs), **K. Fr.**, Cassel, 1770
—Berlin, 1836 ; conductor and dram.
composer.

**Eberwein** (ā'-bĕr-vīn), (1) **Traugott
Maximilian**, Weimar, 1775—Rudolstadt, 1831 ; dram. composer. (2)
**Karl**, Weimar, 1786—1868, bro. of
above ; dram. composer.

**Eccard** (ĕk'-kärt), **J.**, Mühlhausen,
Thuringia, 1553—Berlin, 1611 ; important composer of church-music.

**Eccles** (ĕk'-kĕls), (1) **John**, London (?),
1668—Kingston, Surrey, 1735 ; son
and pupil of the violinist, (2) **Solomon E. C.** His brother (3) **Henry**,
was violinist and composer. (4)
**Solomon Thomas**, bro. of above,
also violinist.

**Eck** (ĕk), (1) **J. Fr.**, Mannheim, 1766—
Bamberg (?), 1809 (1810?) ; violinist
and composer. (2) **Fz.**, Mannheim,
1774—insane, Strassburg, 1804 ; bro.
and pupil of above ; violinist.

**Eckelt** (ĕk'-ĕlt), **J. Val.**, Wernings-
hausen, near Erfurt, 1680—Sondershausen, 1734 ; writer.

**Ecker** (ĕk'-ĕr), (1) **K.**, Freiburg, Bad-
en, 1813—1879 ; composer. (2)
**Wenzel**, pen-name of **W. Gericke**.

**Eckert** (ĕk'-ĕrt), **K. Ant. Florian**,
Potsdam, 1820—Berlin, 1879 ; at 10
c. an opera, at 13 an oratorio ; court-
conductor and dram. composer.

**Ed'dy, Clarence H.**, b. Greenfield,
Mass., June 23, 1851 ; pupil of J. G.
Wilson and Dudley Buck ; 1871 of
Haupt and Löschhorn (pf.) ; toured
in Germany, Austria, Switzerland,

and Holland ; 1874, organist, Chicago ; 1876, dir. Hershey School of Musical Art ; later m. its founder Mrs. S. B. H. ; toured America and Europe, 1879 gave 100 recitals at Chicago without repeating a number; for some years cond. Chicago Philh. Vocal Soc. ; c. organ and church music, etc ; pub. " *The Church and Concert Organist*," " *The Organ in Church* " (1887), and transl. Haupt's " *Cpt. and Fugue* " (1876).

**Ed'son, Lewis,** Bridgewater, Mass., 1748—Woodstock, N. Y., 1820 ; pub. a coll. of hymns, etc.

**Ed'wards, Julian,** b. Manchester, England, 1855 ; pupil Sir H. Oakley, Edinburg, then of Macfarren, London ; 1875, pianist to Carl Rosa Opera Co.; 1877, cond. Royal Eng. Opera Co. and prod. " *Victorian* " Covent Garden. 1880, prod. " *Corinne* " at St. James's Hall, London ; cond. Engl. Opera at Covent Garden, and prod. 2 operas, " *Corinne* " and " *Victorian* " at Sheffield, 1883 ; came to the U. S., 1889, and prod. with success various comic operas, incl. " *Madeleine or the Magic Kiss* " (Boston, 1894), and " *Brian Boru* " (N. Y., 1896); " *The Wedding Day*," " *The Jolly Musketeer*," " *Princess Chic* " (1899), "*Dolly Varden*" (N. Y., 1902), and " *When Johnny Comes Marching Home*"; prod. also romantic opera " *King Réné's Daughter*"; c. gr. opera "*Elfinella*" (MS.), symphonies, overtures, etc.

**Eeden** (ā'-děn), **Jean Baptiste van den,** b. Ghent, Dec. 26, 1842 ; pupil of Ghent and Brussels Cons.; 1st prize for comp. (1869) with the cantata " *Faust's Laaste Nacht* " ; 1878 dir. of Cons. at Mons.; c. opera, "*Numance*" (Antwerp, 1897), 4 oratorios and the trilogy " *Judith*," 2 cantatas with orch., a symph. poem, "*La Lutte au XVI. Siècle*," etc.

**E'gan, Eugene,** Irishman, less than four feet tall ; 1740 built organ in Lisbon Cathedral.

**Egenolff** (or **Egenolph**) (ā'-gěr Chr., ca. 1485 ; a slovenly and ical German mus.-printer.

**Eggeling** (ěg'-gě-lǐng), (Ed Brunswick, 1813—Harzburg, pf.-teacher, writer and composer

**Egghard** (ěg -härt), **Julius** (penof Count Hardegen), Vienna, 1 1867 ; composer.

**Egli** (āl'-yē or ā'-glē), **Johann** I **rich,** Seegraben, canton Zurich, —1810 ; c. " *Oden*," etc.

**Ehlert** (ā'-lěrt), **Louis,** Königs 1825—Wiesbaden, 1884 ; teache critic ; conductor and composer.

**Ehmant** (ā'-mänt), **Anselm,** 18 Paris, 1895 ; conductor, teacher writer.

**Ehnn-Sand** (ān'-zänt), **Bertha** Pesth, 1848 ('45 ?) ; dramatic sopi pupil of Frau Andriessen.

**Ehrlich** (ār'-lǐkh), (1) **Chr. Fr.,** I deburg, 1810—1887 ; conductor, ing-teacher, and dram. composer **Alfred H.,** b. Vienna, Oct. 5, 1 pupil of Henselt, Bocklet, Thal (pf.), and Sechter (comp.) ; c pianist to King George V.; 186 pf.-teacher Stern Cons., and 186 critic in Berlin ; composer and ed

**Eibenschütz** (ī'-běn-shüts), (1) Alb b. Berlin, April 15, 1857 ; pianist ; pil of Reinecke and Paul, Lei Cons., won the Diploma of Hon 1876-80, prof. in Charkoff (Russ 1880-84 at Leipzig Cons., then logne Cons.; 1893, dir. Cologne derkranz ; 1896, 1st pf.-prof. S Cons., Berlin ; c. pf.-sonatas, (2) **Ilona,** Pesth, May 18, 1 cousin of above ; pianist ; at 5 played in a concert with Liszt ; 18 85; pupil of Hans Schmitt ; 1885 studied with Frau Schumann ; l in Vienna and makes tours thence

**Eichberg** (īkh'-běrkh or īch'-bürg) **Julius,** b. Düsseldorf, June 13, 182 Boston, Mass., Jan. 18, 1893 ; vic ist and notable teacher ; c. 4 ope tas, etc. (2) **Oskar,** Berlin, 184 1898 ; singing-teacher, conduc critic, editor, and composer.

hborn (īkh'-bôrn), **H. L.**, b. Breslau, Oct. 30, 1847 ; studied pf., flute, rumpet, horn, etc., at an early age ; t 14 pupil of the trumpeter Ad. cholz ; studied theory with Dr. E. Sohn ; became a Waldhorn virtuoso; 882 inv. the Oktav (or soprano) Valdhorn ; wrote musical essays, tc. ; cond. at Gries, near Bozen ; ditor, writer and composer.

hhorn (īkh'-hôrn), (1) **J. Paul E.**, 787—1823 ; court-musician, Coburg; is sons (2), **J. G. Ernst**, 1822–44, nd (3) **J. K. Ed.**, 1823–97, performed on the vln. respectively at 6 nd 7.

ers (ī'-lĕrs), **Albert**, 1831—Darmstadt, 1896 ; basso cantante.

sfeld (īs'-fĕlt), **Th.**, Wolfenbüttel, pril 11, 1816—Wiesbaden, Sept. 6 (?), 1882 ; important figure in New ork music ; 1848–66 previously conuctor at Wiesbaden ; then of " Concerts Viviennes," Paris.

ssler (īs'-lĕr), (1) **Marianne**, b. Brünn, Nov. 18, 1865 ; violinist, pupil of Hessler ; her sister, (2) **Emma**, a pianist.

ner (īt'-nĕr), **Rob.**, b. Breslau, Oct. 2, 1832 ; pupil of Brosig ; 1853, eacher at Berlin ; est. a pf.-sch., 863 ; important for work in musical terature, and research in 16th and 7th centuries, Dutch music, etc. ; c. Biblical opera," "*Judith*"; overure to *Der Cid* ; etc.

andi (ā-iàn'-dē), **Rita**, b. Cincinnati, ). soprano ; pupil of Marchesi, aris . sang in Italy, Spain, and Germany , created " Santuzza " in "*I Pagliacci*" in English with Carl Rosa Opera Co.; 1900, in N. Y. with American Opera Co.

dering, **Bram**, b. Groningen, Holland, July 8, 1865 ; violinist ; tudied with Poortmann, Hubay, and oachim ; Konzertmeister Berlin Philh. ; then do. in Meiningen ct.-hapel.

ers (ā'-lĕrs) (called **El'erus**), **Fz.**, Jelzen, ca. 1500—1590, Hamburg ; eacher, director, and composer.

**Elewyck** (vän ā'-lŭ-vĕk), **Xavier Victor** (Chevalier) **van**, Ixelles les Bruxelles, Belgium, 1825—in an insane asylum, Zickemont, 1888 ; writer.

**El'gar, Edw. Wm.**, b. Broadheath, Worcester, Engl., June 2, 1857 ; important English composer, violinist, and organist ; cond. Worcester Instrumental Soc., 1882–89 ; 1885–89, organist at St. George's ; 1891, lived in Malvern ; c. oratorio, " *The Light of Life* " (1896) ; " *The Dream of Gerontius* " (1900) ; 2 cantatas ; a choral suite ; concert - overtures, "*Froissart*," and "*Cockaigne*" (1901); 6 Scenes from the Bavarian Highlands, for chorus and orch. (1896) ; Spanish serenade for ch. and orch. ; romance for vln. and orch. ; church-music ; pcs. for vln. and pf. ; organ-sonata ; songs, etc.

**Elias** (ā'-lĭ-äs), **Salomonis**, monk at Saint-Astère, Perigord, wrote in 1274 the oldest extant book of rules for improvised counterpoint.

**Elisi** (ā-lē'-zē), **Filippo**, Italian tenor in London, 1765.

**El'la, John**, Thirsk, Yorkshire, 1802—London, 1888 ; violinist, lecturer and writer.

**El'ler, Louis**, Graz, 1819—Pau, 1862; vln.-virtuoso; c. " *Valse Diabolique*," a " *Rhapsodie Hongroise*," etc., for vln.

**El'lerton, J. Lodge**, Chester, 1807—London, 1873 ; dram. composer.

**El'liott, Jas. Wm.**, Warwick, Engl., Feb. 13, 1833 ; pupil of Macfarren ; organist various churches; since 1874 at St. Mark's, London ; c. 2 operettas, etc.

**El'lis, Alex. J.**, London, 1814—Kensington, 1890 ; writer on musical science.

**Elmblad** (ĕlm'-blät), **Jns.**, b. Stockholm, Aug. 22, 1853 ; bass ; studied with Stockhausen and Garcia ; 1876, Wagner chose him for " Donner " (Rheingold). but his father, a prof. of theology, objected; 1880, he went into opera and sang in various cities, as well as in London and America;

1896, sang " Fafner " at Bayreuth ; since 1897 at ct.-Th., Stockholm.

**Elmenreich** (ĕl'-mĕn-rīkh), **Albert,** 1856, actor in the Court Th. at Schwerin.

**Elsenheimer** (ĕl'-zĕn-hī-mĕr), **Nicholas J.,** b. Wiesbaden, 1866 ; pupil of his father and of Jakobsthal, Strassburg, LL.D., Heidelberg ; 1890, America ; 1891, prof. at Coll. of Music, Cincinnati ; c. cantata " *Valerian,*" with orch. " *Belshazzar,*' etc

**Elsner** (ĕls'-nĕr), **Jos. Xaver,** Grottkau, Silesia, 1769—Warsaw, 1854 ; writer and composer of 19 operas.

**El'son, Louis Chas.,** b. Boston, April 17, 1848 ; writer and teacher ; pupil of Kreissmann (singing), Boston, and Gloggner-Castelli (theory), Leipzig ; edited the *Vox Humana ;* then on the *Music Herald ;* for years critic of the *Boston Courier,* now of the *Advertiser ;* since 1881 prof. of theory and lecturer on the orch. and musical history at N. E. Cons. ; has lectured on music with much success ; pub. " *Curiosities of Music,*" " *The History of German Song,*" " *The Theory of Music,*" " *The Realm of Music,*" " *German Songs and Song-writers,*" " *European Reminiscences,*" " *Syllabus of Musical History,*" and " *Great Composers and Their Work*" (1899), " *The National Music of America* (1900), " *Home and School Songs*"; c. operettas, songs, and instr.-works ; transl. and arranged over 2,000 songs, operas, etc.

**El'terlein, Ernst von.** Vide GOTT-SCHALD.

**El'vey,** (1) **Stephen,** Canterbury, 1805 —Oxford, 1860 ; organist. (2) Sir **George (Job),** Canterbury, 1816— Windlesham, Surrey, 1893 ; bro. of above ; c. oratorios.

**Elwart** (ĕl'-värt), **Antoine Aimable Elie,** Paris, 1808—1877 ; violinist and dram. composer.

**Em'erson, Luther Orlando,** b Parsonsfield, Mass., Aug. 3, 1820 ; cond. and composer.

**Em'ery, Stephen Albert,** Pa Maine, Oct. 4, 1841—Boston, A 15, 1891 ; prof. of harm. and c asst.-ed. *Musical Herald ;* grace composer and pop. theorist.

**Emmerich** (ĕm'-mĕr-ĭkh), **Ro** Hanau, 1836—Stuttgart, 1891 ; c poser.

**Encke** (ĕnk'-ĕ), **H.,** Neustadt, Ba ria, 1811—Leipzig, 1859 ; pia and composer.

**Enckhausen** (ĕnk'-how-zĕn), **H. F** Celle, 1799—Hanover, 1885 ; co organist, pianist and director.

**Engel** (ĕng'-ĕl), (1) **Jn. Jakob,** I chim, Mecklenburg, 1741—1802 ; and composer. (2) **David H** Neuruppin, 1816—Merseburg, 18 organist, writer and dram. compo (3) **K.,** Thiedenweise, near Hanov 1818 —suicide, London, 1882 ; org ist and writer. (4) **Gv. Ed., I** nigsberg, 1823—Berlin, 1895 ; si ing-teacher, composer and theo (5) **Pierre Émile,** b. Paris, Feb. 1847 ; tenor ; studied with Dupr début, Th. Italien, 1869 ; then s in New Orleans Brussels, and si 1889 at Paris.

**En'na, Aug.,** b. Naskov, Denma May 13, 1860; grandson of an Ital soldier in Napoleon s army ; son c shoemaker ; self-taught in pf. and strumentation, and had almost teaching in vln. or theory ; went w a small orch. to Finland (188 played various insts., even a drum fore a circus-tent; returned to Cop hagen ; prod. the operetta " *A V lage Tale*" (1880) in provincial t atres ; played at dancing-lessons, a gave pf.-lessons at 12 cents an ho 1883, cond. for a small provin troupe, for which he wrote act-tun and 10 overtures ; pub. songs, j pcs., an orchl. suite, and a sympho this gained him, through Gade's terest, the Ancker scholarship, ena ling him to study in Germany (188 89). After producing an opere " *Areta,*" he prod. with unequal succ. for a Dane, the opera " *1*

*Vitch,"* 1892, at the R. Opera House, openhagen. The opera "*Cleopa-ra*" (Copenhagen, 1894) failed, but 895, with new cast, was succ. as lso "*Aucassin and Nicolette*" (Co-enhagen, 1896; Hamburg, 1897). pera "*Aglaia,*" in MS. Pub. a ln.-concerto, etc.

och & Co., London music-pub. rm, est. 1869.

ine (dĕ-lā-pé´-nĕ), Francesca Mar-erita de l'., extremely popular alian singer and harpsichordist in ondon, from ca. 1698—1718, when ie m. Dr. Pepusch; her sister sang a London from 1703–1748 as Maria allia.

stein (ĕp´-shtīn), (1) Julius, b. gram, Aug. 14, 1832; pupil of ichtenegger, Halm (pf.), and Rufi-atscha (comp.); from 1867 prof. of f. Vienna Cons. His two daugh-rs, (2) Rudolfine ('cellist), and (3) ugénie (violinist), toured Austria id Germany, 1876–77.

rd (ā´-rär), (1) Sébastien, Strass-urg, April 5, 1752—near Paris, Aug. , 1831; notable piano-maker and in-entor; inv. a "Clavecin Mécan-que"; the "Piano organisé," fin-lly the double-action mechanism, hich made a new instr. of the harp r. D. D.); perfected in 1811 his reatest achievement, the repetition ction of the piano (v. D. D.). His iccessor as a piano-maker was is nephew, (2) Pierre (1796—1855), icceeded by Pierre Schaffer (d. 1878); ie present head is the Count de ranqueville.

atos´thenes, Cyrene, 276 — Alex-ndria, Egypt, 195 B.C.; writer.

 (ĕrp), M. Jos., b. Strassburg, ct. 23, 1860; pupil of St.-Saëns, igout, and Loret, Paris; now lives a Strassburg as teacher and or-anist at the Johanniskirche and ie Synagogue; c. a symphony; symphonic suite; sonatas and dram. episode" "*Der letzte Ruf.*" Strassburg, 1895), with some succ., tc.

Er´ba, Don Dionigi, nobleman and composer at Milan, 1694; Händel appropriated some of his best works.

Erbach (ĕr´-bäkh), Chr., Algesheim, Palatinate, ca. 1560—Augsburg, 1628; composer and organist.

Er´ben, Robert; 1894, conductor at Frankfort-on-M.; 1896, at Mann-heim; prod. the succ. 1-act opera "*Enoch Arden*" (Frankfort-on-M., 1895), and a "fairy comedy," "*Die Heinzelmännchen*" (Mayen e, 1896).

Erdmannsdörffer (ĕrt´-mäns-dĕrf-fĕr), (1) Max, b. Nürnberg, June 14, 1848; pupil Leipzig Cons., and in Dresden of Rietz; 1871–80, ct.-cond., Sondershausen; 1882, dir. Imp. Mus. Soc. at Moscow, and prof. at the Cons.; 1885, founded a students' orch. society; returned to Germany, cond. the Bremen Philh. Concerts till 1895; 1896, cond. Symphony Con-certs St. Petersburg; 1896, cond. at the ct.-Th., Munich; c. "*Prinzessin Ilse,*" "a forest-legend"; and other works for soli, chor. and orch.; over-ture to Brachvogel's "*Narciss,*" etc.; 1874 he m. (2) Pauline Fichtner Oprawik, b. Vienna, June 28, 1847 (1851 ?); pupil of Pirkhert and Liszt; court-pianist.

Erhard (ĕr´-härt) (called Erhar´di), Laurentius, b. at Hagenau, Alsatia, 1598; cantor at Frankfort-on-Main, 1640, etc.

Erk (ĕrk), (1) Adam Wm., Herpf, Saxe-Meiningen, 1779—Darmstadt, 1820; organist and composer. (2) Ludwig (Chr.), Wetzlar, 1807—Ber-lin, 1883; son of above; conductor. (3) Fr. Albrecht, Wetzlar, 1809— Düsseldorf, 1879; bro. of above; pub. the "*Lehrer Commersbuch,*" etc.

Erkel (ĕr´-kĕl), (1) Franz (or Ferencz), Gyula, Hungary, Nov. 7, 1810— Pesth, June 15, 1893; the father of Hungarian opera, conductor and prof., composer of operas incl. "*Hunyády Lázló*" and "*Bank Ban.*" (2) Alexander (or Alexius), Pesth, 1846—1900, son of above;

dir. of Philh. Conc., Pesth, 1875–93;
1896, dir. Royal Opera, Pesth; prod.
opera "*Tempeföi*" (Pesth, 1883).
(3) **Gyula**, son of (1), prof. at Acad.
of Mus., Pesth; conductor for many
years at R. Opera.

**Erlanger** (ĕr-läṅ-zhä), (1) **Camille**, b.
Paris, May 25, 1863; pupil of Délibes,
Paris Cons.; 1888 took Grand prix
de Rome with cantata "*Velleda*"; c.
symphonic piece, "*La Chasse Fantastique*"; dram. legend, "*Saint
Julien L'Hospitalier*" (Paris, 1896);
the succ. lyric drama "*Kermaria*"
(Paris, Op.-Com., 1897), etc. (2)
Baron **Frédéric d'** (pen-names **Fr.
Regnal** or **Federico Ringel**), son
of a banker; prod. succ. opera "*Jehan de Saintré*," Hamburg (1894),
and mod. succ. opera "*Inez Mendo*"
(London, 1897).

**Er'ler**, (1) **Hermann**, b. Radeberg,
near Dresden, June 3, 1844; 1873
est. a mus.-pub. business (now Ries
and Erler); editor and critic. (2)
**Ernst II.**, Duke of Saxe-Coburg-
Gotha, Coburg, 1818—Keinhards-
brunn, 1893; dram. composer. (3)
**Fz. Anton**, Georgenthal, Bohemia, 1745—Gotha, 1805; violinist
and orch.-leader. (4) **H. Wm.**,
Brunn, 1814—Nice, 1865; vln.-vir-
tuoso; toured, then lived in London;
composer. (5) **Heinrich**, b. Dresden,
Sept. 19, 1846; nephew of above;
pupil of Pesth Cons., 1872; barytone
Leipzig Th., then studied with Rebling and became tenor; 1875, Royal
Opera, Berlin. (6) **Alfred**, ca. 1855
—Paris, 1898; writer.

**Errani** (ĕr-rä'-nĕ), **Achille**, Italy, 1823
—New York, 1897; operatic tenor
and notable singing-teacher in N. Y.

**Errera** (ĕr-rä'-rä), **Ugo**, b. Venice, Oct.
25, 1843; composer.

**Ert'mann**, Baroness, ca. 1778—Vienna, 1848; pianist; intimate friend of
Beethoven.

**Eschmann** (ĕsh'-män), **Jn. K.**, Winterthur, Switzerland, 1826—Zurich,
1882; pianist, teacher and composer
at Leipzig.

**Escudier** (ĕs-küd-yä), two broth
of Castelnaudary, Aude, (1) **Ma**
1819—1880, and (2) **Léon**, 182
Paris, 1881; journalists.

**Eslava** (ĕs-lä'-vä), **Don Miguel
Iario**, Banlada, Navarra, 1807—
drid, 1878; court-conductor, ed
and theorist.

**Espagne** (ĕs-päkh'-nĕ), **Fz.**, Müns
Westphalia, 1828—Berlin, 1878;
rector and editor.

**Es'ser**, **H.**, Mannheim, 1818—S
burg, 1872; court-conductor.

**Es'sipoff** (or **Essipova**) (ĕs-sĭ-pôf
**Annette**, b. St. Petersburg, Feb
1851; pianist; pupil of Wielho
and Leschetizky, whom she m. 18
début, 1874, St. Petersburg; tou
Europe with great succ.; tou
America (1876); 1885, pianist to
Russian Court; 1893, pf.-prof.
Petersburg Cons.

**Este** (or **Est**, **East**, **Easte**),
**Thomas**, London music-prir
ca. 1550—1625. (2) **Michael**,
of above; 17th cent. composer.

**Esterházy** (esh'-tĕr-hä-zĕ), Cc
**Nicholas**, 1839—Castle Totis, H
gary, 1897; generous patron of
sic.

**Est'wick**, Rev. **Sampson**, D
1657—1739; English composer.

**Ett** (ĕt), **Kaspar**, Erringen, Bava
1788—Munich, 1847; court-orga
and composer.

**Eulenburg** (tsoo oi'-lĕn-boorkh), **I**
Graf **zu**, b. Königsberg, Feb.
1847; Royal Prussian Ambassa
Stuttgart; c. songs (words and mu

**Eulenstein** (oi'-lĕn-shtīn), **Ch**
b. Heilbronn, Würtemberg, 18
virtuoso on the Jew's harp and gui

**Euler** (oi'-lĕr), **Leonhardt**, Ba
1707—St. Petersburg, 1783; aco
cian.

**Euter'pe**, patroness of flute-play
the Muse of Music.

**Ev'ans**, Chas. S., 1778—1849; E
lish alto and composer.

**Everard** (ĕv-ŭ-rär), **Camille Fr**
b. Dinant, Belgium, Nov. 15, 1
basso; pupil of Liège Cons., I

Cons. (Ponchard), and of Rossi and Manzini, Naples; sang Naples, 1847–50; studied with Lamperti; sang in various cities; 1870–90, prof. of singing St. P. Cons.; 1890, Kiev Conservatoire.

ers (ā'-věrs), K., Hamburg, 1819—Vienna, 1875; pianist and composer.

esham (ēvz'-ăm), Monk of. Vide DINGTON.

r' er & Co., London mus.-publishers; founded 1820 by J. J. Ewer, succeeded by E. Buxton; 1860, W. Witt; 1867, became Novello, Ewer & Co.

yeyck (ā'-vīk), Arthur van, b. Milwaukee, U. S. A., May 27, 1866; studied with Felix Schmidt, Berlin, where he lives as concert and oratorio barytone.

ximenio (ĕx-ī-mā'-nĭ-ō), Ant., Balastro, Aragon, 1732—Rome, 1798; Jesuit priest; had historical controversy with Padre Martini.

bler (ī'-blĕr), Jos. (later, in 1834, Edler von Eybler), Schwechat, near Vienna, 1765—Schönbrunn, 1846; conductor and composer.

ken (ī'-kĕn), (1) Simon van (or Eycken; du Chesne). Vide QUERCU. (2) (Eijken), Jan Albert van, Amersfoort, Holland, 1822—Elberfeld, 1868; organist and composer; c. valuable chorals, etc. (3) Gerard Isaac van, bro. of above; organist and teacher at Utrecht from 1855.

ymieu (ĕm'-yŭ), Henri, b. Saillans Drôme, France, May 7, 1860; a lawyer, but studied with E. Gazier (theory) and Widor (comp.); now lives in Paris as writer and critic for " Le Ménestrel," etc.; c. a stage-piece, " Un Mariage sous Néron" (Paris, 1898), and an oratorio, " Marthe et Marie "(Asnières, 1898), etc.

# F

aber (fä'-bĕr), (1) Nikolaus (Nicol), priest at Halberstadt, 1359–61, built there what is considered the first organ made in Germany. (2) Nikolaus (II.), a native of Botzen, Tyrol; pub. " Rudimenta musicae," Augsburg, 1516. (3) Heinrich, " Magister," d. Lichtenfels, Oelsnitz, Saxony, 1552; rector of a school, whence he was expelled for satirical songs against the Pope; then rector of Brunswick; pub. a pop. book of rudiments. (4) Benedikt, Hildburghausen, 1602—Coburg, 1631; composer.

Fabozzi (fä-bôd'-zē), Genaro, b. Italy; blind pianist; court-pt. to Dowager Queen, prof. at Inst. for Blind, Naples.

Fabio. Vide URSILLO.

Fabri (fä'-brē), (1) Stefano (il maggiore), b. Rome, ca. 1550; 1599—1601, conductor. (2) Stefano (il minore), Rome, 1606—1658; conductor and composer. (3) Annibale Pio (called Balino), Bologna, 1697—Lisbon, 1760; tenor, etc.

Fabricius (fä-brē'-tsĭ-oos), (1) Werner, Itzehoe, 1633—Leipzig, 1679; composer. (2) J. Albert, Leipzig, 1668—Hamburg, 1736, son of above; professor.

Faccio (fät'-chō), Franco, Verona, March 8, 1841—Monza, July 23, 1891; an important composer; criticised as Wagnerite; notable cond.; prof. at Milan Cons. (harmony, later cpt.) Vide BOITO.

Faelten (fĕl'-tĕn), K., b. Ilmenau, Thuringia, Dec. 21, 1846; studied as a school-boy with Montag; for 6 years orchestra-violinist; 1867 studied with J. Schoch, Frankfort, and was for 10 years friend of Raff; 1868–82 Frankfort; 1878 Hoch Cons.; 1882–85 Peabody Institute, Baltimore, U. S. A.; 1885–97 N. E. Cons., Boston; dir. 1890–97; 1897 founded the Faelten Pf.-School (Teachers' Seminary), at Boston; pub. text-books.

Fago (fä'-gō), Nicola (called " Il Tarentino"), Tarento, 1674—1730 (?); c. oratorio, masses; prod. several very succ. operas.

**Fahrbach** (fär'-bäkh), (1) **Jos.**, Vienna, 1804—1883 ; flutist, conductor, and composer. (2) **Ph.** (Sr.), Vienna, 1815—1885 ; conductor and dram. composer. (3) **Wm.**, Vienna, 1838 —1866 ; conductor and composer. (4) **Ph.** (Jr.), Vienna, 1843—1894 ; son of (2) ; conductor.

**Faignient** (fīn-yäṅ), **Noë**, b. Antwerp, ca. 1570, Flemish contrapuntist.

**Fair'lamb, J. Remington**, b. Philadelphia, Jan. 23, 1837 ; studied in Paris and Florence ; 4 years in Zurich as consul ; organist Phila., etc., and from 1884 New York, St. Ignatius ; c. grand opera " *Valérie* " (MS.), etc.

**Faiszt** (fīst), **Immanuel G. Fr.**, Esslingen, Würtemberg, 1823 — Stuttgart, 1894 ; organist.

**Falcke** (fälk), **Henri**, Paris, 1866— May, 1901 ; pupil of Saint-Saëns, Massenet, Dubois, and Mathias, Paris Cons. ; won 1st prizes in pf. and harm. ; studied in Germany ; pub. a useful text-book on arpeggios.

**Falcon** (fäl-kôṅ), **M. Cornélie**, Paris, 1812—1897 ; soprano singer.

**Faliero** (fäl-ĭ-ā'-rō), **Nina**, b. Naples, April 10, 1878 ; studied with Mme. Kraus ; toured widely in concert ; lives at Geneva.

**Falk Mehlig** (fälk mā'-lĭkh), **Anna**, b. Stuttgart, June 11, 1846 ; studied at the Cons., also with Liszt ; toured as concert pianist throughout Germany, England, and America ; court-pianist to the king of Würtemberg.

**Faltin** (fäl'-tēn), **R. Fr.**, b. Danzig, Jan. 5, 1835 ; pupil of Markell, Schneider, and Leipzig Cons. Since 1869 lives at Helsingfors, Finland, as cond.; pub. " *Finnish Folk-Songs* " and a " *Finnish Song-Book.*"

**Faminzin** (fä-mēn'-tsēn), **Alex. Sergievitch**, Kaluga, Russia, 1841— Ligovo, near St. Petersburg, 1896 ; critic and dram. composer.

**Fan'ing, Eaton**, b. Helston, Cornwall, May 20, 1850 ; pupil of the R. A. M., took Mendelssohn Scholarship in 1873 and the Lucas Medal in 1876 ;

1894 Mus. Bac., Cantab.; since ᵭ dir. music at Harrow School ; operettas, cantata for female voi symphony in C minor, overture, " *Holiday*," etc.

**Farabi.** Vide ALFARÂBI.

**Fargas y Soler** (fär'-gäs ē sō-l Antonio, Spanish writer, pub. " *ografias de los Musicos*," etc. (iss since 1866, in parts), etc.

**Farinel'li**, (1) **Carlo Broschi** (br kē), Naples, June 24, 1705—Bolog July 15, 1782 ; famous male soprai début 1722 at Rome ; he sang v the utmost brilliancy and success, ing only once overcome by a r (Bernacchi) from whom he imme ately took lessons ; he joined the position to Händel in London, Händel went into bankruptcy ɑ took to oratorio. He amassed gr wealth and became the chief advi of Philip V. of Spain ; biog. Sacchi (Venice, 1784). (2) **Gɪ** Este, 1769—Trieste, 1836 ; org. ; 60 operas.

**Farkas** (fär'-käsh), **Edmund** (Hun Ödön), b. Puszta-Monostor (Heve Hungary, 1852 ; important figure national Hungarian music ; of nol family, intended to be a civil en; neer ; but studied 3 years at the Mus. Acad., Pesth ; next year ł came dir. at the Cons. at Klause burg, Transylvania ; was for a tiː op. cond. and wrote mus. article 1876, while still studying engineeriṅ he prod. a 1-act opera " *Bayadé* (Pesth) ; won the Haynald prize 300 florins with a mass ; c. al mixed choruses, and the orch. worl " *Dawn*" (*Virradat*), " *Evensonɡ* (*Estidal*), " *Twilight*" (*Alkonɣ* and " *Dies iræ*" ; a pop. sympho and 5 string-quartets ; a prize " *Feᵴ ouvertüre* " ; and the operas " *Faiː fountain*" (*Tünderhorrds*), 1-aᴄ (Klausenburg, 1892) ; " *The Penː tent*"(*Veseklök*) (Pesth, 1893) ; " *Bː lassa Balint*," comic (Pesth, 1896 aᵭd " *The Blood-ordeal*" (*Tetem Hívds*) (not prod.).

mer, (1) **H.**, Nottingham, England,
19—1891 ; violinist and organist.
**J.**, Nottingham, Aug. 16, 1836—
ly, 1901; nephew of above; pupil of
ipzig Cons. and of Spath; teach-
in Zurich for some years ; 1862–85
is.-master at Harrow School, then
ganist at Balliol Coll., Oxford,
here he founded a mus. society;
ited song-books, etc.; c. an orato-
); a fairy opera; comic cantata; a
quiem, etc.

**naby, Giles,** English composer,
80–98.

**rant,** (1) **John,** English organist,
. 1600. (2) **John,** English organist,
lisbury cath., ca. 1600. (3) **Rich-**
**d,** d. Nov. 30, 1580 ; English or-
nist and notable composer of
urch-music.

**renc** (far-ränk), **Jacq. Hipp,**
**ristide,** Marseilles 1794—Paris,
5. teacher and composer. (2)
anne Louise (née Dumont
aris, 1804—1875 ; wife of above,
.-professor.

**well, Arthur,** American composer;
pil of H. A. Norris, Boston, and of
umperdinck ; founded at Newton
enter, Mass., 1901, the " Wawan
ress " for the artistic pub. of supe-
or comps. by Americans ; c. ballade
r vln. and pf., and songs, etc.

**sch** (fäsh), (1) **Jn. Fr.,** Buttlestadt,
ear Weimar, 1688—Zerbst, 1758 (?);
urt-conductor, composer. (2) **K.**
**r. Chr.,** Zerbst, 1736 — Berlin,
800 ; cembalist ; son of above ; conuctor.

**uchey** (fo-she), **Paul,** former " chef
u chant," Op. Com. Paris ; prod.
omic opera, 1897.

**ugues, Vincent** (or **Fauques, Fa'-**
**us, La Fage**) (fog, fok, lä fäzh),
5th cent. contrapuntist.

**ure** (for), **J. Bapt.,** b. Moulins,
llier, Jan. 15, 1830 ; 1841, Paris
Cons.; choir-boy at the Madeleine,
nd studied with Trevaux ; took 1st
rize for comic opera ; 1852–76, at
he Op. Com. as leading barytone
vith great succ.; 1857, teacher in the

Cons.; since 1876 sang in concert ;
pub. " *L'Art du Chant.*"

**Fauré** (fō-rā), **Gabriel Urbain,** b. Pamiers, Ariège, May 13, 1845 ; pupil
of Niedermayer, Dietsch, and Saint-
Saëns ; 1866, organist at Rennes,
then at St.-Sulpice and St.-Honoré ;
1885 took Prix Chartier for chamber-
music ; 1896 organist at the Madeleine, and prof. of comp., cpt., and
fugue at the Cons. (vice Massenet) ;
c. 1-act opera " *L'Organiste* " (1887);
" *La Naissance de Venus,*" for soli,
chorus, and orch.; " *Chœur de
Djinns* " ; requiem; symphony ; vln.-
concerto ; orchestral suite ; 2 pf.-
quartets ; *Élégie,* for 'cello ; *Berceuse
and Romance,* for vln. and rch., a
vln.-sonata (1878), etc.

**Faust** (fowst), **K.,** Neisse, Silesia,
1825—Bad Cudowa, 1892 ; bandm.
and composer.

**Faustina.** Vide HASSE, FAUSTINA.

**Favarger** (la-var-zhä), **Réné,** Paris,
1815—Étretat, 1868 ; composer.

**Favre** (favr), **Jules.** Vide V. M. WAT-
SON.

**Faw cett,** (1) **J.,** Kendal, England, 1789
—Bolton, Lancashire, 1867 ; teacher
and composer. (2) **J. (jr.),** Bolton,
1824—Manchester, 1887, son of above;
organist and composer.

**Fay, Amy,** b. Bayou Goula, Miss., May
21, 1844 ; pianist and teacher, Chicago ; pupil of Tausig, Kullak, Liszt ;
wrote the popular " *Music-Study in
Germany*" (Chicago, 1881).

**Fayolle** (fi-yôl), **Fran. Jos. M.,** Paris,
1774—1852 ; mus. biographer and
lexicographer.

**Fayr fax, Robt.,** Mus. Doc., Cantab
and Oxon, 1504–11 ; organist and
composer.

**Fechner** (fěkh'-něr), **Gv. Th.,** Gross-
Sarchen, Niederlausitz, 1801—Leipzig, 1887 ; writer.

**Fedele** (fā-dā'-lě). Vide TREU.

**Federici** (fā-dā-rē'-chě), **V.,** Pesara,
1764—Milan, 1827 ; went to London,
where he became cembalist ; returned
to Italy in 1803 and prod. many succ.
operas

**Federlein** (fā'-dĕr-līn), **G.** (**H.**), b. Neustadt-an-der-Aisch, near Nürnberg, Nov. 5, 1835; pupil of Munich Cons.; lives in New York; singing-teacher, composer and writer.

**Felstein** (fĕl'-shtīn) (called **Felstinen'sis**), **Sebastian von**, ca. 1530; church-conductor and composer, Cracow.

**Feltre** (dŭ fĕl'tr), **Alphonse Clarke**, Comte de, Paris, 1806—1850; dram. composer, etc.

**Fenaroli** (fā-nä-rō'-lē), **Fedele**, Lanciano, Abruzzi, 1730—Naples, 1818; teacher and composer.

**Fen'ton, Lavinia**, d. Greenwich, 1760; singer and actress at London.

**Feo** (fā'-ō), **Francesco**, b. Naples, ca. 1685; composer and teacher.

**Ferlen'dis** ——, b. Rome, ca. 1778; operatic contralto.

**Fer(r)abosco** (fĕr-rä-bôs'-kō), (1) **Alfonso**, Italy, 1515; c. madrigals. (2) **Dom. M.**, Rome, 16th cent., member Papal Choir; composer. (3) **Cos⁺antino**, court-musician and con.poser at Vienna, 1591. (4) **Alfonso**, Greenwich, England. ca. 1580 —1652; probably son of (1); composer. (5) **John**, d. 1682, son of (4); organist Ely Cathedral.

**Ferrari**, (1) **Benedetto** (called **della Tiorba** "the theorbist") (fĕr-rä'-rĕ dĕl-la tē-ôr'-bä), Reggio d'Emilia, 1597—Modena, 1681; court-conductor and dram. composer. (2) **Domenico**, Piacenza, (?)—Paris, 1780; violinist, conductor and composer. (3) **Carlo**, Piacenza, ca. 1730—Parma, 1789, bro. of above; 'cellist. (4) **Giacomo Gotifredo**, Roveredo, Tyrol, 1759—London, 1842; cembalist, writer, teacher, and composer. (5) **Francisca**, Christiania, ca. 1800—Gross-Salzbrunn, Silesia, 1828; harpist. (6) **Serafino Amadeo de'**, Genoa, 1824—1885; pianist and dram. composer. (7) **Carlotta**, b. Lodi, Italy, Jan. 27, 1837; pupil of Strepponi and Panzini (1844—50) of Mazzucato at Milan Cons.; wrote text and music of succ.

operas "*Ugo*" (Milan, 1857); " . *fia*" (Lodi, 1866); "*Eleanora ... Arborea*" (Cagliari, 1871); a[ masses; a *Requiem for Turin*, 186 etc.

**Ferreira** (fĕr-rä'-ē-rä), **Da Costa, Ro rigo**, d. 1834 (37?); Portuguese writ

**Fer(r)et'ti, Giov.**, b. Venice, ca. 154 composer.

**Ferri** (fĕr'-rē), (1) **Baldassare**, Per gia, 1610—Sept. 8, 1680; one of t most gifted and successful of singer through a boyhood accident becar a male soprano; possessed extrac dinary endurance of breath, flexib ity of voice, and depth of emotio at 65 returned to Perugia; on h death left 600,000 crowns for a pio foundation. (2) **Nicolà**, Mola Bari, Italy, 1831—London, 188( Naples, singing teacher and dran composer.

**Ferrier** (fĕr-rĭ-ā), **Paul Raoul M chel M.**, b. Montpelier, March 2 1843; c. light operas for Paris.

**Ferron** (fĕr'-rôn), **Ad.**, 1892, condu tor Th. Unter den Linden, Berlin 1897 at Carl Th., Vienna; prod. Berlin the burlesque "*Adam ur Eva*" (1891), and other operettas.

**Ferro'ni, V. Emidio Carmine,** ( Tramutola, Italy, Feb. 17, 1858; pu Paris Cons.; 1st prize in harm. an comp., 1880—83; 1881, asst.-prof. ( harm. at the Cons.; since 1888 pro of comp. at Milan Cons., and mu dir. of the "Famiglia Artistica 1897, Chevalier of the Ital. Crown c. operas "*Rudello*" (Milan, 1892) and (text and mus. of) "*Ettore Fi ramosca*" (Como, 1896).

**Fes'ca,** (1) **Fr. Ernst**, Magdeburg 1789—Carlsruhe, 1826; violinist an composer. (2) **Alex. Ernst**, Carl ruhe, May 22, 1820—Brunswick, Fel 22, 1859; son of above; brilliant p anist and dram. composer.

**Fes'ta,** (1) **Costanzo**, Rome, ca. 149 —April 10, 1545; singer and contra puntist. (2) **Giu. M.**, Trani, 1771— Naples, 1839; violinist, conducto and composer. (3) **Francesca**

ples, 1778—St. Petersburg, 1836;
ratic singer; m. Maffei.

ing, **Michael Christian,** Lon-
n (?) 1680—1752; son of a flutist,
same name; conductor, violinist,
l composer.

ler (fĕsh'-lĕr), **Eduard,** b. Neu-
g, Bavaria, Oct. 5, 1841; oper-
c barytone; studied with Fz.
user, Munich.

s (fā-tēs), (1) **François Joseph,**
ons, Belgium, March 25, 1784—
ussels, March 26, 1871; indefatig-
e scholar and historian; he worked
-18 hours a day; his father, organ-
and conductor at the Cathedral,
s his first teacher; he learned the
., and c. at 9 a concerto for vln.
d orch.; the same year became orist to the Noble Chapter of Saint
audra; 1800–03 in the Paris Cons.;
93, Vienna, for study of fugue, and
ster-work of German music; here
gan an investigation of Guido
Arezzo's system and the history of
tation. 1804 he started a short-lived
is. periodical. 1806 he began the
years' task (still unpub.) of revis-
g the plain-song and entire ritual of
e Roman Church. He m. a wealthy
man, and was enabled to pursue
s studies comfortably till 1811,
en her fortune was lost. He re-
ned to the Ardennes and made re-
arches into harmony, which led to
s formulating the modern theory of
nality. 1813, organist and teacher
Douai; wrote "La Science de
Organist," and "Méthode élémen-
ire d'harmonie et d'accompagne-
nt." 1818, Paris, where he prod.
rious operas with succ. 1821,
of. of comp. at the Cons., later li-
arian. 1827–35 founded and edit-
"La Revue Musicale." In 1832
gan historical lectures and concerts.
33, cond. to King Leopold I.,
ussels, and for 39 years dir. of the
ons. Cond., and 1845 member of,
e Belgian Academy. On his wed-
ng-jubilee a Mass of his was sung,
d his bust was unveiled. In 1806,

he began collecting and preparing for
his great "Biographie universelle des
musiciens et bibliographie générale de
la musique" in 8 volumes (1837–1844).
This invaluable monument is, like
everything else of its kind, bristling
inevitably with error, bias, and excess;
yet is a standard of highest repute.
Pub. many treatises and c. 6 operas
(182c–32); 2 symphonies, an overture
for orch.; masses, a requiem, motets,
etc. Biog. in his Dictionary by L.
Alvin (Brussels, 1874); and Gollmick
(Leipzig, 1852). (2) **Ed. L. Fran.,**
b. Bouvignes, near Dinant, May 16,
1812; son of above; editor; for
years libr., Brussels Library; pub.
"Les musiciens Belges" (1848). (3)
**Adolphe L. Eugène,** Paris, 1820—
1873; son and pupil of (1); pianist,
teacher and dram. composer.

**Feurich** (foi'-rĭkh), **Julius,** Leipzig,
1821—1900; founded pf. factory,
1851.

**Fevin** (fū-văň), **Ant. (Antonius) de,**
ca. 1490 (?)—1515 (?); Netherlandish
(?) contrapuntist; contemporary with
Josquin Desprès, and rated second
only to him. (2) **Robert (Robertus),**
Cambrai, 15th cent.; c. masses.

**Fiala** (fē'-ä-lä), Lobkowitz, Bohemia,
1749—Donauschingen, 1816; oboist,
'cellist, composer, and conductor.

**Fibich** (fē'bĭkh), **Zdenko,** Seborschitz,
Bohemia, Dec. 21, 1850—Prague,
Oct. 1900; pupil at Prague, Leipzig
Cons. (1865), and of Lachner; 1876
asst. cond. at the National Th.,
Prague; 1878, dir. Russian Church
Choir; notable Czech dram. composer. Prod. at Prague 6 operas incl.
"Sarka" (1898); c. the symphonic
poems "Othello," "Zaboj and Sla-
voj," "Toman and the Nymph,"
and "Vesna"; "Lustspiel Ouvertüre," etc. "A Night on Kaarl-
stein," and other overtures.

**Fiby** (fē'-bē), **Heinrich,** b. Vienna, May
15, 1834; pupil of the Cons.; from
1857 city mus. dir., Znaim; founded
a music-school and a society; c. 3
operettas; pop. male choruses, etc.

**Ficher** (fēkh'-ĕr), **Fd.**, Leipzig, 1821 —New York, 1865 ; pianist and composer.

**Fiedler** (fēt'-lĕr), **August Max**, b. Zittau, Dec. 3, 1859 ; piano pupil of his father, and studied organ and theory with G. Albrecht ; 1877–80 Leipzig Cons.; won the Holstein Scholarship ; since 1882 teacher, Hamburg Cons.; c. a symphony, etc.

**Field,** (1) **John,** Dublin, July 16, 1782— Moscow, Jan. 11, 1837 ; a great though gentle revolutionist of music, to whom much of Chopin's glory belongs, for Field developed the more lyric manner of pf.-playing and carried it into his composition, in which he gave the piano-song or poem its first escape from the old stiff forms. He created the Nocturne, and many of his comps. in this form have practically every quality and mannerism characteristic of those of Chopin, who excelled him in passion, resource, and harmonic breadth. He was the son of a violinist, and grandson and pupil of an organist, who compelled him to practise so hard that he ran away, but was brought back and later was apprenticed to Clementi as a salesman. He also had lessons from C., and went with him to Paris in 1802, making a great stir with his interpretation of Bach's and Händel's fugues ; he was kept at his salesman's tasks till 1804, when he settled at St. Petersburg as a teacher and pianist of great vogue. After touring Russia, in London, 1832, he played a concerto of his own at the Philh.; then to Paris ; 1833 Belgium, Switzerland, Italy, where he was not a succ. Intemperance and fistula kept him nine months in a Naples hospital; whence he was rescued by a Russian family Raemanow and taken to Moscow, playing in Vienna with greatest succ. ; but his health was lost and he died a few years later and was buried in Moscow. Besides 20 nocturnes (of which only 12 were so named by Field) he c. 7 concertos (No. 4 in E flat the most popular) ·

4 sonatas ; "*Air russe*" ; *russe varié*" (4 hands) ; "*Ch*( *russe varié*," in D min. ; polon " *Reviens, reviens* " Romanza Cavatina in E ; 4 romances ; 7 deaux ; rondeau with 2 vlns., and bass ; variation in C ; 2 tissements with 2 vlns., viola bass ; 2 fantasias ; and pf.-exe in all keys. (2) **Henry,** " Fie Bath " Dec. 3, 1791—May 19, 1 pianist and teacher.

**Fielitz** (fōn fē'-lĭts), **Alexander** b. Leipzig, Dec. 28, 1860 ; pu Dresden of J. Schulhoff (pf.) and schmer (comp.) ; he became c cond. in Zürich, Lübeck, and Le (City Th.) ; a nervous disorder pelled his retirement ; lives in as a composer of sacred cho orch. pcs., songs, etc. His s have attained much solid popul

**Filippi** (fē-lĭp'-pǐ) (1) **Giu. de,** N 1825—Neuilly, near Paris, 1 writer. (2) **Filippo,** Vicenza, —Milan, 1887 ; critic, writer, composer.

**Fill'more, J. Comfort,** Frar Conn., 1843—1898 ; studied at ( lin (O.) Coll., and Leipzig C 1884–95 founder and dir. of So Mus. in Milwaukee ; then mus Pomona Coll., Claremont, Cal ; "*A Study of Omaha Indian M*( (with Miss Fletcher and F. Flesche ; Peabody Museum, 1 etc.

**Filtsch** (fēltsh), **Karl,** Hermanns Transylvania, 1831—Vienna, 1 pianist ; pupil of Chopin and L died at 15.

**Finck** (fĭnk), (1) **Heinrich,** 1482, ductor to John Albert I., Cra( eminent contrapuntist. (2) **Herm** Pirna, Saxony, 1527—Witten 1558, grand-nephew of above ; poser and writer. (3) **Henry** ( **ophilus,** b. Bethel, Missouri, 22, 1854 ; prominent American and essayist ; influential advoca Wagner; lived in Oregon, then (: graduate of Harvard, having st

ory and hist. of mus. with J. K.
ine ; 1876, attended the first Bay-
ath festival, and studied at Munich;
b. the valuable " *Wagner and His
orks*" (N. Y., 1893, 2 vols., Germ.
nsl., Breslau, 1897) ; 1877-78,
died anthropology at Harvard ; re-
ved a Fellowship and spent 3 years
Berlin, Heidelberg, and Vienna,
dying comparative psychology and
ading mus. letters to N. Y. *Nation;*
s since been mus.-ed. of the N. Y.
*ening Post;* pub. " *Chopin, and
er Mus. Essays,*" " *Paderewski
d his Art,*" " *Songs and Song-
riters*" (1901) ; 3 books of travel :
*Pacific Coast Scenic Tour,*" " *Lo-
time in Japan,*" " *Spain and Mo-
co*"; and 2 important books on
e psychology of love, " *Romantic
ve and Personal Beauty,*" having
ched 4 editions ; " *Primitive Love
d Love Stories*" (1900).

ke (fĭnk'-ĕ), **Fritz,** b. Wismar,
ay 1, 1846 ; pupil Leipzig Cons.;
orist and violinist, Frankfort, then
ganist at Wismar ; 1879, teacher of
ging, Peabody Inst., Baltimore ;
iter and composer.

leisen (fĭnt'-ī-zĕn), **Otto,** 1890,
nductor Wilhelm-Th., Magdeburg,
od. succ. operetta " *Der Alte Des-
uer*" (Magdeburg, 1890) ; and the
cc. folk - opera " *Henings von
effenfeld*" (ib. 1891).

ger (fĭng'-ĕr), **Gf.,** b. Olmütz, Ba-
ria ; in England, 1685–1701 ; then
amber-mus. to Queen of Prussia,
1717.

r, **Gf. Wm.,** Sulza, Thuringia,
83—Halle, 1846 ; editor, writer,
d composer. (2) **Chr.,** b. Detting-
, Würtemberg, Aug. 9, 1831; pupil
sslingen Seminary ; Leipzig Cons.,
d Schneider, Dresden ; till 1860
ed as organist and teacher, Leip-
g ; then teacher and organist, Ess-
gen, and prof. in 1862 ; composer.

enstein (shtīn), **Jettka,** b. Seni,
ussia, March 22, 1865 ; alto ; stud-
d at Berlin Hochschule, and with
ardot Garcia ; 1st. alto at Darm-

stadt ct.-theatre till 1891, then
toured ; lives in Breslau.

**Fioravanti** (fē-ôr-ä-vän'-tē), (1) **Valentino,** Rome, 1764—Capua, June 16,
1837 ; opera-cond. and composer.
(2) **Vincenzo,** Rome, 1799—Naples,
1877, son of above ; conductor and
dram. composer.

**Fiorillo** (fē-ô-rēl'-lō), (1) **Ignazio,**
Naples, 1715—Fritzlar, near Cassel,
1787 ; court-conductor and composer.
(2) **Federigo,** b. Brunswick, 1753 (?);
son and pupil of above ; viola player
and composer.

**Fiqué** (fē-kā), **Karl,** b. Bremen, 1861 ;
pupil of Leipzig Cons.; lives in Brooklyn, N. Y.; pianist and composer.

**Fischel** (fĭsh'-ĕl), **Adolf,** b. Königsberg, 1810 ; pupil of Spohr ; cigar-
dealer in Berlin ; violinist and composer.

**Fischer** (fĭsh'-ĕr), (1) **Chr. Fr.,** Lübeck, 1698—Kiel, 1752 ; cantor and
writer. (2) **Jn. Chr.,** Freiburg, Baden, 1733—London, 1800 ; oboist and
composer. (3) **Chr. Wm.,** Konrads-
dorf, near Freiburg, 1789—Dresden,
1859 ; basso buffo. (4) **Ludwig,**
Mayence, 1745—Berlin, 1825 ; operatic bass, of great range (D – a'). (5)
**Michael Gotthard,** Alach, near
Erfurt, 1773—Erfurt, 1829 ; cond.
and composer. (6) **Anton,** Ried,
Swabia, 1777—Vienna, 1808 ; composer. (7) **Ernst Gf.,** Hoheneiche,
near Saalfeld, 1754—Berlin, 1831 ;
prof. and acoustician. (8) **Gf. Emil,**
Berlin, 1791—1841, son of above ;
singing-teacher and writer. (9) **K.
L.,** Kaiserslautern, Bavaria, 1816—
Hanover, 1877 ; court-conductor and
composer. (10) **Ad.,** Uckermunde,
Pomerania, 1827—Breslau, 1893 ; or-
ganist and composer. (11) **K. Aug.,**
Ebersdorf, Saxony, 1828—Dresden,
1892 ; organist. (12) **Fz.,** b. Munich,
July 29, 1849 ; 'cellist, pupil of H.
Müller ; 1870 soloist National Th.,
Pesth, under Hans Richter ; later at
Munich and Bayreuth with Wagner ;
1877-79, court-conductor at Mann-
heim, then Munich. (13) **Paul,**

Zwickau, 1834—Zittau. 1894 ; cantor and writer. (14) **Ad.**, Brussels, 1847 —insane in Brussels, 1891 ; 'cellist. (15) **Ignaz**, 1828—Vienna, 1877 ; conductor ct.-opera, Vienna. (16) **Josef**, 1828—Stuttgart, 1885 ; composer. (17) **Emil**, b. Germany, ca. 1835; notable German basso in Wagnerian rôles ; début 1849 ; sang at Met. Op. N. Y. many years ; 1899 m. Camille Seygard ; divorced 1902.

**Fischhof** (físh'-ôf), **Jos.**, Butschowitz, Moravia, 1804—Vienna, 1857 ; prof., composer and writer.

**Fish, Wm.**, Norwich, 1775—ca. 1863; violinist and oboist.

**Fish'er**, (1) **John A.**, b. Dunstable, 1774, pf.-and organ-virtuoso ; violinist and composer. (2) **Wm. Arms**, b. San Francisco, April 27, 1861 ; pupil of J. P. Morgan (org. and pf.), H. W. Parker, and Dvořák, New York ; also studied singing in London ; lives in Boston as teacher, composer of songs, and editor.

**Fissot** (fís-sō) **Alexis Henri**, Airaines (Somme), 1843—Paris, 1896 ; pf. and organ-virtuoso and composer.

**Fitzenhagen** (fíts'-ĕn-häkh-ĕn), **Wm. K. Fr.**, Seesen, Brunswick, 1848— Moscow, 1800 ; 'cellist.

**Fitzwilliam, Edward F.**, 1824—Jan. 30, 1857 ; English composer.

**Fladt** (flät), **Anton**, b. Mannheim, 1775 ; oboist and composer.

**Flag'ler, Isaac van Vleck**, b. Albany, N. Y., May 15, 1844 ; pupil of Beale at Albany, Batiste in Paris, etc. ; organist various churches, then (1899) a publisher and concert-organist ; Chautauqua-lecturer for 13 years ; teacher at Syracuse and Cornell Universities and Utica Cons. ; composer.

**Flaxland** (fläx-län), **Gve. Alexandre**, Strassburg, 1821—Paris, 1895 ; pub., Paris.

**Flégier** (flā-zhā), **Ange**, b. Marseilles, Feb. 25, 1846 ; pupil of Marseilles Cons. and Paris Cons. 1870 ; returned to Marseilles ; c. 1-act comic opera, "*Fatima*" (Mars. 1875), "*Ossian*,"

and "*Françoise de Rimini*," cant with orch., etc.

**Fleischer** (flī'-shĕr), (1) **Reinhold** Dansau, Silesia, April 12, 18 pupil of the R. Inst. for Chu music, and R. Akademie, at Ber 1870, organist at Görlitz and Singaka emie ; 1885, Royal M Dir. ; c. a cantata, "*Holda*," etc. **Oskar**, b. Zörbig, Nov. 1, 18 studied in Italy on govt. stipe pupil and, since 1896, successo Spitta as Prof. Extraordinary, at Berlin Univ., also custodian of Royal Coll. of Mus. Instrs., teacher of history at the Hochsc für Musik ; pub. a study of neu 1895, etc. (3) **Fleischer-Édel** (ä'-Katharina**, b. Mülheim, Sept. 1873 ; soprano ; studied with Ifi sings at court-opera, Dresden.

**Flem'ming, Fr. Fd.**, Neuhau Saxony, 1778—Berlin, 1813 ; c. "*Integer vitæ*," etc.

**Floersheim** (flärs'-hīm), **Otto**, b. la-Chapelle, March 2, 1853 ; pup Fd. Hiller, Cologne ; 1875, York ; 1880, edited *The Mu Courier*, since 1894 manager o Berlin Branch ; c. "*Prelude Fugue*," "*Scherzo*," for orch., et

**Floridia** (flō-rēd'-yä), (**Napolino**) tro**, b. Modica, Sicily, March 5, 1 pianist, pupil of S. Pietro a Maj Naples ; while there he pub. s pf.-pcs. ; prod. succ. comic o "*Carlotta Clepier*" (Naples, 1 later burned the score, retired 3 years to Sicily ; toured 1885 1888–90, prof. of pf. Palermo Co 1889, his grand symphony won prize of the Soc. del Quartetto, an ; w. text and music of succ. o "*Maruzza*" (Venice, 1894) ; live Milan ; c. (with Luigi Illica) "*L lonia Libera*"; also "*Festouverti serenata*, etc.

**Florimo** (flō'-rĭ-mō), **Fran.**, San G gio Morgeto, Calabria, 1800—Na 1888 ; writer, teacher, and comp

**Flo'rio, Caryl**, pen-name of **Wm. Robjohn.**

izel. Vide REUTER.

ow (flō'-tō), **Friedrich**, Freiherr
1, Teuterdorf, Mecklenburg, April
1812—Darmstadt, Jan. 24, 1883;
nposer of 2 extremely popular and
lodious, also extremely light, op-
s; son of a landed nobleman;
died composition with Reicha,
ris; he fled from the July Revolu-
n to Mecklenburg, where he c. 2
erettas; returning to Paris, he
d. "*Séraphine*," 1836, "*Rob
y*," and the succ. "*Le Naufrage
la Méduse*," 1839, (given Ham-
rg, 1845, as "*Die Matrosen*"), in
ich he collaborated with Paloti and
isa; 3 later works failed, incl. the
llet "*Lady Harriet*" (Opéra,
43); afterwards rewritten with
eat succ. as "*Martha*" (Vienna,
47). "*Alessandro Stradella*"(Ham-
rg, 1844; rewritten from a "pièce
rique, "*Stradella*," Paris, 1837),
ade his name in Germany. He fled
om the March Revolution (1848),
d prod. "*Die Gross-fürstin*" (Ber-
1, 1853), and "*Indra*" (Berlin Op-
a, 1850); 3 later works failed.
56–63, he was intendant of court-
usic, Schwerin, and c. a "Torch-
ance" and excellent music to Shake-
eare's "*Winter's Tale*"; 1863–68,
e prod. 2 operettas, 2 operas, and 2
allets, without succ.; 1868, he re-
red to one of his estates, near Vien-
a, made visits to Vienna, Paris, It-
ly; 1870, "*L'Ombre*" (Paris, Op.
om., 1870; prod. in London, 1878,
s the "*Phantom*") was very succ.;
"*Naïda*" (Milan, 1873) and "*Il
"ior d'Harlem*" (Turin, 1876) were
evisions, and he rewrote "*Indra*" as
"*l'Enchanteresse*" (Paris and London,
878); Italy, "*Alma l'Incancatrice*";
Germany "*Die Hexe*"; after his
death "*Rosellana*," "*Der Graf
Saint-Mégrin*" (Cologne, 1884), and
"*Die Musikanten*" (Hanover, 1887)
were produced.

ow'ers, **Geo. French**, Boston, Eng-
and, 1811—1872, organist, teacher,
composer, and writer.

**Flügel** (flü'-gĕl), (1) **Gustav**, Nienburg
on-Saale, July 2, 1812—Stettin, 1900;
cantor, organist, writer, and composer. (2) **Ernest Paul**, b. Stettin, Aug.
31, 1844; son and pupil of above;
studied at the R. Inst. for Church-
music, and the Akademie, Berlin;
private pupil of von Bülow; 1867,
organist and teacher at the Prenzlan
Gymnasium; in 1879, cantor, Breslau, and founded the "Flügelverein",
writer and composer.

**Fo'dor**, (1) **Jos.**, Vanlos, 1752—1828,
violinist and composer. (2) **Josephine**, b. Paris, 1793; soprano;
retired, 1833; daughter of above;
m. the actor Mainvielle.

**Foerster** (fĕr'-shtĕr), **Ad. Martin**, b.
Pittsburg, Pa., Feb. 2, 1854; important American composer; pupil of his
mother and of Leipzig Cons.; 1875–
76, teacher at Ft. Wayne (Ind.),
Cons., then Pittsburg, Pa., where he
still lives as a teacher of singing and
pf.; c. "*Faust*" overture; march-
fantasia; festival music, 2 suites (No.
1, "*The Falconer*"), festival march
(May festival, 1891, under Seidl);
"*Symphonic Ode to Byron*," and
"*Dedication March*" (Carnegie Hall,
Pittsburg); "*Thusnelda*," etc.

**Foggia** (fôd'-jä), **Fran.**, Rome, 1604–
1688, composer and conductor.

**Fogliani** (fōl-yä'-nē), **Ludovici**, Modena, 15th cent.—ca. 1540; theorist
and composer.

**Foignet** (fwän'-yä), (1) **Chas. Gabriel**,
Lyons, ca. 1750—Paris, 1823; teach-
er. (2) **Fran.**, Paris, ca. 1780—
Strassburg, 1845; tenor, later barytone and dram. composer.

**Földesy** (fŭl'-dĕ-shē), ——, b. Hungary; young 'cellist, succ. in London,
1902; son of a military bandman at
Budapest; pupil of Becker.

**Fo'ley** ("Signor **Foli**"), **Allan Jas.**,
Cahir, Tipperary, Ireland, 1841—
Southport, England, Oct. 20, 1899;
concert and operatic bass.

**Folville** (fôl-vē'-yŭ), (**Eugénie Émi-
lie) Juliette**, b. Liège, Jan. 5, 1870;
brilliant pianist, violinist, teacher,

conductor and composer; pupil of her father, a distinguished lawyer; studied vln. with Malherbes, Musin, and César Thomson; in 1879, début at Liège as concert-violinist; frequently directs her own orchestral works; annually conducts at Liège Cons. a concert of ancient music, and gives clavecin-recitals; prod. 1893, very succ. opera "*Atala*" (Lille, 1892; Rouen, 1893); 1898, pf. prof. at Liège Cons.; c. 3 orchestral suites: "*Scènes* (a) *champêtres*, (b) *de la mer*, (c) *d'hiver*," etc.

**Fon'da**, (Mrs.) **G. A.**, 1837—Louisville, 1897; wrote "*Life of Gottschalk*," etc., under pseud., "Octavia Hensel."

**Fontaine** (fôn'-těn), (1) **Mortier de**, v. MORTIER. (2) **Hendrik**, b. Antwerp, April 5, 1857; concert-bass; pupil of the Cons. and singing-teacher, 1883.

**Fontana** (fôn-tä'-nä), **Giov. Bat.**, d. Brescia, 1630; composer.

**Foote, Arthur Wm.**, b. Salem, Mass., March 5, 1853; prominent American composer; pupil of B. J. Lang (pf.), S. A. Emery, and J. K. Paine (comp.) 1875, A. M. Harvard (for mus.); since 1878, organist of the first Unitarian Ch., Boston; pub. overture, "*In the Mountains*," symphonic prologue, "*Francesca da Rimini*," 'cello concerto; orch. suite and choral works, "*Farewell of Hiawatha*," "*The Wreck of the Hesperus*," and "*The Skeleton in Armour*"; pf.-quintet, quartet in C; pf.-trio in C min.; sonata for pf. and vln.; 2 string-quartets; pcs. for vln. and 'cello, and pf.-pcs.; 2 suites, and songs.

**Forberg** (fôr'-běrkh), **Robt.**, Lützen, 1833—Leipzig, 1880; mus. pub. at Leipzig.

**Forbes, H.**, 1804—1859; Engl. organist, pianist, and dram. composer.

**Forchhammer** (fôrkh'-häm-měr), **Th.**, b. Schiers, Gray Cantons, July 29, 1847; pupil of Stuttgart Cons.; 1885, organist at Magdeburg Cath.; 1888

Royal Mus. Dir.; writer and c poser.

**Ford**, (1) **Thos.**, England, ca. 158 1648; composer and writer. **Ernest A. C.**, b. London, Feb. 1858; pupil of Sullivan and La cond. Empire Th., London; pro operas; comic-opera, "*Jane Anni* a cantata; motet "*Domine De* (for 250th anniv. of Harvard Uni etc.

**For'kel, Jn. Nikolaus**, Meeder, Coburg, 1749 — Göttingen, 18 historian, organist, harpist, teacher.

**For'mes, K. Jos.**, Mülheim-on-Rh 1816—San Francisco, 1889; ope bass. His wife (2) a notable c tralto in N. Y. (3) **Theodor**, N heim, 1826—Endenich, near Bo 1874; tenor, bro. of above.

**Formschneider** (fôrm'-shnī'-děr). V GRAPHÄUS.

**Fornari** (fôr-nä'-rē), **V.**, b. Nap May 11, 1848; pupil of Sira ( and Battista (comp.); c. ope "*Maria di Torre*" (Naples, 18 "*Salammbo*," "*Zuma*" (Nap 1881), and 1-act opera-seria " *Dramma in Vendemmia*" (Floren 1896), succ.

**Fornasari** (fôr-nä-sä'-rē), **Lucia** Italian bass; début ca. 1828; tou widely and retired 1846.

**Förner** (fěr'-něr), **Chr.**, Wettin, 1 —1678; organ-builder; ca. 1675, i the "wind-gauge."

**Forqueray** (fôrk-rě), *fils*, contem rary French composer.

**Forster** (fôr'-shtěr), **G.**, (1) Amberg —Nürnberg, 1568; editor and c (2) **G.**, (II), d. Dresden, 15 double-bass; conductor. (3) **Ni** laus (called **Fortius**), 1499—15 contrapuntist. (4) (or **Förster**) K par, Danzig, 1617—1673; compos theorist and conductor. (5) **W** (Sr.), Brampton, Cumberland, 173 London, 1808; vln.-maker; his and successor was (6), **Wm.**, L don, 1764—1824.

**För'ster** (fěr'-shtěr), (1) v. FORST

(2) **Chr.**, Bebra, Thuringia, ¹3—Rudolstadt, 1745; organist, ιductor and composer. (3) **Eman- Aloys**, Neurath, Austrian Sile- ¸ 1748—Vienna, 1823; theorist ¹ composer. (4) **Jos.**, b. Osojnitz, hemia, Feb. 22, 1833; Prague ¹ool of Organists; organist in various ιrches; since 1887, Prague Cath. ; ₁f. of theory, Prague Cons.; c. masses ¹ requiems, org.-pcs; wrote a trea- ² on harmony. (5) Vide FOERSTER. **Alban**, b. Reichenbach, Saxony, t. 23, 1849; violinist; pupil R. ιme, later of Dresden Cons.; lead- ιet Carlsbad, Breslau, Stettin; 1871, ιrt mus., and cond. Neustrelitz, ₁1, teacher in Dresden Cons., ιd. of the *Liedertafel;* since 1882, ιrt-cond. at Neustrelitz, 1875; c. ιnic operas, ballet pantomime, orch. ¹ chamber music, etc.

ιyth', **Bros.**, mus. publishers, ιndon and Manchester.

ι (fôr'-tē), **Anton**, Vienna, 1790— ¸9; barytone.

ιlage (fôrt'-lä-gĕ), **K.**, Osnabruck, ₁6—Jena, 1881; writer.

ιsch (fĕrtsh), **Jn. Ph.**, Wertheim, ιanconia, 1652—Eutin, 1732; con- ιctor, singer, and dram. composer.

ιter, (1) **Stephen Collins**, Law- ιceville (Pittsburg), Pa., July 4, ₁26—New York, Jan. 13, 1864; ιiefly self-taught as flageolet-play- ι and composer; a writer of words ¹ music of genuine American folk- ιng; he enjoyed enormous vogue, ιeiving $500 for the privilege of ιging "Old Folks at Home" (or ιSuwanee River") before its publi- ιtion; c. 160 songs, incl. "My Old ιentucky Home," "Nellie was a ιιdy," and many war-songs; his ιelody, though simple, was rarely ιnal and has elements of immortal- ι. (2) **(Myles) Birket**, b. London, ιov. 29, 1851; organist and com- ιɒser; pupil of Hamilton Clarke, and ι R. A. M. of Sullivan, Prout, and ΄estlake; 1873-74, organist at Ha- ιeis' Church; 1880-92, at the Found- ling Hospital; then mus.-ed. for Boosey & Co.; c. 2 Evening Ser- vices; symphony, "*Isle of Arran*"; overtures, etc.

**Fouqué** (foo-kā), **P. Octave**, Pau, Bas- ses-Pyrenées, 1844—1883; libr., Paris Cons.; critic and writer.

**Fourneaux** (foor-nō), **Napoléon**, Leard, 1808—Aubanton, 1846; im- prover of the reed instruments.

**Fournier** (foorn-yā), (1) **P. Simon**, Paris, 1712—1768; introducer of round-headed notes, and writer on history of music-types. (2) **Émile Eugène Alex.**, Paris, 1864—Join- ville-le-Pont, 1897; pupil of Délibes and Dubois at Cons.; 1891 took 2d Grand prix de Rome, and 1892 Prix Cressent, for 1-act opera "*Stratonice*" (Gr. Opéra, Paris, 1892); c. opera "*Carloman*," etc.

**Fox, Geo.**, b. 1854, Eng. (?); bary- tone, with various opera troupes in London and the provinces and c. pop. operettas, "*Robert Macaire*," 1887; "*The Corsican Brothers*," 1888, and "*Nydia*," 1892—all prod. at the Crys tal Palace; c. cantatas, songs, etc.

**Fradel** (frä'-dĕl), **Chas.** (**Karl**), b. Vienna, 1821; music-teacher New York, then London; composer.

**Framery** (främ-rē), **Nicolas Ét.**, 1745 —Paris, 1810; writer.

**Francesco.** Vide LANDINO.

**Francesina** (lä frän-chä-sē'-nä), **La** (rightly **Elizabeth Duparc**), French singer in Italy, and, 1738-45, London, where she created Händelian rôles.

**Franchetti** (frän-kĕt'-tē), (1) **Alberto** (Baron); b. Turin, Sept. 18, 1850; pupil of N. Coccon and F. Magi; then of Draeseke, and at the Munich Cons.; prod. "dram. legend" "*Asraële*" (Brescia, 1888); opera, "*Cristoforo Colombo*" (Genoa,1892), "*Fior d'Alpe*" (Milan, 1894), "*Il Signor di Pourceaugnac*" (Milan, 1807), all succ.; c. a symphony, etc. (2) **Valerio**, b. Italy; violinist; nephew of above; opposed by his family he made succ. as "Oliveira"; played with succ. Berlin, 1892.

**Franchinus** (frän-kē′-noos). Vide GAFORI.

**Franchi - Verney** (frän′-kē-vĕr′-nā), **Giu. Ip.**, Conte della Valetta ; b. Turin, Feb. 17, 1848 ; 1874 gave up law for music ; 1875–77 under the pen-name "Ippolito Valetta" contributed to various papers ; 1893 (?), m. Teresina Tua ; c. succ. lyric sketch "Il Valdese" (Turin, 1885), and succ. ballet, "Il Mulatto" (Naples, 1896).

**Franchomme** (frän-shŭm), **Auguste**, Lille, April 10, 1808—Paris, Jan. 21, 1884 ; 'cellist ; teacher at the Cons. and composer.

**Franck** (fränk), (1) **Melchior**, Zittau, ca. 1580—Coburg, June 1, 1639 ; from 1603 court-cond. at Coburg ; a prolific and important c. of secular and church-music, a pioneer in improving instrumental accompaniment ; two of his chorales "Jerusalem, das hochgebaute Stadt," and "Wenn ich Todesnöthen bin," are still sung ; he is said to have written the text for many hymns. (2) **Jn. W.**, Hamburg, 1641—Spain, 1688 (or later) ; opera-cond. ; c. 14 operas. (3) (frän), **César Auguste**, Liège, Dec. 10, 1822—Paris, Nov. 8, 1890 ; important and influential French composer ; pupil Liège Cons., then of Paris Cons., where he took 1st prize for piano, and 2d for comp., also succeeding his organ-teacher, Benoist, as prof. there in 1872, and as organist at Ste. Clothilde ; c. a notable symph. poem with chorus "Les béatitudes," symph. poem "Le chasseur maudit," a symphony in D minor, a succ. com. opera "Hulda" (Monte Carlo, 1894), 2 oratorios, an unfinished opera "Ghisella," a sonata for pf. and vln.; pf.-pcs.; chamber-music, songs, etc. ; biog. by Derepas (Paris, '97), and by Destranges. (4) **Eduard**, Breslau, 1817—Berlin, 1893 ; professor and composer. (5) **Jos.**, b. Liège, ca. 1820 ; bro. of (3) ; organist and teacher, Paris ; pub. Ode to St. Cecilia (with orch.) ; cantatas, etc.

**Francke** (fränk′-ĕ), **Aug. Hn.**, 1 founded Leipzig pf.-factory.

**Fran′co**, a name honoured in men music and probably belonging to perhaps three, men : (1) **F.** of **P** (the elder), cond. at Nôtre-Da Paris, ca. 1100 (?) A.D.; and (2 **of Cologne**, Dortmund and pri the Benedictine Abbey at Cologn 1190, author of 2 treatises.

**Francœur** (frän-kŭr), (1) **Franç** Paris, 1698—1787 ; violinist dram. composer. (2) **Louis** Paris, 1738—1804 ; nephew of ab violinist, conductor and dram. c poser.

**Frank** (1) **Melchior**. Vide FRA (2) **Ernst**, Munich, 1847—(insa Oberdöbling, near Vienna, 1 court-organist and dram. compos

**Franke** (fränk′-ĕ), **Fr. W.**, b. men, June 21, 1862 ; studied B Hochschule ; organist at Strals later at Cologne, also teacher in Cons.

**Frankenberger** (fränk′-ĕn-bĕrkh **H.**, Wümbach, Schwarzburg-Son hausen, 1824—Sondershausen, 18 conductor, violinist, and dram. c poser.

**Frank′lin, Benj.**, Boston, M 1706—Philadelphia, 1790 ; the nent philosopher ; inv. the harmo (v. D. D.), and wrote wittily Scotch and contemporary music

**Franz** (fränts), (1) **K.**, Langenbie Silesia, 1738—Munich, 1802 ; v oso on the waldhorn, and the b ton. (2) **J. H.**, pen-name of C B. von Hochberg. (3) **Robt.**, H June 28, 1815—Oct. 24, 1892 ; 1 changed his family-name Kna by royal permission ; long opp by his parents, he finished his m cal studies 1835–37, under Fr. Sch der, Dessau ; returned to Halle, spent six years studying Bach, 1843, his first album of 12 songs peared, and was cordially rec'd Liszt and Mendelssohn, and by S mann, who wrote about him in periodical. He became organis

e Ulrichskirche, and later cond. of
e Singakademie, and mus. dir. at
alle Univ., which made him Mus.
oc., 1861. In 1868, deafness at-
cked him, and nervous disorders
evented his writing further. His
stress was relieved by the receipt of
5,000, from a series of concerts or-
nised 1872, in Germany, by Helene
agnus, Joachim, Liszt, and in
nerica, by Dresel, Schlesinger, and
J. Lang. His wife (4) **Marie** (née
inrichs, 1828–91), pub. many ex-
llent songs. His supplementing of

the old musical shorthand of Bach
and Händel, by full scores with modern instrumentation has been of invaluable service. He also pub. essays and "open letters" to Hanslick
on Bach and Händel. He pub. 257
songs ; the 117th Psalm, for double
chorus *a cappella ;* Kyrie for soli and
4-part chorus, *a cappella,* a liturgy for
6 chorals, 6 part-songs for mixed
chorus, and 6 do. for male chorus.
Biog. sketches, by Ambros, Liszt,
Dr. W. Waldmann (Leipzig, 1895),
etc.

## Robert Franz.

### By HENRY T. FINCK.

EXT to Schubert, Robert Franz is undoubtedly the most original of
German song-writers. Unlike Schubert, he was a specialist, confining himself almost entirely to the field of art-songs, of which he
te 279. These short songs represent, however, *multum in parvo.* As
imself once remarked, they are " like a mirror reflecting the development
usic from a to z." By their simple strophic structure they remind one
he early folk-song. Many of them are as stately and majestic as the Prot-
nt chorals of the time from Luther to Bach. ¶Like Bach's music, the
oforte parts of Franz's songs are polyphonic ; that is, the melody is not
fined to the voice, but each part of the instrumental accompaniment is a
ody, too, and these diverse melodies are interwoven with magic art. At
same time his harmonies and tone-colours are as modern as Chopin's, espe-
y in the use of chords widely extended with the aid of the pedal. ¶Franz
itted he could never have become what he was, had it not been for Schu-
n and Schubert ; yet his style is entirely different from theirs. He was
more critical than any of his predecessors, retaining in his desks all songs
did not please him ; hence the proportion of good ones is greater in his
than in any other. His songs are a happy blending of the romantic
it and the classical style, of the modern declamatory style and a genuine
*canto.*

nzl (frĕnts'l), (1) **Ignaz,** Mann-
eim, 1734—1803 ; violinist, conduc-
or and composer. (2) **Fd.,** Schwet-
ngen, Palatinate, 1770—Mannheim,
833 ; son and pupil of above ; conuctor and dram. composer.

**Frauenlob** (frow'-ĕn-lōp). Vide voi
MEISSEN.
**Frauscher** (frow'-shĕr), **Moritz,** b.
Mattighafen, Austria, 1861; studied
with Jn. Ress, sang *Pogner* ("*Mei*

*tersinger.*"), Bayreuth, 1892; since 1899. Vienna, ct.-opera.

**Frasi** (frä'-zē), **Giulia**, Italian singer in England, 1743–58 in Händel's works.

**Frederick II.** (the Great), of Prussia; Berlin, 1712—Potsdam, 1786; flute-player and composer of remarkable skill—for a king.

**Frédérix** (frä-dā-rēx), **Gv.**, Liège, 1834—Brussels, 1894; critic.

**Frege** (frä'-gĕ), **Livia** (née **Gerhard**), Gera, b. June 13, 1818; singer; pupil of Pohlenz; début at 15 with Clara Wieck, who was then 13, at the Gewandhaus, Leipzig.

**Freiberg** (frī'-bĕrkh), **Otto**, Naumburg, April 26, 1846; studied, Leipzig Cons.; from 1865, violinist in court-orch., Carlsruhe; studied with V. Lachner; became mus. dir. Marburg Univ.; 1887, mus. dir. and prof. Göttingen.

**Frène** (frĕn), **Eugène H.**, Strassburg, 1860 (?)—Paris, 1896; conductor.

**Frère** (frăr),° **Marguerite Jeanne** (called **Hatto**), b. Lyons, Jan. 30, 1879; soprano; pupil of the Cons., took 2 opera prizes, 1899, début at Opéra, 1899; created "*Floria*" in Saint-Saëns' "*Les Barbares*"; sang at Monte Carlo, etc.

**Freschi** (frĕs'-kē), **Giov. Dom.**, Vicenza, 1640—1690; conductor and dram. composer.

**Frescobaldi** (frĕs-kō-bäl'-dē), **Girolamo**, Ferrara, 1583—(buried) Rome, March 2, 1644; the greatest organist of his time, a revolutionist in harmony and important developer of fugue and notation; he was so famous that 30,000 people attended his first performance as organist of St. Peter's, Rome (1610, or –14); pupil of Luzzacchi; organist at Mechlin probably 1607; c. org.-pcs., fugues, double-choir church-music, etc.; biog. by Haberl.

**Freudenberg** (froi'-dĕn-bĕrkh), **Wm.**, b. Raubacher Hütte, Prussia, March 11, 1838; studied in Leipzig; th.-cond. in various places; 1865, cond. of the Cecilia Singing Society, and the

**Synagogenverein**, Wiesbaden; 1 founded a Cons., and till 1886, c the Singakademie; later opera-c at Augsburg and (1889) Ratisl c. many operas, chiefly comic; syr poem, etc.

**Freund** (froint), **Robt.**, b. Buda-Pe April 7, 1852; pianist; studied Moscheles, Tausig, and Liszt; in Zurich.

**Frey** (frī), **M.**, d. Aug. 10, 1832; linist, court-cond. at Mannheim, dram. composer.

**Freystätter** (frī'-shtĕt-tĕr), **W** 1836—Munich, 1892, critic.

**Frezzolini** (frĕd-zō-lē'-nē), **Ermi** b. Orvieto, 1818; soprano; dé 1838.

**Friberth** (frī'-bĕrt), **K.**, Wullersd Lower Austria, 1736—Vienna, 18 tenor; conductor.

**Frick** (or **Frike**) (frĭk, or frē'- **Ph. Jos.**, near Würzburg, 174 London, 1798; organist and c poser.

**Fricke** (frĭk'-ĕ), **Aug. Gf.**, Brunsw 1829—Berlin, 1894; bass.

**Frickenhaus** (frĭk'-ĕn-hows), **Fa** (née **Evans**), b. Cheltenham, I land, June 7, 1849; pianist; p of G. Mount, Aug. Dupont (Brus Cons.), and Wm. Bohrer; 1869, but, London.

**Friedheim** (frēt'-hīm), **Arthur**, b. Petersburg, Oct. 26, 1859; pia and conductor; pupil of Rubins one year, and of Liszt, 8 years concerto, etc.

**Friedländer** (frēt'-lĕnt-ĕr), **Max.** Brieg, Silesia, Oct. 12, 1852; conc bass and editor; pupil of Mar Garcia and Stockhausen; dé 1880, London; 1881–83, Frankf since in Berlin; 1882, Dr. Phil c. (Breslau).

**Friedrich II.** Vide FREDERICK.

**Fries** (frēs), **Wulf** (**Chr. Juli** Garbeck, Holstein, Ger. Jan. 1825—Roxbury, Mass., April 1902; self-taught 'cellist; at 17 the Bergen Th. orch. and Ole Bu concerts; 1847, Boston, Mass.,

the founders of the Mendelssohn
intet Club ; later a member of the
ethoven Q. Club.
e. Vide FRICK.
mel (frĭm'-mĕl), **Th.**, b. Amstet-
, Lower Austria, Dec. 15, 1853 ;
. D. (Vienna) ; writer.

ze (frĭt'-zĕ), **Wm.**, Bremen, 1842
Stuttgart, 1881 ; conductor, writer,
d composer.

zsch (frĭtsh), **Ernst Wm.**, b.
tzen, Aug. 24, 1840 ; pupil Leip-
Cons. ; acquired the music-pub.
siness of Bomnitz in Leipzig,
ace 1870, ed. the radical "*Musi-
lisches Wochenblatt*," and 1875
arted the "*Musikalische Hausblät-
-*" ; is a member of the Gewand-
us Orch. ; pub. the works of Wag-
r, Grieg, etc., and aided progress.

berger (frō'-bĕrkh-ĕr), **Jn. Jakob,**
05 (?) — Héricourt, France, May
1667 ; chief German organist of
e 17th cent. ; son of a captor at
alle ; studied in Rome with Fresco-
ldi ; court organist at Vienna ; trav-
ed, and in England, being robbed,
came a bellows-treader ; he over-
ew during Chas. II's marriage and
s beaten by the organist Gibbons ;
fell to improvising shortly after,
d was recognised by a pupil who
esented him to the king.

(h)lich (frā-lĭkh), (1) **Jos.**, Würz-
arg, 1780—1862 ; musical director ;
iter and dram. composer. (2) The
me of three sisters b. Vienna, (a)
**anette (Anna),** 1793—? pianist,
acher, and singer. (b) **Barbara,**
97—?, contralto and painter, m. F.
gner. (c) **Josephine,** 1803—1878,
table singer and teacher.

mm (frôm), **Emil,** b. Spremberg,
iederlausitz, Jan. 29, 1835 ; pupil
R. Inst. for Church-music, Berlin ;
66, Royal Mus. Dir. ; 1869, organ-
t and conductor at Flensburg ; c. 2
assion cantatas, an oratorio, etc.

ntini (frôn-tē'-nē), **F. Paolo,** b.
atania, Aug. 6, 1860 ; pupil of P.
atania, and Lauro Rossi ; now
r. Catania Mus. Inst. ; c. succ-

opera "*Malia*" (Bologna, 1893) ;
oratorio "*Sansone*" (1882), etc.

**Froschauer** (frôsh'-ow-ĕr), **Ju.**, printer
at Augsburg ; said to have printed
the first music with movable type in
1498.

**Frost, (1) Chas. Jos.,** b. Westbury-
on-Tyne, Engl., June 20, 1848 ; son
and pupil of an organist at Tewkes-
bury, also pupil of Cooper, Goss, and
Steggall , organist various churches,
1882, Mus. Doc. Cantab. ; 1880 prof.
of organ Guildhall Sch. of Mus. ;
c. oratorio, "*Nathan's Parable*"
(1878) ; a symphony, etc. (2) **H. Fr.,**
London, March 15, 1848—June,1901,
studied organ with Seb. Hart. ; 1865–
91, organist of the Chapel Royal,
Savoy ; 1880–88, pf.-prof. Guildhall
Sch. of Mus. ; from 1877 critic of
"*The Academy*," later of "*The Athenæum*," and "*The Standard*"; pub.
biog. of Schubert, and the "*Savoy
Hymn-tunes and Chants.*"

**Frotz'ler** (frôts'-lĕr), **Carl ("Auer"),**
b. Stockerau, Lower Austria, April
10, 1873 ; pupil of his father ; at 15,
had c. a grand mass, an offertory,
etc. , then entered Vienna Cons.
studying under Krenn ; 1887–93, organist at the Pfarrkirche, Stockerau,
and chamber-pianist to Prince Heinrich Reuss IV ; 1893–97, cond. to
Count Esterházy at Totis, Hungary ;
since, cond. City Th., Linz-on-Danube ; c. operas "*Arnelda*" (Totis,
1894 ; took Philh. Ger.-Amer. Opera
Society's prize) ; "*Der Liebesring*" ,
"*Mathias Corvinus*" (Pesth, Royal
Opera, 1896) ; 3 masses ; a symphony,
etc.

**Frugatta** (froo-gät'-tä), **Giu.,** b. Bergamo, May 26, 1860 ; pianist ; pupil
of Bazzini (comp.) and Andreoli (pf.)
at Milan Cons.; became prof. there ;
also at the "Collegio reale delle Fan-
ciulle"; composer.

**Früh** (frü), **Armin Lebrecht,** Mühlhausen, Thuringia, Sept. 15, 1820—
Nordhausen, Jan. 8, 1894 ; dram.
composer ; inv. 1887, of the "Semeio-
melodicon" (vide D. D.).

**Fruytiers** (froi'-tĕrs), **Jan.**, Flemish composer at Antwerp 16th century.

**Fry, Wm. H.**, Philadelphia, 1813—Santa Cruz, 1864 ; dram. composer ; critic N. Y. *Tribune.*

**Fuchs** (fookhs), (1) **G. Fr.**, Mayence, 1752—Paris, 1821 ; clarinettist and bandm. (2) **Aloys**, Raase, Austrian Silesia, 1799—Vienna, 1853 ; collector and writer. (3) **K. Dorius, Jn.**, b. Potsdam, Oct. 22, 1838 ; pupil of his father and v. Bülow, Weitzmann and Kiel ; Dr. phil., Greifswald; 1871–75, concert pianist, teacher and critic, Berlin ; 1875–79, Hirschberg ; 1879, Danzig; since '86, organist at the Petrikirche, there . Pub. numerous valuable musical treatises. (4) **Jn. Nepomuk**, Frauenthal, Styria, May 5, 1842—Vienna, Oct. 5, 1899 ; from 1893, dir. of Vienna Cons. ; dir. and dram. composer. (5) **Robt.**, b. Frauenthal, Feb. 15, 1847 ; bro. of above ; pupil, since 1875 prof., at Vienna Cons. ; pub. a symphony, 3 valuable serenades, etc.; prod. 2 operas : succ. " Spieloper " " *Die Teufelsglocke* " (Leipzig, 1893) and the succ. com. opera " *Die Königsbraut* " (Vienna, 1889). (6) **Albert**, b. Basel, Aug. 6, 1858 ; pupil of Leipzig Cons. ; 1880, mus. dir. at Trier ; 1889, owner and manager Wiesbaden Cons.; composer. (7) **Anton**, b. Munich, Jan. 29, 1849 ; barytone ; studied with Hey and Milner ; sang at the court-opera ; since 1882 at Bayreuth, first as singer then as manager.

**Füchs** (füks), **Fd. K.**, Vienna, 1811—1848 ; dram. composer.

**Fuentes** (foo-ān'-tĕs), (1) **Don Pasquale**, b. Albayda, Valencia, d. there 1768 ; conductor and composer. (2) **Francisco De Santa Maria de**, Franciscan monk and writer at Madrid, 1778.

**Fuertes, M. S.** Vide SORIANO.

**Führer** (fü'-rĕr), **Robt.**, Prague, 1807—Vienna, Nov., 1861 ; organ-composer.

**Fuhrmann** (foor'-män), (1) **G. Ld.**, wrote work on the lute, Nürnberg,

1615. (2) **Martin H.**, ca. 1670-1736 ; theorist and writer.

**Fulda, Adam von.** Vide ADAM.

**Fulsztynski** (foolsh-tēn'-shkĭ), **bastian**, Polish theorist, 16th c.

**Fumagalli** (foo-mä-gäl'-lē), nam four bros. b. at Inzago, Italy **Disma**, 1826—Milan, 1893 ; pr sor and composer. (2) **Adolfo**, —Florence, May 3, 1856 ; pia (3) **Polibio**, b. Oct. 26, 1830 ; nist and composer. (4) **Luca** May 29, 1837 ; pupil Milan Co concert-pianist ; prod. opera " *L XI* " (Florence, 1875).

**Fumagal'lo, Mario Léon**, b. M Sept. 4, 1864 ; studied with Ce barytone of wide travel.

**Fumi** (foo'-mē), **Vinceslao**, Mo pulciano, Tuscany, 1823—Flore 1880 ; conductor, violinist, d composer and collector.

**Fur'ker**, one of the best vln.-mal London, 1780—1840.

**Furlanetto** (foor-lä-nĕt'-tō), **B** ventura (called **Musin**), Ver 1738 — 1817 ; singing-teacher, ductor and composer.

**Furno** (foor'-nō), **Giov.**, Capua, 17 Naples, 1837 ; professor and d composer.

**Fursch-Madi** (foorsh'-mä-dē), **Em** Bayonne, France, 1847—Warren N. J., Sept. 20, 1894 ; pupil of I Cons., début Paris; came to Ame 1874, with the New Orleans Fr Opera Company ; 1879–81, Co Garden, London ; her final app ance was as " Ortrud," N. Y., 1

**Fürstenau** (fürsht'-ĕ-now), (1) **K** par, Münster, Westphalia, 1772—denburg, 1819 ; flute-virtuoso ; c poser. (2) **Anton B.**, Münster, —Dresden, 1852 ; son and pupi above ; flutist and composer. **Moritz**, Dresden, 1824—1889 ; and pupil of (2) ; flutist and write

**Fürstner** (fürsht'-nĕr), **Ad.**, b. Be Jan. 2, 1835 ; founded (1868) a m pub. house, Berlin.

**Fux** (foox), **Jn. Jos.**, Hirtenf Upper Styria, 1660—Vienna, B

, 1741 ; eminent theorist, organist, d court-conductor and writer ; c. 5 works (few pub.). incl. 18 operas, oratorios, 50 masses, incl. *missa nonica.* He wrote the famous eatise on cpt. "*Gradus ad Parnasm*" in dialogue form ; it is based the church-modes. Biogr. by öchel (Vienna, 1872).

## G.

ler (gäp'-lĕr), **Jn.**, d. ca. 1784 ; or-n builder at Ulm.

riel (1) (gä'-brĭ-ĕl), **Mary Ann irginia**, Banstead, Surrey, Engl., 25—London, 1877 ; c. cantatas, eras, etc. (2) (gä'-brĭ-ĕl), **Max,** 90, cond. Residenz Th., Hanover ; od. the succ. 3-act operettas, *Steffen Langer*" (Magdeburg, 89); "*Der Freiwerber*" (Hanover, 90); "*Der Garde-Uhlan*" (Bres-u, 1892 ; Berlin, 1893, as "*Der ar-de-Husar*").

rieli (gä-brĭ-ā'-lē), (1) **Andrea,** enice, ca. 1510—1586 ; eminent or-nist and teacher and composer of e first "real" fugues (v. D.D.). (2) iov., Venice, 1558—Aug. 12, 1613 cc. to his monument) ; nephew and upil of above, and equally famous ; extraordinary contrapuntist, his symphoniæ sacræ" employing 3 nultaneous choirs independently ndled ; he has been called "the ther of the chromatic style" be-use of his bold modulations. (3) om. (called "Menghino del violon-llo "), Bologna, ca. 1640—ca. 1690; ellist, conductor, and composer.

rielli (gä-brĭ-ĕl'-lē), (1) **Catterina,** ome, Nov. 12, 1730—April, 1796 ; ughter of Prince G.'s cook (and ence called "**La Cochetta,**" or **Cochettina** ") ; one of the most eautiful and brilliant of singers ; her xtraordinarily flexible voice had a thrilling quality" (Burney) ; her prices and her high-handed treat-ent of the nobility and royalty ena-oured of her make her a most pict-

uresque figure ; she sang with great-est succ. all over Europe and retired wealthy. Her sister (2) **Francesca** (called "**La Gabriellina,**" or "**La Ferrarese**"), Ferrara, 1755—Ven-ice, 1795, was a celebrated prima donna buffa. (3) Conte **Nicolo,** Naples, 1814—1891 ; prod. 22 operas and 60 ballets.

**Gabriels'ki,** (1) **Jn. Wm.**, Berlin, 1791 —1846 ; flutist and composer. (2) **Julius,** Berlin, 1806—1878 ; bro. and pupil of above ; flutist. (3) **Ad.**, 1st flutist, Berlin Royal orch., son of (2).

**Gabrilowitsch** (gä-brē-lō'-vĭtsh), **Os-sip,** b. St. Petersburg, Jan. 26, 1878; studied at the Cons. with Tolstoff and Rubinstein ; at 16 took the Ru-binstein prize ; studied with Les-chetizky at Vienna, 1894–96 ; 1896 began touring with success ; 1900–02 America ; c. pf.-pieces.

**Gabussi** (gä-bōōs'-sē), **V.**, Bologna, 1800—London, 1846 ; teacher and composer.

**Gade** (gä'-dĕ), **Niels Wm.**, Copen-hagen, Feb. 22, 1817—Dec. 21, 1890; son of an instr.-maker ; at 15 refused to learn his father's trade, and be-came pupil of Wexschall (vln.) Berg-green (theory) ; at 16 a concert-violin-ist. His overture, "*Nachklänge von Ossian,*" took first prize at the Copenhagen Mus. Soc. competition (1841) and won for him a royal stipend. In 1842 the C min. symphony, and 1846 the cantata "*Comala,*" were prod. by Mendelssohn at the Gewand-haus. He travelled in Italy ; then, 1844, lived in Leipzig as sub-cond. to Mendelssohn, and regular cond. at his death (1847) ; 1848, he returned to Copenhagen as cond. of the Mus. Soc. and as organist ; 1861, court-cond., made Prof. by the King, and Dr. Phil. *h. c.* by the Univ. ; 1886, Commander in the Order of Dane-brog ; 1876 the govt. voted him a life-pension. Autobiog. "*Aufzeich-nungen und Briefe*" (Basel, 1893). Pub. 7 symphonies (D minor, No. with pf.) ; 5 overtures, "*Nach*

*klänge von Ossian,*" " *Im Hoch-*
*lande,*" " *Hamlet,*" " *Michelangelo,*"
octet, sextet, and quartet for strings ;
8 cantatas, " *Elverskind*",(Erl-King's
daughter), " *Frühlingsbotschaft,*"
" *Die Heilige Nacht,*" " *Zion,*"
" *Kalanus,*" " *Die Kreuzfahrer,*"
" *Psyche,*" etc.; 2 vln.-concertos ; pf.
sonata and pcs., songs, etc.

**Gads'by, H. Robt.,** b. Hackney, London, Dec. 15, 1842 ; pupil of Wm.
Bayley, but mainly self-taught ; organist at St. Peter's, Brockley ; 1884,
prof. of harm. Queen's Coll. London;
also at Guildhall Sch. of Mus. ; c.
" *Festival Service* " ; 3 symphonies ;
3 overtures, " *Andromeda,*" " *The
Golden Legend,*" and " *The Witches'
Frolic,*" etc.

**Gad'sky, Johanna,** b. Anclam, Prussia, June 15, 1871 ; soprano, educated at Stettin ; 1892, m. H. Pausch-
er ; sang in U. S. A. for many years,
1899 Covent Garden and as " Eva "
(*Meistersinger*), at Bayreuth.

**Gaforio** (gä-fō'-rĭ-ō) (or **Gafori, Gafu-
ri, Gaffurio**), **Franchino** (Latinized
" Franchinus Gafurius," or " Franchinus "), Lodi, Jan. 14, 1451—
Milan, June 24, 1522 ; priest, eminent theorist, choirmaster and singer.

**Gagliano** (gäl-yä'-nō), (1) **Marco di
Zanobi da,** b. Florence; d. there,
Feb. 24, 1642 ; conductor and composer. (2) A family of Naples vln.-
makers, (a) **Alessandro,** pupil of
Stradivari, worked ca. 1695—1725.
His sons. (b) **Nicolò** (170c—40), and
(c) **Gennaro** (1710—50), and his
grandson, (d) **Ferdinando** (1736—81)
succeeded him ; later descendants est.
factory of strings, still famous.

**Gährich** (gä'-rĭkh), **Wenzel,** Zercho-
witz, Bohemia, 1794—Berlin, 1864 ;
violinist, ballet-master, and dram.
composer.

**Gaïl** (gä-ēl), **Edmée Sophia** (née
**Garre**), Paris, Aug. 28, 1775—July
24, 1819 ; singer and dram. composer.

**Galeazzi** (gä-lä-äd'-zē), **Fran.,** Turin,
1758—Rome, 1819 ; violinist.

**Galerat'ti, Catterina,** Italian cont:
to, in London 1714–21.

**Galilei** (gä-lĭ-lä'-ē), **V.,** Florence,
1533—ca. 1600 ; lutenist, violin
and theorist ; father of the astro-
mer.

**Galin** (gä-lăn̄), **P.,** Samatan Ge
France, 1786—Paris (?), 1821 ; wr
pop. method " *Meloplaste* " (v. D. 1

**Galitzin** (gä-lē'-tshĕn), (1) **Nico
Borissovitch,** d. Kurski, 1866 ;
Russian prince, to whom Beethov
dedicated an overture, and 3 quarte
he advanced Beethoven liberal su
for his dedications ; a skilful 'cell
(2) **G.** (Prince), St. Petersburg, 1
—1872 ; son of above ; compo
and cond. ; maintained in M
cow (1842) a choir of 70 boys ; la
an orchestra.

**Gallay** (gäl-lĕ), (1) **Jacques Fra**
Perpignan, 1795—Paris, 1864 ; ho
virtuoso and composer. (2) **Jul**
Saint-Quentin, 1822—Paris, 18
amateur 'cellist of wealth ; made
searches and pub. valuable treatis

**Gallenberg** (gäl'-lĕn-bĕrkh), **Wen
Robt.,** Graf **von,** Vienna, 178
Rome, 1839 ; c. ballets.

**Galle'tius, Fran.** (rightly **Franç
Gallet** (gäl-lä)), b. Mons, Haina
16th cent.; contrapuntist.

**Gal'li,** (1) **Filippo,** Rome, 1783—Pa
June 3, 1853 ; first most succes
as a tenor ; illness changed his vo
and he achieved great success a
bass. (2) ——, d. 1804; Ita
mezzo-soprano in London from 17

**Gal'lia.** Vide ÉPINE.

**Galliard** (gäl'-lĭ-ärt), **Jn. Ernst,** Ce
Hanover,1687—London, 1749; ob
and organist.

**Gal'lico, Paolo,** b. Trieste, May
1868 ; at 15 gave a pf.-recital
Trieste ; then studied Vienna Co
with Julius Eppstein ; at 18 gradu
ing with first prize and " Ges
schafts " medal ; toured Euro
since 1892 pianist and teacher, N
York.

**Gallic'ulus, Jns.,** contrapuntist
Leipzig. 1520–48.

i-Marié (găl-lĭ măr-yā), Celés-
ie (née Marie de l'Isle), b.
.ris, Nov., 1840 ; mezzo-soprano ;
ughter of an opera-singer ; début
rassburg, 1859 ; sang Toulouse,
6o, Lisbon, 1861, Rouen, 1862 ;
62–78, and 1883–85, Paris Opéra
mique ; she created " Mignon "
866), " Carmen " (1875), etc.

lus, (1) Jacobus (rightly Jacob
ändl, Handl or Hähnel) ; Carnio-
, ca. 1550—Prague, 1591 ; compos-
and conductor. (2) Jns. (Jean le
ocq, Maître Jean, or Mestre
ian), d. before 1543 ; a Dutch con-
apuntist, conductor and composer.
) Vide MEDERITSCH, JN.

ippi (gä-loop'-pĭ), Baldassare
alled Il Buranel'lo), Island of Bu-
no, near Venice, Oct. 18, 1706—
inice, Jan. 3, 1784 ; harpsichord
rtuoso ; organist 1765–68 ; conduc-
r ; c. 54 comic operas.

abale (gäm-bä'-lĕ), Emm., music-
acher, Milan ; pub. " La riforma
usicale " (1840), etc., advocating a
ale of 12 semitones.

ibini (gäm-bē'-nē), Carlo Andrea,
noa, 1819—1865 ; c. operas, etc.

a'ble, John, English violinist and
mposer, 17th century.

iucci (gä-moot'-chē), Baldassare,
orence, 1822—1892 ; pianist and
iter.

assi (gä-näs'-sē), Silvestro, b.
ntego, near Venice, ca. 1500
alled " del Fontego ") ; editor and
iter on graces.

d (gäṅ), Ch. Nicolas Eugène,
, 1826—Boulogne-sur-Seine, 1892 ;
i.-maker. V. LUPOT.

dillot (gäṅ-dē-yō), Léon, b. Paris,
in. 25, 1862 ; writer of comedies
d composer of Parisian vaudevilles.

dini (gän-dē'-nē), (1) A., Modena,
86—Formigine, 1842 ; conductor
d dram. composer. (2) Alessan-
o, Modena, ca. 1807—1871 ; son,
pil (1842) and successor of above ;
am. composer and writer.

ne (găn), L. Gaston, b. Buxières-
-Mines, Allier, April 5, 1862; pupil

of Dubois and Franck, Paris Cons. ;
c. comic opera " Rabelais " (1892),
vaudeville operetta, ballets, etc.

Gänsbacher (gĕns'-bäkh-ĕr), Jn.,
Sterzing, Tyrol, 1778—Vienna, 1844 ;
conductor and composer.

Gan'tenberg (-bĕrkh), H., b. Berlin,
Nov. 29, 1823 ; studied with
Gabrielsky; from 1860 chamber-mus.,
pensioned 1893 ; from 1872 teacher
at the Hochschule.

Gantvoort (gänt'-vōrt), Arnold J.,
b. Amsterdam, Dec. 6, 1857 ; 1876,
in America as teacher in various colleges ; 1894, Coll. of Mus., Cincinnati ; pub. school music-readers.

Ganz (gänts), (1) Ad., Mayence, 1796
—London, 1870 ; violinist and cond.;
his 2 brothers were, (2) Moritz,
Mayence, 1806—Berlin, 1868 ; 'cel-
list ; (3) Ld., Mayence, 1810—Ber-
lin, 1869 ; violinist and composer ;
Adolf's 2 sons were, (4) Eduard,
Mayence, 1827—1869 ; pianist. (5)
Wilhelm, b. Mayence, Nov. 6, 1833;
pianist, professor, conductor.

Garat (gä-rä), P. J., Ustaritz, Basses-
Pyrénées, April 25, 1764 — Paris,
March 1, 1823 ; most remarkable
French singer of his time, a barytone
of great compass and amazing memory and mimicry ; professor and composer.

Garaudé (găr-ō-dä), Alexis de, Nancy, 1779—Paris, 1852 ; professor,
composer and writer.

Garbini (gär-bē'-nē), Edoardo, b.
Parma ; stable-boy there, when discovered ; now pop. tenor in opera.

Garbrecht (gär'-brĕkht), Fr. F. W.
(d. 1875), founded at Leipzig (1862)
a music engraving establishment,
owned since 1880 by Os. Brandstetter.

Garcia (gär-thē'-ä), a notable family of
Spanish vocal teachers. (1) Don
Fran. Saverio (Padre Garcia, called
" lo Spagnoletto "), Nalda, Spain,
1731—Saragossa, 1809 ; conductor
and composer. (2) Manuel del Po-
polo Vicente, Sevilla, Jan. 22, 1775
—Paris, June 2, 1832 ; eminent as
tenor, teacher, and progenitor of sing-

ers ; successful as manager, cond. and composer; took his family, his wife, son (3), and daughter (5) and others to America for a v. succ. opera season, 1825-26. Produced 43 operas and c. others. (3) **Manuel**, b. Madrid, March 17, 1805 ; son of above ; bass (in Paris) ; he was a scientific investigator, and inv. the laryngoscope, receiving Dr. Phil. *h. c.* Königsberg Univ.; 1847, prof. at the Cons., 1850, London, R.A.M. Jenny Lind was one of his pupils; pub. " *Traité complet de l'art du chant,*" 1847. (4) **Eugènie** (née **Mayer**), Paris, 1818—1880 ; wife and pupil of (3) ; soprano and teacher. (5) **M. Félicité,** v. MALIBRAN. (6) **Pauline**, v. VIARDOT GARCIA. (7) **Mariano**, b. Aoiz, Navarra, July 26, 1809 ; not related to the others ; dir. of the Pampeluna School of Music ; composer of church-music.

**Garcin** (gär-săn), **Jules Aug. Salomon,** Bourges, 1830—Paris, 1896 ; violinist, conductor and professor.

**Gardano** (gär-dä'-nō), (1) **A.** (till 1557 called himself **Gardane**), ca. 1500— Venice, 1571 (?) ; early Italian mus.-printer, succeeded by sons, (2) **Alessandro** and (3) **Angelo.**

**Gar'den, Mary,** b. Aberdeen, Feb. 20, 1877; soprano ; as a child brought to America ; pupil of Mrs. Duff ; (1896), Paris with Trabadello and Fugère ; début, 1900, Paris Op. Com.; has created various rôles there, including " Mélisande " in Debussy's " *Pelléas et Mélisande,*" 1902 ; sang at Covent Garden, 1902.

**Gardo'ni,** Italo, b. ·Parma, 1821 ; retired, 1874 ; operatic singer.

**Gargiulo** (gär-joo'-lō), (1) Chevalier **Enrico,** b. Bari, Italy, March 31, 1865 ; mandolinist ; son and pupil of a dram. barytone (2) **Eugenio.**

**Garibol'di, Giu.,** b. Maccerato, Italy, March 17, 1833 ; flutist and composer of operettas.

**Garlan'dia, Johannes de,** ca. 1210–32 ; French theorist.

**Garnier** (gärn-yā), **Fran. Jos., Lauris,**

Vaucluse, 1759—ca. 1825 ; oboist composer.

**Gar'rett, Geo. Mursell,** Winche England, 1834—Cambridge, 1 pianist, conductor, composer and urer.

**Gärtner** (gĕrt'-něr), **Jos.,** Tac Bohemia, 1796—Prague, 1863 ; builder and writer, Prague.

**Gas'par van Weerbeke** (vär'-bĕ b. Oudenarde, Flanders, ca. 1 eminent contrapuntist and teache

**Gaspari** (gäs-pä'-rē), **Gaetano,** logna, 1807—1881 ; librarian, fessor and composer.

**Gasparini** (ŏr **Guasparini**)(gäs-pä nē), (1) **Fran.,** Camaiore, near Lu 1668—Rome, 1737 ; director, ductor and theorist. (2) **Miche gelo,** Lucca, 1685—Venice, 1 male contralto and dram. comp (3) **Don Quirino,** 'cellist at Tu 1749-70 ; conductor and compose

**Gasparo da Salo** (gäs-pä'-rō dä sä (family name **Bertolot'ti**), S Brescia, Italy, ca. 1542—Brescia 1609 ; famous maker of viols.

**Gassier** (gäs-yā), **L. Éd.,** Fra 1822—Havana, 1871 ; barytone.

**Gassmann** (gäs'-män), **Florian** Brux, Bohemia, 1723—Vienna, 1 court-conductor and dram. comp

**Gass'ner, F. Simon,** Vienna, 17 Carlsruhe, 1851 ; violinist, tea editor and composer.

**Gast, Peter. Vide** KOSELITZ.

**Gastaldon** (gäs-täl'-dōn), **Stanis** b. Turin, April 7, 1861 ; at 17 nocturnes, *ballabili,* songs, etc., s of them v. pop.; c· succ. 1-act op seria, " *Il Pater* " (Milan, 1894),

**Gastinel** (gäs-tĭ-něl), **Léon G. C rien,** b. Villers, near Auxonne, / 15, 1823 ; pupil of Halévy, F Cons. ; took first Gr. prix de R with cantata " *Velasquez*" ; p comic operas ; ballet " *Le R* (Gr. Opera, 1890), etc.

**Gastoldi** (gäs-tōl'-dĕ), **Giov. Gia** mo, Caravaggio, ca. 1556—Milan 1622 ; conductor, contrapuntist composer.

res (gă-těz'), (1) **Guill. P. A.**,
s, 1774—1846 ; guitar-player and
poser. (2) **Jos. Léon**, Paris,
;—1877 ; son of above ; harpist,
c and composer. (3) **Félix**, b.
s, 1809 ; bro. of above ; pianist,
ly self-taught ; for 20 years
ed Europe, America and Austra-
c. excellent symphonies and over-
s ; military music, etc.

r (gä-tē), **Aug.**, Liège, 1800—
s, 1858 ; editor, teacher and com-
r.

y, **Alfred Scott**, b. Ecclesfield,
ks., April 25, 1847 ; 1880 Pour-
ant of Arms, Heralds' Coll. Lon-
; c. 2 operettas, many pop. songs,
icularly in imitation of American
tation songs, pf.-pieces.

uier (gōk-yā), **Alard** (rightly
Boyer, Latinized **Nuceus**), called
Gaucquier and **Insulanus** from
e-l'isle, court-bandm. to Maxi-
an II. ; famous 16th cent. contra-
ist.

en'tios, a Greek writer, 1652.

(gôl), **Alfred Robt.**, b. Norwich,
land, April 30, 1837 ; at 9 a
. chorister articled to Dr. Buck ;
g, Mus. Bac. Cantab.; 1887, cond.
sall Philh.; later teacher and
d. at the Birmingham and Mid-
. Inst., etc.; c. oratorio "*Heze-*
*e*" (1861); cantatas, incl. "*Ruth*,"
"*The Holy City*," etc.

btier (gōt-yā), (1) **Jacques** (G.
*ngleterre*, or *l'ancien*), Lyons, ca.
o—Paris, ca. 1670 ; lutenist. (2)
ais (*le jeune*, or *l'illustré*), Mar-
es, 1600(-10 ?)—d. Paris ; cousin
bove, and his partner in a lutenist
ool ; famous lutenist and collector
te-music. (3) **Pierre**, b. Orleans ;
ites for lute (1638). (4) **Enne-
ad**, Vienne, Dauphine, 1635—be-
1680 ; son of (1) ; lutenist. (5)
rre, Cioutat, Provence 1642—
vned, Cette, 1697 ; dram. comer. (6) **Aloysius Éd. Ca-
le**, (Abbé) Italy, ca. 1755—Paris,
8 ; wrote a method for teach-

**Gaunt'lett, H. J.**, Wellington, Shropshire, 1805—London, 1876 ; organist and composer.

**Gauthier** (gōt-yā), **Gabriel**, b. in
Soane-et-Loire, France, 1808 ; became blind when 11 months old ; was
pupil and (1827-40) teacher Paris
Inst. for the Blind, then organist of
St. Étienne-du-Mont, Paris ; pub
treatises.

**Gautier** (gōt-yā), (1) v. GAULTIER. (2)
**J. Fran. Eug.**, Vaugirard n. Paris,
1822—Paris, 1878 ; conductor and
dram. composer.

**Gaveaux** (ga-vō), **P.**, Béziers, Hé-
rault, Aug., 1761—insane, Paris, 1825 ;
tenor ; c. operas, incl. "*Leonore*"
(1788), the same subject afterwards
used in Beethoven's "*Fidelio*."

**Gaviniès** (gă-vēn-yěs), **P.**, Bordeaux,
1726—Paris, 1800 ; violinist, professor and dram. composer.

**Gaztambide** (gäth-täm-bē'-dhě), (1)
**Joaquin**, Tudela, Navarra, 1822—
Madrid, 1870 ; composer, teacher
and conductor. (2) **Xavier**, a young
relative, also c. zarzuelas (see D. D.).

**Gazzaniga** (gäd-zän-ē'-ga), **Giu.**,
Verona, 1743—Crema, 1819 ; conductor and dram. composer.

**Gear** (gēr), **Geo. Fr.**, b. London, May
21, 1857; pianist; pupil of Dr. Wylde
and J. F. Barnett; 1872 scholarship
London Acad. of Mus., now prof.
there ; 1876-92 mus.-dir. German-
Reed Company ; composed scena for
sopr. solo and orch., etc.

**Gebauer** (zhŭ-bō-ā), (1) **Michel Jos.**,
La Fère, Aisne, 1763—1812, on the
retreat from Moscow ; oboist, violinist and viol-player ; also extraordinary virtuoso on the Jew's harp. He
had 3 brothers, (2) **François Réné**,
Versailles, 1773—Paris, 1845 ; bassoonist, prof., writer, and composer.
(3) **P. Paul**, b. Versailles, 1775 ; died
young ; pub. 20 horn-duets. (4) **Ét.
Fran.**, Versailles, 1777—Paris, 1823;
flutist and composer. (5) (gě-bow'-
ěr), **Fz. X.**, Eckersdorf, near Glatz,
1784—Vienna, 1822 ; 'cellist, conductor, teacher and composer.

**Gebel** (gä'-bĕl), (1) **Georg** (Sr.), Breslau, 1685—1750; organist; inv. clavichord with quarter tones and clavicymbalum with pedal-keyboard; composer; he had 2 sons, (2) **Georg** (Jr.), Brieg, Silesia, 1709—Rudolstadt, 1753; son of above; conductor, organist and composer. (3) **Georg Sigismund**, d. 1775; organist and composer. (4) **Fz. X.**, Fürstenau, near Breslau, 1787—Moscow, 1843; conductor, pf.-teacher, and composer.

**Gebhard** (gĕp'-härt), **Martin Anton**, b. Bavaria, 1770; Benedictine monk, then, 1831, a priest at Steinsdorf; theorist.

**Gebhar'di, Ludwig Ernst,**Nottleben, Thuringia, 1787—Erfurt, 1862; organist, composer and teacher.

**Gédalge** (zhä-dälzh), **André,** b. Paris, Dec. 27, 1856; pupil of Guiraud at the Cons.; took 2nd Grand prix de Rome, 1885 wrote lyric drama " *Hélène* " ; c. pantomime " *Le Petit Savoyard* " (Paris, 1891); a succ. 1-act opera-bouffe " *Pris au Piège* " (Paris, 1895); 2 symphonies, etc.

**Gehring** (gä'-rĭng), **F.**, 1838 — Penzing, near Vienna, 1884; writer.

**Geijer** (gī'-ĕr), **Erik Gustaf**, Ransätter, Wermeland, 1783—Upsala, 1847; coll. of Swedish folk-songs.

**Geisler** (gīs'-lĕr), (1) **Jn. G.**, d. Zittau, 1827; writer. (2) **Paul**, b. Stolp, Pomerania, Aug. 10, 1856; grandson and pupil of a mus.-dir. at Mecklenburg; studied also with K. Decker; 1881–82 chorusm. Leipzig City Th., then with Neumann's Wagner Co.; 1883–85 at Bremen (under Seidl); then lived in Leipzig; prod. 5 operas; c. 12 symphonic poems, incl. " *Der Rattenfänger von Hameln* " (1880), " *Till Eulenspiegel,*" etc.

**Geistinger** (gīs'-tĭng-ĕr), **Maria** ("**Marie**") **Charlotte Cäcilia**, b. Graz, Styria, July 26, 1836; soprano, etc.

**Gelinek** (gä'-lĭ-nēk), (1) **Hn. Anton** (called **Cervetti**), Horzeniowecs, Bohemia, 1709—Milan, 1779; ex-

priest, violinist and composer. **Joseph**, Abbé; Selcz, Boh 1758—Vienna, 1825; teacher composer.

**Geller-Wolter** (gĕl'-lĕr-vôl-tĕr), **ise,** b. Cassel, March 27, 1863 era and concert alto; studied Frau Zottmayer and Mme. Mar

**Geminiani** (jĕm-ē-nĭ-ä'-nē), **F** Lucca, 1680—Dublin, Dec. 17, brilliant and eccentric violini great importance in English pro and the author of the first vln. m pub. (1740).

**Gemünder** (gĕ-münt'-ĕr), Ingelfi Würtemberg, March 22, 1814— York, Sept. 7, 1895; a maker v vlns. were of the very highest fection; his sons succeed him.

**Genast** (gĕ-näst'), **Ed.**, Weimar, —Wiesbaden, 1866; barytone composer.

**Genée** (zhŭ-nä), **Franz Frie Richard**, Danzig, Feb. 7, 1 Baden, near Vienna, June 15, 1 pupil of Stalleknacht, Berlin; th conductor various cities; a stu then conductor and operatic comp 1868–78 at Th. an der Wien, Vi wrote libretti for many of his works and for Strauss and ot c. light operas with succ., incl. ' *Geiger aus Tirol,*" "*Nanon,*" et

**Generali** (jä-nĕ-rä'-lē), **Pietro** (r Mercandet'ti), Masserano, mont, 1783—Novara, 1832; co tor and dram. composer.

**Genet** (zhŭ-nä), **Eleazar** (call **Carpentras'so,** or **Carpentras** pän-träs)), Carpentras Vaucluse 1745—Avignon (?), ca. 1532; si then cond., then bishop; his mired masses, etc., were the printed in round notes without ture.

**Gengenbach** (gĕng'-ĕn-bäkh), **N laus**, b. Kolditz, Saxony; cant Zeitz, and writer, 1626.

**Genss** (gĕns), **Hermann**, b. 1 Jan. 6, 1856; pianist; pupil of Royal Hochsch. für Mus., Be teacher in various cities; 1893

Scharwenka-Klindworth Cons.,
n; c. orch. works, etc.

es (zhôrzh), **Alex.**, b. Arras,
ce, Feb. 25, 1850; pupil, now
of harm., Niedermeyer Sch.,
s; c. operas "*Le Printemps*"
3) and "*Poèmes d'Amour*"
2); "*Charlotte Corday*" (1901);
atorios, a mystery "*La Passion*"
2); symph. poem, etc.

d (zhā-răr), **H. P.**, Liège, 1763—
ailles, 1848; teacher and writer.

dy (zhā-răr-dē), **Jean**, b. Lüt-
Dec. 6, 187ᴜ; notable 'cellist;
ed with Bellmann; a pupil of
zmacher; played as a child in
land; at 13 in Dresden; 1899,
toured America; lives at Spa.

er, (1) **H. Nikolaus**, Wenigen-
ch, near Sondershausen, 1702—
lershausen, 1775; organist and
poser. (2) **Ernst L.**, Sonders-
en, 1746—1819; son, pupil and
essor (1775) of above; 'cellist,
nist, lexicographer and compos-

rt (gĕr'-bĕrt), **(von Hornau)**
rtin, Hor-bon-Neckar, Aug. 12,
—St. Blaise, May 13, 1793; col-
r of the invaluable "*Scriptores
siastici de musica sacra potissi-
z*," noteworthy treatises of the
dle Ages, reproduced exactly (the
pilation was continued by Cousse-
er). The work is briefly referred to
nis book as "Gerbert." He be-
e in 1736 cond. at St. Blaise;
n he died, the peasants erecting a
ue to him; pub. also other very
ortant works, and c. offertories,

ke (gā'-rĭ-kĕ), **Wilhelm**, b. Graz,
ia, April 18, 1845; pupil of Des-
Vienna, Cons., then cond. at
z; 1874, 2d. cond. Vienna ct.-
ra (with Hans Richter); 1880,
l. of the "Gesellschaftsconcerte"
e Brahms); also cond. the Sing-
rein; 1884–89, cond. Boston
ss) Symphony Orch., resuming
post 1898 (vice Emil Paur) after
g dir. "Gesellschaftsconcerte" at

Vienna until 1895; pub. several choruses, pf.-pcs. and songs; also c.
operetta "*Schön Hännchen*" (Linz,
1865); a Requiem; a concert-overture, etc.

**Gerlach** (gĕr'-läkh), (1) **Dietrich**, d.
Nürnberg, 1574; music - printer,
1566–1571. (2) **Theodor**, b. Dresden, June 25, 1861; pupil of Wüllner; at 22 prod. a notable cantata,
"*Luther's Lob der Musica*," 1884;
Italy, 1885; cond. Sondershausen
Th., then of German Opera in Posen;
his "*Epic Symphony*" caused his appointment as ct.-cond. in Coburg,
1891; 1894, cond. at Cassel; c. succ.
opera (book and music) "*Matteo Fal-
cone*" (Hanover, '98, Berlin, 1902),
orch. pieces, etc.

**Gerle** (gĕr'-lĕ), (1) **Konrad**, d. Nürnberg, 1521; lute-maker. (2) **Hans**,
d. Nürnberg, 1570; probably son of
above; violinist and vln.-maker.

**Ger'man, J. Edw.**, b. Whitchurch,
Shropshire, England, Feb. 17, 1862;
violin pupil of R. A. M.; 1889, dir.
Globe Th., London; 1901 completed
Arthur Sullivan's unfinished opera
"The Emerald Isle," prod. with
succ. London, 1901; c. operetta; 2
symphonies; various suites, including
the "Gipsy" suite, chamber-music,
songs, etc. His incidental music to
Shakespeare's plays is especially notable.

**Germer** (gĕr'-mĕr), **H.**, b. Sommers-
dorf, Province of Saxony, Dec. 30,
1837; pupil Berlin Akademie; teacher, pianist and writer.

**Gern, August**, organ-builder, London.

**Gernsheim** (gĕrns'-hīm), **Fr.**, b.
Worms, July 17, 1839, of Hebrew
parents; pupil of Rosenhain and
Hauff, Frankfort, and Leipzig Cons.;
1865, teacher of comp. and pf. Cologne Cons.; 1872, Prof.; 1874, dir.
of the Cons. at Rotterdam and cond.
"Winter Concerts"; since 1890 at
Stern Cons., Berlin; c. 4 symphonies,
overtures, etc.

**Gero** (gā'-rō), **Jhan (Johann)** (called
**Maister Jan** or **Jehan**, or **Joannes**

Gallus), **c**onductor and composer at Orvieto Cath., 16th cent.

**Gersbach** (gĕrs'-bäkh), (1) **Joseph**, Säckingen, Baden, 1787—Carlsruhe, 1830; teacher and composer. (2) **Anton**, Säckingen, 1801—Carlsruhe, 1848; bro., pupil and successor of above.

**Gerson** (gĕr-sôṅ), **J. Charlier de**, Gerson, near Rethel, 1363—Lyons, 1429; writer.

**Gerster** (gĕr'-shtĕr), **Etelka**, b. Kaschau, Hungary, June 16, 1857; one of the most remarkable coloraturasopranos of her time; 1874-75, a pupil of Marchesi, Vienna Cons.; v. succ. début Venice, Jan. 8, 1876; m. her impresario Dr. Carlo Gardini and toured Europe and America; lost her voice suddenly and opened (1896) a singing-school, in Berlin.

**Gervasoni** (jĕr-vä-sō'-nē), **Carlo**, Milan, 1762-1819; writer and theorist.

**Gervinus** (gĕr-vē'-noos), **Georg Gf.**, Darmstadt, 1805—Heidelberg, 1871; professor and writer.

**Geselschap** (gĕ-zĕl'-shäp), **Marie**, b. Batavia, Java, 1874 (?); pianist; pupil of X. Scharwenka, Berlin; played in America, etc.; 1895 in London.

**Gesius** (rightly **Göss**) (gä'-sǐ-oos; gĕs), **Bartholomäus**, Müncheberg, ca. 1555—Frankfort-on-Oder, 1613; cantor and composer.

**Gesualdo** (jä-zoo-äl'-dō), **Don Carlo**, Prince of Venosa, d. 1614; one of the most intellectual and progressive mus. of his time; wishing to revive the chromatic and enharmonic genera of the Greeks, he strayed out of the old church-modes and, becoming one of the "chromaticista," wrote almost in modern style.

**Gevaërt** (zhŭ-värt'), **François Auguste**, b. Huysse, near Oudenarde, July 31, 1828; pupil of Sommère (pf.) and Mengal (comp.) at Ghent Cons., taking Gr. prix de Rome for comp.; 1843, organist at the Jesuit church; he prod. 2 operas; lived in Paris (1849-50); then went to Spain and c.

" *Fantasia sobre motivos espa*[  ] still pop. there, for which h[  ] given the order of Isabella la Cat[  ] he sent back reports on Spanis[  ] sic (pub. by the Academy, 185[  ] returned to Ghent 1852, prod. [  ] ras, 2 of them, "*Georgette*" an[  ] *billet de Marguerite*," with muc[  ] cess; in 1857 his festival c[  ] "*De Nationale Verjaerdag*" b[  ] him the Order of Leopold; 1[  ] *chef de chant* Gr. Opéra, Paris; dir. Brussels Cons. (vice Fétis) colls. of Italian music, also the[  ] able fruits of much research plain-song. His "*Traité d'instr*[  ] *tation*" (1863) revised as "*No*[  ] *traité*," etc. (1885), threatens t[  ] plant Berlioz' great work; he also 3 cantatas, "*Missa pro D*[  ] *tis*" and "*Super Flumina*[  ] *lonis*" for male chorus and overture "*Flandre au Lion*," [  ]

**Geyer** (gī'-ĕr), **Flodoard**, Berlin[  ]—1872; prof., critic, theoris[  ] dram. composer.

**Gheyn** (gĕn), **Matthias van den**[  ] mont, Brabant, 1721—Louvain[  ] one of a Flemish family of bell[  ] ers; organist. Of his 17 child[  ] son **Jossé Thos.** (b. 1752) w[  ] successor as organist.

**Ghiselin(g)** (gē-zē-lŭng) (or [  ] **linus**), **Jean**, Netherlandish; [  ] puntist 15-16th cent.

**Ghislanzoni** (gēs-län-tsō'-nē), **A**[  ] co, 1824—Caprino-Bergamasc[  ] barytone and writer.

**Ghizeghem.** Vide HEYNE.

**Ghizzolo** (gēd'-zō-lō), **Gio.**, b.[  ] cia, 1560 (?); monk and comp[  ]

**Ghymers** (gē'-mĕrs), **Jules E**[  ] b. Liège, May 16, 1835; p[  ] Liège Cons.; pianist and critic[  ]

**Gys** (gēs), **Joseph**, Ghent, 18[  ] Petersburg, 1848; violinist, [  ] and composer.

**Giacche** (jäk'-kĕ). Vide BE[  ] **Giacchet'to.** Vide BUUS.

**Giacomelli** (jäk-ō-mĕl'-lē), **Gemi**[  ] Parma, 1686—Naples, 1743; composer.

ni (jäl-dē-nē), **Gialdino,** b. Pes-
Nov. 10, 1843, pupil of Mabel-
Florence, his first opera, "*Ros-
da*," won prize offered by the Per-
Th., Florence, but was unsuc.;
3, prod. 2 "opere buffe" in
aboration, then devoted himself to
d. with great succ.; prod. opera
*Due Soci*" (Bologna, 1892) and
*Pupilla*" (Trieste, 1896) with
ess.

lli (jä-něl'-lē), **Pietro,** (Abbate)
li, Italy, ca. 1770—Venice, 1822
lexicographer.

ttini (jä-nět-tē'-nē) (or **Zanet-
**, A., Venice, 1649—Modena,
: ; dram. composer.

tti (jä-nôt'-tē), **P.,** Lucca—
s, 1765 ; double-bassist, composer
writer.

ini (jär-dē'-nē), **Felice de,** Tu-
1716—Moscow, 1796 ; violinist
dram. composer.

ons, (1) Rev. **Edw.,** ca. 1570—
:650; organist. (2) **Ellis G.,** d. ca.
) ; bro. of above ; organist Salis-
- cath. (3) **Orlando,** Cambridge,
lan d, 1583—Canterbury, June 5,
5 ; bro. of above ; one of the
most of Engl. organists and com-
ers ; Mus. Doc. Oxon ; 1604, or-
1st Chapel Royal ; 1623, organist
stminster Abbey. (4) **Chris-
her,** London, 1615—Oct. 20,
5 ; son of (3), organist and comer.

(gē'-běl) (or **Gibe'lius), Otto,**
nd of Fehmarn (Baltic), 1612—
den, 1682 ; composer.

lini (jē-běl-lē'-nē), **Eliseo,** b. Osi-
Ancona, ca. 1520 ; until 1581
poser and conductor.

t (zhē-bär), **Paul César,** Ver-
es, 1717—Paris, 1787 ; dram.
poser.

t (hē'-běrt) (or **Gisbert, Gispert),
ncisco Xavier,** Granadella,
in—Madrid, 1848 ; priest, cond.
composer.

'ne, **Guillaume Ignace,** b. Lon-
, ca. 1826 ; pianist ; pupil of
scheles ; also dram. composer.

---

**Gide** (zhēd), **Casimir,** Paris, 1804—
1868; composer.

**Gigout** (zhē-goo), **Eugene,** b. Nancy,
France, March 23, 1844; organ-virtuoso, critic, etc.; pupil in the *maîtrise* of Nancy cath.; at 13 entered
Niedermeyer Sch., Paris and was
later teacher there for over 20 years;
studied also with Saint-Saëns; 1863,
organist at the Ch. of St. Augustin;
succ. concert organist throughout
Europe ; 1885, founded an organ-
sch. subsidized by the govt.; commander of the order of Isabella la
Catolica ; 1885, officier of pub. instruction ; 1895, Chev. of the Legion
of Honour ; pub. over 300 Gregorian
and plain-song compositions.

**Gil** (hēl), **Francisco Assis,** b. Cadiz,
1829 ; pupil of Fétis ; prof. of harmony, Madrid ; writer, theorist and
dram. composer.

**Gil y Llagostera** (hēl ē lä-gôs-tā'-rä),
**Caytan,** b. Barcelona, Jan. 6, 1807 ;
first flute at the theatre and cath.,
Barcelona ; c. symphonies, etc.

**Gil'christ, W. Wallace,** b. Jersey
City, N. J., Jan. 8, 1846 ; pupil of
H. A. Clarke at the U. of Penn.;
from 1877 organist and choirm. Christ
Ch., Germantown ; from 1882 teacher Phila. Mus. Acad.; cond. of various choral societies ; c. prize *Psalm
xlvi.* for soli, chorus, orch. and org.
(Cincinnati Festival, 1882), "*Song of
Thanksgiving*" for chorus and orch.;
a cantata " *The Rose* " (1887), etc.

**Giles** (jīlz), **Nathaniel,** near Wor-
cester, Engl., ca. 1550—Windsor,
Jan. 24, 1633 ; organist ; Mus. Doc.
Oxon ; writer and composer.

**Gille** (gēl'-lě), **Karl,** 1897 conductor
at Hamburg City Th.; previously conductor at the Ct.-Th., Schwerin.

**Gilles** (rightly, **G. Brebos)** (zhēl brü-
bŏ), called **Maitre G.,** or "**Mase-
giles,**" d. 1584 ; organ builder at
Louvain and Antwerp.

**Gillet** (zhē-yā), **Ernest,** b. Paris,
Sept. 13, 1856 ; pupil Niedermeyer
Cons.; solo 'cellist Gr. Opéra ; then
lived in London ; c. " *Loin du bal*",

and other pop. and graceful pf.-pieces.

**Gillmeister** (gĭl'-mī-shtĕr), **Carl**, b. Schönebeck, Dec. 25, 1856 ; bass ; studied at the Hochschule, Berlin ; début at Augsburg ; 1888 at Bayreuth, 1900 at Hanover.

**Gil'more, Patrick Sarsfield**, near Dublin, Dec. 25, 1820—St. Louis, Mo., Sep. 24, 1892 ; an immensely popular conductor, some of whose influence went to the popularising of good music ; on occasions he cond. an orch. of 1,000 and a chorus of 10,000, also an orch. of 2,000 and a chorus of 20,000, reinforced with cannon fired by electricity, an organ, anvils, chimes, etc. (cf. Sarti) ; he c. pop. military and dance music.

**Gilson** (zhĕl-sôṅ), **Paul**, b. Brussels, 1869 ; self-taught ; his cantata " *Sinai* " won the Grand prix de Rome, 1892 ; 1896 prod. opera " *Alvar*," Brussels ; completed Ragghianti's opera " *Jean-Marie* " ; c. symph. sketches " *La Mer*," etc.

**Ginguené** (zhăṅ-gŭ-nā), **P. L.**, Rennes, 1748—Paris, 1816 ; writer.

**Giordani** (jôr-dä'-nē), name of a family, father, 3 sisters and 2 brothers, all singers in comic opera at Naples, till 1762 when they came to London (except Giuseppe) ; one of the brothers wrote the still pop. song " *Caro mio ben*." (1) **Tommasa** (rightly **Carmine**), Naples, ca. 1740 — Dublin after 1816 ; dram. composer. (2) **Giuseppe** (called **Giordanel'lo**), Naples, 1744—Fermo, 1798 ; bro. of above ; conductor ; c. 30 operas.

**Giordano** (jôr-dä'-nō), **Umberto**, b. Foggia, Aug. 27, 1867 ; studied with Paolo Cerraos at the Naples Cons. ; notable neo-Italian, living at Milan ; c. operas ; very succ. " *Andrea Chénier* " (La Scala, Milan, 1896 ; also in Berlin, 1898, and U. S.); also " *Marino* " unsucc., " *Regina Diaz* " (Naples, 1894) ; and succ. 3-act melodrama " *Mala Vita* " (Rome, 1892, prod. as " *Il Voto*," Milan, 1897) ; " *Fédora* " and " *Siberia*."

**Giorgi** (jôr'-jē). Vide BANTI.

**Giornovichi.** Vide JARNOVIC.

**Giorza** (jôr'-tsä), **Paolo**, b. [M]1838 ; son and pupil of an or[g] and dram. singer ; studied cpt. La Croix ; lived New York years, later London ; prod. u[n] opera " *Corrado* " (Milan, 1869[)] many very succ. ballets at La S[

**Giosa, Nicola de.** Vide DE GIO[

**Giovanelli** (jō-vä-nĕl'-lē), **Rugg[e]** Velletri, ca. 1560—Rome, ca. 1599 successor of Palestrina as [con]ductor at St. Peter's, Rome ; a[n im]portant composer.

**Giraldoni** (zhē-räl-dō'-nē), **L[** Paris, 1824—Moscow, 1897 ; [bari]tone.

**Girard** (zhē-rär), **Narcisse**, N[a] France, 1797—Paris, 1860 ; co[nduc]tor and violin professor.

**Girardeau** (zhē-rär-dō), **Isab[** called **la Isabella**, Italian sing[er] London, ca. 1700.

**Girelli-Aguilar, ——,** Italian s[inger] in Vienna and London, ca. 1771[.]

**Gismonde** (zhēs-môṅd), **Celest[e** 1735 ; mezzo-soprano.

**Giuglini** (jool-yē'-nē), **Antonio**, [Fos]sane, Pesaro, 1865 ; Italian ten[or.]

**Gizziello** (gĭd-zĭ-ĕl'-lō), **Gioacc[** Vide CONTI.

**Glad'stone, Francis Edw.**, b. [Sum]mertown, near Oxford, May 2, [1845;] pupil of S. Wesley ; one of chief [and] contemporary organists; organist [at vari]ous churches, then became a Ca[tholic] and was until 1894 choir-dir. St. [Mary] of the Angels, Bayswater; 1879 [Mus.] Doc., Cantab ; 1881, prof. of [?]; Trinity Coll., London ; prof[. of] harm. and cpt. R.C.M.; c. an [over]ture, chamber-music, etc.

**Glarea'nus, Henricus** (rightly H[ein]rich **Lo'ris**, Latinised, Lori[tus**]** Glarus, 1488 — Freiburg, Ba[den,] March 28, 1563 ; poet and im[por]tant theorist.

**Glasenapp** (glä'-zĕ-näp), **Karl** [F.,] b. Riga, October 3, 1847 ; st[udied] philosophy at Dorpat ; since [1875] head-master at Riga ; wrote on W[agner]

, a biography in 3 vols., a lexi-
, and a Wagner Encyclopædia,

er (glä'-zĕr), (1) **K. G.,** Weissen-
s, 1784—Barmen, 1829 ; mus. dir.
1 later dealer, composer and
ter. (2) **Fz.,** Obergeorgenthal,
hemia, 1798—Copenhagen, 1861 ;
ductor, violinist, and dram. com-
ser.

(o)unow (glä'-tsoo-nôf), **Alex.,**
St. Petersburg, Aug. 10, 1865 ;
died till 1883 at Polytechnic Inst.,
n took up music ; studied with
nsky - Korsakov ; 1881 his first
nphony was produced, repeated
der Liszt in 1884 at Weimar ; he
nd. his second symphony in Paris,
89 ; his fourth symphony, London
il., 1896–97, with Rimsky-Korsa-
v and Liadov, cond. Russian Sym-
ony Concerts at St. P.; c. 5 sym-
onies, 2 overtures on Greek themes ;
erture "*Carnaval*"; Élegie "*A la
moire d'un héros*"; symphonic
em "*Stenka Rasine*"; symphonic
ture "*The Forest*"; "*Chopini-
a*" orch. suite ; and other orchl.
s., string-quartets, pf.-pcs., suite
S. A. C. H. A. (his nickname) for
, etc.

son (glē'-sŭn), **Fr. Grant,** b.
ddletown, Conn., Dec. 17, 1848 ;
pil of Dudley Buck at Leip-
Cons.; later at Berlin, of Loesch-
, Weitzmann and Haupt ; later
h Beringer (pf.) in London ; 1875
ganist Hartford ; 1877, teacher
rshey Sch. of Music, Chicago ;
tic for years of Chicago *Tribune ;*
(text and music) grand operas
*tho Visconti* " and "*Montezuma*";
atata "*The Culprit Fay,*" with
h.; "Praise-song to Harmony,"
nphonic cantata ; "Auditorium
stival Ode," symph. cantata with
h.; op. 21, "*Edris,*" symphonic
em (after the prologue to "*Ar-
h*" by Marie Corelli), etc.

ch (glīkh), **Ed.,** Erfurt, 1816—
ngebrück, near Dresden, 1898 ;
tic and writer ; c. symphonies.

**Gleichmann** (glīkh'-män), **Jn. G.,**
Steltzen, near Eisfeld, 1685—Ilmenau, 1770 ; organist.

**Gleissner** (glīs'-nĕr), **Fz.,** Neustadt-
on-the-Waldnab, 1760—Munich, after
1815 ; printed songs of his own by
lithographic process, the first music
so printed.

**Gleits** (glīts), **K.,** b. Hetzerode, near
Cassel, Sept. 13, 1862 ; studied Leipzig Cons. and Munich Music School,
and in Berlin ; c. symph.-poem "*Fata Morgana*" (played by Nikisch at
the Berlin Philh. concerts, 1898) ;
"*Ahasuerus,*" "*Venus and Bellona,*"
etc., for orch.; "*Hafbur and Signild,*"
for chorus ; "*Inlichter,*" a pf.-fanta-
sy with orch.; vln.-sonata, etc.

**Glinka** (glĭnk'-ä), **Michail Ivanovitch,** Novospaskoï, near Smolensk,
Russia, June 1 (new style), 1804—
Berlin, Feb. 15, 1857; piano-virtuoso
and composer, father of the new na-
tionalistic Russian Musical School ;
of noble birth ; pupil of Bohm
(vln.), Mayer (theory and pf.), John
Field (pf.). Of very weak health, he
studied vocal composition in Italy ;
1834 with Dehn in Berlin ; prod. at
St. Petersburg, 1836, the first Russian
national opera "*A Life for the Czar*"
(*Zarskaja Skisu* or *Ivan 'Sussanina*),
with succ. still lasting ; the next
opera "*Russlan and Ludmilla*" (St.
P., 1842) was also succ. (book by
Pushkin) ; 1844 in Paris he gave orch.
concerts strongly praised by Berlioz ;
1845–47, Madrid and Seville, where
he c. "*Jota Aragonese,*" a "*Capriccio
brillante*" for orch., and "*Souvenir
d'une nuit d'été à Madrid,*" for
orch.; 1851, Paris ; 1854–55, near
St. Petersburg writing his autobiography, planning a never-attempted
opera ; he visited Dehn at Berlin in
1856, and died there suddenly ; Glinka's other comp. incl. 2 unfinished
symphonies ; 2 polonaises for orch.; a
fantasia, "*La Kamarinskaja*"; a
septet ; 2 string-quartets ; trio for
pf., clar. and oboe ; dramatic scenes ;
vocal-quartets, songs and pf.-pcs.

**Glöggl** (glĕg'-gl), (1) **Fz. .X.**, Linz-on-Danube, 1764—after 1832; conductor, mus. dir.; writer. (2) **Fz.**, Linz, 1797—Vienna, 1872; son of above; est. music business, 1843; writer and mus. director.

**Glover** (glŭv'-ĕr), (1) **Sarah Ann,** Norwich, Engl., 1785—Malvern, 1867; inv. the Tonic Sol-fa system of notation and wrote about it. (2) **Chas. W.,** Feb., 1806—London, 1863; violinist, etc. (3) **Stephen,** London, 1812—Dec. 7, 1870; teacher and composer. (4) **W. Howard,** London, 1819—New York, 1875; violinist and critic; sang in opera. (5) **William,** b. London, 1822; organist, etc.

**Gluck** (glook), **Christoph Wilibald** (Ritter **von**), Weidenwang, near Neumarkt, Upper Palatinate, July 2, 1714—Vienna, Nov. 25, 1787; son of head-gamekeeper to Prince Lobkowitz; at twelve sent to the Jesuit Coll. at Komotau (1726–32), where he learnt the violin, clavecin, and organ, and was chorister in the Ch. of St. Ignaz; at eighteen he went to Prague, earning a living by playing at rural dances, giving concerts and singing and playing in various churches; under the tuition of Father Czernohorsky he mastered singing and the 'cello, his favourite instr.; 1736 entered the service of Prince Melzi, Vienna, who took him to Milan and had him study harm. and cpt. with Sammartini. After four years' study he prod. "*Artaserse*" (La Scala, 1741) with great succ. and was commissioned to c. for other theatres; prod. 8 operas 1742–45. On invitation he went to London 1745 as composer for the Haymarket, in opposition to Händel. "*La Caduca dei Giganti*" was given on the defeat of the Pretender, 1746, "*Artamene*," followed by "*Piramo e Tisbe*," a pasticcio of his best arias had no succ. and led Händel to say that the music was detestable, and that Gluck knew no more counterpoint than his cook.

The operas **G.** had written up t[o that] time were thoroughly Italian. T[he in]-fluence of Händel and Rameau's [work] heard at Paris awakened him [and] led him to that gradual reform [which] made him immortal, thoug[h it] brought on him the most fer[ce] opposition. "*La Semiramide [rico]- nosciuta*" (Vienna, 1748) bega[n the] change to more serious power. [Of] 62 he prod. "*Telemaco*" ([Rome,] 1750), "*La Clemenza di Tito*" ([Na]-ples, 1751), and 4 others. 17[5. . .] he was dir. court-opera Vienna [and] prod. 6 more works. He made [great] succ. in spite of opposition [with] "*Orfeo ed Euridice*" (1762), ["*Al*]-*ceste*" (1767), "*Paride ed E[lena*"] (1769), libretti by Calzabigi. 2[1] inferior works were performe[d by] members of the royal family (176[. .]) the dedicatory prefaces to "*Al[c.*]" and "*Paride ed Elena*," **G[.]** pressed his protest against the I[talian] school, and declared for dramati[c con]-sistency unhampered by rigid f[orm]-læ for arias, duets, etc., and [inter]-polated cadenzas. He had [met] harsh criticism at home and suc[h en]-couragement from du Rollet o[f the] French Embassy at Vienna in [1772] that he went to Paris. But here a[lso he] met such opposition, that all his [di]-macy and all the power of his f[ormer] pupil, Queen Marie Antoinette [bare]-ly availed to bring about the pre[senta]-tion of "*Iphigénie en Aulide*" (1[774] its great succ. was repeated in ["*Or*]-*pheés*" (Aug., 1774), "*Alceste*" (1[776]) and *Armide* (1777). Piccinni [was] brought to Paris as a rival, and [with] "*Roland*" while Gluck was prep[aring] the same subject. Gluck burne[d his] score and published a letter v[hich] precipitated an unimaginably [furious] war of pamphlets. Both men [were] set to composing "*Iphigénie en [Tau]-ride*"; here Gluck forestalled his [rival] by two years (1779), and Picc[ini's] work on appearing was not a s[ucc.] while Gluck's succeeded enorm[ously.] His last opera, "*Echo et Narc[isse*"]

.s not succ. (Sept. 21, 1779); 1780, he
tired to Vienna and lived on his well-
rned wealth, till apoplexy carried
m off. He wrote a De profundis
r chorus and orch., 6 overtures and
an incomplete cantata, "*Das Jüngste
Gericht*," finished by Salieri, and 7
odes for solo voice and pf. Biog. by
A. Schmidt (1854); Marx (1863);
Desnoiresterres (1872).

## Gluck.

### By Ernest Newman.

AKEN up in his twenty-second year by an amateur of Italian music,
and put under Sammartini at Milan, Gluck's earliest models were
Italian. Though his first works showed slight, unconscious traces of
-thern origin, he probably thought, for twenty years, of little more than
ducing opera after opera in the Italian style. The intellectual changes
led to the reform of the opera with *Orfeo* were perhaps due in part to
influence of Rameau and Händel. The French light opera, also, and
own attempts in it, seem to have taught him something of direct, con-
porary expression, as distinguished from the conventional operatic mouth-
of antique sentiments. Apart from these musical influences, he was
ngly swayed by the general æsthetics of the eighteenth century, whose
l of art was the veracious imitation of Nature. He had probably read
arotti's book on the Opera (1763), which advocates many of the reforms
afterwards carried out. ¶ Three rich currents intercrossed in him when
came to consciousness of himself. His Italian practice had given him ease
grace of style; his Northern nature and training made him at home in the
rld of grave and dignified passion; from the French opera he had learned
eek in musical tones the natural correlatives to the verbal idea. To these
ee musical qualities he added the power of penetrating reflection upon the
ence of his art. ¶ The opera, when he took it up, was the laughing-stock
Europe. It left his hands a serious form of art, carefully thought out in
its details, with a new method and unity of purpose. The overture was
de to throw light on the coming drama; the libretto was kept on as high
vel as the taste and subjects of those days would permit; the old distinc-
a of aria and recitative was undermined, the aria becoming more dramatic
ile not ceasing to be lyrical when required, and the recitative being raised
n its previous conventional lines into a living, organic musical speech; the
hestra no longer merely accompanied the singer, but helped in the expres-
n of the emotions of the actor; the senseless vocal ornaments of the Italian
era were discarded, and the singers taught to exist for the opera instead of
opera existing for them; in a word, brains and a purpose occupied the
d hitherto filled only by vanity and imbecility. ¶ Had Europe not under-
ne such startling changes at the end of the last century, Gluck's influence

would have borne great fruit. But the new social and intellectual life bro
in a new world, for which a new music had to be found ; while elsewher
influence was lost sight of in the dazzling artificiality of the later Italian op
Still, all the serious dramatists—Beethoven, Wagner, Weber, Berlioz—
their way made easier by the labour of Gluck. ¶ Like Wagner and B
he stands in a category of his own, seeming almost to be without ance
and without descendants. His place is among the masters of dramatic
and veracious poetic expression. Even yet, indeed, some of his wor
incomparable in these respects.

**Gmeiner** (g'mī'-nĕr), **Lula**, b. Kronstadt, Aug. 16, 1876 ; alto ; studied
vln. with Olga Grigorourcz ; then
studied voice with Gr. Walter and
Emilie Herzog ; lives in Berlin.

**Gnecco** (n'yĕk'-kō), **Francesco**,
Genoa, 1769—Milan, 1810 ; dram.
composer.

**Gobbaerts** (gŭb'-bärts), **Jean Louis**,
Antwerp, 1835—Saint Gilles, near
Brussels, 1886 ; pianist and com-
poser.

**Gobbi** (gôb'-bē), (1) **Henri**, b. Pesth,
June 7, 1842 ; pupil of R. Volkmann,
and Liszt ; music-teacher and critic,
Pesth ; c. a festival cantata celebrating Liszt's public career, etc. (2)
**Aloys**, b. Pesth, Dec. 30, 1844; bro.
of above ; violinist and teacher.

**Göbel** (gā'-bĕl), **K. H.**, Berlin, 1815—
Bromberg, 1879 ; pianist, conductor,
and dram. composer.

**Gockel** (gôk'-ĕl), **Aug.**, Willibadessen,
Westphalia, 1831—1861 ; pianist and
composer.

**Godard** (gō-där), **Benjamin** (**Louis
Paul**), Paris, Aug. 18, 1849—Cannes,
Jan. 11, 1895 ; studied vln. with
Hammer and played in public at 9 ;
then studied with Reber (comp.) and
Vieuxtemps (vln.), Paris Cons.; 1865
pub. a vln.-sonata, later other chamber - compositions ; rec'd the Prix
Chartier from the Institut de France
for merit in the department of chamber-music ; prod. 5 operas, incl. "*Jo-
celyn*" (Brussels, 1888), and the very
succ. posthumous "*La Vivandière*"
(Paris Op.-Com., 1895), the last 2

acts orchestrated by Paul Vida
operas not prod.; he c. also i
mus. and 6 symphonies; "*Le T*
(Tasso), dram. symphony with
and chorus took the city of
prize in 1878 ; concerto for vln
pf.-concerto, songs and pf.-pcs.

**God'dard** (**Davison**), **Arabella**, b.
Servan, near Saint Malo, Britt
Jan. 12, 1838 ; at 4 played in pu
at 6 studied with Kalkbrenne
Paris, at 8 played to Queen Vict
pub. 6 waltzes and studied with
Anderson and Thalberg ; at
played at the Grand National
certs ; 1850–53 pupil of J. W. I
son, whom she m. (1860) ; to
Germany and at 17 played at I
zig Gewandhaus 1855 ; 1873
toured the world ; retired 1880
lived in Tunbridge Wells.

**Godebrye.** Vide JACOTIN.

**Godefroid** (gôd-fwä), (1) **Jules
seph**, Namur, Belgium, 1811—P
1840 ; harpist and dram. compo
(2) **Dieudonné Jos. Guil. Fé**
Namur, 1818—Villers-sur-mer, 1
bro. of above ; harpist and d
composer.

**God'frey**, (1) **Chas.**, Kingston, Su
1790—1863 ; bassoonist and
ductor. (2) **Daniel**, b. Westmin
Engl., Sept. 4, 1831 ; son of ab
pupil R.A.M., later Fellow and I
of Military Mus.; 1856 bandm
the Grenadier Guards ; 1872
1898 toured the U. S. with his ba
composer. ⟨3) **Adolphus Fr**
b. 1837, son of (1) ; conductor.

harles, b. 1839, son of (1) ; con-
ictor.

lowski (gō-dôf'-shkē), Leopold,
Wilna (Vilno), Russian Poland,
eb. 13, 1870 ; pianist ; début and
urs at 9; pupil of Wilna, and 1881–
4 R. Hochschule, Berlin ; at 14
ured America ; 1887–90 studied
ith Saint-Saëns ; 1890–91 toured
merica again ; 1894 dir. pf.-dept.,
road St. Cons., Phila.; 1895–99
ead of pf.-dept., Chicago Cons.;
ien toured Europe ; since 1902 lives
Berlin ; began first comp. at 7 ;
ib. *Moto Perpetuo*, Polonaise in C.;
aborations of Chopin, etc.

pfart (gĕp'-färt), (1) **Chr. H.**, Wei-
ar, 1835—Baltimore, Md., 1890 ;
ganist and composer. (2) **Karl**
duard, b. Weimar, March 8, 1859;
in of above ; since 1891 cond.
aden-Baden Mus. Union ; c. " *Sa-
stro*," a sequel to Mozart's " *Magic
lute*," etc. (3) **Otto Ernst**, b.
'eimar, July 31, 1864 ; bro. of
iove ; since 1888 Weimar town can-
r and composer.

ring (gā'-rĭng), **Th.**, b. Frankfort-
-Main, Oct. 2, 1844 ; critic, 1880–
; Paris, then Munich ; now music
rrespondent Cologne *Zeitung*.

s (gō'-ĕs), **Damião de**, Alemquer,
irtugal, 1501—Lisbon, 1573 ; am-
ssador, theorist and composer.

the (gā'-tĕ), **Walther Wg. von**,
'eimar, 1818—Leipzig, 1885; grand-
n of the poet ; c. 3 operettas, etc.

tschius (gĕt'-shĭ-oos), **Percy**, b.
aterson, N. J., Aug. 30, 1853; pupil
uttgart Cons.; 1876 teacher there ;
85 Royal Prof.; critic for various
erman music papers ; 1890–92 prof.
rracuse (N. Y.) Univ. and Mus.
oc.; 1892–96, taught comp. and
ctured on mus. hist., etc., N. E.
ins., Boston ; since 1896 private
acher Boston, and essayist ; since
97 organist First Parish Ch., Brook-
ie ; pub. important and original
eatises ; c. 2 Concert-Fugues, etc.

tz (gĕts), **Hn.**, Königsberg, Prus-
ı, 1840—Hottingen, near Zurich,

1876 ; 1863, organist and conductor ;
c. operas, songs, etc.

**Gogavi'nus, Ant. Hn.**, Dutch physician at Venice 1552 ; writer.

**Goldbeck** (gōlt'-bĕk), **Robert**, b.
Potsdam, April 19, 1839 ; pupil of
Kohler and H. Litolff ; gave v. succ.
concerts in London and prod. operetta ; 1857–67 in New York as teacher; 1868 founded a Cons. at Chicago;
dir. till 1873 ; cond. the Harmonic
Society, and co-dir. Beethoven Cons.,
St. Louis ; New York, 1885 ; c. 2
operas; cantata, Burger's " *Leonore*,"
etc.

**Goldberg** (gōlt'-bĕrkh), (1) **Jn. G.
(Theophilus)**, Königsberg, ca. 1730
—Dresden (?), 1760 (?) ; organ and
clavichord player. (2) **Jos. Pasquale**, Vienna, 1825—1890; vln.-pupil
of Mayseder and Seyfried, then operatic bass and teacher. His 2 sisters,
(3) **Fanny G.-Marini** and (4) **Catherine G.-Strossi**, are singers.

**Golde** (gōl'-dĕ), (1) **Ad.**, Erfurt, 1830—
1880 ; son and (1872) successor of (2)
**Joseph G.**, dir. Soller Singing-Society, Erfurt.

**Goldmark** (gōlt'-märk), (1) **Karl**, b.
Keszthely, Hungary, May 18, 1830
(not 1832, as usually stated); violinist
and pianist, pupil of Jansa (vln.),
later of Bohm (theory) at the Vienna
Cons., then mainly self-taught ; début 1858, Vienna, with his own pf.-
concerto ; the popular overture "*Sakuntala*" (op. 13); and a Scherzo,
Andante, and Finale for Orch. (op.
19) won him success strengthened by
his opera "*Die Königin von Saba*"
(Vienna, 1875); c. also operas " *Merlin* " (Vienna, 1886) v. succ. ; " *Das
Heimchen am Herd*" based on Dickens' "Cricket on the Hearth" (Vienna, 1896) ; " *Die Kriegsgefangene* "
(Vienna Ct. - opera, 1899) ; " *Der
Fremdling*" (not prod.) and "*Götz
von Berlichingen ;* " c. also 2 symphonies, incl. " *Ländliche Hochzeit*" ;
overtures," *Im Frühling*," " *Prometheus Bound*," and " *Sappho*," etc.
**(2) Rubin**, b. New York City, 1872.

composer; nephew of above; at 7 began to study with A. M. Livonius, with whom he went to Vienna, 1889; studied there also with Door and Fuchs; later in New York with Joseffy and Dvorák; since 1892 lives in Colorado Springs, Colorado; founder and dir. of a Coll. of Mus. there. At 19 c. " *Theme and Variations*" for orch. (performed by Seidl, 1895); c. a pf.-trio, cantata with orch. " *Pilgrimage to Kevlaar*," overture " *Hiawatha* " (played by Boston Symph. Orch.), vln.-sonata, etc.

**Goldner** (gōlt'-něr), **Wm.**, b. Hamburg, June 30, 1839; pupil Leipzig Cons.; lives in Paris as a pianist and composer.

**Goldschmidt** (gōlt-shmǐt), (1) **Sigismund**, Prague, 1815—Vienna, 1877, pianist and composer. (2) **Otto**, b. Hamburg, Aug. 21, 1829; pianist; pupil of Jakob Schmitt and F. W. Grund, Mendelssohn, and Chopin; 1849 London with Jenny Lind, whom he accompanied on her American tour and m. (Boston, 1852); 1852–55 Dresden; 1858–87 London; 1863 vice-principal of the R.A.M., 1875 founded Bach Choir, also cond. mus. festivals at Düsseldorf (1863) and Hamburg (1866); c. oratorio " *Ruth* " (Hereford, 1867); pf.-concerto and trio, etc. (3) **Adalbert von**, b. Vienna, 1853; pupil Vienna Cons.; amateur composer; prod. with great succ. cantata " *Die Sieben Todsünden*" (Berlin, 1875), and succ. opera " *Helianthus* " (Leipzig, 1884); prod. trilogy " *Gaea* " 1889. (4) **Hugo**, b. Breslau, Sept. 19, 1859; 1884 Dr. jur.; studied singing with Stockhausen (1887–90); 1893 co-dir. Scharwenka-Klindworth Cons., Berlin; writer.

**Gold'win, John**, d. Nov., 1719; Engl. organist and composer.

**Golinel'li, Stefano**, b. Bologna, Oct. 26, 1818; pianist; pupil of B. Donelli and N. Vaccai; pf.-prof. Liceo Musicale till 1870; c. 5 pf.-sonatas, etc.

**Gollmick** (gôl'-mǐk), (1) **Fr. K.,** lin, 1774—Frankfort-on-Main, 1 tenor. (2) **Karl**, Dessau, 1 Frankfort-on-Main, 1866; so above; theorist and writer. **Adolf**, Frankfort-on-M., 1825— don, 1883; pianist; son and pu (2); studied also with Riefs 1844; c. comic operas, etc.

**Goltermann** (gôl'-těr-män), (1) **Ed.**, Hanover, 1824—Frankfoi M., 1898; 'cellist and composer **Jn. Aug. Julius**, Hamburg, 1 Stuttgart, 1876; 'cellist. (3) **A** 1826—Schwerin, 1890; court pi

**Gombert** (gôm'-běrt), **Nicolas,** ges, ca. 1495—after 1570; a mos portant 16th cent. composer, o the first to take up secular seriously; a lover of Nature a writer of descriptive and pas songs of much beauty; his " *Paster Noster* " was prod. at by Fétis with impressive effect.

**Gomes** (or **Gomez**) (gö'-mās), **A** nio Carlos, Campinas, Brazil, 11, 1839—Para, Sept. 16, 1896 pil of Rossi, Milan Cons.; D Para Cons.; c. succ. operas " *tor Rosa*," " *Lo Schiavo*," " *A Tudor*," etc.

**Good'ban,** (1) **Thos.**, Canter 1780—1863; writer and cond. 3 sons were (2) **Chas.**, (3) **H Wm.**, 'cellist, and (4) **Thos.**, ist. (5) **Jas. F.**, nephew of (1), ist and organist.

**Good'groome,** (1) **John**, b. ca. composer. (2) **John**, probably s above; organist, 1735. (3) **dore**, Pepys' teacher; probably of (1).

**Good'rich,** (1) **Alfred John**, b. Ohio, May 8, 1847; eminent the except for a year's instruction his father, wholly self-taught; te theory Grand Cons., N. Y., voice, pf. and theory Fort V Cons., Ind.; dir. vocal-dept. Beeth Cons., St. Louis; 2 years at M Washington Coll., Va.; lived in cago, now in New York as tea

꜕. theoretical essays and books of
ical and scholarly nature, the im-
tant products of research and in-
iduality, incl. " *Complete Musical
alysis* " (1889), " *Analytical Har-
ny* " (1894), " *Theory of Inter-
tation.* " (1898), " *Counterpoint.* "
**John Wallace**, b. Boston,
꜕o (?) ; notable organist ; studied
ston, Munich and with Widor,
꜕is ; teacher N. E. Cons., Boston ;
꜕rs in concert ; 1902 chorusmaster
꜕rcester Festival.

ꞁ'son, (1) **Richard**, d. 1718 ; or-
ꞁist and professor at Oxford. (2)
ꞁchard, d. 1741; son and successor
꜕above ; organist.

ꞁ'win, **Amina Beatrice**, b. Man-
꜕ster, Engl.; pupil of her father ;
꜕6 played in public, then studied
ꞁh Reinecke, Jadassohn, Delabord,
꜕zt and Frau Schumann ; 1895
꜕nded a pf.-coll. for Ladies, Lon-
꜕1 ; m. an American, W. Ingram-
ꞁams ; pub. a work on technic and
꜕pf.-pieces.

ꞁaerts (gö'-värts), **Alphonse, J.
André**, b. Antwerp, May 25,
꜕7 ; 1866, assist. librarian, Ant-
꜕rp ; founded an amateur cathedral
꜕ir to cultivate Palestrina and the
ꞁtherland cptists ; 1887 royal ar-
꜕vist, Brussels; writer and composer.

ꞁert (gĕp'-fĕrt), (1) **K. And.**, Rim-
꜕ꞁ, near Würzburg, 1768—Meining-
꜕1818 ; clarinetist and dram. com-
ꞁser. (2) **K. G.**, Weesenstein, near
꜕esden, 1733—Weimar, 1798 ; vln.
ꞁtuoso ; conductor and composer.

ꞁigiani (gôr-dĕd-jä'-nē), (1) **Giov.
ꞁt.**, Mantua, 1795—Prague, 1871;
꜕1 of a musician ; dram. composer.
**Antonio**, a singer. (3) **Luigi**,
꜕dena, 1806—Florence, 1860 ; bro.
꜕(1); dram. composer.

ꞁdon, (1) **John**, Ludgate, 1702—
꜕39 ; Prof. (2) **W.**, Swiss flutist
ꞁEngl. descent ; 1826 began im-
꜕ovements on the flute, which later
꜕hm carried to success, though W.
ꞁwent insane 1836 from discourage-
ꞁent.

34.

**Goria** (gō-rē'-ä), **Alex. Éd.**, Paris,
1823—1860; teacher and composer.

**Gorno** (gôr'-nō), **Albino**, b. Cassalmo-
rano (Cremona), Italy; pupil Milan
Cons., graduating with 3 gold medals ;
pianist and accompanist to Adelina
Patti on Amer. tour 1881–1882 ; then
pf.-prof. Cincinnati Coll. of Music ;
c. opera, cantata " *Garibaldi*," etc.

**Göroldt** (gä'-rôlt), **Jn. H.**, Stempeda,
near Stolberg (Harz), 1773—after
1835 ; mus. dir., writer and composer.

**Gorria, Tobio.** Vide BOITO, ARRIGO.

**Gorter** (gôr'-tĕr), **Albert**, b. Nürnberg,
Nov. 23, 1862 ; studied medicine ;
then music at R. Mus. Sch., Munich ; took 3 prizes for composition ;
studied a year in Italy ; assist. cond.
Bayreuth Festivals ; cond. Breslau,
etc.; 1894–99 assist. cond. Carlsruhe
Ct.-Th., then cond. Leipzig City Th.;
c. (text and mus.) opera " *Harold* "
and comic opera " *Der Schatz des
Rhampsinnit* " (Mannheim, 1894); 2
symphonic poems, etc.

**Goss**, (1) **John Jeremiah**, Salisbury,
1770—1817; alto. (2) Sir **John**,
Fareham, Hants, England; 1800—
London, 1880 ; organist ; knighted,
1872 ; composer and writer.

**Gossec** (gôs'-sĕk) (rightly **Gossé, Gos-
set** or **Gossez**) (gôs-sä), **François
Joseph**, Vergniers, Belgium, Jan.
17, 1734—Passy, near Paris, Feb. 16,
1829; 1741–49 chorister Antwerp
cath.; for 2 years he then studied vln.
and comp.; 1751 Paris, cond. private
orch. of La Popelinière ; then *fer-
mier-général ;* 1754 he pub. his first
symphonies (5 years before Haydn's);
1759 his first string-quartets which
became pop.; 1769 his " *Messe des
Morts* " made a sensation (the " *Tuba
mirum* " being written for 2 orch.,
one for wind. instrs., concealed, a new
effect he repeated in his first oratorio);
1762 cond. of Prince Conti's orch.
at Chantilly ; from 1764 prod. 3-act
operas " *Le Faux Lord*," etc., incl.
succ. " *Les Pêcheurs* " (Comédie It.,
1766) ; 1770 founded Concerts de

Amateurs; 1773 reorganised and cond. the Concerts Spirituels till 1777; 1780–82 assist. cond. Académie de Musique (later Gr. Opera); 1784 founded and dir. École Royale de Chant, the beginning of the Cons. of which (1795) he was an inspector and prof. of comp.; c. 26 symphonies, 3 symphonies for wind, "Symphonie concertante" for 11 insts., overtures, 3 oratorios, etc.; masses with orch.; string-quartets, etc.

**Gost'ling**, Rev. **John**, d. 1733; bass, famous for his range; Purcell wrote for him a song ranging from D–e' (v. PITCH, D. D.).

**Gottschald** (gôt'-shält), **Ernst**, b. Elterlein, Saxony, Oct. 19, 1826; a jurist and writer under pen-name "**von Elterlein**."

**Gottschalg** (gôt'-shälkh), **Alex. W.**, b. Mechelrode, near Weimar, Feb. 14, 1827; pupil Teachers' Seminary, Weimar; succeeding Göpfer there later; court organist, teacher, editor and writer.

**Gottschalk** (gôts'-chôlk), (1) **Louis Moreau**, New Orleans, La., May 8, 1829–Rio de Janeiro, Dec. 18, 1869; brilliant and original pianist and composer; studied in Paris; began c. at 10; c. operas, etc., and 90 pf.-pcs. of distinct and tropical charm. (2) **Gaston**, bro. of above, singer and for years teacher in Chicago.

**Götze** (gĕt'-zĕ), (1) **Jn. Nik. K.**, Weimar, 1791—1861; violinist and dram. composer. (2) **Fz.**, Neustadt-on-Orla, 1814—Leipzig, 1888; tenor, teacher and composer. (3) **Karl**, Weimar, 1836—Magdeburg, 1887; pianist and dram. composer. (4) **H.**, b. Wartha, Silesia, April 7, 1836; studied singing with (2); lost his voice; teacher in Russia and Breslau; 1885 Ziegenhals, Silesia; 1889 Royal Mus. Dir.; wrote 2 technical books; c. a mass with orch., etc. (5) **Auguste**, b. Weimar, Feb. 24, 1840; daughter of (2); teacher Cons., Dresden; founded a school there; 1891 taught at Leipzig Cons.; wrote

under name "**Auguste Wein** (6) **Emil**, b. Leipzig, July 19, pupil of Scharfe, Dresden; 187 tenor Dresden Ct.-Th., then a logne Th., then toured as " 1900 lived in Berlin as court-si (7) **Otto**, 1886, conductor at Esse Ruhr; prod. succ. opera "Risc (Sondershausen, 1896). (8) **Fz.**, prod. Volksoper "Utopia" (St 1892) and 1-act opera "Die Ro. Thiessow" (Glogau, 1895). **Marie**, b. Berlin, Nov. 2, alto, studied Stern Cons. and Jenny Meyer and Levysohn; Berlin opera, then at Hamburg Th.; 2 years in America; 1892 I ct.-opera.

**Goudimel** (goo-dĭ-mĕl), **Claude**, son, near Avignon, ca. 1505—kill St. Bartholomew massacre, L Aug. 24, 1572; pupil perhaps of quin Desprès; est. a school formed Palestrina and other p winning name; "Father of the man School"; a music printer time; his important comp. incl. " Psalms of David," complete.

**Gould**, **Nathaniel Duren**, Che ford, Mass., 1781—Boston, 1 conductor and writer.

**Gounod** (goo-nō), **Charles F** **çois**, Paris, June 17, 1818—Oct 1893; son of a talented painter engraver; his mother taught him pf. and he entered the Lycée S Louis; 1836 studied at the Cons. with Reicha (harm.), Ha (cpt. and fugue), Lesueur and (comp.); took 2nd Prix de R with cantata "Marie Stuart et zio" in 1837; his cantata "Fer da" won the Grand Prix de Rom 1839, and he studied church mus Rome; 1841 his orch. mass was formed; in 1842 he cond. his quiem at Vienna with great su returned to Paris as precentor an ganist of the Missions Étrangè studied theology 2 years, intende take orders and was called l'A **Gounod** by a publisher in 1846;

years of seclusion, parts of his *esse Solennelle* were played with ofound succ. in London ; he prod. symphony, but his opera "*Sappho*" led (Gr. Opéra, 1851) ; revised 84, it failed again ; a gr. opera, *La Nonne Sanglante*" (1854), and comic opera, "*Le Médecin Malgré ui*" (played in London as "The ock Doctor") (1858), both failed ; 52–60 cond. the "Orphéon," Paris, d c. choruses and 2 masses. The era "*Faust*" (Th. Lyrique, 1859) s and still is a great succ. "*Philé on et Baucis*" (1860); "*La Reine de bä*" (in London as "Irène") (1862); *Mireille*" (1864), "*La Colombe*" 866), were not great works, but *Roméo et Juliette*" (1867) still holds e stage ; 1866 member of the Insti- t de France and commander of the gion of Honour. In 1870, during e war he lived in London ; founded unod's Choir. In 1871 he prod. *Gallia*," a cantata based on "Lam- tations" ; 1875 returned to Paris, od."*Cinq Mars*" (Opéra Comique,

1877),"*Polyeucte*" (Gr. Opéra, 1878), and "*Le Tribut de Zamora*" (1881), none succ. The sacred trilogy "*La Rédemption*" (Birmingham, 1882) (music and French words), and "*Mors et Vita*" (Birmingham, 1885) (Latin text arranged by Gounod) are stand- ard. He also c. "*Messe Solennelle à Ste. Cecile*" ; masses; "*Angeli custo des*" (1882); "*Jeanne d'Arc*" (1887); a Stabat Mater with orch.; the orato- rios "*Tobie*," "*Les Sept Paroles de Jésus*," "*Jésus sur le Lac de Tibé- riade*" ; the cantatas "*A la Fron- tière*" (1870, Gr. Opéra), "*Le Vin des Gaulois*," and "*La Danse de l'Épée*," the French and English songs, etc. He left 2 operas, "*Maî- tre Pierre*" (incomplete) and "*Georges Dandin*" (said to be the first comic opera set to prose text, cf. Bruneau). He wrote "*Méthode de cor à pistons*," essays, etc. Biog. by Jules Clarétie (Paris, 1875); Mme. Weldon (London, 1875) ; Paul Voss (Leipzig, 1895) ; "*Mémoires*" (Paris, 1895).

## Gounod.

### BY VERNON BLACKBURN.

OUNOD'S music belongs entirely to a world of its own. In a word, he made that world, and then he set his music in it. You would not say that it was first-rate by any means, and you would not the heart to say that it was second-rate. But, just as the old writers con- ed a condition after death in which man received neither reward nor pun- ent, a sort of midway house where the dross of the flesh had not been nged and where the fire of the spirit had not entirely departed, so Gounod kind of mingled spirit in music. He is the idol of gold with the feet of ¶Yet he had one note, one separate characteristic in his music which certainly divide him from every other musician in the world. None ounded as he has sounded the peculiar note of eroticism which is absolutely al. Instance it by one example (the song of *Marguérite* at the end of second act of "*Faust*," when she throws open the window to give ex- sion to her emotion) as a creation of sexualness which no other song in world has probably possessed. I have heard it said that the performance of Gounod's masses in Paris used to be regarded by ladies of fashion quality as something in the light of an orgy. For this was Gounod's d inant note, his dominant quality. ¶He was not a master of melody, bu wrote quite beautiful melodies. He was not a master—and in each ca am using the word " master " in the superlative sense—of technique, bu had a mystic-second-rate mystic, but, all the same, mystic, quality in work. He was not really dramatic ; *"Philémon et Baucis,"* *"Faust,"* *Roméo,"* are there to prove so much ; but he was charming in just not great way. As a song-writer, though, he often achieved something greatness. The much-hackneyed " *Quand tu chantes,"* "*Nazareth,"* b above all, *"Le Juif Errant,"* prove that in little flights of emotion, sepa swingings into the sky, as it were, Gounod could do as well as anybo But he was not a great master ; he was a great contemporary, as I have s elsewhere, and his death was mourned by contemporaries. Whether fut generations will rank him any higher than Emanuel Bach, time alone prove. ¶Gounod's personality can scarcely be said to have made any pression upon the world, and his influence died like a bright " exhalation the evening." You can prove it to-day only in mediocre song-writers.

---

**Gouvy** (goo-vē)**, Louis Théodore,** Goffontaine, Rhenish Prussia, 1819— Leipzig, 1898 ; pianist and composer.
**Gow,** (1) **Niel,** Strathband, 1727— Inver, Scotland, 1807 ; violinist and composer. (2) **Nathaniel,** 1766 — 1831 ; son of above, also violinist and composer. (3) **Donald,** brother of (1), was a 'cellist. And (4) **Niel, Jr.,** 1795—1823, son of (2), was violinist and composer. (5) **George Coleman,** b. Ayer Junction, Mass., Nov. 27, 1860 ; studied with Blodgett, Pittsfield and Story (Worcester) ; graduate Brown Univ., 1884, and Newton Theol. Seminary, 1889 ; then teacher of harm. and pf. Smith College ; studied with Büssler in Berlin ; 1895 prof. of music Vassar Coll.; composer and writer.
**Graan** (grän)**, Jean de,** Amsterdam, 1852—The Hague, 1874 ; violinist.
**Graben-Hoffmann** (grä'-bĕn hôf'-män), **Gustav** (rightly **Gustav Hoffmann**), Bnin, near Posen, March 7, 1820—Potsdam, May 21, 1900 ; singing teacher, writer and composer.

**Grabert** (grä'-bĕrt), **Martin,** b. A walde, May 15, 1868 ; studied Bargiel and Bellerman, Berlin, R for church-music, 1891 winning M erbeer-stipend, 1894 Mendelss prize; lived in Berlin as organist, c dir. and composer of choruses, et
**Grabu(t)** (grä-bü), **Louis** (or **Lew** French operatic composer at the I lish court, 1666-90.
**Grädener** (grä'-dĕ-nĕr), (1) **K. G.** Rostock, 1812 — Hamburg, 18 dir., conductor, writer, and dr composer. (2) **Hermann (Th. Ot** b. Kiel, May 8, 1844 ; son and p of above; later studied Vienna Cc 1873 teacher harmony Horak's Sch., later Vienna Cons.; from lecturer on harm. and cpt. Vie Univ.; cond. Singakademie ; c. priccietta and Sinfonietta for o (op. 14), etc.
**Graew** (gräv). Vide BACFART.
**Graffigna** (gräf-fēn'-yä), **Achille,** Martino Dal l'Argine, Italy, 18 Padua, 1896 ; conductor, teac and dram. composer.

a'ham, **Geo. F.,** Edinburgh, 1790
–1867 ; composer and writer.

ammann (gräm'-män), **Karl,** Lü-
·eck, 1844—Dresden, 1897 ; dram.
omposer and writer.

andi (grän'-dē), **Ales. de,** Venice (?)
—Bergamo, 1630 ; singer and com-
)oser.

andval (grän-văl), Mme. **Marie
Félicie Clémence de Reiset,**
Vicomtesse **de,** b. Saint-Remy-des-
Monts (Sarthe), France, Jan. 20,
830 ; pupil of Flotow and Saint-
Saëns (comp.) ; prod. the operas
' *Piccolini* " (Op.-Com., 1868), " *Les
Fiances des Rosa* " (Th.-Lyr., 1863),
' *Atala* " (Paris, 1888), " *Mazeppa* "
Bordeaux, 1892) and others ; won
he Prix Rossini with oratorio " *La
Fille de Jaïre.*" " drame sacré,"
" *Sainte-Agnès* " in MS.; has prod.
symph. works and songs ; sometimes
wrote under pen-names " **Tesier,
Valgrand, Jasper, Banger,**" etc.

an'inger, **Chas. Alb.,** b. Cincinnati, Jan. 2, 1861 ; pupil Coll. of
Mus.; dir. several mus. societies ;
prof. in the College for Music.

ranjon (grän-zhôṅ), **Robert,** music-
printer, Paris, Lyons and Rome, 1582.

an'om, **Louis C. A.,** English composer, 1751.

raphäus (grä'-fĕ-oos), **Hieronymus,**
d. May 7, 1556 ; music-printer Nürnberg from 1533.

rassini (gräs-sē'-nē), **Josephina,**
Varese, Lombardy, 1773 — Milan,
1850 ; Italian soprano of remarkable
talent and beauty.

ras (dorü-gräs), Mme. **Julia Aimée
Dorus,** Valenciennes, 1807—retired,
1850 ; operatic singer Paris and London.

rasse (gräs), **Edwin,** b. New York
City, 1874 ( ?) ; blind violinist ; pupil
of Carl Hauser, N. Y.; at 13, of
César Thomson, Brussels, then at
the Cons., taking 1st prize ; 1901
took " Prix de Capacité " ; début
Berlin, Feb. 22, 1902, with great
succ.

rasset (gräs-sä), **J. Jacques,** Paris,

ca. 1767—1839 ; violinist, conductor,
professor, etc.

**Gratiani.** Vide GRAZIANI.

**Graumann** (grow'-män), **Mathilde.**
Vide MARCHESI.

**Graun** (grown), (1) **Aug. Fr.,** 1727–
71, tenor, cantor. (2) **Jn. Gl.,** 1698
—Berlin, 1771 ; bro. of above ; violinist ; pupil of Pisendel and Tartini;
in service of Fredk. the Great and
cond. of Royal band ; c. 40 symphonies, etc. (3) **K. H.,** Wahrenbrück,
Prussian Saxony, May 7, 1701—Berlin, Aug. 8, 1759 ; bro. of above ; organist, singer, court-conductor, and
composer.

**Graupner** (growp'-nĕr), **Chp.,** Kirchberg, Saxony, 1683 — Darmstadt,
1760 ; dram. composer.

**Graziani** (grä-tsē-ä'-nē), (1) (Padre)
**Tommaso,** b. Bagnacavallo, Papal
States ; conductor and composer of
16th cent. (2) (or **Gratiani**) **Boniface,** Marino, Papal States, ca. 1606
—Rome, 1664 ; cond. and composer.
(3) **Ludovico,** Fermo, Italy, 1823—
1885 ; tenor. (4) **Francesco,** Fermo, April 16, 1829—Fermo, June 30,
1901, bro. of above ; barytone, sang
in Italy, Paris, New York.

**Grazzini** (gräd-zē'-nē), **Reginaldo,**
b. Florence, Oct. 15, 1848 ; studied
R. Cons. with T. Mabellini ; op.-
cond. in Florence, later prof. of mus.
theory and artistic dir. Liceo Benedetto Marcello, Venice ; c. symphonies ; a mass with orch., etc.

**Great'orex, Thos.,** North Wingfield,
Derby, Engl., 1758—Hampton, near
London, 1831 ; organist. teacher, and
composer (1789-93) ; then conductor.

**Greco** (grä'-kō) (or **Grec'co**), **Gaetano,**
b. Naples, ca. 1680 (?) ; composer
and teacher.

**Greef** (gräf), (1) **Wm.,** Kettwig-on-
Ruhr, 1809—Mors, 1875 ; organist
and singing teacher. (2) **Greef-An-
driessen.** Vide STAHMER, A.

**Green, Samuel,** London, 1730—Isle-
worth, 1796 ; organ-builder.

**Greene,** (1) **Maurice,** London, 1696
(1695 ?)—1755 ; teacher and compos-

er. (2) **(Harry) Plunket,** b. Old Connaught House, Co. Wicklow, Ireland, June 24, 1865 ; basso ; studied with Hromada and Goetschius, Stuttgart, 1883–86, and 6 months with Vannuccini of Florence ; later with J. B. Welch and Alf. Blume, London ; début, Jan. 21, 1888, in "*Messiah*" ; début in opera at Covent Garden, 1890 ; excels in recitals ; has sung frequently in America.

**Greet'ing, Thos.,** teacher of flageolet, London, latter half 17th cent. ; taught Pepys.

**Grefinger** (or **Gräfinger**) (grä'-fĭng-ĕr), **Jn. W.,** Vienna, 16th cent. composer.

**Gregh** (grĕg), **Louis,** Paris music-publisher ; 1894 prod. pantomime ; vaudeville operettas, etc.

**Gregoir** (grŭg-wär), (1) **Jacques Mathieu Joseph,** Antwerp. 1817—Brussels, 1876 ; teacher and dram. composer. (2) **Éd.,** Turnhout, near Antwerp, Nov. 7, 1822—Wyneghem, June 28, 1890 ; bro. and pupil of above ; pianist, dram. composer and writer.

**Gregoro'vitch, Charles,** b. St. Petersburg, Oct. 25, 1867 ; violinist ; pupil of Wieniawski, Dont and Joachim ; 1896–97 toured Europe and America.

**Greg'ory I.** ("The Great"), Rome, 540–604 ; Pope from 590 ; reformer and reviser of Roman Catholic ritual. v. GREGORIAN and MODES (D.D.).

**Grell, Ed. Aug.,** Berlin, 1800—Steglitz, near Berlin, 1886 ; organist, conductor, prof. and composer.

**Grenié** (grŭn-yä), **Gabriel Jos.,** Bordeaux, 1757—Paris, 1837 ; inv. of the *orgue expressif* (v. HARMONIUM, D. D.), which Érard improved.

**Gresnich** (grĕn-ĭsh), **Ant. Frédéric,** Liège, 1755—Paris, 1799 ; conductor and dram. composer.

**Gréta** (grä'-tä), **Jeanne** (née **Greta Hughes**), b. Lancaster, Mo. ; coloratura soprano ; studied with Gottschalk, Chicago, Agramonte, New York, Mme. La Grange, Critikos.

and Dubulle, Paris ; début St. Ja Hall, London, 1897 ; toured Eng and Scotland with great success, w at a concert before the Princes Teck she caught a severe cold, ne sitating a long retirement ; now s ing again in New York ; 1899, Herbert Witherspoon.

**Grétry** (grä-trwē), (1) **André Err Modeste,** Liège, Feb. 9, 174 Montmorency, near Paris, Sept. 1813 ; dram. composer ; son of a linist. Chorister at 6, but dismi for incapacity at 11, then pupi Leclerc and Renekin. R. failin keep him to the strict course of Moreau later tried with equal fail 1758 he prod. 6 symphonies at Li 1759 a mass for which the Canon Harlez sent him to study in Ro to which he walked ; he studied and comp. with Casali and Mar for 5 years, but was again dismi as impossible ; a dramatic interme "*Le Vendemmiatrice*," was s 1765, but reading Monsigny's "*A et Colas*," he decided that his rest dramatic longings were best adap for French opéra comique. He wa long time finding a fit librettist ("V taire declining his invitation). reached Paris slowly *via* Gene where he taught singing a year ; prod. the succ. 1-act "*Isabelle Gertrude.*" In Paris after 2 ye hardships his "*Les Mariages S nites*" was rehearsed, and though prod., won him a patron in Co Creutz, the Swedish Minister, v secured him as libretto Marmon comedy "*Le Huron.*" This prod. (Op.-com., 1768) with a gr succ., enjoyed also in extraordin degree by an astounding series works, mostly comic and mostly s cessful, the best of which are "*A cile*," "*Le Tableau Parlant*" (17 "*Les Deux Avares*," "*Zémire Azor*" (1771), "*Le Magnifiqu* (1773) ; "*La Rosière de Salen* (1774) ; "*La Fausse Magie*" (17 "*Le Jugement de Midas*" (in wh e satirised the old French music and its rendition at the Académie), and "*L'Amant Jaloux*" (1778); the grand opera "*Andromaque*" 1780) (in which the chief rôle is accompanied by 3 flutes throughout); "*La Double Épreuve*" (or "*Colinette à la cour*") (1782); "*Théodore et Pauline*" (or "*L'Épreuve villa-reoise*"); and "*Richard Cœur de Lion*" (his best work, still played in Paris); the gr. opera "*La Caravane u Caïre*" (1785, performed 506 times; libretto by the Comte de Provence, later Louis XVIII.); "*La Rosière Republicaine*" (1793); "*La Fête de i Raison*" (prod. 1794 during the Revolution); "*Lisbeth*"; "*Anacre-n chez Polycrate*" (1797); c. 50 operas in all, remarkable for sponta-eity, grace and fervour of melody, dramatic effect and general charm, but open to serious criticism as works of formal art. He was called 'the Molière of music." Mozart and Beethoven wrote Variations on themes of his. Once launched, his progress was a triumph of honour of all kinds; in 1802 Napoleon made him Chev-llier of the Legion of Honour with a pension of 4,000 francs. He bought Rousseau's former residence at Mont-morency and retired there; wrote *Memoirs*, etc. He had several chil-dren, including the gifted Lucille (v. *nfra*), all of whom he outlived. He left 6 unprod. operas and c. also 6 symphonies; 6 pf.-sonatas, 6 string-quartets, church-mus., etc. Biog. by his nephew, A. J. G. (1815); Grégoir (1883); Brunet (1884), etc. (2) **Lu-cille**, Paris, 1773-93; daughter of above, who instrumented her opera "*Le Mariage d'Antonio*," written and prod. at the Op.-Com., with succ. when she was only 13; the next year her opera "*Toinette et Louis*" was not a success; she married un-happily and died at 20.

**eulich** (groi'-lïkh), (1) **K. W.**, Kunzendorf, Silesia, 1796 — 1837; teacher and composer. (2) **Ad.,**

Posen, 1819—Moscow, 1868; teach-er and composer. (3) **Ad.**, Schmiede-berg, Silesia, 1836—Bresiau, 1890; conductor, bass., organist and com-poser.

**Grieg** (grēg), **Eduard Hagerup**, b. Bergen, June 15, 1843; pupil of his mother, a pianist; at 15 entered Leipzig Cons.; pupil of Hauptmann and Richter (harm. and cpt.); Rietz and Reinecke (comp.); Wenzel and Moscheles (pf.); then with Gade, Copenhagen. With the young Nor-wegian composer Rikard Nordraak, he conspired, as he said, "Against the effeminate Mendelssohnian-Gade Scandinavianism, turning with enthu-siasm into the new, well-defined path along which the Northern School is now travelling." 1867 Grieg founded a Musical Union in Christiania and was cond. till 1880; 1865 visited Italy, again in 1870, meeting Liszt in Rome. 1879 he performed his pf.-concerto at the Gewandhaus, Leipzig. Since 1880 lives chiefly in Bergen; lately cond. the Christiania Phil.; 1888 played his concerto and cond. his 2 melodies for string-orch. at Lon-don Phil. 1894 Mus. Doc. Cantab. C. concert-overture "*In Autumn*"; op. 20, "*Vor der Klosterpforte*," for solo, female voices and orch.; "*Landerkennung*" for male chorus with orch.; "*Der Einsame*" for bary-tone, string orch. and 2 horns; op. 35, "Norwegische Tänze," for orch.; op. 40, "*Aus Holzberg's Zeit*," suite for string orch.; "*Bergliot*," melo-drama 1 with orch.; "*Peer Gynt*," suites 1 and 2 for orch.; op. 50, "*Olav Trygvason*," for solo, chorus, and orch.; "*Sigurd Jorsalfar*" for orch., etc.; op. 22, 2 songs for male voices and orch.; various pcs. for string orch., string-quartet in G min.; pf.-concerto; pf.-sonatas, 3 vln.-so-natas, a 'cello-sonata, also for pf.-"*Poetische Tonbilder*," Romanzen and Balladen; several sets of "*Ly-rische Stücke*," "*Symphonische Stücke*" (4 hands), "*Norwegische*

*Volkslieder und Tänze," " Bilder aüs dem Volksleben," Peer Gynt* suite No. 1 (4 hands), and many songs, incl. song-cycle to Garborg's " *Ha tussa."* Biog. by Ernest Clos (Fischbacher, Paris, 1892).

## Eduard Grieg.

### By Henry T. Finck.

WHEN Hans von Bülow called Grieg the Norwegian Chopin doubtless had in mind the melodic fertility, the harmonic ori nality and boldness, the eloquence of style, and the almost exc sive devotion to the shorter forms of composition, which these two mast have in common. There is another point of resemblance. For a long ti musicians believed that the striking peculiarities of Chopin's music were c to the influence on him of the Polish folk-music, whereas, in truth, they only the product of his own genius. The same must be said of Grieg w reference to the Norwegian folk-songs, which are generally supposed to ha been the sources of his inspiration. It is only necessary to study these folk-sor of Norway to see how utterly erroneous this idea is. He caught their spirit half melancholy, half wild—but his melodies and harmonies are his own, a they are more beautiful than any folk-music. ¶ As a youth he came und the influence of Schubert, Schumann, Chopin, and Wagner, but in his so (beginning with the third Grieg Album in the Peters edition) he is all Gri and the same is true of his pianoforte and other instrumental pieces. Ap from a concerto for the pianoforte, three sonatas for piano and violin, one piano and 'cello, a few choruses, an overture and a few orchestral sui (among which the two *Peer Gynt* are best known), he has written only sor (120 up to date), and a large number of short pianoforte pieces. Half dozen of his songs have been arranged with pianoforte accompaniments. As a harmonist Grieg is even bolder than Wagner and Liszt; he has spok the last word in modulation. His best productions are still far too lit known. His music has influenced nearly all the younger Scandinavian co posers, and not a few others, who sometimes help themselves to his ideas, the innocent belief that they are simply copying Norwegian folk-melodi A kindred spirit to Grieg is the most original of American composers, Edwa MacDowell.

**Griepenkerl** (grē´-pĕnk-ĕrl), (1) **F. K.**, Peine, Brunswick, 1782—Brunswick, 1849; Prof. (2) **W. Rob.**, Holwyl, 1810—Brunswick, 1868; son of above; teacher and writer.

**Griesbach** (grēs´-bäkh), (1) **John Hy.**, Windsor, 1798—London, 1875; of the 'cellist. (2) **J. C. G.**, pian 'cellist, dir. and writer.

**Griesinger** (grē´-zǐng-ĕr), **G. Aug.**, Leipzig, 1828; writer.

**Griffin,** (1) **Thos.**, English org

uilder 18th cent. (2) **George Eu-ene**, 1781—London, 1863; Engl. anist and composer.

**ll**, (1) **F.**, d. Odenburg, Hungary, a. 1795; composer, etc. (2) **Leo**, Pesth, Feb. 24, 1846; pupil of F. achner; since 1871 teacher of cho-al singing and theory Leipzig Cons.; overture "*Hilarodia*," 1892.

**llet** (grĕ-yä), **Laurent**, b. Sancoins, her, France, May 22, 1851; pupil of .. Martin ('cello), E. Mangin (harm.), nd Ratez (cpt. and fugue); cond. arious theatres; 1886 Nouveau-irque, Paris; writer; c. comic opera "*Graciosa*" (Paris 1892), ballets, etc.

**mm**, (1) **Fr. Melchior**, Baron **von**, Ratisbon, 1723—Gotha, 1807; one f the advocates and controversial-sts for the Ital. *opera buffa*. (2) **Karl**, Hildburghausen, 1819—Frei-urg, Silesia, 1888; 'cellist and com-oser. (3) **K. Konst.**, lived in Ber-in, 1820—1882; harpist. (4) **Ju-ius Otto**, b. Pernau, Livonia, March , 1827; pianist; pupil of Leipzig Cons.; founded vocal society at Göttingen, then R. Mus. Dir. Mun-ster Academy and cond.; c. a sym-phony, 2 suites in canon-form, etc.

**im'mer, Chr. Fr.**, Mulda, Saxony, 1800—1850; composer.

**isar** (grĕ-zăr), **Albert**, Antwerp, Dec. 26, 1808—Asnières, near Paris, June 15, 1869; prolific dram. com-poser; biog. by Pougin, Paris.

**isart** (grĕ-zär), **Chas. J. Bapt.**, prod. light operas in minor theatres, the last "*Le Petit Bois*" (1893) and "*Voilà le Roi*" (1894).

**risi** (grē'-zē), (1) **Giuditta**, Milan, July 28, 1805—near Cremona, May 1, 1840; famous mezzo-soprano; pupil of Milan Cons.; m. Count Barni, 1834. (2) **Giulia**, Milan, July 28, 1811—Berlin, Nov. 29, 1869; sister and pupil of above; famous dra-matic soprano; pupil of Giacomelli, Pasta and Marliani; m. Count Mel-cy, later m. Mario.

**ritzinger** (grĭts'-ĭng-ĕr), **Léon**, b. Bojan, Austria, Sept. 20, 1856;

tenor; studied in Vienna and sang 10 years at the opera house there; then in various cities, 1900 Bruns-wick court-theatre.

**Groninger** (grō'-nĭng-ĕr), **S. van**, b. Deventer, Holland, June 23, 1851; pupil of Raif and Kiel, Berlin; pian-ist; teacher in Zwolle, The Hague; now at Leyden; composer.

**Grosheim** (grōs'-hīm), **G. Chr.**, Cassel, 1764—1847; dram. composer.

**Grosjean** (grō-zhäṅ), (1) **J. Romary**, Rochesson, Vosges, France, 1815—St. Dié, 1888; org. composer and writer. (2) **Ernest**, b. Vagney, Dec. 18, 1844; nephew of above; organist at Verdun.

**Gross** (grôs), **Jn. Benj.**, Elbing, West Prussia, 1809—St. Petersburg, 1848; 'cellist and composer.

**Gros'si** (grôs'-sē), (1) **G. F.** Vide SI-FACE. (2) **Carlotta** (rightly **Char-lotte Grossmuck**), b. Vienna, Dec. 23, 1849; coloratura singer; studied in the Cons. there; 1869-78 at the Berlin Opera.

**Gross'man, Louis**, b. Kalisz, Po-land, 1835; c. overtures "*Lear*" and "*Marie*," and succ. operas "*Fisherman of Palermo*" (Warsaw, 1866) and "*Woyewoda's Ghat*" (1872).

**Grove**, Sir **George**, Clapham, Surrey, Aug. 13, 1820—London, May 28, 1900; civil engineer; Sec. to the So-ciety of Arts; 1852, Sec., and 1873 a member of the Board of Directors, Crystal Palace; edited *Macmillan's Magazine;* later dir. of the Royal Coll. of Mus.; 1883, knighted; 1875 D.C.L. Univ. of Durham; 1885 LL.D., Glasgow; wrote important book "*Beethoven and His Nine Symphonies*" (1896), etc., and was the editor-in-chief 1879-89 of the mu-sical dictionary known by his name.

**Grua** (groo'-ä), (1) **C. L. P.**, court-conductor at Mannheim and com-poser, 1700—1755. (2) **Paul**, Mann-heim, 1754—Munich, 1833; son of above; conductor and dram. com-poser.

**Gruber** (groo'-bĕr), **Jn. Sigismund**, Nürnberg, 1759—1805 ; lawyer and writer.

**Grucnberg** (grün'-bĕrkh), **Eugene**, b. Lemberg, Galicia, Oct. 30, 1854 ; violinist ; pupil at Vienna Cons.; for 10 years member Leipzig Gewandhaus Orch.; then (till 1898) Boston Symph. Orch. ; for 3 years vln.-teacher at the Boston Cons.; later at the N. Engl. Cons.; pub. "Theory of Violin Playing"; studies, essays, etc.; c. a symphony (performed at the Gewandhaus), etc.

**Grün** (grün), **Friederike**, b. Mannheim, June 14, 1836 ; soprano, at first in the opera-chorus, then sang solo parts at Frankfort, later (1863) at Cassel and 1866–69 Berlin ; 1869 m. Russian Baron von Sadler ; studied with Lamperti at Milan and continued to sing with success.

**Grünberg** (grün'-bĕrkh), (1) **Paul Emil Max**, b. Berlin, Dec. 5, 1852 ; violinist ; leader at Sondershausen, later at Prague ; now teacher in Berlin. (2) Vide GRUENBERG.

**Grünberger** (grün'-bĕrkh-ĕr), **Ludwig**, Prague, 1839—1896 ; pianist and composer.

**Grund** (groont), **Fr. Wm.**, Hamburg, 1791—1874 ; conductor and dram. composer.

**Grünfeld** (grün'-fĕlt), (1) **Alfred**, b. Prague, July 4, 1852 ; pianist and composer ; pupil of Hoger and Krejci, later at Kullak's Academy, Berlin ; 1873, chamber-virtuoso, Vienna ; toured Europe and the U. S. (2) **Heinrich**, b. Prague, April 21, 1855 ; bro. of above ; 'cellist; pupil of Prague Cons.; 1876, teacher in Kullak's Academy ; 1886 'cellist to the Emperor.

**Grüning** (grü'-nĭngk), **Wilhelm**, b. Berlin, Nov. 2, 1858 ; tenor, studied Stern Cons.; sang in various theatres ; toured America ; then 1889–97 at Bayreuth as Parsifal, Siegfried, etc.; 1900 Berlin court-opera.

**Grus** (grüs), **Léon**, 1835—Paris, July, 1902. Publisher ; also c. under name "**Elsen.**"

**Grützmacher** (grüts'-mäkh-ĕr), **Fr. Wm. L.**, b. Dessau, March 1832 ; eminent 'cellist ; son and pil of a chamber-musician at Dess later studied with Drechsler ('ce and Schneider (theory) ; at 16 joi a small Leipzig orch.; was "disc ered" by David, and at 17 made 'cello, Gewandhaus orch. and tea er at the Cons.; 1869 Dresden, la Cologne ; 1902 Philadelphia ; c. c certo for 'cello, orch.- and chamb music, pf.-pcs., songs, etc. (2) **L** b. Dessau, Sept. 4, 1835 ; bro. a pupil of above ; studied with Drec ler ('cello) and Schneider (theor played in the Gewandhaus orc Leipzig ; then 1st 'cello Schwe court-orch. ; 1876 chamber vir oso at Weimar. (3) **Friedri** son and pupil of (2) ; 1st 'ce Sondershausen court-orch., then Pe (1890) ; 1892–94 prof. at the Co Pesth ; 1894 in the Gürzenich Or and teacher at the Cons., Cologne

**Guadagni** (goo-ä-dän'-yē), (1) **Gae no**, Lodi, 1725 (?)—1785 (97 ?) ; m contralto (later a soprano) of 1 cent.; Gluck wrote "*Telemaco*" him. (2)—— ; sister of above; san London ; m. F. Alessandri.

**Guadagnini** (goo-ä-dän-yē'-nē), fam of vln.-makers of the Cremona sch (1) **Lorenzo** and (2) **John Baptis** worked 1690–1740. (3) **J. B.**, younger (son of Lorenzo), also m excellent violins.

**Guarducci** (goo-är-doot'-chē), Mon fiascone, ca. 1720 (?) ; Italian sin in London, 1766–71.

**Guarneri** (goo-är-nä'-rē) (Latinis **Guarne'rius**), family of famous vl makers at Cremona. (1) **Pietro A drea**, b. ca. 1630 ; worked 1650–c pupil of N. Amati ; his label *Andr Guarnerius Cremonæ sub titolo S tæ Theresiæ* 16—. (2) **Giuseppe**, 1660 ; son of above ; worked 16g 1730 ; his label *Joseph Guarner filius Andreas fecit Cremonæ sub tolo St. Theresiæ* 16—. (3) **P.**, b. 1670 ; son of (1) ; worked 1690–17

) **P.**, son of (2) ; worked 1725–40.
) **Giuseppe Antonio** (known as
**uarneri del Gesù**, i.e., " the Je-
s," from the " I H S " on his labels),
ne 8, 1683—ca. 1745 ; the best of
e family, nephew of (1) ; his label,
*seph Guarnerius Andreæ Nepos*
*emonæ* 17—, I H S.

**ehus** (goo'-dĕ-hoos), **H.**, b. Alten-
gen, Hanover, March 30, 1845; tenor,
n of a village schoolmaster ; pupil
Frau Schnorr von Karolsfeld at
'unswick ; 1870–73 engaged for the
urt opera, Berlin ; 1872, studied
th Louise Ress, Dresden ; reap-
ared 1875 ; 1880–90 at Dresden
.-opera, creating " Parsifal " at Bay-
uth, 1882 ; in New York 1890–91,
ter at Berlin ct.-opera.

**nin** (gä-näṅ), **Marie Alex.**, Mau-
uge (Nord), France, 1744—Paris,
19 ; violinist and composer.

**rcia** (goo-är-chĕ'-ä), **Alphonso**, b.
aples, Nov. 13, 1831; pupil of Mer-
dante ; dram. barytone for a time ;
nce 1859 vocal teacher, Naples ;
succ. opera "*Rita*" (Naples, 1875),
c.

**rin** (gä-räṅ), **Emmanuel**, b. Ver-
illes, 1779 ; 'cellist.

**rrero** (gĕr-rä'-rō), **Francisco**, Se-
lla, Spain, 1528—1599 ; conductor,
nger and composer.

**st**, (1) **Ralph**, Basely, Shropshire,
42—1830 ; organist and composer.
) **George**, Bury St. Edmunds,
71—Wisbeach, 1831 ; organist and
mposer.

**ymard** (gĕ'-mär), (1) **Louis**, Chap-
nay (Isère), France, 1822—Cor-
eil, near Paris, 1880 ; tenor, 1848–
at the Gr. Opéra. (2) **Pauline**
ée **Lauters**), b. Brussels, Dec. 1,
34 ; wife of above ; mezzo-soprano ;
pil of the Cons.; début 1855, Th.
yrique, Paris ; later at Gr. Opéra.

**lielmi** (gool-yĕl'-mē), (1) **Pietro**,
nd. to Duke of Modena. His son
) **P.**, Massa di Carrara, Italy, 1727
720 ?)—Rome, Nov. 19, 1804 ; con-
ctor, teacher and composer of over
0 operas. (Perhaps the (3) **Signora**

**G.** who sang in London 1770–72 was
the wife he treated so shamefully.)
Rival of Passiello and Cimarosa ;
1793 cond. at the Vatican, composed
only church-music. (4) **Pietro Carlo** (called **Guglielmini**), Naples, ca.
1763—Massa di Carrara, 1827 ; son
of above ; dram. composer, teacher
and conductor.

**Guicciardi** (goo-ēt-chär'-dē), **Giulietta**
(or **Julie**), Countess (or Gräfin),
Nov. 24, 1784—March 22, 1855 ; pianist ; pupil of Beethoven and his
enamoured *inamorata ;* a Viennese
woman, m. Count Gallenberg, 1803.

**Gui de Châlis** (gē dŭ shäl-ēs) (**Guido**), end of the 12th cent.; writer.

**Guidetti** (goo-ē-dĕt'-tē), **Giov.**, Bologna, 1532—Rome, 1592 ; pupil and
assistant of Palestrina ; conductor
and composer.

**Guido d'Arezzo** (goo-ē'-dō där-rĕd'-
zō) (Latinised **Areti'nus**), Arezzo, Italy, ca. 995—Avellano (?), May 17 (?),
1050 (?) ; eminent revolutionist in
music ; a Benedictine monk at
Pomposo, near Ferrara, later perhaps at Arezzo ; his abilities as
a singing-teacher and musician led
Pope John XIX. to summon him
to Rome ; he was later probably
a Prior at Avellano ; though he
is being stripped of many of his
early honours, it seems true that he
introd. the 4-line staff, and ledger-
lines and Solmisation (v. ARETINIAN ;
GAMUT and SOLMISATION, D. D.).

**Guido de Châlis.** Vide GUI DE
CHALIS.

**Guignon** (gēn-yôṅ), **J. P.**, Turin, 1702
—Versailles, 1775 ; violinist and
composer.

**Guilmant** (gēl-mäṅ), (1) **Alex. Félix**,
b. Boulogne, March 12, 1837 ; son
and pupil of the org. (2) **Jean Baptiste G.** (Boulogne, 1793—1800) ;
later pupil of Lemmens and G. Carulli (harm.) ; at 12 substituted for his
father at the church of St. Nicolas ;
at 16 organist at St. Joseph ; at 18
prod. a solemn mass ; at 20 choirm.
at St. Nicholas, teacher in Boulogne

Cons. and cond. of a mus. soc.; 1871 organist of Ste. Trinité; 1893 chev. of Legion of Honour; 1896 org.-prof., Paris Cons.; 1893, 1897-98 toured Europe and U. S. with much succ.; 1901 resigned from Ste. Trinité; c. symphony for organ and orch.; "lyric scene" "Belsazar" for soli. chorus and orch.; "Christus Vincit," hymn for chorus, orch., harps and org.; 4 org. sonatas, etc.

**Guindani** (goo-ēn-dä´-nē), **Ed.**, Cremona, 1854—1897; dram. composer.

**Guiraud** (gē-rō), (1) **Ernest**, New Orleans, June 23. 1837—Paris, May 6. 1892; son of (2) **Jean Baptiste G.** (Prix de Rome, Paris Cons., 1827), at 12 in Paris; at 15 prod. opera "Le roi David" at New Orleans; studied Paris Cons., and took Grand prix de Rome; later prof. of accompaniment Paris Cons. and dram. composer.

**Gulbranson** (gool´-brän-zōn), **Ellen**, b. Stockholm; notable soprano; studied with Marchesi, sang in concert; 1889 entered opera, singing Brünhilde, 1899 Kundry at Bayreuth and other rôles in other cities; lives on her estate near Christiania.

**Gumbert** (goom´-bĕrt), **Fd.**, Berlin, 1818—1896; tenor and barytone; also critic and dram. composer.

**Gumpeltzhaimer** (goom´-pĕlts-hī-mĕr), **Adam**, Trostberg, Bavaria, 1559—Augsburg, 1625; composer and theorist.

**Gumpert** (goom´-pĕrt), **Fr. Ad.**, b. Lichtenau, Thuringia, April 27, 1841; pupil of Hammann; from 1864 1st horn Gewandhaus Orch., Leipzig; writer and composer.

**Gumprecht** (goom´-prĕkht), **Otto**, b. Erfurt, April 4, 1823; studied law, Dr. jur.; 1849 critic and writer.

**Gungl** (or **Gung'l**) (goong´-l), (1) **Joseph**, Zsámbék, Hungary, Dec. 1, 1810—Weimar, Jan. 31, 1889; oboist, bandmaster and composer of pop. dance-music. (2) **Virginia**, daughter of above; opera-singer; début ct.-opera. Berlin, 1871; later at Frankfort.

(3) **Jn.**, Zsámbék, 1828—Pecs, H[ungary], 1883; nephew of (1); c[om]poser.

**Gunn,** (1) **Barnabas**, d. 1743; E[nglish] organist. (2) **Barnaby**, 1730[,] organist. (3) **John**, Edinburgh[,] 1765 (?)— ca. 1824; Chelsea H[os]pital, 1730-53; 'cello-teacher [and] writer.

**Günther** (gün´-tĕr), (1) **Herm[ann]**, Leipzig, 1834-71; a physician[;] opera under name "F. Hesther." [(2)] **Otto**, Leipzig, 1822—1897; bro[ther of] above; dir. (3) **Günther-Ba[ch]mann**, **Karoline**, Düsseldorf, [d.] —Leipzig, 1874; singer.

**Gunz** (goonts), **G.**, Gaunersdorf, L[ow]er Austria, 1831—Frankfort, 18[ ]; tenor.

**Gura** (goo´-rä), (1) **Eugen**, b. Press[ou]n. Saatz, Bohemia, Nov. 8, 18[ ] barytone; pupil of Polytechnic [and] the Akademie, Vienna; then Mu[nich] Cons., début 1865, Munich, 186[ ] Breslau; 1870-76 Leipzig with g[reat] succ.; 1876-83 Hamburg, Mur[ ] 1883-95. His son (2) **Hermann**[,] barytone.

**Gurlitt** (goor´-lĭt), **Cornelius**, A[lto]na, near Hamburg, Feb. 10, 18[ ] Berlin, 1901; pupil of the elder [Re]necke and Weyse; army mus. di[r. in] the Schleswig-Holstein campai[gn;] prof. Hamburg Cons.; 1874 R[oyal] Mus. Dir.; c. 3 operas, incl. "[Die] römische Mauer" (Altona, 18[ ] etc.

**Gürrlich** (gür´-lĭkh), **Jos. Augus[t]**, Munsterberg, Silesia, 1761—Be[rlin,] 1817; organist, bass, court-cond[uct]or and dram. composer.

**Gusikow** (goo´-zĭ-kôf), **Michael J[ef]**, Sklow, in Poland, Sept. 1806—Aix [la] Chapelle, Oct., 1837; remarkable v[irt]uoso on the xylophone.

**Gutmann** (goot´-män), **Ad.**, Hei[del]berg, 1819—Spezia, 1882; compo[ser].

**Gyrowetz** (gē-rō-vĕts), **Adalb[ert]**, Budweis, Bohemia, Feb. 19, 176[ ] Vienna, March 19, 1850; son [and] pupil of a choirm.; c. symphon[ies,] operettas, etc.; court-conductor.

## H

**eneck** (äb'-ĕ-nĕk), **François nt.**, Mézières (Ardennes), France, ne 1 (Jan. 25 ?), 1781—Paris, Feb. 1849 ; son and pupil of a German usician ; studied Paris Cons.; later nd. of its concerts and vln.-prof.; trod. Beethoven's symphonies to the rench public ; composer.

**erbier** (hä'-bĕr-bēr), **Ernst**, Kögsberg, Oct. 5, 1813—Bergen, Noray, March 12, 1869 ; son and pupil an organist ; court-pianist at St. etersburg ; later toured with great ccess ; composer.

**erl** (hä'-bĕrl), **Fz. X.**, b. Oberelnbach, Lower Bavaria, April 12, 840; took orders 1862 ; 1862–67 th. cond. and mus. dir. Passau eminary ; 1867–70 organist, Rome ; 871–82 cath.-cond. at Ratisbon ; 875 founded famous sch. for churchusic; edited Palestrina's works, etc.; 889, Dr. Theol. h. c., Univ. of Würzurg ; 1883, Pope Leo XIII. inusted him with the cataloguing of e invaluable archives of the Sistine hapel, of which he published a noble bibliography and thematic catague ; his pub. works are of the reatest importance in the history of hurch-music.

**bermann** (hä'-bĕr-män), **Fz. Jn.**, önigswarth, Bohemia, 1706—Eger, 783 ; conductor, teacher and comoser.

**bert** (hä'-bĕrt), **Jns. Evangelista**, berplan, Bohemia, 1833—Gmunden, 896 ; editor and collector.

**ckel** (hä'-kĕl), **Anton**, Vienna, 1779 –1846 ; composer.

**ckh** (häk), **Otto (Chp.)**, b. Stuttart, Sept. 30, 1852 ; pupil of Stuttart Cons. and of A. de Kontski (pf.), t New York ; 1872–75 teacher at e Cons.; 1877–78 toured ; 1878 eacher in London ; in 1880–89 Gr. Cons., New York ; later private eacher and composer.

**d'ley**, **Henry K.**, b. Somerville, Iass., U. S. A., 1871 ; notable composer, son and pupil of a musicteacher ; also studied with Chadwick, Heindl and Allen, Boston ; 1894–96 at Vienna with Mandyczewski ; 1896 in charge of music St. Paul's school, Garden City, N. Y.; c. 2 symphonies "Youth and Life" (prod. by Seidl, 1897), and " The Seasons," a ballet, suite, cantata ; 2 comic operas, etc.

**Had'ow, Wm. H.**, b. Ebrington, Gloucestershire, Dec. 27, 1859; composer, lecturer and writer of "Studies in Modern Music," etc.

**Hadria'nus.** Vide ADRIANSEN.

**Häffner** (hĕf'-nĕr), **Jn. Chr. Fr.**, Oberschönau, near Suhl, 1759—Upsala, Sweden, 1833 ; organist, court-conductor, dram. composer and collector.

**Hagemann** (hä'-gĕ-män), (1) **François Wil¹em**, b. Zutphen, Holland, Sept. 10, 182'; 1846 royal organist Appeldoorn; 1848 cond. at Nijkerk, studied 1852 Brussels Cons.; organist and composer at Batavia. (2) **Maurits Leonard**, b. Zutphen, Sept. 23, 1829 ; bro. of above ; violinist and pianist ; pupil of Brussels Cons.; 1865–75 dir. Cons., Batavia ; 1875 founder and dir. of a Cons., Leuwarden ; c. oratorio "Daniel," etc.

**Hagen** (hä'-gĕn), (1) **Fr. H. von der**, Schmiedeberg, Ukraine, 1780—Berlin, 1856 ; prof. and writer. (2) **Jn. Bapt.**, Mayence, 1818—Wiesbaden, 1870 ; conductor and composer. (3) **Ad.**, b. Bremen, Sept. 4, 1851 ; son of above ; violinist ; 1879–82 cond. Hamburg Th.; 1883, court cond. Dresden, and 1884 manager of the Cons.; c. comic cpera " Zwei Komponisten," Hamburg, 1882, etc. (4) **Theodor**, Hamburg, 1823—New York, 1871 ; teacher, critic and composer.

**Hager, Jns.** Vide HASSLINGER-HASSINGEN.

**Hague** (hāg), (1) **Chas.**, Tadcaster, 1769—Cambridge, 1821 ; prof. and composer. (2) **Harriet**, 1793—1816 ; daughter of above ; pianist and composer.

**Hahn** (hän), (1) **Bd.**, Leubus, Silesia, 1780—Breslau, 1852 ; cath.-conductor and writer. (2) **Albert,** Thorn, West Prussia, 1828—Lindenau, near Leipzig, 1830 ; teacher. (3) **Reynaldo,** b. Caracas, Venezuela, Aug. 9, 1874 ; pupil of Massenet, Paris Cons. ; lives in Paris ; c. 3-act " idylle polynésienne " " *L'Ile du Rêve* " (Paris, Op.-com., 1898) ; opera, " *La Carmelite* " (MS.) ; songs of remarkable beauty and originality, etc.

**Hähnel** (hä'-něl). Vide GALLUS, J.

**Haigh, Thos.,** b. 1769 ; Engl. violinist, pianist and composer.

**Haines, Napoleon J.,** London, 1824 — New York, 1900 ; founder of Haines Bros. Piano Mfrs., N. Y.

**Hainl** (ăṅl), **Georges François,** Issoire, Puy-de-Dôme, 1807 — Paris, 1873 ; 'cellist ; conductor, writer and composer.

**Haizinger** (hī'-tsǐng-ěr), **Anton,** Wilfersdorf, Lichtenstein, 1796—Vienna, 1869 ; tenor.

**Hale** (1), **Philip,** b. Norwich, Vt., March 5, 1854 ; notable American critic and essayist ; as a boy, organist Unit. Ch., Northampton, Mass. ; 1876 grad. Yale Univ. ; 1880 admitted to the Albany bar ; pupil of D. Buck, 1876 ; 1882–87 studied organ and comp. with Haupt, Faiszt, Rheinberger and Guilmant, Urban, Bargiel, Raif and Scholz ; 1879–82 organist St. Peter's, Albany ; 1887–89 St. John's, Troy ; since 1889 of First Religious Soc., Roxbury, Mass. ; 1887–89 also cond. of Schubert Club at Albany ; 1889–91 critic successively of the Boston *Home Journal, Post ;* 1891, *Journal ;* 1897–1901 edited *Mus. Record ;* 1901, Ed. *Musical World ;* lecturer on mus. subjects ; 1884 m. at Berlin (2) **Irene Baumgras,** b. Syracuse, N. Y., U. S. A. ; pupil Cincinnati Coll. of Mus. ; taking gold medal 1881 ; then studied with Moszkowski and Raif, Berlin ; ruined her health by overwork ; lives in Boston ; c. songs and pf.-pcs. under pen-name " **Victor René.** "

**Hâle** (or **Halle**). Vide ADAM D: HALE.

**Halévy** (ă-lā-vē), **Jac. Franç. F** mental **Élie,** Paris, May 27, 17 of consumption, Nice, March 1862 ; of Jewish parentage ; pup Cazot, Lambert (pf.), and Be (harm.), Cherubini (cpt.) ; Paris C winning 2nd harmony prize ; and 1817, 2nd Prix de Rome ; won Prix de Rome ; 1827 prof harmony and accomp. at the Co 1833 prof. of cpt. and fugue ; ¤ prod. 2 succ. operas ; 1830 succ. let " *Manon Lescaut* " *;* 1830–46 *de chant* at the Opera ; 1832 he ¢ pleted Herold's " *Ludovic* " succ. ; 1835 he wrote and prod. 2 g successes, his master - piece *Juive* " (Gr. Opéra) and a comic oj " *L'Éclair* " *;* Chevalier of the gion of Honour ; 1836 member of Académie ; 1854, secretary for In 1836 Meyerbeer appeared, and efforts to rival his prestige **H.** w too much with inferior libret among his works being (1841) " *Reine de Chypre.*" He collabora with Adam, Auber and Carafe ¡ operas ; he left 2 unfinished ope " *Vanina d'Ornano* " (completed Bizet) and " *Le Déluge.*" Biogr his brother Léon (1862). etc.

**Halir** (hä'-lēr), (1) **Karl,** b. Hol elbe, Bohemia, Feb. 1, 1859 ; vio ist ; pupil of Bennewitz, Prague Cc and Joachim in Berlin ; 1884 lea of the ct.-orch., Weimar ; 1 toured the U. S. His wife (2) **T resa** (née **Zerbst**), b. Berlin, N 6, 1859, and m. in 1888 ; sopra pupil of Otto Eichberg.

**Hall,** (1) **Henry,** Windsor, ca. 165 1707 ; organist and composer. **Henry, Jr.,** d. 1763 ; son of abo organist and composer. (3) **W** 17th cent. violinist and compo (4) **Chas. King,** London, 1845 (? Sept. 1, 1895 ; organist, dram. c poser. (5) **Glen,** b. Chicago (?), 18 tenor ; pupil of Henschel, etc.

**Halle** (ăl). Vide ADAM DE LA H.

lle (häl'-lĕ), **Jn. Samuel**, Barten-
ein, Prussia, 1730 — 1810; prof.
nd writer.

llé (äl-lā), Sir **Charles** (rightly
.arl **Halle**), Hagen, Westphalia,
pril 11, 1819—Manchester, Oct. 25,
895; pianist and conductor, Paris,
836–48; later pop. cond. at Man-
1ester and dir. of "Gentlemen's
oncerts" there; also closely con-
ected with London Popular Con-
erts; 1888 m. Mme. Neruda (q.
).

len (häl'-lĕn), **Anders**, b. Goten-
1rg, Dec. 22, 1846; pupil of Rei-
ecke, Rheinberger, and Rietz; cond.
* the Mus. Union, Gotenburg; 1892
1nd. Royal Opera, Stockholm; c. 3
peras, "*Harald der Viking*" (Leip-
g, 1881; Stockholm, 1883); v. succ.
*Hexfallen*" ("*Der Hexenfang*")
tockholm, 1896); "*Waldemar*"
tockholm, 1899); 2 Swedish Rhap-
odies; ballad cycles with orch.; sym-
1onic poem "*Ein Sommermär-
en*"; romance for vln. with orch.;
erman and Swedish songs, etc.

ler (häl'-lĕr), **Michael**, b. Neusaat
Jpper Palatinate), Jan. 13, 1840;
64 took orders; studied with
hrems; 1866 cond. "Realinsti-
t"; teacher of vocal comp. and
t. at the Sch. of Church-music;
riter and composer; completed the
st 3rd-choir parts of six 12-part
mps. of Palestrina's.

lström (häl'-strām), **Ivar**, Stock-
olm, June 5, 1826—1901; dram.
mposer; librarian to the Crown
rince, now King of Sweden; 1861
r. of Sch. of Music. His first opera
iled—having 20 numbers in minor
eys; his 2d also; but others were
cc., incl. "*Nyaga*" (1885; book
* "Carmen Sylva").

m (hälm), **Anton**, Altenmarkt,
.yria, 1789—Vienna, 1872; pianist
1d composer.

nbourg (häm'-boorg), **Mark**, b.
ogutschar-Noronez, Russia, June
1879; notable piano-virtuoso;
udied with his father (now a teacher

in London), and with Leschetizky;
has toured widely with brilliant success; 1900, America; lives in London.

**Ham'boys.** Vide HANBOYS.

**Hamel** (ä-mĕl), (1) **M. P.**, Auneuil
(Oise), France, 1786—Beauvais, after
1870; amateur expert in organ-build-
ing; writer. (2) **Eduard**, b. Hamburg, 1811; violinist and pianist;
Grand Opéra orch., Paris; from 1846
at Hamburg as teacher and composer. (3) **Margarethe.** Vide
SCHICK.

**Ham'erik, Asger**, b. Copenhagen,
April 8, 1843; pupil of Gade, Mat-
thison-Hansen and Haberbier; 1862
of von Bülow; c. two operas; 1870 at
Milan prod. an Ital. opera "*La Vendetta*"; 1871 dir. of the Cons. of the
Peabody Institute and of the Peabody symphony concerts, Baltimore,
Md.; 1890 knighted by the King of
Denmark; c. 1866 a festival cantata
to commemorate the new Swedish
constitution, "*Der Wanderer*"
(1872); 1883 "*Oper ohne Worte*";
a choral work "*Christliche Trilogie*" (a pendant to a "*Trilogie ju-
daique*" brought out in Paris); 5
symphonies, etc.

**Ham'erton, Wm. H.**, b. Nottingham,
1795; singing-teacher and composer.

**Ham'ilton, Jas. Alex.**, London, 1785
—1845; writer.

**Hamma** (häm'-mä), (1) **Benj.**, b.
Friedingen, Würtemberg, Oct. 10,
1831; studied with Lindpaintner
(comp.) at Stuttgart; then at Paris
and Rome; till 1870 cond. and teacher at Königsberg; now dir. sch. of
mus. at Stuttgart; dram. composer.
(2) **Fz. X.**, b. Wehingen, Würtemberg, Dec. 3, 1835; bro. of above;
organist at Basel; then at Obersta-
dion; now teacher at Metz; composer.

**Hammerschmidt** (häm'-mĕr-shmĭt),
**Ands.**, Brüx, Bohemia, 1611—Zittau, Oct. 29, 1675; organist, 1639,
at Zittau; c. important and original
concertos, motets, madrigals, etc.

**Hampel** (häm'-pĕl), **Hans,** Prague, 1822—1884 ; organist and composer.

**Han'boys** (or **Hamboys**), **John,** English theorist ca. 1470.

**Hand** (hänt), **F. G.,** b. Plauen, Saxony, 1786—Jena, 1851 ; writer.

**Handel** (or **Händel, Handl**). (1) Vide GALLUS. (2) Vide HÄNDEL.

**Händel** (hĕnt'-l) (**Hendel, Hendeler, Handeler** or **Hendtler**), **Georg Friedrich** (at first spelt **Hendel** in England ; later he anglicised it to **George Frederic Handel** (hăn'-dĕl, the form now used in England), Halle, Feb. 23, 1685—London, April 14, 1759 ; son of a barber (afterwards surgeon and valet to the Prince of Saxe-Magdeburg) and his second wife Dorothea Taust. Intended for a lawyer ; in spite of bitter opposition he secretly learned to play a dumb spinet. At 7 on a visit to his elder step-brother, valet at the court of Saxe-Weissenfels, Händel while playing the chapel-organ, was heard by the Duke, who persuaded the father to give the boy lessons. Zachau, organist of Halle, taught him cpt., canon and fugue, and he practised the oboe, spinet, harpsichord and organ ; he soon c. sonatas for 2 oboes and bass, became assist. organist, and for 3 years wrote a motet for every Sunday. In 1696 his skill on organ and harpsichord won him at Berlin the friendship of Ariosti, and the jealousy of Bononcini. The Elector offered to send him to Italy ; but his father took him back to Halle ; the next year his father died, and he went to Halle Univ. (1702–03) to study law, at the same time serving as organist at the cathedral at a salary of $50 a year. 1703 he went to Hamburg as *violino di ripieno.* He fought a duel with Mattheson, later his friend and biographer, and was saved by a button. When Keiser the dir. fled from debt, **H.** was engaged as clavecinist. He c. a " Passion" and prod. 2 operas, "*Almira*" (succ.) and "*Nero*" (1705) ; he was also commissioned to

write "*Florindo und Daphne*" (17 an opera filling two evenings. 1706, with 200 ducats earned teaching, he went to Italy and m success and powerful acquaintan incl. the Scarlattis. In Flore (1707) he prod. with succ. "*Rodri* (Venice, 1708), and "*Agrippi* with great succ. In Rome he pr 2 oratorios, and in Naples a seren: "*Aci, Galatea . Polifemo,*" in wl is a bass solo with a compass of 2 taves and a fifth. 1709, in Germ as cond. to the Elector of Hanov 1710 visited England on leave of sence. In 2 weeks he c. the op "*Rinaldo,*" a pasticcio of his ol songs. It was prod. at the Hayma Th. with great succ.; 1712 he retur to London on leave ; but stay His first two operas were not suc but an ode for the Queen's birthc and a Te Deum and Jubilate in c bration of the Peace of Utrecht v him royal favour and an annuity £200 ; 1714 who Hanover pat became George I. of England, only the good offices of Baron I manseck and the production of the pieces called the " *Water-Music,*" a royal aquatic fête, restored him favour. 1716–18 he went to Hanc with the King. He there c. his c German oratorio, the "*Passion* 1718 cond. to the Duke of Chan and c. the English oratorio "*Esthe* the secular oratorio "*Acis and Ga tea,*" and the Chandos Te Deums a Anthems. He taught the Princ Wales' daughters, and c. for Princ Anne " *Suites de Pièces*" for har; chord (*The Lessons*) including " *Harmonious Blacksmith.*"

He was dir. of new R. A. of 1720 prod. the succ. opera " *Ra misto* " (prod. 1721 in Hamburg " *Zenobia* "). Now Bononcini a Ariosti appeared as rivals and a mous and lasting feud arose round three after they had prod. one ope " *Muzio Scaevola,*" in which ea wrote an act. B. had rather the l er of it, when he was caught in plagiarism (a crime not unknown i Händel's works (v. LOTTI). B. eft England without reply (1731). Jp to this time **H.** had prod. 12 peras.

1726 he was naturalised. 1729-31 e was in partnership with Heidegger, roprietor of the King's Th., where e prod. "*Lotario*," followed by 4 iore operas. 1732 he prod. his two ratorios revised ; 1733 the oratorios *Deborah*" and "*Athaliah*" at Oxrd, when he was made Mus. Doc. *h.c.* 733 he began a stormy management f opera, quarrelled with the popular inger Senesino, and drove many of is subscribers to forming a rival roupe "The Opera of the Nobility," vith Porpora and afterwards Hasse s composer and conductor; 1737 the ompanies failed, **H.** having prod. 5 peras; the ode "*Alexander's Feast*" Dryden), and the revised "*Trionfo 'el Tempo e della Verita.*" Over-exrtion brought on a stroke of paralyis in one of his hands and he went o Aix-la-Chapelle, returning to Lonlon with improved health. He now rod., under Heidegger, 5 operas, ncl. "*Faramondo*," "*Serse*" (1738), nd "*Deidamia*" (1741).

Now he abandoned the stage and urned to oratorio, producing "*Saul*," nd "*Israel in Egypt*" (1739) ; the "*Ode for St. Cecilia's Day*," and in 740 "*L'Allegro and Il Penseroso*" Milton), and a supplement "*Il Mo-'erato*," written by Chas. Jennens, who lso wrote the text of the Messiah.

1741 he visited Dublin and prod. there his masterpiece the "*Messiah*," April 13, 1742. This re-established him in English favour and raised him from bankruptcy. It was followed by "*Samson*," the "*Dettingen Te Deum*," "*Semele*," "*Joseph*" (1743), "*Belshazzar*," and "*Heracles*" (1744). His rivals worked against him still, and in 1745 he was again bankrupt, writing little for a year and a half, when he prod. with renewed success and fortune his "*Occasional Oratorio*," and "*Judas Maccabaeus*" (1746); "*Joshua*" (1747), "*Solomon*" (1748); "*Susannah*" (1748); "*Theodora*" (1749); "*The Choice of Hercules*" (1750); and "*Jephthah*" (1752), his last. During the comp. of "*Jephthah*" he underwent three unsuccessful operations for cataract. He was practically blind the rest of his life, but continued to play org.-concertos and accompany his oratorios on the organ up to 1759. He was buried in Westminster Abbey. His other comp. incl. the "*Forest Musick*" (Dublin, 1742), etc., for harps.; the "*Fireworks Musick*" (1749) for strings; 6 organ-concertos; concertos for trumpets and horns ; and for horns and side drums (MS.) ; sonatas for vln., viola and oboe, etc. A complete edition of his works in 100 vols. was undertaken in 1856 for the German Händel Soc. by Dr. Chrysander as editor. Biog. by Mattheson (1740); Mainwaring (1760); Forstemann (1844); Schölcher (1857); Rockstro (1883).

## Handel.

### By John F. Runciman.

F Handel cannot be called the greatest of the musicians, he is without doubt the greatest man who ever wrote music. The resource and energy of the man and the splendour of his personality altogether threw the shade the magnificence of his music. The man eclipses the music as sun eclipses the moon ; the music indeed seems merely to reflect a small

part of the light issuing from that miraculous sun, the man. Had he devo
the whole of his life to music, his music would have been a wonder
achievement ; had he devoted his whole life to his business enterpri
and to fighting the aristocracy, it would still seem a life wonderfully a
greatly lived ; and when one remembers that he wrote most of the glori
music the same time that he was fighting aristocracy and trying to run op
in England, he does indeed appear as one of the most astounding phenome
the world has produced and stared at. ¶ Born in Germany towards the e
of the seventeenth century (1685), he promptly entered upon an infan
struggle on the question of whether or not he should become a musici
His father, a doctor, thought it a more honourable—it was everywh
thought a more respectable—proceeding to earn a livelihood by sendi
people slowly or swiftly to the next world than by making them miserable
this, through playing on instruments tuned according to the old " natural
temperament. The fact that the child Handel found a means of carrying
point, is characteristic of the man. He was apprenticed after the old-wo
German fashion to an old-world German organist, Zachau, and learned
play the organ and a few other instruments, studied all the music in use
his master's church or known to his master, and was taught to write anthe
at a moment's notice. When he considered the time ripe he set out on
travels to learn all that could be learned elsewhere. He was for a ti
attached to an opera-house ; he visited Italy, and finally came to Englar
He returned to Germany for a short time after his first English trip, l
returned and made England his permanent home. ¶ He acquired the co
trol of opera, at first having the aristocracy at his back. The aristocra
quarrelled with him and tried to crush him. They started a rival ope
house ; and the result was that the two enterprises failed for want of suffici
support. Handel became bankrupt and lost his health. He took a t
abroad and returned to try his luck with opera once more. His aristocra
rivals never tried again. They were wise. Even Handel, without co
petitors, was not able to succeed. " The Beggar's Opera " was all t
rage. All the world rushed night after night to hear it. Italian opera (o
fashioned Italian opera, of course) was in pretty much the same condition
London, as Middle-Victorian Italian opera is in to-day in London a
America. People were sick of its inanities and went to something not, p
haps, much more reasonable, but at any rate more interesting and intelligib
" The Beggar's Opera " was not a very stimulating concoction ; but co
pare the libretto with the perfectly idiotic drivel that Handel had to set
drivel of which the bulk of his audiences understood nothing save that it z
drivel—and one can easily see why all the world gave it the preferen
So Handel, beaten, not by the aristocracy, but by the changing taste of t

e, reluctantly relinquished opera, and, going in for oratorio, immediately
ame once again a popular favourite and made a fortune. ¶ It is neces-
⁀ to consider these roughly selected details of his life. As has been
cated, no estimate of Handel can afford to leave out the man. Moreover
purely artistic development is very hard to understand if we forget the
led by the man as apart from the life led by the composer. In his youth
acquired the German technique of his day. The same technique as John
astian Bach acquired. That is the foundation of all his art. But whereas
h remained in Germany, an obscure and all but unknown schoolmaster
organist, and evolved his perfected mode of expression out of the German
anique, Handel immediately went to Italy and learned something that
d be added to it. He learned, that is, the value of Italian song; and
lesson immediately bore splendid fruit. ¶ No one ever wrote more
nificently for the voice than Bach; but Handel learned to write beauti-
⁀, simply, plausibly. His first Italian operas are full of wonderful tunes.
an melodic outlines grafted on German harmony, and shaped so as to
me infinitely more dignified and expressive than any Italian music save
strina's had ever been. Then he came to London, where Purcell's
ic was all the vogue, and it was from Purcell that he learned the art of
dling the chorus and of writing picturesque music for chorus or solo voice
rchestra. ¶ Had he never come to England, had he never known Pur-
s music, his name might indeed have lived as the author of a few divinely
red songs, but it is safe to say that Handel, the gigantic chorus writer,
d never have been heard of. ¶ There is scarcely a thing in the later
del, in the Handel all England knows and adores, that does not derive
Purcell. His method of painting musical pictures, as used throughout
portions of " *Israel in Egypt* " as are his own, as used in such " *Mes-*
" choruses as " *All we like sheep have gone astray*," is simply a more
orate development of Purcell's plan of writing a chorus. His trick,
ys certain of its effect, of hurling enormous tone-masses at his hearers had
been extensively used by Purcell. ¶ His music may be said to be made
f the old German technique or trickery in writing flowing parts, of Italian
ble melody, of Purcell, and of Handel. Not that—apart from his
niable thefts—he can be called a thief. These thefts—after all, only so-
d—need not detain us more than a moment. ¶ All his life, as has been
ted out, Handel was greatly occupied by other matters than the writing
usic; he had again and again to throw together an oratorio at a few days'
ce; he did it and probably never thought of " immortality " or any of
*ièces d'occasion* being regarded a centu  ater as masterpieces. If in his
w he put in a few choruses by this, that, or the other German or Italian
tten no- or little- body, he did it quite openly. Of course, as Handel

has turned out to be so much vaster a genius than he himself suspected, i
well that we should know precisely how much of his music really is his ;
now that Dr. Chrysander has finally settled the whole question it might
dropped. ¶ Handel never stole. What he learned from Italy he assi
lated and made his own ; he assimilated and made his own Purcell's metho
and what he brought into music was a very notable thing. It was a spler
radiant spiritual robustness, a magnificent sense of the sublime, and a tend
ness that is not surpassed even by the tenderness of Mozart, Beethoven,
Wagner. There is also a quality of electric speed in many of his choru
and a power of heaping climax on climax until one's very nerves yield to
strain put on them. Two very familiar choruses, " *For unto us a chil*
*born* " and " *Worthy is the Lamb*," exemplify this power in an astound
way. His tenderness, his sheer strength, his sublimity, may all be foun
the well-known oratorio. ¶ But one cannot but believe that in the long
Handel will be better known by his songs than by anything else. It wa
the writing of these songs—of strings of them called Italian operas—that
found his most congenial occupation, and he only gave it up when he
fairly driven out of it. Great as his choruses are, they are not greater t
his songs. There are hundreds of them only waiting to be sung once ag
to be appreciated. Beyond what may be called the strictly personal quali
that Handel brought to music, Handel added nothing. Consequently
left no field unworked for any successors. Consequently, also, Eng
musicians ever since have gone on imitating his successes without any suc
whatever. He killed for many generations any chance there ever was of
Englishman becoming an original composer. Nevertheless, he was a gr
man and even an Englishman may forgive him.

---

**Hand'lo, Robert de,** Engl. theorist of
14th century.

**Hand'rock, Julius,** Naumburg, 1830
—Halle, 1894 ; teacher and composer.

**Hanel von Cronenthal** (hä'-nĕl fōn
krō'-nĕn-täl), **Julia,** b. Graz, 1839 ;
wife of the Marquis d'Héricourt de
Valincourt ; studied in Paris ; c. 4
symphonies, 22 pf.-sonatas, etc.

**Hanfstängel** (hänf'-shtĕng-ĕl), **Marie**
(née **Schröder**), b. Breslau, April
30, 1848 ; soprano ; pupil cf Viardot-
Garcia ; début, 1867, Paris ; studied
1878 with Vannucini ; 1882–97 Stadt-
theatre, Frankfort.

**Hanisch** (hä'-nĭsh), **Jos.,** Ratisbon,

1812—1892 ; organist, teacher a
composer.

**Hanke** (hänk'-ĕ), **K.,** Rosswal
Schleswig, 1754—Hamburg, 18
conductor and composer.

**Hans'com, E. W.,** b. Durham, Ma
U. S. A., Dec. 28, 1848 ; stud
there and in London, Berlin, s
Vienna; organist and composer
Auburn, Maine.

**Hanslick** (häns'-lĭk), **Eduard,**
Prague, Sept. 11, 1825 ; emin
critic and writer ; Dr. Jur., 18
studied piano under Tomaschek
Prague 1848–49 ; critic for the W
*er Zeitung ;* among his many bo
his first is most famous. " *Vom A*

alisch-Schönen " (Leipzig, 1854); a
newhat biassed, yet impressive plea
absolute music as opposed to pro-
mme (v. D. D.) or fallaciously
timental music ; he has been a
ter opponent of all Wagnerianism
1 an ardent Brahmsite ; 1855–64
s. editor *Presse ;* since, of the *Neue
ie Presse ;* lecturer on mus. hist.
1 æsthetics Vienna Univ.; 1851
f. extraordinary, 1870 full prof.;
95 retired.

ssens (häns'-sĕns), (1) **Chas. L.,**
s. (ainé), Ghent, 1777—Brussels,
2 ; conductor and composer. (2)
**as. L.** (cadet), Ghent, 1802—
ssels, 1871 ; conductor, professor,
list and composer.

rdelot (gĕ-dărd'-lō), **Guy (Mrs.
odes),** b. Château d'Hardelot,
r Boulogne, France ; lives in Lon-
1 ; c. operetta " *Elle et Lui* " and
ny pop. songs.

ngton, **Henry,** Kelston, Eng-
d, 1727—1816 ; composer.

*nes.* Vide SENKRAH.

**ns'ton, J. Wm.,** London, 1823—
beck, 1881 ; teacher and compos-

'er, (1) **Thos.,** Worcester, 1787—
ndon, 1853 ; trumpet virtuoso.
s 3 sons were (2) **Thomas,** his
cessor. (3) **Charles,** horn-player.
**Edward,** pianist.

raden, **Samuel,** Cambridge,
gl., 1821 (?)—Hampstead, Lon-
, 1897 ; org -professor.

iers-Wippern (här'-rĭ-ĕrs vĭp'-
n), **Louise** (née **Wippern),** Hil-
heim, 1837—Grobersdorf, Silesia,
8 ; soprano.

is, (1) **Jos. M.,** London, 1799—
nchester, 1869 ; organist and comer. (2) **Augustus** (Sir), Paris,
2—Folkestone, Engl., June 22,
6 ; an actor, début as Macbeth in
nchester, 1873 ; then stage man-
r ; 1879 leased Drury Lane Th.
spectacle ; 1887 he took up
ra and controlled successively H.
's Th., the Olympia, etc., finally
vent Garden. (3) **(Wm.) Victor,**

b. New York, April 27, 1869 ; pupil
of Charles Blum (pf.), Wm. Court-
ney (voice), Fredk. Schilling (harm,
and comp.), Anton Seidl (cond.) ;
1889–95 org. various churches; 1892–
95 *répétiteur* and coach at Met.
Op.; 1893–94 cond. Utica Choral
Union ; 1895–96 asst.-cond. to Seidl,
Brighton Beach Concerts ; now lives
as vocal teacher and accompanist,
N. Y.; c. a pf.-suite, a cantata, an
operetta "*Mlle. Mai et M. de Sem-
bre,*" songs, etc. (4) **Chas. Albert
Edw.,** b. London, Dec. 15, 1862 ;
(son and pupil of (5) **Edwin H.,** organist) ; Ouseley scholar St. Michael's
Coll., Tenbury, 1875 ; 1881 private
organist to the Earl of Powis ; since
1883 he lives with his father at Montreal, Canada, as organist ; c. an opera, a cantata, etc.

Har'rison, (1) **Wm.,** London, 1813—
London, 1868 ; tenor. (2) **Annie
Fortescue** (wife of Lord Arthur
Wm. Hill), contemporary English
composer ; c. operetta (London,
1884), a cantata, songs, etc.

**Hart,** (1) **James,** d. 1718 ; Engl. bass
and composer. (2) **Philip,** d. ca.
1749 ; Gentleman of Chapel Royal ;
son of above (?) ; organist and composer ; wrote music for " *The Morning Hymn* " from Book V. of Milton's
" *Paradise Lost.*" (3) **J. Thos.,**
1805—London, 1874 ; vln. maker.
(4) **George,** London, 1839—1891 ;
son of above ; writer.

**Härtel** (hĕr'-tĕl), (1) Vide BREITKOPF
UND HÄRTEL. (2) **G. Ad.,** Leipzig,
1836—Homburg, 1876 ; violinist,
conductor and dram. composer. (3)
**Benno,** b. Jauer, Silesia, May 1,
1846 ; pupil of Hoppe (pf.), Jappsen
(vln.), Kiel (comp.) ; 1870 teacher of
theory, Berlin Royal High Sch. for
Music ; c. an opera, over 300 canons,
etc. (4) **Luise** (née **Hauffe),** Düben,
1837—Leipzig, 1882 ; pianist ; wife
of (5) **Hermann H.** Vide BREIT-
KOPF.

**Hart'mann,** (1) **Johan Peder Emili-
us.** Copenhagen, May 14, 1805

Copenhagen, March 10, 1900; organist and dram. composer; grandson of a German court-cond. (d. 1763); son of an organist at Copenhagen. (2) **Emil** (jr.) Copenhagen, 1836—1898; son and pupil of above, and court-organist; composer. (3) **Ludwig**, b. Neuss-on-Rhine, 1836; pianist, composer and critic (son and pupil of (4) **Friedrich**, song-composer, b. 1805); also studied at Leipzig Cons. and with Liszt; lives in Dresden; prominent Wagnerian champion; c. an opera, etc. (5) **Arthur**, b. Philadelphia, July 23, 1882; violinist. (6) **Ferdinand**, clarinettist; lives in Munich as court-musician. (7) **Peter**, Franciscan monk of Hochbrunn-on-the-Lahn, prod. succ. oratorio " *Sankt Franziskus* " (Munich, 1902).

**Har'tog**, (1) **Edouard de**, b. Amsterdam, Aug. 15, 1826; pupil of Hoch, Bartelmann, Litolff, etc.; 1852 in Paris as teacher of pf., comp., and harm.; decorated with the orders of Leopold and the Oaken Crown; c. operas, the 43rd psalm with orch., etc. (2) **Jacques**, b. Zalt-Bommel, Holland, Oct. 24, 1837; pupil of Wilhelm and Fd. Hiller; prof. Amsterdam Sch. of Music.

**Hartvigson** (härt'-vĭkh-zōn), (1) **Frits**, b. Grenaa, Jutland, May 31, 1841; pianist; pupil of Gade, Gebauer, Ree, and von Bülow; since 1864, London; 1873 pianist to the Princess of Wales; 1875 prof. at the Norwood Coll. for the Blind; 1887 pf.-prof. Crystal Palace. (2) **Anton**, b. Aarhus, Oct. 16, 1845; bro. of above; pianist; pupil of Tausig and Neupert; lives in London.

**Har'wood**, **Edw.**, Hoddleson, 1707—Liverpool, 1787; composer.

**Hase** (Dr.), **Oskar von**. Vide BREITKOPF UND HÄRTEL.

**Häser** (hä'-zĕr), (1) **Aug. Fd.**, Leipzig, 1779—Weimar, 1844; theorist, conductor, writer and composer. (2) **Charlotte Henriette**, b. Leipzig, 1784; sister of above; singer; m. a

lawyer Vera. (3) **Heinrich**, b. R Oct. 15, 1811; bro. of above; of med. at Jena; writer.

**Hasert** (hä'-zĕrt), **Rudolf**, b. G wäld, Feb. 4, 1826; studied with lack (pf.), and Dehn (comp.); Berlin as teacher; 1873 past Gristow.

**Has(s)ler** (häs'-lĕr), (1) **Hans von**, Nürnberg, 1564 — Frank June 5, 1612; the eldest of 3 so ((2) **Isaac H.**, town-mus., Nürnb pupil of his father; organist and poser. (3) **Jakob**, Nürnberg, —Hechingen (?), 1601; bro. of conductor, organ virtuoso and poser. (4) **Kaspar**, Nürnberg, —1618; bro. of above; organist

**Haslinger** (häs'-lĭng-ĕr), (1) **To** Zell, Upper Austria, 1787—Vi 1842; conductor and publisher. **Karl**, Vienna, 1816—1868; son successor of above; pianist opera " *Wanda*," etc.

**Hasse** (häs'-sĕ), (1) **Nikolaus,** 1650; organist and writer at tock. (2) **Jn. Ad.**, Bergedorf, Hamburg, March 25, 1699—Ve Dec. 16, 1783; famous tenor a succ. operatic cond.; rival of Por c. over 100 operas, etc. (3) **Fau** (née **Bordoni**), Venice, 1693 (17 1783; of noble birth; one o most cultivated mezzo-sopr.; the above 1730, a happy union collaborating in his success. **Gustav**, b. Peitz, Brandenburg. 4, 1834; studied Leipzig Cons., ward with Kiel and F. I settled in Berlin as teacher and poser.

**Has'selbeck**, **Rosa**. Vide SUCH

**Hasselt-Barth** (häs'-sĕlt-bärt), **Maria Wilhelmine** (née van selt), b. Amsterdam, July 15, 1 soprano; début Trieste (1831).

**Hässler** (hés'-lĕr), (1) **Jn. Wm** furt, March 29, 1747 — Mo March 25 (29?), 1822; organist composer; important link be Bach and Beethoven. (2) **So** wife of above; singer.

slinger-Hassingen (häs'-lĭng-ĕr
s'-sĭng-ĕn), Jos., "Hofrath" Frei-
r von Vienna, 1822—1898 ; dram.
nposer. Used pen-name "Jos.
ager."

tings, Thos., Washington,
nn., 1787 — New York, 1872 ;
tor and composer.

treiter (häst'-rĭ-tĕr), Helene, b.
uisville, Ky., Nov. 14, 1858 ; op-
tic contralto, popular in Italy ;
pil of Lamperti, Milan ; m. Dr.
rgunzio ; lives in Genoa.

o. Vide FRÈRE.

ton, J. Liphot, Liverpool, Oct.
, 1809—Margate, Sept. 20, 1886 ;
nd. and dram. composer.

städt (hät'-shtĕt), J. J., b. Mon-
e, Mich., Dec. 29, 1851; studied in
rmany ; pf.-teacher and writer in
troit, St. Louis, and for 11 years,
icago Coll. of Mus.; 1886, dir.
ner. Cons., Chicago.

(c)k (howk), Minnie, b. New
rk, Nov. 16, 1852 (53 ?) ; notable
prano ; pupil of Errani and Moritz
akosch ; début 1869, N. Y., as
Norma "; 1868–72 Vienna ct-opera;
75, Berlin ; has sung with great
cc. in Europe and America. She
court-singer in Prussia, Officier
Académie, Paris, and member of
e Roman Mus. Academy.

er (how'-ĕr), K. H. Ernst, Hal-
rstadt, 1828—Berlin, 1892 ; organ-
a.d composer.

ff (howf), Jn. Chr., Frankfort,
11—1891 ; founder and prof.,
ankfort School of Music ; writer
d composer.

ffe (howf'-fĕ), Luise. Vide HÄR-
L, LUISE.

pt (howpt), K. Aug., b. Kunern,
esia, Aug. 25, 1810—Berlin, July
1891; pupil of A. W. Bach, Klein,
d Dehn ; famous as organist and
acher at Berlin ; composer.

ptmann (howpt'-män), Moritz,
esden, Oct. 13, 1792—Leipzig,
n. 3, 1868 ; violinist ; pupil of
ohr ; famous as theorist and teach-
; from 1842 prof. of cpt. and

comp. Leipzig Cons., and dir. Thomasschule. His canon was "unity
of idea and perfection of form,"
exemplified in his comps., enforced
upon his many eminent pupils
and exploited in many essays and
standard works, incl. "Die Natur
der Harmonik und Metrik" (1833) ;
the posthumous, "Die Lehre von der
Harmonik," 1868, etc.; c. opera,
"Mathilde" (Cassel, 1826) ; quartets, masses, etc.

Hauptner (howpt'-nĕr), Thuiskon,
Berlin, 1825—1889 ; conductor and
composer.

Hauschka (howsh'-kä), Vincenz, Mies,
Bohemia, 1766—Vienna, 1840 ; 'cellist and barytone player ; composer.

Hause (how'-zĕ), Wenzel, b. Bohemia, ca. 1796 ; prof. of double-bass,
Prague Cons.; writer.

Hausegger (hows'-ĕg-gĕr), (1) Fr. von,
b. Vienna, April 26, 1837 ; pupil of
Salzmann and Dessoff ; barrister at
Graz ; 1872 teacher of history and
theory, Univ. of Graz ; writer. (2)
Siegmund von, German composer of
notable symphony "Barbarossa"
(Munich, 1900) ; 2d cond. Munich
Kaim orch.; 1902, cond. Frankfort
Museum (vice Kogel), 1903, 1st
cond. Munich Kaim orch.

Hauser (how'-zĕr), (1) Fz., b. Craso-
witz, near Prague, 1794—Freiburg,
Baden, 1870 ; bass-barytone ; teacher. (2) Miska (Michael), Pressburg, Hungary, 1822—Vienna, 1887;
vln.-virtuoso ; composer.

Häuser (hī'-zĕr), Jn. Ernst, b. Ditt-
chenroda, near Quedlinburg, 1803 ;
teacher, Q. Gymnasium ; writer.

Hausmann (hows'-män), Valentin,
the name of five generations, (1) V.
I., b. Nürnberg, 1484 ; a friend of
Luther ; composer and conductor.
His son (2) V. II., organist and
composer His son (3) V. III., organist at Löbejün, expert in org.-
building. His son (4) V. IV., organist and court-conductor at Köth-
en ; writer. His son (5) V. V. Vide
BARTHOLOMAUS ; Löbejün, 1678—

Lauchstadt, after 1740 ; cath. organist and theorist. (6) **Robt.**, b. Rottleberode, Harz Mts., Aug. 13, 1852 ; 'cellist ; pupil of Th. Müller, and Piatti in London ; teacher, Berlin Royal " Hochschule"; since 1879, member Joachim quartet.

**Hau(l)tin** (ō-tăṅ), **P.**, La Rochelle, ca. 1500—Paris, 1580 ; first French founder of musical types.

**Hav'ergal**, Rev. **Wm. H.**, Buckinghamshire, 1793—1870 ; composer.

**Haweis** (hôẑ), Rev. **H. R.**, Egham, Surrey, 1838—London, Jan. 30, 1901; amateur violinist and popular writer on music.

**Hawes** (hôz), **Wm.**, Engl., London, 1785—1846 ; conductor and composer.

**Haw'kins** (Sir), **J.**, London, March 30, 1719—Spa, May 14, 1789 ; an attorney ; eminent historian of music ; knighted, 1772.

**Haw'ley, Chas. B.**, b. Brookfield, Connecticut, U. S. A., Feb. 14, 1858 ; organist at 13 there ; studied with G. J. Webb, Revarde, Dudley Buck, Mosenthal, etc., N. Y.; bass singer, organist and composer of excellent songs, New York.

**Hay'den**, **Geo.**, Engl., organist and composer, 1723.

**Haydn** (hīd'-'n), (2) (**Fz.**) **Josef**, Rohrau-on-Leitha, Lower Austria, March 31, 1732—Vienna, May 31, 1809 ; second son of a wheelwright who was the sexton and organist of the village church, and a fine tenor, and whose wife, Maria Koler, had served as cook for Count Harrach. She sang in the choir. At 5, **H.** was taken to the home of a paternal cousin, Frankh, who taught him Latin, singing, the vln. and other instrs. He was engaged as a chorister for St. Stephen's, and taught by Reutter the cond., who gave him no encouragement and dismissed him in 1748. At 8, he went to Vienna, and studied singing, vln. and clavier, with Finsterbusch and Gegenbauer. He studied harmony chiefly from Fux' "*Gradus ad Parnas-*

*sum*" and Mattheson's "*Volkommner Kappellmeister.*" At 13 he mass. He obtained a few pup and a Viennese tradesman lent 150 florins, with which he rented attic-room and an old harpsichord. practised C. P. Bach's first 6 son and the vln.; Metastasio taught Italian, and recommended him t Spanish family as teacher for t daughter, who was studying Porpora. From Porpora, in ret for menial attentions, **H.** recei some instruction in comp. and a ommendation to the Venetian amb sador for a stipend of 50 franc month. At 20, he had c. 6 tr sonatas, his first mass, and a co opera "*Der neue krumme Teup* (Stadttheater, 1752), a satire on lame baron Affligi the ct.-opera this work was suppressed but revi afterwards, and he received 24 du for it. He began to make powe friends, and became Musikdire and Kammercompositeur to Co Fd. Maximilian Morzin. 1759 Pri Paul Anton Esterházy heard his symph. and 1760 took him into service as 2d (later 1st) conductor ; same year **H.** m. Maria Anna, elder sister of the girl whom he lo and who had entered a conv This marriage was as unhappy one would expect. Prince Niko Esterházy, who succeeded his bro 1762, retained **H.** as conductor in his service **H.** c. 30 symphon 40 quartets, a concerto for Fre horn, 12 minuets, most of his ope etc. He was soon very pop. thro Europe, and royalty sent him gi 1785 commissioned to write a m "*The Seven Words on the Cro* for the Cath. of Cadiz ; in 1 Prince Nikolaus was succeeded by son Anton, who kept **H.** as co and increased his stipend of 1,000 rins to 1,400. In 1791 on a press invitation brought by Salomon, went to England and was for months the lion of the season.

rd made him Mus. Doc.; and he c.
e so-called "*Salomon Symphonies*,"
r his concerts. On his way home,
e visited his native place to witness
e unveiling of a monument erected
his honour by Count Harrach. In
is year Beethoven became his pu
l. 1794, he revisited London, with
newed triumph, the King urging
m to stay, but, at the invitation of
new Prince Esterházy, he returned.
797, he c. the Austrian national
nthem. At 65, he prod. his great
ratorio "*The Creation*" ("*Die
chöpfung*"); in 1801 "*The Seans*" ("*Die Jahreszeiten*"). His
ealth failing he went into retire-
ent, appearing in public only once
1808, when he was carried in a
air to hear a special performance
f the "*Creation*." His agitation
as so great that he had to be taken
way after the first half; the throng
iving him a sad farewell, and Beet-
oven bending to kiss his hands and
orehead. In 1809, his death was
astened by the shock of the bom-
ardment of Vienna by the French.
Iis astounding list of works in-
ludes besides those mentioned, 125

symphonies and overtures, incl. the
"*Farewell*" ("*Abschiedssymphonie*,"
1772), the "*Fire S.*" (" *Fuer symph.*,
1774), the " *Toy S.*" (" *Kinder-
symph.*), "*La Chasse*" (1870), the
"*Oxford*" (1788), the "*Surprise*,"
("*S. mit dem Paukenschlag*," 1791);
"*S. with the drum-roll*" ("*S. mit
dem Paukenwirbel*," 1795); 51 concertos for harpsichord, vln., 'cello,
lyre, barytone double-bass, flute and
horn; 77 string-quartets; 175 numbers for barytone; 4 vln.-sonatas;
38 pf.-trios; 53 sonatas and diverti-
menti; an oratorio "*Il Ritorno di
Tobia*"; 14 masses; 4 operas; 4
Italian comedies; 14 Ital. opere
buffe, and 5 marionette-operas; music to plays; 22 arias; cantatas, incl.
"*Ariana a Naxos*," "*Deutschlands
Klage auf den Tod Friedrichs des
Grossen*," "*The 10 Commandments*"
in canon-form; 36 German songs;
collections of Scotch and Welsh folk-
songs, etc. Biog. by S. Mayr, 1809;
K. F. Pohl (Leipzig, 1875, 1882;
completed by E. von Mandyczewski).
Haydn's diary is quoted from extensively in Krehbiel's "*Music and
Manners*" (New York, 1898).

## Joseph Haydn.

### By August Spanuth.

WHILE the relative station in musical history of Bach, Händel,
Gluck, Mozart, and Beethoven is universally and definitely agreed
upon, various opinions may still be entertained of the merits and
sequent influence of Joseph Haydn's work as a composer. ¶ This is all
more remarkable as he never met with much opposition. Only at one time
ing his life, a few rather inferior critics earnestly tried to belittle him; now-
r, these were insignificant attempts, wholly unworthy of the closer attention
the historian. Nowhere has the musical public been slow in acknowledg-
Haydn's genius. Even at the time when he was Kapellmeister in the remote
e town of Eisenstadt, his fame spread all over Europe, and his compositions
re loved, played, and sung in all the big and small cities. Nor has there even
n a violent partisanship pro and contra Haydn. All of which is easy enough to
nprehend, inasmuch as he did not offend anybody's taste, even where he was

most progressive in his compositions, and remained with his feet on the gro
when his ideals were ever so lofty.    ¶ The source of his musical inventions
the song and the dance. of the people, yes, one might say, the children's sc
and his artistic development was as slow as it was steady, thus allowing
admirers time to grow with him.    Even where he reaches the very summi
his art, his melodic invention bears the ear-mark of childlike naïveté.    ¶ ⟨
yet it seems impossible to have any two musicians determine the value
Joseph Haydn for the development of music, both entirely alike.    Was h
reformer ?    The one will answer, "Yes," and point out that there was
real symphony before Haydn ; that the old Italian symphony was noth
else but an introduction to, or an interlude during, the opera ; that what th
was of instrumental music before Haydn, was either in the way of fugues,
in the style of the concerto, or purely descriptive music.    He will, furth
more, assert that Haydn created a thoroughly novel oratorio, doing av
almost entirely with the old Italian style, and holding up his individuality
spite of the tremendous influence of the Händel oratorio.    ¶ The other ⟨
will deny him the exalted title of a reformer, and, while he may rea⟨
admit that Haydn has added the Menuetto to the symphony, and fortunat
got rid of the clavicembalo, that he, moreover, succeeded in giving the s⟨
sonata and the string-quartette a concise and plastic shape, he will proba
insist that Haydn has done only very little that was essentially new, and th
in musical history, he can only rank as the man who paved the way for
giant Beethoven.    ¶ But no matter how opinions may differ on this po⟨
one must own of Haydn, that he was the first great musician to introduce
element of subjectiveness into instrumental music.    And in so far one can
deny him the instinct of a reformer, though he hardly was conscious of
He never abandoned traditions just because he had decided to create a n
musical language ; he simply followed the inner voice of his genius.    ¶ A
he could do so all the more freely, since he had never enjoyed a thorough ⟨
severe musical education.    He learned from here and there, he had mo⟨
like Philipp Emanuel Bach, or Porpora, and Händel, etc., but he follow
none of them so closely as to restrict his own individuality in the least.    ⟨
the other hand, there was no trace of the spirit of revolt in his system.    ⟨
very life is a strong proof for his peaceful and benevolent nature.    When
sweetheart took the veil, he allowed himself to be persuaded to marry
older sister, who was three years his senior, and a Xantippe.    This, and
fact that he lived with her for more than forty years, stamps the man as of
almost angelic character.

**Haydn** (hīd´-'n), (2) **Jn. Michael,** Roh-
rau, Sept. 14, 1737—Salzburg, Aug.
10, 1806 ; bro. of above ; soprano
chorister, with compass of 3 octav
at St. Stephen's, Vienna, repla⟨ing
brother Josef. Studied v'n and

n, and became asst. - organist ;
57, cond. at Grosswardein ; 1762,
. to Archbishop Sigismund, Salz-
rg ; 1777, organist of the Cath.
d St. Paul's Ch. He m. Maria
agdalena Lipp, an excellent sopra-
; 1880 he lost his property, by the
ench occupation, but was aided by
s bro. and 2 others, and the Em-
ess Maria Theresa rewarded him
- a mass c. at her command, in
ich she sang the soprano solos. He
unded a school of composition, and
d many pupils, incl. Reicha and
eber. Prince Esterházy twice
ered to make him vice-cond.; but
. refused, hoping to reorganise the
lzburg Chapel. His best works
ere sacred music, which his brother
teemed above his own. He declined
blication, however ; c. 360 church-
mps., incl. oratorios, masses, etc.,
symphonies ; operas, etc. Biog.
Schinn and Otter (Salzburg, 1808).
res (hāz), (1) Wm., Hanbury, Wor-
stershire, Dec., 1706— Oxford, July
7, 1777 ; organist, conductor and
riter. (2) Philip, Oxford, April, 1738
-London, March 19, 1797 ; son and
pil of above, and his successor as
niv. Prof. of Mus. at Oxford ; also
ganist there ; c. oratorio ; a masque;
concertos, etc. (3) Catherine,
eland, 1825 (or 6)—Sydenham, 1861;
nger.

ym (hīm), (1) (or Hennius), Gilles,
elgian composer 16th cent. (2)
alian composer, Aimo (ä'-ē-mō), (3)
iccolò Franc., Rome, ca. 1679—
ondon, 1729 ; 'cellist and librettist.
ynes, Walter B., b. Kempsey,
ngl., 1859 ; studied Leipzig Cons. ;
ganist various churches ; prof.
f harm. and comp., R. A. M.
ys, Wm. Shakespeare, b. Louis-
ille, Ky., July 19, 1837; pub. nearly
oo pop. songs.
ap, Chas. Swinnerton, Birming-
am, Engl., April 10, 1847—June 11,
900 ; won the Mendelssohn scholar-
hip and studied at Leipzig Cons.; also
rgan with Best ; Mus. Doc. Cam-

bridge, 1872 ; cond. Birmingham
Phil. (1870–86), and other societies ;
c. an oratorio " The Captivity " ; cantatas, etc.

Hebenstreit (hāb'-'n-shtrīt), Pantaleon, Eisleben, 1660 (9?)—Dresden,
1750, conductor ; improved the dulcimer as the " Pantalon " (v. D. D.).

Hecht (hĕkht), Ed., Durkheim, Rhine
Palatinate, 1832 — Didsbury, near
Manchester, 1887 ; pianist ; prof.
and composer.

Heckel (hĕk'-ĕl), Wolf, lutenist at
Strassburg, 16th cent.

Heckmann (hĕk'-män), (1) G. Julius
Robt., Mannheim, 1848—Glasgow,
1891 ; violinist. His wife (2) Marie
(née Hartwig), Greiz, 1843—Cologne, 1890 ; pianist.

Hedge land, Wm., organ - builder,
London, 1851.

Hédouin (ād-wăn), P., Boulogne,
1789—Paris, 1868 ; lawyer, writer,
librettist and composer.

Heermann (här'-män), Hugo, b. Heilbronn, March 3, 1844 ; violinist ;
studied with J. Meerts Brussels Cons.
since 1865 ; lives in Frankfort as soloist and teacher at the Hoch Cons.

Heeringen (hā'-rĭng-ĕn), Ernst von,
Grossmehlza, near Sondershausen,
1810—Washington, U. S. A., 1855 ;
unsuccessful innovator in notation
and scoring.

Hegar (hā'-gär), (1) Fr., b. Basel,
Oct. 11, 1841; studied Leipzig Cons.,
1861 ; from 1863 cond. Subscription
Concerts, and of the Choral Soc.,
Zürich ; 1875 founded Cons. at
Zürich ; c. vln.-concerto in D ; succ.,
dram. poem, " Manasse," for soli,
chorus and orch.; " Festouvertüre,"
etc. (2) Emil, b. Basel, Jan. 3, 1843;
bro. of above ; pupil, later 'cello-
teacher at Leipzig Cons., and 1st
'cello Gewandhaus Orch. ; then studied singing, now vocal-teacher Basel
Sch. of Mus. (3) Julius, bro. of
above ; 'cellist at Zürich.

Hegedüs (hĕg-ĕ-dūsh), Ferencz, b.
Hungary, 1872 (?) ; violinist ; succ.
début, London, 1901.

**Hegner** (hākh'-nĕr), (1) **Anton**, b. Copenhagen, March 2, 1861 ; 'cellist; studied Copenh. Cons. ; at 14 played with great succ.; now teacher N. Y.; c. 4 quartets ; 2 concertos for 'cello, etc. (2) **Otto**, b. Basel, Nov. 18, 1876 ; pianist ; pupil of Fricker, Huber, and Glaus ; made début very early at Basel (1888), England and America, at the Gewandhaus, Leipzig, 1890 ; c. pf.-pcs.

**Heide, von der.** Vide VON DER H.

**Heidingsfeld** (hī'-dĭngs-fĕlt), **L.**, b. Jauer, Prussia, March 24, 1854 ; pupil, later teacher Stern Cons., Berlin; composer.

**Height'ington, Musgrave,** 1680 — Dundee, 1774 ; organist and composer.

**Heinefetter** (hī'-nĕ-fĕt-tĕr), (1) **Sabine**, Mayence, 1805 (1809 ?)—(insane) Illenau, 1872 ; noted soprano , m. Marquet; her five sisters also sang with succ. : (2) **Clara** (Mme. **Stöckel**), Mayence, 1816—(insane),Vienna, 1857. (3) **Kathinka,** 1820—1858. (4) **Fatima**, m. a nobleman, Miklowitz. (5) **Eva**, and (6) **Nanette.**

**Heinemeyer** (hī'-nĕ-mī-ĕr), (1) **Chr. H.**, 1796—1872 ; flutist at Hanover ; composer. (2) **Ernst Wm.**, Hanover, 1827—Vienna, 1869 ; son of above ; flutist and composer.

**Heinichen** (hī'-nĭkh-ĕn), **Jn. D.**, Krössuln, near Weissenfels, 1683—Dresden, 1729 ; dram. composer and writer.

**Heinrich** (hīn'-rĭkh), (1) **Jn. G.**, Steinsdorf (Silesia), 1807 — Sorau, 1882 ; organist, writer and composer. (2) **Heinrich XXIV.**, Prince Reuss j. L., b. Dec. 8, 1855 ; pianist ; c. a symphony, a pf.-sonata, etc.

**Heinrichs** (hīn'-rĭkhs), (1) **Jn. Chr.**, b. Hamburg, 1760 ; lives in St. Petersburg ; writer on Russian music. (2) **Anton Ph.**, Schönbüchel, Bohemia, 1781—New York, 1861 ; known as " **Father H.**"; composer.

**Heinroth** (hīn'-rōt), (1) **Chp. Gl.**, for 62 years organist at Nordhausen. (2)

**Jn. Aug. Günther**, Nordhau 1780 — Göttingen, 1846 ; son above ; director and composer.

**Heintz** (hīnts), **Albert**, b. Eberswa Prussia, March 21, 1882 ; orga " Petrikirche," Berlin ; writer Wagner ; composer.

**Heinze** (hīnts'-ĕ), (1) **Wm. H. H.** 1790 ; clarinettist in the Gewandh Orch. (2) **Gv. Ad.**, b. Leipzig, ( 1, 1820 ; son and pupil of above 15 clarinettist in the Gewandha 1844, 2d cond. Breslau Th.. prod. 2 operas (of which his wrote the libretti) ; 1850, Amster as cond. ; c. 5 oratorios, 3 masse overtures, etc. (3) **Sarah** (née **M** **nus**), b. Stockholm, 1839 ; pian pupil of Kullak, Al. Dreyschock, Liszt ; lives in Dresden.

**Heise** (hī'-zĕ), **Peder Arnold,** Cop hagen, 1830 — 1879 ; teacher dram. composer.

**Heiser** (hī'-zĕr), **Wm.**, Berlin, 181 Friedenau, 1897; singer, bandmas and composer.

**Hek'king, Anton,** 'cello virtuoso teacher at the Stern Cons.

**Hel'ler, Stephen,** Pesth, May 1815—Paris, Jan. 14 1888 ; nota composer who, like Chopin, confi his abilities to the pf. Lacking breadth, passion and colour of C pin's, his music has a candour a vivacity and a fascinating quaintr that give it peculiar charm ; études, simpler than Chopin's, are well imbued with art and perso ity. Studied piano with F. Bräu at 9 played in pub. with succ. ; t studied with Czerny and Halm ; 12, gave concerts in Vienna, a toured ; at Pesth studied a li harmony with Czibulka ; at Au burg fell ill, and was adopted b wealthy family, who aided his stud 1838, Paris. Schumann praised first comp. highly. 1849, Lond he played with succ. though in quently because of nervousne thereafter lived in Paris. C. seve hundred pf.-pcs., incl. 4 sonatas a

e famous Etudes. Biogr. by H.
arbadette (1876)

lmesberger (hĕl'-mĕs-bĕrkh-ĕr),
) G. (Sr.), Vienna, 1800—Neuwal-
egg, 1873 ; violinist, conductor and
omposer. (2) G. (Jr.), Vienna,
830—Hanover, 1852 ; son and pupil
above ; violinist and dram. com-
oser. (3) Rosa, daughter of (2),
as a singer, début 1883, ct.-opera.
ienna. (4) Jos. (Sr.), Vienna, 1829
-1893 ; son of (1) ; conductor, vio-
nist and professor. (5) Jos. (Jr.),
, Vienna, April 9, 1855 ; son of (4);
olinist and composer of operettas,
llets, etc. 1902, cond. Vienna
ailh. Orch. (6) Fd., b. Vienna,
an. 24, 1863 , bro. of above ; 'cellist
ct.-orch. from 1879; from 1883 with
s father's quartet ; 1885 teacher at
e Cons.; 1886, solo 'cellist, ct.-opera.

dwig (hĕl'-vĭkh), K. Fr. L., Kü-
ersdorf, 1733—Berlin, 1838 ; conuctor and dram. composer.

m, Theodor, b. Vienna, April 9,
843 ; studied law, entered govt.
ervice ; since 1867 critic for various
urnals, and writer; 1874, teacher of
us. hist. and æsthetics, Horak's
chool of Music.

mholtz (hĕlm'-hôlts), Hermann L.
d., Potsdam, Aug. 31, 182? —
harlottenburg, Sept. 8, 1894 ; emi-
ent scientist ; pub. famous treatises
ich as " Sensations of Tone as a
hysiological Basis for the Theory of
Iusic" (Lehre von den Tonempfin-
ingen als physiologische Grundlage
ir die Theorie der Musik) (Bruns-
ick, 1863 ; English trans. by Ellis,
875) ; this work, the result of much
xperiment, is the very foundation of
iodern acoustics, though Riemann,
ho was in some opposition to H.,
ays his conclusions are not infallible,
d attacks are increasing upon him.
I. inv. also a double harmonium
ith 24 vibrators to the octave ; this
cks the dissonant 3rds and 6ths of
qual temperament (v. D. D.) and
ermits the same modulation into all
eys.

Hel'more, Rev. Thos., b. Kidder-
minster, May 7, 1811 ; composer.

Hen'derson, Wm. Jas., b. Newark, N. J., Dec. 4, 1855 ; prominent American critic and writer ;
graduated Princeton Univ., 1876 ;
mainly self-taught in music ; 1883 re-
porter, from 1887 critic, N. Y. Times;
lecturer on mus. hist. N. Y. Coll. of
Mus.; c. various light operas, songs,
etc.; pub. a " Story of Music," "Preludes and Studies," " What is Good
Music?" (1898), " How Music Developed" (New York, 1899), " The
Orchestra and Orchestral Music"
(1899), " Wagner" (1902).

Henkel (hĕnk'-ĕl), (1) Michael,
Fulda, 1780—1851 ; composer. (2)
G. Andreas, Fulda, 1805—1871 ;
organist and composer. (3) H., b.
Fulda, Feb. 14, 1822 ; son and pupil
of (1), also studied with Aloys
Schmitt, and theory with Kessler and
Anton Andre ; 1849, teacher, etc.,
Frankfort. (4) K., son of (3) ; stud-
ied in Berlin Hochschule ; lives in
London, as violinist.

Hen'ley, Rev. Phocion, Wooten Abbots, 1728—1764 ; English composer.

Henneberg (hĕn'-nĕ-bĕrkh), Jn.Bapt.,
Vienna, 1768—1822 ; organist, conductor and composer.

Hen'nen, (1) Arnold, b. Heerlen, Holland, 1820 ; pianist ; 1845 took first
pf.-prize, Liège Cons.; lives at Heerlen ; composer. (2) Fr., b. Heerlen,
Jan. 25, 1830 ; bro. of above ; 1846
took first vln.-prize Liège Cons.;
1847, medal 1850-71, soloist in various London orchestras ; then retired to Strythagen, near Heerlen ;
composer. (3) Chas., b. Dec. 3,
1861 ; son of (2) ; violinist at Antwerp. (4) Mathias, b. Heerlen,
1828 ; bro. of (1) ; 1852, first pf.-
prize Liège Cons.; since 1860 teacher
at Antwerp, and prof. at the Cons. ;
composer, etc.

Hennes (hĕn'-nĕs), (1) Aloys, b. Aix-
la-Chapelle, 1827 — Berlin, 1889;
pf.-teacher at various places ; composer. (2) Therese, his daughter, b

Dec. 21, 1861 ; pianist ; studied with Kullak.

**Hennig** (hĕn'-nĭkh), (1) **K.**, Berlin, 1819 —1873, organist, dir. and composer. (2) **K. Rafael**, b. Jan. 4, 1845 ; son of above ; pupil of Richter and Kiel ; 1869-75, organist Posen ; 1873, founder of " Hennig " Vocal Soc. ; 1883, Royal Mus. Dir. ; 1892, R. Prof. ; composer and writer.

**Hen'nius.** Vide HAYM, GILLES.

**Henschel** (hĕn'-shĕl), (1) (**Isidor**) **Georg**, b. Breslau, Feb. 18, 1850 ; prominent barytone, pianist, and teacher ; pupil of Wandelt and Schaeffer, Breslau ; of Leipzig Cons. also Kiel and Ad. Schulze (singing); Berlin ; 1877-80, lived in London ; 1831-84, cond. Boston (U. S. A.) Symph. Orch.; since 1885, London ; founded the "London Symphony Concerts"; 1886-88, prof. of singing R. C. Mus. ; c. operas, "Friedrich der Schöne" and "Nubia"; operetta. "A Sea Change, or Love's Castaway"; an oratorio, etc. (2) **Lillian** (née **Bailey**), Columbus, Ohio, Jan., 1860 —London, Nov. 4, 1901 ; pupil and 1881 wife of above ; also studied with C. Hayden and Viardot-Garcia, concert-soprano ; she and her husband gave recitals with great art and success. (3) **Helen**; daughter of above, soprano ; sang N. Y. 1902.

**Hensel** (hĕn'-zĕl), (1) **Fanny Cäcilia** (née **Mendelssohn**), Hamburg, Nov. 14, 1805—Berlin, May 14, 1847 ; eldest sister of FELIX M., whose devoted companion she was, and who died six months after her sudden death. He said she was a better pianist than he, and six of her songs are pub. under his name : viz., his op. 8 (Nos. 2, 3, 12), and op. 9 (7, 10, 12) ; she pub. under her own name " Gartenlieder," part-songs and songs ; c. also pf.-trios and pcs. (2) **Octavia**. Vide FONDA.

**Henselt** (hĕn'-zĕlt). **Ad. von**, Schwanach, Bavaria, May 12, 1814—Warmbrunn, Silesia, Oct. 10, 1889 ; eminent pianist who played with remarkable

sonority and emotion ; to obtain remarkable reach he c. and tised incessantly very difficult stud he c. a famous pf.-concerto, étu etc.

**Hentschel** (hĕnt'-shĕl), (1) **Ernst** lius, Langenwaldau, 1804—Weis fels, 1875. (2) **Fz.**, Berlin, 18 1889 ; teacher and dram. comp (3) **Theodor**, Schirgiswalde, U Lusatia, 1830—Hamburg, 1 conductor, pianist and dram. poser.

**Herbart** (hĕr'-bärt), **Jn. Fr.**, Ol burg, 1776—Göttingen, 1841; w

**Herbeck** (hĕr'-bĕk), **Jn. Fz. von** enna, Dec. 25, 1831—Oct. 28, 1 important cond., mainly self-tau dir. 1866, ct.-cond. at Vienna prof. at the Cons.

**Her'bert, Victor**, b. Dublin, Irel Feb. 1, 1859 ; a grandson of Sa Lover, the novelist; at 7, sen Germany to study music ; 1st t ct.-orch. Stuttgart, and elsewh 1886 solo 'cellist, Metropolitan O New York ; later Theodore Tho and Seidl's orchs. (also assoc cond.) ; 1894, bandm. 22d Regt., Gilmore ; 1898, cond. of Pittsb (Pa.) Orch. (70 performers); c. spi pcs. for orch. and 'cello ; a 'c concerto ; an oratorio, " The tive" (Worcester Festival); and merous comic operas, incl. " P Ananias," a failure, " The Wi of the Nile," v. succ., " The nade," " The Idol's Eye," " Fortune Teller" and "The Sin Girl," all v. succ., in which the usual combination of Irish mu humour and German scholarli justifies their great success.

**Hering** (hä'-rĭng), (1) **K. Gl.**, Sc dau, Saxony, 1765—Zittau, 18 teacher, editor and composer. **K. E.**, b. Oschatz. Saxony, 18 Bautzen, 1879 ; son and pupi above and successor as editor ; dram. composer. (3) **K. Fr. A** Berlin, 1819—Burg. near Magdeb 1889 : violinist and composer.

rion (hä'-rĭ-ōn), **Abraham Adam**, chonau, Odenwald, 1807—Dresden, 893 ; pf.-teacher.

ritte - Viardot (ŭr-ēt-v'yär-dō), ouise Pauline Marie, b. Paris, )ec. 14, 1841 ; daughter of Viardot-Garcia ; vocal-teacher St. Petersburg 'ons.; later at Frankfort, and Bern ; m. Consul-General Heritte ; c. pera "*Lindora*" (Weimar, 1879), nd cantatas.

rmann (hĕr'-män), (1) **Matthias**, alled **Verrecoiensis**, or **Verreco-ensis**, from his supposed birthplace, Varkenz or Warkoing, Holland ; Vetherland cptist. 16th cent. (2) **n. D.**, Germany, ca. 1760—Paris, 846 ; pianist and composer. (3) **n. Gf. Jakob**, Leipzig, 1772—1848 ; vriter. (4) **Fr.**, b. Frankfort, Feb. , 1828 ; pupil of Leipzig Cons., 846–75, viola-player, Gewandhaus nd theatre orchs.; 1848, vln.-teacher t the Cons.; 1883 Royal Saxon Prof.; . symphony, etc.: editor and collec-or. (5) **Rheinhold L.**, b. Prenz-au, Brandenburg, Sept 21, 1849 ; upil of Stern Cons., Berlin ; 1878–81 ir. of it ; 1871–78 singing-teacher nd cond. New York ; 1884, cond. J. Y. "Liederkranz"; 1887, prof. f sacred history at the Theol. Semi-ary ; 1898, cond. Handel and Haydn oc., Boston ; 1900 returned to Ber-in ; c. 4 operas incl. "*Vineta*" Breslau, 1895), and "*Wulfrin*" (Co-ogne, 1896) ; 5 cantatas, overtures, tc. (6) **Robt.**, b. Bern, Switzer-and, April 29, 1869 ; studied Frank-ort Cons ; previously self-taught in ither, pf., comp. and had c. works f much originality in which Grieg ncouraged him ; 1893, studied with Iumperdinck, then went to Leipzig nd Berlin, where (1895) his sym-hony, and a concert-overture were rod. at the Philh., provoking much ritical controversy ; now lives in .eipzig ; c. also "*Petites variations our rire*," for pf. and vln.; etc. 7) **Hans**, b. Leipzig, Aug. 17, 1870, ontrabassist and composer ; left au

orphan, he had a struggle with poverty ; studied with Rust, Kretz, Schoner and von Herzogenberg ; lives in Berlin, and c. string-quartets, pf.-pcs., etc., and many notable songs. (8) **J. Z.** Vide ZENNER. (9) Vide HERRMANN.

**Herman'nus** (called **Contrac'tus** or " **der Lahme**," for his lameness), Graf von Vehrihgen, Sulgau, Swabia, July 18, 1013—Alleshausen, near Biberach, Sept. 24, 1054 ; important writer and theorist.

**Hermes** (hĕr'-mĕs), **Ed.**, b. Memel, May 15 (?), 1818 ; merchant, and composer in Königsberg, Prussia.

**Hermesdorff** (hĕr'-mĕs-dôrf), **Michael**, Trier (Trèves), 1833—1885 ; organist, composer and editor.

**Hermstedt** (hĕrm'-shtĕt), **Jn. Simon**, Langensalza, near Dresden, 1778—Sondershausen, 1846 ; composer.

**Hernandez** (ĕr-nän'-dĕth), **Pablo**, b. Saragossa, Jan. 25, 1834 ; pupil of Madrid Cons.; organist and (1863) auxiliary prof. there ; c. *zarzuelas;* a mass, symphony, etc.

**Hernando** (ĕr-nän'-dō), **Rafael José M.**, b. Madrid, May 31, 1822 ; pupil of R. Carnicer, Madrid Cons.; 1848–53, he prod. several succ. *zarzuelas,* some in collab.; later dir. and composer to Th. des Variétés ; 1852, secretary, later prof. of harm., Madrid Cons.; founded a Mutual Aid Mus. Soc.

**Hérold** (ā-rôl), (1) **Louis Jos. Fd.**, Paris, Jan. 28, 1791—(of consumption) Thernes, near Paris, Jan. 19, 1833 ; son of (2) **Fran. Jos. H.** (d. 1802; pf.-teacher and composer, pupil of P. E. Bach), who opposed his studying music, though Fétis taught him solfège and L. Adam, pf. After his father's death (1802), he studied piano with Louis Adam, Paris Cons. (first prize, 1810) ; harmony with Catel and (from 1811) comp. with Méhul ; 1812 won the Prix de Rome, with cantata " *Mlle. de la Vallière*" : studied at Rome and Naples, where he was pianist to Queen Caroline, and prod. opera ' *La Gioventù di Enrico Quinto* " (1815) ; Paris, 1815, finished Boieldieu's " *Charles de France* " (prod. with succ. 1816, Op. Com.) ; " *Les Rosières* " and " *La Clochette* " followed 1817, both v. succ. ; others followed; the last (1820) failing, he imitated Rossini in several operas, but recovered himself in the succ. " *Marie* " (1826) ; 1824, pianist, later chorusm. at the Ital. Opera, but soon relinquished. 1827 Chef du Chant, at the Gr. Opéra, for which he wrote several succ. ballets, incl. " *La Somnambule*," which gave a suggestion to Bellini ; 1828, Legion of Honour. "*Zampa*" (1831) gave him European rank and is considered his best work by all except the French, who prefer his last work " *Le Pre aux Clercs* " (1832) ; he prod. also " *L'Auberge d'Airey* " (1830) (with Carafa), " *La Marquise de Brinvilliers* " (1831), with Auber, Boieldieu, Cherubini, and 5 others ; and " *La Médicine sans Médecin* " (1832) ; he left " *Ludovic* " unfinished, to be completed by Halévy with succ. ; c. also much pf.-mus. Biogr. by Jouvin (Paris, 1868).

**Herrmann** (hĕr'-män), (1) **Gf.**, Sondershausen, 1808—Lübeck, 1878 ; violinist, pianist, organist and dram. composer. (2) **K.**, d. Stuttgart, 1894, 'cellist. (3) **Klara**, daughter of (2) ; pupil of Leipzig Cons.; pianist ; lives in Lübeck.

**Herschel** (hĕr-shĕl), **Fr. Wm.** (Anglicised, Sir **William Herschel**, K.C. H., D.C. L.), Hanover, 1738—Slough, near Windsor, 1822 ; oboist ; organist at Bath ; astronomy, in which he won such fame, was till 1781 only his diversion.

**Hertel** (hĕr'-t'l), (1) **Jn. Chr.**, Oettingen, Swabia, 1699—Strelitz, 1754 ; singer, viola da gambist, violinist and composer. (2) **Jn. Wm.**, Eisenach, 1727—Schwerin, 1789 ; son and pupil of above ; violinist, conductor and composer. (3) **K.**, 1784—1868 ; violinist. (4) **Peter L.**, Berlin,

1817—1899 ; son of above ; co[mposer].

**Herther** (hĕr'-tĕr), **F.**, pen-name [of] H. Gunther.

**Hertz** (hĕrtz), **Alfred**, b. Frankfort-[on]-Main, July 15, 1872 ; studied R[--] Cons.; from 1895 2d-cond. vari[ous] cities; 1899 cond. city theatre Bresl[au]; 1899 London ; 1902 Met. Op., N. [--]

**Hertzberg** (hĕrts'-bĕrkh), **Rudol[f]** von, Berlin, 1818—1893 ; conduc[tor] and editor.

**Hervé** (rightly **Florimond Rong[é]** (ĕr-vā or rôṅ-zhā), Houdain, n[ear] Arras, June 30, 1825—Paris, Nov. [--] 1892 ; singer, then organist, c[on]ductor ; in Paris acting as librett[ist] composer and actor, and produ[cing] flippant but ingenious little works [in] which French operetta finds a r[eal] origin ; c. over 50 operettas, a[lso] heroic symphony " *The Asha[nti* War*," and ballets. (2) **Gardel, [son]** of above, prod. 1871 operetta " [Ja]ni, c'est fini.*"

**Hervey** (här'-vĭ). **Arthur**, b. of Ir[ish] parents, Paris, Jan. 26, 1855 ; pu[pil] of B. Tours (harm.) and Ed. Marl[--] (instr.) ; intended for the diploma[tic] service, till 1880 ; critic of " *Van[ity] Fair* " ; from 1892, London " *Post*[--]; c. a 1-act opera, a dram. overt[ure] " *Love and Fate*," etc.

**Herz** (hĕrts or ĕrs), (1) **Jacques Simo[n]**, Frankfort, Dec. 31, 1794 — Ni[ce], Jan. 27, 1880 ; of Jewish parentag[e]; studied at Paris Cons. with Pradhe[re]; pianist and teacher in Paris ; th[en] London ; 1857, acting-prof. Pa[ris] Cons.; c. vln.-sonatas, etc. **Henri**, Vienna, Jan. 6, 1806—Pa[ris] Jan. 5, 1888 ; 1st prize pf.-pu[pil] Paris Cons.; very popular as touri[ng] pianist ; succ. as mfr. of pianos ; o[b]tained extravagant prices for [his] comps.; prof. at the Cons. ; writer[--]

**Herzberg** (hĕrts'-bĕrkh), **Anton**, Tarnow, Galicia, June 4, 1825 ; p[ia]nist ; pupil of Bocklet and Prey[er], Vienna ; toured Europe, and receiv[ed] many decorations ; 1866, pf.-teach[er] Moscow ; composer.

**rzog** (hĕr'-tsōkh), (1) **Jn. G.,** b.
chmolz, Bavaria, Sept. 6, 1822;
upil of Bodenschatz, and at Altdorf
eminary; 1842, organist at Munich;
848, cantor; 1850, organ - prof.
t the Cons.; 1854, mus. dir. Er-
angen Univ.; 1866, Dr. Phil.,
ater prof.; retired 1888; lives in
Munich; composer. (2) **Emilie,** b.
Diessenhofen, Thurgau, ca. 1860;
oubrette coloratura - singer; pupil
Zürich Sch. of Mus., then of Glogg-
er, and Ad. Schimon, Munich, début, Münich (1879?); 1889, Berlin
t.-opera.

**rzogenberg** (hĕr'-tsōkh-ĕn-bĕrkh),
1) **H. von,** Graz, Styria, June 10,
843—Wiesbaden, 1900; prof. at
Berlin, etc.; director, professor and
omposer. (2) **Elizabeth** (née **von
Stockhausen**) (?) 1848—San Remo,
892; pianist, wife of above.

**es'eltine, Jas.,** d. 1763; English organist and composer.

**ess,** (1) **Joachim,** organist, writer and
carillonneur, Gouda, Holland, from
1766—1810. (2) **A. H.,** organ-builder
at Gouda; bro. of above. (3) **Willy,**
b. Mannheim, July 14, 1859; violinist, pupil of his father and Joachim;
at 19 Konzertmeister at Frankfort,
1886 at Rotterdam, then England;
1895 1st vln.-prof. Cologne Cons.,
and 1st vln. Gürzenich Quartet.

**esse** (hĕs'-sĕ), (1) **Ernst Chr.,**
Grossen-Gottern, Thuringia, 1676—
Darmstadt, 1762; viola-da-gambist,
conductor. (2) **Ad. (Fr.),** Breslau,
1809—1863; org.-virtuoso and composer. (3) **Julius,** Hamburg, 1823—
Berlin, 1881; introduced the present
measurement for pf.-keys; and pub.
a method. (4) **Max,** b. Sondershausen, Feb. 18, 1858; 1880 founded
mus. pub. house in Leipzig; in 1883,
founded H. und Becker.

**etsch** (hĕtsh), **K. Fr. L.,** Stuttgart,
1806 — Mannheim, 1872; pianist,
violinist and dram. composer.

**euberger** (hoi'-bĕrkh-ĕr), **Richard
Fz. Jos.,** b. Graz, Styria, June 18,
1850; a civil engineer; in 1876 took

3ι

up music, which he had previously
studied; chorusm., Vienna academical Gesangverein; 1878 cond. Singakademie; c. operas "*Abenteuer
einer Neujahrsnacht*" (Leipzig,
1886); "*Manuel Venegas*" (do., 1889),
remodelled as "*Mirjam*" (Vienna,
'94); 2 operettas; overture to Byron's
"Cain," etc.

**Heubner** (hoip'-nĕr), **Konrad,** b.
Dresden, 1860; pupil of the "Kreuzschule" there; 1878–79, at Leipzig
Cons. and writer; with Riemann, later Notteböhm, Vienna; Wüllner,
Nicodé and Blassmann, Dresden;
1882, cond. Leipzig Singakademie;
1884, asst. cond. Berlin Singakademie; 1890, dir. Coblenz Cons. and
Mus. Soc.; c. a symphony, overtures,
etc.

**Heugel** (ŭ-zhĕl), **Jacques Ld.,** La
Rochelle, 1815—Paris, 1883; editor
and publisher.

**Heumann** (hoi'-män), **Hans,** b. Leipzig, Aug. 17, 1870; at 18, double-
bass in orch. at Cassel; studied with
W. Rust, at Leipzig Cons. and
Kretschmer at Dresden; later with
von Herzogenberg at Berlin; lives in
Berlin; pub. a suite in sonata-form
for vln. and pf.; over 100 songs of
all kinds, etc.

**Hew'itt, J. H.,** b. New York, 1801;
from 1845 lived in Baltimore; c.
oratorios, incl. "*Jephtha*," operas,
etc.

**Hey** (hī), **Julius,** b. Irmelshause,
Lower Franconia, April 29, 1832;
studied with Lachner (harm. and
cpt.), and F. Schmitt (singing); later
with von Bülow at the Munich Sch.
of Mus. (estab. by King Ludwig
II. on Wagner's plans); attempted a
reform in the cultivation of singing,
but resigned at Wagner's death
(1883), and pub. important vocal
method, "*Deutscher Gesangsunter-
richt*" (4 parts, 1886), exploiting
Wagner's views. Wagner called him
"the chief of all singing-teachers."
1887, Berlin; later Munich; composer.

**Heyberger** (hī'-bĕrkh-ĕr), **Jos.**, Hettstadt, Alsatia, 1831—Paris, 1892; organist, composer and conductor.

**Heyden** (hī'-d'n), (1) **Sebald**, Nürnberg, 1498 (1494 ?)—1561; cantor, writer. (2) **Hans**, Nürnberg, 1540—1613; son of above; organist; inv. the " Geigenclavicimbal."

**Heydrich** (hī'-drĭkh), **Bruno**, b. Leuben, near Lommatzsch, Saxony, 1865; pupil of Dresden Cons.; 1879–82, took prizes as double-bass player, pianist and composer; for a year in von Bülow's Weimar orch.; 4 years Dresden ct.-orch.; also studied singing with Scharfe, Hey and v. Milde; succ. début as tenor at Sondershausen theatre; prod. v. succ. 1-act opera-drama, with pantomimic prologue, "*Amen*," Cologne, 1895; c. songs.

**Heymann** (hī'-män), (1) **Karl**, pianist, b. Filehna, Posen, Oct. 6, 1854. Son of (2) **Isaac H.** (cantor); pupil of Hiller, Gernsheim, Breunung and Cologne Cons. and of Kiel; ill-health ended his promising career as virtuoso; till 1822, mus. dir. at Bingen; court-pianist to the Landgrave of Hesse, 1877–80, Hoch Cons., Frankfort; c. concerto "*Elfenspiel*" "*Mummenschanz*," "*Phantasiestücke*," etc., for piano.

**Heymann-Rheineck** (hī'-män-rī'-nĕk) (**K. Aug. Heymann**), b. Burg-Rheineck on Rhine, Nov. 24, 1852; pianist; pupil Cologne Cons., and R. Hochschule, Berlin; since 1875, teacher there; composer.

**Heyne Van Ghizeghem** (also **Hayne**, or **Ayne**, "Henry"); Netherland contrapuntist and court-singer, ca. 1468.

**Hiebsch** (hēpsh), **Josef**, Tyssa, Bohemia, 1854—Carlsbad, 1897; teacher and writer in Vienna.

**Hiedler** (hēt'-lĕr), **Ida**, b. Vienna, Aug. 25, 1867; soprano; studied with Ress; début, Berlin ct.-opera, 1887.

**Hientzsch** (hēntsh), **Jn. Gf.**, Mokrehna, near Torgau, 1787—Berlin, 1856; teacher, composer and writer.

**Hieron'ymus de Morvia**, ca. 12 Dominican friar, Paris; writer.

**Hignard** (ēn-yär) (**J. L.**), **Aristi** Nantes, 1822—Vernon, 1898; preface to his "*Hamlet*" writ 1868, not prod. till Nantes, 18 shows him to have attempted a n and serious manner, but he fou production only for comic ope which were usually succ.

**Hildach** (hĭl'-däkh), (1) **Eugen**, b. W tenberg-on-the-Elbe, Nov. 20, 184 barytone; pupil of Frau Prof. Dreyschock. (2) **Anna** (née **Sch bert**, b. Königsberg, Prussia, Oct. 1852; wife of above; mezzo-sopran teacher Dresden Cons., 1880–86.

**Hildebrand** (hēl'-dĕ-bränt), (1) **Z charias**, Saxony, 1680—1743; or builder. His son, (2) **Jn. Gf.**, w equally eminent.

**Hiles** (hīlz), (1) **J.**, Shrewsbury, 18 —London, 1882; organist, wri and composer. (2) **H.**, b. Shrew bury, Dec. 31, 1826; bro. and pu of above; organist various churche 1867, Mus. Doc. Oxon; 1876, le urer; later, prof. R. Manchest Coll. of Music; 1885, editor a writer; c. 2 oratorios, 3 cantatas, historic opera, etc.

**Hilf** (hēlf), (1) **Arno**, b. Bad Elste Saxony, March 14, 1858; vln.-virt oso; son and pupil of (2) **Wm. Ch H.**; from 1872 he also studied wi David. Röntgen, and Schradiec Leipzig Cons.; second concertm 1878, and teacher at Moscow Cons (1888) Sondershausen; 1878, lead Gewandhaus orch., Leipzig; 1st vl prof. at the Conservatorium.

**Hill**, (1) **Wm.**, London, 1800—187c org.-builder. (2) **Wm. Ebsworth** London, 1817—Hanley, 1895; vln maker. (3) **Thos. H. Weist**, Lon don, 1828—1891; violinist, condu tor and composer. (4) **Ureli C** New York, 1802 (?)—1875; violinis (5) **Wm.**, b. Fulda, March 28, 1838 pianist; pupil of H. Henkel ar Hauff; since 1854 lives in Frankfor c. prize-opera "*Alona*"; vln.-son as,' etc. (6) **Junius Welch**, b. Hingham, Mass., Nov. 18, 1840 ; pupil of J. C. D. Parker, Boston, and of Leipzig Cons.; organist various churches ; till 1897, prof. of Mus. at Wellesley Coll.; now teacher and editor. (7) **K.**, Idstein, Nassau, 1840—insane asylum, Sachsenberg, Mecklenburg, 1893 ; barytone ; created "Alberich" at Bayreuth.

**lle** (hĭl'-lĕ), (1) **Ed.**, Wahlhausen, Hanover, 1822—Göttingen, 1891 ; cond. and teacher. (2) **Gv.**, b. Jerichow-on-Elbe, near Berlin, May 31, 1851 ; violinist ; pupil of R. Wüerst (theory), Kullak's Acad., 1869–74 w. Joachim (vln.) ; lives in Berlin, as a solo-player ; 1879, invited to the Mendelssohn Quintet Club, Boston, Mass.; toured ; then teacher at Mus. Acad., Phila.; c. 5 vln.-concertos with orch., etc.

**llenmacher** (hĭl'-lĕn-mäkh-er, or ēl-lĭn-mä-shä), **two brothers.** (1) **Paul Jos. Wm.**, b. Paris, Nov. 25, 1852. (2) **Lucien Jos. Ed.**, b. Paris, June 10, 1860 ; both studied at the Cons., and took the first Grand Prix de Rome, (1) in 1876 ; (2) in 1880. They write all their scores in collaboration. C. symph. legend "Lorely" (1882, City of Paris prize) ; succ. opera "St. Megrin" (Brussels, 1886), etc.; "Orsola" (Gr. Opéra, Paris, 1902).

**ller (Hüller)** (hĭl'-lĕr), (1) **Jn. Adam**, Wendisch-Ossig, near Görlitz, Dec. 25, 1728—Leipzig, June 16, 1804 ; pupil of Hornilius (Kreuzschule) and U. of Leipzig ; flutist in concerts, and teacher ; 1754 tutor to the son of Count Brühl ; 1758, accompanied him to Leipzig, where he lived thereafter ; 1763, revived, at his own expense, the subscription concerts, which developed into the famous "Gewandhaus" concerts, of which he was cond.; 1771, founded a singing-school ; 1789–1801, cantor and dir. Thomasschule. He founded the "Singspiel," from which German "comedy-opera" developed, contemporaneously with *opera buffa* and *opéra comique*. In his dram. works the aristocratic personages sing arias, while the peasants, etc., sing simple ballads, etc. His *Singspiele*, all prod. at Leipzig, had immense vogue, some of the songs being still sung ; 1766–70, he wrote, edited collections, etc.; c. also a Passion cantata, funeral music (in honour of Hasse), symphonies and partitas, the 100th Psalm, etc. Biog. by Carl Peiser (Leipzig, 1895). (2) **Fr. Adam**, Leipzig, 1768—Königsberg, Nov. 23, 1812 ; violinist and tenor ; son and pupil of above ; mus. dir. of Schwerin Th.; 1803, cond. of Königsberg Th.; c. 4 operettas, etc. (3) **Fd. von**, Frankfort, Oct. 24, 1811—Cologne, May 12, 1885 ; of wealthy Jewish parentage ; a pupil of Hofmann (vln.), Aloys Schmitt (pf.) and Vollweiler (harm. and cpt.) ; at 10 played a Mozart concerto in public, at 12 began comp.; from 1825 pupil of Hummel ; at 16 his string-quartet was pub. Vienna ; at 15, he saw Beethoven on his death-bed ; 1828–35, taught Choron's School, Paris ; then independently giving occasional concerts ; 1836, he returned to Frankfort, and cond. the Cäcilien-Verein ; 1839, prod. succ. opera "Romilda," at Milan ; oratorio, "Die Zerstörung Jerusalems" (Gewandhaus, 1840) ; 1841, studied church-music with Baini, Rome ; 1843–44 he cond. the Gewandhaus ; prod. at Dresden, 2 operas ; 1847, municipal cond. at Düsseldorf ; 1850 at Cologne, where he organised the Cons.; cond. Gürzenich Concerts, and the Lower Rhine Festivals ; 1852–53, cond. Opera Italien, Paris ; 1868, Dr. Philh. *h. c.* Bonn Univ. ; 1884 he retired. He was a classicist in ideal of the Mendelssohn type and his comp. are of precise form and great clarity. He was also a lecturer and writer on music. He c. 3 other operas, 2 oratorios, 6 cantatas, 3 overtures, 3 symphonies, a ballad "Richard Löwen-

*herz*," with orch. (1883), etc. (4)
**Paul,** b. Seifersdorf, near Liegnitz,
Nov., 1830; 1870, asst.-organist,
and since 1881 organist St. Maria-
Magdalena, Breslau; composer. (5)
**Emma,** b. Ulm; studied with Sit-
tard and Hromada; court-singer at
Würtemberg.

**Hill'mer,** (1) **Fr.,** Berlin, ca. 1762—
1847; viola-player; a son of his (2)
was a singing-teacher in Berlin.

**Hil'pert, W. Kasimir, Fr.,** Nürnberg, 1841 — Munich, 1896; 'cellist.

**Hil'ton, J.,** d. 1657; English organist
and composer.

**Him'mel, Fr. H.,** Treuenbrietzen,
Brandenburg, 1765 -- Berlin, 1814;
court-cond. and dram. composer.

**Hind'le, J.,** Westminster, 1761—1796;
composer.

**Hine, W.m.,** Oxfordshire, 1687—1730;
composer and organist.

**Hings'ton, J.,** d. 1683; Engl. organist to Chas. I.; and composer.

**Hinke** (hǐnk'-ĕ), (1) **Gv. Ad.,** Dresden,
1844—Leipzig, 1893; oboist. Son of
(2) **Gf. H.,** d. 1851.

**Hinrichs** (hǐn'-rǐkhs), **Fz.,** Halle-on-
the-Saale, ca. 1820—Berlin, 1892;
composer and writer on music. His
sister (2) **Maria.** Vide FRANZ.

**Hip'kins, Alfred Jas.,** b. Westminster, June 17, 1826; writer; an
authority on ancient instrs., etc.;
was for a time in business with
Broadwood; wrote many articles for
the "*Encyclopædia Britannica,*" and
"*Grove's Dictionary of Music,*" also
books on old instr. and pitch.

**Hirn** (hērn), **Gv. Ad.,** Logelbach, near
Colmar (Alsatia), 1815—Colmar, 1890;
writer.

**Hirsch** (hērsh), (1) Dr., **Rudolf,** Napa-
gedl, Moravia, 1816—Vienna, 1872;
critic, poet and composer. (2) **Karl,**
b. Wending, Bavaria, March 17,
1858; studied in Munich; 1885–87,
church mus.-dir., Munich; 1887–92,
Mannheim; then Cologne; since
1893, dir. various societies, etc.; c.
numerous pop. *a cappella* choruses,
cantatas · "*Werinher.*" a dram.

poem with orchestration (op. 1
etc.

**Hirschbach** (hērsh'-bäkh), **H.,** Be
1812—Gohlis, 1888; editor and c
poser.

**Hirschfeld** (hērsh'-fĕlt), **Robt.,** b.
ravia, 1858; studied Vienna Co
later lecturer there; 1884 teache
musical æsthetics; took Dr. 1
with dissertation on "*Johannes
Muris*"; he wrote a pamphlet aga
Hanslick in defence of ancient *a
pella* music, and founded the "1
naissance-Abende" to cultivate it.

**Hitz'ler, Daniel,** Haidenheim, V
tenberg, 1756—Stuttgart, 1635; wri

**Hobrecht** (hō'-brĕkht) (or **Obre
Obreht, Ober'tus, Hober'tus),
kob,** Utrecht, ca. 1430—Antw
ca. 1506; church composer of g
historical importance.

**Hobbs, J. Wm.,** Henley, 1799—C
don, 1877; tenor and composer.

**Hochberg** (hōkh'-bĕrkh), **Bolko, C
von** (pseud. **J. H. Franz**), b. Fürs
stein Castle, Silesia, Jan. 23, 18.
maintained the H. quartet at Dresd
1876 founded the Silesian music fe
vals; 1886, general intendant P
sian Ct. Th.; prod. 2 operas;
symphonies, etc.

**Hod'ges,** (1) **Edw.,** Bristol, Engl., 1
—Clifton, 1867; organist and wri
(2) **Faustina Hasse,** daughter
above, d. New York, Feb., 18
organist and composer. (3) Rev
**Seb. Bach,** D.D., son of abo
rector St. Paul's Ch., Baltimore;
ganist.

**Hoffmann** (hôf'-män), (1) **Euchari
b.** Heldburg, Franconia, cantor
Stralsund; writer and compos
1577–84. (2) **Ernst Th.** (Am
**deus) Wm.** (he added Amadeus fr
love of Mozart), Königsberg, 177(
Berlin, 1822; gifted poet, caricatur
and dram. composer. (3) **H. A**
(called **H. von Fallersleben**), F
lersleben, Hanover, 1798 — Cas
Korvei, 1874; writer. (4) **Richa**
b. Manchester, Engl., May 24, 18;
pianist and teacher: pupil of

ther, and de Meyer, Pleyel, Mosch-
es Rubinstein, Döhler, Thalberg,
d Liszt; since 1847, New York;
lo pianist with Jenny Lind on
urs, etc.; also with von Bülow,
N. Y. (1875); c. anthems, pf.-
s., etc. (5) **Karl,** b. Prague, Dec.
, 1872; violinist; studied Prague
ns.; founder and 1st vln. the faus "Bohemian String-quartet."

**Baptist,** b. Garitz, July 9, 1864;
rytone; studied with Tipka and
ockhausen; 1888—94 at Cologne;
97 ct.-opera, Berlin.

fmeister (hôf'-mī-shtĕr), **Fz. An-
n,** Rotenburg-on-Neckar, 1754 —
enna, 1812; conductor and dram.
mposer, etc.

haimer (hôf'-hī-mĕr) (**Hoffheimer,
offhaimer, Hoffhaymer), Paulus**
n, Radstadt, Salzburg, 1459—Salz-
rg, 1537; eminent organist; luten-
, composer and teacher.

mann (hôf'-män), (1) **Chr.,** ca.
68; cantor at Krossen; writer.
) **H.** (**K. Jn.**), Berlin, Jan. 13,
42—July 19, 1902; pupil of Würst,
ullak's Academy; famous pf.-vir-
oso and teacher; prod. succ. op-
as "*Cartouche*" (Berlin, 1869)
d "*Donna Diana,*" and 4 others;
d succ. orch. works, "*Hungarian
uite*" (1873) and "*Frithjof*" symph.
874); is a Prof., and a member of
e Berlin R. Acad. of Arts; c. 6
her operas, "secular oratorio"
*Prometheus*" (1896); cantatas;
*Schauspiel*" overture; "*Trauer-
arsch,*" etc., for orch.; a vln.-so-
ta, etc. (3) **Richard,** b. Delitzsch,
ussian Saxony, April 30, 1844; son
municipal mus.-dir.; pupil of
reyschock and Jadassohn; lives in
eipzig as teacher; pub. a valu-
le "*Praktische Instrumentations-
hule*" (Leipzig, 1893), a catechism
instrs., etc. (4) **Casimir** (rightly
yszkowski) (wēsh-kôf'-shkĭ), b.
acow, 1842; pianist; prof. of
rm. and comp. at Cons., and cond.
opera, Warsaw. (5) **Josef,** b.
acow, Jan. 20, 1877. Son and

(till 1892) pupil of (4); at 6 played in
public; at 9 toured Europe; at 10
gave 52 concerts in America; then
studied 2 years with Rubinstein and
made new début in Dresden, 1894, and
has toured Europe since and (1899)
America; from being a sensational
prodigy, he has developed into a solid
artist of great power, virtuosity and
charm; lives in Berlin; c. concerto,
etc.

**Hofmeister** (hôf'-mī-shtĕr), (1) **Fr.,**
1781—1864; publisher; his son and
successor (2) **Ad. H.,** ca. 1818—Leipzig, 1870; was succeeded by **Albert
Röthing,** b. Leipzig, Jan. 4, 1845.

**Ho'garth, G.,** Carfrae Mill, near Oxton, Berwickshire, 1783—London.
1870; 'cellist and composer; hi
daughter m. Charles Dickens.

**Hohlfeld** (hōl'-fĕlt), **Otto,** Zeulenroda,
Voigtland, 1854—Darmstadt, 1895;
vln.-virtuoso and composer.

**Hohnstock** (hōn'-shtŏk), **Carl,** Brunswick, 1828—1889; teacher, violinist,
pianist and composer.

**Hol, Richard,** b. Amsterdam, July 23,
1825; pupil Martens (org.) and of
Bertelman (harm. and cpt.); teache
at Amsterdam; 1862, city mus.-dir.,
Utrecht; 1869, cath.-organist; 1875,
dir. Sch. of Mus.; also cond. "Dili-
gentia" Concerts at The Hague, Classical Concerts at Amsterdam; 1878,
officer of the French Academy; c.
oratorio "*David*" (op. 81); 2 operas;
2 symphonies, etc.

**Hol'borne, Antony** and **Wm.,** English composers, 1597.

**Hol'combe,** (1) **H.,** Salisbury, ca.
1690—ca. 1750; singer, teacher and
composer. (2) **Josephine,** soprano,
N. Y., and (3) **Philip G.,** harp-
maker, London, both descendants
of (1).

**Hol'den, Oliver,** Charlestown, Mass.;
before 1792, publisher; composer,
his comp. incl. the hymn-tune "Coronation."

**Hol'der,** (1) Rev. **Wm.,** Nottinghamshire, ca. 1614—Amen Corner, 1697
write , editor and composer. (2)

**Jos. Wm.**, St. John's Clerkenwell, 1764—1823 ; organist and composer.

**Held'rich, Geo. M.**, English org.-builder, 1838.

**Hollander** (hôl'-länt-ĕr), (1) **Jans (de Hollandere)**, or **Jean de Holland**, Netherland contrapuntist (1543–58). (2) **Chr. Janszone**, Dordrecht (?), Holland, ca. 1520—Munich, ca. 1570 ; son of above ; conductor and composer.

**Holländer** (hôl'-lĕnt-ĕr), (1) **Alexis,** b. Ratibor, Silesia, Feb. 25, 1840 ; pianist ; pupil of Schnabel and Hesse at Breslau , cond. of the Gymnasium Singing Society ; 1858–61, studied with Grell and A. W. Bach, and K. Bohmer, Berlin, R. Akad.; 1861, teacher at Kullak's Acad.; 1864, cond.; 1870, cond. the "Cäcilienverein"; 1883, professor ; c. 6 pf. Intermezzi for left hand, etc. (2) **Gv.**, b. Leobschütz, Upper Silesia, Feb. 15, 1855 ; played in public very early ; pupil of David, of Joachim (vln.), and Kiel (theory) ; 1874, principal teacher Kullak's Acad. and royal chamber-mus.; toured .Austria with Carlotta Patti ; 1881, teacher at the Cons., Cologne ; 1884, leader at the Stadttheater ; 1894, dir. Stern Cons., Berlin ; 1896, concertmeister of a new orch., Hamburg ; c. vln. and pf.-pcs. (3) **Victor**, b. Leobschütz, April 20, 1866 ; pupil of Kullak ; c. the succ. 1-act comic operas "Ca1mosinella " (Frankf. - on - M., 1888) ; " The Bey of Morocco " (London, 1891) and piano-pieces.

**Hollangue.** Vide MONTON.

**Hollmann** (hôl'-män), **Josef**, b. Maestricht, Holland, Oct. 16, 1852 ; notable 'cellist ; studied with Gervais ; toured Europe, England and America ; court-mus., Holland, and wears many decorations.

**Hol'ly, Fz. Andrs.**, Luba, Bohemia, 1747—Breslau, May 4, 1783 ; dir. and writer at various theatres ; composer.

**Holmes** (hōmz), (1) **Edw.**, near London, 1797—U. S. 1859 ; pf.-teacher,

editor and critic. (2) **Wm.** Sudbury, Derbyshire, 1812—Lond 1885 ; pianist and professor.

**Alfred**, London, 1837—Paris, 18 son of above ; dram. composer.

**Hy.**, b. London, Nov. 7, 1839 ; I of above ; vln.-prof. R. C. M.; symphonies, etc.

**Holmès** (ôl'-mĕs) (rightly **Holm Augusta Mary Anne**, b. (of I parents) Paris, Dec. 16, 1847 ; first a pianist ; studied comp. v Lambert, Klosé and César Fran 1873, prod. a psalm, " In Exit 1874, a 1-act symphony " Héro Leandre " (Chatelet) ; the symp nies " Lutece " and " Les A nautes," 1883 ; symph. " Irlan 1885 ; unsucc. drama " La Monta Noire " (Gr. Opera), 1895 ; sympho poems, " Roland," " Pologne," " Pays Bleu " ; 2 operas, etc.; sometimes uses pseud. " Herme Zenta."

**Holst** (hôlst), **Edvard**, Copenhag 1843—N. Y., 1899 ; lived in N. was an actor, stage-dancer, danci master and playwright ; also co poser of pop. song and pf.-pcs., c 2,000 works in all.

**Holstein** (hôl'-shtīn), **Fz. (Fr.)** v Brunswick, 1826—Leipzig, 18 dram. composer.

**Holten** (hôl'-tĕn), **K. von**, b. Ha burg, July 26, 1836 ; pianist ; pu of J. Schmitt, Ave-Lallemant a Grädener, and at Leipzig Co since 1874, teacher Hamburg Co c. a Kindersymphonie, etc.

**Holy** (ō'-lē), **Alfred**, b. Oporto, A 5, 1866 ; harp-virtuoso ; son and pil of a cond. and teacher fr Prague ; studied at Prague Co and lived there till 1896, when went to the Berlin ct.-opera.

**Holyoke** (hōl'-yōk), **Samuel**, B ford, Mass., 1771—Concord, N. I 1816 ; teacher.

**Holz** (hôlts), **K.**, Vienna, 1798—18 violinist and composer.

**Holzbauer** (hôlts'-bow-ĕr), **Ignaz**, enna, 1711—Mannheim, 1783 ; cou

nductor and dram. composer ; high-
praised by Mozart.

zel (hĕl'-tsĕl), (1) **K.**, Linz-on-
onau, 1808—Pesth, 1883; composer.
) **Gustav**, Pesth, 1813—Vienna,
83 ; bass and composer.

zl (hĕl'-ts'l), **Fz. Severin**, Malacz-
, Hungary, 1808—Funikirchen,
84 ; conductor and composer.

neyer (hō'-mī-ĕr), name of a mu-
cal family. The most prom. of
em is (1) **Paul Joseph M.**, b. Os-
rode, Harz, Oct. 26, 1853 ; famous
ganist at the Gewandhaus, and
acher Leipzig Cons. (2) **Jn. Just.
dam**, editor. His son (3) **H. H.**
832—1891), was organist at Lam-
ringe ; st. Leipzig Cons.; and also
ith his uncle (4) **J. M. H.** (d. Oct. 5,
94), organist at Duderstadt.

nilius (hō-mē'-lĭ-oos), **Gf. Aug.**,
osenthal, Saxony, 1714—Dresden,
785 ; eminent organist and com-
ser.

od, **Helen**, b. Chelsea, Mass., June
8, 1863 ; pupil of B. J. Lang (pf.)
d Chadwick (comp.), Boston ; and
oszkowski (pf.) ; lives in Boston ;
omposer.

ok, **Jas.**, Norwich,1746—Boulogne,
827 ; organist and composer.

op'er, **Edmond**, Halberton, Deon, ca. 1553—1621 ; composer.

pe'kirk, **Helen**, b. near Edinburgh;
udied with Lichtenstein and A. C.
Iackenzie ; for 2 years at Leipzig,
ater with Leschetizky ; début as
ianist at Gewandhaus, Leipzig,
878 ; gave concerts in Great Britain
nd (1883–84) U. S.; 1897–1901,
eacher N. E. Cons.; now private
eacher, Boston, Mass.; c. Concert-
tück for pf. and orch.; 1894, orch.
cs.; a pf.-concerto ; sonata for pf.
nd vln., and songs.

pffer (hŏp'-fĕr), **L. Bd.**, Berlin, 1840
—Niederwald, near Rudesheim, 1877;
ram. composer.

p'kins, (1) **Edw. J.**, Westminster,
une 30, 1818—London, Feb. 4,
901 ; self-taught organist at various
hurches ; 1843–1898, to the Temple

Ch., London ; wrote " *The Organ ;
its History and Construction* " (Rimbault) ; contributed to Grove's Dict.
of Mus. ; c. 3 prize anthems, hymn-
tunes, chants and church-services.
(2) **Edw. Jerome**, Burlington, Vt.,
1836—Athenia, N. J., 1898 ; self-
taught in harmony ; began composing
at 4 ; organist, editor and lecturer.
(3) **Harry Patterson**, b. Baltimore ;
graduated Peabody Inst., 1896 ;
studied with Dvôrák in Bohemia ;
lives in New York ; c. a symphony,
songs, etc.

**Hoplit.** Vide POHL, R.

**Horák** (hō'-räk), (1) **Wenzel (Václav)
Emanuel**, Mscheno-Lobes, Bohe-
mia, 1800—Prague, 1871 ; organist,
teacher and composer. (2) **Ed.**, Ho-
litz, Bohemia, 1839—Riva, Lake of
Garda, 1892 ; teacher and writer. (3)
**Ad.**, b. Jankovic, Bohemia, Feb.
15, 1850 ; bro. of above and co-
founder, " Horák " Pf.-School, Vienna ; writer.

**Horn**, (1) **K. Fr.**, Nordhausen, Saxony,
1762—Windsor, Engl., 1830 ; organ-
ist, writer and theorist. (2) **Chas.
Edw.**, London, 1786 — Boston,
Mass., 1849 ; son of above ; singer,
teacher, cond., and composer. (3)
**Aug.**, Freiberg, Saxony, 1825 —
Leipzig, 1893 ; dram. composer.

**Horneman** (hôr'-nĕ-män), (1) **Johan
Ole Emil**, Copenhagen, 1809—1870;
composer. (2) **Chr. F. Emil**, b.
Copenhagen, Dec. 17, 1841 ; son and
pupil of above ; studied at Leipzig
Cons.; dir. of sch. of mus. in Copen-
hagen ; c. overtures " *Aladdin* " and
" *Heldenleben*," etc.

**Hornstein** (hôrn'-shtīn), **Robt. von**,
Stuttgart, 1833 — Munich, 1890 ;
dram. composer.

**Hors'ley**, (1) **Wm.**, London, 1774—
1858 ; organist, theorist and composer. (2) **Chas. Edw.**, London,
1822—New York, 1876 ; son and pupil of above ; organist, writer and
composer.

**Horwitz** (hôr'-vĭts), **Benno**, b. Berlin,
March 17, 1855 ; violinist and com-

poser ; pupil of the Rl. Hochschule, and of Kiel and Albert Becker ; c. symph. poem "*Dionysos*," etc.

**Hostinsky** (hô-shtēn'-shkĭ), **Ottokar**, b. Martinoves, Bohemia, Jan. 2, 1847 ; Dr. Phil., Prague ; writer.

**Hoth'by** (or **Hothoous, Otteby,** Fra **Ottobi**), **John** (or **Johannes**), d. London, Nov., 1487; English Carmelite monk ; famous for science.

**Hotteterre** (ôt'-tăr), (1) **Henri**, d. 1683 ; instr.-maker, musette player, ct.-musician. (2) **Louis** (called "**Le Romain**," having lived in Rome) ; son of above ; notable flutist and writer. (3) **Nicolas**, d. 1695 ; noted bassoonist and oboist ; bro. of (2).

**Ho'ven**, J., pen-name of V. **von Putt-Lingen.**

**How'ard**, (1) **Samuel**, 1710—1782 ; English organist and composer. (2) **G. H.**, b. Norton, Mass., Nov. 12, 1843 ; pupil of J. Tufts (theory), and B. F. Baker (singing), also at Leipzig Cons.; teacher in Boston ; 1891, founder and dir. School for Teachers ; composer.

**How'ell**, (1) **Jas.**, b. Plymouth, England, d. 1879 ; singer and double-bass player. His 2 sons : (2) **Arthur**, d. 1885 ; double-bass player and bass singer. (3) **Edw.**, 'cellist.

**How'gill, Wm.**, Engl. organist and composer, 1794.

**Hoy'land**, (1) **J.**, Sheffield, 1783—1827 ; organist and composer. (2) **Wm.**, d. 1857 ; son of above ; organist.

**Hrimaly** (h'rĭm'-ŭ-lē), **Adalbert**, b. Pilsen, Bohemia, July 30, 1842 ; violinist ; pupil of Mildner, Prague Cons., 1861; cond. Gothenburg orch., 1868 ; National Th., Prague ; at the German Th., there in 1873, and at Czernowitz, Bukowina, in 1875 ; his succ. opera "*Der Verzauberte Prinz*" (1871) is still played at Prague.

**Hromada** (h'rä'-mŭ-dŭ), **A.**, Kladno, Bohemia, Dec. 23, 1841—1901 ; notable bass-barytone ; pupil of Pivoda, Stockhausen and Fra Lamperti; début ct.-opera, Stuttgart, 1866; has sung

there since ; has also toured a[*] heavily decorated.

**Hubay** (hoȯ'-bä-ē) (or **Huber**), K., Varjas, Hungary, 1828—1[*] 1885 ; vln.-prof., Pesth Cons.; ductor and dram. composer. Jenö (known as **Eugen Hub[*]** Germany), b. Budapesth, Sept.[*] 1858 ; violinist ; son and pup[*] above, and 1886 his successo[*] prof.; also studied with Joac[*] gave succ. concerts in Hun[*] and at Paris ; 1882 principal prof., Brussels Cons.; 1894, Countess Rosa Cebrian ; c. [*] opera "*Der Geigenmacher von*[*] *mona*" (Pesth, 1893) ; opera "[*] *nor*" (Pesth, 1892) ; succ. Hunga[*] opera "*A Falu Rossza*" (The T[*] loafer) (Budapesth, 1896) ; a [*] phony, etc.

**Huber** (hooˈ-běr), (1) **F.**, d. Be[*] Feb. 23, 1810; poet and song-c[*] poser. (2) **Fd.**, 1791—St. Ga[*] 1863 ; Swiss song-writer. (3)[*] Vide HUBAY. (4) **Jos.**, Sigmarin[*] 1837—Stuttgart, 1886 ; violinist[*] dram. composer. (5) **Hans**,[*] Schönewerd, Switzerland, June[*] 1852 ; pupil Leipzig Cons.; tea[*] at Wesserling for 2 years, the[*] Thann (Alsatia), later Basel M[*] School ; 1892, Dr. Phil. *h. c.*, B[*] Univ. ; 1896, dir. of the Mus. S[*] c. succ. operas "*Weltfrühli*[*] (Basel, 1894) ; and "*Gudr*[*] (Basel, 1896) ; cantatas, sona[*] concerios, overtures "*Lustsp*[*] symph. "*Tell*," etc. (6) **Eug**[*] Vide HUBAY, JENO.

**Hu'bermann, Bronislaw**, Polish [*] linist ; succ. début as prodigy ;[*] tired for five years' study ; re[*] peared, Bucharest, 1902.

**Hubert** (hooˈ-běrt), **Nikolai Alber**[*] **vitch**, 1840—1888 ; prof. and wri[*] at Moscow.

**Huberti** (ü-běr'-tē), **Léon Gve.**,[*] Brussels, April 14, 1843 ; pupil B[*] sels Cons. ; 1865, won Prix de Ro[*] 1874–78, dir. of Mons. Cons. ; 18[*] 89, Antwerp ; since prof. at Brus[*]

1s., and dir. of the Mus.-School of
Josse - ten - Noode - Schaerbeek ;
1, member of the Belgian Aca-
1y ; 1893, chevalier of the
zion of Honour. C. 3 oratorios,
dram. poem "*Verlichting*"
Fiat lux "), with orch.; symphonic
m "*Kinderlust en Leed*," chorus
l orch., etc.; symphonie funèbre,
:ival marches, etc.

bald (hook'-bält, or ük-bäl) (**Hug-
l'dus, Ubal' dus, Uchubal'dus)
S.Amand(o),** ca. 840—St. Amand,
r Tournay, June 25 (or Oct. 21),
b (or June 20, 932). He is perhaps
dited with some works belonging
a monk of the same name living a
tury later, pupil of his uncle,
lo, a mus.-dir., whose jealousy
ve him to Nevers, where he taught
ging ; 872 he succeeded his uncle ;
893, the Archbishop of Rheims
ited him to reform the music of
: diocese. His works (Gerbert)
atain the first known notation
wing difference of pitch on lines.

'son, (1) **Robt.,** 1731 — Eton,
5 ; singer, organist and composer.

**Mary,** daughter of above ; organ-
and composer, 1801.

(ü), **Georges Ad.,** b. Versailles,
iy 6, 1858 ; pupil of Paris Cons.,
ok 1st Grand prix de Rome ; later
ix Cressent ; l. Paris as teacher ;
op. com. "*Les Pantins*" (Op.-
m., 1881) ; "*Rübezahl*," symphonic
gend in 3 parts (" Concerts Cone." 1886) ; succ. "Féerie drama-
ue " "*La Belle au Bois Dormant*"
aris, 1894) ; "épisode sacré"
Ressurrection" ; a symphony, a
mphonic overture ; 2 operas "*Va-
nta*," and "*Le Roi de Paris*" (not
od.), etc.

ffer (hüf'-fĕr), **Francis,** Münster,
-43—London, Jan. 19, 1899 ; 1869,
ed in London ; from 1878, critic of
he Times ; librettist and writer.

to **von Reutlingen** (hoo'-gō fōn
it'-lĭng-ĕn) (called " Spechzhart "),
:85 (1286 ?)—1359 (1360 ?) ; writer.

guenet (üg-nā). Vide GIRARD.

**Huhn** (hoon), **Charlotte,** b. Lüneburg,
Sept. 15, 1868 ; alto ; studied with
Hoppe, Hey, and Marianne Brandt .
sang 2 years at the New York Opera,
then at Cologne ; 1895 Dresden ; 1900
Vienna ct.-opera.

**Hul'lah, John Pyke,** Worcester, June
27, 1812—London, Feb. 21, 1884 ;
professor, conductor, writer and
dram. composer.

**Hüller, J. A.** Vide HILLER.

**Hüllmandel** (hǐl'-mänt-'l), (1) **Nicholas Jos.,** Strassburg, 1751 — London, 1823 ; pianist and harmonica-
player. (2) **Rodolphe,** famous horn-
virtuoso and composer , uncle of
above.

**Hüllweck** (hǐl'-vĕk), (1) **Fd.,** Dessau,
1824—Blasewitz, 1887 ; concert-violinist and composer. (2) **K.,** b. Dresden, April 15, 1852 ; son of above ;
pupil of Fr. Grützmacher ('cello) ;
Reichel and Merkel (harm. and cpt.);
1877–82 'cellist Dresden ct.-orch. ;
'cello-teacher, Dresden Cons. ; composer.

**Hülskamp** (hǐls'-kämp), **Henry** (or
**Gv. Heinrich),** b. Westphalia ; 1850
established a factory at Troy, N. Y.;
1866, N. Y.

**Hume, Lobias,** Engl. viol da gambist,
etc., 17th cent.

**Hum'frey (Humphrey, Humphrys),
Pelham,** London, 1647—Windsor,
July 14, 1674 ; important English
composer. Charles II. sent him to
Paris to study with Lully ; 1672
master Chapel Royal children and
with Purcell ct.-composer.

**Hummel** (hoom'-mĕl), (1) **Jos.,** music-
master Wartberg Military Acad. ;
1786, conductor at Vienna. (2) **Jn.
Nepomuk,** Pressburg, Nov. 14, 1778
—Weimar, Oct.17, 1837; son of above;
a famous pianist and improviser, and
a composer of once popular pieces in
which ornament outweighs matter ;
and form, interest ; protégé of Mozart ; début 1787 ; toured Europe frequently ; 1793 studied with Albrechtsberger ; asst.-cond. to Haydn, 1804–
11 ; 1830 and 1833 cond. German

opera in London ; c. operas, cantatas, ballets, 3 masses, sonatas; he pub.
a notable pf.-method ; c. dram. pcs.,
concertos, sonatas, septet in D minor,
etc.   (3) **Elisabeth** (née **Röckl**),
1783—Weimar, 1883 ; wife of above;
opera-singer.  (4) **Jos. Fr.**, b. Innsbrück, Aug. 14, 1841 ; pupil Munich
Cons., 1861–80 ; th.-cond. Vienna,
since 1880 dir. Mozarteum at Salzburg, and cond. *Liedertafel.*   (5)
**Fd.**, b. Berlin, Sept. 6, 1855 ; son
and pupil of a musician ; at 7 a harp
virtuoso ;   1864–67 toured Europe,
and received a royal grant for study
at Kullak's Akademie, Berlin ; 1871–
75, studied R. High Sch. of Mus.,
then at Akademie; c. succ. operas,
" *Mara* " (Berlin, 1893) ;  " *Ein
Treuer Schelm* " (Prague, 1894) ;
" *Assarpai* " (Gotha, 1898) ; a symphony, sonatas, etc.

**Humperdinck** (hoom'-pĕr-dĭnk), **Engelbert,** b. Siegburg, near Bonn,
Sept. 1, 1854 ; studied architecture,
Cologne, then mus. at the Cons. ;
won Mozart scholarship at Frankfort ; studied 2 years with Franz
Lachner, Munich, also with Rheinberger and Barmann at the Cons. ;
pub. Humoreske for orch. and " *Die
Wallfahrt nach Kevelaar* " for chorus ;   1878 won the Mendelssohn
prize (3,000 marks), 1880 the Meyerbeer prize (7,600 marks) ; 1885–86,
prof. Barcelona Cons.; 1881–82, a
special protégé of R. Wagner in Bayreuth ; made pf.-scores, and aided in
the preparation of " *Parsifal.*"  Returned to Cologne, 1887, went to
Mayence in the employ of Schott &
Co. ;   1890 teacher Hoch Cons.,
Frankfort.  Critic on the Frankfort
*Zeitung,* since lives at Boppard-on-
Rhine.  His first international succ.
was the graceful 2-act fairy-opera
" *Hänsel und Gretel,*" Munich,
1893 (prod. at Milan, 1897, as *Nino
e Rita*) ;  c. also " *Dornröschen*";
" *Die Königskinder* " (1896); " *Saint-
Cyr ;* " " *Die 7 Geieslein* " (" März-
chen-spiel fur die Kleinen ") ; symph.

incid. mus., " *Moorish Rhapso*
for orch., etc.

**Huneker** (hū'-něk-ěr), **Jas. (Gibbo**
b. Philadelphia, Jan. 31, 1[
prominent critic and writer ; at [
intended for the priesthood ; pup
Michael Cross (pf.) at Philadeip
1878, with Th. Ritter and Ld. [
treleau, Paris ;  since 1888 live
New York as pf.-teacher at the I
Cons. ; for some time mus. and di
critic of the *Commercial Adver*
and *The Recorder;* 1901 of the N
*Sun ;* has for many years written
brilliant " Raconteur " departmen
the *Mus. Courier.*   Many of his
says were reprinted with great s
as " *Mezzotints in Modern Mu.*
(New York, 1899) ; his biogr.
critical " *Chopin, the Man and
Music* " (N. Y., 1900) is an im
tant book ; and his " *Melomania*
(1901), studies of musical personal
and moods in the form of short
ries, is a work of unique insight
ingenuity.  He is preparing a life
Liszt.

**Hungar** (hoong'-är) **E-nst**, b. Sch
bach, Aug. 5, 1854 ; barytone ; p
of Stockhausen ; teacher at Dres
and Cologne Cons.; sang at Schw
ct.-opera ; lives in Leipzig.

**Hunkě** (hoon'-kě), **Jos.,** Josephst
Bohemia, 1801—St. Petersburg, 1[
choirm.  Russian ct.-chapel ; c
poser.

**Hünten** (hĭn'-tĕn), (1) **Fz.,** Coble
1793--1878 ;  c. pop. pf.-pcs.,
His brothers, (2) **Wm.,** pf.-teac
Coblenz. and (3) **Peter Ernst,**
Duisburg, also c. pop. pieces.

**Hurel de Lamare** (ü'-rĕl-dŭ-lä-m
**Jacques Michel,** Paris, 1772—Ca
1823 ; 'cellist and composer ;
friend Auber pub. some comp. un
H.'s name.

**Huss** (hoos), (1) **G. J.,** b. Roth, n
Nürnberg, Sept. 25, 1828 ; son
pupil of (2) **Jn. Michael** (pian
also studied org. with Lambrec
1848, America as organist var
churches.  1856, New York, org. [

acher and composer. (3) **H. Hold-**
**a,** b. Newark, N. J., June 21, 1862 ;
ncert-pianist and teacher ; son and
upil of (1) ; studied with O. B.
>ise (cpt. and comp.), also at Mu-
ch Cons.; lives in N. Y. as teacher
pf., comp. and instr.; pub. pf.-
>ncerto, ballade "*Haidenröslein,*"
c.; he has also works in MS., but
erformed with succ.: rhapsody for
. and orch., "*Festival Sanctus*"
>r chorus and organ, with orch.; a
n.-concerto ; romanze and polonaise
>r vln. with orch.; a pf.-trio, "*Cleo-
atra's Death,*" etc.

ch'inson, (1) **J.,** organist and com-
>ser Durham cath., 17th cent. (2)
'rancis, English composer under
seudonym "*Francis Ireland,*"
771.

tschenruijter (hoot'-shĕn-roi-tĕr),
) **Willem,** Rotterdam, 1796—1878 ;
orn- and trumpet-virtuoso ; profess-
r, conductor, director and dram.
omposer. (2) **Willem,** b. March
2, 1828 ; son of above ; horn-virtu-
so.

ttenbrenner (hĭt'-tĕn-brĕn-nĕr),
**Anselm,** Graz, Styria, 1794—Ober-
andritz, 1868 ; pianist, conductor
nd dram. composer.

kaert (or **Ycaert**) (ē-kärt), **Bd.,**
antor in Belgium, ca. 1480 ; theorist
nd composer.

·llested (hŭl'-lĕ-städh), **Aug.,** b. (of
Janish parents) Stockholm, June 17,
858 ; violinist : at 5 played in pub-
ic ; studied with Holger Dahl till
869, and then made succ. tour
hrough Scandinavia ; entered the
Royal Cons. at Copenhagen ; 1876,
>rganist of the Cath., and dir. of a
nus. soc.; 1879, studied with Kullak,
Kiel, and later Liszt ; 1885, toured U.
S.; 1886–91, asst.-dir. Chicago Mus.
Coll.; 1891–94, Gottschalk Lyric
Sch.; 1894–97, toured Europe ; prod.
in London, symph. poem "*Elizabeth,*" with double chorus ; 1897,
Chicago ; c. romantic play "*Die
Rheinnixe,*" orch. "suite romantique," etc.

## I

**Ibach** (ē'-bäkh), (1) **Jns. Ad.,** 1766—
1848 ; pf. and organ-builder. His son
(2) **C. Rudolf** (d. 1862), and (3)
**Richard,** joined the firm ; a third
son (4) **Gustav J.,** founded another
business 1869. (5) **Rudolf** (d. Herren-
alb, Black Forest, July, 1892), son of
(2), continued the pf.-factory, and
**Richard,** the organ-factory.

**Iliffe** (ī'-lĭf), **Fr.,** b. Smeeton-Westerby,
Leicester, Engl., Feb. 21, 1847; since
1883, organist and choirm. St. John's
Coll., Oxford ; cond. of Queen's
Coll. Mus. Soc. 1873, Mus. Bac.
Oxon.; wrote "*Critical Analysis of
Bach's Clavichord*" (London, 1896 ;
4 parts); c. oratorio, "*The Visions
of St. John the Divine*"; cantata
with orch. "*Lara,*" etc.

**Ilinski** (ē-lĭn'-shkĭ), Count **Jan Stanis-
law,** b. Castle Romanov, 1795;
composer.

**Im'myns,** (1) **J.,** 1700 (?)—London,
1764 ; lutenist. (2) **J.,** d. 1794 ; son
of above ; organist.

**Inc'ledon, Chas.,** Bery St. Kevern,
Cornwall, 1763—1826 ; tenor, called
"The Wandering Melodiste."

**Indy** (dän-dē), **Paul M. Th. V. d',**
b. Paris, March 27, 1851; pupil of
César Franck (comp.) and at the
Cons., 1875, chorusm. with Colonne ; played drum-parts for 3 years
to learn instrumentation ; he is pres.
of various concert-societies ; mus.-
inspector of Paris schools ; chev. of
the Legion of Honour ; c. a 3-part
symph. poem "*Wallenstein*" (Part
II., "*I Piccolomini,*" prod. 1874 by
Pasdeloup) ; symphonies (1) "*On a
French mountaineer-song,*" and (2)
"*Jean Hunyadi,*" symphonic legend
"*La forêt enchantée*"; overture to
"*Antony and Cleopatra*"; "*La Che-
vauchée du Cid,*" for orch. ; symphonic pf.-concerto ; prod. 1-act comic opera, "*Attendez-moi sous l'Orme*"
(Op.-com., 1882) ; c. text and mus.;
succ. mus. drama, "*Fervaal*" (Brussels, 1897); "*L'Etranger*" (do. 1901)

**Ingegneri** (ēn-gān-yā'-rē), **Marco A.**, Venice (or Cremona), ca. 1540—Ferrara (?), 1603 ; conductor, composer and publisher.

**Ing'lott, Wm.**, 1544 — 1621 ; Eng. organist.

**Insanguine** (ēn-sän-gwē'-nā), **Giacomo** (called **Monopoli**), Monopilo, 1744—Naples, 1795 ; teacher and dram. composer.

**Ireland, Francis.** Pen name of **Hutchinson** (2).

**Irgang** (ēr'-gäng), **Fr. Wm.**, b. Hirschberg, Schleswig, Feb. 23, 1836 ; pupil of Grell and A. W. Bach, R. Acad., Berlin, 1856—59 ; then teacher in Proksch's Sch., Prague ; 1863, founded sch. at Görlitz ; also organ composer.

**Isaak** (ē'-zäk), **H.** (or **Isaac, Izak, Yzac, Ysack** ; in Italy **Arrigo Tedesco**, Henry the German ; Low ; Lat. **Arrighus**), ca. 1450—ca. 1517 famous contrapuntist doubtless of Netherlandish birth ; conductor and organist.

**'sham, J.**, d. London, 1726 ; organist and composer.

**Isido'rus** (**Hıspalen'sis**), Saint, Cartagena, ca. 570—636; writer (Gerbert).

**Isnardi** (ēs-när'-dē), **Paolo**, b. Ferrara, ca. 1525 ; conductor and composer.

**Isouard** (ē-zoo-ăr), **Niccolò** (called **Niccolo de Malte**), Malta, 1775—Paris, March 23, 1818 ; pupil of Amendola, Sala, and Guglelmi ; organist, conductor and prolific dram. composer.

**Israel** (ēs'-rä-ĕl), **K.**, Heiligenrode, Electoral Hesse, 1841—Frankfort-on-M., 1881; critic and bibliographer.

**I'van(h)off, Nicholas**, b. 1809 ; Russian tenor.

**Ives, Simon**, d. London, 1662 ; Engl. singer and composer.

**Ivry** (dēv-rē), **Paul Xavier Désiré**, Marquis **Richard d'**, b. Beaune, Côte D'Or, Feb. 4, 1829 ; pupil of A. Hignard and Leborne ; since 1854 lives in Paris as amateur ; c. operas, "*Fatma,*" "*Quentin Metzys*" (1854), "*La Maison du Docteur*" (Dijon,

1855), "*Omphale et Pénélopé,*" *Amants de Vérone*" (1867), u the pen-name "**Richard Irvi** revised as "*Roméo et Julie* 1878 ; "*Persévérance D'Amo* (MS.) ; concert-overture, songs, e

**Izac.** Vide ISAAK.

## J

**Jachet.** Vide BERCHEM.

**Jachmann-Wagner** (yäkh'-män). \ WAGNER, JOHANNA.

**Jack'son**, (1) **Wm.**, Exeter, 173 1803 ; organist, writer, and dr composer. (2) **Wm.**, Mash Yorks, Engl., 1815—Bradford, 1 organist, conductor, writer and c poser. (3) **Samuel P.**, Manches Engl., 1818—Brooklyn, N. Y., 1 composer ; son of (4) **James J.**, gan-builder. (5) **Edwin W.**, E lish justice of the peace, pub. German (Leipzig, 1866) a valua manual of finger-gymnastics. (6 P., English writer ; pub. books transl. of Wagner's operas.

**Ja'cob**, (1) **Benj.**, London, 1778—1 organist, conductor and compo (2) **F. A. L.**, Vide JAKOB.

**Jacobs** (zhă-kō), **Édouard**, b. Hal, 1 gium, 1851 ; pupil of Servais, B sels Cons. ; 'cellist Weimar ct. or for some years ; 1885 prof. Bruss Cons.

**Jacobsohn** (yäk'-ôp-zōn), **Simon** b. Mitau, Kurland, Dec. 24, 18 violinist ; pupil Leipzig Cons. ; 1 leader Bremen orch.; 1872, of Th dore Thomas's orch., N. Y.; teac Cincinnati Cons., then Chicago.

**Jacobsthal** (yäk'-ôps-täl), **Gv.**, b. ritz, Pomerania, March 14, 18, 1872, lecturer on music Strassb Univ.; 1875 professor extraordina writer.

**Jacotin** (rightly **Jacques Godebry** (zhăk-ô-tăn) (or gôd-brē), ca. 144 March 24, 1529; famous Flem cptist.; singer and composer at A werp.

quard (zhăk-kăr), **Léon J.,** Paris,
26—1886 ; 'cellist ; composer.

assohn (yä'-däs-zōn), **Salomon,**
reslau, Aug. 13, 1831—Leipzig, Feb.
1901 ; eminent theorist ; pupil of
esse (pf.), Lüstner (vln.) and Bro-
y (harm.) ; later Leipzig Cons., then
ith Liszt, and Hauptmann (comp.);
om 1852 lived in Leipzig ; 1866
ind. " Balterion " choral soc.; 1867—
cond. " Euterpe"; from 1871, prof.
pf., harm., cpt., comp. and instru-
entation at the Cons. 1877, Dr.
ail., *h. c.*; 1893 Royal Prof. He m.
singing-teacher. Wrote occasion-
ly under name " **Lübenau** " (lü'-
-now). Pub. very succ. text-books
l trans. in English. " *Harmonie-
hre* " (Leipzig, 1883) ; " *Kontra-
nkt* " (1884) ; " *Kanon und Fuge*"
884) ; " *Die Formen in den Werk-
 der Tonkunst* " (1889) ; " *Lehr-
ch der Instrumentation* " (1889) ;
*Allgemeine Musiklehre* " (1895).
is comps. are notable for form, par-
cularly his many works in canon
cl. serenade for orch. (op. 35), and
llet-mus.; which have won him the
me " **Musical Krupp** " ; c. also
symphonies ; 2 overtures ; a pf.-
ncerto ; The 100th Psalm, for
uble chorus with orchestration,
c.

in (zhă-dăn), (1) **Louis Emman-
l,** Versailles, 1768—Paris, 1853 ;
of., conductor and dram. compos-
. Son and pupil of (2) **Jean J.,**
olinist. (3) **Hyacinthe,** Versailles,
69—Paris, 1802 ; prof. and com-
ser ; bro and teacher of (1).

ll (yăl), (1) **Alfred,** Trieste, March
1832—Paris, Feb. 27, 1882 ; noted
uring pianist and composer, son of
) **Eduard J.** (d. Vienna, 1849). (3)
ell-Trautmann, Marie, b. Stein-
ltz, Alsatia, 1846 ; wife of (1);
anist, composer and writer.

é (yäf'-fä), **Moritz,** b. Posen, Jan.
1835; violinist; pupil of Ries Boh-
er (harm.), of Maurin and Massard,
aub, Wuerst and Bussler ; c. ope-
s, etc.

**Jahn** (yän), (1) **Otto,** Kiel, June 16
1813 — Göttingen, Sept. 9, 1869 ;
prof. of archæology, Bonn Univ. ;
wrote a model biog. of Mozart (1856-
59, 4 vols.), etc., also composed. (2)
**Wm.,** Hof, Moravia, Nov. 24, 1835—
Vienna, April 21, 1900 ; 1854 conductor ; dir. ct.-opera, Vienna, etc.

**Jähns** (yäns), **Fr. Wm.,** Berlin, 1809
—1888 ; singer, composer and writer.

**Jakob** (yä'-kôp), **Fr. Auff. Leberecht,** Kroitzsch, 1803 — Liegnitz,
1884 ; collector.

**Jakubowski** (yäk-oo-bôf'-shkĭ), **Samson,** b. Kowno, 1801 ; Polish composer; inv. and played the xylophone.

**James,** (1) **J.,** d. 1745 ; Engl. organist and composer. (2) **W. N.,** Eng.
flutist and composer, 1824.

**Janiewicz** (yän-ē-vēch), **Felix,** Wilna, 1762—Edinburgh, 1848 ; violinist
and composer.

**Jan** (yän), (1) **Maistre.** Vide GAL-
LUS, J. (2) **K. von,** b. Schweinfurt,
1836 ; Dr. phil., Berlin, 1859 ; writer.

**Jankó** (yäng'-kō), **Paul von,** b. Totis,
Hungary, June 2, 1856 ; pupil Polytechnic, Vienna, and at the Cons.
with Hans Schmitt, Krenn, and
Bruckner ; 18 1–82, mathematics at
Berlin Univ., pf. with Ehrlich ; inv.
in 1882 the admirable keyboard
known by his name (v. D. D.) ;
taught in Leipzig Cons., etc.

**Jan(n)akoni** (yän-nä-kō'-nē), **Gius.,**
Rome, 1741—March 16, 1816 ; emi-
nent church-composer ; conductor at
St. Peter's ; pupil of Rinaldini and
Carpani.

**Jannequin** (or **Janequin, Jennekin**)
(zhăn-kăn), **Clément,** a French (or
Belgian) contrapuntist of the 16th
cent. ; nothing is known of him except that he lived to be old and poor;
c. genuine " programme " music.

**Janotha** (yä-nō'-tä), **Nathalie,** b.
Warsaw ; pupil of Joachim and Rudorff, Clara Schumann, Brahms, and
Princess Czartoryska, F. Weber
(harm.) and Bargiel ; début at the
Gewandhaus, Leipzig, 1874 ; 1885,
ct.-pianist to the German Emperor

and decorated with many orders;
pub. a trans. with additions of Klec-
zynski's "Cho in"; c. "*Ave Maria*"
(dedicated to Pope Leo), "*Mountain Scenes*" (to Frau Schumann),
gavottes, etc., for piano.

**Janowka** (yä-nôf'-kä), **Thos. Balthasar**, b. Kuttenberg, Bohemia; organist and writer at Prague ca. 1660.

**Jansa** (yän'-sä), **Ld.**, Wildenschwert,
Bohemia, 1794—Vienna, 1875; violinist, teacher and composer.

**Jansen** (yän'-zĕn), **F. Gv**, b. Jever,
Hanover, Dec. 15, 1831; pupil of
Coccius and Riccius; teacher at
Göttingen; 1855, organist Verden
Cath.; 1861, Royal Mus. Dir.; com-
poser and writer.

**Janssen** (yäns'-zĕn), (1) **N. A.**, Car-
thusian monk; organist and writer at
Louvain, 1845. (2) **Julius**, b. Ven-
lo, Holland, June 4, 1852; studied
Cologne Cons.; 1876, cond. Mus.
Soc., Minden; later cond. at Lort-
mund; 1890, city mus. dir.; cond.
the 1st and 2d Westphalian Mus.
Festivals; pub. songs.

**Janssens** (yäns'-zĕns), **Jean Fran.
Jos.**, Antwerp, 1801—insane, 1835;
dram. composer.

**Januschowsky** (yän-oo-shôf'-shkĭ),
(Frau) **Georgine von**, b. Austria, ca.
1859; 1875, soprano in operetta at
Sigmaringen; 1877, soubrette, Th.
an der Wien, Vienna; 1879-80, Leipzig; 1880, Germania Th., New York;
1892, at Mannheim and Wiesbaden;
1893-95, prima donna, Imp. Opera,
Vienna; sang Wagner, etc., as well
as leading soubrette-rôles in over 60
comic operas and operettas; m. Ad.
Neuendorff.

**Japha** (yä'-fä), (1) **G. Jos.**, Königsberg, 1835—Cologne, 1892; violin-
ist. (2) **Louise**, b. Hamburg, Feb.
2, 1826; pianist and composer; pupil of Warendorf (pf.), Gross and
Grund (comp.) and Robt. and Clara
Schumann; 1858, she m. W. Langhans, with whom she gave v. succ.
concerts; since 1874, Wiesbaden;
c. an opera, etc.

**Järnefelt**, —— b. Finland, 1869; s
ied with Massenet, Paris; compo

**Jaquet** (zhă-kä). Vide BUUS.

**Jarecki** (yä-rĕts'-kē), **Henri**, b. V
saw, 1846; dir. at Lemberg;
operas, incl. "*Wanda*," etc.

**Jarnowic** (or **Giornovi(c)chi** (yär'
vĕk, or jôr-nō-vē'-kē), **Giov. M.**,
lermo, 1745—St. Petersburg,
21, 1804; violinist and compo
pupil of Sully whose intolerable
centricities and immorality, as we
virtuosity, he adopted with disast
results; J. B. Cramer challenged
but he would not fight.

**Jar'vis**, (1) **Stephen**, 1834 ?—Lon
1880; composer. (2) **Chas.**
Philadelphia, 1837—1895; pia
and conductor.

**Jay, J.**, Essex, 1770—London, 1
violinist.

**Jean le Coq**, or **Jehan.** Vide GAL
JOHANNES.

**Jedliczka** (yät-lēch'-kä), **Ernest**
Poltawa, Russia, June 5, 1855;
nist; pupil of Moscow Cons.; tea
there till 1888, then teacher Be
Stein Cons.

**Jeff'eries**, (1) **G.**, organist to
I., 1643. Had a son (2) **Ch**
**topher**, organist and composer.
**Stephen**, 1660—1712; Engl. or
ist and composer.

**Jéhin** (zhā-ăṅ), **Léon**, b. Spa,
gium, July 17, 1853; violinist;
pil of Leonard, Brussels Cons.; c
at Antwerp and Vauxhall, Brus
1879-89, asst.-prof. of theory, I
sels Cons.; since cond. at Mon
composer.

**Jéhin (Jéhin-Prume)** (zhā-ăṅ-pr
**Fz. H.**, Spa, Belgium, April
1839—Montreal, May 29, 1899;
of the most eminent violinists of
gian sch.; composer.

**Jelensperger** (yā'-lĕn-shpĕrkh
**Daniel**, near Mühlhausen, Als
1797—1831; writer.

**Jelinek** (yĕ'-lĭ-nĕk), **Fz. X.**, b.
rins, Bohemia, 1818—Salzburg, 1
oboist and composer.

**Jenk'ins**, (1) **J.**, Maidstone, 15

...mberley, Norfolk, 1678 ; court-lu-
...t and lyra-violist to Chas. I. and
... ; composed. "*12 Sonatas for 2
...ns. and a Base, with a Thorough
...se for the Organ or Theorbo*," the
...st Engl. comp. of the sort ; the
...p. "*The Lady Katherine Audley's
...lls*, or *The Five Bell Consort*,"
... . (2) **David**, b. Trecastell, Bre-
...n, Jan. 1, 1849 ; pupil of Dr. Jos.
...rry ; 1878, Mus. Bac. Cantab.;
...85, cond. America ; now prof. Univ.
...ll. of Wales ; c. operetta, 2 ora-
...ios, 3 cantatas, *A Psalm of Life*,
...
**...ekin** (zhĕn-kăń). Vide JANNE-
...IN.

**...en** (yĕn'-sĕn), (1) **Ad.**, Königs-
...rg, Jan. 12, 1837—of consumption,
...den-Baden, Jan. 23, 1879 ; one of
...e most original and poetical of com-
...sers for piano and voice ; his pf.-
...s. have an unexcelled lyricism, al-
...ost an elocution. Self-taught, but
...vised by L. Ehlert and Fr. Mar-
...rg ; before 20 had c. overtures, a
...ing-quartet, sonatas and songs.
...56, teacher in Russia ; then studied
...th Schumann ; 1857, cond. Posen
...ty Th.; 1858–60, studied with
...de ; 1860, returned to Königs-
...rg ; 1866–68, teacher at Tausig's
...h. in Berlin ; compelled by ill-
...alth to retire to Dresden, 1870 to
...az, finally to Baden-Baden. C.
...era "*Turandot*" (finished by
...enzl) ; "*Nonnengesang*," and
...*Brautlied*" for solo and chorus with
...orns, harp and a piano, "*Jephtha's
...ochter*" and "*Adonis-Feier*,"
...*Donald Caird ist wieder da*."
...d other vocal works with orch.;
...ncert-overture ; "*Geistliches Ton-
...ück*"; "*Hochzeitsmusik*," "*Abend-
...usik*," "*Lebensbilder*," 6 "*Silhouet-
...a*," and "*Ländliche Festmusik*,"
...r pf. (4 hands); and "*Innere Stim-
...en*," "*Wanderbilder*," a sonata ; 6
...erman Suites, "*Idyllen*," "*Eroti-
...n*" (7 pcs.), a scherzo, "*Wald-
...ylle*," op. 47, "*Scenes carnava-
...sques*," for pf.-solo ; and 160 solo

songs. Biog. by Niggli. (2) **Gustav**, Königsberg, 1843—Cologne,
1895 ; pupil of Dehn (comp.) and
Laub and Joachim (vln.) ; violinist
Königsberg Th.; 1872–75, prof. of
cpt., Cologne Cons.; c. symphony,
etc.

**Jew'itt, R.**, d. 1675 : Engl. organist
and composer.

**Jimmerthal** (yĭm'-mĕr-täl), **Hn.**, Lübeck, 1809—1886 ; organist, org.-
builder and writer.

**Joachim** (yō'-ä khēm), (1) **Jos.**, b.
Kittsee, near Pressburg, June 28,
1831 ; eminent violinist ; studied at
5 with Szervacinski, Pesth, with
whom he appeared in public at 7;
from 1841, at Vienna Cons. with
Böhm ; at 12, played in Leipzig, and
soon after at the Gewandhaus, with
much succ.; frequently leader of the
Gewandhaus Orchestra ; 1844, made
his first of many appearances in London ; 1849, *Concertmeister* of the
Weimar orch.; 1854, cond. and solo
violinist to the King of Hanover ;
1863 m. Amalie Weiss (v. infra); 1868
head of the new "Hochschule für
ausübende Tonkunst," Berlin ; later
artistic dir.; 1895, dir.; 1877, Mus.
Doc. *h. c.*, Cambridge Univ.; has
had many degrees from German Universities, and various orders of
knighthood ; holds undisputed pre-
eminence as a classicist and solo-per-
former; his famous J. Quartet includes
De Ahna, Wirth and Hausmann. He
c. the notable "Hungarian" concerto,
and 2 others, and famous variations
with orch., also overture to "*Hamlet*"; 4 overtures incl. "*Dem Anden-
ken Kleists*"; Hebrew Melodies, for
vla. and pf.; Op. 14, "*Szene der
Marfa*" (from Schiller's *Demetrius*),
for contralto solo with orch.; three
cadenzas to Beethoven's vln.-concer-
to, etc. (2) **Amalie** (née **Weiss**,
rightly, **Schneeweiss**), Marburg,
Styria, May 10, 1839—Berlin, Feb.
3, 1899 ; eminent concert and operatic soprano ; then contralto and
teacher ; wife of above.

**João IV.** (zhowṅ), King of Portugal, Villa-Vicosa, 1604—Lisbon, 1656; theorist and composer.

**Jöcher** (yĕkh'-ĕr), **Chr. Gl.**, Leipzig, 1694—1758; professor and writer.

**Johan'nes,** (1) **Cotto.** Vide COTTO (2) **Damasce'nus** (rightly **Jns. Chrysorrho'os**), of Damascus, ca. 700—ca. 760; composer, editor and writer. (3) **De Garlan'dia.** Vide GARLANDIA. (4) **De Mu'ris.** Vide MURIS. (5) **Gallus.** Vide GALLUS.

**Johns, Clayton,** b. New Castle, Del., Nov. 24, 1857; pupil of J. K. Paine, and W. H. Sherwood, Boston; later with Kiel, Grabow, Raif, and Rummel (pf.) in Berlin; since lives in Boston, Mass., as a concert-pianist and teacher; c. a Berceuse and Scherzino for string-orch. (played by Boston Symph. orch.); many pop. songs, etc.

**John'son,** (1) **Edw.**, English composer, 1594. (2) **Robert,** Engl. 16th cent. ecclesiastic and church composer. (3) **Robert,** lutenist and prominent composer, 1573—1625.

**Jommelli** (yŏm-mĕl'-lĭ), **Niccolò,** Aversa, near Naples, Sept. 11, 1714 —Naples, Aug. 28, 1774; eminent operatic and church-composer; pupil of Canon Mozzillo, Durante, Feo, Leo, Prato and Mancini. C. ballets and songs, then dram. cantatas; at 23 prod. opera "*L'Errore Amoroso*" (Naples, 1737), under the name "**Valentino**"; its succ. relieved his anxiety and removed his anonymity and he followed it with other succ. works in various cities under various patronage. He was made Dir. of the Cons. del Ospedaletto, Venice; 1748–54 asst. *Maestro* at St. Peter's, Rome, until 1754; cond. to the Duke of Würtemberg. Lived in Germany 15 years and made great succ. He profited artistically by German influence, but when the Stuttgart opera was disbanded and he retired to Italy his style was too serious and perhaps his best works "*Armida Abbandcnata*" (1770), "*Demofoönte*" (1770),

and "*Ifigenia in Tauride*" (1 were failures when prod. at Na The humiliation after such long umph brought on apoplexy (1 from which he recovered only enough to write a cantata on birth of a prince, and his masterp a "*Miserere*." The King of P gal commissioned him to wri operas and a cantata; but he di live to finish them; he c. ove known operas and divertissem and equally fine sacred mus., in oratorios, a magnificat, with echo,

**Jonás** (zhō-näs), (1) **Émile,** b. F March 5, 1827; pupil of Cara the Cons.; from 1847 teacher 1 also mus.-dir. Portuguese synago (2) (hō'-näs), **Alberto,** b. Ma June 8, 1868; pf. pupil of Olave Mendizabal; also at the Cons.; with Gevaert, Brussels Cons.; 1st prize for pf., and later 2 prizes in harm.; début, Brus 1880; 1890, studied St. Peters Cons. under Rubinstein's tuit since toured Europe and Ame 1894 head of the pf.-dep. Uni Michigan; composer and writer.

**Joncières** (zhôṅ-sï-ärs), **F. Lu Victorin de,** b. Paris, April 12, 1 studied painting, then mus. with wart at the Cons.; an ardent Wa rian, he left the Cons. because o wart's adverse opinion; he is 1 "Soc. des Compositeurs de sique," Chev. of the Legion of l our, and officer of public instruc since 1871 critic of *La Liberté*, prod. 4 operas, incl. "*Le Chev Jean*" (Op.-com., 1885), a syı ode, "*La Mer*"; a "*Symphoni mantique*"; "*Li Tsin*," a Chi theme for soli and orch, etc.

**Jones,** (1) **Robt.**, Engl. lutenist composer, 1601–16; one of his so "*Farewell deere love*," is allude in "*Twelfth Night*." (2) V ("of Nayland"), Lowick, Northa tonshire, 1726 — Nayland, Suf 1800; writer and composer. (3 1728—London, 1796; organist

mposer. (4) (Sir) **Wm.**, London,
46—Calcutta, 1794; writer. (5)
dw. (" **Brady Brenin** "), Llander-
., Merionethshire, April 18, 1752—
ondon, April 18, 1824; Welsh
rpist, writer and composer. (6)
riffith Rhys (or **Caradog**), b.
ecynon, Wales, Dec. 21, 1834;
elsh conductor; as a youth cond.
e choir " Cor Caradog," whence his
briquet; 1872–73, cond. the succ.
oir in the Crystal Palace competi-
ns. (7) **Griffith**, British writer,
b. " *A History of the Origin and
ogress of Theoretical and Practi-
l Music*," 1819. (8) **Arthur Bar-
ay**, b. London, Dec. 16, 1869; pupil
Wingham and Banister; and at
uildhall Sch. of Mus., won a schol-
ship; 1889, Associate; 1892, prof.
pf.; c symphony, concert-over-
re, etc (9) **Sidney**, Engl. compos-
of the succ. operetta " *The Gaiety
l*" (London, 1893); " *An Artist's
odel*" (Daly's Th., London, 1895);
*The Geisha*" (ibid., 1896), etc.

lan, **Jules**, b. Willimantic, Conn.,
ov. 10, 1850; studied singing with
good, Boston, Shakespeare, Lon-
n, and Sbriglia, Paris; for 13
ars choirm. of Grace Ch., Province; since 1880 cond. Arion
ub; c. comedy-opera " *Rip Van
inkle*" (pub. 1898); cantata with
ch.; songs, etc.

ffy (yō-zěf'-fĭ), **Rafael**, b. Mis-
cz, Hungary, July 3, 1853; emi-
nt pianist; pupil of Moscheles,
ipzig Cons., and Tausig; toured
rope with succ.; lived in Vienna;
many years at New York; since,
cher Nat. Cons.; c. pf.-pcs.

uin. Vide DESPRÉS.

et (zhoo-rā), (1) **Th.**, Ath, Belgi-
, 1821—Kissingen, 1887; critic and
m. composer. (2) **Léon**, b. Ath,
t. 17, 1828; bro. of above; pupil
ussel Cons. and since 1874 vocal
cher there; c. 2 operas, cantatas,
.

net (zhoor'-nā), **Marcel**, b Paris,
59; bass; pupil of the Cons.: début

Th. de la Monnaie, Brussels; has
sung often at Covent Garden; and
since 1900 at Met. Op., N. Y.

**Jousse** (zhoos), **J.**, Orleans, France
1760—1837; teacher and writer.

**Judenkunig** (yoo'-den-koo-nĭkh),
**Hans**, b. Schwäbisch-Gmünd; lutenist, violist and composer at Vienna,
1523.

**Jue** (zhŭ), **Edouard**, b. Paris, 1794
(?); violinist and writer.

**Jul(l)ien** (zhül-yän), (1) **Marcel Bd.**,
Paris, 1798—1881; writer. (2) **Jean
Lucien Ad.**, b. Paris, June 1, 1845;
son of above; prominent critic and
writer. (3) **Louis Ant.**, Sisteron,
Basses-Alpes, April 23, 1812—insane,
Paris, March 14, 1860; pop. conductor and composer of dance music,
etc. (4) **Paul**, Brest, France, Feb
12, 1841—at sea, 1866; violinist;
pupil Paris Cons., took 1st prize;
toured America, 1853–66.

**Jumilhac** (zhü-mēl-yăk), **Dom P. Benoît de**, near Limoges, 1611—St.-
Germain-des-Pres, 1682; writer.

**Junck** (yoonk), **Benedetto**, b. Turin,
Aug. 24, 1852; pupil of Bazzini and
Mazzucato; lives in Milan; c. string-
quartet, etc.

**Jungmann** (yoong'-män), (1) **Albert**,
Langensalza, Prussia, 1824 — Pan-
dorf, near Vienna, 1892; professor
and composer. (2) **Ludwig** (or
**Louis**), Weimar, 1832—1892; teacher
and composer.

**Jüngst** (yĭnkst), **Hugo**, b. Dresden,
Feb. 26, 1853; studied at Cons. there;
founded the Julius Otto Soc.; and
cond. Male Choral Soc.; 1898 made
prof. by King of Saxony; c. male
choruses.

**Junker** (yoonk'-ĕr), **K. L.**, Öhringen,
ca. 1740—Kirchberg, 1797; writer
and composer.

**Jupin** (zhü-păn), **Chas. Fran.**, Chambéry, 1805—Paris, 1839; violinist,
professor, conductor, and dram. composer.

**Jürgenson** (yür'-gĕn-zōn), **Peter**, b.
Reval, 1836; founded mus.-pub.
house, Moscow, 1861.

37

## K

**Kaan** (kän) ("**Albést-Kahn** ), **H. von,** b. Tarnopol, Galicia, May 29, 1852; pianist; pupil of Blodek and Skuhersky, Prague; since 1890, prof. at the Cons. there; c. ballets, symphonic poem " *Sakuntala* " ; etc.

**Kade** (kä'-dĕ), **Otto,** Dresden, 1825—Schwerin, 1900; ct.-conductor, writer and composer.

**Kaff'ka** (or **Kawka**) (käf'-kä), **Jn. Chr.,** b. Ratisbon, 1759 ; dram. composer.

**Kafka** (käf'-kä), **Jn. Nepomuk,** Neustadt, Bohemia, 1819—Vienna, 1886; composer.

**Kahl** (käl), **H.,** Munich, 1840—Berlin, 1892 ; conductor.

**Kahlert** (kä'-lĕrt), **K. Aug. Timotheus,** Breslau, 1807—1864; writer and composer.

**Kahn** (kän), **Robt.,** b. Mannheim, July 21, 1865 ; pianist ; pupil of Ernst Frank and V. Lachner, Kiel, and Jos. Rheinberger (Munich, 1885); 1891 founded Ladies' Choral Union, Leipzig ; 1893 teacher of pf. Berlin Hochschule für Musik ; c. serenade for orch., etc.

**Kahnt** (känt), **Chr. Fr.,** 1823—Leipzig, 1897 ; mus.-publisher.

**Kaiser** (kï'-zĕr), (1) **K.,** Leipa, Bohemia, 1837—Vienna, 1890 ; founded sch. continued by his son (2) **Rudolf.** (3) **Fr. Emil,** b. Coburg, Feb. 7, 1850 ; regimental bandm. Prague ; prod. 5 operas, incl. " *Der Trompeter von Säkkingen* " (Olmütz, 1882).

**Kajanus** (kä-yä'-noos), **Robt.,** contemporary cond. Philh. Orch. of Helsingfors, Finland.

**Kal'beck, Max,** b. Breslau, Jan. 4, 1850 ; studied Munich Sch. of Mus. ; 1875, writer, critic at Breslau ; now on the *Wiener Montags-Revue,* and the *Neues Tageblatt.*

**Kalisch** (kä'-lĭsh), **Paul,** b. Berlin, Nov. 6, 1855 ; tenor ; studied with Leoni ; sang Berlin ct.-opera ; m. Lilli Lehmann ; sang at Cologne and 6 times in America.

**Kalischer** (kä'-lĭsh-ĕr), **Alfred,** Thorn, March 4, 1842 ; Dr. Pl Leipzig U. ; studied with Bürgel Bohmer : lives in Berlin, as a wr and teacher ; editor *Neue Berli Musikzeitung ;* pub. " *Lessing Musikasthetiker* " ; " *Musik Moral,*" etc.

**Kalkbrenner** (kälk'-brĕn-nĕr),(1) **C** Minden, Hanover, 1755—Paris, 1 writer and dram. composer. (2) **Wm. Michael,** b. on a journey f Cassel to Berlin, 1788—d. of cho Enghien-les-Bains, near Paris, J 10, 1849 ; son and pupil of abc very succ. pianist and teacher ; veloped modern octave-playing, hand technique and pedalling ; w valuable études and other com also studied Paris Cons. and Clementi and Albrechtsberger. **Arthur,** d. near Paris, 1869 ; so (2) ; composer.

**Kalliwoda** (käl' - lĭ - vō - dä), (1) **Wenzel,** Prague, 1801—Carlsr 1866 ; pianist, conductor and dr composer. (2) **Wm.,** Donaueso gen, 1827—Carlsruhe, 1893 ; son pupil of above ; dir., ct.-conduc pianist and composer.

**Kallwitz,** or **Kalwitz.** Vide CA SIUS.

**Kal'tenborn, Fz.,** violinist, conduc member Seidl's and other orches at New York ; asst.-cond. of S Soc., Brooklyn, N. Y.; 1894 foun Kaltenborn quartet ; 1899 foun the succ. K. orchestra, which g summer concerts in N. Y.

**Kamienski** (käm-ĭ-ĕn'-shkĭ), **Math** Odenburg, Hungary, 1734—Wars 1821 ; teacher and composer of first Polish Opera " *The Wret Made Happy* " (1778), etc.

**Kammerlander** (käm'-mĕr-länt-ĕr), Weissenhorn, Swabia, 1828—A burg, 1892; conductor and compe

**Kandler** (känt'-lĕr), **Fz. Sales,** K terneuberg, Lower Austria, 17 Baden, 1831 ; writer.

**Kaps** (käps), **Ernst,** Döbeln, Sax 1826 — Dresden, 1887 ; est. p

ctory, Dresden, 1859; succeeded
his sons.

▪sberger (käps' - bĕrkh - ĕr), **Jn.
ieronymus von**, b. of noble Ger-
an family, d. Rome, ca. 1650,
▪tuoso on theorbo, chitarrone, lute.
▪d trumpet; notable composer.

ajan (kä'-rä-yän), **Th. G. von,**
▪enna, 1810—1873; writer.

asowski (kä-rä-shôf'-shkĭ), **Mo-
tz,** Warsaw, 1823—Dresden, 1892;
▪llist, writer and composer.

ganoff (kär-gän-yôf'), **Genari,**
▪ashetin, Caucasus, 1858—Rostroff-
▪-Don, 1890; pianist and composer.

**l, Tom,** b. Dublin, Jan. 19, 1846;
▪nor; studied with H. Phillips, San-
▪ovanni and Trivulzi; sang in Ital-
▪ opera for years, went to America
th Parepa-Rosa, then with "The
▪stonians" in comic opera many
▪ars, retired 1896; now vocal
▪cher, N. Y.

ow (kä'-rôf), **Karl,** Alt-Stettin,
▪90—Bunzlau, Silesia, 1863; teach-
▪ and composer.

▪kel (käs'-kĕl), Freiherr **K. von,**
▪ Dresden, Oct. 10, 1866; studied
▪w at Leipzig, also mus. in the Cons.
▪th Reinecke and Jadassohn (1886—
▪), and later with Wüllner and Jen-
▪n, Cologne; now lives in Dresden;
▪ succ. 1-act opera "*Hochzeitsmor-
n*" (Hamburg, 1893); v. succ.
▪era "*Sjua*" (Cologne, 1895), etc.

▪smeyer (kĕs'-mī-ĕr), **Moritz,** Vi-
▪na, 1831—1885; violinist; c. 3
▪ring-quartets. some of them hu-
▪orous.

▪tner (käst'-nĕr), (1) **Jn. G.,** Strass-
▪rg, March 9, 1810—Paris, Dec. 19,
▪67; pupil of Maurer and Romer;
▪ 10, organist; at 20, bandm.; at
▪ had prod. 4 operas and was sent
▪ the town council to Paris, to study
▪th Berton and Reicha; 1837,
▪b. treatise "*On Instrumentation*"
▪nong others; also methods adopted
▪ the Paris Cons.; lived there-
▪ter at Paris as teacher, wrote
▪arned essays and an "*Encyclopédie
la musique.*" C. 3 later operas

incl. "*Le dernier roi de Juda,*" his
masterpiece, also 3 symphonies, 5
overtures, 10 serenades for wind;
"*Livres-partitions*" (symphony-can-
tatas, prefaced by brilliant historical
essays, incl. "*Les dances des morts*"),
a vol. of 310 pages; "*La harpe
d'éole*" (1856); "*Les voix de Paris,*"
followed by "*Les cris de Paris,*"
grande symphonie humoristique voc.
et instr. (1857); "*Les Sirènes,*"
etc. Biogr. by Jan (Leipzig, 1886).
(2) **G. Fr. Eugen,** Strassburg, 1852
—Bonn, 1882; son of above; inv.
the pyrophone (v. D. D.), and pub.
work on it. (3) **Emmerich,** b. Vienna, March 29, 1847; editor and
writer.

**Kate** (kä'-tĕ), **André Ten,** Amsterdam, 1796—Haarlem, 1858; 'cellist
and dram. composer.

**Katzmayr** (käts'-mīr), **Marie,** b. Vienna, March 6, 1869; colorature soprano; pupil Frau Niklass-Kempner;
sang in Holland, then at Berlin, etc.

**Kauders** (kow'-dĕrs), **Albert,** critic in
Vienna, and composer of comic opera.

**Kauer** (kow'-ĕr), **Fd.,** Klein-Thaya,
Moravia, Jan. 8, 1751 — Vienna,
April 13, 1831; prolific c. of *Singspiele ;* organist, conductor, 'cellist;
c. 2,000 operas and operettas.

**Kauffmann** (kowf'-män), (1) **Ernst
Fr.,** Ludwigsburg, 1803—Stuttgart,
1856; pianist and composer. (2) **Emil,**
b. Ludwigsburg, Nov. 23, 1836; violinist; son of above; pupil of Stuttgart
Cons.; since musical dir. Tubingen
Univ.; Dr. phil., 1885. (3) **Fritz,** b.
Berlin, June 17, 1855; a druggist,
Leipzig and Hamburg; took up music, 1878, entered the Akademische
Hochschule at Berlin, won Mendelssohn prize for comp. 1881; till 1889,
lived in Berlin as a teacher and cond.
of the "Gesellschaftsconcerte" at
Magdeburg; 1893, Royal Musik-Di-
rector; c. comic opera, "*Die Herz-
krankheit*"; symphony, etc.

**Kaufmann** (kowf'-män), (1) **G. Fr.,**
Ostramondra, Thuringia, 1679—Merseburg. 1735; organist, director.

writer and composer. (2) **Jn. Gf.**, Siegmar, Saxony, 1751—Frankfort, 1818; maker of musical clocks. (3) **Fr.**, Dresden, 1785—1866; son of above; inv. the "Belloneon," etc. His son (4) **Fr. Theodor**, Dresden, 1823—1872, developed the "Orchestrion." (5) **Robert**, b. Basel, and later there studied with Rossi, Duprez and Stockhausen; oratorio tenor; has sung in many capitals.

**Kayser** (kī´-zĕr), (1) **Ph. Chr.**, Frankfort, 1755—Zurich, 1823; pianist. (2) **H. Ernst**, Altona, 1815—Hamburg, 1888, violinist and teacher. (3) **Fr. Emil.** Vide KAISER.

**Kazynski** (kä-zēn -shkī), **Victor**, b. Wilna, Lithuania, Dec. 18, 1812; pupil of Elsner. Warsaw; prod. 3 operas; 1843, cond. Imp. Th. St. Petersburg.

**Kearns** (kärnz), **Wm. H.**, Dublin, 1794—Kennington, 1846; violinist and composer.

**Keck von Giengen** (kĕk fōn gēng´-ĕn), **Jn.**, Benedictine monk at Tegernsee, Upper Bavaria, ca. 1450; writer. (Gerbert.)

**Kee´ble, J.**, Chichester, 1711—1786; organist, teacher and composer.

**Kee´ley**, Mrs **M. A.**, b. Ipswich, 1805; English soprano.

**Keinspec** (or **Keinsbeck, Künspeck**, and wrongly **Reinspeck**) (kīn´-shpĕk), **Michael**, of Nürnberg; pub. one of the first theoretical works printed at Basel, 1496.

**Keiser** (kī´-zĕr), **Reinhard**, Teuchern, near Weissenfels, Jan. 9, 1674—Hamburg, Sept. 12, 1739; the father of German opera, the first to employ popular subjects and to leave the Italian and French pattern; also noteworthy for his instrumentation and dramatic force; pupil of his father; c. 116 operas at Hamburg from 1694; mgr. the opera there, ct. cond. and later canon and cantor; c. also oratorios, masses, etc.

**Keler Bela** (rightly **Albert von Keler**) (kä´-lĕr bā´-lä), Bartfeld, Hungary, Feb. 13, 1820 --Wiesbaden,

Nov. 20, 1882, violinist, condu and composer.

**Kel´ler**, (1) **Gottfried** (called G frey), b. in Germany; teacher writer in London, 1707. (2) **M** Trostberg, Bavaria, 1770—Altött 1855; organist and composer. **K.**, Dessau, 1784—Schaffhau 1855; ct.-flutist, conductor and c poser. (4) **F. A. E.**, inv., 1835, unsucc. "pupître-improvisateur" D D.), and pub. a method.

**Kel´lermann**, (1) **Berthold**, b. N berg, March 5, 1853; pianist; p of his parents and of Liszt, 187 Wagner's secretary; 1882, tea Munich R. Mus. Sch.; conductor ct.-pianist. (2) **Chr.**, Randers, land, 1815—Copenhagen, 1866; list and composer.

**Kel´ley, Edgar Stillman**, b. Spa Wis., April, 14. 1857, one of most original and brilliant of A ican composers; pupil of F. Merriam, Clarence Eddy, and 187 Ledochowski (Chicago), and 187 of Seifriz (comp.). Krüger and S del (pf.) and Fr. Finck (org.) Stuttgart; organist at Oakland San Francisco, Cal., cond. c opera, 1890-91, teacher pf., c and comp. in various schools; la N. Y. Coll. of Mus., critic for *Examiner* San Francisco, 1893-and essayist for various periodic since 1896 lecturer on music for Univ. of New York; 1901-02 Yale University; c. "*Gulliv* humorous symph.; Chinese s "*Aladdin*," for orch.; comic op "*Puritania*" (Boston, 1892); incid. music to *Macbeth* and to *Hur*, both for chorus and or string-quartet, op. 1 (MS.); " *V ding-Ode*," for tenor solo, male ch and orch. (MS.); 6 songs, "*Ph of Love*"; notable songs, "*L rado*" and "*Israfel*," and other

**Kel´lie, Lawrence**, b. London, A 3, 1862; tenor and composer; s ied at R. A. M. and with Randeg début Covent Garden. 1886.

ner, (1) **David**, dir. German ch.
Th. at Stockholm, 1732. (2)
**Peter**, Grafenroda, Thuringia,
5—1788 ; organist and composer.
Jn. **Chp.**, Grafenroda, 1735—
ssel, 1803 ; son of above ; ct.-or-
ist and dram. composer. (4) **G.**
r., d. Sept., 1808 ; teacher and
ter at Mannheim.     (5) **Ernst**
g., Windsor, England, 1792—
ndon, 1839 ; probably a grandson
3); barytone, pianist and organist.
ogg, **Clara Louise**, b. Sumter-
e, S. C., July, 1842 ; noted sono ; 1856–61, studied in New
rk ; début Acad. of Mus. (1861);
ut, London, at H. M's. Th.
57), as Margherita, with great
c.; sang in many capitals.
y, **Michael**, Dublin, 1762—Mar-
e, 1826 ; tenor and dram. compos-
friend of Mozart ; wrote musical
eminiscences.''
vay, (1) **Thos.**, d. 1749 ; Engl.
anist and composer.  (2) **Joseph**,
1782 ; bro. of above ; organist,
psichordist, and composer.
ble, **Adelaide**, b. 1814 ; retired
3 ; daughter of the actor Chas.
nble ; operatic singer.
, (1) **Jos.**, Exeter, 1778—Lon-
, 1824 organist and composer.
**Robert** (called ''Father Kemp''),
llfleet, Mass., 1820 — Boston,
7 ; organised and cond. pop.
ld Folks' Concerts'' ; wrote auto-
graphy.
is, **Nicholas A.**, organist and
poser at Brussels, 1644–50.
ter, (1) **K.**, Limbach, Bavaria,
—Augsburg, 1871 ; conductor.
**Lothar**, b. Lauingen, Bavaria,
. 5, 1844 ; cond., professor, and
n. composer ; son and pupil of
**Fr. K.** (music-teacher) ; studied
nich Univ., then with Rhein-
er ; chorus-dir.; since 1886 prof.
us. theory, Zürich Mus. Sch.
all, **J.**, organist and composer,
don, 1780.
, **P.**, German horn-virtuoso and
poser : 1782 at Paris.

**Ken'nedy, David**, Perth, 1825—1886 singer.

**Kent, Jas.**, Winchester. Engl.,1700–1776 ; organist and composer.

**Kepler** (kā´-plĕr), **Jns.**, Weil, Würtemberg, 1571—Ratisbon, 1630 ; astronomer ; writer.

**Kerle** (kĕrl), **Jacques de**, b. Ypres, Flanders, 16th cent. ; conductor and composer.

**Kerl(l) (Kherl, Cherl), Jn. Caspar**, Gaimersheim, near Ingolstadt, 1621—Munich, Feb. 13, 1693 ; organist, ct.-conductor, teacher, and notable composer of the '' Missa nigra '' (all in black notes), etc.

**Kes** (kās), **Willem**, b. Dordrecht, Holland, Feb. 16, 1856 ; violinist, pupil of Böhm, etc., then of David, and, under royal patronage, of Wieniawski, and Joachim ; 1876, leader Park Orch. and Felix Meritis Soc., Amsterdam ; then cond. '' Society '' concerts, Dordrecht ; 1883–95 cond. at Amsterdam ; 1895 Glasgow orch.; 1898 cond. Philh. and dir. Moscow Cons.

**Kes'sel, Fz.**, th.-cond., 1889, at Freiburg-in-the-Breisgau ; c. a symph. and succ. opera, '' *Die Schwestern* '' (Trier, 1895).

**Kess'ler**, (1) **Fr.**, preacher and writer. (2) **Fd.**, Frankfort-on-Main, 1793—1856 ; violinist and composer. (3) (rightly **Kötzler**) (kĕts´-lĕr), **Jos. Chp.**, Augsburg, 1800 — Vienna, 1872 ; teacher, organist and composer.

**Ket'ten, H.**, Baja, Hungary, 1848—Paris, 1883 ; pianist and composer.

**Kettenus** (kĕt-tä´-noos) (or kĕt-nüs), **Aloys**, Verviers, 1823 — London, 1896 ; violinist and dram. composer.

**Ketterer** (kĕt-tŭ-rä), **Eugène**, Rouen, 1831—Paris, 1870 ; pianist and composer.

**Keurvels** (kŭr´-vĕls), **Edw. H. J.**, b. Antwerp, 1853 ; pupil of Benoît · till 1882, chorusm. Royal Th.; since cond. Nat. Flemish Th., Antwerp c. operas, cantatas, etc.

**Kewitsch** (Kiewics) (kā´-vĭtsh  o

kĕ'-vĕch), (**Karl**) **Theodor**, b. Po-
silge, W. Prussia, Feb. 3, 1834 ; son
and pupil of an organist ; studied
with Maslon ; oboist, then teacher
and organist in different towns ; pensioned 1887, then editor, etc.
**Kiel** (kēl), **Fr.**, Puderbach, near Sie-
gen (Rh. Prussia), Oct. 7, 1821—
Berlin, Sept. 14, 1885 ; notable
teacher and composer of classic sch. ;
self-taught as pianist and composer ;
vln.-pupil of Prince Karl von Wittgen-
stein and later, on stipend from Fr.
Wm. IV., studied with Dehn ; lives
in Berlin ; 1868 " Royal Prof." ; c.
oratorios, etc.
**Kiene** (kē'-nĕ). Vide BIGOT.
**Kienle** (kēn'-lĕ), **Ambrosius**, b. Sieg-
maringen, May 8, 1852 ; Benedictine
monk and writer.
**Kienzl** (kēnts'-'l), **Wm.**, b. Waizen-
kirchen, Upper Austria, Jan. 17,
1857 ; pupil of Buwa, Uhl, Remy,
Mortier de Fontain, Jos. Krejci, and
later, Liszt; 1879 Dr. Phil. at Vienna;
1880 lectured at Munich ; 1881–82
toured as pianist; 1883–84 chief cond.
of German Opera, Amsterdam ; 1886
m. the concert-singer Lili Hoke ;
1886–90 dir. Styrian Musikverein at
Graz and cond.; 1890–92, 1st cond.
Hamburg Opera ; 1892–93, at Munich ; 1899–1901 at Graz as composer. His first opera " *Urvasi*"
(Dresden, 1886) was succ., as was
" *Heilmar, der Narr*" (Munich,
1892), and still more so " *Der Evan-
gelimann*"; c. also " *Heilmann the
Fool*," " *Don Quichote*," a " musical
tragi-comedy " ; he finished Jensen's
" *Turandot*," and c. also 90 songs,
etc.
**Kiesewetter** (kē'-zĕ-vĕt-tĕr), **Raphael G.** (Edler von Wiesenbrunn), Hol-
leschau, Moravia, 1773—Baden, near
Vienna, 1850 ; important coll. of
mus. MSS. and historian of many obscure periods, etc.; later ennobled.
**Kiewics.** Vide KEWITSCH.
**Kim'ball, Josiah**, Topsfield, Mass.,
1761—1826 ; teacher and composer
of psalm-tunes. etc.

**Kind** (kĭnt), **J. F.**, Leipzig, 1[?]
Dresden, 1843 ; librettist of '
*Freischütz*," afterwards compos[?]
**Kindermann** (kĭnt'-ĕr-män), (1)
**Erasmus**, b. Nürnberg, 1616—
1652 ; organist and composer.
**Aug.**, Potsdam, 1817—Munich,
barytone. (3) **Hedwig**, daught[?]
above. Vide REICHER, K.
**King**, (1) **Wm.**, 1624—1680 ; [?]
organist and composer. (2) **R**
d. after 1711 ; Engl. composer.
**Chas.**, Bury St. Edmunds, 1[?]
London, 1748 ; composer. (4)[?]
**thew Peter**, London, 1773—[?]
theorist and dram. composer.
**Oliver A.**, b. London, 1855; pi[?]
pupil of W. H. Holmes, and
necke, Leipzig Cons. ; pianist t[?]
Princess Louise, 1879 ; toured
ada and New York; 1899 pf.-pr[?]
R. A. M.; c. cantatas, 147th P
with orch. (Chester Festival, [?]
a symphony, " *Night*." (6) **J**
Vide RIVE-KING.
**Kink'el, Johanna** (née **Mocke**
vorced **Matthieux**), Bonn, [?]
London, 1858 ; writer and
composer.
**Kipke** (kĭp'-kĕ), **K.**, b. Breslau,
20, 1850 ; editor.
**Kip'per, Hn.**, b. Coblenz, Aug[?]
1826 ; pupil of Anschütz an[?]
Dorn ; teacher and critic at Col
c. operettas.
**Kircher** (kērkh'-ĕr), **Athana**
Geisa (Buchow ?), near Fulda, 1[?]
Rome, 1680 ; Jesuit archæologis[?]
coll. of airs, some of them sup[?]
to have curative effects.
**Kirchl** (kērkh'-'i), **Ad.**, b. Vi[?]
June 16, 1858 ; choirm. " Sch[?]
bund," Vienna ; c. male cho[?]
etc.
**Kirchner** (kērkh'-nĕr), (1) **Fz.**, b.
dam, Nov. 3, 1840 ; pianist ;
Kullak's Acad., where he t[?]
1864–89, then in the Mädchen
sch., Berlin ; c. pf.-pcs., etc
**Hn.**, b. Wolfis, Thuringia, Jan
1861 ; concert-tenor, and compo[?]
Berlin. (3) **Theodor**, b. Neukir[?]

Chemnitz, Saxony, Dec. 10, ...; pupil of J. Knorr (pf.), K. F. ...er (org.), Jn. Schneider, and at ...zig Cons.; 1843–62, organist ...terthur; 1862–72, teacher Zurich ... Sch., and cond.; 1873–75, dir. ...rzburg Cons., Leipzig; 1883, ...sden; 1890, Hamburg; c. 90 pf.- ..., etc.

...mann, (1) **Jacob** (rightly Kirch-...nn), d. London, 1778; founder ...ore 1740) of the firm of harpsi-...rd-makers, K. & Son, the "son" ...g his nephew, (2) **Abraham K. Jan.,** b. Holland, d. Norwich, ...; organist and composer, Lon-..., 1782.

...erger (kērn'-běrkh-ĕr), **Jn. Ph.,** ...feld, Thuringia, 1721 — Berlin, ...; eminent theorist, conductor composer.

(kēst), **Florent Corneille** (Flo-...s Cornelius), Arnheim, 1796—...echt, 1863 · horn-player and flut-...editor, conductor and composer.

...ner, (1) **Fr.,** Leipzig, 1797—1844; ... His son (2) **Julius** succeeded ... (3) **Cyrill,** b. Grossaitingen, ...r Augsburg, March 12, 1848; ...ol-teacher; studied with Wüll-..., Rheinberger, and Fr. Lachner; ... teacher Sondershausen Cons.; ...e 1885 lives in Bad Kissingen as ...cipal of a sch., pub. of text-books, ... "*A Harmony, based on Wag-*..." etc.; c. 2 operas; a succ. ...usical comedy" "*Eulenspiegel*" ...ürzburg, 1893); etc.

...iner, **Wm.,** London, 1775—...7; a wealthy physician; writer ... dram. composer.

...l (kĭt'-tĕl), **Jn. Chr.,** Erfurt, Feb. ...1732—May 9, 1809; J. S. Bach's ...pupil; organist in Erfurt; famous ...ill-paid virtuoso and teacher.

(kĭt'-'l), **Jn. Fr.,** b. Schloss, Wor-...Bohemia, 1806—Lissa, 1868; ...ductor and dram. composer.

...er (kĭts'-lĕr), **Otto,** b. Dresden, ...rch 16, 1834; pupil of Schneider, ...o, and Kummer ('cello), later of ...vais and Fétis, Brussels Cons.;

'cellist in opera-orchs. at Strassburg and Lyons; cond. at various theatres; 1868 dir. Brunn Mus. Soc. and Mus. Sch., also cond. of the Männerge-sangverein; pub. orch.-mus., pf.-pcs., etc.

**Kjerulf** (k'yä'-roolf), **Halfdan,** Sept. 17, 1818—Christiania, Aug. 11, 1868; teacher and composer; gave up the-ology for music; studied at Leipzig; settled in Christiania; c. songs and pf.-pcs.

**Klafsky** (**Lohse-Klafsky**) (kläf'-shkĭ), **Katharina,** St. Johann, Hun-gary, 1855—Hamburg, 1896; sopr.; pupil of Mme. Marchesi; sang in comic opera chorus, later leading Wagnerian rôles in Europe and Amer-ica; m. Otto Lohse.

**Klauser** (klow'-zĕr), (1) **K.,** b. of Swiss parents, St. Petersburg, Aug. 24, 1823; chiefly self-taught; 1850, New York; 1856, Mus.-Dir. Far-mington Cons.; editor. (2) **Julius,** b. New York, July 5, 1854; pupil of Wenzel, Leipzig Cons.; mus.-teacher, Milwaukee; pub. "*The Septonate and the Centralization of the Tonal System*" (1890).

**Klauwell** (klow'-věl), (1) **Ad.,** Langen-salza, Thuringia, 1818 — Leipzig, 1879; teacher, writer, etc. (2) **Otto,** b. Langchsalza, April 7, 1851; nephew of above; pupil of Schulp-forta, and at Leipzig Cons.; Dr. Phil.; 1875 prof. Cologne Cons.; since 1885, dir. Teachers' Seminary; writer and dram. composer.

**Klee** (klā), **L.,** b. Schwerin, April 13, 1846; pupil of Th. Kullak, and until 1875, teacher Kullak's Acad., then dir. of his own sch.; "Musik-Direktor," writer and editor.

**Kleeberg** (klā-bär), **Clotilde,** b. Paris, June 27, 1866; pianist; pupil of Mmes. Retz and Massart at the Cons., won 1st prize; début, at 12, with Pasdeloup orch.; toured Europe with great succ.; 1894, Officier de l'Acad-émie.

**Kleemann** (klā'-män), **K.,** b. Rudol-stadt, Sept. 9, 1842; pupil of Müller;

1878, studied in Italy; then 2nd opera cond. and ct. mus.-dir. Dessau; c. 2 symphonies, etc.

**Kleffel** (klĕf'-fĕl), **Arno**, b. Possneck, Thuringia, Sept. 4, 1840; studied Leipzig Cons., and with Hauptmann; 1863–67, dir. Riga Mus. Soc.; then th. cond. in Cologne; later teacher of theory, Stern's Cons., Berlin; 1895, professor; c. opera, Christmas legend, overtures, etc.

**Klein** (klīn), (1) **Jn. Jos.**, Arnstadt, 1740—Kahla, near Jena, 1823; writer. (2) **Bd.**, Cologne, 1793—Berlin, 1832; teacher and composer. (3) **Joseph**, 1802—62, bro. of above; lived as composer in Berlin and Cologne. (4) **Bruno Oscar**, b. Osnabrück, Hanover, June 6, 1858; son and pupil of (5) **Carl K.** (organist Osnabrück Cath.); (4) studied at Munich Cons.; 1878, gave concerts in America; 1883, New York; 1884, chief pf.-teacher Convent of the Sacred Heart; also, 1884–94, organist St. Francis Xavier, and 1887–92, prof. of cpt. and comp. Nat. Cons.; 1894–95, gave concerts in Germany; prod. succ. gr. opera, "*Kenilworth*" (Hamburg, 1895), vln.-sonata, etc. (6) **Hermann**, b. Norwich, Eng.; critic and teacher: studied law; 1874 singing with Manuel Garcia; 1881–1901, critic London *Sunday Times;* 1887. prof. of singing at Guildhall; 1896, dir. opera-class (vice Weist Hill); 1902, New York.

**Kleinmichel** (klīn'-mĭkh-'l), (1) **Hermann**; (?) 1816—Hamburg, 1894; bandmaster. (2) **Richard**, Posen, Dec. 31, 1846—Sept., 1901; son and pupil of above; studied also at Hamburg and at Leipzig Cons.; teacher, Hamburg; 1876, Leipzig; 1882, mus. dir. City Th.; c. 2 operas; 2 symphonies; chamber-music, valuable études, etc.; m. a dramatic soprano, (3) **Clara Monhaupt**.

**Klengel** (klĕng'-ĕl), (1) **Aug. Alex.** ("Kanon-Klengel"), Dresden, 1784—1852; organist and composer of an attempt to rival Bach's "Well-tem-

pered Clavichord," etc. (2) **Pa** Leipzig, May 13, 1854; pianis violinist; Dr. phil., Leipzig; 86, cond., Leipzig, "Euterpe" certs; 1888–93, 2nd ct.-cond., gart; cond. "Arion," Leipzig; New York. (3) **Julius**, b. Le Sept. 24, 1859; bro. of above; list, pupil of Emil Hegar ('cello) Jadassohn (comp.); 1st 'cello i wandhaus Orch., and teacher a Cons.; composer.

**Kliebert** (klē'-bĕrt), **K.**, b. Pr Dec. 13, 1840; pupil of Rheinb and Wüllner, Munich; 1876, d Sch. of Mus., Würzburg.

**Klinck'erfuss** (-foos), **Johanna** Hamburg, March 22, 1856; pu Beer and Liszt; notable ct.- ist.

**Klindworth** (klĭnt'-vôrt), **K.**, over, Sept. 25, 1830; pianist, nent teacher and editor; self-ta pianist; at 6 played in public; cond. of an opera-troupe; teacher at Hanover; 1852, a J woman advanced him money to with Liszt; 1854, music-début, don; Wagner admired him, and became friends. 1854–68, he concerts and lessons, London; pf.-prof. Imp. Cons. Moscow; here he completed two monu al works, his pf.-scores of Wag "*Ring des Nibelungen*," and a ed. of Chopin. 1882–92, cond Berlin the Wagnerverein and Joachim and Wüllner) the Philh Concerts. Est. a "Klaviersch (Sch. of Pf.-playing), later u with the Scharwenka Cons., when he retired to Potsdam; posed piano-pieces.

**Kling**, **H.**, b. Paris, Feb. 17, 1 prof. Geneva Cons. and teach city schools; writer and dram. poser.

**Klingenberg** (klĭng-ĕn-bĕrkh), **Wm.**, b. Sulau, Silesia, June 6, 1 1840–85, cantor, Peterskirche, litz; c. a symphony, etc.

**Klitzsch** (klĭtsh), **K. Ema**

onhaide, Saxony, 1812—Zwickau,
9 ; writer and composer.

é (klô-zā), **Hyacinthe Eléonore,**
e of Corfu, 1808—Paris, 1880 ;
rinettist and prof., Paris Cons.;
nposer.

s (kloos), **Augusta** (stage-name
ria) ; b. Boston, U. S. A. ; con-
lto ; pupil of Hey, Berlin, 1895,
nnuccini, Florence, and Bax,
ris ; début, Monte Carlo, 1899,
ing name " Doria " ; has sung at
ssels and Rouen.

z (klôts), family of Bavarian vio-
-makers at Mittenwald. The first
Ægidius, sen., the best; his son
**Matthias** (ca. 1660—96). Mat-
as's sons were (3) **Sebastian** and
**Joseph,** and their sons (5) **Georg,**
**Karl,** (7) **Michael,** and (8) Ægi-
s, Jr.

hardt (klookh'-härt), **Aug. (Fr.**
artin), b. Köthen, Nov. 30, 1847 ;
oil of Blassmann and Reichel,
esden ; ct.-cond. at Neustrelitz and
er at Dessau ; prod. 4 operas, the
table symphonic poem, "*Leonore*";
symph. (1. "*Waldweben*"), over-
es "*Im Frühling*"; "*Sophonis-*
" "*Siegesouvertüre,*" and " *Fest-*
vertüre,*" etc.

be (k'nä'-bě), (1) **Wm.,** Kreuz-
rg, Prussia, 1803—Baltimore, 1864;
nder of pf.-factory at Baltimore,
I.; succeeded by his sons (2) **Will-**
n (1841—89) and (3) **Ernest,** and
y by (4) **Ernest J.** (b. July 5, 1869)
I (5) **Wm.** (b. March 23, 1872).

uth (knowt). Vide FRANZ, ROBT.

cht (knĕkht), **Justin H.,** Biberach,
rtemberg, Sept. 30, 1752—Dec. 1,
7; rival of Vogler as organist, and
portant theorist, conductor and
nposer.

sel (knī'-zěl), **Fz.,** b. of German
ents in Roumania, 1865 ; violin-
; pupil of Grün and Hellmesberg-
Vienna ; *Konzertmeister*, Hofburg
.-Orch ; then of Bilse's Orch., Ber-
; since 1885, leader and soloist, Bos-
Symphony Orch.; 1887, founded
"Kneisel Quartet." which has

played with greatest succ. in Amer
ica and Europe ; 1902, cond. Worces
ter (Massachusetts) Festival.

**Kniese** (knē'-zě), **Julius,** b. Roda, near
Jena, Dec. 21, 1848 ; pianist and organist ; pupil of Stade, at Altenburg,
Brendel and C. Riedel, Leipzig ;
1884–89, mus.-dir. at Aix ; 1882,
chorusm. at Bayreuth, where he lived ,
1889, dir. Preparatory Sch. for Stage-
Singers ; c. opera, "*König Witti-*
*chis*"; symphonic poem, "*Frith-*
*jof*," etc.

**Knight** (nīt), **Jos. Philip,** Bradford-
on-Avon, 1812—Great Yarmouth,
1887 ; organist and composer of
songs incl. "*Rocked in the Cradle of*
*the Deep.*"

**Knorr** (knôr), (1) **Julius,** Leipzig, 1805
—1861 ; pf.-teacher and deviser of
standard rudimentary exercises ; pub.
"*Methods,*" etc. (2) **Ivan,** b. Mewe,
West Prussia, Jan. 3, 1853 ; studied
Leipzig Cons. with Richter, Reinecke ; 1883, prof. of theory, Hoch
Cons. Frankfort-on-Main ; c. 2 suites,
etc.

**Kny'vett,** (1) **Chas.,** England, 1752—
London, 1822 ; tenor and organist.
(2) **Chas.,** 1773—1852 ; son of above ;
organist and teacher. (3) **Wm.,**
1779—Ryde, 1856 ; bro. of above ;
composer and conductor.

**Kobbé** (kôb-bā), **Gustav,** b. New
York, March 4, 1857 ; studied pf.
and comp. with Adolf Hagen, Wiesbaden ; later with Jos. Mosenthal,
New York ; 1877, graduated Columbia Coll.; 1879, Sch. of Law ; lives
in Morristown, N. J.; pub. essays in
leading magazines and newspapers ;
also " *Wagner's Life and Works* "
(N. Y., 1890), "*The Ring of the Ni-*
*belung*" (1889), "*Plays for Ama-*
*teurs*" (1892), "*My Rosary and*
*other Poems*" (1896), "*New York*
*and its Environs*" (1891) ; teacher ;
pub. a few songs.

**Kobelius** (kō-bā'-lĭ-oos), **Jn. Augus-**
**tin,** Wählitz, near Halle, 1674—Wei-
senfels, 1731 ; ct.-cond. and dram.
composer.

**Koch** (kōkh), (1) **H. Chp.**, Rudolstadt, 1749—1816; violinist; writer and composer. (2) **Eduard Emil**, Schloss Solitude, near Stuttgart, 1809 —Stuttgart, 1871; writer. (3) **Emma**, b. Mayence; pianist; pupil of Liszt, Moskowski, etc.; since 1898, teacher Stern Cons. (4) **Fr.**, b. Berlin, 1862; pupil of the Hochschule; conductor, 'cellist and c. of 2 operas, "*Die Halliger*" and "*Lea*" (Cologne, 1896), etc.

**Köchel** (kĕkh'-'l), **L.** Ritter **von**, Stein-on-Danube, Lower Austria, 1800—Vienna, 1877; writer.

**Kocher** (kōkh'-ĕr), **Conrad**, Ditzingen, near Stuttgart, 1786—Stuttgart, 1872; mus.-dir. and dram. composer.

**Kocian** (kō'-tsĭ-ŭn). **Jaroslav**, b. Wildenschwert, Bohemia, Feb. 22, 1884; violinist, son and pupil of a school-teacher; studied violin at 3½ years; at 12, Prague Cons. under Sevcik (vln.), and Dvôrák (comp.); début, 1901; has toured Europe with much succ.; 1902, America.

**Koczalski** (kō-chäl'-shkĭ), **Raoul (Armand G.)**, b. Warsaw, Jan. 3, 1885; studied pf. with his mother; then with Godowski at Warsaw; at 4 played in public with great succ.; at 7, played at Vienna, St. Petersburg, etc., 600 concerts up to 1892; ct.-pianist to the Shah of Persia, with annuity of 3,000 francs; c. 1-act operas, "*Hagar*," "*Rymond*," etc.

**Koemmenich** (kĕm'-mĕ-nĭkh), **Louis**, b. Elberfeld, Germany, Oct. 4, 1866; pupil of Anton Krause, Barmen and at Kullak's Acad. 1890, New York, as conductor and teacher; since 1894, cond. Brooklyn Sängerbund; 1898, organised an Oratorio Soc.; c. a cantata, male choruses, etc.

**Koenen** (kā'-nĕn), **Fr.**, Rheinbach, near Bonn, 1829—Cologne, 1887; conductor and composer.

**Kofler** (kôf'-lĕr), **Leo**, b. Brixen, Austrian Tyrol, March 13, 1837; from 1877, organist and choirm. of St. Paul's Chapel, New York; writer and composer.

**Kogel** (kō'-gĕl), **Gv.**, b. Leipzig, 16, 1849; pupil of the Cons.; cond. various cities; 1891–1902, Museum Concerts, Frankfort; and composer.

**Köhler** (kā-lĕr), (1) **Ernst**, Langelau, Silesia, 1799—Breslau, organist and composer. (2) (Louis (H.),** Brunswick, 18 Königsberg, 1886; pianist, te and dramatic composer, also no critic.

**Kohut** (kō-hoot'), **Ad.**, b. Minds Hungary, Nov. 10, 1847; live Berlin; writer.

**Kohout** (kō-hoot'), **Fz.**, b. Ho Bohemia, May 5, 1858; pupil of hersky, Prague Org.-Sch.; now ductor "Deutsches Th." at Pra and organist Weinberger synago c. v. succ. 1-act (German) o "*Stella*" (Prague, 1896), etc.

**Kolbe** (kôl'-bĕ), **Oskar**, Berlin, 18 1878; composer and writer.

**Kolff** (kôlf), **J. van Santen**, Ro dam, 1848—Berlin, 1896; writer

**Kolling** (kôl'-lĭng), **K. W. P.,** Hamburg, Feb. 28, 1831; tea and composer of v. succ. oper "*Schmetterlinge*" (1891, Hamb

**Kollmann** (kôl'-män), **Aug. Fr.** Engelbostel, Hanover, 1756—1 don, 1824; organist, theorist composer.

**Kömpel** (kĕm'-pĕl), **Aug.**, Brücke 1831—Weimar, 1891; violinist.

**Königslöw** (kā'-nĭkhs-läv), (1) **Jn. V Cornelius von**, Hamburg, 17 1833; organist and composer. **Otto Fr. von**, b. Hamburg, Nov 1824; pupil of Fr. Pacius and Hafner, and at Leipzig Cons.; to for 12 years; 1858–81, leader Gu nich Orch., Cologne; vice-dir. vln.-prof. at the Cons.; Royal P retired to Bonn.

**Koning** (kō'-nĭng), **David**, Rotterc 1820—Amsterdam, 1876; pia conductor and composer.

**Konradin** (kōn'-rät-ēn), **K. Fd.**, Helenenthal, near Baden, 1833– enna, 1884; dram. composer.

ski (kônt′-shkē), (1) **Antoine de,**
Cracow, Oct. 27, 1817 ; pianist ;
pil of Markendorf and Field ;
de v. succ. tours ; teacher, Lon-
a ; lived in Buffalo, N. Y. ; at 80
red round the world ; c. an opera,
oratorio ; symph. ; very florid and
o. pf.-pcs., incl. "*Le Réveil du
n*," etc. (2) **Chas.,** 1815—Paris,
7 ; violinist. (3) **Apollinaire de,**
arsaw, 1825—1879 ; violinist ; bro.
l pupil of (2). (4) **Stanislas,**
Cracow, Oct. 8, 1820 ; bro. of
ove ; vln.-teacher and composer,
ris.

ecký (kō-pět′-skē), **Ottokar,** b.
otebor, Bohemia, April 29, 1850 ;
linist ; pupil of Prague Cons. ;
der Philh. Orch., cond. " Shaeffer "
ch., and teacher in the Cons.,
mburg ; now ct.-cond. to King of
eece.

ylow (kō′-pē-lôf), **Alex,** b. St.
tersburg, 1854 ; studied in the Imp.
apel, where he is now vocal teach-
; c. orch.- and pf.-pcs., etc.

oay (kôr′-bä-ē), **Francis Alex,**
Pesth, Hungary, May 8, 1846 ;
or ; pupil of Roger, and pf.-pu-
of Liszt ; 1865–68, Hungarian
era, Pesth ; toured as pianist ;
ce 1871 New York as teacher of
ce and pf. ; composer.

a, Mrs. **Clara A.,** teacher and
mposer ; lives Orange, New Jersey,
S. A.

ier (kĕr′-nĕr), (1) **Chr. Gf.,** Leip-
, 1756—Berlin, 1831 ; composer.
**Gotthilf Wm.,** Teicha, near
alle, 1809 — Erfurt, 1865 ; pub-
her.

chat (kō′-shät), **Thos.,** b. Vik-
ng, near Klagenfurt, Aug. 8, 1845 ;
died science at Vienna ; joined the
-opera chorus, soon became leader ;
74, joined cath.-choir ; 1878, the
ofkapelle. 1871, he began the pub.
original poems in Carinthian dia-
t, which he set to music for male
artets ; these have had great pop-
arity. 1875, founded the famous
Kämthner Quintett " ; prod. 4-act

" Volksstück mit Gesang," "*Die Ro-
senthaler Nachtigall,*" and succ.
"Singspiel "*Der Burgermeister von
St. Anna*" (Prague, 1893), etc.

**Köselitz** (kā′-zĕ-lĭts), **H.,** b. Annaberg,
Saxony, 1854 ; pupil of Richter,
Leipzig Cons. and Nietzsche, Basel,
lived in Italy ; under the name
" **Peter Gast** " prod. opera, "*Die
Heimliche Ehe*" (Danzig, 1891).

**Kosleck** (kôs′-lĕk), **Julius,** b. Neu-
gard, Pomerania, Dec. 3, 1835 ;
trumpet- and cornet-virtuoso ; member of the royal band, Berlin ; teacher.

**Kossak** (kôs′-säk), **Ernst,** Marienwerder, 1814—Berlin, 1880 ; writer.

**Kossmaly** (kôs′-mä-lē), **Karl,** (?) 1812
—Stettin, 1893 ; teacher, conductor
and writer.

**Köstlin** (kĕst′-lēn), (1) **K. Rheinhold,**
Urach, Würtemberg, 1819—1894 ;
prof. and writer. (2) **H. Ad.,** b.
Tübingen, Oct. 4, 1846 ; preacher ;
1875 he united the choirs of three
towns, which became in 1877 the
Würtemberg Evangelical " Kirchen-
gesangverein," and which he cond. ;
1891, Darmstadt ; writer.

**Kotek** (kō′-tĕk), **Jos.,** Kamenez-Po-
dolsk, Govt. of Moscow, 1855—
Davos, Switz., 1885 ; violinist, teacher and composer ; c. vln.-pcs.

**Kothe** (kō′-tĕ), (1) **Bd.,** Gröbnig, Silesia, 1821 — Breslau, 1897 ; teacher
and composer. (2) **Aloys,** b. Gröbnig, 1828 — Breslau, 1868 ; bro. of
above ; teacher and composer. (3)
**Wm.,** b. Gröbnig, Jan. 8, 1831 ; bro.
of above ; pupil of R. Orgel-Inst.,
Berlin, since 1871 ; teacher, writer
and composer, Habelschwerdt, Silesia.

**Kotthoff** (kôt′-hôf), **Lawrence,** b.
Eversberg, Dec. 11, 1862 ; pupil of
Breslaur, Grunike, and Buchholz,
Berlin ; 1886, St. Louis, U. S. A. ;
critic and teacher.

**Köttlitz** (kĕt′-lĭts), (1) **Ad.,** Trier,
1820—Siberia, 1860 ; dir. and composer. His wife (2) **Clothilde** (née
**Ellendt**), 1822–67, was an excellent
singing-teacher.

**Ko(t)že'luch** (kôt'-zě-lookh or kō'-zhě-lookh), (1) **Ja. A.** (rightly **Jan An-tonin**), Wellwarn, Bohemia, 1738—Prague, 1814; mus.-dir.; conductor and dram. composer. (2) **Ld. Anton**, Wellwarn, 1752—Vienna, 1811; pupil and cousin of above; conductor, teacher and composer.

**Kotzolt** (kôt'-tsôlt), **H.**, Schnellewalde, Upper Silesia, 1814—Berlin, 1881; conductor and composer.

**Kotzschmar** (kôtsh'-mär), **Hn.**, b. Finsterwalde. Germany, July 4, 1829; his father taught him various instrs.; studied also with his uncle Hayne and Jul. Otto, Dresden; in the opera-orch.; 1848, America, with Saxonia Band; since 1849 lives Portland, Me.; cond. "Haydn Assoc.," etc.

**Kotzwara** (kôts-vä'-rä), **Fz.. b.** Prague—suicide, Ireland. 1791. tenor-player and composer of "Battle of Prague," etc.

**Kowalski** (kō-väl'-shkĭ), **H.**, b. Paris, 1841; pianist and composer; pupil of Marmontel (pf.) and Reber (comp.); composer.

**Kraft** (kräft), (1) **Anton**, Rokitzan, 1752—Vienna, 1820; 'cellist and composer. (2) **Nicolaus**, Esterház, Hungary, 1778—Stuttgart, 1853; 'cellist and composer; son and pupil of above; became a member of the famous "Schuppanzigh Quartett." (3) **Fr.**, b. Feb. 12, 1807, son of above; for years 'cellist Stuttgart ct.-orch.

**Král** (kräl), **Jn. Nepomuk**, (?) 1826—Tulln, near Vienna, 1895 (?); bandmaster.

**Krantz** (kränts), **Eugen**, Dresden, 1844 — 1898; pianist and critic. teacher and composer.

**Krause** (krow'-zě), (1) **Chr. Gf.**, Winzig, 1719—Berlin, 1770; writer. (2) **Karl Chr. Fr.**, Eisenberg, Altenberg, 1781—Munich, 1832; writer. (3) **Theodor**, b. Halle, May 1, 1833, rector at Berlin; cond. Seiffert Soc.; R. Mus.-Dir., 1887; composer. (4) **Anton**, b. Geitham, Saxony, Nov. 9, 1834: at 6 pupil of cantor Dietrich ·

then of Fr. Wieck, Reissiger. Spindler, Dresden, later L Cons., début, as pianist, Gei 1846; 1853–59, teacher and Leipzig *Liedertafel;* 1859–97, *Singverein* and the *Concert* *schaft* (retired); 1877 Royal Dir.; prof.; c. "*Prinzessin* "Rübezahl Legend." (5) (Prof. **Eduard**, Swinemunde, 1837—B 1892; pianist, teacher and comp (6) (Dr.) **Emil**, Schassburg in sylvania, 1840 — Hamburg, barytone. (7) **Emil**, b. Ham [aly 30, 1840; pupil of L Cons.; since 1860, teacher of pf theory at Hamburg; since 188 the Cons.; c. an Ave Maria etc. (8) **Martin**, b. Lobstedt, Leipzig, June 17, 1853; pianist teacher; son and pupil of a ca then studied with Fuchs Borna T ers' Sem., and at Leipzig Cons.; t Holland and Germany, then nervous prostration 2 years; ha friendship and advice of Lisz years; 1885, with Siloti and o founded the Leipzig "Lisztver 1892, professor; 1901, Munich C

**Kraushaar** (krows'-här), **Otto**, C 1812—1856; writer and compos

**Krauss** (krows), (1) Dr. **Feli** Vienna, Oct. 3, 1870; bass; pu Stockhausen; sang *Hagen* and *nemanz* at Bayreuth, 1899. (2) **brielle Marie**, b. Vienna, Marc 1842; soprano; pupil of Vienna C and Marchesi; 1860–67, Vienna opera; 1867 Th. des Italiens, P 1875–86, Gr. Opéra. Paris since a teacher at Paris and officier d' démie.

**Krebs** (kräps), (1) **Jn. L.**, Buttels Thuringia, 1713—Altenburg, 1 organist and composer. (2) **Aug.** (rightly, **Miedcke**, cha after adoption by his teacher opera-singer **J. B. Krebs**), N berg, 1804—Dresden 1880; c. ras. (3) **Marie** (Frau **Brenn** Dresden, Dec. 5, 1851—June 1900; daughter of above, pi

d teacher. (4) **K.**, b. near Hanse-
rg, Würtemberg, Feb. 5, 1857 ;
idied R. Hochschule, Berlin ; lives
Berlin as critic and writer.

**čman.** Vide KRETSCHMANN.

**hbiel** (krä'-bĕl), **H. Edw.**, b. Ann
bor, Mich., March 10, 1854; prom-
ent American critic ; studied law at
ncinnati, but entered journalism ;
74-78, mus.-critic Cincinnati *Ga-
'te ;* later editor New York *Mus.
view,* and since then critic of the
*ibune;* pub. many succ. books, incl.
*Studies in the Wagnerian Drama*,"
391), " *How to Listen to Music*"
396) ; " *Annotated Bibliography
Fine Art*," with R. Sturgis (1897);
*Music and Manners in the 18th
utury*" (1898), etc.

**hl** (kräl), **Stephen,** b. Leipzig, July
1864 ; studied Leipzig Cons. and
esden Cons., 1889 ; teacher of pf.
d theory, Carlsruhe Cons. ; c. Char-
terstücke, sonata, etc., for piano.

**ipl** (krï'-pl), **Jos.,** 1805—Vienna,
66 ; tenor.

**isler** (krïs'-lĕr), (1) **Jns.** Vide E.
A. HOFFMANN. (2) **Fritz,** b.
enna, Feb. 2, 1875 ; violinist, pupil
Massart and Delibes ; début
ris ; toured Europe and U. S.;
es in Vienna.

**issle von Hellborn** (krïs'-lĕ fôn
l'-bôrn), **H.,** Vienna, 1803—1869 ;
iter ; wrote " *Biog. of Schubert*."

**iči** (krä'-chē), **Josef,** Milostin,
hemia, 1822—Prague, 1881 ; or-
nist and composer.

**mpelsetzer** (krĕm'-p'l-zĕts-ĕr), **G.,**
sbiburg, Bavaria, 1827—1871 ;
nd. and dram. composer.

**mser** (krĕm'-zĕr), **Eduard,** b. Vina, April 19, 1838 ; from 1869,
orusm. the Vienna " Männerge-
ngverein " ; c. operettas, a cantata,
th orch., famous " *Altniederlän-
sche Volkslieder*," and other part-
ngs, etc.

**nn** (krĕn), **Fz.,** Dross, Lower
istria, 1816—St. Andrä vorm Ha-
nthal, 1897 ; organist, composer
d conductor

**Kretschmann** (or **Krečman**) (krĕtch'-
män), **Theobald,** b. Vinos, near
Prague, 1850 ; solo 'cellist, Vienna
ct.-opera.

**Kretschmer** (krĕtsh'-mĕr), (1) **Edmund,** b. Ostritz, Saxony, Aug. 31,
1830 ; pupil of Otto and Schneider,
Dresden ; ct.-organist ; founder and
till 1897 cond. the Cäcilia Singing-
Soc., etc.; teacher in the R. " Ka-
pellknaben-Institut," where his son
(2) **Fz.** succeeded him; E. K. c. text
and music of 2 important operas,
" *Die Folkunger* " (Dresden, 1874)
and " *Heinrich der Löwe* " (Leipzig,
1877) ; operetta, " *Der Flüchtling* "
(Ulm, 1881) ; a romantic opera
" *Schön Rohtraut* " (Dresden, 1887);
" *Geisterschlacht* " (prize, Dresden,
1865) ; 3-part mass for male chorus
(Brussels Acad. prize, 1868) ; an orch.
suite " *Hochzeitsmusik*," etc.

**Kretzschmar** (krĕtsh'-mär) (**Aug.
Ed.**), **Hermann,** b. Olberhau, Saxony, Jan. 19, 1848 ; organist and
conductor ; pupil of Otto at the
Kreuzschule, Dresden, and at Leipzig Cons.; 1871 Dr. Phil. at Leipzig,
with a thesis on notation prior to
Guido d' Arezzo; then teacher of org.
and harm. at the Cons. and cond.
several societies ; 1887, mus.- dir. of
Leipzig Univ. and cond. " Paulus."
1888-97, cond. of the " Riedel-Ver-
ein," retired because of ill-health ;
1890, prof., critic, lecturer and
writer ; c. org.-pcs. and part-songs.

**Kreubé** (krŭ-bä), **Chas. Frédéric,**
Luneville, 1777—at his villa, near St.
Denis, 1846 ; cond. at Paris Op.
com.; c. 10 comic operas.

**Kreu(t)zer** (kroi'-tsĕr), (1) **Conradin,**
Mosskirch, Baden, Nov. 22, 1780-
Riga, Dec. 14, 1849 ; pupil of Rie-
gard, Weibrauch and Albrechtsberger ; toured as pianist; ct.-cond. ; c.
30 operas, incl.  " *Das Nachtlage von
Granada* " (1834) and " *Jerry und
Bätely*," still played, etc. His daughter
(2) **Cäcilie** was an operatic singer.
(3) (pron. in France, krŭt-zär), **Rodolphe** Versailles, Nov. 16, 1766;

—-Geneva, Jan. 6, 1831 ; famous violinist to whom Beethoven dedicated the "*Kreutzer Sonata*"; son and pupil of a German violinist and of Stawitz ; prof. at the Cons.; ct.-violinist to Napoleon and to Louis XVIII., 1802–26 ; prod. at Paris over 40 operas, incl. "*Lodoiska*," also collaborated with Rode and Baillot in a standard method and c. famous vln.-études, etc. (4) **Aug.**, Versailles, 1781 — Paris, Aug. 31, 1832 ; bro. of above, and 1826, his successor as vln.-prof. at the Cons. ; composer. (5) **Léon** (**Chas. Fran.**), Paris, 1817—Vichy, 1868. Son of (3) ; writer and composer.

**Krieger** (krē'-gĕr), (1) **Adam,** Driesen, Neumark, 1634—1666 ; ct.-organist and composer. (2) (**Jn.**) **Philip,** Nürnberg, 1649—Weissenfels, 1725 ; ct.-organist, ct.-cond., and dram. composer. (3) **Jn.**, Nürnberg, Jan. 1, 1652—Zittau, July 18, 1736 ; famous contrapuntist ; bro. and pupil of above, and his succ. as ct.-cond. (4) **Fd.**, b. Waldershof, Franconia, Jan. 8, 1843; studied Eichstatt Teachers Seminary and Munich Cons.; from 1867, teacher Normal Sch. at Ratisbon ; writer and composer.

**Kriesstein** (krēs'-shtīn), **Melchior,** printer at Augsburg (1545).

**Krigar** (krē'-gär), (**Julius**) **H.**, Berlin, 1819—1880 ; pianist, conductor and composer.

**Krisper** (krē'-shpĕr), Dr. **Anton L.**, b. Graz, 1882 ; writer.

**Krizkowsky** (krēsh-kôf'-shkĭ), **Paul,** 1820—Brunn, 1885 ; Czech composer.

**Kroeger** (krä'-gĕr), **Ernest R.**, b. St. Louis, U. S. A., Aug. 10, 1862 ; at 5 studied pf. and vln. ; lives St. Louis as teacher ; c. a symph., 5 overtures, a fugue, etc.

**Kroll** (krôl), **Fz.**, Bromberg, 1820—Berlin, 1877 ; pianist and composer.

**Krolop** (krō'-lôp), **Fz.**, Troja, Bohemia, 1839—Berlin, 1897 ; bass.

**Krommer** (krôm'-mĕr), **Fz.**, Kamenitz, Moravia, 1760—Vienna, 1831 ; violinist, organist and conductor.

**Kronach.** Vide KLITZSCH.

**Kronke** (krônk'-ĕ), **Emil,** b. Dan Nov. 29, 1865 ; pianist ; pupi Reinecke and Paul, Nicodé and Kirchner, Dresden ; 1886 won prize, Dresden Cons.; 1887, dipl of honour ; editor of an editior Liszt's complete works ; also c poser.

**Krü(c)kl** (krük'-'l), **Fz.**, Edispitz, ravia, Nov. 10, 1841—Strassb Jan. 13, 1899 ; barytone, teacher composer.

**Krug** (krookh), (1) **Fr.**, Cassel, 18 Carlsruhe, 1892 ; op. barytone dram. composer. (2) **Dietrich,** H burg, 1821—1880 ; pianist and c poser. (3) **Arnold,** b. Hamb Oct. 16, 1849 ; son and pupil above ; studied also with Gurlitt Reinecke ; won Mozart scholars 1869 ; studied with Kiel and Franck, Berlin ; 1872–77, pf.-tea er, Stern Cons.; won Meyerbeer sc arship, and studied in France Italy ; 1885, ct.-cond. at the H burg Cons.; pub. a symph., syn prologue "*Otello*," and orch. su choral works, etc. (4) (**Wen Jos.** (called **Krug-Waldsee**), Waldsee, Upper Swabia, Nov 1858 ; chiefly self-taught until 1 then studied vln., pf., singing comp. with Faiszt, at Stutt Cons.; 1882–89, cond. at Stuttg 1889, chorusm., mus.-dir. Munic Th., Hamburg ; 1892, th.-cond. v ous cities ; 1889, Munich ; 1 Nürnberg ; 1901, Magdeburg ; important concert-cantatas, "*D röschen*," "*Hochzeitslied*," "*Ge zu Gmund*" and "*Seebilder*"; s opera "*Astorre*" (Stuttgart, 18 "secular oratorio" "*König Roth* etc.

**Krüger** (krü'-gĕr), (1) **Eduard,** L burg, 1807—Göttingen, 1885 ; p and writer. (2) **Wm.**, Stuttg 1820—1883 ; pianist, teacher editor. (3) **Gt.**, Stuttgart, 18 1895 ; bro. of above ; harpist.

**Kruis** (krīs), **M. H. van,** b. O

ter, Holland, March 8, 1861; pupil of Nikolai at The Hague ; 1884,
pianist, teacher and writer, Rotter-
n ; 1886, founded monthly " Het
gel " ; c. an opera " *De Bloem Van
and,*" 3 symph., 8 overtures, etc.

npholtz (kroomp'-hôlts), (1) **Jn.
p.**, Zlonitz, near Prague, ca. 1745
Feb. 19, 1790 ; harpist and com-
ser ; he m. his 16-year old pupil,
M. Meyer, a brilliant harpist ; they
ve concerts together, until her elope-
nt, when he drowned himself in
e Seine. (2) **Wenzel**, 1750—Vina, 1817 ; bro. of above ; violinist
d composer.

se (kroo'-zĕ), **Jn. S.**, b. Mel-
urne, Australia, March 31, 1859 ;
linist ; pupil of Joachim ; leader
the Philh. Orch., Berlin ; 1892,
der, Bremen orchestra.

elik (koo'-bĕ-lĭk), **Johann**, b.
chle, near Prague, July 5, 1880 ;
ominent violinist ; son and pupil of
Bohemian gardener ; pupil for 6
ars of Sevcik, Prague Cons.; studied
at Vienna ; début there 1898 ;
en toured Europe, played at Milan,
ndon, 1900, and 1901 America
th great success ; 1902, London
ilh. Society awarded him its Bee-
oven medal.

harž (koo'-chärzh), **Jn. Bap.,**
otecz, Bohemia, 1751—Prague,
29 ; organist and conductor.

ken (kĭk'-'n), **Fr. Wm.**, Bleck-
e, Hanover, 1810—Schwerin, 1882 ;
mposer of operas and pop. songs ;
some time cond. at Stuttgart.

zynski (koo-chĕn'-shkĭ), **Paul**,
1846 ; Polish composer ; pupil of
n Bülow ; c. succ. cantata "*Ari-
ne.*"

elski (koo-dĕl'-shkĭ), **K. Mat.**,
rlin, 1805—Baden-Baden, 1877 ;
olinist, composer and conductor.

erath (koof'-fĕr-ät), (1) **Jn. Hn.**,
ühlheim-on-the-Ruhr, 1797—Wies-
den, 1864 ; conductor. (2) **Louis**,
ühlheim, 1811—near Brussels, 1882;
anist, teacher and composer. (3)
ubert Fd., Mühlheim, June 11,

1818—Brussels, June 23, 1896 ; noted
pianist ; bro. and pupil of above ;
writer and composer. (4) **Maurice**, b.
Brussels, Jan. 8, 1852. Son and pupil of (3) ; studied with Servais (père
and fils) 'cello ; 1873, editor " *Guide
musicale,*" later, proprietor ; writer
and translator under the name
" **Maurice Reymont.**"

**Küffner** (kĭf'-nĕr), **Jos.**, Würzburg,
1776—1856 ; dram. composer.

**Kugelmann** (koo'-gĕl-män), **Hans**, d.
Königsberg, 1542; trumpeter and
composer.

**Kuhe** (koo'-ĕ), **Wm.**, b. Prague, Dec.
10, 1823 ; pianist ; pupil of Proksch,
Tomaschek and Thalberg; 1845,
London ; from 1886 prof. the R. A.
M.; composer.

**Kuhlau** (koo'-low), **Fr.**, Ülzen, Hanover, Sept. 11, 1786—Copenhagen,
March 13, (18?). 1832 ; ct.-flutist,
dram. composer, teacher and composer of important technical pf.-pcs.,
etc.

**Kühmstedt** (küm'-shtĕt), **Fr.**, Oldis-
leben, Saxe-Weimar, 1809—Eise-
nach, 1858 ; theorist, composer, writer and teacher.

**Kuhnau** (koo'-now), **Jn.**, Geysing,
Saxony, April, 1667 (?)—Leipzig,
June 5, 1722 ; pupil of Henry, Al-
brici and Edelmann ; organist at the
Thomaskirche, Leipzig, and 1700
cantor, before Bach ; pub. the first
sonata for harpsichord, of which he
was a noted player ; also famous Biblical sonatas ; composer and writer.

**Kühner** (kü'-nĕr), **Konrad**, b. Markt-
streufdorf, Meiningen, March 2,
1851 ; pupil Stuttgart Cons. ; lives in
Brunswick as teacher, writer and
composer.

**Kulenkampf** (koo'-l'n-kämpf), **Gus.**, b.
Bremen, Aug. 11, 1849 , concert
pianist and teacher ; pupil of Rein-
thaler, Barth and Bargiel, Berlin
Hochschule, organised the succ.
" Kulenkampscher Frauenchor " ; dir.
Schwantzer Cons. at Berlin for a few
years ; c. succ. comic operas "*Der
Page*" (Bremen, 1890) and "*Der*

*Mohrenfürst*" (Magdeburg, 1892) ; " *Die Braut von Cypern* " (Schwerin, 1897) ; male choruses, etc.

**Kullak** (kool'-läk), (1) **Theodor,** Krotoschin, Posen, Sept. 12, 1818—Berlin, March 1, 1882 ; eminent teacher ; Prince Radziwill had him taught by the pianist Agthe ; at 11 he played at a ct.-concert ; studied with Dehn, Czerny, Sechter and Nicolai ; then teacher to the royal family ; 1846, ct.-pianist, Berlin ; 1850, founded (with Julius Stern and Bern. Marx) the Berlin (later Stern) Cons.; 1855, resigned, established his famous "Neue Akademie der Tonkunst ; " 1861, royal prof. ; wrote standard works, " *Sch. of Octave-playing,*" " *Seven Studies in Octave-playing,*" etc.; c. a concerto, sonata and other brilliant pf.-pcs., etc., incl. " *Kinderleben.*" (2) **Ad.,** Meseritz, 1823—Berlin, 1862 ; bro. of above ; writer and composer. (3) **Fz.,** Berlin, April 12, 1842 ; son and pupil of (1) ; studied with Wieprecht and Liszt ; 1867, pf.-teacher and dir. orch.-class in Acad. of his father, on whose death he became dir. in 1890 ; writer ; c. an opera " *Ines de Castro* " (Berlin, 1877), etc.

**Kummer** (koom'-m'r), (1) **Kaspar,** Erlau, 1795—Coburg, 1870 ; flute-virtuoso. (2) **Fr. Aug.,** Meiningen, Aug. 5, 1797—Dresden, May 22, 1879 ; notable 'cellist and composer for 'cello ; wrote method. (3) **Alex.,** b. Dresden, July 10, 1850 ; son of above ; pupil of Leipzig Cons., vln.-virtuoso ; lives in England.

**Kümmerle** (kĭm'-mĕr-lĕ), **Salomon,** Malmsheim, near Stuttgart, 1838—Samaden, 1896 ; prof. and composer.

**Kündinger** (kĭn'-dĭng-ĕr), (1) **G. Wm.,** b. Königshofen, Bavaria, Nov. 28, 1800 ; 1831 Stadtcantor at Nordlingen ; 1838, Nürnberg ; composer of church music. His 3 sons, (2) **Alex,** b. Kitzingen, Feb. 13, 1827 ; ct.-violinist and composer, St. Petersburg. (3) **Kanut,** b. Kitzingen, Nov. 11, 1830 ; 'cellist, since 1849 in

Munich ct.-orch.; and (4) **Rudo**(l)
Nordlingen, May 2, 1832 ; pia
pupil of his father and Blumr(
since 1850 lives in St. Petersb
teacher at the court and to the
press ; 1879 prof. at the Cons. ;
poser.

**Kunkel** (koonk'-'l), (1) **Fz. Jos.,**
burg, Hesse, 1804 — Frankfor
Main, 1880 ; theorist and comp
(2) **K. Bros.,** music publishers
Louis, Mo.

**Kuntze** (koon'-tsĕ), **K.,** Trier, 18
Delitzsch, Saxony, 1883 ; teacher
composer.

**Kunz** (koonts), **Konrad Max,** Sch
dorf, Bav. Palatinate, 1812—Mu(n)
1875 ; conductor and composer.

**Kunzen** (koonts'-'n),(1) **Jn. Paul,**
nig, Saxony, 1696—Lübeck, 1
organist and composer. (2) **Ad.,**
Wittenberg, 1720—Lübeck, 1781
ganist, pianist and composer.
**Fr. L. Æmilius,** Lübeck, 17
Copenhagen, 1817; ct.-conductor
composer.

**Kupfer-Berger** (koop'-f'r-bĕrk(
**Ludmilla,** b. Vienna, 1850 ; pu(pil)
the Cons.; début Linz-on-Dan(ube)
1868, then at the Berlin Ct.-op(era)
m. the Berlin merchant Kupfer ;
at Vienna, ct.-opera as alternate
Materna.

**Kurpinski** (koor-pĭn'-shkĭ), **Karl (**
**simir**), Luschwitz, Posen, 17
Warsaw, 1857 ; conductor and d(r)
composer.

**Kurth** (koort), (**Martin Alex.**) O
b. Triebel, Brandenburg, Pru
Nov. 11, 1846 ; pupil of Ha
Löschhorn, and Jul. Schneider,
lin ; since 1871, teacher Teac(hers)
Seminary, Lüneburg ; 1885, R. M
Dir.; c. 3 operas, oratorio, ad
cantata, with orch., symph., etc.

**Kus'ser** (or **Cous'ser**), **Jn. S(ig)**
**mund,** Pressburg, ca. 1657—Du(blin)
1727 ; conductor and dram. comp(oser)

**Küster** (kĭs'-tĕr), **Hn.,** Tem(pelberg)
Brandenburg, 1817—Herford, W
phalia, 1878 ; ct.-organist, theo
and composer

ıst (kwäst), **Jas.**, b. Nijkerk, Hol-
ıd, Nov. 23, 1852 ; pianist ; pupil
his father and Fd. Böhme ; Rei-
cke and Richter, Kullak and
ıerst, Brassin and Gevaert, Brus-
s ; 1874 teacher Cologne Cons.;
83, Hoch Cons., Frankfort : com-
ser.

## L

arre (lä-băr), **Th.**, Paris, 1805—
70 ; harpist and dram. composer.

att (lä-bät'), **Leonard**, Stockholm,
38—1897 ; tenor.

itzky (lä-bĭt'-shkĭ), (1) **Jos.**, Schön-
d, near Eger, 18c2 — Carlsbad,
81 ; violinist. Two sons (2) **Aug.**,
Petschau, Saxony, Oct. 22, 1832 ;
pil of Prague Cons., of David and
ıuptmann, Leipzig ; 1853, cond.
d composer at Carlsbad. (3) **Wm.**,
ıinist ; lives in Toronto, Canada.

ıache (lä-blăsh), **Luigi**, son of
ench father and Irish mother,
ıples, Dec. 6, 1794—Jan. 23, 1858;
ınent bass, with powerful and flex-
e voice with compass (E♭ -e') ; pu-
of Valesi, pupil Cons. della Pietà;
ıut Naples as buffo ; later in heroic
es throughout Europe ; wrote
Méthode de chant."

ır (lä'-bôr). **Josef**, b. Horowitz,
hemia, June 29, 1842 ; a blind
ınist and organist ; pupil of Sechter
ı Pirkjer, Vienna Cons.; chamber-
ınist and teacher of the princess of
ınover; c. a Paternoster with orch.;
Ave Maria in canon-form for
ıale voices, etc.

ırde. Vide DELABORDE.

ıaume (lä-shōm), **Aimé,** b. Paris ;
ınist and composer ; came to New
ırk, 1890 (?) ; lives there as teacher,
ompanist, cond. and composer of
ıtomimes, incid. mus., etc.

ımund (läkh'-moont), **Carl V.,** b.
oneville, Mo., U. S. A., 1854 ; at
studied in Cologne with Heller,
ısen and Seiss ; then Berlin, also 4
ırs with Liszt at Weimar ; c. trio
ıyed by Berlin Philh. orch.),
28

"*Japanese*" overture (perf. by
Thomas and Seidl), etc.; lives in
New York as teacher, conductor and
composer.

**Lachner** (läkh'-nĕr), (1) **Theodor, b.**
1798; son of a poor organist at Rain,
Upper Bavaria ; organist at Munich.
(2) **Thekla,** b. 1803; sister of above
organist at Augsburg. (3) **Christi-
ane,** b. 1805 ; sister of above ; organist at Rain. (4) **Fz.**, Rain, April,
2, 1804 — Munich, Jan. 20, 1890 ;
half-brother of above ; studied with
Eisenhofer (comp.), and with Ett ;
1882, organist Protestant Church,
Vienna, and studied with Stadler,
Sechter, and Weigl ; a friend of
Schubert and Beethoven; 1826, cond.
Kärthnerthor Th.; 1834, Mannheim ;
1836, the production of his D minor
symph. at Munich won him the appointment of ct.-cond.; from 1852,
was gen. mus. dir.; 1868 retired with
pension in protest against the growing
Wagnerianism at court ; his eight
orch. suites are his best work, showing his contrapuntal gifts at their
best ; he prod. 4 operas, 2 oratorios,
8 symphs., incl. the "*Appassionata,*"
chamber-music, etc. (5) **Ignatz,**
Rain, Sept. 11, 1807—Hanover, Feb.
24, 1895. Bro. of (4) and his successor
as organist, 1825. 2d cond. of court-
opera, later ct.-mus.-dir.; Stuttgart ;
1858, ct.-cond., Stockholm ; c. operas, pop. Singspiele, etc. (6) **Vincenz,** Rain, July 19, 1811—Carlsruhe, Jan. 22, 1893 ; bro. of above :
his successor as organist and later
successor of **Fz.**, as ct.-cond.; teacher and composer.

**Lacknith** (läk'-nĭt), **L. Wenzel,** b.
Prague, 1746 ; horn-player, and de-
ranger of famous works.

**Lack** (läk), **Théodore,** b. Quimper,
France, Sept. 3, 1846 ; pupil of Marmontel (pf.) and Bazin (harm.) Paris
Cons.; teacher at Paris ; 1881 officier
of the Académie; officier of public instruction ; c. much light and graceful pf.-music.

**Lackowitz** (läk'-ō-vĭts), **Wm.**, Trebbin, near Berlin, Jan. 13, 1837; pupil of Erk, Kullak, and Dehn; editor.

**Lacombe** (lä-kôṅb), (1) **Louis** (**Brouillon - Lacombe**), Bourges, France, Nov. 26, 1818—St. Vaast-la-Hougue, Sept. 30, 1884; pianist; pupil of Paris Cons.; writer and dram. composer. (2) **Paul**, b. Carcássonne, Oude, France, July 11, 1837; studied with Teysseyre, but mainly self-taught; 1880 won the Prix Chartier, for chamber-mus., in which field he is most famous; c. also 3 symphs., a symph. overture, etc.

**Lacome** (lä-kŭm), **Paul** (**P. J. Jac. Lacome de L'Estaleux**), b. Houga, Gers, France, March 4, 1838; lives since 1860, Paris; essayist and composer of many light operas, incl. "*Jeanne, Jeannette et Jeanneton*" (1876); orchestral suites; songs, incl. "L'Estudiantina," etc.

**La'cy**, (1) **J.**, bass, at London, 1818. His wife (2), Mrs. **Bianchi Lacy**, was a soprano. (3) **Michael Rophino**, Bilbao, 1795—Pentonville, 1867; English violinist and composer.

**Ladegast** (lä'-dĕ-gäst), **Fr.**, b. Hochhermsdorf, near Leipzig, Aug. 30, 1818; org.-builder.

**Ladurner** (lä-door'-nĕr), **Ignaz Ant. Fz.**, Aldein, Tyrol, 1766—Villain (Massy), 1839; pianist and composer.

**Lafage** (lä-fäzh), **Juste Adrien Lenoir de**, Paris, 1801—Charenton Insane Asylum, 1862; singing-teacher, conductor, composer and writer.

**Lafont** (lä-fôṅ), **Chas. Philippe**, Paris, 1781—near Tarbes, 1839; violinist and composer.

**La Grange** (lä gräṅzh), **Mme. Anna** (**Caroline**) **de**, b. Paris, July 24, 1825; coloratura soprano of remarkable range and flexibility; pupil of Bordogni and Lamperti; début 1842, at Varese; m. the wealthy Russian Stankowich, has since lived in Paris as teacher.

**La Harpe** (lä-ärp), **J. Fran. de**, Paris, 1739—1803; critic.

**Lahee'**, **H.**, b. Chelsea, England, April 11, 1826; pupil of Bennett, F and J. Goss (comp.); concertist; lives in Croydon as teache 5 cantatas, etc.

**Lahire** (lä-ēr'), **Ph. de**, Paris, 1 1719; writer.

**Laid'law**, **Anna Robena** ( **Thomson**), Bretton, Yorkshire, 30, 1819—May, 1901; successful cert-pianist until her marriage,

**Laïs**. Vide LAYS.

**Lajarte** (lä-zhärt), **Th. Ed. Du de**, Bordeaux, 1826—Paris, writer and dram. composer.

**Lajeunesse**, **M.** Vide ALBANI.

**Lalande** (lä-länd), (1) **Michel F ard de**, Paris, 1657—1726; o ist, conductor and composer. (**Méric-Lalande**) **Henriette mentine**, Dunkirk, 1798—P 1867; brilliant soprano.

**Lalo** (lä-lō), **Ed. (V.)**, Lille, Jar 1823—Paris, April 22, 1892; vio and viola.-virtuoso; c. 2 vln.-co tos; "*Symphonie espagnole*"; sody for orch., opera "*Le Roi d'* chamber-music, etc.

**Lamb**, **Benj.**, Engl. organist cent.

**La Mara**. Vide LIPSIUS, MARIE.

**Lambert** (läṅ-bär), (1) **Michel** vonne, Poitou, 1610—Paris, conductor and composer. (2) cien, b. Paris, Jan., 1861; pup Paris Cons.; 1883, took Prix R w. cantata "*Prométhée Enchat* c. lyric dram. "*Le Spahi*" com., 1897); overture, etc.

**Lambert** (lǎm'-bĕrt), (1) **Jn. H.**, hausen, Alsatia, 1728—Berlin, writer. (2) **Geo.**, b. Beverley, organist there, succeeded by hi (3) **Geo. Jackson** in 1818; re 1874. (4) **Alex.**, b. Warsaw, land, Nov. 1, 1862; son and pu (5) **Henry L.**; (4) studied at V Cons.; graduated at 16; studied Urban, Berlin; toured German Russia; studied some months at mar with Liszt; 1884, Ame since 1888, dir. N. Y. Coll. of ] composer.

berti (läm-bĕr'-tē), **Gius.**, Cuneo,
ly, 1820 (?)—Turin, 1894; dram.
iposer.

beth, **H. A.**, b. Hardway, near
sport, 1822; organist.

billotte (län-bī-yôt), Père **Louis**,
arleroi, Hainault, 1797—Vaugi-
l, 1855; organist, conductor and
iposer.

mers (läm'-mĕrs), **Julius**, Leip-
, 1829—1888; composer and teach-

ond', (1) **Fr. A.**, b. Glasgow, Jan.
1868; concert-pianist (pupil cf
bro. (2) **David**); 1882 at Raff
ns., Frankfort; later with von
ow and Liszt; début, Berlin,
5; toured Europe; 1902, America;
symph., overture "*Aus dem schot-
hen Hochlande,*" etc.

othe (lä-môt), **G.**, France, 1837—
rbevoie, 1894; composer.

oureux (läm-oo-rŭ'), **Chas.**, Bor-
ux, Sept. 28, 1834—Paris, 1900;
inent conductor; pupil of Girard,
is Cons.; later with Tolbecque,
orne and Chauvet; co-founder of
oc. for chamber-mus.; 1872, dir-
ist "Société de musique sacrée;"
6, assist.-cond. Paris Opéra;
8, first cond.; 1872-78, also
ist.-cond. the Cons. Concerts; re-
ned from the Opéra, 1881, and est.
celebrated "Concerts Lamou-
x" (Nouveaux Concerts).

pada'rius, (1) **Jns.**, chapel-singer,
Sophia, Constantinople, 14th
it.; writer. (2) **Petrus**, b. Tripo-
a, Morea, ca. 1730; composer.

padius (läm-pä'-dī-oos), **Wm**
., 1812—Leipzig, 1892; writer.

pe (läm'-pĕ), **J. F.**, Saxony, 1703
Edinburg, 1751; bassoonist and
eratic composer.

peren (län'-pĕ-rän), **Michel**
n, b. Brussels, Dec. 6, 1826; 1859,
r. Brussels Cons.; composer.

pert (läm'-pĕrt), **Ernst**, Gotha,
8—1879; pianist, violinist, ct.-
iductor and dram. composer.

perti (läm-pĕr'-tē), **Fran.**, Sala, Italy, March 11, 1813—Como,

May 1, 1892; eminent singing-teacher; pupil of Milan Cons. and teacher
there, 1850-76; pub. treatises.

**Lampugnani** (läm-poon-yä'-nē), **Giov.
Bat.**, Milan, 1706—ca. 1780; dram.
composer.

**Land** (länt), Dr. **Jan Pieter Nico-
laas**, Delft, 1834—Arnhem, 1897;
professor; pub. important results of
research in Arabian and Javanese
mus., etc.

**Landgraf** (länt'-gräf), **J. Fr. Bd.**,
Dielsdorf, Weimar, 1816—Leipzig,
1885; clarinettist.

**Landi** (län'-dē), **Stefano**, Rome, ca.
1590—ca. 1655; conductor, com-
poser and singer.

**Landino** (län-dē'-nō), **Fran.** (called
**Francesco Cieco** "the blind," or
**Degli Organi**), Florence, ca. 1325—
1390; notable organist and composer.

**Landolfi** (län-dôl'-fē) (or **Landul'-
phus**), (1) **Carlo Fdo.**, 1. Milan,
1750-60; maker of 'cellos, etc. (2)
**Pietro**, instr.-maker at Milan ca.
1760, probably son or bro. of above.

**Lang** (läng), (1) (**Lang-Köstlin**), **Josephine**, Munich, 1815—Tübingen,
1880; composer. (2) **Benj. Johnson**, b. Salem, Mass., Dec. 28, 1837
prominent pf.-teacher and conductor,
pupil of his father and of F. G. Hill
at Boston, Jaell and Satter, later in
Berlin, and with Liszt; since 1852,
organist various churches, Boston;
for over 25 years organist Handel and
Haydn Soc. and cond. since 1895;
also cond. the Apollo Club and the
Cecilia, etc.; c. an oratorio "*David*";
symphs., etc. (3) **Margaret Ruthven**, b. Boston, Nov. 27, 1867;
daughter and pupil of above; studied
also with Schmidt of Boston, Drechsler and Abel (vln.) and Gluth (comp.)
in Munich; pub. many original and
important songs and pf.-pcs. (4)
**Karl**, b. Waiblingen, June 24, 1860;
tenor at Schwerin; pupil of Dr.
Gunz.

**Langbecker** (läng'-bĕk-ĕr), **Emanuel
Chr. Gl.**, Berlin. 1792—1843; writer.

**Lang'don, Richard,** Exeter, Engl., ca. 1729—1803 ; organist and composer.

**Lange** (läng'-ĕ), (1) **Otto,** Graudenz, 1815—Cassel, 1879 ; editor and writer. (2) **Gustav,** Schwerstedt, near Erfurt, 1830—Wernigerode, 1889 ; pianist and composer. (3) **Samuel de,** Rotterdam, Feb. 22, 1840 ; son and pupil of the organist, (4) **Samuel de L.** (1811—1884); later studied with Winterberger, Vienna, and Damcke and Mikuli, Lemberg; 1863 organist and teacher Rotterdam Mus. Sch., often touring Europe ; 1876 teacher Cologne Cons., also cond. 1885-93, cond. at The Hague, later teacher and vice-dir. Stuttgart Cons., and since 1895, cond. ; c. oratorio " *Moses* " (The Hague, 1389), a symph., etc. (5) **Daniel de,** b. Rotterdam, July 11, 1841 ; bro. of above ; studied with Ganz and Servais ('cello), Verhulst and Damcke (comp.), at Lemberg Cons. 1860-63, then studied pf. with Mme. Dubois at Paris ; chiefly self-taught as organist ; 1895, dir. Amsterdam Cons., and cond.; also critic ; c. opera " *De Val Van Kuilenburg*" ; two symphs. ; overture, " *Willem van Holland*," etc. (6) **Aloysia.** Vide WEBER (4).

**Langer** (läng'-ĕr), (1) **Hn.,** Hockendorf, near Tharandt, Saxony, 1819—Dresden, 1889 ; organist, conductor and teacher. (2) **Fd.,** b. Leimen, near Heidelberg, Jan. 21, 1839 ; 'cellist at Mannheim ct.-Th., and later 2nd cond. ; prod. there 5 succ. operas. (3) **Victor,** b. Pesth, Oct. 14, 1842 ; pupil R. Volkmann, and Leipzig Cons.; lives in Pesth as teacher, th.-cond. and editor ; pub. under the name of " **Aladar Tisza** " very pop. songs, etc.

**Langert** (läng'-ĕrt), (1) (**Jn.**) **Aug. (Ad.**), b. Coburg, Nov. 26, 1836 ; dram. composer ; th.-cond. Coburg; 1872, teacher of comp. Geneva Cons.; 1873, ct.-cond., Gotha, reappointed 1893 ; prod. 7 operas.

**Langhans** (läng'-häns), (**Fr.**) V Hamburg, 1832—Berlin, 1892; w

**Langlé** (län'-lä), **Honoré Fran.** Monaco, 1741—Villiers-le-Bel, Paris, 1807 ; mus.-dir., theorist composer.

**Lang'shaw,** (1) **J.,** d. 1798; Eng ganist. (2) **J.,** London, 1763 ganist ; son and successor of abo

**Lanière** (**Lanier** or **Lanieri**) (län län-ēr', or län-ĭ-ā'-rē), (1) **Nich** Italy (?), ca. 1588—London, (1668 ?); son of (2) **Jos.,** and ne of (3) **Nicholas.** (2) and (3) car England, were mus. to Queen I beth. (1) was ct.-musician to Ch I. ; a prolific composer and s who introduced the recitative into England.

**Lanner** (län'-nĕr), (1) **Jos. (Fz.** Oberdöbling, near Vienna, 18 1843 ; violinist, composer and ductor. (2) **Aug. (Jos.**), 1834— son of above ; violinist, cond and dance-composer of promine

**Lans** (**Michael**), **J. A.,** b. Haa July 18, 1845 ; a R. C. priest, 1869 teacher in Voorhout Semir from 1887, pastor at Schiedam ; founded church-mus. periodical 1878, the Gregorian Soc. ; c. a r etc.

**Lapicida** (lä-pĭ-chē'-dä), **Eras** 16th cent. composer.

**Laporte** (lä-pôrt), **Jos. de,** B 1713— Paris, 1779 ; Jesuit a writer.

**Lara** (lä'-rä). **Isidore de** (rightly hen), b. in Ireland, 1862, of En father and Portuguese mother; st at Milan Cons.; took 1st priz comp. at age of 17; has written s and the following operas : "*La dell' Asia*," founded on Sir E Arnold's poem (London, 1 "*Amy Robsart*" (1893) ; "*Mo* (1897) ; "*Messaline*," Monte (1899), very successful.

**Laroche** (lä-rôsh), (1) **Jas.** (c " **Jemmy** "), ca. 1680—singer, don. (2) **Hermann Augustov** b. St. Petersburg, 1845 ; studie he Cons.; since 1866 teacher of heory and history at Moscow Cons.; writer and composer.

**Rue** (lä-rü), **Pierre de** (Latinised **Petrus Platensis**; also called **Perisone, Pierchon, Pierson, Pierzon,** or **Pierazon de la Ruellien**), eminent 16th cent. Netherland contrapuntist and composer; fellow-pupil (with Desprès) of Okeghem; ct.-singer and favourite of Margaret of Austria.

**aruette** (lä-rü-ĕt), **J. L.,** Toulouse, 1731—1792; composer.

**a Salette** (lä-sä-lĕt'), **Joubert de,** Grenoble, 1762—1832; writer.

**asner** (läs'-nĕr), (1) **Ignaz,** Brosau, Bohemia, 1815—Vienna, 1883; 'cellist. (2) **K.,** b. Vienna, Sept. 11, 1865; son of above; 'cellist Laibach Philh. Orch.

**assalle** (läs-säl), **Jean,** b. of French parents, London, 1847; studied Paris Cons.; notable barytone; début, Brussels, 1871; sang at Paris opéra, in America, etc.

**assen** (läs'-sĕn), **Eduard,** b. Copenhagen, April 13, 1830; at 2 was taken to Brussels and at 12 studied in the Cons. there; won first pf.-prize, 1844; harm. prize, 1847; 2nd prize in comp. and 1851 Prix de Rome; travelled in Germany and Italy and made a long stay in Rome; 1858, ct.-mus.-dir. at Weimar; Liszt procured the prod. of his opera "*Landgraf Ludwig's Brautfahrt*" (Weimar, 1857); 1861–95, Liszt's successor as ct.-cond. at Weimar; then pensioned; c. operas "*Frauenlob*" (Weimar, 1860); "*Le Captif*" (Brussels, 1865; in German, Weimar, 1868); 11 characteristic orch.-pcs.; Bible-scenes with orch.; cantatas, 2 symphs., pop. songs, etc.

**asserre** (läs-sär), **Jules,** b. Tarbes, July 29, 1838; pupil Paris Cons.; took 1st and 2nd prize as 'cellist; 1869 Engl. composer.

**asso** (läs'-sō), (1) **Orlando di** (rightly **Roland de Lattre,** Lat. **Orlan'dus Las'sus**), Mons (Hainault), 1520—Munich, June 14, 1594; most eminent of Netherland, and (except Palestrina) of 16th cent, composers and conductors. C. 2,500 compositions, many of which are still beautiful to modern ears, as his melodic suavity was not smothered by the erudition which gave him even among contemporaries the name "Prince of Music." Befriended by various noblemen and given much Italian travel, he became 1541–48 cond. at S. Giovanni in Laterano at Rome; then visited Mons and ca. 1554, England, settling in Antwerp the same year; 1557 joined on invitation the ct.-chapel of Albert V., Duke of Bavaria; from 1562 he was cond. there, full of honours. His complete works (in course of pub. by Breitkopf & Härtel) include his famous "*Psalmi Davidis poenitentiales,*" masses, psalms, and secular compositions of occasionally humorous vein. Biogr. by Dehn (1837), Bäumkehr (1878), and Sandberger. (2) **Fd. di,** d. Munich, Aug. 27, 1609, eldest son of above; ct.-cond. (3) **Rudolf di,** d. Munich, 1625; second son of (1); organist and composer. (4) **Fd. di,** d. 1636; son of (2); conductor and composer.

**Latilla** (lä-tĭl'-lä), **Gaetano,** Bari, Naples, 1713—Naples, 1789; conductor, teacher and composer.

**Latrobe,** (1) Rev. **Chr. I.,** Fulnes, Leeds, 1758—Fairfield, near Liverpool, 1836; composer. (2) **J. Antes,** London, 1792—Gloucester, 1787; son of above; organist and composer.

**Lattre, de.** Vide LASSO.

**Laub** (lowp), **Fd.,** Prague, 1832—Gries, Tyrol, 1875; vln.-virtuoso; teacher and composer.

**Laubner** (lowp'-nĕr), **Julius,** 1896, cond. Municipal Th., Stettin, prod. there succ. 1-act opera "*Gunare.*"

**Laurencin** (low'-rĕn-sĕn), **Graf Fd. P.,** Kremsier, Moravia, 1819—Vienna, 1890; writer.

**Laurens** (lō-räns), **Edmond,** b. Bergerac, France, Sept. 2, 1851; pupil of E. Guiraud, Paris Cons.; c. operas; a suite japonaise, etc.

**Laurent de Rille** (lō-räṅ dü ŕē′-yŭ), **Fran. Anatole,** b. Orleans, France, 1828; pupil of Comoghio and Elwart; inspector of vocal instruction, Paris pub. schools, etc.; wrote a mus. novel "*Olivier l'orphéoniste*"; prod. about 25 operettas, male choruses (chœurs orphéoniques), etc.

**Laurenti** (lä-oo-rěn′-tē), (1) **Bart. Gir.,** Bologna, 1644—1726; violinist and composer. (2) **Gir. Nicolò,** b. Bologna, Dec. 26, 1752; son of above; violinist and composer.

**Lauska** (lä-oos′-kä), **Fz. (Seraphinus Ignatius),** Brünn, Moravia, 1764 —Berlin, 1825; teacher and composer.

**Lauterbach** (low′-těr-bäkh), **Jn. Chr.,** b. Culmbach, Bavaria, July 24, 1832; pupil Würzburg Mus. Sch., and of Fétis and de Bériot at Brussels (1850), won gold medal for vln.-playing, 1851; 1853 Munich Cons.; 1860–77 Dresden Cons.; 1889, pensioned; composer.

**Lavallée** (lä-väl-lä), **Calixa,** Verchères, Canada, 1842 — Boston, Mass., 1891; concert-pianist; toured U. S., singing, giving frequent concerts of American composers' works, 1886–87; c. 2 operas, an oratorio, a symph., etc.

**La'venu, Louis H.,** London, 1818—Sydney, 1859; 'cellist and dram. composer.

**Lavigna** (lä-vēn′-yä), **V.,** Naples, 1777—Milan, ca. 1837; teacher and dram. composer.

**Lavignac** (là-vēn-yăk), **Albert,** prof. of harmony, Paris Cons.; writer; pub. a "*Cours complet théorique et pratique de dictée musicale*," 1882, which led to the general adoption in mus. schs. of courses in mus. dictation; also "*La musique et les musiciens*" (Paris, 1895, Engl. ed., 1899).

**Lavigne** (lä-vēn), (1) **Jacques Émile,** Pau, 1782—1855; tenor. (2) **A. Jos.,** b. Besançon, France, March 23, 1816; oboist; pupil Paris Cons.; from 1841 in Drury Lane Promenade Concerts, later in Halle's Manchester

orch.; he partially adapted Böhr system to the oboe.

**Lavoix** (lä-vwä), **H. M. Fra** Paris, 1846—1897; writer and co poser.

**Law, Andrew,** Cheshire, Conn., 17 —1821; singing-teacher, writer a composer of hymn-tunes, etc.

**Lawes** (lôz), (1) **Wm.,** Salisbury, Wi shire, 1582—killed at the siege Chester, 1645; composer. (2) **H** Dinton, near Salisbury, Dec., 1595 London, Oct. 21, 1662; bro. above; one of the most original a important of song-writers, forestallin in his principles those of Franz, etc in that he made his music respect t poetry he was setting; Milton, He rick and others accordingly prais him. Pupil of Coperario. 162 Epistler and Gentleman, Chap Royal; on Charles I.'s execution lost his places but re-found them the Restoration in 1660; buried Cloisters of Westminster Abbey; the music to Milton's "*Comus*," et

**Lawrowskaja** (or **Lavrovskaja** (lä rôf-shkä′-yä)), **Elizabeth Andre jevna** (Princess Zeretelev), b. Kashir Russia, Oct. 12, 1845; sopr.; pupil Fenzi and of Mme. Nissen-Saloma St. Petersburg Cons.; début as O pheus, 1867.

**Layol(l)e** (or **dell'Aiole, Ajolla** (l yôl′, or ä-yō′-lě), **Fran.,** Florentin composer 16th cent.

**Lays** (rightly **Lay**) (lě(s)), **Fran.** Gascony, 1758—Angers, 1831; note singer and teacher.

**Lazare** (lä-zăr), **Martin,** Brussels 1829—1897; pianist.

**Laz′arus, H.,** London, 1815—1895 clarinettist.

**Lazzari** (läd-zä′-rē), (1) **Sylvio,** b Bozen, 1858; studied with Césa Franck, Paris Cons.; lived in Pari as a teacher; c. opera "*Armor*," pantomimic ballets, etc. (2) **Raf faele,** c. succ. opera "*La Conzsse d'Egmont*" (Trieste, 1902).

**Lazzarini** (läd-zä-rē′-nē), **Gustavo,** b. Padua, or Verona, 1765; singer.

**Leach, Jas.,** Yorkshire, 1762—1797 ; tenor and composer.

**Le Bé** (lŭ-bā), **Guil.,** 16th cent. French type-founder.

**Le Beau** (lŭ-bō), **Louise Adolpha,** b. Rastatt, Baden, April 25, 1850 ; concert-pianist ; pupil of Kalliwoda, Frau Schumann, Sachs, Rheinberger and Fr. Lachner ; lives since 1890 in Berlin ; c. choral works " *Hadu-moth* " (1894), etc.

**Lebeau** (lŭ-bō), **Fran.,** b. Liège, Aug. 4, 1827 ; pupil of Michelot (pf.) and Rosselet (harm.) ; Sec. administration commission Brussels Cons. ; c. opera " *Esmeralda*," text by Victor Hugo (Liège, 1856).

**Lebègue** (lŭ-bĕg), **Nicolas A.,** Laon, 1630—Paris, 1702 ; ct.-organist and composer.

**Lebert** (lā′-bĕrt) (rightly **Levy**), **Siegmund,** Ludwigsburg, near Stuttgart, 1822 — Stuttgart, 1884 ; teacher, writer and composer ; co-founder of Stuttgart Cons. (1856–57).

**Lebeuf** (lŭ-bŭf), Abbé **Jean,** Auxerre, 1687—1760 ; writer.

**Leblanc** (lŭ-bläṅ), **Georgette,** b. Rouen; pupil of Bax ; début Op. Com. Paris, 1893, in " *L'Attaque de Moulin*," 1895, Th. de la Monnaie, Brussels ; then gave song recitals in costume with much effect.

**Leborne** (lŭ-bôrn), (1) **Aimé Ambroise Simon,** Brussels, 1797—Paris, 1866 ; teacher and writer. (2) (or **Le Borne**), **Fd.,** b. Paris, March 10, 1862 ; pupil of Massenet, Saint-Saëns, and Franck, Paris Cons.; lives in Paris as critic ; c. pastoral dramas, " *Hedda*," a symph. légende; symphs., etc.

**Lebouc** (lŭ-book), **Chas. Jos.,** Besançon, 1822—Hyères, 1893 ; 'cello-virtuoso.

**Lebrun** (lĕ-broon′), (1) **L. Aug.,** Mannheim, 1746 — Berlin, 1790 ; greatest oboist of the 18th cent.; composer. (2) (née **Danzi**), **Franciska,** Mannheim, 1756—Berlin, 1791 ; wife of above ; soprano. Their two daughters, (3) **Sophie** and (4) **Rosine,** were distinguished singers.

**Lebrun** (lŭ-brŭṅ),(1) **Jean,** Lyons, 1759 —suicide, Paris, 1809; horn-virtuoso. (2) **Louis Sébastien,** Paris, 1764— 1829 ; tenor and teacher. (3) **Paul H. Jos.,** b. Ghent, April 21, 1861 ; pupil of the Cons. there; 1891 won the Prix de Rome for composition and the Belgian Académie 1st prize for a symphony.

**Le Carpentier** (lŭ kăr-pänt-yā), **Ad. Clair,** Paris, 1809—1869 ; pianist and composer.

**Lechner** (lĕkh′-nĕr), **Ld.,** b. The Etschthal, Switzerland (?)—Stuttgart, 1604 ; ct.-cond. and composer.

**Léclair** (lā-klär), **J. M.,** Lyons, 1697 —assassinated, Paris, 1764 ; violinist ; c. operas, 48 notable vln.-sonatas, etc.; his wife, a singer, engraved his compositions.

**Leclerq** (lŭ-klär), **L.,** b. Paris, 1828 ; wrote under pen name **" L. Celler."**

**Lecocq** (lŭ-kôk), **(Alex.) Chas.,** b. Paris, June 3, 1832 ; studied at the Cons., won 1st prize for harm., and 2d prize for fugue ; his first work, " *Le Docteur Miracle*," in conjunction with Bizet (prod., 1857), won a prize offered by Offenbach for opera buffa ; smaller succ. culminated in " *Fleur de Thé*" (1868); followed by the sensational succ. " *La Fille de Mme. Angot*" (Brussels, 1872 ; Paris, 1873), which ran uninterruptedly over a year ; its succ. was equalled by " *Giroflé-Girofla*" (1874), 1894, chev. of the Legion of Honour ; prod. over 40 operas-bouffes, comic operas and operettas, written with scholarship and brilliant instrumentation ; sacred and other songs, etc.

**Le Couppey** (lŭ koop′-pĕ′), **Félix,** Paris, April 14, 1814—July 5, 1887 ; prof., pf.-teacher and composer.

**Ledebur** (lā′-dĕ-boor), **K. Freiherr von,** b. Schildesche, near Bielefeld, April 20, 1806 ; Prussian cavalry officer and lexicographer.

**Ledent** (lŭ-däṅ), **F. Ét.,** Liège, 1816 —1886 ; pianist and composer.

**Lederer** (lā′-dĕ-rĕr), **Georg,** b. Marienburg, May 2, 1843 ; notable tenor ;

pupil of Mantius and Louise Ress; sang in various cities; 1891–99, Zurich, then at Riga.

**Leduc** (lŭ-dük), **Alphonse,** Nantes, 1804—Paris, 1868; pianist, bassoonist and composer.

**Lee** (lā), (1) **G. Alex.,** 1802—1851; tenor and composer. (2) **Sebastian,** Hamburg, 1805—1887; 'cellist and composer. (3) **Louis,** b. Hamburg, Oct. 19, 1819; bro. of above; 'cellist; pupil of J. N. Prell; at 12 gave concerts; 'cellist in the Hamburg Th.; lived several years in Paris; organist, chamber-mus. soirées. Hamburg; until 1884, teacher in the Cons. and 1st 'cello; c. symphonies, overtures, etc. (4) **Maurice,** Hamburg, 1821—London, 1895; bro. of above; pf.-teacher, and composer. (5) (lē) **Geo. Alex.,** d. 1851, English mgr., tenor and composer.

**Leeves,** Rev. **Wm.,** 1748—Wrighton, 1828; probable composer of "*Auld Robin Grey,*" etc.

**Lefébure** (lŭ-fā-bür), **L. Fran. H.,** Paris, 1754—1840; composer and writer.

**Lefébure-Wély** (lŭ-fā-bür-vā-lē), **L. Jas. Alfred,** Paris, 1817—1869; noted organist; c. opera, masses, etc.

**Lefèbvre** (lŭ-fĕv'-r) (1) (**Le Febvre**), **Jacques** (called **Jacobus Faber**), also **Stapulensis,** from his birthplace, Étaples, near Amiens (?)—Nérac, 1537 (47?); writer. (2) **Chas. Édouard,** b. Paris, June 19, 1843; pupil of Ambr. Thomas, Paris Cons.; 1870, Grand prix de Rome; 1873, after touring the Orient settled in Paris; c. succ. opera, "*Djelma*" (1894); "*Zaïre*" (1887), etc.

**Lefèvre** (lŭ-fĕv'-r), **J. X.,** Lausanne, 1763—Paris, 1829; clarinettist, composer and professor.

**Leff'ler,** Adam, 1808—1857; Engl. bass.

**Lefort** (lŭ-fôr), **Jules,** 1821—Paris, 1898; tenor-barytone.

**Legouix** (lŭ-gwēx), **Isidore Éd.,** b. Paris, April 1, 1834 pupil of Reber

and Thomas at the Cons.; prod. 4 operas, etc.

**Legrenzi** (lā-grĕn'-tsē), **Giov.,** Clusone, near Bergamo, ca. 1625—Venice, 1690; organist, conductor and dram. composer.

**Lehmann** (lā'-män), (1) **T. Marie** (I.) prima donna at Cassel under Spohr; (2) **Lilli,** b. Würzburg, May 15, 1848; daughter and pupil of above; eminent soprano; début at Prague as "First Boy" in "*Die Zauberflöte*"; 1868, at Danzig, and Leipzig, 1870; in the same year obtained a life-engagement at the Royal Opera, Berlin, with the title (1876) of Imp. Chamber-singer; she sang "Woglinde," "Helmwige" and the "Bird," at their first performance, 1876; 1885, broke her contract, and sang in the U. S., etc. (3) **Geo.,** New York, July 31, 1865; violinist; pupil of Leipzig Cons. and of Joachim; won the Helbig prize at the Gewandhaus, 1883; 1886–89, leader of the Cleveland Symph. Orch.; lives in New York as soloist and teacher pub. "*True Principles of the Art of Violin-Playing*" (New York, 1899). (4) **Marie** (II.), b. Hamburg, May 15, 1851, daughter and pupil of (1); at 16 sang in Leipzig City Th.; for many years, till 1897, Vienna ct.-opera; lives in Berlin. (5) **Liza** (Mrs. Herbert Bedford), b. in London; concert-soprano; pupil of Randegger and Raunkilde at Rome (voice) and of Freudenberg (Wiesbaden), and Hamish MacCunn (comp.); début Nov. 23, 1885, at a Monday Pop. Concert; 1887, sang at the Norwich Festival; 1894, m. and retired; c. many songs incl. the very pop. song cycle from Omar Khayyám, "*In a Persian Garden,*" also "*In Memoriam,*" etc.

**Leibrock** (līp'-rôk), **Jos. Ad.,** Brunswick, 1808—Berlin, 1886; writer and composer.

**Leidesdorf** (lī'-dĕs-dôrf), **Max. Jos.** d. Florence, 1840; 1804–27 member of the mus.-pub firm of **Sauer &**

**L.,** which published Schubert's works.

**eighton** (lā'-tŭn), Sir **Wm.**, Engl. composer, 1641.

**eisinger** (lī'-zĭng-ĕr), **Elisabeth,** b. Stuttgart, May 17, 1864; sopr.; studied at the Cons., and later with Viardot-Garcia, Paris; 1884, Berlin ct.-opera.

**eite** (lī'-tĕ), **Antonio da Silva,** 1787—1826; cond. Oporto Cath., and composer.

**eitert** (lī'-tĕrt), **Jn. G.,** Dresden, Sept. 29, 1852—1901; pianist; pupil of Kragen and Reichel (pf.) and Rischpieter (harm.); début Dresden, 1865; studied with Liszt; 1879–81 teacher Horak Mus. Sch., Vienna; composer.

**eitgeb.** Vide LEUTGEB.

**e Jeune** (lŭ-zhŭn), **Claudin,** Valenciennes, ca. 1530—1598 or 1603; French contrapuntist and composer.

**ekeu** (lŭ-kŭ), **Guillaume,** Belgium, 1869—1884; composer whose early death cut short a promising career; c. adagio in C minor for orch. etc.

**emaire** (or **Le Maire**) (lŭ-măr'), (1) ———, French musician, 16th–17th cent.; believed to have advocated the adoption of a seventh syllable of solmisation (v. D. D.). (2) **Théophile,** b. Essigny-le-Grand, Aisne, March 22, 1820; pupil of Paris Cons.; singing-teacher and writer.

**e Maistre** (lŭ-mĕtr) (or **Le Maître**), **Mattheus,** d. 1577; Netherland contrapuntist; ct.-conductor and composer.

**emière de Corvey** (lŭm-yăr dŭ kôr-vĕ'), **J. Fr. Aug.,** Rennes, 1770—Paris, 1832; French officer and dram. composer.

**emmens** (lĕm'-mĕns), **Jacques Nicolas,** Zoerle-Parwys, Belgium, 1823—Castle Linterport, near Malines, 1881; organist, professor and composer.

**emoine** (lŭm-wăn), (1) **Ant. Marcel,** Paris, 1763—1817; publisher, ct.-conductor and writer. (2) **H.,** Paris, 1786—1854; son of above and his successor in business; writer. (3) **Aimé,**

b. 1795 (?); pub. " Méthode du Méloplaste"; teacher.

**Lemoyne** (lŭm-wăn) (rightly **Moyne**) (mwăn), **J. Bap.,** Eymet, Périgord, 1751—Paris, 1796; conductor and dram composer.

**Lenaerts** (lŭ-närts), **Constant,** b. Antwerp, March 9, 1852; pupil of Benoît; at 18 dir. Flemish National Th., now teacher Antwerp Cons.

**Lenepveu** (lŭ-nŭp'-vŭ), **Chas. Fd.,** b. Rouen, Nov. 4, 1840; studied with Servais, in 1861 won 1st prize at Caen; studied with Thomas at the Cons., 1865 took Grand prix de Rome, rt. from Rome; won a prize with opera " *Le Florentin* " (Op.-com., 1874); prod. gr. opera " *Velleda* " (Covent Garden, 1882); 1891 harm.-prof. in the Cons. and 1893 prof. of comp.; 1896, Académie des Beaux-Arts; is Chev. of the Legion of Honour, and officer of pub. instruction; c. lyric drama " *Jeanne d'Arc* " (Rouen Cath., 1886); " *Hymne funèbre et triomphal* " (V. Hugo) (Rouen,1889), etc.

**Len'ton, J.,** d. after 1711; band-musician and composer, London.

**Lenz** (lĕnts), **Wm. von,** Russia, 1804—St. Petersburg, Jan. 31, 1883; pianist; wrote genial and enthusiastic studies of musicians, " *Beethoven et ses trois styles* " (1852), etc., being the first so to divide B.'s art.

**Leo** (lā'-ō), **Leonardo,** Brindisi, 1694—Naples, 1746; eminent pioneer in the Neapolitan Sch. and noted teacher, conductor and organist; pupil of Aless. Scarlatti, Fago, and Pitoni; ct.-organist; c. 60 operas, also religious mus., incl. a noble 8-part " *Miserere*," a cappella.

**Léonard** (lā-ō-när), **Hubert,** Bellaire, near Liège, April 7, 1819—Paris, May 6, 1890; eminent violinist; pub technical studies.

**Leoncavallo** (lā-ôn-kä-väl'-lō), **Ruggiero,** b. Naples, March 8, 1858; studied Naples Cons., and at 16 made a tour as pianist; his first opera " *Tommaso Chatterton*," failed at first but was succ. revived at Rome, 1896 ; a disciple whom Wagner personally encouraged, he spent 6 years in researches, resulting in an " historic " trilogy " *Crepusculum* " (" Twilight "), I. *Medici*, II. *Girolamo Savonarola*, III. *Cezare Borgia* ; toured as pianist through Egypt, Greece, Turkey, etc.; lived in Paris some years and had an opera " *Songe d'une Nuit d'Été*," privately performed, and many songs published ; he prod. 2-act opera seria " *I Pagliacci* " (Milan Dal Verme Th., 1892, in Germany 1893, as "*Der Bajazzo* ") of which he wrote the masterfully constructed libretto as well as the strenuous music that made it a universal succ. The first part of the trilogy, the 4-act "*I Medici*," was not succ. (La Scala, Milan, 1893); the 4-act opera " *La Bohème* " (Venice) was a succ. (cf. PUCCINI); and he c. also a symph. poem, " *Serafitus—Serafita* " ; c. operas " *La Tosca* " and " *Trilby* "; " *Zaza* " (Antwerp, 1902) succ.; in preparation, opera " *Roland*," libretto by Emperor Wilhelm II. of Germany.

**Leonhard** (lā'-ōn-härt), **Julius Emil,** Lauban, 1810—Dresden, 1883 ; professor and composer.

**Leoni** (lā-ō'-nē), (1) **Leone,** cond. Vicenza Cath., 1588—1623, and composer. (2) **Carlo,** Italian composer ; prod. 3-act operetta " *Per un Bacio* " (Siena, 1894), and text and music of succ. comic opera " *Urbano* " (Pienza, 1896). (3) **Franco,** prod. cantata " *Sardanapalus* " (London, 1896) and romantic opera " *Rip V n Winkle* " (London, 1897).

**Leonowa** (or **Leonova**) (lā-ō-nō'-vä), **Dapya Mikailovna,** Russia, 1825— St. Petersburg, 1896 ; contralto.

**Leroux** (lŭ-roo), **X. H. Napoléon,** b. Velletri, Papal States, Oct. 11, 1863; pupil of Paris Cons., took Grand Prix de Rome, 1885; c. opera " *Cléopatre* " (1890), lyric drama " *Evangeline*," a dramatic overture " *Harold*," and operas " *William Ratcliff* " and

" *L'Epavo* " (not prod.) ; " *Astart* (Gr. Opéra, 1901), " *La Reine Fia ette* " (1902), a mass, etc.

**Le Roi** (lŭr-wä), **Adrien, 17th cent** partner of Ballard (q. v.).

**Lesage de Richés** (lŭ-säzh-dŭ-shä), **Philipp Fz.** ; lutenist a composer

**Leschetizky** (lĕ-shĕ-tĭt'-shkĭ), **The dor,** b. Langert, Austrian Polan 1830 ; eminent pfs. teacher ; son a pupil of a prominent teacher in enna ; studied with Czerny (p and Sechter (comp.) ; at 15 beg teaching ; 1842 made succ. tou 1852 teacher in the St. Petersb Cons.; 1878 toured ; 1880 m. former pupil Annette Essipoff, a settled as a teacher in Vienna; c. su opera, " *Die Erste Falte* " (Prag 1867), etc.

**Les'lie,** (1) **H. David,** London, 18 —Wales, 1896 ; 'cellist, cond. a composer. (2) **Ernest,** pen-name **Brown, O. B.**

**Les'sel, Fz.,** Warsaw, ca. 178c Petrikow, 1839 ; composer.

**Less'man (W. J.), Otto,** b. Rüde dorf, near Berlin, Jan. 30, 184 critic and composer ; teacher Stern's Cons.; then at Tausig's Aca until 1871 ; organised a piano-sch. his own ; since 1882 proprietor a ed. *Allgm. Musik-Zeitung.*

**Le Sueur** (lŭ-sŭr) (or **Lesueur**), **Fran.,** Drucat-Plessiel, near Abl ville, France, Jan. 15, 1764—Par Oct. 6, 1837 ; chiefly self-taugh 1786 cond. at Notre Dame, Par where he drew crowds and critici by his progammatic mus.: he pu pamphlets defending " dramatic a descriptive " church-mus.; the opp sition prevailed, however, and he tired to the country for 4 years ; 17 he prod. succ. opera " *La Cavern* followed by others ; 1804 Napole raised him from distress to the p of ct.-cond.

**Leuckart** (loik'-ärt), **F. Ernst Ch** founded mus. business at Bresla 1782, bought 1856 by C. Sanders.

...tgeb (Leitgeb) (līt'-gāp), **Josef**, . Vienna, 1811 ; horn-player ; friend f Mozart.

...asseur (lŭ-văs-sŭr), (1) **P. Fran.**, . Abbeville, France, 1753 ; 'cellist, 'aris Grand Opéra ; composer. (2) . **H.**, Paris, 1765—(?) ; a 'cellist. ...) **Rosalie**, soprano, Paris Opéra, 766–85. (4) **Nicholas Prosper**, b. . Picardy, March 9, 1781 ; dram.- ...ass and professor.

...ens (lŭ-văns), ——, church-cond. ...nd mathematician and theorist at ...ordeaux (1743).

...'eridge, **Richard**, 1670—1758 ; ...ngl. bass singer.

...' ey, **Wm. Chas.**, Dublin, 1837— ...ondon, 1894 ; dram. composer.

...vi (lā'-vē), (1) **Hermann**, b. Gies- ...en, Nov. 7, 1839 ; eminent conduc- ...or ; pupil of V. Lachner and of ...eipzig Cons. ; 1859–61, mus.-dir., ...aarbrucken ; 1861–64, cond. Ger- ...an Opera at Rotterdam ; 1864–72, ...t.-cond. at Carlsruhe ; from 1872, ...t.-cond. at Munich ; 1894, Gen. mus. ...ir. Munich ; 1896, pensioned. (2) ...evi (or **Levy, Lewy**). Vide LE- ...ERT.

...wandowski (lā-vän-dôf'-shkĭ), ...ouis, Wreschen, Posen, 1823— ...erlin, 1894 ; singing-teacher and com- ...oser.

...w'is, **Thos. C.**, org.-builder, Lon- ...on, 1861.

...wy (lā'-vē),(1) **Eduard Constantin**, ...aint-Avold, Moselle, 1796—Vienna, ...846 ; horn-virtuoso and prof. (2) ...os. **Rodolphe**, Nancy, 1804—Ober- ...ssnitz, near Dresden, 1881 ; bro. and ...upil of above ; horn-virtuoso. (3) ...has., Lausanne, 1823—Vienna, ...883 ; son of (1) ; pianist and com- ...oser. (4) **Richard Levy**, Vienna, ...827—1883 ; son of (1) ; horn-player, ...inging-teacher. (5) Vide LEBERT.

...ybach (lī'-bäkh), **Ignace**, Gambs- ...eim, Alsatia, 1817 — Toulouse, ...891 ; pianist, teacher and composer.

...adoff (or **Liadow**) (lē'-ä-dôf), **Ana- ...ole**, b. St. Petersburg, April 29, ...855 ; pupil Johansen (cpt. and

fugue) and Rimsky-Korsakov (form and instr.) at St. P. Cons.; since 1878, prof. of harmony there ; also at the Imp. Chapel ; since 1894, cond. Mus. Soc.; c. brilliant and original pf.-pcs., etc.

**Liapunov** (or **Liapounow**) (lē-ä'-pc— nôf), **Serge Michailovitch**, b. Jan slavi, Russia, Nov. 18, 1859 ; pupil Klindworth and Pabst (pf.) and Hu bert (comp.) Moscow Cons.; sub-dir. Imp. Choir. St. Petersburg, and a member of the Imp. Geographical Soc., which 1893 commissioned him to collect the folk-songs of Vologda, Viatna and Kostroma, which he pub. 1897 ; since 1894, mus.-master to the Grand Duke ; pub. concerto. a symph., etc.

**Libe'lius**, incorrect form of **Sibelius**.

**Lich'field**, **H.**, Engl. composer, 1614.

**Lichner** (lĭkh'-nĕr), **H.**, Harpersdorf, Silesia, 1829—Breslau, 1898 ; organ- ist and conductor.

**Lichtenberg** (lĭkh'-t'n-bĕrkh), b. San Francisco, Cal., Nov. 22, 1861 ; vln.- virtuoso ; pupil of Beaujardin ; at 8 played in public ; at 12 pupil of Wie- niawski, and his aide on a U. S. tour ; studied 6 months with Lambert in Paris, then studied again with Wieniawski 3 years ; won first prize of honour at the " National concourse "; toured America and Europe ; mem- ber of Boston Symph. Orch.; 1899, vln. prof. Nat. Cons., New York.

**Lichtenstein** (lĭkh'-t'n-shtīn), **K. Aug.**, Freiherr **von**, Lahm, Franco- nia, 1767—Berlin, 1845 ; c. operas.

**Lichtenthal** (lĭkh'-t'n-täl), **Peter**, Pressburg, 1780— Milan, 1853 ; dram. composer and writer on mus.

**Lie** (lē), **Erica** (Mme. **Nissen**), b. Kongsvinger, near Christiania, Jan. 17, 1845 ; pianist, pupil of Kjerulf, and of Th. Kullak ; teacher at the Kul- laks' Acad., toured Germany, etc.; member R. Acad., Stockholm.

**Liebau** (lē'-bow), (1) **Julius**, b. Lun- denburg, Feb. 19, 1857 ; tenor-buffo ; studied with Gänsbacher ; won Wag- ner's praise as " Mime " ; 1882, ct.-

opera, Berlin. (2) **Liebau-Globig, Helene,** b. Berlin, March 31, 1866; soprano; sang "Yum-Yum" in *"Der Mikado,"* Berlin, 1889, since 1898 at ct.-opera.

**Liebe** (lē'-bĕ), **Ed. L.,** Magdeburg, Nov. 19, 1819—Coire, Switz., 1900; pianist, organist and dram. composer.

**Liebich** (lē'-bĭkh), **Ernst (Jn. Gottlob),** Breslau, 1830—1884, eminent vln.-maker.

**Liebig** (lē'-bĭkh), (1) **K.,** Schwedt, 1808—Berlin, 1872; staff oboist in a Regt., 1843. est. Berlin "Symphoniekapelle"; 1860. R. Mus. Dir. (2) **Julius** 1838—1885, son of above, cond. at Ems.

**Liebling** (lēp'-lǐng), (1) **Emil,** b. Pless, Silesia, April 12, 1851 concert-pianist, pf.-pupil of Ehrlich and Th. Kullak, Berlin, Dachs, Vienna, Liszt and Dorn, since 1867, America, and since 1872, Chicago, as reviewer and concert-pianist, teacher and writer. Co-ed. in a "*Dictionary of Terms*"; pub. pf.-pcs. and songs. (2) **G.,** b. Berlin, Jan. 22, 1865, pupil of Th., and Fr. Kullak, and Liszt (pf.), H. Urban and H. Dorn (comp.); 1880-85, teacher in Kullak's Acad.; 1881-89 toured Germany and Austria, with success; 1890, ct.-pianist to Duke of Coburg. (3) **Leonard,** pianist; studied in Germany, also writer and humorist on musical topics.

**Lienau** (lē'-now), **Robt.,** b. Neustadt, Holstein, Dec. 28, 1838; mus.-pub., Berlin.

**Liliencron** (lē'-lĭ-ĕn-krōn), **Rochus, Freiherr von,** b. Plon, Holstein, Dec. 8, 1820; prof.; commissioned by the Historical Commission of Munich to collect the mediæval German folk-songs, and pub. them.

**Lillo** (lĭl'-lō), **Gius.,** Galatina, Lecce, Italy, 1814—Naples, 1863; teacher and dram. composer.

**Limnan'der de Nieuwenhove** (nā'-vĕn-hō-vĕ), **Armand Marie Ghislain,** Ghent, 1814—Moignanville 1892; dram. composer.

**Lim'pus, Richard,** 1824—1875; E[...] organist and composer.

**Lincke** (lǐnk'-ĕ), **Jos.,** Trachenbe[...] Silesia, 1783—Vienna, 1837; 'cell[...]

**Linc'oln, H. C.,** 1739—1864; o[...] builder, London.

**Lind** (lǐnt), **Jenny,** Stockholm, Oct[...] 1820—at her villa, Wynds Po[...] Malvern Wells, Nov. 2, 1887; "[...] Swedish Nightingale," one of [...] most eminent and pop. of sopran[...] had a remarkably sympathetic v[...] of great compass (d' –e''', v. CH[...] OF PITCH), remarkable pur[...] breath, endurance and flexibil[...] studied with Berg and Lindblad[...] the court where she made her v[...] succ. début, 1838, in "*Der F[...] schütz*"; 1841, studied with Man[...] Garcia, in Paris, for nine mont[...] 1842, sang at the Opéra, but was [...] engaged; 1844, studied German [...] Berlin, and sang with greatest su[...] in Germany and Sweden; 1847, m[...] a furore in London; 1849, she [...] the operatic stage, and created e[...] greater sensations in concert; 18[...] 52, under the management of P. [...] Barnum, she toured the U. S., ea[...] ing $120,000; 1852, she m. Otto G[...] schmidt in Boston; lived in Dresd[...] 1856, London, appearing especi[...] with the Bach Choir which her h[...] band cond. Her last pub. appe[...] ance was in his oratorio "*Rut[...] Düsseldorf. 1870 Her private [...] was unusually serene, impeccab[...] and generous. Her bust is in We[...] minster Abbey. Biogr. by A. [...] Becher (1847).

**Lindblad** (lǐnt'-blät) **Ad. Fr.,** L[...] vingsborg, near Stockholm, 180[...] 1878; teacher of Jenny Lind; c. [...] cellent Swedish songs and an oper[...]

**Linden** (lǐnt'-'n), **K. van der,** b. D[...] drecht, April 24, 1839, promin[...] Dutch cond., pupil of Kwast (p[...] and F. Böhme (theory); 1860 co[...] Dordrecht; later bandm. the N[...] Guard (1875), cond. Netherla[...] Musicians' Assoc. c cantatas w[...] orch., 2 operas, etc.

ader (lĭn'-dĕr), Gf., b. Ehingen, July
2. 1842, pupil Stuttgart Cons.;
rom 1868 teacher there 1879 pro-
essor; c. 2 operas, overture "*Aus
ordischer Heldenzeit*," etc.

ad ley, (1) Robert, Rotherham,
'orkshire, 1777 — London. 1855;
cellist. (2) Wm., 1802—Manchester.
869; son of above; 'cellist.

adner (lĭnt'-nĕr), (1) Fr., Liegnitz,
a. 1540—Nürnberg, composer. (2)
——, Lobenstein, 1808—Leipzig,
867; horn-player. (3) Ernst Otto
Timotheus, Breslau, 1820—Berlin,
867; conductor and writer. (4)
Aug., Dessau, 1820—Hanover, 1878,
cellist and composer.

adpaintner (lĭnt'-pīnt-nĕr), Peter
os. von, Coblenz. Dec. 8, 1791—
Nonnenhorn, Aug. 21, 1856; emi-
ent conductor, ct.-conductor and
ram. composer.

ad'say, M. (now Mrs. J. W. Bliss),
English composer of pop. songs.

a ley, (1) Thos., Sr., Bath. 1725—
London. 1795, conductor and dram.
omposer, owner with Sheridan of
Drury Lane Th., 1776, he had 3
aughters and 3 sons. (2) Thos.,
r., Bath, 1756—drowned at Grims-
horpe. Lincolnshire, 1778, violinist
nd composer. (3) Eliza Ann,
754—Bristol. 1792, brilliant sopra-
o. (4) Mary, d. 1787, singer.
5) Maria, d. Bath, 1784, singer.
5) Ozias, 1765—1831 organist and
omposer. (7) Wm., ca. 1767—1835,
omposer and editor. (8) Francis.
Doncaster. 1774—1800; organist and
omposer. (9) G., Leeds, 1798—
London 1865; writer and dram.
omposer.

anarz (lĭn'-närts). Robt., b. Pots-
am. Sept. 29. 1851; pupil of Haupt,
Berlin, teacher in Bederkesa semi-
ary; do. at Alfeld; wrote methods,
tc.; c. a festival cantata "*All-
Deutschland*," etc.

atermans (lĭn-tĕr-mäns), Fran.
os., Brussels, 1808—Ixelles, 1895;
anging-teacher and composer.

inski (lĭ-pĭn'-shkĭ), K. Jos., Rad-

zyn, Poland, Nov. 4 (Oct. 30 ?), 1790
—Urlow, near Lemberg, Dec. 16,
1861; noted violinist and composer;
pupil of Paganini; lived in Dresden,
1839-59.

Lipsius (lĭp'-sĭ-oos), Marie, b. Leipzig, Dec. 30, 1837; wrote under pen-
name "La Mara."

Lirou (lē-roo), J. Fran. Espic,
Chev. de, Paris, 1740—1806; writer
and composer; pub. a "*Harmony*"
(1785), the first French book to desert Rameau for the modern laws of
tonality.

Lischin (lēsh'-ĭn), Grigory Andree-
vitch, 1853—St. Petersburg, June
27, 1888; c. operas, incl. "*Don César de Bazan*."

Lissmann (lēs'-män), (1) H. Fritz,
Berlin, 1847—Hamburg, 1894; bary-
tone; m. the sopr. (2) Anna
Marie Gutzschbach.

Listemann (lĭs'-tĕ-män), (1) Fritz, b.
Schlotheim, Thuringia. March 25,
1839; violinist; pupil of his uncle
Ullrich, and of David, Leipzig Cons.,
1858, chamber-virtuoso to the Prince
of Rudolstadt; 1867 lived in New
York; 1871, 1st vln. Thomas Orch.;
from 1878, 1st vln. Philh. Orch.;
1881 – 85 Symph. Orch.; since
taught and toured with "Listemann Concert Co.", c. 2 vln -con-
certos. etc. (2) Bernhard, b. Schlotheim, Aug. 28. 1841; bro. of above;
pupil of Ullrich, and David, Vieuxtemps and Joachim. 1859-67, 1st.
vln. in Rudolstadt ct.-orch.; came to
America with his bro., lived in Bos
ton; 1871-74, leader Thomas Orch.;
1874 founded the "Philharm. Club,"
and toured the country; 1878 founded
Boston Philh.-Orch., cond. till 1881,
then 4 yrs. leader of the New
"Symph.-Orch."; founded "Listemann Quartet"; 1883 – 93, dir.
of the "Listemann Concert Co.";
from 1893, prof. Chicago Coll. of
Mus.; pub. a "*Method*." (3) Paul,
b. Boston, Oct. 24, 1871; son and
pupil of (2); studied also with (1)
and was a member of the Quar-

tet and Concert Co., 1890 – 93;
studied with Brodsky and Hilf, Leipzig, and with Joachim, at Berlin;
leader of the Pittsburg (Pa.) Orch.:
1896, of the "American Orch.," N.
Y.; since soloist of the "Redpath
Concert Co." (4) **Fz.**, b. New York,
Dec. 17, 1873; bro. of above; 'cellist; pupil of Fries and Giese at Boston, of Julius Klengel, Leipzig; and
Hausmann, Berlin; 1st 'cello Pittsburg Orch. for a year, since lives in N.
Y. as teacher and concert-performer.

**Liszt (lyst), Franz** (originally **Ferencz)** Raiding, near Odenburgh,
Hungary, Oct. 22, 1811—Bayreuth,
July 31, 1886; in many ways the
most brilliant of all pianists, and a
composer whose poorest works are
too popular, while he is not granted
the credit due his more solid achievements; as great a patron of art, also,
as he was creator. Son and pupil of
an amateur; at nine played in public,
at Oedenburg, Ries' E♭ concerto. A
group of Hungarian counts sub-
scribed a 6 years' annuity of 600 florins, and the family moved to Vienna,
where **L.** studied with Czerny (pf.),
and Salieri (theory) for 18 months.
Beethoven hearing him play his trio
op. 97, embraced him. At 12 he gave
v. succ. concerts in Vienna and his
father took him to Paris, where he
was refused as a foreigner because
of Cherubini's objections to "infant
phenomena;" hereafter **L.** was his
own teacher, except in comp. which
he studied with Paër and Reicha. At
14, his 1-act operetta, "*Don Sancho*" had 5 performances at the Acad.
royale de musique. On his father's
death in 1827 he supported his
mother by teaching, soon becoming
the salon-idol he always remained.
He was strongly influenced by Chopin, von Weber, Paganini and Berlioz. He had a brilliant series of
heart-affairs, beginning with the literary Countess d'Agoult ("Daniel
Stern"), with whom he lived in
Geneva (1835-39). She bore him a

son and three daughters; Cosi
the youngest, became the wife
von Bülow, later of Wagner. 1
he successfully undertook to ear
concerts money enough for the c
pletion of the Beethoven monun
at Bonn. 1849, ct.-cond. at Wein
with royal encouragement to aid n
progress. He made himself
greatest patron among creative arti
aiding Wagner materially by 1
ductions of his works at Weimar
by pf. - transcriptions, aiding
Raff, Schumann, and Berlioz, fin
resigning before the opposition
and failure of, an opera by Corne
(q. v.). 1859-70, he lived chiefl
Rome, where in 1866 the Pope, I
IX., made him an abbé. 1870
was reconciled with the Weir
Court. 1875 pres. of the new Ac
of Mus. at Pesth; he spent
last years at Weimar, Pesth, a
Rome, followed by a large retinue
disciples and pupils whom he tau;
free of charge. He died durin;
Bayreuth Festival. C. 2 SYMPI
"*Dante*" (after the "Divina Cc
media" with female chorus); "*E
Faustsymphonie*" ("Faust," "G
chen," "Mephistopheles," with m
chorus); SYMPH. POEMS: "*Ce qu
entend sur la montagne*" (Vic
Hugo); "*Tasso, lamento e trionfo*
"*Les Préludes*"; "*Orpheus*
"*Prometheus*"; "*Mazeppa*"; "*F
klänge*"; "*Héroïde funèbre*
"*Hungaria*"; "*Hamlet*"; "*H
nenschlacht*"; "*Die Ideale*" (Sc
ler); and "*Von der Wiege bis z
Grabe*" (Michael Zichy); ALSO 1
ORCH. "*Zwei Episoden aus Len
Faust*" (Der nachtliche Zug, 2 ]
phisto-wälzer), etc. FOR PIAN
2 concertos; "*Danse macabre*" w
orch.; "*Concerto pathétique*";
"*Rhapsodies hongroises*"; "*Rh
sodie espagnole*"; "*Sonata in
Min.*"; · *Fantasia and Fugue
B–A–C–H*"; variations on a the
from Bach's *B-min. mass* · 10 "*H
monies poétiques et réligieuse*

*Années de pèlerinage"; 3 "Apparitions."* 2 ballades ; 6 " *Consolations"*; 2 élégies ; 2 légendes (*St. François D'Assise* and *St. François de Paul*) ; " *Liebesträume* " (Nocturnos) ; " *Études d'éxécution trancendante* "; " *Ab irato, étude de perfectionnement* "; concert-études, " *Waldesrauschen* " and " *Gnomenreigen*"; " *Technische Studien* " (12 books), etc., and many transcriptions of symphs., overtures, 50 songs by Schubert, etc. Vocal comps. : 4 masses, incl. *Missa solennis* (the " Graner " Festival Mass) ; requiem ; 3 oratorios, " *Die Legende von der Heiligen Elisabeth,*" " *Stanislaus,*" and " *Christus*"; Psalms 13th, 18th, etc., with orch. and other church-music ; 3 cantatas with orch.; male choruses, 60 songs, etc. Wrote life of Chopin, of Franz, etc. Complete ed. of his writings in 6 vols. Biogr. by L. Ramann, 1880.

## Franz Liszt.

### By Henry T. Finck.

THERE are two great paradoxes in the career of Liszt. The first is that just as Rossini, the most popular opera composer of his day, ceased writing operas thirty-nine years before his death, so Liszt, the greatest and most adored pianist of all times, ceased playing in public (except for an occasional charitable purpose) about the same number of years before his end came. He had, with his inimitable art, familiarised concert-goers with nearly all the best compositions for the piano, created by other masters. He had transcribed for the same instrument a large number of songs, operatic melodies and orchestral works (the number of these transcriptions at his death was 371), thereby vastly increasing their vogue. He also wrote altogether 160 original compositions for the pianoforte, many of them as new in form as in substance ; unique among them being the fifteen Hungarian rhapsodies—collections of Magyar melodies with gypsy ornaments, moulded by him into works of art, after the manner of epic poets. But—and here is the second paradox—Liszt, the greatest of all pianists, was not satisfied with the piano. In many of his pieces for it, he endeavours to impart to it orchestral power and variety of tonal effect ; and finally, when he became conductor at Weimar (1849), he transferred his attention chiefly to the orchestra. ¶ Of his thirty-four orchestral works, the most important are the *Faust*" and *"Dante"* symphonies, and thirteen symphonic poems, in which he deviated from the old symphonic form in a spirit similar to Wagner's operatic reforms—abolishing the mosaic of unconnected movements and allowing the underlying poetic idea (programme) to shape the form of the music. Of great importance and beauty also are his sixty songs, which represent the climax of the tendency to mirror in the music, not only the general spirit of the poem, but every line and word. The last period of his life was largely given up to the writing of sacred compositions. Among these, the

most original in substance is the *"Legend of St. Elizabeth,"* the most origi
in form *"Christus,"* in which the last remnants of the opera (the aria a
recitative) are eliminated from the oratorio, and little remains besides choru
and instrumental numbers. Liszt's genius in early life was shaped largely
Schubert, Chopin, Berlioz, and Wagner. His own influence on the pian
and orchestral writers of Germany, France, and Russia, can hardly be ov
estimated.

**Litolff** (lē -tôlf), **H. Chas.**, London, Feb. 6, 1818—Paris, Aug. 5, 1891; prominent pianist, conductor, publisher and composer.

**Litta** (lĭt'-tä), Duca **Giulo**, Visconte **Arese**, Milan, 1822—Vedano, near Monza, 1891; dram. composer.

**Litvinne** (lēt'-vĭn), **Felia**, b. Russia; soprano; pupil of Mme. Barth-Banderoli and Maurel; début Th. des Italiens, Paris; later sang Wagner at Met. Op., N. Y.; then in St. Petersburg; sister-in-law of Ed. de Reszké.

**Litzau** (lēt'-tsow), **Jns. Barend**, Rotterdam. 1822—1893; pianist, organist and composer.

**Liverati** (lē-vě-rä'-tē), **Giov.**, Bologna, 1772—after 1817; noted tenor, conductor and dram. composer.

**Lloyd** (loid), (1) **Edw.**, b. London, March 7. 1845; noted concert tenor; choir-boy, Westminster Abbey, with Jas. Turle, till 1860; from 1874, first tenor, Leeds Festival; sang at Cincinnati Festival 1888, and has toured the U. S.; gave farewell concert, London, 1900. (2) **Chas. Harford**, b. Thornbury, Gloucestershire, Engl., Oct. 16, 1849; 1891, Mus. Doc. Oxford; 1876, organist Gloucester Cath.; 1892 precentor and mus.-teacher Eton Coll.; founded Oxford Univ. Mus.-Club; 1877–80, cond. Gloucester Festivals; now Oxford Symph. Concerts; c. 7 cantatas, mus. to *Alcestis* (Oxford, 1887); full cath. service, etc.

**Lobe** (lō'-bĕ), **Jn. Chr.**, Weimar, May 30, 1797—Leipzig, July 27, 1881; flutist, vla.-player, and dram. composer; wrote important treatises.

**Lobkowitz.** Vide CARAMUEL DE ↑

**Lo bo** (or **Lopez**) (lō'-pĕs) (or **Lupi Duarte**, Portuguese composer Lisbon, 1600.

**Locatel'li, Pietro**, Bergamo, 169 Amsterdam, 1764; vln.-virtuoso, garded as marvellous for his dou stopping and effects procured changed accordature (v. D. D.) which Paganini imitated him.

**Locke, Matthew**, Exeter, Engla 1632 (33 ?)—London, 1677; co poser.

**Lock'ey, Chas.**, succ. Engl. ten retired, 1859.

**Lo'der**, (1) **J. Fawcett**, 1812—18 violinist and conductor. (2) **Ed Jas.**, Bath, 1813—London, 186 dram. composer. (3) **J.**, violin d. ca. 1860 (?). (4) **Wm.**, 'celli d. ca. 1860; bro. of above. **Emily Woodyat**, wife of above.

**Loeb** (lāp), **Jules**, b. Strassburg, 18 pupil of Chevillard, Paris Cons., v 1st prize; solo 'cellist at the Opé and the Cons. Concerts; membe the Marsick Quartet, and the "S ciété pour instrs. à vent et à c des."

**Loeffler** (lěf'-lěr), **Chas. Martin T nov**, b. Mühlhausen, Alsatia. 18 violinist and notable composer; pu of Massart, Leonarti Joachim a Guiraud (comp.); played in Pas loup's orch.; later in Prince Dervi orch.; now 2d leader and soloist B ton (U. S. A.) Symph. Orch.; symph. poem "*La mort de Tin giles*" (after Maeterlinck), with vi d'amore obbligato; suite "*Les V lées de l'Ukraine*" (after Gogol)

ln. and orch.; concerto in 1 movement for orch.; divertimento for vln.
with orch.; string quartet; songs
with viola obbl., etc.

eillet (lwä-yä'), **J. Bap**, Ghent—
London, 1728; noted virtuoso on
lute and harp; composer.

ewe. Vide LÖWE.

gier (lö'-jĕr), **Jn. Bd.**, Cassel,
777—Dublin, 1846; flutist, writer
and composer; invented the "chiro-
last."

groscino (lô-grō-shē'-nō), **Nicolà**,
Naples, ca. 1700—1763; professor of
pt.; composer; pupil of Durante;
747, prof. of cpt. at Palermo, then
ved in Naples and prod. some 20
ght operas; he was brilliantly suc-
essful, and was the first to close acts
ith an ensemble.

amann (lö'-män), **Peter**, b.
chwelm, Westphalia, April 24, 1833;
nce 1856, lives in Leipzig; 1858–61,
riter for *Neue Zeitschrift für Mu-
k;* he believes that the drama
nould be of universal appeal without
calism, patriotism or other alleged-
narrowing influence; wrote trea-
ses and several dramas set to music
y Huber, Goebel, etc.

ir (lōr), **Jn.**, b. Eger, May 8, 1828;
g.-virtuoso and teacher; pupil of
s father, and of Pitsch; 1858, or-
anist, Szegedin, Hungary; lives in
esth; played with succ. in London,
871.

ir (lär), (1) **G. Augustus**, Norwich,
ngl., 1821—Leicester, 1897; or-
anist and conductor. (2) **Richard**
I., Leicester, Engl., June 13, 1856;
udied R. A. M. won two medals;
ganist, London; since 1882, con-
ert-pianist; c. oratorios; wrote
*Primer of Music,*" etc.

ise (lö'-zĕ), **Otto**, for years cond.
Iamburg City Th., 1895–96, Dam-
sch Op. Co., in which the prima
nnæ was his wife **Klafsky** (q. v.);
nd. Covent Garden, 1901; now
nd. City Th., Strassburg; prod.
cc. opera "*Der Prinz Wider
Villen*" (Cologne, 1898).

39

**Lolli** (lôl'-lĭ), **Ant.**, Bergamo, ca. 1730
('40?)—Palermo, 1802; violinist and
leader; composer and writer.

**Lomagne, B. de.** Vide SOUBIES.

**Long'hurst**, (1) **Wm. H.**, b. Lambeth, Engl., Oct. 6, 1819; chorister
in Canterbury Cath.; later asst.-or-
ganist, master of the choristers and
lay-clerk; 1873, organist; 1875,
Mus. Doc. and mus.-lecturer; c. oratorios, cath. service, etc. (2) **J.
Alex.**, 1809—1855; operatic and
concert-singer; bro. of above.

**Loo'mis, Harvey Worthington**, b.
Brooklyn, U. S. A., Feb. 5, 1865;
notable composer; pupil of Dvořák
at the National Cons., New York,
1892, winning a 3-years' scholarship;
lives in New York; c. several excellent pantomimes and notable programme music in the form of "musical backgrounds" to poems, original
pf.-pcs. and songs.

**Loose'more**, (1) **H.**, d. 1667; organist
at Cambridge, and composer. (2)
**G.**, son of above; organist. (3) **J.**,
d. 1681; son of (1), org.-builder.

**Lopez.** Vide LOBO.

**Lorenz** (lö'-rĕnts), (1) **Fz.**, Stein, Lower
Austria, 1805—Vienna, 1883; writer.
(2) **Karl Ad.**, b. Koslin, Pomerania,
Aug. 13, 1837; c. quartets, etc., as a
sch.-boy; studied with Dehn, Kiel
and Gehrig, Berlin, and at Berlin
Univ.; 1861, Dr. Phil.; 1866, Municipal Dir., Stettin, cond. symph.
Concerts, etc.; teacher in two gym-
nasiums; founded the "Stettin Musikverein" (for oratorio); 1885, professor; c. 2 succ. operas, overtures.
etc. (3) **Julius**, b. Hanover, Oct.
1, 1862; from 1884, cond. Singakademie, Glogau; 1895, of the "Arion,"
New York; c. an opera "*Die Re
kruten,*" and overtures.

**Lo'ris, Lori'tus.** Vide GLAREANUS.

**Lortzing** (lôrt'-tsĭng) (**Gv.**), **Albert**,
Berlin, Oct. 23, 1803—Jan. 21, 1851;
an actor, son of actors, and m. an
actress, 1823. Had a few lessons
with Rungenhagen; chiefly self-
taught; 1826, actor at Detmold;

prod. 2 vaudevilles with succ.; 1833–
44, tenor at Leipzig th. ; prod. succ.
" *Die beiden Schützen*"; 1837 and
1839, " *Czar und Zimmerman*"; 4
others followed, then " *Der Wild-
schütz*," 1842 ; cond. at Leipzig Op.,
then travelled, producing 6 more operas, incl. "*Undine*" (1845) ; "*Der
Waffenschmied*" (1846) ; his melodious unction keeps those works mentioned still popular, and his "*Regina*"
was posthumously prod. Berlin, 1899,
with succ.; he lived in poverty in
spite of his succ., and a benefit was
needed for his family after his death ;
c. also an oratorio, etc.; biogr. by
Düringer (Leipzig, 1851).

**Löschhorn** (lĕsh′-hôrn), **Albert**, b.
Berlin, June 27, 1819; pupil of L.
Berger, Kollitschgy, Grell and A. W.
Bach at the R. Inst. for Church-music ; 1851, as pf.-teacher there ; 1859,
professor ; noted teacher also ; writer
and composer.

**Los′sen, Magda.** Vide DULONG.

**Los′sius, Lucas,** d. Lüneberg, 1852 ;
writer and composer.

**Lott, Edwin M.,** b. St. Helier, Jersey,
Jan. 31, 1836 ; at 10 yrs. organist ;
later various London churches; c.
sacred mus.

**Lotti** (lôt′-tē), **Ant.,** Hanover (?), ca.
1667—Venice, Jan. 5, 1740; son of
the ct.-cond. at Hanover ; pupil of
Legrenzi ; at 16 prod. an opera at
Venice ; 1697 organist there ; prod.
20 operas with general succ. ; was
noted as an organist, and more
famed as a composer of church-music.

**Lotto** (lôt′-tō), **Isidor,** b. Warsaw,
Dec. 2, 1840 ; pupil of Massart (vln.)
and Reber (comp.), Paris Cons. ;
1862, solo-violinist, Weimar ; 1872,
teacher Strassburg Cons., later at
Warsaw Conservatorium.

**Lotze** (lôt′-tsĕ), **Rudolf Hn.,** Bautzen,
1817—Berlin, 1881 ; professor and
writer.

**Louis** (loo′-ēs), **Fd.,** Friedrichsfelde,
near Berlin, 1772—Saalfeld, 1806 ;
Prince of Russia, nephew of Frederick II. ; composer.

**Loulié** (loo-yā), **Ét.,** 17th cent. ;
the " chronomètre " (forerunner
the metronome) and a " sonomèt.

**Lovattini** (-tē′-nē), **Giov.,** Ital. t
in London, 1767.

**Lov′er, Samuel,** Dublin, 1797—
sey, 1868 ; famous novelist ;
composer.

**Löw** (lāv), **Jos.,** Prague, Jan. 23,
—Oct., 1886 ; pianist and comp
of light pf.-pcs.

**Lowe** (lō), **Edw.,** Salisbury, E
1610 (–15?)—Oxford, 1682 ; orga
professor and composer.

**Löwe** (lā′-vĕ) (Jn.) **Karl (Gf.),** L
jün, near Halle, Nov. 30, 17
Kiel, April 20, 1869 ; son and p
of a cantor ; studied with Türk
royal stipend ; 1821–66 town m
dir. at Stettin ; toured Europe s
ing his own fine " ballades " or
matic solos ; also c. 5 operas
oratorios, etc., wrote a " Selbst-
graphie (1870)."

**Low′thian, Caroline** (Mrs. **Cyril
Prescott**), English composer.

**Lübeck** (lü′-bĕk), (1) **Vincentius,**
dingbüttel, near Bremen, 1654—H
burg, Feb. 9, 1740 ; famous orga
(2) **Jn. H.,** Alphen, Holland, 17
The Hague, 1865; violinist and
conductor. (3) **Ernst,** The Ha
1829—Paris, 1876 ; son of ab
pianist. (4) **Louis,** b. The Ha
1838 ; bro. of above ; pupil of
quard ; 1863–70, 'cello-teacher, I
zig Cons. ; then in Frankfort.

**Lü′benau, L.** Vide JADASSOHN,

**Lubrich** (loo′-brĭkh), **Fritz,** b. I
dorf, July 29, 1862 ; 1890 canto
Peilau, Silesia ; editor and
poser.

**Lucantoni** (loo-kän-tō′-nē), **Giov.
Rieti, Italy, Jan. 18, 1825 ; pup
Milan Cons.; 1857 lived in P
then London as vocal teacher ;
opera, a symph., etc.

**Lu′cas,** (1) **Chas.,** Salisbury, 18
London, 1869 ; 'cellist and comp
(2) **Stanley,** since 1861 secretar
the R. Soc. of Mus.; and 1866–8
the Philh. Soc. (3) **Clarence,** b. (

..a, 1866 ; studied Paris Cons.; c.
pera, "*Anne Hathaway*," etc.
..cca (look´-kä), **Pauline**, b. Vienna,
..pril 25, 1841 ; soprano ; studied
.ith Uschmann and Lewy ; in chorus
.ienna Op.; 1859 won attention as
.irst Bridesmaid in "*Der Frei-
..hütz*," engaged at Olmütz, for
.ading rôles ; Meyerbeer chose her
.o create "Selika" in "*L'Africaine*"
.t Berlin, where she was engaged as
..-singer for life ; sang in London
.nnually, and broke her Berlin en-
.agement to sing in the United
.tates for two years ; 1869 m. Baron
.n Rhaden (divorced, 1872) ; m. von
.allhofen in America ; lives in Vi-
.na.

.cchesma (look-käs´-mä), **Maria A.
..**, Ital. mezzo-soprano, London,
.37.

.ck (lǐk), **Stephan**, Linz-on-Rhine,
.06—Trier, 1883 ; reformer in Cath-
.ic church-music.

.lwig (loot´-vǐkh), **Otto**, Eisfeld,
.huringia, 1813 — Dresden, 1865 ;
.am. composer.

.rsz (loorsh), **K.**, Schwerin, 1834—
.erlin, 1882 ; composer.

.y (rightly **Lulli**) (lül-lē, or lool´-lǐ),
.) **J. Bap. de**, Florence, 1633—
.aris, March 22, 1687. A Franciscan
.onk taught him the violin and gui-
.r. His parents were noble but
.oor ; the Chev. de Guise took the
.oy in 1646 to France to entertain
.lle. de Montpensier, but he was
.t to work in the scullery, where
.ount de Nogent heard him play
.e vln. and placed him in the
.ivate band. **L.**, however, set to
.usic a satirical poem on Mlle. de
... and she dismissed him. He stud-
.d the harps. and comp. with Métri,
.oberdet, and Gigault, and became
. member of the King's private or-
.estra ; 1652, he became head of the
. 24 violins" ; he organised a second
.oup. "les petits violons," of 16
.strs. and made it the best orchestra
. France. 1653, ct.-composer and
.od. masques and ballets in which

Louis XIV. took part and Lully as
"M. Baptiste," danced and acted.
1672, the king held him in such favour
that he gave him letters patent for
an "Académie royale de musique"
(now the Gr. Opéra) ; a rival theatre
was closed by the police (v. CAMPRA).
With this opportunity (cf. Wagner's
Bayreuth, Theatre) the transplanted
Italian proceeded to found French
opera—idiomatic mus. to texts in the
vernacular, and free of the super-
ornamentation of the Italian Sch. He
held the vogue till Gluck put him in
eclipse. **L.** was dir., stage-manager,
conductor, and even at times machin-
ist, as well as composer. He was
fortunate in his librettist, Quinault.
He developed the overture, and introduced the brass into the orch. He
was famous for his temper and once
while cond. furiously struck his own
foot with the baton, producing a
fatal abscess. His works, mainly on
classical subjects, include "*Les Fêtes
de l'Amour et de Bacchus*"; a pastoral pasticcio (1672) ; "*Cadmus et
Hermione*"; "*Alceste*"; "*Thésée*";
"*Le Carnaval*," opera-ballet ; "*Atys,
Isis, Psyche*"; "*Bellérophon*"; "*Proserpine*" ; "*Le Triomphe de
L'Amour*"; "*Persée*"; "*Phaëton*";
"*Amadis de Gaule*" ; "*Roland*" ;
"*Armide et Renaud*"; "*Acis et
Galatée*," historic pastoral (1686),
etc., also symphs., a mass, etc. (2)
**Louis de**, Paris, 1664—after 1713 ;
son of above ; dramatic com-
poser.

**Lum´bye, Hans Chr.**, Copenhagen,
1810—1874; conductor and composer of pop. dance-mus. His son and
successor (2) **G.**, c. opera "*The
Witch's Flute.*"

**Lum´ley, Benj.**, 1812—1875 ; London
operatic manager.

**Lu´pi.** Vide LUPUS.

**Lupi** (loo´-pē), Italianised form of
"Wolf"; frequent 16th cent. surname
worn by **Lupus Lupi, Didier, Johannes (Jean)**, and **Manfred Lupi**,
of whom nothing remains except their

works (detached motets for the greater part). Also see LOBO.

**Luporini** (loo-po-rē'-nē), **Gaetano**, b. Lucca, Italy; pupil of Primo Quilici, graduating from the Pacini Mus. Inst.; c. opera " *Marcella*," succ. lyric comedy, " *I Dispetti Amorosi*" (Turin, 1894); v. succ. opera "*La Colonna di Pasqua*" (Naples, 1896), etc.

**Lupot** (lü-pō), (1) **Nicolas**, Stuttgart, 1758—Paris, 1824 ; chief of a French family of vln.-makers, incl. his great grandfather (2) **Jean;** his grandfather (3) **Laurent** (b. 1696), his father (4) **François**, his bro. (5) **François** (d. 1837), and his son-in-law, **Chas. Fr. Gand** of **Gand & Bernardel**, Paris.

**Lupus** (loo'-poos) (Christian name frequently occurring among 16th cent. composers). Among those who wore it are, (1) **L. Hellinck**, (2) **L. Lupi**.

**Lusci'nius** (Latin form of **Nachtgall** or **Nachtigall** (näkht'-(i)-gäl), " Nightingale "), **Ottomar**, Strassburg, 1487—ca. 1536 ; organist, theorist and composer.

**Lussan** (dŭ lŭs-säň), **Zélie de**, b. New York, 1863 ; pupil of her mother ; début in concert and stage, 1886 ; 1889 Carl Rosa Co., London ; from 1894, Met. Op. N. Y., also in Spain, etc.

**Lussy** (loo-sē), **Mathis**, b. Stans, Switz., April 8, 1828 ; pupil of Businger and Nägeli; pf.-teacher, Paris, and writer.

**Lüstner** (lĭst'-n'r), (1) **Ignaz P.**, Poischwitz, near Jauer, 1792—Breslau, 1873 ; violin teacher. His five sons were (2) **K.**, b. Breslau, Nov. 10, 1834 ; pianist and 'cellist ; since 1872 teacher in Wiesbaden. (3) **Otto**, Breslau, 1839—Barmen, 1889 ; town mus.-dir. at Barmen. (4) **Louis**, b. Breslau, June 30, 1840 ; violinist, and since 1874 cond. at Wiesbaden. (5) **G.**, b. Berlin, 1887 ; 'cellist; ct.-cond. at Berlin. (6) **Richard**, b. Breslau, Sept. 2, 1854 ; harpist and violinist.

**Luther** (loo'-tĕr), **Martin**, Eisleben, Nov 10 1483—Feb. 18, 1546 ; the great reformer concerned himself a with church-mus., issuing " *Form missae*" (1523), and a new or for the German mass. He wrote words of at least 36 chorals, and generally believed to have c. 13 c ral-tunes (incl. the famous " *Ein f Burg ist unser Gott*," and " *Jes den Propheten das gescha*"), his me od being to play them on the fl (which he played well) while friends and assistants, the cond. K rad Rupff and cantor Jn. Walth wrote them out.

**Lütschg** (lĭtshkh), **Waldemar**, b. Petersburg, May 16, 1877 ; piani pupil of his father a prof. at the Co there ; after his father's death toured Germany ; lives in Berlin.

**Lutz** (loots), **Wm. Meyer**, b. M nerstadt, 1829 ; pianist and dra composer ; from 1848, conductor London.

**Lützel** (lüt'-tsĕl), **Jn. H.**, Igglehei near Speyer, 1823—Zweibrucke 1899 ; writer and composer.

**Lutzer, Jenny.** Vide DINGELSTED'

**Lux** (looks), **Fr.**, Ruhla, Thuring 1820—Mayence, 1895 ; conduct organist, pianist and dram. compos

**Luzzi** (lood'-zē), **Luigi**, Olevano Lomellina, 1828—Stradella, 187 dram. composer.

**Lvoff** (or **Lwoff**) (l'vôf), **Alex. v** Reval, 1799—on his estate, Govt. Kovno, 1870 ; violinist and cond tor ; c. the Russian national hymn a 4 operas.

**Lwowezyk** (l'vō'-yĕ-zēk), **Mart (Leopolitas)**, d. 1589, Polish co poser.

**Lynes** (līnz), **Frank**, b. Cambridg Mass., May 16, 1858 ; pupil N. Cons. and Leipzig Cons.; lives Boston as organist, conductor a composer.

**Lyra** (lē'-rä), **Justus W.**, Osnabrūc 1822—Gherden, 1882 ; composer.

**Lysberg** (lēs-bĕrkh) (rightly **Bovy Chas. Samuel**, Lysberg, near G neva, 1821—Geneva, 1873 ; pian and dram. composer.

## M

as (mäs), (1) **Jos.**, Dartford, 1847—
886; tenor. (2) **Louis (Ph. O.)**,
Viesbaden, 1852—Boston, 1889;
anist, conductor and composer.

**bellini** (mä-běl-lē'-nē), **Teodulo**,
istoia, Italy, 1817—Florence, 1897;
.-conductor and dram. composer.

**billon** (mä-bē-yôṅ), **Jean**, St.
ierremont, 1632—St. Germain-des-
rés, 1707; writer and editor.

**cbeth', Allan**, b. Greenock, Scot-
nd, March 13, 1856; pupil of Leip-
g Cons.; organist in Glasgow;
nce 1890, principal sch. of mus.,
lasgow Athenæum; c. an operetta,
cantatas, chamber-mus., etc.

**ccherini** (mäk-kě-rē'-nē), Bologna,
'45—1825, soprano, wife of Anni.

**cCunn', Hamish**, b. Greenock,
otland, March 22, 1868; notable
ritish composer; pupil of Parry, R.
. M., having won a scholarship for
mp.; at 19, several of his orch.-
s. were prod. by Manns; at 20
mmissioned to c. a cantata for the
lasgow Choral Union; gave con-
rts at the studio of John Pettie,
nose daughter he m., 1889; 1888—
., prof. of harm. R. A. M.; 1898,
nd. Carl Rosa Op. Co.; c. operas,
*Jeanie Deans*" (Edinburgh, 1894),
*Diarmid and Ghriné*" (Covent
arden, 1897); 5 cantatas incl. "*The
eath of Parry Reed*" (male chorus
d orch.), overtures "*Cior Mhor*,"
*The Land of the Mountain and the
'ood*" ballad overture, "*The Dowie
ns o' Yarrow*"; ballade, "*The
ip o' the Fiend*," with orch.; 8th
alm with orch., etc.

**cDow'ell, Edw. Alex.**, NewYork,
ec. 18, 1861; eminent American
mposer and one of the most orig-
al and virile of contemporary cre-
ors, having given the sonata a
w enlargement and spontaneity,
d written programme-mus. of espe-
al dignity; pupil of J. Buitrago, P.
esvernine and Teresa Carreño. N.

Y.; 1876, Paris Cons.; 1879, with
Heymann (pf.) and Raff (comp.)
Frankfort; 1881–82, chief pf
teacher at Darmstadt Cons.; at 2;,
Raff (who was deeply interested
in his progress) and Liszt pro
cured the performance of his works
at the annual festival of the "Allgemeiner deutscher Musikverein"; lived
in Wiesbaden; 1888, Boston; 1896,
prof. of mus. in Columbia Univ.,
New York; Mus. Doc. *h. c.*, Princeton Univ. and 1902, Penn. U.
also; he gives frequent pf.-recitals,
and has played his concertos with
the Boston Symph. and other
orchs. ORCHESTRAL COMPOSITIONS:
2 poems "*Hamlet*" and "*Ophelia*";
symph. poems, "*Lancelot and
Elaine*," "*Lamia*" and "*Roland*,"
op. 35, romance for 'cello with orch.;
3 orch. suites incl. "*In October*" and
"*Indian Suite*." FOR PIANO. 4
sonatas "*Tragica*," "*Eroica*"
("*Flos regum Arthurus*"), "*Scandinavian*" and "*Celtic*"; prelude
and fugue, modern suite; forest
idyls, 3 poems, "*Moon-pictures*," 6
poems after Heine, 4 "*Little Poems*";
technical exercises (3 books), and 12
virtuoso-studies, etc., and many songs
of great charm and individuality.

**Mace, Thos.**, 1613—after 1675; Engl
lutenist, inventor and writer.

**Macfar'ren**, (1) Sir **G. Alex.**, London, March 2, 1813—Oct. 31, 1887;
notable English composer and scholar; son and pupil of the playwright
G. Macfarren; also studied with Ch.
Lucas and C. Potter, R. A. M.;
1834, prof. there, even after blindness
overtook him; from 1875 prof. at
Cambridge Univ. Mus. Doc. there
1876; from 1876, also principal of
the R. A. M.; 1883, knighted; c. 13
operas, 9 of them prod.; 4 oratorios,
6 cantatas, 8 symphonies, 7 overtures, incl. "*Chevy Chase*," "*Don
Carlos*," "*Hamlet*" and "*Festival*,"
concertos, sonatas, etc.; wrote text-
books, articles; ed. old texts, etc.;
biog. by Banister (London, '91). **(2)**

**Natalia,** b. Lübeck, wife of above; contralto, translator and writer. (3) **Walter Cecil,** b. London, Aug. 28, 1826 ; bro. and pupil (in comp.) of (1) ; studied with Turle, Holmes (pf.) and Potter (comp.) ; from 1846, pf.-prof. at the R. A. M., of which he is a Fellow ; 1873–80, cond. Acad. Concerts ; dir. and treasurer Philharm. Soc. ; pianist, lecturer, editor, and composer of a symph., 7 overtures, a cantata "*The Song of the Sunbeam*," services, etc.

**Machault** (or **Machau, Machaud, Machut**) (mă-shō), **Guillaume (Gulielmus) de Mascandio,** Machau in the Champagne (?) ca. 1284–1370 ; troubadour ; composer.

**Mächtig** (měkh'-tǐkh), **K.,** Breslau, 1836—1881; organist and composer.

**Macirone** (mä-chē-rō'-ně), **Clara Angela,** b. London, Jan. 20, 1821; pianist ; pupil of R. A. M.; later teacher there and elsewhere ; c. " *Te Deum*" and "*Jubilate*," anthem "*By the Waters of Babylon,*" etc.

**Macken'zie,** Sir **Alex. Campbell,** b. Edinburgh, Aug. 22, 1847 ; notable British composer ; pupil of Ulrich (pf.) and Stein (comp.),Sondershausen Cons.; at 14 a violinist in the Ducal Orch.; 1862, won the King's scholarship, R. A. M., and studied with Sainton, Jewson, and Lucas ; from 1865 teacher and cond. Edinburgh ; 1888 of Cambridge ; 1896 of Edinburgh U., 1894 knighted; since 1888, principal R. A. M. (vice Macfarren); 1892 cond. Philh. Soc.; c. operas, "*Colomba*" (Drury Lane, 1883), "*The Troubadour*" (ibid. 1886), and "*His Majesty, or the Court of Vingolia*" (1897 ; comic). "*Cricket on the Hearth*" (MS ); oratorios, "*The Rose of Sharon*" (Norwich Festival, 1884), and "*Bethlehem*" (1894); cantatas, *Jason* (Bristol Festival, 1882), "*The Bride,*" "*The Story of Sayid*" (Leeds Festival, '86), "*The New Covenant,*" "*The Dream of Jubal,*" "*The Cotter's Saturday Night,*" and "*Veni, Creator Spiritus*"; a

Scottish rhapsodies, a ballad, w orch., " *La belle dame sans merc* overtures " *Cervantes*," " *To a co edy*," " *Tempo di ballo*," " *Twel Night*," " *Britannia* "; a vln.-c certo, a " Pibroch " for vln. a orch.; " *Scottish Concertos* " for p etc.

**Mackintosh** (1) **J.,** 1767—1840 ( bassoonist. (2) **Alphonso,** son above ; violinist.

**McGuck'in, Barton,** b. Dublin, J 28, 1852 ; pupil of Turle and T vulsi ; pop. oratorio and opera tenor.

**McLean, Alick,** b. Eton, Engl., J 20, 1872 ; c. opera " *Quentin D ward* " (London, 1895) ; 1-act op " *Petruccio* " (Covent Garden, 189 Moody Manners prize of £100), e

**McMur'die, Jos.,** London, 1792 Merton, Surrey, 1878 ; composer a director.

**Mader** (mä'-děr), **Raoul (M.),** b. Pre burg, Hungary, June 25, 1856 ; stu ied Vienna Cons.; took 1st prize pf. and comp., and the great silv medal and the Liszt prize as be pianist in the Cons. ; 1882–95, " coach" for solo singers, Vien ct.-opera, also asst.-cond. From 18 cond. Royal Opera, Pesth; c. 2 con operas, 4 ballets, incl. " *Die Sirene insel*," and " *She* " (after Rider Ha gard), parody on Mascagni's *Cav leria Rusticana* (Th. an der Wie 1892), choruses, songs, etc.

**Mag(g)ini** (mäd-jē'-nē) (or **Magin Giov. Paolo,** Botticino - Mari Italy, 1580—Brescia, ca. 1631 ; vl maker, rivalling Stradivari and Gu neri ; his double-basses particula good ; label, " Gio. Paolo Maggi Brescia."

**Mag'nus, Désiré** (rightly **Magn Deutz**), Brussels, 1828 — Pai 1884 ; teacher, composer and critic

**Mahillon** (mä-ē-yôň), **Chas. Vict** b. Brussels, March 10 1841 ; sir 1877 custodian of mus. instrs., Bru sels Cons.; editor and writer ; ma ager wind-inst. factory of his father

ler (mä'-lĕr), **Gus.,** b. Kalisch,
hemia, July 7, 1860 ; studied with
uckner at Vienna Cons.; cond. at
ssel, 1885–86, Leipzig. 1888–91 ;
. Royal Opera Pesth, 1891–97,
nd. Hamburg City Th., 1897, ct.-
nd. Vienna Ct.-Opera, later dir.; c.
era "*Die drei Pintos*" (after
eber's sketches) (Leipzig, 1888) ;
ntata "*Das klagende Lied,*" fairy
ay, 3 notable symphonies, etc.

au (mä-oo), **Stephan,** b. Germany,
-singer and composer, 1538

er (mī'-ĕr), (1) **Jos. Fr. Bd.** Cas-
.r, cantor at Schwäbisch Hall 1718–
. (2) **Julius Jos.,** Freiburg,
den, 1821—Munich, 1889 ; teacher
d writer.

lhac (mĭl'-äk), **Pauline,** b. Vienna,
ay 4, 1858 ; pupil of Uffmann, so-
ano at Carlsruhe many years.

lart (mĭ yär), **Louis** (called
mé), Montpellier, Herault, France,
17—Moulins, Allier, 1871 ; dram.
mposer.

lly (mĭ-yē), **Alphonse J. Ernest,**
Brussels, Nov. 27, 1833 ; pianist,
d organ virtuoso ; pupil of Girsch-
r, Brussels Cons.; 1861 pf.-teacher
ere ; 1868 organ-teacher ; com-
ser.

nzer (mĭn'-tsĕr), **Abbé Jos.,** Trier,
07 — Manchester, 1851 ; singing-
acher, writer and dram. composer.

tland (mät'-lănd) (**J. Alex.**), Ful-
r, b. London, April 7, 1856 ; 1882,
.A. Trinity Coll., Cambridge ;
cturer and critic for various papers,
w of London *Times* ; ed. the Ap-
ndix to Grove's Dict.; pianist at
e Bach choir concerts , wrote
*Masters of German Music*" (1894),
d many authoritative works.

o (mä'-yō), **Fran. di** (called Cic-
o di Majo), Naples, 1745 (?)—
me, 1770 ; organist and noted
mposer of operas and church-mus.

orano. Vide CAFFARELLI.

'colm, **Alex.,** British writer, 1721.

der (mäl'-dĕr). **Pierre van,** Brus-
ls, 1724–1768 ; violinist and com-
ser.

**Malherbe** (mäl-ärb), **Chas. Théodore,** b. Paris, April 21, 1863 ; at
first a lawyer, then studied with Danhauser, Wormser, and Massenet ;
also pub. some original comps., and
transcriptions ; Danhauser's sec. ;
1896, asst.-archivist, Gr. Opéra ;
Officer of the Acad. and of Pub. Instruction ; Chev. of various orders.
Ed. *Le Ménestrel,* and is prolific
writer on Wagner, etc.; owns what is
probably the best private coll. of mus.-
autographs in the world, ed. Rameau's complete works.

**Malibran** (mäl-ĭ-brän), (1) **M. Feli-
cità** (née Garcia), Paris, March 24,
1808—Manchester, Sept. 23, 1836
(from singing too soon after being
thrown and dragged by a horse). In
some respects the greatest of all
women vocalists ; she had a contralto
voice with an additional soprano register and several well-concealed
" head tones" between ; she improvised frequently on the stage, and
also c. ; at 5 she played a child's
part and one evening broke out singing the chief rôle to the amusement
of the audience ; at 7 studied with
Pauseron ; at 15 studied with her
father (v. GARCIA) ; début, London,
1825 ; she had a personality that
compelled extraordinary homage.
She m. Malibran ; when he became
bankrupt she divorced him, and 1836
m. de Bériot, ct.-violinist with whom
she had lived since 1830. (2) **Alex.,**
Paris, 1823—1867; violinist and composer.

**Mallinger** (mäl'-lĭng-ĕr), **Mathilde**
(née **Lichtenegger**), b. Agram,
Feb. 17, 1847 ; soprano : pupil of
Giordigiani and Vogl, Prague Cons.,
and Lewy, Vienna ; début, Munich,
1866, 1868, created "Eva" in the
*Meistersinger* ; m. Baron von Schim-
melpfennig; since 1890 singing-teacher, Prague Cons.

**Malten** (mäl'-tĕn), **Therese,** b. In-
sterburg, East Prussia, June 21, 1855;
soprano ; pupil of Engel (voice), and
Kahle (action), Berlin ; at 18 début,

Dresden as *Pamina*, and engaged there for life ; created "Kundry" (*Parsifal*) at Bayreuth, 1882 ; 1898, ct.-chamber singer.

**Mälzel** (mĕl'-tsĕl), Jn. Nepomuk, Ratisbon, 1772—on a voyage, July 31, 1838 ; mus-teacher ; inv. "panharmonion" (a sort of orchestrion), an automaton-trumpeter, and an automatic chess-player; while experimenting with his "chronometer," a sort of metronome (v. D.D.), he saw Winkel's invention, adopted its chief features and patented the result as Maelzel's metronome (v. D.D.).

**Mancinelli** (män-chï-nĕl'-lĭ), **Luigi**, b. Orvieto, Papal States, Feb. 5, 348 ; intended for commerce, self-aught on the pf., and ran away from home ; was brought back, but permitted to study at 14 with Sbolci (Florence, 'cello) ; at 15, 3rd 'cellist Pergola Th., earning his living the next 8 years ; studied with Mabellini (comp.) ; 1870 in the orchestra of the opera at Rome , 1874, 2nd cond. ; 1875, cond. ; 1881. dir. Bologna Cons., which he made one of the best in Italy ; 1886-88, cond. at Drury Lane, London ; 1888-95, Royal Th. Madrid ; since at Covent Garden, London, and Met. Op., New York ; in Italy called "il Wagnerista" for his advocacy ; c. opera "*Isora di Provenza*" (Bologna, 1884) ; succ. "*Ero e Leandro*" (Madrid, 1897, New York, 1899) ; an oratorio, etc. ; overture and entr'acte-mus. to Cossa's *Cleopatra*.

**Mancini** (män-chē'-nē), (1) **Fran.**, Naples, 1674—1739 ; cond. and dram. composer. (2) **Giambattista**, Ascoli, 1716—Vienna, 1800 ; writer.

**Mancio** (män'-chō), **Felice**, Turin, 1840 — Vienna, 1897 ; singer and publisher.

**Mangeot** (män-zhō), **Ed. Jos.**, Nantes, France, 1834 — Paris, 1898 ; pf.-maker and editor ; inv. piano "à double clavier renversé."

**Mangold** (män'-gôlt), (1) **G. M.**, 1776 —1835 ; violinist. (2) (Jn.) **Wm.**,

Darmstadt, 1796—1875 ; cond and dram. composer. (3) **K. Amand**), Darmstadt, 1813—Ol dorf, Algau, 1889 ; bro. of ab dir., conductor and composer. **K. G.**, 1812—London, 1887; pia composer and teacher.

**Mann**, (1) **Arthur Henry**, b. wich, Engl., May 16, 1850 ; cho at the cath. with Dr. Buck ; org various churches ; since 1876, K Coll., Cambridge ; 1871, F. C 1882, Mus. Doc., Oxford ; H scholar ; with Prout discovered original wind-parts of the *Mess* ed. the *Fitzwilliam Catalogue* Maitland, etc. ; c. "*Ecce H* with orch.; "*Te Deum*," "*Ev Service*," for orch., etc. (2) **Jn Hendrik**, b. The Hague, Ju 1858 ; pupil R. Sch. of Mus. t bandm., Leyden ; composer.

**Man'ney**, **Chas. Fonte** , b. B lyn, 1872 ; studied with Wm. Fisher and J. Wallace Goo Boston ; composed a cantata, s etc.

**Manns** (mäns), **Aug. (Fr.)**, b. St berg, near Stettin, March 21, noted conductor ; son of a blower, who with his sons for quintet (vlns., 'cello, horn, and at 15, apprenticed to Urban, c bing ; later 1st clar. of a regin band, Dantzig ; 1848, at F Wieprecht got him a place as is in Gungl's orch. at Berlin ; 184 cond. Kroll's Garden ; regin bandm. Königsberg and Co (1854) ; joined Crystal Palace London as asst.-cond. to Sch who pub. as his own M.'s arr ment of certain quadrilles ; w upon M. resigned, publicly st the reason ; 1859 he succeeded he later made the band a full giving famous and very popular urday Concerts till 1900, whe public ceased to support it has also cond. 7 Triennial H Festivals, concerts of the Gla Choral Union, 1879-92, etc.

nsfeldt (mäns'-fĕlt), **Hn.**, Erfurt,
33—Ems, 1892 ; conductor.

nstädt (män'-shtĕt), (1) **Fz.**, b.
agen, Westphalia, July 8, 1852 ;
pil Stern Cons., Berlin ; 1874,
nd. at Mayence ; 1876, Berlin
mph. Orch.; 1879, pf.-t. Stern
ns.; 1893–97, cond. Berlin Philh.;
en returned to Wiesbaden, where
had been as conductor and teacher
83–97. (?) (2) **Wm.**, b. Bielefeld,
ay 20, 1837 ; bro. of above ; con-
ctor and stage manager, Berlin
n.; editor ; c. (text and music)
rces and operettas.

nsfeldt, **E.** Vide PIERSON, H. H.

atius (män'-tsĭ-oos), **Ed.**, Schwe-
n, 1806—Bad Ilmenau, 1874 ; tenor.

atovano, **Al.** Vide RIPA.

azuoli (män-tsoo-ō'-lē), **Giov.**, b.
orence, ca. 1725 ; famous soprano-
usico.

pleson, Col. **Jas. H.**, London,
ay 4, 1830—Nov. 14, 1901 ; fa-
ous impresario ; studied R. A. M.,
ondon ; a singer, and vla.-player
an orch.; 1861, managed Italian
pera at the Lyceum ; 1862–68, was
H. M.'s Th.; 1869, Drury Lane ;
77, reopened H. M.'s Th.; gave
pera at Acad. of Mus., New York,
ith varying succ. in different seasons.

ra (mä'-rä), **Gertrud Elisabeth**,
ée **Schmeling**), Cassel, Feb. 23,
49—Reval, Jan. 20, 1833 ; phe-
omenal soprano with compass,
-e''' (v. PITCH, D.D.), who reached a
gh pinnacle of art over difficulties
anging from rickets to the Moscow
e) not surpassed in the wildest fic-
on ; she m. in 1773, the 'cellist
ara, divorced him 1799 ; teacher.

ra, **La.** Vide LIPSIUS, MARIE.

rais (mä-rĕ'), (1) **Marin**, Paris,
arch 31, 1656—Aug. 15, 1728 ; the
eatest viola-da-gambist of his time ;
symphonies, etc. (2) **Roland**,
on of above ; solo gambist ; pub.
es. for gamba.

r'beck, **J.** (or **Merbecke**), 1523—
, 1581; Engl. organist and com-
oser.

**Marceau** (măr-sō), **Jas. Herbert**, b.
Napierville, Canada, Oct. 31, 1859;
studied singing with Willard, N.Y.,
and with de Padilla and Ch. Doual
lier, Paris ; teacher Mansion Sch.
Wollaston, Mass.

**Marcello** (mär-chĕl'-lō), **Benedetto**,
Venice, Aug. 1, 1686—Brescia, July
24, 1739 ; noted composer, pupil of
Gasparini and Lotti ; held gov't positions ; pub. satires, and c. 50 psalms,
etc.

**Marchand** (măr-shän), **Louis**, Lyons,
1669—in poverty, Paris, 1732 ; an
org.-virtuoso whose fame wilted before his failure to meet J. S. Bach in
a duel of virtuosity.

**Mar'chant, Arthur Wm.**, b. London,
Oct. 18, 1850; organist in several
English churches ; 1880–82, St.
John's Cath., Denver, Col.; since
1895, organist, Dumfries, Scotland ;
wrote text-books ; c. Psalm 48, with
orch.; "A Morning Service" and an
"Evening Service," etc.

**Marchesi** (mär-kā'-zē), (1) **Luigi**
("Marchesi'ni"), Milan, 1755—Inzago, Dec. 14, 1829 ; soprano musico. (2) **Salvatore**, Cavaliere **De
Castrone** (dä-käs-trō'-nĕ) (Marchese **Della Rajata**), b. Palermo, Jan. 15, 1822 ; studied mus.
with Raimondi, Lamperti and Fontana ; exiled after the Revolution of
1848, and début as barytone, N. Y.;
then studied with Garcia, London ;
a succ. concert-singer ; 1852 m. Mathilde Graumann (v. infra), and
they sang together in opera, later
taught together at Vienna Cons.,
1865–69, Cologne Cons.; 1869–81,
Vienna, since then in Paris ; pub. a
vocal method, translations, etc.; c.
songs. (3) **Mathilde** (née **Graumann**), b. Frankfort-on-M., March
26, 1826 ; famous singing-teacher :
pupil of Nicolai, Vienna, and Garcia,
Paris ; sang in concert ; wife of above
(q. v.) ; pub. a vocal method, vocalises, and autobiog. "Marchesi and
Music," enlarged from "Aus meinem
Leben" (Dusseldorf, 1887 ?).

**Marchetti** (mär-kĕt'-tĭ), **Filippo**, Bolognola, Italy, Feb. 26, 1835—Rome, Jan. 18, 1902; pupil of Lillo and Conti, Royal Cons., Naples; at 21 prod. succ. opera, "*Gentile da Varano*" (Turin), "*La Demente*" (1857); singing-teacher, Rome; went to Milan and prod. succ. "*Giulietta e Romeo*" (1865), and "*Ruy-Blas*" (La Scala, 1869). From 1881, dir. R. Accad. di Santa Cecilia, Rome; prod. 3 other operas, symphonies, and church-music.

**Marchet'tus of Padua** (**Marchetto da Padova**), lived in Cesena, ca. 1270—ca. 1320; learned theorist. (Gerbert.)

**Marchi** (mär'-kē), **Emilio de**, Chevalier (rightly **Peano**), b. Voghera, Piedmont, 1866; prominent tenor; son of Italian general; entered army and se₁ved with distinction in Africa as lieutenant, then studied voice with Landi, Florence; début, Milan, 1866, as Alfredo in "*La Traviata*"; sang with great success throughout Europe; 1896–97 and 1901–02 in the U. S. 1900 created "Cavardossi" in Puccini's "*La Tosca*."

**Marcolini** (-lē'-nē), **Marietta**; Italian soprano, 1805–18; created Rossini rôles.

**Maréchal** (mär-ā-shǎl), **H. Chas.**, b. Paris, Jan. 22, 1842; pupil of Cons., 1870, won Grand prix de Rome; prod. 1-act op.-com. "*Les Amoureux de Cathérine*" (Op.-Com., 1876); also 3-act op.-com. "*La Traverne des Trabans*" (ibid.,'81); "*Déidamie*" (Gr. Opéra,'93); "*Calendal*" (Rouen, '94); c. sacred drama "*Le Miracle de Naim*" ('91), etc.

**Marek'**, **Louis**, Galicia, 1837—Lemberg (?); pianist, pupil of Liszt.

**Marenco** (mä-rĕn'-kō), **Romualdo**, b. Novi Ligure, Italy, March 1, 1841; violinist; then 2d bassoon, Doria Th., Genoa, where he prod. a ballet, studied cpt. with Fenaroli and Mattei; 1873, dir. of ballet at La Scala, Milan; has prod. 4 operas, and over 20 ballets.

**Marenzio** (mä-rĕn'-tsĭ-ō), **Luca**, ( caglio, near Brescia, ca. 1550—( love disprized") Rome, Aug. 1599; famous composer of madrig also of motets, etc.

**Mareš** (mä'-rĕsh), **John A.**, Chotel Bohemia, 1719—St. Petersburg, 1 invented the Russian "hunting-h mus.," each horn sounding one to

**Maretzek** (mä-rĕt'-shĕk), **M** Brunn, Moravia, June 28, 182 Pleasant Plains, Staten Island, N. May 14, 1897; well-known impr rio; also dram. composer and teac

**Mariani** (mä-rĭ-ä'-nē), **Angelo**, Ra₁ na, Oct. 11, 1822—Genoa, June 1873; famous conductor.

**Marimon** (mă-rē-môṅ), **Marie**, Liège, 1839; pupil of Duprez; but, 1857; soprano.

**Marin** (mă-răṅ), **M. Martin M celle de**, b. Bayonne, France, Se 8, 1769; harpist and composer.

**Marini** (mä-rē'-nē), (1) **Biagio**, B cia—Padua, ca. 1660; violinist ₁ composer. (2) **Carlo A.**, b. Be₁ mo; violinist and composer, 1696.

**Mario** (mä'-rĭ-ō), **Giuseppe**, Conte Candia, Cagliari, Sardinia, Oct. 1810—Rome, Dec. 11, 1883; e₁ nent tenor; pupil of Bordogni ₁ Poncharde; début, Paris Ope 1838; toured Europe and Amer with greatest success; m. Giulia Gr

**Ma'rius**, clavecin-maker, Paris, 1 cent.

**Mark, Paula**, b. ca. 1870; sopran pupil Vienna Cons., début, Le zig, 1890; in 1897 m. the physicia Neusser (who had cured her of throat trouble), and retired from stage.

**Markull** (mär-kool'), **Fr. Wm.**, Rei enbach, near Elbing, 1816—Danz 1887; pianist, critic and dram. co poser.

**Markwort** (märk'-vôrt), **Jn. Ch** Riesling, near Brunswick, 1778 Bessungen, 1866; tenor and writer

**Marmontel** (mär-môṅ-tĕl), **A** **Fran.**, Clermont-Ferrand, Puy-( Dôme, July 18, 18₁6—Paris, Jan. ₁

1898 ; pupil Paris Cons., 1848 ; pf.-
teacher there, noted for famous pupils ; writer of historic and didactic
treatises ; composer.

ar'ny, Elsa ; contralto ; pupil of
Marchesi ; at 8 sang in concert, later
in opera ; 1900 in New York.

arpurg (mär'-poorkh), (1) Fr. Wm.,
Seehausen, Altmark, Oct. 1, 1718—
Berlin, May 22, 1795 : important
theorist ; wrote treatises of great historic and theoretic value, much translated. (2) Fr., Paderborn, 1825—
Wiesbaden, 1884 ; great-grandson of
above ; violinist, pianist, cond. and
dram. composer.

arschner (märsh'-nĕr), (1) H. (August), Zittau, Saxony, Aug. 16, 1795
(not 1796)—Hanover, Dec. 14, 1861;
eminent opera-composer of Weber's
school but great modernity, and remarkable brilliance of instrumentation ; studied piano from age of 6 ;
sang as a boy, then pupil of Bergt
(org ); studied law Leipzig U. 1813,
then turned to mus. entirely ; pupil
of Schicht ; the Graf von Amadée became his patron, and he went to Vienna ; later taught at Pressburg ; c. 3
operas, the last prod. 1820 at Dresden by C. M. von Weber ; 1823, he
became co.-dir. of opera there with
von W. and Morlacchi ; 1826, cond.
Leipzig Th. and prod. "Der Vam-
pyr" (1828) and "Der Templer und
die Jüdin ;" both widely succ. and still
heard , 1831–59, ct.-cond. Hanover,
when he was pensioned ; while ct.-
cond. he prod. "Hans Herling" (Berlin, 1833), also very succ. and still alive;
he prod. 8 other operas ; c. incidental
music, choruses, etc. (2) Fz., b.
Leitmeritz, Bohemia, March 26, 1855;
pupil Prague Cons., and Bruckner,
Vienna ; since 1886, teacher Female
Teachers' Seminary, Vienna · pub. a
treatise on piano-touch.

arsh, J., Dorking, 1750—1828; composer and violinist.

ar'shall, Wm., Oxford, 1806 —
Handsworth, 1875 ; organist, writer
and editor.

Marsick (mär-sĭk), Martin P. Jos., b.
Jupille, near Liège, Belgium, March
9, 1848 ; prominent violinist ; pupil
of Désiré Haynberg, Liège Cons.; at
12 organist of the cath., and a vocalist ; pupil of Léonard, Brussels
Cons., later of Massenet at Paris
Cons. (taking 1st vln. prize) ; and of
Joachim at Berlin ; début, Paris,
1873 ; toured Europe and (1895–96)
U. S.; 1892, vln.-prof., Paris Cons.;
c. 3 vln.-concertos, etc.

Mar'ston, George W., Sandwich,
Mass., U. S. A., 1840—Feb., 1901 ;
studied with Tufts at Portland ; l.
Boston as teacher and composer of
pop. songs and pf.-pcs.

Marteau (mär-tō), H., b. Rheims ;
excellent violinist ; pupil Paris Cons.;
1892, took 1st prize ; toured U. S.,
1893, 1898 ; Russia, 1899 ; then
compelled to spend a year in the
French army ; founded " Marteau
Prize for vln.-sonata c. by a na-
tive-born American " ; 1900 toured
America.

Martelli, E. Vide COTTRAU, T.

Martin (mär-tăṅ), (1) Jn. Blaisé,
Paris, 1769—1837 ; barytone. (2)
P. Alex, d. Paris, Dec., 1879 ; org.-
builder, and inv. of the " percussion"
action in the harmonium. (3) (mär'-
tĭn), Jonathan, 1715—London, 1737;
organist and composer. (4) G. Wm.,
1828 — Wandsworth, 1881 ; Engl.
composer, editor and publisher. (5)
Sir George Clement, b. Lambourne,
Berks, Sept. 11, 1844 ; organist various churches ; teacher in R. Coll. of
Mus.; c. anthems ; knighted, Easter,
1889.

Martin y Solar (mär-tēn'-ē-sō-lär'),
Vicente, Valencia, Spain, 1754—St.
Petersburg, May, 1810 ; organist at
Alicante ; prod. operas in Italy in
succ. rivalry with Cimarosa and Paisiello and in Vienna with Mozart; his
best work was " La Cosa Rara,"
1785 ; 1788–1801, dir. Italian Op. at
St. Petersburg ; then teacher ; c.
operas, ballets, etc.

**Martines** (mär-tē′-něs) (or **Martinez**) (mär-tē′-něth), **Marianne di**, Vienna, 1744—1812; singer, pianist and composer.

**Martini** (mär-tē′-nē), (1) **Giambattista** (or **Giov. Bat.**) (known as **Padre M.**), Bologna, April 25, 1706 —Aug. 3, 1784; son and pupil of a violinist ((2) **Antonio Maria M.**), he studied with Predieri and Riccieri Zanotti and Perti; took orders 1729; cond. from 1725 at church of San Francisco, Bologna; as a composer of church-mus., a theorist and teacher he won European fame; he also pub. a history of ancient mus., and treatises. (3) (rightly **Schwarzendorf**) (shvärts′-ěn-dôrf), **Jean Paul Egide**, Freistadt, Palatinate, 1741—Paris, 1816; dram. composer.

**Martucci** (mär-toot′-chē), **Gius.**, b. Capua, Jan. 6, 1856; son and pupil of a trumpet-player; début as pianist Naples, 1867; studied at the Cons.; 1874, prof. there; cond. the orch. and concerts estab. by Prince d'Ardore, and dir. of the Società del Quartetto; from 1875, toured with succ. as pianist; 1886–1902, dir. Bologna Cons.; 1902, Naples; c. symph., pf.-concerto, etc.

**Marty** (mär-tē), **G. Eugène**, b. Paris, May 16, 1860; studied at the Cons. 1882; won the Grand Prix de Rome with cantata "*Edith*"; since 1894, prof. for ensemble singing there; 1895–96, chorusm. and cond. of the Concerts de l'Opéra; 1901, dir. concerts of the Cons.; c. several suites for orch., pantomime, "*Le Duc de Ferrare*," 3-act opera (1896), etc.

**Marx** (märx), **Ad. Bd.**, Halle, May 15, 1799—Berlin, May 17, 1866 eminent theorist; founded with Schlesinger, "*Berliner allgemeine musikalische Zeitung*"; editor, prof. and mus.-dir., 1832; c. opera; wrote v. succ. and important treatises.

**Marxsen** (märx′-zěn), **Eduard**, Nienstadten, near Altona, 1806—Altona, 1887 (8?); organist and teacher.

**Marzials** (mär-tsī-äls′), **Theodor**, b.

Brussels, Dec. 21, 1850; pupil o L. Lawson, London; studied in Paris and Milan; since 1870, mus.-dept. British Museum; tone and composer of pop. songs

**Marzo** (mär′-tsō). **Ed.**, b. Naples pil of Nacciarone, Miceli and Pa lardo; 1867, New York, as pianist; became opera and con cond., and accompanist. to Car Patti, Sarasate, etc.; organist at Agnes' Church, N. Y.; later at Saints; 1884, knighted by the of Italy; 1892, member of the Acad. of S. Cecilia; l. N. Y. teaches singing; pub. 6 masse with orch.), etc.

**Mascagni** (mäs-kän′-yē), **Pietro** Leghorn, Dec. 7, 1863. Son baker who wished him to study he secretly studied the piano, lat Soffredini's Mus.-Sch.; studied harm., cpt., and comp.; his fa finding him out, locked him in house, whence he was rescued 14 by an uncle; upon the un death he was befriended by C Florestan, while studying with chielli and Saladino, at Milan C He was cond. of various small trou finally cond. of the mus.-soc. at Ce nola; he won the prize offered by mus.-pub. Sonzogno, for a opera, with "*Cavalleria Rustica* which had a sensational succ. (6 tanzi Th., Rome, 1890) and has universally performed; while fier assailed by the critics it has produ a school of short operas showir tendency to excessive realism strenuousness, yet offering a m needed relief from the eternal clas mythologic or costume-play plots bringing serious opera as close h to real life as comic opera; 1 dir. of the Rossini Cons. at saro. M.'s later operas have fared so well as his "*Cavalleria I ticana*"; they include : "*L'A Fritz*" (Rome and Berlin, 18 "*I Rantzau*" (Florence, 1892), f succ. ; "*Guglielmo Ratcliff*" (Mi

a Scala, 1895), "*Silvano*" (ibid.,
895); 1-act "bozzetto" *Zanetto*"
Pesaro, 1896); and the fairly succ.
"*Iris*" (Rome, 1898; revised La
cala, Milan, 1899); "*Le Maschere*"
imultaneously prod. without succ.
n 6 cities in Italy, Jan., 1901, thus
illing six opportunities with one
tone; he c. also (previously to *Cav.
Rust.*) 2-act opera "*Il Filanda*,"
nd Schiller's "*Hymn to Joy*"; also
"*Hymn in Honor of Admiral
Dewey, U. S. N.*" (July, 1899), etc.
902, toured America with his own
pera-troupe.

schek (mä-shāk'), (1) **Vincenz**,
wikovecz, Bohemia, 1755—Prague,
831; pf. and harmonica-virtuoso;
rganist and dram. composer. (2)
aul, 1761—Vienna, 1826; bro. of
bove; pianist.

setti (mä-sĕt'-tē), **Umberto**, b.
Bologna, Feb. 18, 1869; studied at
he Cons., and since 1895 prof. of
inging there; member of the R.
Phil. Acad.; c. the succ. "*Vindice*"
Bologna, 1891); a requiem with
rch., etc.

sini (mä-sē'-nē), **Fran.**, Florence,
804 — in extreme poverty, Paris,
863; c. songs.

son, (1) Rev. **Wm.**, Hull, Engl.,
725—Aston, 1797; writer and com-
oser. (2) **Lowell**, Boston, Mass.,
an. 24, 1792—Orange, N. J., Aug.
1, 1872; pioneer in American comp.
nd teaching; c. v. succ. and remu-
erative colls., principally of sacred
usic. (3) **Wm.**, Boston, Mass.. Jan.
4, 1829; prominent American teacher
nd technician, son of above; studied
ith Henry Schmidt (pf.) in Boston;
t 17, début as pianist there; 1849,
tudied with Moscheles, Hauptmann
nd Richter, at Leipzig; with Drey-
chock at Prague; and Liszt, at Wei-
ar; he played in Weimar Prague,
nd Frankfort, London, and 1854–55
n American cities; since 1855 lives
n New York as teacher; 1872, Mus.
Doc. *h. c.*, Yale; pub. the important
nd influential "*Touch and Tech-*

nic, *a Method for Artistic Piano
playing*"; "*A Method for the Pf.*"
with E. S. Hoadley (1867); "*System for Beginners*" (1871); "*Mason s Pf.-Technics*" (1878); and
"*Memoirs*" (New York, 1901); c :
serenata for 'cello and many pf.-pcs
in classical form. (4) **Luther Whiting**, Turner, Maine, 1828—Buckfield
Maine, 1896; devised the v. succ.
"*National System*" of mus.-charts
and books; wrote "*Die neue Gesangschule.*"

**Massa** (mäs'-sä). **Nicolò**, Calice, Ligure, Italy, 1854—Genoa, 1894; c.
operas.

**Massaini** (mäs-sä-ē'-nē), **Tiburzio**, b.
Cremona, 16th cent.; Augustine
monk; cond. and composer.

**Massart** (mäs-sär'), (1) **Lambert Jos.**,
Liège. July 19, 1811—Paris, Feb. 13.
1892; violinist and prof. Paris Cons.
(2) **Louise Aglæ** (née Masson).
Paris, 1827—1887; wife of above:
pianist and. 1875. teacher at the
Cons.

**Massé** (mäs-sä), **Felix M.** (called
Victor), Lorient, Mar. 7, 1822—Paris,
July 5, 1884; pupil Paris Cons.; won
Grand prix de Rome, prof. of cpt.
there 1872; c. 18 operas, 13 prod..
incl. the still succ. "*Les noces de
Jeannette*" (Op. Com. 1853).

**Massenet** (mäs-nä), **Jules (Émile
Fr.)**, b. Montreaux, near St. Étienne
France, May 12, 1842; eminent
French opera - composer; pupil of
Laurent (pf.), Reber (harm.), Savard
and Ambr. Thomas (comp.) at the
Cons.; took first prizes for piano and
fugue; 1863, the Grand prix de Rome
with cantata "*David Rizzio*"; 1878–
96 prof. of comp. at the Cons.;
1878, member of the Académie, Commander of the Legion of Honour. C.
operas, almost all of them succ. and
constantly in the repertory of the
Paris Opéra and Op. Com., 1-act
comic opera "*La Grand Tanta*"
(1867); the operas, "*Don César de
Bazan*" (1872); "*Le Roi de Lahore*"
(1877); "*Hérodiade*" (.384); "*Ma-*

*non Lescaut"* (one of the greatest successes in the history of the Op.-Com.). " *Le Cid*" (1885); fairy-opera (1889) " *Esclarmonde* "; " *Le Magé*" (1891); " *Werther* " (1892); lyric comedy. " *Thaïs*" (1894); 1-act com.-op. " *Le Portrait de Manon*" (1894); lyric episode, " *La Navarraise*" (London, 1894 ; Paris, 1895) ; " *Sapho*" (Op.-Com., 1897) ; " *Cendrillon* " (Op.-Com., 1899); also 4-act drama " *Marie-Magdeleine* " (Odéon Th., 1873); " *Ève*," a mystery, 1875; oratorio, " *La Vièrge*," 1880 ; conte lyrique " *Griseldis*" (Op. - Com., 1901), opera, " *Le Jongleur de Nôtre-Dame*" (Monte Carlo, 1902) ; orch. suites; overtures incl. " *Phèdre* "; pf.-pcs., songs, etc.

**Massol** (măs-sôl), **J. Etienne A. Lodève,** Herault, 1802—Paris, 1887; tenor.

**Mas'son, Elizabeth,** 1806 — 1865; English mezzo-soprano ; teacher, and composer.

**Masutto** (mä-soot'-tō), (1) **Giov.,** Treviso, 1830—Venice, 1894, critic, and writer. (2) **Renzo,** b. Treviso, April 25, 1858 ; son of above ; bandm. 27th Italian Infantry regiment ; concert-pianist, violinist and dram. composer.

**Maszkowsky** (mäsh-kôf'-shkĭ), **Raphael,** b. Lemberg, 1838 ; pupil of the Vienna and Leipzig Cons. ; 1885, cond. at Schaffhausen ; 1889, mus.-dir. Coblenz ; 1890 cond. of Orch. Soc. Breslau.

**Materna** (mä-tĕr'-nä), **Amalie,** b. St. Georgen, Styria, July 10, 1847; noted soprano ; daughter of a sch.-master ; sang in church and concert at Graz ; début 1865 in opera as soubrette ; m. an actor, K. Friedrich, and sang with him in operetta at the Carl Th., Vienna ; 1869-96 prima donna, Vienna, ct.-opera ; toured America later ; she created " Brünnhiĭde," at Bayreuth, 1876, and " Kundry " in " *Parsifal*," 1882.

**Math'er,** (1) **Wm ,** 1756—1808 ; organist St. Paul's. London. (2) **Sam-**

uel, 1783—1824 ; organist and com poser.

**Math'ews, Wm. Smyth Babcock** b. New London. N H., May 8, 183 prominent teacher and writer ; studie at New London ; later at Lowell an Boston ; 1860-63, pf.-teacher Macor Ga.; 1867-93, organist Chicago; 1868 72, ed. " *Musical Independent*; 1878-86, critic of Chicago " *Times* " *Morning News*,"and " *Tribune* ; 1891, founded and since ed. the mag azine " *Music* ; " pub. many books o educational value.

**Mathias** (mä-tē'-äs), **Georges (Amé dée St. Clair),** b. Paris, Oct. 14 1826 ; pupil of Kalkbrenner an Chopin (pf.) and of Paris Cons.; 1862 pianist and prof. there, c. symph overtures, etc.

**Mathieu** (mät-yŭ), (1) **Adolphe Chas Ghislain,** b. Mons, Belgium, Jun 22, 1840 ; custodian of MSS. Brus sels Library ; writer. (2) **Emil (Louis V.),** b. of Belgian parents Lille, France, Oct. 18, 1844 ; studie Louvain Mus. Sch. and Brussel Cons.; won 1st harm. prize, and 1s pf. prize, 1869, and 1871, won 2n Grand prix de Rome ; 1867-73, prof pf. and harm., Louvain Mus. Sch. 1881-98, dir. Louvain Mus.-Sch. since 1898, dir. R. Cons. at Ghent c. 7 operas, mostly comic, a ballet, cantatas and 2 children's cantatas, (text and music) " *Poèmes lyriques* symphoniques*," 3 symph. poems, etc.

**Mattei** (mät-tā'-ē), (1) Abbate **Stanislao,** Bologna, 1750—1825 ; professor, conductor and writer. (2) **Tito,** b. Campobasso, near Naples, May 24, 1841; pianist to the King of Italy; pupil at 11 and later " Professore, Accad. di Santa Cecilia, Rome; re ceived a gold medal from Pius IX. toured Europe ; 1865, cond. at H. M.'s Th., London ; c. 3 operas incl. " *Maria di Gand* " (H. M's Th., 1880) , ballet, pop. songs, etc.

**Matteis** (mät-tā'-ēs), (1) **Nicolà,** Ital ian violinist, 1672. London. (2) **Nicolà,** d. 1749, son of above ; teacher

tthäi (mät-tä'-ē), H. Aug., Dres-
en, 1781—Leipzig, 1835; violinist
nd composer.

t(t)heson (mät'-tĕ-zōn), Jn., Hamurg, Sept. 28, 1681—April 17, 1764;
n " admirable Crichton " of music ;
singer. composer and player on the
rg. and harps.; operatic tenor ; im-
ortant in the development of the
hurch cantata afterward advanced
y Bach ; the first to introduce women
ito church-service ; pub. valuable
nd controversial and progressive
reatises.

tthias (or Mattheus), Le Maî-
re. Vide LE MAISTRE.

tthieux, Jna. Vide KINKEL.

tthison-Hansen (mät'-tĭ-zōn-hän'-
ĕn), (1) Hans, Flensburg, Den-
ark, 1807—Roeskilde, 1890; organ-
st and composer. (2) Godfred, b.
Roeskilde, Nov. 30, 1832 ; son of
bove ; 1859, organist German Frie-
richskirche, Copenhagen ; 1862,
von the Ancker scholarship, and
tudied at Leipzig ; 1867, organist at
t. John's and organ-teacher Copen-
agen Cons.; from 1877, asst.-organ-
st to his father ; later organist of
Trinity Ch.; c. vln. sonata, 'cello
onata, etc.

ttiolo (mät-tĭ-ō'-lō), Lino, b. Par-
na, Italy. 1853 ; graduated from the
Cons. with high honours ; 'cellist and
inging-teacher at Cincinnati. U. S.
A.; c. songs.

urel (mō-rĕl), Victor, b. Mar-
eilles, June 17, 1848 ; eminent baryone ; studied Marseilles and with
Vauthrot at the Paris Cons., gaining
st prizes in singing and opera ; dé-
ut, 1869 (?), at the Gr. Opéra as " de
Nevers " in " Les Huguenots"; 1870,
ang at La Scala, Milan, then in
New York, Egypt, Russia with Patti,
London, etc.; 1883, co-director Th.
talien, Paris, without succ.; has sung
n all the capitals as the supreme dramatic artist of his operatic generation;
is splendid impersonation and vocal
art carrying conviction after his voice
ost its youth; he created " Iago "

in Verdi's " Otello." 1887, and has
stamped " Don Giovanni " and other
rôles with his own personality as a
criterion.

Maurer (mow'-rĕr). L. Wm., Potsdam. Feb. 8, 1789—St. Petersburg,
Oct. 25, 1878 ; distinguished violinist
and dram. composer.

Maurin (mō-răṅ). Jean Pierre, Avignon, 1822—Paris, 1894; violinist
and teacher.

May, (1) Edw. Collett, Greenwich,
1806—London, 1887 ; vocal teacher
and writer. (2) Florence, pianist,
London ; daughter of above.

May'brick, Michael (pseud. Stephen Adams), b. Liverpool, 1844 ;
opera and concert barytone ; pupil of
Best (org.) and of Leipzig Cons.;
vocal pupil of Nava, Milan ; 1884,
toured the U. S. and Canada ; c.
popular songs, including " Nancy
Lee."

Mayer (mī'-ĕr), (1) Chas., Königsberg,
1799—Dresden, 1862 ; pianist and
composer. (2) Emilie, b. Friedland, Mecklenburg, May 14, 1821;
pupil of Löwe, Marx and Wieprecht;
lives in Berlin ; c. 7 symphonies, 12
overtures, an operetta, " Die Fisch-
erin," etc. (3) Wm. (pseud. W.
A. Remy), Prague, 1831—Graz,
1898 ; excellent teacher of cpt. and
comp.; composer. (4) Vide MAYER.
(5) Karl, b. Sondershausen, March
22, 1852 ; concert barytone ; pupil of
Götze ; lives in Schwerin.

Mayerhoff (mī'-ĕr-hôf), Fz., b. Chemnitz, Jan. 17, 1864 ; pupil Leipzig
Cons.; theatre-cond. various cities ;
from 1885, Chemnitz ; 1888, cantor
Petrikirche, and cond. Mus. Soc.; c.
sacred choruses. etc.

Mayerl (or Maierl) (mī'-ĕrl), Anton
von, Botzen (?)—Innsbruck, 1839 ;
pupil of Ladurner and Ett ; c. a Stabat Mater. etc.

Maylath (mī'-lät). H., b. Vienna, Dec.
4, 1833 ; pupil of his father (pf.) ;
toured, 1865 ; lived in Russia till
1867 ; then New York ; teacher and
composer.

**May'nard, Walter.** Vide BEALE, TH. W.

**Mayr** (or **Mayer**) (mīr), **(Jn.) Simon,** Mandorf, Bavaria, June 14, 1763—blind, Bergamo, Dec. 2, 1845; famous teacher and dram. composer; pupil of Lenzi and Bertoni; lived in Venice as church-composer; 1794 prod. v. succ. opera "*Saffo*," followed by 70 more; 1802, cond. Santa Maria Maggiore, Bergamo, and 1805, dir. Mus. Inst.; wrote a life of Haydn, treatises and verse; he is said to have been the first to use the orchestral crescendo in Italy; biogr. by Alborghetti and Galli (Bergamo, 1875).

**Mayrberger** (mīr'-bĕrkh-ĕr), **K.,** Vienna, 1828—Pressburg, 1881; conductor and dram. composer.

**Mayseder** (mī'-zā-dĕr), **Jos.,** Vienna, Oct. 26, 1789—Nov. 21, 1863; eminent violinist, teacher and composer; 2nd vln. of famous "Schuppanzigh Qua.tet."

**Mazas** (mä-zäs), **Jacques Féréol,** Béziers, France, 1782—1849; violinist, writer and dram. composer.

**Mazzinghi** (mäd-zēn'-gǐ), **Jos.,** of noble Corsican family, London, 1765—Bath, 1844; organist, teacher and dram. composer.

**Mazzocchi** (mäd-zôk'-kǐ), **Dom.,** Cività Castellana, Rome, ca. 1590—ca. 1650; composer.

**Mazzucato** (mäd-zoo-kät'-tō), **Alberto,** Udine, 1813—Milan, 1877; violinist, teacher, editor and composer.

**Mead, Olive,** b. Cambridge, Mass., Nov. 22, 1874; concert-violinist; pupil of J. Eichberg and Fr. Kneisel.

**Mear(e)s, Richard,** d. London, ca. 1743; son and successor of instrument-maker and publisher.

**Mederitsch** (mä'-dĕ-rǐtsh), **Jn.** (called Gailus), b. Nimburg, Bohemia, ca. 1705—after 1830, Lemberg; pianist and composer.

**Meerens** (mā-räns), **Chas.,** b. Bruges, Dec. 16, 1831; 'cellist and acoustician.

**Meerts** (märts), **Lambert (Jos.),** Brussels, 1800—1863; violinist, profes and composer.

**Mees** (māz), **Arthur,** b. Columb Ohio, Feb. 13, 1850; pupil of Kullak (pf.), Weitzmann (theory), H. Dorn (cond.), Berlin; cond. C cinnati May Festival Chorus; as cond. various societies in New Y Albany, etc.; 1896, asst.-cond. Th as Orch., Chicago; since 1901, co Mendelssohn Glee Club, New Yo writes analytical programmes, an pf.-studies; pub. "*Choirs and C ral Music,*" 1901.

**Mehlig** (mā'-lǐkh), **Anna,** b. Stuttg June 11, 1843; pianist, pupil of bert and Liszt; m. Antwerp m chant Falk.

**Mehrkens** (mār'-kĕns), **Fr. Ad.,** Neuenkirchen, near Otterndorf-Elbe, April 22, 1840; pupil, Lei Cons.; lives in Hamburg as piar teacher and conductor; from 18 cond. of the Bach-Gesellschaft; symph., a Te Deum, etc.

**Méhul** (mā-ül), **Étienne Nicol (Henri),** Givet, Ardennes, June 1763—of consumption, Paris, ( 18, 1817; one of the great master French opera, a student of o effects, and a special master of overture; son of a cook; pupil of old blind organist; at 10, stud with Wm. Hauser; at 14, his ass 1778, taught in Paris and stud with Edelmann (pf. and comp Gluck's advice and assistance tur him to dram. comp., after a su cantata with orch. (1782). He ( operas, never prod., and now los 4th was accepted but not perforn until after the succ. of the op.-co "*Euphrosyne et Coraaïn*" (Th. ) lien, 1790); 15 other operas follo with general succ. incl. "*Stratoni* (1792)," *Le Congrès des Rois*" (17 with 11 collaborators; 1705, insp or of the new Cons., and a mem of the Academie; 1797, "*Le Je Henri*" was hissed off as irrever toward Henri IV., though the ↑ overture had been demanded th

nes ; the opera buffa " *L'irato, ou
mporté*" (1801) made great succ.
d lightened the quality of later op-
as ; his best work was "*Joseph*"
807) ; for four years he wrote only
llets ; he left 6 unprod. operas incl.
*Valentine de Milan*," completed by
aussoigne-Méhul, and prod. 1822 ;
c. also inferior symphs. and pf.-
natas, and very pop. choruses
*Chant du départ*," "*C. de victoire*,"
*Chant de retour*," etc. Biogr. by
eillard, 1859, and A. Pougin,
89.

bo:n (mī'-bôm) (or **Meibo'mius**),
Iarcus, Tönning, Schleswig, 1626
—Utrecht, 1711 ; theorist and col-
ctor ; his great work is a valuable
storical coll. of old composers.

fred (mĕ-frä), **Jos. J. P. Émile**,
olmars, Basses-Alps, 1791—Paris,
867 ; horn-virtuoso, professor and
riter.

iland (mī'-länt), **Jakob**, Senften-
erg, Upper Lusatia, 1542—Celle,
577 ; important contrapuntist.

inardus (mī-nar'-doos), **L. Sieg-
ied**, Hooksiel, Oldenburg, 1827—
ielefeld, 1896 ; writer and dram.
omposer.

iners (mī'-nĕrs), **Giov. Bat.**, Milan,
826—Cortenova, Como, 1897 ; conuctor and dram. composer.

issen (mīs'-sĕn), **H. von** (called
'rauenlob, " woman-praise "); 14th
ent. German singer, poet, and re-
uted founder of the Meistersinger
7. D. D.) at Mainz, 1311.

ister (mī'-shtĕr), **K. Severin**, Kö-
igstein (Taunus), 1818—Montabaur,
Westerwald), 1881 ; teacher and
us. director.

l (mĕl), **Rinaldo del**, Flemish
usician, 16th cent.

la (mä'-lä), (1) **del M.** Vide DEL
KELA. (2) **Vincenzo**, Verona, 1821
—Cologna, Vaneta, 1897 ; dram.
omposer.

lani (mä-lä'-nē), **Amelia**, b. Pistoia,
876 ; soprano ; pupil of Galetti ;
ébut, Florence, 1896 (?) ; has sung
isewhere with success.

**40**

**Melba** (mĕl'-bä), **Nellie** (rightly **Mit-
chell**, " Melba " being a stage-name
from her birthplace), b. Melbourne,
Australia, 1865 ; one of the chief
colorature-sopranos of her time, with
a voice of great range, purity and
flexibility ; pupil of Mme. Marchesi :
début Th. de la Monnaie, Brussels,
1887, as " Gilda " in " *Rigoletto* ";
has sung in Europe and America with
greatest succ. in both opera and concert.

**Melcer** (mĕl'-tsĕr), **H. von**, b. Warsaw,
Oct. 25, 1869; pianist and composer ;
1895 won Rubinstein prize with Concertstück for pf. and orch.

**Melchior** (mĕl'-kĭ-ôr), **Edw. A.**, b.
Rotterdam, Nov. 6, 1860 ; teacher
and lexicographer.

**Melchiori** (mĕl-kĭ-ō'-rē), **Ant.**, Parma,
1827 — Milan, 1897 ; violinist and
composer.

**Melgunow** (mĕl'-goo-nôf), **Julius von**,
b. Kostroma, Russia, 1846 ; pupil of
Henselt and the Rubinsteins ; also
of Moscow Cons. and R. Westphal,
whose system he adapted to Bach's ;
pub. a coll. of folk-songs.

**Mell**, **Davis**, English violinist and
composer, 1657.

**Melone**. Vide BOTTRIGARI.

**Meluzzi** (mä-lood'-zē), **Salvatore**,
Rome, July 22, 1813—April 17, 1897;
eminent organist, composer and conductor.

**Membrée** (mäṅ-brä), **Edmond**, Valenciennes, 1820—Château Damont, near
Paris, 1882 ; dram. composer.

**Mendel** (mĕn'-dĕl), **Hn.**, Hatte, 1834
—Berlin, 1876 ; writer and lexicographer.

**Mendelssohn**, (1) **(Jakob Ludwig)
Felix** (rightly **Mendelssohn-Bar-
tholdy**) (mĕn'-d'l-zōn-bär-tôl'-dē),
Hamburg, Feb. 3, 1809—Leipzig,
Nov. 4, 1847 ; eminent composer of
remarkably early maturity. Great-
grandson of a Jewish sch.-master,
Mendel, who adopted Christianity
and had his children reared in the
Christian faith ; grandson of the
prominent philosopher Moses : son of

the banker Abraham M. Pf.-pupil of his mother, Lea Salomon-Bartholdy, as was also his elder sister Fanny (v. HENSEL). The family-life of the Mendelssohns is almost unique in history for its happiness and mutual devotion. **M.** studied also with L. Berger, Zelter (theory), Hennings (vln.) and Mme. Bigot (pf.). At 10 he entered the Singakademie, as an alto ; the same year his setting of the 19th Psalm was performed by the Akademie. Every Sunday a small orch. performed at his father's house, and his comps. were heard here early and often ; he usually cond. these concerts even as a child. 1825 his father took him to Paris to consult Cherubini, who offered to teach him, but the father preferred to have him at home. At 12 he began the series of 44 vols., in which he kept copies of his comps. This year he c. bet. 50 and 60 pcs., incl. a cantata, a mus. comedy, a pf.-trio, 2 pf.-sonatas, a vln.-sonata, songs, etc. At 9 he had played the pf. in public ; at 12 he was a notable improviser (while playing a Bach-fugue at Goethe's request he extemporised the Development which he had suddenly forgotten). At 17 he c. the remarkably original, beautiful and (in advance) Wagnerian overture to "*A Midsummer Night's Dream,*" and the superb octet for strings (op. 20). This same year he matriculated at Berlin Univ. with a translation of Terence, said to be the first German attempt to render Terence in his own metres. He also painted, and was proficient in gymnastics and billiards. At 18 he prod. the succ. opera "*Die Hochzeit des Camacho,*" at the Berlin Opera, in which he used the leit-motif (v. D. D.). At 20 he compelled and conducted the first performance since the composer's death of the Bach "*Passion according to St. Matthew*" at the Singakademie. This was the first step in the great crusade he waged, taking Bach out of obso-

lescence into the pre-eminence now keeps. 1830, **M.** declined chair of mus. at the Berlin Un The year before he had made first of nine voyages to Engla where he has stood next to Hände popularity and influence. He co his symph. in C minor, at the Lond Philh., which gave him his first o cial recognition as a composer. T same year he was invited (in vain) c. a festival hymn for the annivers of the emancipation of the natives Ceylon, and in his letters (in which sunny nature finds free play) he ferred to himself as "Composer the Island of Ceylon." He appear also with brilliant succ. as pianist a organist. He now travelled in Sc land, Switzerland, and elsewhere, a returning to London, conducted t "*Hebrides*" overture, played G min. concerto and B min. Capr cio brillant, and pub. his first "Songs without Words" (c. in V ice, 1830). His race and his amazi energy and succ. made him much position at Berlin, and he was fused the conductorship of the Si akademie in 1833, although he h arranged a series of concerts for t benefit of the Orch. Pension Fu 1833, he cond. the Lower Rh Mus. Festival at Düsseldorf, and came Town Mus. Dir. of the c mus., the opera, and two singing-s cieties, for a salary of 600 Tha (about $450). 1835, he became co of the Gewandhaus Orch., Leipz which (with Fd. David as leader) raised to the highest efficiency ; t Univ. made him, in 1836, Dr. Ph *h. c.*; 1836, he cond. his orato "*Paulus,*" the Lower Rhine Festiv Düsseldorf, in 1837 also at the B mingham Festival. 1837, he Cécile Charlotte Sophie Jeanrena of Frankfort, daughter of a Fren Protestant clergyman. She bore h five children, Karl, Marie, Paul, F lix, and "Lili" (Elisabeth). In 18 Friedrich Wilhelm IV. invited him take charge of the grand orch. and choral concerts at Berlin. The hostility to him was however so general that he wished to resign, but at the King's request organised the cath. mus., later famous as the "Domchor" (cath. choir). He was made R. Gen. Mus. Dir. With Schumann, Hauptmann, David, Becker, and Pohlenz, in the faculty, he organised the since famous Conservatorium of Mus. at Leipzig (since 1876 the "R. Cons."); he again cond. the Gewandhaus Concerts. 1845 he cond. "*Elijah*" at Birmingham. He resigned the Gewandhaus conductorship to Gade, and the piano-dept. to Moscheles, whom he invited from London. Upon hearing the news of the sudden death of his idolised sister, Fanny Hensel, he fell insensible and lived only 6 months.

M. was kept from opera by inability to find a satisfactory libretto. Besides "*Die Hochzeit des Camacho*" he left an unfinished opera "*Lorelei*," an operetta "*Son and Stranger*," and 5 small unpub. operas. He c. 3 oratorios, "*Paulus*" (St. Paul), "*Elias*" (Elijah), and "*Christus*" (unfinished), the symph. cantata "*Lobgesang*," op. 52; the ballade, with orch. "*Die erste Walpurgisnacht*," op. 60; 2 "*Festgesänge*," "*An die Künstler*" (for male chorus and brass), and "*Zur Säcularfeier der Buchdruckerkunst*" ("Gutenberg Cantata"), with orch.; mus. to the plays "*Antigone*" (op. 55), "*Athalie*" (op. 74), "*Œdipus in Colonos*" (op. 93), and "*A Midsummer Night's Dream*" (op. 61); c. also vocal works with orch., hymn, "*Tu es Petrus*," Psalms 114, 115, and 95, prayer "*Verleih' uns Frieden*," and sopr. concert-aria "*Infelice*" (op. 94).

4 SYMPHONIES, in C min.; A min. (or "*Scotch*"); A (or "*Italian*"); D (or "*Reformation*"). OVERTURES, "*Sommernachtstraum*" ("A Midsummer Night's Dream"), op. 21; "*Hebrides*," "*Die Fingalshöhle*" (or "Fingal's Cave"), op. 26; "*Meerstille und glückliche Fahrt*" ("Calm Sea and Prosperous Voyage"), "*Die Schöne Melusine*" ("The lovely Melusine") (op. 32), "*Ruy Blas*" (op. 95), "*Trumpet*" overture, and an overture for wind-band (op. 24); c. also andante, scherzo, capriccio, and fugue, for string-orch. (op. 81), funeral march (op. 103), and march (op. 108); 2 pf.-concertos, in G min. and D min.; capriccio brillant; rondo brillant, and serenade and allegro giojoso, for pf. with orch.; vln.-concerto in E min. (op. 64); a string octet, quartets, 2 quintets, a pf.-sextet, 7 string-quartets, 3 pf.-quartets, 2 pf.-trios, 2 trios for clar., basset horn, and pf.; 2 'cello-sonatas, a sonata for vln., variations concertantes (op. 17) and "*Lied ohne Worte*" (op. 109), for 'cello with pf., religious and secular choruses, 13 vocal duets, and 83 songs. FOR PIANO—3 sonatas; capriccio; Charakterstücke; rondo capriccioso; 4 fantasias, incl. "*The Last Rose of Summer*"; "*Lieder ohne Worte*" ("Songs without Words") in 8 books; "*Sonate écossaise*," 6 preludes and fugues, "*Variations sérieuses*," etc.; 6 Kinderstücke, 3 preludes and 3 studies, op. 104; "*Albumblatt*," "*Perpetuum mobile*," etc. 4-hand variations; 4-hand allegro brillant; duo concertant (with Moscheles), for 2 pfs. on the march-theme in Weber's "*Preciosa*." FOR ORGAN, 3 preludes and fugues; 6 sonatas, op. 65; preludes in C min.

Biogr. by his eldest son Karl (1871); by Hiller (1874); S. Hensel (1879); Eckardt (1888); an extended article by Grove (in his Dictionary), etc. Numerous editions of his letters are published. See also next page.

(2) **Arnold**, b. Ratibor, Dec. 26, 1855; grand-nephew of above; stud. ed with Haupt, Kiel, Grell, Taubert; organist and teacher in the

Univ. at Bonn; then teacher at Cologne Cons.; then at Darmstadt professor. C. operas "*Elsi*" (Cologne

City Th., 1894), and "*Der Bä*
*häuter*," " *Der Hagestolz* " for ch
and orch.

## Mendelssohn.

### BY VERNON BLACKBURN.

FELIX MENDELSSOHN BARTHOLDY almost rivalled Mo
in the precocity of his genius. Music came to him, as it w
straight out of the skies. He played with it from boyhood, and
the age of nineteen wrote his greatest work. I refer, of course, to the o
ture to "*A Midsummer Night's Dream.*" It would be difficult to
exactly whence Mendelssohn derived the leading motives of his musical t
dency. Mozart, of course, did much for him, but he was a brilliant, thou
I should imagine, a superficial, student of the great John Sebastian and of
train of German and Austrian composers, including Haydn, which succee
the period of that great master, Beethoven, with whom, of course, he v
intimate from his childhood. One remembers the story of his playing
of the symphonies to Goethe; but I doubt if Beethoven had a very seri
influence over this gay, companionable, brilliant musician to whom m
was not so much a spiritual as a pantheistic influence. ¶The external wc
to him fired his brain, and his delicate genius responded to the influen
His personality was neither commonplace nor profoundly interesting. Th
is a certain class of German youth which makes a point of exuberance,
high spirits and somewhat boisterous assertiveness of the bright side of li
Such a temperament is usually accompanied by a certain shallowness of spi
and by a certain naïf outlook which is just a trifle irritating to the seri
man. ¶His place in the art of music has not, I should imagine, been qu
definitely settled even at this day. While Sir George Grove would pl
him among the archangels of musical creation, there are others who prefer
rank him as quite in the front rank of the second class. On the whole, r
judgment ranges with the latter, although there are times, of course, when
strayed into the really great things of his art, as for example in the "*Wate*
*man,*" from the "*Hymn of Praise,*" or "*How Lovely are the Messengers*
from "*St. Paul.*" There will be none, however, I imagine, not even
George Grove himself, to rank Mendelssohn with Mozart, John Sebasti
Bach, and Handel, and that alone may be taken as a test as to whether
really may be placed among the great gods. ¶If I were asked to assign
position, in the flash of a phrase, I should call him the Ganymede, the cu
bearer of Jupiter's table. He was in the company of the gods, and he serv
them, he pleased them well; and his dwelling-place was in the palace

e ; but he was not of royal rank, though he wore the livery of the great
ςs of art. And his influence has been confined chiefly to the more elegant
g-writers of the time, to the composers of graceful and forgotten oratorios,
to the brilliant comic opera record of Sir Arthur Sullivan. And this,
ugh Mendelssohn, after arriving at man's estate, never wrote a note that
icates him as possessing one flash of genuine humour. The disciple has
e indeed outstripped the master.

ndès (män-dĕs), **Catulle**, b. Bor-
eaux, May 22, 1841. Poet ; libret-
st of pop. poems and operettas.

ngal (män-gäl), **Martin Jos.**,
ghent, 1784—1851 ; horn-virtuoso
nd dram. composer.

ngelberg (meng'-ĕl-bĕrkh), **Wm.
os.**, b. Utrecht, May 28, 1870 ;
upil of Umland, Hol, Wurff, and
'etré at Amsterdam, then at Cologne
Cons., 1891. dir. at Lucerne, 1895,
Amsterdam ; at 8 began to compose.

ngewein (mĕng'-ĕ-vīn), **K.**, b.
Zaunroda, Thuringia, Sept. 9, 1852 ;
rom 1881–86, teacher at Freuden-
ֵerg's Cons. Wiesbaden ; co-founder
ִf a Cons. at Berlin, 1886 ; c. orato-
io, festival cantata, operetta, over-
ֻure " *Dornröschen*," etc.

ngozzi (mĕn-gôd'-zē), **Bdo.**, Flor-
ִnce, 1758—Paris, March, 1800 ;
ֵenor, writer and composer of 13 op-
ֵras.

ֵnter (mĕn'-tĕr), (1) **Jos.**, Deuten-
ִofen, Bavaria, 1808—Munich, 1856:
ִcellist. (2) (**Menter-Popper**) **So-
ֵhie**, b. Munich, July 29, 1848;
ֵaughter of above ; eminent pianist;
ֵupil of Schönchen, Lebert and Niest;
lébut, 1863; in 1867, studied with
Tausig ; 1869, with Liszt ; 1872, m.
ִhe 'cellist Popper (divorced 1886) ;
ִt.-pianist to the Emperor of Austria;
ἰ878–87, prof. St. Petersburg Cons. ;
ֵives at her country-seat, Castle Itter,
ֵn the Tyrol.

ֵrbecke, **J.** Vide MARBECK.

ֵrcadante (mĕr-kä-dän'-tĕ), **Fran.
Saverio**, Altamura, Sept. 17, 1795—
Naples, Dec. 17, 1870 ; pupil of Zin-
garelli and in 1840 his successor as

dir. of Naples Cons.; in 1819 prod.
an opera with great succ. and followed it with 60 others, incl. " *Elisa
e Claudio*" (Naples, 1866), " *Il Giu-
ramento*" (Milan, 1837) ; he lived in
various cities ; 1833 cond. at Novara
Cath.; 1862 he went blind ; he c. also
2 symphonies, 4 funeral symphonies,
20 masses, etc.

**Mercadier** (mĕr-kăd-yā), **J. Bap.**, Bel-
esta, Ariège, France, April 18, 1750
—Foix, Jan. 14, 1815 ; theorist.

**Merck, Louis**, Landau, 1832—Brussels, April 15, 1900 ; horn-virtuoso.

**Mer᾿cy** (or **Merci**), **Louis**, Engl. virtuoso on the beak-flute, 1735 ; com-
poser.

**Méreaux** (mā-rō), (1) **J. Nicolas
Amédée Lefroid de**, Paris, 1745—
1797 ; organist and dram. composer.
(2) **Jos. N. L. de**, b. Paris, 1767;
son of above ; organist, and pianist.
(3) **J. A. L. de**, Paris, 1803—Rouen,
1874 ; son of above ; pianist, composer and writer.

**Merian** (mā'-rǐ-än), **Hans**, d. Leipzig,
1902 ; writer.

**Méric** (mā-rǐk). Vide LALANDE.

**Mériel** (mā-rǐ-ĕl), **Paul**, Mondoubleau,
1818 — Toulouse, 1897 ; violinist,
cond. and dram. composer ; dir. Toulouse Cons.

**Merighi** (mā-rē'-gē), **Antonia**, Italian
contralto profondo in Händel's operas, London, 1729–38.

**Merk** (mărk), **Jos.**, Vienna, 1795—
Ober-Döbling, 1852 ; violinist and
composer.

**Merkel** (măr'-kĕl), (1) **Gustav (Ad.)**,
Oberoderwitz, Saxony, Nov. 12, 1827
—Dresden, Oct. 30, 1885 ; org. and

composer. (2) **K. L.**, wrote treatises on throat, etc.

**Merklin** (măr'-klēn), **Jos.**, b. Oberhausen, Baden, Jan. 17, 1819 ; org.-builder at Brussels ; son of an org.-builder ; took his brother-in-law, F. Schütze, into partnership, as "Merklin-Schütze," 1858 ; in 1855, est. a branch in Paris.

**Mersenne** (mĕr-sĕn'), **Marie**, Oize (Maine), France, Sept. 8, 1588 — Paris, Sept. 1, 1648 ; writer of mus. treatises.

**Mertens** (măr'-tĕns), **Jos.**, Antwerp, Feb. 17, 1834—Brussels, July, 1901; 1st vln. at the opera there and teacher at the Cons.; 1878–79, cond. Flemish Opera, Brussels ; later, dir. at Royal Th., The Hague ; prod. succ. Flemish and French operettas and operas, incl. "*De Zwarte Kapitein*" (The Hague, 1877).

**Mertke** (mĕrt'-kĕ), **Ed.**, Riga, 1833—Cologne, 1895 ; pianist, violinist, composer and collector.

**Mertz** (mărts), **Jos. K.**, Pressburg, Hungary, 1806—Vienna, 1856 ; guitar-virtuoso.

**Merula** (mā-roo'-lä), **Tarquinio**, b. Bergamo ; violinist and composer, 1623–40.

**Merulo** (mā-roo'-lō) (rightly **Merlot'ti**), **Claudio** (called "**Da Coreggio**"), Coreggio, April 8, 1533 — Parma, May 4, 1604 ; eminent organist, dram. composer and famous teacher ; pupil of Menon and G. Donati ; he was a leader of the Venetian sch. and bordered on the new tonality.

**Merz** (mărts), **K.**, Bensheim, near Frankfort-on-Main, 1836—Wooster, Ohio, 1890 ; teacher and writer.

**Messager** (mĕs-să-zhā), **André** (**Chas. Prosper**), b. Montlucon, Allier, France, Dec. 30, 1853 ; pupil of Niedermeyer School and of Saint-Saëns ; 1874, organist of the choir, St. Sulpice; cond. at Brussels; organist at St. Paul-Saint-Louis ; Paris, cond. at Sainte Marie des Batignolles ; 1898, cond. Op. Com. ; Chev. of the Legion of Honour ; 1901, mus.-dir. Covent Garden, London ; completed B cat's unfinished score, "*Franço Bas Bleus*" (Folies - Dramati 1883), following it with abou other comic operettas, and op incl. the succ. "*Le Chevalier d'. mental*" (Op.-Com., 1896); *Basoche*" (Op.-Com., 1890, Bre 1892, as *Zwei Könige*) ; m. I Temple (q. v.).

**Messerschmidt - Grünner** (mĕs shmĭt-grĭn'-nĕr) (Frau), Vienna 1847—1895 ; founded at Vienna first "Ladies' Orchestra."

**Mestrino** (mās-trē'-nō), **Niccolò**, an, 1748—Paris, 1790 ; violinist, ductor, and composer.

**Metastasio** (mā-täs-tä'-zĭ-ō) (rig **Trapassi**, but changed to **M** pun. on **T.** to please his patron G na), **P. Ant. Dom. Bonavent** Rome, Jan. 3, 1698—Vienna, 12, 1782 ; poet and dramatist ; w librettos set to mus. by Gluck Mozart.

**Methfessel** (māt'-fĕs-sĕl), (1) **Al Gl.**, Stadtilm, Thuringia, 17 Heckenbeck, 1869 ; dram. comp (2) **Fr.**, Stadtilm, 1771—1807 ; of above ; composer. (3) **Er** Mülhausen, 1802—Berne, 1878, ative of above ; conductor. Ernst M., 1811—1886, conduct

**Métra** (mā-trä), (**Jules Louis**) **Oliv** Rheims, 1830—Paris, 1889 ; viol and double-bass player, condu and dram. composer.

**Mettenleiter** (mĕt'-tĕn-lī-tĕr), (1) **G.**, studied Ulrich, near Ulm, 18 Ratisbon, 1858 ; organist and com er. (2) **Dominicus**, Tannenhau Würtemberg, 1822—Ratisbon, 1.8 brother of above; writer and com er. (3) **Bernhard**, cousin of abo composer at Kempten, Bavaria.

**Metzdorff** (mĕts'-dôrf), **Richard** Danzig, June 28, 1844 ; pupil of Geyer, Dehn, and Kiel, Berlin ; c at various cities ; c. opera "*R munde*" (Weimar, 1875); succ. "*I bart und Signe*" (Weimar, 1893) also 3 symph. incl. "*Tragic*" ; o

e "*King Lear*" ; "*Frau Alice*,"
llade, with orch., etc.

zler (měts'-lěr), (1) **& Co.**, Lon-
n, mus.-pubs., founded by **Valen-**
**ke M.**, 1790. (2) **Metzler-Löwy**
ěts'-lěr-lā'-vě), **Pauline**, b. The-
sienstadt, 1850 (?) ; contralto ; 1875—
, Leipzig City Th.; 1881, m. the
,-teacher, (3) **Fd M.**

**rs, de.** Vide MURIS, DE.

**rsius** (mŭr'-sĭ-oos), **Jns.**, Looz-
inen, near The Hague, 1579—
nmark, 1639 ; prof. and writer.

**sel** (moi'-zěl), **Jn. G.**, Eyrichshol,
43 — Erlangen, 1820 ; writer and
itor.

**yer** (mī'-ěr), (1) **Joachim**, Perle-
rg, Brandenburg, 1661—Göttingen,
32 ; prof. and writer. (2) **Ld. von**
alled "**De Meyer**"), Baden, near
enna, 1816—Dresden, 1883 ; pia-
st and composer. (3) **Julius Ed.**,
itenburg, Germany, 1822—Brook-
n, U. S. A., 1899 ; vocal-teacher,
om 1852, at Brooklyn. (4) **Jenney**,
erlin, 1834—1894 ; concert-singer ;
65 teacher, 1888 proprietress Stern
ons. Berlin. (5) **Felix**, b. Berlin,
eb. 5, 1850 ; son of (6) **Bernard**
us.-director) ; pupil of David ; vio-
nist in ct. chapel, Berlin. (7) **Wal-**
emar, b. Berlin, Feb. 4, 1853 ; vio-
nist, pupil of Joachim ; 1873–81,
ember of the Berlin ct. orch. (8)
ustav, b. Königsberg, Prussia,
ine 14. 1859 ; pupil of Leipzig
ons.; cond. various cities ; 1895,
eipzig City Th.; c. 4-act farce, bal-
t-pantomime, etc.

**yerbeer** (mī'-ěr-bār), **Giacomo**
ightly **Jakob Liebmann Beer**,
y adding the name "Meyer" he se-
ired a large inheritance from a
ealthy relative ; he then Italianised
acob" as "Giacomo"), Berlin, Sept.
, 1791 (94 ?)—Paris, May 2, 1864 ;
on of a Jewish banker ; a precocious
nd remarkable pianist ; pupil of
auska and Clementi, at 7 played in
ublic ; studied with Zelter, Anselm,
Veber ; 1810, was invited by Abbé
ogler to live in his house as a son

and pupil ; did so for 2 years, one of
his fellow-pupils being his devoted
friend C. M. von Weber. Here he
c. an oratorio and 2 operas "*Jeph-*
*thas Gelübde*" (Ct.-Op., Munich,
1813) and "*Abimilek*" (Munich,
1813), the first a failure, the latter
accepted for Vienna, whither he went
and made a great succ. as pianist
though his opera was not a succ. In
his discouragement Salieri told him
he needed only to understand the
voice, and advised an Italian journey. He went to Venice in 1815
and, carried away with Rossini's
vogue, c. 6 Italian operas which had
succ., especially "*Il Crociato in Egit-*
*to*" (Venice, 1824). While writing
this last he went to Berlin hoping to
prod. 3-act German opera, "*Das*
*Brandenburger Thor*" ; though he
found no hearing, Weber begged him
not to give himself up to Italian influences. In the 6 years of silence
that followed, occurred his marriage,
his father's death, and the death of
his two children. In 1826, he went to
Paris to live, and made a profound
and exhaustive study of French opera from Lully down, forming his
third style, in which acc. to Mendel
"he united to the flowing melody of
the Italians and the solid harmony of
the Germans the pathetic declamation and the varied, piquant rhythm
of the French." He made a coali-
tion with the sophisticated librettist,
Scribe, and his first French opera,
"*Robert le Diable*" (Gr. Opéra,
1831), was an enormous succ., financially establishing the Opéra itself,
though **M.** had had to pay the manager Véron a large sum to secure its
production. Less pop. succ. at first,
but more critical favour attended
"*Les Huguenots*" (1836) ; its prod.
at Berlin, 1842, led King Fr. Wm. IV,
to call him there as Gen. Mus.-Dir,
His opera "*Das Feldlager in Schle-*
*sien*" (1843), had only mod. succ.
until Jenny Lind sang it in 1844.
1847, he visited Vienna and London

returning to Berlin he prod. Wagner's new work "*Rienzi*"; later he obtained "*The Flying Dutchman*" performance, after its rejection elsewhere. The extent to which he befriended Wagner is matter of bitter controversy, some claiming that he gave only formal assistance while Wagner was obscure, and fought him with underhanded methods and a "press-bureau," when Wagner attained power. At any rate Wagner despised and publicly assailed the music of Meyerbeer. Yet, whether or no Wagner borrowed money from **M.**, he certainly borrowed numberless points of artistic construction from him. In 1849, "*Le Prophète*" (finished 1843) was prod. at the Paris Gr. Opéra (1849) followed by the successes "*L'Étoile du Nord*" (Op.-Com., 1854), some of it taken from his "*Das Feldlager in Schlesien*"; and "*Dinorah, ou le Pardon de Ploërmel*" (Op. Com., 1859). "*L'Africaine*" (worked on with constant and characteristic changes from 1838) was prod. at the Paris Gr. Opéra, 1865, a year after his death. **M.** left by will 10,000 thaler ($7,500) for the foundation of a *Meyerbeer Scholarship*, for which only Germans under 28, and pupils of the Berlin "Hochschule," the Stern Cons., and the Cologne Cons., are eligible. Competitors must submit a vocal fugue *à 8* (for double chorus), an overture for full orch., and a dram. cantata *à 3*, w orch. (text of cantata, and text a theme of fugue being given). fund gives six months in Italy, si Paris, and six more in Vienna, M nich and Dresden together. **M.** also incid. music to "*Struensee*" ( tragedy by his brother, Michael Be Berlin, 1846), choruses to Æschy "*Eumenides*"; festival-play "*I Hoffest von Ferrara*"; monodra "*Thevelindens Liebe*," for sopr. so chorus with clar. obbligato (Vien 1813); cantatas, "*Gutenberg*" a "*Maria und ihr Genius*" (for silver wedding of Prince and Princ Carl of Prussia); "*Der Genius Musik am Grabe Beethoven*"; se nade "*Brautgeleite aus der Heimat* (for the wedding of Princess Louise Prussia) ; ode to Rauch (the sculpto with orch.; 7 sacred odes *a cappell* Festhymnus (for the King of Pr sia's silver wedding); 3 "Fack tänze," for wind-band, also sco for orch. (for the weddings of King of Bavaria, and the Princes Charlotte and Anna of Prussi grand march for the Schiller Cent ary (1859) ; overture in march-fo (for opening of London Exhibiti 1862) ; coronation march for K Wilhelm I. (1863) ; church-mus pf.-pcs., etc. Biog. by A. de I salle (1864) ; H. Blaze de B (1865) ; Ella (1868) ; H. Men (1868), and J. Schucht, 1869.

## Meyerbeer.

### By Irenaeus Prime-Stevenson.

**W**ITHIN a decade or so, especially since the Wagnerian measurin rule was applied right and left, up and down, to almost all t lyric drama, more in enthusiasm than in good judgment, a also since opera-making has come to be talked of as a sort of ex science—Meyerbeer has been ungraciously handled by a certain school criticism. This school is rich in Podsnaps. If we can believe these ar ters and observers, Meyerbeer was a feeble charlatan in French opera, or

kind of opera, a vulgar and bawdy melodist and a commonplace orches-
or. Moreover, we must, by such critics, believe that the public as well
he critics have so thoroughly " found him out," that the popular interest in
works is over ; that " *The Huguenots*," " *L' Africaine*," and " *Le Pro-
te*" are works that bore everybody of true musical intelligence—" the souls
them fumed forth, the hearts of them torn out." ¶ Unfortunately for
e undiscerning prophets, their premises are obviously wrong, and their
lts are short-sighted. Meyerbeer is a composer full of faults. His
nsistencies are a continual irritation. His shortcomings are plain to
ear. His superficial, emotional side, too, is indisputable. He was
er sure of himself, or rarely so ; and that is fatal often to artistic strength.
when all is counted against him, Meyerbeer is still a great composer, an
ratic master to be reckoned with for a long operatic time to come ; and
for the world in general it is far from setting him aside when his best
res are the question. ¶ His splendid subtler mastery of true dramatic effect
after all, as emphatic as his cheaper method of making a point. He does
, alas ! sustain his melodies. He does not work out good themes as
y deserve, over and over. He gives-out, he resorts to noise and clap-
. His favourite rhythm ♩♩♩ ♩ is tedious. ¶ But notwithstanding all,
is a genius in dramatic, pathetic melody. He is constantly able to
ve us legitimately by his beautiful art as an orchestral colourist. He
tes for the operatic actor as a singer, perfectly and consistently, as well
for the operatic artist as a declaimer. He is a king at great musical
ases, words and music so linked that we cannot think of them as not
ether. And as a merely French composer Meyerbeer is of the first
k. A sincere and learned musician himself, especially influenced by
greatest and even severest German and Italian musicians, he is distinctly
escendant in artistic speech of no less than Gluck. One often finds
Gluck-like nobility of phrase in Meyerbeer's dialogue, a Gluck-like out-
rt of melody, to atone for all that is savoury of Offenbach or worse. ¶ As
Meyerbeer's influence on not only the French opera but in far wider range,
t is undeniable. French opera since his day has never set his monitions
de, from Halévy to Reyer : and Wagner (heretical as it sounds to say so)
ver quite drew away from the French principles in dramatic opera that he
en most repudiated—exactly as he repudiates his eternal practical debts to
eyerbeer for no vague kindness. ¶ Meyerbeer is the Scott, the Jokai, of
era, forever. Just as we forgive technical error or error of sentiment in both
re and there, so must we forgive Meyerbeer : and in admiring his best
nes much indeed is to be forgot ! ¶ Personally, he was a large-souled and a
od man as well as a man of finest cultivation and polish. His charities
re numberless and his large bequests have continued them. Take him

all in all, he is a creator and an influencer of, we may say, perma
dignity and honour in the general gallery of the really great, not merely
pseudo-great, operatic sovereigns.

**Meyer-Helmund** (mī'-ĕr-hĕl-moont),
**Erik,** b. St. Petersburg, April 13
(25 new style), 1861; pupil of his father
and of Kiel and Stockhausen; prod.
3 comic operas, incl. the succ. "*Der
Liebeskampf*" (Dresden, 1892); succ.
ballet "*Rübezahl*" (or "*Der Berg-
geist*") (Leipzig, 1893), 1-act burlesque "*Tischka*" (Riga, 1894); and
pop. songs.

**Meyer-Lutz** (mī'-ĕr-loots), **Wm., b.**
Münnerstadt, near Kissingen, 1829;
pupil of Eisenhofer and Keller,
Würzburg, 1848, in England, organist at Birmingham, then Leeds, later
St. George's R. C. Ch., London;
1869. cond. at Gaiety Th.; c. 8 operas, masses, etc.

**Meyer-Olbersleben** (mī'-ĕr-ôl'-bĕrs-
lā-bĕn), **Max, b.** Olbersleben, near
Weimar, April 5, 1850, pupil of his
father, of Müller-Hartung and Liszt,
on whose recommendation he was
given a stipend by the Duke, and
studied with Rheinberger and Wüllner; 1877, teacher of cpt., and comp.
R. Cons. of Mus., Würzburg; 1879,
cond. the "*Liedertafel*"; 1885.
"Royal Prof."; 1896, dir. "*Deutscher Sängerbund*," and co-dir. the Fifth
National *Sängerfest*, Stuttgart; c.
succ. romantic opera "*Cläre Dettin*"
(Würzburg, 1896), and a comic opera "*Der Hauben Krieg*" (Munich
Opera); overtures, "*Feierklänge*"
and "*Festouverture*"; fine choruses;
chamber-mus., etc.

**Mézeray** (māz-rĕ'), **L. Chas. Lazare
Costard de,** Brunswick, 1810—Asnières. near Paris, April, 1887; barytone and dram. composer.

**Miceli** (mē-chā'-lē), **Giorgio,** Reggio di Calabria, 1836—Naples, 1895;
c. 6 operas, 2 biblical operas, etc.

**Michaelis** (mē-khä'-ā-lēs), (1) **Chr. Fr.,**
Leipzig, 1770—1834; writer. (2)

**Gustav,** Ballenstedt, 1828—B
1887; cond. and composer.
**Theodor,** Ballenstedt, 1831—H
burg, 1887; bro. of above; orga

**Micheli** (mē-kā'-lē), **Romano,** R
ca. 1575—ca. 1660; conductor, w
and composer of notable canons,

**Mickwitz** (mĭk'-vĭts), **Harald vo**
Helsingfors, May 22, 1859; pia
pupil of Brassin and Rimsky-Ko
kov, St. Petersburg Cons., an
Leschetizky, Vienna; 1886, pf.-t
Carlsruhe Cons; 1893, Wiesb
Cons; composer.

**Mierźwiński** (mīrzh-vĭn'-shkĭ),
**dislas,** b. Warsaw, Oct. 21, 1
untrained tenor of short-lived far

**Mihalovich** (mē-hä'-lō-vĭch), **Edm**
**von, b.** Fericsancze, Slavonia, S
13, 1842; pupil of Hauptmann
von Bülow; dir. R. Acad. of M
Pesth; c. romantic opera "*Hagb
und Signe*" (Dresden, 1882); s
opera "*Toldi*" (Pesth, 1893);
lads for full orch. ("*Das Gei
schiff*," "*Hero und Leander*," "
ronde du sabbat*," "*Die Nixe*'
symph., etc.

**Miksch** (mēksh), **Jn. Aloys,** Ge
enthal, Bohemia, 1765 — Dres
1845; barytone and celebr
teacher.

**Mikuli** (mē'-koo-lē), **Karl,** Czernov
Bukowina, 1821 — Lemberg, 18
pupil of Chopin and ed. of stand
edition of his works, composer.

**Milanollo** (mī-län-ôl'-lō), (1) **Ter**
b. Savigliano, near Turin, Aug.
1827; at 4 hearing a vln. at ch
she became so frantic for one
she was given lessons, studied
Ferrero, Gebbaro, and Mora, at
rin, and played in public at 6; a
wards touring with great succ. ti
1857 she m. military engineer,
mentier; lived in Toulouse.

ipanion on her tours was her sis-
(2) **Maria,** 1832—(of consump-
i) Paris, 1848. Also a violin-

imeyer (mĭlkh'-mī-ĕr), **Ph.** Ja-
ɔ, Frankfort - on - Main, 1750—
issburg, 1813, pf.-teacher ; inv. a
ianual pf.; composer.

e (mēl'-dĕ), (1) **Hans Feodor**
ı, b. Petronek, near Vienna, April
1821 ; pupil of Hauser and Man-
Garcia ; created " Telramund " in
iengrin, Weimar, 1850 ; life-mem-
of the Weimar ct.-opera. (2)
isa (née **Agthe**), b. Weimar,
ie 25, 1827 ; wife of above ; cre-
i " Elsa," sang at Weimar till
6. (3) **Fz. von,** b. Weimar,
rch 4, 1855 ; son and pupil of (1)
l (2) ; barytone, since 1878 at Han-
r ct.-th. (4) **Rudolf von,** b. Wei-
r, Nov. 29, 1859 ; son and pupil
ı) and (2) ; barytone ; début 1883
he ct.-th. and sang there till 1886,
ı in the New York Opera till 1888 ;
cher Stern Cons. till 1894, then
ig at Dessau ct.-opera ; 1897 sang
iunther " at Bayreuth.

er-**Hauptmann** (mēl'-dĕr-howpt'-
ı), **Pauline Anna,** Constantino-
. 1785—Berlin, 1838 ; soprano ;
thoven wrote the rôle of " Fide-
' for her.

ner (mēlt'-nĕr), **Moritz,** Turnitz,
iemia, 1812—Prague, 1865 ; vln.-
cher.

otti (mē-lē-lôt'-tē), (1) **Leopoldo,**
Ravenna, Aug. 6, 1835 ; studied
Rome and lives there as singing-
cher ; pub. songs and writes. His
ther (2) **Giuseppe,** 1833—1883,
l. 2 operettas.

ard', **Harrison,** b. Boston, Mass.,
ʃ. 27, 1830 ; studied in Italy ;
ɔr concert-singer ; toured Great
tain ; lived in New York from 1856,
singer and teacher ; c. an opera,
ɪd mass ; and many pop. songs,
. " *Waiting.*"

er, **Edw.,** Norwich, 1735—Don-
ier. 1807 ; organist, composer, and
ier.

**Milleville** (mĭl-lĕ-vĭl'-lĕ), (1) **Fran.,** b.
Ferrara, ca. 1565 ; conductor and
composer ; son and pupil of (2) **Alessandro M.,** organist, and composer
to the Ducal Court.

**Mil'lico, Giuseppe,** b. Modena, 1739 ;
male soprano, and dram. composer.

**Millöcker** (mĭl'-lĕk-ĕr), **K.,** b. Vienna,
March 29, 1842 ; pupil of the Cons.;
1864, th.-cond. at Graz ; 1866, Har-
monie-Th., in Vienna ; from 1869,
Th. an der Wien ; c. many graceful
and succ. operettas, and comic op-
eras, incl. 2 prod. at 23, " *Der
todte Gast* " and " *Die beiden Binder* "
(Pesth, 1865); " *Das verwünschene
Schloss* " (1878), with songs in Upper
Austrian dialect ; the widely pop.
" *Der Bettelstudent* " (Dec. 6, 1881 ;
in Italian as " *Il Guitarrera,*" in
English " *The Beggar Student* ");
" *Die sieben Schwaben* " (1887, in
Engl. " The 7 Swabians "); " *Der
arme Jonathan* " (1890, in Engl.
" Poor Jonathan "); " *Das Sonn-
tagskind* " (1892); " *Nordlicht* "
(1897) ; c. also pf.-pcs.

**Mills,** (1) **Sebastian Bach,** Cirences-
ter, England, March 1, 1838—Wiesbaden, Dec. 21, 1898 ; organist ; pf.-
teacher, New York. (2) **Watkin,** b.
Painswich, Engl., ca. 1861 ; oratorio
and concert basso cantante, range
E♭-f' (v. PITCH, D.D.); pupil of Edwin Holland at the R. A. M., and of
F. Blasco, Milan ; of Sir J. Barnby,
Randegger, and Blume ; début, Crystal Palace, 1884 ; in America, 1894-
95.

**Milon** (mē-lôṅ). Vide TRIAL.

**Mil'ton, J.,** d. 1646(7 ?) ; father of the
English poet ; a scrivener in London,
and an excellent musician and composer.

**Mingotti** (mēn-gôt'-tĭ), **Regina** (née
**Valentini**); b. Naples, 1728 ; soprano.

**Minoja** (mē-nō'-yä), **Ambrosio,** Ospedaletto, 1752—Milan, 1825 ; singing-
teacher and composer.

**Mirande** (mē-räṅd), **Hippolyte,** b.
Lyons, May 4, 1862 : pupil of Du-

bois and Guiraud, Paris Cons.; 1886–90, prof. Geneva Cons.; 1890, Sec.-Gen. Gr. Th., Lyons, and prof. of mus. history, Lyons Cons.; critic ; organist at the synagogue ; c. v. succ. ballet, " *Une Fête Directoire* " (Lyons, 1895) ; overtures, " *Rodogune*," " *Frithjof*," " *Macbeth*," " *Prométhée*," and " *La mort de Roland*," etc.

**Mirus** (mē'-roos), b. Klagenfurt, 1856; studied in Italy ; barytone and composer ; since 1891, lives in Vienna.

**Miry** (mē'-rē), **Karel**, Ghent, 1823—1889 ; professor and dram. composer.

**Missa** (mīs'-sä), **Edmond Jean Louis**, b. Rheims, June 12, 1861 ; pupil of Massenet, Paris Cons. ; won Prix Cressent ; lives in Paris, as teacher ; c. an op. com., " *Juge et Partie* " (Op.-Com., 1886), followed by others, also pantomimes, revieus, *Ninon de Lenclos* lyric episode (1895), etc.

**Mitterwurzer** (mĭt - tĕr - voor - tsĕr), **Anton**, Sterzing, Tyrol, 1818—Döbling, near Vienna, 1872 ; barytone.

**Mizler** (mĭts'-lĕr), **Lorenz Chp.** (ennobled as **M. von Kolof**), Heidenheim, Würtemberg, 1711—Warsaw, 1778 ; writer, editor and composer.

**Mlynarski** (m'lē-när'-shkĭ), **Emil**, b. Poland, 1850; violinist ; dir. opera, Warsaw.

**Modernus** (mō-der'-noos), **Jacobus** (rightly **Jacque Moderne**; called **Grand Jacques**, or **J. M. de Pinguento**, because of his stoutness) ; cond. at Notre Dame, Lyons ; pub. and composer, 1732–58.

**Moffat, Alfred E.**, b. Edinburgh, Dec. 4, 1866 ; pupil of L. Bussler, Berlin ; c. cantatas.

**Mohr** (mōr), **Hn.**, Nieustadt, 1830—Philadelphia, 1896 ; composer.

**Möhring** (mä'-rĭng), **Fd.**, Alt-Ruppin, 1816—Wiesbaden, 1887 ; organist, teacher, and dram. composer.

**Moir, Frank Lewis**, b. Market Harborough, Engl., April 22, 1852 ; studied painting at S. Kensington, also mus.; won scholarship Nat. Training Sch. (1876) ; c. a comic

opera, church - services, mad[?] " *When at Chloe's Eyes I G[?]* " (Madr. Soc. prize, 1881), many songs, etc.

**Mol, de.** Vide DEMOL.

**Molique** (mōl-ēk'), **Wm. Bd.**, N[?] berg, Oct. 7, 1802—Cannstadt, 10, 1869 ; eminent violinist ; son pupil of a town-musician ; stu[?] with Rovelli on royal stipend ; r successor of R. as leader of Mu[?] orch.; studied with Spohr ; r " Musik-direktor " at Stuttgart; 1[?] 66, London ; also toured with g[?] succ.; c. an oratorio, 6 famous [?] concertos, etc.

**Mollenhauer** (mōl'-lĕn-how-ĕr), t[?] brothers, b. at Erfurt. (1) **Fr.**, 18[?] 1901; violinist and composer. (2) [?] 1825 ; 'cellist. (3) **Ed.**, April 1827, violinist; pupil of Ernst, ar[?] Spohr; 1853, New York, founde[?] vln.-sch.; one of the originator[?] the " Conservatory System " America ; c. 2 operas ; 3 sympho[?] incl. the " *Passion*," string-quar[?] vln.-pcs., etc. (4) **Emil**, b. Br[?] lyn, U. S. A., 1855 ; son of (1) ; linist at 9, then with Boston Sy[?] Orch., now cond. Boston Ha[?] and Haydn Societies.

**Moller** (or **Möller**) (mōl'-lĕr, or ler), **Joachim**. Vide BURGK.

**Molloy, Jas. Lyman**, b. Corno[?] Ireland, 1837; c. operettas ; Irish melodies with new accom[?] ments and c. pop. songs.

**Momigny** (mō-mēn'-yē), **Jérome de**, Philippeville, 1762—? ; orga[?] theorist and dram. composer.

**Momolet'to.** Vide ALBERTINI, M[?]

**Monasterio** (mō-näs-tā'-rĭ-ò), **G**[?] b. Potes, Spain, March 21, 1 violinist ; début at 9, then pup[?] De Bériot, Brussels Cons.; ma[?] succ. tours ; 1861 founded Qu[?] Soc., Madrid; ct.-violinist, prof., (1894) dir. Madrid Cons.; c. vln.-pcs.

**Monbelli** (môn-bĕl'-lē), **Marie** Cadiz, Feb. 13, 1843 ; soprano ; pil of Mme. Garcia, Paris.

ndonville (môn-dôn-vē'-yŭ), J.
os. Cassanea de (de M. being his
ife's maiden name), Narbonne,
711—Belleville, near Paris, 1772 ;
olinist, conductor and dram. com-
oser.

niuszko (mō-nĭ-oosh'-kō), Stanis-
.w, Ubiel, Lithuania, May 5, 1813
-Warsaw, June 4, 1872 ; pupil of
reyer and Rungenhagen ; l. Berlin,
.en at Wilna ; c. 15 notable Polish
eras, also masses, songs, etc.; or-
.nist, director, professor. Biogr. by
. Walicki (Warsaw, 1873).

ık, (1) Edwin G., b. Frome,
.ngl., December 13, 1819 ; pupil of
. A. Macfarren ; Mus. Doc. Oxon,
56; 1859-83, organist York Minster;
.. choral books, etc.; c. 2 odes,
.ison service, etc. (2) Wm. H.,
.ndon, 1823 — Stoke Newington,
.ndon, 1889 ; organist, professor of
cal mus.; editor.

ipou (môn-poo) (Fran. L.) Hip.,
.ris, 1804—Orleans, 1841 ; c. of
.ht operas and songs.

.ro', H., b. Lincoln, 1774 ; Engl.
.ganist and composer.

.signy (môn-sēn-yē), P. Alex.,
.uquembergue, near St.-Omer, Oct.
, 1729—Paris, Jan. 14, 1817 ; ill-
.ined but melodious French comic
.era writer of noble birth but left
.or on his father's death ; became a
.rk, later steward to the Duke of
.leans ; he had studied the vln. as
.hild and now studied harm. for 5
.nths with Gianotti ; at 30 prod.
.succ. 1-act op., followed by 12
.ers, the last, " Félix, ou l'enfant
.uvé" (1777), the greatest succ. of
; immediately m., ceased to write;
.s stewardship and his royalties had
.ught him riches, which the Revo-
.ion swept away ; he was given a
.nsion of 2,400 francs ($480) a
.ar by the Op. Com.; 1800–02, in-
.ector at the Cons. ; 1813, member
.the Acad.; 1816, Legion of Hon-
.r. Biogr. by Alexandre (1819),
.d Hédouin, 1820.

Montaubry (môn-tō-brē). Achille F.,
Niorte, Nov.12, 1816—Angers, 1898
tenor.

Monte (môn'-tĕ), Filippo (or Philippus de) (Philippe de Mons) (dŭ-
môns), probably at Mons (or Malines), 1521—Vienna, July 4, 1603 ;
conductor and celebrated composer.

Montéclair (môn-tā-klăr), Michel
Pignolet de, Chaumont, 1666—
Saint - Denis, n. Paris, Sept., 1737 ;
double-bass player ; dram. composer
and writer of methods.

Monteverde (môn-tā-vĕr'-dĕ) (he
signed his name, Monteverdi),Clau-
dio (Giov. A.), Cremona (bapt.,
May 15), 1567—Venice, Nov. 29,
1643 ; eminent composer ; when
young, vla.-player in the orch of Duke
Gonzaga, Mantua, and studied cpt.
with Ingegneri. At 17 and at 20
pub. Canzonette à 3, and madrigals,
in which appeared (among many un-
intentional or unbeautiful effects) the
harmonic innovations for which he is
famous and which led Rockstro to
call him " not only the greatest musician of his own age, but the inventor of a system of harmony which
has remained in uninterrupted use to
the present day." His progressions
include the unprepared entrance of
dissonances, the dominant seventh
and the ninth (v. D. D., CHORD, PRO-
GRESSION, SUSPENSION, PREPARA-
TION, etc.). He was bitterly assailed
in pamphlets, particularly by Artuso,
and he replied in kind. The outcome
was his complete triumph and the establishment of the new school of
song and accompaniment. His victory, while salutary for art in general
and dramatic song in particular, was
too complete ; for the bigoted defend-
ers of polyphonic music dragged
down with them in their ruin the
splendid edifice of church-mus. built
to perfection by Palestrina and
others. 1603, M. became his teacher's successor as Maestro to the
Duke and c. for the wedding of the
Duke's son to Margherita of Savoy

the opera "*Arianne*," in which Ariadne's grief moved the audience to tears. In 1608 he prod. his opera "*Orfeo*" with the unheard-of orchestra of 36 pieces (Riemann states that "*Arianne*" was the 2d work and Orfeo the first). *Orfeo* was published in 1609 and in 1615, and the score shows great modernity, Rockstro comparing its preludes with one bass-note sustained throughout to the Introduction to "*Das Rheingold*," and its continual recitative also to that of Wagner.

In 1608 appeared his mythological spectacle "*Ballo delle Ingrate*." Vespers and motets (pub. 1610) gave him such fame that he was in 1613 made Maestro di Cappella at San Marco, Venice, at the unprecedented salary of 300 ducats (the usual salary had been 200), but it was raised to 500 in 1616, and a house and travelling expenses given him. 1621, his very romantic Requiem was given with effect. In 1624, he introduced the then startling novelty of an instrumental tremolo (which the musicians at first refused to play) into his Dramatic Interlude; "*Il Combattimento di Tancredi e Clorinda*"; 1627 he c. 5 dramatic episodes incl. "*Bradamante*" and "*Dido*," for the court at Parma; 1630, opera "*Proserpine Rapita*"; in 1637 in the first opera-house opened at Venice, the Teatro di S. Cassiano, operas having hitherto been performed at the palaces of the nobility (v. PERI), M. prod. the operas "*Adone*" (Venice, 1639); "*Le Nozze di Eneta con Lavinia*" (1641), "*Il Ritorno di Ulisse in Patria*" (1641), and "*L'Incoronazione di Poppea*" (1642). He earned the title of "the father of the art of instrumentation"; was the most popular and influential composer of his time.

In 1663 he joined the priesthood and is heard of no more. C. masses, psalms, hymns, magnificats, motets, madrigals, etc.

**Monticelli** (môn-tĭ-chĕl'-lē). Ar Maria, Milan, 1710—Dresden, soprano musico.

**Montigny-Rémaury** (môn-tēn-y mō-rē), Caroline, b. Pamiers, Ja 1843; sister and pupil of Mme. broise Thomas; studied at the and took 3 prizes; one of the French pianists of her time; 186 Léon M., a journalist.

**Moore,** (1) Thos., Dublin, 1779—Devizes, 1852; famous poet; p and singer. (2) Homer, b. Ame teacher at St. Louis, Mo.; there 1902, opera "*The Purita*

**Moorehead,** J., b. Ireland—d. composer.

**Mooser** (mō'-zĕr), Aloys, Frib 1770—1829; Swiss org.-builder.

**Morales** (mō-räl'-äs) (Cristof Cristofano, b. Sevilla; entere Papal chapel ca. 1540; em Spanish contrapuntist and comp

**Moralt** (mō'-rält), the name of brothers famous at Munich as a tet. (1) Jos., Schwetzingen, Mannheim, 1775—Munich, 1st violinist. (2) Jn. Bpt., M heim, 1777—Munich, 1825; 2d linist; composer. (3) Philipp, nich, 1780—1829; 'cellist. (4 Munich, 1781—1818; vla.-playe

**Moran-Olden** (rightly F. Tap horn) (mō'-rän-ōl'-dĕn), Fanny Oldenburg, Sept. 28, 1855; pup Haas and Götze; début as "F Olden" at the Gewandhaus, 1878, leading sopr., Frankfort; 89, New York; m. in 1879 the K. Moran; 1897, m. Bertram, singer at Munich.

**Morel** (mō-rĕl), Auguste Fran., seilles, 1809—Paris, 1881; dir. o Marseilles Cons. and dram. con er.

**Morelli** (mō-rĕl'-lē), (1) Giacc Venice, 1745—1819; librarian, Marco. (2) Giov., Italian bas London, 1787.

**Morelot** (môr-lō), Stephen, b. D Jan. 12, 1820; from 1845, c "*Revue de la Musique*"; 1847,

y the Ministry of Pub. Instruction
o study church-mus. in Italy ; wrote
work on plain-chant, an attempt to
evive ancient harmonisation, etc.

**ɯet'ti, Giov.**, Naples, 1807—Ceg-
ie, near Naples, 1884; cond. and
.ram. composer.

**r'gan, (1) G. Washbourne**, Glou-
ester, Engl., 1822—Tacoma, U. S.
., 1892; organist and conductor.
2) **J. Paul**, Oberlin, Ohio, 1841—
akland. Cal., 1879 : organist and
omposer.

ri (mō'-rē), (1) **Nicolas**, London,
793—1839; violinist. (2) **Frank**,
. Aug., 1873 ; son of above; com-
oser.

riani (mō-rǐ-ä'-nē), **Napoleon**,
lorence, 1806—1878 ; tenor.

richelli (mō-rǐ-kěl'-lē), **Anna Bo-**
ello, Reggio, 1760 ; violinist ; after
794, opera-singer.

rja, pen-name of **Moriz Jaffe**
v.).

rlacchi (môr-läk'-kē), **Fran.**, Peru-
a, June 14, 1784—Innsbrück, Oct.
, 1841; pupil of Zingarelli, Padre
artini, etc., from 1810 cond. of Ital-
n opera, Dresden ; c. many succ.
eras, also church-music, incl. Tuba
irum, inspired by Michelangelo's
*Last Judgment*"; biog. by Count
ossi-Scotti (1870).

'ley, (1) **Thos.**, 1557—1604; pu-
il of Byrd ; 1588, Mus. Bac., Oxrd ; 1592, Gentleman of the Chapel
oyal ; also Epistler and Gospeller ;
the only contemporary Shakespear-
n song extant, "*It Was a Lover
d His Lass*" from "*As You Like*
" pub. 1600 in one of his very
merous colls.; he wrote the first
iglish treatise on mus. (1597) still
luable, and ed. (1599) a curious
eatise on ensemble playing ; some of
s madrigals and melodious ballets
e still heard. (2) **Wm.**, d. 1731 ;
us. Bac Oxford, 1713 ; 1715, Gent.
the Chapel Royal ; c. one of the ear-
st known double-chants, songs, etc.

n'ington, **Garret Colley Welles-**
**y,** Earl of , Dangan, Ireland, 1735

—1781; father of the Duke of Wellington ; prof. of music at Dublin U.
and composer.

**Morse, Chas. H.**, b. Bradford, Mass.,
Jan. 5, 1853 ; 1873. graduate New
Engl. Cons.; studied with Perabo,
and Baermann, 1879; 1873, teacher N.
E. Cons.; 1875–84, Mus. Dir. Wellesley Coll.; from 1891, organist
Plymouth Church, Brooklyn ; pub.
collections of organ-pieces and composed.

**Mortier de Fontaine** (môrt-yä dǔ
fôñ-těn), **H. Louis Stanislas**, Wis-
niewiec, Russia, 1816—London,
1883 ; pianist.

**Mor'timer, Peter,** Putenham, Surrey,
1750—Dresden, 1828 ; a Moravian
brother ; writer.

**Mosca** (môs'-kä), (1) **Giuseppe**, Naples, 1772—Messina, 1839 ; conductor and dram. composer. (2) **Luigi**,
Naples, 1775—1824 ; bro. of above ;
prof. of singing.

**Moscheles** (mô'-shě-lěs), **Ignaz,**
Prague, May 30, 1794—Leipzig,
March 10, 1870; son of a Jewish merchant ; at 10 pupil of Dionys Weber,
Prague Cons.; at 14 played publicly
a concerto of his own ; studied with
Albrechtsberger and Salieri while
earning his living as a pianist and
teacher ; at 20 was chosen to prepare
the pf.-score of "*Fidelio*" under
Beethoven's supervision ; as a pianist
a succ. rival of Hummel and Meyerbeer ; he could not comprehend or
play Chopin or Liszt, but had large
influence on subsequent technic ;
after tours, he lived in London 1821–
46, when Mendelssohn, who had
been his pupil, persuaded him to join
the newly founded Leipzig Cons., of
which he became one of the pillars ;
c. 8 pf.-concertos, incl. "*fantas-*
*tique*," "*pathétique*" and "*pastor-*
*al*"; "*Sonata*" and "*Sonate sym-*
*phonique*," for pf. 4 hands, and
"*Sonate caracteristique*," "*Sonate*
*mélancolique*," and many standard
studies ; biog. (1872) by his wife
Charlotte (née Embden).

**Mosel** (mō'-zĕl), **Ignaz Fz.**, Edler **von**, Vienna, 1772—1844 ; conductor, writer and dram. composer.

**Mosenthal** (mō'-zĕn-täl), **Jos.**, Cassel, Nov. 30, 1834—New York, Jan. 6, 1896 ; from 1867, cond. Mendelssohn Glee Club, New York, also violinist, organist and composer.

**Moser** (mō'-zĕr), (1) **K.**, Berlin, 1774—1851; violinist and conductor. (2) **Aug.**, Berlin, 1825—(while touring America) 1859 ; son of above ; composer and violinist.

**Mosewius** (mō-zā'-vĭ-oos), **Jn. Th.**, Königsberg, 1788 — Schaffhausen, 1858 ; opera-singer and writer.

**Moson'yi** (rightly **Michael Brandt**), Boldog-Aszony, Hungary, 1814— Pesth, 1870 ; pf.-teacher and com-. poser.

**Mos'sel, Jan.**, b. Rotterdam, April 22, 1870 ; 'cellist ; pupil of Köhler and Eberle ; 1886 toured ; since 1888 lives in Amsterdam as soloist and teacher in the Cons.

**Moszkwa** (môshk'-vä), Prince **de la** (**Jos. Napoléon Ney**), Paris, 1803 —St. Germain-en-Laye, 1857 ; eldest son of Marshal Ney ; a senator, Brigadier Gen. under Napoleon III., also a finished musician ; cond. and dram. composer.

**Moszk wski** (môsh-kôf'-shkĭ), (1) **Morit**. ∖. Breslau, Aug. 23, 1854 ; son of a wealthy Polish gentleman; pupil of Dresden Cons., Stern and Kullak Cons.; teacher Stern Cons. for years ; later début with succ. as pianist, Berlin, 1873 ; until 1897 Berlin then Paris, as a composer, prod. succ. opera, "*Boabdil der Maurenkönig*" (Berlin, 1882) ; symph. poem "*Jeanne d'Arc*" ; "*Phantastischer Zug*" for orch.; 2 orchestral suites and a vln.-concerto ; c. many pop. pf.-pcs., incl. "*Aus. allen Herren Länder*," and "*Spanische Tänze.*" (2) **Alex.**, b. Pilica, Poland, Jan. 15, 1851 ; bro. of above ; critic, editor and writer at Berlin.

**Motti** (môt'-'l), (1) **Felix**, b. Unter-St. Veit, near Vienna, Aug. 24, 1856 ;

prominent conductor ; as a boy-s prano, entered Löwenberg "Ko vikt," then studied at the Vienn Cons., graduating with high honours cond. the Academical Wagnervere for some time ; 1880, ct.-cond. Carlsruhe, also, until 1892, con Philh. *Concerts ; 1893 the Gra Duke app. him Gen. Mus. Dir.; 188 cond.-in-chief, Bayreuth ; invited be ct.-cond. but he declined ; 18 declined a similar call to Munic gives succ. concerts London a Paris ; 1892, he m. (2) **Henriet Standhartner** (b. Vienna, Dec. 1866, now ct. opera singer at Weim and Carlsruhe). He c. succ. oper "*Agnes Bernauer*" (Weimar, 188 and the 1-act "*Fürst und Sänge* (Carlsruhe, 1893), prod. also a "Fe spiel," "*Eberstein*," songs, etc.

**Moun'sey**, (1) **Ann Shephard**, London, 1811 ; composer, teach and organist. (2) **Elizabeth**, b. L don, 1819 ; organist, pianist, guit player and composer.

**Mount-Edg'cumbe**, **Richard**, E of, 1764—Richmond, Surrey, 18 wrote "*Reminiscences of an A ateur*" ; c. opera "*Zenobia.*"

**Mouret** (moo-rā), **J. Jos.**, Avign 1682 — insane asylum, Charent 1738 ; conductor and composer.

**Moussorgsky.** Vide MUSSORGSKI.

**Mouton** (moo-tôn) (**Jean de Holl gue** (ôl'-lăng) (called "Mouton" Holling(?), near Metz—St. Wuen Oct. 30, 1522 ; important contrap tist.

**Mouzin** (moo-zăn), **P. Nicolas** (ca **Édouard**), b. Metz, July 13, 18 studied at Metz branch of the P Cons. ; 1842, teacher there, 18 dir.; 1871, teacher at the Paris Co writer ; c. 2 operas, symphs., etc.

**Mozart** (mō'-tsärt) (originally **M zert**), (1) (**Jn. G.**) **Ld.**, Augsb 1719—Salzburg, 1787 ; father of A. M.; dram composer. (2) (**Ma Anna** (called "**Nannerl**"), S burg, 1751—1829 ; daughter and pil of above ; pianist ; c. org. pcs

(3) **Wolfgang Amadeus** (bap-
ed Jns. **Chrysostomus Wolf-**
ngus **Theophilus**), Salzburg,
n. 27, 1756—Vienna, Dec. 5, 1791 ;
n of (1), and bro. of (2) ; one of
e major divinities of music. Of un-
alled precocity in performance,
mposition, and acoustic sensitive-
ss ; at 3 his talent and his discov-
y of thirds (v. D.D.), led his father
teach him. He began at once to
mpose little minuets which his fath-
and later he himself noted down.
e and his sister made a joint début
Munich, when he was barely 6,
ough he had appeared as a per-
rmer 4 months before in a comedy
the Univ. at Salzburg. He ap-
ared the same year in Vienna, fas-
ating the court. He now learned
e vln. and org. without instruction.
7 he was in Paris, where his first
rks were pub., "*II Sonates pour le
vecin.*" The next year he was in
ndon, delighting royalty, winning
e honest praise of musicians and
ming victoriously out of remark-
le tests of his ability as sight-read-
and improviser. During his fath-
s illness, while silence was required,
c. his first symph. Here his 6
natas for vln. and harps. were
b. and his first symph. performed
equently. He won the friendship
J. Chr. Bach, and was given sing-
g lessons by Manzuoli. Before
ving England he wrote a motet to
nglish words in commemoration of
visit to the British Museum. The
mily stopped at various cities on
e way home, the children playing
courts with constant succ., a con-
rt being given at Amsterdam in
66, at which all the instrumental
sic was **M.**'s. At Biberuch he
mpeted as organist without result
ainst a boy 2 years older, Sixtus
chmann. Returning to Salzburg,
1766, **M.** was set to studying Fux,
c. 1767 he c. an oratorio, 1768, an
era, "*La Finta Semplice,*" at the
nperor's request. Its production

was postponed by the now jealous
musicians till 1769. Meanwhile a
German opera "*Bastien und Basti-
enne*" had been performed, and **M.**
made his début as cond. in 1768 (aged
12), with his solemn mass. The Archbishop made him Konzertmeister,
with salary, but his father wished him
to enjoy study in Italy. His concerts
were sensations, the Pope gave him
the order of the Golden Spur (also
given to Gluck), and at his father's
behest he signed a few compositions
by his new title Signor Cavaliere
Amadeo, but soon dropped this.
After tests he was elected a member
of the Accademia Filarmonica of Bologna. At 14 he gave a concert at
Mantua in which according to the
programme he promises to play " a
Symphony of his own composition ;
a Clavichord-concerto, which will be
handed to him, and which he will immediately play at sight ; a Sonata
handed him in like mann, which he
will provide with variations, and afterwards repeat in another key ; an
Aria, the words for which will be
handed to him, and which he will immediately set to music and sing himself, accompanying himself on the
clavichord ; a Sonata for clavichord on a subject given him by the
leader of the violins ; a Strict Fugue
on a theme to be selected, which he
will improvise on the clavichord ; a
trio, in which he will execute a violin-
part *all' improvviso ;* and finally, the
latest Symphony composed by himself." In Rome, after twice hearing
Allegri's famous "*Miserere,*" long
kept secret, he correctly wrote out the
entire score from memory. At Milan
he prod. 3-act opera seria " *Mitridate,
re di Ponto*" (1770), which had 20 consecutive performances under his direction. 1771, he brought out a
dramatic serenade, " *Ascanio in
Alba,*" for the wedding of Archduke
Ferdinand. 1772 his friendly protec-
tor, the Archbishop of Salzburg, died ;
his successor, Hieronymous, Count of

Colloredo, treated **M.** with the greatest inappreciation, compelling him to sit with the servants (though **M.** was frequently entertained at the houses of the nobility with great distinction); and when **M.** demanded his discharge in 1781, he had him kicked out by a servant. It was for his installation that **M.** had c. the dramatic "*Il Sogno di Scipione*" (1775), "*Lucio Silla*" (1772), and "*La Finta Giardiniera*," prod. at Milan, under his own direction. 1775; later "*Il Re Pastore*" at Salzburg during Archduke Maximilian's visit. 1778 he went with his mother to Paris, where he won little attention in the struggle between Gluck and Piccini. At length after his mother's death he returned to Salzburg as Konzertmeister, and ct.-organist; but settled in Vienna, after prod. the opera "*Idomeneo*" (Munich, Jan., 1781). On commission for the Emperor he wrote ("*Belmonte und Constance, oder) Die Entführung aus dem Serail*," prod. with great succ., despite the machinations of the theatrical clique, 1782; a month later he m. Constance Weber (the sister of Aloysia, whom he had loved in Mannheim). She bore him six children, four sons and two daughters. The small receipts for compositions and concerts were quickly spent on luxuries beyond their means, and as neither was a good manager of resources, many hardships followed. After two unfinished operas he prod. a mus. comedy, "*Der Schauspieldirector*" (Schönbrunn, 1786). May 1, in Vienna, his opera buffa "*Le Nozze di Figaro*" ("Marriage of Figaro") was rescued from intrigues into a very great succ. The then famous librettist Da Ponte next wrote the book for "*Don Giovanni*" (Don Juan), which made a very great succ. at Prague (1787), and led the Emperor to appoint **M.** "chamber composer," at 800 gulden ($400) a year (Gluck, just deceased, had 2,000 gulden). 1789 he accompanied Prince Karl

Lichnowski to Berlin, playing for Dresden court, and at the Thor kirche, Leipzig. King Fr. Wm. hearing him at Potsdam, offered the post of 1st Royal cond. 3,000 thaler ($2,250) a year, **M.** would not abandon his "g Kaiser;" still Fr. Wm. II. ord three quartets, for which he paid ᵥ Hearing this, the Emperor ord the opera buffa "*Così fan Tu* (Vienna, 1790). Soon after its pro tion the Emperor died; his succe Ld. II. cared little for **M.**, lea him in greatest hardship. His voted friend Jos. Haydn now wer London. **M.** made a tour, paw his plate to pay the expenses. the coronation of Leopold II. King of Bohemia, at Prague, he invited to write the festival oᵖ "*La Clemenza di Tito*," perfor 1791. He returned to Vienna an "*Die Zauberflöte*" ("Magic Flu Vienna, Sept. 30, 1791), a worl which are exploited the allegorie the Masonry of which **M.** was a m ber. It made a decided succ. was, however, growing weaker suffering from fainting fits, clain that he had been poisoned. A r terious stranger had commissic him to write a requiem, and **M.** gan it with a superstitious dread the messenger had come from other world to announce his de It has since been learned that he Leutgeb, the steward of Count Walsegg, who gave the work ou his own, not, however, destroying MS. The work was not quite c pleted by Mozart, who had his p Süssmayer fill out the incomp portions. Mozart died of malig typhus. A violent rain-storm cor up in the midst of the funeral, the p turned back leaving the body t interred in some spot, never after covered, in the ground allotte paupers in the St. Mary cemet The profits of a Mus. Festival g by the Frankfort "Liederkra

25, 1838, were devoted to found-
Mozart Scholarship, the interest
nting in 1896 to 1500 marks,
ed quadrennially to the aid of
ted young composers of limited
s. At Salzburg the *Mozarteum*,
nicipal musical institute founded
memory, consists of an orch. soc.
;ed to perform his church-music
e 14 churches of the town, to
12 concerts yearly, and to sus-
a mus.-sch. in which the musicians
e orch. give instruction.
complete ed. of **M.'s** works pub.
eitkopf & Hartel (1876–86), con-
much church-mus. inc. 15 masses,
tas "*Davidde penitente*" (ma-
), "*Maurerfreude*" and "*Kleine
naurrercantate*," etc. ; stage-
s, besides those mentioned, "*Die
ldigkeit des ersten Gebots*" (only
ally his own), "*Apollo et Hyacin-
*" (Latin comedy with mus.);
*ide*" (unfinished); "*Thamos,
g in Aegypten*" (choruses and
actes ; Berlin, 1786) ; "*Ido-
o, re di Creta, ossia Ilia ed Ida-
e.*" ORCH. WORKS : 41 symph.;
mph. movements ; 31 diverti-
i, serenades, and cassations ; 9
hes ; 25 dances, "*Masonic Fu-
l-Music*" ; "*A Musical Jest*" for
g-orch. and 2 horns ; a sonata

for bassoon and 'cello ; phantasie for
Glockenspiel ; andante for barrel-organ, etc.; 6 vln.-concertos, bassoon-
concerto, a concerto for flute and
harp, 2 flute-concertos, horn-concer-
tos, a clarinet-concerto, 25 pf.-con-
certos, a double concerto for 2 pfs., a
triple concert for 3 pfs. CHAMBER-
MUSIC : 7 string-quintets ; 26 string-
quartets ; "*Nachtmusik*" for string-
quintet ; 42 vln.-sonatas, etc. PF.-
MUSIC : for 4 hands ; 5 sonatas, and
an andante with variations ; for 2
pfs., a fugue, and a sonata ; 17 solo
sonatas ; a fantasie and fugue ; 3
fantasias ; 36 cadenzas to pf.-con-
certos ; rondos, etc.; 17 organ sonatas, etc. VOCAL MUSIC : 27 arias, and
1 rondo for sopr. with orch.; German
war-song ; a comic duet ; 34 songs ;
a song with chorus and org.; a 3-part
chorus with org. ; a comic terzet with
pf.; 20 canons.

The best of many biographies
is by Otto Jahn (1856–59, 4 volumes in English, London, 1882),
etc.

His letters have also been published
and translated in two volumes. One
of his two overtures was found at the
Paris Cons. 1901. Six unpublished
sonatas were found in Buckingham
Palace, 1902.

## Mozart.

### BY VERNON BLACKBURN.

HN CHRYSOSTOM WOLFGANG AMADEUS MOZART,
the son of a tolerably good musician, by name Leopold, from his earliest years displayed the most extraordinary sense of musical precocity.
At the age of three years he was able to pick out harmonies on the
chord ; by the time he was seven, he had already burdened his young
ith the responsibility of various compositions which are more interesting
uch compositions might be expected to be. The darling of courts in his
ood (for his father took him early on his travels for purposes of exhibi-
a musical prodigy), the intensely industrious youth, the creator of a
tic art in music, separate and by itself in the world, the greatest master

of melody that this earth has ever seen, the writer of innumerable sympho innumerable songs, innumerable sonatas, the possessor of a musical me such as had never been conferred on the son of man before, he was the iant artist of high spirits, the man who lived life to the very last drop of glass. ¶In a word, a genius, in art and in living, of the highest flower. went down to his grave before he was forty years of age, buried no knows where, deserted of friends, deserted even in his last journey to Vienna cemetery by his wife; abjectly poor, with not a soul to weep him, not a soul to care what became of these sacred relics. Here was deed, a combination of glory and the darkest tragedy which can scarcel found outside the Attic drama. ¶Yet, from the critical point of view, it scarcely be said that Mozart was in any sense a revolutionary; he was glorious link which combined the music of the last century with the musi this. The strictest formalist, the impeccable master of counterpoint, respecter in every way of traditions, you can see him, as it were, on tiptoe of the future, bearing on his brilliant soul, and bearing it lightly, al burdens of the past. ¶But it is as a writer of opera that his fame is like to longest, for it is here that he brought the brilliant qualities of the consum musician to combine with the scarcely less brilliant qualities of the drama Many men who might have written music equally noteworthy could not touched the dramatic significance of it. "*Don Giovanni*," that glory of blood and state, "*Le Nozze di Figaro*," "*Cosi Fan Tutte*," "*Die Zau flöte*," these remain as noble a testimony of his great genius in the mus dramatic world as the centuries are likely to bring forth. Then consider G minor symphony—so different in quality from the quality of Beethove his best, and therefore not comparable to the great nine, but in its way very flower of musical genius. Then again, such work as he brought the *Requiem* declares him to be, as a master of the emotions, of supernat terror, unsurpassed; I would almost say unsurpassable. In a word, was the golden child of music, adding to the simplicity of his childishness complex wisdom of the serpent. ¶Poor Mozart! Yet, who is ordinary that he should say "poor" of such an immortal creature? Poor as it se to us, yet it is not likely that he would have given up one golden momen his glorious inspiration in exchange for the comforts of a Sultan. He wa artist, every inch of him.

(4) **Wolfgang Amadeus,** Vienna, July 26, 1791—Carlsbad, July 30, 1844; son of above; pianist, teacher and composer of pf.-concertos, sonatas, etc.

**Muck** (mook), **K.,** b. Darmstadt, 22, 1859; Dr. Philh., Leipzig; pu Leipzig Cons., cond. at various ci since 1892, ct.-cond. Royal Op.,

lie, **Thos. Molleson**, Chelsea,
)9—London, 1876; teacher, or-
nist and composer.

at (moof'-fät), (1) **G.**, b. Passau,
)4; organist, conductor and com-
ser. (2) **Aug. Gl.**, 1683—Vienna,
·o; son of above; organist and
nposer.

ldörfer (mül'-dĕrf-ĕr), (1) **Wm.**,
·3—Mannheim, 1897; ct.-inspector
:heatres, Mannheim. (2) **Wm. K.**,
Graz, Styria, March 6, 1837; son
above; studied at Linz-on-Dan-
e and Mannheim; actor; 1855, th.-
d., Ulm; 1867–81, 2d cond. at
logne; c. 4 operas, incl. success-
"*Iolanthe*" (Cologne, 1890), over-
es, etc.

lfeld (mül'-fĕlt), **Richard**, b.
zungen, Feb. 28, 1856; clarinet-
for whom Brahms c. a trio and
ata; studied with Büchner at
iningen, where he lived since 1873,
0 1875-96, 1st clarinet at Bay-
th.

ling (mü'-lĭng), **Aug.**, Raguhne,
·6—Magdeburg, 1847; organist
l composer.

lberger-Leisinger (lī'-zĭng-ĕr),
izabeth, b. Stuttgart, May 17,
·3; colorature-soprano; studied
h Viardot-Garcia; début, R. op.
, Berlin; sang in Paris, 1887.

er (mül'-lĕr), (1) **Chr.**, org.-builder
Amsterdam, ca. 1720–70. (2)
m. **Chr.**, Wassungen, Meiningen,
,2—Bremen, 1831; mus. director
l writer. (3) **Aug. Eberhard**,
rdheim, Hanover, 1767—Weimar,
·7; son and pupil of an organist;
·anist, ct.-conductor and dram.
nposer. (4) **Wenzel**, Tyrnau,
·ravia, 1767—Baden, near Vienna,
·5; conductor and composer of
0 operas. (5) **Fr.**, Orlamunde,
·6—Rudolstadt, 1871; clarinettist,
·aductor and composer (6) **Ivan**
**van**), Reval, 1786—Bückeburg,
·54; inv. of the clarinet with 13
·ys. and altclarinet; finally ct.-mus.
**Peter**, Kesselstadt; Hanau, 1791
·angen, 1877; c. operas, and fa-

mous "*Jugendlieder*," etc. (8) Two
famous German quartet parties, (a)
The bros. **K. Fr.** (1797—1873),
**Th. H. Gus.** (1799—1855), **Aug**
**Th.** (1802 — 1875), and **Fz. Fd**
**G.** (1808—1855), sons of (9) **Aegi**
**dius Chp. M.** (d. 1841, Hofmus.
to Duke of Brunswick), all b. Bruns·
wick, and in the orch. there—**K.**
as Konzertmeister, **Th.** 1st 'cello,
**Gv.** symph.-director, and **G.** conductor. (b) The four sons of the
**Karl Fr.** above, who organised 1855
a ct.-quartet. **Hugo**, 2d vln. (1832
—1886); **Bd.**, b. Feb. 24, 1825,
viola; **Wm.**, b. June 1, 1834, 'cello;
**Karl**, jr., b. April 14, 1829, 1st vln.
Since 1823 this last lives in Stuttgart and Hamburg; m. Elvina Berg-
haus and took name **Müller-Berg-**
**haus**, under which he has c. a symph.,
etc. (10) (Rightly **Schmidt**) **Ad.**
Sr., Tolna, Hungary, 1801—Vienna,
1886; singer, conductor and dram.
composer. (11) **Ad.**, Jr., Vienna
1839 — 1901, son of above; 1875,
cond. German opera at Rotterdam,
prod. 4 operas and 5 operettas, incl.
the succ. "*Der Blondin von Namur*"
(Vienna, 1898). (12) **Jns.**, Coblenz,
1801—Berlin, 1858; writer. (13)
**Fz. K. Fr.**, Weimar, 1806—1876;
one of the first to recognise Wagner;
pub. treatises on his work. (14)
**Aug.**, 1810—1867; eminent double-
bass. (15) **K.**, Weissensee, near
Erfurt, 1818—Frankfort, 1894; conductor and composer. (16) **Bd.**,
Sonneberg, 1824—Meiningen, 1883;
cantor. (17) **K. Chr.**, b. Saxe-
Meiningen, July 3, 1831; pupil of
F. W. and H. Pfeiffer (pf. and org.),
Andreas Zollner (comp.) 1854, New
York; since 1879, prof. of harm. N.
Y. Coll. of Mus.; translator, etc.
(18) **Richard**, b. Leipzig, Feb. 25,
1830; pupil of Zollner, Hauptmann
and Reitz; until 1893, cond.
"Arion," then the "Hellas," and the
"Liedertafel;" teacher singing, Ni·
kolai Gymnasium; c. motets, etc
(19) **Jos.**, 1839—Berlin, 1880; writer.

(20) **Wm.**, b. Hanover, Feb. 4, 1845 ; tenor at the ct.-opera, Berlin. (21) **Hans**, Cologne, 1854—Berlin, 1897; prof. and writer. (22) **Gustav.** Vide BRAH-MULLER.

**Mül'ler-Har ung, K.** (**Wm.**), b. Sulza, May 19, 1834 ; pupil of Kuhmstedt, Eisenach ; mus.-dir. and teacher at the Seminary ; 1864, prof.; 1869, opera-cond. Weimar ; 1872, founder and dir. Gr Ducal "Orchester-und-Musikschule ; " wrote a system of music theory (vol. i. "*Harmonielehre*" appeared in 1879) ; composer.

**Müller-Reuter** (roi-tĕr), **Theodor**, b. Dresden, Sept. 1, 1858 ; pupil of Fr. and Alwin Wieck (pf.) ; J. Otto and Meinardus (comp.) ; and the Hoch Cons., Frankfort ; 1879–87, teacher Strassburg Cons.; 1887, cond. at Dresden ; 1892, teacher in the Cons.; c. 2 operas, Paternoster, with orch; "*Hackelberend's Funeral*" for chorus and orchestra (1902), etc.

**Müller von der Werra** (rightly **Fr. Konrad Müller**), Ummerstadt, Meiningen, 1823 — Leipzig, 1881 ; popular poet and ed., founded " Deutscher Sängerbund."

**Münchhoff** (mĭnsh'-hôf), **Mary**, b. Omaha, U.S.A.; colorature soprano ; studied in Germany 1897 ; sang in Austria, etc.; 1902, U.S.A.

**Munck, de.** Vide DEMUNCK.

**Munzinger** (moonts'-ĭng-ĕr), **Edgar**, b. Olten, Switz., Aug. 3, 1847; studied Leipzig Cons. and with Kiel and Ehrlich, Berlin, where he is pf.-teacher, and 1893–98 dir. Eickelberg Cons.; c. 3 symphonies No. 1 " *In der Nacht*," No. 3 " *Nero*," an opera, 2 symphonic poems, etc.

**Muris** (dŭ mü'-rēs), **Jns de** (or **de Meurs**) (dŭ mŭrs), eminent theorist ; wrote treatise " *Speculum Musicae*" (probably ca. 1325) (Coussemaker).

**Murschhauser** (moorsh'-how-zĕr), **Fz. X. Anton**, Zabern, near Strassburg, ca. 1670—Munich, 1724 ; conductor and theorist.

**Murska** (moor'-shkä), **Ilma di**, C tia, 1836—Munich, Jan. 16, 1 famous dramatic soprano, with markable compass of nearly 3 octa

**Musard** (mü-zăr), (1) **Philippe,** F 1793—1859 ; c. pop. dances. **Alfred**, 1828 — 1881 ; orch.-cc and composer ; son of above.

**Musin** (moo-zēn), **Bonavent** Vide FURLANETTO.

**Musin** (mü-zăn), **Ovide**, b. Nan n. Liège, Sept. 22, 1854 ; violi pupil of Liège Cons.; at 11 too vln.-prize ; studied then at Cons.; at 14 won the gold meda solo and quartet playing ; taug year at the Cons. then toured Eu with great succ.; later organis concert-troupe and toured Ame then the world ; 1897, returnee Liège as vln.-teacher at the Cc 1898, vln.-professor.

**Musiol** (moo'-zĭ-ōl), **Robt. Paul** b. Breslau, Jan. 14, 1846; from 1 91 teacher and cantor at Röhrsc Posen ; pub. mus. lexicons ; c. songs, etc.

**Mussorgski** (moos-sôrg'-shkĭ), dest **Petrovitch**, Toropetz, Ru March 28, 1839 — St. Petersb March 28, 1881 ; army officer, pupil of Balakirev; c. operas, " *E Godunoff*" (Imp. Opera, St. P., 18 " *Chovanstchina*" (1893) ; c. pcs., etc.

**Mustel** (müs-tĕl), **Victor**, b. Ha 1815 ; mfr. and improver of the monium.

**Muzio** (moo'-tsĭ-ō), **Emanuele,** Zibello, near Parma, Aug. 25, 1 pupil of Provesi and Verdi, and pf.) of Verdi's first wife, Margh Barezzi ; 1852, cond. It. Op Brussels ; later, London, 187 (Acad. of Mus.) ; 1875 noted sin teacher, Paris ; c. 4 operas, etc.

**Myrzwinski** (mĕrsh-vĭn'-shkĭ), — tenor in Paris.

**Mysliweczek** (mē-slē'-vä-chĕk) (called " Il Boemo," or " Vena ni "), near Prague, March 9, 17: Rome, Feb. 4, 1781 ; prod. abou

. operas in Italy; c. symphs., pf.-
atas praised by Mozart, etc.

# N

f (näf), **Anton E. Aug.**, b. Wei-
trebelitzsch, Bohemia, Nov. 28,
o ; mus. editor and poet at Vi-
a.

baur (näkh'-bowr), **Fz.**, Schloss
ssen, near Friedrichshafen, March
1835—Munich, March 21, 1902 ;
il of Pischek ; sang at theatres in
gue and other cities ; 1866-90,
ammersänger," Munich.

ez (nä'-chĕs) (**Tivadar (Theo-**
-) **Naschitz** (nä'-shĭts)), b. Pesth,
y 1, 1859 ; vln.-virtuoso ; pupil of
atil, Joachim and Leonard ;
red the continent ; lived in Paris
l (1889) London; c. 2 concertos for
., 2 Hungarian Rhapsodies, requi-
mass, with orch., etc.

ud (nä-dō), **Gv.**, Roubaix, France,
. 20, 1820—Paris, 1893 ; cele-
ted poet, composer of chansons ;
c. 3 operettas.

rmann (nä'-dĕr-män), **François**
., Paris, 1773—1835 ; harpist,
cher and composer. (2) **H.**, b.
o; bro. of above and his asst.-
pist in the King's music, and asst.-
fessor.

el (nä'-gĕl), (1) **Julius**, Gotha,
7—St. Petersburg, 1892 ; 'cellist,
cher and composer. (2) Dr. **Wil-
ald**, German writer ; pub. "Ge-
ichte der Musik in England"
97).

eli (nä'-gĕl-ē), **Jn. Hans G.**,
tzikon, near Zürich, 1773—1836 ;
s.-publisher, writer and composer.

ller (nä'-gĭl-lĕr), **Matthäus**,
nster, Tyrol, 1815 — Innsbrück,
4; conductor and dram. composer.

li (näl'-dē), (1) **Giuseppe**, Bologna,
o—Paris, ca. 1820 ; actor. singer,
nist, 'cellist and composer. (2)
—— daughter of above singer ;
ut, 1819 ; retired, 1824 ; m. Conte
Sparre.

**Nal'son**, Rev. **Valentine**, d. 1722 ;
Engl. composer.

**Nanini** (nä-nē'-nē) (incorrectly **Nani-
no**), (1) **Giov. M.**, Vallerano, Italy,
ca. 1540—Rome, March 11, 1607 ;
noted Italian composer ; pupil of
Goudimel ; cond. at Vallerano,
1571-75, at Santa Maria Maggiore,
Rome (vice Palestrina); 1575 founded
a pub. mus.-sch. in which Palestrina
was one of the teachers ; 1577, papal
singer ; 1604 cond. Sistine Chapel ;
his 6-part motet "Hodie nobis cœlo-
rum rex" is still sung there every
Christmas morning. (2) **Giov. Bernardino**, Vallerano, ca. 1560—Rome,
1624; younger bro. (Riemann says
nephew) and pupil of above ; conductor and notable composer.

**Nantier - Didiée** (nänt-yä dĕd-yä),
**Constance Betsy R.**, Ile de la Reunion, 1831—Madrid, 1867 ; v. succ.
mezzo-soprano.

**Napo'léon, Arthur**, b. Oporto, March
6, 1843 ; pianist and cond.; at 9
made a sensation at the courts of
Lisbon, London (1852), and Berlin
1854), then studied with Hallé, at
Manchester ; toured Europe, and N.
and S. America. 1868 (1871 ?) settled
in Rio de Janeiro as mus.-seller, etc.

**Nápravnik (Náprawnik)**, (nä-präf'-
nĕk) **Eduard**, b. Bejst, near König-
gratz, Aug. 24, 1839 ; pupil Prague
Org.-Sch.; from 1856 teacher Maydl
Inst. for Mus., Prague ; 1861, cond.
to Prince Yussupoff at St. Petersburg ; then organist and 2nd cond.
Russian Opera ; from 1869 1st cond.;
1870-82, cond. the Mus. Soc.; c. 4
operas, incl. the succ. "Dubroffsky"
(St. P., 1895) ; symph. poem "The
Demon," overtures, incl. "Vlasta"
(1861), etc.

**Nardini** (när-dē'-nē), **Pietro**, Fibiana,
Tuscany, 1722 — Florence, May 7,
1793 ; noted violinist ; pupil of Tartini ; ct.-musician at Stuttgart and
Florence ; composer.

**Nares** (närz), **Jas.**, Stanwell, Middlesex, 1715—London, Feb. 10, 1783 ;
organist and composer.

**Naret·Koning** (nä'-rĕt-kō-nĭng), **Jn. Jos. D.**, b. Amsterdam, Feb. 25, 1838; violinist; pupil of David, Leipzig: from 1878 leader City Th., Frankfort; pub. songs, etc.

**Nasolini** (nä-sō-lē'-nē), **Sebastiano**, Piacenza, ca. 1768—(?); prod. 30 operas in Italy.

**Natale** (nä-tä'-lĕ), **Pompeo**, choir-singer and composer at S. Maria Maggiore, Rome, 1662.

**Na'than, Isaac,** Canterbury, 1792—Sydney, Australia, 1864; writer.

**Natorp** (nä'-tôrp), **Bd. Chr. L.**, Werden-on-Ruhr, Nov. 12, 1774—Münster, Feb. 8, 1846; reformer of church and sch.-mus.; writer.

**Nau** (na'-oo), **Mana Dolores Benedicta Josefina**, b. of Spanish parents, New York, March 18, 1818; soprano; pupil of Mme. Damoreau-Cinti, Paris Cons., taking 1st prize in 1834; début at the Opéra, 1836; sang minor rôles there 6 years, etc.; 1844–48 and 1851–53, leading rôles, singing in other cities; retired, 1856.

**Naubert** (now'-bĕrt), **Fr. Aug.**, Schkeuditz, Saxony, 1839—Neubrandenburg, 1897; organist and singing-teacher.

**Naudin** (nä'-oo-dēn), **Emilio**, b. Parma, Oct. 23, 1823; tenor; pupil of Panizza, Milan; début, Cremona. Meyerbeer in his will requested him to create the rôle of "Vasco" in "L'Africaine" (1865), which he did.

**Naue** (now'-ĕ), **Jn. Fr.**, Halle, 1787—1868; organist and composer.

**Nauenburg** (now'-ĕn-boorkh), **Gv.**, b. Halle, May 20, 1803; barytone and singing-teacher; writer and composer.

**Naumann** (now'-män), (1) **Jn. Gl.** (Italianised as **Giov. Amadeo**), Blasewitz, near Dresden, April 17, 1741—Dresden, Oct. 23, 1801; pupil of Tartini and Padre Martini; 1764, ct.-cond., Dresden; 1776, cond.; prod. 23 operas and excellent church-music. (2) **Emil**, Berlin, Sept. 8, 1827—Dresden, June 23, 1888; grandson of above; court church

mus.-dir., Berlin; c. an opera, mous oratorio "Christus der densbote"; pub. many valuable tises. (3) **K. Ernst**, b. Frei Saxony, Aug. 15, 1832; grands (1), studied with Hauptmann, Ric Wenzel and Langer, Leipzig (1 Dr. Philh. at the Univ., 1858; ied with Joh. Schneider (org Dresden; mus.-dir. and orgä Jena; prof., 1877; pub. many able revisions of classical work the Bach-Gesellschaft; c. the fir nata for vla., much chamber-mus

**Nava** (nä'-vä), (1) **Ant. Maria,** 1775—1826; teacher and com for guitar. (2) **Gaetano,** M 1802—1875; son and pupil of al prof. at the Cons. and composer

**Navál** (nä-väl'), **Fz.**, b. Laibach, tria, Oct. 20, 1865; tenor at Vie pupil of Gänsbacher.

**Nawratil** (nä-vrä'-tēl), **K.**, b. Vi Oct. 7, 1836; pupil of Notte (cpt.); excellent teacher; pub. I XXX with orch., an overture, c ber mus., etc.

**Nay'lor,** (1) **J.**, b. Stanningly, Leeds, 1838—at sea, 1897; org and composer. (2) **Sidney,** don, 1841—1893; organist.

**Neate** (nēt), **Chas.**, London, 1 Brighton, 1877; pianist, 'cellis composer.

**Nebe** (nä'-bĕ), **Karl,** bass; pu Jahn at Wiesbaden; 1890, at ( ruhe; sang "Alberich" and " messer" at Bayreuth and Lor 1900, Berlin.

**Ned'bal, Oscar,** b. Tabor, Boh March 25, 1874; vla.-player ir "Bohemian" string-quartet; st Prague Cons. (comp. with Dvc c. a scherzo-caprice for orch., e

**Neeb** (näp), **H.**, Lich, Upper I 1807—Frankfort, 1878; conc and dram. composer.

**Need'ler, H.**, London, 1685—pianist, violinist and composer.

**Neefe** (nä'-fĕ), **Chr. Gl.**, Cher 1748—Dessau, 1798; mus.-di ..nd conductor.

(năf), (Dr.) **K.**, Swiss writer; pub.
reatise on the amateur musical as-
ciations of the 17th and 18th cen-
ies.

, **Fritz**, notable composer, lives at
unich; c. "Chorus of the Dead"
th orch. (1902), etc.

rlich (när'-lĭkh), **Chr. Gf.**, Ruh-
id, Upper Lusatia, 1802—Berlin,
58; teacher and writer.

lhardt (nīt'-härt), **Jn. G.**, d. Kö-
rsberg, 1739; writer.

llinger (nīt'-lĭng-ĕr), **Wm. Ha-
ld**, b. Brooklyn, N. Y., July 20,
53; pupil of Dudley Buck and
üller; teacher of singing in Paris,
en Chicago; c. a mass, etc., pop.
ngs and valuable books of mus.
· children.

hardt (nīt'-härt), **Aug. H.**,
hleiz, 1793—Berlin, 1861; oboist,
icher of singing, conductor and
im. composer.

:zel (nīt'-tsĕl), **Otto**, b. Falken-
rg, Pomerania, July 6, 1852; pu-
of Kullak's Acad., Berlin; Dr.
ailh., 1875, at the Univ.; toured as
anist; 1879–81, teacher Moscow
ons.; then Cologne Cons.; since
87, also critic; 3 operas: "
*Angela*" (Halle, 1887), text and mu-
: of, "*Dido*" (Weimar, 1888) and
*Der Alte Dessauer*" (Wiesbaden,
89).

li, **Romilda**, b. Italy, 1882(?);
lorature and operatic soprano; pu-
l of Galletti.

'na, **Pomponio**, b. Bari, Naples;
b. madrigals, 1585—1631.

i (nä'-rē), **Filippo**, Florence, July
, 1515—Rome, May 26, 1595;
eacher in the oratory (It. *oratorio*)
San Girolamo. From the music c.
r illustrations by Animuccia and
alestrina arose the term "oratorio."

uda (nä-roo'-dä), (1) **Jakob**, d.
32; violinist. (2) **Jn. Chrysos-
m**, Rossiez, 1705—1763; violinist;
n of above. (3) **Jn. Baptist G.**,
resden, 1707—1780; composer, son
Jakob. (4) (**Noimann-Neruda**)
r **Lady Hallé**) **Wilma Maria**

**Fran.**, b. Brünn, March 29, 1839;
noted violinist (daughter of (5) **Josef**,
an organist); she studied with Jansa;
at 7 played in public at Vienna with
her sister (6) **Amalie** (a pianist);
then toured Germany with her
father, sister and bro. (7) **Fz.** (a 'cellist); 1864, in Paris, she m. L. Normann; since 1869 has played annually in London; she m. Hallé (q.v.),
1888, and toured Australia with him,
1890–91; 1899, America.

**Ness'ler, Victor E.**, Baldenheim, Alsatia, Jan. 28, 1841—Strassburg, May
28, 1890; studied with Th. Stern at
Strassburg; 1864, prod. succ. opera,
"*Fleurette*"; studied in Leipzig, became cond. of the "Sängerkreis"
and chorusm. City Th., where he
prod. with general succ. 4 operettas
and 4 operas, incl. two still pop. "*Der
Rattenfänger von Hameln*" (1879),
"*Der Trompeter von Säkkingen*"
(1884); c. also "*Der Blumen Rache*,"
ballade, with orch.; pop. and comic
songs, etc.

**Nesvad'ba, Jos.**, Vyskeř, Bohemia,
1824—Darmstadt, 1876; conductor
and dram. composer.

**Nešvera** (nĕsh-vä'-rä), **Jos.**, b. Pros-
koles, Bohemia, Oct. 24, 1842; now
cond. Olmütz Cath.; c. succ. opera
"*Perdita*" (Prague, 1897); masses,
De Profundis, with orch., etc.

**Netzer** (nĕt'-tsĕr), **Jos.**, Imst. Tyrol,
1808—Graz, 1864; teacher, con-
ductor and dram. composer.

**Neubauer** (nä'-oo-bow-ĕr), **Fz. Chr.**,
Horzin, Bohemia, 1760—Bückeburg,
1795; violinist, conductor and composer.

**Neuendorff** (noi'-ĕn-dôrf), **Ad.**, Hamburg, June 13, 1843—New York,
Dec. 4, 1897; at 12 taken to America; pianist, concert-violinist, prominent conductor and composer of comic
operas.

**Neukomm** (noi'-kôm), **Sigismund**,
Ritter **von**, Salzburg, 1778—Paris,
1858; organist, conductor and con-
poser.

**Neumann** (noi'-män), **Angelo**, b. Vi-

enna, Aug. 18, 1838 ; studied singing with Stilke-Sessi, début as lyric
tenor, 1859 ; 1862–76, Vienna ct.-
opera ; 1876–82, Leipzig opera ; as
manager of a travelling company
prod. Wagner operas ; 1882–85, manager Bremen opera ; then German
opera, Prague.

**Neumark** (noi'-märk), **G.**, Langensalza,
1621—Weimar, 1681 ; composer.

**Neusiedler** (noi'-zēt-lĕr) (or **Newsidler**), (1) **Hans,** b. Pressburg, Nürnberg, 1563 ; lute-maker. (2) (or
**Neysidler**) **Melchior,** d. Nürnberg,
1590 ; lutenist and composer at Augsburg ; 2 books of lute mus. (Venice,
1566), etc.

**Nevada** (nĕ-vä'-dä) (rightly **Wixon**),
**Emma,** b. Austen, Nevada, U. S. A.,
1862 ; eminent colorature-soprano ;
pupil of Marchesi in Vienna ; début
London, 1880; sang in various Italian
cities ; 1883 and 1898 Paris, Op.-
Com. ; 1885 sang Opera Festival
Chicago, and again in 1889 ; 1898,
Op.-Com., Paris ; 1885 m. Dr. Raymond Palmer ; sang " Mignon " a
whole year in Paris; 1900 America.

**Nevin** (nĕv'-ĭn), (1) **Ethelbert** (**Wood-
bridge**), Edgeworth, Penn., Nov.
25, 1862—New Haven, Conn., Feb.
17, 1901 ; prominent American composer ; pupil of von der Heide and
E. Günther (pf.) at Pittsburg ; of
von Böhme (voice), at Dresden, 1877–
78 ; of Pearce (N. Y.), B. J. Lang
and Stephen A. Emery (Boston) ;
von Bülow, Klindworth, and K. Bial,
Berlin ; lived in Florence, Venice,
Paris, and New York as teacher and
composer ; after 1900 at Sewickley,
near Pittsburg, Pa.; c. a pf.-suite ;
song-cycles " In Arcady," and a
posthumous " The Quest of Heart's
Desire " ; highly artistic piano pieces
and many song albums of well-de-
served popularity. His songs are
genuinely lyrical, with an exuberance
of musical passion, and accompaniments full of colour. individuality and
novelty. (2) **Arthur,** b. Sewickley,
Pa., 1871; bro. of above, from 1891

studied Boston, then at Berlin
Boise and Klindworth ; lives in
York ; c. songs, etc.

**New'man, Ernest,** b. Liverpool,
30, 1868 ; prominent critic ; stu
for the Indian Civil Service, bu
health broke down from over-st
engaged in business in Liver
where he has since lived , in
wrote " *Gluck and the Opera,*" w
was published in 1895 ; " *A Stu*
*Wagner*" 1899. Has contributed
merous scholarly essays on mu
and other topics to various magaz

**Newsidler, Neysidler.** Vide
SIEDLER.

**Ney.** Vide MOSZKVA.

**Niccolò de Malta.** Vide ISQUA

**Nichelmann** (nĭkh'-ĕl-män), **C**
Treuenbrietzen, Brandenburg,
—Berlin, 1762 ; cembalist and w

**Nicholl** (nĭk'-ôl), **Horace Wadh**
b. Tipton, near Birmingham, E
March 17, 1848 ; notable conte
rary contrapuntist ; son and pup
a musician John N.; studied
Samuel Prince ; 1867–70 organi
Dudley ; 1871 organist at Pittsb
Pa., U. S. A.; 1878 editor New Y
1888–95 prof. at Farmington, Co
contributed to various periodic
pub. a book on harmony ; his
notable compositions are his 12 s
phonic preludes and fugues for or
displaying his remarkable contra
tal ability (1 in quadruple cpt.,
triple, 4 in double) ; he c. al
suite for full orch. (op. 3) , a cycl
4 oratorios with orch.; symph. p
" *Tartarus*"; 2 symphonies ; a
chic sketch " *Hamlet*," etc.

**Nich'olson, Chas.,** Liverpool, 17
London, 1837 ; flutist and compo

**Nick'lass-Kempt'ner, Selma,**
Breslau, April 2, 1849 ; noted col
ture soprano and teacher , studie
Stern Cons.; début, 1867 , sang
Rotterdam 10 yrs. , then tea
Vienna Cons.; 1893, Berlin " *Pro*
*saria.* "

**Nicodé** (nē'-kō-dā), **Jean Louis,**
Jerczik, near Posen, Aug. 12, 18

pil of his father and the organist
rt..as, and at Kullak's Acad.; lives
Beriin as a pianist and teachet.,
78–85 pf.-teacher Dresden Cons.;
97, cond. Leipzig " Riedel Verein";
symph. poem " Maria Stuart";
Faschingsbilder," " Sinfonische
uriationen," op. 27; " Das Meer,"
nph. ode, for full orch.; " Erbar-
en," hymn for alto with orch., etc.

olai (nē'-kō-lī), (1) Otto, Königs-
rg, June 9, 1810—of apoplexy,
rlin, May 11, 1849; son and pupil
a singing-teacher; studied with
lter and Klein, later with Baini at
ome, where he was organist at the
ibassy chapel; 1837 – 38 theatrend. at Vienna; again in Rome,
41–47 ct.-cond. at Vienna and
inded the Phil., 1842; 1847 cond.
the opera and cath.-choir, Berlin;
od. 5 v. succ. operas, incl. " Il
mplario" (Turin, 1840; known in
ermany as " Der Templer," based
Scott's "Ivanhoe"); and the unct-
us and still popular opera " Die
stigen Weiber von Windsor," based
. and known in English as " The
erry Wives of Windsor" (Berlin,
49); he c. also a symph., etc.; biog.
Mendel (Berlin, 1868); his diary
Tagebücher") was pub. Leipzig,
93. (2) Wm. Fr. Gerard, Ley-
n, Nov. 20, 1829—The Hague,
oril 25, 1896; professor; notable
nductor and composer.

colini (nēk-kō-lē'-nē), (1) Giusep-
e, Piacenza, Jan. 29, 1762—Dec.
., 1842; conductor and operatic
mposer. (2) (Rightly Ernest
icholas) Tours, France, Feb. 23,
34—Pau, Jan. 19, 1898, tenor;
86 m. Adelina Patti.

olson, Richard, d. 1639; Engl.
ganist.

cks (nēks), Frederick (Friede-
ch), b. Düsseldorf, March 3, 1845;
cturer, critic, etc.; pupil of Lang-
ns, Grünewald, and Auer (vln.);
but at 12; 1868, organist, Dum-
ies, Scotland, and viola-player in a
iartet with A. C. Mackenzie; stud-

ied in Leipzig Univ. (1877), and
travelled Italy; critic, London; 1891,
Ried Prof. of Mus., Edinburgh Univ.;
pub. notable biog. of " Frederic
Chopin as a Man and a Musician"
(1888); a " Dict. of Mus. Terms,"
etc.

Nieden, Zur. Vide ZUR NIEDEN.

Niedermeyer (nē'-dĕr-mī'ĕr), Louis,
Nyon, Switzerland, 1802 — Paris,
1861; dramatic composer and theorist.

Niedt (nēt), Fr. Erhardt, d. Copenhagen, 1717; writer.

Niemann (nē'-män), (1) Albert, b.
Erxleben, near Magdeburg, Jan. 15,
1831; 1849, without study sang in
minor rôles at Dessau; then studied
with F. Schneider, and the bar.
Nusch; sang at Hanover, then studied with Duprez, Paris; 1860–66,
dram. tenor, Hanover, since at the
ct.-opera, Berlin; Wagner chose him
to create " Tannhäuser" (Paris,
1861), and " Siegmund" (Bayreuth
1876); retired 1889. (2) Rudolf
(Fr.), Wesselburen, Holstein, 1838—
Wiesbaden, 1898; pianist and composer.

Nietzsche (nēt'-shĕ), Fr., Röcken,
near Lutzen, Oct. 15, 1844—(insane)
Aug., 1900; prof. at Basel Univ.;
notable, if eccentric, philosopher; as
a partisan of Wagner he pub. " Die
Geburt der Tragödie aus dem Geiste
der Musik," " Richard Wagner in
Bayreuth"; while " Der Fall Wagner," and " Nietzsche contra Wagner" attack Wagner as violently as
he once praised him; his philosophical work " Also sprach Zarathustra "
provides the title of R. Strauss'
symph. poem.

Niggli (nĭg'-glē), Arnold, b. Aarburg,
Switzerland, Dec. 20, 1843; since
1875 sec. to the Aarau town council;
writer.

Nikisch (nĭk'-ĭsh), Arthur, b. Szent,
Miklos, Hungary, Oct. 12, 1855;
eminent conductor; son of the
head-bookkeeper to Prince Lichtenstein; pupil of Dessoff (comp.) and

Hellmesberger (vln.), Vienna Cons.,
graduating at 19 with prizes for vln.,
and for a string-sextet ; violinist in
the ct.-orch.; then 2nd cond. Leipzig
Th.; 1882–89, 1st. cond.; 1889–93,
cond. Symph. Orch., Boston (U. S.
A.) ; 1893–95, dir. Royal Opera,
Pesth, and cond. Philh. Concerts ;
since 1895 cond. Gewandhaus Concerts, Leipzig (vice Reinecke), also
Phil. concerts, Berlin ; he conducts
usually without score; 1902, dir.
Leipzig Cons.

**Nikita** (nĭ-kē′-tä) (stage-name of
**Louisa Margaret Nicholson**), b.
Philadelphia, Aug. 18, 1872 ; colorature-soprano ; pupil of M. Le Roy,
Washington ; sang in various cities,
with an opera-troupe, then studied
with Maurice Strakosch, Paris ; sang
in concerts with much succ.; 1894,
prima donna soprano, Paris Opéra.

**Nikom′achus** (called **Gerasenus**), b.
Gerasa, Syria ; Greek writer on mus.,
2nd century, A.D.

**Nilsson** (nēls′-sōn), **Christine**, b. on
the estate Sjoabel, near Wexio,
Sweden, Aug. 20, 1843 ; eminent so-
prano, compass 2½ octaves (g–d″) ;
pupil of Baroness Leuhausen and
F. Berwald, Stockholm ; later, in
Paris, of Wartel ; début, 1864, Th.-
Lyrique; Paris, engaged for 3 years
there ; 1868–70, Opéra ; toured
America and Europe ; 1872, she m.
Auguste Rouzaud (d. 1882) ; 1887,
m. Count Casa di Miranda.

**Nini** (nē′-nē), **Ales.**, Fano, Romagna,
1805—Bergamo, 1880 ; cond. and
dram. composer.

**Nisard** (nē-zăr), **Théodore** (pen-name
of Abbé **Théodule Eleazar X.
Norman**), b. Quaregnon, near Mons,
Jan. 27, 1812 ; chorister at Cambrai ;
studied in Douay ; 1839, dir. Enghien Gymnasium, and 1842, 2d *chef
de chant* and organist St.-Germain,
Paris; then confined himself to writing valuable treatises on plain-chant,
etc.

**Nissen** (nĭs′-sĕn), (1) **G. Nicolaus
von,** Hardebsleben, Denmark, 1761

—Salzburg, March 24, 1826 ;
cillor of State ; m. the widow of
zart, 1809, and aided her in prep
his biog. (1828). (2) (**Nissen-S
man**) **Henriette**, Gothenburg,
den, March 12, 1819—Harz
Aug. 27, 1879 ; great singer
teacher ; pupil of Chopin and
nuel Garcia ; début Paris,
1850, m. Siegfried Saloman,
1859 teacher St. Petersburg (
(3) **Erica.** Vide LIE.

**Nivers** (nē-vărs), **Guillaume Gab**
Melun, 1617—after 1701; orga
singer and composer.

**Nix′on**, (1) **H. G.**, Winchester, 17
1849 ; organist and composer.
**Jas. Cassana**, 1823—1842 ; v
ist ; son of above. (3) **H. Co**
b. London, 1842 ; organist and
poser at St. Leonard's.

**Nöb** (nāp), **Victorine**. Vide STO

**Nohl** (nōl), (**K. Fr.**) **L.**, Iser
1831—Heidelberg, 1885 ; 1880,
fessor and writer ; wrote biogs
Beethoven, Mozart, etc., and
lished many colls. of the letter
composers.

**Nohr** (nōr), **Chr. Fr.**, Langens
Thuringia, 1800—Meingen, 1
violinist and dram. composer.

**Norblin** (nôr-blăṅ), (1) **Louis Pĭ
Martin**, Warsaw, 1781—Châ
Conantre, Marne, 1854 ; 'cellist
professor. (2) **Émile**, 1821—1
son of above ; 'cellist.

**Nor′dica**, **Lillian** (stage-name
**Mrs. Lillian Norton (Gov
Doeme**), b. Farmington, Me., 1
pupil of John O'Neill and of N
Cons., Boston ; concert-début,
ton, 1876 ; 1878, toured Europe
Gilmore's Band ; studied opera
San Giovanni, Milan ; début
Brescia, 1880.; 1881. Gr. Op
Paris ; 1882, m. Frederick A. Gov
1885, he made a balloon ascen
and never returned ; she retired
1887, then sang Covent Garden, I
don, 1893 ; since then has sung
ularly in U. S., England, etc.; i
chosen to sing '' Elsa '' at Bayre

896, m. Zoltan F. Doeme, Hunga-
an singer.

·man. Vide NISARD.

·man(n), L., Stockholm, 1831—
884; conductor, professor and com-
oser. Vide NERUDA.

·ris, (1) Wm., d. ca. 1710; Engsh composer. (2) Thos., ca. 1745–
790; English male soprano, organist
nd composer. (3) Homer A., b.
Wayne, Maine, U. S. A.; notable
neorist; studied with Marston, Hale,
hadwick and Emery, Boston; lives
here as teacher; also studied 4
ears in Paris with Dubois, Godard,
igout and Guilmant; c. overture
Zoroaster," cantata "Nain" and
ongs; pub. "Harmony" and
Counterpoint" on French basis.

rth, (1) Francis, Lord Guilford,
ougham. Norfolk, ca. 1640—1685;
mateur musician and writer. (2)
Ion. Roger, Rougham Lane, 1650
–1733; bro. of above; writer.

szkowski (nôsh-kôf´-shkǐ), Sigismund (Zygismunt von), b. Warsaw,
May 2, 1846; pupil of Warsaw Mus.
nst.; inv. a mus.-notation for the
lind, and was sent by the Mus. Soc.
o study with Kiel and Raif, Berlin;
876 cond.; 1881, dir. of the Mus.
oc., Warsaw, and (1888) prof. at the
ons.; prod. succ. opéra "Livia"
Lemberg, 1898); c. symph., overure "Das Meerauge," etc.

szler (nôsh´-lěr), K. Eduard, b.
Reichenbach, Saxony, March 26,
863; pupil of Leipzig Cons.; 1888–
3, organist Frauenkirche, Bremen;
ince 1887, cond. Male Choral Union;
lso (since 1893) organist Bremen
Cath., and since 1896, cond. Neue
ingakademie; c. symph., c. "Lust-
piel-Ouvertüre," etc.

tker (nôt´-kěr) (called Balbulus,
"the stammerer"), 840—912, monk
t St. Gallen; important writer and
omposer of sequences. (V. D. D.)

tot (nǔ-tō), Jos., b. Arras, Pas de
Calais. 1755; d. in England; pupil
f Leclerc, Paris, noteworthy organ-
st there and at Arras; c. important

symphonies, pf.-concertos, sonatas,
etc.

Nottebohm (nôt´-tě-bōm), Martin
Gv., Ludenscheid, Westphalia, 1817
—Graz, 1882; teacher and writer
chiefly of valuable Beethoven works
and discoveries; also composer.

Nourrit (noor-rē), (1) Louis, Montpellier, 1780—Brunoy, 1831; leading
tenor Gr. Opéra, Paris. (2) Ad.,
Paris, 1802—suicide, Naples, 1839;
eminent tenor; son and successor
(1825) of above; pupil of Garcia and
teacher at the Cons.; also composer.

Novello (nō-věl´-lō), (1) Vincent, London, Sept. 6, 1781—Nice, Oct. 9,
1861; son of Italian father and English mother; founded, 1811, the pub.
firm Novello & Co. (now Novello, Ewer & Co., London); notable organist, pianist and composer. (2) Mary Sibilla, London,
1809 — Genoa, 1898; daughter of
above; m. Cowden Clarke; transl.
treatises into English; wrote Shakespeare Concordance, etc. (3) Jos.
Alfred, London, 1810—Genoa, July
17, 1896; son of (1); bass singer
and organist. (4) Clara Anastasia, b. London, June 19, 1818; 4th
daughter of (1); pupil Paris Cons.,
succ. operatic début Padua, 1841,
but made her best succ. in oratorio;
1843, m. Count Gigliucci; retired
1860.

Noverre (nō-vǎr), J. G., Paris, April
29, 1727—St. Germain, Nov. 19,
1810; solo-dancer at Berlin; ballet-
master at the Op.-Com., Paris; inv.
the dramatic ballet.

Nowakowski (nō-vä-kôf´-shkǐ), Jozef,
Mniszck, 1805—Warsaw, 1865; pf.-
teacher, professor and composer.

Nowowiejski (nō-vō-vě´-shkǐ), Felix,
b. Poland; 1902, won Berlin Meyerbeer prize with oratorio "Die Rück-
kehr des verlorenen Sohnes."

Nuceus. Vide GAUCQUIER.

Nux (nüx), Paul Véronge de la, b.
Fontainebleau, June 29, 1853; pupil
of F. Bazin, Paris Cons.; took 2d
Grand prix, 1876; prod. succ. 2-act

grand opera "*Zaïre*" (Opéra, 1889 ; Stuttgart, 1895) ; **c.** music-drama "*Labdacides*," etc.

## O

**Oakeley** (ōk'-lǐ), Sir **Herbert Stanley,** b. Ealing, Middlesex, July 22, 1830 ; while at Oxford, studied with Elvey (harm.), later at Leipzig Cons., with Schneider, Dresden, and Breidenstein, Bonn.; 1865–91, Ried Prof. of Mus., Edinburgh Univ., developing the annual Ried Concerts into a 3-days' Festival ; his org.-recitals had a large influence ; knighted 1876 ; Mus. Doc., Cantab., 1871; Oxon., Dublin, 1887; 1892, Emeritus Professor ; composer to the Queen in Scotland, and since 1887, Pres., Cheltenham Mus. Festival ; pub. a cantata "*Jubilee Lyric*," "*Suite in the Olden Style*," "*Pastorale*," Festival March, and a Funeral March (op. 23) for orch.; pf.-sonata, etc.

**Oberthür** (ō'-běr-tür), **K.**, Munich, 1819—London, 1895 ; harpist, teacher and dramatic composer.

**Obin** (ō-bǎn), **Louis H.**, Ascq., near Lille, 1820—Paris, 1895 ; basso cantante.

**O'Car olan, Turlough,** Newton, Meath, 1670—Roscommon, 1738 ; Irish harpist.

**Ochs** (ôkhs), (1) **Traugott,** b. Altenfeld, Schwerin-Sondershausen, Oct. 19, 1854 ; pupil of Stade, Erdmannsdorfer, Kiel, and the R. Inst. for Church-mus.; 1899, artistic dir. Mus.-Union and the Mus.-Sch., Brünn ; c. "*Deutsches Aufgebot*" for male chorus and orch. ; requiem, etc. (2) **Siegfried,** b. Frankfort-on-Main, April 19, 1858 ; studied R. Hochschule für Musik, Berlin, later with Kiel and Urban, and von Bülow, who brought into publicity a small choral union, the "Philharmonischer Chor," of which he was cond., and which is now the largest singing-society in Berlin ; he is also a singing-teacher and writer, 1901. Munich ; **c.**

succ. comic opera (text and m "*Im Namen des Gesetzes*" (Hamb 1888) ; 2 operettas ; etc.

**Ochsenkuhn** (ôkh'-zān-koon), **Se tian,** d. Heidelberg, Aug. 2, 1 lutenist and composer.

**Ockenheim.** Vide OKEGHEM.

**Odenwald** (ō'-děn-vält), **Robt. `** b. Frankenthal, near Gera, Ma 1838 ; since 1882 teacher Ham and cond. a succ. church-choir Psalms and part-songs.

**O'dington, Walter de** ("Mon Evesham "), b. Odington, Glouce shire ; d. ca. 1316 ; important theo (Coussemaker.)

**O do de Clugny** (dǔ klün -yē) (Sa **became** in 927 abbot of Clugny, w **he d** 942 , writer. (Gerbert.)

**Oeglin** (ākh'-lēn), **Erhard,** 16th c German printer of Augsburg, the to print figured mus. with types.

**Oelschlägel** (āl'-shlā-gěl), **Alfred** Anscha, Bohemia, Feb. 25, 1 Prague Org.-Sch.; th.-cond. at H burg, etc., and Karltheater, Vier later bandm. Klagenfurt ; **c.** op tas "*Prinz und Maurer*" (Kla furt, 1884) ; succ. "*Die Raubrit* (Vienna, 1888) ; succ. *Der L streicher* (Magdeburg, 1893).

**Oelsner** (ěls'-něr), (**Fr.**) **Bruno** Neudorf, near Annaberg, Sax July 29, 1861; pupil of Leipzig C solo-vla., ct.-orch. Darmstadt ; s ied with de Haan (comp.) ; s 1882, vln.-teacher Darmstadt C with title Grand Ducal Cham mus.; prod. at Darmstadt 1-act eras, incl. succ. "*Der Brautga* (1894); also a cantata with orch.,

**Oesten** (ā'-shtěn), **Theodor,** Be 1813—1870 ; pianist and compose

**Oesterle** (äs-těr'-lē), **Otto,** St. L Mo., 1861—Darien, Conn., 18 1st flute Thomas Orch., the Philh New York and Brooklyn, and S Orch.; teacher the Nat. Cons., N

**Osterlein** (ā'-shtěr-līn), **Nikola** 1840—Vienna, 1898 ; maker of coll. known as the "*Wagner* seum."

ettingen (ĕt′-tǐng-ĕn), **Arthur Joachim von**, b. Dorpat, March 28, 1836; 1866, prof. of physics in ordinary there; pres. of the Dorpat Mus. Soc., and cond. an amateur orch.; theorist.

fenbach (ôf′-fĕn-bäkh), **Jacques**, Cologne, June 21, 1819—Paris, Oct. 5, 1880; eminent writer of light opera; studied 'cello at the Cons., then joined Op.-Com. orch., Paris; c. chansonnettes (parodying La Fontaine), played the 'cello in concerts, and c. 'cello-pcs.; 1849, cond. Th.-Français, prod. unsucc. 1-act operetta "*Pepito*" (Op.-Com., 1853); others followed till 1855–66 he had a theatre for his own work; 1872–76, manager Th. de la Gaité; 1877, toured America with little succ. described in his "*Notes d'un musicien en voyage*" (1877); his 102 stage-works include the ballet-pantomime "*Le Papillon*" and the v. succ. operas, "*Orphée aux Enfers*," 1858; "*La Belle Hélène*," 1864; "*Barbe-Bleu*" and "*La Vie Parisienne*," 1866; "*La Grande Duchesse de Gérolstein*," 1867; "*Madame Favart*," 1879.

ʒinski (ō-gēn′-shkǐ), (1) Prince **Michael Cléophas**, Guron, near Warsaw, 1765—Florence, 1833; composer. (2) **Michael Casimir**, Warsaw, 1731—1803; uncle of above; said to have inv. the pedals of the harp.

keghem (or **Okekem, Okenghem, Ockegheim, Ock′enheim**), **Jean de** (or **Joannes**), probably Termonde, East Flanders, ca. 1430—Tours (?), 1495—1513; eminent contrapuntist; the founder of the Second (or New) Netherland Sch. Chorister, Antwerp Cathedral; studied with Dufay; 1454, t.-cond. and composer to Charles VII. at Paris; 1467, royal cond. to Louis XI.; toured Spain and Flanders on stipend; c. masses, motets, anons, etc.

ʒeary (ō-lā′-rǐ), (1) **Arthur**, b. n. Killarney, Ireland, 1834; pianist and

composer. (2) **Rosetta**, wife of above; composer.

**Olib′rio, Flavio Anicio.** Vide J. F. AGRICOLA.

**Ol′iphant, Thos.**, Condie, Perthshire, 1799—London, 1873; theorist and collector.

**Olitz′ka, Rosa**, b. Berlin, Sept. 6, 1873; contralto; studied with Artot and Hey; sang at Brünn, Hamburg, then Covent Garden and New York opera; then in Russia, etc.

**Ol′iver, H. Kemble**, Beverley, Mass., 1800—Boston, 1885; boy soprano; organist, mus. dir. and composer.

**Olsen** (ōl′-zĕn), **Ole**, b. Hammerfest, Norway. July 4, 1851; c. symph. poem "*Asgaardsreien*," 1891, etc.

**Ondriczek** (ôn′-drǐ-chĕk), **Fz.**, b. Prague, April 29, 1859; violinist; pupil of his father, and at 14 member of his small orch. for dance mus.; then studied Prague Cons. and with Massart, Paris Cons., took first prize for vln.-playing; toured Europe and America; lives in Boston.

**Ons′low, G.**, Clermont-Ferrand, France, 1784—1852; grandson of the first Lord Onslow; amateur 'cellist and pianist; prod. 4 succ. comic operas; 34 string-quintets; 36 quartets; and other chamber-music.

**Opelt** (ō′-pĕlt), **Fr. Wm.**, Rochlitz, Saxony, 1794—Dresden, 1863; writer.

**Ordenstein** (ôr′-dĕn-shtīn), **H.**, b. Worms, Jan. 7, 1856; pianist; pupil of Leipzig Cons., also in Paris; 1879–81, teacher at Carlsruhe; 1881–82, at Kullak's Acad., Berlin; 1884, founded Carlsruhe Cons.; made prof. by Grand Duke of Baden.

**Orefice, dell′.** Vide DELL′ OREFICE.

**Orgeni** (ôr-gā′-nē) (**Orgenyi**) (ôr-gān′. yē), **Anna Maria Aglaia**, b. Tismenice, Galicia, Dec. 17, 1843; colorature soprano; pupil of Mme. Viardot-Garcia; début, 1865, Berlin Opera; 1886, teacher Dresden Cons.

**Orlando**, or **Orlandus**. Vide LASSO.

**Orlow** (ôr′-lôf), Count **Gregor Vladimir**, 1777—St. Petersburg, 1826, writer.

**Ornithopar'cus** (Greek form of **Vogelsang**) (fō'-gĕl-zäng), **Andreas**, b. Meiningen; early 16th cent. theorist.

**Orpheus** (ôrf'-yoos), mythical Greek singer; son of Apollo, and best of singers to the lyre, 1350 B. C.

**Or'ridge, Ellen Amelia**, London, 1856—Guernsey, 1883; contralto.

**Ortigue** (ôr-tēg'), **Jos. Louis de**, Cavillon Vaucluse, 1802—Paris, 1866; writer.

**Orto** (ôr'-tō), **Giov. de** (Italian form of **Jean Dujardin**) (dü-zhăr'-dăn); Latinised as **de Hor'to** (called "**Marbriano**"); contrapuntist and composer 15th and 16th centuries.

**Os'borne**, (1) **G. Alex.**, Limerick, Ireland, 1806—London, 1893; composer. (2) (rightly **Eisbein** (īs'-bīn)), **Adrienne**, b. Buffalo, N. Y.; pupil of Auguste Götze and Max Stagemann in Leipzig; dram. soprano; now at Leipzig City Th.; has sung at the Gewandhaus.

**Os'good, Geo. Laurie**, b. Chelsea, Mass., April 3, 1844; graduated Harvard, 1886; dir. of the Glee Club, and the orch. there; studied singing with Sieber and Haupt, and German song and chorals with R. Franz; studied with the elder Lamperti in Italy 3 years; made a succ. tour of Germany; then, under Thomas, of America; since 1872, lived Boston as vocal-teacher and conductor; pub. "*Guide in the Art of Singing*" (8 editions); c. anthems, etc.

**Osiander** (ō'-zē-änt-ĕr), **Lucas**, Nürnberg, 1534—Stuttgart, 1604; writer and composer.

**Othmayer** (ōt'-mī-ĕr), **Kaspar**, Amberg, 1515—Nürnberg, 1553; composer.

**Otho.** Vide ODO.

**Ott(o)** (or **Ottl**), **Hans**, ca. 1533—1550; pub. in Nürnberg.

**Ottani** (ôt-tä'-nē), Abbate **Bernardino**, Bologna, 1735—Turin, 1827; dram. composer.

**Otto** (ôt'-tō), (1) Vide OTT. (2) (**Ernst**) **Julius**, Königstein, Saxony, Sept. 1, 1804—Dresden, March 5,

1877; notable composer of cycles male chorus, songs, operas, etc. **Fz.**, Königstein, Saxony, 18⟨ Mayence, 1841; c. pop. songs. **Rudolph K. Julius**, b. Berlin, A 27, 1829; solo boy-soprano at Domchor, Berlin; from 1848, t⟨ there; 1852, teacher singing S⟨ Cons.; 1873 at R. Hochschule Musik.

**Otto-Alvsleben** (ôt'-tō-älf'-slā-b⟨ **Melitta** (née **Alvsleben**), Dres⟨ 1842—1893; soprano; married, 1

**Oudin** (oo-dăn), **Eugène** (E⟨ **rance**), New York, 1858—Lon⟨ 1894; barytone, pianist and c⟨ poser.

**Oudrid y Segura** (oo-drēdh' ē sä-g rä), **Cristobal**, Badajoz, 1829—M rid, March 15, 1877; conductor dram. composer.

**Oulibichef.** Vide ULIBISHEV.

**Oury.** Vide BELLEVILLE-OURY.

**Ouse'ley**, Sir **Fr. Arthur Gore**, I don, Aug. 12, 1825—Hereford, A 6, 1889; notable theorist and ⟨ poser; pianist and organist rem able for fugal improvisation; w important treatises, etc.; c. an o⟨ at 8; M. A. Oxford, 1840, Mus. I there, 1854; also from Durham Cambridge, 1862; from 1855 Pro Music at Oxford, vice Sir H. Bishop; c. 2 oratorios incl. "⟨ gar."

**O'verend, Marmaduke**, d. 1⟨ Engl. organist and composer of vices, 70 anthems, 18 organ prel⟨ and fugues, etc.; biog. by J⟨ (London, 1896).

**Owst, Wilberfoss G.**, b. Lon⟨ June 13, 1861; pupil of Eaton ⟨ ing and H. Gadsby, and of Stutt Cons., 1893—95; organist, Baltim U. S. A.; pub. Communion Ser⟨ anthems, etc.

# P

**Pabst** (päpst), (1) **Aug.**, Elber⟨ May 30, 1811—Riga, July 21, 1⟨ director and composer of op⟨

**(2) Louis**, b. Königsberg, July 18, 1846; son of above; pianist and composer. From 1899, head pf.-teacher Moscow Philh. Sch. **(3) Paul**, Königsberg, 1854—Moscow, 1897; son of (1); pf.-prof.; director.

**acchiarotti** (päk-kǐ-ä-rôt'-tē), **Gasparo**, Fabriano, Ancona, 1744—Padua, Oct. 28, 1821; one of the greatest and most succ. of 18th cent. singers; soprano-musico.

**achelbel** (päkh'-ĕl-bĕl), **(1) J.**, Nürnberg, Sept. 1, 1653—March 3, 1706; org.-virtuoso and composer. **(2) Wm. Hieronymus**, b. Erfurt, 1685; son of above; organist and composer.

**acher** (päkh'-ĕr), **Jos. Adalbert**, Daubrawitz, Moravia, 1816—Gmunden, 1871; composer.

**achmann** (päkh'-män), **Vladimir de**, b. Odessa, July 27, 1848; notable pianist especially devoted to Chopin's mus.; son and pupil of a prof. at Vienna Univ.; a good violinist; studied also with Dachs, Vienna Cons.; 1869 toured Russia with a great succ. that has followed him throughout Europe and America; in Denmark he received the Order of the Danebrog from the King; since 1896, lives in Berlin.

**achulski** (pä-khool'-shkǐ), **Henry**, b. Poland, Oct. 4, 1859; pupil Warsaw Cons., now prof. Moscow Cons.; c. pf.-pcs., etc.

**ac(c)ini** (pä-chē'-nē), **(1) Andrea**, b. Italy, ca. 1700; male contralto. **(2) A. Fran. Gaetano Saverio**, Naples, 1778—Paris, 1866; singing-teacher, conductor and composer of comic operas. **(3) Giov.**, Catania, Feb. 17, 1796—Pescia, Dec. 6, 1867; son of a tenor; pupil of Marchesi, Padre Mattei and Furlanetto; 1813-35, prod. 40 operas, the last failing, he established a sch. at Viareggio, later Lucca, wrote treatises, etc.; 1840, the succ. of "*Saffo*" set him to work again, and he turned out 40 more operas, also oratorios, a symph.

"*Dante*," etc. **(4) Emilio**, 1810—Neuilly, near Paris, Dec. 2, 1898; bro. of above; librettist of "*Il Trovatore*," etc.

**Pacius** (pä'-tsǐ-oos), **Fr.**, Hamburg, March 19, 1809—Helsingfors, Jan. 9, 1891; violinist; c. the Finnish National Hymn, operas, etc.

**Paderewski** (päd-ĕ-rĕf'-shkǐ), **Ignace Jan**, b. Podolia, Poland, Nov. 6, 1859; eminent pianist and composer; pupil of Raguski (harm. and cpt.) Warsaw Cons., of Urban and Wuerst, Berlin; of Leschetitzky, Vienna. 1878-83, pf.-teacher, Warsaw Cons.; has toured Europe and America with unprecedented succ. financially and with high artistic triumph. His first wife, who died young, bore him a son. 1899, m. Mme. Gorski. 1896 he set aside $10,000 as the Paderewski fund, the interest to be devoted to triennial prizes "to composers of American birth without distinction as to age or religion;" 1. $500 for best orchestral work in symph. form; 2. $300 for best comp. for solo instr with orch.; 3. $200 for best chamber-music work. Lives in Paris and Switzerland; c. succ. opera "*Manru*" (Ct.-Th., Dresden, 1901); Po'ish fantasia for pf. with orch. op. 19, "*Légende No. 2*," for pf. op. 20, and many original and brilliant pf.-pcs. incl. "*Chants du voyageur*," a vln. sonata; vars and fugue on original theme; op. 14, "*Humoresques de concert for pf.*" (*Book 1; Menuet, Sarabande, Caprice; Book 2, Burlesque. Intermezzo polacco, Cracovienne fantastique*); "*Dans le désert, toccata*"; v. pop. Minuet (op. 1); songs, etc.

**Padilla y Ramos** (pä-dēl'-yä ē rä'-mōs), b. Murcia, Spain, 1842; pupil of Mabellini, Florence; barytone at Messina, Turin, etc., St. Petersburg, Vienna and Berlin; 1869, m. Désirée Artot.

**Paër** (pä'-är), **Ferdinando**, Parma, June 1, 1771—Paris, May 3, 1839. 1807, ct.-cond. to Napoleon and cond. Op.-Com; 1812, cond. Th.-

42

Italien (vice Spontini), violinist and c. 43 operas.

**Paesiello.** Vide PAISIELLO.

**Paganini** (päg-ä-nē'-nē), **Niccolò,** Genoa, Oct. 27, 1782—Nice, May 27, 1840; the pre-eminent violin-virtuoso. Studied with G. Servetto and G. Dosta; at 8 he c. a vln.-sonata; at 9 he played in public with greatest succ.; from 1795 he studied with Ghiretti and Aless. Rolla (though **P.** denied this), at Parma. 1798, he ran away from his severe father after a concert at Lucca, and played at Pisa and other places. At 15 he was a passionate gambler, and very dissipated. Fits of gambling alternated with periods when he practised 10 hours a day, the result being a ruined constitution. He pawned his violin to pay a gambling debt, but a M. Levron presented him with a Joseph Guarnerius, which **P.** willed to Genoa. In 1804 he went home, and practised till 1805, when he had extraordinary succ. making a sensation by brilliant performances on the G string alone; soon ct.-soloist at Lucca; then to 1827 he toured Italy, crushing all rivalry with an extraordinary technic; 1827, Pope Leo XII. conferred on him the Order of the Golden Spur; he played at Vienna, receiving from the municipality the great gold medal of St. Salvator; from the Emperor the honorary title of ct.-virtuoso. 1829, Berlin; 1831, Paris; 1831, London. 1833-34, Paris; then retired to his villa at Parma. He lost 50,000 francs on a scheme to establish a gambling house with concert-annex at Paris, the gambling-license being refused. Though his earnings were enormous, he was not generous except spasmodically; he gave Berlioz $4,000 as a compliment for his "*Symphonie Fantastique*" (B. had writtten "*Harold in Italy*" for **P.'s** Stradivari viola). He m. the singer Antonia Bianchi, and he left his son Achille $400,000 (£80,-000). He died of phthisis of the lar-

ynx. His technic was never equa and it provoked superstitious d among his auditors, his ghoulish pearance aiding the impression. was sometimes the charlatan some of his effects were due to cial tunings (scordatures), but virtuosity has never been rival C. 24 caprices for violin-solo; which pf.-transcriptions were m by Schumann and Liszt; 12 sona for violin and guitar (op. 2); do 3); 3 gran quartetti; concerto in (solo part in D, for a vln. tune semitone high); concerto in B m "*La Campanella*," with Rondo à clochette (op. 7); variations on m themes, "*Le Streghe*," "*God save King*," "*The Carnival of Veni* etc.; concert Allegro "*Moto* petuo*" (op. 12); a sonata with comp. of vln., 'cello or pf., and stud etc. Biog. by Fétis (Paris, 1851; E London, 1852); A. Niggli (188 O. Bruni (Florence, 1873).

**Page,** (1) **J.,** England, ca. 1750—L don, 1812; tenor. (2) **Nathan C ford,** b. San Francisco, Oct. 1866; pupil of E. S. Kelley; at c. an opera (prod. at San Francisc incid. mus. for "*Moonlight Blosso* (London, 1898), using Japan themes; c. also an opera "*Villier* a "*Caprice*" developing one 8-me ure theme through 5 movements an orch. suite; a "*Village Sui* for orch., etc.

**Paine** (pān), **J. Knowles,** b. Portlar Me., Jan. 9, 1839; the first Am ican composer of importance; pu of Kotzschmar, at Portland, Hau (cpt.), Fischer (singing), and W precht (instr.), Berlin; gave or concerts in Berlin and Americ cities, then lived in Boston as orga ist West Church; 1862, teacher mus. Harvard Univ., and organist Appleton Chapel, Cambridge; sin 1876, prof. of mus. and organist Harvard; c. an opera (text and mu "*Azara*"; oratorio "*St. Peter* "*Centennial Hymn*," with orch.

open the Philadelphia Exposition, 1876); "*Columbus March and Hymn*" (to open the Columbian Exposition, Chicago, 1893); mus. to Sophokles' "*Œdipus Tyrannus*" for male voices and orch. (prod. at Harvard, 1881); 3 cantatas with orch. "*The Realm of Fancy*," "*The Nativity*," "*Song of Promise*," 2 symphs. op. 23, in C min., and op. 34 in A ("*Spring symph.*"); 2 symph. poems, "*The Tempest*" and "*An Island Fantasy*"; overture to "*As You Like It*"; Domine Salvum with orch.; mass, with orch.; chamber-mus., vln.-sonata, etc.

**aisiello** (pä-ē-sǐ-ěl'-lō) (or **Paesiello**) (pä-ā-sǐ-ěl'-lō), Taranto, Italy, May 9, 1741—Naples, June 3, 1816. At 5 studied at Jesuit sch. in Taranto with a priest Resta; later studied with Durante, Cotumacci and Abos, Cons. di S. Onofrio. at Naples, teacher there, 1759-61. He c. masses, etc., till a comic intermezzo (Cons. Theatre, 1763) won him a commission to c. an opera for the Marsigli Th., at Bologna, where his comic opera "*La Pupilla, ossio il Mondo alla Rovescia*," was prod. 1764. (Grove calls this work 2 operas.) In 12 years he prod. 50 operas mainly succ., though in rivalry with Piccinni and Cimarosa; these include "*Il Marchese di Tulipano*" (Rome, 1766); "*L'Idolo Cinese*" (Naples, 1767) and "*La Serva Padrona*" (Naples, 1769). He was notable also for his jealousy and devotion to intrigue. 1776-84, St. Petersburg, with a splendid salary and on invitation from Empress Catherine. Here he prod. 1776 "*Il Barbiere di Siviglia*," gaining such succ. that the later and better opera by Rossini was received as a sacrilege with great hostility at first; on his return from Russia he prod. at Vienna one of his best works, "*Il Re Teodoro*," and 12 symph. for Joseph II. 1784-99, cond. to Ferdinand IV. of Naples; and prod. various works incl.

"*L'Olimpiade*" (1786) and "*Nina, o la Pazza per Amore*" (1789), "*La Molinara*" and "*Izingari in Fiera*." During the revolution 1799-1801, he won the favour of the Republican govt., also regained the favour of royalty at the Restoration, till Napoleon who had always admired him called him to Paris, 1802-03, as cond. Here **P.** lived in magnificence, lording it over Cherubini and Méhul. 1803-15, he was in Naples again as ct.-cond. In 1815, on the return of Ferdinand IV., he was reduced to a small salary; soon his wife died, and he shortly after. A composer of great prolificity, melodic grace and simplicity, his works are rarely heard now. He c. 100 operas, a Passion oratorio (Warsaw, 1784); 3 solemn masses, Te Deum for double chorus and 2 orch.; requiem with orch. (performed at his own funeral); 30 masses with orch., 40 motets, 12 symphs., and other things in proportion. Biog. by Le Seuer (1816), Quatremère de Quincy (1817), Schizzi (Milan, 1833), Villarosa (Naples, 1840).

**Paix** (pä'-ěx), **Jacob**, Augsburg, 1550—after 1590; organist and composer.

**Paladilhe** (päl-ä-děl), **Émile**, b. June 3, 1844; studied with Marmontel (pf.), Benoît (org.) and Halévy (cpt.), Paris Cons.; won 1st prize for pf. and org., 1857; 1860, Grand prix de Rome, with the cantata "*Le Czar Ivan IV.*" (Opéra, 1860); from Rome, he sent an Italian opera buffa, an overture and a symph.; 1872, prod. the 1-act comic opera "*Le Passant*" (Op.-Com.) followed by 5 operas incl. the still pop. "*Patrie*" (Opéra, 1886; 1889, Hamburg, as "*Vaterland*"; 1895, Milan, as "*Patria*"); and c. also 2 masses, a symph., etc.

**Palestrina** (pä-lěs-trē'-nä) (rightly **Giovanni Pierluigi Sante**, called **da Palestrina**, from his birthplace), Palestrina, near Rome, probably 1514 or 1515 (some say 1528 or 9)—Rome, Feb. 2, 1594. One of the most revered, names in music; he was b. of poor parents, little is known of his early life; he is said to have earned his living first as a church-singer; probably studied in Goudimel's sch., 1540, and was, 1544–51, organist at Palestrina, then magister puerorum (master of the boys), in the Cappella Giula, with title "maestro della cappella della Basilica Vaticana." He dedicated a book of masses to Pope Julius III., who, Jan., 1554, admitted him to the Pontifical Chapel as a singer, against the rules, P. having a wife and no voice. July 30, 1555, Paul IV. dismissed him with a pension of 6 scudi per month. This blow affected him so deeply (he had 4 children to support) that he suffered nervous prostration. On Oct. 1, however, the Pope appointed him cond. at the Lateran. 1560, he prod. his famous "*Improperia*" (v. D. D.) for Holy Week, with such succ., that the Pope secured them for the Sistine Chapel, where they have been performed on every Good Friday since. 1561, he took the better-salaried post of cond. at Santa Maria Maggiore. The Pope was determined to rid church-mus. of its astonishing secular qualities: first, the use of street-ballads, even when indecent, as *canti fermi*, many of the choir actually singing the words; and second, the riotous counterpoint with which the sacred texts and the secular tunes were overrun. The Council of Trent and a committee of 8 cardinals, considering the matter seriously, decided not to revolutionise church-music entirely, and in 1564 commissioned Palestrina, by this time famous, to write a mass which should reform, without uprooting, ecclesiastical polyphony. He wrote three, all noble, the third, the "*Missa papæ Marcelli*," winning the most profound praise. He was called "the saviour of music," and appointed composer to the Pontifical Chapel. 1571, he became and remained till death maestro of St.

Peter's. He also composed for the "Congregazione del Oratorio" (v. NERI); taught in Nanini's sch., and was from 1581 maestro concertator to Prince Buoncompagni. Pope Sixtus V. wished to appoint him maestr of the Sistine Chapel, but the singer refused to serve under a layman. He was, however, commissioned to revise the Roman Gradual and Anti phonal, by Pope Gregory XIII.; h pub. the "Directorium chori" (1582) the offices of Holy Week (1587), an the *Præfationes* (1588), but on th death of his pupil and assist. Giudett he was compelled to leave the wor unfinished. A complete ed. of h works is pub. by Breitkopf and Hä tel: Vols. i.–vii. contain 262 mo tets; Vol. viii., 45 hymns; Vol. ix 68 offertories; Vols. x.–xxiv., 9 Masses; Vol. xxv., 9 Lamentatior each in various arrangements in 3, 5, 6, or 8 parts; Vol. xxvi., 17 Lita nies, Motets and Psalms in 3–1 parts; Vol. xxvii., 35 Magnificats Vol. xxviii., about 90 Italian (sec lar) Madrigals; Vol. xxix., 56 Churcl Madrigals (Latin); Vol. xxx. (fro colls. of 16th–17th cent.), 12 Ca tiones sacræ, 12 Cant. profanæ, an 14 Cant. sacræ; Vol. xxxi. (fro archives of the Pontifical Chape etc.), 56 miscellaneous numbers, mar doubtful, incl. 11, "Esercizi sopra scala"; Vol. xxxii., 60 miscellaneo comp. incl. 8 Ricercari, Response Antiphones, etc.; Vol. xxxiii., Doc ments, Index, Bibliography, et Among his best masses are "*Æterr Christi munera*," "*Dies sanctific tus*," "*O sacrum convivium*," in parts; "*Assumpta est Maria in co lum*," "*Dilexi quoniam*," "*Ecce e Joannes*," "*Papæ Marcelli*" in parts; "*Tu es Petrus*" in 6 part these, the Motet "*Exaudi Domine* 3 Lamentations, also selected M drigals, Canzonets, etc., are pub. se arately. Biog. by Baini (Rome, 1828 A. Bartolini (Rome, 1870); Bäu ker (1877); Cametti (Milan, 1895).

## Palestrina.

### By W. J. Henderson

ꓵALESTRINA'S work in musical history was bringing order out of chaos in church-music, and setting the model for the loftiest purity of style. The music of the Church had become too complex ᴿough the extreme development of rigidly canonic writing. Palestrina, ꓟowing the lead of some of his predecessors, who had begun to write in ᵗe counter-point, showed how this new style could be made to yield the ᵉst possible results in the composition of music for the mass, and other ᴿts of the Roman ritual. By adhering to the ecclesiastical scale and ᴼiding chromatic progressions, by clinging to purely religious thought ᵈ excluding any thing like passion, Palestrina produced works which ꚍe remained to this day the perfect model of church-music. ¶ The ꓠtrapuntal skill in his writing is masterly, but it never parades itself. ꞅ most beautiful effects are produced with apparent spontaneity, and ᵉquent chord harmonies of enchanting loveliness seem to be accidental. ꓠe Roman school of church-composers was founded by Palestrina, and ꞅ influence is even yet perceptible in the music of the Holy City. He has ꓲversally been accorded the position of the greatest of all church-composers.

---

ꞁf'fy, Count **Fd. von Erdöd**, Vien-ᵃ, 1774–1840; amateur musician ᵃnd operatic manager.

ꞁlavicin̄. ꓑäl-lä-vē-chē'-nē), (1) (or Ꝓallavicino) **Benedetto**, Cremona —Mantua (?), after 1616; conductor ᵃnd composer. (2) **Carlo**, Brescia, ᵗ630—Dresden, 1688; conductor and ꓒram. composer.

ꞁlo'ni, **Gaetano**, b. Camerino, Italy, ꓯug. 4, 1831; pupil of Cellini, Fer-ꓟo; organist there, 1854; studied ꚍith Mabellini, Florence, where he ꞁived as a singing-teacher and com-ꝓoser.

ꞁlme (päl'-mě), **Rudolph**, b. Barby-ꝋn-Elbe, Oct. 23, 1834; pupil of Á. ꓚ. Ritter; organist; R. Mus. Dir. ᵃnd organist at Magdeburg; c. con-ᵗcert-fantasias with male chorus, so-ꓠatas, etc., for org.

ꓯlm'er, **Horatio Richmond**, b. Sher-ꓐurne, N. Y., April 26, 1834; pupil ꝋf his father and sister, and studied in New York, Berlin and Florence; at 18, began composing; at 20 chorus-cond.; 1857, teacher at Rushford Acad.; after the Civil War, Chicago; ed. "*Concordia*"; cond. various so-cieties from 1873, cond. New Church Choral Union, giving concerts, some-times with 4,000 singers; since 1877, Dean of the Chautauqua Sch. of Mus.; Mus. Doc. (Chicago Univ. and Alfred Univ.); pub. colls. and treatises.

**Paloschi** (pä-lôs'-kē), **Giov.**, 1824—1892, member of the Milan firm of Ricordi.

**Palot'ta, Matteo**, Palermo, 1680—Vienna, 1758; ct.-composer and writer.

**Paminger** (pä'-mǐng-ěr) (or **Pammigerus, Panni'gerus**), **Leonharḍ**, Aschau, Upper Alsatia, 1484—Passau, 1567; composer.

**Pan**, one of the Greek gods; said to be inventor of the pipe.

**Pan'ny, Jos.**, Kolmitzberg, Loweᵗ

Austria, 1794—Mayence. 1838; violinist, teacher and composer.

**Panofka, H.,** Breslau, 1807—Florence, 1887; violinist, writer and composer.

**Panseron** (pän-sŭ-rôň), **Aug. Mathieu,** Paris, 1796—1859; writer of vocal methods, études, etc.; composer.

**Paolucci** (pä-ō-loot'-chē), **Giu.,** Siena, 1727—1777; conductor, theorist and composer.

**Panthès** (pän-tĕs'), **Marie,** b. of French parents, at Odessa; pupil of Fissot. Paris Cons., taking 1st prize at 14.

**Panzner** (pänts'-nĕr), **K.,** b. Teplitz, Bohemia, March 2, 1866; pupil of Nicodé and Dräeseke; cond. at Sondershausen th.; 2 years later at Elberfeld; 1893; 1st cond. Leipzig city th.; 1899, cond. Philh. concerts, Bremen.

**Pape** (pä'-pĕ), **Jn. H.,** Sarstedt, near Hanover, July 1. 1789—Paris. Feb. 2, 1875; distinguished maker and improver of the piano; he inv. a transposing piano, introd. padded hammers, etc.

**Papier** (pä-pēr'), (1) **Louis,** Leipzig, 1829—1878; organist, singing-teacher and composer. (2) **Rosa,** b. Baden, near Vienna, 1858; mezzo-soprano; Imp. Op., Vienna; 1881, m. Dr. Hans Paumgartner.

**Papillon de la Ferté** (pä-pē-yôň dŭ lä fĕr-tā'), (1) guillotined, Paris, 1793. 1777, Intendant of the "Ménus plaisirs," of Louis XVI.; Inspector "École royale de chant"; dir. of Opera. (2) His son was, 1814, Mus. Intendant-in-chief.

**Papini** (pä-pē'-nē), **Guido,** b. Camagiore, near Florence, Aug. 1, 1847; violinist; pupil of Giorgetti; début at 13; toured Europe; composer.

**Papperitz** (päp'-pĕ-rets), **Benj. Robt.,** b. Pirna, Saxony, Dec. 4, 1826; pupil of Hauptmann, Richter and Moscheles, Leipzig Cons., 1851; teacher of harm. and cpt. there; from 1858-69, also organist of Nikolai-

kirche there; 1882, R. Prof.; ( poser.

**Paque** (päk), **Guil.,** Brussels, 18: London, 1876; 'cello-virtuoso teacher.

**Paradies** (or **Paradisi**) (pä-rä-dē or dē'-sē), **P. Dom.,** Naples, 17: Venice, 1792; pupil of Porp harps.-player and teacher, also di composer.

**Paradis** (pä-rä-dēs'), **Maria Th sia von,** Vienna, May 15, 17: Feb. 1, 1824; a skilful blind or; ist and pianist for whom Mc wrote a concerto; daughter of Imperial Councillor; teacher of and voice; c. an opera.

**Parent** (pä-räň), **Charlotte Fran Hortense,** b. London, March 1837; pianist; pupil of Mme. I renc, Paris Cons.; founded "É préparatoire au professorat," Pa wrote a pf.-method (1872), etc.

**Parepa-Rosa** (pä-rä'-pä-rō'-zä) **Parepa de Boyescu), Euphrosy** Edinburgh, May 7, 1836—Lon Jan. 21, 1874; daughter and p of Elizabeth Seguin, a singer; prominent soprano in opera and orato her strong and sympathetic voice a compass of 2½ octaves reaching d''' (v. PITCH, D.D.); début at Malta; 1865 m. Carl Rosa; tou Europe and America.

**Parish-Alvars, Elias,** Teignmo Engl., Feb. 28, 1810—Vienna, J 25, 1849; of Jewish descent; n harp-virtuoso and composer.

**Parisini** (pä-rĭ-sē'-nē), **Federico,** logna, 1825—Jan. 4, 1891; theo and dram. composer.

**Parke,** (1) **J.,** 1745—1829; Engl. o ist and composer. (2) **Wm. Th** London, 1762—1847; bro. of abc oboist, composer and writer. **Maria Hester,** 1775—1822; dau ter of (1), singer, composer and wri

**Park'er,** (1) **Jas. Cutler Dunn,** Boston, Mass., June 2, 1828; stud Leipzig Cons.; lives in Boston a Brookline; 1862, organist "Par Club," vocal soc.; 1864-91, orga)

'rinity Ch., and for years organist
ſändel and Haydn Soc.; prof. Bos-
ɔn Univ. Coll. of Mus., and Exam-
ɪer N. E. Cons. ; writer and transl.;
" *Redemption Hymn*" (1877) ; can-
ɪta " *The Blind King*" (1886) ;
*St. John*," with orch. ; oratorio,
*The Life of Man*"; church-ser-
ces, etc. (2) **H.**, b. London, Aug.
1845 ; pupil of Leipzig Cons., and
ſ Lefort, Paris ; singing-teacher and
ɔnd. London ; wrote treatise " *The
Voice*"; c. comic opera " *Migno-
ette*" (London, 1889) ; "*Jerusa-
m*," for bass-solo and chorus (Albert
ſall, 1884); gavottes, etc., for orch.;
ſ.-pcs. (3) **Horatio Wm.**, b. Au-
ɪrndale, Mass., Sept. 15, 1863;
ɪrominent American composer ; pupil
ſ his mother, later of Emery (theo-
ɾ), J. Orth (pf.), and Chadwick
ɔmp.), Boston ; organist Dedham
ɪnd Boston ; studied 1882–85 with
ſheinberger (org. and comp.) and L.
ɪbel (cond.), Munich ; organist and
ɪrof. of mus. St. Paul's Sch., Gar-
ɪn City, New York ; 1886, organist
ſ. Andrew's, Harlem ; 1888, Ch.
ſ the Holy Trinity, N. Y.; since
ɪ94, prof. of mus., Yale Univ.;
ɪ99, cond. his notable oratorio
*Hora Novissima*" at Worcester
ɪngl.) Festival with great succ.
ɪrst given at Worcester (U. S. A.)
ɪstival, 1893). Pub. coll. of org.-
ɪs.; c. oratorios, "*Hora Novissi-
ɪa*" (1893), and "*St. Christopher*"
ɪ896) ; cantatas " *King Trojan*"
Munich, 1885), " *The Holy Child*,"
*The Kobold*" and " *Harold Har-
ɪger*," prize-cantata, " *Dream
ɪing*" (1893) ; symph. in C.; con-
ɪrt-overture; heroic-overture " *Reg-
ɪus*"; overture to " *Count Robert of
ɪaris*," " *Cohal Mahr*," for bar.-
ɪlo and orch. (1893) ; " *Commence-
ɪent Ode*," Yale Univ. (1895) ; Mc-
ɪagg prize chorus *a cappella* (1898) ;
ɪ *A Northern Ballad*" for orch.
ɪ899), etc.

ɪrk'inson, **Elizabeth**, b. Missouri ;
ɪupil of Mrs. Lawton, Kansas City,

and Miolan Carvalho and de la Nux,
Paris ; début as "Dinorah," 1896 ;
engaged at Opéra Comique, 1887 ;
has sung there since and elsewhere.

**Par'ratt**, Sir **Walter**, b. Huddersfield,
Feb. 10, 1841 ; at 7 sang in church ;
at 10 knew Bach's " *Well-tempered
Clavichord*" by heart ; at 11, organist Armitage Bridge ; 1872 Magdalen
Coll., Oxford ; 1882, St. George's
Chapel, Windsor Mus. Bac. Oxon.,
1873 ; 1883, organ-prof. R. C. M. ;
knighted 1892; 1893, Master of Mus.
in Ordinary to the Queen ; wrote articles ; c. mus. to "*Agamemnon*"
and "*Orestes*," "*Elegy to Patro-
clus*" (1883), anthems, org.-and pf.-
pcs., etc.

**Par'ry**, (1) **J.**, Ruabon, N. Wales—
Wynnstay, Oct. 7, 1782; Welsh bard,
harper, and composer. (2) **J.** (called
" Bardd Alaw," i. e., master of song),
Denbigh, Feb. 18, 1776—London,
April 8, 1851 ; clarinettist ; cond. of
the Eisteddfod for years; critic, teacher and composer in London ; pub.
colls., etc. (3) **J. Orlando**, London,
1810—E. Molesey, 1879 ; son of
above ; pianist, harpist, singer and
composer. (4) **Jos.**, b. Merthyr
Tydvil, Wales, May 21, 1841 ; the
son of a labourer ; at 10 worked in a
puddling-furnace ; 1854 emigrated to
America with his family, but returned
to Britain, won Eisteddfod prizes for
songs, 1868 studied R. A. M. on a
fund especially raised by Brinley
Richards ; 1871, Mus. Bac. Cambr. ;
prof. of music, Univ. Col., Aberyst-
with ; 1878, Mus. Doc.; 1888, Mus.
Lecturer at Cardiff ; also Fellow R.
A. M. C. 4 operas, cantatas " *The
Prodigal Son*," " *Nebuchadnezzar*,"
and " *Cambria*"; " Druids' Chorus";
an orchestral ballade, overtures, etc.
(5) Sir **Chas. Hubert Hastings**, b.
Bournemouth, England, Feb. 27,
1848 ; eminent English composer ;
from 1861, while at Eton, pupil of
G. Elvy (comp.), was pianist, organist, singer, and composer at the concerts of the Musical Soc. At 18,

while still at Eton, he took " Mus. Bac. " at Oxford, wrote a cantata, " *O Lord, Thou hast cast us out*"; 1867, Exeter Coll., Oxford; founded " Univ. Mus. Club " ; 1874, M. A. ; studied with Bennett and Macfarren, and Dannreuther (pf.), and Pierson, Stuttgart. At 26 prod. " *Intermezzo religioso*," for strings (Gloucester Festival) ; 1883, Choragus of Oxford and Mus. Doc. Cantab.; do. Oxon, 1884, do. Dublin, 1891 ; 1894 dir. R. C. M.; 1898, knighted; 1902 made a baronet ; active as lecturer and writer of essays and books incl. the notable " *Evolution of the Art of Music*"(1896). C. also 4 symphs.; symph vars. ; overtures, " *To an Unwritten Tragedy*" and " *Guillem de Cabestanh*"; oratorios " *Judith*," "*Job*," " *King Saul*"; mus. to Aristophanes' " *Birds*" (1883), and " *Frogs*" (1892) ; and to " *Hypatia*" (1893) ; the following were prod. at prominent festivals : scenes from Shelley's " *Prometheus Unbound*," with orch. (Gloucester festival, 1880); " *The Glories of our Blood and State*"; " *Suite moderne*," " *Ode on St. Cecilia's Day*," " *L'Allegro ed Il Penseroso*," " *De profundis*," with 3 choirs and orch.; chamber-mus.; vln.- and pf.-sonatas, songs, etc.; " *Invocation to Music*"; Magnificat, in Latin.

**Par'sons,** (1) **Robt.**, Exeter, 1563—drowned Newark, 1569 (–70?) ; composer. (2) **J.**, d. 1623 ; probably son of above ; organist and composer. (3) Sir **Wm.**, 1746—1817 ; master of King's Band and teacher. (4) **Albert Ross**, b. Sandusky, O., Sept. 16, 1847 ; noteworthy American teacher; pupil of F. K. Ritter, N. Y., and at Leipzig Cons.; later of Tausig, Kullak, Weitzmann and Würst, Berlin ; 1871, New York ; organist since 1885, Fifth Av. Presb. Ch.; translator, editor, and writer of various works ; c. vocal quartets, songs, etc. (5) **E. A.**, pianist ; from 1894 organist, Ch. of the Divine Paternity, N. Y.; c. pf.-concerto, etc.

**Pasch** (päsh), **Oskar**, b. Frankfort-Oder, March 28, 1844 ; pupil of Inst. for Church-mus. and the A[c] for Comp., Berlin ; 1874, won Michael Beer prize ; wrote Psalm with orch.; 1884, Royal Mus. I[.] organist and singing-teacher at [I] lin ; c. a symph., oratorios, etc.

**Pascucci** (päs-koot'-chē), **Giov. sare,** b. Rome, Feb. 28, 1841; comic operas and operettas in Ror dialect, 2 oratorios, etc.

**Pasdeloup** (pä-dŭ-loop), **Ju Étienne,** Paris, Sept. 15, 1819—F[ tainebleau, Aug. 13, 1887; emir cond.; pianist ; pupil Faris Co 1847-50 ; pf.-teacher, and 1855-teacher of ensemble there ; 18 cond. famous concerts (known f[ 1861 as " concerts populaires ") succ. till 1884, when they fell be[ the popularity of Colonne and moureux ; a benefit festival brou[ him 100,000 francs ($20,000).

**Pash'aloff, Victor Nikandrovit[** Saratoff, Russia, 1841—Kasan, 18 composer.

**Pas'more, H. Bickford,** b. Jacks Wis., June 27, 1857; pupil of J. Morgan (org. and harm.), of Jac[ sohn, Reinecke (pf.), Frau Un[ Haupt (voice), Leipzig and of Shakespeare and R. H. Cummir London ; lives in San Francisco organist and prof. of singing; " *Conclave*" march, overture for or " *Miles Standish*," masses, etc.

**Pasquali** (päs-kwä'-lē), **Nicolò,** Italy—Edinburgh, 1757; writer composer.

**Pasqué** (päs-kā'), **Ernst,** Colog 1821—Alsbach, 1892 ; barytone ; rector and writer.

**Pasquin:** (päs-kwē'-nē), **Bdo.**, Ma di Valdinevole, Tuscany, Dec. 1637—Rome, Nov. 22, 1710; nc organist at San Maria Maggiore ; pil of Vittori and Cesti ; teacher [ composer of 2 operas, an orato etc.

**Pasta** (päs'-tä) (née **Negri**), (1) **G ditta,** Como, April 9 1798—villa

Lake Como, April 1, 1865; a noted Jewish singer; pupil of Asioli; début, 1815, but had no succ.; studied with Scappa, and reappeared with greatest succ. Her powerful voice (range a–d''', v. PITCH, D. D.) had always some irregularities, but her dramatic power was great and she invented embellishments with much skill; m. the tenor (2) **Pasta**, before 1816; she created "La Sonnambula" and "Norma" and earned a fortune.

**astou** (päs-too), **Étienne J. Bapt.**, Vigan, France, 1784—Ternes, near Paris, 1851; singing-prof. and writer.

**a'tey, Janet Monach** (née **Whytock**), London, 1842—Sheffield, 1894; alto.

**a'ton, Mary Ann** (Mrs. Wood), Edinburgh, 1802—Bucliffe Hall, near Wakefield, 1864; prominent soprano; m. tenor Jos. Wood, 1831.

**atti** (pät'-tē), (1) **Carlotta**, Florence, 1840—Paris, June 27, 1889; eminent concert coloratura-soprano; pupil of her father, (2) **Salvatore P.**, a tenor, and her mother, (3) **Caterina** (née **Chiesa**), a soprano. (4) **Adelina (Adela Juana Maria)**, b. Madrid, Feb. 10, 1843· one of the most eminent coloratura-singers in history; sister of (1), and like her a pupil of her parents; sang in public as a mere child; then studied with Max Strakosch (husband of her sister Amelia); début, at 16, New York, Nov. 24, 1859, as "Lucia" (under the stage-name "the little Florinda"); 1861, London, Covent Garden; 1862, Paris Th. Italien; 1868, m. the Marquis de Caux. After making the world her own, she now sings only infrequently in concerts, and lived till recently at her villa Craig y Nos, in Wales. 1886, m. and toured with the tenor Nicolini (d. 1898); 1899, m. a Swedish nobleman, Baron Cederström. (5) **Carlo**, Madrid, 1842 —St. Louis, Mo., March, 1873; bro. of above; violinist.

**Pat'tison, J. Nelson**, b. Niagara Falls, N. Y., Oct. 22, 1845; pianist; pupil of Liszt, Thalberg, Henselt and von Bülow (pf.), and Haupt (harm.); toured U. S. as pianist with Parepa Rosa, etc.; c. symph. for orch. and military band "*Niagara*"; concert overture, etc.

**Patzold** (pät'-tsôlt), **Hn.**, Neudorf, Silesia, 1822—Königsberg, 1861; conductor and composer.

**Pauer** (pow'-ĕr), (1) **Ernst**, b. Vienna, Dec. 21, 1826; noted pianist; son of a prominent Lutheran clergyman; pupil of Th. Dirza, W. A. Mozart, Jr. (pf.), and Sechter (comp.), later of Fr. Lachner, Munich; 1847–51, dir. mus. societies at Mayence; 1851, London; 1859, prof. at the R. A. M.; in 1861, gave historical performances of clavecin and pf.-mus.; 1866, pianist to Austrian Court; 1867, prof. at the Nat. Training Sch.; 1883, R. C. M.; since 1870, lecturer; toured U. S.; ed. the classics; pub. mus. primers, colls. of old clavier-works, and many didactic works; c. a quintet, vln. arrangements of symphs., etc. (2) **Max.**, b. London, Oct. 31, 1866; son and pupil of above; then studied with Lachner, Carlsruhe; 1887, pf.-prof. Cologne Cons.; 1893, chamber-virtuoso to the Grand Duke of Hesse; since 1897, prof. Stuttgart Cons.; 1898, made prof. by the King of Würtemberg; pub. pf.-pieces.

**Paul** (powl), **Oscar**, Freiwaldau, 1836 —Leipzig, 1898; professor and theorist.

**Paumann** (pow'-män), **Konrad**, b. (blind) Nürnberg, ca. 1410—Munich, Jan. 25, 1473; c. the oldest extant book of org.-pcs.

**Paumgartner** (powm'-gärtnĕr), **Dr. Hans**, 1844—Vienna, May 23, 1893; pianist; critic and composer.

**Paur** (powr), (1) **Emil**, b. Czernowitz, Bukovina, Aug. 29, 1855; noted conductor; pupil of his father; at 8 he played vln. and pf. in public; studied with Dessoff (comp.) and Hellmesberger (vln.) Vienna Cons. (fellow pupil with Nikisch and Mottl); graduated with first prizes; 1870, first vln. and assist.-soloist in ct.-opera orch.; 1876, cond. at Cassel; later Königsberg; 1880, 1st ct.-cond. Mannheim; 1891, cond. Leipzig City Th.; 1893–98, cond. Boston (U. S. A.) symph. Orch. (vice Nikisch); 1898, New York Philh. Concerts (vice Seidl); 1899, dir. of the Nat. Cons., N. Y. (vice Dvořák); 1900, cond. German opera of the Met. Op.; c. a vln.-concerto, string-quartet, vln.-sonata, pf.-pcs., songs. (2) **Maria** (née **Burger**), Gengenbach, Black Forest, 1862—New York, 1899; wife of above; pianist; pupil Stuttgart Cons., Leschetizky and Essipoff, Vienna.

**Pauwels** (pow′-vĕls), **Jean Engelbert**, Brussels, 1768—1804; violinist, conductor and dram. composer.

**Pavesi** (pä-vä′-sē), **Stefano**, Crema, 1779—1850; dram. composer.

**Pax′ton**, **Stephen**, d. 1787; Engl. composer.

**Payer** (pī-ĕr), **Hieronymus**, Meidling, near Vienna, 1787--Wiedburg, near Vienna, 1845; conductor and dram. composer.

**Peace**, **Albert Lister**, b. Huddersfield, Engl., Jan. 26, 1844; prominent organist; pupil of Horn and Parratt; 1875, Mus. Doc. Oxon; 1873, organist Glasgow cath.; 1897, of St. George's Hall, Liverpool (vice Best); c. Psalm 138 with orch., org.-music.

**Pearce**, (1) **Stephen Austen**, London, Nov. 7, 1836—April 9, 1900; pupil of J. L. Hopkins; Mus. Doc. Oxford, 1864, same year U. S. and Canada; then organist 2 London churches; 1872, vocal-teacher, Columbia Coll., N. Y., and lecturer Peabody Inst. and Johns Hopkins Univ., Baltimore; 1879–85, organist Collegiate Church, N. Y.; writer and composer of a 3-act opera, a children's opera, an cratorio and a church-cantata in strict fugal style (prod. at Ox-

ford), overture, etc. (2) **Chas. Wr** b. Salisbury, England, Dec. 5, 185 pupil of Ayluard, Hoyte, Read a Pront; 1881, Mus. Bac., 1884 M Doc., Cambridge. From 1871 ganist various London churches. 18 Prof. of Trinity College; co-edit organist and choir-master; wr various text-books, and c. an ora rio.

**Pear′sall**, **Robt. Lucas De**, Clifto Engl., 1795 — Schloss Wartense Lake of Constance, 1856; writer a composer.

**Pearson.** Vide PIERSON.

**Pease** (pēz), **Alfred Humphrie** Cleveland, U. S. A., 1838—St. Lou 1882; pianist and composer.

**Pedrell** (pä′-dhrĕl), **Felipe**, b. Spai ca. 1835; lives in Madrid; 18 prof. of Mus. History and Æstheti Royal Cons., Madrid; editor, crit lexicographer and writer; c. 2 op ras, symphonic "*Scene*," a mass, e

**Pedrotti** (pä-drôt′-tē), **Carlo**, Veron Nov. 12, 1817 — suicide, Oct. 1 1893; conductor and composer of operas, etc.

**Pellegrini** (pĕl-lā-grē′-nē), (1) **Felic** Turin, 1774 — Paris, 1832; bass buffo and composer. (2) **Giuli** Milan, 1806—Munich, 1858; bass serio.

**Pelletan** (pĕl-täṅ), **Fanny**, Paris ( 1830—1876; singer and writer.

**Pembaur** (päm′-bowr), **Jos.**, b. Inn bruck, May 23, 1848; studied V enna Cons., later at Munich R. Sc of Mus.; since 1875 dir. and hea master, Innsbruck Mus. Sch.; pro v. succ. opera "*Zigeunerleben* (1898), choral works with orch symph. "*Im Tyrol*," etc.

**Peña y Goni** (pän′-yä ē gō′-nē), **Ant** nio, San Sebastian, Spain, 1846 Madrid, 1896; critic and composer.

**Pen′field**, **Smith Newell**, b. Oberli Ohio, April 4, 1837; pupil of Ja Flint, New York, and of Leipz Cons.; also studied in Paris; founde Savannah (Ga.) Cons., and Moza Club; also "Arion" Cons., Brool

, N. Y.; since 1882, lives in New
rk ; organist Broadway Taber-
cle ; 1884, Mus. Doc. Univ. of the
y of N. Y.; 1885, pres. of the
T. N. A.; c. psalm 18, with
ch.; overture, etc.

na, **Lorenzo,** Bologna, 1613—
ola, 1693 ; conductor and compos-

enrieder (pĕn'-tĕn-rē-dĕr), **Fz.**
, Kaufbeuren, Bavaria, 1813—
unich, 1867 ; organist and dram.
mposer.

asch (pä'-poosh), **John Chr.** (**Jn.
ap.**), Berlin, 1667—London, July
, 1752 ; violinist, composer and
iter ; pupil of Klingenberg and
osse ; held a position at the Prus-
an Court, but 1697 seeing the king
ll an officer without trial he went
London. 1710 founded the fa-
ous " Academy of Antient Music ; "
12 organist and composer to Duke
Chandos (succeeded by Händel),
r. Lincoln Inn's Theatre, for which
c. 4 masques, the music to the
ormously pop. *" Beggar's Opera,"*
c.; 1730 m. de l'Épire, the singer.

abo (pä'-rä-bō), (**Jn.**) **Ernst,** b.
iesbaden, Germany, Nov. 14,
45 ; at 7 brought to New York ;
upil of his father ; then of Mosche-
s and Wenzel (pf.), Papperitz,
ichter, and Hauptmann (harm.),
nd Reinecke (comp.), Leipzig Cons.,
turned to America, 1865; succ. con-
rt-pianist ; lives in Boston as teach-
and pianist ; c. arrangements, etc.

'cy, **J.,** d. 1797 ; Engl. composer
ballads, incl. *" Wapping Old
tairs."*

eira (pä-rä'-ē·rä), (1) **Marcos
oares,** Ciminha, Portugal—Lisbon,
n. 7, 1655 ; c. a mass, etc. (2) **Do-
ingos Nuñes,** Lisbon—Camarate,
ear Lisbon, 1729 ; cond. and com-
oser.

epelitzin (pä-rĕ-pĕ-lēt'-shēn), **Po-
ycarp de,** Odessa, Dec. 14, 1818 ;
ussian colonel ; pupil of Lipinski
vln.) ; writer and composer.

ez (pä'-rĕth), **Davide,** of Spanish
parents, Naples, 1711—Lisbon, 1778;
cond. at Palermo Cath.; 1752, ct.-
cond., Lisbon ; rival of Jomelli as c.
of operas. incl. *" Demofoonte";* c.
also notable church-mus.

**Perfall** (pĕr'-fäl), **K.,** Freiherr ant, b.
Munich, Jan. 29, 1824 ; studied mus.
with Hauptmann, Leipzig ; 1854–64
founded and cond. the still succ.
" Oratorio Soc." ; in 1864, Intendant
ct.-mus. ; 1867–1893, Intendant Ct.-
Th., writer and composer of 4 operas, 3 fairy cantatas, etc.

**Perger** (pĕr'-gĕr), **Richard von,** b. Vienna, Jan. 10, 1854; pupil of Brahms ;
1890–95, dir. and cond. Rotterdam
Cons.; 1895, cond. " Gesellschaftsconcerte," Vienna ; prod. (text and
mus.) succ. comic opera *" Der
Richter von Granada"* (Cologne,
1889), a vaudeville, vln.-concerto, etc.

**Pergolesi** (pĕr-gō-lä'-sē), **Giov. Bat.,**
Jesi, Papal States, Jan. 4, 1710—(of
consumption) Pozzuoli, near Naples,
March 16, 1736, eminent composer.
At 16 entered the Cons. dei Poveri
di Gesù Cristo, Naples, and studied
with de Matteis (vln.), Greco (cpt.),
Durante, and Feo (cpt.). He speedily won attention by novel harmonies
and threw off contrapuntal shackles
early. His last student-work, the
biblical drama *" San Guglielmo
D'Aquitania"* (prod. with comic
intermezzi at the convent of S. Ag-
rello Maggiore, Naples, 1731) shows
the beginnings of vivid and original
fancy. He prod. at Naples in 1731,
the excellent and novel opera *" Sal-
lustia,"* and the intermezzo *" Amor
Fa l' Uomo Cieco,"* which had no
succ., while the opera seria *" Rici-
mero"* was a distinct failure. But he
found a patron in the Prince of Stig-
liano, for whom he wrote 30 terzets
for vln. with bass ; he was commissioned to compose a solemn mass for
Naples, which was performed after
the earthquake of 1731, as a votive
offering to the patron saint of the
city. It brought him immediate
fame. After four stage-works, prod.

in 1732 the intermezzo " *La Serva
Padrona* " (Naples, 1733) ; won him
note as a dramatic composer and has
served as a model of comic operas
since ; it has only 2 characters and
the accompaniment is a string-quartet with occasional support of horns.
His subsequent 6 operas were received without interest (except for
the intermezzo to " *Adriano* " first
given as " *Livietta e Tracollo* " and
later as " *La Contadina Astuta*," ,"
though after his death they were revived with immense enthusiasm, and
their harmonic novelty, sweetness,
delicacy and melodic charm were
recognised, " *La Serva Padrona* "
and " *Il Maestro di Musica* " becoming standards in France. Of the
failure of " *L'Olimpiade*," v. DUNI.
Irregular habits due to regular dis-
appointments undermined Pergolesi's
constitution, and he died of consumption at the baths of Pozzuoli,
finishing five days before his deata
his masterpiece, the celebrated " *Stabat Mater* " for soprano and alto
with string orch. and org. He c.
also 3 masses with orch.; Dixit for
double chorus and orch.; a Kyrie
cum gloria; a Miserere, and a Lau-
date with orch., etc.; an oratorio,
" *La Natività*," a cantata " *Orfeo* "
for solo voice and orch.; a cantata,
" *Giasone* "; 6 cantatas with string-
accomp.; 30 trios, etc. Biog. by Bla-
sis (1817) ; Villarosa (1831).

**Peri** (pā'-rē), (1) **Jacopo** (called " Il
Zazzerino," i.e., the long-haired),
Florence, ca. 1560—ca. 1630; of
noble birth; pupil of Malvezzi;
court-cond. at 3 successive courts;
an enthusiast in everything classic,
he haunted the salons of Count Bardi and Corsi, where he joined the attempt at revival of Greek musical recitative, with Caccini and Corsi ; he
set to mus. Rinuccini's text of " *Dafne*"; this was doubtless the first opera ever written ; its effort at repro-
ducing the supposed manner of
Æschylos. Sophokles, etc., was called

" stile rappresentativo"; the op
was given only once, and privatel
Bardi's house, but it won Peri a co
mission to set Rinuccini's text "*
ridice*" for the wedding of Maria
Medici and Henry IV. of Fra
(1600) ; an ed. of his works was p
1603, incl. madrigals, etc.

**Achille,** Reggio d'Emilia, Ita
1812—1880; conductor and dr
composer.

**Perisine.** Vide LA RUE.

**Perk'ins,** (1) **Wm. Oscar,** Sto
bridge, Vt., May 23, 1831—Bost
1902 ; pupil of Wetherbee, Bost
and of G. Perini, Milan ; 1879, M
Doc., Hamilton Coll.; lives in Bos
as teacher and composer. (2)
**Southwick,** b. Stockbridge, 
March 20, 1833 ; bro. of abo
graduate, 1861, Boston Mus. S
1890, founded Chicago Nat. Coll
Mus.; cond. many festivals and c
mentions ; 1875, studied with Wa
at Paris and Vannuccini, Floren
ed. colls. and composed. (3) Jul
**Edson,** Stockbridge, 1845—M
chester, Engl., 1875 ; bro. of abo
bass; 1874, m. Marie Roze (la
Mrs. Mapleson).

**Perne** (pärn), **Fran. L.,** Paris, 177
May 26, 1832 ; pupil of Abbé d'H
dimont (harm. and cpt.); 1792, c
rus-singer at the Opéra ; 1799, do
le-bass player in the orch.; 18
prod. a grand festival mass ; the r
year he c. a triple fugue to be s
backwards on reversing the pa
1811, prof. harm. at the Cons.; 18
Inspector Gen.; 1819, libr.; 18
retired to an estate near Laon;
returned to Paris a few weeks bef
he died ; he was indefatigable in
search, and an authority on Gr
notation, the troubadours, etc.; wr
and composer.

**Perosi** (pä-rō'-sē), Don **Lorenzo,**
Tortona, Italy, Dec. 23, 1872 ;
young priest and organist who
attracted much attention by his
cred mus., though critics are divi
as to its value ; it aims to use m

n resources and ancient principles;
pil of Saladino, Milan Cons.; 1894,
Haberl's Domchorschule, Ratis-
n; 1895, cond. at Imola; from
97, at San Marco, Venice; his sa-
ed trilogy "*La Passione di Cristo*"
, "*La Cena del Signore*"; b,
*L'Orazione al Monte*"; c, "*La
'orte del Redentore*"), Milan, 1897, at
e Ital. Congress for Sacred Mus.,
eated a sensation, and has been
dely performed; 1898, Pope Leo
III. made him honorary *maestro* of
e Papal Choir; c. also 15 masses;
also oratorios, "*La Transfigu-
zione del Nostro Signore Gesù
-isto*" (1898), "*La Risurrezione di
azaro*" (Venice, July 27, 1898, in
a Fenice Th., by special permission),
*Il Natale del Redentore*" (Como,
899); "*Mosè*" (Rome, 1902).

oti'nus, **Magnus,** Magister; 12th
nt. composer; conductor at Nôtre-
ame, Paris. (Coussemaker.)

otti (pä-rôt'-tē), **Giov. Ag.,** Ver-
lli, 1760—Venice, 1855; writer and
mposer.

rin (pĕr-răn), **Pierre** (called *l'abbé*,
ough never ordained), Lyons, ca.
20—Paris, 1675; librettist of the
st French operas.

ron (pĕr'-rōn), **Karl,** b. Franken-
al, June 3, 1858; barytone; stud-
d with Hey and Hasselbeck and
ockhausen; concert-début, 1880;
84–91, Leipzig City th.; then at
resden ct.-opera.

'ry, (1) **G.,** Norwich, 1793—Lon-
on, 1862; director and composer.
) **Edw. Baxter,** b. Haverhill,
ass., Feb. 14, 1855; pianist; blind
om an early age; pupil of J. W.
ill, Boston; later of Kullak, Clara
chumann, Pruckner and Liszt;
ayed before the German Emperor;
10 years he gave 1,200 concerts in
merica; originated the "lecture-re-
tal"; c. fantasia "*Loreley*," "*The
ost Island*," etc., for piano.

siani (pĕr-sĭ-ä'-nē), (1) (née **Tac-
hinardi)** (täk-kĭ-när'-dē), **Fanny,**
ome, Oct. 4, 1812—Passy, near

Paris, May 3, 1867; daughter and pupil of the tenor-singer Nicolà T.:
one of the most noted and succ. colo
rature-sopranos of the century; lack
ing in appearance and possessed of a
faulty voice, she compelled homage
by her perfect technic; in 1830 she m.
(2) **Giuseppe Persiani** (1804—1869),
a composer of operas.

**Persuis** (pĕr-swēs), **Louis Luc Loi-
seau de,** Metz, 1769—Paris, 1819;
violinist, conductor, prof. and comp.

**Perti** (pĕr'-tē), **Jacopo A.,** Bologna,
June 6, 1661—April 10, 1756; one of
the chief 17th cent. composers of operas; pupil of Padre Franceschini;
at 19 prod. a mass; church-conductor
and composer of oratorios, etc., also
21 operas.

**Pescetti** (pä-shĕt'-tē), **Giov. Bat.,** Venice, 1704—(probably) 1766; organ-
ist and dram. composer.

**Peschka-Leutner** (pĕsh'-kä-loit'-nĕr),
**Minna,** Vienna, 1839—Wiesbaden,
1890; soprano.

**Pessard** (pĕs-săr), **Émile Louis For-
tuné,** b. Montmatre, Seine, May
28, 1843; pupil of Paris Cons.; won
1st harm. prize; 1866, Grand Prix de
Rome, with cantata "*Dalila*" (Opéra,
1867); 1878–80, inspector of singing,
Paris schools; 1881, prof. of harm.
at the Cons.; dir. of mus. instruction
in the Legion of Honour; since
1895, critic; prod. 10 comic operas
and operettas, incl. "*Le Capitaine
Fracasse*" (Th. Lyr., 1878); c. also
masses, etc.

**Pes'ter-Pros'ky,** (1) **Bertha,** b. Frankfort-on-Main, March, 1866; soprano
there, then Berlin in operetta; studied
with Frau Dreyschock and reappeared
as dramatic soprano; 1894 m. the
harpist (2) **Reinhold Pester** and
toured with him; 1899 at Cologne
City Theatre.

**Peters** (pā'-tĕrs), (1) **Carl Fr.,** Leipzig
pub. firm, founded 1814 by C. F.
Peters; 1893, a large library was
opened to the public as the "Bibliothek Peters." (2) **Max Abraham,** is,
since 1863, sole proprietor

**Petersen** (pā'-tĕr-zĕn), (1) **Peter Nikolaus,** Bederkesa, 1761—Hamburg, 1830 ; player on, improver of, and composer for, the flute. (2) **Margarete,** b. Amager, near Copenhagen, Oct. 1, 1869 ; alto ; pupil of Geistingers and Schytte ; toured and lives in Copenhagen.

**Petersilea** (pā'-tĕr-sē'-lā-ä), **Carlyle,** b. Boston, Mass., Jan. 18, 1844 ; pianist and teacher ; pupil of his father, and at Leipzig Cons., winning the Helbig prize for pf.-playing , toured Germany with succ., lives in Boston, est. 1871 " The Petersilea Acad. of Mus." ; 1886, teacher New Engl. Cons.; 1884 studied with Liszt at Weimar, and gave a concert at the Singakademie, Berlin ; pub. pf.-studies.

**Petit, Adrien.** Vide COCLICUS.

**Petrejus** (pā-trä'-yoos), **Jns.,** Langendorf, Franconia — Nürnberg, 1550 ; mus.-printer.

**Petrella** (pā-trĕl'-lä), **Errico,** Palermo, Dec. 10, 1813 — in poverty, Genoa, April 7, 1877 ; v. succ. Italian composer of operas, rivalling Verdi's popularity, " *Marco Visconti* " and " *La Contessa d'Amalfi* " most succ.; pupil of Saverio del Giudice (vln.) and Naples Conservatorium.

**Petri** (pā'-trē), (1) **Jn. Samuel,** Sorau, 1738—Bautzen, 1808 ; cantor and writer. (2) **H.,** b. Zeyst, near Utrecht, April 5, 1856 ; violinist ; pupil of David ; 1882 – 89 leader Gewandhaus Orch. with Brodsky, then leader Dresden Ct.-orch.; composer.

**Petrini** (pā-trē'-nē), **Fz.,** Berlin, 1744 —Paris, 1819 ; harpist and theorist.

**Petrucci** (pā-troot'-chē), **Ottaviano dei,** Fossombrone, June 18, 1466 —May 7, 1539 , inv. of mus.-printing with movable types ; in 1498 received from the Council of the Republic of Venice a 20 years' monopoly of mus.-printing by his method ; 1511–23 at Fossombrone with a 15 years' privilege for the Papal States , his method, which required 2 impres-sions, one of the lines, one of notes, was beautifully managed a specimens are valuable ; he p[  ] many of the most important com of his time and of previous comp ers.

**Petrus de Cruse (Pierre de Croix)** (pā-troos dŭ krüz or pĭ-ăr lä krwä), of Amiens ; a 13th ce writer. (Coussemaker.)

**Pe'trus Platen'sis.** Vide LA RUE.

**Petschke** (pĕtsh'-kĕ), Dr. **Hn. Thꞁ bald,** Bautzen, 1806—Leipzig, 18[ ] director and composer.

**Petsch'nikoff, Alex.,** b. Jeletz, R sia, Feb. 8, 1873 ; violinist ; p[ ] Moscow Cons.; at 10 entered M cow Cons. and took prize ; tou[ ] Europe with great succ., 1895–[ ] America, 1899 ; lives in Berlin.

**Pet'tit, Walter,** b. London, Ma[ ] 14, 1836 ; pupil R. A⹁ M.; 'cell[ ] Philh. orch. and in the court band

**Petzmayer** (pĕtsh'-mī-ĕr), **Jn.,** b. enna, 1803 ; zither virtuoso.

**Petzold** (pĕt'-tsôlt), (1) **Chr.,** Kön stein, 1677—Dresden, 1733 ; ct.-ganist and composer. (2) (or **Pe** **hold), Wm. Leberecht,** b. Lic enhain, Saxony, 1784 ; piano-ma[ ] (3) **Eugen K.,** Ronneburg, Alt[ ] burg. 1813—Zofingen, Switz., 188 director and organist.

**Pevernage** (pŭ-vĕr-nǎzh), **André Andreas),** Courtray, Belgium, 1ꞁ —Antwerp, 1591 ; choirm. Nôt Dame and composer.

**Pezel** (pā'-tsĕl) **(Peze'lius Jn.),** to[ ] musician at Bautzen and Leipz[ ] writer and composer 1674.

**Pezze** (pĕd'-zĕ). **Ales.,** b. Mila 1835 ; 'cellist ; in London from 18[ ] pupil Merighi.

**Pfeiffer** (pfīf'-fĕr), **K.,** 1833 (?)—ꞁ enna, 1897 ; dram. composer. (pfĕf-fä), **Jean Georges,** b. V sailles, Dec. 12, 1835 ; pianist ; p[ ] of Maleden and Damcke ; 1862 but ; won Prix Chartier for chamb mus. ; critic ; member of the firm Pleyel, Wolff et Cie., Paris ; c. symph., a symph. poem, "*Jean*

*Arc"*; pf. concertos, 3 operettas,
·atorio "*Hagar*," etc.

il (pfīl), **H.,** b. Leipzig, Dec. 18,
\35 ; since 1862, ed. "*Sängerhalle*"
he organ of the Sängerbund) ; c.
ale choruses.

zner (pfīts'-něr), **Hans Ehrich,** b.
·oscow, May 5, 1869 ; pupil of
.och Cons., Frankfort ; 1892–93,
acher of pf. and theory, Coblenz
ons.; 1894–95, asst.-cond. City
h., Mayence ; and prod. his succ.
us. drama "*Der arme Heinrich*"
Iayence, 1895) ; also incid. mus. to
osen's "*Festival on Solhaug*"; 
\97–98, teacher in Stern Cons., Ber-
1 ; c. scherzo for orch.; ballad
·*Herr Oluff*" for bar. and orch.
:refeld, 1902) ; pf.-trio, etc.

ighaupt (pflookh'-howpt), (1)
obt., Berlin, 1833 — Aix-la-Cha-
·lle, 1871 ; pianist and composer.
) **Sophie** (née **Stschepin**), Dün-
·urg, Russia, 1837—Aix-la-Chapelle,
\67 ; pianist.

hl (pfōl), **Fd.,** b. Elbogen, Bohe-
·ia, Oct. 12, 1863 ; critic ; studied
·us. at Leipzig (1885) ; c. an orch.
.ite, etc.

·ndt (pfoont), **Ernst Gotthold
·enj.,** Dommitzsch, near Torgau,
·\06—Leipzig, 1871 ; tympanist ;
·v. the "machine-head ;" wrote
·ethod for kettle-drum.

·lèse (fă-lěz'), **P. (Petrus Phale'-
·us),** b. Louvain, ca. 1510 ; 1545, est.
·mus.-publishing business ; 1579 re-
·oved to Antwerp, as "Pierre Phal-
·e et Jean Bellère."

·lps, **Ellsworth C.,** b. Middle-
·wn, Conn., Aug. 11, 1827 ; self-
·ught ; at 19 organist ; from 1857,
·rooklyn ; teacher in pub. schools
·r 30 years ; c. 2 comic operas ;
·mphs. "*Hiawatha*," and "*Eman-
·pation ;*" 4 symphonic poems ;
·salm 145, with orch., etc.

·lidor (rightly **Danican**) (fē-lī-dôr
·' dǎ-nǐ-kän). A famous French
·mily called usually **Danican-Phil-
·or,** the name Philidor being taken
·om a remark of the King comparing

**Jean D.** with his favourite oboist
Philidor. There seem to have been
two named **Michel,** (1) the first,
b. Dauphine—d. Paris, ca. 1650, the
oboist whom the King praised ; the
other (2) **Michel,** d. 1659, ct.-mus.
(3) **Jean,** d. Paris, Sept. 8, 1679, in
the King's military band. (4) **André D.-P.** (l'aîné), b. Aug. 11, 1730 ;
cromorne-player, and composer. He
had 16 children. (5) **Jacques** (le
cadet), Paris, 1657—Versailles, 1708 ;
bro. of (4), oboist, etc., favourite of
Louis XIV.; c. military music, etc.;
he had 12 children, four of whom
were musicians, the best known being
(6) **Pierre,** 1681—1731 ; flutist ; c.
suites, etc., for flutes. (7) **Anne,**
Paris, 1681 — 1728 ; eldest son of
(4) ; flute-player, and conductor ; before he was 20, prod. operas at court.
(8) **Michel,** b. Versailles, 1683, 2nd
son of (4); a drummer. (9) **Fran.,**
Versailles, 1689—1717(18 ?), 3rd son
of (4); oboist and bass-violist ; c. flute-
pcs. (10) **Fran. André,** Dreux,
Sept. 7, 1726—London, Aug. 31,
1795 ; last and greatest of the family,
the youngest son of (4) ; remarkable
chess-player of European fame ; musical pupil of Campra.   At 30 he suddenly began to prod. operas with
great succ., his best works being the
following (among 25 notable for orch.
and harm. brilliance) : "*Le Diable à
quatre*" (Op.-Com., 1756) ; "*Le
Maréchal*" (1761), performed over
200 times ; "*Le Sorcier*" and "*Tom
Jones*" (only 8 weeks apart, in 1704 ;
the latter containing the then novelty
of an unaccompanied quartet) ; the
grand opera, his best work, "*Erne-
linde,*" 1767 (revised, 1769, as "*Sando-
mir*"). Biog. by Allen (Philadelphia,
1863). He had four sons all ct. mus.:
(11) **Pierre,** Paris, 1681—1740(?) ;
oboist, flutist and violist ; c. suites and
prod. a pastorale at court. (12)
**Jacques,** 1686—1725, oboist. (13)
**François,** 1695—1726, oboist. (14)
**Nicolas,** 1699 — 1769 ; played the
serpent, etc.

Phil'ipp, Isidor (Edmond), b. Pesth, Sept. 2, 1863; pianist; a naturalised French citizen; came to Paris as a child; at 16 pupil of Georges Mathias, at the Cons.; won 1st. pf.-prize, in 1883; studied with Saint-Saëns, Stephen Heller, and Ritter; played with succ. in European cities; est. concerts (with Loeb and Berthelier), producing modern French chamber-comps.; reorganised the "Société des instr. à vent"; cofounder and pres. of the "Soc. d'Art"; pub. a "Suite fantastique," a "Rêverie mélancolique," a "Sérénade humoristique," for orch., etc.

Philippe, (1) de Caserte. Vide CASERTA. (2) de Mons. Vide MONTE. (3) de Vitry. Vide VITRY.

Phil'ipps, (1) Peters (or Petrus Philip'pus, Pietro Filip'po), England, ca. 1560—April, 1625; organist and composer. (2) Arthur, b. 1605, organist at Oxford, prof., and composer. (3) Henry, Bristol, 1801—Dalston, 1876; bass-barytone. (4) Wm. Lovell, Bristol, 1816—1860; 'cellist and composer. (5) Adelaide, Stratford-on-Avon, 1833—Carlsbad, 1882; noted contralto, taken to America as a child; pupil of Garcia; début, Milan, 1854.

Philomath'es, Wenzeslaus (called "de Novadomo," because born at Neuhaus, Bohemia), pub., 1512, a treatise.

Philp (fïlp), Elizabeth, Falmouth, 1827—London, Nov. 26, 1885; singer and writer.

Phil'pot, Stephen Rowland, living Engl. composer; pupil of Macfarren, R. A. M., c. operas (not prod.), etc.

Piatti (pē-ät'-tē), (1) Carlo Alfredo, Bergamo, Jan. 8, 1822 — Bergamo, July 19, 1901; 'cello-virtuoso (son of a violinist, (2) Antonio P., d. Feb. 27, 1878); pupil of his grand-uncle, Zanetti, and of Merighi, Milan Cons.; début, Milan, 1838; at 7 had played in an orch., 1849, 1st 'cello It. opera, London; from 1859 at Monday and Saturday Pop. Concerts

of chamber-mus.; pub. a method for 'cello, 2 'cello-concertos, vocal mus with 'cello obbligato, etc.

Piccinni (or Piccini or Picinni) (pït chïn'-nē), (1) Nicolà, Bari, Jan. 16 1728—Passy, near Paris, May 7 1800; operatic composer, famou as a rival of Gluck. Son of a mu sician who opposed his tastes. Th Bishop of Bari recognising his talen and irrepressible passion for mus overcame opposition, and at 14 h entered the Cons. di San Onofri Naples, remaining for 12 years, a favourite pupil of Leo and Durant He entered into competition with th popular Logroscino, and prod. th v. succ. opera-buffa "Le Donne D pettose" (1754), followed by (175 "Gelosia per Gelosia" and "Il Cur oso del suo proprio Danno"; whi had the unprecedented run of fo years, "Alessandro nelle Indie (Rome, 1758), and ".Cecchina Zit la, o La Buona Figliuola" (Ron 1760), the most success. work of kind in Europe, though written in weeks, were hailed as masterwor His new dramatic fervour and his e tended duets and varied finales ga him such prestige that he is said have c. 133 dramatic works, incl. " Re Pastore"(1760); "L'Olimpiae (1761) previously though less su set by Pergolesi, Galuppi and Jom li; revised 1771; "Berenice"(176 "Le Cecchina Maretata" (176 "Didone abbandonata"(1767); " tigone" (1771). 1773, the Ron public favoured his pupil Anfossi, a hissed one of P.'s operas, which pr trated him with grief; on recover he regained favour with ' I Via atori." In response to flattering vitations in 1776 he removed with family to Paris, spent a whole y learning the tongue and writing first French opera, "Roland" (Op 1778), which had a succ. said to due largely to the necessity the a Gluck faction was under to find a val. The war betwen the "Gl

s" and "Piccinists" was violent
d incessant, though **P.** regretted
s position and made a vain effort
er Gluck's death, to raise a fund
r annual concerts in his memory.
e had succ. with the following
ench operas, " *Le fat méprisé*"
779), " *Atys*" (1780), " *Didon*,"
*Le dormeur éveillé*," and " *Le faux*
*rd*" (all 3 in 1783). In 1778, as
r. It. Opéra, whose performances
ternated with the French company
the Opera, he produced his best
alian works with succ. The man-
ement simultaneously commissioned
th Gluck, and **P.** to set the opera
*Iphigénie en Tauride*"; **P.** had
s libretto rewritten by Ginguené,
d his version was delayed till
ter Gluck had made a triumph
d left Paris. **P.**'s opera, though
ually called a failure, ran 17 nights
spite of having an intoxicated
ima donna on the first night to start
e joke " *Iphigénie en Champagne*".
alf a dozen others failed or were
ver performed. A new rival, Sac-
ini, now appeared. When this sec-
d succ. rival died, the large-hearted
ccinni delivered a glowing funeral-
logy over him. 1784, he was Maî-
e de chant at the new " École roy-
e de musique et déclamation." His
st operatic attempts in French were
succ. At the outbreak of the Rev-
ution he lost his positions, and reed to Naples, on a pension. But
s daughter m. a young French rad-
al, and **P.**, suspected of republican-
n, was kept a prisoner in his own
ouse for four years, in extreme pov-
ty. 1798, he returned to France,
as fêted at the Cons., presented
th 5,000 francs and small irregular
nsion. He was prostrated for some
onths by paralysis ; a sixth inspec-
rship was created at the Cons. for
m, but he soon fell ill and died.
) **Luigi**, Naples, 1766 — Passy,
ly 31, 1827 ; son and pupil of above;
-cond. at Stockholm and dr. com-
ser. (3) **Louis Alex.**, Paris, 1779

—1850 ; grandson and pupil of (1) ;
conductor and dram.-composer.

**Piccolomini** (pĭk-kō-lō'-mē-nē), **Maria,** b. Siena, 1836 ; mezzo-soprano
of "hardly one octave and a half-
compass" (Chorley), but so excellent
an actress, that she became a great
ragé; pupil of Mazzarelli and Raimondi, Florence ; début there 1852,
with great succ., sang in Italy, London, Paris and New York (1858) ;
1863, m. the Marquis Gaetani, and
retired from the stage.

**Pichel** (or **Pichl**) (pĕsh'-'l), **Wenzel,**
Bechin, Bohemia, 1741—Vienna,
1805 ; violinist ; c. 700 works.

**Picinni** Vide PICCINNI.

**Piel** (pēl), **Peter,** b. Kessenich, near
Bonn, Aug. 12, 1835 ; from 1868,
teacher Boppard-on-Rhine ; 1887,
R. Mus.-Dir.; wrote a harm.; c. 8
Magnificats (in the church-modes),
etc.

**Pieragon,** or **Pierchon.** Vide LA
RUE.

**Pierné** (p'yĕr-nā) (**H. Constant**) **Gabriel,** b. Metz, Aug. 16, 1863 ; pupil of Marmontel, César Franck and
Massenet, Paris Cons.; won 1st prize
(1879), do. for cpt. and fugue (1881),
do. for organ (1882) and Grand prix
de Rome (1882); 1890, organist Ste.
Clothilde (vice César Franck); 1893,
prod. spectacle " *Bouton d'or*"; opera, "*Izéil*" (1804) ; succ. " *Vendée*"
(Lyons, 1897); a hymn to the Russian
visitors, " *La Fraternelle*," 1893,
etc.

**Pierre** (pĭ-ăr'), **Constant,** b. Passy,
Aug. 24, 1855; pupil of Paris Cons.;
bassoon-player ; assist. sec. at the
Cons.; ed. "*Le Monde musical*";
wrote a history of the Opéra orchestra (for which the " Soc. des compositeurs" awarded a prize, 1889), etc.

**Pier'son, (1)** or **Pier'zon.** Vide LA
RUE. (2) (rightly **Pearson**), **Henry
Hugo** (early pen-name "**Edgar
Mansfeldt**"), Oxford, 1815—Leip-
zig, 1873 ; prof. of mus.; prod. in
Germany 4 operas. (3) **Pierson-
Brethol** (brā'-tŏl), **Bertha,** b. Vienna.

July 15, 1861; soprano; studied with Laufer, Varesi and Lamperti, début, Graz; toured U. S. 1882–84; 1884–88 in Italy singing Wagner, etc.; then Berlin 1882; retired 1897; wife of (4) **Henry**, 1851?—Berlin, Feb. 17, 1902; opera-director; from 1889, court-dir. at Berlin.

**Pieterez** (pē'-tĕ-räs), **Adrian**, b. Bruges, early 15th cent.; first known org.-builder in Belgium.

**Piéton** (pǐ-ä-tôṅ), **Loyset**, French contrapuntist, 1531.

**Pig'gott**, (1) **Francis**, d. 1704; Engl. organist at Oxford; composer. (2) **Francis**, Jr., d. 1736; son and succ. of above.

**Pilk'ington**, **Francis**, Engl. lutenist and composer, 1595–1614.

**Pilotti** (pē-lôt'-tē), **Giuseppe**, Bologna, 1784—1838; son and succ. of an org.-builder; professor, writer and dram. composer.

**Pinel'li**, **Ettore**, b. Rome, Oct. 18, 1843; violinist; pupil of Ramaciotti and Joachim; 1866, founded (with Sgambati) soc. for classical chamber-mus.; 1874, the " Società Orchestrale Romana," which he cond.; since 1877, in the Liceo Musicale; also cond. ct.-concerts alternately with Sgambati; c. overture " *Rapsodia italiana*," etc.

**Pin'ner**, **Max**, New York, 1851—Davos, Switzerland, 1887; pupil Leipzig Cons. and of Tausig; pianist and teacher.

**Pinsuti** (pǐn-soo'-tē), **Ciro**, Sinalunga, Florence, 1829—Florence, 1888; famous vocal teacher at the R. A. M., London, from 1856; composer of operas and very popular songs.

**Pintt**, (1) **Thos.**, b. Engl., d. Ireland, 1773; remarkable pianist. (2) **G. Fred.**, Lambeth, 1786—Little Chelsea, 1806; grandson of above; violinist, pianist, singer and composer.

**Piozzi** (pē-ôd'-zē), **Gabriel**, b. Florence; d. Engl., 1809; teacher and composer; immortal chiefly for having married Dr. Samuel Johnson's Mrs. Thrale, 1784.

**Pipegrop** (pē'-pĕ-grôp) (called **Ba phonus**), **H.**, Wernigerode, 158 Quedlinburg, 1655; town-cantor theorist.

**Pipelare** (pē-pĕ-lä'-rĕ), **Matthæ** 16th cent. Belgian composer.

**Pirani** (pē-rä'-nē), **Eugenio**, b. logna, Sept. 8, 1852; pianist; p of Golonelli, Bologna Liceo Music and of Th. Kullak (pf.) and I (comp.); 1870–80 in Kullak's Ac: lived in Heidelberg till 1895, t Berlin; wrote essays; c. sym poem, " *Heidelberg*," etc.

**Pisa** (pē'-zä), **Agostino**, wrote earl known treatise on conducting, (2d ed., Rome, 1611).

**Pisari** (pē-sä'-rĕ), **Pasquale**, Ro 1725—1778; bass-singer and c poser, whom Padre Martini ca the " Palestrina of the 18th cent."

**Pisaroni** (pē-sä-rō'-nē), **Benede Rosamonda**, Piacenza, 1793—18 high soprano; after an illness beca a contralto.

**Pischek** (pē'-shĕk), **Jn. Ba** Mscheno, Bohemia, 1814—Sig ringen, 1873; barytone.

**Pisendel** (pē'-zĕnt-ĕl), **Jn. G.**, Ka burg, 1687—Dresden, 1755; violii and composer.

**Pistocchi** (pēs-tôk'-kē), **Fran. A** Palermo, 1659—Bologna, after 17 founder of famous Sch. of Singing Bologna; c. operas.

**Pitoni** (pē-tō'-nē), **Gius. Ottavîo**, eti, Italy, March 18, 1657—Ro Feb. 1, 1743; an eminent teac and composer; pupil of Natale Froggia; from 1677 cond. Coll. San Marco, Rome; c. a Dixit in parts for 4 choirs, etc.

**Pitt'man**, **Josiah**, 1816; organ composer, writer and lecturer.

**Pittrich** (pǐt'-trĭkh), **G. Washingt** b. Dresden, Feb. 22, 1870; stud Dresden Cons., graduating with h honours; from 1890, chorusm. D den ct.-opera, also cond. operas, b lets, etc., and taught chorus-sing in the Cons.; 1898, cond. Hamb opera; 1899, 1st cond. Cologne

a ; c. 1-act opera "*Marga*" (Dres-
n, Feb. 8, 1894) ; incid. mus., a
rinet-concerto, etc.

:ti (pē-oot'-tē), (1) **K.**, Elgersburg,
uringia, April 30, 1846—Leipzig,
ne 17, 1902; notable organist ; pu-
l, and from 1875, teacher Leipzig
ns.; 1880, also organist Thomas-
che ; wrote a harm.; c. 6 fugal
itasias, 8 preludes, "*Wedding So-
ta*," etc., for organ. (2) **Max.**,
usenhail, near Erfurt, 1852—Jack-
n, Mich., 1885 ; brother of above ;
iter, teacher and composer.

**s** (pēx'-ēs), (1) **Fr. Wm.**, Mann-
im, 1786—Prague, 1842 ; violinist
d conductor. (2) **Jn. Peter**,
annheim, 1788 — Baden - Baden,
74 ; bro. of above ; pianist, teach-
and dram. composer.

:i (pĭd'-zē), **Emilio**, b. Verona,
b. 2, 1862 ; pupil of Ponchielli and
zzini, Milan Cons., graduating
84 ; took 1st prize Milan, 1885, for
ict opera "*Lina*"; 1st and 2d
ize, Florence, for 2 string quartets ;
ize of 5,000 francs, Bologna, 1889,
r succ. grand opera "*Guglielmo
itcliff*" (Bologna, 1889) ; 1897, dir.
mus.-sch. at Bergamo and at church
S. Maria Maggiore ; c. also 2
ct operas "*Gabriella*" and "*Ro-
lba*" (written for Adelina Patti,
93–96), etc.

**dy** (plĭ'-dē), **Louis**, Huberts-
rg. Saxony, Nov. 28, 1810—Grim-
a, March 3, 1874 ; eminent pf.-
icher ; pupil of Agthe and Haase ;
first a violinist ; 1843, invited by
endelssohn to teach at the then new
eipzig Cons., and did so till 1865 ;
ote text-books.

**ik** (plänk), **Fritz**, b. Vienna, Nov.
1848 ; studied with F. Schmitt
d Gänsbacher ; sang at Carlsruhe
d lives there ; sang at Bayreuth
ice 1884, "Hans Sachs," etc.

**iquette** (plän-kĕt), (**Jean**) **Robert**,
Paris, July 31, 1850 ; studied
mp. with Duprato, Paris Cons., c
ansons and "*Saynètes*" for "ca-
s-concerts"; prod. succ. 1-act op-

eretta "*Paille d'Avoine*" (1874) followed by others incl. the still pop.
comic opera, "*Les Cloches de Corne-
ville*" (Folies - Dramatiques, 1877),
given over 400 times, consecutively,
and widely popular elsewhere (known
in Engl. as "Chimes of Normandy");
later works incl. "*Mam'zelle Quat'
sous*" (Gaité, 1897) and for London
"*The Old Guard*" (1887), and
"*Paul Jones*" (1889).

**Plantade** (plän-tăd), (1) **Chas. H.**,
Pontoise, 1764—Paris, 1839 ; prof. of
singing at Paris Cons.; ct.-conductor
and dram. composer. (2) **Chas.
Fran.**, Paris, 1787—1870 ; son of
above ; composer.

**Planté** (plän-tā), **Fran.**, b. Orthez,
Basses Pyrénees, March 2, 1839 ; pianist ; pupil of Marmontel at Paris
Cons.; won 1st prize after 7 months'
tuition ; pupil of Bazin (harm.) then
self-taught for 10 years ; reappeared
with succ.; c. transcriptions.

**Plantania** (plän-tā'-nĭ-ä), **Pietro**, b.
Catania, April 5, 1828 ; pupil of P.
Raimondi at the Cons. there ; 1863,
dir. Palermo Cons.; later cond. Milan (1888), dir. R. Coll. of Mus. at
Naples ; wrote a treatise on canon
and fugue ; c. 5 operas ; a symph.
"*L'Italia*"; funeral symphony in
memory of Pacini, festival symph.
with choruses to welcome King Hum-
bert in 1878, etc.

**Platel** (plă-tĕl), **Nicolas Jos.**, Versailles, 1777—Brussels, 1835 ; 'cellist;
prof. and composer.

**Pla'to**, eminent Greek philosopher, 429
—347 B.C.; formulated in his "*Ti-
maeus*" a system of harm., interpret-
ed in Th. H. Martin's "*Études sur
les Timée de Platon*," etc.

**Play'ford**, (1) **John**, 1623 — 1693 ;
London mus.-publisher. (2) **Henry**,
his son and successor, 1657—1710.

**Ples'ants**, **Thos.**, 1648 — 1689 ; organist at Norwich.

**Pleyel** (plĭ'-ĕl, or plĕ'-yĕl), (1) **Ignaz
Jos.**, Ruppertshal, near Vienna,
June 1, 1757—at his estate near Paris,
Nov. 14, 1831 ; pianist, c. cond.;

founded,1797,at Paris a piano factory still known as Pleyel, Wolff & Co.; c. 29 symphs., sonatas, etc. (2) **Ca-mille,** Strassburg, 1788—Paris, 1855; son, pupil and successor of above ; a pianist and composer ; his successor in business was August Wolff. (3) **Marie Félicité Denise,** Paris, 1811 — St.-Josse-ten-Noode, 1875 ; wife of (2) ; pianist and teacher.

**Plüddemann** (plüt'-dĕ-män), **Martin,** Kolberg, 1854—Berlin, 1897 ; conductor and singing teacher, writer and composer.

**Plutarch (Plutar'chos)** (ploo'-tärk), Chaeronea, Boeotia, ca. 50 A.D.—120 (131 ?) ; the Greek biographer ; wrote treatises '' *De musica,*'' containing important data.

**Poenitz** (pä'-nĭtsh), **Fz.,** b. Bischofswerda, Aug. 17, 1850; harpist ; studied with Weitzmann, Berlin ; since 16 at the ct. opera ; composer.

**Pohl** (pōl), (1) **K. Fd.,** Darmstadt, 1819—Vienna, 1887 ; writer. (2) **Richard,** Leipzig, 1826 — Baden-Baden, 1896 ; ed. and writer (penname '' Hant ''). (3) **Bd.** Vide POLLINI.

**Pohlenz** (pō'-lĕnts), **Chr. Aug.,** Saalgast, Niederlausitz, 1799—Leipzig, 1843 ; organist, conductor and composer.

**Poise** (pwäz), **Jn. Alex. Fd.,** Nîmes, 1828—Paris, 1892 ; dram. composer.

**Poisot** (pwä-zō), **Chas. Émile,** b. Dijon, France, July 8, 1822; pianist; pupil of Paris Cons.; co.-founder '' Soc. des Compositeurs''; founder and dir. Dijon Cons., also from 1872 cond. Soc. for Sacred and Classical Mus.; dram. composer and writer.

**Poiszl** (poish'-'l), **Jn. Nepomuk,** Freihe. von, Haukenzell, Bavaria, 1783 — Munich, 1865 ; dram. composer.

**Pölchau** (pĕl'-khow), **G.,** Cremon, Livonia, 1773—Berlin, 1836 ; librarian and collector.

**Pole, Wm.,** b. Birmingham, Engl., April 22, 1814 ; Mus. Doc. Oxon., 1864 ; 1876–90, examiner in Mus.

London Univ.; writer ; c. Psalm in cantata-form, etc.

**Polidoro** (pō-lĭ-dō'-rō), (1) **Giusep** d. Naples, 1873 ; singing - teac Naples Cons. (2) **Federico,** Naples, Oct. 20, 1845 ; scn and pil of above ; studied with L Conti and d'Arienzo, essayist historian under pen-name '' Acut

**Polko** (pôl'-kō) (née **Vogel), Él** Wackerbarthsruhe, near Dresc 1826—Munich, 1899 ; mezzo-sopr and writer of romantic musical says.

**Pollarolo** (pôl-lä-rō'-lō), (1) **C** **Fran.,** Brescia, 1653—Venice, 17 organist and dram. composer. **Ant.,** Venice, 1680—1750; son successor of above, and dram. c poser.

**Polledro** (pôl-lä'-drō), **Giov. B** Piovà, n. Turin, 1781—1853 ; vic ist, cond. and composer.

**Pollini** (pôl-lē'-nē), (1) **Fran.,** Laib Carniola, 1763 — Milan, Sept. 1846 ; pianist and pf.-prof., 1809, lan Cons.; perhaps the first to w pf.-music on 3 staves. (2) **Ed.** (rig **Pohl),** Cologne, Dec. 18, 18 Hamburg, Nov. 27, 1897 ; te later barytone ; but more famous manager; his second wife was Bia Bianchi. (3) **Cesare,** Cavaliere b. Padua, July 13, 1858 ; stuc with Bazzini, Milan ; 1883–85 dir a Cons. at Padua ; resigned to w and compose.

**Pollitzer** (pôl'-lĭts-ĕr), **Ad.,** b. Pe 1832 ; violinist ; pupil of Böhm ( and Preyer (comp.), Vienna ; tos Europe, then studied with Alard Paris ; 1851 leader H. M.'s London ; later New Philh. Sc prof. of vln., London Acad. of M since 1890, director.

**Polonini** (pō-lō-nē'-nĭ), (1) **Entin** Italian bass ; début, London, 18 (2) **Aless.,** d. 1880 ; son of abo barytone.

**Ponchard** (pôn-shär), (1) **L. A** **Éléonore,** Paris, 1787—1866 ; te and prof. at the Cons. (2) **Ch**

ris, 1824—1891 ; son of above ;
cher at the Cons.

chielli (pôn-kĭ-ĕl'-lē), **Amilcare,**
derno Fasolaro, Cremona, Aug.
1834—Milan, Jan. 16, 1886 ; op-
, composer ; pupil Milan Cons. ;
ganist, then bandmaster,1881;cond.
cenza Cath. from 1856; c. 10 op-
s, incl. "*La Giaconda,*" widely
pular ; 1902 his son discovered a
5. opera "*I Mori di Valenza*"
mposed, 1878–79).

atowski (pō-nĭ-ä-tôf'-shkĭ), **Jozef
ichal Xawery Franciszek
n),** Prince of Monte Rotondo,
me. 1816 — Chiselhurst, Engl.,
3 ; tenor and dram. composer.

tz (pä'-nĭts), **Fz.,** b. Bischofs-
rda, W. Prussia, Aug. 17, 1850 ;
oil of L. Grimm ; from 1866,
pist Berlin royal orch.; 1891
hamber-virtuoso ;" c. opera "*Cle-
tra,*" etc.

s (pōns), **José,** Gerona, Catalonia,
68—Valentia, 1818 ; composer.

te, **Lorenzo da.** Vide DA PONTE.

écoulant (pôn-tä-koo-läň), **L.
l. le Doulcet,** Marquis **de,** Paris,
24 — Bois Colombe, near Paris,
32 ; writer.

coglio (pôn-tōl'-yō), **Cipriano,**
umello - del - Piano, Italy, 1831—
lan, 1892 ; dir. ; c. operas. .

e, **Elizabeth,** b. London, April
1820 ; mezzo-soprano and violin-

per (pôp'-pĕr), **David,** b. Prague,
ne 18, 1845 ; prominent 'cellist ;
pil of Goltermann, Prague Cons.;
nember of Prince von Hechingen's
h., at Löwenburg ; since 1863 has
ured Europe with greatest succ. ;
68–73, 1st 'cello, Vienna ct.-orch.;
72 m. Sophie Menter (divorced,
86) ; c. excellent and pop. 'cello-
s., a concerto, etc.

ges (pôr'-gĕs), **H.,** b. Prague,
ov. 25, 1837 ; pupil of Müller (pf.),
mmel (harm.) and Zwonar (cpt.) ;
63 co.-ed. "*Neue Zeitschrift fur
usik*"; friend and champion of
agner ; lived in Vienna; 1867 was

called to Munich by King Ludwig
II.; pf.-teacher R. Sch. of Mus. and
since 1871 R. Musikdirector ; writer
and composer.

**Por'pora, Niccolò A.** (wrote his name
" Niccolà," printed it as here),
Naples, Aug. 19, 1686—1766 (or 67);
eminent vocal teacher at London,
1729–36 ; ct.-conductor ; as dram.
composer, rival of Händel, c. about
50 operas.

**Porporino** (-rē'-nō). Vide UBERTI.

**Porta** (pôr'-tä), (1) Padre **Costanzo,**
Cremona, ca. 1530—Padua, 1601 ;
writer and composer. (2) **Fran.
della,** Milan, ca. 1590—1666 ; composer. (3) **Giov.,** Venice, ca. 1690—
Munich, 1755 ; ct.-cond. and dram.
composer.

**Por'ter,** (1) **Walter,** d. London, 1659;
tenor and composer. (2) **Samuel,**
Norwich, 1733—1810 ; organist and
composer. (3) **Frank Addison,**
b. Dixmont, Maine, Sept. 3, 1859 ;
graduate, N. E. Cons., Boston, later
piano prof. there ; studied later at
Leipzig ; since 1892 also supt. Normal Course for pf.; pub. a pf.-meth-
od, etc. ; c. prelude and fugue, etc.

**Port'mann,** (1) **Richard,** organist
Westminster Abbey, 1633, etc. (2)
**Jn. Gl.,** Oberlichtenau, Saxony, 1739
—Darmstadt, Sept. 27, 1798 ; singer
and theorist.

**Portugal (Portogallo)** (pôr-tŭ-gäl' or
pôr-tō-gäl'-lo), i.e., " The Portuguese"), **Marcos A.** (acc. to Vasconcellos, rightly "**Portugal da Fon-
seca,**" not **M. A. Simão** as in Fétis).
Lisbon, March 24, 1762—of apoplexy,
Rio de Janeiro, Feb. 7, 1830 ; the
most eminent of Portuguese composers ; studied Italy and prod. 3 operas
there ; 1790 ct.-cond. Lisbon, also
theatre cond. and produced 20 operas
1810 followed the court to Rio and
prod. operas ; 1813 dir. of a Cons.
at Vera Cruz.

**Pothier** (pōt-yä), **Dom Jos.,** b. Bouze-
mount, near Saint-Dié, Dec. 7, 1835 ;
1866, prof. of theology Solesmes
monastery ; writer and theorist.

**Pott, August,** b. Nordheim, Hanover, Nov. 7, 1806 ; violinist and composer, pupil of Spohr.

**Pot'ter, Philip Cipriani Hambly,** London, Oct. 2, 1792—Sept. 26, 1871 ; pianist, writer and composer.

**Pougin, Fran. Aug. Arthur (Paroisse),** b. Châteauroux, Indre, France, Aug. 6, 1834 ; pupil Paris Cons.; 1856–59, asst.-cond. Folies-Nouvelles ; till 1863, violinist at Op.-Com., then important critic, essayist and biographer ; ed. the supplement to "*Fétis*" (1878).

**Pow'ell, Walter,** (1) Oxford, 1697—1744, counter-tenor. (2) **Maud,** b. Illinois, 1868 ; first notable American woman violinist ; pupil of Lewis, later in Paris and of Schradieck, Leipzig, and of Joachim ; has toured widely with success Europe and America.

**Pradher** (rightly **Pradère**) (präd-ā, or prä-dăr'), **Louis Barthélemy,** Paris, 1781— Gray, Haute-Saone, 1843 ; noted teacher at the Cons. and the court ; pianist, and dram. composer.

**Präger** (prä'-gĕr), (1) **H. Aloys P.,** Amsterdam, 1783—Magdeburg, 1854; violinist and conductor. (2) **Fd. Chr. Wm.,** Leipzig, Jan. 22, 1815—London, Sept. 1, 1891 ; son and pupil of above ; 'cellist, later pianist and writer ; c. symph. poem "*Life and Love, Battle and Victory,*" overture "*Abellino,*" etc.

**Prätorius** (prä - tō' - r ǐ- oos) (Latinised form of **Schulz(e)**), (1) **Gottschalk,** Salzwedel, 1528 — Wittenberg, 1573 ; writer. (2) **Chp.,** b. Silesia(?) ; pub. a funeral song on Melanchthon (1560). (3) **Hieronymus,** Hamburg, 1560—1629 ; son of an organist ; organist ; c. churchmus., etc., with his son (4) **Jakob,** d. 1651 ; organist. (5) **Bartholomäus,** composer, Berlin, 1616. (6) (or **Praetorius**), **Michael,** Kreuzberg, Thuringia, Feb. 15, 1571(72)—Wolfenbüttel, Feb. 15, 1621 ; conductor and ct.-organist. Eminent as a composer of church- and dance-mus.;

wrote valuable historical "Synta; musicum."

**Pratt,** (1) **J.,** Cambridge, Engl., 177 1855 ; organist and composer. **Chas. E.,** Hartford, Conn., 184 New York, 1902 ; pianist, cond. composer. (3) **Silas Gamaliel,** Addison, Vt. Aug. 4, 1846 ; Pro nent American composer for orc at 12 thrown on his own resour became a clerk in mus.-houses ; st ied with Bendel, and Kullak (p Wuerst and Kiel (comp.) ; 1871 ganised Apollo Club, Chicago ; 18 returned to Berlin, and studied w H. Dorn ; prod. "*Anniver:s Overture*" there 1876; 1877, Chi go ; gave symph. concerts, 1878, a prod. his opera "*Zenobia,*" 184 1885, gave concerts of his o comp. Crystal Palace, London ; si 1890, pf.-prof. N. Y. Metropoli Cons.; c. lyric opera "*Lucille*" (1 cago, 1887) ; "*The Last Inca,*" c tata with orch. which ran for th weeks ; 2 symphs. (No. 2 the nota "*Prodigal Son*"), "*Magdale: Lament*" (based on Murillo's pict for orch.; an excellent symph. su "*The Tempest*" ; a grotesque s "*The Brownies*"; cantata " lumbus," etc.

**Prat'ten,** (1) **Robt. Sidney,** Bri: 1824— Ramsgate, 1868 ; flutist composer. (2) **Fr. S.,** d. 1873 ; I of above ; contrabassist.

**Predieri** (prä-dǐ-ā'-rē), (1) **Giaco Cesare,** d. after 1711 ; from 1 cond. at Bologna Cath. ; c. ora rios, motets, etc. (2) **Luca Ant.,** logna, 1688—1769 ; ct.-cond. dram. composer.

**Preindl** (prīnt' 'l), **Jos.,** Marbach, L er Austria, 1756 — Vienna, 18 conductor, writer and collector.

**Preitz** (prīts), **Fz.,** b. Zerbst, A 12, 1856 ; concert-organist ; pupi Leipzig Cons., singing-teacher, Ze Gymnasium, and cantor at the church ; pub. a requiem, etc.

**Prell** (prĕl), (1) **Jn. Nicolaus,** H. burg, 1773—1849; 'cellist and teacl

**(2) Aug. Chr.,** b. Hamburg, Aug. 1, 1805 ; son and pupil of above ; from 1822, 2nd 'cello at Meiningen ; from 1825 1st 'cello, Hamburg ; pensioned 1869.

**elleur** (prĕl'-lŭr), **Peter,** d. before 1758 ; Engl. organist, writer and composer.

**en'tice, Thos.** Ridley, Paslow Hall, Ongar, Essex, 1842—Hampstead, 1895 ; teacher, pianist and writer.

**es'sel, Gv Ad.,** Tübingen, 1827—Berlin, 1890 ; dram. composer.

**es'ser, Theodore,** b. Pittsburg, Pa., July 3, 1848 ; Philadelphia publisher ; 1883, founded and has since ed. "The Etude," transl. text-books, etc.; c. instructive pf.-pcs., etc.

**évost** (prā-vō), **Eugène Prosper,** Paris, Aug. 23, 1809—New Orleans, Aug. 30, 1872 ; conductor and singing-teacher ; prod. operas in Paris and New Orleans.

**evosti** (prā-vôs'-tē), **Francheshina,** b. Livorno, 1865 ; her mother was English ; she studied with Rononi at Milan and début at La Scala ; toured widely ; from 1890 in Germany winning especial succ. in "La Traviata."

**eyer** (prī'-ĕr), (1) **Gf.,** Hausbrunn, Lower Austria, May 15, 1809—Vienna, 1901 ; organist ; pupil of Sechter ; 1838, prof. of harm. and cpt. at the Cons.; 1844–48, dir.; 1844, also ice ct.-cond.; 1846, ct.-organist ; 1853, con. at St. Stephen's ; 1876, pensioned as "Vice-Hofkapellmeister"; prod. 3 operas, masses, etc. (2) **Wm. Thierry,** b. Manchester, Engl., July 2, 1841, studied Bonn Univ. ; 1869–94 prof. of physiology, Jena ; acoustician.

**ipp** (prĕ'-lĭp), **Camille,** mus. sell- at Paris, c. 400 pf.-pcs., some very pop. under pen-name C. "Schubert.

**l** (prĭl), **K.,** b. Berlin, Oct. 22, 1864, son and pupil of a mus.- r., and pupil of Helmich, Wirth, and Ioachim (at the Hochschule);

violinist ; 1883–85 leader Bilse's orch.; 1885 at Magdeburg ; from 1891, of the Gewandhaus Orch., Leipzig ; later at Nürnberg ; 1901, at Schwerin (vice Zumpe).

**Prime-Stevenson** (originally **Stevenson), Edw. Irenaeus,** b. Madison, N. J.; prominent writer and critic ; grad. Freehold Inst., N. J., 1881 book reviewer and critic N. Y. "Independent"; also from 1895 of "Harper's Weekly"; 1899, because of an inheritance added "Prime" to his name and lives abroad, chiefly at Vienna ; writer of mus. novels, "A Matter of Temperament," "Sylvester Sand"; also "White Cockades,"etc., and a coll. of sketches, "Some Men and Women, and Music."

**Pring,** (1) **Jacob C.,** Lewisham, Eng., 1771—1799 ; organist and composer. His 2 brothers were (2) **Jos.,** Kensington, 1776—Bangor, 1842; organist, writer and composer. (3) **Isaac,** Kensington, 1777—Oct. 18, 1799 ; organist.

**Printz** (prĭnts), **W. Caspar,** Waldthurn, Upper Palatinate, 1641—Sorau, 1717 ; cantor and theorist.

**Proch** (prōkh), **H.,** Böhmisch-Leipa, June 22, 1809—Vienna, Dec. 18, 1878 ; noted vocal teacher and conductor ; c. comic opera and famous vocal variations.

**Prochaska** (prō-khäs'-kä), **Ludwig,** Prague, 1835 (?)—July 18, 1888 ; singing teacher and composer of pop. Bohemian dances and songs.

**Proksch** (prôksh), (1) **Josef,** Reichenberg, Bohemia, 1794—Prague, 1864 ; pianist, writer and composer; founded a pf.-school ; his children and successors were (2) **Theodor,** 1843—1876 ; and (3) **Marie.**

**Prony** (prô-nē), **Gaspard Claire Fran M. Riche,** Baron de, Chamelot, France, 1755 — Paris, 1839 ; harpist and writer.

**Proske** (prôsh'-kĕ), **K.,** Gröbnig, Upper Silesia, 1794—Ratisbon, 1861 ; canon, conductor, publisher, editor and composer.

**Prout** (prowt), (1) **Ebenezer**, b.
Oundle, Northamptonshire, March
1, 1835; prominent theorist and composer. Save for a few piano lessons
as a boy, and with Chas. Salaman,
wholly self - taught. B.A. London
Univ., 1854; 1859 took up music;
1861–73, organist Union Chapel, Islington; 1861–85, pf.-prof. at the
Crystal Palace Sch. of Art; from
1876 prof. of harm. and comp. at the
Nat. Training Sch.; 1879, at the R.
A. M. (vice A. Sullivan), also cond.
1876–90, the Hackney Choral Assoc.;
1874 Critic on the "Acad."; 1879,
on the "Athenaeum." Contributed
53 articles to Grove's "*Dictionary.*"
1894, prof. of mus., Dublin Univ.;
1895, Mus. Doc. *h. c.* Dublin and
Edinburg Univ. Has pub. many
valuable and original treatises, incl.
"*Harmony*" (1889, 10 editions);
"*Counterpoint, Strict and Free*"
(1890); "*Double Counterpoint and
Canon*" (1891); "*Fugue*" (1891);
"*Fugal Analysis*" (1892); "*Musical Form*" (1893); "*Applied Forms*"
(1895); "*The Orchestra*" (1898–
1900); c. 4 symphs., 2 overtures,
"*Twelfth Night*" and "*Rokeby;*"
suite de ballet for orch.; suite in D;
cantatas; a Magnificat, Evening
Service, Psalm 126 (St. Paul's, 1891);
Psalm 100 "*The Song of Judith*"
(Norwich, 1867), "*Freedom*" (1885),
all with orch., 2 organ-concertos, 2
prize pf.-quartets, etc. (2) **Louis
Beethoven**, b. London, Sept. 14,
1864; son of above; from 1888,
prof. of harm. Crystal Palace Sch. of
Art; pub treatises; c. Psalm 93.
**Pruckner** (prook'-něr), (1) **Dionys**,
Munich, May 12, 1834—Heidelberg,
Dec. 1, 1896; pianist and teacher.
(2) **Caroline**, b. Vienna, Nov. 4,
1832; succ. operatic soprano; 1855,
suddenly lost her voice; 1870 opened
a Sch. of Opera; pub. a vocal treatise
(1872) for which she was made Prof.
**Prudent** (prü-dän) (**Beunie-Prudent**),
**Émile**, Angoulême, 1817 — Paris,
1863; pianist and composer.

**Prume** (prüm), (1) **Fran. Hube**
Stavelot, near Liège, 1816—184
ct.-prof. and composer. (2) **Fz. F**
nephew of the above. Vide JEH.
PRUME.
**Prumier** (prüm-yä), (1) **Ant.**, Par
1794—1868; harpist; prof. at
Cons. and composer. (2) **An**
**Conrad**, 1821 (?)—Paris, 1884; s
pupil and successor of above.
**Psellos** (psěl'-lōs), **Michael**, theo
at Constantinople, ca. 1050.
**Ptolemy** (tǒl'-ǔ-mē), **Claudius**,
celebrated astronomer in the
century; wrote treatise on mus.
**Puccini** (poot-chē'-nē), (1) **Giacon**
b. Italy, 1712; pupil of Padre M
tini; organist; c. church-music.
**Antonio**, b. 1747; son of above
church-music and (acc. to Fétis) o
ras; m. di capp. to Republic of
Lucca; his son and successor (3) **I**
**menico**, 1771—1815; c. church-m
and many comic operas; his son
**Michele**, 1812—1864; pupil of N
cadante; lived at San Lucca
church and opera-composer; his
(5) **Giacomo**, b. Lucca, Italy, 18
pupil of Angeloni at Lucca; the
A. Ponchielli, Milan Cons., grad
ing with a "*Capriccio sinfonic*
1893, prof. of comp. there; prod. 1
opera "*Le Villi*" (Milan 1884);
tended later to 2-acts and prod
La Scala; succ. "*Edgar*" (La Sc
Milan, 1889); succ. lyric dr
"*Manon Lescaut*" (Turin, 18
widely popular opera seria "*La
hème*" (Turin, 1896); succ. "
*Tosca*" (London, Covent Gar
1900); "*Madame Butterfly.*"
**Pucitta** (poo-chǐt'-tä), **V.**, Civita
chia, 1778—Milan, 1861: cemb
and dram. composer.
**Puchat** (poo'-khät), **Max**, b Bres
1859; pianist, pupil of Kiel, at
lin; 1884, Mendelssohn prize;
symph. poems "*Euphorion*" (1
and "*Tragödie eines Künst*
(1894); overture; a pf.-concerto,
**Puchtler** (pookh'-tlěr), **Wm.**
Holzkirchen, Franconia, 1848—1

**r**; teacher, conductor and composer.

**r** (poo'-dôr), (1) **Jn. Fr.**, Desch, Saxony, 1835 — Dresden, **7**; from 1859 proprietor Dresden **ns.** (2) Dr. **H.**, b. ca. 1860; son **d** successor of above in the Cons., **ich** he sold 1890 to E. Krantz; **te** many essays.

**te** (poo-ĕn'-tě), **Giuseppe del,** **ples,** April, 1845—Philadelphia, S. A., May 25, 1900; operatic **rytone** and teacher.

**et** (pü-zhā), **Paul Chas. M.,** b. **ntes,** June 25, 1848; pupil of **ris** Cons., took Grand Prix de **me**; prod. comic opera "*Le Sig-* **l**" (Op. Com., 1886); mod. succ. **era** "*Beaucoup de Bruit Pour* **en**" ("*Much Ado about Nothing*") **id.,** 1899); incid. mus. to "*Loren-* **cio,**" etc.

**nani** (poon-yä'-nē), **Gaetano,** Tu**n,** Nov. 27, 1731—July 15, 1798; **nous** violinist, dram. composer **d** conductor.

**ni** (poon'-yē), **Cesare,** Milan, **05**—St. Petersburg, 1870; dram. **mposer.**

**no** (pün-yō), **Raoul,** b. Montrouge, **ine,** France, June 23, 1852; prom**ent** pianist; st. Paris Cons.; 1866 **ok** 1st pf.-prize, 1867, 1st harm.**ize**; 1869, 1st org.-prize; organist **d** cond. Paris; from 1896, prof. of **ano** at the Cons. 1897–98, toured **.** S. with succ.; Officer of the Aca**mie**; prod. an oratorio, "*La Re-* **rrection de Lazare*" (1879); comic **era** "*Ninetta*" (1882); 2 opéras **uffes,** 3 1-act vaudev.-operettas **La Petite Poucette*" (1891; Berlin, **93,** as "*Der Talisman*"); pan**mime,** etc.; 1902 toured U. S. **zain** with increased success.

**iti** (poo-lē'-tē), **Leto,** Florence, **18**—1875; composer.

**ato, G.** Vide STICH.

**po** (poop'-pō), **Gius.,** Lucca, June **2,** 1749—in poverty, Florence, April **9.** 1827; an eccentric violinist, con**uctor** and composer.

**Purcell** (pŭr'-sĕl), (1) **H.,** d. London, 1664; gentleman of the Chapel Royal, and Master of the Choristers at Westminster Abbey. (2) **Henry** (called "the younger"), London 1658—of consumption, Dean's Yard, Westminster, Nov. 21, 1695; son of above. Most eminent of strictly English composers. Chorister Chapel Royal, and studied with Cooke, Humfrey, and Dr. Blow; at 18 c. mus. for Dryden's tragedy, "*Aurungzebe,*" and Shadwell's comedy "*Epsom Wells*"; pub. a song; at 19 an overture, etc., to Aphra Behn's tragedy, "*Abdelazor,*" and an elegy on Matthew Locke; at 20 c. music to Shadwell's version of "*Timon of Athens*"; 1680, incid. mus., and a short opera "*Dido and Æneas*" written to order for Josias Priest for his "boarding sch. for young gentlewomen"; c. also the "*Ode or Welcome Song for his Royal Highness*" Duke of York, and "*A song to Welcome home His Majesty from Windsor.*" From 1680 organist Westminster Abbey, where he is buried. 1682, organist Chapel Royal; 1683, composer-inordinary to the King. His first pub. chamber-mus. is dated the year 1683. He c. "*Odes*" to King Charles 1684, and to King James in 1685, 28 in all. He c. mus. for 35 dram. works of the time. 1695 he pub. his first real opera, "*Dioclesian.*" The Purcell Society (organised, 1876) has issued many of his works and given frequent performances of them in London. The Mus. Antiq. Soc. has pub. others; his widow pub. in 1697 "*A Collection of Ayres Composed for the Theatre and upon other Occasions*"; also songs for 1–3 voices, from his theatrical works and odes; and the "*Orpheus Brittanicus*" in 2 parts (Part i, 1698, Part ii, 1702). Playford's "*Theatre of Musick*" (1687), and other colls. contain many of his works; "*Purcell's Sacred Music*" is pub. in 6 vols. (Novello). (3) **Edw.,** 1689—174?; son of above;

organist and composer. (4) **Daniel,** London, 1660—Dec. 12, 1718; bro. of above; 1688, organist; 1695, succ. his bro. as dram. composer; c. i mus. to ten dramas; odes, incl neral ode for his brother, etc.

## Purcell.

### By John F. Runciman.

MODERN English musicians scarce count, and by their achievem up to the present can scarce hope to count, in the history of world's music. When, however, the world was younger the English race was fresher, things went differently. Before the res Europe had produced anything worth long consideration to-day, the Eng had brought forth a strong race of musicians; and while the rest of Eur was striving hard to catch up with the English, the English school was rea ing a magnificent culmination in Purcell. Many influences went to the sh ing of him. Behind was the contrapuntal English school, of which Tallis Byrde were exemplars; more immediately behind was Pelham Humphr who brought to England all that France knew; and it is as good as cer that he knew what the Italians, with Corelli at their head, had accomplish That is to say, he must have learned how to handle many parts in a cho or orchestral movement; learned how to write recitative and expressive so learned what could be done in the way of chamber-music; and such orch tral colouring as was possible at that day. ¶ To these acquired masteries brought a native ear for miraculous colour in music—as witness his *Tem* music, written for the worst libretto that the world has not listened to glorious invention of expressive or picturesque melody, though chiefly pic resque; a fine instinct for the dramatic, and for expressing it in music; a the most noble sense of the splendid effects to be gained by throwing ab masses of vocal tone in the manner afterwards appropriated and made entir his own by Handel. ¶ Those who have studied Purcell's scores will be tonished by the extent to which Handel took his themes and modes of us them. In that lies his sole contribution to what must be called the "pr ress" of music. Later English composers, to their shame, and certainly their utter confusion, copied Handel instead of developing on Purcell's lin They profited nothing; and Purcell remains as the last of the tribe of genuinely creative English musicians. He was determined to excel in eve thing he touched; and he excelled in everything. His forms are at on broad and flexible; his harmonies are as daring as Sebastian Bach's; themes have a great dignity and vigour; and on everything he wrote there re an early morning freshness. No music has preserv d its freshness better; dew is still on it. ¶ Born just before the Restoration, he felt to the

anti-Puritan reaction ; he shared in the revival of the sheer joy of being
; and his music is filled with a cheerful health such as one finds in no
c written since his day.    But he experienced the deeper emotions ; and.
may find in his works profound utterances of grief and sorrow, of the
:ery and terror of all life.    He was entirely pagan, and wrote no real re-
us music—religious as we use the word when we speak of Sweelinck,
strina, or Byrde.    But power is there, and delicacy, and marvellous
ty ;   and above all that external freshness and picturesque quality
:h  give his music the character that stamps and marks it off as his

a'nus, Ericius (Latinised form of
, Van de Putte) (poot´-tĕ) (Galli-
ed to Dupuy), Venloo, Holland,
74—Louvain, 1646 ; professor and
iter.
, Kellow J., Exeter, Feb. 9, 1812
Exmouth, Sept. 22, 1901; pianist
d composer.
e (pīn), (1) Geo., 1790—1877, Engl.
ıle alto.    (2) Jas. Kendrick, d.
57;   Engl.  tenor.  (3)  Louisa
ınny, b. England, 1832 ; soprano,
ughter of (2) ;   pupil of Sir G.
ıart ; début, Boulogne, 1849; 1868,
Frank Bodda, a barytone.
ıag'oras, Samos, Greece, ca. 582,
č.—Metapontum, ca. 500 B. C.;
nous philosopher and mathemati-
ın ; developed an elaborate sys-
n of musical ratios.

### 2.

dri (kwä´-drē),  Dom.,  Vicenza,
o1—Milan, 1843 ;   teacher and
eorist.
drio (kwä´-drĭ-ō), Fran. Saverio,
ınte, Valtellina, 1695—Milan, 1756;
eorist.
gliati (kwäl-yä´-tē),  Paolo,  d.
ɔme, ca. 1660; cembalist ;  c. one
the earliest mus. dramas (1611).
ndt (kvänt),  Chr. Fr., Herrnhut,
ıxony, 1766—Niesky, near Görlitz,
n. 30, 1806 ; writer.

Quantz (kvänts),  Jn. Joachim, Ober-
scheden, Hanover, 1697—Potsdam,
1773 ; noted flutist ; inv. the second
key and sliding top for tuning the
flute ; taught Frederick the Great ; c.
500 flute pcs.
Quaranta (kwä-rän´-tä),  Fran.,  Naples, 1848—Milan, 1897 ;  singing-
teacher and dram  composer.
Quarenghi (kwä-rän´-gē), Guglielmo,
Casalmaggiore, 1826—Milan, 1882 ;
'cellist, professor, conductor and
dram. composer.
Quarles (kwärls), Chas., d. 1727; organist at York Minster and composer.
Quatremère de Quincey (kăt-rŭ-măr´-
dŭ-kăń-sē´),   Ant.  Chrysostome,
Paris, 1755—1849 ; writer.
Quef (kĕf), Ch., French organist ; 1900,
choir-org. at La Trinité, Paris ; 1902,
organist (vice Guilmant).
Queisser (kvīs´-sĕr), Carl T., Döben,
n. Leipsic, 1800—1846 ; noted trombonist.
Quercu (kvĕr´-koo), Simon de (Latinised from Van Eycken or Du
Chesne), b. in Brabant ; theorist and
ct.-chapel-singer, Milan, ca. 1500.
Quidant (kē-dän), Alfred (rightly Jos.),
Lyons, France, 1815—Paris, 1893 ;
pianist.
Quinault (kē-nō), (1) Philippe, Paris,
1635—1688 ;  Lully's librettist. (2)
J. Bap. Maurice, d. Gien, 1744 ;
singer, actor and composer of ballets,
etc.

# R

**Ra(a)ff** (räf), Holzem, 1714—Munich, 1797; tenor.

**Rachmaninoff** (räkh-mä'-nē-nôf), **Sergei Vassilievitch**, b. Novgorod, Russia, 1873 ; pianist and composer ; pupil of Siloti (pf.) and Arensky (theory), Moscow Cons.; 1891, took great gold medal ; c. succ. 1-act opera "*Aleko*" (Moscow, 1893), pf.-concerto ; a popular " *Prelude*," and other notable pf.-pieces.

**Radecke** (rä'-dĕk-ĕ), (1) **Rudolf**, Dittmannsdorf, Silesia, 1829—Berlin, 1893 ; conductor, teacher and composer. (2) (**Albert Martin**), **Robert**, b. Dittmannsdorf, Oct. 31, 1830; bro. of above ; pupil of Leipzig Cons.; 1st vln. in Gewandhaus ; then pianist and organist, Berlin ; later mus.-dir. ct.-th.; 1871–84, ct.-cond.; 1883–88, artistic dir. Stern Cons.; 1892, dir. R. Inst. for Church-mus., Berlin ; c. 1-act " *Liederspiel*," " *Die Monkguter*" (Berlin, 1874); a symph., 2 overtures, etc. (3) **Ernst**, b. Berlin, Dec. 8, 1866 ; son of above ; Dr. Phil. at Berlin U., 1891; 1893, town mus.-director and teacher, Winterthur, Switzerland. (4) **Luise**, b. Celle, Hanover, June 27, 1847; soprano ; pupil of Marchesi ; début, 1867, Cologne ; 1876, m. Baron von Brummer.

**Radoux** (rä-doo), **Jean Théodore**, b. Liège, Nov. 9, 1835 ; pupil at the Cons.; 1856, teacher of bassoon there ; 1859, won Prix de Rome with cantata " *Le Juif Errant*;" studied with Halévy, Paris ; 1872, dir. Liège Cons.; pub. biog. of Vieuxtemps (1891); prod. 2 comic operas, oratorio " *Cain*" (1877), cantata " *La Fille de Jephté*" with orch., 2 symph. tone-pictures, symph. overture, Te Deum, etc.

**Radziwill** (rät'-tsē-vĭl), Prince **Anton H.**, Wilna, 1775—Berlin, 1833 ; singer and composer ; patron of Beethoven and Chopin.

**Raff** (räf), (1) Vide RAAF. (2) **Joachim**, Lachen, Lake of Zu May 27, 1822—Frankfort-on-M June 25, 1882 ; eminent comp particularly in the field of prog matic romanticism. Son of an o ist ; too poor to attend a Uni became a sch.-teacher ; was taught in comp. and vln.; 184 sent some comps. to Mendelss who recommended them to a pul er. **R.** accompanied Liszt on a cert-tour as far as Cologne (1 where he lived for a time, writing views ; later von Bulow played "*Concertstück*"; his opera "*K Alfred*" was accepted at the ct. but forestalled by the Revolutio 1848 ; it was prod. in revised for Weimar by Liszt. He pub. (1 a pamphlet " *Die Wagnerfr* 1854, m. the actress Doris Ge and obtained vogue at Wiesbade a pf.-teacher. 1863, his first syn "*An das Vaterland*," won the of the Viennese ' Gesellschaft Musikfreunde ;" 1870, his comic era " *Dame Kobold*," was pro Weimar. 1877, dir. Hoch Cons Frankfort. He was a very pr and uneven composer. The Memorial Soc. pub. at Fran. (1886), a complete list of his w which incl. 11 symphs.: No. 1, ' *das Vaterland*"; famous No. 3 F, "*Im Walde*" (1869) ; No. 5. 177 in E, the noted "*Lenore*"; N op. 189 in D min., " *Gelebt, gest gelitten, gestritten-gestorben, um ben*"; No. 7, op. 201 in B♭, " *In Alpen*"; No. 8, op. 205, A, " *F lingsklänge*"; No. 9, op. 208 min., " *Im Sommer*"; No. 11, 214, A min., " *Der Winter*" (p humous); a sinfonietta ; 4 su No. 2, "*In ungarischer Wei No. 3, " Italienisch*"; No. 4, " *I ringer*"; 9 overtures, the "*J Fest*" and " *Concert - ouvertü "Festouverture*" for wind ; " *feste Burg*," " *Romeo and Jul " Othello*," " *Macbeth*," and "

*Tempest ;"* festival cantata *" Deutschlands Auferstehung"; De profundis* in 8 parts, op. 141; *"Im Kahn"* and *"Der Tanz";* for mixed chorus *" Morgenlied"* and *"Einer Entschlafenen"; " Die Tageszeiten"; " Die Jägerbraut und die Hirtin,"* 2 scenes for solo voice ; all with orch ; the oratorio *" Weltende, Gericht, Neue Welt"* (Revelations) (Leeds, 1882); *" Die Sterne"* and *"Dornröschen"* (MS.) ; 4 unperformed operas, *"Die Eifersüchtigen"* (text and music) ; *" Die Parole," " Benedetto Marcello"* and *" Samson";* mus. to Genast's *" Berhard von Weimar"* (1858) ; *" Ode au printemps"* for pf. and orch.; *" La fête d'Amour "* suite for vln. with orch.; 2 'cello-concertos · much chamber-mus., incl. op. 192 (3 nos., "Suite älterer Form," "Die schöne Müllerin," "Suite in canonform "); 5 vln. sonatas ; 'cello-sonata ; 2 pf.-sonatas, suites, sonatinas ; *"Homage au néo-romantisme," "Messagers du printemps," "Chant d'Ondine"* (arpeggio tremolo étude), Ungarische Rhapsodie, Spanische Rhapsodie, 2 études mélodique, op. 130 (" Cavatina," and the famous "La Fileuse "), many paraphrases ; many songs, incl. 2 cycles, " Maria Stuart " and " Blondel de Nesle " ; 30 male quartets, etc.

**agghianti** (räg-gĭ-än'-tē), **Ippolito,** Viareggio, near Pisa, 1866—1894 ; violinist.

**aif** (rīf), **Oscar,** The Hague, 1847—Berlin, 1899 ; pianist, teacher and composer.

**aillard** (rī-yăr), **Abbé F.,** b. Montormentier, France, 1804 ; teacher of science.

**aimondi** (rä-ē-môn'-dē), (1) **Ignazio,** Naples, 1733—1802 ; violinist and composer. (2) **P.,** Rome, Dec. 20, 1786—Oct. 30, 1853 ; extraordinary contrapuntist, rivalling the ancient masters in ingenuity ; prof. of cpt., and cond. at St. Peter's ; prod. 54 operatic works and 21 ballets, 4 masses w. orch. and 5 oratorios, be-

sides the monumental trilogy " *Giuseppe*" (*Joseph*) consisting of 3 oratorios ("*Potifar,*" " *Giuseppe,*" " *Giacobbe*"), performed at Rome, 1852 separately, then all at once by 400 musicians, producing such frantic excitement that the composer fainted away ; he c. also an opera buffa and an opera seria performable together; 4 four-voiced fugues which could be combined into one fugue *à 16,* etc., incl. a fugue for 64 parts in 16 choirs; he wrote essays explaining his methods.

**Rainforth, Elizabeth,** 1814—Redland, Bristol, 1877, Engl. soprano.

**Ramann** (rä'-män), **Lina,** b. Mainstockheim, near Kitzingen, June 24, 1833 ; pupil of Franz and Frau Brendel, Leipzig ; 1858, founded a mus.-seminary for female teachers, 1865, a mus.-sch. at Nürnberg ; pub. treatises and composed.

**Rameau** (rä-mō), (1) **J. Philippe,** Dijon, Sept. 25, 1683—of typhoid Paris, Sept. 12, 1764 ; eminent as theorist, composer and organist. At 7 he could play at sight on the clavecin any music given him ; from 10 to 14 he attended the Jesuit Coll. at Dijon; but taking no interest in anything but music was dismissed and left to study music by himself. He was sent to Italy, 1701, to break off a love affair, but did not care to study there, and joined a travelling French operatroupe as violinist. Later he became organist at two churches in Paris, 1717. He studied org. with Louis Marchand, who found his pupil a rival, and in a competition favoured his competitor, Daquin, as organist of St. Paul's ; **R.** went as organist to Lille, later to Clermont (where lived his brother (2) **Claude,** a clever organist, and his father (3) **Jean Fran.,** a gifted but dissipated organist and poet). After 4 years he returned to Paris, and pub. a treatise on harm. which attracted some attention. He became organist Sainte-Croix-de-la-Bretonnerie ; and c. songs and dances for pieces by Piron, at the Op.-Com.; 1726, he pub. his epoch-making "*Nouveau système de musique théorique*," based on his own studies of the monochord (v. D. D.); in this work among many things inconsistent, involved and arbitrary (and later modified or discarded) was much of remarkable even sensational, novelty, such as the discovery of the law of chord-inversion. He founded his system on (1) chord-building by thirds; (2) the classification of chords and their inversions to one head each, thus reducing the consonant and dissonant combinations to a fixed number of root-chords; (3) a fundamental bass ("basse fondamentale," not our thorough-bass), an imaginary series of root-tones forming the real bases of all the chord-progressions of a composition. His theories provoked much criticism, but soon won him pupils from far and wide and the pre-eminence as theorist that he enjoyed as organist. He followed his first theoretic treatises with 5 other treatises. He now obtained the libretto "*Samson*" from Voltaire (whom he strikingly resembled in appearance) but the work was rejected on account of its biblical subject. "*Hippolyte et Aricie*," libretto by Abbé Pelegrin, was prod. at the Opéra, 1733, with so little succ. that he was about to renounce the stage, but his friends prevailed and he prod., 1735, the succ. ballet-opera "*Les Indes Galantes*," and at the age of 54 his masterpiece "*Castor et Pollux*," a great succ. as were most of his later works for 23 years, "*Les Fêtes d'Hébé*" (1739), "*Dardanus*" (1739), "*La Princesse de Navarre*," "*Les Fêtes de Polhymnie*," and "*Le Temple de la Gloire*" (1745), "*Les Fêtes de l'Hymen et de l'Amour, ou les Dieux d'Egypte*" (1747), "*Zaïs*" (1748), "*Pygmalion*" (1748), "*Platée ou Junon jalouse*," "*Neis*" and "*Zoroastre*" (the "*Samson*" music with another libretto) (1749), ' *Acanthe et Céphise*,"

"*La Guirlande*," and "*La Naissance d'Osiris*" (1751), "*Daphnis et Églé*," "*Lycis et Délie*" and "*Le Retour d'Astrée*" (1753), "*Anacréon*," "*Les Surprises de l'Amour*," and "*Les Sybarites*" (1757), "*Les Paladins*" (1760). He c. also others not prod. His mus. is full of richness, novelty and truth, though he wrote only fairly for the voice. He said himself that were he younger he would revolutionise his style along the lines of Pergolesi. 1745 the King made him chamber-composer. His patent of nobility was registered, just before his death. He c. also many books of mus. for claveein, etc.; of these a complete ed. is pub. by Steingräber. Biog. by du Charger (1761), Nisard (1867), Grique (1876).

**Ramm** (räm), **Fr.**, b. Mannheim, 1744; eminent oboist.

**Ram'sey, Robt.**, organist and composer at Cambridge, 1628–44.

**Ran'dall**, (1) **J.**, 1715—1799; singer, professor at Cambridge and composer. (2) **Richard**, 1736—1828; tenor in Händel's oratorios.

**Randegger** (rän'-dĕd-jĕr), **Alberto**, b. Trieste, April 13, 1832; pupil of Lafont (pf.), and Ricci (comp.); at 20 prod. 2 ballets and an opera, "*Il Lazzarone*," in collab. with 3 others, at Trieste; then th.-cond. at Fiume, Zara, Sinigagli, Brescia and Venice, where he prod. grand opera "*Bianca Capello*" (1854); ca. 1854, London, as a singing-teacher; 1868 prof. of singing, R. A. M.; later dir. and a member of the Committee of Management; also prof. of singing R. C. M. 1857 cond. It. Opera, St. James's Th. 1879–85, Carl Rosa company; and from 1881, the Norwich Triennial Festival. Wrote "*Primer on singing*." C. comic opera "*The Rival Beauties*" (London, 1864); the 150th Psalm with orch. and org. (Boston Jubilee, 1872); dram. cantata "*Fridolin*" (1873, Birmingham); 2 dram. scenes "*Medea*" (Leipzig, 1869) and "*Saffo*" (London, 1875); canta'a

" *Werther's Shadow* " (Norwich, 1902), etc.

**andhartinger** (ränt-härt'-ĭng-ĕr), **Benedikt,** Ruprechtshofen, Lower Austria, 1802—Vienna, 1894 ; at 10 soprano ; conductor and composer of over 600 works.

**ansford, Edwin,** Gloucestershire, 1805—London, 1876 ; barytone.

**aoul de Coucy.** Vide COUCY.

**appoldi** (räp-pôl'-dē), (1) **Eduard,** b. Vienna, Feb. 21, 1839 ; pupil at the Cons.; 1854–61, violinist ct.-opera ; then leader at Rotterdam, then teacher Hochschule, Berlin ; then leader opera-orch., Dresden, and since 1893 head vln.-teacher at the Cons.; c. chamber-mus., etc. (2) **Laura Rappoldi-Kahrer** (kä'-rĕr), b. Mistelbach, near Vienna, Jan. 14, 1853 ; wife of above ; pianist ; pupil of Vienna Cons. and of Liszt.

**astrelli** (räs-trĕl'-lē), (1) **Jos.,** Dresden, 1799—1843 ; ct.-conductor and dram. composer ; son and pupil of (2) **Vincenzo,** 1760—1839.

**as(o)umovski** (rä-zoo-môf'-shkĭ), Count (from 1815 Prince) **Andrei Kyrillovitch,** Nov. 2, 1752—Sept. 23, 1836 ; Russian ambassador at Vienna, 1793–1809 ; to whom Beethoven dedicated the 3 quartets, op. 59.

**atez** (rä-tĕs), **Émile P.,** b. Besançon, Nov. 5, 1851 ; pupil of Bazin and Massenet at Paris Cons.; vla.- player, Op.-Com.; chorusm. under Colonne ; 1891, dir. the Lille branch of the Paris Cons.; prod. 2 operas " *Ruse d'Amour* " (Besançon, 1886), and succ. " *Lydéric* " (Lille, 1895) ; c. a symph. poem with soli and chorus, " *Scènes héroiques,*" etc.

**athgeber** (rät'-gā-bĕr), **Valentin,**ca. 1690—after 1744, Benedictine monk at Banz, Franconia ; composer.

**atzenberger** (rät'-sĕn-bĕrkh-ĕr), **Th.,** Grossbreitenbach. Thuringia, 1840— Wiesbaden, 1879 ; teacher and comp.

**auchenecker** (row'-khĕ-nĕk-ēr), **G. Wm.,** b. Munich, March 8, 1844 ; pupil of Th. Lachner, Baumgartner

and Jos. Walter (vln.) ; dir. Avignon Cons.; then 1873, mus.-dir. at Winterthur ; 1874, prod. prize cantata, " *Niklaus von der Flüe* " (Zurich Music Festival) ; for one year cond. Berlin Philh. Concerts ; 1889, mus. dir. at Elberfeld, where he prod. 3 succ. operas, " *Die letzten Tage von Thule*" (1889), " *Ingo* " (1893), and " *Sanna* " (1-act, 1893) ; c. also " *Le Florentin*" (not prod.) ; a symph., etc.

**Rauscher** (row'-shĕr), **Max,** b. Wettstetten, Bavaria, Jan. 20, 1860 ; 1884, took holy orders ; from 1885, cond. Ratisbon Cath.

**Rauzzini** (rä-ood-zē'-nē), (1) **Venanzio,** Rome, 1747—Bath, Engl., 1810; tenor and dram. composer. (2) **Matteo,** d. 1791; bro. of above ; dram. composer.

**Ra'venscroft,** (1) **Thos.,** 1582 (?)— London, 1635 (?) ; prominent early English composer and writer. (2) **John,** d. 1740 ; violinist, London.

**Ravera** (rä-vā'-rä), **Niccolò Teresio,** b. Alessandria, Italy, Feb. 24, 1851; pupil Milan Cons.; won first prizes for pf., organ and comp.; now cond. Th.-Lyrique de la Galérie-Vivienne, Paris ; c. 4 operas.

**Ravina** (rä-vē'-nä), **J. H.,** b. Bordeaux, May 20, 1818 ; pianist ; pupil of Zimmermann (pf.) and Laurent (theory) at Paris Cons., won first pf.-prize, 1834 ; 1st harm.-prize, 1836 ; asst.-teacher there till 1837, and also studied with Reicha and Leborne ; made tours ; 1861, chev. of the Legion of Honour ; c. a concerto, etc.

**Raw'lings,** (1) **Thos.,** 1703—1767; Engl. organist. (2) **Robt.,** 1742— 1814 ; son of above ; violinist. (3) **Thos. A.,** 1775 ; violinist, teacher and composer. Son of (2).

**Raymond** (rĕ'-môn̂), **G. M.,** Chambéry, 1769—1839 ; acoustician.

**Rea** (rā), **Wm.,** b. London, March 25, 1827; articled pupil of Josiah Pittmann ; at 16, organist ; studied wi h Sterndale Bennett (pf., comp. **and**

instr.), then at Leipzig and Prague; returned to London, and gave chamber-concerts; 1856, founded the Polyhymnian Choir; organist at various churches; since 1878, at St. Hilda's, South Shields; c. anthems, etc.

**Read, Daniel,** Rehoboth, Mass., 1757—New Haven, Conn., 1836; mus.-teacher and composer.

**Reading** (rĕd'-ĭng), (1) **John,** 1645—Winchester, Engl., 1692; organist and composer of "Dulce domum," etc. (2) **John,** 1677—London, Sept. 2, 1764; son of above; organist and composer; the " *Portuguese Hymn*," " *Adeste Fideles*," is credited to him. (3) **John,** 1674—1720; organist. (4) ——, singer at Drury Lane, 1695. (5) Rev. **John,** Prebendary of Canterbury Cath.; pub. " *A Sermon, concerning Church Musick* " (1663).

**Reay** (rā), **Samuel,** b. Hexham, Engl., March 17, 1822; a pupil of Henshaw and Stimpson; 1841, organist St. Andrew's, Newcastle; since songschoolmaster, Newark Parish Ch. and cond. Philh. Soc.; c. Psalm 102, with string-orch.; Communion Service, etc.

**Rebel** (rŭ-bĕl), (1) **J. Ferry,** Paris, 1669—1747; conductor and composer. (2) **Fran.,** Paris, 1701—1755; violinist and dram. composer.

**Rebello** (rā-bĕl'-lō), **João Lourenço (João Soares),** Caminha, 1609—San Amaro, Nov. 16, 1661, eminent Portuguese composer.

**Reber** (rŭ-bā), **Napoléon H.,** Mühlhausen, Alsatia, Oct. 21, 1807—Paris, Nov. 24, 1880; 1851, prof. of comp., Paris Cons.; pub. one of the best French harm. treatises (1862); c. comic operas, etc.

**Rebicek** (rā'-bĭ-tsĕk), **Josef,** b. Prague, Feb. 7, 1844; violinist; pupil Prague Cons.; 1861, Weimar ct.-orch.; 1863, leader royal th., Wiesbaden; 1875, R. Mus.-Dir.; 1882, leader and op.-dir. Imp. Th. Warsaw; 1891, cond. Nat. Th., Pesth; 1893, at Wiesbaden; 1897, cond., Berlin Philh. Orch.

**Rebling** (rāp'-lĭng), **Gv.,** b. Barby Magdeburg, July 10, 1821; pupil ( Fr. Schneider at Dessau; 1856, Mus.-Dir.; 1858, organist Johanni kirche; 1846, founded and cond. church choral soc.; 1897, c. Psalm " *a cappella*," 'cello-sonata, etc. ( **Fr.,** b. Barby, Aug. 14, 1835; pup of Leipzig Cons. and of Götz (sing ing); 1865-78, tenor at various the tres; from 1877, singing-teacher Lei zig Cons.

**Reckendorf** (rĕk'-ĕn-dôrf), **Alois,** Trebitsch, Moravia, June 10, 184 studied Leipzig Cons.; since 187 teacher of pf. and theory there composer.

**Redan, K.** Vide C. CONVERSE.

**Redeker** (rā'-dĕk-ĕr), **Louise Doret Auguste,** b. Duingen, Hanove Jan. 19, 1853; contralto; studi Leipzig Cons.; début, Bremen, 187

**Red'ford, J.,** organist and compos St. Paul Cath., 1491-1547.

**Red'head, Richard,** Harrow, Eng 1820—May, 1901; studied at Ma dalen Coll., Oxford; organist of S Mary Magdalene's Ch., Londo ed. colls.; c. masses, etc.

**Ree** (rā), **Anton,** Aarhus, Jutlan 1820—Copenhagen, 1886; piani teacher and writer.

**Reed,** (1) **Thos. German,** Bristol, 18 —Upper East Sheen, Surrey, 188 pianist and singer. In 1844 he m. **Priscilla Horton** (1818—1895), fine actress and contralto. Th entertainments were continued their son (3) **Alfred German** London, March 10, 1895). (4) **Rob Hopké,** and (5) **Wm.,** bros of ( 'cellists.

**Reeve, Wm.,** London, 1757—181 c. operettas.

**Reeves,** (1) **(John) Sims,** Woolwi Sept. 26, 1818 (acc. to Gro Shooters Hill, Oct. 21, 1822)—L don, Oct. 25, 1900; noted tenor; 14 organist of North Cray C learned the vln., 'cello, oboe and b soon; and studied with J. B. Cra (pf.) and W. H. Callcott (harm

ut as barytone, 1839; studied
h Hobbs and Cooke, and sang
ior tenor parts at Drury Lane,
n studied with Bordogni, Paris,
1 Mazzucato, Milan, sang at La
ala, 1846, Drury Lane, 1847, with
at succ.; début in Italian opera,
48, at H. M.'s Th., also in orato-
at the Worcester and Norwich
stivals, the same year; retired in
91, but on account of reverses, re-
peared in 1893; and 189 made
c. tour of South Africa; pub. "*Life
d Recollections*" (London, 1888);
m., 1850, (2) **Emma Lucombe**,
era and concert soprano. (3)
erbert, his son and pupil, studied
Milan; concert-début, 1880.

an, **Anna.** Vide SCHIMON-REGAN.
er (rä'-gĕr), **Max**, b. Brand, Ba-
ria, March 19, 1873; pupil of
idner and H. Riemann; c. 'cello-
iata, etc.

ibo (rä'-zhē-bō). **Abel B. M.**, b.
naix, Belgium, April 6, 1835; or-
nist, pianist, and composer.

ino (rä-jē'-nō) (**Prumiensis**), d.
5; Abbot of Prum monastery, near
ier, 892; writer. (Gerbert.)

is (rä'-zhĕs), **Jns.**, Belgian cptist.;
ntemporary of Okeghem.

nal, **Fr.** Vide FR. D'ERLANGER.

nart (or Regnard) (rĕkh'-närt),(1)
.cob, Netherlands, 1540—Prague,
. 1600; imp. vice-cond.; popular
mposer. His brothers (2) **Fz.**, (3)
., and (4) **Pascasius**, also c. songs.
ondi (rä-gôn'-dē), **Giulio**, Geneva,
22—Engl., 1872; guitar, and con-
tina-virtuoso; composer.

baum (rä'-bowm), **Theobald**, b.
rlin, Aug. 7, 1835; pupil of H.
ies (vln.) and Kiel (comp.), l. Wies-
den; c. 7 operas incl. "*Turan-
t*" (Berlin, 1888), etc.

berg (rä'-bĕrkh), (1) **Willy**, b.
orges, Switz., Sept. 2, 1863; pian-
; son and pupil of (2) **Fr. R.** (a
is.-teacher); later studied at Zurich
us.-Sch and Leipzig Cons.; pf.-
acher there till 1890; 1888–90,
nd. at Altenburg since 1890, head

**44**

pf -teacher Geneva Cons.; since 1892,
also cond. Geneva Municipal Orch.
c. vln.-sonata, pf.-sonata, etc.

**Rehfeld** (rä'-fĕlt), **Fabian**, b. Tuchel,
W. Prussia, Jan. 23, 1842; violinist;
pupil of Zimmermann and Grünwald,
Berlin, 1868, royal chamber-mus.;
1873, leader ct.-orch.

**Reicha** (rī'-khä), (1) (rightly **Rejcha**,
rä'-khä), **Jos.**, Prague, 1746—Bonn,
1795; 'cellist, violinist, and cond. at
Bonn. (2) **Anton (Jos.)**, Prague,
Feb. 27, 1770—Paris, May 28, 1836;
nephew and pupil of above; flutist,
vla.-player, and teacher. Notable in
his day as a theorist and an ingenious
and original contrapuntist; c. an opera, etc.

**Reichardt** (rī'-khärt), (1) **Jn. Fr.**,
Königsberg, Nov. 25, 1752—Giebich-
enstein near Halle, June 27, 1814;
cond., editor and dram. composer;
pupil of Richter and Veichtner; 1775,
ct.-cond. to Frederick the Great,
later to Fr. Wm. II. and III., then
to Jerome Bonaparte; he prod. many
German and Italian operas and influential Singspiele; also c. 7 symphs., a
passion, etc., and notable songs. (2)
**Luise**, Berlin, 1788 — Hamburg,
1826; daughter of above; singing-
teacher. (3) **Gv.**, Schmarsow, near
Demmin, 1797—Berlin, 1884; conductor; c. pop. songs. (4) **Alex.**,
Packs, Hungary, 1825 — Boulogne-
sur-Mer, 1885; tenor.

**Reichel** (rī'-khĕl), (1) **Ad. H. Jn.**, b.
Tursznitz, W. Prussia, 1816; pupil of
Dehn and L. Berger; Berlin; pf.-
teacher, Paris; 1857–67, taught comp.
at Dresden Cons.; 1867, municipal
mus.-dir. Berne, Switz.; c. pf.-con-
certos, etc. (2) **Fr.**, Oberoderwitz,
Lusatia, 1833—Dresden, 1889; can
tor and org.-composer.

**Reicher-Kindermann** (rī'-khĕr-kĭn'-
dĕr-män), (1) **Hedwig**, Munich, 1853
—Trieste, 1883; soprano; daughter
of the barytone, A. Kindermann; m.
(2) **Reicher**, an opera singer.

**Reichert** (rī'-khĕrt), **Mathieu André**,
b. Maestricht, 1830; flute-virtuoso;

pupil Brussels Cons., took 1st prize in 1847; toured Europe and America; composer.

**Reichmann** (rīkh'-män), **Th.**, b. Rostock, March 18, 1849; barytone, pupil of Mantius, Elsler, Ress and Lamperti; 1882-89, ct.-opera Vienna; 1882, created "Amfortas" in "*Parsifal*," Bayreuth; 1889-90, New York; then Vienna.

**Reid** (rēd), General **John**, Straloch, Perthshire, 1721(?)—London, 1807; a musical amateur, founded a chair of mus. Edinburgh Univ.

**Reijnvaan** (or **Reynwaen**) (rĕn'-vän), **Jean Verschuere**, LL.D.; Middleburg, Holland, 1743—Flushing, May 12, 1809; organist and composer.

**Reimann** (rī'-män), (1) **Mathieu** (**Matthias Reymannus**), Löwenberg, 1544—1597; composer. (2) **Ignaz**, Albendorf, Silesia, 1820—Rengersdorf, 1885; composer. (3) **H.**, b. Rengensdorf, March 14, 1850; son and pupil of (2); since 1887 asst.-libr., R. Library, Berlin; organist to the Philh. Soc.; teacher of organ and theory, Scharwenka-Klindworth Cons., and (since 1895) organist at the Gnadenkirche; prominent critic and writer; c. sonatas and studies for organ.

**Reinagle** (rī'-nä-gĕl), (1) **Jos.**, b. London; son of a German mus., hornplayer and composer, 1785. (2) **Hugh**, d. young at Lisbon; bro. of above; 'cellist. (3) **Alex. R.**, Brighton, 1799 —Kidlington, near Oxford, 1877; organist and composer; son of (1).

**Reinecke** (rī'-nĕk-ĕ), (1) **Ld. K.**, Dessau, 1774—Güsten, 1820; leader and dram. composer. (2) **K. (H. Carsten)**, b. Altona, June 23, 1824; noteworthy pianist and teacher; son and pupil of a music-teacher; at 11, played in public; at 19 toured Denmark and Sweden; at Leipzig advised by Mendelssohn and Schumann; ct.-pianist at Copenhagen; 1851 teacher Cologne Cons.; 1854-59 mus.-dir. Barmen; 1859-60 mus.-dir. and cond. Singakademie, Bres-

lau; 1860-95 cond. Gewandh[ ] Concerts, Leipzig; also prof. of [ ] playing and free comp., Leip[ ] Cons.; 1897 "Studiendirektor" th[ ] Dr. Phil. *h. c.*, Leipzig Univ.; R[ ] Professor; toured almost annu[ ] with great succ., c. 2 masse[ ] symphs., 5 overtures "*Dame* [ ] *bold*," "*Aladin*," "*Friedensfei[ ]* "*Festouvertüre*" "*In memoria[ ]* (of David), "*Zenobia*," introd. [ ] fugue with chorus and orch; fun[ ] march for Emperor William I., [ ] certos for vln., 'cello and harp.; p[ ] grand opera "*König Manfr[ ]* (Wiesbaden, 1867); 3 comic oper[ ] fairy opera "*Die Teufelchen* [ ] *der Himmelswiese*" (Glarus, 189[ ] mus. to Schiller's "*Tell*"; orat[ ] "*Belsazar*"; 2 cantatas "*Ha[ ] Jarl*," and "*Die Flucht n[ ] Ægypten*," with orch.; 5 fairy can[ ] tas, 4 concertos, many sonatas; "[ ] *der Jugendzeit*," op. 106; "*Ne[ ] Notenbuch für Kleine Leute*," [ ] 107; concert-arias, 20 canons f[ ] female voices, and excellent so[ ] for children.

**Reiner** (rī'-nĕr), (1) **Jacob**, Altd[ ] Würtemberg, ca. 1560—1606; c[ ] poser. (2) **Ambrosius**, Altdorf-W[ ] garten, 1604—1762; ct.-conduct[ ] son of above.

**Reinhard** (rīn'-härt), **B. Fran.**, Stra[ ] burg, mus.-printer, 1800; the first stereotype music plates.

**Reinhold** (rīn'-hōlt), (1) **Thos.**, D[ ] den, 1690—Soho, 1751; singer. **Chas. Fred.**, 1737—Somers Tov[ ] 1815; Engl. bass and organist. **Hugo**, b. Vienna, March 3, 18[ ] composer.

**Reinholdt** (rīn'-hōlt), **Th. Chr[ ] lieb**, d. Dresden, March 24, 17[ ] cantor, teacher and composer.

**Reinke(n)** (rīn'-kĕn) (or **Reinick[ ]** **Jn. Adam**, Deventer, Holland, A[ ] 27, 1623—Hamburg, Nov. 24, 17[ ] noted organist and composer.

**Reinsdorf** (rīns'-dôrf), **Otto**, Kösel[ ] 1848—Berlin, 1890; editor.

**Reinthaler** (rīn'-täl-ĕr), **K. (Marti[ ]**

Erfurt, 1832—Bremen, 1896; sing-ng-teacher, organist, conductor and dram. composer.

isenauer (rī'-zĕ-now-ĕr), **Alfred**, b. Königsberg, Nov. 1, 1863; pianist; pupil of L. Köhler and Liszt; début, 1881, Rome, with Liszt; toured, composer.

iser (rī'-zĕr) **Aug. Fr.**, b. Gammeringen, Würtemberg, Jan. 19, 1840, 1880–86 ed Cologne " *Neue Musikzeitung* ", c 2 symphs., choruses, ncl. " *Barbarossa*," for double ch., tc.

iset. Vide DE GRANDVAL.

iss (rīs),(1) **K. H. Ad.**, b Frankfort-n-Main, April 24, 1829; pupil of Hauptmann, Leipzig, chorus-master nd cond. various theatres; 1854, st cond. Mayence; 1856, 2d., later st cond. at Cassel (vice Spohr). 1881–86, ct.-th., Wiesbaden; prod. opera, "*Otto der Schütz*" (Mayence, 1856). (2) **Albert**, b. Berlin; Wagnerian tenor; studied law, then became an actor, discovered by Pollini; pupil of Liebau and Stolzenberg; début in opera at Konigsberg, later t Posen and Wiesbaden, famous as 'Mime" and " David." 1902–3, N. Y.

issiger (rīs'-sĭkh-ĕr), (1) **Chr. Gl.**, . 1790; comp. (2) **K. Gl.**, Belzig, near Wittenberg, Jan. 31. 1798—Dresden, Nov. 7, 1859; son of above; pupil f Schicht and Winter; singer, pianist and teacher; 1826, on invitation, organised at The Hague the still ucc. Cons.; ct.-cond. Dresden (vice Weber); c. 8 operas, 10 masses. (3) Fr. **Aug.**, Belzig, 1809—Frederiksald, 1883; bro. of above; military andm.; composer.

issmann (rīs'-män), **Aug.**, b. Frankenstein, Silesia, Nov. 14, 1825; studied there and at Breslau; 1863–80, lectured at Stern Cons., Berlin; hen lived in Leipzig (Dr. Phil., 875), Wiesbaden and Berlin; writer of important historical works, and exicographer, c. 3 operas, 2 dram. scenes, an oratorio, etc.

iter (rī'-tĕr), **Ernst**, Wertheim,

Baden, 1814—Basel, 1875; vln.-prof. and dram. composer.

**Relfe** (rĕlf), (1) **Lupton**, d. 1803; for 50 years organist Greenwich Hospital. (2) **John**, Greenwich, 1763—London, ca. 1837; son of above; noted teacher; theorist.

**Rellstab** (rĕl'-shtäp), (1) **Jn. K. Fr.**, Berlin. 1759—1813; son and successor of owner of a printing-establishment; critic, teacher, and composer. (2) (**H. Fr.**) **L.**, Berlin, 1799—1860; the noted novelist, son of above; wrote biog., libretti and criticisms which got him twice imprisoned; c. part-songs. (3) **Karoline**, b. 1793 (or '94); sister of above; singer of unusual compass.

**Remenyi** (rĕm'-ān-yĕ), **Eduard**, Heves, Hungary, 1830—on the stage, of apoplexy, San Francisco, Cal., May 15, 1898; noted violinist; pupil of Böhm, Vienna Cons.; banished for his part in Hungarian Revolution; toured America; 1854, solo violinist to Queen Victoria; 1860, pardoned by Austrian Emperor and made ct.-violinist; toured widely, 1866 round the world; c. a vln.-concerto, transcriptions, etc.

**Remi d'Auxerre** (rä-mē dō-săr) (**Remigius Altisiodorensis**), monk at Rheims, 893; writer.

**Remmers** (rĕm'-mĕrs), **Jn.**, Jever, 1805—The Hague, Jan. 28, 1847; violinist.

**Rem'mert, Martha**, b. Gross-Schwerin, near Glogau, Sept. 13, 1854; pianist; pupil of Kullak, Tausig and Liszt; lives in Berlin.

**Rémusat** (Rémuzat) (rä-mü-zä), (1) **Jean**, Bordeaux, 1815—Shanghai, 1880; flute-virtuoso; writer and composer. (2) **Bd. Martin**, b. Bordeaux, 1822; bro. of above; flutist.

**Remy, W. A.** Vide MAYER, WM.

**Rénard** (rä-năr), **Marie**, b. Graz, Jan. 18,1864; soprano; début, Graz, 1882, 1885–88, Berlin ct.-opera; then Vienna ct.-opera.

**Renaud** (rŭ-nō), (1) **Albert**, b. Paris, 1855; pupil of Franck and Délibes;

organist St. François-Xavier; critic, "*La Patrie*"; c. 4-act "féerie," "*Aladin*" (1891); opéra comique "*À la Houzarde*" ('91); operetta "*Le Soleil de Minuit*" (1898); ballets, etc. (2) **Maurice,** b. Bordeaux, 1862; notable bass; pupil of Paris Cons.; 1883–90, at R. Opera, Brussels; 1890–91, Op.-Com., Paris; from 1891–1902, Gr. Opéra; equally fine in comic and serious works; has a repertory of 50 operas.

**Rendano** (rĕn-dä'-nō), **Alfonso,** Carolei, Calabria, April 5, 1853; pianist; pupil of Naples Cons., Thalberg and Leipzig Cons. (1871); toured; c. piano-pcs.

**Ren'ner, Josef,** Schmatzhausen, Bavaria, 1832—Ratisbon, 1895; editor.

**Reszké.** Vide DE RESZKÉ.

**Réty** (rā-tē), **Chas.,** ca. 1826—Paris, 1895; under the pseud. "Chas. Darcours," critic for twenty-five years.

**Reubke** (roip'-kĕ),(1) **Ad.,** Halberstadt, 1805—1875; org.-builder at Hausendorf, near Quedlinburg. (2) **Emil,** Hausneindorf, 1836—1885; son and successor of above. (3) **Julius R.,** Hausneindorf, 1834—Pillnitz, 1858; bro. of above; pianist and composer. (4) **Otto R.,** b. Nov. 2, 1842; bro. of above; pupil of von Bülow and Marx; mus.-teacher and conductor, Halle; 1892, mus.-dir. at the University.

**Reuling** (roi'-lĭng), **(L.) Wm.,** Darmstadt, 1802—Munich, 1879; conductor and dram. composer.

**Reuss** (rois), (1) **Eduard,** b. New York, Sept. 16, 1851; pupil of Ed. Krüger and of Liszt; 1880, teacher at Carlsruhe. His wife, (2) **Reuss-Belce** (-bĕl'-tsĕ) **Louise,** b. Vienna; soprano; pupil of Gänsbacher; début as "Elsa," Carlsruhe, 1884; later at Wiesbaden, and Bayreuth as one of the "Norns" and "Walküre" for years; 1900 sang Wagner in Spain, 1901, Met. Op., N. Y. (3) **H. XXIV.,** Prince of Reuss-Köstritz; b. Trebschen, Brandenburg, Dec. 8, 1855; pupil of Herzogenberg and

Rust, Leipzig; c. 2 symphs., a m etc.

**Reuter** (roi'-tĕr), **Florizel** (known "Florizel")**;** b. 1890 (?); boy linist; pupil of Bendix, Chicago, of Marteau, in Europe; has tou America with popular success.

**Reutter** (roit'-tĕr), (1) **G.** (Seni Vienna, 1656—Aug., 1738; thec ist, ct.-organist and conductor. **(Jn. Adam), G.** (Junior), Vien 1708—1772; son and (1738) suc sor of above as ct.-conductor; opera, etc.

**Rey** (rĕ), (1) **J. Bap.,** Lauzerte, 1 —Paris, 1810; conductor, profes of harm. and dram. composer. **L. Chas. Jos.,** bro. of above; 40 years 'cellist, Gr. Opéra. (3) **Bap.** (II.), b. Tarascon, ca. 17 from 1795 till 1822, 'cellist, Opéra, and theorist. (4) **V. F. S.** Lyons, ca. 1762; theorist. (5) V REYER.

**Reyer** (rĕ-yā) (rightly **Rey**), **L. É enne Ernest,** b. Marseilles, Dec 1823; prominent French compos studied as a child in the free mu ipal sch. of mus.; while in the Go financial bureau at Algiers, c. a emn mass and pub songs; the Re lution of 1848 deprived him of position and he retired to Pa where he studied with his aunt, M Farrenc; librarian at Opéra (v Berlioz); 1876, Académie; cr "*Journal des Débats*"; 1862, Ch of the Legion of Honour; 18 Officier. Prod. a symph. ode w choruses "*Le Sélam*" (Th. Ital 1850); 1-act comedy-opera "*M tre Wolfram*" (Th.-Lyrique, 185 a ballet-pantomime "*Sacounta* (Opéra, 1858); comedy-opera "*Statue*" (Th.-Lyr., 1861, revived the Opéra 1878 without succ.);unsu opera "*Erostrate*" (Baden-Bad 1862); the still pop opera "*Sigur* (Brussels, 1884), and "*Salammb* (Brussels, 1890). C. a cantata "*V toire*" (1859); a hymn, "*L'Un des Arts*" (1862), a dram. sce

*La Madeleine au Dese,* " (1874);
ale choruses; also some hurch-
aus. Pub. a volume of essays, 875.

znicek (rĕz'-nĭ-tsĕk), Emil Nico-
aus, Freiherr von, b. Vienna, May
, 1861; studied Leipzig Cons.; th.-
onductor various cities; 1896, 1st
ond. ct.-th., Mannheim; prod. at
rague operas "*Die Jungfrau von
rleans*" (1887)," *Satanella*" (1888),
" *Emerich Fortunat*" (1889), comic
pera (text and music), "*Donna
Diana*" (1894), all very succ.; Volks-
per, " *Till Eulenspiegel*" (Berlin,
903). C. also a requiem (1894), a
ymph. suite, etc.

aw (Rhau) (row), G., Eisfeld, Fran-
onia, 1488—Wittenberg, 1548; mus.-
rinter and composer.

einberger (rīn'-bĕrkh-ĕr), Jos.
Gabriel), Vaduz, Lichtenstein,
March 17, 1837—(of nerve and lung
roubles) Munich. Nov. 25, 1902; 
:minent teacher and composer. At
; played the piano; at 7 a good organist; studied R. Sch. of Mus.,
Munich; 1859, teacher of theory
here; also organist at the ct.-
church of St. Michael, and cond.
Oratorio Soc. 1865–67, " *Repetitor*"
:t.-opera; Royal Prof. and Inspector
of the Sch. of Mus.; from 1877 ct.-cond.
Royal Chapel-Choir; m. Franziska
von Hoffnas, a poetess (1822—1892);
prod. romantic opera " *Die 7 Raben*"
(Munich, 1869); comic opera " *Des
Thürmers Töchterlein*" (Munich,
1873); " *Christophorus*," a mass for
double choir (dedicated to Leo XIII.);
mass, with orch.; requiem for soldiers
of the Franco-Prussian war; 2 Stabat Maters; 4 cantatas with crch.;
2 choral ballades; " *Floren.ine*"
symph.; symph. tone-picture " *Val-
lenstein*"; a symphonic fantasia; 3
overtures " *Demetrius,*" " *The Tam-
ing of the Shrew,*" " *Triumph*"; 2
organ - concertos; pf. - concertos,
chamber-music; vln.-sonatas; pf.-
sonatas ("symphonique"; op. 47;
" romantic," op. 184), etc., notably
18 important org.-sonatas; left un-

finished mass in A minor (finished by
his pupil L. A. Coerne).

Riccati (rĭk-kä'-tē), Count Giordano, b. Castelfranco, 1709—Treviso,
1790; theorist.

Ricci (rĭt'-chē), (1) Luigi, Naples,
1805 — insane, in asylum, Prague,
1859; conductor and dram. composer, m. (2) Lidia Stoltz, who
bore him two children, of whom (3)
Adelaide sang at Th. des It., Paris,
1867, and died soon after. (4) Federico, Naples, 1809 — Comegliano,
1877; bro. of (1) and collaborator in
4 of his operas; also c. others.

Riccius (rĕk'-tsĭ-oos), (1) Aug. Fd.,
Bernstadt, Saxony, 1819—Carlsbad,
1886; conductor, critic, singing-teacher and composer. (2) K. Aug.,
Bernstadt, July 26, 1830—Dresden,
July 8, 1893; nephew of above; conductor, violinist and composer of
comic operas, etc.

Rice, Fenelon B., Green, Ohio, Jan.
2, 1841—Oberlin, Ohio, Oct. 26, 1901;
studied Boston, Mass., later Leipzig;
for 3 years organist, Boston; from
1871, dir. Oberlin (Ohio) Cons. of
Mus.; Mus. Doc. Hillsdale (Mich.)
Coll.

Rich'ards, (H.) Brinley, Carmarthen,
Wales, Nov. 13, 1817 — London,
May 1, 1885; pop. composer and
pianist.

Rich'ardson, (1) Vaughan, d. 1729;
organist and composer, London. (2)
Jos., 1814—1862; flutist and composer, London.

Richault (rē-shō), (1) Chas. Simon,
Chartres, 1780—Paris, 1866; mus.-
publisher, succeeded by his sons (2)
Guillaume Simon (1806 — 1877)
and (3) Léon (1839—1895).

Riche, A. Le. Vide DIVITIS.

Richter (rĭkh'-tĕr), (1) Fz. X., Hole-
schau, Moravia, 1709—1789; cond.,
writer and composer. (2) Jn. Chr.
Chp., Neustadt-am-Kulm, 1727 —
Schwarzenbach - on - Saale, 1779;
Father of Jean Paul R.; organist.
(3) Ernst H. Ld., Thiergarten,
Prussian Silesia, 1805—Steinau-on-

Oder, 1876 ; notable teacher ; c. an opera, etc. (4) **Ernst Fr. (Eduard)**, Gross Schönau, Saxony, Oct. 24, 1808—Leipzig, April 9, 1879 ; eminent theorist ; pupil of Weinlig, and self-taught ; 1843 teacher at Leipzig Cons. newly founded ; 1843-47, conductor Singakademie ; organist various churches 1863 mus.-dir. Nikolaikirche ; 1868 mus.-dir. and cantor Thomaskirche ; Prof.; wrote a standard "*Lehrbuch der Harmonie*" (1853), and "*Lehrbuch der Fuge*"; c. an oratorio, masses, etc (5) **Alfred**, b. Leipzig, April 1, 18.., son of above ; teacher at the Cons., 1872-83 ; then lived in London ; 1897, Leipzig ; pub. supplement to his father's "*Harmonie*," and "*Kontrapunkt*"; also "*Das Klavierspiel für Musikstudierende*" (Leipzig, 1898). (6) **Hans**, b. P.ao, Hungary, April 4, 1843; em.... conductor; son of the cond. of ..e local cath. ; his mother was a prominent sopr. and later a distinguished teacher ; choirboy in the ct.-chapel, Vienna ; studied with Sechter (piano-playing), and Kleinecke (the French horn), at the Cons.; horn-player in Kärnethor Th. orch.; then with Wagner, 1866-67 in Lucerne, making a fair copy of the "*Meistersinger*" score. On W.'s recommendation, 1867, chorusm., Munich Opera. 1868-69 ct.-cond. under von Bülow. Cond. first performance of "*Lohengrin*" (Brussels, 1870); again at Lucerne with Wagner, making fair copy of the score of the "*Nibelungen Ring*"; 1871-75, cond., Pesth National Th.; then cond. of the Imp. Opera, Vienna ; 1893, 1st cond. ; since 1875 also cond. "*Gesellschaft der Musikfreunde*" excepting 1882-83. Selected by Wagner to cond. the "*Ring des Niebelungen*" (Bayreuth, 1876), and alternate cond. with Wagner at the Wagner Concerts, Albert Hall, London. 1877 ; chief-cond. Bayreuth Festivals, and since 1879, annually cond. Philh. concerts at London. Cond. several Lower Rhe-

nish Festivals and (since 1885) Birmingham Festivals. In 18 Mus. Doc. *h. c.*, Oxford Univ. 1898 the freedom of the city of enna was given him.

**Ricieri** (rē-chā'-rĕ), **Giov. A.**, Ven 1679—Bologna, 1746 ; male sopr. and composer.

**Ricordi** (rē-kôr'-dē), (1) **Giov.**, Mil 1785—1853 ; founder of the m publishing firm in Milan ; violi and conductor ; succeeded by his (2) **Tito** (1811—1888); the pres head is (3) **Giulio** (b. Milan, Dec. 1840); also ed. of the "*Gazetta M sicale.*"

**Riechers** (rē'-khĕrs), **Aug.**, Hanov 1836—Berlin, 1893 ; maker and pairer of vlns.; writer.

**Riedel** (rē'-d'l) (1) **Karl**, Kronenbe Oct. 6, 1827—Leipzig, June 3, 188 pupil Leipzig Cons.; 1854, found the noted social society Riedel rein ; pres. Wagnerverein, et pub. colls. (2) **Hn.**, b. Burg, ne Magdeburg, Jan. 2, 1847; pupil V enna Cons.; ct.-cond. Brunswic composer. (3) **Furchtegott Ern Aug.**, b. Chemnitz, May 22, 185 pupil Leipzig Cons.; from 18 town cantor, Plauen, Saxony, a cond.; c. cantatas, etc.

**Riedt** (rēt), **Fr. Wm.**, Berlin, 1712 1784 ; flute-virtuoso ; writer and co poser.

**Riehl** (rēl), **Wm. H. von**, Biebric 1823—Munich, 1897; director, writ and composer.

**Riem** (rēm), **Fr. Wm.**, Kolleda, Th ringia, 1779—Bremen, 1857; orga ist, conductor and composer.

**Riemann** (rē'-män), (1) **Jakob**, at Ca sel 18th cent.; ct.-composer. ( **Aug.**, Blankenham, Thuringia, 177 —Weimar, 1826 ; 1st violinist ct orch. (3) **Hugo**, b. Grossmehlr near Sondershausen, July 18, 184 notable theorist. Son of a farme who taught him the rudiments mus., and who had prod. an ope and choral pcs. at Sondershausen but opposed his son's mus. ambi

ns ; the youth, however, studied
eory with Frankenberger, and piano
th Barthel and Ratzenberger, at
ndershausen. Studied law, then
ilosophy and history, at Berlin and
ibingen ; after serving in the cam-
ign of 1870—71, entered Leipzig
ons.; 1873, Dr. Phil. Göttingen ;
ote dissertation "*Musikalische*
*gik*"; until 1878, a cond. and
acher at Bielefeld, then lecturer
eipzig Univ.; 1880–81, teacher of
us. at Bromberg ; then till 1890,
amburg Cons , then the Wiesbaden
ons. ; 1895, lecturer at Leipzig
niv. ; m. in 1876. Notable at times
ader pseud. **"Hugibert Ries"**
an essayist, writer of theoretical
eatises of much originality, also an
aportant historian and lexicographer;
us.-ed. of Meyer's "*Konversations-
xikon*" and ed. a valuable "*Mu-
k-Lexikon*" (1882; Engl. ed. 1893);
chamber-mus., vln.-sonata, etc.

menschneider (rĕ´-mĕn-shnī-dĕr),
., b. Stralsund, April 1, 1848 ; pu-
l of Haupt and Kiel ; th.-cond. Lü-
eck (1875) and Danzig ; later cond.
reslau concert-orch.; c. operas
*Mondeszauber* " (Danzig, 1887),
ad "*Die Eisjungfrau*" (symphonic
cture), "*Julinacht*," etc.

pel (rĕ´-pĕl), **Jos.,** Horschlag, Up-
r Austria, 1708—Ratisbon, 1782 ;
aamber-musician, theorist and com-
oser.

s (rēs), (1) **Jn.,** Benzheim, 1723—
86 (7); ct.-trumpeter and violinist
the Elector of Bonn ; also conuctor (2) **Anne Maria,** daughter
above ; ct.-soprano, Bonn, 1764—
794 ; m. a violinist Fd. Drewer.
.) **Fz.** (der alter), Bonn, 1755—
remen, 1846 ; bro. of above ; lead-
, later ct.-mus. dir., Bonn. (4)
d., Bonn, Nov. 29, 1784—Frank-
rt-on-Main, Jan. 13, 1838 ; noted
anist ; pupil of Beethoven (of **whom**
e wrote a valuable sketch) and Al-
rechtsberger ; toured, 1813–24,
ondon , m. an English woman ;
om 1830, l. Frankfort as cond.: c. 8

operas, 6 symphs., etc. (5) **Peter
Jos.,** 1790—London, 1882 ; bro. of
above ; Royal Prussian Prof. (6)
**Hubert,** Bonn, April 1, 1802—Berlin, Sept. 14, 1886 ; bro. of above ;
violinist, teacher and composer of
valuable method, studies, etc., for vln.
(7) **Louis,** b. Berlin, Jan. 30, 1830;
son of (6), vln.-teacher, London. (8)
**Ad.,** b. Berlin, Dec. 20, 1837; bro.
of above ; pf.-teacher, London ; composer. (9) **Fz.,** b. Berlin, April 7,
1846 ; son and pupil of (6); studied
with Massart at Paris Cons. and with
Kiel (comp.) ; concert-violinist till
1875 when he retired because of ner-
vousness, and entered mus.-publishing
(Ries & Erler, Berlin) , c. excellent
orch. and chamber-mus., etc. (10)
**Hugibert.** Vide HUGO RIEMANN.

**Rieter-Biedermann** (rē´-tĕr-bē´-dĕr-
män), **J. Melchior,** 1811—Winterthur, Switz., 1876 ; founded pub.-
house, 1849; 1862, branch at Leipzig.

**Rietz** (rēts), (1) **Jn. Fr. R.,** d. Berlin,
1828 ; vla.-player, royal chamber-
mus. (2) **Eduard,** Berlin, 1802—
1832 ; son of above , violinist and
tenor ; founded the Berlin Philh.
Soc., 1826 ; was its cond. till death.
(3) **Julius,** Berlin, Dec. 28, 1812—
Dresden, Sept. 12, 1877; son of (1) ;
'cellist and cond.; pupil of Schmidt,
Romberg and Ganz ; 1834, asst.-
cond. to Mendelssohn, Düsseldorf opera ; 1835, his successor ; 1847, cond.
Singakademie, Leipzig, later also
cond. Gewandhaus and prof. of comp.
at the Cons.; 1860, ct.-cond. at Dresden ; later dir. of the Cons.; editor
of scores ; c. 4 operas, 3 symphs.,
various overtures, masses, etc.

**Riga** (rē´-gä), **Frantz (François),**
Liège, 1831—Schaerbeek, near Brussels, 1892 ; conductor and composer
of male choruses, etc.

**Rig´by, Geo. Vernon,** b. Birmingham (?), Jan. 21, 1840 ; notable operatic and concert tenor ; toured Engl.,
Ger. and Italy.

**Righini** (rē-gē´-nē), **V.,** Bologna, Jan.
22, 1756—Aug. 19, 1812 : tenor,

singing-teacher and court-cond. at Mayence, later Berlin ; c. 20 operas, etc., incl. vocalises.

**Rille.** Vide LAURENT DE RILLE.

**Rimbault** (rĭm'-bōlt), (1) **Stephen Francis**, organist and composer, 1773—1837. (2) **Edw. Fran.**, London, June 13, 1816—Sept. 26, 1876 ; son and pupil of above ; organist and noted lecturer, editor, essayist and writer of numerous valuable historical works based on research.

**Rimsky-Korsakov** (rĭm'-shkĭ-kôr'-sä-kôf), **Nikolas Andrejevitch**, b. Tikhvin, Novgorod, May 21 (new style), 1844 ; notable Russian composer ; studied at the Naval Inst., Petersburg ; also took pf.-lessons ; 1861, took up mus. as a profession after study with Balakirev ; at 21 prod. his first symph.; 1871, prof. of comp. and instr. at Petersb. Cons., also 1873—84 inspector of Marine Bands; 1874—87, dir. Free Sch. of Mus., and until 1881, cond. there ; 1883, asst. cond. (to Balakirev) of the Imp. Orch.; from 1886, cond. Russian Symph. Concerts ; 1889, cond. 2 Russian concerts at the Trocadero, Paris. He orchestrated the posthumous operas : Dargomyzsky's "Commodore," Mussorgsky's "Khovanstchyna" and Borodin's "Prince Igor"; pub. coll. of Russian songs and a harmony. C. operas "Pskovitjanka" ("The Girl from Pskov") (St. Petersburg, Imp. Th. 1873) ; "A May Night" (do. 1880); "Snegorotchka" ("The Snowy Princess") (do. 1882); "Mozart und Salieri" (Moscow); opera ballet "Mlada" (Petersburg, 1892); opera "Christmas Eve" (1895) ; 3 symphs. incl. "Antar" (1881), sinfonietta; "Russian" overture ; Servian fantasia , mus. tableau "Sadko" (1876) : pf. concerto, etc. ; opera "Zarskaja Newjesta" (1901).

**Rinaldi** (rē-näl'-dē), **Giov.**, Reggiolo, Italy, 1840—Genoa, 1895 ; pianist.

**Rinck** (rĭnk), **Jn. Chr. H.**, Elgersburg, Thuringia, Feb. 18, 1770—Darmstadt, Aug. 7, 1846 . famous organist, writer and composer ; pupil Kittel, etc.; town organist Gies then, 1805, at Darmstadt, where also taught in the seminary ; 1 ct.-organist there ; autobiog. (Br lau, 1833).

**Ringel, Federico.** Vide F. D'ERL. GER.

**Ringler** (rĭng'-lĕr), **Eduard**, b. Nü berg, Jan. 8, 1838 ; pupil of H mann; but did not adopt mus. till then studied with Grobe, and Dup at Nürnberg ; cond. the "Singv ein" ; from 1883 choir-dir. in synagogue, and from 1890, cond. excellent "Verein für klassisch Chorgesang"; singing-teacher a critic ; c. succ. "Volksoper" " pelein von Gailigen" (Nürnberg,189 grand opera "Frithjof," songs, et

**Rinuccini** (rē-noot-chē'-nē), **Ottav** Florence, 1562—1621 ; the librett of the first opera ever performe Peri (q. v.) and Caccini's "Dafn (1594), also of Peri's "Euridic (1600), and Monteverde's "Arian a Nasso" (1608).

**Riotte** (rĭ-ôt), **Phillip J.**, St. Mend Trèves, Aug., 1776—1856 ; condu or and dram. composer.

**Ripa** (rē'-pä), **Alberto de** (called berto Mantovano), b. Mantua— ca. 1580 ; lutist and composer.

**Rischbieter** (rĭsh'-bē-tĕr), **Wm.** bert, b. Brunswick, 1834 ; pupil Hauptmann, theory ; violinist Leipzig and other cities ; from 18 teacher harm. and cpt., Dresd Cons., pub. treatises, etc.; c. symph overtures etc.

**Risler** (rēs'-lĕr), **Edouard**, b. Bade Baden, Feb. 23, 1873 ; notable p nist ; pupil of Diemer and d'Albe Stavenhagen, etc.; lives in Paris.

**Ristori** (rēs-tō'-rē), **Giov. Albert** Bologna, 1692 — Dresden, Feb. 1753 ; organist and conductor ; c of the earliest comic operas, a church-music.

**Rit'ter,** (1) **G. Wenzel**, Mannhei April 7, 1748—Berlin, June 16, 18c bassoonist. Berlin ct.-orch.; compo

, (2) **Aug. Gf.**, Erfurt, Aug. 25, 11—Magdeburg, Aug. 26, 1885; gan-virtuoso, editor and composer. ) **Alex**, Narva (or Reval), Russia, ne 27 (new style), 1833—Munich. oril 12, 1896; violinist; c. succ. erettas, etc. (4) **Frédéric Louis**, rassburg, June 22, 1834—Antwerp, lly 22, 1891; prof. of mus. and nductor at Loraine; 1856, Cincinti (U. S. A.), organist Philh. orch. d Cecilia Soc.; 1861 New York, nd. the Arion; 1867 prof. Vassar ol.; wrote " *Music in England*," d " *Music in America* " (both N. ., 1883); and other historical orks; c. 5 symphs., etc. (5) **(Raymond-Ritter), Fanny**, b. Philadelia, 1840; wife of above; writer d translator. (6) (rightly **Bennet) héodore**, near Paris, 1841—Paris, 886; pianist and composer. (7) ermann, b. Wismar, Sept. 16, 849; violinist; studied Berlin with achim, etc.; invented and played a ola alta; for 20 yrs. teacher at Vürzburg. (8) **Josef**, b. Salzburg, ct. 3, 1859; barytone at Vienna. (9) **titter-Götze (gĕt-'tsĕ), Marie**, b. erlin, Nov. 2, 1865; mezzo-sopr.; upil of Jenny Meyer and Levysohn; ébut R. Opera, Berlin; later Hamurg for 4 years; sang at Met. Op. nd in concert U. S. A. 1890–02; en Berlin R. Opera.

é-King (rē'-vā-kǐng), **Julie**, b. incinnati, Ohio, Oct. 31, 1857; oteworthy pianist; toured the world ith great succ.; c. pop. pf.-pcs.

ière (rĕv-yăr), **Jules**, 1809—Paris, Dec. 26, 1900; conductor.

b'inson, (1) **J.**, 1682—1762; Engsh organist and composer. (2) **Ann** née Turner, d. 1741; singer; wife ⸺ above. (3) **Anastasia**, 1750; Engl. inger; m. Earl of Peterborough. 4) **Margaret**, sister of (1); singer ⸺ Händel's oratorios. (5) **Francis**, rofessor at Dublin, 1810. His four ons were (6) **Francis**, tenor; (7) **Wm.**, bass; (8) **J.**, tenor and organst; (9) **Jos.**, b. Aug., 1816; famous

cond. and composer; his wife, (10) **Fanny Arthur**, 1831—1879, was a singer and composer.

**Rob'erts, J. Varley**, b. Stanningly, near Leeds, Sept. 25, 1841; organist and composer; from 1868 at Halifax; 1876 Mus. Doc. Oxford; c. cantata " *Jonah*," etc.

**Rob'john, Wm. Jos.**, b. Tavistock, Devon, Nov. 3, 1843; self-taught mus.; at 14 went to America; has been organist various churches; c. various operettas, etc.; wrote under pen-name **Caryl Florio**.

**Robyn** (rō'-bǐn), (1) **Alfred G.**, b. St. Louis, Mo., April 29, 1860; son of (2) **Wm. R.** (who organised the first symph. orch. west of Pittsburgh); at 10 **A.** succeeded his father as organist at St. John's Church; at 16 solo-pianist with Emma Abbott's Co.; prod. comic opera " *Jacinta*" (1894); c. pf.-concerto, etc., also very pop. songs (incl. " *Answer* "), etc.

**Rochlitz** (rôkh'-lǐts), **Jn. Fr.**, Leipzig, Feb. 12, 1769—Dec. 16, 1842; composer, editor and prominent writer of essays, biog. and librettos.

**Rock, Michael**, d. March, 1809; English organist and composer.

**Röckel** (rĕk'-ĕl), (1) **Jos. Aug.**, Neumburg-vorm-Wald, Upper Palatine, 1783—Anhalt-Cöthen, 1870; singer, prof. and operatic dir. at Aix; 1829–32, of a German co. at Paris; 1832, London. (2) **Aug. Gratz**, 1814—Buda-Pesth, 1876; joint-conductor at Dresden opera (with Wagner); 1848, abandoned mus. for politics. (3) **Edw.**, b. Trèves, Nov. 20, 1816; pupil of his uncle, J. N. Hummel; toured as pianist; from 1848 lived Bath, Eng.; c. pf.-pcs. (4) **Jos. (Ld.)**, b. London, April 11, 1838; bro. of above; pupil of Eisenhofer, Götze, and of his father and bro. Eduard (pf.); lives in Bristol, as teacher and pianist; c. cantatas, pf.-pcs., pop. songs, etc.

**Rock'stro** (rightly **Rackstraw), Wm. Smyth**, North Cheam, Surrey, Jan. 5, 1823—London, July 2, 1895; no

table historian ; pupil Leipzig Cons.;
pianist and teacher, London ; 1891,
lecturer R. A. M. and R. C. M.;
wrote treatises, biog. and " *General
History of Music* " (1886); c. overture, cantata " *The Good Shepherd*,"
etc.

**Roda** (rō'-dä), **Fd. von**, Rudolstadt,
1815—near Kriwitz, 1876 ; mus.-dir.
and composer.

**Rode** (rôd), **(Jacques) P. (Jos.)**, Bordeaux, Feb. 16, 1774—Château-
Bourbon, near Damazon, Nov. 25,
1830 ; notable violinist ; pupil of Fau-
vel and Viotti ; début, Paris, 1790 ;
toured ; prof. at the Cons.; 1800, soloist to Napoleon, later to the Czar ;
c. 13 concertos, famous études, etc.;
wrote a method (with Baillot & Kreutzer).

**Rode** (rō'-dĕ), **(1) Jn. Gf.**, Kirch-
scheidungen, Feb. 25, 1797—Potsdam, Jan., 1857 ; horn-virtuoso ; c.
tone-pictures, etc. **(2) Th.**, Potsdam, 1821—Berlin, 1883 ; son of
above ; singing-teacher and writer.

**Röder** (rä'-dĕr), **(1) Jn. Michael**, d.
ca. 1740 ; Berlin org.-builder. **(2)
Fructuo'sus**, Simmershausen, March
5, 1747—Naples, 1789 ; notable organist. **(3) G. V.**, Rammungen,
Franconia, 1780—Altötting, Bavaria,
1848 ; ct.-cond. and composer. **(4)
Carl Gl.**, Stötteritz, near Leipzig,
1812—Gohlis, 1883 ; 1846, founded
the largest mus. and engraving establishment in the world ; in 1872, his
sons-in-law, C. L. H. Wolf and C. E.
M. Rentsch, became partners. **(5)
Martin**, Berlin, April 7, 1851—Boston, Mass., June 7, 1895 ; pupil R.
Hochschule ; conductor and teacher
of singing in various cities, incl. Dublin and Boston ; critic and writer under pseud. **" Raro Miedtner ";**
wrote essays, librettos, etc.; c. 3 operas, a symph., 2 symph. poems, etc.

**Rodio** (rō'-dǐ-ō), **Rocco**, b. Calabria,
ca. 1530 ; famous Neapolitan contrapuntist and theorist.

**Rodolphe** (rō'-dôlf) (or **Rudolph**),
**Jean Jos.**. Strassburg, Oct. 14, 1730

—Paris, Aug. 18, 1812 ; horn-v
oso and violinist ; pub. treati
prod. operas.

**Rogel** (rō'-hĕl), **José**, b. Orihuela,
cante, Dec. 24, 1829 ; conductor
composer of 61 zarzuelas, etc.

**Roger** (rō-zhā). **Gve. Hip.**, La (
pelle St.-Denis, near Paris, Dec.
1815—Paris, Sept. 12, 1879 ; ne
tenor ; created "*Le Prophète*"; 1
prof. of singing at the Cons.
**Victor**, b. Montpellier, France,
21, 1854 ; pupil École Niederme·
critic of "*La France*"; prod. ab
20 operettas, etc., incl. "*La P·
Tâche*" (1898); succ. "*Poule Blan·
(1899) ; and succ. " *Mlle. Georg*
**(1900).**

**Rogers** (rä'-jĕrs), **(1) Benj., Wind**
1614—Oxford, 1698 ; organist
Dublin ; later at Windsor ; c.
hymn sung annually at 5 A. M., M
1, on the top of Magdalen tov
Oxford. **(2) John**, d. Aldersg
ca. 1663 ; lutenist to Chas. II.
Sir **John Leman**, 1780—1847 ; c·
poser ; pres. Madrigal Soc.
**Clara Kathleen** (née **Barnett**)
Cheltenham, Engl., Jan. 14, 18
daughter and pupil of John Barne
pupil of Leipzig Cons.; studied
singing with Götze and Sangiovar
at Milan ; début Turin, 1863 (un
name **"Clara Doria"**); sang
Italy, then in London concer
1871, America with Parepa-Rosa C
1872-73, also with Maretzek C
since then lived in Boston as sin
and teacher ; 1878, m. a Boston l·
yer, Henry M. R.; pub. "*The F
losophy of Singing*" (New Yo
1893), c. songs, sonata for pf. a
vln., etc. **(5) Roland**, b. W
Bromwich, Staffordshire, Nov.
1847; at 11, organist at St.·Pet·
there ; 1871-91, organist a Ban·
Cath. and cond. of the Penrhyn a
Arvonic Choirs, teacher in Wa
1875, Mus. Doc. Oxford ; c. can
tas "*Prayer and Praise*" (with orcl
" *The Garden*" (prize, Llandud
1896) ; and " *Florabel*"; Psalm 1

r soli, chorus and strings ; a symph.,
c. (6) **James H.,** b. Fair Haven,
onn., U. S. A., 1857; at 18 studied
Berlin with Löschorn, Haupt, Ehr-
h and Rohde, and at Paris with
rsot, Guilmant and Widor ; lives in
eveland, Ohio, as organist, pianist
d composer of notable songs. (7)
**ella,** b. Denver, Colorado, ca.
69 ; soprano ; pupil of Mme. de la
ange and Léon Jancey (French
ction) ; début, St. Petersburg ; has
ng at La Scala, Milan, in Rouma-
a, Turkey, etc.

**none** (rôn-yō'-nĕ), (1) **Riccardo,**
Milanese violinist. His son (2)
**ran.,** pub. a vln. method, 1614,
.

**de** (rō'-dĕ), **Eduard,** Halle-on-
ale, 1828—Berlin, March 25, 1883 ;
iter of pf.-method ; singing teacher
d composer.

**leder** (rō'-lā-dĕr), (1) **Jn.,** pastor at
iedland, Pomerania ; pub. a trea-
e, 1792. (2) **Fr. Traugott,** Pas-
at Lahn, Silesia ; pub. articles on
urch-mus. (1829–33).

**itansky** (rō-kĭ-tän'-shkĭ), **Victor,**
eiherr **von,** Vienna, 1836—1896 ;
b. treatises on singing.

**ndt** (rō'-länt), **Hedwig** (stage-
me ʒi Hedwig **Wachutta**), b.
az, Sept. 2, 1858 ; soprano ; pu-
of Frau Weinlich-Tipka, Graz ;
but Wiesbaden, 1877; 1883, m.
e merchant Karl Schaaf.

**la, Ales.,** Pavia, April 22, 1757
Milan Sept. 15, 1841 ; violinist
d teacher ; prof. of vln. and vla.·
ganin was his pupil.

**e** (rôl ĭĕ), **Jn. H.,** Quedlinburg,
c. 23 1718—Magdeburg, Dec. 29,
85 ; son and successor of the town
is.-dir. of Magdeburg ; 1741–46,
.-player, Berlin ct.-orch.; c. 4
ssion 20 oratorios, etc.

**ig** (rĕl' lĭkh), **K. Ld.,** Vienna,
51—March 4, 1804 ; harmonica-
yer, inv. of the " Orphika " and
Kanorphika " (v. D. D.) ; wrote
atises on them ; c. comic opera.

**aniel.o** (rō-män-ĭ-ĕl'-lō), (1) **Lui-**

gi, b. Naples, Dec. 29, 1860 ; pianist ; pupil of his father, his brother (2) **Vincenzo,** and at Naples
Cons.; graduating with highest honours ; dir. of the pf.-dept. there,
later member of the Soc. del Quartetto, also pianist Ferni Quartet ; instructor in the R. " Educandato di
San Marsellino " and critic ; Chev. of
the Italian Crown ; has made tours
and pub. a pf.-method (prize at Naples, 1886) ; c. 3 operas, symphonic
poems " *Corsair* " and " *Manfred,*"
2 symphs., etc.

**Romanina.** Vide ALBERTINI, G.

**Romanini** (rō-mä-nē'-nē), **Romano,** b.
Parma, 1864 ; pupil of Mandovani
(vln.) and Dacci (comp.) at the Cons.;
1st vln. Teatro Regio ; then cond.
concert and theatre-orch. at Savigliano ; 1890, prof. of vln.; since 1897,
director " Instituto Venturi," Brescia ; c. succ. opera "*Al Campo*"
(Brescia, 1895), symph., etc.

**Romano,** (1) **Alessandro** (q. v.). (2)
**Giulio.** Vide CACCINI.

**Romberg** (rôm'-bĕrkh), (1) **Anton** (a)
and (2) **H.,** two brothers, lived in
Berlin, 1792. (3) **Anton** (b), Westphalia, 1745—1812 (1742—1814,
acc. to Riemann); bassoonist. (4)
**Gerhard H.,** b. 1748 ; clarinettist
and mus.-dir. at Münster. (5) **Bd.,**
Dincklage, near Münster, Nov. 11,
1767—Hamburg, Aug. 13, 1841; the
head of the German sch. of 'cellists ;
prof.; ct.-cond., 1815–19 ; c. many
operas, incid. mus.; 9 excellent concertos. (6) **Andreas** (**Jakob**),
Vechta, near Münster, 1767—Gotha,
1821 ; vln.-virtuoso ; son of (7) **Gerhard H.,** b. 1748 ; dir. and clarinettist. (8) **Cyprian,** Hamburg, 1807
—1865 ; son of (6) and pupil of (5),
'cellist and composer. (9) **Anton** (c),
b. 1777; bassoonist ; son of (3). (10)
**Therese,** b. 1781; pianist ; sister of
(6).

**Romer, Emma,** 1814—Margate, 1868,
Engl. soprano.

**Ronchetti - Monteviti** (rôn-kĕt'-tē
môn-tā-vē'-tē), **Stefano,** Asti, 1814—

Casale Monferrato, 1882 ; pupil of
B. Neri, Milan ; 1850, prof. of comp.
at the Cons.; 1877, dir.; c. an opera,
a motet, etc.

**Ronconi** (rôn-kō'-nē), (1) **Dom.**, Len-
dinara, Rovigo, July 11, 1772—Mi-
lan, April 13, 1839 ; singer and famous vocal-teacher ; tenor ; 1809,
dir. of the ct.-opera, Vienna ; 1819–
29 ; singing-master to the princess,
Munich ; 1829, founded a singing-
sch. at Milan ; pub. vocal exercises.
(2) **Giorgio,** Milan, 1810—1890 ;
son of above ; barytone ; 1863, teacher at Cordova, Spain ; from 1867,
New York ; composer. (3) **Felice,**
Venice, 1811—St. Petersburg, 1875 ;
singing-teacher and writer. (4) **Sebastiano,** b. Venice, 1814 ; barytone,
violinist and teacher, Milan.

**Rong** (rông), **Wm. Fd.,** d. Berlin ;
said to have been living in 1821,
aged 100 ; chamber-musician of Prussia ; mus.-teacher, writer and composer.

**Rönisch** (rā'-nǐsh), **K.,** Goldberg, Silesia, 1814—Blasewitz, 1894 ; piano-
manufacturer at Dresden.

**Röntgen** (rĕnt'-gĕn), (1) **Engelbert,**
Deventer, Holland, 1829—Leipzig,
1897 ; violinist. (2) **Julius,** b. Leipzig, May 9, 1855 ; pianist ; son of
above ; pupil of Hauptmann and E. F.
Richter, Plaidy, Reinecke and Fr.
Lachner ; at 10 began to c.; at 17
pub. a vln.-sonata ; début as pianist,
1878 ; teacher mus.-sch., Amsterdam ; 1886–98, cond. to the Soc. for
the Promotion of Mus., also Felix
Meritis Soc.; co-founder (1885) of
the Cons.; c. "*Toskanische Rispetti,*"
an operetta for voices and pf.; a pf.-
concerto, etc.

**Rooke, Wm. M.,** Dublin, 1794—London, 1847 ; teacher, pianist, violinist
and dram. composer.

**Root,** (1) **G. Ed. Fr.,** Sheffield, Mass.,
Aug. 30, 1820—Barley's Island, Aug.
6. 1895 ; teacher of singing and conductor ; pupil of Webb, Boston ;
studied Paris, 1850 ; c. "*Battle-cry
of Freedom,*" "*Tramp, Tramp,*

*Tramp,*" "*Just before the Ba[ttle]
Mother,*" etc. (2) **Fr. Woodm[an]**
b. Boston, Mass., June 13, 1[8]
son and pupil of above ; pupi[l of]
Blodgett and Mason, New York ;
ganist ; 1869–70, studied in Eur[ope]
later lecturer, writer and teache[r]
large vocal classes.

**Rooy, van.** Vide VAN ROOY.

**Roquet** (rō-kā), **Ant. Ernst,** Nan[tes]
1827—Paris, 1894 ; amateur, who [un-]
der pen-name "**Ernest Thoin[an]**"
(twä-nän) pub. valuable histo[ric]
works based on research.

**Rore** (rō'-rĕ), **Cipriano de,** Mec[heln,]
1516—Parma, 1565 ; eminent [com-]
poser of Venetian sch.; pupil of [Wil-]
laert, 1550, and his successor, 1[5 ..]
ct.-conductor.

**Rorich** (rō'-rǐkh), **Carl,** b. Nürnb[erg,]
Feb. 27, 1869 ; pupil of R. Sch[ ...]
Mus., Würzburg ; from 1892, tea[cher]
Gr. Ducal Sch. of Mus., Weimar[ ; c.]
an overture "*Märchen,*" a s[ ...]
"*Waldleben,*" etc.

**Ro'sa,** (1) **Salvato're,** Aranella, [Na-]
ples, 1615—Rome, 1673 ; fam[ous]
painter and poet ; wrote a satir[e on]
mus., etc.; composer. (2) **C[ ...]**
(rightly **Carl Rose**), Hamburg, [ ...]
—Paris, 1889 ; violinist ; 1867, [m.]
Parepa-Rosa, and with her organ[ized]
an English opera-company ; to[ok ...]
with great frequency, especially [at ...]
head of an Engl. opera syndicate[ ...]

**Rosé** (rō'-zā), **Arnold Josef,** b. Ja[ssy,]
Oct. 24, 1863 ; pupil of Heissler[, Vi-]
enna Cons.; 1st vln. Rosé Quar[tet]
since 1881, soloist, Vienna ct.-or[ch.,]
and since 1888, leader Bayreuth [fes-]
tivals.

**Roseingrave** (rōz'-ǐn-grāv), **Th[os.,]**
Dublin—London, 1750 ; 12 y[rs.]
organist at St. George's, Han[over]
Square ; composer and writer.

**Rosel** (rō'-zĕl), **Rudolf Arthur,** [b.]
Münchenbernsdorf, Gera, Aug. [ ...]
1859 ; pupil of Weimar Mus.-S[ch.,]
later of Thomson ; 1877–79, 1st [vln.]
various cities ; from 1888 in the W[ei-]
mar ct.-orch.; also teacher at M[us.]
Sch.; c. fairly succ. "lyric st[age" ...]

play " " *Halimah* " (Weimar, 1895),
ymph. poem " *Frühlingsstürme*," a
otturno for horn with orch., a not-
urno for oboe with orch., etc.

sellen (rō-zĕl-län), **H.**, Paris, 1811
—1876 ; pf.-teacher, writer and composer.

senhain (rō'-zĕn-hīn), (1) **Jacob
Jacques**), Mannheim, 1813—Baden-
Baden, 1894 ; pianist and dram. composer. (2) **Eduard**, Mannheim,
818—Frankfort, 1861; bro. of above;
pianist, teacher and composer.

senmüller (rō'-zĕn-mĭl-lĕr), **Jn.**,
615—Wolfenbüttel, 1682 ; mus.-di-
ector and composer.

senthal (rō'-zĕn-täl), **Moriz,** b.
Lemberg, 1862 ; brilliant pianist ; at
his ability enlisted the aid of Miku-
; at 10, pupil of R. Joseffy ; at 14,
ave a concert Vienna ; Royal Pian-
st ; 1876–86, pupil of Liszt ; from
887, toured America and Europe ;
896–97, tour of U. S. interrupted
y illness ; pub. (with L. Schytte)
*Technical Studies for the Highest
Degree of Development.*"

ses (rō'-zĕs), **Jose**, Barcelona, 1791
—1850; organist, composer and
eacher.

setti (rō-sĕt'-tē), **Fran. Ant.**
Fz. **Anton Rössler**, rĕs-lĕr), Leitmeritz, Bohemia, 1750—Ludwigslust,
792 , ct.-conductor and composer.

sler (räs'-lĕr). **Gv.**, 1819—Dresden,
882 ; teacher and dram. composer ;
rod. succ. opera (Dessau)

ss, **J.**, b. Newcastle-on-Tyne 1764,
rganist and composer.

ssaro (rōs-sä'-rō), **Carlo**, Crescen-
no, Vercelli. 1828—Turin, 1878 ,
anist and dram. composer.

setor, **Phillip**, Engl. lutenist and
omposer, 1616.

ssi (rōs' sē). (1) **Giov. Bat.**, Gen-
ese monk : theorist, ca. 1618. (2)
bbate **Fran.**, b. Bari, Italy, ca.
645 , canon and dram. composer.
) **Gaetano**, Verona 1780—1855 ;
rettist. (4) **Luigi Felice**, Bran-
zzo, Piedmont 1804—Turin, 1863 ,
sayist and translator. (5) **Lauro,**

Macerata, 1812 — Cremona, 1885 ;
wrote a harmony and c. operas. (6)
**Giov. Gaetano**, Borgo, S. Donino,
Parma, 1828—Genoa, 1886 ; c. 4
operas.

**Rossini** (rôs-sē'-nē), **Gioacchino A.**,
Pesaro, Feb. 29, 1792—Ruelle, near
Paris, Nov. 13, 1868; eminent Italian
opera-composer. His father was inspector of slaughter-houses and also
horn - player in strolling troupes in
which the mother (a baker's daughter) was *prima donna buffa.* Left in
charge of a pork-butcher, **R.** picked
up some knowledge of the harpsichord
from a teacher, Prinetti ; 1802 studied with Angelo Tesci ; this began
his tuition ; he made rapid progress,
and sang in church, and afterwards
joined his parents as a singer, horn-
player and accompanist in the theatre.
At 14 he studied comp. with Padre
Mattei, and 'cello with Cavedagni at
the Bologna Liceo. At 15 he prod.
a cantata " *Il Pianto d'Armonia per
la Morte d'Orfeo*," which won a
prize. Mattei soon told him that,
though he had not enough cpt. to
write church-mus., he knew enough
to write operas, and he ceased to
study. At 17 he prod. a succ. 1-act
opera buffa ' *La Cambiale di Matrimonio*" (Venice, 1810) ; next year, a
succ. 2-act opera buffa " *L'Equivoco
Stravagante*," Bologna.. He received
various commissions, writing 5 operas
during 1812. 1813, his " *Tancredi* "
(Fenice Th., Venice) was an immense succ. and " *L'Italiana in Algeri*," an opera buffa (San Benedetto
Th.), was also succ. Two failures
followed with disheartening effect,
but " *Elisabetta* " (its libretto curiously anticipating Scott's " *Kenilworth* ") was a succ. (Naples, 1813),
and in it he dropped *recitativo secco.*
A failure followed and on the first
night of the next work the public re-
sentment at his daring to set to mus.
the text of one of Paisiello's operas
led to its being hissed. This work
" *Almaviva* " (Rome, 1816) was

better received the second night and gradually est. itself in its subsequent fame under the title " *Il Barbiere di Seviglia* "; 1815–23 he was under contract to write two operas yearly for Barbaja, manager of La Scala at Milan, the Italian opera, Vienna, and Neapolitan theatres. His salary was 12,000 lire (about $2,400). During these 8 years he c. 20 operas, travelling from town to town and working under highest pressure. 1821 he m. Isabella Colbran (d. 1845), who had sung in his operas. The ill-succ. of his most carefully written " *Semiramide* " (Venice, 1823) and an offer from Benelli, a mgr., led him to London where he was lionised and in 5 months earned £7,000. For 18 months he was mgr. of the Th. Italien at Paris, and prod. several operas with artistic, but not financial succ. He was however " Premier compositeur du roi " and " Inspector-général du chant en France," sinecures with a salary of 20,000 francs ($4,000). He lost these in the Revolution of 1830, but afterwards on going to law received a pension of 6,000 francs.

At the Gr. Opéra he prod. with su revisions in French, of earlier Ital succs. 1829 he gave there his grea succ. masterpiece " *Guglielmo Te* At the age of 37, having prod. un his direction Meyerbeer's first op and having heard " *Les Huguenot* R. foreswore opera and never wr again anything more dramatic than famous " *Stabat Mater* " (1832), performed entire till 1842 ; " *Pe messe solennelle*," with orch.; a c tata for the Exposition of 1867 ; a pf.-pcs. with burlesque names. retired to Bologna and Florence, turning to Paris in 1855. 1847 he Olympe Pelissier. He c. 35 ope 16 cantatas, canzonets and ari "*Gorgheggi e solfeggi per soprano rendere la voce agile*," " *Chant Titans* " for 4 basses with orc " *Tantum ergo* " for 3 male voi with orch.; " *Quoniam* " for solo b with orch.; " *O salutaris* " for s quartet, etc. Biog. by Stend (1823), Azvedo (1865), H. S. I wards (London, 1869), Zano (1875), Struth (Leipzig), Dr. A. I hut (Leipzig, 1892).

## Rossini.

### By Irenaeus Prime-Stevenson.

IT is like a page of goldenest sunshine in the volume of musical person to review the brief, brilliant, artistic story of Rossini's activity or glance at his long and happy life. Almost from the first came to h fame, fortune, and opportunity for that amazing fecundity of mind which w so curiously sorted with his indolence of body. Few men of genius ha lived and worked and rivalled and succeeded, of whom so little is curre that is ungracious or discreditable. ¶As to Rossini's place in art, albeit huge fraction of his operas are empty to our ears, and bore us with th flowery ornamentation and feeble dramatic substructure, we have no right predict that thorough neglect will soon deliver to darkness and dust su scores as " *L'Italiana in Algeri*," " *Il Barbiere di Seviglia*," " *Gug elmo Tell*,"—and possibly " *Semiramide* " ; for the world will have l too completely a natural irresistible feeling for melody, for restrained elegan

chestral diction, and above all for the perfect expression of true comedy
usic. Only in one other master, Mozart, to whom Rossini felt that he
d so much, and to whom he declared himself so far inferior, do we meet
l sincerity, taste, and eloquence as prolifically put into operatic song and
estration. ¶ And as to "*Tell*," with that noble and serious work, a
ing variant from the old Italianistic Rossini, a work by a mature and
us-minded composer of the first order, all the great and the little musical
d will long have to reckon. ¶ The great influences on Rossini were
: Mozart, whose greatest successor in Italian operatic comedy Rossini
inly is ; and a mixture of French form and French dramatic spirit with
man importance in every detail of the orchestra. ¶ It cannot be said
Rossini founded a school. He " said it all himself," as the phrase goes ;
his imitators either gave over copying (often with most happy and sig-
ant advantages to great individualities for themselves, as in the instances
Meyerbeer and Donizetti and Verdi), or else they were not of substance
eir efforts to eclipse the dazzling master of Pesaro. His effect upon the
le operatic public of Europe was for a time almost demoralising, paralys-
to all other music. ¶ Immediately after the striking renunciation of his
er, at only thirty-seven years of age, came the Wagner movement, which
owing not unwelcome signs of sluggishness and eventual disappearance.

---

sler, **F. A.** Vide ROSETTI, F. A.

t (ròst), (1) **Nicolas,** pastor at
osmenz, Altenburg ; composer,
83–1614. (2) **Fr. Wm. Ehren-**
ed, Bautzen, 1768—Leipzig, 1835;
riter.

h (rōt), (1) **Ph.,** Tarnowitz, Sile-
a, 1853—Berlin, 1898 ; 'cellist. (2)
ertrand, b. Degersheim, St. Gal-
n, Feb. 12, 1855 ; pianist ; pupil of
eipzig Cons. and Liszt ; teacher
och Cons., Frankfort, co-founder.
aff Cons., 1882 ; 1885–90, Dresden
ons.; then opened a private mus.-
h. there.

hmühl (rōt'-mül), **Nikolaus,** b.
arsaw, March 24, 1857: tenor ; pu-
l of Gänsbacher ; début, Dresden
.-theatre, then Berlin, etc.; toured
dely, incl. America ; then at Stuttart ct.-opera.

h-**Ronay** (rōt-rō'-nä-ē), **Kalman,**
Veszprein, Hungary, July 20, 1869;
otable violinist ; pupil Grün, Vien-
a Cons., took 1st prize gold medal

for vln.; studied comp. at Leipzig
Cons., then with Joachim, Berlin.
1893–94, leader Covent Garden ;
toured Europe ; decorated by King
of Hungary, King of Servia, Prince
of Bulgaria and the Sultan ; pub. a
few songs ; c. also sonatas for vln.
and piano, etc.

**Rotoli** (rò-tō'-lē), **Augusto,** b. Rome,
Jan. 7, 1847; pupil of Lucchesi ;
founded and cond. "Società corale
de' concerti sagri," 1876, singing-
master to Princess Margherita ; 1878,
maestro, Capella reale del Sudario ;
1885, invited to Boston, Mass., as
teacher in the N. E. Cons.; Chev. of
the Ital. Crown, etc. C. mass for the
funeral of Victor Emmanuel, 1878 ;
" *Salmo elegiaco*," with orch. (1878),
etc.

**Rot'tenberg** (-bĕrkh), Dr. **Ludwig,** b.
Czernowicz, Oct. 11, 1864 ; studied
vln. and piano with Fuchs, and theory with Mandyczewski ; début as
pianist ; 1888, director ; 1891, cond.

at Brunn, then 1st opera cond. at Frankfort.

**Rotter** (rôt'-tĕr), **L.**, Vienna, 1810—1895 ; pianist, conductor, theorist and composer.

**Rottmanner** (rôt'-män-nĕr), **Ed.**, Munich, 1809—Speyer, 1843 ; organist.

**Rouget de l'Isle** (roo-zhā dŭ-lĕl), **Claude Jos.**, Lons-le-Saulnier, Jura, May 10, 1760—Choisy-le-Roy, June 27, 1836 ; composer of the " *Marseillaise*," military engineer, poet, librettist, violinist and singer ; wrote "*La Marseillaise*," picking out the air on his vln. ; he called it "*Chant de Guerre*," but it grew popular first in Marseilles, and was brought to Paris by Marseillaise volunteers in 1792 ; **R.** was imprisoned for refusing to take an oath against the crown, but was released, and lived in Paris in great poverty.

**Rousseau** (roos-sō), (1) **Jean Jacques,** Geneva, June 28, 1712—Ermenonville, near Paris, July 3, 1778. The great writer ; mainly self-taught in mus , but aiming to reform notation by the substitution of numerals for letters and note-heads, read before the Académie, 1742, a " *Dissertation sur la musique moderne*" (1743) ; his opera, "*Les Muses Galantes*," had one private representation (1745); his revision of the intermezzo " *La Reine de Navarre*" (by Voltaire and Rameau) was a failure ; but his opera "*Le Devin du Village*" (Gr. Opéra, 1752) was succ. for 60 years. He wrote mus. articles for the "*Encyclopédie*," which were roughly handled by Rameau and others, but revised and re-pub. as " *Dictionnaire de musique*" (1768). In 1752 he participated in the " Guerre des Bouffons," between the partisans of French and Italian opera, **R.** siding with the Italianists and declaring that a French national music was impossible and undesirable ; for which the members of the opera burned him in effigy. " *Pygmalion*" (1773) was v. succ. being a novelty—a melodrama,

all the dialogue spoken, the or furnishing interludes and backgrou Six new arias for " *Le Devin du V lage*," and a coll. of 100 roman and duets " *Les consolations des sères de ma vie*" (1781), and fr ments of an opera, " *Daphnis Chloé*," were pub. (1780). (2) **Je** violinist in Paris ; pub. valuable te books (1678—87) ; composer.

**Samuel Alex.**, b. Neuvemais Aisne, June 11, 1853 ; pupil of Pa Cons., 1878, won the Prix Cresse and 2d Grand Prix de Rome ; pr 1-act comedy-opera " *Dianora* (Op.-Com., 1879) ; 1891, won Prize of the City of Paris, with op " *Merowig*" ; 1892, 1st cond. Lyrique ; 1898, prod. fairly su lyric drama "*La Cloche du Rhin* c. also a solemn mass, etc.

**Roussier** (roos-sĭ-ā), Abbé **P. Jo** Marseilles, 1716—Écouis, Norman ca. 1790 ; canon and theorist.

**Rovel'li,** (1) **Giu.**, Bergamo, 175 Parma, 1806 ; 'cellist. (2) **P.**, B gamo, 1793—1838 ; nephew of abo violinist and composer.

**Rovet'ta, Giov.**, d. Venice, 1668 ; pil of Monteverde, and his succes (1644) at San Marco ; c. operas, e

**Row'botham, John F.**, b. Edinbur April 18, 1854 ; studied Oxfc Berlin, Paris, Vienna, Dresd wrote numerous histories of mu biogs., etc.

**Roze** (rôz), Abbé **Nicolas,** Bou Neuf, near Châlons, 1745—St.-M dé, near Paris, 1819 ; composer a writer.

**Rozkošny** (rōz'-kōsh-nē), **Josef Ri ard,** b. Prague, Sept. 21, 18 pianist ; pupil of Jiranek, Tomasc and Kittl ; toured, then lived Prague ; prod. there 9 Bohemian eras ; c. also overtures, 2 masses, e

**Rubini** (roo-bē'-nē), **Giov. Bat., I** mano, Bergamo, April 7, 1795— his castle, near Romano, March 1854 ; famous tenor, said to ha been the first to use the vibrato a the sob, both since abused ; his ra

as from E–b' (with a falsetto regis-
er to f'. v. PITCH, D.D.); Bellini
rote many operas for him; toured
ith Liszt, earning by one concert
ver $10,000; had one of the largest
ortunes ever amassed by a singer.

binstein (roo'-bĭn-shtīn), (1) **Anton**
**regorovitch**, of Jewish parents,
Vechwotynecz, Bessarabia, Nov. 30,
830—Peterhof, near St. Petersburg,
ov. 20, 1894; one of the greatest
f the world's pianists. Early taken
o Moscow, where his father est. a
encil factory, he was at first a pupil
f his mother; at 7, of Alex. Vil-
ing, who was his only pf.-teacher.
t 9 he made a tour with Villoing as
r as Paris, where, in 1840, he played
efore Chopin and Liszt, who ad-
sed him to study in Germany. He
oured further and returned to Mos-
ow in 1843. His brother, Nikolai
. below), was also musical, and
1844 both were taken to Berlin,
here Anton studied comp. with
ehn. Returning to Russia after a
our through Hungary, with the flut-
t Heindl, he lived in Petersburg
nder the patronage of the Grand
uchess Helen; he prod. 2 Russian
peras; 1854-58, with the assistance
Count Wielhorski and the Grand
uchess, he made a wide tour, finding
mself now well known as composer
d pianist; 1858, ct.-pianist and
nd. of ct.-concerts, Petersburg;
359, dir. Russian Mus. Soc.; 1862,
unded the Imp. Cons. at Peters-
urg, and was its dir. until 1867;
365, he m. Vera Tchekuanoff.
867-70, he toured Europe, with
eatest imaginable succ.; 1872-73,
e gave in America 215 concerts, from
hich he earned $40,000 (£8,000);
ut he could never be induced to
oss the ocean again, though offered
25,000 (£25,000) for fifty con-
rts. 1887-91, again dir. Petersburg
ons., then lived in Berlin; 1891, in
resden. The Czar bestowed on
m the Order of Vladimir carrying
ith it nobility, and the title of Imp.

Russian State Councillor; he was an
officer of the Legion of Honour, a
Knight of the Prussian Ordre pour le
mérite, etc. He instituted the *Rubinstein prizes* of 5,000 francs each for
pf.-playing and composition open
every 5 years to men between 20 and
26 of any nationality.

He wrote his " *Memoirs*," also
" *Die Musik und ihre Meister* "
(1892), " *Gedankenkorl* " (1892).

As a pianist **R.** is second only to
Liszt, whom he perhaps excelled in
fire and leonine breadth. He was,
however, frequently inaccurate in his
performance. He chiefly wished to
be remembered as a composer and
placed great hope in the creation of
what he called "Sacred Opera" (oratorio to be enacted with costume and
scenery). In this "new form" he c.
" *The Tower of Babel*," " *Paradise
Lost*," " *Moses*," " *Christus*." Besides the noteworthy operas " *Nero* "
(Hamburg, 1879), " *The Demon* " (Russian, P., 1875), and " *Die Mak-
kabäer* " (German, Berlin, 1875), he c.
11 other operas, a ballet " *La Vigne* "
(*Die Rebe*), and 2 cantatas with orch.
C. also 6 symphs. (incl. the famous
" *Ocean*," op. 42, in C, in 7 movements); op. 95, in D min. ("*Dramatic*"); op. 107, in G min. (in
memory of Gr. Duch. Helen).
"Character-pictures" " *Faust*,"
" *Ivan IV.*," and " *Don Quixote*";
3 concert-overtures, incl. op. 43
(" *Triomphale*"), and op. 116 ("*Anthony and Cleopatra* "); a Suite in 6
movements, op. 119 (his last work);
symph. poem " *La Russie*,"; 5 pf.-
concertos; fantasia eroica with orch.;
vln.-concerto; romance and caprice
for vln. with orch.; 2 'cello-concertos;
vln.-sonatas; vln.-sonata (arr. for
vln. by David), etc. FOR PIANO
SOLO: suite; 4 sonatas, 6 preludes,
6 études, 5 barcarolles; " *Kamenoi-
Ostrow* " (" *Isle of Kamenoi* " in the
Neva, a series of 24 "pictures");
" *Soirées de St. P.*," " *Miscellanies*,"
" *Le Bal*," 10 pcs. op. 14; " *Album*

45

*de Peterhof*," etc. FOR PF. 4 HANDS, sonata, "*Bal Costumé*," 6 Charakt-erbilder, fantasia for 2 pfs.; over 100 songs, 18 duets, choruses, etc. Autobiog. " *Memoirs*" (St. P. 1889; Leipzig, 1893). Biogr. by MacArthur (London, 1889).

(2) **Nikolai**, Moscow, June 2, 1835—(of consumption), Paris, March 23, 1881; bro. of above, who declared **N.** to be the better pianist of the two; founder Moscow Mus. Soc.; dir. Moscow Cons. from its foundation. 1864; c. pf.-pcs. etc. (3) **Jos.**, Staro-Constantinow, Russia, Feb. 8, 1847—(suicide) Lucerne, Sept. 15, 1884; pianist for rehearsals at Bayreuth; composer. (4) **Jacques**, Russia, 1874—Paris, 1902; son of (1).

**Rubner** (roop'-nĕr), **Cornelius**, b. Co-penhagen, Oct. 26, 1853; pianist; pupil of Gade and Reinecke; 1892, cond. Carlsruhe Philh. Soc.; c. a symph. poem; " *Festouvertüre*," etc.

**Ruckers** (rook'-ĕrs), family of clavecin-makers at Antwerp, superior to all others. (1) **Hans** (Senior), d. ca. 1640; father of (2) **Fz.**, b. 1776. (3) **Hans** (Junior), b. 1578. (4) **Andries** (senior), b. 1579. (5) **Anton**, b. 1581; the last mfr. was (6) **Andries** (Junior), 1607-67.

**Rucsicska.** Vide RUZICKA.

**Rudersdorff** (roo'-dĕrs-dôrf), **Hermine**, Ivanowsky, Ukraine, Dec. 12, 1822—Boston, Mass., Feb. 26, 1882; noted soprano and teacher.

**Rudolph, Jn. J. R.**, Arch-duke of Austria, Florence, 1788 — Baden, Vienna, 1831; pianist and composer; pupil and intimate friend of Bee-thoven.

**Rudorff** (roo'-dôrf), **Ernst Fr. K.**, b. Berlin, Jan. 18, 1840; pupil of Bar-giel (pf.), and Leipzig Cons.; pri-vate pupil of Hauptmann and Rei-necke; 1865, pf.-teacher, Cologne Cons.; 1867 founded the Bach-verein, 1869 head pf.-teacher Berlin Hoch-schule; 1880-90 cond. Stern Gesang-verein; c. 2 symphs., 2 overtures, etc.

**Ruegger** (rüg'-gĕr), **Elsa**, b. [L]cerne, Dec. 6, 1881; 'cellist; stud[ied] with Jacobs and Anna Campowski[?] the Cons. there, taking 1st prize 13; began touring widely Amer[ica] and Europe.

**Rüfer** (rü'-fār), (1) **Ph. (Barthé[le]-my)**, b. Liège, June 7, 1844; son [of] a German organist. (2) **Philipp** pupil of Liège Cons.; 1869-71, m[us.] dir. at Essen; pf.-teacher Ste[rn] Cons., Kullak's Cons., and fr[om] 1881 Scharwenka's, Berlin, c. o[pe]-ras " *Merlin*" (Berlin, 1887); su[ng] "*Ingo*" (Berlin, 1896); symph. F.; 3 overtures, etc.

**Ruffo** (roof'-fō), **V.**, b. Verona; ma[es]-tro of the Cath.; composer (15[77-] 88).

**Rufinatscha** (roo'-fĭ-nät-shä), [J.,] Tyrol, 1812—Vienna, May 25, 18[78;] composer.

**Ruggeri (Ruggieri)** (rood-jā'-rē) Cremonian family of vln.-makers, **Fran.**, flourished, 1668—1720. **Giov. Bat.** (1700—1725), and **P.** (1700—1720), probably his so[ns] (4) **Guido** and (5) **V.**, both of C[re]-mona in 18th cent. **R.** violins [re]-semble Amatis. (6) **Giov. M.**, [Ve]-netian composer; prod. operas t[here] 1696—1712.

**Ruggi** (rood'-jē), **Fran.**, Naples, [1767] —1845; conductor, professor [of] dram. composer.

**Rühlmann** (rül'-män), (**Ad.**) Jul[ius] Dresden, 1817 (16?)—1877; co[urt] trombonist; professor, writer [and] composer.

**Rumford, R. Kennerly**, b. Lon[don,] Sept. 2, 1871; concert baryto[ne;] studied in Frankfort, Berlin [and] Paris; m. Clara Butt, 1900.

**Rummel** (room'-mĕl). (1) **Chr. (Fz. Fr. Alex.)**, Brichsenstadt, Bava[ria,] 1787—Wiesbaden, 1849; clarinet[ist] and composer. (2) **Josephine**, M[a]-yares, Spain, 1812—Wiesbaden, 1[877;] daughter of above; ct.-pianist. **Jos.**, Wiesbaden, 1818 — Lon[don,] 1880; son and pupil of (1); ct.-p[ian]-ist and composer. (4) **Franzis[ka**

esbaden, 1821—Brussels, 1873; ct.-
ger; sister of above; m. Peter
ott, the pub. (5) **Aug.**, Wies-
len, 1824—London, 1886; pian-
(6) **Fz.**, London, Jan. 11, 1853
May, 1901; pianist; son of (3);
pil of Brassin, Brussels Cons., win-
g 1st prize, 1872; 1877–78, toured
lland with Ole Bull; toured Amer-
3 times; teacher Stern's Cons.,
n Kullak's, Berlin; 1897 " Profess-
' from the Duke of Anhalt.

ciman, **John F.**, b. England,
6 , prominent critic. Educated
he science school (now Rutherford
lege), Newcastle-on-Tyne; orist from childhood; 1887, took
ition in London; from 1894 musi-
critic " *Saturday Review* "; later,
il 1898 also acting editor and man-
ng director; also editor of the quar-
y " *The Chord*," and of the " *Mu-
an's Library* "; for some years
respondent Boston " *Musical Rec-
*"; 1901, of New York " *Musical
rier* "; some of his essays were
blished as " *Old Scores and New
dings* " (1899); has also written a
graphical study of Purcell.

; (roongk), **Henrik**, Copenhagen,
7—1871; conductor and dram.
poser.

enhagen (roong´-ĕn-hä-gĕn),
**Fr.**, Berlin, 1778—1851; Profess-
conductor and dramatic compos-

**f.** Vide LUTHER, M.

sell, (1) **Wm.**, London, 1777—
3; pianist. (2) **Henry**, Sheer-
s, 1813—London, Dec. 6, 1900;
pop. Engl. song-composer. (3)
uis Arthur, b. Newark, N. J.,
. 24, 1854; pupil of S. P. War-
, G. F. Bristow, and C. C. Mul-
New York; also studied, London,
8–95; organist and choirm., New-
; since 1879, cond. Schubert
al Soc.; since 1885, Easton (Pa.)
ral Soc.; 1885, founded the New-
Coll. of Mus., of which he is dir.
l teacher; 1893, organised Newark
nph. Orch.; wrote various books;

c. cantata with orch., " *A Pastoral
Rhapsody*," etc.
**Rust** (roost), (1) **Fr. Wm.**, Wörlitz,
near Dessau, July 6, 1739—Dessau.
Feb. 28, 1796; violinist; bro. and pupil
of an amateur violinist in J. S. Bach's
orch. at Leipzig; ct.-mus. director;
c. stage pieces, etc. (2) **Wm. K.**,
1787—1855; son of above; pupil of
Türk; organist and composer. (3)
**Wm.**, Dessau, Aug. 15, 1822—
Leipzig, May 2, 1892, nephew of
above. composer; notable organist
and teacher; cond. Berlin Bach-
Verein and editor of Bach's text.
**Ruta** (roo´-tä), **Michele**, Caserta, 1827
—Naples, Jan. 24, 1896; theorist
and dram. composer.
**Ruthardt** (root´-härt), (1) **Fr.**, 1800—
1862; oboist and composer. (2)
**Julius**, b. Stuttgart, Dec. 13, 1841;
son of above; violinist, th.-conductor
since 1885 at Bremen; c. incid. mus.
songs. (3) **Ad.**, b. Stuttgart, Feb.
9, 1849; bro. of above; pupil of the
Cons.; 1868–85, teacher in Geneva,
then Leipzig Cons.; writer and composer.
**Ruzicka (Rucsicska, Rutschitsch-
ka, etc.)** (root-shētsh´-kä), **Wenzel**,
Jaumentz, Moravia, 1758—Vienna,
1823; bandm. and dram. composer
and ct.-organist; Schubert was his
pupil.
**Ry´an**, (1) **Michael Desmond**, Kilkenny, 1816—London, 1868 from
1836 critic and librettist in London.
(2) **Thos.**, b. Ireland, 1827; at 17
went to the U. S.; studied Boston.
1849; co-founder " Mendelssohn
Quintet Club," with which he toured
America; clarinet and vla.-virtuoso;
c. quintets, quartets, songs, etc.;
wrote " *Recollections of an old Musician* " (New York, 1890).
**Ryba** (rē´-bä), **Jakob Jan.**, Przestitz,
Bohemia, 1765—Roczmittal, 1815; c.
6 comic operas, etc.
**Ry´der, Thos. Philander**, b. Cohas-
set, Mass., June 29, 1836; pupil of
Gv. Satter; organist Tremont
Temple, Boston; c. pf.-pieces.

# S

**Saar** (zär), (**Louis**) **Victor Fz.**, b. Rotterdam, Dec. 10, 1868 ; studied with Rheinberger and Abel, Munich Cons.; then with Brahms ; 1891 took the Mendelssohn composition prize for a pf.-suite and songs ; 1892–95, opera-accompanist, New York ; 1896–98, teacher, comp. and cpt., National Cons., N. Y.; 1898, Coll. of Mus.; critic and composer for piano.

**Sabbatini** (säb-bä-tē'-nē), (1) **Galeazzo**, b. Pesaro ; ct.-maestro and composer (1627–39). (2) **Luigi A.**, Albano Liziale, Rome, 1739—Padua, 1809 ; maestro, writer and composer.

**Sacchi** (säk'-kē), Don **Giovenale**, Barfio, Como, 1726—Milan, 1789; writer.

**Sacchini** (säk-kē'-nē), **A. M. Gasparo**, Pozzuoli, near Naples, June 23, 1734—Paris, Oct. 8, 1786 ; eminent Neapolitan opera composer, son of a poor fisher. Discovered and taught by Durante and others; 1756, prod. succ. intermezzo "*Fra Donata*," followed by others in Neapolitan dialect ; 1762–66, at Rome in a keen rivalry with Piccini ; 1772–82, London, succ. as composer but not as financier. Fled from creditors to Paris where he had succ. and prod. many works, incl. "*Œdipe à Colone*," his best work. He c. over 60 operas, 6 oratorios, etc.

**Sachs** (zäkhs), (1) **Hans**, Nürnberg, Nov. 5, 1494 — Jan. 19, 1576 ; a cobbler ; chief of the Meistersinger (v. D.D.) and hero of Wagner's opera of that name ; he wrote over 4,000 poems, 1.700 tales and 200 dramatic poems ; also c. melodies. (2) **Julius**, Waldhof, Meiningen, 1830—Frankfort-on-Main 1888 ; pianist. (3) **Melchior Ernst**, b. Mittelsinn, Lower Franconia, Feb. 28, 1843 ; pupil Munich Cons. and of Rheinberger ; 1868–72, cond. "Liederkranz"; 1871, teacher of harm. Sch. of Mus.; founded and still cond. "Tonkünstlerverein" concerts ; c. opera, ballade with orch., etc.

**Sachse-Hofmeister** (zäkhs'-ĕ-hōf'-

**mī-shtĕr**), **Anna**, b. Gumpe kirchen, near Vienna, July 26, 18 soprano.

**Saffieddin'**, **Abdolmumin**, Ben chir el Ormeve el Bagdadi, Arabic and Persian theorist of 13th and 14th cents., author of standard work "*Shereffie*."

**Safonoff**, **W.**, b. Istchóry, Cauca Feb. 6 (new style), 1852 ; pupi Leschetizki and Zaremba ; the Brassin, Petersburg Cons., ta gold medal, 1881–85, teacher th 1885, Moscow; 1889, dir. of the C there, and since 1890 conductor.

**Ságh** (säkh), **Jos.**, b. Pesth, March 1852; Hungarian lexicographer; 1 founder and editor of mus. p "*Zenelap*."

**Sagitta'rius**. Vide SCHÜTZ.

**Sahla** (zä'-lä), **Richard**, b. Graz, S 17, 1855 ; violinist ; pupil of Da Leipzig Cons.; début, Gewandh 1873 ; 1888, ct.-cond. Bückeb founded an oratorio-soc. there ; Roumanian Rhapsody, etc.

**Saint-Amans** (săn-tä-mäṅ), **L. J** Marseilles, 1749—Paris, 1820 ; ductor at Brussels and dram. c poser.

**Saint Aubin** (săn-tō-băṅ), (1) **Jea Charlotte** (née **Schroeder**), P 1764—1850 ; notable operatic sin Her three children : (2) **Jean De** Lyons, 1783—Paris, 1810 ; viol and composer. (3) **Cécile**, b. Ly 1785 ; retired, 1820 ; singer. **Alexandrine**, b. Paris, 1793 ; tired, 1812 ; sister of above ; si of great promise.

**Saint-Georges** (săṅ-zhôrzh), (1) – Chev. **de**, Guadeloupe, 1745—P 1799 (or 1801) ; mulatto violinist composer. (2) **Jules H. Ver** Marquis **de**, Paris, 1801—1875 brettist of many works, especial collaboration with Halévy.

**Saint-Huberty** (săṅ-tü-bĕr-tē), **A** **nette Cécile Clavel** (called **St.** **berty**, rightly **Clavel**), Toul, ca. 1 —London, 1812, noted soprano, Opéra, Paris. 1777–89 ; 1790, m

Count d'Entraigues ; they were assassinated at their country seat, near London, 1812 (probably from political motives).

**int-Lambert** (săn-län-băr), **Michel le**, Parisian harpsichord-teacher ; wrote methods (1680–1700).

**int-Lubin** (săn-lü-băn), **Léon de**, Turin, 1805—Berlin, 1850 ; violinist nd dram. composer.

**inton** (săn-tôn), (1) **Prosper (Ph. Catherine)**, Toulouse, 1813—London, 1890 ; violinist and composer. 2) **Sainton-Dolby, Charlotte Helen** (née **Dolby**), London, 1821—885 ; contralto-singer.

**int-Saëns** (săn-sän), **Chas. Camille**, b. Paris, Oct. 9, 1835 ; eminent French composer. Began to study the piano before 3 ; at 5 played Grétry opera from the score ; at 7 entered the Cons., pupil of Stamaty pf.), Maleden and Halévy (comp.), and Benoist (org.); 1st org.-prize, 851; at 16, prod. a symph.; 1853, organist Saint-Méry; 1858, the Madeleine ; also till 1870 pf.-teacher Niedermeyer Sch.; made frequent tours. He is a writer of unusual gifts. 894, Commander of the Legion of Honour. C. operas: 1-act "*La Princesse Jaune*" (Op.-Com., 1872) ; "*Le Timbre d'Argent*," 4-acts (Th.-Lyr., 877) ; the very succ. "*Samson et Dalila*" (Weimar, 1877, often sung as an oratorio) ; "*Proserpine*" (Op.-Com., 1887) ; "*Ascanio*" (Opéra, 890) ; comic "*Phryne*" (Op.-Com., 893) ; "*Parisatis*" (Béziers, 1902) ; wrote the last 2 acts of Guiraud's unfinished "*Frédégonde*" (Opéra, 1895). C. ballets, music to "*Antigone*" (Comédie-Française) ; and Gallet's "*Déjanire*" (Béziers, 1898, with orch. of 50, chorus of 200, and ballet of 60 in open air). C. also a Christmas oratorio ; the "Biblical opera" "*Le Déluge*"; 2 masses ; ode "*La Lyre et la Harpe*" (Birmingham Fest., 879) ; "*La jota aragonese*" for orch.; 5 pf.-concertos ; 3 vln.-concertos ; 'cello-concerto ; cantata "*Les*

*Noces de Prométhée*" (1867) ; Psalm 19, with orch. (London, 1885) ; **5** symphs., 4 symphonic poems, "*Le rouet d'Omphale*," "*Phaëton*," "*Danse macabre*," "*La jeunesse d'Hercule*"; 2 orch. suites, the first "*Algérienne*," etc.

**Sala** (sä'-lä), **Nicola**, near Benevento, Italy, 1701—Naples, 1800 ; Maestro theorist and dram. composer.

**Sal'aman, Chas. Kensington**, London, March 3, 1814—July, 1901 ; pianist ; pupil of Rimbault and Chas. Neate ; début 1828, then studied with H. Herz, Paris ; 1831, teacher in London ; 1840, founded a choral soc.; 1858, founded the Mus. Soc. of London ; also the Mus. Assoc., 1874 ; critic and essayist ; c. orch. pcs., etc.

**Sal'blinger** (**Salminger**) (zäl'-mïng-ĕr), **Sigismund**, monk, at Augsburg; composer, 1545.

**Saldoni** (säl-dō'-nē), **Don Baltasar**, Barcelona, 1807—1890 ; organist, singing-teacher, writer and dram. composer.

**Sale** (säl), (1) **Fran.**, Belgian ct.-tenor and composer, 1589. (2) (säl), **John**, London, 1758—1827; bass, conductor and composer. (3) **John B.**, Windsor, 1779—1856 ; organist, bass, teacher and composer ; son of above. (4) **Geo. Chas.**, Windsor, 1796—1869 ; organist ; son of (2).

**Saléza** (säl-ā-zä), **Albert**, b. Bruges, Béarn, 1867; notable tenor ; pupil Paris Cons.; 1st prize in singing, 2d. in opera ; début Op.-Com., 1888; 1889–91, at Nice ; from 1892, engaged at the Opéra, Paris ; 1898, Met. Op., New York.

**Salieri** (säl-ĭ-ā'-rē), (1) **Ant.**, Legnago, Verona, Aug. 19, 1750—Vienna, May 7 (12 ?), 1825 ; noted operatic composer and organist ; pupil of his brother (2) **Francesco** (violinist) and of Simoni, Pascetti and Pacini; taken to Vienna by Gassman ; his successor as ct.-composer and cond. of Italian opera ; he prod. many operas there, then one at Paris under Gluck's name, G. kindly confessing the ruse

when the opera was a succ.; 1788, ct.-
cond. Vienna ; was a rival of Mozart
and unjustly accused of poisoning
him ; c. 40 operas, 12 oratorios, etc.

**Salimbeni** (säl-ĭm-bā'-nē), **Felice**,
Milan, ca. 1712—Laibach, 1751; soprano-musico.

**Salinas** (sä-lē'-näs), **Fran.**, Burgos,
Spain, ca. 1512—1590 ; professor.

**Sallantin** (säl-läṅ-täṅ), **A.**, Paris, 1754
—after 1813; oboe-virtuoso, teacher
and composer.

**Salminger.**   Vide SALBLINGER.

**Salmon** (säm'-ŭn), **Eliza**, Oxford,
1787—Chelsea, 1849 ; soprano.

**Salò, Gasparo da.**   Vide GASPARO.

**Saloman** (zä'-lō-män), **Siegfried**,
Tondern, Schleswig, 1818—Stockholm, 1899 ; violinist, lecturer and
dram. composer.

**Salomé** (säl-ō-mā), **Th. César**, Paris,
1834—St.-Germain, 1896 ; composer
and organist.

**Salomon** (zä'-lō-mōn), (1) **Jn. Peter**,
Bonn, Jan., 1745—London, Nov.
28, 1815 ; vln.-virtuoso ; from 1781,
London ; 1786, organised famous
Salomon concerts for which Haydn,
whom he brought over, c. special
works.    (2) **Moritz**, mus.-dir. at
Wernigerode, Harz ; pub. a treatise
against Natorp, 1820, and mus.
novels.   (3) **M.**, Besançon, 1786—
1831; guitar-player ; composer, inv.
the "harpolyre."   (4) **Hector**, b.
Strassburg, May 29, 1838 ; pupil of
Jonas and Marmontel (pf.), Bazin
(harm.) and Halévy (comp.); in 1870,
2d chorusm., later *chef de chant*, Gr.
Opéra ; c. operas, etc.

**Salter** (sôl'-tĕr), **Sumner**, b. Burlington,
Iowa, June 24, 1856; studied at Am-
herst Coll. and music in Boston; organist and mus. dir., N. Y.; ed. *"The Pianist and Organist,"* N.Y.; c. church-mus.

**Salvayre** (säl-vâr) **(Gervais Bd.),
Gaston**, b. Toulouse, June 24, 1847;
studied at the cath.-maîtrise, then at
Toulouse Cons.; later Paris Cons.,
taking the Grand prix de Rome,
1872, with cantata " *Calypso*"*;* 1877,
chorusm. at the Opéra-Populaire ,

1894 in Servia ; later critic of " (
*Blas* "*;* Chev. of the Legion
Honour ;  c. operas " *Le Brav*
(1877), "*Richard III.*"  (Pete
burg, 1883), " *Egmont* " (Op.-Co
1886), " *La Dame de Montsorea*
(Opéra, 1888), etc.; c. also Bibli
symph., " *La Resurrection*," 11;
Psalm with orch., etc.

**Samara** (sä-mä'-rä), **Spiro**, b. Cor
1861; pupil of Enrico Stancampia
in Athens ;  later of Délibes, Pa
Cons.;  prod. v. succ. opera, " *Fl*
*Mirabilis*" (Milan, 1886) ; "*Med*
(Rome, 1888) ;  " *Lionella* " (Mila
1891) ;  " *La Martire*" (Napl
1894 ; Paris, 1898) ; " *La Furia*
*mata*" (Milan, 1895) ; " *Histo*
*d'amour*" (Paris, 1902).

**Sammartini** (säm-mär-tē-nē),
**Pietro**, ct.-mus. at Florence, e
(1635-44).  (2) **Giov. Bat.**, Mila
ca. 1705—ca. 1775 ; organist, c
ductor and composer.  (3) **Giu.**,
London, 1740 ; oboist ; bro. of abo

**Samuel** (säm-wĕl), **Ad.**, Liège, 182
Ghent, 1898 ; theorist and dra
composer.

**Sanctis, de.**   Vide DE SANCTIS.

**Sandberger** (zänt'-bĕrkh-ĕr), **Ad.**,
Würzburg, Dec. 19, 1864 ; studied
the R. Sch. of Mus. there, and
Munich, also with Spitta ; 1887, 1
Phil.; mus. libr., Munich Libra
and lecturer at the Univ.; 1898 pr
of mus. at Prague Univ.; ed. Orlan
di Lasso's complete works ; wr
biog., hist., essays, etc.; c. v. su
opera " *Ludwig der Springer* " (C
burg, 1895), overture, etc.

**Sanders, C.**   Vide LEUCKART.

**San'derson**, (1) **Jas.**, Workingt
Durham, 1769—ca. 1841 ; violin
teacher and composer.  (2) **Lilli**
b. Sheboygan, Wis., U. S. A., O
13, 1867 ;  concert mezzo-sopran
pupil of Stockhausen, Frankfort-
Main ; début Berlin, 1890 ; tou
Europe ; m. Fz. Rummel ; lives
Berlin.  (3) **Sibyl**, b. Sacramen
Cal., 1865 ; soprano, opera-sing
pupil of de la Grange and Masser

cc. début, Op.-Com., 1889 ; sang
ere for years ; 1898 in New York
et. Op., and variously in Europe.
**doni.** Vide CUZZONI.
**dow** (zän'-dō), (1) **Eugen,** b. Ber-
a, Sept. 11, 1856; violinist ; pupil
ohne, W. Müller, and K. Hoch-
hule ; from 1879 court chamber-
us. His wife (2) **Adelina** (née
**erms**), b. Friesack, Oct. 14, 1862 ;
ager and teacher.
**dt** (zänt), **Max van de,** Rotter-
am, Oct. 18, 1863 ; pianist ; pupil
his father and Liszt ; toured
urope ; 1889, pf.-teacher Stern
ons., Berlin.
**dys** (sänds), **Wm.,** 1792—1874 ;
nglish writer on music.
**ger-Sethe** (zĕng'-ĕr-zā-tĕ), **Irma,**
Brussels, April 28, 1876 ; notable
olinist ; daughter of Dutch father
ad German mother ; began violin at
; pupil of her mother, of Joachim,
ilhelmj, and Ysaye, took 1st prize
the Cons.; début London, 1895 ;
ured Europe with great success ; m.
r. Sänger, 1897, and lives in Berlin.
**giovanni** (sän-jō-vän'-nē), **A.,**
ergamo, 1831—Milan, 1892 ; prof.
singing.
**tini** (sän-tē'-nē), Abbate **Fortu-**
**ato,** Rome, 1778—? ; coll. a noble mus.-library.
**t'ley,** (1) **Chas.,** b. Liverpool,
eb. 28, 1834 ; noted operatic and
oncert barytone ; pupil Nava, Mi-
n, Garcia, London ; début, 1857 ;
on pre-eminence in England at
stivals, etc. ; operatic début, Cont Garden, 1859 ; 1875 with Carl
osa Co. ; 1871 and 1891, America ;
tired 1900 ; also a painter ; c. a
ass with orch.; a berceuse for orch.
890) ; songs (pub. under the pseud.
**Ralph Betterton**"), etc. His wife,
) **Gertrude Kemble** (Charles
emble's granddaughter) (d. 1882),
as a soprano ; their daughter (3)
**dith** was a successful soprano, till
er marriage in 1884 with the Hon.
. H. Lyttleton.
**tucci** (sän-toot'-chē), **Marco,**

Camajore, 1762—Lucca, 1843 ; conductor and composer.
**Sapell'nikoff, Wassily,** b. Odessa,
Oct. 21, 1868 ; pianist ; pupil of Fz.
Kessler, and then (with a stipend from
the city of Odessa) of L. Brassin and
Sophie Menter, Petersburg Cons.;
1888, début Hamburg ; toured.
**Saran** (zä'-rän), **Aug. (Fr.),** b. Alten-
plathow, Province of Saxony, Feb.
28, 1836 ; pupil of Fr. Ehrlich and
of R. Franz ; teacher, army-chap-
lain (1873) ; 1885 cond. of a church-
choral soc. at Bromberg ; writer and
composer.
**Sarasate** (sä-rä-sä'-tĕ), **Pablo (Mar-**
**tin Meliton Sarasate y Navas-**
**cuez**) **de,** b. Pamplona, Spain,
March 10, 1844 ; eminent violinist ;
at 10 played before the Queen, who
presented him with a Stradivari ;
after succ. concerts in Spain he studied with Alard (vln.) and Reber
(comp.), Paris Cons., taking 1st vln.-
prize 1857, and a *premier accessit*,
1859, in harm.; he has made very
wide and very succ. tours ; 1889,
America. For him Lalo c. his 1st
vln.-concerto and the "Symph. espagnole"; Bruch, his 2nd concerto
and the Scotch Fantasia ; A. C.
Mackenzie, the "Pibroch" Suite. **S.**
has pub. "*Zigeunerweisin*" for vln.
and orch.; "*Spanische Tänze*" for
vln. and pf., fantasias, etc.
**Sarmiento** (sär-mĭ-ĕn'-tō), **Salvatore,**
Palermo, 1817—Naples, 1869 ; conductor and dram. composer.
**Saro** (sä'-rō), **J. H.,** Jessem, Saxony,
1827—Berlin, 1891 ; bandmaster and
writer.
**Sarrette** (sär-rĕt), **Bd.,** Bordeaux,
1765—Paris, 1858 ; founder and director till 1814 of the Paris Cons.
which he gradually developed from
a sch. started by the band of the
Paris National Guard.
**Sarri** (sär-rē), **Dom.,** Trani, Naples,
1678—after 1741 ; conductor and
dram. composer.
**Sarti** (sär'-tĕ), **Giuseppe** (called **Il**
**Domenichino**) (ēl dō-mĕn-ĭ-kē' -nŏ),

Faenza, Dec. 1, 1729—(of gout) Berlin, July 28, 1802 ; pupil of either Vallotti or Padre Martini; 1748–50 organist Faenza Cath. ; 1751 he prod. at Faenza, succ. opera "*Pompeo in Armenia*," followed by "*Il Re Pastore*" (Venice, 1753) and others so succ. that at 24 he was called to Copenhagen as dir. Italian opera and court-cond.; he was summarily dismissed for political reasons; 1775–99, dir. Cons. dell' Ospedaletto, Venice ; in competition (with Paisiello and others) he won the position of cond. at Milan Cath.; he prod. from 1776–84, 15 operas, he also prod. grand cantatas and several masses, etc. Catherine II. invited him to Petersburg. As he passed Vienna, he was received by the Emperor, and met Mozart, complaining, however, of the " barbarisms " in M.'s quartets and finding 19 mortal errors in 36 bars. Lived at Petersburg 18 years, excepting a brief period of disgrace, due to Todi, during which exile he founded a fine sch. at Ukraine. 1793 he was restored to the Empress' favour, and placed at the head of a Cons. He raised the Italian opera to high efficiency, inv. a very accurate machine for counting vibrations and was ennobled in 1795. In a Te Deum (on the taking of Otchakow by Potemkin) the music was reinforced by fireworks and cannon. He set the libretto "*Hega*" by the Empress. He c. 40 operas, masses, some still performed, etc.

**Sartorio** (sär-tō'-rĭ-ō), **A.**, Venice, ca. 1620—ca. 1681; conductor and dram. composer.

**Sass** (săs) (at first sang under the name **Sax**), **Marie Constance**, b. Ghent, Jan. 26, 1838 ; a chansonette-singer in a Paris café, found and taught by Mme. Ugalde; début Th.-Lyrique, 1859, as soprano, 1860–71, at the Opéra, then in Italy; 1864, m. Castelmary, divorced 1867.

**Satter** (zät'-tĕr), **Gustav**, b. Vienna, Feb. 12. 1832; pianist , studied Vi-

enna and Paris ; 1854–60 toured U. S. and Brazil ; returned to Pa where Berlioz warmly praised compositions ; lived in various citi c. opera " *Olanthe*," overtures " *L lei*," " *Julius Cesar*," " *An Freuae*," 2 symphs., a symph. to picture " *Washington*," etc.

**Sattler** (zät'-lĕr), **H.**, Quedlinbu 1811—Brunswick, 1891 ; writer a composer.

**Sauer** (zow'-ĕr), (1) **Wm.**, b. Fr land, Mecklenburg, 1831 ; o builder from 1857 at Frankfort-Oder. (2) Vide LEIDESDORF. **Emil**, b. Hamburg, Oct. 8, 186 notable pianist ; pupil of his mot of N. Rubinstein at Moscow, 18 and of Liszt at Weimar ; from 1 toured Europe and 1898–99 U.S.v great succ. ; 1901, head of pf.-de Vienna Cons.; c. suite moderne, "*lichten Tagen*," 2 piano concert concert-étude, etc.

**Saurel** (sä'-oo-rĕl), **Emma**, b. Pa mo, 1850 ; opera - singer ; dét Pisa ; has toured widely.

**Sauret** (sō-rā), **Emile**, b. Dun-le-l Cher, France, May 22, 1852; nota violinist ; pupil of Paris Cons. and de Bériot, Brussels Cons.; at 8 be succ. European tours ; America 18 and frequently since ; 1880–81, Kullak's Acad., Berlin ; lived Berlin till 1890, then prof. R. A. London ; wrote " *Gradus ad Par sum du violoniste*" (Leipzig, 189 c. 2 vln.-concertos, etc.

**Sauter** (zow'-tĕr), **Severin S.**, G many, 1822—St. Louis, Mo., Ma 24, 1901; cond.; came to America refugee, 1848.

**Sauveur** (sō-vŭr'), **Jos.**, La Flèc 1653—Paris, 1716 ; a deaf-mute, v learned to speak at 7, and becam notable investigator in acous (which word in fact he invented) ; was the first to calculate absolute bration-numbers, and to explain o tones; pub. many treatises (1700–

**Sauzay** (sō-zĕ'), **Chas.) Eugè** Paris, July 14, 1809—1901 ; violin

upil of Vidal; later of Baillot at the
ons.; won 1st and 2nd vln.-prize, and
rize for fugue ; 2nd vln. and after-
ards vla. in Baillot's quartet, and m.
..'s daughter (a pianist); 1840 solo vio-
nist to Louis Philippe ; later leader
f 2nd vlns. Napoleon III.'s orch.;
860 vln.-prof. at the Cons.; pub. a
eatise ; c. a string-trio, "*Études
armoniques*," etc.

**vard** (să-văr), **M. Gabriel Aug.**,
aris, 1814—1881 ; prof. of harm.
nd thorough-bass at the Cons.; pub.
eatises.

**vart** (să-văr), **F.**, Mézières, 1791—
aris, 1841 ; acoustician.

**vile** (săv'-Il), **Jeremy**, English com-
oser, 1653.

**x** (săx), (1) **Chas. Jos.**, Dinant-sur-
Meuse, Belgium, 1791—Paris, 1865 ;
tudied flute and clarinet, Brussels
Cons.; from 1815 managed an instr.-
actory at Brussels, making a spe-
ı᠎  ̃ ᷾ of brass instrs.; he made many
nprovements ; 1853 he joined his
on Ad. in Paris. (2) **(Ant. Jos).**
**Adolphe**, Dinant, Nov. 6, 1814—
aris, Feb. 9. 1894 ; son of above ;
minent maker and inv. of instrs.; he
ıv. the family of instrs. called the
axophone (v. D. D.) ; in Paris he con-
inued to make improvements invent-
ıg the saxhorns, saxotromba, etc.;
857 teacher of the saxophone, Paris
Cons. and pub. a saxophone method;
e had much litigation over the prior-
cy of his inventions, but always won.
3) **Alphonse**, bro. and co-worker of
bove. (4) **Marie.** Vide SASS.

olci (s'bôl'-chē), **Jefte**, Florence,
833—1895 ; 'cellist and teacher.

acchi (skäk'-kē), **Marco**, b. Rome ;
t.-conductor 1618–48 ; writer and
omposer.

alchi (skäl'-kē), **Sofia**, b. Turin,
Nov. 29, 1850 ; alto or mezzo-sopra-
io of unusua. range f-b'' (v. PITCH
». D.) ; pupil of Boccabadati ; début
Mantua (1866); she has sung through-
ut Europe, often in North and South
America with much succ.; 1875 m.
Signor Lolli.

**Scaletta** (skä-lĕt'-tä), **Orazio**, Crema
—Padua, 1630 ; conductor and composer.

**Scandel'li, Ant.**, Brescia, 1517—Dresden, 1580 ; conductor and composer.

**Scaria** (skä'-rĭ-ä), **Emil**, Graz, 1840—
Blasewitz, 1886 ; bass ; created
"Wotan" at Bayreuth, 1876 and
"Gurnemanz" (*Parsifal*), 1882.

**Scarlatti** (skär-lät'-tē), (1) **Alessandro**, Trapani, Sicily, 1659—Naples,
1725 ; founder of the "Neapolitan
Sch."; noted teacher and an important innovator in opera (he prod. over
115) ; in 1680 he is first heard of as
conducting his own opera ; he introduced the innovation of the orchestral
ritornello, and a partial *recitativio
obbligato* (v. D.D.); 1684 court-cond.;
1703, 2nd cond. S. Maria Maggiore,
Rome ; 1707–09, 1st. cond.; teacher at 3 conservatories, San Onofrio ;
de' Poveri di Gesù Christi, and the
Loreto. (2) **Domenico (Girolamo)**,
Naples, 1683 (5 ?)—1757 ; son and
pupil of above ; studied also with
Gasparini ; eminent virtuoso and
composer for harpsichord ; founded
modern pf.-technic ; devised many
now familiar feats ; the first to compose in free style without contrapuntal elaboration and mass ; in a
competition with Händel he proved
himself equal as a harpsichordist, but
confessed himself hopelessly defeated
as an organist ; he was thereafter a
good friend, almost an idolater, crossing himself when he mentioned Händel ; 1715–19 he was maestro at St.
Peter's, 1720 at London ; 1720 court-
cembalist Lisbon ; his gambling left
his family destitute; from 1710 he prod.
operas, incl. the first setting of "*Amleto*" (1715). (3) **Giuseppe**, Naples,
1712—Vienna, 1777; grandson of (1);
dram. composer. (4) **Fran.**, c. a
melodrama in MS. at Rome. (5)
**Pietro**, c. opera "*Clitarro*," with
intermezzi by Hasse.

**Schaab** (shäp), **Robt.**, Rotha, near
Leipzig, 1817—1887 ; organist and
composer.

**Schachner** (shäkh'-nĕr), **Rudolf Jos.,** Munich, 1821—Reichenhall, 1896; pianist, teacher and composer.

**Schacht** (shäkht), **Matthias H.,** Viborg, Jutland, 1660—Kierteminde, 1700; lexicographer.

**Schack** (**Cziak**) (shäk or chäk), **Benedikt,** Mirowitz, Bohemia, 1758—Munich, 1826; tenor and dram. composer.

**Schad** (shät), **Jos.,** b. Steinach, Bavaria, 1812—Bordeaux, 1879; pianist and composer.

**Schade** (shä'-dĕ), (1) (**Schadaus**) **Abraham,** pub. a valuable coll. of 384 motets (1611-16). (2) **Carl,** singing-teacher and writer (1828-31).

**Schäffer** (shĕf'-fĕr), (1) **Aug.,** Rheinberg, 1814—Berlin, 1879; dram. composer. (2) **Julius,** b. Crevese, Altmark, Sept. 28, 1823; studied with Dehn, Berlin; 1855 mus. dir. to the Grand Duke at Schwerin; founded and conducted the "Schlosskirchenchor;" 1860 mus.-dir. at the Univ. and cond. Singakademie, Breslau; 1871, "R. Mus.-Dir."; 1878 prof.; Dr. Phil. *h. c.* (Breslau), 1872; wrote defence of his friend Franz' accompaniments to Bach and Händel; composer.

**Schafhäutl** (shäf'-hī-tl), **K. Fz. Emil von,** Ingolstadt,1803—Munich, 1890; professor and theorist.

**Schalk** (shäl'k), **Josef,** b. Vienna and studied at the Cons.; notable cond., first at Graz, then 1st cond. at the Prague Opera and Philh. concerts; since 1899 1st cond. ct.-opera, Berlin; 1898 at Covent Garden, 1899 gave the complete Wagner Ringcycle in New York.

**Scharfe** (shär'-fĕ), ——, Grimma, Saxony, 1835—Dresden, 1892; barytone, teacher and composer.

**Scharfenberg** (shär'-fen-bĕrkh), **Wm.,** Cassel, Germany, 1819—Quogue, N. Y., 1895; pianist, teacher and editor.

**Scharnack** (shär'-näk), **Luise,** b. Oldenburg, ca. 1860; mezzo-soprano;

pupil of von Bernuth, Hamb Cons.; début, Weimar.

**Scharwenka** (shär-vĕn'-kä), (1) **Philipp,** b. Samter, Posen, Feb. 1847; pupil of Würst and Kuli Acad., Berlin, also of H. Do 1870, teacher of theory and comp the Acad.; 1880 founded (with bro. Xaver) the "Scharwenka Con 1891, accompanied his bro. to N York; returned, 1892, as co-dir. the Cons., later, 1893, merged in Klindworth Cons.; he is also a car turist and illustrated a satire by A Moskowski (Berlin, 1881); 1c R. Professor; c. "*Herbstfeier*" "*Sakuntala*," for soli, chorus a orch., 2 symphs.,"*Arkadische Su* and "*Serenade*" for orch., fest overture, Trio in G, op. 112, etc. (**Fz.**) **Xaver,** b. Samter, Jan. 1850; bro. of above; distinguis pianist and composer; pupil of K lak and Würst, Kullak's Acad.; 18 teacher there; at 19 gave public c cert at the Singakademie, with su for 10 years he gave annually 3 cha ber-concerts there (with Sauret a H. Grünfeld); cond. of subscript concerts; 1874, toured Europe a America; 1880, co-founder the "I lin Scharw. Cons.," dir. till 18 then founded a Cons. in New Yo 1898, Berlin, as dir. Klindwor Scharwenka Cons.; ct.-pianist to Emperor of Austria, "Prof." fr the King of Prussia; c. succ. op "*Mataswintha*" (Weimar, 189 symph., 3 pf.-concertos, etc.

**Schauensee** (show'-ĕn-zä), (**Fz. J Leonti**) **Meyer von,** Lucerne, 1; —after 1790; organist and dra composer.

**Schebek** (shä'-bĕk), **Edmund,** Pete dorf, Moravia, 1819—Prague, 18c amateur authority on vln.-constr tion, etc.

**Schebest** (shä'-bĕst), **Agnes,** Vien 1813—Stuttgart, 1869; mezzoprano.

**Schechner - Waagen** (shĕk'-nĕr-v gĕn), **Nanette,** Munich, 1806—18(

noted soprano; 1832, m. Waagen, a painter

**heibe** (shī'-bĕ), (1) **Jn.,** d. Leipzig, 1748; celebrated org.-builder. (2) **Jn. Ad.,** Leipzig, 1708—Copenhagen, 1776; son of above; organist, editor and composer.

**heibler** (shī'-blĕr), **Jn. H.,** Montjoie, near Aix-la-Chapelle, 1777—Crefeld, 1838; acoustician and inventor.

**heidemann** (shī'-dĕ-män), (1) **Heinrich,** Hamburg, ca. 1596—1663; organist; pupil and successor of his father (2) **Hans S.,** organist Katherinenkirche.

**heidemantel** (shī-dĕ-män-tĕl), **K.,** b. Weimar, Jan. 21, 1859; pupil of Bodo Borchers; sang at the ct.-th., 1878–86; pupil of Stockhausen; 1885, "Kammersänger"; since 1886, Dresden ct.-opera; 1886, sang "Amfortas" in "*Parsifal*" at Bayreuth.

**heidt** (shīt), **Samuel,** Halle-on-Saale, 1587—1654; famous organist and composer; pupil of Sweelinck; organist of Moritzkirche and ct.-conductor; c. notable chorals, etc.

**hein** (shīn), **Jn. Hermann,** Grünhain, Saxony, 1586—Leipzig, 1630; soprano; ct.-conductor and composer.

**helble** (shĕl'-blĕ), **Jn. Nepomuk,** Hüfingen, Black Forest, 1789—Frankfort-on-Main, 1837; notable cond. and singing-teacher; tenor; c. operas, etc.

**helle** (shĕl'-lĕ), (1) **Jn.,** Geisingen, Saxony, 1648—Leipzig, 1701; cantor Thomaskirche. (2) **K. Ed.,** Biesenthal, near Berlin, 1816—Vienna, 1882; critic, lecturer and writer.

**heller** (shĕl'-lĕr), **Jacob,** b. Schettal, Bohemia, 1759; vln.-virtuoso.

**helper** (shĕl'-pĕr), **Otto,** b. Rostock, April 10, 1844; an actor, later baryone in opera, at Bremen; 1872–76, Cologne, then sang leading rôles, Leipzig City Theatre.

**henck** (shĕnk), (1) **Jean (Johann),** gamba-player and dram. composer, 1688–93, Amsterdam. (2) **Jn.,**

Wiener-Neustadt, Lower Austria, 1761 (1753?)—Vienna, 1836; c. operettas. (3) **Hugo,** 1852 (?)—Vienna, 1896; conductor and composer.

**Scherer** (shā'-rĕr), **Sebastian Anton,** organist at Ulm Minster and composer, 1664.

**Scherzer** (shĕr'-tsĕr), **Orto,** Ansbach, 1821—Stuttgart, 1886; violinist and organist.

**Schetky** (shĕt'-kē), **Chp.,** Darmstadt, 1740—Edinburgh, 1773; 'cellist and composer.

**Schicht** (shĭkht), **Jn. Gf.,** Reichenau, Saxony, 1753—Leipzig, 1823; pupil of an uncle (org. and pf.); pianist, conductor and writer; c. 4 oratorios, chorals, etc.

**Schick** (shĭk) (née **Hamel**), **Margarete Luise,** Mayence, 1773—Berlin, 1809; soprano; pupil of Steffani and Righini; début, Mayence, 1791; from 1794, Royal Opera, Berlin.

**Schiedermayer** (shē'-dĕr-mī-ĕr), **Jos. Bd.,** d. Linz-on-Danube, Jan. 8, 1840; cath.-organist; wrote a text-book on chorals and a vln.-method, c. symphs., sacred mus., org.-pcs., etc.

**Schiedmayer** (shēt'-mī-ĕr) & **Söhne,** Stuttgart firm of piano-makers, founded in Erlangen, 1781. (1) **Jn. D.,** removed to Stuttgart 1806. The present head is (2) **Ad.** (b. 1847), a great-grandson of (1).

**Schikaneder** (shē'-kä-nä-dĕr), **Emanuel Jn.,** Ratisbon, 1751—Vienna, 1812, the librettist of Mozart's "*Zauberflöte*" in which he created "Papageno"; a manager, actor and singer.

**Schildt** (shĭlt), **Melchior,** Hanover (?), 1592—1667; organist.

**Schiller** (shĭl'-lĕr), **Madeline,** b. London, Engl.; pianist and teacher; a pupil of Isaacs, Benedict and Hallé, but mainly self-taught; début, Gewandhaus, with great succ., repeated in London; toured Australia; m. M. E. Bennett of Boston, Mass., where she lived several years making many tours, incl. Australia and Europe; later lived in New York.

**Schilling** (shĭl-ling), **Gv.,** Schwiegershausen, near Hanover, 1803—Nebraska, U. S. A., 1881; wrote textbooks and treatises, etc.

**Schil'lings, Max,** b. Düren, April 19, 1868; notable composer; studied with Brambach and von Königslöw; 1892, stage-manager at Bayreuth; 1890 while studying law, at Munich, c. the opera "*Inguelde*" (prod. by Mottl, Carlsruhe, 1894); played in many other cities; c. also opera "*Der Pfeiertag*" (Schwerin, 1901); 2 symph. fantasias "*Meergruss*," 1895, and "*Seemorgen*," etc.

**Schimon** (shē'-mōn), **Ad.**, Vienna, 1820—Leipzig, 1887; singing-teacher, accompanist and dram. composer, etc.; 1872, m. the soprano (2) **Anna Regan**, Bohemia, 1842—Munich, 1902; pupil of Manuel Garcia and Stockhausen; sang in Italy and Germany; court-singer in Russia; 1874, teacher of singing Leipzig Cons.; 1877–86, R. Sch. of Mus., Munich; again at Leipzig Cons.; also after death of her husband, singing-teacher at Munich.

**Schindelmeisser** (shĭn'-dĕl-mīs-sĕr), **L.,** Königsberg, 1811—Darmstadt, 1864; ct.-conductor and dram. composer.

**Schindler** (shĭnt'-lĕr), **Anton,** Medl, Moravia, 1796—Bockenheim, near Frankfort, 1864; violinist and conductor; friend and biographer of Beethoven.

**Shintlöcker** (shĭnt'-lĕk-ĕr), (1) **Philipp,** Mons, Hainault, 1753—Vienna, 1827; 'cellist. (2) **Wolfgang,** b. Vienna, 1789; 'cellist and composer; nephew and pupil of above.

**Schira** (shē'-rä), **Fran.,** Malta, 1809 —London, 1883; professor, conductor and dram. composer.

**Schirmacher** (shēr'-mäkh-ĕr), **Dora,** b. Liverpool, Sept. 1, 1862; pianist; pupil of Wenzel and Reinecke, Leipzig Cons., winning Mendelssohn prize; début Gewandhaus, 1877; c. a suite, sonata, etc.

**Schirmer** (shēr'-mĕr). (1) **Gustav,** Königsee, Saxony, 1829- Einsbach,

Thuringia, 1893; son and grands of court piano-makers at Sonde hausen; 1837 came to New Yo founded pub. firm, Beer & Schirm 1866 **S.** obtained the entire busin since known as G. Schirmer; si 1893 incorporated under managem. of (2) **Rudolf E.** and (3) **Gusta** sons of above.

**Schladebach** (shlä'-dĕ-bäkh), **Juli** d. Kiel, 1872; wrote treatise on voice.

**Schläger** (shlä'-gĕr), **Hans,** F kirchen, Upper Austria, 1830—Sa burg, 1885; conductor and dra composer.

**Schlecht** (shlĕkht), **Raimund,** Ei stadt, 1811—1891; priest and writ

**Schleinitz** (shlī'-nĭts), **H. Conra** Zechanitz, Saxony, 1807—Leipz 1881; dir. Leipzig Cons. (vice M delssohn).

**Schlesinger** (shlä'-zĭng-ĕr), two mu pub. firms. (a) at Berlin, found 1810 by (1) **Ad. Martin,** from 18 managed by his son (2) **Heinri** (d. 1879); since 1864 under R. L nau. (b) at Paris, founded 1834 (3) **Moritz Ad.,** son of (1); un Louis Brandus in 1846. (4) **Seba tian Benson,** b. Hamburg, Se 24. 1837; at 13 went to U. S.; stu ied at Boston with Otto Dresel; 17 years Imp. German Consul Boston; now lives in Paris; p many pop. songs and piano-pieces.

**Schletterer** (shlĕt'-tĕr-ĕr), **Ha Michel,** Ansbach, 1824—Augsbu 1893; mus.-dir., writer and compos

**Schlick** (shlĭk), (1) **Arnold,** ct.-orga ist to the Elector Palatine, and co poser, 1511. (2) **Jn. Konrad,** Mü ster (?), Westphalia, 1759 — Got 1825; 'cellist and composer.

**Schlimbach** (shlĭm'-bäkh), **G. C Fr.,** b. Ohrdrof, Thuringia, 176 organist, writer on org.-building, e

**Schlösser** (shlĕs'-sĕr), (1) **Lou** Darmstadt 1800—1886; ct.-condu or and dram. composer. (2) (1 **Wm.) Ad.,** b. Darmstadt, Feb. 1830; son and pupil of above; piani but Frankfort, 1847; toured; from '54, teacher in London; c. pf.-quartet and trio, etc.

**lottmann** (shlôt'-män), **Louis**, b. erlin, Nov. 12, 1826; concert-anist, pupil of Taubert and Dehn; 'ed in Berlin as teacher; 1875, R. us.-Dir.; c. overture to "*Romeo nd Juliet*," "*Trauermarsch*" for ch., etc.

**medes** (shmā'-dĕs), **Erik**, b. Co-nhagen, 1868; pianist; then stud-d singing with Rothmühl; sang as arytone in various theatres; studied th Iffert and, 1898, sang tenor rôles Vienna; 1899 "Siegfried" and Parsifal " at Bayreuth.

**meil** (shmīl), ———, teacher at agdeburg, inv. "notograph."

**melzer**(shmĕl'-tsĕr), **Jn. H.**, Prague, 55—d. after 1695 at Vienna; ct.-nd. and composer.

**mid(t)** (shmĭt), (1) **Bd.**, organist at rassburg, 1560. He was succeeded y (2) **Bd. Schmid**, the younger. ) **Anton**, Pihl, Bohemia, 1787—57; mus. libr. Vienna Library; riter.

**midt** (shmĭt), (1) **Jn. Phil. Samuel**, önigsberg, 1779—Berlin, 1853; ovt. official, critic, writer and dram. mposer. (2) **Jos.**, Bückeburg, 1795 -1865; violinist, ct.-conductor and mposer. (3) **Hermann**, Berlin, 310—1845; ballet-conductor and .-composer; c. operetta. (4) **Gus-av**, Weimar, 1816 — Darmstadt, 382; ct.-conductor and dram. com-oser. (5) **Arthur P.**, b. Altona, er., April 1, 1846; est. mus.-pub. usiness, Boston and Leipzig, 1876.

**mitt** (shmĭt), (1) **Jos.**, 1764—rankfort-on-Main, 1818; writer, olinist and composer. (2) **Niko-aus**, b. Germany; bassoonist and mposer; from 1779, *chef de mu-que* of the French Guards at Paris. ) **Aloys**, Erlenbach, Bavaria, 1788 -Frankfort-on-Main, 1866; eminent acher, pianist, writer and dram. mposer. (4) **Jacob (Jacques)**, bernburg, Bavaria, 1803—Ham-

burg, 1853; bro. and pupil of above; wrote a method and c. (5) **(G.) Aloys**, Hanover, Feb. 2, 1827—Dres-den, Oct., 1902; pianist and cond.; son and pupil of (3); pupil Voll-weiler (theory), Heidelberg; toured; then th.-cond. at Aix-la-Chapelle, etc.; 1857–92, ct.-cond. at Schwerin; from 1893, dir. "Dreyssig'sche Sing-akademie," Dresden. He c. 3 op-eras, incl. "*Trilby*" (Frankfort, 1845); incid. music; overtures, etc. He arranged the fragments of Mo-zart's C minor mass into a complete work; died of an apoplectic stroke while conducting his own "*In Mem-oriam*." (6) **Hans**, b. Koben, Bo-hemia, Jan. 14, 1835; piano-teach-er and oboist; pf.-pupil of Dachs, Vienna Cons., taking the silver medal; later, teacher there; wrote a vocal method; c. important instructive pcs., etc.

**Schmölzer** (shmĕl'-tsĕr), **Jakob Ed.**, Graz, 1812—1886; teacher and com-poser.

**Schnabel** (shnä'-bĕl), (1) **Jos. Ignaz**, Naumburg, Silesia, 1767—Breslau, 1831; conductor and composer. (2) **Michael**, Naumburg, 1775—Breslau, 1842; bro. of above; founded at Breslau (1814) a piano factory, car-ried on by his son (3) **K.** (1809—1881); pianist and composer.

**Schnecker** (shnĕk'-ĕr), **Peter Aug.**, b. in Hessen-Darmstadt, 1850; pupil of Oscar Paul, Leipzig; came to America; lives in New York as teacher and organist; pub. collec-tions; c. pf.-pcs. and much pop. church-mus.

**Schneegass** (shnä'-gäs) **(Snegas'-sius)**, **Cyriak**, Buschleben, near Go-tha, 1546—1597; theorist and com-poser.

**Schneevoigt** (shnä'-foikht), **Georg**, b. Wiborg, Nov. 8, 1872; Finnish 'cellist; studied with Schröder, Klengel and Jacobs; lives in Hel-singfors as teacher in the Cons., etc.

**Schneider** (shnī'-dĕr), (1) **Jn.**, Lauder, near Coburg, 1702—Leipzig, ca

1775 ; famous improviser and organist. (2) **G. Abraham,** Darmstadt, 1770—Berlin, 1839 ; horn-virtuoso ; conductor, composer of masses, etc. (3) **Louis,** Berlin, 1805—Potsdam, 1878 ; son of (2); writer. (4) (**Jn. G.**) **Wm.,** Rathenow, Prussia, 1781—Berlin, 1811 ; pianist, teacher, composer and writer. (5) **Wm.,** Neudorf, Saxony, 1783 — Merseburg, 1843 ; organist and writer. (6) **Jn. Gottlob,** 1753 — Gernsdorf, 1840 ; organist. (7) (**Jn. Chr.**) **Fr.,** Alt-Waltersdorf, Saxony, Jan. 3, 1786—Dessau, Nov. 23, 1853 ; son and pupil of (6) ; at 10 c. a symphony ; 1821 ct.-conductor at Dessau ; wrote text-books and c. 15 oratorios, incl. famous "*Das Weltgericht*"*;* biog. by F. Kempe. (8) **Jn.** (**Gottlob**), Alt-Gersdorf, Oct. 28, 1789—Dresden, April 13, 1864 ; bro. of above ; eminent organist and teacher. As a boy a soprano of remarkable range (to f" acc. to Riemann, v. PITCH, D.D.); later, tenor ; 1825 ct.-organist, Dresden, also conductor ; made tours ; c. fugues, etc., for organ. (9) **Jn. Gottlieb,** Alt-Gersdorf, 1797 — Hirschberg, 1856 ; bro. of above ; organist. (10) **Theodor,** b. Dessau, May 14, 1827 ; son and pupil of (7) ; pupil of Drechsler ('cello) ; 1845, 'cellist, Dessau ct.-orch.; 1854 cantor and choir-dir. court and city churches; 1860—96 cantor and mus.-dir. Jakobikirche, Chemnitz ; also cond. (11) (**Jn.**) **Julius,** Berlin, 1805—18?5 ; pianist, organist and mus.-director ; and c. operas ; son of (12) **Jn. S.,** pf.-mfr. at Berlin. (13) **K.,** Strehlen, 1822—Cologne, 1882 ; tenor. (14) **K. Ernst,** Aschersleben, 1819—Dresden, 1893 ; writer.

**Schnitger** (shnĭt'-gĕr), (1) **Arp.,** Godswarden, Oldenburg, 1648—Neuenfelde, ca. 1720 ; org.-builder. His son, (2) **Fz. Caspar** (d. 1729), and an elder bro., worked at Zwolle, Holland.

**Schnorr von Karolsfeld** (shnôr fŏn kä'-rŏls-fĕlt), (1) **L..** Munich, 1836—

Dresden, 1865 ; noted tenor ; cre[ Wagner's " Tristan "; c. opera Munich (1865), his wife, (2) **Ma na** (née **Garrigues**), creating " de "; she took a fatal chill on occasion.

**Schnyder von Wartensee** (shnē' fŏn vär'-tĕn-zä), **X.,** Lucerne, 17[ Frankfort-on-Main, 1868 ; teac writer and composer.

**Schoberlechner** (shō'-bĕr-lĕkh-r **Fz.,** Vienna, 1797—Berlin, 18 pianist, conductor and dram. c poser.

**Schöberlein** (shä'-bĕr-līn), **L.,** K[ berg, Bavaria, 1813—Göttingen,1[ writer.

**Schobert.** Vide SCHUBART (3).

**Schoenefeld** (shā-'nĕ-fĕlt), **H.,** b. [ waukee, Wis., Oct. 4, 1857; son pupil of a musician ; later stud Leipzig Cons. ; winning a prize f[ chorus with orch. performed at Gewandhaus ; then studied with Lassen (comp.), Weimar ; tou Germany as a pianist ; from 18 Chicago, as pianist and teacher, a cond. the " Germania Männerch C. " *The Three Indians* " ode v orch.; 2 symphs. ("*Rural*," "*Spri time* ") *;* 2 overtures, " *In the Su South*" (a notable work based Ethiopian themes) and " *The Am ican Flag*"*;* vln.-sonata (Henri M teau prize, 1899), pf.-pcs., etc.

**Schöffer** (shĕf'-fĕr), **Peter** (the you er), mus.-printer at Mayence a Strassburg, 1530—39.

**Schœlcher** (shĕl-shär) **Victor,** Pa 1804—1893 ; writer, :atesman a biographer of Händel.

**Scholtz** (shôlts), **Hn.,** b. Bres[ June 9, 1845 ; pianist and teach pupil of Brosig, of C. Riedel a Plaidy at Leipzig, and v. Bülow, a Rheinberger, R. Sch. of Mus., N nich ; 1870—75, teacher there ; t[ in Dresden ; 1880 " R. Saxon cha ber-virtuoso " ; ed. Chopin's worl c. pf.-concerto, sonata, etc.

**Scholz** (shôlts), (1) **F.,** important c[ poser of Russian music, taught cor[

Moscow, 1830. (2) **Bd. E.**, b. May-
nce, March 30, 1835 ; pupil of Ernst
Pauer, Mayence, and of Dehn, Ber-
lin ; 1856 teacher R. Sch. of Mus.,
Munich; 1859–65, ct.-conductor Han-
over Th.; 1871–78, cond. Breslau
Orch. Soc.; 1883, dir. of the Hoch
Cons., Frankfort (vice Raff) ; Dr.
Phil. *h. c.* (Breslau Univ.), " Royal
Prussian Professor," etc.; pub. es-
says " *Wohin treiben wir ?* " (Frank-
fort, 1897) ; prod. 5 operas incl. succ.
" *Ingo* " (Frankfort, 1898). C. " *Das
Siegesfest* " and " *Das Lied von der
Glocke* " for soli, chorus and orch.;
symph. poem " *Malinconia* "; symph.
vertures " *Iphigenia* " and " *Im
Freien*," etc.

**hön** (shän), **Moritz**, Kronau, Mo-
avia, 1808—Breslau, 1885 ; violinst, conductor and writer.

**hönberger** (shän'-bĕrkh-ĕr), **Benno,**
. Vienna, Sept. 12, 1863 ; pianist ;
upil of Vienna Cons., studied also
vith Liszt ; toured ; 1885 teacher,
Vienna ; later in Sweden (1886), then
London ; 1894 toured America; c. 3
f.-sonatas, 3 rhapsodies, etc.

**hondorf** (shōn'-dôrf), **Jns.**, b. Rö-
el, Mecklenburg, 1833 ; pupil of
tern-Kullak Cons., Berlin ; since
864 organist Pfarrkirche, Güstrow ;
inging-teacher Cath. Sch., and conuctor ; c. " *Vaterländische Ge-
änge*," " *Kaiserhymne*," etc.

**hönfeld** (shän'-fĕlt), **Hermann**, b.
Breslau, Jan. 31, 1829 ; cantor and
R. Mus.-Dir. there ; c. cantatas, a
ymph.; 3 overtures, etc.

**hörg** (shĕrkh), **Fz.**, b. Munich, Nov.
5, 1871 ; violinist ; pupil of Ysaye ;
oured ; lives in Brussels.

**hott** (shôt), (1) **Bd.**, d. 1817; found-
d (Mayence, 1773) the mus.-pub.
rm of B. Schott, carried on by his
ons (2) **Andreas** (1781—1840) and
3) **Jn. Jos.** (1782—1855), under the
rm-name of " B. Schott's Söhne ;
he present manager at Mayence and
he London branch are Fz. von Land-
ehr and Dr. L. Strecker. (4) **An-
on,** b. Schloss Staufeneck, Swabian

Alp, June 25, 1846 ; tenor ; 1865–71
an artillery officer in the French cam-
paign ; then studied with Frau Sche-
best-Strauss ; 1871, Munich opera ;
1872–75 Berlin opera ; leading tenor
at Schwerin and Hanover, made
concert-tours ; 1882 in Italy with
Neumann's Wagner troupe.

**Schradi(e)ck** (shrä'-dĕk), **Henry,** b.
Hamburg, April 29, 1846 ; noted
violinist ; pupil of his father and of
Leonard, Brussels Cons., David,
Leipzig ; 1864–68 teacher Moscow
Cons., then leader Philh. Concerts,
Hamburg ; 1874–82, co-leader, Ge-
wandhaus Orch. and theatre-orch.,
Leipzig, also teacher for a time at the
Cons. 1883–89, prof. of vln., Cin-
cinnati Cons., U. S. A.; returned to
Germany as leader of the Hamburg
Philh. Soc.; afterward head vln.-
prof. Nat. Cons., N. Y., and later
Broad St. Cons., Philadelphia ; pub.
excellent technical studies for vln.

**Schramm** (shräm), **Melchior,** German
organist and contrapuntist, 1595.

**Schreck** (shrĕk), **Gustav,** b. Zeulenroda, Sept. 8, 1849 ; pupil of Leipzig
Cons.; 1885 teacher of theory and
comp., Leipzig Cons.; 1892, mus.-
dir. and cantor, and cond. of the
" Thomanerchor "; prod. concert-
cantatas, oratorio, " *Christus der
Auferstandene* " (Gewandhaus,1892),
church-music, etc.

**Schrems** (shrĕms), **Jos.**, Warmen-
steinach, Upper Palatinate, 1815—
Ratisbon, 1872 ; conductor, editor
and teacher.

**Schröder** (shrä'-dĕr), (1) **Hermann,** b.
Quedlinburg, July 28, 1843 ; violinist, writer and composer ; pupil of A.
Ritter, Magdeburg; from 1885,
teacher R. Inst. for Church-mus.,
Berlin, and at a mus.-sch. of his
own. (2) **Karl,** b. Quedlinburg.
Dec. 18, 1848 ; bro. of above ; 'cellist and composer ; pupil of Drechsler, Dessau and Kiel, Berlin ; at 14,
1st 'cello ct.-orch. at Sondershausen,
and teacher in the Cons.; 1873, 'cello, Brunswick ct.-orch.; 1874, solo

'cellist Gewandhaus Orch., and th.-
orch., Leipzig, also teacher at the
Cons., and made tours ; 1881, ct.-
cond., Sondershausen ; cond. German
Opera at Amsterdam ; until 1888,
Berlin ct.-opera ; till 1890, the Hamburg Opera ; returned to Sondershausen as ct.-cond. and dir. "Fürst-
liches Conservatorium ;" wrote 'cello-
method, catechism on conducting and
the 'cello. C. succ. opera "*Aspasia*"
(Sondershausen, 1892) ; a succ. 1-act
opera "*Der Asket*" (Leipzig, 1893) ;
succ. operetta "*Malajo*" (Bunzlau,
1887) ; 1871, founded the "Schröder
Quartett," with his brothers (1)
**Hermann** (3) **Fz.** and (4) **Alwin**,
b. Neuhaldensleben (Magdeburg),
June 15, 1855 ; pupil of his father and brother Hermann, also of
André (pf.), and De Ahna (vln.), W.
Tappert (theory) ; self-taught as a
'cellist, as which he has won his
fame ; 1875, 1st 'cello in Liebig's
"Concert-Orchester," later under
Fliege and Laube (Hamburg) ; 1880,
Leipzig, as asst. of (1), whom he succeeded, 1881, in the Gewandhaus,
theatre and Cons.; 1886, Boston, as
first 'cellist Symph. Orch.; member
of the "Kneisel Quartett." (5) **Konrad (Gv. Fd.)**, b. Marienwerder, W.
Prussia, July 7, 1850; pupil of Kullak's Acad., Berlin, also of O. Kolbe
(comp.); teacher in the Acad.;
pf.-teacher, Berlin. C. the first
"Low German" opera (after Fritz
Reuter), the v. succ. 1-act comic opera "*Du dröggst de Pann weg*"
(Schirenn, 1897); pub. 50 songs. (6)
**Fr.**, d. 1818 ; barytone, the first to
sing Mozart's "*Don Giovanni*" in
German.

**Schröder-Devrient** (shrä'-děr-dā'-
frĭ-ĕnt). **Wilhelmine**, Hamburg, 1804
—Coburg, 1860 ; eminent soprano ;
daughter of (6) above, and of a celebrated actress, Antoinette Sophie
Bürger Devrient (divorced 1828, after bearing him 4 children; married
twice afterward) ; pupil of Mazatti ;
début, Vienna, 1821 ; m. the actor

Karl D.; she created the rôle of "A
ano Colonna" in the "*Rienzi*"
Wagner, whose style she deeply
fected.

**Schröder-Hanfstängl.** Vide HA
STÄNGL.

**Schröter** (shrä'-tĕr), (1) **Leonha**
Torgau, ca. 1540—Magdeburg, a
1580; eminent contrapuntist.
**Chp. Gl.**, Hohenstein, Saxony, 169
Nordhausen, 1782 ; noted organ
claimed in a pamphlet (1763) to h
invented, 1717, the pianoforte,
was forestalled by Cristofori ; c
poser. (3) **Corona (Elisabeth V
helmine)**, Guben, 1751—Ilmen
1802 ; celebrated soprano ; pupi
her father, (4) **Joh. Fr. S.**, cha
ber-singer. (5) **Joh. Samuel**, V
saw, 1750—London, 1788, son
(4) ; pianist. (6) **Joh. H.** (b. V
saw, 1762), son of (4) ; violinist.

**Schubart** (shoo'-bärt), (1) **(Chr. I
Daniel**, Sontheim, Swabia, 173
Stuttgart, 1791 ; poet ; organist a
composer. (2) **L.**, son of abo
editor of his father's "*Ideen zu ei
Æsthetik der Tonkunst*" (18
(3) (also **Schobert**, or **Chob**
(sho'-bĕrt) (————), first name
known), Strassburg, 1720—Pa
1768 ; a relative of above ; orga
at Versailles ; 1760, chamber-mus
Prince de Conti ; very pop. pia
and composer.

**Schubert** (shoo'-bĕrt), (1) **Jos.**, Wa
dorf, Bohemia, 1757—Dresden, 18
violinist, and dram. composer.
**Jn. Fr.**, Rudolstadt, 1770—Colog
1811; violinist, writer and compo
(3) **Fd.**, Lichtenthal, near Vien
1794—Vienna, 1859; elder bro.
the great composer (4) and passi
ately devoted to him ; dir. Nor
Sch., Vienna ; c. church-mus., a
quiem for his brother, etc.

(4) **Franz (Peter)**, Lichtentl
near Vienna, Jan. 31, 1797—of
phus, Vienna, Nov. 19, 1828 ; on
the most eminent of the world's c
posers. One of the 14 children c
schoolmaster at Lichtenthal, ▪

taught him the vln. ; also studied with Holzer there ; at 10, first soprano in the church-choir, and c. songs and little instrumental pcs. 1808, a singer in the Vienna court choir, and also in the "Convict" (the training-sch. for the court singers). He played in the sch.-orchestra, finally as first vln., and studied theory with Ruczizka and Salieri. His earliest extant composition is a 4-hand fantasia of 12 movements written when he was 13. He had a frenzy for writing, and a fellow-pupil, Spaun, generously furnished him with mus.-paper, a luxury beyond the means of Schubert. At 15 he had written much, incl. an overture ; at 16 he c. his first symph. ; 1813, his voice broke and he left the "Convict," where the unrestrained license allowed him in his compositions accounts for the crudeness of some of his early works and the faults of form that always characterised him, as well as for his immediate and profound individuality ; at 17 he c. his first mass. In order to escape military conscription he studied a few months at the Normal Sch. and took the post of elementary teacher in his father's sch. He taught there until 1816, spending his leisure in studying with Salieri, and in comp. particularly of songs, of which he wrote as many as 8 in one day—144 in his 18th year (1815), including "Der Erlkönig"; 1814-16, he also c. 2 operettas, 3 Singspiele and 3 incomplete stage-pieces, 4 masses. 1816, he applied, without succ., for the directorship of the new State mus.-sch. at Laybach (salary $100 (£20) a year). From 1817 he lived in Vienna, except two summers (1818 and 1824), spent at Zelész, Hungary, as teacher in Count Esterházy's family. How **S.** existed is a matter of mystery, except for the help of such friends as Fz. von Schober, who aided him with the utmost generosity. The famous tenor Michael Vogl, popularised his songs. By his 21st year (1818) **S.** had c. six

of his symphs. and a great mass of work. His mus. farce "Die Zwillingsbrüder" was prod. (Kärnthner thor Th., 1820, but ran only six nights). 1821, after he had written over 600 compositions, his "Erlkönig" was sung at a public concert of the "Musikverein" and elsewhere, with a wide sale that attended most of his subsequent publication of songs and pf.-pcs.; though he was sadly underpaid by his publishers, sometimes receiving only a gulden (20 cents, less than a shilling) for them. In 1822 he declined the post of organist at the court chapel; but could never obtain a salaried position, though many efforts were made. At 31 he gave his first concert of his own works, with good succ. (1828). In 1822, he had finished a grand opera "Alfonso und Estrella," the libretto bad, the scoring too difficult for the musicians at Graz, where it was put in rehearsal ; it was withdrawn, not to be prod. till 1854 under Liszt and in 1881 when Jn. Fuchs rewrote the libretto and prod. it at Carlsruhe with great succ. In 1825 a work, "Rosamunde," was prod. at the Th. an-der-Wien, with applause for the music, but it was withdrawn after a second performance. Other works of his had not even productions, his stubborn refusal to alter a note preventing the profitable performance of dram. scenes, etc. His health finally broke under the strain of composition all day on a little food and revelry till late at night. He died of typhus and was buried, at his own request, in the "Ostfriedhof" at Währing, near Beethoven.

A complete critical edition of his works is pub. by Breitkopf & Härtel. These incl., besides those mentioned, an opera "Adrast" (unfinished), 3-act operettas "Der Teufels Lustschloss" and "Der Spiegelritter"; SINGSPIELE : "Der Vierjährige Posten," "Fernando"; "Claudine von Villabella" (unfinished); "Die

*Freunde von Salamanca*" and "*Der Minnesänger*"*;* all written 1814—1816 ; none performed ; 3-act melodrama, "*Die Zauberharfe*" (Aug. 19, 1820) ; 3-act opera, "*Sakontala*" (not finished or performed) ; 1-act operetta, "*Die Verschworenen, oder der häusliche Krieg*" (Vienna, 1861) ; 3-act opera, "*Fierabras*" (Vienna, 1861) ; "*Die Burgschaft,*" 3-act opera (c. 1816 ; prod. by Fz. Lachner, Pesth, 1827) ; unprod. operas "*Der Graf von Gleichen*" (1827) and "*Die Salzbergwerke*"*;* 6 masses; "*Deutsche Messe*"*;* unfinished oratorio "*Lazarus,*" 2 "*Tantum ergo*" (with orch.); 2 "*Stabat Mater,*" etc. CHORAL WORKS WITH ORCH., OR INSTRS.: "*Miriams Siegesgesang*"*;* prayer, "*Vor der Schlacht*"*;* hymn, "*Herr unser Gott,*" "*Hymne an den Heiligen Geist,*" "*Morgengesang im Walde,*" "*Nachtgesang im Walde*" and "*Nachthelle,*" "*Schlachtlied,*" "*Glaube, Hoffnung und Liebe,*" several cantatas and part-songs. ORCH. AND CHAMBER-MUS.: 10 symphs., No. 8 the "unfinished" in B min., 7 overtures (Nos. 2 and 5 "in the Italian style") ; vln.-concerto ; rondo for vln. with orch.; octet ; pf.-quintet ("*Forellenquintet,*" with double-bass); string-quintet with 2 'celli ; 20 string-quartets ; 2 pf.-trios ; 2 string-trios ;

rondo brilliant, phantasie in C, sonata, 3 sonatinas, nocturne for 'cello and pf.; introd. and vars. for flute and pf.; 17 pf.-sonatas (incl. op. 78, fantasia), 3 grand sonatas, posthumous ; 8 impromptus, 6 moments musicals ; many variations, many waltzes, incl. "*Valses sentimentales,*" "*Homage aux belles Viennoises,*" "*Valses nobles,*" 12 "*Grätzer Wälzer,*" "*Wanderer-Fantasie*"*;* FOR PF., HANDS : 2 sonatas, "*Divertissement ó l'hongroise,*" "*Grand rondo,*" "*Notre amitié,*" rondc in D, "*Lebensstürme,*" fugue, polonaises, variations, waltzes 4 Ländler ; marches, incl. "Trauer marsch" and "héroique."

SONGS WITH PIANO : "*Erlkönig,*" op. 1 ; "*Gretchen am Spinnrade,*" op. 2 ; "*Heidenröslein,*" op. 3 "*Der Wanderer*" and "*Der du von dem Himmel bist,*" op. 4 ; Suleika songs, Mignon's songs, 2 song cycle by Wilhelm Müller, "*Die Schön Müllerin*" and "*Die Winterreise,*" containing 20 and 24 numbers ; songs from "*Fräulein vom See* (Scott's "*Lady of the Lake*"), 9 song from "*Ossian*"*;* 6 songs by Heine i the "*Schwanengesang,*" etc.

Biog. by von Hellborn (Vienna 1861, 1865) ; Reissman (Berlin, 1873 A. Niggli (1880) ; Barbedette (Paris 1866) ; Max Friedländer.

---

## Schubert.

### BY H. A. SCOTT.

FRANZ SCHUBERT was very nearly the greatest of all composers If he had lived longer, been more carefully trained when young and received greater appreciation in his lifetime—three very reason able "might-have-beens"—who shall set limits to the heights which h might have won ? He died at thirty-one. If others of the masters had bee cut off at this age what treasures the world would have lost !—in the case say of Handel, every one of his oratorios ; in that of Beethoven, his seve greatest symphonies ; in that of Wagner, all his operas after "*Tannhäuser* and "*Lohengrin*" : in that of Brahms, the "*German Requiem*" and a s symphonies. ¶ It does not follow that Schubert would necessarily have eveloped in any like manner. But, at least, there are reasons for thinking at he might have done so. We know that in the last year of his life he ontemplated taking lessons in counterpoint, that on his death-bed he spoke " " entirely new harmonies and rhythms " running through his head, and at he had the loftiest of ambitions. As it was, and taking his works as ey stand, certain weaknesses distinguish them which there is no overlooking. hat fabulous fertility which could beget six of the " *Winterreise* " songs at single sitting, three of the pianoforte sonatas in as many weeks, and eight peras in a year, was not counterbalanced by a like faculty in the matter of lf-criticism and concentration. Too many of his bigger works lack form id proportion. He did not trouble sufficiently to work out and make the ost of the inspired thoughts which came to him in such unparalleled abun- ance. He was a stupendous genius, it might almost be said, with an infi- te capacity for *not* taking pains—whose " profuse strains of unpremeditated t " were at once too profuse and too unpremeditated. ¶ But even so only ne or two of the very greatest names can stand before his in music's history e occupies a position only one degree short of the very highest. In the tual quality of his inspiration indeed perhaps there is not one who could be nked before him. No composer in the whole history of music was more ondrously endowed by nature, whether one considers either the surpassing eauty of his ideas or the profusion of their supply. ¶ In Schubert's music : its best there is a haunting and unutterable loveliness, an exquisite blending f tenderness, sweetness, and purity, with strength, nobility, and grandeur, which, for the true Schubertian, there is perhaps no equivalent in the works f all the other masters put together. And this applies, it should be said, ot less to his instrumental pieces than to his songs. ¶ The notion that chubert is great only in his songs is one of those stock judgments which, once ccepted, it seems almost impossible to eradicate. In point of fact nothing could e wider of the mark than this belief. Schubert left imperishable works in early every branch of music. His songs comprise no doubt his most char- cteristic and distinctive achievements, inasmuch as nothing like them had ver been so much as attempted before. But, so far as concerns the specific uality of their music, they were equalled, if not surpassed, by such works s the symphonies, his chamber compositions, and those exquisite one-move- ent pieces for the pianoforte, the " *Impromptus* " and " *Moments Musicals*," vhich in their way, be it said, were only a degree less epoch-making than ie songs. ¶ What then is the distinctive place in music of this divinely- ifted tone-poet ? His distinction is twofold : he created the song as we now it, and more than any other composer he influenced the development f the romantic movement. As the greatest of all song-writers, Schubert's

position is assured. It seems safe to say that his noblest achievements und
this head will never be surpassed. The Schubert song, of which the te
throughout is mirrored in the accompaniment, in which every bar of t
music is conditioned by the words, thoughts, and dramatic or emotion
content of the poem illustrated, was a distinctive creation in its way not o
whit less wonderful than, say, the Beethoven symphony or the Wagneria
music-drama. Such songs as "*Der Erlkönig*," "*Die junge Nonne,*
"*Der Tod und das Mädchen,*" "*Der Atlas,*" "*Der Doppelgänger,*"
"*Gruppe aus dem Tartarus,*" to name but half-a-dozen almost at random fro
his more descriptive examples, were a totally new thing in music, the influ
ence of which upon all succeeding composers, not only of songs but of ever
kind of dramatic or illustrative music, not excluding opera, it would l
hard to over-esteem. ¶ And more remarkable still perhaps is the fact th
this superb emotional and dramatic expressiveness was attained without th
smallest sacrifice of qualities specifically musical—nay, took shape in mus
of the greatest beauty, richness, variety and charm, as music alone and with
out reference to the text. Schubert's creation of the song in truth partake
almost of the miraculous, for he not only invented an absolutely new kind
song, but developed its utmost possibilities, one might almost say, at a blov
—in a word did this new thing at the first time of asking and did it supremel
well. ¶ Schubert's influence as song-writer it would be hardly possible t
exaggerate. It was truly not a reform which he introduced but a revolution
As to his influence on the composers of the romantic school one has only t
consider in general the whole character of his music with its all-pervadin
poetry, and emotional expressiveness, and in particular such works as thos
already named, his "*Impromptus*" and "*Moments Musicals*" to wit, t
realise the character of the connection. Here also, in these last-name
works, he did that which no one before him had attempted, inventing nev
forms for the expression of moods too delicate, too intimate, and too persona
for treatment in the larger movements of established type, and once again le
behind him creations of an entirely novel kind, which later composers have
striven in vain to improve upon. ¶ Perhaps in the whole range of pianofort
music there are no passages more ravishingly beautiful—more enchanting to
the ear, regarded from the purely sensuous standpoint—than some to be found
in these inspired works. Had Schubert left nothing further than this slender
volume of "*Impromptus*" and "*Moments Musicals*" for the pianoforte hi
name would live forever in the records of the art. ¶ If Schubert's essays in
the larger forms—the symphony and the sonata—are to a certain exten
impaired by the qualities alluded to, this is by no means to deny their enormous significance and importance. Schubert in these larger works may have
been diffuse at times, may not always have developed to the full the von

s ideas which came to him in such abundance, his works may sometimes proportion ; but what qualities are theirs by way of comparison !—what th of melody ! what intoxicating harmonies ! what irresistible rhythms ! t magical modulations ! Recall such creations as the C major and the inor symphonies, the quintet in C major, the D minor, A minor, and G r quartets, and the sonatas in A minor, B flat, and G among his larger o works, and of what account seem the dry-as-dusts' and analysts' strict- in the face of such imperishable compositions as these ? Nor should it verlooked that in these larger works also, Schubert's methods, if he kept in the recognised forms, were all his own, and as such were full of ence upon his successors. Apart from such technical matters as his onies, modulations, instrumentation, and the like, under all of which s he made striking advances, he breathed into these established forms also rit of romance, a yearning, wistful, personal note of lyric tenderness fervour, whereby they are distinguished from all earlier compositions heir kind. ¶Well might it be said by Grove of Schubert that " there r has been one like him and there never will be another " ; by Liszt he was " le musicien le plus poète que jamais " ; and by the inscription is tomb that " Die Tonkunst begrub hier einen reichen Besitz aber noch schönere Hoffnungen."

(5) **Fz. Anton,** 1768—1824 ; vio- ist ; R. Konzertmeister. (6) **Fz.,** resden, 1808—1878 ; son and pupil (5) ; violinist, Konzertmeister R. ch. and composer. (7) **Maschin-** , wife of (6) and daughter of G. Schneider, 1815—Dresden, 1882 ; prano. (8) **Georgine,** Dresden, 40—Potsdam, 1878 ; daughter and pil of (7) ; pupil also of Jenny Lind d Garcia ; sang in many European ies. (9) **Louis,** Dessau, 1828— resden, 1884 ; violinist ; singing- acher and composer. (10) **Oskar,** Berlin, Oct. 11, 1849 ; clarinettist ; America 2 years ; since at Berlin. ı) **Camille,** pen-name of Camille ilipp.

uberth (shoo'-bĕrt), (1) **Gottlob,** arsdorf, 1778—Hamburg, 1846 ; oist and clarinettist. (2) **Julius** 'd. G.), Magdeburg, 1804—Leip- , 1875 ; son of above; founded firm " J. Schuberth & Co.," Hamburg, 26 ; Leipzig branch. 1832 ; New

York, 1850. His brother (3) **Fr. Wm.** (b. 1817), took the Hamburg house, 1853 (under firm-name " Fritz Schuberth") ; 1872, at Weimar founded the mus.-library " Liszt - Schuberth Stiftung" ; 1891 succeeded by Felix Siegel ; New York branch now owned by J. H. F. Meyer. (4) **L.,** Magdeburg, 1806—St. Petersburg, 1850 ; son and pupil of (1) and von Weber ; at 16 dir. Stadt Th. at Mag- deburg ; conductor Oldenburg, 1845; cond. German opera, St. Petersburg; c. operas, symphs., etc. (5) **K.,** Magdeburg, 1811 — Zurich, 1863 ; bro. of above ; noted 'cellist ; pupil of Hesse and Dotzauer ; toured widely ; soloist to the Czar; ct.-cond., dir. at the U.; c. 2 'cello-concertos.

**Schubiger** (shoo'-bĭkh-ĕr), **Anselm,** Uznach, Canton of St. Gallen, 1815 —1888 ; important writer.

**Schuch** (shookh), (1) **Ernst von,** b. Graz, Styria, Nov. 23, 1847 ; pupil of E. Stoltz and O. Dessoff ; 1872, cond.

Pollini's It. Op.; from 1873 ct.-cond. Dresden, then R. Ct.-Councillor and Gen. - Mus. - Dir. (2) **Clementine Proska**, b. Vienna, Feb. 12, 1853; wife of above; 1873, colorature-sopr., Dresden ct -theatre.

**Schucht** (shookht), **Jean F.**, Holz-thalleben, Thuringia, 1832—Leipzig, 1894; critic and composer.

**Schücker** (shĭk'-ĕr), **Edmund**, b. Vienna, ca. 1856; harpist; pupil of Zamara, Vienna Cons.; 1884, teacher Leipzig Cons., and harpist Gewand-haus Orch.; 1890, ct.-harpist to Duke of Saxe-Altenburg; 1891, Chicago Orchestra.

**Schulhoff** (shool'-hôf), **Julius**, Prague, 1825—Berlin, 1898; notable pianist; pupil of Kisch, Tedesco and Toma-schek; début, Dresden, 1842; lived in Paris as teacher, then Dresden and Berlin; c. pf.-pcs., etc.

**Schultesius** (shool-tā'-zĭ-oos), **Jn. Paul**, Fechheim, Saxe-Coburg, 1748 —Leghorn, 1816; theorist and com-poser.

**Schultheiss** (shoolt'-hīs), **Benedict**, d. 1693; organist and composer, Nürnberg.

**Schultz** (shoolts), **Edwin**, b. Danzig, April 30, 1827; barytone; pupil of Brandstätter, Berlin; singing-teacher there; also cond. the " Monstre Con-certe " given 1864—71, for the ben-efit of wounded soldiers; in 1880 the Prussian Ministry of War com-missioned him to compile songs; c. 7 prize male choruses, etc.

**Schultze** (shoolt'-tsĕ), (1) **Jn.**, organ-ist and composer, Dannenberg, Brunswick, 1612. (2) **Chp.**, cantor, etc., Delitzsch, Saxony (1647—1668). (3) Dr. **Wm. H.**, Celle, Hanover, 1827—Syracuse, N. Y., 1888; violin-ist and professor. (4) **Ad.**, b. Schwe-rin, Nov. 3, 1853; pianist; pupil of Kullak's Acad., Berlin; teacher there; 1886–90 ct.-cond., Sonders-hausen and dir. of the Cons.; later in Berlin; c. a pf.-concerto, etc.

**Schulz** (shoolts), (1). Vide PRÄTORI-US. (2) **Jn. Abraham Peter**, Lüne-

burg, March 30 (31 ?), 1747—Schw June 10, 1800; important prede sor of Schubert as a song-wri pupil of Kirnberger, Berlin; tea there. 1780, ct.-cond. at Rheinsb 1787–94, ct.-cond. Copenhagen; theorist; c. operas, oratorios, (3) **Jn. Ph. Chr.**, Langensalza, ringia, 1773—Leipzig, 1827; c and composer. (4) **K.**, Subrecto Fürstenwalde; wrote pop. books, 1812 and 1816. (5) **Otto Fr. Wm.**, b. Gortz, Brandenb March 25, 1805; pupil of Klein Zelter, Berlin; organist at Pr lau; R. Mus.-Dir.; pub. metl and c. sacred music, etc. (6) Berlin, 1817—1884; violinist composer. (7) **Fd.**, Kossar, 18: Berlin, 1897; 1856 conductor, m dir., singing-teacher and compo (8) **August**, b. Brunswick, June 1837; violinist; pupil of Zinkei Leibrock, and Joachim; leader the Ducal Orch. there; c. pop. r quartets.

**Schulz-Beuthen** (shoolts-boi'-tĕn), b. Beuthen, Upper Silesia, 19, 1838; pupil of Leipzig Co and of Riedel; since 1881, pf.-te er, Dresden Cons.; c. 3 opera symphonies, " Haydn," " Frühli feier," E♭, " Schön Elizabe " Reformation-S." (with org " König Lear," and a " Kinder-fonie "; symph. poem, " Die Toa insel "; 3 overtures, incl. " Ina ischer Kriegstanz "; cantatas orch., " Befreiungsgesang der bannten Israels," and " Harald," quiem and Psalms 42, 43, and with orch. Psalm 13 a cappella n choruses, etc.

**Schulz-Schwerin** (shoolts-shvā'-r K., Schwerin, Jan. 3, 1845; pian pupil of Stern Cons., Berlin; pianist to Grand Duke of Meck burg; since 1885 lived in Ber c. a symph., overtures " Torq Tasso," " Die Braut von Messi and " Triomphale "; Sanctus, B dictus. etc., with orch., etc.

ılze (shoolts'-ĕ), (1) **Jn. Fr.**, Mil-
z, Thuringia, 1793 — Paulinzelle,
58 ; org.-builder with his sons at
ühlhausen. (2) **Ad.**, b. Mannhagen,
ar Molln, April 13, 1835 ; concert-
ss ; pupil of Carl Voigt, Hamburg,
d Garcia, London ; head-prof. of
ging R. Hochschule, Berlin.

ımacher (shoo'-mäkh-ĕr), (Peter)
ıul (H.), Mayence, 1848—1891 ;
nductor, critic, teacher and com-
ser.

ımann (shoo'-män), (1) **Robert**
lex.), Zwickau, Saxony, June 8,
10—insane, Endenich, near Bonn,
ly 29, 1856 ; one of the most in-
vidual and eminent of composers.
ıungest son of a book-seller (of lit-
ıry taste and author of a biog.
llery to which R. contributed at 14).
.pil of a local organist, Kuntzsch
.), who prophesied immortality for
m ; at 6 he began to compose, at
, untaught, he c. for chorus and
ch. At 17 he set poems of his own
mus. 1820–28, attended Zwickau
mnasium ; then matriculated at
ipzig Univ. to study law and phi-
ophy. 1829 Heidelberg, where he
o studied mus., practising the piano
ıours a day ; played once in public
th great succ. 1830, Leipzig,
ıere he lived with Friedrich Wieck,
th whom he studied the piano ; he
ıo studied comp. with H. Dorn.
trying to acquire independence of
ı fingers by suspending the fourth
ıger of the right hand in a sling
ıile practising with the others he
ıppled this finger and foiled his am-
ıion to be the chief virtuoso of his
ıe. He now made comp. his first
ıbition. In 1833, his first symph.
ıs performed with little succ., the
ıst movement having been played in
ıblic by Wieck's 13-year old daugh-
r, Clara, with whom **S.** fell in love.
ıe father liked **S.** as a son, but not
a son-in-law, and put every ob-
ıcle in his way, until in 1840, after a
ıar's law-suit, the father was forced
consent and the two lovers, both

now distinguished, were united in one
of the happiest marriages known in
art ; she giving his work publicity in
her very popular concerts ; he devoted to her and dedicating much of
his best work to her. 1834 he founded the " Neue Zeitschrift für Musik,"
and was its editor till 1844. His
essays and criticisms (signed FLORES-
TAN, EUSEBIUS, MEISTER RARO, 2,
12, 22, ETC., JEANQUIRIT, etc.) are
among the noblest works in the history of criticism, particularly in the
matter of recognising new genius and
heralding it fearlessly and fervently.
(Chopin, Berlioz, and Brahms, profited by this quality. Of Wagner he
did not altogether approve.) In his
writings he constructed an imaginary
band of ardent young Davids attacking the Goliath of Philistinism. He
called this group the " Davidsbünd-
ler." His pen-name " EUSEBIUS,"
represents the vehement side of his
nature, " FLORESTAN," the gentle
and poetic side. His paper had
some succ., which was not bettered
by a removal to Vienna, 1838–39, and
a return to Leipzig. 1840, Dr. Phil.,
Jena. 1840 was mainly devoted to
his important song-composition; 1841
to symph. work ; 1842 to chamber-
mus., incl. his pf.-quintet (op. 44)
which gave him European fame.
1843 was choral, " *Das Paradies und
Peri* " (from Moore's "Lalla Rookh"),
having a great succ.; he also began
his choric mus. for " *Faust.*" The
same year, on the invitation of his
warm personal friend Mendelssohn,
he became teacher of pf. and comp.,
and of playing from score at the
newly founded Leipzig Cons.; 1844,
after going with his wife on a concert-tour to Russia, he removed to
Dresden and resigned the editorship
of the " *Neue Zeitschrift* "; lived at
Dresden until 1850 teaching and composing such works as the great **C**-
major symph, 1846, and the opera
" *Genoveva* " (1848 ; prod. 1850
without succ.; its exclusion of recita♦

tive displeasing the public). 1847 cond. of the "Liedertafel"; 1848 organised the "Chorgesangverein." 1850, Düsseldorf as town mus.-dir. (vice Fd. Hiller). 1853, signs of insanity, first noted in 1833 and more in 1845, compelled him to retire. 1854 he threw himself into the Rhine, whence he was rescued by some boatmen; he was then taken to an asylum at Endenich near Bonn, where he remained in acute melancholia, varied by intervals of complete lucidity, when he composed as before. A complete ed. of his comps. is edited by Clara Schumann and publ. by Breitkopf & Härtel. It includes, besides the works mentioned, mus. to Byron's "Manfred," Goethe's "Faust," cantatas, "Der Rose Pilgerfahrt," with orch.; "Adventlied," for sopr., chorus and orch.; "Abschiedslied," chorus with wood-wind or pf.; requiem for "Mignon"; "Nachtlied," for chorus and orch.; ballades "Der Königssohn," "Des Sänger's Fluch" (op. 139), "Vom Pagen und der Königstochter," "Das Glück von Edenhall," and "Neujahrslied"; Missa sacra, and requiem mass, with orch.; 4 symphs. (No. 3, op. 97, in E♭ the "Rheinische," or "Cologne," symph.); "Ouvertüre, Scherzo und Finale," op. 52; 4 concert overtures "Die Braut von Messina," "Festouvertüre," "Julius Cæsar" and "Hermann und Dorothea"; pf.-concerto; Concertstück, and concert-allegro, 'cello-concerto; fantasia for vln. with orch., etc.

Much remarkable CHAMBER MUSIC. incl. pf.-quintet in E♭ op. 44; 3 pf.-trios, etc.; 6 org.-studies in canon-form,"Skizzen für den Pedal-flügel"; 6 org.-fugues on B-A-C-H, op. 60. FOR PF.: Op. 1, Variations on

A-B-E-G-G (the name of a y[oung] woman); op. 2 "Papillons"; o[...] "Studies after Paganini's Capri[...] op. 5, "Impromptus on theme b[...] Wieck"; op. 6, "Davidsbün[...] tänze"; op. 9, "Carnaval"; op[...] "Studies on Paganini's Capri[...] op. 15, thirteen "Kinderscenen" 16, "Kreisleriana"; op. 21, "N[...] letten" (4 books), 3 sonatas 3 "Concert sans orchestre"), 3 sonatas for the young; o[...] "Nachtstücke"; op. 26 "Fasch[...] schwank aus Wien"; op. 68, "[...] bum für die Jugend," a cano[...] "An Alexis." FOR PF. 4 HANDS: 66, "Bilder aus Osten," after R[...] ert, 12 "Clavierstücke für klein[e] grosse Kinder"; op. 109, "[...] scenen." Many choruses a capp[...] many songs and duets, incl. ten [...] nische Liebeslieder, with 4-han[d] comp., op. 138; Liederkreis (He[...] song-cycle, op. 24, and Lieder [...] (12 poems by Eichendorff), op. [...] "Myrthen," op. 25; Lieder und [...] sänge, 5 sets; 12 poems (Kör[...] op. 35; 6 poems (Rückert), in co[...] oration with his wife, op. [...] 'Frauenliebe und Leben," op. [...] 'Dichterliebe," op. 48; "Lied[...] bum für die Jugend," op. 7[...] songs from Byron's "Hebrew [...] dies," op. 95 (with pf. or harp); [...] Lieder und Gesänge from "Wi[...] Meister," op. 98a, etc.

His writings are pub. in 4 v[...] 1854; 4 vols. in English, Lon[...] 1875; and his letters ed. by his [...] (1885) and (1880) by Jansen.

Biogr. by von Wasielewski (1[...] Reissmann (1865), Ambros (1[...] L. Mesnard (Paris, 1876), H. [...] mann (1887), H. Erler (1887)[...] Bagge (1879), Waldersee (1880)[...] by Ph. Spitta (1882).

## Schumann.

### By Richard Aldrich.

CHUMANN'S music falls into three groups or periods as easily as Beethoven's. There is first, the product of his early, exuberant style, those wonderful series of short piano pieces, slight in form, but ng into imaginative power; saying little, but vaguely hinting at much. The nd period is one of more self-centred activity, of greater poise, of more ervative methods ; his ideal had expanded, and was leading him to com- in a larger mould, with a broader sweep of imagination, and with a ter regard for form as itself an element of beauty. And, in his last period, must group those of his works that show the failing powers, the exhausted gination of an intellect already overshadowed by its approaching doom. chumann's beginnings in music were as nearly the spontaneous outpour- of himself as can well be thought of. It is difficult to derive the sources even his first attempts from the music of his predecessors. He studied e of Hummel's works, and greatly admired Moscheles, and, the critics that the "*Abegg*" variations, *Opus 1*, are in the Hummel-Moscheles e. He was devoted to Schubert from his early years, and played his little o pieces, especially the dances, with great love; perhaps the traces of this be found in the *Papillons, Opus 2*. But even here, the influence, if there any, related more to the concise and sententious form, the poetic content, to the fibre of the music itself. It is not the kind of resemblance that will find to Mozart and Haydn all through the earliest works of Beetho- . Bach, too, formed a part of young Schumann's musical daily bread ; may perhaps discern that influence in the instinctive feeling for contra- tal movement—though of a very free, and, as it were, untechnical sort— those earliest piano pieces ; but here again comparison of the specifically cal style reveals nothing. ¶There is one influence, however, that cannot be rlooked in computing the forces bearing on Schumann's formative period ; t is Jean Paul Richter. All readers of Schumann's letters know how steeped was in the spirit of this singular German fantastic, this overwrought romantic nbolist, a story-teller, philosopher, and poet in one. He was all in all to umann ; not only the young man's literary style—he was already a copi- writer—but his very ideals in music, were moulded on Jean Paul's, and ckly overlaid with his mannerisms. For, in these early years of Schumann's , music and poetry seem to meet on common ground, and to take their pulse from one and the same starting-point. In Jean Paul, all that charm- crew of "*Davidites*," with "*Florestan*" and "*Eusebius*" as their fore-

front, have their prototypes ; and their appearance in the early *Zeitsc*
articles is no more characteristic of this influence than their appearance in
"*Carnéval*" and the "*Davidsbündlertänze.*" ¶ With his attainme
his heart's desire in his marriage with Clara Wieck, in 1840, there seem
have come a mellowing, a ripening force in Schumann's musical inspiratio
if you will, a conservative force that led him to see the significance and v
of those musical forms to which he had at first been indifferent. Some o
ardent companions in the revolutionary parties of the earlier years saw in
a backsliding from his professions. But the fact that he parted company v
"*Florestan*" and "*Eusebius,*" and erased their names from the reissue
musical works once signed by them, can be for us naught but an indicatio
intellectual growth. We enjoy those romantic and engaging figures, but
see greater things than they were concerned with in the symphonies,
piano-quintette, the string-quartettes, the piano-concerto, the third part
"*Faust,*" and "*Paradise and the Peri.*" ¶ The contributions of Sc
mann to the development of the art are important and permanent. Wha
did to develop the expressive power of the pianoforte is all his own.
wrote for the instrument in a new way, calling for new and elaborate advan
in technique—not the brilliant finger-dexterity of Chopin and Liszt, bu
deeper underlying potency of expression through interlacing parts, skilf
disposed harmonies, the inner voices of chords, and through new demand
to variety of tone quality, contrasts of colour and the enrichment of the wh
through pedal effects. It has been called a crabbed style, but it is no
idiomatic of the piano than the more open and brilliant manner that v
developed at the same period by the virtuoso-school of pianoforte-playing a
composition. ¶ Schumann's use of short pieces, in connected series, as an
position of what is really a single poetic idea running through them all, is
own creation, and one that succeeding composers have made the most
So is his idealised form of programme-music—music, that is, expressing so
definite, concrete, external idea. But his wise judgment on music of
kind must always be kept in mind, that it must always be beautiful and in
ligible as music without the need of explanation through titles, in which he s
only an aid or stimulus to the hearer's imagination. Space is lacking to c
cuss his later experiments in modifying or developing the classical or son
form to increase its unity and its emotional potency, such as are to be fou
in the D-minor and C-major symphonies, and the piano-quintette. Sch
mann added something peculiarly his own to the Lied, in his enhancement
the accompaniment's significance, increasing its power of expression in
operation, sometimes almost on equal terms with the voice, and, in ma
instances, giving its ritournelles or instrumental postludes an independent el
oration and meaning of their own. ¶ Schumann came of a well-to-

ily, and his early genera. education and socia. surroundings had been far
ond those of most musicians. The fact that he was not only well read,
a writer himself of peculiar charm and individuality, a critic of quickening
ght and generous discernment, reacted, as it needs must, on his music.
ough he was, early in his youth, of a lively character, he was always dis-
ed toward moodiness; and by the time he reached manhood he had fallen
o a state of remarkable taciturnity and introspection. Wrapped in his own
ughts, he would, when in the company of friends or fellow-musicians, sit
nt hour after hour, with his head leaning on his hand, often with an incip-
t smile upon his face, and with his lips pursed, as though to whistle.
s letters show him to have been of a sweet and affectionate nature toward
family and intimates; kindly and generous in his estimate and treatment
others, yet roused to anger by a wrong, and capable of deep and glowing
entment. ¶ Schumann's place in modern music was slowly won, both
is native land and elsewhere, but there is little sign yet, of its being shaken.
s symphonies suffer unduly, through their unskilful orchestration, in the
mation of a generation to whom fine feeling for orchestral colour is essential,
the magnificent elegance of the two great overtures (to "*Manfred*" and
*Genoveva*") is little discounted in this way; the string-quartettes and the
no-quintette and quartette seem to lose none of their beauty as they recede in
orical perspective; the piano concertos, and a great number of the songs are
rd repeatedly, every year, with unremitted joy. His solo piano-pieces
eal less and less to the taste of the latter-day piano-virtuoso who cannot utilise
sic calling so little for nimbleness of finger and brilliancy of effect; but it
mpossible to deny that these pieces are still competent, as few others are,
serve deep and sincere music lovers "for the enjoyment of god at home."
umann will always have a commanding hold, a commanding place in the
eteenth century, the century of evolution, the century that struck off the
demic bonds from art. * In the noble band of romantic adventurers into
v and unexplored realms of music, Schumann was a leader, but he never
ed in his bold and chivalrous championship of the rectitude of his art.

(2) **Clara (Josephine)**, née **Wieck**,
Leipzig, Sept. 13, 1819—Frankfort-
on-Main, May 20, 1896; eminent
pianist; wife of above (q. v.). She
played in public at 9; at 11 at the
Gewandhaus; toured from 1832;
Vienna (1836) received the title of
Imp. Chamber-virtuoso. On Sept. 12,
1840. m. Schumann (q. v.). After he
died she went with her children to
Berlin; 1863 to Wiesbaden, resuming her public career as a concert-
pianist; 1878–92 pf.-teacher Hoch
Cons., Frankfort. Besides editing
Schumann's works, his early letters
and finger-exercises from Czerny,
she c. pf.-concerto, preludes and
fugues, pf.-trio, Vars. on a theme
by Schumann, many songs, incl. 3
in Schumann's op. 37 (Nos. 2, 4,
and 11). Biog. by Litzmann, 1902.
(3) **Georg (Alfred)**, b. Königstein,

Saxony, Oct. 25, 1866 ; pianist , son and pupil of the city mus.-dir., pupil of his grandfather, a cantor, and of K. A. Fischer, B. Rollfuss, and Fr. Baumfelder Dresden, then of Leipzig Cons., where he c. 2 symphs., a serenade for orch., a pf.-quintet, a vln.-sonata, etc., taking the Beethoven prize, 1887 ; lived 2 years in Berlin; 1892–96, cond. at Danzig, since then Bremen Philh. Orch. and chorus; c. also choral work, " *Amor und Psyche* " (Leipzig, 1888), orch.-suite " *Zur Karnevalszeit*," etc.

**Schumann-Heink** (shoo'-män - hĭnk), **Ernestine** (née **Rössler**), b. Lieben, near Prague, June 15, 1861 ; contralto ; pupil of Marietta von Leclair, Graz ; début Dresden, 1878, in " *Il Trovatore ;*" sang there 4 years ; 1883 Hamburg City Th.; 1896, sang " Erda," " Waltraute," and the First Norn at Bayreuth; m. Herr Heink, 1883; m. Paul Schumann, 1893 ; from 1898, in America with Met. Op. troupe.

**Schund** (shoont), **Joachim**, org.-builder, Leipzig, 1356.

**Schunke** (shoonk'-ĕ), (1) **K.**, Magdeburg, 1801—suicide, Paris, 1839 ; pianist ; son and pupil of a horn-virtuoso. (3) **Michael S.**, composer. (3) **L.**, Cassel, 1810—Leipzig, 1834 ; pianist and composer ; pupil of his father, the horn-virtuoso. (4) **Gottfried S.**

**Schuppanzich** (shoop'-păn-tsĭkh), **Ignaz**, Vienna, 1776—1830 ; violinist, conductor and teacher.

**Schürer** (shü'-rĕr), **Jn. G.**, Raudnitz, Bohemia, ca. 1732—Dresden, 1786 ; dram. composer.

**Schurig** (shoo'-rĭkh), (**Volkmar**) **Julius** (**Wm.**), Aue, Saxony, 1802—Dresden, 1899 ; composer and teacher.

**Schuster** (shoo'-shtĕr), **Jos.**, Dresden, 1748—1812 ; ct.-conductor ; c. pop. operas, symphs., etc.

**Schütt** (shüt), **Eduard**, b. Petersburg, Oct. 22, 1856 ; pianist ; pupil of Petersen and Stein, Petersb. Cons.:

studied at Leipzig Cons.; now co Akademischer Wagnerverein, Vier c. fairly succ. comic opera " *Si Formica* " (Vienna, 1892) ; c. concerto, etc.

**Schütz** (shüts), (**Sagitta'rius**) " The father of German mus Köstritz, Saxony, Oct. 8, 1585—D den, Nov. 6, 1672 ; in 1607 ente Marburg Univ. to study law, 1609, was sent to Venice by La grave Moritz of Hesse-Cassel to st with Giov. Gabrieli; 1612 returnee Cassel as ct.-organist ; 1615 cond the Elector of Saxony at Dresd he frequently revisited Italy, whe he brought much to modify and large German mus. ; also made visits to Copenhagen as ct.-co 1627, on royal invitation for the w ding of Princess Sophie of Saxony c. the first German opera, the libr being a transl. from the " *Daf* of Peri (q. v.) ; this work is lost, a also the ballet, " *Orpheus und E* *dice*," 1638, for the wedding of Georg II. of Saxony. Carl Ri revived interest in **S**. by pub. producing " *Die 7 Worte Christi Kreuz*," and a " *Passion*." A c plete ed. of **S**'s works is pub. Breitkopf and Härtel in 16 vols.; t include sacred and secular mus. great historical importance as predecessor whom Händel and B rather developed than discarded ; was born just a hundred years fore them and shows great dram force and truth in his choral w combining with the old polyph structure a modern fire that ma many of his works still beauti Biog. by Ph. Spitta, and Fr. Sp (1886).

**Schwab** (shväp), **Fran. M. L.**, Str burg, 1829—1882 ; conductor dram. composer.

**Schwalm** (shvälm), (1) **Robt.**, b. furt, Dec. 6, 1845 ; pupil of Pf haupt and Leipzig Cons.; cond. Königsberg ; c. opera, male chor with orch., oratorio, etc. (2) Os

urt, Sept. 11, 1856; pupil of Leip-
Cons.; 1886–88, proprietor of
hn's pub.-house in Leipzig; also
ic for the " *Tageblatt*," etc.; c. an
rture; pf.-pcs., etc.

**y'ler, Wm.**, b. St. Louis, U. S.
, May 4, 1855; lives there as ama-
r composer, largely self-taught; c.
cellent songs, notably to Stephen
ane's " *Black Riders*."

**wanberg** (shvän'-běrkh), **Jn. Gf.**,
olfenbüttel, 1740 — Brunswick,
04; ct.-conductor and dram. com-
ser.

**wantzer** (shvän'-tsěr), **Hugo,**
erlogau, 1829—Berlin, 1886; or-
nist, teacher and composer.

**warbrook** (shvär'-brook), **Thos.,**
r. org.-builder in England, 1733–
52.

**warz** (shvärts), (1) **Ands. Gl.,**
ipzig, 1743—Berlin, 1804; bassoon-
in London. (2) **Chp. Gl.**, b.
68; son of above; bassoonist. (3)
'm., Stuttgart, 1825—Berlin, 1878;
ger and teacher. (4) **Max**, b.
anover, Dec. 1, 1856; son of above;
pil of Bendel, Bülow, and Liszt;
anist; 1880–83, teacher Hoch
ns., Frankfort; then co-founder,
er Raff's death, of the Raff
ns.; since 1885 its dir. (5) **Bi-
ca.** Vide BIANCHI. (6) **Wenzel,**
Brunnersdorf, Feb. 3, 1830; pu-
Prague Cons.; from 1864 lived in
enna, proprietor of a mus.-insti-
te; writer.

**wedler** (shvät'-lěr), **(Otto) Maxi-
lian,** b. Hirschberg, Silesia, March
, 1853; flutist; pupil of Fr. Meinel,
resden; in Leipzig municipal and
ewandhaus Orch.; since 1895, 1st
te; inv. the " Schwedler flute ";
ote a pamphlet on it and c. tran-
riptions, etc.

**weitzer** (shvät'-lěr),——, Coburg,
'37—Gotha, 1787; conductor and
mposer.

**weizer** (shvīt'-tsěr), **Otto,** b. Zü-
h, May 26, 1846; pianist; pupil
Moscheles and Wenzel, Leipzig
ns.; since 1870 Edinburgh, also

pf.-teacher at Athenæum Sch., Glasgow; c. 2 pf.-suites, etc.

**Schwencke** (shvěnk'-ě), (1) **Jn. Gl.,**
1744—1823; bassoonist. (2) **Chr.
Fr. Gl.**, Wachenhausen, Harz, 1767
—Hamburg, 1822; son of above;
cantor and mus.-dir. (3) **Jn. Fr.,**
Hamburg, 1792—1852; son and pupil of (2); composer. (4) **K.**, Hamburg, 1797—?; pianist; son of (2).
(5) **Fr. Gl.**, Hamburg, 1823—1896;
virtuoso on the pf. and organ; com
poser.

**Schytte** (shět'-tě), **L. (Th.)**, b. Aarhus, Jutland, April 28, 1850; druggist, then studied with Ree, Neupert,
Gebauer, Gade, Taubert, and Liszt
(comp); 1887–88 teacher Horák's
Institute, Vienna; lived in Vienna as
concert-pianist and teacher; c. 2
comic operas; pf.-concerto; pantomimes for 4 hands, sonata, etc.

**Scontrino** (skôn-trē'-nō), **A.**, b. Trapani, 1851; pupil of Plantania, Palermo; lived in Milan as teacher;
since 1897 prof. of cpt. at Florence
Cons.; c. 5 operas, incl. succ. 1-act
" *Gringoire* " (1890), and " *La Cor-
tigiana* " (Milan, 1896); c. " *Sinfonia
marinaresca* " (Naples, 1897).

**Scot'son Clark,** the Rev., London,
Nov. 16, 1840—1883; pupil of his
mother (a pupil of Chopin); then
at Paris; at 14 organist; studied
with J. Hopkins and at R. A. M.; after
serving as organist various places, he
studied at Leipzig and Stuttgart;
1873, returned to London as teacher,
organist and composer of many pop.
works.

**Scott, John,** England, ca. 1776—
Jamaica, 1815.

**Scotto** (skôt'-tō), (1) **Ottaviano,** and
his son (2) **Girolamo,** mus.-printers
at Venice, 1536–39, and 1539–73, respectively, the latter was also a composer.

**Scriabine** (skrē'-ä-bē-ně), **Alex,** b.
Moscow, Jan. 6 (new style), 1872;
brilliant pianist; pupil of Safonoff
(pf.) and Tanejev (comp.) at the
Cons.; toured Europe from 1895; c.

sonata, prelude and nocturne for left hand alone ; pf.-impromptus, preludes, etc.

**Scribe** (skrēb), **Eugène**, Paris, 1791—1861 ; most prolific of French dramatists, and wrote over 100 librettos, incl. " *Fra Diavolo*," " *Prophète*," " *L'Africaine*."

**Scuderi** (skoo-dā'-rē), **Salvatore**, b. Terranova, Italy, Jan. 3, 1845 ; c. pop. songs.

**Scudo** (skoo'-dō), **Paolo**, Venice, 1806—insane, Blois, 1864 ; writer.

**Sebald** (zā'-bält), (1) Frau **von** (née **Schwadke**); contralto, Berlin, 1791 ; her daughters (2) **Amalie**, soprano ; for some time the object of Beethoven's affections; (3) **Auguste**, sister of above ; also soprano.

**Sebastiani** (sā-bäs-tǐ-ä'-nē), **Jn.**, b. Weimar, 1622 ; conductor and composer.

**Sebor** (shā'-bôr), **K.** (**Karel**), b. Brandeis, Bohemia, July 18 (Aug. 13 ?), 1843 ; pupil Prague Cons. and of Kittl; 1864–67, cond. Nat. Opera ; from 1871 military bandm., Vienna ; prod. at Prague 5 Czech operas; c. symphs., overtures, etc.

**Sechter** (zĕkh'-tĕr), **Simon**, Friedberg, Bohemia, Oct. 11, 1788—Vienna, Sept. 10, 1867 ; eminent contrapuntist and teacher, ct.-organist, prof. of harm.; wrote valuable treatises ; c. burlesque opera " *Ali Hitch-Hasch*."

**Sedlmair** (zāt'l-mīr), **Sofia Offeney**, b. Hanover, Jan. 25, 1863 ; soprano in various cities.

**Seeling** (zā'-lǐng), **Hans (Hanuš)**, Prague 1828—1862 ; piano-virtuoso and composer.

**Seger(t)** (zā'-gĕrt), **Jos.**, Repin, Bohemia, 1716—Prague, 1782 ; organist and composer.

**Seghers** (sŭ-gärs'), **Fran. J. Bap.**, Brussels, 1801 — Margency, near Paris, 1881 ; violinist and conductor.

**Segond** (sŭ-gôǹ), **L. A.**, a physician at Paris ; studied singing with Manuel Garcia, and wrote " *Hygiène du chanteur* " (1846), etc.

**Segouro'la, Andres Perello de**, b.

Spain ; studied law Madrid U practised a year at Barcelona ; took up singing with success.

**Seguin** (sĕg'-wǐn), (1) **Albert E S.**, London, 1809—New York, 1 bass (2) **Elizabeth**, his s mother of Parepa Rosa. (3) **Childe**, wife of (1) ; operatic er ; début, 1828 ; retired and New York, 1880. (4) **Wm. H.**, —1850 ; bro. of (1) ; bass.

**Seibert** (zī'-bĕrt), **Louis**, b. Clee near Wiesbaden, May 22, 1833 ; teacher Wiesbaden Cons.; c. c ber-mus., etc.

**Seidel** (zī'-dĕl), (1) **Fr. L.**, Tre brietzen, Brandenburg. 1765—C lottenburg, 1831 ; organist and d composer. (2) **Jn. Julius**, Bre 1810—1856 ; organist and writer

**Seidl** (zīt'-'l), (1) **Anton**, Pesth, 7, 1850—New York, March 28, 1 eminent cond., particularly of V nerian mus.; pupil Leipzig C 1870 chorusm. Vienna opera ; 1 79, assisted Wagner in score of " *belungen Ring*"; 1879–83 cond Neumann's Wagner-troupe ; 188 cond. Bremen opera (m. there soprano (2) Frl. **Krauss**); 188 Met. Op., N. Y., also from 189 cond. N. Y. Philh. Orch.; 1886 1897 cond. at Bayreuth ; 1897 c Covent Garden, London. (3) thur, b. Munich, June 8, 1863; R. Sch. of Mus. at Ratisbon an Paul, Stade, Spitta, and Bellerm Dr. Phil., Leipzig, 1887 ; live Dresden ; writer.

**Seifert** (zī'-fĕrt), **Uso**, b. Rom Thuringia, Feb. 9, 1852 ; pup Dresden Cons.; teacher there an ganist ; wrote pf.-method, pf.- etc.

**Seifriz** (zī'-frǐts), **Max**, Rott Würtemberg, 1827—Stuttgart, 1 violinist, ct.-cond. and composer

**Seiler** (zī'-lĕr), **Jos.**, Lügde, near mont, 1823—1877 ; organist, w and composer.

**Seiss** (zīs), **Isidor (Wm.)**, b. Dres Dec. 23, 1840 ; pianist ; pupi

pzig Cons.; since 1871 pf.-teacher
ogne Cons.; 1878 Prof.; con-
:tor Musikalische Gesellschaft ; c.
dies in bravura, etc.
; (zīts), (1) **Robt.**, Leipzig, 1837—
•9 ; mus.-publisher and editor. (2)
, **(Fritz)**, b. Günthersleben, Go-
, June 12, 1848 ; violinist ; pupil
Uhlrich ; since 1884 leader Dessau
orch.

n (sä-zhän), **Nicolas**, Paris, 1745
-819 ; famous organist ; 1772,
tre Dame; 1783, St. Sulpice ; 1783,
al chapel ; teacher and composer.
•ls (zä′-kĕls), **Bd.**, pupil, now t. of
np. Hoch Cons., Frankfort ; c.
gs.

•y, **Bertram Luard,** b. Kent,
gl., Feb. 12, 1853 ; organist,
isbury Cath.; then of St. Barna-
s, London ; c. 2 operas ; a 1-act
eretta ("duologue"), successful
*Weather or No*" (London, 1896),
·lin as " *Das Wetterhäuschen*,"
06; org-sonatas, etc.

;mann (zā′-lĭkh-män), **Hippolyte**
**osper,** Paris, 1817—Monte Carlo,
32 ; 'cellist and composer.
e (zĕl′-lĕ), **Thos.**, Zorbig, Saxony,
09—Hamburg, 1663 ; cantor and
nposer.

ıer (zĕl′-nĕr), **Jos.**, Landau, Ba-
:ia, 1787—Vienna, 1843 ; oboe-
tuoso, teacher, writer and compos-

**brich** (zĕm′-brĭkh), **Marcella**
ghtly **Praxede Marcelline Ko-**
**anska,** Sembrich being her moth-
s maiden name), b. Wisnewszyk,
.licia, Feb. 15, 1858 ; eminent col-
·ature soprano ; pupil (later the
fe) of Wm. Stengel (piano), Lem-
·rg Cons.; studied with Epstein at
·enna, and singing with Victor Ro-
ansky. and with G. B. Lamperti,
, at Milan; début, May, 1877, at
hens ; studied German opera at
·rlin with Lewy; sang for 18 months
·esden ct.-th.; from June, 1880,
ondon, and, 1883–84, toured Eu-
·pe and America ; 1884, studied
th Francesco Lamperti, Sr.; from

1898 has sung at Met. Op. and in
concert in America with greatest
succ.; 1900, managed her own opera
co. in Germany.

**Semet** (sŭ-mā), **Théophile (Aimé**
**Émile),** Lille, 1824—Corbeil, near
Paris, 1888 ; drummer and dram.
composer.

**Semler** (zĕm′-lĕr), **Fz. X.,** 1772—1859;
vla.-soloist in Berlin.

**Senesino** (sän-ĕ-sē′-nō), **Bernardi**
**Francesco** (called the Sienese), Siena,
1680—ca. 1750; male contralto or
mezzo-sopr.; sang in Händel's operas
till 1729, where he quarrelled with
H. and went over to Bononcini; made
a fortune and returned to Siena.

**Senff** (zĕnf), **Bartholf,** Friedrichshall,
near Coburg, 1818—Leipzig, 1895 ;
founder Leipzig mus.-pub. house
(1850), also editor.

**Sen(f)fl** (zĕnf′l) (or **Senfel**), **L.,** Basel-
Augst, 1492 — Munich, ca. 1555 ;
eminent contrapuntist. ct.-cond. and
composer.

**Senkrah** (zän′-krä) (rightly **Hark′ness**),
**Arma Leorette,** New York, 1864
—suicide, Weimar, Aug. 4, 1900; vio-
linist ; pupil of Arno Hilf, Leipzig;
Wieniawski, and Massart, Paris
Cons.; toured with succ.

**Serafino** (sä-rä-fē′-nō), (1) **Santo,** vln.-
maker at Venice, 1730-45 ; his label
is " Sanctus Seraphin Utinensis fecit
Venetiis, Anno, 17—". (2) **Grego-**
**rio**, his nephew, also was a vln.-
maker, label " Georgius Seraphin
Sancti nepos fecit Venetiis, 17—."

**Serassi** (sä-räs′-sē), Italian family of
org.-builders at Bergamo. The founder (1) **Giuseppe** (*il vecchio*), Gor-
dano, 1694—Crema, 1760. His son
(2) **Andrea Luigi,** 1725—1799. (3)
**Giuseppe** (*il giovane*), Bergamo,
1750—1817; succeeded by his sons (4)
**Carlo** and (5) **Giuseppe.**

**Sering** (zā′-rĭng), **Fr. Wm.,** Fürstenwalde, near Frankfort-on-Oder, Nov.
26, 1822—1901; from 1871 teacher at
Strassburg, where he organised a Gesangverein ; pub. treatises, also an
oratorio, male choruses, etc.

**Sermisy** (sĕr-mē-sē), **Claude de** (called **Claudin**, not **Claudin Lejeune**), ca. 1530–60 ; French ct.-cond. and composer.

**Serov** (or **Sjeroff, Syeroff** (s'yä-rôf)); **Alex. Nikolajevitch**, Petersburg, May 11, 1820—Feb. 1 (new style), 1871 ; important Russian composer and critic ; a lawyer, studied 'cello with Karl Schuberth ; 1863 prod. grand opera (text and mus.) "*Judith*," and the Czar granted him a pension ; he was a lecturer on mus. at Moscow and Petersb. Universities and wrote his own librettos ; 1865 prod. "*Rogneda*" with succ. ; laid aside 2 unfinished operas to finish "*Wrazyiasiela*" but died before it was done. Soloviev finished it and it was prod. with succ.

**Serpette** (sĕr-pĕt), **(H. Chas. A.) Gaston**, b. Nantes, Nov. 4, 1846 ; pupil of Thomas, Paris Cons. ; 1871, taking 1st Grand prix de Rome, wrote cantata "*Jeanne d'Arc*"; 1874, prod. opera-bouffe "*La Branche Cassée*" (Bouffes-Parisiens), followed by 30 other light works.

**Serrao** (sĕr-rä'-ō), **Paolo**, b. Filadelfia, Catanzaro, in 1830 ; pupil of Naples Cons. ; political troubles prevented the prod. of his opera "*L'Impostore*" in 1852, and another in 1857, but he prod. "*Pergolesi*" and "*La Duchessa di Guisa*" (1865), and "*Il Figliuol prodigo*" (1868) ; c. also an oratorio, a requiem, a funeral symph. (for Mercadante), etc.

**Servais** (sĕr-vĕ), (1) **Adrien Fran.**, Hal, near Brussels, 1807—1866 ; eminent 'cellist and teacher ; pupil of his father and of Platel, début Paris, 1834 ; 1848, Prof. Brussels Cons. and soloist to the King ; toured widely ; c. 3 concertos for 'cello, etc. (2) **Jos.**, Hal, 1850—1885 ; son and pupil of above ; 'cellist and prof. Brussels Cons.

**Sestini** (sĕs-tē'-nē), **Giovanna**, prima buffa in London, 1783.

**Sevcik** (sĕv'-tsĭk), **Pan** ; notable Bohemian violin teacher.

**Sev'ern, Thos. H.**, London, 18[ ] Wandsworth, 1881 ; conductor, [ ] lisher and dram. composer.

**Sew'ard, Theodore Frelinghuy[ ]** d. New York, Oct. 30, 1902 ; t[ ] er, ed. and composer of slave s[ ] and "spirituals."

**Seydelmann** (zī'-dĕl-män), **Fz.**, [ ] den, 1748—1806 ; cembalist, [ ] ductor and dram. composer.

**Seyffarth** (zīf'-färt), **Ernst Hn[ ]** Crefeld, 1859 ; pupil of Col[ ] Cons. and of Kiel ; from 1892, [ ] ductor Neuer Singverein, Stutt[ ] c. dram. scene "*Thusnelda*," "*T[ ] erfeier beim Tode einer Jungf[ ]* symph., sonatas, MS. opera "[ ] *Bells of Plurs*," etc.

**Seyfried** (zī'-frēt), **Ignaz X. [ ] von**, Vienna, 1776—1841 ; condu[ ] writer and dram. composer.

**Seygard** (sā'-gärd), **Camille**, b. [ ] land ; went early to Russia ; pu[ ] her father and of Marchesi ; d[ ] 1888, Covent Garden as "Zerli[ ] sang at Opera Comique, later in [ ] sterdam ; has sung in concert [ ] opera in Europe, and since 18[ ] America.

**Sgambati** (sgäm-bä'-tē), **Giovann[ ]** Rome, May 18, 1843 ; importan[ ] anist and conductor ; pupil of [ ] ga, Barbieri and Natalucci, late[ ] Liszt ; at 6 played in public, sar[ ] Church and cond. small orches[ ] later he toured Italy and Germ[ ] 1877, head-teacher Accad. di S. [ ] cilia, Rome ; 1896, founded "N[ ] Società Musicale Romana " ; adr[ ] and friend of Wagner ; c. req[ ] with orch. (1896), 3 symphs., [ ] tures, pf.-concerto, an octet, 2 [ ] quintets, a string-quartet (op. 17) [ ] piano pcs., etc.

**Shakespeare, Wm.**, b. Croy[ ] Engl., June 16, 1849 ; choir-boy [ ] 13 organist ; pupil of Molique (cor[ ] 1866, won King's scholarship R[ ] M., and studied there with Ben[ ] 1871, took Mendelssohn Schola[ ] for pf.-playing and comp. ; stu[ ] with Reinecke, Leipzig ; 1872, sir[ ]

Milan; from 1875, concert and ora-
rio-singer; 1878, prof. of singing,
A. M.; in 1880, 1886, cond. of
e concerts there; resigned; has
on high reputation as a singing-
acher; c. overtures, a symph., pf.-
ncerto, etc.

rpe, **Herbert Francis,** b. Hali-
x, Yorkshire, March 1, 1861;
ueen's Scholar, Nat. Training Sch.,
ondon; gave pf.-concerts; 1884,
of. R. C. M.; 1890, examiner;
ote "*Pianoforte Sch.*" (with Stan-
y Lucas); c. comic opera, etc.

w, (1) **Oliver,** b. Middleboro',
ass., d. 1848; a blind singing-
acher and public singer. (2)
ary, London, 1814—Suffolk, 1876,
ntralto and teacher.

d'lock, **John South,** b. Reading,
ngl., 1843; graduate, London,
niv., 1864; pupil of E. Lübeck
f.) and Lalo (comp.), Paris; teach-
and concert-pianist, London, 1879;
tic for the "*Athenæum*"; also lect-
ed at the R. A. M.; pub. articles,
*The Pianoforte Sonata, Its Origin
d Development*" (London, 1895);
itor and translator; c. string-quar-
, etc.

l'ley, **Harry Rowe,** b. New
aven, Conn., June 8, 1858; pupil
Stoeckel at Yale, Dudley Buck,
ogrich and Dvořák (New York);
ganist various churches, also teach-
of theory and comp. Metropolitan
ollege, N. Y.; c. "*The Inheritance
ivine,*" sacred cantata, 2 symphs.
ae first E♭, performed, N. Y., 1897),
n.-concerto (1891), cantata "*Vexil-
Regis*" (N. Y., 1894), and suite
*Baden-Baden,*" etc., for orch.;
urch-mus., pf. and org.-pcs. and
ngs, many very pop.

p'ard, (1) **Thos. Griffin,** b. Madi-
n, Conn., April 23 1848; pupil of
W. and J. P. Morgan; organist
rious churches in New Haven; in-
ructor, Yale Glee Club and cond.
ratorio Soc., also dir. Apollo Club
ale voices); teacher and critic; c.
mic opera, Christmas cantata, etc.

(2) **Frank Hartson,** b. Bethel,
Conn., Sept. 20, 1863; pupil of
Thayer, Boston; organist various
towns; 1886–90, studied Leipzig
1888, organist English Chapel there
1891, est. a sch. at Orange, N. J.
organist there; writer of text-books
and treatises.

**Sher'rington, Jose.,** b. Rotterdam,
Oct. 27, 1850; sister of Mme. Lemmens - Sherrington; concert - soprano
with remarkable range (a–e''').

**Sher'wood,** (1) **Edgar Harmon,** b.
Lyons, N.Y., Jan. 29, 1845; pianist;
served in the Union Army 1862–65,
and then took up mus.; lives in Rochester, N. Y., as pianist, teacher and
composer. (2) **Wm. Hall,** b. Lyons,
N. Y., Jan. 31, 1854; noteworthy
pianist and teacher, bro. of (1); son
and pupil of Rev. L. H. Sherwood,
founder of Lyons Mus. Acad.; pupil
also of Heimberger, Pychowski and
Wm. Mason; studied 5 years under Th. Kullak, Weitzmann, Wuerst
and Deppe (Berlin), Richter (Leipzig), K. Doppler and Scotson Clark
(Stuttgart) and Liszt (Weimar); début with succ., Berlin; returned 1876
to the U. S., and has toured with great
succ.; teacher N. E. Cons., Boston,
later, New York; 1889, Chicago, as
head of the pf.-section of the Cons.;
1897, founded "Sherwood Piano
Sch."; 1887 he m. his pupil, Estella F. Adams, also pianist; pub.
pf.-pcs. (3) **Percy,** b. of English
parents, Dresden, May 23, 1866; pupil of Hermann Scholtz (pf.); later
of Dresden Cons.; concert-pianist and
teacher, Dresden Cons.; c. pf.-pcs.

**Shield, Wm.,** Whickham, Durham,
1748—London, 1829; violinist, writer
and composer.

**Shin'ner, Emily,** Cheltenham, July 7.
1862—Aug., 1901; concert violinist,
England. 1889, m. Capt. Liddell;
founded S. Quartet (female).

**Shore,** (1) **Matthias,** d. 1700, English ct.-trumpeter; reputed inventor
of the tuning-fork. (2) **Wm.,** d.
1707, son and successor of above.

17

(3) **Catherine,** ca. 1668—ca. 1730; sister of above; stage-singer, 1693, m. Colley Cibber. (4) **John,** 1660—1750; bro. and successor of (2).

**Shudi.** Vide BROADWOOD.

**Shut'tleworth, Obadiah,** d. ca. 1735; English organist and violinist.

**Sibelius** (sē-bā'-lǐ-oos), **Jean,** b. Tavastehus, Finland, Dec. 8, 1865; studied Mus. Inst. Helsingfors; and with Becker and Goldmark; since 1893, teacher theory, Mus. Inst. and the Orch. Sch., Helsingfors; c. The first Finnish opera " *Tornissa Olija Impi* " (Helsingfors, 1896); also for orch. " *The Swan of Tuenela* " and " *Lemmin Kainen.*"

**Siboni** (sē-bō'-nē), (1) **Giu.,** Forli, 1780—Copenhagen, 1839; tenor. (2) **Erik (Anton Waldemar),** Copenhagen, 1828—1892; pianist, organist, teacher and dram. composer. (3) **Johanna Frederika** (née Crull), b. Rostock, Jan. 30, 1839; pianist; pupil of Moscheles; 1866 m. above.

**Sicard** (sē-kǎr), **Michel de,** b. of French parents, Odessa, 1868; violinist, pupil of Cons. at Kiev; début at 9; 1884, pupil Paris Cons.; 1886, 1st. vln-prize, then pupil of Joachim (vln.), and Bargiel (comp.); has toured Europe.

**Sieber** (zē'-běr), **Fd.,** Vienna, 1822—Berlin, 1895; famous singing-teacher.

**Siegel** (zē'-gěl), (1) **E. F. W.,** d. 1869; founded, 1846, mus.-pub. firm at Leipzig, now owned by R. Linnemann. (2) **F.** Vide SCHUBERTH, J.

**Siehr** (zēr), **Gv.,** 1847—Munich, 1896; bass; created " Hagen," Bayreuth, 1876.

**Sieveking** (zē'-vě-kǐng), **Martinus,** b. Amsterdam, March 24, 1867; notable pianist; pupil of his father, of J. Röntgen, Leipzig Cons., and Coenen (harm.); 1890 played in London; made v. succ. tours; 1895 Boston; 1896–97 American tour; c. a suite (played by Lamoureux, Paris), etc.

**Siface** (sē-fä'-chě) (rightly **Grossi),** **Giov. Fran.,** robbed and murdered in Northern Italy, ca. 1699;

soprano-musico; ca. 1675 mem Papal Chapel.

**Sighicelli** (sē-gǐ-chěl'-lē), family violinists. (1) **Filippo,** San Cesa Modena, 1686 — Modena, 17 violinist. (2) **Giu.,** Modena, 173 1826; son of above; violinist. **Carlo,** Modena, 1772—1806; son (2), also attached to court. (4) Modena, 1802—1883; son of eminent violinist and conductor. **V.,** b. Cento, July 30, 1830; son pupil of (4); pupil of Hellmesber Mayseder, and 1849 solo-violinist 2nd ct.-cond. Modena; since 18 teacher Paris; c. vln.-fantasias, e

**Sigismondi** (sē-jǐs-môn'-dē), **G** Naples, 1739—1826; singing-teac and dram. composer.

**Silas** (sē'-läs), **Eduard,** b. Amsterd Aug. 22, 1827; pianist; début A sterdam, 1837; pupil of Neher, K brenner, etc.; later of Benoist Halévy, Paris Cons.; winning prize for org. playing, 1849, in c petition with Saint-Saëns and Col since 1890 lives in England as ganist; 1866 Assemblée générale Catholiques en Belgique awarded 1st prize (gold medal and 1, francs) for a mass; later prof. harm. Guildhall Sch. and the Lon Acad. of Mus.; c. oratorio " *Joa.* (Norwich Fest., 1863), Kyrie Eleis with orch., 3 symphs., 3 overtu etc.

**Silbermann** (zēl'-běr-män), (1) **And as,** Klein-Bobritzsch, Saxony, 1 —Strassburg, 1734; org.-builde Strassburg. (2) **Gf.,** Klein britzsch, 1683—Dresden, 1753; bro above and his apprentice; the first ( man to manufacture pianofortes, preceded by Cristofori; inv. *cen d'amour* (V. D. D.). (3) **Jn. And as,** Strassburg, 1712—1783; son (1); org.-builder. (4) **Jn. Dan** 1717—Leipzig, 1766; son of (1), cessor of (2). (5) **Jn. H.,** Strassbu 1727—1799; son of (1); pf.-ma (6) **Jn. Fr.,** 1762—1817; son of org.-builder, organist and compos

er (zĭl´-khĕr), **Fr.**, Schnaith,
rtemberg, 1789—Tübingen, 1860;
ed song-composer; pupil of his
er and of Auberlen; teacher at
ttgart, 1817; mus.-dir. at Tübin-
Univ.; pub. a text-book and
ected and c. chorals, etc.

(sē´-lō-ä), **Giulio,** pupil of Acad.
St. Cecilia, Rome; c. "*Carmen
ulare*" for soli, chorus and orch.
02).

i (sē´-lō-tē), **Alex.,** b. Charkov,
ssia, Oct. 10, 1863; pianist; pupil
`Zwereff and of N. Rubinstein and
aikovsky, Moscow Cons.; win-
g a gold medal; début, Moscow,
o; studied with Liszt 3 years;
7–90, prof. Moscow Cons.; since
Paris; has made v. succ. tours
8–90, America; c. pf.-pieces.

(zĕl´-vä), (1) **Andreas de,** 16th
t. contrapuntist; c. motets, etc.
**David Poll de,** St. Esprit, near
onne, 1834 — Clermont, Oise,
5; blind; pupil of his mother
o c. operas, oratorios, etc.; wrote
his comp. by dictation.

r (sĕl-vär) **Chas.,** Paris, April 16,
8; pupil of Dubois and Massenet
the Cons.; won Grand prix de
ne with cantata "*L'Interdit*"; c.
retta, elegiac poem "*Raïs*"; 4-
fairy opera "*La Belle au Bois
rmant*" (Paris, 1895), oratorio
*obie,*" etc.

ndl (zē´-mänt'l), **Fz.,** 1st double-
s Vienna court orch.; since 1869
cher at the Cons.; pub. method
contra-bass.

.o. Vide PORTUGAL.

n (zē´-mōn). (1) **Jn. Kaspar,** Can-
and organist at Nordlingen, 1750–
; composer. (2) **Chr.,** Schern-
g, 1809 — Sondershausen, 1872;
ble-bass.

n (sē´-môṅ), (1) **Jean Henri,** Ant-
p. 1783 — 1861; violinist. (2)
non - Girard, **Julie Josephine
roline** (née **Girard**), b. Paris,
9; pupil of Cons.; début 1877
ating Offenbach's "Colinette,"
8, "Mme. Favart," and many

other rôles; m. Simon; later m.
Hugenette.

**Simons-Candeille.** Vide CANDEILLE.

**Simp´son (or Sympson),** (1) **Chp.,**
d. London, ca. 1677; player on the
viola da gamba; pub. text-books.
(2) **Thos.,** b. England; from ca.
1615, violinist in Germany; composer.

**Sim´rock,** (1) **Nicolaus,** b. Bonn,
1755; founded there 1790 mus.-pub.
house; 1805 Berlin branch founded
by his son (2) **Peter Jos.;** since 1870
in Berlin under (3), **Fritz,** 1841—
Lausanne, Sept., 1901.

**Sina** (sē-nä), **Louis,** 1778—Boulogne,
1859; violinist.

**Sin´clair** (sĭnk´-lĕr), **J.,** near Edinburgh, 1790—Margate, 1857; tenor.

**Sinding** (zĭnt´-ing), **Chr.,** b. Kong-
bery, Norway, Jan. 11, 1856; notable
composer; pupil of Reinecke, Leipzig Cons., later with Royal Scholarship, studied at Dresden, Munich,
and Berlin; l. Christiania as organist
and teacher; c. symph., 2 vln.-sona-
tas, chamber-mus., a pf.-concerto, pf.-
pcs., and **songs.**

**Singelée** (săṅzh-lä), **J. Bap.,** Brussels,
1812—Ostend, 1875; violinist and
composer.

**Singer** (zĭng´-ĕr), (1) **Peter,** Häfelgehr
(Lechthal), 1810 — Salzburg, 1882;
monk; inv. (1839) the "Pansym-
phonikon" (v. D. D.); composer. (2)
**Edmund,** b. Totis, Hungary, Oct.
14, 1831; violinist; pupil of Ellinger,
at Pesth, then of Kohne; toured, then
studied with Jos. Böhm, Vienna, and
at Paris Cons.; 1853–61 leader at
Weimar; then leader at Stuttgart,
and prof. at the Cons. (3) **Otto,**
Sora, Saxony, 1833—New York, 1894;
pianist, conductor, teacher and composer. (4) **Otto,** Jr., b. Dresden,
Sept. 14, 1863; violinist; studied in
Paris, in Berlin under Kiel, and in
Munich under Rheinberger; 1890
teacher in Cologne Cons., and conductor; since 1892 lives in Leipzig;
c. vln.- Concertstück, etc.

**Sinn** (zĭn), **Chp. Albert,** wrote treatise on "*Temberament,*" 1717.

**Sir´men (Syrmen)**, (1) **Luigi**, violinist and cond. at Bergamo ; his wife, (2) **Maddalena Lombardini de**, b. Venice, 1735 — d. towards end of cent.; prominent violinist ; pupil of Tartini ; later singer and composer.

**Sistermanns** (zĭst´-ĕr-mäns), **Anton**, b. Herzogenbusch, Holland, Aug. 5, 1867; bass ; pupil of Stockhausen ; 1899, sang " Pogner " at Bayreuth ; lives in Frankfort.

**Sitt** (zĭt), **Hans**, b. Prague, Sept. 21, 1850; violinist ; studied Prague Cons.; 1867, leader theatre-orch., Breslau ; 1869, cond. there, later in Prague, etc.; 1883, teacher of vln. Leipzig Cons. and vla.-player Brodsky Quartet; cond. of various societies ; c. 3 vln.-concertos, a vla.-concerto, a 'cello-concerto, etc.

**Sittard** (sĭt-tăr), **Josef**, b. Aix-la-Chapelle, June 4, 1846 ; pupil, Stuttgart Cons., later teacher of singing and pf. there ; lecturer on mus.; since 1885, critic ; 1891, prof. ; writer and composer.

**Sivori** (sē-vō´-rē), **Ernesto Camillo**, b. Genoa, 1815—1894; famous violinist and composer; début at 6 ; pupil of Costa and **Paganini** ; toured widely.

**Sjögren** (shäkh´-rĕn), (**Jn. Gv.**) **Emil**, b. Stockholm, 1853 ; pupil of the Cons. there ; later of Kiel (cpt.) and Haupt (org. at Berlin) ; since 1890, organist Johankirke, Stockholm ; c. sonatas, etc.

**Skroup** (or **Skraup**) (shkroop or shkrä´-oop), (1) **Fz.** (**František**), Vosic, Bohemia, 1801—Rotterdam, 1862 ; conductor and dram. composer. (2) **Jan Nepomuk**, Vosic, 1811 -—Prague, 1892 ; bro. of above ; conductor, singing-teacher, writer and dram. composer.

**Skuherský** (skoo´-hĕr-shkē), **Fz.** (**František**) **Sdenko**, Opocno, Bohemia, 1830—Budweis, 1892 ; organist, conductor, theorist and composer.

**Siátinn** (slä´-tĭn). **Ilja Ilitch**, b. Belgorod, Russia, July 7, 1845 ; pupil

St. Petersburg Cons. and of Th. lak and Wuerst, Berlin ; dir. ( kow section, Imp. Russian Soc.

**Slaughter** (slôt´-ĕr), **A. Walter**, rister at St. Andrew's, Wells London ; pupil of A. Cellier Jacobi ; cond. Drury Lane an( James's Th.; prod. comic o (1890), and a succ. mus.-co " *The French Maid* " (1897), et

**Slavik** (slä´-vĕk), **Jos.**, Jince, mia, 1806—Pesth, 1833 ; violini

**Slivinski** (slĭ-vēn´-shkĭ), **Jos. vo** Warsaw, Dec. 15, 1865 ; pia pupil of Strobl, Leschetizky an( ton Rubinstein ; début, 1890 ; A ica, 1893 ; toured with Leipzig I orch. ; lives Paris.

**Slo´per** (**Edw. Hugh**), **Lindsay**, don, 1826—1887 ; pianist, tea writer and composer.

**Small´wood**, **Wm.**, b. Kendal, I 1831—1897; organist ; writer composer.

**Smareglia** (smä-räl´-yä), **A.**, b. Istria, May 5, 1854 ; studied V and at the Milan Cons., gradu with a symph. work " *Eleano* prod. 6 operas, incl. " *Prez* (Milan, 1879), " *Bianca da Ce* (Milan, La Scala, 1882), " *Il V lo di Szigeth*" (Vienna, 1889, as *Vasall von Szigeth*," New 1890), and " *La Falena*" (V 1897.

**Smart**, (1) Sir **G.** (**Thos.**), Lo 1776—1867; noted conductor ; of Dupuis and Arnold ; knig 1811 ; cond. Phil. Soc., 181 (2) **Henry**, Dublin, 1778— bro. of above ; violinist ; leader ry Lane, 1812–21 ; piano-ma ture:. (3) **Henry**, London, Oc 1813—(blind) July 6, 1879 , son pupil of (2) ; studied with K( organist in London from 1836 ; opera "*Bertha*" (1855), many ( tas, etc.

**Smetana** (smä´-tä-nä), **Fr.** (**Bed** Leitomischl, Bohemia, 1824—in Prague, 1884 , noted composer

nist ; pupil of Proksch and Liszt ;
.8, organised a sch. at Prague ;
6–74, cond. Nat. Theatre Prague.
afness caused his resignation and
eternal ringing of one note in his
d brought on insanity. He made
s note the motif of a prophetic
iposition. C. a string-quartet, 7
ras, incl. *"Prodaná nevěsta"*
*The Bartered Bride"*), 1866 ; 9
iph. poems, incl. a cycle of 6
*Iá Vlast"* (*" My Country "*),
iph. of *" Triumph,"* etc.

h'ergell, **Wm.**, pianist, organist,
ter and composer, London, 1794.

h, (1) **Bd.** (**Bd. Schmidt**) (called
ather Smith"), Germany, ca.
o—London, 1708 ; ct. org.-build-
(2) **Robt.**, Cambridge, 1689—
8 ; acoustician. (3) **J. Chris-**
**her** (**Johann Chr. Schmidt**),
sbach, 1712—Bath, 1795 ; dram.
·r ver. (4) **Johann Stafford**,
acester, Engl., ca. 1750—Lon-
, 1836 ; organist and composer.
**Edw. Woodley**, 1775—1849,
vicar at Windsor. (6) **Geo.**
wnshend, Windsor, 1813—Here-
l, 1877 ; son of above ; composer.
**Montern**, bro. of above ; singer.
**Samuel**, b. Eton, 1821 ; bro. of
ve ; organist. (9) **John**, Cam-
lge, 1795—1861 ; composer and
f. (10) **Robt. Archibald**, Read-
, 1780—1829 ; composer and vio-
st. (11) **Alice Mary** (Mrs. Mead-
White), London, 1839—1884 ;
iposer. (12) **Sydney**, Dorchest-
Engl., 1839—London, 1889 ; pi-
st, teacher, writer, etc. (13) **Wil-**
**G.**, b. Elyria, Ohio, Aug. 19,
5 ; notable composer ; pupil of
o Singer, at Cincinnati ; at Ber-
1880–82, of Kiel, the Scharwen-
Neumann, Moszkowski and
f ; since 1882, lives in Cleveland
teacher of pf., voice and comp. ;
. numerous graceful pf.-pcs. and
gs, also *" Octave Studies "* and
er valuable technical works. (14)
rit, b. Hagerstown, Maryland
. **11**, 1859 ; graduate (M. A. and

Mus. Doc.) Hobart College, Geneva,
N. Y.; pupil of Stuttgart Cons.; then
of S. P. Warren, New York ; organist, Buffalo ; also studied with Eugene Thayer (org.), and W. H
Sherwood (pf.), and one year in Ber
lin with Haupt and Rohde ; then
organist, Albany ; since 1885, at the
South Ch., N. Y.; music-prof.; prof.
Union Theol. Seminary ; c. cantata
*" King David."* choruses, graceful
pf.-pcs. and songs.

**Smolian** (shmō'-lǐ-än), **Arthur,** b.
Riga, Dec. 3, 1856 ; pupil of Munich
Cons.; cond. at various theatres ;
teacher, Wiesbaden ; 1890, teacher
Carlsruhe Cons.; and critic ; compos-
er.

**Smyth, Ethel,** b. England ; c. text
and music of opera *" The Forest "*
(*Der Wald*), prod. Berlin, 1902, and
London, 1902.

**Snel** (sněl), **Jos. Fran.,** Brussels, 1793
—Koekelberg, near Brussels, 1861;
violinist, conductor and dram. composer.

**Snetzler** (shněts'-lěr), **John,** Passau,
1710—London, end of 18th cent.;
org.-builder, England.

**Snow,** (1) **Moses,** d. 1702 ; member
of the Chapel Royal. (2) **Valen-**
**tine,** d. 1772 ; English trumpeter in
Händel's works.

**Soáres, João.** Vide REBELLO.

**So'binof,** ——, favourite Russian
tenor at Petersburg.

**Sobolevsky** (sō-bō-lěf'-shkǐ), ——
prof. at St. Petersburg ; ed. Russian
folk-songs (1895).

**Södermann** (sä'-děr-män), **August**
**Johan,** Stockholm, 1832—1876;
theatre-conductor there ; pupil of
Hauptmann and Richter ; c. Swedish
operetta, a notable mass with orch.,
etc.

**Soffredini** (sôf-frě-dē'-nē), **Alfredo,**
from 1896, ed.-in-chief, Milan *"Gaz-*
*zetta Musicale";* prod. (text and
mus.) 2-act children's opera *" Il Pic-*
*colo Haydn "* (Pavia, 1893), etc.

**Sokolov** (sō'-kō-lôf), **Nicholas,** b.
Petersburg, 1858 ; pupil at the Cons.;

taught harm. in the Imp. Chapel; c. an elegy (op. 4), and intermezzo for orch., etc.

**Soldat** (zōl'-dät), **Marie** (Frau **Soldat-Roger**), (b. Graz, March 25, 1864; violinist; pupil of Pleiner and Pott, and of Joachim, 1889; m. Herr Roger (Vienna).

**Solié** (sōl-yā) (rightly **Soulier**), (1) **J. P.**, Nîmes, 1755—Paris, 1812; barytone; c. comic operas, many pop. (2) **Chas.**, son of above; conductor; prod. a comic opera (Nice, 1877).

**Solle** (zôl'-lĕ), **Fr.**, Zeulenroda, Thuringia, 1806 — 1884; cantor and writer.

**Soloviev** (or **Solowiew**) (sō'-lō-vēf), **Nicolai Feopometovitch**, b. Petrosavodsk, Russia, April 27 (May 9), 1846; pupil of N. J. Zaremba (theory), Imp. Cons. at Petersburg; since 1874 prof. there; also critic, editor and Councillor of State; c. comic opera "*Vakula, The Smith*" (Petersb., 1875), and grand opera "*Cordelia*" (Petersb., 1883, in German, Prague, 1890); finished Seroff's opera "*The Demon's Power*"; c. symph. picture, "*Russia and the Mongols*" (Moscow, 1882); prize chorus "*Prayer for Russia*" (Imp. Russ. Mus. Soc., 1876), cantata '*The Death of Samson*" (1870).

**Som'erset**, Lord **H. (Richard Chas.)**, b. Dec. 7, 1849; amateur composer.

**Som'ervell**, **Arthur**, b. Windermere, Engl.; pupil Berlin Hochschule and of Stanford and Parry, R.C.M.; c. mass, with orch. (Bach Choir, 1891), "*A Song of Praise*" (1891), "*The Forsaken Merman*" (Leeds Fest., 1895), "*The Power of Sound*" (1895), elegy for alto with orch., suite for small orch. "*In Arcady*," song cycle on Tennyson's "*Maude*," etc.

**Somis** (sō'-mēs), **Giov. Bat.**, Piedmont, 1676—Turin, 1763; violinist, teacher and conductor.

**Sommer** (zôm'-mĕr), (1) Dr. **Hans** (rightly **Hans Fr. Aug. Zincke**) (tsĭnk'-ĕ), b. Brunswick, July 20, 1837;

pupil of Meves and J. O. Gr... graduate, later prof. at Gött Univ.; from 1888 lived in Wei c. succ. opera "*Lorelei*" (Bruns 1891), 1-act "*Bühnenspiel*," *Foix*" (Munich, 1894), 1-act " *Meerman*" (Weimar, 1896), ". *zahl*" (1902). (2) **Karl**, sing ct.-opera, Vienna.

**Sonnleitner** (zôn'-līt-nĕr), (1) **Ch**... Szegedin, 1734—Vienna, 1786; of jurisprudence, Vienna; com... (2) **Jos.**, Vienna, 1765—1835; s above; 1827, discovered the fa 9th cent. Antiphonary of St. (in neume-notation. (3) **Ld.** Vienna, 1797 — 1873; nephe... above; devoted friend of Schub...

**Sontag** (zôn'-täkh), **Henriette trude Walpurgis**), Coblenz, 3, 1804—of cholera, Mexico, 17, 1854; famous colorature-s no, her voice taking e'' easily; d ter of two actors; operatic si... 1823 created von Weber's "... anthe."

**Sontheim** (zôn'-tīm), **H.**, b. B... hausen, Feb. 3, 1820; notable début Carlsruhe, 1839; 1872, sioned.

**Sor** (rightly **Sors**) (sôr), **Fdo.**, I... lona, 1778—Paris, 1839; guita... uoso and dram. composer.

**Sorge** (zôr'-gĕ), **G. Ands.**, M... bach, Schwarzburg, 1703 — L... stein, 1778; famous organist theorist; ct.-organist and com...

**Soriano**, (1) **Fran.** Vide SURIAN... **Soriano - Fuertes** (sō-rĭ-ä'-n ĕr'-tĕs), Don **Mariano**, Murcia —Madrid, 1880; son and pupil dir. royal chamber-mus. (1841); several zarzuelas, aiming to national opera; conductor and of historical works.

**Sormann** (zôr'-män), **Alfred (Ri... Gotthilf**), b. Danzig, May 16, pianist; pupil of R. Hochs... Berlin, and of Liszt; début 1889, ct.-pianist to Grand Du Mecklenburg-Strelitz; c. con... etc.

ies (soo-bĭ-ĕs), **Albert,** b. Paris,
y 10, 1846 ; mus.-historiographer
critic ; a lawyer, then pupil of Sa-
d and Bazin (harm. and comp.) at
Cons.; 1874 he revived the faus "*Almanach des spectacles,*
*n. Duchesne*"*;* for this the Aca-
nie, 1893, awarded him the Prix
rac ; 1876, critic for "*Le Soir,*"
ler name "*B. de Lomagne*"*;*
cer of public instruction, and Le-
n of Honour, also of the Russian
er Stanislas ; writer of valuable
orical works, etc.

re (soobr), **Etienne Jos.,** Liège,
3—1871; director and dram. comp.

aitty (soo-ĕt-tē'), **J. Jac.,** Fran-
an monk at Paris, the first to use
res for popular notation, 1665-78.

er (soo-yä). Vide SOLIÉ.

a (soo'-sä), **John Philip,** b.
shington. D. C., Nov. 6, 1856 ;
of a Spanish trombonist in the
S. Marine Corps band. Pupil of
n Esputa and G. F. Benkert
rm. and comp.) ; at 17 cond. of
velling theatrical troupes ; 1877,
inist in Offenbach's orch. in Amer-
; dir. "Philadelphia Church-choir
afore Co."; 1880–92, bandm.
S. Marine Corps ; resigned and
anised the military band bearing
own name, which has toured
erica and Europe with greatest
:. ; (1900), Paris, Exposition.
npiled, by Govt. order, "*National
riotic and Typical Airs of all Coun-
s*"*;* wrote instruction-books for
mpet and drum, and for vln. C. 7
ic operas incl. v. succ. "*El Capi-
,*" succ. (text and music) '*The
de Elect,*" "*The Charlatan*" and
*hris and the Wonderful Lamp,*"
mph. poem "*The Chariot Race*"
m ("*Ben Hur*"); 3 suites, "*The
t Days of Pompeii,*" "*Three Quo-
ons,*" and "*Sheridan's Ride*"*;*
many immensely succ. marches
ular throughout the world,
*Vashington Post,*" "*High School
ets,*" "*Stars and Stripes For-
-*" "*Imperial Edward,*" etc.

**Sovinsky** (sô-vĭn'-skĭ), **Albert (Czyli
Wojech),** Ladyzyn, Ukraine, 1803
(1805 ?)—Paris, March 5, 1880 ; pianist, teacher and dram. composer.

**Soyer** (swä-yä), **Berthe,** b. Chalon-
sur-Saône, May 12, 1877; contralto ;
pupil of Paris Cons., took 1st prize
Paris Cons., 1899 ; début same year
at Opéra as "Amneris."

**Spangenberg** (späng'-ĕn-bĕrkh), (1)
**Jn.,** Hardeisen, near Göttingen, 1484
—Eisleben, 1550 ; theorist and composer. (2) **Cyriak,** Nordhausen,
1528 — Strassburg, 1604 ; son of
above ; writer.

**Spark,** Dr. **Wm.,** Exeter, Engl., Oct.
28, 1823 — Leeds, June 16, 1897;
noted organist and editor ; wrote autobiography and memoirs; composer.

**Spataro** (spä-tä'-rō) (or **Spat'arus,
Spada'ro, Spada'rius),** **Giov.,** Bologna, ca. .1460 — 1541 ; conductor
and theorist.

**Spazier** (shpä-tsēr'), **Jn. Gl. K.,** Berlin, 1761—Leipzig, 1805 ; theorist
and composer.

**Speer** (shpär), **Daniel,** cantor at Waiblingen, 1692 ; composer.

**Speidel** (shpī'-dĕl), (1) **Konrad,** d.
Ulm, Jan. 29, 1880 ; singer and conductor. (2) **Wm.,** Ulm, 1826—
Stuttgart, 1899; son of above; pianist,
conductor and composer. (3) **Maria,** b. Stuttgart, Oct. 13, 1872 ;
daughter of above ; singer ; pupil of
Pollini and Nicklass-Kempner.

**Spengel** (shpĕng'-ĕl), **Julius H.,** b.
Hamburg, June 12, 1853 ; pupil of
Cologne Cons. and Berlin Hochschule, taught in Hamburg, and
studied with Gradener and Armbrust;
1878, cond. Cäcilienverein ; singing-
teacher and organist ; c. symph.,
'cello-sonata, etc.

**Spen'ser, Willard,** b. Cooperstown,
N. Y., July 7, 1856 ; self-taught ;
prod. v. succ. operettas, text and
music, "*The Little Tycoon*" (Philadelphia, 1886), and "*Princess Bonnie.*"

**Speyer (Speier)** (shpī'-ĕr), **Wilhelm,**
Frankfort, 1790—1878 ; violinist and
composer.

Spicker (shpĭk'-ĕr), **Max**, b. Königsberg, Prussia, Aug. 16, 1858 ; pupil
of Louis Köhler, then of Leipzig
Cons.; theatre conductor various
cities ; 1882–88, cond. "Beethoven
Männerchor," New York ; 1888–95
Dir. Brooklyn Cons.; since teacher
Nat. Cons., New York ; c. orch.
suite, cantata with orch., etc.

Spiering (shpē'-rĭng), **Theodor**, b.
St. Louis, Missouri, 1871 ; violinist ;
pupil of H. Schradieck, Cincinnati ;
then of Joachim, Berlin ; founder and
1st vln. "Spiering Quartet," Chicago.

Spies (shpēs), **Hermine**, Lohnberger
Foundry, near Weilburg, 1857—
Wiesbaden, 1893 ; concert-contralto.

Spiess (shpēs), (1) **Jn. Martin**, organist and composer (1745–61). (2)
**Meinard**, Honsolgen, Swabia, 1683
—Yrsee Monastery, ·1761 ; prior,
theorist and composer.

Spindler (shpĭnt'-lĕr), **Fritz**, b. Würz-
bach, near Lobenstein, Nov. 24,
1817 ; pianist ; studied mus. with
Fr. Schneider at Dessau ; from 1841,
lived in Dresden as teacher ; c. 3
symphs., pf.-concerto, v. pop. salon-
pcs., etc.

Spinelli (spĭ-nĕl'-lĭ), **Nicolà**, b. Turin, 1865 ; notable neo-Italian ; pupil
of Naples Cons.; 1890 took 2nd Sonzogno prize with 1-act opera "*Co-
billa*," Mascagni winning 1st prize ;
prod. v. succ. 3-act lyric drama "*A
Basso Porto*" (1894, New York,
1899), vide "Stories of the Operas."

Spin'ney, English family of musicians.
(1) **Thos. Edw.**, b. June 24, 1824 ;
pupil of Sir Henry Bishop ; organist St. Edmund's, Salisbury, and cond.
Orpheus Soc.; c. cantata, church-
mus., etc. (2) **Mattie** (Mrs. Bees-
ley), daughter of above ; pianist ;
pupil of Benedict, Bennett, and von
Bülow ; début, London, 1875 ; organist, at Banbury. Her four brothers, (3) **Eugene**, 1845—1867 ; 1862,
organist, Banbury. (4) **Frank**, 1850
—1888 ; organist, conductor and
composer. (5) **Walter**, 1852—1894 ;

organist various cities ; c. org.
etc. (6) Rev. **T. Herbert**, b.
13, 1857 ; pupil of Arnold
Bridge ; won harm.-prize, T
Coll., London, 1876 ; at 16 c
ist, Salisbury, later at Exeter
Oxford ; F.R.C.O.; 1882, ord
priest ; 1885, vicar, Burton-on-T
composer.

Spiridio (spē-rē'-dĭ-ō), **Bert**
monk, organist and composer,
berg, 1665–91.

Spirid'ion. Vide XYNDAS.

Spitta (shpĭt'-tä), (1) (**Julius**
**Philipp**, Wechold, near Hoya,
over, Dec. 27, 1841—Berlin, Ap
1894 ; teacher and prof. musica
tory ; wrote many essays and a
able life of J. S. Bach (2 vols.,
80), etc. (2) **Fr.**, b. Wittingen,
over, Jan. 10, 1852 ; bro. of a
prof. of theology, Strassburg U
ed. works of Schütz and pub.
able treatises.

Spof'forth, (1) **Reginald**, Notting
Southwell, 1769—Kensington,
c. glees, etc. (2) **Samuel**, 1
1864 ; bro. of above ; organist
composer.

Spohr (shpōr), **Ludwig** (in his
biography he calls himself **L**
Brunswick, April 5, 1784—C
Nov. 22, 1859 ; eminent violinis
conductor ; notable composer
teacher. Son of a physician wh
moved to Seesen, 1786 ; pupil o
mother, and at 5 studied with
menschneider (vln.) and Du
then with Kunisch, Hartung
Maucourt, Brunswick ; at 14
played a concerto of his own at 6
He became a member of the
Orch.; 1802 pupil of Fz. Eck,
he accompanied to St. Peters
1803, returned to the Ducal C
1804 toured with great succ. ;
leader Duke of Gotha's orch.
Dorette Scheidler (d. 1834), the
player and toured with her, 1807
1809. 1836 he m. the pianist
anne Pfeiffer (d. 1892) ; 1812,
brilliant concerts at Vienna, lead

e Th. an der Wien ; 1815, toured
uly (playing a concertante of his
'n with Paganini at Rome) ; 1817–
, opera-cond. at Frankfort ; prod.
re succ. opera "*Faust*"; 1820,
ited England with his wife, played
Philharm. Concerts, and prod.
ere two symphs.; introducing into
ngland the habit of conducting with
bâton. Gave concerts at Paris
th little succ. From 1822 ct.-cond.
Cassel ; 1857, retired for political
isons on a reduced pension. Dur-
g his period as a cond. he prod.
agner's "*Fliegende Holländer*"
842). and "*Tannhäuser*" (1853),
t could not overcome the oppo-
ion to a production of "*Lohen-
in.*" He soon recognised Wagner
the greatest living dramatic com-
ser. but did not care for Beethoven
Weber. He is among the first of
e second-best composers, his high-
: attainments being the opera "*Jes-
nda*" (Cassel, 1823), the oratorio
*Die Letzten Dinge*" (Cassel, 1826 ;
England as "*The Last Judg-
nt*"); the grand symph. "*Die
eihe der Töne*" ("*The Consecra-
n of Tone,*" 1832) and the clas-
vln.- concertos. His "*Violin-
hool*" (1831 in 3 parts), is a stand-
d. He c. 11 operas in all; dram.
ntata, "*Das Befreite Deutsch-
nd*"; a mass etc., with orch. 9
mphs. No 4 op. 86 in F ("*Weihe
Töne*"); No 6 op 116. G ("*His-
rical*", dedicated to the London
ilh Soc ) 7 op. 121. C ("*Irdisch-
und Göttliches im Menschen-
en*") for 2 orchs. 8 op. 137. G
n. (ded to the London Philharm.);
op. 143, B min. (*Die Jahreszeit-
*). 8 overtures and 15 vln.-con-
rtos No 8 (op. 47. in A min.,
*in modo d'una scena cantante*")
quartet-concerto ' for 2 vlns. vla.,
d cello with orch.; 2 concertantes
r 2 vlns. with orch., grande polo-
ise for vlns. with orch.. 2 clar.-
ncertos mucn chamber mus.
itobiogr (Cassel. 1860. 61 2 vols.);

Biogr. by Malibran (Frankfort, 1860);
by H. M. Schletterer (1881).

**Spontini** (spôn-tē´-nē), **Gasparo
(Luigi Pacifico)**, Majolati Ancone,
Nov. 14, 1774—Jan. 24 1851 noteworthy cond. and dram. composer,
Son of poor peasants who intended
him for the church, he ran away, and
an uncle. at San Vito, provided him
with teaching At 17 entered the
Cons. della Pietà de' Turchini at Naples. 1796 commissioned to write
an opera for the Teatro Argentina at
Rome. its director having heard some
of his church-mus. in Naples. he left
the Cons. without permission and
prod. succ. opera, "*I Puntigli delle
Donne*"; Piccinni secured his rein-
statement and gave him valuable advice. He prod. operas with succ. in
various cities and in Palermo, where
he was cond. to the Neapolitan court
which had fled before the French.
After having produced 16 light Italian operas. he went to Paris (1803),
where three successive failures and
a study of Mozart's works. led him
to change his style. After supporting himself as a singing-teacher he
won succ. with his substantial 1-act
opera "*Milton*" (Th. Feydeau, Nov.
27. 1804) the Empress Josephine. to
whom he had dedicated the score. appointed him "chamber-composer."
He c. a cantata "*L'eccelsa Gara,*"
celebrating the victory of Austerlitz.
The Empress's power secured a hearing for his opera "*La Vestale,*" which
after three years of delay and polish-
ing. was prod. with greatest succ. 1807;
by a unanimous verdict of the judges,
Méhul. Gossec and Grétry Napoleon's prize for the best dram work
of the decade was awarded to it. It
was followed with equal succ. by the
grand opera "*Fernand Cortez,*"
1809. 1810, dir. It. opera; dismissed for financial irregularity ;
1814 Louis XVIII. appointed him
ct.-composer He c. 2 stage-pieces
in glorification of the Restoration.
The opera "*Olympie*" was prod

1819 without succ., though when revised and prod. 1826 it prospered. 1820, he became ct.-composer and gen. mus.-dir. at Berlin; he prod. his old operas with succ., and c. the festival play "*Lalla Rukh*" (1821), remodelled as "*Nurmahal*" (1822); "*Alcidor*" (1825) and "*Agnes von Hohenstaufen*" (1829), none of which were widely succ. A period of violent jealousies and quarrels with the Intendant Brühl, and virulent intrigues, culminated after a score of stormy years in his being royally reprimanded, and finally driven out of the theatre by a hostile audience. He retired in 1841 on full pay. He went to Paris, then to Italy. 1844 the Pope gave him the rank and title of "Conte di Sant' Andrea"; he was a knight of the Prussian "Ordre pour le mérite." member of the Berlin Akademie (1839), and Paris Académie, and Dr. Phil., Halle Univ. Biog. by L. de Loménie (1841); Montanari (1851); Raoul-Rochette (1882).

**Spor'le** (rightly Burnett), **Nathan J.,** 1812—1853; English tenor and composer.

**Squire, Wm. Henry, b.** Ross, Herefordshire, Aug. 8, 1871; 'cellist; son and pupil of an amateur violinist; début at 7; won scholarship at the R. C. M., and studied with Powell and Parry; second début. 1891; c. 'cello-concerto.

**Stabile** (stä'-bē-lĕ), **Annibale,** d. Rome, ca. 1595; . conductor and composer.

**Stade** (shtä'-dĕ), (1) **H. Bd.,** Ettischleben, 1816—Arnstadt, 1882; organist and composer. (2) **Fr. Wm., b.** Halle, Aug. 25, 1817; organist, pupil of Fr. Schneider, Dessau; mus.-dir. and Dr. Phil. *h. c.* Jena Univ.; 1860–1891, ct.-organist and cond. at Altenburg; c. 2 symphs.; Festouvertüre, music to "*Orestes*"; cantatas, with orch.; choral works; vln.-sonata; "*Kindersonate*" (4 hands), etc. (3) **Dr. Fritz** (L. Rudolf), **b.** Sonders-

hausen, Jan. 8, 1844; pupil of and Richter, Leipzig, and te there; pub. an answer to Hans "*Vom Musikalisch-Schönen*," e

**Staden** (shtä'-dĕn), (1) **Jn.,** Nürn ca. 1579—1634; organist and poser. (2) **Sigismund Gl.,** so successor of above; c. "*Seele* the earliest extant German opera H. SCHUTZ' opera "*Dafne*").

**Stadler** (shtät'-lĕr), **Maximi** Melk, Lower Austria, 1748—Vi 1833; composer and writer.

**Stadlmayer** (shtät'-'l-mī-ĕr), **Jn.,** sing, Bavaria, 1560—Innsbruck, 1646; conductor and composer.

**Stadtfeldt** (shtät'-fĕlt). **Alex., V** baden, 1826—Brussels, 1853, d composer.

**Stagemann** (shtä'-gĕ-män), **Ma** Freienwalde-on-Oder, May 10, 1 pupil of Dresden Cons.; bar and "chamber-singer" at Han 1877, dir. of Königsberg Th.; 1 manager Leipzig City Th.

**Stag'gins, Nicholas,** d. 1705; lish composer and professor.

**Stagno** (stän'-yō), **Alberto,** Pale 1836—Genoa, 1897; tenor.

**Stahlknecht** (shtäl-k'nĕkht), two b ers, (1) **Ad.,** Warsaw, 1813—B 1887; violinist and dram. comp (2) **Julius,** Posen, 1817—B 1892; 'cellist royal orchestra.

**Stahmer-Andriessen** (shtä'-mĕ drēs-sĕn), **Pelagie** (now Greef-A Vienna, June 20, 1862; pupil of Cons., and of Frau Dreyschock prano in Neumann's troupe; 188 Leipzig town-theatre; 1890, m. a itect Ende; later m. Greef.

**Stainer** (or **Steiner**) (shtī-nĕr), **Ja** Absam, Tyrol, 1621—1683; inve and manufacturer of instrs. **Markus,** his brother, also vln.- vla.-maker.

**Stainer** (stä'-nĕr), Sir **John, Lor** June 6, 1840—Verona, April, 1 chorister at St. Paul's; studied Bayley (harm.) and Steggal (c and later Cooper (org.); 1854–6c ganist various places then Univ

ist at Oxford; (1859) Bac. Mus.,
1 (1865) Mus. Doc.; 1866, Exam-
r for mus. degrees; 1872–88, or-
aist of St. Paul's, resigning on
ount of his eyesight; 1876, prof.
org. and harm. Nat. Training
a. for Mus.; 1881, principal in
C. M.; 1883, again at Oxford;
32, Govt. Inspector of Mus. in
Training-Sch.; 1878, Chev. of
Legion of Honour; knighted,
38; 1889, prof. of mus. at Oxford
iv.; pub. treatises and (with Bar-
) a "*Dict. of Mus. Terms*," 1875;
oratorio "*Gideon*," cantatas "*The
ughter of Jairus*" (Worc. Fest.,
78), "*St. Mary Magdalene*"
loucester, 1883), and "*The Cruci-
ion*" (London, 1887), 4 services,

r, **Martha Greene** ("Patty"),
Cleveland, O.; pianist; pupil of
Bassett, there; lives there as con-
t pianist, organist and composer.

naty (stă-mä-tĕ), **Camille M.,**
me, 1811—Paris, 1870; pianist
d composer.

nitz (shtä'-mĭts), (1) **Jn. K.,**
utsch - Brod., Bohemia, 1717—
annheim, 1761; notable violinist
d composer. (2) **Anton Thad-
us,** Deutsch-Brod., 1721—Altbunz-
g, 1768; bro. of above; canon;
llist, Mannheim. (3) **K.,** Mann-
m, 1746—Jena, 1801; violinist
d viole d'amour - performer, con-
ctor and composer. (4) **Anton,**
annheim, 1753—Paris, bro. of above;
linist and composer.

'ford, **Chas. Villiers,** b. Dublin,
pt. 30, 1852; pianist and notable
mposer; pupil of Sir Robt. Stew-
and Arthur O'Leary (comp.), and
nst Pauer (pf.), London; 1870 won
an scholarship at Queen's Coll.,
mbridge; 1873–92, organist of
inity Coll., Cambridge, also cond.
iv. Mus. Soc. (till 1893); 1875-
studied comp. with Reinecke at
ipzig, and Kiel, Berlin. M.A.,
ntab., 1878; Mus. Doc., Oxford,
3, Cambridge, 1888; 1883, prof.

of comp. and cond., R.C.M.; 1885
cond. Bach Choir; 1887, prof. of
Mus. at Cambridge; 1897, cond.
Leeds Philh. Soc. C. operas, "*The
Veiled Prophet of Khorassan*" (Han-
over, 1881); "*Savonarola*" (Ham-
burg, 1884); "*The Canterbury Pil-
grims*" (London, Covent Garden,
1884); v. succ. "*Shamus O'Brien*"
(London, 1896); "*Much Ado about
Nothing*" (Covent Garden, 1901,
Leipzig, 1902); incid. mus.; crato-
rio, "*The Resurrection*" (1875);
"*The Three Holy Children*" (Bir-
mingham, 1885); Psalm 96 (1877);
"*Elegiac Ode*" (Norwich, 1884);
"*The Revenge*" (Leeds, 1886);
"*Jubilee Ode*" (1887), etc. "*The
Bard*" (Cardiff, 1895); "*Phaudrig
Crochoore*" (Norwich, 1896); re-
qüiem, 3 Morning and Evening
Services; a Communion Service, etc.;
5 symphs. "*Elegiac*," in D min.
(No. 3) "*Irish*," (No. 4) "*Thro'
Youth to Strife, Thro' Death to
Life*"; and No. 5 "*L'allegro ed il
penseroso*"; 2 overtures, a pf.-con-
certo; "*Irish Rhapsody*" (1902), etc.

**Stange** (shtäng'-ĕ), **Hermann,** b. Kiel,
Dec. 19, 1835; pupil of Leipzig Cons.;
organist at Rossal College, Engl.;
since 1878, mus.-dir., and since 1887
prof. Kiel Univ.

**Stan'hope, Chas.,** Third Earl of.
1753—London, 1816; writer.

**Stan'ley,** (1) (**Chas.**) **John,** London,
1713—1786; organist and conduct-
or. (2) **Albert Augustus,** b. Man-
ville, Rhode Island, May 25, 1851;
studied in Providence, and at Leipzig; organist, Providence; 1888,
prof. of mus. Univ. of Michigan. C.
"*The City of Freedom*," ode, with
orch. (Boston, 1883); Psalm 21 (Providence, 1892), and Commemoration
Ode "*Chorus triumphalis*," with
orch; symph. "*The Awakening of
the Soul*"; symph. poem "*Altis*,"
etc.

**Stans'burg, Geo. F.,** Bristol, 1800—
1845; pianist, viol'nist, flutist, singer
and composer.

**Starck, Ingeborg.** Vide BRONSART.

**Stark** (shtärk), **L.,** Munich. 1831—Stuttgart, 1884 ; teacher. editor and composer.

**Starke** (shtärk'-ĕ), **Fr.,** Elsterwerda, 1774—Döbling, near Vienna, 1835 ; bandm., writer and composer.

**Stasny** (shtäs'-nē), (1) **L.,** Prague, 1823 — Frankfort. 1883 ; conductor and dram. composer. (2) Vide STIASTNY.

**Staudigl** (shtow'-dēkh-'l) (1) **Josef,** Wöllersdorf, Lower Austria, 1807—(insane), Michaelbeuerngrund, near Vienna, 1861 ; bass and ct.-conductor. (2) **Josef,** b. Vienna, March 18, 1850 ; son of above, barytone; pupil of Rokitansky at the Cons.; chamber-singer to the Grand Duke at Carlsruhe and a member of the ct.-opera. His wife (3) **Gisela,** singer ; pupil of Marchesi, 1899 Wiesbaden ct.-opera.

**Stavenhagen** (shtä'-fĕn-hä-gĕn), (1) **Bd.,** b. Griez, Reuss, Nov. 24, 1862; pianist ; pupil of Kiel, at the Meisterschule, and of Rudorff. at the Hochschule, Berlin, 1880, won the Mendelssohn prize for pf.; pupil of Liszt, 1885, toured Europe with succ. and the U. S. (1894-95) ; 1890. ct.-pianist and ct.-conductor at Weimar ; Knight of the White Falcon order, from 1898 ct.-cond. at Munich, c. pf.-pcs. (2) **S. Denis Agnes,** b. Winsen, Sept. 3, 1862 ; soprano ; pupil of Frau Prof. Schultzen and Frau Jachmann-Wagner, chamber-singer.

**Stcherbatcheff** (stchĕr'-bät-chĕf), **Nicolas de,** b. Russia, Aug. 24, 1853 ; prominent figure in the neo-Russian sch.; c. " *Deux idylles pour orchestre* "; ' *Féeries et pantomimes,*" " *Mosaique, album pittoresque,*" etc., for pf.; songs " *Au soir tombant,*" etc.

**Stecker** (shtĕk'-ĕr), **K.,** b. Kosmanos, Bohemia, Jan. 22. 1861, pupil of Prague Org.-Sch.; 1885-89 teacher of org. there; then prof. of cpt., and history at the Cons., from 1888 also

lecturer at the Univ.; pub. trea c a Missa solemnis, etc

**Steffani** (stĕf-fä'-nē), Abbate **Ag no,** Castelfranco, Venetia, 1 Frankfort-on-Main. 1730 ; em composer of daring originality great power both in instrument and general construction, ct. chamber-musician and ct.-orga prod. 20 operas.

**Steffens** (shtĕf'-fĕns), **Julius,** Star Pomerania. 1831—Wiesbaden, 'cellist and composer.

**Steffkins,** (1) **Theodore,** prof. and viol. in London. 1672; his b er (2) **Dietrich** was in the ct.-l 1641, (3) **Fr.,** and (4) **Chr.,** so (1) ; violinists.

**Steggall,** (1) **Chas.,** London, Ju 1826 ; pupil of Bennett, R. A 1851; prof. of org. and harm. t Mus. Bac. and Mus. Doc., Cambr from 1864, organist Lincoln's Chapel ; wrote method for org. colls., and c. Psalms 105, an with orch. services, etc. (2) **R nald,** b. London. April 7, 1867 and asst.-organist of above ; p R.A.M.; from 1895. prof. of there ; c. mass with orch. and or " *Festival Evening Service* " orch., a symph., 3 overtures, etc

**Stegmann** (stäkh'-män), **K, Da** Dresden. 1751—Bonn, 1826; t cond. and dram. composer.

**Stegmayer** (shtäkh'-mī-ĕr), **Fd., V** na, 1803—1863 ; conductor, sin teacher and composer.

**Stehle** (shtä'-lĕ), **Gv. Ed.,** b. S hausen, Würtemberg. Feb. 17, 1 cond. at St. Gallen Cath.; c. syr tone-picture " *Saul,*" for org.

**Steibelt** (shtī'-bĕlt) **Daniel,** Be 1765—St. Petersburg 1823 ; v. unvirtuous virtuoso. Under pat age of the Crown Prince, a pup Kirnberger, early début; 1790, vourite pianist. teacher and c poser at Paris, prod. v. succ. o " *Roméo et Juliette* " (1793). seems to have suffered from klc mania and general dishonesty w with his insolence, snobbery, and his debts, forced him to leave Paris in 1797, for London, where he was equally succ.; the "*Storm Rondo*" (or the finale of his 3rd concerto "*L'Orage, précédé d'un rondeau pastoral*"), rivalling the notorious "*Battle of Prague*," by Koczwara. 1799, he toured Germany, challenging Beethoven at Vienna with disastrous results. He carried Haydn's "*Creation*" back to Paris and prod. it, 1800, with great succ., with himself as cembalist; but had to leave Paris again, remaining in London, until 1805, when he revisited Paris for 3 years; 1808 toured and settled in Petersburg; 1810, Imp. ct. - cond. and cond. of French Opera; here prod. 2 new operas, as well as earlier ones. In spite of his odious personality, his virtuosity was remarkable, and his compositions show much originality in modulation and scoring. He wrote a pop. pf.-method; c. 6 operas, 5 ballets, and much pianomus., including 50 études, many programme - pcs. of extraordinary vogue.

ein (shtīn), (1) **Jn. Andreas**, Heidesheim, Palatinate, 1728—Augsburg, 1792; inv. "German (Viennese) pf.-action"; organist and famous pf.-maker. Succeeded by son (2) **Matthäus Andreas** (Augsburg, 1776—Vienna, 1842), who 1802 set up for himself in Vienna. (3) **Maria Anna** or **Nanette Streicher**), Augsburg, 1769—Vienna, 1835; daughter of (1); a devoted friend of Beethoven; also a manager of the pf.-factory. Her son (4) **Jn. Bapt.** (b. Vienna, 1795), was her successor. (5) **Fr.**, Augsburg, 1781—(of consumption) Vienna, 1808; bro. of above; prominent pianist. (6) **Karoline** (née **Haar**), pianist and teacher. (7) **K. Andreas**, Vienna, 1797—1863; son and successor of (2); pupil of Förster, t.-pf.-maker and composer. (8) **Eduard**, Kleinschirma, Saxony, 1818—Sondershausen, 1864; ct. - con-

ductor and composer. (9) **Theodor**, b. Altona, 1819; pianist; début at 12; since 1872, pf.-prof. Petersburg Cons. (10) **Gertrude May**, b. Albany, U. S. A.; pupil C. A. White; 1891, toured with the Juch Opera Co.; prominent American contralto; 1901 m. L. A. Bailey.

**Steinbach** (shtīn'-bäkh), (1) **Emil**, b. Lengenrieden, Baden, Nov. 14, 1849; pupil Leipzig Cons.; 1877, cond. Mayence town-orch; c. orch. and chamber-mus., etc. (2) **Fritz**, b. Grünsfeld, Baden, June 17, 1855; bro. and pupil of above; also pupil Leipzig Cons.; won Mozart Scholarship; 1880–86, 2nd cond. at Mayence; since 1886 ct.-cond. Meiningen; pub. a septet, 'cello-sonata, songs.

**Steindel** (shtīn'-děl), (1) **Bruno**, b. Zwickau, Saxony, ca. 1864; 1st 'cello, Berlin Philh.; later in the Chicago Orch. (2) **Bruno**, b. München-Gladbach, Germany, 1890; pianist; son and pupil of mus.-dir. in that town; played in public at 6; has played since in Germany and London.

**Steiner.** Vide STAINER.

**Steingräber** (shtīn'-gräp-ěr), **Theodor**, b. Neustadt-on-the-Orla, Jan. 25, 1830; founder of Hanover mus.-pub. firm; since 1890 in Leipzig; wrote a pf.-method under the pseud. "**Gustav Damm.**"

**Stein'way & Sons**, firm of pf.-makers, New York and Hamburg; founded by (1) **H. Engelhard Steinweg** (shtīn'-vākh), Wolfshagen, Harz, 1797—New York, 1871; journeyman org.-builder, Seesen, ca. 1820; he worked at night on his first piano, which combined the good points of Old English and recent German instrs.; it made immediate succ.; after the Revolution of 1848, he emigrated to New York in 1850 with four sons, (2) **Chas.**, Seesen, 1829—1865. (3) **H.**, Seesen, 1829—New York, 1865. (4) **Wm.**, Seesen, 1836—New York, 1896; (5) **Albert**, Seesen, 1840—

New York, 1877 ; leaving the business in charge of (6) **Theodor** (Seesen, 1825—Brunswick, 1889). Father and sons worked in different
factories till 1853, when they combined as Steinway & Sons. In 1865
Theodor, who had moved to Brunswick, sold the business to the firm
Grotrian, Helferich & Schulz, Theodor Steinwegs Nachfolger (i. e. " successors ") (v. STEINWEG), and became a partner in the N. Y. firm,
now the largest of its kind in the
world.

**Steinweg,** Original form of " Steinway " (q. v. No. 6).

**Stelzner** (shtĕlts'-nĕr), Dr. **Alfred,** b.
Wiesbaden ; lives in Dresden ; inv.
the violotta and cellone, etc. (v.
D.D.) ; they were used in the orch. of
his fairy opera " *Rübezahl* " (Dresden, 1902). " He was diffident as a
performer, but his compositions for
the 'cello must render his name immortal, for though the list of his
works only amount to 13, the originality and purity of them entitle him
to rank among the very first writers.
He is often called the Beethoven of the
violoncello, nor can that be considered too high praise" (George Herbert).

**Ste'phens,** (1) Dr. **John,** d. 1780 ; organist Salisbury Cath.; composer.
(2) **Catherine,** London, 1791 (94?)
—1882 ; opera and concert-soprano.
(3) **Chas. Edw.,** London, 1821—
1892 ; nephew of above ; pianist ;
teacher, organist and composer.

**Sterkel** (shtĕr'-kĕl), Abbé **Jn. Fz. X.,**
Würzburg, 1750—Mayence, 1817 ;
conductor, organist and composer.

**Ster'ling,** (1) **Antoinette,** b. Ster-
lingville, N. Y., Jan. 23, 1850 ; concert and oratorio contralto, range
*e* flat—*f''* (v. PITCH, D. D.) ; pupil
of Mme. Marchesi, Viardot-Garcia
and Manuel Garcia ; sang for a time
in Henry Ward Beecher's Ch., at
Brooklyn ; from 1873, London ; 1875,
m. John MacKinlay. (2) **Win-
throp S.,** b. Cincinnati, 1859 ; pupil

of Coll. of Mus. and Leipzig Cons
also under R. Hoffman (comp.) a
Frau Unger-Haupt (voice), later
London under Turpin, Behnke a
Shakespeare ; organist West Lond
Tabernacle ; from 1887, prof. Ci
cinnati Coll. of Mus.

**Stern** (shtĕrn), (1) **G. Fr. Théophi**
Strassburg, 1803 — 1886 ; organ
and composer. (2) **Julius,** Bresla
1820—Berlin, 1883 ; cond., teach
and composer. (3) **Margaret**
(née **Herr**), b. Dresden, Nov. 2
1857 ; pianist ; pupil of Karl Krage
Liszt and Frau Schumann ; 1881, s
m. the poet Dr. Adolph Stern, Dre
den. (4) **Leo,** b. Brighton, Eng
1870 ; 'cellist ; pupil of Piatti and
Klengel and Davidoff, Leipzig ; fi
tour, 1888 (with Piatti) ; made su
tours in France ; 1897, America ;
'cello pieces, etc.

**Sternberg** (stĕrn'-bĕrkh), **Constant
(Ivanovitch),** Edler **von,** b.
Petersburg, July 9, 1852 ; piani
pupil of Leipzig Cons., Berlin Al
demie, and of Liszt ; conductor
rious churches ; from 1877, tou
widely ; 1880, United States ; fr
1890, dir. " Sternberg Sch. of Mus
Philadelphia ; c. 2 pf.-trios, " *Dan
cosaques* " for vln., 'cello-fantas
etc.

**Ste'vens,** (1) **Richard J. Samu**
London, 1757—1837 ; organist, cc
poser and prof. (2) **Kitty.** V
STEPHENS (2).

**Ste'venson,** (1) Sir **J. Andrew,** D
lin, ca. 1762—1833 ; Mus. Doc.;
Irish operas ; son of (2) **John** (
linist in the State-Band at Dubl
(3) **E. Irenaeus.** Vide PRIME-ST
ENSON.

**Stew'art,** Sir **Robt. Prescott,** D
lin, 1825—1894 ; organist, profess
conductor, and composer.

**Stiastny** (**Stastný**) (sht'yäst'-nē),
**Bd. Wenzel,** Prague, 1760—18
'cellist, professor and composer.
**Fz. Jn.,** Prague, 1764—Mannhe
ca. 1820 ; bro. and pupil of abo
'cello-virtuoso and composer.

h (stĭkh), **Jan Václav** (or **Jn.
enzel**) (Italianised as "**Giovan-
Punto**"), Zchuzicz, Bohemia, 1748
Prague, 1803 ; eminent horn-virtu-
o, writer and composer.

hl (shtēl), (1) **H. (Fz. Daniel)**,
beck, 1829—Reval, 1886 ; organ-
conductor and dram. composer.
**K. Jn. Chp.**, b. Lübeck, 1826 ;
o. of above ; organist and compos-
; from 1878, conductor and critic
beck ; and mus.-custodian in the
rary ; pub. historical works on
beck.

hle (shtē′-lĕ), **L. Maximilian**
d., b. Frankfort, Aug. 19, 1850 ;
olinist ; pupil of Vieuxtemps, Her-
nn and Joachim ; lives at Basel.

elli (rightly **G. Stiegele**) (stĭ-gĕl′-
or shtē′-gĕ-lĕ), **Giorgio**, Ingstet-
n, 1819—at his villa n. Monza,
aly, 1868 ; tenor and composer.

np′son, **Jas.**, b. Lincoln, 1820 ;
ganist various churches in Engl.;
of. of mus. Blind Inst.; editor, or-
nist and composer.

′ling, **Elizabeth**, Greenwich, 1819
London, 1895 ; organist and com-
oser.

bäus (shtō′-bā-oos), **Jn.**, Graudenz,
. Prussia, 1580—Königsberg, 1646;
ss, conductor and composer.

ckhausen (shtôk′-how-zĕn), (1)
z., 1792—1868 ; harpist and com-
oser. His wife (2) **Margarethe**
ée Schmuck), Gebweiler, 1803—
olmar, 1877; pupil of Cartruffo,
aris ; concert-soprano ; toured with
er husband. (3) **Julius**, b. Paris,
uly 22, 1826 ; barytone and eminent
acher ; son of above ; pupil of
aris Cons. and of Manuel Garcia ;
cc. concert-singer ; 1862–67, cond.
hilh. Concerts and Singakademie,
Hamburg ; 1869–70, chamber-
nger at Stuttgart ; 1878–79 and
382–98, teacher of singing, Hoch
ons., Frankfort ; since private
acher ; pub. a Method. (4) **Fz.**,
Gebweiler, Jan. 30, 1839 ; pupil of
lkan and of Leipzig Cons.; 1868–
9, cond. at Strassburg ; from 1871,

teacher Strassburg Cons.; 1892, R.
Prof.

**Stojowski** (stō-yôf′-shkĭ), **Sigismund**,
b. Strelce, Poland, May 2, 1870 ; pianist ; pupil of L. Zelenski at Cracow, and at Paris Cons., winning 1st
prizes for pf. and comp.; studied
with Paderewski ; lives in Paris, as
teacher ; comp. pf.-concerto, suite
and variations for orch., songs, pf.-
pcs., etc.

**Stokes, Chas.**, b. 1784, Engl.; organist, pianist, teacher, composer and
theorist.

**Stoltz**, (1) **Rosine** (rightly **Victorine
Nöb**) (shtôlts or năp), Paris, Feb. 13,
1815—(?) ; pupil of Choron's Sch.;
mezzo-soprano ; 1837–47, Gr. Opéra,
Paris ; other stage-names "**Mme.
Ternaux**," "**Mlle. Héloise**,"
"**Rose Niva**" ; m. successively a
baron and 2 princes ; c. 6 songs. (2)
**Therese**, Trieste, 1838 ?—Milan,
1902 ; soprano ; début, La Scala,
1865 ; created "*Aïda*" in Italy ; intimate friend of Verdi ; married after
1875 and retired.

**Stoltzer** (shtôlts′-ĕr), **Thos.**, Silesia,
ca. 1490—Ofen, 1526 ; ct.-conductor
and composer.

**Stölz(e)l** (shtĕlts′-ĕl), **Gf. H.**, Grün-
städtl, Saxony, 1690—Gotha, 1749 ;
ct.-conductor and dram. composer.

**Stolzenberg** (shtôl′-tsĕn-bĕrkh), **Benno**, b. Königsberg, Feb. 25, 1829 ;
tenor ; pupil of Mantius and H.
Dorn ; début, Königsberg, 1852 ;
dir. Danzig City Th.; teacher, Berlin ; 1885, Cologne Cons.; from 1896,
dir. of a vocal sch. at Berlin.

**Stöpel** (shtā′-pĕl), **Fz. (David Chp.)**,
Oberheldrungen, Saxony, 1794—
Paris, 1836 ; theorist.

**Sto′nard, Wm.**, d. 1630 ; organist
and composer at Oxford.

**Stör** (shtär), **K.**, Stolberg, Harz, 1814
—Weimar, 1889 ; violinist, cond.
and dram. composer.

**Sto′race**, (1) **Stephen**, London, 1763
—(of gout) 1796, prod. 18 stage-
works; son and pupil of (2) **Stefano
S.**, an Italian double-bass-player,

(3) **Anna Selina** (1766—1817), famous colorature-sopranc; daughter and pupil of (2); sang in public at 8; then début, Florence, 1780; created " Susanna " in Mozart's " *Figaro*."

**Storch** (stôrkh), **M. Anton**, Vienna, 1813—1888; conductor and composer.

**Stöwe** (shtä'-vĕ), **Gv.**, Potsdam, 1835—1891; dir. and composer.

**Stradella** (strä-dĕl'-lä), **Alessandro,** probably Naples or Venice, ca. 1645 —Genoa, after 1681 (the date of his last cantata); important Italian composer, of whom little is actually known, though he is the hero of an extraordinarily melodramatic legend of jealous nobility, paid assassins, and love pursued. In a work by Bonnet-Bourdelot (1715), it is said that his name was Stradel and being engaged to write an opera for Venice, he eloped with the mistress of a nobleman who sent paid *bravi* to assassinate him in Rome. These men were overcome by the beauty of an oratorio of his and warned him of his danger. He fled to Turin with the woman who passed for his wife, and after being followed here and there, and recovering from numerous wounds, was finally slain in Genoa. Flotow made an opera of this story, in which there is much that is incredible. **S.** was also credited with being a singer and poet, and a wonderful harpist. In any case, 148 of his works exist in MS. in the Modena Library, and others elsewhere, incl. 8 oratorios, many cantatas, madrigals, duets, etc. The church-aria " *Pietà, Signore*," and the arias " *O del mio dolce ardor*" and " *Se i miei sospiri*," are probably wrongly attributed to him. Monographs by P. Richard, " A. Stradella " (1866), and Calelane.

**Stradivari (Stradivarius)** (sträd-Y-vä'-rē, or vä'-rÝ-oos), (1) **Antonio,** Cremona, 1649 (1650 ?)—Dec. 17 (18 ?), 1737; maker of vlns., vlas., 'cellos, etc., who established a type and pro-

portion never improved ; his to: also supreme among vlns. (witl possible exception of those of Guarneri) ; he probably worked Niccolò Amati, 1667—79; 1680 purchased the house in which workshop thereafter was situa 1700–25, is his best period, bu worked to 1736; his label reads ' tonius Stradivarius Cremone Fecit Anno . . . (A † S)." his eleven children, 2 sons, (2) **F** (1671—1743) and (3) **Omobono** ( —1742), were his assistants. M graphs, by Lombardini (1872), (1856) ; Wasielewski, and Ri ers.

**Straeten, van der.** Vide VANI STRAETEN.

**Strakosch** (shträ'-kôsh), (1) **Mo**r Lemberg, Galicia, 1825 (1830 Paris, Oct. 9, 1887 ; pianist and presario ; c. operas ; teacher of lina, and husband of Carlotta, P (2) **Max,** d. New York, 1892 ; of above and equally famous as presario. (3) **Phoebe ;** sopra niece of above ; début in op Trieste, 1896; has sung at Co Garden, Met. Op., etc.

**Stratton, Geo. W.**, Swanzey, N. U. S. A.—Berlin, 1901 ; lived Bos as composer.

**Straube** (strow'-bĕ), **C. ;** pupil of I mann, Rufer, and A. Becker ; 1 organist Thomaskirche (vice Piatti).

**Strauss** (shtrows), (1) **Jos.**, Brü 1793—Carlsruhe, Dec. 1 (2 ?), 18 violinist, mus.-director, ct.-cond or ; c. operas. (2) **Jn.** (Sr.), Vier March 14, 1804—(of scarlet fe Sept. 25, 1849, " The Father of Waltz " ; son of proprietor of a l and dance-hall ; conductor and c poser of 152 waltzes all more or famous. (3) **Jn.** (Jr.), Vienna, ( 25, 1825 — June 3, 1899 ; " Waltz-King "; son of above, who posed the mus. tastes of the th sons, for whom the mother secu secret instruction. In 1844 cond or of court - balls and very succ. orch. concerts. He had c. a waltz at 6, and his later comps. eclipsed the success of those of his father, after whose death he united the two orchestras. 1862, he m. the singer Henriette Treffz (d. 1878), and later the singer Angelica Dittrich ; c. 400 pcs. of dance-music ; his waltzes "*The beautiful blue Danube,*" "*Künstlerleben,*" "*Wiener Blut,*" "*The 1001 Nights,*" "*Wine, Women and Song,*" etc., are dance-rhapsodies whose verve and colour have deserved and won the highest praise of severe musicians. His light operas rival his waltzes in charm and succ. and incl. the v. succ. "*Die Fledermaus*" ('74). (4) **Jos.**, Vienna, April 25, 1827—July 22, 1870; bro. of above, during whose illness in 1853 he served as cond.; later formed an orch. of his own and learned the vln.; on a tour to Warsaw he was maltreated by Russian officers for whom he had refused to play, and died in the arms of his wife (whom he had m. in 1857) ; he c. 283 dances. (5) **Eduard**, b. Vienna, Feb. 14, 1835 ; bro. and succ. of Johann as cond. of the ct.-balls and orch.; took his orch. to America 1892 and 1900 ; c. dance-mus. (6) **Ludwig**, b. Pressburg, March 28, 1835—Cambridge, Engl., 1899 ; violinist. (7) **Victor von**, Royal opera conductor, Berlin, 1902. (8) **Richard**, b. Munich, June 11, 1864 ; composer ; daring and brilliant musical adventurer ; son of (8) **Fz. S.** (chamber-mus. and horn-player) ; studied also with W. Meyer. At 4

he c. a polka. He took a regular Gymnasium course 1874–82, and spent two years at the univ. At 17 his first symph. was prod. by Levi ; his "*Serenade*" for 13 wind-instrs. had much succ. with the Meiningen orch. under von Bülow, to whom **S.** became asst., and (1885) successor as ct.-mus. dir. at Meiningen ; 1886, 3rd cond. at Munich ; 1889, ct.-cond. at Weimar under Lassen; 1894, cond. at the ct.-opera, Munich, also 1894, cond. Berlin Philh., and from 1898, cond. at Berlin Royal Opera. He m. the soprano, Pauline de Ahna, who created "Freihilde" in his opera "*Guntram*" (Weimar, 1894, Munich, '95). His 1-act opera "*Feuersnoth*" ("Fire-Famine"), libretto by Wolzogens, was prod. Dresden, Nov. 21, 1901, with much success. He has also cond. with great succ. in various cities. C. symph. op. 12 ; symphonic fantasie "*Aus Italien,*" "*Wanderers Sturmlied*" (Goethe), for 6-part chorus, and full orch.; tone - poems, "*Don Juan,*" op. 20 ; "*Macbeth,*" op. 23; "*Tod und Verklärung,*" op. 24, the symph. poems "*Also sprach Zarathustra*" (after Nietzsche),"*Ein Heldenleben*" (op. 40), and "*Don Quixote*"; op. 28, Orchester-Rondo "*Till Eulenspiegel's lustige Streiche*"; chamber-mus.; vln.-concerto ; 5 "*Stimmungsbilder*" for pf.; concerto for Waldhorn ; "*Enoch Arden,*" melodrama for pf. and recitation, and songs. 16-part *a cappella* chorus "*Der Abend*" (1902), ballad for chorus and orch. "*Taillefer*" (1902). Biog. by Dr. Arthur Seidl (Prague).

## Richard Strauss.

### By James Huneker

THAT Richard Strauss was the son of the famous horn-player, may explain his predilection for the beautiful instrument. ¶At Meiningen he met Alexander Ritter, a pupil of Wagner, and this friendship, with Von Bülow's daily coaching, decided Richard Strauss's tendency in

art. He became a composer of the future, a man of the new school.
travelled much—he went to Greece, Italy, and Egypt for incipient
trouble—and on " guesting " tours, on which he was received with
thusiasm, for he is a modern conductor in all the implications of the ph
A man of good physique, Scandinavian in appearance, Strauss is w
cultured and well read in classical and modern literature. ¶In music h
true descendant of Berlioz, Liszt, and Wagner, though early in his care
showed marked traces of a devotion to Brahms. This is more noticeal
his piano and orchestra *Burleske in D minor*, in the solo sonata and in
" *Wanderer's Sturmlied*," *opus 14*, for six-voiced chorus and orche
But the Richard Strauss we know to-day stands for all that is revolutic
in the art. ¶He has in his symphonic forms pushed to the verge o
sublime—or the ridiculous,—or both—the poetic programme ( Vide D.
"program music "). His " *Don Juan*," "*Macbeth*," "*Death and T.
figuration*," "*Till Eulenspiegel's Merry Pranks*," " *Thus Spake Zara
tra*," " *Don Quixote*," and " *Ein Heldenleben* " are tokens of lal
almost Balzacian in their intensity. An emotional strenuousness, a ma
lous mastery of the orchestral apparatus, an abnormal colour and rhyt
sense, combined with poetic feeling, bizarre, even grotesque methods o
terance, an utter defiance of formalism either classic or romantic, an
thematic invention not commensurate with his other gifts—all these c
ties jumbled in amazing juxtaposition and flavoured by a powerful indi
ality, easily made Richard Strauss the leader of the New German School
a formidable figure in the musical arena. ¶Since his flaming utteranc
" *Don Quixote*" and " *A Hero's Career* " the faith of some of his
ardent disciples has been rudely shaken. " Either retreat or madness
the critical cry, and Strauss is not a man to be moved by prayer or ass
So we find his two new solos for barytone and orchestra, sung at the Le
Rhine Festival, June, 1900, in Aix-la-chapelle, more eccentric than
¶A brilliant composer, a strikingly intellectual man, Richard Strauss to
may be fairly called the leader of the musical Decadence. As a song-w
his various collections have met with the greatest success, for he has a h
method of welding music and poem into a perfect, if somewhat start
whole. Form he abandons utterly, striving to capture the idea as he
ceives it, in its full bloom. *Opera* 10, 15, 17, 127, 29, 32, are favour
the newer songs are very difficult and almost cryptic in sentiment and ex
tion. Richard Strauss is the greatest living master of the orchestra.

---

**Streabbog.** Vide GOBBAERTS.
**Street** (shtrāt), **G. Ernest,** b. of
French parents, Vienna. 1854 ; pupil

of Bizet and Damcke, Paris ;
there ; since 1898, of " *L'Écla*
c. operettas, 1-act mimod

*ides*" (Op.-Com., 1894), 3-act
era "*Mignonette*," parody of
omas's "*Mignon*" (1896), ballet,
*Scaramouche*" with Messager, 1891,

*cher* (shtrī'-khĕr), (1) **Jn. Andre-**
, Stuttgart, 1761—Vienna, 1833;
no-maker and professor; 1793 inv.
pf.-action which drops the ham-
r from above; succeeded 1832 by
son (2) **Jn. Bapt.**, 1794—1871,
o was succeeded by his son (3)
nil.

*ezki* (strĕ-lĕt'-shkĭ), **Anton** (pen-
me of a Mr. **Burnand** (?)), b.
oydon, Engl., Dec. 5, 1859; pupil
Leipzig Cons., and of Frau Schu-
nn; c. popular songs, and pf.-
s.

*pponi*. Vide VERDI.

*ggio* (strĭd'-jō), **Ales.**, b. Mantua,
, 1535, lutenist, composer and
aductor.

*nasacchi* (strē-nä-säk'-kē), **Regi-**
, Ostiglia, near Mantua, 1764—
23; violinist.

*gers*, **Nicholas,** English organ-
and composer, 1685.

*hmeyer* (shtrō'-mī-ĕr), d. Weimar,
45; bass.

*ng*, **G. Templeton,** b. New
rk, ca. 1855; pupil of Leipzig
ns., and lives in Berlin; c. symph.
*In den Bergen*"; symph. poem
*Undine*" (op. 14); "*Gestrebt—*
*wonnen—Gescheitert*", f. orch. with
.-obbligato; choral works with
ch.; pf.-pcs., etc.

*ud*, **Chas.**, 1705—1726, Engl.
ganist and composer.

*zzi* (strôd'-zē), (1) **Pietro,** b. Flor-
ce, 16th cent.; co-founder of the
*le rappresentativo* (v. PERI); set
music Caccini's "*La Mascarada*
*gli Accecati*," 1595. (2) Abbate
*regorio*, apostolic protonotary at
aples, composer, 1683.

*ibe* (shtroo'-bĕ), **Gustav,** b. Ballen-
edt, Harz, March 3, 1867; violin-
; pupil of his father; at 10 in
allenstedt orch.; at 16 pupil of Leip-
g Cons.; played in the Gewand-

haus Orch.; later prof. at Mannheim
Cons.; 1889, Boston, Mass., in
Symph. Orch.; c. symph., etc.

**Struck** (shtrook), **Jn. Bapt.** (called
**Batistin**), Florence, ca. 1680—Paris,
1755; 1st 'cellist that ever played in
Paris Opéra orch.; c. operas.

**Strungk** (or **Strunck**) (shtroonk), **Nikolaus Adam,** Celle, Hanover, 1640
—Leipzig, 1710; violinist, organist
and dram. composer.

**Struss** (shtroos), **Fz.,** b. Hamburg,
Nov. 28, 1847; violinist; pupil of
Unruh, Auer, and Joachim; 1870,
member Berlin ct. - orch.; 1885,
"chamber-virtuoso"; 1887, ct.-Con-
zertmeister; also teacher Klindworth-
Scharwenka Conservatorium.

**Stumpf**(f) (shtoompf), (1) **Jn. Chr.,**
bassonist at Paris, ca. 1785; composer. (2) **K.,** b. Wiesentheid, Lower
Franconia, April 21, 1848; lives in
Munich; theorist.

**Stuntz** (shtoonts), **Jos. Hartmann,**
Arlesheim, near Basel, 1793—Munich,
1859; dram. composer.

**Stürmer** (shtĭr'-mĕr), **Heinrich,** 1811
—Leipzig, 1902; operatic bass.

**Succo** (zook'-kō), **Reinhold,** Görlitz,
1837 — Breslau, 1897; organist,
teacher and composer.

**Such** (zookh), **Percy,** b. June 27, 1878;
'cellist; studied with Robt. Haas-
manns; toured; lived in Berlin.

**Sucher** (zoo'-khĕr), (1) **Josef,** b. Dor-
bor, Hungary, Nov. 23, 1844; emi-
nent cond.; studied singing and the
vln., Vienna; pupil of Sechter
(comp.); vice-cond. of the acad. Gesangverein; coach for solo singers
at the ct.-opera; 1876, cond. Leipzig
City Th.; 1877, m. the distinguished
Wagnerian soprano, (2) **Rosa
Hasselbeck** (b. Velburg, Upper
Palatinate); 1878–88 they were engaged by Pollini at Hamburg; later
as cond. of the Royal Opera at Berlin (retired 1899), and prima donna
(retired 1898). Frau **S.** was daughter of a musician and sang small rôles
at Munich and elsewhere at first,
later prominent in Wagner opera.

which she sang at Bayreuth and in America.

**Sudds, Wm., b.** London, Engl., March 5, 1843; at 7 moved with his parents to a farm in Gouverneur, N. Y.; self-taught; a bandm. during the Civil War, and later pupil of Eugene Thayer (org.), and J. Eichberg (vln. and comp.), Boston Cons. of Music; lives in Gouverneur as teacher and pub. of various methods; c. 4 overtures, many dances, marches, church mus., etc., for pf., incl. cantata " *The Star of Bethlehem.*"

**Suk (sook), Josef, b.** Křečovic, Bohemia, Jan. 4, 1874; violinist; pupil and son-in-law of Dvôrák at Prague Cons., 1896, 2nd vln. "Bohemian String-Quartet"; c. a dramatic overture " *Winter's Tale,*" symphony in E; suite for orch. op. 16 " *Ein Märchen* " (1898), etc.

**Sul'livan, Sir Arthur Seymour,** London, May 14, 1842—Nov. 22, 1900; eminent composer of national English comic opera; v. succ. in church-mus. also; at 12 a chorister under Helmore, Chapel Royal; at 13 pub. a song; 1856, the first Mendelssohn Scholar at the R. A. M.; studied also at Leipzig Cons., etc. At 18 cond. his overture " *Lalla Rookh*"; at 20 prod. his mus. to " *The Tempest*" (Crystal Palace); at 22 his notable cantata " *Kenilworth*" (Birmingham festival); cond. of the London Philharm. (1885–87); and from 1880, the Leed's Festivals. 1876–81, principal, and prof. of comp. at the Nat. Training Sch. for Mus.; Mus. Doc. *h.c.*, Cambridge (1876), and Oxford (1879); Chev. of the Legion of Honour, 1878; grand organist to the Freemasons, 1887; knighted, 1883. C. symphony (played at the Gewandhaus, Leipzig, etc.) overtures " *In Memoriam* " (on his father's death), " *Marmion,*" "*Di ballo,*" and " *Sapphire Necklace* "; oratorios and cantatas, incl. "*The Golden Legend*" (1886); " *A Festival Te Deum*" (1872), Ode " *I Wish to Tune my*

*Quivering Lyre,*" with orch., succ. incid. mus. to 8 of Shakespeare's plays and others; c. much succ. church-mus. of all kinds. operas include the grand c " *Ivanhoe* " (1891), the rom opera, "*Rose of Persia*" (1 neither a succ.

His chief contribution to m was his brilliant series of truly lish comic operas, with the ec brilliant librettos of W. S. Gi Some of these had a world succ., and " *Patience*" was a of equal effectiveness with Mol " *Les Précieuses Ridicules.*" A 16 comic operas were the follo great successes: " *Cox and* (1867), " *Trial by Jury*" (1 " *H. M. S. Pinafore* " (1878), *Pirates of Penzance* " (1880), ' *tience*" (1881), "*Iolanthe* " (1 " *The Mikado* " (1885), "*Ruddig* (1887), " *The Yeomen of the Gu* (1888), " *The Gondoliers,*" " *U* (*Limited*)" (1893); " *Contraba ta* " (1867, revised 1894 as " *Chieftain* "), " *The Emerald* (1901), finished by Edw. Germ libretto by Basil Hood.

**Sulzer (zool'-tsĕr), (1) Jn. G., W** thur, 1719—Berlin, 1779; writer professor. (2) **Salomon,** of J parents, Hohenems, Vorarlberg, —Vienna, 1890; prof. of singing composer. (3) **Julius,** Vienna, —1891; son of above; violinist conductor, and c. operas. His si (4) **Marie** and (5) **Henriette** singers.

**Sun'derland, Mrs. ———, b.** Br house, Yorkshire, 1819; soprano tired, 1864.

**Suppé, Fz. von** (fōn-zoop'-pā), S to, Dalmatia, 1820—Vienna. 22, 1895; very popular operetta poser; pupil of Padua, Cigala, Ferrari; at first unpaid cond. a Josephstädter Th.; then at Press and Baden and at Vienna; he grand operas, a symph.. a Missa matica, a requiem, " *L'estremo g* *zio*," overtures (incl. the immensely pop. " *Dichter und Bauer*," pub. for 59 combinations). Of his Singspiele, comediettas, etc., some (like " *Tan-...nhauser*" and " *Dinorah*") are parodies, of the others the most succ. are " *Fatinitza*" (Vienna, 1876), and " *Die Afrikareise*" (1883).

**urette** (sū-rĕt'), **Thos. Whitney**, b. Concord, Massachusetts, Sept. 7, 1862 ; graduated Harvard, 1891 ; pupil there of Arthur Foote (pf.), and J. K. Paine ; organist, Baltimore ; then University Extension lecturer (Phila., Pa.) ; wrote treatises, etc.; pub. 2 - act operetta " *Priscilla*" (given over 500 times), etc.

**uriano** (or **Soriano**) (soo'- (or sō') rĭ-ä-nō), **Fran.**, Rome, 1549—Jan., 1620 ; conductor and notable composer ; pupil of Nanini and Palestrina ; cond. S. Maria Maggiore, and 1603, at St. Peter's, Rome.

**ur'man, Jos.**, 1803—1871 ; English tenor, conductor and composer.

**usato.** Vide TYLMAN SUSATO.

**Süssmayer** (züs'-mī-ĕr), **Fz. X.**, Steyr, Upper Austria, 1766—Vienna, 1803 ; conductor and dram. composer.

**Svendsen** (svĕnt'-zĕn), (1) **Oluf**, Christiania, 1832—London, 1888 ; flutist. (2) **Johan** (**Severin**), b. Christiania, Sept. 30, 1840; important, though eclectic composer ; son of a bandm.; at 11 c. vln.-pcs.; at 15 enlisted in the army and was soon bandm., and played flute, clarinet, and vln.; with a stipend from Charles XV., he studied vln.; at 23 he became pupil of David and Hauptmann, Richter, and Reinecke, Leipzig Cons.; toured 1868–69, in Musard's orch.; and at the Odéon, Paris ; 1869, Leipzig ; 1871, m. an American in New York ; 1872–77, and 1880–83, cond. Christiania Mus. Assoc.; 1883, ct.-cond. at Copenhagen ; from 1896, cond. Royal Th. there. C. 2 symphonies, overture to Björnson's " *Sigurd Slembe*"; " *Romeo and Juliet*," funeral march for Charles XV., corona-

tion march (for Oscar II.), wedding-cantata, etc., with orch.; op. 16, " *Carnaval des artistes norvégiens*," humorous march ; 4 " *Norwegian Rhapsodies*" for orch.; vln. and 'cello concertos, chamber-music and songs, etc.

**Swan, Timothy**, Worcester, Mass., 1758—Northfield, 1842 ; teacher and composer.

**Sweelinck** (or **Swelinck**, the best 2 of the 7 spellings) (svā'-lĭnk), (1) **Jan Pieter** (called **Jan Pieters-zoon**), Amsterdam, 1562—Oct. 16 1621 ; chief of Dutch organists. Son and (1577–81) successor, probably also pupil, of (2) **Pieter** (d. 1573), who had won pre-eminence as the org.-virtuoso and teacher of his own time· (1) was the first to employ the pedal in a real fugal part, and originated the org.-fugue.

**Sweet'hand, W.**, org.-builder, Bath, Engl., 19th cent.

**Swert, Jules de.** Vide DESWERT.

**Swieten** (svē'-tĕn), **Gf.**, Baron **von**, 1734—Vienna, 1803; eminent patron, but unimportant composer, of music; c. 6 symphs.

**Swinnerton, Heap.** Vide HEAP.

**Swoboda** (svō-bō'-dä), **August**, d. 1901; teacher in Vienna ; pub. text-books (1826–32).

**Sylva** (sĕl'-vä), **Eloi**, b. Geeraerds-bergen, Belgium, Nov. 29, 1847 ; noted tenor ; studied Brussels Cons., and with Duprez ; début, Nantes ; sang 7 years Paris Opéra, then in Russia, England and America ; 1889 Berlin.

**Sympson.** Vide SIMPSON.

**Szalit** (shä'-lēt), **Paula** ; b. 1886 (?) : pianist ; pupil of Leschetizki.

**Szarvady.** Vide CLAUSZ-SZARVADY.

**Székely** (shā'-kĕ-lē), **Imre** (**Emeric**), b. Malyfalva, Hungary, May 8, 1823 ; pianist ; studied in Pestn ; toured 1846 ; from 1852 teacher Pesth ; c. Hungarian fantasias on national airs ; pf.-concertos, etc.

**Szumowska** (shoo-môf'-shkä), **Antoinette**, b. Lublin, Poland, Feb. 22,

1868 ; pianist ; pupil of Strobel and Michalowski at Warsaw, and of Paderewski at Paris ; has played with great succ. at London, Paris, New York, Boston, etc.; m. Joseph Adamowski ; lives in Boston.

**Szymanowska** (shē-mä-nôf'-shkä), **Maria** (née **Wolowska**), Poland, 1790—(of cholera), Petersburg, 1831 ; pianist ; pupil of Field at. Moscow ; ct.-pianist at Petersburg ; Goethe was infatuated with her and she with him ; c. 24 mazurkas, etc.

## T

**Tabourot** (tă-boo-rō), **Jean**, Dijon, 1519—Langres, 1595 (?) ; a priest and writer under the pseud. " **Thoinot Arbeau**."

**Tacchinardi** (täk-kĭ-när'-dē), (1) **Nicola**, Florence, 1772—1859 ; at 17 a violinist ; later a tenor of greatest European popularity, even singing " Don Giovanni" (transposed) with succ., though he was hideous and a hunchback. His daughter (2) **Fanny Tacchinardi-Persiani** (v. PERSIANI). His daughter (3) **Elisa** was a pianist.

**Tadolini** (tä-dō-lē'-nē), (1) **Giov.**, Bologna, 1793—1872 ; dram. composer ; m. (2) **Eugenia Savorini** (b. Forli, 1809), a singer.

**Taffenel** (täf'-fŭ-něl), **Claude Paul**, b. Bordeaux, Sept. 16, 1844 ; flutist, pupil of Dorns (flute) and Reber (comp.) ; 3rd cond. Grand Opéra, Paris ; 1892, dir. Paris Cons. concerts—resigned, 1901 ; 1893, prof. of flute there.

**Tag** (täkh), **Chr. Gotthilf**, Bayerfeld, Saxony, 1735—Niederzwonitz, 1811; composer.

**Tagliafico** (täl-yä-fē'-kō), (1) **Jos. Dieudonné**, b. Toulon, Jan. 1, 1821: operatic singer and stage-manager in London ; married (2) ——**Cottis**, a singer.

**Tagliana** (täl-yä'-nä), **Emilia**, b. Milan, 1854 ; pupil of the Cons. there,

also of Lamperti ; colorature-sopra in various cities ; 1873-77, Vienn pupil of Hans Richter ; 1881-8 chamber-singer, Berlin.

**Täglichsbeck** (tākh'-lĭkhs-běk **Thos.**, Ansbach, 1799—Baden-B den, 1867; violinist, conductor ar dram. composer.

**Taglioni** (täl-yō'-nē), **Fdo.**, b. Naple Sept. 14, 1810; son of the famo ballet-master **Salvatore T.** (1790 1868). 1842-49, cond. at Lazianc till 1852, leader San Carlo Th., N ples ; editor and conductor ; founde a sch. for choral singing ; pub pamphlets and sacred songs.

**Talexy** (tă-lěx-ē), **Adrien**, Paris, 182 —1881; pf.-teacher and composer.

**Tal(l)ys** (or **Tallis**), **Thos.**, ca (1520-29)—London, Nov. 23, 1585 an early English composer whose re markable contrapuntal ability an harmonic richness place him close t Palestrina. His training is not knowr 1540, he ceased to be organist at Wal tham Abbey and joined the Chape Royal ; he was co-organist with Byr and shared his monopoly of mus. paper and printing ; he c. notabl church mus. for both Catholic an English services, also a song in 4 parts, etc.

**Tamagno** (tä-män'-yō), **Fran.**, b. Tu rin, 1851; robust tenor ; débu:, Paler mo ; sang with great succ. at L Scala, Milan, 1880. Has sung through out Europe and in both Americas 1887, he created Verdi's " Otello."

**Tamaro** (tä-mä'-rō), **Josef**, Barcelona 1824—New York, March 3, 1902 noted tenor ; pupil of Lamperti from 1876 teacher in America.

**Tam'berlik**, **Enrico**, Rome, 1820 Paris, 1889 ; famous tenor ; pupil o Borgna and Guglielmi ; début, Na ples, 1841; he had a powerful high c'''.

**Tamburini** (täm-boo-rē'-nē), **A.**, Faen za, March 28, 1800—Nice, Nov. 9 1876. Next to Lablache, perhaps the most succ. of male singers ; a lyric bass with compass of 2 octaves :

the son and pupil of a bandm. A horn-player first, then pupil of Boni and Asioli ; début, Centi, 1818.

**Tanaka** (tä-nä'-kä), **Shohé,** Japanese theorist ; pupil of Spitta ; inv. the enharmonium with just intonation.

**Tanejeff** (tä'-nä-yĕf), **Sergei,** b. Russia, Nov. 13, 1856 ; pupil of N. Rubinstein and Tchaikowski ; prof. of theory and comp. Moscow Cons.; prod. 3-act opera " *Oresteia* " (St. Petersburg, 1895).

**Tansur** (tän'-sŭr), **Wm.,** Dunchurch or Barnes? ca. 1700—St. Neots, 1783 ; organist, teacher, writer and composer.

**Tappert** (täp'-pĕrt), **Wm.,** b. Ober-Thomaswaldau, Silesia, Feb. 19, 1830 ; important theorist ; a schoolmaster, then 1856, studied with Dehn theory ; Kullak's Acad.; lived in Berlin from 1866 as a writer, editor and composer.

**Tarchi** (tär'-kē), **Angelo,** Naples, 1760—Paris, 1814 ; dramatic composer.

**Tarditi** (tär-dē'-tē), **Orazio,** d. after 1670 ; from 1648, maestro Faenza Cath.; composer.

**Tartini** (tär-tē'-nē), **Giuseppe,** Pirano, Istria, April 8, 1692—Padua, Feb. 16, 1770; eminent violinist, composer and scientist ; at first he studied for the priesthood at his father's wish ; then law, finally mus.; apparently self-taught as a violinist. A charge of abduction, due to his secret marriage with a niece of Cardinal Cornaro, led him to take refuge in the Franciscan monastery at Assisi, where for two years he practiced the vln. and studied comp. After a reconciliation he returned to Padua. Later he heard the violinist Veracini at Venice, and sending his wife to relations, retired to Ancona for further study. 1714, he discovered the combinational tones (v. D. D. " RESULTANT ") and utilised them in perfecting intonation; 1721, solo-violinist and cond. at St. Antonio, Padua ; 1723-25, chamber-mus. to Count Kinsky, Prague; 1728,

founded a vln.-school at Padua ; pub. treatises on harm. and acoustics; c. over 200 vln.-concertos, 50 sonatas with bass, etc., incl. the famous, posthumous " *Il Trillo del Diavolo,*" an effort to reproduce a sonata played to him by the devil in a dream. Biog. Fanzago (Padua, 1770); J. A. Hiller (1784), Fayolle (1810).

**Tasca** (täs'-kä), **P. Ant.,** neo-Italian ; c. opera " *A Santa Lucia,*" succ. in Germany, 1902.

**Taskin** (täs-kăn), (1) **Pascal,** Theux (Liège), 1723—Paris, 1795 ; celebrated instr.-maker in Paris ; introd. the piano-pedal worked by the foot instead of the knee ; inv. leather tangents for clavichord, the armandine, etc. (2) **Jos. Pascal,** 1750—1829 ; nephew of above ; keeper of the King's Instruments. (3) **H. Jos.,** Versailles, 1779—Paris, 1852 ; son of above ; organist. (4) (**Émile**) **Alex.,** Paris, 1853—1897 ; grandson of (3); barytone.

**Taubert** (tow'-bĕrt), (1) (**K. Gf.**) **Wm.,** Berlin, 1811—1891 ; noted pianist and composer of operas, incid. mus to Shakespeare, etc.; pupil of Neidthardt, Berger and Klein; ct.-cond. at Berlin. (2) **Otto,** b. Naumburg-on-Saale, June 26, 1833 ; pupil of O. Claudius and " prefect" of the cath.-choir ; 1863, prof., cantor and cond. at Torgau ; pub. treatises ; composer. (3) **Ernst Eduard,** b. Regenwalde, Pomerania, Sept. 25, 1838; studied at the Stern Cons., Berlin ; Prof., 1898 ; pub. chamber-mus., etc.

**Taudou** (tō-doo), **A. (Antonin Barthélémy),** b. Perpignan, France, Aug. 24, 1846 ; violinist ; pupil of Paris Cons., winning Grand prix de Rome, 1889; member of the Opéra-orch.; from 1883, prof. of harm. at the Cons.; c. vln.-concerto, etc.

**Tausch** (towsh), (1) **Fz.,** Heidelberg, 1762—Berlin, 1817; clarinettist and composer. (2) **Julius,** Dessau, 1827—Bonn, 1895 ; pianist, conductor, composer and writer.

**Tausig** (tow'-zĭkh), (1) **Aloys**, 1820—1885 ; pianist and composer, pupil of Thalberg. (2) **Karl**, Warsaw, Nov. 4, 1841—(of typhoid fever), Leipzig, July, 1871 ; remarkable piano-virtuoso ; son and pupil of above; and of Liszt; début, Berlin, 1858; lived Dresden and Vienna as notable cond.; 1865 founded a sch. at Berlin ; c. brilliant exercises, transcriptions, etc.

**Tauwitz** (tow'-vĭts), **Eduard**, Glatz, Silesia, 1812—Prague, 1894 ; conductor ; c. more than 1,000 comps. incl. 3 operas.

**Tavecchia** (tä-věk'-kĭ-ä), **Luigi** ; notable buffo ; début in concert Milan ; in opera at La Scala ; has sung in Europe and America.

**Tav'erner**, (1) **John**, d. Boston, England; organist and composer at Oxford, 1530. (2) Rev. **J.**, d. Stoke Newington, 1638 ; organist and composer.

**Tayber.** Vide TEYBER.

**Tay'lor**, (1) **Edw.**, Norwich, Engl., 1784—Brentwood, 1863 ; bass, conductor, critic, lecturer and writer. (2) **Franklin**, b. Birmingham, Engl., Feb. 5, 1843 ; pianist and teacher ; pupil of C. Flavell (pf.) and T. Redsmore (org.) ; also of Leipzig Cons.; 1876–82, prof. Nat. Training Sch., and from 1883, at the R. C. M.; Pres. of Acad. for the Higher Development of pf.-playing ; writer and translator.

**Tchaïkovsky** (or **Tschaïkowski**, etc.) (tshä-ē-kôf'-shkĭ), **Peter Iljitch**, Wotinsk, in the Government of Wiätka, Dec. 25, 1840—(of cholera) Petersburg, Nov. 6, 1893 : eminent Russian composer. Studied law, and entered the government civil service ; did not take up mus. seriously till 22 ; then entered the newly founded Petersburg Cons., under Zaremba and A. Rubinstein,

1865, winning a prize medal for Schiller's ode " *An die Freude* " (also used in Beethoven's 9th symph.); 1866–77, instructor of harm. there ; then lived Petersburg, Italy, Switzerland, as composer. He visited England and appeared at Phil. Concerts, 1888 and '89 ; visited New York for the dedication of the new Carnegie Music Hall, and cond. his own compositions. 1893, Mus. Doc. *h.c.*, Cambridge. Writer, and translator of harm. text-books. C. 11 Russian operas, incl. " *The Voyevode* " (Moscow, 1869)," *Opritchnnyk* " (Petersb., 1874) " *Vakula, the Smith* " (Petersb. 1876) ; " *Jevgenjie Onegin*"; 1879 " *Eugene Onegin*," in German (Hamburg, 1892), and posthumous " *Pique Dame* " (Vienna ct.-th., 1902) ; 3 ballets, " *Le Lac des Cygnes* " (op. 20), " *La Belle au Bois Dormant* " (1890), and " *Le Casse-Noisette* " (op. 71); a coronation cantata with orch. ; 2 masses ; 6 symphs., incl. No. 6 in B minor, the famous " *Pathétique*"; symph. poems, " *The Tempest*, " *Francesca da Rimini*," " *Manfred*," " *Romeo and Juliet* " (a fantasy-overture) ; " *Hamlet*," " *Fatum*," and " *Le Voyevode* " (symph. ballad) ; 4 orch. suites incl. " *Mozartiana* ;" 3 overtures " *1812* " (op. 49) " *Triomphale*" on the Danish natl hymn; " *L'Orage*"; " *Marche slave*," coronation march ; 3 pf.-concertos ; pf.-fantasia with orch.; vln.-concerto capriccio for 'cello with orch.; string sextet " *Souvenir de Florence*," string-quartets, a pf.-trio, pieces for vln. and 'cello; and pf.-pcs., incl. " *Souvenir de Hapsal*," sonata " *The Seasons*," 12 characteristic pcs. " *Kinder Album*"; 6 duets, Russian songs, etc. Also pub. a harmony ; his " *Erinnerungen* " and translations of Gevaert, etc.

## Tschaikowsky.

### By Ernest Newman.

HALF French in his ancestry, Tschaikowsky's prenatal influences were a blend of East and West. While Westerns regard him as typically Russian, his compatriots think him less "native" than her Russian composers. Like most Slavs, he drew sustenance more from France than Germany. Brahms he thought dull ; Wagner he never really understood. He loved music, he said, that came from the heart, that expressed "a deep humanity," like Grieg's. To the delicate brain and nerves of the modern man he added the long-accumulated eruptive passions of his race. He takes the language made by the great Germans, and uses it to express the complex pessimism of another culture. The colour of life in his music ranges from pale grey to intense black, with here and there a note of angry scarlet tearing through the mass of cloud. Almost all his work, like Tourgenieff's, lies within the one scale of emotions ; but from relatively few elements he evokes an infinite variety and complexity. In his songs, for example, though melancholy is the dominant note of nine out of ten, each hints a different shade of the generic mood. ¶ More interested in personal, dramatic emotion than in music of abstract beauty, he worked his way through and beyond the ordinary symphonic form, to the symphony with a human significance or the symphonic poem pure and simple. His phrases, coloring his general conceptions, are vital, emotional, intimate. Music, he held, must always interest in the first place ; and so he avoids the cold displays of technical artifice which Brahms, for example, so often gives us, preferring rather to repeat the old matter with variations of ornamentation. His real contribution to the history of music, apart from the general beauty and expressiveness of his work, is the modification of the symphonic form in obedience to a poetic idea. He takes up the suggestions bequeathed by Berlioz and Liszt, and turns them into accomplished realities.

---

ebaldini (tä-bäl-dē'-nē), **Giovanni,** b. Brescia, 1864 (?) ; pupil of Paolo Chimeri ; at 15 organist of Brescia Cath., and chorusm. Guillaume Th.; later studied at Milan Cons.; expelled 1886 for criticising a mass written by a prof.; after wandering as organist and journalist, studied at Ratisbon ; maestro, "Schola Cantorum," San Marco, Venice ; 1894, maestro, Padua Cath.; 1897, dir. Parma Cons. ; wrote org.-method (v.

bossi) ; c. opera "*Fantasia Araba,*" "*Messa funèbre*" with Bossi, etc.

**Tedesca** (tä-děs'-kä), **Fernanda,** near Baltimore, U. S. A., 1860—August, 1885 ; violinist.

**Tedesco** (tä'-děs'-kō), **Ignaz (Amadeus),** Prague, 1817—Odessa, Nov. 13, 1882 ; brilliant pianist ("the Hannibal of octaves") ; composer.

**Telemann** (tā'-lě-män), (1) **G. Philipp,** Magdeburg, March 14, 1681—Hamburg, July 23, 1767 ; mainly self-taught; conductor; 1709, ct.-cond.; he overshadowed J. S. Bach in contemporary esteem and was one of the most prolific and facile composers ever known; c. opera; autobiog., 1731. (2) **G. Michael,** Plon, Holstein, 1748—Riga, 1831; grandson of above; cantor, theorist and comp.

**Telle** (těl'-lě), **K.,** 1826—Klosterneuburg, 1895; ballet-composer.

**Tel'ford.** Vide FRANCIS BOOTT.

**Tel'lefsen, Thos. Dyke Acland,** Trondheim, Norway, 1823 — Paris, 1874; pianist and composer.

**Tem'ple, Hope,** b. 19th cent. of English parents, Dublin; pupil of J. F. Barnett, and E. Silas, London, and of A. Messager, whom she m.; c. operetta " *The Wooden Spoon,*" and numerous pop. songs.

**Tem'pleton, J.,** Riccarton, Scotland, 1802—New Hampton, near London, 1886; tenor.

**Tenaglia** (tā-näl'-yä), **Anton Fran.,** b. Florence; conductor at Rome; c. the first known opera using an aria da capo, " *Clearco,*" 1661.

**Ten Brink.** Vide BRINK, TEN.

**Tenducci** (ten-doot'-chē), **Giusto F.,** b. Sienna, 1836; famous male operatic soprano.

**Ten Kate.** Vide KATE TEN.

**Ternina** (tăr-nē'-nă), **Milka,** b. Begišĕe, Croatia, Dec. 19, 1864; notable dramatic soprano; studied with Gänsbacher; début Leipzig, 1883; then sang Graz and Bremen; 1890 Munich, named " court-singer"; sang in Bayreuth and in America from 1899.

**Terpan'der,** b. Antissa, Lesbos, 7th cent. B.C.; called the " Father of Greek music."

**Terradellas** (**Terradeglias**) (tĕr-rädĕl'-läs or däl'-yäs), **Domingo** (**Domenico**), Barcelona, Spain (baptised, Feb. 13, 1711)—Rome, 1751; dram. composer.

**Terschak** (tĕr'-shäk), **Ad.,** Prague, April 21, 1832—1901: flutist; pupil of Zierer, Vienna Cons.; toured; c. flute-pcs.

**Terziani** (tĕr-tsї-ä'-nē), **Eugen** Rome, 1825—1889; prof., condu or and dram. composer.

**Teschner** (tĕsh'-nĕr), **Gv. Wr** Magdeburg, 1800—Dresden, 188 teacher, composer and editor.

**Tesi-Tramontini** (tä'-zē-trä-môn-t nē), **Vittoria,** Florence, ca. 169 Vienna, 1775; famous contralto.

**Tessarin** (tĕs'-sä-rēn), **Fran.,** b. V ice, Dec. 3, 1820; pianist and tea er; pupil of A. Fanno and G. Ferrari; c. opera " *L'Ultimo Ab cerragio* " (Venice, 1858); a canta etc.

**Tessarini** (tĕs-sä-rē'-nē), **Carlo,** Rimini, 1690; famous violin writer and composer.

**Testori** (tĕs-tō'-rē), (1) **Carlo Gi** vln.-maker at Milan, ca. 1687—17 with his sons (2) **Carlo A.** and **Paolo A.**

**Teyber** (or **Tayber**) (tī'-bĕr), (1) **A ton,** Vienna, 1754—1822; conduct cembalist and composer. (2) **F** Vienna, 1756—1810; bro. of abo organist and dram. composer.

**Thadewaldt** (tä'-dĕ-vält), **Herman** b. Bodenhagen, Pomerania, April 1827; 1850—51, bandm. at Düss dorf; 1893—95, cond. at Diepp 1857 at Berlin.

**Thalberg** (täl'-bĕrkh), **Sigismun** Geneva, Jan. 7, 1812—Naples, A 27, 1871; famous piano-virtuoso a composer. " Being the son of Prin Dietrichstein, who had many wi without being married, **T.** had seve brothers of different family name (Grove). His mother was the Bar ess von Wetzlar. Both of the paren took the greatest interest in his ed cation. He was intended for a di lomatic career, but after his succ. a pianist at 14, gave himself up mus. He had some tuition fr Hummel (pf.) and Sechter (comp but chiefly from Mittag, a bassoo ist. At 16 three florid compositio appeared; at 18 a pf.-concerto. T same year he toured Germany wi much succ. 1834, ct.-pianist at Vie na ; 1835, he conquered Paris, and later the rest of Europe. 1843, he m. Mme. Boucher, daughter of Lablache ; 1851, his first opera "*Florida*," failed in London, and 1855, "*Cristina di Svezia*" failed in Vienna. He then toured Brazil (1855), and 1856, United States ; retiring in 1858 to his villa at Posilippo, near Naples. 1862, Paris and London ; 1863, second Brazilian tour ; 1864, retired again. He was remarkable for his legato effects and for the singing-tone, Liszt saying " Thalberg is the only artist who can play the violin on the keyboard." He originated the subsequently abused scheme of dividing a central melody between the two thumbs, and enveloping it in arpeggiated ornament. His comps. include many florid transcriptions of opera-tunes, also a grand concerto, 6 nocturnes, "*La Cadence*," and "*Marche funèbre variée*," etc.

**Thal'lon, Robt.**, b. Liverpool, March 18, 1852 ; taken to New York at 2 ; studied in Stuttgart, Leipzig, Paris, and Florence ; lives in Brooklyn, N. Y., as organist and mus.-teacher.

**Thayer** (thā'-ĕr), (1) **Alex. Wheelock**, South Natick, Mass., Oct. 22, 1817—Trieste, July 15, 1897 ; graduated Harvard, 1843 ; was librarian there for some years ; 1849 went to Europe and began materials for life of Beethoven ; 1862, America as journalist ; 1854 returned to Germany and frequently afterwards as his means permitted ; 1862, U. S. consular agent at Vienna ; later, till death, consul at Trieste ; besides many articles he wrote a great but unfinished life of Beethoven ; though written in English it has been pub. only in a German trans. by H. Deiters, in 3 vols. (Berlin, 1866-1879). Though incomplete, his biog. of Beethoven is his monument. (2) **(Whitney) Eugene**, Mendon, Mass., 1838—Burlington, Vermont, 1889; organist, editor, lecturer and composer. (3) **Arthur Wilder**, b Dedham, Mass., Aug. 26, 1857 ;

pupil of Guilmette and Adams (singing), Chadwick and Zerrahn ; cond. choral societies in Lowell, Worcester, etc.; 1882 at Dedham, 1885 at Milton ; then mus.-dir. Eliot Ch., Newton ; c. part-songs, etc.

**Theile** (tī'-lĕ), **Jn.**, Naumburg, 1646—1724 ; conductor and composer.

**Theo'deri'cus, Sixtus.** Vide DIETRICH.

**Thern** (tărn), (1) **Karl (Karolý)**, Iglo, Upper Hungary, 1817—Vienna, 1886; conductor, professor and dram. composer. His sons and pf.-pupils (also pupils of Moscheles and Reinecke), (2) **Willi** (b. Ofen, June 22, 1847), and (3) **Louis** (b. Pesth, Dec. 18, 1848), were teachers.

**Thibaud** (tē'-bŏ), (1) **Jos.**, b. Bordeaux, Jan. 25, 1875 ; pianist ; pupil of L. Diémer, Paris Cons., taking 1st prize for pf.-playing, 1892; 1895-96, accompanied Marsick to America. (2) **Jacques**, b. 1880; French pianist.

**Thibaut IV.** (tē-bō-kătr), King of Navarre ; Troyes, 1201—Pamplona, 1253 ; composer.

**Thibaut** (tē'-bowt), **Anton Fr. Justus**, Hameln, 1774 — Heidelberg, 1840 ; professor and writer.

**Thiele** (tē'-lĕ), (1) **Ed.**, b. Dessau, Nov. 21, 1812 ; mus.-dir. at Kothen, organist and prof. at the Seminary ; 1855, Dessau ; 1860, Hofkapellmeister , c. a mass, etc. (2) **K. L.**, Harzgerode, near Bernburg, 1816—Berlin, 1848 ; organist and composer.

**Thieme** (called **Thiémé**) (tē'-mĕ, or t'yā'-mā), **Fr.**, Germany (?)—Bonn, 1802 ; publisher of text-books, and composer.

**Thierfelder** (tēr'-fĕlt-ĕr), **Dr. Albert (Wm.)**, b. Mühlhausen, April 30, 1846; pupil of Leipzig Univ. and Dr. Phil.; studied with Hauptmann, Richter and Paul ; cond. various cities ; from 1887 mus.-dir. and prof. Rostock Univ.; writer of important treatises ; prod. 5 operas, incl. succ. "*Der Heirathstein*" (text and music) (Rostock, 1898), "*Zlatorog*," and

" *Frau Holde*," for soli, chorus, and orch., and 2 symphs., etc.

**Thieriot** (tē′-rĭ-ôt), (1) **Paul Emil**, Leipzig, 1780 — Wiesbaden, 1831 ; violinist. (2) **Fd.**, b. Hamburg, April 7, 1838 ; pupil of E. Marxsen, and Rheinberger ; mus.-dir. at Hamburg, Leipzig, and Glogau ; lives in Hamburg ; c. symph. fantasy "*Loch Lamond*," vln.-concerto, etc.

**Thillon** (tē-yôṅ), **Anna** (née **Hunt**), b. London, 1819; very succ. soprano; pupil of Bordogni, Tadolini, and Thillon, marrying the last named at 15 ; début, Paris, 1838 ; 1844, Auber's "*Crown Diamonds*" was written for her; 1850–54, in America, the first to produce opera in San Francisco ; retired 1867 to Torquay.

**Thimus** (tē′-moos), **Albert**, Freiherr **von**, Cologne, 1806—1846 ; writer.

**Thirlwall**, (1) **J. Wade**, Shilbottle, Northumbria, 1809 — 1875 ; critic, conductor and composer. (2) **Annie**, daughter of above ; soprano.

**Thoinan**, **E.** Vide ROQUET.

**Thoma** (tō′-mä), **Rudolf**, b. Lehsewitz, near Steinau-on-Oder, Feb. 22, 1829 ; pupil of R. Inst. for Churchmus., Berlin ; 1857, cantor, Hirschberg, then Breslau, 1870, "R. Music Dir." ; founder of a singing-soc., dir. of a sch.; c. 2 operas, 2 oratorios, etc.

**Thomas** (tō′-mäs), **Chr. Gf.**, Wehrsdorf near Bautzen, 1748—Leipzig, 1806 ; writer.

**Thomas** (tō-mäs) (**Chas. Louis**), **Ambroise**, Metz, Aug. 5, 1811— Paris, Feb. 12, 1896; pupil of Paris Cons.; winning 1st pf.-prize, 1829 ; harm., 1830 ; Grand prix de Rome (1832), with cantata "*Hermann et Ketty.*" After 3 years in Italy, returned to Paris, and up to 1843, prod. nine stage-pcs., at the Opéra and Op.-Com. with fair succ. The failure of the last was retrieved after a silence of 5 years by "*Le Cid*"(1849), "*Le Songe d' Une Nuit d'Été*" (1850, both at the Op.-Com.). 1851 elected to the Académie. The next 6

operas were only moderately suc but "*Mignon*" (Op.-Com., 18 made a world-wide succ. and "*H let*" (Opéra, 1868) a lasting succ Paris, where it is still sung. "*Gil Gillotin*" (1874), "*Françoise de mini*" (1882), and the ballet, " *Tempête*" (Opéra, 1889), were his dram. works ; 1871, dir. of the Co 1845, Chev. ; 1858, Officier ; 18 Commander of the Legion of H our. C. also cantatas; messe so nelle (Nôtre-Dame, 1865) ; m excellent "chœurs orphéoniqu (3-part male choruses), etc.

**Thomas** (täm′-üs), (1) **J.**, b. Brige Glamorganshire, March 1, 18 1861 made " Pencerdd Gwalia," i Chief Bard of Wales ; pupil at R. A. M.; 1851, harpist, R. It. ( era ; toured Europe, 1852–62 pla at the Gewandhaus, etc. 1862, co of the first annual concert of We mus., with a chorus of 400, and harps ; 1871, harpist to the Quee leader in the Eisteddfodau, and ha prof. R. C. M. C. dram. cant "*Llewelyn*" (1863) ; a Welsh sce "*The Bride of Neath Valley*" (18 patriotic songs, with harp ; 2 ha concertos, etc. (2) **Lewis Wn** Bath, April, 1826—London, 18 concert-bass, editor and critic. sons are : (3) **W. Henry** (b. Ba May 8, 1848), prof. of singing,Gui hall and R. A. M.; and (4) **Fra L.**, conductor and organist Bromley. (5) **Harold**, b. Chelte ham, July 8, 1834 ; pianist ; pupil Sterndale Bennet, C. Potter, a Blagrove ; début 1850 ; pf.-pr R. A. M. and Guildhall Sch., Lc don ; c. overtures, etc. (6) **The dor(e)**, b. Esens, East Frieslar Oct. 11, 1835 ; eminent cond., ed cator and stimulator of mus. taste America; son and pupil of a violin at 6 played in public ; at 10 w brought to New York, where he so entered an orch.; 1851, toured soloist, later with Jenny Lind, Gri etc.; 1855, began the Mason a

Thomas Soirées (with Dr. Wm. Mason); 1864–69 cond. "Symph. Soirées"; 1869 made concert-tour with an orch. of 54 ; 1876 at Philadelphia Centennial with ill-succ. leading to disbandment ; 1878–80, pres. Cincinnati Coll. of Mus.; 1880, cond. New York, Philh. Orch.; from 1888, dir. Chicago Cons., also cond. Chicago Orch. (7) **Arthur Goring**, Ralton Park, near Eastbourne, Sussex, Nov. 21, 1850—London, March 20, 1892 ; took up music at 24 and studied with Émile Durand, later with Sullivan and Prout R. A. M., London, winning Lucas Prize, 1879; lived in London. C. 2 operas, v. succ. "*Esmeralda*" (Drury Lane, 1883, New York, 1900) ; "*Nadeshda*" (1885) ; "*The Golden Web*" (score finished by Waddington, Liverpool, 1893) ; a choral ode, "*The Sun Worshippers*" (Norwich, 1881), v. succ. cantata, "*The Swan and the Skylark*" (Birmingham, 1894, instrumented by C. V. Stanford) ; psalm with orchestra (1878) ; 3 vocal scenes, "*Hero and Leander*" (1880), etc.

**homas Aqui′nas** (Saint Thomas of Aquino), Rocca Sicca, near Aquino, Italy, 1225 (27?)—Fossa Nuova, near Terracina, 1274 ; famed theologian and philosopher ; he c. a notable communion service.

**homé** (tō-mā), **Francis** (rightly **François Luc. Jos.**), b. Port Louis, Mauritius, Oct. 18, 1850 ; pupil of Marmontel (pf.), and Duprato (theory), Paris Cons.; lives in Paris as teacher and critic ; c. "*Roméo et Juliette*"(1890); a mystery, "*L'Enfant Jésus*" (1891) ; symph. ode "*Hymne à la Nuit*" and many pop. songs and pf.-pcs.

**homson** (tăm′-sŭn), (1) **Geo.**, Limekilns, Fife, 1757—Leith, 1851 ; notable coll. and pub. of Scotch, Welsh and Irish melodies, to which he had special instrumental accompaniments written by Beethoven, Pleyel, etc. (2) **J.**, Sproutson, Roxburgh, 1805—

Edinburgh, 1841; conductor and dram. composer.

**Thomson** (tôṅ-sôṅ), **César**, b. Liège, March 17, 1857; notable iolinist ; from 7 pupil of Liège Cons.; at 11, winning the gold medal ; then pupil of Vieuxtemps, Léonard, Wieniawski and Massart ; 1873–83, chambermus. to Baron von Derwies at Lugano, and a member of Bilse's orch., Berlin ; 1883–97, teacher at Liège Cons.; 1898, vln.-prof. Brussels Cons (vice Isaye) ; has toured widely ; 1894 United States.

**Thorndike, Herbert Elliot**, b. Liverpool, April 7, 1851; concert-bass ; début, Cambridge, 1878 ; 1887, Drury Lane.

**Thorne** (thôrn), (1) **Edw. H.**, b. Cranborne, Dorset, May 9, 1834 ; pianist and org. ; chorister under Elvey ; organist various churches ; from 1891, at St. Anne's, Soho, London ; cond. St. Anne's Choral and Orch'l Soc. C. Psalm 57, with orch. (1884) ; Magnificat and Nunc dimittis with orch. and organ ; an overture ; "*Sonata elegia*" for pf. (2) **Thos. Pearsall**, American composer of comic operas, "*Leandro*" (New York, 1898), etc.

**Thuille** (too-ē′-lě), **L. (Wm. Ands. M.)**, b. Bozen, Tyrol, Nov. 30, 1861; pupil of Jos. Pembaur (pf., cpt.), at Innsbruck ; Baermann (pf.) and Rheinberger (comp.) Munich Mus. Sch.; from 1883, teacher of pf. and theory there ; also cond. "*Liederhort*"; 1891, R. Prof. of Mus.; c. succ. opera "*Theuerdank*" (Munich, 1897, Luitpold Prize), opera "*Lobetanz*" (Carlsruhe and Berlin, 1898) ; "*Romantic*" overture, sextet for piano and wind, sonatas, etc.

**Thun′der, H. G.**, near Dublin, 1832—New York, 1891 ; pianist, organist and composer.

**Thürlings** (tür′-lĭngks), **Ad.**, since 1877, prof. of Old-Catholic theology at Bonn ; Dr. Phil., Munich, with dissertation, "*Die beiden Tongeschlechter und die neuere mus. Theo* *rie"* (1877) (advocating harmonic dualism).

**Thru'nam, Ed.,** Warwick, 1825—188—; organist and composer.

**Thurner** (toor'-nĕr), **Fr. Eugen,** Montbeliard, 1785 — Amsterdam, 1827; oboe-virtuoso; composer.

**Thurnmayer.** Vide AVENTINUS.

**Thurs'by, Emma,** b. Brooklyn, N. Y. Nov. 17, 1857; famous concert-soprano; pupil of Meyer (Brooklyn), Errani (New York) and Mme. Rudersdorff (Boston), then of Lamperti and San Giovanni, Milan; concert-début, America, Plymouth Church, Brooklyn, 1875; sang in concert and oratorio, and with Gilmore (1875); frequently toured Europe and America with great succ.; compass c'–e''' (v. PITCH, D. D.).

**Tichatschek** (tēkh'-ät-shĕk), **Jos. Aloys,** Ober-Weckelsdorf, Bohemia, 1807—Dresden, 1886; tenor; created Wagner's "*Rienzi*" and "*Tannhäuser.*"

**Tieffenbrücker.** Vide DUIFFOPRUGGAR.

**Tiehsen** (tē'-zĕn), **Otto,** Danzig, 1817—Berlin, 1849; c. comic opera.

**Tiersch** (tērsh), **Otto,** Kalbsrieth, Thuringia, 1838—Berlin, 1892; singing-teacher and theorist.

**Tiersot** (tĭ-ĕr'-sō), **(J. Bapt. Elisée) Julien,** b. Bourg, Bresse, France; pupil of Franck, Paris Cons.; from 1883, asst. libr. there; pub. essays, incl. "*Histoire de la chanson populaire en France,*" Bordun Prize, 1885; c. "*Hellas*" for soli, chorus and orch.; rhapsodies on popular airs, etc.

**Tietjens** (rightly **Titiens**) (tēt'-yĕns), **Therese Johanne Alex.,** of Hungarian parents, Hamburg, July 17, 1831—London, Oct. 3, 1877; famous soprano; teachers unknown; début, Hamburg, 1849; from 1858, chiefly in London in grand and comic opera.

**'il'borghs, Jos.,** b. Nieuwmoer, Sept. 28, 1830; theorist; pupil of Lemmens (org.) and Fétis (comp.), Brussels Cons.; from 1882, prof. of org.,

Ghent Cons.; and of cpt. Antw Mus.-Sch.; comp. organ-pieces a motets.

**Tilman** (tĕl'-män), **Alfred,** Brusse 1848—1895; composer and pianist

**Tilmant** (tĕl'-män), (1) **Théoph Alex.,** Valenciennes, 1799—Asnièr 1878; conductor. His brother Alex., 1808—Paris, 1880; 'cellist

**Timanoff** (tē'-män-ôf), **Vera,** b. U Russia, Feb. 18, 1855; pianist; p pil of L. Nowitzky, A. Rubinste Tausig and Liszt; lived in Pete burg, Prague (1871) and Vien (1872).

**Timm** (tĭm), **Henry Christian,** Ha burg, Germany, 1811—New Yo 1892; pianist and org.-composer.

**Timm'ner, Christian,** b. 1860; (too) violinist; pupil of Wirth; toure then retired 1894 for eight yea practice; reappeared in Berlin, 19

**Tinc'toris, Johannes** (called **Jo Tinctor;** or **Giov. Del Tintor** rightly **Jean de Vaerwere** (vär'-w rĕ)), Poperinghe, 1434 (or 35, some s 1450)—Nivelles, 1511; canon; wro 1477, the earliest known dict. of m (ca. 1475), etc.; composer.

**Tinel** (tē-nĕl'), **Edgar,** b. Sinay, B gium, March 27, 1854; pianist a composer; son and pupil of a po school-teacher and organist; pu also of Brussels Cons.; 1st pf.-pri 1873, and pub. op. 1, 4 nocturn for solo-voice with pf.; 1877, w Grand prix de Rome w. cant "*Klokke Roeland*" (op. 17); 188 dir. Inst. for Sacred Mus. at M lines; 1888, prod. very succ. oratori "*Franciscus*" (op. 36); 1889, i spector State mus. schs.; 1896, pro of cpt. and fugue, Brussels Cons pub. a treatise on Gregorian chan and prod. a "*Grand Mass of t Holy Virgin of Lourdes,*" for 5 pa (op. 41), Te Deum, Alleluia, mote and sacred songs incid. mus., pf pcs., etc.

**Tiraboschi** (tē-rä-bôs'-kē), **Girolam** Bergamo, 1731 — Modena. 179 writer.

**Tirindelli** (tē-rĭn-dĕl'-lē), **P. Adolfo,** b. Conegliano, Italy, 1858 ; violinist; pupil Milan Cons., then of Boniforti; cond. at Gorizia 3 years, then studied with Grün and Massart ; 1887, vln.-prof. Liceo Benedetto Marcello, Venice ; 1893, dir., also cond. " Verdi Orchestra "; made Cavaliere, 1894; played with the Boston Symph. Orch. in 1895 ; c. 1-act opera " *L'Atenaide* " (Venice, 1892), etc., now prof. Cincinnati Cons.

**Titl** (tēt'-'l), **Anton Emil,** Pernstein, Moravia, 1809—Vienna, 1882 ; conductor and dram. composer.

**Titoff** (tē'-tôf), **Nicolai Alexeijevitch,** St. Petersburg, 1801—1876 ; c. songs.

**Ti(e)tze** (tēt'-tsĕ), **L.,** 1797—1850; tenor at Vienna.

**Todi** (tō'-dē), **Luiza Rosa** (née de **Aguiar**), Setubal, Portugal, Jan. 9, 1753—Lisbon, Oct. 1, 1833 ; famous mezzo-soprano ; an actress at 15, then pupil of Perez ; sang London, 1712 ; 1777 v. succ. at Madrid ; 1783 provoked a famous rivalry with Mara ; 1780 ct.-singer, Berlin. When she died she left her 2d husband and her 8 children $80,000 and much jewelry.

**Todini** (tō-dē'-nē), **Michele,** b. Saluzzo, ca. 1625 ; musette-player and instr.-maker, at Rome.

**Toedt** (tāt), **Theodore J.,** b. New York, Feb. 4, 1853 ; choir-boy, Trinity Parish, 1861–71 , pupil of Mrs. Horn - Rust ; singer in oratorio, church, and concert ; lives in New York as a vocal teacher ; blind from 1895.

**Toeschi** (tō-äs'-kē) (in German tä'-shē), (1) **Carlo Giu.** (rightly **Toesca della Castella-Monte**), Romagna, 1724—Munich, 1788, ct.-mus., director and composer. (2) **Jn. Bapt.,** Mannheim, ca. 1745—Munich, May, 1800 ; son and successor of above ; noted violinist ; c. 18 symphs., etc.

**Tofts,** Mrs. **Katherine,** first Englishwoman to succeed in Italian opera ; most successful soprano ; accumu-lated a fortune, lost her reason 1709, and d. after 1735 ; m. Jos. Smith.

**Tolbecque** (tôl'-bĕk), four Belgian brothers. (1) **Isidore Jos.,** Hanzinne, 1794—Vichy, 1871 ; conductor and composer. (2) **Jean. Bapt. Jos.,** 1787—Paris, 1869 ; violinist and conductor. (3) **Aug. Jos.,** 1801 —Paris, 1869 ; violinist. (4) **Chas. Jos.,** Paris, 1806 —1835 ; violinist and conductor. (5) **Aug.,** b. Paris, March 30, 1830 ; 'cellist ; pupil of the Cons., and 1849 took 1st prize ; 1865–71, teacher Marseilles Cons. ; later 'cellist in the Paris Cons. concerts ; pub. " *La Gymnastique du Violoncelle* " (op. 14) ; prod. succ. 1-act comic opera " *Après la Valse* " (Niort, 1895). His son (6) **Jean,** b. Niort, Oct. 7, 1857 ; 'cellist ; pupil Paris Cons. ; 1873, took 1st 'cello-prize.

**Tol'let, Thos.,** English pub. and composer, 1694.

**Tomaschek, Jn. Wenzel** (rightly **Jan Václav Tomášek**) (täm'-ä-shĕk), Skutsch, Bohemia, April 17, 1774—Prague, April 3, 1850; notable pianist, organist ; also c. operas and pf.-pcs.

**Tomasini** (tō-mä-sē'-nē), (1) **Luigi (Aloysius),** Pesaro, 1741—Esterház, 1808 ; violinist and director ; he had two daughters who sang in opera at Eisenstadt and 2 sons, (2) **Luigi,** Esterház, 1779—after 1814 ; violinist. (3) **Anton,** Eisenstadt, 1775—1824, viola-player and leader.

**Tombelle** (tôn-bĕl), **Fd. de la,** b. Paris, Aug. 3, 1854 ; pupil of Guilmant and Dubois, Paris Cons. ; his quartet and symph. won 1st prize of the " Société des compositeurs " ; Officer of Pub. Instruction, Paris ; c. orch.-suites, etc.

**Tomeoni** (tō-mä-ō'-nē), (1) **Florido,** Lucca, 1757—Paris, 1820 ; teacher and theorist. (2) **Pellegrino,** b. Lucca, ca. 1729 ; bro. of above ; teacher and writer in Florence.

**Tom'kins,** (1) Rev. **Thos.,** Engl. composer, Gloucester, 1600. His son

(2) **J.**, d. 1638 ; organist and composer. (3) **Thos.**, d. 1656 ; organist at Worcester cath. ; composer ;
son of (1). (3) **Giles**, d. 1668 ; bro.
and succ. of above. (4) **Robt.**, son of
(2); 1641 one of the King's musicians.

**Tom'lins, Wm. Lawrence**, b. London, Feb. 4, 1844 ; pupil of Macfarren, and Silas ; 1869, America, from
1875 singing-t. and cond. Apollo Glee
Club, Chicago ; pub. " *Children's
Songs, and How to Sing Them*"
(1885 ?).

**Tommasi** (tôm-mäs'-sē), **Giu. M.**,
Cardinal, Alicante, Sicily, 1649 —
Rome, 1713 ; writer.

**Töpfer** (tĕp'-fĕr), **Jn. Gl.**, Niederrossla,
Thuringia, 1791—Weimar, 1870; or-
ganist, writer and composer.

**Torchi** (tôr'-kē), **Luigi**, b. Mordano,
Bologna, Nov. 7, 1853 ; graduate,
Bologna Cons., 1876, then studied
with Serrao (comp.) at Naples Cons.
and at Leipzig Cons. where he c. a
symph., an overture, a string quartet;
1885–91, prof. of mus. history, Liceo
Rossini, Pesaro ; then at Bologna
Cons.,since 1895 also prof. of comp.;
has begun a great 34-vol. coll. of the
chief Italian works of the 15–18 centuries, " *L'arte musicale in Italia.*"

**Torelli** (tō-rĕl'-lē), **Giu.**, Verona, ca.
1660—Ansbach, 1708 ; violinist and
composer ; originator of the " concerto grosso."

**Tor'rance**, Rev. **G. Wm.**, b. Rath-
mines, near Dublin, 1835 ; chorister,
Dublin ; organist at St. Andrew's,
and St. Anne's ; studied at Leipzig,
1856 ; 1866, priest; 1869, Melbourne,
Australia; since 1895, incumbent at
St. John's there ; Mus. Doc., *h. c.*
Dublin, 1879 ; c. succ. oratorios,
"*Abraham*" (Dublin, 1855), " *The
Captivity* " (1864), and " *The Reve-
lation*" (Melbourne, 1882), services,
an opera, etc.

**Torri** (tôr'-rē), **Pietro**, ca. 1665—Munich, 1737 ; court - conductor and
dram. composer.

**Tor'rington, Fr. Herbert**, b. Dudley Engl., Oct. 20, 1837 ; pianist

and conductor ; articled pupil of J[
Fitzgerald ; at 16 organist at Be[
ley ; 1856–68, organist, Great
James's Church, Montreal, Canad
also solo-violinist, cond. and ba
master; his orch. represented Cana
at the Boston Peace Jubilee, 186
then teacher New Engl. Cons.;
vln. Handel and Haydn, and ot
socs.; from 1873, organist Met
politan Ch., Toronto, Canada, a
cond. Toronto Philh. Soc.; 1886,
ganised the first Toronto mus. fe
val ; 1888, founded Toronto Coll.
Mus.; c. services, etc.

**Tosel'li, Enrico**, b. Florence, 18[
pianist ; pupil of Sgambati and M
tucci ; début Monte Carlo, 18[
played in London and America,19[

**Tosi** (tō'-zē), **Pier Fran.**, Bologr
1647 — London, 1727 ; celebrat
contralto musico and singing-teach

**Tosti** (tôs'-tē), **Fran. Paolo**, b. Or
na, Abruzzi, April 9, 1846 ; pupil
the R. C. di S. Pietro a Majel
Naples; sub-teacher there till 186
then ct.-singing-teacher at Rom
1875 sang with great succ. Londo
and has since lived there as a teache
1880, singing-master to the Roy
family ; 1894, prof. R. A. M.; pu
à coll. of " *Canti popolari abruzzes*
(Milan), and c. pop. songs.

**Tottmann** (tôt'-män), **Carl Albert**,
Zittau, July 31, 1837; studied Dr[
den, and with Hauptmann, at Le
zig Cons.; violinist in the Gewar
haus Orch.; teacher of theory a[
history at Leipzig, also lecture
1873, Prof., for his valuable compe
dium of vln.-literature ; pub. a[
essays, etc.; c. a melodrama " *Do[
röschen,*" Ave Maria, etc.

**Toulmouche** (tool-moosh), **Fr.**,
Nantes, Aug. 3, 1850 ; pupil of V
tor Massé ; 1894, dir. theatre " M
nus-Plaisirs"; since 1882, prod. ma[
operettas.

**Tourjée** (toor-zhā), Dr. **Eben, W[
wick, Rhode Island, 1834—Bostc
1890 ; organist, teacher and foun[
of N. E. Cons.

**Tours** (toors), **Berthold,** Rotterdam, Dec. 17, 1838—London, March 11, 1897; violinist, composer and editor; pupil Brussels and Leipzig Conservatory.

**Tourte** (toort), **Fran.,** Paris, 1747—1835; famous maker of vln.-bows; est. the standard since followed.

**Tow′ers, J.,** b. Salford, Feb. 18, 1836; pupil of R. A. M. and of Marx, Berlin; conductor and organist, Manchester, England.

**Tracy, Minnie,** b. New York; soprano; sang with Hinrich's Opera Co., Philadelphia; later at Geneva and elsewhere; 1900 with Am. Op. Co., Met. Op., N. Y.

**Traetta** (trä-ĕt′-tä) (not **Trajetta**), (1) **Tommaso (Michele Fran. Saverio),** Bitonto, Naples, March 30, 1727—Venice, April 6, 1779; pupil of Durante; 1758, maestro to Duke of Parma; 1765, given a life-pension by the Spanish King; 1768, ct.-composer at Petersburg; he prod. 37 operas, many of them v. succ.; c. also an oratorio, masses, etc. (2) **Filippo,** Venice, 1777—Philadelphia, 1854; son of above; from 1799 in America as an exile; wrote a vocal method; c. opera, oratorios, etc.

**Trasuntino** (trä-soon-tē′-nō), **Vito,** harps.-maker and inv., Rome, 1555—1606.

**Trautmann, Marie.** Vide JAEL, AL-FRED.

**Trautwein** (trowt′-vīn), **Traugott,** founded (1820) mus.-pub. business, at Berlin, transferred in 1840 to J. Guttentag, and by him to Martin Bahn (1858).

**Travenol** (trä-vŭ-nôl), **Louis,** d. 1783; vln.-maker and writer, Paris.

**Trav′ers, J.,** d. 1758; English organist and composer.

**Trebelli** (trā-bĕl′-lē), **Zella** (rightly **Guillebert**), Paris, 1838—Étretât, Aug. 18, 1892; noted mezzo-soprano; pupil of Wartel; début, Madrid, 1859; 1863, m. Bellini; sang in Europe and (1884) U. S. with great succ.

**Tree, Anna M.,** London, 1802—1862 mezzo-soprano.

**Treiber** (trī′-bĕr), **Wm.,** Graz, 1838-Cassel, 1899; pianist.

**Tren′to, Vittorio,** b. Venice, 1761 (or 1765); d. after 1826; mus.-dir. and dram. composer.

**Treu** (Italianised **Fedele**) (troi, or fā-dā′-lĕ), **Daniel Gl.,** b. Stuttgart, 1695; violinist, conductor and dram. composer.

**Tréville** (trä-vē-yŭ), **Yvonne de** (rightly **Le Gièrce**), b. Texas, of French father and American mother; notable soprano; pupil of Marchesi; début, New York, in "La Falote," later for years with Castle Square Opera Co.; 1890 went abroad for rest and study; 1901 sang in Spain; June, 1902, at Paris Opéra Comique.

**Trial** (trī-ăl), (1) **Jean Claude,** Avignon, 1732—Paris, 1771; dir. Paris Opéra and dram. composer. (2) **Antoine,** 1736—suicide, 1795; bro. of above; tenor; his wife (3) **Marie Jeanne** (née **Milon**) was a colorature-sopr. Their son (4) **Armand Emmanuel,** Paris, 1771 — 1803; dram. composer.

**Triébert** (trī′-ā-bĕr′), (1) **Chas. L.,** Paris, 1810—July 1867; oboist and professor and manufacturer of instrs. (2) **Frédéric,** 1813—1878; bro. and partner of above, and maker of bassoons. (3) **Frédéric,** son of (2); oboist.

**Trito′nius, Petrus,** German composer, Augsburg, 1507.

**Tritto, Giacomo,** Altamura, Naples, 1735—Naples, 1824; professor of cpt. and dram. composer.

**Tromboncino** (trôm-bôn-chē′-nō), **Bartholomaeus,** c. at Verona, 1504-10.

**Tromlitz** (trôm′-lĭts), **Jn. G.,** Gera, 1726 — Leipzig, 1805; flute-player, maker and teacher.

**Trotter** (**Trotère**)(trō-tăr′),**Henry,** b. London, Dec. 24, 1855; c. pop. songs.

**Troutbeck,** Rev. **J.,** Blencowe, Cumberland, 1832—London, 1899; pub. psalters and transl. libretti.

**Troyers** (troi'-ĕrs), **Fd.**, Count **von**, amateur clarinettist and patron, Vienna, 1821-47.

**Troyte** (troit), **Arthur H. D.**, Devon, 1811—1857; composer.

**Truhn** (troon), **Fr. Hieronymus**, Elbing, 1811—Berlin, 1886; conductor, writer and composer.

**Tschaikowsky.** Vide TCHAIKOVSKY.

**Tschirch** (tshĕrkh), six brothers, (1) **Hermann**, Lichtenau, Silesia, 1808—Schmiedeberg, 1829; organist. (2) **K. Ad.**, Lichtenau, 1815—Guben, Silesia, 1875; writer. (3) **Fr. Wm.**, Lichtenau, 1818—Gera, 1892; ct.-conductor and dram. composer. (4) **Ernst Lebrecht**, Lichtenau, 1819—Berlin, 1854; conductor and dram. composer. (5) **H. Julius**, Lichtenau, 1820—Hirschberg, Silesia, 1867; R. Mus.-Dir. and composer. (6) **Rudolf**, Lichtenau, 1825—Berlin, 1872; mus.-dir. and composer.

**Tschudi.** Vide BROADWOOD.

**Tua** (too'-ä), **Teresina**, b. Turin, May 22, 1867; violinist; pupil of Massart, Paris Cons., took 1st prize 1880; toured Europe, and, 1887, America, with great succ. 1891 (?), m. Count Franchi-Verney della Valetta.

**Tubbs**, (1) **Frank Herbert**, b. Brighton, Mass., Nov. 16, 1853; pupil of Leavitt, Petersilea and W. F. Apthorp, Boston; and (in singing) of Davis and Wheeler, Boston, Manuel Garcia, E. Behnke, and Shakespeare, London, San Giovanni and Lamperti in Italy; choirm. various churches; founded N. Y. Vocal Inst.; writer of essays and books on the voice. (2) **Jas.**, head of a family of vln. bowmakers in London, 1890.

**Tucher** (too'-khĕr), (1) **Gl.**, Freiherr **von**, Nürnberg, 1798—1877; writer. (2) Rev. **Wm.**, d. 1675; Engl. composer.

**Tuck'erman**, **Samuel Parkman**, Boston, Mass., 1819—Newport, 1890; organist, editor and composer.

**Tuczek** (toots'-zĕk), **Fz.**, Prague, ca. 1755—Pesth, 1820; tenor; conductor and dram. composer.

**Tud'way, Thos.**, England, ca. 166—London, 1730; organist and pro fessor, Cambridge, 1704-26; Mus Doc. there, 1705; made a coll. o contemporary services, also c. se vices, etc.

**Tulou** (tü-loo), **J. L.**, Paris, Sept 1786—Nantes, 1865; chief flutist o his time; at 14 at the Opéra; 1826 56, flute-prof. at the Cons.; compo er.

**Tuma** (too'-mä), **Fz.**, Kostelecz, B hemia, 1704—Vienna, 1774; gamba virtuoso and composer.

**Tunder** (toon'-dĕr), **Fz.**, 1614—L beck, 1667; organist Marienkirch as predecessor of Buxtehude.

**Tunsted(e)** (tŭn'-stĕd) (or **Dunstede Simon**, b. Norwich, Bruisyard, Su folk, 1369; writer. (Coussemaker.

**Turini** (too-rē'-nē), (1) **Gregori** Brescia, ca. 1560—Prague, ca. 1600 singer, cornet-player and compose (2) **Fran.**, Brescia, ca. 1590—1650 son of above; organist and comp.

**Türk** (tŭrk), **Daniel Gl.**, Claussnit Saxony, Aug. 10, 1756—Halle, Au 26, 1813; eminent organist and teac er, theorist and composer.

**Turle** (tŭrl), (1) **Jas.**, Somerton, Eng 1802—London, 1882; organist, co ductor, editor and composer. (2 **Robt.**, 1804—1877; bro. of abov organist. (3) **Wm. Taunton**, b. 179 cousin of above; organist.

**Turley** (toor'-lī), **Jn. Tobias**, Treue brietzen, Brandenburg, 1773—182 org.-builder.

**Tur'ner**, (1) **Wm.**, 1651—1740; En lish Mus. Doc. Cambridge; co poser. (2) **Austin T.**, b. Brist 1823, cond. and composer; fr 1854 in Australia. (3) **Alfred Du ley**, St. Albans, Maine, 1854—188 pianist, teacher and composer.

**Turnhout** (tŭrn'-hoot), (1) **Gerard** (rightly **Gheert Jacques**), Tu hout, Belgium, ca. 1520—Mad 1580; cond. at Antwerp Cath. a to the Court at Spain 1572; c poser. (2) **Jean**, son of above; conductor and composer, ca. 1595

**Tur'pin, Edmund Hart,** b. Nottingham, May 4, 1835 ; concert-organist; lecturer, editor and writer ; pupil of Hullah and Pauer, London ; organist various London churches ; from 1888 at St. Bride's ; in 1889 Mus. Doc.; then c. masses, 2 oratorios, cantatas, symph. " *The Monastery*," overtures, etc.

**Turtshaninoff** (toort-shä'-nĭ-nôf), **Peter Ivanovitch,** St. Petersburg, 1779 —1856 ; composer.

**Tye** (tī), **Christopher,** d. Westminster, 1572 ; 1554–61, organist Ely cathedral and composer.

**Tylman, Susato** (also **Tilman, Tielman, Thieleman**) (tēl'-män), mus.-printer at Antwerp from 1543 ; composer.

**Tyn'dall, J.,** Leighlin Bridge, Ireland, 1820—Haslemere, Engl., 1893 ; famous scientist and acoustician.

# U

**Ubaldus.** Vide HUCBALD.

**Uber** (oo'-bĕr), (1) **Chr. Benj.,** Breslau, 1746—1812 ; dram. composer. (2) **Fr. Chr. Hermann,** Breslau, 1781—Dresden, 1822 ; son of above; opera-conductor and composer. (3) **Alex.,** Breslau, 1783—Carolath, Silesia, 1824 ; bro. of (2) ; 'cellist, conductor and composer.

**Uberti** (oo-bĕr'-tē) **(Hubert) A.,** Verona, 1697 (?)—Berlin, 1783; brilliant soprano-musico and teacher of Malibran, Grisi, etc.

**Uccellini** (oo-chĕl-lē'-nē), **Don Marco,** conductor and composer at Florence, 1673.

**Uchbaldus, Uchubaldus.** Vide HUCBALD.

**Ugalde** (ü-găld), **Delphine** (née **Beauce**), b. Paris, Dec. 3, 1829 ; soprano at Op.-Com., etc.; 1866, also managed the Bouffes-Parisiens; twice m.; c. an opera.

**Ugolini** (oo-gō-lē'-nē), **V.,** Perugia, ca. 1570—1638 ; teacher and important composer ; pupil of Nanini ; 1620–26 *maestro* at St. Peter's.

**Ugolino** (oo-gō-lē'-nō), **Biagio,** monk in Venice ; pub. treatise, 1744.

**Uhl** (ool), **Edmund,** b. Prague, Oct. 25, 1853 ; pupil of Leipzig Cons. winning Helbig pf.-prize, 1878; since teacher at the Freudenberg Cons., Wiesbaden ; organist at the Synagogue ; and critic ; c. Romance for vln. with orch., etc.

**Uhlig** (oo'-lĭkh), **Th.,** Wurzen, Saxony, 1822—Dresden, 1853 ; violinist, theorist and composer.

**Ulibisheff** (in French **Oulibischeff**) (oo-lē'-bĭ-shĕf), **Alex. d',** Dresden, 1795 — Nishnij Novgorod, 1858 ; diplomat and writer of biographies.

**Ulrich** (ool'-rĭkh), **Hugo (Otto),** Oppeln, Silesia, 1827 — Berlin, 1872 ; teacher and dram. composer.

**Umbreit** (oom'-brīt), **K.Gl.,** Rehstedt, near Gotha, 1763—1829 ; org.-virtuoso and composer.

**Umlauf** (oom'-lowf), (1) **Ignaz,** Vienna, 1756—Meidling, 1796 ; music director ; asst.-conductor to Salieri. (2) **Michael,** Vienna, 1781—1842; son of above ; conductor and dram. composer.

**Umlauft** (oom'-lowft), **Paul,** b. Meissen, Oct. 27, 1853; pupil Leipzig Cons., with Mozart scholarship 1879–83 ; c. succ. 1-act opera "*Evanthia*" (Gotha, 1893) (won Duke of Coburg-Gotha's prize) ; dram. poem "*Agandecca*," with orch. (1892) ; "*Mittelhochdeutsches Liederspiel*," etc.

**Unger** (oong'-ĕr), (1) **Jn. Fr.,** Brunswick, 1716—1781 ; inventor. (2) (in Ital. **Ungher**) **Caroline,** Stuhlweissenburg, Hungary, 1803 — at her villa, near Florence, 1877 ; soprano ; 1840, m. Sabatier. (3) **G.,** Leipzig, 1837—1887 ; tenor.

**Up'ton, G. Putnam,** b. Boston, Mass., Oct. 25, 1835 ; graduate Brown Univ., 1854 ; 1861–85, on the editorial staff, Chicago "*Tribune*"; founder (1872) and first pres. Apollo Club; translator and writer of valuable essays, incl. "*Standard Operas*"

(1890); "*Standard Oratorios*" (1891); "*Standard Symphs.*" (1892), etc.

**Urban** (oor'-bän), (1) **Chr.**, b. Elbing, 1778 ; mus.-director, theorist and composer. (2) **H.**, Berlin, Aug. 27, 1837—Nov. 24, 1901; pupil of Ries, Laub, Helman, etc.; violinist and theorist; 1881, teacher at Kullak's Acad.; c. symph. "*Frühling*," overtures to "*Fiesco*" (Schiller), "*Scheherazade*," and "*Zu einem Fastnachtsspiel*," etc. (3) **Fr. Julius**, b. Berlin, Dec. 23, 1838 ; bro. of above ; solo boy-soprano in the Domchor ; pupil of H. Ries, and Helmann (vln.), Grell (theory), Elsner and Mantius (singing) ; singing-teacher, Berlin ; wrote vocal methods and songs.

**Urbani.** Vide VALENTINI.

**Urfey** (dŭr'-fĭ), **Thos.** d', Exeter, ca. 1649—London, 1723 ; pop. playwright, whose plays were set by Purcell ; also a singer and composer.

**Urhan** (ür-äṅ), **Chrétien**, Montjoie, 1790—Paris, 1845 ; eccentric and gifted player on stringed instrs., ancient and modern ; organist and composer.

**Urich** (oo'-rĭkh), **I.**, b. Alsace ; pupil of Gounod ; prod. operas "*Der Lootse*," "*Hermann und Dorothea*," and 2-act "*Le Carillon*" (Berlin, 1902).

**Urio** (oo'-rĭ-ō), **Fran. A.**, b. Milan, 1660 ; writer and composer.

**Urquhart** (ŭr'-kärt), **Thos.**, vln.-maker, London, 1675.

**Ursillo** (oor-sĭl'-lō), **Fabio** (or simply **Fabio**), 18th cent. archlute virtuoso and composer at Rome.

**Urso** (oor'-sō), (1) **Camilla**, Nantes, France, 1842—New York, Jan. 20, 1902 ; vln.-virtuoso (daughter of (2) **Salvator**, organist and flutist; pupil of Massart ; she played in America with great succ. at 10 ; toured the world; m. Fr. Luères.

**Urspruch** (oor'-sprookh), **Anton**, b. Frankfort-on-Main, Feb. 17, 1850; pupil of Ignaz Lachner and M. Wallenstein, Raff and Liszt ; pf.-teacher Hoch Cons.; from 1887 at Raff

Cons.; c. opera "*Der Stur* (based on Shakespeare's "*Tempe* Frankfort, 1888), comic opera (t and music) "*Das Unmöglichste Allem*" (Carlsruhe, 1897), a symp pf.-concerto, etc.

**Ursus.** Vide BÄHR.

**U(u)tendal** (or **Utenthal, Uut dal**) (ü'-tĕn-däl), **Alex.**, d. In bruck, May 8, 1581 ; Flemish c ductor and composer.

## V

**Vaccai** (väk-kä'-ē), **Niccolò**, Tole tino, Papal States, 1790 — Pesa 1848 ; noted singing-teacher ; pr of comp. Milan Cons.; c. an opera, funeral c tata, etc.

**Vaet** (vät), **Jacques**, d. Vienna, 15 Flemish conductor and composer.

**Valentini** (vä-lĕn-tē'-nē), (1) **Gio** ca. 1615 ; organist and compos (2) **Giov.**, Naples, 1779—1788; dra composer. (3) **P. Fran.**, Rome, 1570—1654 ; eminent contrapunti pupil of Nanini. (4) (Rightly **V lentino Urbani**) (oor-bä'-nĕ), ce brated contralto-musico ; later a t or ; London, 1707. (5) **Giu.**, Florence, ca. 1690; violinist a composer.

**Valentino** (väl-äṅ-tē'-nō), **Henri J** tin Armand Jos., Lille, 1785—V sailles, 1865; conductor Paris Opé 1820–31, then at Op. Com. till 18;

**Valet'ta, Ippolito.** Vide FRANC VERNEY.

**Valle'ria, Alwina** (rightly **A. V. Lo mann**), b. Baltimore, U. S. A.,18. soprano ; pupil R. A. M., Lond and of Arditi ; début, 1871 ; fr 1882 in oratorio, England ; tour Europe and America (range *b* flat d′′′, v. PITCH. D. D.).

**Vallotti** (väl-lôt'-tē), **Fran. A.**, V celli, June 11, 1697—Padua, Jan. 1780; noted organist, theorist a composer

**Van Bree** (vän brä), **Jn. B.**, Amst

n, 1801—1857 ; violinist, conduct-
and composer.

**Cleve, J. Smith,** b. Maysville,
., Oct. 30, 1851 ; pianist and
cher, pupil of Nothnagel (Colum-
, O.), Lang and Apthorp (Boston),
l W. Steinbrecher (Cincinnati) ;
9—97 as teacher, critic, writer and
urer Cincinnati Cons. and the
l. of Mus. ; then Chicago ; later
urned to Cincinnati ; composer.

den Eeden (ā'-dĕn), (1) **Gilles,** d.
2 ; first teacher of Beethoven; son
nephew of (2) **Heinrich** ; ct.-mus.
the Elector of Cologne.

der Heiden (hī'-dĕn), d. Besan-
, 1902 ; noted Belgian 'cellist.

erlinden (vän'-dĕr-lēn-dĕn), **C.,**
Dordrecht, 1839 ; pupil of Böhme
rm. and cpt.) and Kwast (pf.) ;
ductor Dordrecht Philh. Soc.,
tional Guard band, and societies ;
2 operas, overtures, etc.

der **Straeten** (strä'-tĕn), **Ed-**
**nd,** Oudenaarden, Belgium, 1826
895; writer of valuable treatises
sed on research and c. an opera, etc.

der **Stucken** (vän'-dĕr-shtook'-
, **Frank (Valentin),** b. Frede-
ksburg, Gillespie Co., Texas,
t. 15, 1858, of Belgian father and
rman mother; notable composer and
ductor ; at 8 taken by his parents
Antwerp, studied with Benoit, later
h Reinecke, Sänger and Grieg;
81—82, cond. at Breslau City Th.;
83, in Rudolstadt with Grieg, and
Weimar with Liszt ; prod. opera
*Vlasda* " (Paris, 1883) ; 1884,
led to be mus.-dir. of the " Arion,"
w York ; from 1895 dir. Cincin-
i Cons., and 1st cond. Cincinnati
nph Orch.; c. symph. prologue
*William Ratcliff*" (Cincinnati,
99) ; orch. episode, " *Pagina d'a-*
*re*," with choruses and songs;
*estival March*," for orch., " *Pax*
*iumphans*" (Antwerp, 1902), etc.

**Duyze** (vän doi'-zĕ), **Florimond,**
Ghent, Aug. 4, 1853 ; lawyer and
ateur ; pupil of Ghent Cons., win-
g Grand prix de Rome, 1873,

with cantata " *Torquato Tasso's
Dood*"; prod. 7 operas, Antwerp and
Ghent ; c. also ode-symphonie " *Di*
*Nacht.*"

**Van Dyck** (vän dĭk), **Ernest (Marîe
Hubert),** b. Antwerp, April 2, 1861 ;
noted tenor; studied law, was then a
journalist at Paris ; studied singing
with St. Yves ; début Paris, 1887, as
" Lohengrin "; 1892 sang " Parsifal "
at Bayreuth ; 1888 engaged for the
Vienna ct.-opera ; has sung in the
chief capitals, London, and 1899
New York.

**Van Hal.** Vide WANHAL.

**Vanneo** (vän-nä'-ō), **Stefano,** b. Re
canati, Ancona, 1493 ; monk and
writer.

**Van Os** (vän ōs), **Albert,** earliest known
org.-builder called " A. the Great,"
at Utrecht, 1120.

**Van Rooy** (vän rō'-ĭ), **Anton,** b.
Rotterdam, Jan. 12, 1870 ; notable
barytone ; pupil of Stockhausen at
Frankfort ; sang in oratorio and con-
certs ; later at Bayreuth, 1897 ; then
at Berlin ct.-opera ; sang with succ.
London (1898), from 1898 in New
York annually ; his greatest rôle is
" Wotan."

**Van Westerhout** (wĕs'-tĕr-howt), **Niccolo** (of Dutch parents), Mola di Bari,
1862—Naples, 1898 ; dram. composer.

**Varney** (văr-nē), (1) **P. Jos. Alphonse,**
Paris, 1811—1879 ; conductor and
composer of operettas. (2) **Louis,**
b. Paris(?) ; son and pupil of above ;
lives in Paris, and has since 1876
prod. over 30 operettas, comic operas,
" revues," etc.

**Vasconcellos** (văs-kōn-sĕl'-lōs), **Joa**
quim de, contemporary Portuguese
lexicographer and historian.

**Vasseur** (văs-sŭr), **Léon (Félix Aug.
Jos.),** b. Bapaume, Pas-de-Calais,
May 28, 1844; studied École Nieder-
meyer ; from 1870 organist Versailles
Cath.; cond. Folies-Bergères and the
Concerts de Paris (1882) ; since 1872
prod. over 30 light operas ; c. also
masses, etc.

**Vaucorbeil** (vō-kôr-bě'), **Aug. Emanuel,** Rouen, 1821—Paris, 1884; 1880. dir. the Opéra ; c. comic-opera, etc.

**Vaughan** (vôn), **Thos.,** Norwich, 1782 —Birmingham, 1843 ; tenor.

**Vavrinecz** (vä'-vrē-něts), **Mauritius,** b. Czegled, Hungary, July 18, 1858 ; studied Pesth Cons., and with R. Volkmann; cath. cond. at Pesth ; c. 4-act opera "*Ratcliff*" (Prague, 1895), succ. 1-act opera "*Rosamunda*" (Frankfort-on-Main, 1895), oratorio, 5 masses, a symph., etc.

**Vecchi(i)** (věk'-kē-(ē) ), (1) **Orazio,** Modena, 1551 (?)—Feb. 19, 1605 ; noted composer; from 1596 maestro Modena cath. ; his "mus.-comedy" "*Amfiparnasso*," in which the chorus joined in all the mus., even the monologues, appeared the same year as PERI'S (q. v.) "*Dafne*"; c. also madrigals, etc. (2) **Orfeo,** Milan, ca. 1540—1613 ; maestro, and composer. eit (vīt),ₗ**Wenzel H. (Václav Jindřich),** Repnic, near Leitmeritz, Bohemia, 1806—Leitmeritz, 1864 ; composer.

**Velluti** (věl-loo'-tē), **Giov. Bat.,** Monterone, Ancona, 1781—San Burson, 1861 ; the last of the great male soprani.

**Venatorini.** Vide MYSLIWECZEK.

**Venosa,** Prince of. Vide GESUALDO.

**Ven'to,** (1) **Ivo de,** b. Spain ; ct -organist at Munich and composer (1561-91). (2) **Mattia,** Naples, 1739—London, 1777 ; c. operas.

**Venturelli** (věn-too-rěl'-lē), **V.,** Mantua, 1851—(suicide) 1895 ; essayist and dram. composer.

**Venzano** (věn-tsä'-nō), **Luigi,** Genoa, ca. 1814—1878 ; 'cellist and teacher ; c. opera, pop. songs, etc.

**Veracini** (vä-rä-chē'-nē), (1) **A.,** violinist at Florence (1696). (2) **Fran. Maria,** Florence, ca. 1685—near Pisa, ca. 1750; nephew and pupil of above ; notable violinist, the greatest of his time ; composer.

**Verdelot** (vărd-lō) (Italianised, **Verdelot'to),** **Philippe,** d. before 1567 ; famous Flemish madrigal-composer

and singer at San Marco, Ven between 1530-40 in Florence.

**Verdi** (věr'-dē), **(Fortunio) Giuse (Fran.),** Le Roncole, near Buss Duchy of Parma, Oct. 9, 181 Milan, Jan. 27, 1901 ; eminent ian opera composer. Son of an keeper and grocer ; pupil, anc 10 successor of the village orga Baistrocchi, for three years pup Provesi at Busseto ; 1831 with aid of his father's friend, Bare he went to Milan, where he was fused admission to the Cons. by sili, who thought him lacking mus. talent. He became a pupi Lavigna, cembalist, at La Sc 1833, cond. Philh. Soc., and org ist at Busseto ; 1836 m. Bare daughter Margherita. 1839, his era "*Oberto*" was prod. with succ. at La Scala, Milan. He commissioned by Merelli, the m ager, to write three operas, one e eight months, at 4,000 lire ($80 £160) apiece, and half the c right. The first was a comic o "*Un Giorno di Regno*," which fa (1840), doubtless in part because two children and wife had died w in three months. V.'s combined tress drove him to rescind his ag ment and renounce compositio over a year, when he was persua by Merelli to set the opera "*Na co*" ("Nebuchadrezzar"), prod. at Scala, 1842, with great applause, chief rôle being taken by Giusep Strepp.oni (1815-97), whom he m 1844. "*I Lombardi alla pr Crociata*" (La Scala, 1843) was more succ. and is still played in I (in Paris as "*Jérusalem*"). "*nani*" (Venice, 1844) was prod. 15 different stages in 9 months. unsucc. works followed, incl. "*I Foscari*" (Rome 1844), "*Macbe* (Florence, 1847, revised Paris, 18 and "*I Masnadieri*' (after Schil "*Robbers*" London, H. M. 1847). "*Luisa Miller*" (Nap 1849) was well received and is

ig in Italy. "*Stiffelio*" (Trieste,
50) ; later as "*Guglielmo Weling-
de*"; also with another libretto as
*Arnoldo*" (1857), was three times a
lure. "*Rigoletto*," c. in 40 days
enice (also given as "*Viscardel-
*"), began a three years' period of
iversal succ., it was followed
the world-wide successes "*Il
ovatore*" (Rome, 1853) and "*La
raviata*" (Venice Th., 1853 ; also
ven as "*Violetta*"), a fiasco at
st because of a poor cast ; "*Les
Vêpres Siciliennes*" (Paris Opéra,
55 ; in Italian "*I Vespri Sicili-
i*"; also given as "*Giovanna di
uzman*") was fairly succ.; "*Simon
occanegra*" (Venice, 1857 ; succ.
vised, Milan, 1881), "*Un Ballo in
aschera*" (Rome, 1859), "*La For-
del Destino*" (Petersburg, 1862),
d "*Don Carlos*" (Paris, Opéra,
67), made no deep impression,
ough they served as a schooling and
arked a gradual broadening from
ere Italian lyricism to a substantial
rmony and orchestration. "*Aïda*"

(written for the Khedive of Egypt)
was prod. Cairo, 1871, at La Scala,
Milan, 1872, and has had everywhere
a great succ. The Khedive gave him
£3,000 for it. His "Manzoni Requiem" (1874) made a sensation in
Italy ; "*Otello*" (Milan, 1887) was a
work worthy of its composer, and in
his last opera "*Falstaff*," written at
the age of eighty, he showed not
only an unimpaired but a progressive
and novel style. He also c. 2 symphs.,
6 pf.-concertos, "*Inno delle Nazi-
oni*," for the London Exhibition
(1862), songs, etc.

In 1893 he was given the title "Marchese di Busseto." He lived at his
villa Sant' Agata, near Busseto. His
funeral brought 100,000 witnesses,
though his will ordered that it should
be simple and quiet. He left the
bulk of his fortune to the home for
aged and outworn musicians.

Biog. by Gino Monaldi (only in
German, transl. by L. Holthof Leip-
zig, 1898) ; Checchi, 1887 ; Blanche
Roosevelt (London, 1887).

## Giuseppe Verdi.

### By W. J. Henderson.

VERDI has been the representative Italian opera composer of his time
and his personal development in art is that of his country, which has
followed his dominating influence. He began to write in the prev-
t style of the old Italian school, but even in his early works, which had
ing resemblances to those of Donizetti and Bellini, he showed a rude
ur not possessed by either of them. ¶ This vigour came conspicuously
notice in his "*Ernani*," though the most familiar example of his style
is period of his development is "*Rigoletto*." The early works show fecun-
of melodic invention, but a close adherence to the elementary
hms used by the Neapolitan school. The dramatic element and the virile
er of the man, however, continually pressed toward the front till in
*ida*," in which the Egyptian subject lured him away from conventions
originality of colour, he entered upon a new field and established himself
new individuality in music. He idealised the old aria, employed all the
urces of modern instrumentation in the orchestral part, and sought for

truthful dramatic expression as none of his predecessors had. *"Aïda"* been the model of the younger Italian school and its influence can be tra through the works of such writers as Mascagni, Leoncavallo, and Pucc ¶ In *"Otello"* Verdi left the old Italian patterns still further behind him, without ceasing to be Italian in style or individual in ideas. The voice p are dominant and essentially melodious at all times, but the determination the composer to be faithful to the spirit of the text is more manifest than e before. The work is a monument of genius. In his *"Falstaff"* V produced a comic opera which stands next to Mozart's *"Nozze di Figar* and Wagner's *"Die Meistersinger."* The freshness and spontaneity of score, the marvellous eloquence of the orchestral details and the infinite nificance of the recitative make this work one of the masterpieces of mod times. The advance of Verdi from the "drum and trumpet" operas of youth to the highly organised, subtly significant and opulent scores of his age, is the feature of his artistic career, and where he has led, Italy has lowed. He was the master and the moulder of Italian musical thought half a century.

**Verdonck', Cornelius,** Turnhout, Belgium, 1564—Antwerp, 1625; composer.

**Vere-Sapio** (văr-sä'-pĭ-ō), **Clementine (Duchêne) de,** b. Paris; soprano; daughter of a Belgian nobleman, and an English-woman; pupil of Mme. Albertini-Baucarde, Florence; début there at 16, sang at leading theatres, Europe, later in concert, also in the United States; 1896, she returned to opera; 1899, toured U. S. with an opera troupe of which her husband, Signor Sapio, was mgr.; 1900-1901 at Metropolitan, N. Y., and Covent Garden

**Verhulst** (vĕr-hoolst'), **Jns. (Josephus Herman),** The Hague, 1816—1891; cond.; famous composer; pupil of Volcke at the Cons. there, later R. mus.-dir.; cond. many societies, etc.; intimate friend of Schumann; c. symphony, 3 overtures, etc.

**Vernier** (vĕrn-yā), **Jean Aimé,** b. Paris, 1769 (?); harpist and composer.

**Ver'non, Jos.,** d. South Lambeth, 1782; male soprano; then tenor; composer.

**Véron** (vā-rôṅ), **Désiré,** Paris, 17 1867; critic, writer and manage the Opéra.

**Verovio** (vā-rō'-vĭ-ō), **Simone,** first copper-plate mus.-printer, Rc ca. 1586—1604.

**Vertov'ski,** c. the first Russian o *"Askold's Grave"* (*Askoldova gila*), based on folksongs.

**Vesque von Püttlingen** (vĕsk pĭt'-lĭng-ĕn), **Jn.,** Opole, Pol 1803—Vienna, 1883; pianist of gian parentage; c. 6 operas; pen-name **" J. Hoven."**

**Ves'trio, Lucia E.,** London, 17 Fulham, 1856; opera-singer.

**Viadana** (vē-ä-dä'-nä) **Ludovico** (rightly **L. Grossi**), Viadana, Mantua, 1564 — Gualtieri, 1 noted church-composer; maestr Mantua cath.; important early fi in the development of basso cont (v. D. D.).

**Vian'na da Mot'ta, José,** b. Isl St. Thomas, Africa, April 22, 1 Portuguese pianist; st Lisbon Scharwenka Cons., Berlin; later Schäffer, Liszt and von Bü toured Europe; lives Paris.

esi (vē-ä-nä′-zē), **Auguste Chas.
éonard François**, b. Leghorn,
ov. 2, 1837; studied in Paris 1859,
nd. Drury Lane, London; then at
ew York, Moscow and Peters-
rg; 12 years cond. at Covent Gar-
n; also in other cities; 1887, 1st
nd. Gr. Opéra, Paris; cond. New
ork, 1891–92.

rd-Louis (vĭ-ăr-loo-ē), **Jenny**, b.
arcassonne, Sept. 29, 1831; con-
rt-pianist and teacher, London.

rdot-Garcia (vĭ-ăr′-dō-gär-thē′-ä),
) **(Michelle Fde.) Pauline**, b.
aris, July 18, 1821; famous mezzo-so-
ano and teacher; daughter of Man-
l Garcia (q.v.), studied pf. with Vega
Mexico Cath., then with Meysen-
rg and Liszt, and Reicha (harm.);
d singing with her father and
other; concert début, Brussels,
37; opera début, London, 1839,
gaged by Viardot, dir. Th. Italien,
aris, and sang there until 1841,
hen she m. him and made Europe-
a tours with him. In 1849 she creed "Fides" in "*Le Prophète*,"
aris, "Sapho" (Gounod's opera),
51; 1863, retired to Baden-Baden;
om 1871 lived in Paris as teacher.
er voice had the remarkable com-
ass of more than 3 octaves from bass
-f′′′. Wrote a vocal method and c.
operas, 60 songs, and also 6 pcs.
or pf. and vln. Biogr. by La Mara.
) Mme. **Louise Héritte Viardot**,
, Paris, Dec. 14, 1841; daughter of
bove; singing-teacher Hoch Cons.,
rankfort (till 1886); then est. a
ch. at Berlin; c. 2 comic operas, a
f.-quartet, etc. (3) Mme. **Chame-
ot**, and (4) **Marianne V.**, daughters
f (1) were concert-singers. (5) **Paul**,
, Courtavent, July 20, 1857; violin-
t; son of (1). pupil of Léonard;
93, temporary cond. Paris Opéra.

entino (vē-chĕn-tē′-nō), **Nicola**,
icenza, 1511 — Milan, ca. 1576;
onductor, theorist and composer;
v. "archiorgano."

torio. Vide VITTORIA.

al (vē-dăl), (1) **B.**, d. Paris, 1880;

guitar-virtuoso, teacher and composer. (2) **Jean Jos.**, Sorèze, 178?
—Paris, 1867; violinist. (3) **Louis
A.**, b. Rouen, July 10, 1820; 'cellist
and writer; pupil of Franchomme;
pub. important historical works. (4)
**François**, b. Aix, July 14, 1832;
poet and writer. (5) **Paul Antonin**,
b. Toulouse, June 16, 1863; pupil of
Paris Cons., winning first Grand
prix de Rome, 1881; 1894, taught
solfège there; from 1896, cond. at
the Opéra; prod. 3-act lyric fantasy
"*Eros*" (1892), a ballet "*La Mala-
detta*" (1893), 2 1-act operettas;
lyric drama "*Guernica*" (Op. Com.,
1895); orch. suite, "*Les mystères
d'Eleusis*," etc.

**Vierdank** (fēr′-dänk), **Jn.**, organist
and composer at Stralsund 1641.

**Vierling** (fēr′-lĭng), (1) **Jn. Gf.**, Metz-
els, near Meiningen, 1750—Schmalk-
den, 1813; organist and composer.
(2) **Jacob V.**, 1796—1867, organist.
(3) **Georg**, Frankenthal, Palatinate,
Sept. 5, 1820 — Wiesbaden, June,
1901; son and pupil of above, also
of Rinck (org.), Marx (comp.); 1847,
organist at Frankfort-on-Oder; 1852–
53, cond. Liedertafel, Mayence;
then lived in Berlin, founder and for
years cond. Bach-verein; prof. and
R. Mus.-Dir.; c. notable secular
oratorios, "*Der Raub der Sabine-
rinnen*" (op. 50), "*Alarichs Tod*"
and "*Konstantin*"; Psalm 137, with
orch.; and other choral works; a
symph.; 5 overtures, incl. "*Im
Frühling*"; capriccio for pf. with
orch., etc.

**Vieuxtemps** (v'yŭ-tän), (1) **Henri**, Verviers, Belgium, Feb. 20, 1820—Mus-
tapha, Algiers, June 6, 1881; eminent violinist and composer; son and
pupil of a piano-tuner and instr.-
maker, then pupil of Lecloux, with
whom he toured at 8 · then pupil of
de Bériot (vln.). Sechter (harm.),
Reicha (comp.); he toured Europe
with great succ., and three times
America (1844, 1857 and 1870); 1845,
m. Josephine Eder, a Vienna pianist;

1846–52, solo-violinist to the Czar and prof. at the Petersburg Cons.; 1871–73, prof. at the Brussels Cons.; then paralysis of his left side stopped his playing. He c. 6 concertos, several concertinos, an overture on the Belgian national hymn (op. 41), fantaisie-caprice, with orch.; fantaisies on Slavic themes, "*Homage à Paganini*," caprice, sonata, vars. on "*Yankee Doodle*," 2 'cello-concertos, a grand solo duo for vln. and 'cello (with Servais), etc. Biog. by Randoux (1891). (2) **Jules Jos. Ernest**, Brussels, March 18, 1832—Belfast, March 20, 1896; bro. of above; solo-'cellist It. Opera, London; also in Hallé's orch. at Manchester.

**Viganò** (vē-gä-nō'), **Salvatore**, Naples, 1769—Milan, 1821; balletdancer and succ. composer of ballets.

**Vilbac(k)** (vēl-băk),**(Alphonse Chas.) Renaud de**, Montpellier, 1829—Paris, 1884; pianist and organist; c. comic operas.

**Villanis** (vēl-lä'-nēs), **Luigi Alberto**, b. San Mauro, near Turin, June 20, 1863; LL.D. Turin Univ., 1887, then pupil of Thermignon, and Cravero (comp.); 1890 prof. of mus. æsthetics and history, Turin Univ.; critic and writer.

**Villarosa** (vēl-lä-rō'-sä), **Carlantonio de Rosa**, Marchese di, Naples, 1762 —1847; Royal Historiographer, 1823, and writer on music.

**Villars** (vē-yärs). **Fran. de**, Ile Bourbon, 1825—Paris, 1879; critic and historian.

**Villebois** (vē'-yŭ-bwä), **Constantin Petrovitch**, Warsaw, 1817—1882; composer.

**Vil'loing, Alex**, b. Petersburg, d. there 1878; pf.-teacher; wrote method and c. pf.-pcs.

**Villoteau** (vē'-yô-tō), **Guillaume André**, Bellême, 1759—Tours, 1839; tenor and writer.

**Vincent** (văṅ-säṅ), (1) **Alex. Jos. Hydulphe**, Hesdin, Pas-de-Calais, 1797—Paris, 1868; pub. treatises

claiming that the Greeks used ha[r] etc.

(fĭn'-tsĕnt), (2) **H. Jos.**, Theilh[e] near Würzburg, Feb. 23, 1819—1[ ] gave up theology and law and bec[a] a tenor in theatres at Vienna (18.[ ] Halle and Würzburg; from 18[ ] singing-teacher and conductor; li[ ] at Czernowitz, Bukowina and late[ ] Vienna; pub. treatises advoca[t] the "Chroma" (v. D.D.) Theory operas, operettas, and pop. songs.

(vĭn'-sĕnt), (3) **Chas. John**, Houghton-le-Spring, Durham, E[n] Sept. 19, 1852 (son and pupil of **Chas. J.**, organist at St. Michae[l] studied Leipzig Cons.; Mus. [ ] Oxon, 1885; 1883–91, organist Ch[ ] Ch., London; ed., writer; c. o[v] ture "*The Storm*"; oratorio "*Ru[ ]* 3 cantatas with orch.; choral fu[ ] in 8 parts, etc. (5) **G. Fr.**, b. Ma[ ] 27, 1855; bro. of above; pupil Leipzig Cons.; from 1882, organis[ ] St. Thomas's, Sunderland, also co[ ] societies there; c. operettas, a c[ ] tata with orch. "*Sir Humphrey* [ ] *bert*," etc.

**Vinci** (vēn'-chē), (1) **Pietro**, b. Nico[ ] Sicily, 1540; maestro and compo[ ] (2) **Leonardo**, Strongoli, Calab[ ] 1690 — Naples, 1732; maestro [ ] dram. composer.

**Vi'ning, Helen Sherwood**, b. Bro[ok]lyn, N. Y., July 4, 1855; wrote te[ ] books, etc.

**Vin'ning, Louisa**, Newton (?), Dev[ ] harpist and singer in London; m[ ] S. C. Heywood, 1865.

**Viola** (vē-ō'-lä), (1) **Alfonso della**, composer at Ferrara, 1541–63 [ ] Ercole II. (2) **Fran.**, pupil of V[il]laert; maestro at Ferrara, and c[ ] poser, 1558–73.

**Viole** (fē'-ō-lĕ), **Rudolf**, Schochw[ ] Mansfeld, 1815—Berlin, 1867; [ ] nist and composer.

**Viotta** (fē-ôt'-tä), **Henri**, b. Ams[ter]dam, July 16, 1848; studied Colo[gne] Cons.; also a lawyer, 1883; foun[ ] and cond., Amsterdam Wagner S[oc] etc.; 1889, ed. "*Maandblad* [ ] *uzie*; 1896, dir. Cons. at The ague; publ. a "*Lexicon der Toon-ust*" (1889).

cti (vē-ôt'-tē), **Giov. Bat.**, Fontato da Pò, Vercelli, Italy, May 23, 53—London, March 10 (?), 1824; n of a blacksmith; at first self-ight, then, under patronage of Prince lla Cisterna, studied with Pugnani Turin; soon entered the ct.-orches-a; 1780 toured with Pugnani, was vited to become ct.-violinist to atherine II., but went to Paris, then ondon, playing with greatest succ.; 83 an inferior violinist drew a larger dience, and in disgust he retired om concerts and became a teacher d accompanist to Marie Antoinette d cond. to the Prince de Soubise. ailing to be dir. of the Opera, 1787, joined Léonard, the Queen's hair-esser, and est. It. Opéra, 1789; ospering till the Revolution. He ent to London as a violinist and ayed with great succ. 1795, mgr. . Opera and dir. Opera Concerts ere; failing he went into the wine-ade. Later returned to Paris, and came dir. of the Opéra, 1819–22, en pensioned with 6,000 francs. e pub. 29 vln.-concertos (the first ritten in the modern sonata-form, d supported with broadened or-estration). C. also 2 Concertantes r 2 vlns., 21 string-quartets, 51 vln.-os, 18 sonatas, etc. Biogr. by ayolle (Paris, 1810); Baillot (1825), c.

dung (fēr'-doongk), **Sebastian**, iest and organist at Basel, 1511; riter and composer.

etti (vē-sĕt'-tē), **Alberto Ant.**, b. palato, Dalmatia, May 13, 1846; upil of Mazzucato, Milan Cons., oncert-pianist at Nice; then Paris, nd. to the Empress Eugénie; on e fall of the Empire, vocal teacher the R. C. M., London; pub. a *History of the Art of Singing*," nd translations.

ali (vē-tä'-lē), (1) **Filippo**, b. Flor-nce, singer and composer. 1631. (2)

**Giov. Bat.**, Cremona, ca. 1644—Modena, Oct. 12, 1692; 2d ct.-cond. and composer of important sonatas, ballets, etc. (3) **Tomaso**, b. Bologna, middle of 17th cent.; leader there, and c. a chaconne.

**Vitry** (vē-trē), **Philippe De (Philippus di Vitria'co)**, b. Vitry, Pas-de-Calais; d. 1316, as Bishop of Meaux; theorist.

**Vittori** (vĭt-tō'-rē), **Loreto**, Spoleto, ca. 1588—Rome, 1670; composer.

**Vittoria** (vĭt-tō'-rĭ-ä), **Tomaso Ludovico da** (rightly **Tomas Luis De Victoria**), Avila (?), Spain, ca. 1540—Madrid, (?) ca. 1608; went to Rome early; 1573 maestro Collegium Germanicum; 1575, of S. Apollinaris; friend and disciple of Palestrina; 1589–1602 vice ct.-conductor, Madrid; c. notable works incl. a requiem for the Empress Maria, 1605.

**Vivaldi** (vē-väl'-dē), Abbate **Ant.**, Venice, ca. 1675—1743; celebrated violinist; from 1713 dir. Cons. della Pietà; c. notable vln.-concertos and sonatas.

**Vivier** (vēv-yā), (1) **Albert Jos.**, b. Huy, Belgium, Dec. 15, 1816; pupil of Fétis; c. opera and wrote a harmony. (2) **Eugène Léon**, b. Ajaccio, 1821; remarkable horn-virtuoso; he always refused to tell how he produced three or four notes at once, making it possible to play the parts for three horns on one; pupil of Gallay, then joined orch. at Paris Opéra; made many tours, was a favourite of Napoleon III., then retired to Nice; a great wit and a composer of excellent songs. (3) **Albert Jos.**, b. Huy, Belgium, Dec. 3, 1816; theorist and composer.

**Vleeshouwer** (flās'-hoo-vĕr), **Albert de**, b. Antwerp, June 8, 1863; pupil of Jan Blockx; prod. 2 operas, "*L'École des Pères*" (1892) and "*Zryni*" (Antwerp, 1895), symphonic poem, "*De wilde Jäger*," etc.

**Vockerodt** (fôk'-ĕ-rōt), **Gf.**, Mülhausen, 1665—Gotha, 1727; theorist.

**Vogel** (fō'-gĕl), (1) **Jn. Chr.**, Nürnberg, 1756—Paris, 1788 ; dram. composer. (2) **L.,** flutist and composer. Paris, 1792—1798. (3) **Fr. Wm. Fd.,** b. Havelberg, Prussia, Sept. 9, 1807; pupil of Birnbach, Berlin ; toured as organist ; from 1852, at Bergen, Norway ; pub. a concertino for org. with trombones ; symph., overture, 2 operettas, etc. (4) **(Chas. Louis) Ad.,** Lille, 1808—Paris, 1892 ; violinist and dram. composer. (5) **(Wm.) Moritz,** b. Sorgau, near Freiburg, Silesia, July 9, 1846; pianist ; pupil of Leipzig Cons.; teacher, critic and conductor of choral socs., Leipzig ; pub. pf. method, c. rondos, etc. (6) **(Ad.) Bd.,** Plauen, Saxony, 1847 — Leipzig, 1898 ; journalist, writer and composer. (7) **Emil,** b. Wriezen-on-Oder, Jan. 21, 1859 ; Dr. Phil., Berlin, 1887; 1883, sent to Italy by the govt. as Haberl's asst. in studying Palestrina's works ; from 1893, lib. Peters Mus. Library, Leipzig ; pub. monographs, etc.

**Voggenhuber** (fôg'-gĕn-hoo-bĕr), **Vilma von** (Frau **V. Krolop),** Pesth, 1845—Berlin 1888 ; dram. soprano at Berlin ct.-opera 1868–88.

**Vogl** (fôkh'-'l), (1) **Jn. Michael,** Steyr, 1768—Vienna, 1840 ; tenor and conductor (v. FZ. SCHUBERT). (2) **Heinrich,** Au, Munich, Jan. 15, 1845— on the stage, Munich, April 21, 1900; famous tenor ; début Munich ct.-opera, 1865 ; sang there thereafter ; eminent in Wagnerian rôles at Bayreuth ; prod. an opera *" Der Fremdling"* (Munich, 1899). (3) **Therese** (née **Thoma),** Tutzing, Lake of Starnberg, Nov. 12, 1845 ; from 1868, wife of above, and like him, eminent in Wagner opera ; dram. soprano ; pupil of Hauser and Herger, Munich Cons.; 1864, Carlsruhe ; 1865–92, Munich. then retired.

**Vogler** (fôkh'-lĕr), **Georg Jos.** (**"Abbé Vogler "),** Würzburg, June 15, 1749 —Darmstadt, May 6, 1814 ; famous organist ; theorist and composer; pupil of Padre Martini and Vallotti ; took orders at Rome ; 1786 ?? court-con-

ductor Stockholm ; 1807, ct.-con Darmstadt ; he was eminent teacher of radical methods ; to widely as a concert organist with " orchestrion"; he wrote many tises ; c. 10 operas, a symphony,

**Vogrich** (fō'-grĭkh), **Max (V Carl),** b. Szeben (Hermannsta Transylvania, Jan. 24, 1852 ; pia at 7 he played in public, then p of Leipzig Cons.; 1870–78, to Europe, Mexico and South Amer then U. S. with Wilhelmj ; 1882 in Australia, where he m.; s 1886, lives in New York ; c. 3 g operas (text and music) incl. *"Wan* (Florence, 1875) ; c. also an orat *" The Captivity "* (1884 ; Met. 1891); 2 cantatas, Missa Solem 2 symphs., vln.-concerto, etc

**Vogt** (fōkht), (1) **Gustave,** Str burg, 1781—Paris, 1879 ; obe professor and composer. (2) **(Jean),** Gross-Tinz, near Leig 1823—Eberswalde, 1888 ; pianist composer.

**Voigt** (foikht), (1) **Jn. G. Herma** Osterwieck, Saxony, 1769—1811; ganist and composer. (2) **K., H** burg, 1808—1879 ; conductor. **Henriette** (née **Kunze),** 1809–( 15, 1839 ; distinguished amateur sician at Leipzig ; intimate friend Schumann.

**Volckmar** (fôlk'-mär), **Wm. (Val tin),** Hersfeld. Cassel, 1812—H berg, near Cassel, 1887; mus.-tea er, organist, writer and composer.

**Volkert** (fôl'-kĕrt), **Fz.,** Heimersd Bohemia, 1767—Vienna, 1845 ; ganist and conductor ; c. over comic operas, Singspiele, etc.

**Volkland** (fôlk'-länt), **Alfred,** Brunswick, April 10, 1841; p Leipzig Cons.; ct.-pianist at Sond hausen ; from 1867, ct.-cond. th 1869–75, cond. Leipzig Euterpe, a co-founder the Bach-Verein ; si 1875, cond. at Basel ; 1889, Phil. *h. c.* (Basel Univ.).

**Volkmann** (fôlk'-män), **(Fr.) Rol** Lommatzsch, Saxony, April 6, 1

-Pesth, Oct. 30, 1883 ; notable composer ; son and pupil of a cantor ; studied with Friebel (vln. and 'cello), Knacker (comp.) and K. F. Becker, at Leipzig ; 1839-42, taught mus. at Prague ; thereafter lived in Pesth, excepting 1854-58, Vienna ; for years prof. of harm. and cpt. at the Nat. Acad. of Mus., Prague ; c. 2 symphs.; serenades for strings ; 2 overtures, incl. "*Richard III*." *;* concerto for 'cello, Concertstück for pf. and orch.; 2 masses with orch.; Christmas carol of the 12th cent.; old German hymns for double male chorus ; 6 duets on old German poems ; 2 wedding-songs ; alto solo with orch., "*An die Nacht*"; dram.-scene for soprano with orch., "*Sappho*"; pf.-pcs. and songs. Biog. by Vogel (Leipzig, 1875).

**Ilhardt** (fôl'-härt), **Emil Reinardt**, b. Seifersdorf, Saxony, Oct. 6, 1858 ; pupil of Leipzig Cons.; cantor Marienkirche and cond. at Zwickau ; c. motets and songs.

**Ilweiler** (fôl'-vī-lĕr), **K.**, Offenbach, 1813 — Heidelberg, 1848 ; pianoteacher and composer.

**Iumier** (vō-lüm-yā), **J. Bapt.**, Spain, 1677—Dresden, 1720 ; ct.-violinist and ball-cond., Berlin and Dresden.

**Inderheide** (fōn'-dĕr-hī'-dĕ), **J. Fr.**, b. Cincinnati, Feb. 28, 1857 ; public singer and violinist at 10 ; at 17 he knew nearly all instrs. of the orch.; taught 3 years in Pittsburg ; studied voice-culture and piano in Cincinnati and Europe ; 1882-84, dir. Buffalo Sch. of Mus.; 1885-91, N. Y. Conservatory.

**pelius** (fô-pā'-lĭ-oos), **Gf.**, Herwigsdorf, n. Zittau, 1645—Leipzig, 1715, cantor and composer.

**retzsch** (vō'-rĕtsh), **Jns. Felix**, b. Altkirchen, July 17, 1835 ; pianist and conductor.

**oss**, (1) **(Vos'sius) Gerhard Jn.**, Heidelberg, 1577—Amsterdam, 1649 ; writer on mus. (2) **Isaak**, Leyden, 1618—Windsor, Engl., 1689 ; son of above ; canon and writer. (3) **Chas.**,

Schmarsow, Pomerania, 1815—Verona, 1882 ; pianist and composer.

**Vowles** (vōlz), **W. G.**, succ. J. Smith. org.-builder, est. Bristol, 1814.

**Vredemann** (frä'-dĕ-män), (1) **Jakob**, teacher and composer, Leuwarden, ca. 1600 — 1640. (2) **Michael**, teacher and theorist, Arnheim, 1612.

**Vroye** (vrwä), **Th. Jos. De**, Villers-la-Ville, Belgium, 1804—Liège, 1873 ; canon and theorist.

**Vuillaume** (vwē-yōm), family of French vln.-makers. (1) **Claude** (1771 — 1834); had 4 sons who followed him, the most famous (2) **Jean Baptiste**, Mirecourt, Dept. of Vosges, France, Oct. 7, 1798—Paris, March 19, 1879; 1821-25, in partnership with Lete ; he was v. succ. and a remarkable imitator of Stradivari ; inv. 1851, "octobasse" (v. D. D.); 1855, a larger viola "contre-alto" ; in 1867 a mute, the "pedale sourdine" ; also a machine for manufacturing gut-strings of unvaried thickness, etc. His brothers were : (3) **Nicolas** (1800—1871), (4) **Nicolas Fran.** (1802—1876), and (5) **Claude Fran.** (b. 1807), also an org.-builder. (6) **Sebastian** (1835—1875), vln.-maker.

**Vulpius** (fool'-pĭ-oos), **Melchior**, Wasungen, ca. 1560—Weimar, 1616 ; cantor and composer.

## W

**Wach** (väkh), **K. Gf. Wm.**, Löbau, 1755 — Leipzig, 1833 ; double-bass player.

**Wachs** (wäsh), **Paul**, b. Paris, Sept. 19, 1851 ; pianist, pupil of Paris Cons.; won 1st prize for organ, 1872; c. pf.-pieces.

**Wachsmann** (väkhs'-män), **Jn. Jacob**, early 19th cent. mus.-director, Magdeburg Cath.; composer, writer of methods, etc.

**Wachtel** (väkh'-tĕl), (1) **Theodor**, Hamburg, 1823—Frankfort-on-Main, 1893 ; noted tenor ; son and successor of a livery-stable keeper, then "discovered" ; studied with Frl. Grandjean. H·s son (2) **Th.** (d. Dessau, 1875) was for a time a tenor.

**Wachter** (väkh'-tĕr), **Ernst,** b. Mühlhausen, May 19, 1872; bass; studied with his father and Goldberg; 1894, Dresden opera; from 1896 Bayreuth, as " Fasolt," etc.

**Wade, Jos. Augustine,** b. Dublin-- d. London, 1845; violinist, conductor and composer.

**Waelput** (väl'-poot), **Hendrik,** Ghent, 1845—1885; cond., professor and dram. composer.

**Waelrant** (wäl'-ränt), **Hubert,** Tongerloo, Brabant, ca. 1517—Antwerp, 1595; a mus.-pub. and teacher; introduced " Bocedisation " (v. D.D.); c. motets, etc.

**Wagenseil** (vä' - gĕn - zīl), (1) **Jn. Chp.,** Nürnberg, 1633 — Altdorf, 1708; writer. (2) **G. Chp.,** Vienna, 1715—1777; teacher and composer.

**Wagner** (väkh'-nĕr),(1) **Gotthard,** Erding, 1697—Benedictine monastery, Tegernsee, 1739; composer. (2) **G. Gf.,** Mühlberg, Saxony, 1698— Plauen, 1760; cantor and composer. (3) **Jn. Joachim,** 18th cent. org.-builder at Berlin. (4) Bros. **Jr.** and (5) **Michael,** org.-builders at Schmiedefeld, 18th cent. (6) Two bros. **Chr. Salomon** and (7) **Jn. Gl.,** harpsichord-makers Dresden, 1774. (8) **K. Jakob,** Darmstadt, 1772—1822; horn-virtuoso, concert-conductor; c. operas. (9) **Ernst David,** Dramburg, Pomerania, 1806—Berlin,1883; cantor, organist, mus.-director and composer; pub. essays.

(10) **(Wm.) Richard,** Leipzig, May 22, 1813—(of eyrsipelas) Venice, Feb. 13, 1883; eminent opera composer; son of a clerk in the city police-court, who died when **W.** was six months old; the mother m. an actor and playwright, Ludwig Geyer of Dresden. **W.** attended the Dresden Kreuzschule until 1827; he †transl. 12 books of the Odyssey, and at 14 wrote a bombastic and bloody Shakespearean tragedy; 1827, he studied at the Nikolai Gymnasium,

Leipzig, where the family lived w' his sister Rosalie was engaged at City Theatre there. Wagner ' impelled music-ward by hearing Beethoven symph. and took Logir's " Thoroughbass." He t studied theory with the organist G lieb Müller and c. a string-quarte sonata and an aria. 1830, after triculation at Leipzig Univ., studied six months with Th. Wei (comp.) and c. a pf.-sonata, and hand polonaise. He studied Beet ven's symphs. very thoroughly. 19 he c. a symph. in 4 movemer prod. at the Gewandhaus, Leip: 1833. He wrote the libretto for opera, " *Die Hochzeit,*" an int duction, septet, and a chorus 18 but his sister Rosalie thought it moral and he gave it up; 1833 brother Albert, stage-manager a singer at the Würzburg Theatre vited him to be chorusm. there.

c. a romantic opera in 3 acts " *Feen,*" to his own libretto (after " *Donna serpente,*" by Gozzi); it accepted but never performed, by Leipzig th.-dir. Ringelhardt (given Munich, 1888). 1834, he beca cond. at the Magdeburg Th. H he c. (text and music) " *Das Lie verbot* (after Shakespeare's "*Meas for Measure*"), performed by a ba rupt troupe, 1836. Th.-cond. Königsberg, and m. (1836) an tress Wilhelmine Planer, who d. 18 after they had separated in 1861.

He c. an overture " *Rule Brit nia.*" 1837 cond. Riga opera. Mov by Meyerbeer's triumphs at the Opéra at Paris, **W.** went there, Ju 1839, by sea. The voyage lasted weeks and was very stormy; the perience suggested to him the op " *Flying Dutchman.*" Meyerb gave him letters to musicians a pubs. in Paris; here he suffered p erty and supported himself by sor writing, arranging dances for pia and cornet, preparing the pf.-sco of Halévy's "*Reine de Chypre,*" a writing articles. His operas were scornfully rejected and he could get no hearing till the v. succ. " *Rienzi* " was prod., Dresden, 1842, and " *Der Fliegende Holländer*," Jan. 2, 1843. The novelties in this work provoked a furious opposition that never ceased. 1843-49 he was cond. of Dresden Opera, also cond. Dresden Liedertafel, for which he wrote a biblical scene, " *Das Liebesmahl der Apostel*," for 3 choirs, a cappella, later with full orch. " *Tannhäuser* " was prod., Dresden, 1845, with succ. in spite of bitter opposition. In 1848 " *Lohengrin* " was finished ; but the mgr. of the Opera did not care to risk the work. He now wrote out a little sketch " *Die Nibelungen, Weltgeschichte aus der Sage*"; a prose study on " *Der Niebelungen-Mythus als Entwurf zu einem Drama* " (1848), and a 3-act drama with Prologue, written in alliterative verse, " *Siegfried's Tod*," preparations for the great work to follow. A rashly expressed sympathy with the revolutionary cause (1849) made flight necessary ; he went to Weimar with Liszt, but had to go on to Paris to escape the order for his arrest. 1849 he proceeded to Zurich, were he wrote a series of remarkable essays : " *Die Kunst und die Revolution*" (1849), " *Das Kunstwerk der Zukunft*," " *Kunst und Klima*," " *Das Judenthum in der Musik*" (1850), " *Oper und Drama*," " *Erinnerungen an Spontini*," a prose drama " Wieland der Schmiedt," and the 3 poems of the Niebelungen trilogy (privately printed 1853). The music of " *Das Rheingold* ' was finished 1854, " *Die Walküre*," 1856. He cond. orch. concerts with much succ., lectured on the mus. drama, prod. " *Tannhäuser* " (Zurich, 1855) ; 1855 he cond. 8 concerts of the London Philh. Soc. 1857 he left "*Siegfried* "unfinished and c. " *Tristan und Isolde*." 1860 he gave concerts of his own works, winning many enthusiastic enemies and some

valuable friends. The French Emperor ordered " *Tannhäuser* " to be prod. at the Gr. Opéra, March 13, 1861. It provoked such an elaborate and violent opposition (for omitting the ballet) that it was withdrawn after the third performance.

**W.** was now permitted to return to Germany ; " *Tristan* " was accepted at the Vienna ct.-opera, but after 57 rehearsals the singers declared it impossible to learn. In 1863, he pub. text of the "*Nibelung Ring*" despairing of ever completing the mus. When his financial state was most desperate, King Ludwig II. of Bavaria (1864) invited him to Munich and summoned von Bülow as cond. to prod. "*Tristan und Isolde*" (June 10, 1865) ; but opposition was so bitter that **W.** settled at Triebschen, Lucerne, and completed the scores of "*Die Meistersinger*" (prod. Munich, 1868) and " *Der Ring des Nibelungen*," "*Siegfried*" (1869) and "*Götterdämmerung*" (1874).

1870 he m. Cosima, the divorced wife of von Bülow and natural daughter of Liszt. Since his death she has had charge of the Bayreuth Festivals. Though King Ludwig's scheme for a special Wagner Theatre in Munich was given up, there were by this enough Wagner-lovers and societies throughout the world, to subscribe funds for a theatre at Bayreuth, where the corner-stone was laid in 1872, on his 60th birthday. In August, 1876, complete performances of "*Der Ring des Nibelungen*" were given there under most splendid auspices, but with a deficit $37,500, paid off by a partially succ. festival in London, 1877, and by the setting aside of the royalties from performances at Munich. He now set to work on the " *Bühnenweihfestspiel*" (Stage - consecrating - festival - play). "*Parsifal*," finished, and prod. in 1882. The same year ill-health sent him to Venice, where he d. suddenly. His writings (extravagantly praised and condemned) are pub. in various eds. There is an English translation in 8 volumes, by Wm. Ashton Ellis. Besides his operas and the other works mentioned he c. a symph. (1832); 6 overtures, incl. "*Konzert-ouvertüre ziemlich fugirt*," "*Polonia*," "*Columbus*," "*Rule Britannia*"; "*New Year's Cantata*"; incid. mus. to Gleich's farce "*Der Berggeist*" (Magdeburg, 1836); "*Huldigungsmarsch*" (1864, finished by Raff); "*Siegfried Idyll*" (1870, for his son then a year old), "*Kaisermarsch*" (1870), "*Festival March*" (for the Centennial Exposition Philadelphia, 1876), "*Gelegenheits-Cantata*" (for unveiling a statue of King Friedrich, August, 1843), "*Gruss an den König*" (1843, pf.), "*An Weber's Grabe*" (Funeral March for wind-instrs. on motives from Weber's "*Euryanthe*," and double quartet for voices, 1844). FOR PF.: sonata; polonaise, for four hands; fantaisie, "*Al-*

*bumsonate, für Frau Mathilde Wesendonck*" (1853); "*Ankunft bei den Schwarzen Schwanen*" (1861); "*Ein Albumblatt für Fürstin Metternich*" (1861), "*Albumblatt für Frau Betty Schott*" (1875). SONGS: " *Carnavalslied*" from "*Das Liebesverbot*" (1835–36); " *Dors, mon enfant,*" "*Mignonne,*" "*Attente*" (1839–40) "*Les deux Grenadiers*" (1839); "*Der Tannenbaum*" (1840); " *Kraftliedchen*" (1871), "*Fünf Gedichte;*" 1 " *Der Engel*"; 2, "*Stehe still*"; 3 " *Im Treibhaus*"; 4, "*Schmerzen*" 5, "*Träume*" (1862).

Biog. by C. F. Glasenapp (1876) F. Hueffer (1881); R. Pohl (1883) W. Tappert (1883); H. v. Wolzogen (1883); Ad. Jullien (1886); H. T. Finck (1893); H. S. Chamberlain (1897); E. Dannreuther, F. Praeger (1893); G. Kobbé; Glasenapp an Ellis (1900). There are many treatises on his works. His letters have also been published in various forms

---

## Wagner.

### BY HENRY T. FINCK.

WHEN Richard Wagner was living as a political refugee in Switzerland, at the age of thirty-six, he elaborated his theory of the "art work of the future" in a long essay. Reduced to one sentence this theory was, that music, poetry, painting, sculpture, and architecture had run their course as separate arts, and that the art-work of the future was be a combination of them. At a later period he tried to make Beethoven responsible for this theory, so far at least as the union of poetry and music concerned. Beethoven, he argued, wrote his first eight symphonies for instruments alone, but when he composed the Ninth, the greatest of them a he reached a point in the last movement, where the orchestra no longer sficed for his purposes, so he called in the aid of the human voice and poe—Schiller's " *Ode to Joy*." This symphony thus became "the gospel the art-work of the future"; and beyond it, Wagner maintained, progress was possible only in the direction of the genuine music-drama; " the key which was thus forged by Beethoven." And when the corner-stone for Bayreuth Theatre—in which the "art-work of the future" was to be p

:ed to the world—was laid, Wagner significantly made it the occasion for
performance of this epoch-making *Ninth Symphony*. ¶ Undoubtedly it
s a stroke of genius on the part of Wagner thus to turn the tables on his
:mies—who had decried him as a heretic and a foe to music—by claim-
their very idol as the sire of his new doctrine. In truth, however, it is
at all probable that Beethoven had in mind any such purpose as Wagner
putes to him. There is no reference to anything of the kind among the
:graphic documents, whereas, it is known, on the other hand, that Bee-
ven had been intending nearly all his life to set to music Schiller's "*Ode
Joy*." According to Czerny, he subsequently even pronounced this ex-
iment of incorporating the Ode in his symphony a mistake (*Missgriff*).
e voice, in truth, was never congenial to him. "Songs I do not like to
ite," he said to Rochlitz, in 1822, the very time when he was at work
the "*Ninth Symphony*." In both this work and the "*Missa Solennis*,"
the same period, Beethoven, moreover, uses the human voice like an in-
ument, and it is probable that in each case his object in employing it was
: so much to secure an alliance with poetry as to increase the power of his
sical forces, and to enlarge the variety of tone-colours by adding to the
hestra the human voice, alone, concerted, and in massive choral combina-
n. ¶ Wagner's musical pedigree must therefore be sought elsewhere.
s ancestry might be traced back as far as Peri and the other originators of
lian opera who (strange as it may seem to us who know only the later
lian opera which Wagner reviled) represented a protest in favor of poetry
inst the tyranny of music in the marriage of these arts. Wagner's whole
was such a protest, and his more immediate progenitor in this respect was
uck, who found that Italian opera had gradually become ridiculous through
: "vanity of singers and the unwise compliance of composers ; " and who,
refore, endeavoured to reduce operatic music to its proper function ; that of
onding the poetry and deepening the feeling it arouses. Gluck's idea that
: relation of poetry to music was much the same as that of a sketch to the
lour, "which animates their figures without altering their outlines" was cor-
lly endorsed and adopted by Wagner. ¶ The next step in the evolution
Wagnerism is represented by Weber, his indebtedness to whom Wagner
nkly acknowledged in several places. He declared that the last scenes in
eber's "*Euryanthe*" realised the ideal of musico-dramatic art, as here the
hestra "interpenetrates the recitatives as the blood does the veins of the
dy." What Weber himself wrote about this opera : "'*Euryanthe*' is a
rely dramatic work, which depends for its success solely on the co-opera-
n of the sister arts, and is certain to lose its effect if deprived of their as-
tance," shows that his ideal was the same as Wagner's. Had he lived
iger, and had he possessed Wagner's pugnacity and iron will, he might

50

have been the man to annihilate the old-fashioned opera and triumphantly
tablish the modern music-drama. He even made use of leading motives [ v
D. D.]. His early opera *"Abu Hassan"* has a melody which is afterwa
repeated in a reminiscent way. The *"Freyschütz"* has eleven recurr
melodies, and *" Euryanthe"* has eight. ¶ While the germs and n
principles of Wagnerism may thus be found in Peri, Monteverde, Gluck, a
Weber, it remained for Wagner's genius to develop and apply them. Gluc
operas were still far from being perfect works of art. To cite Wagn
own words : " In Gluck's operas we find the aria, the recitative, the ba
still placed side by side without any connection ; " while opera in gen
remained after him, as before, a mere variety show, with here a pretty tu
there a graceful skip of a dancer or a brilliant feat of vocalisation, here a d
zling scenic effect, there a volcanic outburst of the orchestra, and the wh
without artistic coherence. If a painter put on a canvas a number of hum
figures and diverse objects totally unrelated to each other, no one would c
it a work of art, however well done each figure might be in itself. T
opera before Wagner was such a canvas. He was the first who made a ge
uine picture of it—an art-work organically united in all its parts. He c
this by means of the leading motives—the typical melodies and chara
teristic harmonies which accompany each of the *dramatis personæ* througho
the score, just as their social and moral character accompanies them, w
such modifications as the situation calls for. Weber had used leading motiv
as we have seen, but only in an elementary way. It remained for Wagn
to make them the very framework of the music-drama. He thus taug
music to speak a definite language, so that we can almost tell by listening
the orchestra alone what is going on on the stage. ¶ His whole aim a
desire was to make the drama impressive and intelligible. For this reason
discarded the tuneful style of vocalism in vogue in Italian opera and develop
a new vocal style—a sort of melodious declamation or " speech-song.
This led to the ridiculous accusation that there was " no melody " in
operas, whereas the orchestral score usually bubbles over with melodies—ofte
two or more at a time. After the singers had begun to master the new voc
style, it was found, moreover, that an artist like Lilli Lehmann or Jean c
Reszké can make this speech-song sound smooth, and melodious, too—as smoo
and melodious as the bel canto of Rossini and Mozart. And after the singe
had learned how to act, and to enunciate distinctly, opera-goers learned th
Wagner had written stage-works which were quite as impressive poetically a
they were musically. He had an immense advantage over all other com
posers in being able to write his own poems. His best ten operas—" Th
*Flying Dutchman,"* " *Tannhäuser,"* " *Lohengrin,"* " *Rheingold,"*
"*Walküre,"* ' *Siegfried,"* "*Götterdämmerung,"* " *Tristan,"* " *Meister*

ger," and "Parsifal"—apart from the music, rank among the best plays
er written in Germany ; though to be sure they must not be judged apart
m the music any more than the music must be judged apart from the poems.
e ludicrous opinions on these works formerly expressed by so many pro-
sional musicians and critics were due chiefly to the fact that they did not
ar this in mind, though Wagner protested on every possible occasion that
must not be judged from the stand-point of the separate arts, but of the
mbined arts.   The greatest defects in the present-day performances of his
eras is owing to this, that few stage-managers have yet learned that he
pects them to be artistic, too, familiar with every detail of the work, so that
ey can show how every incident on the stage is mirrored and emphasised
the orchestral score.   There is much delightful pantomimic music in these
eras, the meaning of which is lost if the stage-manager is a bungler, and the
gers poor actors.   ¶ With all these reforms and innovations, Wagner
ver could have become the most commanding figure in the modern music-
orld had he not been endowed at the same time with the faculty for creat-
g an extraordinary abundance of ideas, melodic and harmonic.   Wilhelm
appert has truly observed that there is more melody in Wagner's " Meis-
-singer " than in all the operas of the melodious Mozart.   In the field of
rmony and modulation Wagner was an innovator of unprecedented origi-
lity.   There can be no tragic expression without discord, and he was the
eatest of all masters of discord—the musical tragedian par excellence.   In
chestration, too—the art of clothing his ideas in beautiful garbs of various
lours—he was without a rival.   ¶ As Schubert influenced all song-writers
er him, Chopin all the pianoforte-composers, and Beethoven all the sym-
onists, so Wagner has cast his spell on every writer for the stage.   " Wag-
r is the oxygen, the atmosphere which modern opera breathes," writes
rdinand Pfohl ; and he hardly exaggerates when he adds that " modern
era, apart from Wagner's art is an empty word, a phantom.   It does not
ist."   The minor composers of all countries have been indulging for nearly
lf a century in a very bacchanal of plagiarism at his expense, while even the
eatest of living masters—Dvořák, Grieg, Saint-Saëns, Richard Strauss—
ve honestly profited by his example in various branches of music.   Rubinein committed suicide by trying to swim against the current.   The German
hool of opera, the French, and even the Italian have followed Wagner in
andoning colorature song and elaborate arias, in giving greater coherence
their scores, and in showing a decent regard for their texts.   In these
spects even Verdi, greatest of the Italians, has in his last period, paid homage
Wagner's genius.

(11) **Siegfried**, b. Triebschen, Lucerne, June 6, 1869; only son of above; attended a polytechnic sch., but took up mus. as pupil of Kniese and Humperdinck; since '893, a concert-cond. in Germany, Austria, Italy and England; he conducts with his left hand; lives at Bayreuth; cond. at the Festivals; c. a symph. poem "*Sehnsucht*" (Schiller), text and music of mod. succ. comic-romantic opera "*Der Bärenhäuter*" (Munich Ct. Th., 1899), unsucc., "*Herzog Wildfang*" (1901). (12) (**Jachmann - Wagner**), **Johanna**, near Hanover, Oct. 13, 1828—Würzburg, Oct. 16, 1894; niece of (10); dram. soprano; created "Elizabeth," 1845; m. a judge Jachmann. (13) **Paul Emil**, b. Neise, June 28; teacher at Paderborn; c. operettas, orch.-pcs., etc.

**Wainwright**, (1) **J.**, d. 1768; organist, Manchester. (2) **Robt.**, 1748—1782; son of above; organist and composer, Liverpool. (3) **Richard**, 1758—1825; bro. and succ. of above. (4) **Wm.**, d. 1797; double-bass virtuoso and singer; bro. of above.

**Waissel** (vīs'-sěl), (**Waisse'lius**) **Matthias**, b. Bartenstein. Prussia; lutenist and composer at Frankfort, 1573.

**Walcker** (väl'-kěr), (1) **Eberhard Fr.**, Cannstadt, 1794—Ludwigsburg, 1872; son of a skilled org.-builder; himself a noted org.-builder; succeeded by his five sons, (2) **H.** (b. Oct. 10, 1828), (3) **Fr.** (b. Sept. 17, 1829), (4) **K.** (b. March 6, 1845), (5) **Paul** (b. May 31, 1846), and (6) **Eberhard** (b. April 8, 1850).

**Waldersee** (väl'-děr-zā), **Paul**, Count **von**, b. Potsdam, Sept. 3, 1831; a Prussian officer from 1848–71, then took up mus.; co-editor of Beethoven and Mozart.

**Wa'ley**, **Simon**, London, 1827—1875, pianist and composer.

**Walkeley** (wôk'-lǐ), **Antony**, 1672—1717(18); Engl. org. and composer.

**Walker** (wôk'-ěr), (1) **Jos. Cooper**,

Dublin, 1760—St.-Valéry, Fra 1810; writer. (2) **Jos. and S** org. - builders, London. (3) **Edw.**, b. Marylebone, London, 17, 1835; tenor; chorister Ch Royal; prof. of singing, R. A. 1883, cond. Brixton Philh. Soc. **Edith**, b. New York; contra studied Dresden Cons. with Org engaged at the Vienna opera fo years as 1st alto; sings also in cert.

**Wal'lace, Wm. Vincent**, Waterf Ireland, June 1, 1814—Château Bages, Haute Garonne, Oct. 1865; violinist; wandered over world; c. very pop. pf.-pcs. and operas includ. the very succ. "*M tana*" (London, 1845); and "*L line*" (do. 1860).

**Wallaschek** (väl'-lä-shěk), **Richa** lecturer at Lemburg Univ.; p 1886, valuable treatise "*Æsth der Tonkunst.*"

**Wallenstein** (väl'-lěn-shtīn), **Mart** Frankfort-on-Main, 1843—1896; anist; c. comic opera.

**Wallerstein** (väl'-lěr-shtīn), **Ant** Dresden, 1813—Geneva, 1892; v linist and composer.

**Wall'is, J.**, Ashford, Kent, 161 London, 1703; acoustician.

**Walliser** (väl'-lǐ-zěr), **Chp. Tho** Strassburg, 1568—1648; mus.-d theorist and composer.

**Wallner** (väl'-něr), **Leopold**, b. K Russia, Nov. 27, 1847; writer a mus.-teacher in Brussels.

**Wallnöfer** (väl'-nä-fěr), **Ad.**, b. Vi na, April 26, 1854; pupil of Wa müller, Krenn and Dessoff (com Rokitansky (singing); barytone Vienna; 1882, with Neuman troupe; 1897–98, N. Y.; c. su op. "*Eddystone*" (Prague, 1889), e

**Walmisley** (wämz'-lǐ), (1) **Th** **Forbes**, London, 1783—1866; ganist and composer. (2) **Th Attwood**, London, 1814—Hastin 1856; son of above; professor a composer.

**Wa'lond**, (1) **Wm.**, organist and co

oser, Oxford, 1759. (2) **Wm.**, d.
336 ; son of above ; organist, Chi-
iester, 1775.

**lsh, John,** d. London, 1736 ; mus.-
ublisher.

**lter** (väl'-tĕr), (1) **Ignaz,** Rado-
itz, Bohemia, 1759—Ratisbon, ca.
830 ; tenor and composer. (2) **Ju-
ane** (née **Roberts**), wife of above ;
singer. (3) **G. Anton,** b. Germany ; pupil, R. Kreutzer ; 1792,
pera conductor at Rouen ; compos-
r. (4) **Albert,** b. Coblentz ; from
795, clarinettist and composer in
'aris. (5) **Aug.,** Stuttgart, 1821—
3asel, Jan. 22, 1896 ; mus.-director
nd composer. (6) **Jos.,** Neuberg-
n-Danube, 1833 — Munich, 1875 ;
ln.-teacher. (7) **Gustav,** b. Bilin,
3ohemia, Feb. 11, 1836 ; tenor ;
/upil of Prague Cons. ; début in
3runn, 1856–87, principal lyric tenor
t Vienna ct.-opera. (8) **Benno,** Mu-
iich, June 17, 1847—Oct. 23, 1901 ;
/ro. and successor of above ; violinst ; pupil of Munich Cons. ; from
863 member of the ct.-orch. (9)
wôl'-tĕr), **Wm. H.,** b. Newark, N.
., July 1, 1825 ; organist as a boy ;
rom 1856, organist Columbia Coll.,
N. Y.; Mus. Doc., 1864; c. 2 masses.
10) **Geo. Wm.,** New York, b. Dec.
6, 1851; son and pupil of (9), also
/upil of J. K. Paine (Boston), S. P.
Warren (New York) ; l. Washing-
on since 1869. (11) **K.,** b. Crans-
berg, Taunus, Oct. 27, 1862 ; pupil
of Meister and Schmetz ; later Ratisbon Sch. for Church-mus. ; then
eacher and organist at Biebrich-on-
Rhine ; from 1893, mus.-teacher at
Montsbaur Seminary ; wrote essays ;
c. motets, a prize triple fugue, etc.
12) **Fr. Wm.,** b. Mannheim, Sept.
3, 1870 ; Dr. Phil., Heidelberg,
1892 ; lives in Mannheim as writer
and critic.

**alther von der Vogelweide** (väl'-
er fōn dĕr fō'-gĕl-vī-dĕ), in the Ty-
ol (?), ca. 1160—Würzburg, after
1227; the chief Minnesinger and
/yric poet of mediæval Germany.

**Walther** (väl'-tĕr), (1) **Jn.,** Thuringia,
1496 — Torgau, 1570 ; singer and
composer ; ct.-conductor. (V. MAR-
TIN LUTHER.) (2) **Jn. Jakob,** b.
Witterda, near Erfurt, 1650 ; ct.-
musician. publisher and composer.
(3) **Jn. Gf.,** Erfurt, 1684—Weimar,
1748 ; organist, writer and composer.
(4) **Jn. Chp.,** Weimar, 1715—71;
organist and composer.

**Wälzel** (vĕl'-tsĕl), **Camillo,** Magdeburg, 1829—Vienna, 1895 ; librettist,
(pseud. **F. Zell**).

**Wambach** (väm'-bäkh), **Émile (X.),**
b. Arlon. Luxembourg, Nov. 26. 1854:
pupil of Antwerp Cons.; c. symph.
poem, "*Aan de boorden van de
Schelde,*" orch. 1 fantasias, Flemish
drama "*Nathan's Parabel*"; 2 oratorios ; a hymn for chorus and orch.,
etc.

**Wangemann** (väng'-ĕ-män), **Otto,** b.
Loitz-on-the-Peene, Jan. 9, 1848 ;
pupil of G. Flügel, Stettin and Fr.
Kiel at Berlin ; since 1878, organist
and singing-teacher Demmin Gymnasium ; wrote org. treatise.

**Wanhal (Van Hal)** (vän'-häl), **Jn.
Bapt.,** Neu-Nechanitz, Bohemia,
1739—Vienna, 1813 ; composer.

**Wanski** (vän'-shkĭ), (1) **Jn. Nepomuk,** b. ca. 1800 (?); son of (2) **Jan**
(a pop. Polish song-composer) ; violinist ; pupil of Baillot ; toured widely, then lived at Aix ; wrote a vln.
method and c. études, etc.

**Ward,** (1) **J.,** d. before 1641 ; English
composer. (2) **J. Chas.,** b. Upper
Clapton, London, March 27, 1835 ;
1846, soloist on the concertina ; since
1852, organist at several London
churches ; c. a motet, and a Sanctus
for double-choir ; cantata " *The
Wood*"; "*A Psalm of Life,*" with
orch.; orch. fugue on "*The Sailor's
Hornpipe,*" etc.

**Warlamoff** (vär'-lä-môf), **Alex.** Jego-
rovitch, Moscow, 1810—1849 ; singing-teacher and composer

**Warnots** (vär-nō), (1) **Jean Arnold,**
(1801—1861). (2) **Henri,** Brussels,
1832—1893 ; opera-tenor ; son and

pupil of above; c. operetta. His
daughter and pupil (3) **Elly,** b.
Liège, 1862; soprano; début, Brussels, 1879; sang there, then at Florence, Paris Op.-Com., etc.

**War′ren,** (1) **Jos.,** London, 1804—
Kent, 1881; organist, pianist, violinist, composer and writer. (2) **G.
Wm.,** Albany, N. Y., Aug. 17,
1828—New York, 1902; self-taught
organist; from 1870, organist St.
Thomas's Ch., New York; prof.
Columbia Univ.; c. church-mus. (3)
**Samuel Prowse,** b. Montreal, Canada, Feb. 18, 1841; organist; pupil
of Haupt, Gv. Schumann (pf.) and
Wieprecht (instr.); 1865–67. organist of All Souls' Ch., New York;
later at Trinity Ch.; c. church-mus.,
org.-pcs., etc. **Richard Henry,** Albany, N. Y., Sept. 17, 1859; son and
pupil of (2), also studied abroad;
from 1886 org. at St. Bartholomew's,
N. Y.; founder and cond. of church
choral soc., which gave many important works their first hearing;
Parker's "*Hora Novissima*" was
written for this society. C. anthems,
services, a comic opera, songs, etc.

**Wartel** (vär-těl), (1) **Pierre Fran.,**
Versailles, 1806—Paris, 1862; tenor.
(2) **Atala Thérèse** (née **Adrien**), b.
Paris, July 2, 1814; wife of above;
1831–38, prof. at Paris Cons.; c. pf.-
studies, etc (3) **Emil,** son of above;
sang for years Th. Lyrique, then
founded a sch.

**Wasielewski** (vä-zē-lěf′-shki), **Jos.
W. von,** Gross - Leesen, Danzig,
1822—Sondershausen, 1896; violinist, conductor, critic, composer, and
important historical writer.

**Wassermann** (väs′-sĕr-män), **H. Jos.,**
Schwarzbach, near Fulda, 1791—
Richen, n. Basel, 1838; violinist and
composer.

**Wassmann** (väs′-män), **K.,** vln.-
teacher, Carlsruhe Cons.; pub. technical works.

**Wat′son,** (1) **Thos.,** Eng. composer,
1590. (2) **Wm. Michael,** Newcastle-on-Tyne, 1840—E. Dulwich,

London, 1889; teacher and comer under pen-name **Jules Favre.**
**John Jay,** Gloucester, Mass., S
23, 1830—Boston, Aug. 5, 19
very succ. vt. and cond.

**Webb,** (1) **Daniel,** Taunton, 17
Bath, 1815; writer. (2) **G. J**
Rushmore Lodge, near Salisb
Engl., 1803—Orange, N. J., 1
organist and editor. (3) **Fr**
**Rush,** b. Covington, Indiana,
8, 1851; pupil of N. E. Cons.,
ton; organist; since 1883, tea
at Staunton, Va.; c. 200 pcs.
military bands, etc.

**Webbe** (wĕb), (1) **Samuel,** Sr., N
orca,1740—London, 1816; ed. co
etc. (2) **Samuel,** Jr., London, 1
—1843; son of above; writer
composer.

**Weber** (vä′-bĕr). (1) **Fridolin**
Zelli, 1733—d. 1764), and his
(2) **Fz. Anton** (b. 1734 ?), were
linists in the orch. of the Elector
Theodor **Fz.** became cond.
Eutin town orch. His four daugh
were (3) **Josepha** (d. 1820), sopra
m. the violinist Hofer, 1789, late
a bass. Meyer. For her Mozar
"The Queen of the Night"
the "*Magic Flute*." (4) **Aloys**
1750—Salzburg, 1839. Mozart's
love; she m. an actor Lange, 1
and toured as a singer. (5) **C
stanze,** Zell, 1763—Salzburg, 18
Mozart's wife (1782); 1809,
Nissen. (6) **Sophie,** 1764—S
burg, 1843; m. the tenor Haibl.
**Fr. Aug.,** Heilbronn, 1753—18
physician and c. (8) **Bd. Anse**
Mannheim, April 18, 1766—Be
March 23,1821; pianist,conductor.
dram. composer. (9) **(Fr.) Dion**
Welchau, Bohemia, Oct. 9, 176
Prague, Dec. 25, 1842; dir. Pra
Cons.; c. operas, etc. (10)
theorist and composer, Freinshe
near Mannheim, 1779—Kreuzn
Sept. 21, 1839, amateur pianist,
ist and 'cellist, also cond.; wrote
says and valuable treatises; c
masses, a requiem and a Te De

with orch. and pf.-sonata. (11) **Fri-dolin** (II.), b. 1761; son of (2), and step-broth. of (12); pupil of Haydn; singer and mus.-director.

(12) **K. Maria (Fr. Ernst)**, Frei-herr **von**, Eutin, Oldenburg, Dec. 18, 1786—(of consumption) London, June 5, 1826; son of the second wife of (2) and cousin, by marriage, of Mozart; the founder of German national opera (Wagner shows his in-fluence deeply), and of the Romantic Sch.; perhaps the most widely influ-ential German composer of the cent. More important, in cold fact, as a path-finder, and an influence, than as an artistic individuality; he was also a notable pianist (he could stretch a 12th), and a pioneer in modern pianistic composition. At first a pupil of his step-bro. (11). His mother, Genoveva (d. 1798, of consumption), was a dram. singer, and the family led a wandering life. At 10 he became pf.-pupil of J. P. Heuschkel. As a chorister in the cathedral at Salzburg, 1797, he had gratuitous lessons in comp. from Mi-chael Haydn, to whom he dedicated his first published comps., six fughet-tas (1798). 1798–1800, at Munich, he studied singing with Valesi, and comp. with Kalcher. At 12 he c. an opera (the MS. lost or burned). He also appeared as concert-pianist. He met Aloys Senefelder, the inv. of lithography, and engraved his own op. 2, 1800, and made improvements in the process. At 13 he c. and prod. with succ. the opera "*Das Wald-mädchen*" (Freiberg; also played at Chemnitz, Prague, Vienna and St. Petersburg). In 1801, he c. a third opera "*Peter Schmoll und seine Nachbarn*" (Augsburg, 1803 ?); 1803, in Vienna, he became a pupil of Abbé Vogler. 1804, cond. Breslau City Th.; resigned 1806; supported him-self by lessons, then mus.-intendant to Duke Eugen of Würtemberg; 1807, private secretary to Duke Lud-wig at Stuttgart, and mus.-master to

his children. In a turmoil of intrigue and dissipation he forgot his art, until he became involved in a quarrel lead-ing to his banishment in 1810. This sobered him and awoke his better self. Going to Mannheim, he prod. his first symph.; then rejoined Abbé Vogler, at Darmstadt. His opera "*Silvana*" was prod. (Frankfort-on-Main, 1810), and "*Abu Hassan*," a comic Singspiel (Munich, 1811). He made a concert-tour to various cities. 1813, cond. of the Landständisches Th. at Prague, where he reorganised the opera, and won such note that in 1816 the King of Saxony called him to Dresden to reorganise the Royal Opera. At 20 he began "*Der Frei-schütz*," but gave it up till later (the incid. mus. to Wolff's "*Precio-sa*" took 3 weeks). In 1817, he m. the singer Karoline Brandt, a mem-ber of his company to whom he had long been engaged. They toured together as pianist and singer. "*Der Freischütz*" was prod. with tremendous succ., Berlin, 1821; its strong nationalism provoking a frenzy of admiration. But "*Euryanthe*" (Vienna, 1823) had much less succ. 1824, he was commissioned to write "*Oberon*," for Covent Garden, Lon-don, but consumption delayed its completion; it was prod. (London, 1826) with much succ. He lived only eight weeks longer; his body was taken to the family vault at Dres-den. [See also pages 785 and 786.]

DRAMATIC WORKS: Besides the operas already mentioned he c. "*Rü-bezahl*" (begun 1804, not completed); "*Die Drei Pintos*" (completed by G. Mahler, written and prod. Leip-zig, 1888). Incid. mus. to Schiller's "*Turandot*," Müllner's "*König Yn-gurd*," Gehe's "*Heinrich IV*," and Houwald's "*Der Leuchtthurm*." C. also cantatas, incl. "*Der erste Ton*" (1808); and "*Kampf und Sieg*" (on the battle of Waterloo), with orch. (1815); "*Natur und Liebe*," 1818; hymn, "*In seiner Ordnung schaff der Herr,"* with orch.; (1812), 2 masses and 2 offertories, with orch.; some very pop. songs, four scenes and arias for soprano with orch.; 2 scenes and arias for tenor, chorus and orch.; 19 part-songs, some very pop.; and children's songs ; 6 canons à 3-4; duets (op. 31); 2 symphs. (both in C); Jubel-Ouvertüre ; 2 clarinet-concertos ; bassoon-concerto; adagio and rondo ungarese for bassoon with orch.; variations for many instrs.; chamber-mus.; 2 pf.-concertos, Concertstück with orch., 10 sonatas, a 4-hand sonata, the famous waltz *"Aufforderung zum Tanze"* (*"Invitation to the Dance"*), op. 65 ; 12 Allemandes ; 6 Ecossaises ; 18 *"Valses favorites de l'impératrice de France";* several sets of Variations, etc. The so-called *"Weber's Last Waltz"* (*Thought or Farewell*) was written by Reissiger ; a MS. copy of it being found in **W.**'s papers. Biog. by Barbedette (Paris, 1862, Leipzig, 1864-68) · Jähns (Leipzig, 1873) ; Carl v. Weber (**W.**'s grandson) pub. his beautiful letters to his wife (1886); Th. Hell (1828). An almost ideal biog. is that of **W.**'s son the Baron Max Maria von W. (in 3 vols., 1866-68).

(13) **Edmund von,** Hildesheim, 1786—Würzburg, 1828 ; mus.-director and composer. (14) **Ernst H.,** Wittenburg, June 24, 1795—Leipzig, Jan., 1878, with his brother (15) **Wm. Ed.** (1804—1891), prof. at Göttingen ; writer on acoustics, etc. (16) **Fz.,** Cologne, 1805—1876 ; organist, conductor and composer. (17) **Eduard W.,** town-musician, Frankenberg. (18) **K. H.,** b. Frankenberg, Aug. 9, 1834 ; son of above ; pupil of Leipzig Cons., 1866-70 ; from 1877, dir. Imp. Russian Mus. Soc. at Saratov ; pub. a pf.-method. (19) **G. Victor,** b. Ober-Erlenbach, Upper Hesse, Feb. 25, 1838 ; pupil of Schrems, Ratisbon ; took orders ; since 1866, cond. at Mayence Cath., expert and writer on org.-building ;

composer. (20) **Gustav,** Münchenbuchsee, Switzerland, 1845—Zurich, 1887; organist, conductor and composer. (21) **Miroslaw,** b. Prague, Nov. 9, 1854 ; violinist ; pupil of his father ; at 10 played before the Austrian Emperor, and toured ; pupil of Blazek, Prague ; also of the Cons.; Konzertmeister, royal orch. at Wiesbaden, and 2nd cond. at the opera (resigned, 1893) ; 1889, R. Mus.-Dir. C. incid. mus. to ballet *"Die Rheinnixe"* (Wiesbaden, 1884), 2 string quartets (the 2nd taking prize at Petersburg, 1891), etc. (22) **Constantine Otto,** Germany, 1847 (?)—New Orleans, La., Nov. 13, 1901 pupil Leipzig Cons.; from 1860 in New Orleans as org., dir., teacher and composer.

**Web'ster, Jos. Philbrick,** Manchester, N. H., 1819—Elkhorn, Wis. 1875 ; composer.

**Weckerlin** (vĕk-ĕr-lăñ), **Jean Bapt Th.,** b. Gebweiller, Alsatia, Nov. 9 1821; entered his father's business o cotton-dyeing ; in 1844, studied singing with Ponchard and comp. with Halévy at the Paris Cons., prod. heroi choral symph. *"Roland,"* 1847; gav mus.-lessons ; 1853, prod. succ. 1-ac opera, *"L'Organiste dans l'embarras* (100 performances, Th.-Lyrique) followed by several privately per formed operettas, 2 comic operas i Alsatian dialect, 1-act opera *"Apr Fontenot"* (Th.-Lyrique, 1877) 1869, asst.-libr. Paris Cons.; 187 libr.; wrote bibliogr. and other a ticles and treatises, and ed. valuab colls. C. *"Symphonie de la forêt,* an oratorio *"Le Jugement Dernier* 2 cantatas, incl. *"Paix, Chari Grandeur"* (Opéra, 1866) ; the od symphonie *"Les Poèmes de la Mer* etc.

**Weelkes** (wĕks), **Thos.,** organi Chichester Cathedral ; c. notab madrigals, etc., 1597.

**Wegeler** (vä'-gĕ-lĕr), **Fz. Gerhar** Bonn, 1765—Koblenz, 1848 ; phys cian and biographer of Beethoven.

dekind (vā'-dĕ-kĭnt), **Erica**, b.
anover, Nov. 13, 1872 ; soprano ;
pil of Dresden Cons. and Fr. Or-
ni ; début Dresden ct.-opera, 1894,
ng there 5 years, then toured widely
concert and opera ; 1898, m. Herr
schwald.

gelius (vā-gā'-lĭ-oos), **Martin**, b.
elsingfors, Nov. 10, 1846 ; pupil of
bl, Vienna, and Richter and Paul,
eipzig ; 1878, opera cond. and dir.
the Cons. at Helsingfors ; pub.
xt-books ; c. overture " *Daniel
jort* "; a ballade with orch; " *Mig-
n* " for sopr. with orch., etc.

hle (vā'-lĕ), **K.**, Prague, 1825—
aris, 1883 ; pianist and composer.

ichler (vīkh'-lĕr), **Maximilian**,
utist, Gewandhaus orch., Leipzig ;
ub. a flute text-book (1897).

idenbach (vī'-dĕn-bäkh), **Jns.**, b.
resden, Nov. 29, 1847 ; pupil of
eipzig Cons.; since 1873 pf.-teacher
ere.

idt (vīt), **K.**, b. Bern, March 7,
857; 1889 cond. at Klagenfurt; lives
Heidelberg ; c. male choruses.

igl (vīkh'-'l), (1) **Jos.**, Eisenstadt,
ungary, 1766—Vienna, 1846 ; ct.-
onductor and dram. composer. (2)
Taddäus, Vienna, 1774 (?)—1844 ;
ro. of above ; c. operettas.

einberger (vīn'-bĕrkh-ĕr), (1) **K.**
r., b. Wallerstein, 1883 ; teacher
nd cath. cond. at Würzburg. (2)
Karl, b. Vienna, April 3, 1861; lives
here ; c. 9 succ. operettas, incl.
' *Die Ulanen*" (Vienna, 1891),
' *Lachende Erben*" (1892), " *Die
Blumen-Mary*" (ib., 1897). ' *Adam
und Eva*" (ib., 1898).

eingartner (vīn'-gärt-nĕr) **(Paul)
Felix**, b. Zara, Dalmatia, June 2,
863 ; notable conductor ; pupil of
W. A. Remy; later of Leipzig Cons.,
winning Mozart prize ; friend of
Liszt at Weimar, where his opera
" *Sakuntala*" was prod. 1884 ; until
1889, theatre cond. at Königsberg,
Danzig, and Hamburg, Mannheim ;
1891-97, 2nd cond. Berlin ct.-opera,
also cond. symph. concerts at the

Royal orch.; from 1898 lives in Munich as cond. Kaim concerts as well
as the R. Orch. Berlin ; wrote
treatises " *Uber das Dirigieren*"(Berlin, 1896), etc. C. operas " *Sakun-
tal* "(1884), " *Malawika*" (Munich,
1886), " *Genesius* " (Berlin, 1893),
withdrawn by the author because of
press attacks and revived with succ.
at Mannheim and elsewhere ; " *Orestes* " (Berlin, June 15, 1902) ; c. a
symph. ; symph. poems " *König
Lear*," " *Das Gefilde der Seligen*,"
etc.

**Weinlig** (or **Weinlich**) (vīn'-lĭkh), (1)
**Chr. Ehregott**, Dresden, 1743—
1813 ; organist and composer. (2)
**(Chr.) Th.**, Dresden, 1780—Leipzig,
1842 ; nephew and pupil of above ;
cantor, theorist and composer.

**Weinwurm** (vīn'-voorm), **Rudolf**, b.
Schaidldorf-on-the-Thaja, Lower
Austria, April 3, 1835 ; chorister, ct.-
chapel, Vienna ; 1858, studied law
and founded the Univ. Gesangverein;
mus.-dir.; 1880 mus.-dir. of the Univ.;
pub. treatises and composer.

**Weinzierl** (vīn'-tsĕrl), **Max**, Ritter
**von**, Bergstadl, Bohemia, 1841—
Mödling, near Vienna, 1898 ; conductor and dram. composer.

**Weis** (vīs), **Karl**, notable contemporary composer ; prod. with succ. 2-
act opera " *The Polish Jew* " (Berlin,
1902) ; comic opera " *The Twins* "
(Frankfort, 1903 ?).

**Weisheimer** (vīs'-hī-mĕr), **Wendelin**, b. Osthofen, Alsatia, 1836; pupil
of Leipzig Cons.; 1866, theatre-cond.
at Würzburg, later Mayence; teacher
at Strassburg ; wrote essays ; c.
grand opera " *Theodor Körner* "
(Munich, 1872), and " *Meister Martin und seine Gesellen*" (Carlsruhe.
1879).

**Weiss** (vīs), (1) **K.**, Mühlhausen, ca.
1738—London, 1795 ; composer. (2)
**K.**, b. 1777, son and pupil of above ;
writer and composer. (3) **K.**, bro.
of above ; prod. the opera " *Twelfth
Night* " (Prague, 1892). (4) **Fz.**,
Silesia. 1778—Vienna, 1830 ; viola-

virtuoso and composer. (5) **Julius,** b. Berlin, July 19, 1814 ; violinist ; pupil of Henning ; teacher, writer and critic ; pub. instructive works for vln. (6) **Amalie.** Vide AMALIE JOACHIM. (7) **Josef,** b. Kaschau, Hungary, Nov. 5, 1864 ; pf.-virtuoso ; c. a concerto, etc.

**Weissbeck** (vīs'-bĕk), **Jn. Michael,** Unterlaimbach, Swabia, 1756—1808; cantor and organist ; writer of satirical pamphlets ; composer.

**Weist-Hill, H.,** b. London, 1830 ; violinist ; pupil R. A. M.; cond. various concerts with much hospitality to novelties ; 1880 principal Guildhall Sch.

**Weitzmann** (vīts'-män), **K. Fr.,** Berlin, 1808—1880 ; eminent theorist ; c. operas, etc.; wrote valuable treatises.

**Welch, J. Bacon,** b. Northampton , 1839 ; prominent Engl. singing-teacher.

**Welcker von Gontershausen** (vĕl'-kĕr fōn gôn'-tĕrs-how-zĕn), **H.,** Gontershausen, Hesse, 1811—Darmstadt, 1873 ; ct.-pf.-maker and writer.

**Wel'don,** (1) **J.,** Chichester, Engl., 1676—London, 1736 ; organist and composer. (2) **Georgina,** b. Clapham, May 24, 1837 ; singer and composer.

**Wels** (vĕls), **Chas.,** b. Prague, Aug. 24, 1825, pupil of Tomaschek; 1847, ct.-pianist; 1849, New York as concert-pianist and teacher ; c. concert-overture and suite for orch.; a pf.-concerto, etc.

**Welsh** (1) **Thomas,** Wells, Somerset, 1770—Brighton, 1848; bass and singing-teacher. (2) **Mary Anne** (née **Wilson**), 1802—1867 ; wife and pupil of above ; v. succ. soprano, earning £10,000 ($50,000) the first year of her short career.

**Wenck** (vĕnk), **Aug. H.,** violinist ; pupil of G. Benda ; lived in Paris (1786), and Amsterdam (1806) ; inv. a metronome ; c. pf.-sonatas, etc.

**Wenckel** (vĕnk'-ĕl), **Jn. Fr. Wm.,** Niedergebra, 1734—Ulzen, 1792 ; organist and composer.

**Wendling** (vĕnt'-lǐng), (1) **Jn. Bap** from 1754 – 1800 flutist in Ma heim ; band composer. His wife **Dorothea** (née **Spurni**), Stuttga 1737—Munich, 1809, was a sing (3) **K.,** d. 1794 ; violinist in Ma heim band. His wife (4) **Augus Elizabethe,** was a singer. (5) **I** b. Frankenthal, Rhine Palatina Nov. 14, 1857 ; pianist ; pupil Le zig Cons.; performer on Jankó ke board ; teacher of it from 1887 Leipzig Cons.; ct.-pianist to Prin of Waldeck.

**Wendt** (vĕnt), (1) **Jn. Gl. (Amadeu** Leipzig, 1783—Göttingen, 1836. **Ernst Ad.,** Schwiebus, Pruss 1806—Neuwied, 1850 ; composer. **Ed.,** Berlin, 1807—Magdeburg,18g violinist and composer.

**Wennerberg**(vĕn'-nĕr-bĕrkh),**Gunna** Linköping, Sweden, 1817 — ( poet, critic, statesman. and compose c. an oratorio and pop. psalms a songs.

**Wenzel** (vĕn'-tsĕl), (1) **Ernst F** Walddorf, near Lobau, 1808—B Kösen, 1880 ; pf.-teacher and write (2) **Leopold,** b. Naples, Jan. 2 1847 ; pupil of the Cons. S. Pietro Majella ; at 13 toured as violini 1866 joined Métra's orch. at Ma seilles ; 1871, conductor ; later con of the Alcazar, Paris ; 1883, Londo from 1889 cond. at the Empire Th prod. operettas, many ballets, etc.

**Werbecke, Gaspar van.** Vide GA PAR.

**Werckmeister** ( vărk'-mī-shtĕr **Ands.,** Beneckenstein, 1645—Hal erstadt, 1706 ; organist, importa theorist and composer.

**Werkenthin** (vär'-kĕn-tēn), **Alber** b. Berlin, March 6, 1842 ; pianis pupil of von Bülow, Weitzmann, U rich and Stern ; pub. a method ; pf.-pcs. and songs.

**Wermann** (vär'-män), **Fr. Oskar,** Neichen, near Trebsen, Saxon April 30, 1840 ; pianist and organis pupil of Leipzig Cons.; 1868, teach R. Seminary. Dresden ; 1876, mu

r. 3 churches and cantor at the
reuzschule there ; c. "*Reforma-
ns-Cantate*," mass in 8 parts, etc.

rneburg (vär′-ně-boorkh), **Jn. Fr.
hr.**, Gymnasium teacher at Weimar;
eorist and composer, 1796.

rner (vär′-něr), (1) **Georgius Jos.,**
·05—Eisenstadt, 1766 ; conductor
·d composer. (2) **Jn. Gottlob,**
·oyer, Saxony, 1777—Merseburg,
·22; organist, mus.-director, teacher
·d composer. (3) **H.,** near Erfurt,
·00—Brunswick, 1833 ; composer.
·) **K.,** Breslau, 1822—1884 ; organ-
·t. (5) **K. Ludwig,** b. Mannheim,
·pt. 8, 1862 ; pupil of Hanlein and
·ischer ; organist at Baden-Baden.
·) **Josef,** b. Würzburg, June 25,
·37 ; ′cellist ; pupil of the Cons.
·ere ; teacher Munich School of
·usic; pub. a method ; c. pcs. for
·ello, etc.

·rstovski (věr-shtôf′-shkǐ), **Alexei
·ikolajevitch,** Moscow, 1799—
·62 ; dram. composer.

·rt (värt), **Jacob van,** b. Nether-
·nds, 1536—Mantua, 1596 ; con-
·uctor and composer.

·ry (vä-rē), **Nicolas Lambert,**
·uy, near Liège, 1789—Bande,
·uxembourg, 1867 ; solo-violinist,
·acher and composer.

·sembeck. Vide BURBURE DE W.

·s′ley, (1) **Chas.,** Bristol, Engl.,
·ec. 11, 1757—London, May 23,
·34; nephew of the evangelist John
·V.; teacher, organist and composer.
·) **Samuel,** Bristol, Engl., 1766—
·ondon, 1837; bro. and pupil of
·bove ; organist and composer. (3)
·amuel Sebastian, London, Aug.
·4, 1810—Gloucester, April 19, 1876 ;
·on of above ; organist.

·essel (věs′-sěl), **Chr. R.,** Bremesia,
·797—Eastbourne, 1885 ; mus.-pub-
·sher, London.

·esselack (věs′-sě-läk), **Jn. G.,** Sat-
·elpeilestein, Upper Palatinate, 1828
·—Ratisbon. 1866 ; editor and com-
·oser.

·essely (věs′-sě-lē), (1) **Jn.,** Frauen-
·urg, Bohemia, 1762—Ballenstedt,

1814 ; violinist ; c. comic operas. (2)
**(K.) Bd.,** Berlin, 1768—Potsdam,
1826 ; dram. composer.

**West, J. Ebenezer,** b. South Hackney, London, Dec. 7, 1863 ; concert-
organist and pianist ; pupil of Bridge
and Prout, R. A. M.; since 1891, organist S. Hackney Parish Ch.; c. 2
cantatas ; Psalm 130 ; services, etc.

**West′brook, Wm. Jos.,** London,
1831—Sydenham, 1894 ; organist,
conductor and composer.

**West′lake, Fr.,** Romsey, Hampshire,
1840—London, 1898 ; composer.

**Westmeyer** (věsht′-mī-ěr), **Wm.,**
Iburg, near Osnabrück, 1832—Bonn,
1880 ; c. operas.

**Westmore′land, J. Fane,** Earl of,
London. 1784 — Apthorpe House,
1859 ; dram. composer.

**Westphal** (věsht′-fäl), **Rudolf (G.
Hn.),** Oberkirchen, Lippe-Schaum-
burg, 1826 — Stadthagen, 1892 :
writer.

**West′rop, H. J.,** Lawenham, Suffolk,
1812—1879 ; pianist, violinist, singer,
organist and composer.

**Wetzler** (věts′-lěr), **Hermann Hans,**
b. Frankfort-on-Main, Sept. 8, 1870 ;
pupil of Frau Schumann (pf.), B.
Scholz (comp.), Ivan Knorr (cpt.),
H. Heerman (vln.), and Humperdinck (orchestration) ; 1893, New
York, as pianist and teacher; asst.-
org. Trinity Ch.; from 1902 cond.
his own symphony orch.

**Wexschall** (věx′-shäl), **Fr. Forkild-
son,** Copenhagen, 1798—1845 ; pupil of Spohr, teacher and solo-violinist in royal band.

**Weyrauch** (vī′-rowkh), **Aug. H. von,**
composer of whom nothing is known
except that he c. and pub. 1824 the
song "*Adieu*" wrongly attributed to
Schubert from 1840.

**Weyse** (vī′-zě), **Chp. Ernst Fr.,** Altona, 1774 — Copenhagen, 1842 ;
dram. composer.

**Wheat′stone, Chas.,** inv. the concertina, 1829.

**Whelp′ley, Benj. Lincoln,** b. East-
port, Maine, U. S. A., Oct. 23, 1865,

studied with B. J. Lang, etc., at Boston, 1890 in Paris; lives in Boston as teacher and composer.

**Whistling** (wĭst'-lĭng), **K. Fr.**, bookseller and lexicographer in Leipzig.

**Whit'aker, J.**, 1776—1847; organist and composer, London.

**White,** (1) **Robt.**, d. Westminster, Nov. 7 (11 ?), 1574; organist at Ely Cath. (1562–67); noted in his day as organist and composer. Often confused with (2) **Wm.** (c. fantasias or "fancies" for org., etc.) and (3) Rev. **Matthew,** Mus. Doc. 1629; c. anthems and catches. (4) **Alice Mary, Meadows** (née **Smith**), 1839—1884; pupil of Bennett, and Macfarren, London; c. symphs., cantatas, etc. (5) **J.,** W. Springfield, Mass., March 12, 1855—Bad Neuheim, Germany, July 18, 1902; pupil of Dudley Buck; then of Haupt (org. and cpt.), Rheinberger; gave org.-concerts in various German cities; 1887–96, organist, New York; from 1897 lived in Munich; pub. Missa Solemnis; O salutaris; c. an oratorio "*Alpha and Omega,*" etc. (6) **Maude Valérie,** b. of English parents, Dieppe, June 23, 1855; pupil of O. May and W. S. Rockstro, and of R. A. M., Mendelssohn Scholar, 1879, also studied in Vienna; now lives in London; c. mass (1888); 14 pf.-pcs.; "*Pictures from Abroad*" and pop. songs, etc.

**White'hill, Clarence,** b. America; bass; début in "*Roméo et Juliette,*" Brussels, 1899; engaged for Paris Op. Com.; 1900 at Met. Op., N. Y.

**Whi'ting,** (1) **G. Elbridge,** b. Holliston, Mass., Sept. 14, 1842; organist at Worcester when 13; later at Hartford, Conn. (where he founded the Beethoven Soc.); later organist in various Boston churches; studied with G. W. Morgan, New York, and Best, Liverpool; Haupt and Radecke, Berlin; till 1879, teacher at the N. E. Cons., Boston; then till 1882, at the Cincinnati Coll. of Mus.; since at the N. E. Cons.; c. masses with orch. and organ (1872), cantatas,

ballade with orch., "*Henry of N̶ varre,*" pf.-concerto, etc. (2) **Art̶ Battelle,** b. Cambridge, Mass., J̶ 20, 1861; nephew of above; pf.- pil of W. H. Sherwood; début at ̶ Boston; studied with Chadwick a̶ J. C. D. Parker; then with Rh̶ berger, in Munich; lived in Bost̶ now New York, as teacher of pf. a̶ comp.; c. fantasy with orch., c̶ cert-overture, concert-étude, chur̶ service, concerto, song cycles, etc.

**Whit'more, Chas. S.,** Colchest̶ 1805—1877; amateur Engl. co̶ poser.

**Whitney, Samuel Brenton,** b. Wo̶ stock, Vermont, June 4, 1842; ̶ ganist; pupil of Chas. Wells and ̶ K. Paine; since 1871, organist, ̶ of the Advent, Boston; conductor ̶ church-choir festivals; org.-pr̶ and lecturer, Boston U. and N. Cons.; c. anthems, org.-sonatas, e̶

**Whyt'horne (or Whitehorne), Tho̶** b. 1528; Engl. composer.

**Wiborg** (vē'-bôrkh), **Elisa,** b. K̶ gerö, Norway; soprano; stud̶ with Natalie Hänisch and Frau H̶ lacher; engaged at Schwerin, th̶ other cities; sang "Elisabeth" ̶ Bayreuth; 1900 at Stuttgart ̶ theatre.

**Wichmann** (vĭkh'-män), **Hermann,** Berlin, Oct. 24, 1824; studied at ̶ Akademie; also with Taubert, M̶ delssohn and Spohr; then lived ̶ Berlin; c. symphs., sonatas, etc.

**Wichtl** (vĭkht'-l), **G.,** Trostberg, B̶ varia, 1805—Bunzlau, Silesia, 187̶ violinist, conductor and dram. co̶ poser.

**Wickede** (vĭk'-ĕ-dĕ), **Fr. von,** b. D̶ mitz-on-Elbe, July 28, 1834; arm̶ officer, then post-office official; p̶ pil of J. Vieth; lived in Munich; ̶ opera "*Ingo,*" overture "*Per aspe̶ ad astra*" (1875), songs, etc.

**Widmann** (vēt'-män), (1) **Erasm̶** poet-laureate, organist and conduct̶ at Weikersheim; publisher and co̶ poser (1607). (2) **Benedikt,** ̶ Bräuntlingen, March 5, 1820: rect̶

t Frankfort ; theorist and composer.
3) **Jos. Victor,** b. Nennowitz, Moravia, Feb. 20, 1842 ; at 3 taken to
Switzerland ; wrote librettos and
biog. of Brahms.

dor (vē-dôr), **Chas. (M.),** b. Lyons,
Feb. 22, 1845 ; distinguished organ-
t ; son of an Alsatian of Hungarian
escent (organist at Lyons) ; studied
ith Lemmens (org.) and Fétis
comp.), Brussels ; at 15 organist
t St. François, Lyons, and since
869, organist at St. Sulpice, Paris ;
890, teacher at the Paris Cons.;
om 1896 prof. of cpt., fugue and
omp.; critic (under pen-name " **Au-**
etes ") and dir. of the soc. "La Con-
ordia," c. v. succ. ballet "*La Korri-*
*ane*" (Opéra, 1880) ; music to
*Conte d'Avril*" (Odéon, 1885) ;
*Les Jacobites*" (Odéon, 1885) ; un-
ucc. lyric drama "*Maître Ambros*"
Op.-Com., May 6, 1896) ; 3 panto-
aimes ; a mass for 2 choirs and 2 orgs.;
'salm 112, with orch. and org.; "*La*
*uit de Walpurgis*," for chorus and
rch.; 2 symphs.; 10 org. symphs.
ncl. "*Gotique*," a concerto for vln.,
'ello, and pf., org.-sonatas, etc.

eck (vēk), (1) **Fr.,** Pretzsch, near
'orgau, 1785—Loschwitz, near Dres-
en, 1873 ; est. a pf.-factory and li-
rary at Leipzig ; eminent pf.-teach-
r ; also singing-teacher and compos-
r; teacher also of his daughter (2)
**Clara.** (Vide SCHUMANN.) (3) **Al-**
**vin,** Leipzig, 1821—1885 ; son of
(); pupil of David ; violinist at St.
'etersburg ; later pf.-teacher at Dres-
en. (4) **Marie,** b. Leipzig, Jan.
7, 1835 ; pianist ; daughter of (1) ;
layed in public at 8 ; 1858, ct.-pian-
st to the Prince of Hohenzollern ;
oured ; est. a sch. in Dresden.

edemann (vē-dě-män), **Ernst Jn.,**
Iohengiersdorf, Silesia, 1797—Pots-
am, 1873 ; organist, teacher and
omposer.

ederkehr (vē-děr-kār), **Jacob Chr.**
**Michael,** Strassburg, 1739—Paris,
823 ; 'cellist, bassoonist, tambourin-
st and composer.

**Wiegand** (vē'-gänt), **Josef Anton H.,**
Frankisch-Crumbach in the Oden-
wald, 1842—Frankfort, 1899 ; bass.

**Wielhorski.** Vide WILHORSKI.

**Wiener** (vē'-něr), **Wm.,** Prague, 1838;
violinist and leader.

**Wieniawski** (v'yä-nē-äf'-shkǐ), (1) **H.,**
Lublin, Poland, July 10, 1835—Mos-
cow, March 31, 1880 ; eminent violinist and composer ; début, at Petersburg, at 13 ; studied with Clavel and
Massart, and Colet (harmony) Paris
Cons.; won 1st vln.-prize, 1846; 1860,
solo-violinist to Czar, and 1862–67,
teacher at the Petersburg Cons.;
1875–77, vln.-prof. Brussels Cons.
(vice Vieuxtemps) ; toured widely,
1872 U. S. with Rubinstein ; c. 2
concertos, etc. (2) **Jos.,** b. Lublin,
May 23, 1837 ; famous pianist ; at 10
pupil of Paris Cons.; at 13 toured
with his brother, then studied with
Marx at Berlin ; 1866, teacher at the
Moscow Cons.; est. a pf.-sch. of his
own ; later teacher in Brussels Cons.;
c. 2 overtures, suite romantique for
orch., pf.-concerto, etc.

**Wieprecht** (vē'-prěkht), **Fr. Wm.,**
Aschersleben, 1802—Berlin, 1872 ;
famous trombonist and violinist ; inv.
the bass tuba (1835).

**Wiétrovetz** (vē-ā'-trō-větsh), **Ga-**
**briele,** b. Laibach, Jan. 13, 1869 ;
violinist ; pupil of Joachim and Wirth.
Toured and lives in Berlin.

**Wihan** (vē'-hän), **Hans (Hanus),** b.
Politz, near Braunau, June 5, 1855 ;
'cellist ; pupil of Prague Cons. ; 1873,
prof. of 'cello, Mozarteum, Salzburg ;
1877–80, chamber-virtuoso to Prince
Schwarzburg-Sondershausen ; 1880,
1st solo-'cellist Munich ct.-orch.;
1888, prof. at Prague Cons., a member " Bohemian String Quartet."

**Wihtol** (vē'-tôl), **Jos.,** b. Wolmar,
Livonia, 1863 ; studied at Mitau ;
then with Johansen (harm.) and
Rimsky-Korsakov (comp. and instrumentation) Petersburg Cons.; since
1886, prof. of harm. there ; c. "*La*
*fête Ligho*," symph. picture, "*Dram*
*atic*" overture, etc.

**Wilbye** (wïl'-bï), **J.**; lutenist and teacher, London, 1598 ; most brilliant composer of madrigals.

**Wild** (vēlt), **Fz.**, Niederhollabrunn, Lower Austria, 1792—Oberdöbling, near Vienna, 1860 ; tenor.

**Wilder** (vēl-dăr), **Jérome Albert Victor van**, Wettern, near Ghent, 1835 —Paris, 1892 ; writer and translator.

**Wilhelm** (vēl'-hĕlm), **K.**, Schmalkalden, 1815—1873; "R. Prussian Mus. Dir."; c. "*Die Wacht am Rhein*," etc.

**Wilhelm von Hirsau** (fōn hēr'-zow), d. June 4, 1091; abbott and theorist at Hirsau, Schwarz-wald.

**Wilhelmj** (vēl-hĕl'-mē), (1) **Aug.** (**Emil Daniel Fd.**), b. Usingen, Nassau, Sept. 21, 1845 ; eminent violinist ; pupil of Fischer at Wiesbaden ; played in public at 8 ; at 16 recommended to David by Liszt as a young Paganini ; he studied 1861–64, with David (vln.), Hauptmann and Richter, Leipzig Cons.; 1862, the Gewandhaus ; 1864, studied with Raff at Frankfort ; from 1865, toured the world ; 1876, leader of Bayreuth orch.; lived for years at Biebrich-on-Rhine, where he est. (with R. Niemann) a " Hochschule " for vln.; 1886, lived at Blasewitz, near Dresden ; 1894, head-prof. Guildhall Sch., London ; 1895, he m. the pianist Miss Mausch ; c. "*Hochzeits-Cantate*" with orch., vln.-pcs., etc. His son (2) **Anton**, 1898, vln.-prof. at Belfast Cons. (3) **Maria** (née **Gastell**), b. Mayence, July 27, 1856 ; sister-in-law of (1) ; concert-soprano, pupil of Viardot-Garcia.

**Wilhem** (rightly **Bocquillon**) (vēl-än or bôk-ē-yôn), **Guillaume Louis**, Paris, 1771—1842 ; dir.-gen. of all Paris schools ; founder of the great system of popular singing societies or " Orphéonistes " (v. D. D.) ; pub. many treatises on his method of " mutual instruction " and a 10-vol. coll. of comps.

**Wi(e)lhórski** (vēl-hôr'-shkï), (1) Count **Matvéi Júrjevitch**, Volhynia, 1787

— Petersburg (?), 1863 ; 'cell His brother (2) Count **Michaíl J jevitch**, Volhynia, 1788—Mosc 1856 ; composer.

**Wilke** (vēl'-kĕ). **Chr. Fr. Gl.**, Sp dai, 1769—Treuenbrietzen, 18. organist and govt. expert on o building.

**Willaert** (wïl'.lärt) (**Wigliar'd Vigliar, Vuigliart**), **Adrian** (cal **Adriano**), Flanders, ca. 1480 Venice, 1562 ; eminent composer a teacher ; called the founder of Venetian Sch.; a very prolific c poser ; pupil of Mouton and J quin Desprès ; 1516 at Rome, la at Ferrara ; then mus. to the K of Bohemia ; Dec. 12, 1527, maes at San Marco, Venice, where he ganised a famous sch.; c. 5 mass many motets, psalms, madrigals,e the first to write for two choirs.

**Willent-Bordogni** (vē-yän - bôr-l yē), **Jean Bapt. Jos.**, Douai, 180 Paris, 1852 ; bassoon-virtuoso, tea er, writer and dram. composer. 18 m. the daughter of Bordogni.

**Wil'liams**, (1) **G. E.**, 1784—18 organist and composer. (2) **Ann** b. London ; début, 1872 ; sopra Also two sisters b. at Bitterl England. (3) **Anne** (b. 1818), prano and (4) **Martha**, b. 1853, c tralto.

**Willing** (wïl'-lĭng), (1) **Jn. L.**, Kü dorf, 1755---Nordhausen, 1805 ; ganist and composer. (2) (wïl'-lï **Chr. Edwin**, b. London, Feb. 1830 ; organist various Lond churches, conductor and teacher.

**Wil'lis**, (1) **H.**, b. England, April 1821; prominent org.-builder and i prover. (2) **Richard Storrs**, B ton, Mass., Feb. 10, 1819—Detr May 7, 1900 ; bro. of N. P. Wi the poet ; critic and editor in N. later Detroit ; composer.

**Will'man**, (1) **Thos. Lindsay**, Engl., 1840 ; famous clarinettist. (vïl'-män), **Maximilian**, b. Forc enberg, near Würzburg, 1812 ; 'c list. (3) ———, oldest daughter

bove; pianist. (4) **Magdelena**, d.
801; famous soprano; her brother,
5) **K.**, violinist. (6) Mme. **Tribolet**
nd wife of (1), d. 1812; opera-singer.
') **Caroline**, debut, 1811; daughter
f (6); pianist and singer.

llmers (vĭl′-mĕrs), **H. Rudolf**,
erlin, 1821—Vienna, 1878; pianist
nd composer.

l′ly, **J. L.**, London, 1812—1885;
iolinist.

lm (vĭlm), **Nicolai von**, b. Riga,
larch 4, 1834: pianist; studied
eipzig Cons.; 1857, 2nd cond. Riga
ity Th.; then Petersburg, 1860;
acher of pf. and theory Imp. Nico-
i Inst.; 1875, Dresden; 1878,
iesbaden; c. pop. s⁺ring-sextet,
ello and vln.-sonatas, male-cho-
ses, etc.

lms (vĭlms), **Jan Willem**, Witz-
elden, Schwarzburg-Sondershausen,
772—Amsterdam, 1847; teacher and
rg.-composer.

lsing (vĭl′-zĭng), **Daniel Fr. Ed.**,
. Horde, near Dortmund, Oct. 21,
809; 1829–34, organist in Wesel,
en Berlin; c. oratorio "*Jesus
'hristus*," in 2 parts (Bonn, 1889);
De profundis *à* 16 (gold medal for
rt, Berlin); pf.-sonata, etc.

l′son, (1) **J.**, Faversham, Kent,
594—London, 1673; famous luten-
t and composer. (2) **J.**, Edin-
urgh, 1800—(of cholera) Quebec,
849; tenor. (3) **Mary Ann**, 1802;
upil of Thos. Welsh (q. v.).

nderstein (vĭn′-dĕr-shtīn), **Hans
Wm. Gv.**), b. Lüneburg, Oct. 29,
856; violinist; pupil of Leipzig
ons.; also playing in Gewandhaus
rch.; 1880–84, leader in Baron von
)erwies' orch. at Nice; till 1887,
.n.-teacher at Winterthur (Switzer-
nd) Cons., then cond. at Nürnberg;
893–96, dir. Philh. Orch., at Mu-
ich, and at the Kaim Concerts;
896, organised and conducted the
Winderstein Orch."; 1898, cond.
eipzig Singakademie; c. Trauer-
arsch, Valse-Caprice and Ständchen
r orch.; orch. suite, etc.

**Winding** (vĭn′-dĭng), **Aug. (Henrik)**.
b. Taaro (Laaland), Denmark, March
24, 1825; pianist; pupil of Reinecke,
Ree, Dreyschock and Gade; dir.
and prof. Copenhagen Cons.; c. vln.-
concerto, sonatas, etc.

**Wing′ham, Thos.**, London, 1846—
1893; organist and composer.

**Winkel** (vĭnk′-ĕl), **Dietrich Nikolaus**, Amsterdam, ca. 1780—1826;
a mechanician; inv. the "compo-
nium" and "metronome," which
later Mälzel (q. v.) appropriated.

**Winkelmann** (vĭnk′-ĕl-män), **Hermann**, b. Brunswick, 1845; tenor;
pupil of Koch at Hanover; début
Sondershausen, 1875; sang at Altenburg, Darmstadt and Hamburg;
then at ct.-opera, Vienna; 1882,
created "Parsifal" at Bayreuth.

**Winn**, (1) **Wm.**, Bramham, Yorkshire,
May 8, 1828; bass and teacher. (2)
**Florence**, 1857, daughter of above;
contralto.

**Win′ner, Septimus**, Philadelphia,
1826—Nov. 23, 1902; writer of pop.
songs and methods; said to have
written 200 technical books on instruments and to have c. and arranged
over 2,000 pcs. for vln. and piano;
also wrote for Graham's Mag., when
Poe was editor. His songs include
"*Listen to the Mocking Bird*," and
"*Give us Back our old Commander*";
founder of Musical Fund Soc.

**Winogradsky** (vē-nō-grät′-shkĭ),
**Alex.**, b. Kiev, Russia, Aug. 3 (new
style), 1854; noted cond.; pupil of
Soloviev, Petersb. Cons.; 1884–86, dir.
Imp. Sch. of Mus. at Saratov; since
1888, of Imp. Soc. of Mus. at Kiev;
in Paris, 1894, he cond. Russian programmes at the concerts "d'Harcourt" and "Colonne," 1896.

**Winter** (vĭn′-tĕr), **Peter von**, Mannheim, 1754—Munich, 1825; studied
with Abbé Vogier, but mainly self-
taught; violinist and ct.-conductor;
composer of v succ. operas, 38 in
all; c. 9 symphs. incl. "*Die Schlacht*"
and much church-mus.

**Winterberger** (vĭn′-tĕr-bĕrkh-ĕr),

**Alex.,** b. Weimar, Aug. 14, 1834;
pianist; pupil of Leipzig Cons. and
of Liszt. 1861, pf.-prof. at Petersburg Cons.; 1872, lived in Leipzig;
c. pf.-pcs. and songs.

**Winterfeld** (vĭn'-tĕr-fĕlt), **K. G. Aug.
Vivigens von,** Berlin, 1784—1852;
libr. and writer of valuable historical
works.

**Wippern** ( vĭp'-pĕrn), **Louise (Har-
riers - Wippern),** Hildeshiem (or
Bückeburg), 1835(7) — Gorhersdorf,
Silesia, 1878; operatic singer.

**Wirth** (vērt), **Emanuel,** b. Luditz,
Bohemia, Oct. 18, 1842; violinist;
pupil of Prague Cons., 1864–77;
teacher at Rotterdam Cons., and
orch.-leader; then vla.-player in the
Joachim Quartet, Berlin, and vln.-
prof. at the Hochschule; Royal Prof.

**Wise, Michael,** England, 1648 ?—
in a street brawl, Salisbury, 1687;
tenor and notable early composer of
anthems, etc.

**Wit** (vēt), **Paul de,** b. Maesticht,
Jan. 4, 1852; 'cellist and viola·da
gambist; coll. of ancient instrs.

**Witásek** (vĕ'-tä-shĕk), **Jn. Nepomuk
Aug.,** Horzin, Bohemia, 1771—
Prague, 1839; conductor, director
and pianist.

**Witek** (vĕ'-tĕk), **Anton;** concertmaster and soloist, Berlin Philh. orch.,
1902.

**With'erspoon, Herbert,** b. New
Haven, Conn.; notable basso can-
tante; graduated Yale Univ pupil of
J. W. Hall, N. Y., and Dubulle,
Paris; sang in opera, Castle Square
Co., N. Y., and with Boston Symph.
and other orchs. throughout U. S.;
v. succ. début in recital, N. Y., 1902.

**Witt** (vĭt), (1) **Fr.,** Halten-Bergstetten,
1771—Würzburg, 1837; violinist,
conductor and dram. composer. (2)
**Julius,** b. Königsburg, Jan. 14,
1819; singing-teacher there, and c.
pop. male choruses. (3) **Theodor
de,** Wesel, 1823—(of consumption)
Rome, 1855; organist and composer.
(4) **Wm.,** Hamburg, 1826—London,
1900; violinist and publisher. (5)

**Fz.,** Walderbach, Bavaria, 183
Schatzhofen, 1888; editor and writ
(6) **Jos. von,** Prague, 1843—Ber
1887; tenor.

**Witte** (vĭt'-tĕ), (1) **Chr. Gl. Fr.,**
1873; org.-builder. (2) **G. H.,**
Utrecht, Nov. 16, 1843; son of abo
pupil of R. Mus. Sch. at The Hag
then of Leipzig Cons.; teacher
Leipzig till 1867, then in Alsatia, 18
cond. at Essen, 1882; R. Mus. D
c. pf.-quartet (prize at Florenc
grand Elegy for vln. and orch., et

**Wittekopf** (vĭt'-tĕ-kôpf), **Rudolf,**
Berlin, Dec. 11, 1863; studied St
Cons.; début, Aix,1888; sang Leipz
1889–96; later in other cities, ir
London in the " *Nibelungen Ring*

**Wittich** (vĭt'-tĭkh), **Marie,** b. Giess
May 27, 1868; soprano; stud
with Frau Otto-Ubridy; sung vari
cities; 1901 Dresden ct.-opera.

**Wohlfahrt** (vōl'-färt), (1) **H.,** Kö
nitz, near Apolda, 1797—Connew
1883; noted teacher, writer and cc
poser. His sons (2) **Fz.,** Frau
priesnitz, 1833—Gohlis, 1884.
**Robt.,** b. Weimar, Dec. 31, 182
violinist, teacher and writer of te
books.

**Woikù** (vói'-koo), **Petresoù,** b. R
mania, 1885 (?); violinist; pupil
Barmas, Stern Cons., Berlin, for
years.

**Woldemar** (vôl-dŭ-măr) (rightly **N
chel,** Orléans, 1750—Clermont-F
rand, 1816; conductor and compos
wrote methods; inv. a mus.-stenog
phy " *Tableau mélotachigraphiqu*
and mus.-correspondence " *Notog
phie.*"

**Wolf** (vôlf), (1) **Ernst Wm.,** Gr
heringen, 1735—Weimar, 1792; «
conductor; c. 42 pf.-sonatas. (2)
**Fr.,** Hainrode, 1762—Wernigero
1814; conductor, theorist and co
poser. (3) **Fd.,** Vienna, 1796—18
writer. (4) **L.,** Frankfort-on-Ma
1804—Vienna, 1859; pianist, viol
ist and composer. (5) **Max,** Mo
via, 1840—Vienna, 1886; c. oper
tas. (6) **Wm.,** b. Breslau, April

838; pupil of Kullak, teacher of
mus.-history, Berlin, also writer and
composer. (7) **Hugo,** Vienna, March
3, 1860—1902; composer; already
here is in Berlin a H. W.-verein; at
studied vln. and piano with his
father; at 8 studied at Vienna Cons.;
rod. succ. comic opera " *Der Cor-*
*egidor* " (Mannheim, 1896) ; c. cho-
ic works with orch. " *Die Christ-*
*acht*" and " *Der Feuerreiter*";
male choruses and about 500 songs,
many of them importantly original.
olff (vôlf), (1). Vide WOLF (4). (2)
**douard,** Warsaw, 1816—Paris, 1880;
ianist and composer. (3) **Auguste**
**Désiré Bd.,** Paris, 1821—1887; pia-
ist, pf.-teacher and maker ; head of
rm " Pleyel-Wolff." (4) **Hermann,**
Cologne, 1845—Feb. 3, 1902 ; pupil
f Fz. Kroll and Würst ; editor, con-
ert-agent and mgr. at Berlin ; c. pf.-
cs. and songs.
i f(f)l (vělf'-'l)(**Woelfel, Woelfle),**
os., Salzburg, 1772—London, 1812;
omposer; his enormous hands and
reat contrapuntal skill made him a
f.-virtuoso whose rivalry with Bee-
hoven divided Vienna into factions ;
ut the rivals had mutual respect and
W. dedicated his op. 6 to B.; c. light
peras (1795-98).
olfram (vôl'-främ), (1) **Jn. Chr.,**
. 1835; organist and writer at Gold-
ach, near Gotha. (2) **Jos. Maria,**
Dobrzan, Bohemia, 1789—Teplitz,
839; conductor and dram. composer.
olfrum (vôl'-froom), **Philipp,** b.
chwarzenbach - am -Wald, Bavaria,
Dec. 17, 1855; pupil Munich Sch. of
Mus.; mus.-dir. Heidelberg Univ.;
Dr. Phil. *h. c.* (Leipzig, 1891); c.
*Grosses Halleluja*," and other cho-
uses, pf.-pcs., etc.
ollanck (vôl'-länk), **Fr.,** Berlin,1782
-1831; amateur composer of an opera.
ollenhaupt (vôl'-lěn-howpt), **H.**
Ad.,** Schkeuditz, near Leipzig, 1827
-New York, 1863; pianist, teacher
nd composer; from 1845 in New
ork.
ollick (vôl'-lĭk) (**Volli'cius, Bolli'-**

cius), **Nicolas,** b. Bar-le-Duc;
teacher and writer at Metz, 1501-12.
**Wolzogen (und Neuhaus)** (vôl'-tsō-
gĕn oont noi-hows), (1) **K. Aug.**
**Alfred,** Freiherr **von,** Frankfort,
1833—San Remo, 1883; writer. (2)
**Hans (Paul),** Freiherr **von,** b. Potsdam, 1848; son of above; lived as
writer at Potsdam till 1877. Wagner
made him editor of the "*Baireuther*
*Blätter*."
**Wonneger (or Vuonnegger** (vôn'-nĕ-
gĕr) ), **Jn. L.,** friend of Glarean ;
pub. an epitome of G.'s "*Dodeka-*
*chordon*" (1557).
**Wood,** (1) Mrs. **Mary Ann.** Vide
PATON. (2) **Henry J.,** b. London,
1869; prominent cond.; pupil of his
father ; at 10 an organist ; 1883-85,
gave org.-recitals ; then st. at R.
A. M. with Prout and others ; then
cond. societies ; 1891-92, Carl Rosa
Op. Co.; 1894, Marie Roze Co.;
1895-1902, Queens Hall Prom. Concerts, London. C. oratorio "*Doro-*
*thea*" (1889), operettas, masses,
songs, etc.; wrote treatise on singing ;
1900, cond. a concert in Paris. His
wife, (3) a Russian, is a singer, début
London, 1900. (4) **Mary Knight,**
b. Easthampton, Mass., April 7,
1857; pianist; pupil of B. J. Lang,
A. R. Parsons, J. H. Cornell, and
H. H. Huss ; lived in New York; pub.
about 30 songs, many very popular.
**Wood'man, Raymond Huntington,**
b. Brooklyn, N. Y., Jan. 18, 1861 ;
pf.-pupil of his father, of Dudley
Buck, and César Franck ; 1875-79,
asst.-organist to his father, at Flushing, L. I.; 1894-97, mus.-editor
" *N. Y. Evangelist*"; since 1880,
organist First Presb. Ch., Brooklyn ;
since 1889, head of org.-dept. Metr.
Coll. of Mus., N. Y., etc. ; c. pf.-
and org.-pcs., etc.
**Woolf, Benj. Edw.,** London, Feb.,
1836—Boston, Feb., 1901 ; at 3
taken to America by his father
who taught him various instrs.;
studied with G. R. Bristow (org.):
cond. theatre-orchs. in various cities;

critic. Boston "*Globe*," later "*Sat. Evening Gazette*"; prod. operatic comedietta, comic operas "*Pounce & Co.*" (Boston, 1883), "*Westward Ho!*" (Boston, 1894), overture to "*Comedy of Errors*" (1887), etc.

**Wormser** (vôrm-zăr), **André (Alphonse Toussaint)**, b. Paris, Nov. 1, 1851; pupil of Marmontel (pf.) and Bazin, Paris Cons. taking 1st pf.-prize, 1872; Grand prix de Rome, 1875; lives in Paris; c. the opéras-comique "*Adèle de Ponthieu*" (Aix-les-Bains, 1877), "*Rivoli*" (Paris, 1896); v. succ. pantomime "*L'Enfant Prodigue*" (Paris, 1890, London, 1891, New York, 1893); pantomime "*L'Idéal*" (London, 1896); ballet, "*L'Étoile*" (Paris, 1897), etc.

**Worgan**, (1) **Jas.**, d. 1753; Engl. organist. (2) **J.**, d. 1794; bro. and succ. of above; also composer.

**Work, H. Clay**, Middletown, Conn., 1832—Hartford, 1884; c. "*Grandfather's Clock*," "*Marching through Georgia*," and other pop. songs.

**Wot'ton**, (1) **Wm.**, org.-builder, 15th cent., Engl. (2) **Wm. B.**, Torquay, Sept. 6,1832; bassoonist, saxophonist, oboist.

**Wouters** (voo'-tărs), **(Fran.) Adolphe**, b. Brussels, May 28, 1841; pupil, and since 1871, pf.-prof. at the Cons.; 1886, organist Nôtre-Dame de Finistère, and cond. at Saint-Nicolas; c. 3 masses solennelles (under pseud. "**Don Adolfo**"), a grand Te Deum, overture, etc.

**Woycke** (voi'-kě), **Eugen (Adalbert)**, b. Danzig, June 19, 1843; pianist; pupil Leipzig Cons.; lived in Edinburgh as teacher; pub. 7 pf.-sonatas. He married in 1871, (2) **Emily Drechsler** (née **Hamilton**), concert-violinist, playing in public since 11. (3) **Victor**, b. Edinburgh, 1872; son and pupil of above; début as violinist, 1889; 1892, teacher at the Nat. Cons., New York.

**Woyrsch** (voirsh) **Felix von**, b. Troppau, Austrian Silesia, Oct. 8, 1860; studied with A. Chevallier, Ham-

burg, but mainly self-taught; si... 1895, organist and conductor at tona; c. 4 comic operas incl. su "*Wikingerfahrt*" (Nürnberg, 189 4 choral works with orch.; symp symph. prologue to "*Divina Com dia*," etc.

**Wranitzky** (frä-nět'-shkǐ), (1) **Pa** Neureusch, Moravia, 1756—Vien 1808; violinist, conductor and dra composer. (2) **Anton**, Neureus 1761—Vienna, 1819; violinist; b and pupil of above; conductor a composer.

**Wrede** (vrā'-dě), Hanover, 182 Frankfort-on-the-Oder. 1899; pi ist, conductor, singing-teacher a composer.

**Wright on, W. T.**, 1816—Tunbri Wells, 1880; English song-cc poser.

**Wüerst** (vü'-ěrst), **Richard (F** Berlin, 1824—1881; teacher, cr and dram. composer.

**Wüllner** (vǐl'-něr), (1) **Fz.**, M ster, Jan. 28, 1832—Cologne, Se 8, 1902; noted conductor; stud Münster, later at Berlin, Brussels, ( logne, Bremen, Hanover and Le zig, and gave concerts as pi ist; 1854, pf.-teacher Munich Cor 1858, town mus.-dir. at Aix-Chapelle; 1861, "R. Mus.-Di 1864, 1882, 1886 and 1890 conducted the Lower Rhine M Fest.; cond. the ct.-chapel, M nich; 1867, dir. choral classes the Sch. of Mus.; in 1869, cor ct.-opera and the Acad. Conce (vice von Bülow), giving Wagne "*Rheingold*" and "*Walküre*" th first hearing. 1870, 1st ct.-con R. Prof. 1875; in 1877, ct.-co at Dresden, and artistic dir. the Cons.; 1883–84, cond. Be Philh.; 1884, dir. Cologne Cor was Dr. Phil. Leipzig U.; c. cant "*Heinrich der Finkler*," with or (1st prize, Aix-la-Chapelle "Lied tafel" 1864); new arrangem (with added recitatives) of von V ber's "*Oberon*"; Psalm 125. w

rch.; Miserere and Stabat Mater,
or double chorus, masses, chamber-
mus., etc. (2) **Ludwig,** b. Münster, Aug. 19, 1858; son of above;
Dr. phil., then studied Cologne Cons.;
888, dir. a church choir; became
a actor in spite of a vocal impedi-
ment, then a tenor singer in concert,
also in opera (as "Tannhäuser,"
c.).

**Inderlich** (voon'-děr-lǐkh), **Jn. G.,**
ayreuth, 1755—Paris, 1819; flute-
rtuoso and prof. Paris Cons.; also
omposer.

**rfel** (vür'-fěl), **Wm.,** Planian, Bo-
emia, 1791—Vienna, 1852; pianist,
rof., conductor and dram. composer.

**rm** (voorm), (1) **Wm.,** b. Bruns-
ick, 1826; virtuoso on the cornet-à-
stons; from 1847, lived in Pe-
rsburg, from 1862 teacher at the
ons., and from 1869 bandm.-in-
ief of the Russian Guards; c. cor-
et-pcs. (2) **Marie,** b. Southamp-
n, Engl., May 18. 1860; pianist;
pil of Pruckner and Stark, Anna
ehlig, Mary Krebs, Jos. Wieniaws-
, Raff and Frau Schumann; 1884,
n the Mendelssohn Scholarship;
udied with Stanford, Sullivan,
ridge and Reinecke; played with
cc. Leipzig, Berlin, etc.; c. an
erture; a pf.-concerto; sonatas,
c.

**lde** (wīld), **H.,** Bushy, Hertford-
ire, 1822—London, 1890; pianist,
ganist and teacher.

**man, Addison P.,** Cornish, N. H.
J. S. A.), 1832 — Washington,
nn. 1872; teacher of vln. and com-
ser.

**nne** (wǐn), **Sarah E.,** b. Holy-
ell, Huntingdon, March 11, 1842;
nger, held Westmoreland scholar-
ip R. A. M.; début, London, 1862;
. Aviet Agabeg, 1875, and since
en teacher.

**ns** (vēns), **Charlotte Félicie,** b.
Flemish parents, Paris, Jan. 11
68, mezzo-sopr.; pupil Paris Cons.,
king in 1892 3 first prizes, singing,
era and opéra comique; engaged

at the opéra, but débuted Op. Com
as *"Mignon";* later at Th. de la
Monnaie, Brussels, returning to Op.
Com. in 1899; m. Ed. de Bruijn.
1899.

**Wyszkowski.** Vide HOFMAN, C.

# X

**Xanrof** (ksän-rôf) (rightly **Léon Four-
neau**), b. Paris, Dec. 9, 1867; lawyer,
critic and amateur composer of song;
for Yvette Guilbert, also of light
stage-pcs.

**Xylander** (rightly **Holtzmann**) (ksē'-
länt-ěr or hôlts'-män), **Wm.,** Augsburg, 1532 — Heidelberg, 1576,
writer.

**Xyndas** (ksēn'-däs), **Spiridion,** Corfù
1812—(in poverty) Athens, 1896;
Greek composer of succ. ballad-op-
eras.

# Υ

**Yonge** (yŭng). Vide YOUNG.

**Yost** (yôst), **Michel,** Paris, 1754—
1786; celebrated clarinettist and
composer.

**Young,** (1) (or **Yonge**), **Nicholas,** b.
Lewes, Sussex; d. 1619; pub. *"Mu-
sica Transalpina,"* colls. of Italian
madrigals, 1597. (2) Rev. **Matthew,** Roscommon, 1750—1800;
acoustician. (3) **Thos.,** Canterbury, 1809—Walmouth, 1872; the
last prominent male altoist. (4) **J.
Matthew Wilson,** Durham, Engl.,
1822—W. Norwood, 1897; organist
and composer.

**Yradier** (ē-rädh'-ĭ-är), **Sebastian,** b.
Vittoria, 1865; Spanish song-composer.

**Yriarte** (ē-rĭ-är'-tĕ), Don **Tomas de,**
Teneriffe, ca. 1750—Santa Maria,
near Cadiz. 1791; writer.

**saye** (ē-sī'-yŭ), **Eugène,** b. Liège,
July 16, 1858; prominent violinist,
son and pupil of a cond. and violinist, then pupil of Liège Cons., and of

Wieniawski and Vieuxtemps; later
with govt.-stipend studied in Paris;
till 1881, leader in Bilse's orch., Berlin, since has made v. succ. tours
throughout Europe and N. America;
from 1886, head prof. of vln. Brussels Cons., and leader "Ysaye Quartet"; 1893, Chev. of the Legion of
Honour; his quartet played in London 1900–01; c. 6 vln.-concertos;
variations on a theme by Paganini;
Poème élégiaque for vln. with orch.
(or pf.), etc.

**Yussupoff** (yoos'-soo-pôf), Prince **Nicolai,** b. Petersburg, 1827; violinist; pupil of Vieuxtemps; writer
of treatises, and c. a programme-
symph. *"Gonzalvo de Cordova,"* with
vln. obbligato; *"Concerto symphonique,"* for vln., etc.

**Yzac** (ē'-zäk). Vide ISAAC.

# Z

**Zabalza y Olaso** (thä-bäl'-thä ē ō-lä'-
sō), **Don Damaso,** Irurita, Navarre,
1833—Madrid, 1894; pianist and
teacher; prof. Madrid Cons.; c.
studies.

**Zabel** (tsä'-běl), **Karl,** Berlin, 1822—
Brunswick, Aug. 19, 1883; cond.
and composer.

**Zacconi** (tsäk-kō'-nē), **Ludovico,** b.
Pesaro, 1540—ca. 1600; monk and
important theorist.

**Zachariä** (tsäk-ä-rē'-ä), **Eduard,** b.
Holzappeler-Hütte, Nassau, June 2,
1823; pastor at Mazsaya; inv.
" Kunstpedal " (v. D.D.).

**Zachau** (tsäkh'-ow), (1) **Peter,** town-
musician, Lübeck, composer for viola
da gamba, 1693. (2) **Fr. Wm.,**
Leipzig, 1663—Halle, 1712; Händel's teacher; organist and composer.

**Zajic** (zä'-yēch), **Florian,** b. Un-
hoscht, Bohemia, May 4, 1853; violinist; son of poor parents; on a
stipend studied at Prague Cons.;
member theatre-orch., Augsburg;
1881, leader at Mannheim and Strassburg; 1889, at Hamburg; 1891,

teacher Stern Cons., Berlin; later
Klindworth-Scharwenka Cons.;
toured widely and was made cha[...]
ber-virtuoso 1885 and given Russ[...]
order of Stanislas.

**Zamminer** (tsäm'-mē-něr), **Fr.,** Da[...]
stadt, 1818 (?)—Giessen, 1856; aco[...]
tician.

**Zanardini** (tsä-när-dē'-nē), **Ange[...]**
Venice, 1820—Milan, 1893; c. ope[...]
also writer and translator of librett[...]

**Zandt van** (fän-tsänt), **Marie,**
New York, Oct. 8, 1861 (daugh[...]
of (2) **Jeanie van Z.,** singer forme[...]
in Royal and Carl Rosa Com[...]
nies); pupil of Lamperti, Milan;
but, Turin, 1879; sang in Lond[...]
then from 1880 at Op.-Com., Pa[...]
with great succ.; 1884, tempor[...]
loss of voice due to prostrat[...]
brought on her such violent critici[...]
that she took a leave of absence a[...]
sang with succ. at St. Petersbu[...]
etc.; on her return, 1885, she met[...]
same opposition and sang therea[...]
in England, etc.; compass a·f'''.

**Zanettini.** Vide GIANETTINI.

**Zang** (tsäng), **Jn. H.,** Zella St. Bla[...]
1733—Mainstockheim, 1811; cant[...]
pianist.

**Zange** (tsäng'-ě) **(Zang'ius), Ni[...]
laus,** d. Berlin, before 1620; c[...]
ductor and composer.

**Zani de Ferranti** (dsä'-nē dä fěr-rä[...]
tē), **Marco Aurelio,** Bologna, 1[...]
—Pisa, 1878; guitar-virtuoso.

**Zanobi.** Vide GAGLIANO.

**Zarate** (thä-rä'-tě), **Eleodoro Or[...]
de,** b. Valparaiso, Dec. 29, 18[...]
pupil of Collegio di San Luis the[...]
1885 won 1st govt. prize, and stud[...]
Milan Cons. with Saladino; won p[...]
1886, for opera " *Giovanna la P[...]
za ";* studied in Italy; 1895, pr[...]
the first Chilian opera, the succ. "[...]
*Fioraia de Lugano* " (Santiago, Ch[...]
Nov. 10).

**Zaremba** (tsä-räm'-bä), **Nicolai Iva[...]
ovitch de,** 1824—Petersburg, 18[...]
teacher.

**Zarembski** (tsä-rěmp'-shkǐ), **Jules [...]**
Shitomir, Russian Poland, 185[...]

885; pianist, pf.-prof. and com-
oser.

rlino (dsär-lē'-nō), **Gioseffo** (called
**arlinus Clodiensis**), Chioggia,
Iarch 22, 1517—Venice, Feb. 14,
590; eminent theorist, conductor
nd ccmpòser ; a Franciscan monk ;
upil of Willaert at Venice; from
565 cond. at San Marco, also chap-
in at San Severo ; his comps. are
most all lost; he was commissioned
y the Republic to write mus. in cel-
oration of Lepanto, a mass for the
lague of 1577 and in welcome of
lenri III., 1574, on which occasion
e also c. a dram. work " *Orfeo* ";
is theoretical ability is shown by the
reat work " *Instituzioni harmo-
iche* " (1558).

·zycki (zär-zēk'-ē), **Alex**, Lem-
erg, Austrian Poland, 1831—War-
aw, 1895; pianist, conductor and
ram. composer.

7(e)rtal (tsä'-vĕr-täl), Bohemian
amily, (1) **Josef R.,** b. Folep, Nov.
, 1819; horn-player and leader. (2)
**Venceslas H.,** Polep, Aug. 31,
321; clarinettist and composer. (3)
adislas, b. Milan, Sept. 29, 1849 ;
on of above; conductor; 1871 t. at
lasgow, 1881 at Woolwich; prod.
peras " *Una notte a Firenze* " and
*Myrrha*," both at Prague, 1886.

·tz (dsä'-ēts), **Giovanni von,** b.
iume, 1834; pupil of Lauro Rossi,
Iilan Cons.; since 1870 theatre-con-
uctor and singing-teacher at the
ons. at Agram; c. the first Croa-
an opera "*Nicola Subic Zrinjski*"
876), also 20 German Singspiele,
asses, etc.

:kwer (tsĕk'-vär), **Richard,** b.
tendal, Prussia, April 30, 1850; pian-
t; pupil Leipzig Cons.; from 1870
rganist at Philadelphia, U. S. A. ;
370 teacher Phila. mus. acad.; since
376 director, composer.

elandia (tsä-län'-dĭ-ä), **Henricus**
e, Netherland theorist and composer
. 1400.

denrust (tsĕl'-dĕn-roost), **Eduard,**
, Amsterdam, June 5, 1865; pianist:

pupil of Robert Collin ; at 13 entered
Cologne Cons. under Fd. von Heller
for 5 yrs.; then studied with Kwast
and Gernsheim in Rotterdam ; later
with Marmontel, Paris Cons.; toured
Europe and America.

**Zelenka** (zĕ-lĕn'-kä), **Jan Dismas,**
Lannowicz, Bohemia, 1679—Dres-
den, 1745; conductor and composer.

**Želenski** (zhĕ-lĕn-shkĭ), **Ladislas,** b.
on the family estate Gradkowice, Ga
licia, July 6, 1837; pupil of Mirecki
at Cracow, Krejči at Prague, and
Damcke at Paris; prof. of comp.,
later dir., Warsaw Cons.; c. a symph.,
2 cantatas, etc. for orch.; succ. opera
" *Goplana* " (Cracow, 1896), etc.

**Zell, F.** Vide WÄLZEL.

**Zellner** (tsĕl'-nĕr), (1) **Ld. Alex.,**
Agram, 1823—Vienna, 1894; son and
pupil of an organist; editor, professor, writer and composer. (2) **Julius,**
Vienna, 1832—Würzzuschlag, Styria,
1900 ; c. 2 symphs., etc.

**Zelter** (tsĕl'-tĕr), **Karl Fr.,** Berlin,
Dec. 11, 1758—May 15, 1832; son of
a mason; studied with Kirnberger and
Fasch, to whom he was assistant and
1800 successor as cond. of the Singakademie; 1809 he founded the
" Liedertafel " from which grew the
great " Deutscher Sängerbund " of
50,000 members, for which he c.
famous male choruses; 1819, founder
and dir. R. Inst. for church-mus. ;
friend of Goethe, whose songs he set;
c. also oratorios, etc.

**Zemlinsky** (zĕm-lĭn'-shkĭ), **Alex.,** b.
of Polish parents, Vienna, 1877; pupil of Fuchs, Vienna Cons.; took
" Gesellschaft der Musikfreunde "
prize with a symph. 1897; his opera
" *Sarema*," took a 2nd prize, 1894,
and was prod. with succ., Munich,
1897.

**Zenger** (tsĕng'-ĕr), **Max,** b. Munich,
Feb. 2, 1837 ; pupil of Stark, and
Leipzig Cons.; 1860, cond. at Ratisbon; 1869 mus.-dir. Munich ct.-op-
era; 1878–85, Munich Oratorio Soc.,
etc.; Dr. Phil. *h. c.*, 1897; c. 3 operas: succ. oratorio " *Kain* " (after

Byron, Munich, 1867), cantatas with orch., "tragic" symph., etc.

**Zenta.** Vide AUGUSTA HOLMES.

**Zeretelev.** Vide LAWROWSKAJA.

**Zerr** (tsĕr), **Anna,** Baden-Baden, 1822 —on her estate, near Oberkirch, 1881; singer.

**Zerrahn** (tsĕr-rän'), **K.,** b. Malchow, Mecklenburg, July 28, 1826; distinguished conductor; studied with Fr. Weber and at Hanover and Berlin; 1848, America, as a member of Germania Orch.; 1854–95, cond. Handel and Haydn Soc., Boston; also cond. Harvard Symph. Concerts, and prof. of harm., instr. and singing, N. E. Cons.

**Zeugheer** (tsoikh'-hār), **Jakob** (known as **J. Z. Hermann**), Zurich, 1805— Liverpool, 1865 ; violinist and conductor.

**Zeuner** (tsoi'-nĕr), **K. Traugott,** Dresden, 1775—Paris, 1841; pianist, teacher and composer.

**Ziani** (dsē-ä'-nē), (1) **P. Andrea,** Venice, ca. 1630—Vienna, 1711 ; organist and dram. composer. (2) **Marco A.,** Venice, 1653—Vienna, 1715; nephew of above; ct. conductor and dram. composer.

**Zichy** (tsē'-shē), Count **Géza,** b. Sztáva, Hungary, July 22, 1849 ; noted left-handed piano-virtuoso; having at 17 lost his right arm ; pupil of Mayrberger, Volkmann and Liszt; holding high legal positions; also made tours for charity. 1890–94, Intendant Nat. Th. and Opera, Pesth. C. succ. operas, "Aldr" (Pesth, 1896); "Meister Roland" (Pesth, 1899, Magdeburg, 1902), cantata, etc.; pf.-pcs., for the left-hand and studies (with preface by Liszt), etc.

**Zimmer** (tsĭm'-mĕr), (1) **Fr. Aug.,** Herrengosserstädt, Thuringia, 1826— Zehlendorf, 1899 ; mus.-director and writer. (2) **Otto,** Priskorsine, Silesia, 1827—Breslau, 1896 ; organist and editor (3) **Robt.,** Berlin, 1828 —1857 ; writer and teacher.

**Zimmermann** (tsĭm'-mĕr-män), (1) **Anton,** Pressburg, 1741—1781; con-

ductor, composer and organist.

**Pierre Jos. Guillaume,** Pa March 19, 1785—Oct. 29, 1853 ; mous pf.-teacher ; pupil, later, 18 48, at Paris Cons.; c. co opera and many pf.-pcs. (3) **Agn** b. Cologne, July 5, 1847; piani at 9 pupil of London R. A. M., w ning King's Scholarship twice, a also silver medal ; début, Crystal I ace, 1863 ; toured with great su has ed. scores and c. a pf.-trio, etc

**Zingarelli** (tsĭn-gä-rĕl'-lē), **Nicola** Naples, April 4, 1752—Torre Greco, near Naples, May 5. 18 violinist, teacher and eminent co poser ; the succ. of his operas a the greater succ. of his grand eras throughout Europe was alm equalled by his noble and vout sacred mus.; pupil of Fenar and Speranza ; his first opera v prod. at 16, and followed by anot at 21, but he had no succ. till "\_ sinda," written in 7 days (La Sca Milan, 1785); he followed this w many others, incl. his best, "Giulie e Romeo" (ibid., 1796) ; 1792, co at Milan Cath.; 1794, at Loret 1804 at St. Peter's, Rome ; 1811, i prisoned for refusal to conduct a s vice in honour of the King of Rom the son of Napoleon, who took him Paris, released him, and paid him w for a mass ; 1813, dir. Naples Con 1816, cond. at the cath.; he was notable teacher; c. 31 operas, mas of all kinds in a series "Annuale Loreto" for every day in the year, magnificats, etc.

**Zinkeisen** (tsĭnk'-ī-zĕn), **Konrad Dietrich,** Hanover, 1779—Bru wick, 1838 ; violinist, conductor a composer.

**Zipoli** (dsē'-pō-lē), **Dom.,** organi Jesuit Church, Rome ; pub. importa clavier-sonatas, treatises, etc. (172

**Zoeller** (tsĕl'-lĕr), **Carl,** Berlin, 18 —London, 1889 ; writer and notal composer.

**Zoilo** (dsō'-ē-lō), **Annibale,** conduct at Laterano, Rome, 1561–70, 15

ger, Papal Chapel ; c. madrigals, c.

ner (tsĕl'-nĕr), (1) K. H., Oels, lesia, 1792—Wandsbeck, near amburg, 1836 ; org.-virtuoso, writer d dram. composer. (2) K. Fr., ittelhausen, Thuringia, March 17, oo—Leipzig, Sept. 25, 1860; famous composer of male choruses; pil of Schicht, Thomasschule. Leipg ; vocal-teacher there, founded a Ledertafeln " Zöllner-verein," other cs. of similar nature, organised 1859 form a " Z-band." (3) H., b. Leipg, July 4, 1854 ; son of above ; pu-l Leipzig Cons.; 1878, mus.-dir. orpat Univ.; 1885, Cologne Cons. d conductor various vocal socs.; 89, toured Italy with a male chos ; from 1840, cond. New York Deutscher Liederkranz"; 1898, us.-dir. Leipzig University and nd. " Paulinerchor"; c. 4 operas, choral works with orch., cantata Die neue Welt" (won international ize, Cleveland, Ohio, 1892), a mph., oratorio, male choruses, etc. ) Andreas, Arnstadt, 1804—Meingen, 1862 ; mus.-dir. and comp.

ff (tsôpf), Hermann, Glogau, 1826 -Leipzig, 1883 ; editor, writer and am. composer.

hiesche (tshē'-shĕ), Aug., Berlin, 800—1876 ; dram. bass.

hocher (tshôkh-ĕr), Jn., Leipzig, 21—1897 ; pianist.

calmaglio (dsook·käl·mäl'·yō), nton Wm. Florentin von, Wal-ol, 1803—Nachrodt, Westphalia, 869 ; contributor to Schumann's eriodicals.

mpe (tsoom'-pĕ), Hermann, b. aubenheim, Upper Lusatia, April 1850 ; grad. Seminary at Bautzen ;

taught a year at Weigsdorf ; from 1871 at Leipzig ; also studied with Tottmann ; 1873-76, at Bayreuth, as copyist and asst. to Wagner ; thereafter th. cond. various cities ; 1891, ct.-cond. at Stuttgart ; 1895, ct.-cond. Munich ; later at Schwerin 1901, Meiningen , c. 2 operas ; v. succ. operettas "Farinelli" (Vienna 1886), "Karin" (Hamburg, 1888). and "Polnische Wirthschaft" (Berlin, 1891); overture " Wallenstein's Tod," etc.

Zumsteeg (tsoom'-shtäkh), (1) Jn. Rudolf, Sachsenflur, Odenwald, 1760 —Stuttgart, 1802 ; 'cellist and ct.-conductor ; c. operas and important " durch-komponirten " ballads, before Löwe (q. v.). His daughter (2) Emilie, Stuttgart, 1797—1857, was a pop. song-composer.

Zur Mühlen (tsoor-mü'-lĕn), Raimund von, b on his father's estate, Livonia, Nov. 10, 1854 ; concert-tenor ; studied at Hochschule, Berlin, with Stockhausen at Frankfort, and Bussine at Paris.

Zur Nieden (tsoor nē'-dĕn), Albrecht, Emmerich - on - Rhine, 1819 — Duisburg, 1872 ; mus.-director, conductor and composer.

Zvonař (tsvō'-närzh), Jos. Ld., Kublov, near Prague, 1824—Prague, 1865 ; teacher, theorist and dram. composer.

Zweers (tsvärs), Benhard, b. Amsterdam, and lived there as composer of 4 symphs., sonatas, etc.; studied with Jadassohn.

Zwintscher (tsvĭnt'-shĕr), (1) Bruno, b. Ziegenhain, Saxony, May 15, 1838 ; pianist ; pupil of Julius Otto, then of Leipzig Cons.; 1875-98, teacher there; writer. (2) Rudolf, pianist in London.

# Supplementary Dictionary of Musicians

## A

..co, correct dates Verona, July
., 1675 — Munich, July 12, 1742.

..é (ăb-bā), **Joseph Barnabe de**
..t. **Sevin,** Agen, France, June 11,
..27 — Charenton, 1787; violinist
..d c.; son of Philippe **Abbé.**

..ndroth (ä'-běnt-rōt), **Irene, b.**
..emberg, July 14, 1872; soprano
..oyal Opera, Dresden, 1899-1908;
.. T. Thaller.

..rt (ä'-běrt), **Hermann, b.** Stutt-
..art, March 25, 1871; son of **J. J.**
.., historian.

..ram, **John,** b. Margate, Aug. 7,
..40, English organist; c. oratorio
..he *Widow of Nain,* cantata *Jeru-
..lem,* etc.

..rányi, (1) **Kornel,** d. Budapest,
..ec. 20, 1903. His son (2) **Emil,** b.
..udapest, 1880 (?); c. operas *Monna
..anna* (Budapest, 1907), *Paolo and
..rancesca* (do. 1912), etc.

..hscharumov (äsh-tshä'-roo-môf),
..emetrius Vladimirovitsch, b.
..dessa, Sept. 20, 1864; violinist and
..; pupil of Auer.

..ktê (ăk'-tā), **Aïno,** b. Helsingfors,
..inland; soprano; sang at Paris
..péra, 1904-5, sang Met. Op., New
..ork.

..alid y Gurréa ( ä-dhä'-lēdh-ē-
..oo-rā'-ä), **Marcel del.,** Coruna,
..ug. 26, 1826 — Longara, Dec. 16,
..881; pianist; pupil of Moscheles
..nd Chopin; c. opera, etc.

..am, **K. F.,** correct date of birth,
..onstappel, Saxony, Dec. 22, 1806.

..anassiev (ä-fä-näs'-sĭ-ěv), **Nikolai
..akovlevich,** Tobolsk, 1821 — St.
..etersburg, June 3, 1898; violinist
..nd c.

..fer'ni, **Ugo,** b. Florence, Jan 1,
..871; pianist and cond.; studied at
..Frankfort and Leipzig; m. the vio-

linist Mary Brammer, 1872; c. an
opera, etc.

**Agincourt** (dă-zhăn'-koor), **Francois d',** Rouen, 1714 — Paris, June
18, 1758; court organist and c.

**Agrenev** (ä-grä'-něv), **Demetrius A,**
1838 — Rustchuk, Bulgaria, July,
1908; organized a choir under the
name Slavjanski, with which he
toured Europe and America, presenting folk-songs.

**Aguilar** (ä'-gē-lär), **Emanuel Abra-
ham,** London, Aug. 23, 1824 —
London, Feb. 18, 1904; pianist of
Spanish origin; c. 2 operas, 3 symph.

**Ahlström, Olof**(not **A. J. R.**), correct
dates Aug. 14, 1756 — Aug. 11, 1835.

**À Kem'pis,** (1) **Nicholas,** organist
and c., at Brussels, ca. 1628. (2)
**Jean Florent,** org. at Brussels,
ca. 1657; c. requiem (pub. Antwerp,
1650) etc.

**Alabiev, A. A.,** correct dates, Moscow, Aug. 16, 1787 — March 6, 1851.

**Albanesi** (äl-bä-nä'-zē), **Luigi,** b.
Rome, March 3, 1821 — Naples, Dec.
4, 1897; pianist and composer.

**Albert, Eugen d',** add that he c.
further operas *Kain* and *Der Improvi-
sator* (both Berlin, 1900), *Tiefland*
(Prague, 1903), *Flauto solo* (Prague,
1905), *Tragaldabas* (Hamburg, 1907),
*Die Verschenkte Frau* or *The Bartered Wife* (1912, Munich). His opera
*Tiefland* (based on Guimera's play,
*Marta of the Lowlands*) has had
immense success; in Berlin alone
(prod. 1907) it reached its 400th performance in Feb., 1912; it was sung at
the Met. Op., N. Y., and throughout
Europe. He married Hermine Finch,
the singer, in 1895. His edition of
Bach's *"Well Tempered Clavier"* was
pub. 1907.

**Alfvén** (älf'-věn), **Hugo,** b. Stockholm, May 1, 1872; violinist; studied

at the Cons, and with César Thomson; 1900 received Jenny Lind scholarship for 3 years foreign study; from 1904 prof. of comp. Stockholm University: from 1910 mus. dir. Upsala Univ. in 1912 conducting a concert of Upsala students in Berlin; c. 3 symphonies; symph. poem *"Aus den Schären"*; cantata *"The Bells," "The Lord's Prayer,"* for chorus; scene with orch., male choruses, etc.

**Al'len, Hugh Percy,** b. Reading, Dec. 23, 1869; organist at 11, 1887 — 1892 org. Chichester Cathedral; since 1901 at Oxford, where he was made Mus. Doc. 1898, and University Choregus since 1909; since 1908, mus. dir. Reading University College.

**Al'lison, Horton Claridge,** b. London, July 25, 1846; pianist; pupil R. A. M. and Leipzig Cons.; Mus. Doc. (Dublin), c. piano and organ music and songs.

**Alois** (ä'-lō-ês), **Ladislaus,** b. Prague, 1860; 'cellist; pupil Paris Cons.; soloist Royal orch., St. Petersburg; c. concertos, etc.

**Alphéraky** (ăl-fä-rä'-kĕ), **Ach. N.,** b. Charkov, Russia, 1846; c. piano pieces, including *"Sérénade lévantine";* and songs.

**Alt'mann, Wilhelm,** b. Adelnau, April 4, 1862; editor and historian.

**Alvarez** (ăl-vä'-rĕth), (1) **Fermin Maria,** b. Saragossa; d. Barcelona, 1898; c. popular songs, etc. (2) (ăl-vä-rĕz), stage name of **Albert Raymond Gourron;** b. Bordeaux; tenor; pupil of A. de Martini; début at Ghent, later at Paris Opéra as leading tenor for many years; 1898, Met. Op. House of New York.

**Al'wood, Richard,** flourished ca. 1550; English priest; c. mass and organ pieces.

**Amato** (ä-mä'-to), **Pasquale,** barytone; début Naples, 1900; sang at Milan, then after a period of financial distress sang at Trieste, etc., 1909, Manhattan Opera; from 1911 Met. Op.

**Am'brosch, Joseph Karl,** Kruman,

Bohemia, 1759—Berlin, Sept. 8, 1 operatic tenor; c. songs.

**Ames, Philip,** 1837 — Durham, 10, 1908; organist Durham Cathe 1861–1906; prof. of music, Durh from 1897.

**Amft, Georg.,** b. Oberhannse Silesia, Jan. 25, 1873; music teac pupil at Royal Inst. for church r Berlin; teacher in Habelschue editor and composer.

**Amicis, De,** vide **De Amicis.**

**Amps, William,** d. Cambridge, M 20, 1909; English organist and co

**Andersen** (1) **Joachim,** Cop hagen, April 29, 1847 — May 7, 19 Soloist at 13. Toured widely; co musician, Copenhagen, Petersb and Berlin; for 8 years solo flutist assistant conductor of Berlin P Orch., of which he was one of founders; 1895–1909, the ruling mu cal force in Copenhagen, as condue of the Palace concerts, the Ti Orchestra, the Municipal Sum concerts, his orchestral school, a Inspector (with rank of Captain) all the military music of Denma Made Knight of Dannebrog Or by King Charles IX; received "Palms" of the Acad. from the Pr of France, and was made "Prof." King Frederik of Denmark.

**Vigo,** Copenhagen, April 21, 1852 Chicago, Jan. 29, 1895; solo flu with Thomas orch.; brother of (1)

**Anderson, Thomas,** Birmingha England, April 15, 1836 — Sept. 1903; critic, organist and c.

**Andrieu** (dän-drĭ-ŭ'), **Jean Fr.** Paris, 1684 — Jan. 16, 1740; o and comp.; 1724 royal cond. at Pa

**Angeli** (dän-jä'-lē), **Andrea d',** Padua, Nov. 9, 1868; historian; opera *"L'Innocente"* (Bologna), 8

**An'gerer, Gottfried,** Waldsee, F 3, 1851 — Zürich, Aug. 19, 1909; male choruses.

**Androt** (än-drō), **Albert August** Paris, 1781 — Aug. 9, 1804; c. ope requiem, etc.

**Angrisani** (än-grē-sä′-nē), **Carlo**, b. Reggio, ca. 1760; bass; sang in Italy and Vienna; 1817 at London; c. songs.

**Ansorge** (än-sôr′-gĕ), (1) **Max**, b. Striegau, Silesia, Oct. 1, 1862; organist; son of a cantor; studied at Berlin; c. songs, motets, etc. (2) **Konrad (Eduard Reinhold)**, b. Buchwald, Silesia, Oct. 15, 1862; pianist; pupil Leipzig Cons. and of Liszt; toured America; c. for orchestra, and piano.

**Antino′ri, Luigi,** b. Bologna, ca. 1697; tenor; sang in London, 1725–1726.

**An′tipov, Constantin,** b. Russia, Jan. 18, 1859; c. symph. allegro for orch., and piano pieces.

**Antoniot′to, Giorgio,** lived at Milan, 1740; theorist and c. of ′cello-sonatas.

**▲rbós** (är′-vōs), **E. Fernandez,** b. Madrid, Dec. 25, 1863; violinist; his grandfather and father were bandmasters in the army; pupil Madrid Cons.; took prizes at 12; then studied with Vieuxtemps, Gevaërt and Joachim; cond. Berlin Phil. Society; taught at Hamburg, Madrid, and Royal College, London; c. comic opera, *El Cientro de la Tierra,* Madrid, 1895; also for violin and orch.

**rchangel′ski, Alexander A.,** b. Pensa, Russia, Oct. 23, 1846; organist and cond. since 16; c. 2 masses, a requiem.

**rensky, A. S.,** b. July 31, 1861; d. Tarioki, Finland, Feb. 25, 1906.

**r′gent, W. I.,** d. May 18, 1908; organist and cond.; c. masses, etc.

**rk, Karl Van,** 1842 — St. Petersburg, 1902; pianist and teacher.

**rl′berg, Georg Ephraim, F.,** Letsand, Sweden, 1830 — Christiania Feb. 21, 1896; barytone.

**rms′heimer, Ivan Ivanovitch,** b. St. Petersburg, March 19, 1860; pupil at the cons.; c. 1-act opera *Sous la feuillée* (French text); 2-act opera *Der Oberhofer* (German text); 3-act opera *Jaegerliv* (Danish text); cantatas, songs, etc.

**rnaud** (är-nō), **Germaine,** b. Bordeaux, Dec. 20, 1891; pianist; pupil of Paris Cons., winning second piano prize, 1904; first prize, 1905; touredas virtuoso, 1908, with Boston Symph.

**Arres′ti, Giulio Cesare,** ca. 1630 — ca. 1695; organist and c. at Bologna.

**Ars,**(or **Volkov**), **Nikolai,** b. Moscow, 1857; composer; cond., studied at Geneva and Milan Cons.; c. operettas, symph. poem, etc.

**Ath′erton Percy Lee,** b. Roxbury, Mass., Sept. 25, 1871; composer; graduated Harvard, 1893, studying music under Paine; studied two years in Munich with Rheinberger and Thuille, then a year in Berlin with O. B. Boise; 1900 studied with Sgambati and Widor; lives at Boston; c. symph., tone poem for orch., *Noon in the Forest,* opera-comique *The Maharaja,* comic opera, and many songs of great importance.

**At′kins, Ivor Algernon,** b. Cardiff, Nov. 29, 1869; organist and cond.; son and pupil of an organist; later pupil and assistant of C. L. Williams; since 1897, org. Worcester Cath.

**Att′water, J. P.,** d. April 10, 1909, age 46. org. and cond. in England.

**Aubry** (ō-brē), **Pierre,** b. Paris, Feb. 14, 1874; historian of liturgical music.

**Auguez** (ō-gā), **Numa,** Saleux (Somme), 1847 — Paris, Jan. 27, 1901; prof. at the Cons.; barytone.

**Aus′tin,** (1) **Frederic,** b. London, Mar. 30, 1872; barytone; organist at Liverpool for some years; then teacher at the College of Music, there till 1906; then studied voice with Lunn; début, 1902, favorite in oratorio and in Wagner operas; c. overture *Richard II* (Liverpool, 1900): rhapsody *Spring* (Queens Hall, 1907), symph. poem *Isabella,* etc. His brother (2) **Ernest,** b. London, Dec. 31, 1874; on the Board of Trade till 33 years old, then studied comp. with J. Davenport; c. symph., idyll, march; *Love Songs from Don Quixote,* for voices and orch.; piano sonata, etc.

**Auxcousteaux** (dō-koo-tō), **Arthur d′,** b. Beauvais, France; d. 1656;

cond. Ste. Chapelle, Paris; c. sacred music.

**Avena'rius, Thos.,** org. and c. at Hildesheim, 1614–1640.

**Ayres, Frederic,** b. Binghamton, N. Y., March 7, 1876; composer; spent a year at Cornell U., 1892; music pupil of E. S. Kelley and Arthur Foote; 1901 went to New Mexico on account of health, since 1902 at Colorado Springs, Col., c. songs and pf. pieces.

## B

**Bache,** (bātch) **Constance;** correct dates, Edgbaston, March 11, 1846— Montreux, June 28, 1903.

**Bac(k)haus** (bäk'-hows), **Wilhelm,** b. Leipzig, March 26, 1884; pianist; pupil of Reckendorf and at the Cons., later of d'Albert; from 1900 toured; 1905, piano teacher R. C. M., Manchester, but won the Rubinstein prize and toured again; 1911 the U. S.; from 1907 has taught mastercourses at Sondershausen Cons.

**Badiali** (bä-dǐ-ä'-lē), **Cesare,** Imola, 1810 — Nov. 17, 1865; basso; début, Trieste, 1827; sang throughout Italy; 1859 in London; said to have been able to sing a scale while drinking a glass of claret.

**Baltzell, Willard J.,** b. Shiremanstown, Penn., Dec. 18, 1864; graduated Lebanon Valley College; at 24 took up music, studied with Emery and Thayer; later in London with Bridge and Parker, later with H. A. Clarke, Philadelphia, as editor; taught musical history and theory at Ohio Wesleyan University one year, then returned to Philadelphia. The previous statement of his death is an exaggeration; he is an editor in Boston and has edited a *"Dictionary of Musicians"* (1911).

**Bantock, Granville,** add that 1898 he founded the New Brighton Choral Society; 1900 Principal Birmingham and Midland Inst. School of Music and cond. various societies; 1908 succeeded Elgar in Peyton Chair of Music at Birmingham Univ.; 1898 he married Helena von Schweitzer. He c. *Omar Khayyam* for voices and orch. Part I (Birmingham Fest, 1906) Part II (Cardiff Fest., 1907), Part III (Birmingham Fest., 1909); 7 tone-poems for orch.; 2 symphonic overtures, comedy overture, *The Pierrot of the Minute,* 1908; overture to *Oedipos at Kolonos* (Worcester Fest. 1911); mass for male voices, 1903; chamber music etc.

**Bar'bi, Alice,** b. Bologna, ca 1860; mezzo-sopr.; pupil of Zamboni, Busi, and Vannucceni; début, Milan, 1882; toured Europe in concert; also a violinist and poet.

**Barcewicz** (bär'-tsĕ-vǐts), **Stanislaus,** b. Warsaw, April 16, 1858; violinist; pupil of Moscow Cons.; opera cond. at Warsaw; since 1885 violin prof. at the Cons.; c. violin pieces.

**Bar'nekov, Christian,** b. St. Sauveur, France, July 28, 1837; organist; of Danish parentage; pianist and organist; pupil of Helfstedt, Copenhagen; c. women's choruses with orch.; chamber music and songs.

**Bart'muss, Richard,** b. Bitterfeld, Dec. 23, 1859; organist; pupil of Grell, Haupt, Löschorn; 1896 royal music director; 1902, professor; c. oratorio *Der Tag des Pfingsten;* 4 organ sonatas and much sacred music.

**Bartz, Johannes,** b. Stargard, Jan. 6, 1848; organist; pupil Leipzig Cons.; since 1872 org. at Church of Sts. Peter and Paul, Moscow; c. opera, *Evangelisches Requiem;* oratorio, *Der Himmelsbote,* etc.

**Bary** (bä'-rē), **Alfred F. von,** b. Malta, Jan. 8, 1873; tenor; studied and practised medicine at first; 1902 appeared Dresden Royal Opera; sang Parsifal, Tristan, etc., at Bayreuth.

**Bath, Hubert,** b. Barnstaple, England, Nov. 6, 1883; 1901 pupil of Beringer and Corder at R. A. M., London; 1904, won Goring Thoma scholarship; c. 1-act opera, "*The Spanish Student*"; symph. poems; cantata *The Wedding of Shon Maclean;* variations for orch. (1904), and many songs.

**Bat'ka, Richard,** b. Prague, Dec. 14, 1868; critic, historian and librettist.

**Bax, Arnold E. Trevor,** b. London, Nov. 8, 1883; pupil of Matthay and Corder at the R. A. M.; c. a symphony, symph. pictures, *Eire;* string quintet, *Celtic Song Cycle,* etc.

**Bayer** (bī'-ĕr), (1) **Aloys,** Sulzbach, July 3, 1802 — Grabenstädt, July 7, 1863; tenor; (2) **Josef,** b. Vienna, Mar. 6, 1852; composer of ballets and operettas; studied at Vienna Cons.; cond. at Court Opera.

**Bay'ley, John Clowes,** d. Oct. 10, 1909, age 75. English composer of anthems and part songs.

**Beach, John,** b. Gloversville, N. Y., Oct. 11, 1877; composer; graduated at New England Cons., 1898; studied further with Clayton Johns, and in Paris with Harold Bauer. Taught piano and theory, Univ. of Minnesota, two years; in New Orleans three years; then in Boston. Since 1910 in Paris studying with Gédalge, c. operettas, *Gipsy Trail* for bar. and orch., songs, etc.

**Beauvarlet = Charpentier** (bō-vär-lā-shär-pänt-yā), (1) **Jean Jacques,** Abbeyville, 1730 — Paris, 1794; organist and comp. (2) **Jacques Marie,** Lyons, July 3, 1776 — Paris, Nov. 1834; organist and comp., son of (1).

**Beck'er, Hugo,** b. Strassburg, Feb. 13, 1864; 'cellist; son of **Jean B.;** pupil of his father, Grützmacher, Piatti, etc.; 'cellist at the Opera Frankfort, 1884–86 and 1890–1906; 1896, Royal Prof.; succeeded Piatti as 'cellist at London Monday concerts.

**Beck'mann, Wm. Gv.,** b. Bochum, Jan. 16, 1865; pupil Royal Inst. for church mus.; Berlin; organist, critic, and teacher at Berlin.

**Beck'with, John Charles,** 1778 —

Oct. 11, 1819; son and successor of **J. Christmas B.** as organist, Norwich Cathedral.

**Beechgard** should be **Bechgaard,** on p. 409.

**Beethoven, Ludwig van,** add that a symphony supposed to be a youthful work of his was discovered 1911 in the library of the University of Jena, by Prof. Fritz Stein, was performed there Jan 17, 1910, and published 1911; performed in Leipzig, Nov. 1911, and by Boston Symph., 1912. It is not generally accepted as Beethoven's but is found weak and uninteresting, of Haydnlike simplicity, with echoes of Mozart.

**Behaim** (bĕ-hīm'), **Michel,** Sulzbach, 1416 — murdered there, 1474; soldier and minnesinger.

**Belch'er, William Thomas,** d. Birmingham, May 6, 1905, age 78. mus. d.; organist.

**Bell, William Henry,** b. St. Albans, Aug. 20, 1873; pupil at the R. A. M.; won Goss scholarship, 1889; since 1903, prof. of harmony, there c. symphonies *Walt Whitman* (1900), and *The Open Road,* 3 symph. poems to the *Canterbury Tales;* symph. poems, *Love Among the Ruins* (1908); *The Shepherd* (1908), etc.

**Bellaigue,** (bĕl-lĕg), **Camille,** b. Paris, May 24, 1858; critic and essayist; pupil of Paladilhe and Marmontel.

**Bellincioni, Gemma,** add that she was b. Como, Italy, Aug. 18, 1866; widow of the tenor, Stagno.

**Bendix** (1) **Otto,** correct birth date, July 26, 1845. (2) **Victor,** correct birth date, May 17, 1851. (3) **Fritz,** b. Copenhagen, Jan. 12, 1847; brother of (1) and (2); 'cellist; pupil of Grützmacher; plays in Royal Orch. at Copenhagen.

**Benoit** (bŭn-wä), **Camille,** pupil of César Franck; 1888–1895, assistant conservator at the Louvre; since 1895 conservator; c. overture, 1880; text and music of opera *Cléopatre,* etc. author of *Souvenirs,* 1884, and

*Musiciens, poetes et philosophes*, 1887; also translator.

**Ber'ber, Felix,** b. Jena, March 11, 1871; violinist; pupil of Dresden Cons. and Leipzig Cons.; concertmaster in various cities; 1904–1907 prof. Royal Acad., Munich; 1907 at Frankfort-on-Main; since 1908 at Geneva Cons.; toured widely; 1910, America.

**Bern'eker, Constanz,** Darkehmen, E. Prussia, Oct. 31, 1841 — Königsberg, June 6, 1906; conductor and comp.

**Bernhardt, August,** b. St. Petersburg, Jan. 15, 1852; pupil at the Cons. and since 1898, director.

**Berteau, (Berteaud or Berthau),** (bĕr'-tō), (1) **Martin,** Valenciennes, (?) — Paris, 1756; the first important 'cellist; c. violin sonatas. (2) **Gabriel,** c. 'cello concerto about 1800.

**Beständig** (bĕ-stĕn'-dĭkh), **Otto,** b. Striegau, Silesia, Feb. 21, 1835; cond. and comp.; pupil of Mettner, etc. in Breslau; founded a conservatory in Breslau; c. oratorio *Der Tod Baldurs* and *Victoria Crucis*, etc.

**Betts, Thomas Percival Milbourne,** d. Aug. 27, 1904, age 53. English critic.

**Beyschlag** (bī'-shläkh), **Adolf,** b. Frankfort-on-Main, March 22, 1845; cond. pupil of V. Lachner; conductor at Frankfort, later at Belfast, Manchester, Leeds; since 1902 at Berlin; 1907 made Royal Prof.; author and comp.

**Biaggi,** correct birth date is 1819.

**Bibl** (bēb-'l), (1) **Andreas,** Vienna, 1797–1878 organist and composer. His son and pupil (2) **Rudolf,** Vienna, Jan. 6, 1832 — Aug. 2, 1902; pupil of Lechter; organist and composer of organ sonata, etc.

**Bidez** (bē-dĕs), **L. Aloys,** b. Brussels, Aug. 19, 1847; teacher and composer of operetta *The Stratagem;* piano concerto, etc.; lived in the U. S., 1876–1901; then returned to Brussels.

**Bie** (bē), **Oskar,** b. Breslau, Feb. 9, 1864; critic; pupil of Ph. Scharwenka;

1886, Dr. Phil.; 1890, Privat Docent at Technical High School, Berlin; author of books; also comp.

**Biehr** (bēr), **Oskar,** b. Dresden, 1851; violinist; pupil of David; for twenty-five years member of Munich court orchestra.

**Biernacki** (bē-ĕr-nät'-skē), **Michael Marian,** b. Lublin, Sept. 9, 1855 comp.; pupil of Warsaw Cons.; director there; comp. 2 masses, *Prologu* for orch., etc.

**Bin'der, Fritz,** b. Baltimore, 1873 pianist; at 7 toured Europe in concert; studied with Leschetizky and at Cologne Cons.; from 1901, dir. o the Danzig Singakademie.

**Bird, Henry Richard,** b. Nov. 14 1842; organist; son of **George B.** an organist; at 9, became org.; pupi of Turle; since 1872 org. at St. Mary Abbots, London; conducted concerts and won prominence as accompanist

**Bishop, Ann,** or **Anna,** London 1814 — New York, March 18, 1884 soprano; daughter of Jules Rivière married Sir Henry Bishop, 1831 deserted him for the harpist Bochsa with whom she toured the world i concert; after his death, in 1856, sh married a Mr. Schulz.

**Bishop, John,** 1665 — Winchester Dec. 19, 1737; organist and composer

**Bispham, David,** correct birth dat is Philadelphia, Jan. 5, 1857.

**Bitt'ner, Julius,** composer of opera *Die Rote Grat* (Vienna, 1907), and *De Musikant* (Dec. 2, 1911, Leipzig Opera

**Black, Andrew,** b. Glasgow, Jar 15, 1859; barytone; at first an organ ist; then pupil of Randegger an Scafati; sang at the Crystal Palace 1887; toured America; famous : *"Elijah";* 1893, Prof. of singin R. C. M., Manchester.

**Black'burn, Vernon,** d. Paddin ton, London, Feb. 14, 1907, age 4 Prominent English critic; for mar years on the *"Westminster Gazette,* London; author of *"The Fringe of Art."*

Blanc (blän), **Claudius** (rightly **Claude**), Lyons, March 20, 1854—June 13, 1900; pupil of Paris Cons., winning first harmony prize, 1875, 2nd Prix de Rome, 1877; Dir. Mus. school Marseilles, 1887–9, then chorus master, Paris Op.; c. *"Ste. Geneviève de Paris"* for orch. and songs.

**Blaser'na, Pietro,** b. Fiumicello, Feb. 29, 1836; teacher and theorist.

**Blauvelt, Lillian Evans,** correct birth date is Brooklyn, N. Y., March 16, 1873; she made her début in opera in *"Faust"* at Covent Garden, 1903, with success.

Blavet, (blă-vā), **Michel,** Besançon, Mar. 13, 1700 — Paris, Dec. 28, 1768; composer of comic operas, etc.

Bleech, (blākh) **Leo,** b. Aachen, April 22, 1871; conductor; pupil of Berlin Hochschule; 1893–1896, cond. at Municipal Theatre, Aachen, and pupil of Humperdinck; 1899–1906, cond. German Laudestheatre at Prague; 1906, Royal Opera, Berlin; 1908, cond. first East-Prussian Festival at Königsberg; c. 3 symph. poems, very successful 1-act opera, *Das War Ich*, (Dresden, 1902); 3-act opera *Aschenbrödel* (Prague, 1905); *Versiegelt* (Hamburg, 1908; New York, 1912), etc.

Bleichmann (blīkh'-män), **Julius Ivanovitch,** b. St. Petersburg, Dec. 5, 1868; conductor; pupil at the Cons., and of Reinecke and Jadassohn; cond. various orchs. at St. Petersburg; c. 2 operas, chamber music, etc.

Bleyle (blī'-lĕ), **Karl,** b. Feldkirch, May 7, 1880; pupil of Wehrle and de Lange; later at Stuttgart Cons. and of Thuille; gave up violin on account of nervous affliction of the arm; lives in Munich; c. symph., *An den Mistral* (from Nietzsche), for mixed chorus and orch., *Lernt lachen* (from Nietzsche's *"Zarathustra"*), do.; symph. poem *Flagellantenzug*, Berlin; Munich, 1908; Berlin, 1911, etc.

Blind Tom," vide **Wiggins.**

Blon (blôn), **Franz Von,** b. Berlin, July 16, 1861; cond.; pupil of Stern's Cons.; 1898, c. operettas *Sub rosa* (Lübeck, 1887); *Die Amazone* (Magdeberg, 1903), etc.

Blondeau (blôn-dō), **Pierre Auguste Louis,** Paris, Aug. 15, 1784–1865; viola-player at the Opéra; pupil of the Cons., taking the Prix de Rome, 1808; c. opera, ballet, etc.

Blu'menberg, **Franz,** b. Remagen, Feb. 28, 1869; organist at Cologne; c. songs, male choruses, etc.

Blumenfeld, (1), **Felix M.,** correct birth date to April 19; since 1898 cond. Imperial Opera, St. Petersberg. His brothers are (2), **Stanislaus,** Kiev, 1850–1897, pianist and teacher; (3) **Sigismund,** b. Odessa, Dec. 27, 1852; song-composer, living in St. Petersburg.

Blumenschein (bloo'-mĕn-shīn), **William Leonard,** b. Brensbach, Dec. 16, 1849; pupil of Leipzig Cons.; since 1879 organist, teacher and cond. at Dayton, Ohio; 1891–96, chorus master at the Cincinnati May Festivals; c. anthems, piano pieces, etc.

**Blumenthal, Jacques,** correct birth date is 1829, d. Chelsea, May 17, 1908.

Blumer, (bloo'-mĕr), **Fritz,** b. Glaris, Aug. 31, 1860. Swiss pianist; pupil of Geneva and Leipzig Cons. and of Liszt; since 1886 teacher at, Strassburg Cons.

Bodenstein (bō'-dĕn-shtīn), **Hermann,** Gandersheim, March 27, 1823 —Braunschweig, April 12, 1902; organist.

Bodin, (bō-dăn), **François Étienne,** Paris, March 16, 1793—Aug. 13, 1862; teacher of theory at Paris Cons.; author of a treatise.

**Bodi'nus, Sebastian,** flourished 1725–1756; born in duchy of Altenburg; violinist and composer.

Böheim, (bä'-hīm), **Joseph Michael,** Prague, 1748 — Berlin, July 4, 1811; actor and singer.

Boismortier (bwä-môrt-yā), **Josef**

**Bodin De,** Perpignan, ca. 1691 — Paris, ca. 1765; c. ballet operas, cantatas, etc.

**Bölsche** (běl'-shě), **Franz,** b. Wegenstedt, near Magdeburg, Aug. 20, 1869; theorist; pupil Berlin Royal Hochschule; 1896, teacher Cologne Cons.; c. overture *Judith*, etc.

**Bonci** (bôn'chē), **Alessandro,** b. Cesena, n. Bologna, 1870; famous lyric tenor; at 7 sang in choir, studied singing with Coen at Pesaro Lyceum for 5 years; then member of choir at Loreto; operatic début in *"Falstaff"*; sang with great success at Covent Garden, 1900, and in 1908; sang at Metropolitan Opera House; toured U. S., 1911–1912; sings in Italy.

**Bo'niforti, [Carlo,** Arona, Sept. 25, 1818 — Trezzo d'Adda, Dec. 10, 1879; organist and comp.

**Bonini** (bō-nē'-nē), **Severo,** b. Florence, 17th century; Benedictine monk, one of the first writers in monodic style; c. madrigals, etc., 1607–1613.

**Booth, Robert,** b. St. Andrews, Dec. 29, 1862; English organist; c. for orch.; church music, etc.

**Bopp, Wilhelm,** b. Mannheim, Nov. 4, 1863; pupil of Leipzig Cons., and of Emil Paur; 1884, dir. in Freiburg; 1886, assistant to Mottl at Bayreuth; 1889, teacher at Mannheim Cons.; 1900, opened a High School of Music; 1907 dir. Royal Cons., Vienna; cond. His wife, born **Glaser,** is a court opera singer at Stuttgart.

**Borchers** (bôr'-khěrs), (1) **Bodo,** 1835 — Leipzig, June 6, 1898; opera singer and teacher in Leipzig. (2), **Gustav,** b. Braunschweig, Aug. 18, 1865; pupil Leipzig Cons.; cantor and teacher of song; since 1898, directed a singing-school at Leipzig.

**Bordes** (bôrd), **Charles,** Vouvray-sur-Loire, May 12, 1863; — Toulon, Nov. 8, 1909; composer; important figure in the revival of French church music; pupil of César Franck; 1887,

church - conductor at Nogent - sur - Marne; 1889 commissioned by the govt. to collect Basque folk music; from 1890 chapel-master at St. Gervais, Paris; founder of the *"Association of the Singers of St. Gervais"* and of the *"Schola Cantorum de St. G.,"* 1898 with d'Indy and Guilmant; 1905 retired to Montpellier and founded a *Schola* there; 1909 went to Nice to give a concert and died on his way home. He resuscitated many forgotten master works, and wrote many articles on them; c. *Phantasie* and *Rapsodie Basque* for orch.; opera *Les trois Vagues,* religious music, choruses, and songs and piano pieces.

**Bo'rek, Christoph,** d. 1557; Polish composer and conductor.

**Bo'ri** (rightly **Borgia**), **Lucrezia,** soprano; studied at Milan; 1911–12 at La Scala. In 1910 singing in Paris with the Met. Op. Co. of N. Y. She was engaged for New York 1912–13.

**Born'hardt, Johann,** Braunschweig, March 19, 1774 — April 19, 1840; c. Singspielen, etc.

**Borosini** (bôr-ō-sē-nē), (1), **Francesco,** b. Bologna, ca. 1695; operatic tenor in 1723 at the Grand Opera, Prague, and 1724–1725 in London, with his wife (2), **Leonora d' Ambreville,** a contralto of French birth.

**Bosch, Pieter Joseph,** Hoboken Holland, 1736 — Antwerp, Feb. 19 1803; organist at Antwerp Cathedral c. sonatas.

**Boschetti** (bôs-kět'-tē), **Viktor,** b. Frankfort-on-Main, Aug. 13, 1871 pupil of Prague Cons.; from 1896 organist at Vienna and Dir. Cour Opera, 1900–3; c. 5 operas, church music, etc.

**Botelho** (bō-těl'-yō), **Manuel Joaquim Pedro,** Lisbon, 1795 — Apr 9, 1873; flutist and teacher of theory

**Bottini** (bôt-tē'-nē), **Mariann Andreozzi,** the Marchesa, Lucca Nov. 7, 1802 — Jan. 24, 1858; she composed masses, overtures, etc.

**Boucheron** (boosh-rôṅ), **Raimondo**, Turin, Mar. 15, 1800 — Milan, Feb. 28, 1876; cond., theorist and composer.

**Bouhy** (boo'-ē), **Jacques**, b. Pepinster, Belgium, 1848; barytone; pupil at Liège Cons., then Paris Cons.; 1871, the Opéra Paris; after 1872 at Opéra Comique, creating the Toreador rôle in "Carmen," etc.; 1885–89, director of New York Conservatory; returned to Paris Opéra; later a famous teacher; c. songs.

**Bouman** (boo'-män), **Martin T.**, b. Herzogenbusch, Holland, Dec. 29, 1858; pupil of Brée and Holl; city director at Gouda; c. operas, masses, etc.

**Bouval** (boo-văl), **Jules Henri**, b. Toulouse, June 9, 1867; pupil of Paris Cons., taking first harmony prize 1889; org. St. Pierre de Chaillot; c. 1-act operas, ballets "*La Chaine d'Amour*" for voice and orch., songs, etc.

**Bo'wen**, **York**, b. London, Feb. 22, 1884; composer and pianist; 1898–1905, pupil of the R. A. M.; c. 3 concertos; symph. fantasia for orch. brought out by Richter; concerto and sonata for the viola, etc.

**Boyle**, **Geo. Frdk**, b. Australia; teacher at Peabody Cons., Baltimore; c. piano concerto, which he cond. with success Feb. 1912 at New York Phil.

**Boyvin** (bwä-văṅ), **Jacques**, d. Rouen, ca. 1706; organist there in 1674; c. organ music.

**Brad'ford**, **Jacob**, b. London, June 3, 1842; organist; pupil of Goss and Steggal; Mus. Doc. Oxford, 1878; since 1892 organist at St. Mary's, Newington; c. oratorio "*Judith*"; *Sinfonia Ecclesiastica* with double chorus; overtures, etc.

**Brady**, **Sir Francis**, d. Co. Tyrone, Ireland, 1909; well-known amateur musician and one of the founders of the Royal Irish Academy of Music; c. several songs, etc.

**Brandl**, **Johann**, b. Kirchenbirk, Bohemia, Aug. 30, 1835; c. operettas.

**Brandram**, **Rosina** (**Mrs. Butcher**), d. Southend-on-Sea, Feb. 28, 1907, age 61. Noted contralto in Gilbert and Sullivan operas.

**Brandt**, **Herman**, Hamburg, 1852 — New York, Dec. 27, 1910; pupil Leipzig Cons.; settled in San Francisco; later cond. the Philh. orch. there; then taught in N. Y.; at one time was concertmaster Theodore Thomas Orch.

**Bran'dukov**, **Anatol Andrejevitch**, b. Moscow, Jan. 6, 1859; 'cellist; pupil Moscow Cons.; spent many years in Paris; founded a quartet there with Marsick; 1890 returned to Moscow; c. for 'cello and orch., etc.

**Brassart**, **Johannes**, priest, composer and singer; in Papal Choir in 1431; probably same as **Johannes de Ludo**; c. sacred music.

**Braun**, (1) **Anton**, Cassel, Feb. 6, 1729–1790; violinist and c.; perhaps the son of (2) **Braun**, whose flute compositions were pub. in Paris 1729–1740. His brother (3) **Johann**, Cassel, 1753 — Berlin, 1795, violinist and comp. (4) **Johann Fr.**, Cassel, 1759 — Ludwigslust, 1824; oboist and comp.; father of (5) **Karl A. P.**, b. Ludwigslust, 1788; oboist; and of (6) **Wilhelm**, b. Ludwigslust, 1791; oboist, whose wife was his cousin (7) **Kathinka B.**, a singer.

**Bredal** (brä'-däl), (1) **Niels Krog**, Drontheim, 1733 — Copenhagen, Jan. 26, 1778; theatre-director and comp. of cantatas. (2) **Ivar Frederick**, Copenhagen, June 17, 1800 — March 25, 1864; viola player; c. operettas; cantata "*Judas Iscariot*," etc.

**Breithaupt**, (brīt-howpt) **Rudolf, Maria**, b. Braunschweig, Aug. 11, 1873; critic and teacher; pupil Leipzig Cons., 1897; c. songs.

**Brend'ler**, **Erich**, b. 1800 — Stockholm, 1831; c. opera "*Ryno*" with Prince Oskar of Sweden (prod. Stockholm, 1834), etc.

**Brescianello** (brĕ'-shä-nĕl'-lō), **Giuseppe Antonio**, Mus. Director at

Stuttgart, 1717-1757; published violin concertos, etc.

**Bress'ler=Gianoli** (jä-nō'-lē) **Mme.** b. Geneva, 1870(?); d. there after operation for appendicitis, May 12, 1912. Operatic mezzo-sopr; studied Paris Cons., début Geneva, at 19; 1900, Paris Op. Com., 1903 with New Orleans Op. Co., from 1907 sang with success at Manhattan Opera, N. Y.; 1910 with Metropolitan Opera, N. Y.; her "Carmen" was famous.

**Breton y Hernàndez** (brā-tôn ē ĕr-nän'-dĕth), **Tomas,** b. Salamanca, Dec. 23, 1850; leading Spanish composer of zarzuelas, an oratorio *Apocalypsia* (1882), for orch. "*Andalusian scenes*"; funeral march for Alfonso XII, etc.

**Bréval, Lucienne,** Add that her correct name is **Berthe A. L. Schilling,**correct birth date, Berlin, Nov. 4, 1869; pupil of Warot at Paris Cons.; début, Opéra, 1892; sang there till 1900, then at Op. Com.; 1902 returned to the Opéra.

**Bréville** (brā-vēl), **Pierre Onfroy de,** b. Bar-le-Duc, France, Feb. 21, 1861; composer and critic, diplomatic career; then studied at Paris Cons. and with César Franck; teacher at the Schola Cantorum; c. masses, sacred chorus with orch., *Sainte Rose de Lima;* symph. poem, *Nuit de décembre;* overture, *Princesse Maleine,* music for *Les sept Princesses,* and *Sakuntala,* etc., orch. fantasie "*Portraits des Musiciens*"; songs, etc.

**Bridge,** (1) **Sir John Frederick;** 1902, made member of the Victorian Order; 1903, King Edward Prof. of Music, London University; (2) **Frank,** b. Brighton, Feb. 26, 1879; viola player; pupil of R. A. M., gaining a scholarship in composition; c. prize quartet in E. Minor (Bologna competition); string quartet "*Three Idylls*"; rhapsody for orch. and symp. poem, "*Isabella*" (1907).

**Briesemeister,** ( brē'- zĕ-mī-stĕr ), **Otto,** Arnswalde, May 18, 1866 —

Berlin, June 17, 1910; tenor; at first a doctor, then a pupil of Wiedemann; début, 1893, Detmold.

**Bright, Dora Estella,** b. Sheffield, Aug. 16, 1863; pianist; pupil R. A. M., London; 1892 married Capt. Knatchbull; c. 2 piano concertos ; variations with orch., etc.

**Bron'ner, Georg,** Holstein, 1666 — Hamburg. 1724; organist ; c. for the Hamburg Opera "*Echo and Narcissus,*" "*Venus,*" etc.

**Brons, Simon,** b. Rotterdam, April 19, 1838; composer; teacher and writer; author of theoretical works; lives at The Hague.

**Broschi, Carlo;** real name of the great male soprano called Farinelli perhaps after his uncle who was a composer.

**Brounoff** (broo'-nôf), **Platon,** b. Elizabethgrad, Russia, 1869; composer pupil of Rubinstein and Rimsky Korsakov, St. Petersburg Cons. cantata "*The Angel*" prod. at court lives in New York as cond. of Russian choral society, etc.; c. piano suite and songs.

**Bruch, Max.** Add that he received in 1908 the Prussian order for merit in art and learning, and many honors from England, France, etc. His further compositions include the secular oratorio, *Gustav Adolf* (1898) *Nal und Damajant* (1903); *Die Macht des Gesanges,* for barytone, mixed chor. and orch. (1912.)

**Bru'dien, Juan,** Spanish priest cond, at Cathedral of Urgel, 158 later at Barcelona; c. madrigals, etc

**Bruneau, Alfred.** Note that Octave Seré, in his *Musiciens français d'aujourd'hui* (Paris, 1911), gives the date of Bruneau's birth as March 1st not 3rd. Add to his compositions the operas, all to Zola's texts: *L'Ouragan* (Op. Com. 1901); lyric comedy 3 acts, *L'Enfant Roi* (Op. Com. 1905 1-act lyric drama *Lazare* (1905 incid. music to *La Faute de l'Abbé Mouret* (Odéon, 1907); lyric drama

*aïs Micoulin* (Monte Carlo, 1907);
*es Quatre Journées* (accepted at
ie Op. Com.); also songs, etc.

**ıns,** (broons) (**Molar**) **Paul,** b.
Verden, June 13, 1867; tenor, baryone, and teacher; studied in Leipzig
nd Italy; gave historic song-recitals;
nce 1902 teacher of singing in Berlin;
uthor of a vocal method, etc.

**chmayer** (bookh'-mī-ĕr), **Rich-
rd,** b. Zittau, April 19, 1857; pupil
)resden Cons.; later piano teacher
here; 1907 Royal Saxon Prof.; gave
nany concerts of ancient clavier
nusic and then devoted himself to
nusical history.

**chner** (bookh'-nĕr), (1) **Hans,**
Ravensburg, Dec. 26, 1483–1540;
rganist and comp. (2) **Philipp Fr.,**
Vertheim, 1614 — Würzburg, 1669;
ond. and comp.

**chner** (bükh'-nĕr), b. Pyrmont,
825; flutist and composer; from
856, soloist at St. Petersburg Royal
)pera, and Prof. at the Cons.

**ck,** (1) **Dudley;** retired from
hurch work 1903; d. Brooklyn, N. Y.
)ct. 6, 1909. (2) **Percy Carter,**
). West Ham., March 25, 1871; pupil
.t R. A. M., London; won scholarship
891–4, organist at Oxford; 1893,
Mus. Doc.; 1896–9, organist Wells
Cathedral, 1899–1901, Bristol Cathe-
lral; 1910, prof. of music Dublin
Jniversity, vice-Pres.; c. overture
*"Coeur de Lion";* chamber music, etc.

**ıhl** (bül), **Joseph David,** b. Am-
)oise, 1781; famous trumpet-player
.t Paris; author of trumpet-method.

**ıllerian** (bool-lā'-rĭ-än), **Rudolf,**
). Berlin, Jan. 13, 1858; director;
)upil Stern Cons.; played in orches-
ras from his 16th year; 1884,
nunicipal director at Göttingen; 1890
n Russia, settling at Moscow, con-
lucting in other cities; since 1902 in
America.

**ımler** (bĭm'-lĕr), **Georg Heinrich,** Berneck , Oct. 10, 1669 —
Ansbach, Aug. 26, 1745; cond. and
comp. of church music.

**Buonamici, Carlo,** b. Florence,
June 20, 1875; pianist; son and pupil
of Giuseppe (q. v.), later studied at
Würzburg Royal Musicsch., with
Van Zeyl, taking first prize; after
year in the army, settled in Boston,
1896, as teacher and pianist with
Boston Symph. Orch., etc.; 1908
toured Europe.

**Buongiorno** (boo-ōn-jȯr'-nō), **Cres=
cenzo,** Bonito, 1864 — Dresden,
Nov. 7, 1903; c. operas.

**Busoni, F.,** add that in 1907 he succeeded Sauer as teacher of the master
class at Vienna Cons.; 1911 toured
America, c. symph. tone-poem
*"Pojohla's Tochter,"* festival overture, 1897; music to *"Berceuse élégiaque,"* for orch.; Schiller's *"Turandot";* transcribed Bach's organ works
for piano; wrote *"Entwurf einer neuen
Aesthetik der Tonkunst."* His opera,
*"Der Brautwahl,"* was prod. Hamburg, April 13, 1912, based on Hoffman's *"Serapeons' Brüder."*

**Butler, Thomas Hamly,** London,
1762 — Edinburgh, 1823; comp.

## C

**Cabezon** (kǎ'-bā-thōn), (1) (**Felix**),
**Antonio De,** Santander, March
30, 1510 — May 26, 1566; composer;
cembalist and organist to Philip II;
called "The Spanish Bach"; blind
from birth; c. harp and flute pieces,
published in 1578 by his son (2)
**Hernando,** who succeeded him.

**Cad'man, Charles Wakefield,** b.
Johnstown, Pa., 1881; at 13 began
piano studies, at 19 composed a
comic opera, prod. at Pittsburg, but
did not study composition till 20;
pupil of W. K. Steiner (organ), Luigi
von Kunits (orchestration), with
critical advice from Emil Paur; took
up Indian music, 1906 published
"Four Indian Songs"; 1909 spent
summer among the Omaha Indians,
taking phonograph records and
transcribing them; gives lecture-

recitals on Indian music. c. *Three Moods* for symph, orch.; chamber music; cantata for male voices *The Vision of Sir Launfal*, Japanese romance for two voices, *Sayonara;* three *Songs to Odysseus;* Indian songs, etc.

**Cahier** (kä-hĕr'), **Mme. Charles** (née **Walker,** ), contralto; b. Tennessee; sang in concert as Mrs. Morris Black, then studied with Jean de Reszké; début in opera as "*Orfeo*" (Nice, 1904); sang in other cities and from 1909 at Vienna Royal Opera. 1912 at Met. Op., N. Y.

**Caland** (kä'-länt), **Elizabeth,** b. Rotterdam, Jan. 30, 1862; teacher and author of piano methods.

**Camar'go,** (1) **Felix Antonio,** b. Guadalajara, 16th cent.; cathedral cond. at Valladolid; c. remarkable hymn to St. Iago, etc. (2) see **Cupis**

**Camerloher** (käm'-ĕr-lō-ĕr), (1) **Placidus Von,** Murnau, 1710 — Freising, 1776; c. operas, etc.; his brother (2) **Anton,** d. Munich, 1743; c. opera.

**Calvé, Emma,** b. Décazeville,'France — not at Madrid, 1863 (1866?); married the tenor Mario Gaspary, 1912.

**Camet'ti, Alberto,** b. Rome, May 5, 1871; organist; pupil at Academy of St. Cecilia; organist of the French church of St. Louis at Rome; historian of music and comp.

**Campanini** (käm-pä-nē'-nē), **Cleofonte,** conductor; pupil Milan Cons., later teacher there; cond. at La Scala, Covent Garden, and 1906–11 at Manhattan Opera House, New York, 1912 at London; married Eva Tetrazzini, operatic soprano (sister and teacher of Luisa).

**Campbell = Tipton, Louis,** b. Chicago, Nov. 21, 1877; studied in Chicago, Boston and Leipzig; lives in Paris;his important compositions have been much played abroad, notably his "*Heroic*" sonata for piano, piano suites, "*The Four Seasons,*" "*Suite Pastorale,*" for piano and violin.

**Canal** (kä'-näl), **Abbate Piet** Crespano, April 13, 1807 — Dec. 1883; historian and comp.

**Canale (or Canali)** (kä-nä'- **Floriano,** organist at Bres 1585–1603; c. church music.

**Canob'bio, Carlo,** violinist at perial Theatre, St. Petersburg, 17 1800; c. 2 operas, ballets, etc.

**Cantor, Otto,** b. Creuznach, Rh ish Prussia, 1857.

**Capel'len, Georg,** b. Salzuf Lippe, April 1, 1869; theorist a comp.; took up music in 1901; aut of important works on modern h monic analysis.

**Caplet,** (kăp-lā), **André,** b. Hav 1879; pupil of Wollett; violinist Havré Theatre, 1896; pupil Leroux at Paris Cons., winning fi harmony prize, 1898, and Prix Rome, 1901; lived in Rome, then Germany; acted as assistant Colonne, 1898; 1900, was the fi to cond. Debussy's *Martyre de S Sebastien;* 1911–12 cond. at Bost Op.; c. prize quintet for wind inst etc.

**Capri,** (kä-prē) **Julius,** b. Marseill 1837; pianist and teacher in St. F tersburg after 1853; pupil Marseil Cons.; c. opera *Leonore,* etc.

**Capuzzi** (kä-pood'-zē), **Giusepp Antonio,** Brescia, 1753–1818; 5 operas, etc.

**Cara** (kä'-rä), **Marco,** called **Ma chetto,** court composer at Mantu 1495–1525.

**Carlez** (kăr-lĕs), **Jules Alexis,** Caen, Feb. 10, 1836; organist, h torian and comp.

**Car'nall, Arthur,** Petersboroug May 7, 1852 — Penge, June 30, 190 from 1873 organist at St. John Penge; c. overture, 2 quintets, et

**Caro** (kä'rō), **Paul,** b. Breslau, De 25, 1859; pupil of Schäffer ar Scholz, and Vienna Cons.; c. 2 opera 4 symph., 30 string-quartets, etc.

**Caron** (kä-rôn), (1) **Firmen,** shoul be **Philippe;** (2) **Rose Lucile** (ne

**Meuniez**), b. Monerville, France, Nov. 17, 1857; soprano; after her marriage entered Paris Cons., 1880, as pupil of Tharset, later of Marie Sasse; début Brussels, 1883; 1885–8, Paris Opéra; 1888–90, Brussels; from 1890, Opéra Paris; also at the Op. Com., from 1902 prof. at the Cons. She created many of the chief rôles in modern French Opéra and in French versions of Wagner. She sang Salammbô at the Opéra, 1908.

**Car'penter, John A.** b. Park Ridge, Ill., 1876; pupil of his mother (a pupil of Marchesi and Shakespeare), Amy Fay, Seeboeck; then graduated at Harvard, 1897, studying music under Paine and taking highest musical honours, submitting a piano sonata; 1907; studied with Elgar in Rome, and thereafter in Chicago with Bernhard Ziehn; c. violin and piano sonata (1912) and many songs.

**Carse, A. Von Ahn,** b. Newcastle-on-Tyne, May 19, 1878; pupil R. A. M., with the Macfarren scholarship; made an associate there in 1902; c. symph. in C minor (prod. 1906); symph. in G minor (1908), revised and prod. 1909, symph. poem, "*In a Balcony*" (1905); concert overture (1904), etc.

**Carter, Thomas,** Dublin, May, 1769 — Nov. 8, 1800; mus. director at Calcutta; c. songs.

**Caruso** (kä - roo'- sō ), **Enrico,** b. Naples, Feb. 25, 1873; famous Italian tenor; pupil of Vergine; début, 1895, winning gradual success in Italy (Naples, 1898; 1899 La Scala), and creating the tenor rôles in Giordano's "*Fedora*," Cilea's "*Lécouvreur*," and Franchetti's "*Germania*"; 1899–1903 sang in St. Petersburg, and Buenos Ayres; 1902, appeared with Melba at Monte Carlo, began his tremendous vogue; 1902 at Covent Garden; 1903, Met. Op. House, N. Y. Since then he has sung at both operas almost every year with unrivalled favor; 1908, his voice was

threatened, but an operation restored it. He created the tenor rôle in Puccini's "*Girl of the Golden West*," and has sung throughout Europe always with sensational effect and unequalled prices. He is an ingenious caricaturist, and has composed songs, one of them being sung in the farce "*The Million*" (New York, 1912), by a character called "The Bowery Caruso."

**Casals', Pablo,** b. Beudrell, Spain, Dec. 30, 1876; 'cellist; pupil of Jose Garcia, Rosereda and Breton; since 1897, prof. at Barcelona Cons.; toured widely; c. *La Vision de Fray Martin,* for chorus and orch.; 'cello pieces, etc.

**Casati** ( kä-sä'-tē ), **Gasparo,** d. Novara, 1643; cond. at Novara Cathedral; c. church music.

**Case, George Edward,** d. Nov. 29, 1909, age 54. Writer and prof. of trombone at R. C. M., London.

**Casimiro** (kä-sē-mē'-rō), **da Silva Joaquim,** Lisbon, May 30, 1808— Dec. 28, 1862; Portuguese comp. of church music.

**Castillon** (kăs-tē-yôṅ), **Alexis de, Vicomte de Saint Victor,** Chartres, Dec. 13, 1838 — Paris, March 5, 1873; composer ; pupil of Massé and César Franck; c. symphony; overture, *Torquato Tasso, Psalm 84* with orch.; piano concerto and important chamber music.

**Cas'tro, Ricardo,** Durango, 1866–1908; dir. Nat. Cons. of Mexico.

**Catalani** [(kät-ä-lä'-nē), **Alfredo,** Lucca, June 19, 1854 — Milan, Aug. 6, 1893; pupil of his father, an organist; at 14, c. a mass sung at the cathedral; pupil of Magi, and of Paris Cons. and Milan Cons.; c. operas "*La Falce*" (Milan, 1875); "*Elda*" (Turin, 1880; revised as "*Loreley*," 1890); "*La Wally*" (La Scala, 1892); c. symph. poem "*Ero e Leandro*," etc.

**Catoir** ( kăt-wär ), **Georg L., b.** Moscow, April 27, 1861; pupil of Klindworth, Willborg, and Liadov; c. symphony; symph. poem. *Mzyri;* cantata, *Russalka,* etc.

Çaudel′la, (1) Franz, d. Jassy, Roumania, 1868; ′cellist and dir. of the Jassy Cons.; his son (2) Eduard, b. Jassy, June 3, 1841; violinist; pupil of his father, and of Alard, Massart, and Vieuxtemps; 1894–1901, dir. of education at Jassy; c. opera, etc.

Chabran (shä-brän), or Ciabrano (cha-brä′-nō), Francesco, b. Piedmont, 1723; violinist and comp.; 1751, toured Europe with success.

Chabrier, A. E., add that after his death in 1894 his unfinished opera "Briséis," was given at the Opéra Paris, 1899; his opera "Gwendoline" (text by Catulle Mendès), at the Op. Com., 1911.

Chad′field, Edward, Derby, Aug. 1, 1827 — Hastings, March 31, 1908; organist at Derby; pupil of Smart, Rosellen and Korbach.

Chadwick, G. W., add that the following compositions were played in the Boston Symph. Orch., overtures "Adonais," (1900); "Euterpe" (1904); "Cleopatra" (1906); symphonic sketches (1908); theme variations and fugue for organ and orch. (1909); Sinfonietta (1910); Suite Symphonique for orch. winning $700 prize of Nat. Federation of Clubs (1910); c. also "Noel" (1909); "Lochinvar," ballad for barytone and orch., 1909. "Judith" lyric drama, Worcester Feast 1900 incid. music to "Everywoman" (1911); symph. poem "Aphrodite" (Norfolk. 1912), In 1905 a concert of his comps. was was given by the Leipzig Concordia Verein.

Chaîne (shĕn), Eugène, b. Charléville, Dec. 1, 1819; pupil and after 1875 teacher at Paris Cons.; c. 2 symph., and important violin pieces.

Chaliapine (shäl-yä′-pĕn), Fedor Ivanovich, b. Kazan, Feb. 11, 1873. Russian bass; pupil of Oussatov, in Tiflis; sang in various cities, finally at Moscow, and with immense success in European capitals; 1908, New York.

Champs (dŭ-shän), Ettore de, b. Florence, Aug. 8, 1835 ; pianist and c. of operas, masses, etc.

Chapi (y Lorente) (chă-pē′ē lō-rĕn′-tĕ) Ruperto, Villena, March 27, 1851 — Madrid, March 25, 1909; pupil Madrid Cons.; c. operas and 78 zarzuelas; also a symph.; oratorio, etc.

Charlier (shărl-yā), Théo., b. Seraing, Belgium, July 17, 1868; trumpet-virtuoso and teacher; c. opera, ballets, etc.

Chausson (shōs-sôn), Ernest, Paris, June 21, 1855—(killed in bicycle accident), Limay n. Nantes, June 10r 1899; pupil of Massenet and Césa, Franck; c. symph.; symph. poems Viviane and Les caprices de Marianne; opera Hélène, Le roi Arthus (Brussels, 1903; text by the composer); songs and piano pieces.

Chemin = Petit ( shŭ-măn-pŭ-tĕ′ ), (1) Maurice, c. opera, "Alfred the Great," (Halle, 1858). (2) Hans c. operas, including "Der Liebe Augustin" (Brandenburg, 1906).

Chesh′ire, John, d. New York, Sept. 21, 1910, age 73. English harpist; pupil and later teacher in Royal Academy of Music; prolific composer for harp.

Chessin ( chĕs′-sēn ), Alexander Borissovich, b. St. Petersburg Oct 19, 1869; conductor; pupil of the Cons., and of Nikisch at Leipzig; since 1901, cond. at St. Petersburg and since 1903 of Philharmonic concerts at Moscow; c. cantata, etc.

Chevillard, Camille, add that in 1898 he acted as substitute cond for Lamoureux, called abroad; on the death of L. Dec. 21, 1899; he became cond. of the Association des Concerts Lamoureux. Add to his comps. incid mus. to La Roussalka (1903); allegr for horn and piano, 1905; piano piece and songs.

Chop (khôp), Max, b. Greuszen Thuringia, May 17, 1862; Mus. writer critic in Berlin, under the nam

Monsieur Charles;" c. piano con-
erto, etc.

opin, Fr., The controversy as to the
ate of his birth has been recently
ided by the discovery of the certifi-
ate, establishing it as Feb. 22, 1810.

rétien (krāt - yäṅ), Hedwige
,ouise Marie, b. Compiègne,
ily 5, 1859; pupil Paris Cons., taking
rst harmony prize, 1881; first
)unterpoint and fugue, 1887; teacher
iere, 1890–2; c. orch. pieces, cho-
ises, songs, etc.

rist (krēst), Wilhelm, Geisen-
eim, Aug. 2, 1831 — Munich, Feb.
, 1906; historian and theorist.

ueca ( chwä'- kä ), Federico, 1846
- Madrid, June 20, 1908; composer
: zarzuelas.

va'la (shvä'-lä), Emanuel, b.
rague, Jan. 1, 1851; pupil of Förster
id Fibich; historian and c. of cham-
er music, etc.

ybiński (khe-bĕn'-yĕ-shkĭ), Ad-
lf, b. Cracow, March 29, 1880; his-
)rian of Polish music.

onia (chĭ-kōn'-yä), Johannes,
inon at Padua about 1400; theorist
id comp.

ĕa ( chĕ' -lĕ- ä ), Francesco, b.
almi, July 29, 1866; leading Italian
)era comp.; at 9 had c. a notturno
id a mazurka; at 15 entered the
aples Cons.; while yet a student he
id success with a suite for orch., and
3-act opera Gina, (1889); 1896–
)04, professor at Royal Institute,
lorence; c. operas La Tilda, (1892);
'Arlesiana (Milan, 1896); Adrianna
écouvreur (Milan, 1902, Covent
arden, 1904); Gloria, (La Scala,
ïilan, 1907).

ri (chĕr'-rē), (1) Ignazio, organ-
t and comp.; his son (2) Giovanni
aptista, b. Forli, ca. 1740; 'cellist;
ient many years in London, then
eturned to Italy; c. important
ello music.

uss'nitzer, Paul, b. Nieder-
:höna, near Freiberg, Dec. 9, 1867;
racher and comp.

Clavé (klä-vä'), José Anselmo,
Barcelona, April 21, 1824 — Feb.,
1874; founder of male choral societies
in Spain; c. very popular songs and
choruses.

Clavijo Del Castillo (klä-vē'-hō
dĕl kăs-tēl'-yō), Bernardo, d. Madrid, Feb. 1626; Spanish organist
and comp.

Clay'ton, Thomas, ca. 1670 — ca.
1730. English manager and comp.

Clem'ens, Charles Edwin, b.
Plymouth, England, March 12, 1856;
organist; 1889–1895, organist at the
English church, and to Empress
Frederick in Berlin, and teacher at
Scharwenka Cons.; then moved to
Cleveland, Ohio; author of organ-
methods.

Clement (or Clemens or Clementi), Johann Georg, b. Breslau ca. 1710; cond. at Breslau, 1735,
till after 1785; c. masses etc.; left two
sons — one at Vienna, the other a
violinist and cond. at Carlsruhe, 1793,
taking the name Clementi.

Clemm, (1) John (Johann Gottlieb Klemm ), Dresden, 1690 —
Bethlehem, Pa., 1762; organ builder,
came to America, 1736; built first organ for Trinity Church, N. Y., 1741,
of which his son (2) John was the
first organist.

Clérambault (klā-räṅ-bō), Louis
Nicolas, Paris, 1749; organist and
comp.

Cleve (klĕv), (1) Johannes De,
Cleve (?) 1529 — Augsburg, 1582;
court tenor at Vienna and Prague; c.
church music;(2) Halfdan, b.Kongs-
berg, Norway, Oct, 5, 1879; pianist;
pupil of his father and of Raif and
the two Scharwenkas at Berlin; c.
piano-concertos, etc.

Cliffe (klĭf), Frederick, b. Lowmoor,
May 2, 1857; organist; pupil of
Sullivan, Stainer, and at R. C.
M.; toured Europe with success;
c. 2 symph.; symph poem "Clouds
and Sunshine"; alto solo with orch.,
"The Triumph of Alcestis," etc.

**Clough=Leiter** (klŭf-lī'-tĕr) (1) **Henry**, b. Washington, D. C.; 1874; composer and musical editor; pupil of his mother, Edw. Kimball, H. Xander, and Dr. J. H. Anger; org. at Washington and various churches at Providence, R. I. c. *Lasca* for tenor and orch.; 4 cantatas, *A Day of Beauty*, for string quintet; 200 songs of unusual color and sweep, etc. His wife, (2) **Grace Cotton Marshall**, b. Nineveh, Ind., Aug. 20, 1885; pupil of her mother; 1902—5 completed seven-year course at Met. School of Music, Indianapolis, graduating with highest honors; studied then in Boston with Carlo Buonamici and H. C. L., whom she married. She has published many piano pieces and songs under the name **G. Mar= schal=Loepke**.

**Coates, John**, b. Girlington, June 29, 1865; tenor; sang in his father's choir at 5; pupil of Burton and Bridge later of Shakespeare; sang in light opera, London and America, as barytone, 1893–1899; decided he was a tenor; studied and made début, 1900, at Covent Garden; favourite festival tenor; also in opera in Germany and 1910 chief tenor at Beecham's season.

**Cob'bold, William**, St. Andrew, Norwich, Jan. 5, 1559–60 — Beccles, Nov. 7, 1639; org. and comp.

**Coccia** (kôt'-chä), **Maria Rosa**, Rome, Jan. 4, 1759 — after 1783; woman composer of great importance in her own day; c. *Magnificat*, etc.

**Coignet** (kwän-yā), **Horace**, Lyons, 1736 — Paris, Aug. 29, 1821; comp.

**Colborne, Langdon**, London, Sept. 15, 1837 — Hereford, Sept. 16, 1899; organist at Hereford Cathedral, 1877–1899; c. oratorio *"Samuel,"* etc.

**Cole**, (1) **Belle**, d. London, Jan. 6, 1905, age 60. American contralto. (2) **Rossetter, G.**, b. near Clyde, Mich. Feb. 5, 1866; composer; 1888,

graduated from Michigan Un taking musical courses also; at graduation the Univ. Mus. performed his cantata with o *"The Passing of Summer"*; 1888— he taught English and Latin in schools; 1890—92 in Berlin, winn competitive scholarship at R Master-school, and studying Max Bruch; 1892—4, prof. of m Ripon College; 1894—1901, I College; from 1902 in Chicago teacher, and from 1908 also in ch of summer music classes of Colum Univ., N. Y. c. *"King Rober Sicily,"* and *"Hiawatha's Wooi* as musical backgrounds for rec tion, ballade for 'cello and o sonata for violin songs, etc.

**Coleridge = Taylor, Samuel,** that he was made cond. Har Society, 1904; his *"Hiawatha"* developed as a trilogy, *"Hiawat Wedding Feast,"* (R. C. M., Lon 1898), *"The Death of Minneha* (North Staffordshire Fest., 1 *"Hiawatha's Departure"* (Lond 1900), the overture the same year also for voices and orch., *"The B Girl of Castel-Cuillé,* (Leeds F 1901), *"Meg Blane,"* (Sheffield F 1902), *"The Atonement,"* (Here Fest., 1903), *"Kubla Khan,"* (H del Society, 1906); incid. music Stephen Phillips's plays, *"Hero "Ulysses," "Nero,"* and *"Fau* (1908); concert march, *"Ethio Saluting the Colors";* 5 ballads Longfellow, with orch., (Norw Fest., 1905); *"A Tale of Old Japa* voices and orch. (London, 1912), He died Sept. 1, 1912, in London

**Colom'bi, Giuseppe,** Modena, 16 1694; conductor and comp.

**Colombini** (kō-lôm-bē'-nē), U b. Milan, 1878; tenor; sang at M Royal Theatre, Madrid, and I Operas in Russia; 1910–11, Montr

**Colyns** (kō-lăńs), **Jean Baptis** Brussels, Nov. 25, 1834 — Oct. 1902; violinist and comp.

**Com'fort, Ambrose H.**, d. April 26, 1905 at Cape Town, age 42. Pianist and teacher.

**Conried** (kän'-rēd), **Heinrich**, Bielitz, Silesia, Sept. 13, 1855—Meran, April 27, 1909; impresario; in 1873 an actor at the Vienna Burgtheater, came to New York 1878; founded German company from 1887 at Irving Place Theatre; 1901, succeeded Grau as manager of the Metropolitan Opera House, where in 1903 he made the first production outside Bayreuth of "*Parsifal*"; 1905, Franz Leopold decorated him and gave him the privilege of the prefix "von"; ill health forced his retirement in 1908.

**Conseil** (kôn-sā), **Jean De**, d. Paris, 1535; composer, and 1526 singer in Papal chapel.

**Con'solo, Frederigo**, Ancona, 1841 — Florence, Dec. 14, 1906 ; violinist and comp.

**Co'nus** (or **Conius** or **Konius**), (1) **George Edwardovich**, composer; b. Moscow, Dec. 1, 1862 ; theorist; pupil of the Cons. ; 1891-9 teacher of theory there; since 1902 prof. at the Opera School; c. symph. poem "*From the Realm of Illusions*," orch. suite, "*Child-Life*," cantata, etc. His brother, (2) **Julius**, b. Moscow, 1869; gold medallist at the Cons. and later teacher of violin there; c. violin concerto, etc. (3) **Leo**, pianist; pupil at the Cons.; later founded a school of his own.

**Converse, Frederick Shepherd**, b. Newton, Mass., Jan. 5, 1871; composer; graduated at Harvard University and studied music with Bährmann and G. W. Chadwick; 1896-8 with Rheinberger, then taught theory and comp. at the New England Cons.; c. operas "*The Pipe of Desire*" (in concert form, Boston, 1906, as an opera, Met. Op., N. Y. 1910, Boston Op., 1911); symph. 1907); overtures, "*Youth*" and "*Euphrosyne*"; orch. romance, "*The*

*Festival of Pan*"; orch. fantasie, "*The Mystic Trumpeter*"; symph. poem "*Ormazd*," (Boston Symph. Orch., 1912); violin concerto and sonata, etc.

**Conver'si, Girolamo**, b. Correggio, 16th cent.; c. madrigals, etc.

**Coquard, Arthur**, add that his birth date is May 26th; c. operas "*Jahel*" (Lyons, 1900), "*La troupe Jolicoeur*" (1902), etc.

**Cornette** (kôr-nĕt), **Victor**, Amiens, 1795 — Paris after 1850; Mus. Director; pupil Paris Cons.; cond. and comp. for wind instruments; author of many methods.

**Coronaro** (1) **Antonio**, b. Vincenza, 1860; brother of **Gaetano C.**, and comp. of operas; his son was (2) **Arrigo**, Vincenza, 1880 — October, 1906; c. opera *Turiddu* (Turin, 1905).

**Corri=Paltoni, Frances**, b. Edinburgh, 1801; mezzo-soprano; niece of Domenico R. Corri; toured Europe till after 1830.

**Cortellini** (kôr-tĕl-lē'-nē), **Camillo**, called "Il violino" from his skill; at Bologna, 1583, as municipal musician and comp.

**Cortesi** (kôr-tā'-zē), **Francesco**, Florence, 1830 — Jan. 3, 1904; conductor, composer of operas, and teacher of voice;

**Cossoul** (kôs'-sool), **Guilherme Antonio**, Lisbon, April 22, 1828 — May 26, 1880; 'cellist and comp.

**Cotes** (kō'-tĕs), **Ambrosio De**, d. Seville, Sept. 9, 1603; Spanish composer and cond.

**Cre'ser, William**, b. York, Sept. 9, 1844; organist and composer; pupil of Macfarren; 1880, Mus. Doc. Oxford; 1881, org. at the Parish church, Leeds; conducted performances of Bach; 1891-1902, org. Chapel Royal; St. James; and comp. to Chapel Royal: married Amelia Clarke a prominent mezzo-soprano; c. oratorio, ("*Micaiah*"; cantatas "*Eudora*" (Leeds, 1882); "*The Sacrifice of Freia*" (Leeds, 1889), etc.

**Crevel'li, Domenico,** Brescia, June 7, 1793 — London, Feb. 11, 1857; comp.

**Cro'mer,** (1) **José Antonio,,** Lisbon, March 11, 1826 — Sept. 28, 1888; flutist; his brother, (2) **Raphael José,** Lisbon, March 26, 1828 — Cascaes, Sept. 22, 1884; clarinettist and oboist.

**Cul'bertson, Sasha,** b. 1893; violinist ; pupil of Suchorukoff; at 9 entered Cons. at Rostoff; in 1905 pupil of Sevcik, Prague; début, Vienna 1908; toured Europe and America.

**Culp** (koolp), **Julia,** b. Amsterdam; mezzo-soprano; well known Liedersinger; pupil of Amsterdam Cons. and of Etelka Gerster; has toured Europe with great success; engaged, 1912, to tour America.

**Culwick** (kŭl'-lĭk), **James, C.,** West Bromwich, April 28, 1845 — Dublin, Oct. 5, 1907; organist, theorist and comp. Prof. Alexandria College, Dublin; cond. Dublin Philharmonic Soc., etc. 1903, Mus. Doc. Univ. of Dublin.

**Cupis** (kü-pē), (1) **(François de Camargo),** Brussels, 1719 — Paris, 1764; violinist and comp. His son, (2) **Jean Baptiste,** Paris ca. 1741 — ca. 1794; 'cellist and comp.

**Cur'ry, Arthur Mansfield,** b. Chelsea, Mass., Jan. 27, 1866; violin pupil of Franz Kneisel, and of MacDonald in harmony; teacher and cond. in Boston; c. overture *"Blomidon"* (Worcester, Mass., Fest. 1902); symph. poem *"Atala"* (Boston Symph., 1911); *"The Winning of Amarac";* Keltic legend for a reader, chorus and orch.

**Cursch = Bühren** (koorsh-bü'-rĕn), **Franz Theodor,** Troppau, Jan. 10, 1859 — Leipzig, March 11, 1908; cond., editor and comp. of Singspiele, including *"E-mol-As,"* a satire on R. Strauss's *"Salomé"*

**Cut'ter, Benjamin,** Woburn, Mass., Sept. 6, 1857—Jamaica Plains, Mass., May 10, 1910; composer; violin pupil of Eichberg in Boston, 1877; 1881 of

Singer in Stuttgart, studied harmony with Emery, Goetschius and Seifriz; member of Boston Symph. Orch. many years. c. important mass in D; trio for piano, violin and 'cello, etc.

**Czapek** (chä'-pĕk), (1) **Joseph,** b Prague, March 9, 1825; organist and director; pupil of the Cons.; c. symphonies, masses, etc. (2) pen-name under which J. L. Hatton c. many songs.

**Czernohorsky** ( chĕr-nō-hôr'-shkĭ) **Bohuslav,** Nimburg, Bohemia Feb. 26, 1684 — Graz, July 2, 1740 Franciscan monk, organist and comp

## D

**Daff'ner, Hugo,** b. Munich, Ma 2, 1882; author and comp.; pupil o Thuille, Schmid-Lindner and Ma Reger; 1904, Ph.D.; c. symph sonatas, etc.

**Dahl** (däl), **Balduin,** b. Copen hagen, Dec. 6, 1834; dir. of Tivo concerts at Copenhagen, and comp. c dance-music.

**Dalcroze** (dăl-krôz), **Emile Jaque:** b. Vienna, July 6, 1865, of Swi parentage; important Swiss con poser; pupil of Fuchs, Bruchn and Délibes; teacher, lecturer ar critic at Geneva Cons.; c. lyric com dies *"Janie"* (Geneva, 1893), a *Sancho Panza* (1897); *Poème Alpest* for voices and orch. (1896, Londo 1897); a violin concerto of great or inality played by Marteau on I tours, and Swiss songs of great pop larity and national feeling.

**Dale, Benjamin James,** b. Crou Hill, London, July 17, 1885; orga ist; pupil of R. A. M.; c. improm 2 overtures, successful piano sona in D Minor, etc.

**Dalmorès,** (dăl-mŏ'-rĕs), **Charl** b. Nancy, France, Jan. 1, 18 tenor; pupil Paris and Lyons Cor sang in France; 1896, at Manhat' Opera, N. Y.; since then at Met politan, N. Y.

'mon (or **Daman**), **William,**
a. 1540 — ca. 1592; musician to
Queen Elizabeth; c. psalm tunes, etc.

. **Mot'ta, José Vianna,** b. Isle
St. Thomas, Africa, 1868; Portuguese
pianist; studied at Lisbon; début there
1881, then studied Scharwenka Cons.,
with Liszt and Von Bülow; toured
widely; c. symph. "*An das Vater-
und,*" 5 Portuguese rhapsodies on
native melodies, etc.; also critic and
author.

mse (däm'-sĕ), **Joseph,** Soko-
ov, Galicia, Jan. 23, 1788 — Rudno,
ear Warsaw, Dec. 15, 1852; clari-
ettist; c. operas, masses, and popu-
ar Polish songs and dances.

ndrieu or **Dandrieu,** vide **Andrieu.**

nnström (dän'-sträm), **Isidor,**
tockholm, Dec. 15, 1812 — Oct. 17,
397; barytone in opera, teacher and
omp.

vaux (dă-vō), **Jean Baptiste,**
ôte-St-André, 1737 — Paris, Feb.
2, 1822; c. many symphonics, cham-
er music, etc.

vey, **Henry,** b. Brighton, Nov.
), 1853; historian and writer on
usical topics.

utresme (dō-trĕm), **Lucien,** El-
euf, Normandy, May 21, 1826 —
aris, Feb., 1892; senator; c. 2 operas,
c.

vis, **John David,** b. Edgbaston,
ct. 22, 1869; pupil Raff Cons., and
russels Cons.; since 1889, teacher at
irmingham; c. opera "*The Cossacks*"
antwerp, 1903), also symph. varia-
ons, (London, 1905), symph. bal-
de "*The Cenci*"; symph. poem
*The Maid of Astolat*"; chamber
usic; prize "*Coronation March*"
902), etc.

v'son, **Frederick H.,** b. Leeds,
ly 16, 1868; pianist, pupil of his
ther, a pianist, and of Hallé.

', (1) **John,,** March 7, 1830 — Pim-
o, Nov. 4, 1905; organist and for 53
ars violinist in Queen Victoria's
ivate band. (2) **Charles Rus-**

sell, Horstead, Norfolk, 1860 —
killed Feb. 18, 1900, in the battle of
Paardeberg; major in British army
and writer of books on musical instruments.

**Dayas, W. H.,** correct birth date,
1863; d. Manchester, England, May
3, 1903.

**De Amicis** (dā ä-mē'-chĕs), (1) **Anna
Lucia,** b. Naples, c. 1740 — d.
after 1789; sang in London, 1763–
1771; in 1773 created the rôle of
Giunia in Mozart's *Lucio Silla;* m.
Buonsollazzi, secretary of King of
Naples; (2) **Domenico,** brother or
husband of (1), sang with her in London in 1763.

**Debefve** (dŭ-bŭv'), **Jules,** b. Liège
Jan. 16, 1863; pianist; pupil and later
teacher at the Cons.; c. opera, rhapsody for orch., etc.

**De Boeck** (dĕ-book), **Auguste,** b.
Merckem, Belgium, May 9, 1865;
organist, son of an organist; pupil of
Brussels Cons., later a teacher there;
c. symph., *Rhapsodie Dahomienne* for
orch., organ music, etc.

**Debussy, A. C.,** add that the correct
birth date is St. Germain, Paris, Aug.
22, 1862; he re-wrote his cantata
"*L'Enfant Prodigue*" for the Sheffield
Fest., 1908; his opera "*Pelléas et
Mélisande*" has been widely played,
1907, Berlin, 1909, New York, etc.; c.
also incid. mus. to "*Dionysos*"
(Orange, 1904); operas "*Chimène,*"
"*Tristan and Isolde,*" "*As You Like
It,*" 3 nocturnes for women's voices
and orch., "*Nuages, Fêtes, Sirènes*";
a series of three "*Images*" for orch.,
I, "*Gigue triste*" (NS), II, "*Ronde des
Printemps*" (Paris, 1910, N. Y. Phil.,
1910, Boston Symph., 1910), III,
"*Iberia*" (Paris Colonne orch., 1910,
N. Y., Phil., 1911, Boston Symph.,
1911), etc.

**Deck'er = Schenk, Johann,** b.
Vienna, 1826; singer, guitar-virtuoso,
and director of operas in St. Petersburg; c. for guitar, balalaika, etc.

**Degner** (dĕkh'-nĕr), **Erich Wolf-**

near Chemnitz, April 8, 1858 — Weimar, Nov. 18, 1908; organist, theorist and teacher; c. symph., choral work *"Martha and the Mother";* overture, etc.

**Degtarev,** (děkh'-tä-rěv), **Stepoan Ankiewitsch,** 1766–1813 ; Russian director in St. Petersburg and Italy; c. 60 concertos, and church choral music.

**Deichmann** (dīkh'-män), **Carl,** d. July 5, 1908, age 81. For 60 years well known violinist in England.

**Del'ius, Frederick,** b. Bradford, England, 1863, of German parentage; important composer, largely self-taught; from 1883 on an orange plantation in Florida; later studied at Leipzig Cons. with Jadassohn and Reinecke; from 1890 lives in France; 1897 his incid. music to Norwegian plan *"Folkeraadet"* with burlesque of national anthem led a spectator to fire several shots at the composer; c. operas *"Koanga,"* based on G. W. Cables *"The Grandissimes"* (Elberfeld 1904); *"Romeo und Julia auf dem Dorfe"* (Berlin 1907; London Covent Garden 1910); 1-act. *"Margot la Rouge";* 5 symph. poems *"Life's Dance"* (1898), *"Paris"* (1899), *"Appalachia"* (1903, London 1907), *"Brigg Fair"* (London 1908) *"In a Summer Garden"* (London 1908); for soli, chor and orch. *"A Mass of Life"* (London 1909), *"Sea Drift"* based on Walt Whitman, for barytone, chor. and orch. (1904), songs, etc.

**Del'ler, Florian,** Württemberg, ca. 1730 — Munich, 1774; court comp. of ballets, etc.

**Delmas** (děl-mäs), **Jean Fr.,** b. Lyons, France, April 14, 1861; bass; pupil Paris Cons.; 1886, joined the Opéra where he created many rôles with great success.

**Delune** (dŭ-lün), **Louis,** b. Charleroi, March 15, 1876; Belgian cond. and pupil at Brussels Cons., winning prize, 1900, and Prix de Rome, 1903; c. sonatas and songs.

**Demar** (dā'-mär), **Josef Se**[...] Gauafschach, Bavaria, June 1763 — Orleans, 1832 ; org. a[...] comp.

**Dercks, Emil,** b. Donnerau, Sile[...] Oct. 17, 1849; organist and con[...]

**Dereyne,** (dě-rěn'), **Fély,** b. M[...] seilles, May 12, 1883; pupil of Blasi[...] début, Marseilles, 1903, sang then[...] Nice, Vichy, etc.; 1907 sang at B[...] ton Opera; 1908–9, Covent Gard[...] also at Met. Op., N. Y., has sung[...] Lisbon, Buenos Ayres, and 1[...] again in Boston.

**Deruyts** (dě-roits'), **Jean Jacqu**[...] Liège, 1790—April 11, 1871 ; teac[...] of César Franck; c. church mus[...]

**Deslandres** (dě-län'-drŭ), **Adolp**[...] **Eduard Marie,,** b. Paris, J[...] 22, 1840 ; organist ; pupil Pa[...] Cons.; organist at St. Marie at B[...] ignolles, where his father was dir[...] tor; c. operettas and church music[...]

**Dessoir** (děs-swär), **Susanne** (a[...] **Triepel),** b. Grünberg, Silesia, J[...] 23, 1869; pianist at first, then pupil[...] Amalie Joachim; singer of Lied[...] married, 1899, Dr. Max Dess[...] (b. Berlin, Feb. 8, 1867), author[...] works on musical æsthetics.

**Destinn, Emmy,** add that her [...] name was Kittl — she chose "D[...] tinn" in honour of her teacher; [...] sang at Bayreuth, 1891; from 1[...] she has had great success at the M[...] Op., N. Y., also at Covent Gard[...] and Berlin Royal Op., she created[...] rôle of *"Minnie"* in Puccini's *"F*[...] *ciulla del West."*

**Dib'bern, Karl,** b. Altona, June[...] 1855; conductor, later regisseur[...] the Amsterdam Opera; c. libret[...] and music of operas and operettas[...]

**Dieckmann** (děk'-män), **Ern**[...] b. Stade, July 17, 1861; organ[...] pupil of Haupt and Löschorn; si[...] 1900 cathedral organist in Verd[...] c. choral works and songs.

**Diepenbrock,** (dě'-pěn-brök,)[...] **J. M.,** b. Amsterdam, Sept. 2, 18[...] teacher and comp. of church mu[...]

1a (dĕ'-mä), **George,** b. Cronadt, Oct. 10, 1847; teacher and cond. Roumanian societies there; c. ngs, etc.

'pel, **Andreas,** after many years success as tenor, became imesario; associated with Gattiasazza in management of Metrolitan Opera House, New York, 08; since then directed opera seans in Chicago and Philadelphia.

on, **George,** Norwich, June 1820 — Finchley, June 8, 1887; ganist, c. of church music.

rn (dōrn), **Georg,** b. Bahrenrf, near Magdeburg, May 23, 1867; nd.; at first lawyer, then pupil ologne Cons., since 1901 at Breslau cond. and director of the Singademie.

nanievski ( dō - män - yĕf'- shkĭ ), oleslaus, b. Gronówek, Poland, 59; famous Polish piano teacher; ipil of Jos. Wieniawski and Rubinein; 1890–1900, prof. at Cracow ons., since, director Warsaw Music chool; author of piano methods.

nnich (dŏm'-nĭkh), (1) **Hein-ch,** Würzburg, May 13, 1767 — aris, June 19, 1844; horn virtuoso; st teacher of the horn at Paris Cons., '95; author of methods. His brothers so played the horn. (2) **Jakob,** b. 758, went to America. (3) **Arnold,** ürzburg, 1771 — Neiningen, 1834.

naudy (dō-nä'-oo-dē), **Stefano,** Palermo, Feb. 21, 1879; c. operas olchetto (Palermo, 1892); *Theodor örner* (Hamburg, 1902), and *Sperti nel Buio* (Palermo, 1907).

et (dō-rā), **Gustave,** b. Aigle. rance, 1866; studied violin with achim and Marsick, and composion at Paris Cons.; lives at Paris as nd.; c. operas *Les Armailles* (Op. om., 1906), and *Le nain de Hassli,* Geneva, 1908), oratorio, etc.

go'ni, **Giovanni Andrea,** Menola, ca. 1540 — Rome, 1598; comoser; pupil of Palestrina; cond. at ne Lateran.

**Drese,** (drā'-zĕ), **Adam,** Thüringen, Dec. 1620 — Arnstadt, Feb. 15, 1701; director and comp.

**Dreyer** (drī'-ĕr), **Alexis De,** b. Russia, 1857; c. piano pieces.

**Drozdovski** (drōsh-dôf'-shkĭ), **Jan,** b. Cracow, Feb. 2, 1858; piano teacher, pupil Vienna Cons.; since 1889, prof. at Cracow Cons.; author of methods.

**Druffel** ( droof'- fĕl ), **Peter,** b. Wiedenbrück, Oct. 8, 1848; composer of old German Liederspiel *"Der Erlöser,"* etc.

**Drys'dale,** **F. Learmont,** Edinburgh, 1866 — June 18, 1909; pupil of R. A. M., won Lucas prize, 1890; c. prize overture, *"Tam o' Shanter"; "The Plague,"* a mystic play (1896, Edinburgh); *"The Red Spider"* (Dundee, 1898), and light operas.

**Ducasse** ( dü - kăs ), **Roger,** pupil Paris Cons., with Gabriel Fauré, winning Prix de Rome, 1902; from 1909 inspector in elementary schools; c. *suite française* for orch. (Colonne concerts, 1909, twice. Boston Symph., 1910); *"Variations plaisantes sur un thème grave"* for harp and orch. (Colonne concerts, 1909), piano pieces, etc.

**Dukas** (dü-kăs), **Paul,** b. Paris, Oct. 1, 1865; one of the most original of French composers; pupil at the Cons. of Dubois, Mathias and Guiraud; won prize in counterpoint, 1888, second Prix de Rome with cantata *"Velleda"*; spent a year in Rome, then a year of military service; his overture *"Polyeucte"* was played by Lamoureux in 1892; his symphony, 1896, and elsewhere; 1897 *"L'Apprenti Sorcier";* 1900, piano sonata; 1906, *Villanelle* for horn and piano; 1907, his opera *"Ariane et Barbe Bleue"* made a great stir and was played in Vienna, 1908, Met. Op., N. Y., 1912, etc. He is prof. of instrumentation at the Cons. and a critic; has edited texts of Rameau, and c. for piano *"Variations, Interlude et Final,"* on a theme of

Rameau's 1902; *Prelude élégiaque* on the name of Haydn, 1909; also a ballet *La Péri* dance-poem in one act (Paris 1911).

**Dulichius** ( dō - lǐkh' - ĭ - oos ) also **(Deulich** or **Deilich) Philip,** Chemnitz (christened Dec. 19), 1562 — March 25, 1631; teacher and comp.

**Dumont** (dü-môn), **Henri,** Villers, near Liège, 1610 — Paris, May 8, 1684; organist and comp.

**Dunc′an, William Edmond-stoune,** b. Sale, Cheshire, 1866; organist; at 16 an associate of the Royal College of Organists; 1883, obtained scholarship at R. C. M., pupil of Parry, Stanford and Mac-farren; critic for some years, then prof. at Oldham College; c. successful odes with orch., notably "*Ye Mariners of England*" (1890), etc.

**Dun′ham, Henry Morton,** b. Brockton, Mass., July 27, 1853; graduated New England Cons., as pupil of G. E. Whiting, (organ), J. C. D. Parker (Piano), Emery and Paine (theory); held various church positions till 1911, and gave organ recitals on the Great Organ at Boston, at St. Louis Exposition, etc.; prof. of organ at N. E. Cons.; author of an organ method; c. symph., poem "*Easter Morning*," a book of organ studies, Meditation for organ, harp and violin; 3 organ sonatas, etc.

**Dunkl** (doonk′-′l), **Joh. Nepomuk,** b. Budapest, 1832; pianist; pupil of Liszt and Rubinstein.

**Dunkler** ( doonk′-lĕr ), **François,** Namur, 1816 — Hague, 1878; military director.

**Duparc** ( dü-păr ), (**Fouques Duparc**), **Henri,** b. Paris, Jan. 21, 1848; pupil of César Franck; soldier in war of 1870–71; ill health led to a life of seclusion to César Franck's great regret; c. symph. poem *Lenore*, an orch. suite rehearsed in 1873, but found impossible; other pieces destroyed and many songs of the highest importance.

**Dupuis** ( dü-pwē ), (1) **Thom‖ Sanders,** London, Nov. 5, 173‖ July 17, 1796; comp. and organist Chapel Royal London; of Fre‖ parentage, but lived in London, an‖ buried in Westminster Abbey. **Albert,** b. Verviers, France, 18‖ prod. opera *L'Idylle,* (Vervi‖ 1896); *Bilitis* (Verviers, 1899); w‖ Prix de Rome at Brussels with op‖ *Hans Michel,* 1903; c. cantata, etc.

## E

**Eaton, Louis H.,** b. Taunton, Ma‖ May 9, 1861; organist; pupil of G‖ mant; from 1901, org. at San Fra‖ cisco.

**Ebert** (ā′-bĕrt), **Ludwig,** b. K‖ drau, Bohemia, April 13, 1834; ′‖ list; pupil Prague Cons.; 1854–‖ first 'cellist at Oldenburg; 1875–‖ teacher at Cologne Cons.; 18‖ founded Cons. at Koblenz; c. 'c‖ pieces.

**Ebner** (āp′-nĕr), **Wolfgang,** Au‖ burg, ca. 1610 — Vienna, Feb., 16‖ organist and comp.

**Eck′ardt Johann Gottfried,** Au‖ burg, 1735 — Paris, Aug., 1809; cor‖

**Edelmann** (ā′-dĕl-män) **Joh. F‖** Strassburg, May 6, 1749 — Pa‖ July 17, 1794; c. opera, ballets, etc‖

**Edwards,** (1) **Henry Sutherlar‖** b. London, Sept. 5, 1829; wri‖ historian and critic for many ye‖ of the *St. James Gazette;* **Frederick George,** London, N‖ 11, 1853 — Nov. 28, 1909; organ‖ ed. "*Musical Times.*" (3) **Her‖ John,** b. Barnstaple, Feb. 24, 18‖ son and pupil of an organist, t‖ pupil of Bennett, Macfarren; 18‖ Mus. Doc. Oxford; c. oratorios, ‖

**Egidi** (ā′-khē-dē), **Arthur,** b. Ber‖ Aug. 9, 1859; organist; pupil of ‖ and Taubert; teacher at the H‖ Cons., Frankfort-on-Main; si‖ then org. at Apostel Paulus Chu‖ Berlin, and Royal Prof.; c. overtu‖ etc.

**hner** (īkh'-nĕr), **Ernest,** Mann-
-im, 1740 — Potsdam, 1777; c.
portant symphonies, concertos, etc.
ken (ī'-kĕn) (or **Eyken**), **van** (1)
**an Albert,** Amersfoort, Holland,
pril 25, 1822 — Elberfeld, Sept. 24,
.68; organist and comp.; his broth-
, (2) **Gerhard Isaak,** b. May
1832; organist and teacher in
trecht; (3) **Heinrich,** Elberfeld,
ly 19, 1861 — Berlin, Aug. 28,
.08; son of Jan.; pupil of Leipzig
ons.; teacher of theory; c. songs
th orch.
kens (ī'-kĕns), **Daniel Simon**
ntwerp, Oct. 13, 1812 — Oct. 9,
.91; composer.
er vide **Eysler.**
.ar, **Sir Edward,** add that as
rt of his early training he was
ndmaster 1879–1884 at the Coun-
Lunatic Asylum with attendants
musicians; he retired to Malvern in
.91 discouraged with his prospects
London; lived as teacher and oc-
sionally cond. His "*King Olaf*"
896) brought his first real success,
nich his orch. variations, (1899),
creased and the "*Dream of Geron-
us,*" (1900) established; Cambridge
ade him Mus. Doc. that year;
rauss cond. "*Gerontius*" in Ger-
any, 1902; 1904 an Elgar Festival
.as given for 3 days at Covent
arden, and the same year he was
nighted. He c. Imperial March,
military marches, called "*Pomp and
rcumstance,*" "*Sea Pictures,*" con-
alto and orch.; Coronation Ode
902), "*The Apostles*" (Birming-
m Fest., 1903); Symphony No. 2
E flat "*To the Memory of Edward
II,*" (London Mus. Fest., 1911,
.d the same year by Cincinnati
ymph., N. Y. Phil., Boston Symph.,
c.).
.nson, **Hans,** b. Stuttgart; tenor;
chimney sweep in Stuttgart be-
iended by Karl Muck; pupil of
lli Lehmann, Vogel and Schwarz;
but 1906 at Erfurt; engaged as

leading tenor at Vienna Royal Opera;
renewed for 1911–16.
**El'icott, Rosalind Frances,** b.
Cambridge, Nov. 14, 1857; daughter of the Bishop of Gloucester and
Bristol; studied at R. A. M., and with
T. Wingham; c. "*Dramatic Overture,*"
(Gloucester Fest., 1886), concert
overture (London, 1886); cantata
"*Elysium*" (Gloucester Fest., 1889);
also chamber music and songs.
**El'man, Mischa,** b. Stalnoje, Russia, Jan. 20, 1892 (some say Jan. 21,
1891); violinist; played at 5 in public;
studied 16 months at Odessa with
Fidelmann, 1903 invited by Auer to
become his pupil; début at St. Petersburg, 1904, and greeted as a
great artist though only 12; toured
widely; 1908, America; 1911–12 toured
America for third time, playing 12
times with Boston Symph. Orch.; c.
songs, etc.
**El'wes, Gervase Cary,** b. Northampton, Nov. 15, 1866; tenor; studied
Vienna, Paris, etc.; at first in diplomatic life; professional début, 1903;
has sung in Europe and America;
excels in Brahms songs.
**Endler** (ĕnt'-lĕr), **Wm. Gottfried,**
(also **Endele** (**in**) ), Bayreuth, May 21,
1722–1793; composer.
**Enesco** ( ā-nĕs'-koo), **Georges,**
b. Cordaremi, Roumania, Aug. 7,
1881; violinist; at 4 played and
composed, at 7 was admitted to
Vienna Cons., by Hellmesberger, in
whose family he lived; at 11, took
first prizes for violin and harmony;
1896, studied in Paris Cons. with
Marsick and Faure; in 1897, he took
second accessit for counterpoint and
fugue, and a concert of his works was
given in Paris, including a violin
sonata, a piano suite, quintet, 'cello
pieces and songs; 1898, Colonne prod.
his "*Poème Roumain*" for orch.; 1899,
he took first violin prize at the Cons.;
toured and became court violinist to
the Roumanian Queen; c. symph.
(Colonne orch.,1906; N. Y. Phil.,1911)

2nd symph. in E flat, op. 13 (Berlin 1912) Pastoral fantasie for orch. (Colonne orch., 1899); Dixtuor, or symphony for wind instrs., do. for 'cello and orch. (Lamoureux orch., 1909); for suite orch. (Boston Symph., 1911); 3 Rhapsodies Roumaines, (1911), etc.

**Engelsberg, E. S.,** (pen-name of **Dr. Ed. Schön**), Engelsberg, Silesia, Jan. 23, 1825—Mähren, May 21, 1879; councillor of the ministry, Dr. Schön published many humorous male quartets under the pen-name; he was a pupil in theory of Storch; he c. also orchestral works.

**Erlebach** ( ĕr'-lĕ-bäkh ), **Ph. H.,** Essen, July 25, 1657 — Rudolstadt, April 17, 1814; court-cond.; c. overtures, etc.

**Ernst, Henry Wilhelm,** Brünn, Moravia, May 6, 1814 — Nice, Oct. 8, 1867; violinist; pupil Vienna Cons. and with Bohm and Mayseder; followed Paganini about to learn his methods; 1832–38 lived at Paris; 1838–44 toured Europe with greatest success; c. violin-concerto, etc.

**Er'tel, Jean Paul,** b. Posen, Jan. 22, 1865; critic and composer; pupil of Tauwitz, Brassin and Liszt; self-taught in instrumentation; teacher at Brandenburg Cons.; 1897–1905, edited the "*Deutsche Musiker Zeitung*"; c. symphony "*Harald*"; symph. poems "*Maria Stuart,*" "*Der Mensch,*" "*Belsazar,*" "*Hero und Leander*" (1909); a double fugue for orchestra and organ, etc.

**Espo'sito, Michele,** b. Castellammare, near Naples, Sept. 29, 1855; pianist; pupil of Naples Cons., under Cesi; 1878–82, at Paris; from 1882, piano-prof., Royal Irish Acad. of Music, Dublin; 1899 organized and cond. an orchestra in Dublin; c. cantata "*Deirdre*" winning Feis Ceoil prize (1897); operetta, "*The Post-bag,*" "*Irish*" symph. (Feis Ceoil prize, 1902), etc.

**Eulambio,** (ā-oo-läm'-bĭ-ō) **Michele A.;** young Italian composer, pupil

Leipzig Cons. where he c. a p[
concerto; his 2-act opera *Ninon Lenclos* was prod. with success Leipzig City Opera, April 27, 191

**Expert** (ĕx-pär), **Henri,** b. Borde May 12, 1863; pupil of César Fra and Gigout; authority on 15–1 century music and editor of m important texts; from 1909 libra Paris Cons., succeeding Weckerlin

**Eysler** (īs'-lĕr), or **Eisler, Edmu** b. Vienna, Mar. 12, 1874; c. opere "*The Feast of Lucullus*" (Vie 1901), and "*Brother Straubing* (1903), "*Vera Violetta,*" 1907, ε

# F

**Fährmann** (fär'-mǎn) **Ernst Ha** b. Beicha, Dec. 17, 1860; orga 1892, teacher at Dresden Cons organ sonatas, etc.

**Falchi** ( fäl'-kē ), **Stanislaus,** Terni, 1855; composer of operas; *trillo del diavolo*" (Rome, 1899),

**Falkenberg** (fäl-kän-bär), **Georg** b. Paris, Sept. 20, 1854; compo teacher of piano.

**Fall, Leo,** composer of light ope "*Irrlicht*" (Mannheim, 1905), " *Rebell*" (Vienna, 1905), "*Der f Bauer*" (Mannheim, 1907), " *Dollar Princessin,*" (Vienna, 1 London and America as "*The Dc Princess*"), etc.

**Fal'ler, Nikola Von,** b. Iwa wetz, Croatia, April 22, 1862; p of Bruckner in Vienna, Massenet Délibes in Paris; since 1887 at Ag as teacher in the Cons.; opera di tor and comp.

**Fanel'li** — b. 1861 ; studied P Cons. ; violinist; played in ca dance halls, acted as music copyist to obtain such work in 1912 showec symphony "*Tableaux Symphoniqu* written in 1883; had its first p March 16, 1912, by the Colonne or received with greatest approval. is based on Th. Gautier's "*Rom of a Mummy.*"

na (fä-rē'-nä), **Carlo**, b. Man-
a; one of the earliest of violin
rtuosos; 1625 court chamber musi-
n at Vienna; c. violin pieces.

**jeon, Harry**, b. Hohokus, N. J.,
ay 6, 1878; composer; of English
rentage, and taken to England in
ancy; pupil of Landon Ronald,
orer, and 1895–1901, R. A. M.;
od. operetta "*Floretta*," 1899; from
o3, prof. of theory at the R. A. M.;
piano concerto, orch. suite "*Hans
adersen*"; symph. poems, "*Mow-
,*" and "*Summer Vision*"; cham-
r music, songs, etc.

**mer**, (1) **John**, important En-
sh composer of madrigals; author
a treatise pub. 1591, and madrigals,
99–1602. (2) **Thomas**, d. 1694 (?);
mposer; graduated at Cambridge,
84; published songs, stage music,
., 1675–1695; Purcell wrote an elegy
Nahum Tate's words, on his death.

**rar', Geraldine**, b. Melrose,
ass., Feb. 28, 1882; soprano; at 12,
pil of J. H. Long, Boston; later of
abadello and Lilli Lehmann; 1901,
but Berlin Royal Opera; with great
ccess has sung there since, and in
e chief European capitals; regularly
gaged also at the Op. Com., Paris,
d since 1906, at the Met. Op.
ouse in N. Y., creating the rôle
the Goosegirl in Humperdinck's
*Königskinder*."

well, **Arthur**, correct birth date
St. Paul, Minn., April 23, 1872. He
nducted the important Wa-Wan
ess publications till 1912, bringing
light much otherwise hidden
nerican genius. He has done
luable work in New York and
ewhere in developing municipal
usic, free concerts in parks, piers,
:. His comps. include for orch.
*awn*," "*The Domain of Hurakan*,"
*Navajo War-Dance*" (all in Indian
emes). "*Cornell*" overture, and
*ove Song*"; for piano many pieces
Indian theme and numerous fine
ags.

**Fauré, Gabriel U.**, add that 1905
he became Director of the Paris
Cons.; c. music to "*Prométhée*"
(Béziers, 1900), "*Julius Cæsar*"
(1905), "*Pelléas et Mélisande*," 1898;
arranged as an orch. suite, 1901; also
much chamber music, and religious
choruses, piano pieces and many
highly important songs.

**Felix** (fā-lĕks), **Dr. Hugo**, b. Vienna,
Nov. 19, 1866; c. operettas "*Husaren-
blut*," Vienna, 1894; "*Rhodope*,"
Berlin, 1900; "*Mme. Sherry*" (Berlin,
1902, since with great success in
America, 1910).

**Fel'ton, Rev. Wm.**, Cambridge, 1713
— Dec. 6, 1769; vicar, harpsichordist and comp.

**Fenell'** (or **Ffinell**), d. Dublin,
Sept. 20, 1709; Irish composer; organist at St. Patrick's Cathedral, 1689–
1694, and buried there.

**Ferling** (fĕr'-lĭnk), (1) **Franz Wm.**
Halberstadt, Sept. 20, 1796 — Braunschweig, Dec. 18, 1874; oboist; his sons
(2) **Gustav**, b. Braunschweig, July
8, 1835; oboist at Stuttgart, and
teacher at the Cons.; (3) **Robert**,
Braunschweig, July 4, 1843 — St.
Petersburg, Mar. 24, 1881; royal
chamber musician at St. Petersburg.

**Ferra'ri, Gabrielle**, b. Paris; pupil
of Ketten, Duprato, later of Gounod
and Leborne; at 12 début as pianist, Naples; c. opera "*Le Colzar*,"
given at Monte Carlo in one act, enlarged to two (Paris Opéra, 1912);
also orch. suites and many popular
songs.

**Fet'terode, L. Adrian van**, b.
Amsterdam, July 25, 1858; pupil of
Coenen and Heinze; teacher at
Amsterdam; c. piano suite, fantasie
for 2 pianos, etc.

**Fiebach** (fē'-bäkh), **Otto** b. Ohlau,
Silesia, Feb. 9, 1851; director of an
institution at Königsberg; royal conductor; c. operas, and an oratorio;
author of "*Die Physiologie der
Tonkunst*" (1891).

**Fiedler, Max**; in 1903, became director of the Hamburg Cons.; 1904 cond. the Philharmonic concerts; 1908–12, cond. Boston Symphony Orchestra with great success during the leave of absence of Karl Muck (q. v.), c. 'cello sonata (Boston, 1909), chamber music, etc.

**Fil'by, Wm. Chas.,** b. London, 1836; organist; studied in Paris; since 1884 organist at St. Paul's; c. masses, etc.

**Fil'ke, Max,** b. Staubendorf-Leobschütz, Silesia, Oct. 5, 1855; organist and singing teacher; pupil of Brosig and Leipzig Cons.; since 1891, cathedral cond. at Breslau, teacher at the Priest's Seminary, and since 1893 at the Royal Inst. for Church music; 1899, Royal Music director; c. works of great importance in modern Catholic music, several masses with orch.; *Salve Regina*, op. 102; choruses, etc.

**Fil'lunger, Marie,** b. Vienna, Jan. 27, 1850; soprano; pupil at Vienna Cons. and of Marchesi, and after 1874 at the Berlin Hochschule; sang in oratorio and concert with great success in Europe, and from 1889 in London, where she afterward settled; toured Australia, 1891; South Africa, 1895; from 1904 teacher at R. C. M., Manchester.

**Filtz (Fieltz, Fils, Filsl or Filz), Anton,** b. probably in Bohemia, ca. 1725; d. 1760 at Mannheim, where he was court 'cellist; c. many important symphonies, 2 masses, etc.

**Finch, Edward,** 1664—Feb. 14, 1738; composer of church music; son of Earl of Nottingham, and prebendary of York.

**Fioc'co,** (1) **Domenico,** early composer of a mass; dates unknown. (2) **Pietro, Antonio,** d. Brussels, Nov. 3, 1704; composer of masses, etc., came from Venice; court musician at Brussels, 1696; from 1706 cond.; his two sons (3) **Jean Josef,** succeeded Pietro as cond., in 1714, and was succeeded by his brother **Gioseffo Hector,** prominent as harpsichordist and composer; died after 1737.

**Fiore** (fĭ-ō'-rĕ) **Stefano Andr** Milan, 1675 — Turin, 1739; comp of operas.

**Fisch'er, Johann Kaspar Fer nand,** ca. 1650 — ca. 1738; imp tant composer for organ and clav cond. to Markgraf Ludwig in hemia, 1688; his works were publis 1695 — 1715; his "*Ariadne Mus Neo-Organoedum per XX Fugas, et* 1702, includes preludes and fugue all modern keys except five, rese bling and preceding Bach's "*W tempered Clavichord,*" which was begun till after 1723, and not p lished till 1810.

**Fitelberg** (fē'-tĕl-bĕrkh), **Geo** b. Dünaburg, Oct. 18, 1879; imp tant Polish composer; pupil War Cons., taking Paderewski prize v a violin sonata, 1896, and 1901 Zamoyski prize with a piano t concertmaster, and 1908 condu Warsaw Philharmonic; 1912, enga for 6 years to cond. Vienna Ro Opera; c. 2 symphonies, including Minor (1905); symph. poems "*Song of Falken*" (1906), and "*Pro ilas and Leodamia,*" etc.

**Flecha** (flĕ'-chä), **Juan,** m teacher; Catalonia, 1483–1553; C melite monk and teacher; his neph (2) **Fray Matheo,** 1520 — F 20, 1604, was an abbot and co to Charles V at Prague; both w composers.

**Flesch, Karl,** b. Moson, Hunga Oct. 9, 1873; violinist; pupil of Gr at Vienna, and Marsick at Paris Co com. 1897–1902 prof. at Buchar Cons.; and chamber musician to Roumanian Queen; 1903–8, teache Amsterdam Cons.; since at Berlin

**Flin'tof, Rev. Luke,** Worces (?) — London, Nov. 3, 1727; i Gentleman of the Chapel Roy buried in Westminster Abbey; s to have invented the double chan which his is the first known examp

**Flo'derer, Wilhelm,** b. Brünn, N 10, 1843; composer of operas.

n'dor, Theodor Joh. Von., d.
·rlin, June 24, 1908; Roumanian
·mposer of operas.

·rence, Evangeline, b. Cam-
idge, Mass., Dec. 12, 1873; stage
.me of Miss Houghton, soprano of
·markable compass, g–c''''; married
·ex. Crerar, 1894.

·idia, Pietro, add that his real
.me is Baron Napolino di San
·esto. He came to America in 1904,
.s for a year piano-prof. at Cin-
·nati Cons., and was commissioned
· write the opera "Paoletta," for the
·position of 1910; the opera had
·eat success. His symphony, con-
·lered the representative symphony
· Italy, has been much played by
·e Cincinnati Symph. Orch., 1910,
·.; c. also opera "The Scarlet Letter,"
·splendid "Madrigal" for barytone
·d orch., songs, etc.; lives in New
·rk; his opera "Maruzza" has had
·00 performances in Italy.

·v'er, Eliza, Harlow, Essex, April
·, 1803 — Dec. 12, 1846; composer
· hymns.

·iani (or Fogliano or Folia=
·ıs), (2) Giacomo, Modena,
·73 — April 4, 1548; brother of
·ıdovici F., organist and comp.

·lström (föl'-strām), Alma, b.
·lsingfors, Jan. 2, 1861; concert
·prano, pupil of Mme. Nissen-
·loman in St. Petersburg.

·te, Arthur, add that he gave
· the organ of the First Unitarian
·urch in 1910 after 32 years; still
·ıching piano in Boston; lectured
·ring summer of 1911 at University
· California. Later comps. include
·ch. suite in D minor (played in
·ston, London, N. Y., etc.) Suite
· strings (do.); 4 character pieces
· orch. (Thomas Orch., Boston
·mph, 1912, etc.) "Bedouin Song,"
·ıle chorus sung very widely; organ
·'te in D (played by Guilmant on
·nerican tour); two piano suites, 5
·ems from Omar Khayyám for
·tho, songs, etc.

Fornia, Rita (P. Newman), b.
San Francisco, July 17, 1879; soprano;
pupil of Jean de Reszké and Frau
Kempner; début, 1901, Hamburg
Stadttheater; sings at Covent Gar-
den and Met. Op., N. Y.

Fos'ter, Muriel, b. Sunderland, Nov.
22, 1877; contralto of remarkable
range, g to b'' flat; pupil of Anna Williams at the R. A. M., winning a
scholarship, 1897; début 1896 in
oratorio; sang with her sister Hilda
in 1899; and at frequent festivals
since; has sung also in Germany,
Russia and America.

Fowles, Margaret F., Ryde, Isle
of Wight, 1846 — Detroit, Michigan,
August 6, 1907; pianist; organist;
cond.

Fragerolle (frä-zhĕ-rŭl), Georges
Auguste, b. Paris, March 11, 1855;
pupil of Guiraud; c. patriotic songs,
operettas, pantomimes, etc.

Franchetti, Alberto, his opera
"Germania" (prod. Milan, 1902),
has been performed widely at Covent
Garden 1907 and 1911 at the Metropolitan Opera House, N. Y.

Frank'o, (1) Sam, b. New Orleans,
Jan. 20, 1857; violinist, pianist,
and cond.; pupil of Wilhelmj, Joachim
and Vieuxtemps; toured with Patti;
cond. concerts of ancient music in
New York, 1912, Berlin; his brother,
(2) Nahan, b. New Orleans, July
23, 1861; violinist and cond.; at 8,
toured the world with Patti; later
studied with Rappoldi, De Ahna,
Wilhelmj, and Joachim; member of
Met. Op. orchestra, N. Y.; from 1883
concertmaster; 1905–7 conductor;
since has cond. his own orchestra.

Fraschini (fräs-kē'-nē), Gaetano,
Pavia, 1815 — Naples, May 24, 1887;
tenor in Italy and England.

Fremstad (frĕm'-shtät), Olive (Anna Olivia), b. Stockholm; dramatic soprano; at 9, a pianist;
brought to America by her parents,
at 12; 1890, soloist at St. Patrick's
Cathedral, N. Y.; 1893–94, pupıȷ oȷ

Lilli Lehmann at Berlin; 1895, début;
1896 sang at Bayreuth; 1897–1900
Vienna Royal Opera; later at Munich,
Covent Garden and since 1903 at
Met. Op. House, N. Y.; officer of the
French Academy, and 1907 of Public
Instruction.

**Freudman, Ignatz,** vide FRIEDMAN.

**Friderici (or Friederich) Daniel,**
Eisleben (?) before 1600— after 1654;
cantor at Rostock ; c. madrigals, etc.

**Fried** (frēt), **Oskar,** b. Berlin, Aug.
10, 1871; pupil of Humperdinck; since
1904 director Stern Gesangverein and
the Gesellschaft der Musikfreunde;
c. choral works with orch., double
fugue for strings; a work for 13 wind
instruments and 2 harps, etc.

**Friedenthal** (frē'-děn-täl), **Albert,**
b. Bromberg, Sept. 25, 1862; pianist; pupil of Fr. and W. Stein-
brunn, and of Kullak; has toured the
world.

**Friedheim, Arthur,** add that he
spent many years in America as
teacher and pianist; later prof. at
R. C. M., Manchester, England, till
1904; c. opera *"Die Tänzerin"*
(Cologne, 1905); toured America,
1911–1912.

**Friedman,** (frēt'-män), **Ignaz,** b.
Podgorze, near Cracow, Feb. 14, 1882,
pianist; pupil of his father and of
Leschetizki; toured Europe with success; c. piano pieces and songs.

**Friedländer** (frēt'-lěn-děr), **Thekla,**
soprano; pupil of Hiller and
Schneider; début, Leipzig, Dec. 11,
1873; popular in England, 1875–1886.

**Frischen,** (frĭsh'-ĕn), **Josef,** b.
Garzweiler, July 6, 1863; singing
teacher; pupil Cologne Cons.; 1888,
city musical director at Lucerne;
1892, dir. Musikakademie, Hanover;
teacher and Royal Director at
Braunschweig; c. choral works, etc.

**Fris'kin, James,** b. Glasgow, Mar.
3, 1886; pianist; pupil of London R.
C. M., winning scholarship in 1900
and composition scholarship 1905; c.

successful piano quintet in C mi
(1907), 'cello sonata, etc.

**Fritz (or Friz), Gaspard, Gen**
1716–1782; violinist; c. 6 symphon
etc.

**Fuenllana** ( fwĕn-lĭ-än'-nä ), **M**
**uel de,** flourished 1554 in Sp
lute-virtuoso and court compo
blind from birth.

**Fugere** (fü-zhăr), **Lucien,** b. Pa
March 3, 1848; barytone; pupil
Raguenau; début, 1870.

## G

**Gabriel** (gä'-brĭ-ĕl), **Richard,**
Zackenzin, Pomerania, Sept. 3, 18
organist; pupil Royal Inst. for chu
music and Humperdinck's Mas
school; since 1902 org. at Sagan
spring overture, choral work w
orch., *"Nach Walhall,"* etc.

**Gabrilowitsch, Ossip,** add t
in 1912 he cond. the Konzertve
orch., Munich.

**Gailhard** (gī'-yăr), **Pierre,** b. T
louse, Aug. 1, 1848; bass; p
Paris Cons.; début 1867, Op. C
Paris; later at the Opéra, of which
was director 1899–1907.

**Gal'eotti,** (1) **Stefano** (or **Sal**
**tore**), c. 'cello sonatas pub. in L
don, Paris and Amsterdam, 17
–60; (2) **Cesare,** b. Pietrasa
June 5, 1872; c. opera *"Anto*
(La Scala, Milan, 1900).

**Gal'kin, Nikolai Vladimirovi**
St. Petersburg, Dec. 18, 1856
May 21, 1906; violinist and c
poser for violin; pupil of Kan
sky, Auer, Joachim, Sauret
Wieniawski; toured Europe and a
1877 was cond. in St. Petersburg
from 1880 teacher at the Cons.; f
1892, prof.

**Gall, Jan,** b. Warsaw, Aug. 18, 18
pupil of Krenn and Rheinbe
1886, teacher of song at Cracow C
then pupil of Mme. Lamperti, la
director of the Lemberg *"Ec*
society; composer of some 400 v
numbers.

let'ti = Gianoli (jä-nō'-lē), Isa=
ella, Bologna, Nov. 11, 1835 —
ilan, Aug. 31, 1901; operatic so-
ano; later contralto.

nsbacher (gĕns-bäkh-ĕr), Josef,
29 — Vienna, June 5, 1911; famous
aging teacher;

iz (gänts), Rudolph, b. Zürich,
77; début at 10 as 'cellist, at
as pianist; then pupil of his
cle, Eschmann-Dumur, and later of
soni; début as pianist and composer
rlin, 1899; 1901–5 succeeded
iedheim in Chicago; has toured
dely; c. "Lake" cycle of songs
06), etc.

'diner, H. Balfour, b. Lon-
n, Nov. 7, 1877; pupil of Knorr at
ankfort; c. symph. (Queens Hall
04 and 1908); "Fantasy" (1908);
erture, chamber music, etc.

es, Bernard, ca. 1685 —North
ton, Nov. 15, 1773; English singer
d comp.

ti=Casazza (gät'-tĭ kä-sät'-sä),
iulio, b. Ferrara, Feb. 5, 1869; at
st a naval engineer; 1894–8 dir.
unicipal Theatre at Ferrara; 1898–
09, dir. La Scala, Milan, making it
home of modern opera; 1909 co-
rector with A. Dippel of the Metrolitan Opera House, N. Y.; since
10 in full charge; he has prod. three
tive American operas, and given
e first prods. anywhere of Humper-
nck's "Königskinder," and Puccini's
Girl of the Golden West."

ty, Nicholas Comyn, b. Brad-
ld, Sept. 13, 1874; composer; critic,
ganist and comp., pupil R. C. M.,
here he produced orch.-variations
a "Old King Cole"; from 1907
itic on "Pall Mall Gazette"; assist-
t at Covent Garden; c. 1-act operas
Greysteel" (Sheffield, 1906), and
Duke or Devil " (Manchester, 1909);
ilton's "Ode on Time," for chorus
orch., (Sheffield Festival, 1905).

ron'ski, Woitech, b. Seimony
ar Wilna, June 27, 1868; pupil War-
w Mus. Inst.; toured Russia, taught

in Orel and Warsaw; c. symph.; 2
operas and a string quartet, (Paderewski prize, Leipzig, 1898).

Gayarré (gĕ-yär-rā'), Julian, Roncal
(?), Jan. 9, 1844 — Madrid, Jan. 2,
1890; operatic tenor, son of a blacksmith.

Gebhard (gĕp'-härt), Heinrich,
b. Sobernheim, near Bingen, July 25,
1878; pianist; taken to America at
10; pupil of Clayton Johns, début,
1896, Boston; playing his violin and
piano sonata, then studied with
Leschetizky and Heuberger; 1899
reappeared Boston with symph. orch.
1900–4, pianist of Longy Club; c.
quartet, piano pieces, etc.

Gehrmann (gär'-män), Hermann,
b. Wernigerode, Dec. 22, 1861; historian and theorist; pupil Stern Cons.,
Berlin; 1908, Royal Prof.; c. string-
quartet and songs.

Gep'pert, Liberatus, b. Jauering
(Austrian Silesia) Feb. 15, 1815 —
Feb. 7, 1881; c. 40 masses, 10 re-
quiems, etc.

Ger'hardt, Paul, b. Leipzig, Nov.
10, 1867; organ-virtuoso; pupil at the
Cons.; since 1898 org. at Zwickau;
c. organ works, etc.

Gerhäuser (gĕr'-hī-zĕr), tenor; début Munich; sang there and at
Carlsruhe; 1902, Met. Op., N. Y.;
gave up singing, became stage-direc-
tor, Stuttgart Royal Op.

Giacobbi (jäk-kŏb'-bē), Girolamo,
Bologna, ca. 1575 — Nov. 30, 1630;
church cond. and one of the first composers of opera; "Andromeda," (1610)
also church music.

Giarda (jär'-dä), Luigi Stefano,
b. Cassolnovo, Pavia, March 19, 1868;
'cellist; pupil Milan Cons.; teacher at
Padua, 1893–7; after, at Royal Cons.,
Naples; c. opera "Rejetto" (Naples,
1898), 'cello-music and method.

Gib'son, George Alfred, b. Nottingham, Oct. 27, 1849; violinist;
pupil of his father and of Henry
Farmer; soloist at 12; from 1871 at
Covent Garden; 1893, leader of the

Queen's private band; prof. at R. A. M., and Guildhall.

**Gigault** (zhē-gō), **Nicolas,** b. Brie, ca. 1645; organist at Paris and composer.

**Gilbert** (1) **Alfred,** Salisbury. Oct. 21, 1828 — London, Feb. 6, 1902; organist and composer; his brother, ▸(2) **Ernest Thos. Bennett,** Salisbury, Oct. 22, 1833 — London, May 11, 1885; organist, teacher and composer. (3) **Walter Bond,** b. Exeter, April 21, 1829; organist; pupil of Wesley and Bishop; 1886, Mus. Doc. Oxford; 1889, came to New York; c. oratorios, etc. (4) **Henry Frank= lin Belknap,** b. Somerville, Mass., Sept. 26, 1868; violin pupil of Mollenhauer; studied harmony with G. H. Howard and for 3 years with MacDowell; 1892–1901 in business, then took up con. position. His work is full of originality, and character; c. Comedy Overture on negro themes (Boston Symph., 1911); *American= esque, Two Episodes, I, Legend; II, Negro Episode,* Boston (1896, and often elsewhere); *"Salammbo's Invocation to Tanith"* for soprano and orch. (1906); *"American Dances in Rag-Time"* for orch.; fantastic symph. poem, *"The Dance in Place Congo"*; for piano *"Indian Scenes," "Negro Episode"*, etc., many beautiful songs, including the well-known *"Pirate Song."*

**Gille** (gǐl'-lě), **Karl,** b. Eldagsen, Hanover, Sept. 30, 1861; pupil of J. Fischer, Bott and Metadorf; theatre-cond. in various cities; 1891–7 court cond., Schwerin; 1897 succeeded Mahler at Hamburg Stadttheater; 1906, first cond. Vienna Volksoper, and during the summer of 1908–9, at the Gura-Opera, Berlin.

**Gil'man, Lawrence,** b. Flushing, N. Y. July 5, 1878; critic for *"Harper's Weekly"*; biographer of MacDowell (1905), author of numerous books showing an enthusiasm for modernity which appears also in his own compo-sitions, such as the musical ba ground to Yeats' poem *"The Curle*

**Gil'son, Paul,** correct birth d Brussels, June 15, 1865; since 1 teacher of harmony Antwerp Co and critic of the *"Soir"*; has beco one of the most important Belg composers, with his operas, *"C de mer,"* (based on Victor Hu, novel, Brussels, 1902; Antwerp, 1( and *"Prinses Zonnenschijn,"* (; twerp, 1903); ballet, *"La Captiv* Brussels, 1902; symph. *"La Me* 1892; orch. fantasy on Canadian fe songs, symph. poems, etc.

**Ginera** (hē-nā'-rä), **Salvado** Valencia, Jan. 17, 1832 — Nov. 1911; pupil of Gascons; dir. Valen Cons.; c. a symph. *"The Four S sons,"* operas, etc.

**Giordano, Umberto,** prod. op *"Fédora"* (Milan, 1898), *Sibe.* (do, 1903, Leipzig, 1907), and *M cella,* (Milan, 1907).

**Giorgetti** (jôr-jĕt-tě), **Ferdinan** Florence, 1796–1867; violinist, teac and comp.

**Glaz(o)unow, Alex. Constan novich,** add that from 1899 was prof. of instrumentation, Petersburg Cons.; from 1909 director, also dir. the Imperial M cal Society. He has c. 7 symp 4 overtures, a symph. poem, *"Ste Rasin,"* a symphonic fanta *"Through Night to Light,"* and a gr number of other orch. works, cham music in large quantity and h quality, cantatas, the *"Memoria* (Leeds, Fest., 1901), ballets, vic concerto (1904), etc.

**Glickh** (glĭkh), **Rudolf,** b. Vien Feb. 28, 1864; 'cellist; c. ope etc.

**Glière** (glē-är), **Reinhold Mori ovich,** composer; b. Kiev, L 30, 1874 (O. S.), or Jan. 11, 18 (N. S.); pupil of Moscow Cons., w ning gold medal; c. 2 popular sy phonies, chamber music, etc. latest symphony *"Ilia Mourom* as prod. at Moscow, April 1912, with great success.

**over, J. Wm.,** Dublin, June 19, 1815 — Jan. 15, 1900; violinist and choir-master at the Cathedral from 1860; opera *"The Deserted Village"* (London, 1880), etc.

**uck** (glook), **A l m a** (née **Reba Pierson**), b. Bucharest, Rouma-ia, May 11, 1866; taken to New York at 6; pupil of Bouzzi-Peccia, ébut New Theatre, N. Y., 1909, the same year at the Met. Op.; has sung here since, and in concert.

**uth** (gloot), **V i c t o r,** b. Pilsen, May 6, 1852; pupil Royal Akademie er Tonkunst, Munich; c. operas *"Zlatorog"* and *"Horand und Hilde."*

**dowsky, Leopold,** add that he has achieved a place as one of the world's most brilliant pianists and teachers; succeeded Busoni in 1910, as head of the Master-School of the Vienna Imperial Academy; 1904, he married Frieda Saxe; gives frequent recitals in Europe; c. symphonic Dance-pictures from Strauss *"Fled-rmaus";* sonata E minor, for piano; left-hand transcriptions of Chopin Études, 50 études on Chopin's Études, and many brilliant piano works.

**hler** (gä'-lĕr), **Karl Georg,** b. Zwickau, June 29, 1874; author and comp.; pupil of Vollhardt and Leip-zig Cons.; 1896, Ph.D.; from 1898 director of the Riedelverein, also from 1903 court cond. at Altenburg; 1907–9 at Carlsruhe; c. 2 symphs.; orch. suite *"Indian Songs."*

**miz** (gō'-mĕth) **Jose Melchior,** Valencia, Jan. 6, 1791 — Paris, July 26, 1836; military bandmaster and singing teacher at Paris; c. operas and patriotic songs.

**mólka** (gō-mool'-kä), **Nikolaus,** Cracow, (?) 1539 — Jazlowiec, March 5, 1609. Polish composer and court musician;

**om'pertz, Richard,** b. Cologne, April 27, 1859; violinist; pupil at the Cons., and of Joachim; toured, then invited to teach at Cambridge Uni-versity; from 1883, teacher at R. C. M., 1895, prof.; from 1899 at Dres-den; c. violin sonatas, etc.

**Good'son, Katharine,** b. Watford, England, June 18, 1872; pianist; at 12 pupil at the R. A. M., till 1892, then four years with Leschet-izky — début, 1896, London Pop. Concerts; has toured widely; 1903, married Arthur Hinton (q.v.).

**Goossens** (gōs'-sĕns), **Eugene,** Bel-gium, 1845(?)—, Liverpool, Dec. 31, 1906; choirmaster; cond.; studied at Bruges; prize winner Brussels Cons.; prof. music, Liverpool.

**Gorczycki** (gŏr-chĕt'-skĭ), **Gregor Gabriel,** before 1650—Cracow, 1734; mus. dir. at the Cathedral; c. church music.

**Görner** (gĕr'-nĕr), (1) **Jno. Gott-lieb,** Penig, 1697 — Leipzig, 1778; organist; his brother, (2) **J. N. Val-entin,** b. Penig, 1702, cond. at Hamburg Cathedral; c. songs.

**Gott'hard,** (1) **J n . P e t e r,** b. Drahanovitz, Moravia, Jan. 19, 1839; cond. at Vienna; c. operas; with his brother (2) **Franz Pázdirek,** pub-lished a musical hand book.

**Gourron** vide ALVAREZ(2).

**Grabov'sky** (or **Graboffsky**), (1) **Countess Clementine,** Posen, 1771 — Paris, 1831; anist; pianist and comp. (2) **Stanislaus,** d. Vienna, 1852; piano-prof. and c. popular polonaises, etc. (3) **Adolph,** b. Hamburg, Oct. 14, 1867, violinist and teacher at Sondershausen Cons.

**Graf** (gräf), (1) **Fr. H a r t m a n,** Rudolfstadt, 1727 — Augsburg, 1795; flutist and comp.

**Grahl** (gräl), **Heinrich,** b. Stralsund, Nov. 30, 1860; concert tenor in Ber-lin; pupil of Frl. Schmidt.

**Grainger** (grān'-jĕr), **P e r c y,** b. Brighton, Australia, July 8, 1882; pianist; pupil of Louis Pabst; at 11 gave recitals and earned money for European study with Kwast and Busoni, settling in London, 1900, playing at important concerts; chosen by Grieg to introduce his piano concerto; toured Australia and South Africa; made piano arrangements of folk-songs, etc.

**Granados y Campina** (grä-nä'-dhōs e käm-pē'-nä), **Enrique**, b. Lerida, July 27, 1867; pianist; c. operas and songs.

**Grandjean** (grän-zhän), **Axel**, b. Copenhagen, March 9, 1847; pupil of the Cons. there; 1869, début in opera, retired after one season; c. operas, etc.

**Grau** (grow), **Maurice**, Brunn, Austria, 1848—Paris, March 13, 1907; impresario of Met. Op. House, N. Y.

**Gray, Alan**, b. York, Dec. 23, 1855; organist; studied law, then music under Dr. E. G. Monk; 1883–92, musical dir. Wellington College; then org. Trinity College, Cambridge, and cond. of the University Musical Society; c. cantatas "*Arethusa*" (Leeds Festival, 1892), and "*A Song of Redemption*" (do., 1898), etc.

**Greatheed, Rev. Samuel Stephenson**, b. Weston-super-Mare, Feb. 22, 1813; pupil of W. C. Ball; 1838 ordained; then spent some months studying music with Schwarz at Berlin; 1844 took up counterpoint; c. oratorio "*Enoch's Prophecy*," (1856) organ fugue in the Dorianmode, etc.

**Grechaninoff** (grä-chä'-nē-nôf), **Alex. Tikhonovich**, b. Moscow, Oct. 26, 1864; composer; pupil of Safonoff at the Cons.; later at St. Petersburg Cons., under Rachmaninoff; c. prize string quartet (1894); symph.; succ. opera "*Dobringa Nikitich*" (Moscow, 1903); incidental music to Tolstoi's "*Feodor*," and "*Ivan*," and to Ostroski's "*Snow-Maiden*" songs, etc.

**Greenwood, John**, d. Preston, April 1, 1909; organist, pianist, composer, member of the firm of John G. & Son, Preston.

**Greith** (grīt), **Karl**, Aarau, Feb. 21, 1828 — Munich, Nov. 17, 1887; organ. and comp. of church music.

**Gretschaninow**, vide GRECHA NOFF.

**Griesbacher** (grēs'-bäkh-ĕr), **Pet** b. Egglham, March 25, 1864; pi and teacher at Regensburg; c. masses, and other church mu also cantatas, etc.

**Griffith, Frederick,** b. Swan Nov. 12, 1867; at 14 won prize a Welsh national Eisteddfod; pupil a A. M.; 1889–91 with Svendsen, la with Jaffanel, Paris; toured wide flutist at Covent Garden, and p at R. A. M.

**Grigny** (grēn'-yē), **Nicolas** Reims, 1671–1703; organist comp.

**Grill'parzer, Fz.**, Vienna, 15, 1791 — Jan. 21, 1871; friend Beethoven and Schubert. Comp.

**Grisart, J. B.**, b. 1848; d. Compiè France, Mar. 1904.

**Gris'wold, Gertrude**, d. Lond July 14, 1912. American sopra pupil of Agramonte, N. Y., and Paris Cons., where she was the f American to win the first gra opera prize; début as "Opheli Paris Opéra, sang there a year, la in oratorio and concert, and w Patti at the Met. Op. N. Y. c.; son

**Grodz'ki, Boleslas**, b. St. Pete burg, Oct. 25, 1865; studied law first, then pupil of Sokolov; c. vio and piano works and songs.

**Grönland** (grün'-land), **Peterse** Schleswig, 1760 — Altona, 1834; ganist and comp.

**Grunewald** (groo'-nĕ-vält), (1) **Got fried**, d. Dannstadt, ca. 1739; sin and comp. (2) **Gottfried**, b. Qu stadt, near Eisleben, 1859; c. opera

**Grüters** (grē'-tĕrs), (1) **Augu** d. Urdingen, Dec. 7, 1841; Mus. I rector; pupil of his father, of Colog Cons., and of Ambroise Thoma 1878, Royal director at Frankfo on-Main; 1908, retired. His broth (2) **Hugo**, b. Ürdingen, Oct. 8, 18 pupil Cologne Cons.; conductor various cities.

**ido d'Arezzo,** born near Paris nd later joining the monastery; later nvestigations identify him with a Benedictine monk in the Monastery f St. Maur des Fosses; his probable irth date would be ca. 990. He thus becomes a Frenchman who went to taly, not an Italian.

**illemain** (gē'-yŭ-măn), **Gab= iel,** Paris, Nov. 15, 1705 — (sui- ide) Oct. 1, 1770; c. violin pieces.

**l'bins, Max,** b. Kammetschen, uly 18, 1862; organist and comp. of horal works.

**lbranson, Ellen,** correct birth late, Stockholm, March 3, 1863.

**illi** (gool'-lē), **Luigi,** b. Scilla, une 17, 1859; pianist; pupil Royal College of Music, Naples, under Cesi; eacher at Rome, where he founded he Gulli Quintet Society, which has oured with much success.

**inke** (goonk'-ĕ), **Joseph,** Joseph- tadt, Bohemia, 1801 — St. Peters- burg, Dec. 17, 1883; violinist, theorist .nd organist; c. oratorio, mass, etc.

**itheil=Schoder** (goot'-hīl-shō'- lĕr), **Marie,** b. Weimar, Feb. 10, .874; mezzo-soprano; pupil of Vir- finia Gungl, and Weimar Music School; 1891-1900 at Weimar court pera; frequently at Vienna court pera; her husband Gustav Gutheil s conductor at Vienna Volksoper.

**izman,** (gooth'-măn), **Juan Bau= tista,** b. Alday, Valencia, Jan. 19, .846; pupil of Úbeda; organist; joined he Benedictine order; c. songs, etc.

### H

**aack** (häk), **Karl,** Potsdam, Feb. :8, 1751 — Sept. 28, 1819; violinist .nd teacher; court cond. to Fr. Wilhelm II at Potsdam; c. violin pieces.

**ias** (häs), **Alma Holländer,** b. Ratibor, Silesia, Jan. 31, 1847; pianist; pupil of Wandelt and Kul- ak; 1872, m. Ernest Haas, prof. of Sanskrit (d. 1882); from 1886 teacher at King's College.

**Hack'l, N. Lajos** b. Siegraben, June 11, 1868; pupil of Kössler; teach- er at Pest Cons.; c. songs, etc.

**Had'dock,** (1) **Thomas,** Leeds, 1812 — Liverpool, Sept. 22, 1893; 'cellist; his brother (2) **George,** Killingsbeck, near Leeds, July 24, 1824—Leeds, Sept. 12, 1907; violinist, author of method; founded Leeds College of Music with his sons (3) **Edgar A.,** b. Leeds, Nov. 23, 1859; violinist; (4) **George Percy,** b. Leeds, Oct. 10, 1860; pianist, organist, 'cellist and comp.

**Hadley, Henry K.,** add that he spent some years abroad, as cond. in various cities, including the Mayence Opera, where his opera "*Safié*" was prod. in 1909. In that year he be- came cond. of Seattle symph. orch.; 1911, San Francisco orch.; add to his comps. two symphs. His 2nd symph. took two prizes simultaneously in 1901, the Paderewski and the New England Cons. His fourth symph. "*North, East, South and West*" he cond. himself with the London Philh. Boston Symph., and other orch.; c. overtures "*Hector and Andro- mache,*" (Boston, 1901); "*In Bohemia*" (1903), "*Herod,*" symph. fantasie "*Salome*" (Boston Symph., 1907, Monte Carlo, 1907; Warsaw, 1908, Cassel, 1908); lyric drama "*Merlin and Vivien,*" piano quintet, (1907), etc. poetic rhapsody, "*The Culprit Fay*" (N. Y., 1912); a music drama, "*The Atonement of Pan,*" (San Fran- cisco, 1912), etc.

**Haesche,** vide HÄSCHE.

**Hagel** (hä'-gĕl), **Karl',** b. Voigts- tedt, Thuringia, Dec. 12, 1847; con- ductor; 1874-77 military cond. at Munich; 1878-1905, municipal cond. and director of the Music School at Bamberg, then pensioned; c. 4 symph., etc. His son and pupil (2) **Richard,** b. Erfurt, July 7, 1872; cond. and teacher in various cities; 1902 cond. at Leipzig Stadt- theater.

**Hägg** (hăg), (1) **Jacob Adolf,**
b. Gotland, Sweden, 1850; Swedish
composer; pupil of Van Booms, Gade,
and Kiel; c. Norse symphony, and
"*Norse Songs Without Words*" suites
in ancient style; sonatas, etc. (2)
**Gustaf,** b. 1868; studied abroad
with municipal stipend; later organ-
prof. at Stockholm Cons.; organist
and comp. of orch. and organ works.

**Hahn,** (1) **Reynaldo,** add that his
opera "*La Carmélite*" was prod. at
the Opéra Comique, Paris, 1902;
incidental music to C. Mendés'
"*Scarron*," Racine's "*Esther*," and
V. Hugo's "*Angelo*," (all in 1905);
2–act ballet "*La fête chez Thérèse,*"
(Opéra, 1910). (2) **William,** Bavaria 1837 — Philadelphia, 1903;
teacher.

**Hähnel** (hä'-něl), **Amalie,** Gross-
hübel, Bohemia, 1807 — May 2,
1849; favourite contralto at Berlin
Royal Opera.

**Hall, Marie** (Mary Paulina), b.
Newcastle-on-Tyne, April 8, 1884;
violinist; as a child played in Bristol
streets; pupil of her father and Hilde-
garde Werner; later of J. Kruse; at
15 won an exhibition at the R. A. M.;
from 1901, pupil of Sevčik; toured
widely.

**Hallwachs** (häl'-väkhs), **Karl,** b.
Darmstadt, Sept. 15, 1870; Mus. Director; pupil at Royal Music-School;
Munich; 1895 – 7 directed Academy Singing Society; 1899 – 1900
cond. at Aachen Stadttheater; 1900–
02 at Saarbrüchen; after 1902 in
Kassel as director of Oratorio Society
and Liedertafel; c. opera" *Nainaka*,"
songs, etc.

**Halm, August,** obscure composer
of important symphony in D minor
for string orch.; performed Stuttgart, 1907; Boston Symph., 1910;
studied theology at Tübingen, then
music; a teacher at Hanbinda, later
at Wickersdorf, Thuringia; c. comedy
overture; piano-concerto in style of
Bach, chamber music, etc.

**Hambourg, Mark,** correct bir
date is May 31, 1879. He has co
tinued to tour and has maintained
high position as a virtuoso.

**Ham'ilton, Sir Edward Walte**
d. Brighton, Sept. 2, 1908 ; co
poser ; Bachelor of Music, C
ford, 1867.

**Ham'merich, Mark,** b. Cope
hagen, Nov. 25, 1848; 'cellist; pupil
Rüdinger and Neruda; 1896 prof.
musical science Copenhagen U
versity; brother of Asger Hamer
(q. v.).

**Ham'merstein, Oscar,** b. Berl
1847; composer and impresario; ca
to America at 16; made a fortune
the invention of a cigar-maki
machine; wrote a comic opera in
hours on a wager, and produced it
his own theatre; built five theatres
N. Y. and the Manhattan Ope
House; where he gave opposition
the Metropolitan, 1906–8; built al
an opera house in Philadelphia; so
out his interests to the Metropolit
Co., and built opera house in Londo
opened, 1912.

**Hanff, J. Nicolaus,** Wechma
1630 — Schleswig, 1706; cathedr
organist at Schleswig and importa
predecessor of Bach in choral-writir

**Han'sel, Peter,** Leipa, Nov. 29, 17
— Vienna, Sept. 18, 1881; violin
and comp.

**Harcourt** (där-koor), **Eugene c**
b. Paris, ca. 1855; composer; pu
Paris Cons., and of Schulze a
Bargiel, in Berlin; 1890 gave co
certs in his own Salle Harcourt; 19
gave oratorios at St. Eustache;
mass (Brussels, 1876); opera "*Tass
(Monte Carlo, 1903); 3 symph., et

**Hard'ing, Henry Alfred,** b. Sal
bury, July 25, 1855 ; organist ; pu
of Corfe ; 1882 Mus. Doc., O
ford; cond. and org. at Bedford;
church music.

**Harris, Clement Hugh Gilber**
Wimbledon, July 8, 1871 — in t
battle of Pentepigadia, Greece, Ap

3, 1897; pianist pupil Frankfort
Cons., and of Mme. Schumann; being
a Greece at the outbreak of the
Turkish war he joined the Greek
army, and was killed in battle; c.
brilliant symph. poem *"Paradise
Lost"* (prod. Birmingham, 1905);
concert studies for piano; songs; etc.

rrison, Samuel, Belper, Derbyshire, Sept. 8, 1760 — London, June
5, 1812; tenor.

c'rold, Orville, tenor; discovered
nging in vaudeville, by Oscar Hammerstein, N. Y., taught by Oscar
Saenger, 1909–10; début Manhattan
p., N. Y., 1910; sang with Mme.
Trentini in comic opera; 1911 at
Hammerstein's London Opera.

rt'inger, Martin, Ingolstadt,
Feb. 6, 1815 — Munich, Sept. 6, 1896;
tenor and teacher at Royal Music-
school, Munich.

rtmann, Arthur, b. Maté
szalka, Hungary, July 23, 1881;
taken to Philadelphia at the age of
two months; violinist; all his schooling in America; has toured Europe
and America with great success.
1911, soloist with Colonne orch.,
Paris; c. orch. works, violin pieces, etc.

rty, Hamilton, b. Hillsborough,
Co. Down, Ireland, Dec. 4, 1879;
organist; pupil of his father; at 12,
organist, later in Belfast and Dublin;
n London from 1900 as an accompanist; c. *"Irish"* symph., *"Comedy
Overture,"* *"Ode to a Nightingale"* for
soprano and orch. (Cardiff Festival,
1907), his wife, Mme. Agnes Nicholls,
singing the solo; c. also important
violin concerto (1909), chamber music
and songs.

r'wood, Basil, b. Woodhouse,
Gloucestershire, April 11, 1859; pian-
t; pupil of Roeckel, Risley, Corfe, and
at Leipzig Cons.; 1880, Mus. Bac.,
Oxford; 1896 Mus. Doc.; organist
various churches; from 1892 at Christ
Church, Oxford; 1896–1900 cond.
Oxford Orch. Association; 1900 chora-
us; c. psalm *"Inclina, Domine,"*

voices and orch. (Gloucester Fest.,
1898), church music, etc.

**Häsche** (hĕsh'-ĕ), **William Ed-
win,** b. New Haven, April 11, 1867;
pupil of Listemann, Perabo, and
Parker; dir. New Haven Symph.
Orch.; since 1903 teacher of instru-
mentation at Yale cond. N. H. Choral
Union (250 voices); c. symph., symph.
poems, *"Waldidylle,"* *"Fridjof and
Ingeborg";* cantata *"The Haunted
Oak,"* etc.

**Hässler** (hess'-lĕr), (1) **Jn. Wm.,**
Erfurt, March 29, 1747 — Moscow,
March 29, 1882; organist and famous
teacher; toured widely; 1892–4 royal
cond. St. Petersburg; then teacher
at Moscow; c. important piano and
organ pieces; his wife, (2) **Sophie,**
was a singer who travelled with him.

**Hath'erly, Stephen Georgeson,**
b. Bristol, Feb. 14, 1827; Greek
priest; organist of various churches;
1857 at the Greek Church, Liverpool;
1871 at Constantinople; author of
works on Byzantine music.

**Hausegger** (hows'-ĕg-gĕr), **Siegmund Von,,** b. Graz, Aug. 16, 1872;
pupil of his father, of Degners and
Pohlig; 1896 cond. at Graz; 1899 of
the Kaim concerts at Munich; 1903–6
the Museum Concerts at Frankfort-
on-Main; c. mass, an opera *"Hel-
frid"* (Graz, 1893); *"Zinnober"* (Munich, 1898); *"Dionysian Fantasie"* for
orch., (Munich, 1899); symph. poems,
*"Barbarossa,"* (1902), *"Wieland der
Schmied,"* 1904.

**Hauss'man, Valentin,** organist and
composer at Gerbstadt, Saxony,
1588 to 1611.

**Haw'don, Matthias;** d. Newcastle
1787, where he had been organist
from 1776; composer.

**Hay, Walter C.,** 1828 — Claremont
Bank, Oct. 1, 1905; pupil R. A.
M.; bandmaster Twelfth Lancers;
many years Prof. Music Shrewsbury;
organist, 1861–1883.

**Hay'ter, Arthur Upjohn,** Brooklyn, 1833 — June 19, 1909; organist.

**Hegyesi** (hĕg'-yā-zē), **Louis,** Arpad, Hungary, 1853 — Cologne, Feb. 1894; 'cellist.

**Hein** (hīn), **Karl,** b. Rendsburg, 1864; 'cellist; pupil Hamburg Cons.; 1885–90 'cellist Hamburg Philharmonic Orch.; 1890 teacher in New York at German Cons.; 1903, joined with a fellow-pupil from the Hamburg Cons., August Francke, in its direction.

**Hein'rich, Max,** b. Chemnitz, Saxony, June 14, 1853; barytone, pupil of Klitzsch and at Dresden Cons.; 1873, moved to Philadelphia; 1876–82 to Marion, Ala. became very popular on concert tours ; 1888–93 prof. at London R. A. M.; then Chicago, where he gave a farewell recital, 1903; c. songs.

**Hei'linck, Joannes Lupus** (often called Lupus or Lupi), d. 1541; Flemish choir master at Cambrai, and Bruges; c. many masses, influencing Palestrina; important motets, hymns and songs.

**Hei'sted,** (1) **Eduard,,** Copenhagen, Dec. 8, 1816–1903; violinist at the Royal Chapel; from 1869, teacher at the Cons.; c. ballets, etc.; his brother (2) **Karl Adolf,** b. Copenhagen, Jan. 4, 1818; flutist, teacher at the Cons.; c. 2 symph., etc.; his son (3) **Gustav,** b. Copenhagen, Jan. 30, 1857; pupil of Gade, etc.; c. symph. orch. suite, etc.

**Hem'pel, Frieda,** b. Leipzig, 1884 (daughter of a janitor); soprano; studied the piano at Leipzig Cons., 1903–5; then voice with Frau Lempner; début in Stettin; 1906, at Bayreuth; 1907 Covent Garden; has sung in Paris Opéra, Brussels, Vienna, etc.; from 1908 Berlin Royal Opera; engaged for Met. Op. N. Y. 1912.

**Hemp'son** (or **Hampson**), **Denis,** Craigmore, 1695 — Magilligan, 1807 (at the age of 112); one of the greatest and latest of the Irish bards; a harper, blind from his third year; wandering afar; 1745 played for the Pretender at Edinburgh.

**Henrion** (än-rĭ-ôn), **Paul, Pa** July 29, 1819 — Oct. 26, 1901; operettas and over a thousand po lar songs.

**Henriques** (hĕn-rē'-kĕs), **Fini B demar,** b. Copenhagen, Dec. 1867 ; violinist; pupil of To Svendsen, and Joachim; member court orch. at Copenhagen; c. in dental mus. to "*Wieland der Schmie* (1898), piano pieces, etc.

**Hen'sel, Heinrich,** b. Neusta 1880 (?); tenor; pupil of Wal in Vienna, and Emerich in Mil début Freiburg, 1897, sang there three years; from 1900 at Frankfe on-Main; 1906, Royal Opera, W baden; sang "*Parsifal*," etc., at B. reuth, 1910; 1911 at Covent Gard

**Hep'worth,** (1) **George,** b. mondbury, England, 1825; organ' at 22 went to Germany; since 1 cathedral organist and court-dir. Schwerin; c. organ music, etc.; his (2) **William,** b. Hamburg, 18 organist and writer at Chemni 1908, church-dir.; c. string quart etc.

**Herbert, Victor.** Add that conducted the Pittsburg orch. 1904, then founded and cond. Victor Herbert Orch., with which toured widely. Later comic ope included the following great s cesses: "*Babes in Toyland*," 19 "*The Red Mill*," 1905, "*Naug Marietta*," 1910, "*The Enchantres* 1911. He c. also the grand op "*Natoma*," libretto by Jos. D. R ding, which was prod. by the Ph delphia Opera Co., 1911 in Ph delphia and at the Met. Op., N. the same year.

**Herbst, Andreas,** Nuremberg, 1 — Frankfort, 1666; theorist a comp.

**Herites** (hĕ-rē'-tĕs), **Marie,** Wodnian, South Bohemia, 1884 ( violinist; pupil of Sevcik at Prag Cons.; toured Europe.

**Herms, Adeline,** b. Friesack, O

4, 1862; mezzo-soprano; pupil of Frau
Breidenhoff, and O. Eichberg; married
the cellist, Eugen Sandow, 1895.

**r'ner, Karl,** Rendsburg, Jan. 23,
1836 — Hanover, July 16, 1906;
violinist and comp.

**rzfeld** (hĕrts'-fĕlt), **Victor von,**
., Pressburg, Oct. 8, 1856; violinst; pupil Vienna Cons., taking prizes
or comp. and violin ; pupil later
f Grell, Berlin; 1886, prof. at Pest; c.
hamber music, etc.

**ss,** (1) **Willy,** add that he was
made Royal Prof., 1900; 1903–4 he
was violin prof. R. A. M., London;
esigned and became concertmaster
Boston Symph. Orch., and leader of
he Quartet; 1908 co-founded the
Hess-Schroeder Quartet. (2) **Lud-**
**vig,** b. Marburg, March 23, 1877;
upil Berlin Royal Hochsch. and
idal in Milan; toured as concert
nger; from 1907 succeeded Felix
Mottl as dir. Munich Konzertgesell-
chaft; c. symphony "*Hans Mem-*
*ing,*" an epic "*Ariadne,*" and other
works for voices and orch.; songs, etc.;
912 engaged to tour America.

**user** (hoi'-zĕr), **Ernst,** b. Elber-
eld, April 9, 1863; pianist; teacher at
Cologne Cons.; c. opera, etc.

**yse** (hī'-zē), **Karl,** b. St. Petersburg, May 10, 1879; organist; pupil of
Homeyer and H. Seifert; 1907, org.
t Frankfort-on-Main, and teacher
t the Hoch Cons.

**n'ton, Arthur,** b. Beckenham,
Nov. 20, 1869; violinist; pupil R. A.
M., later with Rheinberger at Mu-
ich Cons., where his first symph. was
layed; his second symph. was played
n London, 1903; c. also opera "*Tam-*
*ra*"; operettas for children, and piano
ieces played by his wife, Katherine
Goodson, whom he married in 1903.

**ll,** (1) **Henry,** London, July 2, 1808
— June 11, 1856; viola player of
reat ability. (2) **Edwin Burl-**
**ngame,** b. Cambridge, Mass., Sept.
, 1872; graduated at Harvard, 1894,
with highest honors in music, pupil

of B. J. Lang (piano), F. F. Bullard
(theory), Arthur Whiting (piano),
later with Widor (comp.), in Paris, and
G. W. Chadwick (instrumentation);
1887–1902 taught piano and harmony
in Boston, then took up writing for
magazines; 1908–12, musical instructor at Harvard; c. fantastic pantomime
for orch. "*Jack Frost in Midsummer*"
(Chicago Orch. 1907, N. Y. Symph.
1908); women's chorus with orch.
"*Nuns of the Perpetual Adoration*"
(Musical Art Society, 1907, Birmingham, England, Orch., etc.); dramatic lyric for tenor and orch., 3
piano sonatas, songs, etc.

**Hilton,** (1) **John,** d. before 1612;
organist at Cambridge, 1594; perhaps the father of (2) **John,** 1599 —
1656–7; organist at Westminster; c.
anthems, madrigals, etc.

**Hirsch'mann, Henri,** b. St. Maudé,
1872; composer, under pen-name of
**V. H. Herblay,** of operas, "*L'*
*Amour à la Bastille,*" (Paris, [1897),
"*Lovelace*" (do., 1898), "*Hernani*"
(do., 1909); operettas "*Das Schwal-*
*benrest*" (Berlin, 1904, in Paris, 1907,
as *Les hirondelles); "La petite Bo-*
*hême*" (Paris, 1905); in Berlin 1905,
as "*Musette*"), etc.

**Hit'zelberger,** (1) **Sabina,** Randers-
sacker, Nov. 12, 1755 — after 1807;
soprano of 3-octaves range ; wife
of the 'cellist H., her maiden name
unknown. Her daughters (2) **Ku-**
**nigunde,** soprano ; (3) **Johanna,**
alto ; wife of violinist Bamberger ;
(4) **Regina,** 1789 — Munich, May
10, 1827; married **Lang,** and bore a
daughter, **Josephine Lang-Kost-**
**lin,** who composed songs.

**Hlawatsch,** (hlä'-väch), **Woizech**
**Ivanovitch,** b. Leditsch, Bo-
hemia, 1849; organist; pupil Paris
Organists' School; cond. in various
Bohemian cities; from 1871 in St.
Petersburg, as cond. of students or-
ganizations; 1900, organist of the
court orch.; c. comic opera "*Oblava,*"
Roumanian rhapsody for orch., etc.

**Hol'brooke, Josef (or Joseph),** b. Croyden, July 6, 1878; English composer; pupil of the R. A. M., till 1898 ; c. symph. poems *"The Raven"* (Crystal Palace, 1900); *"Ode to Victory," "The Skeleton in Armor," "Ulalume"* (London Symph., 1904), *"Queen Mab"* (Leeds Fest., 1904), *"The Masque of the Red Death,"* overture, *"The New Renaissance,"* etc. His opera *"The Children of Don"* (libretto by Lord Howard de Walden), was prod. at the London Op., June 15 1912 with Nikisch conducting without success.

**Hollander** (hôl'-lĕn-dĕr), **Benno,** b. Amsterdam, June 8, 1853; violinist; played as child, then studied with Massart and Saint-Saëns at Paris Cons., winning first violin prize, 1873; after 1876 toured, then settled in London as viola player; 1882, cond. German Opera season; 1887 violin prof. at the Guildhall; cond. London Symph. Concerts; 1903, organized the Benno H. Orchestral Society; c. symph. *"Roland"*; violin concertos, pastoral fantasia played by Ysaye, 1900, etc.

**Hol'lingshead, Frederick Edward,** d. July 5, 1907; organist at Bath; Fellow Royal College of Org.

**Hol'lins, Alfred,** b. Hull, Sept. 11, 1865; pianist, and org.; blind from birth; pupil of Hartvigson; played Beethoven concerto as a boy; at 16 played for the Queen; pupil of Bülow, later at Raff Cons.; played for crowned heads, and toured America; 1884, org. at Redhill; 1888 at People's Palace; 1897 at Edinburgh, Free St. George's Church; c. 2 overtures, organ music, etc.

**Holst, Gustav Von,** b. Cheltenham, Sept. 21, 1874; dir. Morley College; pupil R. C. M.; c. operas *"Sita"* and *"Savitri"; scene w. orch. "The Mystic Trumpeter," "Ave Maria"* for women's voices, etc.

**Ho'mer,** (1) **S i d n e y,** b. Boston, Mass., Dec. 9, 1864; prominent American song-composer; pupil G. W. Chadwick, then of Rh[e]berger, O. Hieter and Abel in G[er]many; 1888–96 teacher of theory [?] Boston; c. many important so[ngs] In 1895 he married (2) **Lou[ise]** (**Dilworth Beatty**), b. Pi[tts]burgh, Pa.; famous operatic contra[lto] pupil of Miss Whinnery and M[?] Goff, W. L. Whitney, and of her h[us]band in theory; then studied in P[aris] with Fidèle Koenig; début, 1898 [at] Vichy; from 1899 at Covent Gard[en] and regularly at the Metropoli[tan] Opera House as leading contra[lto] with especial success in Wagner[ian] rôles, also as *"Orfeo,"* etc.; 1912 c[re]ated title-rôle in *"Mona."*

**Hop'kinson, F r a n c i s,** compos[er] 1737–91; one of the earliest Ameri[can] composers; inventor of the *"Bell[?] monica."*

**Horváth** (hôr'-vät), **Géza,** b. K[?] áron, Hungary, May 27, 1868; pu[pil] of L. Schytte, etc.; teacher in Vien[na] c. popular piano-pieces.

**Hösel** (hä'-zĕl), **Kurt,** b. Dresd[en] Jan. 20, 1862; Mus. Director a[nd] composer; pupil of the Cons.; co[nd.] Wagner Concerts there from 1895 a[nd] founded the Philh. chorus; c. m[ale] and mixed choruses, etc.

**Hoy'a, Amadeo Von Der,** b. N[ew] York, March 13, 1874; violinist; pu[pil] of Joachim, Halir, etc., in Berlin; c[on]certmaster, N. Y. Symph. Orc[h.] 1894–6 cond. court opera at B[ay]reuth; from 1901 concertmaster [at] Linz; author of a method.

**Huë, Georges Adolphe,** add t[hat] his opera *"Le roi de Paris"* was pr[od.] 1901, *"Titania"* 1903.

**Huhn, Bruno (Siegfried),** b. L[on]don, 1871; org. and pianist; pupil [of] Sophie Taunton, later in New Y[ork] of S. B. Mills and L. Alberti; [?] toured Europe as pianist; promin[ent] accompanist in New York; c. *"[Te] Deum"* with orch., and many son[gs]

**Hull, Alexander,** b. Columbus, [?] Sept. 15, 1887; pupil of his moth[er] nd (by correspondence, later in person) of Dr. Hugh A. Clarke; studied 'cello with Michael Brandt, Cincinnati, voice with H. A. Preston nd H. B. Turpin, Columbus; took music bachelor degree Univ. of Penna; teacher in Pacific College, Oregon; c. orch. suites, 'cello pieces, ongs, etc.

Isteyn (hŭl'-shīn), Joai'n C. Van, b. Amsterdam, 1869; violinist upil at Liège Cons. of César Thomson; won first prize; played in Lamoureux orch., Paris; prof. at Peaody Inst., Baltimore.

mbert (ŭn-băr), Georges, b. St. Croix, Switzerland, Aug. 10, 1870; organist; pupil Leipzig and Brussels Cons., and of Bargiel; teacher of mus. history at Geneva Cons. and org. at Nôtre Dame; from 1893 at Lausanne.

mperdinck, Engelbert, add hat in 1900 he became dir. of Master-School of the Berlin Royal Acad. of Arts. His "Königskinder" written in 1896 and played in excerpt at concerts), was prod. at Met. Op., N. Y., 1910 with greatest success, later in Europe. "Dornröschen" was prod. Frankfort-on-Main (1902), com. op. "Die Heirat wider Willen" (Berlin, 1905), incid. music to Aristophanes' "Lysistrata," (do., 1908); Shakespeare's "Winter's Tale," and "Tempest," (do. 1906).

ur'ka, Friedrich Franz, Merklin, Bohemia, Feb. 23, 1762—Berlin, Oct. 10, 1805; tenor and comp. of songs.

url'ebusch, (1) Harris Lorenzo, b. Hanover, July 8, 1666; organist; his son (2) Konrad Fr., Braunschweig, 1696 — Amsterdam, Dec. 16, 1765; organist; and cond.: c. 72 odes, etc.

url'stone, Wm. Yeates, London, Jan. 7, 1876 — May 30, 1906; composer; at 9 pub. 5 waltzes; at 18 held scholarship at R. A. M.; later Prof. there of harmony and counterpoint; c. piano concerto, etc.

Huss, Henry Holden, add that he and his wife, the soprano, Hildegard Hoffman, have given joint recitals throughout America, and 1910 in London. His piano concerto in B major has been played with the composer as soloist by the N. Y. Philh., Boston Symph., Pittsburgh and Cincinnati Symph, orch's. and by the Monte Carlo Symph., with Pugno as soloist; his violin sonata has been played by Kneisel, Spiering, etc.; his "The Recessional" for mixed chorus, organ, and orch. (Worcester, Mass. Festival, 1911); string quartet in E minor (Kneisel Quartet); 'cello sonata much played; songs, etc.

Huszla (hoosh'-lä), Victor, St. Petersburg, Oct. 16, 1857 — Lisbon, Nov. 14, 1899; violinist; pupil of Schradieck and César Thomson; 1887 cond. Royal Academy of Music Lovers, Lisbon; c. 3 Portuguese rhapsodies, Portuguese suite, etc.

Hutch'eson, (1) Francis, b. Glasgow, 1720; physician and comp. of glees, etc., under pen-name Francis Ireland. (2) Ernest, b. Melbourne, Australia, July 20, 1871; pupil of Leipzig Cons., 1886–1892, winning Mozart prize with a trio; toured Australia; studied with Stavenhagen; 1898 married Baroness von Pilsach; from 1900 teacher Peabody Cons., Baltimore; c. symph. poem "Merlin and Vivien" (Berlin, 1899); orch. suite (do.), piano concerto (1899).

Huygens (hī'-gĕns), Constantin, The Hague, Sept. 4, 1596 — March 28, 1687; poet and military secretary to William II and William III; also skilful performer; c. over 700 airs for lute, theorbo, etc.; his son (2) Christian, The Hague, April 14, 1629 — June 8, 1695; mathematician and musician.

Hy'att, Nathaniel Irving, b. Lansingburgh, N. Y., April 23, 1865; pupil of White and Jefferey at Troy; from 1887 at Leipzig Cons.; 1892 settled in Troy as teacher; 1895-9 prof. of piano and theory, Syracuse University; then head teacher at St. Agnes School, Albany, N.Y.; c. symph. overture "*Enoch Arden,*" chamber music, songs, etc.

## I

**If'fert, August,** b. Braunschweig, May 31, 1859; singer and teacher in various cities; author of a vocal method.

**Igumnoff** (ē-goom'-noff), **Konstantin Nikolajavich,** b. Lebedjana, Tambouv, May 1, 1873; Russian pianist; pupil of Svereff, Siloti and Pabst; 1898, teacher in Tiflis; 1900 Prof. at Moscow Cons.

**Iljinski** (ēl-yēn'-shkǐ), **Alexander Alexandrovich,** b. Tsarkoe Selo, Jan. 24, 1859; composer; pupil of Kullak and Bargiel; 1885 Prof. of theory at the Philharmonic Music School in Moscow; c. opera "*The Fountain of Bastchi-Sarai*"; symph.; symphonic scherzo; incidental music to Sophokles' "*Oedipos*" and "*Philoktetes;*" overture to Tolstoi's "*Czar Feodor,*" etc.

**Imbart de la Tour** (ăṅ-bär dŭ lä toor), **Georges,** b. Paris, May 20, 1865; operatic tenor; pupil of the Cons.; début 1891, Geneva; sang at the Opéra Comique, Paris, and Th. de la Monnaie, Brussels; 1901 sang in the U. S.

**India, Sigismondo d',** flourished 1608-1621; born of a noble family in Palermo; court mus. director in various Italian cities; c. madrigals, etc.

**Indy, Vincent d',** add that while 1851 is the birth year in the Paris Cons. records, the composer gave Philip Hale the year 1852 as correct; 1896 he became prof. of Composition at Paris Cons.; 1896 with Bordes and Guilmant founded the *Schola Cantorum,* and became director; c. "*Le chant de la cloche,*" dramatic legend in seven pictures, with his own te for soli, double chorus and orc Festival cantata "*Pour l'inaugu tion d'une Statue*" for baryton chorus and orch.,"*Ode à Valence,*" symph. in B flat 1902; *Jour d'été la montagne,* 1905; *Souvenirs* for or 1906; songs, piano pieces a choruses, author of a *Cours de Co position Musicale,* 1902, and a life César Franck, 1906.

**Ippolitov-Ivanov**(ēp-pō'-lē-tôf-ē'-v nôf), **Mikhail Mikhailovitch,** Gatchina, Nov. 19, 1859; added mother's name to Ivanoff, to d tinguish him from Ivanoff (2); pu of Rimsky-Korsakov; at St. Peter burg Cons.; 1882 dir. of the Mus School and cond. in Tiflis; 18 cond. at the Imperial Theatre; fro 1893 prof. of theory at Moscow Con from 1899 cond. the Private Opera; operas "*Ruth,*" (Tiflis, 1887),"*Asja,*" (Moscow, 1900); and "*Saba Putjatischna,*" (St. Petersburg, 1901 overtures "*Jar Chmel,*" "*Spring,*" and "*Medea*"; orch. suite, "*Caucasio Sketches*"; violin-sonata (rearrange as a Sinfonietta); character-picture for chorus and orch.; cantatas "*I Memory of Pushkin*" of Gogol an Shukovski, and "*Legend of the Whi Swan of Novgorod,*" etc.; author a book on Georgian folk-songs.

**I'rons, H. S.,** Canterbury, 1838 – Nottingham, June 29, 1905. Organ ist and prolific comp. of church musi

**I'vanov, (1) Nicholas Kusmich** Poltava, Oct. 22, 1810 — Bologna July 7, 1880; tenor; popular in Lor don, 1834-37; accumulated a fortun in Italy and Paris and retired in 1845 (2) **Michael Mikhailovich,** Moscow, Sept. 23, 1849; pupil o Tchaikovsky and Dubuque at th Cons.; critic and comp.; 1870-76 a Rome; then critic for the *Novc Vremya;* c. symph. "*A Night in May*" symph. prologue "*Savonarola*"; fou operas including "*Potemkin's Feast*" (1888), and "*Sabava Putjatischna*"

(Moscow, 1899); incidental music to "*Medea*," etc. His opera "*Treachery*" (Moscow, Feb. 1911), made great success.

# J

**chimecki** (yäkh-ĭ-mĕt'-skĭ), **Lad=islav**, b. Lemberg, July 7, 1882; pupil of Schönberg and Grädener; author and composer in Cracow.

**co'bi, Georges**, Berlin, Feb. 13, 1840 — London, Sept. 16, 1906); violinist; pupil of De Bériot, Massart, etc., at Paris Cons.; 1861, violinist at the Opera when "Tannhauser" was first performed; cond. light opéra and ballets, first in Paris, and for 26 years ('72–'95) at the Alhambra, London; c. operas and a hundred ballets and divertissements, many of them performed in America, Brussels, Berlin, Munich, Rome, Paris.

**cques** (jä'-quĕz), **Edgar F.,** London, March 27, 1850 — Brighton, Dec. 30, 1906; organist and critic.

**ffé** (yäf'-fä), **Sophia,** b. Odessa, Feb. 26, 1872; violinist; pupil of Auer; later at Paris Cons. where she won first prize; toured Germany with success but inheriting a fortune, left the concert stage.

**iger** (yä'-gĕr), **Fd.,** Hanan, Dec. 25, 1838 — Vienna, June 15, 1902; tenor at Vienna and Bayreuth; notable as *Siegfried* and *Parsifal*.

**irnefelt** (yärn'-ĕ-fĕlt), **Armas,** b. Wiborg, Finland, 1869; pupil of Helsingfors Cons., later of Becker in Berlin, and Massenet in Paris; cond. of court opera in Stockholm; 1906 dir. of Helsingfors Cons.; c. symph. poem "*Korsholm*"; fantasie "*Heimat Klang*" for orch.; important piano pieces, etc.

**arno** (yär'-nō), **Georg,** b. Pesth, June 3, 1868; composer; cond. at Breslau city theatre, c. operas "*Die Schwaıze Kaschka*" (Breslau, 1895), "*Der Richter von Zalamea*," (do., 1899), "*Der Zerbrochene Krug*," (Hamburg, 1900), "*Der Goldfisch*,"

(Breslau, 1907), and "*Die Förster-Christel*" (Vienna, 1907).

**Jaspar** (zhäs-pär), **Maurice,** b. Liège, June 20, 1870; pianist; pupil and later teacher at the Cons.; c. piano pieces and songs.

**Jenner** (yĕn'-nĕr), **Gustav,** b. Keitum, Island of Sylt, Dec. 3, 1865; pupil of Stange and Gänge in Kiel, of Brahms and Mandyczewski in Vienna; from 1895 director in Marburg; c. songs and quartets for women's voices.

**Jentsch** (yĕntsh), **Max,** b. Ziesar, Saxony, Aug. 5, 1855; pianist and teacher; pupil of Stern Cons.; toured the Orient; 1884–89 in Constantinople; later in Berlin; from 1894 in Vienna; c. symphony, "*Elysium*" for chorus and orch., 2 operas, etc.

**Jiránek** (yē'-rä-nĕk), (1) **Anton** ca. 1712 — Dresden, Jan. 16, 1761; studied at Prague; later joined the royal chapel at Warsaw. (2) **Josef,** b. Ledec, Bohemia, March 24, 1855; pianist; pupil of Smetana, and of the organ school at Prague; studied the harp with Stanek, the violin with Hrimaly, and was a harpist at first; 1877–91 piano teacher at Charkov; thereafter prof. at Prague Cons.; c. "*Ballade*" and "*Scherzo fantastique*" for orch., piano pieces; author of methods. His brother (3) **Aloys,** b. Ledec, Sept. 3, 1858; pupil of Prague Organ School, and in composition of Fibich; from 1881, piano teacher at Charkov; c. opera "*Dagmar*," etc.

**Johnson,** (1) **John,** d. 1594–5; musician to Queen Elizabeth; c. lute-music; (2) **William Lyman,** b. Boston; studied there, graduated from Harvard, 1897; c. Persian serenade for tenor, chorus and orch.; 5 preludes for orch., etc. (3) **William Spencer,** b. Athol, Mass., Dec. 7, 1883; pupil of Perabo, and Goetschius, Boston; 1901–7 of Reinecke and H. Riemann, Leipzig; from 1910, teacher at Quincy, Ill.; c. songs.

**Jomelli** (yō-mĕl'-lē), **Jeanne,** b. Amsterdam, May 18, 1879; soprano; pupil of Meschaert, Stockhausen and Massenet; début Amsterdam Opera, 1897; toured in concert; 1905 (?), Met. Op., N. Y.; 1907-8 Manhattan Op., N. Y.

**Josephson** (yō'-zĕf-zōn),**Jacob Axel,** Stockholm, March 27, 1818—Upsala, March 29, 1880; Swedish cond. and composer.

**Juon** (zhwôṅ), **Paul,** b. Moscow, March 8, 1872; violinist; pupil of Hrimaly, Taneiev and Arensky, later of Bargiel in Berlin, where he won the Mendelssohn Scholarship; 1896 taught theory at Baku; 1897 settled in Berlin; from 1906 teacher of composition at the Royal High School for music; c. 2 symph., the second prod. with much interest at Meiningen, 1903, and in London, 1904 and 1905; fantasie for orch., *"Wächterweise,"* on Danish folk-themes, orch. suite, *"Aus meinem Tagebuch"; chamber* music, *"Satyrs and Nymphs,"* and other piano pieces.

**Juul** (yool), **Asger,** b. Copenhagen, May 9, 1874; pupil of Hansen, Rosenhoff and Riemann in Leipzig; from 1906 teacher and critic at Copenhagen; c. piano pieces and songs.

## K

**Kad'letz, Andreas,** b. Dobrisch, Bohemia, Feb. 18, 1859; violinist; concertmaster at Imperial Russian Opera, St. Petersburg, and teacher; pupil Prague and St. Petersburg Cons.; c. opera, ballets, and violin pieces.

**Kahl** (käl), **Oscar W.,** Thuringia, 1862 — Baltimore, Dec. 29, 1910; teacher in Peabody Cons., Baltimore.

**Kajanus** (kä-jä'-noos), **Robert,** b. Helsingfors, Dec. 2, 1856; Finnish composer; pupil Leipzig Cons.; returned to Helsingfors, founded an orchestra school, and developed the Phil. orch.; 1897 mus. director

of the University; c. 2 Finnish rha sodies, symph. poems *"Aino" a "Kullervo"; orch.* suite *"Summ Memories,"* cantata, etc.

**Kalafati** (kä-lä'-fä-tē), **B.,** b. E patoria, Crimea, 1869; Russian cor poser of songs and piano sonatas, et

**Kam'mel, Anton,** Hanna, Bohem 1740 — London, before 1788; violin and composer; pupil of Tartini; masses, violin duets, etc.

**Kaempfert** (kĕmp'-fĕrt), **Max,** Berlin, Jan. 3, 1871; studied Paris and Munich; 1899 cond. a Palm Garden, Frankfort-on-Main; opera, 3 rhapsodies for orch., etc.

**Kalin'nikov, Vassili Sergeievich** Voina, Jan. 13, 1866 — Jalta, Crime Jan. 11, 1901; pupil of Iljinski an Blaramberg at Moscow; 1893 a sistant cond. at the Italian Oper there; compelled to retire fro pulmonary trouble and go south; 2 symph., the first in G. minor, muc played; 2 symph. poems, *"Tl Nymphs"* and *"Cedar and Palm'* music to Tolstoi's *"Czar Boris,* (Little Theatre, Moscow, 1899 *"Russalka,"* ballade with orch., ca tata, *"St. John of Damascus,"* etc.

**Kap'pey, Jacob Adam,** Binge 1826 — Chatham (?) Dec. 6, 190; went to England 1848; 1857 banc master Royal Marines; c. opera an cantata. Author of a history c wind instrumental bands, (1894).

**Karg=Elert** (kärkh-ā'-lĕrt), **Sigfrid** b. Oberndorf, Nov. 21, 1879; pup Leipzig Cons.; teacher and compose especially for the harmonium.

**Karlovicz** (kärl'-yō-vĭch), **Mieczy slav,** Wisznievo, Lithuania, Dec. 11 1876 — (in an avalanche), Zakopane Galicia, Feb. 10, 1909; composei studied in Warsaw and Berlin; c symph., symphonic-trilogy *"Thre Ancient Songs"* (1907), *"Lithuaniai Rhapsody"* (1908), also publishec Chopin letters and documents (War saw and Paris, 1905).

**Kasachen'ko, Nicolai Ivanovich**

b. Russia, May 3, 1858; cond.; pupil St. Petersburg Cons.; 1883 chorus master at the Imperial Opera; cond. "*Russian Concerts*" in Paris, 1898, c. symph., 2 oriental suites, 2 operas, "*Prince Serebrianni*" (St. Petersburg, 1892), and "*Pan Sotkin,*" (do., 1902).

**asan'li, Nicolai Ivanovich,** b. Tiraspol, Dec. 17, 1869; Russian composer; pupil Odessa Music school and St. Petersburg Cons.; has cond. Russian symph. concerts in Germany, Bohemia, etc.; c. symph., sinfonietta, cantata "*Russalka*" (Munich, 1897), and "*Leonore*" (do.).

**asch'in, Daniel Nikitich,** Moscow, 1773–1844; composer of Polish folk and patriotic songs; also three operas.

**aschinski** (kä-shǐn'-ski), **Viktor,** Wilna, Dec. 30, 1812–1870; pupil of Elsner in Warsaw; cond. at St. Petersburg; c. operas.

**ash'perov, Vladimir Nikitich,** Simbirsk, 1827 — Romanzevo, July 8, 1894; Russian composer; pupil of Voigt and Henselt; and comp. an opera in 1850, then went to Berlin to study with Dehn; thence with Glinka to Italy, where he produced various operas. "*Maria Tudor*" (Milan, 1859), "*Rienzi*" (Florence, 1863), "*Consuelo,*" (Venice); 1866–72 he was singing teacher at Moscow Cons., and organized chorusclasses; c. also operas "*The Weather*" (St. Petersburg, 1867), and "*Taras Bulba*" (Moscow, 1893).

**at'zer, Karl August,** Berge, near Bautzen, Dec. 3, 1822 — May 19, composer; 1904; composer of Wendina songs and dances.

**aulich** (kow'-lǐkh), **Josef,** Florisdorf, near Vienna, Nov. 27, 1827– 1900; composer of 7 masses, also military music.

**aun** (kown), **Hugo,** b. Berlin, March 21, 1863; pupil at Royal High school under Grabau and Fr. Schulz; also with K. and O. Raif, and Fr.

Kiel; 1887 took up residence in Milwaukee, Wis., as teacher and cond.; 1900 returned to Berlin; 1912, elected to Berlin Royal Academy; c. symph. "*An Mein Vaterland,*" symph. prolog "*Marie Magdalene*"; symph. poems; festival march "*The Star Spangled Banner,*" chamber music with orch., "*Normannen Abschied*"; 1-act opera "*Der Pietist*" or "*Oliver Brown,*" and important songs and piano pieces.

**Kelly, Thomas Alex., Sixth Earl of Erskine,** Sept. 1, 1732 — Brussels, Oct. 9, 1781; pupil of Stamitz; c. popular overture "*The Maid of the Mill,*" minuets, etc.

**Keussler** (kois'-lěr), **Gerhard von,** b. Schwanenburg, Livonia, July 6, 1874; pupil Leipzig Cons.; cond. 2 singing societies in Prague; c. symph. poems, etc.

**Kiall'mark** (1) **George,** Kings, Lynn, Feb. 1781 –— Islington, March 1835; violinist; and comp. His son (2) **George Frdk.,** Islington, 1804 — London, 1887, was a pianist.

**Kiefer** (kē'-fěr), **Heinrich,** b. Nuremberg, Feb. 16, 1867; 'cellist; pupil of Royal Cons., 1883 at Munich, 1884, Stuttgart, 1887–90, Frankforton-Main with Cossmann; 1896; soloist of Leipzig, Phil.; 1898 do. of Berlin Phil.; 1900, teacher at Stern Cons.; from 1902, co-founder of the Munich string quartet; tours widely.

**Kienzl, Wm.,** his opera, "*Kuhreigen*" (Vienna Volksoper, Nov. 25, 1911) has been a great suc. in Europe.

**Kin'der, Ralph,** b. Stalybridge, Lancashire, Jan. 27, 1876; organist in Bristol R. I.; 1888–1897 studied in London with Dr. Pearce, Dr. Turpin, and E. H. Lemare; from 1899 in Philadelphia, Holy Trinity; toured U. S.; c. church music, etc.

**Kirbye** (kěr'-bǐ), **George,** d. Bury St. Edmunds, Oct. 1634; popular English composer of madrigals 1592–1634.

**Kit'ziger, Frederick E.,** Saxony. 1850 — New Orleans, Feb. 3, 1903; teacher.

**Kleefeld** (klā'-fĕlt), **Dr. Wilhelm,**
b. Mayence, April 2, 1868; author and
comp.; pupil of Radecke, Härtel and
Spitta; 1891 cond. in Mayence, etc.;
1897 Ph. D., 1898–'01 teacher at the
Klindworth-Scharwenka Cons.; c.
opera "*Anarella*" (Königsberg, 1896)
string suite, etc.

**Klenov'ski, Nicholas Semeno-
vich,** b. Odessa, 1857; pupil Moscow Cons.; leader of private concerts
there 1883–93; when he became cond.
at the Imperial Theatre, then a
teacher at Tiflis till 1902, then assistant cond. of the Imperial Chapel
at St. Petersburg; c. ballets, "*Hasheesh*" Moscow, 1885; "*Salanga*"
(St. Petersburg, 1900); orch. suite
"*Fata Morgana,*" cantatas, etc.

**Klička** (klĭtch'-kä), **Josef,** b. Klattau, Bohemia, Dec.15, 1855; organist;
pupil Prague Cons. and later Prof.
there; c. an opera, organ music, etc.

**Klose** (klō'-zĕ), **Friedrich,** b. Karlsruhe, Nov. 29, 1862; composer;
pupil of Lachner, Ruthardt and
Bruckner; 1907 teacher of comp. at
the Akademie der Tonkunst, Munich;
c. dramatic symph. "*Ilsebill,*" or "*The
Fisher and his Wife*" (Karlsruhe,
1903); mass with orch.; symph. poem
in three parts "*Das Leben ein Traum*"
with organ and women's chorus,
(Karlsruhe, 1899), etc.

**Knap'ton, Philip,** York, 1788–1833;
assistant cond. of York Festivals
and comp.

**Knüpfer** (k'nĭp'-fĕr), **Sebastian,**
Asch, Saxony, 1633 — Leipzig, 1676;
editor and comp.

**Kochetov** (kō'-chĕ-tôf), **Nicholas
Razoumnikovich,** b. Oranien-
baum, July 8, 1864; mainly self-
taught; critic and comp. of a symph.
(1895) an opera and piano pieces.

**Köckert** (kĕk'-ĕrt), **Adolph,** b.
Magdeburg, Oct. 27, 1828; violinist;
pupil Prague Cons.; 1857–1881 in
business, then returned to composition; c. oratorios, etc.

**Koenen,** (koo'-nĕn), **Tilly,** b. Java,
of Dutch parents, her father a cava[l]
general and Governor of the Provin[c]
pupil of the Amsterdam Cons. a[t]
with Cornelie van Zanten; 18[9]
sang in London, Berlin, etc.; 1909
the U. S.

**Koessler,** (kĕs'-lĕr) **Hans,** b. Walde[c]
Jan. 1, 1853; organist; pupil Muni[ch]
Cons. 1877 teacher at Dresden Con[s.]
and. cond. of the Liedertafel; 18
teacher at Budapest; c. Psalm for
voices, winning a prize at Vienna;
symph., an opera "*Der Münzenfran[z]*
(Strasburg, 1902), etc.

**Kolachev'ski, Michail Nicolaie[v-]
ich,** b. Oct. 2, 1851; pupil Le[ip-]
zig Cons.; c. "*Ukranian*" symp[h.]
and church music.

**Kolakov'ski, Alexei Antonovic[h]**
b. Podolia, 1856; violinist; pupil [St.]
Petersburg Cons., winning go[ld]
medal; and government funds f[or]
foreign study; teacher at Mosc[ow]
Cons., and solo violinist at the I[m-]
perial Theatre; 1897 teacher in Ki[ev.]

**Kolb** (kôlp) **Karlmann,** Kostla[r,]
Bavaria, 1703 —Munich, 1765; Ben[e-]
dictine monk; organist at the Abb[ey]
of Aschbach, later tutor in Munic[h;]
c. church music.

**Köler** (kā'-lĕr), **David,** Zwicka[u,]
Saxony (2) — July, 1565; compose[r;]
1563 cond. at Gustrov in Meckle[n-]
burg; then cantor at Zwickau till h[is]
early death; c. important work "*T[he]
Psalms*" (Leipzig, 1554).

**Komorovski** (kôm-ō-rôf'-ski), **Igna[z]
Marzel,** Warsaw, 1824 — Oct. 1
1858; composer; Polish song compose[r.]

**Königsperger** (kā'-nĭkhs-pĕrkh-ĕ[r])
**Marianus,** Roding, Bavaria, Dec.
1708—Ratisbon, Oct. 9, 1769. Ben[e-]
dictine monk who devoted the procee[ds]
of his very successful works to t[he]
Abbey; c. church music, also oper[a.]

**Konius,** vide CONUS.

**Könnemann** ( kĕn'-nĕ-män ), **A[r-]
thur,** b. Baden-Baden, March 1
1851; composer; pupil of his father [a]
cond. of the Kur-orchestra), Kr[a-]
selts and Deeckes; theatre-cond[.]

various cities; from 1887 **in** Mährisch-Ostrau as director of a conservatory and cond. c. the Luitpold-prize opera "*Der tolle Eberstein*" (Munich, 1898); symph. suite "*Indien*" etc.

**optjajev** (kôpt′-yä-yĕf), **Alexander Petrovich**,, b. St. Petersburg, Oct. 12, 1868; author and composer of "*Oriental Dances*" and "*Elégie,*" for orch., etc.

**orestchenko** (kôr-ĕsht-chĕn′-kō), **Arseni Nicholaievich**, b. Moscow, Dec. 18, 1870; pupil of the Cons., winning a gold medal in 1891; later teacher there and in the School of the Synod; c. 1-act opera "*Belshazzar's Feast*" (Moscow, 1892), 2-act "*The Angel of Death*," "*The Ice Palace*" (Moscow 1892); two "*Symphonic Pictures,*" "*Symphonie Lyrique*" (op. 23), chamber music, etc.

**or′ganov, Gennari Ossipovich,** Kwarelia, May 12, 1858 — Rostov, April 12, 1890; pianist and composer; pupil of Leipzig and St. Petersburg Cons.; c. piano pieces, etc.

**orn′gold, Erich Wolfgang,** b. Vienna, May 29, 1897; remarkable boy composer and pianist; at a concert in Berlin, March 1911, his trio in D Major, op. I., composed at the age of 13, was played; also portions of two piano sonatas, and a series of "*Fairy Pictures*"; he c. a ballet given at the Royal Opera and elsewhere; trio (Rosé Quartet, Berlin); serenade and pantomime, "*The Snowman,*" (London, 1912).

**otshetov,** vide KOCHETOV.

**ovařovic** (kō-vär′-zhō-vǐts), **Karl**, b. Prague, Dec. 9, 1862; pupil of the Cons., and of Fibich; from 1899 cond. at the Bohemian Landestheater in Prague; where many of his operas have been given from 1884 to "*Fraquita*" (1902); c. ballet "*Hasheesh,*" piano concerto, etc.

**ozlovski** (kôs-l′yôf′-ski), **Joseph Antonovich,** Warsaw, 1757 — St. Petersburg, Feb. 11, 1831; teacher in the household of Prince Oginski;

went to the Turkish war, attracting the notice of Prince Potemkin, who took him to St. Petersburg, where he became director of the court balls, and c. a war song which was for a long time the Russian national anthem; c. also requiem to the Polish King Stanislas, and the Czar Alexander I, etc.

**Kramm, Georg,** b. Kassel, Dec. 21, 1856; violinist of court orch. at Kassel, from 1880 in Düsseldorf, where his opera "*Leonore*" was prod. 1903.

**Kraus** (krows), (1) **Joseph Martin,** Miltenberg, 1756 — Stockholm, 1792; pupil of Abt Vogler; 1778 director and cond. at Stockholm opera; c. operas, symphs., etc. (2) **Ernst,** b. Erlangen, Bavaria, June 8, 1863; tenor; pupil of Galliera and Frau Schimann-Regan; 1893 sang at Mannheim; from 1896, Berlin Royal Opera; (3) **Felix von,** (not **Krauss** as given), b. Vienna, Oct. 3, 1870; bass; pupil of Stockhausen for two months, but largely self-taught; sang Hagen and Gurnemanz at Bayreuth; from 1908 teacher at Royal Akad. der Tonkunst, Munich. His wife (4) **Adrienne,** (Osborne) b. Buffalo, N. Y., 1837; pupil of Marie Götze.

**Kreider** (krī′-dĕr), **Noble Wickham,** b. Goshen, Ind.; composer; pupil from 15th year of Clarence Forsyth, Indianapolis; visited Europe; lives at Goshen; c. orch. works, and important piano pieces, ballads, consert studies, etc.

**Krem′berg, Jakob,** Warsaw, ca. 1650 — London (?) after 1718; composer; court poet and comp. at Halle, Stockholm, Hamburg, Warsaw and London; c. songs of unusual melodiousness.

**Kreuz** (kroits), **Emil,** b. Elberfeld, May 25, 1867; viola player; pupil of Japha at Cologne; 1883, won an open scholarship at the R. A. M., London; studied there till 1888, when he made début as viola-soloist in Berlioz' "*Harold in Italy*"; member of the

Queen's Band 1900–3, then assistant at Covent Garden; c. viola concerto, prize quintet, etc.

**Kroeger, E. R.** add that his orch. suite "*Lalla Rookh*" has been played by the Thomas, Herbert, Damrosch and other orch's. His comps., include a piano sonata op. 33, concert studies for the piano, violin and piano sonata; and many other piano pieces, songs, etc.

**Krogulski** (krō-gool′-skĭ), **Joseph,** Tarnov, 1815 — Warsaw, Jan. 9, 1842; composer; pupil of Elsner; c. 10 masses, an oratorio, etc.

**Krohn** (krōn), **Ilmari Henrik Rheinhold,** b. Helsingfors, Nov. 8, 1867; Finnish author and comp. of sacred songs, piano sonatas, etc.

**Kroy′er, Theodor,** b. Munich, Sept. 9, 1873; author, critic and comp. studied theology, then music at the Akadamie der Tonkunst; 1897, Ph. D. Munich University; c. 2 symphonies with chorus and soli, chamber music, etc.

**Kruse** (kroo′-zĕ), **Georg Richard,** b. Greiffenberg, Jan. 16, 1856; studied in Leipzig; opera cond. in Germany and America; 1891–4 critic of the *Herold,* Milwaukee; then conducted tour of "*Hänsel und Gretel*" till 1896, when he was cond. in Switzerland; 1901 settled in Berlin as biographer; c. incid. mus. to "*As You Like It,*" etc. (2) **Johann Secundus,** add that from 1897 he cond. Sunday and Monday concerts in London.

**Kunwald** (koon′-vält), **Ernst,** b. Vienna, April 14, 1868; studied law there, then music at Leipzig Cons.; became correpetitor at the city theatre; 1895, cond. operetta at Rostock, 1901–2 at Teatro Real, Madrid, where he gave Wagner's Ring cycle complete and was decorated by the Queen of Spain; 1902, cond. at opera Frankfort. 1906 cond. at Nuremberg city theatre; conducting two concerts of the New York Phil. as

guest, Feb.1906; 1907 director of t Berlin Phil. orch.; 1912 engaged conduct the Cincinnati Symph. Orc

**Kupsch** (koopsh), **Karl Gusta** Berlin (?) — Naumberg, July 3 1846; cond. and teacher in Leipz Dresden; 1838–45 Rotterdam, d Singakademie; then director of theat in Naumberg. Robert Schuma was his pupil in composition.

## L

**Labey** (lä-bĕ′), **Marcel,** b. De Besinet, France, 1875; studied law Paris, then with d'Indy at the Sch *Cantorum;* c. symph. (1903), fantas for orch., sonatas, etc.

**Laborde** (lä′-bôrd) (rightly **Bediez Rosine,** Paris, May 30, 1824 Chézy-sur-Marne, Sept. 1, 190 soprano; sang as *Rosalie Villau* till 1843 when she married the ten Laborde (rightly Dur); pupil Pa Cons.; début Op. Com., 1840; 1848– she and her husband sang in Americ 1850–7, Paris Opera; from 18 teacher.

**Ladmirault,** (läd-mē-rō), **Pa Émile,** b. Nantes, Dec. 8, 187 began to study at the Cons. pian violin, organ, and harmony at 7, a to compose at 8; at 15 his 3-act ope *Gilles de Retz,* was given at Nant (1893); the next year he refused allow its repetition; he took fir harmony prize at the Nantes Cor and 1895 entered Paris Cons. und Taudou, winning first harmony pri 1899. After a year of military se vice, he entered the classes of Fau and Gédalge; failing three times win the Prix de Rome, he left t Cons. His comps., include *Le Choe des âmes de la Forêt* (1903), *Su Bretonne* for orch. (1904), a *Tant Ergo* (1907) crowned by the Socié des Compositeurs de Musique; p lude symphonique, *Brocéliande Matin* (1909); this is a portion o dramatic work *Myrdhin* not y roduced; a symphony in c. major, 910; songs, piano pieces, and pieces or military band.

**duchin** (läd′-oo-chēn), **Nikolai Mikailovich**, b. St. Petersburg, Oct. 3, 1860; violinist and pianist; pupil of Taneiev at Moscow Cons.; symphonic variations; 100 children's songs, "*Liturgy of Johann Slatoust*" for chorus, etc.

**Forge, Frank**, b. Rockford, Ill., Oct. 22, 1877; pupil of his sister-n-law, Mrs. Ruth La Forge, then of Harrison M. Wild of Chicago, 1900 -04, Leschetizky, Vienna, and Josef Labor (theory); since accompanist to Gadski and Sembrich on their tours; c. piano pieces and many successful songs.

**hèle** (or **Helle**) (dŭ lă ĕl), **George de**, Antwerp after 1550 — Madrid, 1589; chorister in Royal Chapel, Madrid; 1576 won a silver lute and a silver harp in a competition in Normandy in which in 1575 Orlando di Lasso had won a prize; 1578 cathedral choirmaster at Tournai; from 1580 dir. Royal Chapel, Madrid; c. volume of 8 remarkable masses (*Octo Missae*, Antwerp, 1578) on themes by other composers.

**alande** (lä-länd), **Désiré**, Paris, 1867 — London, Nov. 8, 1904; solo-oboist of the Queen's Hall and other orchestras.

**alevicz** (lä-lä′-vĭch), **Georg von**, b. St. Petersburg, Aug. 21, 1876; piano teacher; pupil of the Cons.; 1900, won the Rubinstein competition in Vienna; 1902–5 prof. in Odessa Cons., after that at Cracow.

**ambrino** (läm-brē′-nō), **Télémaque**, b. Odessa, Oct. 27, 1878 (of Greek parents); studied there at the Royal Akad. der Tonkunst, Munich, and with Teresa Carreño; from 1900 lived in Leipzig, from 1908 teacher at the Cons.

**amoureux, Chas.**, the correct date of his death is Dec. 21, 1899.

**amper′ti, Giovanni Battiste,**

d. Berlin, March 18, 1910. Famous singing master; lived in Dresden and wrote "*The Technic of Bel Canto*," 1905.

**Lamping** (läm′-pĭnk), **W.**, b. Lingen, Hanover, 1861; pupil of Kullak's Academy; from 1886, director of the "*Arion*" and org. at Beilefeld; edited Bach works; 1907 Royal Prof.

**Lancia** (län′-chä), **Florence, (Ladbrake Clarke),** 1840 — Tunbridge Wells, May 24, 1905; operatic and concert vocalist.

**Lan′di, Camilla,** b. Geneva 1866; mezzo-soprano, daughter and pupil of singers; début 1884 Florence; 1886–92 in Paris, then in London where her mother taught; toured widely and returned to Geneva.

**Landormy** (län-dôr-mē), **Paul Charles René,** b. Issy, near Paris, Jan. 3, 1869; studied singing with Sbriglia and Plançon; published philosophical works; 1902 took up composition and musical biography.

**Lange** (läng′-ĕ), **(Langius,)** (1) **Hieronymus Gregor,** Havelberg, Brandenburg — Breslau, 1587; in 1574 cantor at Frankfort-am-Oder; paralysis sent him to the Breslau Alms House, but did not prevent his composition of Latin motets and songs. (2) **Hans,** b. Constantinople, Feb. 14, 1884; pupil there of Brassin and Wondra; then of Prague Cons.; début Berlin, 1903.

**Lange=Müller** (läng′-ĕ-mĭl-lĕr), **Peter Erasmus,** b. Frederiksberg, Dec. 1, 1850; Danish composer; pupil of Copenhagen Cons.; c. operas "*Tove*" (to his own libretto 1878); "*The Spanish Students*," (1883); "*Frau Jeanna*" (1891) and "*Vikingeblod*" (Copenhagen and Stockholm, 1900); symph. "*Autumn*"; incid. music to "*Fulvia*" and "*Es war einmal*"; orch. suite "*Alhambra*" and songs of decidedly national feeling.

**Langey** (läng′-ĭ), **Otto,** b. Leichholz, Oct. 20, 1851; 'cellist; pupil of Specht, Cabisius, etc.; 1877 went to

London, playing in the orchestras of Hallé and Richter; 1889, went to New York; published many methods.

**Lanzetti** (län-tsĕt'-tē), **Salvatore,** Naples, ca. 1710 — Turin, ca. 1780; one of the earliest 'cello virtuosi; c. 'cello sonatas and a method.

**Laroche** (lä-rôsh), **Hermann,** St. Petersburg, May 25, 1845 — Oct. 18, 1904; critic and comp.; pupil of the Cons. and of Tchaikovski, whose friend and biographer he was; prof. at Moscow, later at St. Petersburg Cons.; c. overture, etc.

**Lasso, Orlando di,** Haberl's claim that he was born in 1532, seems to be accepted as conclusive, in spite of Vinchant's contemporary statement that 1520 was the date, and Quichelberg's contemporary statement that 1530 was the date. His family seems to have used the name Lassus for some time before him; he signed his own name variously.

**Las'son,** (1) **Bredo,** b. Feb. 24, 1838; Norwegian composer of piano pieces, songs, etc. His brother (2) **Per,** April 18, 1859 — June 6, 1883.

**Lat'zelsberger, Josef,** b. Allhartsberg, Austria, Jan. 11, 1849; pupil of Vienna Cons.; choirmaster and comp. of church music.

**Lavignac** (lä-vēn-yăk) (**Alex. Jean**), **Albert,** b. Paris, Jan. 21, 1846; pupil of the Cons., and from 1882 prof. there; author of many important works on Wagner, etc.

**Lazzari** (läd-zä'-rē), **Silvio,** Italian composer of operas "*La Lépreuse*" (Op. Com., Paris, 1912), "*Moelenis,*" etc.; c. lyric drama "*Armor*" (prelude at Lamoureux concerts, 1895 — prod. at opera Lyons 1903, revived 1912); c. also symphonic pieces, trio, etc.

**Lee, Cordelia,** b. America of Norwegian parents; pupil of Auer in St. Petersburg; played in Germany 1910, and with the Blüthner Orch., Berlin, 1912.

**Lehár** (lĕ-här'), **Franz,** b. Komorn, Hungary, April 30, 1870; composer of

the world sweeping operetta "*I Lustige Witwe*" (Vienna, 1905, New York and London as "*T Merry Widow*"); lives in Vien as cond. of the Tonkünstlers orc c. also operas "*Kukuska,*" Leipz 1896, revised as "*Tatjana,*" Brü 1905; operettas "*Wiener Fraue* (Vienna, 1902; revised as "*I Schüssel zum Paradiese,*" Leipz 1906); "*Mitislav*" (Vienna, 190 "*Edelweiss und Rosenstock*" (190' "*Peter and Paul reisen ins Schla affenland*" (Vienna, 1906); "*L Mann mit den drei Frauen*" (190

**Lehmann-Osten,** (lā'-män-ôs-tĕ **Paul,** b. Dresden, April 16, 18( pupil of Spindler, Scholtz and Schu Beuthen; from 1892 dir. Ehrli Cons. at Dresden; c. piano pieces, e

**Leichner** (līkh'-nĕr), **Ludwig,** 18 — Berlin, April 1912; singer Wagnerian rôles at Stuttgart, et left the stage, became a manufa turer, and accumulated a gre fortune.

**Leichtentritt** (līkh'-tĕn-trīt), **Hug** b. Pfleschen, Posen, Jan. 1, 18; at 15 taken to America, where studied with J. K. Paine, Bosto then at the Royal Hochschule, B lin; 1901, Ph.D.; wrote theoretical a historical works and c. chamb music and songs.

**Le Jeune** (lŭ-zŭhn), **George F** d. New York, April 11, 1904, age 6 Organist and comp. of church musi

**Lekeu, Guillaume.** The corre date of his birth is Jan. 20, 1870, a of his death Jan. 21, 1894. His dea at 24 left many unfinished works, b enough were complete to assure h fame, among them 3 *études sy phoniques* (1889, 1890); adagio f quatuor and orch. (1891), *epithalam* for string quintet, organ and 3 tror bones; introduction and adagio f orch. with tuba solo; *fantaisie sy phonique sur deux airs populair angévins,* 1892; 2 lyric comedie *Barberine Andromède* (2nd Prix

Rome at Brussels, 1891); chamber music, including sonata for piano and 'cello, finished by V. d'Indy, 1910, and a quatuor finished by the same; sonata for piano and violin (ded. to and played by Ysaye), etc.

**maire** (lŭ-măr), **Jean Eugène Gaston**, b. Château d'Amblainvilliers (Seine-et-Oise) Sept. 9, 1854; pupil Niedermeyer School; critic; c. symph. poem "*Jeffick*," orch. works, ballets, songs, etc.

**mare** (lĕ-măr'), **Edwin Henry**, b. Ventnor, Isle of Wight, Sept. 9, 1865; organist; pupil R. A. M. London, with Goss Scholarship, then made an associate, later a fellow; 1884 fellow Royal College of Organists; occupied various church positions, and gave recitals; 1902–04, organist at Carnegie Hall, Pittsburg, Pa.; 1905, again in London; c. symph., a pastorale and much organ music.

**m'mens = Sher'rington, Helen,** Preston, Oct. 4, 1834 — Brussels, May 9, 1906; operatic singer 1850–1891; prof. Brussels Cons., later R. A. M., London and R. C. M., Manchester.

**oncavallo, Ruggiero,** add that his opera "*Zaza*" was prod. Milan, 1900 with some success and was played in various European capitals; the libretto of "*Roland*" was by Leoncavallo, not by the Kaiser, though he commissioned the work which was not a success when prod. at the Royal Opera Berlin, 1904. L. wrote the libretto for "*Mario Wetter*" by the Portuguese composer Machado. His opera "*Maja*" (Berlin Royal Op., 1911) was a failure. "*Regnetta della Rosa*" (Florence July 15, 1912); "*The Gypsies*" (London, Sept. 16, 1912); "*La Foresta Mormora*" not prod.

**eoni'nus, Magister,,** 12th Century Mus. Director in Paris, at the church of the B. M. Virginis; before Notre Dame was built: one of the earliest masters of the Paris school.

**Leono'va, Daria Mikhailovna,** in the Russian Govt. of Twer, 1825 — St. Petersburg, Feb. 9, 1896; alto; début at 18 in Glinka's "*Life for the Czar*"; sang for many years at the National Opera, and toured around the world.

**Leopo'lita** (or **Lvovczyk**) (l'vôf'-chĕk), **Martin**, Lemburg, 1540 — Cracon, 1589; from 1560 Polish court composer; c. masses, chorales, etc.

**Ler'ner, Tina,** b. Russia 1891 (?); pianist; toured Europe; from 1908, toured America; played with London Phil. orch. three successive seasons; 1911, with Moscow Phil.

**Leva** (dĕ lä'-vä), **Enrico de,** b. Naples, Jan. 18, 1867; singing teacher pupil of Puzone and Ariengo; c. opera "*La Camargo*," (Naples, 1898); serenade "*A Capomonte*" and popular Neapolitan canzonets.

**Levadé** (lŭ-vă-dā'), **Charles Gaston,** b. Paris, Jan. 3, 1869; pupil of Massenet at the Cons.; c. opera "*Les Hérétiques*" (Béziers, 1905), operetta "*L'Amour d'Héliodora*" (Paris, 1903), pantomime, suites, etc.

**Lewalter** (lĕ-văl'-tĕr), **Johann,** b. Cassel, Jan. 24, 1862; pupil Leipzig, Cons.; from 1886 music teacher and essayist; c. fugues, songs, etc.

**Lewinger** (lā'-vĭng-ĕr), **Max,** Sulkov, near Cracow, March 17, 1870—Dresden, Aug. 31, 1908; violinist; pupil of Cracow and Lemberg Cons.; and with Grüns Scholarship, at the Vienna Cons.; from 1892 toured; teacher at Bucharest Cons.; thence to Helsingfors as concertmaster; 1897, do. at the Gewandhaus Orch., Leipzig; 1898 Royal Court concert master in Dresden.

**L'Héritier** (lā-rĭt-yä), (1) **Jean,** flourished 1519–1588; French pupil of Deprès; c. masses and songs. (2) **Antoine,** court musician to Charles V. at Toledo, 1520–1531; (3) **Isaac,** probably the same as **Jean.**

**Lhévinne** (lā-vēn), **Joseph,** b. Moscow, Dec. 3, 1874; pianist; pupil

## 790 THE MUSICAL GUIDE

of his father (first cornet soloist in
Moscow Royal Orch.), and of Chrysander; début at 8; pupil of Safonoff
at the Cons.; 1885, winning highest
honours; 1895 won Rubinstein prize;
1902–6 teacher at the Cons., and
toured Europe; 1905, the U.S.; again,
1912.

**Liadoff** (or **Ljadow**), add that correct pronunciation is "l'yä'-dôf."
His birthdate is May 12th, new style,
as given old style; add that in 1908 he
resigned on account of the expulsion
of Rimsky-Korsakov (q.v.) and was
later reinstated in the Cons.; c.
scherzo for orch. *"The Inn Mazurka"*
scene for orch. polonaise in memory
of Pushkin; *"Baba-Yaga"* tone-
picture (1905, Boston Symph., 1910),
8 folk-songs for orch.; suite *"To
Maeterlinck"* for orch., choruses with
orch.; *"The Music Box,"* and other
piano pieces and songs.

**Libon** (lē'-bōn), **Felipe**, Cadiz,
Aug. 17, 1775 — Paris, Feb. 5, 1838;
violinist and comp. for violin.

**Lichey** (lēkh'-ī), **Rheinhold**, b. Neumark, near Breslau, March 26, 1879;
organist; pupil of Baumert and
Rudnick, later at the Royal High
School in Berlin; from 1907 org.
Königsberg; c. organ pieces, choruses,
etc.

**Lick'l**, (1) **Johann Georg**, Korn-
nenburg, April 11, 1769 — May 12,
1843; church dir.; c. Singspielen for
Schikaneder's theatre. His sons (2)
**Karl Georg**, b. Vienna, Oct. 28,
1801, performer on the Physhar-
monica and composer for it; (3)
**Agidius Fd. K.**, b. Vienna, Sept. 1,
1803; guitarrist; c. oratorio.

**Lidon** (lē'-thôn), **José**, Bejar, Salamanca, 1752 — Madrid, Feb. 11, 1827;
organist; 1808, royal chapel organist
and royal cond. at Madrid; c. operas,
church music, etc.

**Lie** (l'yä), **Sigurd**, May 23, 1871 —
Sept. 30, 1904; important Norwegian
conductor and composer; pupil Leipzig
Cons.; 1894 cond. in Bergen, studied

again in Berlin; cond. of vocal socie
in Christiania; c. symph., Marc
symphonique; orch. suite, *"Orient
isk,"* cantatas, chorals and songs.

**Liebling, Leonard**, add that
was b. Feb. 7, 1874. He writes '
died in 1899; that is when I became
critic." Since that time he has wr
ten the column of the **N . Y.** *Music
Courier* formerly written by Jam
Huneker; c. sonata, barcarolle, r
manza and valse petite for pian
trio for piano, violin, 'cello, etc.

**Lier** (văn lēr), **Jacques Van**, b. T
Hague, April 24,1875; pupil of Hart
Giese and Eberle; 1891 first 'celli
Amsterdam Palace Orch.; 18
Berlin Phil. Orch.; teacher at Klin
worth-Scharwenka Cons.; 'cellist
the Dutch Trio and the Dutch Stri
Quartet; author of methods.

**Liguori** (lē-goo-ō'-rē), **Alfonso d**
1696 — 1787; Neapolitan comp.

**Lim'bert, Frank L.,** b. New Yor
Nov. 15, 1866; at 8 taken to Ge
many; pupil of Hoch Cons. and
Rheinberger; 1894 Ph.D. Berli
1901 cond. of the Düsseldorf Singir
Society, and teacher at the Con
1906, at Hanau; c. choral works wit
orch., etc.

**Lind'egren, Johan,** Ullared, Swede
Jan. 7, 1842 — Stockholm, June
1908; teacher of theory and contra
puntist; from 1884 cantor at th
Stockholm Storkyrka; c. and edite
church music.

**Lin'demann**, (1) **Ole Andrea**
Surandalen, Norway, 1769 — Dror
theim, 1859; organist; teacher an
comp. His sons (2) **Fr. Christian**
1804 — Drontheim 1867, organist, (3
**Jacob Andreas,** 1806—Sognepraes
1846, organist at Christiania; (4
**Matthias,** 1812 — Christiania, Ma
23, 1887; collector of Norwegian folk
music; c. songs; (5) **Just,** b. 182
from 1858 cathedral org. at Drontheim

**Lissenko** (or **Lysenko**), **Nikola
Vitalievich,** b. Grinjki, March 2
1842; popular Little Russian comp

pupil of Panochiny, Dimitriev and Vilczek; then of Leipzig Cons.; 1868, teacher at Kiev; c. 6 operas; children's opera, and popular songs.

**ladow,** vide LIADOFF.

**o'der, Kate Fanny (Lady Thompson)** Bath; Aug. 21, 1886—London, Aug. 30, 1904; pianist, cousin of E. J. Loder (q. v.); pupil of the R. A. M., London, winning the King's scholarship, 1839 and 1841; from 1844 Prof. of harmony there; played with great success at Phil. concerts and elsewhere; 1851 married the surgeon Henry Thompson, afterward knighted; c. an opera, overture, violin sonata, etc.

**oeffler, C. M. T.,** add that he was born Jan. 30, 1861; resigned from the Boston Symph. Orch., 1903, to give his time entirely to composition; c. also fantastic concerto for 'cello and orch. (1894); divertimento for violin and orch. (1897); his symph. poem for 2 viole d'amore *La Mort des Tintagiles* was prod. by the Boston Symph. 1897; he revised it for one viola d'amore and it was prod. 1901, with the composer as the soloist; his *Divertissement Espagnol* for saxophone, and orch. was prod. 1901; his 2 symph. poems. "*Avant que tu ne t'en ailles*" (after Verlaine's "*La bonne chanson*,") and "*Villanelle du diable*" (after Rollinat) were prod. 1902; his "Pagan Poem" for orch. piano, 3 trumpets and Engl. horn 1907; c. also choral works and important songs.

**öbmann,** (läp'-män), **Hugo,** b. Schirgiswalde, Dec. 19, 1864; Catholic music teacher; organist at Trinity Church, Leipzig; c. songs.

**öhlein** (lä'-lln), **Georg Simon,** Neustadt, 1727 — Danzig, 1782. pianist and teacher;

**o'makin, Gabriel Joakimovich,** St. Petersburg April 6, 1812 — Gatschina, May 21, 1885; teacher in St. Petersburg; where he founded the Free School of Music, with Balakirev; c. 10 "*Cherubinische*" songs, etc.

**Longy** (lôn-zhē), **Gustave Georges Léopold,** b. Abbéville, Aug. 29, 1868, pupil Paris Cons. taking second oboe prize 1885, first prize 1886; oboist with Lamoureux and at Op. Com.; from 1898 first oboist Boston Symph., founding 1900 the Longy Club, (flute, oboe, clarinet, horn, bassoon, piano), and giving important concerts.

**Loquin** (lō-kǎn), **Anatole,** b. Orléans, Feb. 22, 1834; composer and theorist at Bordeaux.

**Loren'te, Andres,** Anchuetos, April 15, 1624 — Alcala, Dec. 22, 1703; Spanish organist and writer.

**Lorraine,** (lôr-rĕn'), **Alys,** American soprano, gave recital in London; coached by Massenet; début, The Hague as "*Marguerite*," engaged for Paris Opéra; début there 1912; has sung also at Monte Carlo and Marienbad, 1909.

**Lossius, Lucas,** Vacha, Hesse-Cassel, Oct. 18, 1508; — Lüneberg 1582; rector, theorist and compiler.

**Louis** (loo'-ē), **Rudolf,** b. Schwetzingen, Jan. 30, 1870; pupil at Geneva and Vienna, where he was made Ph.D., studied conducting with Mottl; theatre-cond. at Landshut and Lübeck; c. symph. fantasie "*Proteus*" (Basel, 1903).

**Loewengard** (lä'vĕn-gärt), **Max Julius,** b. Frankfort-on-Main, Oct. 2, 1860; writer and composer; pupil of Raff, then teacher at Wiesbaden Cons.; 1904 critic in Hamburg and 1908 teacher at the Cons.; author of text books in theory; c. comic opera "*Die 14 Nothelfer.*"

**Löwenstern** (lä'-vĕn-shtĕrn) (or **Leuenstern** or **Leonastro**), **Matthaeus Apelles von,** Neustadt, 1594 — Bernstadt, 1648; poet and composer; son of a saddler named Löwe; became a privy councillor and was ennobled by Ferdinand II, taking the name of von Loewenstern; c. words and music of "*Früh-*

*lings-Morgen*" (30 sacred songs), oratorio "*Judith*" (1646), etc.

**Lowe** (lō), **Thomas,** English, popular tenor; début, 1740, at Drury Lane; d. London, March 1, 1783.

**Lucchesi** (look-kä'-zē),**Andrea,** Motta, May 28, 1741 — Italy, ca. 1800; organist and cond.; 1771 theatre dir. of an Italian troupe in Bonn; 1774-94 royal cond. there; **c.** symphonies, etc.

**Lucia** (dě-loo-chē'-ä), **Fernando de,** b. Naples, about 1860; dramatic tenor; said to have been a trombone-player, largely self-taught; début Lisbon; 1887 London Opera at Drury Lane, with little success, but on his reappearance, 1893, at Covent Garden, as the first to sing "*I Pagliacci*" in London, he made a sensation with his fervor; later became a favourite at the Met. Op., New York, rather as an actor than a singer; 1905, in London again.

**Ludwig,** (1) **August,** b. Waldheim, Saxony, Jan 15, 1865; critic and comp. pupil of Cologne and Munich Cons.; attracted attention by risking the completion of Schubert's Unfinished symph., with a "*Philosophic scherzo*," and a "*March of Fate*"; **c.** also an overture "*Ad Astra,*" etc. (2) **Joseph** b. Bonn, April 6, 1844; violinist; pupil Cologne Cons., and of Joachim; from 1870 in London as teacher and naturalized subject; plays in a quartet; **c.** 2 symph., etc., His son (3) **Paul,** b. Bonn, Aug. 11, 1872; 'cellist; pupil of R. A. M., London and of Piatti; soloist and quartet player; (4) **Frederich,** b. Potsdam, May 8, 1872; historian of music; docent at Strassburg Universty; (5) **William** (rightly **Wm. Ledwidge,**), b. Dublin, ca. 1850; Irish barytone; from 1877, with Carl Rosa Co., especially successful in "*The Flying Dutchman*"; 1896 sang Hans Sachs; a fine Elijah.

**Luft** (looft), **Heinrich,** Magdeburg, 1813 – 1868; oboist and comp.

**Lugert** (loo'-gĕrt), **Josef,** b. Frohnau,

Bohemia, Oct. 30, 1841; teach· pupil of Prague Organ School, a· violinist in German Landestheat there; later piano teacher at Prag Cons.; 1905 Royal Music Inspect· organized orchestra schools, and w fame as a teacher; **c.** symph., se· nades for orch., "*In Memoriam*" f full orch. with English horn so. also wrote technical books.

**Luigini** (lwē-zhē'-nē), **Alexand (Clément L. Jos.)** Lyons, Mar 9, 1830 — Paris, July 29, 1906; pu· and prize-winner at the Cons.; 18 leader in Grand Théâtre, Lyons, a· founder of the Cons. concerts a· Prof.; 1897 cond. at Op. Comiqu Paris; **c.** comic operas, *Les capri· de Margot* (Lyons, 1877), *Faub·* (1881), ballets, etc.

**Lunn,** (1) **Henry Charles,** L· don, 1817 — Jan. 23, 1894; edit and author; pupil Royal Mu· Akademie, later teacher; 1863–· edited *The Musical Times,* Lond· (2) **John Robert,** Cleeve Pri· 1831 — Morton, Yorkshire, Ap· 1899; vicar there from 1867; **c.** o· torio "*St. Paulinius of York,*" e· His brother (3) **Jan,** Birmingha· 1838–1906; singer, teacher and auth· of books on the voice. (4) **(Louis· Kirkby,** b. Manchester, Nov. 8, 18· mezzo-soprano; pupil of J. H. Gre· wood, then of Visetti, R. A. M., L· don, gaining a scholarship in 18· Appeared in a student performance Schumann's *Genoveva,* 1893, with su· success that she was engaged by · Augustus Harris; 1897–9 contral· of Carl Rosa Company; then marri· W. J. K. Pearsen; sang in conce· 1901 began an uninterrupted engag· ment at Covent Garden; sang mu· at festivals; 1902 at Met. Op. Hou· New York and with Boston Symp· and other orchs., 1907 created *Ku· dry* in first English performance "*Parsifal*" by the Henry W. Sava· Company.

**Lustig** (loos'-tĭkh), **Jacob Wm·

Hamburg, Sept. 21, 1706-1796; organist and theorist.

**ython** (or **Luiton**) (lī-tôn), **Carl,** Antwerp (?) — Prague, 1620; important composer of madrigals, masses, fugues, etc.; 1576 court organist to Maximilian II and to Rudolf II.

**zzaschi** (lood-zäs'-kē), **Luzza=sco,** d. Ferrara, 1607; court organist; pupil of Ciprian de Rore, and teacher of Frescobaldi; c. Madrigals, etc.

**ne, Felice,** b. Kansas City, Mo.; 1892 (?); soprano; 1906-11 pupil of Marchesi, de Reszké and d'Aubigny, Paris; 1910 engaged by Hammerstein to sing "Hans the Flute-Player"; 1911 appeared at the London Opera in *Rigoletto* and other operas.

**ssenko,** vide LISSENKO.

# M

**accar'thy, Maud,** b. Clonmel, Ire., July 4, 1884; violinist; pupil of Arbos, début London, 1894; toured America.

**'Cor'mack, John,** b. Athlone, 1884; tenor; pupil of Sabatini, Milan; début Covent Garden, 1907, with great success; 1910 sang with Philadelphia Opera Co.; 1911 Chicago Opera Co., and at Met. Op. N. Y.; toured Australia, 1912, with the Melba Opera Co. and sang in concert with immense success.

**acdon'ald,** (1) **Peter,** Sutherland, Scotland, 1729 — Kilmore, 1824; violinist and collector of Highland melodies; minister. His brother (2) **Joseph,** 1739 — India, 1762; was also a musician.

**acDowell, E. A.,** add that in Jan. 1904, he resigned his professorship at Columbia University from dissatisfaction with the faculty's attitude toward music as a high art. He was succeeded by Cornelius Rübner (q. v.). He had cond. the Mendelssohn Glee Club for two years. In 1905 he fell a prey to cerebral trouble that ended his beautiful career. Faithfully tended by his wife, he lingered under increasing clouds, till his death, Jan. 23, 1908, at New York. So great was his hold upon the American public that a MacDowell Club with many branches was formed to carry on his ideals of art and to aid the struggling musician; a choral branch under the leadership of Kurt Schindler has attained a very high standard; taking the title of "Schola Cantorum" in 1912; a biography of MacDowell was written by Lawrence Gilman, 1905.

**Marschal-Loepke,** vide CLOUGH-LEITER (2).

**M'Ew'en, John Blackwood,** b. Hawick, April 13, 1868; Scots composer and pupil R. A. M., Glasgow, later Prof. there; c. symph., 2 overtures, "*Hellas*" for women's voices and orch. "*The Last Chantey,*" chorus and orch. Milton's "*Nativity,*" do.; also Highland dances for strings, violin, etc.

**Macfar'lane, W. Chas.,** b. London, Oct. 2, 1870; organist; brought to New York at 4; pupil of his father and of S. P. Warren; c. anthems, etc.

**M'Gib'bon, William,** d. Edinburgh, Oct. 3, 1756; studied violin under Corbett, London; cond. "*Gentlemen's Concerts*" in Edinburgh; collected Scots melodies and c. sonatas.

**Mackaý, Angus,** drowned near Dumfries, March 21, 1859; Highland Piper to Queen Victoria; collected pipe tunes.

**Mack'intosh,** (1) **John,** London 1767 — March 23, 1844; bassoonist. (2) **Robert,** d. London, 1807; Scots violinist and teacher; composer of strathspeys, and cond. at Edinburgh. His son (2) **Abraham,** Edinburgh, 1759 — Newcastle after 1807.

**M'Leod** (măk-lowd'), **Peter,** West Calder, 1797 — Bonnington, 1859; Scots composer and violinist; collected Scottish melodies.

**Macmil'len, Francis,** b. Marietta, Ohio, Oct. 14, 1885; violinist; pupil of Listemann, Chicago; at 10, pupil of Markees, Berlin; at 15 of César Thomson at Brussels Cons.; sharing first violin prize 1902 and taking Van Hal prize; played in Brussels, etc.; 1903 London; 1906 toured U. S.

**Macpher'son,** (1) **Charles Stewart,** composer; b. Liverpool, March 29, 1865; pupil of R. A. M., London, with a scholarship; gained also the Balfe scholarship and medals; 1887 prof. there; 1892 a fellow; 1903 prof. Royal Normal College for the Blind; c. symph., 2 overtures, a fine mass with orch. (1898); "*Concerto alla fantasia*" for violin, etc.; wrote theoretical text books, (2) **Charles,** b. Edinburgh, May 10, 1870; 1890 pupil R. A. M., winning Lucas prize 1892; later teacher of counterpoint there; 1895, sub-organist at St. Paul's, London; c. overture "*Cridhe an Ghaidhil*" (London, 1895); orch. suites, "*Highland*" and "*Hallowe'en*"; *Psalm* 187 for choir and orch., etc.

**McWhood, Leonard B.,** b. New York, Dec. 5, 1870; graduated from Columbia University 1893; after various posts, 1904 prof. of music there; conductor, lecturer; c. unpublished works.

**Macque** (măk), **Jean de,** Flemish choirmaster in Rome 1576–82; 1610 at Royal Chapel Naples; c. madrigals and motets.

**Madin** (mă-dăṅ) (rightly **Madden**), **Henri,** Verdun, 1698 — Versailles, 1748; clergyman of Irish parentage; cond. at the cathedral of Tours; from 1737 in the Chapel of the King; c. motets.

**Magnard** (mĭn-yăr), **Lucien D. G. A.,** b. Paris, June 9, 1865; composer; pupil of the Cons. (winning first harmony prize 1888), then of d'Indy; c. 3 symph., overture, suite in ancient style; hymns to "*Justice*".

and to "*Venus,*" 1-act opera " ] lande" (Brussels, 1892); 3-act "*Gu cœur*"; important chamber mus etc.

**Mahler, Gustav,** add that he v dir. of the Court Opera Vienna 1907, when he resigned; and co Met. Op., N. Y., for two seaso 1909 was elected to cond. Philh. Orc N. Y., with the highest salary ev paid a cond. ($30,000 a year); nervous breakdown in 1911 ended I work, and he sailed for Europe in Ap dying in Vienna May 18, 1911. I comps. include 8 symph., the last fi written, 1901, 1904, 1906, 1908, 191 His eighth was prod. in Munich, 191 and Leipzig, 1912, requiring a chor and orch. of 1,000 members. A nim symph. is said to have been finishe His "*Das Lied von der Erde,*" a symp in six parts, for tenor and alto a orch. (text from Hans Bathg Chinese flute) was given at Munic Nov. 20, 1911.

**Maichelbeck,** (mīkh'-ĕl-bĕk), **Fran Anton,** Reichenau, 1802 — Freibu 1750; c. important sonatas, etc., f clavier.

**Maillard** (mī-yăr), **Jean,** 16th ce tury French composer; pupil Deprès; c. important motets a masses, from one of which Palestri took themes for a mass of his own.

**Maikapar** (mă'-kä-pär), **Samue** b. Chersson, Russia, Dec. 18, 186 pianist; pupil of the Cons., and Leschetizky; settled in Moscow; piano pieces.

**Mair, Franz,** Weikersdorf Marshfel 1821 — Vienna, 1893; composer a founder of the Schubertbund.

**Major** (mä'-yôr), **Julius J.,** Kaschau, Hungary, Dec. 13, 185 pupil of the Landes-Musik Akad. Pest; founded a music school ar singing societies there; c. a symph operas, "*Lisbeth*" and "*Erysika* (Pest, 1901), *Szechi Maria* (Klause burg, 1906), etc.

**Maksylevich** (măk-sē'-lĕ-vĭch), V

cent, 1685 — Cracow, 1745; church cond. at Cracow; c. church music.

**alash'kin, Leonid Dimitrie= vitch,** 1842 — Moscow, Feb. 11, 1902; Russian composer of an opera, a symph., songs, etc.

**al'ling,** (1) **Jörgen,** Copenhagen, 1836 — July 14, 1907; important Danish composer and teacher; from 1875 in Vienna. His brother (2) **Otto (Vlademar),** b. Copenhagen, June 1, 1848; pupil of Gade and Hartmann at the Cons., later teacher there; organist and founder of concert association; c. symph.; violin fantasie with orch., overture, chamber music, and valuable organ pieces.

**alm'qvist** (mälm'-kwĭst), **Julius,** b. Copenhagen, June 16, 1819 — Hirscholm, Aug. 4, 1859; Danish composer of male quartets, operettas, etc.

**alvezzi** (mäl-vĕd'-zē), **Christo= fano,** Lucca, 1547 — Florence, 1597; canon in Florence; and chapel master to the Grand Dukes of Tus- any; collected and composed dra- matic intermezzi, 1591, etc.

**ancinelli, Luigi,** add that his cantata "Saint Agnes" was prod. at Norwich Festival 1905; his opera "Paolo e Francesca" (Bologna, 1907).

**anc'nus, Thomas,** Schwerin, 1550 — Wolfenbüttel ca. 1620; Dutch composer of Passions according to St. Matthew and St. John; cond. to Duke of Brunswick.

**andl** (mänt'-'l), **Richard,** b. Ross- itz, Moravia, 1862; pianist; pupil Vienna Cons., later of Delibes, Paris, where he settled 1886; c. 1-act. opera "Rencontre Imprévue" (Rouen, 1889); Chanson Provençal for voice and orch., orch. scherzo (Lamoureux con- certs, 1894); important symph. poem, with organ, mezzo-sopr. and female chorus; "Griselidis" (Vienna, 1906?); overture "To a Gascon Knight drama" (Wiesbaden, 1910), piano pieces, etc.

**andyczevski** (män-dē-chĕf'-skĭ), **Eusebius,** b. Czernovitz, Aug. 18,

1857; pupil of Fuchs and Notte- bohm; from 1897 teacher Vienna Cons.; writer and editor of Schubert's works, for which he was made Ph. D., Leipzig.

**Manén** (mä'-nän) **Joan De,** b. Barcelona, March 14, 1883; Spanish composer; travelled as prodigy pianist, then took up violin; pupil of Alard; c. operas "Giovanni di Napoli" (Bar- celona, 1903), "Akté" (do.); "Der Fackeltanz" (Frankfort-o n-Main 1909); symph. poem "Nuova Catalo- nia," violin concert, etc.

**Manfredini** (män-frĕ-dē'nē), (1) **Francesco,** b. Pistoja, 1688; violin- ist; 1711 cond. at Monaco; c. ora- torios, concertos, etc. His son (2) **Vincenzo,** Pistoja, 1737 — St. Pe- tersburg, 1799, as court cond., c. sonatas, etc.

**Mangin** (män-zhăn), **Edouard,** Paris, 1837 — May 24, 1907; founded Cons. at Lyons, 1870; also the Popular Concerts; from 1893 cond. the Opéra, Paris.

**Mann, Frederick A.,** Norwich, March 23, 1844 — April 11, 1903; violinist; cathedral organist and dir.; brother of **Arthur Henry M.** (q. v.).

**Man'ners,** (1) **Charles** (rightly **Southcote Mansergh**), b. London, Dec. 27, 1857; bass; pupil Dublin Academy and R. A. M., London, and of Shakespeare; début 1882; 1890 Covent Garden; 1893 toured America; 1896 South Africa; 1897, organized Moody-Manners Opera Co. touring the provinces with three companies, two seasons at Covent Garden. In 1890 he married (2) **Fanny Moody,** b. Redruth, Nov. 23, 1866; soprano; pupil of Mme. Sainton Dolby; début 1887 with Carl Rosa Co., since 1890 has sung with her husband.

**Maquarre** (mä-kär), **André,** b. Molenbeck, St. Jean, Belgium, Jan. 13, 1875; pupil Paris Cons., took first flute prize 1893; played in Co- lonne and Lamoureux orchs.; from

1898 first flute Boston Symph.; c. opera "*Dolores*," two comic operas, "*Indian suite*" for orch., overture "*On the Sea Cliffs*" (Boston Symph., 1909), etc.

**Marchesi, Mathilde,** add that in 1912, at the age of 90, she sold her school and moved to London, to join her daughter Blanche.

**Marchisio** (mär-kē'sĭ-ō), **Barbara,** b. Turin, 1834; opera singer in Paris and London; sang usually with her sister. (2) **Carlotta,** Turin, 1836 — Turin, 1872.

**Marks, Dr. Jas. Chr.,** Armagh, May 4, 1835 — Grand Spa, Clifton, July 17, 1903; organist and conductor.

**Mar'schalk, Max,** b. Berlin, April 7, 1863; composer of 2-act opera "*In Flammen*" (Gotha, 1896); musical piece "*Aucassin und Nicolette*" (Stuttgart, 1907); incid. music to "*Und Pippa tanzt*" (Berlin, 1906), and to Maeterlinck's "*Sister Beatrice*" (Berlin, 1904).

**Marsh,** (1) **Alphonso,** Westminster, 1627–1681; gentleman of Chapel Royal and composer. His son (2) **Alphonso,** d. Westminster, 1692; gentleman of the Chapel Royal from 1676; c. songs. (3) **William,** Fochabers, 1748 — Dandaleith, 1833; Scots violinist; c. strathspeys, etc.

**Marshall, John Patton,** b. Rockfort, Mass., Jan. 9, 1877; pupil of B. J. Lang, MacDowell, Chadwick, and Norris; 1903 Prof. of Music, Boston University, also org. at St. John's; c. songs and piano pieces.

**Marteau, Henri,** add that he was born at Rheims, March 31, 1874; from 1900 teacher at Geneva Cons.; 1908 successor to Joachim at the Royal Hochschule für Musik, Berlin.

**Martinel'li, Giovanni,** tenor; at first an instrumentalist in Milan; début 1912, Covent Garden in "*La Tosca*" with great success.

**Mascagni, Pietro,** add that he was dir. of Pesaro Cons. 1895–1903, when he toured the U. S. with an opera co., and was supplanted a[t] the Cons.; 1909, cond. at Teatr[o] Costanzi, Rome; c. also "*Amica*[" (Monte Carlo, 1905, Cologne, 1907[;] 1910 he c. opera "*Isabeau*" for th[e] U. S. but not completing it on tim[e] became involved in a lawsuit. Th[e] opera was prod. at Venice and Mila[n] simultaneously, 1912, with much su[c]cess and has been widely sung sinc[e.] His next work is announced a[s] "*Parisina*" with libretto by d'A[n]nunzoo.

**Mascheroni** (mäs-kĕ-rō'-nē), **Edo**[?]**ardo,** b. Milan, Sept. 4, 1857[;] cond. and composer; pupil of Bouc[h]eron; 1883 theatre cond. at Leghor[n] later at Teatro Apollo, Rome; 18[9?] chosen to cond. Verdi's "*Falstaff*" [at] La Scala; c. important *Requiem* f[or] King Victor Emanuel, also by Roy[al] command another *Requiem* for t[he] royal chapel; c. operas "*Lorenza*[?]" (Rome,1901), very successful throug[h]out Europe and South America; "*[?]Perugina*," etc.

**Mason, Daniel Gregory,** b. Broo[k]line, Mass., Nov. 20, 1873; pu[pil] of Clayton Johns, E. Nevin, [?] Whiting, J. K. Paine, G. W. Cha[d]wick and Percy Goetschius; gra[d]uated Harvard, 1895; author [of] articles and books on musical topic[s;] c. violin and piano sonata (191[?]) piano variations on "Yank[ee] Doodle"; quartet in A major; pa[s]torale for violin, clarinet and pian[o;] elegy for piano (played by Gabril[o]witsch in Berlin, London a[nd] America), songs, etc.

**Massart,** (mäs-sär) **Nestor, H.** [?] tenor opera singer; Ciney, Belgiu[m] 1849 — Ostende, 1899; operat[ic] favourite in Europe and America.

**Massenet,** add that his "*Jongle*[ur] *de Nôtre Dame*," (Monte Carlo, 190[?]) has been sung widely; Covent Ga[r]den, 1906, New York Manhatt[an] Opera, 1910; "*Cherubin*" (Op. Co[?] Paris, 1905); "*Ariane*" (190[?] "*Thérèse*" (Monte Carlo, 19[?]

*Don Quichotte"* (Paris, 1911); *"Rona"* (Paris, Opéra, 1912); oratorios *'La Terre Promise"* (Paris, 1900); piano concerto (1903); ballets, *"La Cigale"* (Paris, 1903), *"Espada"* (Monte Carlo, 1908), etc., after suffering for years from cancer, he died suddenly at his home, Paris, Aug. 13, 1912.

**aszynski** (mä-shĭn'-shkĭ), **Peter,** b. Warsaw, 1855; pianist and composer; pupil of Mikhalovski, Roguski and Noskovski; his *"Chor zniviarzy"* won a prize at Cracow; teacher at the Musical Institute; cond.; c. violin sonata, incid. music, a cantata in honor of the jubilee of Sienkiewicz, etc.

**atthay'**, **Tobias Augustus,** b. London, Feb. 19, 1858; pianist; pupil R. A. M., teacher there; c. *'Hero and Leander,"* for chorus and orch., etc.

**auduit** (mō-dwē), **Jacques,** Paris, Sept. 16, 1557 — Aug. 21, 1627; lute player and composer of chansons and a requiem for the poet Ronsard.

**auke** (mow'-kĕ), **Wilhelm,** b. Hamburg, Feb. 25, 1867; pupil of Löw and Huber; then at Munich Akad. der Tonkunst, acted as critic; c. symph. poem *"Einsamkeit"* (after Stuck and Nietzsche), opera, etc.

**auricio** ( mä-oo-rē'-sĭ-ō ), **José,** Coimbra, 1752 — Figueira, 1815; Portuguese composer of church music.

**azzolani** ( mäd-zō-lä'-nē ), **Antonio,** Ruina, Ferrara, Dec. 26, 1819 — Ferrara, Jan. 25, 1900; composer of successful operas and choruses.

**eisel** (mī'-sĕl), ‖ **Carl,** Germany, 1829—Boston, Dec. 27, 1908; came to America in 1852; violinist in Boston Symph. Orch. at its foundation.

**elar'tin, Erik,** b. 1875; Finnish composer of excellent songs; pupil of Wegelius.

**elchissédec** ( mĕl-shĭs-sä-dĕk ), **Léon,** b. May 7, 1843; barytone;

pupil Paris Cons. and from 1894 teacher there; 1866–1891 sang at Opéra Comique, Paris.

**Mel'lon, Alfred,** London, April 17, 1821 — March 27, 1867; cond. at Covent Garden, and Liverpool Phil.; c. operas.

**Meltz'er, Charles Henry,** b. London, June 7, 1853 of Russian parentage; critic; pupil of the Sorbonne, Paris, later journalist on various New York papers; author and translator of plays and librettos; press representative Met. Op. House, 1911, critic New York *American.*

**Ménil** (dŭ-mä-nēl), **Félicien, de,** b. Boulogne-sur-Mer, July 16, 1860; historian and comp.; after much foreign travel, settled in Paris, 1899, as teacher of musical history at the Niedermeyer Church Music School; c. opera *"La Janelière"* (Op. Com., Paris, 1894); operetta *"Gosses"* (1901) and ballets.

**Mergner** (mĕrkh'-nĕr), **Adam Fr. Chr.,** Regensburg, Oct. 19, 1818 —near Ansbach, Jan. 7, 1891; priest and church composer.

**Merikant'o, Oscar,** b. Finland, 1868; organist and composer of opera, etc.

**Meschaert** (mā'-shärt), **Johannes,** b. Hoorn, Holland, Aug. 22, 1857; barytone; pupil of Schneider, Stockhausen and Wüllner; teacher and cond. in Amsterdam; tours widely.

**Messager, André,** add that he remained as cond. of the Op. Com. till 1903, and as director of Covent Garden from 1901 to 1907, in which year he became director of the Opéra at Paris, and from 1908 cond. of the concerts of the Cons. Add to his operettas; *"Mirette"* (Savoy, London, 1894); *Les P'tites Michu* (Paris, 1894) enormous success; *Véronique* (1899); *Fortunio* (Op. Com. 1907); also ballets and songs.

**Mess'ner, Georg,** b. Berlin, Sept. 22, 1871; pupil of H. van Eijken; artillery officer at Breslau; c. songs and male choruses.

**Mest'dagh** (mĕst'-däkh), **Karel**, b.
Bruges, Oct. 22, 1850; pupil of
Waelput, Gheluwe and Gevaert;
c. overture "*Les noces d'Attila*"
choruses with orch., etc.

**Michael** (mē'-khä-ĕl), (1) **Simon**,
musician to Emperor Ferdinand I.
His son (2) **Rogier**, d. Dresden,
ca. 1619; tenor and cond. to the
Elector; c. motets. His son (3)
**Tobias**, b. Dresden, 1592; church
cond. Leipzig; c. church music, etc.

**Middelschulte** (mid'-dĕl-shool-tĕ),
**Wilhelm**, b. Werwe, Westphalia,
April 3, 1863; organist; pupil of
the Berlin Inst. for church music;
from 1888 organist there; in 1891
settled in Chicago; from 1894 org. of
the Thomas orch. and of St. James;
c. canons and fugue on "*Our Father
in Heaven*"; organ concerts on a
theme of Bach's; canonic fantasie on
Bach, etc.

**Mielck** (mēlk), **Ernst**, Wiborg,
Oct. 24, 1877 — Locarno, Oct. 22,
1899; Finnish composer, who, in spite
of his pitifully brief life of 22 years,
gained a place of national importance;
pupil of Tietse, Radecke and Bruch;
c. Finnish symph.; overture "*Macbeth* "; Finnish fantasie for chorus and
orch.; Finnish orch. suite, etc.

**Miersch** (mērsh), (1) **Carl Alex.
Johannes**, b. Dresden, 1865;
violinist; pupil of the Cons. and of
Massart; 1888–90 teacher in Aber-
deen, then for a year with the Boston
Symph. Orch.; 1894–8 artistic dir. of
the Athens Cons. and court violinist;
1902, returned to the U. S.; from
1910 at Cincinnati Coll. of Music. His
brother (2) **Paul Fr.**, b. Dresden,
Jan. 18, 1868; 'cellist, pupil of Royal
Akad., Munich; from 1892 in New
York, for five years soloist N. Y.
Symph. Orch., 1898, soloist Met.
Opera; c. Indian rhapsody, for orch.,
'cello and violin concertos. etc.

**Mignard** (mēn-yăr), **Alexander
Konstantinovich** (rightly
**Scheltobrjuchov**), b. Warsaw

Aug. 13, 1852; pupil of the Cons. a[nd]
of Saint Saëns at the Paris Cons.; la[w]-
yer and statesman at Warsaw;
operas, overtures, 2 symph., etc.

**Mil'denberg**, **Albert**, b. Broo[k]-
lyn, Jan. 13, 1873; pupil of Josef
Bruno Oskar Klein and C. C. Müll[er]
c. orch. suites, etc.

**Millet** (mēl'-yĕt), **Luis**, b. Bar[ce]-
lona, April 18, 1867; pupil of Vidie[l]
and Pedrell; founded and cond. t[he]
Orféo Catalá society; c. choruses a[nd]
orch. fantasies on folk-themes.

**Mil'ligen**, **Simon Van**, b. Rott[er]-
dam, Dec. 14, 1849; organist; pupil[of]
Nicolai, Bargiel, etc.; for many yea[rs]
municipal dir. of Gouda, later [at]
Amsterdam as critic and teacher;
operas "*Brinio*" and "*Darthul[a*"]
(The Hague, 1898), etc.

**Minc'us**, **Ludwig**, b. Vienna, 18[ ]
violinist and cond. in St. Petersbu[rg]
1872, bailet composer at the Imper[ial]
Opera; then retired to Vienna;
ballets, including "*La Source*"
collaboration with Delibes.

**Mirecki** (mē-rets'-kē), **Franz**, C[ra]
cow, April 1, 1791 — May [ ]
1862; pupil of Hummel and Che[ru]-
bini; after 1838 director of school [of]
opera singing in Cracow; c. oper[as,]
ballets, etc.

**Mit'terer**, **Ignaz Martin**, b. St. J[us]-
tina, Tyrol, Feb. 2, 1850; compo[ser]
and director; pupil of his un[cle]
**Anton M.**, (a choirmaster), and [of]
Father Huber; 1874 became a prie[st,]
studied at Regensburg under Jak[ob]
Haberl and Haller; 1880 chaplain [at]
Rome; 1882–5, cathedral cond. [at]
Regensburg, later at Brixen as dir.; [in]
the cathedral; his compositions sh[ow]
the influence of Palestrina; c. mas[ses]
with orch., offertories and a gr[eat]
amount of church music.

**Mlynarski** (m'lē-när'-shkĭ), **Em[il]**,
b. Kibarty, Suvalki, July 30, 18[ ]
pupil St. Petersburg Cons.; 1893 co[nd.]
and teacher at Warsaw; 1894 [at]
Odessa; from 1899 cond. at Op[era]
House, Warsaw; also cond. P[hil.]

ch.; 1904–7 director of the Cons.;
en in London; c. violin concerto
'aderewski prize at Leipzig, 1898),
peras, etc.

cquereau (môk-rō), André,
La Tessouale, France, June 6, 1849;
riter; 'cello pupil of Dancla; from
875 Benedictine monk, teacher of
noral singing at the Abbey of Soles-
es, later prior; founder and editor of
ne "Paléographie musicale"; in 1903
n the exile of the order, moved to the
le of Wight, continuing the publi-
tion of his great work; authority on
regorian chant, on which he wrote
Rythmique Grégorienne" (vol. I,
908), etc.

isisovics (mō-sē'-sō-vĭch), Rod-
rich von, b. Graz, May 10, 1877;
npil of Degner, and of the Cologne
ons., and Munich Akad.; 1903 cond.
various cities; c. symph. "In the
ps," symph. poem "Stella," "Chorus
yslicus" from Faust for soli, double
norus, organ and orch., etc.

ck, Heinrich, Grosz-Himstedt,
825 — Hanover, 1889; composer
d organist.

'ter, Johann Melchior, mus.
rector in Durlach, 1733; amazingly
rolific writer; c. 169 symph., 14
rertures, etc.

n'day, Joseph, 1851 — January
, 1909; English organist and conuctor.

nhaupt (môn'-howpt), Franz, b.
ckelsthal, near Friedland, Aug.
, 1854; director of the Prague
mshouse for some years, then school
rector in Bohemian Leipa; c. opera,
ch. suite, piano quintet, etc.

nn, Georg Matthias, Lower
ustria, 1717 — Vienna, Oct. 3, 1750;
ganist and comp. of highly impor-
nt instrumental works, symphonies,
c., marking a transition to the
odern style.

nnet (mŭn-nā), Jean, b. Con-
ieux, 1700 — Paris, 1785; 1743 and
52–8 cond. Opéra Comique, Paris.

nod (mŭ-nō), Edmond, b.

Lyons, Feb. 4, 1871; author and
teacher; pupil of Roth, Stepanov and
Leschetizky; 1899–1906 teacher in
Berlin; 1907 Prof. at Geneva Cons.;
c. songs.

**Montanari** (môn-tä-nä'-rē), **Francesco,** Padua (?) — Rome, 1730;
violinist at St. Peter's, Rome; c. 12
violin sonatas.

**Montefiore** (môn-tĕ-fĭ-ō'-rē), **Tommaso Mosè,** composer; b. Livorno,
1855; pupil of Mabellini; critic under
the pen-name of "Puck," editor;
c. operas "Un bacio a portatore"
(Florence. 1884), and "Cecilia"
(Ravenna, 1905).

**Moody, Fanny,** vide MANNERS
(2).

**Moor** (môr), (1) **Karl,** Bohemian
comp. of 1-act opera "Vij" (Prague,
1903), and "Hjördis" (do., 1905).
(2) **Emanuel,** c. symph. concertos
and operas "Die Pompadour" (Cologne, 1902), and "Andreas Hofer"
(do. 1902); "Hochzeitsglocken" (Cassel, 1908).

**Moraës** (mō-räⁿs), **João da Silva,**
Lisbon, Dec. 27, 1689 — ca. 1747;
important Portuguese composer of
church music; cond. at the Cathedral.

**Morena** (mō-rā'-nä), **Berta,** b. Würzburg, Jan. 27, 1878; pupil of Frau
Röhr-Brajnin and Mme. de Sales;
début at Munich Court Theatre; has
sung there since, and from 1908 with
Met. Op., N. Y.; also in concert with
Boston Symph., 1909, etc.

**Möricke** (mä'-rĭk-ē), **Oscar,** b. Coburg, Aug. 10, 1839; bassoon player
there in the Opera orch., 1856–66;
1878–82 teacher in Munich, then in
Berlin; c. 2 symphs., etc.

**Morigi** (mō-rē'-jē), **Angelo,** Rimini,
1752 — Parma, 1788; violinist; pupil
of Tartini and Valotti; court cond.;
c. violin sonatas, etc.

**Mor'nington, Earl of (Garrett C.
Wesley or Wellesley,)** Dangan,
Ireland, July 19, 1735 — May 22,
1781; founded Academy of Music,
1757; 1764 Mus. Doc. (Dublin) and

Prof.; 1760; created M. Viscount Wellesley and Earl of M.; c. well-known chant in E flat, and prize glees and madrigals; one of his sons was the Duke of Wellington.

**Mor'telmans, Lodevijk,** b. Antwerp, 1868; pupil of the Cons. and Brussels Cons.; c. symph. "*Germania,*" symph. poem "*Wilde Jagd,*" etc.

**Mo'sel Giovanni Felice,** b. Florence, 1754; violinist; pupil of Nardini and his successor as court cond., 1793; c. violin music, etc.

**Mo'ser, Marie,** 1848 — Vienna, May 17, 1911; singer in Wagner rôles; wife of General von Steinitz.

**Motta, José Da,** vide **Da Motta.**

**Mottl, Felix,** add that he resigned at Carlsruhe, 1903, and cond. in New York at the Met. Op., directing the first performances of "*Parsifal*" outside Bayreuth; 1904 he became co-director of the Royal Academy of Music, Munich; he was cond. the United Royal Operas there, when he fell ill of arteriosclerosis and died in July, 1911. Shortly before his death he was divorced from his first wife and married Sdenka Fassbender, of the Munich Opera.

**Muck, Karl,** add that in 1899 he cond. German Opera in London; 1903–5 alternated with Mottl as cond. of the Vienna Phil.; 1906–8 on leave of absence he cond. Boston Symph. during the winters; appearing also at Paris, Madrid, etc.; 1901, 2, 4, 6, and 8 cond. "*Parsifal*" at Bayreuth. By arrangement with the Boston Symph. he continued his contract, sending Max Fiedler to conduct in his place 1909–12; and returning 1912.

**Muffat, (1) Georg,** Schlettstadt, correct birthplace, ca. 1645; d. Passau, Feb. 23, 1704. (2) **Aug. Gottlieb,** Passau, April, 1690 — Vienna, Dec. 10, 1770.

**Mugellini** (moo-gĕl-lē'-nē), **Bruno,** b. Potenza, Dec. 24, 1871; pianist; pupil of Tofano, Busi and Martucci; 1898 teacher at the Bologna Lyceum;

c. prize symph. poem "*Alle fonte Clitumno*"; 'cello sonata, etc.; ed Bach, Czerny and Clementi.

**Mulert** (moo'-lĕrt), **Fr. von,** Mitau, 1859; 'cellist; pupil of Petersburg Cons.; prof. at Kiev orch. suites, and piano pieces.

**Mun'dy, (1) William,** d. 1591 gentleman of the Chapel Royal, 1 c. anthems, etc. His son (2) **Jo** d. Windsor, 1630; where he had b organist from 1585; c. madrigals a fantasia describing the weather.

**Münnich** (mĭn'-nĭkh), **(1) Rud** b. Friedenau, Berlin, June 18, 18 song-composer. His son and p **(2) Richard,** pianist; author singing teacher in Berlin.

**Munzinger,** (moon'-tsĭng-ĕr) **Ka** Balsthal, Sept. 23, 1842 — Be Switzerland, Aug .17, 1911; pupi Leipzig cons.; dir. music school Berne till retirement in 1909; c. p cantata "*Murtenschlacht.*"

**Mustafà,** (moos-tä'-fä), **Domeni** Montefalco (?) — 1912; singer at Vatican and composer of chu music; succeeded by Perosi, 1898.

**Müthel** (mē'-tĕl), **Johann Go fried,** Mölln, 1720 — Riga, a 1790; organist; c. sonatas and so

## N

**Navrátil** (nä-vrä'-tēl), **Carl,** b. Prag April 24, 1867; violinist; Bohem composer; pupil of Adler and O řiček; c. symph.; symph. poe "*Jan Hus,*" "*Zalco,*" etc.; op "*Salammbô,*" lyric drama, "*I mann*"; violin concerto, etc.; w biog. of Smetana.

**Nay'lor, Edward Woodall,** Scarborough, Feb. 9, 1867; compo pupil of his father, Dr. John N. v.); and at the R. C. M., Lond organist at various churches; 1 made Mus. Doc. by Cambridge U versity, where he had taken degrees of B. A., M. A., and Mus. organist from 1897 at Cambri

manuel College); lecturer there
om 1902; c. Ricordi prize opera
*The Angelus*" (Covent Garden,
09); cantata "*Arthur the King*"
Harrogate, 1902), church music, etc.

elong (nā'-bĕ-lông), **Johan
endrik,** b. Copenhagen, Nov. 9,
47; pupil of Holm, Thielemann and
arth; from 1881 organist at Copen-
gen, founder of organist pension
nd; c. patriotic songs, etc.

'bal, **Oscar,** add that he was
r. Bohemian Phil., Prague 1896–
06; thereafter cond. Vienna Volk-
per, also the Tonkünstler orch.;
ballet "*Der faule Hans*" (Vienna,
03), scherzo caprice for orch.,
olin sonata, etc.

'le, **Wilhelm,** b. Schwöbber, near
ameln, May 9, 1849; preacher,
ganist and historian of church
usic; pupil of Robert Franz.

'son, **Sydney,** London, Jan. 1,
00 — April 7, 1862; publisher and
mposer of ballads, etc.

u'da, **Franz,** b. Brünn, Dec. 3,
43; 'cellist, son of **Josef N.,**
d brother of **Normann N.,** (q. v.)
pil of Royal Chapel at Copen-
gen; from 1892 successor of Gade
, dir. of the Copenhagen Music
ociety; also dir. of Stockholm
usic Society; 1894, Prof., c. "*Slo-
k*" march, orch. suite "*From the
ohemian Forest,*" 'cello pieces, etc.

t'ler, **August Julius,** b. Grum-
ach, Dec. 3, 1851; teacher, founder
f a musical institute in Leipzig,
878 (assisted by his son **Amadeus**);
880 teacher at the Royal Gymna-
um; 1892 Royal Musical director; c.
ymn with orch., etc.

pert (noi'-pĕrt), **Edmund,** Chris-
ania, April 1, 1842 — New York,
ne 22, 1888; pianist; pupil of
ullak's Academy and teacher at
tern Cons.; 1861 at Copenhagen
ons.; 1888 at Moscow Cons.; from
883 at New York; c. piano studies,
tc.

ville (nŭ-vē'-yĕ), **Valentin,** b.

Rexpoede, French Flanders, 1863;
organist; pupil of Brussels Cons.;
org. at Lyons; c. 2 symph., an oratorio "*Nôtre Dame de Fourvières,*"
6 operas, including "*Les Avegules*"
(1901), and "*Les Willis*" (1902).

**Neve** (dĕ nā'-vĕ), **Paul de,** b.
Steglitz, Berlin, Jan. 24, 1881; pupil
of Ph. Scharwenka, Berger and Goldschmidt; from 1893 cond. at Wiesbaden Court Theatre, then in Aschersleben; c. opera, chamber music, etc.

**Nevin, Arthur.** Add that his correct birthplace is Vine Acre, Edgeworth, Pa., April 17, 1871. Add
to the list of his teachers, Humperdinck in Berlin, and Goetschius,
Boston. He spent the summers of
1903 and 1904 among the Blackfeet
Indians in Montana, collecting material for his Indian opera "*Poia,*"
libretto by Randolph Hartley (prod.
in concert form by the Pittsburg
Orch. and as an opera at the Royal
Opera, Berlin); c. also 1-act opera
"*Twilight*" (accepted by Met. Op.
N. Y. but not produced); orch,
suites "*Lorna Doone*" (prod. by
Karl Muck in Berlin), and "*Love
Dreams*" (Pittsburg Orch.); c. also
songs.

**Nibelle** (nē-bĕl), **Adolphe André,**
Gien, 1825 — Paris, 1895; pupil Paris
Cons.; lawyer and composer of
operettas, etc.

**Nich'olls, Agnes,** b. Cheltenham,
July 14, 1877; soprano; pupil of
Visetti at the R. C. M., London, with
a scholarship; début 1895 in a revival
of Purcell's "*Dido and Aeneas*";
studied also with John Acton; 1901,
and 1904–6 sang at Covent Garden;
has sung much in concert and oratorios, and at the Cincinnati Festival,
1904; in which year she married
Hamilton Harty (q. v.).

**Nich'ols, Marie,** b. Chicago, Oct. 16,
1879; violinist; pupil of E. Mollenhauer (Boston), Halir and Debroux;
début 1899; has toured Europe and
America.

**Nich'olson, Henry,** 1825—Leicester, Sept. 14, 1907; age 82; celebrated flutist; from 1877 with Birmingham Festival Orch.

**Nicolau** (nē'-kō-lä-oo), **Antonio,** b. Barcelona, June 8, 1858; pupil of Pujol and Balart; cond. of Catalonian Concert Society in Paris, then dir. municipal music school at Barcelona; c. opera, choral works, etc.

**Nicolini** (nē-kō-lē'-nē), **Nicolino Grimaldi detto,** Naples, ca. 1673 — Venice, (?) after 1726; tenor, whom Addison called "perhaps the greatest performer in dramatic music that ever appeared upon a stage"; he was a contralto in Italy as early as 1694 and was decorated with the Order of St. Mark; from 1708–1716 in England rousing a furore; created "Rinaldo" in Handel's opera, 1711; returned to sing in Italy.

**Nidecki** (nē-dět'-skǐ), **Thomas,** Warsaw, 1800–1852; pupil of the Cons., and on government funds at Vienna; 1841 director Warsaw Opera; c. 3 masses, burlesques, etc.

**Nielsen** (nēl'-sĕn), (1) **Carl,** b. Nörre-Lyndelse, Fünen Island, June 9, 1865; important Danish composer; pupil of Gade, member of the Copenhagen court orch., and from 1904 assistant cond. succeeding Svendsen; c. 2 symph., No. 2 "The Four Seasons," overture, "Helios," opera "Saul and David" (Copenhagen, 1902); chorus with orch., "Hymnus amoris"; chamber music, etc. (2) **Ludolf,** b. Nörre-Tolde, Zealand, Jan. 29, 1876; pupil Copenhagen and Leipzig Cons.; viola player in Andersen's orch.; c. opera "Mascarade" (Copenhagen 1906).

**Nieviadomski** (n'yäv-yä-dôm'shkǐ), **Stanislav,** b. Soposzyn, Galicia, Nov. 4, 1859; pupil of Mikuli, Krenns, and Jadassohn; teacher at Lemberg Cons.; critic; c. songs, etc.

**Nikisch, Arthur,** add that he was dir. Leipzig Cons. till 1907; 1905–6 dir. the Stadttheater, has toured

widely with the Berlin Phil., acted as guest cond. in many capit April, 1912, he toured the U. S cond. of the London Phil. v immense success. He c. a sympl cantata "Christnacht," orch. tasie "Der Trompeter"; etc. His **Amélie** (née Heuser), b. in Bruss was a soubrette in Cassel and Lei operas, and has composed music.

**No'ack, Sylvain,** b. Rotterdam, 21, 1881; at first a pianist, then vi pupil of André Spoor, Amsterd at 17 entered the Cons., as a pup Elderling, winning first prize, 1 and becoming a teacher there; 1 settled in Rotterdam, and tou widely; 1906 concertm. at Aix Chapelle; from 1908 second conc master Boston Symph.

**No'ble, Thomas Tertius,** b. B. May 5, 1867; composer; pupil the R. C. M., London, winnin; scholarship, and later teaching th org. at Cambridge, Ely Cathedral, from 1898 at York Minster, founc the York Symphony Orch.; c. chu music with orch., cantata "Gl Domini," music to Aristophai "Wasps," etc.

**No'dermann, Presben,** b. Hjorr Denmark, Jan. 11, 1867; teacl studied at Helsingborg; organist : 1894 Ph.D., University of Lu Sweden, in which city he has b since 1903, cathedral org.; c. op "König Magnus" (Hamburg, 18ç operetta "Prinz Inkognito" (Cop hagen, 1909), etc.

**No'lopp, Werner,** Stendal, June 1835 — Magdeburg, Aug. 12, 19 teacher and composer of male cl uses.

**Nolthenius** (nôl-tä'-nǐ-oos), **Hu** b. Amsterdam, Dec. 20, 1848; pu of Viotta and Auerkamp; cond. m cal societies; 1888–91 at Utrec editor and author.

**Nordqvist** (nôrt'-kwǐst), **Joh Conrad,** b. Venersborg, April 1840; Swedish composer; pupil Stc

olm Musikakademie; 1864 military
andmaster, then with state funds
udied in Dresden and Paris; from
875 organist and teacher at Stock-
olm; 1881 teacher of harmony at the
Iusikakad.; 1885 court cond.; c.
:ch. works, etc.

·draak (nôr'-dräk), **Rikard,**
hristiania, June 12, 1842 — Berlin,
Iarch 20, 1876; composer whose early
eath ended a promising career; pupil
: Kiel and Kullak; c. incid. music
) Björnson's "*Maria Stuart*" and
*Sigurd Slembe,*" piano pieces, etc.

**ren, Heinrich Gottlieb,** b.
·raz, Jan. 6, 1861; violinist; pupil of
Iassart; concertmaster in various
ountries; from 1896–1902 in Crefeld,
·here he founded a Cons.; teacher at
tern Cons., in Berlin; later in Dres-
en; c. orch variations "*Kaleido-
kop*" (Dresden, 1907), serenade for
rch., etc.

**ronha** (nō-rōn'-yä), **Francisco
)e Sá,** Vianna do Castello, Feb.
4, 1820 — Rio de Janeiro, Jan. 23,
881; Portuguese violinist, and self-
aught composer of operettas and
iolin pieces.

**tz, Franz,** b. Cannstadt, 1867;
·upil of Stuttgart Cons.; from 1901
eacher in Insterberg; c. choral
*Liedlegende,*" etc.

**uguès** (noo-gĕs), **Jean,** b. 1874;
omposer of operas "*Yannha* (Bar-
elona, 1897); "*Thamyris*" (Bor-
leaux, 1904); "*Quo Vadis*" (Paris
;aîté, 1910, Berlin Royal Op., 1912);
·*Chiquito,*" "*L'Eclaircie,*" "*La
)anseuse de Pompeii*" (Rouen).

**·váček** (nō'-vä-chĕk), **Ottokar,**
·ehértemplom, Hungary, May 13,
:866 — New York, Feb. 3, 1900;
·iolinist; pupil of his father, of Dont,
ınd at Leipzig Cons., where he won
:he Mendelssohn prize, 1889; 1891
nember Boston Symph. Orch.; 1892
-3 Damrosch Orch., N. Y.; heart-
·rouble forced his retirement; c.
:hamber music, Bulgarian dances
ınd other violin pieces.

**No'vák, Vítězslav,** b. Kamenitz,
Bohemia, Dec. 5, 1870; important
Bohemian composer; pupil of Prague
Cons. under Dvôřák, later teacher
at Prague; from 1909 teacher of
composition at the Cons.; c. overture
"*Maryscha,*" symph. poems "*On
the High Tatra,*" and "*Eternal Longing*"; "*Slovak*" suite, four Moravian
ballads with orch., chamber music,
piano sonata "*Eroica,*" etc.

**Novot'ny, Wenzel,** b. Pocáterl, Bohemia, Sept. 17, 1849; music editor,
translator of Wagner; pupil Prague
Organ School; c. songs, violin pieces,
etc.

**Nowowiejski, Felix,** add that he
was b. Wartenburg, 1875; pupil of
Stern Cons., and Regensburg Church
Mus. Sch., etc.; c. 2 symph.; opera
"*Quo Vadis*" (1907); oratorio "*Die
Auffindung des Kreuzes*" (Lemberg,
1906). "*Quo Vadis*" was given as
an oratorio New York, 1912.

**Nunn, J. H.,** Bury St. Edmunds, Nov.
10, 1827 — Penzance, Oct. 17, 1905;
pupil R. A. M., London, later Fellow;
org. and cond.

**Nu'no, Jaime,** Spain (?) — Bayside,
L. I., July 19, 1908; composer of
Mexican National Anthem; educated
in Spain, went to Cuba as military
bandmaster, invited to Mexico, 1851,
by President Santa Anna; fled from
revolution and settled in Buffalo,
N. Y., as teacher for 52 years; 1901
invited to Mexico and received with
great honours, gold crown, and a
purse; returned to Buffalo, where he
is buried.

**Nunczy** (noon'-chē), **Louis,** d. Budapest, April 18, 1910. Hungarian
violinist.

### O

**O'berhoffer, (1) Heinrich,** Pfalzeln,
Dec. 9, 1824 — Luxembourg, May
30, 1885; organist at Luxembourg,
c. church music. (2) **Emil,** b.
Munich, Aug. 10, 1867; pupil of
Kistler, and I. Philipp; settled in

Minneapolis, Minn.; cond. Phil.
Club. and from 1903 Minn. Symph.
Orch., with which he toured the U.
S., 1912; c. church music, songs, etc.

**Obermeyer** (ō'-bĕr-mī-ĕr), **Joseph,**
Nezabudicz, Bohemia, 1749 — Prague
after 1816; violinist to Count Waldstein; pupil of Kamel and Tartini.

**Obrecht,** vide **Hobrecht.**

**O'brist, Aloys.** b. San Remo, March
30, 1867; pupil of Müller Hartung at
Weimar; cond. in various cities; from
1900 at Weimar; mus. director and
coll. of mus. instruments.

**Oldberg, Arne.** b. Youngstown, Ohio,
July 12, 1874; began piano studies
with his father at 5; at 6 was playing
Haydn symphonies in duet form;
pupil of Aug. Hyllested, Chicago;
1893-5 of Leschetizky, Vienna; from
1895 in Chicago with Middelschulte
(counterpoint); Ad. Koelling (instrumentation) and F. G. Gleason;
1898 with J. Rheinberger, Munich;
from 1899 teacher at Northwestern
Univ., Ill.; c. 2 symphs. (F minor,
winning National Federation prize
1911); overture "*Paola and Francesca*" (played 3 times by Thomas
Orch.); Festival Overture, 12 orch.
variations, horn concerto, chamber
music, piano sonata, etc.

**Ollone** (dôl-lŭn), **Max d',** b. Besançon, June 13, 1875; pupil Paris
Cons., taking the Prix de Rome,
1897; c. cantata "*Frédégonde,*" lyric
scene "*Jeanne d'Arc à Domrémy,*" etc.

**Ölschlegel** ( ĕl'-shlä-gĕl ), **Alfred,**
b. Anscha, Bohemia, Feb. 25, 1847;
pupil Prague Organ School; cond.
various theatres, finally at Franzens-
bad; c. operettas, and opera "*Ky-
nast*" (Altenburg, 1898).

**Olth'off, Statius,** Osnabruch, 1555
— Rostock, 1629; composer; cantor
and con-rector; set Buchanan's Latin
version of the Psalms (1585).

**O'Mara, Joseph,** b. Limerick, July
16, 1866; tenor; pupil of Perini and
Moretti, and Holland; début 1891
Royal English Opera House; 1894 at

Drury Lane and Covent Gard
1896 created the rôle of "*M
Murphy*" in "*Shamus O'Brien*"
England and America; toured v
Moody-Manners Co.

**O'Neill,** (1) **Norman,** b. Kens
ton, March 14, 1875; cond., pup
Somervell and Hoch Cons. at Fra
fort; c. incid. music to "*Ham
(1904), "King Lear*" (1908), ."
*Blue Bird*" (1909); overture
*Autumn,*" "*In Springtime*"; fant
for voices and orch. "*Woldemo
Scotch rhapsody; ballade with or
"*La belle dame sans merci*" (Lond
1910), etc.; 1899, he married
**Adine Rückert,** pianist; pupi
Clara Schumann and Mme. Cla
Szavardy.

**Opienski** (ôp-yĕn'-shkĭ), **Heinri**
b. Cracow, June 13, 1870; p
of Zelénski there, of d'Indy
Urban; critic in Warsaw, then p
of Riemann in history, and of N
isch in conducting; from 1907 teac
of history at the Warsaw M
School, and from 1908 cond. of
Opera; c. prize cantata in honou
Mickiewicz; opera "*Maria,*" sym
poem "*Lilla Weneda*" (1908), etc.

**Orlan'di, Fernando,** Parma, I
— Jan. 5, 1848; 1809-28 sing
teacher at Milan Cons.; then
Munich Music School; c. 26 ope

**Orlandini** (ôr-län-dē'-nē), **Giusep
Maria,** Bologna, 1685 — Floren
ca. 1750; opera composer, c. 44 o
ras, 3 oratorios, etc.

**Orologio** (ôr-ō-lō'-jĭ-ō), (1) and (
**Alessandro,** two contempor
madrigal composers of the same nar
one of them in 1603 became vi
chapelmaster to Emperor Rudo
at Prague; the other vice-chap
master to the Electoral Court
Dresden the same year.

**Orth,** (ôrt), (1) **John,** b. near A
weiler, Bavaria; teacher; brought
America at the age of one; pupil of
father; at 16 taught and earned fur
for study abroad; from 1875 tea

Boston; c. piano pieces, etc. In
883 he married (2) **Lizette E.
lood,** composer of children's op-
-ettas, songs, etc., under name
L. E. Orth."

:iz (ôr-tĕth), **Diego,** b. Toledo,
a. 1530; from 1558 chapelmaster to
)uke of Alva; c. important book of
acred music (pub. Venice, 1565).

:orn=Hannah, Jane,** soprano,
ifter concert career, became pupil of
.osa Sucher in 1903; 1904 engaged
)r Leipzig Opera by Nikisch; sang
)r 3 years there, appearing also as
)loist at the Gewandhaus concerts;
as sung in other German cities, at
'ovent Garden, London; 1909, Met.
)p. N. Y.; from 1910 with Chicago-
'hiladelphia Opera Co. in Wag-
erian rôles.

;ul'livan, Denis,** San Francisco,
.pril 25, 1868 — Columbus, Ohio,
'eb. 1, 1908; barytone of Irish decent; pupil of Talbo and Formes;
ater of Vannucini, Santley and
hakespeare; début 1895 in concert;
lso in opera with Carl Rosa Co.; 1896
reated the title rôle in Stanford's
*Shamus O'Brien*" and sang it in
.ngland and America; created other
ôles in light and serious opera; in
907 sang in America in *"Peggy
Tachree"* of which his wife wrote the
ibretto; suffering with appendicitis
.e persisted in struggling through
'erformances and died on tour in a
.otel.

'wald, James,** d. Knebworth
an. 1769; Scots composer of
)opular tunes, to whom Kidson
redits the composition of *"God
.ave the King";* dancing-master at
)umferline, 1734; later in Edinburgh;
rom 1741 in London; c. songs.

hegraven (ō'-tĕ-grä-vĕn), August
von,** b. Cologne, June 2, 1864; music
)rofessor; pupil of the Cons. and
rom 1889 teacher there; c. fairy
)lay *"The Sleeping Beauty"* (Cologne, 1907), songs, etc.

'ter, Franz Joseph,** Nadlstadt,

Bavaria, 1760 (1764?)—Vienna, Sept.
1, 1836; violinst; pupil of Nardini;
violinist with his brother Ludwig at
Salzburg Cathedral; 1803-7, then
pensioned; taught and conducted in
Vienna.

**Otterstroem** (öt'-tĕr-strŭm), **Thor-
vald,** b. Copenhagen, July 17, 1868;
composer; piano pupil of Sophie
Menter, St. Petersburg; from 1892 in
Chicago; c. 24 preludes and fugues
for piano, chamber music, etc.

**Ot'to,** (1) **Georg,** b. Torgau, ca. 1544;
from 1588-1619 at Cassel as cond.
to the Landgrave; c. sacred music;
(2) **Valentin,** cantor at Leipzig,
1564-94. (3) **Valerius,** organist at
Prague, 1607; c. church music. (4)
**Stephan,** b. Freiburg, Saxony, ca.
1594; cantor there and at Schandau;
c. church music.

# P

**Pacchioni** (päk-kĭ-ō'-nē), **Antonio
Maria,** Modena, 1654-1738, priest,
court chaplain; c. oratorios, etc.

**Pacelli** (pä-chĕl'-lē), **Asprilio,** Varci-
ano, ca. 1570 — Warsaw, May 3,
1623; Italian choirmaster; 1604.
called to Warsaw as chapelmaster to
the King; c. motets, etc.

**Pache** (päkh'-ĕ), (1) **Johannes,** b.
Bischofswerda, Dec. 9, 1857 — Limbach, Dec. 1, 1897; organist and composer of male choruses, etc. (2)
**Joseph,** b. Friedland, Silesia, June
1, 1861; pupil Royal Akad., Munich,
and of Scharwenka Cons., and Max
Bruch; settled in New York and
founded 1903 an oratorio society;
from 1904 dir. oratorio society in
Baltimore.

**Pachler=Koschak** (päkh'-lĕr-kō'-
shäk), **Marie Leopoldine,** Graz,
Oct. 2, 1792 — April 10, 1855; pianist
and composer; friend of Beethoven,

**Paderewski, I. J.,** add that he
settled at Morges, Switzerland, continuing to tour the world; 1912, in
South Africa; 1909 director Warsaw

Cons.; c. opera *"Sakuntala"* (text by C. Mendès), a symphony in memory of the revolution of 1864, (1908; Boston Symph., 1909; Richter, London, 1909); a second symph., an hour and twenty minutes long (1912); piano sonata, variations, and fugue for piano (1907), etc.

**Pagin** (pä-zhäṅ), **André Noel**, Paris, 1721–1770; composer and violinist.

**Palmer** (päm'-ẽr), **Bessie (Elizabeth Annie)**, b. London, Aug. 9, 1831; contralto; pupil R. A. M., and of Garcia; début, 1854; sang in oratorio and concert; from 1870 in opera; from 1877–1886 teacher.

**Panor'mo,** (1) **Vincenzo Trusaino,** Monreale, 1734—London, 1813; violin maker, as were his two sons, (2) **Joseph,** London, 1773 — ca. 1825, and (3) **George Lewis,** London, 1774 — ca. 1842.

**Pancera** (pän-chä'-rä), **Ella,** b. Vienna, Aug. 15, 1875 (of Italian parents); pianist; pupil of Epstein and Vockner; début at 13; toured widely.

**Panizza** (pä-nĭd'-zä), **Ettore,** b. Buenos Ayres, Aug. 12, 1875; c. opera *"Il fidanzeto del mare"* (Buenos Ayres, 1897); the trilogy *"Medioevo latino"* (Geneva, 1900) *"Aurora,"* (Buenos Ayres, 1908).

**Paolucci** (pä-ō-loo'-chē), **Giuseppe,** Siena, May 25, 1726 — Assisi, April 26, 1776; Franciscan monk; c. church music.

**Paravicini** (pä-rä-vē-chē'-nē), **Signora,** Turin, 1769 — after 1830; violinist; pupil of Viotti; 1797, befriended by Empress Josephine, and made great success in Paris and other cities.

**Pardew, John,** 1855 — Plymouth, April 13, 1910, organist, conductor and teacher.

**Par'ker, Horatio W.,** add that in May, 1911, his opera *"Mona,"* libretto by Brian Hooker (b. N. Y. Nov. 2, 1880, a graduate of Yale, 1902, and instructor there 1905–10), won the $10,000 prize offered by the

Met. Op. Co. for the best grand o[p] in English by an American. It prod. with success.

**Par'low, Kathleen,** b. Calg[ary] Canada, 1890; violinist; taken [to] California at 5, and studied there [with] Conrad and Holmes; début ther[e] 6; at 15 gave a recital in London appeared with the London Sy[mph] Orch.; then studied with Auer; [then] began to tour.

**Parry, Sir C. Hubert H.,** that in 1908 his health forced resignation of the Oxford Profes[sor]ship; c. also Processional Music [for] the coronation of Edward VII (19[11]) a simfonia sacra for soli, chorus orch. (Gloucester Festival, 19[ ]) music to Aristophanes' *"Clo[uds"]* (Oxford, 1905); Browning's *"[Pied] Piper"* with orch. (Norwich F[est.] 1905); symph. poem *"The Visio[n of] Life"* (Cardiff Fest., 1907); can[tata] (Worcester Fest., 1908); revisio[n of] 4th symph., (Philharmonic, 19[ ]) wrote important work on Ba[ch] *"The Music of the 17th Centu[ry"]* for the Oxford History of M[usic] (1902), etc.

**Par'ry, Joseph Haydn,** Penn[syl]vania, 1864 — London, March [ ] 1894; composer; son and pupil of Jos. Parry; 1890 prof. Guild[hall] School; c. operas, *"Cigarette,"* 18[ ] *"Miami"* (London, 1893), etc.

**Pashálov** (pä-shä'-lôf), **Victor N[ik]androvich,** Saratov, 1847 — Kas[an,] 1885; Russian; composer of songs.

**Pashkevich** (päsh'-kä-vĭch), **Vass[ili]** violinist; chamber musician; c[a.] cond. to Catherine II; 1789, dir. c[omic] balls; c. operas, etc., one of th[em] *"Oleg"* to Catherine II's text.

**Pasterwitz** (päs'-tẽr-vĭtz), **Geo[rg]** Passau, 1730 — Kremsmünster, 18[ ] priest, and cond.; c. fugues, etc.

**Pa'tey, John George,** Stoneho[use,] Devonshire, 1835 — Falmouth, D[ec.] 4, 1901; bass at Covent Garden; h[us]band of **Janet Monach P.** (q. v[.])

**Pauer, Max,** add that he beca[me]

dir. of Stuttgart Cons. 1908: gives annual recitals in European capitals.

**ul, William,** England, 1868 (?) — St. Louis, Feb. 5, 1903, teacher.

**ulli** (pow'-lē), **Simon Holger,** Copenhagen, Feb. 22, 1810 — Dec. 21, 1891; violinist and court cond.; c. overture, operettas, etc.

**ur, Emil,** add that he returned to Europe, 1903; cond. concerts in Madrid; 1904, returned to the U. S. as cond. Pittsburgh Symph. Orch. His symph. was published in 1909.

**chatschek** (pĕkh'-ä-chĕk), (1) **Francois,** conductor in Vienna; c. popular dance music, ballets and operas. His son (2) **Francois,** Vienna, July 4, 1793 — Carlsruhe, Sept. 15, 1840; violin-virtuoso, court dir. at Boden; c. violin concerto, etc.

**drell, Felipe,** add that he was born in Tortosa, Spain, Feb. 19, 1841, and c. operas, including *"Quasimodo"* (Barcelona, 1875), a trilogy *"Los Pinneos"* (Barcelona, 1902), *"La Celestina"* (1904), *"La Matinada"* (1905), a Gloria mass with orch.; also wrote and edited important historical works.

**ñalosa** (pĕn-yä-lō'-sä), **Francisco,** Spanish composer, 1470–1535; cond. to Ferdinand the Catholic, then singer in Papal Chapel.

**navaire** (pä-nä-vär), **Jean Gré-goire,** Lesparre, Sept. 15, 1840 — Paris, Sept. 1906; composer; theatre-cond. at Nantes; c. overtures *"Tasso," "Cervantes";* symph. poem with chorus, *"La vision des Croisées,"* comic opera and ballets.

**erez** (pĕr'ĕth), **Juan Ginez,** Orihuela, Murcia, Oct. 17, 1548 — Valencia after 1601; royal chaplain and comp. of church music.

**erosi, Don Lorenzo,** add the later compositions; oratorios *"Leo the Great"* (1902), *"Il Giudizio Universale"* (The Last Judgment), Rome, 1904; and *"In Patris Memoriam"* (1910); orch. variations (1904), cantatas *"Anima"* (1908), and *"Dies*

*Iste";* a series of 10 symphonies each devoted to an Italian city; requiem for Leo XIII (1909), etc.

**Per'singer, Louis,** b. Rochester, Ill., 1887; violinist; at 12 taken to Leipzig and studied with Hans Becker; later pupil of Ysaye, Thibaud and at Leipzig Cons.; concertm. Blüthner Orch., Berlin; played in concerts abroad, engaged for American tour, 1912.

**Peterson=Berger** (pä'-tĕr-son-bĕrkh-ĕr), **Wilhelm,** b. Ingermanland, 1867; composer; studied in Dresden and in Stockholm where he has been since 1894 critic and regisseur at the opera; c. dramatic works *"Ran"* (Stockholm, 1903), etc.

**Petrie, George,** Dublin, 1789 — Jan. 17, 1866; collector of Irish airs.

**Petrov** (pä'-trôf), **Ossip Afanass-jevich,** b. Elisavetgrad, Nov. 15, 1807 — St. Petersburg, Mar. 14, 1878; famous Russian barytone-bass, with remarkable compass of nearly four octaves (B-g''); discovered on the stage of a country fair, by Lebedev; created Sussanin in *"Life for the Czar";* Glinka wrote *" Ruslan "* for him, and he created rôles in many of the chief Russian operas, singing up to four days before his death in his seventy-first year.

**Petsch'nikov, Alexander,** b. Teletz, Feb. 8, 1873; violinist; pupil of Moscow Cons.; lives in Berlin.

**Petz'et, Walter,** b. Breslau, Oct. 10, 1866; pupil of Kleffel, Rheinberger and von Bülow; 1887–96 piano teacher in America, then at Helsingfors Cons., and 1898 at Karlsruhe Cons.; c. an opera, piano pieces, etc.

**Peurl** (Bäwerl, Bäurl, or Beurlin), **Paul,** organist at Steyer; important composer of suites, etc., (1611–20).

**Pfannstiehl** (pfän'-shtĕl), **Bernhard,** b. Schmalkalden, Thuringia, Dec. 18, 1861; blind organist; pupil Leipzig Cons., winning the Mendelssohn prize three times; from 1903 org. at Chemnitz.

**Phip'son, Thomas Lamb,** b. Birmingham, May 5, 1833; violinist and author.

**Pierné, Gabriel,** add that from 1910 he cond. the Colonne concerts Paris; he c. very successful choral work, *"Croisade des Enfants"* (1905), *"La coupe enchantée"* (Paris, 1895; Stuttgart, 1907); opera *"La fille de Tabarin"* (Op. Com., 1901); oratorio *"Les enfants de Bethlehem"* (1907); *"Les Fioretti de St. Francis d'Assise"* (Paris, 1912), etc.

**Pilati** (pē-lä'-tē), **Auguste** (rightly **Pilate**), Bouchain, Sept. 29, 1810 — Paris, Aug. 1, 1877; c. operettas under name of A. P. Juliano.

**Pinel'lo de Gherardi** (gā-rär'-dē), **Giov. Bat.,** Genoa, ca. 1540 — Prague, 1587; court cond. and composer.

**Pir'ro, André,** b. St. Dizier, Feb. 12, 1859; organist and historian; from 1896, teacher at the Schola cantorum, Paris.

**Pique** (pēk), **Louis François,** Roret, 1758 — Charenton-St. Maurice, 1822; violin maker at Paris.

**Pišna** (pǐsh'-nǎ), **Johann,** Bohemia, June 15, 1826 — Prague, 1896; teacher at Moscow and Prague; c. piano exercises.

**Pitsch** (pǐtsh), **Karl Franz,** b. Senftenberg, Bohemia, 1789—Prague, 1858; organist; c. organ pieces.

**Pitt, Percy,** b. London, Jan. 4, 1870; organist and prominent English composer; pupil of Reinecke, Jadassohn and Rheinberger; 1896 organist Queen's Hall; 1902 adviser and cond. Covent Garden; c. sinfonietta, (Birmingham Fest., 1906); symphonic prelude *"Le sang des crépuscules,"* (1900); ballade for violin and orch.; orch. suites, etc.

**Plançon** (plän-sôṅ), **Pol Henri,** b. Fumay, Ardennes, June 12, 1854; famous barytone; pupil of Duprez and Sbriglia; début, 1877, at Lyons; 1883–93, at the Paris Opéra; 1891–1904, Covent Garden annually, and 1893–1906, at Met. Op. House, N. Y.

**Platz'becker, Heinrich Augus** b. Merzenhausen, Sept. 13, 186 editor at Dresden; c. operettas, e

**Pochhammer** (pŏkh'-häm-měı **Theodor,** b. Rheine, Nov. 16, 184 pupil of Hamburg Cons., teacher Wiesbaden Cons.; studied singi from 1902; teacher in Aachen; c.son;

**Podbert'sky, Theodor,** b. M nich, Nov. 16, 1846; cond. Muni Männergesangverein; from 1887, Fürstenfeldbrück; c. opera *"I Liedes Ende,"* and male choruses.

**Poglietti** (pōl-yĕt'-tē), **Alessandr** from 1661 court organist; murder by the Turks in the siege of Vienı 1683; c. clavier pieces.

**Pohlig** (pō'-lǐkh), **Karl,** b. Tepli Feb. 10, 1864; pupil of Liszt; coı Graz Hamburg, Covent Garden, et 1907 — 1912, Philadelphia Symp Orch; c. orch. pieces and songs.

**Poirée** (pwä'-rā), **Elie Emile G briel,** b. Villeneuve, St. Georges, O 9, 1850; librarian, author; c. stri quartet, etc.

**Polac'co Giorgio,** b. Venice, 187 pupil Milan Cons.; cond. in Londo Italy, Spain, South America; 19c Royal Op., Weisbaden; 1908, Berl Royal Op.; 1911–12, cond. H. V Savage's prod. of *"Girl of the Gold West";* 1912, engaged for Met. O N. Y.; c. 2 operas, *" Rahab "* (Buc pest), and *" Fortunatus."*

**Polaro'li** (or **Pollarolo,** (1) **Car Francesco,** Brescia, ca. 1653 Vienna, 1722; composer; organist aı assistant-cond. at St. Mark's; c. oratorios, 68 operas, etc. His son aı pupil (2) **Antonio,** Venice, 16: — Venice, 1746; 1723, cond. at S Mark's; c. operas.

**Poldini** (pōl-dē'-nē), **Eduard,** b. Pes June 13, 1869; composer of ope. *"Vagabond and Princess,"* (Pes 1903), and children's operas.

**Polleri** (pōl-lā'-rē), **Giov. Bat** b. Genoa, 1855; organist; from 188 teacher in the U. S.; 1894, in Genoa

om 1898 dir. of the Cons.; c. organ
ieces, etc.

nasan'ski, Ivan Alexandro=
ich, b. near Kiev, April 11, 1848;
arpist and composer; pupil St.
etersburg Cons.; from 1868 harpist
nd chorus — master at the Imperial
)pera; c. cantata *"The Death of
amson"*; Russian overture and songs.

ole, vide BACON.

p'ov, Ivan Gegorovich, b. Eka-
erinodar, 1859; pupil Moscow Phil.
chool, from 1900, director of society
1 Stavropol, Caucasus; c. symph.,
rmenian rhapsody; symph. poem
*Freedom,"* overture, *"Ivan the Ter-
ible,"* etc.

r'ro, Pierre, Béziers, 1750 —
Montmorency, 1831; guitar-virtuoso
nd teacher at Paris; c. pieces for the
nstrument, etc.

rsile (pôr-sē'-lĕ), Giuseppe, b.
Naples, 1672 — Vienna, 1750; court
ond.; c. 6 operas, etc.

ttgiesser (pôt'-gēs-sĕr), Karl, b.
Dortmund, Aug. 8, 1861; pupil of H.
Riemann: c. opera *"Heimkehr,"*
Cologne, 1903), a Festspiel, choruses,
tc.; chapter 1 of *St. Paul's First Epis-
le,* for voices, organ and orch.; orato-
io *"Gott ist der Liebe"*; choruses, etc.

ueigh, (poo-ā) (Marie Octave
léraud) Jean, b. Toulouse, Feb. 24,
876; studied with the Jesuit fathers
t Toulouse; at 19 took up harmony
vith Huguonenc of the Cons., which
e entered in 1897, receiving the
econd harmony prize 1898; he then
tudied in Paris with Caussade,
Lenepveu and Fauré, receiving
riticisms from d'Indy. His comps.
nclude sonata for piano and violin
performed by Enesco and Aubert
1906); orch. suite *Fünn* (1906 and
1908 at Lamoureux concerts), poem
with orch. *"Sentellière de Rêve"*
1907); dramatic poem for solos, choir
nd orch. *Les Lointains* (1903); 5-
ct lyric drama, *Le Meneur de Louves,*
not prod. *Le Soir rôde* (song with
orch. 1910), etc.

Poznan'ski, Barrett Isaac, Charles-
ton, Va., Dec. 11, 1840 — London,
June 24, 1896; violinist and composer;
pupil of Vieuxtemps; c. violin
pieces, etc.

Powell, Maud, add that her birth
place was Peru, Ill.; played piano
and violin in public at 9; début
Berlin Phil., 1885; the same year in
America with Theo. Thomas orch.
married H. Godfrey Turner.

Pren'dergast, A. H., Dalrymple,
June 28, 1833 — Kensington, July 13,
1910; choral cond. and composer.

Pres'cott, Oliveria Luisa, b. London, Sept. 3, 1842; pupil of Macfarren;
singing teacher; c. string quartets, etc.

Pressen'da, Johannes Franciscus,
Laquio-Berria Jan. 6, 1777 — Turin,
Sept. 11, 1854; violin maker.

Pribik (prē'-bĭk), Joseph, b. Bohemia, 1853; pupil Prague Cons.;
director of opera in various cities;
from 1894 of Odessa Symph. Orch.
c. orch. suites, etc.

Primavera (prē-mä-vā'-rä), Giovanni Leonardo, b. Barletta;
from 1573 concertmaster at Milan; c.
madrigals, etc.

Pri'oris, Johannes, organist at St.
Peter's, Rome, 1490; 1507, cond. to
Louis XII of France; c. motets, etc.

Procházka (prō-khäz'-kä), (1) Lud=
wig, correct birth date, Klattau,
Aug. 14, 1837; (2) Rudolf, Freiherr
von, Prague, Feb. 23, 1864; composer; pupil of Fibich and Grünberger;
magistrate in Prague; author of biographies; c. dramatic tone story.
*"Das Glück"* (Vienna, 1898); sacred
melody *"Christus,"* etc.

Pro'fe, (or Profius) Ambrosius,
Breslau, Feb. 12, 1859 — Breslau,
Dec. 27, 1661; organist; c. church
music.

Puccini, Giacomo, add that his
correct birth date is Lucca, June 22,
1858; *"Madame Butterfly,"* (La Scala,
Milan, 1904), was a dire failure and
withdrawn after one performance;
revised and brought out at Brescia

the same year with a success that has spread all over the world, being sung throughout America in English by the Henry W. Savage Company. It was based on a play by John Luther Long and David Belasco. His next opera was also based on a play of Belasco's, *"The Girl of the Golden West,"* (*"La Fanciulla del West"*), and first prod. New York Met. Op., 1910, with much success and later in Italy, England, etc. He is said to be working on an opera with Franz Hals as hero, and an Andalusian story by Quinteros, *"Anima Allegra."*

**Puchalski** (poo-chäl'-shkĭ), **Vladimir V.,** b. Minsk, April 2, 1848; pupil at St. Petersburg Cons.; pianist; from 1876 director Imperial Music School in Kiev; c. Little-Russian fantasie for orch., an opera, etc., etc.

**Puget** (pü-zhä), **Loisa,** b. Paris, ca. 1810; composer; pupil of A. Adam; c. popular songs and operetta *"Le mauvais oeil"* (Paris Op. Com., 1836), and *"LaVeilleuse"*; married Lemoine.

**Pujol** (poo'-hôl), **Juan Bautista,** Barcelona, 1836 —Dec., 1898; pianist, author of a method; c. piano pieces.

**Pur'day, Charles Henry,** Folkstone, Jan. 11, 1799 — London, April 23, 1885; composer, lecturer and writer; c. *"Lead, Kindly Light,"* etc.

**Pychovski** (pē-khôv'-skĭ), **Jan Nepomucene,** Grazen, Bohemia, April 8, 1818 — Hoboken, N. J., March 18, 1900; pianist and teacher; pupil Prague Cons. and of Tomaschek; 1850 moved to New York; from 1855 in Hoboken; c. violin sonata, etc.

## Q

**Quadflieg** (kvät'-flēkh), **Gerhard Jakob,** b. Breberen, Aug. 27, 1854; pupil Church Music School, Regensburg; from 1881, teacher; from 1898, rector at Elberfeld; also cond. and organist; c. 7 masses, many motets, etc.

**Quil'ter, Roger,** b. Brighton, Nov.

1, 1877; composer; pupil of Kn Frankfort; c. serenade for or (London, 1907), part songs, etc.

## R

**Raabe** (rä'-bĕ), **Peter,** b. Frankfc am-Oder, Nov. 27, 1872; pupil Bargiel; cond. at various theat 1899 at the Opera, Amsterdam; 19 dir. Kaim orch., Munich; from 1ς court cond. Weimar; c. song a piano pieces.

**Rachmaninoff, S. V.,** add corr birth date, April 2 (N. S.), 18 in 1899 appeared in London conductor and pianist; from 1ς piano prof. Maryinski Inst. for Gir Moscow; 1912, appointed chief co of the Opera St. Petersburg; c. sym] (1895); cantata *"Spring,"* fanta for orch., *"The Rock,"* Gipsy priccio; 2 piano concertos; chaml music, incl. Elegiac trio in memory Tchaikovsky; 'cello sonata, etc.

**Radeglia** (rä-däl'-yä), **Vittorio,** Constantinople, 1863; composer; operas *"Colombo"* (Milan, 188 *"Amore occulto"* (Constantinop 1904), etc.

**Radicati** (rä-dĭ-kä'-tē), **Felice** **Maurizio di,** Turin, 1778—Vienr April 14, 1823; violinist, court co poser and 1815 cond. at Bologr c. operas and important chamb music.

**Raida** (rī'-dä), **Karl Alex.,** b. Par Oct. 4, 1852; pupil Stuttgart a Dresden Cons.; theatre-cond. in va ous cities; 1878–92, in Berlin; fro 1895, Munich; c. operettas, balle etc.

**Rand'les, Elizabeth,** Wrexham, Au 1, 1800 — Liverpool, 1829; pianis prodigy, playing in public before t age of two; daughter of a blind har ist; pupil of John Parry; later teacher in Liverpool.

**Randolph, Harold,** b. Richmon Va., Oct. 31, 1861; pupil of M Auerbach and Carl Faelten, at Pe body Cons., Baltimore; from 1898 i director; pianist, has played with Boston Symph., etc.

**Rap'pold, Marie** (née **Winteroth**), b. Brooklyn, N. Y.; sang in London at 10; m. Dr. Julius Rappold of Brooklyn; studied with Oscar Saenger and sang in concert; from 1905 Met. Op.

**Rase'lius, Andreas,** Hahnbach, upper Palatinadte, 1562–64 — Heidelberg, Jan. 6, 1602; court cond. and comp.

**Ravel', Maurice,** b. Ciboure, March 7, 1875; pupil of Fauré, Pessard and De Bériot at Paris Cons.; important French composer; he won the 2nd Prix de Rome 1901 with cantata *"Myrrha"; c.* overture *"Shéhérazade,"* (1898), Spanish Rhapsodie for orch., etc.; operetta *"L'heure espagnole"* (Op. Com. 1911); opera *"La cloche engloutie"* (after Hauptmann's *"Sunken Bell"*), string quartet, strikingly individual songs such as *"Histoires naturelles"* (1906), and piano pieces including the 5 pieces called *"Miroirs"* (1905).

**Raway** (rä'-vĭ), **Erasme,** b. Liège, June 2, 1850; priest, teacher and cathedral cond. at Liège; c. church works, Hindu scenes, a dramatic dialog. *"Freya,"* 1908, etc.

**Rebikov** (rĕb'-ĭ'-kôf), **Vladimir Ivanovich,** b. Krasnojarsk, Siberia, June 1 (N. S.), 1866; pupil Moscow Cons., and in Berlin; 1897–1902 cond. in Kishinev; later in Berlin and Vienna; theorist and composer of daring originality, as in his famous piece *"Satan's Diversions,"* his *"Melomimik,"* lyric scenes in pantomime, 1-act fairy opera, *" Der Christbaum,"* etc.

**Reger, Max,** add that he has come to be recognized as one of the most important of living composers, especially in chamber music and sacred music; 1891–96 he was teacher at Wiesbaden Cons., then took his year of military service. After a severe illness he settled in Munich, 1901, and married there; 1905 he taught

counterpoint at the Royal Academy; 1907–8 taught composition at Munich Cons., and was University music dir.; 1908 was named Royal Prof. and Dr. Phil. by Jena; 1910 Mus. D. Berlin U. in 1911, he became General Music Dir. at Meiningen, cond. Meiningen orch., continuing to teach one day a week at Leipzig Cons. He toured with the orch., 1912. His compositions are exceedingly numerous, and include a sinfonietta, op. 90, symph. prologue to a tragedy, op. 108, *"Lustpiel"* overture (1911), violin concerto; a vast amount of chamber music, sonatas for piano, organ, violin, clarinet, 'cello, variations, fugues, canons in all keys, left hand studies, and transcriptions for piano; much organ music; *"Gesang der Verklärten"* for choir and orch., *"An die Hoffnung"* for contralto and orch. (1912); three orch. pieces *"Nocturne," "Elfenspuk,"* and *"Helios"* (1912); organ fantasie and fugue, B-A-C-H; violin suite op. 103, sonata op. 42, for violin alone; tone-forms for pianos, *"Aus meinem Tagebuch";* cantatas, male and mixed choruses, and many beautiful sacred and secular songs.

**Reggio** (rĕd'-jō), **Pietro,** Genoa — London, July 23, 1685; private lutenist to Christina of Sweden; from 1677 at Oxford; c. songs, etc.

**Reichwein** (rīkh'-vīn), **Leopold,** director and composer; b. Breslau, May 16, 1878; cond. 1909 of the Court Opera at Carlsruhe; c. operas *"Vasantasena,"* (Breslau, 1903), *"Die Liebenden von Kandahar"* (1907), and music for *"Faust"* (Mannheim, 1909).

**Rein'hardt, Heinrich,** b. Pressburg, April 13, 1865; c. operettas for Vienna *"Das süsse Mädel"* (1901); *"Ein Mädchen für Alles"* (Munich, 1908).

**Reiter** (rī'-tĕr), **Josef,** b. Braunau, Jan. 19, 1862; composer; Viennese composer of operas, including *"Der Totentanz"* (Dessau, 1908), symph., cantatas, male choruses, etc.

**Rembt,** (rĕmpt), **Johann Ernst,** Suhl, 1749–1810; organist and composer.

**Rheineck** (rī'-nĕk), **Christoph.** Memmingen, Nov. 1, 1748 — July 29, 1797; c. operas.

**Rice, Elihu S.,** Genesee Co., N. Y., 1827 — Logansport, Ind., May 1912; merchant; lived Logansport from 1838; c. pop. hymns, "*Shall we Meet Beyond the River,*" etc.

**Richafort** (rēsh-ä-fôr), **Jean,** important Flemish composer of masses, motets and songs; pupil of Deprès: 1543, choirmaster in Bruges.

**Rid'dell,** (1) **John,** Ayr, 1718–1795; blind Scots, composer of dance music, (2) **Robert,** d. Friar's Carse, 1794; captain, friend of Burns; c. dances and songs.

**Rider=Kelsey, Corinne,** b. Le Roy, N. Y., Feb. 24, 1880; soprano; studied with L. A. Torrens, Chicago, Mr. and Mrs. Toedt, N. Y.; sang widely in concert and oratorio; 1908, début in opera at Covent Garden; returned to concert work.

**Rietsch** (rētsh), **Heinrich,** b. Falkenau, Sept. 22, 1860; professor and composer; pupil of Krenn, Mandyczevski, and Fuchs; from 1892 teacher in Vienna; from 1900 prof. at the German Univ., Prague; author, and historian; c. opera, chamber music, etc.

**Rimsky=Koraskov, N. A.,** add that he died at St. Petersburg, June 21, 1908; in 1901 he ceased to cond. Russian symph.; 1905 he wrote a letter protesting against the use of armed force in the Cons. to repress students' political expression, and he was dismissed; Glazounoff, Liadov, and others at once resigned, public feeling was aroused, and his opera "*Kotschei*" was prod. at the Theatre du Passage, 1905, with great acclaim; later he was reinstated and Glazounoff chosen director. His opera "*Kitesch*" was prod. the same year, and "*Zolotoi Pietouchok*" (1909); his

symphonic suite, "*Schêhêrazad...*" (Boston Symph., 1897), was used the Russian ballets in Paris, 19... with immense success.

**Rinal'do di Capua,** ca. 1700 (?) Rome, after 1771; important Ital... composer of 30 or more light oper... popular in Italy, France,and Engla...

**Rip'fel, Karl,** Mannheim, 1799 Frankfort-on-Main, March 8, 18... 'cellist and composer.

**Rip'pon, John,** Tiverton, 1751 London, 1836; clergyman; c. orato... "*The Crucifixion.*"

**Riseley** (rĭz'-lĭ), **George,** b. Brist... Aug. 28, 1845; organist; pupil Corfe, later his successor at t... Cathedral; cond. orch. societi... pensioned, 1898, then cond. Lond... c. *Jubilee Ode,* 1887, etc.

**Rivarde** (rē-vär'-dĕ), **Serge Achil...** b. New York, Oct. 31, 1865 Spanish father, American mothe... violinist; at 11 taken to Euro... pupil of Dancla, Paris Cons.; dividi... first prize, 1879, with Ondriček; 188... 90, solo violinist Lamoureux orc... from 1899, prof. R. C. M., London.

**Rob'erts, John,** Wales, 1822 Aberdare, 1877; composer of chur... music; founder of festivals.

**Röckel, Jane Jackson,** d. Clift... August 27, 1907, age 73; wife J... Leopold R. (q. v.); pupil Pau... Hallé, Mme. Schumann; pianist a... teacher; c. piano pieces with p... name "Jules de Sivrei." Inventor "*Pamphonia,*" appliance for learni... staves and clefs.

**Rod'well, George Herbert Bon... parte,** London, (?), 1800–1852; pu... of Novello and Bishop; from 18... prof. of harmony R. C. M.; numerous operettas, farces, etc.

**Roguski** (rŏ-goo'-skĭ), **Gustav,** Warsaw, 1839; pupil there and Marx, Kiel, and Berlioz; from 18... prof. of composition at the Warsa... Cons.; c. symph., 2 masses, chamb... music, etc.

**Röhr,** (rär), **Hugo,** b. Dresden, Fe...

13, 1866; pupil of the Cons.; cond. in various cities; from 1896 royal court cond. at Munich Court Opera; c. oratorio "*Ekkehard*," opera "*Vater unser*" (Munich, 1904), etc.

**Rolland** (rŭl-läṅ), **Romain,** b. Clamecy, Jan. 29, 1868; teacher of history at the Ecole normale supérieure, at Paris; 1900 organized an international congress of music; historian at Paris; author of many historical and critical works, dramatic poems, and the musical romance "*Jean Christophe*" (1905-1908).

**Róman, Johann Helmich,** Stockholm, 1694 — near Calmar, 1710, called the father of Swedish music; pupil of Handel in London with a municipal stipend; 1727, court cond. at Stockholm; c. funeral march for King Fredrik (1751), coronation march for King Adolph Fredrik; 2 symphonies, etc.

**Roo'tham,** (1) **Daniel Wilberforce,** b. Cambridge, Aug. 15, 1837; pupil of Walmesley and Schira; 1865-77, cathedral org., Bristol; cond. Bristol madrigal society. His son (2) **Cyril Bradley,** b. Bristol, Oct. 5, 1875; Mus. B. at Cambridge, 1900; from 1901, organist there, St. John's College; pupil also at R. C. M., London; c. overture "*The Spirit of Comedy*," (1909), and vocal works with orch. "*Albert Graeme's Song*" (1904); "*Andromeda*" (Bristol Festival, 1908), "*Coronach*," etc.

**Ropartz** (rō-pärs), **J. Guy,** b. Quingamp, France, June 15, 1864; pupil of Dubois, Massenet, and César Franck; from 1894, dir. Nancy Cons., and cond. symph. concerts; c. symph. on a Breton chorale, 1895; incid. music to Loti's "*Pêcheur d'Islande*" (Paris, 1893); suite "*Dimanche breton*" (1898); *Psalm 136* for organ and orch. (Nancy, 1898), etc.

**Rösch** (rěsh), **Friedrich,** b. Memmingen, Dec. 12, 1862; author and conductor of male choruses, etc.; pupil of Wohlmuth and Rheinberger;

lived in various cities; from 1898 in Berlin.

**Rosé** (rō-zā), **Marie,** singer and teacher in Paris; from 1912 also in London. Her son (2) **Raymond,** 1911, cond. London Op. House; cond. His Majesty's Theatre, and c. incid. music for Beerbohm Tree's prods. of Shakespeare "*Macbeth*," etc., c. text and music of operas "*Joan of Arc*" (in concert form Queen's Hall, 1911); "*Antony and Cleopatra*"; a symph. poem on the same subject (Queen's Hall, 1911); songs, etc.

**Ro'seingrave,** (1) **Daniel,** d. Dublin, 1727; English composer of anthems; pupil of Blow and Purcell; 1679-98 org. at various cathedrals; 1698 at St. Patrick's, Dublin; father of (2) **Thomas** (q. v.), and of (3) **Ralph,** Salisbury, ca. 1695 — Dublin, 1746; pupil of his father and his successor as organist at St. Patrick's, Dublin; c. anthems.

**Ro'senfeld, Leopold,** Copenhagen, July 21, 1850 — July 19, 1909; studied in Germany; critic and teacher in Copenhagen; c. vocal works with orch., "*Henrik og Else*," "*Liden Helga*," "*Naar Solen daler*," songs, etc.

**Ro'senhoff, Orla,** b. Copenhagen, Oct. 1, 1845; pupil of Lund and Gade; from 1880 teacher of theory at the Cons.; c. chamber music, etc.

**Rosenzweig,** (rō'-zěnts-vīkh) **Max,** b. Roumania, 1900; violinist; brought to America at 7; son of a barber; he studied at the Music Settlement under David Mannes, then with Sinsheimer; début at MacDowell Club banquet March 10, 1912, with such success that subscription was taken up to send him abroad to study.

**Ro'ser, (von Reiter) Franz de Paula,** Naarn, 1779 — Pest, 1830; cond. in theatres; c. 100 operettas, ballets, etc

**Ros'si** (1) **Carlo,** b. Lemberg, April 4, 1839; pupil of Menzel; from 1851 in Venice; c. symph., etc. (2) **Cesare,** b. Mantua, 1864; c. operas "*I fugitivi*"

(Trient, 1896), and *"Nadeya"* (Prague, 1903); (3) **Arcangelo,** suicide, San Francisco 1905 (?); buffo barytone; pupil Milan Cons.; sang at Covent Garden and Met. Op. House, N. Y.; toured with the latter troupe and was injured at San Francisco in the earthquake; lost his voice and his mind.

**Rössl** (rĕs'-l), **Damian von,** b. Belts, Russia, July 13, 1852; pianist; pupil of Liszt; from 1882 teacher in Odessa.

**Röthig** (rā'-tĭkh), **Bruno,** b. Ebersbach, Oct. 7, 1859; pupil of Riedel Papperitz and G. Weiss; 1889, cantor in Leipzig; 1908 royal cond.; founder and cond. *"Solo Quartet for Church Songs,"* with which he has toured widely; c. songs.

**Roth'well, Walter Henry,** b. London, Sept. 22, 1872; conducted the first English performance of *"Parsifal"* in America; pupil Vienna Royal Acad.; cond. in various cities, and at Amsterdam Royal Opera; 1903, America to conduct English productions of *"Parsifal,"* and *"Madame Butterfly";* 1908 cond. Minneapolis symph. orch.

**Roussel,** (roos'-sĕl) **Albert.** b. Tourcoing, April 5, 1869; composer; at first attracted to the navy and a naval student, he made a voyage to China as an ensign; but resigned in 1894 and took up music, studying harmony with Gigout; 1898 entered the Schola Cantorum and studied under d'Indy till 1907; since 1900 he has been prof. of counterpoint at the Schola Cantorum. His comps. include symph. prelude, *Résurrection* (after Tolstoi's novel); symph. sketch, *Vendanges;* symphony, *Le poème de la Forêt* (1904–6); symph. sketches *Evocations* (1910–11), poem for orch. *La Menace* (1907), etc.

**Różycki** (roo-zhēt'-skĭ), (1) **Jacet,** Polish court cond. and composer to John Sobieski at Warsaw, 17th century. (2) **Ludomir von,** b. Warsaw, 1883; pupil of the Cons. and of

Humperdinck; from 1908 teacher the Cons. in Lemberg and cond. the Opera; c. opera *"Boleslas a Kühne"* (Lemberg, 1909); symp poem *"Stanczyk,"* etc.

**Ru'bensohn, Albert,** Stockhol Dec. 20, 1826–1901; violinist; pupil David; 1872 dir. of the Stockho Cons.; c. symph., incid. music Björnson's *"Halte Hulda,"* etc.

**Rubert** (roo'-bĕrt), **Johann Ma tin,** Nuremberg, 1614 — Stralsun 1680; organist and comp.

**Rubinel'li, Giovanni Battist** Brescia, ca. 1753–1829; Italian ope singer; début at 18, Stuttgart.

**Rubinstein, Anton,** the corr birth date is Nov. (16) 28, 18 Rubinstein having been in en himself until 1889.

**Rübner,** (1) **Cornelius,** add th he succeeded MacDowell as prof. music Columbia University, N. 1905; c. 3-act dance legend *"Pr Ador"* (Carlsruhe, 1903), etc.; h given piano recitals, often with h daughter (2) **Dagmar,** pian début Carlsruhe, playing the Sch mann concerto under Mottl; tou the U. S.; c. songs.

**Rückauf** (rĭk'-owf), **Anton,** Schl Alt-Erler, Prague, March 13, 1855 Sept. 19, 1903; composer of i portant songs; pupil of Proks and teacher at his institute, th pupil of Nottebohm and Navra at Vienna: c. opera *"Die Rose thalerin"* (Dresden, 1897), etc.

**Rudnick** (root'-nĭk), **Wilhelm,** Dammerkow, Pomerania, Dec. 1850; pupil of Kullak's acad., and Dienel; org. at Liegnitz; c. ope *"Otto der Schütz"* (1887); orato *"Judas Ischariot"* *"Der Verlore Sohn,"* etc.

**Ru'dolph, Fd.,** d. Wiesbaden, M 23, 1911; barytone at the ope 1872–1904; famous as "Beckmesser

**Ruffo,** (roof'-fo) **Titta,** b. Tuscar eminent barytone; pupil of St. Ceci Cons., Rome; after two years d missed and advised to give up singing; then Cassini of Milan taught him gratis; he won his first success at Rio Janeiro and throughout South America, then triumphed in Italy, later in Vienna; 1912 a sensation in Paris and engaged for Chi.-Phil. Opera Co., appearing Philadelphia Nov. 4, 1912.

**Runge,** (roong'-ĕ) **Paul** b. Heinrichsfeld, Posen, Jan. 2, 1848; pupil of church music Institute, Berlin, and J. Schneider; from 1873 at Colmar as historian and comp.

**Rünger,** (rĭng'-ĕr), **Julius,** b. Holics, Hungary, July 26, 1874; barytone; first studied organ and conducting at Prague, then voice with Giannini and Vogl; sang in various cities; toured the world; c. songs, etc.

**Rüter** (rē'-tĕr), **Hugo,** b. Hamburg, Sept. 7, 1859; pupil of the Cons.; from 1897 singing teacher and cond. at Wandsbeck; c. symph.; 2 operas, etc.

**Rutini** ( roo-tē'-nē ), **Giovanni Marco,** Florence, ca. 1730—ca. 1797; c. operas and clavier sonatas.

**Rybakov** (rē'-bä-kôf), **Sergei Gav=rilovich,** b. 1867; pupil of St. Petersburg Cons.; author; c. songs.

**Ryder, Arthur H.** b. Plymouth, Mass., April 30, 1875; pupil of his mother, F. H. Rowse, Loraine Holloway, and at Harvard, of J. K. Paine and W. R. Spalding; from 1894, org. and dir. at various churches in Boston and Providence, R. I.; editor of musical texts; c. organ and piano pieces, etc.

**Ryelandt** (rē'-länt), **Joseph,** b. Bruges, April 7, 1870; composer; pupil of Tinel; c. choral works with orch., "*St. Cécile,*" and "*Purgatorium,*" chamber music, etc.

## S

**Saar, Louis Victor,** add that he has been principal of the dept. of theory at Cincinnati College of Music from 1906; 1903 he won Kaiser prize for composition, Baltimore; c.

piano quintet (Chicago 1912), "*Hymn to Venus*" (Cincinnati 1912), etc.

**Sachsenhauser** (zäkh'-zĕn-how-zĕr), **Theodor,**July 27, 1866 — Munich, Feb. 25, 1904; comp.

**Sack** (zäk), **J.Ph.,** Harzerode, Anhalt, 1722 — Berlin, 1763; organist at Berlin Cathedral; important composer of songs and clavier pieces.

**Sacks,** (1) **Woldemar,** b. Riga, 1868; teacher and critic in Leipzig; c. songs. His wife and pupil (2) **Elly Schel=lenberg=S.,** b. Nannhof, near Leipzig, 1879; concert soprano; pupil Leipzig Cons.

**Sacrati** (sä-krä-tē), **Francesco,** d. Modena, May 20, 1650; court cond. and important early composer of opera.

**Safonoff, Wassily Ilich,** add that in 1906 he visited London and cond. the Phil. orch. once; 1906–9 he cond. the Philh. orch., New York City, with great success, then returned to Russia. He conducts without a bâton.

**Sahlender** (säl'-ĕn-dĕr), **Emil,** b. Ibenhain, Thuringia, March 12, 1864; cond. at Heidelberg; pupil Leipzig Cons.; c. operas, choruses, etc.

**Saint=Leon** (săñ-lā-ŏñ), **Ch. V. A.,** Paris, 1821–1870; ballet dancer and violinist; c. concertos.

**Salazar** ( săl=ä-thär ), **Don Juan Garcia,** d. 1710 at Zamora, where he was cond. at the Cathedral; c. motets.

**Saint=Saëns, Chas. Camille,** add that he c. operas "*Lola,*" (1901), "*Les Barbares*" (1901), "*Andromaque*" (1903), "*Hélène*" (Monte Carlo, 1904), "*L'Ancêtre*" (do., 1906), "*Dejanire*" (1911); cantata "*La feu céleste*" (1900); fantaisie for violin and harp (1907); "*La Muse et le Poète*" for violin and orch. 1909; "*Overture de Fête,*" op. 133, 1909: songs, piano pieces, etc.

**Salter,** (1) **Sumner,** add that since 1905 he has been mus. dir. at Williams College. (2) **Mrs. Mary**

née **Turner,** b. Peoria, Ill., March 15, 1856; studied singing with Alfred Arthur, Burlington, Ia., where she sang in church; then pupil of Max Schilling, John O'Neill, and Mme. Rudersdorf, Boston; 1877 succeeded Emma Thursby as soprano of Broadway Tabernacle, N. Y.; 1879, soprano Trinity Church, New Haven, teaching also at Wellesley College. 1881, married Sumner Salter, who was her teacher in composition; 1893 retired from church and concert work, devoting her time to teaching and composition of songs.

**Samar'off** (née **Hickenlooper**), **Olga,** b. San Antonio, Texas, Aug. 8, 1880 (of German-Russian parents); pianist; at 9 pupil of Von Sternberg, later of Marmontel, Widor, and the Paris Cons.; studied again with Ernest Hutcheson and with Jedlicka; début, N. Y., 1905; 1906, London; has toured widely; 1911 married L. Stokovski.

**Samazeuilh** (săm-ä-zŭ'-ē), **Gustave,** b. Bordeaux, June 2, 1877; Parisian critic and composer; pupil of Chausson and d'Indy; c. "*Poème*" for violin and orch., "*La barque*" for voice and orch., songs, etc.

**Sammar'co,** **Mario,** b. Palermo, 1873; barytone; pupil of Cantelli; début Milan; from 1904 at Covent Garden; from 1907 also at New York Manhattan Opera House, and later at Metropolitan; has sung also in Russia, South America, etc.

**Sances** (sän'-chĕs), **Giovanni Felice,** Rome, 1600—Vienna, Nov. 24, 1679; tenor and court cond. at Vienna; one of the first to write "cantatas"; c. operas, oratorios, etc.

**San'den, Aline,** dramatic soprano, member of the Leipzig Opera since 1909; has sung as guest at Berlin, 1912, Dresden and Braunschweig court operas with sensational success as "*Salome*," "*Elektra*," under Strauss' direction, "*Carmen*," etc.

**San'ford, Samuel Simons,** Bridge-port, Conn., March 15, 1849 — New Haven, Conn., Jan. 6, 1910. Professor of applied music Yale University.

**Sank'ey, Ira David,** Edinburg, Pa., 1840 — Brooklyn, Aug. 14, 1909; world-famous singer of gospel hymns as the singing colleague of the late D. L. Moody at their mission services; ed. a coll. of mission hymns "*Sacred Songs and Solos*," which had an enormous circulation.

**Sauer, Emil,** add that he resigned his professorship at the Master School of Vienna Cons., 1907, and moved to Dresden.

**Savage,** (1) **William,** 1720 — London, 1789; singer in Chapel Royal; c. church music. (2) **Henry W.,** b. Boston, Mass.; impresario; graduate of Harvard; as a builder and real estate owner in 1895 took over the Castle Square Theatre, Boston, and organized a stock co. which gave light and serious operas for many years in Boston, New York, etc.; produced many new American operettas as well as plays; made the immensely successful productions of "*Parsifal*" and "*Madame Butterfly.*"

**Savard** (să-văr), **M. A.,** b. Paris, May 15, 1861; pupil of the Cons.; taking the Prix de Rome, 1886; from 1902 dir. Lyons Cons.

**Saw'yer, F. H.,** Brighton, June 19, 1857 — April 29, 1908. Bachelor of music, Oxford, 1877; Mus. Doc., 1884, Fellow R. C. of organists; organist for over 30 years; prof. of singing; c. oratorio, "*Mary, the Virgin*" (1884); recast as "*Star of the East*" (1889); cantatas, etc.

**Sbriglia** (sbrēl'-yä), **Giovanni,** b. Naples, 1840; tenor and famous teacher; pupil of De Roxas; début Naples, 1851; sang throughout Italy and toured America with Patti and others; became a very successful teacher in Paris, numbering the De Reszkés, Plançon, Nordica, Sanderson, etc., among his pupils.

**Schäfer** (shä'-fĕr), **Alex. Nikolaje-**

**vich,** b. St. Petersburg, Sept. 11, 1866; pupil of the Cons., teacher and cond., c. operas, 2 symph., etc.

**Schaffrath** (shäf'-rät), **Christoph.**, Hohenstein, 1709—Berlin, 1763; court composer.

**Schall** (shäl), **Klaus,** Copenhagen, April 28, 1757 — Aug. 10, 1835; violinist; c. 30 ballets, etc.

**Schaub** (showp), **Hans F.,** b. Frankfort, Sept. 22, 1880; pupil of Knorr, Humperdinck, and A. Mendelssohn; teacher and editor; c. symph. prologue "*Monna Vanna*," etc.

**Scheinpflug** (shīn'-pflookh), **Paul,** b. Loschwitz, Dresden, Sept. 10, 1875; pupil of the Cons.; from 1909 cond. at Königsberg; c. "*Frühlings symph.*" (1907), chamber music, etc.; overture to a comedy of Shakespeare (based on English melody of 16th century), Boston Symph. Orch., 1909; tone-poem for orch. (Bremen, 1908), songs, etc.

**Schel'ling, Ernest (Henry),** b. Belvedere, N. J., July 26, 1876; pianist; played in public before he was five; pupil of Mathias, Moszkowski, Leschetizky, and for four years of Paderewski; toured widely; c. symphonic legend, orch. suite, violin sonata, etc.

**Schenk** (shěnk), **Peter Petrovich,** b. St Petersburg, Feb. 23, 1870; pupil of the Cons., and of Saloviev; librarian and critic; c. operas, 3 symph., etc.

**Schering** (shä'-rĭnk), **Arnold,** b. Breslau, April 7, 1870; violinist and historian, pupil of Joachim and Succo.

**Schiefferdecker** (shēf'-fěr-děk-ěr), **Jn. Chrn.,** d. Lübeck, 1732; organist; c. operas, etc.

**Schiever** (shē'-věr), **Ernst,** b. Hanover, March 23, 1844; violinist; pupil of Joachim, later member of his quartet; from, 1878 in Liverpool as cond. of the Richter orch. and the Schiever quartet.

**Schjelderup** (shělt'-ěr-oop), **Gerhard,** b. Christiansand, Norway, Nov. 17, 1859; 'cellist; pupil of

Franchomme, Savard and Massenet; c. operas "*Norwegische Hochzeit*" (Prague, 1900), and "*Frühlings Nacht*," a symph. and orch. works, "*Eine Sommernacht auf dem Fjord*," etc.

**Schlemüller** ( shlä'-mǐl-lěr ), (1) **Gustav,** Königsberg, Nov. 7, 1841 —Leipzig, May 22, 1900; teacher and critic. His son (2) **Hugo,** b. Königsberg, Oct. 2, 1872; 'cellist and teacher in Leipzig; pupil of Schröder, Klengel and Becker; teacher; c. 'cello music.

**Schlögel** ( shlä'-gěl ), **Xavier,** b. Brillonville, Belgium, 1854 — Ciney, 1889; pupil Liège Cons.; c. mass with orch., chamber music, etc.

**Schmeidler** (schmīt'-lěr), **Karl,** b. Kattowitz, Silesia, Aug. 21, 1859; teacher in Berlin; c. piano pieces, etc.

**Schmitt,** (shmēt) **Florent.** b. Blâmont, France, Sept. 28, 1870; studied at Nancy; 1889, entered Paris Cons. winning second Prix de Rome 1897; first 1900, with cantata *Sémiramis*. He sent from Rome a symph. poem *Combat des Raksasas et Délivrance de Sita,* a symph. ètude based on Poe's "*Le Palais hanté*" and the *46th Psalm,* which was later played with success, 1906, increasing to furore (1910 and Colonne Concerts, 1912); his piano quintet (1909) has won great fame; his *Tragédie de Salomé* was danced by Loie Fuller 1907; his symph. poem *Sélamlik* (1904), much chamber music, piano pieces, and songs have given him a high place in France.

**Schmittbauer** ( schmǐt'-bow-ěr ), **Joseph Alois,** Bamberg, 1718 — Carlsruhe, 1809; cond. and composer.

**Schneider, Edward Faber.** b. Omaha, Neb., Oct. 3, 1872; pupil of X. Scharwenka in N. Y., and O. B. Boise, Berlin; from 1900 in San Francisco. Dean of mus. dept. of Mills College; c. music-drama "*Triumph of Bohemia,*" text by George Sterling, (Bohemian Club, 1907);

symph. "The Autumn Time" (San
Francisco Orch. 1912), songs, etc.
**Schönberg** (shän'-bĕrkh), **Arnold,**
b. Vienna, Sept. 13, 1874; composer
of startling originality; pupil of
Zemlinsky; c. symph. poem "*Pelleas
und Melisande,*" etc. His music is
written without bars and has aroused
great hostility and great enthusiasm.
His string quartet in D minor, op.
7, played in Berlin, 1912, was actually
hissed as well as applauded; in London, 1912, 5 orch. pieces provoked a
storm; also wrote treatise on harmony.
**Scholtz** (shôlts), (1) **Adolf,** 1823
— Breslau, 1834; trumpet virtuoso.
(2) **Hermann,** b. Breslau, June 9,
1845; pianist; pupil of Brosig, Liszt,
von Bülow and Rheinberger; teacher
in Dresden, 1880 chamber virtuoso;
c. concerto; edited Chopin's text.
**Schön, Ed.,** vide ENGELSBERG.
**Schop** (shôp), **Johann,** d. Hamburg,
ca. 1665; court violinist in Denmark, 1615–19; from 1621 cond. at
Hamburg; c. instrumental works.
**Schöpf** (shĕpf), **Franz,** b. Girlau,
1836; organist at Bozen; c. an opera
and church music.
**Schor** (shôr), **David,** b. Simferopol,
1867; pianist; pupil of Amenda and
Safonoff; at St. Petersburg; member
of the Moscow Trio at Moscow.
**Schos'takovski, PeterAdamovich,**
b. 1853; pianist; pupil St. Petersburg
Cons., and of Kullak and Liszt; prof.
at Moscow Cons.; 1894–98 dir. Italian
opera at Moscow.
**Schroeder, Alwin,** add that in
1903 he resigned from the Boston
Symph. Orch., and joined the Kneisel
Quartet; 1905–7, teacher at New
York Institute of Musical Art; 1907,
first 'cello teacher at Hoch Cons.,
Frankfort-on-Main; 1908, returned
to Boston as co-founder of Hess-
Schroeder Quartet; 1910, first 'cellist
of Boston Symph; resigned 1912 for
concert tours.
**Schultz-Adaievski** (shoolts-ä-da-

yĕf'-ski), **Ella von,** b. St. Petersburg, Feb. 10, 1846; pupil of Henselt
and the St. Petersburg, Cons.; pianist;
toured and from 1882 lived at
Venice; c. opera "*Die Morgenröte der
Freiheit*" (1881); "*Sonate grecque*"
for clarinet and piano, etc.
**Schumann=Heink, Ernestine,**
add that 1899-1904 she sang at Berlin Royal Opera as well as at Met.
Op., N. Y.; 1904 she starred in a comic
opera, "*Love's Lottery*"; 1909 she
created "*Clytemnestra*" in Strauss's
"*Elektra*" at Dresden; Paul Schumann, d. 1904; she m. William Rapp,
Jr., 1905; divorced him, 1912; she has
sung in concert with enormous success in America and in opera abroad;
became naturalized American, 1908.
**Schuppan** (shoop'-pän), **Adolf,** b.
Berlin, June 5, 1863; pupil of B.
Härtel; c. chamber music.
**Schwindel** (shvĭnt'-l), **Fr.,** d. Carlsruhe, 1786; violinist; c. operettas,
symphonies, etc.
**Scott,** (1) **Lady John Douglas**
(née Alicia Ann Spottiswoode); Spottiswoode, 1810 — March 12, 1900;
composer of "*Annie Laurie,*" and
other songs, (2) **Cyril Meir,** b
Oxton, Sept. 27, 1879; pupil of Hoch
Cons.; c. a symph., 3 overtures
vocal works with orch., songs, etc.
**Scot'ti, Antonio,** b. Naples, 1869
barytone; début Malta, 1889; sang ir
various cities; from 1899 at Coven'
Garden and Met. Op. House, N. Y.
regularly; famous as "*Don Giovanni.*'
**Scriabine** (or **Skrjabin**), **Alex.**
add that according to Rosa New
march he was born Jan. 10, not 6
he was piano prof. at Moscow Cons
1898-1903, then devoted himself t
composition; played in New York
1906, his own concerto; 3 symph., th
first with choral finale "*Rêverie*" an
"*Poème de l'Extase*" for orch., 3 pian
sonatas, etc. He gave recitals of hi
own works, Berlin, 1911. His wif
**Vera,** is also a pianist.
**Sebald** (zā'-bält), **Alex.,** b. Pest, Apr.

29, 1869; violinist; pupil of Saphir and C. Thomson; member of Gewandhaus orch., Leipzig, and toured with Gewandhaus Quartet; toured widely from 1903; was concertm. Berlin Royal Orch.; 1906 taught in Chicago; 1907 opened a school in Berlin; wrote a method and c. violin pieces, etc.

**Seck'endorff, Karl Siegmund, Freiherr von**, Erlangen, Nov. 26, 1744 — Ansbach, May 6, 1809; c. a monodrama and songs to Goethe's texts.

**Seeg(e)r** (sā'-gĕr) (or **Segert** or **Zeckert**), **Joseph Norbert**, Rzepin, Bohemia, March 21, 1716 — Prague, April 22, 1872; composer; famous organist and teacher; c. toccatas, masses, etc.

**Segni** (sān'-yē), **Giulio**, (called Giulio da Modena), Modena, 1498 — Rome, 1561; organist.

**Seiffert** (zīf'-fĕrt), **Max**, b. Beeskow, Feb. 9, 1868; historian and composer; pupil of Spitta; from 1891 at Berlin as author and 1907 Royal Prof.

**Seixas** (sā'-shăs), **José Ant. Carlos de**, organist and composer; Coimbra, June 11, 1704 — Aug. 25, 1742; organist and church composer.

**Sekles** (zĕk'-lĕs), **Bernhard**, b. Frankfort-on-Main, June 20, 1872; pupil of Hoch Cons., later theory teacher there; c. symph. poem "Die Gärten der Semiramis," songs, etc.

**Sel(e)neccer** (sā'-lĕ-nĕk-kĕr), **Nikolaus**, Hersbruch, n. Nuremberg, 1528 — after 1587; organist and composer of hymns.

**Selmer, Julius**, Hamburg, 1817 — Glasgow, May 4, 1903; teacher and conductor; founder of Glasgow Soc. of Musicians, and for 14 years its president.

**Selmer, Johann**, Christiania, Jan. 20, 1844 — Venice, July 21, 1910; Norwegian composer; cond. and author; pupil of A. Thomas, Paris, Richter and Paul, Leipzig; 1883–6 cond. Phil. orch., Christiania; driven

south by pulmonary trouble; c. Norwegian Festival March, "Scène funèbre," Finnish Festival Bells, "In the Mountains," ' Carnival in Flanders,' etc., for orch., choral works with orch., songs, etc.

**Senaillé** (sŭn-ĭ-yā), **Jean Baptiste**, Paris, Nov. 23, 1687 — April 29, 1730; famous violinist; at court of Louis XV; c. violin sonatas, etc.

**Senger=Bettaque** (zĕng'-kĕr-bĕt-täk-vĕ), **Katharina**, b. Berlin, Aug. 2, 1862; soprano; a ballet dancer at the Imperial Opera, Berlin, then studied with Dorn, and 1879 appeared on the same stage in soubrette rôles; sang in various cities, 1888 in Bayreuth as "Eva"; 1895 married the actor Alex. Senger.

**Serato** (sā-rä'-tō), **Amigo**, b. Bologna, Feb. 7, 1877; violinist, son and pupil of a violinist and prof. at the cons.; later pupil of Sarti; has played with success in Germany and elsewhere.

**Serran'o** (or **Serrão**), **Emilio**, b. Vitoria, 1850; court pianist at Madrid; prof. at the Cons., and dir. of Royal Opera; c. operas.

**Servais** (sĕr-vĕ'), **Franz** or **François**, (**Matthieu**), 1844 — Asnières, Jan. 14, 1901; cond. at Brussels; c. opera "L'Appolonide" or "Ion" (Carlsruhe 1899). Son of Adrien Fr. (g. v.)

**Ševcik** (shĕf'-chĭk), **Otokar**, b. Horaždowitz, Bohemia, March 22, 1852; famous violin teacher; pupil of Prague Cons.; from 1870 concertmaster various cities; 1875 prof. at Kiev; 1892 at Prague Cons.; teacher of Kubelik, Kocian, etc.; author of methods; c. Bohemian dances, variations, etc.

**Sévérac** (sā-vā-răk), **Déodat de**, b. Saint Felix, July 20, 1874; writer and composer; pupil Toulouse Cons., and the Schola cantorum, Paris; a concert of his works was given in 1905 with success; c. 2-act lyric drama "Le Coeur de Moulin" (Op. Com. Paris, 1909); lyric tragedy

*"Héliogabale"* (Arènes de Beziers, 1910); *"Muguetto"* (1911); *"Hélène de Sparte"* (Paris 1912); symph. poems, *"Nymphes au Crépuscule"* and *"Didon et Enée"*; a piano sonata, etc.

**Seydel, Irma.** b. Boston (?) 1896 (?); violinist; pupil of her father, Theodore S. (contrabass of Boston Symph.) Strube, C. M. Loeffler, and Maquarre; début at Cologne 1910; played with Boston Symph. 1912.

**Seyfert** (zī'-fĕrt), **Johann,** b. Prague, 1837; 'cellist; pupil Prague Cons.; from 1859, teacher at St. Petersburg Cons.

**Shaliapin,** vide CHALIAPINE.

**Sharpe, Ethel,** b. Dublin, Nov. 28, 1872; pianist; pupil R. Irish Acad., and of R. C. M., London; début London 1891; 1895 married Alfred Hobday, viola-virtuoso.

**Shepherd, Arthur.** b. Paris, Idaho, Feb. 19, 1880; 1892, pupil at N. E. Cons. Boston, of Dennée and Faelten (piano), Benj. Cutter (harmony); Goetschius and Chadwick (comp.); graduated 1897, and settled in Salt Lake City as teacher; cond. Salt Lake Symph. Orch.; from 1909, teacher of piano, harmony and cpt. at N. E. Cons.; 1902, won Paderewski prize with *"Ouverture Joyeuse"*; 1909 won two Nat. Fed. prizes with piano sonata, and song, *"The Lost Child"*; c. also barytone solo with chor. and orch., songs and piano pieces.

**Shir'reff, Jane,** 1811 — Kensington, Dec. 23, 1883; singer at Covent Garden; 1838 toured America.

**Sibelius, Jean,** add that he became the principal of the Helsingfors Cons. and has increased his fame as a composer of remarkable nationalism, though he denies that he uses folk - music. Add to his compositions 2 symphs., overture and suites, *"Karelia,"* tone-poems for orch. *"En Saga,"* and *"Finlandia"*; orch. suite, *"Pelleas and Melisande,"* symphonic fantasias, *"Pohgolas'*

*Daughter,"* *"Belshazzar's Feast,"* incid. music to *"Kuolema,"* etc.

**Sichra** (sĭkh'-rǎ), **Andreas Ossipovich,** Wilna, 1772 — St. Petersburg, 1861; guitarist and composer.

**Sick** (sĭk), **Theodor Bernhard,** b. Copenhagen, Nov. 7, 1827; artillery officer and composer of chamber music.

**Siefert** (zē'-fĕrt), **Paul,** Danzig, 1586–1666; organist and composer.

**Simon** (sē-môñ), **Anton Yulievich,** b. France, 1851; composer; pupil of Paris Cons.; 1871 theatre cond. in Moscow; 1891 prof. at Phil. Society School; c. 6 operas, symph. poems, etc.

**Simonet'ti, Achille,** b. Turin, June 12, 1859; violinist; pupil of Sivori, Dancla, and Massenet; member of the *"London Trio"*; c. violin sonatas, etc.

**Sinclair** (sĭnk'-lĕr), **George Robertson,** b. Croyden, Oct. 28, 1863; organist; pupil Ouseley, Stewart, and Lloyd; at 17 was organist of Truro Cathedral; from 1889 at Hereford Cath., cond. the H. Festivals, 1891–1906; 1899 Mus. Doc. from Archbishop of Canterbury; 1904 fellow of R. Coll. of Organists.

**Sinding, Christian,** add that he c. 2 symph.; the first was played by the Boston Symph., 1899 and 1906 *"Episodes chevaleresques"* for orch. (based on a poem by Holgar Drachmann), *"Rondo infinito"* for orch. (1898, Theo. Thomas, Chicago, 1900) piano concerto, 2 violin concertos, chamber music, piano pieces, a song cycle, *"Heimfahrt,"* etc.

**Sin'ico, (1) Francesco,** Trieste 1810–1865; conductor and composer. His son (2) **Giuseppe,** Trieste, Feb. 10, 1836 — Dec. 31, 1907, c. opera.

**Sinigaglia** (sē-nĭ-gäl'-yä), **Leone,** b. Turin, Aug. 14, 1868; pupil of the Cons. and of Mandyczewski; c. violin concerto, rhapsody *"Piemontese,"* for violin and orch., string quartet, concert étude for quartet, overture *"Le baruffe chiozzotte,"* etc.

ádek (slä'-děk), **Wendelin,** d. Prague, July 1, 1901; contrabassist; composer and teacher at Prague Cons.

nieton, (1) **John More,** Dundee, 1857 — Broughty Ferry, July 13, 1904. Before the age of 10, c. songs, piano pieces and produced cantata "*Peace.*" Pupil of Sir Herbert Oakeley. In collaboration with his brother, (2) **James,** prod. several choral works.

nith, **David Stanley,** b. Toledo, Ohio, July 6, 1877; pupil of Horatio W. Parker, at Yale, where he graduated 1900 with a "Commencement Ode" for barytone (Herbert Witherspoon), chorus and orch.; studied then with Thuille and Widor abroad; 1903 Mus. Bac. Yale; from 1904 teacher, later asst. prof. at Yale; c. symph., symph. poem "*Darkness and Dawn,*" overture "*Joyeuse*" (Boston Symph. Orch., 1904); 1909, won Paderewski Prize with "The Fallen Star," for chorus and orch.

nolen'ski, **Stephan V.,** Kasan, 1848 — St. Petersburg, Aug. 6, 1909; prof. of history of Russian church music at Moscow Cons.; 1901 cond. court chapel at St. Petersburg; author of important historical works.

nul'ders, **Karl Anton,** b. Maestricht, May 8, 1863; pupil of Liège Cons.; c. piano pieces, etc.

nyth, **Ethel Mary,** add that she was born London, April 23, 1858; daughter of Artillery general; pupil of Leipzig Cons. and of Herzogenberg. Her string quintet was played there 1884; her violin sonata 1887; c. orch. serenade (London, 1890), overture "*Antony and Cleopatra*" (do.); *Mass in D* (London, 1893 under Barnby), and operas, "*Fantasio*" (her own libretto, Weimar 1898, Carlsruhe, 1901); 1-act "*Der Wald*" (her own German libretto, Dresden, 1901, Covent Garden, 1902 and 1903, Met. Op., N. Y., 1903); 3-act "*Les Naufrageurs*" (book by Leforestier), given at Leipzig, 1906, as "*Strandrecht*" (Prague, do.); c. also songs with orch.

**Snoer** (snoor), **Johannes,** b. Amsterdam, June 28, 1868; harpist at Leipzig and Bayreuth; pupil of Schuëcker; c. harp pieces.

**Sokal'ski,** (1) **Peter Petrovich,** Charkov, Sept. 26, 1832 — Odessa, April 11, 1887; author and composer of operas and piano pieces. His nephew and pupil (2) **Vladimir Ivanovich,** b. Heidelberg, April 6, 1863; lawyer and composer of a symph. (1894), a children's opera, "*The Turnip,*" a dramatic fantasie for orch., etc.

**Sokolov, Nikolai Alexandrovich,** add correct birth date, St. Petersburg, March 26, 1858; from 1896 teacher at the Cons.; c. incid. music to Shakespeare's "*Winter's Tale,*" ballet, "*The Wild Swans,*" 3 string quartets, songs, etc.

**Sol'dene, Emily,** Islington, 1844 — London, April 8, 1912; at first a music hall singer; 1871 appeared in "*Geneviève de Brabant,*" 1873 "*La Fille de Mme. Angot,*" touring America and Australia; she wrote a novel and contributed to journals.

**Sol'nitz, Anton Wilhelm,** 1722 — Amsterdam, 1758; c. symphonies, etc.

**Soltys** (sôl'-tĕs), **Mieczyslaw,** b. Lemberg, Feb. 7, 1863; pupil of Krenn and Gigout; director and teacher Lemberg Cons.; c. operas, symph., oratorio, etc.

**Som'born, Theodor Karl,** b. Barmen, Nov. 16, 1851; pupil of Rheinberger and Wüllner; from 1882 teacher, Strassburg Cons.; c. operas "*Philenor*" (Strassburg, 1903), "*Die Flamme*" (1908), etc.

**Son'neck, Oskar Geo. Th.,** b. Jersey City, N. J., Oct. 6, 1873; author; at 20 studied at Heidelberg, Munich and Italy; 1899 returned to America as music librarian at the Library of Congress.

**Spagnoletti** (spän-yō-lĕt'-tē), **Paolo** (rightly **P. Diana),** Cremona-

1768 — London, 1834; violinist and
cond.; pupil Naples Cons.; from 1802
in London in the King's theatre orch.;
1812 cond. Italian Opera, 1817 cond.
King's theatre orch.; gained immense
popularity in London.

**Spanuth** (spän'-oot), **August**, b.
Brinkum, Hanover, March 15, 1857;
pianist and critic; pupil of Hoch
Cons., Frankfort-on-Main; 1886–1893
Chicago as pianist and teacher; then
in New York as critic; 1906 returned
to Berlin as editor.

**Speer**, (1) **Charlton T.**, b. Cheltenham, Nov. 21, 1859; pupil R. A. M.
London, winning a scholarship; from
1885 prof. of piano there, also organist
at various churches; c. 2 operas,
*"The Battle of Lake Regillus,"* for
chorus and orch ; symph. poem,
*"King Arthur,"* etc. His cousin
(2) **William Henry**, b. London,
1863; organist; pupil of Lloyd and
the R. C. M.; 1906 Mus. Doc. Cambridge; c. symph., overture, orch.,
rhapsody, ballad, *"The Jackdaw of
Rheims,"* etc.

**Spielter** (shpēl'-tĕr), **Hermann**, b.
Bremen, April 26, 1860; pupil Leipzig Cons.; from 1894 in New York as
composer and teacher.

**Sporck, Georges**, b. Paris, April
9, 1870; pupil of the Cons. and of d'
Indy; c. symph. poems, symphonie
*"Vivaraise,"* *"Esquisses symphoniques,"* etc.

**Spring'er, Max**, b. Schwendi, Dec.
19, 1877; pupil of Schachleiter and
Klička; joined the Benedictine abbey
of Saint Emaus at Prague; organist
and composer there.

**Squarcialupi** ( skwär-chä-loo'-pē ),
**Antonio**, famous 15th century
organist and composer of the
Florentine School.

**Squire, William Barclay**, b.
London, Oct. 16, 1855; historian and
author, educated at Cambridge, 1879,
B. A.; 1902, M. A.; critic, librettist
and antiquarian.

**Stamm**, (shtäm), **Thomas Oswald**,

b. Uthleben, April 17, 1868; pupil
Jadassohn and Radecke; teach
and cond. at Weissenfels; c. sy
phony, etc.

**Stanford, Sir Chas. Villiers**, a
that he was knighted, 1901, a
made cond. of the Leeds Festiv
resigning the Bach Chair, 1904; co
posed motet with orch., *"The L*
*of Might"* (1903); symphony No.
*"In Memoriam G. F. Watts,"*
symphony (London Phil., Fe
1912), *"Stabat Mater,"* with or
(Leeds Fest., 1907); *"Wellington*
for voices and orch., incid. mus.
*"Attila"* (1907), overture *"*
*atque Vale"* (Haydn Centena
1909), etc.

**Stan'iforth, T. W.**, Sheffield, Ju
7, 1845 — March 25, 1909; piani
organist and composer.

**Starczewski** (stär-chĕf'-skĭ), Feli
b. Warsaw, 1868; critic and auth
pupil of the Music Institute and
Humperdinck, Fleischer, and d'Ind
c. orchestral pieces, etc.

**Starzer** (shtär'-tsĕr), **Josef**, Vie
na, 1726 — April 22, 1787; from 17
court conductor at St. Petersburg;
ballets, c atorio, etc.

**Statkov's.ii, Roman von**, b. ne
Kalisch, Dec. 24, 1859; pupil of Zele
ski, and of St. Petersburg Con
teacher of instrumentation and h
tory at Warsaw Cons. His ope
*"Philaenis"* took an internatior
prize in London and was prod., Wa
saw, 1904; c. also opera *"Mar*
(Warsaw, 1906); fantasie and polo
aise for orch., piano pieces, etc.

**Stefani** (stä'-fä-nē), (1) **Jan.** Pragu
1746 — Warsaw, Feb. 24, 182
Mus. Director; director at Wa
saw Cathedral; c. opera *"Die Krak*
*witer und die Bergvölker,"* 1794, a
others, also masses and polonais
His son (2) **Josef**, Warsaw, Ap
16, 1800 — (?); pupil of Elsner;
ballets, operettas, also 10 masses, et

**Stef'fan, Joseph Anton**, Cop
dino, Bohemia, March 14. 1726 -

Vienna, 1800; court piano teacher at Vienna, numbering among his pupils Marie Antoinette and Queen Caroline of Naples; c. piano pieces and songs.

**Steigleder** (stīkh-lā-dĕr), **Johann Ulrich**, Lindau, 1580 — Stuttgart, 1635; from 1605 court organist and composer at Stuttgart.

**Stein** (shtīn), **Fritz**, b. Heidelberg, Dec. 17, 1879; theologian at first, then studied music; organist and cond. at Heidelberg, 1906; musical dir. of Jena University, cond. academic concerts.

**Steinhauer** ( shtīn'-how-ĕr ) **Karl**, b. Düsseldorf, May 29, 1852; pupil of Leipzig Cons.; singing teacher and cond. at Düsseldorf; from 1901 at Oberhauser; c. male choruses with orch., etc.

**Stendhal** (stän-dăl), pen-name of **Marie Henri Beyle** (bĕl),Grenoble, Jan. 23, 1783 — Paris, March 23, 1842; French consul at Civitavecchia, 1831–42, and author of numerous books in music.

**Sten'hammar,** (1)**Fredrika,** Wisby, 1836 — Stockholm, 1880; operatic soprano; born Andrée. (2) **Ulrik,**Stockholm, 1829–1875; composer of oratorio "*Saul,*" etc. His son (3) **Wilhelm,** b. Stockholm, Feb. 7, 1871; pianist; pupil of the Cons., and of H. Barth; from 1898 cond. Phil. Society in Stockholm; from 1900 assistant cond. at the Royal Theatre; c. symph., "*Prinsessan och Svennen*" for voices and orch., music. dramas " *Tirfing* " (Stockholm, 1898), and "*Das Fest auf Solhaug*" (Stuttgart, 1899), overture "*Excelsior,*" and many important songs.

**tephani** (stä'-fă-nē), **Hermann,** b. Grimma, June 23, 1877; from 1906 director and organist at Eisleben; pupil Leipzig Cons.; c. Fest. overture, etc.

**tierlin** (shtēr'-lĭn), **Joh. Gottfr. Adolf.,** b. Adenau, Oct. 14, 1859; bass; pupil of F. Schmidt; 1897 founded a Cons. in Münster; c. operas ballets, etc.

**Stock, Fr. Wm. Aug.,** b. Dülich, Nov. 11, 1872;composer;son and pupil of a military bandmaster; then studied with Humperdinck, Zöllner, Jensen and Wüllner, at the Cologne Cons.; 1891–5 violinist in the City Orch.; then joined the Thomas Orch. in Chicago; 1899 became assistant cond. to Theodore Thomas, on whose death in 1905 he was chosen as conductor; c. symphonic poems, symph., variations, chamber music, songs, etc.

**Stojowski, Sigismund,** add that he has lived in New York since 1906 as piano prof. Musical Art Inst., giving frequent recitals. Add to his comps. symph. (Leipsiz, 1898); romance for violin and orch.; chor. with orch. "*Spring*"; Polish Rhapsodie for piano and orch.; violin concerto (1908); violin and piano sonata op. 37 (New York, 1912).

**Stokowski,** (stō-kôf'-skĭ) **Leopold.** b. London, of Polish parentage; graduated at Oxford; studied at Paris Cons., acted as cond. there 1905–8 mus. dir. St. Bartholomew's, N. Y.; 1908, cond. in London; 1909–12, cond. Cincinnati Symph. Orch; 1912, cond. Philadelphia Orch., vice Carl Pohlig; 1911, married the pianist Olga Samaroff.

**Stolze** (shtôl'-tsĕ), (1) **G. Chr.,** Erfurt, 1762–1830; organist. His son (2) **H. Wm.,** Erfurt, 1801—Celle, 1868; organist; c. oratorio, cantatas, etc.

**Stradal** ( strä - däl ), **August,** b. Teplitz, 1860; pupil of Door, Bruckner,and Liszt; pianist and composer.

**Stran'sky Josef,** b. Bohemia, 1873, of German parents; studied medicine at first; and then music while at the Universities of Vienna, Leipzig and Prague; début as cond. at Prague Opera, succeeding Muck, later succeeded Mahler at Hamburg; cond. Blüthner orch., Berlin; 1911, succeeded Mahler as cond. N. Y. Phil.

**Straus** (shtrows), **Oskar,** b. Vienna, April 6, 1870; pupil of Grädener and

Max Bruch; cond. theatres in various cities; c. overture "*Der Traum ein Leben*," chamber music and many operas, some of them extremely successful, especially "*Ein Walzertraum*" (Vienna, 1906; London and America as "*The Waltz Dream*"); "*Der tapfere Soldat*" (Vienna, 1908), "*Little May*" (Paris, 1909), etc.

**Strauss, Richard,** Add that a Strauss Festival was given in London, 1903, with S. conducting the Amsterdam Orch.; 1904 he was made general musical director of the Berlin Royal Opera; c. 2 symphonies, F moll. op. 12 and *Sinfonia Domestica* (1904); operas "*Salomé*" (1 act after Oscar Wilde, Dresden, 1905, and throughout Europe; prod. at Met. Op., N. Y.; it was withdrawn by the subscribers' request after one performance); "*Elektra*" (Dresden, 1909, and in many other capitals); "*Der Rosenkavalier*" (Dresden, June 26, 1911, and throughout Europe); "*Circe*," "*Ariadne auf Naxos.*" (Stuttgart, Oct. 25, 1912).

**Strube, Gustave,** add that the Boston Symph. Orch. of which he is still a member, has played compositions of his as follows; symphony in C minor (1896), in B minor (1909 and 1912); overtures "*The Maid of Orleans*" (1895); "*Fantastic*" (1904); "*Puck*" (1910); symph. poems "*Longing*" (1905 and 1908); "*Fantastic Dance*" (1908); concertos, violin (1897, 1905, 1906); 'cello (1909), etc.; 1909 he became a cond. of the Worcester Festivals.

**Strungk, Delphin,** 1611 — Brunswick, 1694; organist and composer; father of **Nikolaus S.** (q. v.).

**St(s)cherbatschev** ( sht - chĕr' - bǎt-shĕf), (1) **Nikolai Vladimirovich,** b. Aug. 24, 1853; Russian composer of songs & piano pieces; c. also Serenade op. 33 and 2 Idylls for orch., (2) **Andrew. V.,** b. Pultava, Jan. 29, 1869; pupil St. Petersburg Cons.; c. orch. march, piano sonata, songs, etc.

**Such, Henry,** b. London, March 31, 1872; violinist in public at eight: pupil of the Hochschule, Berlin, 1885–92; then toured, studied further with Wilhelmj; 1898 prof. at Guildhall School.

**Suter** ( zoo' - tĕr ), **Hermann,** b. Kaiserstuhl, Switzerland, April 28, 1870; pupil of his father, an organist, and of the Stuttgart and Leipzig Cons.; from 1892, organist and cond. in Zürich, from 1902 in Basel as cond.; c. quartets and choruses.

**Sutor** ( zoo' - tôr ), **Wilhelm,** Edelstetten, 1774 — Linden, Sept. 7, 1828; court cond. at Hanover; c. operas, etc.

**Swoboda** (svō'-bō-dä), (1) **August,** Bohemia, 1787 — Prague, May 17, 1856; teacher of theory, at Vienna. His son (2) **Adalbert Viktor,** Prague, Jan. 26, 1828 — Munich, May 19, 1902; historian and editor.

**Szamotulski,** vide WENZEL.

### T

**Tanejew** (or **Taneiev**), (1) **Sergei Ivanovich,** add that he composed a cantata "*John of Damascus*," 1884; four symphonies, No. 1 pub. 1902, a Russian overture, seven string quartets. His uncle (2) **Alexander Sergeivich,** b. St. Petersburg, Jan. 5 1850; statesman and high chancellor; was a pupil of Reichel and later of Rimsky-Korsakov and Petrov; c. two symphs.; symph. poem "*Alecha Popovich*"; 1-act opera, etc.

**Taubmann** ( towp' - män ), **Otto,** b. Hamburg, March 8, 1859; mus director; pupil Dresden Cons.; 1886–c dir. Wiesbaden Cons. 1891 theatre cond. in St. Petersburg; from 1895 in Berlin as critic; c. mass with orch (1898), choral drama "*Sängerweihe*" (Elberfeld, 1904), "Psalm 13" with orch., etc.

**Taund** (shĕl-townt), **Eugen von Schyll,** b. Pressburg, July 17, 1856 opera composer; c. operettas prod at Vienna.

**Tchaikovsky,** The correct birth

date is May 7 (new style), April 25 (old style), 1840.

**Tebaldini** (tā-bäl-dē'-nē), **Giovanni**, b. Brescia, Sept. 1864; historian; pupil Milan Cons., and in musical history of Amelli, Haberl and Haller; 1889 cond. at St. Mark's, Venice; 1894 at San Antonio, Padua; from 1897, dir. Parma Cons., wrote historical works, and c. Arabian fantasie for orch., also church music.

**Teichmüller** (tīkh'-mĭl-lĕr), **Robert**, b. Braunschweig, May 4, 1863; piano teacher; pupil of his father and of Leipzig Cons.; later teacher there; 1908 Royal Prof.

**Tempia** (tĕm'-pē-ä), **Stefano**, Racconizi, Dec. 5, 1832 — Turin, Nov. 25, 1878; violin teacher at Turin Cons. and composer of masses, etc.

**Terrabugio** (tĕr-rä-boo'-jō), **Giuseppe**, b. Primiera, May 13, 1842; writer; pupil of Rheinberger, etc.; from 1883 editor of "*Musica Sacra*" at Milan, and active in the reform of church music; author of organ methods; c. overtures, 12 masses, and much church music.

**Ter'ry, Richard Runciman**, b. Ellington 1865; organist; 1890 — 2 at Elston School, then in Antigua, West Indies, at St. John's Cathedral; 1896–1901 Downside Abbey; from 1901 at Westminster Cathedral; active in reviving early English Catholic music.

**Tetrazzini** (tĕt-rä-tsē'-ne), **Luisa**, b. Florence; pupil of Ceccherini, and her sister Eva, wife of Cleofonte Campanini; début 1895 as *Inez* in "*L'Africaine*," Teatro Pagliano, Florence; later at Rome and elsewhere, touring widely in Russia and South America; a favourite in San Francisco, her fame had not reached eastward till after a season of great success at Covent Garden, she made a sensation at the Manhattan Opera, N. Y. She has since held a foremost position among the world's sopranos in opera and concert. Her

voice is one of extraordinary grace and flexibility in coloratura rôles.

**Theindl** (tīnt'-'l), **J. N.**, d. Pest, Dec. 30, 1902; pianist.

**Thiard=Laforest** (tē-ăr-lă-fôr-ā), **Josef**, Püspöki, March 16, 1841 — Pressburg, March 2, 1897; from 1881 cond. at Pressburg Cathedral.

**Thibaud** (tē-bō), **Jacques**, b. Bordeaux, Sept. 27, 1880; violinist; pupil of Marsick at Paris Cons., winning first prize at 16; played at the Café Rouge and was engaged for Colonne's orch., became soloist 1898; has toured widely in Europe and America.

**Thiébaut** (t'yā'-bō), **Henri**, b. Schaerbeck, near Brussels, Feb. 4, 1865; teacher and critic in Brussels; founded, 1896, a music-school developed 1907 into the "Institut des hautes études musicales et dramatiques"; c. orch. works, songs, etc.

**Thiele**, (1) **K. L.**, should be **Johann Fr. Ludwig**. His son (2) **Eugen Felix Richard**, Berlin, Oct. 29, 1847 — April 25, 1903; organist at English church; composed pantomimes, etc. (3) **Edvard**, d. Dessau, Jan. 10, 1895.

**Thirion** (tē-rĭ-ôn), **Louis**, b. Baccarat, 1879; piano teacher at Nancy Cons.; c. symph.; played by Colonne's orch., under Pierné, 1911, with success.

**Thomelin** (tŭm-lăn), **Jacques**, famous organist in Paris; ca. 1667 chapel organist to Louis XIV; c. organ works, etc.

**Thompson, Lady**, vide LODER.

**Thoost** (tost), **Willem Frans**, Amsterdam, July 10, 1829 — Rotterdam, Aug. 27, 1900; pupil of Dupont, Hauptmann and Richter; founded the German opera at Rotterdam, 1860; c. choral prize symphony, "*Karl V*" (1861); 3 other symphs., an opera, etc.

**Thor'ley Handel**, d. Manchester, Jan. 20, 1910, age 87; bass singer, chorister; double bass in Halle orch. over 40 years.

**Thorne John of York**, d. York,

Dec. 7, 1573; important English musician; c. motet, etc.

**Thouret** (too-rā), **Georg**, b. Berlin, Aug. 25, 1855; historian, especially of German military music.

**Thrane** (trä-ně), **Waldemar**, Christiania, 1790–1828; violinist; c. overtures, etc.

**Tierie** (tē'-rē), **Anton H.**, b. Wageningen, April 4, 1870; organist. teacher in Amsterdam Cons.; cond. oratorio society.

**Till'metz, Rudolf**, b. Munich, April 1, 1847; flutist; pupil of Bohm; 1864 soloist in court orch.; 1883 teacher in Royal Musichsch., and cond. to Prince Ludwig Fd.; c. flute works.

**Tim'mermans, Armand**, b. Antwerp, 1860; pupil of the Cons., and teacher in Antwerp; c. prize winning choral works.

**Tischer** (tǐsh'-ěr), **Johann Nikolaus**, 1731–66 organist at Schmalkalden; pupil of **J. S. Bach**; c. clavier-pieces, orch. works, etc. (2) **Gerhard**, b. Lübnitz, Nov. 10, 1877; historian, Ph.D., Berlin, 1903; from 1904 teacher of musical history in Cologne.

**Titelouze** (tēt-looz), **Jean**, St. Omer, 1563 — Rouen, Oct. 25, 1633; organist; called the "founder of French organ music"; 1585 org. at St. Jean Rouen, from 1588 at the cathedral there; c. mass, and organ works.

**Titov** or **Titoff** (tē'-tôf), (1) **Vassili**, 17th century church composer. (2) **Alexei Nikolaievich**; 1769 — St. Petersburg, Nov. 20, 1827; Russian cavalry general; c. 13 operas. His brother (3) **Sergei N.**, b. 1770; c. operas and ballets. (4) **Nikolai Alexeivich**, St. Petersburg, May 10, 1800 — Dec. 22, 1875; son of (2) called the "grandfather of Russian song"; a lieutenant-general, whose songs were the first to obtain foreign vogue; c. also popular dances and marches.

**Tiv'endell, Frederick**, b. Eng-

land, 1825; organist at Liverpool; 1843 pupil of Spohr and Leipzig Cons.; popular as accompanist to Spohr, Jenny Lind, etc.

**Tod** (tōt), **Eduard Adolf**, Neuhausen, 1839 — Stuttgart, 1872; organist and composer.

**Todt** (tōt), **Joh. Aug. Wilhelm**, b. Düsterort, July 29, 1833 — Stettin, Oct. 26, 1900; organist, cantor and composer.

**Tofano** (tō-fä'-nō), **Gustavo**, Naples, Dec. 22, 1844 — June 30, 1899; pupil at the Bologna Cons. and prof. there; pianist and composer.

**Tofft, Alfred**, b. Copenhagen, Jan. 2, 1865; pupil of Nebelong and Bohlmann; c. opera "*Vifandaka*" (Copenhagen, 1898), songs, etc.

**Tofte** (tŏf'-tě), **Lars Waldemar**, Copenhagen, Oct. 21, 1832 — June, 1907; court violinist and teacher at the Cons.

**Tol'lius, Jan.** b. Amersfort, 1550 — Copenhagen, 1603 (?); church-cond. in Italian cities; 1601 court-cond. at Copenhagen; c. motets, madrigals, etc.

**Tolstoi** (tŏl'-stō-ē), **Count Theophil Matveievich**, 1809 — St. Petersburg, March 4, 1881; critic under pen-name "Rostislav" and composer studied singing with Rubini, comp with Fuchs, Miller, Raimondi and Hebel; 1832 prod. opera "*Birichine di Parigi*," Naples; 1835 at St Petersburg, its failure led Nichola I to forbid the Italian singers to appear in Russian works. He c. also songs.

**Tolstov** (tŏl'-stôf), **Victor Paulo vich**, b. St. Petersburg, Dec. 5, 1843 pianist; pupil of Leschetizky; fror 1878 teacher at St. Petersburg Cons. 1889 prof. there.

**Tonassi** (to-näs'-sē), **Pietro**, Venice Sept. 1801 — Nov. 4, 1877; compose of church music, etc.

**Tonel'li, Antonio**, Carpi, Italy Aug. 19, 1686 — Dec. 25, 176; important early 'cellist; pupil of h mother and of Pace; after a wande

ing life including (perhaps) three years in Denmark, he was made cond. at the Cathedral in Carpi; c. opera "*Lucio Vero*" (Alassio, 1740). After some years the Wanderlust carried him off to and from Carpi, where he died; c. oratorio, cantatas, etc.

**Töpler** (tĕp'-lĕr), **Michael,** Ullersdorf, Jan. 15, 1804 — Brühl, Nov. 12, 1874; teacher and composer of church music.

**Torrance, Canon Geo. Wm.,** add that he returned to Ireland, 1897, and 1900 became canon at Kilkenny, where he died Aug. 20, 1907. His madrigal "*Dry be that tear,*" won Molyneux prize and London Madrigal Society medal, 1903.

**Toscanini** (tôs-kä-nē'-nē), **Arturo,** b. Italy; pupil Milan Cons.; won eminence as conductor at La Scala, and since 1908 has cond. with greatest success at the Met. Op. House, N. Y., not only Italian operas, but Wagnerian and French.

**Töschi** (tĕsh'-ē), **Carlo Giuseppe,** Romagna, 1724 — Munich, April 12, 1788; court dir. and composer. His son and successor (2) **Johann Baptist,** Mannheim, ca. 1745 — Munich May 1, 1800; c. 18 symphs., etc.

**Tournemire** (toorn-mēr), **Charles Arnould,** b. Bordeaux, Jan. 22, 1870; organist and successor of César Franck at Ste. Clothilde; pupil of the Paris Cons. (winning first organ prize 1891); then of d'Indy. The City of Paris prize was awarded to his "*Le Sang de la Sirène,*" for voices and orch. 1904, and it has been given in various cities; c. symph., lyric tragedy "*Nittetis,*" chamber music, etc.

**'o'vey, Donald Francis,** b. Eton, July 17, 1875; pianist; pupil of Sophie Weisse (piano), Parratt, Higgs and Parry (comp.); graduated at Oxford, 1898; began to compose at 8; at 19 gave a concert at Windsor with Joachim; from 1900 played in London and on the continent; 1903 and 1906 performed his own piano con-

certo under Wood and Richter; c. military band music, chamber music, sonata for clarinet and piano, etc.

**Trautner** (trowt'-nĕr), **Fr. Wm. Lorenz,** b. Buch-am-Forst, May 19, 1855; cantor and organist at Nördlingen; c. Reformation cantata, "*Martin Luther,*" "*Sängers Gebet*" for voices and orch., etc.

**Traver'sa, Gioachimo,** prominent 18th century violinist to Prince Carignan; pupil of Pugnani.

**Trem'bath, Henry Gough,** d. Herne Bay, July 31 1908, age 65; pupil R. A. M., organist and composer.

**Tricklir** (trēk-lēr), **Jean Balthasar,** Dijon, 1745 — Dresden, 1813; 'cellist; from 1783 in Dresden court chapel; c. 'cello works.

**Trneček** (tŭ-rŭ-nĕ'-chĕk), **Hans,** b. Prague, May 16, 1848; harpist; pupil of the Cons.; from 1882–8 harpist at Schwerin Court Theatre, then prof. of piano and harp at Prague Cons.; virtuoso on the Jankó Keyboard; c. piano and harp music and operas "*Der Geiger von Cremona*" (Schwerin, 1896), "*Amaranth*" (Prague 1890), and "*Andrea Crini*" (Prague, 1900).

**Trunk,** (troonk) **Richard.** b. Baden-Baden, 1879; composer and conductor; studied at the gymnasium there; 1896–1901, at Royal Music Academy, Munich, under Jos. Rheinberger, winning gold medal; founded the Gemischter Volkscor Union; dir. also of the Munich Burgers Saenger-Zunft; 1912 elected director Arion Singing Society of New York.

**Tscherepnin** (chĕr-ĕp'-nēn), **Nikolai Nikolaievich,** b. 1873; composer; studied law at first, then at St. Petersburg Cons. under Rimsky-Korsakov; c. valuable male and mixed choruses, overture "*La Princesse lointaine,*" "*Sappho's Song*" for soprano and orch., lyric poem for violin and orch., choruses with orch., etc.

**Tscheschichin** ( chĕsh - ē' - chēn ), **Vsevolod Ievgrafovich,** b. Riga, Feb. 18, 1865; critic and author at Riga.

**Tura** (too'-ra), **Gennaro de,** tenor, sang at Milan and in Europe; début May, 1912, with great success at Hammerstein's London Op.

**Tur'ban, Charles Paul,** b. Strasburg, Oct. 3, 1845 — Paris, May 11, 1905; clarinet soloist at the Opéra; pupil and frequent prize winner at the Cons.; from 1900 prof. there.

**Tutkov'ski, Nikolai Apollono- vich,** b. Lipovetz, Feb. 17, 1857; pianist; pupil of Puchalski; from 1881–90 teacher of history at St. Petersburg Cons.; from 1893 dir. of Cons. in Kiev; c. symph. "*Pensée élégiaque*" and "*Bachanale bohém- ienne*" for orch., etc.

### U

**Überlée** (ü'-bĕr-lā), **Adelbert,** Berlin, June 27, 1837 — Charlottenberg, March 15, 1897; organist and royal director; c. opera, oratorio, etc.

**Udbye** (oot'-bē), **Martin Andreas,** b. Drontheim, 1820; pupil of Haupt- mann and Becker; organist at Dron- theim; c. operas, cantatas, songs, etc.

**Ujj** (oo'-yǐ), **Bela von,** b. Vienna, 1875; Hungarian composer, blind from his 7th year; c. opera "*Der Bauernfeind*" (Baden, near Vienna, 1897); operettas "*Der Herr Profes- sor*" (Vienna, 1903), "*Kaisermanö- ver*" (do., 1907), and "*Der Müller und sein Kind*" (Graz, 1907).

**Urbach** ( oor'-băkh ), **Otto,** b. Eisenach, Feb. 6, 1871; composer; pupil of Müller-Harting, Staven- hagen, Scholz, Knorr and Humper- dinck; won the Liszt stipend, 1890, and the Mozart stipend 1896, and studied with Draeseke and Klind- worth; from 1898 piano teacher at the Dresden Cons.; c. opera "*Der Müller von Sanssouci*" (Frankfort, 1896);

overture "*Bergfahrt,*" string quarte "*Haliba,*" etc.

**Urbanek** ( oor' - bä' - nĕk ), **Jan,** Slanin, Bohemia, Jan. 31, 1809; vic linist; pupil Prague cons.; concert master in Berlin.

**Urlus** (oor'-loos), **Jacques,** teno sang many years at Leipzig Stadt theater; 1912 Boston Op.; engaged t sing at Met. Op., 1912–13.

**Usiglio** (oo-sēl'-yō), **Emilio,** Parma Jan. 8, 1841 — Milan, 1910; operati composer.

### V

Note: For names not found under V consult W.

**Vaccari** ( väk - kä' - rē ), **François** Modena, 1775— Portugal, after 182 violin-virtuoso of astonishing power pupil of Nardini; toured Europe wit great success; acted as court musicia in Spain; c. medleys, etc.

**Vacher** (or **Levacher**) (lŭ-vă-shā **Pierre Jean,** Paris, 1772–181 violinist at Paris Opera; c. trios, et

**Vachon** (vă-shôṅ), **Pierre,** Arle 1731 — Berlin, 1802; violinist an composer of sonatas, chamber musi etc.; toured widely; 1784–98 cou cond. to the Emperor in Germany.

**Vacqueras** (vă-kä'-răs), **Beltram** 1481 singer at St. Peter's, Rom 1483–7 papal chapel singer; c. motet etc.

**Val** or **Duval** (dü-văl), **Françoi Du,** d. Paris, 1738; violinist to Lou XIV; the first Frenchman to wri violin sonatas in the Italian styl with *basso continuo.*

**Valente** (vä-lĕn'-tĕ), **Antoni** *il cieco*), blind organist and compos at Naples, 1580. (2) **Vincenzo,** Corigliano, near Cosenza, 1855; operas and songs.

**Van Den Eeden** (văn den ā'-dĕ **Jean Baptiste,** b. Ghent, De 26, 1842; pupil of the Cons., an of Brussels Cons., where he won prize with a cantata, "*Fausts laas Nacht*"; from 1878 dir. music scho at Mons.; c. symph. poem *"La lutte au XVI siècle"* cantatas, a 3-part work *"Judith"* or *"Le siège de Béthulie,"* etc.

**Van der Stucken, Frank,** add that he was dean of the Cincinnati College of Music 1897–1901; cond. Cincinnati Symph. 1895–1907, when he returned to Germany, retaining the conductorship of the Cincinnati May Festivals.

**Van'nius,** vide WANNENMACHER.

**Var'lamov (or Warlamoff), Alex= ander Igorovich,** Moscow, Nov. 15 (27), 1801 — St. Petersburg, Oct. 1848; singer in the court chapel as youth, later director of it; then teacher in Moscow; c. the famous melody *"The Red Sarafan,"* and many other songs.

**Vasquez y Gomez** (văs'-kĕth ē gō'-mĕth), **Marino,** Granada, Feb. 3, 1831 — Madrid, June 1894; concertmaster at Madrid Royal Theatre; c. zarzuelas, etc.

**Vassilen'ko, Sergei Nikiforovich,** b. Moscow, 1872; writer; pupil of the Cons., winning gold medal, 1901; c. cantata *"The Legend of the Sunken City of Kitesch"* (given as an opera, Moscow, 1903); *"Epic Poem"* for orch., choral works *"Nebuchadnezzar,"* and *"Daphnis,"* etc.

**Vatielli** (vä-tĭ-ĕl'-lē), **Francesco,** b. Pesaro, Jan. 1, 1877; pupil of Liceo Rossini; 1905 librarian at Bologna, teacher and writer on history; c. intermezzi, etc.

**Vau'tor, Thomas,** English song composer of early 17th century; probably a musician to Sir George Villiers; 1616 Mus. Bac. Oxford; published songs in 1619.

**Vecsey** (vĕt'-chĕ-ē), **Franz von,** b. Budapest, March 23, 1893; violinist; at 8, pupil of Hubay; at 10 accepted by Joachim as a great musician, and toured Germany, England and America with immense success; toured South America, 1911; reappeared in London, 1912.

**Venth** (vĕnt), **Karl,** b. Cologne, Feb. 10, 1860; pupil of the Cons. and of Wieniawski; from 1880 in New York as concertmaster at Met. Op. House; founded 1888 a cons. in Brooklyn; c. Schiller's *"Bells"* for chorus and orch., etc.

**Venturini** (vĕn-too-rē'-ne), **Fran= cesco,** d. Dresden (?) April 18, 1745; from 1698 in the Hanoverian court chapel as cond.; c. concertos, etc.

**Venzl** (fĕnts'-'l), **Josef,** b. Munich, March 26, 1842; pupil of the Royal Music Sch.; c. violin pieces and method.

**Ver'rinder, C. G.,** d. Ealing, June 27, 1904; organist; Bachelor of Music Oxford; 1873 Doctor of Music by Archbishop of Canterbury; c. cantata *"Israel,"* Hebrew services and Psalter; Anglican church music, etc.

**Verstovsky (or Werstowski), Ale= xei Nikolaievich,** Tambov, Feb. 18 (March 1), 1799 — Moscow, Nov. 5 (17), 1862; composer; while studying civil engineering at the Institute in St. Petersburg, he was also a pupil of John Field and Steibelt (piano), Böhm (violin), Tarquini (voice), Brandt and Tseiner (theory); c. a vaudeville at 19, and soon acquired a vogue; at 25 was inspector of the Imp. Opera, Moscow; at 29, c. a succ. opera, *"Pan Tvardovski,"* followed by five others, including *"Askold's Tomb"* (1835), which had enormous success and was revived in 1897; was accepted as a beginning of national opera and had undoubted influence on its development. He c. also cantatas and 29 popular songs.

**Vetter** (fĕt-tĕr), (1) **Nikolaus,** Königsee, 1666 — Rudolfstadt, 1710; court organist and important choral composer; (2) **Hermann** b. Grossdrebnitz, Saxony, July 9, 1859; pupil Dresden Cons.; from 1883 teacher there; 1907 Royal Prof.; c. technical studies, etc.

**Verhey** (vĕr'-hī), **F. H. H.,** b.

Rotterdam, 1848; pupil of the Royal Music Sch., at The Hague and of Bargiel; teacher at Rotterdam; c. operas, a mass, chamber music, etc.

**Vieuxtemps, Jean Joseph Lucien,** Verviers, July 5, 1828 — Brussels, Jan. 1901; pianist and composer; pianist, teacher, and c. of piano pieces, brother of **Henri** and **Jules V.** (q. v.).

**Vigna** (vēn'-yä), **Arturo** cond. Met. Op. House, N. Y., 1903–7; pupil Milan Cons.

**Vilain** (vē-lăṅ), **Léandre,** b. Trazegnies, Belgium, 1866; pupil of Lemmens, and von Mailly; from 1890 organist at Ostend; from 1902 teacher at the Ghent Cons.

**Vilano'va, Ramon,** Barcelona, Jan. 21, 1801 — May, 1870; cathedral cond.; c. church music.

**Vilar** (vē'-lär), **Joseph Teodor,** Barcelona, Aug. 10, 1836 — Oct. 21, 1905; pupil of Vilanova and in Paris of Herz, Bazin and Halévy; later cond. at Teatro Principal; c. zarzuelas, etc.

**Vilda,** vide WILT.

**Villafiorita** (vĭl-lä-fē-ō-re'-tä), **Giuseppe Burgio di,** Palermo, March 22, 1845 — Milan, Nov. 1902; composer of operas.

**Vi'ner, William Letton** (or **Litton**), Bath, 1790 — Westfield, Mass., 1867; organist; from 1859 in America; c. popular hymn tunes.

**Vizentini** (vē-zĕn-te'-nē), **Louis Albert,** Paris, |Nov. 9, 1841 — Oct. 1906; violinist; pupil of the Paris and Brussels Cons.; critic on the *Figaro;* cond. in theatres in various cities; c. operettas, ballets, etc.

**Vock'ner, Josef,** Ebensee, March 18, 1842 — Vienna, Sept. 11, 1906; organ teacher at the Cons.; c. oratorio, organ fugues, etc.

**Volbach** (fôl'-bäkh), **Fritz,** b. Wipperfürth, Dec. 17, 1861; organ-virtuoso; pupil of Cologne Cons. for a year; studied philosophy, then took up music again at the Royal Inst. for church mus., Berlin; from 1887 teacher there; 1892 cond. at Mainz; 19 at Tübingen; has written biogs. a. edited musical texts; c. symph. symph. poems, *"Ostern"* (Easte for organ and orch. (Sheffield Fes 1902); *"Es waren zwei Königskinder "Alt Heidelberg, du Feine,"* a series vocal works with orch. which cond. in London, 1904, etc.

**Volkov,** vide WOLKOW.

**Vos** (väs), (1) **Eduard de,** b. Ghen Jan. 19, 1833; director and teach at the Cons.; c. songs. (2) **Isidor** Ghent, 1851—March 31, 1876; dyi just after he won the Prix de Ron with his cantata *"De Meermin";* also piano pieces, etc. His broth (3) **Franz,** is teacher at the Cons.

**Vreuls** (vrŭls), **Victor,** b. Vervie Feb. 4, 1876; pupil Liège Co and of d'Indy, at whose Schola ca torum he became teacher of harmon 1903 won the Picard prize of t Belgian Free Academy; c. symphon poems, *"Triptyque"* for voice a orch., chamber music and songs.

## W

Note: For names not found under V consult V.

**Waack** (väk), **Karl,** b. Lübec March 6, 1861; pupil of Grand-duc School, Weimar,; cond. in Finla and at Riga; 1890 studied with I Riemann, returned to Riga as edit cond. and author.

**Wad'dington, Sidney Peine,** Lincoln, July 23, 1869; compose pupil R. C. M., London; later teach there and pianist to Covent Garde c. *"John Gilpin"* for chorus a orch. (1894); *"Ode to Music,"* d violin and 'cello sonatas, etc.

**Waefelghem,** ( vä' - fĕl - khĕm vä-fĕl-gäṅ), **Louis Van,** Bruge Jan. 13, 1840 — Paris, June 19, 19 violinist and virtuoso on the viole amour; pupil Brussels Cons.; solo at Budapest Opera; 1888 violaist 'aris Opéra, and in Lamoureux's rch.; after 1893 soloist on the viole l'amour, for which he composes.

**.genaer** (väkh'-ĕ-när), **Johann,** ⁆. Utrecht, Nov. 1, 1862; organist at he Cathedral; c. "*Fritjofs Meer-ıhrt*" and "*Saul and David*" for ʼrch., overture "*Cyrano de Bergerac*," tc.

**.gner, Siegfried,** add that from 898 he was teacher in Vienna; 1901 ond. Acad. Singing Society, and Ƭonkünstler Orch.; 1912, cond. pecial concert of the London Sym-h orch. c. 8 operas "*Der Kobold*" Hamburg, 1904), "*Bruder Lustig*" do., 1905), "*Das Sternengebot*" (do., 1908), "*Banadietrich*" (Elberfeld, 910) and "*Schwarzschwanenreich*" Black-swan Country), c. also male nd female choruses, etc.

**.kefield, Augusta Mary,** b. ˌedgwick, Aug. 19, 1853; contralto; ⁆upil of Randegger, Alari and ⁆gambati; 1885 organized the so-alled Wakefield Competition Festi-ˌals, said to be "the most vital ₁ovement in the musical life of Ƈngland to-day;" from 1890 she ₑctured; c. songs, etc.

**.ldauer** (väl'-dow-ĕr), **August,** 825 — St. Louis, Dec. 26, 1900; ⁆under and dir. Beethoven Cons.

**.ldmann** (vält'-män), **Madame,** ⁆. Vienna; contralto; made sensation ₁ London, 1875.

**.ldteufel** (vält'-toi-fĕl), **Emil,** b. ˌtrasburg, Dec. 9, 1837; pupil Paris Ƈons.; pianist to Empress Eugènie; . immensely succ. waltzes.

**.lk'er, Ernest,** b. Bombay, July 15, ₁870; composer; Mus. Bac. Ox-ord, 1893; Mus. Doc. 1898; from 900, dir. at Balliol College; mainly ₑlf-taught as composer of "*Stabat Ɱater*," "*Hymn to Dionysus*," and "*Ode to Nightingale*" for voices and ₁rch.; overture, chamber music, songs ₑtc.

**.ll'ace, William,** b. Greenock, July ₅, 1860; at first a surgeon; in 1889

took up music and studied at the R. A. M., London, till 1890; c. symph. "*The Creation*" (New Brighton, 1892); choral symph. "*Koheleth*"; 6 symph. poems, "*The Passing of Beatrice*" (Crystal Palace, 1892), "*Amboss oder Hammer*" (do., 1896), "*Sister Helen*" (do. 1899), "*Greeting to the New Century*" (London Phil., 1891), "*Sir ⫽William Wallace*" (Queen's Hall, 1905), "*François Villon*" (New Symph., 1909; also by New York Phil., 1910, 1912), overtures, suites, song cycles, 1-act lyric tragedy "*Brassolis*," etc. He is author of poetry and a critical work, "*The Threshold of Music.*"

**Wall'worth, Thos. Adlington,** 1834 — Brixton, Jan. 7, 1904, age 70; pupil, later singing prof. R. A. M., London; pupil of Crevelli; sang with Pyne & Harrison Opera Co.

**Walpurgis** (väl-poor'-gēs), **Antonia,** 1724–1780; Saxon Crown Princess; c. an overture "*Talestria Regina dell' Amazone*," revived at a concert of women's compositions by the German Lyceum Club, Berlin, 1912, cond. by Elizabeth Knyper.

**Wal'thew, Richard H.,** b. London, Nov. 4, 1872; pupil of the Guildhall and with scholarship at R. C. M. under Parry; 1907 prof. at Queen's College, and cond. opera class at the Guildhall; 1909 cond. at Finsbury. c. "*Pied Piper*" for chorus and orch; (1893); piano concerto (1894), two operettas, etc.

**Wannenmacher** (vän'-nĕn-mäkh-ĕr) (or **Vannius**), **Johannes,** d. Interlaken, ca. 1551; important Swiss church composer; and canon, renounced Catholicism, was tortured, and banished.

**Ware, Harriet.** b. Waupun, Wis.; graduated at Pillsbury Cons. Owatonna, Minn., 1895; pupil of Wm. Mason, N. Y. for 2 years, then of Stojowski (piano and comp.) and Juliana, Paris, later of Hugo Kaun, Berlin; c. "*The Fay Song*," 1905;

cantata *"Sir Olaf"* (New York Symph. 1910), piano pieces and many successful songs.

**Warnke** (värn'-kĕ), **Heinrich,** b. Wesselbüren, Aug. 30, 1871; 'cellist; son and pupil of his father, a violinist; later at Hamburg Cons.; début there, then studied with Klengel at Leipzig; member of various orchs., finally with the Kaim orch., Munich, for 10 years; from 1905 with Boston Symph. Orch.

**Warot** (vă-rō), (1) **Charles,** Dunkirk, Nov. 14, 1804 — Brussels, July 29, 1836; violinist and theatre-cond.; pupil of Fridzeri; c. operas, 3 grand masses, etc. His brother (2) **Victor,** Ghent, 1808 — Bois Colombes, 1877; cond. and teacher; c. operettas, a mass, etc. (3) **Constant Noël Adolphe,** Antwerp, 1812—Brussels, 1875; 'cello-teacher, Brussels Cons.; c. 'cello-pieces, etc. (4) **Victor Alex. Jos.,** Verviers, 1834 — Paris, 1906; son of **Victor** (2); opera tenor, later teacher at Paris Cons.

**War'rum Helen,** b. Washington, D. C. (?); soprano; pupil of Oscar Saenger; engaged for Chicago Opera, 1912.

**Warwick** (wär'-ĭk), (1) (or **Warrock**), **Thomas,** organist Hereford Cathedral, 1586–9; 1625 org. at Chapel Royal; c. anthems, etc. (2) **Giula,** d. June 13, 1904; pianist and opera singer, then prof. of singing Guildhall School of Music, later founded vocal academy.

**Web'ber, Amherst,** b. Cannes, Oct. 25, 1867; studied music at Oxford, then at Dresden with Nicodé and at Paris Cons.; pianist to Covent Garden and Met. Op., N. Y.; c. symph. (Warsaw Phil., 1904, Boston Symph., 1905); 1-act opera *"Fiorella"* (London, 1905), songs, etc.

**Web'er, Frederick,** Würtemberg, Nov. 5, 1819 — London, Feb. 16, 1909; organist and author of works on the pianoforte.

**Wecker** (vĕk'-ĕr), **Georg Kaspar,** Nuremberg, 1632–1695; organ teacher and composer.

**Weckmann** (vĕk'-män), **Matthi** Oppershausen, 1621—Hamburg, 16 organ-virtuoso and comp.

**Wedekind** (vā'-dĕ-kĭnt), **Erika,** Hanover, Nov. 13, 1869; colo tura soprano; pupil of Orgeni Dresden Cons.; 1894–1909 at co opera Dresden, then at Berlin Co Opera.

**Weeber** (vā'-bĕr), **Johann Ch** b. Warmbronn, 1808 — Nürting 1877; court mus. director and co poser.

**Weed, Marion,** b. Rochester, Y., soprano; 1903–4 Met. Op., N.

**Wehrle** (vär'-le), **Hugo,** b. D aueschingen, July 19, 1847; violini pupil of Leipzig Cons. and Paris Cor toured and played in Singer's Qu tet till nervous trouble lamed hand; 1898 retired to Freiburg; violin pieces.

**Weidig** (vī'-dĭkh), **Adolf,** b. Ha burg, Nov. 28,1867; pupil of the Co and winning Mozart stipend, pupi Rheinberger; from 1892, teacher Chicago and co-director of American Cons.; c. orch. and cha ber music.

**Weingartner, Felix,** add that 1⁓ he succeeded Mahler as dir. Vien Royal Opera; Jan. 4, 1911, he sign contract for 3 years with Berlin Pl Orch., resigning directorship of Ro Opera; he married Marie Juiller. in 1903 he married Baroness Feode von Dreifus; author of *"Über Dirigieren* (1895, 3rd edition 190 *"Die Symphonie nach Beethove* (1897, also in English), a dram *"Golgotha"* (1908), etc.; c. 3 symp *"Frühlingsmärchenspiel"* (Weim 1908), music to *"Faust"* (do., 1908 his 3rd symph. was played by N York Phil., Dec. 28, 1911.

**Weismann** (vīs'-män), **Julius,** Freiburg, Dec. 26, 1879; pupil Royal Musicschool, Munich, th with Herzogenberg and Thuille; fre o5 in Freiburg as composer of oral works, a symph., etc.

**ssheimer** (vīs'-hī-měr), **Wenelin**, b. Osthofen, Feb. 26, 1838; us. director and composer; pupil eipzig Cons., teacher and theatrend. in various cities; c. 2 operas, *Theodor Körner*" (Munich, 1872), ıd "*Meister Martin und seine esellen*" (Carlsruhe, 1897), bass lo with orch., "*Das Grab in usento*," etc.

**l'ings, (Joseph) Milton,** b. andsworth, n. Birmingham, Eng., ec. 4, 1850; c. popular songs and *The Dancing Master*" (London, 94).

**ndel** (věn'-děl), **Ernst,** b. Bresu, 1876; violinist and director; pil of Wirth, Joachim, Lucco and argiel; 1896 joined Thomas Orch., hicago; 1898 cond. Königsberg usikverein; 1909 cond. Bremen hil.; c. choruses with orch., etc.

**nzel von Gamter (or Szamoulski)** (shä-mō-tool'-skř), Gamter, 525 — Cracow, 1572; Polish comoser of church music,

**rschbilovich** (věrsh-bē'-lō-vřch), **lex. Valerianovich,** b. Jan. 8, 350; 'cellist; pupil of Davidov and is successor at the Italian Opera in t. Petersburg; from 1885 prof. at the ons.

**ssely** (věs'-sě-le), **Hans,** b. Vienna, ec. 23, 1862; violinist; pupil of the ons.; toured with success; from 1889 rof. R. A. M., London, leader of ıe W. Quartet.

**tzel** (vět'-tsěl), **Hermann,** b. yritz, Pomerania, March 11, 1879; acher at Riemann Cons. 1905-7; ıen in Potsdam as teacher and a ıthor; c. songs, etc.

**weler** (vā'-vě-lěr), **August,** b. Recke, Westphalia, Oct. 20, 1868; omposer; pupil Leipzig Cons.; c. fairy operas "*Dornröschen*" (Kassel, 1903), omic opera "*Der grobe Märker*" Detmold, 1908), etc.

**eymarn** (vī'-märn,) **Paul Pla-**

**tonovich,** b. St. Petersburg, 1857; son of a lieut.-general and himself an officer; gave up the army for music; writes biographies, criticisms, 'cellopieces, etc.

**White, (1) John,** York, 1779 — Leeds, 1831; organist and assist.-cond. of Leeds Festivals. (2). **Carolina,** b. Dorchester, Mass., Dec. 23, 1883; pupil of Weldon Hunt; concert début, 1905; 1907 studied with Sebastian at Naples; début at San Carlo Theatre, 1908; sang in Italy, and from 1910 with Chicago Op. Co.; 1911 with Boston Op.; married, 1910, Paul Longone, dir. San Carlo Theatre.

**Whitehouse, William Edward,** b. London, May 20, 1859; 'cellist; pupil of Pettit and R. A. M., winning prize, 1878; and from 1882 teacher there; later prof., member of Ludwig Quartet and London Trio.

**Whit'ney, (1) Myron William,** Ashby, Mass., Sept. 5, 1835 — 1910; bass; pupil of Frost, Randegger, and Vannucini; début Boston, 1858; sang with greatest success in concert and oratorio and for a time in opera with the Boston Ideals, and the American Opera Co.; retired 1900; his son (2) **Myron, Jr.,** is a popular bass.

**Wichern** (věkh'-ěrn), **Karoline,** Horn, near Hamburg, Sept. 13, 1836 — March 19, 1906; soprano; led choruses at the houses of correction for 20 years, then for 15 years taught in Manchester, returning 1896 to her previous task; 1900 cond. at Hamburg a concert of her own orchestral works; c. vocal works of many sorts, etc.

**Wickenhausser** (vřk'-ěn-hows'-sěr), **Richard,** b. Brünn, Feb. 7, 1867; pupil of Leipzig Cons.; 1894 was given a stipend on the advice of Brahms and Hanslicj; 1895 leader of a singing society in Brünn; 1902 in Graz; 1907 dir. Vienna Singakademie, c. choral works in great numbers, also 2 piano sonatas, a violin sonata, etc.

**Wiedermann** (vē'-dĕr-män), **K. Fr.,** b. Görisseiffen, Dec. 25, 1856; organist and Royal Dir., in Berlin; c. overture, songs, etc.

**Wiehmayer** (vē'-mī-ĕr), **Theodor,** b. Marienfeld, Westphalia, Jan. 7, 1870; pianist; pupil Leipzig Cons. and of Krause; début Leipzig, 1890; teacher there; 1902–6 at the Cons.; from 1908 at Stuttgart Cons., 1909 prof.; c. piano pieces and songs.

**Wiemann** (vē'-män), **Robert,** b. Frankenhausen, Nov. 4, 1870; pupil Leipzig Cons.; cond. various theatre orchs. and singing societies; from 1899 in Osnabrück; c. orch. works, "*Erden wallen,*" "*Kassandra,*" etc.; choral works with orch., etc.

**Wietrowetz** (vē'-trō-vĕtz), **Gabrielle,** b. Laibach, Carmola, Jan. 13, 1866; violinist; pupil of Joachim, winning Mendelssohn prize at Berlin Hochsch.; début 1885 at Münster; toured and from 1904, teacher at the Berlin Hochsch., the first woman so employed.

**Wig'gins, Thomas** ("Blind Tom"), Columbus, Ga., May 24, 1849 — Hoboken, N. J., June 13, 1908; phenomenal pianist; a negro slave imbecile in all except music; son of slaves and exploited by the former owners of his parents; played in public for forty years, with enormous financial success, and revealed extraordinary gifts for musical mimicry and repetition of pieces performed in his hearing, though of course his powers were greatly exaggerated.

**Wilhelmj, Adolf** (not **Anton**), correct birth date is March 31, 1872.

**Williams,** (1) **Charles Lee,** b. Winchester, May 1, 1853; organist; pupil of Arnold; 1882–98 org. at Gloucester Cathedral; cond. of five festivals; c. cantatas, church music, etc. (2) **Charles Francis Abdy,** b. Dawlish, July 16, 1855; took music degrees at both Cambridge and Oxford; later pupil Leipzig Cons.; organist at various posts; authority on

Greek music and Plain song: c. chu music, choruses for "*Alcestis*" "*A gone,*" and "*Agamemnon.*" (3) **Ral Vaughan,** b. Down Amprey, Oct. 1872; studied music at Cambri and the R. C. M.; later at Berlin w Max Bruch and with Ravel in Pa organist at South Lambeth, 1896 c. "*A Sea Symphony*" (Walt W man) for voices and orch.; sympho impression "*In the Fen Count* (London, 1909), three Norfolk Rh sodies (1906–7), cantata "*Wil Wood*" (Liverpool, 1909), "*Tou the Unknown Region*" (Walt Wl man), chorus and orch. (Leeds Fe 1907), etc.

**Wille** (vĭl'-lĕ), **Georg,** b. Gr Sept. 20, 1869; 'cellist; from 1 court-concertmaster at Royal Cha in Dresden and teacher in the Coi pupil of Leipzig Cons.

**Wil'son, Grenville Dean,** Plymo Conn., Jan. 26, 1833—Nyack, N. Sept. 20, 1897; teacher and s composer.

**Wilt** (vĭlt), **Marie** (née Liebe **thaler**), Vienna, Jan. 30, 188 (suicide) Sept. 24, 1891; fam operatic soprano; début 1865 Graz; sang throughout Europe, a popular in concerts. In 1866–7 sang at Covent Garden under name "**Vilda,**" again in 1874–75

**Wiltberger** (vĭlt'-bĕrkh-ĕr), **Heinrich,** b. Sobernheim, Aug. 1841; son of an organist; 1872–1 teacher in Alsace; co-founder the Cecilia society and composer church music. and favourite Alsat composer of male-choruses. brother (2) **August,** b. Sobernhe April 17, 1850; teacher in vari towns; 1884 at Brühl; author of organ method, a theory, and c. c torios "*Cecilia*" and *Bonifaciu* cantatas, etc.

**Winkelmann** (1) **Hermann,** ter correct birth date is Braunschw March 8, 1849; (2) **Hermann** Frankfort - on - Main, March

1899; organist and teacher at Raff Cons.

**Winkler** (vĭnk'-lĕr), (1) **Theodor**, d. Weimar, Dec. 21, 1905; flutist at the court chapel; c. concerto, etc. (2) **Alex. Adolfovich**, b. Charkov, March 3, 1865; pianist; studied at Charkov and at Vienna under Leschetizky and Navrátil; teacher at Charkov; from 1896 at St. Petersburg Cons.; c. prize-winning string quartet. op. 7, piano pieces, etc.

**Winneberger** (vĭn'-nĕ-bĕrkh-ĕr), **Paul**, d. Hamburg, Feb. 8, 1821; 'cellist and composer.

**Winter=Hjelm** (vĭn'-tĕr-hyĕlm), **Otto**, b. Christiania, Oct. 8, 1837; organist at Christiania; pupil Leipzig Cons. and of Kullak and Wüerst; dir. Phil. concerts; c. 2 symph., 50 Psalms, 46 Norwegian *"Fjeld melodier"* or mountain songs, etc.

**Wirtz** (vērts), **Charles Louis**, b. The Hague, Sept. 1, 1841; pupil of the Cons.; later piano teacher there;. c. church music.

**Wis'ke, Mortimer**, b. Troy, N. Y., Jan. 12, 1853; from 1872 organist and dir. Brooklyn; c. church and organ music.

**Witek** (vē'-těk), **Anton**, b. Saaz, Bohemia, 1872; violinist; pupil of Bennewitz; concertmaster of Berlin Phil.; also toured; later became concertm. Boston Symph.; married (2) **Witek, Vita** (née **Gerhardt**), b. Copenhagen; at first a violinist; pupil of Gade and Joachim; decided to be a pianist, studied with Leschetizky and Carreño.

**Witherspoon, Herbert**, add that his correct birthplace is Buffalo, N. Y., July 21, 1873; in 1908 he coached with Lamperti in Berlin; in 1908 he joined the Met. Op., N. Y., and has sung there with increasing success, making especially deep impression in the rôles of *Gurnemanz*, *King Mark*, etc. Gave recitals in London with great success,

1910, and has continued his concert and oratorio appearances.

**Witkowsky** (vĭt-kôf'-skĭ), **G. M.**, lieutenant in French Army; pupil of d'Indy; c. symph., (Paris 1901) quintet, etc.

**Wittkowska** (vĭt-kôf'-skä), **Marta**, b. Poland; contralto; brought to America as a child; studied at Syracuse, N.Y., University with a scholarship; pupil of Emma Thursby, then of Colonogi; début at Perugia; sang in various Italian cities, then at Covent Garden; 1911 Chicago Opera Co.

**Witting** (vĭt'-tĭnk), **Karl**, Jülich, Sept. 8, 1823 — Dresden, June 28, 1907; tenor singer; pupil of Reichel in Paris; teacher in various cities; c. 'cello sonata, etc.

**Woikowski=Biedau** (voi-kôf'-skĭ-bē'-dow), **Victor Von**, b. Nieder-Arnsdorf, Sept. 2, 1866; pupil of B. Wolff and W. Berger; c. operas *"Helga"* (Wiesbaden, 1904), and *"Der lange Kerl"* (Berlin, 1905).

**Wolf, Hugo**, correct birthplace is Windischgräz, Styria, March 13, 1860; correct death date is Vienna, Feb. 22, 1903; add that he was expelled from the Vienna Cons. as incorrigible, and suffered constantly from poverty and hunger, giving occasional piano and violin lessons; 1886–90 he was critic to the *Salonblatt;* 1888–89 he c. 200 songs, then wrote no more for 3 years; his opera *"Der Corregidor"* though praised was never repeated; he was at work on another *"Manuel Venegas"* when his mind failed; after some months in an asylum, he was released only to be taken back as a violent maniac in 1898; paralysis followed, but he lived for five years. His songs continue to deepen their impression and he seems to be safely established among the greatest composers of lyrics.

**Wolf=Ferrari** (vôlf'-fĕr-rä'-rē), **Ermanno**, b. Venice, Jan. 12, 1876; important and versatile composer;

son of a painter; largely self-taught; later pupil of Rheinberger, Munich; 1902 dir. Liceo Benedetta Marcello, Venice; resigned 1909 and settled in Germany; c operas "*La Sulamita*" (Venice, 1889), "*Cenerentola*" (Venice, 1900 as "*Aschenbrödl*," Bremen, 1902), comic opera based on Goldoni, "*Le Donne Curiose*" given at Munich as "*Die neugierigen Frauen*," Munich, 1903, also with great success Chicago and Met. Op., N. Y., 1912 and throughout Europe; "*Die vier Grobiane*" (Munich, 1906), the very successful '*I Giojelli della Madonna*" or "*Der Schmuck der Madonna*" (Berlin Royal Op., 1911, Chicago and Met. Op., N. Y., 1912), "*The Secret of Susanne*" (do., 1912), c. also the important oratorio "*La Vita Nuova*" (text from Dante), 1903 a symphony da camera, violin sonata, piano quartet, etc.

**Wolkenstein**, (vôl'-kĕn-shtīn), **Oswald von**, Tyrol, ca. 1377 — Aug. 2, 1445; a knight, ambassador, and wanderer, "the last of the Minnesinger," c. poems and melodies.

**Wolkow** (vôl'-kôv), **Feodor Grigorievich**, Kostroma, 1729 — St. Petersburg, 1763; "founder of the Russian theatre, 1756, and the first Russian opera composer", according to Riemann; he wrote the first original Russian libretto "*The Charitable Titus*" for Araja, 1751; and c. an opera "*Tanjuscha*" (St. Petersburg, Dec. 9, 1756).

**Wolle** (vôl'-lĕ) **John Frederick**, b. Bethlehem, Pa., April 4, 1863; founder of a choir of Moravians among the Bethlehem steel-workers with which from 1900 he gave remarkable productions of the works of Bach; in 1901 at a three-day festival the Christmas oratorio, *Passion According to St. Matthew*, and Mass in C. minor were given entire; 1904, a nine-day festival of Bach's works was given; from 1905 prof. University of California and cond. symph. con-

certs at the Open Air Greek Thea at Berkeley, Cal.

**Wol'stenholme, William,** b. Bla burn, Feb. 24, 1865; organist, bl from birth; pupil of Dr. Do Mus. B. Oxford, 1887, from 1 organist in London; toured the U. 1908; c. organ music of all kin piano sonata, choral ballad, " Humphrey Gilbert," etc.

**Wood,** (1) **Charles** b. Armagh, Ju 15, 1866; pupil of T. O. Marks, a at R. C. M., London, winning Morley scholarship, later teac there, and cond. Cambridge U. Mu cal Society; Mus. Doc. Cambrid 1894; L L. D. Leeds, 1904; c. "*Ode the West Wind*," voices and orc (1890); incid. music to Greek pla "*Dirge for Two Veterans*" (Lee Fest., 1901), "*Ballad of Dundee* (do., 1904); symphonic variations "*Patrick Sarsfield*" (London, 190 songs, etc. (2) **Henry J.,** corre birth date is London, March 3, 18; he was appointed cond. of the Sh field Festivals in 1902 and of t Norwich Festivals in 1908.

**Woodward, Richard,** Dublin, 17 — Nov. 22, 1777; composer of chur music; org. at St. Patrick's Cat 1765; vicar-choral from 1772.

**Wool'ridge, H. Ellis,** b. Wincheste March 28, 1845; writer; historian; first a painter and 1895 Slade Pr of Fine Arts at Oxford; took musical history and has written e tensively on mediæval music.

**Worobkiewicz** (vôr-ôp-k'-yā'-vĭch **Isidor,** Czernowitz, 1836 — Sep 18, 1903; priest in the Greek churc and pupil on stipend at Vienna Cons later teacher of church music Czernowitz and author; c. 8 Ro manian songs, etc.

**Wot'quenne, Alfred,** b. Lobbe Hennegau, Jan. 25, 1867; pup Brussels Cons.; from 1894 librarian

**Wright** (rīt), **Thomas,** Stockton on-Tees, 1763–1829; organist, con poser and inventor.

dow (or **Wedow, Widow, Wy-
ewe**) (wĭd'-ō), **Robert,** called
Grammaticus"; Thaxted, Essex (?)
- Buckland Newton, Oct. 4, 1505;
music master to Edward IV of
England; first Mus. Bac. of Oxford;
ector and vicar.

ssotzki (vĕs-sŏt'-skĕ), **Michael
h.,** 1790 — Moscow, Dec. 28, 1837;
guitar-virtuoso, teacher and com-
oser.

### Y

w, **Ellen Beach,** b. Boston, Sept.
8, 1868, concert soprano of remark-
ble range (to c''''); has toured
Europe and America; pupil of delle
Sedie, Paris concert début St Paul,
894; operatic début Rome 1897.

### Z

bel, (tsä'-bĕl) **Albert,** Berlin, 1835
— St. Petersburg, 1910; harpist; pupil
Berlin Royal Inst. for church mus.;
soloist Berlin Opera from 1851 at
Royal Ballet orch. St. Petersburg;
from 1862 prof. at the Cons.; c. harp
concertos, etc.

ch (tsäkh), **Johann** Czelakowicz,
1699 — Irrenhause, 1773; director at
Mayence and composer of church
music.

cherevich (tsä-chĕ-rā'-vĭch),
**Michael,** b. Ostroff, Russia, Aug. 26,
1879; violinist; début Odessa at 15,
under auspices of Tchaikovski, who
secured funds for his study with
Sevčik at Prague, also with Ysaye;
has toured widely.

hn (tsän), **Johannes,** Espenbach,
Franconia, Aug. 1, 1817 — Neudet-
telsau, Feb. 17, 1895; historian of
church music, and compiler of hymn
books, etc.

ajicek (zä'-ĭ-tsĕk), **Julius,** b. Vienna, Nov. 2, 1877; composer of opera
"*Helmbrecht*" (Graz, 1906).

amara (tsä-mä'-rä), (1) **Antonio,**
Milan, June 13, 1829 — Hietzing,
near Vienna, Nov. 11, 1901; harp-

virtuoso, pupil of Sechters; teacher at
Vienna Cons.; c. for harp, flute, etc.
(2) **Alfred Maria,** b. Vienna, April
28, 1863; c. operettas.

**Zandonai** (tsän-dō-nä'-ē), **Riccardo,**
b. Sacco (Trentino) 1883; pupil of
Gianferrai at Trento; from 1899 at
Rossini Cons., Pesaro, in 1902 winning comp. prize with symph. poem
for voices and orch.; c. also "*Serenata
Mediœvale*" for cello, 2 harps, and
strings; "*Ave Maria*" for female
voices, harp, and strings; "*O Padre
Nostro*" (from Dante's Purgatorio),
for chorus, orch., and organ; operas,
"*Grillo del Focolare*" (Cricket on the
Hearth) (Turin, 1908), and with
great success elsewhere, and the
highly succ. "*Conchita*" (based on
Pierre Lovÿ's "*Femme et le Pantin*"
(Milan, 1911, Covent Garden, 1912,
etc.); "*Melœnis*" (Milan, 1912).

**Zanella** (tsä-nĕl'-lä), **Amilcare,** b.
Monticelli d'Ongina, Sept. 26, 1873;
pupil of Parma Cons. and from
1903 director, after years as operatic
cond. in South America, etc.; c. a
symph. fantasie and fugue for piano
and orch., 2 operas, etc.

**Zan'ten, Cornelie Van,** b. Dordrecht, Aug. 2, 1855; operatic soprano.
pupil of Geul, Schneider, and Fr;
Lamperti; début in Turin, sang
throughout Europe, and with the
"National Opera" in America; then
sang at Amsterdam and taught in
the Cons.; from 1903 teacher in Berlin.

**Zel'ler** (tsĕ'-lĕr), **Dr. Karl,** St. Peter-
in-der-Au, Lower Austria, July 19,
1842 — Baden, near Vienna, Aug. 17,
1898; c. operettas.

**Zenatello** (tsĕn-ä-tĕl'-lō), **Giovanni,**
b. Verona; very popular operatic
tenor, appearing first at Covent Garden 1905, and singing there annually;
from 1907 in America each year, 1909
at Manhattan Op., N. Y.

**Zepler** (tsĕp'-lĕr), **Bogumil,** b. Breslau, May 6, 1858; composer; a
physician at first then pupil of
Urban, in Berlin; c. parody on

*"Cavalleria Rusticana"* as *"Cav. Berolina"* 1891, c. various operettas and ballets.

**Ziehn,** (tsēn), **Bernhard,** Erfurt, Jan. 20, 1845 — Chicago, Sept. 8, 1912; theorist; came to Chicago 1868; teacher and organist; author of important works: *" Harmonie und Modulations lehre "* (Berlin, 1888), *" Five and Six Part Harmonies "* (Milwaukee, 1911), etc.

**Ziehrer** (tsē'-rĕr), **Carl Michael,** b. Vienna, May 2, 1843; military bandmaster; toured; c. 600 dances and an operetta *"Ein tolles Mädel"* (Nuremberg, 1908).

**Zilcher** (tsĭlkh'-ĕr), **Hermann,** b. Frankfort-on-Main, Aug. 18, 1881; pupil of the Hoch Cons.; lives in Berlin; c. concerto for 2 violins with orch., violin concerto, etc.

**Zimbalist** ( tsĭm' - bä - lĭst ), **Efrem,** b. Rostov, Russia, May 7, 1889; violinist; pupil of his father, a conductor; 1901–7 at St. Petersburg Cons. under Auer, winning gold medal and scholarship; toured Europe and 1911 America; c. 3 Slavish dances, *"Old Folks at Home,"* etc., for violin.

**Zinck** (tsĭnk), **Harnack Otto Konrad,** Husum, 1746 — Copenhagen, 1832; singer, teacher and composer.

**Zingel** (tsĭng'-ĕl), **Rudolf Ewald,** b. Liegnitz, Sept. 5, 1876; pupil Berlin Royal Hochsch.; from 1899 dir. Singakad. at Frankfort-on-Oder; from 1907 at Greifswald; c. operas *"Margot"*(Frankfort-on-Main, 1902), *"Liebeszauber"* (Stralsund, 1908), *"Persepolis"* (Rostock, 1909).

**Zoboli** (tsō-bō'-lē), **Giovanni,** b. Naples, July 22, 1821; pupil of the Cons.; teacher; c. operas and church music.

**Zocca** ( tsôk' - kä ), **Gaetano,** Ferrara, 1784 — Sept. 14, 1834; violinist and cond.

**Zois=Edelstein** (tsō'-ēs'-ä'-dĕl-shtīn) **Hans Freiherr von,** b. Graz, Nov. 14, 1861; c. popular songs and operettas.

**Zuschneid** (tsoo-shnīt'), **Karl,** b Oberglogau, Silesia, May 29, 1856 pupil Stuttgart Cons.; director o societies in various towns; from 190 dir. Mannheim Hochschule; c. mal choruses with orch., etc.

**Zwyssig** (tsvēs'-sĭkh), **P. Alberich** (rightly **Joseph**), b. Bauen, Nov. 17 1808; Cistercian abbey Mehrerau entered the Cistercian order 1826; c the famous *"Swiss Psalm"* (1841) etc.

# Necrology

(NOTE. This list contains the names of those who are included in the Biographical Dictionary and have died since the original publication.)

Allitsen, Frances, d. London, Oct. 1, 1912.
Altès, E. E., d. St. Dye, July 8, 1899.
Anderton, Thomas, d. Edgbaston, Sept. 18, 1903.
Appel, K., d. Dessau, Dec. 9, 1895.
Arditi, Luigi, d. Brighton, Eng., May 1, 1903.
Armingaud, J., d. Paris, Feb., 1900.
Artot, Desirée, d. Vienna, Apr. 3, 1907.
Attrup, Karl, d. Copenhagen, Aug. 5, 1892.

Bach, L. E., d. London, Feb. 15, 1902.
Bacon, Mrs. Elizabeth (née Poole), d. Jan. 15, 1906.
Balakirew, M. A., d. St. Petersburg, May 30, 1910. (Born Dec. 21, 1836.)
Baptie, David, d. Mar. 26, 1906.
Bargheer, Adolf, d. Basel, Mar. 10, 1901.
Bargheer, K. Louis, d. Hamburg, May 19, 1902.
Bartay, Ede, d. Pest, Aug. 31, 1901.
Bassford, W. K., d. New York, Dec. 22, 1902.
Batta, d. Versailles, Oct. 8, 1902.
Bechstein, Fr. W. K., d. Berlin, Mar. 6, 1900.
Becker, Jeanne, d. Mannheim, Apr. 6, 1893.
Beer, Max J., d. Vienna, Nov. 25, 1908.
Behr, Franz, d. Dresden, Feb. 15, 1898.
Bellermann, J. G., d. Potsdam, Apr. 10, 1903.
Berger, Wilhelm, d. Meiningen, Jan. 16, 1911.
Bergson, M., d. London, Mar. 9, 1898.
Bernard, Emile, d. Paris, Sept. 11, 1902.
Bernsdorf, E., d. Leipzig, June 27, 1901.
Bernuth, J. von, d. Hamburg, Dec. 24, 1902.

Berwin, Adolf, d. Rome, Aug. 29, 1900.
Betz, Franz, d. Berlin, Aug. 11, 1900.
Bevignani, Enrico, d. Naples, Aug. 29, 1903.
Biese, W., d. Berlin, Nov. 14, 1902.
Bibl, Rudolf, d. Vienna, Aug 2, 1902.
Bilse, B., d. Berlin, July 13, 1902.
Blanc, Adolphe, d. Paris, May, 1885.
Blockx, Jan, d. Antwerp, May 22, 1912.
Boott, Francis, d. Cambridge, Mass., Mar., 1904.
Boulanger, H. A. A. E., d. Paris, Apr. 14, 1900.
Bourgault-Ducoudray, L. A., d. Vernouillet (Seine-et-Oise), June 4, 1910.
Braga, Gaetano, d. Milan, Nov. 21, 1907.
Brambach, Joseph, d. Bonn, June 19, 1902.
Brinsmead, Edgar, d. Nov. 28, 1907.
Brooks, Walter M., d. Mar. 14, 1907.
Bruch, Max, d. Vienna, Sept. 17, 1907.
Brull, Ignaz, d. Vienna, Sept. 17, 1907.
Bruyck, Karl Debrois van, d. Waidhofen, Aug. 1, 1902.
Büchner, Emil, d. Erfurt, June 9, 1908.
Buck, Dudley, d. Brooklyn, N. Y., Oct. 6, 1909.
Bullard, F. F., d. Boston, June 24, 1904.
Bürgel, Konstantin, d. Breslau, July 1, 1909.
Busoni, Anna Weiss, d. Trieste, Oct. 3, 1909.

Cahen, Albert, d. Cap d' Ail, Mar. 1903.
Callaerts, J., d. Antwerp, Mar. 3, 1901.
Calkin, J. B., d. London, May 15, 1905.
Chaumet, William, d. Gajac, Gironde, Oct. 1903.
Choudens, A., d. Paris, 1902.
Chrysander, Fr., d. Bergedorf, Sept. 3, 1901.
Clauss-Szarvady, Wilhelmine, d. Paris. Sept. 2, 1907.
Cobb, G. F., d. Cambridge, Mar. 31, 1904.

Coccon, Nicolo, d. Venice, Aug. 4, 1903.
Coenen, (1) J. M. d. Amsterdam, Jan. 9,
1899. (2) Franz, d. Leyden, Jan. 24,
1904.
Cohen, Jules, d. Paris, Jan. 14, 1901.
Coleridge-Taylor, S., d. London, Sept.
1, 1912.
Colonne, Ed., d. Paris, Mar. 28, 1910.
Coquard, Arthur, d. 1910.
Courvoisier, Carl, d. 1908.
Cossmann, B., d. Frankfurt, May 7,
1910.
Czartoryska, Marcelline, d. Cracow,
June 8, 1894.

Dancla, J. B. C., d. Tunis, Nov. 8, or 9,
1907.
Danks, H. P., d. Philadelphia, Nov. 20,
1903.
Dannreuther, Edward George, d. Pim-
lico, Feb. 12, 1905.
Deffès, L. P., d. Toulouse, June 10,
1900.
Deiters, D. H., d. Coblenz, May 11,
1907.
Delle Sedie, Enrico, d. Paris, Nov. 28,
1907.
Dick, Charles G. C., d. 1895.
Dienel, Otto, d. Berlin, Mar. 10, 1905.
Dietrich, A. H., d. Berlin, Nov. 20, 1908
Doppler, Karl, d. Stuttgart, Mar. 10,
1900.
Dörffell, A., d. Leipzig, Jan. 22, 1905.
Dorn, Alexander, Julius Paul, d. Berlin,
Nov. 27, 1901.
Drobisch, M. W., d. Leipzig, Sept. 30,
1896.
Dupont, Joseph, d. Brussels, Dec. 31,
1899.
Durand, Auguste, d. Paris, May 31,
1909.
Durand, Émile, d. Neuilly, May 6, 1903.
Duvernoy, V. A., d. Paris, March 7,
1907.
Dvořák, Antonin, d. Prague, May 1,
1904.

Edwards, Julian, d. 1910.
Ehrlich, A. H., d. Berlin, Dec. 30, 1899.
Eitner, Robert, d. Templin, Jan. 22,
1905.

Erdmannsdörfer, Max von, d. Muni
Feb. 14, 1905.
Erkel, Gyula (or Julius), d. Pest, M
22, 1909.

Fernandez, Caballero, Manuel (f
nän-děth käv'-äl-lä'-rō), d. Madr
Feb. 20, 1906. See Caballero.
Fétis E., d. Brussels, Jan. 31, 1909.
Fleischer, Reinhold, d. Görlitz, Feb.
1904.
Fornari, V., d. Naples, Aug. 1900.
Fritzsch, E. W., d. Leipzig, Aug.
1902.
Fuchs, Albert, d. 1910.
Fumagalli, P., d. Milan, June 21, 19

Gadsby, Henry R., d. Putney, Nov.
1907.
Garcia, Manuel, d. Cricklewood, Lo
don, July 1, 1906.
Geistinger, Marie, d. Rastenfeld, Sep
29, 1903.
Gevaert, Fr. A., d. Brussels, Feb.
1908.
Gleason, F. G., d. Chicago, Dec. 6, 19
Godfrey, Daniel, d. Beeston, June 3
1903.
Goldschmidt, Otto, d. South Kensin
ton, Feb. 24, 1907.
Goldschmidt, Adalbert von, d. Vienn
Dec. 21, 1906.
Götze, Emil, d. Charlottenburg, Sep
28, 1901.
Grieg, Edvard, d. Bergen, Norwa
d. Sept. 4, 1907.
Grimm, J. O., d. Münster, Westphali
Dec. 7, 1903.
Grossi, Carlotta, d. May 28, 1900.
Grützmacher, Fr., d. Dresden, Feb. 2
1903.
Gudehus, H., d. Dresden, Oct. 9, 190
Guercia, Alfonso, d. 1890.
Gumprecht, Otto, d. Meran, Feb.
1900.
Gura, Eugen, d. Aufkirchen, Bavari
Aug. 26, 1906.
Gurlitt, C., d. Altona, June 17, 1901.

Haberl, F. X., d. Regensburg, Sept.
1910.

Halir, Karl, d. Berlin, Dec. 21, 1909.
Hanslick, Eduard, d. Baden near Vienna, August 6, 1904.
Härtel, Benno, d. Berlin, Aug. 4, 1909.
Hartmann, Ludwig, d. 1910.
Häser, Charlotte H., d. Rome, May, 1871.
Hasse, Gustav, d. Berlin, Dec. 31, 1889.
Hatton, Jno. d. Leptrot, Sept. 20, 1886.
Hausegger, Fr. von., d. Graz, Feb. 23, 1899.
Hausmann, Robert, d. Vienna, Jan. 19, 1909.
Hegner, Otto, d. Hamburg, Feb. 27, 1907.
Heilf, Arno, d. Bad Elster, Aug. 2, 1909.
Heinze, G. Ad., d. Muiderberg, near Amsterdam, Feb. 20, 1904.
Heinze, Sarah, d. Dresden, Oct. 7, 1901.
Held, Leo, d. Vienna, May 16, 1903.
Henkel, H., d. Frankfort-am-Main, Apr. 10, 1899.
Hey, Julius, d. Munich, Apr. 23, 1909.
Hill, Wilhelm, d. Homburg, May 6, 1902.
Hillemacher, Lucien, d. Paris, June 2, 1909.
Hipkins, A. J., d. London, June 3, 1903.
Hol, Richard, d. Utrecht, May 14, 1904.
Holmes, Augusta, d. Paris, Jan. 28, 1903.
Holmès, Henry, d. San Francisco, Dec. 9, 1905.
Homeyer, Paul, d. Leipzig, 1908.
Horwitz, Benno, d. Berlin, June 3, 1904.
vry, Marquis Richard, d', d. Hyères, Dec. 18, 1903.
ackson, John P., d. Paris, Dec. 1, 1897.
acobsohn, Simon E., d. Chicago, Oct. 3, 1902.
acques-Dalcroze, vide Dalcroze, 1865.
adassohn, Salomon, d. Leipzig, Feb. 1, 1902 (not 1901).
ansen, Gustav F., d. Hanover, May 3, 1910.
apha, Louise, d. Wiesbaden, Oct. 13, 1910.
edliczka, Dr. Ernst, d. Berlin, Aug. 3, 1904.

Joachim, Joseph, d. Berlin, Aug. 15, 1907.
Joncières, Felix-Ludger, d. Paris, Oct. 25, 1903.
Jürgensen, P., d. Moscow, Jan. 6, 1904.
Kauffmann, Emil, d. Lubingen, June 18, 1909.
Kirchner, Fritz, d. Potsdam, May 14, 1904.
Kirchner, The., d. Hamburg, Sept. 18, 1903.
Kistler,Cyrill, d. Kessingler, Jan. 1, 1907
Klein, Bruno Oscar, d. New York, June 22, 1911.
Kleinmichel, Richard, d. Charlottenburg, Aug. 18, 1901.
Klingenberg, Fr. W., d. Sirlan, Silesia, Apr. 2, 1888.
Klughardt, A. F. M., d. Dessau, Aug. 3, 1902.
Kontski, A, de., d. Ivanitshi. near Akulovka, Dec. 2, 1899.
Kretschmer, Edmund, d. Dresden, Sept. 13, 1908.
Krauss, Gabrielle, d. Paris, Jan. 6, 1906.
Krug, Arnold, d. Hamburg, Aug. 4, 1904.
Kuczinski, Paul, d. Berlin, Oct. 21, 1897.
Kuhe, Wm., d. Kensington, Oct., 1912.

Labitzky, August, d. Reichenhall, Aug. 29, 1903.
Lamoureux, Charles, d. Paris, Sept. 21, 1899.
Lang, B. J., d. Boston, Apr. 4, 1909.
Langer, Victor, d. Pest, Mar. 19, 1902.
Lassalle, Jean, d. Paris, Sept. 7, 1909.
Lassen, Eduard, d. Weimar, Jan. 15, 1904.
Lasserre, Jules, d. Tarbes, Feb. 19, 1906.
Lavigne, A. J., d. (in the almshouse), Manchester, Eng., Aug. 1, 1886.
Lenepven, Chas. Fd. d. 1910.
Levasseur, J. H., d. Paris, 1823.
Levi, Hermann, d. Munich, May 13, 1900.
Lie, Erica, d. Christiania, Oct, 27, 1903.
Longhurst, H., d. Harbledown, Canterbury, June 17, 1904.

Löschhorn, Albert, d. Berlin, June 4, 1905.
Lübeck Louis, d. Berlin, Mar. 8, 1904.
Lucas, Stanley, d. So. Hampstead, July 24, 1903, aged 69.
Lucca, Pauline, d. Vienna, Feb. 28, 1908.
Lussy, Mathias, d. 1910.
Lutz, W. M., d. W. Kensington, Jan. 31, 1903.

Macbeth, Allan, d. Glasgow, 1910.
MacDowell, Edward, d. New York, Jan. 24, 1908.
Macfarren, Walter Cecil, d. London, Sept. 2, 1905.
Mahler, Gustav, d. Vienna, May 18, 1911.
Mann, J. G. H., d. Amsterdam, Feb. 1904.
Manns, Sir August, d. Norwood, Mar. 1, 1907.
Martucci, G., d. Naples, June 3, 1909.
Marty, G. E., d. Paris, Nov. 11, 1908.
Mason, William, d. New York, July
Massenet, Jules, d. Paris, Aug. 13, 1912. 14, 1908.
Maszkowsky, Raphael, d. Breslau, Mar. 14, 1901.
Mathias, Georges, d. Pontoise, 1910.
Mathews, W. S. B., d. Denver, Col., Apr. 8, 1912.
Maylath, H.,d. NewYork,Dec. 31,1883.
Mehrkens, Fr. Ad., d. Hamburg, May 31, 1899.
Merklin, Jos., d. Nancy, July 10, 1905.
Meyer-Lutz, William, d. London, Jan. 31, 1903.
Milanollo,Teresa, d. Paris,Oct. 25,1904.
Milde, Hans F. von, d. Weimar, Dec. 10, 1899.
Millöcker, Karl, d. Baden, Dec. 31, 1899.
Moir, Frank Lewis, d. Deal, England, July 14, 1904.
Monasterio, Gesù,d. Santander, Sept.. 28, 1903.
Molloy, J. L., d. Wooleys, Bucks, Feb. 4, 1909.
Monk, E. G., d. Radley, England, Jan. 3, 1900.

Mottl, Felix, d. Munich, July (?) 1911.
Mounsey, Elizabeth, d. London, Oct. 3, 1905.
Mühlfeld, Richard, d. Meiningen, June 1, 1907.
Müller, Richard, d. Leipzig, Oct., 1904.
Musiol, R. P. J., d. Fraustadt, Posen, Oct. 18, 1903.
Neumann, Angelo, d. Prague, Dec. 20, 1910.
Nixon, H. C., d. Bromley, Dec. 25, 1907.
Norman-Neruda, (Lady Hallé), d. Berlin (?) Apr. 15, 1911.
Noszkowski, Sigismund, d. Warsaw, July 24, 1909.
Novello, Clara, d. Rome, Mar. 12, 1908.
Novello, Mary Sabilla, d. Genoa, Jan. 8, 1904.
Oakeley, Sir Herbert Stanley, d. Eastbourne, Oct. 26, 1903.
Odenwald, R. T., d. Hamburg, Apr. 22, 1899.
O'Leary, Mrs. Arthur, d. June 17, 1909
Paine, J. K., Cambridge, Mass., Apr. 25, 1906.
Papperitz, Robert, d. Leipzig, Sept 29, 1903.
Parratt, H. L., d. Huddersfield, Feb. 15 1904.
Parry, Joseph, d. Penarth, Feb. 17 1903.
Pauer, Ernst, d. Jugenheim, Darmstadt May 9, 1905.
Petersilea, Carlyle, d. Tropico, near Lo Angeles, Cal., June 11, 1903.
Pfeiffer, Jean Georges, d. Paris, Feb. 14 1908.
Pfeil, Heinrich, d. Leipzig, Apr. 17 1899.
Piccolomini, Maria, d. near Florence Dec. 1899.
Planquette, Robert Jean, d. Paris, Jai 28, 1903.
Planté, François, d. Prigueux, July 1898.
Poisot, Charles (Emile), d. Dijon, Mar 1904.

e, William, d. London, Dec. 30, 1900.

idoro, Federigo, d. S. Giorgia a Cremano, near Naples, Aug. 14, 1903.

litzer, Adolf, d. London, Nov. 14, 900.

ges, H., d. Munich, Nov. 17, 1900.

yer, G. von, d. Vienna, May 9, 1901.

ut, Ebenezer, d. Hackney, Dec. 5, 909.

ne, Louisa F., d. London, Mar. 20, 904.

ndegger, Alberto, d. London, Dec. 911.

ppoldi, Eduard, d. Dresden, May 6, 1903.

uscher, Max, d. Pfarring, Mar. 14, 895.

a, William, d. Newcastle-on-Tyne, Mar. 8, 1903.

ay, Samuel, d. Newark-on-Trenk, uly 21, 1905.

bicek, Josef, d. Berlin, Mar. 24, 1904.

bling, Friedrich, d. Leipzig, Oct. 15, 900.

bling, Gustav, d. Madgeburg, Jan. ), 1902.

ichel, A. H. J., d. Berne, Mar. 4, 896.

ichmann, Theodor, d. Marbach, Switzerland, May 22, 1903.

inecke, Carl, d. Leipzig, Mar. 10, 910.

isenauer, Alfred, d. Libau, Silesia, Oct. 3, 1907.

issmann, August, d. Berlin, Dec. 1, 903.

uss, Edward, d. Dresden, 1911.

yer, Ernst, d. Le Lavandon, near Toulon, Jan. 15, 1909.

Leinberger, Joseph, d. Munich. Nov. 25, 1901.

cordi, Giulio, T., d. Milan, June 6, 1912.

msky-Korsakov, Nicholas Andneievitch, d. St. Petersburg, June, 21, 1908.

tter, Josef, d. Salzburg, Austria, June 21, 1911.

ockel, Edw., d. Bath, Nov. 2, 1899.

oger, Victor, d. Paris, Dec. 2, 1903.

Rotoli, A., d. Boston, Nov. 26, 1904.

Rosseau, Samuel, d. Paris, Oct. 1, 1904.

Ryan, Thomas, d. New Bedford, Mass., Mar. 25, 1903.

Salaman, C. K., d. London, June 23, 1901.

Sanderson, Sibyl, d. Paris, May 16, 1903.

Sarasate, Pablo, d. Biarritz, Sept. 20, 1908.

Sauzay, Eugène, d. Paris, Jan. 27, 1901.

Schäffer, Julius, d. Breslau, Feb. 10, 1902.

Schitler, Madeline, d. New York, July 3, 1911.

Schimon-Regan, Anna, d. Munich, Apr. 18, 1902.

Schnecker, P. A., d. New York, Oct. 3, 1903.

Schneider, Theodor, d. Zittau, June 15, 1909.

Schneider, Theodor, d. Zettan, June 15, 1909.

Schnorr von Karolsfeld, Malwina, d. Karlsruhe, Feb. 8, 1904. (aged 72).

Schytte, Ludwig, d. Berlin, Nov. 10, 1909.

Seibert, Louis, d. Eisenberg, near Wetzlar, July 29, 1903.

Seiss, Isidor, d. Cologne, Sept. 25, 1905.

Serpette, Gaston, d. Paris, Nov. 3, 1904.

Sherwood, William H., d. Chicago, Jan. 7, 1911.

Silas, Eduard, d. West Kensington, Feb. 8, 1909.

Singer, Edmund, d. Stuttgart, Jan. 23, 1912.

Sittard, Josef, d. Hamburg, Nov. 23, 1903.

Slaughter, W., d. London, Mar. 2, 1908.

Smith, Gerrit, d. Greenwich, Conn., July 21, 1912.

Smolian, Arthur, d. Leipzig, Nov. 5, 1911.

Sontheim, Heinrich, d. Stuttgart, Aug. 2, 1912, aged 92.

Spicker, M., d. New York, Oct. 16, 1912.

Spindler, Fritz, d. Lössnitz, near Dresden, Dec. 26, 1905.

Spinelli, Nicolo, d. Rome, 1909.
Stade, F. W., d. Altenburg, Mar. 25, 1902.
Stainer, Sir John, d. Verona, Mar. 31, 1901.
Steggall, Charles, d. London, June 7, 1905.
Steingräber, Theodor, d. Lepzig, Apr. 5, 1904.
Stehle, G. Ed., d. St. Gallen, Apr. 11, 1896.
Sterling, Antoinette, d. Hampstead, Jan. 10, 1904.
Stern, Leo, d. London, Sept. 3, 1904.
Stern, Margarethe, d. Dresden, Oct. 4, 1899.
Stiehle, L. M. A., d. Mulhaüsen, Alsatia, July 6, 1896.
Stoltz, Rosine, d. Paris, July 31, 1903.
Stockhausen, Julius, d. Frankfort-on-Main, Sept. 22, 1906.
Sucher, Josef, d. Berlin, Apr. 4, 1908.
Sunderland, Mrs. Susan Sykes, d. Brighthouse, May 7, 1906.
Svendsen, J. S., d. Copenhagen, June 13, 1911.
Székely, Imre, d. Pest, Apr., 1887.

Taffanel, Paul, d. Paris, Nov. 22, 1908.
Tamagno, Francesco, d. Varese, Aug. 31, 1905.
Tappert, Wilhelm, d. Berlin, Oct. 27, 1907.
Taubert, Otto, d. Torgau, Aug. 1, 1903.
Thallon, Robert, d. 1910.
Thiele, Eduard, d. Dessau, Jan. 10, 1895.
Thomas, Theodore, d. Chicago, Jan. 4, 1905.
Thomé, François, d. Paris, Nov. 16, 1909.

Thuille, Ludwig, d. Munich, Feb. 5, 1907.
Trotère, Henry, d. London, April 10, 1912.
Tinel, Edgar, d. Brussels, Oct. 28, 1912.
Turpin, Dr. E. H., d. London, Oct, 25, 1907.

Ugalde, Mme. D., d. Paris, July 18, 1910.
Verdi, Giuseippina, d. Busetto, Nov. 14, 1897.
Vianesi, Auguste, d. New York, Nov. 11, 1908.
Viard-Louis, J. Jenny, d. Auteuil, Paris, Jan. 27, 1904.
Viardot-Garcia, Mme. Michelle, d. Paris, May 18, 1910.
Vidal, L. A., d. Paris, Jan. 7, 1901.
Vincent, H. Jos. d. Vienna, May 20, 1901.
Walter, Gustav, d. Vienna, Feb., 1910.
Weber, Miroslaw, d. Munich, Jan. 2, 1906.
Weckerlin, J. B., d. Trottberg (Alsace), May 20, 1910.
Willing, Chris. Edwin, d. St. Albans Dec. 1, 1904.
Willis, Henry, d. London, Feb. 11, 1901
Winkelmann, Hermann, d. Vienna Jan. 19, 1912.
Wood, Mrs. Henry J. (née Olga Narishkin), d. London, Dec. 20, 1909.
Wurm, Wilhelm, d. St. Petersburg June 20, 1904.

Zerrahn, Karl, d. Milton, Mass., Dec 29, 1909.
Zumpe, Hermann, d. Munich, Sept. 4, 1903.

# The
# Stories of the Operas

# The
# Stories
## *of the*
# OPERAS
## told by Acts, Entrances and Songs; with the Casts of the Original Creators

*BEETHOVEN, LUDWIG VON.*

**Fidelio,** *oder die eheliche Liebe* (fē-dāl'-yō, ō'-dĕr dē ā'-ĕ-lĭkh-ĕ lē'-bĕ). Fidelio, or Conjugal Love.

Two-act opera. Book by Joseph Sonnleithner and Treitschke after Bouilly's romance "Léonore, ou l'Amour Conjugal."

Produced in three acts, Vienna, Nov. 20, 1805, without success. Revised by Breuning and produced as "Leonore" in 2 acts without success. Revised by Treitschke and produced as "Fidelio," Vienna, May 23, 1814, with success. For this work Beethoven composed four overtures. That called "No. I," was composed third, in 1807. The "Leonore," or "No. 3" was composed second in 1806; the "No. 2" was written first, in 1805; the "No. 4" or "Fidelio," in 1814.

### CHARACTERS AND THEIR CREATORS.

DON FERNAN'DO,
 *Minister* ............ Weinkoff, bar.
DON PIZARRO (dôn pē-tsär'-rō),
 *Governor of a State*
 *Prison* .............. Meier, bar.
FLORESTAN (flôr'-ĕs-tän),
 *A prisoner* ......... Demmer, tenor.
ROC'CO,
 *Chief jailer* ................ Rothe.
ʲAQUINO (yäk-wē'-nō),
 *Turnkey* ................... Cache.
CAPTAIN OF THE GUARD ......... Meister.

LEONORE (lā-ô-nō'-rĕ),
 *known as* FIDELIO, *wife*
 *of Florestan* ......... Frl. Milder.
MARZELLINE (mär-tsĕl -lē'-nĕ),
 *Rocco's daughter* ....... Frl. Müller.

Act I.—Scene. Courtyard of the Prison. Marzelline ironing, worried and beset by Jaquino, who makes love to her, with interruptions of someone knocking. Rocco calls him and he goes, jealously mentioning Fidelio, who has entered Rocco's service and whom Marzelline loves, thinking her to be a man. Left alone the girl rejoices in hope that Fidelio will marry her (in an aria "Die Hoff'nung"). Jaquino enters with Rocco, inquiring for Fidelio, who enters in man's garb, laden with provisions and a box of letters. Rocco and Marzelline hint of marriage, and Fidelio secretly expresses her uneasiness. In a famous quartet ("Mir ist so wunderbar "—in canon-form) their varying feelings find vent. Rocco tells of the importance of money to wedded bliss. Fidelio asks to be allowed to help him in his prison duties, and he consents that she shall have admittance to all but the dungeon, where a certain wretch has lain two years. The two women depart on the announcement that Pizarro is coming. He enters with a guard, and Rocco gives him the letters. One of them is a secret warning that Don Fernando is going to make an unannounced inspection of the prison, having

847

heard that there are several prisoners unjustly held. Pizarro plans to put his old rival, Florestan, out of the way. He sends an officer to watch from a tower for Fernando's approach ; then orders Rocco to kill Florestan. Rocco refuses, and is ordered by Pizarro to dig the doomed man's grave, while Pizarro himself commits the murder. When they have gone, Fidelio enters ; she has overheard the plot, and pours out her horror (in the great aria " Abscheulicher ! "). Her rage changes to grief, then to hope in God. When she has gone, Marzelline and Jaquino enter, quarrelling. Rocco appears, rebukes Jaquino for hoping to marry his daughter, and orders him to release the minor prisoners for their breath of air. The prisoners rejoice in the sun, and Rocco tells Fidelio that she may come and help him dig the grave of the mysterious prisoner whom Pizarro is going to kill. Fidelio is overcome with horror at having to dig her husband's grave. Marzelline and Jaquino hurry in, saying that Pizarro is coming in a rage. After them enters Pizarro, storming at Rocco's letting the prisoners out. They are ordered back to their cells.

Act II.—Scene I. The dungeon. Florestan, chained, bemoans his fate : he sees his wife in a vision, but sinks down exhausted and oblivious of the entrance of Rocco and Fidelio. She cannot see the prisoner's face, but believes it is her husband, and vows to save him in any case. She gives feeble aid to Rocco in digging the grave, and when Florestan, waking, calls for drink, she lifts a pitcher of wine to his lips and gives him a crust of bread. Pizarro enters and orders Fidelio away. She does not obey, but when Pizarro starts to stab Florestan she protects him and declares herself his wife. She draws a pistol and threatens Pizarro. A trumpet is heard. Jaquino enters, announcing the coming of Don Fernando. Pizarro hurries away, and Rocco follows him, after pressing the hands of the reunited lovers, who join in a rapturous duet (" O Namen-

lose Freude "). Rocco returns, saying that all the prisoners are to have a hearing, and leads them out. Scene 2. The square before the castle. The Minister frees the rejoicing prisoners. Rocco leads in Florestan and Fidelio, for whom he pleads. Pizarro is sent away in disgrace, and all join in praise of the wife's fidelity.

## BELLINI, VINCENZO.

**Nor'ma.**

Two-act lyric tragedy. Book by Romani. Produced in Milan, 1832.

CHARACTERS AND THEIR CREATORS.

POLLIO'NE,
*A Roman Pro-Consul*, Donzelli, tenor.
FLAVIO (flä'-vĭ-ō),
*His friend*...................tenor.
OROVESO (ôr-o-vā'-so),
*Druid Chief*.................bass.
NOR'MA,
*His daughter, a Druidess*.....sopr.
ADALGISA (ä-däl-gē'-zä),
*A young priestess*............sopr.
CLOTILDE (klō-tēl'-dĕ),
*Norma's confidante*..........scpr.
Two children of Norma and Pollione.

Act I.—Scene I. Night in the Sacred Druid Forest in Gaul ; in the centre the Oak of Irminsul. The Druids enter in religious procession. Oroveso bids them strike the bell thrice when the moon appears. They wait for Norma to cut the sacred branch, and give the signal for the defeat of the Roman invaders. When they have passed on Pollione and Flavio steal in. Pollione confesses that, though he has loved Norma, who has broken all her vows and borne him two children, he has tired of her, and loves Adalgisa, a priestess vowed to virginity. He tells of a dream (" Meco all' altar di Venere ") in which Norma blights his vision of joy with Adalgisa. The sacred shield resounds, calling the Druids back, and the two Romans slip away, Pollione vowing to wipe out their religion. The Druids welcome Norma, who enters with a retinue of priestesses, but in place of calling them to fight the impious Romans, she rebukes their wrath and bids them keep peace (" Sediziose voci "), saying that Rome will perish from its own vices. She cuts the sacred mistletoe, and, kneeling, calls on the moon's "chaste goddess" ("Casta diva ") to shed peace upon them. They demand Pollione's life, and she promises them revenge, but aside confesses her love for him (" Ah bello a me ritorno "). When the Druids have left, Adalgisa appears, dreaming of her love for Pollione (" Sgombra è la sacra selva "). In contrition she kneels before the altar she has forgotten. Pollione, appearing, reproaches her for praying to the god (" Va, crudele "), and begs her to go to Rome with him (" Dove è amor "), and she consents. Scene 2. Norma's dwelling. Norma and Clotilde speak of the two children of her secret and forbidden love. Hearing someone approach, she has Clotilde conceal the children. Adalgisa appears and, prostrating herself, confesses her unholy love. Norma grants her forgiveness and then asks her lover's name. Adalgisa points to Pollione, who appears. Norma, in her rage, has no blame for Adalgisa, but covers Pollione with reproaches, and, hearing the temple bell, leaves him. Adalgisa also repulses him.

Act II.—Scene 1. Norma's dwelling. Her children are asleep on a couch. She enters with a dagger to kill her children in revenge on Pollione. But a revulsion of motherly feeling leads her to embrace them. She sends Clotilde to bring Adalgisa, who enters and is asked to take the children to Pollione (" Deh, con te li prendi ") and become his wife, while Norma kills herself. Adalgisa pleads with Norma to seek her own happiness (" Mira, O Norma "). Adalgisa and Norma pledge friendship. Scene 2. A solitary place where the Gauls chant of war. Oroveso says that Pollione is to return to Rome and be replaced by a still more cruel pro-consul ; he counsels delay, however, before they

take up arms. Scene 3. Temple and altar of Irminsul. Norma is hopefully waiting Adalgisa's mission begging Pollione to return to the mother of his children. Clotilde comes to say Pollione has refused, and even vows to take Adalgisa by force from the temple. Norma, in high frenzy, strikes the shield of Irminsul three times, and the Druids and Gallic warriors assemble excitedly. Norma cries for immediate war on the Romans (" Guerra, guerra ! "). Clotilde runs in to say that a Roman warrior has been caught in the temple. Pollione is brought in, and Norma is given the sword to kill him for his impiety. Her hand trembles, and she begs all to withdraw while she questions the culprit. Alone with Pollione, she tells him his life is in her power (" In mia mano alfino tu sei "). She says Adalgisa will be burned for breaking her vows. He kneels and prays that she be spared. Norma summons the Druids back and says that one of the priestesses has broken her vows and must be burned alive. The Druids demand her name. Pollione implores mercy, and is dumbfounded when Norma announces herself as the guilty one. In a sudden recrudescence of his old passion he climbs the funeral pyre with her (" Qual cor tradisti "). Her last prayer is that her father protect her children (" Deh, non volerli "). The Druids throw over her the black veil, and she and Pollione look forward to bliss beyond this life.

## BELLINI, VINCENZO.

**La Sonnambula** (lä-sôn-näm'-boo-lä). The Somnambulist.

Two-act opera. Book by Felice Romani, after a vaudeville by Scribe. Milan, March 6, 1831.

CHARACTERS AND THEIR CREATORS.

ELVINO (ĕl-vē'-nō),
    *A rich farmer* ....... Rubini, tenor.
RODOL'FO,
    *A young lord incognito,*
                        Mariano, bar.

ALES'SIO,
*A peasant, in love with Lisa* ...bass.
AMINA (ä-mē'-nä),
*An orphan, Teresa's ward,*
                    Mme. Pasta, sopr.
LISA (lē'-zä),
*An innkeeper*...Mme. Toccani, sopr.
TERESA (tä-ra'-sä),
*The miller's wife*..........m.-sopr.

Act I.—Scene. In front of a mountain inn. The peasants gather, singing a welcome to the bride Amina. Lisa, who loves Elvino, the bridegroom, alone is jealous amidst the joy ("Tutto è gio-ja"). Her lover, Alessio, cannot quiet her envy, though he speaks of his own approaching marriage with her. After a song of Switzerland ("In Elvezia non v'ha rosa"), Amina enters, grateful for the welcome and her serene future ("Come per me sereno" and "Sovra il sen la man mi posa"). She embraces her foster-mother and the grudging Lisa. The notary comes, and then Elvino, who had stopped to implore the Virgin to send his wife perfect virtue. He gives her the ring ("Prendi, l'annel ti dono") and violets. He invites everybody to be present at the wedding at dawn the next morning. The noise of post-horses is heard, and Rodolfo enters to ask the way to the castle. He recalls the familiar scenes ("Vi ravviso o luoghi ameni"), but he is not recognised by the others. He flatters the bride's bright eyes ("Tu non sai con quei begli occhi"), and Elvino feels a pang of jealousy. The sunset makes it dangerous to proceed up the mountain to the castle, and Rodolfo is warned of the phantom that appears at night ("A fosco cielo"). He decides to stop at Lisa's inn. When he has gone, Elvino jealously rebukes Amina. She tries to calm his jealousy ("Son geloso del zefiro amante"), and they are tenderly reconciled ("Mai più dubbi").

Act II.—Scene I. A bedroom in the inn. Lisa comes to welcome the Count, whom she has recognised. She slips into a cabinet on hearing someone approach, but leaves her shawl behind her. Amina enters in a nightdress, walking in her sleep. Rodolfo realises her condition, but Lisa, seeing her, hurries away scandalised. Amina lies down and sleeps on Rodolfo's bed, while he leaves by the window. The villagers come tiptoeing in to welcome the Count, who has been away so many years. Lisa leads in Elvino and Teresa, who see Amina and believe her guilty. She wakes and is repulsed by Elvino. Teresa alone believes her innocence. Scene 2. A shaded valley. Peasants pass on their way to the castle to plead with the Count to clear Amina's good name. Amina and Teresa enter, and, later, Elvino, who again covers her with scorn, though he longs for the time of his old trust ("Ah, perchè non posso odiarti").

Act III.—Scene. The village green ; ? mill in the distance. Alessio is pleading with Lisa not to love Elvino, but she scorns him. Villagers enter to say that Lisa is chosen as bride to Elvino; he comes himself to tell her. Rodolfo appears and explains Amina's presence in his room, but Elvino refuses to hear him. Teresa comes, saying that the distraught Amina has at last fallen asleep. She brings Lisa's shawl, and accuses her of visiting the Count. The Count will not speak of her guilt, but persists in defending Amina, who is seen coming out of the mill. She is again walking in her sleep, and passes across a plank over the very mill-wheel. All watch her in suspense, but she crosses in safety dreaming of Elvino's cruelty. He gives her back the ring he took from her, and she wakes in his arms. She gives voice to her rapture ("Ah non giunge uman pensiero"), and all rejoice with her.

### BIZET, GEORGES.

**Carmen** (kär-mān).

Four-act opera. Book by Henri Meilhac and Ludovic Halévy (after Prosper Mérimée's romance).

Produced, Paris Opéra Comique, March 3, 1875, with Mme. Galli-Marié as "Carmen," Mlle. Chapuy as " Michaela."

### CHARACTERS.

DON JOSÉ (dôn zhô-zā ; in Spanish
hō-zā'),
A brigadier................tenor.
ZUNIGA (tsü-nē'-gä),
An officer................bass.
MORALES (mô-rä'-lĕs),
A brigadier................bass.
ESCAMILLO (ās-kä-mēl'-yō),
A toreador................bar.
IL DANCAIRO (el-dän-kī'-rō), IL
REMENDADO (ēl rä-mĕn-dä'-dhō),
Smugglers................tenor, bar.
LILLAS PASTIA (lēl'-yäs päs-tē'-ä),
Innkeeper................
CARMEN,
A cigarette girl................m.-sopr.
MICHAELA (mē-kä-ā-lä'),
A peasant girl................sopr.
FRASQUITA (frä-skē'-tä), MER-
CEDES (mĕr-thä'-dĕs),
Cigarette girls................m.-sopr.

Act I.—Scene. A crowded square
in Seville, in front of a cigarette factory
near a bridge. Michaela enters, looking
for Don José ; she is advised by Morales to wait inside the guard-house.
The guard is relieved (" Noi con la
guardia "), under command of Zuniga
and José. An officer chaffs José about
Michaela, and José says none of the
cigarette girls can compare with her.
The bell rings for the noon-hour and
the girls enter smoking and singing of
life as all one vanity of smoke (" Seguir
l'occhio in aria "). Carmen saunters in,
gay and impudent, teasing her loving
admirers with an old Spanish Habanera
(composed by Pradier and called " El
Aveglito ") (" Amor, misterioso Angelo "). The bell rings and as the cigarette
girls return to work, she tosses a flower
at the bewildered José. Michaela appears and timidly tells that his mother
has sent him by her a letter, some
money, and also—a kiss (" La madre

tua con me "). José is moved by memories of his mother (" Mia madre io la
rivedo "), and feels that her letter has
saved him from the tempter Carmen.
He gives Michaela loving messages
and the girl goes. A riot is heard in
the factory ; thither all rush in panic,
discussing a fight between Manuelita
and Carmen, who is brought out by
officers. She mocks their questions and
finally strikes one of them. They decide to tie her hands with a rope and
leave José to guard her. On him she
practises all her wiles, and asks him to
meet her at Lillas Pastia's inn near the
bastion (a seguidilla, " Pressa il bastion
di Siviglia "). He at length unties her
hands, but she pretends, when the officer returns, that they are still tied.
When José starts to lead her across the
bridge, however, she pushes him down
and escapes.

Act II.—Scene. Lillas Pastia's inn,
two months later. Cigarette girls, gypsies and others including Zuniga, are
making merry and Carmen sings and
dances with the rest (" Vezzi e anella
scintillar "). Frasquita brings word that
the inn must close ; Zuniga invites Carmen to go, but seeing her sad, tells her
that Don José, who has suffered impris-
onment and reduction to the ranks for
conniving at her escape, is now free. A
procession in honour of the toreador Escamillo passes and the famous bullfighter is invited in. He sings of the
delights of the arena (" Toreador, at-
tento "). He flirts with Carmen, she
banters him, and Lillas Pastia clears
the inn of all except the gypsies and
Carmen and closes it up. The two smugglers appear and confess the usefulness
of women in their profession (a quintet
" Abbiam in vista "). Carmen declines
to join them, and they blame it to love.
José is heard singing (" Dragon d'Alca-
là ") and they decide that he would
make a good smuggler. Carmen consents to try to win him over, and the
others withdraw. José enters and she
levels all her witchery on him, dancing
and singing (" Voglio danzar per tuo

piacer"). He hears the "retreat" sounded at the distant barracks, but her pouting coquetry restrains him; he shows her the flower she gave him at their first meeting (" Il fior che avevi ") and she pleads with him to give up the army and lead a gypsy life with her. He recoils at the thought of being a deserter, and is rushing away when Zuniga returns. He reproaches Carmen for preferring a private such as José to himself, an officer ; and orders José back to the barracks. José, infuriated, defies him and draws his sword ; the gypsies enter, cover Zuniga with their pistols and lead him away. José has no resource but to join the smugglers.

Act III.—Scene. The smugglers' lair in the mountains. They are rejoicing at their luck, but José is restless and thinks of his mother. Carmen tells him he would better go back home. He threatens her with his knife. She turns her back on him and the gypsies fall to telling fortunes with cards (" Mischiam ; alziam "). Carmen finds always Death in her cards; she takes the omen jauntily. The smugglers move off followed by José. Michaela enters in great fear (" Io dico no "). She hides when a gun-shot is heard and Escamillo enters with a bullet hole through his hat. José appears and challenges the toreador, who says he comes to find his sweetheart Carmen who is tired of her dragoon lover. The rivals prepare to fight with knives, but Carmen saves Escamillo in the nick of time and he is sent away. Michaela tells José that his mother is dying with grief for him (" Io ti vengo a cercar "), and Carmen advises him to go. He jealously refuses at first to leave Carmen, but finally goes, glaring threateningly at the fickle siren, who hears with joy the distant song of the bullfighter.

Act IV. Scene. A square in Seville outside the arena. A great crowd seethes about the place. Dancers whirl (" Danziam, danziam ! "). The procession of bull-fighters of all classes passes into the arena with ceremony, and Carmen accompanies the idolised Escamillo Frasquita and Mercedes warn Carme that José is looking for her, but sh pluckily waits for him after the crow has entered the arena. He begs her go away with him and threatens h when she refuses ruthlessly. As sh taunts him with her weariness of h love, the noise of the spectators roa out from the arena. She wishes to ent but he blocks the way, and when sh throws at him the ring he gave her, h stabs her and she dies without a wor The crowd pouring out of the aren find him kneeling lovingly at her side.

### BOITO, ARRIGO.

**Mefistofele** (mā-fē'-stō-fā-lĕ). Mephi topheles.

Grand opera in prolog, four acts an epilog. Book and music by Boito. L Scala, Milan, 1868.

#### CHARACTERS.

MEFISTOFELE...................bass
FAUST, later HENRICO (fowst, ĕn-rē'-kō)...teno
WAGNER (väkh'-nĕr)............teno
NEREO (nā'-rā-ō)................teno
MARGHERITA....................sop
MARTA, *her mother*............cont
ELENA, Helen of Troy..........sop
PAN'TALIS.....................cont

In the attempt to cover the scope o Goethe's whole poem " Faust," the op era exchanges continuity for picturesqu episodes. It opens with a " Prologue i the Heavens," a cloud-scene in whic Satan interrupts the songs of the invis ble angel-choirs, and parleys with th unseen Jehovah for the soul of Faus which he boasts he can win.

Act I.—Scene I. Holiday street-scen in Frankfort. The Elector passes wit retinue. Faust and his friend Wagne stroll about, followed by Mefistofel disguised as a gray friar, whom Faus dreads, but Wagner ridicules. Scene 2

'aust's laboratory. The gray friar conceals himself in an alcove ; Faust enters
and begins to read his Bible, the dread
of which betrays Mefistofele, who declares himself and assumes the form of
knight. He bargains for Faust's soul,
ffering him all earthly pleasures. Faust
cccepts, and steps on Mefistofele's cloak
o be spirited away.

Act II.—Scene I. The garden of Mar-
herita, who engages in amorous dal-
iance and promise with her lover, Faust
Enrico), while her mother, Marta,
irts ludicrously with Mefistofele. Scene
. The wild gorge of the Brocken, where
vil spirits of all sorts hold the varie-
ated orgy appropriate to the witches'
abbath. Faust, under the guidance
f Mefistofele, is shown a vision of the
etrayed Margherita's sorrow, and Me-
stofele pictures the world in a declama-
on over a globe of glass.

Act III.—Scene. The prison where
Margherita, who has killed the child of
er shame, is awaiting her execution.
'aust appears and begs her to fly with
im. With her dying breath she refuses,
nd as the day breaks he is haled away
y Mefistofele, who declares Margherita
oomed. But the angelic chorus (given
 the orchestra) declares her to be for-
iven and saved.

Act IV.—Scene I. The moonlit banks
f the river Peneus, on "The Night of
Classical Sabbath." Pantalis and the
'rens sing of the moon, and Helen of
'roy describes the capture and pillage
f the old Homeric city. Faust wakens
rom slumber and appears on his rest-
ess pleasure hunt, and, watched by Me-
stofele, finds in Helen a quick re-
ponse to his ardor. Scene 2. Faust's
aboratory, in which he muses on his dis-
nal hunt for earthly pleasure, and longs
or Heaven. Mefistofele tries to per-
uade him to continue the hunt, but the
eavenly music is heard. Mefistofele
nvokes seductive sirens to counteract
he better influence, but Faust clings
 his Bible, and, praying and redeemed,
:es in a shower of roses, which scorch
nd foil Mefistofele.

## CHARPENTIER, GUSTAV.

## Louise.

Four-act opera. Book by the composer. Produced, Opéra Comique,
Paris, February 2, 1900. [The story
of this opera, by Annie C. Muirhead.]

PRINCIPAL CHARACTERS AND THEIR
CREATORS.

JULIEN,
    An artist.........Maréchal, tenor.
THE FATHER.............Fugère, bar.
LOUISE,
    Mdlle. Marthe Rioton, dram. sopr.
THE MOTHER,
    Mme. Deschamps-Jehin, mez.-sopr.

*Other Characters (all with singing
parts).*

*Men.*

{ The Night Walker and
{ Master of the Revels.
An old Bohemian. A Song-writer.
First Philosopher. Second Philosopher.
A painter. A sculptor. A young poet.
A student. A ragpicker. A jack-of-
all-trades. First policeman. Second
policeman. An apprentice. A street
urchin.

*Women.*

Irma,
Camille,
Gertrude,   } Sewing-girls.
Elise,
Dressmaker's apprentice.
Dressmaker's forewoman.
Blanche,
Suzanne,
Marguerite,   } work-girls.
Madeleine,
A ragpicker. A street-sweeper. A
milk-girl. A newspaper-girl. A ciga-
rette-gatherer.

The street-cries : Sellers of chick-
weed, green peas, potatoes, brooms,
barrels, old clothes.
Place of action : Paris. Time : the
present day.
Act I.—Scene. Room in a tenement.

Louise at the window talking with Julien outside. He urges her to elope, since her parents prevent their marriage. She refuses to grieve them so. She asks how he fell in love with her. He tells. The mother, entering, listens angrily to their mutual confidences, then pulls Louise back and dismisses Julien. A violent scene follows between Louise and her mother, who talks of Julien's alleged bad character. The father enters, holding a letter, and tenderly greets Louise. While he reads the letter, which is from Julien, Louise anxiously scans his face ; they embrace without a word (the orchestra, during this pantomime, is notably expressive). The family sup, the father talking contentedly of his lot, the mother making bitter allusions to artists and idlers. After supper, the parents discuss the letter. The father sympathises, the mother fiercely opposes. Then the father reasons with Louise about her inexperience and Julien's bad reputation. He asks whether she has ever spoken with him. Louise says no. The mother ironically mimics the talk she heard between the lovers. The father makes Louise promise to have no more dealings with Julien ; says she will soon get over her pain, and sets her to reading aloud the newspaper. She breaks down at the word " Paris."

Act II.—Orchestral Prelude. " Paris awakening." Scene 1. On the Hill of Montmartre. All sorts of workers beginning their day's toil. The Nightwalker enters and talks beguilingly to the girls. He throws off his cloak, appearing garbed as Spring ; explains that he represents the Pleasures of Paris, and runs off, knocking over an old ragpicker as he goes. This old man tells, weeping, how his daughter was formerly tempted away by the Nightwalker. An old street-sweeper tells how she once was rich and gay—it was paradise. An urchin asks for the address of her paradise. She points to Paris. Julien enters with Bohemian friends, and describes how he means to abduct Louise.

The young men sing gaily of love and a free life. Julien, left alone, sings passionately of his love and wonders whence help will come. As he pauses, the street-cries of Paris are heard. He listens with growing emotion ; then breaks out in praise of city life. Work-girls pass chattering. Julien hides. Louise and her mother appear and separate for the day's work. Julien waylays Louise and entreats her to go with him, but she refuses. He sorrowfully departs. Street - cries resound on all sides. Scene 2. Interior of dressmaker's shop. Girls sewing, and quarrelling. Louise sits among them, pensive. The others note her sadness and talk among themselves, telling how severely her parents treat her, even striking her. Then they teasingly accuse her of being in love. Gertrude, an old maid, talks sentimentally (hurdygurdy in the distance). Camille moralises on the strong attraction of men for girls. Irma describes enthusiastically the charms of city life. Sounds of street-music are heard. The girls flock to the window and recognise Julien singing to his guitar. Each girl, thinking the serenade is for her, is loud in praise, till Julien missing Louise, breaks his strings impatiently and sings in sadder vein ; then the girls feign boredom. The pathos of the singer moves Louise's heart. She rises to go, pleading illness. As the girls watch from the window, they see Louise walking away with Julien.

Act III.—Scene 1. Julien and Louise in the garden of a little house on the summit of Montmartre. Panorama of Paris in the background. Twilight. Louise rejoices that her happiest dream has come true. She regrets nothing—at home, her father treated her as child, her mother with blows. Julien calls them Mother Routine and Father Prejudice. Louise tells how they wished her to be guided by their experience instead of by her heart. Julien declaims against experience. He asserts that everyone has a right to freedom and love. Louise asks whether anyone has ne right to break another's heart. He answers that her parents' selfishness must be met with selfishness. He says her character has been developed by city life. They join in a rhapsody over Paris. The city begins to light up. The lovers exult in a pæan of liberty, echoed by voices from the city. Then they sing ecstatically of love and life. Scene 2. A crowd of their Bohemian friends arrive, and with dancing and ceremonies crown Louise "Muse of Montmartre." The mother suddenly appears. At her sad aspect, the revelers scatter in dismay. She comes humbly to tell of the Father's illness, and beg Louise to return home. The old ragpicker passes by, alluding to his lost daughter. Julien, touched, lets Louise go on the promise of her return.

Act IV.—Scene same as Act I. A summer evening. The father seated, broken down and sombre, gradually muses to talk bitterly of the injustice of fate; of rearing children only to suffer from their ingratitude. Louise at the window merely looks out into the night. Her Mother calls her to help in the kitchen and argues with her, while the father eagerly listens, hoping she will be convinced. Louise recalls their promise that she should be free. The Mother refuses to let her return to a life of sin. Louise bids her father goodnight coldly. He draws her passionately to him and rocks her on his knee like a child, in forced gaiety singing a lullaby, promising that if the child will be good, she shall have whatever she wants. Louise answers that if they want her to be happy they must let her go to her lover, and repeats Julien's words of the individual's right to freedom of choice. Joyous voices heard from the town increase her longing. She declares Paris calls her. The Father coming infuriated chases her from the house; then immediately repents and calls her back—in vain. He shakes his fist at the city, ejaculating bitterly "O Paris!"

## DÉLIBES, LÉO.

**Lakmé** (lăk-mā).

Three-act opera. Book by E. Gondinet and Ph. Gille.

Produced, Opéra Comique, April 14. 1883.

Act I.—Scene. A garden in India at dawn. A chorus in morning homage to Brahma. Nilakantha appears and invokes maledictions on the English conquerors, Lakmé joins the prayers. Her father tells her he must go to another temple for the day, and leaves Lakmé in charge of Mallika and Hadji. Lakmé lays her jewels on a table, sings of the beauty of the stream, and sets forth with Mallika in a little boat. The English enter laughing and chattering. They talk of the Hindus and of Lakmé's beauty, and force their way through the hedge. Frédéric explains that in trespassing on the garden of a Brahman they commit sacrilege, and are liable to a deadly revenge. The women hurry away, leaving Gérald the design of Lakmé's jewels. He hides as Lakmé returns. She muses on love and seeing Gérald gives a cry. The servants

enter hastily but she says it was nothing
and sends them away. She upbraids
Gérald when they have gone, but he
wins her love by his flattery. Seeing
her father return, she makes him steal
away unseen. Her father finds the
hedge broken, however, and vows revenge on the trespassers.

Act II.—Scene. A market-place full
of people. The English enter, much
bothered by the merchants. The
bell for closing sounds ; and soldiers
clear the market-place. A fête begins,
and bayadères dance. Nilakantha
and Lakmé pass, he clothed as a peni-
tent. Frédéric tells Gérald that their
regiment moves at dawn to put down an
uprising. The English leave, and Nilakantha explains to Lakmé that he is disguised searching for revenge. A crowd
gathers and Lakmé sings to them a
legend of Vishnu and a Hindu maid.
The English officers return. Nilakantha recognises them and orders Lakmé
to sing the legend again. Gérald recognises her, but she pretends not to know
him. The English soldiers pass and
the officers go. Nilakantha plots with
the other Hindus, leaving Lakmé with
Hadji. Gérald returns. They exchange
vows of love. The crowd returns for the
Brahmin rites, but soon withdraws again.
Nilakantha stabs Gérald and disappears.
Lakmé bends over him and seeing that
he is not mortally wounded calls the
faithful Hadji to her aid.

Act III.—Scene. The heart of a forest. Gérald asleep, watched by Lakmé.
Songs of lovers are heard in the distance,
Lakmé goes to bring him sacred water.
Frédéric appears ; he has followed Gérald by the drops of blood. He reminds him of his betrothal to Ellen and
makes him promise to return to her.
He leaves, and when Lakmé returns
with the consecrated water in a cup
she notes a change in Gérald's manner.
He hears the soldiers singing in the distance, and she eats the leaf of a poison
plant. Nilakantha returning finds them
embracing. Lakmé tells her father that
Gérald, having drunk of the sacred

water, is consecrated. She offers herself as a sacrifice in his place and dies.

## DONIZETTI, GAETANO.

**La Favorita** (lä fä-vō-rē´-tä). The
Favourite.

Four-act opera. Book by Royer and
Waëtz (based on the play " Le Comte
de Commingues").

Produced, Paris, Dec. 2, 1840.

### CHARACTERS AND THEIR CREATORS.

ALFON´SO, *King of Castile* . . . . . . . . .bar.
BALDASSARE (sä´-rĕ) . . . . .Baroelhst, bass.
FERNAN´DO . . . . . . . . . . . .Duprez, tenor.
DON GASPARE (gäs-pä´-rĕ)
LEONORA (lä-ō-nō´-rä), Mme. Stolz, sopr.
INES (ē´-nĕs) . . . . . . . . . . . . . . . . . .contr.

Act I.—Scene I. Interior of a monastery. Chorus of monks passing. Fernando, in distraction, tells Baldassare
that he has fallen in love with a maid-
en, an angel of heaven (" Una vergine,
un angel di dio "). Baldassare is horrified and bids him begone (" Deh
vanne ! "). Scene 2. A flowery island.
Ines and other women gathering flowers.
A boat arrives with Fernando, blindfolded. His bandage is removed, but
his questions are not answered. At
length Leonora enters, and the lovers
have a rapturous reunion. She shows
him a parchment which will lead him to
glory provided he gives her up. He refuses passionately. Ines enters to say
that the King Alfonso has arrived. Leonora, in agitation, gives Fernando the
parchment and hurries away. Ines
warns him to be cautious. Left alone
he finds the parchment to be a commission with a title, and he welcomes his
chance for military fame (" Si, che u-
tuo solo accento ").

Act II.—Scene. The Palace of the Alcazar. The King is rejoicing with Don
Gaspare in the victory over the Moors,
giving the credit to the brave Fernando

om he is now waiting to load with
nours. An attendant announces a
essage from the chief churchman, and
aspare retires. The King broods over
e plots of his courtiers, but swears
ey shall never separate him from Le-
nora, his favourite ("Vien, Leonora,
piedi tuoi"). Don Gaspare returns,
d is sent to invite the court to the
te. Leonora enters with Ines, who is
nt away. The King pours out his
ve ("Ah, l'alto ardor"), but Leonora
proaches him with betraying her
d decoying her from home on false
omises. He tries vainly to console
r with her rich surroundings. The
urt gathers. Don Gaspare, in much
itation, gives the King an intercepted
ve-letter to Leonora. The King de-
ands the lover's name, which Leonora
thholds. Baldassare is led in. He
ars a mandate from the Pope, ordering
lfonso to put away Leonora and return
his queen. The King refuses fiercely,
it Baldassare's threats of excommuni-
tion terrify him, and Leonora flees.

Act III.—Scene. A room in the palace.
ernando, dreaming only of Leonora,
es the King and Don Gaspare enter.
he King has decided to yield to the
ope, and sends for Leonora. He wel-
omes Fernando and offers him whatever
may ask. He asks for Leonora. Leo-
ora enters, and the King reproaches
r ("A tanto amor"), but demands
at she marry Fernando at once. Le-
nora, left alone, is enraptured, and can-
ot believe the truth ("Fia dunque ve-
?") that she is to possess her lover
"O mio Fernando"), but she thinks it
shonourable for her, disgraced as she
, to wed him, and decides to die. She
aves Ines to tell him the whole truth.
When she is gone, Ines is arrested and
d away. The courtiers gather. The
ing gives Fernando a title and the
nd of Leonora, who, thinking Ines
as told Fernando of her past, consents
d is led to the altar. The courtiers,
vercome with the shame of making the
nknown Fernando a nobleman, and
en marrying him off to the King's dis-

carded mistress, treat him with contempt
on his return from the altar. He is infuriated, and challenges Gaspare. Baldassare enters to make peace, and Fernando embraces him. Baldassare tells
Fernando the truth, and he, in wild
rage, rebukes the King, who returns
with Leonora. Baldassare declares the
marriage null, and Fernando refuses to
keep his title and decorations. The
King orders him into exile, and Leonora
learns that Ines is under restraint.

Act IV.—Scene (composed in four
hours). Convent cloisters. Monks digging their graves and chanting ("Sca-
viam l'asilo"). Fernando, in dejection
returns to the monastery. Baldassare
welcomes him, then leaves to console a
youth who, he says, has just come as a
novice. Fernando, alone, bewails his
trust in hope, the gentle zephyr ("Spirto
gentil"). He is led into the chapel.
Leonora, clad as a monk, appears when
he has gone, and scans the faces of
the other monks. She has come to implore Fernando's forgiveness. Inside
the church he is heard taking his vows.
She sinks before the cross, and he, returning, finds her and bids her leave
("Ah, va, t'invola"). She tells him the
truth and begs his forgiveness ("Cle-
mente al par di Dio"). He takes her in
his arms ("Vieni, ah, vieni") and offers
to fly the cloisters once more with her.
She dreads such a step, and dies be-
seeching him to be faithful to his vows.
The monks, entering, are bidden to pray
for the dead young novice.

**La Figlia del Reggimento** (lä fēl'-yä
děl rěd-jĭ-měn'-tō), *I.*, La fille du
Régiment, *F.*, Marie, die Tochter des
Regiments, *G.* The Daughter of the
Regiment.

Two-act opera. Book by Bayard and
St. Georges.

Produced, Paris, February 11, 1840.

### CHARACTERS.

MARIA, created by Mme. Anna
Thillon....................sopr.

Marchesa di Birkenfeld (or Mag-
giorivoglio).............m.-sopr.
To'nio,
A young Swiss..............tenor.
Orten'sio,
Steward to the Marchesa.......bar.
Caporale.....................bass.
Sulpizio (sool-pe'-tsĭ-ō),
A sergeant..................bass.
Pesa'no.

Act i.—Scene. The Tyrolese mountains during the French occupation.
Peasants gather for war; women pray
to the Virgin. The Marchioness and
Ortensio are anxiously waiting news.
Peasants enter to say the enemy are re-
treating. All withdraw. Sulpizio, a
French sergeant, enters, followed by
Maria, the "daughter" of the Regiment and its vivandière. She rejoices
in having first seen the light of day on a
battle-field (" Apparvi alla luce sul campo guerrier "). Sulpizio proudly claims
credit for finding her on the battle-field
and adopting her. He speaks of the letter
he found with her; she speaks of the
young Swiss who saved her life and
whom she has learned to love. This
very Swiss now enters as a captive.
The French are about to kill him, but
she saves him and he joins in a toast.
Maria sings the song of the Regiment,
which has no equal as " everybody says
and knows " (" Ciascun lo dice ; ciascun
lo sà "). A drum calling to roll-call is
heard and the soldiers hurry away, taking Tonio under guard. He returns,
however, having eluded the others.
Maria and he are on cordial terms,
she welcoming his ardent vows (" A
voti cosi ardente "). They stroll away
together and Sulpizio and the Marchioness appear. She is reading the letter
found with Maria many years before.
It is addressed to her by the child's
father, and she recognises Maria as her
daughter by an early secret marriage
with Captain Roberto. But she tells
Sulpizio that Maria is her niece. The
soldiers return and Tonio enters, having

decided to enlist with the French fo
Maria's sake. He asks the Regimenta
fathers for her hand, and they grant it
But Sulpizio tells them that her aun
has appeared to claim her. Maria bid
her friends a fond farewell (" Convie
partir "), to the disgust of the Mar
chioness.

Act ii.—Scene. A salon. Sulpizi
wounded. Maria dressed as become
her new station, is mutinous against he
training. The Marchioness makes he
sing a romance by Caffariello (" Sorgev
il di ") but Sulpizio prefers the regimen
tal rataplan, in which Maria joins
the Marchioness leaves angrily. Or
tensio calls Sulpizio away to see a sol
dier who has come. Maria hears th
familiar music and the Regiment reap
pears, Maria welcoming all, particularl
Tonio, now an officer. The soldier
are sent to broach a cask of wine, an
the Marchioness finds Maria with Toni
and says the girl is engaged to the Duk
of Krakenthorp. Tonio goes, vowin
he will have Maria, who withdraw
weeping. The Marchioness reads t
Sulpizio a confession of her own secre
marriage and begs him to aid her i
marrying Maria to the Duke withou
telling the truth to the world. Th
mother of the Duke appears, he bein
unable to appear, and the contract i
about to be signed when Tonio leads th
Regiment in to protest against the bar
tering of its daughter (" Ti rincor
amata figlia "). Maria avows her grati
tude to the soldier who saved her fror
death (" Quando il destino "). Th
Marchioness relents and gives Maria t
Tonio, to the joy of the Regiment.

**Lucia di Lam'mermoor** (loo-chē'-
dē). Lucy, The Bride of Lammer
moor.

Three-act opera. Book, from Si
Walter Scott's novel, by Cammara
no.

Produced, Naples, 1835, with Pers
ani as " Lucia " and Duprez as " Ec
gardo."

## CHARACTERS.

ENRICO (ĕn-rē′-kō)...............bar.
  *Lord Henry Ashton of Lammermoor.*

EDGARDO...................tenor.
  *Sir Edgar Ravenswood.*

RAIMONDO (rä-e-môn′-dō).........bass.
  *Raymond Bide-the-Bent, Tutor.*

ARTURO (är-too′-rō)............tenor.
  *Lord Arthur Bucklaw.*

NORMANNO ....................tenor.
  *Warrior-chief of Ravenswood.*

LUCIA .........................sopr.
  *Lucy, Ashton's sister.*

ALISA (ä-lē′-sä)................sopr.
  *Alice, her maid.*

Time, Scotland, about 1670.

Act I.—Scene I. A vestibule. Norman and others are searching the tower. Henry enters brooding and tells Norman that he has lost his fortune and that his sister Lucy who can by marrying Arthur restore the Lammermoor prestige, refuses and spends her time mourning her dead mother. Meanwhile his enemy Edgar triumphs. Norman tells Henry that Lucy is in love; he tells how she was saved from a furious bull by a shot fired by Edgar, whom she now loves. At this Henry is insane with rage (" Cruda funesta smania "). A chorus of hunters enter and tell (" Come vinti la stanchezza ") how they had seen a mysterious horseman stealing from the tower. It was Edgar. Henry threatens revenge (" La pietade in suo favore "). Scene 2. A Park. Lucy and Alice. Lucy is longingly awaiting Edgar (" Regnava nel silenzio "). Edgar enters to say he is ordered to France as an ambassador. He tells how Henry has killed his father and robbed him of his heritage; he had sworn revenge on his father's tomb (" Sulla tomba che rinserra "), but Lucy's love has changed his ideal. The act ends in a love-duet.

Act II.—Scene. A room in the castle. Henry and Norman are waiting for Lucy. They speak of intercepting Edgar's letters and poisoning Lucy's mind against him. Henry asks Norman for the forged letter and bids him summon Arthur. As Norman goes, Lucy enters. Reproached for her gloom, she accuses him of cruelty; he shows her the letter and she believes Edgar false; he begs her to marry Arthur, who is even now coming with nuptial splendour. They quarrel in a duet (" Se tradirmi tu portrai ") and he threatens to kill Edgar if she persists. She prays for death. She leaves as Arthur enters with a great crowd, but is led back by Henry; intimidated by threats he utters under his breath, she signs the marriage contract. Suddenly Edgar appears and there are mutual reproaches in a powerful sextet (" Chi mi frena "). Raymond pleads that there be no bloodshed. Edgar, seizing the marriage contract, furiously upbraids Lucy for her faithlessness and will not listen to her explanation.

Act III.—Scene I. A room in the Castle on Wolf's Crag. Edgar alone rejoices in the storm. Henry enters and the men confront each other; they agree to fight at dawn, and pray for the sun to rise (in a duet " O sole, più rapido "). Scene 2. The chorus sings a song of jubilant victory (" D'immenso giubilo "). Raymond bids them cease their mirth, he tells how he had heard a groan from the bridal-chamber (" Dalle stanze ove Lucia ") and entering had found Arthur dead and Lucy with his bloody sword in her hand; she had gone insane. The mad girl now appears, thinking she is about to wed Edgar. She sings the famous mad-song (" O gioja che si senti "). Henry enters and sees her frenzy with bitter remorse. Scene 3. Outside the castle at night. Edgar alone before the tomb of his ancestors begs for speedy death from his sorrows (" Tombe degli avi miei "). People enter to say that Lucy has gone mad: he determines to see her; Raymond enters with the news that she is dead, and Edgar stabs himself.

## GLUCK, CHRISTOPH VON.

**Orfeo e Euridice** (ôr'-fā-ō ā ā'-oo-rē-dē'-chĕ), *I.*, Orphéus et Eurydice, *F.* Orph'eus and Euryd'ice.

Three-act opera. Book by Calzabigi. Produced, Vienna, October 5, 1762, in two acts. Revised and extended. Paris Académie, August 2, 1774 (with the rôle of Orfeo transposed for the tenor Legros. In 1859 restored by Berlioz for the alto Viardot-Garcia).

### CHARACTERS.

ORFEO (Orpheus) ...............alto.
L'OMBRA FELICE (*The Happy Shade*)
  (lôm'brä fä-lē'chĕ)...........sopr.
L'AMORE (lä-mō'-rĕ). *The God of Love* ......................sopr.
EURIDICE.......................sopr.

Act I.—Scene 1. A lonely wood with the tomb of Eurydice and a statue of Hymen. Rustics and nymphs dance about, calling on Eurydice to come back to life and her inconsolable husband, Orpheus. Orpheus, lost in sorrow, bids them leave him to his grief (" Chiamo il mio ben così "). He muses on his great loss (" Euridice ! ombra cara "). At length the God of Love enters and offers his aid. Even Jupiter has been moved to grant Orpheus the privilege of descending into the abode of the dead to bring back his wife, provided he promises not to look back at her till he has safely led her to the upper world. The god bids Orpheus restrain his ardour (" Gli sguardi trattieni ") and all will be well. The god vanishes and Orpheus sets forth boldly on his quest.

Act II.—Scene 1. The gates of Inferno. Demons and furies gather and the sound of Orpheus' lyre sets them to dancing and crying out with wrathful amazement at the hardy wanderer in Erebus (" Chi mai dell' Erebo "). The barking of the three-headed hound Cerberus is hinted in the orchestra. Orpheus begs them to be calm ; he tells them of the thousand pangs that rend

his heart (" Mille pene ") ; and the furies melt before him. They order the gates to open and the minstrel enters. Scene 2. Elysium and the blessed shades, who wreathe a blissful dance under the leadership of one of them. As they withdraw Orpheus enters rejoicing in the pure sky and peace of the region ("Che puro ciel !"). When he cries out for Eurydice, the happy shades tell him she is there, and bid him come to the realm of repose (" Vieni ai regni del reposo "). They lead in Eurydice, veiled.

Act III.—Scene. A cavernous egress from Inferno. Orpheus enters leading Eurydice. She rejoices at the reunion, but is distressed at his anxiety and his refusal to look at her. She is angered at his mysteriousness, and deeply grieves (" Che fiero momento "). At length he turns and looks at her. She falls down lifeless, and Orpheus in despair at the thought of losing her, cries " What can I do without Eurydice ! " (" Che farò senza Euridice "). He determines to kill himself that he may join her eternally. The God of Love entering stays his hand and restores Eurydice to life. The two embrace amidst a chorus of rejoicing at Love's triumph (" Trionfi amore ").

## GOUNOD, CHAS. FRANÇOIS.

**Faust** (fowst ; in *F.* fōst), in Germany this opera is called Margarete (mär-gä-rā'-tĕ), in Italy, Faust e Margherita (ā mär-gä-rē'-tä).

Five-act opera. Book from Goethe's poem, Part I, by Jules Barbier and Michel Carré.

Produced, Théâtre Lyrique, Paris, March 19, 1859.

### CHARACTERS AND THEIR CREATORS.

FAUST, *An old scholar*....Barbot, tenor.
MÉFISTOFELE ( mā-fē-stō-fĕl ), MEPHIS-
  TOPHELES,
  *The Evil Spirit*.....Balanqué, bass
VALENTIN (văl-än-tän), *Valentine*,
  *Brother of Marguerite*..Regnal, bar

WAGNER (văg-nẽr),
[in the German version,
BRANDER].....................tenor.

IEBEL (sĭ-ĕb-ĕl),
*A youth in love with Marguerite,*
Mlle. Faivre, m. sopr.

MARGUERITE (mär-gŭ-rēt),
*A village beauty,*
Mme. Miolan-Carvalho, sopr.

MARTHA (mär-tä)...Mme. Duclos, alto.

Act I.—Scene I. The study of the decrepit scholar Faust, who soliloquises on the vanity of research ("Interrogo invano"); he decides to kill himself and pours out poison. Bursts of song heard from peasant girls and men passing by, embitter his reflections on old age, and in his rage he calls on Satan, who to his amazement, appears and bargains for his soul, Faust asking for youth and pleasure ("Io voglio il piacer"). When Faust has signed, Mephistopheles shows him in a vision Marguerite at her spinning-wheel. Faust drinks to her, and is transformed to a richly dressed youth, who hurries away with the Evil One.

Act II.—Scene. A Fair, or Kermesse. Students, soldiers, etc., sing of wine, old men sing of peace, and young girls of love. Valentine enters wearing a medallion ("O santa medaglia") given by his sister; he is about to go to the wars and commends Marguerite to the charge of Siebel. As Wagner is singing a ballad of an old rat, Mephistopheles appears and joins the fun with a song of the calf of gold ("Dio del' or"). He tells fortunes, saying that Wagner will fall in battle, and that every flower Siebel touches will wither; he draws wine from the sign of the inn and as the goblet flares up, he drinks to Marguerite. Valentine indignantly knocks down the glass, and they draw swords. Mephisto draws a circle about him and Valentine's blade is shattered. When, however, the soldiers hold up their sword-hilts as crosses ("Tu puoi la spada frangere") the Evil One cowers while they pass. Faust arrives

and asks to see Marguerite; a bevy of students and girls waltz in ("Come la brezza") and Marguerite appears. Siebel moves toward her but is kept away by Mephisto, while Faust offers her his arm; she declines it with meekness and passes on. Faust and Mephisto follow her.

Act III.—Scene. The garden of Marguerite. Siebel is plucking a bouquet for his beloved Marguerite ("La parlate d'amor"); each flower withers at his touch till he dips his fingers in holy water; as he passes on in his search, Faust and Mephisto look in and see him place the flowers at Marguerite's window. When he has gone, Faust apostrophises the pure and lowly dwelling of his love ("Salve! dimora casta e pura," or "Salut, demeure!"). Mephisto reappears with a casket of jewels which he places on the steps, then draws Faust back into the shrubbery. Marguerite enters alone; she is humming a folk-song ("C'era un re di Thule"—"Es war ein König im Thule" in Goethe's Faust) which she intermits with memories of Faust. She spins awhile, then rises wearily and sees Siebel's nosegay, but drops it in ecstasy over the jewels, in which she decks herself ("Ah, è strano poter"). Martha, an old neighbour, enters and tells her they were doubtless left by a suitor. Mephisto and Faust appear and Mephisto by flirting desperately with the giddy crone leaves Faust a chance to woo Marguerite, who tells of her loneliness, the absence of her brother ("Al campo è il fratel"), and the death of her little sister. Siebel appears and Martha drives him away and goes home. Mephisto watches the crescent passion of the lovers ("Sempre amar"). As night falls Marguerite begs Faust to be gone, and enters her home. Mephisto drives Faust back, and when she opens her window to tell her love to the night-wind ("Ei m'ama"), Faust takes her in his arms, while Mephisto chuckles in the shadow.

Act IV.—Scene I (often omitted). A room in Marguerite's house. The betrayed and deserted girl, taunted by passers-by, reflects that her shame is due to love alone (" Nascose eran "), but when Siebel tries to console her with promise of revenge (" Quando a te lieta ") she determines to go to the church and pray for her false lover and for her unborn child. Scene 2. The square before the cathedral. The soldiers returned from war chant of victory and peace (" Deponiam il brando "). Valentine greets Siebel cordially, but is met only with embarrassment and evasion, and at last a plea that he forgive Marguerite. The soldiers pass on and Valentine gloomily enters his house. Faust appears full of remorse ; Mephisto tries sardonically to win her forth with a burlesque serenade to " Catterina " (" Tu che fai l'addormentata "). Valentine comes out and demands the cause of the serenade, sends Mephisto's mandolin flying with his sword, and falls to fighting with the reluctant Faust. Valentine throws away disdainfully his sister's medallion and Faust with Mephisto's aid wounds him mortally and flies. The citizens gather excitedly and finally Marguerite, on whom the dying Valentine invokes maledictions (" Stammi adascoltar "). When his body is borne away she prays for heavenly mercy, but Mephisto taunts her with despair and claims her while a chorus of monks combat with a chorus of demons.

Act v.—Scene 1 (often omitted). The Walpurgis revel in the Brocken, with a vision of Marguerite shown. Scene 2. A prison, Marguerite lying asleep in a heap of straw. Faust and Mephisto enter and Mephisto, who has procured the keys, urges Faust to waken the girl and make her fly with him. Faust is torn with repentance and blames himself for Marguerite's fall and for the madness in which she killed her new-born child (" Penetrato è il mio cor "). She wakes and greets him as her rescuer (" Pur fra il riso beffardo "). Her mind wanders and she lives over their first meetings. Mephisto tries to drag Faust away before the dawn be-

trays his presence, and Faust tries to lead Marguerite with him, but seeing the Evil One, she falls on her knees and prays (" O del ciel angeli "). She repulses Faust with her dying breath and a chorus of angels welcomes her re-deemed soul to heaven. A tableau (often omitted) shows her in Paradise, Faust, seeing her, prays and Mephisto falls beneath an Archangelic sword.

**Roméo et Juliette** (rôm-ā-ō ā zhü-yĕt'), *F.*, Romeo e Giulietta (rō'-mā-ā jool-yĕt'-tä), *I.* Romeo and Juliet

Five-act grand opera. Book by Barbier and Carré, a⁴ter Shakespeare.

Produced, Théâtre Lyrique, Paris, April 27, 1867.

Characters as in Shakespeare with the addition of Stephano, Romeo's page (played by a mezzo-soprano), and Gregorio, a watchman.

Act i.—Scene. The masked ball at Capulet's palace. Romeo disguised as a pilgrim meets and makes love to the young Juliet, who later confides her ecstasy in a famous waltz-song to her nurse. Her cousin Tybalt recognising the presence of his family enemy Romeo, is only restrained from inter-rupting the festivity by Capulet himself.

Act ii.—Scene. Juliet's balcony where Romeo finds her, and though in-terrupted by the impatience of the nurse and the tour of Gregorio and his watch-men, plights his troth.

Act iii.—Scene 1. The cell of Friar Laurence (or Lorenzo) who marries the young runaways. Scene 2. Street before Capulet's palace. Stephano in flippant serenade, provokes a street brawl between the retainers of the rival families, in which Tybalt kills Romeo's cousin Mercutio. Romeo coming from the church wishes to avoid a duel with Tybalt, now his kinsman, but taunted into a fight, kills him. Capulet appearing cries for " justice " from the Duke who enters. Romeo, to his wild grief, banished, but determines to see Juliet

ct IV.—Scene I. Juliet's chamber at
break. Her husband Romeo is
ding her farewell. When he has
en away, her father Capulet enters
h Friar Laurence and declares that
iet must marry Paris at once. The
ar secretly gives her a potion to keep
as one dead till Romeo can be sum-
ned to spirit her away. Scene 2
ually omitted). The wedding cele-
tion, in the midst of which Juliet
oons and is thought to have died.
ct V.—Scene. The tomb of the Cap-
ts, where Juliet lies in state. Romeo,
orant of the plot, has come to die at
side and takes poison. She wakens
see him perish in helpless regret and
s herself with his dagger.

## UMPERDINCK, ENGELBERT.

nsel und Gretel (hĕn'-zĕl oont grā'-
ĕl).

airy opera in Three "Pictures."
ok by the composer's sister, Frau
lheid Wette.

roduced, Weimar, 1895.

### CHARACTERS.

ER (pā'-tĕr),
  broom-maker ................bar.
RTRUD (gĕr'-troot),
  His wife .................m.-sopr.
NSEL,
  Their son (played by a girl)..m.-sopr.
TEL, Their daughter .........sopr.
KNUSPERHEXE (knoos'-pĕr-hĕx-ĕ),
  witch ....................m.-sopr.
DMÆNNCHEN (zänt'-mĕn-khĕn),
  The sandman, or sleep-fairy ...sopr.
USENDMÆNNCHEN (tow'-zĕnt-mĕn-
  hĕn), The dew man, or dawn-
  airy ..........................sopr.

ased on one of Grimm's stories,
graceful opera imports Wagnerian
s into the nursery.
ct I.—Scene. The home of Peter.
hungry children left alone bewail
r poverty, then fall to frolic. Their
mother finding them idle, in her eagerness
to punish them knocks over the only jug
of milk in the house. She sends them to
the woods to pick berries for supper and
falls asleep. Her husband returns slightly tipsy but burdened with provisions.
On learning of the errand of the children
he is terrified lest they fall into the
clutches of the Witch who lives on the
Ilsenstein in a honey-cake house and
bakes into gingerbread all the children
she can capture. Peter and Gertrud
rush out to rescue their children.

Act II.—Scene I. The depths of a fir
forest near the Ilsenstein. The children, at first delighting in the woods
and their liberty, suddenly realise as it
grows dark that they are lost. At length
they fall asleep under the spell of the
Sandman after they have said their
prayers invoking the fourteen angels,
who appear coming down a Jacob's ladder to guard the children.

Act III.—Scene. The Witch's House.
The angels and the forest have vanished, and the Dew-fairy appearing
wakens Gretel by sprinkling her with
dew from a bluebell. She wakens Hänsel by tickling him. They discover the
Witch's House with its oven and cage,
and a fence of gingerbread. They are
nibbling bits of this when the Witch
appears, takes the children captive and
gallops about on her broomstick weaving incantations. She prepares the
oven and tells Gretel to crawl in and
see if the cakes are ready. The shrewd
Gretel, however, has already used the
Witch's wand to release Hänsel from
the spell, and now pretending stupidity,
begs the Witch to show her the way.
The Witch bends over the oven and
the children pop her into it and close
the door on her. The fire roars within
at such a rate as the children dance with
glee, that finally the oven falls to pieces.
The gingerbread figures now lose their
honey-crust and prove to be children
whom Hänsel restores to life with the
wand. The jubilation is increased by the
entrance of Peter and Gertrud, and finds
its climax in the discovery that the

Witch has been turned into a huge
gingerbread-cake. A hymn of gratitude
ends the quaint masterpiece.

### LEONCAVALLO, RUGGIERO.

I **Pagliacci** (ē păl-yät'-chē), *I.* The
Strolling Players. Der Bajazzo (děr
bä-yät'-sō), *G.*

Two-act drama ; text and music by
Leoncavallo.

Produced, Milan, May 21, 1892.

#### CHARACTERS.

*Strolling Players :*

| | |
|---|---|
| Canio (kä'-nĭ-ō) | tenor. |
| To'nio | bar. |
| Bep'pe | tenor. |
| Ned'da, *Canio's wife* | sopr. |
| Sil'vio, *A villager* | bar. |

The scene is in Calabria on the Feast
of the Assumption, about 1865. It develops a play within a play, a tragedy
within a farce, and concerns the domestic crisis of a group of strolling players,
presenting the venerable story of Harlequin, Columbine & Co., to the peasants
of Italy.

After a brief orchestral flourish, Tonio, a hunchback, the clown of the
troupe, sticks his head through the curtain and begs permission to revive the
old Greek prologue. He steps forward
as Prologue and explains that the play
is a draught from real life, and shows
that actors have their genuine, as well
as their mimic tragedies. The pur-
port of this famous number may be expressed in an inversion of Shakespeare's
lines : " All the stage is a world, and
all the players merely men and women."

Act I.—At Tonio's signal the curtain
opens disclosing a cross-roads with a
rude portable theatre. The distant
sounds of a cracked trumpet and a be-
laboured drum call the peasants together
and they greet with joy the familiar
characters in whose costumes Canio,
Nedda and Beppe enter in a donkey-
cart. Silencing the crowd with his drum,

Canio announces the play for the eve
ing. Canio descends and boxes
ears of Tonio who loves Nedda a
has hastened to assist her. The cro
laugh at Tonio who wanders off angr
Beppe leads the donkey out and a vil
ger invites the players to drink. Bep
throws down his whip and goes
change his clothes. Tonio says he m
stay to clean the donkey. The villa
hints that Tonio lingers to flirt w
Nedda. Canio takes it as a joke.
says it is his place to play the ho
winked husband on the stage, but
the stage—the end of the joke would
different (" Un tal gioca "). He lo
his wife. After kissing Nedda, he g
with the men. The other peasants st
away to Mass on hearing the church-b
Nedda left alone broods over
fierce look Canio gave her. She w
ders if he suspects her. The sunli
thrills her with a vague ecstasy, and
revels in the song and sport of
birds (" Ballatella "). At the end
her rhapsody she finds that the hide
Tonio is listening. He makes ard
love (" So ben che difforme "—" I kr
I'm deformed "). She laughs him
scorn and advises him to save his lo
making for the stage. He pursues h
however, and she, picking up Bep
whip, slashes him across the face with
He curses her, swears revenge, a
stumbles away. Now her secret lov
Silvio, a villager, steals in over the w
In an ardent love-scene he pleads w
her to leave her hateful life, and j
him. She begs him not to tempt
(" Non mi tentar "), but promises
meet him that night after the play
over. Tonio, having seen them, hurr
away and returns with Canio. Sil
escapes, however, unrecognised in
thicket, while Tonio taunts Ned
Canio returns and demands the lov
name. He threatens to kill Nedda,
she will not speak. Beppe rushes
and disarming Canio implores him
dress for the play as the people are e
now approaching. Tonio hints that
lover may appear at the play. L

ne, Canio bewails his bitter fate donically, "On with the motley! Vesti la giubba") the people pay I want to laugh. If Harlequin steal ır Columbine—laugh, Punchinello, I everyone will applaud. Laugh at ır own frenzied love! laugh at the e that is rending your heart." In d grief Canio gropes his way into the atre.

Act II.—Same scene in the evening, ppe and Tonio beat the drum and w the horn, and the people crowd o their places. Nedda collects the ney and whispers a word of warning I promise to Silvio. The crowd ws impatient and at length the cur- n of the theatre opens showing a crude le room. Nedda (as Columbine) is tlessly waiting. The servant Taddeo away at market. She hears someone ing a guitar outside and the voice of ppe (as Harlequin) is heard outside a serenade (" O Columbina, il tenero o arlecchin"). As Columbine flut- s with delight, the loutish Taddeo ayed by Tonio) enters with a market- sket and makes ludicrous love. Har- uin entering the window kicks him. ddeo finding a rival generously sur- ders Columbine and promises to act sentinel. Columbine and Harlequin st gaily on the bird and wine fetched Taddeo. He gives her a sleeping tion to mix with her husband's (Pun- nello's) drink. Taddeo enters to rn the lovers, and Harlequin steals t of the window. Punchinello (played Canio) enters the door just in time hear Columbine promise to meet Har- uin at midnight. Canio's self-pos- ssion is shattered by the similarity of ese words with those he had heard in ıl life a few hours before. He goes with increasing difficulty. Columbine ws that no one has been with her, d Taddeo substantiates her story. nio lays such an ironic stress on the aise of Nedda's virtue that Canio ain forgets himself and frantic with alous rage demands the name of her er. Nedda tauntingly calls him

Punchinello, but he declares that he is a man again, not a puppet; and tells how he had taken her up as a starving orphan and loved her. He breaks down and the audience is much affected by the realism of the acting. Canio bursts out again in furious denunciation of Nedda's infidelity. The crowd ap- plauds. Nedda volunteers to leave, but Canio says she shall not get to her lover so easily, and again demands the man's name. Nedda tries to resume the play with a flippant air (" Suvvia, così terri- bile"). Canio shrieks with rage at her manner and once more demands her lover's name, which she solemnly swears on her mother's soul that she will not tell. Tonio appears at the back of the stage restraining Beppe. Nedda, de- termined to escape, dashes toward the audience, but Canio seizing her stabs her. As she dies, she cries Silvio's name, and he rushing forward is also stabbed to death. Canio gasps to the horrified crowd, "The comedy is fin- ished."

### MASCAGNI, PIETRO.

**Cavalleria Rusticana** (kä-väl-lĕ-rē′-ä roos-tĭ-kä′-nä). Rural Chivalry.

One-act melodrama. Book by Tar- gioni-Fozzetti and G. Menasci (based on a story by Giovanni Verga).

Produced, Rome, May 20, 1890.

CHARACTERS AND THEIR CREATORS.

TURIDDU (too-rĭd′-doo),
  *A peasant*....Roberto Stagno, tenor.
ALʹFIO, *A carrier*.. ............bar.
SANTUZZA (sän-tood′-zä),
  *A peasant girl*,
  Gemma Bellinconi, sopr.
LUCIA (loo-chē′-ä),
  *Turiddu's mother* ..........contr.
LOʹLA, *Alfio's wife* .........m.-sopr.

Scene.—A village square in Sicily on Easter Day. Before the curtain rises, Turiddu is heard carolling a *Siciliana* to Lola whom he loves. At rise of the curtain peasant men, women, and children enter the church. There is a chorus of May and love. The deserted Santuzza enters and going to Lucia's cottage asks where Turiddu is. Lucia says he has gone to Francofonte, but Santuzza says he was seen in the village. She cannot enter Lucia's house, being excommunicated. The whip and bells of the carrier are heard and Alfio appears singing of the joys of the road ("Il cavallo scalpita"), and also of the fidelity of his wife. He asks Lucia for wine. She says Turiddu has gone to the next town to fetch it. Alfio says he had seen him that very morning near his own cottage. Lucia is curious but Santuzza signs her to be silent. The Easter hymn is sung and all enter the church but Santuzza and Lucia. Lucia asks why Santuzza warned her to keep silent. Santuzza tells her, "Well, you know, mother" ("Voi lo sapete, O mamma"), how Turiddu, going to war had plighted troth with Lola, returning to find her wedded. He then won the heart and the honour of Santuzza, only to be reconciled with Lola, leaving Santuzza to despair. Lucia goes into the church sadly. Turiddu comes and when asked, says he has been to Francofonte. Santuzza gives him the lie, she had seen him at dawn leaving Lola's house. He denies that he loves her, but scorns Santuzza. Lola is heard singing a light flower-ballad ("Fior di giaggolo"). Lola comes and finding the two together, scornfully enters the church. Turiddu reviles Santuzza for awaking Lola's jealousy. She pleads with him frantically but vainly ("No, no, Turiddu"). He casts her off and enters the church. In her fury she tells Alfio, who enters, that Turiddu has betrayed him. Alfio swears revenge.

After an instrumental *Intermezzo*, the same scene. An Easter chorus of people returning from church. Turiddu speaks to Lola, but she is hurrying home expecting her husband. Turiddu invites all to join him in wine ("Viva il vino spumeggiante"). Alfio comes.

Turiddu invites him to drink with them. He says it would be poison to him. The women in alarm lead Lola away. Turiddu offers Alfio satisfaction and the men embrace, Turiddu according to custom biting Alfio's ear as a challenge. Turiddu begs Alfio not to blame Lola and thinks sadly of the lorn Santuzza. Alfio moves on to await Turiddu, who calls his mother and asks her blessing and her care for Santuzza if he does not return. He hurries away leaving her mystified and anxious. Santuzza and others appear. Confused voices are heard, then a woman screaming, "Turiddu is killed!" Santuzza and Lucia swoon.

## MASSENET, JULES E. F.

**Le Cid** (lŭ cēd). The Cid (Commander).

Four-act opera. Book (after Corneille) by Messrs. D'Ennery, Gallet and Blau.

Produced, Paris, November 30, 188—

CHARACTERS AND THEIR CREATORS

CHIMÈNE (shē-mĕn),
   *Daughter of De Gormas,*
         Mme. Fidès-Devriès, sop
THE INFANTA.....Mme. Bosman, sop
RODRIGUE (rôd-rēg'), *Son of Don Dièg—*
         M. Jean de Reszke, ten—
DON DIÈGUE (dôn dē-ĕg'),
         M. Edouard de Reszke, ba—
THE KING...Melchissédec, bar. or ba—
THE COMTE DE GORMAS (kônt dŭ Gôr-mä—
         M. Plançon, bass or b—
SAINT JAMES...M. Lambert, bass or b—
THE MOORISH ENVOY,
         M. Ballerory, bass or b—
DON ARIAS (don ă-rē-ăs), M. Girard, ten—
DON ALONZO (don ă-lôn'-zō),
         M. Sentein, ba—

Act 1.—Scene 1. Hall in the Com— de Gormas's palace. The Count a— his friends hear a trumpet fanfare su— moning them to be present at the knigh—

g of the young Rodrigo. The friends
y flatteringly that while honours are
the air, it were fitting the Count
ere appointed tutor to the King's
n. The Count says how much he
.ould value the honour. Chimène
nnot contain her joy at the rejoic-
gs in honour of Rodrigo. Her father
milingly accuses her of a tender in-
rest in the hero of the day, and ap-
auds her choice. Chimène, left alone,
joices in being able to love openly.
he Infanta, coming to visit her, reals her own love for Rodrigo ; but
eing Chimène's consternation, bids
er love on untroubled, as a princess
is not the right of loving whom she
ill. Scene 2. Gallery leading from
alace to Cathedral. Priests and peo-
e intone a psalm of thanksgiving
r deliverance from the Moors. The
ing announces his intention to knight
odrigo, though his valour is yet un-
roved, in compliment to Don Diègue.
odrigo enters, his noble bearing ad-
ired by the assemblage. The King
lministers the oath of knighthood and
resents the sword. Rodrigo apostro-
hises his sword, and invokes the aid of
is patron St. James, and, gazing at Chi-
iène, of his guardian angel. Chimène
ejoices in this sign of his love for her.
he King dismisses Rodrigo to the ca-
hedral. As a further proof of his re-
ard for Don Diègue, appoints him tutor
the Infanta. The friends of De Gor-
as express dissatisfaction. The King
ebukes them, and goes. Diègue returns
ask the hand of Chimène for his son.
he jealous Count repulses him, and
nds by striking him. The old man,
rawing his sword to avenge the insult,
easily disarmed by the Count, and
taunted by the others. Left alone,
e bewails his age and dishonour.
Iearing the voice of Rodrigo taking
ne oaths in the cathedral, he remembers
nat he has a champion in his son.
Vhen Rodrigo appears, he is told of
ne insult, which he angrily swears to
venge, and demands the offender's
ame. He is horrified to hear the

name of Chimène's father. She appears from the church at that moment.
His struggle between love and filial
duty is fierce, but duty triumphs. He
joins with his father in swearing vengeance.

Act II.—Scene I. Moonlight street in
Burgos with the Count's palace. Rodrigo enters, bemoaning his cruel fate,
and meditating suicide ; but overcomes
his weakness, meets the Count, and
challenges him. The Count disdains so
untried a foe, but Rodrigo forces him
to fight, and kills him. Diègue enters
with friends and commends his son,
who, however, is distracted with grief.
Diègue sympathises with his distress.
Chimène enters and wildly inquires
her father's murderer, going from one
to another, till she sees by Rodrigo's face
that he is the guilty one. She swoons.
A Requiem is heard chanted within.
Scene 2. Square in Burgos. Scene
of popular rejoicing. The Infanta goes
from group to group, distributing alms.
The King enters and is received with
acclamation, to his daughter's joy. Suddenly Chimène rushes in and calls excitedly for justice ; followed by Don
Diègue and his friends who give their
explanation of the Count's death. All,
in chorus, express varied emotions ; interrupted by a Moorish envoy, who
brings a defiant message from the
returning enemy. He is answered
proudly by the King and withdraws.
Then the King reproaches Rodrigo for
having deprived him of his best general
in this extremity. Diègue boldly suggests that Rodrigo take the place of
leader, and is seconded by the crowd
and Rodrigo himself, who begs a chance
of proving his valour before he dies.
The King consents.

Act III.—Scene I. Chimène alone in
her chamber at night, mourning her
dead father and her lost lover (" Pleurez,
pleurez, mes yeux ! "). To her surprise,
Rodrigo enters. They sing sadly of the
bygone days of their happiness. Rodrigo, enraptured to find that Chimène
still loves him, bids farewell before he

goes to die. Chimène, reproaching him for thinking of death, urges him to return victorious, so that his past may be forgiven; then shocked with herself at this disloyalty to her father, tries to take it back, and flees, ashamed. But Rodrigo, glorying in her love, feels that no enemy can be too strong for him. Scene 2. Rodrigo's camp. Soldiers amusing themselves. Rodrigo entering reproaches them for frivolity in the face of death, and announces that an overwhelming army is upon them. Some counsel flight; it is indignantly repudiated by Rodrigo, who, however, lets the cowards go. He thanks the brave few who remain. Scene 3. Rodrigo praying in his tent. St. James appears and promises him victory. Scene 4. The battle-field at sunrise. Rodrigo assures his soldiers of victory.

Act IV.—Scene I. Hall in the palace at Grenada. The runaway soldiers tell that Rodrigo has been overpowered and slain and they alone escaped. Diègue accuses them of cowardice, and says he had rather see his son dead than living as they. The ladies, entering, hear the bad news and cry out in grief. The Infanta tenderly consoles the old father, Chimène mourns her twice-broken heart, then publicly proclaims that she still loves Rodrigo, and is glad he knew it before he died. The King entering inquires the meaning of their distress when the town is joyful. Sounds of acclamation are heard, and Chimène understands at once that Rodrigo is alive, and a conqueror. Scene 2. Court of the palace. The King, etc., enter and take their places, while the crowd sings praises of the Cid. Procession of soldiers, captives, etc., lastly Rodrigo. He proffers his sword to the King, who tells him to keep it and name his reward. Rodrigo sadly answers that the only reward he craves is not in the King's power to grant. The King, understanding, bids Chimène answer, and is echoed by the people. Chimène complains that she should be asked to reward

her father's murderer, and the people fear she means to sentence him to death; but she can neither condemn nor forgive. Rodrigo, to relieve her, prepares to kill himself, but Chimène just in time prevents him, and confesses her love. General rejoicing.

## MEYERBEER, GIACOMO.

**L'Africaine** (läf-rĭ-kĕn), *F.*, Die Afrikanerin (dē äf-rĭ-kä'-nĕr-ĭn), *G.* The African.

Five-act opera. Book by Scribe. The Académie, Paris, April 28, 1865.

CHARACTERS AND THEIR CREATORS.

SELIKA (sā-lē'-kä), *An African queen in slavery,*
           Mme. Marie Saxe, sopr.
INEZ (ē-nĕs), *Daughter of Don Diego*....Mlle. Marie Batte, sopr.
ANNA, *Her attendant*............contralto.
VASCO DI GAMA (gä'-mä), *Portuguese naval officer,*
           Naudin, tenor.
NELUSKO (nä-loos'-kō), *A slave*...............Faure, bass.
DON PEDRO (pā'-drō), *President of the Royal Council*...Belval, bass.
DON DIEGO (dē-ā'-gō), *Member of the Council and Admiral*.....bass.
DON ALVAR', *Member of the Council and Admiral*.......bass.
GRAN SACERDOTE DI BRAMA (sä-chĕr-dō'-tĕ), *High Priest of Brama*...............Obin, bass.
GRANDE INQUISITORE (grän'-dĕ ĕn-kwēz-ä-tō'-re) *and Inquisitors.*

Begun in 1838 the opera was not finished till 1863, nor produced till two years after Meyerbeer's death.

Act I.—Scene. Royal Council chamber. Inez and Anna appear; Inez, who loves the absent Vasco, has been summoned by her father, who comes to tell her that she is to marry Don Pedro. He tells her that Vasco is lost at sea, and she hurries away. The council assembles to discuss further explorations. Vasco appears. He has escaped alone from the shipwreck at the Cape of Storms, but begs a new ship to try the passage again, explaining that he has bought in Africa two slaves, members of a race not conquered by the Spaniards. Selika and Nelusko are brought in. Questioned as to their country, they refuse to tell. Vasco, persisting in his request for a ship, is arrested, and is condemned for impiety.

Act II.—Scene. The prison of the Inquisition at Lisbon. Vasco asleep. Selika declares her love for him, but hides as Nelusko enters to kill him as a Christian and enemy. She intervenes and pleads for him, but is forced to wake him, whereupon Nelusko conceals his dagger and leaves. Vasco studies his map and she warns him against dangerous capes. He expresses his gratitude, just as Don Pedro and Inez enter with his pardon. Inez suspects that Vasco loves Selika; to allay her suspicions he presents Selika to her as a slave. Don Pedro announces that he has won the royal commission to make the exploration Vasco planned. He also announces that he is to wed Inez, who has consented in order to secure Vasco's freedom. The treacherous Nelusko is to go as Pedro's pilot. Vasco is left alone in despair.

Act III.—Scene. The "between-decks" of a ship. Sailors' chorus and prayer. Inez, now Pedro's wife, is with him. Nelusko appears and gives commands. Accused of treachery, he denies it, but gleefully sings of Adamastor, the god of the typhoon, whom he trusts to destroy the Portuguese. A strange ship is sighted and a boat puts out. Vasco comes aboard and tells Pedro that he is drifting into the same trap he himself fell into; that the ship will fall prey to the storm and to a horde of savages from the shore. Pedro scornfully orders him to be tied to a mast and shot. Selika threatens to stab Inez if Vasco is not released. She is hoodwinked, over-

powered and ordered to be scourged. But now the hurricane dashes on them, and in the panic, the ship is invaded by savages who overpower the crew.

Act IV.—Scene. Space between an Indian temple and a palace. The coronation ceremony of Selika. All the Portuguese have been condemned to death except Vasco, who had been found in chains. When all have departed, Vasco enters, guarded. He is overcome with the beauty of the place, an earthly Paradise. The Brahmans and soldiers are about to kill him, when Selika appears and rescues him, declaring that she has been plighted to wed him. Nelusko is overcome with grief at losing his beloved Selika. Vasco, in loving gratitude, consents gladly to the marriage, and the rites begin, when the mournful wails of Inez and her women are heard in the distance. He attempts to rush to her rescue, but the bridesmaids surround him and hale him to the altar.

Act V.—Scene I. The queen's gardens. Inez, under guard, is upbraided by the enraged Selika, because Vasco has found his way to her. Inez confesses that she and Vasco are lovers still, and begs to be killed; but Selika's anger subsides into anguish, and when Nelusko enters with soldiers, she orders Inez and Vasco to be put on board a ship and sent home. Scene 2. A promontory on which is a large tree—the manchineel, whose perfume produces an ecstasy ending in death. The lone Selika appears and, inhaling the odour, breaks into a rapturous delirium of love for Vasco, as she falls asleep. The sound of a distant cannon awakens her. Nelusko enters joyfully announcing that Vasco has sailed. With a despairing cry her soul departs, and Nelusko dies of grief at her feet.

**Les Huguenots** (lä-zǖg′-nō), _F._, Gli Ugonotti (lē oo-gō-nôt′-tē), _I._, Die Hugenotten (de hookh′-ĕ-nôt-tën), _G._ The Huguenots.

Four-act opera. Book by Scribe and Deschamps.

Académie, Paris, February 29, 1836.

CHARACTERS AND THEIR CREATORS.

VALENTINE (văl-ăṅ-tēn),
*Daughter of St. Bris,*
Mlle. Falçon, sopr.

MARGUERITE DE VALOIS (dŭ văl-wä),
*Betrothed to Henry IV.,*
Mme. Dorus-Gras, sopr.

URBAIN (ür-băṅ),
*Her page,* Mlle. Flécheux, sopr.; now
a contr. rôle.

COMTE DE ST. BRIS (săṅ-brē),
*Governor of the Louvre*.......Leda.

COMTE DE NEVERS (kôṅt dŭ-nŭ-
vĕr)....................Derivis.

RAOUL DE NANGIS (rä-ool dŭ näṅ-
zhē), *A Protestant*..Nourrit, tenor.

MARCEL (măr-sĕl),
*His servant*........Levasseur, bass.

MAUREVERT (mō-rŭ-văr).

TAVANNES (tă-văn).

DE RETZ.

MERU (mŭ-rü).

Act I.—Scene I. A feast at the castle of De Nevers. The revellers persuade Raoul to tell of a beautiful stranger he had once rescued from a crowd of boisterous students, and had since loved though he does not know her name. His servant, a stern old Protestant soldier, appears and is persuaded to sing an anti-Popery song, which the Catholic noblemen take good-naturedly. A servant, followed by Valentine, heavily veiled, whispers to De Nevers, who leaves with the veiled woman. Raoul recognises her as his mysterious love. De Nevers returns. The page Urbain appears and with much flourish delivers to Raoul a letter, which he passes about; though not signed, it is recognised as Marguerite's writing and is an invitation to come blindfolded to Court. The noblemen shower the puzzled Raoul with congratulations. Scene 2. The château and gardens of Marguerite.

Surrounded by her attendants, she is rhapsodising over love, "A questa voc sola." Valentine enters. She has become a favourite of Marguerite and at her request has asked De Nevers t absolve her from the promise of mar riage arranged by her father. Urbain laughingly announces that a cavalier with eyes blindfolded is waiting. Raoul is led in. Marguerite bids him remove the veil, and he is overcome by her beauty. She exacts of him a promise to de as she bids. The Gentlemen of the Court, including Valentine's father, St Bris and De Nevers enter. She make them all take an oath of peace and friendship. Marguerite, who is eage to reconcile the Catholics and Protes tants, who are already drifting toware the St. Bartholomew massacre, an nounces that Raoul is to wed a lady o her choice. St. Bris brings in his daugh ter, and Raoul recognising her as the veiled woman who had called on De Nevers, suspects her honesty, and firml declines to wed her. De Nevers and St. Bris swear revenge, and Valentine i overcome with humiliation.

Act II.—Scene. Two inns and a chapel on the bank of the Seine. Cath olic students at one tavern and Hugue not soldiers at the other are making holiday. A bridal procession appears leading De Nevers and Valentine and St. Bris and Maurevert. Valen tine remains at the chapel to pray. De Nevers leaves. Marcel enters and delivers a letter to St. Bris, who finds in it a challenge. He plots with Maure vert to assassinate Raoul, and is over heard by Valentine, who warns Marcel and leaves. St. Bris and Raoul arrive and prepare for the duel, when Marcel seeing Maurevert appear with soldiers, summons the Huguenot soldiers from the inn. The Catholics hasten from theirs and a riot is brewing. Marguerite and Urbain appear, and the com batants begin recrimination. Valentine appears and Marguerite explains to Raoul the purpose of Valentine's visit to De Nevers. He learns with grie that she has now become the wife of De Nevers, who appears in a barge and takes her away.

Act III.—Scene. The château of De Nevers. Valentine, alone, bemoans her lot, wedded to De Nevers, loving Raoul. Raoul appears. She conceals him behind a curtain just before the entry of St. Bris, De Nevers and others, who have met to plan the annihilation of all the Huguenots. There is an impressive scene, " The Blessing of the Poignards." De Nevers refuses to stoop to assassination ; he breaks his sword and is led away. St. Bris bids them await the signal of the bell for the general massacre. Monks enter with a basket of white scarves. They bless the swords. When all have gone, Raoul steps out, eager to warn his friends and slay the conspirators. Valentine pleads with him not to go lest her father and her husband perish. She clings to him lovingly and he echoes her passion till the distant bell announces the slaughter ; they look out into the street and see the St. Bartholomew massacre in full course. She faints with terror for him and he leaves by the window. [The performance usually ends here.]

Act IV.—Scene. A cemetery and church. Within the church are Huguenot women and children preparing to die for the faith. Raoul meets Marcel, who falls wounded. Little remains to them but to die bravely. De Nevers has been killed for interceding. Valentine appears, dishevelled and breathless. She begs Raoul not to die but to live for her. Her husband is dead. Marcel will join them in marriage. The religious hymns from the church are interrupted by sounds of musketry and the fury of the assassins. After a silence the three begin to sing Protestant hymns. The Catholics appear. St. Bris leading a company of soldiers. Though Valentine tries to restrain him, Raoul declares that he is a Huguenot. Valentine and Marcel cry, " And we also." St. Bris gives the command to fire, not seeing his daughter. She dies

declaring that she will intercede for her father in heaven.

[In some versions there is a scene in which Raoul makes wild but vain appeals to Marguerite to put a stop to the massacre.]

**Le Prophète** (lŭ prô-fĕt), *F.*, Il Profeta (ĕl prō-fä′-tä), *I.*, Der Prophet (dĕr prô-fāt′), *G.* The Prophet.

Five-act opera. Book by Scribe.

Produced, Paris, April 16th, 1849, with Mme. Viardot-Garcia as *Fides*, and Roger as the *Prophet.*

### CHARACTERS.

JEAN DE LEYDEN (zhôń dŭ lĕd-äń),
*An innkeeper. The Prophet*...tenor.

COMTE D'OBERTHAL (kôńt d'ô-bĕr-täl).

GIO'NA, MA'THISEN, ZACCA'NA,
*Three Anabaptist Leaders of the Revolt.*

FIDÈS (fē-dĕs),
*Mother of Jean*..............alto.

BERTA,
*His betrothed.*................sopr.

*Note.*—The hero of the opera is John of Leyden, an historical personage, who led a religious revolt that succeeded for a time in Holland, 1534.

Act I.—Scene. Dordrecht. Peasants and millers are at breakfast. Berta and Fidès meet. Berta, a poor orphan, is to be wed to Jean ; the bridegroom even now waits her. Berta says she cannot wed without the consent of Oberthal, the lord of the domain. They start to ask this, but meet with three Anabaptists, who enter, and by talk of liberty arouse the peasants to attack the Castle. Oberthal appears at the gates and scornfully reviles Giona as his late thievish cellar-keeper. This cools the mob's fury. Berta and Fidès interrupt to ask Oberthal's consent to the girl's marriage, but he, smitten with her beauty, refuses it, and has her and Fidès dragged into the Castle. In the distance the hymn of the Anabaptists is heard.

Act II.—Scene. Jean's inn at Leyden. A soldier and peasants drinking. Jean serves them, but dreams of Berta's return. The three Anabaptists enter. They are struck by Jean's likeness to the image of the patron saint of the city of Münster. They learn from a peasant that he is also brave and versed in the Scriptures. Left alone with Jean, they question him. He tells them of dreams that have disturbed him by showing the people kneeling and hailing him king, while he reads in blazing letters a warning against drawing the sword; then a sea of blood envelops him and as he tries to climb to the throne it is swept away; demon-voices roar round him, but give way to a soft voice whispering "Mercy." They hail him as their leader, but he prefers Berta and lowly peace, and they leave him. A sound of horses is heard and Berta rushes in in terror, hiding, just before Oberthal and soldiers hasten after her. Oberthal demands the delivery of Berta, and vows otherwise to take the life of Fidès, who is dragged in and threatened with a soldier's axe. Jean turns toward Berta, who comes from concealment, but cannot see his mother killed, and in despair surrenders Berta to Oberthal, who drags her away swooning. Fidès pours out her gratitude (in a famous air "Ah, mon fils" or "O figlio mio") and leaves him to his misery. The Anabaptists enter and offer him the crown and sword. He accepts with fire, but when they tell him he must give up all his family ties and depart without seeing his mother again, he wavers; at length, however he follows them.

Act III.—Scene 1. The Anabaptist Camp, near a frozen lake in Westphalia. A battle is heard in the distance, and Anabaptist soldiers drag in a monk and other prisoners whom they and their women taunt. A band of skaters arrive with food, for which the soldiers

barter spoils. Zaccana sends the visitors away and sends the soldiers to sleep. Scene 2. Zaccana's tent. He and Mathisen meet. They decide to assault Münster at once before Oberthal's father can bring up reinforcements. Oberthal is brought in as prisoner. He is not recognised in the dark and offers to join them, swearing to help destroy the abbeys and the nobility. They declare that he must help destroy his father, and he consents. Giona strikes a light gaily and they at recognise Oberthal. They order him at once to the gallows, as Jean enters. He is determined to see his mother, and Zaccana says she will be killed if he attempts it. Oberthal is led past, but Jean demands his safety and, left alone with him, learns that Berta had leaped into the river to save her honour, and had escaped to Münster. A mutiny is threatened now by the soldiers chafing at Jean's inaction, till he, after prayer and exhortation and the seeing of heavenly vision, sets forth with them to the assault.

Act IV.—Scene 1. A square in Münster. The citizens are paying tribute of gold to the victorious Anabaptist and secretly cursing the impostor Prophet, who is to be proclaimed Emperor of Germany. Fidès enters, disguised as a beggar. The citizens give her alms and depart; Berta enters as a Pilgrim. Recognising Fidès by her voice, she tells of her flight from Oberthal, her rescue by a shepherd, her return to the inn, where she learned Jean and Fidès had gone to Münster. Fidès says that Jean is dead; she had found blood-stained clothes of his and she believed the mysterious Prophet had killed him. Berta vows to kill the Prophet in revenge. Scene 2. Interior of the Cathedral. The coronation procession of Jean passes across. Fidès kneeling has not seen him and prays for his destruction, unwitting who he is. Jean re-enters as all kneel, and takes the crown. Fidès and he recognise each other. Mathisen tells him that if he acknowl edges her, she dies, and he disavows her. When she proclaims herself his mother, he says she is insane. She is about to be killed, but he intervenes, saying she has lost her reason. He then declares that if she still calls him her son, his followers must kill him. Faced by this crisis, Fidès denies him, and he is hailed as a miracle-worker for restoring the reason of Fidès, who is made prisoner.

Act v.—Scene 1. Prison in Münster Palace. The three Anabaptists meet; and learning that the true Emperor is marching on the town to recapture it, discuss a paper sent offering them clemency if they surrender Jean. Soldiers lead in Fidès, who, left alone, broods bitterly over her son's faithlessness to her. Jean enters, and she makes him kneel to implore her pardon. She demands that he renounce his power and repent. He consents. An officer enters to announce that the city is betrayed to the Emperor, and that a frantic woman was found trying to set fire to the palace. Berta is dragged in. Learning Jean's identity, she is revolted by his bloody ambition, and cursing him, stabs herself. Jean sends his mother away to safety, and determines to revenge himself on the traitors. The scene changes to 2. The Banquet Hall. Jean after sending two officers secretly to close the gates as soon as the Emperor's forces enter, joins wildly in the revel. The three Anabaptists now rush in, leading the hostile troops. They claim Jean as their prisoner. He cries that they are his. A great explosion rends the wall and all perish in the flames. Fidès rushes in to forgive her son, and dies with him.

**Robert le Diable** (rō-băr lŭ dĭ-ăbl'), *F.*, Rober'to il Dia'volo, *I.*, Robert der Teufel (toi' fĕl), *G.*, Robert the Devil.

Five-act opera. Book by Scribe and Delavigne.

Produced, Paris, Académie, November 21. 1831.

CHARACTERS AND THEIR CREATORS.

ROBERT,
    *Duke of Normandy*, Nourrit, tenor.
BERTRAM (băr-trän),
    *His friend* ........Levasseur, bass.
RAIMBAUT (răn-bō),
    *A Norman peasant*...Lafont, tenor.
ALBERT,
    *A knight*.....................bar.
ISABELLE,
    *Princess of Sicily*,
        Mme. Cinti-Damoreau, sopr.
ALICE,
    *A Norman peasant*, Mlle. Dorus, sopr.
THE ABBESS.........Signora Taglioni.

[Next to Die Zauberflöte, probably the worst libretto in existence.]

Act I.—Scene. A tented space near the port of Palermo. The Sicilian knights are drinking. Robert introduces himself and joins the chorus. A Norman minstrel (Raimbaut) appears and being asked to sing, tells the history of Robert the young duke ("Regnava un tempo"). According to this the Princess Bertha was won and wedded by a fiend in human disguise; their son was Robert called "the fiend." Robert in rage, declares himself the subject of the song, and orders his servants to hang the minstrel; he spares the man's life, however, when he learns that Raimbaut's betrothed has a message for him. Alice is shown in, Robert's heart softens toward her and he orders the boisterous knights away. Alice, his foster-sister, tells him his mother is dead, and dying had told her to go to her son ("Vanne, disse, al figlio mio") and beg him to reform his ways, and, on the day he felt worthy, to read the scroll which Alice shows: Robert feels unworthy to read. He tells Alice he has fallen in love with the Princess Isabelle, and in attempting to carry her off, was set upon by the knights of the court, and only saved by Bertram. Alice advises him to write to the Princess, whom he has not since seen. He dictates a letter and gives it to Alice to deliver, promising to consent to her marriage with Raimbaut. As she goes, she meets Bertram, who terrifies her by his resemblance to a picture of Satan she had seen. Robert confesses to Bertram he thinks his influence evil, but is persuaded to join the gambling knights, singing a Sicilian luck-song ("Sorte amica"). He loses everything he possesses in the game and receives only jeers from the others.

Act II.—Scene. Alone the Princess muses on her ill-fated love ("Dell' umana grandezza"). Alice and others enter with petitions, and Alice gives the Princess Robert's letter, which she receives with delight ("Ah, vieni"). She leaves just as Robert and Bertram enter. Robert has challenged the Prince to a bout at arms. A herald announces that the Prince desires the combat to be mortal; he leads Robert away to the forest. Isabelle and the King, Bertram, Alice, Raimbaut, and others assemble. After dances and song, the herald announces to Isabelle that the Prince wishes her to arm him. She gives his squires the arms, but secretly wishes Robert success. Bertram aside gloats over the fact that Robert is lost in the woods and will not come. The others wait anxiously for him, but he does not appear, and the procession moves away.

Act III.—Scene I. A gloomy place with a ruined temple, a cavern and a cross. Raimbaut has come to meet Alice here, but Bertram appears and giving him gold advises him not to be hasty about marrying Alice. The minstrel goes away in doubt. Bertram alone gloats demon-like over the approaching doom of Robert, who is actually his son. The chorus of fiends is heard ("Demoni fatali," the "Valse Infernale") and Bertram enters their fiery cave. Alice comes down the mountain dreaming of Normandy ("Nel lasciar la Normandia"). She is

terrified by the sounds from the cavern, but hearing Robert's name called she stops, embraces the cross and swoons. Bertram enters in confusion; the demons have warned him that if he does not win Robert's soul before midnight, he loses him forever. Seeing Alice, he threatens her and her betrothed and all her friends with death if she discloses what she has heard. Robert comes gloomily and Bertram orders her away. She goes reluctantly, and Bertram tells Robert she is agitated with jealousy of Raimbaut; he tells Robert that the Prince has used sorcery and must be met with it. Scene 2. Mysterious vaults. Bertram entering calls statues of nuns to life and bids them entice Robert when he comes, and make him pluck the branch of magic power. When he withdraws, the nuns dance a wild Bacchanale and surround Robert, who enters, but in terror seeks to fly. After the ballets of "Intoxication," and "Gaming," and "Love," he seizes the branch.

Act IV.—Scene. Isabelle is in her apartments surrounded by bridesmaids; she is to marry the Prince. As he enters, Robert appears and with his magic branch puts all to sleep, then awakens Isabelle. She rebukes him for not being present at the combat, and pleads with him to throw off the infernal influence ("Roberto, o tu che adoro," or "Robert, toi que j'aime"). He consents, breaks the branch, and kneels at her feet. The court awakens from its sleep and Robert is seized and dragged away. Alice prays for him and the Princess swoons.

Act V.—Scene. Cloisters. A chorus of monks. Robert enters, dragging in the reluctant Bertram. Bertram promises him success after all if he will sign a scroll. As he is about to do so, he hears a hymn sung in the chapel, and his childhood faith wakes in him. Bertram tries to win him away to despair, and at last declares himself Robert's father. Alice enters and struggles for Robert with the fiend-father; as he finally produces a parchment and a stiletto, Alice presents the mother's will; in it Robert reads a warning not to trust the counsels of the fiend. As he still hesitates, the clock strikes twelve. Bertram vanishes in despair and a chorus of angels and men sing a hymn of joy.

## MOZART, WOLFGANG AMADEUS.

**Il Dissolu'to Puni'to ; ossia il Don Giovanni** (dôn jō-vän'-nē), *I.*, Don Juan (dôn hwän in *Sp.*, in *F.* dôñ-zhwäñ, in *E.* dän joo'-än).

Two-act opera buffa. Book by Lorenzo da Ponte (from Tirso de Molina's story, "El combidado de piedra"). Composed in great haste and produced, Prague, October 29, 1787.

CHARACTERS AND THEIR CREATORS.

Don OTTA'VIO........Baglioni, tenor.
Don GIOVANNI.......Luigi Bassi, bar.
LEPOREL'LO,
  *His servant*...Felice Ponziani, bass.
Don PEDRO (pā'-drō),
  *Il Commendatore* (in German, Der Komthur), Commandant of Seville.
MASET'TO, *A peasant.* } Loli, bass.
DONNA ANNA,
  *Daughter of Don Pedro,*
    Signora Teresa Saporitti, sopr.
DONNA ELVIRA (ĕl-vē'-rä) ..Micelli, sopr.
ZERLINA (tsĕr-lē'-nä).....Bondini, sopr.

Act I.—Scene I. Seville Square before the Commendatore's palace at night. Leporello complains of working for his master night and day ("Notto e giorno faticar"). Don Giovanni now enters ; he has attempted outrage upon Donna Anna, and being frustrated is taking flight ; she clings to him to discover who he is and calls for help. Her father, the Commendatore, hurrying to her rescue, is killed by Don Giovanni, who slinks away undiscovered, followed by his disgusted and terrified servant.

Ottavio, Anna's fiancé, enters with servants and torches. He and Donna Anna swear revenge against the murderer ("Fuggi crudele"; Schwur-Duett). Scene 2. A street. Don Giovanni enters hastily. Leporello protests against his master's mode of life, but is threatened and cajoled, and told of a new amour. Donna Elvira is seen coming and the men withdraw to one side, while she bewails her lost honour and Don Giovanni's perfidy ("Ah chi mi dice"). Not recognising her, the Don comes forward flirtatiously, only to be bitterly rebuked. The Don referring her to Leporello, steals away. Leporello tells her that she is only one of a long list of victims to the Don's gallantry ; he unrolls a catalogue of them ("Madamina, il Catalogo"; Register-Arie), a thousand or more of all countries, ages and conditions. When he has gone, she breaks out into a prayer for revenge ("Mi tradi quell' alma ingrata"). Scene 3. The country near the Don's palace. Zerlina and Masetto, about to be married, make merry with the other peasants ("Giovenette, che fate"). The Don and his servant appear, and the Don questions Zerlina and orders the others to his palace for refreshment. Masetto, in spite of his jealous dread, is dragged away by Leporello. The Don promises the terrified girl that he will marry her, and after some fluttering she accepts the decoy (in a duet, "La ci darem"). They are confronted by Donna Elvira, who leads the girl away from danger. Ottavio and Anna in deep mourning enter. The Don now attempts to play the gallant to Anna, and pretends he does not know the cause of her mourning. Elvira returns and denounces him ("Non ti fider, O misera"), whereupon he declares that she is insane. Ottavio and Anna are deceived for the moment, but when, after inviting them to his palace, he follows Elvira away, Anna tells Ottavio that she believes Don Giovanni to be the mysterious man who had entered her room at night, and in his flight had killed her father. She describes the scene in detail and declaring to Ottavio " Now you know the villain" (" Or sai che l'indegno "), she bids him revenge her. When they have gone, Leporello enters, deciding to quit his distasteful service, and when Don Giovanni enters, he tells him how he has filled Masetto and the others with food and drink only to have Zerlina return with Elvira, who had told the company of the Don's misdeeds. Leporello tells how he finally got her out of the house, and the Don decides that a carousal with the peasants will please him (" Finchè dal vino "). Scene 4. A garden. Zerlina is trying to console the indignant Masetto, finally crying, " Beat me, beat me" (" Batti, batti "). Just as he is won over, the Don's voice is heard; Masetto and she hide and the Don enters with the peasants; they pass on and the Don discovers Zerlina; as he pleads with her, he also descries Masetto and with presence of mind invites him to join them at the feast. When they have gone Ottavio enters with Anna and Elvira, all three in dominoes and masks. In the " Mask-Trio" they disclose their plan to learn the true character of the Don who with Leporello appears and invites them in. Scene 5. A great ball-room. The peasants are revelling in the hospitality of the Don, and the attentiveness of his servant. Both master and man flirt outrageously, and Masetto is in torment, as the Don drags Zerlina away. Her voice is heard crying for help, and the three masked people entering realise the Don's blackness of heart. Zerlina escapes and throws herself on their protection. The Don tries to throw the blame on Leporello, but the three remove their masks and denounce his crimes. Thunder is heard foreboding his doom, but the Don laughs at fate.

Act II.—Scene I. A street at evening. Leporello is trying to get away from his master, who finally bribes him with money to carry out his plot. He exchanges cloaks and hats with the reluctant servant, and when the love-lorn Elvira appears at a window, the Don from concealment implores her to forgive him and come down. She is overwhelmed with joy at his return and descends. Leporello imitates his master's voice, and makes such love to her that when the Don makes a noise as if killing someone, she flees hastily with Leporello. The coast is now clear for the Don's plot against Zerlina, and he sings a serenade to bring her to the window (" Deh vieni alla finestra "). But Masetto enters with his friends armed with cudgels and guns. Thinking the Don to be the servant, he tells his plan to kill the libertine ; the Don sends the villagers on a wild-goose chase, beats the stupid Masetto and gets safely away. Zerlina entering tries to appease her distracted and aching lover by her tenderness (" Vedrai carino "). Scene 2. Portico of Donna Anna's palace. Leporello and Elvira enter, he wondering how to get rid of the tenacious servants and torches. Ottavio is trying to comfort Anna. Leporello in eluding Elvira comes upon Masetto and Zerlina, but after pleading for pardon escapes by running. Ottavio declares himself convinced of the Don's guilt, and promises to console Anna " his treasure" (" Il mio tesoro ") with speedy revenge. Scene 3. A square with a statue of the Commendatore. The Don and Leporello groping along, meet in the dark. The Don laughingly tells of an amorous encounter he had with some strange woman who thought him to be Leporello. The statue speaks warningly. Leporello is terrified, but the Don only mystified ; he has Leporello read the inscription " On the impious wretch who caused my death. here I wait revenge." He laughs and says : " Tell the old buffoon, that I expect him to dinner to-morrow evening" ; he is greatly amused at Leporello's terror, and asks the statue itself. " Will you come to dinner?" The statue answers " Yes," and the Don, amazed, drags the trembling Leporello home. Scene 4. A garden. Ottavio is trying to pacify Donna Anna with hopes of speedy revenge, but when he talks of love she bids him wait (" Non mi dir "). Scene 5. Banquet-hall in Don Giovanni's palace. Musicians play while the Don eats, served by Leporello, who steals many mouthfuls meanwhile. (In this scene Mozart alludes to and parodies an aria from his rival Martin's opera, " La Cosa Rara," and later parodies his own " Non più andrai " from " Le Nozze di Figaro.") Elvira enters to plead with him to repent. the last proof of her love (" L'ultima prova "), but he ridicules her and she leaves her. As she goes, she gives a scream of terror. The Don sends Leporello to learn the cause. He cries out and fastens the door. The musicians take flight, and Leporello explains as he shivers, that the statue has come. Its knock is now heard, and the Don goes to the door while Leporello crawls under the table. The Don ushers in the statue and orders Leporello to bring him food, but the statue says he does not feed on mortal food ; he has come to invite the Don to sup with him. In spite of Leporello's pleading, the Don jauntily accepts. The statue takes his hand, and in this chill clutch the Don learns fear for the first time. He refuses the statue's pleading that he repent, however, and is enveloped in flames and haled by demons down to eternal punishment.

**Le Nozze di Figaro** (lä nôd'-zĕ dē fē'-gä-rō), *I.*, Die Hochzeit des Figaro (dē-hôkh'-tsīt dĕs fē'-khä-rō), *G.*, Le Mariage (or Les Noces) de Figarò (lŭ mär-ĭ-äzh (or lä nôs) dŭ *F.*), *F.* The Marriage of Figaro.

Four-act opera buffa. Book by Lorenzo da Ponte (after the comedy by Beaumarchais).

Composed, December, 1785—April, 1786. Produced, Vienna, May 1, 1786.

CHARACTERS AND THEIR CREATORS.

CONTE ALMAVIVA (kôn'-tä äl'-ma-vē-vä),
Mandini, bar.
FIGARO,
His valet ............Benucci, bass.
DR. BARTO'LO..........Occheley, bass.
BASILIO (bä-sē'-lĭ-ō),
A singing-master....Bussani, tenor.
ANTO'NIO,
Gardener.....................bar.
DON CURZIO (dôn koor'-tsĭ-ō),
A magistrate...............tenor.
CHERUBINO (kä-roo-bē'-nō),
The Count's page,
Signora Mandini, sopr.
LA CONTES'SA,
The Countess (in German Die Gräfin) (dē grä'-fĭn),
Signora Storace, sopr.
SUSAN'NA,
Her maid......Signora Laschi, sopr.
MARCELLINA (mär-chĕl-lē'-nä),
Dr. Bartolo's housekeeper,
Signora Bussani, m.-sopr.
BARBARINA (bär-bä-rē'-nä),
Antonio's daughter,
Frau Gottlieb, sopr.

[The story is really a sequel to that in Rossini's " Barber of Seville."]

Act I.—Scene. A half-furnished room in the Count's castle near Seville. Figaro and Susanna talk of their coming marriage. He thinks the room very convenient ; " ding-ding ! " he can soon answer his master's bell ; " dong-dong ! " she can soon answer that of her mistress. Susanna suggests that the bell may send him three miles away while the Count comes in his place. She tells the jealous Figaro of the Count's attention to herself. She is called away and he fumes and threatens to lead the Count a dance he will not like. When he has gone, Bartolo and Marcellina enter, with a document, Figaro's former agreement to marry her. She is planning to break up the match between Susanna and Figaro, so that she can marry him herself ; Bartolo, in love with Susanna, seeks revenge ("La Vendetta ") on his successful rival. He goes and Susanna enters. The two women cast aspersions on each other ironically, and Marcellina leaves. Cherubino the page enters, and says the Count has threatened to discharge him for flirting with Barbarina ; he is really in love with the Countess, and the Count is jealous of him. He says that he is a madman over love, and has written a poem (he sings "Non so più cosa son "). The Count is heard coming and he has just time to hide behind a great chair. Basilio is next heard and Susanna just manages to conceal the Count behind the chair and Cherubino in it. Basilio retails a deal of gossip about the page and the Countess till the Count rises angrily. Susanna pretends to swoon, and the two men support her with great solicitude. The Count tells how he discovered the page hiding under the table at Barbarina's. In illustration he lifts the cloth Susanna had thrown over Cherubino, and again discovers the page. The Count is first consternated, then angry. Peasants come in to deck the bridal-chamber, and the Count declares that he will send Cherubino to the war with a commission as Captain. Figaro gloats over the terrified boy, " No more you'll flit, amorous butterfly," etc. (" Non più andrai ").

Act II.—Scene. The Countess's chamber. She is alone and sings a sad love-wail (" Porgi, amor "). Susanna enters, then Figaro, who tells a plan to torment the Count with jealousy by sending him a warning letter. He leaves and Cherubino appears. He shows his commission ; they make him sing his poem, " You who know what love is " (" Voi che sapete "). They then dress him in women's clothes, Susanna bidding him kneel (" Venite inginocchiatevi "). Suddenly the Count is heard outside. Cherubino flies to the closet. The Count is suspicious and shows his letter ; he hears the page in the closet,

but his wife will not unlock the door. He makes her go with him while he hunts a crowbar. While they are gone Cherubino steals forth and jumps out of the window and Susanna takes his place in the closet. As the Count is about to break the door in, the Countess confesses that Cherubino is there and is overcome with grief. Susanna walks out to the astonishment of all. The Countess taunts the apologetic Count, and tells him Figaro wrote the letter. Figaro enters and is accused of the letter, but denies it. The gardener, half-drunk, enters complaining that some man had jumped out of the window and ruined his flowers, then run away. Figaro says it was he, in terror of the Count. The gardener says that he dropped some papers, among them Cherubino's commission. This is recognised and the Count is frenzied. To complete Figaro's discomfiture, Marcellina enters with his document promising to marry her. Bartolo and Basilio are witnesses. All ends in confusion.

Act III.—Scene I. A large room decorated for a wedding. The Count, alone, plans to compel Figaro to marry Marcellina. Susanna, overhearing, pretends to have come for the Countess's smelling-salts ; she says she has overheard the Count's scheme, but consents to meet him in the garden at night. He starts to go, and she tells Figaro, who enters, that he has won his cause. They hurry out ; the Count, who has overheard her, ponders suspiciously ; he miserably asks " Shall I behold, while I sorrow, my servant happy ? " (" Vedrc, mentr' io sospiro "). Don Curzio enters with Figaro, Marcellina, and Bartolo. He says that Figaro must marry Marcellina or pay her a forfeit. Figaro proves that he is of good birth, and shows a mark on his arm by which Marcellina recognises him as her own son by Dr. Bartolo. They are all embracing when Susanna enters with the money to buy Figaro's liberty. Her indignation is soon assuaged and all leave. Scene 2. The Countess enters alone, musing over the plan to disguise herself as Susanna and meet the Count in the garden ; she bewails the lost devotion of her husband who had wooed her so ardently (see Rossini's opera "The Barber of Seville"). She moans "Where now are those blessed moments" ("Dove sono i bei momenti"). Susanna enters and the Countess dictates to her a letter (in a duet "The Zephyr"), telling the Count to meet her where the zephyr breathes in the pines. Cherubino enters in girl's clothes, and a chorus of country girls present the Countess with flowers. Antonio and the Count enter and recognise Cherubino. Figaro tries to calm the Count, the Wedding March is heard ; Figaro sings ("Ecco la Marcia") and all leave except the Count and Countess, who remain and wait coldly till the double wedding-procession returns with Figaro and Susanna and Bartolo and Marcellina. Susanna (observed by Figaro) slips the note to the Count, who bids all make merry.

Act IV.—Scene. The garden. Basilio and Bartolo ponder the Count's duplicity and the folly of love. Basilio tells how "in those years when inexperienced" ("In quegli anni"), love had made him mad, till finally age and experience protected him with the skin of an old ass. They withdraw and Figaro entering grieves over Susanna's treachery and woman's frailty ("Ah, che il fidarsi a donna"). He hides, but is observed by Susanna, who enters with the Countess and Marcellina. To torment Figaro Susanna sings "Come, love, do not delay" ("Deh, vieni non tardar"), and leaves ; Cherubino enters in regimentals looking for Barbarina ; he sees the Countess in Susanna's garb and thinking her to be actually Susanna tries to flirt with her. He escapes into the pavilion on the left as the Count enters. Seeing Figaro, the Count whispers the supposed Susanna to hide with him in a pavilion on the right. Susanna enters in the Countess's gown and explains herself to the delighted Figaro. The

Count reappears and seeing Figaro kneeling before the supposed Countess is infuriated and calls the servants. Figaro and Susanna escape into a pavilion on the left. Basilio and others enter with torches. The Count entering the pavilion on the left unearths Cherubino and Barbarina, Marcellina and Bartolo, and Susanna, who, pretending still to be the Countess, hiding her face, pleads for pardon, which the Count will not grant. The Countess herself now appears and the Count kneeling begs her forgiveness. She grants it and a chorus of general contentment ("Ah, tutti contenti") cuts the Gordian knot of complications.

**Die Zauberflöte** (dē tsow'-bĕr-flā-tĕ). Il Flauto Magico (ēl flä'-oo-tō mä-jē'-kō). The Magic Flute.

Two-act opera. Book by Emanuel Schickaneder. Composed, 1791.

Produced, Vienna, September 30, 1791, under the management of the librettist, who also played the rôle of Papageno.

CHARACTERS AND THEIR CREATORS.

SARASTRO (sä-räs'-trō),
  *High-Priest of Isis.*,
      Schickaneder, sr., bass.
PAPAGENO (pä-pä-gä'-nō),
  *A bird-catcher.*
      Schickaneder, jr., bass.
TAMINO (tä-mē'-nō),
  *A fisher*............Schack, tenor.
MONOSTATOS,
  *A Nubian prince*.......Gorl, tenor.
BAMBOLODA,
  *His slave.*
MANES (mä'-näs),
  *And other priests of Isis.*
KÖNIGIN DER NACHT (kä'-nĭkh-ēn dĕr näkht), *Queen of Night*
      Frau Hofer sopr
PAMINA (pä-mē'-nä),
  *Her daughter, a net-worker*,
      Frl. Gotlieb, sopr.

PAPAGE'NA,
   *Slave of Monostatos*...Frau Gorl, —
THREE FAIRIES,
   *Disguised as women and guides.*

NOTE.—The opera is sadly complicated by the vanity and gaucherie of the librettist and his desire to drag in certain allusions to Freemasonry, in which he and Mozart were enthusiasts.

Act I.—Tableau I. A rocky path past a fairy cavern. Tamino in the toils of a serpent (or in some versions Gnomes) calls for help just as he falls asleep under the spell. The Fairies rescue him and discuss how he, a fisher, played his sweetheart such sweet tunes that the Queen of Night herself loved him. As her love is fatal, they plan to save him by getting him into the Temple of Isis. They retire as Papageno runs in ; he meets Papagena and tells her who he is (" Der Vogelfänger bin ich ja," or " Sono un gaio uccellator ") ; she tells him she is in the power of Monostatos. Tamino wakes as from a dream and asks the way to the Temple ; he tells of his beloved Pamina and shows a miniature of her (" Dies Bildniss ist bezaubernd schön "—" O cara immagine "). Papagena tells him that Monostatos has just bought Pamina as a slave. They decide to hunt for her, but cannot find the path ; as they look for it, the Queen of Night appears to Tamino and sings to him a love-song, " Oh, fear not, dear youth " (" O zittre nicht, mein lieber Sohn "—" Giovane amato, non temer "). She pledges him to rescue her daughter Pamina and vanishes. The three Fairies offer to show the lost ones the path ; but the price must be the power of speech or that of memory. Papagena loses memory and Papageno is rendered dumb, but later restored on swearing never to lie again, and given a magic bell, while Tamino is given a flute of magic power. They are then shown the path, after a quintet known as the " Padlock." Tableau 2. The Harem of Monostatos. Bamboloda drags Papagena in ; in her absence Pamina has

escaped. Monostatos enters and the recaptured Pamina is brought in and chained. Papageno appears and frightens Monostatos away. They sing a duet of love's power (" Bei Männern, welche Liebe füllen "—" Del cor gli affanni ") ; he shakes his bell, the gates open and they escape. Tableau 3. An Avenue. The Fairies tell that Pamina has fallen in Sarastro's power ; appearing to Tamino disguised as Guides, they point him a path and leave him. He is warned by voices and by Manes, who tells him that he is moved by desire for revenge on Sarastro, and refuses to tell him where Pamina is. Tamino plays on his flute and sirens gather round ; he wanders sadly away, searching. Papageno enters with Pamina and answers Tamino's distant flute with his own ; encountering Monostatos and slaves, he compels them to dance away to his magic bell. Sarastro enters with retinue, and welcomes the two to his Temple. Monostatos drags in Tamino, who embraces Pamina. Sarastro orders Monostatos to be flogged and Tamino and Papageno to be veiled and led in.

Act II.—Tableau 4. The Hall of Initiations. Sarastro and the Priests invoke Isis and Osiris (" O Isis und Osiris ! "—" Possenti Numi "). Tamino and Papageno are brought in and asked if they will undergo the rites ; they are advised by two priests to avoid false beauty and they are left alone and find that their flute and bell have been taken. The three Fairies appear and warn them not to undergo the rites, but they resist the blandishments of the women, whose presence in the sanctuary causes the fall of the altar. Tableau 5. A Tent in a garden. Monostatos steals in, guided by Bamboloda. He is furious at being beaten, but dreams of the beloved Pamina (" Alles fühlt der Liebe Freuden "—" Regna amor "). Pamina is discovered in the tent ; he tries to take her away, and she escapes only to be confronted by the Queen of Night, her mother. who hates her for her devotion to the noble Sarastro, who is trying to save the girl's soul. The Queen curses her in tremendous fury (" Der Hölle Rache kocht "—" Gli angui d'inferno "). Sarastro enters and declares that only peace and love rule in these sacred precincts (" In diesen heil'gen Hallen "—" Qui sdegno "). He leads the girl away and the Queen and Monostatos plot the death of Pamina. When they have gone, the three Fairies enter ; they have overheard the plot but decline to aid it. Tamino and Papageno enter ; the Fairies appear as the Guides and restore the magic talismans in a trio. Papageno shakes his bell and calls for Papagena, only to see her flirting with Bamboloda. He shakes the bell again and summons Pamina ; she enters and embraces Tamino, but he is under pledge and does not answer her. She sings sadly that no joy is for her (" Ach ! ich fühl's es ist verschwunden "—" Ah, lo so "). Sarastro enters and removing the pledge reunites the lovers ; he bids Tamino hasten across the sacred forest to complete his rites. There is a trio of farewell and Tamino leaves. Tableau 6. The Sacred Forest. Papageno alone sings a love-song (" Ein Mädchen oder Weibchen "—" Colomba o tortorella "). Papagena enters, she does not remember him, and he reproaches her. She flees, and the three Fairies tell him of Tamino's ordeal. He leaves, and Pamina enters with a dagger ; she would kill herself, but the Fairies prevent her. Tableau 7. The Crypt of the Temple. Tamino is taking his final vows ; Pamina is brought in, and the two undergo the ordeal of fire and water, the evil spirits being chased by Tamino's flute. He is hailed by the Priests as a victor. Tableau 8. The Portal of the Temple. Papageno in despair for Papagena is about to hang himself ; the Fairies advise him to summon her with his bell. She appears and they have a joyful duet (" Pa-pa-pa-pa-geno "). When they have gone, the Queen of Night and Monostatos steal in to murder Sarastro before her

power vanishes with dawn. The gates of the Temple open, revealing the votaries kneeling, and the lovers united before Isis. The Queen vanishes in helpless rage before the dawn and the chorus of reverent joy.

## PADEREWSKI, IGNACE JAN.

### Manru.

Three-act opera. Book by Dr. Alfred Nossig. Produced, Court Theatre, Dresden, May 29, 1901.

CHARACTERS AND THEIR CREATORS.

MAN'RU,
   *A gipsy*.............Anthes, tenor.
UROK (oo'-rôk),
   *A dwarf*.......Scheidemantel, bar.
JAGU (yä'-goo),
   *A gipsy fiddler*........Rains, bass.
O'ROS,
   *A gipsy chief*..........Hopfl, bass.
ULANA (oo-lä'-nä),
   *A Galician girl*....Frl. Krull, sopr.
HEDWIG (hāt'-vĭkh),
   *Her mother*,
      Frl. von Chavanne, m. sopr.
ASA (ä'-zä),
   *A gipsy girl*....Frau Kammer, sopr.

The opera begins and ends with a single voice. It has no overture at all, and only seventeen measures of prelude. The scene is the Tatra Mountains between Galicia and Hungary.

Act I.—The widow Hedwig sits before her hut and bemoans in a folksong the fate of the dove that took no heed of the hawk's approach till she felt his sharp claws. The dove is Hedwig's daughter, Ulana ; the hawk, the heathen gipsy who carried her off. As she sings maidens dance about, adorning the village green for the festival. The dwarf, Urok, appears. The maidens call him " dragon's-egg, an adder, monster, wood-dwarf, tadpole, and horn-owl." Urok takes these as a great joke. Then he asks Hedwig of her daughter "She is dead to me," says Hedwig. Urok tells of meeting the "dead" Ulana. The maidens greet her name with jeers ; the mother, with a vow never to receive her until she gives up her gipsy. Hedwig returns to her hut ; Urok rebukes the maidens, and they mock him as a rejected lover of Ulana. Ulana herself now appears in great dejection and the villagers rail at her. She says she still loves her gipsy, and he her. But they taunt her with a proverb :

" Ere the full moon starts to wane
Every gipsy goes insane,
Leaves his child and leaves his wife
And scoots for his dear life."

This jingle reappears all through the opera. The maidens leave Ulana to her grief. Against Urok's advice, she knocks at her mother's door. Hedwig comes. After some reproach she offers to take Ulana and her child back if she will give up Manru. Urok and Hedwig insist that Manru will leave her, anyway, when the gipsies come again. But Ulana refuses. Hedwig shuts her door on her. Urok prophesies Manru's perfidy and proffers his own love. But she prevails on him to brew her a philter to bring back Manru's wavering fancy. The village men and maidens gather and dance. They surround Ulana. Manru appears and demands that they let her go, but they scout him as a heathen. Hedwig comes out of her hut and a hush falls on the mob. She bitterly denounces the pair as lepers, and the people fall back from them.

Act II.—Scene. The curtain rises at once on Manru's home in the mountains, where the gipsy, turned blacksmith, is fighting a losing battle against his Wanderlust. Ulana is singing a lullaby to her baby in the hut. Manru admires, but cannot imitate, her steadfastness. In a frenzy he belabours the anvil with his sledge. Ulana hurries out to calm his fury, but whispers uneasily :

" Ere the full moon starts to wane
Every gipsy goes insane."

This brings down on her own head all his violence, and he is about to strike her when Urok appears and stays his hand. Both Manru and Ulana accuse him of being a sorcerer, but he claims only a knowledge of the human heart and a few herbs. He admits that he can evoke a spell to carry Manru away. Listen ! In the distance a Romany fiddler is heard. Manru breaks away and flies toward the siren music. Ulana would run after him, but Urok holds her back, gives her a potion for Manru, and keeps her in hiding while Manru returns with an old gipsy fiddler, Jagu. Jagu offers Manru the leadership of the tribe. He refuses. Jagu mentions the fair Asa, who longs for Manru but must soon wed Oros, his old rival. Manru, about to go, sees Ulana, and refuses, ordering the tempter away. Left alone, Manru and Ulana marvel at the travel-frenzy that spurs him. With a noble effort to return to his duty he takes up his sledge. But Urok teases him with a vivid picture of Asa. Manru drives him away and Ulana brings him a potion, which he drains. This rouses him to an ecstasy of love in which she joins.

Act III. has a long prelude. The rise of the curtain reveals a summer landscape of storm and night. Manru is alone and stifling with restlessness. "All is dark," he cries, "but I *feel* the moon which sweeps past behind the clouds." Voices of gipsies are heard in the distance and he sinks down asleep. There follows an orchestral nocturne. Now and then the full moon breaks from the clouds and Manru grows restless in his sleep, till it is veiled again. Gipsies troop in, among them Asa. They discover Manru and sprinkle his face with water. When he wakes, it is Asa that first welcomes him. Oros protests angrily that Manru should be an outcast as he is a renegade. He quarrels with Asa ; but Manru insists that he cannot follow them. Asa pleads with him. The people fall to dancing and Asa joins them to allure

Manru. Oros protests wrathfully and the tribe are won to his wrath. Then Jagu enters and turns the tide for Manru, who is hailed as a repentant kinsman. Oros, in a rage, throws down his staff of office and goes. The revel begins anew, but Manru refuses the chieftainship. Then the musicians under Jagu try their skill, and Manru's last scruple melts in an outburst of joy. Urok appears and gleefully reviles Manru's treason to his wife and child. He is driven away by the crowd. Manru's conscience gnaws him again, but is smothered by Romany-rapture. He embraces Asa, and the tribe marches away (the stage remaining empty during most of a barbaric march-tune). Ulana follows, crying for her husband, and Urok tells her of his perfidy. She cries to Manru to come back. She sends Urok up into the hills to find him. He answers that he has gone past recall. With a last shriek she leaps into the lake. Later, upon a cliff, Asa and Manru reappear in each other's arms. Oros rushes upon Manru and crying, "You rob me of Asa; you'd replace me as chief!" hurls him into the gorge. Asa screams. Urok laughs fiendishly. Oros roars "The place is mine!" [In a later version it is Urok who hurls Manru over the cliff.]

## PUCCINI, GIACOMO.

**La Bohême** (lä bō-ĕm'), *F.*, Die Bohême (dē bō-hā'mĕ), *G.* Bohemia.

Four-act opera. Words by C. Giacosa (after Murger's "Scènes de la Vie de Bohême").

Produced, Regio Theatre, Turin, February 1, 1896.

### CHARACTERS.

RUDOLPHE (rü-dôlf),
    *Poet*...........................tenor.
MARCEL (mär-sĕl),
    *Painter* .....................bar.
SCHAUNARD (shō-när),
    *Musician*...................bar.
COLLINE (kŭ-lēn),
    *Philosopher*.................bass.
BERNARD (bĕr-när),
    *Landlord* ...................bass.
PARPIGNOL (pär-pēn-yŭl),
    *Toy-seller* ................tenor.
ALCINDOR (ăl-săn-dôr)...........bass.
SERGEANT AT TOLL-HOUSE..........bass.
MIMI (mē-mē).................... .sopr.
MUSETTE (mü-zĕt)...............sopr.

Place of action, Paris. Time, about 1830.

Act I.—Scene. A bare and cold garret. Marcel and Rudolphe at their work. Rudolphe brings a MS. tragedy of his to burn in the stove for warmth. Colline enters and assists. Then Schaunard comes to the rescue with food and wine and fuel, which they enjoy. The landlord enters to demand rent. They make him drink and chaff him about his flirtations ; then, in simulated righteous indignation, eject him. The young men go pleasure-seeking, leaving Rudolphe to finish his writing. Mimi, an embroiderer and fellow-lodger, enters to ask for a light. As the door opens to let her out again, a gust of air extinguishes all the lights. She drops her key and they both grope for it in the dark. Rudolphe finds it, but promptly pockets it and continues groping till he catches Mimi's hand. He engages her in talk, tells her he is a poet, and she tells about herself and her work. The others call impatiently from below, where they wait. Rudolphe opens the window to answer. The moonlight streaming in irradiates Mimi's beauty. Rudolphe and Mimi confess their mutual love.

Act II.—Scene. Christmas Eve in the Latin Quarter. A throng of holiday-makers, in front of the Café Momus, buying, eating, etc. Rudolphe, Mimi wearing a becoming pink hood, Marcel, Schaunard, and Colline mix with the crowd. A waiter brings out a table for the young men. Rudolphe introduces Mimi and they sit down together. Their

orders to the waiter mingle with the outcry caused by the entry of Parpignol,
surrounded by eager children, whose
mothers try to lead them away. Musette, richly dressed, enters with the elderly and infatuated Alcindor. They
sit at an adjacent table. She is indignant that Marcel, her former lover,
takes no notice of her, and talks loudly
for his benefit, while Alcindor vainly
tries to quiet her, thinking her talk is
meant for himself. Musette, seeing
that she has at last moved Marcel, pretends her shoe hurts and sends Alcindor to buy a new pair. Then she and
Marcel embrace and are reconciled.
The bill is presented, but none of the
party has money. Musette bids the
waiter add it to her bill and leaves it
for Alcindor to pay. A military procession marches across the scene. The
friends fall in line behind and exeunt;
Musette having only one shoe, is carried by Marcel and Colline, followed by
the rest keeping step. Alcindor returning, is shown the bill and sinks horrified
into a chair.

Act III.—Scene. The Barrière d'En-
fer. Market-women, etc., paying toll.
Mimi enters, coughing, and asks for Marcel at the inn where he lives with Musette. He comes out and she tells him Rudolphe threatens to leave her, and asks
in despair what to do. As Rudolphe just
then comes out of the inn, she hides behind a tree. Rudolphe tells Marcel he
means to leave Mimi. At first he pretends it is on account of jealousy ; finally he confesses it is because he sees she
is dying of consumption and, though he
still loves her, he has no money to keep
her in comfort. Marcel tries to lead
Rudolphe out of earshot, but Mimi, la-
menting, hears her death-sentence. A
fit of coughing betrays her hiding-place.
Rudolphe, startled, soothes and caresses
her. Musette is heard within, laughing
and flirting. Marcel, jealous, rushes
inside. Mimi bids Rudolphe farewell,
telling him to keep her pink hood as a
keepsake. Marcel and Musette emerge
quarrelling, and the four voices mingle

in contrasting colloquies. The disput-
ing lovers go in again, leaving the others to end their pathetic farewell.

Act IV.—Scene. Same as Act I. Marcel and Rudolphe at their work tell how
each has seen the beloved of the other
riding in a carriage, well-dressed, etc.
Both express contentment, but are in-
wardly jealous and cannot work. Marcel takes out a ribbon Musette gave him,
and Rudolphe presses Mimi's hood to his
heart, each concealing his emotion from
the other. Schaunard and Colline enter with frugal provisions. They try to
forget their woes in merrymaking. Suddenly Musette enters, saying that Mimi
is close behind, and explains that Mimi
has left her Count and returned to Rudolphe to die. Mimi enters in the last
stage of consumption. She says how
much better she feels to be back there,
but that her hands are cold and she
would like a muff. Rudolphe tries to
warm them in his. The others are
overcome with compassion. Musette
gives her jewels to Marcel to sell to
get a doctor, etc., for Mimi ; then declares she must also get her a muff, and
goes with him. Colline bids farewell to
his faithful old coat and carries it to
pawn, taking Schaunard with him that
the lovers may be alone. Mimi, who
had apparently been asleep, now rouses,
and the two renew memories of their
happy past. Mimi, rejoiced to see her
hood, makes Rudolphe put it on her.
The others return and Mimi delights in
the muff. Soon she falls asleep and
dies. Rudolphe in despair throws himself on her corpse.

### ROSSINI, GIOACCHINO.

**Il Barbiere di Siviglia** (ēl bär-bĭ-
ā'-rĕ dē sē-vēl'-yä), *I.* The Barber of
Seville.

Two-act lyric comedy. Book (from
Beaumarchais's comedy) by Sterbini.
Composed in three weeks. Produced,
Rome, Argentina Theatre, February 5,
1816.

## CHARACTERS AND THEIR CREATORS.

FIGARO (fē'-gä-rō),
  *A barber*........Luigi Zamboni, bar.
IL CONTE ALMAVIVA (äl-mä-vē'-vä),
  *A young count*........Garcia, tenor.
DOTTO'RE BARTO'LO,
  *Rosina's guardian*...Botticelli, bass.
BASILIO (bä-sēl'-yö),
  *Music-master*........Vittarelli, bass.
FIORELLO (fē-ō-rĕl'-lō),
  *A servant*..................tenor.
ROSINA (rō-zē'-nä),
  *Dr. Bartolo's ward*,
  Signora Giogi Righetti, sopr.
BER'TA,
  *Her governess* (in Germany MARCEL-
  LINE).......Signorina Rossi, sopr.

NOTE.—This opera is taken from the same source as an opera by Paesiello, and Mozart's "Nozze di Figaro," to which it is precedaneous in action. It was originally called "Almaviva, ossia l'inutile precauzione," "The Useless Precaution."

Act I. — Scene I. Dawn in a Seville street. Fiorello leads along several musicians for a serenade. The Count enters and sings a serenade or aubade under Rosina's window (" Ecco ridente il cielo "). He pays the musicians liberally and drives them away, vexed at their profuse thanks. Figaro bustles gaily by to his work (singing " Largo al factotum "), rejoicing in his importance as the general factotum and go-between of the town. The Count stops him, tells him he has fallen in love with the ward of Dr. Bartolo, and is flirting with her desperately under the name of Lindoro. Rosina appears on the balcony to drop the Count a note, but, Bartolo appearing, she pretends it is a paper that has slipped out of her hand, and asks him to go down and get it. While he disappears in the house, the Count gets the note and lets Figaro read it. It reveals a Juliet-like desire to know more of the stranger. Bartolo comes out, then stops to call back instructions that none is to be admitted to the house save Basilio ; he says he himself will marry Rosina that very day. The Count offers Figaro a reward if he can help him to win Rosina, and Figaro, always prolific in schemes, bids him disguise as a tipsy soldier. He tells the Count how to find his shop (" La bottega ") and after a duet on love (" A che d'amore ") Figaro enters Bartolo's house and the Count hurries away. Scene 2. A room in Bartolo's house. Rosina ponders how to get a letter past her lynx-eyed guardians (in the brilliant air " A voice has made my heart resound," " Una voce poco fa "). Figaro enters, but seeing Bartolo coming, postpones his message, and they leave in opposite directions. Bartolo and Basilio come in. Basilio tells the anxious Bartolo that Rosina's unknown lover is the Count Almaviva. They decide to efface him with calumny (" La calunnia "), whose growth from a whisper to a tempest Basilio pictures vividly. They depart and Figaro steals in, soon meeting Rosina, who questions him about the Count, and persuades him to bear a note to him. She has it already written; he takes it and goes, after a duet (" E il maestro io faccio "). Bartolo comes in and cross-questions her as to the note she dropped from the balcony and the one he suspects she has given Figaro. She blames the ink on her finger to a design she was drawing. They go their ways and Berta, hearing loud knocking, enters. The Count disguised as a soldier bursts in, pretending to be drunk, but anxiously looking for Rosina while he embraces and worries Bartolo. Rosina entering, the two steal a few words surreptitiously ; he bids her drop her handkerchief, while Bartolo angrily hunts a paper giving him exemption from soldierly visits. The Count lets fall a note, Rosina drops her handkerchief on it, but Bartolo observes the ruse and snatches the note, only to find it a mere list of names. He apologises, but the Count jostles him about and also Basilio and Berta, who enter. Fi.

garo appears with a basin and is amazed at the noise, which finally brings the police. The Count shows his order of nobility and avoids arrest.

Act II.—Scene. Bartolo is alone in a room, and bitterly reflects that he is not safe in his own house. The Count enters disguised as a music-teacher. He annoys Bartolo with over-effusive greetings and says Basilio was too ill to come, and sent him. He lets slip a word about Rosina's note, and to cover the slip tells Bartolo that he has happened on a note written to the Count by Rosina, and he suggests that if he can talk with Rosina he might convince her that the Count is only a faithless rake. Bartolo gladly brings in Rosina, who recognises the alleged teacher and sings for him. (The music written for this place by Rossini was lost, and the prima donna is at liberty to introduce any song she prefers.) Figaro arrives to shave Bartolo, who resists, but finally sends Figaro to his room to get the cloth, giving him the keys, one of which Rosina whispers him is the key to the balcony. Now Basilio enters, to the exquisite confusion of the Count, who tries to make Basilio think he is ill and to send him home. A purse opens Basilio's eyes to the plot and he goes. As the Count and Rosina pretend to study music and really plot an elopement, Bartolo overhears in spite of Figaro's efforts to keep him engaged. He disperses the group. Berta enters alone complaining of the noisy house always in uproar, and the old dotard's love (" Il vechietto cerca moglie "—based on a Russian air, and called the " Aria di Sorbetto," because the audiences chose it as a good time to eat sherbets). She leaves, and Bartolo brings on Basilio, who tells him that the music-teacher was the Count and there is to be a marriage that night at Figaro's house. When he has gone, Bartolo plans a bold coup, and calls Rosina, whom he tells that the Count is unfaithful to her; showing her the note she had written him as proof. Rosina, infuriated, consents to marry

Bartolo at once, confessing to him her plan to elope. Bartolo hurries away to find the police to arrest the Count when he comes. The Count and Figaro steal in from the balcony as soon as he has gone, and Rosina is soon convinced of his love. He reveals himself as the Count Almaviva. They decide to elope, and tip-toe stealthily with a " Hush, hush " (" Zitti, zitti "). They find the ladder gone and see persons coming with a lantern. They conceal themselves and Basilio enters with a notary. The Count, by softly threatening Basilio with death, gets himself married to Rosina. Bartolo enters with soldiers, but too late. He gives the two their blessing and all ends happily.

**Guglielmo Tell** (gool-yĕl′-mō tĕl), **Guillaume** (gē-yōm), or **Wilhelm** (vĕl′-hĕlm), or **William, Tell.**

Three - (originally five-) act opera Book by Étienne Jouy, revised by Hippolyte Bis, after Schiller's drama The Académie, Paris, August 3, 1829.

CHARACTERS AND THEIR CREATORS.

MATHILDE VON HAPSBURG,
　*Gessler's daughter*,
　　　　Mme. Damoreau-Cinti, sopr.
HEDWIG,
　*Tell's wife*.....Mlle. Mori, m. sopr.
JEM′MY,
　*Tell's son*.....Mme. Dabodie, sopr.
GESS′LER,
　*Austrian Governor of Switzerland*,
　　　　　　　　Prévost, bass.
RUDOLF DER HARRAS.....Massol, tenor.
TELL.................Dabodie, bar.
WALTHER FÜRST......Levasseur, bass.
MELCH′THAL (mĕltch′-täl),
　*An old man*.........Dupont, bass.
AR′NOLD,
　*His son*..............Nourrit, bar.
LEUTHOLD (loit′-hōlt),
　*A peasant*.............Prévôt, bar.
A FISHER.................. ...tenor

Act I.—Scene. Switzerland, thirteenth century. Shore of a mountain-lake. Peasants enjoying a wedding festival are joined by Tell, who bemoans the tyranny oppressing his country. Arnold, who has loved Gessler's daughter since he saved her life, promises nevertheless to aid Tell in freeing Switzerland. The peasant Leuthold appears. He has killed an Austrian soldier who tried to abduct his daughter, and is now pursued by the soldiers. He begs to be rowed across the lake, but the rising storm dismays the fishermen. Tell takes the oars and puts out into the storm just before the soldiers enter, led by Rudolf, who, finding no one who will reveal the identity of Leuthold's rescuer, seizes old Melchthal as an inciter of rebellion. Act II.—Scene. A forest. Huntsmen and shepherds meet and disperse. Princess Mathilde passes, returning from a hunt. She meets Arnold and reciprocates his love. She leaves him when Tell comes up with Walther Fürst, who tells Arnold that his father has been killed by the Austrian. Arnold, putting aside his thoughts of love, joins the other two men in an oath of dire revenge. The deputies of three cantons appear successively and Tell persuades them to join the oath and free Switzerland. Act III.—Scene I. A love-duet between Mathilde and Arnold. Scene 2. The market-place of Altdorp. Gessler has set his hat up on a pole and the indignant citizens are compelled to salute it. Tell and his son enter and scorn such humility. They are seized and the father ordered to prove his vaunted archery by shooting an apple from his son's head. After an anxious prayer, he accomplishes this. Gessler seeing that he has another arrow, asks what it is for. Tell declares that if he had missed the apple and hurt his son, his second arrow would have been shot at Gessler. For this defiance he is fettered, despite Mathilde's plea. Scene 3. The Swiss revolutionists meet in a storm, Mathilde asks to be admitted to the band, and gives her hand to Arnold. Success follows the battles of the Swiss, and Tell enters; he has escaped from prison and slain Gessler; the country has now won liberty, which is celebrated in a hymn of freedom.

## SPINELLI, NICOLLA.

**A Bas'so Por'to.** At the Lower Harbour.

Three-act lyric drama of the slums. Book by Eugenio Checchi.

### CHARACTERS.

MARI'A,
A widow.................m. sopr.
SESEL'LA,
Her daughter...............sopr
LUIGINO (loo-ē-jē'-nō),
Maria's son, a gambler.......tenor
CICILLO (chē-chǐl'-lō),
A government spy.............bar
PASQUALE (päs-kwä'-lě),
An innkeeper................bass.
PICILLO (pē-chǐl'-lō)............tenor.

Act I. — Scene. An open market-place near the lower harbor of Naples ; time 1860. Maria and Sesella are wearily at work on one side, on the other in front of a tavern Luigino is gambling away their hard earnings. Maria pleads with him but ends by paying his gambling debts. Cicillo appears. He is posing as the leader of the Cammoristi, an anarchistic society, but is really spying on them and trying to foist on another member the treachery that has been betraying them. Luigino hates Cicillo but Sesella loves him ; and he is plotting to seduce her ; he takes an opportunity to ask her to elope with him since the Cammoristi hate him. Luigino sees her kiss him and tries to stab him, but Maria intervenes and sends her children away. She and Cicillo have a bitter interview, in which it transpires that, years before, Cicillo had betrayed Maria and deserted her for another woman, against whom Maria had conspired, securing the arrest of both. The girl had been put to death, though Cicillo had escaped to vow vengeance against Maria, who meantime had married. Though she is now a widow, he still plots to bring her son to the gutter and her daughter Sesella to the streets. Maria pleads and threatens for an end to the feud, but Cicillo mocks her. The Cammoristi rush in in excitement ; another member has been arrested and they swear to hunt out and kill the traitor. Cicillo's momentary uneasiness is seen by Maria.

Act II.—Scene. A low tavern filled with hilarious smugglers, girls, etc. Luigino sings a gay song. Cicillo enters and strikes him across the face. He explains that he believes Luigino to be the traitor. He is to meet Sesella and will try to wring the truth from her. They leave him alone and his remorseful soliloquy is interrupted by Sesella's entrance. He poisons her mind against her mother, and she consents to elope with him at midnight. When he has gone, Maria enters and pleads with her daughter, finally confessing her own past and proclaiming Cicillo a spy. Sesella is won back and determines to betray Cicillo. She calls in the landlord and the others and accuses the absent Cicillo. Luigino, however, is brought to trial by the Cammoristi, but Maria saves him by swearing that she has seen Cicillo take government pay. Cicillo is condemned to die, and Luigino chosen to assassinate him, in spite of Maria's frantic appeals.

Act III.—Same scene as Act I. Night. Maria, alone, prays heaven to save her children. Cicillo enters and she warns him that she alone can save him from the Cammoristi and begs him to give up his plot to ruin her children. He laughs at her and says that in a moment he will have the soldiers all about the place. Singing and mandolin-playing in the distance indicate the signal to kill him, but he will not accept her offer, and brushes past her to call the soldiers, whereupon she stabs him, to save her son from the blood-guilt. The Cammoristi rush in as he dies

## THOMAS, AMBROISE.

**Mignon** (mēn-yôṅ).

Three-act opera. Book by Barbier & Carré (based on Goethe's " Wilhelm Meister ").

Produced, Opéra Comique, Paris, November 17, 1866.

CHARACTERS AND THEIR CREATORS.

GUGLIELMO (gool-yĕl'-mō),
  in German, WILHELM MEISTER,
                    Achard, tenoɪ
LOTARIO (lō-tä'-rĭ-ō)......Bataille, bar.
FEDERICO (fā-dĕ-rē'-kō)........tenor.
LAËRTE (lä-ĕr'tĕ)........Conders, bar.
GIARNO (jär'-nō)............bass.
ANTO'NIO,
MIGNON.....Mme. Galli-Marié, m. sopr.
FILINA (fē-lē'-nä)....Mme. Cabel, sopr.

Act I.—Scene. Courtyard of a German inn. Townsfolk seated drinking. The old minstrel Lotario enters almost distracted with grief at the loss of his child, who has disappeared, and whom seeking he wanders disconsolately. A band of gipsies appear, and dance for pennies, watched from a balcony by two actors, Filina and Laerte. The savage chief Giarno orders the child Mignon to dance. When she proudly rebels, he threatens her with a cudgel, and the old minstrel tries to protect her. He is pushed aside, but Guglielmo entering cows the gipsy. Mignon gives flowers to both of her rescuers. When the others withdraw, Filina admiringly sends Laerte to scrape acquaintance with Guglielmo. She follows soon, and begins to flirt with great sophistication. Guglielmo gives her the flowers Mignon gave him. Filina and Laerte leave, and Mignon, seeing that Giarno is asleep, steals forward to pour out her gratitude. She tells Guglielmo that her childhood is a mystery. She remembers being stolen. When he asks her the name of her country she can only ask, " Knowest thou the land where the citrons bloom " (in Goethe's words, "*Kennst du das Land wo äie Citronen blüh'n "*). He judges from her other phrases that her land must be Italy. Giarno reappearing, offers to sell Mignon for what he paid for her. Guglielmo enters the inn to close the bargain. Mignon tells the old minstrel of her new freedom, and when he says he must follow the swallows northward, she sings a swallow-song ("Leggiadre rondinelle"). They withdraw and Filina appears, teasing Federico, her lover. Guglielmo returns, having bought Mignon. Filina introduces him to Federico. A letter comes ordering the troupe of players to appear at the castle of Federico's uncle; and Guglielmo is invited to go as poet. Mignon seizes an opportunity to ask what is to become of her, and begs to follow Guglielmo in disguise as a page; though the old minstrel pleads for her, Guglielmo consents to take her. She notes with a pang that he has given her flowers to Filina. The troupe set out for the castle.

Act II.—Scene I. The boudoir of Filina who is gaily preparing her charms for further conquest ("A maraviglia!"). Laerte, and later Guglielmo, enter. Laerte, about to leave, finds Mignon jealously waiting; Guglielmo treats her with kindly impatience, and she seems to fall asleep before the fire. Guglielmo makes love to Filina. They leave; and Mignon, after brooding morosely, looks about with interest and falls to powdering and rougeing her face, hoping to captivate Guglielmo by her beauty ("Son io che mi specchio?" or "Ist das Mignon wohl?"). She disappears just as Federico enters at the window singing a Rondo-Gavotte. Guglielmo, coming back to seek Mignon, falls to altercation with Federico. They draw swords, but Mignon rushes between. She is garbed in one of Filina's gowns, and Federico retires laughing. Guglielmo sadly tells Mignon she must leave him ("Addio, Mignon"). Filina entering, Mignon fiercely tears off the gown and rushes away. Laerte announces that the play is about to begin and they

leave, Mignon and Federico jealously watching Guglielmo's devotion to Filina. Scene 2. The park of the castle. Mignon alone in her grief is about to throw herself into the lake, when she hears the harp of the minstrel. He appears and tries to console her. She frantically wishes that the fires of heaven would consume the hated castle, and hurries away. The half-insane minstrel ponders her wish and disappears. The guests flock out from the play, "The Midsummer. Night's Dream," and Filina rejoices in her success as Titania ("Io son Titania bionda"). Guglielmo searches for Mignon. She appears, and the minstrel tells her that he has set fire to the castle. She represses her horror, and when Filina asks her to get a bouquet which Guglielmo had given her, and which she had left in the castle, Mignon goes. The flames break forth, while the old minstrel chants to his harp. Guglielmo rushes into the castle and rescues Mignon against her will.

Act III.—Scene. Gallery of a manor-house. A chorus of sailors is heard in the distance. The minstrel appears; later Guglielmo, and Antonio who explains that all the other houses of the region are illuminated in honour of the festival, but this house alone remains dark since, ten years ago, the daughter of the count who owned it was drowned. The count has since been a wanderer, and Antonio offers to sell the house to Guglielmo, who plans to buy it. He tells the minstrel, who, hearing the name, seems to recall a forgotten past, and enters a long-sealed door. Guglielmo, alone, muses on the discovery he has made that Mignon secretly loves him ("Ah, non credea l'afflito"). A note comes telling that Filina is following him. He is not interested. Mignon appears, very pale and feeble; she seems to remember her surroundings vaguely. Guglielmo tells her he has learned to love her. Filina's voice is heard, and she is terrified again. Now the minstrel enters richly garbed. He has returned to his right mind. He welcomes them to the house as his own. He brings out a casket of jewels belonging to his lost child. In it is a Prayer Book. Mignon reads a few lines and, letting the book fall, recites the rest of the child's prayer by heart. The Count recognises her as his child. She faints with delight, but recovers and sings with joy the last of the "Mignon's Song" of Goethe, "Kennst du das Land."

### VERDI, GIUSEPPI.

**Aïda** (ä-ē'-dä).

Four-act opera. Book by A. Ghizlandoni, from de Locle's version of an old Egyptian tradition. The opera was composed on a commission from the Khedive and first produced at Cairo, December 27, 1871.

#### CHARACTERS.

AÏDA,
*An Ethiopian princess in slavery,*
sopr.
AMNERIS (äm-nä'-rēs),
*Princess of Egypt, in love with*
RADAMES.................contr.
RADAMES (rä'-dä-mäs),
*Egyptian Captain in love with*
AÏDA.....................tenor.
AMONAS'RO,
*Ethiopian King, father of* AÏDA, bar.
RAMFIS (räm'-fēs),
*High Priest of Isis*..........bass.
KING OF EGYPT.
MESSENGER.

Act I.—Scene I. Hall in the Palace. Ramfis speaks to Radames of the hostile movements of the Ethiopian king; he hints that Radames will lead the Egyptian force. When he has gone, Radames rejoices in the hope of winning glory, all for the sake of Aïda ("Céleste Aïda"). Princess Amneris, entering, notes his joy and hopes it is for her. Aïda enters and the Princess greets her kindly but suspects her of being Radames' sweetheart. Aïda weeps for the woes of her country. The King and

retinue appear and Ramfis and other Priests; a messenger follows to speak of the Ethiopian incursion led by Amonasro. The Priest declares Radames the leader chosen of Isis, and after a chorus all leave except Aïda, who is torn between love for her father and for Radames ("Retorna vincitor"), ending in a prayer ("Numi, pieta"). Scene 2. The Temple of Phthah at Memphis. Priests and Priestesses chant and dance before the altar. Radames enters and is veiled and armed by Ramfis (two actual Egyptian themes are employed in the harp music and the dance).

Act II.—Scene I. Amneris' apartments. Her slaves sing while she broods on love. Aïda enters and the slaves retire. Amneris wrings from Aïda the secret of her love by saying that Radames is dead. She upbraids the girl with high fury. The army is heard returning in pomp (duet "Alla pompa"). Scene 2. An open place. The victorious army returns loaded with trophies and is welcomed with all ceremony. Aïda, cowering at Amneris' feet, sees Radames triumphant; among his captives she sees her father, who whispers her not to tell his rank; but he decides to announce it himself, appealing for mercy ("Questa assisa"). The Priests and people demand his death but Radames wins clemency from the King, who releases the other prisoners but retains Amonasro. The act ends with a paean ("Gloria all' Egitto").

Act III.—Scene. Shore of the Nile, before a Temple of Isis, wherein the worshippers are heard singing. Ramfis enters the Temple; Amneris follows to pray Isis for Radames' love. Aïda steals in, veiled, to meet Radames; she muses on the beauty of the sky and on her far-off home ("O cieli azzurri"). Amonasro appears; he tells Aïda he has discovered her passion for Radames; he tells her she can see her home again and have her lover too ("Rivedro le foreste"). She must win Radames to treachery, or at least learn from him the name of the pass by which his troops will march. When she protests, he paints a wild picture of the havoc the Egyptians have wrought in Ethiopia and threatens her with his curse. At the height of her terror, Radames appears, Amonasro hiding near by. Radames tells Aïda that the Ethiopians have risen again, he intends to defeat them again and then claim Aïda's hand from the King. Aïda says Amneris would seek vengeance, that only one course is open to their love, and that is, flight (" Fuggiam gli ardori "). He is horrified, but she mentions Amneris and says that she and her father will be put to death. In an access of love he consents to fly. She asks him the name of the pass ; he tells her, and is overheard by Amonasro, who is discovered by Radames. Amneris, who has overheard, charges Radames with being a traitor. Amonasro is about to stab her, but is prevented by Radames, who surrenders to Ramfis, while Aïda and Amonasro escape.

Act IV.—Scene I. A hall in the palace. Amneris alone broods over Aïda's escape and Radames' trial for treachery ; she wishes to save him. Radames is led in ; she pleads with him to love her and be saved, but he is faithful to Aïda, though he learns that her father has been killed. He will not renounce her though Amneris demands it (" Chi ti salva "). He is led away and Amneris gives way to despair (" Ohimè, morir mi sento "). She sees the Priests descending into the subterranean hall, then hears their voices as they pray for divine guidance ; she hears Ramfis calling on Radames to speak, but he will make no defence, and they condemn him to be buried alive under the altar. As the priests return, Amneris assails them insanely. Scene 2. Same as Act I, Scene 2, save that the vault below the altar is also shown. Radames is in the crypt, dreaming of Aïda. Suddenly she appears, saying that she foresaw his doom and stole into the crypt unobserved to die with him. They bid farewell to life (" O terra addio "), while the chant of the Priests and the dance of the Priestesses goes on over them. Amneris, in black, enters the Temple to pray Heaven to accept Radames into bliss.

## Otel'lo. Othello.

Four-act lyric drama. Book from Shakspere's play by Arrigo Boïto.

Produced at Milan, La Scala, February 5, 1887.

CHARACTERS AND THEIR CREATORS.

OTELLO,
*A Moorish general in the Venetian army*...........Tamagno, tenor.
IAGO,
*His ensign*............Maurel, bar.
CASSIO, *Otello's lieutenant.*
RODERIGO (rō-dĕ-rē'-gō),
*A Venetian gentleman in love with Desdemona.*
LODOVICO (lō-dō-vē'-kō),
*Venetian ambassador.*
MONTA'NA,
*Otello's predecessor as Governor of Cyprus.*
A HERALD.
DESDEMO'NA,
*Otello's wife,*
Signorina Pantaleoni, sopr.
EMIL'IA, *Iago's wife.*

Act I.—Scene. A stormy quay. All the men except Otello are present and watching a storm-tossed ship. It is Otello's. Women enter, and pray for the ship's safety. The ship reaches the harbour at length ; Otello lands with news of a great victory, and passes into the Castle. A bonfire is built, and Iago talks to Roderigo of Desdemona, saying she will soon weary of the Moor ; he says he hates him for promoting Cassio over him. The soldiers rejoice in the fire (" Fuoco di gioia ") and in wine. Iago plies Cassio with wine and talks of Desdemona, bidding Roderigo beware of Cassio as a rival. Iago sings a wine-song, and Cassio grows drunk.

He is easily provoked to a fight by Roderigo, and sets on Montano who tries to be a peacemaker. At Iago's advice Roderigo steals away and rings the alarm, bringing the people and Otello, later Desdemona. Otello reduces Cassio to the ranks, and all disperse save Otello and Desdemona; they have a love-scene and she praises him as a great warrior ("Mio superbo guerrier"). He exclaims that death were welcome in such bliss ("Venga la morte").

Act II.—Scene. Hall in the Castle; garden at the back. Iago is promising the despondent Cassio restoration, advising him to appeal to Desdemona; left alone, Iago soliloquises over his cynical creed of cruelty and deceit ("Credo in un Dio crudel"). Later Cassio finds Desdemona in the garden and they talk together. Otello enters and Iago slyly provokes his jealousy. Sailors, children, and others appear to load Desdemona with flowers and gifts; she dismisses them graciously, and comes forward to plead for Cassio. Otello blames his uneasiness to headache; Desdemona is about to bind his head with her handkerchief; he throws it away; Emilia unobserved picks it up, and Iago snatches it from her, while Otello broods. When the women have gone, Otello upbraids Iago for instilling suspicion in him, and finally throttles him, then demands proof. Iago whispers that he heard Cassio talking in his sleep of trysts with Desdemona; he mentions the handkerchief, and says he saw it in Cassio's possession. Otello vows a terrible revenge.

Act III.—Scene. A large hall with portico. The Herald announces the arrival of ambassadors from Cyprus, and goes. Iago advises Otello to watch Cassio's gestures when later Iago talks to him. He goes, and Desdemona enters; Otello asks for her handkerchief; she says it is mislaid; he warns her that it has a strange significance, but she impatiently persists in pleading for Cassio. He makes her swear she is faithful, then drives her from him. Left alone he muses on his grief ("Dio, mi potevi scagliar"). Iago enters to say Cassio has come, and Otello hides. Iago then talks softly to Cassio of Bianca, and he is moved to laughter; he speaks of finding a strangely broidered handkerchief mysteriously left at his lodgings and produces that of Desdemona. Trumpets and a gun announce the arrival of the ambassadors and Cassio hastens away. The ambassadors enter to deliver official praises to Otello. Desdemona appears and Otello sends for Cassio, bidding Iago watch how Desdemona looks when he comes. He announces that Cassio is to stay in Cyprus as its Governor, while Otello is recalled to Venice. He mistakes Desdemona's distress at her husband's manner, for grief at the loss of Cassio, and hurls her to the ground, where she cowers. Iago tells Otello that he will kill Cassio; he then whispers Roderigo to kill Cassio so as to keep Otello at Cyprus longer, when Roderigo may still hope for Desdemona's favour. Otello rising in supreme wrath orders everyone away, curses his wife, and swoons with rage. As the cries of "Long live Otello" resound outside, Iago gloats over the prostrate "lion."

Act IV.—Scene. A bedroom. Desdemona and Emilia. Desdemona in deep sorrow as she undresses sings a sad ballad ("Willow"), of a girl, Barbara, whose lover had gone mad. When Emilia is gone, she kneels and prays to the Virgin, then lies down on the bed and sleeps. Otello enters with a scimitar. He puts out the candle, and gazing at Desdemona kisses her; she wakes and he orders her to pray. He accuses her of unfaith with Cassio, saying that he has been killed; when she weeps, he thinks his suspicions verified and smothers her. Knocking is heard. Emilia enters to say Cassio has killed Roderigo, and lives. Desdemona with her dying breath says she has killed herself. Emilia calls for help, and the others enter. The truth of the handkerchief is explained. Iago escapes. Otello tries to kill himself with his scimitar, but Lodovico prevents him. Gazing on Desdemona he draws a dagger and kills himself.

**Rigoletto** (rē-gō-lĕt'-tō).

Three-act opera. Book by F. M. Piave. (Based on Victor Hugo's "Le toi s'amuse.") Produced, Venice, March 11, 1851.

CHARACTERS AND THEIR CREATORS.

IL DUCA DI MANTO'VA.... Mirate, tenor.
RIGOLETTO,
  *His court fool*.........Varesi, bar.
SPARAFUCILE (foo'-chī-lĕ),
  *A bravo*...............Ponz, bass.
IL CONTE DI MONTERO'NE... Damini, bar.
MARUL'LO,
  *A cavalier*..........Kunerth, bar.
BOR'SA,
  *A courtier*..........Zuliani, tenor.
IL CONTE DI CEPRANO (chĕ-prä'-nō),
                        Bellini, bass.
COURT USHER.............Rizzi, tenor.
GILDA (jēl'-dä),
  *Rigoletto's daughter*,
      Signorina T. Brambilla, sopr.
MADDALENA (lä'-nä),
  *Sister of Sparafucile*,
            Casaloni, contr.
GIOVANNA (jo-vän'-na),
  *Gilda's nurse*.......Saini, m. sopr.
LA CONTESSA DI CEPRANO,
            Marselli, m. sopr.
PAGE OF THE DUCHESS,
      Modes Lovati, m. sopr.

Act I.—Scene 1. A fête in the Duke's palace. The Duke tells Borsa of his infatuation for an unknown maiden whom he has seen at church, and traced to her home where an unknown man visits her nightly. He sings of the fickleness of his heart for this or that woman ("Questa o quella"). The Countess Ceprano appears and though watched by her jealous husband permits the Duke to lead her away. Rigoletto, the Duke's favourite and the go-between of his intrigues, laughs at the Duke's flirtations, and Marullo says he learns that even the hunchbacked Rigoletto has a sweetheart. The Duke reappears and Rigoletto advises him to elope with Ceprano's wife. He taunts Ceprano, who plots with other courtiers to put the hunchback out of the way. The Count Monterone forces his way in and denounces the Duke's crimes. Rigoletto mocks him because he makes such ado over the loss of his daughter's honour; but Monterone frightens the hunchback by a father's curse before he is led away. Scene 2. A dark, secluded street at night. Rigoletto, stealing in, is accosted by Sparafucile, who offers to put any rival out of the way, either by a single thrust in the street, or by decoying the victim into his house with the aid of his sister. Rigoletto declines the man's service with thanks, and in a soliloquy compares the bravo's sword to his own wit as a weapon. He enters the walled yard of his house, out of which Gilda comes and embraces her father. He keeps her in this seclusion from the corruptions of court life, and she does not even know his name. She asks to know who her mother was He begs her not to ask ("Deh non parlare"). Gilda assures him she has never left the house except for church, and her nurse Giovanna corroborates her. Father and daughter sing a loving duet ("Veglia o donna"). The Duke in disguise appears outside. Rigoletto goes out to see who is there, and the Duke manages to steal inside unobserved and throw a purse to the nurse. Rigoletto returning warns Gilda to let no one in on any account, and, not seeing the Duke, locks the gate from the outside and goes away. The Duke appears, motions the nurse to retire, and kneeling before Gilda, declares his love for her ("E il sol dell' anima"), pretending he is a poor student named Gaultier Maldé. She promises him her love and he goes away.

Left alone Gilda muses on his dear name ("Caro nome") and enters the house. Outside appear three courtiers to steal Rigoletto's supposed mistress. Rigoletto appears and is told they are going to steal Ceprano's wife. His fears for his own daughter thus set at rest, he enters the plot with zest, and is given a mask, which blindfolds him, and is set to hold a ladder by which the courtiers ascend his own wall to steal Gilda. Though she manages to scream, he does not recognise her voice. Tearing off the bandaging mask, he discovers too late that he has aided in the violation of his own home, and remembering Count Monterone's malediction, he swoons.

Act II. — Scene. The Duke's palace. He is brooding over the abduction of Gilda whom he truly loves ("Parmi veder"). The courtiers enter to tell him of stealing Rigoletto's mistress ("Scorrendo uniti remota"). The Duke recognises from their story that it is Gilda whom they have stolen, and exclaiming that the voice of love calls him ("Possente amor"), hurries away. Rigoletto enters, trying to conceal his anxiety from the taunting courtiers. The Duchess's page enters, asking for the Duke. They try uneasily to explain his absence. Rigoletto suspects that Gilda is with the Duke and confessing that she is his daughter tries vainly to force his way through the courtiers. He curses them bitterly ("Cortigiani, vil razza dannata"), and breaks down weeping. Gilda appears and rushes to her father. The courtiers withdraw, and Gilda tells of her humble lover and her abduction. Rigoletto weeps with her ("Piange, fanciulla"). The Count Monterone passes in chains, confessing that his cursing of the Duke has been vain, but Rigoletto fiercely vows to administer the curse, though Gilda pleads against his frenzy ("No, vecchio, t'inganni").

Act III.—Scene. An old weatherworn house on the bank of the Mincio. Inside Sparafucile cleaning his belt. Outside Gilda pleads with her father who has plotted the death of the Duke.

She persists that the Duke is faithful to her. The Duke, dressed as a soldier, now appears inside the house, and calls for wine. He sings recklessly of "fickle woman" ("La donna è mobile"), and when Maddalena, Sparafucile's sister, appears, makes violent love to her, not knowing that Gilda and her father are watching through crevices in the walls. The varying emotions are combined in the famous quartet ("Bella figlia dell' amore"). Sparafucile steps out and bargains with Rigoletto, who wants him to kill the Duke and put the body in a sack which Rigoletto will throw into the river at midnight. He pays half the sum agreed and promises more. He has sent Gilda on ahead to don boy's clothes to aid their flight, and now follows her out. A storm rises, and the Duke decides to spend the night where he is. He goes up to a room, and Maddalena pleads with Sparafucile not to kill him. Gilda, who has stolen back in boy's clothes, overhears the plea. The assassin says he will spare the Duke if he can get someone else to put in the sack. Gilda, to save her faithless lover, knocks at the door and asks lodging. As she is admitted, the lights are put out. Rigoletto appears; the clock strikes twelve. Sparafucile comes out with a heavy sack, receives the money, and goes. As Rigoletto is dragging the sack toward the river, he hears the Duke pass in the distance singing "La donna è mobile." In amazement he tears open the sack and finds his daughter. She asserts with dying breath her devotion to the Duke, and promises to pray for her father in heaven ("Lassu in cielo"). She dies, leaving him in frantic grief and loneliness, confessing the fulfilment of Monterone's malediction.

**La Traviata** (lä trä-vĭ-ä'-tä). The Erring One.

Three-act opera. Book by Piave, after Dumas fils' "La Dame aux Camélias" or "Camille" (with names of

characters changed, and time placed
back in 1700).

First produced disastrously, Venice,
March 6, 1853, the failure being largely
due to the embonpoint of the soprano,
whose wasting away was not convinc-
ng.

CHARACTERS AND THEIR CREATORS.

VIOLETTA VALERE (vä-lā'-rĕ),
   Mme. Donatelli, **sopr.**
FLORA BERVOIX (bĕr-vwä),
 *Her friend*..................**sopr.**
GEORGIO GERMONT (jĕr'-mônt),
    Vavesi, **bar.**
ALFREDO GERMONT,
 *His son*....................**tenor.**
BARON DAUPHOL (dä'-oo-fôl)......**bass.**
GASTONE DE LETORIÈRES (gäs-tō'-nĕ
 dä lä-tō-rĭ-ā'-rĕs).........**tenor.**
DOTTORE GRENVIL (dôt-tō'-rĕ grän'-vēl),
    **bass.**
MARQUIS D'OBIGNY (dō-bēn'-yē) ...**bass.**

Act I.—Scene. The rich apartments
of Violetta, a demi-mondaine doomed
to die of consumption. She is giving
a dinner-party. Gastone introduces
Alfredo, who has conceived a deep passion for her. He is prevailed on to
sing a wine-song, but shows deep sympathy when, the dinner finished, she
faints on the way to the ball-room.
She gives him a flower and he departs,
followed soon after by the other guests.
Left alone she thinks that she has at
last found a sincere lover, and falls into
ecstatic revery (" Ah, fors è lui "), " Per-
hance 'tis he that my fancy has been
painting in its loneliness."

Act II.—Scene I. A country house
near Paris. Alfredo enters, rejoicing in
the blissful seclusion in which he is living with Violetta. Her maid returns
from Paris, and betrays the fact that
Violetta has been pawning her resources to keep up the country place.
He is overcome with the humiliation of
his position, and leaves for Paris to secure funds. Violetta enters, and re-

ceiving a letter from Flora inviting her
back to the old gaiety, laughs at the
thought. An elderly man is shown in.
He announces himself to be Alfredo's
father. He has come to plead with her
to give up Alfredo as otherwise the
lover of Alfredo's sister will break off
the match because of the scandal. After
a bitter struggle, she consents, and he
embraces her and goes into the garden.
She writes a letter and Alfredo surprises her. She leaves him, in great
agitation. Soon a messenger appears
with a letter, and he learns that Violetta has fled. In his grief, his father
appears and endeavours to console him,
reminding him of his home in sunny
Provence; but Alfredo reading Flora's
letter determines to follow Violetta and
revenge himself. Scene 2. Flora's
mansion. Some of her guests are gambling, others pass in masquerade as
gipsies. Gastone leads a group of bull-
fighters, and recites the romance of the
Matador Piguillo. Flora and her devoted but quarrelsome Marquis have
various disagreements. Alfredo appears, and dejectedly joins the card-
players. Violetta enters upon the arm
of the Baron. Alfredo as he plays
makes slighting references to the fickleness of the broken-hearted Violetta.
Dinner is announced, and all leave the
room save Violetta, who calls Alfredo.
She warns him of the Baron's fury.
He says he will go if she will go with
him, but she refuses, and he summons
all the guests and furiously denounces
Violetta as a mercenary wretch; to pay
his debt to her he flings a purse at her.
She faints in the arms of her Doctor.
Alfredo's father enters and leads him
away.

Act III.—Scene. Violetta's bedroom.
She is asleep and her maid Annina
sleeps near the fireplace. The Doctor
arrives and tells Annina that Violetta
has only a few hours to live. When he
has gone, Violetta sends Annina to give
ten of her remaining twenty louis to the
poor, who are making holiday outside.
Left alone she reads an old letter from

Alfredo's father, who has been moved by her suffering to send for his son to return from the foreign country. She fears that he will be too late. Annina enters hastily, trying to prepare her for the coming of Alfredo. They have a rapturous reunion and decide to flee from "dear Paris" (" Parigi caro "). But weakness overcomes her, and she accepts her fate. The Doctor and Alfredo's father enter, but can be of no help. She gives a medallion of herself to Alfredo as a memorial, and dies.

**Il Trovatore** (ĕl trō-vä-tō'-rĕ). The Troubadour.

Four-act opera. Book by S. Commarano, from a drama by Garcia de la Vega. Produced, Rome, January 19, 1853.

CHARACTERS.

| | |
|---|---|
| Il Conte di Luna | bar. |
| Manrico (män-rē'-kō) | tenor. |
| Ferran'do | bass. |
| Ruiz (roo'-ēts) | tenor. |
| An Old Zingaro (Gipsy) | bass. |
| Un Messo | tenor. |
| Leono'ra | sopr. |
| Azucena (ä-tsoo-chä'-nä) | m.-sopr. |
| Ines (ē'-nĕs) | sopr. |

Act I.—Scene I. Vestibule to the apartments of the Count. Ferrando tries to keep awake the other servants by telling them the story of the Count's younger brother, who had been bewitched in his cradle by a gipsy. For this the gipsy had been burned. Her daughter, and the Count's baby brother then simultaneously disappeared. It was believed that he had been burned. Ferrando hopes some day to meet this younger gipsy. Scene 2. The gardens of the Queen's palace. Leonora, her maid of honour, tells her friend Ines how she fell in love with a cavalier at a tournament. He appeared again one placid night (" Tacea la notte placida "), and sang to her as a Troubadour. She confesses her love for him (" Di tale amor che dirsi "). The two women with-

draw, and the Count di Luna appears breathing love for Leonora. Outside h hears the voice of a Troubadour singing Leonora rushes out and mistaking th Count for the singer, embraces him The Troubadour appearing upbraid Leonora's faithlessness, but she ex plains her mistake. The Count cha lenges Manrico to combat, and th men withdraw, Leonora fainting wit terror.

Act II.—Scene I. A ruined house a dawn. Azucena, a gipsy, near a larg fire ; near her Manrico. Gipsies gathere about. The men working with thei hammers sing the famous " Anvil cho rus " (" Vedi le fosche "). Azucena sings a fierce song of burning a woma at the stake (" Stride la vampa ! ") The others disperse to their tasks, leav ing Azucena and Manrico together She tells him the dismal story of he mother's death for sorcery, and how she, mad for revenge, had seized th Count's younger brother, as sh thought, and burned him to death only to find that she had burned he own child. Manrico exclaims, " The I am not your son." But Azucena denies her own words and says sh was raving. Manrico tells her that h has once more met his old enemy th Count, this time not in battle but i duel ; he had defeated him, but ha spared his life. Azucena command him never again to spare the Count. A messenger appears and summons Man rico to the command of the troops. H bids Azucena farewell and goes. Scen 2. Convent cloisters at night. Th Count with his followers has come t kidnap Leonora, whose beauty h cannot resist (" Il balen del su sorriso "). A chorus of nuns is heard Leonora and Ines appear, and Leonor declares her intention to take the vei The Count seizes her, but Manric appears and later some of his fol lowers. Leonora consents to go wit Manrico.

Act III.—Scene I. Camp of Coun di Luna, outside a besieged castle errando and chorus sing a martial ong ("Squilli, eccheggi la tromba guerera"). The Count appears and is told nat a spying gipsy has been captured. Lzucena is brought in. She says her ome is Biscay and the Count says his ounger brother was stolen there. Ferando recognises her, she is seized, and alls on Manrico her son to save her. The Count rejoices at this double re-enge. Scene 2. A room near a hapel in the castle. Leonora and Manico together. He rejoices in her love s an aid in battle ("Ah, se ben mio"). They are about to be married in the hapel when Manrico's friend Ruiz rings news that Azucena is taken, and s to be burned. Manrico in horror 'Di quella pirra") rushes to rescue er.

Act IV.—Scene I. Outside a palace ower at night. Leonora and Ruiz nter. Manrico has been captured; she ends him hope and comfort "on love's osy wings" ("D'amor sull' ali rose"). A death-knell is tolled and voices are eard chanting a "Miserere." She hears Manrico bewailing his fate ("Ah, che la norte ognora"), and she vows to save im at all costs ("Tu vedrai che amore n terra"). She withdraws as the Count nters, then accosts him and begs for Manrico's life with bitter tears ("Mira, li acerbe lagrime"). She finally offers erself as payment for Manrico's life. The Count gives the order to release Manrico, and Leonora takes poison from ring, then follows the Count. Scene . A prison; Azucena and Manrico. Azucena sees in terrible vision her own nother's death at the stake. She falls sleep watched by Manrico. The Count nd Leonora enter. She offers him free-lom and begs him to fly. He curses er; but she dies before him and he nderstands her fidelity. The Count, hus foiled, orders Manrico out to death. Ie awakes Azucena and drags her to he window, and shows her Manrico's lead body. She exclaims, "He was our brother! Thus thou art avenged, ) mother mine!"

## WAGNER, WILHELM RICHARD.

[Who wrote all of his own librettos.]

**Der Fliegende Holländer** (děr flē'-gĕn-dĕ hôl'-lĕnt-ĕr). The Flying Dutchman. In French as "Le Vaisseau Fantôme" (le vĕs-sō fäṅ-tōm). In Italian, first as "L'Ollando'se danna'to" then as "Il Vascello Fantas'ma" (ēl vä-shĕl'-lō) or "The Phantom Ship."

Three-act opera, book and music by Wagner. Conceived during a very stormy three-weeks sea-voyage in 1839. Begun, 1841. Produced, Dresden, January 2, 1843.

CHARACTERS AND THEIR CREATORS.

DALAND (dä'-länt),
   *Norwegian sea-captain*........bass.
ERIK (ā'-rēk),
   *A huntsman*...............tenor.
DAS STEUERMANN (däs shtoi'-ĕr-män),
   *Daland's pilot*..............tenor.
THE HOLLANDER........Wechter, bar.
SENTA (zän'-tä),
   *Daland's daughter*,
     Frau Schröder-Devrient, sopr.
MARY (mä'-rē)..............m.-sopr.

Act I.—A rocky shore. Under a heavy storm a Norwegian ship has cast anchor close to shore. The sailors are heard singing as they furl the sails. Daland on the rocks grumbles at being driven inshore so near his port, so near home and his dear old child Senta. The storm subsides and Daland (with grand opera license) is able to step aboard as easily as he stepped ashore. He orders the sailors below to rest and leaves the pilot to take the watch. Left alone, the pilot sings a love-song of his sweetheart ("Mein Mädel") and the southwind that brings him home. He gradually falls asleep. The storm wakens and a ship with blood-red sails and black masts appears and drops anchor with a crash; then the uncanny crew furl the sails without noise, and go below. The captain landing, exclaims that the seven-year terror is past

and he may come ashore a little while.
He bewails his lot, cursed to sail on
forever till the Day of Judgment unless
some woman perchance may love him
unchangingly. He feels the futility of
such hope and cries to heaven to destroy him. On Daland's ship there is a
scene of excitement. Daland, coming
on deck, finds his pilot asleep and a
strange ship near; he goes ashore and
meets the newcomer, who tells him of
his sad lot and begs a home for a time;
he has a chest brought from his ship
and offers the pearls it contains for a
night's hospitality, and still greater
wealth for the hand of the daughter
Daland mentions. The canny Daland
accepts, and the two captains going
aboard cheerfully make sail for Daland's port.

Act II.—Scene. Interior of Daland's
home. Among charts, pictures, etc., on
the wall is a portrait of a pale, black-
bearded man in Spanish garb. The
room is filled with girls at spinning
wheels. Senta and Mary are among
them. Senta alone of all is sad, and the
merry spinning chorus ("Summ' und
brumm'") does not enliven her. Mary
rebukes Senta for gazing at the portrait. They finally persuade her to sing
the ballad of the "Flying Dutchman,"
whose portrait it is. She sings of the
ship with blood-red sails and black
mast and her sleepless spectral captain,
who must sail on and on forever because in trying to round a cape in the
teeth of a gale he swore, " I will keep on
trying to all eternity." Satan heard him
and condemned him to sail eternally
till some maiden should love him faithfully. He may land once in seven years
to hunt for such a wife. At the end of
the ballad Senta excitedly cries out
that she herself would be that faithful
woman. Her lover Erik enters, and,
hearing the words, is deeply hurt at her
resolve. When the spinners finish the
task and leave, he pleads for her love;
but she puts him off, eager to welcome
her father, whose ship has been sighted.
Erik is jealous of the picture and tells

her that he has dreamed of seeing h[e]
father coming home and bringing th[e]
Flying Dutchman; in the dream 'Sent[a]
embraced the stranger and sailed awa[y]
with him. On hearing this drea[m]
Senta exclaims that she feels the Flyin[g]
Dutchman to be her destiny. Eri[k]
rushes away in horror. Senta, remain[-]
ing gazing at the picture, suddenly see[s]
her father enter with—the Dutchma[n]
himself! Her father, amazed at h[e]
stupor, tells her that the stranger ha[s]
come to find a home and a wife. Com[-]
mending each to each, he goes away[,]
leaving them together. The Dutchma[n]
muses on her beauty and she on h[is]
sorrow. He asks her to be his wife an[d]
she vows to follow him through al[l]
Daland returning is rejoiced at the ou[t]
come.

Act III.—Scene. A bay at night[,]
on shore, Daland's house; in the ba[y]
Daland's and the Dutchman's ships a[t]
anchor. Daland's sailors are makin[g]
merry on deck singing " Pilot, leave th[e]
watch" ("Steuermann, lass di[e]
Wacht"). Girls come from the hous[e]
with food and drink for the sailors[.]
They are surprised at the unnatura[l]
gloom and silence on the Dutch shi[p]
They can get no response to thei[r]
taunts. At length a strange blue flam[e]
appears on the Dutch ship, and gradu[-]
ally a storm rocks the weird craft, leav[-]
ing the bay and the other ship calm[.]
The Dutch sailors now bestir themselve[s]
and chant a sardonic song of the van[-]
ity of the Dutchman's hopes. Th[e]
Norwegian sailors and women ar[e]
frightened and try to drown the uncann[y]
song with their own, but vainly, an[d]
finally go below in terror, and silenc[e]
takes the Dutch ship again. Erik an[d]
Senta come from the house, he pleadin[g]
with her frantically and imploring he[r]
to remember the day of their youn[g]
love ("Willst jenes Tag's"). Th[e]
Dutchman entering hears his plea an[d]
thinking Senta false, cries out in despair[,]
and orders his crew to set sail, weig[h]
anchor and away. Senta pleads wit[h]
him, in spite of Erik's prayer, but th[e]

Dutchman mocks her. He proclaims his identity and, going aboard his ship, puts to sea. Senta is restrained from following him by her father and others who rush out. But she breaks away, and with a last cry, " Here am I, faithful unto death ! " leaps into the sea. The Dutch ship sinks, and in the sunset glow Senta and the Hollander are seen rising, transfigured in each other's arms.

## Die Meistersinger von Nürnberg
(dē mī′-stěr-zǐng-ěr fōn nürn′-běrkh). Les Maîtres Chanteurs (lā mětr shäṅ-tŭr). I maestri cantori di Norimburga (ē mä-ä′-strē kän-tō′-rē). The Mastersingers of Nuremburg.

A 3-act Comic Opera. First sketched in Vienna, 1845, the text finished and published, Paris, 1862, music finished, 1867.

Produced, Munich, June 21, 1868.

CHARACTERS AND THEIR CREATORS.

HANS SACHS (häns zäkhs),
*A cobbler and famous writer,*
Betz, bass.
VEIT POGNER (fīt pôkh′-něr),
*A goldsmith*.................bass.
SIXTUS BECKMESSER (zēx′-toos běk′-měs-sěr),
*Town clerk*..........Hölzel, bass.
FRITZ KOTHNER (frǐts kōt′-něr),
*A baker*....................bass.
EIGHT OTHER TRADESMEN.
WALTHER VON STOLZING (väl′-těr fōn shtôl′-tsǐng),
*A young Franconian Knight,*
Nachbauer, tenor.
DAVID (dä′-fēt),
*Apprentice to Hans Sachs,*
Schlosser, tenor.
EVA (ā′-fä),
*Pogner's daughter, in love with Walter,* Frl. Mallinger, sopr.
MAGDALENE (mäkh-dä-lā′-ně),
*Eva's maid, in love with David.*
Frau Dietz, m. sopr.
A. NIGHT WATCHMAN.

NOTE.—This semi-historical opera concerning the guild of Mastersingers is a comic companion-piece to Tannhäuser (q. v., Note a), but without supernatural personages. It is also a satirical answer to Wagner's academical critics. Hans Sachs is an actual figure in early German literature.

Act I.—Scene. Interior of St. Katherine's church. A service is just closing. Walter gazes at Eva, who flirts with him, and when, as the congregation disperses, he speaks to her, she gains time by sending her nurse back for a scarf-pin, then her prayer-book. The anxious nurse tells the ardent lover that Eva must marry the victor in the next day's song-tourney. David enters and busies himself drawing curtains to shut off the nave. Eva, comparing Walter to the painter Dürer's picture of the Biblical David, is misunderstood by Magdalene to refer to the awkward apprentice. David and other apprentices are preparing the room for the Mastersingers ; they are about to undergo the examination that will admit them to the guild. Walter decides to try the examination. David with his shoemaking companions, tells him how a song must be cut, soled and heeled to fit the rigid requirements of the guild. With many interruptions from the skylarking apprentices, David tells Walter of the various steps : first the thirty-six musical tones and modes must be learned, they make a long list most arbitrarily named as " short, long, crimson, luscious, nightingale, secret, glutton, pelican, etc." Once these are known, they must be sung with proper voice production and correct embellishment. Having thus become " a scholar " and " a singer," one must pass the examination as " Poet," manipulating rimes adroitly but strictly within limits of the rules. To become a " Mastersinger " one must sing both poetry and music of his own composing, and do all three feats without breach of the thirty-three canons. A blackboard is brought in. On this one of the judges, called the " Marker," chalks down each mistake —seven are allowed ; if more are made the candidate is declared " outsung and outcast." Pogner and Beckmesser enter, the latter, a grotesque old pedant, begging Pogner to plead with his daughter on his behalf, Pogner having declared that though Eva is to be the prize, she must add her consent before she will be made to marry the victor. Walter announces himself as a candidate for Mastership. Beckmesser is jealous, but the rest welcome the young nobleman. The roll is called, Pogner announces the prize he offers for the next song contest—his daughter, who must add her verdict to that of the judges. Hans Sachs suggests that the public also be given a voice in the decision. He defends their right to be considered, lest art grow too severe and hidebound. He enrages Beckmesser by hinting that only the young bachelors be allowed to vie for the girl's hand. Walter is brought forward, and asked who has been his teacher. He says the books of the old Minnesinger Walter von der Vogelweide (vide Tannhäuser) have taught him poetry ; he has learned music of the birds in the woods. His tuition is received with scepticism save by Sachs, and he prepares for the trial. Beckmesser goes to the Marker's box. Kothner summarises to him the rules, and Walter begins a joyous song of spring and love. Beckmesser is heard scratching down the marks, and at the end shows the blackboard quite covered. The other masters ridicule the formless composition, and Walter is allowed to sing his second stanza only when Sachs has outwrangled Beckmesser, who insults him as a poor cobbler. The spontaneous lilt of the second attempt Beckmesser finds guilty of breaking every rule, and despite Sachs' plea for genius unfettered, a vote throws Walter out, and the meeting disperses in confusion.

Act II.—Scene. A Street, on one **side** Hans Sachs' Shop : on the other

Pogner's residence, in front of it a lime tree and shrubs. It is evening and the apprentices are putting up the shutter and thinking of the next day's festiva Magdalene enters with a basket of sweets for David ; on learning of Walter's rejection, she snatches it away and hurries into the house. The apprentices mock him, and Sachs, on his way to his shop, stops an impending brawl. Pogner and Eva enter ; he says she must wed none but a master, and enters the house. Eva and Magdalene after deciding to consult Hans Sachs follow Pogner. Sachs appears and sit down at his bench to make shoes for Beckmesser ; he falls to musing on the strange, lawless charm of Walter's song Eva steals across to him, but being timid of direct questioning, gets nothing from him but vexation and bante and reproval of the aristocrat, who would not study the rules. He withdraws to his shop, leaving his door slightly ajar. Magdalene tells Eva to prepar for a serenade from Beckmesser, who hopes so to soften her heart to him Walter appears and tells Eva of his humiliation. The watchman passes, ordering all lights out. Eva slips into the house, and Walter hides behind the lime-tree. Hans Sachs has overheard, and, fearing an elopement, turns a bright light across the street. Eva slips out in Magdalene's cloak, but she fears to cross the light. Beckmesser is now seen approaching, and the lovers hide behind the shrubbery. Sachs, resuming his work, sings lustily a song of Eve driven barefoot out of Paradise, and needing the aid of a cobbler. The cunning allusion to Eva's own plan to become an exile is not lost on the girl hidden with her lover behind the shrubbery. Beckmesser, seeing Magdalene at an upper window, sings to her his idea of an artistic serenade, pretending to Sachs, whom he cannot get rid of, that he is singing merely to get Sachs' opinion. The cobbler now plays Marker, noting each mistake with a thwack of his hammer on the shoe. Beck messer lays the stress on the wrong syllables, adds tawdry flourishes, etc. Sachs finds so many mistakes that the shoe is finished before the song. The neighbours now begin to complain. David appears and cudgels Beckmesser. The whole town falls into a riot, and Walter decides to clear a way through. He and Eva make a dash, but Sachs seizes Walter, and Pogner appearing drags Eva inside the house. Sachs drives David in, and forces Walter also into his house. And the watchman appearing disperses the crowd.

Act III.—Scene I. Interior of Sachs' workshop. Sachs is reading. David enters with a basket full of ribbons and edibles, which he hides from his master. He tells Sachs that he and 'Lena have made up, but Sachs does not hear him. At length he closes his book, and has David rehearse his trial-song. David begins with Beckmesser's tune, but corrects himself. Sachs dismisses the apprentice more gently than usual, and falls into reverie on the troublesome little things of life. Walter appears, having slept ill. Sachs counsels him that his passionate spring song was all very well, but that life and wedlock demand more serious art and science. In a long scene he now writes down and corrects and guides the composition of a song as Walter improvises it. Two sections or "bars" being shaped, Sachs says Walter can fashion the third later, and goes with him to dress for the festival. Beckmesser limps in and, finding Sachs' manuscript of Walter's song, slips it in his pocket. Sachs re-enters only to be reviled as a rival and conspirator against Beckmesser. In proof he shows the song. Sachs says he may keep it, and use it. Beckmesser is overcome with delight at having a poem by the gifted Sachs, and hurries away to compose his music. Eva enters, pretending to be troubled by a tight shoe ; but she cannot tell where it pinches. She is evidently scheming to see Walter, who soon appears. Sachs draws off her shoe

and pretends to be busy with it, while Walter sings to Eva the third bar of his prize-song. As Sachs sighs ironically of the miseries of his trade, Eva tells him that she could have loved him had not Walter appeared. But Hans Sachs alludes to the fate of the old husband, who intervened between Tristan and Isolde (the love-motive of that opera being quoted in the music). Magdalene and David enter. Sachs says a new mode of art has been created by Walter, and with a box on the ear he raises David to a journeyman. The five unite in a song of hope for Walter's success—this glorious quintet is well known. Eva and Magdalene go home, and the scene changes to 2. The banks of the river Pegnitz ; a stage has been erected for the contest, and the "Corporations" arrive in the following order : Shoemakers, Instrument makers, Tailors and Bakers. The apprentices gather. David waltzes with a girl till someone mentions Magdalene. The Masters gather, and Pogner leads in Eva. Sachs steps forward, but the affectionate people break out into one of his own songs. Sachs then tells of the unusual prize of the contest. Beckmesser is the first to sing, and is received with laughter. He sings Walter's verses to his old serenade tune. The words fit it so ill, that he becomes confused, mixes his metaphors and words and sings arrant nonsense. He at length breaks down and, accusing Sachs of the fault, rushes away. Sachs says the song is not his, and only needs good music. To prove it, he asks Walter to sing it ; Walter takes his place and wins the enthusiasm of the throng by his art. The people at last vote him the prize. Pogner welcomes him as a Master. Sachs gives him counsel in the glory of German poetry and song, and places the golden chain about his neck. Eva takes the Master's wreath from Walter's head and places it on that of Sachs. Walter and she embrace the cobbler, whom all hail with affectionate homage.

**Lohengrin** (lō'-ĕn-grēn).

Three-act opera. Begun in 1845. Produced, Weimar, August 28, 1850 (Goethe's birthday).

CHARACTERS AND THEIR CREATORS.

LOHENGRIN . . . . . . . . . . . . . . Beck, tenor.
HEINRICH DER VOGLER (hīn'-rĭkh dĕr fōkh'-lĕr) (" Henry the Fowler "), *Emperor* . . . . . . . . . . . . . Hofer, bass.
FRIEDRICH VON TELRAMUND (frēt'-rĭkh fōn tĕl'-rä-moont) . . . . . . . . Millde, bar.
THE HERALD of the King . . . . . . . . bass.
ELSA VON BRABANT (ĕl'-zä fōn brä'-bänt), Frau Agathe, sopr.
ORTRUD (ôr'-troot), *Wife of Count Telramund,* Frl. Fastlinger, alto.

Act I.—Scene. The banks of the Scheldt in Brabant near Antwerp, Tenth Century. After the Herald's message the Emperor Henry announces that he has come to Brabant to gather forces to repel the Hungarians ; he learns that the people are in discord. He calls on Telramund to explain, and is told by him that the late Duke had died, leaving two children in Telramund's charge. The son and heir has disappeared and he accuses the sister Elsa of putting him out of the way. He therefore claims the Duchy as next kinsman. The accused is summoned to trial, and she enters, answering the King's questions by telling a dream she had of an angelic knight and defender. Telramund offers to undergo the ordeal of battle (which was then the procedure of the courts) and Elsa says she will have no champion save the one she dreamed of. Four trumpeters sound North, South, East, and West, but no one appears to champion her. She kneels in prayer ; from the distance comes a knight in a boat drawn by a swan. All are amazed except Ortrud, who is terror-stricken. The knight (who is Parsifal's son Lohengrin, one of the semi-deified Knights of the Holy Grail period of King Arthur) bids farewell to the swan, which departs. He announces himself Elsa's champion, but makes one stipulation : that she shall ask no questions of who or what he is, or whence come. She promises and is embraced as his betrothed. The ground is now prepared for the fight and with due ceremony the contest begins. Telramund is soon beaten down, but his life is spared, and he and his wife are crushed with shame, while the Knight is hailed with joy by the others.

Act II.—Scene. Night outside the palace. On the steps of the Minster opposite, cower Telramund and his wife. Under the ban of confiscation and exile they linger in rags. He reviles her as the cause of his disgrace, the lying accuser of Elsa and the source of the whole plot. She promises in one day to ruin Elsa by making her ask Lohengrin the forbidden question. She relies on witchcraft for success. Elsa appears on the balcony in blissful reverie. Ortrud with mock meekness addresses her, craving pity, which Elsa bestows. She comes down to take into shelter the outcast noblewoman, promising to add Lohengrin's forgiveness to her own. She invites her to attend the wedding, and Ortrud, pretending gratitude, says she would save Elsa from impending ill, and hints that Lohengrin may depart as easily as he came. Elsa, ill at ease, takes her into the house, and Telramund watches gloatingly. Day begins with the bustle of servants and the sounding of trumpets to gather the people. The Herald publishes Telramund's exile, Lohengrin's accession to his estates, his wedding to Elsa, and the departure the next day of all the warriors to battle. Four noblemen, angry at being called on for service, find Telramund and conceal him. The wedding procession forms, Elsa entering with Ortrud richly garbed. As Elsa is about to ascend the Minster step, Ortrud angrily darts in front of her, demanding precedence. She casts aspersion on the mysterious Knight. The King and Lohengrin press through the crowd, and Lohengrin, rebuking Ortrud as an evil sorceress, starts to lead Elsa up the steps. Telramund confronts him, demanding his name and station. Lohengrin sees with grief that Elsa is disheartened and afraid. Telramund whispers to her that if the Knight but lose even a finger-joint, he must tell all. Elsa hesitating, finally falls on Lohengrin's bosom and enters the Minster with him. Act III.—Scene 1. The bridal chamber. The procession enters and Lohengrin and Elsa are divested of their outer robes. Left alone they exchange words of bliss, and she says her only regret is that she may not know and speak his name. She persists in her questioning, despite his entreaties. Suddenly Telramund and the four nobles rush in with swords drawn. Elsa seizes Lohengrin's sword and hands it to him quickly. He kills Telramund with it and bids the nobles, who yield, to take the body to the King. Elsa swoons and he summons her women and bids them take her also before the King. He promises there to give her the answer she has asked; and sadly departs.—The scene changes to that of Act I. The armies gather and the King promises them success in battle. Telramund's body is brought in, followed soon by the tottering and dejected Elsa, then by the mournful Lohengrin. He tells the King he cannot go to the war with the armies: he says that Telramund was slain as a midnight assassin, and that Elsa has been lured into breaking her vow. He says he has no shame of birth to conceal, and describes the Temple of the Holy Grail (i.e., the second cup or grail, from which Christ drank at the Last Supper, which contained the blood He shed on the cross, and which is preserved and renewed yearly by the Holy Ghost, as it is guarded by Knights chosen for blameless life). Lohengrin declares that he is the son of Parsifal (see the story of that opera), and has been sent to rescue the maiden. The swan reappears and Lohengrin announces that the Grail is

recalling him. He says that Elsa's brother will return to her, and gives her for him his sword, horn, and ring, which ensure her brother's success. Ortrud exultantly confesses that Elsa's brother is the swan, changed to that shape; if the Knight had remained, the swan would have been freed of the spell. Lohengrin listening kneels in the boat to pray. A dove descends, Lohengrin joyfully removes the chain from the swan, which sinks. In its place appears Elsa's brother. Ortrud falls with a shriek. Elsa greets the boy with such delight that she does not see the dove taking the chain and drawing the boat away. The nobles kneel to the returned boy, but Elsa seeing Lohengrin already far in the distance, faints with a last cry, " My husband ! "

**Tristan und Isolde** (trēs'-tän oont ē-zōlt'-ĕ). Tristram et Yseult (trēsträn ā ē-sŭl), *F*. Tristram and Isolde.

Three-act " Action." Composed 1857–59. Produced, Munich, June 10, 1865.

CHARACTERS AND THEIR CREATORS.

TRISTAN,
  *Cornish Knight,*
Ludwig Schnorr von Carolsfeld, tenor.
KURWENAL (koor'-fĕ-näl),
  *His squire*.......Mitterwurzer, bar.
KÖNIG MARKE (kā'-nĭkh mär'-kĕ),
                      Zoltmayer, bass.
MELOT (mā'-lôt),
  *King of Cornwall*...........tenor.
STEERSMAN......................bar.
YOUNG SAILOR.................tenor
SHEPHERD.....................tenor
ISOLDE,
  *Daughter of the king of Ireland,*
  Frau Schnorr von Carolsfeld..sopr.
BRANGÄNE (bräng-ā'-nĕ),
  *Her attendant*.....Frl. Deinet, sopr.

Act I.—Scene. A pavilion on the forward deck of a ship; a tapestry closing from view the portion aft. Isolde reclining on a couch, Brangäne gazing

out over the sea. The voice of an unseen sailor singing of his Irish love.
Isolde starts up in a sudden fury. Brangäne is distressed. Isolde calls for air.
Isolde throws back the tapestry, showing sailors and knights and Tristan looking off seaward. Isolde speaks scornfully of Tristan to Brangäne, who defends
him. Sent to summon Tristan, Brangäne finds him reluctant to come ; he
says his only duty is to take the bride
Isolde, willing or not, to King Marke,
who awaits her. The devoted Kurwenal emphasises this point, but is re-
proved by Tristan, while Brangäne
draws the curtains again. The insulted
Isolde tells her of the first meeting when
once, years before, she had found Tristan
wounded in Ireland and had nursed him
to health, though she should have killed
him, since he had killed her kinsman
and betrothed lover Thorold. He had
made love to her and she had forgotten
the blood-feud between them ; then he
had sailed away, only to return to demand her hand for his king and lead
her away as bride to another. She
curses Tristan. Brangäne tries to calm
her, but at Isolde's order brings out a
coffer of medicines and poisons. Isolde
indicates a deadly draught. The crew
is heard greeting the land. Kurwenal
appears to bid them prepare to disem-
bark. She tells him to send Tristan to
her. Brangäne pleads frantically, but is
silenced as Tristan enters. He explains
that honour has kept him far from her,
and she bitterly reminds him that she
should have slain him for killing Thorold. He offers her his sword, but now
she pretends to have forgiven him and
asks her to seal the peace with a
draught ; she offers him the cup and he
drinks ; she snatches it away from him
and drains the rest. Instead of both dying as Isolde expects, the draught, which
Brangäne has surreptitiously changed
to a love-potion, makes them lovers,
madly impassioned and blind to all that
goes on about them. They do not observe even the bustle of landing, and the
approach of King Marke from shore.

Act II.—Scene. A garden with steps
leading up to Isolde's chamber. A
torch burns. In the distance the horns
of far-away hunters are heard. Isolde is
awaiting Tristan. Brangäne warns her
that Melot, her pretended friend, is
actually spying on them ; she bitterly
regrets her mixture of the love-potion,
but Isolde says it is destiny. She
quenches the torch as a signal, and
beckons to Tristan, who hurries in.
They have a long scene of unrestrained
ecstasy, the voice of Brangäne, who
watches unseen from the tower, falling
on their ears with unheeded warning.
At last she screams. Kurwenal rushes
in to warn Tristan, but King Marke,
and Melot and others appear and confront the lovers. Tristan in a daze tries
to conceal Isolde, who is overcome with
shame. Melot is violent with accusa-
tions, but King Marke is only bewildered and mystified. Tristan confesses
equal bewilderment, is ready to die,
however, and asks Isolde if she will die
with him. She says she will follow him
anywhere ; he kisses her. Melot draws
his sword. Tristan rebukes him as a
false friend, draws and attacks, but lets
himself be wounded, and falls in Kurwenal's arms. Isolde throws herself on
his breast.

Act III.—Scene. A castle garden on
the cliffs. The mortally wounded Tristan lies sleeping on a couch watched by
the anxious Kurwenal. A shepherd
playing a melancholy air on a pipe
pauses to inquire of Tristan's welfare.
He is watching for a ship—Isolde's, if
he sees it, he will pipe merrily. Tristan wakes drearily. Kurwenal explains
how he had carried the wounded Tristan away to his own long-deserted castle. Tristan tells a dream he had of
Isolde. Kurwenal says he has sent for
her to come and heal the wound. This
enraptures Tristan for a moment, but
he sinks back under the spell of the
shepherd's wailing song. He wakens
again, however, and the shepherd plays
a brighter melody. A ship is sighted.
Isolde leaps ashore, and Kurwenal

hastens down the steep to bring her up. Tristan, left alone in a delirium of joy, desires to meet Isolde again as when she first saw him—with bleeding wounds. He tears the bandage from his wound, staggers toward her, and dies in her arms with a last sigh "Isolde!" The shepherd now warns Kurwenal that another ship has landed with King Marke and Melot. They barricade the gate. Kurwenal kills Melot and resists Marke and his followers, not heeding Brangäne's appeals, and is wounded to death. Brangäne tries to explain to Isolde that she has told the story of the love-potion. The King, understanding all, has come to reunite the lovers. Isolde, however, oblivious of everything, falls into a state of exaltation and seems to see Tristan rising in an apotheosis of bliss. In a transfiguration of rapture, she sinks upon his body, and King Marke invokes a blessing on the dead lovers. This swan-song of Isolde is called the "Liebestod" (lē'-bĕs-tōt), or "Love's-death."

## Tannhäuser und der Sängerkrieg auf Wartburg (tän-hä'-ē-zĕr oont dĕr zĕng'-ĕr-krēkh owf värt'-boorkh). Tannhaeuser and the Singer's Contest at the Wartburg.

Three-act opera; book and music by Wagner. Produced, Dresden Royal Opera, October 20, 1845, with Frau Schröder-Devrient and Niemann as Elizabeth and Tannhäuser.

### CHARACTERS.

*Knights and Singers:*

HERMANN,
  *Landgrave of Thuringia* .... bass.
TANNHÄUSER OR HEINRICH ...... tenor.
WOLFRAM VON ESCHENBACH (vôl'-främ fōn ĕsh'-ĕn-bäkh) ......... bar.
WALTER VON DER VOGELWEIDE (väl'-tĕr fōn dĕr fō'-gĕl-vī-dĕ) ..... tenor.
BITEROLF (bē'-tĕr-ôlf) .......... bar.
HEINRICH DER SCHREIBER (hīn'-rĭkh dĕr shrī'-bĕr) .............. tenor.
REINMAR VON ZWETER (rīn'-mär fōn tsvä'-tĕr) ................. bass.

ELIZABETH (ā-lē'-zä-bāt),
  *Niece of the Landgrave* ...... sopr.
VENUS (fā'-noos),
  *Goddess of love* .............. sopr.
A YOUNG SHEPHERD ............. sopr.

NOTE.—(a) Like "Die Meistersinger," this opera has a semi-historical basis in the ancient contests between Germanic singers. The Minnesänger (mĭn'-nĕ-zĕng-ĕr) or love-bards were noblemen who sang poems and music of their own in praise of pure love, to their own harp accompaniment. They flourished in the twelfth and thirteenth centuries. The Mastersingers, usually tradesmen, who succeeded them in the fourteenth to the sixteenth centuries, made more elaborate rules for composition. (b) The goddess Freia or Holda (v. "Das Rheingold"), Goddess of Youth and Spring, was believed to have been driven by Christianity to take refuge in the caverns of a mountain near Eisenach. She became confused, and finally identified, with the Greek Venus of similar attributes, and the mountain came to be called the Venusberg. This mountain is not far from the castle of the Wartburg, where the old landgraves held vocal contests of the sort described in this opera.

Act I.—Scene I. The subterranean palace of Venus. Surrounded and beguiled by singing and dancing nymphs and sirens, Venus reclines in voluptuous languor, gazing wonderingly at Tannhäuser, who is dreaming of the upper air and homesick for the life he left for her. At her insistence he sings in her praise, but begs for his freedom. At first resentful, she then tries to charm his restlessness away, but grows furious again and tells him that his Christian God will never forgive him. She vanishes and he finds himself (scene 2) in a sunny valley before a shrine of the Virgin. A young shepherd pipes and sings of Holda, the Goddess of Spring. Seeing a file of elderly Pilgrims wandering Rome-wards, he asks their blessing. Tannhäuser himself kneels and joins their chant (known as the Pilger-chor, " The Pilgrims' Chorus "). They disappear in the distance, and the Land-grave, entering with his retinue of Bards, on a hunt, finds his long-lost favorite and welcomes him back. Tannhäuser speaks vaguely of travel in strange lands and wishes to avoid them, but Wolfram tells him that Elizabeth has been pining for him and his all-surpassing minstrel-sy. Tannhäuser, at the memory of her, gladly rejoins them and they set off for the castle of the Wartburg.

Act II.—Scene. The Hall of Apollo in the Castle. Elizabeth enters and greets it with joy since now Tann-häuser's voice is to glorify it again. Wolfram ushers in Tannhäuser and he and Elizabeth are fervently reunited. The Landgrave welcomes Elizabeth to the hall she has shunned so long and announces her as the queen of the con-test. The court gathers with much pomp. The Minnesingers enter. The Landgrave announces that love is the subject of the prize-songs. Four pages collect the names of the Bards in a cup and draw lots. Wolfram, the first chosen, sings of the fountain of clean-hearted love, to much applause. Tann-häuser interrupts with a praise of pas-sion, but is received in chill silence. Walter sternly contradicts him, and is applauded. Tannhäuser reiterates his view and Biterolf angrily rebukes him. Tannhäuser returns the abuse, and Wolfram tries to calm the rising excite-ment by imploring heaven's interven-tion. Tannhäuser madly declares that Venus alone can teach love. The women leave the Hall hastily and the men advance against Tannhäuser, whom the Landgrave declares eternally condemned, for his unholy life in the Venusberg. The rash minstrel is about to be cut to pieces by the infuriated mob, but Elizabeth protects him and pleads that he may have a chance to re-pent. Tannhäuser is now overcome with shame and prays God to accept him. The Landgrave bids him join a band of young Pilgrims who seek absolu-tion at Rome. He rushes away hope-fully.

Act III.—Same as scene 2 of Act I. Elizabeth is praying before the shrine. Wolfram muses on her incessant prayer that Tannhäuser may return forgiven. The returning elderly Pilgrims are heard approaching and she rises. They pass, singing joyfully, and she scans them anxiously, but Tannhäuser is not with them. Crushed with grief, she sinks to her knees begging to die. In an apo-theosis of soul she departs. When Wolfram offers her escort, she points silently to heaven whither she now is tending. The faithful Wolfram, left alone, sings to the Evening-star to bless and guide her. (Romance of the Even-ing Star—" O du mein holder Abend-stern.") In the thickening night, Tann-häuser staggers by in tattered Pilgrim garb. Wolfram asks him how he dares return unshriven, and he declares wildly that he is on his way to the Venusberg again. He tells how the Pope had ab-solved all the other Pilgrims, but had likened him in his unholy acquaintance with the Venusberg to the Pope's own dead staff, which could never again put forth leaf or flower. The excommu-nicated Tannhäuser can find shelter nowhere but with Venus. She now appears to him in a rosy cloud, but Wolf-ram struggles to restrain the maniacal Tannhäuser and finally breathes Eliza-beth's name. Tannhäuser cries her name wildly, and the goddess vanishes frustrated. A funeral procession enters bearing the dead Elizabeth. At sight of her, Tannhäuser, imploring her to pray for him in heaven, dies of grief. The younger Pilgrims now enter, chanting of the miracle they have seen. The Pope's staff has blossomed, showing heaven's forgiveness of Tannhäuser.

**Der Ring des Nibelungen** (děr rĭng däs nē'-běl-oong-ĕn). The Ring of the Nibelung.

" A stage-festival for three days and a Fore-evening."

This great work is a trilogy with prologue, or rather a tetralogy, bearing a close resemblance to Greek tragedies, which were groups of three plays set to music by the author of the text, and declaimed with choral interspersions much after the manner of Wagnerian opera, except that the harmonic resources in which this latter is so rich were practically unknown in the music of the tragedies of Æschylos, Sophokles, etc.

The stories of these four works have a continuity, but, though they were meant for performance on consecutive evenings, they contain many repetitions. The plots are adapted with much license from that great collection of German legend and mythology, the epic " Das Nibelungenlied " or " Song of the Nibelungs," a race of hideous gnomes living in the heart of the earth in the Nebelheim or " home of mists."

The tetralogy follows the baleful effect of a piece of consecrated gold stolen from the Rhine, made into a ring and then fought for by gods, Nibelungs, and heroes, bringing disaster to all its possessors, until it finally returns to the Rhine after compassing the destruction of the old dynasty of gods, with Wotan as their chief and Walhalla as their home. There is much room for moralising and allegory in the work, and commentators have not lost sight of the opportunity to confuse the complex with further obscurities. There is enough, however, in these librettos as dramatic and poetic works to occupy the interest and the attention.

The Prologue or " Vorabend " (fôr-ä'-bĕnt), or Fore-Evening of the trilogy :

**I. Das Rheingold** (däs rīn'-gôlt). The Rhine-gold.

One-act music-drama. Begun 1852, finished 1856. Produced (at public dress-rehearsal, Munich, August 25, 1869) ; with the entire trilogy, Bayreuth. August 13, 1876.

CHARACTERS AND THEIR CREATORS
(at Weimar).

*Gods :*
WOTAN (vō'-tän)..........Betz, bar.
DONNER (dôn'-nĕr),
*Thunder*..............Gura, bar.
FROH (frō), Joy........Unger, tenor
LOGE (lō'-gĕ),
*Demi-god of fire and trickery*,
Vogl, tenor.

*Nibelungs :*
ALBERICH (äl'-bĕ-rĭkh)......Hill, bar.
MIME (mē'-mĕ)......Schlösser, tenor

*Giants :*
FASOLT (fä'-zôlt).......Eilers, bar.
FAFNER (fäf'-nĕr),
von Reichenberg, bass.

*Goddesses :*
FRICKA (frĭk'-ä),
*Wotan's wife*,
Frau von Grün-Sadler, m. sopr.
FREIA (frī'-ä), or HOLDA (hôlt'-ä),
*Goddess of love and youth*,
Frl. Haupt, sopr.
ERDA (ĕr'-dä),
*The Earth-mother*..Frl. Jäida, alto.

*Rhine Daughters :*
WOGLINDE (vōkh'-lĭn-dĕ),
Frl. Lilli Lehmann, sopr.
WELLGUNDE (vĕl'-goon-dĕ),
Frl. Marie Lehmann, m. sopr.
FLOSSHILDE (flôs'-hĭl-dĕ),
Frl. Lammert, alto.

Scene I.—The orchestral prelude, based on a single musical pattern, indicates the gloomy flow of the depths of the Rhine, which are disclosed on the rising of the curtain. The Rhine daughters or nymphs gather and disport around a great central rock where rests the sleeping Rhine-gold, which their father has set them there to sentinel. Alberich appears from a chasm and makes sensual love to them and tries to clutch them. They make sport of him and decoy him to violent scrambling and wrath. Suddenly the Rhine-gold " awakes" and gleams. The fascina ed Alberich asks what it is, and the Rhine-girls laughingly taunt him with his ignorance of the fact that this gold if seized and fashioned into a ring would confer boundless power on the thief, who must, however, they add tauntingly, forswear love before he can take it. Alberich's love is turned to hate by their scorn, and climbing the rock he wrenches the gold loose. In the gloom that follows, he laughs at their frantic pursuit and disappears into the earth. By a scenic transformation, the first scene is modulated skilfully, as are all the scenes of this opera, into the next. Scene 2.—An open space among cliffs, one of which bears the new castle Walhalla. Wotan and Fricka awake from sleep. He revels in the beauty of the vast achievement just finished in the building of a fit home for the gods. She reminds him that he must now pay the builders, for he had promised the two Giants his wife's sister Freia. Fricka upbraids him for his ruthless ambitions and his roving infidelity. He reminds her that he gave one of his eyes to win herself and that he will not give Freia up to the Giants as he promised, but trusts in Loge to slip him out of the compact by trickery, since the whole compact was Loge's idea. Freia now hurries in, terrified with fear that the Giants are to have her. The Giants follow shortly. They say they have come for their wages. Wotan tells them she is not his to give. The Giants are furious, Fasolt saying they had counted on her beauty, Fafner preferring the golden apples of youth that grow in her garden. They propose to seize Freia, but Froh and Donner appear to shelter her. Donner threatens them with his thunderous hammer, but Wotan intervenes. The anxiously awaited Loge now appears and all suspect him of trickery as he flits flame-like about. He finally tells how he has ransacked the earth for a ransom for Freia, but nowhere could he find anything rated so high as woman and love—only one being in the universe has other preference, and that is

Alberich. He tells of the theft of the gold and of the ring Alberich has made from it. Wotan now covets the ring and so do the Giants. Loge says the ring can only be got by theft. The Giants offer to accept it as ransom. Meanwhile they take away the screaming Freia as hostage. Immediately the Gods grow wan and old and Loge says that the apples of youth which renew the universe and the gods, are withering in Freia's deserted garden; a pallid mist rises. Wotan resolves to wrest the gold from Alberich, and Loge leads him into a cleft of the earth whence sulphurous vapours spread, veiling the transformation to Scene 3. A subterranean cavern. Alberich drags in the squealing Mime, who pretends not to have finished his appointed task of making the Tarnhelm (a helmet conferring invisibility on the bearer). Inadvertently he lets it fall. Alberich puts it on and vanishes into mist; invisible now, he beats Mime, then is heard as he departs to the forge-room beneath. Loge leads in Wotan and they question the whimpering Mime, who tells them that Alberich has usurped a despotism over them all and makes them slaves to his greed. He tells of the new helmet of darkness and the beating he had. Alberich comes in, visible now, the Tarnhelm at his girdle, he drives in a herd of Nibelungs who heap up gold; he then scourges them back to their work. He gives his new guests bitter greeting and says he will soon have them all in his grasp, gods and women. Loge hints that the gold might be stolen in his sleep. Alberich trusts in the Tarnhelm to hide him. They question his power to change his shape. To prove it he becomes a great serpent. Loge hints that he cannot change himself to anything small like a toad. Alberich ingenuously makes this change. Wotan puts his foot on the toad, Loge snatches the Tarnhelm, thus bringing Alberich back to his natural shape. They tie him up and drag him back to the upper ir and to scene 4, the same as scene 2. They offer him freedom for all his gold ; he murmurs to his ring a summons to his dwarfs, who appear and heap up the gold. Loge, in spite of his protest, adds the Tarnhelm to the heap. Wotan espies the ring and wrenches it from Alberich's finger. Alberich, released, curses the ring and loads its power with a heritage of death, misery, envy, sleeplessness, and crime to its possessor. He then returns to his forge. (The too-consistent mind will wonder why a ring which conferred "measureless might" on its wearer, could not get him out of an ordinary rope ; but myths, like metaphors, "must not be squeezed till they squeal".) The Gods and the Giants assemble. The Giants demand that the gold be heaped up to hide the beautiful Freia whom they are so loth to surrender. They stick their staves in the ground in front of her, and Loge and Froh heap up the gold. The Giants can still see her hair shining through and the Tarnhelm must be added to the heap. Even now they can see one of her eyes, and demand the ring on Wotan's finger. He furiously refuses it. Now, in a rocky cleft appears the awesome Erda, mother of the three Norns or Fates ; she implores Wotan to keep his faith and yield the ring. She vanishes, and after some resistance he throws the ring on the heap. Immediately the Giants quarrel for it, and Fafner kills Fasolt, places the treasure in a sack, and stalks away. The Gods watch him with horror and Wotan resolves to visit Erda again. Donner, hating the mists that veil Walhalla, disappears in storm clouds ; he swings his thunder hammer and the lightning clears the mists. Froh spans the gorge with a rainbow bridge to Walhalla. The Gods move toward the castle. Loge, the flame demi-god, looks scornfully after those whom he has saved, and is tempted to turn against them, but follows for the nonce. The wail of the forlorn Rhine daughters is heard from the deeps of the valley, but the Gods mock it with laughter.

**2. Die Walküre** (dē väl-kü′-rě). The Valkyrs.

Music-drama in three acts. Begun, 1852. Finished, 1856.

Produced at public dress-rehearsal, Munich, june 24, 1870. With the trilogy, Bayreuth, August 14, 1876.

CHARACTERS AND THEIR CREATORS
(at Munich).

*Volsungs :*

SIEGMUND (zēkh′-moont), Vogl, tenor.
SIEGLINDE (zēkh-lĭn′-dě),
  *His sister, Hunding's wife,*
                          Frau Vogl, sopr.
HUNDING (hoont′-ĭng),
  *A Neidung*.....Bauserwein, bass.

*Gods :*

WOTAN (vō′-tän), Kindermann, bar.
FRICKA (frĭk′-ä),
        Frl. Kauffmann, m. sopr.

*Valkyrs :*

BRUENNHILDE (brĭn-hĭl′-dě),
                          Frl. Stehle, sopr.
ROSSWEISE (rôs′-vī-zě) ..........sopr.
GRIMGERDE (grēm′-gĕrt-ě).......sopr.
HELMWIGE (hĕlm′-vē-khě)....m. sopr.
GERHILDE (gĕr′-hĭl-dě).......m. sopr.
ORTLINDE (ôrt′-lĭn-dě).......m. sopr.
WALTRAUTE (vält′-row-tě).......alto.
SIEGRUNE (zē′-groo-ně)..........alto.
SCHWERTLEITE (shvĕrt′-lī-tě).....alto.

With this work, the trilogy proper begins. As gradually transpires : since the events of " Das Rheingold," the fickle Wotan has been wandering over the now populated earth under the name Wälse (vĕl′-zě). The children of his roving amours have formed a tribe called Wälsungen, or Volsungs, who are at war with the tribe of Neidungs (nī′-doongs). A Volsung woman had borne to Wotan the twins Siegmund and Sieglinde, but the children were soon separated. Over the conflicts of humanity Wotan eagerly watches, and those who prove heroes and are killed in battle are carried aloft to form a blissful garrison for the defence of Walhalla. Over every battlefield hover, for this purpose, the heavenly horse-women, or Valkyrs, who are all illegitimate daughters of Wotan by Erda, whom he had seduced with a love-potion.

Act I.—Scene. The interior of a primitive hut built round a great tree in which a sword has been thrust up to the hilt. Siegmund breathlessly enters from the storm outside. Sieglinde not knowing him, gives him a horn of mead, and treats him kindly; her husband Hunding, one of the Neidungs, enters and confirms her hospitality but with suspicion. Siegmund, asked to tell who he is, describes his vile life in the woods with his father, a Volsung, his mother and twin-sister having been carried off by the Neidungs. To-day he has fought single-handed in defence of a woman. Hunding recognises him as the wretch his tribe is hunting, and says that on the morrow he must fight out the feud. He gives Siegmund sanctuary for the night, but warns him to have weapon and resolution for the morning. Siegmund, left alone, broods over the misfortune that hounds him, but remembers that his father had said a sword would be at hand in direst need. Sieglinde enters, having drugged her husband, and tells him of the sword in the tree, thrust there by a strange wanderer (Wotan). No one has ever been able to draw it out. She longs for someone to unsheath it, and revenge her. The door springs open, showing moon-lit night outside. Siegmund says that the mysterious visitor is the Spring itself, and sings a rapturous idyll. Sieglinde calls him the Spring she has longed for. Not knowing that they are brother and sister, they grow ardent in love. He proclaims Wälse (Wotan) as his father, and with a mighty effort, plucks out the sword, which is called "Nothung" (nōt-oong), i.e., need. Sieglinde proclaims herself his sister. He embraces her fervently as both sister and bride for the restoration of the Volsung lineage.

Act II.—Scene. A gorge in the mountains. Wotan sends Brünnhilde to watch an impending battle. Fricka comes angrily in. She plays the Xanthippe. To her as goddess of wedlock, Hunding had appealed to punish Siegmund and Sieglinde, who have fled. After a bitter quarrel she compels Wotan to swear that Siegmund shall die under Hunding's sword, even if he must intervene himself. When she has gone, Brünnhilde reappears and tries to console her dejected father. He tells her the story of the Rhine-gold; of Fafner who holds the ring, of his betraying Erda for his purpose, and of his one hope that some unaided hero shall of his own volition and resource win the world-power. He bewails his oath to Fricka, but when Brünnhilde hints that she will save Siegmund, he threatens her wrathfully. When they have left in opposite directions, Siegmund and Sieglinde enter, both overcome with fatigue, and she also with shame at yielding to him. In the distance the horses of their pursuers are heard. She swoons in her anguish. Brünnhilde appears and bids Siegmund follow her to Walhalla, but he refuses to be separated from Sieglinde. He even threatens to kill her and himself first, and Brünnhilde passionately vows to preserve them both. She disappears, and a great storm arises. Siegmund leaves Sieglinde to meet Hunding. They fight. Brünnhilde protects Siegmund with his shield; but Wotan appears, and with his spear shatters the sword of Siegmund whom Hunding slays. The disobedient Brünnhilde, in terror, escapes with Sieglinde, and Wotan after slaying Hunding with one scornful glance, follows her.

Act III.—Scene. A mountain peak and cavern. The Valkyrs gather, each with a slain hero across her horse. They await Brünnhilde, who appears finally in great panic with Sieglinde on her saddle. She tells what she has done and begs shelter. Sieglinde pleads to be allowed to die, but Brünnhilde reminds her that in her womb she bears

Siegmund's son, to be called Siegfried [here first appears the motive "Siegfried and the sword"). Sieglinde now wishes to live, and they decide that a cave near Fafner's lair would be safe from Wotan's discovery. She gives Sieglinde the pieces of Siegmund's sword, and bids her save them for her son. Sieglinde hurries away, just before Wotan appears and denounces Brünnhilde bitterly. He disowns her, and tells his plan to disgrace her by making her a prisoner on this mountain. The maidenhood which is the pride of the Valkyrs, shall be the prey of whosoever finds her. He sends the other Valkyrs away, and Brünnhilde pleads earnestly that she protected Siegmund because she knew Wotan really loved him and wished him to win; but she cannot alter his resolve. She begs to be surrounded with flames that only a fearless hero may reach her to make her his own. Wotan grants this wish, and bids her a tender farewell, kisses her divinity away and lays her fast asleep with closed helmet on a bank of moss. He places her long shield over her, and invokes Loge, who sends a circle of fire to guard the sleeping Valkyr. He vanishes after a last charm: "He who feareth my spear, shall never fare through this fire" (in which again the "Siegfried and the sword" motive appears).

### 3. Siegfried (zēkh'-frēt).

Three-act music-drama. Begun, 1856, finished, 1869. Produced, Bayreuth, August 15, 1876.

CHARACTERS AND THEIR CREATORS.

SIEGFRIED..............Unger, tenor.
MIME (mē'-mĕ).......Schlosser, tenor.
DER WANDERER (dĕr vän'-dĕr-ĕr),
Betz, bar.
ALBERICH (äl'-bĕr-ĭkh)........Hill, bar.
FAFNER (fäf'-nĕr), Von Reichenberg, bar.
ERDA (ĕrt'-ä).........Frau Iäida, alto.
BRÜENNHILDE (brĭn-hĭl'-dĕ),
Frau Friedrich Materna, sopr.

Act I.—Scene. A cave-dwelling with primitive forge and anvil. The dwarf Mime is forging a sword, but grumbles that the boy Siegfried breaks the strongest blade he can make. If he could only forge the pieces of Siegmund's sword Nothung, that would be unbreakable; with it Siegfried might even slay Fafner who, shaped like a dragon, guards the all-powerful Ring. Mime would then possess himself of the Ring. But he winces at his inability to forge Nothung. The boyish Siegfried romps in with a bear and terrifies the dwarf, and breaks with a blow the latest sword he has forged. Mime sobs that all his fatherly care of the boy meets only hate and rebuff. Siegfried confesses an unconquerable repugnance to the dwarf; he only tolerates him for the knowledge he has. He has learned that all animals have father and mother; he asks who his mother was, and Mime claims the double honour of being both father and mother to the boy. Siegfried has seen his own image in a brook, and gives Mime the lie. He chokes the dwarf into telling him of a nameless woman who had come to the cave and died in bearing a child. She entrusted him to Mime after naming him Siegfried. He tells over in little slices the story of his devoted care for the boy, and finally produces the broken sword. Siegfried orders him to forge it anew and dashes out into the woods. Mime, despairing of hoodwinking the lad to his own purposes, views with suspicion the entrance of Wotan, who is disguised as a wanderer. In a long colloquy, which re-tells the stories of the previous operas, they enter into a contest in which each is to ask three questions; the one failing to answer forfeits his head. Mime asks (1) What race dwells in the earth? (2) What on the surface? (3) What in the clouds? Wotan answers (1) The Nibelungs, whom Alberich subjugated with the Ring. (2) The Giants, of whom Fafner guards the Ring. (3) The Gods, of whom Wotan is the chief, ruling all with his spear. He strikes the spear on the ground and a thunder rumbles. Wotan, recognised, asks Mime three questions : (1) What race does Wotan persecute though he loves them? Mime answers correctly, " the Volsungs." (2) What sword must Siegfried use to slay Fafner? Mime answers, " Nothung." (3) Who will forge that sword anew? Mime can find no answer. Wotan laughs and says that only one who knows no fear can forge it ; to that hero he bequeathes Mime's head. When he is gone, Siegfried returns to find Mime hysterical with fright. He tries to teach Siegfried fear, a thing the boy has never felt ; as a last resort he will show him the dragon. Siegfried resolves to forge the sword himself and with growing ecstasy works away. Mime watches him and plans his own ambitions, brewing the while a poison for Siegfried when he has won the Ring. The sword at length is made and Siegfried exultantly splits the anvil in twain with its resistless edge.

Act II.—Scene. The heart of a forest at night. Alberich lies brooding. The Wanderer enters. The ancient enemies quarrel. They speak of Siegfried who is coming to slay Fafner. Alberich calls to the dragon Fafner, whose cave is near by, offering to protect him if he will give him the Ring. Fafner yawningly declines. Wotan advises Alberich to try Mime next, and vanishes. Alberich hides as in the dawning light Mime enters with Siegfried. His descriptions of the dragon fail to terrify Siegfried, who finally orders him away. The boy, alone, muses on his father and his mother. The bird-choir charms him. He cuts a reed, fashions a pipe and tries to imitate them on it and on his horn. Fafner thrusts out his hideous head and gapes. Siegfried laughs. After some banter he closes to the attack and kills the fire-breathing dragon, who with his dying breath warns the boy against conspiracy. The dragon's blood on the boy's hand burns him. He lifts it to his lips. Instantly he understands the bird-

voices. A wood-bird tells him of the Tarnhelm and the Ring and he enters the cave. Mime and Alberich steal in ; they wrangle, but retire when Siegfried reissues with the ring and Tarnhelm. The wood-bird tells him to beware of Mime, whose hypocrisy he can see through, thanks to the taste of dragon's blood. Mime enters and while trying to dissemble, actually tells his basest motives. Siegfried finally slays him and, throwing the body in the cave, calls again to the wood-bird for counsel. The bird tells him that his future wife sleeps on a lofty peak flame-girdled. He bids the bird lead on and joyfully hastens after.

Act III.—Scene 1. The mouth of a craggy cavern at night. Wotan appearing summons Erda to a long, but bootless conference, in which he expresses his resignation to his coming doom. Erda vanishes and Siegfried comes along the path. Wotan questions him and is told all that has happened. He reproaches the boy for his frank insolence and tries to check him, but has his spear hewn in two for his counsel, and vanishes. Siegfried, blowing his horn, plunges into the mist and flames and the scene is changed to the same as Act III. of " Die Walküre," where Brünnhilde still lies sealed in sleep under her long shield. Siegfried, seeing her, thinks her a man till he has opened her helmet and lifted her breastplate. He is overcome with an emotion which he thinks may be fear, but at length kisses her. She wakes and greets the sunlight, and knows him to be Siegfried. Her joy changes to fear and grief as she remembers her lost Valkyr estate, but his ardour and bravery win her back to rapture in his arms.

4. **Götterdämmerung** (gĕt'-tĕr-dĕm'-mĕr-oongk). The Gloaming (or Dusk or Twilight) of the Gods.

Music-drama in three acts and Prologue. Begun, 1867. Finished, 1876. Produced, Bayreuth, August 16, 1876.

## CHARACTERS AND THEIR CREATORS.

SIEGFRIED (zēkh'-frēt).....Unger, tenor.
GUNTHER (goon'-tĕr).......Gura, bar.
HAGEN (hä'-gĕn),
      Von Reichenberg, bass.
ALBERICH (äl'-bĕr-ĭkh).......Hill, bar.
BRUENNHILDE (brĭn-hĭl'-dĕ),
    Frau Friedrich Materna, sopr.
GUTRUNE (goo-troo'-nĕ), Frl. Weckerlin.
WALTRAUTE (vält'-row-tĕ), Frau Jäida.
THE THREE NORNS, OR FATES.
THE THREE RHINE-DAUGHTERS.

*Prologue.*—Scene, on the Valkyrs' rock, same as the last scenes of "Die Walküre" and "Siegfried." The three Norns sit idle and gloomy under a fir-tree. The first Norn fastens a golden rope to the tree, and tells of the coming of Wotan long before, and how ne had paid one of his eyes to drink at the spring of wisdom, and broke a spear from the World-ash tree; thereafter the tree and the spring failed. She throws the rope to the second Norn, who winds it round a rock and tells how Siegfried shattered Wotan's spear, and Wotan had sent his Walhalla heroes to chop up the World-ash tree. She casts the rope to the third Norn, who tells that the Gods and heroes will gather in Walhalla round a fire made of the World-ash boughs, and the fire will waste Walhalla and leave the Gods in eternal night. As the rope is passed forward and back, they talk of Loge's plots against Wotan and of Alberich; the sacred rope grows frayed and finally parts. They wind the strands about them and moaning that eternal wisdom and wise counsel are lost forever to the world, sink into the earth. Day dawns. Siegfried comes from the cave, full-armed, followed by Brünnhilde leading her horse Grane, which had been preserved in sleep during her own long slumbers. Siegfried having made Brünn-hilde his own, and learned from her the story of the Gods and the meaning of the holy runes, is now eager for new deeds. He promises to remember her faithfully, and gives her the Ring itself as a pledge. She gives him the horse to carry him back to the world, and they part in mutual idolatry.

Act I.—Scene I. The Hall of the Gibichungen (gē'-bĭkh-oong-ĕn), on the banks of the Rhine. Three of the Gibichs or Gibichungs, a race of heroes, are seated in earnest counsel: Gunther (who is wifeless and longs for Brünnhilde, whom he believes to be still surrounded by the terrifying flames which Siegfried had pierced), his sister Gutrune (who is husbandless and longs to wed Siegfried, whose fame has reached them), and their half-brother, the vicious Hagen (whom their mother Grimhilde had borne when seduced by Alberich's gold). Hagen is suggesting that they persuade Siegfried to marry Gutrune, then ask him to bring Brünnhilde through the flames to wed Gunther. Siegfried's horn is heard and they see him rowing on the river. They invite him to land. He does so, and they lead his horse Grane to a stall. He tells them that he has left the useless gold of Alberich in the dead dragon's cave, and brought away only the Tarnhelm and the Ring. Now, Hagen's father Alberich had charged him to recover the Ring (v. "Das Rheingold"), and he learns that Siegfried has given it to Brünnhilde. Gutrune brings in a horn full of a magic liquor which effaces all remembrance. Siegfried, draining it, forgets Brünnhilde utterly, and becomes so infatuated with Gutrune that he asks for her hand. Gunther tells of the fire-guarded Brünnhilde, and Siegfried promises to win her for Gunther by means of the Tarnhelm. The two men prick their arms with their swords, drop blood into their wine-horn, and swear blood-brotherhood, and Hagen cuts the horn in two to complete the pact. When asked why he has not joined the two, he evades the question. Siegfried and Gunther set forth to find Brünn-hilde, while Hagen stays to guard the house, and bide his time to seize the

Ring. Scene 2, same as the Prologue. Brünnhilde, alone, is visited by her sister Waltraute (v. " Die Walküre"). Asked why she had broken the ban their father Wotan has put on Brünnhilde, she says that she has fled from Walhalla in terror. The Valkyrs no longer seek heroes slain on battlefields ; Wotan has come home with his spear hewn asunder ; the sacred ravens have flown away ; Wotan has made a great pile of logs from the shattered World-ash tree and sits with his heroes waiting the general doom. Waltraute has wrung from him the word that if the Ring could be found and flung back into the Rhine whence it was stolen, and cursed by Alberich (v. " Das Rheingold ") the doom would be averted. Brünnhilde, despite Waltraute's frenzied pleading, sternly refuses to throw back into the Rhinewaves the pledge of love Siegfried has given her, and Waltraute rushes away in wild despair. Siegfried's horn is heard, and he enters in Gunther's form with the Tarnhelm hiding his face. The terrified Brünnhilde threatens the stranger with the Ring. Siegfried says it shall be her wedding-ring, and takes it from her after a struggle. He orders her into the cave, and drawing his sword Nothung to lay between them as a proof of faith to Gunther, follows her in.

Act II.—Scene. The river-bank before the Hall of the Gibichungs. Hagen is seated, asleep. Alberich, his father, is talking to him in his dreams, urging him on to revenge his ancient wrongs on the ignorant Siegfried. Hagen vows and Alberich vanishes. Siegfried enters in the dawn and removes the Tarnhelm. Hagen wakes, Gutrune enters, and Siegfried tells how he had won Brünnhilde, but kept the sword between them till he gave her over to Gunther, who was waiting at the foot of the mountains. Siegfried had then willed himself back to the Hall by his Tarnhelm's power. Hagen summons the vassals with his horn ; they come expecting a battle, but are told of the wedding festivities. Gunther and Brünn-

hilde arrive in a boat. Brünnhilde is dumbfounded at seeing Siegfried, and swoons in his arms, but he still fails to recognise her. Then she sees the Ring on his finger. Gunther confesses he had not given it to Siegfried. Hagen tells Brünnhilde that Siegfried had won the ring from Gunther by wiles, and Brünnhilde in supreme rage accuses Siegfried of having possessed her body as well as her soul when he conquered her. Siegfried swears to Gunther on Hagen's spear that Brünnhilde's accusation is false. Brünnhilde on the same spear swears her own statement, and hallows the point to pierce Siegfried's heart in revenge. Siegfried tries to reassure Gunther, and embraces Gutrune. Hagen promises the distracted Brünnhilde revenge, and she tells him that he must stab Siegfried in the back, his only vulnerable point. Gunther, overcome with his own position, and believing that Siegfried has played him false, is drawn into the plot. Hagen plans to kill Siegfried out of Brünnhilde's sight at a hunt. The three then vow the death of Siegfried, who enters, wreathed as a bridegroom.

Act III.—Scene 1. A valley through which the Rhine sweeps. In the stream the Rhine-daughters drift, waiting the hero who shall restore them the lost Rhine-gold. Siegfried appears ; he has lost his way, following a bear. The Rhine-daughters tease him and try to win the Ring from him, but their prayers are futile, and threats do not avail to frighten him, so they swim away. The hunters now gather with their booty ; they drink, and Siegfried, under the memory-waking spell of a herb Hagen has put in his drink, tells them the whole story of his life, and how he came to learn the language of birds, and how he won Brünnhilde. The sacred ravens fly past, Siegfried starts up and looks after them. Hagen thrusts his spear into his back. Siegfried turning, swings his shield high to crush Hagen, but with sudden weakness, drops it, and falls on it. Hagen stalks away. Siegfried, seeing Brünnhilde in a vision welcoming him, dies in a rapturous delirium. His body is raised and carried homeward. Scene 2. The Hall of the Gibichungs at night. Gutrune is waiting for Siegfried. Hagen storms in, announcing Siegfried's return, saying that a wild boar has killed him. Gutrune faints as the body is brought in. Gunther declares Hagen's guilt. Hagen admits it, and claims the Ring. Gunther opposes him, and is killed. As Hagen moves to take the Ring, the dead Siegfried's arm rises threateningly and all fall back in terror. Brünnhilde enters. She proudly claims the dead hero as her husband, and Gutrune now realises for the first time the truth. While a funeral pyre is being raised and decked, Brünnhilde muses upon Siegfried, and the tangled net of lies that has enmeshed his pure soul and brought her shame. She understands all Fate now, and taking the Ring from Siegfried's hand, places it on her own. His body is put upon the pyre. She calls to the Rhine-maidens that they will find the ring burned free of its curse in her own ashes. She seizes a firebrand, and sets the pyre ablaze. The ravens fly up and disappear. She bids all look to the north when she is dead, to see the burning of Walhalla. Her horse has been brought in. Addressing him and bidding him neigh gladly to rejoin Siegfried his lord and her husband, she warns mankind to trust only to love and not to gain or to treachery, and dashes into the flames. In a great flash the Hall of the Gibichungs catches fire and is ruined. The pyre dies out and collapses. The Rhine overflows and comes rippling across the Hall. The Rhine-daughters swim in on the waves. Hagen, who rushes in to struggle for the Ring, is dragged down to death by two of them while the third holds up exultantly the Rhine-gold that has returned home at last from its devastating travels. In the north a great glow appears. It is the flash of the flames consuming Walhalla. With the palace built by deceit and broken faith, the fire destroys the race of gods and heroes, and their merciless, honourless dynasty, leaving Freewill and Love as the inspiration of mankind.

## *VON WEBER, CARL MARIA.*

**Der Freischütz** (děr frī'-shüts), *G.*, Il Franco Arciero (är-chä'-rō), *I.* In French first produced as " Robin des Bois " ; later with recitatives by Berlioz as " Le Franc Archer " (lŭ-frän-kăr-shä). The Free Shot.

Three-act Romantic opera. Book by Friedrich Kind. Produced, Berlin, June 18, 1821.

CHARACTERS AND THEIR CREATORS.

GRAF OT'TOKAR.......Rubinstein, bar
KUNO (koo'-nō),
   *His chief forester*.....Waner, bass.
KAS'PAR,
   *A forester*....Heinrich Blume, bass.
MAX (mäx),
   *A forester* (in Italian, Giulio),
              Karl Stümer, tenor.
ZAMIEL (zäm-ĭ-ĕl'),
   *A demon.*
A HERMIT................Gern, bass.
KIL'LIAN,
   *A peasant*.......Wiedemann, tenor.
AGATHE (ä'-gä-tě),
   *Kuno's daughter*,
      Frl. Karoline Seidler, sopr.
AENNCHEN (ěn'-khěn),
   *Her friend*,
      Frl. Johanna Eunike, sopr.

Act I.—Scene. Before an inn. The peasants are congratulating Killian, the winner of a shooting-match ; he taunts Max, who has lost. Kuno and Kaspar enter and learn of Max's humiliation. Kuno tells how his own grandfather was made head-ranger to the prince by a lucky shot that saved the life of a man bound to a stag ; he will give his own daughter to the best marksman, and make him his successor. He hopes Max may win. Killian speaks of a certain enchantment with seven magic bullets of which he has heard. A trio concerning the morrow's match is followed by a hunting chorus, and the men and women dance away. Max alone, bewails his recent bad luck and his fear of losing Agathe (" Durch die Waldes, etc."), while Zamiel, the demon, hovers about unseen. Kaspar appears and persuades Max to drink, singing a boisterous vine-song (" Hier im ird'-schen Jammerthal "). He persuades the sceptical Max to shoot at an eagle almost invisible aloft ; the eagle falls just as the clock strikes seven ; Kaspar says that more of the magic bullets may be had, and after winning from Max a promise to meet him in the Wolf's Glen at midnight, he sings a song of diabolic triumph.

Act II.—Scene I. A room in Kuno's house. Agathe preparing for her wedding is gloomy with foreboding ; a picture had fallen from the wall and cut her forehead just as the clock struck seven. Aennchen teases her and sings a little ballad of a young lover (" Kommt ein schlanker Bursch gegangen "). But Agathe speaks of a hermit who frightened her with his prophecies. Aennchen goes, and Agathe leaning out into the moonlight has a blissful reverie (" Leise, leise, fromme Weise "). She sees her lover coming ; he enters, and Aennchen returns. Max learns with dread that Agathe's forehead was cut by the picture just the moment he killed the eagle with the magic bullet. He tells her he must go to bring a slain stag from the Wolf's Glen, and in spite of her horror of the place he goes. Scene 2. The wild ravine of the Wolf's Glen. A chorus of invisible demons. Kaspar appears and summons Zamiel. The demon appears to him ; he appeals to be released from his unholy compact —he is to die the next day ; he offers as a bribe to Zamiel to bring a new victim who wishes the magic " free bullets." Zamiel accepts, saying that six of the bullets shall hit, but the seventh shall betray. Kaspar asks that the seventh may kill Agathe so that both her lover and her father shall go mad and fall in

Zamiel's power. Zamiel consents, saying, " Thou or he to-morrow must be mine." He vanishes. Max enters in much terror. They set about casting the bullets from unhallowed materials ; as they count them an echo repeats their words. After the fifth, the demons cry out ; after the sixth the echo cries " Beware," but Max summons Zamiel, who appears as the seventh is cast.

Act III.—Scene I. Agathe's room. The bride is still sad and praying. Aennchen enters and Agathe tells of the fierce storm that raged at midnight ; she dreamed she was a dove ; a huntsman appeared ; the dove vanished and an eagle fell dead. Aennchen tries to reassure her by telling comically a frightful dream her grandmother had, all caused by the family dog getting into her room. The bridesmaids appear and sing (" Wir winden dir den Jungfern Kranz "). When, however, the bridal garland is produced, it proves to be a funeral wreath ; but she remembers in her gloom the roses left for her by the hermit and plucks up courage. Scene 2. The Forest. The Graf and others assembled. A Hunters' Chorus (" Was gleicht wohl auf Erden dem Jägervergnügen "). Kaspar watching from behind a tree. The match has taken place and the Graf accepts the victorious Max as Kuno's successor ; he asks Max as a last test (this is his seventh shot) to bring down a white dove flitting about in the branches. Agathe's sudden absence is noted. Max calls on his last bullet to find its mark, and Kaspar invokes Zamiel. Agathe, standing near the tree where Kaspar hides, cries, " I am the dove ! " She is stunned but is saved by the hermit's wreath ; Kaspar is killed and dies cursing as Zamiel appears to him. Max confesses his league with Zamiel and the Graf banishes him in spite of the entreaties of all. The hermit appears, however, and pleads for him as it was his first sin ; he suggests the abolition of the trial-shot, a year's penance for Max, and then his wedding to Agathe The opera ends in rejoicing and religious fervour.

# Supplementary Stories of the Operas

# Errata.

## (Not corrected in the supplement.)

Page 309, col b......................Ssafiddin should be Safieddin.
Page 311, col. b......................Agrel should be Agrell.
Page 372, col. a......................Breuning should be Breunung.
Page 374, col. b., line 34.............Kerim should be Kérim.
Page 375, col. a., line 9.............Bebroid should be Debrois.
Page 379, col. a., line 30.............kä-bäl-lä-ro should be kă-văl-lä'-rō.
Page 383, col. a., line 16.............Firmin should be Philippe.
Page 384, col. a., line 30.............London should be Dublin.
Page 389, col. a., line 3.............February 22, 1810 is correct. See supplement.
Page 389, col. a., line 12.............Zwyny should be Zywny.
Page 394, col. a., line 31.............1882 should be September 2, 1907.
Page 411, col. b., line 46.............Eminy should be Emmy.
Page 437, col. b., line 48.............1807 should be 1897.
Page 493, col. a., .....................Hillenmacher should be Hillemacher.
Page 512, col. a., line 38............. omit "Helmann the Fool."
Page 525, col. a., line 24.............1900 should be December 21, 1899.
Page 531, col. a., line 24.............1884 should be 1894.
Page 533, col. a., line 39.............1804 should be 1802.
Page 533, col. a., line 50.............Lē-a-dôf should be L'yä'-dôf.
Page 540, col. a., line 26.............1852 should be 1582.
Page 549, col. b., line 42.............Solar should be Soler.
Page 549, col. b., line 44.............May, 1810, should be March 3, 1806.
Page 560, col. a., line 15.............July should be June 30.
Page 583, col. b., line 23.............1898 should be January 8, 1904.
Page 586, col. b., line 4.............Mayence, 1841, should be Mannheim, April 30, 1842.
Page 610, col. b., line 37.............1863 should be 1893.
Page 640, col. b., line 18.............1818 should be 1816.
Page 666, col. a., line 29.............Serrao should be Serrão.
Page 668, col. a., line 39.............1847 should be 1837.
Page 685, col. b., line 10.............1710 should be 1700.
Page 690, col. a., line 40.............December 25 should be April 25 (or May 7, N. S.).
Page 693, col. b., line 36.............K. L. should be J. F. L.
Page 700, col. b., line 27.............1756 should be 1750.
Page 736, col. a., line 48.............1827 should be 1822.

# Supplementary Stories of the Operas

## MASSENET, JULES.

**Thaïs** (tä-ēs)

A three-act lyric comedy. Book by Louis Gallet (based on the novel by Anatole France).

Produced at the Opéra, Paris, 1894.

### CHARACTERS.

| | |
|---|---|
| ATHANAEL (ä-tä′-nä-ĕl) | bar. |
| NICIAS (nē′-sĭ-ăs) | ten. |
| PALEMON (pä-lā-môn) | bass. |
| THAÏS | sopr. |
| ALBINE (ăl-bēn) | |
| CROBYLE (krō-bēl) | |
| MYRTALE (mēr-tăl) | |

Place of action: Egypt, in the early Christian Era.

Act I.— Scene I. A settlement of hermit Cenobites on the Nile. Twelve holy men are eating their frugal meal, among them Palémon. They are awaiting the return of Athanaël. He returns from Alexandria fagged and dejected, and describes the power of a priestess of Venus named Thaïs, whom he had known in his youth and whom now he wishes to save. Palémon and the others warn him not to meddle with such evil, and Athanaël falls asleep. In a vision he beholds a crowded theatre where the half-naked Thaïs postures. As the vision vanishes, he awakens with horror and vows to save her, praying for aid to the God of Pity (*Toi qui mis la pitié dans nos âmes*). The Cenobites anxiously bid him farewell.

Scene II. The terrace of the palace of Nicias. Athanaël with difficulty persuades a slave to summon his master. While he waits, he contemplates the panorama of the terrible city (*Voilà donc la terrible cité*). He calls upon the angels to purify its corruption, as Nicias appears laughing with two slave girls, Crobyle and Myrtale. He welcomes Athanaël as an old friend. Athanaël speaks of Thaïs, for whom Nicias has bankrupted himself. He warns Athanaël against her, but consents to arrange their meeting. In fact she is expected for supper this night. Athanaël asks for decent raiment, and the slave girls laughingly adorn and perfume him, until they find him beautiful as a young god. A great throng of revellers and philosophers pour in, preceding Thaïs. She arrives for her last visit with Nicias after "one whole long week of constancy." She meets Athanaël and demands why he is so severe (*Qui te fait si sévère*). She swears that nothing is real but love, and invites him to wreathe his head with roses and watch her posturing again as Aphrodite. But he flees in horror.

Act II.— Scene. The home of Thaïs. She dismisses her friends wearily, and, left alone, begs her faithful mirror to reassure her that she will always be beautiful (*Dis-moi que je suis toujours belle*). She sees Athanaël, who declares that he loves her, but not as she understands. A duel between sacred and profane love ensues, and each begins to influence the other strangely. Thaïs sprinkles incense on the altar of Venus, and Athanaël trembles. But he tears away his gorgeous robe and reveals himself as a monk, cursing her life and bidding her forsake it. She throws herself at his feet and the voice of Nicias heard in the distance fills her with loathing. Athanaël tells her that he will wait for her on her doorstep until dawn, but she turns against him and drives him out; then falls weeping on her pillows.

After a symphonic interlude in the form of religious meditation, the scene changes to a square before her house.

In the moonlight Athanaël is seen lying on the steps. In the distance, the home of Nicias is brilliant and noisy with revelry.

Thaïs appears and Athanaël promises to lead her to a monastery in the desert. But first she must destroy all the monuments of her shame. She must burn her house and her goods. She consents, but asks only to save one little ivory image of Cupid, for "Love is a virtue rare" (*L'amour est une vertu rare*). She wishes to take this image to the convent; it was a gift from Nicias. Athanaël hurls the statuette to the ground. Thaïs meekly submits and they go within to burn the palace. Nicias and a crowd of revellers fill the square. The two slave girls sing of a new charmer, who is more beautiful than the Queen of Sheba (*Celle qui vient est plus belle*). At the end of this duet and during the dance, Athanaël appears with a lighted torch, leading Thaïs meanly clad and followed by her sorrowful slaves. While the palace burns, the crowd turns on Athanaël and Thaïs and would stone them, but Nicias saves them from violence by throwing gold into the mob.

Act III.— Scene I. The oasis, with the white cells of the retreat of the nuns of Albine. Thaïs and Athanaël, greatly fatigued, struggle in. He is rough with her until she swoons; then a change comes over him and his heart bleeds for her bleeding feet, which he kisses, hailing her as a saint. He goes to the well for water, and she blesses him as a messenger from God (*O messager de Dieu*). He brings her water and fruits while the white nuns of Albine appear singing a Latin hymn. Athanaël greets Albine and presents Thaïs to her. Thaïs bids Athanaël farewell forever. The word shocks him, and as he sees her led away in Albine's arms, a cry of anguish escapes him.

Scene II. The Cenobite settlement again with a night of storm coming on. Athanaël has returned and spent twenty days of fasting. He comes out of his hut and asks Palémon to confess him. In saving the soul of Thaïs, he has lost his own. His mind is filled with visions of Aphrodite. He falls asleep and sees her again in all her fleshly charms. The vision vanishes in strident laughter, giving place to a new vision, the Monastery of Albine, where Thaïs, all in white, is dying, surrounded by the kneeling nuns. Athanaël awakens in a frenzy of revolt and dashes out to reclaim her.

The scene changes to the Convent garden, where Albine and the nuns moan over the saintly Thaïs, who has saved her soul, but worn out her life with her penances. Athanaël appears and is greeted with respect as a venerable saint. He drags himself on his knees to the side of Thaïs, who weakly reminds him that his promise of Heaven and redemption are fulfilled. She sees the angels and God. But Athanaël protests that nothing is true but life and love. And when she dies, he falls to the ground with a terrible cry.

## SMETANA, FRIEDRICH

**The Bartered Bride.** Prodana Nevesta (prō'-dä-nä něv-yěs'-tä) *B.* Die Verkaufte Braut (dē fěr-kowf'-tě browt) *G.*
  A comic opera in three acts. Book by Karl Sabina.
  Produced, National Theatre, Prague, May 30, 1866.

CHARACTERS

HANS ........................ten.
WENZEL (věn'-tsěl) .............ten.
KEZAL (kā'-tsäl) ...............bar.
KRUSCHINA (kroo-shē'-nä) .... bass.
SPRINGER ....................bar.
MUFF
MICHA (mē-khä)
MARIE .......................sopr.
KATHINKA (ka-teenk'-a) ....mez-sopr.
ESMERAL'DA
AGNES

Act I.— Scene. The Square of a Bohemian village during a Spring Church Festival. The chorus is rejoicing in the coming of Spring, but Marie is sad. Hans, her lover, asks her why, and is told that she is to be the bartered bride of the son of Micha. She is puzzled at the calmness of Hans, and asks him to explain the mystery of his origin. He tells her that he is the son of a rich man, but he left home on the death of his mother. He bids her to be of good cheer and goes. She hides as her father and mother, Kruschina and Kathinka, come in with the marriage broker, Kezal. Kezal has arranged a marriage for Marie with the son of Micha, whose elder son has disappeared. Kezal sings the praises of the younger son, Wenzel. Marie appears and refuses the match declaring her love for Hans. Kezal shows the agreement with Micha, but Marie knocks it out of his hand. Kezal promises to talk to Hans, and the act ends with a country dance, called "the hen."

Act II.— Scene. A room in the inn, Hans at one table, Kezal at another. A beer-chorus is sung and Hans toasts love, while Kezal toasts cash. After a wild dance called a "furiant" the scene is emptied, and Wenzel enters stuttering a song about his mother's advice to her "Dear Son" (*Theu' . . . theurer Sohn*). Marie appears and is amused at her prospective bridegroom, but Wenzel does not suspect her identity. She persuades him that Marie will be a wretched wife, and promises to find him another. He repeats her oath that he will forswear Marie, and follows her when she runs away. Kezal drags Hans in and begs him not to interfere with the wedding. Kezal described love as a folly (*Wer in Lieb' entbrannt*). He promises to get Hans another bride and to give him three hundred gulden. Hans consents on one condition, that Marie shall marry no one but Micha's son. The duped Kezal hurries away in delight to draw up the contract, and Hans rejoices in the happiness awaiting him (*Es muss gelingen*). Kezal returns with the others and reads the marriage contract by which Hans gives up all claims to Marie in favour of the son of Micha. Hans signs the paper while the villagers revile him for selling his bride.

Act III.— Scene. The same room. Wenzel is grieving that Marie has escaped him, when Springer, a circus man, arrives with his troupe, including Esmeralda, the tight-rope walker, a wild Indian chief and a great trained bear. A brief performance is given and Wenzel falls in love with Esmeralda. The Indian chief tells Springer that the actor who plays the trained bear is drunk. In his desperation Springer appeals to Wenzel to join the troupe and promises him a life of joy with Esmeralda, who teaches him how to dance as a bear. His mother, Agnes, his father, Micha, and Kezal arrive to lead him to the ceremony; but he declines the marriage. Marie rushes in in an agony of grief because Hans has betrayed her and sold her. Left alone, she broods upon her sorrow (*Wie fremd und todt ist Alles umher*). Hans rushes to her, but is repulsed, and she announces that she will marry Wenzel. Kezal appears and Hans still appeals for trust (*Gesegnet, wer da liebt und auch vertraut!*) The others return and Hans is recognized by his father and mother. Marie, understanding his plot rushes to his arms, and Kezal dashes away from the general ridicule. Loud cries are heard that the bear has escaped and there is a general panic, but the bear exclaims "Don't be afraid! I'm only We-We-Wenzel!" and the opera ends in cries of "Long life to the Bartered Bride."

## STRAUSS, RICHARD.

**Salomé** (săl-ō-mä') *F.* (să-lō'-mĕ) *E.*
Drama in one act. German text by Frau Hedwig Lachmann (founded on

the drama written in French by Oscar Wilde).

Produced, Dresden, Dec. 9, 1905; New York, 1907, the subscribers demanding its withdrawal.

### CHARACTERS

| | |
|---|---|
| HER'OD AN'TIPAS | ten. |
| IOKANAAN (yō-kän'-än) | bar. |
| NAR'RABOTH, | |
| *A young Syrian; Captain of the Guard* | ten. |
| TIGELLI'NUS, | |
| *A young Roman* | |
| A CAPPADO'CIAN | bass. |
| A NUBIAN | |
| THE PAGE | contr. |
| NAAMAN (nä'-män), | |
| *The executioner* | |
| HEROIDIAS | mez-sopr. |
| SALOMÉ | sopr. |

The story is based upon the account in the New Testament. Salome is the daughter of Herodias by her first husband, Herod Phillip. The second husband, Herod Antipas, has imprisoned Iokanaan (John the Baptist) in a well because he denounced Herod for marrying his own brother's wife.

Scene. A terrace of Herod's palace above the banquet hall. At the back, an old cistern. Soldiers are leaning over the balcony and watching the banquet, discussing the beauty of Salome, the quarrelsomeness of the Jews and the gloom of Herod. Narraboth, a young Syrian, Captain of the Guard, stares with idolatry at Salome. The voice of Iokanaan is heard from the well, prophesying the coming of a mightier than he. The Cappadocian thinks that the cistern is a strange prison for a man, but a soldier tells him that Herod kept his elder brother, the first husband of Herodias, imprisoned there for twelve years, and then sent his ring to the executioner, Naaman, who strangled him. Narraboth exclaims that Salome is leaving the table, and

Salome enters, complaining that she could not endure the strange stare of Herod. She is glad to be in the garden away from the crowds; she hears the voice of Iokanaan, and asks about him. A slave comes from Herod to beg her to return, but she refuses, and insists that the soldiers bring Iokanaan forth from the cistern. They are afraid, but she beguiles Narraboth into disobeying Herod's orders, and the Prophet is brought forward, denouncing Herod and Herodias. He terrifies, yet fascinates, Salome, and she speaks to him. He denounces her and her mother, but she grows all the more amorous of him. Again he rebukes her as a daughter of Babylon. She turns upon him in fury, only to grow ardent again. She longs to caress and to kiss him. Narraboth's heart breaks with jealousy and he slays himself and falls between Salome and Iokanaan. The young page of Herodias, who had foreseen omens in everything on this fateful evening, bewails the death of Narraboth, but Salome does not even see the body, so fiercely is she pleading for the lips of Iokanaan. He reviles her, and bids her go seek One whom she will find by the Sea of Galilee, but she will not cease demanding his love, and he curses her and returns to the well.

Herod and Herodias and the Court appear, Herod demanding why Salome had not returned to the banquet as he commanded. He notes that the moon has a strange look like a mad woman. Herod calls for torches and wine that he may do honour to Tigellinus, the Ambassador of Cæsar. He slips on the blood of Narraboth, and finds that an ill omen. He sees the corpse of Narraboth and learns that he has slain himself. Herod remembers that Narraboth looked too much at Salome. Herodias says that Narraboth is not the only one who looked too much at Salome, and bids him go within. But he calls again for wine which Cæsar himself sent him, and asks Salome to sip from his cup.

She refuses, and he calls for fruit, but she will not eat. Herodias in fury denounces Herod as the son of a camel driver. He invites Salome to share his throne. The voice of the Prophet comes from the well denouncing Herod. The Jews ask that Iokanaan be delivered into their hands, but Herod answers that Iokanaan is reputed to be the prophet Elias returned. Iokanaan predicts the coming of the Saviour of the World. Tigellinus protests that this is a title of Cæsar's. Other Jews describe the miracles of Christ, and Herod wishes Jesus apprehended and forbidden to raise the dead. The Prophet's voice still thunders from the well, and Herodias demands his life, but Herod refuses it. He stares always at Salome and begs her to dance. She refuses. He commands her. She refuses. He pretends indifference and loudly declares himself happy and content. But again he begs Salome to dance away his gloom, promising her whatsoever she may ask, even to the half of his kingdom. Salome takes off her sandals in spite of her mother's protests. Herod warns her that she will dance upon the blood on which he has slipped: but she dances "The Dance of the Seven Veils."

Herod, overjoyed, now asks her her fee, and she, to her mother's delight, calls for the head of Iokanaan on a silver charger. Herod is aghast and protests and pleads, but Herodias and Salome remind him of his oath. He offers jewels and fifty white peacocks, but she is immovable. He warns her of the evil omens and promises her all manner of gifts, even to the Veil of the Sanctuary, but she repeats, "Give me the head of Iokanaan." At last he yields. He draws from his hand the ring of death and gives it to a soldier who bears it to the executioner. The executioner, with a look of terror, descends into the cistern. Salome leans over the edge and describes what she sees. The executioner is afraid and will not strike. But

at last, his huge black arm comes forth from the cistern, bearing on a shield the head of Iokanaan. Salome seizes it as Herod hides his head in his cloak.

Herodias smiles and the Nazarenes kneel in prayer.

Salome gloats over the head, and taunts it with having refused the kisses she demanded. She kisses the helpless lips of the dead Iokanaan, and cries out her love for him.

Herod sickens and cries out against her as a monster. He orders the torches quenched, and as the cloud hides the moon and the hideous courtship of Salome, Herod cries, "Kill that woman!" The soldiers hurl their shields upon her.

## STRAUSS, RICHARD

### Elek′tra

Tragic opera in one act. Book by Hugo Hoffmannsthal.

Produced, Dresden, January 25, 1909; New York, February 1, 1910.

#### CHARACTERS

ELEK′TRA.......................sopr.
CHRYSOTHEMIS (krē-sŏth′-ā-mĭs) .sopr.
KLYTAEMNESTRA (klē-tĕm-nĕs′-trä)
.....................mez-sopr.
AEGISTHUS (ē-jĭs′thŭs)..........ten.
ORES′TES..................bar.
FOSTER FATHER OF ORESTES.....bass.
A YOUNG SERVANT..............ten.
AN OLD SERVANT...............bass.
THE CONFIDANT................sopr.
OVERSEER OF THE SERVANTS....sopr.
TRAINBEARER .................sopr.
FIVE SERVING WOMEN

The story is based upon the Greek legends somewhat as treated in the tragedies by Sophokles and Euripides.

Elektra was the daughter of King Agamemnon and his wife, Klytaemnestra. During the absence of Agamemnon at the Trojan war his wife carried on an intrigue with Aegisthus. When Agamemnon returned home he was slain in his bath by his wife and her paramour. The Queen treated her children, Elektra and Orestes, with great cruelty, and they finally conspired to murder her and her lover.

The German author has introduced the character of Chrysothemis as a sister of Elektra.

Scene. A courtyard of the palace showing the servants' quarters and a well. Five serving maids are grouped about the well under the direction of the Overseer. They are discussing the ferocious and uncanny behaviour of Elektra, who is a veritable wildcat. Some of the maids have sympathy for her because she is beaten and treated like a beast. When they have gone, Elektra appears, brooding over the murder of her father, which she sees enacted before her. She longs for the day when her father shall be revenged, and when she shall dance over the bodies of her guilty mother and the wicked Aegisthus. Her sister, Chrysothemis, appears and warns Elektra that she is to be thrown into a dungeon. Chrysothemis longs for a life of love and motherhood, but Elektra rebukes her for her weakness and sends her away, as Klytaemnestra appears with torches and retinue. Klytaemnestra is worn out with guilt and sleeplessness, and asks Elektra if there is no rest for her. Elektra answers in riddles which imply that Klytaemnestra's repose shall only come when the right blood shall flow under the axe; when a certain woman and a certain man shall be slain by another man. Elektra asks if Orestes may not be allowed to return from his years of exile, and accuses her mother of trying to have him murdered. Elektra warns her that she will die for her crime.

As the two women confront each other, the Queen's confidant hurries in and whispers news to her which gives her great joy. As she hurries away, Chrysothemis comes in screaming that Orestes is dead, and that two strangers, an old man and a young man, have brought word that he had been trampled to death by his horses.

A young servant darts in demanding a horse, as he must carry a message quickly. Elektra pleads with Chrysothemis to join her in the vengeance which the dead Orestes should have wreaked. She praises the younger sister for her strength and beauty, and offers to be her slave if she will aid her. Chrysothemis is afraid and reluctant, and flees. Elektra creeps toward the house to do the slaughter herself, but meets Orestes himself, who enters. Brother and sister do not recognize each other at first, because he has grown to manhood and she has lost her beauty. An old servant prostrates himself before Orestes' feet, and Elektra embraces him with joy. Orestes' foster-father hurries in to warn the brother and sister not to betray themselves. A servant appears to invite Orestes to the presence of Klytaemnestra, who does not suspect him. Orestes enters the palace and shortly afterward the wild shrieks of Klytaemnestra are heard as she is being slain. Elektra braces herself against the door and keeps out the servants, who are in a panic. Aegisthus arrives hastily and Elektra, taking a torch, invites him to enter, and pays him ironical homage, dancing before him. Much puzzled, Aegisthus enters the house and is heard crying for help. He appears at the window, struggling and tearing down the curtain. He is dragged away and his cries are silenced. Chrysothemis speaks to Elektra and tells her that the palace is in an uproar, the retainers of Orestes having attacked the partisans of Aegisthus. Elektra crouches by the door brooding with uncanny rapture over the great revenge. She tries to dance, but falls prostrate.

## HUMPERDINCK, ENGELBERT

**Königskinder** (kä'-nĭkhs-kĭnt-ĕr)

A fairy opera in three acts. Book by Ernest Rosmer.

Produced, Metropolitan Opera House, New York, Dec. 28, 1910.

## CHARACTERS AND THEIR CREATORS

DER KOENIGSSOHN (kā'-nĭkhs-zōn),
*The King's Son*
Hermann Jadlowker, ten.

DIE GAENSEMAGD (gĕn'-zĕ-mäkht),
*The Goose-girl*, Geraldine Farrar, sopr.

DER SPIELMANN (shpēl'-män),
*The Fiddler*........Otto Goritz, bar.

DIE HEXE (hĕx'-ĕ),
*The Witch*.....Louise Homer, contr.

DER HOLZHACKER (hŏlts'-häk-ĕr),
*The Wood-cutter*.Adamo Didur, bass.

DER BESENBINDER (bā'-zĕn-bĭn-dĕr),
*The Broom-maker*..Albert Reiss, ten.

ZWEI KINDER
*Two Children*
Edna Walter, Lottie Engel,

DER RATSAELTESTE (räts'-ĕl-tĕs-tĕ),
*The Senior Councillor*
Marcel Reiner, bar.

DER WIRT (vērt),
*The Inn-keeper*
Antonio Pini-Corsi, bass.

DIE WIRTSTOCHTER (vērts'-tôkh-tĕr),
*The Inn-keeper's Daughter*
Florence Wickham, mez-sopr.

DER SCHNEIDER (schnī'-dĕr),
*The Tailor*........Julius Bayer, ten.

DIE STALLMAGD (shtäl'-mäkht),
*The Stable-maid*
Marie Mattfeld, contr.

*The Two Gate-keepers*
Herbert Witherspoon,
William Hinshaw, } bar's.

The action takes place in the Hella Forest, and in the neighbouring town of Hellabrunn.

Act I. — Scene. A glade near the Witch's hut. The Goose-girl is neglecting her flock, and idly humming to herself, when the Witch pops her head out, berates her for letting her geese stray, then calls her into make a poisoned pasty of acorns. The Goose-girl stares at a stunted lily and wonders why her flowers will not grow as others do. She asks of her own childhood, begs her "Grandmother" to let her go forth into the world, but the Witch tells her she has cast a spell over bush and briar, and she cannot escape. The girl, left alone, sings to the beloved linden tree (*O liebe Linde*) and to her own reflection in the water. The King's son appears in a shabby hunting costume, with a bundle on his shoulders. She questions him ignorantly, and he finds her beautiful. She asks what a King is, and he tells her that a King guards his people as she guards her geese; but that he, being youthful, has found the life of a Prince too gloomy and fettered and has fled (*Fort! Hinaus!*) She longs to go with him, and he takes her in his arms, asking her, "Wilt thou go maying with me?" (*Willst du mein Maienbuhle sein?*) The wind blows the wreath from her hair, and he puts it in his doublet as a token. He unties his bundle and takes out a golden crown, but she refuses it and he tosses it aside. He takes her hand to lead her away, but she feels the charm and is frightened. He is angry and finds her unworthy with her beggar's blood (*Königsblut und Bettelblut*). He dashes away and leaves her weeping. She hears the Witch calling, and fearing lest the crown betray her, begs one of the geese to hide it, and hangs it on the goose's neck. The Witch quizzes her closely, and she confesses that she has seen a man. The Fiddler is heard singing, "Three fools went out one day for an egg that a cock did lay" (*Drei Narren zogen aus*). The Witch drives the girl into the house and follows her in. The Fiddler, the Wood-cutter and the Broom-maker appear. They knock at the door loudly, and when the Witch finally appears, the Fiddler sings an ironical love song to her beautiful red eyes (*Deine schönen roten Augen*). He and his friends have come to say that the King of Hellabrunn had died and his heir had disappeared. They ask her whom they shall choose to rule over them. The Witch says that at the Hella feast the next day, when the noon strikes, the gate of the city must be open, and whosoever enters the town must wear the crown. The Broom-maker and the Wood-cutter go back to the city, but the Fiddler, having caught a glimpse of the Goose-girl, demands that she be given her liberty. When she appears, he questions her. He thinks that she is of royal blood, but the Witch sneers that she is the shameful child of a hangman's daughter. Nevertheless, the Fiddler hails her as royal, and she calls to the gray goose to bring back the crown. She puts it upon her head as she kneels in prayer and the light of a star falls upon the stunted lily, which opens wide in full bloom. Crying that she is free, the Goose-girl darts away, followed by her geese and the Fiddler. The Witch knocks down the lily with her staff.

Act II. — Scene. A square near the gate of the city. The Gate-keepers are on guard and the Inn-keeper's daughter is quarrelling with the Stable-maid, as the King's son comes out of the inn yawning. He has slept with the swine, and the girls treat him with contemptuous familiarity. The Inn-keeper's daughter brings him food, but it is too coarse for his palate. She makes love to him and advises him to marry, but he asks if it is a linden tree under which they sit. She embraces him, but he pushes her hands away and she boxes his ears. He turns to leave the hateful town, when he finds in his doublet the Goose-girl's wreath. The leaves seem to whisper to him, "Do not go." The townspeople appear, and the Gate-keepers keep them from the gates lest one of them claim the crown. There is a Spring dance. The King's son asks the Inn-keeper for employment. He is offered the post of swineherd and reluctantly accepts. The Broom-maker appears, followed by his thirteen daughters, each of the children riding a broom and trying to sell it. The

youngest child of the Broom-maker asks the King's son to play with her, and they dance a ring-around-a-rosy. The Councillors and the rich Burghers with their families arrive and seat themselves in the Tribune. The Wood-cutter describes for them his journey to the Witch's hut, which he dresses up with dangers and wild animals. He announces that at the opening of the gates the King will arrive in glory upon a golden car. The King's son asks if the King might not come in rags, but everybody laughs at the idea. He describes what a true King should be, but they mock him; the Inn-keeper demands pay for the food which the King's son could not eat. He is about to be roughly handled by the crowd, when the first bell rings. The crowd is hushed with awe. At the twelfth stroke the Gate-keepers throw open the gates, and the Goose-girl enters with her flock, followed by the Fiddler. The King's son hails her as his Queen, and she him as her King, but the crowd bursts into derisive laughter at her bare feet and his rags. The King's son draws his sword and protects the girl, and the Fiddler proclaims them King and Queen, but the mob drives them out all three with sticks and stones. The Broom-maker's littlest daughter weeps. The Senior Councillor asks her if she weeps because her broom has vanished. She answers, "No, it was the King and Queen you banished."

Act III. — Scene. The same as the first act, but it is now bleak winter. The water trough is frozen and the linden tree is bare. The Witch's hut is dilapidated, for she has been burned at the stake on account of her prophecy. The Fiddler has been jailed and broken on the rack for defending the two pretenders. He is living alone in the hut, hoping for the return of the two children. He feeds the doves that gather, and questions them for knowledge of the outcast royal children, but they flutter away. The Wood-cutter and the

Broom-maker appear, shivering with the cold. The Broom-maker brings his littlest daughter, and the Fiddler greets her with gratitude because when he was perishing in jail she was the only one to bring him bread. The Wood-cutter brings word that the town has forgiven the Fiddler, and the children, who have followed, beg him to come back and play for them, promising him cakes and kisses, but he has sworn an oath not to revisit the hateful town. The Broom-maker describes the desolation that has fallen upon the city, the hostility of the children toward their parents. The little child tells the Fiddler that the children know the King and Queen were driven away. They want them brought back. The Fiddler says he hopes that when the Spring comes he can go forth and find them. The child says that May is a hundred years away, and the Fiddler, taking up his fiddle limps off into the wood with the children. The Wood-cutter and the Broom-maker remain and search the hut, while the Fiddler is heard singing, "Whither hast thou wandered, oh, my Royal Maid" (*Wohin bist du gegangen*). His voice dies out, and the King's son and the Goose-girl enter, starved and chilled. The King's son goes to the door of the hut and knocks. The Wood-cutter opens the window, but slams it shut when the King's son asks for bread. The Goose-girl regrets that they have left the cave where they have been in hiding, but the King's son explains that hunger was their compulsion, and that he was lured back to his rightful realm. He contrasts the gayety with which he ran away from home and the sorrow of his exile. To cheer him, she throws off her fatigue, and dropping her cloak and tearing her furs from her feet, she dances barefooted in the snow until she drops at the foot of the linden tree. He wraps her in her cloak and in his own robe. He resolves to sell the useless crown for bread, but breaks it in two lest any one else should wear it. · He knocks at the hut door and the Wood-cutter and the Broom-maker, who have found nothing in the hut but the poisoned pasty, greedily exchange it for the gold. The King's son takes it to the Goose-girl, and they quarrel lovingly over which shall have the larger share. They eat, and as the poison fills their veins they dream of Spring and happiness. Wrapped in each other's arms and kissing, they fall asleep. The snow begins to fall more heavily and gradually covers them over.

The Fiddler comes back with the children, and the Wood-cutter and the Broom-maker shows the pieces of the crown and describe the ragged outcast from whom they had taken it. The Fiddler calls wildly into the woods, "Königskinder!! Königskinder!" A dove circles about the Fiddler, and flies to the linden tree, where the Fiddler finds the royal children in the sleep of death. The children from the town gather about and place the two bodies on a bier of pine branches, on which they are borne away to a royal grave on the mountain, the Fiddler vowing to sing them one last song, then fling away his fiddle forever.

## WAGNER, WILHELM RICHARD

**Parsifal** (pär'-sĭ-fäl)

"A consecration festival-drama" in three acts.

In 1848 Wagner made plans for a work, "Jesus von Nazareth," which were gradually modified into the project for "Parsifal," on which he was engaged as early as 1854. But the poem was not finished until 1877, in which year it was published. He began the music the next year at the age of 65. The prelude was privately performed at Bayreuth, Christmas, 1878, but the work was not completed until January 13, 1882. The first performance was at Bayreuth, July 28, 1882; sixteen performances were given during the following month.

It was Wagner's earnest wish that the work should never be given except in the theatre to which it was sacred, though it was performed almost entire in concert form in London in 1884, under Sir Joseph Barnby. After much controversy and an effort at legal prevention, the work was performed at the Metropolitan Opera House, under Conried's management, with Burgstaller as Parsifal, Blass as Gurnemanz, Van Rooy as Amfortas, and Ternina as Kundry. In 1905 it was produced at Amsterdam.

At its original production there were alternating casts as follows:

### CHARACTERS

PARSIFAL. Winkelmann, Gudehus, Jaeger..........................ten.
AMFOR'TAS. Reichmann, Fuchs...bar.
GURNEMANZ (goor'-nĕ-mänts). Scaria, Siehr........................bass.
KLINGSOR (klĭnk'-zôr). Hill, Degele, Plank .....................bar.
TITUREL (tee'-too-rĕl).
KNIGHTS OF THE GRAIL
FOUR SQUIRES
KUNDRY (koon'-drē). Materna, Marianne Brandt, Malten ....sopr.
FLOWER MAIDENS

The story concerns the legend of the Holy Grail (the chalice from which Jesus drank at the Last Supper, and in which blood from His wounded side was caught and kept). The Grail and the spear that pierced Christ's side fell to the care of the Knights Templars, whose chief, Titurel, built the castle Montsalvat for their sanctuary. The power of the Grail was renewed annually by the Holy Ghost, in the form of a dove, from which the Knights also received miraculous virtues.

The Knight Klingsor, failing to obtain admission to the circle, laid violent hands on himself, and avowed undying enmity to the Grail Knights In the wilderness near Montsalvat he established, by evil magic, a garden filled with flower-women of infernal charm. Among his enchantresses was Herodias, who laughed at Christ on His way to crucifixion and was cursed. She now exists as Kundry, only partly under the spell of Klingsor. At his behest she works evil sorceries, for which she tries to atone when she is free.

The Knights know her only as the wild Kundry, but it was she who, under Klingsor's spell, once enchanted Amfortas, the son of Titurel, who had abdicated in Amfortas' favour. During Amfortas' enchantment Klingsor had robbed him of the sacred spear, and with it inflicted on him a wound which could not be cured save by the same spear, which should be recaptured by a pure-souled fool. Meanwhile, Klingsor has continued to entice away the Knights one by one, and the Castle of the Grail is the home of despair.

Act 1.—Scene 1. A forest near a lake, in the demesne of Montsalvat, the castle of the Keepers of the Holy Grail. The elderly Gurnemanz is asleep at the foot of a tree and two squires are asleep at his feet. A reveille of trombones wakes them; they kneel in prayer. Two Knights enter and Gurnemanz asks after Amfortas' health. He is about to be brought to his bath though Gurnemanz says that his only hope is in one man.

Kundry enters like a witch, bringing a small flask of balsam which she has fetched from Arabia. Amfortas is brought in on a litter, bewailing his wound. He thanks Kundry for her gift and is carried on to his bath. The squires revile Kundry, but Gurnemanz defends her, and outlines to the squires the whole previous history as described above, and the prophetic dream of the guileless fool (*der reine Thor*).

A commotion is heard from the lake, and a wounded swan flutters dying to the ground. Other squires drag in the half-witted Parsifal, whose arrow has slain the swan. Gurnemanz reproaches him for the wanton cruelty. Parsifal, now first realizing what he has done, weeps and breaks his bow and arrows. The swan is borne away in state. Gurnemanz, questioning Parsifal, learns that, though he has no name himself, his mother was called Heart's-Grief (*Herzeleide*). Kundry hoarsely explains that he was born after his father, Gamouret, had been slain in battle, and was reared in solitude by his timorous mother. Parsifal says that he was lured from home by seeing a glittering company of Knights ride by, and had had to defend himself from wolves and robbers.

Kundry says that she saw his mother die. At this news Parsifal, in a frenzy, seizes Kundry by the throat. Gurnemanz takes him away and rebukes him. He turns faint and Kundry restores him with water from a brook; then Kundry, unnoticed, struggles in vain against the slumber that marks Klingsor's spell, and falls behind a thicket.

The Knights return with Amfortas and pass on. Gurnemanz, half-hoping that Parsifal is indeed the pure-souled fool, invites him to the castle; magically the woods flow back beneath their feet, till they arrive in Scene II, a lofty cathedral, on whose shrine stands the Holy Grail. Parsifal, overawed, stands in motionless wonder throughout the long ceremony of the Eucharist. Knights and squires gather at tables singing, and Amfortas is brought in. From an unseen crypt comes the voice of the aged Titurel ordering his son to celebrate the feast. Amfortas in an agony of pain and remorse reluctantly consents, crying aloud for forgiveness or death. The Grail is unveiled and placed before him, and, in a shaft of light from heaven, Amfortas elevates the Host.

The cups of the Knights are seen to be filled with wine. Gurnemanz motions Parsifal to sit by him and partake of the Communion, but Parsifal does not move. At the end of the repast Amfortas' pain breaks out afresh and he is carried out, and the others withdraw. Gurnemanz, finding Parsifal still stupefied, asks him if he understands what he saw. Parsifal shakes his head. Gurnemanz in disgust orders him off, with a warning to leave the swans alone and seek the geese, since he is one.

Act II. — Scene. Klingsor's Magic Castle. In the inner keep of a tower, Klingsor stands amid his magic implements, and with necromancy summons Kundry. Her form rises from the earth, resisting vainly and protesting. Klingsor exultantly commands her to change her form and enchant Parsifal, whom he sees approaching. The other enchanted Knights are heard resisting him, but in vain. With triumphant hopes of possessing the very Grail itself, Klingsor sends Kundry to her task, and sinks into the earth with his tower, revealing Scene II: the flowery terraces of the palace, and Parsifal staring into the garden. From all sides beautiful women rush upon him with caresses and laughter, each proffering him her love. At first fascinated, he grows colder, and is about to flee when he hears Kundry's voice call him by the name "Parsifal." The word reminds him of his mother's voice and he pauses.

Kundry in the form of a beautiful woman on a flowery couch dismisses the other enchantresses. Parsifal asks her how she came to call him, the nameless one, "Parsifal." She tells him of his mother, her loneliness for her son, and his death. Thus she brings Parsifal to his knees at her side. Then she offers him the consolation of her own love, and kisses him. Her lips burn him, and he remembers Amfortas' pain and his outcry against the enchantress whose charms ensnared him. He denounces Kundry as the destroyer of Amfortas.

Kundry tries all her wiles, appealing for pity because of her ancient sufferings since she laughed at Christ, and

can only be healed by the returning
Christ. She begs Parsifal to take her
to his arms and redeem her, but he cries
that her love would only make him
share her damnation. She seizes him,
but he breaks from her. She curses his
pathway and calls for help, and the
enchantresses rush out. Klingsor also
appears on the castle wall. He raises
the sacred spear and hurls it at Parsifal.
But it pauses in air over his head.
Parsifal, reaching upward, grasps it,
makes the sign of the cross, and the
palace and garden fall into instant ruins.
Parsifal calls to the prostrate Kundry,
"Thou knowest where alone thou see'st
me again."

Act III.— Scene I. A meadow and
grove in Montsalvat. A hut wherein
dwells Gurnemanz, now much older and
in hermit's garb. Hearing groans, he
comes out and finds Kundry lying
among brambles. He restores her to
life with difficulty, and her only answer
is the words "To serve! To serve!"
As she brings water from the spring,
she sees a strange warrior approaching
in complete black armour, with visor
down. The mysterious Knight will not
answer Gurnemanz' questions save by
noddings of the head. Gurnemanz informs him that the day is Good Friday,
and that he should disarm. He does so
slowly and in silence, kneeling before his
own spear. Gurnemanz tells Kundry
softly that the stranger is the fool he
had banished long ago. Parsifal rises,
recognizes Gurnemanz, and tells him of
his long, long wanderings. Kundry's
curse upon his pathway had kept him
from finding his way back till now. He
shows the sacred spear which he has
carried undefiled. Gurnemanz welcomes him with rapture, and tells him
that since the day of his departure
Amfortas would no more elevate the
Host, and the Grail has remained un-
revealed. Lacking its aid, the Knights
have grown old and weak, and Titurel
has died.

Parsifal, blaming himself for his long

delay to return, grows faint. Kundry,
like a Magdalen, washes his feet and
anoints them, and dries them with her
hair, while Gurnemanz, like a John the
Baptist, baptizes him, and at Parsifal's
behest anoints his head, for Parsifal is to
be the King. Parsifal now baptizes
Kundry and redeems her.

Seeing how fair the landscape is, Parsifal wonders that nature should not
grieve on the day of agony, but Gurnemanz answers that everything glows
with gratitude to the Saviour. (This
scene is known musically as The Spell
of Good Friday and the Flowering
Meadow intermezzo.) Parsifal kisses
the brow of Kundry, and the peal of
bells in the distance calls him. Gurnemanz brings out armour and a mantle
of the Grail Knights, and he and Kundry fasten them on Parsifal. Once
more the landscape flows magically beneath their feet, but in the opposite
direction from Act I. Once more the;
arrive in the Hall, Scene II: but now the
Communion tables are missing.

The Knights bring in Titurel's body
in its coffin, and Amfortas in his litter,
preceded by the covered shrine of the
Grail. Amfortas has consented once
more to reveal the Grail. He blames
himself now for his father's death and
implores the dead body to mount to
heaven and pray: "Saviour, give my
son peace."

The Knights demand the uncovering
of the Grail, but he asks them rather
to slay him. Baring his wound, he begs
them to thrust in their swords and slay
him. They shrink back, but Parsifal,
advancing with the sacred spear, puts it
forth and touches Amfortas' wound,
saying that only the weapon that made
the wound can heal it. Amfortas, released from pain, thrills with ecstasy as
Parsifal announces that he himself will
reign thereafter. The Grail glows and
a halo of glory streams down from
heaven, in which a white dove descends
and hovers over Parsifal's head. He
rises and elevates the Grail. Kundry

sinks slowly. into a blissful death. Amfortas and Gurnemanz kneel in homage to the guileless fool.

## PUCCINI, GIACOMO

**Madama Butterfly**
A Japanese tragedy in two acts. Libretto by L. Illica and G. Giacosa (after the book and play by John Luther Long and David Belasco).

Produced La Scala, Milan, 1904, in two acts and hooted off the stage. Withdrawn after one performance and revised in three acts. Produced again at Brescia with an immediate success. Repeated at Covent Garden, 1905, and throughout the world.

### CHARACTERS

MADAMA BUTTERFLY
(Cho-Cho-San)..............sopr.
SUZUKI,
Her Servant..............mez-sopr.
KATE PINKERTON ........mez-sopr.
B. F. PINKERTON,
Lieutenant in the United States
Navy ....................ten.
SHARPLESS,
United States Consul at Nagasaki .bar.
GORO,
A Marriage Broker............ten.
PRINCE YAMADORI...............bar.
THE BONZE,
Cho-Cho-San's Uncle..........bass.
YAKUSIDE.....................bar.
THE IMPERIAL COMMISSIONER....bass.
THE OFFICIAL REGISTRAR.......bar.
CHO-CHO-SAN'S MOTHER...mez-sopr.
THE AUNT ...............mez-sopr.
THE COUSIN...................sopr.
TROUBLE,
Cho-Cho-San's Child

Place of action at Nagasaki, Japan.

Act I.— Scene. A Japanese house and garden, with the harbour in the background. A United States naval officer, Lieutenant B. F. Pinkerton, has hired a Japanese marriage broker, Goro, to procure for him the pretty Japanese girl, Cho-Cho-San, with whom he has become infatuated. The broker has arranged the contract and leased this house — both leases for nine hundred and ninety-nine years, and both breakable at will. At the rise of the curtain, Goro is explaining to Pinkerton the conveniences of the little house and the conveniences of Japanese marriage-law. The two servants come in and prostrate themselves, but are dismissed with scant courtesy by Pinkerton. Goro explains that the bride's relatives must be present in large numbers at the ceremony. Sharpless, the American Consul, comes in, out of breath with the climb. Refreshments are served and Pinkerton gayly exalts the Yankee spirit, but Sharpless warns him that his course is dangerous. Pinkerton describes his infatuation — "love or whim" (*Amore o grillo*)? Sharpless begs Pinkerton not to crush this butterfly. Pinkerton laughs at his old-fogy notions, and drinks to the day when he will marry "in true marriage an American."

Butterfly enters singing of the breath of Spring (*Spira sul mare*). She kneels and orders her friends to kneel. Sharpless asks her of her people, and learns that she comes of a wealthy family whose sudden poverty drove her to the life of a geisha. Her father is dead, but she has two uncles; one of them is a toper; the other is the Bonze, a great man. She is fifteen years old.

The High Commissioner and the official Registrar and the relations now arrive. Pinkerton laughs at the farce (*Che burletta*). Refreshments are served and the papers are drawn up. Meanwhile, Butterfly takes from her big sleeves her possessions. She throws away her jar of paint at his protest. She has brought also the sword the Emperor had sent to her father with instructions to commit hara-kiri; brings out the images of the souls of her ancestors; to please him she has gone to the mission, forsworn her religion and taken his; and now she throws the images away.

The marriage bond is signed, and the guests are dispersing, when the Bonze enters in a rage and demands of his niece what she was doing at the mission. Learning that she has renounced her religion, he curses her and, gathering the relatives together, leads them all away, renouncing her. Butterfly weeps. Pinkerton consoles her tenderly, the servants close the sliding walls, and Butterfly, aided by her maid, Suzuki, prepares her toilet. Pinkerton muses on her ways of a little squirrel (*Con moti di scojattolo*), her childlike charms (*Bimba dagli occhi*). She compares herself to the moon-goddess (*La piccola Dea della luna*), tells of her fear of him when the marriage-broker proposed marriage to a foreign barbarian, and now of her love. She begs him to be good to his butterfly and not to thrust a needle through her heart, as Americans do with butterflies. She points to the star-filled night (*Dolce notte! Quante stelle!*) and he leads her to the marriage chamber.

Act II.— Scene. Three years later. Inside the same house. Suzuki is praying and ringing a prayer-bell. Butterfly says that the God of her husband must have overlooked them, for they are near to starvation and Suzuki has only a few coins left. Butterfly is sure that her husband will return, and quotes his promise to come back when the robins nest. "Some fine day we'll see the smoke of his ship" (*Un bel di, vedremo*). Sharpless and Goro appear. The Consul brings a letter from Pinkerton. She asks when robins nest in America. "They have already nested thrice in Japan; perhaps they nest less often in America." Goro laughs and Butterfly explains that as soon as Pinkerton left her, Goro tried to bribe her to marry the Prince Yamadori, who enters now and declares his love. They insist that Butterfly is already

divorced through her husband's desertion. Goro whispers that Pinkerton's ship is already signalled. Sharpless has had a letter asking him to break the news to Butterfly that Pinkerton is married and does not want to see her. Yamadori rejected again, goes away dejected and Sharpless reads the letter to Butterfly, trying to prepare her. But she is furious and orders him out, then begs his forgiveness, and to prove that she could not be forgotten, brings in her baby, born after Pinkerton left her. Surely the mother of so wonderful a child could not go back to the geisha life.

Sharpless rises in despair, kisses the child and asks its name. Butterfly says his name is "Trouble" till his father returns; then it shall be "Joy." When Sharpless goes, Suzuki drags in Goro, saying that he has been spreading a scandal that nobody knows who is the baby's father. Butterfly is about to kill him with her father's sword, but spurns him and he slinks away. A cannon is heard from the harbour. Butterfly mad with joy, gets her telescope and reads the name of Pinkerton's ship, the *Abraham Lincoln.*

Flowers are gathered and scattered everywhere. She is made beautiful, and her wedding *obi* donned. They make three little holes in the wall to watch for Pinkerton. The vigil is prolonged till Suzuki and the child fall asleep, but Butterfly stands like a statue. The slow passage of the night is indicated by the orchestral intermezzo, accompanied by the humming of an unseen chorus.

Dawn comes, sailors are heard in the distance, Suzuki wakens and begs Butterfly to rest. She takes the child up the stairs, crooning to it (*Dormi amor mio*). Sharpless arrives with Pinkerton. Pinkerton will not let Suzuki call Butterfly. She sees a woman in the garden. It is Pinkerton's American wife. Sharpless explains that she is willing to adopt the child and rear it.

Suzuki refuses to carry the proposal to Butterfly. Pinkerton looks about at the flowers, in remorse (*Oh! l'amara fragranza*). He cannot face Butterfly, but gives the Consul money for her and hurries away.

His wife, Kate, comes in and Butterfly returns, hearing voices. Kate explains the situation. Butterfly is majestic in her grief, and promises that Pinkerton shall have his child if he will come for it himself in half an hour. Sharpless and Mrs. Pinkerton go, and Butterfly, driving out the heartbroken Suzuki, prays to Buddha, takes her father's sword and reads the legend on the blade, "With honour die whoso cannot with honour live." She is about to kill herself when Suzuki thrusts the child into the room. She embraces the child frantically (*Tu, tu, piccolo Iddio*) and tells him that she is dying for his sake, that he may cross the ocean. She begs him to remember her, then seats him with an American flag and a doll, and bidding him play, goes behind the screen. The sword is heard to drop, and she comes from behind the screen with a white veil wrapped around her throat. She falls at the child's side, and as Pinkerton rushes in with the Consul, she points to the child and dies.

## PUCCINI, GIACOMO

### La Tosca

"A melodrama" in three acts. Libretto by L. Illica and G. Giacosa. (After the play by Sardou.)

Produced Costanzi Theatre, Rome, January 14, 1900.

#### CHARACTERS

FLORIA TOSCA,
  *A Celebrated Songstress* ........ sopr.
MARIO CAVARADOSSI,
  *A Painter* .................... ten.
BARON SCARPIA,
  *Chief of Police* ............... bar.
CESARE ANGELOTTI ........... bass.
A SACRISTAN ................... bar

SPOLETTA,
  *Police Agent* ................. ten.
SCIARRONE,
  *Gendarme* ................... bass.
A GAOLER .................... bass.
A SHEPHERD BOY ............ contr.
ROBERTI,
  *Executioner*

The action takes place at Rome, June, 1800, and concerns the activities of the Baron Scarpia, Chief of the Police in his efforts to recapture Angelotti, the Consul of the fallen Roman Republic. Just before the rise of the curtain Angelotti has escaped from the prison of San Angelo, and has made his way to the Church of Sant' Andrea alla Valle, where his sister has concealed in the Attavanti Chapel a woman's costume to aid his escape. It happens that a painter, Mario Cavaradossi, who has been painting frescoes in this chapel, has made a sketch of Angelotti's sister as she has knelt at prayer. This hasty portrait is the cause of a quarrel with Mario's sweetheart, the celebrated singer, Floria Tosca; and her jealousy is the weapon which Scarpia uses for the eventual destruction of everybody concerned.

Act I.— Without any overture, the curtain rises with the first music from the orchestra. Angelotti in convict garb steals into the empty church, finds a key at the foot of the Madonna's statue, and lets himself into the Attavanti Chapel, just as the Sacristan, who is cleaning Mario's paint brushes, comes in followed by the painter, who ascends the dais and uncovers the picture of Mary Magdalen, which is the portrait of Angelotti's sister. The Sacristan recognizes the likeness and Mario confesses that he has made the sketch without the model's knowledge. As he paints, however, he takes out a miniature of La Tosca and, comparing the two, avows his heart's fidelity to La Tosca (*Recondita armonia*). The Sacristan points out to him the basket of food, but Mario tells him to leave it and go.

Later Angelotti, thinking the church empty, comes from concealment and is discovered by Mario, to whom he tells his story. Mario gives him the basket of food and he hurries back into hiding as La Tosca enters, jealously insisting that she heard voices. Mario only partially convinces her, but she tells him to meet her at the stage door after the performance that they may retreat together to their villa in the country (*Oh al tuo fianco sentire*). She catches sight of the portrait, recognizes it, and her jealousy is again suppressed with difficulty. He swears he prefers her black eyes to the blue eyes in the portrait (*Quale occhio al mondo*), and she departs after a duet of love. Angelotti returns from the chapel with the woman's costume his sister has left for him, but Mario thinks it unnecessary for him to put it on and offers the protection of his own villa. A cannon shot is heard announcing the prisoner's escape, and the two men hurry away as the Sacristan and the choir-boys enter with the glorious news that Napoleon has been defeated. Their joy is silenced by the unexpected entrance of Scarpia, with his aide, Spoletta. Scarpia finds that the Attavanti Chapel has been opened with a new key, and inside he finds a fan with the family coat of arms. He recognizes also the portrait on the easel, and discovers that the basket of food brought for Mario has been emptied, although the Sacristan insists that Mario refused to eat it. Tosca returns, and Scarpia, who loves her, devises a scheme to play upon her jealousy for a double purpose: to make her betray Mario and to bring her into his own power. He shows her the fan, which he claims to have found upon the easel, and convinces her that the blue-eyed woman has been meeting Mario secretly. She swears revenge and hurries out, and Scarpia, giving instructions to Spoletta to follow her in a closed carriage, remains to exult over his triumph and then to kneel in prayer.

Act II. — Scarpia's apartments in the Farnese Palace. Scarpia is dining alone and rejoicing over the assured capture of Mario and Angelotti. He has sent word to Tosca, who is to sing for Queen Caroline in the Palace, that she must come to his apartments at once "for the sake of her Mario." His gendarme, Sciarrone, is sent to bring Spoletta, who comes to say that he has arrested Mario, and searched his villa, but has been unable to find Angelotti. Scarpia orders Mario brought into his presence, and stands listening to the music which is being sung for the Queen, and in which Tosca's voice is audible.

Mario is brought in with Roberti, the executioner, and a judge. Mario is indignant at his arrest and denies all knowledge of Angelotti. Tosca is brought in in great alarm and, as she embraces Mario, he warns her to say nothing. Scarpia orders him taken away, and murmurs to the executioner that he is to be tortured. Then he turns to Tosca with suave politeness and questions her about what she has learned at Mario's villa. She says that her jealousy about the fan was unfounded and that Mario was entirely alone when she arrived at his villa. Unable to move her otherwise, he tells her that Mario is being tortured with a steel band about his temples. He is heard groaning and she calls to him, but he warns her to keep silence. At last, however, Scarpia permits her to look into the torture chamber and she is overcome by what she sees. She confesses that Angelotti is concealed in an old well in the garden. Mario is brought in swooning, and Spoletta is ordered to go search the well in the garden. Mario, overhearing, accuses Tosca of treachery and repulses her. Sciarrone brings word that Napoleon has won the battle of Marengo and the royal troops have been defeated.

This brings a cry of joy from Mario. Scarpia orders him hanged. He is dragged away, and Tosca remains to plead for his life. Scarpia will save it if she will pay the price — herself. He pours out his love for her with ardour that she detests. She repulses him until she hears the drums of the death march, and is told that the gallows awaits her lover outside the window. Spoletta enters to say that Angelotti took poison when captured, and Scarpia orders Mario shot. Tosca consents with a silent nod to pay Scarpia's price, and he promises that there shall be a mock execution with blank cartridges. He instructs Spoletta that Mario's execution is to be conducted "like that of Palmieri." Spoletta, understanding his duplicity, hurries away. Tosca insists that Scarpia must write a safe conduct to take her and Mario out of the country. While Scarpia is writing it she picks up a sharp knife, and when Scarpia moves to take her in his arms, she stabs him to death. As soon as he is dead she forgives him, and finding the safe conduct clenched in his fingers, takes it from them, and puts out all the lights, except two candles, which she places on either side of him. She removes also a crucifix from the wall, and, placing it on his breast, slinks out of the room.

Act III. A platform of the castle with a trap-door and a flight of steps. It is almost daybreak and the voice of a shepherd leading his flock to the hills is heard dying in the distance. Mario is brought in under guard. The jailer records Mario's name and grants his request for the privilege of writing a letter of farewell. As he begins to write he muses upon Tosca coming into his garden under the starlight (*E lucevan le stelle*). He breaks down and weeps as Spoletta appears, followed by Tosca, who rushes to him and shows him the safe conduct. Perceiving the signature of Scarpia, he demands what price she paid. She says that he demanded "your blood or my love," and describes how she had killed him. He wonders at such a deed at such gentle hands (*O dolci mani*). She explains the plan of escape and informs him that he must simulate death after the volley. There is a love duet (*Amaro sol per te*).

The firing party enters. Mario is led to one side. He refuses to have his eyes bandaged. The soldiers fire. Mario falls. The soldiers are led away, leaving Tosca alone. She hurries to Mario bidding him to make haste. She finds that he is actually dead, Scarpia has duped her after all; she throws herself upon his body in agony of grief. Spoletta and others return, exclaiming that Scarpia has been assassinated by Tosca. As Spoletta rushes to seize her, she springs upon the parapet and leaps to her death.

## PUCCINI, GIACOMO

**La Fanciulla** (fän-chool'-lä). **Del West.** *I.* The Girl of the Golden West.

An opera in three acts. Book by C. Zangarini and G. Civinini (after the drama by David Belasco).

Produced, Metropolitan Opera House New York, December 10, 1910.

CHARACTERS AND THEIR CREATORS

| | |
|---|---|
| MINNIE | Emmy Destinn, sopr. |
| JACK RANCE, Sheriff | Pasquale Amato, bar. |
| DICK JOHNSON, Ramerrez | Enrico Caruso, ten, |
| NICK, Bartender | Albert Reiss, ten. |
| ASHBY, Agent of the Wells-Fargo Transport Co. | Adamo Didur, bass. |

| | | |
|---|---|---|
| SONORA | | Dinh Gilly, bar. |
| TRIN | | ten. |
| SID | | bar. |
| HANDSOME | Miners | bar. |
| HARRY | | ten. |
| JOE | | Glen Hall, ten. |
| HAPPY | | A. Pini-Corsi, bar. |
| LARKENS | | bass. |

BILLY JACKRABBIT,
*An Indian*. . . Georges Burgeois, bass.
WOWKLE,
*Billy's Squaw,*
Marie Mattfeld, mez-sopr.
JAKE WALLACE,
*Travelling camp-minstrel,*
A. de Segurola, bar.
JOSÉ CASTRO . . . . . . . . . . . . . . . . . . bass.
*A Greaser from Ramerrez' gang*
A POSTILION . . . . . . . . . . . . . . . . . . ten.
MEN OF THE CAMP

Place of action, California in the days of the gold fever, 1849–1850.

Act I.— Scene. Interior of the "Polka," a barroom and dance hall. On the wall a placard offering a reward of five thousand dollars for the stage-robber, Ramerrez. The room is full of miners gambling and drinking. From the distance comes the homesick voice of Jake Wallace, singing his song of "Way Back Yonder" (*Là lontano*). Larkens, another miner, breaks down with homesickness and a subscription is taken up for him. Sid is caught cheating at faro. Jack Rance, the Sheriff, saves him from being lynched, but pins a badge on him in token of dishonour and has him kicked out. Rance and others play poker as Ashby, the Wells-Fargo agent enters. Ashby tells them that he is hard on the track of Ramerrez and expects to catch him soon. Nick enters with whiskey and glasses, telling the boys that Minnie has sent it to them. They all join in drinking to Minnie. Rance impressively tells them that Minnie will be Mrs. Rance shortly. Sonora bursts out with rage that Minnie is only fooling Rance, whereupon ensues a fight, which is stopped by Minnie's entrance. She separates and subdues them all.

The boys gather around her, giving her presents. Sonora hands her a little bag of gold to clear up his debt to the bar, and Minnie signs for it and places it in the barrel. She then takes out her

Bible and holds her school for the boys, treating them all as little children. The pony-express boy enters with letters, and tells Nick that a greaser has been seen hanging around, and to be on his guard. Ashby asks him if he knows an adventuress by the name of Nina Micheltorena. Minnie interposes that she has heard of this creature, who tries to make love to all the boys. Ashby tells the Sheriff that he will catch Ramerrez that night, as Nina has betrayed his movements.

As the boys read scraps of their home letters aloud, Rance makes love to Minnie and asks her to marry him. Minnie asks him what will become of the wife he already has. He tells her that for her sake he will desert his wife. Minnie, drawing a pistol, warns Rance to cease his dishonourable proposals. Rance goes angrily to the faro table, and Minnie follows to say that she has only done what she was taught down at her home in Soledad (*Laggiù nel Soledad*).

Nick reënters with Ramerrez, alias Dick Johnson, whom Minnie greets and seems to remember. They recall to each other their meeting on the road to Monterey and vow that neither ever would or ever could forget. He asks her to dance with him; some of the others follow. Sounds of shots are heard and Ashby enters dragging José Castro. Castro, seeing Johnson's saddle, believes that his master is captured, but when he is questioned by Rance concerning Ramerrez he gives them a false scent; and they decide to follow it. The door opens and Castro meets the eyes of Johnson and secretly tells him that Johnson's following are near at hand and will give the signal when they are ready to come to him. Rance and the others gallop away on the false scent, taking Castro. Nick goes into the dance hall to put out the lights. Minnie and Johnson talk together. A whistle is heard and Johnson realizes it is the signal of his men. Minnie is frightened and tells Johnson that the gold, representing all the labour of the boys, is in the barrel under her care, but she will fight for it with her life. Johnson is so moved that he cannot take the gold as he intended. He tells her that he wants to come and see her in her cabin by the hillside, and that she has the face of an angel. He goes, and Minnie is left alone, repeating as the curtain falls, "The face of an angel."

Act II.— Scene. The interior of Minnie's cabin. The act opens with Wowkle, the Indian woman, singing to her baby (*Il mio bimbo*). Billy, the Indian, enters and they discuss marriage till Minnie appears and makes preparation to receive Johnson. Johnson enters and they have a love-scene. Minnie sings "You should see my little pony" (*Ho un piccolo polledro*). Wowkle enters with candles and Minnie sends her home, telling Johnson that he may stay for an hour longer. During their further love-scene, the snowstorm increases, till Minnie tells Johnson that it will be impossible for him to go at all. Minnie sends him to rest on her bed, while she wraps herself in a blanket to sleep by the fire.

Nick is heard knocking and calling at the door. Minnie forces Johnson to hide, as she fears the jealous Rance has come and brought the others. As she opens the door, Rance, Nick, Ashby, and Sonora enter. They tell Minnie that they feared for her safety, and that Johnson is in reality Ramerrez, who had come to the "Polka" to rob it. Rance convinces Minnie that Johnson is Ramerrez, and has been betrayed by his woman, Nina Micheltorena, showing her the picture of Johnson given them by Nina. Minnie, concealing her jealous agony, sends them away, and then orders Johnson to come out of hiding. She accuses him violently, and Johnson bursts out in self-defence, confessing "I am Ramerrez, vagabond by birth," (*Sono Ramerrez: nacqui vagabondo*). Minnie, moved at the story of

his life, says that she could forgive him anything but his having taken her first kiss: that she cannot forgive; she sends him out into the blizzard. He goes and immediately after, shots are heard. Minnie opens the door and Johnson staggers in wounded. He struggles to go away again, but Minnie helps him to hide in the loft, declaring that she loves him. Rance, knocking excitedly, Minnie runs to admit him, feigning surprise as Rance declares he has tracked Ramerrez to her cabin. Minnie denies having seen Johnson, and Rance makes violent love to her. As she repulses him, a drop of blood falling on his hand from above leads to the discovery of Johnson. Minnie helps Johnson down the ladder, and as he faints, she bargains to gamble with Rance — she is to have Johnson's life if she wins; she gives herself to Rance if she loses. During the game, Minnie contrives to exchange her cards for others hidden in her stocking. Rance, believing that she has fairly won, goes and Minnie is left sobbing on the inert body of her lover.

Act III.— Scene. Early dawn on the edge of the great California forest. Nick and Rance talk of Johnson, cursing his love for Minnie. Men come and go on horseback and there is pursuit. Sonora rides in with the news of Johnson's capture. Rance exulting, sings "Your turn to weep now Minnie" (*Minnie, ora piangi tu*)! The men dance and sing pointing to the tree where Billy is preparing the noose for hanging. Johnson appears in the midst of a crowd of horsemen. Ashby hands him over to Rance and demands that justice be done without delay. The men insult Johnson. He tells them that he does not fear to die, but only begs that Minnie shall not know. He sings "Let her believe me free and far away" (*Ch'ella mi creda libero e lontano*). As they take him to the tree where Billy holds the noose, Minnie rides in wildly crying, followed by Nick. She throws herself in front of Johnson, holding a pistol toward the men, who close in threateningly. She pleads with them: "I claim this man as mine" (*Ora quest' uomo è mio*). So appealing to them each in turn for some favour or service she has rendered in the past she melts their hearts. Sonora frees Johnson, and together Johnson and Minnie take up the trail toward the mountains singing "Good-bye, My California."

## DEBUSSY, CLAUDE ACHILLE

**Pelléas et Mélisande** (pĕl'-lā-ăs ă mā-lē-sänd
Lyric drama in five acts. From the play by Maurice Maeterlinck.
Produced Opéra Comique, Paris, April, 30, 1902.

### CHARACTERS

ARKEL, *King of Allemonde*......bass.
PRINCE GOLAUD (gō-lō),
    *His grandson*.................bar.
PELLÉAS,
    *Half-brother of Golaud*..........ten.
MÉLISANDE.....................sopr.
GENEVIEVE (zhŭn--vyĕv),
    *Pelléas' mother*............mez-sopr.
YNIOLD (ēn-yôl'),
    *Golaud's son.*
A PHYSICIAN

Act I.— Scene I. A forest in Allemonde. Mélisande is seated by a fountain weeping. Prince Golaud, who is hunting and has lost his way, asks her why she weeps. She shrinks from him. She has dropped into the fountain her crown, but will not let him regain it. He persuades her to let him lead her away, as the night is coming on. Scene II. A room in the castle. King Arkel is listening to a letter read to him by his queen. It is Golaud's letter to his half-brother, Pelléas, telling how he had found Mélisande and later married her, and now fears to bring her home lest Arkel refuse to receive her. Golaud has been a widower devoted to his little son, Yniold. Pelléas enters to say that he is called away by the illness of

his friend Marcellus. Arkel tells him he must await Golaud's arrival. Scene III. In front of the castle. Mélisande is complaining to Geneviève of the gloom of the surrounding forests. Pelléas appears and they watch a ship putting out with the coming storm. Geneviève leaves them and Pelléas helps Mélisande to descend. She hopes that he will not go away.

Act II.— Scene I. A fountain in the park. Pelléas and Mélisande enter, and Mélisande tries to reach down into the dark depths. She plays with the ring Golaud gave her. It falls and is lost. She is afraid and wonders what to tell Golaud. Pelléas says "The truth, the truth, the truth!" Scene II. An apartment. Golaud is ill; his horse has thrown him. Mélisande stands by his bed, she begins to weep. She is not happy at the castle. She wants Golaud to take her away. He questions her closely of Pelléas. He notes that his ring is gone. She is confused and tells him she lost it in the sea while gathering shells for Yniold. He bids her go hunt for it. She is afraid of the dark. He tells her to take Pelléas with her; she goes weeping. Scene III. Before a grotto. Pelléas would lead Mélisande within so that she may describe it as the place where she lost the ring. The moon reveals three poor old men asleep. She is afraid and will not enter.

Act III.— Scene I. A tower. Mélisande at a window sings as she combs her long hair (*Mes longs cheveux descendent*). Pelléas appears and praises her hair. He tells her he must leave on the morrow, and would kiss her hand. As she bends over, her hair falls about him; he embraces and kisses it. It "inundates" him, it "loves" him. To hold her prisoner, he ties it to a willow. Two doves are frightened by her outcry and fly off. Golaud appears and calls them mere children. He leads Pelléas away. Scene II. A vault under the castle. Golaud leads Pelléas in, speaking of the odour of death and the deep abyss. Pelléas feels suffocated and they go. Scene III. A terrace. Pelléas comes gasping from the vaults. Golaud warns him that there must be no more of these games of children. Scene IV. In front of the castle under Mélisande's window. Golaud takes his little son Yniold on his knees, questions him of his stepmother, Mélisande. The child says that Pelléas is always with her. Golaud's grasp makes the child cry. Golaud promises him toys. Yniold says that Pelléas and Mélisande do not send him away. They are afraid not to have him there. They are always afraid. Did they ever kiss? Once when it was raining. Now a light appears in the window above. Golaud lifts the child so that he can see into Mélisande's room. He sees Pelléas there, but the two are apart, just gazing at one another.

Act IV.— Scene I. A corridor. Pelléas meets Mélisande. He has just come from talking with Arkel, who has advised him to set out on his voyage. He has made up his mind to go. Arkel enters and speaks tenderly to the sorrowful Mélisande. Golaud appears. His forehead is bleeding. He says he tore it on a thorn. He repulses Mélisande and demands his sword. He seizes Mélisande by the hair and drags her about; then strides away. Mélisande sighs "He loves me no more. I am not happy." Scene II. A dark terrace. Yniold is trying to lift a rock behind which his ball has rolled; he pauses to watch a flock of sheep driven by in a panic. Scene III. A fountain. Pelléas broods over the snares of destiny. Mélisande comes. She is fearsome, but he suddenly seizes her in his arms and she confesses her love. In the midst of their mutual rapture they hear the noise of the castle gates closing. They hear some one approaching. They kiss as Golaud rushes upon them with drawn sword. Pelléas falls and Mélisande flees in wild terror with Golaud in pursuit.

Act V.— Scene I. An apartment. Mélisande lies in a bed. A physician tells Golaud and Arkel that she should not die from so little a wound. Golaud is bitterly remorseful, "They were embracing like little children — and I did it in spite of myself. I did it in spite of myself." Mélisande wakens. Arkel tells her she has been a little delirious for days, and she has borne a child. She asks Golaud to come close. He asks the others to withdraw and begs her forgiveness. As she is about to die, he implores her to tell him truthfully if she loved Pelléas. She says that she loved him, but there was no guilt in them. Golaud cannot believe her. The servants gather unbidden with an ominous prescience. Golaud begs again to question her; but Arkel tells him not to disturb her, "The human soul is very silent. The human soul loves to steal away alone." He leads the sobbing Golaud from the room. "It was a little being, peaceful, so timid, so taciturn. It was a poor little mysterious thing, like everybody else. She lies there as if she were the elder sister of her child. It must live in her place. It is the little one's turn now."

*WOLF-FERRARI, ERMANNO*

**I Giojelli Del'la Madon'na** (ē jō-yĕl'-lē) *I*. The Jewels of the Madonna.

Three-act opera. Book by the composer. Lyrics by C. Zangarini and E. Golisciani.

Produced Berlin, December 23, 1911.

### CHARACTERS

GENNARO (gĕn-nä'-rō),
  *A blacksmith* ................ten.
CARMELA (kär-mä'-lä),
  *His mother* ............. mez-sopr.
MALIELLA (mäl-yĕl'-lä),
  *Her foster-child* .............. sopr.
RAFAELE (rä-fä-ā'-lĕ),
  *Head of the Camorra* ........... bar.
BIASO (bĕ-ä'-sō)
  *A scribe* ................. buf-ten.

CICCILLO⁻ (chē-chǐl'-lō) ⎰ Cam-　　　ten.
ROC'CO　　　　　　　 ⎱ orrists　bass.
STELLA　　　　　　　⎱　　　　 sopr.
CONCETTA　　　　　 ⎰ Friends　 sopr.
(kôn-chĕt'-tä)　　 ⎰ of the
　　　　　　　　　　⎱ Camor-
SERENA　　　　　　⎰ rists　　contr.
(sā-rā'-nä)
GRAZIA (gräts'-yä)
　Known as "la biondina"
TOTON'NO,
　A young man of the peasant class..ten.

Place of action: Naples. Time:
The present day.

Act I.— Scene. A small open square
by the sea; Carmela's house, Gennaro's
workshop, Biaso's hut and tavern. It
is the afternoon of the festival of the
Madonna, and the square is crowded
with merrymakers of all sorts. The
Children of St. John and others pass by
in procession. When the crowd is
somewhat dispersed, Gennaro works at
his anvil on a wrought-iron candela-
brum. Totonno quizzes him for being
so serious. When he is gone, Gennaro
kneels before the anvil as at an altar and
pledges the gift to the Madonna (Madonna, con sospiri). Maliella rushes
out of the house in disarray, rebuked by her foster-mother, Carmela.
Gennaro, her foster-brother, protests
against her recklessness, and she accuses
him of jealousy. Biaso, the scribe,
gives her a paper cap and she sings the
"Canzone di Cannetella," while a chorus
of Camorrists come over the bay.
Then Maliella dashes out followed by a
crowd of young men; and Gennaro pours
out to his mother, Carmela, his jealous
anguish. The mother tells how, when
Gennaro was a sick baby about to die,
she vowed to adopt an infant girl begot-
ten in sin if the Madonna would spare
Gennaro's life (T'eri un giorno ammalato
bambino). Maliella has turned out
badly, but Carmela hopes that marriage with an honest man will reform
her. Gennaro goes out with his candel-

abrum, as the Camorrists chase Biaso
and threaten him because he has protested against their pursuit of Maliella.
Among them is Rafaele, their chief.
He seizes the girl in his arms with a
song of love (Si, perchè t' amo, bella
assassina). She tries to escape, but
they surround her and sing a mock
serenade (Olà Plam, Plam!) She defends herself with a sharp hatpin, and
stabs Rafaele in the hand. He kisses
the wound made by her "kiss of steel"
(Bacio di lama), and thrusts a flower in
her bosom. She throws the flower down.
　The crowd now appears to watch the
procession of children in white, preceding the image of the Madonna. During the procession Rafaele pours out his
love and asks her if she wishes to be
adored kneeling (Adorarti in ginocchio)
and if she wishes him to steal the Jewels
of the Madonna for her. Gennaro appears and warns her against Rafaele.
When Maliella defends him, Gennaro
orders her into the house, and is about
to attack Rafaele; but the procession
reappears, and all must kneel. Rafaele
throws a flower to Maliella. She picks
it up, puts it in her lips and hurries into
the house.
　Act II.— The garden of Carmela's
house in the evening a few hours later.
Maliella stands near the railing looking
longingly toward the sea. She is still
holding the flower. Carmela bids them
good-night and goes in. Maliella turns
on Gennaro saying that she is sick of
this gloom and is going away. She
goes inside and can be seen at her window packing her things, as she sings a
popular love song (E ndringhete,
ndranghete). She comes out with her
bundle and Gennaro checks her, lovingly
embraces her and pours out his devotion
(Si, perchè t'amo, t'adoro). She is
astounded, but says she could love only
a man of reckless courage like the one
who had offered to steal for her the
Jewels of the Madonna. Gennaro is
horrified, but when she starts to go,
prevents her, and she storms back to her

room in a rage, leaving him alone with a sacrilegious temptation. At last, he goes to a tool chest and taking out skeleton keys and files, steals away like a thief.

A group of serenading Camorrists, among them Rafaele, appear and call upon Maliella to open her window (*Aprila, o bella, La finestrella*). Maliella appears, and Rafaele makes love to her, and promises to make her queen of his band. At last she embraces him through the bars of the gate just as a warning is given that Gennaro is returning. Rafaele disappears as Gennaro comes back in a mood of horror. He carries a bundle, which he opens at Maliella's feet. It contains the Jewels of the Madonna. Maliella is terrified, but Gennaro, with mystical passion declares "The Madonna knows that I am guiltless" (*No, la Madonna sa che non l'offesi*). Irresistibly fascinated, Maliella takes up the necklace and notes that it smells of incense. She puts on the diadem and the bracelets, wishing that Rafaele might see her so. Gennaro embraces her with wild fervour and she, almost in a trance of horror, thinking him to be Rafaele yields herself to him.

Act III.— Scene. The headquarters of the Camorra. Among the crude and vulgar ornaments is a fresco of the Madonna, and a little altar behind a curtain. The Camorrists are drinking stupidly, and three women join in their revel. When Rafaele appears, the girls twit him with his infatuation for Maliella, but he sings in her praise. "You don't know Maliella's charm" (*Non sapete — di Maliella*). A curtain is drawn in front of the fresco of the Madonna, and a wild orgy begins. In the midst of it Maliella pounds on the door and rushes in, appealing for help against Gennaro and revenge. She faints in Rafaele's arms, and he orders the Camorrists to bring him Gennaro alive or dead. "Were you his?" Rafaele demands. She covers her face and sobs. The others ridicule him. He

turns against Maliella, crying, "You belong to Gennaro, go to him," and hurls her to the ground. As she falls, her shawl falls open and exposes the jewels. The other women surround Maliella in amazement, not knowing whence the jewels had come. In the distance Gennaro is heard bewailing his sin. Then the noise of the attack upon him is heard and he bursts into the room pursued by the Camorrists. He bares his breast, calling on them to kill him. Rafaele rushes upon him in a rage, but is dragged away. Gennaro, seeing Maliella, moves toward her with a despairing cry, but she looks on him with loathing, tearing off the jewels and flinging them at his feet, crying to all the crowd that Gennaro had stolen them from the Madonna. The men recoil, and the women drop to their knees mumbling the Litany. Rafaele cries out that Maliella's soul is damned, and she dashes out to drown herself. Rafaele protects Gennaro from the attacks of the Camorrists, saying that he shall be left to die there like a dog. In the distance the church bells ring the alarm, showing that the theft is discovered. The women flee in terror; the men, bowing before the Madonna's fresco, retreat backward, leaving Gennaro alone. He gathers up the jewels, kisses them with reverence and staggers to the altar, where he lays them before the portrait of the Madonna begging her pity. A ray of light from the rising sun shines through the window and falls on the jewels. Gennaro takes it for a sign of forgiveness and in his delirium seems to hear the angels of paradise. Finding a knife on the ground, he calls aloud for his mother not to weep for him, and in a mystical ardour, slowly presses the knife into his breast. As he falls, he sees Maliella's scarlet wrap on the ground. He kisses it, and pillows his dying head on it as the birds break out into song. The angry mob appears at the door, but halts on the threshold seeing Gennaro dead.

## WOLF-FERRARI, ERMANNO

**Le Donne Curiose** (lā dôn'-nā koo-rĭ-ō'-sā). *I.* Inquisitive Women. A musical comedy in three acts. Book by Luigi Sugana (based upon Carlo Goldoni's comedy).

First produced in Munich, 1903, as Die Neugierigen Frauen (dē noi-gē'-rĭ-gĕn frow'-ĕn).

### CHARACTERS

OTTAVIO (ôt-täv'-yō) . . . . . . . . . . . . bass.
BEATRICE (bā-ä-trē'-chĕ) . . . . mez-sopr.
ROSAURA (rō-zä-oo'-rä) . . . . . . . . . . sopr.
FLORIN'DO . . . . . . . . . . . . . . . . . . . . . ten.
PANTALONE (pän-tä-lō'-nĕ) . . . . buf-bar.
LELIO (lā'-lĭ-ō) . . . . . . . . . . . . . . . . . bar.
LEAN'DRO . . . . . . . . . . . . . . . . . . . . . ten.
COLOMBI'NA . . . . . . . . . . . . . . . . . . sopr.
ELEONO'RA . . . . . . . . . . . . . . . . . . . sopr.
ARLECCHINO (är-lĕk-kē'-nō) . . buf-bass.
ASDRUBALE (äz-droo-bä'-lĕ) . . . . . . ten.
ALMO'RO . . . . . . . . . . . . . . . . . . . . . ten.
ALVISE (äl-vē'-zĕ) . . . . . . . . . . . . . . ten.
LUNAR'DO . . . . . . . . . . . . . . . . . . . . bass.
MO'MOLO . . . . . . . . . . . . . . . . . . . . . bass.
MENEGO (mĕ-nā'-gō) . . . . . . . . . . . bass.

The action concerns a men's club in Venice, whose mottoes are "No Women Admitted" and "Friendship" (*L'amicizia!*) and the efforts of the members to discover what goes on in the club.

Act I.— Scene I. A room in the club-house. The members are variously engaged at chess and arguments. Florindo is sighing like a furnace for his sweetheart, Rosaura, the daughter of Ottavio. The members describe the efforts of their wives and daughters to find out the secrets of the organization, but Florindo sings of his sweetheart (*Ma, allor ch'io vedo tremulo*). Leandro, who is a bachelor, suggests a dinner for the evening, and they all agree to allow old Pantalone to pay for it. He comes in and falls into the trap. His servant, Arlecchino appears and is told to order a fine supper for that evening at ten

o'clock. Pantalone reminds him that the club's secrets must be kept from the women.

Scene II. A room in the home of Ottavio, who is late for dinner, detained, of course, at his horrid club. His wife, Beatrice, and his daughter, Rosaura, are complaining. Beatrice is sure they gamble there. Rosaura's theory is that they meet women there. Eleonora a neighbour, appears, and she is positive that the men are alchemists trying to discover the philosopher's stone. She sings of her tragic experience with the dressmaker (*A trovare la mia sarta*). Colombina, a maid, runs in breathlessly and announces that she has discovered that the club is engaged in digging for buried treasure (*Ne ha di belle*). And now Arlecchino, who is secretly courting Colombina, comes in. The women pounce on him with their theories as to the object of the club and he agrees to all of them. They turn upon him in a rage and he runs out, leaving the women as mystified as ever, but each still positive of her own theory. Ottavio comes home and announces that Florindo will dine with him. He is figuring out some accounts in his notebook, and his wife tries to wheedle from him the secrets of the club. He leaves in a huff and she follows him. Florindo appears, but Rosaura will not give him her heart until he tells her the secret of the club. He pleads for mercy (*Io sento, ahimè*). Colombina returning, suggests to Rosaura that she should try the effect of swooning. She pretends to faint. Florindo is frantic and Colombina advises him that the only way to regain Rosaura's affections is to tell her the secrets of the club. She manages to wheedle from him the rule of the club that no women shall be admitted, the motto "Friendship," the fact that there is to be a supper at ten o'clock, and that every member has his own key. Colombina then gets rid of him and speedily resuscitates Rosaura.

Act II.— Scene I. A room in the house of Lelio. His wife is going through the pockets of his clothes (*Che bestion di marito*). She finds two new keys with a letter from Pantalone saying that the locks have just been changed. She cries "Victory! Victory!" and restores the letter, but not the keys. Lelio comes in and she asks him if he is going back to the alchemist's furnace. He is furious at her quizzing, and they storm out at opposite doors.

Scene II. A room in Ottavio's house. Colombina announces all that she has learned. Only one thing is lacking — the key to get in with. Ottavio and Florindo appear and Beatrice tries to get her husband to change his coat so that she may search the pockets of it, and Colombina, as if by accident, spills coffee on Ottavio's coat. And now Ottavio takes it off to have the spots removed. Ottavio begins to sneeze while waiting for another coat. Colombina brings back the things she has found in the pockets, but secretly informs Beatrice that she has substituted the cellar keys for the club keys, and Ottavio goes with Florindo leaving the women rejoicing in their triumph. Beatrice seizes the keys and tells Rosaura that she is too young to go to a men's club. Rosaura, left alone, muses over Florindo (*Ah, tutto per te, mio bene*). He steals back. but she refuses to relent unless he gives her the keys. He pours out his despair (*Voi lacerate il mio povero cuore*), but finally yields to her determination, and they are reconciled in a duet (*Il cor nel contento*).

Act III.— Scene I. A street in Venice before the clubhouse. At the back is a canal. Pantalone comes out of the clubhouse looking for Arlecchino, who appears with bottles, but has forgotten the candles. Arlecchino goes inside to unload before he returns for them, and Pantalone follows him in. A gondola draws up to the landing and Eleanora steps from it as Arlecchino comes from the clubhouse. Eleonora in her terror drops her keys and runs. Arlecchino pockets them and goes on his way, as Colombina, disguised as a man, enters with Beatrice from a side street. Beatrice hides as Pantalone comes out, and seeing Colombina gives the password, "Friendship." He soon discovers that Colombina is only a disguised woman, and snatches the keys from her. She runs off, leaving Pantalone to wonder who is the traitor who has given up the club keys into women's keeping. Pantalone goes back into the club. Lelio and Ottavio come up. Lelio is puzzled at not finding his keys in his pocket. Florindo appears. Ottavio twits him about his love for the capricious Rosaura (*Bravo mio genero*). Ottavio, about to open the club door, finds that he has the cellar keys instead. He turns to Florindo for his. Florindo in some confusion says that he left them at home. The three locked out members knock, and Pantalone comes to the door in a bad temper and shows the keys that have been found. Lelio and Ottavio follow him into the club, but Florindo remains, seeing a servant with a lantern preceding a woman. He conceals himself and Rosaura, masked, follows her servant in. The servant is about to put the key in the door when Florindo snatches it from him. Rosaura drops her mask and the servant runs away. Florindo reproaches Rosaura for trying to betray him, and entering the Club, slams the door behind him. Arlecchino, who has seen this quarrel, catches Rosaura as she faints. While he is wondering what to do with his burden, Beatrice and Eleonora appear. Beatrice, recognizing her daughter, faints in Arlecchino's other arm. Colombina runs and prepares to faint also, but Arlecchino reminds her that he has not arms enough for three. The women recover and begin to cry, reviling the door that will not open. They now turn upon Arlecchino. Colombina tries to bribe him with caresses. Beatrice offers him money; Rosaura offers him earrings; Colombina offers him a dinner and kisses. But he refuses them all. Then they turn upon him with their finger-nails, and he surrenders the keys. They open the club door and enter while Arlecchino picking up the lantern looks up and down the street, ironically calling out, "Are there any others who want to get in?"

Scene II. A room in the clubhouse, with an opaque door leading to the dining room. The members of the club are saluting Pantalone, who warns them not to give to a woman the keys to a door or to their hearts. Arlecchino announces supper and the members enter the banquet room. When the door is closed the four women steal from their hiding places, somewhat surprised to find that the mysterious activity of the club consists of a simple stag supper. The men are heard laughing and the women, taking turns at the keyhole, describe what is going on. They grow hungry at the sight of the banquet, and when Arlecchino comes in at a side door with a dish of tarts, they rob him of them. They begin now to struggle so frantically for the privilege of peeping through the keyhole, that they push the door open. The club members arise in amazement from the table, and Pantalone exclaims that he has heard of showers of frogs and showers of larks, but never before showers of women (*Piova de sorzi*). The women apologize for their suspicions and are forgiven. One of the members begins to play the spinet and Pantalone chucks Colombina under the chin. Arlecchino protests that her hand belongs to him, and she gives it to him — over the ear. A minuet is begun, and it gradually develops into a livelier and livelier dance, during which Pantalone gives Arlecchino a clip over the head and sends him face downward into a large dish of whipped cream. The dance breaks up with a general cry of the club's motto, "Friendship" (*Amicizia*).

## MASSENET, JULES

### Manon

An opera in five acts. Book by H. Meilhac and Ph. Gille, (after the romance by the Abbé Prévost).

Produced Opéra Comique, Paris, January 19, 1884.

#### CHARACTERS

THE CHEVALIER DES GRIEUX (shŭ-văl-yā′ dā grē-ŭ′)..............ten.
THE COUNT DES GRIEUX,
  *His father,*
LESCAUT (lĕs-kō),
  *Of the Royal Guards, cousin of*
      Manon............ ....bar.
GUILLOT MORFONTAIN (môr-fôṅ-tăṅ),
  *Minister of finance, an old beau,*
DE BRÉTIGNY (dŭ brā-tēn-yē′),
  *A nobleman*
AN INNKEEPER
MANON (mă-nôṅ)..............sopr.
POUSETTE, (poo-sĕt), )
JAVOTTE (zhă-vôt), }*Actresses*
ROSETTE. )

Place of action, Amiens in the year 1721.

Act I.—Scene. Courtyard of an Inn. Morfontain, the old Minister of Finance, and Brétigny with three actresses are demanding food and drink. The host appears and they order dinner. The landlord leads them to a pavilion. A bell rings and the townsfolk gather to see the coach arrive. Among them is Lescaut, who has come to meet his cousin, Manon. The coach appears and the passengers descend and wrangle with the porters. Manon is among them and greets her cousin with a kiss. She describes her impressions of the voyage and tells how one moment she wept and another she laughed (*Je suis encore tout étourdie*). Her cousin goes in search of her luggage, and Morfontain, seeing Manon, starts an immediate flirtation. She is amused rather than offended. His companions join in the merriment. As Morfontain in a low voice states that his carriage is at her service, Lescaut returns. He advises her to be prudent and good (*Ne bronchez pas, soyez gentille*) and returns to his brother officers. Manon resolves to go to the convent and have done with her dreams (*Voyons, Manon, plus de chimères*). Suddenly she sees in the pavilion Morfontain and the actresses, and she envies their jewels and their splendours, their life of pleasure. The young Chevalier Des Grieux appears on his way to meet his father. Seeing Manon, he is greatly struck with her and makes her acquaintance with little difficulty. She explains that she is only a simple maid, not wicked, but longing for happiness and now on her way to a convent. He cannot endure the thought of her being so entombed, and offers her his protection. She accepts and they decide that they will live in Paris together (*Nous vivrons à Paris tous les deux*). At her suggestion they will elope together in the carriage that Morfontain has placed at her disposal. They hurry away, leaving Morfontain and Lescaut to amazement and wrath.

Act II.— Scene. An apartment in Paris. Des Grieux is writing at his desk. He reads his letter to her. It is a description of her charms written to his father. He goes to mail the letter, but notices some flowers, and she explains quickly that they were thrown in at her window. He promises not to be jealous. The maid enters to announce that two officers are present. One of them is Lescaut and the other De Brétigny. They come in and Lescaut denounces Des Grieux for dishonouring his family. He demands that Des Grieux marry Manon, and is shown the letter just written. As the men read it together at the window, De Brétigny warns Manon that her lover is to be kidnapped that evening by his father's order, and advises her to let him be taken, lest poverty engulf them. Once she is free, he will make her the

Queen of Beauty. The two visitors depart and Manon is troubled, though Des Grieux is full of rapture and love. He goes to post the letter and she makes up her mind that for his sake she must sacrifice him, especially as she is not worthy of him. She hears a voice which calls her (*J' entends cette voix qui m' entraine*). He returns and tells her of a dream he had, seeing a little cottage (*En fermant les yeux je vois là-bas*). A loud knock is heard at the door and he is about to answer it, but she is overcome with fear for him and tries to restrain him. He releases himself and going to the door is gagged and dragged away. She runs to the window crying, "Oh, my poor Chevalier!"

Act III.— Scene. The promenade of the Cours la Reine. It is a holiday and there are booths and a dancing pavilion, where the three actresses beckon to youths to join them. Lescaut appears singing of his Rosalinda. Morfontain sees the actresses and greets them, complaining that not one of the three is faithful to him. De Brétigny ironically begs him not to rob him of Manon. Morfontain says that he has heard that De Brétigny refused Manon a favour, and steals away. Later Manon appears on the arm of De Brétigny and receives much homage. She is delighting in her conquests, and advises everybody to heed the call of love and youth. As she moves on, the Count Des Grieux, father of the Chevalier appears and tells De Brétigny that his son has taken holy orders and become an Abbé. Manon seizes an opportunity to speak to the Count and is told that her lover has learned his lesson and forgotten her. She determines to see him and orders her chair to take her to the Seminary of Saint Sulpice.

Scene II. The parlour of the Seminary. The Count congratulates his son on the eloquence of his sermons, but begs him not to take final orders; rather to find some worthy maiden and marry her, especially as the next day he will receive a fortune from his mother. Des Grieux, left alone, is tormented by the image of Manon (*Ah, fuyez, douce image*). Soon she appears and hearing the choir within, says a prayer. On seeing Des Grieux, she appeals for his forgiveness. He warns her that she cannot speak of love in such a place, but she clings to him, and at length he throws his arms about her, defying heaven's vengeance.

Act IV.— Scene. A fashionable gambling house. Lescaut is playing and winning, but the sharpers are watching him hopefully. The three actresses appear, and he tells them that his sweetheart is the queen of spades (*C'est ici que celle que j'aime*). Des Grieux and Manon appear, and Des Grieux tells her that he both hates and loves her. She has brought him here to recoup their squandered fortunes. Lescaut encourages him to play. Morfontain challenges Des Grieux to a game, and as they gamble Manon revels in the excitement, which is life to her (*A nous les amours et les roses*). Morfontain accuses Des Grieux of cheating, and the crowd turns against him just as the place is raided by the police. Morfontain denounces Des Grieux and Manon as accomplices. The Count enters and orders his son and Manon arrested. He tells his son that he shall be released at once, but that Manon must "go where many of her sort have gone."

Act V.— Scene. The road to Havre. Des Grieux is seated by the roadside to watch Manon pass by under guard; for she is to be transported to a penal settlement. Lescaut appears and Des Grieux discusses with him their plan to release Manon. The soldiers are heard singing (*Capitaine, ô gué, es-tu fatigué?*) Des Grieux is desperate enough to attack the guard single handed, but Lescaut drags him behind some bushes, promising him that he shall see Manon. The soldiers appear and Lescaut leads

one of the sergeants aside. The soldiers move on, dragging with them the women who are prisoners. Later Manon comes down the path greatly exhausted. She is remorseful for her fickleness and feels at last a pure flame in her heart (*Ah! je sens une pure flamme*). The evening stars appear To her coquettish heart they are jewels. "You know I was always fond of jewels." She grows weaker and weaker, and dies of exhaustion murmuring "This is the story of Manon Lescaut."

## MASSENET, JULES

**Le Jongleur De Nôtre Dame** (lŭ zhôn-glĕr' dŭ nōt-rŭ däm) *F.* The Juggler of Nôtre Dame.

A "miracle" in three acts. Book by Maurice Lena (based on an old miracle play).

Produced, Monte Carlo, February 18, 1902.

### CHARACTERS

JEAN (zhän),
   *The juggler*............ten. or sopr.
BONIFACE (bôn-ē-fäs),
   *Cook of the abbey*..............bar.
THE PRIOR....................bass.
THE MUSICIAN MONK
THE SCULPTOR MONK
THE POET MONK
THE PAINTER MONK

The part of the Juggler, though originally sung by a tenor, was taken by Miss Mary Garden on its production at the Manhattan Opera House in New York.

Place: Paris. Time of action: Fourteenth Century.

Act I.— Scene. The Place Cluny, in front of the abbey with a statue of the Madonna over the door. It is market day and the Square is filled with merchants, and with merry-makers who dance in honour of the Madonna and the "Dauphin, Jesus." The sound of a vielle is heard approaching. It is recognized as the music of a Juggler Joyous anticipations are quenched by the appearance of the meagre and poverty-stricken Jean. He is hailed as "His Majesty, King Famine." He plays for them to dance, holding out his cup with little success. They ridicule him, and when he suggests the various songs that he knows, they refuse to hear any of them. They demand a drinking song, and he consents to sing "The Hallelujah of Wine," first praying the Virgin to pardon his sacrilege, for though his heart is Christian, his stomach is pagan. As he is singing reluctantly, the Prior rushes out of the abbey, and all flee except the Juggler, who drops to his knees craving pardon. This the Prior refuses, declaring that the gate of hell is yawning for him. Jean weeps in terror, and the Prior, relenting, tells him he can save himself, but only by taking holy orders. Jean recoils at the thought of renouncing Liberty, his heart's mistress (*C'est elle que mon coeur pour maitresse a choisie*). The Prior warns him that Liberty will let him starve, while the convent will feed both soul and body. He points to Boniface, the cook, who arrives on a donkey laden with flowers, food and wine. The cook sings of the three: the flowers for the Virgin, the food and the wine for her servants (*Pour la Vierge d'abord*). The breakfast bell rings in the abbey, and the monks are heard reciting the Benedicite in the refectory. The Prior invites Jean to the feast, and he enters taking with him the Juggler's outfit.

Act II.— Scene. Study room and garden of the abbey. Among the monks is a Sculptor who has finished a statue of the Virgin, which the Painter is colouring. A Musician monk is rehearsing the others in a hymn to the Virgin, which he has composed for the occasion; Assumption morning (*Ave cœleste lilium*). Jean is bemoaning the fact that he cannot join their praises because he does not know Latin, but only profane songs in the vulgar tongue. The monks joke with Jean because he is taking on flesh, but he regrets that he is only an ignorant monk who can simply eat and drink and do nothing in honour of the Virgin (*Depuis qu'en ce couvent prospère*). He asks to be turned out into the world again, but the Sculptor advises him to study sculpture, pointing with pride to his statue (*Vois: des flancs du marbre se lève*). The Poet monk cries "Not so; give poetry the place of honour (*Non pas la place d' honneur*). The Musician upholds music as the direct echo of the great mystery (*Pour moi, je me figure*). The Painter joins the quarrel until the Prior silences them all and compels them to be reconciled. They carry the statue out into the Chapel, leaving Jean alone with Boniface the cook. Boniface declares that the art of the cook is the true glory (*S'il faut s'enfler de gloire*). He tries to console Jean with the statement that the Virgin understands French as well as Latin, and tells the legend of the rose and the sage-plant (*Marie avec l'Enfant Jesus*). As for himself, he serves the Virgin by looking to his oven. Jean is uplifted with a sudden ray of light (*Quel trait de soudaine lumière*), and hopes that perhaps the Virgin will accept a Juggler's offering.

Act III.— Scene. The chapel of the Abbey. In the distance the monks are singing the new hymn to the Virgin. The painter is alone before the statue he has coloured, taking a last look at it. He sees Jean dressed as a monk, but carrying his vielle and his kit. Jean approaches and appeals to the Mother of Jesus (*Mère adorable de Jesus*), to accept his homage. Throwing off his monk's robe, he appears in the Juggler's costume, spreads his carpet and begins to play on his vielle while the Painter hurries out to warn the Prior. Jean, declaring himself to be the King of Jugglers from force of habit, begins to pass his cup about a circle of imaginary bystanders, but stops in confusion. He begins to sing a song of war, but fears it will frighten the Virgin. He tries two other songs, but his memory fails him, and sings the eternal pastoral of Robin and Marion (*A l'oré du joli bocage*). As he sings, the Prior, the Painter and the cook appear. The cook restrains the Prior from interfering, and Jean, not knowing he is observed, jovially offers to evoke flying devils for Her. He apologizes to the statue and permits himself the honour of dancing before her. The cook reminds the indignant Prior that David danced before the Ark, and Jean dances a bourrée faster and faster until he falls exhausted, kneeling in adoration. The other monks have gathered and are furious at the blasphemy. They are about to attack Jean when the cook orders them back, "The Virgin protects him." A strange light begins to shine on the statue, and on the mouth a smile is about to awake. The voices of angels are heard singing "Hosannah! Glory to Jean." The Prior and the monks approach the Juggler reverently. Startled from his prayer, Jean kneels for forgiveness from the Prior. But the Prior says that it is Jean who should forgive them, for he is a great saint. Thinking they are mocking him, he is horrified, but they point to the intense radiance now illuminating the altar and the aureole, which descending from the hands of the Virgin, gleams on the head of the Juggler. Jean swoons with ecstasy. When the monks have chanted the Kyrie Eleison, he says feebly, "At last I understand Latin." He swoons again while two unseen angels sing of Heaven's Gate opening before him. There is a snow of lilies and bluebells about him and a cloud of incense. The Virgin mounts to the skies and Jean sees her surrounded by the angels in Heaven. In his death ecstasy, he sees Paradise welcoming him (*Spectacle radieux*) and the Virgin beckoning him. He dies in his rapture.

**Ariane et Barbe-Bleue** (är-yän′ ā-bär-bŭ-blĕ′). Ariane and Blue Beard.

A lyric story in three acts. Book by Maurice Maeterlinck.

Produced, Opéra Comique, Paris, 1907.

### CHARACTERS

ARIANE...................................sopr.
THE NURSE
SÉLYSETTE (sā-lē-zĕt)
YGIANE (ē-zhän)
MÉLISSANDE (mā-lĭs-sänd)
BELLANGÈRE (bĕl-län-zhär)
ALLADINE (äl-lä-dēn)
BLUE BEARD

Act 1.— Scene. A hall in Blue Beard's castle, showing six doors with silver locks. Outside the window the angry peasants are threatening to kill Blue Beard for bringing home another wife. The windows close magically as Ariane enters with the nurse. The nurse is terrified because the peasants insist that Blue Beard killed his first five wives. Ariane feels sure that they are not dead, but alive, and thinks Blue Beard loves her so much that she will gain his secret. She shows the keys her husband has given her; six silver keys, which she is permitted to use, and one gold key, which is forbidden to her. Woman-like, she throws away the silver keys and keeps the gold one. The nurse, picking up the keys, opens the doors in succession. Out of them tumble great heaps of precious stones; first, amethysts, second, sapphires third, pearls, fourth, emeralds, fifth, blood-red rubies, and sixth, a cataract of diamonds. These last fascinate Ariane and she bedecks herself with them. (*O mes clairs diamants!*) Inside this cell she finds a door with a golden lock and, in spite of the nurse's terror, opens it. From the depths a smothered chant arises from the five imprisoned wives, the five daughters of Orlamonde (*Les cinq filles d'Orlamonde*). Blue Beard enters in a rage. The imprisoned wives have all disobeyed him just as Ariane has done: some of them after a few days; the last of them after a year. "It was the last one alone that deserved to be punished," said Ariane. Blue Beard seizes her, but she and the nurse scream so loudly that the peasants come to the rescue. Blue Beard draws his sword, but Ariane gently pushes the peasants back and says: "What do you want? — He hasn't done me any harm."

Act II.— Scene. The dungeon. Ariane, with a lamp, and the nurse move forward till they discover in a huddle the five wives. Ariane rushes to them with kisses and caresses, crying: "Ah! I have found you" (*Ah! Je vous ai trouvées*). She is sure that they are beautiful, but they are in rags and unkempt and frightened. She asks their names and comforts them. A drop of water from the dank roof extinguishes the lamp, but the wife, Sélysette is used to the dark and leads the others to a trap door. Ariane breaks it open, and the music of wind and sea, mingled with the song of birds and the sound of shepherd bells invades the room. Sélysette waves her long hair as a signal flag to a distant peasant, and as the clock strikes noon the women scramble out joyously.

Act III.— Scene. The same hall as in the first act. Open coffers are overflowing with gorgeous robes. The wives before large mirrors are dressing their hair and donning gleaming raiment, while Ariane goes from one to the other assisting them. They have been unable to escape from the castle walls, but Ariane hopes to make them so beautiful that Blue Beard will fall in love with them again. The nurse appears with the terrifying news that Blue Beard is returning. But the peasants are armed and lying in wait for him. From the window they see Blue Beard arrive with warriors who fight the peasants. At length the peasants conquer, and tying the wounded Blue Beard, they burst into the hall with their prisoner. They deliver him to the wives for punishment. When the peasants have gone, Ariane and the wives, overcome with pity, release Blue Beard and dress his wounds, kissing him furtively. He stares at his victims, but turns to Ariane. She tells him farewell and asks the other wives if they will go with her. She points to the open door and the moonlit sky (*Vois, la porte est ouverte*), but they prefer to remain with Blue Beard, and she leaves them, wishing them happiness.

*A*

# TABLE *of* PRONUNCIATIONS

Giving the Code of Symbols used in this
Book; and also a Guide to the Pronunciations of sixteen Languages, arranged
in a novel Tabular Form by Letters

| | A | B | C |
|---|---|---|---|
| p row gives the phonetic ing ot the letters and sym- AS USED IN THIS K. | as used in this book: ä as in father; ā as in fate: ä as in fat; an and ăn, see Note 1. | as in bob. | see ch, at end of the alphabet. |
| AN : very difficult even ojourners among the peo- | as in fat; before r as in far. | as in bob. | as in English; ch like German ch, see Note 3. |
| MIAN : See Note 4. In hongs the vowels are pro-ced separately, as in Ital- | as a in fun; á as in father. | as in bob. | c like ts, or German z; č like ch in child. |
| SH : doubled vowels are ly prolonged. | as in father; aa as a in fall. | as in bob. | like Swedish c. |
| H : e in be and ge; i be-k, g and ng; and ij in the lijk are silent. | when short as in half; also before h; when open as in father: aa, aai (see ai), prolonged as in father. | beginning a syllable, as in bet; ending, as p in trap. | only in foreign words; like s before e, i and y; like k, otherwise. |
| ISH : dead as a literary uage, but of great historic rtance. | a or ă, as in father or mica; aa or ae, the same prolonged. | as in bob. | like k; ch like German ch. |
| CH : a silent final conso-is usually sounded with following word when that is with a vowel. This is d liaison. French sylla-have duration rather than nt; the tendency is, to give ght stress to the final syl-. In this book accent is y marked. | as in făt; â as in father; see ai, au, and Note 1. | as in bob. | as s before e, i and y; as k otherwise, except that ç is always s. See ch. |
| AN : long words usually nt the first syllable most gly, and give a lesser ac-to one or more of the rs. | as in father; ä, see Note 2; ä is sometimes spelled ae; ai = i in bite; for äu and aeu, see au. | beginning a syllable, as in bet; ending a syllable, as p in trap. | like ts in hats before e, i and ä; like k before a, o and u; ch. See Note 3. |
| ARIAN : long and short els are so rather in dura-than in sound. There are lent letters and no accents. | as in what; á is prolonged, as in father. | as in bob. | cs = ch in church; cz = ts, as in hats. |
| AN : doubled consonants distinctly pronounced, as do. Doubled vowels are separately pronounced. | as in father and mica; á as in far. | as in bob. | before e and i as ch in chime; cc before e and i = tch, as wretched; ch = k. |
| EGIAN : | a as in father; aa as o in no; au as o in no. | as in bob. | only in foreign words; as s before e, i and y; as k otherwise. |
| H : consonants strongly ded are accented thus: b, 7 7 1 7 1 m, n, p, s, w, z. | as in father: ǫ as in ball. | as in bob. | c = ts, as in hats; ch = German ch; cz = ch in church. |
| UGUESE : a very difficult uage; placed usually just of the teeth. The nasal els are also unique. Note 5. | as in father; when two as occur in a word the first is more like a in fat; ă, see Note 5. | nearly as in bob; but softer. | like s before e, i and y; k otherwise; ç always like s; in cc the first c is like k, the second is determined by the following letter. |
| AN : has 36 letters, in-ing 12 vowels. It is usu-written phonetically in nan pronunciation as fol- | when accented, as in father; unaccented, as in bat; at the beginning, as ya in yacht; if unaccented, as in yank. | this letter resembling our f is pronounced v, as in vane, or f, as in foe; the equivalent of our b sounds as b or p in bet or trap. | as in cent or zone; ch = German ch at the end; at the beginning, as in chest. |
| ISH : a language of ideal larity and precision; all els are separately pro-aced. | as in father or in hat; å as in father. | like v in very. | before e or i, as th in think; otherwise as k; ch as in church; cu as qu in quart. |
| DISH : | as in father or in mica; å as o in go, when long; when short, as a in what; ä as in hare. | as in bob. | before e, i or y, as in cent; otherwise as in cash; cu = k, except in foreign words. |
| SH : all vowel combina-s are separately pro-aced; the letter w = oo oon. | as in fat; â as in dare. | as in bob. | always like k; ch = German ch, see Note 3. |

| D | E | F | G |
|---|---|---|---|
| as in deed; *dh* as *th* in these; *dj* as in adjoin. | *ĕ* as in bean; *ĕ* as in pet—at the end of words almost like *ŭ*. | as in fife. | as in gig. |
| soft like Italian *d*. | as in prey; *ĕ* as in pet. | as in fife. | as in gig. |
| as in deed. For *d'*, *dĕ* and *di*, see Note 4. | as in pet; *é* as in ere; *ĕ* = *ya*, as in beatitude. See also Note 4. | as in fife. | as in gig. |
| beginning a syllable as in date; ending as *th* in bathe; after *l*, *n*, and *r*, silent; *ds* = *ss* in hiss. | as in prey and there; *ej* like *i* in bite. | as in fife. | as in gig; after *e* or *ĕ* like yoke; between vowels mute. |
| at the beginning of syllables as in date; at the end as *t* in hot. | when short as in met; when open as in prey; *ee* simply prolongs the sound; see also *eu*. | as in fife; *fl* as in flow; *fr* as in fresh. | like German *g*; *ng* as in ing. |
| like German *d* and *dt*. | *e* or *é* as in pet; *eu* like French *eu*; *e* after a vowel usually simply prolongs it; *ee* = *a* in fate or as in seen; see *eu*. | as in fife. | as German *g*, very guttu[...] |
| at the beginning or in the middle as *d* in deadlock; usually silent at the end of the word; in liaison it becomes *t*. | as *e* in father or *u* in cut; as a final syllable generally silent; *é* as in prey when it has stress, otherwise as in pet; *è* as *ai* in fair; *ê* as in pet; see *ei*, *d*, *s*, *t*, *z*, *r*. | as in fife, not silent at the ends of words. except in clef; in liaison it becomes *v*. | as in gate except befor[e] and *y*, then as *s* in ple[...] (marked here as *zh*); when final, becoming [...] liaison; *gn* as *ni* in min[...] |
| beginning a syllable as in date; ending a syllable as *t* in hat; *dt* = *t* in hat. | when long as in prey; when short as in pet; *ei* = *i* in right; see *eu*. | as in fife. | at the beginning of a sy[...] as in gate, but softer; [...] end. see Note 3; *ng* [...] final vanishes in a fa[...] sound as sang = zangk[...] |
| *s* in deed; *dj* same as *'gy*; *djs* = *j* in judge. | before *m* or a sharp consonant as in fat; otherwise as *e* in ten; *é* as in prey. | as in fife. | as in gig; *gy* = *d* in du[...] doo); *ggy* = *gygy* or a[...] |
| as in deed, but softer and more palatal. | as in prey when long; when short as in pet; *è* as in pet. | as in fife. | before *e* and *i* as in gem[...] as *dj* in adjoin; *gli*[...] like *ll* in million, *gn* or *ni* in pinion; *gu* = [...] *gui* = *wē*. |
| as in deed. | as in prey; but when final as *e* in father. | as in fife. | as in gig, but before *j* [...] as *y* in yoke. |
| as in deed; *dz* as in adze; *dž* as *dge* in judge, | *e* as in met; *ē* = French in, see Note 1; *ê* = *a* as in pate. | as in fife. | as in gig. |
| as in deed. | *e* and *é* usually as in prey; *è* has a curious closed sound. | as in fife. | as in gate; but before *e*, *y* as in gem. |
| as in deed. | at the beginning of words = *yo* in yolk if accented; if unaccented as *ye* in yesterday; otherwise as *e* in pet. | usually represented by the German *v* or *w*. | at the beginning usually [...] go; sometimes at the [...] ning, always at the e[...] German *ch*; see Note[...] |
| much like *th* in those (marked in this book by *dh*); when two *ds* occur in a word, only the second has this sound, the first a[s] in date. | as in prey when long; when short as in pet; *é* as in prey or pet. | as in fife. | as in gate; but before *e* a[...] as a very harsh *h* in [...] *gue* = *ga* as in gate, *g*[...] *ge* as in gear; *gn* as [...] nite; *gl* as in glow. |
| as in deed, but silent in *ndn* and *nds* and before *j* or *t*. | as in film when long; when short as in pet; *er* as *ar* in bare. | as in fit at the beginning of syllables or after a short vowel; at end of syllable like *v* in slave; before *v* silent. | as in gate; before *ä*, *e*, *i*, and after *l* and *r*, like yoke; silent before *i*; *ng* in sing. |
| as in date; *dd* as *th* in these. | as in pet; *ĕ* as in bean. | like *v* in revive; *ff* like *f* in off. | as in gate; *ng* as in wron[g] |

| ...ic meaning ...the letters ... symbols ...USED IN ...S BOOK. | **H** as in hate. | **I** ɪ as in fight; ĭ as in pin. | **J** as in jug. | **K** as in kick; kh = German ch or g; see Note 3. |
|---|---|---|---|---|
| AN : | strongly aspirated at end or beginning of a word. | as in pin; i as in bird. | as in jug. | strongly guttural. |
| MIAN : | as in hate. | as in pin; i as in machine. | like y in yes; after vowels it prolongs their sounds somewhat as y in day, whey, etc. | as in kick. |
| SH : | as in hate but silent before j and v. | as in machine; after a, e, o, ö, and u like y in yoke. | even with vowels aj, ej, like y in yoke. | as in kick. |
| H : | as in hate. | when short as in pin; when open as e in rely; ie prolongs the open sound only before r, otherwise as e in rely; ij same as ei. | as y in yoke. | as in kick; ks = x in fix; kw = qu in quart. |
| ISH : | as in hate. | i or i as in pin; ü or ie the same prolonged; ieu sounds like ē-ŭ. | as y in yoke. | as in kick; ks = x in fi. |
| CH : | always silent. | as in pin, see ei, oi; i as i in machine, but see ai. | as s in measure (marked in this book as zh). | as in kick. |
| AN : | as in hate. | as in machine; ie as in believe. | as y in yoke. | as in kick. |
| ARIAN : | as in hate. | as the quick e in rely; i as in machine. | as y in yoke; jj as y in paying. | as in kick. |
| AN : | silent; after c or g it has simply a hardening effect. | as in machine, but when short as in pin; at the beginning of words like y in yoke. | same as i; at the beginning of words like y in yoke; as a vowel like i in machine. | .................... |
| EGIAN : | as in hate. | as in machine; at the beginning as y in yoke. | as in yoke. | as in kick; before i and y like h; kv = qu in quarter. |
| H : | as in hate; see c, l and n. | i as in machine; after a consonant it has the effect of the imaginary y in due (not doo); iu = u in gun. | as y in yoke. | as in kick. |
| UGUESE : | silent. | as in machine. | as in jug. | only in foreign words, as in kick. |
| AN : | used only in a few native words, and in foreign derivations. | as in machine, but well back in the throat; after labials (b, f, m, p and v) as i in pin. | as y in yet. | as in kick; before k, l and ch softly as in German ch. |
| ISH : | usually silent or very slight; see c. | as in machine when long; when short as in pin; i as in machine. | as a very harsh h in hate; almost like German ch. | ..................... |
| ISH : | as in hate; silent before j or v. | as in machine. | as y in yoke. | as in kick but before ä, e, i, ö and y in the same syllable like ch. |
| H : | as in hate. | as in machine. | ..................... | as in kick. |

| **L** as in lull. | **M** as in mum. | **N** as in nun; ñ, see Note 1. | **O** ð as in note; oi as in noise; oo as in moon or foot; ð as in wrong; ow as in cow; ðñ, see Note 1. | **P** as in pop. |
|---|---|---|---|---|
| as in lull. | as in mum. | as in nun. | as in note; ö = German ö, see Note 2. | as in pop. |
| as in lull. | as in mum. | as in nun; ñ as in cañon. | as in note; ó as in wrong. | as in pop. |
| as in lull. | as in mum. | as in nun. | when open as in bother; when closed as in move; φ = French eu closed as in peu; ö = the same open as in coeur; see Note 2. | as in pop. |
| as in lull, but when followed by another consonant a short e is interpolated, as if elk were spelt elek. | as in mum. | as in nun. | as in bother when short, when long as in over; oo = o in over; ooi = o in over followed by i in pin; see oe. | as in pop; f. |
| as in lull. | as in mum. | as in nun. | o as in note or not; oo or oe usually the same prolonged, sometimes like wa in was, oei or oey as ō-ē. | as in pop. |
| as in lily, t sometimes l (called "l mouillé") is liquid, as y in yoke or paying. | at the beginning, as in mate. See note 1. | at the beginning, as in name. See Note 1. | as in not; often almost as ŭ in nut; ð as in note; see oi. | at the beginning and middle in paper; = almost ph = f; when final |
| as in lull. | as in mum. | as in nun. | as in wrong; ö see Note 2; ð is sometimes spelled oe. | as in pop. |
| as in late; ll' or ly = y in paying. | as in mum. | as in nun; ny = n as in new (not noo); nny = nyny, or n' n'. | o as in note; ð is prolonged as in slow; ö = French eu; ö or ö = German long ö. | as in pop. |
| as in lull; see g. | as in mum. | as in nun; see g. | as in note; ð as in wrong. | as in pop. |
| as in lull. | as in mum. | as in nun. | as u in full, but often as o in note or not; oe = a in sale; ö like French eu long or short. | as in pop. |
| as in lull; t is sounded by closing the teeth on the tip of the tongue as l is pronounced. | as in mum. | as in nun. | o as in note; ð is between note and move. | as in pop. |
| as in lull; lh like lli in million. | as in meet, but at end of syllables or after e, like French nasal n. See Note 1. | as in note; but at end of syllables or after e, like French nasal n, see Note 1; nh = ni in minion. | as in note or in not; ö see Note 5. | as in pop; f. |
| as in lull; before a or o, as il in collar. | as in mum. | as in nun. | as in not. | as in pop. |
| as in look; ll like lli in billiards. | as in mum. | as in nun; ñ divides into ny as ni in minion, thus cañon = canyon. | when long as in note; when short o as in not; ó as in note. | as in pop; before s, t. |
| as in lull, but usually silent before j. | as in mum. | as in nun; gn = ng in sing. | as in move or not, according to complex rules; ö = German ö. | as in pop. |
| as in look; ll has a curl as mingling of th and l. | as in mum. | as in nun. | as in gone; ð as in bone; the sound oo is represented by w. | as in pop; f. |

| Phonetic meaning of the letters and symbols AS USED IN THIS BOOK. | Q | R as in roar. | S as in sense. | T as in tot; th as in think. |
|---|---|---|---|---|
| ABIAN : | .................. | as in roar. | as in sis; ss strongly hissed; sh as in show. | strongly palatal. |
| HEMIAN : | as qu in quart. | as in roar; ř = rzh or rsh as in "for sure," thus Dvořák is dvôr-zhäk. | s as in sis; š as sh in show. | as in tot; see also Note 4. |
| NISH : | qv = qu in quart. | as in roar. | as in sense; ski or sky as in skim. | as in tot. |
| TCH : | qu as in quart. | as in hurry. | sharply as in sense; sj = sh in show; see sch. | after a hard vowel it is soft as in note, otherwise as in hot. |
| EMISH : | qu as in quart. | as in roar. | as in suppose. | as in tot; dt as t in hat. |
| NCH : | qu always as k in kick; cq as k. | commonly rolled on the back of the tongue; in Paris almost like w in bower; as a final letter it is sounded except after e; er = a in sale. | as in suppose; when final it is silent except in proper names; in liaison it becomes z. | as t in tub; like s in such suffixes as -tion: almost always silent when final; et = a in sale. |
| M.AN : | qu as kv; thus quart = k'värt. | usually rolled and always strongly sounded. | beginning a syllable before a vowel usually as z in zone; as the end of a syllable as in this; sp and st = shp and sht; sch = sh. | as in tot; th = t in hat. |
| GARIAN : | .................. | always trilled. | as sh in show; sz = sh. | as in tot; ty strongly as t in tube; tty = ty' ty' or t' t'; ts = ch. |
| IAN : | qu as in quart. | usually trilled. | as in suppose; sce = shā; sci = shē; sch = sk. | as in tot; ti usually = tsi. |
| WEGIAN : | qu as in quart. | as in hurry. | as in sis; ski = sh in show. | as in tot. |
| SH : | .................. | as in roar; rz = French j or s in measure. | as in sense; sz = sh in show. | as in tot. |
| UGUESE : | qua as in quart; before e or i, qu is like k. | as in roar and hurry. | as in suppose; having the z sound between vowels. | as in tot. |
| IAN : | .................. | with a burr as rr in worry. | as in sense; sh as in show; ski = shk; sz = sh. | as in tot; ts beginning or ending as in hats; tsch as shtch in washt-church. |
| ISH : | qu as k in kick. | as in roar. | as in sense. | as in tot. |
| ISH : | qv = k in kin. | as in hurry. | as in sense; sk, sy, and stj all = sh in show. | as in tot; tj = ch in church; but if followed by a or e = ts in hats; th = t in tot. |
| E : | .................. | as in roar. | as in sense. | as in tot; th as in think. |

| U | V | W | X | Y |
|---|---|---|---|---|
| **U**<br>always with the sound of you; *ŭ*, see Note 2. | **V**<br>as in revive. | **W**<br>as in will. | **X**<br>as in fix. | **Y**<br>as in yoke. |
| as in full. | as in revive. | as in will. | .................... | as in why. |
| as in full; *ū* or *ú*, as in rule. | as in revive. | as in will: *w* is silent before *z* and another consonant, as *wzd.* | as in fix. | as *i* in pin, *ý* as *i* in chine. |
| as in rule or full. | as in revive; silent after *l* and *r*. | only in foreign words. | as in xebec. | like *u* in fur. |
| when short, as in cut: when long, as in rule; *uu* as *oo* in moon. | at the beginning, as in vote at the end, as *f* in off. | as in will. | as in fix. | as in why. |
| like a short German *ü*, see Note 2 : *uu* or *ue*, the same prolonged: see *uï*. | as in revive. | as in will. | as in fix. | like *i* in machine; s times nasal like Fr *in*, see Note 1, see a |
| see Note 2. | as in revive. | in foreign words only, and sounded like *v* in vote; *wh* sounded as *w* in was. | as in fix or exile; silent when final; becoming *z* in liaison. | when alone or when a sonant precedes or fo it, as *e* in bear. Wh lies between two vow may be said to be di into two sounds. Aft *a* or *e* it is sounded in pet followed by yoke (thus rayon bec ré-yôn); with an sounds like *wä* in wa lowed by *y*, as in (thus joyeux bec zhwä-yŭ); with *u* comes *ē — y'* (thus a ant becomes ăp-pwē |
| *oo* in moon or foot; *ü* (sometimes spelled *ue*), see Note 2. | like *f* in fife. | like *v* in revive, but with a soft trace also of the *w* in was. | as in fix, even at the beginning of a syllable. | as *e* in bean, sometime *ü*; see Note 2. |
| *u* as in pull; *ú* as in rule: *ü* = French *u*; *ŭ* or *ü* the same prolonged. | as in revive. | .................... | .................... | see *g*, *l*, *n* and *z*. |
| as in rule; *ü* as in full. | as in revive | .................... | .................... | .................... |
| as in rule. | as in revive; *v* = *qu* in quart. | .................... | as in fix. | like French *u*. |
| as in rule; preceded by *i* it is the French *u*. | .................... | as *v* in revive. | as in fix. | *yj* = *e* in bean. |
| as in rule; *ŭ*, see Note 5. | as in revive. | .................... | after *e*, as in vex: otherwise as *sh* in show. | as *i* in machine. |
| as in due, or as *oo* in moon, except in words of French or German origin, then as French *u*. | as *f* in far or off. | as *f* in far or off. | .................... | same as Russian *z*. |
| as in rule, when long, when short, as in full; *ú* as in rule or full; *ue* = *wa* in wait. | as in revive. | .................... | as in fix; even at the beginning; in some proper names as *k* in hate. | as *i* in machine. |
| as in rule; or in full. | as in revive. | like *v* in revive. | .................... | like French *u*; see N |
| a little broader than *i* in this; *ä* = *ee* in seen. | .................... | sounded like *oo* in moon. | .................... | as *u* in turn; at the e syllable as in prett |

| | Z | Æ | AI | AU | EUA |
|---|---|---|---|---|---|
| | as in zone and buzz. | | | | |
| ABIAN : | as in zone. | | | | |
| GERMAN : | as in zone; ž as in azure. | | | | |
| NISH : | only in foreign words, then like *s* in sis. | like *ai* both in sail and in said. | like *i* in bite. | as *ow* in cow. | |
| TCH : | as in zone. | | *aai* combines *a* in father with a quick *e* in meet, almost like *y* in why. | combines *a* in *iat* with *oo* in moon; sharper than *ow* in cow. | |
| EMISH : | as in zone; often used interchangeable with *s*. | same as *aa* = *a* prolonged ; *aei* or *aey* = *ai* prolonged. | *ai* and *ay* as *ai* in said ; *aei* or *aey* the same prolonged. | | |
| RNCH : | as in zone. | | *ai, aî, ay* as *e* in pet. | as *o* in zone. | as *o* in zone. |
| RMAN : | like *ts* in hats, even at the beginning of a syllable. | only another spelling of *ä*. See Note 2. | like *i* in bite. | as *ow* in cow; *äu* almost like *i* in bite (actually *ah—ē*). | |
| NGARIAN : | as in zone; *zs*, see *d*. | | | | |
| ALIAN : | *z* as *ts* in hats; *zz* as *ds* in Windsor. | in vowel combinations the vowels are always separately pronounced in Italian. | | | |
| RWEGIAN : | like *ts* in hats. | | | like *o* in note. | |
| LISH : | as in zone; *ž* = *s* in measure ; *zg* = *g* preceded by a buzz. | | | | |
| RTUGUESE : | as in zone; but at the end of syllables like *s* in this. | | | | |
| SSIAN : | as German *z* = *ts* ; or as French *z* = *g* in menagerie. | same | as | German | diphthongs. |
| ANISH : | as *th* in think. | | | | |
| EDISH : | like *s* in sis. | | | | |
| ?? : | | | | | |

| EI | EU | IE | OE | OI as in noise. | OU |
|---|---|---|---|---|---|
| combines *e* in met with *i* in pin; in the suffix heid = *a* in fate. | same as German short *ö*, see Note 2; *eeu* = *a* in fate, with a whispered *v* after it. | see *i*; *ieu* = *a* in fate, with a soft *w* after it. | same as *oo* in moon; *oei* = *oo* followed by a short *i*. | | combines ... in ... with *u* in ru... softer than, often confu... with, *au*. |
| | same as French *eu*; *eeu* the same prolonged. | | as *oo* in moon; sometimes a simple prolonged *ō*; or like *wa* in was; *oei* or *oey* = *we*. | | |
| as *i* in pet. | like *e* in father when short; when long, the same sound prolonged; it lies between *e* in pet and *u* in cut, and resembles German *ö*. See Note 2. | | *oe* = *wa* in was; *oeu* like *eu*. | *oi* or *oy* = *wa* in was; *oin* = *w* followed by the nasal in. See Note 1. | *ou* = *oo* in bo... *ouin* = *oin*; *oi* and Note ... |
| like *i* in bite. | almost like *i* in bite with a hint of *oi* in noise. | as in believe. | only another spelling of *ō*. See Note 2. | | |
| | | | | | |
| | | | | | |
| | | like *a* in sale. | | | |
| | | | | | |
| | | | | | almost as *o* in rou... |
| same | as | the | German | diph- | thongs. |
| | | | | | |
| | | | | | |
| | | | | | |

| netic meaning the letters n d symbols s USED IN HIS BOOK. | UE | UI | CH as in church; German *ch* is represented by *kh*, see Note 3. | SCH | SP |
|---|---|---|---|---|---|
| ABIAN : | | | like German *ch*. | | |
| EMIAN : | | | | | |
| NISH : | | | as *k*, except in foreign words. | | |
| CCH · | | almost *y* in why; but verging on the French *eu*. | like German *ch*, but more palatal at the beginning of foreign words; as *sh* in show. | beginning a syllable, as *stch*; at the end, as simple *s* in this. | as in span. |
| MISH : | same as a prolonged *u*. | *ui* and *uy* like German *eu*. | like German *ch*. See Note 3. | | |
| ENCH : | *uei* like *eu*. | | as *sh* before a vowel; before a consonant as *k*. | | |
| RMAN : | only another spelling of *ü*. See Note 2. | | see Note 3. | like *sh* in show. | like *shp* in dish-pan. |
| NGARIAN : | | | | | |
| LIAN : | | | as *k* in kin. | as *sk* in skip. | as in span. |
| RWEGIAN : | | | | | |
| LISH : | | | like German *ch*, see Note 3. | | |
| RTUGUESE : | | | | | |
| SSIAN : | | | | | |
| ANISH : | | | as in church. | | |
| EDISH : | | | | | |
| LSR : | | | like German *ch*, see Note 3. | | |

| ST | TH | NOTES |
|---|---|---|
| | as in *thing*; the *th* in *those* is represented by *dh*. | |

<table>
<tr><td>ST</td><td>TH</td></tr>
<tr><td>................</td><td>................</td></tr>
<tr><td>................</td><td>................</td></tr>
<tr><td>................</td><td>................</td></tr>
<tr><td>as in stone.</td><td>................</td></tr>
<tr><td>................</td><td>................</td></tr>
<tr><td>*ve sh? in* washtub.</td><td>like *t* in tot.</td></tr>
<tr><td>................</td><td>................</td></tr>
<tr><td>as in stone.</td><td>................</td></tr>
<tr><td>................</td><td>................</td></tr>
<tr><td>................</td><td>................</td></tr>
<tr><td>................</td><td>................</td></tr>
<tr><td>................</td><td>like *t* in tot.</td></tr>
<tr><td>................</td><td></td></tr>
</table>

## NOTES

**No. 1.**—The French nasal sounds are easily obtained:
(1) Though spelled with an *m* or *n* (and indicated in this book by an *n̄*) they have really no *n* sound in them, much less the *ng* sound that some foreigners give them. Though variously spelled they are reducible to four vowel sounds pronounced as we say, "through the nose," though actually with closed nasal passages. If one will pronounce or rather snort the word "wrong" without producing the final *g* at all one will have exactly the French *on* (1); the word "thank" similarly sounded without the *k* will give the French *in* (2); the word "trunk" without the *k* gives the French *un* (3); the word "donkey" (not pronounced like monkey) contains the French *en* (4). These four are indicated in this book by (1) *ôn* ; (2) *än* ; (3) *ün* (4) *än*.
The French nasals may be grouped as follows: Those pronounced like (1) are *om*, *on*, and *eon* after *g* ; like (2), *ïm*, *in*, *aim*, *ain*, *ein* and also *en* as an ending; like (3) *um*, *un* and *evm* ; like (4) *am*, *an*, *ean*, *aen*, *aon* and *en* at the beginning of words.
These letters *m* and *n*, however, lose their nasal quality when doubled or when preceding a vowel; *onne* is pronounced as *one* in done, *ome* or *omme* as in come, *em* as in *em* in them, etc.

**No. 2.**—French *u* (which is the same as the German *ü* when long) is easily pronounced if one will pucker his lips to say *oo*, as in moon; and keeping them strongly puckered say *e* as in bean. Those who have eaten green persimmons, or had their lips distended with peach fuzz, have the correct position for this *e* sound. There is really no *oo* sound in the French *u* at all, and if one cannot say the *u* correctly he will come much nearer the truth if he uses a plain English long *e*, as in bean, rather than the sound of *u*, as the spelling might suggest.
The German *ü* when short is formed by keeping the lips puckered and saying *i* as in fit, instead of *e* in serene.
The other German modified (or umlauted) vowels are (2) *ä*, pronounced, when long almost like *a* in sale, but verging on *a* in care (it is marked here simply as *ā*); when short much like *e* in pet; (3) *ö* when long can be secured by puckering the lips for round, full *o*, as in note and then saying *a* as in sale (it is marked in this book simply as *ā* to avoid the danger of saying a plain *o*); when it is short the lips should be puckered for the round *o*, and a short *e* as in pet then pronounced. The caution must be emphasised that in the experiments the lips must be firmly kept in the first, or puckered position, in spite of the temptation to alter it.

**No. 3.**—German *ch* is not difficult, once caught. Our sound *th* as in think will be found if prolonged to be produced by the simple device of holding the tip of the tongue lightly between the teeth and then breathing. The German *ch* results from pressing the two sides of the tongue firmly against the bicuspid teeth (the two upper teeth on each side back of the canine or eye teeth) and leaving the tip of the tongue free, then breathing the necessary vowel as in *ach. ich*, etc. German *g* is much the same but even softer. Both are indicated in this book by *kh*.

**No. 4.**—Certain Bohemian letters and combinations insert the sound *y* closely allied to a consonant, as in the French *diable* and *tien*, or the English "How *d'ye* do?" or "I've caught*ye*." Bohemian *d*, *n* and *t* are given this *d'y* and *t'y* sound when followed by *e* or *i* or by an apostrophe as *d'*, *n̄* or *t'*.
Many Bohemian combinations of consonants seem unspeakable because they are spelt with no vowels between. They are no harder to say, however, than such words of ours as "twelfths." Among such consonant chains are *drn*, *kb*, *kd*, *krl*, *prs*, *skrz*, *sr*, *wl* and *zr*. They must be run together as smoothly as possible.

**No. 5.**—Portuguese diphthongs are of three sorts: the first two cannot be distinguished here, they are simply combinations of vowels (sometimes of three vowels or triphthongs) in which each vowel is sounded independently; in the first class the first vowel takes the accent, in the second class the second vowel is accented. The third class contains a nasal vowel marked *ã*, *õ* or *ũ*, and pronounced with a strong nasal twang.

**No. 6.**—In vowel combinations other than those specially mentioned here, the vowels are pronounced separately, each in its own way.

**No. 7.**—Combinations of consonants other than those mentioned here will be found under their first letter.

**No. 8.**—As Greek and Latin pronunciations are matters of controversy and personal taste, no system is attempted here. Chinese, Japanese, Hebrew, Hindu, and various other languages are usually spelled phonetically, but on such different national personal standards that they can hardly be generalised.